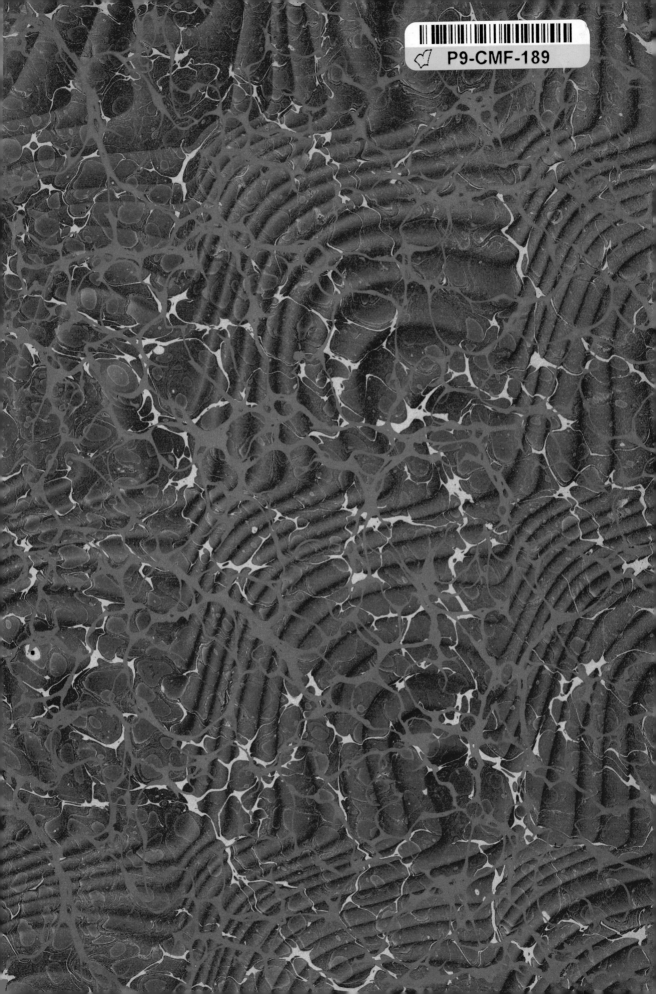

THE POPULAR AND CRITICAL

BIBLE ENCYCLOPÆDIA

AND

SCRIPTURAL DICTIONARY

FULLY DEFINING AND EXPLAINING ALL RELIGIOUS TERMS

INCLUDING

Biographical, Geographical, Historical
Archæological and Doctrinal Themes

Superbly Illustrated with Over 600 Maps and Engravings

EDITED BY

RT. REV. SAMUEL FALLOWS, A. M., D. D., LL. D.

ASSOCIATE EDITORS

ANDREW C. ZENOS, A. M., D. D.
(McCormick Theological Seminary)

HERBERT L. WILLETT, A. M., PH. D.
(University of Chicago)

VOLUME II

CHICAGO
THE HOWARD-SEVERANCE COMPANY
1902

F

FABLE (fā'b'l), (Gr. μῦθος, *moo'thos ;* Lat. *fabula*) parable.

Fable is a form of narrative in which plants and animals, or even lifeless objects, are represented as endowed with some of the attributes of man, as the gift of speech and rational action. Sometimes the fable is designed to teach moral and practical truths, and sometimes only to interest and entertain. Neander, *Life of Christ,* thus distinguishes between the parable and fable: "The parable is distinguished from the fable by this, that in the latter qualities or acts of a higher class of beings may be attributed to a lower, e. g., those of men to brutes; while in the former the lower sphere is kept perfectly distinct from that which it seems to illustrate. The beings and powers thus introduced always follow the law of their nature, but their acts, according to this law, are used to figure those of a higher race."

To illustrate: What the fable relates is not real and cannot occur, as trees speaking (Judg. ix: 8); while that which the parable relates may and does take place, as the sower sowing seed in soil of various degrees of productiveness (Matt. xiii: 3). The fable was often used in ancient heathen as in modern Christian literature. In the Bible there is only one fable (Judg. ix :7-15), where Jotham represents the trees as seeking a king and asking, one by one, the olive and others to reign over them, till the bramble finally consents. This is often erroneously called a parable.

Fables are referred to in the New Testament as *inventions, falsehoods* (2 Pet. i :16); and in 1 Tim. i:4, etc., as "cunningly devised" or foolish systems and opinions, etc.

FACE (fās), (Heb. פָּנִים, *paw-neem'*).

(1) Face, in Scripture, is often used to denote *presence* in the general sense, and, when applied to the Almighty, denotes such a complete manifestation of the divine presence, by sound or sight, as was equivalent, in the vividness of the impression, to the seeing of a fellow-creature 'face to face.' The 'face of God' therefore denotes in Scripture any thing or manner by which God is wont to manifest himself to man. Thus, when it is said that Adam and Eve hid themselves from 'the face of Jehovah,' we understand that they hid themselves from his presence, however manifested; for *pawneem* not only signifies *presence,* as well as (literally) *face,* but is the very word for *presence,* however manifested. There is no other word to denote presence in the Hebrew language. Whenever 'presence' occurs in our translation, the word in the original is the same which is rendered 'face' in other places.

(2) It was a very ancient and common opinion that our mortal frame could not survive the more sensible manifestations of the Divine presence, or 'see God face to face and live' (Gen. xxxii :30), hence, in this passage, the gratitude and astonishment of Jacob that he still lived after God had manifested himself to him more sensibly than by dreams and visions. This impression was confirmed to Moses, who was told, 'Thou canst not see my face: no man can see my face and live' (Exod. xxxiii :20); which clearly signifies that no one can in this present state of being endure the view of that glory which

belongs to Him (1 Cor. xiii:12; 1 Pet. iii:12; Rev. xxii:4).

(3) The *physical* manifestations of the Divine presence appear to have been made through the Angel of whom it is said *"My name is in him"* (Exod. xxiii :21; xiv:19). We are to bear in mind that God is usually represented to us in Scripture under a human form; and it is indeed difficult for even more spiritualized minds than those of the Hebrews to conceive of Him apart from the form and attributes of the highest nature actually known to us. The Scripture sanctions this concession to the weakness of our intellect, and hence arise the anthropomorphous phrases which speak of the face, the eyes, the arm of God. The appearances of the angels in the Old Testament times were generally in the human form (Judg. xiii :6, etc); and from this cause alone it would have been natural, in the imagination, to transfer the form of the messengers to Him by whom they were sent. (See ANTHROPOMORPHISM.)

(4) God's "face" is used to express his favor and love, and the gracious displays thereof; this is always meant when his face is said to "shine," or it is represented as a mercy to behold and enjoy it or a misery to be deprived of it (2 Chron. xxx :9; Ps. xxxi :16; lxxx :7; Dan. ix :17). It is used also to denote wrath, and the providential display thereof (Ps. xxxiv :16).

(5) Christ's "face" denotes: (1) His person and office as the image of the invisible God (2 Cor. iv:6). (2) His gracious, glorious, or terrible appearances (Rev. xx :11).

FACES, BREAD OF (fās'ĕz, brĕd ŏv), is the shewbread which was always in the presence of God. (See SHEKINAH.)

FAIN (fān), (Gr. ἐπιθυμέω, *ep-ee-thoo-meh'o,* from θυμέω, to breathe hard), to have earnest longings, hence to set the heart upon, desire (Luke xv:16).

It thus properly means *glad* or *gladly,* as John xii:21; Tyndale, "We wolde fayne se Jesus." But the commonest meaning has always been 'glad under the circumstances,' and that is its meaning in A. V.; Job xxvii:22 'he would fain flee out of his hand.' (Hastings' *Bib. Dict.*)

FAIR (fâr), (Heb. טָהוֹר, *taw'hore,* Zech. iii:5), pure; clean in a physical, ceremonial or moral sense.

It also is used for *beautiful* (Acts vii :20) and for *plausible* (Gal. vi :12).

FAIR HAVENS (fâr hā'v'nz), (Gr. Καλοὶ Λιμένες, *kal-oy' lee-men'es,* good harbors), a harbor or roadstead of Crete, the unsafeness of which to winter in occasioned that attempt to make for Phenice, on the other side of the island, which led to the eventual loss of the vessel in which Paul sailed for Rome (Acts xxvii :8).

As the name of Kaloi Limenes is still preserved, there is no difficulty in fixing the situation to a small bay a little to the northeast of Cape Leon, the present Cape Matala. (Smith, *Voyage and Shipwreck of St. Paul,* 2d Ed., pp. 80 ff.; Conybeare and Howson, *Life and Epistles of St. Paul,* ii :320).

FAIRS (fârz), (Heb. עִזְּבוֹנִים, *iz-zeh-bow-neem',* Ezek. xxvii:12, 33).

This word is found only in Ezekiel, and does not mean *fairs,* but *wares,* as the R. V. renders it, and as the A. V. has it in verse 33.

FAITH (fāth), (Gr. πιστις, *pis'tis*), belief, trust—especially in a higher power.

(1) General. Faith in every language, spoken by Christian, Jew, or Mohammedan, seems everywhere to convey the fundamental ideas of 'fixedness, stability, steadfastness, reliability.' What the ultimate conception is which underlies these ideas remains somewhat doubtful, but it would appear to be rather that of 'holding' than that of 'supporting' (although this last is the sense adopted in *Oxf. Heb. Lex.*)

(2) Old Testament. The extreme rarity of the noun 'faith' in the Old Testament may prepare us to note that even the verb 'to believe' is far from common in it. In a religious application it occurs in only some thirteen Old Testament books, and less than a score and a half times. But the prin-

was a religion of faith in a far more specific sense than this, and that not merely because faith was more consciously its foundation, but because its very essence consisted in faith, and this faith was the same radical self-commitment to God, not merely as the highest good of the holy soul, but as the gracious Savior of the sinner, which meets us as the characteristic feature of the religion of the New Testament. Between the faith of the two Testaments there exists, indeed, no further difference than that which the progress of the historical working out of redemption brought with it.

(3) New Testament. The word in the New Testament denotes: (1) The truth of the gospel of Christ and the kingdom of God (Acts vi:7; xxiv:24; Rom. i:5; Gal. i:23; Phil. i:27; 1 Tim. iii:9; Jude, ver. 3), "the faith which was once delivered to the saints," for the truth and faithfulness of God (Rom. iii:3), and for the persuasion

Fair Havens of Crete.

ciple is there designated by other terms, such as to "look" to God (Is. xlv:22), to "wait on" him (Ps. xxvii:14), and to "trust" in him (Nah. i:7).

Abraham is "the father of the faithful," because unbounded trust in God was the very essence of his piety. (Comp. Rom. iv:1). Paul derives the theme of his Epistle to the Romans from the passage of Habakkuk: "The just shall live by faith" (Rom. i:17; comp. Hab. ii:4). The Epistle to the Hebrews gives a bright catalogue of the heroes of faith under the old dispensation (xi: 1 ff).

To believe in God, in the Old Testament sense, is thus not merely to assent to his word, but with firm and unwavering confidence to rest in security and trustfulness upon Him.

Despite the infrequency of the occurrence on its pages of the terms 'faith,' 'to believe,' the religion of the Old Testament is thus obviously as fundamentally a religion of faith as is that of the New Testament. There is a sense, to be sure, in which all religion presupposes faith (Heb. xi:6), and in this broad sense the religion of Israel, too, necessarily rested on faith. But the religion of Israel

of the mind as to the lawfulness of things indifferent (Rom. xiv:22, 23.)

(2) The act by which we lay hold of and appropriate the truths of the gospel and Jesus Christ, and rely for salvation upon the work done by him in our stead. This is the prevailing sense of the word (Matt. viii:10; John iii:16; Rom. i:16, etc.; and all through John and the Pauline Epistles).

(4) Saving Faith. (1) In the breadth of its idea, faith is thus the going out of the heart from itself and its resting on God in confident trust for all good. But the scriptural revelation has to do with, and is directed to the needs of, not man in the abstract, but sinful man; and for sinful man this hearty reliance on God necessarily becomes humble trust in him for the fundamental need of the sinner—forgiveness of sins and reception into favor. In response to the revelations of his grace and the provisions of his mercy, it commits itself without reserve and with abnegation of all self-dependence to him as its sole and sufficient Savior, and thus, in one act, empties itself of all claim on God and casts itself upon his grace alone for salvation.

(2) This appears to be the plain scriptural representation of this doctrine; and we may infer from it (a) that the faith by which we are justified is not a mere assent to the doctrines of the gospel, which leaves the heart unmoved and unaffected by a sense of the evil and danger of sin and the desire of salvation, although it supposes this assent; nor (b) is it that more lively and cordial assent to, and belief in, the doctrine of the gospel, touching our sinful and lost condition, which is wrought in the heart by the Spirit of God, and from which springeth repentance, although this must precede it; nor (c) is it only the assent of the mind to the method by which God justifies the ungodly by faith in the sacrifice of his Son, although this is an element of it; but it is (d) a hearty concurrence of the will and affections with this plan of salvation, which implies a renunciation of every other refuge, and an actual trust in the Savior, and personal appropriation of his merit; such a belief of the gospel by the power of the Spirit of God as leads us to come to Christ, to receive Christ, to trust in Christ, and to commit the keeping of our souls into his hands, in humble confidence of his ability and his willingness to save us.

Faith therefore apprehends Christ, and takes actual hold of him and all his benefits. Hence he who believes in Christ has already eternal life (John iii:36).

(3) By faith we "put on" Christ. It is by faith that we are justified, and not by works. The work of salvation was all accomplished when the Savior uttered the words, "It is finished."

The *saving power* of faith resides thus not in itself, but in the Almighty Savior on whom it rests. It is never on account of its formal nature as a psychic act that faith is conceived in Scripture to be saving—as if this frame of mind or attitude of heart were itself a virtue with claims on God for reward, or at least especially pleasing to him (either in its nature or as an act of obedience), and thus predisposing him to favor, or as if it brought the soul into an attitude of receptivity or of sympathy with God, or opened a channel of communication from him. It is not faith that saves, but faith in Jesus Christ; faith in any other savior, or in this or that philosophy or human conceit (Col. ii:16, 18; 1 Tim. iv:1), or in any other gospel than that of Jesus Christ and him as crucified (Gal. i:8, 9), brings not salvation, but a curse. It is not, strictly speaking, even faith in Christ that saves, but Christ that saves through faith. The saving power resides exclusively, not in the act of faith or the attitude of faith, or the nature of faith, but in the object of faith; and in this the whole biblical representation centers, so that we could not more radically misconceive it than by transferring to faith even the smallest fraction of that saving energy which is attributed in the Scriptures solely to Christ himself.

(4) But a living faith will be accompanied by works, as much as a rose must diffuse perfume, and a good tree bring forth good fruit. As our Lord said, "Thy faith hath made thee whole," so Paul says, "By grace are ye saved through faith; and that not of yourselves; *it is* the gift of God" (Eph. ii:8).

But "faith without works is dead" (James ii: 26). Faith is operative in love (Gal. v:6).

B. B. Warfield, Hastings' *Bib. Dict.*; Schaff, *Bib. Dict.* See works on systematic theology.

FAITHFULNESS (fāth'ful-nĕs), (Heb. אֱמוּנָה, *em-oo-naw'*, faithfulness, stability).

(1) Faithfulness is a divine attribute, and denotes the certainty of the accomplishment of all that the Divine Being has declared, in the promises which he has made to his people. (1) In respect to temporal blessings (1 Tim. iv:8; Ps. lxxxiv:11; Is. xxxiii:16). (2) To spiritual blessings (1 Cor. i:9): In supporting them in temptation (1 Cor. x:13); encouraging them under persecution (1 Pet. iv:12, 13; Is. xli:10); sanctifying afflictions (Heb. xii:4-12); directing them in difficulties (1 Thess. v:24); enabling them to persevere (Jer. xxxi:40); bringing them to glory (1 John ii:25). (Buck, *Theolog. Dict.*)

(2) Faithfulness is also used regarding men: "He was a *faithful* man" (Hebrew, *trustworthy, reliable* (Neh. vii:2); "who then is that faithful (trusty) and wise steward?" (Luke xii:42, etc.) *"The Faithful"* was the general and favorite name in the early Church to denote baptized persons and specifically applied to them, as distinguished from the clergy, catechumens, penitents, and sinners.

FAITHLESS (fāth'lĕs), (Gr. ἄπιστος, *ap'is-tos*, Matt. xvii:17; John xx:27), disbelieving, or without Christian faith, with special reference to the heathen.

FAITH, RULE OF (fāth, rul ŏv). In the early Church the summary of doctrines taught to catechumens, and to which they were obliged to subscribe before baptism. It was afterward applied to the Apostles' Creed.

(1) **Protestant Doctrine.** One of the chief doctrinal elements of the Reformation was the sufficiency of the Scriptures for faith and salvation.

(2) **Roman Catholic.** The teaching of the Roman Catholic Church is contained in the *Catechism of the Council of Trent,* which, in the *Preface,* declares that "all the doctrines of Christianity in which the faithful are to be instructed are derived from the word of *God,* which includes Scriptures and tradition."

FAITH, THE CHRISTIAN. To those who receive the light, in the sense of not refusing it, revelation is one whole, and all its glorious system of truth is received and surely believed. To them it is both objectively and subjectively the faith; and, inasmuch as Christianity has brought it in all fullness into the world, it is to them the Christian faith. This phrase has therefore a larger meaning. It signifies that it is not their philosophy simply, the glory of their reason, the tradition they have derived from their fathers, but the rich inheritance which the Holy Spirit has given to that one supreme faculty of their souls, the faith which is the *evidence of things not seen.* It is a body of truth which, as reason did not give it, so reason cannot take it away. It is a region in which they walk by faith, which their faith habitually visits, in which their faith lives, and moves, and has its being" (Pope, *Compend. Christian Theol.,* p. 45). (Quoted in Barnes' *Bib. Cyc.*)

FALCON (fa'k'n).

A diurnal bird of prey other than a vulture. The family includes among its genera falcons strictly so called, hawks, kites, eagles. The word is used in R. V. to render the Hebrew *'Ayyah* (Job xxviii:7; in A. V. vulture), an unclean bird (Lev. xi:14; Deut. xiv:13; in A. V. kite). Several varieties are mentioned by Tristram as occurring in Palestine; the hobby hawk (*Falco subbuteo*), the red-legged hobby (*F. vespertinus*), the Eleanora falcon (*F. eleanoræ*). (See VULTURE.)

FALL OF MAN (fal ŏv măn). A theological term which denotes the loss of those perfections and that happiness which his Maker bestowed on him at his creation, through transgression of a positive command, given for the trial of man's obedience, and as a token of his holding everything of God, as lord paramount of the creation, with the use of everything in it, exclusive of the fruit of one tree.

(1) **Account in Genesis.** The account in Genesis is that a garden having been planted by the Creator, for the use of man, he was placed in it, "to dress it, and to keep it;" that in this garden two trees were specially distinguished, one as "the tree of life," the other as "the tree of the knowledge of good and evil;" that from eating of the latter Adam was restrained by positive interdict, and by the penalty, "In the day thou eatest thereof, thou shalt surely die;" that the serpent, who was more subtle than any beast of the field, tempted the woman to eat, by denying that death would be the consequence, and by assuring her that her eyes and her husband's eyes "would be opened," and that they would "be as gods, knowing good and evil;" that the woman took of the fruit, gave of it to her husband, who also ate; that for this act of disobedience they were expelled from the garden, made subject to death, and laid under other maledictions.

(2) **Varied Interpretations.** The character of the primitive record in Genesis has been the subject of much discussion. Some have contended that the account is purely literal; others, that it is figurative, poetic, or allegorical; still others, rationalistic or semirationalistic, relegate the whole matter to the realm of the mythical. This last view, of course, cannot be consistently held by anyone who accepts the Scriptures as of divine authority.

It must be admitted that the account leaves room for many questions both as to its form and its meaning in relation to incidental details. But still the great, underlying, essential facts are sufficiently clear, especially when the account is taken in connection with other Scriptures. They are as follows (Barnes' *Bib. Dict.*):

Those holding the orthodox view maintain that the account of Moses is to be taken as a matter of real history, and according to its literal import.

It is claimed that this is established by two considerations, against which, as being facts, nothing can successfully be urged. (1) The first is that the account of the fall of the first pair is a part of a continuous history. Either, then, the account of the fall must be taken as history, or the historical character of the whole five books of Moses must be unsettled. (2) The second consideration, as establishing the literal sense of the history, is that, as such, it is referred to and reasoned upon in various parts of Scripture (Job xx:4, 5; xxxi:33; xv:14).

"Eden" and "the garden of the Lord" are also frequently referred to in the prophets. We have the "tree of life" mentioned several times in the Proverbs and in the Revelation. "God," says Solomon, "made man upright." The enemies of Christ and his church are spoken of, both in the Old and New Testaments, under the names of "the serpent," and "the dragon;" and the habit of the serpent to lick the dust is also referred to by Isaiah.

If the history of the fall, as recorded by Moses, were an allegory, or anything but a literal history, several of the above allusions would have no meaning; but the matter is put beyond all possible doubt in the New Testament, unless the same culpable liberties be taken with the interpretation of the words of our Lord and of St. Paul as with those of the Jewish lawgiver (Matt. xix:4; 5; 1 Cor. xv:22; 2 Cor. xi:3; 1 Tim. ii:13, 14; Rom. v:12-19). (3) When, therefore, it is considered that these passages are introduced, not for rhetorical illustration, or in the way of classical quotation, but are made the basis of grave and important reasonings, which embody some of the most important doctrines of the Christian revelation, and of important social duties and points of Christian order and decorum, it would be to charge the writers of the New Testament with the grossest absurdity, nay, with even culpable and unworthy trifling, to suppose them to argue from the history of the fall as a narrative, when they knew it to be an allegory. (4) By the act of disobedience of our first parents "sin entered into the world and death by sin." Shame and alienation from God were the first visible consequences. The image of God, which contained among its features "righteousness and true holiness," was marred and broken, though not completely lost. (See IMAGE OF GOD.) Expulsion from Eden followed. The ground was cursed on account of sin. Sorrow and toil and struggle with the evil in human nature became the lot of mankind. (For a full presentation of the subject see ADAM. For distinctively doctrinal, Calvinistic and Arminian views, see PREDESTINATION.)

FALLOW DEER (făl'lŏ dēr), a wrong rendering of Heb. יַחְמוּר, *yakh-moor'*, Deut. xiv:5; 1 Kings iv:23), which is correctly rendered by R. V. "roebuck." (See ROEBUCK.)

FALLOW GROUND (făl'lŏ ground), (Heb. נִיר, *neer*), a field plowed up and left for seeding; as summer fallow, intelligently carried on, is a sure method of destroying weeds (Jer. iv:3; Hos. x:12).

FALLOW YEAR (yēr). See SABBATH.

FALSE CHRISTS (fals krīsts), (Gr. ψευδόχριστοι, *psyoo-dokh'ris-toi*), those who falsely claim to be Messiah: foretold by Jesus (Matt. xxiv:24; Mark xiii:22).

FALSE PROPHET (fals prŏf'ĕt), a pseudo-prophet pretending to be sent from God, a false teacher (Matt. vii:15; xxiv:11, 24, etc.) "The false prophet" (Rev. xvi:13) is used for the second "beast," the mythological system of paganism.

FAMILIAR SPIRIT (fà-mĭl'yĕr spĭr'ĭt), (Heb. אוֹב, *obe*).

The spirit of a dead person which professed mediums claimed to summon to consultation (Deut. xviii:11), and which appeared to speak from the earth (Is. xxix:4), or to dwell in the controlling medium (Lev. xx:27, in Hebrew). The medium was called the possessor or lord of a spirit (1 Sam. xxviii:7, in Hebrew). (See DIVINATION.)

FAMILY (făm'ĭ-lў).

(1) The idea of the family in Greece was that of the nucleus of society or of the state. The idea of the Christian family, on the contrary (Eph. iii:15), is a communion resting on an ethico-religious foundation, and forming the closest of all human relationships. It is a copy of the highest and most perfect union, that of the church with Christ, its head. (McC. and Str. *Bib. Cyc.*)

(2) The influence of the Christian religion upon the customs and habits of family life was very considerable, even from the first; although it did not aim at making any abrupt or sudden changes, except in those things which were necessarily sinful.

The great Christian doctrines which so powerfully affect the feelings, hopes, and whole inner life of those who heartily receive them, led at once to the renunciation of idolatry in all its forms, and of the excesses and licentiousnesses then so common and so little thought of; and inculcated new principles of thought and action, which operated more or less powerfully in every direction. But the ordinary usages of domestic life, which were not directly connected with the religious and moral obliquities of the old polytheism, were apparently left untouched by any positive interference or command. Christianity proved itself the salt of the earth by gradually interpenetrating the surrounding mass of pagan civilization, and not by shrinking from all contact with it.

The elevation of the female sex was one of the most conspicuous of the indirect results which rapidly followed the reception of the new religion. The position of women among the Jews, and the manner in which Jesus had received them as his disciples and friends, must have taught the apostles, if they needed any such teaching, what place women were entitled to hold in the social economy of the church. And accordingly, wherever Christ was proclaimed, women were invited and welcomed into the Christian communities, and were admitted equally with men to all Christian privileges. Hence in a Christian family the wife and mother held an honorable place; and the conjugal union, the source of all other family relationships, being thus honored, communicated a happy influence throughout the household.

(3) Before Christianity became the prevailing and established religion, families were in continual danger of being molested by popular violence, and of being utterly broken up in times of legalized persecution. But, besides these dangers and troubles, there were sometimes others hardly less painful within the family itself, when only a part of the household had become Christians. The antagonism and consequent discomfort, if not positive misery, must then have been almost perpetual; and the difficulty of maintaining religious faithfulness, without losing family affection or breaking family ties, must have been very great. Jesus himself had warned his disciples beforehand that "a man's foes might be those of his own household;" and that his religion, in such a case, might bring "not peace but a sword." St. Paul, while desirous that this difference of religion should not actually separate a husband and wife, admitted that it would and must sometimes have this effect. Tertullian (ad Uxor. ii:4) describes in detail the sort of hindrances, opposition and ridicule which a Christian woman must expect if she married a husband who was an unbeliever; and how impossible she would find it to fulfill in peace, if she could fulfill at all, her Christian duties—even if nothing worse occurred. But in times of persecution, or of any strong excitement of anti-Christian feeling, it was not merely difficulties and discomforts that had to be encountered. The strongest words of Christ were then often literally realized, when the most powerful natural affections were shattered, and Christians were betrayed and denounced by their nearest relatives and given up to the persecutor's sword. See an early instance of this in Justin Martyr, Apol. ii:2.

(4) Parental obligations include the maintenance of children (1 Tim. 5:8) and their education in its fullest sense (Exod. xii:26, 27; Deut. vi:6, 7; Eph. vi:4).

The filial obligations are obedience (Luke ii:51; Eph. vi:1; Col. iii:20), reverence (Exod. xx:12; comp. Eph. vi:1, 2), and grateful requital (1 Tim. v:4; comp. John xix:26).

(5) The entire life of the Christian family is a continuous act of worship in the more extended sense of the term. Hence the importance of *family worship*.

FAMINE (făm'ĭn), (Heb. רָעָב, *raw-awb'*). We have an account of at least eight famines in Palestine and the neighboring countries.

They were among the judgments of God for national sins, and were often prophetically announced. Two famines occurred in the lifetimes of Abraham and Isaac (Gen. xii:10; xxvi:1); another in Jacob's time (Gen. xli:56).

The first mention of a famine which occurs in Scripture is in Gen. xii:10, where we read that so early as the days of the patriarch Abraham 'there was a famine in the land,' which is described as so grievous as to compel the father of the faithful to quit Canaan. The country to which he resorted was, as we might expect, the land of Egypt, the early and lasting fertility of which is a well-known historical fact. In Gen. xxvi:1 this famine is designated as 'the first,' that is, the first known, or of which there was any record. The same passage informs us of another famine, as stated above, which afflicted 'the land' in the days of Isaac, who seems to have contemplated a descent into Egypt; but who, being instructed of God, removed to a part of Arabia Petræa (Gen. xxvi:17), named Gerar, a city of the Philistines, whose monarch's name was Abimelech.

The famine in Egypt while Joseph was governor lasted seven years. The ordinary cause of dearth in Egypt is connected with the annual overflow of the Nile. If the rise of the waters is in any year below a certain standard, the country affords scanty supplies of food, and may for the greater part remain a desert. But more than local causes must have been in operation in the case before us; for we are told that 'the famine was sore in all lands,' that 'the famine was over all the face of the earth.' By the foresight and wisdom of Joseph, however, provision against the evil had been made in Egypt, while other countries were left to suffer the unmitigated consequences of their neglect. The provision made by Joseph must have been of a most abundant nature, since the period during which the dearth lasted was no less than seven years, and the people of other parts sought and received supplies in Egypt—'all countries came in to Egypt to buy corn.' Among other lands, Canaan suffered from the famine; which was the immediate occasion of Jacob sending his sons down into Egypt, of the discovery which they made of their lost brother, and of the settlement in that land of the descendants of Abraham, an event of the highest consequence in the sequel, and serving to illustrate the benignity and wisdom of Divine Providence in the evils with which, under its influence, the world is afflicted.

This famine was made by Joseph the occasion of one of the greatest social revolutions which history records. The details may be found in the book of Genesis; and it is enough to say here that, as the special administrator of the affairs of the country, Joseph got into his hands all the property of the kingdom, including the land, excepting that which belonged to the priests, and gave the same back to the people as tenants at will, on condition of their paying to the king 'the fifth,' probably of the annual produce. (See Joseph.)

Famines are mentioned in the time of the

judges (Ruth i:1), and in the time of King David (2 Sam. xxi:1), but it is not until the time of Elijah that any account is given of the failure of the pasturage and springs. 'There shall not be dew nor rain these years, but according to my word' (1 Kings xvii:1). 'And Ahab said unto Obadiah: Go through the land, unto all the fountains of water, and unto all the brooks; peradventure we may find grass and save the horses and mules alive, that we lose not all the beasts' (xviii:5).

Several causes of famine are given: (1) God's blessing withheld (Hos. ii:8, 9; Hag. i:6); (2) want of seasonable rain (1 Kings xvii:1; Jer. xiv:1-4; Amos iv:7, *sq.*)

The most terrible results of famine related in the Bible are due to the hand of man, and this was well recognized by King David. 'And David said unto Gad, I am in a great strait; let us fall now into the hand of the Lord, for his mercies are great; and let me not fall into the hand of man' (2 Sam. xxiv:14). 'And he shall eat the fruit of thy cattle, and the fruit of thy ground, until thou be destroyed; which also shall not leave thee corn, wine or oil, the increase of thy kine, or the young of thy flock, until he have caused thee to perish' (Deut. xxviii:51). 'And thou shalt eat the fruit of thine own body, the flesh of thy sons, and of thy daughters, which the Lord thy God hath given thee, in the siege, and in the straitness, wherewith thine enemies shall straiten thee' (verse 53). 'And there was a great famine in Samaria, and, behold, they besieged it, until an ass's head was sold for fourscore pieces of silver, and the fourth part of a cab of dove's dung for five pieces of silver' (2 Kings vi:25). 'And she answered, This woman said unto me, Give thy son, that we may eat him to-day, and we will eat my son to-morrow' (verse 28).

Figurative. The prophets and our Lord himself use highly figurative language regarding famine, in their righteous endeavors to turn wicked men and wicked nations from the evil of their ways (Ezek. vi:11; Matt. xxiv:7). In Amos viii:11 *sq.*, a heavier woe than even the want of bread is appropriately spoken of under the appellation of a famine: 'Behold, the days come, saith the Lord God, that I will send a famine in the land; not a famine of bread nor a thirst for water, but of hearing the word of the Lord; and they shall wander from sea to sea, and from the north even to the east, they shall run to and fro to seek the word of the Lord, and shall not find it; in that day shall the fair virgins and the young men faint for thirst.' In Zeph. ii:11 it is symbolical of the destruction of idols.

FAN (făn), (Heb. זָרָה, *zaw-raw'*, to *toss* about; מִזְרֶה, *miz-reh'*; Gr. πτύον, *ptoo'on*).

An instrument used in the East for winnowing corn. Fans are of two kinds—one a sort of fork, having teeth, with which they throw up the corn to the wind, that the chaff may be blown away; the other is formed to produce wind when the air is calm (Is. xxx:24; Luke iii:17).

Figurative. (1) God's judgments are compared to a *fan;* by these he turns up persons and nations to the winds of his retributive providences, and scatters and disperses them for their sins, and his thus scattering and overturning them is called his *fanning* of them (Jer. xv:7; comp. Is. xxx:24). (2) The Medes, Persians and others, by whose means he executed his scattering and overturning judgments, are called *fanners* (Jer. li:2). (3) Christ's *fan is in his hand,* with which he *will thoroughly purge his floor;*

by the gospel dispensation and spiritual influence which he introduced, men were or shall be put to the trial, and the evil be separated from the good (Matt. iii:12).

FANNERS (făn'nērs), (Heb. זוּר, *zoor*, strangers), rendering in the A. V. (Jer. li:2); but properly "strangers," and so translated in the R. V.

FARE (fâr), (Heb. שָׁלוֹם, *shaw-lome'*, 1 Sam. xvii:18, welfare, prosperity; Gr. εὐφραίνω, *yoo-frah-ee'no*, Luke xvi:19, to make glad, to make merry).

FARM. See AGRICULTURE.

FARTHING (fär'thĭng). Two names of coins in the New Testament are thus translated: (1) Gr. κοδράντης, *kod-ran'tace*, Matt. v:26; Mark xii:42. It was equivalent to two lepta (A. V. "mites"). Its value was about 3.8 mills. (2) Gr. ἀσσάριον, *as-sar'ee-on*, Matt. x:29; Luke xii:6. Its value is estimated at three-fourths of a penny English money, or one and a half cents of American. (See MONEY.)

FASHION, FASHIONING (Gr. εἶδος, *i'dos*, Luke ix:29). "The fashion of his countenance was changed."

(1) **Appearance.** The *appearance* of a thing, as Jas. i:24, Tyndale, 'For assone as he hath loked on him silfe, he goeth his waye, and forgetteth immediattlie what his fassion was.' So in A. V., Luke ix:29, as he prayed, the fashion of his countenance was altered.' Especially denoting outward visible appearance in contrast with inner reality, as Shaks. *Merch. of Venice,* iv:1, 18—
'Shylock, the world thinks, and I think so too,
That thou but leadst this fashion of thy malice
To the last hour of act; and then 'tis thought
Thou'lt show thy mercy and remorse more strange
Than is thy strange apparent cruelty.'

(2) **Form, etc.** And being found in *fashion* as a man, he humbled himself, etc. (Phil. ii:8).

Fashion has here its original sense of *make, shape, form*—a wider meaning than that which it now bears.

FASTS, FASTING (făsts, făst'ing), (Heb. צוּם, *tsoom*, to *cover* the mouth; Gr. νηστεύω, *nace-tyoo'o*, to abstain), has, in all ages and among all nations, been practiced in times of mourning, sorrow and affliction.

It is in some sort inspired by nature, which, under these circumstances, refuses nourishment, and suspends the cravings of hunger. We see no example of fasting, properly so called, before Moses; whether the patriarchs had not observed it, which yet is difficult to believe, since there were great mournings among them, which are particularly described, as that of Abraham for Sarah, and that of Jacob for Joseph, or whether he did not think it necessary to mention it expressly, is uncertain.

(1) **Among the Israelites.** It appears by the law that devotional fasts for expiation of sins were common among the Israelites. There seems, however, no reason to doubt that 'to afflict the soul' bore with it the meaning of fasting. To a mere English reader the phrase seems to comprise all kinds of voluntary mortifications, but 'soul' in Hebrew not seldom denotes the 'appetite' (Prov. xxvii:7). Accordingly the words regard immediately abstinence from food, and most probably (so far as they go) nothing more.

The sole fast required by Moses was on the great day of annual atonement. This observance seems always to have retained some prominence as 'the fast' (Acts xxvii:9), but what the observance of the enjoined duty involved we are nowhere expressly informed.

(2) Other General Fasts. Other general fasts, however, were in course of ages introduced, which were celebrated at fixed times every successive year. In the reign of Zedekiah, Nebuchadnezzar besieged and captured Jerusalem, which calamity led to the establishment of a fast on the seventeenth day of the fourth month (Thammuz, July) (Jer. lii:6, 7; Zech. viii:19). In the last passage other fasts are enumerated, namely, 'the fast of the fifth, and the fast of the seventh, and the fast of the tenth.' That of the fifth month (Ab, August) was held on the ninth day, in mournful commemoration of the burning of the city by Nebuzar-adan, a servant of the king of Babylon, who 'burnt the house of the Lord, and the king's house, and all the houses of Jerusalem, and every great man's house' (2 Kings xxv:8, sq.; Jer. lii; 12; Zech. vii:3-5; viii:19). The fast of the seventh month (Tishri, October) was established to bewail the murder of Gedaliah at Mizpah (Jer. xli:1, sq.; 2 Kings xxv:25). That of the tenth month (Tebeth, January) was held on the tenth day to commemorate the commencement of the siege of Jerusalem on the part of Nebuchadnezzar (2 Kings xxv:1; Zech. viii:19; see also Hieron. ad. Zech. c. viii., and Hieros. Taanith, 68; Reland, p. 471).

(3) Particular Occasions. On particular and signal occasions extraordinary fasts were appointed. Thus when Naboth was condemned for blasphemy because he would not give up the inheritance of his fathers to Ahab, Jezebel, as a part of her plan for gratifying the evil desires of her royal husband, ordered a fast to be proclaimed (1 Kings xxi:9; comp. Jer. xxxvi:9; 2 Chron. xx:3). So in Judges xx:26, the children of Israel 'came unto the house of God and wept, and sat there before the Lord and fasted until even, and offered burnt-offerings and peace-offerings before the Lord,' when they had suffered a calamitous defeat at the hands of the Benjamites. Other instances of fasting on occasion of loss in battle may be found in 1 Sam. xxxi:11-13; Baruch i:5. In Joel i-ii a fast is enjoined with a view to turn away the wrath of God as displayed in the terrible consequences of the invasion of the land of Judæa by an army of devastating locusts (Credner's Joel). The idea also prevailed that a special fast might have the effect of averting the divine displeasure and securing the divine co-operation in any great undertaking (Jonah iii:5; 1 Sam. vii:5, 6, 8, 10, 12; 1 Macc. iii:47; 2 Macc. xiii:12; Judith iv:11; vi:19). Local fasts are at a later period sometimes held in order to avert calamity or procure a favor from heaven; and the Sanhedrim ordered general fasts when the nation was threatened with any great evil, such as drought or famine (Joseph. Vit. sec. 56; Taanith, i:5), as was usual with the Romans in their supplications (Liv. iii:7; x:23; Smith's Dict. of Greek and Roman Antiq.).

(4) Private Fasts. There were also private fasts, though the Mosaic law did not require them. They were held in connection with individual or family incidents, and agreed in aim and tendency with fasts of a general and public nature. Examples may be found in 1 Sam. i:7; xx:34; 1 Kings xxi:9; Ezra x:6; Neh. i:4.

After the exile private fasts became very frequent (Lightfoot, p. 318), awaiting the call of no special occasion, but entering as a regular part of the current religious worship (Suet. Aug. 76; Tacit. Hist. v:4, 3).

The parable of the Pharisee and Publican (Luke xviii:9; comp. Matt ix:14) shows how much the Pharisees were given to voluntary and private fasts—'I fast twice a week.' The first was

on the fifth day of the week, on which Moses ascended to the top of Mount Sinai; the second was on the second day, on which he came down (Taanith, ii:9; Hieros. Megillah, 75, 1). The Essenes and the Therapeutæ also were much given to such observances (Philo, Vit. Contempl. p. 613; Euseb. Præp. Evan. ix:3).

Fasts were considered as a useful exercise in preparing the mind for special religious impressions. Thus Dan. x:2, sq., 'In those days I Daniel was mourning three full weeks., I ate no pleasant bread, neither came flesh nor wine in my mouth. Then I lifted up my eyes and looked, and behold a certain man,' etc. (see also Acts xiii:3; xiv:23). From Matt. xvii:21, 'Howbeit this kind (of demons) goeth not out but by prayer and fasting,' it would appear that the practice under consideration was considered in the days of Christ to act in certain special cases as an exorcism.

(5) Mourning. Fasting was accompanied by the ordinary signs of grief among the Israelites, as may be seen in 1 Macc. iii:47, 'Then they fasted that day and put on sackcloth, and cast ashes upon their heads and rent their clothes.' The fast ordinarily lasted from evening to evening, but was not observed on the sabbath or on festival days (Joseph. Antiq. iii:10, 3; Judith viii:6; Mischn. Taanith, ii:10). The abstinence was either partial or total. In the case of the latter food was entirely foregone, but this ordinarily took place only in fasts of short duration; and abstinence from food in eastern climes is more easy and less detrimental (if not in some cases positively useful) than keeping from food would be with us in these cold, damp, northern regions (Esther iv:16). In the case of partial abstinence the time was longer, the denial in degree less. When Daniel (x:2) was 'mourning three full weeks,' he ate no 'pleasant bread, neither came flesh nor wine in my mouth.'

(6) Duration. There does not appear to have been any fixed and recognized periods during which these fasts endured. From one day to forty days fasts were observed. The latter period appears to have been regarded with feelings of peculiar sanctity, owing doubtless to certain events in Jewish history. Thus Moses 'was with the Lord on Mount Sinai forty days and forty nights, he did neither eat bread, nor drink water' (Exod. xxxiv:28). So, also, Elijah (1 Kings xix: 8) 'arose and did eat and drink, and went in the strength of that meat forty days and forty nights unto Horeb the mount of God.' The same was the number of days that our Lord fasted in the desert in connection with his temptation (Matt. iv:1-11; Mark i:12, 13; Luke iv: 1-13). In the latter case the abstinence appears to have been entire, for Luke expressly declares he ate nothing, καὶ οὐκ ἔφαγεν οὐδέν, and he did not eat anything. In Dan. i:10, 16, a passage is found which shows that abstaining from meat and wine did not imply total abstinence, for Daniel and his friends had 'pulse to eat and water to drink' (Wetstein, p. 270; De Wette, Kritik der Mos. Ges. p. 245).

(7) Abuses. We have already seen how qualified the sanction was which Moses gave to the observance of fasting as a religious duty. In the same spirit which actuated him, the prophets bore testimony against the lamentable abuses to which the practice was turned in the lapse of time and with the increase of social corruption (Is. lviii:4, sq.; Jer. xiv:12; Zech. vii:5). Continuing the same species of influence and perfecting that spirituality in religion which Moses began, our Lord rebuked the Pharisees sternly for their outward and hypocritical pretences in the fasts which they observed (Matt. vi:16, *sq.*), and actually abstained from appointing any fast whatever as a part of his own religion (Matt. ix:14).

From the passages referred to it is at least clear that Jesus ascribed to fasts no essential worth, nor required any such observance from his followers. Whether and how far he *allowed* fasting as a means of religious improvement is a question which our space does not permit us to discuss (Neander, *Leben Jesu*).

(8) Early Christians. That the early Christians observed the ordinary fasts which the public practice of their day sanctioned is clear from more than one passage in the New Testament Scriptures (Acts xiii:2; xiv:23; 2 Cor. vi:5); but in this they probably did nothing more than yield obedience, as in general they thought themselves bound to do, to the law of their fathers so long as the Mosaic institutions remained entire. And though the great body of the Christian Church held themselves free from all ritual and ceremonial observances when God in his providence had brought Judaism to a termination in the rasure of the Holy City and the closing of the Temple, yet the practice of fasting thus originated might have easily and unobservedly been transmitted from year to year and from age to age.

On fasting in the Christian Church consult Bingham, *Orig. Eccl.* bk. xxi, chap. i-iii; Coleman, *Ancient Christianity*, p. 552 ff.).

FAT (făt), **(1)** (Heb. יֶקֶב, *yeh'keb*, Joel ii:24; iii:13), elsewhere rendered wine press. A. S. *foet*, a vessel. In Coleridge, *Gloss.*, it is found as "fet." Fat, meaning a large vessel for holding liquids, has been displaced by 'vat' in literary English. The difference between the spellings, says Skeat (*Etymol. Dict. s. v.*), is one of dialect only, 'fat' being northern and 'vat' southern. Fat occurs in A. V. (Joel ii:24), 'the fats shall overflow with wine and oil,' and Joel iii:13; in the compound 'winefat' in Is. lxiii:2; Mark xii:1 (A. V. 1611 'wine fat' as two words); and 'pressfat' (1611 'presse-fat'), Hag. ii:16.

(2) (Heb. חֵלֶב, *khay'leb*). In Lev. iii there are minute details of the parts of victims which were to be specially appropriated to the altar. Among these all the internal *fat* is minutely specified, particularly the fat of the kidneys; and of external parts the tail of the sheep, which, in the common species of Western Asia, is a mass of fat (iii:4, 9, 10, 15); and the whole concludes with 'All the fat is the Lord's; ye shall eat neither fat nor blood' (iii:17). The reason assigned, namely, that the fat was consecrated to the altar, could only apply with respect to that of animals used in sacrifice, which were also usually employed for food. One point seems to have been very generally overlooked, which is, that not fat absolutely but particular fat parts only are interdicted. They might eat the fat involved in the muscular tissue—in short, fat meat; and we know that animals were actually fattened for food (1 Kings iv:23; Jer. xlvi:21; Luke xv:23). This was, however, not a usual practice; and even at this day in the East, domestic cattle seldom undergo any preparatory feeding or fattening before being killed. Hence there is little fat in the carcass, except that belonging to the parts specified in the prohibition, which is all more or less of the nature of suet.

Various reasons have been assigned for this somewhat remarkable restriction. The secondary cause, that the fat was consecrated to the altar and therefore was to be abstained from, is not all, for it is usually considered that it was thus consecrated to give a religious sanction to a prohibition expedient on other grounds.

The truth probably is that this suet or suet-like fat is not particularly wholesome or digestible in warm climates, if anywhere, and is particularly unsuitable for persons subject to cutaneous diseases, as the Israelites appear to have been at the time of their leaving Egypt.

Figurative. (1) The Hebrews used the word which we render *fat* to signify the best of anything, and, next to blood, it was the sign of healthfulness and vigor; hence we read of the *fat* of wheat; the *fat* of the land; the *fat* of the flock (Ps. lxxxi:16 and cxlvii:8, 9; Gen. xlvii:6; iv:4). (2) Wicked men are represented as *fat;* as *fatlings;* as *enclosed in their own fat*, when they abound in honor, power and wealth (Deut. xxxii:14, 15; Ezek. xxxix:18; Ps. xvii:10). (3) Their heart is *fat*, or *gross*, when men are self-conceited, stupid, careless, and unteachable (Ps. cxix:70; Is. vi:10). (4) They perish as the *fat of lambs* when they are easily and quickly wasted and destroyed (Ps. xxxvii:20). (5) Great men are represented as *fat ones*, because of their large possessions, joy and pleasure (Is. v:17 and x:16; Ezek. xxxiv:16, 20; Ps. xxii:29). (6) Saints are fat when they abound much in spiritual graces and comfort (Ps. xcii:14; Prov. xi:25; xiii:4; xv:30 and xxviii:25). (7) The sword of the Lord is *fat with fatness* when his judgments cut off multitudes of men, great and wealthy (Is. xxxiv:6).

FATHER (fä'thẽr), (Heb. אָב, *awb*, ancestor, source, inventor), this word, besides its obvious and primary sense, bears, in Scripture, a number of other applications, most of which have, through the use of the Bible, become more or less common in all Christian countries.

(1) The Divine Father. The term Father is very often applied to God himself (Gen. xliv:19, 20; Deut. xxxii:6; 2 Sam. vii:14; Ps. lxxxix:27, 28; Is. lxiii:16; lxiv:8). The New Testament leaves little room to question that it is the intention of the sacred record to set God before us as the Father of all men, in the general sense of creator and preserver of all men, but more especially of believers, whether Jews or Christians. To the same effect is also a passage in Josephus's paraphrase of the law (Deut. xxi:18-21), respecting rebellious sons, *'because he (God) is himself the father of the whole human race'* (*Antiq.* iv:8, 24).

Without doubt, however, God is in a more especial and intimate manner, even as by covenant, the Father of the Jews (Jer. xxxi:9; Is. lxiii:16; lxiv:8; John viii:41; v:45; 2 Cor. vi:18); and also of Christians, or rather of all pious and believing persons, who are called 'sons of God' (John i:12; Rom. viii:16, etc.). Thus Jesus, in speaking to his disciples, calls God their Father (Matt. vi:4, 8, 15, 18; x:20, 29; xiii:43, etc.). The Apostles, also, for themselves and other Christians, call him 'Father' (Rom. i:7; 1 Cor. i:3; 2 Cor. i:2; Gal. i:4; and many other places).

(2) Ancestors. *Father* is applied to any ancestor near or remote, or to ancestors ('fathers') in general. The progenitor, or founder, or *patriarch* of a tribe or nation, was also pre-eminently its father, as Abraham to the Jews. Examples of this abound. See, for instance, Deut. i:11; 1 Kings xi:12; Matt. iii:9; xxiii:30; Mark xi:10; Luke i:32, 73; vi:23, 26; John vii:22, etc.

(3) Chief or Ruler. *Father* is also applied as a title of respect to any head, chief, ruler, or elder, and especially to kings, prophets, and priests (Judg. xvii:10; xviii:19; I Sam. x:12; 2 Kings ii:12; v:13; vi:21; xiii:14; Prov. iv:1; Matt. xxiii:9; Acts vii:2; xxii:1; 1 Cor. iv:15, etc.).

(4) Author or Source. The author, source, or beginner of anything is also called the Father of the same, or of those who follow him. Thus Jabal is called 'the father of those who dwell in tents, and have cattle;' and Jubal, 'the father of all such as handle the harp and the organ' (Gen. iv:21, 22; comp. Job xxxviii:28; John viii:44; Rom. iv:12). This use of the word is exceedingly common in the East to this day, especially as applied in the formation of proper names, in which, also, the most curious Hebrew examples of this usage occur. (See Ab.)

(5) The Father's Authority. The authority of a father was very great in patriarchal times; and although the power of life and death was virtually taken from the parent by the law of Moses, which required him to bring his cause of complaint to the public tribunals (Deut. xxi:18-21), all the more real powers of the paternal character were not only left unimpaired, but were made in a great degree the basis of the judicial polity which that law established. The children and even the grandchildren continued under the roof of the father and grandfather; they labored on his account, and were the most submissive of his servants. The property of the soil, the power of judgment, the civil rights, belonged to him only, and his sons were merely his instruments and assistants.

(6) Filial Duty. Filial duty and obedience were, indeed, in the eyes of the Jewish legislator, of such high importance that great care was taken that the paternal authority should not be weakened by the withdrawal of a power so liable to fatal and barbarous abuse as that of capital punishment. Any outrage against a parent—a blow, a curse, or incorrigible profligacy—was made a capital crime (Exod. xxi:13, 17; Lev. xx:9). If the offense was public it was taken up by the witnesses as a crime against Jehovah, and the culprit was brought before the magistrates, whether the parent consented or not; and if the offense was hidden within the paternal walls, it devolved on the parents to denounce him and to require his punishment.

It is a beautiful circumstance in the law of Moses that this filial respect is exacted for the mother as well as for the father. The threats and promises of the legislator distinguish not the one from the other; and the fifth commandment associates the father and mother in a precisely equal claim to honor from their children. The development of this interesting feature of the Mosaical law belongs, however, to another head (see Woman). (Lane, *Mod. Egypt*, i:84; Atkinson, *Travels in Siberia*, p. 559).

FATHER, GOD THE (fä'thēr, gŏd thē). See Father, I.

FATHER-IN-LAW (fä'thēr-ĭn-lạ'). **1.** *Khawm* (Heb. חָם, from חָמָה, *khaw-maw'*), to join in affinity (Gen. xxxviii:13, 25).

2. *Khaw-than'* (Heb. חָתַן, *to marry*), one giving a daughter in marriage (Exod. iii:1; iv:18; xviii: 1-27, Num. x:29, etc.).

3. *Pen-ther-os'* (Gr. πενθερός), strictly one related by affinity, a wife's father (John xviii:13).

FATHER'S BROTHER (fä'thēr's brŭth'ēr), Heb. דּוֹד, *dode*), strictly *one beloved* (Is. v:1); an

uncle (Num. xxxvi:11; 2 Kings xxiv:17); in Exod. vi:20 used in the feminine as a father's sister, or aunt.

FATHER'S HOUSE (fä'thēr's hous), the name denoting *families* among the Israelites (Josh. xxii:14; comp. vii:14; xvi:18). (See Israel, Constitution of.)

FATHOM (făth'ŭm). See Table of Weights and Measures, p. 42, Appendix.

FATLING (făt'lĭng). **1.** An animal fatted for slaughter (Heb. מְרִיא, *mer-ee'*, 2 Sam. vi:13).

2. A *marrowy* sheep, particularly of the fat-tailed variety (Heb. מֵחַ, *may'akh*, Ps. lxvi:15).

3. A wrong rendering of *Mish-neh'* (Heb. מִשְׁנֶה, *repetition*, 1 Sam. xv:9). These were "animals of the *second birth*, which were considered superior to the others" (K. and D. *Com.*, in loco.)

FATTED FOWL (Heb. בַּרְבֻּרִים אֲבוּסִים, *bar-boo-reem' ay-boo-seem'*), are referred to among the daily provisions for Solomon's table (1 Kings iv: 23).

The meaning of *bar-boo-reem'* is uncertain. The earlier translators render it birds or fowls, others "geese" (from the Heb. בָּרַר, *baw-rar'*, "to be pure," because of their white feathers). A special variety of fowl may be meant.

FEASTS (fēsts), (Heb. מִשְׁתֶּה, *mish'teh*). The root idea of the word is to be found in what we should term the pleasures of the table, the exercise of hospitality.

(1) Early Hospitality. To what an early date the practices of hospitality are referable may be seen in Gen. xix:3, where we find Lot inviting the two angels; 'and they entered into his house; and he made them a feast;' which was obviously of a religious nature, since it is added, 'and did bake *unleavened* bread, and they did eat' (Judg. vi:19). It was usual not only thus to receive persons with choice viands, but also to dismiss them in a similar manner; accordingly Laban, when he had overtaken the fleeing Jacob, complains (Gen. xxxi:27), 'Wherefore didst thou steal away from me and didst not tell me, that I might have sent thee away with mirth, and with songs, and with tabret, and with harp?' See also 2 Sam. iii:20; 2 Kings vi:23; 1 Macc. xvi: 15. This practice explains the reason why the prodigal on his return was welcomed by a feast (Luke xv:23). Occasions of domestic joy were hailed with feasting; thus, in Gen. xxi:8, Abraham 'made a great feast the same day that Isaac was weaned.' Birthdays were thus celebrated (Gen. xl:20). 'Pharaoh, on his birthday, made a feast unto all his servants' (Job i:4; Matt. xiv: 6; comp. Herod. i:133). Marriage feasts were also common. Samson (Judg. xiv:10) on such an occasion 'made a feast,' and it is added, 'for so used the young men to do.' So Laban, when he gave his daughter Leah to Jacob (Gen. xxix:22), 'gathered together all the men of the place, and made a feast.' These festive occasions seem originally to have answered the important purpose of serving as evidence and attestation of the events which they celebrated, on which account relatives and neighbors were invited to be present (Ruth iv:10; John ii:1).

(2) Harvest Celebrations. Those processes in rural occupations by which the Divine bounties are gathered into the hands of man have in all ages been made seasons of festivity; accordingly, in 2 Sam. xiii:23, Absalom invites all the king's sons, and even David himself, to a sheep-shearing feast, on which occasion the guests became 'merry with wine' (1 Sam. xxv:2, *sq.*)   The vintage was also celebrated with festive eating and drinking (Judg. ix:27).

(3) **Funeral Feasts.** Feasting at funerals existed among the Jews (2 Sam. iii:33). In Jer. xvi:7, among other funeral customs, mention is made of 'the cup of consolation, to drink for their father or their mother,' which brings to mind the indulgence in spirituous liquors to which our ancestors were given, at interments, and which has not yet entirely disappeared (Carleton's *Irish Peasantry, England in the Nineteenth Century,* vol. ii). To what an extent expense was sometimes carried on these occasions may be learned from Josephus (*De Bell. Jud.* iv, i:1), who, having remarked that Archelaus 'mourned for his father seven days, and had given a very expensive funeral feast to the multitude,' states, 'which custom is the occasion of poverty to many of the Jews,' adding, 'Because they are forced to feast the multitude, for if any one omits it he is not *esteemed a holy person.*'

(4) **Sacrificial Feasts.** As among heathen nations, so also among the Hebrews, feasting made a part of the observances which took place on occasion of animal sacrifices (Deut. xii:6, 7; 1 Sam. ix:19; xvi:3, 5; 2 Sam. vi:19). These sacrificial meals were enjoyed in connection with peace offerings, whether eucharistic or votive. The kidneys, and all the inward fat, and the tail of the lamb, were burnt in the daily sacrifice; the breast and right shoulder fell to the priest; and the rest was to be eaten by the offerer and his friends, on the same day if the offering were eucharistic, on that and the next day if it were votive (Lev. iii:1-17; vii:11-21; 29-36; xix:5-8; xxii:29, 30). To the feast at the second tithe of the produce of the land, which was to be made every year and eaten at the annual festivals before Jehovah, not only friends, but strangers, widows, orphans, and Levites, were to be invited as well as the slaves. If the tabernacles were so distant as to make it inconvenient to carry thither the tithe, it was to be turned into money, which was to be spent at the place at which the festivals were held in providing feasts (Deut. xiv:22-27; xii:14; Tobit i:6). Charitable entertainments were also provided, at the end of three years, from the tithe of the increase. The Levite, the stranger, the fatherless and the widow were to be present (Deut. xii:17-19; xiv:28, 29; xxvi:12-15). At the feast of Pentecost the command is very express (Deut. xvi:11), 'Thou shalt rejoice before the Lord thy God, thou, and thy son, and thy daughter, and thy man servant, and thy maidservant, and the Levite that is within thy gates, and the stranger, and the fatherless, and the widow, that are among you.' The Israelites were forbidden to partake of food offered in sacrifice to idols (Exod. xxxiv:15), lest they should be thereby enticed into idolatry or appear to give a sanction to idolatrous observances (1 Cor. x: 28). (See AGAPE; FESTIVALS; Riddle, *Christian Antiquities,* p. 648; Bingham, *Orig. Eccles.* bk. xx).   J. R. B.

FEEBLE KNEES (Gr. τὰ παραλελυμένα γόνατα), a term employed to express the results of overexertion, as in an athletic contest, and, figuratively, of *weariness of mind, depression, low spirits* (Heb. xii:12),

Men are said to have *weak hands,* and *feeble knees,* when they have small courage and vigor (Is. xxxv:3).

FEEBLE-MINDED (mīnd'ĕd), (Gr. ὀλιγόψυχος, ol-ig-op'soo-kos, little spirited), a term frequently used in the Bible, and signifies one who is laboring under such trouble that his heart sinks within him (1 Thess. v:14, R. V. "fainthearted").

FEELING (fēl'ing). (1) In Eph. iv:19 we find this, "who being past feeling have given themselves over to lasciviousness," etc. The Greek word ἀπαλγέω, *ap-alg-eh'o,* means "to become insensible to pain, callous, and so indifferent to truth, honor, or shame."

In the epistle to the Hebrews we are told "we have not a high-priest which cannot be touched with the feeling of our infirmities' (Heb. iv: 15). The Greek term συμπαθέω, *sum-path-eh'o, to feel for, to have compassion on,* is employed.

(2) Religious feelings are those sensations or emotions of the mind produced by the views we have of religion. While some enthusiasts boast of, depend on, and talk much of their feelings, there are others who are led to discard the term, and almost to abandon the idea of religious feeling; but it is evident that however many have been misguided and deceived by their feelings, yet there is no such thing as religion without them. For instance, religion consists in contrition, repentance, and devotion; now what is contrition but a feeling of sorrow for sin? What is repentance, but a feeling of hatred to it, with a relinquishing of it? What is devotion but a feeling of love to God and his ways? Who can separate the idea of feeling from any of these acts? The fact is this: Religious feelings, like everything else, have been abused; and men, to avoid the imputation of fanaticism, have run into the opposite evil of lukewarmness, and been content with a system without feeling its energy.

(3) Such as keep God's commandments *feel no evil,* meet with nothing that really tends to their hurt (Eccl. viii:3). The heathen *feel after God* when, amid great ignorance and mistake, they search out and perceive his existence, and some of his perfections (Acts xvii:27). They are past *feeling,* who have their conscience so seared that they can commit the most horrid crimes without the least conviction or remorse (Eph. iv:19).
                                                      Brown.

FEET (fēt). See FOOT.

FELIX (fē'lĭx), (Gr. φῆλιξ, *fay'lix,* happy), a Roman procurator of Judea, before whom Paul so 'reasoned of righteousness, temperance, and judgment to come,' that the judge trembled, saying, 'Go thy way for this time; when I have a convenient season I will call for thee'(Acts xxiv:25).

The context states that Felix had expected a bribe from Paul; and, in order to procure this bribe, he appears to have had several interviews with the Apostle. The depravity which such an expectation implies is in agreement with the idea which the historical fragments preserved respecting Felix would lead the student to form of the man.

The year in which Felix entered on his office cannot be strictly determined. From the words of Josephus (*Antiq.* xx:7, 1), it appears that his appointment took place before the twelfth year of the Emperor Claudius. Eusebius fixes the time of his actually undertaking his duties in the eleventh year of that monarch.

(1) **Elevation and Crimes.** Felix was a remarkable instance of the elevation to distinguished station of persons born and bred in the lowest condition. Originally a slave, he rose to little less than kingly power. For some unknown, but probably not very creditable services, he was manumitted by Claudius Cæsar (Sueton. *Claud.* 28; Tacit. *Hist.* v:9); on which account he is said to have taken the prænomen of Claudius. In .

Tacitus, however (*loc. cit.*), he is surnamed Antonius, probably because he was also a freedman of Antonia, the emperor's mother. The character which the ancients have left of Felix is of a very dark complexion. The country was ready for rebellion, and the unsuitable remedies which Felix applied served only to inflame the passions and to incite to crime. Josephus (*Antiq.* xx:8, 5) reports that under Felix the affairs of the country grew worse and worse. The land was filled with robbers and impostors who deluded the multitude. Felix used his power to repress these disorders to little purpose, since his own example gave no sanction to justice. Thus, having got one Dineas, leader of a band of assassins, into his hands, by a promise of impunity, he sent him to Rome to receive his punishment. Having a grudge against Jonathan the high-priest, who had expostulated with him on his misrule, he made use of Doras, an intimate friend of Jonathan, in order to get him assassinated by a gang of villains, who joined the crowds that were going up to the temple-worship—a crime which led subsequently to countless evils, by the encouragement which it gave to the Sicarii, or leagued assassins of the day, to whose excesses Josephus ascribes, under Providence, the overthrow of the Jewish state. Among other crimes, some of these villains misled the people under the promise of performing miracles, and were punished by Felix. An Egyptian impostor, who escaped himself, was the occasion of the loss of life to four hundred followers, and of the loss of liberty to two hundred more, thus severely dealt with by Felix (Joseph. *Antiq.* xx:8. 6; *De Bell. Jud.* ii:13, 5; comp. Acts xxi:38).

(2) **Marriage.** While in his office, being inflamed by a passion for the beautiful Drusilla, a daughter of King Herod Agrippa, who was married to Azizus, king of Emesa, he employed one Simon, a magician, to use his arts in order to persuade her to forsake her husband and marry him, promising that if she would comply with his suit he would make her a happy woman. Drusilla, partly impelled by a desire to avoid the envy of her sister, Berenice, was prevailed on to transgress the laws of her forefathers, and consented to a union with Felix. In this marriage a son was born, who was named Agrippa; both mother and son perished in an eruption of Mount Vesuvius, which took place in the days of Titus Cæsar (Joseph. *Antiq.* xx:7, 2). With this adulteress was Felix seated when Paul reasoned before the judge, as already stated (Acts xxiv:24). (See DRUSILLA.)

(3) **Hears Paul.** Paul, being apprehended in Jerusalem, was sent by a letter from Claudius Lysias to Felix at Cæsarea, where he was at first confined in Herod's judgment hall till his accusers came. They arrived. Tertullus appeared as their spokesman, and had the audacity, in order to conciliate the good will of Felix, to express gratitude on the part of the Jews, 'seeing that by thee we enjoy great quietness, and that very worthy deeds are done unto this nation by thy providence' (Acts xxiii; xxiv). Paul pleaded his cause in a worthy speech; and Felix, consigning the Apostle to the custody of a centurion, ordered that he should have such liberty as the circumstances admitted, with permission that his acquaintance might see him and minister to his wants. This imprisonment the Apostle suffered for a period of two years (Acts xxiv:27).

(4) **Summoned to Rome.** Felix was recalled to Rome; A. D. 60 and Festus was sent in his room. To do the Jews a pleasure, he left Paul bound; this, however, did him no service; numbers of them followed him to Rome, and complained of his extortion and violence. He would have been punished with death, had not his brother Pallas, by his credit at court, preserved his life (Acts xxiii and xxiv).

FELLER (fĕl'lēr), (Heb. כָּרַת, *kā-rath'*, to cut off, to fell), a cutter of wood.

This is an old Anglo-Saxon word and is used in Is. xiv:8, where David represents the cedars of Lebanon as rejoicing over the fall of Sennacherib, who had been their great destroyer.

FELLOES (fĕl'lōs), (Heb. חִשֻּׁק, *khish-shook'*, conjoined spokes of a wheel, 1 Kings vii:33), probably means 'spokes' that connect the hub and rim, rather than the rim itself. It is kindred to the word translated "fillet," *joinings* (Ex. xxvii:10).

FELLOW (fĕl'lō).

1. A term of contempt denoted by the Heb. אִישׁ, *eesh*, (1 Sam. xxix:4), and Gr. ἀνήρ, *an-ayr'*, words for *man*.

2. The translation of *ray'ah* (Heb. רֵעַ, *friend, associate*, etc., Exod. ii:13; Judg. vii:13, etc.), and of *khaw-bare'* (Heb. חָבֵר, Eccles. iv:10).

3. The translation of *aw-meeth'* (Heb. עָמִית, *neighbor*) in that peculiar passage, "Awake, O sword, against my shepherd, and against the man that is my *fellow*" (Zech. xiii:7).

FELLOWSHIP.

1. The translation of the Hebrew *tes-oo-meth'*, תְּשׂוּמֶת, *deposit* (Lev. vi:2); something handed over as a *pledge*.

2. Joint interest (Heb. חָבַר, *khaw-bar'*, to be joined, Ps. xciv:20; Gr. κοινωνία, *koy-nohn-ee'ah, fellowship, communion*, Acts ii:42 et al.; μετοχή, *met-okh-ay', partnership*, 2 Cor. vi:14).

(1) The saints have *fellowship* with God; they are interested in whatever he is and has, and are allowed intimate familiarity with him (1 John i:7; Eph. ii:18). (2) They have *fellowship* with Christ in his sufferings; he suffered in their room; these sufferings are imputed to them, and the virtue thereof experienced by their hearts (Phil. iii:10). (3) The *fellowship of the gospel* is the mutual interest and intercourse of saints and ministers, in the profession of the truths, experience of the blessings, and observance of the rules and ordinances of the gospel (Phil. i:5). (4) There is no *communion* or *fellowship* between Christ and Belial, sin and holiness; i. e., neither mutual interest nor friendly intercourse (2 Cor. vi:14, 15). The bread and wine in the Lord's supper are the *communion* of the body and blood of Christ; they signify, seal, and apply the same; and are means of our partaking of Christ's person, righteousness, and fullness, for the nourishment of our souls and for promoting the *fellowship* of believers (1 Cor. x:16).

FENCE (Heb. גָּדֵר, *gaw-dare'*, an inclosure).

The Hebrew fences were of two kinds. One was the outer thorny fence of the vineyard; and the other, the inner wall of stones surrounding it (Prov. xv:19; xxiv:31). The Phœnicians called any enclosed place *guddir*, and particularly gave this name to their settlement in the southwestern coast of Spain, which the Greeks from them called *Gadeira*, the Romans *Gades*, and the moderns, *Cadiz*. In Ezek. xiii:5; xxii:30 *gadêr* appears to denote the fortifications of a city.

Figurative. The wicked are as a *tottering fence*, and *bowing wall;* their ruin comes on them very suddenly (Ps. lxii:3).

FENCED CITIES. See FORT, FORTIFICA-
TIONS, ETC.

Walls of Antioch.

FERRET (fĕr'rĕt), (Heb. אֲנָקָה, *an-aw-kaw'*, lizard, R. V., Lev. xi:30, for A. V. "ferret").

This lizard is named from the sound which it
emits. Its scientific name is *Ptyodactylus Hassel-
quistii*. It is frequently found in houses. It is
not very probable that the Hebrew original of
this word signifies the *ferret,* which is so called
with us. (See LIZARD.)

FERRYBOAT (fĕr'rȳ bōt), (Heb. עֲבָרָה, *ab-aw-
raw'*, crossing), mentioned only in 2 Sam. xix:18,
"A ferryboat for the king's house."

FESTIVALS (fĕs'tĭ-vals), (Heb. חַג, *khag*, from
the verb signifying to *dance*, and מוֹעֵד, *mo-ade'*, a
set time or *assembly*, *place of assembling*), were
occasions of public religious observances, recurring at certain set and somewhat distant intervals.

1. Divine Institutions. Those which owe
their existence to the authority of God are, the
seventh day of the week, or the Sabbath; the
Passover; Pentecost; the Feast of Trumpets;
the Day of Atonement; the Feast of Tabernacles;
the New Moon. Festivals which arose under
purely human influences are, the Feast of Lots,
or Purim; the Death of Holofernes; the Dedication; the Sacred Fire; the Death of Nicanor.

At the daily service two lambs of the first year
were to be offered at the door of the tabernacle;
one in the morning, the other in the evening, a
continual burnt-offering. With each lamb was
to be offered one-tenth of an ephah of flour, mingled with one-fourth of a hin of fresh oil, for a
meat-offering, and one-fourth of a hin of wine
for a drink-offering. Frankincense was to be
placed on the meat-offering, a handful of which,
with the frankincense, was to be burnt, and the
remainder was to be eaten by the priest in the
holy place, without leaven. The priests were to
offer daily the tenth of an ephah of fine flour, half
in the morning and half in the evening, for

themselves. The high-priest was to dress the
lamps in the tabernacle every morning, and light
them every evening; and at the same time burn
incense on the altar of incense. The people
provided oil for the lamps which were to burn
from evening to morning; the ashes were removed by a priest, dressed in his linen garment
and his linen drawers, and then carried by him
out of the camp, in his common dress. Great
stress was laid on the regular observance of these
requirements (Num. xxviii:1-8; Exod. xxix:38-
42; Lev. vi:8-23; Exod. xxx:7-9; xxvii:20; Lev.
xxiv:1-4; Num. viii:2).

(1) The Sabbath. Labor was to last not
longer than six days. The seventh was a Sabbath, a day of rest, of holy convocation, on which
no one, not even strangers or cattle, was allowed
to do any servile work. The offender was liable
to stoning.

On the Sabbath two lambs of the first year,
without blemish, were to be offered for a burnt-
offering, morning and evening, with two-tenths
of an ephah of flour, mingled with oil, for a
meat-offering, and one-half of a hin of wine for a
drink-offering, thus doubling the offering for
ordinary days. Twelve cakes of fine flour were
to be placed every Sabbath upon the table in the
tabernacle, in two piles, and pure frankincense
laid on the uppermost of each pile. These were
to be furnished by the people; two were offered
to Jehovah, the rest were eaten by the priests in
the holy place (Exod. xvi:23; Lev. xxiii:3; xxvi:
2; Num. xxviii:9, 10).

(2) New Moon (Heb. רֹאשׁ חֹדֶשׁ, *roshe kho'desh*,
beginning of month, Num. x:10; xxviii:11).

At the *New Moon* festival, in the beginning of
the month, in addition to the daily sacrifice, two
heifers, one ram, and seven lambs of the first year,
were to be offered as burnt-offerings, with three-
tenths of an ephah of flour, mingled with oil, for
each heifer; two-tenths of an ephah of flour, mingled with oil, for the ram; and one-tenth of an
ephah of flour, mingled with oil, for every lamb,
and a drink offering of half of a hin of wine for a
heifer, one-third of a hin for the ram, and one-
fourth of a hin for every lamb. One kid of the
goats was also to be offered as a sin-offering.

**(3) The Seventh New Moon, or Feast of
Trumpets** (Heb. יוֹם תְּרוּעָה, *yome ter-oo-aw'*, day
of blowing).

The first day of the *seventh month* was to be a
Sabbath, a holy convocation, accompanied by the
blowing of trumpets. In addition to the daily and
monthly sacrifices, one ram and seven lambs were
to be offered as burnt-offerings, with their respective meat-offerings, as at the usual New Moon
festival (Num. xxviii:11-15; xxix:1:6; Lev.
xxiii:23-25).

Three times in the year—at the Feast of Unleavened Bread, in the month Abib; at the Feast
of Harvest, or of Weeks; and at the Feast of Ingathering, or of Tabernacles—all the males were
to appear before Jehovah, at the place which he
should choose. None were to come empty-handed,
but every one was to give according as Jehovah
had blessed him; and there before Jehovah was
every one to rejoice with his family, the Levite, the
stranger, the fatherless, and the widow (Exod.
xxiii:14-17; xxxiv:22-24; Deut. xvi:16-17).

(4) The Passover. The Hebrew word פֶּסַח,
peh'sakh (from פָּסַח, *paw-sakh'*, to *leap over*,
figuratively, to *spare, show mercy*) denotes: (1)
An overstepping; (2) The *paschal sacrifice* by
virtue of which the *passing over* was effected

(Exod. xii:21, 27, 48; 2 Chron. xxx:15). The first of these three great festivals, that of Unleavened Bread, called also the Passover, was kept in the month Abib, in commemoration of the rescue of the Israelites by Jehovah out of Egypt, which took place in that month. (See PASSOVER).

In order to make the season more remarkable, it was ordained that henceforward the month in which it took place should be reckoned the first of the national religious year (Exod. xii:2). From this time, accordingly, the year began in the month Abib, or Nisan (March—April), while the civil year continued to be reckoned from Tishri (September—October) (Exod. xii:3, 14, 27; 43-49; Lev. xxiii:5; Num. xxviii:16; Deut. xvi:1-7). The Passover lasted one week, including two Sabbaths (De Wette, *Archæol*, p. 214). The first day and the last were holy, that is, devoted to the observances in the public temple, and to rest from all labor (Exod. xii:16; Lev. xxiii:6; Num. xxviii:18; Deut. xvi:8).

On the day after the Sabbath, on the Feast of Passover, a sheaf of the first fruits of the barley harvest was to be brought to the priest to be waved before Jehovah, accompanied by a burnt-offering. Till this sheaf was presented, neither bread nor parched corn, nor full ripe ears of the harvest, could be eaten (Exod. xii:15-20; xiii:6-10; Lev. xxiii:6-8; Deut. xvi:2-8; Num. xxviii:17-25).

(5) Pentecost. (Gr. Πεντηκοστή, *pen-tay-kos-tay', fiftieth*, i. e., *day*). The Feast of Pentecost or of Weeks was kept to Jehovah at the end of seven weeks from the day of the Festival of Unleavened Bread, on which the sheaf was presented. On the morrow after the seventh complete week, or on the fiftieth day, two wave loaves were presented as first fruits of the wheat-harvest, together with a burnt-offering, a sin-offering, and a peace-offering, etc. The day was a holy convocation, in which no servile work was done. The festival lasted but one day. It is said to have been designed to commemorate the giving of the law on Mount Sinai (Brown's *Antiquities of the Jews*, vol. i, p. 494; Deut. xvi:9-16; Num. xxviii:20-31; xv:17-21).

(6) Tabernacles, Feast of, the third of the great annual feasts, the other two being the Passover and Pentecost. These were:

I. *The Festival of Tents* (Heb. חַג הַסֻּכּוֹת, *khag has-sook-kohth'*, A. V. "Feast of Tabernacles, 2 Chron. viii:13; Ezra iii:4; Zech. vii:19, 20, 21; Gr. σκηνοπηγία, *skay-nop-ayg-ee'ah*, John vii:2, because the Israelites were commanded to live in booths during its continuance (comp. Lev. xxiii: 43).

2. *The Feast of Ingathering* (Heb. חַג הָאָסִף, *khag haw-aw-seef'*; Exod. xxiii:16; xxxiv:22), because it was held after the ingathering of the harvest and fruits.

3. *The Festival of Jehovah* (Heb. חַג יְהֹוָה, *khag yeh-ho-vaw'*, Lev. xxiii:39), or simply *the festival* (1 Kings viii:2; 2 Chron. v:3), because it was the most important or well known. This Feast of Ingathering or of Tabernacles began on the fifteenth day of the seventh month, and continued eight days, the first and last being Sabbaths. During the feast all native Israelites dwelt in booths made of the shoots of beautiful trees, palm-branches, boughs of thick-leaved trees, and of the willows of the brook, when they rejoiced with their families, with the Levite, the stranger, the fatherless, and the widow, before Jehovah. Various offerings were made. At the end of seven years, in the year of release, at the Feast of Tabernacles, the law was required to be read by the priests in the hearing of all the Israelites (Deut. xvi:13-15; xxxi:10-13; Lev. xxiii:39-43; 33-36; Num. xxix:12-38, 40).

The Feast of Tabernacles was appointed partly to be an occasion of annual thanksgiving after the ingathering of the harvest (Exod. xxxiv:22; Lev. xxiii:39; Deut. xvi:13), and partly to remind the Israelites that their fathers had lived in tents in the wilderness (Lev. xxiii:40-43). This feast took place in the end of the year, September or October.

(7) Day of Atonement. (Heb. יוֹם הַכִּפֻּרִים, *yome hak-kip-poor-eem'*). The tenth day of the seventh month was the Day of Atonement—a day of abstinence, a day of holy convocation, in which all were to afflict themselves. Special offerings were made. (See ATONEMENT, DAY OF.) (Lev. xxiii:26-32; xvi:1, 31; Num. xxix:7-11; Exod. xxx:10.)

On these solemn occasions food came partly from hospitality (a splendid instance of which may be found in 2 Chron. xxxv:7-9), partly from the feasts which accompanied the sacrifices in the temple, and partly also from provision expressly made by the travelers themselves. Lodging, too, was afforded by friends, or found in tents erected for the purpose in and around Jerusalem (Helon's *Pilgrimage;* Brown's *Antiquities*, p. 520 ff).

The three great festivals have corresponding events (but of far greater importance) in the new dispensation. The Feast of Tabernacles was the time when our Savior was born, some suppose; he was crucified at the Passover; while at Pentecost the effusion of the Holy Spirit took place.

The rest and recreation would be the more pleasant, salutary, and beneficial, because of the joyous nature of the religious services in which they were, for the greater part, engaged. These solemn festivals were not only commemorations of great national events, but they were occasions for the reunion of friends, for the enjoyment of hospitality, and for the interchange of kindness. The feasts which accompanied the sacrifices opened the heart of the entire family to joy, and gave a welcome which bore a religious sanction, even to the stranger, the fatherless, and the widow (Michaelis, *Mos. Recht,* art. 199).

How much, too, would these gatherings tend to foster and sustain a spirit of nationality! By intercourse the feelings of tribe and clan would be worn away; men from different parts became acquainted with and attached to each other; partial interests were found to be more imaginary than real; while the predominant idea of a common faith and a common rallying-place at Jerusalem, could not fail to fuse into one strong and overpowering emotion of national and brotherly love, all the higher, nay, even the lower feelings, of each Hebrew heart.

'If,' says Michaelis (*Mos. Recht,* art. 198, Smith's Transl.), 'any of the tribes happened to be jealous of each other or involved in civil war, their meeting together in one place for the purposes of religion and sociality, had a tendency to prevent their being totally alienated; and even though this had happened, it gave them an opportunity of reuniting.' He adds that 'the separation of the ten tribes from the tribes of Judah under Rehoboam and Jeroboam could never have been permanent, had not the latter abrogated one part of the law of Moses relative to festivals. In order to perpetuate the separation, he prohibited the annual pilgrimages to Jerusalem, and appointed two places for divine service within his own territories' (1 Kings xii:27-30). 'He also,' adds Michaelis,

42

'transferred the celebration of the Feast of Tabernacles, and probably the other two festivals likewise, to a different season from that appointed by Moses' (1 Kings xii:33).

Another effect of these festivals Michaelis has found in the furtherance of internal commerce. They would give rise to something resembling our modern fairs. Among the Mahometans similar festivals have had this effect.

These festivals, in their origin, had an obvious connection with agriculture. Passover saw the harvest upon the soil; at Pentecost it was ripe; and Tabernacles was the festival of gratitude for the fruitage and vintage (Michaelis, art. 197). The first was a natural pause after the labors of the field were completed; the second, after the first-fruits were gathered; and the third, a time of rejoicing in the feeling that the Divine bounty had crowned the year with its goodness.

2. Human Institutions. (*De Feriarum Hebræorum origine ac ratione*, auctore H. Ewald; Gottingæ, 1841; and Creuzer. *Symbol.* ii:597.)

(1) **Purim.** (Heb. פּוּרִים, *poo-reem'*, lots). The Feast of Purim or of Lots originated in the gratitude of the Jews in escaping the plot of Haman, designed for their destruction. It took its name from the lots which were cast before Haman by the astrologers, who knew his hatred against Mordecai and his wish to destroy his family and nation (Esther iii:7; ix:2, 5). The feast was suggested by Esther and Mordecai, and was celebrated on the 13th, 14th and 15th days of the twelfth month (Adar). The 13th was a fast, being the day on which the Jews were to have been destroyed; and on the 14th and 15th were a feast held in commemoration of their deliverance. The fast is called the Fast of Esther, and the feast still holds the name of Purim. Prideaux (*Connex.*) styles it the Bacchanalia of the Jews. (Brown, *Antiq.* i:575.)

(2) **Death of Holofernes.** The killing of Holofernes by the hand of Judith, the consequent defeat of the Assyrians, and the liberation of the Jews, were commemorated by the institution of a festival (Judith xiv: xv).

(3) **Feast of Dedication.** The Feast of Dedication was appointed by Judas Maccabæus, on occasion of the purification of the temple, and reconstruction of the altar, after they had been polluted by Antiochus Epiphanes (1 Macc. i; 2 Macc. v; Prideaux, *sub* A. C. 167-8, 170).

The new dedication took place on the 25th day of the ninth month, called Chislev, in the year before Christ, 170. This would be in December. The day was chosen as being that on which Antiochus, three years before, had polluted the altar by heathen sacrifices.

In John x:22 this festival is alluded to when our Lord is said to have been present at the Feast of Dedication. The historian marks the time by stating 'it was winter.'

(4) **Festival of Fire.** The festival 'of the Fire' was instituted by Nehemiah, to commemorate the miraculous rekindling of the altar-fire. The circumstances are narrated in 2 Macc. i:18.

(5) **Defeat of Nicanor.** The defeat by Judas Maccabæus of the Greeks when the Jews 'smote off Nicanor's head and his right hand which he stretched out so proudly,' caused the people to 'rejoice greatly, and they kept that day a day of great gladness; moreover, they ordained to keep yearly this day, being the thirteenth day of Adar' —February or March (1 Macc. vii:47).

Some other minor fasts and festivals may be found noticed in Brown's *Antiquities*, i:586; and in Simon's *Dictionnaire de la Bible*, art. Fêtes;

Bähr, *Symbolik des Mosæischen Cultus*, bk. iv; Raphall, *Festivals of the Lord*).

FESTUS, PORCIUS (fĕs'tus pôr'shĭ-us), (Gr. Πόρκιος Φῆστος, *por'kee-os face'tos*).

Porcius Festus was the successor of Felix as the Roman governor of Judea, to the duties of which office he was appointed by the emperor Nero (Joseph. *Antiq.* xx:8, 9; *De Bell. Jud.* ii: 1, 1), in the first year of his reign. One of his first official acts was hearing the case of the apostle Paul, who had been left in prison by his predecessor. He was at least not a thoroughly corrupt judge; for when the Jewish hierarchy begged him to send for Paul to Jerusalem, and thus afford an opportunity for his being assassinated on the road, he gave a refusal, promising to investigate the facts at Cæsarea, where Paul was in custody, alleging to them, 'it is not the manner of the Romans to deliver any man to die before that he which is accused have the accusers face to face, and have license to answer for himself concerning the crime laid against him' (Acts xxv:16). On reaching Cæsarea he sent for Paul, heard what he had to say, and, finding that the matters which 'his accusers had against him' were 'questions of their own superstition, and of one Jesus which was dead, whom Paul affirmed to be alive,' he asked the apostle whether he was willing to go to Jerusalem, and there be tried, since Festus did not feel himself skilled in such an affair. Paul, doubtless because he was unwilling to put himself into the hands of his implacable enemies, requested 'to be [r]e[....] unto the hearing of Augustus,' and was [in] [con]sequence kept in custody till Festus had [op]portunity to send him to Cæsar. Agripp[a], [how]ever, with his wife Bernice, having come [to] salute Festus on his new appointment, expressed a desire to see and 'hear the man.' Accordingly Paul was brought before Festus, Agrippa and Bernice, made a famous speech, and was declared innocent. But having appealed to Cæsar, he was sent to Rome.

Festus, on coming into Judea, found the country infested with robbers, who plundered the villages and set them on fire; the Sicarii also were numerous. Many of both classes were captured, and put to death by Festus.

King Agrippa had built himself a splendid dining-room, which was so placed that, as he reclined at his meals, he commanded a view of what was done in the Temple. The priests, being displeased, erected a wall so as to exclude the monarch's eye. On which Festus took part with Agrippa against the priests, and ordered the wall to be pulled down. The priests appealed to Nero, who suffered the wall to remain, being influenced by his wife Poppæa, 'who was a religious woman' (Joseph. *Antiq* xx:8, 11). Festus died shortly afterwards. The manner in which Josephus speaks is favorable to his character as a governor (*De Bell. Jud.* iv:14, 1).

FETTERS (fĕt'tērs). Three Hebrews words are thus translated:

1. *Nekh-o'sheth*, נְחֹשֶׁת, expresses the material of which they are made, *brass;* and also from the dual number, that they were made in pairs (Judg. xvi:21; 2 Sam. iii:34; 2 Kings xxv:7; 2 Chron. xxxiii:11; xxxvi:6; Jer. xxxix:7; lii:11).

2. *Kebel*, כֶּבֶל Ps. cv:18; cxlix:8) may apply to the link connecting the fetters.

3. *Zikkim*, זִקִּים, frequently translated chains (Ps. cxlix:8; Is. xlv:14; Nah. iii:10), but it refers to the "contraction" of the feet by a chain (Gesen

Thes. p. 424). Iron fetters are doubtless meant in Mark v:4; Luke viii:29. (Wilkinson, *Ancient Egypt*, i:410.)

FEVER (fē'vẽr),(Heb. קַדַּחַת,*kad-dach-ath'*, burning heat). Both the Hebrew, *kaddachath*, and the Greek, πυρετός, *pu-ree-tos'*, burning fire, are derived from the association of burning heat, the ordinary symptom of a febrile attack (Deut. xxviii:22; Matt. viii:14; Mark i:30; Luke iv:38; John iv:52; Acts xxviii:8).

FIDELITY (fī-dĕl'ĭ-tў), (Gr. πίστις, *pis'tis*, strict adherence to one's promise or trust).

Thus our Lord says, 'Who then is that faithful and wise steward,' etc (Luke xii:42). Paul gives the description of the faithful servant as 'showing all good fidelity' (Tit. ii:10).

FIELD (Heb. שָׂדֶה, generally *saw-deh'*, smoothness).

The English word does not fully represent the Hebrew term. They both mean cultivated land, but *sawdeh* is applied specificially to what is *un-inclosed*, the opposite of the notion conveyed by the word **field**. The separate plots of land were divided by stones, which might be removed (Deut. xix:14; xxvii:17; cf. Job. xxiv:2; Prov. xxii:28; xxiii:10). Stray cattle could enter (Exod. xxii:5), and therefore the flocks and herds must be constantly watched (Wortabet. *Syria*, i:293). From the absence of enclosures the term "field" might be applied to a plot of ground of limited area, or a man's whole property (Gen. xxiii:13, 17; Is. v:8; Lev. xxvii:16 ff; Ruth iv:5; Jer. xxxii:9, 25; Prov. xxvii:26; xxxi:16). The practice of leaving the fields unfenced, and separated only by a foot-path explains how seeds, in sowing, could fall on the hard unplowed earth and be exposed to the birds (Matt. xiii:4); and how the Saviour, with his disciples,could pass through the cornfields along these dividing paths, plucking the ears of corn, which, according to the Jewish custom, was not a violation of the rights of property (Luke vi:1 ff). (See Rob. *Bibl. Res.* ii:192.) It also explains how Ruth gathered grain "in a part of the field belonging to Boaz" (Ruth ii:3).

FIG TREE (fĭg), (Heb. תְּאֵן, *teh-ane'*, or תְּאֵנָה, *teh-ay-naw'*; Gr. σύκον, *soo'kon*), the fruit of the well-known tree.

Figs and Fig Leaves.

(1) The first notice of the fig-tree occurs in Gen. iii:7, where Adam and Eve are described as sewing fig-leaves together, to make themselves aprons. The common fig-leaf is not so well suited, from its lobed nature, for this purpose; but the practice of sewing or pinning leaves together is very common in the East even in the present day, and baskets, dishes and umbrellas are made of leaves so pinned or sewn together. The fig-tree is enumerated (Deut. viii:8; comp. Is. xxxiv:4) as one of the valuable products of Palestine, 'a land of wheat, and barley, and vines, and fig-trees, and pomegranates.'

(2) It has been cultivated in Palestine from remote times, and is also found in a wild state. It does not grow to a great height, but throws out a profusion of very spreading branches, and the trunk is often three feet in diameter. Five-lobed leaves luxuriantly clothe these limbs, and often convert this tree into a beautiful natural arbor (1 Kings iv:25; 2 Kings xviii:31; Is. xxxvi:16; Mic. iv:4; Zech. iii:10; John i:48).

The fruit is pear-shaped, and the small green figs appear before the leaves. When these figs have attained some size, their interior will be found filled with minute white flowers. This curious provision leads to the common impression that this tree never blossoms. When the leaves have appeared, if there be no fruit among them, the fig-tree will be barren for the present season (Matt. xxi:19).

(3) Figs are much used as food in all Eastern lands. Two kinds of this fruit are mentioned in the Bible. (a) The early fig, or *boccôre*, of which a few ripen and are gathered in June (Is. xxviii:4; Hos. ix:10; Mic. vii:1), while the most of this early fruit falls off before it is perfected (Rev. vi:13). (b) The main crop, or *kermouse*, ordinarily does not ripen till August. These are the "green figs" of Cant. ii:13. "Bethphage" means "house of green figs." A long dark-colored kermouse sometimes hangs upon the trees all winter.

These various kinds of figs are eaten as they come from the tree, and are also dried in masses or cakes (1 Sam. xxv:18). They seem to have been an ordinary article of food, and to have possessed medicinal properties (2 Kings xx:7; 1 Chron. xii:40).

The putting forth of the fig-tree was one of the earliest indications of summer (Cant. ii:13; Matt. xxiv:32; Luke xxi:29; and a failure of its fruit was a great calamity (Jer. v:17; viii:13; Joel i:7, 12; Hab. iii:17, 18).

Figurative. (1) The *fig-tree* is referred to as one of the signs of prosperity (1 Kings iv:25). 'And Judah and Israel dwelt safely, every man under his vine and under his fig-tree.' (2) And its failure is noted as a sign of affliction (Ps. cv:33). 'He smote their fig-trees and broke the trees of their coasts.' (3) The Jewish nation is likened to a *barren fig-tree*, spared another year at the request of the dresser. When our Savior came into the world, and for more than three years exercised his public ministry among them, how barren were they, and how ripe for destruction! But by His intercession and the prayers of His apostles, they were spared till it was seen that the preaching of the gospel had no good effect on the greater part of them; and were afterward cut off with terrible destruction (Luke xiii:6-9). (4) They were also shadowed forth by the *fig-tree* with fair leaves, but no fruit, which Jesus cursed into barrenness and withering; they had many showy pretenses to holiness and zeal, but were destitute of good works and refused to believe in and receive the promised Messiah (Matt. xxi:19). (5) The cursing of the fig-tree by our Savior (Mark xi:13, 21) has occasioned great perplexity. This incident occurred about the beginning of April, when, as the evangelist states, the time for figs had not come. Why, then, should Christ seek figs upon the tree and, as it were, blame its barrenness? The best reply seems to be: because the

FIGURE 660 FIR

tree was in leaf; and when the tree was in this state, abnormal though it were, fruit might be expected. Dr. Thompson, as the result of his observation, considers it not at all impossible that the early variety of this tree might have ripe fruit in the warm, sheltered ravines of Olivet at Easter. If there was no fruit on this leafy tree it might justly be condemned as barren; and hence the propriety of the lesson it was made to teach—that those who put forth in profusion only the leaves of empty profession are nigh unto cursing.

FIGURE (fĭg'ûr), the translation of the following words: *Seh'mel* (Heb. סֶמֶל), an idol, as otherwise; *mik-lah'ath* (Heb. מִקְלַעַת), a carving; *tab-neeth'* (Heb. תַּבְנִית), likeness or model; *an-teet'oo-pon* (Gr. ἀντίτυπον, 1 Peter iii:21), antitype; the verb *met-askh-ay-mat-id'zo* (Gr. μετασχηματίζω).

(1) Deut. iv:16, 'Lest ye corrupt yourselyes, and make you a graven image, the similitude of any figure,' (Driver, '*statue*'). The word is found also (2 Chron. xxxiii:7, 15) 'idol,' and (Ezek. viii:3, 5) 'image.' The meaning 'statue' is confirmed by the Phœnician inscriptions.
(2) 1 Kings vi:29, 'He carved all the walls of the house round about with carved figures of cherubim' and the next: vi:18 'was carved,' *i. e.*, 'was carving of;' vi:32 'carvings;' vii:21 'gravings.' These 'carved figures' were representations of the cherubim cut in relief on the wood of the doors.
(3) Is. xliv:13, 'The carpenter . . . maketh it [the image] after the figure of a man (*tabhnith*). The Hebrew is frequent for the outward appearance of a person or thing.
(4) In Acts vii:43 the meaning is 'representations' or 'images of gods;' in Rom. v:14 it is 'type.'
(5) Heb. ix:24, 'Christ is not entered into the holy places made with hands, *which are* the figures of the true; but into heaven itself.'
(6) 1 Cor. iv:6, 'And these things, brethren, I have in a figure transferred to myself and to Apollos.' The Greek verb 'in a figure transferred' elsewhere means to change one's form or appearance into some other form (2 Cor. xi:13, 14, 15) (A. V. 'transform,' R. V. 'fashion into' or 'fashion as'), and Phil. iii:21 (A. V. 'change,' R. V. 'fashion anew'). Here it is the truth stated that is to change its application; applied by the apostle to himself and Apollos, it really applies to the Corinthians. (Hastings' *Bib. Dict.*) (See TYPE.)

FILE (fīl), is the improper translation in the A. V. of the Heb. פְּצִירָה פֶה, *pets-ee-raw' peh* (1 Sam. xiii:21), literally signifying a bluntness of the mouth, i. e., *edge* of tools.

FILLET (fĭl'ĕt), an incorrect translation in the A. V. of two words:
1. *Khash-oo-keem'* (Heb. חֲשֻׁקִים, joinings, Exod. xxxviii:17, 28; xxvii:17), the rods which joined together the tops of the pillars round the court of the Tabernacle (q.v.) and from which the curtain was suspended (Exod. xxvii:10, 11, etc.).
2. *Khoot* (Heb. הוּט, thread, as elsewhere rendered), i. e., a measuring line (Jer. lii:21).

FILTH, FILTHY (filth, fĭl'thy̆), the translation of several Hebrew and Greek words and meaning "foul matter," "anything that soils or defiles." In 2 Chron. xxix:5 and Ezra. vi:21, it denotes the filth from which the Jews were to cleanse the Temple.

Figurative. (1) Filth represents *moral impurity* (Ezek. xxxvi:25; 2 Cor. vii:1; James i:21, etc.).
(2) That the *filthiness* of it may be molten in it"

(Ezek. xxiv:11) seems to mean that the pot was to be placed empty upon the fire that the rust may be burned away by the heat. The *filthiness* of the pot was the rust upon it. (3) The apostles were made as the *filth of the world; its offscourings, or outsweepings.* They were by wicked men accounted and used as if most base and contemptible (1 Cor. iv:13). (4) Sinful pollutions of the heart or practice are often called *filth* and *filthiness;* they render men corrupt and abominable to God and to good men (Is. iv:4; Ezek. vi:21). (5) Men are represented as *filthy,* and *filthiness,* on account of their being infected and defiled with sin (Rev. xxii:11; Ezek. xxii:15). (6) *Filthy lucre* is gain basely and sinfully gotten; as when ministers make their salaries their great aim in their work (Tit. i:7, 11; 1 Pet. v:2).

FIN (Heb. סְנַפִּיר, *sen-ap-peer*), a distinctive mark of such fish as might be eaten under the Mosaic law (Deut. xiv:9, 10; Lev. xi:9, 10, 12).

FINE (fīn). Under the Mosaic law the amount of indemnification was fixed by the one injured in certain cases; in others by the judge (Ex. xxi:19-36; xxii:6; Deut. xxii:19, 29.)

FINER (fīn'ĕr), (Heb. צָרַף, *tsaw-raph*, to refine), a worker of gold and silver (Prov. xxv:4).

FINGER (fĭn'gēr), (Heb. אֶצְבַּע, *ets-bah'*; Gr. δάκτυλος, *dak'too-los*). Besides referring to the member of the human body it has a specific meaning as *Digit* (Heb. אֶצְבַּע, *ets-bah'*), the smallest measure among the Hebrews, and equal to the breadth of the human finger. We find the thickness of the solid parts of Solomon's pillars measured by *fingers* (Jer. lii:21).

Figurative. (1) The *finger of God* denotes his power, his operation. Pharaoh's magicians discovered the finger of God in some of the miracles of Moses (Exod. viii:19). (2) That legislator gave the tables written with the *finger* of God to the Hebrews (Exod. xxxi:18). The heavens were the work of God's fingers (Ps. viii:3). (3) Our Lord says, he casts out devils with the finger of God; meaning, perhaps, by his authority (Luke xi:20). (4) To put forth one's finger, is a bantering gesture (Is. lviii:9). (5) To "teach with the *fingers,*" imported a concealed and indirect method of exciting others to iniquity (Prov. vi:13). (6) To bind God's law *on the fingers,* is to have it constantly in our eye as the rule and reason of our whole practice (Prov. vii:3). (7) Rehoboam's *little finger* being thicker than his father's loins, meant, that the easiest exertion of his power and authority, should be more rigid and grievous than any servitude or hardship they had suffered under his father (1 Kings xii:10; 2 Chron. x:10).

FINGER NAIL signatures were common among the Chaldeans. "An indentation was made with the finger nail on one of the sides of the (soft clay) tablet, and this mark, followed or preceded by the mention of a name, 'Nail of Zabudamik,' 'Nail of Abzii,' took the place of more or less complicated sign-manuals" (Maspero, *Dawn of Civilization,* p. 731). (Barnes' *Bib. Cyc.*)

FINISHER (Gr. τελειωτής, *tel-i-o-tace'*, completer), spoken of Jesus (Heb. xii:2) as one who in his own person raised faith to its perfection and so set before us the highest example of faith (Grimm, *Gr. Lex.*, s. v.).

FIR (Heb. בְּרוֹשׁ, *ber-ōsh'*), probably the *cypress, Cupressus sempervirens,* L. This tree fulfills all the conditions of the various passages in which *fir* occurs (1 Kings vi:15, 34; 2 Chron. iii:5; Ezek. xxvii:5). The tall trunk of this tree is well adapted for masts.

FIRE (fīr), (Heb. אֵשׁ, *aysh;* Gr. πῦρ, poor).

The uses of fire among the Hebrews were various:—

(1) **Domestic.** The domestic use, for cooking, roasting, and baking. (See BREAD; FOOD.)

(2) **Warmth.** In winter they warmed themselves and their apartments, by 'a fire of coals' (Jer. xxxvi:22, 23; Luke xxii:55). In the rooms it would seem that a brazier with charcoal was usually employed, as is still the case in western Asia, although the ovens and fire-places used in baking bread might have been, and doubtless were, as now, often employed to keep rooms properly warm. (See BREAD; COAL.)

(3) **Religious.** The religious use of fire was for consuming the victims on the altar of burnt-offerings, and in burning the incense on the golden altar; hence the remarkable phrase in Is. xxxi:9—'the Lord, whose fire is in Zion, and his furnace in Jerusalem.'

In the sacerdotal services no fire but that of the altar of burnt-offerings could lawfully be used. That fire was originally kindled supernaturally and was ever after kept up. From it the fire used in the censers for burning incense was always taken; and for neglecting this and using common fire, Nadab and Abihu were struck dead by 'fire from heaven' (Lev. x:2, *sq.;* Num. iii:4; xxvi:61).

(4) **War.** In time of war torches were often carried by the soldiers; which explains the use of torches in the attack of Gideon upon the camp of the Midianites (Judg. vii:16). This military use of torches was very general among ancient nations, and is alluded to by many of their writers (Statius, *Theb.* iv:5, 7; Stobæus, *Serm.* p. 194; Michaelis, in *Symbol Liter. Bremens,* iii: 254).

Towns were often destroyed by fire. This, as a war usage, belongs to all times and nations; but among the Hebrews there were some particular notions connected with it, as an act of strong abhorrence, or of devotement to abiding desolation. The principal instances historically commemorated are the destruction by fire of Jericho (Josh. vi:24); Ai (Josh. viii:19); Hazor (Josh. xi:11); Laish (Judg. xviii:27); the towns of the Benjamites (Judg. xx:48); Ziklag, by the Amalekites (1 Sam. xxx:1); Jazer, by Pharaoh (1 Kings ix:16); and the temple and palaces of Jerusalem by Nebuchadnezzar (2 Kings xxv:9). Even the war-chariots of the Canaanites were burnt by the Israelites, probably on the principle of precluding the possibility of recovery, by the enemy, of instruments of strength for which they had themselves no use. The frequency with which towns were fired in ancient warfare is shown by the very numerous threats by the prophets that the towns of Israel should be burned by their foreign enemies. Some great towns, not of Israel, are particularly named; and it would be an interesting task to trace, as far as the materials exist, the fulfillment of these prophecies in those more marked examples. Among the places thus threatened we find Damascus (Is. xliii:12, 13), Gaza, Tyre, Teman (Amos i:7, 10, 11). The temples and idols of a conquered town or people were very often burned by the victors, and this was enjoined as a duty to the Israelites (Deut. vii:5, 25; xii:3; xiii:16; Is. xxxiii:12).

(5) **Special Regulations.** (1) There were some special regulations respecting the use of fire among the Israelites. The most remarkable of these was the prohibition to light fire on the Sabbath (Exod. xxxv:3). As the primary design of this law appears to have been to prevent the proper privileges of the Sabbath day from being lost to anyone through the care and time required in cooking victuals (Exod. xvi:23) it is doubted whether the use of fire for warmth on the Sabbath day was included in this interdiction. In practice it would appear that the fire was never lighted or kept up for cooking on the Sabbath day, and that consequently there were no fires in the houses during the Sabbaths of the greater part of the year; but it may be collected that, in winter, fires for warming apartments were kept up from the previous day. Michaelis is very much mistaken with respect to the climate of Palestine in supposing that the inhabitants could, without much discomfort, dispense with fires for warmth during winter (*Mosäisches Recht,* iv:195). The modern Jews, although there is no cooking in their houses, have fires on the Sabbath day, which are attended to by a Christian servant, or a charwoman is hired to attend to the fires of several houses, which she visits repeatedly during the day. (2) Another law required the damage done by a conflagration in the fields to be made good by the party through whose incaution it had been kindled (Exod. xxii:6). This was a most useful and necessary law in a country where the warmth and drought of summer soon render the herbage and underwood highly combustible, so that a fire once kindled often spreads most extensively, and produces disastrous consequences (Judg. ix:15; xv:5). This law was calculated to teach caution in the use of fire to the herdsmen in the fields, who were the parties most concerned. And it is to be remembered that the herdsmen were generally substantial persons, and had their assistant shepherds, for whose imprudence they were made responsible. Still no inference is to be drawn from this law with regard to fires breaking out in towns, the circumstances being so very different.

(6) **Punishment.** Burning criminals alive does not appear to have been known to the Hebrews; but as an additional disgrace the bodies were in particular cases burnt after death had been inflicted (Josh. vii:25; compare verse 15); and it is in this sense that the allusions to burning as a punishment are to be understood, except when the reference is to a foreign usage, as in Dan. iii:22, 24, *sq.*

Figurative. (1) 'Fire from heaven,' 'fire of the Lord,' usually denotes lightning in the Old Testament; but, when connected with sacrifices, the 'fire of the Lord' is often to be understood as the fire of the altar, and sometimes the holocaust itself (Exod. xxix:18; Lev. i:9; ii:3; iii:5, 9; Num. xxviii:6; 1 Sam. ii:28; Is. xxx:30; Mal. i:10. (2) Fire was a symbol of the Lord's presence and the instrument of his power, either in the way of approval or of destruction (Exod. xiv:19, 24; Num. xi:1, 3, etc.). Thus Jehovah appeared in the burning bush and on Mount Sinai (Exod. iii:2; xix:18). In the midst of fire he showed himself to Isaiah, Ezekiel, and John (Is. vi:4; Ezek. i:4; Rev. i:14), and will so appear at his second coming (2 Thess. i:8). (3) Fire is the comparison of intense love (Cant. viii:6); of the injuring tongue (Ps. cxx:4; Prov. xvi:27; Jas. iii:5), and of godlessness (Is. ix:18). (4) God is compared to *fire* because of his purity, majesty, terribleness (Deut. iv:24; Heb. xii:29; Is. x:17). (5) Christ is compared to *fire;* he tries the children of men, purifies and comforts his people, and destroys his enemies (Mal. iii:2; Ezek. viii:2, and i:27). (6) The Holy Ghost is likened to *fire,* to denote his enlightening, purifying, sin-destroying, and holy love-enkindling influences (Matt. iii:11; Acts ii:3; Is. iv:4). (7) Angels are compared to *fire;* they are pure in their nature, and their execution of God's command is irresistible, awful and speedy (Ps. civ:4). (8) The church of God is likened to *fire;* she is often full of troubles; but, eventually she shall prevail over her opposers (Obad. 18). (9) The wicked are like *fire;* they are very dangerous and destructive to others, and hateful to God (Prov. vi:27; Is. lxv:5), and God makes them like a *fiery oven,* when he inflicts his judgments on them (Ps. xxi:9). (10) God's word is like *fire;* it tries the states and conditions of men; and it warms, melts and purifies the heart, and its threatenings are fulfilled (Jer. v:14, and xxiii:29).

FIRE BAPTISM. See BAPTISM OF FIRE; MOLECH.

FIREBRAND (fīr-brănd).

1. *Lap'peed* (Heb. לַפִּד, torch, Judg. xv:4). The firebrand used by Samson was probably a torch made of resinous wood or other material that would hold fire.

2. *Zake* (Heb. זֵק, Prov. xxvi:18), i. e., arrows fitted with combustibles (comp. Eph. vi:16).

3. *Ood* (Heb. אוּד, Is. vii:4; Amos iv:11), the burnt ends of wooden pokers (literally, fire stirrers), which would blaze no longer, but only continue smoking.

FIREPAN (fīr-păn), (Heb. מַחְתָּה, *makh-taw'*), a vessel used in the temple service (Ex. xxvii:3, xxxviii:3; 2 Kings xxv:15; Jer. lii:19). In Ex. xxv:38; xxxvii:23; Num. iv:9, the word is translated "snuff-dish," and in Lev. x:1; xvi:12; Num. xvi:6 ff, "censer." The first mentioned must have been like a chafing dish, to carry coals for burning incense; the other like a snuffer-dish to trim the lamps.

FIRES (fīrz), (Heb. אוּר, *oor*). In Is. xxiv:15 we read, "Glorify ye the Lord in the fires," but which is better rendered in the R. V. "East." The lands of the Asiatic East were called *oo-reem,* "the lands of light," i. e., the sun-rising, as opposed to the West, i. e., the "from the sea" (verse 14). (Barnes' *Bib. Dict.*).

FIRE, STRANGE. See FIRE, 3.

FIRE WORSHIP or PYROLATRY. The custom which prevailed among the ancient Persians and Medes, and which also obtained among the Carthaginians, Scythians, the ancient Germans and the ancient inhabitants of Great Britain.

Reville, *Religions of Mexico and Peru,* pp. 162 and 163, says: Among the Peruvians "fire, considered as derived from the sun, was the object of profound veneration. Strange as it may seem at first sight, the symbol of fire was stones. But . . . stones were thought to be animated by the fire that was supposed to be shut up within them, since it could be made to issue forth by a sharp blow. A perpetual fire burned in the Temple of the Sun and in the abode of the Virgins of the Sun. It was supposed that fire became polluted and lost its divine nature by too long contact with men. The fire must be renewed from time to time, and this act was performed yearly by the chief priest of Peru, who kindled wood by means of a concave golden mirror.

FIRKIN (fĕr'kĭn). See WEIGHTS AND MEASURES.

FIRMAMENT (fĕr'mȧ-ment), (Heb. רָקִיעַ, *raw-kee'ah,* expanse), the pure and transparent expanse of ether which envelops the globe. This is the

word which is translated as "the firmament of the heavens." It is explained in Gen. i:14, 15, 17, as that which is distended, expanded—the *expanse* of heaven. (See marginal reading.)

With some old astronomers the *firmament* is considered the region of the fixed stars, or the highest of all the heavens. But in Scripture, and in common language, it is used for the middle regions, the space or expanse appearing like an arch immediately above us in the heavens. Many of the ancients, and of the moderns also, account the firmament a fluid substance; but science has yet to find a better name than the term which Moses used so long ago, viz., *expanse.*

The Hebrews seem to have considered the *firmament* as transparent, like a crystal or sapphire (Ezek. i:22; Dan. xii:3; Exod. xxiv:10; Rev. iv:6).

FIRSTBORN (fẽrst' bôrn'). The rendering of several words from Heb. בָּכַר, *baw-kar',* to burst forth; Gr. πρωτοτόκος, *pro-tot-ok'os,* applied both to animals and human beings.

By the firstborn, in a religious point of view, we are to understand the first of a mother's offspring (Exod. xii:12). (See INHERITANCE.)

Figurative. The term *firstborn* denotes that which is most excellent. (1) Christ, the *firstborn* of every creature, and the *first-begotten* from the dead, who, as he was begotten from eternity, is dignified above all creatures, has a double portion of power, authority and fullness; is the great high priest consecrated for evermore, and is the first, the only person, who ever did or will rise from the dead by his own power. He is the head of all his chosen, the preserver of his father's name, and the sanctifier of his people (Col. i:15, 18; Rev. i:5). (2) The *firstborn of the poor* are those who are exceedingly wretched, having a double share of poverty (Is. xiv:30). (3) The *firstborn of death* is an accursed and most wretched and tormenting death (Job xviii:13).

FIRSTBORN, DESTRUCTION OF. See PLAGUES OF EGYPT.

FIRSTBORN IN ISRAEL.

(1) **Consecrated.** The first-born male of every Jewish family and of all beasts was consecrated to God in commemoration of the judgment which God brought upon the firstborn of Egypt (Ex. xiii:2). Several provisions of the Jewish law relate to the firstborn.

(2) **Privileges.** He received a double portion of the estate (Deut. xxi:17) and officiated as priest of the family in the father's absence or death. The privileges of the firstborn were obviously great in the cases of Esau and Reuben (Gen. xxvii:19, 32; 1 Chron. v:1, 2), but might be forfeited, as these two cases show. The religious pre-eminence of the firstborn ceased when the priesthood was committed exclusively to the tribe of Levi (Num. iii:12, 13). It was then required that a certain piece of money (5 shekels, about $2.50) should be paid for the redemption of all the firstborn of succeeding generations; and this redemption money became part of the sacred revenue (Num. viii:17; xviii:16).

(3) **Beasts.** The firstborn of all beasts used in sacrifice were devoted to the Lord (Ex. xiii:2), but the firstborn of unclean animals might be redeemed with the addition of one-fifth of the value (Lev. xxvii:13); otherwise they were sold, exchanged, or destroyed (Ex. xiii:13; Lev. xxvii:27). It is supposed that dogs were never redeemed (Deut. xxiii:18). (See BIRTHRIGHT.)

FIRST FRUIT (fẽrst frụt), (Heb. רֵאשִׁית, *ray-sheeth'*).

No doubt the leading object, as far as regards the offering of the first fruits to God, was, that all the after fruits and after gatherings might be consecrated in and through them, and it was not less the dictate of a natural impulse that the first fruits should be offered to God in testimony of thankfulness for his bounties. Hence we find some analogous customs among most nations in which material offerings were used. There are, however, some particulars in the Mosaical regulations which these considerations do not adequately explain.

1. First Fruits of Fruit Trees. It was directed that the first fruits of every tree whose fruit was used for food should, for the first three years of bearing, be counted 'uncircumcised,' and regarded as unclean (Lev. xix:23, 24). It was unlawful to sell them, to eat them, or to make any benefit of them. It was only in the fourth year of bearing that they were accounted 'holy,' and the fruit of that year was made an offering of first fruits, and was either given to the priests (Num. xviii:12, 13), or, as the Jews themselves understand, was eaten by the owners of it 'before the Lord,' at Jerusalem,' as was the case with second tithe. After the fourth year all fruits of trees were available for use by the owner. As the general principle of the law was, that only that which was perfect should be used in offerings, it is an obvious inference that the fruits of trees were considered imperfect until the fourth year, and if so, the law may have had the ulterior object of excluding from use crude, immature, and therefore unwholesome fruits. Michaelis (iii:267-8), indeed, finds a benefit to the trees themselves in this regulation.

2. First Fruits of Yearly Increase. Of these there were two kinds—(1) *The first fruits in the sheaf* (Lev. xxiii:10). (2) *The first fruits in the two wave-loaves* (Lev. xxiii:17). These two bounded the harvest, that in the sheaf being offered at the beginning of the harvest, upon the 15th of the month Nisan; the other at the end of the harvest, on the Feast of Pentecost. Both of these are called תְּנוּפָה, *ten-oo-faw'* (undulation), wave offerings.

(1) **Heave Offerings.** (1) *The first of the dough,* being the twenty-fourth part thereof, which was given to the priests (Num. xv:20), and this kind of offering was not neglected even after the return from Babylon (Neh. x:37). (2) *The first fruits of the threshing floor.* These two are together called תְּרוּמָה, *ter-oo-maw'*, (raised), 'heave offerings;' the one, the 'heave offering of the threshing floor,' the other, 'the heave offering of the dough.' The words *tenuphoth* and *terumoth* both signify 'shake offering,' 'heave offering,' or 'wave offering.'

(2) **First Fruits of Corn, Wine, etc.** The *second* sort consisted of corn, wine, oil and whatever other produce was fit for the support of human life. Under this class of first fruits was included the first of the fleece, by which the priests were provided with clothes, as by the other offerings with food. The hair of goats, which are shorn in the East, was included under this denomination.

(3) **Ceremonies.** The first fruits were brought up to Jerusalem with great pomp and ceremony. All the people of a given district assembled on an appointed day in one of the towns, and lodged in the streets. On the following morning the chief of the party gave the signal for departure.

When the party came to the mount of the Temple every one then, however high or noble, took his own basket upon his shoulder, and went forward till he came to the court of the Temple. The offerer, having the basket still upon his shoulder, then began to recite the passage, 'I profess this day,' etc. (Deut. xxvi:3-10). It was usual with those who were liberally disposed to hang turtledoves or pigeons about their baskets, and these formed part of the offering. The first fruits became the property of the course of priests which was in actual service. The party who brought them was obliged to spend the night following his offering in Jerusalem, but was at liberty to return home the ensuing morning.

It is obvious that this and some other of the apparently onerous obligations of the law, cannot be properly appreciated or understood when regarded in the 'dry light' of abstract duties or exactions. They were surrounded by engaging and picturesque associations, calculated to make their observance a matter of privilege and pleasure to all the parties concerned.

Figurative. (1) The ancient patriarchs were the *first fruits* of the Jewish nation, by whose means their posterity were blessed, and set apart to God (Rom. xi:16). (2) The Hebrews were the *first fruits of God's increase;* were long his peculiar people, before the gentiles were gathered to Shiloh (Jer. ii:3). (3) The *first fruits of the Spirit* are such communications of his grace on earth, as fully ensure the full enjoyment of God hereafter (Rom. viii:23). (4) The first fruits were typical of Jesus, the principal *first fruits,* who was before all things, who has in all things the preëminence, and by his consecration, oblation, and resurrection on the second day of unleavened bread his people are sanctified to God, and their resurrection and eternal happiness secured (1 Cor. xv:20), and whose Spirit descending at Pentecost, began to gather the nations to Christ (Acts ii). (5) They represent the saints, who, as *first fruits* to God, were chosen to his service; in the day of power devote themselves to him; are by grace rendered more excellent than their neighbors, and are a means of preserving and converting the nations to Christ. (6) Those who are first converted to Christ in a country are represented as the *first fruits* of it (Rev. xiv:4; Jam. i:18; 1 Cor. xvi:15).

FISH (fĭsh), (Gr. ἰχθύς, *ich-thoos'*, Gen. ix:2; Num. xi:22; Jonah ii:1, 10; Matt. vii:10; xiv:17; xv:34; Luke v:6; John xxi:6, 8, 11).

(1) Fishes, strictly so called, that is, oviparous, vertebrated, cold-blooded animals, breathing water by means of gills or branchiæ, and generally, provided with fins, are not unfrequently mentioned in the Bible, but never specifically.

(2) In the Mosaic law (Lev. xi:9-12), distinction of them is made into clean and unclean, according as they have fins and scales or are without them. Of the numerous species of fish which inhabit the lakes and rivers of Palestine and the adjacent sea, Solomon possessed some knowledge (1 Kings iv:33), but not a single variety has its name recorded in the Bible. (The whale is not a fish!)

(3) An aggravation of the first plague of Egypt was the destruction of fish—an important part of the food of the people. In the wilderness the Israelites murmured for the fish of their old home (Num. xi:5). It was a sad prophecy for Egypt that by the falling of her waters the fishermen should mourn, and that they should be disappointed who make ponds and sluices for fish (Is. xix:5-10; comp. Ezek. xxix:4-10).

(4) Most of the still and running waters of Palestine swarm with fish. Josephus first called attention to the similarity of the fish of the Sea of Galilee and those of the Nile. Of those in the former water Tristram says: the density of the shoals can scarcely be conceived by those who have not witnessed them. Frequently these shoals cover an acre or more of the surface, and the fish, as they slowly move along in masses, are so crowded, with their back-fins just appearing on the level of the water, that the appearance at a little distance is that of a violent shower of rain pattering on the surface. We obtained fourteen species of fish in the lake, and probably the number inhabiting it is at least three times as great.

But not all of these fish of Galilee are savory eating (Matt. xiii:47, 48). On this lake four of the disciples toiled as fishermen (Matt. iv:18-21).

(5) But the Hebrews could draw only a small supply from the lake of Tiberias and the affluents of the Jordan. On the coast the great sea-fisheries were in the slack waters, within the dominion of the Phœnicians, who must have sent the supply into the interior in a cured or salted state; although the fact involves the question how far in that condition, coming out of Pagan hands, consumption by a Hebrew was strictly lawful; perhaps it may be presumed that national wants had sufficient influence to modify the law. The art of curing fish was well understood in Egypt, and unquestionably in Phœnicia, since that industrious nation had early establishments for the purpose at the Golden Horn or Byzantium, at Portus Symbolorum in Tauric Chersonesus, and even at Calpe, in the present Bay of Gibraltar.

(6) The usual method of catching fish was either by casting the net (Hab. i:15; Ezek. xxvi:5, 14; xlvii:10; Matt. iv:18, 20, 21; Mark i:16, 18, 19; Luke v:2 ff; John xxi:6 ff), or dragging it (Is. xix:8; Matt. xiii:47). See Tristram, *Land of Israel*, pp. 245, 426, 485, 529, 544. The language of Matt. vii:10, and Luke xi:11, implies that one in need might ask a fish as a gratuity and expect to receive it.

(7) The Hebrews seem to have classified together all creatures living in the waters, whether 'whales' A.V. or 'sea-monsters' R.V. (Gen. i:21; Heb. *tunnînîm*), or 'great fish' (Jonah i:17; *dâg gâdhâl*), or the 'living creature that moveth' (Gen. i:21), or 'fish' (ver. 28). (See JONAH.)

(8) The fish was an object of idolatry in all the ancient world. The Philistines worshiped Dagon, the fish-god (1 Sam. v:4), who was represented with the body of a man and the tail of a fish (see DAGON). Hence it was forbidden to make an image of a fish (Deut. iv:18), which to the Hebrew included, as before said, all living creatures in the water (Ex. xx:4).

(9) The form of a fish (*Notius Poseidon*) was from remote ages, a type of protective dominion, as above indicated. As the symbolizing spirit of the ancients it passed into Christian observance, as appears from Eusebius (*Life of Constantine*), and St. Augustine (*De Civitate Dei*). On the walls of the oldest catacombs of Rome the representation of the fish is frequently discernible, and always interpreted as an emblem of the Savior.

Figurative. (1) Men are compared to *fishes* and *fishes of the great sea;* they are very numerous; their tempers and courses are very different; they often live in a very confused and disorderly manner; they prey on one another; they are frequently taken in the net of temptation and trouble, and sometimes in the net of the gospel. At last, by the providence of God, they are drawn to the shore of the eternal state; and the good fishes are separated from the sea (Ezek. xlvii:9, 10;

Eccl. ix:12; Matt. xiii:47-50). **(2) Ministers** are *fishers of men;* by casting the net of the gospel among them, with great labor and care they draw them to Christ and his church (Matt. iv:16; Ezek. xlvii:10). **(3)** The Chaldeans are called *fishers;* they ensnared, apprehended and carried out of their country multitudes of men (Jer. xvi:16; Hab. i:15).

FISHER (Heb. דָּוָג, *dav-vawg';* Gr. ἁλιεύς, *hal-ee-yoos'*).

In addition to the usual meaning, the Lord called his disciples "fishers of men" (Matt. iv:19; Mark i:17). (See FISHHOOK.)

FISH GATE (fish gāt), (Heb. שַׁעַר הַדָּגִים, *shah'ar had-dawg-yeem'*, gate of the fishes), the name (2 Chron. xxxiii:14; Neh. iii:3; xii:39) of one of the gates of Jerusalem. (See JERUSALEM.)

FISHHOOK (fish'hŏŏk), (Heb., plural סִירוֹת דּוּגָה, *see-roth' doo-gaw'*, horns of fishing, Amos iv:2; comp. Jer. xvi:16).

The method of taking fish with hooks was doubtless known in the early ages of the world (Job xli:1). The spear was also used (Job xli:7).

The usual way, however, was by a net—either a casting-net (Ezek. xxvi:5; xlvii:10; Hab. i:15; Matt. iv:20, 21; Mark i:18, 19; Luke, v:2; John xxi:6 ff.) or a drag net (Is. xix:8; Hab. i:15; Matt. xiii:47). In the latter case a boat was necessarily used. Such fishing was done, by preference, at night (Luke v:5). Angling was a favorite recreation in ancient Egypt. The reference in Job xli:2 is to the custom of putting a ring through the gill of a fish, and then by a line attaching it to a stake, the object being to keep it alive in the water until required for use. Besides amateur there were professional fishermen. Such were many of the apostles. (Schaff, *Bib. Dict.*)

FISHING (Heb. דִּיג, *deeg;* Gr. ἁλιεύω, *hal-ee-yoo'o*). For modes of fishing see FISHHOOK.

FISH POOL (fish pōōl), (Heb. בְּרֵכָה, *ber-ay-kaw'*, pool), in general a pond or reservoir (Cant. vii:4); a mistranslation for "pools" simply. There is no reference to fish. (See HESHBON.)

FITCHES (fich'ĕz), the rendering of two different words.

1. *Keh'tsakh* (Heb. קֶצַח, Is. xxviii:25, 27), which refers to the fruit of the *nutmeg flower, Nigella sativa,* L. It is a plant of the buttercup family.

Some species are cultivated in our flower gardens under such names as "love-in-a-mist." Fitches are grown for their small black, hot-tasting seeds, which are sprinkled over the flat cakes of the Syrians before they are baked. These tender seeds are still beaten out with a stout staff, as described in Is. xxviii:27.

2. *Koos-seh'meth* (Heb. כֻּסֶּמֶת, Ezek. iv:9), which should be *vetch* or *kirsenneh,* or as in the margin, "spelt." (See RYE; KETZACH.)

FLAG (flăg), (Heb. אָחוּ, *aw'khoo*).

Probably used, as by us, somewhat indefinitely (Ex. ii:3). If any special plant was intended it may have been the edible rush or the flowering rush, both of which abound in Egypt, and the latter in Palestine.

The Hebrew original, אָחוּ, is rendered (Gen. xli:2, 18) A. V. "meadow," R. V. "reed grass." It would be better to render it in all the passages *fens.* Another word, *soof* (Exod. ii:3, 5), is well translated "flags." (See ACHU.) For Flag, an Ensign, see STANDARDS.

FLAGON (flăg'ŭn), (Heb. אֲשִׁישָׁה, *ash-ee-shaw'*, a thin cake).

1. The word thus rendered in the A. V. (2 Sam. vi:19; 1 Chron. xvi:3; Hos. iii:1; Cant. ii:5) means rather a *cake*, especially of dried figs or raisins, pressed into a particular form. (See FRUITS.)

2. In Is. xxii:24 occurs the word *nebel*, which was used for a bottle or vessel, at first of skin, later of pottery (Is. xxx:14). The same word means a musical instrument; the "psaltery" of the A. V., or "viol."

FLAKE (flāk), (Heb. מַפָּל, *map-pawl'*, pendulous), the dewlaps or flabby parts on the belly of the crocodile (Job xli:23), which are firmly attached to the body and do not hang loosely as on the ox.

FLAME (flām). See FIRE.

FLANK (flănk), (Heb. כֶּסֶל, *keh'sel*, loin), in the plural the internal muscles of the loins near the kidneys, to which the fat adheres (Lev. iii:4, 10, 15; vii:4); hence the viscera in general, figuratively for the inmost feelings (Ps. xxxviii:7, "loins"). (See REINS.)

FLAX (flăx), (Heb. פִּשְׁתָּה, *pish-taw'*), a well-known plant, *Linum sativum,* L.

The fibers of the bark, when separated, twisted, bleached and woven, are *linen.* In the raw state they are "tow" (Judg. xvi:9; Is. i:31). Somewhat twisted, tow constitutes a "wick" (R. V. marg. Is. xlii:3; xliii:17). (See PISHTAH.)

Egyptian Flax.

It was produced of the best quality in Egypt (Is. xix:9), and was an article of extensive commerce.

At the present day, as in ancient times, flax is laid upon the housetop in the heat of the sun to dry (Josh. ii:6). It was anciently the labor of the most noble ladies (Prov. xxxi:13, 19, 24. (See LINEN.)

FLEA (flē), (Heb. פַּרְעשׁ, *par-oshe*, pulex irritans), occurs only 1 Sam. xxiv:14; xxvi:20, where David

thus addresses his persecutor Saul at the cave of Adullam: 'After whom is the king of Israel come out? after whom dost thou pursue—after a flea?' 'The king of Israel is come out to seek a flea.'

In both these passages the Hebrew means 'to pursue after, to seek *one* or a *single* flea.' David's allusion to the flea displays great address. It is an appeal founded upon the immense disparity between Saul as the king of Israel and himself as the poor, contemptible object of the monarch's laborious pursuit. Hunting a flea is a comparison, in other ancient writings, for much labor expended to secure a worthless result. However, the reference (1 Sam. xxvi:20) is considered by some an error in the text. Owing to the habits of the lower orders, fleas abound so profusely in Syria, especially during the spring, in the streets and dusty bazaars, that persons of condition always change their long dresses upon returning home. There is a popular saying in Palestine that 'the king of the fleas keeps his court at Tiberias;' though many other places in that region might dispute the distinction with that town (Kitto's *Physical History of Palestine,* p. 421).

J. F. D.

FLESH (flĕsh), (Heb. בָּשָׂר, *baw-sawr'*, fleshiness). This word bears a variety of significations in Scripture:

(1) Whole Animal Creation. It is applied, generally, to the whole animated creation, whether man or beast; or to all beings whose material substance is flesh (Gen. vi:13, 17, 19; vii:15, etc.).

(2) Humanity. But it is more particularly applied to 'mankind;' and is, in fact, the only Hebrew word which answers to that term (Gen. vi: 12; Ps. xlv:3; cxlv:21; Is. xl:5, 6). In this sense it is used somewhat figuratively to denote that evil principle which is opposed to the spirit, and to God, and which it is necessary to correct and subdue (Gen. vi:5; Job x:4; Is. xxxi:3; Matt. xvi: 17; Gal. i:16, etc.).

(3) Opposed to Soul. The word 'flesh' is opposed to *nephesh,* 'soul,' or 'spirit,' just as we oppose *body* and *soul* (Job xiv:22; Prov. xiv:30; Is. x:18).

(4) Ordinary Sense. The ordinary senses of the word, namely, the flesh of men or beasts (Gen. xli:2, 19; Job xxxiii:25), and flesh as used for food (Exod. xvi:12; Lev. vii:19), are both sufficiently obvious; and with respect to the latter see FOOD.

(5) General Term. The word 'flesh' is also used as a modest general term for the secret parts, in such passages as Gen. xvii:11; Lev. xii:3; Ezek. xxiii:20; 2 Peter ii:10; Jude 7. In Prov. v:11 the 'flesh of the intemperate' is described as being consumed by infamous diseases.

FLESH AND BLOOD (blŭd), (Gr. σάρξ καὶ αἷμα), an expression denoting man as fallible, liable to err (Matt. xvi:17; comp. Gal. i:16; Eph. vi:12).

Figurative. (1) "*Flesh and blood* cannot inherit the kingdom of God;" human nature, in its frail and corrupt condition, is not capable of the immediate enjoyment of God (1 Cor. xv:50). (2) We are not born again by the will of *flesh* or *blood;* that is, by natural descent from godly parents, or by any, however vigorous and careful, cultivation of our natural powers (John i:13). (3) *Flesh and blood,* that is, merely human means, did not reveal Jesus' true character as the Christ, the Son of the living God, to Peter (Matt. xvi:17). (4) Paul, when converted, conferred not with *flesh* and *blood;* consulted not earthly friends, inclinations or views regarding his true interest and duty (Gal. i:16).

FLESH HOOK (flĕsh'hŏŏk), (Heb. מַזְלֵג, *maz-layg'*, and מַזְלֵגָה, *maz-law-gaw'*), an instrument with a number of prongs bent backward to catch and draw the flesh from the fire when it was being roasted in the sacrificial service (1 Sam. ii:13, 14; Exod. xxvii:3; xxxviii:3; Num. iv:14; 1 Chron. xxviii:17; 2 Chron. iv:16). The hook mentioned in Samuel is three tined, and was probably only an ordinary culinary fork.

FLESHPOT (flĕsh'pŏt), (Heb. סִיר הַבָּשָׂר, *seer hab-baw-sawr'*, pot of the flesh), probably of bronze, standing on three legs, and suitable for cooking purposes (Exod. xvi:3).

FLIES (flīz), (Heb. זְבוּב, *zeb-oob'*, fly). The immense number of flies in the East is one of its most striking characteristics. The Heb. *zeb-oob'*, which is part of the name of the god of Ekron, Baal-zebub, is generic, but as the house fly is the most familiar representative it would be most frequently thought of in connection with this name. In speaking of the plague of flies the word used is עָרֹב, *aw-robe'*. (See FLY.)

FLINT (flĭnt), (Heb. חַלָּמִישׁ, *khal-law-meesh'*, perhaps hardness). The Heb. word צֹר, *tsor*, for צוּר, *tsoor*, is rendered "rock" (Job. xxviii:9).

Flint is a form of silica, a mineral which occurs in its purest condition as quartz. Flint is found in bands and nodules in certain calcareous rocks, notably in chalk, in various parts of the world. It is exceedingly hard, and breaks with a glassy fracture and sharp edges. When pieces of it are struck together, or against steel, sparks are emitted, and this method of obtaining fire has been used from the earliest times. It is probably alluded to in 2 Macc. x:3. Flints are often dark colored owing to impurities. Their origin is one of the problems of geology not yet completely solved, but it is supposed that the siliceous framework of certain marine organisms was dissolved, and afterward deposited in cavities, or actually substituted for the material of other organic remains. (Jas. Patrick, Hastings' *Bib. Dict.*)

Flint proper was the material almost everywhere employed in early prehistoric time for edge tools and weapons, prior to the use of metals. Its hardness, and the peculiar sharpness of its edges when broken or "flaked," rendered it all important for such purposes to primitive man, and hence the science of prehistoric archæology has dealt very largely with the study of flint implements, in their wide distribution, their varied forms and their stages of evolution from ruder and more finished types. All this lies back of any Old Testament references. (Barnes' *Bib. Dict.*)

Figurative. In Is. l:7 it signifies the firmness of the prophet against his persecutors. In Ezek. iii:9, the Hebrew *tsor* is translated "flint" in the same sense. The hoofs of horses are likened to flint (Is. v:28) in hardness.

FLOAT (flōt), of uncertain derivation. A *raft* for conveying bulky substances like timbers, etc., by water. Thus Solomon contracted with Hiram, king of Tyre, to have cedars cut on the western side of Mount Lebanon and floated to Joppa or Jaffa, and then carried overland to Jerusalem (1 Kings v:9). Sometimes spelled "flote" (2 Chron. ii:16).

FLOCK (flŏk).

Figurative. (1) Armies, nations and companies of men are likened to *flocks;* they are numerous, and are inspected, governed, and, as it were, fed and folded by their respective rulers (Jer. xlix:20 and li:23). (2) The chief ones of the *flock* are men distinguished in honor, power and wealth (Jer. xxv:34, 35). (3) The Jews are represented as the *Lord's flock;* they were peculiarly chosen, redeemed and governed by him; and a *beautiful flock* that made a glorious appearance at their solemn feast (Jer. xiii:17, 20); a *holy flock,* as they were separated to the service of God, and not a few of them sanctified by his Holy Spirit (Ezek. xxxvi:38); and a *flock of slaughter,* as in Christ's time, they were condemned to, and ripened for, judgments of God (Zech. xi:4). The Lord himself, and, under him their magistrates, prophets, priests and teachers, were their shepherds (Ps. lxxx; Ezek. xxxiv). (4) The church is likened to a *flock,* because of the number, the order and agreeable society of her members (Is. xl:11; Acts xx:28).

FLOOD (flŭd), (Heb. מַבּוּל, *mab-bool;* Gr. κατακλυσμός, *kat-ak-looce-mos'*). See DELUGE.

FLOOR (flōr), (Heb. גֹּרֶן, *go'ren*, to smooth), a level, or open area, as the "place" or square near the gates of oriental cities (1 Kings xxii:10; 2 Chron. xviii:9; A. V. "void place" in both passages). (See HOUSE; PAVEMENT; THRASHING FLOOR.)

FLOTES (flōtz). See FLOAT.

FLOUR (flour), rendered in the A. V. for the following: *Keh'makh* (Heb. קֶמַח, to grind, Judg. vi: 19; 1 Sam. i:24; xxviii:24, etc.); *So'leth* (Heb. סֹלֶת, to strip), from a *stripping off* the hull; the finest and purest of the meal, usually rendered "fine flour." (See BREAD; MEAL, etc.)

FLOWERS (flou'ērz). See PLANT.

FLUTE (flūt). See MUSIC.

FLUX, BLOODY (Gr. δυσεντερία, *doos-en-ter-ee'ah,* dysentery, Acts xxviii:8). This was a complaint which is often epidemic in the East. This was probably the disease of Jehoram (2 Chron. xxi:15,19).

FLY (flī), (Heb. זְבוּב, *zeb-oob*).

(1) The word occurs Exod. viii:21, 22, 24, 29, 31; Ps. lxxviii:45, and cv:31; all which passages relate to the plague of flies inflicted upon Pharaoh and his people. In the Septuagint it is uniformly rendered κυνόμυια, or the dog-fly.

(2) Philo, in his *Life of Moses* (i:23, p. 401, ed. Mangey), expressly describes it as a biting, insidious creature, which comes like a dart, with great noise, and rushing with great impetuosity on the skin, sticks to it most tenaciously. All the ancient translators understood by the original word, a mixture of noxious creatures. More modern writers, reasoning on other senses of the Hebrew word, and which are very numerous, have proposed several different insects. Thus, one of the meanings of the word is 'to darken,' and Mouffet observes that the name cynomyia agrees with no kind of flies, better than with those *black,* large, compressed flies, which boldly beset cattle, and suck out blood from beneath, and occasion great pain. He observes that they have no proboscis, but, instead of it, have double sets of teeth, like wasps, which they infix deeply in the skin, and adds that they greatly infest *the ears of dogs* (*Theat. Insect.* cxi). Others have proposed the blatta Orientalis or Ægyptia of Linnæus, as answering considerably to the characteristics of voracity, intrusion into houses, etc., etc. (Forskal, *Descrip. Animal.,* Præf., p. 22). The miracle involved in the plague of flies consisted, partly at least, in the creature being brought against the Egyptians in so great an

abundance during *winter*. The particular species is, however, at present undetermined.

FOAL (fōl), (Heb. עַיִר, *ah'yeer*, Gen. xlix:11; בֵּן, *bane*, son, Zech. ix:9; Gr. υἱός, son, Matt. xxi:5), an ass's colt. (See Ass.)

FOAM (fōm), (Heb. קֶצֶף, *keh'tsef*, something broken, a splinter). The original word is rendered "foam" in Hos. x:7, "As for Samaria, her king is cut off as the *foam* upon the water." It means a broken branch, a dry twig, or splinter.

FODDER (fŏd'dēr), (Heb. בְּלִיל, *bel-eel'*, Job vi: 5). The word properly signifies a mixture, a medley, and is rendered "corn" in Job xxiv:6, and "provender" in Is. xxx:24.

FOLD (fōld). Several Hebrew and Greek words are thus translated.

1. *Ghed-ay-raw'* (Heb. גְּדֵרָה, walled in, Num. xxxii:16, 24, 36). See HEDGE.

2. *Mik-law'* (Heb. מִכְלָה, a pen, Hab. iii:17; Ps. l:9; lxxviii:70).

3. *Raw-bats'* (Heb. רְבֵץ, to recline, Is. xiii:20). These three words, with the Gr. αὐλή, *ŏw-lay'*, signify a small inclosure for flocks to rest in.

4. The following terms, *Do'ber* (Heb. דֹּבֶר, Is. v:17; Mic. ii:12), and *Naw-veh'* (Heb. נָוֶה, at home, 2 Sam. vii:8; 1 Chron. xvii:7; Jer. xxiii:3, etc.), signify *pasture*.

In the passage in John x:6 the Greek word ποίμνη, *poym'nay*, means the *flock* itself. (See FLOCK.) There shall be one *flock* and one shepherd. The *folds* of the Christian Church may be many; the *flock* is one.

FOLDEN (fōld'en), (Heb. סָבַךְ, *saw-back'*).

This earlier participle of the verb *to fold* is found in Nah. i:10, 'while they be folden together as thorns' (R. V., 'like tangled thorns;' American R. V., 'entangled'). The meaning is that the thorns are intertwined so as to form an impenetrable hedge.

FOLLOWER (fŏl'lō-ēr), (Gr. μιμητής, *mim-ay-tace'*, an imitator).

St. Paul says to the Corinthian Christians: "Be followers of me," etc., meaning that they were to imitate him in all good things (1 Cor. iv:16; xi:1, etc.) ; also to take God as an example (Eph. v:1). In Phil. iii:17 the "followers" were to be co-imitators of him.

FOLLY (fŏl'lў), (mostly Heb. אִוֶּלֶת, *iv-veh'leth* and נְבָלָה, *neb-aw'law*).

The first word means *silliness*, as in Prov. v:23, etc.; the second word *emptiness* (Gen. xxxiv:7, and many others).

1. Folly denotes, in general, weakness of understanding (Ps. xiv:1; 1 Cor. i:27; iv:10), and sometimes sin or wickedness (Ps. xxxviii:5; Josh. vii:15). The transgression and disobedience of Adam were the height of folly, as is the sin of humanity generally. Foolish talking, jesting, foolish and unlearned questions, etc. (2 Tim. ii:23), are such as are vain, frivolous, or have no useful tendency.

2. The phrase "Thou fool" (Matt. v:22), implies not only an angry temper and foolishness, but probably also impiety and wickedness, in allusion to Ps. xiv:1, where the atheist is called a fool. (See FOOL.)

FOOD (fōōd), (Heb. לֶחֶם, *lekh-em*, bread, food).

The productions of a country, at an early period of the world, necessarily determined its food. Pal-estine abounded with grain and various kinds of vegetables, as well as with animals of different species. Such, accordingly, in general, was the sustenance which its inhabitants took.

(1) In Early Times. Bread formed 'the staff of life' to the ancient Hebrews even more than to ourselves; but the modes of preparing it have been noticed under other heads. (See BREAD; MILL.)

On a remarkable occasion a calf, tender and good, is taken, slain, dressed (roasted, most probably, Judg. vi:19; Gen. xxvii:7; 1 Sam. ii:13; Exod. xii:8, 9; boiling was not known till long afterward), and set before the guests, while the entertainer (Abraham) respectfully stood at their side, doubtless to render any desirable service. The sauce or accompaniments on this occasion were butter and milk. From Gen. xix:3 it may be inferred that the bread was unleavened.

The cases, however, to which reference has been made were of a special nature; and from them, as well as from what is recorded touching Isaac and Esau and Jacob, it appears that flesh meat was reserved as food for guests, or as a dainty for the sick; lentils, pulse, onions, grain, honey and milk being the ordinary fare.

The agreeable, and perhaps in part the salubrious, qualities of salt were very early known and recognized. In Lev. ii:13 it is expressly enjoined: 'Every oblation of thy meat-offering shalt thou season with salt; with all thine offerings shalt thou offer salt.'

Locusts were a permitted (Lev. xi:22) and a very common food. At the present day they are gathered by the Bedouins in the beginning of April, and, being roasted on plates of iron, or dried in the sun, are kept in large bags, and, when needed, eaten strewed with salt by handfuls.

Of four-footed animals and birds the favorite food were sheep, goats, oxen and doves. There are few traces of the eating of fish, at least in Palestine (Num. xi:15; Lev. xi:9-22). In the last passage a distinction is made between certain fish which might be eaten and others which were forbidden. 'These shall ye eat of all that are in the waters; whatsoever hath fins and scales in the waters, in the seas, and in the rivers, them shall ye eat; and all that have not fins and scales they shall be an abomination unto you.'

(2) Among the Egyptians. The distinction of clean and unclean animals, and of animals which might and those which might not be eaten, is found to have existed to a great extent in ancient Egypt. Among fish the oxyrrhynchus, the phagrus, and the lepidotus were sacred, and might not even be touched. The inhabitants of Oxyrrhynchus objected to eating any fish caught by a hook, lest it should have been defiled by the blood of one they held so sacred. The phagrus was the eel; and the reason of its sanctity, like that of the oxyrrhynchus, was probably owing to its unwholesome qualities; the most effectual method of forbidding its use being to assign it a place among the sacred animals of the country.

Neither the hippopotamus nor the crocodile appears to have been eaten by the ancient Egyptians. Some of the Egyptians considered the crocodile sacred, while others made war upon it (Herod. ii:69). In some places it was treated with the most marked respect, fed, attended, adorned, and after death embalmed. But the people of Apollinopolis, Tentyris, Heracleopolis and other places held the animal in abhorrence; how far they carried their dislike may be seen in Juvenal (*Sat.* xv), though something, probably, must be deducted from the account, in consideration of poetic license.

Cats as well as dogs were held in high esteem by the ancient Egyptians. The former especially were objects of superstitious regard. When a cat died in a house a natural death, a general mourning throughout the family ensued, and to kill one of these revered animals was a capital offense.

Though it appears that swine frequently formed part of the stock of an Egyptian farmyard, yet the animal was unclean and an abomination in the estimation of the Egyptians. Herodotus. tells us (ii:47) that if any one but touched a pig in passing he was compelled to bathe himself and wash his garments; and those of the natives who were swineherds were a degraded caste, with whom others would not intermarry.

(3) The Mosaic Law. The Mosaic laws which regulated the use of animal food may be found in Lev. xi. and Deut. xiv. The grounds of many of these regulations may be ascertained with a greater or less degree of probability, provided the student is well acquainted with the mind and spirit of Hebrew antiquity. Considerations drawn from idolatrous usages, regard to health, the furtherance of agriculture and established customs and tastes, had in each case an influence in the promulgation of these laws.

(4) Beverages. In the earliest times water was the common drink. That wine of an intoxicating tendency was drunk at a very early period appears from what happened to Noah (Gen. ix: 20), who seems to have made as well as drunk wine. Bread and wine are spoken of in Gen. xiv:18, as offered for refreshment to Abraham by Melchizedek, king of Salem. Water was sometimes put to the wine; at others a strong drink was made by mixing with the wine aromatic herbs (Ps. lxxv:8; Is. v:22), or a decoction derived from them; myrrh was used for this purpose. Date-wine was in use, and probably the Egyptian or malt wine, ζῦθος, οἶνος κρίθινος (Herod. ii:77). Jerome (*Opp.* iv. 364, ed. Bened.) says that 'drink, called by the Hebrews *Sikera,* is every kind which can inebriate, or that which is made from grain, or of the juice of apples, or when the honeycomb is made (decoquuntur) into a sweet and barbarous beverage, or the fruit of the palm expressed into a liquor, and when water receives a color and a consistency from prepared herbs.' 'The common people' (Mark xii:37) drank an acrid sort of wine, which is rendered vinegar in our English Version (Ruth ii:14; Matt. xxvii: 48). The Orientals frequently used wine in excess, so as to occasion intoxication, whence are drawn many striking figures in Holy Writ (Is.

v:11; xxviii:1; xlix:26; Jer. viii:14; ix:15; Deut. xxxii:42; Ps. lxxviii:65). That indulgence in wine was practiced in very ancient days is manifest from there being in the court of Pharaoh, at the time of Joseph, state officers who had charge of the wine, and served the monarch with it when he drank (Gen. xl:1, 2, 11; comp. Neh. i:11; 1 Kings x:5; 2 Chron. ix:4.) (See PALM TREE.)

(5) Drinking Cups. For drinking vessels there were used the cup and the bowl (Jer. xxxv:5; Amos vi:6; Zech. ix:15; Num. vii:13, 84). The cup was generally of brass covered with tin, in form resembling a lily, sometimes circular. It is still used by travelers, and may be seen in both shapes in the ruins of Persepolis (1 Kings vii:26). The bowl (Exod. xxv:33) assumed a variety of shapes, and bears many names. Some of these 'chargers' appear, from the presents made by the princes of Israel (Num. vii.), to have been of large size and great splendor; some were silver, some gold (1 Kings x:21).

(6) Meal Hours. In Eastern climes the chief meal, or what we term dinner, is, in consequence of the heat of the middle period of the day, deferred till towards evening, a slight repast being taken before noon (Adam, *Rom. Antiq.* p. 377, ed.

Major; Potter, ii. 625; Chardin, iv.; Jahn, i:2). But from Gen. xliii:16, 25, it appears to have been the custom to dine at noon in the days of the patriarchs. The same seems to have been the case in Palestine at a later period (1 Kings xx:16; comp. Acts x:10; Luke xi:37). Convivialities, however, were postponed till evening, and sometimes protracted to the following morning (Is. v:11; Mark vi:21; Luke xiv:24).

(7) Giving of Thanks. The meal was preceded by washing of hands (Luke xi:38; Mark vii:2), which the mode of eating rendered necessary, and by an invocation of the divine blessing (1 Sam. ix:13); in Greek, εὐλογία εὐχαριστία, *blessing,* giving of thanks (Luke ix:16; John vi:11). Similar customs prevailed among the Greeks and Romans. Jahn (*Bib. Antiq.,* p. 68) has given the short prayer, as preserved in the Talmud, which the Jews used, as follows: 'Blessed be Thou, O Lord our God, King of the world, who hast produced this food (or this drink) from the earth (or the vine)' (Matt. xiv:19; xv:36; xxvi:27).

(8) Table Customs. The Hebrews, like the Greeks and Romans in their earlier history, ate sitting (Gen. xxvii:19; Judg. xix:6; 1 Sam. xx: 25). A carpet was spread, on which the meal was partaken. At a later period, however, particularly when Palestine came under the influence of Roman manners, the Jews reclined on cushions or couches (Esth. i:6; Amos vi:4; Luke vii:37; ἀνεκλίθη, *reclined,* not 'sat,' as in the common translation). The custom of giving preference in point of seat or position to guests of high consideration appears from 1 Sam. ix:22, to have been of ancient date (Amos. iii:12). In the time of Christ (Luke xiv:8) the Pharisees, always eager for distinction, coveted the place of honor at meals and feasts. Women were not admitted to eat with the men, but had their meals supplied in their own private apartment (Esth. i:6-9). In Babylon and Persia, however, females mingled with males on festive occasions (Dan. v:2). In general the manner of eating was similar to what it is in the East at the present day. Special care was taken of favored persons (Gen. xliii:34;

1 Sam. i:4; ix:22; John xiii:26). Knives, forks and spoons were not employed for eating. The food was conveyed from the dish to the mouth by the right hand. The parties sat with their legs bent under them round a dish placed in the center, and either took the flesh meat with their fingers from the dish, or dipped bits of their bread into the savory mess, and conveyed them to their mouths. In Ruth ii:14, Boaz says to Ruth, 'Dip thy morsel in the vinegar,' which explains the language of our Lord (John xiii:26), 'He it is to whom I shall give a sop when I have dipped it.' This presenting of food to a person is still customary, and was designed originally as a mark of distinction, the choice morsels being selected by the head of the family for the purpose. Drink was handed to each one of the guests in cups or goblets, and at a very ancient period, in a separate cup to each person. Hence the word cup is used as equivalent to what we term a man's lot or destiny (Ps. xi:6; lxxv:8; Is. i:22; Matt. xxvi:39). J. R. B.

FOOL (fōōl), (Heb. אֱוִיל, *evil*, fool).

The fool of Scripture is not an idiot, but an absurd person; not one who does not reason at all, but one who reasons wrong; also any one whose conduct is not regulated by the dictates of reason and religion. Foolishness, therefore, is not a privative condition, but a condition of wrong action in the intellectual or sentient being, or in both (2 Sam. xiii:12, 13; Ps. xxxviii:5). In the Proverbs, however, 'foolishness' appears to be sometimes used for lack of understanding, although more generally for perverseness of will. (See Folly.)

FOOT (fōōt), (Heb. כֵּן, *kane*, a stand, with reference to the laver (which see); Heb. רֶגֶל, *reh'gel*; Gr. πούς, *pooce*, the human foot).

Of the various senses in which the word 'foot' is used in Scripture, the following are the most remarkable. Such phrases as the 'slipping' of the foot, the 'stumbling' of the foot, 'from head to foot' (to express the entire body), and 'foot-steps' (to express tendencies, as when we say of one that he walks in another's footsteps), require no explanation, being common to most languages. The extreme modesty of the Hebrew language, which has perhaps seldom been sufficiently appreciated, dictated the use of the word 'feet,' to express the parts and the acts which it is not allowed to name. Hence such phrases as the 'hair of the feet,' the 'water of the feet,' 'between the feet,' 'to open the feet,' 'to cover the feet,' all of which are sufficiently intelligible, except perhaps the last, which certainly does not mean 'going to sleep,' as some interpreters suggest, but to 'dismiss the refuse of nature.'

Figurative. **1.** 'To be under any one's feet' denotes the subjection of a subject to his sovereign, or of a servant to his master (Ps. viii:6; comp. Heb. ii:8; 1 Cor. xv:25), and was doubtless derived from the symbolical action of conquerors, who set their feet upon the neck or body of the chiefs whom they had vanquished, in token of their triumph. This custom is expressly mentioned in Scripture (Josh. x:24), and is figured on the monuments of Egypt, Persia and Rome.

2. In like manner, 'to be at any one's feet,' is used for being at the service of any one, following him, or willingly receiving his instructions (Judg. iv:10). The passage, in which Paul is described as being brought up 'at the feet of Gamaliel,' will appear still clearer, if we understand that, as the Jewish writers allege, pupils actually did sit on the floor before, and therefore at the

feet of the doctors of the law, who themselves were raised on an elevated seat.

(3) 'Lameness of feet' generally denotes affliction or calamity, as in Matt. xviii:8; xxxviii:17; Jer. xx:10; Micah iv:6, 7; Zeph. iii:9.

(4) 'To set one's foot' in a place signifies to take possession of it, as in Deut. i:36; xi:25, and elsewhere.

5. 'To water with the feet' (Deut. xi:10) implies that the soil was watered with as much ease as a garden, in which the small channels for irrigation may be turned, etc., with the foot. (See Garden.)

6. An elegant phrase, borrowed from the feet occurs in Gal. ii:14, where St. Paul says: 'When I saw that they walked not uprightly'—literally, 'not with a straight foot,' or 'did not foot it straightly.'

7. Nakedness of feet expressed mourning (Ezek. xxiv:17). This must mean appearing abroad with naked feet; for there is reason to think that the Jews never used their sandals or shoes within doors. The modern Orientals consider it disrespectful to enter a room without taking off the outer covering of their feet. It is with them equivalent to uncovering the head among Europeans. The practice of feet washing implies a similar usage among the Hebrews. Uncovering the feet was also a mark of adoration. Moses put off his sandals to approach the burning bush where the presence of God was manifested (Exod. iii:5). Among the modern Orientals it would be regarded the height of profanation to enter a place of worship with covered feet. The Egyptian priests officiated barefoot; and most commentators are of opinion that the Aaronite priests served with bare feet in the tabernacle, as, according to all the Jewish writers, they did it afterward in the temple, and as the frequent washings of their feet enjoined by the law seem to imply. (See Sandals.)

8. The passage, 'How beautiful upon the mountains are the feet of him that bringeth glad tidings, that publisheth peace' (Is. lii:7), appears to signify that, although the feet of messengers and travelers are usually rendered disagreeable by the soil and dust of the way, yet the feet of these blessed messengers seemed, notwithstanding, even beautiful, on account of the glad tidings which they bore.

Respecting the 'washing of feet,' see Ablution and Washing.

FOOTMAN (fōōt-man), (Heb. רַגְלִי, *ragli*, from *regel*, a foot).

1. A word used to distinguish the men who fought on foot from cavalrymen and charioteers.

2. A term applied to swift runners attached to the king (1 Sam. xxii:17). The same word is rendered guard (margin, "runners" (1 Kings xiv: 27, 28; 2 Chron. xii:10, 11; 2 Kings xi:4, 6, 11, 13, 19). There are many allusions in the Bible to the valuable accomplishment of swift running, though obscured by the translation of *gibbor* in the A. V. (Ps. xix:5; Job xvi:14; Joel ii:7), as "giant," "mighty man," "strong man."

FOOTSTEPS (fōōt'stĕps), (Heb. פַּעַם, *pah'am*, Ps. xvii:5; עָקֵב, *aw-kabe'*, Ps. lxxxix:51; Cant. i:8). To watch one's footsteps is to seek a cause for accusation (Ps. xvii:5, 11).

FOOTSTOOL (fōōt'stōōl), (Heb. כֶּבֶשׁ, *keh'besh*, something *trodden* upon); a support for the feet when on an exalted seat or throne (2 Chron. ix:18).

Such the ark was represented to be (1 Chron. xxviii:2; Ps. xcix:5; cxxxii:7); and the earth is God's footstool (Ps. cx:1; Is. lxvi:1; Matt. v:35).

FORBEAR (fŏr'bâr), **FORBEARANCE** (fŏr-bâr'ạns), (Gr. ἀνοχή, *an-okh-ay'*, a holding back, delaying, Rom. ii:4, iii:25).

The words mean: (1) To let alone (2 Chron. xxv:16). (2) To neglect (Num. ix:13). God's *forbearance* is the continued exercise of his patience, whereby he lets men alone, at least for a time, without punishing them (Rom. ii:4, and iii:25). Christian *forbearance,* required of us, is a patient letting of others alone, not resenting the injuries which they have done us, nor oppressing their conscience with a rigid imposition of our notions, or pattern, as their rule (Eph. iv:2; Col. iii:13). By long *forbearing* a *prince is persuaded;* by mild representations, repeated and submissive remonstrances and patient waiting, he is persuaded to do that which he would not had it been haughtily and rashly suggested to him (Prov. xxv:15).

FORCES (fōrs'ĕz), (Heb. חַיִל, *khah'yil*, strength, especially in a military point of view). It is applied to army, fortifications, etc. (Is. lx:5, 11).

FORD (fōrd), (Heb. מַעֲבָר, *mah-ab-awr'*, and מַעֲבָרָה, *mah-ab-aw-raw'*, a pass), a shallow place where a stream might be crossed easily by wading (Gen. xxxii:23; Josh. ii:7; Is. xvi:2). The Hebrew word also refers to the mountain pass at Michmash (1 Sam. xiv:4; Is. x:29). The fords of the Jordan seem to have been few and well known (Josh. ii:7; Judg. iii:28; xii:5, 6, A. V. "passages").

FOREFRONT (fŏr'frŭnt') is used in its present sense as the foremost part or place, e. g., the *forefront* of a building or of a battle (Ex. xxvi:9; 2 Sam. xi:15, etc.).

FOREHEAD (fŏr'ĕd), (Heb. מֵצַח, *may'tsakh*, to shine).

The practice of veiling the face in public for women of the higher class—especially married women—in the East, sufficiently stigmatizes with reproach the unveiled face of women of bad character (Gen. xxiv:65; Jer. iii:3). Reference is

made to this when Israel is called "impudent;" that is, "hard of forehead" (Ezek. iii:7, 8, 9).

Marks upon the forehead, for the purpose of distinguishing the holy from the profane, are mentioned in Ezek. ix:4, and again in Rev. vii:3.

The classical idolaters used to consecrate themselves to particular deities on the same principle. The marks used on these occasions were various. Sometimes they contained the name of the god; sometimes his particular ensign, as the thunder-

bolt of Jupiter, the trident of Neptune, the ivy of Bacchus, etc.; or else they marked themselves with some mystical number whereby the god was described.

If this analogy be admitted the mark on the forehead may be taken to be derived from the analogous custom among the heathen of bearing on their forehead the mark of the gods whose votaries they were. Some, however, would rather understand the allusion to refer to the custom of marking cattle, and even slaves, with the sign of ownership.

Figurative. (1) The saints having a mark or seal in their *foreheads* denotes their having full direction and protection amid terrible calamities (Ezek. ix:4; Rev. vii:3). (2) The saints having God's name in their *foreheads* denotes their open and bold profession of his truth, obedience to his law and conformity to his image (Rev. xiv:1 and xxii:4). (3) The *forehead* of an abandoned woman and a stiff *forehead* imports their shameless obstinacy in idolatry and other wickedness (Jer. iii:3; Ezek. iii:8). (4) God's setting a jewel on their *forehead* signifies his giving them public and great honor and wealth, and openly placing his tabernacle, temple and ordinances among them (Ezek. xvi:12).

Men's having the mark of the beast in their *forehead* denotes their open profession of the heresies and their bold attachment to superstition and idolatry (Rev. xiii:16 and xx:4).

FOREIGNER (fŏr'ĭn-ēr), (Heb. נָכְרִי, *nok-ree'*, stranger, Deut. xv:3; Obad 11; תּוֹשָׁב, *to-shawb'*, Exod. xii:45, dweller, as distinguished from a native; Gr. πάροικος, *par'oy-kos*, dwelling near, Eph. ii:19), one living in a country of which he is not a native, i. e., in the Jewish sense, a Gentile.

Toleration and special privileges were granted the heathen or alien people who dwelt among the Jews. For these they were required to observe certain regulations. They were not to blaspheme the name of Jehovah (Lev. xxiv:16); not to indulge in idolatrous worship (Lev. xx:2); not to commit acts of indecency (Lev. xviii:26); not to do any work on the Sabbath (Exod. xx:10); not to eat leavened bread during the Passover (Exod. xii:19); not to eat any manner of blood or flesh of animals that had died a natural death or had been torn by wild beasts (Lev. xvii:10, 15). Under such circumstances the law accorded to foreigners not only protection and toleration, but equal civil rights with the Israelites.

Figurative. The saints are termed *foreigners* or *strangers* on earth; they are born from above; have their possession and "conversation," i. e., their *citizenship* in heaven (1 Pet. ii:11; see also Ps. xxxix:12; Heb. xi:13).

FOREKNOWLEDGE (fŏr-nŏl'ĕj).

As an attribute of God, foreknowledge is simply a special case or aspect of omniscience. God knows all things, therefore not only the present and the past, but the future also, must lie open to His sight. This is implied in all His *promises,* whether they refer to the individual only, as where offspring is promised to Abraham (Gen. xviii:14), or are on a national scale, as when the glory of Abraham's descendants is foretold (Gen. xviii:18). It is implied also in the *warnings* which God gives, or causes to be given, as in the story of Lot and Sodom (Gen. xix), or in that of Moses before Pharaoh (Exod. viii-xi). To an earlier Pharaoh God shows in a dream 'what he is about to do' (Gen. xli:25), and similarly, at a later period, to Nebuchadnezzar 'what shall be in the latter days' (Dan. ii:28, 29).

It is, however, in its application, not to events generally, but to *salvation,* and that both of the individual and of the community, that the question of the divine foreknowledge has arrested the attention, engaged the thoughts, and sometimes tried the hearts of men. True piety refers all things to God, and rejoices to see in the individual life of faith and love the manifestation of divine activity. It seems to it that, were the case otherwise, there could be no assurance of salvation, and the peace which is the most priceless possession of God's children would be impossible to them. It is argued that, as God is both able and willing to bring about the salvation of the individual, He must know beforehand, not only His purpose to do so, but its fulfillment. We refer salvation, along with all other events, to the Divine Will; but, as God is not only Supreme Will, but Supreme Intelligence, before, or accompanying the forthputting of that will, there must be an act of knowledge. Thus foreknowledge comes to be associated with ELECTION and PREDESTINATION (which see) as a constitutive element in the ultimate ground of the salvation made known in Christ. (See the article GOD, 4.) (A. Stewart, Hastings' *Bib. Dict.*)

FOREORDINATION (fōr-ôr'dĭ-nā'shŭn). See ELECTION; PREDESTINATION.

FORERUNNER (fōr-rŭn'nēr), (Gr. πρόδρομος, *prod'rom-os*), one who is sent before to take observations or act as a spy, a scout, a light-armed soldier. In Heb vi:20 it is used in the sense of one who comes in advance to a place whither the rest are to follow, viz., Jesus Christ (John xiv:2), and also to make arrangements for them to follow.

FORESHIP (fōr'shĭp), (Gr. πρώρα, *pro'ra,* Acts xxvii:30, 41, "forepart"), the prow of a ship. (See SHIP.)

FORESKIN (fōr'skĭn), (Heb. עָרְלָה, *or-law' ;* Gr. ἀκροβυστία, *ak-rob-oos-tee'ah*), the prepuce, which was taken off in circumcision. (See CIRCUMCISION.)

FOREST (fŏr'ĕst), (Heb. יַעַר, *yah'ar,* a thicket). Tracts of woodland are mentioned by travelers in Palestine, but rarely what we should call a forest. The word translated by 'forest' is יַעַר, *ya'ar,* which does not necessarily mean more than 'woodland.' There are, however, abundant intimations in Scripture that the country was in ancient times much more wooded than at present, and in parts densely so. The localities more particularly mentioned as woods or forests are:

1. *The forest of cedars on Mount Lebanon* (1 Kings vii:2; 2 Kings xix:23; Hos. xiv:5, 6) which must have been much more extensive formerly than at present.

2. The name of *'House of the Forest of Lebanon'* is given in Scripture (1 Kings vii:2; x:17, 21; 2 Chron. ix:16, 20) to a palace which was built by Solomon in, or not far from, Jerusalem, and which is supposed to have been so called on account of the quantity of cedar trees employed in its construction, or, perhaps, because the numerous pillars of cedar wood suggested the idea of a forest of cedar trees.

3. *The forest of oaks,* on the mountains of Bashan. The trees of this region have been already noticed under ALLON and BASHAN.

4. *The forest or wood of Ephraim,* already noticed under EPHRAIM 4.

5. *The wood of Bethel* (2 Kings ii:23, 24). This was situated in the ravine which descends to the plain of Jericho.

6. The wood through which the Israelites passed while pursuing the Philistines (1 Sam. xiv:25).

7. The wood in the wilderness of Zeph, where David hid himself (1 Sam. xxiii:15 ff.).

8. *The forest of Hareth,* in the south of Judah, to which David withdrew to avoid the fury of Saul (1 Sam. xxii:5). The precise situation is unknown.

Figurative. (1) Forest is used symbolically to denote a city, kingdom, polity, or the like (Ezek. xv:6). Devoted kingdoms are also represented under the image of a forest, which God threatens to burn or cut down. See Is. x:17, 18, 19, 34, where the briers and thorns denote the common people; 'the glory of the forest' are the nobles and those of highest rank and importance. See also Is. xxxii:19; xxxvii:24; Jer. xxi:14; xxii:7; xlvi:23; Zech. xi:2. (2) The forest is the image of unfruitfulness as contrasted with a cultivated field or vineyard (Is. xxix:17; xxxii:15; Jer. xxvi:18; Hos. ii:12). (3) The Assyrian army is called a *forest,* how numerous and how stately was their appearance! but how soon were they consumed by the wrath of God! (Is. x:18, 19, and xxxii:19). (4) Egypt and her numerous cities, of their large army, under Pharaoh-necho, is called a forest (Jer. xlvi:23). (5) Jerusalem is called the *forest of the south field;* it lay near the south of Canaan; the Chaldeans marched southward to it, and its houses and inhabitants were numerous.

FORGIVENESS (fŏr-gĭv'nĕs), (Heb. כָּפַר, *kawfar',* to cover, to hide, to purge, to do away, Deut. xxi:8, et al.; נָשָׂא, *naw-saw',* to lift up, to take away, Gen. l:17, et al.; סָלַח, *saw-lakh',* and ἀφίημι, *af-ee'ay-mee,* to send away, let off, Ps. ciii:3, et al., Matt. vi:12, and most of the New Testament places; χαρίζομαι, *khar-id'zom-ahee,* to give gladly or freely, Luke vii:42, et al.). (Barnes, *Bib. Dict.*)

Forgiveness is an act of God toward man, and of man toward his fellow. To forgive sin is the exclusive prerogative of God, of whose law sin is the transgression (Ps. cxxx:4). Our Lord, by virtue of his Divine nature, assumed the prerogative and exercised the power of forgiving sins, which the scribes and Pharisees, viewing him merely as a man, made the occasion of a charge of blasphemy (Mark ii:5). The gospel makes known not only that there is forgiveness with God, but also how such forgiveness is made compatible with the Divine justice.

Forgiveness, full, free and everlasting, is offered to all who will believe and obey the gospel (Acts xiii:38, 39; 1 John ii:12). The duty of mutual forgiveness is urged upon man with the most solemn sanctions.

While Christ forbids retaliation and revenge, he does not command us to forgive, in the strict sense of the word, only on condition of repentance; but when this takes place the forgiveness must be prompt and cordial (Luke xvii:3, 4). We are bound to this, under the penalty of not having our own sins forgiven by God; or the canceling of the act of forgiveness if we have been pardoned (Matt. vi:12-15; xviii:15-35). The *forgiving spirit* Christ enjoins.

FORK (fŏrk), (Heb. קִלְּשׁוֹן שְׁלֹשׁ, *shel-oshe' killesh-one',* three of prongs), a three-pronged fork for pitching hay, or straw (1 Sam. xiii:21).

FORMER (fŏr'mēr), (Heb. קַדְמֹנִי, *kad-mo-nee'*); as to time it is anterior, and as to place it refers to the "East." R. V. has it "eastern" (Zech. xiv:8).

FORNICATION (fŏr'nĭ-kā'shun), (Heb. תַּזְנוּת, *taz-nooth' ;* Gr. πορνεία, *por-ni'ah*).

In Scripture this word occurs more frequently in its symbolical than in its ordinary sense.

Figurative. (1) In the Prophets woman is often made the symbol of the church or nation of the Jews, which is regarded as affianced to Jehovah by the covenant on Mount Sinai. In Ezek. xvi there is a long description of that people under the symbol of a female child, growing up to the stature of a woman, and then wedded to Jehovah by entering into covenant with him. Therefore when the Israelites acted contrary to that covenant, by forsaking God and following idols, they were very properly represented by the symbol of a harlot or adulteress, offering herself to all comers (Is. i:2; Jer. ii:20; Ezek. xvi; Hos. i:2; iii:1). And thus fornication, or adultery (which is fornication in a married state), became, and is used as the symbol of idolatry itself (Jer. iii:8, 9; Ezek. xvi:26, 29; xxiii:37). (2) Antirepresented on Egyptian monuments, though dating back to a period of fifteen centuries before the Christian era, bear evidence of an advanced state of fortifications—of walls built of squared stones, or of squared timber judiciously placed on the summit of scarped rocks, or within the circumference of one or two wet ditches, and furnished on the summit with regular battlements to protect the defenders.

(2) **More Ancient System.** All these are of later invention than the accumulation of unhewn or rudely chipped, uncemented stones, piled on each other in the form of walls, in the so-called Cyclopean, Pelasgian, Etruscan and Celtic styles, where there are no ditches, or towers, or other gateways than mere openings occasionally left between the enormous blocks employed in the work. As the first three styles occur in Etruria, they show the progressive advance of military archi-

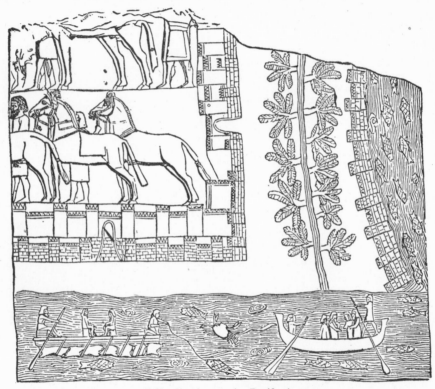

Tablet Showing Assyrian Fortifications.

christ is called the *great whore* and *mother of harlots and abominations,* because of its noted apostasy and idolatry, and decoying others into it; and such apostasy is called *fornication, whoredom,* or *adultery* (Rev. xvii, and xix:2). (3) Tyre *sang as a harlot* when by fair speeches the Tyrians enticed the nations to renew their trade with them (Is. xxiii:15).

FORT, FORTIFICATIONS, 'FENCED CITIES' (fôrt, fôr'tĭ-fĭ-kā'shuns). Several Hebrew words are thus translated: *Maw-tsood'* (מָצוֹר, net), a *fastness* (2 Sam. v:9; xxii:2, and five times in the Psalms); *maw-ooz'* (מָעוֹז, Dan. xi:19), a *stronghold,* fortified by nature and art; *daw-yake'* (דָּיֵק, 2 Kings xxv:1; Jer. lii:4).

Inventions for the defense of men in social life are older than history.

(1) **Egyptian.** The walls, towers and gates tecture, and may be considerèd as more primitive, though perhaps posterior to the era when the progress of Israel, under the guidance of Joshua, expelled several Canaanitish tribes, whose system of civilization, in common with that of the rest of Western Asia, bore an Egyptian type, and whose towers and battlements were remarkably high, or rather were erected in very elevated situations. When, therefore, the Israelites entered Palestine, we may assume that the 'fenced cities' they had to attack were, according to their degree of antiquity, fortified with more or less of art, but all with huge stones in the lower walls, like the Etruscan. Indeed, Asia Minor, Armenia, Syria and even Jerusalem still bear marks of this most ancient system. Stones from six to fifty feet in length, with suitable proportions, can still be detected in many walls of the cities of those regions, wherever quarries existed, from Nineveh, where beneath the surface there still remain ruins

and walls of huge stones, sculptured with bas-re-liefs, originally painted, to Babylon, and Bassorah, where bricks, sun-dried or baked, and stamped with letters, are yet found, as well as in all the plains of the rivers where that material alone could be easily procured. The wall was some-times double or triple (2 Chron. xxxii:5), suc-cessively girding a rocky elevation, and 'building a city' originally meant the construction of the wall.

In Biblical times the general distinction be-tween a city and village was that the former was surrounded by one or more walls, while the lat-ter was not. These walls were often crowned with battlements and parapets, with towers placed at frequent intervals (2 Chron. xxxii:5; Jer. xxxi:38). Engines of war were mounted on them, and, in times of war, a constant watch was kept (2 Chron. xxvi:9, 15; Judg. ix:45; 2 Kings ix:17). (Layard, *Nineveh.*) The walled towns of Palestine seldom served to check the invasion of an enemy, though they often prolonged the struggle (2 Kings xviii:10; xxv:3).

Figurative. (1) 'Sitting in the gate' of the fortress was, and still is, synonymous with the possession of power, and even now there is com-monly in the fortified gate of a royal palace in the East, on the floor above the doorway, a coun-cil-room with a kind of balcony, whence the sov-ereign sometimes sees his people, and where he may sit in judgment. (2) The Lord is the *fortress or stronghold* of his people. To him they flee in times of danger; in him they trust and find preservation from hurt (Ps. xviii:2; Nah. i:7). (3) "*The fortress* also shall cease from Ephraim" (Is. xvii:3), is an expression signifying that she loses her fortified cities, which were once her defense. (4) To *overthrow one's fortress* is to rob it of defense, to humiliate (Is. xxv:12). (5) Of the righteous man it is said, "his place of de-fense shall be the munitions of rocks" (Is. xxxiii: 16), i. e., God's protection shall be to him as the impregnable walls of a fortress upon a rock. "I have set thee for a tower and a *fortress* among my people," etc. (Jer. vi:27).

FORTH (Gr. ἐκδίδωμι, *ek-did'o-mee*), out, to let out, to deliver over (Luke xx:9).

In the following examples 'out' is distinctly the modern word, with *put* (Acts ix:40), 'Peter put them all forth' (Gen. viii:9; Judg. vi:21; Matt. ix:25); with *break* (2 Sam. v:20), 'The Lord hath broken forth upon mine enemies;' with *give* (Ezek. xviii:8, 13), 'He that hath not given forth upon usury;' with *set* (Ezek. xxvii:10), 'they set forth thy comeliness;' with *spread* (Ezek. xlvii: 10), 'a place to spread forth nets' (R. V., 'for the spreading of nets'); with *cast* (Jonah i:5, 12, 15); *let* (Luke xx:9), 'A certain man planted a vine-yard, and let it forth to husbandmen' (R. V., 'out'); *look* (Cant. ii:9), 'he looketh forth at the windows (R. V., 'in'); or omitted altogether, as in John ii:11, 'Jesus . . . manifested forth his glory.' (Hastings' *Bib. Dict.*)

FORTUNATUS (fôr'tū-nā'tus), (Gr. Φορτουνάτος *for-too-nat'os, from Latin,* fortunate), a disciple of Corinth, of Roman birth or origin, as his name indicates, who visited Paul at Ephesus, and re-turned, along with Stephanus and Achaicus, in charge of that apostle's first Epistle to the Corin-thian church, B. C. 59 (1 Cor. xvi:17).

FORUM APPII (fō'rum ăp'pi-ī). See APPII-FORUM.

FORWARDNESS (fôr'wĕrd-nĕs).

1. Gr. Σπουδή, *spoo-day'*, literally *haste,* and gen-erally of *earnestness* in accomplishing (2 Cor. viii:8; in ver. 7 "diligence").

43

2. Gr. Προθυμία, *proth-oo-me'ah* (2 Cor. ix:2; R. V. "readiness"), literally *predisposition.*

FOUNDATION (foun-dā'shŭn).

1. The lower part of any structure, as of a house, wall, mountain, etc., which supports the rest (Ezra iv:12; 2 Sam. xxii:16; Deut. xxxii:22).

2. The beginning of a thing; thus, the *founda-tion of the world* denotes the beginning of it (Matt. xiii:35).

Figurative. (1) Christ is a *foundation;* on his person, office and work is his church, and the whole of our salvation erected and supported (Is. xxviii:16; 1 Cor. iii:11; Matt. xvi:18). (2) He is likened to twelve *foundations* of precious stones; he is infinitely precious, adapted to every case, and exhibited in the doctrine of his twelve apostles (Rev. xxi:14, 19, 20). (3) God's truths, pub-lished by the prophets and apostles, are a *founda-tion;* on them the saints found their faith and hope (Eph. ii:20). (4) The first principles of Divine truth are a *foundation,* as they ought to be first known, in order to understand the rest, which depend on them (Heb. vi:1, 2). (5) Teaching these Divine truths is called a *foundation.* (6) Paul studied so to preach Christ as not to build on another man's *foundation;* i. e., to preach Christ where nobody had before taught the first princi-ples of Christianity (Rom. xv:20). (7) Magis-trates, and the principal constitutions of their gov-ernment, are the *foundations* of a state that support and establish the rest (Ps. lxxxii:5 and xi:3; Mic. vi:2). (8) The righteous are an everlasting *foun-dation;* being fixed in Christ, their persons, and holy and happy state and condition, are stable and fixed, and they are great means of supporting and establishing nations and churches (Eph. ii:20). They lay up a good *foundation* for the time to come; the *good foundation* they lay up is the heav-enly glory itself, which is fixed and stable, and on that account is called a city having foundations (1 Tim. vi:19; Heb. xi:10). (9) The *founda-tion of God* that *standeth sure, having this seal. The Lord knoweth them that are his,* i. e., the fundamental truths of the gospel, that cannot be overthrown; or the saints themselves, divinely fixed in their new covenant state (2 Tim. ii:19). (10) The *foundations* or *pillars* of heaven are the mountains on which the skies seem to rest (2 Sam. xxii:8).

FOUNTAIN (foun'tĭn), the rendering of several Hebrew words and one Greek word.

1. *Ah'yin* (Heb. עַיִן, *eye*), a natural source of *living* water (Gen. xvi:7; Deut. viii:7, xxxiii:28; 1 Sam. xxix:1; Prov. viii:28, etc.).

2. *Mah-yawn'* (Heb. מַעְיָן), a spring of running water (Lev. xi:36; Josh. xv:9; Ps. lxxiv:15; Prov. xxv:26); a well-watered place (Ps. lxxxiv:6); A. V. "well"; R. V. "a place of springs."

Figurative. (1) God is called a *fountain of living waters* and with him is the *fountain* of liv-ing waters; he is the unsearchable and unfailing source of all our happiness and comfort (Jer. ii: 13; Ps. xxxvi:9). (2) Jesus Christ is an open fountain, a *fountain of gardens, a well of living waters,* and *streams* from Lebanon (Zech. xiii). (3) The church is a *spring shut up,* and *fountain sealed* (Is. lviii:11). All the saints' *springs are in her;* in her dwells God, the fountain of living wat-ers; Jesus, the smitten, the water-yielding Rock of Ages; the Holy Ghost, that *river* of life, issuing from under the throne of God, and the Scrip-tures and ordinances. (4) Spiritual knowledge and wisdom, and the fear of the Lord, are a *foun-tain,* or *well-spring of life;* a delightful means of promoting the temporal and spiritual happiness of ourselves and others (Prov. xvi:22; xviii:4; xiii:14) and (xiv:27). (5) Wives are called *fountains and wells;* they bring forth children, that, as streams, are dispersed in the streets, and are a great means of happiness and comfort to their husbands (Prov. v:15, 18). (6) Children are *fountains,* and the offspring of Jacob, *his fountain;* they are means of help and comfort to their parents, and, in due time, produce children of their own (Prov. v:16; Deut. xxxiii:28). (7) *Fountains* and *springs* also denote prosperity and the means thereof (Hos. xiii:15). Thus, to turn dry land into springs of water is to afford great prosperity to a distressed nation, or to grant plenty of ordinances and powerful influences to a church or people that had been barren and withered (Ps. cvii:35; Is. xxxv:7; xli:11, and xlix:10). (8) To turn *springs* and *rivers* into a wilderness is not only to alter the soil of fields to the worse, as God has done in Idumea, Canaan, Egypt, etc., but to change great prosperity into sad adversity (Ps. cvii:33).

FOUNTAIN-GATE (foun'tĭn-gāt). See JERUSALEM.

FOWL (foul).

In the New Testament "fowls" is the frequent rendering of the Greek τὰ πετεινά, which comprehends all kinds of birds (Matt. xiii:4; Mark iv:4, etc.). (See BIRDS; COCK, etc.)

FOWLER (foul'ẽr), (Heb. יָקוֹשׁ, *yaw-koosh',* to lay snares, Ps. xci:3; Prov. vi:5; Jer. v:26; Hos. ix:8), one who took birds by means of nets, snares, decoys, etc.

Among the Egyptians "fowling was one of the great amusements of all classes. Those who followed this sport for their livelihood used nets and traps, but the amateur sportsman pursued his game in the thickets and felled them with the throw-stick . . . The throw-stick was made of heavy wood, and flat, so as to offer little resistance to the air in its flight, and the distance to which an expert could throw it was considerable. It was about one foot and a quarter to two feet in length and about one and a half inches in breadth, slightly curved at the upper end. They frequently took with them a decoy bird, and, in order to keep it to its post, a female was selected, whose nest, containing eggs, was deposited in the boat" (Wilkinson, *Ancient Egyptians,* i:234, *sq*). By a humane and just regulation Moses forbade anyone finding a bird's nest, to take the mother with the eggs or young (Deut. xxii:6, 7) lest the species be extinguished; or, perhaps, to impress upon men the sacredness of the relation between parent and young.

FOX. In several places it is uncertain whether Heb. שׁוּעָל, *shoo-awl';* Gr. ἀλώπηξ, *al-o'pakes,* signifies *fox* or *jackal* (Lam. v:18; Ezek. xiii:4; Cant. ii:15). In others it probably means *jackals* (Judg. xv:4; Ps. lxiii:10).

Under this term, as above indicated, the jackal is included—indeed, most of the references seem to be to that animal. The Orientals at the present time do not distinguish in common language between the two creatures. Both are common in Palestine. The fox (*Vulpes vulgaris*) is smaller than the jackal (*Canis aureus*), and is of a reddish hue, while the latter is yellowish; hence its scientific name, meaning "the golden dog." It is the latter also, and not the fox, which devours the dead and follows the armies that he may feed on human bodies left behind (Ps. lxiii:10). Both animals are omnivorous, but the jackal, which goes in packs, is even more destructive to the

vineyards than the other (Cant. ii:15). The crafty, artful nature of the fox is proverbial (Ezek. xiii:4; Luke xiii:32). He prowls singly for his prey of birds or small quadrupeds, which he takes by stratagem. Jackals are concealed by hundreds

Jackal.

among the ruins, caves and gardens of Syria (Lam. v:18). At sunset they come forth, and both then and at intervals through the night the traveler hears their cry, resembling the confused wailing of many infants. (See SHUAL.)

Figurative. (1) False prophets and teachers are likened to *foxes;* how crafty! how obstinate in their evil way! how uneven and inconsistent their doctrine and practice! (Ezek. xiii:4; Cant. ii:5). (2) Tyrants and other wicked men are likened to *foxes* for their craft, obstinacy in sin, and ruinous designs against others (Luke xiii: 32). (3) Inward sinful lusts resemble *foxes;* how crafty, stubborn, abominable and ruinous to the souls of men! and how hurtful to the graces of the saints! (Cant. ii:15). (4) To be the *portion of foxes* is for men to have their land or habitation rendered desolate and ruinous, and themselves left unburied (Ps. lxiii:10). (5) The fox's fondness for grapes is alluded to in Cant. ii:15.

FRAME (Heb. יֵצֶר, *yay'tser,* form), as of the human body (Ps. ciii:14); "thing framed" (Is. xxix:16); and "the *frame* of a city" (Heb. מִבְנֶה, *mib-neh',* Ezek. xl:2), a city building.

It denotes in general:

1. To contrive, to manage (Judg. xii:6), 'he could not frame to pronounce it right.'

2. To direct (Hos. v:4), 'They will not frame their doings to turn unto their God.'

3. To form (Is. xxix:16), 'Shall the thing framed say of him that framed it, He had no understanding?'

4. To fit together, make (Eph. ii:21), 'all the building fitly framed together.'

5. To devise (Ps. l:19), 'thy tongue frameth deceit'; (xciv:20), 'which frameth mischief'; (Jer. xviii:11), 'Behold, I frame evil against you.'

FRANKINCENSE (frănk'ĭn-sĕns), (Heb. לְבֹנָה, *leb-o-naw',* whiteness).

A dry, resinous, aromatic substance of a white or yellowish color, bitter and acrid to the taste, burning for a long time with a clear, steady and very odoriferous flame. Several trees (of the genus *Boswellia*) which grow in India, Arabia and Africa, yield this gum from incisions in the bark. Along the coast of Hadramaut, a district of Arabia, as Carter has shown, frankincense (the olibanum of commerce) is produced, as was affirmed by Herodotus, Celsius, other ancient writers and the Bible (Is. lx:6; Jer. vi:20). The Arabian species (*B. Carterii*) somewhat resembles, especially in its pinnate leaves when young, the mountain ash. This gum, in the above and other passages, is mentioned simply as "incense." It is

Frankincense Plants, Etc.

called *frank* because of the freeness with which it burns and gives forth its odors; and the pure incense is that which is first obtained and is freest from foreign admixture.

"Sweet incense" (Exod. xxx:7) might as well be rendered "incense of spices," and is the composition mentioned in Exod. xxx:34.

The use of incense in the Jewish worship may be learned from Exod. xxx:7 and Lev. xvi:12, 13, and it is figuratively employed to represent lovely and agreeable qualities (Cant. iii:6; iv:6, 14), and devotional fervor (Ps. cxli:2; Mal. i:11; Rev. viii:3). (Schaff, *Bib. Dict.*) (See OFFERING; SACRIFICE.)

FRANKLY (fränk'lĭ), (Gr. χαρίζομαι, *khar-id'-zom-ahee*, Luke vii:42).

The English word 'frankly' is used, not in the modern sense of *candidly, openly,* but in the old and literal sense of *freely, unrestrainedly,* as in Elyot, *The Governour,* ii:234, 'puttynge out of their citie their women and all that were of yeres unhabill for the warres, that they mought more frankely sustayne famyne;' and in Shakes. *Meas. for Meas.,* III, i:106:

'O, were it but my life,
I'd throw it down for your deliverance
As frankly as a pin.'

Wycliffe 1380, "he sat freely." R. V. omits the word altogether.

FRAY (Heb. חָרַד, *khaw-rad'*, to frighten, Deut. xxviii:26; Jer. vii:33; Zech. i:21), an old word, signifying to frighten, to scare away, as the driving of wild beasts from a dead body.

FRECKLED SPOT (frĕk'k'ld spŏt), (Heb. בֹּהַק, *bo'hak,* Lev. xiii:39), an "efflorescence on the skin, not uncommon in the East, consisting of spots of a palish white, resembling the leprosy, but harmless, and neither contagious nor hereditary." It was a tetter or "a wen of white color," Tyndale. (Gesenius, *Lex.,* s. v.)

FREEDOM (frē'dŭm), (Heb. חֻפְשָׁה, *khoof-shaw',* liberty; Gr. πολιτεία, *pol-ee-ti'ah,* citizenship, Acts xxii:28). See LIBERTY; SLAVE.

FREEDOM OF GOD and FREEDOM OF MAN. See LIBERTY; WILL.

FREEDOM YEAR. See JUBILEE.

FREEMAN (frē'man), (Gr. ἀπελεύθερος, *ap-el-yoo'ther-os,* one set free), a person who had been freed (I Cor. vii:22). Especially 'the Lord's freeman' (R. V. 'freedman'), so as to bring out the spiritual emancipation and to distinguish from the natural 'freeman' following. In Gal. iv:22, 23, 30, a strong distinction is drawn between the freewoman and the bondmaid. (See SLAVE.)

FREEWILL OFFERING (frē'wĭl ŏf'fēr-ĭng). See OFFERING.

FRET (Heb. פָּחֶתֶת, *pekh-eh'theth,* Lev. xiii:55, to wear a hole by corrosion, to eat like moth or mildew; Heb. חָרָה, *khaw-raw',* Ps. xxxvii:1, primitive root, to grow warm, glow, vex, displease in the sense of vying with a rival).

FRIEND (Heb. רֵעַ, *ray'ah,* associate), a person with whom one has friendly intercourse (Gen. xxxviii:12, 20; 2 Sam. xiii:3; Job. ii:11; xix:21, etc.); also a *lover, one beloved* of a woman (Cant. v:16).

1. *Het-ah'ee-ros* (Gr. ἑταῖρος, comrade, Matt. xi: 19, A. V. "fellow"), used in kindly address (Matt. xx:13; xxii:12; xxvi:50).

2. *Pi' tho* (Gr. Πείθω, Acts xii 20), is used in the sense of to *pacify,* to *win one's favor.*

3. *Fee' los* (Gr. φίλος), one attached by affection; frequently used in the New Testament, as Jas. ii:23; iv:4. (Barnes' *Bib. Dict.*)

(a) Christ's *friends* and *neighbors,* whom he invites to rejoice with him at the conversion of his elect, are angels, ministers, and saints, who ardently love him and his Father, promote his honor and cause, and have much intimacy with him Luke xv:6, 9; James ii:22; John xv:15). (b) In allusion to the *friend* at marriages, who performed the honors of the wedding, and led the bride to the nuptial bed, John Baptist, and other ministers, are *friends of the Bridegroom;* they, by their preaching and example, direct and conduct sinners to Christ (Judg. xiv:20; John iii:29). (c) Judas, and the man without the wedding garment were but pretended *friends;* or the word is used as a term of discreet address (Matt. xxvi:50, and xxii:12. (d) The *friendship* of this world, which is enmity with God, is a superlative love and desire of earthly and sinful things, and a study to obtain the favor of worldly men, by conformity to them in their evil courses (James iv: 4; Matt. vi:24; Luke xvi:13).

FRINGE (frĭnj), (Heb. גְּדִל, *ghed-eel',* twisted thread, i. e., a tassel, Deut. xxii:12; צִיצִת, *tsee-tseeth',* flowery, bloomlike, and so tassel, Num. xv: 38, 39).

Fringes were a part of the outer garment, and the same as the hem or border of the garment (Deut. xxii:12; Matt. ix:20; xiv:36).

The children of Israel were enjoined to wear them by Moses (Num. xv:38), and to place them on the four borders or edges of their outer garment, which was usually rectangular in shape. They were of a blue color.

The object of the fringes was to remind the children of Israel of the commandments of God (Num. xv:39). In the time of our Lord they had become objects of parade and show, so that he finds an evidence of the hypocrisy of the Pharisees in their practice of "enlarging the borders of their garments." The "hem of the garment" which the woman with the issue of blood touched (Matt. ix:20), was the ancient fringe enjoined by Moses. (See CLOTHING.)

FROG (frŏg) (Heb. צְפַרְדֵּעַ, *tsef-ar-day'ah*, frog, Exod. viii:2).

Although the common frog is so well known that no description is needed to satisfy the reader, it may be necessary to mention that the only species recorded as existing in Palestine is the green (*Rana esculenta*), and that of all the authorities we have been able to consult, Dr. Richardson alone refers the species of Egypt to the green-speckled grey frog (*Rana punctata*). But considering the immense extent of the Nile from south to north, and the amazing abundance of these animals which it contains in the state of spawn, tadpole, and complete frog, it is likely that the speckled is not the only species found in its waters, and that different species, if they do not occur in the same locality, are at least to be met with in different latitudes. The speckled species is found westward, even to the north of France. It is lively, but no strong swimmer, the webs on the hinder toes extending only half their length; hence, perhaps, it is more a terrestrial animal than the common green frog, and, like the brown species, is given to roam on land in moist weather.

Frog.

Although it is very hazardous in transactions of an absolutely miraculous nature to attempt to point out the instruments that may have served to work out the purposes of the Almighty, we may conjecture that, in the plague of frogs, a species, the one perhaps we have just mentioned, was selected for its agility on land, and that, although the fact is not expressly mentioned, the awful visitation was rendered still more ominous by the presence of dark and rainy weather —an atmospheric condition never of long duration on the coast of Egypt, and gradually more and more rare up the course of the river.

We have ourselves witnessed, during a storm of rain, frogs crowding into our cabin, in the low lands of Guiana, till they were packed up in the corners of the apartment, and continually falling back in their attempts to ascend above their fellows; and the door could not be opened without others entering more rapidly than those within could be expelled. Now, as the temples, palaces and cities of Egypt stood, in general, on the edge of the ever dry desert, and always above the level of the highest inundations, to be there visited by

a continuation of immense number of frogs was assuredly a most distressing calamity; and as this phenomenon, in its ordinary occurrence within the tropics, is always accompanied by the storms of the monsoon or of the setting in of the rainy season, the dismay it must have caused may be judged of when we reflect that the plague occurred where rain seldom or never falls, where none of the houses are fitted to lead off the water, and that the animals appeared in localities where they had never before been found, and where, at all other times the scorching sun would have destroyed them in a few minutes. Nor was the selection of the frog as an instrument of God's displeasure without portentous meaning in the minds of the idolatrous Egyptians, who considered that animal a type of Pthah—their creative power—and also an indication of man in embryo. The magicians, indeed, appeared to make frogs come up out of the waters; but we must not understand that to them was given also the power of producing the animals. The effect which they claimed as their own was a simple result of the continuation of the prodigy effected by Moses and Aaron; for that they had no real power is evident, not only from their inability to stop the present plague, the control of which even Pharaoh discovered to be solely in the hands of Moses, but also the utter failure of their enchantments in that of lice, where their artifices were incompetent to impose upon the king and his people.

C. H. S.

FRONTIER (frŏn'tēr), (Heb. קָצֶה, *kaw-tseh'*, Ezek. xxv:9), the extremity or border of a country.

FRONTLET (frŭnt'lĕt), (Heb. טוֹטָפָה, *to-taw-faw'*, to bind, only in Exod. xiii:16; Deut. vi:8; xi: 18).

FROST (frŏst), (Heb. כְּפוֹר, *kef-ore'*, so called from *covering* the ground, "hoar frost," Exod. xvi:14). Light frosts are frequent in certain parts of Palestine and the pools become covered with thin ice (Barclay, *City of the Great King*, p. 50).

FROWARDNESS (frō'wĕrd-nĕs), (Heb. תַּהְפֻּכָה, *tah-poo-kaw'*), perverseness (Deut. xxxii:20); falsehood, deceit (Prov. ii:12; vi:14, etc.).

FRUITS (frŭtz), (Heb. פְּרִי, *peri*, fruit), in general, vegetable or animal (Deut. vii:13, *bis*; xxviii:51, *bis*).

It originated the English word 'fruit,' by the פ being sounded as *ph*, and subsequently converted into *f*. Under this head may perhaps be most appropriately noticed a classification of produce of great importance to a right understanding of the Bible, since the beauty and force of more than forty passages of the sacred record are impaired by inattention to it.

(1) **Summer Fruits.** The term *kayits*, 'summer-fruits,' appears to denote those less important species of fruit which were adapted only to immediate consumption, or could not be easily or conveniently conserved for winter use (Jer. xl:10, 12). *Kayits* may have been included as a species under the head of orchard-fruit; it would seem to indicate either the existence of some contrasted term, as 'winter-fruits,' or to imply that the products of the class under which it ranked as a species were generally distinguished by their capability of being preserved throughout the year. It is conceived that the products denoted by the third of the generic terms now to be considered were chiefly characterized by their capacity of being stored up and *preserved*. The three terms spoken of as being so frequently associated in the Scriptures, and expressive of a most comprehen-

sive triad of blessings, are Dagan, Tirosh, and Yitzhar.

(2) Fruit of the Field. *Dagan,* 'fruit of the field,' or agricultural produce. Under this term the Hebrews classed almost every object of field culture. (See AGRICULTURE.) Dr. Jahn says, 'the word is of general signification, and comprehends in itself different kinds of grain and pulse, such as wheat, millet, spelt, wall-barley, barley, beans, lentils, meadow-cummin, pepper-wort, flax, cotton, various species of the cucumber, and perhaps rice' (*Bib. Antiq.,* sec. 58). There is now no doubt among scholars that *dagan* comprehends the largest and most valuable species of vegetable produce; and therefore it will be allowed that the rendering of the word in the common version by '*corn*,' and sometimes by '*wheat*,' instead of '*every species of corn*' or field produce, tends to limit our conceptions of the divine bounty, as well as to impair the beauty of the passages where it occurs.

(3) Fruit of the Vine. *Tirosh,* 'the fruit of the vine,' in its natural or its solid state, comprehending grapes, moist or dried, and the fruit in general, whether in the early cluster or the mature and ripened condition (Is. lxv:8), which is rendered by βότρυϊ, *grape,* in the Septuagint, refers to the young grape; while (Judg. ix:13), where 'the *vine* said, Shall I leave my *tirosh* (fruit) which cheereth God and man?' as evidently refers to the ripened produce which was placed on the altar as a first-fruit offering in grateful acknowledgment of the divine goodness. 'Sometimes,' says Dr. Jahn, 'the grapes were dried in the sun and preserved in masses, which were called *gnenabhim, eshishah, tzimmookim*' (1 Sam. xxv:18; 2 Sam. xvi:1; 1 Chron. xii: 40; Hos. iii:1); (*Bib. Antiq.* sec. 69). *Tirosh* is derived from the verbal noun *yarash,* 'to possess by inheritance' (whence Latin *hæres,* English *heir*), and was very naturally applied to designate the vintage-fruit, which, next to *dagan,* constituted one of the most valuable 'possessions' of the Jews.

It is also distinctly referred to as the *yielder* of wine, and therefore was not wine itself, but the raw material from which it was expressed or prepared. Dr. Conquest's amended translation of (Micah vi:15), is, 'Thou shalt sow, but thou shalt not reap, thou shalt *tread* the olives, but thou shalt not anoint thee with oil (*shemen,* not *yitzhar*); and the *grape* (*tirosh*), but shalt not drink wine' (*yayin*). As the treading of the *olive* is represented as yielding *oil,* so is *tirosh* represented as that which, being trodden in the vat, should yield *wine,* which flowed out from an opening into the *lacus* or receptacle beneath. Archbishop Newcome, in his version of this text, has '*the grape of* the choice wine;' while Julius Bate, M. A., observes on this passage—'Hence it is plain that *tirosh* is what is pressed, *the grapes.*'

Dr. Jahn's definition of *tirosh* as the juice which flows from the trodden grapes, is also negatived by the fact that another word exactly expressive of the same thing already exists, namely, *ausis,* from *ausas,* 'to tread down together.' Neither is it likely that it should be a generic name for wine, since such a term is found in יין, *yayin*.

(4) Orchard Fruits. *Yitzhar,* 'orchard-fruits,' especially winter or keeping fruits, as dates, figs, olives, pomegranates, citrons, nuts, etc. The etymology of *yitzhar* (whence perhaps the Saxon *ortgeard,* and the old English word *hortsyard* now *orchard*) quite accords with the claim advanced for it, as denoting a large and valuable class of fruits. Lexiconists properly refer it to the root *tzhar,* expressive of a bright, glowing and shining appearance.

As we distinguish *dagan* from *hhittahh* (wheat) and *tirosh* from *ausis* and *yayin,* so must we *yitzhar* from *shemen,* 'oil.' which are unfortunately confounded together in the common version. *Shemen,* beyond question, is the proper word for *oil,* not *yitzhar*.

Figurative. (1) Christ is the fruit *of the earth;* his human body sprung of it (Is. iv:2). (2) The *twelve manner of fruits* which he bears, and which are better than gold, are his various blessings of righteousness, peace, pardon, acceptance, adoption, sanctification, comfort, and eternal glory, sufficient for all the tribes of the chosen Israel (Rev. xxii:2; Prov. viii:19). (3) The *fruits of the Spirit* are the gracious qualities, tempers, comforts, and good works, which his inhabitation and influence produce in the saints (Gal. v:22-24; Eph. v:9). (4) The *fruits of the Gospel,* are turning from idols, and other wickedness, to God, believing on Christ, and the bringing forth of good works (Col. i:6; Rom. i:13). (5) Saints are represented as *fruit* gathered (Is. xxvii:6; John iv:36); their *good fruit* is the exercise of their graces and their good works; they are *fruits of righteousness* produced by the application of Jesus' righteousness to their souls (Matt. vii:18 and xii:33; Gal. v:22-24; Prov. xi: 30; Phil. i:11; Jam. iii:18). (6) They are *fruits meet for repentance;* i. e., such as mark the truth and sincerity of, and answer to a profession of it (Matt. iii:8); and *fruit unto holiness* and life; they mark the truth of our inward sanctification, and promote our holiness in themselves; and they are a means of promoting life temporal, spiritual, and eternal, in ourselves and others (Rom. vi:22). (7) The *fruit of the lips* is either the comfortable doctrines of the gospel published by ministers; or the saints' praises and thanksgiving to God; or their pious conferences and counsels (Is. lvii: 19; Heb. xiii:15; Prov. xii:14). (8) The *fruit* of the wicked is their evil works, in thought, word, or deed (Matt. vii:16); it is *fruit unto death,* as it tends to promote the spiritual and eternal death of themselves and others (Rom. vii:5, 13; Jam. i:15). Even their good-like fruit is *fruit to themselves;* springs from selfish principles, is performed in their own strength, and directed to selfish ends (Hos. x:1; Zech. viii:5); and it is *withering fruit,* which is not continued in, but they fall away, and grow worse and worse (Jude 12). (9) The *fruit* of the stout heart of the king of Assyria, was his insolent blasphemies against God (Is. x:12). (10) Liberal donations to such as are in need are called *a fruit;* they proceed from a benevolent disposition, and are refreshing to such as receive them (Rom. xv:28; Phil. iv:17). (11) The *fruit* of men's ways or deeds, is the reward or punishment that follows on good or evil works (Prov. i:31; Is. iii:10).

Fruit is also employed symbolically in many other ways in the Scriptures, as of offspring, children (Exod. xxi:22; Ps. xxi:10; Hos. ix:16); also in such phrases as "fruit of the womb" (Gen. xxx:2; Deut. vii:13, etc.); "fruit of the loins" (Acts ii:30); "fruit of the body" (Ps. cxxxii:11; Mic. vi:7).

FRYING PAN (frī'ĭng păn), (Heb. מַרְחֶשֶׁת, *markheh'sheth*), properly a boiler. It was a deep vessel so that the oil could not become ignited upon the fire (Lev. ii:7; vii:9).

FUEL (fū'ĕl), (Heb. מַאֲכֹלֶת, *mah-ak-o'leth*, and אָכְלָה, *ok-law'*, both meaning to be consumed).

In most Eastern countries there is a scarcity of wood and other materials used by us for fuel. Consequently almost every kind of combustible matter is eagerly sought for, such as the withered stalks of herbs and flowers (Matt. vi:28, 30), thorns (Ps. lviii:9; Eccles. vii:6), and animal excrements (Is. ix:5, 19; Ezek. iv:12-15; xxi: 32). At present wood or charcoal is employed in the towns of Syria and Egypt, although the people of Palestine use anthracite coal to some extent. (Mc. & Str. *Cyc.*) (See COAL.)

FUGITIVE (fū'jĭ-tĭv), the rendering of several Hebrew words, meaning to wander, a refugee, deserter, vagabond, etc. (Gen. iv:12, 14).

FULFILL (fṵl-fĭl), (Heb. from מָלָא, *maw-law'*, to fill; Gr. πληρόω, *play-ro'o*), a term generally used with reference to the accomplishment of prophecy.

FULLER (fṵl'ẽr), (Heb. כָּבַס, *kaw-bas'*, to wash; Gr. γναφεύς, *gnaf-yuce'*, a clothes dresser).

At the transfigurations, our Saviour's robes are said to have been white, 'so as no fuller on earth could white them' (Mark ix:3). Elsewhere we read of 'fullers' soap' (Mal. iii:2), and of 'the fullers' field' (2 Kings xviii:17). Of the processes followed in the art of cleaning cloth and the various kinds of stuff among the Jews we have no direct knowledge. In an early part of the operation they seem to have trod the cloths with their feet, as the Hebrew *Ain Rogel*, or En-rogel, literally Foot-fountain, has been rendered, on Rabbinical authority, 'Fullers' fountain,' on the ground that the fullers trod the cloths there with their feet. A subsequent operation was probably

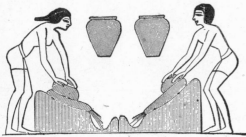

Fullers Cleansing Cloth.

that of rubbing the cloth on an inclined plane, in a mode which is figured in the Egyptian paintings, and still preserved in the East. Fullers were warned to be careful to avoid a mixture of clothes sent to be cleaned, such as was forbidden by the law (Lev. xix:19; Deut. xxii:11).

FULLER'S FIELD (fṵl'ẽrs fēld), (Heb. כָּבַס שָׂדֶה, *seh-day' kaw-bas'*).

A locality near Jerusalem (2 Kings xviii:17, 26; Is. xxxvi:2; vii:3). Some locate it on the northern side of the city, others on the west, near the modern pool *Birket el Mamillah*. It took its name doubtless from the fact that the fullers spread their garments here after cleaning them in the neighboring pool, as they do to this day (Williams' *Holy City*, i suppl. p. 122 Robinson *Bibl. Sacra*. iii: 646 ff.) (See EN-ROGEL.)

FULLERS' FOUNTAIN. See EN-ROGEL.

FULLERS' SOAP. See BORITH.

FUNERALS (fū'nẽr-ạlz). See BURIAL; MOURNING.

FURLONG (fûr'long). See WEIGHTS AND MEASURES.

FURNACE (fûr'nås).

In Neh. iii:11; xii:38, the word applies to the baker's oven. In Gen. xv:17 and Is. xxxi:9 it is used in a broader sense. Smelting ovens and calcining furnaces were also known and used (Gen. xix:28; Exod. ix:8-10; xix:18). The Hebrews also evidently understood the use of the lime kiln (Is. xxxiii:12; Amos ii:1). Refining is frequently mentioned and the furnaces were doubtless like those used in Egypt (Prov. xvii: 3; xxvii:21; Ezek. xxii:18 ff; Deut. iv:20; 1 Kings viii:51; Is. xlviii:10; Jer. xi:4). The furnace of Dan. iii:22, 23, was built like a brick-kiln, with an opening at the top to put in the materials and a floor at the bottom where the metal might be extracted (verse 26). These were used by the Persians as an instrument of capital punishment (Dan. iii; Jer. xxix:22; Hos. vii:7).

FURNACES, THE TOWER OF (fûr'nås-ĕz, thē tow'ẽr ŏv), (Heb. מִגְדַל הַתַּנּוּרִים *mig-dal' hat-tannoo-reem'*, Neh. iii:11; xii:38).

This was one of the towers of the middle or second wall of Jerusalem, at its northwest angle, adjoining the "corner gate," and near the intersection of the present line of the Via Dolorosa with the street of Stephen. Possibly it may be the "Baker's Street" (Jer. xxxvii:21).

FURNITURE (fûr'nĭ-tŭr).

1. The rendering in the A. V. of the Heb. כַּר, *kar*, pad, a camel's litter or canopied saddle, in which women usually travel in the East at the present day (Gen. xxxi:34).

2. *Kel-ee'* (Heb. כְּלִי, something prepared). The name given to the sacred articles in the tabernacle and their utensils (Exod. xxxi:7, *sq.*; xxxv:14; xxxix:33). In Nah. ii:9 it is translated "ornamental vessels." (See TABERNACLE; HOUSE; etc.)

FURROW (fŭr'rō), (Heb. גְּדוּד, *ghed-ood'*, an incision, Ps. lxv:10), a trench in the soil made by a plow in the process of tilling (Ps. lxv:10; Hos. x:4).

Figurative. Grievous injuries done to the church and saints of God, are likened to *long furrows* made upon the back; how barbarous and painful (Ps. cxxix:3). The Israelites' *'two furrows,'* may either denote their principal transgressions, revolting from the family of David, by rebellion, and from God, by idolatry; or their two countries; or their hard service under the Assyrians (Hos. x:10). The marginal translation has it, "When I shall bind them for their two transgressions, or in their two habitations." The Chaldee compares Israel under bondage to their enemies, as a pair of yoked heifers drawing the plow. By some it is thought that reference is here made to the practice of saying that two persons at enmity, when reconciled, are plowing in two furrows; that is, acting in accordance. So Israel would fall in heartily with idolaters. The passage is confessedly obscure.

FURY (fū'rў), (Heb. חֵמָה, *khay-maw'*, heat; or חָרוֹן, *khaw-rone'*, burning), intense anger, attributed to God metaphorically, or speaking after the manner of men (Lev. xxvi:28; Job xx:23; Is. lxiii:3, etc).

FUTURE LIFE (fū'tŭr lĭf). See LIFE; IMMORTALITY.

G

GAAL (gā'al), (Heb. גַּעַל, *gah'al*, miscarriage, loathing), son of Ebed.

He went to Shechem with his brothers when the inhabitants became discontented with Abimelech, and so engaged their confidence that they placed him at their head. At the festival at which the Shechemites offered the first-fruits of their vintage in the temple of Baal, Gaal, by apparently drunken bravadoes, roused the valor of the people, and strove yet more to kindle their wrath against the absent Abimelech. It would seem as if the natives had been in some way intimately connected with, or descended from, the original inhabitants; for Gaal endeavored to awaken their attachment to the ancient family of Hamor, the father of Shechem, which ruled the place in the time of Abraham (Gen. xxxiv:2, 6), and which seems to have been at this time represented by Gaal and his brothers. Although deprived of Shechem, the family appears to have maintained itself in some power in the neighborhood; which induced the Shechemites to look to Gaal when they became tired of Abimelech. Whether he succeeded in awakening among them a kind feeling towards the descendants of the ancient masters of the place, does not appear; but eventually they went out under his command, being assisted doubtless by his men, to intercept and give battle to Abimelech, when he appeared before the town. Gaal, however, fled before Abimelech, and his retreat into Shechem being cut off by Zebul, the commandant of that place, he went to his home, and we hear of him no more. The account of this attempt is interesting, chiefly from the slight glimpse it affords of the position, at this period, of what had been one of the reigning families of the land before its invasion by the Israelites (Judg. ix:26-48). (B. C. 1319.)

GAASH (gā'ash), (Heb. גַּעַשׁ, *ga'ash*, quaking), a mountain of Ephraim, north of which stood Timnath-Serah, celebrated for Joshua's tomb (Josh. xxiv:30; Judg. ii:9), which, Eusebius says, was known in his time. A brook or valley (2 Sam. xxiii:30; 1 Chron. xi:32).

Dr. Eli Smith discovered Timrath-Serah in the modern Tibneh, six miles northeast of *Jufua,* and within its precincts a high hill on "the north side" of which are some remarkable ruins of tombs of great antiquity. There can be but little doubt that this spot is the site of the ancient tomb of Joshua.

GABA (gā'bà). The same as Geba. The broader vowel sound occurs in the pause (Josh. xviii:24; Ezra ii:26; Neh. vii:30). (See GEBA).

GABATHA (găb'a-thà). See BIGTHAN.

GABBAI (găb'ba-ī), (Heb. גַּבָּי, *gab-bah'ee*, tax gatherer), head of a Benjamite family of note in Jerusalem (Neh. xi:8), B. C. 536.

GABBATHA (găb'ba-thà), (Gr. γαββαθά, *gab-bath-ah';* Chald. גַּבְּתָא, knoll), the place mentioned in John xix:13 where the Evangelist states that Pontius Pilate, alarmed at last in his attempts to save Jesus, by the artful insinuation of the Jews, 'If thou let this man go, thou art not Cæsar's friend,' went into the prætorium again, and brought Jesus out to them, and sat down once more upon the βῆμα, *tribunal,* in a place called Λιθόστρωτον, *stone-paved,* but in the Hebrew Gabbatha.

The Greek word, signifying literally *stone-paved,* is an adjective, and is generally used as such by the Greek writers; but they also sometimes use it to denote a pavement formed of ornamental stones of various colors, commonly called a *tesselated* or *mosaic pavement.* The partiality of the Romans for this kind of pavement is well known (Casaubon, *ad Sueton.* p. 38, etc., edit. 1605). From this fact it has been inferred by many eminent writers, that the *stone-paved place* where Pilate's tribunal was set on this occasion, was covered by a tesselated pavement, which, 'as a piece of Roman magnificence, was appended to the prætorium at Jerusalem. The emphatic manner in which St. John speaks of it agrees with this conjecture. It further appears from his narrative that it was *outside* the prætorium; for Pilate is said to have 'come out' to the Jews, who, for ceremonial reasons, did not go into it, on this as well as on other occasions (John xviii:28, 29, 38; xix:4, 13). Besides which, the Roman governors, although they tried causes, and conferred with their council (Acts xxv:12), *within* the prætorium, always pronounced sentence in the open air. Probably this tesselated pavement, on which the tribunal was now placed, was inlaid on some part of the terrace, etc., running along one side of the prætorium, and overlooking the area where the Jews were assembled, or upon a landing-place of the stairs, immediately before the grand entrance.

It has been conjectured that the pavement in question was no other than the one referred to in 2 Chron. vii:3, and by Josephus, *De Bell. Jud.* vi: 1, 8, as in *the outer court of the temple;* but that he would *adjourn* the whole assembly, consisting of rulers of every grade, as well as the populace, to *any* other place, is very unlikely; and the supposition that such place was any part of the temple is encumbered with additional difficulties.

J. F. D.

GABRIEL (gā'bri-el), (Heb. גַּבְרִיאֵל, *gab-ree-ale',* the mighty one or hero of God), the heavenly messenger who was sent to Daniel to explain the vision of the ram and the he-goat (Dan. vii), and to communicate the prediction of the Seventy Weeks (Dan. ix:21-27).

Under the new dispensation he was employed to announce the birth of John the Baptist to his father Zechariah (Luke i:11), and that of the Messiah to the Virgin Mary (Luke i:26). Both by Jewish and Christian writers, Gabriel has been denominated an archangel. The scriptures, however, affirm nothing positively respecting his rank, though the importance of the commissions on which he was employed, and his own words 'I am Gabriel, that stand in the presence of God' (Luke i:19), are rather in favor of the notion of his superior dignity. But the reserve of the Inspired Volume on such points strikingly distinguishes its angelology from that of the Jews and Mohammedans, and, we may add, of the Fathers and some later Christian writers. In all the solemn glimpses of the other world which it gives, a great moral purpose is kept in view. Whatever is divulged tends to elevate and refine; nothing is said to gratify a prurient curiosity.

GAD (găd), (Heb. 🔲, *gawd*, fortune).

(1) The Seventh Son of Jacob. By his concubine Zilpah, the handmaid of Leah; so called, to signify that a *troop,* or *good fortune,* was coming (Gen. xxx:9-11). He had seven sons—Ziphion, Haggai, Shuni, Ebzon, Eri, Arodi, Areli; all of whom were fathers of numerous families (Gen. xlvi:16; Num. xxvi:15-18). (B. C. 1915.)

(2) The Tribe of Gad. When this tribe came out of Egypt, under their prince Eliasaph, the son of Deuel, it amounted to 45,650; but it decreased 5,150 in the wilderness. Their spy to search the Promised Land was Geuel, the son of Machi (Num. xiii:15). They, along with the Reubenites, petitioned for, and obtained their inheritance from Moses, on the east of Jordan, between the Reubenites on the south and the Manassites on the north (Deut. xxxii; xxxiii:20, 21). Their warriors assisted in conquering Canaan westward of Jordan; and from Mount Ebal they gave their assent to the curses of the law (Deut. xxvii:13; Josh. i:12; iv:12). After seven years they returned to their homes (Josh. xxii). Eleven captains of this tribe, swimming through Jordan when high swollen, came to David in the hold, and routed some Arabs, or Philistines, whom they found in the valley of Jordan; and great numbers of them attended at David's coronation to be king of Israel (1 Chron. xii:8-15, 37, 38).

The Gadites were a warlike people, and were compelled to be continually armed and on the alert against the inroads of the surrounding Arabian hordes (comp. Gen. xlix:19; Deut. xxxiii:20; 1 Chron. v:19, *sq.*) About the time of Jeroboam II, they cut off a prodigious number of the Arabian Hagarites, and seized on their cattle and country (Gen. xlix:19; Deut. xxxiii:20). When Tiglath-pileser transported the Gadites and Reubenites to Assyria, the Ammonites and Moabites seized on their country (1 Chron. v:18-26; Jer. xlviii:18-24; xlix:1).

(3) The Land of Gad. As a reward for their having formed the vanguard in war of the army of the tribes collectively, they were allowed to appropriate to their exclusive use some pastoral districts beyond the Jordan (Num. xxxii:17, sq.).

The inheritance of this tribe, called the *land of Gad* (1 Sam. xiii:7; Jer. xlix:1), was situated beyond the Jordan in Gilead, north of Reuben, and separated on the east from Ammon by the river Jabbok. According to 1 Chron. v:11, the Gadites had extended their possessions on the east as far as Salcah, though the latter had been allotted by Moses to Manasseh (Deut. iii:10, 13); a proof how difficult it is to draw a strong line of demarcation between the possessions of pastoral tribes. The territory of Gad forms a part of the present Belka (Burckhardt, *Syria,* ii:598).

In Josh. xiii:25, the land of Gad is called 'half the land of the children of Ammon;' not because the latter were then in possession of it, but probably because the part west of the Jabbok had formerly borne that name (comp. Judg. xi:13).

The principal cities of Gad are called by the general appellation, the Cities of Gilead (Josh. xiii:25).

(4) The Prophet. A prophet contemporary with David, and probably a pupil of Samuel, who early attached himself to the son of Jesse (1 Sam. xxii:5). Instances of his prophetic intercourse with David occur in 2 Sam. xxiv:11, sq.; 1 Chron. xxi:9, sq.; xxix:25. Gad wrote a history of the reign of David, to which the author of the 2nd book of Samuel seems to refer for further information respecting that reign (1 Chron. xxix:29). (B. C. 1062-1017.)

(5) An Idol. (Heb. 🔲, gad), the god (Is. lxv:11, A. V. "troop") of good fortune. Properly "the Gad," with the article. In the A. V. of Is. lxv:11 the clause "that prepare a table for that troop" has in the margin instead of the last word the proper name "Gad," which evidently denotes some idol worshiped by the Jews in Babylon, though it is impossible positively to identify it. Huetius would understand by it Fortune as symbolized by the Moon, but Vitringa, on the contrary, considers it to be the sun. Gesenius, Münter, and Ewald, consider Gad to be the form under which the planet Jupiter was worshiped as the greater star of good fortune (see especially Gesenius. *Comment. über der Iesaia,* ad loc.). J. W.

(6) A Plant. (Heb. 🔲, gad) occurs in two places in scripture, in both of which it is translated *coriander,* viz. (Exod. xvi:31). 'And it (manna) was like coriander (*gad*) seed, white; and the taste of it was like wafers made of honey' (Num. xi:7), 'And the manna was as coriander seed, and the color thereof as the color of bdellium.' The manna which fell in the desert, and on which the Israelites were fed during their sojourn there, is usually described, from a collation of the different passages in which it is mentioned, as white, round, and like *gad,* which last has almost universally been considered to mean 'coriander' seed, though some prefer other seeds. The coriander is an umbelliferous plant, the *Coriandrum sativum* of botanists. The fruit, commonly called seeds, is globular, greyish-colored, about the size of peppercorn, having its surface marked with fine striæ. Both its taste and smell are agreeable, depending on the presence of a volatile oil, which is separated by distillation. (See CORIANDER.) J. F. R.

GADARA (găd'a-rà), (Gr. Γαδαρά, *gad-a-rah'*).

(1) Gadara was the chief city or metropolis of Peræa, lying in the district termed Gadaritis, some small distance from the southern extremity of the sea of Galilee, sixty stadia from Tiberias, to the south of the river Hieromax, and also of the Scheriat-al-Mandhur (Joseph. *Antiq.* xiii:13, 3; Polyb. v:71, 3; Joseph. *De Bell. Jud.* iv:8, 3; Plin. *Hist. Nat.* v:15). It was fortified, and stood on a hill of limestone. Its inhabitants were mostly heathens. Josephus says of it, in conjunction with Gaza and Hippos, 'they were Grecian cities' (*Antiq.* xvii:11, 4). After the place had been destroyed in the domestic quarrels of the Jews, it was rebuilt by Pompey, in order to gratify Demetrius of Gadara, one of his freedmen (Joseph. *De Bell. Jud.* i:7, 7). Augustus added Gadara, with other places, to the kingdom of Herod (Joseph. *Antiq.* xv:7, 2); from which, on the death of that prince, it was sundered, and joined to the province of Syria (Joseph. *De Bell. Jud.* ii:6, 3). At a later period it was the seat of an Episcopal See in Palæstina Secunda, whose bishops are named in the councils of Nice and Ephesus.

(2) Identification. There can be no doubt that we find Gadara in the present village of Om-keis, or Un-keis.

The city formed nearly a square. The upper part of it stood on a level spot, and appears to have been walled all round, the acclivities of the hill being on all sides exceedingly steep. The eastern gate of entrance has its portals still remaining. Among the ruins Buckingham found a theater, an Ionic temple, a second theater, besides traces and remnants of streets and houses. The prevalent orders of architecture are the Ionic and the Corinthian.

Burckhardt also found near Gadara warm sulphurous springs. They were termed Thermæ Heliæ, and were reckoned inferior only to those of Baiæ (Euseb. *Onomast.*) According to Epiphanius (*Adv. Hæres.* i:131) a yearly festival was held at these baths (Reland, p. 775).

(3) Scene of a Miracle. Gadara is the scene of the miracle recorded in Matt. viii:28; Mark v:1; Luke viii:26. The text of the original narratives which record the cure of the Gadarene demoniac, or demoniacs (see DEMONIAC), has more than its share of difficulty in regard to the name of the locality where the

GADI (gā'dī), (Heb. גָּדִי, *gaw-dee'*, a Gadite), father of Menahem, who deprived Shallum of the throne of Israel (2 Kings xv:14, 17), B. C. bef. 741.

GADITES (găd'ītz), (Heb. גָּדִי, *gaw-dee'*), descendants of Gad, the son of Jacob. See GAD.

GAHAM (gā'hăm), (Heb. גַּחַם, *gah'kham*, to burn), son of Nahor (brother of Abraham), by his concubine Reumah (Gen. xxii:24), B. C. about 2200.

GAHAR (gā'här), (Heb. גַּחַר, *gah'khar*, lurker), the sons of Gahar were among the Nethinim who returned from Babylon with Zerubbabel (Ezra ii: 47; Neh. vii:49), B. C. 536.

GAIUS (gā'yŭs), (Gr. Γάϊος, *gah'ee-os*).

1. An inhabitant of Corinth, the host of Paul,

Gadara.

event took place. Mark and Luke indeed agree in describing it as 'the country of the Gadarenes,' but Matthew calls it 'the country of the Gergesenes.' One various reading gives 'of the Gerasenes,' another 'of the Gadarenes.' But Gerasa (see GERASA) lay at a wide distance from the lake of Galilee, and possibly the difficulty which hence arose was that which led Origen to conjecture that the reading should be 'of the Gergesenes,' for with Origen this reading took its rise (Rosenmüller, ii:2, 22; Reland, pp. 774, 806). Indeed to him the place as well as the name owes its existence. Gergesa is found in some maps, but the best authorities omit it (Kiepert's *Atlas*); for it is not found either in the Bible or Josephus. (See GERGESA.) J. R. B.

GADARENE (găd'a-rēne'), (Gr. Γαδαρηνός, *gad-ar-ay-nos'*), an inhabitant of Gadara (Mark v:1; Luke viii:26, 37). (See GADARA.)

GADDI (găd'dī), (Heb. גַּדִּי, *gad-dee'*, fortunate), son of Susi, of Manasseh, sent by Moses to explore the land (Num. xiii:11), B. C. 1209.

GADDIEL (găd'di-el), (Heb. גַּדִּיאֵל, *gad-dee-ale'*, fortune of God), son of Sodi, of the tribe of Zebulun, one of the spies (Num. xiii:10), B. C. 1209.

and in whose house the Christians were accustomed to assemble (Rom. xvi:23). He was baptized by Paul (1 Cor. i:14).

2. A Macedonian missionary, associate of Paul. When the apostle went into Asia, Gaius and Aristarchus accompanied him to Ephesus, where they abode some time with him; so that in the sedition raised there about the great Diana, the Ephesians ran to the house of Gaius and Aristarchus, and dragged them to the theater (Acts xix:29). (A. D. 54.)

3. The person to whom the apostle John directed his third epistle. In the opinion of several commentators he is the same as **4.** The apostle commended him for his goodness (3 John i:6). (A. D. about 92.)

4. One of those who accompanied Paul from Corinth, or Philippi, to Asia on his last trip to Palestine. He was a native of Derbe (Acts xx: 4), and perhaps to be identified with **3.** The name was such a common one that it is difficult to differentiate them. (A. D. 55.)

GALAL (gā'lăl), (Heb. גָּלָל, *gaw-lawl'*, perhaps weighty), three Levites by this name are mentioned.

1. Son of Asaph (1 Chron. ix:15). (B. C. before 536.)

2. Son of Jeduthun (Neh. xi:17).

3. One of the family of Elkanah (1 Chron. ix: 16). (B. C. before 536.)

GALATIA (ga-lā'shĭ-à), (Gr. Γαλατία, gal-at-ee'-ah).

Galatia was a province of Asia Minor, bounded on the north by Bithynia and Paphlagonia, on the south by Lycaonia, on the east by Pontus and Cappadocia, and on the west by Phrygia and Bithynia.

It derived its name from the Gallic or Keltic tribes who, about 280 years B.C., made an irruption into Macedonia and Thrace. At the invitation of Nicomedes, king of Bithynia, they passed over the Hellespont to assist that prince against his brother Ziboeta or Zipœtes. Having accomplished this object, they were unwilling to retrace their steps; and strengthened by the accession of fresh hordes from Europe, they overran Bithynia and the neighboring countries, and supported themselves by predatory excursions, or by imposts exacted from the native chiefs. After the lapse of forty years, Attalus I, king of Pergamus, succeeded in checking their nomadic habits, and confined them to a fixed territory. Of the three principal tribes, the Trocmi settled in the eastern part of Galatia near the banks of the Halys; the Tectosages in the country round Ancyra; and the Tolistobogii in the southwestern parts near Pessinus. They retained their independence till the year B. C. 189 when they were brought under the power of Rome by the consul Cn. Manlius (Livy, xxxviii; Polybius, xxii:24), though still governed by their own princes. In the year B. C. 25 Galatia became a Roman province. Under the successors of Augustus the boundaries of Galatia were so much enlarged that it reached from the shores of the Euxine to the Pisidian Taurus. In the time of Constantine a new division was made, which reduced it to its ancient limits, and by Theodosius I or Valens it was separated into *Galatia Prima,* the northern part, occupied by the Trocmi and Tectosages, and *Galatia Secunda* or *Salutaris:* Ancyra was the capital of the former, and Pessinus of the latter.

From the intermixture of Gauls and Greeks Galatia was also called Gallo-Græcia (Strabo. xii: 5), and its inhabitants Gallo-Græci. But even in Jerome's time they had not lost their native language. The gospel was introduced into this province by the Apostle Paul. His first visit is recorded in Acts xvi:6, and his second in Acts xviii:23.   J. E. R.

"Few Jewish or Jewish-Christian inscriptions can be detected in South Galatian cities, because the names are usually unrecognizable and few emblems or Jewish formulæ are employed.

"Christian inscriptions are comparatively numerous in Galatic Phrygia and Lycaonia, especially in the country that lies north and northwest of Iconium; and, though none are dated, yet style indicates that some must be as early as the third century." (W. M. Ramsay, Hastings' *Bib. Dict.*)

GALATIANS (ga-lā'shanz), (Gr. Γαλάται, gal-ah'tai, Galatia), the people to whom St. Paul wrote his Galatian Epistle (Gal. iii:1).

They were a mixed people; Phrygians, Gauls, Greeks, Romans and Jews made up the population in a more or less amalgamated form. Quickness of apprehension, prompt action, impressibility and eager craving for knowledge marked their character; but, true to their racial disposition, they were fickle. This perhaps accounts for the readiness with which they discarded their own religious system and embraced the teachings of St.

Paul. But the pure spiritual teaching soon ceased to satisfy, and they sought a more ritualistic and external form which the Apostle rebukes, saying to them "having begun in the spirit are ye now made perfect by the flesh?" (Gal. iii:3).

GALATIANS, EPISTLE TO THE.

(1) Pauline Origin. The Pauline origin of this epistle is attested not only by the superscription which it bears (i:1), but also by frequent allusions in the course of it to the great Apostle of the Gentiles (comp. i:13-23; ii:1-14). and by the unanimous testimony of the ancient church (Lardner, *Works,* vol. ii:8vo.). It is corroborated also by the style, tone, and contents of the epistle, which are perfectly in keeping with those of the Apostle's other writings.

(2) To Whom Addressed. The parties to whom this epistle was addressed are described in the epistle itself as 'the churches of Galatia' (i: 2; comp. iii:1). Into this district the gospel was first introduced by Paul himself (Acts xvi: 6; Gal. i:8; iv:13, 19). Churches were then also probably formed; for on revisiting this district some time after his first visit it is mentioned that he 'strengthened the disciples' (Acts xviii: 23). These churches seem to have been composed principally of converts directly from heathenism, but partly, also, of Jewish converts, both pure Jews and proselytes. Unhappily, the latter, not thoroughly emancipated from early opinions and prepossessions, or probably influenced by Judaizing teachers who had visited these churches, had been seized with a zealous desire to incorporate the rites and ceremonies of Judaism with the spiritual truths and simple ordinances of Christianity. So active had this party been in disseminating their views through the churches of Galatia that the majority at least of the members had been seduced to adopt them (i:6; iii:1, etc.). To this result it is probable that the previous religious conceptions of the Galatians contributed; for, accustomed to the worship of Cybele, which they had learned from their neighbors the Phrygians, and to the theosophistic doctrines with which that worship was associated, they would be the more readily induced to believe that the fullness of Christianity could alone be developed through the symbolical adumbrations of a very elaborate ceremonial (Neander, *Apostol. Zeitalter,* S. 400, 2te, Aufl.). From some passages in this epistle (*e. gr.* i:11-24; ii:1-21) it would appear also that insinuations had been disseminated among the Galatian churches to the effect that Paul was not a divinely-commissioned Apostle, but only a messenger of the church at Jerusalem; that Peter and he were at variance upon the subject of the relation of the Jewish rites to Christianity; and that Paul himself was not at all times so strenuously opposed to those rites as he had chosen to be among the Galatians. Of this state of things intelligence having been conveyed to the Apostle, he wrote this epistle for the purpose of vindicating his own pretensions and conduct, of counteracting the influence of these false views, and of recalling the Galatians to the simplicity of the gospel which they had received. The importance of the case was probably the reason why the Apostle put himself to the great labor of writing this epistle with his own hand (vi:11).

(3) How Divided. The epistle consists of *three* parts. (1) In the *first* part (i.-ii.), after his usual salutations, Paul vindicates his own Apostolic authority and independence as a directly-commissioned ambassador of Christ to men, and especially to the Gentile portion of the race;

asserting that the gospel which he preached was the only gospel of Christ,—expressing his surprise that the Galatians had allowed themselves to be so soon turned from him who had called them to a different gospel,—denouncing all who had thus seduced them as troublers of the church, perverters of the doctrine of Christ, and deserving, even had they been angels from heaven, to be placed under an anathema instead of being followed,—maintaining the Divine origin of his Apostolic commission, which he illustrates by the history of his conversion and early conduct in the service of Christ,—and declaring that, so far from being inferior to the other Apostles, he had ever treated with them on equal terms, and been welcomed by them as an equal. (2) Having in the close of this part of the epistle been led to refer to his zeal for the great doctrine of salvation by the grace of God through faith in Christ, he enters at large, in the *second* part (iii.-iv.), upon the illustration and defense of this cardinal truth of Christianity. He appeals to the former experience of the Galatians as to the way in which they had received the Spirit, to the case of Abraham, and to the testimony of scripture in support of his position that it is by faith and not by the works of the law that men are accepted of God (iii:1-9). He proceeds to remind them that the law has brought a curse upon men because of sin, a curse which it has no power to remove, and from which the sinner can be redeemed only through the substitutionary work of Christ, by whose means the blessing of Abraham comes upon the Gentiles. And lest any should object that the law being of more recent origin than the covenant must supersede it, he shows that this cannot be the case, but that the covenant must be perpetual, while the law is to be regarded only in the light of a temporary and intercalary arrangement, the design of which was to forward the fulfillment of the promise in Christ (iii:10-29). The relation of the Jewish church to the Christian is then illustrated by the case of an heir under tutors and governors as contrasted with the case of the same person when he is of age and has become master of all; and the Galatians are exhorted not willingly to descend from the important and dignified position of sons to that of mere servants in God's house— an exhortation which is illustrated and enforced by an allegorical comparison of the Jewish church to Ishmael, the son of Hagar, and of the Christian to Isaac, the son of Sarah, and the Child of Promise (iv:1-31). (3) The *third* part of the Epistle (v.-vi.) is chiefly hortatory and admonitory; it sets forth the necessity of steadfast adherence to the liberty of the gospel in connection with obedience to the moral law as a rule of duty, the importance of mutual forbearance and love among Christians, and the desirableness of maintaining a firm adherence to the doctrine of Christ and him crucified. The apostle concludes with benedictions and prayers.

(4) **Time and Place.** Respecting the time when and the place where this epistle was written, great diversity of opinion prevails. Marcion held this to be the earliest of Paul's epistles (Epiphanius, *Adv. Hæres.* xlii:9); and Tertullian is generally supposed to favor the same opinion, from his speaking of Paul's zeal against Judaism displayed in this epistle as characteristic of his being yet a neophyte (*Adv. Marc.* i:20).

Michaelis also has given his suffrage in favor of a date earlier than that of the Apostle's second visit to Galatia, and very shortly after that of his first. Koppe's view (*Nov. Test.* vol. vi. p. 7)

is the same, though he supposes the Apostle to have preached in Galatia *before* the visit mentioned by Luke in Acts xvi:6, and which is usually reckoned his first visit to that district. Others, again, such as Mill (*Proleg. in Nov. Test.* p. 4), Calovius (*Biblia Illust.* t. iv. p. 529), and, more recently, Schrader (*Der Ap. Paulus,* th. i. s. 226), place the date of this epistle at a late period of the Apostle's life.

The majority, however, concur in a medium view between these extremes, and fix the date of this epistle at some time shortly after the Apostle's second visit to Galatia. This opinion has decided support from the epistle itself. From the Apostle's abrupt exclamation in ch. i:6, 'I marvel that ye are *so soon* removed from him that called you,' etc., it seems just to infer that he wrote this epistle not very long after he had been in Galatia for the second time, and perhaps while he was residing at Ephesus (Gal. i:6; iv:13; comp. Acts xviii:23; xix:1 ff.).   W. L. A.

(5) **Difficulties.** Among the difficulties connected with the Epistle are the apparent discrepancies made by St. Paul in Galatians ii. and Acts ix:23. Comp. also Galatians i:23; Acts ix: 27, 28. To these objections it has been answered by Pfleiderer (*Hibbert Lect.* p. 103, comp. p. 111), that 'the agreement as to the chief points is in any case greater than the discrepancies in the details, and these discrepancies can be for the most part explained simply by the difference of the standpoint of the relaters.'

"It is further objected that the conduct ascribed to St. Paul in the Acts is inconsistent with the attitude he assumes and the principles he maintains in Galatians. In Acts he is represented as circumcising Timothy (xvi:3), as shaving his head in fulfillment of a vow (xviii:18), as attending the Jewish feasts (xx:16), and as being at charges for four men who had a vow on them (xxi:23, 24). Such acts of conformity to the law are, it is thought, incompatible with the principle St. Paul lays down in the Epistle, 'If ye be circumcised, Christ shall profit you nothing.' The solution is obvious. When St. Paul makes this strong statement, what he means is, If you observe the ordinances of Moses because you believe them to be necessary to salvation, Christ shall profit you nothing. Together with this fundamental principle he held also as an ethical maxim, that it is right to become all things to all men, a Jew to the Jew if need be. And when he observes the Mosaic ordinances in the temple, it is not because he believes they have any virtue for salvation, but because he wishes to give no offense to his Jewish brethren. These Jewish observances have become to him matters of indifference, and only when they are lifted out of their proper position and considered essentials do they become dangerous. 'Neither is circumcision anything, *nor uncircumcision*' (Gal. vi:15; comp. I Cor. vii:18). That he did not yield when it was demanded of him as a matter of principle that he should circumcise Titus, is perfectly consistent with his circumcising Timothy as a concession to expediency. (Marcus Dodds, Hastings' *Bib. Dict.*)

GALBANUM (găl′bȧ-nŭm). See CHELBENAH; FRANKINCENSE; ETC.

GALEED (găl′e-ĕd), (Heb. גַּלְעֵד, *gal-ade′*, heap of witnesses), a name given by Jacob and Laban to the heap they made on Mount Gilead in witness of the covenant they agreed upon (Gen. xxxi:47, 48; comp. verses 23, 25).

GALILÆAN or GALILEAN (găl'ĭ-læ'an or găl'ĭ-lē'an), (Gr. Γαλιλαῖος, *gal-ee-lah'yos*, Galilæan), an inhabitant of GALILEE (which see) (Mark xiv: 70; Luke xiii:1, 2, xxii:59, xxiii:6; John iv:45; Acts ii:7, and in the Greek, Matt. xxvi:69; Acts i:11, v:37).

GALILEE (găl'ĭ-lē), (Heb. גָּלִיל, *gaw-lee-law'*, circle region district), the Greek form of the name given to one of the three principal divisions of Palestine, the other two being Judæa and Samaria.

(1) Name. This name of the region was very ancient. It occurs in the Hebrew forms of *Galil* and *Galilah* (Josh. xx:7; xxi:32; 1 Kings ix:11; 2 Kings xv:29), and in Is. ix:1, we have 'Galilee of the nations' (1 Macc. v:15; Matt. iv:15).

(2) Geography. Galilee was the northernmost of the three divisions, and was divided into Upper and Lower. The former district had Mount Lebanon and the countries of Tyre and Sidon on the north; the Mediterranean Sea on the west; Abilene, Ituræa, and the country of Decapolis on the east; and Lower Galilee on the south. This was the portion of Galilee which was distinctively called 'Galilee of the nations,' or of the 'Gentiles,' from its having a more mixed population, *i. e.* less purely Jewish, than the others. Cæsarea Philippi was its principal city. Lower Galilee had Upper Galilee on the north, the Mediterranean on the west, the Sea of Galilee or Lake of Gennesareth on the east, and Samaria on the south. Its principal towns were Tiberias, Chorazin, Bethsaida, Nazareth, Cana, Capernaum, Nain, Cæsarea of Palestine, and Ptolemais.

(3) Home of Christ. This is the district which was of all others the most honored with the presence of our Savior. Here he lived entirely until he was thirty years of age; and although, after the commencement of his ministry, he frequently visited the other provinces, it was here that he chiefly resided (Matt. iv:13; ix:17). Here also he made his first appearance to the apostles after his resurrection; for they were all of them natives of this region, and had returned hither after the sad events at Jerusalem (Matt. xxviii: 7).

(4) Disciples Called Galileans. Hence the disciples of Christ were called 'Galileans' (Acts i:11; ii:7; John i:46; vii:52). They were easily recognized as such; for the Galileans spoke a dialect of the vernacular Syriac different from that of Judæa, and which was of course accounted rude and impure, as all provincial dialects are considered to be, in comparison with that of the metropolis. It was this which occasioned the detection of St. Peter as one of Christ's disciples (Mark xiv:70; Matt. xxvi:73). The Galilean dialect (as we learn from Buxtorf, Lightfoot, and others), was of a broad and rustic tone, which affected the pronunciation not only of letters but of words.

(5) A Seditious People. The Galileans are mentioned by Josephus (*Antiq.* xvii:10, 2; *De Bell. Jud.* ii:10, 6; iii:3, 2) as a turbulent and rebellious people, ready on all occasions to rise against the Roman authority. This character of them explains what is said in Luke xiii:1, with regard to 'the Galileans whose blood Pilate had mingled with their sacrifices.' Josephus, indeed, does not mention any Galileans slain in the Temple by Pilate; but the character which he gives that people sufficiently corroborates the statement. The tumults to which he alludes were, as we know, chiefly raised at the great festivals, when sacrifices were slain in great abundance; and on all such

occasions the Galileans were much more active than the men of Judæa and Jerusalem, as is proved by the history of Archelaus (Joseph. *Antiq.* xvii:9, 10); which case, indeed, furnishes an answer to those who deny that the Galileans attended the feasts with the rest of the Jews.

The seditious character of the Galileans also explains why Pilate, when sitting in judgment upon Jesus, caught at the word Galilee when used by the chief priests, and asked if he were a Galilean (Luke xxiii:6). To be known to belong to that country was of itself sufficient to prejudice Pilate against him, and to give some countenance to the charges, unsupported by impartial evidence, which were preferred against him, and which Pilate himself had, just before, virtually declared to be false. (Porter, *Handbook.*)

GALILEE (găl'ĭ-lē), **MOUNTAIN IN,** where Christ showed himself to certain of his disciples after his resurrection (Matt. xxviii:16; perhaps 1 Cor. xv:6). It is quite impossible to know to which mountain the Evangelist refers. It is, however, generally conjectured that it was Mt. Tabor.

GALILEE, SEA OF. See SEA.

GALL (gal).

1. *Mer-ay-raw'* (Heb. מְרֵרָה), or *mer-o-raw'* (Heb. מְרֹרָה), denotes etymologically "that which is bitter;" occurs in its *primary* and *proper* meaning, as denoting the substance secreted in the gall-bladder of animals, commonly called bile, in the following passage: (Job xvi:13) 'He poureth out my gall,' *mererah;* Sept. τὴν χολήν μου, *my gall;* Vulg. *viscera mea.* The metaphors in this verse are taken from the practice of huntsmen, who first surround the beast, then shoot it, and next take out the entrails. The meaning as given by Bp. Heath, is, 'he entirely destroyeth me.' Job xx:14 as describing the remorse of a wicked man.

2. *Roshe* (Heb. רֹאשׁ, or רֹושׁ), generally translated "gall" by the A. V. is in Hos. x:4 rendered "Hemlock;" in Deut. xxxii:33 and Job xx:16 *roshe* denotes the "poison" or "venom" of serpents.

Gall (Quercus.)

It refers to 'the gall of adders,' which according to the ancients is the seat of their poison (Plin. *Hist. Nat.* ii:37). See, also, Job xx:25, where, to describe the certainty of a wicked man's destruction, it is said, 'the glittering sword cometh out of his gall.' Sept., out of *his vitals.* In the story of Tobit the *gall* of a fish is said to have been used to cure his father's blindness (Tobit vi:8; xi:10, 13). Pliny refers to the use of the same substance for diseases of the eye. Galen and other writers praise the use of the liver of the *silurus* in cases of dimness of sight.   J. F. D.

3. *Khol-ay'* (Gr. χολή, perhaps *greenish*), the bitter secretion gall. It is related that the Roman soldiers offered our Lord, just before his crucifixion, "vinegar (R. V. 'wine') mingled with gall" (Matt. xxvii:34), and "wine mingled with myrrh" (Mark. xv:23). This was intended as a stupefying draught.

Figurative. (1) Injustice, oppression, and like wicked works, are likened to *gall;* how offensive and detestable to God! how hurtful and ruinous to men (Deut. xxxii:32; Amos vi:12). (2) A state of sin is called the *gall of bitterness* and "bond of iniquity" (Acts viii:23). Most grievous troubles are called "gall" (Jer. viii:14; ix:15; Lam. iii:5, 19). (3) The wicked man's meat, and other outward enjoyments, are turned into the *"gall of asps"* within him; they tend to ruin and destroy him; and often is his conscience terribly tormented for the unlawful manner of procuring them (Job xx:14).

GALLANT (găl'lant), (Heb. אַדִּיר, *ad-deer'*, large, mighty). "But there the glorious Lord *will be* unto us a place of broad rivers *and* streams; wherein shall go no galley with oars, neither shall gallant ship pass thereby" (Is. xxxiii:21).

GALLERY (găl'lẽr-ȳ), the rendering of two Hebrew words:

Rekh-eet' (Heb. רָחִיט, probably panel work or fretted ceiling); the term denotes a portico or veranda. *At-took'* signifies *projection* of a story.

In Cant. i:17 the Hebrew means *panelling,* and in Ezek. xli:15; xlii:3, it seems to signify a pillar used in supporting a floor. In Cant. vii:5 the term is applied to the regularly arranged, flowing locks of the hair, in their likeness to the channels of running water. So it is doubtful if the Hebrew words mean "galleries" in our sense of the word.

GALLEY (găl-lȳ), (Heb. אֳנִי, *on-ee-yaw'*, conveyance). A low, flat built vessel with one or more banks, *i. e.,* rows of oars (Is. xxxiii:21; 2 Macc. iv:20). (See SHIP.)

The enemies of the Jews, and the Assyrian army are compared to *galleys* or *gallant* vessels; that is, large and magnificent ships (Is. xxxiii:21).

GALLIM (găl'lim), (Heb. גַּלִּים, *gal-leem'*, fountains, or perhaps heaps).

1. The name of the place from which Phalti came to whom Saul gave Michal, David's wife (1 Sam. xxv:44).

2. One of the places terrified by the approach of Sennacherib (Is. x:30). In both instances the place is mentioned in connection with towns in the tribe of Benjamin and not far from Jerusalem.

GALLIO (găl'li-o), (Gr. Γαλλίων, *gal-lee'own*, Gallion). Junius Annæus Gallio, elder brother of Seneca the philosopher.

His name was originally M. Ann. Novatus, but changed to Jun. Ann. Gallio in consequence of his adoption by Jun. Gallio the rhetorician ('pater Gallio.' Quintil. *Inst. Orat.* iii:1; sec. 21; ix: 2; sec. 91). Seneca dedicated to him his treatise *De Vita Beata,* and in the preface to the fourth book of his *Naturales Quæstiones* describes him as a man universally beloved; and who, while exempt from all other vices, especially abhorred flattery. According to Eusebius, he committed suicide before the death of Seneca, but Tacitus speaks of him as alive after that event (*Annal.* xv:73), and Dion Cassius states that he was put to death by order of Nero. He was *Proconsul* (ἀνθυπατεύοντος), of *Achaia* (Acts xviii:12) under the Emperor Claudius, when Paul first visited Corinth,

and nobly refused to abet the persecution raised by the Jews against the Apostle. Dr. Lardner has noticed the strict accuracy of Luke in giving him this designation, which is obscured in the Auth. Vers. by the use of the term *deputy* (*Credibility.* part i. book i. ch. i.; *Works*, i:34). (See PAUL).

J. E. R.

GALLOWS (găl'lŏz), (Heb. עֵץ, *ayts*, a tree of wood, Esth. vi:4). In Gen. xl:19; Deut. xxi:22, "a tree." Hanging seems to have been a punishment inflicted by the Egyptians.

GAMALIEL (ga-mā'li-el), (Heb. גַּמְלִיאֵל, *gam-lee-ale'*, reward of God).

1. Son of Pedahzur, and the captain of the tribe of Manasseh (Num. vii:54; x:23), who was appointed to assist Moses in numbering the people at Sinai (i:10; ii:20). He made an offering, as tribe prince, at the dedication of the altar (vii:54), and was chief of his tribe at starting on the march through the wilderness (x: 23). (B. C. 1210.)

2. A doctor and member of the Sanhedrim in the early times of Christianity, who, by his favorable interference, saved the Apostles from an ignominious death (Acts v:34). He was the teacher of the Apostle Paul before the conversion of the latter (Acts xxii:3). He bears in the Talmud the surname of *hazoken,* 'the old man, and is represented as the son of Rabbi Simeon, and grandson of the famous Hillel; he is said to have occupied a seat, if not the presidency, in the Sanhedrim during the reigns of Tiberius, Caligula, and Claudius, and to have died eighteen years after the destruction of Jerusalem.

There are idle traditions about his having been converted to Christianity by Peter and John (Phot. *Cod.* clxxi. p. 199); but they are altogether irreconcilable with the esteem and respect in which he was held even in later times by the Jewish Rabbins, by whom his opinions are frequently quoted as an all-silencing authority on points of religious law. Neither does his interference in behalf of the Apostles at all prove—as some would have it —that he secretly approved their doctrines. He was a dispassionate judge, and reasoned in that affair with the tact of worldly wisdom and experience, urging that religious opinions usually gain strength by opposition and persecution (Acts v:36, 37), while, if not noticed at all, they are sure not to leave any lasting impression on the minds of the people, if devoid of truth (ver. 38); and that it is vain to contend against them, if true (ver. 39). That he was more enlightened and tolerant than his colleagues and contemporaries, is evident from the very fact that he allowed his zealous pupil Saul to turn his mind to Greek literature; which, in a great measure, qualified him afterwards to become *the* Apostle of the Gentiles; while by the Jewish Palestine laws, after the Maccabæan wars, even the Greek *language* was prohibited to be taught to the Hebrew youth (Mishna, *Sotah,* ix:14).

Another proof of the high respect in which Gamaliel stood with the Jews long after his death is afforded by an anecdote told in the Talmud respecting his tomb, to the effect that Onkelos (the celebrated Chaldæan translator of the Old Testament) spent seventy pounds of incense at his grave in honor of his memory. (*Youchasin,* 59; Conybeare and Howson, *Life of St. Paul,* ed. 2, vol. i. p. 69, ff.)

E. M.

GAMES (gāms).

If by the word are intended mere secular amusements, which are the natural expression of vigorous health and joyous feeling, fitted, if not designed, to promote health, hilarity, and friendly feeling, as well as to aid in the development of the corporeal frame, we must look to other quarters of the globe, rather than to Palestine, for their origin and encouragement.

1. Among the Hebrews. The Hebrew temperament was too deep, too earnest, too full of religious emotion, to give rise to games having a national and permanent character. Whatever of amusement, or rather of recreation, the descendants of Abraham possessed, partook of that religious complexion which was natural to them; or rather the predominant religiousness of their souls gave its own hue, as to all their engagements, so to their recreations.

(1) **Amusements of Children.** Zechariah (viii :5) alludes to the sportiveness of children in the streets as a sign and consequence of that peace and prosperity which are so free from alarm that the young take their usual games, and are allowed entire liberty by their parents :—'and the streets of the city shall be full of boys and girls playing in the streets thereof' (comp. Jer. xxx :19). An interesting passage illustrative of these street-amusements is found in Matt. xi :16 :—'This generation is like unto children sitting in the markets and calling unto their fellows, We have piped unto you and ye have not danced, we have mourned unto you and ye have not lamented.'

That the amusement of playing with tamed and trained birds was not unusual may be learned from Job xli :5 :—'Wilt thou play with him (leviathan) as with a bird?' Commenting on Zech. xii :3, Jerome mentions an amusement of the young, which we have seen practiced in more than one part of the north of England. 'It is customary,' he says, 'in the cities of Palestine, and has been so from ancient times, to place up and down large stones to serve for exercise for the young, who, according in each case to their degree of strength, lift these stones, some as high as their knees, others to their middle, others above their heads, the hands being kept horizontal and joined under the stone.'

(2) **Amusements of Young People.** Music, song, and dancing were recreations reserved mostly for the young or for festive occasions. From (Lam. v :16), 'the crown is fallen from our head' (see the entire passage on the subject of Games), it might be inferred that, as among the Greeks and Latins, chaplets of flowers were sometimes worn during festivity. To the amusements just mentioned frequent allusions are found in holy writ, among which may be given Ps. xxx :11 ; Jer. xxxi :13 ; Luke xv :25. In Is. xxx :29, a passage is found which serves to show how much of festivity and mirth was mingled with religious observances ; the journey on festival occasions up to Jerusalem was enlivened by music, if not by dancing : 'Ye shall have a song as in the night when a holy solemnity is kept ; and gladness of heart, as when one goeth with a pipe to come into the mountain of the Lord, to the Mighty One of Israel.' A passage occurs in 2 Sam. ii : 14, which may indicate the practice among the ancient Israelites of games somewhat similar to the jousts and tournaments of the middle ages. On the subject of dancing see Michaelis, (*Mos. Recht,* art. 197). No trace is found in Hebrew antiquity of any of the ordinary games of skill or hazard which are so numerous in the western world.

2. Grecian Games. The Grecian influence which made itself felt after the Exile led to a great change in the manners and customs of the Hebrew nation. They were soon an almost different people from what we find them in the days of their national independence and primitive simplicity.

(1) **Gymnasium.** In Macc. i :14, we find evidence that the Grecian games were introduced ; and that a gymnasium was built under Antiochus Epiphanes—'They built a place of exercise at Jerusalem, according to the custom of the heathen.' Compare 2 Macc. iv :12, 13, 14, where special mention is made of the prevalence of 'Greek fashions,' and 'the game of Discus ;' though, as appears clearly from the last passage (v :17), these practices were considered contrary to the Mosaic institutions, and were hateful to pious Israelites.

(2) **Theaters and Amphitheaters.** The Herodian princes had theaters and amphitheaters built in Jerusalem and other cities of Palestine, in which were held splendid games, sometimes in honor of their Roman masters. The drama does not appear to have been introduced, but Jews were in foreign countries actors of plays (Joseph. *Vita,* sec. 3). The passage already cited (see the original) is full of evidence how distasteful these heathenish games were to the more soundminded part of the nation.

These facts make it the less surprising that allusions should be found in the New Testament writings to the Grecian games.

The fact that, as we have seen, the games of the amphitheater were celebrated even in Jerusalem, serves to make it very likely that Paul, in 1 Cor. xv :32; iv :9, alludes to these detestable practices, though it is not probable that the apostle was himself actually exposed to the fury of the raging animals. Contrary to the opinion of some writers, the reference to these combats appears to us very clear, though it was only metaphorically that Paul 'fought with beasts at Ephesus.'

3. Barbarous Sports. The word which the Apostle (1 Cor. xv :32) uses is emphatic and descriptive, ἐθηριομάχησα, *I fought with wild beasts.* The θηριομαχία or *beast-fight* (venatio in Latin) constituted among the Romans a part of the amusements of the circus or amphitheater. It consisted in the combat of human beings with animals. The persons destined to this barbarous kind of amusement were termed θηριομάχοι, *beast-fighters.* They were generally of two classes.

(1) **Volunteers.** Voluntary, that is, persons who fought either for amusement or for pay; these were clothed and provided with offensive and defensive weapons.

Beast-fight.

(2) **Martyrs.** Condemned persons, who were mostly exposed to the fury of the animals unclothed, unarmed, and sometimes bound (Cic. *Pro Sext.* 64; *Ep. ad Quint. Frat.* ii. 6; Senec. *De Benef.* ii :19; Tertull. *Apol.* 9). As none but the vilest of men were in general devoted to these beast-fights, no punishment could be more condign and cruel than what was frequently inflicted on the primitive Christians, when they were hur-

ried away 'to the lions' (as the phrase was), on account of their fidelity to conscience and to Christ, its Lord. Ephesus appears to have had some unenviable distinction in these brutal exhibitions (Schleusner, *in voc.*), so that there is a peculiar propriety in the language of the Apostle.

Olympic Games.

4. Sacred Games of Greece. Some of these games stood far above the rest, bearing the appellation of ιεροι, 'sacred,' and deriving their support from the great Hellenic family at large, though each one had special honor in its own locality.

(1) Olympic. The Olympic games were held in the highest honor. The victors at them were accounted the noblest and happiest of mortals, and every means was taken that could show the respect in which they were held. These games were celebrated every five years at Olympia, in Elis, on the west side of the Peloponnesus. Hence the epoch called the Olympiads.

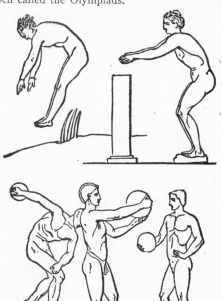

Vaulting and Quoits.

At the Olympic games the prize was simply a chaplet made of wild olive. The crowns were laid on a tripod, and placed in the middle of the

course, so as to be seen of all. On the same table there were also exposed to view palm-branches, one of which was given into the hand of each conqueror at the same time with the chaplet. The victors, having been summoned by proclamation, were presented with the ensigns of victory, and conducted along the stadium, preceded by a herald, who proclaimed their honors, and announced their name, parentage, and country.

The real reward, however, was in the fame which ensued. A chaplet won in the chariot-races at Olympia was the highest of earthly honors. What congratulations from friends; how was the public eye directed to the fortunate conqueror; what honor had he conferred on his native city, and for what office was such an one unfit!

In order to perpetuate the memory of these great men, their names and achievements were entered into a public register, which was under the care of suitable officers. A no less privilege was that of having a statue of themselves placed either at the expense of their country or their friends, in the sacred grove of Jupiter. A perhaps still greater honor awaited the victor on his return home. The conquerors at the Isthmian games were wont to be received in their chariots, superbly attired, amid thronging and jubilant multitudes.

Wrestling.

(2) The Pentathlon. The Pentathlon was made up of the union of leaping, running, quoiting, wrestling, and hurling the spear.

Boxing.

(3) Boxing. The Pankration consisted of wrestling and boxing.

(4) Foot Races. *Racing* may be traced back to the earliest periods of Grecian antiquity, and may be regarded as the first friendly contest in which men engaged. Accordingly the Olympic and Pythian, probably also the other games, opened with foot races. Foot racing, perfected by systematic practice, was divided into different kinds. If you ran merely to the end of the course (στάδιον), it was called *stadium;* if you went thither and back, you ran the *double course* (δίαυλος). The longest course was the δόλιχος, *long course*, which required extraordinary speed and power of endurance.

It may well be supposed that the competitors employed all their ability, and displayed the greatest eagerness to gain the prize. The nearer, too, they approached to the goal, the more did they increase their efforts. Sometimes the victory de-

Foot Racing.

pended on a final spring; happy he that retained power enough to leap first to the goal. The spectators, also, used every encouragement in their power, these favoring one competitor, those another. All these remarks go to show how wisely Paul acted in selecting the figure, and how carefully he has preserved the imagery which belongs to it. A word employed in the Common Version, I Cor. ix :27, 'Lest when I have *preached* to others I myself should be a castaway'—namely, *preached*, mars the figure. The original is κηρύξας, *keruchsas* 'acted the part of herald' whose business it was to call the competitors to the contest and proclaim their victory, functions which Paul spent his life in performing.

(5) The Isthmian. In writing to the Christians at Corinth there was a special propriety, on the part of the Apostle, in making allusions to the public games. Corinth was the place where one of the four Greek national games was celebrated, namely, the Isthmian. These games were so called from being held on the isthmus which joins northern with southern Greece—a spot of land most celebrated in Grecian history, alike in martial and commercial matters.

At the Isthmian games the prize was parsley during the mythic periods. In later ages the victor was crowned with a chaplet of pine leaves. Parsley, however, appears to have been also employed. If the conqueror had come off victorious in the three great divisions—music, gymnastics, and racing—he was in the Pythian, as well as in the other sacred games, presented also with a palm-branch. The names of about seventy persons are preserved who gained honors at the Isthmian games, among which occurs that of the emperor Nero, who is recorded to have gained the victory in the character of harper and that of herald.

Section of the Chariot Race. Circus Maximus.

(6) Chariot Races. The Corinthians appear to have been inordinately fond of these amusements. They were held every three years. They comprised three leading divisions—musical, gymnastical, and equestrian contests. In the first the ty-

rant Nero carried off a crown, by destroying his too highly-gifted antagonist. The gymnastic contests were the same as those of which we have already spoken. A few words, however, may here be introduced as to the horse racing, which has not been hitherto described. Generally the same kinds prevailed as at the Olympic and Pythian games. Chariot races seem to have been practiced in the earliest heroic times, since chariots were as early as this used in battle, and the notices which have come down to us refer this kind of sport to the early period now indicated. It stood

Horse Racing.

pre-eminently before other games. The skill and outlay which it required prevented any but persons of distinction—the wealthy, governors, princes, and kings—from engaging in its enjoyments. The number of chariots that might ap-

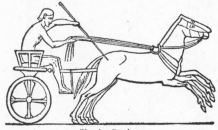

Chariot Racing.

pear on the course at once cannot be accurately determined. Pindar (*Pyth.* v. 46) praises Arkesilas of Cyrene for having calmly brought off his chariot uninjured, in a contest where no fewer than forty took part. The course had to be gone over twelve times. The urgency of the drivers, the speed and exhaustion of the horses, may easily be imagined. The greatest skill was needed in turning the pillar which marked the extremity of the course, especially when the contending chariots were numerous.

5. New Testament Allusions. The New Testament, in several places, contains references to the celebrated Grecian Games, though it may be allowed that some commentators have imagined illusions where none were designed. As might, from his learning, be expected, it is Paul who chiefly supplies the passages in question. In Gal. ii:2, 'Lest by any means I should run in vain;' v:7, 'Ye did run well, who did hinder you?' Phil. ii:16, 'That I may rejoice in the day of Christ, that I have not run in vain nor labored in vain;' Heb. xii:1, 'Run with patience the race set before us;' xii:4, 'Ye have not resisted unto blood, striving against sin' (ἀνταγωνιζόμενοι); Phil. iii:14, 'I press toward the mark for the prize;' 2 Tim. ii:5, 'If a man strive he is not crowned except he strive lawfully.' The most signal passage, however, is found in I Cor. ix:24-25, 'Know ye not that they which run in a race run all, but one receiveth the prize? So run that ye may obtain. And every man that striveth for the mastery is temperate in all things. Now they do it to obtain a corruptible crown; but we an incorruptible.'

6. Literature. On the subject here treated, see West's *Odes of Pindar*, 2d edit.; Potter's *Antiquities of Greece;* Harper's *Dict. of Classical Antiq.*

GAMMADIM (găm'ma-dĭm), (Heb. גַּמָּדִים, *gam-maw-deem'*, brave, valiant warriors, Ezek. xxvii: 11). The word occurs but once and is of uncertain meaning, some connecting it with the word *cubit*, in the sense of *cubit-high men;* others treat it as a geographical name. The best explanation is that of *warriors*, in a general sense (Gesenius, *Thes.* p. 292).

For other views see Spencer, *de Leg. Heb. Rit.* ii. Cap. 24; Fuller, *Miscell.* vi:3; Hitzig, *Comm.* in loco.

GAMUL (ga'mul), (Heb. גָּמוּל, *gaw-mool'*, rewarded), a priest who had charge of the 22d course in the temple service (1 Chron. xxiv:17), B. C. after 1000.

GAOLER (jāl'ēr), (Gr. δεσμοφύλαξ, *des-mof-oo'-lax*, Acts xvi:23), a keeper of a prison. (See JAILER.)

GAP (găp), (Heb. פֶרֶץ, *peh-rets*, breach), an opening in a wall (Ezek. xiii:5); "breaches" (Amos iv:3).

The Jewish false prophets did not *stand in the gap*, or make up the hedge: they did nothing tending to stop the course of wickedness, which opened a door for the vengeance of God to break in upon their nation, nor did they, with effectual fervent prayer, intercede with God to turn away his providential judgments (Ezek. xiii:5, and xxii:30).

GARDEN (gär'd'n), (Heb. גַּן, *gan;* גַּנָּה, *gan-naw';* גִּנָּה, *gin-naw';* Gr. κῆπος, *kay'pos*). *Gan* and its derivatives have the same generic meaning in Hebrew as their English equivalent *garden.*

Several gardens are mentioned in the Scriptures, as the garden of Eden (Gen. ii:8, 9, 10, 15), Ahab's garden of herbs (1 Kings xxi:2), the royal garden near the fortress of Zion (2 Kings xxi: 18; xxv:4), the royal garden of the Persian kings at Susa (Esther i:5; vii:7, 8), the garden of Joseph of Arimathea (John xix:41), and the garden of Gethsemane (John xviii:1). It is clear, from Lam. ii:6, that gardens were generally hedged or walled, as indeed Josephus expressly states respecting the gardens near Jerusalem (*De Bell. Jud.* v. 7). In Neh. ii:8, and John xx:15, gardeners and keepers of gardens by occupation are indicated.

Gardens were planted not only with fragrant and beautiful plants, but with various fruit-bearing and other trees (Gen. ii:9; Jer. xxix:5; Amos ix:14). Thus we find mention of nut-gardens (Cant. vi:11), pomegranate-gardens (Cant. iv: 13), olive-gardens (Deut. viii:8; 1 Chron. xxvii: 28), vine-gardens (Cant. vii:12). Here, however, we are not to suppose that the gardens were exclusively occupied by these fruits, but that they were severally predominant in the gardens to which they gave name. The distinction, for instance, between a vine-garden and a vineyard would be, that, in the latter, the vine was cultivated solely for use, whereas in the former it was planted for solace and ornament, to cover walls, and to be trained in arbors and on trellises.

Gardens were, when possible, planted near streams, which afforded the means of easy irri-

gation. This explains such passages as Gen. ii:9, *sq.* and Is. i:30.

Gardens were dedicated to various uses among the Hebrews, such as we still find prevailing in the East. One most essential difference between them and our own is that they are not attached to or in any way connected with the residence, but are situated in the suburbs. We have known gardens from half a mile to a mile distant from the houses of the persons to whom they belonged. It is manifest that all the gardens mentioned in scripture were outside the several towns. This is, however, to be understood of regular gardens, for shrubs and flowers were often planted in the open courts of the dwelling-houses.

People repair to their suburban gardens to take the air, to walk, and to refresh and solace themselves in various ways. For their use there is mostly in each garden a kind of summer-house or pavilion, fitted up with much neatness; gaily painted, and furnished with seats, where the visitants may sit and enjoy themselves. Here sometimes banquets were and are still given, attended by singing and music (Is. li:3; lxv:3). The custom of burying the dead in gardens is indicated in Gen. xxiii:19, 20; 1 Sam. xxv:1; Mark xv:46; and still occurs sometimes in the East, but is not very prevalent. We find it also among the Greeks (Heliodorus, *Æthiop.* i. 2, p. 35), and the Romans (Suetonius, *Galba,* 20).

It is evident that the gardens of the Hebrews were in a very considerable degree devoted to the culture of medicinal herbs, the preparation of which in various ways was a matter of much solicitude with them (Jer. viii:22). This is still the case in the East, where vegetable simples are as much employed in medicine as they were in this country in the times of Gerarde and Culpepper.

It would seem that the Jews were much in the habit of performing their devotions in gardens (Gen. xxiv:63; Matt. xxvi:36; John xviii: 1, 2). This interesting practice, however, was idolatrously abused; for the worship of idols in these shady seclusions was not of unfrequent occurrence, and is often mentioned in scripture (1 Kings xiv:23; 2 Kings xvi:4; xviii:10; Is. i: 29; lxv:3; lxvi:17; Jer. ii:20; iii:6; Ezek. xx: 28).

The Jews in their ceremonial treatises have frequent occasion to mention gardens, chiefly for the purpose of showing what plants or seeds might or might not be planted or sown together under the law against heterogeneous propagations (Lev. xix:9; Deut. xxi:9-11).

GARDENER (gär'd'n-ēr), a class of workmen alluded to in Job xxvii:18, and mentioned in John xx:15. (See GARDEN.)

GARDEN HOUSE (gär'd'n hous), the rendering (2 Kings ix:27) of Heb. בֵּית הַגָּן, *bayth hag-gawn'*, "Ahaziah fled by the way of the garden house."

"The 'garden house' cannot have formed a portion of the royal gardens, but must have been at some distance from the city of Jezreel, as Ahaziah went by the road thither, and was not wounded till he reached the height of *Gur*, near Jibleam" (Keil, *Com.*)

GAREB (gā'reb), (Heb. גָּרֵב, *gaw-rabe'*, scabby).

1. A hill near Jerusalem (Jer. xxxi:39), the situation of which is not known. Ewald would identify it with Golgotha (*Geschichte Christus*, p. 485); Gesenius with *Bezetha* (add. ad *Thesaur.* p. 80).

2. An Ithrite, descendant of Jethro or Jether, and one of David's thirty heroes (2 Sam. xxiii: 38; 1 Chron. xi:40). (B. C. about 1000.)

44

GARLAND (gär'land), (Gr. στέμμα, stem'mah, wreath). Garlands of flowers brought by the priest of Jupiter, at Lystra, together with oxen, when the people were about to offer worship to Paul and Barnabas (Acts xiv:13).

GARLIC (gär'lĭk), (Heb. שׁוּם, shoom, odor), a well-known vegetable, more agreeable to Oriental than to most European palates. It is mentioned in Num. xi:5.

GARMITE, THE (gär'mīte, the), (Heb. הַגַּרְמִי, with the art. hag-gar-mee' ; an appellation of Keilah, a descendant of Gerem, in the genealogies of Judah (1 Chron. iv:19).

GARNER (gär'nẽr), (Heb. מֶזֶו, meh-zev', to gather), a place for storing grain, a granary (Ps. cxliv:13; Joel i:17; Matt. iii:12).

GARNISH (gär'nĭsh), (Heb. צָפָה, tsaw-faw'). (1) To adorn, to decorate with ornamental additions (2 Chron. iii:6; Job xxvi:13; Matt. xii:44; xxiii:29; Luke xi:25; Rev. xxi:19). (2) (Heb. שִׁפְרָה, shif-raw', brightness), i. e., with which the heavens are clothed (Job xxvi:13).

GARRISON (gär'rĭ-s'n), (Heb. נְצִיב, nets-eeb', 1 Sam. xiii:23; xiv:1, 4, 12, 15; 2 Sam. xxiii:14; 1 Chron. xi:16).

In 2 Sam. viii:6, 14; 1 Chron. xviii:13; 2 Chron. xvii:2, the Hebrew means "officers" placed over a conquered people, by which "garrison" is implied. There was a garrison at Jerusalem in later times known as the acropolis, or castle, or barracks (Acts xxi:34, 37). This stood on the northwest corner of the temple area, and is memorable as being the refuge of the Apostle Paul (Acts xxiii:10). It had a tower seventy cubits high which overlooked the temple and its courts. This arrangement explains how the Chiliarch could so quickly interfere and rescue Paul from the fury of the mob (Acts xxii:3 ff). At Damascus there was a garrison (2 Cor. xi:32) employed to prevent Paul's escape.

GASHMU (găsh'mu), (Heb. גַּשְׁמוּ, gash-moo'), given as a variation of GESHEM by the lexicons (Neh. vi:6).

GATAM (gā'tam), (Heb. גַּעְתָּם, gah-tawm', puny), grandson of Esau and fourth son of Eliphaz (Gen. xxxvi:11; 1 Chron. i:36), and a "duke" of Eliphaz (Gen. xxxvi:16), B. C. after 1740.

GATE (gāt), (Heb. שַׁעַר, shah'ar), the entrance to enclosed grounds, buildings, dwelling houses, towns, etc.

1. Various Names. Thus we find mentioned:
(1) **Cities.** Gates of cities, as of Jerusalem, its sheep-gate, fish-gate, etc. (Jer. xxxvii:13; Neh. i:3; ii:3); of Sodom (Gen. xix:1); of Gaza (Judg. xvi:3).
(2) **Palaces and Temples.** Gates of royal palaces (Neh. ii:8). Gates of the Temple. The temple of Ezekiel had two gates, one towards the north, the other towards the east; the latter closed (Ezek. xliv:1, 2), the other must have been open.
(3) **Tombs and Prisons.** Gates of tombs (Matt. xxvii:60). Gates of prisons. In Acts xii:10, mention is made of the iron-gate of Peter's prison (xvi:27). Prudentius (Hymn. v. 346) speaks of gatekeepers of prisons.
(4) **Caverns and Camps.** Gates of caverns (1 Kings xix:13). Gates of camps (Exod. xxxii:26, 27; see Heb. xiii:12). The camps of the Romans had generally four gates. The camp of the Trojans is also described as having had gates (Virgil, Æn. ix.724).

2. Material. We do not know of what materials the enclosures and gates of the temporary camps of the Hebrews were formed. In Egyptian monuments such enclosures are indicated by lines of upright shields, with gates apparently of wicker, defended by a strong guard. As the gates of towns served the ancients as places of security (see FORTIFICATIONS, etc.), durable material was required for them, and accordingly we find mentioned:
(1) **Iron and Brass.** Gates of iron and brass (Ps. cvii:16; Is. xlv:2; Acts xii:10). It is probable that gates thus described were, in fact, only sheeted with plates of copper or iron (Faber, Archæol, p. 297); and it is probably in this sense we are to interpret the hundred brazen gates ascribed to the ancient Babylon. Thevenot (Voyage, p. 283) describes the six gates of Jerusalem as covered with iron: which is probably still the case with the four gates now open. Other iron-covered gates are mentioned by travelers, such as some of the town gates of Algiers (Pitt's Letter, viii. p. 10), and of the towers of the so-called iron bridge at Antioch (Pococke, vol. ii. pt. 1. p. 172). The principal gates of the great mosque at Damascus are covered with brass (Maundrell, p. 126). Gates of iron are also mentioned by Hesiod (Theog. 732), by Virgil (Æn. i. 482; vii:609), and by Ovid (Metam. vii:126).
(2) **Stones and Pearls.** Gates of stone, and of pearls, are mentioned in Is. liv:12, and Rev. xxi:12, which, it has justly been supposed, refer to such doors, cut out of a single slab, as are occasionally discovered in ancient countries. At Essouan (Syene), in Upper Egypt, there is a granite gateway bearing the name of Alexander, the son of Alexander the Great (Wilkinson, iii. 403). The doors leading to the several chambers of one so-called 'Tombs of the Kings' near Jerusalem, were each formed of a single stone seven inches thick, sculptured so as to resemble four panels: the styles, muntins, and other parts were cut with great art, and exactly resembled those of a door made by a carpenter at the present day—the whole being completely smooth and polished, and most accurate in their proportions. The doors turned on pivots, of the same stone of which the rest of them were composed, which were inserted in corresponding sockets above and below, the lower tenon being of course short. (See Giant Cities of Bashan.)
(3) **Wood.** Gates of wood (Judg. xvi:3). They had generally two valves, which, according to Faber's description (Archæol. p. 300), had sometimes smaller doors, or wickets, to afford a passage when the principal gate was closed—a fact which he applies to the illustration of Matt. vii:13.

3. General Features and Purposes.
(1) **Protection.** Gates were generally protected by some works against the surprises of enemies (Jer. xxxix:4). Sometimes two gates were constructed one behind another, an outer and inner one; or there were turrets on both sides (2 Sam. xviii:24, 33; see Faber's Archæol. p. 301). The gates of the ancients were generally secured with strong heavy bolts and locks of brass or iron (Deut. iii:5; 1 Sam. xxiii:7; 1 Kings iv:13; 2 Chron. viii:5; Jer. xlix:31; Ps. cxlvii:13). This was probably done with a view to the safety of the town, and to prevent hostile inroads (Harmer's Observations, vol. i. p. 188). The keys of gates, as well as of doors, were generally of wood; and Thevenot observes that gates might be opened even with the finger put

into the keyhole—from which Harmer elucidates the passage in Cant. v:4.

The gates of towns were kept open or shut according to circumstances: in time of war they were closed against the inroads of the enemy (Josh. ii:5), but they were opened when the enemy had been conquered. On festive occasions they were also thrown wide open; to which Ps. xxiv:7 alludes. This opening of the gates, as well as closing them, was done by means of keys. That near the gates towers were often constructed, serving for defense against attacks of the enemy, may be inferred from Deut. iii:5; 2 Sam. xviii:24; Judg. ix:35, comp. with verse 52. Enemies, therefore, in besieging towns were most anxious to obtain possession of the gates as quickly as possible (Deut. xxviii:52; Judg. ix:40; 2 Sam. x: 8; 1 Kings xvii:10; Job v:4; Is. xxii:7; xxviii: 6); and generally the town was conquered when its gates were occupied by the invading troops (Deut. xxviii:57; Judg. v:8). In or near the gates, therefore, they placed watchmen, and a sufficiently strong guard, to keep an eye on the movements of the enemy, and to defend the works in case of need (Judg. xviii:16; 2 Kings vii:3; Neh. xiii:22).

(2) Place of Judgment. Gates are often mentioned in Scripture as places at which were holden courts of justice, to administer the law and determine points in dispute: hence *judges in the gate* are spoken of (Gen. xix:1; xxiii:10, 18; xxxiv: 60; Deut. xvi:18; xvii:8; xxi:19; xxv:6, 7; Josh. xx:4; Ruth iv:1; 1 Sam. iv:18; 2 Sam. xviii:24; xix:8; 1 Kings xxii:10; Job. xxix:7; Prov. xxii: 22; xxiv:7; Lam. v:14; Amos v:12; Zech. viii: 16). The reason of this custom is apparent; for the gates being places of great concourse and resort, the courts held at them were of easy access to all the people; witnesses and auditors to all transactions were easily secured (a matter of much importance in the absence or scanty use of written documents); and confidence in the integrity of the magistrate was ensured by the publicity of the proceedings. There was within the gate a particular place, where the judges sat on chairs, and this custom must be understood as referred to when we read that courts were held *under the gates,* as may be proved from 1 Kings xxii:10; 2 Chron. xviii:9. Apart from the holding of courts of justice, the gate served for reading the law, and for proclaiming ordinances, etc. (2 Chron. xxxii:6; Neh. viii:1, 3). We see from Prov. xxxi:23; Lam. v:14, that the inferior magistrates held a court in the gates, as well as the superior judges (Jer. xxxvi:10); and even kings, at least occasionally, did the same (1 Kings xxii: 10; comp. with Ps. xxvii:5). The gates at Jerusalem served the same purpose; but for the great number of its inhabitants, many places of justice were required. Thus we find that Nehemiah (iii:31) calls a particular gate of this city the counsel-gate, or justice-gate, *the gate Miphkad,* which seems to have had a preference, though not exclusive since courts must have been held in the other gates also.

(3) Place of Proclamations. In Palestine gates were, moreover, the places where, sometimes at least, the priests delivered their sacred addresses and discourses to the people; and we find that the prophets often proclaimed their warnings and prophecies in the gates (Prov. i:21; viii:3; Is. xxix:21; Jer. xvii:19, 20; xxvi:10; xxxvi:10). On an uproar having broken out at Jerusalem, the heads of the people met under the New-gate (Jer. xxix:26), where they were sure to find insurgents. The town-gates were to the ancient Orientals what the coffee-houses, exchanges, markets, and courts of law, are in our large towns: and such is still the case in a great degree, although the introduction of coffee-houses has in this, and other respects, caused some alteration of Eastern manners.

Figurative. (1) *Gates* are put figuratively for public places of towns and palaces. (2) *The gates of a town* are also put instead of the town itself (Gen. xxii:17; xxiv:60; Deut. xii: 12; Ps. lxxxvii:2). (3) *Gates of brass, and bars of iron,* import strong help and full protection; or impediments apparently insurmountable (Ps. cxlvii:13, and cvii:16). (4) The *gates of death* and of *hell* occur in Job. xxxviii:17; Ps. ix:14; Micah. ii:13. Doors and gates of hell are chiefly introduced (Prov. v:5; Is. xxxviii:10; Matt. xvi: 19); and the Jews go so far in their writings as to ascribe real gates to hell (Wagenseil, *Sota,* p. 220). Virgil (*Æn.* vi. 126) also speaks of infernal gates. The origin of this metaphorical expression is not difficult to explain; for it was very common to use the word gates as an image of large empires (Ps. xxiv:7; and in pagan authors the abode of departed souls is represented as the residence of Pluto (see Virgil, *Æn.* vi. 417, *sq.*). In the passage, then, Matt. xvi:19, by 'gates of hell' must be understood all aggressions by the infernal empire upon the Christian church. (5) The *gates* of the river may be the bridges on it (Nah. ii:6).

GATH (găth), (Heb. גַּת, *gath,* a wine fat).

It was one of the five princely cities of the Philistines, of which mention is made in Josh. xiii:3. It was one of the cities upon which the ark is said to have brought calamity (1 Sam. v: 8, 9), and which offered in connection therewith a trespass-offering, each one a golden emerod (1 Sam. vi:17). Goliath, of the family of giants which Joshua spared (Josh. xi:22), of which other members may be found mentioned in Scripture (1 Chron. xx:5-8; 2 Sam. xxi:19-22), has rendered Gath a word familiar from our childhood; but it is not certain whether Goliath was a native or merely a resident of Gath (1 Sam. xvii:4). To Achish, king of Gath, David fled for fear of Saul (1 Sam. xxi:10; xxvii:2-7; Ps. lvi). At his own entreaty David received from Achish the city of Ziklag. David dwelt in the country of the Philistines 'a full year and four months.' It was conquered by David, and fortified both by him and by Rehoboam (2 Sam. viii:1; Chron. xviii:1; 2 Chron. xi:8). From 2 Sam. xv:18, it appears that David had a band (600 men) of Gittites in his service at the time of the rebellion of Absalom. Their devotedness to him under Ittai their leader forms a beautiful episode in the history of David's varied fortune (2 Sam. xv:19, *sq.*) Shimei's visit to Gath and its fatal consequences to himself may be read in 1 Kings ii:39-46. In the reign of Solomon mention is made of a king of Gath (1 Kings iv:24), who was doubtless a tributary prince, but powerful enough to cause apprehension to Solomon, as appears from the punishment he inflicted on Shimei. Under Jehoash, Hazael, king of Syria, took Gath (2 Kings xii:17); from his successor, Benhadad, the place was recovered (2 Kings xiii:24). It must, however, have soon revolted; for Uzziah (2 Chron. xxvi:6), finding it necessary to war against the Philistines, 'broke down the wall of Gath.' Probably the conquest was not of long duration. This constant withstanding of the power of Jerusalem shows that Gath was a place of great resources and high eminence—a conclusion which is confirmed by the language employed by the prophets (Amos vi: 2; Micah i:10). 'Gath,' says Jerome (*on Micah* i), 'is one of the five Philistine cities lying near the confines of Judah, on the road from Eleutheropolis to Gaza; now it is a very large village.' On Jer. xxv the same authority declares that Gath was not far from Azotus. (Reland, *Palæst.* p. 785, *sq.*; Porter, *Handbook,* p. 252; Thomson, *Land and Book,* ii. 360.)

GATH-HEPHER (găth-hē′pher), (Heb. with the article גַּת־הַחֵפֶר, *gath-hah-khay′ fer,* wine press of the well).

There was a Gath-hepher belonging to the children of Zebulun (Josh. xix:10, *sq.*), the birthplace of the prophet Jonah (2 Kings xiv:25), lying not far from Sepphoris on the road to Tiberias. This location corresponds with the village of el-Meshhed or Meshhad, three miles north-

47). It is a very ancient place, as we find it mentioned in Gen. x:19, where it is given as one of the border-cities of the Canaanites. In Deut. ii: 23, it is found as the place unto which the Avims dwelt. Joshua smote the Canaanites as far as Gaza (Josh. x:41), but spared the Anakims (giants) that dwelt there (Josh. xi:21, 22). In the division of the land, Gaza fell to the lot of Judah (Josh. xv:47), and was taken by him with the coast thereof (Judg. i:18), but its inhabitants were not exterminated (Judg. iii:3) Gaza was one of the five Philistine cities which gave each a golden emerod as a trespass-offering to the Lord (1 Sam. vi:17). Solomon's kingdom extended as far as Gaza (1 Kings iv:24). But the place appears always as a Philistine city in scripture (Judg. iii:3; xvi:1; 1 Sam. vi:17; 2 Kings xviii: 8). Hezekiah smote the Philistines as far as Gaza (2 Kings xviii:8). Gaza fell into the hands of

Gaza.

east of Nazareth. Here one of Jonah's tombs exists, its chief rival being at the site of ancient Nineveh. (Thomson, *Land and Book,* ii. 122.)

GATH-RIMMON (găth′rĭm′mon), (Heb. גַּת־רִמּוֹן, *gath-rim-mone′,* wine press of Rimmon).

1. This place lay in the territory of Dan, and was given to the Levites (Josh. xxi:24; 1 Chron. vi:69). It was apparently not far from Joppa (Josh. xix:45).

2. A town of the half tribe of Manasseh, west of the Jordan (Josh. xxi:25). Raumer (*Palästina*) supposes it to be another Levite city; but Winer (*Handwörterbuch*), with more likelihood, ascribes its origin to a mistake of the transcriber, who took the word from the preceding verse.

J. R. B.

GAULANITIS (gaul′ăn-īts). See GOLAN.

GAZA (gā′zà), (Heb. עַזָּה, *az-zaw,* stronghold).

Gaza lies on the road leading from Akabah to Hebron, which passes along nearly the whole length of the great Wady-el-Arabah. It is on the seacoast, in lat. 31d. 29m, long. 34d. 29m. (Robinson), in the country of the Philistines (Josh. xv:

the Egyptians, probably Pharaoh-Necho (Jer. xlvii:1; comp. Herod. ii:159). The prophets speak in severe terms against it (Jer. xlvii:5; Amos i:6, 7; Zeph ii:4; Zech. ix:5). After the destruction of Tyre it sustained a siege of two months against Alexander the Great (Joseph. *Antiq.* xi:8, 4). Jonathan Maccabæus (1 Macc. xi:61) destroyed its suburbs; Simon Maccabæus (1 Macc. xiii:43) took the city itself, though not without extraordinary efforts. Alexander Jannæus spent a year in besieging it and punishing its inhabitants (*Antiq.* xiii:13, 3). The place was rebuilt by Gabinius (*Antiq.* xiv:5, 3). It was among the cities given by Augustus to Herod (*Antiq.* xv:7, 3), after whose death it was united to the province of Syria (*Antiq.* xvii:11, 4).

Gaza is celebrated for the exploit recorded of Samson (Judg. xvi:1-3), who 'took the doors of the gate of the city, and the two posts, and went away with them, bar and all, and put them on his shoulders, and carried them up to the top of a hill that is before Hebron.' The Philistines afterwards took Samson, and put out his eyes, and brought him to Gaza, and bound him with fetters of brass, and he did grind in the pris-on-house: he, however, pulled down the temple of Dagon, god of the Philistines, and slew, together with himself, 'all the lords of the Philistines,' besides men and women (Judg. xvi:21-30). It was near Gaza—on the road from Jerusalem to that place—that Philip baptized the eunuch 'of great authority under Candace, queen of the Ethiopians' (Acts viii:26, sq.).

Gaza lay some distance from the sea (Arrian, ii:26), though it had a port on the sea, called 'Gaza on the sea,' called also Majuma (ὁ Μαιούμας), which Constantine called Constantia, from the name of his son, giving it, at the same time, municipal rights. Julian took away this name and ordered it to be called the port of Gaza. Subsequent emperors restored the name and the privileges of the place. It was afterwards called the sea-coast of Gaza. (*Literature*, Porter, *Handbk. of Syria and Palest.* i. 262. ff.; Gage's Transl. of Ritter, *Geog. of Palest.*; Van de Velde, *Syria and Palest.* ii. 179-189; Thomson, *Land and Book,* ii. 331 ff.)

GAZATHITES (gā'za'h-ītez), (Heb. הָעַזָּתִי, *haw-az-zaw-thee'*), a designation (Josh. xiii:3) of the inhabitants of the city of Gaza; rendered Gazites (Judg. xvi:2).

GAZELLE (gȧ-zĕl'). See ANTELOPE.

GAZER (gā'zer), (Heb. גֶּזֶר, *gaw'zer*, precipice). The same as GEZER. The emphatic Hebrew accent has been retained (2 Sam. v:25; 1 Chron. xiv: 16) in the A. V., which accounts for difference of form.

GAZEZ (gā'zez), (Heb. גָּזֵז, *gaw-zaze'*, shearer), son of Caleb and his concubine Ephah (1 Chron. ii: 46). In the same passage he is mentioned as the son of Haran and the Ephah. The second is in all probability only a repetition of the first (B. C. about 1856).

GAZITES (gā'zītes), (Heb. הָעַזָּתִים, *haw-az-zaw-theem'*, Judg. xvi:2), inhabitants of Gaza. Elsewhere the form is GAZATHITES (which see).

GAZZAM (găz'zam), (Heb. גַּזָּם *gaz-zawm'*, devouring). Founder of a family of Nethinim who returned with Zerubbabel (Ezra ii:48), B. C. 536.

GEBA (gē'bà), (Heb. גֶּבַע, *gheh'bah*, in pause *ga-ba*, a hill).

It is often stated that Geba and Gibeah were names of the same place. The two names are indeed only masculine and feminine forms of the same word, signifying 'hill;' but that they were two different places is evident from Josh. xviii: 24; comp. 28; 1 Sam. xiii:2; comp. 3; Is. x:29. Geba belonged to the tribe of Benjamin (Josh. xviii:24), and was assigned to the priests (Josh. xxi:17; comp. chap. xvi:24). The Philistines were smitten from Geba unto Gazer by David (2 Sam. v:25); Asa rebuilt Geba and Mizpeh with the stones of Ramah (1 Kings xv:22; 2 Chron. xvi:6). 'From Geba (in the north) to Beersheba' (in the south) (2 Kings xxiii:8), expressed the whole extent of the separate kingdom of Judah, just as 'from Dan to Beersheba' expressed the whole length of Palestine. It would seem, from the manner in which Geba (Gaba) and Ramah are coupled in Neh. vii:30, that they were very near each other, but the site of Geba is now unknown, although a village still bearing the old name, marks the site, six miles north-northeast of Jerusalem and two miles southwest of Michmash. The form Gaba (Josh. xviii:24 and elsewhere) is due to the Hebrew emphasis. (See GABA.)

GEBAL (gē'bal), (Heb. גְּבָל, *gheb-awl'*, a line).

1. A name occurring in connection with Ammon and Amelek, Moab and Edom. Gebal signifies a mountain, and apparently belongs not to the most ancient times, as it does not occur when the Israelites were actually in this quarter, but is first found in Ps. lxxxiii:7, which was probably written in the time of Jehoshaphat to encourage him and the people to resist the invasion of the Moabites, Ammonites, and others. This would connect the Gebal of Ezekiel xxvii:9, with (2).

2. A city of Phœnicia, between Sidon and Orthosia, on the Mediterranean, in the country north of the Dead Sea and on the west of El Ghor, which is called Gebalene by Josephus and Jerome (Ps. lxxxiii:7). Gebal was called Byblos by the Greeks, and so the Septuagint has it. It was an important place, and celebrated for the birth and worship of Adonis, the Syrian Thammuz. Pliny and other Roman authors call it Gabale (*Hist. Nat.* v. 20). The town is still standing under the name of Jebail. It is seated on a rising ground near the sea, at the foot of Lebanon, which here approaches close to the coast. It became a Christian See in the patriarchate of Antioch (Reland, Palæst. i. p. 214 ff.). (See Maundrell, *Early Travels in Palest.,* by Wright, p. 494.)

GEBER (gē'ber), (Heb. גֶּבֶר, *gheh'ber*, warrior).

1. The son of Uri, governor of Gilead, in the reign of Solomon (1 Kings iv:19), B. C. 1013.

2. Son of Geber, who had charge of the Havoth-Jair, and the district of Argob (1 Kings iv:13). These are taken by some to be the same persons.

GEBIM (gē'bim), (Heb. גֵּבִים, *gay-beem'*), springs, cisterns; in Is. xxxiii:4, "locusts;" in Jer. xiv:3, "pits."

A village north of Jerusalem, apparently between Anathoth, the modern *Anata,* and Nob. It is one of the places from which the inhabitants fled on the approach of Sennacherib (Is. x:31). Exact site unknown.

GECKO (gĕk'ŏ), the rendering of the Hebrew אֲנָקָה, *an-aw-kaw'*, a ceremonially unclean animal which the Hebrews classed with creeping things (Lev. xi:30, R. V.)

The gecko is a wall lizard. It has white spots on its back; and it emits a plaintive wail, whence the Hebrew name. The common gecko or fanfoot (*Ptyodactylus gecko*) is very common in Palestine. It frequents houses, running over the walls and ceiling. It is able to do this by reason of the peculiar construction of its toes, which are provided with plates under which a vacuum is created when the animal walks, thus causing it to adhere. (Davis, *Bib. Dict.*)

GEDALIAH (gĕd'a-lī'ah), (Heb. גְּדַלְיָהוּ, *ghed-al-yaw'*, made great by Jehovah).

1. The son of Ahikam, and appointed by Nebuchadnezzar, governor of Judea, after the destruction of Jerusalem. He was probably of the number of those who quitted the city at the instance of the prophet, justly despairing of the successful defense of a place which God had abandoned. Gedaliah had inherited his father's respect for Jeremiah (Jer. xl:5, *sq.*), and was moreover enjoined by Nebuzaradan to look to his safety and welfare. He established the seat of his melancholy government at Mizpah in the tribe of Benjamin: and there the Jews, who had fled at the advance of the Chaldæan armies, or when the troops of Zedekiah were dispersed in the plains of Jericho, quitting their retreats, began to gather

around him. Gedaliah wisely counseled them to submission and quietness; and he promised on that condition to ensure them the undisturbed enjoyment of their possessions, and of the produce of the ground. In this hope the labors of the field were resumed, and the extraordinary returns of that season seemed as if specially given to repair the recent injuries of war. But this calm was of short duration. Among those who returned was a member of the royal family, named Ishmael, who had taken refuge with Baalis, king of the Ammonites. He appears to have been irritated at seeing one who was not of the house of David seated upon even the shadow of David's throne; and some of the friends of Gedaliah believed him to be in a plot with Baalis to take away his life. But the noble-minded governor refused to entertain such a suspicion, and rejected with horror the proposal of an over-zealous friend, who offered to assassinate Ishmael. The suspicion which he thus generously repelled was, however, correct. He was murdered in the midst of a repast by this very Ishmael, whom he had received as a friend. This event happened about two months after the destruction of Jerusalem, and by it the present ruin of Judea seemed to be consummated (B. C. 588) (2 Kings xxv:22-26; Jer. xxxix:14; xl:5; xli:18).

2. Son of Amariah, and grandfather of the prophet Zephaniah (Zeph. i:1). (B. C. before 635.)

3. One of the six sons of Jeduthun, the Levite, who played a harp in the temple service (1 Chron. xxv:3, 9). (B. C. 1013).

4. A priest of the time of Ezra (Ezra x:18). (B. C. 458.)

5. One of those who conspired to imprison Jeremiah (Jer. xxxviii:1). (B. C. 589.)

GEDEON (gĕd'e-on), (Gr. Γεδεών, ghed-eh-own'). This is the Greek form of GIDEON (Heb. xi:32). (See GIDEON.)

GEDER (gē'der), (Heb. גֶּדֶר, gheh'der).

This word signifies a *wall, enclosure,* or *fortified* place. Geder itself was the name of an ancient town of the Canaanites, in the plain country of Judah (Josh. xii:13), whose king was one of the thirty-one conquered by Joshua, west of the Jordan. It may be the same as Gedor (1 Chron. iv:39).

GEDERAH (ge-dē'rah or gĕd'e-rah), (Heb. גְּדֵרָה, ghed-ay-raw', sheep-cote), a city of Judah with a Phœnician title. It is the feminine form of Geder (Josh. xii:13) and its plural is Gederoth (xv:41).

GEDERATHITE, THE (gĕd'e-rath-īte, thē), (Heb. הַגְּדֵרָתִי, hag-ghed-ay-raw-thee'), the designation of Josabad (1 Chron. xii:4). He could not have been a native of the Gederah in the lowlands of Judah, for he was of Saul's own tribe (1 Chron. xii:2).

GEDERITE, THE (gē'de-rite or gĕd'e-rīte), (Heb. הַגְּדֵרִי, hag-ghed-ay-ree'). Baal-hanan, who had charge of the olive and sycamore groves of the low country of Judah for David, was thus called (1 Chron. xxvii:28). He perhaps belonged to Gederah mentioned (Josh. xv:36).

GEDEROTH (gē-dē'roth or gĕd'e-roth), (Heb. גְּדֵרוֹת, ghed-ay-roth', fortresses), a city in the plain country of Judah (Josh. xv:41), and one of those which the Philistines took from King Ahaz (2 Chron. xxviii:18). Its site, or that of Gederah,

is commonly fixed at Katrah, called in 1 Macc. xv:39 Kidron, in the maritime plain about four miles southwest by south of Ekron.

GEDEROTHAIM (gĕd'e-ro-thā'im), (Heb. גְּדֵרֹתַיִם, ghed-ay-ro-thah'yim, double wall), a town in the low country of Judah named next to Gederah (Josh. xv:36).

GEDOR (gē'dôr), (Heb. גְּדוֹר, ghed-ore', a wall).

1. An ancient city in the mountains of Judah (Josh. xv:58), a few miles north of Hebron. Robinson identifies it with *Jedûr* (iii:283).

2. Apparently a town of Benjamin, the native place of Joelah and Zebadiah, who came to David at Ziklag (1 Chron. xii:7).

3. Son of Jehiel and an ancestor of Saul (1 Chron. viii:31; ix:37). (B. C. about 536.)

4. A name occurring twice in the genealogies of Judah (1 Chron. iv:4, 18).

5. A city apparently in the south of the mountains of Judah, surrounded by fat pastures, and formerly occupied by the Amalekites (1 Chron. iv:39).

GEHAZI (ge-hā'zī), (Heb. גֵּיחֲזִי, gay-khah-zee', valley of vision).

The servant of Elisha, whose entire confidence he enjoyed. His history is involved in that of his master (see ELISHA). He personally appears in reminding his master of the best mode of rewarding the kindness of the Shunamite (2 Kings iv:14). He was present at the interview in which the Shunamite made known to the prophet that her son was dead, and was sent forward to lay Elisha's staff on the child's face, which he did without effect (2 Kings iv:31). (B. C. about 887). The most remarkable incident in his career is that which caused his ruin. When Elisha, with a noble disinterestedness, declined the rich gifts pressed upon him by the illustrious leper whom he had healed, Gehazi felt distressed that so favorable an opportunity of profiting by the gratitude of Naaman had been so wilfully thrown away. He therefore ran after the retiring chariots, and requested, in his master's name, a portion of the gifts which had before been refused, on the ground that visitors had just arrived for whom he was unable to provide. He asked a talent of silver and two dresses; and the grateful Syrian made him take two talents instead of one. Having deposited this spoil in a place of safety, he again appeared before Elisha, whose honor he had so seriously compromised. His master asked him where he had been? and on his answering, 'Thy servant went no whither,' the prophet put on the severities of a judge, and having denounced his crime, passed upon him the terrible doom, that the leprosy of which Naaman had been cured, should cleave to him and his forever. 'And he went forth from his presence a leper as white as snow' (2 Kings v:20-27). (B. C. 894.)

We afterwards find Gehazi recounting to king Joram the great deeds of Elisha, and, in the providence of God, it so happened that when he was relating the restoration to life of the Shunamite's son, the very woman with her son appeared before the king to claim her house and lands, which had been usurped while she had been absent abroad during the recent famine. Struck by the coincidence, the king immediately granted her application (2 Kings viii:1-6).

GEHENNA (gē-hĕn'nà), (Gr. Γέεννα, gheh'ennah, for the Heb. הִנֹּם, hin-nome', the *Valley of Hinnom*). See HINNOM.

GELILOTH (gĕl'i-loth), (Heb. גְּלִילוֹת, *ghel-ee-lowth'*, circles), one of the marks of the south boundary of the tribe of Benjamin (Josh. xviii:17).

In the description of the north boundary of Judah at this point Gilgal is substituted for Geliloth (Josh. xv:7). As Geliloth does not appear again, it is likely that Gilgal is the right reading. The word, however, is used in a topographical sense (Josh. xiii:2; xxii:10, 11; Joel iii:4) for "borders," "coast," which may be the sense here (Stanley *S. and P.*, 1st ed. Appendix, sec. 13).

GEMALLI (ge-măl'lī), (Heb. גְּמַלִּי, *ghem-al-lee*, camel driver), father of Ammiel, the "ruler" of Dan, who was among the spies chosen to explore the land of Canaan (Num. xiii:12), B. C. before 1209.

GEMARA (gĕ-mä'rà). See TALMUD.

GEMARIAH (gĕm'a-rī'ah), (Heb. גְּמַרְיָה, *ghem-ar-yaw'*, God-perfected).

1. The son of Shaphan, and a scribe of the temple in the time of Jehoiakim. Baruch read aloud the prophecies of Jeremiah to the people at the official chamber of Gemariah, which was attached to the new gate of the temple built by King Jotham (Jer. xxxvi:10; comp. 2 Kings xv:35). Gemariah's son Michaiah having reported this to his father, Baruch was invited to repeat the reading at the scribes' chamber in the palace, before Gemariah and other scribes and councillors, who gave an account of the matter to the king (Jer. xxxvi:10-26). (B. C. 607.)

2. The son of Hilkiah, who, with Elasah, son of Shaphan, was sent to Babylon by king Zedekiah with his tribute-money for Nebuchadnezzar. He also took charge of a letter from Jeremiah to the Jewish captives at Babylon, warning them against the false prophets who deluded them by promises of a speedy return to their own land (Jer. xxix:3, 4). (B. C. 599.)

GEMS. See AMETHYST; RUBY; SAPPHIRE; etc.

GENEALOGY (jĕn'ĕ-ăl'ō-jў), (from the Greek γενεαλογία, tracing a family, compounded of γένος, *race*, and λόγος, *discourse*), signifies a list of ancestors set down both in their direct and collateral order.

(1) Care of Records. We read of no nation which was more careful to frame and preserve its genealogical tables than Israel. Their sacred writings contain genealogies which extend through a period of more than 3,500 years, from the creation of Adam to the captivity of Judah. Indeed, we find from the books of Ezra and Nehemiah that the same care in this matter was observed

after the captivity; for in Ezra ii:62 it is expressly stated that some who had come up from Babylon had sought their register among those that were reckoned by genealogy, but were not found; therefore were they, as polluted, removed from the priesthood. The division of the whole Hebrew nation into tribes, and the allotment to each tribe of a specified portion of the land of Canaan as an inalienable possession, rendered it indispensable that they should keep genealogical tables. God had, however, a still higher object than that of giving stability to property in Israel, in leading successive generations of His people thus to keep an accurate list of their ancestry. That they should do this was especially required from the moment that the voice of prophecy declared that the promised Messiah should be of the seed of Abraham, of the posterity of Isaac, of the sons of Jacob, of the tribe of Judah, and of the family of David.

The Rabbins affirm that after the Captivity the Jews were most careful in keeping their pedigrees (*Babyl. Gemar. Gloss.* fol. xiv:2). Josephus (*De Vita sua*, p. 998, D) states that he traced his own descent from the tribe of Levi by *public registers*. And he informs us that, however dispersed and depressed his nation were, they never neglected to have exact genealogical tables prepared from the authentic documents which were kept at Jerusalem; and that in all their sufferings they were particularly careful to preserve those tables, and to have them renewed from time to time. Since, however, the period of their destruction as a nation by the Romans, all their tables of descent seem to be lost, and now they are utterly unable to trace the pedigree of any one Israelite who might lay claim to be their promised, and still expected, Messiah. Hence Christians assert, with a force that no reasonable and candid Jew can resist, that *Shiloh must have come.*

We find traces of the existence of the public tables of descent, to which Josephus refers, in the New Testament: the taxation spoken of by St. Luke ii:2 3, would clearly indicate this; for how could each one be able to go to his own city, unless he knew the specific tribe to which he belonged? Hence it was, we think, that St. Paul was able with confidence to appeal to the Hebrews concerning the lineage of Christ; 'for it is evident,' says he, 'that our Lord sprung out of Judah' (Heb. vii:14; 2 Tim. ii:8). To evince this beyond reasonable doubt, it pleased God to give us by his inspired servants, St. Matthew and St. Luke, the following genealogies:

MATTHEW i:2-16.

1 Abraham	1 Solomon	1 Jechonias, *i. e.*, Jehoiachin.
2 Isaac	2 Roboam	2 Salathiel.
3 Jacob	3 Abia	3 Zorobabel.
4 Judas	4 Asa	4 Abiud.
5 Phares	5 Josaphat	5 Eliakim.
6 Esrom	6 Joram	6 Azor.
7 Aram	7 Ozias	7 Sadoc.
8 Aminadab	8 Joatham	8 Achim.
9 Naasson	9 Achaz	9 Eliud.
10 Salmon	10 Ezekias	10 Eleazar.
11 Booz	11 Manasses	11 Matthan.
12 Obed	12 Amon	12 Jacob.
13 Jesse	13 Josias	13 Joseph, the husband of Mary,
14 David	{ 14 Jechonias, *i. e.*, Jehoiakim or Eliakim	{ 14 Jesus.

· GOD.   LUKE iii:23-38.

1 Adam	1 Thara	1 Eliakim	1 Joanna.
2 Seth	2 Abraham	2 Jonan	2 Juda.
3 Enos	3 Isaac	3 Joseph	3 Joseph.
4 Cainan	4 Jacob	4 Juda	4 Semei.
5 Maleleel	5 Juda	5 Simeon	5 Mattathias.
6 Jared	6 Phares	6 Levi	6 Maath.
7 Enoch	7 Esrom	7 Matthat	7 Nagge.
8 Mathusala	8 Aram	8 Jorim	8 Esli.
9 Lamech	9 Aminadab	9 Eliezer	9 Naum.
10 Noe	10 Naasson	10 Jose	10 Amos.
11 Sem	11 Salmon	11 Er	11 Mattathias.
12 Arphaxad	12 Booz	12 Elmodan	12 Joseph.
13 Cainan	13 Obed	13 Cosam	13 Janna.
14 Sala	14 Jesse	14 Addi	14 Melchi.
15 Heber	15 David	15 Melchi	15 Levi.
16 Phalec	16 Nathan	16 Neri	16 Matthat.
17 Ragau	17 Mattatha	17 Salathiel	17 Heli.
18 Saruch	18 Menan	18 Zorobabel	18 Joseph.
19 Nachor	19 Melea	19 Rhesa	19 Jesus.

(2) Genealogy of Christ.
We do not find that there was any objection made to these genealogies, either by Jew or Gentile, during the first century. Had any difficulty on this head existed, we may reasonably suppose that the Jews, of all others, would have been but too ready to detect and expose it. We may therefore fairly conclude that, whatever difficulty meets us now in harmonizing our Lord's pedigree as given by the two Evangelists, it could have had no place in the first age of the Christian church.

(3) Objections. In subsequent ages, however, objections were and still are made to the genealogies of Matthew and Luke. The chief ground of objection is the alleged inconsistency of the Evangelists with each other. The first solution of these apparent discrepancies is that of Africanus, which, he informs us (Euseb. *Hist. Eccles.* i. 7), he received from the relatives of our Lord, who, because of their consanguinity to him, were called des-pos'vo-noi, *belonging to the Master.* It is to the effect that Matthan, the third in the list from Joseph, in Matthew's genealogy, and Melchi, the third in Luke's list, married successively the same woman, by whom the former begat Jacob, and the latter Heli. Heli dying without issue, his maternal brother took his widow to wife, by whom he had Joseph, who, according to law (Deut. xxv: 6), was registered by Luke as the son of Heli, though naturally the son of Jacob as Matthew records him. This is the explanation which was generally admitted by Eusebius, Nazianzen, the writer of *Ad orthodoxos,* and others, *for ages.*

Grotius, however, availing himself of the tradition that Heli and Jacob were both sons of the same mother, but of different fathers (Matthan and Melchi), supposes that *Luke* traces the *natural* pedigree of Christ, and Matthew the *legal.* This he argues on two grounds. First, that Salathiel *could not* have been the natural son of *Jechonias,* who was *childless*—according to the declaration of God by Jeremiah (xxii:30)—and was, therefore, as Luke states, the son, properly so called, of Neri, of Nathan's line; and, secondly, that the *Levirate* law imposed no necessity on Jacob to marry Heli's widow they being only *uterine* brothers. But both the reasons assigned by Grotius for differing from the solution of Africanus would seem to be founded on a *petitio principii.* It does not appear an ascertained fact that Salathiel was not the natural son of Jechonias, nor yet that the law which obliged a man to marry the widow of his deceased brother might be departed from when they were only *maternal* brethren; for even in cases of distant relationship the

law seemed obligatory, as we see in the case of Boaz marrying Ruth, the widow of his distant kinsman.

Dr. Barrett objects to the above theory as given by Africanus and altered by Grotius, on the ground principally, that it refers entirely to the descent of Joseph from David without attempting to prove that the son of Mary was the son of David. Dr. Barrett then states his own hypothesis, viz., that Matthew relates the genealogy of Joseph, and Luke that of Mary. He supposes a sufficient reason, that after Matthew had given his genealogical table another should be added by St. Luke, fully to prove that Christ, according to the flesh, derived his descent from David, not only by his supposed father Joseph, but also by his real mother Mary.

(4) Reckoned Only by Males. In constructing their genealogical tables, it is well known that the Jews reckoned wholly by males, rejecting, where the blood of the grandfather passed to the grandson through a daughter, the name of the daughter herself, and counting that daughter's husband for the son of the maternal grandfather (Num. xxvi:33; xxvii:4-7). On this principle Joseph, begotten by Jacob, marries Mary, the daughter of Heli; and in the genealogical register of his wife's family, is counted for Heli's son. Salathiel, begotten by Jeconiah, marries the daughter of Neri, and, in like manner, is accounted his son: in Zorobabel, the offspring of Salathiel and Neri's daughter, the lines of Solomon and Nathan coalesce; Joseph and Mary are of the same tribe and family; they are both descendants of David in the line of Solomon; they have in them both the blood of Nathan, David's son. Joseph deduces his descent from Abiud (Matt. i:13), Mary from Rhesa (Luke iii:27) sons of Zorobabel. The genealogies of Matthew and Luke are parts of one perfect whole, and each of them is essential to the explanation of the other. By Matthew's table we prove the descent of Mary, as well as Joseph, from Solomon; by Luke's we see the descent of Joseph, as well as Mary, from Nathan. (See CHRONOLOGY.)

(5) Literature. Yardley, *On the Geneal. of Jesus Christ;* Dr. Mill, *Vindication of the Geneal.* For the genealogy of the ancient Hebrews see Auberlen, *Göttlich Offenbarung; ein Apologetischer Versuch.* (Trans. in the Bibl. Sacra. 1865, pp. 395-405.)   J. W. D.

GENEALOGY OF JESUS CHRIST. See GENEALOGY (2); CHRONOLOGY, NEW TESTAMENT; JESUS.

GENERALLY (jĕn'ēr-ạl-lўͺ), (Heb. כֹל, *kole*).

The adverb 'generally' means (1) *universally* in every place, Jer. xlviii:38 'There shall be lamentation generally upon all the housetops of Moab' (כֻּלֹה, lit. 'all of it' (see Driver on 2 Sam. ii:9; R. V. 'everywhere'). Cf. Art. XVII. (*XXXIX. Articles*). 'Furthermore, we must receive God's promises in suchwise, as they be generally set forth to us in Holy Scripture' (*ut nobis in sacris literis generaliter proposita sunt*); Hooker, *Eccl. Polity*, v. lv. 1, 'God in Christ is generally the medicine, which doth cure the world;' Prayer Book, *Catechism*, 'How many Sacraments hath Christ ordained in his Church? Two only, as generally necessary to salvation;' and Chaucer *Troilus and Criseyde*, i:86—

   'The noyse up roos, whan it was first aspyed,
   Through al the toun, and generally was spoken,
   That Calkas traytor fled was, and allyed
   With hem of Grece.'

GENERATION (jĕn'ēr-ā'shŭn), (Heb. תּוֹלְדָה, *to-led-aw'*; Gr. γένεσις, *ghen'es-is*, birth, nativity; Gr. γέννημα, *ghen'nay-mah*, offspring; Heb. דּוֹר, *dore*; Gr. γενεά, *ghen-eh-ah'*, period).

1. Considerable obscurity attends the use of this word in the English Version, which arises from the translators having merged the various meanings of the same original word, and even of several different words, in one common term, 'generation, instead of bringing out the *abstract* and *concrete* ideas of the word. The following instances seem to require the original words to be understood in some or other of their *derivative* senses—(Gen. ii:4), 'These are the generations,' *toledaw* (Vulg. *generationes*), rather 'origin,' 'history,' etc. The same Greek words (Matt. i:1), are rendered 'genealogy,' etc., by recent translators: Campbell has 'lineage' (Gen. v:1), 'The book of the generations' is properly *a family register,* a history of Adam.

The same words (Gen. xxxvii:2), mean a history of Jacob and his descendants: so also (Gen. vi:9; x:1), and elsewhere. (Gen. vii:1), 'In this generation' is evidently 'in this age.' (Gen. xv:6), 'In the fourth generation' is an instance of the word in its concrete sense. (Ps. xlix:19), 'The generation of his fathers' Gesenius renders 'the *dwelling* of his fathers,' *.i e.,* the grave, and adduces (Is. xxxviii:12; Ps. lxxiii:15), 'The generation of thy children' is 'class,' 'order,' 'description;' as in Prov. xxx:11, 12, 13, 14. Is. liii:8, 'Who shall declare his generation?' is rendered, "Who can describe his length of life?" (Seiler), or "who of his contemporaries reflected?" (Gesenius and Rosenmüller).

In the New Testament, Matt. i:17, γενεαί, *generations* is a series of persons, that is a succession from the same stock. The passage in Matt. iii: 7, is well rendered by Doddridge and others 'brood or vipers.' Matt. xxiv:34, ἡ γενεὰ αὕτη, means the generation or persons *then* living *contemporary with Christ* (see Macknight's *Harmony* for an illustration of this sense.) (Luke xvi:8), 'in their generations,' etc., wiser in regard to their dealings with the *men* of their generation. Rosenmüller gives, *inter se.* The passage found in 1 Pet. ii:9, is a 'chosen people,' quoted from the Sept. Version of Is. xliii:20. The ancient Greeks, and, if we may credit Herodotus and Diodorus Siculus, the Egyptians also, assigned a *certain period* to a generation. The Greeks reckoned three generations for every hundred years. This is nearly the present computation. The ancient Hebrews also reckoned by the

generation, and assigned different spaces of time to it at different periods of their history. In the time of Abraham it was one hundred years (comp. Gen. xv:16, 'in the fourth generation they shall come hither'). This is explained in verse 13, and in Exod. xii:40, to be four hundred years. Caleb was *fourth* in descent from Judah, and Moses and Aaron were fourth from Levi. In Deut. i:35; ii:14). Moses uses the term for thirty-eight years. In later times 2) (Baruch vi., in the Epistle of Jeremiah, verse 2) γενεά, *generation*, clearly means ten years. In Matt. i:17, it means a single descent from father to son. (See GENEALOGY.)   J. F. D.

2. (Gr. γέννημα, *ghen'nay-mah*, Luke iii:7), progeny, offspring, brood. "O generation of vipers."

GENESIS (jĕn'ē-sĭs), (Sept. Γένεσις, *ghen'es-is*, beginning), the first book of the Pentateuch, is, in Hebrew, called בְּרֵאשִׁית, *ber-ee-sheeth'*, from the word with which it begins.

This venerable monument, with which the sacred literature of the Hebrews commences, and which forms its real basis, is divided into two main parts; one universal, and one special. The most ancient history of the whole human race is contained in chapters i-xi., and the history of Israel's ancestors, the patriarchs, in chapters xii-l. These two parts are, however, so intimately connected with each other that it would be erroneous to ascribe to the first merely the aim of furnishing a universal history. The chief aim which pervades the whole is to show how the theocratic institution subsequently founded by Moses was rendered possible and necessary. The book, therefore, takes its starting-point from the original unity of the human race, and their original relation to God, and proceeds thence to the interruption of that relation by the appearance of sin, which gradually and internally wrought an external and internal division in the human race for want of the principles of divine life which originally dwelt in man in general, but which had subsequently been preserved only among a small and separate race—a race which in progress of time became more and more isolated from all the other tribes of the earth, and enjoyed for a series of generations the special care, blessing, and guidance of the Lord. The Mosaical theocracy appears, therefore, by the general tenor of Genesis, partly as a restoration of the original relation to God, of the communion of man with God, and partly as an institution which had been preparing by God himself through a long series of manifestations of his power, justice, and love. Genesis thus furnishes us with the primary view and notion of the whole of the theocracy, and may therefore be considered as the historical foundation without which the subsequent history of the covenant people would be incomplete and unintelligible.

1. Unity and Authenticity. The *unity* and *composition* of the work, which is a point in dispute among the critics in regard to *all* the books of the Pentateuch, have been particularly questioned in the case of Genesis.

(1) Objections. Some suppose that Genesis is founded on two principal original documents, distinguished by the terms *Elohim* and *Jehovah*, the names which they respectively give to God. That of *Elohim* is closely connected in its parts, and forms a whole, while that of *Jehovah* is a mere complementary document, supplying details at those points where the former is abrupt and deficient, etc. These two documents are said to have been subsequently combined by the hand of an editor, so ably as often to render their separation difficult, if not altogether impossible.

But Ranke, Hengstenberg, Drechsler, Hävernick, and others, maintain that Genesis is a book closely connected in all its parts, and composed by only one author, while the use of the two different names of God is not owing to two different sources on which Genesis is founded, but solely to the different significations of these two names. The use of each of the two names, Jehovah and Elohim, is everywhere in Genesis adapted to the sense of the passages in which the writer has purposely inserted the one name or the other. This point of view is the more to be considered, as it is the peculiar object of the author to point out in Genesis the gradual and progressive development of the divine revelations.

The opponents have in vain attempted to discover in Genesis a few contradictions indicative of different documents in it; their very admission, that a fixed plan and able compilation visibly pervade the whole of the book, is in itself a refutation of such supposed contradictions, since it is hardly to be conceived, that an editor or compiler who has shown so much skill and anxiety to give unity to the book should have cared so little about the removal of those contradictions. The whole of Genesis is pervaded by such a freedom in the selection and treatment of the existing traditions, such an absence of all trace of any previous source or documents which might in some measure have confined the writer within certain limits of views and expressions, as to render it quite impracticable to separate and fix upon them specifically, even if there were portions in Genesis drawn from earlier written documents.

(2) **Authorship and Date.** That first question concerning the unity of the book is closely connected with another question, respecting its authenticity, or whether Moses was the author of Genesis. We confine ourselves here to only a few remarks on the authenticity of Genesis in particular, and refer the reader for further information to the article Pentateuch.

Some critics have attempted to ascertain the period when Genesis was composed, from a few passages in it, which they say must be *anachronisms,* if Moses was really the author of the book (see, for example, Tuch, *Commentar über Genesis,* p. lxxxv. *sq.*).

Among such passages are, in particular, Gen. xii :6; xiii :7; 'And the Canaanite was then in the land.' This remark, they say, could only have been made by a writer who lived in Palestine after the extirpation of the Canaanites.

But the sense of the passage is not that the Canaanites had not as yet been extirpated, but merely that Abraham, on his arrival in Canaan, had already found there the Canaanites. This notice was necessary, since the author subsequently describes the intercourse between Abraham and the Canaanites, the lords of the country. According to the explanation given to the passage by the opponents, such an observation would be quite a superfluous triviality.

Also the name *Hebron* (Gen. xiii :18; xxiii :2), they say, was not introduced till after the time of Moses (Josh. xiv :15; xv :13). This, however, does not prove anything, since *Hebron* was the original Hebrew name for the place, which was subsequently changed into *Arba* (by a man of that name), but was restored by the Israelites on their entrance into Canaan.

The opponents also maintain that the name of the place Dan (Gen. xiv :14) was given only in the post-Mosaical period (Josh. xix :47; Judg.

xviii :29). But the last two passages speak of quite a different place. There were two places called *Dan;* Dan-*Jaan* (2 Sam. xxiv :6), and Dan-*Laish,* or *Leshem.*

In Genesis, they further add, frequently occurs the name *Bethel* (xii :8; xxviii :19; xxxv : 15) ; while even in the time of Joshua, the place was as yet called Luz (Josh. xviii :13). But the name *Bethel* was not first given to the place by the Israelites in the time of Joshua, there being no occasion for it, since Bethel was the old patriarchal name, which the Israelites restored in the place of Luz, a name given by the Canaanites.

Another passage in Genesis (xxxvi :31), 'Before there reigned any king over the children of Israel,' is likewise supposed to have been written at a period when the Jews had already a king over them. But the broachers of these objections forget that this passage refers to those promises contained in the Pentateuch in general, and in Genesis in particular (comp. Gen. xxxv: 11), that there should hereafter be kings among the Israelites as an independent nation. In comparing Israel with Edom (Gen. xxxvi), the sacred writer cannot refrain from observing that Edom, though left without Divine promises of possessing kings, nevertheless possessed them, and obtained the glory of an independent kingdom, long before Israel could think of such an independence; and a little attention to the sense of the passage will show how admirably the observation suits a writer in the Mosaical period.

The passage (Gen. xv :18) where the land of Israel is described as extending from the river of Egypt (the Nile) to the great river (Euphrates), it is alleged, could only have been penned during the splendid period of the Jews, the times of David and Solomon. *Literally* taken, however, the remark is inapplicable to any period, since the kingdom of the Jews at no period of their history extended so far. That promise must, therefore, be taken in a rhetorical sense, describing the central point of the proper country as situated between the two rivers.

2. Historical Character. In its historical character *Genesis* is a book consisting of two contrasting parts.

(1) **The Creation.** The first part introduces us into the greatest problems of the human mind, such as the Creation and the fall of man; and the second, into the quiet solitude of a small defined circle of families. In the former, the most sublime and wonderful events are described with childlike simplicity; while, in the latter, on the contrary, the most simple and common occurrences are interwoven with the sublimest thoughts and reflections, rendering the small family circle a whole world in history, and the principal actors in it prototypes for a whole nation, and for all times. The contents in general are strictly religious. Not the least trace of mythology appears in it. It is true that the narrations are fraught with wonders. But primeval wonders, the marvelous deeds of God, are the very subject of Genesis. None of these wonders, however, bear a fantastical impress, and there is no useless prodigality of them. They are all penetrated and connected by one common leading idea, and are all related to the counsel of God for the salvation of man. This principle sheds its lustrous beams through the whole of Genesis; therefore the wonders therein related are as little to be ascribed to the invention and imagination of man as the whole plan of God for human salvation. The foundation of the Divine theocratical institution throws a strong light upon the early patri-

archal times; the reality of the one proves the reality of the other, as described in Genesis.

(2) Biblical Cosmogony. The separate accounts in Genesis also manifest great internal evidence of truth if we closely examine them. They bear on their front the most beautiful impress of truth. The *cosmogony* in Genesis stands unequaled among all others known in the ancient world. (See COSMOGONY.) No mythology, no ancient philosophy, has ever come up to the idea of a *creation out of nothing*. All the ancient systems end in Pantheism, Materialism, emanation-theory, etc. But the Biblical cosmogony occupies a place of its own, and therefore must not be ranked among, or confounded with, any of the ancient systems of mythology or philosophy. The mythological and philosophical cosmogonies may have been derived from the Biblical, as being later depravations and misrepresentations of Biblical truth; but the contents of Genesis cannot, *vice versâ*, have been derived from mythology or philosophy. (See Babylonian Creation Story, BABYLONIA, 16.)

(3) Fall of Man. The historical delineation also of the Creation and of the fall of man does not bear the least national interest or coloring, but is of a truly universal nature, while every mythus bears the stamp of the national features of the nation and country where it originated and found development. All myths are subject to continual development and variations, but among the Hebrews the accounts in Genesis stand firm and immutable for all times, without the least thing being added or altered in them for the purpose of further development, even by the New Testament. What a solid guarantee must there be in this foundation of all subsequent revelations, since it has been admitted and maintained by all generations with such immovable firmness!

The ancient heathen traditions coincide in many points with the Biblical accounts, and serve to illustrate and confirm them. This is especially the case in the ancient traditions concerning the Deluge (Gen. vi:9), and in the list of nations in the tenth chapter; for instance (Gen. x:4), Tarshish is called the son of Javan. This indicates that the ancient inhabitants of Tarshish or Tartessus in Spain were erroneously considered to be a Phœnician colony like those of other towns in its neighborhood, and that they sprang from Javan, that is, Greece. That they were of Greek origin is clear from the account of Herodotus (i. 163). Also (verse 8), Nimrod, the ruler of Babel, is called the son of *Cush,* which is in remarkable unison with the mythological tales concerning *Bel* and his Egyptian descent (comp. Diodor. Sic. i. 28, 81; Pausan, iv:23-5). *Sidon* alone is mentioned (verse 15), but not *Tyrus* (comp. xlix:13), which arose only in the time of Joshua (Josh. xix:29); and that *Sidon* was an older town than *Tyrus,* by which it was afterwards eclipsed, is certified by a number of ancient reports (comp. Hengstenberg, *De Rebus Tyriorum,* pp. 6, 7). (See FALL OF MAN.)

(4) Patriarchal History. With the patriarchal history (xii. *sq.*) begins an historical sketch of a peculiar character. The circumstantial details in it allow us to examine more closely the historical character of these accounts. The numerous descriptions of the mode of life in those days furnish us with a very vivid picture. We meet everywhere a sublime simplicity quite worthy of patriarchal life, and never to be found again in later history. One cannot suppose that it would have been possible in a later period, estranged

from ancient simplicity, to invent such a picture.

(5) Fidelity of Author. The authenticity of the patriarchal history and the fidelity of the author everywhere exhibits itself. Neither the blemishes in the history of Abraham, nor the gross sins of the sons of Jacob, among whom even Levi, the progenitor of the sacerdotal race, forms no exception, are concealed.

The same author, whose moral principles are so much blamed by the opponents of Genesis, on account of the description given of the life of Jacob, produces, in the history of Abraham, a picture of moral greatness which could have originated only in facts.

The faithfulness of the author manifests itself also especially in the description of the expedition of the kings from Upper to Western Asia; in his statements concerning the person of Melchizedek (Gen. xiv); in the circumstantial details given of the incidents occurring at the purchase of the hereditary burial-place (ch. xxiii); in the genealogies of Arabian tribes (ch. xxv); in the genealogy of Edom (ch. xxxvi); and in many remarkable details which are interwoven with the general accounts. In the history of Joseph the patriarchal history comes into contact with Egypt; and here the accounts given by ancient classical writers, as well as the monuments of Egypt, frequently furnish some splendid confirmations. For instance, the account given (xlvii: 13-26) of the manner in which the Pharaohs became proprietors of all the lands, with the exception of those belonging to the priests, is confirmed by Herodotus (ii. 109), and by Diodorus Siculus (i. 73). The manner of embalming described in Gen. l. entirely agrees with the description of Herodotus, ii, 84, etc. For other data of a similar kind, compare Hengstenberg (*Die Bücher Mosis und Aegypten,* p. 21, *sq.*) (See PENTATEUCH.)

H. A. C. H.

3. Literature. Conant, *The Bk. of Genesis;* Quarry, *Gen. and Its Authorship;* Lange, *Die Genesis* (Am. ed. by Lewis); Hävernick, *Introd. to the Old Testament;* Driver, *Introd. to Lit. of Old Testament;* Keil, *Introd. to Old Testament;* Driver, Addis, *Documents of the Hexateuch;* Fripp, *Composition of the Book of Genesis;* C. J. Ball, '*Book of Genesis;*' and Spurrell, *Notes on the Text of Genesis.* The fullest complete commentaries are those by Dillmann and Delitzsch (both now translated into English; Edinburgh: T. & T. Clark). Sayce, *Higher Crit. and the Mon.* and the writings of George Smith, Maspero, Pinches, Haupt, and others. On the Theology of Genesis: the *Old Testament Theology* of Schultz, Oehler, Riehm.

The reader may also consult Miss Wedgwood, *Message of Israel;* Watson, *The Book Genesis;* Ottley, *Aspects of the Old Testament;* Westcott, *Faith of the Gospel;* Ryle, *Early Narratives of Genesis.*

GENNESARET (gen-nĕs'a-rĕt), (Gr. Γεννησαρέτ, *ghen-nay-sar-et',* garden of riches). See CHINNERETH.

GENNESARET, LAKE OF (gen-nĕs'a-rĕt), (Gr. Γεννησαρέτ). See SEA.

GENTILES (jĕn'tils), (Heb. גּוֹיִם, *go-yeem'*), a word which, both in the Hebrew *Goyim,* and in the Anglo-Latin 'Gentile,' by which we translate it means literally, 'the nations.'

It was applied by the Hebrews to all individuals or communities not under the law—that is, all the nations of the world excepting the Jews (Neh. v:

8; in Lev., Deut., Ps. it is applied to **various** heathen nations). But in later times some small states, and many individuals, embraced the law; and they were distinguished from the Gentiles, as well as from the Jews, by the name of Proselytes (προσήλυτοι). In some places our authorized version has the word 'Gentiles' where the original has Ἕλληνες (Rom. ii:9, 10; iii:9; John vii:33; 1 Cor. x:32), which is usually and properly rendered 'Greeks' (Acts xiv:1; xvii:4; Rom. i:16; x:12), thus failing in consistency in the treatment of this word.

GENTILES, COURT OF THE. A court in the Temple where strangers might assemble. (See TEMPLE HILL.)

GENTILES, ISLES OF THE (Gen. x:5) denotes, in a most general way, the people of the far western islands and Europe.

GENTLENESS (jĕn't'l-nĕs), (Heb. עֲנָוָה, an-aw-vaw', condescension, Ps. xviii:35; Gr. ἐπιείκεια, ep-ee-i'ki-ah, clemency, 2 Cor. x:1).

"All God's going back from the strictness of his rights as against men, all his allowing of their imperfect righteousness and giving a value to that which, rigidly estimated, would have none; all his refusal to exact extreme penalties; all his remembering whereof we are made and measuring his dealings with us thereby" (Trench, *Syn. of New Testament*).

In other words, God's *gentleness* is his grace, goodness, and mercy, and favors proceeding therefrom (Ps. xviii:35).

GENUBATH (ge-nū'bath), (Heb. גְּנֻבַת, ghen-oo-bath', perhaps theft), an Edomite, son of Hadad. His mother was an Egyptian princess, the sister of Tahpenes, who was the wife of that Pharaoh ruling in the latter part of the reign of David (1 Kings xi:20), B. C. about 1036. Genubath was born in Pharaoh's palace, and became a member of the royal establishment.

GEOGRAPHY (jĕ-ŏg'rà-fў). It is the Hebrews who present us with the earliest written information of a geographical kind.

In the account of creation mention is made of a spot called Eden, out of which a river, after watering Paradise, ran, and 'from thence it was parted, and became into four heads' (fountains) which sent forth as many rivers, Pison, Gihon, Hiddekel, Phrat or Euphrates. Of these the last is the only stream that is identified. The highlands of Armenia would appear to have been the first known to the human family. Descending from these some may have gone eastward, others westward. The latter alone are spoken of in scripture. Coming south and west the progenitors of the world first became acquainted with the countries lying between the Euphrates and the Tigris, roughly termed Mesopotamia, whence they advanced still more south and west into Aram or Syria, Arabia, Canaan, and Egypt.

Professor Sayce says: "The geography of Genesis starts from the north. It was upon the mountains of Ararat or Armenia that the ark rested, and it was accordingly with this region of the world that our primitive chart begins." He claims that the tenth chapter of Genesis is ethnographical rather than ethnological. "It is descriptive merely of such races of men as fell within the horizon of the writer from a geographical point of view. We shall never understand the chapter rightly unless we bear in mind that its main purpose is geographical. In Hebrew as in other Semitic languages, the relation of a mother state to its colony, or of a town or country to its

inhabitants, was expressed in genealogical form. The inhabitants of Jerusalem were regarded as 'the daughters of Jerusalem;' the people of the east were 'the children' of the district to which they belonged.

"When therefore we are told that 'Canaan begat Sidon his first born,' and 'Heth,' all that is meant is that the city of Sidon and the Hittites to whom reference is made were alike to be found in the country called Canaan. It does not follow that there was any ethnological kinship between the Phœnician builders of Sidon and the Hittites from the north. Indeed we know from modern research that there was none. But the Hittite and the Sidonian were both inhabitants of Canaan, or as we should say, Canaanites; they were both accordingly 'the children of Canaan.' " (*Races of the Old Testament*, pp. 39-40.)

We know that the Hebrews were widely acquainted with the then known world, since colonies and individuals of their nation were spread over nearly the entire surface covered by ancient civilization, and identified with the Roman empire. The occasional, if not periodical, return of the Jews thus scattered abroad, or at least the relations which they would sustain with their mother country, must have greatly widened, and made less inaccurate, the knowledge entertained in Palestine of other parts of the world. Accordingly we read (Acts ii:5, *sq.*), that, at the effusion of the Holy Spirit on the day of Pentecost, 'there were dwelling at Jerusalem Jews out of every nation under heaven.'   J. R. B.

GEPHEN (gē'fĕn), (Gr. ἄμπελος, am'pe-los). See VINE.

GERA (gē'rà), (Heb. גֵּרָא, gay-raw', grain), the name of at least three Benjamites.

1. Son of Bela, a descendant of Benjamin, who is mentioned as living at the time of Jacob's migration into Egypt. (B. C. 1706.) (Gen. xlvi: 21; 1 Chron. viii:3). The passage in Chron. is very corrupt and the different Geras there seem to merge themselves into the Gera, son of Bela (comp. 1 Chron. viii:5, 7).

2. Father of Ehud, the Judge (Judg. iii:15). Possibly identical with 1. (B. C. 1170.) (See EHUD.)

3. Father or ancestor of Shimei, the man who abused David (2 Sam. xvi:5; xix:16, 18; 1 Kings ii:8). Perhaps identical with both 1 and 2. (B. C. 966.) (See SHIMEI.)

GERAH (gē'rah), (Heb. גֵּרָה, gay-raw', a kernel). The smallest piece of money among the Hebrews. Twenty made a shekel; one of them would therefore be worth three cents, according to the present value of silver (Exod. xxx:13).

GERAR (gē'rär), (Heb. גְּרָר, gher-awr, a region, a lodging place).

A city and district on the southernmost borders of Palestine, in the country of the Philistines, and not far from Gaza. It was visited by Abraham after the destruction of Sodom (Gen. xx: 1), and by Isaac when there was a dearth in the rest of Canaan (Gen. xxvi:1). The incidents of their sojourn show that the district was very fertile. It was the seat of the first Philistine kingdom we read of, and gave name to it. The intercourse, differences, and alliances of the Hebrew fathers with the king and people of Gerar form a very curious and interesting portion of patriarchal history. It was still an important place in later times, as we may gather from 1 Chron. xiv:13, 14. According to the ancient accounts Gerar lay in or near a valley, which appears to be no other than the great Wady Sheriah, called by some Wady Gaza (or one of the branches of it), that comes down from Beersheba; besides we know that it was in the land of the Philistines, and that it was not far from Beersheba when Isaac resided there (Gen. xxvi:1, 20, 23, 26-33; comp. xx:1). The name continued to exist (perhaps as a matter of tradition) for several centuries after the Christian era. Thomson in *The Land and the Book*, vol 2, p. 349, says "the Rev. J. Rowlands writes that near Joorf el Gerar are the traces of an ancient city called Khirbet el Gerar—the Ruins of Gerar." These ruins are between Gaza and Khalasa.

GERAR, VALLEY OF (gē'rär, văl'ley ŏv). See GERAR.

GERASENES (gĕr'ā-sēnz').

The people of Gerasa (R. V. of Mark v:1 and Luke viii:26, 37; manuscripts vary between Gerasenes, Gadarenes, Gergesenes). See GERGESA OR GERASA.

GERGESA or GERASA (gĕr'as-a), (Gr. Γέρασα, *gher'as-ah*), now Jerash (not named in the Bible), was in the Decapolis, and formed the eastern boundary of Peræa. It lay on elevated ground, according to Ptolemy, in 68° 15' = 31° 45'. Its inhabitants were mostly heathen.

After the Roman conquests in the East, the country in which Gerasa lies became one of their favorite colonies, and ten principal cities were built on the east of the Jordan, giving the name of Decapolis to the land in which they stood. The place was taken by storm by Alexander Jannæus, who was actuated by a desire of gaining a large treasure (Joseph. *De Bell. Jud.* i:4, 8; *Antiq.* viii:2, 3). Alexander died near it while besieging Regaba (*Antiq.* xv:5). Before the place had time to recover from this calamity, it was included among the number of those cities which were burnt by the enraged Jews in their vengeance on the Syrians, and on the Roman power generally, for the massacre of a number of their nation at Cæsarea (Joseph. *De Bell. Jud.* ii:18, 1). A terrible revenge was taken by other cities, but Gerasa is honorably excepted (*De Bell. Jud.* ii:18, 5). Annius, general under Vespasian, took the city; 'after which he set fire to their houses,' 'and what was remaining was all burnt down' (*De Bell. Jud.* iv:9, 1). Its ruins were first discovered by Seetzen, and have often been subsequently visited They have been pronounced superior to those of Palmyra (Burckhardt, *Syria*, p. 252-64; Kelley, *Syria*, p. 448 ff.; Buckingham, *Palestine*, p. 405).

           J. R. B.

GERGESENES (gĕr'ge-sēnez'), (Gr. Γεργεσηνός, *gher-ghes-ay-nos'*). The inhabitants of GERGESA (which see).

GERIZIM, MOUNT (gĕr'i-zĭm, mount), (Heb. □יְרִזִ, *gher-ee-zeem'*). See EBAL and GERIZIM, MOUNTS.

GERIZITES (gĕr'iz-ītes), (1 Sam. xxvii:8). See GERZITES, THE.

GERMAN EVANGELICAL SYNOD OF NORTH AMERICA.

This Synod is based on the union between the two great branches of Protestantism—the Lutheran and the Reformed Church, as the same was effected since 1817 in the different German states. The founders of the Evangelical Synod were missionaries, sent during the third decade of the nineteenth century to America by the Mission Houses of Basel and Barmen. These two institutions are supported alike by Lutherans and Reformed Congregations in Germany and Switzerland, and both

denominations are also represented in the Board of Directors. It was therefore only natural for the pupils of these schools to organize a church here in America as similar as possible to their mother church in Germany. On October 15, 1840, seven of these missionaries assembled at Gravois Settlement, near St. Louis, Mo., and organized an association, which has become known as The German Evangelical Synod of North America.

(1) Doctrine. The following declaration of faith was adopted by the founders and still serves as its confessional basis: "The German Evangelical Synod of North America means by the term Evangelical Church *that* church community which acknowledges the Holy Scriptures of the Old and New Testament as the Word of God, and as the only true and infallible standard of Christian doctrines and precepts (1) and accepts as its confession that interpretation of the Holy Scriptures which is laid down in the symbolic books of the Lutheran and Reformed Churches, among which the Augsburg Confession, Luther's Minor and Major Catechism, and the Heidelberg Catechism are the principal ones, so far as they agree; but in points of difference the German Evangelical Synod adheres solely to the passages of Holy Scriptures alluding to them, observing that liberty of conscience existing in the Evangelical Church."

According to these articles of faith the German Evangelical Synod accepts as its doctrine the *consensus fidei* of the Lutheran and Reformed Churches. We confess, in entire harmony with the Church of the Reformation, God as the Almighty Creator of heaven and earth; his omnipresent providence in the guidance of men; the doctrine of the fall of man, of original sin, of redemption through the atoning blood of Christ; and the Christology, as the same was formed by the ecumenical councils of the first centuries. We confess that sanctification is not our work, but is initiated by the agency of the Holy Spirit, by means of the Divine word and the sacraments, and is a process that reaches its end only with the close of life. This declaration expresses the union of the Lutheran and Reformed branches of protestantism. As is well known, both have always agreed in all fundamental doctrines of Christian life and faith, and on all subjects and facts clearly expressed and stated in the Holy Scriptures, and on all articles of faith pertaining to our salvation. The controversy between the two *German* denominations centers around the doctrine of the Lord's Supper. (2) Our position on this question is the following: The German Evangelical Synod believes and confesses, that in the Holy Supper the faithful and penitent communicant receives in the bread and wine the body and the precious blood of Christ and therewith forgiveness of sins, life and salvation; but the unbeliever and unworthy receives damnation. The other question: *How* is this done? *how* is it possible? *how* is this miracle performed? the Synod leaves unanswered, since the Scripture gives us no explanation. But we believe in the fact, in the actuality of the miracle; we believe that bread and wine in the Holy Supper is the body and the blood of Christ, for Christ plainly said so.

(2) Polity. Every congregation binds itself voluntarily to the doctrine and precepts as laid down in the statutes of the German Evangelical Synod, when it joins that body.

Our relation toward other churches has ever been governed by the so-called Augustine motto: "*In necessariis unitas, in dubiis libertas, in omnibus charitas.*" We show friendly interest in all undertakings for a confederation of different denominations such as the International Evangelical Alliance, and prior to that organization the "Evanglischer Kirchentag" in Germany. We support international Bible associations and like work in different directions.

Let us say a few words on the management of our Church. Every congregation is independent in its local affairs; the Synod acts more in the character of a counsellor or adviser. A number of congregations within certain geographical boundaries constitute a "district," whose ministers and lay delegates meet annually in a district conference. All the districts meet together in the "General Synod," which is composed of one out of every nine ministers, and one lay delegate out of every nine congregations, elected at district conferences. It convenes every three years.

(3) Institutions. The Synod owns a theological seminary founded 1850 at Marthasville, Mo., removed to St. Louis, Mo., 1883. The preparatory college for students purposing to enter the theological seminary is at Elmhurst, Ill. It was founded 1871. In connection with the college is the seminary for the education of teachers for our parochial schools.

The German Evangelical Synod has its own mission field in the Central Province of India. There are seven missionaries and fifty native preachers. The annual expense is about $10,000, while a much larger sum is expended for home missions. A harbor mission in Baltimore, Md., for the benefit of emigrants, has been during the last ten years a blessing to many. There are orphanages at Detroit, Mich.; at Chicago, Bensenville, and Hazleton, Ill.; at St. Louis, Mo.; and at Lincoln, Neb.; also deaconess homes in seven of the states. Edĕn Publishing House is at St. Louis, Mo., and publishes all kinds of church papers and books of worship. The official organ is the *"Friedensboten,"* with a circulation of 25,000, besides which are seven other papers.   F. M.

GERSHOM (gēr'shom), (Heb. גֵּרְשֹׁם, *gay-resh-ome'*, expulsion).

1. The elder of the two sons (the other was Eliezer) who were born to Moses in the land of Midian by Zipporah (Exod. ii:22; xviii:3). These sons of the great lawgiver held no other rank than that of simple Levites, while the sons of their uncle ᴧaron enjoyed all the privileges of the priesthood (1 Chron. xxiii:15). The glory of being the children of such a father doubtless availed them more than the highest dignities; but we must nevertheless admire the rare disinterestedness of Moses in making no public provision—as he might so easily have done—for his own children. (B. C. 1698.)

2. The form of *Gershon*, as it appears (1 Chron. vi:16, 17, 20, 43, 62, 71; xv:7).

3. One of those who returned with Ezra from Babylon, as a representative of the priestly family of Phinehas (Ezra viii:2). (B. C. 459.)

GERSHON (gēr'shon), (Heb. גֵּרְשׁוֹן, *gay-resh-one'*, expulsion), eldest of the three sons of the patriarch Levi, born in Canaan before the going down into Egypt.

He is only known from his name having been given to one of the three great branches of the Levitical tribe. The office of the Gershonites, during the marches in the wilderness, was to carry the veils and curtains of the tabernacle, and their place in the camp was west of the tabernacle (Gen. xlvi:11; Exod. vi:16; Num. iii:17). (B. C. about 1706.) Gershon's sons were Libni and

Shimi (Exod. vi:17; Num. iii:18, 21; 1 Chron. vi:17).

GERSHONITES, THE (gēr'shon-ītes).

1. Descendants of Gershon (Num. iii:21, 23, 24; iv:24, 27; xxvi:57; Josh. xxi:33; 1 Chron. xxiii:7; 2 Chron. xxix:12). (See GERSHON).

As to the office and duties of the Gershonites, see LEVITES.

2. "The Gershonite," a name applied to Laadan (1 Chron. xxvi:21), and Jehiel (1 Chron. xxix:8).

GERZITES, THE (gēr'zītes), (Heb. with the art. הַגִּרְזִי, *hay-girzi*), a tribe living between Egypt and the south of Palestine in the time of Saul (1 Sam. xxvii:8, marg.) Our translators adopted the form Gizrites (or rather Gezrites) as corrected by the Masorets.

GESHAM (gē'sham), or rather **GESHAN** (Heb. גֵּישָׁן, *gay-shawn'*, filthy, or else firm, strong), the third son of Jahdai, among the descendants of Caleb (1 Chron. ii:47), B. C. after 1210.

GESHAN (gē'shan), (Heb. גֵּישָׁן, *gay-shawn'*, filthy, Ges), in A. V. Gesham, an error which crept in the later editions, the original of 1611 having Geshan.

GESHEM (gē'shem), (Heb. גֶּשֶׁם, *gheh'shem*, shower), an Arabian (Neh. ii:19; vi:1), and one of the enemies of the Jews on the return from the exile, especially in the plots against the life of Nehemiah (vi:2), B. C. 445.

He was probably a Samaritan, although on some account or other designated an Arabian (Neh. ii:19), and seems to have been a subaltern officer at Jerusalem. He opposed the designs of the Jewish governor, talking of them as seditious, and turning them into ridicule. Eventually he took part in the plots of Tobiah against the life of Nehemiah (Neh. ii:19; vi:2-9). (B. C. about 445.)

GESHUR (gē'shur), (Heb. גְּשׁוּר, *ghesh-oor'*, bridge), Syria (2 Sam. xv:8; 1 Chron. ii:23), which adjoined, on the east side of the Jordan, the northern border of the Hebrew territory, and lay between Mount Hermon, Maachah, and Bashan (Deut. iii:13, 14; Josh. xii:5).

According to the boundaries of the Holy Land, as defined by Moses, Geshur would have formed part of it; but in Josh. xiii:2, 13, it is stated that the Israelites had expelled neither the Geshurites nor the Maachathites, but dwelt together with them. That the Hebrews did not afterwards permanently subdue Geshur appears from the circumstance that, in David's time, this district had a king of its own, called Talmai, whose daughter, Maacah, was one of the wives of David (2 Sam. iii:3). She was the mother of Absalom, who took refuge with his grandfather after the murder of Amnon, and remained three years in Geshur (2 Sam. xiii:37; xv:8). The word *Geshur* signifies a bridge, and corresponds with the Arabic *Jisr*, and in the same region where, according to the above data, we must fix Geshur, between Mount Hermon and the lake of Tiberias, there still exists an ancient stone bridge over the upper Jordan, called Jisr-Beni-Jakub, or 'the bridge of the children of Jacob,' *i. e.*, the Israelites.

GESHURI (gĕsh'u-ri), (Heb. גְּשׁוּרִי, *ghe-shoo-ree'*, Deut. iii:14; Josh. xiii:2), or **GESHURITES** (Heb. גְּשׁוּרִים, *ghe-shoo-reem'*, Josh. xii:5; xiii:11, 13; 1 Sam. xxvii:8), the inhabitants of GESHUR, bordering on Aram, to the east of Jordan. (See GESHUR).

GETHER (gē'ther), (Heb. גֶּתֶר, *gheh'ther*, derivation uncertain). The third of the sons of Aram (Gen. x:23), no trustworthy identification of the people sprung from him has been made.

GETHSEMANE (geth-sĕm'a-ne), (Gr. Γεθσημανῆ, *gheth-say-man-ay'*, seemingly from oil press), the

The Garden of Gethsemane.

name of a small field, or garden, just out of Jerusalem, over the brook Kidron, and at the foot of the Mount of Olives.

That which is now pointed out as the garden in which our Lord underwent his agony, occupies part of a level space between the brook and the foot of the Mount, and corresponds well enough in situation and distance with all the conditions which the narrative requires. It is about fifty paces square, and is enclosed by a wall of no great height, formed of rough loose stones. Eight very ancient olive-trees now occupy this enclosure, some of which are of very large size, and all exhibit symptoms of decay clearly denoting their great age. The garden belongs to one of the monastic establishments, and much care has been taken to preserve the old trees from destruction. Dr. Robinson admits the probability that this is the site which Eusebius and Jerome had in view; and, as no other site is suggested as preferable, we may be content to receive the traditional indication. Thomson, however (*The Land and the Book*, vol. ii. pp. 483-4), says: "The position is too near the city, and so close to what must have always been the great thoroughfare eastward, that our Lord would scarcely have selected it for retirement on that dangerous and dismal night." He believes Gethsemane to have been in a secluded vale several hundred yards northeast of the traditional site. Barclay thinks it evident that the present enclosure, from its narrow dimensions, can occupy only in part the site of the ancient garden, and finds a better position higher up in the valley. Porter states that the Greeks, envious of the Latins, have recently enclosed a piece of ground a little north, beside the Virgin's tomb, and contend that this is the true garden.

GEUEL (ge-ū'el), (Heb. גְּאוּאֵל, *gheh-oo-ale'*, majesty of Gad), son of Machi, and ruler of the tribe of Gad. He was among the spies sent to explore the promised land (Num. xiii:15), B. C. 1657.

GEZER (gē'zēr), (Heb. גֶּזֶר, *gheh'zer*, a precipice).

Formerly a royal city of the Canaanites, and situated in what became the western part of the tribe of Ephraim. The Canaanites were not expelled from it at the conquest (Josh. x:33; xvi: 5, 10; Judg. i:29). It was, nevertheless, assigned to the Levites (Josh. xxi:21; 1 Chron. vi:67). In after times, having been, on some occasion, destroyed by the Egyptians, it was rebuilt by Solomon (1 Kings ix:16). M. Clermont Ganneau identified the site by inscriptions; one of which, perhaps as old as the Herods, marked the limits of Gezer, and gave in Hebrew letters the actual name. It is now called Tell Jezar and is situated about eighteen miles west-northwest of Jerusalem, and nearly six east of Ekron.

GEZRITES (gĕz'rītes), (Heb. הַגִּזְרִי, *hagh-ghiz-ree'*, strictly "the Gizrite"), is the rendering of the *geri* of 1 Sam. xxvii:8, where the kethîbh has הגרזי, which may be Girzite, Gerizite, or Gerizzite. (See GERZITES, THE.)

GIAH (gī'ah), (Heb. גִּיחַ, *ghee'akh*, fountain), a place named (2 Sam. ii:24), which Ammah was said to face. No trace of this place has been found.

GIANTS (jī'ants), (Heb. גִּבּוֹר, *ghib-bore'*, for mighty, strong one). The English word is derived immediately from the Latin *gigas*, which is only Greek in Roman letters; and γίγας, *giant*, itself is, in all likelihood, made up of γινέσθαι, *to be born*, and γέα, the earth, thus signifying 'the earth-born,' in allusion to classical fable.

These beings of unusual height are found in the early history of all nations, sometimes of a purely human origin, but more frequently supposed to have partaken also, in some way, of the supernatural and the divine.

(1) Nephilim. In Gen. vi:4, we have the first mention of giants (Heb. נְפִילִם, *nef-ee-leem'*, causing to fall), 'There were giants in the earth in those days; and also after that, when the sons of God came in unto the daughters of men, and they bare children to them, the same became mighty men which were of old, men of renown.'

In our judgment the bearing of the passage obviously favors the common notion of giants, and that the rather because their origin is traced to some unexplained connection with 'the sons of God,' that is, with beings of high endowments, if not of a superior nature.

(2) Rephaim. In Gen. xiv:5, we meet with a race termed Rephaim (Heb. רְפָאִים, *ref-aw-eem'*, strong), as settled on the other side of the Jordan, in Ashteroth-Karnaim, whom Chedorlaomer defeated.

Of this race was Og, king of Bashan, who alone remained, in the days of Moses (Deut. iii:10), of the remnant of the Rephaim. This race gave their name to a valley near Jerusalem.

(3) Anakim. The Anakim (עֲנָקִים, *an-aw-keem'*, sons of Anak). In Num. xiii the spies sent by Moses before his army to survey the promised land, report among other things—'The people be strong that dwell in the land; and, moreover, we saw the children of Anak' (verse 28).

This indirect mention of the children of Anak shows that they were a well-known gigantic race. In the 32d and 33d verses the statement is enhanced—'It is a land that eateth up the inhabitants; and all the people that we saw in it are men of great stature. And there we saw the giants, the sons of Anak which came of the giants; and we were in our own sight as grasshoppers, and so we were in their sight.' However much of exaggeration fear may have given to the description, the passage seems beyond a doubt to show the writer's belief in a race of giants (Deut. ix:2). From Deut. ii:10, it appears that the size of the Anakim became proverbial, and was used as a standard with which to compare others. In the time of Moses they dwelt in the environs of Hebron (Josh. xi:22).

(5) Emim. Another race is mentioned in Deut. ii:10, the Emim (אֵימִים, *ay-meen'*), who dwelt in the country of the Moabites. They are described as a people 'great and many, and tall as the Anakims, which were also accounted giants' (Gen. xiv:5).

(6) Zamzummim. The Zamzummim also (זַמְזֻמִּים, *zam-zum-meem'*, Deut. ii:20) had their home in the land of Ammon—'that also was accounted a land of giants. Giants dwelt therein of old time, and the Ammonites called them Zamzummims, a people great and many, and

Old Olive Trees in the Garden of Gethsemane.

They consisted of three branches or clans—'Ahiman, Sheshai, and Talmai—the children of Anak' (Num. xiii:22). They were destroyed by Joshua (Josh. xi:21; Judg. i:20).

(4) Goliath. From this remnant of the Anakim thus left in Gath of the Philistines, proceeded the famous Goliath (גָּלְיָת, *gol-yath'*, exile, 1 Sam. xvii:4). This giant is said to have been in height six cubits and a span.

Other giants of the Philistines are mentioned in the passage before cited, 2 Sam. xxi:16, *sq.*, namely:—(1) 'Ishbi-benob, which was of the sons of the giant, the weight of whose spear weighed three hundred shekels of brass, he being girded with a new sword, thought to have slain David; but Abishai, the son of Zeruiah, succored him, and smote the Philistine and killed him.' (2) Saph (2 Sam. xxi:18), which was of the sons of the giant who was slain by Sibbechai. (3) 'A man (2 Sam. xxi:20) of great stature, that had on every hand six fingers and on every foot six toes, four and twenty in number, and he also was born to the giant; and when he defied Israel, Jonathan, the son of Shimeah, the brother of David, slew him.' These four were sons of the giant in Gath, that is, probably of the Goliath of Gath whom David slew (1 Kings xx:8; 2 Sam. xxi:19; 1 Sam. xvii:4).

tall as the Anakims; but the Lord destroyed them before them, and they (the Israelites) succeeded them, and dwelt in their stead.'

From this enumeration it is clear that the scriptures tell of giants in the olden time, and of races of giants; that primitive races greatly excelled all others in size; and that, though giants are mentioned as something singular and consequently as comparatively rare, they appear to have been, relatively to the numbers of the population, of frequent occurrence. (See BASHAN; REPHAIM.)

The possibility of a race of giants cannot well be denied. There is a known tendency in the human frame to perpetuate peculiarities which have been once evolved. Why not extraordinary 'procerity' as well as any other? In fact, the propagation of stature, whether high or low, is a phenomenon which we all see presented daily before our own eyes. Tall parents give birth to tall children. The tallness is found to remain in families; and, doubtless, did not circumstances intervene to reduce the stature by intermarriage with short persons, the unusual height would be perpetuated in any given line. The inhabitants of Potsdam, descended to a great extent from the famous regiment of tall grenadiers which Frederick of Prussia took so much pains to bring together, are said to be still remarkable for exceeding the average height. The family of Scaligers appears to have been unusually tall.   J. R. B.

GIBBAR (gĭb'bar), (Chal. גִּבָּר, *ghib-bawr'*, a hero), ninety-five of "the sons of Gibbar" returned from captivity with Zerubbabel (Ezra ii:20). In the parallel passage of Neh. vii:25, the name is Gibeon.

GIBBETHON (gĭb'be-thŏn), (Heb. גִּבְּתוֹן, *ghib-beth-one'*, a height), a city of the Philistines, which was included in the territories of the tribe of Dan (Josh. xix:44), and was assigned to the Levites (Josh. xxi:23).

It was still in the hands of the Philistines in the time of Nadab, king of Israel, who besieged it, and was slain under its walls by Baasha, one of his own officers (1 Kings xv:27; xvi:15). Nothing is known of its site.

GIBEA (gĭb'e-à), (Heb. גִּבְעָא, *ghib-aw'*, hill), occurs among the names of places, among the descendants of Judah (1 Chron. ii:49). This would seem to identify Gibea with GIBEAH of Judah (Burrington, i. 216).

GIBEAH (gĭb'e-ah), (Hebrew same as above). There were several places of this name, which, as before remarked (see GEBA), is the feminine form of the word Gibeah, and signifies a *hill*. Without doubt all the places so named were situated upon hills.

(1) Gibeah of Judah. Gibeah in the mountains of Judah (Josh. xv:57), which, under the name of Gabaatha, Eusebius and Jerome place twelve Roman miles from Eleutheropolis, and state that the grave of the prophet Habakkuk was there to be seen. Dr. Robinson (*Researches*, ii: 327) identifies it with the village of Jebah, which stands upon an isolated hill, in the midst of Wady-el-Musurr, about ten miles southwest of Jerusalem.

(2) Gibeah at Kirjath-jearim. The place where the ark rested after it was returned by the Philistines, until its removal by David (2 Sam. vi:3, 4; comp. 1 Sam. vii:1, 2).

(3) Gibeah of Benjamin is historically the most important of the places bearing this name. It is often mentioned in Scripture. It was the scene of that abominable transaction which involved in its consequences almost the entire extirpation of the tribe of Benjamin (Judg. xix:14, *sq.*). It is without doubt identical with the next.

(4) Gibeah of Saul, which was the birthplace of Saul, and continued to be his residence after he became king (1 Sam. x:26; xi:4; xv:33; xxiii: 19; xxvi:1); and here was the scene of Jonathan's romantic exploit against the Philistines (1 Sam. xiv). It was doubtless on account of this intimate connection with Saul that the Gibeonites hanged up here his seven descendants (2 Sam. xxi:6). Jerome speaks of Gibeah as, in his time, level with the ground (*Ep.* 86, *ad Eustoch.*), and since then it does not appear to have been visited by travelers till recently. Dr. Robinson, who made many valuable observations in this neighborhood, detected Gibeah in the small and half-ruined village of Jeba, which lies upon a low, conical, or rather round eminence, on the broad ridge which shelves down towards the Jordan valley, and spreads out below the village in a fine sloping plain. The views of the Dead Sea and the Jordan, and of the Eastern mountains, are here very extensive. Among the ruins some large hewn stones, indicating antiquity, are occasionally seen. This place is about five miles north by east from Jerusalem.

(5) Gibeah in Mount Ephraim, called Gibeah of Phineas, where the high-priest Eleazar, son of Aaron, was buried by his son Phineas (Josh. xxiv:33). The *Onomasticon* makes it five Roman miles from Gophna, on the road to Neapolis (Shechem); which was itself fifteen Roman miles north of Jerusalem. Dr. Robinson finds it in a narrow valley called Wady-el-Jib, the Geeb of Maundrell, lying just midway on the road between Jerusalem and Shechem.

(6) Gibeah in the Field, a place to which ran one of the highways out of Gibeah of Benjamin (Judg. xx:31). The place has not been identified.

(7) Other Gibeahs. The name of several places given in the A. V. in their translated form (1) "Hill of the foreskins" (Josh. v:3), between the Jordan and Jericho. It took its name from the circumcision which took place there. It seems to have been called Gilgal, afterwards. (2) The "hill of Moreh" (Judg. vii:1). (3) The "hill of God" on the route of Saul (1 Sam. x:5). (4) The "hill of Hachilah" (1 Sam. xxiii:19; xxvi:1). (5) The "hill of Ammah" (2 Sam. ii: 24). (6) The "hill of Gareb" (Jer. xxxi:39).

GIBEATH (gĭb'e-ăth), (Heb. same as Gibeah), enumerated among the towns of Benjamin, next to Jerusalem (Josh. xviii:28). It is very probably not the same as Gibeah of Benjamin, as has been suggested, because the latter place was five or six miles north of Jerusalem, and near to Gibeon and Ramah, with which it would have been enumerated. (See GIBEA; GIBEAH.)

GIBEATHITE, THE (gĭb'e-ath-īte), (Heb. גִּבְעָתִי, *ghib-aw-thee'*, a native of Gibeah; applied to Shemaah, the father of two Benjamites under Saul, who joined David), (1 Chron. xii:3).

GIBEON (gĭb'e-on), (Heb. גִּבְעוֹן, *ghib-hon'*, hill city).

A town celebrated in the Old Testament, but not mentioned in the New. (1) It was 'a great city,' as one of the royal cities; and to its jurisdiction originally belonged Beeroth, Chephirah, and Kirjath-jearim (Josh. ix:17; x:2). It is first mentioned in connection with the deception practiced by the inhabitants upon Joshua, by which, although Canaanites (Hivites), they induced the Jewish leader not only to make a league with them, and to spare their lives and cities, but also, in their defense, to make war upon the five kings by whom they were besieged. (2) It was in the great battle which followed that 'the sun stood still upon Gibeon' (Josh. x:12, 1-14). (3) The place afterwards fell to the lot of Benjamin and became a Levitical city (Josh. xviii:25; xxi:17), where the tabernacle was set up for many years under David and Solomon (1 Chron. xvi:39; xxi:29; 2 Chron. i:3), the ark being at the same time at Jerusalem (2 Chron. i:4). (4) It was here, as being the place of the altar, that the young Solomon offered a thousand burnt-offerings, and was rewarded by the vision which left him the wisest of men (1 Kings iii:4-15; 2 Chron. i:3-13). (5) This was the place where Abner's challenge to Joab brought defeat upon himself, and death upon his brother Ashael (2 Sam. ii:12-32), and where Amasa was afterwards slain by Joab (2 Sam. xx:8-12). (6) None of these passages mark the site of Gibeon; but there are indications of it in Josephus (*De Bell. Jud.* ii:19, 1), who places it fifty stadia northwest from Jerusalem; and in Jerome (*Ep.* 86, *ad Eustoch.*); which leave little doubt that Gibeon is to be identified with the place which still bears the name of El-Jib. (7) El-Jib is a moderately sized village, seated on the summit of a hill, five miles north by west

45

from Jerusalem. The houses stand very irregularly and unevenly, sometimes almost above one another. They seem to be chiefly rooms in old massive ruins, which have fallen down in every direction. (8) One large building still remains, probably a former castle or tower of strength. Towards the east the ridge of the hill sinks a little, and here, a few rods from the village, just below the top of the ridge towards the north, is a fine fountain of water. It is in a cave, excavated in and under the high rock, so as to form a large subterranean reservoir. Not far below it, among olive-trees, are the remains of an open reservoir, about one hundred and twenty feet in length by one hundred in breadth. It was doubtless designed to receive the superfluous waters of the cavern, and there can be little question but that this was 'the Pool of Gibeon' mentioned

such, and preferably employed upon the shipping which formed the glory and strength of Tyre. The term is Gebalites in the R. V.

GIDDALTI (gid-dăl'tĭ), (Heb. גִּדַּלְתִּי, *ghid-dal-tee'*, I have made great), a Kohathite Levite, son of Heman, "the king's seer" (1 Chron. xxv:4, 29), B. C. 1013. He with his thirteen brothers played the horn in the temple service (verses 5, 7). He also conducted the 22d course (verse 29).

GIDDEL (gĭd'del), (Heb. גִּדֵּל, *ghid-dale'*, large).

1. The children of Giddel returned with the Nethinim from captivity under Zerubbabel (Ezra ii:47; Neh. vii:49).
2. Sons of Bene-Giddel, servants of Solomon, returned from Babylon with Zerubbabel in the same caravan (Ezra ii:56; Neh. vii:58).

Gibeon.

in 2 Sam. ii:13; and, in the whole, we find the 'Great (or many) waters of Gibeon' of Jer. xli: 12.

GIBEONITES, THE (gĭb'e-on-ītes), (Heb. גִּבְעֹנִים, *ghib-o-neem'*, the people of Gibeon: Hivites). (See GIBEON.) Individual Gibeonites are ISMAIAH (1 Chron. xii:4); Melathia (Neh. iii:7); Hananiah, son of Azur (Jer. xxviii:1, 10, 13, 17).

GIBLITES (gĭb'lites), (Heb. גִּבְלִי, *ghib-lee'*, the inhabitants of the city and district of Gebal in Phœnicia, 34° 7′ N. lat., 35° 42′ E. long., on the shore of the Mediterranean, under Mount Lebanon.

'The land of the Giblites,' with 'all Lebanon,' was assigned to the Israelites by the original appointment (Josh. xiii:5); but it does not seem that they ever possessed themselves of it. The Giblites are denoted by the word rendered 'stone-squarers' in 1 Kings v:18; from which it would seem that they were then subject to, or in close connection with, Tyre. It is doubtful whether this Gebal, or the one in Edom, is that mentioned in Ps. lxxxiii:7. But in Ezek. xxvii:9, the Phœnician Giblites are distinctly mentioned as

GIDEON (gĭd'e-on), (Heb. גִּדְעוֹן, *ghid-ohn'*, tree feller, i. e., warrior or destroyer).

He was surnamed Jerubbaal or Jerubbesheth, fifth Judge in Israel, and the first of them whose history is circumstantially narrated. He was the son of Joash, of the tribe of Manasseh (Judg. vi: 11), and resided at Ophrah in Gilead beyond the Jordan.

(1) Condition of Israel. The Midianites, in conjunction with the Amalekites and other nomade tribes, invaded the country every year, at the season of produce, in great numbers, with their flocks and herds. They plundered and trampled down the fields, the vineyards, and the gardens; they seized the cattle, and plundered man and house, rioting in the country, after the manner which the Bedouin Arabs practice at this day.

(2) Call of Gideon. After Israel had been humbled by seven years of this treatment, the Lord raised up a deliverer in the person of Gideon. He was threshing corn by stealth, for fear of its being taken away by the Midianites, when an angel of God appeared before him, and thus saluted him:—'The Lord is with thee, thou mighty man of valor.' Gideon expressed some doubt whether God was still with a people subject to such affliction, and was answered by the most unexpected commission—'Go in this thy might, and thou shalt save Israel from the hand of the Midianites; have not I sent thee'? Gideon still urged, 'Wherewith shall I save Israel? Behold my family is poor in Manasseh, and I am the least in my father's house.' The 'Wherewith' was answered by 'Surely I will be with thee.' He then demurred no more, but pressed his hospitality upon the heavenly stranger, who, however, ate not of what was set before him, but directing Gideon to lay it out upon the rock as upon an altar, it was consumed by a supernatural fire, and the angel disappeared.

(3) Destroys Baal's Altar. Assured by this of his commission, Gideon proceeded at once to cast down the local image and altar of Baal; and, when the people would have avenged this insult to their false god, their anger was averted through the address of his father, who, by dwelling on the inability of Baal to avenge himself, more than insinuated a doubt of his competency to protect his followers. This was a favorite argument among the Hebrews against idolatry. It occurs often in the prophets, and was seldom urged upon idolatrous Israelites without some effect upon their consciences.

(4) The Sign of the Fleece. Gideon soon found occasion to act upon his high commission. The allied invaders were encamped in the great plain of Jezreel or Esdraelon, when he blew the trumpet, and thus gathered round him a daily increasing host, the summons to arms which it implied having been transmitted through the northern tribes by special messengers. The inquietude connected with great enterprises is more sensibly felt some days before than at the moment of action; and hence the two miraculous signs which, on the two nights preceding the march, were required and given as tokens of victory. The first night a fleece was laid out in the middle of an open threshing-floor, and in the morning it was quite wet, while the soil was dry all around. The next night the wonder was reversed, the soil being wet and the fleece perfectly dry (Judg. vii).

(5) Midianites Defeated. Encouraged by these Divine testimonies, Gideon commenced his march, and advanced to the brook Harod, in the valley of Jezreel. He was here at the head of 32,000 men; but, lest so large a host should assume the glory of the coming deliverance, which of right belonged to God only, two operations, remarkable both in motive and procedure, reduced this large host to a mere handful of men. First, by Divine direction, proclamation was made that all the faint-hearted might withdraw; and no fewer than 22,000 availed themselves of the indulgence. The remaining 10,000 were still declared too numerous; they were therefore all taken down to the brook, when only those who lapped the water from their hands, like active men in haste, were reserved for the enterprise, while all those who lay down leisurely to drink were excluded. The former numbered no more than 300, and these were the appointed vanquishers of the huge host which covered the great plain (Judg. vii:1-8).

The overheard relation of a dream, by which Gideon was encouraged (Judg. vii:9-14), and the remarkable stratagem, with pitchers and torches, by which he overcame (verses 15-23), are well known.

The routed Midianites fled towards the Jordan, but were pursued with great slaughter, the country being now roused in pursuit of the flying oppressor.

(6) The Ephraimites. The Ephraimites rendered good service by seizing the lower fords of the Jordan, and cutting off all who attempted escape in that direction, while Gideon himself pursued beyond the river those who escaped by the upper fords. Gideon crossed the Jordan a little below where it leaves the lake of Gennesaret, in pursuit of the Midianitish princes Zeba and Zalmunna. On that side the river, however, his victory was not believed or understood, and the people still trembled at the very name of the Midianites.

(7) Destroys Succoth and Penuel. Hence he could obtain no succor from the places which he passed, and town after town refused to supply even victuals to his fatigued and hungry, but still stout-hearted troop. He pronounced vengeance upon them, but postponed its execution till his return; and when he did return with the two princes as his prisoners, he by no means spared those towns which, like Succoth and Penuel, had added insult to injury (Judg. viii:4-17).

(8) Avenges His Brethren. In those days captives of distinction taken in war were almost invariably slain. Zeba and Zalmunna had made up their minds to this fate; and yet it was Gideon's intention to have spared them, till he learned that they had put to death his own brothers under the same circumstances; upon which, as the avenger of their blood, he slew the captives with his own hand (Judg. viii:18-21). Among the fugitives taken by the Ephraimites were two distinguished emirs of Midian, named Oreb and Zeeb, whom they put to death. They took their heads over to Gideon. which amounted to an acknowledgment of his leadership; but still the always haughty and jealous Ephraimites were greatly annoyed that they had not in the first instance been summoned to the field; and serious consequences might have followed, but for the tact of Gideon in speaking in a lowly spirit of his own doings in comparison with theirs (Judg. vii:14; viii:4).

(9) Refuses the Crown. Gideon having thus delivered Israel from the most afflictive tyranny to which they had been subject since they quitted Egypt, the grateful people, and particularly the northern tribes, made him an offer of the crown for himself and his sons. But the hero was too well acquainted with his true position, and with the principles of theocratical government, to accept this unguarded offer: 'I will not rule over you,' he said, 'neither shall my son rule over you; Jehovah, he shall rule over you.' He would only accept the golden earrings which the victors had taken from the ears of their slaughtered foes (see EARRINGS); and a cloth being spread out to receive them, the admiring Israelites threw in, not only the earrings, but other ornaments of gold, including the chains of the royal camels, and added the purple robes which the slain monarchs had worn, being the first indication of purple as a royal color. The earrings alone weighed 1,700 shekels, equal to seventy-four pounds four ounces, and worth, at the present value of gold, about £3,300, or $16,500.

(10) Remaining Deeds and Death. With this 'Gideon made an ephod, and put it in his city, even in Ophrah; and all Israel went thither a whoring after it; which thing became a snare unto Gideon and to his house.' An ephod, at least that of the high-priest, was an outer garment like a sleeveless tunic, to which was attached the oracular breast-plate, composed of twelve precious stones set in gold, and graven with the names of the twelve tribes. Another plainer description of ephod was worn by the common priests. The object of Gideon in making an ephod with his treasure is not very clear. Some suppose that it was merely designed as a trophy of Israel's deliverance; if so, it was a very strange one. It is more probable that as Gideon had, on his being first called to his high mission, been instructed to build an altar and offer sacrifice at this very place, he conceived himself authorized, if not required, to have there a sacerdotal establishment—for at least the tribes beyond the river—where sacrifices might be regularly offered. In this case the worship rendered there was doubtless in honor of Jehovah, but was still, however well intended, highly schismatical and irregular. Even in his lifetime it must have had the effect of withdrawing the attention of the people east of the Jordan from the Tabernacle at Shiloh, and thus so far tended to facilitate the step into actual idolatry, which was taken soon after Gideon's death. The probability of this explanation is strengthened when we recollect the schismatical sacerdotal establishments which were formed by Micah on Mount Ephraim, and by the Danites at Laish (Judg. xvii:5-13; xviii:29-31).

The remainder of Gideon's life was peaceable. He had seventy sons by many wives, and died at an advanced age, after he had 'ruled Israel' (principally the northern tribes and those beyond the river) for forty years (B. C. about 1100 to 1080.) He is mentioned in the discourse of Samuel (1 Sam. xii:11), and his name occurs in Heb. xi:32, among those of the heroes of the faith.

GIDEONI (gĭd'e-ō'nī), (Heb. גִּדְעֹנִי, *ghid-o-nee'*, warlike).

The father of Abidam, who was chief in the tribe of Benjamin at the time of the taking of the census in the wilderness of Sinai (Num. i: 11; ii:22; vii:60, 65; x:24). (B. C. about 1220.)

GIDOM (gī'dŏm), (Heb. גִּדְעֹם, *ghid-ohm,'* a cutting down, desolating), a place to which Benjamin went in pursuit after the battle of Gibeah (Judg. xx:45). It is evidently situated between Gibeah (*Tuleil-el-Ful*) and the cliff Rimmon; but no trace of it has been found.

GIER-EAGLE (jēr'ē'g'l), (The A. V. uses this term for Heb. רָחָם, *raw-khawm'*, Pharaoh's chicken, *Neophron percnopterus*. R. V. uses it for פֶּרֶס, *peh'res*, which may be translated ossifrage).

An unclean bird mentioned in Lev. xi:18; Deut. xiv:17. This is probably the *racham* of the Arabs or the Egyptian vulture (*neophron percnopterus*), a bird of disgusting appearance and habits; but a faithful scavenger. (Shaw, *Travels*, p. 388; Russell, *Natural Hist. of Aleppo*, ii:195, 2d ed.)

GIFT (gĭft), the translation of several Hebrew and Greek terms.

1. From the Hebrew root נָתַן (*naw-than'*) we have words, meaning a *gratuity* (Prov. xix: 6); to secure favor (Prov. xviii:16; xxi:14), in religious thankfulness (Num. xviii:11), or in dowry (Gen. xxxiv:12), in inheritance (Gen. xxv:6; 2 Chron. xxi:3; Ezek. xlvi:16, 17), or as a bribe (Prov. xv:27).

2. From the Heb. נָשָׂא (*naw-saw'*, to raise) we have terms expressive of *pecuniary assistance* (Esth. ii:18) and of a *present* in token of respect (2 Sam. xix:42).

3. More distinctly in the sense of a votive offering is *min-khaw'* (Heb. מִנְחָה), an *oblation* or propitiatory gift (2 Sam. viii:2, 6; 1 Chron. xviii:2, 6, etc.), and in several other passages where the word has the accessory idea of *tribute* elsewhere usually rendered offering.

4. Other words are mercenary in character. Thus *show'khad* (Heb. שֹׁחַד) is a gift for the purpose of escaping punishment presented either to a judge (Exod. xxiii:8; Deut. x:17) or to a conqueror (2 Kings xvi:8).

5. In Greek the usual terms are generally derived from δίδωμι (*did'o-mee*, to give), and have a very wide meaning as did the Hebrew. (Mc. & Str. *Cyc.*)

6. There are specific uses of the term as follows: (1) Christ is the *unspeakable gift of God;* his excellence, usefulness, and fullness of office, righteousness, and salvation, cannot be expressed or conceived by any creature; and God freely gave him for us as our ransom, and gives him to us as our husband and portion (2 Cor. ix:15). (2) His righteousness and the benefits purchased by it, are *the free gift,* and *gift of righteousness* (Rom. v:15-17). (3) The Holy Ghost, and his miraculous influences, are the *gift of God* (Acts viii:20). Eternal life, offices in the church, and qualifications for the discharge of them, and every saving blessing are represented as *gifts.* Such of them as are necessarily connected with union to Christ are *gifts* given to his children, never to be recalled; and such as are separable from real grace are *gifts* given to servants to be recalled (Rom. vi:23; Jam. i:17; Ps. lxviii:18; Eph. ii:8; iv: 8; Ezek. xlvi:16, 17; Rom. xi:29; 1 Cor. xii:1, 4, 9, 31, and xiv:1, 12; Heb. vi:4).

GIFT OF TONGUES. An ability given by the Holy Spirit to the apostles and others, of readily and intelligibly speaking a variety of languages which they had never learned. This was a glorious and decisive attestation to the gospel, as well as a suitable, and indeed, in their circumstances, a necessary qualification for the mission for which the apostles and their coadjutors were designed. Nor is there any reason to understand it as merely an occasional gift so that a person might speak a language most fluently one hour, and be entirely ignorant of it the next; which neither agrees with what is said of the abuse of it, nor would it have been sufficient to answer the end proposed (Acts ii). Some appear to have been gifted with one tongue, others with more. To St. Paul this endowment was vouchsafed in a more liberal degree, than to many others; for, as to the Corinthians, who had received the gift of tongues, he says, "that he spake with tongues more than they all."

GIFTS, SPIRITUAL (gĭfts, spĭr'ĭt-ū-al), (Gr. χαρίσματα, *khar-is'mah-tah*, gifts of grace).

1. *Charismata* means those "graces" which are the effects of grace; that is of the outpouring of the Holy Ghost, consequent on the ascension of our Lord into heaven,—all, properly speaking, subjective: yet St. Paul calls the pardon of sin in one place (Rom. v:15), and eternal life in another (*ib.* vi:23), a "*charisma;*" that is, a gracious or free gift on the part of God through Christ.

2. Again, subjective graces have been distinguished into two classes: (1) those conferring mere power (*gratiae gratis datae*); and (2) those which affect the character (*gratiae gratum facientes*). The *locus classicus* for both is 1 Cor. xii to the end of ch. xiv (on which see Bloomfield, Alford, Cornelius à Lapide, and others), where they are thrown together without much system or classification.

(a) Of the former class, some were neither permanent nor universal, as the gift of healing: others, as for instance, that which he affirms elsewhere to be in Timothy by the laying on of his hands (2 Tim. i:6; comp. 1 Pet. iv:10); in other words, the gift conferred upon all ministers of the gospel at their ordination, fitting them for their respective posts, were permanent, but not universal. Both were bestowed primarily for the edification of the whole body; not but that it would fare better or worse with each individual possessed of them according to the way in which they were used. "The manifestation of the Spirit is given to every man, to profit withal."

(b) Of the latter class all were permanent and universal, being designed primarily for individual sanctification; all had them therefore without exception; and anybody might double or quadruple his share of them by his own exertions. Where they lay dormant in any, the fault was his own. Wherever they were cultivated, they would bring forth, some thirty, some sixty, and some a hundredfold.

(c) "Follow after charity," says the Apostle. Then, in substance, he goes on to say: This is a gift of the same character with faith and hope, permanent and bestowed on all. Therefore the degree to which you may become possessed of it rests with yourselves. As you follow after it, so you will obtain it. For those gifts which are not given to all you can only pray; still I enjoin you to pray; and of these "pray rather that ye may prophesy;" in other words that ye may "understand the scriptures" (compare Luke xxiv:45), and be able to interpret them for the benefit of others, as well as your own;—a gift which is permanent, and for the good of all, like charity. Of ordinary gifts, I have devoted a whole chapter to show that charity should occupy the first place: of extraordinary gifts, I proceed to show in the ensuing chapter my reasons for considering prophecy, taken in its widest sense, to be first also; one is for practice, the other for information: to understand the scriptures, and to act upon them aright, for general as well as for private profit and edification, is to fulfill every purpose for which grace is vouchsafed.

(d) Prophecy, therefore, will mean here the gift of expounding, rather than of foretelling (Corn. à Lap. ad. l.), and to the nine extraordinary "charismata" set down here, correspond the nine ordinary, described as "the fruit of the Spirit," in the Epistle to the Galatians (v:22). To these last three more have been added, making twelve in all; while faith, hope, and charity have been contrariwise classified by themselves as the three theological virtues.   E. S. F.

(e) Concerning spiritual gifts Cremer says: "Their number is as various as the needs of the Church, and neither the enumeration of 1 Cor. xii, nor of Eph. iv, nor Rom. xii can be regarded as exhaustive. But those are permanent which are necessary for the government of the Church, and those temporary which had a miraculous element, as the miraculous gifts of the apostles. But among the latter is not to be included the 'gift of proclaiming the gospel so as to produce faith' (Weiss). The apostolic charismata bear the same relation to those of the ministry that the apostolic office does to the pastoral office, and consist in the power to lay the foundations of the Church. They are therefore not repeated, as the Irvingites hold, for there are no circumstances calling for their repetition." (See article in Schaff-Herzog.)

GIHON (gī'hŏn), (Heb. גִּיחֹון, *ghee-khone'*).

1. A fountain near Jerusalem. The place outside the city to which the young Solomon was taken to be anointed king was called Gihon, but its direction is not indicated (1 Kings i:33, 38). Subsequently King Hezekiah 'stopped the upper water-course (or upper out-flow of the waters) of Gihon, and brought it straight down to the west side of the city of David (2 Chron. xxxii: 30; xxxiii:14). This was, perhaps, on occasion of the approach of the Assyrian army under Sennacherib, when, to prevent the besiegers from finding water, great numbers of the people labored with much diligence in stopping the water of the fountains without the city, and in particular of 'the brook that ran through the midst of the land' (2 Chron. xxxii:3, 4). The author of the book of Sirach (xlviii:17) also states, that 'Hezekiah brought water into the midst of the city; he dug with iron into the rock, and built fountains for the waters.' The fountain of Gihon is also mentioned by Josephus. From a comparison of these passages the conclusion has been reached, since confirmed by Dr. Robinson (*Researches*, i. 313), that there existed anciently a fountain of Gihon, on the west side of the city, which was 'stopped', or covered over by Hezekiah, and its waters brought by subterraneous channels into the city. Before that time it would naturally have flowed down through the valley of Gihon, and probably formed the brook which was stopped at the same time. Captain Sir Charles Warren claimed to have traced the diverted water course and secured the stone plug, twelve inches in length, with which the drain was stopped (see Harper, *Bible and Mod. Disc.*) The fountain may have been stopped, and its waters thus secured very easily by digging deep and erecting over it one or more vaulted subterranean chambers.

2. Upper Gihon is commonly identified with Birket Mamilla, and lower Gihon with Birket es-Sultan. The former of these pools is less than half a mile west, the latter not the third of a mile south, of the Jaffa gate. These pools, however, are not now fed by living springs. Largely on this account the question has been raised in recent years whether Gihon should not be identified with the fountain of the Virgin, on the eastern slope of Ophel, and distant some 400 yards from the pool of Siloam, with which it is connected by an ancient tunnel. (Comp. Robinson's *Researches*, i. 352, 512-514, Thomson, *The Land and the Book*, vol. ii. pp. 494-523, 526-7.)

3. The name of one of the rivers of Paradise. (See PARADISE.)

GILALAI (gĭl'a-lāi), (Heb. גִּלֲלַי, *ghil-al-lah'ee*, dungy or weighty), one of a number of priests' sons, who played an instrument in the company under Ezra at the time the wall of Jerusalem was consecrated (Neh. xii:36), B. C. 446.

GILBOA (gil-bō'à), (Heb. גִּלְבֹּעַ, *ghil-bo'ah*, bubbling fountain), a mountain memorable for the defeat of Saul by the Philistines, where his three sons were slain, and where he himself died by his own hand (1 Sam. xxviii:4; xxxi:1-8; 2 Sam. i:6-21).

The circumstances of the narrative would alone suffice to direct our attention to the mountains which bound the great plain of Esdraelon on the southeast, and are interposed between it and the Jordan valley. Here there are a number of ridges, with a general direction from northwest to southeast, separated by valleys running in the same direction. The largest of these valleys is the southernmost: it is a broad deep plain about two miles and a half wide, and leading direct into the Jordan valley. This is supposed to be distinctively (for the plain of Esdraelon is sometimes so called) the Valley of Jezreel. The mountains which bound it on the north appear to be those of Little Hermon; and the higher mountains which bound it on the south undoubtedly form Mount Gilboa. There is still, indeed, an inhabited village, in whose name of Jelbon that of Gilboa may be recognized. (Van de Velde, *Travels in S. and P.* ii. 368 ff.; Porter, *Handbook*, ii. 355 ff.; Thomson, *The Land and the Book*.)

GILEAD (gĭl'e-ad), (Heb. גִּלְעָד, *ghil-awd'*, mound of witness).

1. Mountain Range. A group of mountains connected with Lebanon by means of Mount Hermon. It begins not far from the latter, and extends southward to the sources of the brooks Jabbok and Arnon, thus enclosing the whole eastern part of the land beyond the Jordan (Gen. xxxi:21; Cant. iv:1). According to Michaelis (*Mos. Recht.* i. 86), this mountain, which gave its name to the country so called, must be situated beyond the region sketched in our maps, and somewhere about the Euphrates.

2. Beyond the Jordan. (*a*) The name of a large district beyond the Jordan, continually mentioned in the Scriptures in contradistinction to, or apart from, Bashan (Deut. iii:13; Josh. xii: 5; xiii:11; xvii:1; 2 Kings x:33; 1 Chron. v: 16; Mic. vii:14); though, to judge from its geographical position (as given Num. xxxii:26; Deut. iii:12), it must have comprised the entire possessions of the two tribes of Gad and Reuben, and even the southern part of Manasseh (Deut. iii: 13; Num. xxxii:40; Josh. xvii:1-6). The cities Ramoth, Jabesh, and Jazer, are usually designated as lying in Gilead.

This region was distinguished for its rich pastures (Num. xxxii:1) and aromatic simples; from which latter different sorts of balsam were prepared—facts confirmed by modern travelers, Seetzen, Burckhardt, etc., with the addition that the whole region is covered with groups of limestone mountains, intersected by fertile valleys.

(*b*) The name of the whole eastern part of the Jordan (Deut. xxxiv:1; comp. 2 Kings x:33; Judg. xx:1). The name *Gilead* continued to be used, in a general and geographical sense, even after the exile (1 Macc. v, etc.). Josephus (*Antiq.* xiii:13, 5) designates it as a part of Arabia, while its special and topographical name was *Peræa*.

3. A City. A city of this name is apparently mentioned Hos. vi:8; so, at least, it is given in most of the ancient and modern versions, though the meaning may only be that Gilead is (like) a city full of iniquity, *i. e.* a union of iniquitous people.

GILEAD (Heb. as above).

1. Son of Machir (Num. xxvi:29, 30). (B. C. between 1874 and 1668.)

2. Father of Jephthah (Judg. xi:1, 2). Perhaps the name is used as a personification of a community (verses 7, 8). (B. C. before 1256.)

3. A descendant of Gad, and ancestor of the Gadites of Bashan (1 Chron. v:14). (B. C. before 781.) E. M.

GILEAD and BASHAN (gĭl'e-ad and bā'shan), as connected with the pre-Mosaic Manassite conquest.

(1) Legal Rights of Women. "Then came the daughters of Zelophehad . . . and they stood before Moses . . . saying, 'Our father died in the wilderness . . . and had no sons . . . Give us therefore a possession among the brethren of our father.' And Moses brought their case before the Lord. And the Lord spake unto Moses, saying, 'The daughters of Zelophehad speak right. Thou shalt surely give them a possession of an inheritance among their father's brethren; and thou shalt cause the inheritance of their father to pass unto them'" (Num. xxvii:1-8). This decision became the basis of a law in Israel in relation to the rights of daughters. The incident of these heiresses occurs in the tribe of Manasseh, after the later of the two "numberings," and this "numbering" had shown that the tribe of Manasseh had an increase of more than thirty-three per cent. over the highest increase which had been shown by any other tribe.

(2) Pre-Mosaic Share of Manasseh. The claim of the heirs and the great increase of this tribe seem both to have resulted from the same antecedent, and this antecedent was the conquest and annexation of the kingdoms of Sihon and Og.

In that conquest it seems evident that the tribe of Manasseh had a pre-Mosaic share. Immediately after that conquest, Moses received a request from the two preëminently pastoral tribes Gad and Reuben only, to be allowed to settle in the newly acquired territory. Their wish was granted on the ground of their possession of "much cattle," but in that concession is also included "the half tribe of Manasseh," although no petition seems to have come from the leaders of this tribe. The request comes from two tribes, and the concession is made to two and a half. The half of Mount Gilead and all of Bashan, the kingdom of Og being awarded to the half tribe of Manasseh (Deut. iii:13). In connection with this allotment it will be noted that "the inheritance of their fathers" which is awarded to the daughters is spoken of as if it were ready for them, not future, but waiting to be filled. It appears that there was some clearly established title which was so well known at the time as not to require any explanation; and what could the Manassite title to eastern territory be founded upon, if not upon pre-Mosaic conquests?

The name of Gilead which is borne by a portion of the country is another very significant point. Gilead was the third in descent from Joseph, Manasseh being his grandfather, and the "sons of Gilead" in Num. xxvi:30 appear as "male children of Manasseh." If on the older historical theory that the Manassite line shared the oppression in Egypt, went out at the Exodus, and merely took part in the Sihon-Og campaign with the rest of Israel, how can we account for the fact that this region bears the name of a Manassite prince who had been dead long ago and was buried in Egypt?

But suppose Machir, the grandson of Joseph and his heir by adoption, to have led a victorious settlement north eastward from the Egyptian frontier, with all of his grandfather's Egyptian influence to second him, and we can see at once why his eldest son should share the name of the region which he first won by conquest. This would be similar to the case of Cain who called "the name of the city" which "he builded" after "the name of his son Enoch" (Gen. iv:17).

We need not suppose that the whole of the region of Gilead and Bashan had been previously won and held by Machir and his sons, but merely that so far as those areas had been conquered, the achievement had been Manassite.

There is an old pæan of victory recorded in Num. xxi. Verse 27 is the beginning of the exultation of Sihon the Amorite over Moab, but later comes the triumph of Israel over Sihon. Sihon and his people were exterminated (Deut. ii:34). How then was this Amorite pæan preserved? The conquered Moabites would not have treasured up Sihon's song of victory over them and passed it on to the Israelites, of whom they had a fear and a jealousy (Num. xxii:4). But if there was a Manassite settlement there which had witnessed the crushing defeat of Moab, and heard the song on the lips of the victorious Amorites, the whole difficulty vanishes.

(3) Points in Deuteronomic Law. There are some points in Deuteronomic law which may be considered in connection with this matter: It has often been urged against the law of "the landmark" and the curse against who "removes" it, and especially in reference to the phrase "which they of old time have set in thine inheritance," that such a law implies the long settled habits of land in traditional possession, and therefore is inconsistent with legislation for lands which are yet to be won.

But suppose that the Manassites were *resuming* their heritage, from which they had been temporarily expelled by the Amorites, and with all the old landmarks still in place, and we have exactly the situation of all others to call for such a law. (See LANDMARK.)

The same or nearly so, may be said of the law forbidding usury (Deut. xxiii:19-20) between Israelites but permitting it towards aliens. The situation is that of nearly one third of the nation newly and suddenly settled by conquest, while the remainder has its heritage yet to win. All the available capital of this remainder might be employed by the newly settled portion; while the alien races with whom Israel had been brought into contact, Edom, Moab and Ammon offered a similar field for loans with interest. Eastern Manasseh having the advantage of earlier possession and domestication on the spot might readily avail themselves of this condition. Thus if ever a law in reference to usury was necessary it would be now.

(4) Property Regranted to Heirs of Early Owners. The conquests of Sihon and Og must have narrowed or absorbed the Machir-Jair territory, but the earlier settlement of this people is indicated in Num. xxxii:34. We are there told that the Gadites and Reubenites "build" (perhaps rebuild after the havoc of war) certain cities, but no such thing is said of the Manassites, only their conquests are recited. The Manassites probably did not rebuild, because their cities were not destroyed, they, the former owners being present on the spot to reclaim their lost ownership.

Thus what Moses did was to regrant, either the whole, or a large part of the earlier Manassite area to the posterity of Machir and Gilead. And thus the Mosaic and the Joshuan narratives harmonize with each other and all obscurities are cleared as soon as we comprehend the fact of this earlier conquest.

(5) Testimony of Jephthah. A little later we find Jephthah "the Gileadite" arguing with the children of Ammon, and claiming that *for three hundred years* "Israel dwelt in Heshbon and her towns, and in Aroer and her towns, and in all the cities that be along by the coasts of Arnon" (Judg. xi:26). And this was a portion of the very region which Moses had obtained by the Sihon-Og conquest. We read in Judges xi:1,

that "Gilead begat Jephthah" and Jephthah would of course have kept the tradition of his fathers.

(6) The Song of Deborah. The designation of the great elder branch of Joseph's house by its sub-patriarch Machir is confirmed by that early document, the Song of Deborah (Judg. v: 14-17). When "Gilead abode beyond Jordan," and Reuben hesitated, "out of Machir there came down chieftains" to aid the cause of western patriotism. Machir dominates the western, and Gilead the eastern branch of the tribe, and they each held their own policy. This suggests that Machir ben-Manasseh never lost the supremacy of his whole tribe. Having established his son in "the Gilead" and given him its name, he may have returned to Goshen.

(7) Havoth-Jair of Bashan. We now see why Moses in Deut. iii:14 speaks of the "Havoth-Jair of Bashan" being so called *unto this day,* a phrase singularly frigid, if the whole series of events concerned had happened since the death of Aaron, and one which has furnished an opportunity for the "higher criticism" to impugn a Mosaic Deuteronomy, but the phrase recovers its suspended animation the moment the light of rectified history falls upon it.

(8) Reunion of a Severed Tribe. We also see now why the total of the Manassite tribe jumps up sixty-three and more per cent. at the second census (Num. xxvi:34, 35). It was evidently by the reunion of long severed members.

(9) Machir. We see also why Machir becomes an eponymous hero, and why he is singled out and erected into a patriarchal status in Numbers, Deuteronomy, Joshua and Judges. He was in fact the morning star of eastern conquest, preluding the brilliant campaign of Moses and in his posterity conducing to its completeness. In the case of Zelophehad's daughters, they claimed to represent and embody the title of descent from Machir, Gilead and Hepher to a heritage which had come down through some two centuries of user, and had only been interrupted through an intrusive hostile possession. That intrusion having ceased, their patrimony lies before them in concrete fact, and they claim to be invested with it. On its settlement in their favor follows the further one of limiting their right of matrimonial choice (Num. xxxvi:6).

(10) Conclusion. The case emerges exactly where we ought to find it, if the main lines of the Exodus history are true. The numbering of Numbers xxvi brought the main stock and the disseyered branch of "Joseph" together in conscious unity. The latter comes into touch with the hopes and fortunes of Israel as a whole; and therefore the question is settled, not by any court of mere tribal elders, but by the highest jurisdiction of the nation now realizing its corporate capacity. The broad side light thus shed on the narrative of the ensuing Joshuan occupation cannot be without important exegetical influence as we read, for indeed it is shed from a lost page of patriarchal history. (See *Gilead and Bashan, or the Pre-Mosaic Manassite Conquest,* by Henry Hayman, D. D., *Bibliotheca Sacra,* Jan., 1898.)

GILEADITES, THE (gil'e-ad-ītes), (Heb. גִּלְעָדִי, *ghil-aw-dee'*), descendants of Gilead who formed a branch of the tribe of Manasseh (Judg. xii:4, 5; x:3; 2 Sam. xvii:27; xix:31; 1 Kings ii:7; Ezra ii:61; Neh. vii:63). They had a long standing feud apparently with the Ephraimites (Judg. xii:4).

GILGAL (gĭl'găl), (Heb. גִּלְגָּל, *ghil-gawl'*, circle, wheel).

1. The place where the Israelites formed their first encampment in Palestine, and which continued for some time to be their headquarters while engaged in the conquest of the land (Josh. iv: 19, 20; ix:6; x:6, 7, etc.). It was here that they set up the twelve stones which they took out of the bed of the Jordan (iv:19). (See STONES.) It is uncertain whether this town or another place of the name was on Samuel's circuit (1 Sam. vii: 16), and where, it may be judged, Saul, the opposition to him having ceased, was made king and the kingdom renewed (xi:15). At any rate, it was at Gilgal in the Jordan valley where a muster of the people took place to form an army which should encounter the Philistines then oppressing the land, when Saul, finding it difficult to hold the people together until Samuel should come and offer sacrifice, himself offered burnt offerings (xiii: 4, 7, 8; comp. 12-15). For his disobedience the forfeiture of his kingdom was announced to him (13, 14). There, too, Saul incurred a second rebuke for his disobedience in sparing Agag (xv: 12, 21, 33; comp. 34). It was to Gilgal also that the representatives of the tribe of Judah went to welcome David back after the death of Absalom (2 Sam. xix:15, 40). Like other holy places, it became a focus of idolatry under the kings who succeeded Jeroboam, and it was in consequence denounced by the prophets (Hos. iv:15; ix:15; xii:11; Amos iv:4; v:5). It is probably the house of Gilgal or Bethgilgal mentioned after the captivity (Neh. xii:29). Its site is Jiljûlieh, a ruin two miles east of Jericho. (Davis, *Dict. of the Bible*.)

2. A place in the region of Dor, whose king was subdued by Joshua (Josh. xii:23). The Gilgal of Neh. xii:29, and 1 Macc. ix:2, is probably the same as this; as well as the ancient Galgala, which Eusebius and Jerome place six Roman miles north of Antipatris. In this neighborhood there is still a village called Jiljûlieh, which probably represents the ancient site.

3. A place on the northern boundary of Judah (Josh. xv:7). In the parallel list of Josh. xviii: 17, it is given as Geliloth, probably Jiljûlieh, a little north of the brook Kânah, and five miles northeast by north of Antipatris.

4. The place where Elisha worked the miracle of healing on the poisonous pottage (2 Kings iv: 38). It was also the last scene of the life of Elijah. There is a ruin fifteen miles from Diospolis, called Jiljûlieh, which probably marks the location of the ancient Gilgal. (See Van de Velde's *Map*, and Rob. iii:139.)

GILOH (gī'loh), (Heb. גִּלֹה, *ghee-lo'*, exile), a city of Judah (Josh. xv:51). It was the native place of Ahithophel (2 Sam. xv:12), and to which he returned to take his life (2 Sam. xvii:23).

GILONITE, THE (gī'lo-nīte), (Heb. גִּילֹנִי, *ghee-lo-nee'*,) a native of Giloh, used only of Ahithophel (2 Sam. xv:12; xxiii:34).

GIMEL (gī'mĕl or gĭm-ĕl), (Heb. ג).

The third letter of the Hebrew alphabet. The Greek letter gamma, and consequently the English C have the same origin; but in the spelling of Hebrew and Greek names in the English versions, gimel and gamma (though not these letters only) are represented by G, their approximate equivalent in sound and a form fabricated out of C.

Gimel stands at the head of the third section of Ps. cxix in several versions, since each verse of the section begins with this letter in the original. (Davis, *Bib. Dict.*)

GIMZO (gĭm'zo), (Heb. גִּמְזוֹ, *ghim-zo'*, a place fertile in sycamores), a city in the south of Judah, which the Philistines took from Ahaz (2 Chron. xxviii:18). The name remains in the modern *Jimzu*, two and a half miles south of Lydda (Rob. ii:249).

GIN (jĭn), an old English word for *trap*, which is represented by two Hebrew words.

1. *Mo-kashe'* (Heb. מוֹקֵשׁ, a noose or "snare," as elsewhere rendered (Ps. cxl:5; Amos iii:5).

2. *Pakh* (Heb. פַּח), a plate of metal, hence a trap (Job xviii:9; Is. viii:14); elsewhere "snare."

GINATH (gī'nath), (Heb. גִּינַת, *ghee-nath'*, derivation uncertain), father of Tibni, who disputed with Omri for the Kingdom of Israel (1 Kings xvi:21, 22), B. C. before 926.

GINNETHO (gĭn-ne-thō), (Heb. same as GINNETHON), one of the heads of the priests who returned from captivity with Zerubbabel (Neh. xii:4), B. C. 536-410.

GINNETHON (gĭn'ne-thŏn), (Heb. גִּנְּתוֹן, *ghinneth-one'*, a gardener), one of the priests who sealed the covenant with Nehemiah (Neh. x:6). He was head of a family of which a member is mentioned at a late period (Neh. xii:16). Probably the same as Ginnetho.

GIRDLE (gẽr'd'l). See ARMS, ARMOR; DRESS; PRIEST, HEBREW PRIESTHOOD; ABNET.

Figurative. (1) God's *girding himself* imports his giving noted displays of his almighty power, and his readiness to act (Ps. xciii:1 and xlv:3). (2) His *girding* others with strength or gladness is his exciting and enabling them to do great exploits, and his filling their hearts with joy and pleasure (Ps. xviii:32, 39, and xxx: 11). (3) He *girded* Cyrus; encouraged and enabled him to conquer the nations (Is. xlv:5); but he *looses the bond* of kings, and *girds their loins with a girdle*, when he strips them of their power and authority, and reduces them to the condition of servants (Job xii:18). (4) Christ's love, power, equity, and faithfulness are the *girdle* of his breast or loins, whereby he is qualified for the discharge of his priestly and kingly office; and whereby we hold him by faith (Is. xi:5; Dan. x:5; Rev. i:13). (5) The Jews are likened to a *linen girdle* hid in the bank of the river Euphrates, and *marred:* after God had caused them to cleave to him by covenant, by profession, and receipt of special favors, he, for their sins, marred them; and by the Chaldean troops, and in the Chaldean captivity, reduced them to a very low condition (Jer. xiii:1-14). (6) The saints have their *loins girded* when they are in constant readiness to receive God's gracious favors, and obey his laws (Luke xii:35; 1 Pet.i:13). (7) Their *loins are girt about with truth*, when they are thoroughly established in the faith and experience of Divine truth; are filled with inward candor and sincerity; and pay an exact regard to their promises and vows; how excellently this qualifies them to fight the Lord's battles (Eph. vi:14). (8) The seven angels that pour out destructive vials on Antichrist are *girded with golden girdles;* they are fully furnished with strength and courage, and are ready for and zealous in their work (Rev. xv:6).

GIRGASHITES (gir'ga-shītes), (Heb. גִּרְגָּשִׁי, *hag-ghir-gaw-shee'*, "the Girgashite"), one of the families of Canaan, who are supposed to have been settled in that part of the country which lay to the east of the Lake of Gennesaret.

The Girgashites are conjectured to have been a part of the large family of the Hivites, as they are omitted in nine out of ten places in which the nations or families of Canaan are mentioned, while in the tenth they are mentioned, and the Hivites omitted. Josephus states that nothing but the name of the Girgashites remained in his time (*Antiq.* i. 6, 2). In the Jewish Commentaries of R. Nachman, and elsewhere, the Girgashites are described as having retired into Africa, fearing the power of God. The notion that the Girgashites did migrate seems to have been founded on the circumstance that, although they are included in the list of the seven devoted nations either to be *driven out* or destroyed by the Israelites (Gen. xv:20, 21; Deut. vii:1; Josh. iii:10; xxiv:11), yet they are omitted in the list of those to be utterly destroyed (Deut. xx:17), and are mentioned among those with whom, contrary to the Divine decree, the Israelites lived and intermarried (Judg. iii:1-6). "The Girgashite" as an appellation of the fifth son of Canaan (Gen. x:16). Elsewhere the term is tribal.

GIRL (gẽrl), (Heb. יַלְדָּה, *yal-daw'*, literally, one born), in the ordinary sense (Joel iii:3; Zech. viii:5), a marriageable girl was called "damsel" (Gen. xxxiv:4).

GISPA (gĭs'pa), (Heb. גִּשְׁפָּא, *ghish-paw'*), an overseer of the Nethinims after the return from Babylon (Neh. xi:21), B. C. 446.

GITTAH-HEPHER (gĭt'tah-hē'pher), (Heb. גִּתָּה־חֵפֶר, *ghit-taw-khay'fer*, Josh. xix:13). See GATH-HEPHER.

GITTAIM (gĭt'ta-ĭm or gĭt-tā'ĭm), (Heb. גִּתַּיִם, *ghit-tah'yim*, two winepresses), a place to which the inhabitants of Beeroth fled for refuge apparently (2 Sam. iv:3). Beeroth was a town of the Gibeonites (Josh. ix:17), and the cause of the flight may have been the persecutions of Saul (2 Sam. xxi:2).

GITTITES (gĭt'tītes), (Heb. גִּתִּי, *ghit-tee'*), inhabitants or natives of Gath (Josh. xiii:3). Obed-edom, although a Levite, is called a Gittite (2 Sam. vi:10), possibly because he had been with David when at Gath, but much more probably from his being a native of Gath-rimmon, which was a city of the Levites.

There seems no reason for extending this interpretation to Ittai (2 Sam. xv:19), seeing that David expressly calls him 'a stranger' (foreigner), and, what is more, 'an exile.' He was at the head of 600 men, who were also Gittites, for they are called (verse 22) his 'brethren.' They appear to have formed a foreign troop of experienced warriors, chiefly from Gath, in the pay and service of David; which they had perhaps entered in the first instance for the sake of sharing in the booty obtainable in his wars. We can conceive that the presence of such a troop must have been useful to the king in giving to the Hebrew army that organization and discipline which it did not possess before his time.

GITTITH (gĭt'tith), (Heb. גִּתִּית, *hag-git-teeth'*), a word which occurs in the title of Ps. viii., lxxxi., lxxxiv. (See PSALMS, BOOK OF.)

The conjectures of interpreters as to its import are various. Some think it signifies a sort of musical instrument, invented at Gath; others that the Psalms with this title were sung during the vintage. The word *Gath*, from which this is the feminine gentile form, signifies *wine-press*.

GIZONITE, THE (gĭ'zo-nīte), (Heb. גִּזוֹנִי, *ghee-zo-nee'*), an appellation of Hashem, whose sons belonged to David's guard (1 Chron. xi:34). No place of this name is known. Kennicott suggests that this name should be *Gouni* (*Dissert.* pp. 199-203).

GIZRITES (gĭz'rītes). See GERZITES, THE.

GLASS (glås), (Heb. גִּלָּיוֹן, *ghil-law-yone'*, Is. iii:23), mirrors, polished metal plates.

(1) How Discovered. Glass, according to Pliny (*Hist. Nat.* xxxvi:26), was discovered by what is termed accident. Some merchants kindled a fire on that part of the coast of Phœnicia which lies near Ptolemais, between the foot of Carmel and Tyre, at a spot where the river Belus casts the fine sand which it brings down; but, as they were without the usual means of suspending their cooking vessels, they employed for that purpose logs of niter, their vessel being laden with that substance; the fire fusing the niter and the sand produced glass. The Sidonians, in whose vicinity the discovery was made, took it up, and having in process of time carried the art to a high degree of excellence, gained thereby both wealth and fame. Other nations became their pupils; the Romans especially attained to very high skill in the art of fusing, blowing, and coloring glass.

(2) Known to the Egyptians. Wilkinson, in his *Ancient Egyptians* (iii:88, *sq.*), has adduced the fullest evidence that glass was known to and made by the Egyptian people at a very early period of their national existence. Upward of 3,500 years ago, in the reign of the first Osirtasen, they appear to have practiced the art of blowing glass. The process is represented in the paintings of Beni Hassan, executed in the reign of that monarch. In the same age images of *glazed* pottery were common. Ornaments of glass were made by them about 1,500 years B. C.; for a bead of that date has been found, being of the same specific gravity as that of our crown glass. Many glass bottles, etc., have been met with in the tombs, some of very remote antiquity. Glass vases were used for holding wine as early as the exodus. Such was the skill of the Egyptians in this manufacture, that they successfully counterfeited the amethyst, and other precious stones. It was sometimes used by the Egyptians even for coffins. They also employed it, not only for drinking utensils, and ornaments of the person, but for mosaic work, the figures of deities, and sacred emblems, attaining to exquisite workmanship, and a surprising brilliancy of color. The art too of cutting glass was known to them at the most remote periods; for which purpose, as we learn from Pliny (*Hist. Nat.* xxxvii:4), the diamond was used. That the ancients had mirrors of glass is clear from the above cited words of Pliny; but the mirrors found in Egypt are made of mixed metal, chiefly copper. So admirably did the skill of the Egyptians succeed in the composition of metals, that their mirrors were susceptible of a polish which has been but partially revived at the present day. The mirror was nearly round, having a handle of wood, stone, or metal. The form varied with the taste of the owner. The same kind of metal mirror was used by the Israelites, who, doubtless, brought it from Egypt. In Exod. xxxviii:8, it is expressly said that Moses 'made the laver of brass of the looking-glasses (brazen mirrors) of the women.'

(3) Known to the Hebrews. It would be justifiable to suppose that the Hebrews brought glass, and a knowledge how to manufacture it, with them out of Egypt, were not the evidence of history so explicit that it was actually discovered and wrought at their own doors. Whether it was used by them for mirrors is another question. That glass, however, was known to the Hebrews appears beyond a doubt. In Job xxviii: 17, זְכוֹכִית, zek-oo-keeth, is believed to mean glass, though it is rendered 'crystal' in the English Version.

(4) New Testament References. In Rev. xxi:18, we read 'The city was pure gold, like unto clear *glass;*' ver. 21, 'as it were transparent glass' (compare c. iv:6). 'Molten glass' also occurs in Job xxxvii:18, but the original is Heb. רְקַע, *raw-deed,'* spreading. Winer, referring to Beckman (*Beiträge zur Gesch. der Erfindung,* iii: 319), expressly denies that glass mirrors were known till the thirteenth century—adding that they are still seldom seen in the East. That in the New Testament a mirror is intended in Jam. i:23, 'beholding his natural face in a glass,' appears certain; but the signification of the other passage in which the word ἔσοπτρον, *mirror,* occurs, is by no means so clear. If by ἔσοπτρον a metal *mirror* is to be understood, the language employed is not without difficulties. The preposition διά, 'through,' is in such a case improper; 'face to face' presents an equally improper contrast, for in a mirror 'face answers to face' (Prov. xxvii:19). So the general import of the passage seems to require an imperfectly transparent medium, through which objects are beheld. It may have been the *lapis specularis,* or a kind of talc, of which the ancients made their windows. This opinion is confirmed by Schleusner, who says that the Jews used a similar mode of expression to describe a dim and imperfect view of mental objects. J. R. B.

There are instances, however, both in the classic Greek of Sophocles and Xenophon, and often in the Greek of the New Testament, wherein *dia* means *by means of,* and expresses mere instrumentality. See Acts xx:28; Eph. i:7; Col. i:22; Heb. ix:26; many more may be cited.

Figurative. The figurative use of glass already referred to may be further amplified as follows: (1) The word and ordinances of God are a *glass;* in them we see our own sins, wants, or graces; have imperfect views of Jesus and his Father, and of eternal things, and have our heart warmed by them (Jam. i:23, 25; 2 Cor. iii:18). (2) When the ceremonial and gospel ordinances are compared, the former are called a *shadow,* which gives a very imperfect view of the thing represented; but the latter are called a *glass,* in which we see spiritual things much more clearly (Col. ii:17; Heb. x:1; 2 Cor. iii:18). (3) The new Jerusalem is like unto *transparent glass,* for its beauty and glory, and the delightful views of Divine things enjoyed in it (Rev. xxi:18, 21). (4) The *sea of glass* mingled with fire before the throne of God, on which the saints stand, may denote the righteousness of Jesus mingled with flaming love and fiery sufferings, and which indeed is the support and encouragement of the saints before God; or the glorious gospel, attended with the influences of the Holy Ghost, to uphold and embolden them; or a pure and holy church actuated with burning zeal for the glory of God (Rev. iv:6, and xv:2).

GLEAN (glēn), (Heb. לָקַט, *law-kat',* to pick up; עָלַל, *aw-lal'*).

The Hebrews were not permitted to go over their trees or fields a second time, to gather the fruit or the grain, but were to leave the gleanings for the poor, the fatherless, and the widow (Lev. xix:10; xxiii:22; Deut. xxiv:21; Ruth ii:7, 8, 15; Judg. viii:2).

GLEDE (glēd), (Deut. xiv:13), is an obsolete name for the common kite, adopted in our version for רָאָה, *raw-aw',* or, as Gesenius thinks, דָּאָה, *dâ'âh.*

It is a species that rises to a towering height, hangs apparently motionless in the sky, and darts down with immense velocity; but the legs and claws being weak, it is cowardly, and feeds upon carrion, fish, insects, mice, and small birds. The bill of this species is dark; head and throat whitish, with brown streaks; body above dark gray brown, pale ferruginous below; tail but slightly forked; legs yellow. It is found in hieroglyphic paintings, colored with sufficient accuracy not to be mistaken. The other species, which may be held as the *Milvus ater,* is the black kite, *Falco melanopterus,* Daudin; *Elanus Cæsius,* Savigny; *Falco Souninensis,* Lath.; *Le Blac,* Le Vaill., and *Kouhieh* of the Arabs. It has the head, neck, and back dark rusty gray; scapulars bordered with rusty; wing-coverts and primaries black, the last-mentioned tipped with white; tail rusty gray above, white beneath; bill dark; legs yellow. The manners of both species are much the same; it is likely that they are equally abundant at Cairo, and spread into Palestine. (See HAWK.) C. H. S.

GLISTER, GLISTERING (glĭs'tēr-ĭng), (Gr. ἐξαστράπτω, *ex-as-trap'to*), to be radiant (Luke ix: 29; compare 1 Chron. xxix:2).

The three verbs 'glisten,' 'glister,' and 'glitter' come from the same Teutonic base, *gli,* to shine, 'glitter' being traced to the Scandinavian, 'glisten' and 'glister' being apparently English in their earliest form. 'Glister' is simply a frequentative form of 'glisten.' It has been superseded by the modern "glitter." "All that *glisters* is not gold " —Shakespeare.

GLORIFY (glō'rĭ-fī), (Heb. same as GLORY).

1. To make glorious or honorable, or to cause to appear so (John xii:28; xiii:31, 32; xv:8; xvii: 4, 5; xxi:19; Acts iii:13). In this view it particularly refers to the resurrection of Christ, and his ascension to the right hand of God (John vii:39; xii:16).

2. The change which shall pass upon believers at the general resurrection, and their admission into heaven (Rom. viii:17).

3. To *glorify* (1 Cor. vi:20) is to "show forth his praise" by obedience to his law. Thus the "heavens declare the glory of God" in obedience to the law of creation, and much more do men glorify him by willing obedience to the moral law (1 Cor. x:31; John xvii:5).

4. To *glorify one's self* is to claim or boast of honor not due to one (Heb. v:5, and Rev. xviii: 7).

GLORY (glō'rў), in the A. V. represents the Heb. word כָּבוֹד, *kaw-bode',* weight, and the Gr. δόξα, *dox'ah.*

Full details as to the various Hebrew words must be sought in the Hebrew lexicon or in commentaries on the various passages. Generally speaking, the English term is sufficiently clear from the context in spite of the number of the Hebrew words which it renders.

The *appearances* of what is termed 'the glory of Jehovah,' Sept. δόξα Κυρίου, the Shechinah of the Rabbins, so often referred to in the Old Testament, seem to have originated certain uses of the word, in the sense of *light*, and *visible splendor* and numerous applications of these senses among the Hellenistic writers. It is first *distinctly* called by this term in Exod. xvi:7, 10. It is described as being like a *bright fire* (Exod. xxiv:17), and as *attended* with a cloud (Exod. xl:34, 35). It is probable that the *tradition* of these phenomena influenced the representations of heathen poets, who so often describe the appearances of the deities as attended by a cloud, with a brightness in it (see Taubmann's *Notes on Virgil*). It is believed that the classical Greek writers never use δόξα in the sense of *light* or *splendor*. The nearest instance yet adduced is from Plutarch (*Nicias*, tom. i. p. 538, E), who speaks of 'the glory of Plato shining forth.' It answers very frequently, in the Sept., to the Hebrew *Kawbode* (Exod. xxiv:17, 40; xxxiv:35; Deut. v:24, etc.), down to the Captivity.

The following instances are offered of the Hellenistic uses, allusions, or applications of the word, *originated* by the events above mentioned: (1) Matt. vi:29, 'Solomon in all his *glory*; i. e. *visible* magnificence, as opposed to the *clothing*, called 'array' of the lilies. (2) 1 Cor. xv:41, 'the glory, *i. e., luster*, of the sun, moon, and stars.' (3) Jesus is called (Heb. i:3), ἀπαύγασμα τῆς δόξης, 'the effulgence of his (the Father's) glory,' an evident allusion to Ezek. x:4). (4) Rom. i:23, 'the glory of God' is 'the glorious *form* of God.' (5) 2 Thess. i:9, 'the *presence* of the Lord and the *glory* of his power.' (6) 1 Tim. vi:16, 'dwelling in light.' (7) 1 Cor. xi:7, 'man is the image and *glory* of God,' metonym, that which *exhibits* or *reflects* this glory, i. e., *symbol, demonstrations*. (8) Other *events* would also conduce to such peculiar uses of the word as *the shining of the face of Moses* (comp. Exod. xxxiv:29; 2 Cor. iii:7, 8; iv:6). (9) The splendor attending the *appearance* of *angels*, especially in later ages (Matt. xxviii:3, etc.) (10) *The transfiguration of Jesus*, in which it is said that Peter, James and John saw his *glory* (Luke ix:32; comp. John i:14; 2 Pet. i:17, 19). (See Macknight on *Phil.* iii:21.) (11) And since the appearances, etc., alluded to, are connected with the Deity, the Savior, angels, etc., the same word is also *consistently* adopted to denote the *participation* in the *glory and blessedness* of these beings which is reserved for the faithful. Col. iii:4, 'appear with him in glory;' 2 Cor. iv:17, 18; 2 Thess. ii:14, 'the obtaining of the glory of our Lord Jesus Christ.'

Figurative and Analogical. (1) The Hebrew *kawbode* is susceptible of the various *analogical* meanings which are derived from its root, viz., 'to be heavy,' 'honored,' 'rich,' etc. (1) In Gen. xxxi:1, 'all this glory;' Is. x:3, 'your glory;' lxvi:12, 'the glory of the Gentiles,' all meaning *wealth, abundance*. (2) Ps. lxxix:9, 'the glory of thy name,' i. e. *honor, reputation*. (3) Is. xxxv:2; lx:13, comp. x:18, 'the glory of Lebanon,' i. e., *ornament*. (4) Is. viii:7, 'the king of Assyria and all his glory,' is rendered by Lowth 'and all his *force*.'

(2) To be heavy is the *primary* meaning of the root; hence *kaw-bed* means 'the liver,' the *heaviest* of all the viscera; just as the lungs, the *lightest* of all, are in our language called *the lights* (Taylor's *Heb. Concord*). In some passages it conveys the ideas of the ancients respecting the bodily seat of certain passions. Among others, they thought *the liver* to be the seat of *anger*

and *love*. Thus Horace (*Carm.* i:13, 4), describing jealous anger or resentment—Fervens difficili bile tumet *jecur*,—'My burning *liver* swells with angry bile' (see notes of the Delphin edition. Comp. Persius, *Sat.* v:129; Juvenal, *Sat.* vi:647). Thus Ps. xvi:9, 'My heart is glad and' literally, 'my liver rejoiceth.' Gen. xlix:6, 'mine honor' is rendered by Sept. τὰ ἥπατά 'μου, 'my liver.' Lam. ii:11, is literally rendered by our translators 'My liver is poured upon the earth,' indicating *violent grief*.

(3) In some instances the literal rendering of the Hebrew idiom in our version is attended with obscurity. (1) 1 Sam. ii:8, 'throne of glory' is 'a glorious throne.' (2) Ps. xxiv:7, 8, 'the king of glory' is 'the glorious or majestic king.' (3) Ps. xxix:3, 'the God of glory' is 'the glorious God,' and is so rendered in the Prayer Book Version. (4) In the New Testament (Luke ii:9), 'the glory of the Lord shone,' is *an extreme splendor* (see also Acts vii:2). (5) In 1 Cor. ii:8, 'Lord of glory' is 'glorious or illustrious Lord.' (6) Rom. viii:18, 'spirit of God' and 'spirit of Christ,' are 'a godly and Christian spirit, temper, or disposition.'   J. F. D.

GLUTTON (glŭt't'n), (Hebrew from לָלַל, *zawlal'*, to shake, hence to be loose, morally), a debauchee, a voluptuary (Deut. xxi:20; Prov. xxiii:21); "riotous" in Prov. xxiii:20, xxviii:7. "Gluttonous" (Matt. xi:19; Luke vii:34) is a free or fast liver.

GNASH (năsh), (Heb. חָרַק, *khaw-rak'*, to grate the teeth; Gr. βρύχω, *broo'kho*), "to gnash with the teeth," and "gnashing of teeth", are expressions denoting rage or sorrow (Job xvi:9; Lam. ii:16; Matt. viii:12; Acts. vii:54).

GNAT (năt), (Gr. κώνωψ, *koh'nohps*, Vulg. *culex;* Order, *diptera*, Linn., *culicidæ*, Latr.; occurs in Matt. xxiii:24).

It is a small insect abounding in marshes and vexatious by reason of its bite, from which the Egyptians protected themselves at night by sleeping under nets (Herod. ii:95). It is evidently some species of *Culex*, a genus known by its hairy antennæ, plumed in the males, its proboscis, its slender body, its two gauzy wings, its long legs and its blood-sucking propensities.

Figurative. Our Savior's allusion to the gnat is a kind of proverb, either in use in his time, or invented by himself, 'Blind guides, who strain *out* a gnat, and swallow down (*bolt*, as we say) a camel.' He adopts the antithesis of the *smallest insect* to the *largest animal*, and applies it to those who are superstitiously anxious in avoiding small faults, yet do not scruple to commit the greatest sins. The typographical error, 'strain *at* a gnat,' first found its way into King James' translation, 1611. It is 'strain out' in the previous translations. The custom of filtering wine, among the Jews, for this purpose, was founded on the prohibition of 'all flying, creeping things' being used for food, excepting the *saltatorii* (Lev. xi:23). The custom seems alluded to by the Sept., which, in Amos vi:6, reads in the Hebrew, 'filtered wine'—a passage having a similar scope. According to the Talmud, eating a gnat incurred scourging or excommunication.

     J. F. D.

GNOSTICISM (nŏs'tĭ-sĭz'm), (Gr. γνῶσις, *no'sis*, knowing).

(1) **The Decline and Fall of Philosophy.** In the whole history of the human mind there is not a more instructive chapter, at once strange and sad, interesting to our curiosity and mortifying to our pride, than the history of Platonism

sinking into Gnosticism, or, in other words, of Greek philosophy merging in Oriental mysticism; showing, on the one hand, the decline and fall of philosophy, and, on the other, the rise and progress of syncretism. According to Dr. Burton, formerly Regius Professor of Divinity at Oxford, Gnosticism is attributed principally to the writings of Plato, as studied at Alexandria.

(2) The Gnosis of Plato. Though the wisdom of Egypt may have influenced the Greeks and Romans through the mysticism of Pythagoras, though the Oriental doctrines of Babylon may have made their way amongst the Jews both at Jerusalem and Alexandria by means of their Cabbala and Talmuds, and though some sects of declared Gnostics may have gone still more directly to the metaphysical, or rather mystical, genealogies of the Eastern Magi, still it is the opinion of Dr. Burton that it was the Greek writings of Plato which gave the extraordinary impulse of their genius, and, if we may use the word, of their fashion, to the lost writings of the Gnostics, as well as to those which remain to us of Philo and Plotinus; in a word, that Platonist, Philonist, and Gnostic, are but emanations at different distances from the Gnosis of Plato.

(3) The Gnostic Heresy. The greatest danger to which Christianity was exposed, in its very early years, arose from that great Gnostic Heresy, which was long the rival, and too often the corrupter of its purer doctrines. Gnosticism was not by any means a new and distinct philosophy, but made up of selections from almost every system. Thus we find in it the Platonic doctrine of ideas, and the notion that every thing in this lower world has a celestial and immaterial archetype. We find in it evident traces of that mystical and cabalistic jargon which, after their return from captivity, deformed the religion of the Jews; and many Gnostics adopted the Oriental notion of two independent co-eternal principles, the one the author of good, and the other of evil. Lastly, we find the Gnostic theology full of ideas and terms which must have been taken from the gospel; and Jesus Christ, under some form or other of Æon, emanation, or incorporeal phantom, enters into all their systems, and is the means of communicating to them that knowledge which raised them above all other mortals, and entitled them to their peculiar name.

(4) Varied Opinions. The genius and very soul of Gnosticism was mystery: its end and object was to purify its followers from the corruptions of matter, and to raise them to a higher scale of being, suited only to those who were to become perfect by knowledge. We have a key to many parts of their system, when we know that they held matter to be intrinsically evil, of which, consequently, God could not be the author. Hence arose their fundamental tenet, that the Creator of the world, or Demiurgus, was not the same with the supreme God, the Author of good, and the Father of Christ. Their system allowed some of them to call the Creator *God,* but the title most usually given was *Demiurgus.* Those who embraced the doctrine of two principles supposed the world to have been produced by the evil principle; and in most systems, the Creator of the world, and not the Father of Christ, was looked upon as the God of the Jews, and the author of the Mosaic law. Some, again, believed that angels were employed in creating the world: but all were agreed in maintaining that matter itself was not created; that it was eternal; and that it remained inactive till the world was formed out of it by the Creator. The supreme God, according to the Gnostics, had dwelt from all eternity in a pleroma of inaccessible light: and beside the name of first Father, or first Principle, they called him also Bythos, as if to denote the unfathomable nature of his perfections. This Being, by an operation purely mental, or by acting upon himself, produced two other beings of different sexes, from whom by a series of descents, more or less numerous according to different schemes, several pairs of beings were formed, who were called *æons,* from the periods of their existence before time was, or *emanations,* from the mode of their production. These successive æons or emanations appear to have been inferior each to the preceding; and their existence was indispensable to the Gnostic scheme, that they might account for the creation of the world without making God the author of evil. These æons lived through countless ages with their first Father. But the system of emanations seems to have resembled that of concentric circles, and they gradually deteriorated as they approached nearer and nearer to the extremity of the pleroma. Beyond this pleroma was matter, inert and powerless, though co-eternal with the supreme God, and, like him, without beginning. At length one of the æons passed the limits of the pleroma, and, meeting with matter, created the world after the form and model of an ideal world, which existed in the pleroma, or the mind of the supreme God.

(5) Inconsistencies. Here it is that inconsistency is added to absurdity in the Gnostic scheme. For let the intermediate æons be as many as the wildest imagination could devise, still God was the remote, if not the proximate cause of creation. Added to which, we are to suppose that the Demiurgus formed the world without the knowledge of God, and that, having formed it, he rebelled against him. Here again we find a strong resemblance to the Oriental doctrine of two principles, good and evil, or light and darkness. The two principles were always at enmity with each other. God must have been conceived to be more powerful than matter, or an emanation from God could not have shaped or molded it into form: yet God was not able to reduce matter to its primeval chaos, nor to destroy the evil which the Demiurgus had produced. What God could not prevent he was always endeavoring to cure; and here it is that the Gnostics borrowed so largely from the Christian scheme. The names, indeed, of several of their æons were evidently taken from terms which they found in the gospel. Thus we meet with Logos, Monogenes, Zoe, Ecclesia, all of them successive emanations from the supreme God, and all dwelling in the pleroma. At length we meet with Christ and the Holy Ghost, as two of the last æons which were put forth. Christ was sent into the world to remedy the evil which the creative æon, or Demiurgus, had caused. He was to emancipate men from the tyranny of matter, or the evil principle; and by revealing to them the true God, who was hitherto unknown, to fit them, by a perfection and sublimity of knowledge, to enter the Divine pleroma. To give this knowledge was the end and object of Christ's coming upon earth: and hence the inventors and believers of the doctrine assumed to themselves the name of *Gnostics.*

(6) Summary. Professor Burton gives a brief and clear summary of the Gnostic doctrines in the following passage, which well deserves to be retained in the memory:—'The system was stated to have begun with Simon Magus; by which I would understand that the system of uniting Christianity with Gnosticism began with that heretic; for the seeds of Gnosticism, as we shall see presently, had been sown long before. What Simon Magus began was brought to perfection by Valentinus, who came to Rome in the former part of the second century; and what we know of Gnosticism is taken principally from writers who opposed Valentinus. Contemporary with him there were many other Gnostic leaders, who held different opinions; but in the sketch which I have given, I have endeavored to explain those principles which, under certain modifications, were common to all the Gnostics. That the supreme God, or the Good Principle, was not the creator of the world, but that it was created by an evil, or at least an inferior being; that God produced from himself a succession of æons or emanations, who dwell with him in the pleroma; that one of these æons was Christ, who came upon earth to reveal the knowledge of the true God; that he was not incarnate, but either assumed an unsubstantial body, or descended upon Jesus at his baptism; that the God of the Old Testament was not the father of Jesus Christ; that there was no resurrection or final judgment. This is an outline of the Gnostic doctrines as acknowledged by nearly all of them.' J. P. P.

GO ABOUT (gō à-bout'), (Gr. ζητέω, *dzay-teh'o*, Rom. x:3, to seek); R. V., "seeking to establish."

GOAD (gōd).

1. (Heb. מַלְמָד, *mal-mawd'*), an instrument for guiding oxen, the long handle of which might be used also as a formidable weapon (Judg. iii:31).

"Shamgar the son of Anath, which slew of the Philistines six hundred men with an oxgoad: and he also delivered Israel."

2. (Heb. דָּרְבוֹן, *dor-bone'*), anything pointed and the context of Eccles. xii:11 requires rather the sense of a peg or nail, anything in short which can be *fastened*, while in 1 Sam. xiii:21 the point of the *plowshare* is more probably intended.

Figurative. "It is hard for thee to kick against the pricks" (Acts ix:5, A. V.), is the metaphor of a recalcitrant animal injuring itself against the *oxgoad*. The words of the wise are as *goads;* they penetrate into men's minds, and stir them up to the practice of duty (Eccles. xii;11).

GOAT (gōt), (Chaldee, *izza;* Phœnician, *aza;* Arabic, *jidda* and *hedzjaz*).

I. A SPECIES OF ANIMALS common to mountainous regions. Of the several Hebrew denominations of this animal there is no doubt, for the simple manners of the ancient Semitic nations multiplied the names of the few objects they had constantly before their eyes; and their domestic animals, in particular, received abundant general and distinctive appellations, according to sex, age, race, and conditions of existence or purpose. Among these terms are the (Heb. אָקֹּו, *ak-ko'*, slender; יָעֵל, *yaw-ale'*, climbing; עֵז, *aze*, strong; עָתוּד, *attood'*, prepared, and so leader; שָׂעִיר, *saw-eer'*, shaggy; Gr. ἐρίφιον, *er-if'ee-on;* τράγος, *trag'os*).

1. *Races of Goats.* The races either known to or kept by the Hebrew people were probably:

(1) Syrian. The domestic Syrian long-eared breed, with horns rather small and variously bent; the ears longer than the head, and pendulous; hair long, often black.

(2) Angora. The Angora, or rather Anadoli breed of Asia Minor, with long hair, more or less fine.

(3) Egyptian. The Egyptian breed, with small spiral horns, long brown hair, very long ears.

(4) Hornless. A breed from Upper Egypt, without horns, having the nasal bones singularly elevated, the nose contracted, with the lower jaw protruding the incisors, and the female with udder very low and purse-shaped. This race, the most degraded by climate and treatment of all the

Syrian Goat.

domestic varieties, is clad in long coarse hair, commonly of a rufous brown color, and so early distinct, that the earlier monuments of Egypt represent it with obvious precision.

(5) Wild Goats. Beside the domestic goats, Western Asia is possessed of one or more wild species—all large and vigorous mountain animals, resembling the ibex or bouquetin of the Alps. Of these, Southern Syria, Arabia, Sinai, and the borders of the Red Sea, contain at least one species, known to the Arabs by the name of Beden or Beddan, and Taytal—the *Capra Jaela* of Ham. Smith, and *Capra Sinaitica* of Ehrenberg. We take this animal to be that noticed under the name of *Yawal*, Jaal or Jol, in the plural yoh-lim (1 Sam. xxiv:2; Job xxxix:1; Ps. civ:18; Prov. v: 19). The male is considerably taller and more robust than the larger tame he-goats, the horns forming regular curves backwards, and with from fifteen to twenty-four transverse elevated cross ridges, being sometimes near three feet long, and exceedingly ponderous; there is a beard under the chin, and the fur is dark brown; but the limbs are white, with regular black marks down the front of the legs, with rings of the same color above the knees and on the pasterns. The females are smaller than the males, more slenderly made, brighter rufous, and with the white and black markings on the legs not so distinctly visible. This species live in troops of fifteen or twenty, and plunge down precipices with the same fearless impetuosity, which distinguishes the ibex. Their horns are sold by the Arabs for knife handles, etc.; but the animals themselves are fast diminishing in number. In Deut. xiv:5 *Akko* is translated 'wild goat.' Schultens (*Origines Hebraicæ*) conjectures that the name arose from its shyness, and consequent readiness to fly.

2. *Uses.* **(1) Sacrifice.** The goat was employed by the people of Israel in many respects as their representative. It was a pure animal for sacrifice (Exod. xii:5), and a kid might be substituted as equivalent to a lamb. Regarding sacrificial offerings we are told that Aaron took two he-goats for a sin-offering for the children of Israel (Lev. xvi:5). These he placed before the Lord at the door of the tabernacle (xvi:7). He cast lots upon them; one lot 'for the Lord' and

Wild Goat of Sinai.

one lot 'for Azazel' (xvi:8). The goat upon which the lot for the Lord fell (xvi:9) he offered for a sin-offering. After the expiation was completed, the second goat, on which fell the lot for Azazel, was brought forward (xvi:10). (See GOAT II., SCAPEGOAT.) He was first placed before the Lord to absolve him. Then Aaron laid his hands upon his head, and confessed over him the (forgiven) iniquities, transgressions, and sins of the children of Israel, put them upon his head, and gave him to a man to take away, in order that he might bear the sins of the people into a solitary land (xvi:22), into the desert, for Azazel (xvi:10). Then Aaron offered a burnt-offering for himself, and one for the people.

(2) Food. The goat formed a principal part of the Hebrew flocks; and both the milk and the young kids were daily articles of food. Among the poorer and more sober shepherd families, the slaughter of a kid was a token of hospitality to strangers, or of unusual festivity; and the prohibition, thrice repeated in the Mosaic law, 'not to seethe a kid in its mother's milk' (Exod. xxiii: 19; xxxiv:26; and Deut. xiv:21), may have originated partly in a desire to recommend abstemiousness, which the legislators and moralists of the East have since invariably enforced with success, and partly with a view to discountenance a practice which was connected with idolatrous festivals, and the rites they involved.

(3) Bottles. It is from goatskins that the leathern bottles to contain wine and other liquids are made in the Levant. For this purpose, after the head and feet are cut away, the case or hide is drawn off the carcass over the neck, without opening the belly; and the extremities being secured, it is dried with the hair in or outside, according to the use it is intended for. The old worn-out skins are liable to burst: hence the obvious propriety of putting new wine into new bottles (Matt. ix:17).

Harmer appears to have rightly referred the allusion in Amos iii:12 to the long-eared race of goats: 'As the shepherd taketh out of the mouth

of the lion two legs or a piece of ear, so shall the children of Israel be taken out that dwell in Samaria and Damascus.' C. H. S.

Figurative. (1) Princes and great men are likened to he-goats (Jer. l:8; Zech. x:3). (2) The Greeks, who were also called Ægeans—that is, *goatish people*—when banded under Alexander the Great, are likened to a *he-goat* with one horn, that, without touching the earth, ran against, and trode down a pushing ram. Under their sovereign, they, with incredible speed, marched into Asia, and overthrew the Persian empire (Dan. viii:5). (3) Devils and wicked men are likened to *goats* (2 Chron. xi:15). (4) In Matt. xxv:32, 33, sheep and goats are used to represent the righteous and the wicked respectively. "The wicked are here conceived of under the figure of *goats,* not on account of the wantonness and stench of the latter (Grotius), or in consequence of their stubbornness (Lange), but generally because these animals were considered to be comparatively worthless (Luke xv:29); and hence, in Matt. xxv:33, we have the diminutive τὰ ἐρίφια for the purpose of expressing contempt" (Meyer, *Com.,* Matt. xxv:32, 33).

11. SCAPEGOAT (scāp'gōt), (Heb. עֲזָאזֵל, *az-az-el';* meaning is doubtful). The account of the remarkable ceremony, respecting the two goats, one of which was to be sacrificed and the other allowed to escape, is contained in Lev. xvi, in verses 1-10, and then follows, in verses 11-28, the explanation of separate points.

(1) General Meaning. As to the meaning of the word Azazel there has been much discussion. Some have regarded it as a designation of the goat itself, supposing it to mean 'the goat sent away,' or 'let loose.' Others, with Bochart, regard the word as referring to a place to which the goat was sent; translating it in the general sense of 'desert places.' Many take Azazel for the name of a person; either some false deity, who was to be appeased by the offering of a goat; or an evil spirit, such as the devil.

(2) Symbolic Signification. According to this view the doctrinal signification of the symbolical action, as far as it has reference to Azazel, is this, that Satan, the enemy of the people of God, cannot harm those forgiven by God, but that they, with sins forgiven of God, can go before him with a light heart, deride him, and triumph over him. There exists here a peculiar trait, which in Hengstenberg's opinion makes it certain that there is an Egyptian reference, namely, the circumstance that the goat was sent to Azazel into the desert. The special residence of Typhon was in the desert, according to the Egyptian doctrine, which is most intimately connected with the natural condition of the country. There, accordingly, is Azazel placed in our passage, not in the belief that this was literally true, but merely symbolically. Finally there is the explanation, less objectionable, if it is not completely satisfactory, which would render the word designating the lot, 'for *complete* sending away.' This view is held by Tholuck, Bähr and Winer.

Perhaps we shall get a truer meaning if we regard the slain goat as symbolizing the act of sacrifice; and the goat that carried off the load of sin, as symbolizing the cleansing influence of faith in that sacrifice. The two goats were parts of one and the same sin-offering, and they form together but one symbolic expression. One alone could not convey the whole of the spiritual truth: this may account for the presence of the two goats (see Maurice, *On Sacrifice*, p. 85; Lightfoot,

Temple Service; Spencer, *De Leg. Heb. Rituali-bus* iii. Dissertatio viii; Hengstenberg, *Egypt and the Books of Moses;* Thomson, *Bampton Lectures,* iii. note).

GOATH (gō′ăth), (Heb. עָגָה, *go-aw′,* lowing), a place evidently in the neighborhood of Jerusalem, (Jer. xxxi:39), accurately the name is *Goah.*

GOAT'S HAIR, GOAT'S SKIN. See DRESS; TABERNACLE.

GOB (gŏb), (Heb. גֹּב, *gobe′,* a pit), a plain where two battles were fought between the Hebrews and Philistines (2 Sam. xxi:18,19). In 1 Chron. xx:4, we read Gezer instead of Gob. The LXX in some copies, read Nob instead of Gob; and in others Gath. Site unknown.

GO BEYOND (Gr. ὑπερβαίνω, *hoop-er-bah′ee-no*), R. V. "transgress," or "overreach" 1 Thess. iv:6.

GOBLET (gŏb′lĕt), (Heb. אַגָּן, *ag-gawn′,*), a trough or receptacle for washing garments; thus any laver, basin, bowl (Cant. vii:2; comp. Exod. xxiv:6, "basin;" Is. xxii:24, "cup"). In form and material the goblet was probably like those found in the Egyptian ruins, of silver, gold, bronze, porcelain and sometimes of wood.

GOD (gŏd).

1. Names of God. The two principal Hebrew names of the Supreme Being (St. Jerome and the Rabbins enumerate ten, but they belong rather to his attributes) used in the Scriptures are יְהֹוָה, *yeh-ho-vaw′, Jehovah,* and אֱלֹהִים, *el-o-heem′, Elohim.* Dr. Hävernick proposes the reading יַהְוֶה, *Jahveh,* instead of יְהֹוָה, *Jehovah,* meaning 'the existing one,' while he derives *Elohim* from an ancient Hebrew root, אָל, *al,* now unused and thinks that the plural is used merely to indicate the abundance and super-richness existing in the Divine Being.

(1) Use of Names in Pentateuch. Both names, he admirably proves, are used by Moses discriminately, in strict conformity with the theological idea he wished to express in the immediate context; and, pursuing the Pentateuch nearly line by line, it is astonishing to see that Moses never uses any of the names at mere random or arbitrarily, but is throughout consistent in the application of the respective terms. (See GENESIS.) *Elohim* is the abstract expression for absolute *Deity* apart from the special notions of unity, holiness, substance, etc. It is more a philosophical than devotional term, and corresponds with our term *Deity,* in the same way as *state* or *government* is abstractedly expressive of a king or monarch. *Jehovah,* however, he considers to be the revealed Elohim, the Manifest, Only, Personal, and Holy Elohim: Elohim is the Creator, Jehovah the Redeemer, etc.

(2) Later Writers. To Elohim, in the later writers, we usually find affixed the adjective חַיִּים, *cha-yim′,* 'the living' (Jer. x:10; Dan. vi:20, 26; Acts xiv:15; 2 Cor. vi:16), probably in contradistinction to *idols,* which might be confounded in some cases with the true God, the linguistical difference in the Hebrew existing only in the plural, the former being called *Elilim* instead of *Elohim* (Lev. xix:14; xxvi:1; Hab. iii:18). In the Anglo Saxon, God means good.

2. The Name Defined. "The true and genuine idea of *God* in general is this—a perfect conscious understanding being (or mind), existing of itself from eternity, and the cause of all other things.

"The true and proper idea of *God,* in its most contracted form, is this—a being absolutely perfect; for this is that alone to which necessary existence is essential, and of which it is demonstrable."

"I define God thus—*an essence or being, fully and absolutely perfect.* I say fully and absolutely perfect, in contradistinction to such perfection as is not full and absolute, but the perfection of this or that species or kind of finite beings, suppose a lion, horse, or tree. But to be fully and absolutely perfect, is to be at least, as perfect as the apprehension of a man can conceive without a contradiction." (Cudworth, *Intell. Syst.*)

3. The Knowledge of God. As to man's knowledge of God two questions have been the subjects of much controversy: the first relating to the possibility of true knowledge of the Divine Being, the second the source or method of such knowledge.

(1) Can God Be Known? The Scriptures declare that God is incomprehensible (see Job xi:7; xxi:14; xxxvi:26; Ps. lxxvii:14; Rom. xi:33). Perfect or complete knowledge of God is not attainable by man. But equally true it is that the scriptures represent God as revealing himself to man, and that a sufficient though limited measure of true knowledge of God is put within the reach of human beings. The important distinction to be maintained at this point is that between partial and perfect knowledge. We cannot comprehend God, and yet we can truly apprehend or know him. Our blessedness, our eternal life even, is in such knowledge (see Matt. xii:28; John xvii:3; Rom. i:19, 20; Eph. i:17; Col. i:10; 1 John v:20). (Barnes, *Bib. Dict.*)

(2) Regarding the Source of Knowledge of God, whether *innate or acquired,* Locke's arguments are of great value.

(*a*) Though God has given us no innate ideas of himself, yet, having furnished us with those faculties our minds are endowed with, he hath not left himself without a witness; since we have sense, perception, and reason, and cannot want a clear proof of him as long as we carry ourselves about us. To show, therefore, that we are capable of knowing, that is, of being certain that there is a God, and how we may come by this certainty, I think we need go no farther than ourselves, and that undoubted knowledge we have of our own existence.

(*b*) I think it is beyond question, that man has a clear perception of his own being; he knows certainly that he exists, and that he is something. In the next place, man knows, by an intuitive certainty, that bare nothing can no more produce any real being, than it can be equal to two right angles. If, therefore, we know there is some real Being, it is an evident demonstration, that from eternity there has been something; since what was not from eternity had a beginning; and what had a beginning must be produced by something else.

(*c*) Next it is evident, that what has its being from another must also have all that which is in and belongs to its being from another too; all the powers it has must be owing to, and derived from, the same source. This eternal source, then, of all being, must be also the source and original of all power; and so this eternal Being must be also the most powerful.

(*d*) Again: man finds in himself perception and knowledge: we are certain, then, that there is not only some Being, but some knowing, intelligent Being in the world. There was a time, then, when there was no knowing Being, or else there has been a knowing Being from eternity. **If it** be said there was a time when that eternal Being had no knowledge, I reply that then it is impossible there should have ever been any knowledge; it being as impossible that things wholly void of knowledge, and operating blindly, and without any perception, should produce a knowing Being, as it is impossible that a triangle should make its three angles larger than two right ones.

(*e*) Thus from the consideration of ourselves, and what we infallibly find in our own constitutions, our reason leads us to the knowledge of this certain and evident truth, that there is an eternal, most powerful, and knowing Being, which, whether any one will call God, it matters not. The thing is evident; and from this idea, duly considered, will easily be deduced all those other attributes we ought to ascribe to this eternal Being. From what has been said, it is plain to me, that we have a more certain knowledge of the existence of a God, than of anything our senses have not immediately discovered to us. Nay, I presume I may say that we more certainly know that there is a God, than that there is any thing else without us. When I say we *know*, I mean there is such a knowledge within our reach, which we cannot miss, if we will but apply our minds to that as we do to several other inquiries.

The Old Testament as little thinks of arguing or proving that God may be known as it thinks of arguing that he exists. Its position is here again, so to speak, far in front of such an argument. How should men think of arguing that God could be known when they were persuaded they knew him, when they felt they were in fellowship with him, when their whole mind was filled and aglow with the thought of him, and when his spirit was within them? The expression 'to see God' (Job xix:26; xxxiii:26; Is. xxxviii:11) sometimes signifies merely to experience his help; but in the Old Testament scriptures it more usually denotes the approach of death (Gen. xxxii:30; Judg. vi:23; xiii:22; Is. vi:5).

4. *Attributes of God.* **(1) Ascribed by Moses.** The attributes ascribed to God by Moses are systematically enumerated in Exod. xxxiv:6-7, though we find in isolated passages in the Pentateuch and elsewhere, additional properties specified, which bear more directly upon the dogmas and principles of religion, such as *e. g.* that he is not the author of sin (Gen. i:31), although since the fall, man is born prone to sin (Gen. vi:5; viii:21, etc.) But as it was the avowed design of Moses to teach the Jews the Unity of God in opposition to the Polytheism of the other nations with whom they were to come in contact, he dwelt particularly and most prominently on that point, which he hardly ever omitted when he had an opportunity of bringing forward the attributes of God (Deut. vi:4; x:17; iv:39; ix:16, etc.; Num. xvi; xxii; xxxiii:27, 29; Exod. xv:11; xxxiv:6, 7, etc.)

(2) By the Prophets. In the Prophets and other sacred writers of the Old Testament, these attributes are still more fully developed and explained by the declarations that God is the first and the last (Is. xliv:6), that he changes not (Hab. iii:6), that the earth and heaven shall perish, but he shall endure (Ps. cii:26)—a distinct allusion to the last doomsday—and that he is Omnipresent (Prov. xv:3; Job xxxiv:22, etc.)

(3) In the New Testament. In the New Testament also we find the attributes of God systematically classified (Rev. v:12 and vii:12), while the peculiar tenets of Christianity embrace, if not a further, still a more developed idea, as presented by the Apostles and the primitive teachers of the church.

The New Testament doctrine of God is distinguished from that of the Old, first, in that it presents with peculiar distinctness and fullness the divine fatherhood. Second, it declares likewise the divine sonship of Jesus Christ, "God manifest in the flesh." The God-man is the fullest disclosure of the divine nature, and the Redeemer and Savior of mankind. Third, the distinct Divine personality and peculiar office of the Holy Ghost is brought most clearly into view. And thus comes what at most was but intimated in the Old Testament, the doctrine of the Trinity. (See TRINITY.)

The attributes of God as revealed in the scriptures may be summed up as follows: Spirituality, Infinity, Eternity, Immutability, Self-sufficiency, Perfection, Freedom, Omnipotence, Omnipresence, Omniscience, Justice, Truth, Love, Mercy, and Grace. For discussion of *Attributes* see separate heads.

(4) God, Children of or Sons of. The teaching of St. John on this subject combines the elements of the Pauline and Petrine and uses the term 'children' rather than sons of God. The keynote to it may be found in the Prologue to the gospel (John i:12, 13), 'to as many as received him (the Logos) he gave the right to become children of God, even to them that believe on his name: which were begotten, not of blood nor of the will of the flesh, nor of the will of man, but of God.' Here we have the right to become children of God bestowed by Christ, which answers to St. Paul's statement, 'God sent forth his Son . . . that we might receive the adoption of sons.' The word 'adoption' is not employed; but the right to become children expresses the same thing in less technical language. Further, this is said to be given to those who receive Christ by believing on his name. St. Paul had also written, 'Ye are all sons of God by faith in Jesus Christ; for as many of you as have been baptized into Christ have put on Christ' (Gal. iii:26, f.). Thus for St. John, as well as for St. Paul, our sonship to God is through union to Christ the only-begotten Son, and that union is effected by faith.

But St. John adds to this the conception found in St. James and St. Peter of a birth or begetting of God, which he emphatically distinguishes from the natural birth in every aspect of it. Those who believe in Christ's name are they who were begotten of God; and that this is not done by the process of natural generation is shown by a threefold contrast: not of blood, *i. e.* they did not become sons of God through or in virtue of their being of the one blood of which God has made all mankind. Neither was it by any movement or impulse of their own nature, whether the spontaneous tendencies of its animal faculties ('the will of the flesh'), or even the voluntary acts of personality ('the will of man'). The contrast is more briefly and pointedly expressed in our Lord's discourse with Nicodemus as between being begotten of the flesh and of the Spirit (John iii:6). St. John seems to conceive the Divine Spirit as a principle or power of life and holiness proceeding from God, given to Jesus Christ in all its fullness and by him communicated to his disciples. It is not unworthy of notice that Irenæus and Tertullian apply John i:13 to Christ, apparently reading the verb in the singular ('who was born'); and though that reading is only found in some Lat. MSS. and cannot be received, yet in 1 John v:18 our Lord, according to the

most natural interpretation, is called 'he that was begotten of God.' (J. S. Candlish, Hastings' *Bib. Dict.*) (See CHILD, CHILDREN, *Figurative.*)

GOD FORBID (Gr. μή, *may*, Rom. iii:4), a primitive particle of qualified negation distinguished from οὐ, *oo*, which expresses unqualified denial, and γίνομαι, *ghin'om-ahee*, to come to be.

A. V. and R. V. translate *hâlîlâh* by 'God forbid' ('The Lord forbid,' 1 Sam. xxiv:6; xxvi:11; 1 Kings xxi:3, and 'My God forbid it me,' 1 Chron. xi:19), everywhere except Gen. xviii:25; 1 Sam. ii:30; xx:9; xxii:15; 2 Sam. xx:20; xxiii:17, where the Wyclifite phrase 'Far be it from' or 'Be it far from' has been retained. This phrase Amer. R. V. prefers throughout the Old Testament.

The Greek μὴ γένοιτο is only one of the renderings of *hâlîlâh* in LXX. Of the others μηδαμῶς occurs twice in New Testament, Acts x:14; xi:8, ('Not so, Lord,') and ἵλεώς σοι once, Matt. xvi:22 ('Be it far from thee, Lord'). But μὴ γένοιτο is found fifteen times, all but Luke xx:16 being in St. Paul's Epistles, and in twelve of St. Paul's fourteen instances it is used to express the apostle's abhorrence of an inference which he fears may be falsely drawn from his argument. (See Burton, *N. T. Moods and Tenses*, 2, p. 79).

GODHEAD (gŏd'hĕd), (Gr. θεῖος, *thi'os*, godlike, Acts xvii:29; θειότης, *thi-ot'ace*, divinity, Rom. i:20; θεότης, *theh-ot'ace*, divinity, Col. 2:9), the divine nature or essence, the nature or essential being of God (Acts xvii:29; Rom. i:20; Col. ii:9).

In Acts xvii:29 τὸ θεῖον, 'the Divine,' is chosen by St. Paul in his speech to the Athenians as a familiar philosophical expression which enables him to carry their thoughts easily with him. Even they, with scarcely a personal conception of God, ought not to debase their conception to the level of men's handiwork. Hence R. V. margin 'that which is divine' is better than text 'the Godhead,' though 'the Divine' would have been better. Wycliffe errs on the other side when he offers 'godly thing' (after Vulg. *Divinum*). Tyndale gave 'godhead,' and was followed by all the Versions except the Rhemish, which has 'the Divinitie,' though 'Godhead' is given as an alternative in the Annotation to the verse. The Greek expression occurs nowhere else in Biblical Greek, though the adjective θεῖος is common in LXX and occurs in 2 Pet. i:3, 4. (Hastings' *Bib. Dict.*)

GODLINESS is in the New Testament the equivalent of the Gr. term εὐσέβεια, *yoo-seh'by-ah* (1 Tim. ii:21; iii:16; iv:7, 8; vi:3, 5, 6, 11; 2 Tim. iii: 5; Tit. i:1; also Acts iii:12, R. V., 2 Pet. i:3, 6. 7; iii:11), except in one passage (1 Tim. ii:10), where θεοσέβεια is used. 'It properly denotes,' says Ellicott, 'only' "well-directed reverences" (Trench, *Synon.*, sec. 48), but in the New Testament is practically the same as θεοσέβεια, "the spirit of piety in the life itself either external or internal."

It may therefore be considered as piety resulting from the knowledge and love of God, and leading to the cheerful and constant obedience of his commands (2 Pet. iii:11).

In 1 Tim. iii:16 it imports the *substance of revealed religion.*

GODS (Heb. אֱלֹהִים, *el-o-heem'*).

(1) Angels are called *gods,* on account of their superior excellence, and their declaring God's mind, and executing his work as his deputies; and they were required to worship Christ, when the heathen idols were destroyed (Ps. xcvii:7; Heb. i:6). (2) In Exodus (xxii:28, A. V.) is the command, "Thou shalt not revile the *gods.*" Some understand the term *gods* to be applied to rulers by way of *respect.* (3) The usual notion of the

ancients, that the royal dignity was derived from God, may here be traced to its source; hence the Homeric διογένης βάσιλευς, *dee-og-en'ace bas'-ee-looce.* This notion, entertained by the Oriental nations with regard to kings, made the latter style themselves *gods* (Ps. lxxxii:6; comp. John x:34). (4) On the other hand with regard to this particular passage Exod. xxxi:28, it is claimed that the more correct rendering (and so given in the R. V.) is "Thou shalt not revile God." "Elohim does not mean either the gods of other nations, or the rulers, but simply God, . . . whose majesty was despised in every breach of the commandments of Jehovah, and who was honored in the persons of the rulers (see Prov. xxiv:21; 1 Pet. ii:17)" (K. and D., *Com.,* in loco). (5) Moses is called a *god,* because God's deputy in delivering the Israelites (Exod. iv:16, and vii:1). (6) Satan is called the *god of this world;* he is believed, obeyed, and adored, under various forms, by most of the inhabitants of it (2 Cor. iv:4). (7) Idols are called *gods,* because adored, worshiped, and trusted by their votaries (1 Kings xi:33). They are *strange,* or *other gods;* the Hebrews were not originally in covenant with them (Deut. xxxii: 16; Judg. ii:12); and the most devoted among them, out of detestation, declined pronouncing their names, and hence substitute *Bosheth* or *Besheth,* i. e. *shame,* instead of *Baal,* in naming some persons; thus, for Eshbaal, Meribaal, and Jerubbaal, they said Ishbosheth, Mephibosheth, and Jerubbesheth; and sometimes called the idols Elhim, *no-things,* or *not-gods;* and often Gilulim, *rolling excrements* (Ezek. xxx:13), etc.

GODS, FALSE. These are the beings, whether real or imaginary, adopted as objects of worship among men instead of Jehovah. Fear, lust, malignity or pride, evidently predominate in the conception and choice of such objects of adoration. Nothing like pure and elevating devotional sentiment could, or did attach to them.

The principal of the ancient gods, whom the Romans called *dii majorum gentium,* and Cicero celestial gods, Varro select gods, Ovid *nobiles deos,* others *consentes deos,* were Jupiter, Juno, Vesta, Minerva, Ceres, Diana, Venus, Mars, Mercury, Neptune, Vulcan, and Apollo. Jupiter is considered as the god of heaven; Neptune, as god of the sea; Mars, as the god of war; Apollo, of eloquence, poetry, and medicine; Mercury, of thieves; Bacchus, of wine; Cupid, of love, etc. A second sort of gods, called demi-gods, *semidii, dii minorum gentium, indigetes,* or gods adopted, were men canonized and deified. As the greater gods had possession of heaven by their own right, these secondary deities had it by merit and donation, being translated into heaven because they had lived as gods upon earth.

The heathen gods may be all reduced to the following classes: (1) Created spirits, angels, or demons, whence good and evil gods; Genii, Lares, Lemures, Typhones, guardian gods, infernal gods, etc. (2) Heavenly bodies; as the sun, moon, and other planets; also, the fixed stars, constellations, etc. (3) Elements; as air, earth, ocean, Ops, Vesta; the rivers, fountains, etc. (4) Meteors. Thus the Persians adored the wind; thunder and lightning were honored under the name of Geryon; and several nations of India and America have made themselves gods of the same. Castor, Pollux, Helena, and Iris, have also been preferred from meteors to be gods; and the like has been practiced in regard to comets; witness that which appeared at the murder of Cæsar. (5) They fashioned minerals or fossils into deities. Such was the bætylus. The Finlanders adored stones; the Scythians, iron; and many nations, silver and gold. (6) Plants have been made gods. Thus leeks and onions were deities in Egypt; the Sclavi, Lithuanians, Celtæ, Vandals, and Peruvians, adored trees and forests; the ancient Gauls, Britons, and Druids, paid a particular devotion to the oak; and it was no other than wheat, corn, seed, etc., that the ancients adored under the names of Ceres and Proserpina. (7) They took themselves gods from among the waters. The Syrians and Egyptians adored fishes; and what were the Tritons, the Nereids, Syrens, etc., but fishes? Several nations have adored serpents; particularly the Egyptians, Prussians, Lithuanians, Samogitians, etc. (8) Insects, as flies and ants, had their priests and votaries. (9) Among birds, the stork, raven, sparrowhawk, ibis, eagle, grison, and lapwing, have had Divine honors; the last in Mexico, the rest in Egypt and at Thebes. (10) Fourfooted beasts have had their altars; as the bull-dog, cat, wolf, baboon, lion, and crocodile, in Egypt and elsewhere; the hog in the island of Crete; rats and mice in the Troas, and at Tenedos; weasels at Thebes; and the porcupine throughout all Zoroaster's school. (11) Nothing was more common than to place men among the number of deities; and from Belus or Baal, to the Roman emperors before Constantine, the instances of this kind are innumerable; frequently they did not wait so long as their deaths for the apotheosis. Nebuchadnezzar procured his statue to be worshiped while living; and Virgil shows that Augustus had altars and sacrifices offered to him; as we learn from other hands that he had priests, called *Augustales,* and temples at Lyons, Narbona, and several other places; and he must be allowed the first of the Romans in whose behalf idolatry was carried to such a pitch. The Ethiopians deemed all their kings gods; the Velleda of the Germans, the Janos of the Hungarians, and the Thaut, Woden, and Assa, of the northern nations, were indisputably men. (12) Not men only, but every thing that relates to man, has also been deified; as labor, rest, sleep, youth, age, death, virtues, vices, occasion, time, place, numbers, among the Pythagoreans; the generative power, under the name of Priapus. Infancy alone had a cloud of deities; as Vagitanus, Levana, Rumina, Edula, Potina, Cuba, Cumina, Carna, Ossilago, Statulinus, Fabulinus, etc. They also adored the gods Health, Fever, Fear, Love, Pain, Indignation, Shame, Impudence, Opinion, Renown, Prudence, Science, Art, Fidelity, Felicity, Calumny, Liberty, Money, War, Peace, Victory, Triumph, etc. Lastly, Nature, the universe, or *Pan,* was reputed a great god.

Hesiod has a poem under the title of *Theogonia,* that is, "The Generation of the Gods," in which he explains their genealogy and descent, sets forth who was the first and principal, who next descended from him, and what issue each had; the whole making a sort of system of heathen theology. Beside this popular theology, each philosopher had his system, as may be seen from the "Timæus" of Plato, and Cicero *"De Natura Deorum."* Justin Martyr, Tertullian, Arnobius, Minutius Felix, Lactantius, Eusebius, Augustine, and Theodoret, show the vanity of the heathen gods. It is very difficult to discover the real sentiments of the heathens with respect to their gods; they are exceedingly intricate and confused, and even frequently contradictory. They admitted so many superior and inferior gods, who shared the empire, that every place was full of gods. Varro reckons up no less than thirty thousand adored within a small extent of ground, and yet their number was every day increasing. In modern Oriental paganism, as in India, China, etc., they amount to many millions, and are, in fact, innumerable.

GODSPEED is the translation of the Greek salutation χαίρω, *khah'ee-ro,* from a primary verb signifying to be cheerful, *to hail* (2 John ver. 10, 11), through the Ang. Sax. *gôd-spêdig,* "good speed."

GOD, THE UNKNOWN (Gr. 'Αγνώστῳ Θεῷ). Paul, in his address on Mars' Hill, said that he had seen in Athens "an altar with this inscription, 'To the unknown God' " (Acts xvii:22, 23).

Considerable difficulty has been found by many interpreters to reconcile this with the fact, that no mention is made by the classic authors of any altar in Athens bearing this inscription, whilst we are informed by Pausanias (*Attic.* i:4; *Eliac.* v:14) and Philostratus (*Vit. Apollonii Tyan.,* vi:3), that there were several altars inscribed ἀγνώστοις Θεοîς, in the plural; and different suppositions have been made to account for the Apostle's language (Kuinoel, *in Act.* xvii: 23). But why should we not receive the apostle's own testimony on this subject, as reported by the inspired historian? It is certain that no one is in circumstances to affirm that no altar existed in Athens bearing such an inscription at the time Paul visited that city; and when, therefore, Paul publicly addressing the Athenians, says he saw such an altar, why should we hesitate for a moment to take his words for what they literally mean? Besides, there is nothing in what Pausanias and Philostratus affirm that appears incompatible with Paul's assertion. It is to be observed that neither of them says there were altars, *on each of which* the inscription was in the plural number, but only there were 'altars of gods called unknown' (βωμοὶ Θεῶν ὀνομαζομένων ἀγνώστων); so that for aught that appears to the contrary, each altar might bear the **inscription** which Paul says he saw upon one.

GOEL (gō'ĕl). See BLOOD-REVENGE.

GOG (gŏg), (Heb. גוֹג, *gohg*; Gr. Γώγ, *gogue*).

1. This name occurs in Ezek. xxxiii:3, 14, and xxxix:11, as a proper name; that of a prince of *Magog* (מָגוֹג), a people that were to come from the North to invade the land of Israel, and be there defeated. In a different sense, but corresponding with the assertions of other Oriental authors, in whose traditions this people occupy an important place, *Gog* occurs in Rev. xx:8, as the name of a country.

Interpreters have given very different explanations of the terms Gog and Magog; but they have generally understood them as symbolical expressions for the heathen nations of Asia, or more particularly for the Scythians, a vague knowledge of whom seems to have reached the Jews in Palestine about that period. Prof. Sayce says: "For an explanation of Magog we must go to the prophet Ezekiel. He tells us (xxxviii: 2) that Magog was the land of Gog, 'the chief prince of Meshech and Tubal.' Gog is the Gugu of the Assyrian inscriptions, the Gyges of the Greeks; and in Magog therefore we must see a title of Lydia. The name is evidently a compound of that of Gog" (*Races of the Old Testament,* p. 45).

As a collective name, *Magog* seems also to indicate in the Hebrew the tribes about the Caucasian mountains. According to Reinegge (*Descrip. of the Caucasus,* ii. 79) some of the

Caucasian people call their mountains Gog, and the highest northern points Magog.

2. A Reubenite, son of Shemaiah (1 Chron. v:4).

GO IT UP (Is. xv:5) is a transposition of the preposition and its case,—not unfrequent in old writers,—meaning *ascend it.*

GOLAN (gō'lan), (Heb. גּוֹלָן, go-lawn', captive).

A Levitical town of Bashan, in the tribe of Manasseh (Deut. iv:43; Josh. xx:8; xxi:27; 1 Chron. vi:71), from which the small province of Gaulonitis (Γαυλωνῖτις) took its name. The word is recognized in the present Jolan or Djolan, mentioned by Burckhardt (*Syria*, p. 286), as giving name to a district lying east of the lake of Tiberias, and composed of the ancient Gaulonitis, with part of Bashan and Argob. Some difficulty has been suggested as arising from the fact, that the Judas whom Josephus (*Antiq.* xviii:1, 1) calls a Gaulonite, is called by St. Luke (Acts v:37) a Galilæan. This is the more remarkable, as Josephus elsewhere (ex. gr. *De Bell. Jud.* ii:20, 4) carefully distinguishes Galilee and Gaulonitis. Yet he himself elsewhere calls this very Judas a Galilæan (*Antiq.* xx:5, 2; *De Bell. Jud.* ii:9, 1). It is, from this, probable that Judas had a double cognomen, perhaps because he had been born in Gaulonitis, but had been brought up or dwelt in Galilee.

GOLD (gōld). The Hebrew word זָהָב, *zaw-hawb,* yellow, golden).

1. Mineralogical Names. This is merely the mineralogical name of this metal. Several Hebrew words are used to denote the metal.

(1) *Seg-ore'* (Heb. סְגוֹר, treasured, i. e., fine gold, (Job xxviii:15; 1 Kings vi:20, vii:49). (2) *Beh'tser* (Heb. בֶּצֶר, clipping, dug out), properly metal in a crude state, "golden ore." (3) *Pawz* (Heb. פַּז, pure or native gold (Job xxviii:17; Cant. v:15; Ps. xix:10; xxi:3; Prov. viii:19; Is. xiii:12; Lam. iv:2).

2. Poetical Terms. (1) *Keh'them* (Heb. כֶּתֶם, also implying something concealed) (Job xxviii:16, 19; xxxi:24; Dan. x:5, etc.). (2) *Khaw-roots'* (Heb. חָרוּץ, derivation not clear) is referred to the verb *khaw-rats'* (חָרַץ, to cut off, make pointed), and is applied to gold as eagerly sought for. From a kindred root *khaw-mas'* (חָמַס, to wrong, oppress), comes the noun *khaw-mawce'* (חָמָס, violence), used by metaphor (Amos iii:10) for wealth gotten by wrong and oppression.

Gold was known and valued in very early times. Abraham was rich in gold (Gen. xiii: 2; xxiv:35), and female ornaments were made of gold (Gen. xxiv:22).

To judge from 1 Chron. xxii:14; xxix:4, the Jews must have been, in their palmy days, in possession of enormous quantities of this metal, considering the many tons of gold that were spent in the building of the temple alone, though the expression, *plenteous as stones* (2 Chron. i:15), may be considered as hyperbolical. It is, however, confirmed by the history of the other Asiatic nations, and more especially of the Persians, that the period referred to really abounded in gold, which was imported in vast masses from Africa and the Indies (Heeren, *Ideen.* i. 1, 37, *sq.*). The queen of Sheba brought with her (from Arabia Felix), among other presents, 120 talents of gold (2 Chron. ix:9). E. M.

Figurative. Gold is often employed in Scripture as an emblem of what is divine, pure,

precious, solid, useful, incorruptible, or lasting and glorious. (1) The *gold* of the temple and tabernacle might represent the divine excellencies of Christ, and the precious and incorruptible ordinances of his church, and graces of his people. His head is as *most fine gold;* his hands *like gold rings,* set with the beryl; he is *gold tried* in the fire; his girdle, censer, and crown are of *fine gold.* How divine, precious, solid, pure, and incorruptible, are his Godhead and government, power and work, person and fullness, and his preparation for, and readiness to execute his office! how valuable and glorious his everlasting reward (Dan. x:5; Rev. iii:18; viii:3; xiv:14). (2) God is likened to *gold;* what a pure, precious, enriching, and everlasting portion is he to his people (Job xxii:25; A. V. *silver,* Marg, *gold*). (3) God's word, and his ordinances, especially if more spiritual, are likened to *gold;* how precious, lasting, enriching, and capable of enduring a trial (Ps. xix:10; Is. lx:17; Zech. iv:12; 1 Cor. iii:12; Rev. xxi:15). (4) Saints, and their graces of faith, hope, love, etc., or even their trials, are likened to *gold* (Job xxiii:10; Ps. xlv:13; 1 Pet. i:7). (5) The vials of God's wrath are *golden;* divine, pure, and unmixed with partiality or passion (Rev. xv:7). (6) That which is wealthy, pompous, and enticing is called *golden;* so antichristian Rome is said to have in her hand a *golden cup* (Rev. xvii:4).

GOLDEN CANDLESTICK. See CANDLESTICK.

GOLDEN CITY (Heb. מַדְהֵבָה, *mad-hay-baw'*), a term used in reference to Babylon (Is. xiv:4) and occurring nowhere else.

"Not one of the early translators ever thought of deriving this word from the Aramæan *dehab* (gold), but translated the word as if it were *marhebah* (haughty, violent treatment). We understand it, according to *madmenah* (dunghill) in Is. xxv:10, as denoting the place where they were reduced to pining away, i. e., as applied to Babylon as the house of servitude where Israel had been wearied to death" (Delitzsch, *Com.,* in loco).

GOLDEN WEDGE. See WEDGE.

GOLDSMITH (gōld'smith), (Heb. צוֹרֵף, *tsorafe'*, Neh. iii:8, 32; Is. xl:19; xli:7), a melter of gold. (See HANDICRAFT.)

GOLGOTHA (gŏl'go-thà), (Gr. Γολγοθά, *gol-goth-ah'*, place of a skull).

The original word signifies 'a skull,' as does its Latin representative, *Calvaria, Calvary.* Different opinions have prevailed as to why the place was so termed. Many have held that Golgotha was the place of public execution; and that hence it was termed the 'place of a skull.' Another opinion is that the place took its name from its shape, being a hillock of a form like a human skull. The last is the opinion to which the writer of these remarks inclines. That the place was of some such shape seems to be generally agreed, and the traditional term *mount,* applied to Calvary, appears to confirm this idea. And such a shape, it must be allowed, is in entire agreement with the name—that is, 'skull.' To these considerations there are added certain difficulties which arise from the second explanation. So far as we know there is no historical evidence to show that there was a place of public execution where Golgotha is commonly fixed, nor that any such place, in or near Jerusalem, bore the name Golgotha. Matthew calls it 'a place called Golgotha; that is to say a place of a skull' (Matt. xxvii:33);

Mark, 'the place Golgotha; which is being interpreted, the place of a skull' (Mark xv:22); Luke, 'the place which is called Calvary' (Luke xxiii:33); John, 'a place called of a skull, which is called in the Hebrew Golgotha' (John xix:17; Matt. xxvii:33). In truth, the context seems to show that the Roman guard hurried Jesus away, and put him to death at the first convenient spot; and that rather because there was no small fear of a popular insurrecion, especially as he was attended by a crowd of people. But where was the place?

(1) Tradition. The traditionary recollection of this remarkable spot was undoubtedly strengthened by the erection of the Temple of Venus on the place, after the capture of Jerusalem by the Romans. The temple thus takes up the tradition and transmits it in stone and marble to coming ages. This continuation of the tradition is the more important because it begins to operate at a time when the Christians, were driven from Jerusalem. But the absence of the Christians from the holy city was not of long duration, and even early in the third century we find pilgrimages from distant places to the Holy Land had already begun, for the express purpose of viewing the spots which the presence and sufferings of the Savior had rendered sacred and memorable (*Hist. Hierosol.* p. 591; Euseb. *Hist. Eccles.* vi: 11). A century later, Eusebius (A. D. 315) informs us that Christians visited Jerusalem from all regions of the earth for the same object. So early and so decided a current towards the holy city presupposes a strong, wide-spread, and long pre-eminent feeling—an established tradition in the church touching the most remarkable spots; a tradition of that nature which readily links itself with the actual record in Hebrews.

Early in the fourth century Eusebius and Jerome write down the tradition and fix the locality of Calvary in their writings. Pilgrims now streamed to Jerusalem from all parts of the world, and that site was fixed for Golgotha which has remained to the present hour.

This was done not merely by the testimony of these two learned fathers, but by the acts of the Emperor Constantine and his mother Helena. This empress, when very far advanced in life, visited Jerusalem for the express purpose of erecting a church on the spot where the Lord Jesus had been crucified. On her arrival at Jerusalem she inquired diligently of the inhabitants. Yet the search was uncertain and difficult, in consequence of the obstructions by which the heathen had sought to render the spot unknown. These being all removed, the sacred sepulcher was discovered, and by its side three crosses, with the tablet bearing the inscription written by Pilate (Robinson, *Bib. Res.* ii. 14; Theodoret, i. 17). On the site thus ascertained, was erected, whether by Constantine or Helena, certainly by Roman influence and treasure, a splendid and extensive Christian temple. This church was completed and dedicated A. D. 335. It was a great occasion for the Christian world. In order to give it importance and add to its splendor, a council of bishops was convened, by order of the emperor, from all the provinces of the empire, which assembled first at Tyre and then at Jerusalem.

J. R. B.

The evidence of locality to be gathered from the gospel statements as to the place of the crucifixion and tomb of our Lord is as follows: If the judgment hall of Pilate was at the northwest angle of the Harem area, where the house of the Turkish pasha stands, then the soldiers would lead Jesus out in a northwest direction to be crucified.

The combination of statements shows that it lay just outside the city walls. The original place was where criminals were executed, and the modern argument is that the hill with the openings on the south very strikingly resembles a human skull. The Romans were accustomed to execute their criminals in a conspicuous place. "And when they were come to a place called Golgotha, that is to say, the place of a skull," there they crucified him. A skull-shaped hill outside the city walls, near the city, near a rock-hewn sepulcher which was in a garden, and near some frequented road, are the facts furnishing the data of the problem. If the traditional site where the Church of the Holy Sepulcher stands is rejected as not answering these conditions, another spot, a hill a little northeast of the Damascus gate, becomes most prominent. Skull Hill was originally a part of the Mount Moriah ridge, extending northward from it in a short and narrow spur. It contained white limestone. Here a quarry was opened, probably as early as the building of Solomon's temple. An excavation was made right through the hill, separating Skull Hill from the south ridge, leaving a rounded knoll on the north. The hill is now quite bare; not a tree or shrub exists on it. The hillock is rounded on all sides but the south, where the yellow cliff is pierced by two small caves high up on the sides, which look in the distance like the eye sockets of a human skull. The hill is certainly outside the most northern wall existing in the days of Herod, or what is known as the second wall. Again; it is near a frequented road which may have been the present Nablus road from the Damascus gate, or a military road from Castle Antonio to Cæsarea. which Dr. Merrill says ran north of the hill, and infers that the place of the execution would be near it. Edward L. Wilson made a thorough study of the place, and has left his record thus:

"A few rods northeast of the Damascus gate the wall rests partly upon the natural rock. Beneath is the old-time quarry known as the "Cotton Grotto." On the opposite side of the road is "the grotto of Jeremiah." Farther, on the left, is a hill, the face of which, with the horrid semblance of deep-sunken eyes and broken visage, looks like a human skull. Its locality and surrounding features have led modern explorers to accept it as Calvary. It is without the gates. It commands an extensive view of the city, and of the whole way to the summit of Olivet. The populace assembled on two sides of the city could see an execution on this hill."

A garden was near the scene of the crucifixion, and a new sepulcher in that garden. In the western face of Skull Hill is a large tomb, one also in the northwest, and one a little further off of large proportions. Again, the Jews now residing at Jerusalem affirm that this hill is the place where Christ was crucified, and their tradition may be as valuable as the claim for the long accepted site within the city.

(2) Opinion of Bishop S. M. Merrill. Bishop S. M. Merrill, after making a careful study of the locality on the ground, says: "From reading the Scriptures, and from reasonable conjecture as to what the authorities would or would not do in the matter of public executions, we incline to the belief that the three crosses were planted farther from the heart of the city than is the site of the Church of the Holy Sepulcher, and that it must have been outside of the wall, and north from the Damascus gate. Of course, if the topography or physical conditions in that direction were out of harmony with the facts and the phenomena in the narratives, this would be baseless conjecture. But, instead of being out of harmony, they are exactly in harmony, and in some respects answer to the narratives better than any other locality. Here has ever been a public road; here are the requisite distance and space; and here the garden, the rock-cut tombs, and the skull-shaped hill. On the right hand side of the road, going north from the Damascus gate, there is a ridge or an uneven elevation of ground overlooking the Damascus road on one side, and the Kedron valley on the other side; and out on this ridge beyond the grotto of Jeremiah, which is in the west side of this ridge, is a hill, or elevation of ground, which is considerably higher than the ridge; and on the lower ground, between the road and this hill, is the site of an ancient garden (still used as a garden,) and extending to the base of the hill; and in the base of the hill itself, facing the garden, are rocks with ancient excavations of tombs, not well preserved. One could not better describe the shape of this hill than by comparing it to a human skull sitting on a level space. Whether it was ever designated as the "place of a skull" or not is now unknown; and the same is true of every other spot which has been supposed to be the Calvary. We have a "Mount Calvary" in our hymns and songs, but, of course, there has never been any such mountain, unless this little skull-shaped hill out near the Damascus road was such. The preponderance of testimony, it seems to me, favors this locality as the place of the crucifixion—not that the crosses stood on the top of this hill, but near by on the low ground, between the hill and the road, and outside of the garden. If this is correct, then the burial place was in some of the unknown excavations along the side of this hill or ridge."

But however strong the arguments for the site outside the north wall, there still remains the old, old claim that reaches back to the days of Constantine, when it was said: "Not the least doubt was entertained where the sepulcher was situated." And this historical argument in its favor has not as yet been set aside. Modern opinions are about equally divided. Strong efforts have been made of late to determine what the early fathers said about the site of Calvary, but they are generally silent. If the old theory is continued, then a new and undeveloped plan of the wall must be presented in a light that will harmonize with the facts of scripture, which the old site does not, and never has in view of any known location of the walls of Jerusalem. (*The Story of Jesus*, by Rev. John O. Foster, A. M. 1894.)

(3) Opinion of Lieut.-Gen. Sir Chas. Warren.
Gen. C. Warren in Hastings' *Bib. Dict.* sums up the case as follows: "There are many arguments in favor of the traditional site of Golgotha, but, until it can be ascertained whether it is within or without the city wall of the time of Christ, the whole question must still remain in doubt. The road from the tower of Antonia leading into the old road from the city to Jaffa would probably have passed close to the site, and on this road, outside the Jaffa gate, public executions have taken place in quite recent years, up to 1868. There are rock-cut tombs in the immediate neighborhood, including that of the Holy Sepulcher.

"During recent years several sites to the north of the city have been suggested as the site of Golgotha, in order, apparently, to comply with the view that the place of execution should be situated on the north side of the city (Lev. i:10, 11); but, though this may have been necessary

for the Jewish place of stoning, there is nothing to indicate that the place of crucifixion during the Roman occupation was located according to Jewish ritual, or that it was identical with the place of stoning.

"A knoll above 'Jeremiah's grotto' has been suggested by Otto Thenius in 1849 (followed by General Gordon, Colonel Conder, and others) as the genuine Calvary, on the ground principally that it is the place of stoning according to modern Jewish tradition."

GOLIATH (go-li'ath), (Heb. גָּלְיָת, *gol-yath'*, exile).

1. The giant whom David slew at Ephes-dammim (1 Sam. xvii). In the account of the fight he is spoken of as a Philistine from Gath. He was so politically, but it does not follow that he was of the ordinary Philistine blood. Presumably, he was of the *rephaite* or giant breed, elsewhere spoken of as living at Gath (2 Sam. xxi: 15-22; 1 Chron. xx:4-8), and was descended from the ancient Avim or Anakim. (See ANAKIM; AVIM; GIANTS; RAPHA; REPHAIM.)
The Hebrew text makes him six cubits and a span in height. Josephus and some MSS. of the Septuagint reduce this to four cubits and a span. On general principles the Hebrew reading is the more authoritative, and it fits best the figures given for the tremendous weight of his armor and weapons. Counting the cubit at twenty-one inches, this would make him over eleven feet high, and over nine feet high if we count the cubit a handbreadth shorter. If he was measured in his armor, from the ground to the top of his helmet-crest, this is not incredible, though he is probably the largest man of whom we have any authentic record. (W. J. Beecher, Hastings' *Bib. Dict.*)
For forty days he went out from the camp of the Philistines, and haughtily defied the Hebrews to produce a man that durst engage him in a single combat. He offered to decide the subjection of the one nation to the other on the victory by this single combat. The Hebrews were terrified at the very sight of him; but David, coming to the camp, undertook to attack him with a staff, a sling, and a few small stones. With disdain Goliath cursed him by his idols, and bade him come on, and he would give his flesh to the fowls of the air; meanwhile David slung a stone, which, penetrating by the hole left in the helmet for the giant's eye, or while he was tossing up his forehead, and leaving it bare, in contempt of his puny antagonist, sank into his head, and brought him to the ground, flat on his face. David then ran up to him, and with his own sword cut off his head (1 Sam. xvii). Perhaps, on occasion of this victory, he composed the 9th and 144th Psalms. Four of his brethren were afterward slain by David's warriors (2 Sam. xxi; 1 Chron. xx). (See GIANTS.)
2. The Goliath of 2 Sam. xxi:19 is probably a different person.

GOME (gōm), (Heb. גֹּמֶא, *go'meh*), translated 'rush' and 'bulrush,' is mentioned in four places of Scripture, from which there is no doubt that it was a plant growing in moist situations in Egypt, and employed in the construction of vessels of different kinds, intended to float upon the water, such as the ark in which Moses was hid, and vessels for transit (Job viii:11; Is. xxxv:7; Exod. ii:3; Is. xviii:2). Though other plants are adduced by translators and commentators as the *gome* of Scripture, yet it is evident that only the *papyrus* can be meant, and that it is well suited to all the passages.

The *papyrus* is now well known: it belongs to the tribe of *sedges* or *cyperaceæ*, and is not a bush or bulrush, as in the Authorized Version. It may be seen growing to the height of six or eight feet, even in tubs, in the hothouses of this country, and is described by the ancients as growing in the shallow parts of the Nile. The root is fleshy, thick, and spreading; the stems triangular, eight or ten feet in height, of which two or so

Papyrus Antiquorum.

are usually under water, thick below but tapering towards the apex, and destitute of leaves; those of the base broad, straight, and sword-shaped, but much shorter than the stem. This last is terminated by an involucel of about eight leaves, sword-shaped and acute, much shorter than the many-rayed umbel which they support. The secondary umbels are composed only of three or four short rays, with an involucel of three awl-shaped leaflets. The flowers are in a short spike at the extremity of each ray.

The *papyrus* was well known to the ancients as a plant of the waters of Egypt. '*Papyrum nascitur in palustribus Ægypti aut quiescentibus Nili aquis, ubi evagatæ stagnant*' (Pliny, xiii:11). Theophrastus, at a much earlier period, described it as growing, not in the deep parts, but where the water was of the depth of two cubits, or even less. It was found in almost every part of Egypt inundated by the Nile, in the Delta, especially in the Sebennytic nome, and in the neighborhood of Memphis, etc.

The plant is sweet, and was used by the Egyptians for food and for making many sorts of vessels; the root was burned for fuel. The construction of *papyrus* boats is mentioned by Theophrastus. That the *papyrus* was employed for making paper is also well known, and Wilkinson mentions that from ancient paper being found at Thebes and elsewhere, it is evident that this application of it was much anterior to the time of Alexander the Great. (See PAPYRUS; REED.)

J. F. R.

GOMER (gō'mer), (Heb. גֹּמֶר, *go'mer*, perfection).

1. The eldest son of Japheth, son of Noah (B. C. after 2414), whose descendants Bochart (*Phal.* iii. 8) supposes to have settled in Phrygia (Gen. x:3; comp. 1 Chron. i:5). Most of the interpreters take him to be the ancestor of the Celtæ, and more especially of the *Cimmerii*, Κιμμέριοι, who were already known in the time of Homer (*Odyss.* xi:14). To judge from the ancient historians (Herodotus, Strabo, Plutarch, etc.), they had in early times settled to the north of the Black Sea, and gave their name to the Crimea, the ancient *Chersonesus Taurica*. But the greater part of them were driven from their territories by the Scythians, when they took refuge in Asia Minor in the seventh century before Christ (Herod. iv:12).

They attacked the northern frontier of the Assyrian empire in concert with the Minni, the Medes, the people of Sepharad (Sapardâ), and other populations whose territories they had already overrun; but in B. C. 677 their leader, Teuspa (Teispes), was defeated by Esarhaddon, and they were driven partly eastward, where they overthrew the old kingdom of Ellipi and built Ecbatana, partly westwards into Asia Minor. Here they sacked Sinôpê and Antandros, which they held for 100 years, and finally invaded Lydia. Gyges or Gugu, the Lydian king, sent an embassy to Nineveh for help; in the end, however, he was slain in battle, and his capital, Sardis, captured by the invading hordes. His successor, Ardys, succeeded in exterminating or driving them out of the country. (A. H. Sayce, Hastings' *Bib. Dict.*)

In the Scriptures, however, the people named Gomer would seem to imply rather an obscure and but vaguely known nation of the barbarous north (Rosenmüller, *Alterth,* i. 1. 235, *sq.*).

Josephus (*Antiq.* i:6, 1) says expressly, that the ancestor of the Galatians, a Celtic colony, was called Gomer (Michael. *Suppl.* p. 335, *sq.*). The Gomeri are generally considered to have been identical with the Cimbri of Roman times, and the Cymry of Wales. Cambria and even Cumberland still preserve the memory of their name.

2. The name of the daughter of Diblaim, a harlot who became the wife or concubine (according to some, in vision only) of the prophet Hosea (Hos. i:3), B. C. about 785.

GOMORRAH (go-mŏr'rah), (Heb. עֲמֹרָה, *am-o-raw'*, a submersion; Gr. Γόμορρα, *gom'or-rhah*, Matt. x:15, etc.), one of 'the cities of the plain' destroyed along with Sodom.

Its position along with that of Sodom and the other three is now pretty generally admitted to have been in the Arabah, or plain, which lies to the north of the Dead Sea. Of the five original cities, all but Zoar (or Bela) were destroyed by fire from heaven (Gen. xix:3-29). The situation has been verified by Tristram, who, on placing himself in the required positions, was able to recognize the view described as it was regarded by Lot on selecting his future residence (Gen. xiii:10), and by Abraham during the destruction of the doomed cities (xix:27). (See SODOM.)

GOMORRHA (go-mŏr'rhâ), the form which appears (Matt. x:15; Mark vi:11; Rom. ix:29; 2 Pet. ii:6) for the foregoing place.

GOODLY, GOODLINESS (Heb. תֹּאַר, *to'ar;* outline, i. e., figure or appearance, beautiful).

Though 'goodly' was at one time used adverbially also, it is employed in A. V. as an adjective only. There it is found with two different meanings (and the modern meaning, *considerable, pretty large,* 'a goodly number,' is not one of them).

Fair to look upon, fine, handsome. In this sense it is applied to *persons,* as Gen. xxxix:6 'Joseph was a goodly *person,* and well favored;' of garments, as Exod. xxxix:28 'goodly bonnets of fine linen;' of trees, as Ps. lxxx:10 'the boughs thereof were like the goodly cedars' (אַרְזֵי־אֵל, lit. as A. V. marg. and R. V. 'cedars of God') ; of cities (Deut. vi:10), mountains (Deut. iii:25), horses (Zech. x:3) ; and not only of majestic things, but of vessels (2 Chron. xxxvi:10, 19), precious stones (Matt. xiii:45; Luke xxi:5), and even 'heritages' (Ps. xvi:6; Jer. iii:19). It is also used of a price (Zech. xi:13) paid for a slave, 'a handsome price!' spoken ironically there. (Hastings' *Bib. Dict.*)

GOODLY TREES (gōōd'lў trēs), (Heb. עֵץ הָדָר, *ates haw-dawr'*, trees of ornament).

The Israelites were directed to take "boughs of goodly trees" (i. e., carry about in festive procession) on the first day of the Feast of Tabernacles (see FESTIVALS), in memory of their having dwelt in booths (Lev. xxiii:40). The expression, "goodly trees," probably included not only the orange and citron, which were placed in gardens for ornament rather than for use, but also myrtles, olive trees, palms, and others which had beauty or pleasant odor" (K. and D., *Com.,* in loco).

GOODMAN (gōōd'măn), (Gr. οἰκοδεσπότης, *oy-kod-es-pot'ace*, Matt. xx:11; xxiv:43; Mark xiv:14; Luke xxii:11), rendered "master of the house" (Matt. x:25; Luke xiii:25; xiv:21); "householder" (Matt. xiii:27; xx:1, etc.) "Goodman" (Prov. vii:19) is the rendering of the Hebrew אִישׁ, *eesh, man.* i. e., husband.

The word is a combination of 'good' and 'man' (not, says Skeat, a corruption of Anglo-Saxon *gumman* as suggested by Aldis Wright) ; and it is probable that the meaning 'master' arose from the meaning 'husband,' in which, it must be remembered, it is one of many similar combinations, as good-father, good-sister, etc.; in fact, all relatives by marriage were once so designated in England, and are still so designated in Scotland, especially when speaking of persons below the rank of what are called the gentry.

GOPHER WOOD (gō'fẽr wōōd), (Heb. גֹּפֶר, *go'-fer*), is mentioned only once in Scripture, as the material of which Noah was directed to build the ark (Gen. vi:14), 'Make thee an ark of gopher wood; rooms shalt thou make in the ark, and shalt pitch it within and without with pitch' (*khemar,* probably 'bitumen').

In endeavoring to ascertain the particular kind of wood which is mentioned in the above passage, we can get assistance only from the name, the country where the wood was supposed to have been procured, or the traditional opinions respecting it. That nothing very satisfactory has been ascertained is evident from the various interpretations that have been given of this word, so that some have preferred, as in our Authorized Version, to retain the original Hebrew. The greatest number of writers have been of opinion that by the gopher wood we are to understand the cypress; and this opinion is supported by such authorities as Fuller in his *Sacred Miscellanies;* Bochart (*Geogr. Sacra*); as well as by Celsius.

GORGIAS (gôr'ji-ăs). A Syrian general under Antiochus IV.

In 166 B. C. he led a detachment of troops from Emmaus, in the Philistine plain, where the main army was encamped, to make a night attack on Judas Maccabæus; but Judas, having learned of the plan, withdrew his forces and led them to a successful attack on Gorgias' own camp. When Gorgias returned, his followers saw their camp in flames and fled (1 Macc. iii:38; iv: 25). A little more than a year later Gorgias was commanding at Jamnia, and he met and defeated Joseph and Azarias, who in the absence of Judas had charge of the troops in Judæa, and were advancing to attack the town (v. 55-62). (Jos. *Antiq.* XII. viii:6.)

In 2 Macc. xii:32-37 this defeat is barely mentioned, but we are told how Judas defeated Gorgias and how the accursed (τὸν κατάρατον) Gorgias himself was nearly taken prisoner by a Jewish horseman named Dositheus. The description of Gorgias in 2 Macc. xii:32 as 'governor of Idumæa' is perhaps an error for 'governor of Jamnia' (So Grotius, and comp. Jos. *Antiq.* XII, vi:8).

GORTYNA (gor-tŷ'nà), (Gr. Γορτῦνα, *gor-tu'na,* 1 Macc. xv:23). The most important city in Crete, after Gnossus, situated about midway between the two ends of the island.

GOSHEN (gō'shen), (Heb. גֹּשֶׁן, *go'shen*).

1. A province or district of Egypt in which Jacob and his family settled through the instrumentality of his son Joseph, and in which they and their descendants remained for a period of 430 years (Gen. xlv:10; xlvi:28; xlvii:27; l:8; Exod. viii:22; ix: 26). The Bible does not present any definite information as to the precise locality of Goshen, and of course later authorities possess only an inferior value. There are, however, incidental expressions, allusions, and implications in the scriptures, which afford aid in determining the spot. That Goshen lay on the eastern side of the Nile may be justifiably inferred from the fact that Jacob is not reported to have crossed that river; nor does it appear that the Israelites did so in their flight out of Egypt. With this inference all the language employed (see the passages as given above), to say the least, agrees, if it does not afford an indirect evidence in its favor. It would appear from Exod. xiii:17, 18, that Goshen bordered on Arabia (see Gen. xlv:10, Sept. Γεσέμ Ἀραβίας, *Goshen of Arabia*) as well as Palestine, and the passage of the Israelites out of Egypt shows that the land was not far removed from the Red Sea. It appears probable that we may fix the locality of Goshen in Lower Egypt, on the east side of the Pelusiac branch of the Nile, in the district around Heroopolis. (Bellermann, *Handb. d. Bibl. Lit.* iv. 191-220; Jablonsky, *Dissert.* viii. *de Terra Gosen.*)

This district was suitable for a nomadic people, who would have been misplaced in the narrow limits of the valley of the Nile. We are not, however, to expect evidences of luxuriant fertility. The country was chosen for its pre-eminent fitness for shepherds. If a nomadic tribe had wide space and good pasture-grounds, they would have 'the best (for themselves) of the land,' and these advantages this district abundantly supplied in ancient times, when the waters of the Nile were more liberally dispensed than at present in the eastern side of the country. Nothing is needed but water to make the desert fertile. 'The water of the Nile soaks through the earth for some distance under the sandy tract (the neighborhood of Heliopolis), and is everywhere found on digging wells eighteen or twenty feet deep. Such wells are very frequent in parts which the inundation does not reach. The water is raised from them by wheels turned by oxen and applied to the irrigation of the fields. Whenever this takes place the desert is turned into a fruitful field. In passing to Heliopolis we saw several such fields in the different stages of being reclaimed from the desert; some just laid out, others already fertile. In returning by another way more eastward, we passed a succession of beautiful plantations wholly dependent on this mode of irrigation' (Robinson's *Palestine,* vol i. p. 36).

2. A district in Southern Palestine (Josh. x:41; xi:16). According to the first passage it was between Gaza and Gibeon, and therefore in the low country; in the second passage the low country is mentioned in addition to Goshen. Exact situation is unknown.

3. A city and the territory around it in the mountains of Judah (Josh. xv:51). Exact site unknown.

GOSPEL (gŏs'pĕl), (Anglo-Sax. *Godspell*—'*God story*', not '*good* story'), the translation from Anglo-Sax. times of εὐαγγέλιον in New Testament. In Homer, in the sing., and in Attic Gr., in the pl., it signified a *reward* or a *thank-offering for good tidings.* In later Greek (Plutarch, in the pl., Lucian, in the sing.) it signified also the *good tidings* itself. In LXX, 2 Sam iv:10, the Attic meaning and the plural occur. (Hastings' *Bib. Dict.*)

The central point of Christian preaching was the joyful intelligence that the Savior had come into the world (Matt. iv:23; Rom. x:15); and the first Christian preachers, who characterized their account of the person and mission of Christ by the term εὐαγγέλιον, *gospel,* were themselves called εὐαγγελισταί, evangelists (Eph. iv:11; Acts xxi:8). The former name was also prefixed to the written accounts of Christ.

Four Gospels. We possess four such accounts; the first by Matthew, announcing the Redeemer as the promised King of the Kingdom of God; the second by Mark, declaring him 'a Prophet mighty in deed and work' (Luke xxiv: 19); the third by Luke, of whom it might be said that he represented Christ in the special character of the Savior of sinners (Luke vii:36-50; xv:18-19, *sq.*); the fourth by John, who represents Christ as the Son of God, in whom deity and humanity became one. The ancient church gave to Matthew the symbol of the lion, to Mark that of man, to Luke that of the ox, and to John that of the eagle; these were the four faces of the cherubim. The cloud in which the Lord revealed himself was borne by the cherubim, and the four Evangelists were also the bearers of that glory of God which appeared in the form of man.

(1) Order and Chronology. Concerning the order which they occupy in the scriptures, the oldest Latin and Gothic Versions, as also the Codex Cantabrigiensis, place Matthew and John first, and after them Mark and Luke, while the other MSS. and old versions follow the order given to them in our Bible. As dogmatical reasons render a different order more natural, there is much in favor of the opinion that their usual position arose from regard to the chronological dates of the respective composition of the four gospels: this is the opinion of Origen, Irenæus, and Eusebius. All ancient testimonies agree that Matthew was the earliest, and John the latest

evangelist. The relation of the gospel of John to the other three gospels, and the relation of the gospels of Matthew, Mark, and Luke to each other, is very remarkable. With the exception of the history of the Baptist, and that of Christ's passion and resurrection, we find in John not only narratives of quite different events, but also different statements even in the above sections, the strongest of which is that relating to the crucifixion of Christ, which—according to the first three gospels—took place on the first day of the Passover, while, to judge from John xiii:1, 29; xviii:28; xix:14, 31, it would appear that it had taken place on the eve of the day on which the passover was to be eaten, but which was either not eaten at all by our Lord, or was anticipated by him by a day. On the other hand, the first three evangelists not only tolerably harmonize in the substance and order of the events they relate, but correspond even sentence by sentence in their separate narratives (comp. *ex. gr.* Mark i: 21-28 with Luke iv:31-37; Matt. viii:31-34; Mark vi:34; v:17; Luke viii:32-37, etc.) The thought that first suggests itself on considering this surprising harmony is, that they all had mutually drawn their information from one another. Thus Grotius, *ex. gr.,* is of opinion that Matthew was the oldest source, and that Mark drew his information both from Matthew and Luke; again, according to Büsching, Luke was the oldest, and Matthew made use of Luke and Mark; while most critics in Germany have adopted the view of Griesbach, that Matthew was the oldest, and was made use of by Luke, and that Mark derived his information both from Matthew and Luke. Following the suggestion of Rore, some of the most modern critics, such as Weisse, Wilke (in his work entitled *Ur-evangelist,* 1838), and Bauer, are, on the other hand, of opinion that Mark was the original evangelist, and that Matthew and Luke derived their information from him. The difference of these opinions leads to the suspicion that none of them are right, more especially when we consider that, notwithstanding the partial harmony of the three evangelists in the choice of their *sentences,* there is still a surprising difference in them as regards the *words* of those sentences; a fact which compelled the critics who suppose that the evangelists made use of each other's writings, to account everywhere for such deviations, and frequently to have recourse to the most trivial and pedantic arguments. To us these differences in word and phrase would appear inconceivable were we disposed to assume that the evangelists had copied from each other.

(2) Substantial Truth Under Circumstantial Variety. As the three evangelists mutually supply and explain each other, they were early joined to each other, by Tatian, about A. D. 170, and by Ammonius, about A. D. 230, and the apparent discrepancies among them early led to attempts to reconcile them. An essay of this kind was written by Augustine in his book *De Consensu Evangelistarum.* Starting from the principle of a *verbal inspiration* in the gospels, every difference in expressions and facts was considered as a proof that the speeches and facts had repeatedly occurred. This opinion is advanced for instance, in Andreas Ossiander's *Harmonia Evangelistarum.* The subject is, however, more freely handled by Calvin, Chemnitz, Kaiser, Gerhard, and others, in their respective works, *De Harmonia Evangelistarum.* Gerhard's book, in three folio volumes, is one of the most comprehensive exegetical works on the four gospels. (See also *Examination of the Testimony of the Evangelists* by Simon Greenleaf, LL. D., late Dane Professor of Law in Harvard University.) Strauss has drawn his principal argument against the historical character of the gospels from these discrepancies; but he is in the first instance wrong in supposing that the Evangelist had the intention of relating the particulars of events scrupulously in a chronological order; nor is he less wrong in seeing in every deviation a contradiction, and in the attempts at reconciliation, productions of mere dogmatic prejudice, while he is himself guilty of prejudice, by the very aversion he shows against every attempt at such reconciliation!

When we consider that one and the same writer, namely, Luke, relates the conversion of Paul (Acts ix:22, 26), with different incidental circumstances, after three various documents, though it would have been very easy for him to have annulled the discrepancies, we cannot help being convinced that the evangelists attached but little weight to minute preciseness in the incidents, since, indeed, the historical truth of a narration consists less in them, in the relation of minute details, than in the correct conception of the *character* and *spirit* of the event. An exposition and refutation of the most recent attacks against the truth of the Evangelical history on account of this discrepancy, may be seen in Tholuck's *Glaubwürdigkeit der Evangelischen Geschichte;* and in his *Review of Strauss's Life of Christ* in *Literarischer Anzeiger,* 1838; also in Ebrard's *Wissenschaftliche Kritik der Evangelischen Geschichte,* 2 vols. 1842. This last work is a compendium of all critical investigations into the history contained in the gospels. (*Literature:* Fisher's *Essays on the Supernatural Origin of Christianity,* N. Y., 1866; N. C. Burt, *Hours Among the Gospels,* Philadel.; Tischendorf, *Wann Wuerden unsere Evangelien verfasst?* Leipz., Eng. trans. by Gage, Boston; Row, *The Historical Character of the Gospels tested by an Examination of their Contents,* Journl. Sacred Lit. 1865-6; Warren, *New Testament with Notes,* Boston; Trench, *Notes on the Parables, Miracles, and Studies in the Gospels;* Lange, *Bibelwerk,* Am. ed.; Nast's *Commentary;* Cowper, *Apocryphal Gospels;* Rushbrooke, *Synopticon,* 1880; A. Wright, *A Synopsis of the Gospels in Greek,* 1896; S. Davidson, *Introduction to the Study of the New Testament,* 2d ed. 1882, 3d ed. revised and improved, 1894; Sanday, '*A Survey of the Synoptic Question,*' arts. in the *Expositor,* 1891, *Inspiration,* Lect. vi. 1893; *Introductions to the Synoptic Gospels in Book by Book;* A. J. Jolley, *The Synoptic Problem for English Readers,* 1893; Westcott, Prolegomena in *Commentary on St. John,* 1881; Sanday, *The Authorship and Historical Character of the Fourth Gospel,* 1872; Watkins, *Modern Criticism considered in its relation to the Fourth Gospel,* 1890.)

GOSPELS, SPURIOUS (gŏs'pĕls, spū'rĭ-ŭs). See APOCRYPHA.

The canon of the New Testament, as we have already seen, having been finally settled before the close of the fourth century, the rejected writings which bore the names of the Apostles and Evangelists soon sunk into oblivion, and few, if any, have descended to our times in their original shape. From the decree of Gelasius and a few other sources we have the names and a few detached notices of a good many of these productions. We shall first speak of those which are still extant.

(1) Joseph the Carpenter. The history of Joseph the carpenter, which has been preserved in the East in an Arabic translation, was first made known in Europe in the commencement of the sixteenth century by Isidore de Isolanis in his *Summa de donis Sti. Josephi.*

(2) The Gospel of the Infancy was first published by Henry Sike, at Utrecht, in 1697, from an Arabic MS. Sike's Latin version was republished by Fabricius, who divided it into chapters. The Arabic was divided into corresponding chapters by Thilo, in 1832.

There are several MSS. of this gospel extant, the oldest of which known is that in the Medicean Library, written in 1299. The narratives which it contains were current in the second century, and the account contained in this gospel respecting Christ's learning the alphabet is mentioned by Irenæus (*Adv. Hæres.* i:20) as a fabrication of the Marcosians. The Gospel of the Infancy is found in the catalogue of Gelasius, and it is especially remarkable from the fact that it was most probably this gospel which was known to Mohammed, who seems to have been unacquainted with any of the canonical scriptures, and who has inserted some of its narrations in the Koran. The original language was probably Syriac. It is sometimes called the Gospel of Peter, or of Thomas.

(3) Gospel of Thomas. The gospel of Thomas the Israelite (Greek), a work which has flowed from the same source with the former, was first published by Cotelerius.

This gospel relates the fable of Christ's learning the *Greek* alphabet, in which it agrees with the account in Irenæus. In other gospels of the Infancy (as in that published by Sike) he is represented as learning the *Hebrew* letters. It has been questioned whether this is the same work which is called the Gospel of Thomas, by Origen, Ambrose, Bede, and others. This gospel probably had its origin among the Gnostics, and found its way from them, through the Manichees, into the church.

(4) The Protevangelion of James has descended to us in the original Greek. Although this work is styled by Postell the *Protevangelium,* there is no MS. authority for this title, nor for the fact of its being ascribed to St. James the Apostle. It only appears that the author's name is James. The narrations of this gospel were known to Tertullian (*Adv. Gnost.,* c. viii.), Origen (*Com. in Matt.* p. 223), Gregory Nyssen (*Orat. in diem Nat. Christ. Opp.* vol. iii. p. 346), Epiphanius (*Hær.* 79. sec. 5), the author of the *Imperfect Work on Matt.,* Chrysost. (*Opp.* tom. vi. p. 24), and many others among the ancients.

(5) The Gospel of the Nativity of Mary, which most probably, in its present form, dates its origin from the sixth century, has been even recommended by the pretended authority of St. Jerome. It is from these Gospels of the Infancy that we have learned the names of the parents of the Blessed Virgin, Joachim (although Bede reads Eli) and Anna. The narratives contained in these gospels were incorporated in the *Golden Legend,* a work of the thirteenth century, which was translated into all the languages of Europe, and frequently printed. There are extant some metrical accounts of the same in German, which were popular in the era of romance. These legends were, however, severely censured by some eminent divines of the Latin church, of whom it will be sufficient to name Alcuin, in his *Homilies,* in the ninth, and Fulbert and Petrus Damianus (bishop of Ostia) in the eleventh century. 'Some,' says the latter, 'boast of being wiser than they should be, when, with superfluous curiosity, they inquire into the names of the parents of the

Blessed Virgin, for the evangelist would surely not have failed to have named them if it were profitable to mankind' (*Sermon on the Nativity*). Eadmer, the monk, in his book on the *Excellence of the Virgin*, writes in a similar strain (cap. ii, Anselm. *Opp*. p. 435, Paris, 1721). Luther also inveighs against the readers of these books (*Homil*. ed. Walch. tom. xi; and *Table Talk*, ch. vii, tom. xxii, p. 396).

There were several editions of Jerome's pretended translation published in the fifteenth century, one of them by Caxton. It is printed by Thilo from a Paris MS. of the fourteenth century, and divided by him into twenty-four chapters, after a MS. of the fifteenth century in the same library. One of the chief objects of the writer of these gospels seems to be to assert the Davidical origin of the Virgin, in opposition to the Manichees.

It has been supposed that the first author of these ancient legends was a Hellenistic Jew, who lived in the second century, but that they were added to and interpolated by Seleucus at the end of the third, who became their reputed author; and that still further additions were made by the Nestorians, or some late Christians in India. Lardner (*Credibility*, vol. viii) so far differs from Mr. Jones as to believe the author not to have been a Jew. The Gospel of the Nativity of Mary was received by many of the ancient heretics, and is mentioned by Epiphanius, St. Augustine, and Gelasius. The Gnostics and Manichees endeavored to found on its authority some of their peculiar opinions (such as that Christ was not the Son of God before his baptism, and that he was not of the tribe of Judah, but of that of Levi).

(6) Gospel of Marcion. Although the gospel of Marcion, or rather that of St. Luke as corrupted by that heretic in the second century, is no longer extant, Professor Hahn has endeavored to restore it from the extracts found in ancient writers, especially Tertullian and Epiphanius. This work has been published by Thilo.

(7) Greek Gospel of St. John. Thilo has also published a collation of a corrupted Greek gospel of St. John, found in the archives of the Knights Templars in Paris. This work was first noticed (in 1828) by the Danish Bishop Muenter, as well as by Abbé Grégoire, ex-bishop of Blois. It is a vellum MS. in large 4to, said by persons skilled in palæography to have been executed in the thirteenth or fourteenth century, and to have been copied from a Mount Athos MS. of the twelfth. The writing is in gold letters. It is divided into nineteen sections, which are called *gospels*, and is on this account supposed to have been designed for liturgical use. These sections, corresponding in most instances with our chapters (of which, however, the twentieth and twenty-first are omitted, are subdivided into verses, the same as those now in use, and said to have been first invented by Robert Stephen (See VERSES). The omissions and interpolations (which latter are in barbarous Greek) represent the heresies and mysteries of the Knights Templars. Notwithstanding all this, Thilo considers it to be modern, and fabricated since the commencement of the eighteenth century.

(8) Gospel of Nicodemus. One of the most curious of the apocryphal gospels is the Gospel of Nicodemus, or Acts of Pilate. It is a kind of theological romance partly founded on the canonical gospels. The first part, to the end of ch. xv., is little more than a paraphrastic account of the trial and death of Christ, embellished with fabulous additions. From that to the end (ch. xxviii) is a detailed account of Christ's descent into hell to liberate the spirits in prison, the history of which is said to have been obtained from Lenthius and Charinus, sons of Simeon, who were two of those 'saints who slept,' but were raised from the dead, and came into the holy city after the resurrection. This part of the history is so far valuable, that it throws some light upon the ancient ideas current among Christians on this subject. It is therefore considered by Birch (*Auctarium*, Proleg. p. vi.) to be as valuable in this respect as the writings of the Fathers.

(9) Lost Gospels. Of the gospels no longer extant, we know little more than that they once existed. We read in Irenæus, Epiphanius, Origen, Eusebius, and other ecclesiastical writers, of the Gospels of Eve or of Perfection, of Barnabas (ancient and modern), of Bartholomew, of Basilides, of Hesychius, of Judas Iscariot, of the Valentinians, of Apollos, of Cerinthus, of the Twelve Apostles, and several others. Some of these were derived from the Gnostics and other heretics; others, as the Gospel of Matthias, are supposed by Mill, Grabe, and most learned men to have been genuine gospels now lost. Those of which we have the fullest details are the *Gospel of the Egyptians* and that of the Nazarenes. This latter is most probably the same with that of the Hebrews, which was used by the Ebionites. It was supposed by St. Jerome to have been a genuine Gospel of St. Matthew, who, he says, wrote it in the Hebrew language and letters. He copied it himself from the original in the library of Cæsarea, translated it into Greek and Latin, and has given many extracts from it. Grabe conceived this gospel to have been composed by Jewish converts soon after our Lord's ascension, before the composition of the canonical Gospel of St. Matthew. Baronius, Grotius, Father Simon, and Du Pin, look upon it as the Gospel of St. Matthew—interpolated, however, by the Nazarenes. Baronius and Grabe think that it was cited by Ignatius, or the author of the Epistles ascribed to him. Others look upon it as a translation altered from the Greek of St. Matthew. Mr. Jones thinks that this gospel was referred to by St. Paul in his Epistle to the Galatians. It is referred to by Hegesippus (Euseb. *Eccl. Hist.* iv: 22), Clemens Alexandrinus (*Strom.* ii, p. 280), Origen (*Comm. on John; Hom.* viii, *in Matt.*), and Eusebius (*Hist. Eccl.* iii:25, 27, 39). Epiphanius (*Hær.* secs. 29, 30) acquaints us that it was held in great repute by the ancient Judaizing Christians, and that it began thus: 'It came to pass in the days of Herod king of Judæa that John came baptizing with the baptism of repentance in the river Jordan,' etc. It consequently wanted the genealogy and the first two chapters.

(10) The Gospel of the Egyptians is cited by Clemens Alexandrinus (*Strom.* iii, pp. 445, 452, 453, 465), Origen (*Hom. in Luc.* p. 1), Ambrose, Jerome (*Præf. to his Comm. on Matt.*), and Epiphanius (*Hæres.* lxii, sec. 2). Grabe, Mill, Du Pin, and Father Simon, who thought highly of this gospel, looked upon it as one of the works referred to by St. Luke in the commencement of his gospel. Mill ascribes its origin to the Essenes, and supposes this and the former gospel to have been composed in or a little before A. D. 58. It is cited by the Pseudo-Clement (*Second Epistle to the Corinthians*, or Chevallier's Translation, 1833), who is generally supposed to have written not before the third century. (See Car. Chr. Schmidt's *Corpus omnium vet. Apocr. extra Biblia*; Kleuker, *De Apoc. Novi Testamenti*;

Hencke, *De Pilati actis probab.*; W. L. Brunn, *De indole, ætate et usu libr. Apocr. vulgo inscripti Evangel. Nicodemi*, Berlin, 1794; Birch's *Auctorium*, Fasc. I, Hafn. 1804. Hone's *Apocryphal New Testament,* London, 1820, which in its external form was designed to be an imitation of the English New Testament, is of no critical use. The *Orthodoxographa* of Grynæus, 7 vols. in 2, fol. Basil, 1569, of which there was formerly a copy in the British Museum, which exists there no longer, but there is a fine copy in Mr. Darling's valuable Clerical Library.)   W. W.

GOSPELS—OLDEST SYRIAC, AND OTHER DOCUMENTS.

When in 1894 the oldest version of the gospels was uncovered amidst the debris of the Greek Convent of Mount Sinai, it was as much the result of faithful research as if it had been found amidst the ruins of buried cities. This discovery was due to the zeal and faithfulness of Mrs. Agnes Smith Lewis, who had conceived the idea that there might be literary treasures here which had not been noticed by Tischendorf and other scholars. She therefore took a long and very tiresome journey accompanied by her sister only, and took up her abode in this old retreat. She went well prepared for serious work, carrying with her a camera and a few necessary books. She could read Syriac and could converse in Greek, and she slowly won the confidence and respect of the monks by her ability to talk with them in their native tongue, and also by the evident sincerity of her character and mission. After a time they gave her access to the library and her long and patient searching was at last rewarded by the discovery of an invaluable palimpsest, which is a manuscript, or rather a parchment, that has been twice written upon, the first writing having been erased with more or less success to make room for the second. Under the later writing of this old parchment Mrs. Lewis found a very old Syrian text of the gospels. She took careful photographs of it and it was afterward found that they represented a text of the gospels not like that of the Peshito Version, but quite similar to what is known as the "Curetonian Fragments."

Soon after this important discovery was made known a new expedition was planned for the study of the manuscripts, and the result is a valuable publication by the Cambridge Press bearing the endorsement of such men as F. Crawford Burkitt, Robert L. Bensly, and J. Rendel Harris.

This old manuscript proved to be the most ancient version of the four gospels, or the larger portion of them, representing a translation from Greek into Syriac which is considerably older than the Peshittâ Syriac, although this had hitherto been considered the oldest and most authoritative for textual purposes of all the versions of the New Testament.

The immense importance of this discovery will be manifest if we consider for a moment the relations of this Sinaitic Syriac text with other versions.

The Syriac Peshittâ had been considered the oldest until Mr. Cureton discovered the most puzzling fragments of another Syriac version in a Nitrian monastery. This Curetonian Syriac version was accepted as an earlier version than the Peshittâ, but no other very early manuscript was discovered which contained the larger part of the gospels until this longer one found by Mrs. Lewis, if we except the famous Sinaitic manuscript of the whole New Testament belonging to the fourth century.

In the meantime, however, the Diatessaron of Tatian, or Tatian's harmony of the Four Gospels in Syriac, was found in Armenian and Arabic versions, and it appeared that in many respects this Diatessaron agreed with the Curetonian rather than with the Peshittâ. In the opinion of the scholars who have devoted the most time to this manuscript the new discovery adds greatly to the value of the Curetonian by attesting its purity and fixing its very early age. The Peshittâ probably goes back to the third century, but Tatian's Diatessaron apparently came into use in the Syriac churches between 170 and 180 A. D. It became so popular that it was read in the Syriac capital and other churches in various portions of the country.

Whether or not the Curetonian was older than the Diatessaron has been a problem which is even yet by no means easy of solution, but the study of the newly discovered manuscript shows it to have a text which is purer than the Curetonian manuscript which is considered older than the Diatessaron; that is, it must go back to about 150 A. D., if not earlier.

Destructive criticism has assailed the age of the manuscripts and has attempted to show that the gospels belong to a much later period than the events which they record, but the weight of scholarship endorses their early production. (See *Historic Origin of the Bible,* by Bissell.) Even Renan admits the force of the arguments along this line. He says: "About the year 100 . . . all the books of the New Testament became fixed very nearly in the form in which we read them." (*Life of Jesus,* 1st page of Int.) Again he says: "It would appear that we are very near the truth in supposing that the Acts were written about the year 80 . . . . Striking indeed is the contrast between this narrative and the Apocalypse written in the year 68, replete with memories of the infamies of Nero." (*The Apostles,* pp. 21-22.)

Each new discovery has tended to corroborate the fact of their early composition. The finding of the text contained in the Diatessaron was a discovery of great value, for it dated back to a period which probably considerably preceded 170 A. D., as its author, who was a Syrian Christian father, died before A. D. 172. But now we have another version going back to about A. D. 150, while back of this again we must place the period during which the sacred books gained their currency and were translated out of the original Greek into the Syriac for church use. This brings us very near to the lifetime of the Apostles, and quite into the generation of men who, like Polycarp, listened to their teachings.

Thus the possibility of error in ascribing these books to their reputed authors is reduced to a minimum.

Besides the discoveries which contain the actual texts of the early manuscripts of the gospels we are now in possession of other parchments which date back to an early period, and which contain quotations from Biblical books which of course must have been in existence for some time before they were quoted.

For instance, we have a complete Greek copy of the "Epistle of Barnabas," which was discovered in 1859 by Tischendorf, and this work goes back nearly, if not quite, to the beginning of the second century. • It quotes Matthew under the formula: "It is written." We have also the "Philosophumena" of Hippolytus, who was martyred in the year 235. This important work gives an account of the heretical sects of the first and second centuries, and is very valuable for the quotations it makes from Valentinus and Basilides, who were heretics in A. D. 125, and from whose writings quotations are given from John's gospel. We have also a valuable work called the "Teaching of the Apostles" which has been recently discovered, and which probably goes back to the early years of the second century, and very likely to the last part of the first century. It gives us that which was probably the first manual which was written for the Christian churches. This work, which has been so remarkably preserved, and at last recovered, casts a clearer light than any other on the origin of the officers in the church, and the early character of its services and teachings. It also quotes considerable portions of the Sermon on the Mount.

But going back to a date earlier than these is "The Epistle of Clement," of *Rome.* This work, which was discovered only a short time ago, was probably written about A. D. 97, and it gives quotations from the Apostle Paul.

Such discoveries are of the utmost importance, and our own generation has been especially rich with them, even the famous Sinaitic manuscript of the whole New Testament, which belongs to the fourth century, having been recovered within the last thirty years.

The researches of our own times have thus thrown a flood of light upon the hitherto dark period which separated the days of the Apostles from the days of Irenæus and Clement of Alexandria. They answer most satisfactorily questions of critical doubt which have been raised by skeptical scholars. They remove many difficulties and carry the gospel of John, as well as other portions of the New Testament, back to the very days of the Apostle John before he died in Ephesus. Every discovery has only confirmed the faith of the church in its accepted scriptures. To doubt that they are the product of the same period to which the events which they record belong, in these days indicates either willful skepticism, or profound ignorance of the subject. (See *Historic Origin of the Bible* by Edwin Cone Bissell; also Ward, in *Hom. Review,* Jan. 1895; Bagster's *Bible of Every Land; Revision of Translations of the Holy Scriptures,* by Henry Burgess; *Scholastic History of Canon,* by John Cosin.)

GO TO (too), (Heb. יָהַב, *yaw-hab',* come on, Gen. xi:3; Gr. ἄγε, *ag' he,* lead, or come on, James iv:13). An interjection of incitement or exhortation, as in Gen. xi:3, 4, 7; or challenging attention, as in Eccl. ii:1; Is. v:5; James iv:13; v:1.

GOURD (gōrd). 1. (Heb. קִיקָיוֹן, *kee-kaw-yone',* nauseous), occurs only in Jonah iv, where it is several times mentioned, as in verses 6, 7, 9, 10.

It is translated *gourd* in our Authorized Version, probably from the κολοκύνθη of the Septuagint, often rendered *cucurbita.* In the margin of the English Bible, *Palm-Christ* is given. In the Vulgate *kikayon* is translated *hedera,* 'ivy.' Neither the gourd nor ivy is considered by modern writers to indicate the plant intended; which is remarkable for having given rise to some fierce controversies in the early ages of the Church. The difficulties here, however, do not appear to be so great as in many other instances. But before considering these, it is desirable to ascertain what are the characteristics of the plant as required by the text. We are told, 'The Lord God prepared a *gourd* (*kikayon*), and made it

to come over Jonah, that it might be a shadow over his head,' etc. (ver. 6). 'But God prepared a worm when the morning rose the next day, and it smote the gourd that it withered' (ver. 7). And in ver. 10 it is said of the gourd that it 'came up in a night, and perished in a night.' Hence it appears that the growth of the *kikayon* was miraculous, but that it was probably a plant of the country, being named specifically; also that it was capable of affording shade, and might be easily destroyed. There does not appear anything in this account to warrant us in considering it to be the ivy, which is a plant of slow growth, cannot support itself, and is, moreover, not likely to be found in the hot and arid country of ancient Nineveh, though we have ourselves found it in more southern latitudes, but only in the temperate climate of the Himalayan Mountains. The ivy was adduced probably only from the resemblance of its Greek name, κισσός, to *kikayon.* That the *kikayon* was thought to be a gourd seems to have arisen from the *kiki* of the Egyptians being the *kherwa* of the Arabs, often incorrectly written *keroa,* that is, without the aspirate, which makes it very similar to *kura,* when written in Roman characters; which last in the East is applied to the gourd or pumpkin (Avicenna, c. 622), and is probably the *Lagenaria vulgaris.* Many modern authors mistake the one for the other. To this plant, no doubt, the following passages refer, 'The Christians and Jews of Mosul (Nineveh) say it was not the *keroa* whose shadow refreshed Jonah, but a sort of gourd, *el-kera,* which has very large leaves, very large fruit, and lasts but about four months' (Niebuhr, *Arabia,* as quoted by Dr. Harris). So Volney: 'Whoever has traveled to Cairo or Rosetta knows that the species of gourd called *kerra* will, in twenty-four hours, send out shoots near four inches long' (*Trav.* i:71).

With regard to the miraculous growth of Jonah's gourd, Dr. Harris states that the passage may mean, 'Son of the night it was, and as a son of the night it died;' and that, therefore, we are not compelled to believe that it grew in a single night, but rather, by a strong Oriental figure, that it was of rapid growth. This, there is no doubt, it is highly susceptible of in warm countries where there is some moisture. It attains a considerable size in one season; and though in Europe it is only known as an herb, in India it frequently may be seen, especially at the margins of fields, the size of a tree. So at Busra, Niebuhr saw an *el-keroa* which had the form and appearance of a tree. The stems are erect, round, and hollow; the leaves broad, palmate, 5 to 8 or 10 lobed, peltate, supported on long foot-stalks. The flowers in terminal panicles; the lower, male; the upper, female. Capsule tricoccous, covered with spines. The seeds are oblong, oval, externally of a grayish color, but mottled with darker-colored spots and stripes. From the erect habit, and the breadth of its foliage, this plant throws an ample shade, especially when young. From the softness and little substance of its stem, it may easily be destroyed by insects, which Rumphius describes as sometimes being the case. It would then necessarily dry up rapidly. As it is well suited to the country, and to the purpose indicated in the text, and as its name *kiki* is so similar to *kikayon,* it is doubtless the plant which the sacred penman had in view.   J. F. R.

Celsius, on the other hand (*Hierob.* ii:273), states that it was the *kharwa',* Ricinus communis, L., the *castor-oil tree.* The grounds for this opinion are philological. Dioscorides (iv, 164) describes the κρότων, *i. e.*, the *castor-oil tree*, under the name of κίκι, and the Talmud calls castor-oil קִיק שֶׁמֶן, *shemen kîk*. The former opinion, however, has the greater weight, that the plant which God provided to overshadow Jonah,

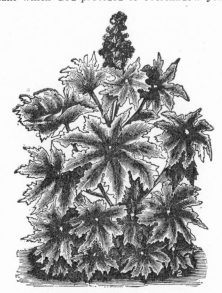

Castor-Oil Plant (*Ricinus Communis*).

was a *vine*, which seems from the context to have trailed over his arbor, and not a small tree like the castor-oil plant, which could not, by any stretch of the imagination, be regarded as a vine. (G. E. Post, Hastings' *Bib. Dict.*)

Colocynthus, or Wild Gourd (*Citrullus Colocynthus*).

2. (Heb. פַּקֻּעָה, *pak-koo-aw'*, bursting or splitting open).

The wild gourds eaten by the sons of the prophets (2 Kings iv:38-41) were doubtless the handsome fruit of the colocynth (*Citrullus colocynthus*), from which the medicine of that name is obtained. The plant bears a fruit resembling an orange in size and shape, but very hard and having its yellow rind marbled with green and white. It resembles the watermelon, and belongs to the same family. For various reasons it is thought that the "knops" used in the ornamental work of Solomon's temple were imitations of the colocynth (1 Kings vi:18). "This plant is very common, and its pulp is a drastic cathartic,

and in large quantities an irritant poison. But the castor-oil plant cannot, with any propriety, be called a *vine*. It is an erect herb, with a brittle, stiff stem and branches, and is quite destitute of tendrils." (G. E. Post, Hastings' *Bib. Dict.*)

GOVERNOR (gŭv'ẽrn-ẽr), the translation of several different Hebrew and Greek words.

1. *Al-loof'* (Heb. אַלּוּף, gentle, familiar), the 'chief' of a tribe or family (Ex. xviii:21; Num. i:16; Gen. xxxiv, 'Dukes' of Edom).

2. *Kho-kake'* (Heb. חֹקֵק, Judg. v:9), and *Mekh-o-kake'* (Heb. מְחֹקֵק, Judg. v:14), denotes a ruler in his capacity of *lawgiver* and dispenser of justice (Gen. xlix:10; Prov. viii:15; comp. Judg. v:14 with Is. x:1).

3. *Mo'shel* (Heb. מֹשֵׁל, having dominion), a ruler having power over property and person (Josh. xii:2; Ps. cv:20; Gen. xxiv:2; xlv:8, 26; 2 Chron. xxiii:20).

4. *Naw-gheed'* (Heb. נָגִיד, a commander), signifies the King as a military and civil chief (2 Sam. v:2; vi:21; 1 Chron. xxix:22; 2 Chron. xxxii:21, xix:11; 1 Kings iv:6, xviii:3, etc.).

5. *Naw-see'* (Heb. נָשִׂא, an exalted one), the *head* or *chief* of a tribe as (Gen. xvii:20; Num. ii:3, etc.).

6. *Peh-khaw'* (Heb. פֶּחָה, a petty chieftain, 1 Kings x:15; 2 Chron. ix:14, etc.).

7. *Paw-keed'* (Heb. פָּקִיד, one who held an office by appointment, Gen. xli:34; Judg. ix:28; 2 Chron. xxiv:11; Neh. xi:14, 22; 2 Kings xxv:19; Jer. lii:25).

8. *Shal-leet'* (Heb. שַׁלִּיט, a man of authority, Gen. xlii:6; Dan. ii:15; v:29).

9. *Sar* (Heb. שַׂר, a chief in any capacity, Gen. xxi:22; 1 Kings xvi:9; xi:24, etc.).

10. *Eth-nar'khace* (Gr. ἐθνάρχης, 2 Cor. xi:32), an officer of high rank.

11. *Hayg-em-ohn'* (Gr. ἡγεμών, Matt. xxvii:2, etc.), a procurator.

12. *Oy-kon-om'os* (οἰκονόμος), Gal. iv:2, a steward.

13. *Ar-khee-tree'klee-nos* (Gr. ἀρχιτρίκλινος, John ii:9), a governor of the feast.

14. *Yoo-thoo'none* (Gr. εὐθύνων, one leading, a guide). "[The ships] are turned about with a very small helm, whithersoever the *governor* listeth" (Jas. iii:4). In this passage the word *governor* means a *pilot*, the man at the helm who *governs* the ship.

GOZAN (gō'zan), (Heb. גּוֹזָן, *go-zawn'*, quarry), a river of Media, to the country watered by which Tiglath-pileser first, and afterwards Shalmaneser, transported the captive Israelites (1 Chron. v:26; 2 Kings xvii:6).

It is now generally admitted that the Gozan is no other than the present Ozan, or, with the prefix, Kizzil-Ozan (Golden River), which is the principal river of that part of Persia that answers to the ancient Media. This river rises eight or nine miles southwest of Sennah, in Kurdistan. It runs along the northwest frontier of Irak, and passes under the Kafulan Koh, or Mountain of Tigris, where it is met by the Karanku. These two rivers combined, force a passage through the great range of Caucasan, and, during their course, form a junction with the Sharood. The collective waters, under the designation of Sifeed Rood or White River, so named from the foam occasioned by the rapidity of its current, flow in a meandering course through Ghilan to the Caspian Sea (Sir John Macdonald Kinneir's *Geograph. Memoir of the Persian Empire*, pp. 121, 122, Morier's *Second Journey*, p. 208; Ker Porter's *Travels*, i. 267).

GRACE (grās), (Heb. חֵן, *khane;* once, in Ezra ix:8, תְּחִנָּה, *tekh-in-naw';* Gr. χάρις, *khar'ece;* once, in Jas. i:11, εὐπρέπεια, *yoo-prep'i-ah*), a word of various meanings.

1. Physical beauty (i. e., *grace* of form and person) (Prov. i:9; iii:22).

2. Favor, goodness of God toward man, or of men toward each other (Gen. vi:8; 2 Sam. x:2; 2 Tim. i:9).

3. God's forgiving mercy, as gratuitous and opposed to merit (Rom. xi:6; Eph. ii:5; Col. i:6, etc.)

4. The gospel generally, as opposed to law (John i:17; Rom. vi:14; 1 Pet. v:12, etc.)

5. Certain gifts of God, freely bestowed; as miracles, prophecy, tongues, etc. (Rom. xv:15; 1 Cor. xv:10; Eph. iii:8, etc.)

6. Christian virtues; e. g., charity, liberality, holiness, etc. (2 Cor. viii:7; 2 Pet. iii:18).

7. The glory to be revealed, or eternal life (1 Pet. i:13).

8. Besides the meaning as given above there are others, among them the following: (1) Spiritual edification of others is called *grace;* it displays the favor of God, and conveys his gracious influences to men (Eph. iv:29). (2) Speech is, with *grace, seasoned with salt,* when it is concerning the favor or truths of God, and tends to promote the edification and holiness of such as hear it (Col. iv:6). (3) To be *called to the grace of Christ* is to have his gospel published to us; and to be invited to the enjoyment of the fullness of God (Gal. i:6).

GRACIOUS (grā'shŭs), (Heb. חֵן *khane*), kindness, favor (Prov. xi:16; Jer. xxii:23). Once used in a passive sense as comely and of fair proportions; attractive; winning.

1. How *gracious shalt thou be, when pains come upon thee!* How *comely, how winning,* when the Chaldeans come and murder, or carry thee away captive (Jer. xxii:23).

2. "A gracious woman retaineth honor" (Prov. xi:16), literally 'a woman of grace;' LXX γυνὴ εὐχάριστος; Vulg. '*mulier gratiosa;*' 'a gracious woman' is Wycliffe's translation, and all the versions agree with him. The meaning is 'a woman of grace of appearance.'

3. 'The words of a wise man's mouth are gracious,' literally 'are grace' (Eccl. x:12), as in A. V. margin; comp. Luke iv:22 below).

4. 'And all bare him witness and wondered at the gracious words which proceeded out of his mouth' (ἐπὶ τοῖς λόγοις τῆς χάριτος, R. V. 'words of grace'). The meaning here, says Plummer, is 'winning words.' He adds, 'The very first meaning of χάρις (χαίρω) is "comeliness," "winsomeness,"' Hom. *Od.* viii:175. (Eccl. x:12; Ps. xliv:3; Sirach xxi:16; xxxvii:21; Col. iv:6); 'and in all these passages it is the winsomeness of *language* that is specially signified.'

Bacon uses the term in the sense of winning. "In beauty that of favor [countenance] is more than that of color, and that of decent [becoming] and *gracious* motion, more than that of favor." Bacon's *Essays.* (Hastings' *Bib. Dict.;* Swinton's *Bib. Word Book.*)

GRAFT, GRAFF (grȧft, grȧf), (Gr. ἐγκεντρίζω, *eng-ken-trid'zo,* to *prick in*).

Grafting is the process in horticulture by which a portion of a plant is made to unite with another plant, whether of the same kind or of another variety or species. The plant upon which the operation is performed is called the stock; the portion inserted or joined with it, the scion or graft. Hence the figure used by the Apostle Paul (Rom. xi:17, 24). It is peculiarly appropriate to the olive tree. God's word is *ingrafted,* as it is put into and planted in our hearts, that it may bring forth the fruit of good works in our life (James i:21).

GRAIN (grān), (Heb. צְרוֹר, *tser-ore',* packed, i. e., kernel; Gr. κόκκος, *kok'kos,* kernel), used (Amos ix:9; Matt. xiii:31, etc.) in the singular and not in a collective sense. (See CORN.)

Figurative. The least *grain* shall not fall to the earth; the weakest believer in God shall not be hurt or ruined amidst sifting and trying providences (Amos ix:9).

GRANARY (grăn'ȧ-rў). See STOREHOUSE.

GRAPE (grāp). See VINE.

GRASS (grȧs), a term used in Scripture in an indefinite sense, referring to *green herbage* in general. All the four Hebrew words, *yerek, hâzîr, dêshe,* and '*esebh,* translated "grass," have this wide meaning.

Grasses are very numerous in Bible lands. In Palestine and Syria they are represented by 90 genera and 243 species. Few of them grow in masses. Turf is almost unknown. With the exception of the cereals, none of the grasses are *cultivated* in these lands. (See CHATZIR; HAY.)

GRASSHOPPER (grȧs'hŏp'-pēr), (Heb. חָגָב, *khaw-gawb'*).

The creature denoted by this Hebrew word so evidently belongs to the class of '*flying* creeping things' (Lev. xi:21, 22) that the *grasshopper,* according to the common acceptation of the word, can scarcely be the proper translation. Other reasons render it most probable that *a species of locust* is intended. (See LOCUST.)　　J. F. D.

GRATE (grāt), (Heb. מִכְבָּר, *mak-bare'*), a *network* of brass at the bottom of the altar of sacrifice (Ex. xxvii:4; xxxv:16; xxxviii:4, 5, 30; xxxix: 39), to allow a draft.

GRAVE (grāv), (properly Heb. קֶבֶר, *keh-ber,* a sepulcher; Gr. μνῆμα, *mnay'mah,* or μνημεῖον, *mnay-mi'on,* literally remembrance, and so tomb). (See BURIAL AND SEPULCHERS.)

GRAVE CLOTHES (grāv klōz), (Gr. κειρία, *ki-ree'ah,* winding sheet). From early times the body was washed (Acts ix:37), then wrapped in a linen cloth (Matt. xxvii:59), or the limbs separately bound round with strips of linen (John xi:44).

GRAVEL (grăv'ĕl), (Heb. חָצָץ, *khaw-tsawts',* Prov. xx:17; Lam. iii:16; מְעָה, *may-aw',* thought by some to mean *interior, belly,* Is. xlviii:19), small stones or pebbles; comminuted rock, coarser than sand.

Wycliffe used 'gravel' as a synonym for 'sand.' Thus Gen. xxii:17 'I shal multiply thi seed as sterris of hevene, and as gravel that is in the brenk of the see'; Matt. vii:26, 'And every man that herith these my wordis, and doth hem nat, is liche to a man fool, that hath bildid his hous on gravel, *or soond*' (Acts xxvii:41) ; 'And whanne we felden into a place of gravel gon al aboute with the see, thei hurtliden the schipp.' In A. V. also there is practically no distinction between 'gravel' and 'sand,' unless it is made by the addition of 'stones.' (Hastings' *Bib. Dict.*)

GRAVEN IMAGE (grā'v'n ĭm'ȧj), (Heb. פֶּסֶל, *peh'sel,* or פָּסִיל, *pes-eel',* a carving), a figure made of wood or stone (Exod. xx:4; Deut. xxvii:15), to represent Jehovah. (See IDOLATRY.)

GRAVING, ENGRAVING (grāv'ĭng, ĕn-grāv'-ĭng). **1.** *Khaw-tsab'* (Heb. חָצַב, to cut, to hew), although once translated "graven" (Job xix:24), is generally used to indicate the rougher work of hewing stone. (See HEWING.)

2. *Khaw-rash'* (Heb. חָרַשׁ, to scratch), used to describe "engraving" (Jer. xvii:1).

3. *Khaw-kak'* (Heb. חָקַק, to hack), a branch of art more nearly coinciding with *our* idea of engraving. The word is used of engraving a plan or map upon a clay brick (Ezek. iv:1, "portrayed"), of inscribing upon a tablet of stone or metal (Job xix: 24), while in Ezek. xxiii:14 it seems to indicate painting.

4. *Peh-sel'* (Heb. פֶּסֶל, graven image) refers to the operation of the carver or sculptor. For

GREAT SEA (grāt sē), (Heb. גָּדוֹל, *gaw-dole'*; יָם, *yawm*, Num. xxxiv:6). The Mediterranean Sea; called also "utmost sea" and "the hinder sea" (Joel ii:20; Zech. xiv:8). (See SEA.)

The Mediterranean was essentially the 'Great Sea' and 'Hinder Sea' to the writers of the Bible; being the western boundary of the Holy Land, beyond which their geographical knowledge did not far extend. Maritime adventure and commerce was not the direction in which Israelitish ambition extended, except perhaps for a short period during the reign of Solomon; and although the lands allotted to the tribes of Judah, Dan, Ephraim, Manasseh, Zebulun, and Asher touched the coast of the Mediterranean at various points, the waters of the Great Sea were seldom traversed by their ships. This was due to several causes; first, the history of the Israelites previous to the

Sketch Map of Greece.

curious details of the fabrication of idols, see Isaiah (xxx:22; xl:19; xliv:12-15).

5. *Paw-thakh'* (Heb. פָּתַח, to open) would appear to describe figures in *relief*, rather than statues, such as the cherubic figures on the temple walls.(2 Chron. iii:7).

6. *Mik-lah'ath* (Heb. מִקְלַעַת, a sculpture) is rendered "carved figures" (1 Kings vi:29), (Mc. & Str. *Bib. Cycl.*)

Figurative. (1) The *engraving* of the names of the twelve tribes in the stones of the high-priest's shoulder and breastplate denoted Christ's perpetual remembrance, esteem, and support of his people, and the impossibility of their separation from him (Exod. xxviii:11, and xxxix: 14. (2) God's *engraving the graving* of the choice stone may denote his conferring on Christ every saving office, his preparing for him a human nature adorned with all gracious excellences (Zech. iii:9). (3) So the saints are *graven* on the palms of God's hands; he perpetually thinks of, cares for, and does them good (Is. xlix:16).

GRAY (grā). See HAIR.

GREASE (grēs), (Ps. cxix:70), elsewhere rendered fat. See FAT.

GREAT OWL (grāt oul). See OWL.

Exodus was essentially of an inland character; secondly, during and after the invasion of Palestine their efforts were too much directed towards dispossessing the inhabitants and retaining their hold on the countries they had conquered, to give them time and opportunity for extending their sway beyond the coast; thirdly, the absence of natural commodious harbors on the Mediterranean seaboard; and lastly, the presence of the Phœnicians on the north, and of the Philistines on the south, along the coast-line. These nations, especially the former, had command of the sea, and rendered adventure in that direction either useless or impracticable to the children of Israel. (Hastings' *Bib. Dict.*)

GREAVES (grēvz), (Heb. מִצְחָה, *mits-khaw'*, 1 Sam. xvii:6), a piece of defensive armor reaching from the knee to the foot.

GRECIA (grē'ci-à), (Heb. יָוָן, *yaw-vawn'*), usually rendered JAVAN (which see); the Latin form (Dan. viii:21; x:20; xi:2) of GREECE (which see).

GREECE (grēes), (Heb. יָוָן, *yaw-vawn'*; Gr. Ἑλλάς, *hel-las'*), properly that country in Europe inhabited by the Greeks (1 Macc. i:1), but in Acts xx:2 apparently designating only that part of it included in the Roman province of MACEDONIA (which see). The relations of the Hebrews with the Greeks were always of a distant kind until the Macedonian conquest of the East; hence in the Old Testament the mention of the Greeks is naturally rare.

(1) Occasional Mention. 'Tubal and Javan,' in connection, are named four times, Dan and Javan once (Ezek. xxvii:19), and Javan, translated by us Greece and Greeks, five times, of which three are in the book of Daniel. Of these passages, that which couples Dan and Javan is generally referred to a different tribe (see JAVAN); in the rest Javan is understood of Greece or its people. The Greek nation had a broad division into two races, Dorians and Ionians; of whom the former seem to have long lain hid in continental parts, or on the western side of the country, and had a temperament and institutions more approaching to the Italic. The Ionians, on the contrary, retained many Asiatic usages and tendencies, witnessing that they had never been so thoroughly cut off as the Dorians from Oriental connection.

(2) Dealings of Greeks with Hebrews. The few dealings of the Greeks with the Hebrews seem to have been rather unfriendly, to judge by the notice in Zech. ix:13. In Joel iii:6, the Tyrians are reproached for selling the children of Judah and Jerusalem to the Grecians; but at what time, and in what circumstances, must depend on the date assigned to the book of Joel (See JOEL). With the Greeks of Cyprus or Chittim, the Hebrews were naturally better acquainted; and this name, it would seem, might easily have extended itself in their tongue to denote the whole Greek nation. Such at least is the most plausible explanation of its use in 1 Macc. i:1, and viii:1.

(3) Religious Ceremonies. Whatever the other varieties of Greek religious ceremonies, no violent or frenzied exhibitions arose out of the national mind; but all such *orgies* (as they were called) were imported from the East, and had much difficulty in establishing themselves on Greek soil. Quite at a late period the managers of orgies were evidently regarded as mere jugglers of not a very reputable kind (see Demosth. *De Coronâ*, sec. 79, p. 313); nor do the Greek States, as such, appear to have patronized them. On the contrary, the solemn religious processions, the sacred games and dances, formed a serious item in the public expenditure; and to be permanently exiled from such spectacles would have been a moral death to the Greeks. Wherever they settled they introduced their native institutions, and reared temples, gymnasia, baths, porticoes, sepulchers, of characteristic simple elegance. The morality and the religion of such a people naturally were alike superficial; nor did the two stand in any close union. Bloody and cruel rites could find no place in their creed, because faith was not earnest enough to endure much self-abandonment. Religion was with them a sentiment and a taste rather than a deep-seated conviction. (See GREECE, RELIGION OF.)

(4) Arts of Peace and War. Among the Greeks the arts of war and peace were carried to greater perfection than among any earlier people. In navigation they were little behind the Tyrians and Carthaginians; in political foresight they equaled them; in military science, both by sea and land, they were decidedly their superiors; while in the power of reconciling subject-foreigners to the conquerors and to their institutions, they perhaps surpassed all nations of the world. Their copious, cultivated, and flexible tongue carried with it no small mental education to all

who learned it thoroughly; and so sagacious were the arrangements of the great Alexander throughout his rapidly acquired Asiatic empire, that in the twenty years of dreadful war between his generals which followed his death, no rising of the natives against Greek influence appears to have been thought of. Without any change of population adequate under other circumstances to effect it, the Greek tongue and Greek feeling spread far and sank deep through the Macedonian dominions. Half of Asia Minor became a new Greece; and the cities of Syria, North Palestine, and Egypt, were deeply imbued with the same influence. Yet the purity of the Hellenic stream deteriorated in various places; and some account of the mixture it underwent will be given in the article HELLENISTS (which see).

(5) Missionary Field. When a beginning had been made of preaching Christianity to the Gentiles, Greece immediately became a principal sphere for missionary exertion. The vernacular tongue of the Hellenistic Christians was understood over so large an extent of country, as almost of itself to point out in what direction they should exert themselves. The Grecian cities, whether in Europe or Asia, were the peculiar field for the Apostle Paul; for whose labors a superintending Providence had long before been providing, in the large number of devout Greeks who attended the Jewish synagogues. Greece Proper was divided by the Romans into two provinces, of which the northern was called Macedonia, and the southern Achaia (as 2 Cor. ix:2, etc.); and we learn incidentally from Acts xviii. that the proconsul of the latter resided at Corinth.

(6) Cities of Note. Of the cities celebrated in Greek history, none are prominent in the early Christian times except Corinth. Laconia, and its chief town Sparta, had ceased to be of any importance: Athens was never eminent as a Christian Church. In Macedonia were the two great cities of Philippi and Thessalonica (formerly called Therme); yet of these the former was rather recent, being founded by Philip the Great; the latter was not distinguished above the other Grecian cities on the same coast. Nicopolis, on the gulf of Ambracia (or Arta), had been built by Augustus, in memory of his victory at Actium, and was, perhaps, the limit of Achaia on the western coast (Tacitus, *Annal.* ii, 53). It had risen into some importance in St. Paul's days, and as many suppose, it is to this Nicopolis that he alludes in his epistle to Titus. (See further under ACHAIA and NICOPOLIS.) F. W. N.

GREEK, an inhabitant of Greece.

GREECE, RELIGION OF.

1. Greek Worship: Local Institutions.

The earlier history of Greek worship discloses a point of view decidedly different from that of the Christian church, especially in its Protestant branches. We have not uncommonly suffered the idea of the religious community to fall into the background, in the emphasis that we have laid on the salvation of the individual. The earlier established worship of Greece was wholly a matter for the local community, or for such social groups as the family, the phratry, or the state. And when an individual sought help for his own needs, he naturally turned to the god of some local sanctuary—the sanctuary where he might be, if away from home; if at home, the sanctuary of the family or state to which he belonged. Thus all worship centered about particular localities at which particular gods were thought to be present. When one race displaced another, it brought the worship of its patron gods to the new locality, but at the same time it adopted from its forerunners there the shrines where they had worshiped. Each local shrine had its own forms of worship, its own priesthood, its own traditions of the gods there honored. Such local cults were the starting-point of Greek religion; they continued through all its growth to be the ground in which it was rooted; and when Christianity was introduced, some of these local gods were transformed into Christian saints, still to be worshiped under a new title.

The different stages in the history of Greek religion may best be understood from this standpoint. It began in the worship by wandering had arisen thus, so that they were exposed to the criticism both of philosophy and of a developed religious sense. Greek religion could not rise out of itself. It brought to the religion which supplanted it a philosophy about God that reached far beyond any Greek god, and a sense of religious need that no Greek worship could satisfy.

The local shrine was very simple in its origin. In the *Odyssey* (IX., 197) we read of Maron, priest of *Apollo*, who frequented Ismaros, dwelling with his wife and child in the wooded grove of the god. Chryses (Iliad, i :36-42) served *Apollo Smintheus,* building temples to please him, and burning fat thighs of bulls and goats on his well-built altar at Chryse. The oldest localities of worship were sacred spots, marked by an altar and often by a grove where a god was wont to

Temple of Poseidon, at Pæstum.

tribes of their patron gods; and as soon as a tribe became attached to any locality, the worship of its gods was also localized there. As intercourse developed between the different Greek tribes or races, these gods became more widely known. It was the province of civilization to unify the culture of all the elements which entered into it. Politically it was attended by the rise of larger political groups, the early kingdoms of Greece; it tended to bring the gods also, as well as men, into one world—*e.g.*, to bring together heaven-gods into a *Zeus,* and herd-gods into an *Apollo,* the son of *Zeus*—so that the way was paved for the creation of the pantheon which appears in the Homeric poems. The life of historic Greece found expression in city-states, and the religious cults of a city shared all its progress and glory. *Athena* became, as we have seen, the exponent of the highest culture of Athens, and to her worship pilgrims gathered from all the Greek world. There remained, however, many heterogeneous elements in the nature of gods that be worshiped. The only priests mentioned in the Homeric poems conducted the worship at such local shrines.

In the historic period sacred precincts varied greatly in size and character. The whole Krissaean plain near Delphi was sacred to *Artemis, Leto,* and *Athena Pronaia,* and its cultivation was entirely forbidden. Or, again, the spot of sacred ground was scarcely more than large enough for a small chapel. Entrance into the sanctuary was forbidden to those who had not complied with the local requirements, and some places were entirely closed. The more sacred spots were carefully marked, and often enclosed by a wall of stone. Rarely the sacred land was kept from cultivation; commonly it was cultivated and the rent derived from its use was devoted to the maintenance of the temple and its worship. Such leases were very carefully drawn up, and describe in detail the manner of cultivating the sacred land, of caring for its forest ground, and of keeping the sacred herds of cattle. From these sources, from tithes and other taxes levied by the state, and from gifts consecrated to the gods, the income of a shrine might become very large.

All that was necessary for worship was an altar. Before the dwelling house and often in each room was a sort of obelisk, on which fruit and incense were offered to the family gods; in the public squares, in the places of assembly, and on the acropolis stood altars to the gods of the city; the altar was the most important feature of the sacred precinct, and in the temple itself there might be a small altar for offerings that were not burned. The altars for offerings of fruits, flowers, cakes, etc., were small pillars, sometimes round, sometimes with paneled sides, and capable of high ornamentation. The altars for burnt offerings were still more various in character. One sacred altar at Olympia was a heap of ashes from former sacrifices, on top of which the thighs of new victims were burned. A pile of stones or a brick structure served as an altar at some sanctuaries, but often the structure was elaborate, with carved marble sides and architectural ornaments at top. The great altar of Zeus at Pergamon was about forty feet high, and its sides were ornamented with a beautiful frieze representing the battle of the gods and giants.

The temple was situated on some spot already made sacred by worship, either on the acropolis of the city, or on some other site a little removed from the bustle of daily life. Only the more important cities had temples, and these varied in size from very small chapels to the great temple of *Artemis* at Ephesus. Approaching a temple from the east, and going up a flight of steps, the worshiper entered a hall enclosed only by pillars in front, from which opened the sanctuary proper, the *naos* (Latin *cella*). Larger temples had also a back room, *opisthodomos*, opening from the opposite end, and they were surrounded by one or two rows of columns. The front room, *Pronaos*, was used for votive offerings, while in the *naos* stood the image of the god. At first this was a rude object of wood or stone, but later the best art of Greece gave expression to the Greek thought of its gods in marble or in bronze. In few instances, as in the Parthenon at Athens, the statue was constructed of gold, with ivory to represent the flesh parts.

It has been said that the temples existed more for the god than for man. Originally, they were built to protect the holy image and the treasure of the divinity; and while this continued to be their main object, they were always centers of worship, for in them was felt the presence of the god. The temple differs from the church in that there is no assembly room for worship. The great altar stood outside, and here the victims were slain and the thigh pieces burned. Meantime, however, the worshiper would visit the god in his temple, and the feast which was so important a part of worship was held about temple and altar in the sacred precinct.

In regard to priests, but one general statement holds true, viz., that they were public officials rather than sacred persons. Each shrine had its own regulations as to age, sex, and other characteristics of its priests. The priesthood might belong to a particular family, or it might be acquired by lot, by election, or even by purchase. Selection did not depend on purity of life or religious devotion, though certain sins might render a man ineligible. The office of course conferred a certain degree of sacredness on those who held it, but the priests were primarily the officials of the city or of the local shrine, whose duty it was to direct the worship there.

(1) Forms of Worship. Religious worship in Greece was connected with certain specified days, as well with definite localities. The Athenians boasted that they were the most religious people of Greece because they observed more sacred days than any other people. Certain days of every month were sacred, the seventh to *Apollo,* the fifth to the *Erinyes,* if Hesiod's statement (*Erg.* 802) be true also of Athens, and the great festivals of the gods increased the number to approximately the number of holy days observed by the Christian church. In speaking of particular gods, we have mentioned some of the elements that entered into the worship of these days. Athletic games were a very ancient method of honoring the Greek gods, and the forms of the athlete were transferred to the types of the gods themselves. Music was a constant element in worship. Processions were accompanied by music, worship at the altar took the form of song and dance, the prayer that accompanied sacrifice was commonly a hymn of praise and supplication; even the contestants for prizes in music were often bound to sing or play in praise of the god. The drama was a development of *Dionysos*-worship, nor were its religious origin and meaning ever forgotten. Processions and splendid pageants were an important element in worship. They were an exhibition of the glory of the god, as well as an indication of man's desire to serve the god. The central point of worship, however, was the festal sacrifice.

It is a fair assumption that the pious Greeks recognized the gods whenever a domestic animal was slain for food. Certainly, when the farmer killed his own stock, he burned certain parts to the gods, just as at the great religious festivals animals were slain as a sacrifice, and parts of them were consumed by fire; and it is probable that the pious Athenian would have felt scruples about the use of flesh bought from a butcher had not similar rites been observed. (Such flesh was therefore "food offered to idols," (1 Cor. viii:4). Thus it is true that the sacrifices were feasts, and also that at every feast the flesh had been in a sense consecrated to the gods. The religious occasions for sacrifice included, first, the recurring feasts of the gods; secondly, the fulfillment of vows made in time of danger, and thirdly, times when the help of the gods was specially needed, as before a battle or a journey. The animals chosen for the sacrifice must be in every way sound. Farther than this, the choice of the animal and its age depended on the particular god to whom it was offered, *Poseidon* preferring bulls, *Apollo* young lambs, *Athena* heifers, and *Dionysos* goats.

In preparation for the sacrifice the offerers clothed themselves in fresh garments and put on wreaths as for a feast, and the animals were adorned with flowers and garlands. The procession brought the animals, together with the implements of sacrifice, to the altar, barleycorns were scattered on the altar and on the animal, and a lock of the animal's hair was thrown into the flame. Meantime all present observed silence, while music of flutes accompanied the prayer-hymns to the gods. The animal's throat was cut —in the case of oxen, after they had been stunned by an axe or club—and the blood was either allowed to flow on the altar, or collected in a vessel and poured on the altar. Parts of the entrails were burned on the altar, with fat to help the flame; and after it was entirely cut up, the thigh bones, and in particular localities other parts also, were burned to the gods. All present joined in pouring libations of wine on the altar to the music of hymns and of flutes. The remainder of the flesh was roasted and eaten by priests and offerers in sacrificial meal, with further libations to the gods. On great festal occasions large numbers of victims were slain, and thus the worship culminated in a general feast to the gods.

Other minor sacrifices may be briefly mentioned. Whenever men were eating or drinking, libations of wine mixed with water were poured out to the gods. In Homer we read many times of libation and prayer, especially before men set out on some important undertaking. Special libations also are offered to the dead and to the gods beneath the earth. In the simple worship of the household, flowers, fruits, and cakes are placed on altars for the gods. In spite of the general preference for animal victims, there were some shrines to which they would be a profanation, and at these men offered fruits or sacred cakes. Again, as the use of incense was introduced into Greece, and men enjoyed its fragrance in their own houses, it came to be used both at the feasts of the gods and in the regular temple ritual.

Sacrifice to Athena at a Wedding.

Votive offerings, *anathemata,* form a class by themselves, to which the name sacrifice is not strictly applicable. They were devoted to a god in memory of some distinct blessing that had been received. The sick man, on regaining health, would dedicate an image of the part that had been diseased—a foot or an ear, it might be—and many of these offerings have been recovered by excavation. After returning from a journey, offerings were brought to the gods. Thus upon the successful return of the ten thousand, a sum of money was dedicated, a part of which Xenophon later used to found a shrine in Elis for the Ephesian Artemis. Trophies won in the games were often devoted to the gods; *e.g.,* the tripods received as prizes in the dramatic contests at Athens were set up as votive offerings. Slaves were dedicated to a Divinity, to be his servants; later, this became a regular method for the manumission of slaves, in which cases they received the protection of the god, though no regular service was

required of them. It was always customary to dedicate to a god small copies of his temple image, or of the animal that was his symbol, however we may interpret this usage. Finally, the *anathemata* included religious taxes, or revenues which were dedicated by states to their patron divinities.

It is not always easy to determine the religious intent of this worship. Votive offerings are the simplest to explain, for clearly they express the worshiper's desire to honor the god by a gift, just as a subject would honor his king by bringing him a gift of value. Libations, cakes, fruits, etc., were also gifts, not valuable in themselves, but nevertheless the correct offering when ancient custom declared that they were what the god wanted then and there of his servant. The last statement applies equally to all sacrifices; viz., they were the right way to express one's desire to honor the god, because they were the way prescribed by tradition. Nevertheless we can analyze somewhat more closely the religious sentiment expressed in the sacrificial feast. The banquet still binds together those who share it, so that it is used by all sorts of associations to arouse a sentiment of union; and among many races this bond has in itself something sacred. Moreover, the banquet has a direct effect on the disposition, which we express by saying that it kindles "good feeling." The physical stimulus of meat and wine is very powerful on human nature. The sacrificial banquet bound Greek worshipers together, and awakened on each occasion a new feeling of union with one another and with the god they worshiped. It was the god who gave the banquet to entertain his worshipers; he was himself present at the sacrifice, so that those who shared it gained a sense of communion with him. The very physical stimulus of the banquet was utilized to produce religious feeling. It was combined, however, with other stimuli, which prevented the sentiment from becoming gross or material.

The splendid procession, solemnly bearing the image or some symbol of the god, the music on some theme consecrated by long use in worship, the artistic surroundings of the perfect temple and statue embodying religious ideals in form for the eye to see them—all these combined to stir the æsthetic nature of this people and to give fitting expression to the feelings which they aroused. The study of Greek worship indicates clearly that religion appealed to the artistic side of the Greek nature, and that it met any reaching toward God by the perfect forms of its manifold art.

(2) Worship in Time of Need. Nowhere is the objective character of Greek religion more apparent than in its attitude toward sin. The normal worship that has just been considered has been called *mechanical* because it proceeds on the supposition that, if man offers food and other objects to the gods, then the gods will grant him prosperity; it may more truly be called *social,* in that theoretically man honors the gods as he would honor a human ruler, and regards divine blessings and the divine rule as he would regard the rule of a righteous king. If, however, the student uses the word social, he should not forget that the social relations between man and the gods in Greece must be conceived as far broader and far more intimate than those between man and any human king.

In such a religion it is impossible that the sense of sin should occupy a fundamental place. It was not indeed difficult or unusual for men to incur the displeasure of the gods. But what impressed the Greek was the judicial side of the matter, the fact that disaster followed wrong-doing as its penalty. No stress was laid on repentance; the Greek gods found no satisfaction in extreme self-humiliation; the wrong was conceived as in the outward act, not so much in the disposition from which the act sprang, so that the only remedy lay in the practice of certain outward rites by which at length divine favor might be regained.

The origin and motives of wrong-doing were carefully analyzed in Greek poetry. It was the presumption of Agamemnon that incurred the wrath of *Artemis,* his ambition which led him to appease her wrath by the sacrifice of his daughter that he might lead the expedition against Troy. The ambition and lust of Aigisthos led him to marry Agamemnon's wife and to slay the king on his return. Pride, becoming presumption, brought severe penalty on such heroes of Greek legend as Marsyas and Niobe. The two great moral thoughts of Greek tragedy are: that sin breeds sin as its penalty and that laws sometimes conflict so that the observance of higher law makes one subject to the penalty of another law, as in the stories of Orestes and Antigone.

Thus the supplicant did not pray for forgiveness of inward guilt, but sought immunity from the penalty of sin in the same spirit that he asked the divine help in evils which he had done nothing to bring on himself. Of the rites by which individuals sought to soothe the anger of the gods and escape disaster we know but little. When in peril at sea or in battle, men sought protecting favor by vows of sacrifices to be paid if they survived. Before a journey they sacrificed to *Hermes,* the traveler's god, and to their own family gods, to prevent disaster. In sickness they vowed sacrifices to some patron deity or hero, or had sacrifices performed in their behalf to some god of healing, such as *Paian* or *Asklepios.*

Sophocles gives us a picture of the rites by which a city sought relief from the plague. An embassy is sent to Delphi to learn what should be done, and meantime processions kindle sacrifices on all the altars of the city. In time of extreme need even human sacrifices were practiced, though rarely, in the hope that the anger of the gods might be satisfied by one victim instead of many. It was the regular practice to offer sacrifices before battle and before an expedition set out from home, and the will of the god was ascertained from the appearance of the victim. The victims for sacrifice in time of calamity or of peril were not always domestic animals, as in the case of ordinary sacrifices, but dogs, asses, wild animals, and birds were also occasionally offered. Nor was the ritual of sacrifice the same; for apparently libations were omitted, the animal was slain in a slightly different manner, and its body was completely burned. At such times men could not seek communion with the gods, but by peculiar sacrifices sought to avert their wrath.

These sacrifices were offered not only to the great gods that ordinarily protected a city, but particularly to the special gods of each locality—the gods closely connected with the soil, and the so-called heroes. The gods of the soil were worshiped mainly by the peasantry, and often represented an older type of deity than the Olympian gods of the ruling classes. To the peculiar rites of such worship men turned in time of need, when the customary forms did not seem efficacious. The *hero* may be defined as a god worshiped only in a limited locality, and with no place among the Olympian gods of mythology. Often

they, too, were old gods whose worship continued only in one place, so that they were reduced to the rank of local spirits. The myths about some of these gods were taken up in the Greek epic, where the term hero (*herōs*) had something of its English meaning; the general use of the term, however, in literature as well as in religion, had to do simply with local divinities. The worship of heroes filled a large place in practical religion. Not that cities celebrated great feasts in their honor, though such was sometimes the case, but for a smaller group of worshipers the hero was more of a real divinity than were the gods themselves. Calamity was attributed to the anger of some hero who had been neglected; and on the other hand, special blessings were expected from their favor. Like the saints of Europe, they stood much nearer the worshiper than the great state gods; they sympathized better with his needs, and so he paid them a truer worship.

Closely related in form to the sacrifices in time of need (*sphagia*), which have just been considered, were the rites of purification for murder and for sacrilege. In the Homeric poems there is no trace of these sacrifices. In later times the murderer must flee out of the land, and, unless the murder were accidental, he could never return. If, however, the act were unintentional, he must first seek purification in a foreign land. The man who conducted the rites slew some animal, preferably a young pig, and applied its blood to the murderer, after which its body was burned and other sacrifices were offered to the gods. Before engaging in certain religious rites, *e.g.,* in the mysteries celebrated at Eleusis, it was also necessary for the individual to purify himself with the blood of a young pig. In contrast with this, the impurity which came from contact with the dead required only ceremonial washings to set it aside.

If it were a city that demanded purification, the rites were far more complex. It was first necessary to remove the cause of impurity, as the graves were all removed from the island of Delos, or again as the Alkmaionidai were all driven from Athens before the city could be purified from their sacrilegious act. In the latter instance, we read, the next step was to bring black and white sheep to the altars where the sacrilegious murders had been committed; there they were released, and wherever one lay down it was sacrificed on the spot to the god in whose precinct it was. A human sacrifice is also mentioned by some writers. By these means the city was purified and the plague was stayed.

Thus by water and by blood, as in special cases by different herbs or by burning sulphur, the taint of evil was removed, and men might again expect favor from the gods.

2. General Character of Greek Religion—Its Place in the History of Religion.

It is the work of religion to explain the world in its spiritual meaning as science explains it from the purely intellectual side.

In the first place, Greek religion furnished a spiritual interpretation of nature. The nature side of most of the greater gods has been so obscured that we cannot be confident what it was; indeed, in many instances, we cannot be quite sure that they ever did represent powers of nature. We do know, however, that the Greek peopled all nature with spiritual beings; the hills and the woods, the rivers, the sea, the winds he regarded as the expression, in each instance, of a life like his own, only superior. Thus he felt a kinship between all that was useful, beautiful, wonderful, terrible, in nature and his own spirit. The world was made intelligible and human by religion; to use the happy phrase of a recent writer, religion made man at home in the world. In such a world not only could his mind work freely and use the objects of nature with confidence, but the spiritual side of his nature could also expand. For the Greek gods were not merely personified powers of nature, but full and complete persons, with the emotions and passions of man, so that a broad spiritual relation connected them with man. Man felt himself also to be a part of nature, and the deification of his own powers—his love in *Aphrodite,* his intellect in *Athena,* his warlike impetuosity in *Ares*—contributed farther to "make him at home in the world."

Secondly, Greek religion met man's needs directly by creating beings which watched over particular phases of his life and activity. *Sosipolis, Orthopolis, Alalkomeneis* were "city-protecting divinities;" *Auxesia, Phytos, Phorbas,* gods of growth, as *Erichthonios,* "earth-breaker," was a god of plowing; *Mylas, Himalis, Alphito* were named from the grinding of the wheat, *Iatros* and

Ruins of the Temple of Victory, Athens.

Paian from their aid in healing; *Taraxippos* kept the charioteer's horses from fright, and *Telesidromos* brought them speedily to the goal of the race. Such gods find no distinct place in the Greek pantheon, although as *Kourotrophos,* "child-nurturer," became one phase of *Demeter's* being, so many of these special gods were in a manner taken up into the great gods of Greece. And these gods, like the divinities of nature, furnished an environment for the development of man's spiritual nature.

Thirdly, the social order was reflected in the world of the gods. All the elements of civilization and of culture were taken up into the Greek gods, so that they became the embodiment of all that was truly Greek, the concrete expression of the excellencies, and the faults also, of Greek life. The gods were so closely connected with the state that patriotism received the sanction of religion; art and literature became all but religious modes of expression; and at length philosophy made the daring attempt to re-create the gods—an attempt that was logical enough, for the gods were what man had made them, but yet it was necessarily all-destructive. The result of the intimate relation between Greek culture and the Greek gods was a

peculiar sympathy between god and worshiper. Greek religion not only brought order into the world, but this order was along the lines of everyday Greek life, and it responded to every act of the individual, intellectual, æsthetic, or distinctly religious. As the natural world developed the body and the senses, so the divine world was a home for man's spirit.

With all its beauty and all its harmony with Greek culture, Greek religion had many weaknesses. In fact, its chief weakness lay along the very line of its strength. The gods were so truly Greek that they copied the frailties of the Greek nature all too well; these ideals of generous, beautiful life lacked the moral fibre of a sterner race; moreover, Greek religion was rooted in the past, so that popular worship, holding to traditional rites, could not rise to the idea of the gods which it had itself suggested. At length it could no longer satisfy religious thought and the needs of the religious life, so that the time was fully ripe for the introduction of Christianity.

Greek religion fulfilled its mission and in large measure disappeared. Estimated historically: (1) It prepared the way for the introduction of Christianity; (2) its sacred places and sacred rites exercised a direct influence on Christianity; and (3) it offered a permanent contribution to the development of religion.

(1) When Christian missionaries came preaching that the world was lost in wickedness, and that men needed salvation (*sōteria*) both for this life and for the life to come, it was a familiar message to their Greek hearers. Earnest minds in Greece had been seeking just this *sōteria* for centuries. A sense of spiritual need had been developed which neither Greek religion nor Greek art nor Greek philosophy could entirely satisfy; and what the Greeks had ignorantly sought, that Christianity declared unto them. A conception of God had been wrought out that was infinitely beyond any Greek god; poets and philosophers entertained a firmly-rooted belief in the righteous government of the universe and in a moral law at its foundation; Greek worship taught men to look to the gods for communion and sympathy only to disappoint them, for their gods were not equal to what men sought in them. These needs and these ideals were met by Christianity, and the new religion found a rich soil in the remains of an earlier growth.

(2) Although Greek religion disappeared, many features of it remained and were taken up into Christianity. Many local shrines were consecrated to the use of Christianity. The very Parthenon became at length a Christian church. Heroes and gods of local worship in many instances continued to be, and still are, worshiped as Christian saints. Some of the old feasts and processions, especially the processions by which help was sought in time of need, became consecrated to Christian use. The old mystery rites were consistently fought by Christian leaders, but we can see that before they entirely disappeared the Christian sacraments of baptism and the Lord's Supper had come to be celebrated somewhat as the mysteries were celebrated, simply be-

cause the mysteries had done so much to define the ideas of solemn ritual for the Greek mind. Thus there were many threads of connection between the old worship and the new.

(3) Certain phases of religion were developed in Greece more perfectly than they had been developed before, and the modern world still has something to learn from Greece along this line. Greece developed the human side of religion to a high degree. Human experiences were reflected in the Divine world so that men might feel a peculiar sympathy with their gods. The gods were in closest touch with human life in all its phases. Their life was in the life of men; the work of the farmer and the smith, the experiences of the traveler by land or sea, the daily life of the market, the activity of the state—all this was the sphere of Greek religion. It made all of life brighter and better by lending to it a spiritual side. A. F.

GREEN (grēn). See COLORS.

GREETING (grēt'ĭng). See SALUTATION.

GREYHOUND (grā'hound'), a very doubtful rendering of Heb. זַרְזִיר מָתְנַיִם, zar-zeer' mawth-na'yeem, slender in the loins (Prov. xxx:31).

That a "greyhound" does not answer to the meaning of the Hebrew is generally agreed. The most probable rendering yet suggested is that of a "wrestler" girded for the fight; others explain it of the war horse, which is so poetically described in the book of Job (xxxix:19-25).

GRIEF (grēf), (Heb. חֳלִי, khōl-ee'), disease, sickness, anxiety. Used in a bodily as well as a mental sense to indicate pain. The Hebrew word rendered grief in Is. liii:3, 4, 10, is elsewhere translated sickness (Deut. vii:15: xxviii:59, 61; 2 Kings i:2). (See MOURNING; SORROW, etc.)

GRIEVANCE, GRIEVOUSLY (grēv'ans, grēv'ŭs-lў), (Heb. עָמָל, aw-mawl', wearing effort, worry, Hab. i:3), human misery either of mind or body.

GRINDERS (grīnd'ērs), in Eccl. xii:3, represent the double teeth used in mastication.

GRINDING (grīnd'ĭng). See MILL.

Figurative. (1) The millstones were hard, the nethermost especially, which was fixed; and so the heart of Leviathan is likened to a piece of it, to represent his undaunted courage and obstinacy (Job xli:24). (2) The ceasing of the *sound of the millstones* implied the turning of the place into a desolation (Jer. xxv:10; Rev. xviii:22). (3) Christ's falling on men, and *grinding them to powder,* denotes his rendering them utterly miserable for their contempt of him; thus he did *grind* the Jewish nation, when their city and temple were utterly ruined, and multitudes slain and enslaved in the most wretched manner (Matt. xxi:44). (4) To *grind the face of the poor* is cruelly to oppress and afflict them (Is. iii:15). (5) Let *my wife grind to another; let her become a slave to work at the mill; or let her be defiled by another* (Job xxxi:10).

GRISLED or GRIZZLED (grĭz''ld or grĭz'z'ld), (Heb. בָּרֹד, baw-rode', spotted), partly colored or variegated, as goats (Gen. xxxi:10, 12), or horses (Zech. vi:3, 6).

GROVE (grōv), (Heb. אֲשֵׁרָה, ash-ay-raw', fortunate).

1. It is generally admitted that this word cannot mean either a green tree or a *grove,* for the sim-

ple reason that the word *to make* (1 Kings xiv:15; 2 Kings xvii:16, etc.), *to set up* (2 Kings xvii:10), *to stand up* (2 Chron. xxxiii:19), and *to build* (1 Kings xiv:23), used to denote the erection of an Asherah, are not one of them suitable to a tree or grove. On the other hand the Asherah is spoken of as being set up under, or by the side of, the green tree. Asherah is, in all probability, a name for ASHTORETH (which see), and the idol (a wooden column) was by the side of the altars of Baal. This Asherah was often set up in a grove, because thus would be given that seclusion necessary to the cruel and indecent rites which marked, among Oriental nations, the worship of false divinities.

2. *Ay'shel* (Heb. אֵשֶׁל, rendered "grove," Gen. xxi:33), really means the *tamarisk* tree, which with its long life, hard wood, and evergreen leaves, was a type of the ever-enduring grace of the faithful covenant-keeping God. A celebrated oak stood by the sanctuary at Shechem (Josh. xxiv:26; Judg. ix:6).

GRUDGE (grŭj), (Heb. לִין, leen), primitive root, to stay permanently; hence, in a bad sense, to be obstinate; not as in our sense, to covet or begrudge (Ps. lix:15). The Revised Version translates it, "tarry all night."

The modern meaning of the word is found twice in A. V., in the phrase 'bear a grudge against,' and in the adverb 'grudgingly;' Lev. xix:18 'Thou shalt not avenge, nor bear any grudge against the children of thy people;' 2 Cor. ix:7 'Every man according as he purposeth in his heart, *so let him give;* not grudgingly, or of necessity: for God loveth a cheerful giver' (ἐκ λύπης, literally 'out of sorrow,' as R. V. margin).

GUARD (gärd), (Heb. טַבָּח, tab-bawkh').

1. The words so translated commonly have reference to the duties of a king's body-guard. *Tab-bawkh'* originally meant "cook;" but as this officer usually did the butchering it acquired the meaning of 'executioner' and is used of the body-guard of the kings of Egypt and Babylon (Gen. xxxvii:36; 2 Kings xxv:8; Jer. xxxix:9; xl:1; Dan. ii:14).

2. *Rats* (רָץ, a runner), also means body-guard (2 Sam. xv:1; 1 Kings i:5; 1 Sam. xxii:17; 2 Kings x:25; xi:6; 2 Chron. xii:10).

3. *Mish-meh'reth,* מִשְׁמֶרֶת, meant to 'watch,' or a 'watcher' (Neh. iv:9, 22; vii:3; xii:9; Job vii:12).

GUARDIAN ANGELS (gärd'ĭ-an ān'jĕlz). See ANGEL.

GUDGODAH (gŭd'go-dah or gud-gō'dah), (Heb. גֻּדְגֹּדָה, gud-go'daw, cutting, cleft), the fortieth station of the Israelites, between Mt. Hor and Jotbath (Deut. x:7). The name appears to be preserved in the present wady *Ghudhagidh.* (See HOR-HAGIDGAD.)

GUEST (gĕst). See HOSPITALITY.

GUEST CHAMBER (gĕst chām'bēr), (Gr. κατάλυμα, kat-al'oo-mah, to break up, i. e., a journey), any room for the entertainment of guests (Mark xiv:14; Luke xxii:11), rendered *Inn* in Luke ii:7. (See HOUSE.)

GUILT (gĭlt). See SIN.

GUILTY (gĭlt'ў), **GUILTY OF BLOOD** (Num. xxxv:27, 31); **GUILTY OF DEATH** (Matt. xxvi:66; Mark xiv:64). This phrase in the last two passages means "deserving of death;" in the former it means simply "guilty of blood-shedding."

GULF (gŭlf), (Gr. χάσμα, *khas'mah*, chasm), figuratively an impassable space, such as is represented to exist between the abode of Abraham and the lost rich man (Luke xvi:26).

The Rabbinical conception of the separation between the two parts of Hades was a thin wall, a mere hand or finger-breadth (Weber, *Lehre des Talmud*, 326 f.). (Hastings' *Bib. Dict.*)

GUNI (gū'nī), (Heb. גּוּנִי, *goo-nee'*, colored, dyed).

1. A descendant of Gad, and father of Abdiel (1 Chron. v:15). (B. C. between 109 and 782.)

2. Son of Naphtali, founder of the family of Gunites (Gen. xlvi:24; 1 Chron. vii:13). (B. C. before 1856.)

GUNITES (gū'nītes), (Heb. הַגּוּנִי, *hag-goo-nee'*), a general name of the descendants of GUNI (which see), of the tribe of Naphtali (Num. xxvi:48).

GUR (gûr), (Heb. גּוּר, *goor*, a whelp as abiding in the lair), an ascent at which Ahaziah was killed while flying from Jehu (2 Kings ix:27), B. C. 883. It was said to be at Ibleam, between Jezreel and Beth-haggan, but has not been identified.

GURBAAL (gûr'bā'al), (Heb. גּוּר־בַּעַל, *goor-bah'al*), a district inhabited by Arabians (2 Chron. xxvi:7). It seems to have been situated between Palestine and the Arabian peninsula.

GUTTER (gŭt'tẽr), (Heb. צִנּוֹר, *tsin-noor'*).

1. A dam or trough for watering flocks or herds (Gen. xxx:38, 41), but the "gutter" through which one might enter the city of Jerusalem was perhaps some privy entrance, by which the filth of the city ran out (2 Sam. v:6-8), or probably a water course.

2. *Rah'hat* (Heb. רַהַט, drinking troughs, Exod. ii:16), into which Jacob placed peeled rods when the sheep came to drink (Gen. xxx:38, 40).

In 2 Sam. v:6-8 we have in the Authorized Version as follows: "And the king and his men went to Jerusalem unto the Jebusites, the inhabitants of the land: which spake unto David, saying, Except thou take away the blind and the lame, thou shalt not come in hither: thinking, David cannot come in hither. Nevertheless David took the stronghold of Zion; the same is the city of David. And David said on that day, Whosoever getteth up to the *gutter*, and smiteth the Jebusites, and the lame, and the blind, that are hated of David's soul, he shall be chief and captain." This has been considered by all commentators for many years as very obscure, and while we will not attempt a full discussion of the subject, we may perhaps understand it better by observing the following points: (1) The two clauses "except thou take away the lame and the blind," and "thou shalt not come in hither" are improperly transposed, and the transposition renders the next clause meaningless. (2) Instead of "except thou take away the lame and the blind," read, "the lame and the blind shall turn thee away." (3) In verse 8 there is also a transposition of the two clauses, "whosoever getteth up to the gutter, and smiteth the Jebusites." (4) Instead of "the Jebusites," with definite article "the" it should be rendered "a Jebusite." (5)

The word translated *gutter* would be here very properly rendered *watercourse*. It comes from a verb expressing the sense of rushing water, and is found only in one other place in the Bible (Ps. xlii:8), and is there translated "waterspouts." The following we believe to be a fair and correct rendering of the same by De Wette:

"And the king and his men went to Jerusalem, to the Jebusite inhabiting the land. And he spoke to David, saying: Thou shalt not come in hither; but the blind and the lame will turn thee away, saying, David shall not come in hither. And David took the stronghold of Zion; that is, the city of David. And David said on that day, Any one that smites a Jebusite and gets to the water course, and the lame and the blind hated of David's soul, he shall be chief and captain." The Jebusites had long held this stronghold and were so confident that no one could come in thither that they contemptuously shouted, "The lame men and the blind men can easily keep the place." David, however, with a keen, strategic eye saw if his men only got to the "gutter" or waterway and shut off the water supply the Jebusite would soon be compelled to surrender. His men soon took the gutter, or waterway, and the impregnable fortress was surrendered and became the stronghold of Zion. And by being the first to climb up to the waterway, Joab became the commander in chief or captain of David's army, according to David's promise.

GYMNASIUM (jim-nā'zi-ŭm), (Gr. γυμνάσιον, in A. V. place of exercise).

A public place in Jerusalem for athletic exercise and exhibitions, below the western cloister of the temple (Josephus, *Bell. Jud.* iv:9, 12; vi:3, 2; 6, 2), below the palace of the Asmonæans (*Antiq.* xx:8, 11; *Bell. Jud.* ii:16, 3), below the citadel or acropolis (2 Macc. iv:12, 27; not the Syrian fortress called the Acra, which was erected later, 1 Macc. i:33). It was situated near the council house, by the first or innermost wall, and at the end of the bridge which led from the temple across the Tyropœon valley (*Bell. Jud.* v:4, 2; cp. vi:6, 2). It was erected by Hellenizing Jews, under the leadership of Jason, by permission of Antiochus Epiphanes (1 Macc. i:10, 14; 2 Macc. iv:7 *sq.*). The essential features of a gymnasium were:

(a) An open court for boxing, wrestling, pitching quoits and throwing the javelin (2 Macc. iv: 14, palæstra, discus). (b) A stadium or course for the foot race. (c) A colonnade for a place of recreation and for athletic exercises in winter. (*Antiq.* and *Bell. Jud., passim:* its Greek name was *xystos*). (d) A bathroom.

The gymnasium at Jerusalem was condemned by strict Jews because it introduced heathen customs; led Jewish youth to wear the hat of Hermes, to exercise stark naked in public, and to be ashamed of the mark of their religion; and infected even the priests and caused them to neglect their official duties (1 Macc. i:14, 15; 2 Macc. iv:13-17). It existed until the overthrow of the city by Titus; and was not only resorted to for athletic sports, but was also occasionally used for popular assemblies (Josephus, *Bell. Jud.* ii: 16, 3), (Davis, *Bib. Dict.*)

H

HA (hà). The Heb. interjection הֶאָח, *heh-awkh'*, is once translated 'ha, ha,' Job xxxix:25 'He saith among the trumpets, Ha, ha,' referring to the neighing of the war horse.

The revisers have changed this into 'Aha!' and have been taken to task for giving the horse a human cry. The older versions were still more 'human,' as Wycliffe (1382) 'Fy!' or (1388) 'Joie!' Coverdale 'tush,' Douay, 'Vah.' 'Ha, ha' comes from the Geneva Bible (Hastings' *Bib. Dict.*)

HAAHASHTARI (hā'a-hăsh'ta-rī).

(Heb. הָאֲחַשְׁתָּרִי, *haw-akh-ash-taw-ree'*, perhaps courier, messenger or a mule driver), a man or family descended from Ashur, by his second wife Naarah (1 Chron. iv:6), B. C. after 1618.

HABAIAH (ha-bā'yah), (Heb. חֲבַיָּה, *khab-ah-yaw'*, in Neh. חֲבָיָה, *khab-aw-yaw'*, [but MSS. and editions vary in both places] whom Jehovah protects), the descendants of Habaiah returned among the sons of the priests from Babylon with Zerubbabel, but because their genealogy was imperfect they were not allowed to serve (Ezra ii:61; Neh. vii:63), B. C. about 536.

HABAKKUK (hab'ak-kŭk or ha-băk'kuk), (Heb. חֲבַקּוּק, *khab-ak-kook'*, embrace, or perhaps the name of a garden plant).

1. The Prophet. One of the most distinguished Jewish prophets, the eighth in order of the minor class, who flourished about 610 B. C., the name denoting, as observed by Jerome, as well a 'favorite' as a 'struggler.' Of this prophet's birthplace, parentage and life we have only apocryphal and conflicting accounts. The Pseudo-Epiphanius (*De Vitis Prophet.* Opp.. tom. ii:18, p. 247) states that he was of the tribe of Simeon, and born in a place called Βηθζοκήρ, *Baythzokār;* that he fled to Ostrarine when Nebuchadnezzar attacked Jerusalem, but afterwards returned home and died two years before the return of his countrymen. But rabbinical writers asserts that he was of the tribe of Levi, and name different birthplaces (Huetius, *Dem. Evang.* Prop. iv. p. 508). Eusebius notices that in his time the tomb of Habakkuk was shown in the town of Ceila, in Palestine; and this is repeated also by Nicephorus (*Hist. Eccles.* xii:48), and Sozomen (vii:29); still there are other writers who name different places where, according to common opinion, he had been buried (Carpzov, *Introd. ad libros canonicos V. T.,* p. 402).

2. Book of Habakkuk. A full and trustworthy account of the life of Habakkuk would explain his imagery, and many of the events to which he alludes; but since we have no information on which we can depend, nothing remains but to determine from the book itself its historical basis and its age.

(1) **Contents.** Now, we find that in chapter i the prophet sets forth a vision, in which he discerned the injustice, violence and oppression committed in his country by the rapacious and terrible Chaldæans, whose oppressions he announces as a Divine retribution for sins committed; consequently he wrote in the Chaldæan period, shortly before the invasion of Nebuchadnezzar which rendered Jehoiakim tributary to the king of Babylon (2 Kings xxiv:1). (1) When he wrote the first chapter of his prophecies, the Chaldæans could not yet have invaded Palestine, otherwise he would not have introduced Jehovah, saying (i:5), 'I *will work* a work in your days, which ye will not believe, though it be told you' (verse 6); 'for I raise up the Chaldæans, that bitter and hasty nation, which *shall march* through the breadth of the land to possess the dwelling-places that are not theirs.' From verse 12 it is also evident that the ruin of the Jews had not then been effected; it says 'the Lord ordained them for judgment, established them for correction.' (2) Agreeably to the general style of the prophets, who to lamentations and announcements of Divine punishment add consolations and cheering hopes for the future, Habakkuk then proceeds in the second chapter to foretell the future humiliation of the conquerors, who plundered so many nations. He also there promulgates a vision of events shortly to be expected (verse 3); 'the vision is yet for an appointed time, but at the end *it shall speak,* and not lie; though it tarry, wait for it, because it *will surely come;* it will not tarry.' (3) This is succeeded in the third chapter by an ode, in which the prophet celebrates the deliverances wrought by the Almighty for his people in times past, and prays for a similar interference now to mitigate the coming distresses of the nation, which he goes on to describe, representing the land as already waste and desolate, and yet giving encouragement to hope for a return of better times. (4) Some interpreters are of opinion that chapter ii was written in the reign of Jehoiachin, the son of Jehoiakim (2 Kings xxiv:6), after Jerusalem had been besieged and conquered by Nebuchadnezzar, the king made a prisoner, and, with many thousands of his subjects, carried away to Babylon, none remaining in Jerusalem, save the poorest class of the people (2 Kings xxiv:14). But of all this nothing is said in the book of Habakkuk, nor even so much as hinted at; and what is stated of the violence and injustice of the Chaldæans does not imply that the Jews had already experienced it. The prophet distinctly mentions that he sets forth what he had discerned in a vision, and he, therefore, speaks of events to be expected and coming. It is also a supposition equally gratuitous, according to which some interpreters refer chapter iii to the period of the last siege of Jerusalem, when Zedekiah was taken, his son slain, his eyes put out, the walls of the city broken down and the temple burned (2 Kings xxv:1-10). There is not the slightest allusion to any of these incidents in the third chapter of Habakkuk, and from the sixteenth verse it appears that the destroyer is only coming, and that the prophet expresses fears, not of the entire destruction of the city, much less of the downfall of the state, but only of the desolation of the country. (5) It thus appears beyond dispute that Habakkuk prophesied in the beginning of the reign of Jehoiakim, about the year stated above. Carpzov (*Introductio ad libr. canon. V. T.,* pp. 79, 410) and Jahn (*Introd. in libros sacros V. T.,* ii sec. 120) refer our prophet to the reign of Manasseh, thus placing him thirty odd years earlier; but at that time the Chaldæans had not as yet given just ground for apprehension, and it would have

been injudicious in Habakkuk prematurely to fill the minds of the people with fear of them. Some additional support to our statement of the age of this book is derived from the tradition, reported in the apocryphal appendix to Daniel and by the Pseudo-Epiphanius, that Habakkuk lived to see the Babylonian exile; for if he prophesied under Manasseh he could not have reached the exile at an age under ninety years; but if he held forth early in the reign of Jehoiakim he would have been only fifty odd years old at the time of the destruction of Jerusalem and of the exile. He was, then, a contemporary of Jeremiah, but much younger, as the latter made his first appearance in public as early as B. C. 629, in the thirteenth year of Josiah. Ranitz (*Introductio in Hab. Vatic*, pp. 24, 59), Stirkel (*Prolog. ad interpr. tertii cap. Hab.* pp. 22, 27), and De Wette (*Lehrbuch der Historisch-kritischen Einleit.* Berlin, 1840, p. 338) justly place the age of Habakkuk before the invasion of Judea by the Chaldæans.

(2) Literary Style. His representations are not inferior to those of the most flourishing age of prophecy, in independent strength, in perfect beauty of arrangement of the parts, and in skillfully rounded discourse, and they combine the greatest force and fullness with the loftiest flights of thought. The style is distinguished by carefully selected and unusual words and turns of expression, which are in some measure quite peculiar to himself. (Keil, *Introd. to O. T.*, vol. i, p. 412.)

Delitzsch Com. on Hab., p. xiii: "Nowhere else do we find the form of *alternate discourse* (between God and the prophet) carried out so far, or *prophecy* so intimately connected with *lyric poetry* (to the extent which we see in the structure of the strophes in chapter ii, and the musical arrangement in chapter iii). Like Isaiah, he is comparatively far less dependent than other prophets on his predecessors, in respect of both form and matter. Everything still mirrors the most flourishing age of the prophetic order—that age in which prophetic poetry took the place of the holy lyric poetry that had hitherto been the mode of utterance for the religious life of the church, and having been laid hold of mightily by God, came with her trumpet voice to awaken anew the consciousness of God in the church now spiritually dead."

(3) Teaching. The central and distinctive teaching of the book lies in the declaration of Hab. ii:4, and, as indicated above, the true sense of this is, that while the wild excesses of the tyrant carry in them the germ of certain ruin, the 'faithfulness' of the righteous (not his *faith*) will be to him a principle of life. It is evident that this declaration is no *solution* of the moral anomaly which the prophet discerns. The Chaldæan might indeed, in virtue of his very nature, be doomed ultimately to perish, but his empire survived for seventy years; and meanwhile Habakkuk's compatriots, so far from abiding in peace and security, experienced the indescribable hardships of siege and exile. But 'live' is here used in the full and pregnant sense which it sometimes has in the Old Testament (*e. g.* Ezek. xviii), of living in the light and consciousness of the Divine favor, and what Habakkuk thus promises is not *mere* material prosperity, but the moral security—of course, often not unaccompanied by material benefits—which righteousness brings with it even in the midst of external calamities (cf. Is. xxxiii:14-16), and the sense of Divine approval which even then does not desert it. It is enough for the prophet if he can mitigate the difficulty which pressed upon him, as it pressed

no doubt upon many of his contemporaries, by recalling to them these two truths of God's providence, the doom which, at least ultimately, overtakes the tyrant, and the moral security enjoyed by the righteous. (S. R. Driver, Hastings' *Bib. Dict.*)

3. Literature. A. B. Davidson, in the *Camb. Bible for Schools;* F. W. Farrar, in the *Minor Prophets* ('Men of the Bible'); A. F. Kirkpatrick, *Doctrine of the Prophets;* Keil, *Introd. to O. T.*

HA-BARKANIM or BARKANIM (ha-bär'-ka-nim or bär'ka-nim). See THORNS.

HABAZINIAH (hăb'a-zi-nī'ah), (Heb. חֲבַצִּנְיָה, *khab-ats-tsan-yaw'*, perhaps lamp of Jehovah; according to Fürst, collection of Jehovah), father of a certain Jeremiah, and grandfather of the chief Rechabite Jaazaniah, whom the prophet Jeremiah tested with the offer of wine (Jer. xxxv:3), B. C. before 609.

HABAZZELETH (ha-băz'ze-leth). See CHABAZZELETH.

HABERGEON (hà-bēr'jĕ-ŏn), (Heb. שִׁרְיָה, *shir-yaw'*, an old English word for breastplate). See ARMS; ARMOR.

HABITATION (hăb'ĭ-tā'shŭn), the rendering of several Hebrew and Greek words, and used in the general sense of a place to dwell in (Ps. lxix:25; civ:12; Acts i:20, etc.)

Figurative. (1) God is the *habitation* of his people; in him they find the most delightful rest, safety and comfort (Ps. xci:9). (2) Justice and judgment are the *habitation* or *establishment* of God's throne; all his royal acts are founded on judgment and justice; he takes pleasure to execute them (Ps. lxxxix:14). (3) The land of Canaan, the city of Jerusalem, the tabernacle and temple, heaven and the heart of the saints are represented as the *habitation* of God; there he did or does signally show himself present, work by his power, or bestow his favor and influence (Jer. xxv:30; Ezra vii:15; Exod. xv:2; Ps. cxxxii:5, 13; Eph. ii:22). (4) Eternity is represented as his *habitation;* he is eternal in a manner no other is, nor does his duration increase as that of angels and men (Is. lvii: 15). (5) He *inhabited* the praises of Israel; he dwelt in the temple where they praised; he owns, deserves, is the object of, and kindly accepts the praises of his people (Ps. xxii:3). (6) Their first *habitation* which sinning angels left was their original state of holiness and happiness, and their mansions in heaven (Jude verse 6). (7) A body, soul or family exercised in holiness is called a *habitation of righteousness* (Job viii:6). (8) The state of heavenly glory is everlasting *habitations* (Luke xvi:9). (9) The firmament is the *habitation* of the sun and the moon (Hab. iii:11).

HABOR (hā'bôr), (Heb. חָבוֹר, *khaw-bore'*, joining together).

1. A country of Media, to which portions of the ten tribes were transported, first by Tiglath-pileser (1 Chron. v:26), and afterward by Shalmaneser (2 Kings xvii:6, xviii:11). It is thought by some to be the same mountainous region between Media and Assyria, which Ptolemy (*Geog.* vi:1) calls *Chaboras* (Χαβώρας.) This notion has the name, and nothing but the name, in its favor. Habor was by the river Gozan, and as we accept Major Rennell's conclusions that Gozan was the present Kizzil-Ozan (see GOZAN), we are bound to follow him in fixing the position of Habor at the town of Abhar, which is situated on a branch of that river and has the reputation of being very ancient. At this place Mr.

Morier found ruins composed of large sun-dried bricks compacted with straw, like some of those found at Babylon. As this kind of construction is an infallible sign of remote antiquity, it so far affords a most important corroboration of Major Rennell's conjecture.

2. A river. There seems to be good ground for making the river the modern *Khabour,* which empties into the Euphrates (Rawlinson, *Ancient Monarch.* i:247). The name of the Habor is found in the Assyrian inscriptions. "Tiglath-pileser I (B. C. about 1120) boasts of having killed ten mighty elephants in the land of Haran and 'on the banks of the Habor.' Assurnazir-apli (B. C. 885-860) crossed the Tigris, conquered the district of the Harmis (or *Har-rit* or *Harsit*), then marched to the Euphrates after subjugating the district around the mouth of the Habor (*piāte sa nâr Habur*), 'the mouths of the river Habor,' from which it would seem that the river flowed into the Euphrates through several outlets" (I. A. Pinches, Hastings' *Bib. Dict.*).

HACHALIA (hăk'a-lī'ah), (Heb. חֲכַלְיָה, *khak-al-yaw'*, the darkness of Jehovah), father of Nehemiah (Neh. i:1; x:1), B. C. before 447.

HACHILAH (hăk'i-lah), (Heb. חֲכִילָה, *khak-ee-law'*, dark).

A mountain about ten miles south of Jericho, where David concealed himself from Saul (1 Sam. xxiii:19; xxvi:3). Jonathan Maccabæus built here the castle of Massada.

HACHMONI (hăk'mo-nī), (Heb. חַכְמוֹנִי, *khak-mo-nee'*, skillful).

A man known only as the father (or ancestor, comp. 1 Chron. xxvii:2) of Jashobeam, the chief of David's warriors (1 Chron. xi:11), where *son of Hachmoni* is rendered "Hachmonite," for which the parallel passage (2 Sam. xxiii:8) has "Tachmonite," and also of Jehiel, the companion of the princes in the royal household (1 Chron. xxvii:32). (See EZNITE).

Hachmon, or Hachmoni, was no doubt the founder of a family to which these men belonged. Zabdiel was the real father of Jashobeam (1 Chron. xxvii:2), and is said to have been a Korhite (1 Chron. xii:6). (See Kennicott, *Diss.*, pp. 72, 82.)

HACHMONITE, THE (hăk'mo-nīte). See HACHMONI.

HADAD (hā'dăd), (Heb. הֲדַד, *had-ad'* fierce).

The name of the chief deity of the Syrians, and borne, with or without additions, as a proper name, or more probably as a title, like 'Pharaoh' in Egypt, by several of the kings of Southern Syria.

(1) Kings of Edom. (1) Hadad, king of Edom, who defeated the Midianites in the intervening territory of Moab (Gen. xxxvi:35; 1 Chron. i:46). This is the only one of the ancient kings of Edom whose exploits are recorded by Moses. (2) Another king of Edom of the same name is mentioned in 1 Chron. i:51 (B. C. before 1618).

(2) King of Syria. Hadad, king of Syria, who reigned in Damascus at the time that David attacked and defeated Hadadezer, king of Zobah, whom he marched to assist, and shared in his defeat (B. C. about 1040). This fact is recorded in 2 Sam. viii:5, but the name of the king is not given. It is supplied, however, by Josephus (*Antiq.* vii:5, 2), who reports, after Nicolas of Damascus, that he carried succors to Hadadezer as far as the Euphrates, where David defeated them both.

(3) Prince of Edom. Hadad, a young prince of the royal race of Edom, who, when his country was conquered by David, contrived, in the heat of the massacre committed by Joab, to escape with some of his father's servants, or rather was carried off by them into the land of Midian, B. C. about 984 (1 Kings xi:14). Thence Hadad went into the desert of Paran, and eventually proceeded to Egypt. He was there most favorably received by the king, who assigned him an estate and establishment suited to his rank, and even gave him in marriage the sister of his own consort, by whom he had a son, who was brought up in the palace with the sons of Pharaoh. Hadad remained in Egypt till after the death of David and Joab, when he returned to his own country in the hope of recovering his father's throne (1 Kings xi:14-22). The Scriptures do not record the result of this attempt further than by mentioning him as one of the troublers of Solomon's reign, which implies some measure of success. After relating these facts the text goes on to mention another enemy of Solomon, named Rezin, and then adds (verse 25), that this was 'besides the mischief that Hadad did; and he abhorred Israel and reigned over Syria.' The A. V. seems to make this apply to Rezin, but the Septuagint refers it to Hadad, reading *Edom,* instead of *Arawm* or *Syria,* and the sense would certainly be improved by this reading, inasmuch, as it supplies an apparent omission; for without it we only know that Hadad left Egypt for Edom, and not how he succeeded there, or how he was able to trouble Solomon. The history of Hadad is certainly very obscure. Adopting the Septuagint reading, some conclude that Pharaoh used his interest with Solomon to allow Hadad to reign as a tributary prince, and that he ultimately asserted his independence.

(4) Son of Ishmael. A son of Ishmael (Gen. xxv:15; 1 Chron. i:30), whose descendants probably occupied the western coast of the Persian Gulf.

HADADEZER (hăd'ad-ē'zer), (Heb. הֲדַדְעֶזֶר, *had-ad-eh'zer,* Adad his help), or Hadadrezer, king of Zobah.

He was a powerful monarch in the time of David and the only one who seems to have been in a condition seriously to dispute with him the predominancy in Southwestern Asia. He was defeated by the Israelites in the first campaign (B. C. about 984) in the neighborhood of the Euphrates, with a great loss of men, war chariots and horses, and was despoiled of many of his towns (2 Sam. viii:3; 1 Chron. xviii:3). This check not only impaired, but destroyed his power. A diversion highly serviceable to him was made by a king of Damascene-Syria (whom the Scripture does not name, but who is the same with Hadad, 3), who, coming to his succor, compelled David to turn his arms against him, and abstain from reaping all the fruits of his victory (2 Sam. x:6, *sq.;* 1 Chron. xix:6, *sq.*). The breathing-time thus afforded Hadadezer was turned by him to such good account that he was able to accept the subsidies of Hanun, king of the Ammonites, and to take a leading part in the confederacy formed by that monarch against David. The first army brought into the field was beaten and put to flight by Abishai and Joab, but Hadadezer, not yet discouraged, went into the countries east of the Euphrates, and got together the forces of all his allies and tributaries, which he placed under the command of Shophach, his general. To confront so formidable an adversary, David took the field in person, and in one great victory so completely broke the power of Hadadezer that all the small tributary princes seized the opportunity of throwing off his yoke, of abandoning the Ammonites to their fate, and of submitting quietly to David, whose power was thus extended to the Euphrates.

HADAD-RIMMON (hā'dad-rǐm'mon), (Heb. הֲדַדְרִמּוֹן, had-ad-rim-mone'), a place in the valley of Megiddo (Zech. xii:11) where a national lamentation was held for the death of King Josiah in the last of the battles which made the plain of Esdraelon famous (2 Kings xxiii:29; 2 Chron. xxxv:23). It is now called Rummâneh, and is about a mile northwest by west of Taanach.

HADAR (hā'dar), (Heb. הֲדַר, khad-ar', perhaps chamber).
1. See HADAD, (3).
2. See HADAD, (4).

HADAREZER (hăd'ar-ē'zer), (Heb. הֲדַרְעֶזֶר, had-ar-eh'zer, Adad his help, 2 Sam. x:16, 19).

He was a son of Rehob (2 Sam. viii:3). He was the king of Zobah whom David overtook and defeated (1 Chron. xviii:3, 4). The captured shields of gold were taken by David to Jerusalem (xviii: 7), and dedicated to Jehovah (B. C. about 1035). Hadarezer made another campaign (1 Chron. xix: 16; 2 Sam. x:15) and was again defeated by David. The name is written Hadadezer in 2 Sam. viii:3-12 and 1 Kings xi:23.

HADAS (hā-dăs'), (Heb. הֲדַס, had-as'), always translated 'myrtle,' occurs in several passages of the Old Testament as in Isaiah xli:19; lv:13; Neh. viii:15; Zech. i:8, 10, 11.

The Hebrew word *hadas* is identical with the Arabic *hadas*, which in the dialect of Arabia

Myrtle.

Felix signifies the myrtle tree (Richardson's *Pers. and Arabic Dict.*). The myrtle is, moreover, known throughout eastern countries.

The repute which the myrtle enjoyed in ancient times it still retains, notwithstanding the great accession of ornamental shrubs and flowers which has been made to the gardens and greenhouses of Europe. This is justly due to the rich coloring of its dark-green and shining leaves, contrasted with the white, star-like clusters of its flowers, affording in hot countries a pleasant shade under its branches and diffusing an agreeable odor from its flowers or bruised leaves.

HADASHAH (hăd'a-shah), (Heb. חֲדָשָׁה, khad-aw-shaw', new), one of the towns of Judah in the low country placed between Zenan and Migdal-gad (Josh. xv:37). It has not been satisfactorily identified. (See Schwarz, *Phys. Descript. of Pal.* p. 103).

HADASSAH (ha-dăs'sah), (Heb. הֲדַסָּה, had-as-saw,' myrtle), the earlier Jewish name of Esther (Esth. ii:7). (See ESTHER.)

HADATTAH (ha-dăt'tah), (Heb. חֲדַתָּה, khad-at-taw', new),
One of the towns in the extreme south of Judah (Josh. xv:25); but the Masoret accents of the Hebrew connect the word with the one preceding it, making it "New Hazor." Both Eusebius and Jerome speak of a "New Hazor," and Mr. Tristram (*Land of Israel*) speaks of some ruins in the south of Judah which the Arabs said were Hadâdah. This may be the Hadattah of Joshua (xv:25). The exact site is unknown.

HADES (hā'dēz), a Greek word ᾅδης, hah'dāce, not to be seen), by which the Septuagint translates the Hebrew שְׁאוֹל, sheol.

(1) Definition. It denotes the abode or world of the dead, in which sense it occurs frequently in the New Testament, where it is usually rendered 'hell' in the English version. The word *hades* means literally *that which is in darkness*. In the classical writers it is used to denote *Orcus*, or the infernal regions.

According to the notions of the Jews, *sheol* or *hades* was a vast receptacle where the souls of the dead existed in a separate state until the resurrection of their bodies. The region of the blessed during this interval, or the inferior paradise, they supposed to be in the upper part of this receptacle; while beneath was the abyss or *gehenna* (Tartarus), in which the souls of the wicked were subjected to punishment.

(2) Interpretation. The question whether this is or is not the doctrine of the Scriptures is one of great importance, and has, first and last, excited no small amount of discussion. It is a doctrine received by a large portion of the nominal Christian church, and it forms the foundation of the Roman Catholic doctrine of Purgatory, for which there would be no ground but for this interpretation of the word *hades*.

The question therefore rests entirely upon the interpretation of this word, and as the Septuagint gives this as the meaning of the Hebrew word *sheol*, the real question is, what is the meaning which *sheol* bears in the Old Testament, and *hades* in the New?

(3) The Grave. A careful examination of the passages in which these words occur will probably lead to the conclusion that they afford no real sanction to the notion of an intermediate place of the kind indicated, but are used by the inspired writers to denote *the grave*—the resting place of the bodies both of the righteous and the wicked; and that they are also used to signify *hell,* the abode of miserable spirits. But it would be difficult to produce any instance in which they can be shown to signify the abode of the spirits of just men made perfect, either before or after the resurrection.

In the great majority of instances *sheol* is in the Old Testament used to signify *the grave,* and in most of these cases is so translated in the Authorized Version. It can have no other meaning in such texts as Gen. xxxvii:35; xlii: 38; 1 Sam. ii:6; 1 Kings ii:6; Job xiv:13; xvii: 13, 16, and in numerous other passages in the writings of David, Solomon and the prophets. But as the grave is regarded by most persons, and was more especially so by the ancients, with awe and dread, as being the region of gloom and darkness, so the word denoting it soon came to be applied to that more dark and gloomy world which was to be the abiding place of the miserable. Where our translators supposed the word to have this sense, they rendered it by 'hell.' Some of the passages in which this has been done may be doubtful; but there are others of which a question can scarcely be entertained. Such are those (as Job xi:8; Ps. cxxxix:8; Amos ix:2) in which the word denotes the opposite of heaven, which cannot be the grave, nor the general state or region of the dead, but hell. Still more decisive are such passages as Ps. ix:17; Prov. xxiii: 14; in which *sheol* cannot mean any place, in this world or the next, to which the righteous as well as the wicked are sent, but the penal abode of the wicked, as distinguished from and opposed to the righteous. The only case in which such passages could by any possibility be supposed to mean the grave, would be if the grave —that is, extinction—were the *final* doom of the unrighteous.

(4) Future Conditions. In the New Testament the word *hades* is used in much the same sense as *sheol* in the Old, except that in a less proportion of cases can it be construed to signify the grave. There are still, however, instances in which it is used in this sense, as in Acts ii:31; 1 Cor. xv:55, but in general the *hades* of the New Testament appears to be no other than the world of future punishments (e. g. Matt. xi:23; xvi:18; Luke xyi:23).

The principal arguments for the intermediate *hades,* as deduced from Scripture, are founded on those passages in which things 'under the earth' are described as rendering homage to God and the Savior (Philip. ii:10; Rev. v:13, etc.). If such passages, however, be compared with others (as with Rom. xiv:10, 11, etc.), it will appear that they must refer to the day of judgment, in which every creature will render some sort of homage to the Savior, but *then* the bodies of the saints will have been already raised, and the intermediate region, if there be any, will have been deserted.

(5) Spirits in Prison. One of the seemingly strongest arguments for the opinion under consideration is founded on 1 Pet. iii:19, in which Christ is said to have gone and 'preached to the spirits in prison.' These spirits in prison are supposed to be the holy dead—perhaps the virtuous heathen—imprisoned in the intermediate place, into which the soul of the Savior went at death, that he might preach to them the Gospel. This passage must be allowed to present great difficulties. The most intelligible meaning suggested by the context is, however, that Christ by his spirit preached to those who in the time of Noah, while the ark was preparing, were disobedient, and whose spirits are *now* in prison, abiding the general judgment. The prison is doubtless *hades,* but what *hades* is must be determined by other passages of Scripture; and whether it is the grave or hell, it is still a prison

for those who yet await the judgment day. This interpretation is in unison with other passages of Scripture, whereas the other is conjecturally deduced from this single text.

(6) Destruction of Death and Hades. Another argument is deduced from Rev. xx:14, which describes 'death and *hades*' as 'cast into the lake of fire' at the close of the general judgment—meaning, according to the advocates of the doctrine in question, that *hades* should then cease as an intermediate place. But this is also true if understood of the grave, or of the general intermediate *condition* of the dead or even of hell, as once more and forever reclaiming what it had temporarily yielded up for judgment —just as we every day see criminals brought from prison to judgment, and after judgment returned to the prison from which they came.

(7) Incomplete Reward. It is further urged, in proof of Hades being an intermediate place other than the grave, that the Scriptures represent the happiness of the righteous as incomplete till after the resurrection. This must be admitted, but it does not thence follow that their souls are previously imprisoned in the earth, or in any other place or region corresponding to the Tartarus of the heathen. Although at the moment of death the disembodied spirits of the redeemed ascend to heaven, and continue there till the resurrection, it is very possible that their happiness shall be incomplete until they have received their glorified bodies from the tomb, and entered upon the full rewards of eternity.

(8) Immediate Transition. A view supported by so little force of Scripture seems unequal to resist the contrary evidence which may be produced from the same source, and which it remains briefly to indicate. The effect of this is to show that the souls of the redeemed are described as proceeding, after death, at once to heaven—*the place* of final happiness, and those of the unredeemed to *the place* of final wretchedness.

In Heb. vi:12 the righteous dead are described as being in actual inheritance of the promises made to the fathers. Our Savior represents the deceased saints as already, before the resurrection (for so the context requires), 'like unto the angels,' and 'equal to the angels' (Matt. xxii:30; Luke xx:36), which is not very compatible with their imprisonment even in the happier region of the supposed Hades. Our Lord's declaration to the dying thief, 'This day shalt thou be with me in Paradise' (Luke xxiii:43), has been urged on both sides of the argument; but the word is here not Hades, but Paradise, and no instance can be produced in which the paradise beyond the grave means anything else than that 'third heaven,' that 'paradise' into which the apostle was caught up, and where he heard 'unutterable things' (2 Cor. xii:2, 4). In the midst of that paradise grows the mystic 'tree of life' (Rev. ii:7), which the same writer represents as growing near the throne of God and the Lamb (xxii:2). In Eph. iii:15 the Apostle describes the whole church of God as being at present in heaven or on earth. But, according to the view under consideration, the great body of the church would be neither in heaven nor on earth, but in Hades—the intermediate place. In Heb. xii:21-24 we are told that in the city of the living God dwell not only God himself, the judge of all, and Jesus, the mediator of the new covenant, and the innumerable company of angels, but also 'the spirits of just men made perfect'— all dwelling together in the same holy and happy place. To the same effect, but, if possible, still more conclusive, are the various passages in which the souls of the saints are described as being, when absent from the body, present with Christ in heaven (comp. 2 Cor. v:1-8; Philip. i:23; 1 Thess. v:10). To this it is scarcely necessary to add the various passages in the Apocalyptic vision, in which St. John beheld, as inhabitants of the highest heaven, around the throne of God myriads of redeemed souls even before the resurrection (Rev. v:9, vi:9, vii:9, xiv:1, 3). Now the 'heaven' of these passages cannot be the place to which the term Hades is ever applied, for that word is never associated with any circumstances or images of enjoyment or happiness. (See HEAVEN.)

(9) **Tartarus.** As these arguments seem calculated to disprove the existence of the more favored region of the alleged intermediate place, a similar course of evidence militates with equal force against the existence of the more penal region of the same place. It is admitted by the stanchest advocates for the doctrine of an intermediate place that the souls of the wicked, when they leave the body, go immediately into punishment. Now the Scripture knows no place of punishment after death but that which was prepared for the devil and his angels. This place they *now* inhabit; and this is the place to which, after judgment, the souls of the condemned will be consigned (comp. 2 Pet. ii:4; Matt. xxv:41). This verse of Peter is the only one in Scripture in which any reference to the word Tartarus occurs. But from the other text we can be quite certain that the Tartarus of Peter is no other than the hell which is to be the final, as it is, in degree, the present doom of the wicked. That this hell is Hades is readily admitted, for the course of the argument has been to show that Hades is hell, whenever it is not the grave. 'Whether the righteous and the wicked, after the judgment, will go literally to the same places in which they were before situated, it is not material to inquire. But, both before and after the judgment, the righteous will be in the same place with their glorified Savior and his holy angels, and this will be heaven; and before and after the judgment the wicked will be in the same place with the devil and his angels; and this will be hell.' (Dr. Enoch Pond, *On the Intermediate Place,* in *American Biblical Repository* for April, 1841; comp. Knapp's *Christian Theology,* sec. 104; Meyer, *De Notione Orci ap. Hebraeos,* Lub. 1793; Bahrens, *Freimüthige Unterss. über d. Orkus d. Hebraer,* Halle, 1786; Bickersteth, *Hades and Heaven,* 1865; *Jour. Sac. Lit.,* 1852-1853.)

The notion repelled in this article was entertained by Justin Martyr, Irenæus, Tertullian and many other of the early Christian fathers. This, however, proves nothing in its favor, as the same notion was common among the Jews themselves, in and before the time of Christ. It may even have been entertained by the Seventy when they translated the Hebrew *sheol* by the Greek *hades.* The question connected with Hades has indirectly brought under view two of the three notions respecting the state of the soul after death. The third notion is that of those who hold that the soul is in a perfectly quiescent condition until the resurrection. This requires notice under another head. (See SOUL; see also HEAVEN; HELL.)

HADID (hā'did), or **CHADID** (Heb. חָדִיד, *khaw-deed'*, pointed), a city of Benjamin (Ezra ii:33; Neh. vii:37; xi:34).

Eusebius and Jerome speak of two cities called Aditha, or Adi, one near Gaza, the other near Diospolis, or Lydda, which latter was probably Hadid. Van de Velde has pretty positively identified it with the present *El-Haditheh,* three miles east of *Ludd,* or *Lydda.*

HADLAI (hăd'la-ī), (Heb. חֶדְלָי, *khad-lah'ee,* resting, or keeping holiday), a man of Ephraim, whose son, Amasa, was a chief of the tribe in the reign of Pekah (2 Chron. xxviii:12), B. C. before 758.

HADORAM (ha-dō'ram), (Heb. הֲדוֹרָם, *had-o-rawm',* Hadar is high), possibly *fire worshipers.*

1. A son of Joktan (Gen. x:27; 1 Chron. i:21), whose settlements have not been identified.

2. Son of Tou, or Toi, king of Hamath, who went as his father's messenger to congratulate David on his victory over Hadarezer (1 Chron. xviii:10), B. C. about 984. In 2 Sam. viii:10 the name is given as Joram, a contraction of Jehoram, which is an Israelitish appellation, and Hadoram is doubtless the correct form of the name (Jos. *Ant.* vii:5, sec. 4).

3. The intendant of taxes under David, Solomon and Rehoboam (2 Chron. x:18). In Kings the name is Adoniram (1 Kings iv:6), but in 2 Sam. xx:24, Adoram. Josephus writes it Adoram in both places.

HADRACH (hā'drak), or **ADRA** (Heb. חֲדְרָךְ, *khad-rawk'*), a city mentioned by Zechariah (ix:1), who denounced dreadful threatenings against it. Ptolemy notices a city called Adra, in lat. 68 ⅔, long. 32 ¼. It could not be far from Damascus; for Zechariah calls Damascus the bulwark, defense and confidence of Hadrach. Exact situation unknown. Hengstenberg, *Christology of the O. T.* iii, 371 ff.

HAFT (håft), Heb. נֶצֶב, *nits-tsawb',* fixed), an old form of handle, e. g., of a dagger (Judg. iii:22).

HAGAB (hā'găb), (Heb. חָגָב, *khaw-gawb',* a locust).

The sons of Hagab were among the Nethinim, who returned from the captivity with Zerubbabel (Ezra ii:46), B. C. before 536.

HAGABA (hăg'a-bà), (Heb. חֲגָבָא, *khag-aw-baw',* also חֲגָבָה, a locust, Ez. ii:45).

The sons of Hagaba were among the Nethinim who returned with Zerubbabel from Babylon (Neh. vii:48). In Ezra ii:45 the name appears as Hazabah (B. C. before 536).

HAGABAH (hăg'a-bah), (Heb. חֲגָבָא, *khag-aw-baw',* locust). See HAGABA.

HAGAR (hā'gar), (Heb, הָגָר, *haw-gawr',* derivation uncertain, perhaps stranger).

(1) **Name.** A native of Egypt and servant of Abraham; but how or when she became an inmate of his family we are not informed. The name Hagar, which is pure Hebrew, signifying *stranger,* having been probably given her after her arrival, and being the one by which she continued to be designated in the patriarch's household, seems to imply that her connection with it did not take place till long after this family had emigrated to Canaan; and the presumption is that she was one of the female slaves presented to Abraham by Pharaoh during his visit to Egypt (Gen. xii:16). But some derive the name from a Hebrew word signifying *to flee,* and suppose it to have been applied to her from a remarkable incident in her life, to be afterwards mentioned.

(2) **Abraham's Concubine.** The long continued sterility of Sarah suggested to her the idea (not uncommon in the East) of becoming a mother by proxy through her handmaid, whom, with that view, she gave to Abraham as a secondary wife. (See ABRAHAM; ADOPTION; CONCUBINAGE).

The honor of such an alliance and elevation

was too great and unexpected for the weak and ill-regulated mind of Hagar; and no sooner did she find herself in a delicate situation, which made her an object of increasing interest and importance to Abraham, than she openly indulged in triumph over her less favored mistress, and showed by her altered behavior a growing habit of disrespect and insolence. The feelings of Sarah were severely wounded, and she broke out to her husband in loud complaints of the servant's petulance; and Abraham, whose meek and prudent behavior is strikingly contrasted with the violence of his wife, leaves her with unfettered power, as mistress of his household, to take what steps she pleases to obtain the required redress. In all Oriental states where concubinage is legalized, the principal wife has authority over the rest; the secondary one, if a slave, retains the former condition unchanged, and society thus presents the strange anomaly of a woman being at once the menial of her master and the partner of his bed. In like manner Hagar, though taken into the relation of concubine to Abraham, continued still, being a dotal maidservant, under the absolute power of her mistress, who, after her husband had left her to take her own way in vindication of her dignity as the principal wife, was neither reluctant nor sparing in making the minion reap the fruits of her insolence.

(3) Flight of Hagar. After a time the maid fled from the face of her mistress, starting in the direction of her own country. This route led her to what was afterwards called Shur, through a long tract of sandy uninhabited country, lying on the west of Arabia Petræa, to the extent of 150 miles between Palestine and Egypt. In that lonely region she was sitting by a fountain to replenish her skin-bottle and recruit her wearied limbs, when the angel of the Lord appeared, and in the kindliest manner remonstrated with her on the course she was pursuing, and encouraged her to return by the promise that she would ere long have a son, whom Providence destined to become a great man, and whose wild and irregular features of character would be indelibly impressed on the mighty nation that should spring from him.

(4) Birth of Ishmael. Obedient to the heavenly visitor, and having distinguished the place by the name of Beer-lahai-roi, 'the well of the visible God,' Hagar retraced her steps to the tent of Abraham, where in due time she had a son; and having probably narrated this remarkable interview to Abraham, that patriarch, as directed by the angel, called the name of the child Ishmael, 'God hath heard' (Gen. xvi:11).

(5) Birth of Isaac. Fourteen years had elapsed after the birth of Ishmael when an event occurred in the family of Abraham by the appearance of the long-promised heir, which entirely changed the prospects of that young man, though nothing materially affecting him took place till the weaning of Isaac, which, as is generally thought, was at the end of his third year. Ishmael was then a lad of seventeen years of age, and being fully capable of understanding his altered relations to the inheritance, as well as having felt perhaps a sensible diminution of Sarah's affection towards him, it is not wonderful that a disappointed youth should inconsiderately give vent to his feelings on a festive occasion, when the newly weaned child, clad according to custom with the sacred symbolic robe, which was the badge of the birthright, was formally installed heir of the tribe (see *Biblioth. Bibl.* vol. i.; Vicasi, *Annot.* 32; Bush on Gen. xxvii:15). The harmony of the weaning feast was disturbed by Ishmael being dis-

covered mocking. The Hebrew word פֹּצַק, *tsaw-khak'*, though properly signifying 'to laugh,' is frequently used to express strong derision, as in Gen. xix:14; Neh. ii:19; iv:1; Ezek. xxiii:32; accompanied, as is probable on some of the occasions referred to in these passages, with violent gestures; and in accordance with this idea the Chaldee and Septuagint versions render it by 'I play,' which is used by the latter in 2 Sam. ii:14-17, as synonymous with boxing, whence it might very justly be characterized as persecution (Gal. iv:29).

(6) Expulsion of Hagar and Ishmael. This conduct gave mortal offense to Sarah, who from that moment would be satisfied with nothing short of his irrevocable expulsion from the family, and as his mother also was included in the same condemnation there is ground to believe that she had been repeating her former insolence, as well as instigating her son to his improprieties of behavior. So harsh a measure was extremely painful to the affectionate heart of Abraham; but his scruples were removed by the timely appearance of his divine counselor, who said: 'Let it not be grievous in thy sight, because of the lad, and because of thy bondwoman; in all that Sarah hath said unto thee, hearken unto her voice;' 'for,' adds the Targum of Jonathan, 'she is a prophetess.'

Accordingly, what she said is called the Scripture (Gal. iv:30), and the incident affords a very remarkable instance of an overruling Providence in making this family feud in the tent of a pastoral chief 4,000 years ago the occasion of separating two mighty peoples, who, according to the prophecy, have ever since occupied an important chapter in the history of man. Hagar and Ishmael departed early on the day fixed for their removal, Abraham furnishing them with the necessary supply of traveling provisions. The Septuagint, which our translators have followed, most absurdly represents Ishmael as a child, placed along with the traveling-bags on the heavily-loaded shoulders of Hagar. But a little change in the punctuation, the observance of the parenthetical clause, and the construction of the word 'child' with the verb 'took' remove the whole difficulty, and the passage will then stand thus: 'And Abraham rose up early in the morning, and took bread, and a bottle of water (and gave it unto Hagar, putting it on her shoulder), and the child, and sent her away.'

In spite of their instructions for threading the desert, the two exiles missed their way. Overcome by fatigue and thirst, increasing at every step under the unmitigated rays of a vertical sun, the strength of the young Ishmael, as was natural, first gave way, and his mother laid him down in complete exhaustion under one of the stunted shrubs of this arid region in the hope of his obtaining some momentary relief from smelling the damp in the shade. The burning fever, however, continued unabated, and the poor woman, forgetting her own sorrow, destitute and alone in the midst of a wilderness, and absorbed in the fate of her son, withdrew to a little distance, unable to witness his lingering sufferings, and there 'she lifted up her voice and wept.' In this distressing situation the angel of the Lord appeared for the purpose of comforting her, and directed her to a fountain, which, concealed by the brushwood, had escaped her notice, and from which she drew a refreshing draught, that had the effect of reviving the almost lifeless Ishmael (Gen. xxi:19).

Of the subsequent history of Ishmael we have no account further than that he established himself in the wilderness of Paran, in the neighborhood of Sinai, was married by his mother to a countrywoman of her own, and maintained both himself and family by the produce of his bow.

R. J.

For the truthfulness to nature of the story of Hagar, see Blunt's *Veracity of the Books of Moses.* On Hagar, see Williams' *Holy City,* i:463 ff; Weil, *Bib. Legends,* p. 82.

HAGAR (hā'gar), (Gal. iv:25), a local name applied to Mount Sinai in Arabia.

HAGARENES, HAGARITES (hā'gar-ē-nēz, hā'gar-ītes), (Ps. lxxxiii:6, Heb. הַגְרִים, Hagarenes, marg. Hagrites; 1 Chron. v:10, הַהַגְרִאִים, Hagrites.) (See ARABIA.)

HAGERITE, THE (hā'ger-īte), (Heb. הַהַגְרִי, *ha-hag-ree'*, was an appellation of Jaziz, a descendant of Hagar, who tended David's flocks (1 Chron. xxvii:31).

HAGGAI (hăg'ga-ī),(Heb. חַגַּי, *khag-gah'ee,* festive).

1. The Prophet. One of the twelve minor prophets, and the first of the three who, after the return of the Jews from the Babylonian exile, prophesied in Palestine.

Of the place and year of his birth, his descent, and the leading incidents of his life, nothing is definitely known. He began to prophesy in the second year of Darius Hystaspes (Hag. i:1). Together with Zechariah, he pressed vigorously the renewal of the building of the temple, which had been suspended after the reign of Cyrus, and obtained the permission and assistance of the king (Ezra v:1, vi:14). Animated by the high courage of these devoted men, the people prosecuted the work with energy and the temple was completed and dedicated in the sixth year of Darius, B. C. 520.

2. Haggai, Book of. These prophecies of Haggai are comprised in a book of two chapters and consist of discourses, brief and summary (Eichhorn, *Einleitung in das A. T.,* iii, sec. 598; Jahn, *Introduction in libros sacros Vet. Fœd.* edit. 2, Viennæ, 1814, sec. 156). Their object generally is to urge the rebuilding of the Temple, which had indeed been commenced as early as B. C. 535 (Ezra iii:10), but was afterward discontinued, the Samaritans having obtained an edict from the Persian king, which forbade further procedure, and influential Jews pretending that the time for rebuilding the Temple had not arrived, since the seventy years predicted by Jeremiah applied to the Temple also, from the time of the destruction of which it was then only the sixty-eighth year. As on the death of Pseudo-Smerdis, and the consequent termination of his interdict, the Jews still continued to wait for the end of the seventy years, and were only engaged in building splendid houses for themselves, Haggai began to prophesy in the second year of Darius (B. C. 520).

His prophecy is divided as follows: (1) His first discourse (chap. i), delivered on the first day of the sixth month of the year mentioned, foretells that a brighter era would begin as soon as Jehovah's house was rebuilt; and a notice is subjoined, stating that the address of the prophet had been effective, the people having resolved on resuming the restoration of the Temple. (2) The second discourse (chap. ii:1-9), delivered on the twenty-first day of the seventh month, predicts that the glory of the new Temple would be greater than that of Solomon's, and shows that no fear need be entertained of the Second Temple not equaling the first in splendor, since, in a remarkable political revolution the gifts of the Gentiles

would be brought thither. (3) The third discourse (chap. ii:10-19), delivered on the twenty-fourth day of the ninth month, refers to a period when building materials had been collected, and the workmen had begun to put them together, for which a commencement of the Divine blessing is promised. (4) The fourth and last discourse (chap. ii:20-23), delivered also on the twenty-fourth day of the ninth month, is exclusively addressed to Zerubbabel, the political chief of the new Jewish colony, who, it appears, had asked for an explanation regarding the great political revolutions which Haggai had predicted in his second discourse; it comforts the governor by assuring him they would not take place very soon and not in his lifetime.

(1) Style of Writer. The style of the discourses of Haggai is suitable to their contents; it is pathetic when he exhorts; it is vehement when he reproves; it is somewhat elevated when he treats of future events, and it is not altogether destitute of a poetical coloring, though a prophet of a higher order would have depicted the splendor of the second temple in brighter hues. The language labors under a poverty of terms, as may be observed in the constant repetition of the same expression.

(2) Scripture References. The prophetical discourses of Haggai are referred to in the Old and New Testament (Ezra v:1; vi:14; Heb. xii: 26; comp. Hagg. ii:6, 7, 8, 22). In most of the ancient catalogues of the canonical books of the Old Testament, Haggai is not, indeed, mentioned by name, but as they specify the twelve minor prophets, he must have been included among them, as otherwise their number would not be full. Josephus, mentioning Haggai and Zechariah (*Antiq.* xi:4, sec. 5, p. 557), calls them δύο προφῆται, *two prophets.* (See generally Rosenmüller, *Scholia in Vet. Test.* vii:4, p. 74; Jahn, *Einleitung in die göttlichen Bücher des Alten Bundes,* ii:2, p. 658; Bertholdt, *Einleitung,* iv, p. 169; Henry Cowles, *Minor Prophets, N. T.;* G. R. Noyes, *New Trans. of the Heb. Prophets;* J. Pye Smith, *Scripture Testimony to the Messiah,* i, 283 ff.; Keil, *Introd. to O. T.*)

G. H. A. v. E.

HAGGERI (hăg'ge-rī), (Heb. הַגְרִי, *hag-ree',* Hagarite), whose son Mibhar was one of David's "thirty" (1 Chron. xi:38). This is probably a corruption of the Hebrew for "Bani the Gadite," which appears in the parallel passage (2 Sam. xxiii:36). (See Kennicott *Dissert.* p. 214.)

HAGGI (hăg'gī), (Heb. חַגִּי, *khag-ghee',* festive), second son of Gad (Gen. xlvi:16; Num. xxvi:15), the founder of the family by the same name (B. C. probably before 1784).

HAGGIAH (hag-gī'ah), (Heb. חַגִּיָּה, *khag-ghee-yaw',* festival of Jehovah), a Levite, descendant of Merari (1 Chron. vi:30), B. C. before 1043.

HAGGITES (hăg'gītes), Heb. הַחַגִּי, *ha-khag-gee'),* were descendants of Haggi, second son of Gad (Num. xxvi:15).

HAGGITH (hăg'gĭth), (Heb. חַגִּית, *khag-gheeth',* festive), David's fifth wife, mother of Adonijah (1 Kings i:5, 11; ii:13; 1 Chron. iii:2; 2 Sam. iii:4), whose birth happened at Hebron (2 Sam. iii:2, 5). He was like Absalom, renowned for his handsome appearance (B. C. before 1053).

HAGIOGRAPHA (hā'jĭ-ŏg'ra-fà), (Gr. Ἁγιόγραφα, *hag-ee-og'ra-phah,* holy writings, sacred writings). The word *Hagiographa* is first found in Epiphanius (*Panarium,* p. 58), who used it to denote the third division of the Scriptures, called by the Jews the *Writings*, consisting of *five books* (see VERSIONS OF SCRIPTURE, *Targums*), viz. the three *poems*, Job, Proverbs, and the Psalms, and the two books of Chronicles.

(1) Classifications. These divisions are found in the Talmud (*Bava Bathra*, fol. 1, ed. Amsterd.), where the sacred books are classified under the *Law*, the *Prophets*, and the *Writings* (*Cetubim*). The last are thus enumerated (*l. c.*): Ruth, the book (*sepher*) of Psalms, Job, Proverbs, Ecclesiastes (*Koheleth*), the Song of Songs, Lamentations, Daniel, and the books (*megilloth*) of Esther, Ezra, and Chronicles. The Jewish writers, however, do not uniformly follow this arrangement, as they sometimes place the Psalms, or the book of Job, as the first of the Hagiographa. Jerome gives the arrangement followed by the Jews in his time. He observes that they divided the Scriptures into five books of Moses, eight prophetical books (viz., 1. Joshua; 2. Judges and Ruth; 3. Samuel; 4. Kings; 5. Isaiah; 6. Jeremiah; 7. Ezekiel; 8. the twelve prophets), and nine *Hagiographa* (viz., 1. Job; 2. David, five parts; 3. Solomon, three parts; 4. Koheleth; 5. Canticles; 6. Daniel; 7. Chronicles; 8. Esdras, two books, viz., Ezra and Nehemiah; 9. Esther). 'Some, however,' he adds, 'place Ruth and Lamentations among the Hagiographa rather than among the prophetical books.'

(2) Early Notice. (1) The earliest notice which we find of these divisions is that contained in the prologue to the book of Ecclesiasticus, written B. C. 130, the author of which refers to the Law, the Prophets, and the *other* books, by which last were most probably meant the Hagiographa. Philo also speaks of the Laws, the Prophets, the Hymns, and the other books, but without classifying them. (2) In the New Testament we find three corresponding divisions mentioned, viz., the Law, the Prophets, and the Psalms, which last book has been supposed to have given its name to the third division from the circumstance of its then being the first in the catalogue (Luke xxiv: 44). Hävernick, however (*Handbuch*, p. 78), supposes that Luke calls the Hagiographa by the name of Psalms, rather on account of the poetical character of several of its parts (3) The 'book of the Prophets' is referred to in the New Testament as a distinct volume (Acts vii:42), where the passage indicated is Amos v:25, 26. It is well known that the second class was divided by the Jews into the early Prophets, viz., Joshua, Judges, Samuel, and Kings; and the later Prophets, viz., Isaiah, Jeremiah, Ezekiel (called the major prophets), and the book of the twelve (minor) prophets. When this division of books was first introduced it is now impossible to ascertain. Probably it commenced after the return from the exile, with the first formation of the canon. Still more difficult is it to ascertain the principle on which the classification was based. (4) It has been concluded from Matt. xxiii:35 and Luke xi:51; comp. with Luke xxiv:44, that as the Psalms were the first, so were Chronicles the last book in the Hagiographa (Carpzov, *Introd.* iv. p. 25). If, when Jesus spoke of the righteous blood shed from the blood of Abel (Gen. iv:8) to that of Zechariah, he referred, as most commentators suppose, to Zechariah the son of Jehoiada (2 Chron. xxiv:20, 21), there appears a peculiar appositeness in the appeal to the first and the last books in the canon. The book of Chronicles still holds the last place in the Hebrew Bibles, which are all arranged according to the threefold division. The late date of Chronicles may in some measure account for its separation

from the book of Kings; and this ground holds good whether we fix the era of the Chronicler, with Zunz, at about B. C. 260, or with the eminent Roman Catholic, Professor Movers, the able defender of the antiquity and authenticity of the book, we conceive him to have been a younger contemporary of Nehemiah, and to have written about B. C. 400 (*Kritische Untersuchung über de Biblische Chronik*, Bonn, 1834). The circumstance of the existence of a few acknowledged later additions, such as 1 Chron. iii:19-24, does not militate against this hypothesis. De Wette conceives that the genealogy in this passage comes down only to the third generation after Nehemiah. (5) The Alexandrian translators have not been guided by the threefold division in their arrangement of the books of Scripture. Luther was the first who separated the canonical from the other books. Not only do the Alexandrian translators, the Fathers, and Luther differ from the Jews in the order of succession of the sacred books, but among the Jews themselves the Talmudists and Masorites and the German and Spanish manuscripts follow each a different arrangement.

W. W.

HAI (hā'ĭ). See AI.

HAIL (hāl), **1.** (Gr. χαῖρε, *khah'ee-reh*, be cheerful, rejoice), a salutation, (Luke i:28); in mockery (Matt. xxvii:29).

2. Frozen rain (Heb. בָּרָד, *baw-rawd'*). When a very cold current of air encounters a hot and humid one, the vapor of the latter is suddenly condensed into drops, and sometimes these are frozen into irregular spheroids of porous ice, which fall to the earth as hail.

This phenomenon is more frequent in temperate than in tropical regions, and usually occurs in summer and at the hottest hour of the day. Hail rarely falls except during thunderstorms, and hence the Bible commonly mentions it in connection with fire (lightning), as in Ps. cxlviii:8. Hail occasionally falls in Egypt (Exod. ix:22-25) between December and April. It is more frequent in Palestine (Josh. x:11; Hag. ii:17). The area affected by a hailstorm is generally a long, narrow line, so that of two places near each other one may be in and the other out of the storm. Thus Goshen might escape it, whilst the adjacent district of Egypt to the westward might be in its track and suffer severely (Exod. ix:26); and a pursuing army might be untouched by the storm and yet see their fleeing foes beaten down by the falling stones (Josh. x:11). (Davis, *Bib. Dict.*).

Figurative. Hail is the symbol of Divine vengeance upon kingdoms and nations, as the enemies of God and his people (Is. xxviii:2, 17, xxxii:19; Hag. ii:17).

HAILSTONE (hāl'stōn), (Heb. בָּרָד אֶבֶן, *eh'ben-baw-rawd'*, a stone of hail (Josh. x:11). See above.

HAIR (hâr), (properly Heb. שֵׂעָר, *say-awr'*; Gr. θρίξ, *threeks*), is frequently mentioned in Scripture and in scarcely anything has the caprice of fashion been more strikingly displayed than in the various forms which the taste of different countries and ages has prescribed for disposing of this natural covering of the head.

(1) The Greeks. The Greeks let their hair grow to a great length, and their natural fondness for this attribute of beauty has been perpetuated not only by the frequently recurring references of Homer, but by the circumstance of the other poets and the artists of that ancient people representing even the gods themselves with long hair.

(2) The Egyptians. The early Egyptians,

again, who were proverbial for their habits of cleanliness, removed the hair as an incumbrance, and the almost unavoidable occasion of sordid and offensive negligence. All classes amongst that people, not excepting the slaves imported from foreign countries, were required to submit to the tonsure (Gen. xli:14).

(3) The Hebrews. Different from the custom both of the Greeks and the Egyptians, that of the Hebrews was to wear their hair generally short and to check its growth by the application of scissors only. The priests at their inauguration shaved off all their hair, and when on actual duty at the temple, were in the habit, it is said, of cutting it every fortnight. The only exceptions to this prevailing fashion are found in the case of the Nazarites, whose hair, from religious duty, was *not* to be cropped during the term of their vow; of young persons, who, during their minority, allowed their hair to hang down in luxuriant ringlets on their shoulders; of such effeminate persons as Absalom (2 Sam. xiv:26), and of Solomon's horse-guards, whose vanity affected a puerile extravagance and who strewed their heads every day with particles of gold-dust (Josephus, *Antiq.* viii:7). Although the Hebrews wore their hair short they were great admirers of strong and thickset locks, and so high a value did they set on the possession of a good head of hair that they deprecated nothing so much as baldness (2 Kings ii:23). To prevent or remedy this defect they seem, at an early period, to have availed themselves of the assistance of art, not only for beautifying the hair but increasing its thickness; while the heads of the priests were anointed with an unguent of a peculiar kind, the ingredients of which, with their various proportions, were prescribed by Divine authority, and the composition of which the people were prohibited, under severe penalties, from attempting to imitate (Exod. xxx: 32). This custom spread till anointing the hair of the head became a general mark of gentility and an essential part of the daily toilet, the usual cosmetics employed consisting of the best oil of olives mingled with spices, a decoction of parsley-seed in wine, and more rarely of spikenard (Ps. xxiii: 5, xlv:7; Eccles. ix:8; Mark xiv:3). The prevailing color of hair among the Hebrews was dark; 'locks bushy and black as a raven' being mentioned in the description of the bridegroom as the perfection of beauty in mature manhood (Cant. v:11). Hence the appearance of an old man with a snow-white head in a company of younger Jews, all whose heads, like those of other Eastern people, were jet black—a most conspicuous object —is beautifully compared to an almond tree, which in the early part of the year is in full bloom while all the others are dark and leafless (Eccles. xii:5).

(4) Dyeing the Hair. The Romans were in the habit of using artificial means to disguise the silver hue of age. From Rome the fashion spread into Greece and other provinces, and it appears that the members of the church of Corinth were, to a certain extent, captivated by the prevailing taste, some Christians being evidently in the eye of the Apostle, who had attracted attention by the cherished and womanly decoration of their hair (1 Cor. xi:14-16). To them the letter of Paul was intended to administer a timely reproof for allowing themselves to fall in with a style of manners which, by confounding the distinctions of the sexes, threatened a baneful influence on good morals; and that not only the Christian converts in that city, but the primitive church generally, were led by this admonition to adopt simpler habits, is evident from the remarkable

fact that a criminal, who came to trial under the assumed character of a Christian, was proved to the satisfaction of the judge to be an impostor, by the luxuriant and frizzled appearance of his hair (Tertullian, *Apol.;* Fleury, *Les Mœurs des Chrétiens*).

(5) Eastern Women. With regard to women, the possession of long and luxuriant hair is allowed by Paul to be an essential attribute of the sex—a graceful and modest covering provided by nature, and yet the same Apostle elsewhere (1 Tim. ii:9) concurs with Peter (1 Pet. iii:3) in launching severe invectives against the women of his day for the pride and passionate fondness they displayed in the elaborate decorations of their head-dress. As the hair was preëminently the 'instrument of their pride' (Ezek. xvi:39, margin), all the resources of ingenuity and art were exhausted to set it off to advantage and load it with the most dazzling finery, and many, on the approach of death, caused their longest locks to be cut off and placed separately in an urn, to be deposited in their tomb as the most precious and valued relics.

Figurative. Various metaphorical allusions are made to hair by the sacred writers, especially the prophets. (1) *Cutting off the hair*' is a figure used to denote the entire destruction of a people by the righteous retributions of Providence (Is. vii:20). (2) *'Gray hairs* here and there on Ephraim' portended the decline and fall of the kingdom of Israel (Hos. vii:9). (3) *'Hair like women's'* forms part of the description of the Apocalyptic locusts, and historically points to the prevailing head-dress of the Saracens, as well as the voluptuous effeminacy of the Antichristian clergy (Rev. ix:8). (4) And, finally, *'hair like fine wool'* was a prominent feature in the appearance of the deified Redeemer, emblematic of the majesty and wisdom that belong to him (Rev. i:14). What was least valuable in man's person was represented by no *hair* (1 Sam. xiv:45; 2 Sam. xiv:11; 1 Kings i:52; Matt. x:30; Luke xii:7; xxi:18).

HAKKATAN (hăk'ka-tăn), or rather **KATAN** (Heb. יָקָטָן, *kaw-tawn'*, little or junior). His son, Johanan, returned from captivity with Ezra (Ezra viii:12). He was chief of the Bene-Azgad. The name is probably Katan with the definite article prefixed. (B. C. before 459.)

HAKKOZ (hăk'kŏz), (Heb. הַקּוֹץ, *hak-kotse'*, the nimble). 1. The chief of the seventh course of priests in the Temple service appointed by David (1 Chron. xxiv:10). In Neh. iii:4, 21; Ezra ii:61, the name appears as Koz, without the article, and no doubt correctly. (B. C. 1014.)
2. A man of Judah (1 Chron. iv:8), B. C. probably 1612.

HAKUPHA (ha-kū'phȧ), (Heb. חֲקוּפָא, *khak-oo-faw'*, crooked, incitement). Sons of Hakupha were among those returning from captivity with Zerubbabel (Ezra ii:51; Neh. vii:53), B. C. before 536.

HALAH (hā'lah), (Heb. חֲלַח, *khal-akh'*), signification unknown.
A city or district of Media, upon the River Gozan, to which, among other places, the captives of Israel were transplanted by the Assyrian kings (2 Kings xvii:6; xviii:11; 1 Chron. v:26). Many, after Bochart (*Geog. Sacra,* iii:14, p. 220), have conceived this Halah or Chalach to be the Calachene which Ptolemy places in the north of Assyria. But if the River Gozan be the Kizzil-Ozan Halah must needs be sought elsewhere, and near

48

that river. Accordingly, Major Rennell indicates as lying along its banks a district of some extent, and of great beauty and fertility, named Chalchal, having within it a remarkably strong position of the same name, situated on one of the hills adjoining to the mountains which separate it from the province of Ghilan (*Geog. of Herod.* p. 396; Rawlinson, *Ancient Mon.*, i:246).

HALAK (hā'lăk), **THE MOUNT** (Heb. קָלָק, *khaw-lawk'*, bare). The Smooth or Bald Mountain named as the southern limit of Joshua's conquests. (Josh. xi:17, xii:7).

HALHUL (hăl'hul). A city of Judah (Josh. xv:58), near Hebron. A hamlet called Alula still remains about three or four miles north of Hebron. (Wilson, *Lands of Bib.*, i:384; Schwarz, Palestine, p. 107.)

HALI (hā'lī), **CALI or CHALI** (Heb. חֲלִי, *khal-ee'*, jewel, necklace.) A city of Phœnicia, in Asher (Josh. xix. 25), named between Helkath and Beten. Its situation is not known.

HALING (hāl'ing), (Gr. κατασύρω, *kat-as-oo'ro*, Acts viii:3). It meant to arrest by force, as we use the word haul.

HALL, (hạl), (Αὐλή, *ow-lay'*, yard.) Open court used of the high priests' house (Luke xxii:55).

It is an inclosed or fortified space, often uncovered, into which the apartments of the house looked. It is incorrectly translated palace (Mark xiv:66; Matt. xxvi:69).

HALLEL (hăl-lĕl), (Heb. הַלֵּל, *hal-lale'*; Gr., ὕμνος, *hoom'nos*, praise), the name of a particular part of the hymnal service chanted at certain festivals.

The name 'great Hallel' is sometimes given to this group as a whole, but it is usually applied to Ps. cxxxvi (or Ps. cxx-cxxxvi), with its twenty-six times repeated refrain of praise. Ps. cxiii-cxviii or cxv-cxviii are called the 'Egyptian' or the 'common' Hallel. During the continuance of the temple the Hallel was recited on eighteen days in the year, but on one night alone, that of the Passover. On that occasion it was taken in parts, Ps. cxiii and cxiv being sung before the meal, just before the drinking of the second cup, and Ps. cxv-cxviii after the filling of the fourth cup. It is to this sacred song that reference is made to the phrase ὑμνήσαντες, 'when they had sung an hymn,' used of our Savior and his disciples in Matt. xxvi: 30 and Mark xiv:26.

HALLELUJAH (hăl'lĕ-lū-yà), (Heb. הַלְלוּ־יָהּ, *hal-leh-loo'yah, praise ye Jah*, i. e., Jehovah; Gr. ἀλληλούϊα, *al-lay-loo'-ee-ah*).

A word which stands at the beginning of many of the Psalms. From its frequent occurrence in this position it grew into a formula of praise and was chanted as such on solemn days of rejoicing. This expression of joy and praise was transferred from the synagogue to the church, and is still occasionally heard in devotional psalmody. In the great hymn of triumph in heaven over the destruction of Babylon the large multitude in chorus, like the voice of mighty thunderings, burst forth: "Allelujah, for the Lord God omnipotent reigneth," in response to the voice from the throne, saying: "Praise our God, all ye his servants" (Rev. xix:1-6).

HALLOHESH (hal-lō'hesh) or rather **LO-CHESH** (lō'kĕsh), (Heb. הַלּוֹחֵשׁ, *hal-lo-khashe'*, enchanter), one of those who with Nehemiah sealed the covenant (Neh. x:24). The name is Lochesh without the article. (B. C. about 410).

HALLOW, HALLOWED (hăl'lō, hăl'lōd), (Heb. קָדַשׁ, *kaw-dash'*, to set apart, consecrate; Gr. ἁγιάζω, *hag-ee-ad'zo*, to make sacred).

'Who,' says Trench, 'would now affirm of the verb "to hallow" that it is even obsolescent? Yet Wallis 200 years ago observed: "It has almost gone out of use" (*fere desuevit*).' He is condemning (in *English Past and Present*, p. 139 f.) the American Bible Union for dismissing from their new version words that have a suspicion of age upon them. And it is still quite true that 'hallow' *as a biblical word*, is in active use, so that the revisers felt no necessity for excluding it from either the New Testament of 1881 or the Old Testament of 1885. (Hastings' *Bib. Dict.*)

It is used in the A. V. of a *person* who consecrates himself to God (Num. vi:11); of Christ undergoing death to consecrate himself to God (John xvii:19; comp. x:36; Gal. i:15); of *things*, e. g., the altar, the temple (Exod. xxix:36; Lev. viii: 15; Num. vii:1; 1 Kings viii:64); the *Sabbath* in keeping it holy (Exod. xx:8, etc.) In general Christians are the hallowed (Acts xx:32, xxvi:18, A. V. "sanctified"), as those who, freed from impurity, have been brought near to God through their faith and sanctity. (See SANCTIFICATION.)

HALOHESH (ha-lō'hesh), father of Shallum. The latter was ruler of half of Jerusalem at the time Nehemiah repaired the walls (Neh. iii:12). The Hebrew is identical with HALLOHESH in spelling.

HALT (hạlt), (Heb. צָלַע, *tseh'-lah*, Gen. xxxii: 31, to limp). (Gr. χωλός, *kho-los'*, Matt. xviii:8, crippled).

Figurative. *Halting* denotes falling into snares and trouble (Ps. xxxviii:17; Jer. xx:10), or continuing in doubt which to choose (1 Kings xviii: 21). *Her that halteth;* i. e., Jews weak and unresolved to return to their own land (Mic. iv:6; Zeph. iii:19).

HAM (hăm), (Heb. חָם, *khawm*, swarthy, hot).

1. The youngest son of Noah (Gen. v:32; comp. ix:24), B. C. after 2613. Having provoked the wrath of his father by an act of indecency towards him, the latter cursed him and his descendants to be slaves to his brothers and their descendants (ix:25). To judge, however, from the narrative, Noah directed his curse only against Canaan (the fourth son of Ham) and his race, thus excluding from it the descendants of Ham's three other sons, Cush, Mizram, and Phut (Gen. x:6). The general opinion is that all the Southern nations derive their origin from Ham (to which the Hebrew root *Khawm*, not unlike the Greek Αἰθίοπες, *burned faces*, lends some force). *Cush* is supposed to have been the progenitor of the nations of East and South Asia, more especially of South Arabia, and also of Ethiopia; *Mizraim*, of the African nations, including the Philistines and some other tribes which Greek fable and tradition connect with Egypt; *Phut*, likewise of some African nations, and *Canaan*, of the inhabitants of Palestine and Phœnicia (see Rawlinson, *Five Grt. Mon.* i. chap. iv; Max Müller, *Sci. of Lang.* p. 2690). On the Arabian traditions concerning Ham. *vid.* D'Herbelot (*Bibl. Orient.* art. 'Ham').

2. A poetical name for the land of Egypt (Ps. lxxviii:51; cv:23, 27; cvi:22).

3. In Gen. xiv:5 occurs a country or place called *Ham*, belonging to the *Zuzim*, but its geographical situation is unknown.   E. M.

4. The original inhabitants of the valley of Gedor are said to be "of Ham" (1 Chron. iv:40).

This may indicate either a Hamite tribe or an Egyptian settlement.

HAMAN (hā'man), (Heb. הָמָן, *haw-mawn*, celebrated or magnificent, a name of the planet Mercury; Sept. Ἀμάν, *aman*), a favorite of the king of Persia, whose history is involved in that of Esther and Mordecai.

He is called an Agagite; and as Agag was a kind of title of the kings of the Amalekites (see AGAG), it is supposed that Haman was descended from the royal family of that nation. He or his parents probably found their way to Persia as captives or hostages; and that the foreign origin of Haman was no bar to his advancement at court is a circumstance quite in union with the most ancient and still existing usages of the East. Joseph, Daniel and Mordecai afford other examples of the same kind. His intrigues against Mordecai and the Jews, the discovery of his plot, and his own execution, are graphically delineated in the book of Esther. Prideaux (*Connexion, anno* 453) computes the sum which he offered to pay into the royal treasury at more than two million pounds sterling (ten million dollars).

In later times, at the Feast of Purim, it seems to have been customary to hang an effigy of Haman; but as the gibbet was sometimes made in the form of a cross, riots between Jews and Christians were the result, and a warning against insults to the Christian faith was issued by the emperor Theodosius II (*Cod. Theod.* XVI. viii:18; comp. 21). (See ESTHER; MORDECAI.)

HAMATH (hā'math), (Heb. חֲמָת, *kham-awth'*, fortress), one of the smaller kingdoms of Syria, having Zobah on the east and Rehob on the south. This last kingdom, lying within the greater Mount Hermon, is expressly said to have been taken possession of by the Israelites, and, like Dan, or Laish, which is represented to have been in the valley of Bethrehob (Judg. xviii:28), is used to denote the northern boundary of the Holy Land (Num. xiii:21). The approach to it from the south is by an opening or mountain pass, called 'the entrance of Hamath,' and 'the entering in of Hamath,' which, being the passage from the northern extremity of the land of Israel into Syria, is sometimes used to describe the boundary of the former in this direction, as 'from the entering in of Hamath to the river of Egypt' (1 Kings viii:65).

The kingdom of Hamath, or, at least, the southern or central portions of it, appear to have nearly corresponded with what was afterward denominated Cœle-Syria; but northward it stretched as far as the city Hamath on the Orontes, which seems to have been the capital of the whole country. This city was called Epiphania by the Greeks, under which name it was known to Josephus (*Antiq.* 1:6, 2; comp. Michaelis *Spicil.* ii:52) and Jerome (*Quæst* in Gen. x:18; *Comment.* in Ezek. xlvii:15, 16); but it has now resumed its more ancient denomination, which indeed was probably never lost among the native population. Toi was king of Hamath at the time when David conquered the Syrians of Zobah, and it appears that he had reason to rejoice in the humiliation of a dangerous neighbor, as he sent his own son Joram to congratulate the victor (2 Sam. viii:9, 10). In the time of Hezekiah the town, along with its territory, was conquered by the Assyrians (2 Kings xvii:24, xviii:34, xix:13; Is. x:9, xi:11), and afterward by the Chaldæans (Jer. xxxix:2, 5). Abulfeda, the Arabian geographer, who was prince of Hamath in the fourteenth century, correctly states (*Tab. Syriæ*, p. 108) that this city is mentioned in the books of the Israelites. Hamath is still a picturesque town, of considerable circumference and with wide and convenient streets. The western part of this district forms the granary of Northern Syria, though the harvest never yields more than a tenfold return, chiefly on account of the immense numbers of mice, which sometimes completely destroy the crops.

In 1812, when Burckhardt visited Hamath, he saw the 'Hamath stones' (so-called Hittite inscriptions in relief on black close-grained basalt), and the enormous water wheels, used for bringing the waters of the Orontes to the houses and gardens situated on the hill above the river. He does not, however, mention the catacombs, said to have existed high up on the right bank.

The Hamath stones were afterward rediscovered by Sir Richard Burton and Tyrwhitt Drake, and of which squeezes were shown in London in 1872. The town, which is divided into four quarters, *Hadher, el-Jisr, el-Aleyat, and el-Medine* (the quarter of the Christians), contained at Burckhardt's visit about 4,446 houses and nearly 11,000 male inhabitants.

Literature. Pococke, *Travels*, ii:209; Burckhardt, *Travels in Syria*, p. 249; Richter, *Wallfahrten*, p. 231; comp. Rosenmüller's *Bib. Geography*, ii:243-246; Irby and Mangles, *Travels*, p. 244; Stanley, *Sinai and Pal.*, pp. 406, 407; and Thomson, *The Land and Book*, vol. ii, p. 279.

HAMATHITE (hā'math-īte), (Heb. חֲמָתִי, *kham-aw-thee'*), a descendant of Canaan who probably settled in Hamath (Gen. x:18; 1 Chron. i:16).

HAMATH-ZOBAH (hā'math-zō'bah), (Heb. חֲמַת צוֹבָה, *kham-ath' tso-baw'*, fortress of Zobah, 2 Chron. viii:3), supposed to be the same as HAMATH (which see) a place said to have been captured by Solomon (2 Chron. viii:3).

HAMMATH (hăm'math), (Heb. חַמַּת, *khammath'*, warm springs), a fortified city in the country allotted to Naphtali (Josh. xix:35), no doubt near Tiberias.

This place seems to be called Hammoth-dor (Josh. xxi:32), and still further altered to Hammon (1 Chron. vi:76). (Thomson, *Land and Book*, ii:66.)

HAMMEDATHA (ham-měd'a-thà), (Heb. הַמְּדָתָא, *ham-med-aw-thaw'*), father of Haman and commonly called the Agagite (Esth. iii:1, 10; viii:5; ix:24).

Gesenius takes the name to be Medatha without the definite article. (See also Fürst, *Handwb.*, B. C. before 474).

HAMMELECH (hăm'me-lĕk), (Heb. הַמֶּלֶךְ, *ham-meh'lek*, the king).

The A. V. renders this as a proper name (Jer. xxxvi:26; xxxviii:6), but it undoubtedly refers to Jehoiakim and Zedekiah. This rendering would enable Jerahmeel and Malchiah to be connected with the royal house of Judah, who do not so appear in the A. V. (B. C. 589.)

HAMMER (hăm'mer).

A tool, called in Hebrew פַּטִּישׁ, *pat-teesh'*, used for smoothing metals and for breaking rocks (Is. xli:7; Jer. xxiii:29). It serves as a figure for any crushing power. Babylon was the hammer of the whole earth (Jer. l:23). God's word is like a hammer that breaketh the rock in pieces (xxiii:29). Other names for an implement of the same class are מַקָּבָה, *mak-kaw-baw'*, and מַקֶּבֶת, *mak-keh'beth*, which was used for driving the tent pin (Judg. iv:21) in building operations (1 Kings vi:7), and in the manufacture of idols (Is. xliv:12;

Jer. x:4). The name Maccabees is generally derived from this latter word.

HAMMOLEKETH (ham - mŏl' e - kĕth), (Heb. הַמֹּלֶכֶת, *ham-mo-leh'keth*, the queen), a woman given in the genealogies of Manasseh (1 Chron. vii:17, 18). The Targum translates the word *who reigned.*

The Jewish tradition is that she ruled all of Gilead, and on that account her lineage has been preserved. (B. C. bet. 1874 and 1658.)

HAMMON (hăm'mon), (Heb. חַמּוֹן, *kham-mone'*, hot or sunny).

1. A Levitical city of Naphtali assigned to the Gershonites (1 Chron. vi:76), and answering to the similar names of *Hammath* and *Hammoth-dor.*

2. A town in Asher (Josh. xix:28). Its site is uncertain. Schultz suggested '*Ain Hamûl*, some 10 miles south of Tyre but Robinson lays no great stress upon this identification. Renan (*Mission de Phénicie*, 708 ff.) found at *Khurbet Ummel-'Amud*, near the coast immediately north of the Ladder of Tyre, two Phœnician inscriptions in honor of Baal Hammon.

HAMONAH (ha-mō'nah), (Heb. חֲמוֹנָה, *ham-o-naw'*, multitude), a city where Ezekiel (xxxix:16) foretold the burial of Gog and his people would be.

We do not know any town of this name in Palestine. Hamonah signifies *multitude;* and the prophet intended to show that the slaughter of Gog's people would be so great that the place of their burial might be called *Multitude.*

"Cornill would read 'and it is all over with this multitude.' If the words are an interpolation, the allusion may be to the city of Bethshean, which may have derived its name Scythopolis from the Scythian invasion in the seventh century, B. C. (See Bertholet, *Das Buch Hesekiel,* 193)." C. R. Conder, Hastings' *Bib. Dict.*

HAMMOTH-DOR (hăm'moth-dôr), (Heb. חַמֹּת דֹּאר, *kham-moih'dore*, hot springs of Dor), a city of the Levites, in Naphtali, ceded to the family of Gershon (Josh. xxi:32).

This is identical with HAMMATH unless there were two places in Naphtali by the same name. The suffix *Dor* may refer in some way to its situation.

HAMON-GOG (hă'mon-gŏg), (Heb. הָמוֹן גּוֹג, *haw-mone'gogh*, multitude of Gog, or ravine of Gog's multitude), the name that was to be given to a valley where were to be buried "Gog and all his multitude" (Ez. xxxix:11, 15).

HAMOR (hă'mor), (Heb. חֲמוֹר, *kham-ore'*, a he-ass), prince of Shechem; father of young Shechem, who ravished Dinah, the daughter of Jacob (Gen. xxxiv:2). (See SHECHEM.)

Jacob, returning from Mesopotamia, set up his tents at Shechem, and bought of Hamor, for the price of a hundred *kesitahs,* or pieces of silver (about £40 or $200), that part of the field where he had pitched his tents (Gen. xxxiii:18, *sq*). The bones of Joseph were afterwards buried there (Josh. xxiv:32; Acts vii:16).

For the wrong which had been done Dinah, Shechem made an offer to take her as his wife; and was supported in his claim by his father, Hamor, who proposed also that there should be freedom of marriage between the families of Jacob and Hamor (Gen. xxxiv:14-17).

To this the sons of Jacob gave their consent on condition that the Shechemites accept the rite of circumcision. The Shechemites agreed to the terms, and were circumcised (Gen. xxxiv:24). On the third day, when the Shechemites were unable through illness to defend themselves, Simeon and Levi and their followers fell upon them, murdered Hamor and Shechem, and carried away Dinah to her own home.

HAMUEL (ha-mū'el), (Heb. חַמּוּאֵל, *kham-moo-ale'*, heat, angel of God), son of Mishma, a man of Simeon, of the family of Shaul (1 Chron. iv:26).

From him evidently sprang that part of the tribe of Simeon located in Palestine. (B. C. before 1046.)

HAMUL (hă'mul), (Heb. חָמוּל, *khaw-mool'*, pitied, spared), son of Pharez (Gen. xlvi:12; 1 Chron. ii:5), and head of the family by his name (Num. xxvi:21), B. C. bet. 1870 and 1856.

HAMULITES (hă'mul-ītes), (Heb. חָמוּלִי, *khaw-moo-lee'*), the descendants (Num. xxvi:21) of Hamul. The family of HAMUL (which see).

HAMUTAL (ha-mū'tal), (Heb. חֲמוּטַל, *kham-oo-tal'*, kinsman of the dew), daughter of Jeremiah of Libnah, wife of king Josiah, and mother of Jehoahaz and Zedekiah, kings of Judah (2 Kings xxiii:31; xxiv:18; Jer. lii:1), B. C. 632-619.

HANAMEEL (ha-năm'e-el), (Heb. חֲנַמְאֵל, *khan-am-ale'*, perhaps God has given), the son of Shallum and a kinsman of Jeremiah, to whom, before the siege of Jerusalem, he sold a field which he possessed in Anathoth, a town of the Levites (Jer. xxxii:6-12).

If this field belonged to Hanameel as a Levite, the sale of it would imply that an antient law had fallen into disuse (Lev. xxv:34) ; but it is possible that it may have been the property of Hanameel in right of his mother. The transaction was conducted with all the forms of legal transfer, and was intended to evince the certainty of restoration from the approaching exile, by showing that possessions which could be established by documents would yet be of future value to the possessor (B. C. 587).

HANAN (hă'nan), (Heb. חָנָן, *khaw-nawn'*, merciful).

1. One of the chiefs of the tribe of Benjamin (1 Chron. viii:23), B. C. between 1612 and 1050.

2. Sixth son of Azel, descendant of Saul (1 Chron. viii:38; ix:44), B. C. 588.

3. Son of Igdaliah (Jer. xxxv:4), B. C. before 606.

4. Son of Maachah and one of David's "thirty" (1 Chron. xi:43), B. C. 1000.

5. The sons of Hanan returned, among the Nethinim, with Zerubbabel from Babylon (Ezra ii:46; Neh. vii:49), B. C. before 536.

6. A Levite who assisted Ezra in instructing the people in the law (Neh. viii:7). In Neh. x:10, the same person is doubtless mentioned again (B. C. about 410).

7. One of the chiefs of the people who took part in sealing the covenant (Neh. x:26), B. C. about 410.

8. Another chief of the laymen who took part in sealing the covenant (Neh. x:22), B. C. about 410.

9. The son of Zaccar who was keeper of the tithes under Nehemiah (Neh. xiii:13).

HANANEEL (ha-năn'e-el), (Heb. חֲנַנְאֵל, *khan-an-ale'*, God has favored), an Israelite who gave name to one of the towers of Jerusalem (Neh. iii:1; xii:39; Jer. xxxi:38; Zech. xiv:10). (See HANAN-EEL, TOWER OF.)

HANANEEL, TOWER OF (ha-năn'e-el, tou'-ēr ŏv), (Heb. חֲנַנְאֵל, *khan-an-ale'*, God has favored), a tower which formed part of the wall of Jerusalem (Neh. iii:1; xii:39).

From these two passages, particularly from the former, it might almost be inferred that Hananeel was but another name for the Tower of Meah; at any rate they were close together, and stood between the sheep gate and the fish gate. This tower is further mentioned in Jer. xxxi:38. The remaining passage in which it is named (Zech. xiv:10) also connects this tower with the "corner gate," which lay on the other side of the sheep-gate (Smith, *Bib. Dict.*) (See HANANEEL.)

HANANI (ha-nā'nī), (Heb. חֲנָנִי, *khan-aw-nee'*, gracious).

1. Son of Heman, David's Seer, who was head of the 18th course in the Temple service (1 Chron. xxv:4, 25), B. C. 1014.

2. A prophet under the reign of Asa, king of Judah, by whom he was seized and imprisoned for announcing that he had lost, from want of due trust in God, an advantage which he might have gained over the king of Syria (2 Chron. xvi:7). The precise occasion of this declaration is not known. This Hanani is supposed to be the same who was father of another prophet, named Jehu (1 Kings xvi:7); but circumstances of time and place seem adverse to this conclusion. (B. C. 928.)

3. A priest in the time of Ezra who had 'strange' wives (Ezra x:20), B. C. 459.

4. A brother of Nehemiah, who went from Jerusalem to Shushan, being sent most probably by Ezra, and brought that information respecting the miserable condition of the returned Jews which led to the mission of Nehemiah. Hanani came back to Judæa, probably along with his brother, and, together with one Hananiah, was appointed to take charge of the gates of Jerusalem, and see that they were opened in the morning and closed in the evening at the appointed time. The circumstances of the time and place rendered this an important and responsible duty, not unattended with some danger (Neh. vii:2, 3), B. C. 455.

5. A priest, one of the musicians who officiated in the ceremonial of purifying the walls of Jerusalem when they had been rebuilt (Neh. xii:36), B. C. 445.

HANANIAH (hăn'a-nī'ah), (Heb. חֲנַנְיָה, *khan-an-yaw'*, Jehovah's goodness).

1. A chief captain of the army of King Uzziah (2 Chron xxvi:11), B. C. 803.

2. Son of Heman and chief of the 16th course of Levites (1 Chron. xxv:4, 5, 23), B. C. 1014.

3. A false prophet of Gibeon, who, by opposing his prophecies to those of Jeremiah, brought upon himself the terrible sentence, 'Thou shalt die *this year*, because thou hast taught rebellion against the Lord.' He died accordingly (Jer. xxviii:1, *sq.*), B. C. 596.

4. Father of Zedekiah, and a prince in the reign of Jehoiakim, King of Judah (Jer. xxxvi:12), B. C. 605.

5. Grandfather of Irijah (Jer. xxxvii:13), B. C. before 589.

6. Head of a Benjamite house (1 Chron. viii:24), B. C. 605.

7. (See SHADRACH.)

8. Son of Zerubbabel from whom Christ was descended (1 Chron. iii:19), B. C. after 536.

9. Sons of Bebai who returned from captivity with Ezra (Ezra x:28), B. C. 459.

10. A priest who had the charge of making the ointments (Exod. xxx:22-38; 1 Chron. ix:30). He built a part of the wall in the time of Nehemiah (Neh. iii:8). Perhaps the same as the one mentioned in verse 30. (B. C. 446.)

11. The person who was associated with Nehemiah's brother Hanani in the charge of the gates of Jerusalem. The high eulogy is bestowed upon him, that 'he was a faithful man, and feared God above many' (Neh. vii:2). (See HANANI 2.)

12. Head of the priestly course of Jeremiah under Joiakim the high-priest (Neh. xii:12), B. C. 446.

13. An Israelite mentioned (Neh. x:23). (See ANANIAS.)

HAND (hănd), Heb. יָד, *yawd*, the open palm; כַּף, *kaph*, the hollow of the hand; Gr. χείρ, *khire*).

The organ of feeling, and rightly denominated by Galen the instrument of instruments, since by its position at the end of the fore-arm, its structure and its connection with the mind, the hand admirably executes the behests of the human will, and acquires and imparts to man incomparable skill and power. By the peculiarities of its conformation—the inclination of the thumb to the palm, the comparative length of the thumb and of the fingers, 'the hollow of the hand,' and the fleshy protuberances by which that hollow is mainly formed—this member is wonderfully adapted to the purposes for which it was designed, and serves to illustrate the wisdom and providence of the great Creator (*The Hand, its Mechanism, and vital Endowments, as evincing Design*, by Sir Charles Bell).

The hand itself serves to distinguish man from all other terrestrial beings. No other animal has any member comparable with the human hand. The trunk of the elephant unites the attributes of skill and power to a surprising extent, but yields the palm to the hand.

Of the two hands the right has a preference, derived from natural endowment. Its universal use, as the chief instrument in acting, serves to show that its superiority is something more than an accident. But the preference which it holds is only a part of the general advantage which the right side has over the left, not only in muscular strength, but also in its vital or constitutional properties (Bell).

From the properties already described, the student of Scripture is prepared to see the hand employed in holy writ as a symbol of skill, strength, and efficacy.

As the hand is the great instrument of action, so is it eminently fitted for affording aid to the mind, by the signs and indications which it makes. Thus to lay the hand on any one was a means of pointing him out, and consequently an emblem of setting any one apart for a particular office or dignity. *Imposition of hands* accordingly formed, at an early period, a part of the ceremonial observed on the appointment and consecration of persons to high and holy undertakings. (See Num. xxvii:18-23; Acts viii:15-17; 1 Tim. iv:14; 2 Tim. i:6.) A corruption of this doctrine was, that the laying on of hands gave of itself divine powers, and on this account Simon the magician (Acts viii:18), offered money, saying 'Give me also this power, that on whomsoever I lay hands he may receive the Holy Ghost,' intending probably to carry on a gainful trade by communicating the gift to others. (See HANDS, IMPOSITION OF.)   J. R. B.

Customs. (1) *Pouring water on one's hands* denoted serving of him (2 Kings iii:11). (2) *Washing of hands* imported profession of innocence (Deut. xxi:6; Matt. xxvii:24); or a solemn purgation of one's self in Jesus' blood, and a resolution to maintain a holy practice (Ps. xxvi:6). (3) *Kissing of the hand* to a thing imported adoration of it (Job xxxi:27). (4) The consecration of the priests was called a *filling of their hands,* because part of the consecrated offerings was put into their hands (1 Kings xiii:33). (5) *Leaning on one's hand* imported the familiarity of a superior with his inferior (2 Kings v:18, and vii:17). (6) *Striking of hands* imports undertaking as surety for one's debt or good behavior (Prov. xvii:18, and xxii:26). (7) *Putting the hand under the thigh* was an ancient form of swearing and subjection to the person under whose thigh the hand was put (Gen. xxiv:2, and xlvii:29). (8) *Giving of the hand* imports making a covenant with one, or serving him (2 Kings x:15; Lam. v:6; 1 Chron. xxix:20). (9) *Witnesses laid their hands on the head of the person accused;* importing their solemn charging him with guilt, or their readiness to be the first in stoning him (Deut. xiii:9, and xvii:7). (10) The Hebrews' *laying their hands on their sacrifices* before they were slain denoted the solemn confession of their sin, and of their deserving to die; their ceremonial translation of their guilt on the victim (Lev. i:4, and xvi:21). (11) *Laying on of hands* was used in setting apart men to an office; thus Moses publicly set apart Joshua to the office of governor (Num. xxvii:18). So the Levites under the Old Testament, and ministers under the New, were set apart to their offices by laying on of hands (Num. viii:10; Acts xiii:3; 1 Tim. iv:14). This form was also used in blessing of persons; so Jacob blessed Joseph's children (Gen. xlviii:14), and so Jesus blessed the little children brought to him (Mark x:16). (12) The miraculous gifts of the Holy Ghost were conferred by laying on of the apostles' hands (Acts viii:17, and xix:6). (13) *Stretching out the hand to God* imports earnest prayer for his favors, and solemn dedication of ourselves to him (Ps. lxviii:31, and cxliii:6). (14) *Lifting up the hand* in affirmation was a form of solemn swearing much used anciently (Gen. xiv:22). (15) *Lifting up the hands* in prayer, or by the priests in blessing, denoted the solemn wishing of blessings to come from God (Lev. ix:22).

Figurative. (1) To *lift up the hand* against a superior is to rebel against him (2 Sam. xx:21). (2) To *put forth the hand* against one is to kill him (1 Sam. xxiv:10). (3) To *put our hand to* our neighbor's goods is to steal them (Exod. xxii:8, 11). (4) To *lay the hand* on the mouth imports silence and an acknowledgment of guilt (Job xl:4; Mic. vii:16). (5) To *lay hands angrily* on persons is to apprehend and smite them (Exod. xxiv:11); or seize on their country (Is. xi:14). (6) *Hiding the hand* in the bosom denotes great inactivity or sluggish aversion to do or receive anything (Prov. xix:24). (7) *Clapping of hands* denotes great joy and rejoicing (Ps. xlvii:1; and the *clapping of hands* by trees and floods denotes universal joy and gladness (Is. lv:12; Ps. xcviii:8); but sometimes it denotes contempt and noisy derision (Ezek. xxv:6; Job xxxiv:37). (8) With respect to station, the *seat on the right hand* was honorable, that on the left not so much so (Matt. xx:21). (9) With respect to the points of the heavens, the *left hand* signifies the north, and the *right hand* the south; and yet sometimes it may only signify different quarters (Gen. xiii:9); and so our not *turning from God's law to the left hand or to the right* imports our following it most exactly in every point, neither indulging ourselves in neglect of what it requires,

nor pretending to go beyond it (Josh. i:7, and xxiii:6; Prov. iv:27). (10) God's *standing at men's right hand* imports his regard to them, and readiness to plead their cause and assist and comfort them (Ps. xvi:8, and cix:31). (11) Satan's *standing at men's right hand* imports his accusing of them, hindering them from their proper work; and his readiness to torment them (Zech. iii:1; Ps. cix:6). (12) In giving alms we are *not to let our left hand know what our right hand doth;* i. e. we are to bestow them with all proper secrecy, and with no proud ostentation (Matt. vi:3). (13) Though *hand join in hand,* i. e. though all men should use their most vigorous and united efforts to protect a wicked man, he shall not go unpunished (Prov. xi:21). (14) To *be in the hand* of persons is to be in their possession, or under their management, or under their power and dominion (Job xii:6; Gen. xxxix:6; 2 Kings xxi:14; Ps. xxxi:15). (15) A darling and apparently pleasant and profitable lust to be mortified is likened to a *right hand,* or foot, or eye, to be cut off or plucked out (Matt. v:29, 30, and xviii:8, 9). (16) To have *one's life or soul in his hand* is to be in extreme hazard of death (1 Sam. xix:5; Job xiii:14; Ps. cxix:109). (17) As hands are the instruments of acting, doing, or receiving, they are often the emblems of power, and work. God's *hand,* or *right hand,* signifies his power and the exertion thereof, either in a way of mercy or wrath (Ps. lxiii:8; Deut. xxxii:40). So his powerful influence to instruct or support a prophet is called his *hand* being on or with him (1 Kings xviii:46; Ezek. i:3, and iii:14). His judgments executed are called his *heavy hand* (1 Sam. v:11). His *stretching out his hand* imports the exertion of his power to protect and deliver his friends, or terribly to punish his foes (Exod. iii:20); or his continuing to threaten men with further strokes (Is. ix:12, and xiv:26, 27). *He will not stretch out his hand to the grave, though they cry in his destruction.* Let friends mourn ever so bitterly, God will not by his power bring me or any other dead man to life again; nor will he pursue me further than the grave with his judgments (Job xxx:24). (18) God *plucks his hand out of his bosom* when he exerts his power for the deliverance of his people, and *withdraws* it when he forbears to help, comfort, or deliver them (Ps. lxxiv:11). (19) *Christ sits at God's right hand;* he is enthroned in his highest favor, and in the highest honor and authority (Rom. viii:34). (20) Christ *stretching out his hands* to men, in the offer of the gospel, denotes his earnest calling of them, his readiness to receive them and supply them out of his fullness (Is. lxv:2; Prov. i:24). (21) Length of days is in his or Wisdom's *right hand,* and in *his left* riches and honor. In receiving and walking in him in a wise and well-ordered conversation, there is to be had life and happiness both here and hereafter (Prov. iii:16). He has the stars or ministers in his *right hand;* he supports, protects, and governs them (Rev. i:16). (22) Angels and ministers have the *hands of a man;* they act with knowledge and affection (Ezek. i:8). (23) *Hands weak or hanging down* denote persons dispirited and unfit for action (Job iv:3; Heb. xii:12). (24) To *lift up the hands* to God's commandments is to be devoted to and earnest in obeying God's law in our practice (Ps. cxix:48). (25) *Clean* and *holy hands* denote a blameless and holy practice (Ps. xxiv:4; 1 Tim. ii:8). (26) *Hands defiled* and *bloody* denote a practice corrupt and murderous (Ezek. xxiii:37; Is. i:15). (27) *Slack hands* import a careless inactive practice (Prov. x:4). (28) To do a thing *by the hand* of others is to do it by their assistance (Exod. iv:13; Lev. viii:36;

x:11, and xxvi:46, etc.) : and so wicked men are called the *hand of God;* as by them he executes much of his providential work on earth, particularly in correcting his people (Ps. xvii:14). (29) In Col. ii:13, 14, 'the law of commandments contained in ordinances' (Ephes. ii:15), is designated '*the handwriting* of ordinances that was against us,' which Jesus blotted out, and took away, nailing it to his cross; phraseology which indicates the abolition, on the part of the Savior, of the Mosaic law.

HANDBREADTH (hănd'brĕdth), (Heb. מֶפַח,

teh'fakh, 2 Chron. iv:5; Ps. xxxix.5; טֹפַח, *to'fakh,* Exod. xxxvii:12).

The breadth of the hand, a palm (Exod. xxv: 25). (See CUBIT.) It is used by the Psalmist figuratively of human life, especially when life closes prematurely (Ps. xxxix:5).

HANDBROAD (hănd'brạd).

Measuring a handbreadth (Ezek. xl:43; in R. V. handbreadth). (See HANDBREADTH.)

HANDICRAFT (hănd'ĭ-krȧft).

In the early periods to which the Scriptural history refers we do not meet with those artificial feelings and unreasonable prejudices against hand-labor which prevail and are so banefully influential in modern society. The entire circle of achievement which man had effected in the natural world, was, in ancient times, too immediately and too obviously connected with the labor of the hands, which is, in truth, the great primary source of wealth, for any feeling regarding it to prevail but one of high estimation. Accordingly, even the creation of the world is spoken of as the work of God's hands, and the firmament is said to show his handiwork (Ps. viii:3; xix:1; Gen. ii:2; Job xxxiv:19). (See HAND, *Figurative.*) The primitive history, too, which the Bible presents is the history of hand-laborers. Adam dressed the garden in which God had placed him (Gen. ii:15), Abel was a keeper of sheep, Cain a tiller of the ground (Gen. iv:2), Tubal-Cain a smith (Gen. iv:22).

The life which the patriarchs previously led in their own pasture-grounds, was not favorable to the cultivation of the practical arts of life, much less those by which it is embellished. Egypt, in consequence, must have presented to Joseph and his father a land of wonders, of rich and attractive knowledge.

The maritime and commercial Phœnicians were to the Hebrews another source of knowledge of handicrafts. Commerce and navigation imply great skill in art and science; and the pursuits to which they lead largely increase the skill whence they emanate. It is not, therefore, surprising that the origin of so many arts has been referred to the northeastern shore of the Mediterranean Sea; nor is there any difficulty in understanding how arts and letters should be propagated from the coast to the interior, as well before as after the settlement of the Hebrew tribes in the land of promise.

The skill of the Hebrews during their wanderings in the desert does not appear to have been inconsiderable; but the pursuits of war and the entire absorption of the energies of the nation in the one great work of gaining the land which had been given to them, may have led to their falling off in the arts of peace; and from a passage in 1 Sam. xiii:20 it would appear that not long after they had taken possession of the country they were in a low condition as to the instruments of handicraft. A comparatively settled state of society, however, soon led to the revival of skill by the encouragement of industry. A more minute division of labor ensued. Trades, strictly so called, arose, carried on by persons exclusively devoted to one pursuit. Thus in Judg. xvii:4 and Jer. x:14, 'the founder' is mentioned, a trade which implies a practical knowledge of metallurgy; the smelting and working of metals were well known to the Hebrews (Job. xxxvii: 18); brass was in use before iron; arms and instruments of husbandry were made of iron. In Exodus, xxxv:30-35, a passage occurs which may serve to specify many arts that were practiced among the Israelites, though it seems also to intimate that at the time to which it refers artificers of the description referred to were not numerous.

'See, the Lord hath called by name Bezaleel, and hath filled him with the spirit of God, in knowledge and all manner of workmanship, and to devise curious works, to work in gold, and in silver, and in brass and in the cutting of stones, to set them, and in carving of wood, to make any manner of cunning work; and he hath put in his heart that he may teach; both he and Aholiab; them hath he filled with wisdom of heart to work all manner of work of *the engraver;* and of the cunning workman, and of *the embroiderer* in blue and in purple, in scarlet and in fine linen, and of *the weaver.*'

From the ensuing chapter (Exod. xxxiv:34) it appears that gilding was known before the settlement in Canaan. The ark (Exod. xxxvii:2) was overlaid with pure gold within and without. The cherubim were wrought, 'beaten' (Exod. xxxvii:7) in gold. The candlestick was of beaten gold (verses 17, 22). Wire-drawing was probably understood (Exod. xxxviii:4; xxxix:3). Covering with brass (Exod. xxxviii:2) and with silver (Prov. xxvi:23) was practiced. Architecture and the kindred arts do not appear to have made much progress till the days of Solomon, who employed an incredible number of persons to procure timber (1 Kings v:13, *sq.*); but the men of skill for building his temple he obtained from Hiram, king of Tyre (1 Kings v:3, *sq.;* 1 Chron. xiv:1; 2 Chron. ii:7). (Scholz, *Handb. der Bib. Archäol.* p. 390, *sq.;* De Wette, *Lehrb. der Archäol,* p. 115, *sq.;* Winer, *Realwört,* art. 'Handwerke').

The intercourse which the Babylonish captivity gave the Jews seems to have greatly improved their knowledge and skill in both the practical and the fine arts, and to have led them to hold them in very high estimation. The arts were even carried on by persons of learning, who took a title of honor from their trade (Rosenmüller, *Morgenl.* vi, 42). It was held a sign of a bad education if a father did not teach his son some handicraft. (Lightfoot, p. 616; Mish. Tr. *Pirke Aboth,* ii, 2; Wagenseil's *Sota,* p. 597; Othon. *Lex. Rabb.* 491).

In the Apocrypha and New Testament there are mentioned tanners (Acts ix:43), tent-makers (Acts xviii:3); in Josephus (*De Bell. Jud.* v: 4. 1), cheese-makers; domestics (κουρεῖς, *barbers Antiq.* xvi:11, 5); in the Talmud, with others we find tailors, shoemakers, blood letters, glaziers, goldsmiths, plasterers. Certain handicraftsmen could never rise to the rank of high-priest (Mish. Tr. *Kiddush,* 82, 1), such as weavers, barbers, fullers, perfumers, cuppers, tanners; which pursuits, especially the last, were held in disesteem (Mishna, Tr. *Megillah,* iii:2; Othon. *Lex. Rabb.* 155; Wetstein, *N. T.* ii: 516). In large cities particular localities were set apart for particular trades, as is the case in the East to the present day. Thus in Jeremiah xxxvii:21 we read of 'the bakers' street.' So in the Talmud (*Mishna,* v. 169, 225) mention is made of a flesh market;

in Josephus (*De Bell. Jud.* v. 4. 1) of a cheese market; and in the New Testament (John v:2) we read of a sheep-market. (See Iken, *Antiq. Heb.* iii-ix. p. 578, *sq.;* Bellermann *Handb.* i, 22, *sq.*) J. R. B.

HANDKERCHIEF, NAPKIN (hăn'ker-chǐf, năp'kǐn), (Gr. σουδάριον, *soo-dar'ee-on,* sweat cloth; Vulg. *sudarium*), occurs in Luke xix:20; John xi: 44; xx:7; Acts xix:12.

The Greek word is adopted from the Latin, and probably at first had the *same* meaning; and, being derived from *sudo,* to perspire, corresponds to our word *handkerchief.*

In the first instance of its use (Luke xix:20) it means a wrapper, in which the 'wicked servant' had laid up the pound entrusted to him by his master. For references to the custom of laying up money, etc., in the Soudaria, both in classical and rabbinical writers, see *Wetstein's N. T.,* on Luke xix:20. In the second instance (John xi:44) it appears as a kerchief, or cloth attached to the head of a corpse. It was perhaps brought round the forehead and under the chin. In many Egyptian mummies it does not *cover the face.* In ancient times among the Greeks it *did.* Nicolaus (*De Græcor. Luctu,* c. iii: sec. 6, Thiel. 1697). Maimonides, in his comparatively recent times, describes the *whole face* as being covered, and gives a reason for the custom (Tract *Efel,* c. 4). The next instance is that of the σουδάριον, *napkin,* which had been 'about the head' of our Lord, but which, after his resurrection, was found rolled up, as if deliberately, and put in a place separately from the linen clothes, *wrapped up apart in a place by itself.* The last instance of the Biblical use of the word occurs in the account of 'the special miracles' wrought by the hands of Paul (Acts xix:11) ; 'so that *soudaria (handkerchiefs, napkins, wrappers, shawls, etc.)* were brought from his body to the sick; and the diseases departed from them, and the evil spirits went out of them.' The Ephesians had not unnaturally inferred that the apostle's miraculous power could be communicated by such a mode of contact; and certainly cures thus received by parties at a distance, among a people famed for their addictedness to 'curious arts,' *i. e.,* magical skill, etc., would serve to convince them of the truth of the minds. But it is not said that Paul sent these napkins.

HANDLE (hăn'd'l), (Heb. plural כַּפּוֹת, *kappoth',* literally hands), the thumb pieces or latch to a door. (See LOCK.)

HANDMAID (hănd'mād), (Heb. שִׁפְחָה, *shif-khaw',* or אָמָה, *aw-maw',* Gen. xvi:1; Ruth iii:9, etc.; Gr. δούλη, *doo'lay,* Luke i:38, etc.), a maidservant. (See SERVICE.)

HANDS, IMPOSITION OF.

(1) Old and New Testament. Laying on hands, or imposition of hands, is understood in different ways both in the Old and New Testament. It is often taken for ordination and consecration of priests and ministers, as well among the Jews as Christians (Num. viii:10; Acts vi:6; xiii: 3; 1 Tim. iv:14). It is sometimes also made use of to signify the establishment of judges and magistrates, on whom it was usual to lay hands when they were intrusted with these employments. Thus when Moses constituted Joshua his successor, God appointed him to lay his hands upon him (Num. xxvii:18). Jacob laid his hands on Ephraim and Manasseh, when he gave them his last blessing (Gen. xlviii:14). The high-priest stretched out his hands to the people as often as

he recited the solemn form of blessing (Lev. ix: 22). The Israelites, who presented sin-offerings at the tabernacle, confessed their sins while they laid their hands upon them (Lev. i:4). This testified that the person acknowledged himself worthy of death, that he laid his sins upon the sacrifice, that he trusted in Christ for the expiation of his sins, and that he devoted himself to God. Witnesses laid their hands upon the head of the accused person, as it were to signify that they charged upon him the guilt of his blood, and freed themselves from it (Deut. xiii:9; xvii:7). Our Savior laid his hands upon the children that were presented to him, and blessed them (Mark x:16). And the Holy Ghost was conferred on those who were baptized by the laying on of the hands of the apostles (Acts viii:17; xix:6).

(2) Ecclesiastical Uses. In the rites of the early church the imposition of hands was used in confirmation, which generally was an accompaniment of baptism, and symbolized the reception of the Holy Ghost. It was also practiced in ORDINATION (which see). In the modern church the Roman Catholics use the imposition of hands in the ceremonies which precede extreme unction, in ordination and confirmation, in both of which services it has received a sacramental efficacy. In the mass, previous to the consecration of the elements, the priest extends his hands over the people in blessing. The Church of England, the Protestant Episcopal, and the Reformed Episcopal churches employ it as a symbolical act in baptism and confirmation. The Methodist Episcopal, the Presbyterian, and Congregational Churches employ it only in ordination. (Barnes' *Bib. Dict.*) (See HAND.)

HANDSTAFF (hănd'stàf), (Heb. מַקֵּל, *makkale',* a rod or staff), a javelin (Ezek. xxxix:9). (See ARMS, ARMOR).

HANDWRITING (hănd'rīt'ǐng), (Gr. χειρόγραφον, *khi-rog'raf-on,* what one has written with his own hand), specially a note of hand, or writing in which one acknowledges that money has either been deposited with him or lent to him by another, to be returned at an appointed time.

Figurative. The ceremonial law is called a *handwriting* against men, R. V. *bond;* its rites witnessed guilt and desert of punishment; and it was a means of shutting out the gentiles from the church of God (Col. ii:14).

HANES (hā'nēz), (Heb. חָנֵס, *khaw-nace'*), a place in Egypt only mentioned in Is. xxx:4, which has not been definitely located, but probably in the neighborhood of Zoan. It must not be confounded with Taphanes.

HANGING (hăng'ǐng). See PUNISHMENTS.

HANGING, HANGINGS. Three Hebrew words are translated thus. In relation to the temple we find:

1. *Keh'lah* (Heb. קֶלַע, a screen). The "hangings" were used for covering the walls of the court of the tabernacle, just as tapestry was in modern times (Exod. xxvii:9; xxxv:17; xxxviii:9; Num. iii:26; iv:26).

2. *Maw-sawk'* (Heb. מָסָךְ), the "hanging" was a curtain or "covering" to close an entrance; one was placed before the door of the tabernacle (Exod. xxvi:36, 37; xxxix:38, etc.). The term is also applied to the veil that concealed the holy of holies (Exod. xxxv:12; xxxix:34; xl:21; Num. iv:5).

3. In relation to heathenism *bawt-teem'* (Heb. בָּתִּים, marg. "houses"), "hangings" (2 Kings xxiii: 7), probably means small tent temples woven by the women for Asherah (comp. 2 Kings xvii:29).

HANIEL (hăn'i-el), the form of Hanniel which is used in 1 Chron. vii:39. (See HANNIEL.)

HANNAH (hăn'nah), (Heb. חַנָּה, *khan-naw'*, grace, favor), wife of Elkanah (a Levite of Ephratah) and mother of Samuel.

(1) A Childless Wife. She was very dear to her husband, but being childless was much aggrieved by the insults of Elkanah's other wife, Peninnah, who was blessed with children. The family lived at Ramathaim-zophim, and, as the law required, there was a yearly journey to offer sacrifices at the sole altar of Jehovah, which was then at Shiloh. Women were not bound to attend; but pious females free from the cares of a family often did so, especially when the husband was a Levite. Every time that Hannah went there childless she declined to take part in the festivities which followed the sacrifices, being then, as it seems, peculiarly exposed to the taunts of her rival.

(2) An Earnest Prayer. At length, on one of these visits to Shiloh, while she prayed before returning home, she vowed to devote to the Almighty the son which she so earnestly desired (1 Sam. i:11). It seems to have been the custom to pronounce all vows at the holy place in a loud voice, under the immediate notice of the priest (Deut. xxiii:23; Ps. lxv:1); but Hannah prayed in a low tone, so that her lips only were seen to move. This attracted the attention of the high-priest, Eli, who suspected that she had taken too much wine at the recent feast. From this suspicion Hannah easily vindicated herself, and returned home with a lightened heart.

(3) Birth of a Son. Before the end of that year Hannah became the rejoicing mother of a son, to whom the name of Samuel was given, and who was from his birth placed under the obligations of that condition of Naziriteship to which his mother had vowed him. (B. C. 1171.)

(4) Taken to Shiloh. Hannah went no more to Shiloh till her child was old enough to dispense with her maternal services, when she took him up with her to leave him there, as, it appears, was the custom when one already a Levite was placed under the additional obligations of Naziriteship. When he was presented in due form to the high-priest, the mother took occasion to remind him of the former transaction: 'For this child,' she said, 'I prayed, and the Lord hath given me my petition which I asked of him' (1 Sam. i:27). Hannah's gladness afterwards found vent in an exulting chant, which furnishes a remarkable specimen of the early lyric poetry of the Hebrews, and of which many of the ideas and images were in after times repeated by the Virgin Mary on a somewhat similar occasion (Luke i:46, *sq.*).

(5) Annual Visits. After this Hannah failed not to visit Shiloh every year, bringing a new dress for her son, who remained under the eye and near the person of the high-priest. (See SAMUEL.) That great personage took kind notice of Hannah on these occasions, and bestowed his blessing upon her and her husband. The Lord repaid her abundantly for that which she had, to use her own expression, 'lent to him;' for she had three sons and two daughters after Samuel.

HANNATHON (hăn'na-thŏn), (Heb. חַנָּתֹן, *khan-naw-thone'*, probably favored), a place on the northern boundary of Zebulun (Josh. xix:14), apparently about midway between the Sea of Galilee and the valley of Jiphthah-el.

HANNIEL (hăn'ni-el), (Heb. חַנִּיאֵל, *khan-nee-ale'*, grace of God).

1. Son of Ephod and assistant in the division of the Promised Land (Num. xxxiv:23). B. C. 1618.

2. An Asherite, son of Ulla (1 Chron. vii: 39, where the name is less correctly HANIEL), before B. C. 720.

HANOCH (nā'nok), (Heb. חֲנוֹךְ, *khan-oke'*, initiated.

1. The third child of Midian, a descendant of Abraham and Keturah (Gen. xxv:4). The name is Henoch in the parallel passage (1 Chron. i:33).

2. Eldest son of Reuben and founder of the family by his name (Gen. xlvi:9; Num. xxvi: 5; 1 Chron. v:3). Hanoch and Enoch are the same in the Hebrew.

HANOCHITES (hā'nok-its), (Heb. הַחֲנֹכִי, *hak-khan-o-kee'*), a family founded by HANOCH, 2.

HANUN (hā'nun), (Heb. חָנוּן, *khaw-noon'*, favored).

1. A son and successor of Nahash, king of the Ammonites. David, who had in his troubles been befriended by Nahash, sent, with the kindest intentions, an embassy to condole with him on the death of his father, and to congratulate him on his own accession. The rash young king, however, was led to misapprehend the motives of this embassy, and to treat with gross and inexpiable indignity the honorable personages whom David had charged with this mission. Their beards were *half* shaven, and their robes cut short by the middle, and they were dismissed in this shameful trim, which can be appreciated only by those who consider how reverently the beard has always been regarded by the Orientals (see BEARD). (B. C. 1038). When the news of this affront was brought to David, he sent word to the ambassadors to remain at Jericho till the growth of their beards enabled them to appear with decency in the metropolis. He vowed vengeance upon Hanun for the insult; and the vehemence with which the matter was taken up forms an instance, interesting from its antiquity, of the respect expected to be paid to the person and character of ambassadors. Hanun himself looked for nothing less than war as the consequence of his conduct; and he subsidized Hadarezer and other Syrian princes to assist him with their armies. The power of the Syrians was broken in two campaigns, and the Ammonites were left to their fate, which was severe even beyond the usual severities of war in that remote age. (See AMMONITES; DAVID). (2 Sam. x; 1 Chron. xix), about B. C. 1034.

2. A man who assisted in repairing the ravine-gate in the wall of Jerusalem (Neh. iii:13), B. C. 446.

3. The sixth son of Zalaph, who assisted in repairing the wall of Jerusalem, apparently on the east side (Neh. iii:30), B. C. 446.

HAP (hăp), (Heb. מִקְרֶה, *mik-reh'*, Ruth ii:3), generally now used in composition with other words; as, mishap, perhaps, haply, hapless (2 Cor. ix:4). It is a Saxon word meaning *luck, chance*.

HAPHRAIM (haph-rā'im), (Heb. חֲפָרַיִם, *khaf-aw-rah'yim*, double pit), a city of Issachar (Josh. xix:19). Eusebius says there was a place called Apharaïm six miles from Legio. At present there is a village, *el-Afûleh*, about six miles northeast of Lejun, which may represent the Ancient Haphraim.

HAPLY (hăp'lў), (Gr. ἄρα, ar'ah).

Haply is 'by hap.' 'Happily' is the same word under a different spelling, and had formerly the same meaning, though it has now come to mean 'by *good* hap.' Happily meaning simply 'by hap,' 'perchance,' is common in Shakespeare, though modern editions usually spell it 'haply.' Thus *Hamlet*, II, ii, 402—

'*Ham.* That great baby you see there is not yet out of his swaddling-clouts.
Ros. Happily he's the second time come to them.'

Hence, it will be observed that the word means *by chance.*

In Acts v:39 the passage reads: "Lest haply ye be founde to stryve agaynst God."—Tyndale.

HAP-PIZZEZ (hăp-pĭz'zĕz), in A. V. *Aphses*, (Heb. פִּצֵּץ, *pits-tsates'*, the dispersion).

A descendant of Aaron. His family became the eighteenth of the twenty-four courses into which David divided the priests (1 Chron. xxiv: 15).

HARA (hā'rà), (Heb. הָרָא, *haw-raw'*, a Chaldee form for mountain, Gesenius; Vulg. *Ara*).

One of the places to which the tribes beyond the Jordan were carried away by Tiglath-pileser. The word occurs only in a single passage (1 Chron. v:26); in the Septuagint and Syriac version it is altogether omitted. The Chaldee Paraphrast renders it *mountains of darkness.* Bochart and Gesenius conjecture that it is a name for the northern part of Media (Herod. vii:62; Bochart, *Geog. Sacra*, iii. 14. p. 194; Gesenius, *Thesaurus, s. v.*, Michaelis, *Supplementa ad Lex. Heb.*, vol. i, p. 570). J. E. R.

W. Max Müller, in Hastings' *Bib. Dict.*, questions the correctness of the conjecture.

HARADAH (hăr'a-dah), (Heb. חֲרָדָה, *kharaw-daw'*, place of terror), the twenty-fifth camp or station of the Israelites (Num. xxxiii:24). It has not been identified. (See WANDERING, THE.)

HARAM (hā'ram). See HOUSE.

HARAN (hā'ran), (Heb. הָרָן, *haw-rawn'*, mountaineer).

1. One of the three sons of Terah, brother of Abraham and Nahor, and father of Lot, Milcah and Iscah. He died before his father Terah; which, from the manner in which it is mentioned, appears to have been a much rarer case in those days than at present (Gen. xi:27, *sq.*), B. C. 2223.

2. A Gershonite Levite of the family of Shimei, in the time of David (1 Chron. xxiii:9), B. C. 1014.

3. More properly *Charan* (Heb. חָרָן, *khawrawn'*, parched), called by the Greeks Charran, and by the Romans Charræ. It was situated in the northwestern part of Mesopotamia, on a river of the same name running into the Euphrates. It is supposed to have been so called from Haran, the father of Lot and brother of Abraham; but there appears no ground for this conclusion except the identity of names. Abraham, after he had been called from Ur of the Chaldees, tarried here till his father, Terah, died, when he proceeded to the land of Canaan (Gen. xi:31, 38; Acts vii:4). The elder branch of the family still remained at Haran; which led to the interesting journeys thither described in the patriarchal history—first, that of Abraham's servant to obtain a wife for Isaac (Gen. xxiv) and next, that of Jacob when he fled to evade the wrath of Esau (Gen. xxviii: 10). The plain bordering on this town is cele-

brated in history as the scene of a battle in which the Roman army was defeated by the Parthians, under the Triumvir Crassus killed.

This place is not at all connected with the modern Hârân-el-awamâd, east of Damascus, as maintained by Dr. Beke. Haran still retains its ancient name in the form of Harran, and is only peopled by a few families of wandering Arabs, who are led thither by a plentiful supply of water from several small streams. It is situated in a flat and sandy plain 36 deg. 40 min. N. lat., 39 deg. 2 min. 45 sec. E. long.

It is mentioned by Ezekiel (xxvii:23) among the places which traded with Tyre. This trade would be very natural, as Haran was the frontier town of Babylon, commanding both the roads and fords of the Euphrates. "It was the city of the moon god, the foundation of whose temple went back to prehistorical times, and was restored by Nabonidus" (Sayce, *Higher Crit. and Mon.*, p. 507, *sq.*)

4. Son of Caleb by his concubine, Ephah (1 Chron. ii:46), B. C. 1618.

HARARITE (hā'ra-rīt), (Heb. הֲרָרִי, *ha-hah-raw-ree'*).

1. A designation of *Agee* (2 Sam. xxiii:11).

2. The name of his son *Shammah* (2 Sam. xxiii:33), which Kennicott suggests should be the reading in 1 Chron. xi:34.

3. The designation of *Sharar* (2 Sam. xxiii:33), or Sacar, which Kennicott regards as more correct (1 Chron. xi:35).

HARBONA (har-bō'nà), (Heb. חַרְבוֹנָא, *khar-bonaw'*, ass driver; in Esth. vii:9 חַרְבוֹנָה), one of the eunuchs of Ahasuerus or Xerxes (Esth. i:10). In vii:9 the name is Harbonah (B. C. 483-473).

HARBONAH (har-bō'nah). The same as above.

HARD (härd). The various meanings of 'hard,' whether as adj. or adv., may be given as follows:

1. Literally, *not soft*, only Job xli:24; Ezek. iii:9; Wisdom of Sol. xi:4; Sirach xl:15, xlviii: 17.

2. *Unfeeling, cruel* (Ps. xciv:4), 'How long shall they utter and speak hard things?' (R. V. 'They prate, they speak arrogantly').

3. *Trying, exacting* (Exod. i:14) 'hard bondage' (R. V. 'hard service'); (2 Sam. iii:39), 'The sons of Zeruiah be too hard for me;' (Ps. lxxxviii:7) 'Thy wrath lieth hard upon me;' (Prov. xiii:15) 'The way of transgressors is hard' (R. V. 'The way of the treacherous is rugged'); (Matt. xxv:24) 'Lord, I knew thee that thou art an hard man;' (John vi:60) 'This is an hard saying; who can hear it?;' (Acts ix:5) 'It is hard for thee to kick against the pricks').

4. *Obdurate* (Jer. v:3) 'They have made their faces harder than a rock;' (Ezek. iii:9) 'As an adamant harder than flint haye I made thy forehead.' Comp. Shaks. *Ant. and Cleop.* III, xi: 111—

'But when we in our viciousness grow hard,
(O misery on't) the wise gods seal our eyes.'

5. *Strenuous* only (Jonah i:13) 'The men rowed hard.'

6. *Difficult* as (Gen. xviii:14) 'Is anything too hard for the Lord?' (R. V. margin, 'wonderful'); (1 Kings x:1) 'She came to prove him with hard questions;' (Mark x:24) 'How hard is it for them that trust in riches to enter into the kingdom of God!' (Hastings' *Bib. Dict.*)

Figurative. (1) *Hardness of spirit* expresses great inward sorrow and trouble (1 Sam. i:15). (2) *Hardness of heart* signifies stupidity and obstinacy in sinning (Ezek. iii:7). (3) *The way of transgressors is hard;* they are obstinate in their sin, and their course is disagreeable and dangerous (Prov. xiii:15). (4) *Manifold troubles* are called *hardness,* because difficult to be borne (2 Tim. ii:3). (5) *God's hardening men* denotes his justly withholding his gracious influences from them, but not in an arbitrary manner. He permits them in harmony with their own free wills to go on in the way of sinning (Exod. iv:21; vii:3; xiv:4, 17; xix:12, and x:10, 27). (6) *Men harden their heart,* face, or neck when they grow more and more obstinate and impudent in wickedness, and refuse to be reclaimed (1 Sam. vi:6; Jer. v:3; Prov. xxix:1). *To harden oneself in sorrow* is with bravery to endure violent pains from an eager desire of death (Job vi:10).

HARDNESS OF HEART (härd'nĕs ŏv härt), (Gr. σκληροκαρδία, *sklay-rok-ar-dee'ah,* Matt. xix:8; Mark iii:5; Gr. πώρωσις, *po'ro-sis,* callousness), destitution of feeling. (See HARD, *Figurative.*)

HARE (hâr), (Heb. אַרְנֶבֶת, *ar-neh'beth*), occurs in Lev. xi:6, and Deut. xiv:7, and in both instances it is prohibited from being used as food, because it chews the cud, although it has not the hoof divided.

The animal which is now called the hare does not actually chew the cud, but has incisor teeth above and below, set like chisels, and calculated for gnawing, cutting, and nibbling, and when in a state of repose the animals are engaged in working the incisor teeth upon each other. This practice is a necessary condition of existence, for the friction keeps them fit for the purpose of nibbling, and prevents their growing beyond a proper length. As hares do not subsist on hard substances, like most of the genera of the order, but on tender shoots and grasses, they have more cause, and therefore a more constant craving, to abrade their teeth; and this they do in a manner which, combined with the slight trituration of the occasional contents of the cheeks even modern writers, not zoölogists, have mistaken for real rumination.

It follows that both with regard to the Shaphan and the Hare we should understand the original in the above passages, rendered 'chewing the cud,' as merely implying a second mastication, more or less complete. The act of 'chewing the cud' and 're-chewing' being considered identical by the Hebrews, the sacred law-giver, not being occupied with the doctrines of science, no doubt used the expression in the sense in which it was then understood. C. H. S.

"The Arab of the present day regards the hare as a ruminant, and for that reason eats its flesh. As Tristram well says, 'Moses speaks of animals according to appearances, and not with the precision of a comparative anatomist, and his object was to show why the hare should be interdicted, though to all appearance it chewed the cud, viz.: because it did not divide the hoof. To have spoken otherwise would have been as unreasonable as to have spoken of the earth's motion, instead of sunset and sunrise.' " (G. E. Post, Hastings' *Bib. Dict.*)

There are two distinct species of hare in Syria, one, Lepus Syriacus, or Syrian hare, nearly equal in size to the common European, having the fur ochery buff, and Lepus Sinaiticus, or hare of the desert, smaller and brownish. They reside in the localities indicated by their trivial names, and are distinguished from the common hare, by a greater length of ears, and a black tail with white fringe. There is found in Egypt, and higher up

the Nile, a third species, represented in the outline paintings on ancient monuments, but not colored with that delicacy of tint required for distinguishing it from the others, excepting that it appears to be marked with the black speckles which characterize the existing species.

HAREPH (hā'reph), (Heb. חָרֵף, *khaw-rafe',* reproachful), the "father" of Bethgader and "son" of Caleb in the genealogy of Judah by one of his legitimate wives (1 Chron. ii:51), B. C. about 1190.

HARETH (hā'reth), (Heb. חֶרֶת, *kheh'reth,* thicket). This is the place in the wooded mountain to which David fled from Saul (1 Sam. xxii:5).

HARHAIAH (här'ha-ī'ah), (Heb. חַרְהֲיָה, *khar-hah-yaw'*), a man whose son, Uzziel, assisted in repairing the walls of Jerusalem under Nehemiah (Neh. iii:8), B. C. before 446.

HARHAS (här'has), (Heb. חַרְחַס, *khar-khas',* glitter, splendor), ancestor of Shallum, the husband of Huldah, a prophetess in the time of Josiah (2 Kings xxii:14), called Hasrah in 2 Chron. xxxiv:22. The two names differ in Hebrew in the second H, and not merely in *transposition of letters.*

HARHUR (här'hur), (Heb. חַרְחוּר, *khar-khoor',* burning fever), one of the Nethinim whose posterity returned from Babylon with Zerubbabel (Ezra ii:51; Neh. vii:53), B. C. before 536.

HARIM (hā'rim), (Heb. חָרִם, *khaw-reem',* flat-nosed).

1. A priest who had charge of one of the divisions in the Temple worship under David (1 Chron. xxiv:8), B. C. 1014.

2. The "sons" of Harim to the number of 1,017, went up from Babylon with Zerubbabel (Ezra ii:39; Neh. vii:42). The name occurs among those who sealed the covenant with Nehemiah (Neh. x:5), and among those who had taken foreign wives (Ezra x:21). The name also occurs as the descendants of those who went up with Zerubbabel in the days of Joiakim son of Jeshua (Neh. xii:15).

3. Another family, to the number of 320, who returned from Babylon with Zerubbabel (Ezra ii:32; Neh. vii:35). They seem to have been among those who took foreign wives (Ezra x:31), and sealed the covenant (Neh. x:27), B. C. about 446.

HARIPH (hā'riph), (Heb. חָרִיף, *khaw-reef',* autumnal), one early born, strong, autumnal rain).

1. An Israelite, whose descendants (or possibly a place whose inhabitants), to the number of one hundred and twelve, returned from Babylon with Zerubbabel (Neh. vii:24). Probably the same with Jorah (Ezra ii:18), B. C. before 536.

2. A chief of the people who gave his hand to the covenant made by Nehemiah (Neh. x:19), B. C. 445.

HARLOT (här'lŏt), (Heb. זוֹנָה, *zo-naw'*; קְדֵשָׁה, *ked-ay-shaw',* whore, strange woman, etc.; נָכְרִיָּה, *nok-ree-yaw'*; זָרָה, *za-raw',* etc.).

The first of these English words, to which various etymologies have been assigned, signifies a prostitute for lust or gain. The *mercenary* motive is more evident in the second.

The first Hebrew word (*zo-naw'*) occurs frequently and is often rendered in our version by the first of these English words, as in Gen. xxxiv:31, etc., and sometimes, without apparent reason for the change, by the second, as in Prov. xxiii:27, and elsewhere. The first English word is also applied to *different* Hebrew words, whereby important distinctions are lost. Thus in Gen. xxxviii:15, the word is *zonaw'*, 'harlot,' which, however, becomes changed to *ked-ay-shaw'*, 'harlot,' in vers. 21, 22, which means, literally, a *consecrated* woman, a female (perhaps priestess) devoted to prostitution in honor of some *heathen* idol. The distinction shows that Judah supposed Tamar to be a *heathen:* the facts, therefore, do not prove that prostitution was then practiced between *Hebrews.* The following elucidation is offered of the most important instances in which the several words occur :

(1) The Veil. First *zonaw.* From the foregoing account of Judah it would appear that the 'veil' was at that time peculiar to harlots. Judah thought Tamar to be such, *'because* she had covered her face.' Mr. Buckingham remarks, in reference to this passage, that 'the Turcoman women go unveiled to this day' (*Travels in Mesopotamia,* 1:77). It is contended by Jahn and others that in ancient times all females wore the veil (*Bibl. Archäol.p.* 127). Possibly some peculiarity in the size of the veil, or the mode of wearing it, may have been (Prov. vii:10) the distinctive dress of the harlot at that period (see New Translation, by the Rev. A. De Sola, etc. pp. 116, 248-9). The priests and the high-priest were forbidden to take a wife that was (*had been,* Matt. xxi:31) a harlot. Josephus extends the law to all the Hebrews, and seems to ground it on the prohibition against oblations arising from prostitution (Deut. xxiii:18) (*Antiq.* iv:8, 23).

(2) Rahab. The celebrated case of Rahab has been much debated. She is, indeed, called by the word usually signifying *harlot* (Josh. ii:1; vi:17; Sept. πόρνη; Vulg. *meretrix;* and in Heb. xi:31; James ii:25); but the word may also mean an innkeeper. (See RAHAB.)

(3) A Foreigner. The next instance introduces the epithet of 'strange woman.' It is the case of Jephthah's mother (Judg. xi:2), who is *also* called a harlot, (πόρνη; *meretrix*); but the epithet 'strange woman' merely denotes *foreign extraction.* The representation given by Solomon is no doubt founded upon facts, and therefore shows that in his time prostitutes plied their trade in the 'streets' (Prov. vii:12; ix:14, etc.; Jer. iii:2; Ezek. xvi:24, 25, 31).

(4) Consecrated Prostitute. *Kedayshaw*, occurs Gen. xxxviii:15, 21, 22; Deut. xxiii:17; Hos. iv:14. It has been already observed that the proper meaning of the word is *consecrated prostitute.* The prohibition in Deut. xxiii:17, 'there shall be no קְדֵשָׁה, "whore," of the daughters of Israel,' is intended to exclude such *devotees* from the worship of Jehovah (see other allusions, Job xxxvi:14; 1 Kings xiv:24; xv:12). The strange woman is further alluded to (1 Kings xi:1; Prov. v:20; vi:24; vii:5; xxiii:27; Sept. ἀλλοτρία; Vulg. *aliena, extranea*). It seems probable that some of the Hebrews in later times interpreted the prohibition against fornication (Deut. xxii:14) as limited to females of their own nation, and that the 'strange women' in question were Canaanites and other Gentiles (Josh. xxiii:13).

(5) New Testament. In the New Testament πόρνη, *harlot, occurs* in Matt. xxi:31, 32; Luke xv:30; 1 Cor. vi:15, 16; Heb. xi:31; James ii:25. In none of these passages does it *necessarily* imply prostitution for gain. The likeliest is Luke xv:30.   J. F. D.

(6) Old English Use. In the old English use of the term harlot meant originally a vagabond. R. C. Trench says it was used of both sexes alike,

and for the most part a term of slight and contempt. (See MARRIAGE; PROSTITUTION, SACRED.)

Figurative. (1) It is used symbolically for a city in Rev. xvii:1, 5, 15, 16; xix:2, where the term and all the attendant imagery are derived from the Old Testament. It may be observed in regard to Tyre, which (Is. xxiii:15, 17) is represented as 'committing fornication with all the kingdoms of the world upon the face of the earth,' that these words, as indeed seems likely from those which follow, may relate to the various arts which she had employed to induce *merchants* to trade with her' (*Patrick, in loc.*). So the Sept. understood it, *she will be an emporium for all the kingdoms on the face of the earth.* Schleusner observes that the same words in Rev. xviii:3 *may* also relate to *commercial dealings.* (2) Since the Hebrews regarded Jehovah as the husband of his people, by virtue of the covenant he had made with them (Jer. iii:1) ; therefore, to *commit fornication* is a very common metaphor in the Scriptures to denote defections on their part from that covenant, and especially by the practice of idolatry. (See FORNICATION.) Hence the degeneracy of Jerusalem is illustrated by the symbol of a harlot (Is. i:21), and even that of heathen cities, as of Nineveh (Nah. iii:4). Under this figure the prophet Ezekiel delivers the tremendous invectives contained in ch. xvi, xxiii. (3) In the prophecy of Hosea the illustration is carried to a startling extent. The prophet seems commanded by the Lord to take 'a wife of whoredoms and children of whoredoms' (ch. i:2), and to 'love an adulteress' (ch. iii:1). It has, indeed, been much disputed whether these transactions were real, or passed in vision only; but the idea itself, and the diversified applications of it throughout the prophecy, render it one of the most effective portions of Scripture. (See HOSEA.) (4) Tyre *sang as a harlot* when, by fair speeches, the Tyrians enticed the nations to renew their trade with them (Is. xxiii:15). (5) *Antichristian Babylon* is called the *great whore*, and *mother of harlots, and abominations*, because of its noted apostasy and idolatry, and decoying others into it: and such apostasy is called *fornication, whoredom,* or *adultery* (Rev. xvii and xix:2).

HARMAGEDON (här-măg'e-don). See ARMAGEDDON.

HARMONIES (här'mŏ-nĭz). The object of Harmonies is to arrange the Scriptures in chronological order, so that the mutual agreement of the several parts may be rendered apparent, and the true succession of events clearly understood. With this view various scholars have compiled harmonies of the Old Testament, of the New, and of particular portions of both. Harmonies of the Old Testament exhibit the books disposed in chronological order, as is done by Lightfoot in his *Chronicle of the Times, and the Order of the Texts of the Old Testament,* and by Townsend in his *Old Testament Arranged in Historical and Chronological Order.* Harmonies of the New Testament present the gospels and epistles distributed in like order, the latter being interspersed among the Acts of the Apostles. In this way Townsend has proceeded in his valuable work entitled, *The New Testament arranged in Chronological and Historical Order.* Books, however, of this kind are so few in number, that the term *harmony* is almost appropriated by usage to the *gospels.* It is this part of the New Testament which has chiefly occupied the attention of those inquirers whose object is to arrange the Scriptures in their true order. The memoirs of our Lord written by the four Evangelists have chiefly occupied the thoughts of those who wish to show that they all agree, and mutually authenticate one another. Accordingly, such compositions are exceedingly numerous. To adopt any one implicitly, is more than the enlightened inquirer can consent to do. We should therefore recommend a minute examination of the works prepared by Newcome, Greswell, Michaelis, De Wette and Lücke, Clausen, Robinson, Andrews, etc.

S. D.

HARNEPHER (här'ne-pher), (Heb. רֶנֶפֶר, *khar-neh'fer*, derivation uncertain, perhaps snoring), an Asherite, son of Zophah (1 Chron. vii:36).

HARNESS, HARNESSED (här'nĕs, här'nĕst), (Heb. אָסַר, *aw-sar'*, to fasten), the act of fastening animals to a cart or vehicle, e. g., *yoking* cattle (1 Sam. vi:7, 10; A. V. "tie"), or horses (Jer. xlvi:4).

In A. V. harness always means armor, and to harness means to put on armor, R. V. gives 'armor' in 1 Kings xx:11; 2 Chron. ix:24, and 'armed in Exod. xiii:18; while R. V. prefers 'armor' also in 1 Kings xxii:34; 2 Chron. xviii:33; both have left Jer. xlvi:4 untouched: 'Harness the horses.' The meaning is not (as Cheyne and most others) 'yoke the horses to the chariots,' but put on their accouterments. (Hastings, *Bib. Dict.*)

HAROD (hā'rod), (Heb. חֲרֹד, *khar-ode'*, trembling or terror).

A brook not far from Jezreel and Mount Gilboa. The name, as given above, means 'palpitation,' and it has been suggested that it originated in consequence of the alarm and terror of most of the men who were here tested by Gideon (Judg. vii:1-3); but this supposition seems very farfetched, and the name more probably arose from some peculiarity in the outflow of the stream. (Porter *Handbook for Sinai and Pal.* ii:355.) It is identical with the present fountain *Ain Julad*, a mile east from Jezreel, and opposite Shunem.

HARODITE (hā'rod-īt), (Heb. חֲרֹדִי, *khar-o-dee'*), a designation of Shammah and Elika in David's guard (2 Sam. xxiii:25), no doubt derived from the name of a place.

HAROEH (hăr'o-ēh), (Heb. רֹאֶה, *ro-ay'*: Haroeh, including the article: means prophet), a name given in the genealogical lists of Judah as son of Shobal (1 Chron. ii:52). (See REAIAH.)

HARORITE (hā'ro-rīt), (Heb. הֲרֹרִי, *har-o-ree'*), a designation of Shammoth, one of David's guard (1 Chron. xi:27). In 2 Sam. xxiii:25 the name appears slightly changed. (See HARODITE.)

HAROSHETH (hă-rŏ'shĕth) **OF THE GENTILES** (Heb. חֲרֹשֶׁת, *khar-o'sheth*), a city in the north of Palestine.

It was the dwelling place of Sisera (Judg. iv:2), from which he advanced against Barak (verse 13) and to which he fled after his defeat (verse 16). The descriptive epithet 'of the Gentiles' is obscure; it may have been given to distinguish this place from a neighboring *Israelite* Harosheth. Harosheth is generally identified (by Moore rather doubtfully) with *el-Harathiyeh*, on the right bank of the lower Kishon, at a point which commands the entrance to the Great Plain from the Plain of Acre and the commercial roads that led through it. (Thomson, *Land and Book* ii:143.)

HARP (härp), (Heb. כִּנּוֹר, *kin-nore'*). See MUSICAL INSTRUMENTS.

HARROW (hăr'rŏ), (Heb. חָרַץ, *khaw-reets'*, 2 Sam. xii:31; 1 Chron. xx:3).

The word so rendered in the above passages is probably a thrashing machine. In Is. xxviii:24; Job xxxix:10; Hos. x:11, the word correctly expresses the breaking of clods.

HARSHA (här'shà), (Heb. חַרְשָׁא, *khar-shaw'*, enchanter), one of the Nethinim whose descendants were among the Nethinim who returned with Zerubbabel from Babylon (Ezra ii:52; Neh. vii:54), B. C. before 536.

HART (härt), the Hebrew אַיָּל, *ah-yawl'*, and not *yahmôr* (Deut. xiv:5; 1 Kings iv:23), is the *fallow deer*. The female is called Hind.

Hind.

It was one of the clean animals (Deut. xii:15; xiv:5; xv:22). From 1 Kings iv:23, it seems to have been frequently killed for food. Its activity is referred to (Is. xxxv:6), though the hind is more often mentioned in such similes. In Lam. i:6, the true rendering is "rams." (See also FALLOW DEER.)

Hart.

Figurative. (1) The saints are likened to *harts panting* for water-brooks, to mark the earnestness of their desire after God, and the ordinances of his grace, when hunted by Satan, and persecuted by the world (Ps. xlii:1). (2) The

Chaldeans were like *chased roes*, when with terror and dread they fled from the fury of the Medes and Persians, not knowing what to do Is. xiii :14). (3) Wives are likened to *hinds and roes,* to mark their comeliness and affection, and the delight their husbands should take in them (Prov. v :19).

HARUM (hā'rum), (Heb. רֻם, *haw-room',* exalted).

A name given in a very obscure portion of the genealogies of Judah (1 Chron. iv :8).

HARUMAPH (hā-ru'maph), (Heb. חֲרוּמַף, *kharoo-maf',* slit-nosed).

He had a son, Jedaiah, who assisted in the repairing of the wall of Jerusalem (Neh. iii :10), B. C. before 446.

HARUPHITE (hā-ru'phīt), (Heb. חֲרוּפִי, *kharoo-fee'),* a designation of Shephatiah, the Korhite, who came to David at Ziklag (1 Chron. xii :5).

HARUZ (hā'ruz), (Heb. חָרוּץ, *khaw-roots',* earnest).

The father of Meshullemeth, who was mother of Amon, king of Judah (2 Kings xxi :19), B. C. before 664.

HARVEST (här'vĕst), (Heb. קָצִיר, *kaw-tseer',* severed).

The period of harvest in ancient Palestine may be divided into two portions : that of barley and that of wheat harvest, the former preceding the latter by about a fortnight (Ruth ii :23). Its beginning was consecrated by the bringing of the sheaf of first fruits (Lev. xxiii :10). It began in the lowlands before the crops were ripe on the hills. In the hot Jordan valley barley harvest commenced in April, when the Jordan was full (Josh. iii :15 ; comp. v :10), at the close of the rainy season (1 Sam. xii :17, 18 ; Prov. xxvi :1). Wheat harvest lingered in the uplands to the month of June. It was a hot time of the year (Prov. xxv :13 ; Is. xviii :4. When the harvest was completed, and the produce gathered in, there were great rejoicings (Is. ix :3). The feasts of unleavened bread, of weeks or harvest, and of ingathering, had all a relation to the season of reaping. (See YEAR.) (Davis, *Bib. Dict.*)

HASADIAH (hăs'a-dī'ah), (Heb. חֲסַדְיָה, *khasad-yaw',* Jehovah loves), a descendant of the royal line of Judah, and apparently son of Zerubbabel (1 Chron. iii :20). Perhaps he was one of those born after the restoration (B. C. about 536).

HASENUAH (hăs'e-nū'ah), (Heb. הַסְּנֻאָה, *hassen-oo-aw',* pointed), a man belonging to one of the chief families of Benjamin (1 Chron. ix :7), B. C. before 536.

HASHABIAH (hăsh-a-bī'ah), (Heb. חֲשַׁבְיָה, *khash-ab-yaw',* Jehovah regards).

1. Three Merarite Levites (1 Chron. vi :45 ; ix : 14 ; Ezra viii :19), B. C. before 440.
2. Son of Jeduthun, who had charge of the twelfth course and was one of David's harp players (1 Chron. xxv :3, 19), B. C. 1014.
3. A descendant of Hebron, who, with the 1700 men of his kindred looked after David's interests on the west of the Jordan (1 Chron. xxvi :30 ; xxvii :17), B. C. 1014.
4. Son of Kemuel, prince of the tribe of Levi in the time of David. Perhaps the same as 3 (1 Chron. xxvii :17), B. C. 1014.
5. A Levite, who assisted in the passover-feast of King Josiah (2 Chron. xxxv :9), B. C. 623.
6. One of the chiefs of the priests who returned with Ezra from Babylon (Ezra viii :24), B. C. 536.

7. A ruler of half the environs of Keilah, who repaired a part of the wall of Jerusalem under Nehemiah (Neh. iii :17), B. C. 446-410.
8. Three Levites : one sealed the covenant with Nehemiah (Neh. x :11) ; another was son of Bunni (Neh. xi :15 ; the third was an attendant in the Temple (Neh. xi :22).
9. A priest of the family of Hilkiah under Joiakim, son of Jeshua (Neh. xii :21), B. C. before 440.

HASHABNAH (ha-shăb'nah), (Heb. חֲשַׁבְנָה, *khash-ab-naw',* probably for Hashabiah), one of the chiefs of the people who sealed the covenant of reformation (Neh. x :25), B. C. about 410.

HASHABNIAH (hăsh'ab-nī'ah), (Heb. חֲשַׁבְנְיָה, *khash-ab-neh-yaw',* thought of Jah, Jehovah regards).

1. Father of Hattush, who assisted in repairing the wall (Neh. iii :10), B. C. before 446.
2. A Levite who assisted in the great fast under Ezra and Nehemiah when the covenant was sealed (Neh. ix :5), B. C. before 410.

HASHBADANA (hash-băd'a-nà), (Heb. חַשְׁבַּדָּנָה, *khash-bad-daw'naw,* intelligence in judging), one of those who took part in the reading of the law to the people by Ezra (Neh. viii :4), B. C. 410.

HASHEM (hā'shem), (Heb. הָשֵׁם, *haw-shame',* wealthy).

His sons were among David's guard (1 Chron. xi :34). In 2 Sam. xxiii :32, Kennicott suggests that "sons of Jashen" should read "sons of Hashem" (B. C. before 1014).

HASHMONAH (hash-mō'nah), (Heb. חַשְׁמֹנָה, *khash-mo-naw',* fatness), a station in the wandering before Moseroth (Num. xxxiii :29), which latter was near Mount Hor (Num. xx :28 ; Deut. x :6).

HASHUB (hā'shub), (Heb. חַשּׁוּב, *khash-shoob',* intelligent), properly Hasshub.

1. Son of Pahath-Moab, who rebuilt a part of the wall of Jerusalem (Neh. iii :23). (B. C. 410.)
2. Another of the same name, who assisted at another part of the wall (Neh. iii :11). (B. C. 410.)
3. One who sealed the covenant with Nehemiah ; perhaps either 1 or 2 (Neh. x :23). (B. C. 446.)
4. A Merarite Levite (Neh. xi :15). In 1 Chron. ix :14, the name appears as Hasshub. (B. C. 440.)

HASHUBAH (ha-shu'bah), (Heb. חֲשֻׁבָה, *khashoo-baw',* esteemed or associated), one of the children of Zerubbabel, born probably after the restoration (1 Chron. iii :20), B. C. about 536.

HASHUM (hā'shum), (Heb. חָשֻׁם, *khaw-shoom',* enriched, rich, distinguished).

1. The sons of Hashum to the number of 223 returned with Zerubbabel (Ezra ii :19 ; Neh. vii : 22). Seven of them had married foreign wives (Ezra x :33). The chief of the family sealed the covenant with Nehemiah (Neh. x :i8). B. C. before 536.
2. One of the priests of the Levites who was present while Ezra read the law to the people (Neh. viii :4), B. C. 410.

HASHUPHA (ha-shu'phà), (Neh. vii :46), see HASUPHA. One of the families of the Nethinim who returned from Babylon in the first caravan (Neh. vii :46. The name appears accurately, Hasupha, in Ezra ii :43.

HASRAH (hăs'rah), (Heb. חַסְרָה, *khas-raw',* poverty). See HARHAS.

HASSENAAH (hăs'se-nā'ah), (Heb. הַסְּנָאָה, *khas-sen-aw-aw'*, thorny), the sons of Hassenaah rebuilt the fish-gate (Neh. iii:3). The name is probably the same as the place SENAAH with the definite article (Ezra ii:35; Neh. vii:38).

HASTE (hāst), (Heb. אוּץ, *oots*, Exod. v:13), to be close, narrow, to hurry; the verb being used transitively. (Comp. Is. xvi:5.)

HASUPHA (ha-sū'pha), (Heb. חֲשׂוּפָא, *khas-oo-faw'*, uncovered, naked).

The sons of Hasupha were among the Nethinim who returned with Zerubbabel (Ezra ii:43), B. C. before 536.

HAT (hăt), (Chald. כַּרְבְּלָא, *kar-bel-aw'*, Dan. iii:21).

Hats are mentioned once in A. V. (Dan. iii:21), but it is quite certain that this is a mistranslation. When Shadrach, Meshach and Abed-nego were about to be cast into the fiery furnace they were 'bound in their coats, their hosen, and their hats' (R. V., their hosen, their tunics, and their mantles').

HATACH (hā'tăk)) (Heb. הֲתָךְ, *hath-awk'*, perhaps *verity*, an eunuch in the palace of Xerxes, appointed to wait on Esther.

By his means Esther learnt from Mordecai the details of Haman's plot against the Jews (Esth. iv:5, 6, 9, 10), B. C. about 478.

HATE (hāt), (Heb. שָׂנֵא, *saw-nay'*; Gr. μισέω, *mis-eh'o*).

In the root of the Hebrew word is the idea of ugliness, deformity; hence to regard with feelings contrary to love; to loathe, to abhor, to cherish resentment or dislike to. In both the Hebrew and Greek words we find the above meaning in several places (e. g., 2 Chron. xviii:7; Ps. xlv:7; Matt. xxiv:10, etc.); while in others the meaning is "to regard with less love" (e. g., Deut. xxi:15, 16; Prov. xiii:24; Mal. i:3; Rom. ix:13).

The command to hate father and mother, wife and children, etc., and one's own life (Luke xiv:26), means that all earthly ties and love must be subordinate to love for Christ. Real hate to men is unchristian.

HATHATH (hā'thăth), (Heb. חֲתַת, *khath-ath'*, terror, as in Job vi:21), son of Othniel and grandson of Kenaz, of the tribe of Judah (1 Chron. iv:13), consequently also grandnephew and grandson of Caleb (verse 15; comp. Judg. i:13), B. C. probably after 1170.

HATIPHA (hăt'i-phà or ha-tī'phà), (Heb. חֲטִיפָא, *khat-ee-faw'*, robber), the sons of Hatipha were among the Nethinim who returned under Zerubbabel (Ezra ii:54; Neh. vii:56), B. C. before 536.

HATITA (hăt'i-tà or ha-tī'tà), (Heb. חֲטִיטָא, *khat-ee-taw'*, exploration). The sons of Hatita were a division of the Levites who returned under Zerubbabel (Ezra ii:42; Neh. vii:45), B. C. before 536.

HATSI HAM MENUCHOTH (hăt'si hămmĕn'ū-koth), (1 Chron. ii:52, margin). See MANAHETHITES, THE.

HATTIL (hăt'tĭl), (Heb. חַטִּיל, *khat-teel'*, waving), one of the descendants of "Solomon's servants" whose descendants returned from Babylon with Zerubbabel (Ezra ii:57; Neh. vii:59), B. C. before 536.

HATTUSH (hăt'tush), (Heb. חַטּוּשׁ, *khat-toosh'*, derivation uncertain).

1. A descendant of the kings of Judah (1 Chron. iii:22), B. C. after 406. (See Lord Hervey, *Genealogies*, pp. 103, 307, 322.)

2. Son of Hashabniah. He assisted in the rebuilding of the wall (Neh. iii:10), B. C. 446.

3. A descendant of David who accompanied Ezra to Jerusalem (Ezra viii:2), B. C. 459.

HAUNT (hänt), (Heb. רֶגֶל, *reh'gel*).

To haunt is in older English simply to frequent, to make one's stay, be familiar with, and conveys no reproach. Thus (John iii:22, Tyndale): 'After these thinges cam Jesus and his disciples into the Jewes londe, and ther he haunted with them and baptised' (A. V. 'tarried'). (Ps. xxvi: 4) Geneva Version, "I have not *haunted* with vain persons." (Comp. 1 Sam. xxx:31.)

HAURAN (hau'ran), (Heb. חַוְרָן, *khav-rawn'*), a province on the northeastern boundary of the Promised Land (Ezek. xlvii:16, 18).

In the passage in Ezekiel the Jordan is made the border line between Haurân, Damascus, and Gilead on the one hand, and the Land of Israel on the other. Haurân is there the whole district between Damascus and Gilead, from the lip of the Jordan Valley eastward. This practically corresponds with the province under the Turkish governor of Haurân to-day, whose seat is in el-Merkez, and whose jurisdiction includes Jedûr, Jaulân, and part of the hill country south of the Jarmuk, as well as the region now specially called Haurân.

Little was known of Haurân previous to 1854. The works of Porter, 1855, Graham, 1858, Wetstein, 1860, Burton and Drake, 1872, and Selah Merrill of the American Palestine Exploration Society, 1877, have thrown much light on its extent, nature, and history, but a thorough exploration of the country yet remains to be made. When the Israelites conquered the land, the whole of this region appears to have been subject to Og, the king of Bashan (Num. xxi:33-35; Deut. iii:1-5) and a large portion of it was alloted to Manasseh. The district would then include the Argob, the slope of the Haurân Mountains, where the Israelites found sixty fortified cities with walls and gates and a fertile tract. (See BASHAN.) In the Roman period the country was divided into five provinces, Ituræa, Gaulanitis, Batanæa (applied also to the whole region), Trachonitis, and Auranitis.

The natives now say that Haurân consists of three parts, viz.: en-Nukrah, el-Lejâ, and el-Jebel. These are clearly defined districts.

The ruins scattered over the region are very extensive and remarkable; those built in the caverns are regarded by Wetstein as the most ancient, and possibly reaching back to the times of the Rephaim (Gen. xiv:5; xv:20, and Deut. iii:11). The villages are chiefly of stone houses, having gates and doors of large slabs of dolerite; the gateways of the larger buildings are ornamented with sculptured vines and inscriptions. The Arabs, according to Wetstein, from near Yemen settled in the Haurân at about the beginning of the Christian era; later, a second immigration from south Arabia took place, and these controlled the country for five centuries, and they probably erected most of the stone buildings now in so good a state of preservation. A large number of inscriptions in various characters are yet to be deciphered, which will throw much light, no doubt, upon the ancient history of this wild region. Wetstein states that the eastern section of the Lejah and the slopes of the Haurân Mountains contain at least 300 ruined cities and towns. Selah Merrill says that an important ruin is found in every half hour of travel, and that among these ruins, he has himself visited and examined sixty ruined churches, and eleven of thirteen theaters, including one vast naumachia where mock sea fights were held. (Schaff, *Bib. Dict.*)

"In the beginning of the first century before Christ, the western Haurân was under the Jew Alexander Janneus, while the Nabateans occupied everything else to the east, including Damascus, the rest of Haurân, and the Leja. When the Romans came, in B. C. 64, besides freeing the Greek cities of Gaulanitis and Gilead from the Jews, they drove the Nabateans to the southern edge of Haurân, but did not occupy Haurân itself." (Smith, *Bib. Dict.*)

Under the Romans, civilization advanced, and, as evinced by the remains of churches and inscriptions, Christianity made rapid progress. In A. D. 632 the Moslem hordes from Arabia burst over the province like a tornado, and the blight swiftly fell, which lies heavy on the land to-day. The latest notice of a Christian building is an inscription found by the Rev. William Ewing, D. D., at el-Kufr, which records the foundation of a church in A. D. 720.

HAVE (hăv), (Heb. אָצָא, *yaw-tsaw'*, 2 Kings xi: 15), to take, conduct, guide, escort, bring, as in Shakespeare, "Your mistress sent to *have* me home to dinner." Used with various prepositions; as, to have away, to have forth, etc. (2 Kings xi:15; 2 Chron. xxiii:14; 2 Sam. xiii:9).

Such phrases may be considered as, 'Have in one's heart to,' (1 Chron. xxviii:2; comp. Phil. i:7) 'I have you in my heart'; 'I would have you with out carefulness' (1 Cor. vii:32): 'I would not have you ignorant,' (2 Cor. i:8) 'Who will have all men to be saved,' (1 Tim. ii:4), (ὃς θέλει, R. V. 'Who willeth that all men should be saved'). Comp. John xxi:22, Tyndale: 'Yf I will have him to tary tyll I come, what is that to the?'

HAVEN (hā'v'n), (Heb. חוֹף, *khofe*), from an unused root, mean. to *cover; a cove* (as a *sheltered* bay), coast [of the sea], haven, shore, [sea-] side. This word is rendered 'haven' by A. V. and R. V. in Gen. xlix:13, and by R. V. in Judg. v:17 (A. V. 'shore').

Havens are seldom mentioned in the Bible, probably for the reason that Palestine proper scarcely possesses any harbors, and the Israelites were not a maritime nation. The harbors in Old Testament times on the Mediterranean coast were in possession of the Phœnicians and the Philistines. (See GREAT SEA; SEA.)

HAVILAH (hăv'i-lah), (Heb. חֲוִילָה, *khav-ee-law'*, circular).

1. A district in Arabia Felix, deriving its name from the second son of Cush (Gen. x:7), or, according to others, from the second son of Joktan (Gen. x:29; comp. xxv:18). There can be no doubt, however, of the existence of a double Havilah; one founded by the descendant of *Ham*, and the other by that of *Shem*. Niebuhr (*Beschr. von Arab.*, pp. 270, 280) actually found in Yemen two districts called *Chaulân* or *Haulân*, one between Saana and Mecca, and the other a few leagues southeast from Saana; which latter Büsching (*Erdbeschr.* v. i. 601) considers to be the Havilah founded by the son of Cush, as mentioned Gen. x:7 (Michaelis, *Spicil.* i, 189, *sq.;* ii, 202). From Gen. xxv:18, it would appear that the land of Havilah formed the eastern boundary of the Israelites, and so likewise from 1 Sam. xv:7, where it seems, moreover, to have been a possession belonging to the Amalekites.

2. A land rich in gold, bdellium, and shoham, mentioned in Gen. ii:11 in the geographical description of Paradise. Some identify this with the preceding; but others take it to be *Chwala* on the Caspian Sea, from whence that sea itself is said to have derived the Russian name of *Chwalinskoy more* (Sea of Chwala); and others suppose it a general name for India (*T. Hieros*). E. M.

"A district of Khaulân (Haulân) is mentioned in the inscriptions of South Arabia; this is either Khaulân in Tihâmah, between Mecca and Saana, or another Khaulân southeast of Saana. Niebuhr further found a Huwailah on the Persian Gulf. The name, in fact, was widely spread in Arabia, and Yakut states that Hawîl was the name of a dialect spoken by the people of Mehri in the east of Hadramaut. The Mehri is the modern representative of the language of the Sabæan inscriptions." (A. H. Sayce, Hastings' *Bib. Dict.*)

HAVOTH JAIR (hā'voth jā'ir),(Heb. חַוּוֹת יָעִיר, *khav-vothe' yaw-eer'*, huts or hamlets of Jair), such as belonged to the Arabians, and a collection of which is regarded as forming a hamlet or village.

The district of Havoth-jair (*Jair's hamlets*), mentioned in Num. xxxii:41, and Deut. iii:14, was beyond the Jordan in the land of Gilead, and belonged to the half-tribe of Manasseh. (See also Josh. xiii:30; 1 Chron. ii:22, 23; 1 Kings iv:13; Judg. x:4.) (See JAIR.)

HAWK (hạk), (Heb. נֵץ, *nayts*, Lev. xi:16; Deut. xiv:15; Job xxxix:26; תַּחְמָס, *takh-mawce'*, an unclean bird), night hawk; by some rendered *ostrich*, by others *owl*.

The English name is an altered form of the old word fawk or falk. Western Asia and Lower Egypt, and consequently the intermediate territory of Syria and Palestine, are the habitation or transitory residence of a considerable number of spe-

Hawk (Falco Saker).

cies of the order *Raptores*, which, even including the shortest winged, have great powers of flight, are remarkably enterprising, live to a great age, are migratory, or followers upon birds of passage, or remain in a region so abundantly stocked with pigeon and turtle-dove as Palestine, and affording such a variety of ground to hunt their particular prey—abounding as it does in mountain and forest, plain, desert, marsh, river and sea-coast.

Falcons, or the 'noble' birds of prey used for hawking, have for many ages been objects of great interest, and still continue to be bought at high prices. They are consequently imported from distant countries, as Central Asia, Iceland, Barbary, etc. Their love of liberty often renders them irreclaimable when once on the wing; and their powers and boldness, independent of circumstances, and the extent of range which the long-winged species in particular can take, are exemplified by their presence in every quarter of the globe. The *Falco communis,* or Peregrine falcon, is so generally diffused as to occur even in New Holland and South America.

Next we may place *Falco Aroeris* of Sir J. G. Wilkinson, the sacred hawk of Egypt. This, if it be not in reality the same as, or a mere variety of, the Peregrine, should have retained the ancient epithet of *Hierax,* and the hawkers' name of *Sacre.* Innumerable representations of it occur in Egyptian monuments.

The Hobby, *Falco subbuteo,* is no doubt a second or third species of sacred hawk, having similar gernonia. Both this bird and the tractable Merlin, *Falco æsalon,* are used in the falconry of the inferior Moslem landowners of Asiatic Turkey.

Besides these, the Kestrel, *Falco tinnunculus,* occurs in Syria, and *Falco tinnunculoides,* or lesser Kestrel, in Egypt; and it is probable that both species visit these two territories according to the seasons.

To the 'noble' birds we may add the Gerfalcon, *Falco gyrfalco,* which is one-third larger than the Peregrine; it is imported from Tartary, and sold at Constantinople, Aleppo, and Damascus.

HAY (hā), (Heb. חָצִיר, *khaw-tseer'*).

This word in Prov. xxvii :25, and elsewhere, does not denote dried grass, as it does with us. The management of grass by the Hebrews as food for cattle was entirely different from ours. It was never dried and stored for winter use, but was cut green as it was wanted; and the phrase "mown grass" (Ps. lxxii: 6) would be more properly rendered "grass that has just been fed off." So in Prov. xxvii :25 the word translated "hay" means the first shoots of the grass; and the whole passage might properly be rendered, "The grass appeareth, and the green herb showeth itself, and the plants of the mountains are gathered." And in Is. xv :6 "hay" is put for "grass," and "grass" is put for the "green herb." The tenderness of grass, the rapidity of its growth, and the early period at which it is cut down and consumed afford the sacred writers some striking and beautiful illustrations (Ps. ciii :15; Is. xl :6; 1 Cor. iii :12). (See CHATZIR.)

HAZAEL (hăz'a-el), (Heb. חֲזָאֵל, *khaz-aw-ale'*, vision of God).

(1) Consults Elisha. An officer of Benhadad, king of Syria, whose eventual accession to the throne of that kingdom was made known to Elijah (1 Kings xix :15); and who, when Elisha was at Damascus, was sent by his master, who was then ill, to consult the prophet respecting his recovery. He was followed by forty camels bearing presents from the king. When Hazael appeared before the prophet, he said, 'Thy son Benhadad, king of Syria, hath sent me to thee, saying, 'Shall I recover of this disease?' The answer was, that he *might* certainly recover. 'Howbeit,' added the prophet, 'the Lord hath showed me that he shall surely die.' He then looked steadfastly at Hazael till he became confused:

on which the man of God then wept; and when Hazael respectfully inquired the cause of this outburst, Elisha replied by describing the vivid picture then present to his mind of all the evils which the man now before him would inflict upon Israel. Hazael exclaimed, 'But what! Is thy servant a dog that he should do this great thing?' The prophet explained that it was as king of Syria he should do it. Hazael then returned, and delivered to his master that portion of the prophetic response which was intended for him.

(2) Kills Benhadad. But the very next day this man, cool and calculating in his cruel ambition, took a thick cloth, and, having dipped it in water, spread it over the face of the king, who, in his feebleness, and probably in his sleep, was smothered by its weight, and died what seemed to his people a natural death (2 Kings viii :8, etc.), B. C. about 885. We are not to imagine that such a project as this was conceived and executed in a day, or that it was suggested by the words of Elisha. His discomposure at the earnest gaze of the prophet, and other circumstances, show that Hazael at that moment regarded Elisha as one to whom his secret purposes were known. In that case, his cry, 'Is thy servant a dog,' etc., was not, as some suppose, a cry of joy at the first view of a throne, but of horror at the idea of the public atrocities which the prophet described.

(3) King and Wars. The further information respecting Hazael which the Scriptures afford is limited to brief notices of his wars with Ahaziah and Joash, kings of Judah, and with Jehoram, Jehu, and Jehoahaz, kings of Israel (2 Kings viii :28; ix :14; x :32; xii :17; xiii :3; 2 Chron. xxii :5). It is difficult to distinguish the several campaigns and victories involved in these allusions, and spread over a reign of forty years; but it is certain that Hazael always had the advantage over the Hebrew princes. He devastated their frontiers, rent from them all their territories beyond the Jordan, traversed the breadth of Palestine, and carried his arms into the states of the Philistines; he laid siege to Jerusalem, and only retired on receiving the treasures of the temple and the palace. The details of these conquests redeemed to the very letter the appalling predictions of Elisha. This able and successful, but unprincipled usurper left the throne at his death to his son Benhadad (B. C. about 815).

Hazael figures more than once in the cuneiform inscriptions. Shalmaneser II, who in the early part of his reign had defeated an alliance formed by *Dadidri* (Ben-hadad II), Ahab of Israel, and other kings, and again in the fourteenth year of his reign had a second time worsted *Dadidri,* states that in his eighteenth year (B. C. 842) he joined battle with Hazael of Damascus, who had assembled a large army and entrenched himself upon the mountain of Sanir in the Anti-Lebanon. Here he awaited the Assyrian onslaught. Six thousand of his soldiers were killed in battle, while 1,121 of his chariots and 470 horses, with his camp equipage, were taken. Hazael fled to Damascus, and was pursued and besieged by the Assyrians. But it appears that, powerful though he was, Shalmaneser was not able to take Damascus, and had to content himself with a thoroughly characteristic conclusion of the campaign. He cut down the trees about the city, and then marching southward, entered Hauran, where he wasted and burned the cities. (Obelisk, lines 97-99 and Fragmentary Text, III R. 5, No. 6, 40-65. See translations by Rogers, *op. cit.* pp. 220, 221; See Rogers, *Hist. of Bab. and Assyr.,* p. 82.)

HAZAIAH (ha-zā'iah or ha-zā'yá), (Heb. חֲזָיָה, khaz-aw-yaw', Jehovah beholds), a man of Judah, descended from Shelah (Neh. xi:5), B. C. before 536.

HAZAR (hā'zar), (Heb. חָצֵר, khaw-tsare', an inclosure).

It is a term employed to denote the dependence of certain towns or villages upon a noted spot. Gesenius (Heb. Lex. s. v.) states that Hazar is "spoken also of the movable villages or encampments of nomadic tribes, who usually pitch their tents in a circle, or so as to form an inclosure." The African Arabs, who originally emigrated from Arabia, have retained many of their ancestral customs. "When these Arabs are in a region where they are liable to attacks from enemies, they pitch their tents in a circle, with their cattle and goods in the center. The whole is then fenced in with a low wall of stones, in which are inserted thick bundles of thorny acacia, the tangled branches and long needle-like spikes forming a perfectly impenetrable hedge around the encampment," Trumbull, Kadesh-Barnea, p. 281. (See HAZAR-ADDAR; HAZAR-ENAN; HAZAR-GADDAH; etc.)

HAZAR-ADDAR (hā'zar-ăd'dar), (Heb. אַדָּר חָצַר, khats-ar' ad-dawr', a village of Addar), a place in the southern desert part of Palestine, between Kadesh-barnea and Amon (Num. xxxiv:4).

It appears to be the same as HEZRON (which see) of Josh. xv:3, which in the latter passage is connected with but separated from Addar.

HAZAR-ENAN (hā'zar-ē'nan), (Heb. עֵינָן חֲצַר, khats-ar' ay-nawn', village of fountains).

One of the northern boundaries of the Promised Land (Num. xxxiv:9; Ez. xlvii:17; xlviii: 1). Mr. Porter (Damascus, i:252; ii:358) would identify this with the modern Kuryetein, sixty miles northeast of Damascus. Buhl and Bertholet suggest that it is identical with the well-known Banias, while Kasteren would locate it at el-Hadr farther to the east, on the way from Banias to Damascus, but C. R. Conder says these sites appear to be too far south.

HAZAR-GADDAH (hā'zar găd'dah), (Heb. גַּדָּה חָצַר, khats-ar' gad-daw', village of fortune; Josh. xv:27), a town in the extreme south of Judah. Perhaps identified with Wady Mubughik and its extensive ruins, but exact site is unknown.

HAZAR-HATTICON (hā'zar hăt'ti-kŏn), (Heb. הַתִּיכוֹן חֲצַר, khats-ar' hat-tee-kone', middle village), named in the prophecy of Ezekiel (xlvii:16) as the ultimate boundaries of the land. Its site is not known.

HAZARMAVETH (hā'zar-mā'veth), (Heb. חֲצַרְמָוֶת, khats-ar-maw'veth, village of death), one of the sons of Joktan (Gen. x:26; 1 Chron. i:20), or a district of Arabia Felix settled by him. Its identity with the modern Hadramaut is certain, and Hazarmaveth is probably also the same as the land of the Χατραμωτῖται, one of the four chief tribes of South Arabia as described by Strabo (XVI, iv:2)! They were celebrated for their traffic in frankincense. The modern Hadramaut is not so extensive as the ancient. (J. A. Selbie, Hastings' Bib. Dict.) (See ARABIA.)

HAZAR-SHUAL (hā'zar shu'al), (Heb. שׁוּעָל חֲצַר, khats-ar' shoo-awl', village of jackals), a town in southern Judah lying between Hazar-gaddah and Beersheba (Josh. xv:28; xix:3; 1 Chron. iv:28).

It is also mentioned after the return from captivity (Neh. xi:27). Wilton suggested Beni-Shail, near Gaza, as its site, but Van de Velde and Conder, with greater probability, locate it at Saweh, between Beersheba and Moladah. The ruins are on a high bluff; a wall built of flint blocks surrounds the site, and justifies the name Hazar ("enclosure").

HAZAR-SUSAH (hā'zar-sū'sah), (Heb. סוּסָה חֲצַר, khats-ar soo-saw', village of horses), a city in the south of Judah allotted to Simeon (1 Chron. iv:31; Josh. xix:5), also Hāzar-sū'im, Wilton believes it was in Wady es-Sunieh, near Gaza, but Conder proposes Beit Susin, south of Beit Jibrin.

HAZAZON-TAMAR (hăz'a-zŏn-tā'mar). See HAZEZON-TAMAR.

HAZEL (hā'z'l), (Heb. לוּז, looz), (Gen. xxx:37).

It is generally supposed that the almond tree is intended in this passage. The original word is thought to be susceptible of this rendering. The R. V. has almond. (See LUTZ.)

HAZELELPONI (hăz'e-lĕl-pō'nī), or rather **ZELELPONI** (Heb. הַצְלֶלְפּוֹנִי, hats-tsel-el-po-nee', shade-facing). The name has the definite article, "the Hazelelponi;" sisters of the sons of Etam in the genealogies of Judah (1 Chron. iv:3), B. C. about 1612.

HAZER (ha'zer), (Heb. חָצֵר, khaw-tsare'), an enclosure), in composition has the form of HAZAR (which see).

HAZERIM (ha-zē'rim), (Heb. חֲצֵרִים, khats-ay-reem', villages).

In Deut. ii:28 we read that the Avim dwelt in Hazerim, even unto Azzah or Gaza; and the notice of the Avites in Josh. xiii:3, 4 as the most southern of the tribes inhabiting the Canaanitish country clearly identifies their land with the mountains of Azazimeh. (See Palmer's Desert of the Exodus, Amer. ed., p. 360).

S. R. Driver, Hastings' Bib. Dict. says: "There is no doubt that the word is not really a proper name, but that it should be rendered (as it is in R. V.) by villages. The clause describes how the Avim dwelt, until they were expelled by the immigrant Caphtorim (or Philistines); they did not dwell in fortified cities, but in villages, or unwalled settlements (Lev. xxv:31), consisting, probably, of rudely-built huts of mud or stone, roofed with leaves or grass. (See HAZAR.)

HAZEROTH (ha-zē'roth), (Heb. חֲצֵרוֹת, khats-ay-roth', villages), the third station of the Israelites after leaving Sinai, and either four or five days' march from that mountain.

It was there that Miriam and Aaron murmured against Moses (Num. xi:35; xii:16). 'Ayn el-Hudera, about 36 miles northeast of mount Sinai, was suggested by Burckhardt, and adopted by Robinson and others, as the site. The identification rests, however, solely on the similarity of the name, and is uncertain. Palmer found at the spot many stone circles, which evidently marked the site of an encampment formed by a pastoral people.

HAZEZON-TAMAR (hăz'e-zŏn-tā'mar), (Heb. תָּמָר חַצְצוֹן, khats-ets-one' taw-mawr', pruning of the palm trees), the ancient name of Engedi (Gen. xiv:7) in 2 Chron. xx:2, called Hazazon-tamar.

It is a city as old as the oldest in Syria, the contemporary of Sodom and Gomorrah, and already a city when Hebron was first founded (Tristram's *Land of Israel*, p. 285). (See EN-GEDI.)

HAZIEL (hā'zi-el), (Heb. חֲזִיאֵל, *khaz-ee-ale'*, vision of God), a "son" of the Gershonite Shimei, and chief of the family of Laadan (1 Chron. xxiii:9), B. C. about 960.

HAZO (hā'zo), (Heb. חֲזוֹ, *khaz-o'*, a seer), one of the sons of Nahor by Milcah (Gen. xxii:22), B. C. after 2250.

HAZOR (hā'zôr), (Heb. חָצוֹר, *khaw-tsore'*, village, enclosure or castle).

1. A chief city of north Palestine (Josh. xi:10), near Lake Merom (Huleh), the seat of Jabin, a powerful Canaanitish king, as appears from the summons sent by him to all the neighboring kings to assist him against the Israelites. He and his confederates were, however, defeated and slain by Joshua, and the city burnt to the ground (Josh. xi:1, 10-13; Joseph. *Antiq.* v. 5, 1). But by the time of Deborah and Barak the Canaanites had recovered part of the territory then lost, had rebuilt Hazor, and were ruled by a king with the ancient royal name of Jabin, under whose power the Israelites were, in punishment for their sins, reduced. From this yoke they were delivered by Deborah and Barak, after which Hazor remained in quiet possession of the Israelites, and belonged to the tribe of Naphtali (Josh. xix:36; Judg. iv: 2). Hazor was one of the towns rebuilt or much improved by Solomon (1 Kings ix:15), and was one of the fortified places of Galilee which the Assyrians under Tiglath-pileser first took, on invading Palestine from the north (2 Kings xv: 29). Several places have been suggested as the site: *Tell Khureibeh,* a rocky peak near Kedesh, by Robinson; and Conder points out the name *Hadireh,* the Arabic equivalent of Hazor, near this; modern *Hazere,* where are ruins, by Thomson; but doubtless it is to be found at *Khŭrbet Harrah,* two and a half miles southeast of Kedesh, as proposed by the Palestine Memoirs. Remains of ancient walls, towers, and a fortress are to be found, and also broken glass and pottery.

C. R. Conder, Hastings' *Bib. Dict.,* says: From Hazor two letters of the Tel el-Amarna collection were written in the 15th century B. C. to the king of Egypt. They are much damaged, but they speak of an attack on the place, and ask for aid. In one of them the king's name is given; and though the first syllable is damaged, it may be read *I-eba-enu, i. e.,* 'Jabin.' Hazor is also noticed, with places in Upper and Lower Galilee, by the *Mohar* (an Egyptian traveler of the 14th century B. C.) on his way from the seacoast to the Lake of Tiberias. (See *Memoirs of Sur. of W. Pal.* vol. i. ch. iv.)

2. A city in the extreme south of Judah (Josh. xv:23).

3. (Josh. xv:25) "Hezron which is Hazor" probably means that the name had been changed.

4. The residence of the Benjamites after the return from captivity (Neh. xi:33), probably north of Jerusalem.

5. Apparently a region of Arabia (Jer. xlix:28-33).

HAZOR HADATTAH (ha'zôr ha-dăt'tah), "New Hazor" (Josh. xv:25). (See HADATTAH.)

HE (hē). The form of this letter is ה.

The fifth letter of the Hebrew alphabet. The English letter E has the same origin, but is a vowel. Where "he" preserves its power as a consonant in Hebrew names, and properly at other times, it is represented by "h" in the English form; as in Abraham.

It stands at the head of the fifth section of Ps. cxix, since each verse in the section begins with this letter in the original.

Through some similarity of form combined with careless writing and slight effacement of the text, it was sometimes misread as aleph on the one hand and tau on the other. (Davis, *Bib. Dict.*)

HEAD (hĕd), (Heb. רֹאשׁ, *roshe;* Gr. κεφαλή, *kef-al-ay'*).

As the head is the topmost part of the human body, it came derivatively to signify that which is highest, chief, the highest in position locally being regarded as highest in office, rank, or dignity: whence, as the head is the center of the nervous system, holds the brain, and stands above all the other parts, Plato regarded it as the seat of the deathless soul; and it has generally been considered as the abode of the intellect or intelligence by which man is enlightened and his walk in life directed; while the heart, or the parts placed near it, have been accounted the place where the affections lie (Gen. iii:15; Ps. iii:3; Eccles. ii:14). The head and the heart are sometimes taken for the entire person (Is. i:5). Even the head alone, as being the chief member, frequently stands for the man (Prov. x:6). The head also denotes sovereignty (1 Cor xi:3). Covering the head, and cutting off the hair, were signs of mourning and tokens of distress, which were enhanced by throwing ashes on the head, together with sackcloth (Amos viii:10; Job i:20; Lev. xxi: 5; Deut. xiv:1; 2 Sam. xiii:19; Esther iv:1); while anointing the head was practiced on festive occasions, and considered an emblem of felicity (Eccles. ix:8; Ps. xxiii:5; Luke vii:46). It was usual to swear by the head (Matt. v:36).

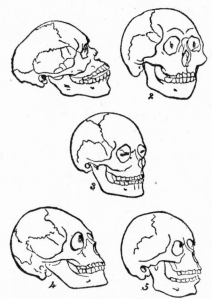

1. Ethiopian; 2. Mongolian; 3. Caucasian; 4. Malay; 5. American.

The general character of the human head is such as to establish the identity of the human race, and to distinguish man from every other animal. At the same time different families of mankind are marked by peculiarities of construction of the head, which, though they run one into the other to the entire loss of distinctive lines, in individual cases, and when extremes are compared together, yet are in the main broadly contrasted one with the other. These peculiarities in the structure of the skull give rise to and are connected with other peculiarities of feature and general contour of face. In the union of cranial peculiarities with those of the face, certain clear marks are presented, by which physiologists have been able to range the individuals of our race into a few great classes, and in so doing to afford an unintentional corroboration of the information which the Scriptures afford regarding the origin and dispersion of mankind.

Physiologists have established five classes of heads corresponding with five great families. (1) The Caucasian family, comprising the nations of Europe, some of the Western Asiatics, etc., have the head of the most symmetrical shape, almost round, the forehead of moderate extent, the cheek bones rather narrow, without any projection, but a direction downwards from the molar process of the frontal bone; the alveolar edge well rounded; the front teeth of each jaw placed perpendicularly; the face of oval shape, straight, features moderately prominent; forehead arched; nose narrow, slightly arched; mouth small; chin full and round. (2) The second is the Mongolian variety. (3) Ethiopian. (4) Malay and South Sea Islanders. (5) American.

J. R. B.

Customs. *Anointing the head* was a common practice amongst the Jews (Ps. xxiii:5; Matt. vi: 17; xxvi:7; Mark xiv:3; Luke vii:46). (See ANOINTING.)

To cover (חָפָה) *the head* was a token of mourning (2 Sam. xv:30). David and his men when fleeing from Absalom (Jer. xiv:3; Esth. vi:12). The same was expressed by *putting the hand upon the head* (2 Sam. xiii:19 Tamar after Amnon's outrage), or putting *ashes* (אֵפֶר) or *earth* (אֲדָמָה) upon it (Josh. vii:6; 1 Sam. iv:12; 2 Sam. i:2; xiii:19; Lam. ii:10).

The *head of one under a vow* was not shaven till its completion (Num. vi:18, ff.; Acts xviii:18; xxi:24). (See NAZARITE.)

The Israelites were forbidden to 'round the corners of their heads' (Lev. xix:27) in token of mourning (comp. Deut. xiv:1, where 'making baldness between the eyes' refers to the custom of shaving the front part of the head).

The *head was bowed;* in worshiping God (Gen. xxiv:26; Exod. iv:31), and as a token of respect (Gen. xliii:28).

Figurative. (1) Blessings come on the *head,* the whole person of the just (Prov. x:6); and men have their way recompensed on their *head* (Ezek. ix:10). (2) To endanger one's *head,* is to expose his life (Dan. i:10). (3) *Covering of the head,* imports protection, as with a helmet (Ps. cxl:7); or grief and mourning (2 Sam. xv: 30); or modesty and subjection, in the case of women (1 Cor. xi:5, 6). (4) To *lift up one's own head,* is to rejoice (Luke xxi:28); or to grow proud, rebel against God, in a bold and daring manner (Ps. lxxxiii:2). (5) To *lift up the head* of another, is to exalt him to honor (Gen. xl:13; Jer. lii:31). (6) *Shaking* or *wagging* of the *head* at one implies contempt, mockery, insult (Ps. xxii:7). (7) Having her *crown of twelve stars on her head,* imports the bold and open profession of divine truth by the church, preached by the twelve apostles (Rev. xii:1). (8) The *head of the serpent which Christ bruises,* is his power, authority, and chief interests (Gen. iii:15). (9) The *head of the leviathan,* which God broke in the waters, is the king of Egypt, and his mighty host, drowned in the Red Sea (Ps. lxxiv:13, 14; Is. li:11). (10) A husband is the *head* of a wife, to protect, rule, and direct her (1 Cor. xi:3). Kings and great men are the *heads of a nation,* who excel the rest in power and dignity, and rule and protect them (Exod. xviii:25; Mic. iii:1; Is. i:5). (11) Capital cities are the *head of a kingdom* (Is. vii: 8). (12) *Iniquities going over our head,* imports that our guilt is very great, and our apprehension of it, and our affliction for it, likely to sink us (Ps. xxxviii:4). (13) Men *riding* over our *heads,* imports great oppression and slavery (Ps. lxvi:12). (14) Whatever is more excellent, or has power over, or gives influence and direction to others, is called the *head.* (15) God is the *head* of Christ; he set him up in his mediatorial office, and gave him his power and authority (1 Cor. xi:3). (16) *Christ is the head of the corner,* and *head of his church,* excelling in dignity, governing her, and communicating light, life, provision, and comfort to her; and he is the head of all things to her, as he rules and governs them for her advantage (Col. i:18; Eph. i:22). (17) *The whole head is sick, and the whole heart is faint, there is nothing but wounds and bruises;* men of power, of wisdom, of professed piety, and the more poor and indigent, are all corrupted, and every man is thoroughly tainted in all his powers, with sin (Is. i:5, 6).

HEADBAND (hĕd'bănd), the rendering of the Hebrew קִשֻּׁר, *kish-shoor',* encircle, band (Is. iii:20, in R. V. a sash; Jer. ii:32, in A. V. attire). It is an article of female attire.

HEADDRESS (hĕd'drĕs). See DRESS.

HEAD OF THE CHURCH (hĕd, chûrch).

On account of the very intimate relation that exists between Christ and the Church he is called the head (Eph. iv:15; v:23), and the Church his body (iv:12), inseparably united.

HEADSTONE (hĕd'stōn), (Zech. iv:7). See CORNER STONE.

HEADY (hĕd'y̆), (Gr. προπετής, *prop-et-ace',* falling forward).

This is the translation in 2 Tim. iii:4 A. V., which in Acts xix:36, its only remaining occurrence in the New Testament is translated 'rashly' (R. V. 'rash'). Heady is from Tyndale; and has been adopted by all the revises thereafter, except Rheims V. 'stubburne,' and R. V. which uses its modern equivalent in this sense, 'headstrong.'

HEAL (hēl), (Heb. רָפָא, *raw-phaw'*).

1. To cure the ailments of one's body (Matt. iv:24).

2. To cure the maladies of men's souls, by forgiving their sins, turning them from sin to God, and filling them with spiritual comfort (Ps. vi:2; Rev. xxii:2).

Figurative. (1) God's *saving health* is his salvation, or his Son in his saving offices (Ps. lxvii:2); and he is the *health* of his people's countenances, as by vouchsafing his salvation, he cheers and exhilarates them (Ps xlii:11). (2) To *heal* nations and churches, is to redress their grievances, purify their corruptions, and reduce them to a fixed and regular state (Jer. xiv:19); and their *health and cure,* is their civil and religious prosperity (Jer. viii:22; xxx:17; li:8, 9). (3) False prophets *heal* by flattering men in their sins, and encouraging them in false hopes of deliverance and prosperity (Jer. vi:14; viii:11).

HEAP (hēp), the translation of several Hebrew words, with the general meaning of a collection of things so as to form a pile or elevation.

The term was applied to a mass of earth or stones covering over or marking the place of a grave (Josh. vii:26; viii:29; 2 Sam. xviii:17); to the ruins of walls and cities (Job viii:17; Is. xxv:2; Jer. ix:11); a pile (e. g., of rubbish, Neh. iv:2; of grain, Cant. vii:2, of sheaves, Ruth iii:7; Hag. ii:16, etc.).

HEART (härt), (Heb. mostly לֵב, *labe;* Gr. καρδία, *kar-dee'ah*).

The heart, among the Hebrews was regarded figuratively and poetically not only as the seat of the passions and emotions, as of love, pleasure, and grief, but also of the intellectual faculties—the mind, the understanding. In the original Scriptures, as well as in the English and other translations, the word 'heart,' therefore, constantly occurs where 'mind' is to be understood, and would be used by a modern English writer. We say modern because the ancient usage of the English word 'heart' was more conformable that the present to that of the Hebrews.

Figurative. All the phrases, more or less metaphorical, in which this word occurs, are rendered intelligible by the following examples:

(1) "A *perfect heart*" follows after what is true and good with candor and sincerity (Is. xxxviii:3; Luke viii:15; Heb. x:22), and it is "of flesh," when pliable and ready to receive the impressions of God's word and providence (Ezek. xxxvi:26). (2) It is "*broken and contrite*" when filled with sorrow and perplexity, on account of guilt, prevalence of corruption, divine hiding, and the like (Is. lxi:1; lxvi:2). It is "*tender*" when easily affected, and afraid of sin (2 Chron. xiii:7; xxxiv:27). (3) It is "*large*" when one knows much, or is filled with spiritual liberty and joy (1 Kings iv:29; Ps. cxix:32). (4) It is "*double, divided, deceitful*" when men try to serve God and idols at once; pretend one thing, and desire and seek after another (Ps. xii:2; Hos. x:2). (5) It is "*stony, hard, stout, froward, perverse,*" when it can scarce be impressed with God's word or providence, and is obstinate in sinning and rebelling against the Lord (Ezek. xi:19; Is. xlvi: 12). (6) It is "*gross and fat as grease*" when void of feeling, stupid, filled with sensual pleasure and unconcern about, and inattention to, eternal things (Ps. cxix:70; Acts xxviii:27). (7) To "*say in the heart*" is inwardly to think, reason (Rom. x:6), or earnestly desire (Ps. xiv:1). (8) To "*speak to the heart*" is kindly to encourage, comfort, and persuade (Hos. ii:14). (9) To do a thing "*with the heart*" is to do it with much affection and diligence (Matt. xxii:37). (10) Persons having their "*heart*" towards anything, or having persons in their "*heart*," denote a fixed remembrance of, desire after, and care for them (2 Cor. vii:3). (11) As "*heart*" denotes a fixed standing, courage, and activity, the Israelites were without it, when they had no sense of, no care and concern about, their real welfare (Hos. vii:11). (12) *God's* "*heart*" is his will, purpose, and love (Is. lxiii:4); but the "turning of his heart" within him, and "kindling of his repentings," denote only the greatness of his mercy and compassion (Jer. xxxi:20; Hos. xi:8). (13) God's law is in Christ and his people's "*heart;*" they understand, remember, love, and are careful to fulfill it (Ps. xl:8; cxix:11). (14) What people think, love or purpose, is said to be in "their heart"; so, false prophets prophesy "*out of their own heart*", say what their vain imaginations and corrupt affections prompt them to (Ezek. xiii:2). (15) In allusion to the heart of animals being in the midst of the body, the midst

of anything, or being within it, is called the "heart"; so Tyre was "in the heart" of the sea, being on an island (Ezek. xxvii:4); and Christ, in the grave, was "in the heart of the earth" (Matt. xii:40).

HEARTH (harth). Several Hebrew words are thus translated:

1. *Awkh* (Heb. אָח, a brazier, or portable furnace, in which fire was made in the king's winter apartment (Jer. xxxvi:22, 23).

2. *Kee-yore'* (Heb. כִּיּוֹר), a fire pan or basin for holding fire (Zech. xii:6), for roasting (1 Sam. ii:14).

3. *Mo-kade'* (Heb. מוֹקֵד, a burning, so rendered in Is. xxxiii:14), a fagot for fuel (Ps. cii:3).

HEAT, HOT (hēt, hŏt), the translation of several Hebrew and Greek words, having besides their ordinary meanings several peculiar uses in Scripture.

Figurative. (1) God's *hot* wrath, displeasure, or *heat* of his anger, is his holy and high displeasure against sin, displayed in the most fearful and tormenting judgments (Exod. xxii:24; Deut. ix:19; Judg. ii:19). Such as are lively, zealous, and active in religion are *hot* (Rev. iii: 15). (2) *One's heart is hot,* when filled with tormenting trouble, impatience, and passion (Ps. xxxix:3); and so Ezekiel went to prophesy in the *heat of his spirit,* with great reluctance and fretting (Ezek. iii:14). (3) The *hottest of the battle,* is where it is most fierce, dangerous and destructive (2 Sam. xi:15). *To pursue one hotly,* is to do it in great wrath, and with much speed (Gen. xxxi:36). (4) The *heat of the sun* is symbolical of tribulation, temptation, or persecution (Matt. xiii:6, 21; Luke viii:6-13). (5) A *gentle heat* of the sun signifies the favor and bounty of the prince, while a fierce heat denotes punishment (see Ps. cxxi:6). (6) "*Heat of the day*" (Matt. xx:12) is united with burden to denote severe toil.

HEATH (hēth), (Heb. עֲרוֹעֵר, *ar-o-ayr'*, Jer. xvii:6; xlviii:6).

No true heath is found in Palestine. There is great probability that the dwarf juniper or savin (*Juniperus sabina*), which grows in the most sterile and desolate parts of the desert, is the plant intended. "Its gloomy, stunted appearance, with its scale-like leaves pressed close to its gnarled stems and cropped close by the wild goats, as it clings to the rocks about Petra, gives great force to the contrast suggested by the prophet between him that trusteth in man, naked and destitute, and the man that trusteth in the Lord, flourishing as a tree planted by the waters." (Tristram.) (See OROR.)

HEATHEN (hē'th'n). The Hebrew words *gôy,* גּוֹי, *go-yeem'*, גּוֹיִם, together with their Greek equivalents ἔθνος, ἔθνη, have been somewhat arbitrarily rendered "nations," "gentiles" and "heathen" in the A. V.

It will be interesting to trace the manner in which a term, primarily and essentially general in its signification, acquired that more restricted sense which was afterwards attached to it. Its development is parallel with that of the Hebrew people, and its meaning at any period may be taken as significant of their relative position with regard to the surrounding nations.

(1) The Nations. While as yet the Jewish nation had no political existence, *gôyim* denoted generally the nations of the world, especially including the immediate descendants of Abraham (Gen. xviii:18; comp. Gal. iii:16). The latter, as they grew in numbers and importance, were distinguished in a most marked manner from the nations by whom they were surrounded, and were provided with a code of laws and a religious ritual, which made the distinction still more peculiar. They were essentially a separate people (Lev. xx:23); separate in habits, morals, and religion, and bound to maintain their separate character by denunciations of the most terrible judgments (Lev. xxvi:14-38; Deut. xxviii). On their march through the desert they encountered the most obstinate resistance from Amalek, "chief of he *gôyim*" (Num. xxiv:20), in whose sight the deliverance from Egypt was achieved (Lev. xxvi: 45).

(2) Idolaters. But, even in early Jewish times, the term *gôyim* received by anticipation a significance of wider range than the national experience (Lev. xxvi:33, 38; Deut. xxx:1), and as the latter was gradually developed during the prosperous times of the monarchy, the *gôyim* were the surrounding nations generally, with whom the Israelites were brought into contact by the extension of their commerce, and whose idolatrous practices they readily adopted (Ezek. xxiii:30; Amos v:26). Later still, it is applied to the Babylonians who took Jerusalem (Neh. v:8; Ps. lxxix:1, 6, 10), to the destroyers of Moab (Is. xvi:8), and to the several nations among whom the Jews were scattered during the Captivity (Ps. cvi:47; Jer. xlvi:28; Lam. i:3, etc.), the practice of idolatry still being their characteristic distinction (Is. xxxvi:18; Jer. x:2, 3; xiv: 22).

As the Greek influence became more extensively felt in Asia Minor, and the Greek language was generally used, Hellenism and heathenism became convertible terms, and a Greek was synonymous with a foreigner of any nation. This is singularly evident in the Syriac of 2 Macc. v:9, 10, 13; comp. John vii:35; 1 Cor. x:32; 2 Macc. xi:2 (Smith, *Bib. Dict.*)

(3) Dwellers in the Heath. As the word heathen may mean *"dweller in the heath,"* the word suggests the fact that the gospel first rooted itself in towns, the inhabitants of which became Christians, while the dwellers on heaths remained worshipers of false divinities. The word Pagan, from Latin *Paganus,* belonging to a village, rustic, has a somewhat similar reference.

HEAVEN (hĕv"n), (Heb. גַּלְגַּל, *gal-gal'*, rolling cloud), the state and place of blessedness in the life to come.

As we can have no distinct conception of those joys which never have been and never will be experienced by us here in their full extent, we have of course no words in human language to express them, and cannot therefore expect any clear description of them even in the Holy Scriptures. Hence the Bible describes this happiness sometimes in general terms, designating its greatness (as in Rom. viii:18-22; 2 Cor. iv:17,18); and sometimes by various figurative images and modes of speech, borrowed from everything which we know to be attractive and desirable.

(1) Terms for. The following are the principal literal terms which are applied in Scripture to the condition of future happiness:

Among such appellations we find ζωή, *life,* ζωή αἰώνιος, *eternal life,* which, according to Hebrew usage, signify 'a happy life,' or 'eternal well being,' (Matt. vii:14; xix:16, 29; xxv:46): δόξα, δόξα τοῦ Θεοῦ, 'glory,' 'the glory of God'. (Rom. ii:7, 10; v:2); and

εἰρήνη, 'peace' (Rom. ii:10). Also αἰώνιον βάρος δόξης, 'an eternal weight of glory' (2 Cor. iv:17); and σωτηρία, σωτηρία αἰώνιος, 'salvation,' 'eternal salvation' (Heb. v:9, etc.).

(2) Conditions in. Besides being exempt from all earthly trials, and having a continuance of that happiness which we had begun to enjoy even here, we have good reason to expect hereafter other rewards and joys, which stand in no natural or necessary connection with the present. In the doctrine of the New Testament, however, positive rewards are considered most obviously as belonging to our future felicity, and as constituting a principal part of it. For it always represents the joys of heaven as resulting strictly from *the favor of God,* and as being *undeserved* by those on whom they are bestowed. Hence there must be something more added to the natural good consequences of our actions, something which cannot be considered as the necessary and natural consequences of the good actions we may have here performed. But, on this subject, we know nothing more in general than this, that God will so appoint and order our circumstances, and make such arrangements, that the principal faculties of our souls—reason and affection, will be heightened and developed, so that we shall continually obtain more pure and distinct knowledge of the truth, and make continual advances in holiness. Some theologians have supposed that the saints in heaven may be taught by *immediate divine revelations lumen gloriæ*); especially those who may enter the abodes of the blessed without knowledge, or with only a small measure of it; *e. g.* children and others who have died in ignorance, for which they themselves were not to blame.

(3) With Christ. In the Scripture revelation respecting heaven, Christ is always represented as one who will be *personally visible* to us, and whose personal, familiar intercourse and guidance we shall enjoy. Herein Christ himself places a chief part of the joy of the saints (John xiv, xvii, etc): and the apostles often describe the blessedness of the pious by the phrase *being with Christ.* To his guidance has God entrusted the human race, in heaven and on earth. And Paul says (2 Cor. iv:6), we see 'the brightness of the divine glory in the face of Christ,' he is 'the visible representative of the invisible God' (Col. i:15). According to the representation contained in the Holy Scriptures, the saints will dwell together in the future world, and form, as it were, a kingdom or state of God (Luke xvi:22; xx:38; Rom. viii:10; Rev. vii:9; Heb. xii:22). They will there partake of a common felicity. Their enjoyment will doubtless be very much heightened by friendship, and by their confiding intercourse with each other.

(4) Knowledge of. All that we can with certainty know or infer from Scripture or reason respecting the blessedness of the life to come, may be arranged under the following particulars:— We shall hereafter be entirely freed from the sufferings and adversities of this life. Our future blessedness will involve a continuance of the real happiness of this life.

(5) Deliverance from Evil. The entire exemption from suffering and all that causes suffering here, is expressed in the Scripture by words which denote rest, repose, refreshment, after performing labor and enduring affliction. But all the terms which are employed to express this condition, define (in the original) the promised 'rest,' as rest after labor, and exemption from toil and grief; and not the absence of employment, not inactivity or indolence (2 Thess. i:7; Heb. iv:9, 11; Rev. xiv:13; comp. vii:17).

This deliverance from the evils of our present life includes:

1. Deliverance from this earthly body, the seat of the lower principles of our nature and of our sinful corruption, and the source of so many evils and sufferings (2 Cor. vi:1, 2; 1 Cor. xviii:15).

2. Entire separation from the society of wicked and evil-disposed persons, who, in various ways, injure the righteous man and embitter his life on earth (2 Tim. iv:18). It is hence accounted a part of the felicity even of Christ himself in heaven to be 'separate from sinners' (Heb. vii: 26).

3. Upon this earth everything is inconstant, and subject to perpetual change; and nothing is capable of completely satisfying our expectations and desires. But in the world to come it will be different. The bliss of the saints will continue without interruption or change, without fear of termination, and without satiety (Luke xx:36; 2 Cor. iv:16, 18; 1 Pet. i:4; v:10; 1 John iii:2, *sq.*)

Figurative. Among the figurative representations, we may place the word 'heaven' itself. The abode of departed spirits, to us who live upon the earth, and while we remain here, is invisible and inaccessible beyond the bounds of the visible world, and entirely separated from it. There they live in the highest well-being, and in a nearer connection with God and Christ than here below. This place and state cannot be designated by any more fit and brief expression than that which is found in almost every language, namely, 'heaven,' —a word in its primary and material signification denoting the region of the skies, or the visible heavens. It is there that the highest sanctuary or temple of God is situated, *i. e.* it is there that the omnipresent God most gloriously reveals himself. This, too, is the abode of God's highest spiritual creation. Thither Christ was transported: he calls it the house of his Father, and says that he has therein prepared an abode for his followers (John xiv:2).

This place, this 'heaven,' was never conceived of in ancient times, as it has been by some modern writers, as a particular planet or world, but as the wide expanse of heaven; high above the atmosphere or starry heavens; hence it is sometimes called the *third* heaven, as being neither the atmosphere nor the starry heavens.

Another figurative name is 'Paradise,' taken from the abode of our first parents in their state of innocence, and transferred to the abode of the blessed (Luke xxiii:43; 2 Cor. xii:4; Rev. ii:7; xxii:2).

Again, this place is called 'the heavenly Jerusalem' (Gal. iv:26; Heb. xii:22; Rev. iii:12), because the earthly Jerusalem was the capital city of the Jews, the royal residence, and the seat of divine worship; the 'kingdom of heaven' (Matt. xxv:1; Jam. ii:5);the 'heavenly kingdom' (2 Tim. iv:18; the 'eternal kingdom' (2 Pet. i:11). It is also called an 'eternal inheritance' (1 Pet. i:4; Heb. ix:15), meaning the possession and full enjoyment of happiness, typified by the residence of the ancient Hebrews in Palestine. The blessed are said 'to sit down at table with Abraham, Isaac, and Jacob,' that is, to be a sharer with the saints of old in the joys of salvation; 'to be in Abraham's bosom' (Luke xvi:22; Matt. viii:11), that is, to sit near or next to Abraham (see ABRAHAM'S BOSOM); 'to reign with Christ' (2 Tim. ii:11), *i. e.,* to be distinguished, honored, and happy as he is—to enjoy regal felicities; to enjoy 'a Sabbath,' or 'rest' (Heb. iv:10, 11), indicating the happiness of pious Christians, *both* in this life and in the life to come.

HEAVE OFFERING. See FIRST FRUIT; FESTIVALS.

HEAVE SHOULDER. See FIRST FRUIT; FESTIVALS.

HEAVING and WAVING. See FIRST FRUIT; FESTIVALS.

HEAVY, HEAVINESS (hĕv'ў, hĕv'ĭ-nĕs), (Heb. כָּבֵד, *kaw-bade',* weight).

Many other words are thus translated. Heaviness occurs often, but always with the meaning of grief. Thus (Prov. x:1) 'A wise son maketh a glad father; but a foolish son is the heaviness of his mother;' (Prov. xii:25) 'Heaviness in the heart of man maketh it stoop; but a good word maketh it glad;' (Is. lxi:3) 'To appoint unto them that mourn in Zion, to give unto them beauty for ashes, the oil of joy for mourning, the garment of praise for the spirit of heaviness.' 'Ye are in heaviness,' R. V. 'Ye have been put to grief' (1 Pet. i:6); 'For he longed after you all, and was full of heaviness,' ἀδημονῶν, R. V., 'Was sore troubled' (Phil. ii:26). In their preface the A. V. translators say of the Scriptures, 'If we be ignorant, they will instruct us; if out of the way, they will bring us home; if out of order, they will reforme us; if in heaviness, comfort us; if dull, quicken us; if colde, inflame us.' The older versions have the word very often, as John xvi:6 Wycliffe's V., 'sorwe, or *heuynesse*, hath fulfillid youre herte;' Ps. xxx:5 Coverdale's V., 'Hevynesse maye well endure for a night, but joye commeth in the mornynge.'

Figurative. We learn from the preceding passages that whatever is burdensome or afflicting to body or mind, is called *heavy.* (1) As *the hand or judgments of God* (1 Sam. v:6). (2) *An oppressive tax* (Neh. v:18; 1 Kings xii:4). (3) *Bad news* (1 Kings xiv:6). (4) And *the outrageous wrath of a foolish man* (Prov. xxvii: 3). (5) A *heart is heavy,* when it is sad and displeased (1 Kings xxi:4). (6) *Eyes are heavy* when they can scarce look up for drowsiness (Matt. xxvi:43). (7) *Ears are heavy,* when men are dull and inattentive (Is. vi:10). (8) *Hands are heavy,* when one is wearied with holding them up (Exod. xvii:12). (9) *Christ was very heavy,* when his spirit was oppressed and filled with sorrow under the unspeakable pressure of his Father's wrath (Matt. xxvi:37).

HEBER (hē'ber), (Heb. עֵבֶר, *ay'ber,* of the other side, i. e., of the river, immigrant).

1. The son of Salah, who became the father of Peleg at the age of 34 years, and died at the age of 464 (Gen. x:24; xi:14; 1 Chron. i:25). His name occurs in the genealogy of Christ (Luke iii:35), B. C. 2448-1984. There is nothing to constitute Heber a historical personage; but there is a degree of interest connected with him from the notion, which the Jews themselves entertain, that the name of Hebrews, applied to them, was derived from this alleged ancestor of Abraham. No historical ground appears why this name should be derived from him rather than from any other personage that occurs in the catalogue of Shem's descendants; but there are so much stronger objections to every other hypothesis, that this perhaps is still the most probable of any which have yet been started.

2. Grandson of Asher (Gen. xlvi:17; 1 Chron. vii:31; Num. xxvi:45), B. C. before 1873.

3. One of the tribe of Judah (1 Chron. iv:18). B. C. after 1612.

4. A Gadite (1 Chron. v:13), B. C. between 1612 and 1093.

5. A descendant of Hobab, son of Jethro, and brother of the wife of Moses. His wife was the Jael who slew Sisera (B. C. 1409), and he is called Heber the Kenite (Judg. iv:11, 17; v:24), which seems to have been a name for the whole family (Judg. i:16). Heber appears to have lived separate from the rest of the Kenites, leading a patriarchal life, amid his tents and flocks. He must have been a person of some consequence, from its being stated that there was peace between the house of Heber and the powerful king Jabin. At the time the history brings him under our notice his camp was in the plain of Zaanaim, near Kedesh in Naphtali. (See JAEL; KENITES.)

6. A Benjamite (Chron. viii:17), B. C. about 518.

7. Also a Benjamite (1 Chron. viii:22), B. C. before 598.

HEBERITES (hē'ber-ītes), (Num. xxvi:45). See HEBER, 4.

HEBREWESS (hē'brü-ĕs), a Hebrew woman (Jer. xxxiv:9).

HEBREW LANGUAGE (hē'brụ lăn'gwăj).

The Hebrew language is that which was the notional idiom of those descendants of Eber which received the distinctive name of the People of Israel, and, as such, was that in which all the books of the Old Testament (with the exception of the few Chaldee passages occurring in those after the Babylonian captivity) were originally composed.

(1) Semitic. It belongs to the Semitic, or, as it is more appropriately called, the Syro-Arabian family of languages; and it occupies a central point amidst all the branches of this family, as well with reference to the geographical position of the country in which it prevailed, as with reference to the degree of development to which it attained.

(2) Jewish. If we except the terms 'lip or language of Canaan,' in Is. xix:18, the only name by which the Hebrew language is mentioned in the Old Testament is 'Jewish יְהוּדִית, *yeh-hoo-deeth'* used adverbially, *Judaicè, in Jewish* (2 Kings xviii:26, 28; Is. xxxvi:11, 13).

In a strict sense, however, 'Jewish' denotes the idiom of the kingdom of Judah, which became the predominant one after the deportation of the ten tribes. It is in the Greek writings of the later Jews that 'Hebrew' is first applied to the language, as in the ἑβραϊστί, *in the Hebrew language*, of the prologue to Ecclesiasticus, and in the γλῶσσα τῶν Ἑβραίων, *language of the Hebrews*, of Josephus.

The best evidences which we possess as to the form of the Hebrew language, prior to its first historical period, tend to show that Abraham, on his entrance into Canaan, found the language then prevailing among almost all the different tribes inhabiting that country to be at least dialectically in affinity with his own. This is gathered from the following facts: that nearly all the names of places and persons relating to those tribes admit of Hebrew etymologies; that, amidst all the accounts of the intercourse of the Hebrews with the nations of Canaan, we find no hint of a diversity of idiom; and that even the comparatively recent remains of the Phœnician and Punic languages bear a manifest affinity to the Hebrew.

(3) History Preceding the Exile. The history of the Hebrew language, as far as we can trace its course by the changes in the diction of the documents in which it is preserved, may be here conveniently divided into that of the period preceding, and that of the period succeeding, the Exile. If it be a matter of surprise

that the thousand years which intervened between Moses and the Captivity should not have produced sufficient change in the language to warrant its history during that time being distributed into subordinate divisions, the following considerations may excuse this arrangement. It is one of the signal characteristics of the Hebrew language, as seen in all the books prior to the Exile, that notwithstanding the existence of some isolated, but important, archaisms, such as in the form of the pronoun, etc. (the best collection of which may be seen in Hävernick, *Einleit.*, p. 183, *sq.*), it preserves an unparalleled general uniformity of structure. The extent to which this uniformity prevails may be estimated, either by the fact that it has furnished many modern scholars, who reason from the analogies discovered in the changes in other languages in a given period, with an argument to show that the Pentateuch could not have been written at so remote a date as is generally believed (Gesenius, *Gesch. der Hebr. Sprache,* sec. 8); or, by the conclusion, *a fortiori,* which Hävernick, whose express object it is to vindicate its received antiquity, candidly concedes that 'the books of Chronicles, Ezra and Nehemiah are the *earliest* in which the language differs sensibly from that in the historical portions of the Pentateuch' (*Einleit.* i. p. 180).

In the canonical books belonging to the first period, the Hebrew language appears in a state of mature development. Although it still preserves the charms of freshness and simplicity, yet it has attained great regularity of formation, and such a precision of syntactical arrangement as ensures both energy and distinctness.

(4) Second Period. The Babylonian captivity is assigned as the commencement of that decline and corruption which mark the second period in the history of the Hebrew language; but the Assyrian deportation of the ten tribes, in the year B. C. 720, was probably the first means of bringing the Aramaic idiom into injurious proximity to it. The Exile, however, forms the epoch at which the language shows evident signs of that encroachment of the Aramaic on its integrity, which afterwards ended in its complete extinction. The diction of the different books of this period discovers various grades of this Aramaic influence; and in some cases approaches so nearly to the type of the first period, that it has been ascribed to mere imitation.

HEBREW OF THE HEBREWS (hē'brụ ŏv the hē'brụz), (Gr. Ἑβραῖος ἐξ Ἑβραίων, *Hebraios eks Hebraion*), emphatically a Hebrew, one who was so by both parents, and that by a long series of ancestors, without admixture of Gentile or even proselyte blood. So speaks Paul (Phil. iii:5) of himself.

Of this the Jews were as proud as were those Christians in Spain, who called themselves Old Christians, of having no mixture of Moorish blood.

HEBREWS (hē'brụz), (Heb. עִבְרִי, *ib-ree'*; plural עִבְרִים, *ib-reem'*; Gr. Ἑβραῖος, *heb-rah'yes*), a designation of the people of Israel.

(1) Its Derivation. (1) Some ascribe the origin of the word to *Ay-ber'* (Heb. עֵבֶר); Eber, the ancestor (Gen. x:21); see also the use of Eber as a national name (Num. xxiv:24). (2) Others trace the name to the Hebrew *aw-bar'* (עָבַר, to *pass over*), so that a Hebrew would mean the "man from the region beyond," and supposed to have been applied to Abraham, as having crossed the Euphrates to the westward. This last derivation is generally admitted. It seems to imply nothing more than that Abraham was an immigrant into Canaan—not a native.

(2) Scripture Application. This name is never applied in Scripture to the Israelites except when the speaker is a foreigner (Gen. xxxix:14, 17; xli:12; Exod. i:16; ii:6; 1 Sam. iv:6, 9, etc.), or when the Israelites speak of themselves to one of another nation (Gen. xl:15; Exod. i:19; Jonah i:9, etc.), or when they are contrasted with other peoples (Gen. xliii:32; Exod. i:3, 7, 15; Deut. xv:12; 1 Sam. xiii:3, 7).

(3) Tribes Embraced. The appellation *Hebrews* may, indeed, originally have embraced more tribes than the Israelites, as it appears from Genesis (x:21, 25) that the descendants of Joktan had some claim to it. Nevertheless, it was soon appropriated to the Israelites as their distinctive name *as a nation* in the earlier periods

tained some hints as to the condition of mind or other occasion in the readers which called it forth. It would not be impossible, perhaps, to account for the lack of one or two of these essential features of a letter, but the absence of all of them is not easily conceivable, in case it was meant to be addressed to a single congregation or even a circle of congregations.

As a homily, its structure and content are easily explained. It characterizes itself as "a word of exhortation" (xiii:22). It begins with a clearly drawn contrast of the old revelation of God to the fathers through the prophets, with the new revelation of God to the times of the writer through his Son (i:1). This immediately leads to the pointing out of the highly exalted character and office of the Son. He existed in eternity and took part in the creation of the universe (i: 2), and was the very image and effulgence of God, but (appearing as man) made purification for sin, and was once more exalted (i:3). He

Group of Hebrew Types Showing Costumes.

of their history, and (after giving place, in the intervening centuries, to that of *Israel,* and, subsequently to the deportation of the ten tribes, to that of *Jews*) was at length revived not long before the Christian era—when, however, it also served to distinguish the Jews of Palestine from the Hellenist Jews—and passed over, together with that of *Jews,* to the classical writers.

HEBREWS, EPISTLE TO THE.

(1) Form and Content. This writing has always been called an epistle. On closer examination, however, it is seen to be such only in form. It is not an epistle in the sense in which, in the New Testament, for instance, the letters to the Romans, Corinthians, and Galatians are epistles. It is rather a homily or practical religious treatise, aimed at a definite end. It is planned and written with the sole object of presenting and defending a clear idea of the New Covenant. As an epistle, it should have had, in accordance with literary customs of its environment, the name of the writer and the name of the party addressed. It should have been pervaded by the sense of personal relationships, and con-

occupies a much higher place than the angels (i:5; ii:18). This last position is established by a series of citations from the Old Testament Scriptures. While still in the process of his argument, the author interrupts it in order to make a homiletical application of the idea in a practical exhortation to perseverance (ii:1-4).

But Christ was superior not alone to angels, but also to others believed to be mediators of the Old Covenant; *i. e.,* to Moses and the Levitical priesthood (iii:1; viii:13). His superiority over Moses is that of the maker of a house to the house (iii:1-4), and that of the Son to the servant (iii:5, 6). At this point the author again interrupts his argument in order to introduce a practical exhortation, re-enforced by an appeal to the history of Israel as recorded in the Pentateuchal account of the Exodus (iii:7; iv:13). Returning to the argument, he then proves that Christ is superior to the Levitical priesthood, because his order is higher than that of Aaron, being the same as that of Melchizedek. In order to establish this position, he first shows that Christ is a true priest, being taken from among men (iv:1-3), and appointed by God (iv:4-10).

At this point, once more, the author stops to make some homiletical uses of what he had already proved, v:11; vi:20. After this he proceeds to show the implications of Christ's appointment under the order of Melchizedek. Melchizedek entered into the sacred narrative in a preternatural manner and is therefore above Levi vii:1-3. Melchizedek was recognized to be of a higher order than Levi historically; for the sons of Levi are allowed to receive tithes of their kindred only, whereas his authority was broader in that he tithed Abraham, a stranger. Furthermore, the sons of Levi, as represented in their ancestor Abraham, paid tithes to him, thus yielding him priority (vii:4-10). But was such a broader priesthood necessary? The author argues from the weakness of the old and the necessity of frequent changes caused by death that it was (vii:11-25). He then concludes this part of the argument by showing Christ's fitness for the new high-priesthood and recapitulates (vii:25; viii:13). In the second part of the writing, the author proves the superiority of the new Covenant itself to the old. The argument is here mainly a contrast between the weakness of the old as to its sanctuary, furniture, and rites, and the strength of the new in its purification, its sacrifice, its spiritual power, and its finality (ix:1; x:18). Having shown this superiority the author suspends argument in order to give opportunity to an exhortation (x:19-39). On resuming the argument he then enters upon an eloquent presentation of the emphatic and central principle of faith as it is fully developed under the new Covenant, showing by a long list of illustrations that whatever was good in the old was due to the operation of this principle (xi:1-40). At this point, the argument is closed. The rest of the writing is practical and hortatory. The lessons of the argument as developed are first enforced (xii:1-29) and some indirect or inferential lessons of conduct appended (xiii:1-17). The author then requests prayer from and invokes a blessing upon his readers (xiii:18-21) and closes with allusion to some personal items and a final benediction (xiii:22-25).

(2) Design. From this plan and outline, it appears that the Epistle to the Hebrews is a homily cast into the mold of a letter for the sake of convenience mainly. The question may now be asked, what the purpose of the epistle was. Bruce (*Epistle to the Hebrews,* 1899) takes the ground that it was put forth as a defense of the Christian faith and calls it the "First Apology for Christianity." This, however, it can only be in a very general sense, just as any other writing intended to show the excellencies of the Christian faith in order to secure perseverance in it may be called an apology. It is not an apology in the sense that it was intended as a vindication of the Christian faith at the bar of reason, or a defense of it against some definite attack made from the intellectual side. Milligan (*Theology of the Ep. to the Heb.,* 1899), finds the design to be the further instruction of believers in the true character of their new faith. So also Reuss takes the view that it was intended as a theological treatise, expounding in general the nature of the new Covenant as contrasted with the old. With this view agrees also substantially that of Ménégoz (*Theologie de l'Epistre aux Hebreux*), who adds to it the idea of a practical end in view. The author, according to this scholar, sets himself to prove the superiority of Christianity in order to retain the believers in the church. Such a view, of course, comes practically to the same thing as our characterization of the writing as a homily with its exposition

of doctrine in order to a practical end. If this be accepted as the design and nature of the writing, it will be unnecessary to suppose with B. W. Bacon (*Intro. to the N. T.,* 1900) that the first paragraph of the writing was lost, for being not strictly a letter, but a discourse, it needed no self-naming and thanksgiving, but begins properly with a reminder of God's former revelation of his will. Such a beginning is itself natural, and only the effort to make it conform to the procrustean ideal of a perfect letter can demand the supposition of the omission of a first section.

(3) Audience. The primary audience of the Epistle, for we may continue to give it that name at least out of deference to custom and convenience, may have been (1) the Christian community at large (So Biesanthal), or (2) that section of it which was of Jewish antecedents (Schwegler, Guericke, Baumgarten), or (3) a circle of congregations such as those in Palestine or in Alexandria and Egypt, or at Rome and in Italy, or (4) finally a particular congregation: i. e., the church at Jerusalem, or that at Rome, or that in Alexandria.

It will be needless to discuss the full merits of each of these views as to the first community for whose benefit the Epistle was written. Suffice it to say that each of them has its advocates and each is supported by plausible considerations. But the very possibility of their all being held and argued for is an evidence that the writer had in mind a catholic or comprehensive as distinguished from a local and particular audience. Those views, therefore, which make some local church, such as that at Rome or Jerusalem or Alexandria, the primary audience of the homily may be set aside as not fully satisfying the conditions.

Nevertheless, the author of Hebrews was not writing for the church universal in its broadest sense. The persons he addresses are a distinct class living "in the same general circumstances of age, position, and opinion" (Westcott). They hold the same views and are exposed to the same dangers. Such general similarity of circumstances is consistent only with a rather restricted audience, yet not necessarily so narrow as a single congregation.

When we pass to the question of the nationality of this audience, we are met at once with the traditional superscription—"To the Hebrews." But it is undeniable that this title formed no part of the original writing. And even if it did, it would not lead us beyond the conclusion that the persons addressed were of Jewish antecedents or Jews. The term Hebrew ('Εβραῖος) is sometimes applied to the Jews of Palestine who used the Aramaic language as their vernacular in order to distinguish them from the Jews of the dispersion who spoke Greek, and sometimes to the Jews of all shades of variety to distinguish them from the Gentiles also called Greeks or Hellenes. The title would be consistent with an audience of either kind of "Hebrews." (See HEBREWS.) It enables us to begin with the understanding that this audience was of Jewish antecedents.

Against this inference some recent scholars (Weizsäcker, *Das Apostolische Zeitalter* p. 473, von Soden, *Hand Komment.* vi, p. 11; Jülicher, *Einl. in das N. T.* p. 110; and McGiffert, *Hist. of Christ in the Apostolic Age,* p. 465 ff.) have pitted the view that the author was addressing an audience either purely of Gentile Christians or of Christians irrespective of antecedents. The support for this view is found in passages like vi: 1, 2; ix:14; xiii:4, 24. But on closer examination, these passages do not furnish the evidence necessary to establish the new view. On the contrary, every internal mark points to the corroboration of the title. The writer, who was evidently himself a Jew, speaks of "the fathers," of "the seed of Abraham," and of "the people of God" as the literal and lineal ancestors of himself and readers (i:1; ii:16; iv:9). And throughout the whole work, the nature of the argument is such as would appeal with fullest force only to those who were possessed by the feeling of the pride of Jewish ancestry.

Can we narrow the circle further and locate the Christian Jews addressed to a special locality or region of the known world? From the earliest times, many have pointed at Palestine as the place in which the Epistle was to be first used. In favor of this idea, one could, of course, cite the predominance of the temple-idea and the effort to build upon the ceremonial so manifest in the writing. In Palestine and Jerusalem Christians would be most exposed to the attacks against which the writer seeks to arm his readers and here alone, if anywhere, would there exist a general Christian community consisting mainly of converts from Judaism. These considerations are not absolutely conclusive, and on the contrary, certain indications, such as the Greek diction of the writing and the habit of quoting the Old Testament in the LXX version seem to exclude Palestine as the destination. Therefore, many have sought for the more particular location of the community in question in Egypt and Alexandria. The reasons which are cited against Palestine are naturally arguments for the location of the destination in Egypt. Here the temple built by Onias at Leontopolis and the ritual observed in it furnished the basis for the reasoning of the writer from the ritual. Moreover the style and diction and the use of the Alexandrian recension of the LXX are in favor of this theory. But these latter considerations point rather to the Alexandrian origin of the author than to the Egyptian destination of the writing. And as against the view it is to be borne in mind that in Alexandria the Epistle was always regarded as addressed to Palestinians. Hence, a third view has recently found favor among scholars to the effect that Rome and its Italian environment are the territory sought for in this inquiry. The facts upon which this view is based are the allusions to the persecutions of Christians, which were endured at Rome, the allusion to Timothy (xiii:23) in whom neither the Palestinian nor Egyptian Christians had, as far as we know, any special interest, and finally the allusion to them "of Italy" (xiii:24), this being understood as a message of some exiled members of the Roman community to their fellow citizens. To these considerations others of less weight could be and have been added inclining many to the view in question. Upon the whole, however, the arguments for this view are neither conclusive in themselves nor strong enough to overbalance those in favor of the Palestinian destination, and our conclusion must be that the Epistle was written with the Christian Jewish public of Palestine and its needs in immediate view.

(4) Date. The date of the writing of the Epistle is fixed by those who believe it to have been composed for the benefit of the churches in Italy and Rome at some time between 50 A. D.—the date of the expulsion of the Jews from Rome—and 64 A. D.—the date of the Neronian persecution. If that destination and object be accepted, the date is a very reasonable one. The sufferings of the Jews under Claudius may in such a case be referred to in x:32 as the "former days," whereas, the impending bloody persecution would naturally be the cause of the fear and probable falling away against which the audience is warned. But if the Palestinian destination of the writing be the correct one, the year 70 A. D., or at the latest one or two years earlier, would be the most probable date of the writing. It is not easy to believe that the author could have omitted all reference to the great catastrophe of the destruction of the temple had he written after that event. Neither could he have written much earlier, for in such a case, he could not have appealed to his readers as he does in ii:3 as men of the second generation of Christians. We shall not be far out of the way therefore, if we set aside as untenable those views which ascribe it to the reign of Domitian (about 90 A. D.), and of Trajan (about 116 A. D.), and assign the Epistle to 68 or 69 A. D.

(5) Place. As to the place whence the writing was issued no data are available. The subscription in the received text—"written to the Hebrews from Italy by Timothy"—is manifestly untrustworthy. Corinth, Ephesus, Cæsarea, and Alexandria have all been advocated as seats of the origin of the writing, but altogether on conjectural grounds. If the author was living in his native environment when he wrote, Alexandria would have better right to the claim set up in its behalf, inasmuch as the style and quality of his thought prove the writer to have been an Alexandrian.

(6) Author. But who was the author? This question is one of the few bequeathed to the modern world by the earliest biblical students. Of other similar questions of authorship it may be said, they are creatures of modern criticism, but not of the authorship of Hebrews. The question was evidently discussed in the earliest days of the church and up to the time of Origen no general agreement had been reached. Origen himself was unable to come to a conclusion and sums up the condition of thought in his day in the words: "But who it was that wrote the Epistle God only knows certainly. The account that has reached us is (manifold) some saying that Clement, who became bishop of Rome, wrote it, while others assign it to Luke, the author of the Gospel and the Acts." (Eusebius, *H. E.* vi :25.)

The divergence of view reflected in this passage disappeared to some extent during the middle ages. But it was rather through lack of real interest in the question that men acquiesced in a view which they had not thoroughly tested, than through the power of a conviction based upon thorough investigations. Accordingly, as soon as this period of slothful thought in biblical questions passed away, the original diversity of view on the authorship of Hebrews revived. At present there may be said to be four general theories on this point: (a) That of Pauline authorship; (b) that of composite authorship in which Paul is assigned a share; (c) that of authorship by another than Paul; and (d) that of suspended judgment or inability to reach a conclusion.

(a) That Paul was the author of Hebrews is still held by many, though not prominent scholars. The grounds for holding this opinion are partly traditional and partly *a priori*. On the traditional side, it is said that the Alexandrian Church fathers ascribe the writing to Paul. On the *a priori* side it is argued that the importance and dignity of the thought are consistent only with the composition of the epistle by a "man of first magnitude;" and none other than Paul was such in the Apostolic age of Christianity. To these considerations is added the general resemblance of the doctrinal system of the Epistle to the doctrinal system of the genuinely Pauline epistles and also of some characteristics of style and diction to the style and diction of Paul. But neither do these resemblances strike scholars forcibly enough to convince them, nor are the considerations of a traditional and *a priori* nature conclusive.

On the contrary, a large array of facts are pointed out as decisively opposed to this view. These have been generally classified as pertaining to the style, form and content. First of all, then, the style of the Epistle is radically different from that of the Pauline Epistles in several particulars. (*a*) It is characterized by rhythm, euphony, and rhetoric. There is through the writing, a stately movement and parallelism or balance of clauses and sentences very different from Paul's abrupt and fragmentary expressions. Farrar has likened the difference between the two authors at this point to the difference between the stately, dignified, and measured steps of the priest at service in the temple and the agile and swift movements of the athlete in the arena. (*b*) It is less Hebraistic, more literary, more idiomatic in construction than Paul's. This feature of it was noticed as early as the days of Clement of Alexandria and Origen. (*c*) The diction is unique. Paul's favorite expressions are lacking. The phrase ἐν Χριστῷ, *in Christ*, which occurs seventy-eight times in the Epistles of Paul, does not occur in Hebrews. So also the phrase Κύριος Ἰησοῦς Χριστός, *the Lord Jesus Christ*, which occurs in every one of Paul's letters (eighty times in all) is not found in Hebrews. The word εὐαγγέλιον, *gospel*, used by Paul sixty times, is not used in this epistle. The word πατήρ, *father*, applied to God thirty-six times by Paul (exclusive of the instances in which God is called the Father of Jesus Christ), and occurring in all of his epistles, is used in that sense only once in Hebrews (xii:9). (*d*) The choice of words is also non-Pauline. There is a frequent use of verbs compounded with παρά and ὑπέρ which is not found in Paul's writings. The same is true of verbs in ἴζω, of substantives in σις, and of the relatives ὅθεν, ὅσος τοσοῦτος. Certain words and phrases finally, which are favorites of the author of Hebrews, are never found in the Pauline Epistles; such as μισθαποδοσία, διαπαντός, εἰς τὸ παντελές, εἰς τὸ διηνεκές, μέτοχον εἶναι. It is not a sufficient explanation to say of these phrases that Paul has no occasion to use them elsewhere, for he does use their equivalents, as μισθός, πάντοτε, κοινωνὸν εἶναι, etc. Nor is it satisfactory to say that all of these peculiarities can be accounted for upon the supposition of the lapse of a considerable interval of time. So far as we are acquainted with the life of the Apostle, there is no room for such an interval. Nor again is there a tendency in Paul's style towards the change indicated by the difference. And, finally, the assumption that Paul, writing to the Jews, purposely adopted this style is not satisfactory, inasmuch as the Jews were not especially in a situation to appreciate finished Greek diction, certainly not as much so as the Corinthians or Ephesians. Of the theory which strives to account for these facts through the mediation of an amanuensis, it will not be necessary to speak at this point; for this view accounts for nothing if it is construed to mean that the amanuensis simply wrote down what Paul dictated; but if more freedom is given by the supposition to the amanuensis, he is thereby raised to a joint author and the theory falls under another class. Secondly, there are some considerations growing out of the form of the writing that indicate non-Pauline authorship. Such are: (*a*) The absence of a salutation, self-naming and thanksgiving. The reason why Paul should have resorted to this change of form is not apparent and the difference is remarkable in view of the uniform way in which all his acknowledged epistles follow the type of his literary production. (*b*) The arrangement of the writing. In his other writings, Paul masses the doctrinal, ethical, and practical parts of his message into sections. In the Epistle to the Hebrews, the practical or hortatory part is broken and its parts interspersed through the writing. (*c*) The confession of dependence upon others for information (ii:3 f.). Paul everywhere insists on the originality of his message. This he considers an essential feature of his apostleship. He has received the Gospel by revelation. The author of Hebrews has heard it from those that heard Jesus. (*d*) The use of the Old Testament. Both quote from the LXX. But Paul quotes with reference to the context, whereas this author quotes without such reference. Paul quotes from the Vatican recension; this author quotes from the Alexandrian. Paul quotes as if from memory; this author, as if copying the text from a MSS. before him. Paul introduces his quotations as "Scripture;" this author as the "word of God." Paul is satisfied simply to cite the words quoted; this author "improves" or makes use of the words (ii:6-9; iii:1-4, 10; vii: 1-25) notes silence (vii:3) and supplements them (iv:6-9; xi:13-16). In general, the use of the Old Testament in Hebrews is half mystical, half spiritualistic in its method. Thirdly, the argument and type of thought of the Epistle to the Hebrews is unlike that of Paul. There are indeed resemblances to the Pauline type which have led many to characterize it as "deutero-Pauline," but in general, the differences are more striking. Paul's idea of faith as the sinner's trust in Christ gives place in Hebrews to faith as an assurance of the reality of invisible things and therefore trust in God's word. Paul's idea of justification as a forensic act declaring the sinner guiltless at the bar of God, yields to the doctrine of perfection (τελείωσις). Vice versa, Paul's conception of sanctification as a moral process equivalent to growth in inner holiness finds its parallel in the doctrine of external sanctification or consecration by a priestly act (ἁγιασμός). Paul's general conception of Christianity is that it stands in sharp antithesis to Judaism, whereas in Hebrews it is the development and consummation of the Old Testament system. While these differences are not irreconcilable and might have been consistent with Pauline authorship if found alone, their occurrence together with the differences already pointed out in the other classes leads to the conclusion that the Epistle to the Hebrews was not written by Paul, to say the least with as little mediation on the part of amanuenses as the other letters of the Apostle.

(**b**) Was Hebrews, then, written by Paul conjointly with some assistant? The affirmative answer to this question takes two forms. According to the first, the Apostle dictated the treatise to some one in Hebrew, and it was translated by this person to its present Greek form. This view was propounded by Clement of Alexandria in order to account for the difference of style between the Epistle to the Hebrews and Paul's other letters. But, though it has been and is held by some, yet it has against it the facts that it is not in style alone that Hebrews differs from Paul's writings, but in form and content also. Furthermore, Hebrews was evidently written in Greek and is no translation.

According to the second variety of the theory of composite authorship, Paul is supposed to have delivered the substance of the writing to some one of his followers, who then worked it over in his own way, supplying form and diction. To the further question who this follower was, some adherents of this general view answer Luke and some, Clement of Rome. That Luke took and re-stated Paul's message to the Hebrews is argued by Delitzsch, upon the ground of the alleged sim-ilarity of language between this treatise and the third Gospel and the book of Acts. But this sim-ilarity is very general, and extends no further than the use of certain words and expressions which were probably common to all Hellenistic writers. Differences between Luke and the au-thor of Hebrews have also been pointed out, and, upon the whole, they overbalance the similarities referred to.

Clement of Rome was first suggested by Ori-gen as the mediator between Paul and the audi-ence to which Hebrews is addressed, and has been accepted as such by some on the ground of the numerous citations of the Epistle to the He-brews in the first Epistle of Clement to the Cor-inthians. But a careful study of the two writings leaves no room for doubt that Clement is using Hebrews as the work of some other man, and that, aside from this, there is no other relation-ship between the two productions. The author of Hebrews is undoubtedly a more forceful and original thinker than Clement. Moreover, the ar-gument from style is fatally against the identifi-cation of the two.

By way of mere suggestion in more recent times, Mark and Aquila have been also named as possible partners with Paul in the writing of Hebrews. But as these suggestions cannot rise above the level of mere conjecture, they have not been seriously considered by scholars.

(c) If Pauline authorship cannot be ascribed to Hebrews, either directly or through the mediation of an assistant, the question next occurs whether some other well-known person of the Apostolic age can be identified as the author. Three such well-known characters have been singled out and assigned this role. (1) The first of these is Silas (so Goder). Silas was a prominent member of the Christian community of Jerusalem, a Jewish Christian prophet and a Roman citizen. He was a companion of Paul on his second missionary journey (Acts xv:40; xviii-xxii), and associated with the Apostle in his letters (1 Thess. i:1; 2 Thess. i:1; 2 Cor. ii:19) under the name of Sil-vanus. The fact that he was acquainted with Timothy, taken with the mention of Timothy in Heb. xiii:23, has led some to think that he wrote the Epistle to the Hebrews. But, on the other hand, no trace of an external tradition ascribing the epistle to him is to be found, and, as he left us no other writings, and we cannot thus reach a conclusion regarding his style and type of thought, and as we are not informed that he had an Alexandrian education, it is not possible to test the value of the hypothesis that ascribes one Epistle to him. (2) The second person to whom the epistle has been ascribed is Apollos. This was the opinion favored by Luther (Works, Ed. of Erlangen, Vol. XI, p. 130, ad Gen. XVIII, 20). Regarding Apollos, the book of Acts informs us that he was a Jew, an Alexandrian, an eloquent man, versed in the Old Testament Scriptures, converted to the faith and active as a preacher and defender of the Messiahship of Jesus among the Jews. He joined Paul and his companions at Ephesus (Acts xviii:24), and was very helpful to those who had believed. He had been selected by one of the factions of Corinth as their head and representative, undoubtedly without his con-sent or knowledge (1 Cor. i:12). Here are char-acteristics which appear also in the author of

Hebrews: i. e., first of all, independence, talent in disputation, precision in thought, fervor, gift of graceful and persuasive use of language, knowledge of Scripture. On the ground of these, many have followed Luther (De Wette, Bleek, Tholuck, Lünemann, Kurtz, Farrar, Alford, Pres-sense, Davidson, Hilgenfeld, and, with hesitation, Pfleiderer) in ascribing the writing to Apollos. On the other side, however, it is necessary to re-member that Apollos was not a Christian of the second generation, as Heb. ii:3 demands that its author should have been, but of about the same age as Paul; neither is it likely that, after taking as important a part in the Judaistic-Pauline con-troversy, he should have made no allusion to that subject, especially in writing for Judæochris-tians. (3) The only other prominent leader of the Apostolic age named in this connection is Barnabas. The view which makes Barnabas the author of Hebrews is perhaps the most widely accepted at the present day (Ullman, Wieseler, Volkmar, B. Weiss, Keil, Salmon, Renan, Zahn, and Harnack). The reasons that lead to this conclusion are, first of all, the ancient tradition attested by Tertullian that Barnabas wrote He-brews (de Pudicitia, 20); then Barnabas was from Cyprus, and thus in close touch with Alex-andria. He was also a companion of Paul, a fact that may explain the Pauline elements of the thought, in Hebrews, and a Levite possessing an intimate acquaintance with the ceremonial law. All of these characteristics undoubtedly belong to the author of Hebrews also. But it may be asked, Could Barnabas have classified himself with the second generation of Christian believers? And, further, as a Levite, was he not better ac-quainted with the Hebrew than appears to be the author of Hebrews? Finally, an epistle bearing the name of Barnabas is extant. Antiquity ad-mitted this, whether correctly or not, it is of no consequence. But having admitted one letter, why should it have scrupled about conceding him also the Epistle to the Hebrews? These questions make the claim in behalf of Barnabas a difficult one to establish.

(d) Accordingly, many scholars, (Eichhorn, Ewald, Köstlin, Lipsius, von Soden, Holtzmann, Ménégoz, Jülicher, Rendall, Dods, Westcott, A. B. Davidson, Bruce, and Milligan) feel compelled to ascribe the writing to an unknown author of Alexandrian training, if not birth. Bishop West-cott finds in the anonymousness of the writing an evidence of the spiritual wealth of the Apostolic age. In any case, the divine authority and canon-icity of the epistle are "self-attested and ratified by the illuminated consciousness of the Christian Society, and that apart from any certitude as to the name and identity of the writer."

Helps to the Study of the Epistle to the Hebrews.

Of the older commentaries on Hebrews, Cal-vin's (In Novum Testamentum Commentarii, Berl. 1838) and Owen's An Exposition of the Epistle to the Hebrews, may still be mentioned as full of value. The Epistle has been more re-cently commented on, and foremost in the list of later works must stand Westcott's Ep. to the Heb. 2nd Ed., London, 1892. Other works of impor-tance are T. C. Edwards, Ep. to the Heb. (in the Expositor's Bible). Lünemann, Handbook to the Ep. to the Heb. (in Meyer's Commentary, Eng. Tr. Edinb. 1882). Rendall, The Ep. to the Heb. in Greek, London, 1883, and The Ep. to the Heb. in Eng. 1888. Delitzsch, Com. on the Ep. to the Heb. (Eng. tr. 1868). A. B. Davidson (in Hand-

books for Bible Classes) Edinb. 1882. Farrar (in *Camb. Bible* for schools) Lond., 1883. A. B. Bruce, *The Ep. to the Heb.* Edinb., 1899. W. Kay (in the *Speaker's Commentary*) Lond., 1881. J. B. McCaul, *The Ep. to the Heb.* Lond., 1871. W. F. Moulton (in Ellicott's *New Test. Com.*) C. J. Vaughan, *The Ep. to the Heb.* Lond. 1890. F. D. Maurice (Warburton Lectures) Lond., 1846.

Of commentaries in the German language, Bleek, *Der Brief an die Hebr.* Berl. 1828-1840, still holds a prominent place. In addition we may name Ewald's (Götting, 1870), Holtzheuer (Berl. 1883), Keil's (Leip. 1885), Kurtz (Mitau, 1869), Schaefer's (Catholic; Münster, 1893). Weiss, (Götting, 1888). On the theology of the Epistle to the Hebrews, Riehm's *Der Lehrbegriff des Hebraerbriefes,* in German. Ménégoz, *La Theologie de l'Epitre aux Hebreux,* in French, and George Milligan, *The Theology of the Epistle to the He-*

erary treatment were ready to their hand in such lyric fragments as the matchless Song of Deborah, or the poetic utterances of King David (2 Sam. i :19-27), in the popular stories about the heroes and leaders of the nation, and in the abundant records of one kind and another, traditional, legal and annalistic, which they seem to have preserved.

There is good reason for thinking that attempts had been made in David's time, and even earlier, to gather up these materials and to unify them into literary wholes. The book of Jasher "the Excellent" (Josh. x:13; 2 Sam. i:18) and the book of the Wars of Jehovah (Num. xxi:14) were collections of popular poetry. The works referred to in 1 Chron. xxix:29 indicate that minor histories were attempted. The structure of such books as Leviticus or Exodus indicates that the Mosaic enactments existed in subordinate

The Sea of Tiberias.

brews, in English, are the most useful. On the authorship, date, and design of the epistle consult the current works on N. T. Introduction.

A. C. Z.

HEBREWS, LITERATURE OF THE.

1. Its Beginning. The Hebrews have held a place in the history of nations since about 1000 B. C. Prior to David's time the conditions of life with which the people struggled were such as to preclude any real unity of action or thinking and any self-developed activity outside of the arts of war, agriculture or government. The most important steps toward a real literature were taken when the tribes were welded into a united nation under David, and the prophetic and priestly orders became definite and important factors in its development. These organized bodies became in Palestine, as they were in Babylonia and elsewhere, a class with the motive impulses and ideals and with the leisure essential to the development of a national literature. Materials for lit-

groupings. Nevertheless it seems clear that these productions were only preparatory. The distinctive literary development of the Hebrew nation was in the interest of ideas which did not get hold of the national mind much earlier than the eighth and ninth century B. C., the age of the great historians and of the notable quartet of prophets, Amos, Hosea, Isaiah and Micah. Under the stimulus of these brilliant thinkers, the accumulated records and memories of the past were utilized to illustrate to the nation the significance of its history.

2. External Influences. The Hebrews were so situated as to make a literary development natural. They belonged to the Semitic family of nations, each one of which under the proper conditions has developed a literature. They spoke a language closely related to that of the Babylonians and Assyrians. Right across the center of their territory passed the stream of international traffic between the two great centers of culture and commerce in that day, the Tigris-Euphrates basin and the valley of the Nile. Thus the more active minds among the Hebrews were kept in close touch with the problems and achievements of the western Asiatic world. The Tel-el-Amarna Tablets give evidence that the culture of Babylonia was paramount in Syria—Palestine in the fifteenth century B. C. and earlier. During the centuries that followed this influence was less direct, but still appreciable. About 600 B. C., during the Great Captivity, when the Hebrews were compelled to make their homes in Babylonia for half a century, a second great impulse to literary productiveness was received.

3. Classification. To separate Hebrew literature into periods of development is unsatisfactory. A less usual but more practical classification will be by three artificial groupings, the literature preserved in the Hebrew or English Old Testament, the extra-canonical literature and the Rabbinic literature.

The Old Testament fairly represents the choicest productions of the Hebrew mind down to about the second century B. C. The Great Captivity (B.C. 586-538) made an alteration in the circumstances of the nation for the next four hundren years, which marked the literature. In Hebrew literature, however, form is so fully subordinated to idea that the unity of Biblical literature is far more marked than its diversity. We can only treat the Old Testament as a literary whole.

The activity of the Hebrew mind did not cease with the completion of the Canon. Numberless writings were put forth between the second century B. C. and the corresponding date of our era. Many of these are worthy of mention.

A peculiar development of Judaism is represented by the Targums, the Mishna and the Talmud, which will require brief attention.

4. Biblical Literature. The literature preserved in the Old Testament constitutes the most representative section of Hebrew literature. It is the choicest portion of a literary output of considerable extent through many centuries. Its collections of psalms and proverbs are anthologies which include specimens, centuries apart in time of origin. Its histories have grown out of earlier histories. Its wisdom writings are masterpieces in their class. Owing to this gradual selection of the fittest, the literature of the Bible is remarkable for its permanent and satisfying character. It rewards examination from the purely literary point of view.

(1) The Historical Writings of the Old Testament are thirteen in number. The Biblical histories are exactly like modern histories, in that they are compilations, made from earlier historical sources long after the date represented by those sources and intended to instruct the people of the compiler's day. They differ from modern histories in that instead of sketching the rise and progress of a people they illustrate an idea. They are reviews of religious progress, histories of Divine Providence. To effect this there is large use of the historic story, which Moulton calls the "epical style" of narrative. The story of Joseph is such a prose epic; the narrative of Elijah is another; the story of Balaam mingles prose, epic and verse. They do more than store the mind; they touch the imagination and the emotions. One of the finest examples of Hebrew history is the book of *First Samuel*. One who follows closely its treatment of the period of Saul's reign will notice that the historical facts as such are rapidly passed over, the personal descriptions are mere sketches, stress is laid on crises and the way in which Jehovah met them by rais-

ing up the right man at the proper time and on his care of these agents. Thus the whole book becomes a sermon on God's providential care for Israel. At the same time it is a model of terse, instructive narrative.

Closely allied to this type of history is the partly imaginative narrative represented by the books of Ruth or Esther or Jonah. In these the historical or prophetic purpose is attained more strikingly by the skillful use of the novelist's art. The prologue of the Book of Job illustrates this. The story is so skillfully told that we are as certain of Job's innocence as of his unexampled calamities.

(2) Old Testament Poetry is peculiar. We may feel its charm without understanding the secret of it. Only the Hebrew student can catch some of its minor devices, such as assonance, alliteration and the alphabetical acrostic. The English reader may, however, catch the most distinctive element of form, that symmetrical arrangement of clauses in a verse called *parallelism*. Compare Job xxxix: 19-25 or Job xxviii, passages which owe their rhythmic effect to this cause. The various poetical forms were well understood by the Hebrews. The Song of Deborah (Judges v) or the Song of Moses (Exod. xv) are notable examples of the ode. The book of Lamentations, when properly rendered, illustrates the elegiac rhythm, a long line followed by a short one. This and other peculiarities are obscured by the method of printing followed in the English Bible. The Psalter is a great storehouse of lyrics, elegies, odes and corresponding literary forms.

(3) The Wisdom or Philosophical writings of the Hebrews are represented by Proverbs, Job, Ecclesiastes, and the Song of Songs. Their variety is such as to indicate that the Hebrews loved to dwell on the problems of life and developed a rich literature of reflection, which made free use of literary devices. The simple proverb, the proverb cluster (Prov. xxv:2-7), the connected composition or essay on some theme (Eccles. iii: 1 ; iv:8) ; the dramatic dialogue as in the Book of Job; the dramatic monologue (Proverbs viii)—all are used with great skill and to good effect.

The most distinctive class of writings in the Old Testament are those which we call *Prophetic*. No other national literature contains their equivalent. They owe their preservation primarily to their contents rather than their form. They are sermons. The prophetic writings embody a variety of literary forms, for the prophets were men of extraordinary versatility, who pressed their messages home with consummate skill. Notice the graphic manner in which Joel describes the devastation of his land and the onset of the locust army on the Day of Jehovah, the magnificent oration or rhapsody of Isaiah on Jehovah's Rod and Reign (xi:4), the stirring ode of judgment in Habakkuk iii. These writings owe not a little of their impressiveness to the fact that, while they preserve the vigor and directness of an address, they are actually carefully edited abstracts of the utterances of a prophet during a considerable period of time. Comp. Jer. xxv:3-13, where the "book" represents about ten chapters.

5. The Special Value of Biblical Literature. Its superiority over contemporary ancient literature can hardly be disputed. This is not because it is rich in literary forms, not because it is distinctively religious in its tone, but because of its lack of trivialness, the high plane of the motives which inspired it, the unselfish spirit which breathes throughout it, and the noble ideals to which it gives expression. It therefore becomes by human as well as divine right the literature of culture, of inspiration and of life.

6. The Extra-Canonical and Rabbinic Literature. The extra-canonical literature was copious. Most of the works available for us are those which were admitted into the Greek Old Testament and have come down to us as "Apocrypha." They include such histories as First and Second Maccabees, such stories as Judith, Tobit and First Esdras, such wisdom writings as Ecclesiasticus and the Wisdom of Solomon, such varied productions as the Psalter of the Pharisees or the book of Enoch or of Baruch. Some of these were written in Greek, but they are truly Hebraistic and belong to an account of Hebrew literature. With one or two exceptions they are distinctly below the literary level of the biblical books.

By the second century A.D. the lines had been closely drawn between Judaism and Christianity. Each followed a distinct development. Judaism dropped out of touch with the world and gave itself, through its great scholars, to a gathering up in exact form of the established paraphrasings of the Hebrew of the Old Testament into the spoken Aramaic, thus producing the *Targums,* and of the decisions of the older Rabbis on subjects of religious importance, thus developing the chapters of the *Mishna.* The Talmud is not easily described. One might call it a vast storehouse of tradition, interpretation, stories, discussions, meditations—a collection containing much rubbish along with considerable material of value. It is a cyclopedia in all but arrangement; it is a literature only in measurement. It marks the close of the literary activity of the ancient Hebrews.

F. K. S.

HEBREWS, RELIGION OF THE (hē'brŭs rē-lĭj'ĭn).

(1) The Pre-Mosaic Period. (1) The ancient Hebrews belonged to the Semitic group of nations, having its original home in northern Arabia, from which region migrations into the Mesopotamian valley formed the eastern branch, including the Babylonians and Assyrians. From Mesopotamia came the northern Semites or Arameans, and the western Semites, including the Phœnicians, Canaanites and Hebrews. Of these westward migrations, that of the Hebrews, was among the latest, including, as it did, clans that later broke off into separate nations, such as Moab, Ammon and Edom. The memorials of Hebrew history and religion that have been preserved are found in the Old Testament. The books composing that collection are of varying dates, from the eighth to the second centuries B. C. But several of them contain documents much older. Traditions and legends of the past are incorporated, and the effort is made by later writers to reconstruct the origins of the nation, as well as the early history of the world. But the purpose of these narratives is rather religious than historical. The materials are chosen seemingly with the object of illustrating the growth of the religion, and not of giving a connected recital of the national experiences. It therefore becomes a matter of difficulty to discover the religious character of the earliest period, colored as it is by the ideas of the later days when the narratives received their present form. But this material deals with the earliest traditions of the race in a spirit marked by an earnestness and sobriety in striking contrast with similar accounts produced by other nations. (2) The Hebrew people brought with them from their earlier home in the east the religious conceptions common to the Semitic races, and these appear to some extent in the narratives of the early period, though modified and given other meanings by later writers. Yet from the first a new force was operating in this national history. That peculiar factor which distinguished Israel from other nations appeared early, even before the days of Moses. Those Semitic elements which this people had in common with its neighbors were used, modified, or eliminated in the development of that particular type of religion which the Old Testament alone discloses. Two processes were at work: the natural growth of religious ideas, as among other nations, and the providential evolution of those unique elements whose fuller disclosure appears in Christianity. (3) Studied in the light of their heredity and environment, the Hebrews exhibit religious characteristics in striking contrast to those of their ancestors or the kindred tribes about them. But those peculiar forces make their appearance but slowly, and under the leadership of rare men. These men gave to the national life its chief significance. There is always a temptation, however, to observe only the unique features of Israel's religious life and to forget the thorough Semitism of this people and the features of its earliest cult, which is possessed in common with the other races of the Semitic family. These nations were polytheists, offered sacrifices, even human sacrifices, practiced circumcision, to some extent at least, erected sanctuaries for their gods, believed that certain places were sacred to the gods, had religious festivals like the Sabbath and other sacred seasons, used images in worship or as family teraphim, and believed in a dim underworld into which the dead descended. Many, perhaps it may be said all, of these features are exhibited by the earliest Hebrew religion, and some continue and are developed, while others fall quite out of sight. But even from the earliest beginnings of the national life there is a difference between Israel and the rest. This is most strikingly illustrated in the conceptions of deity held by this people. From this the higher ethical character of the nation arose. The earliest ideas may have been polytheistic, as the plural form of the word *Elohim* (God) hints, and there may appear rare indications of such an idea (Gen. iii:22), but they are slight. There are no traces of a Hebrew pantheon. This is the more surprising when it is observed that the neighboring and kindred tribes of Edom, Ammon, and Moab, descended indeed from the traditional ancestors of the Hebrews, were polytheists. In the case of Moab the evidence is found in the mention of at least two gods on the celebrated "Moabite Stone" of King Mesha. But while the worship of more than one god is not traceable in the religion of Israel, that religion is not, in its earlier stages, a pure monotheism, but rather monolatry, *i. e.,* the worship of a national God for Israel, while admitting the existence of other gods for other nations (Judg. xi:24; I Sam. xxvi:19). There are certain interesting characteristics of the Hebrew idea of God which mark the being they worshiped as quite different from the gods of the nations about them. He had no goddess or consort, nor was his worship attended by any of those degrading rites connected so largely with the worship of goddesses. Fire was his symbol (Ex. iii:4; Judg. xiii:20; 2 Kings i:10). He could be seen only with peril to the beholder (Judg. xiii:22), and sacred places and objects could be approached only with danger (I Sam. vi:19; 2 Sam. vi:6 *sq.;* Ex. xix:21 *sq.*). He led his people in war (Ex. xv:3), and their achievements in battle were his own (Num. xxi:14), while cities taken in his name and devoted to him were destroyed. In these and other elements of the faith are discerned the harsher and fiercer characteristics of the age. Righteousness was, however, the dominant feature of his nature, and to this belief much of the high ethical tone of the Hebrew religion is to be traced. (4) Abraham is the traditional ancestor of this people, and the one to whom the earliest disclosures of the divine character are made. Whatever the legendary nature of the traditions regarding this man, there can be little doubt of his reality and impress upon the national life. Faith in God is his motive. He comes westward to a new land in obedience to a divine impulse (Gen. xii:1 sq.). He erects altars wherever he stops (Gen. xii:8; xiii:4), and constantly lives in communion with God. He is even willing to offer his son in sacrifice (Gen. xxii), according to the custom of his day, but is forbidden to carry out his purpose, and thus the ban is placed on the practice, though it does not disappear. The patriarchs whom the early traditions introduce to us are not demi-gods, but men—men of very imperfect character, like Abraham and Jacob, and typical sheiks of the Orient, whose counterparts might be found there to this day, but, withal, men with a moral purpose, if we may trust the outlines of their lives, a purpose never obscured in Abraham's case, gradually attained in that of Jacob, and preparing for a fuller disclosure of the divine purpose in later days.

In this period many of the elements of Semitic religion are discovered. Altars were built on hills and under trees, sacrificial meals and sacred festivals were celebrated, circumcision was introduced, and probably abstinence from blood and the taboo of certain kinds of food were practiced. With these went the customs of blood revenge, polygamy, concubinage, and slavery. Images for worship, called teraphim, were not unknown, even in the families of the patriarchs (Gen. xxxi:19), and sacred stones were set up and anointed with oil (Gen. xxxv:14, 15; Josh. iv:20), while certain places were deemed especially sacred, as Hebron, Shechem, the Oak of Moreh, and Beersheba.

(2) The Religion of Moses. (1) After an indefinite period of residence in Canaan, the Hebrew clans moved southward into Egypt, following the leadership of the tribe of Joseph. The monuments mention many migrations of this character into a country that was the granary of the world at the time, but no certain identification of the Hebrews in any inscriptions can be made. A period of prosperity in which the Joseph clan came to prominence was followed by a reversal of policy toward foreigners, and the hardships of servitude were experienced. After a stay of about four centuries, the emancipation of the Hebrews was wrought by a leader named Moses. His first attempt to rouse the nation to action was unsuccessful, and he was compelled to quit the country (Ex. ii:11-15; Acts vii:23-25). He betook himself to the territory of Midian, and entered into alliance with that tribe. After a time the divine impulse came upon him to renew his effort in behalf of his oppressed countrymen. Mount Sinai was the mountain of God, the reputed home of deity (Ex. iii:1-5; xix:2; Judg. v:5), and here Moses was commissioned to undertake the difficult task. He returned to Egypt, and at last succeeded in the plan of deliverance, which was greatly aided by a series of disasters that fell upon Egypt at that time, and which were ever believed by the Hebrews to mark the wrath of God against their oppressors. The departing host made its way toward the friendly land of Midian, and, crossing an arm of the Gulf of Suez at low water, the Egyptian army sent in pursuit was overthrown and destroyed. This deliverance was celebrated in perhaps the oldest fragment of Hebrew literature (Ex. xv), and was forever regarded as the decisive sign of the divine care of the nation.

Moving on to the sacred mountain Sinai, Moses, whose place as a leader had been firmly established by the remarkable experiences of the past, seized the opportunity to lay the foundations of national life by the promulgation of certain institutes of political and religious character suited to the people he was leading. No attempt was made to break with the past (Ex. iii:6; iv:5; vi:2, 3; vii:16). The Hebrews already possessed a religion which differed in no small degree from that of other nations, but in the centuries of serfdom in Egypt much of the patriarchal practice, simple as it was, may have been forgotten. But the people were passing from clan life to nationality. The purpose of Moses was to prepare for a future such as had been foreseen by none of his ancestors. Looking at the work which Moses accomplished for this people, taking them at a time of such utter lack of organization and of such elementary religious ideas; witnessing the lofty character of the ideals which he lifted before them, however little they were realized for centuries, the question naturally rises, What is the explanation of his unique personality and his conceptions of God and righteousness, so greatly in contrast with the philosophy of the Egyptian priesthood and the barbarism and immorality of the common life in his day? The response is to be found alone in that divine choice of this nation, not for its own sake, but for the disclosure it might make through its history of the divine purposes regarding men. This disclosure could only be made through chosen men intrusted with leadership, and among these one of the most conspicuous is Moses. (2) Our sources tell us that a new name for God sprung up in this period. The indefinite *Elohim* no longer sufficed to represent the covenant God of the Hebrew people, who had made himself known to their fathers. The new name is *Jehovah*, or more correctly *Jahveh* (also written *Yahva* or *Yahway*, and pronounced in accordance with the latter form), the living, self-existent (Ex. vi:1-4). Whether this name originated with Moses, or was used in Midian and brought back by him, or was used in his family, as the name of his mother might suggest (Ex. vi:20), or in the tribe of Joseph, as Joshua (Je-Hoshua) might argue, in any case the name first appears at the time of Moses' return from Midian, and was connected in Hebrew traditions with an epiphany at Sinai. The name continued to be employed to the close of the Old Testament literature. It is not claimed as yet that *Jahveh* is the only God, but that he alone must be worshiped by Israel. Other nations may have their deities, but the Hebrews must have no god beside *Jahveh*. It will be seen that it is a far cry from this idea of monolatry to the pure monotheism of the post-exilic period; but the religious education of Israel was a long and painful process, and one thing had to be learned at a time. (3) The code of laws promulgated by Moses (Ex. xx:23, 34) dealt with the situation in which Israel found itself in the period of its unsettled life, and served as the basis of all the legislation that grew up in later times. So largely was the Mosaic spirit preserved and continued in all the legislative material ever produced by Israel that the phrase, "The Law of Moses" was never felt to be a misnomer in describing the body of statutes, the most of which, as a matter of fact, came into existence centuries subsequent to the time of Moses. The first code, called the Book of the Covenant (Ex. xx:23, 34), and including the Decalogue in its primitive form, is a striking interpretation of the character of *Jahveh*, the national God. There is little in common with either the nature-worship of the times or the speculative character of the Egyptian religion, from which it might be supposed leading elements would be drawn. *Jahveh* is righteous and holy, and he demands these characteristics in his people. There is an utter lack of the sensuous elements of other religions. No images are to be employed. Altars of earth at places selected furnish a sufficient means of worship. But *Jahveh* alone must be the object of this service. The element of sternness, not to say fierceness, which the Hebrews associated with the character of God, appears. *Jahveh* is capable of fierce wrath when his will is not honored (Ex. xxii :23, 24; xxxiv: 7), and he will not lightly overlook transgression xxiii :21). His jealousy of other gods who may receive the affection of his people is carried to the extent of forbidding any covenant with other nations, and of commanding the total destruction of all symbols of worship not connected with the national cult (Ex. xxxiv :12-16). The nations are to be driven out before Israel (Ex. xxiii :22-24). This stern spirit appears in certain of the laws regulating social life. The *lex talionis* is to be enforced (Ex. xxi :24). The man who kills another, or smites or curses his father or mother, is to be put to death. Yet there is a note of great tenderness in the laws of this primitive code. Care for the life and honor of servants, mitigation of the severities of the blood feud, care for the property and welfare of all the community, kind treatment of strangers, even help to an enemy in distress, are enforced. The seventh day and year are made sacred, and three annual religious feasts are instituted. The standard of morality and worship is high for the age. Indeed, it was the first serious attempt to unite morality with religion. Justice and purity, as elements in the divine character, were demanded of the people; and if there was a sternness and harshness in the character of *Jahveh* which seems incompatible with a moralized idea of deity, they might easily be found to co-exist in the mind of a teacher like Moses, with the profound conviction that God is sternly just and demands justice and holiness in his followers. (4) In providing for the future of the nation Moses made use of those ancestral religious elements which commended themselves to his divinely illumined judgment. Circumcision, altar sacrifice, the sabbatic periods, the fundamental laws of morality were all accepted as sanctioned by *Jahveh*. With them certain features in the Egyptian and Midianitish religions were incorporated, such as the idea of the sanctuary and sacred palladium or ark, the priesthood, and the Urim and Thummim. Moses established a tent of meeting at Kadesh, and the function of priestly service he assigned to his own tribe of Levi. This office of priest and that of judge he probably derived from the practice he had observed in Midian (Ex. xviii :1, 17-25). The priesthood was much more than a mere order of sacrificers. The latter function was not confined to them till a much later period. Kings, prophets, and common citizens had the right of sacrifice (Judg. vi :24-26; xiii :19; 1 Sam. xiv :34, 35; 2 Sam. vi :17, 18; 1 Kings xviii). The priests were the spiritual teachers and leaders of the nation, and the interpreters of the will of God. They had a Torah, or law, which grew up around the Decalogue and the Book of the Covenant given by Moses. This Torah grew as experience widened the application of the primitive code. Moses' actual contribution to the literature of Israel was probably small. Jesus, the founder of Christianity, wrote nothing. Nevertheless, Moses stands as the most striking figure of the early history, a figure so important and lofty that his influence is plainly traced through-

out all the subsequent history as the great prophet and spiritual leader, the organizer of Israel's national life.

(3) The Conquest and the Judges. (1) About the year 1250 B. C. the Hebrew nation, having spent some time in the less desirable regions to the south and east of the Dead Sea, began their entrance and conquest of Canaan. The experiences of the desert had developed the qualities of national life and prepared a generation of warriors. After the conquest of the east-Jordan districts the river was crossed and the serious business of occupying the rich lands to the west was undertaken. Canaan was ever the coveted goal of the desert tribes, and Israel was neither the first nor last of the nations that attempted its possession. The inhabitants already represented a variety of elements, the result of successive inroads, and against these older and higher civilizations Israel prepared to do battle. The success with which this purpose was attained was the result, in no small degree, of the hardships of the desert, which had toughened the national fiber, and of the personality and work of Moses, who had given something of form and national spirit to the band of refugees who had so recently escaped Egyptian serfdom. In a series of rapid and aggressive campaigns, under the leadership of Joshua, some of the most important cities were taken, and the united opposition of the Canaanites was broken (Josh. vi :12-27; viii :10-29; x: 11), while a portion of the population succeeded in making terms with the invaders (Josh. ix :11-19). It is evident, however, that scarcely more than a foothold was secured at the time, and that the only thing needed to inspire the native population to renewed hostilities was the removal of Joshua and the decay of the strong military force organized under his hand. Much of the land was not really conquered (Josh. xiii :1-6). The best that could be done was to secure a possession in the land and wait for greater strength. But this period was yet far ahead. The strong cities were in Canaanite hands, and for the most part the Israelites were obliged to content themselves with the smaller towns and open country. War was carried on for many years, but with varying success (Judg. i), and not infrequently the people were reduced to desperate straits (Judg. iv :3; vi : 3 *sq.*). The tribes were not united. Each was seeking to hold its own ground. Moreover, between the northern tribes, at whose head, in the days when any united action was attempted, stood the strong tribe of Ephraim, and the southern tribes, the most powerful of which was Judah, there was little common interest, and neither section gave much heed to the welfare of the other. These sectional jealousies often appeared, and culminated in the rupture of the nation at the close of Solomon's reign.

(2) In all this series of national experiences the belief in *Jahveh* as the god of the people is never obscured. It was he who brought them into the land, after the wanderings in the desert (Josh. iii :5-7; he gave directions for the campaigns (Josh. i :1-9), and under his leadership cities were taken and battles won. Even the laws of nature were believed to have been set aside in answer to appeals to him on one memorable occasion (Josh. x :12-14), and the inhabitants of conquered places were devoted to destruction in his honor by the imposition of the *herem* or ban (Josh. vi :18-21; viii :21-29), the breaking of which, even by one individual, might cause disaster to the army and bring upon the offender and his family the ban itself (Josh. vii). Soon after the arrival in Canaan, Gilgal was selected as a sacred camp, and

there circumcision and the keeping of the Passover feast were enjoined (Josh. iv:19; v:12).

(3) The period that followed the first tide of warfare was one of retrogression and decline, both in organization and religion. The excitement of the events connected with the last years of Moses and the leadership of Joshua was followed by a reaction. The age of these two leaders was full of stirring experiences that kept the people measurably united and keyed up to high enthusiasm for their national honor and their God. The loosing of ties incident to the removal of competent leadership permitted much disorder that would have been impossible before. The people, unable to conquer the inhabitants of the country, settled down on friendly terms with them, and soon, as a matter of course, adopted from them many of their religious and social customs, and a fairly close intimacy was preserved for generations. The worship of *Baal* and his consort *Astarte,* Phœnician deities, was more or less prevalent in Canaan, and soon the Israelites were tainted with this practice. *Baal* was the god of fire, and his worship was attended with fire offerings, in which the sacrifice of children had a frequent part. Each town where the worship prevailed had its sanctuary and image of *Baal,* and these local *Baals* or *Baalim* were a constant temptation to Israel. In connection with the *Baal sanctuary* there was usually a grove, tree, pillar, or obelisk sacred to *Astarte* or *Ashera* (plural *Ashtaroth*), whose seductive and licentious cult proved the most debasing influence of the age.

(4) That the Israelites were often led away into this worship and that of other gods there is abundant evidence, as well as that later writers saw in this fact ample explanation of the frequent calamities which overtook the nation (Judg. ii:11-19; iii:7, 8; vi:1-28; viii:33; x:6, 7, etc.). Moreover, even where the worship of *Jahveh* was retained, the elements of the *Baal* worship were mixed with it. High places like Bethel, Beersheba, Shechem, Hebron, Gilgal, Penuel, Ramah, and Mizpeh were resorted to as sacred. Children were named for *Baal* even in families where *Jahveh* was worshiped (see JERUBBAAL), and it is not unlikely that the word *Baal,* i. e., "lord," may have been applied to *Jahveh* through custom. Micah, the Danite, a worshiper of *Jahveh,* uses an ephod and a teraph which the writer of the narrative explains as images, the one graven and the other molten, representing probably *Jahveh* and the dead ancestor of the family, as was usually the case with teraphim (Judg. xvii:1-6). Gideon is reproached for making an image (ephod) with the golden spoil of battle, which was used as an object of worship (Judg. viii: 24-27). The Danites carried off these same images and set up one in their new sanctuary at upper Dan (Judg. xviii:14-31). At the same time it must be noted that the pure imageless worship of *Jahveh* was carried on at Shiloh, where the tent of meeting, with its ancient ark and its Levitical priesthood, was established after their removal from Gilgal (Josh. xviii:1, *sq.;* 1 Sam. i:3). The leadership of *Jahveh* was recognized, and this was especially the case in times of war. In peace there might be relapses into the seductive cult of their neighbors, but when a war was to be waged *Jahveh* alone was the God of Israel (Judg. i:19, 22; iv:6, 15). The Song of Deborah, one of the oldest fragments of the national literature (Judg. v), bears witness to the lofty religious enthusiasm of the people on occasion. Indeed such enthusiasm reveals the power of the true religion manifesting itself in the midst

of such unfavorable conditions; and in its power to inspire high ideals, not alone of heroism, but of moral conduct, lay the supremacy of this faith.

The principle of monolatry is recognized. *Jahveh* is the God of Israel, and should alone be worshiped by his people; but outside of this nation other gods have sway, and bring their people into possession of their territories, as in the case of *Chemosh* and the Ammonites (Judg. xi:24).

(5) It was an age of contradictions. Cruelty, violence, feuds, license in conduct, polygamy and deceit were permitted. Yet along with these go hospitality, even at the risk of life, and vengeance taken on an inhospitable city; gentleness toward neighbors and friends, a forgiving spirit toward a runaway wife, love for the customs and ideas of Israel. It is, in a word, an age in which the normal characteristics of simple and joyous life appear. However late the Book of Ruth may be, the picture which it gives of these times seems truthful and lifelike, and it is like a charming glimpse into the inner life of the people, whose career at first glance seems to be marked at this time only by the elements of storm and struggle.

(6) It has been said that it was a period of retrogression; yet it was also a period of progress. While the enthusiastic spirit of the days of Moses and Joshua had passed away, there were influences at work preparing for better things. The work of the Judges, disconnected and transient as it seemed, prepared the people for the closer organization of the monarchy. The character and ideals of *Jahveh* as the true God were more firmly fixed in the heart of the people. It was one of those periods of silence when energies are maturing for a larger activity ahead. Such times are ever the birth-hours of great forces. With much that was barbarous and debased there was also much that was noble and inspiring. Taken all in all, it may be said that real progress was made under the Judges, and this progress came to its full disclosure under the ministry of Samuel, the last of the Judges.

(4) Samuel, David, and Solomon. (1) Under the leadership of Samuel the nation passed from the anarchy and confusion of the period of the Judges to the organization and order of the days of David. Samuel was as prophet a worthy successor to Moses; and in him it seems that the promise of a line of prophets, which may be as early as the time of Moses, was beginning to be fulfilled (Deut. xviii:15). The picture of worship at the time he first appears is simple and natural, yet corrupted by the vicious practices of the priests in office. The tent in which the ark was kept at Shiloh was lighted at night by a lamp, and in it slept the priest and his attendants (1 Sam. iii:1-3). Samuel, though not of the tribe of Levi, but of Ephraim (1 Sam. i:1), was taken into the tabernacle service and ministered often throughout his life in priestly offices, as did others of non-Levitical families (Judg. xvii:1, 5; 2 Sam. viii:18, R. V.). After the death of Eli, the priest in office, and the temporary loss of the ark, Samuel undertook the leadership of Israel, and for a score of years worked silently toward the realization of national ideas. Little appreciated at first, and regarded as a mere clairvoyant whose advice might be sought by those in trouble (1 Sam. ix:6-9), he came at length to be regarded as the real leader of the people. Perhaps the sincerest compliment ever paid him was the popular demand for a king, which indicated the sense of unity, solidarity and national pride fostered by him, so foreign to the days of the Judges. Whatever may have been the reluctance felt by Samuel, as set down in one of our sources

(1 Sam. viii :6), the step was a wise one, and Saul, whatever his limitations, served to set the type of royalty, tried unsuccessfully and for but a brief period in the days of Gideon and his son Abimelech (Judg. viii :22, 23; ix :6).

(2) It was a period of transition. The old and the new were meeting, and Saul was not equal to the emergency. Probably few men would have been. But above the tall figure of the king towers evermore Samuel, the prophet of the Lord. His work is no mere political revolution. It was far more a religious reformation. From his home in Ramah he went on visits, almost pastoral in their character, to places of ancestral sacredness, like Gilgal, Mizpeh, Bethlehem and Bethel, where sacrificial feasts were held and the sanctions of the true faith laid upon the hearts of the people (1 Sam. vii :5, 9; x :8; xvi :4, 5). No use was made of the ark in this time. It remained quietly at Kirjath Jearim. The members of the tribe of Levi found livings wherever they might, some as private or tribal priests, as in the case of the grandson of Moses (Judg. xviii :30, R. V.). In connection with the work of Samuel we first learn of the Schools of the Prophets. These companies of men present little that is attractive at first. They seem to have been dervish-like groups of men devoted to the national God, but closely resembling the similar order of men in the service of Baal, of whom we catch a glimpse at a later time (1 Kings xvii :22-29). In Israel the bands of prophets in the early days of Samuel were of this character, made up of enthusiasts who went about the country rousing themselves to a high pitch of ecstasy by means of the wild music of the time, and no doubt preaching the religion of *Jahveh* in the fierce spirit of the age. In the circle of such "prophesying" the bystander might be seized with the same enthusiasm, utter similar words, and fall unconscious on the ground; and these manifestations were believed to be divinely induced (1 Sam. x :5-13; xix :18-24). Nothing speaks more eloquently for the wisdom of Samuel than the fact that with all his loftiness of purpose he did not despise the good these bands of men might accomplish, repulsive as might be their practices. He even identified himself with them in a measure, and by assuming their leadership (1 Sam. xix :20) he gradually made of them organizations effective in the propagation of the saner and loftier conceptions of *Jahveh* and his religion, which appeared in his own work and that of his successors. Such prophets as Elijah and Elisha in later days made large use of the Schools of the Prophets. There was, to be sure, an element of fanaticism and fierce zeal in Samuel's character, as is shown by his command to Saul to exterminate the Amalekites (1 Sam. xv :1-3), and his killing of Agag, their king, with his own hands (1 Sam. xv :32, 33), in both of which acts he believed himself fulfilling the divine will. But these are rare blemishes in a splendid career of many years, in one of the most critical periods of the history. No loftier prophetic note was ever struck than that uttered in his famous words, "To obey is better than sacrifice, and to hearken than the fat of rams" (1 Sam. xv :22).

Under divine direction he raised up Saul, and then rejected him from the kingship, and the dark close of the gigantic king's career only makes the character of the great prophet more impressive by contrast. His reforms underlay the throne of David. New disclosures of divine truth had come through him, and the vision of God and righteousness was enlarged.

(3) David's contribution to the religious thought of his times is somewhat problematical, and the solution of the problem depends upon the amount of Psalm material we may assign him. Depending alone on the records of his life, however embellished by later writers, we discover him to have been a man marked by strikingly variant qualities. His unfavorable traits are in ample evidence. Among them are found duplicity (1 Sam. xxi :2), a spirit of revenge and cruelty in war (1 Sam. xxx :17; 2 Sam. viii :2; xii :29-31), and his sin with Bathsheba (2 Sam. xi), which wrought such havoc in his family. These were the faults of his age, and he must be judged by its standards, not those of our own day. Yet he was brave, generous (1 Sam. xxiv :1-16; xxvi :5-9), and intent upon the establishment of religion in his capital. He brought up the ark, which had lain in obscurity through the reign of Saul, and established it in Jerusalem (2 Sam. vi). Moreover, he honored Nathan the prophet, and made instant confession of his sin upon that prophet's rebuke (2 Sam. xii :1-10). If the fifty-first Psalm may be considered Davidic, we have in that beautiful utterance, which has become the world's confessional, another proof of his repentance.

(4) There is abundant proof of superstition and imperfect religious ideas in this time. Saul gave to his children names compounded with *Baal*. A teraph was owned by Michal, his daughter, David's wife (1 Sam. xix :13). Saul, though he had rigorously enforced the law against witchcraft, consulted a necromancer in his last distress (1 Sam. xxviii). An accident on the journey of the ark to Jerusalem was interpreted as a sign of divine wrath (2 Sam. vi :6, 7). In a time of continued drought David was informed that the reason lay in an injustice done the city of Gibeon by Saul, and the king, in response to a demand made by the citizens of that place, hung seven of Saul's descendants (2 Sam. xxi :1-14). The belief that the divine sanction could be given to such an atrocity marks a degree of superstition above which even David did not rise.

(5) David was a devoted follower of *Jahveh*. There could be no suspicion of idolatry in his nature. The reverence paid to the prophet Nathan shows that his office was held in higher honor than even the kingship. Levitical priests were established by the king at the sanctuary in Jerusalem, though he performed their functions at times and made his sons priests (2 Sam. vi :12-14; 2 Sam. viii :18, R. V.) David's sincere love for God and desire to promote religious ideals cannot be questioned. If he as a prophet misjudged in some degree the divine character, it is only an added proof of the gradual disclosure of God's nature through the centuries. The fiercer and darker elements inherited from the past were slow to disappear. But little by little the larger vision came. David's ambition to build a costly temple to *Jahveh* was not gratified. Approved at first by Nathan, it was later discouraged with reasons that must have satisfied the king, but back of which there could hardly fail to lie the fear in the prophet's mind that the inauguration of the more costly ritual of such a building as David had in mind would work disaster to the simpler faith of which Samuel had been the exponent.

(6) Solomon had no such scruples. The work committed to him by his father was pushed with vigor, and soon the temple was complete in all its beauty, and its ritual inaugurated upon a most elaborate scale. One need not question the sincerity of the king. A most favorable view is given us of his early years and the happy choice he made (1 Kings iii :4, 14). Yet it is easy to see

that the result of the temple cult was the secularization of religion. The building and its surroundings became one of the sights of the kingdom. The enormous sacrifices (1 Kings viii:5) emphasized the external elements of the religion, but the essentials were too largely disregarded. Very soon the same spirit of ostentation led him to erect shrines to other gods in his capital, under the influence of his foreign wives, and the prophets who saw deepest into the situation perceived that drastic measures alone could remedy the evil case. The prophets were neglected and the priests were elevated in Solomon's reign. There must be a change or the true faith would suffer beyond remedy. The older sanctuaries were being forgotten. The tendency was to substitute an expensive ritual in one place for righteousness everywhere. Samuel's words were being forgotten: "To obey is better than sacrifice." If nothing else could avail, the pride of king and people must be humbled, and the secularization of the nation by commerce and conquest must cease. The only question was when the decisive blow should be struck. The death of Solomon and the elevation of his son Rehoboam furnished the occasion.

(5) Religion In the Kingdom of Israel.
(1) Ahijah of Shiloh was at the moment of Rehoboam's coronation the leader of the prophetic party. He had already set himself to the work of fomenting rebellion, and had opened his plans to a young officer of Solomon's building force—Jeroboam, the son of Nebat of the tribe of Ephraim. Promising him success in his efforts, Ahijah had induced him to take up arms against the king (1 Kings xi:26-40); but the first attempt was not successful, and Jeroboam was obliged to take refuge in Egypt. Returning, however, in answer to the summons of his friends at the death of Solomon, he placed himself at the head of the malcontents from the northern tribes, who demanded lighter taxation (1 Kings xii:1-20). The request was refused, and the breach between the two sections, which had always been apparent, was now widened into a chasm that was never closed, by the election of Jeroboam to the kingship of the northern tribes. Much was naturally expected of the new king by the prophets who had been his advisers in the important steps already taken. But statecraft was stronger than religion in Jeroboam's character, and the prophets were bitterly disappointed. Fearing that the old sanctuaries would not be attractive enough to keep his people away from the new temple at the capital of his rival, he organized two sanctuaries at the extremes of his kingdom, Bethel and Dan, and, instead of the imageless worship which had been the only officially recognized order of things hitherto, he set up two images of *Jahveh* in the form of bulls (1 Kings xii:26-33). The representation of deity in this manner was not new. As the symbol of strength and creative power the bull was regarded as sacred in Egypt and among other nations; and perhaps in remembrance of Egyptian customs, the Israelites once before fell into the practice (Exod. xxxii:1-6). It is to be noticed that in neither case was *Jahveh* set aside as the national God. It was simply an effort to gratify the craving for a visible symbol of deity, a craving which had manifested itself in the use of images in previous periods, but against which the purer idealism of prophets like Moses and Samuel had set itself like a flint. With this reversion to a lower type of religion came other departures from the form of worship recognized in the period, such as the appointment of non-Levitical priests and the designation of other feasts than those already celebrated.

(2) The prophets were always the advocates of the policy of national seclusion. All that tended to bring Israel into contact with other nations, whether war or commerce, met with their disapproval. The secret of this feeling was their fear of foreign religious ideas gaining a foothold by such means. To kings like Solomon, intent upon the enrichment of his realm, this seemed a narrow policy. National prosperity was to be attained only through friendly relations with other peoples, and to this end alliances by marriage were secured with foreign courts. But the purity of the religion of *Jahveh* was dependent upon insulation until it should have time to take firmer hold on the people. The two principles are admirably represented by Ahab and Elijah. The former reigned over Israel from 875 to 853 B. C. He entered into alliance with Ethbaal of Zidon, and married his daughter Jezebel, giving her religion, the worship of *Baal* and *Astarte,* official sanction beside the religion of *Jahveh,* in his capital, Samaria (1 Kings xvi:29-34), the prophets of *Astarte* being supported by the queen (1 Kings xviii:19). While it is improbable that Ahab went so far as to renounce the faith of his nation, yet the worshipers, and especially the prophets, of *Jahveh* were subjected to ill-treatment and, perhaps, actual persecution (1 Kings xviii:3, 4). Under the favor of the court the foreign cult made rapid progress, till it might have seemed that the whole nation had been swept away by the seductive Phœnician worship (1 Kings xix:14).

(3) But the counter-movement came. Its center was in the prophetic circle, and its leader was Elijah. His first effort at reformation was only partially successful (1 Kings xviii:19), and he learned that abrupt and bloody methods were not always wisest (1 Kings xix:11, 12). The prophets of *Baal* had been slaughtered, but the queen remained. His next plan was a change of rulers (1 Kings xix:15, 16), and this was accomplished shortly after (2 Kings ix:1), though not till after the close of Elijah's career. This prophet represents the rugged, inflexible character of the prophets of Samuel's type, with the fierce zeal for their faith that would sanction any deed of blood in its behalf (1 Kings xviii:40). His relation and that of his friend Elisha to the prophetic bands is marked (1 Kings xx:35-43; 2 Kings ii:3, 5; vi:1-7; ix:1), and probably these groups of men were capable of great service in behalf of the religion of Israel, which was, as a matter of fact, never so near extirpation as the despondent Elijah at one time thought (1 Kings xix:18). Its vitality was greater than he knew. But doubtless in a very true sense he stood for that reaction which weakened the worship of *Baal* in the land, and left its final overthrow as an officially recognized worship to the violent and bloody measures of Jehu, who soon came to the throne (2 Kings ix:10). In a true sense, therefore, Elijah, as the champion of justice (1 Kings xxi) and the defender of the faith, was the guardian of Israel, its "chariots and horsemen" (2 Kings ii:12). It is noticeable, however, that he is not reported as protesting against the bull worship of Bethel and Dan; and Jehu, who might be supposed to stand as the royal patron of the prophetic party, is upbraided by the later prophets for following to that extent in the path of Jeroboam (2 Kings x:29-31). Perhaps it was considered a sufficient step to preserve the worship of *Jahveh* as against that of *Baal* without so much regard to its character.

(4) It was in the reign of Jeroboam II (781-840 B. C.) that the period of greatest importance for religion in the northern kingdom began. This reign witnessed the work of Amos, and the first part of that of Hosea, the earliest prophets who have left writings. This new phase of prophecy may almost be called a new beginning, for here we are able for the first time to study the materials that reveal the true condition of the kingdom, and exhibit the new tone of the prophetic work. Amos and Hosea are not a new order of men. They recognize the fact that they are continuing the work of others before them (Amos ii:11; iii:7), but the tone of the prophetic ministry is higher and the vision of the divine nature and purpose wider. The Schools of the Prophets remain, but the fierce enthusiasm of the past has given way to a professionalism, which makes preaching a mere source of revenue, and causes a true prophet to shrink from being classed with such men (Amos vii:14). Social and religious conditions are reflected in their writings. There is a growing separation between rich and poor, and the sins that grow out of such conditions are set down (Amos ii:78; iii:12, 15; v:7, 10, 11; vi:4-6). The popular religion is of a low and formal character, and it is hard to tell at times whether the description is that of degraded *Jahveh* worship, or the heathen customs that have crept in (Amos ii:12; iv:4, *sq.;* v:21; viii:5). Amos was a native of the Southern Kingdom, and came to Bethel for only a short time (Amos i:1; vii:14). (See AMOS.) Hosea was a resident of the north. (See HOSEA.) The one speaks a message of warning and denunciation of coming judgment; the other, of the love and mercy of God. This lesson has come to him through a tragic experience in his own life which he has come to feel was providential (Hos. i:3). To Amos, Israel is a chosen nation, selected by *Jahveh*, the universal ruler of the world. But this cannot be ground of pride, but rather strict accountability (ii:11; iii:2, 7). Monotheism is distinctly recognized. Heathen nations are under the government of *Jahveh* (Amos ii), and are condemned for cruelties that were freely committed by David, while Israel is held even to a higher law than they (i:3, 6, 9, 11, 13; ii:1, 4, 6, 12). Nothing could more plainly mark the growth of prophetic ideals. In a similar manner Hosea denounces the slaughter wrought by Jehu the reformer at Jezreel (i:4). The worthlessness of religious ritual without righteousness is emphasized (Amos v:21-24). The doctrine of divine love preached by Hosea is an immeasurable advance over any previous prophetic message and shows the clearer vision of God now enjoyed. Such ideals were found nowhere else in this period save in this chosen nation. Natural development will not produce an Amos or a Hosea, much less an Isaiah. The divine purpose is the only explanation. Slowly disclosing itself in the lives of men as they were prepared to understand and embody it, the centuries witnessed among the Hebrew people the most remarkable manifestation of moral and spiritual development which history records, a development whose end was not the elevation of one nation alone, but of all the world. After the days of Amos and Hosea, the Northern Kingdom hastened to its fall, and the work of the prophets centered wholly in Jerusalem.

(6) Judah Before the Exile. (1) The religion of *Jahveh* had always the advantage in Judah after the disruption, for the temple without an image was there, and the regular order of services under the Levitical priesthood went on without interruption, though probably on a much diminished

scale, owing to the narrower resources of the state. But the temple never displaced the high places in popular affection till late in this period, and sacrifices were offered to *Jahveh* both at Jerusalem and at these ancestral sanctuaries. But along with this legitimate worship of the high places, which fell under the ban of disapproval at a later time, there were darker features of a heathenish character mingled with the provincial worship, such as the use of obelisks, and even sacred prostitution. (See PROSTITUTION, SACRED.) This was the condition in the reign of Rehoboam (B. C. 937-920) (1 Kings xiv:21-24). Asa (B. C. 917-876) abolished the more objectionable features, and destroyed an image of *Astarte,* which the queen-mother had set up (1 Kings xv:9-14). (See ASA.) With the accession of Jehoram (B. C. 851-843) there came the introduction of the *Baal* worship from Samaria, through the influence of the queen, Athaliah, a daughter of Ahab and Jezebel. A temple was built to *Baal*, and his images and shrines were set up in many places. A check was given to this cult by the zeal of Jehoiada the priest, who organized a movement centering at the temple of *Jahveh,* and by the overthrow and death of Athaliah swept away for a time the danger that threatened the true faith (2 Kings xi:). The temple was repaired by Joash (B. C. 856-796), directed by Jehoiada (2 Kings xii). In this instance it was the priests, not the prophets, who organized resistance to the foreign cult.

(2) With Ahaz, however, other foreign elements appear (B. C. 735-715). The horrible rite of human sacrifice is enforced by royal example, and an altar of foreign fashion is introduced into the temple (2 Kings xvi:1-4, 10-18). The custom of human sacrifice seems not to have been unknown in earlier periods (Gen. xxii: Judg. xi:30,31; R. V., margin), and was practiced among neighboring nations, the Israelites sharing in the opinion that it was effective (2 Kings iii:27). It also made its appearance in the northern kingdom, probably under the influence of the worship of *Baal* (2 Kings xvii:17). But at Jerusalem and in the royal family the practice is suggestive of the inroad of heathen ideas. With Hezekiah (B. C. 715-686) a new era of reform was ushered in, suggested, no doubt, by the preaching of the prophets Isaiah and Micah. The obelisks and images were overthrown and the brazen serpent, now become an object of veneration, was destroyed (2 Kings xviii:1-5). Hezekiah is reported to have abolished the high places as well, though these had remained undisturbed and seemingly approved through all the past, including the most strenuous periods of reform (1 Kings xv:14; xxii:43; 2 Kings xii:3; xv:4, 35; xvi:4). It was only later writers occupying the standpoint of the law of Josiah's time, who disapproved of the country sanctuaries. Perhaps their evil effects had begun already to manifest themselves to the prophets.

(3) The work of Isaiah and Micah brings a new influence to bear on the life of Judah. The former belonged to the higher circles in Jerusalem, and for forty years (B. C. 737-701) was prominent in the religious and political life of the people. Micah, as a countryman, was not so closely identified with the life of the court. With these preachers prophecy reaches its highest level, as an effort to save the nation from the consequences of its misdeeds. The picture of the times is graphic. Foreign relations have caused the bringing in of manners and customs unsuitable for the people of God. Jerusalem is full of luxury and idols (Is. ii:5-11). Monopolists, skeptics, perverters, and corrupt judges abound (v:8-24). The images to which the prophet refers, not so much in wrath

as in contempt, seem not to have been the representations of other deities, but the means by which the worship of *Jahveh* was reduced to a mere superstition. The service of the temple was kept up carefully, but it could not be accepted as a substitute for righteousness (Is. i:10-17). The vision by which Isaiah had been called to his prophetic work (Is. vi) gave him the keynote of his message—the holiness of God. *Jahveh* is for him henceforth the "Holy One of Israel," not in the later sense of mere ceremonial separation, but of moral purity and spiritual grandeur. The rising power of Assyria, he predicted, would be permitted to come against Judah as a chastisement of her offenses. The Assyrian king, as an instrument of God, would be used to humble the pride of the nation and bring it to repentance (x:5 *sq.;* v:26-30). Throughout the period of Assyrian activity in the western lands, the prophet made his sermons revolve about the one theme of judgment, emphasizing the four points—the people have sinned, they shall be punished, a good remnant shall remain, and the future will be prosperous and glorious under Messianic rule (viii:19-22; xi:1; xii:6). The character of God was disclosed by the preaching of Isaiah as never before. What he felt and saw of the divine life he gave to the nation, and it became an inestimably precious spiritual inheritance for the future. The long reign of Manasseh (B. C. 686-641) was a time of disheartening reaction. The king was the patron of every foreign religious fad. Altars were erected for *Baal* and *Astarte*, the Babylonian planet worship was brought in and even given a place in the temple, bronze horses and chariots in honor of the sun were set up, and every form of divination was encouraged; the king himself offered his son in sacrifice, and a bitter persecution of the faithful began (2 Kings xxi:1-16). In such a period little could be done, and prophecy was silent. The inroad of the Scythians through the coast-lands (B. C. 627) gave occasion for the denunciation by Zephaniah of more terrible judgments to come.

(4) Presently Josiah (B. C. 639-609) came to the throne, and gave promise of better things. (See JOSIAH.) The work of repairing the temple was undertaken, and during the process discovery was made of a book of law. This code is now recognized to have been the Deuteronomic law, which, based upon the Book of the Covenant, had gradually grown up in the period of the kingship, and being put into final form by some priest or priests, and perhaps also prophets, was laid away until the dark days, which the reigns of Manasseh and Amon brought, should pass away. The most radical element in the new code was the centralization of worship at Jerusalem. Idolatry in its worst forms was creeping in. Isaiah had only alluded to idols with the contempt of one who saw in them a minor source of evil as compared with the prevailing immorality and corruption of his day. But the days of Manasseh had revealed the full horror of the worship of false gods, and the reformers set themselves to meet the evil. The temple could easily be controlled with a pious king on the throne. (See MANASSEH.) Even the desecrations introduced by Manasseh could be removed and forgotten. But the local sanctuaries throughout the land, which had hitherto been viewed as quite legitimate, were less easily supervised, and had shown themselves to be the elements of danger. The remedy was drastic. The local sanctuaries, with all their ancestral memories, were abolished at a stroke, and the temple alone made the center of all religious service (Deut. xii:1-28). Other portions of the code that

appear to hint especially at existing conditions were those referring to pillars and obelisks (xvi: 21 *sq.*), the "host of heaven" (xvii:2-7), *Moloch* worship (xviii:10), and religious prostitution (xxiii:17 *sq.*). (See PROSTITUTION, SACRED.) Laws already uttered in the legislation of the Mosaic age, others growing out of traditions concerning the great lawgiver and his work, and still others recent and dealing with the present situation, were included in the collection, and were set into a framework of Mosaic exhortation. The effect of this discovery could be nothing less than startling to a man of Josiah's nature (2 Kings xxii:11). The work of reformation into conformity with the new law was begun at once, and in this thoroughgoing process (2 Kings xxiii) he was ably assisted by the priests, to whose order Jeremiah, the great prophet of Judah's decline and fall, belonged (Jer. i:1). (See JEREMIAH.) If Josiah could have lived till his reforms were thoroughly understood and established, the sequel might have been different. But his untimely death in a needless battle left the reforming party without assistance, filled the questioning with doubt, and gave the advocates of the old regime a strength that the better leaders of the nation could not overcome. The end came on apace. Jeremiah, the saddest of the prophets, faced the coming darkness, and gave the people the only divine message that could come in such an hour: "Too late! The nation must die that it may be reborn. Captivity in Babylon is inevitable."

(7) **The Exile.** (1) In B. C. 597 Nebuchadrezzar, king of Babylon, came westward and laid siege to Jerusalem. Jehoiachin, the king, a grandson of Josiah, gave himself into the hand of the Babylonian, who took him, together with some ten thousand captives from the better classes of Jerusalem, and, plundering the treasures of the palace and the temple, returned with the spoil, leaving Zedekiah (B. C. 597-586), a son of Josiah, on the throne. In the ninth year of his reign, Nebuchadrezzar returned and beseiged the city, reducing it at last and destroying the temple, and ended the existence of the city for half a century, taking another company of the people to Babylon. A wretched remnant was left in the land, and a company of refugees made their way into Egypt, taking with them the unwilling Jeremiah. During these eventful years, he had stood constantly as the champion of God and righteousness in the midst of a vicious court and a worldly people, and more than once his life had been in danger. There is a deep pathos in the life and writings of this prophet, whose unhappy lot it was to be placed at a time when the tide of disaster could not be turned, and only the experiences of the exile could avail. His life came to its close among the refugees in Egypt. Among the exiles who went out to Babylonia in the first deportation was a young man named Ezekiel, a priest. (See EZEKIEL.) He was taken to Tel-Abib, on the river Chebar, where presently the divine call came to him to be the mouthpiece of *Jahveh* among his brethren (Ezek. i:3). Both Jeremiah and Ezekiel express the conviction that no other prophets of the true faith are to be found, though both in Jerusalem and Babylon the professional prophets were numerous (Jer. xxiii). It is noticeable that both these prophets are from the priestly order.

(2) The problems which the destruction of the city and the transportation of the people brought were perplexing. Few could appreciate the high spiritual plane occupied by Jeremiah, or his doctrine that purification was to be wrought by suffering. To those who had sunk into idolatry it was a seeming proof that *Jahveh* was not as powerful

as the gods of Babylon, or he would have saved his city. To the faithful it was a paralyzing shock, for did it not mean that God had abandoned his people? And then the monolatristic idea, so largely prevalent, prevented hope that now the people were removed from the land, they could be longer under the protection or within the hearing of *Jahveh,* for was he not localized at Jerusalem, above the ruins of the dismantled city? To such troubled questions the vision by which Ezekiel was called addressed itself. The chariot of God, moving about on the wings of the storm, with the dreadful wheels full of eyes, was a symbol to show prophet and people that their God was no mere local deity, but the Lord of the world, and that in Babylon they were as near him as in Jerusalem. During all the years between the first deportation and the final fall of the city, the two prophets, Jeremiah in Jerusalem, and Ezekiel upon the Chebar, labored to convince the misguided people that the city must fall and the exile be prolonged. Jeremiah wrote a letter to the exiles, assuring them that their hopes of early return were delusive, and advising preparations for a permanent stay (Jer. xxix:1 *sq.*). Ezekiel had labored with his fellow exiles to the same end, assuring them that as long as Jerusalem was the scene of such practices as defiled the true faith she could not avert the coming doom (Ezek. viii). It was not till a refugee from Palestine brought him the tidings of the actual fall of the city (Ezek. xxxiii:21) that the tone of the prophet changed. From that time on, he devoted himself to the kindling of hope for a final return and future for the nation, in which the reconstructed temple, to which he devoted the closing chapters of his book, plays an important part.

(3) Another voice, even more clear than Ezekiel's, was raised during the latter portion of the exile, speaking of the coming redemption. The Evangelical Prophet, whose message is contained in the last chapters of the book of Isaiah (Is. xl-lxvi), brought a much needed encouragement to the people. (See ISAIAH.) When the days were growing very long, and the voices of Jeremiah and Ezekiel had both been long hushed, the promise comes that the nation shall soon go back to Jerusalem, for *Jahveh,* who is the only God, the Creator of the ends of the earth, is concerned for his own sake as well as for his people's sake, to bring them back to national life in Jerusalem (Is. xl). This prophet was not a preacher, as his predecessors had been, but only a writer, who, probably from the necessities of the case, sent out his exhortations and promises in the form of fly leaves or tractates. It would hardly be possible to boldly preach such treasonable doctrines as these chapters contain, and perhaps the anonymity of the material is thus to be accounted for. But a new philosophy of history is set forth. Cyrus is already on the frontier. Through him, as an instrument in God's hands, deliverance is to come to the nation (Is. xli:25; xliv:27, 28; xlv:1 *sq.*; xlvi:11). But deliverance is not enough. The nation is a chosen order of people for a particular purpose. It is the Servant of *Jahveh* (Is. xli:8; xlii:1 *sq.;* xlii:18 *sq.;* xliii:1-10; xliv:21; xlv:4). But the nation as a whole is unable to accomplish the work of bringing redemption to the world. They cannot even save themselves, and gradually a select portion is seen to represent the idea rather than the full nation. This remnant, or nucleus, is not only to save the remainder, but the world as well (Is. xlix:1-6). Then, just as gradually, there emerges from this remnant the figure of a Messianic Servant, the representative of the nation and the remnant, who, personified as the nation,

despised, rejected, misunderstood, is still successful in the redemptive work to which God had called him (Is. lii:13; liii:12). In this section, and one or two later which describe the breadth and character of the Servant's work (Is. lv and lxi), prophecy reaches its very highest levels. Israel's sufferings are not for its own sins so much as for the world. All redemption is through suffering, and thus a philosophy of history was fashioned which included not one nation alone, but all, and the Servant of *Jahveh,* Israel, remnant and Messiah successively, as the messenger of a world-wide ministry of divine love. The possibility, nay, the certainty, of return to Jerusalem; the national programme which makes such a return necessary; and the purification of the people, by which preparation for the return may be accomplished—these are the great themes of this prophet.

(4) The exile was a period of great importance to the people. Deprived of the temple and law, the literary spirit in the nation turned back upon the past and produced history, such as Samuel-Kings, and recast other narratives of former days; revised the law on the basis of the existing codes and the praxis that had grown up since Deuteronomy, and codified the so-called Priest Code contained in the latter portion of Exodus and in Leviticus and Numbers; turned in upon its own spirit and tried to answer doubts, as in Job, or give expression to praise and longing, as in the Psalms. There must have been a strong grasp upon the fundamentals of the faith by large classes of the people to explain the firmness with which they clung to it in the midst of the taunts of their masters and the ridicule of apostate countrymen. Though many lost faith and hope, and others were led away into forbidden practices (Ezek. xx:30), yet the core of the nation remained sound, and there may even be said to have been decided progress in some directions. Monolatry gave way finally to monotheism, and idolatry was eradicated. Sabbath observances and circumcision became more binding, prayer and fasting were recognized as never before as aids in the religious life, and the doctrine of individual accountability was emphasized. At the same time, a growing tendency towards particularism and legalism manifested itself, the fruit of which appeared later.

(8) The Restoration. (1) The predictions of the prophets regarding the termination of the exile came to fulfillment B. C. 538. In that year Cyrus, having conquered Media and Lydia, entered Babylon, and the map of the world was again transformed. It is not necessary to suppose that Cyrus was influenced by a special admiration for the religion of that small fragment of people held captive in his capital province. His motive in permitting the exiles to return to Jerusalem is amply explained by the desire to provide a strong and friendly base of operations in any future trouble with Egypt, and such an opportunity was offered by the situation of Jerusalem. (See CYRUS.) The royal permission was accordingly given, a company of Jews numbering nearly fifty thousand was gathered for the journey, and the remaining vessels, brought from the temple at Jerusalem, were placed in their hands (Ezra i: 2). By no means all the exiles came back. Many had grown up in their eastern home and preferred to remain, and among these not a few even of the priestly class. The company was placed in charge of a Persian officer named Sheshbazzar, but with him was associated a council of leading men, chief among whom were Zerubbabel, the grandson of Jehoiachin, and Joshua, the grandson of the last priest in Jerusalem, who lost his

life at the sack of the city. As soon as the caravan reached Jerusalem, an altar was set up on the
site of the temple, and the feasts resumed (Ezra
iii :2-4). As soon as preparations could be made
the foundations of the new temple were laid (B.
C. 534) amid the mingled shouts of the more
hopeful and lamentations of those who contrasted
the meager present with the glorious past of the
city (Ezra iii :7-12). The work of building was,
however, soon interrupted. The descendants of
the old Israelites on the north desired a share in
the work. But the exclusive spirit prevailed, and
the waiting help was rejected, which fostered a
bitterness that hindered the building of the temple for many years. Two tendencies must have
manifested themselves among the people. There
was the broader, more tolerant attitude, which
looked on other nations with friendliness and
would welcome relations with foreigners, for the
sake of the ministry of redemption for the world
with which Israel was charged. Then there was
the more narrow and exclusive spirit, that made
Jewish particularism the fundamental article in
its creed, and was unconscious of any duty to
others. The latter attitude could claim the sanction of Ezekiel; the former, of the Evangelical
Prophecy. In the end the narrow party won.
Perhaps this was a necessary phase of the movement. The narrowing of the channel compelled
the deepening of the stream, but the ungracious
features of the more conservative and exclusive
Judaism were the outcome of this tendency.

(2) After nearly twenty years, the work was
resumed under the exhortation of two prophets,
Haggai and Zechariah, and after royal aid had
been given, brought to completion B. C. 515 (Ezra
v :6). But it is evident that conditions were far
from satisfactory. The hopes raised by the prophets were not being fulfilled. The city was small
and poor, and the prospects were disheartening.
It could not be that this meager situation was all
that God intended for his people. The belief
seems to have gained ground that a political crisis
was imminent, a breaking up of the empire, by
which Judah would profit. The horizon was anxiously scanned for signs of the coming upheaval
(Zech. i :10-12). But no crisis came, and in the
sinking of heart that hope deferred produced
many grew indifferent to all religious obligations.
The worship at the temple, while still carried on,
was not made the first concern, and poor offerings
were presented. It is this situation which is set
before us in the anonymous prophecy named
from its most suggestive word, "My Messenger"
(Mal. iii :1). There was danger of a still deeper
pessimism and despair. The chief comfort lay in
the company of the faithful who continued in the
service of God amid all discouragements (Mal.
iii :16-18). (See MALACHI.) The appeal of this
prophet, like that of Haggai and Zechariah, is to
a renewed devotion to the law and the ritual. No
longer are the great sanctions of righteousness
and morality made the first concern, but the
Torah and the temple are the chief consideration.
Thus the tone of prophecy has changed since the
days of Isaiah and the great prophet of the exile,
and who could say for the better?

(3) It is evident that a new factor had been
introduced into the national life just previous to
the date of "Malachi," from which assistance
was hoped by the religious leaders in Jerusalem.
And this is found to have been the case. There
had been from the time of the first return a bond
of sympathy between the Jews in Jerusalem and
those who remained in Babylonia. Meantime a
company of the latter had been carrying forward
the work of expanding the Divine law in the

spirit of Ezekiel, and now, when tidings reached
them that affairs had approached a serious crisis
in the little community in Judea, another company
was organized to swell the population of Jerusalem, and under the leadership of Ezra, a scribe,
the first named of that important order which
had so much to do with the enlargement, teaching,
and enforcement of the law in the later days, they
left Babylon, B. C. 459, to the number of 1,700.
Their leader brought with him the new law (Ezra
vii :14, 25, 26), prepared to put it into operation.
(See EZRA.) On arrival in Judea Ezra found the
work of reform difficult, for the people did not
take readily to the legal regulations insisted upon,
so much more exacting in some directions than
any known before. Ezra was compelled, indeed,
to give up the effort for a time, and it was not
till the arrival of Nehemiah, a Babylonian Jew,
who, having obtained a position in the Persian
court, requested the vacant governorship of Judea,
that the work of reform could be prosecuted with
a zeal that was backed up with the royal authority, and that overcame all opposition. The city
was repaired, the walls built, and then at a great
gathering of the people, the law was promulgated
by Ezra (Ezra viii) to an audience that requested
the reading, and that was profoundly impressed
by the regulations set forth in the code. The
religious education implied in the popular feeling
of sin, as compared with the strict demands of the
law now proclaimed, is profoundly interesting
(Ezra ix :8-12). The law that was brought by
Ezra from Babylon, and read to the people, was
the Priest Code, of which mention has already
been made as the work of priests in Babylon during and after the exile. The particulars in which
it most vitally differed from the earlier codes, the
Book of the Covenant and Deuteronomy, were
its separation of priests from other Levites and
its emphasis upon the rules of "holiness," i. e.,
ceremonial, not moral, purity. The business of
this law is to make a holy community in which
God may dwell. God is honored by such institutions as secure a regulation of the external religious life of man. The community has a purely
religious end. The nation, disappointed in its
political hopes, turns now to a purely religious
ideal within itself, and seeks there its satisfaction. The temple became, in a new and deeper
sense, the center of Jewish thought and life. Its
services and its offices were the most important
concerns of the people. Under the direction of
Ezra and Nehemiah the exclusive particularism
of the more conservative party became triumphant, and the community was started on the narrow path toward the later Judaism.

(9) The Rise of Judaism. (1) The history
of the Old Testament closes with the return from
Babylon, but fortunately the literature which it
comprises gives us some light on the period from
the exile to the advent. The movement which
Ezra had started went on with increased force.
Gradually the literature of the nation was gathered into a collection, to which, however, additions were made up to within a century and a half
of the Christian era. The love of the Scriptures,
and especially the law which had now been put
into one collection, the Pentateuch, grew in the
hearts of the people, as salvation was more and
more believed to be found in its possession. One
finds expression of this feeling in the psalms of
the period (e. g., cxix).

(2) Closely related to the pride in the Scriptures
was that inspired by the temple and its services.
No other nation had such possessions as these,
and all the world might well envy the Jew these
Divine gifts. Thus Judaism came to be more and

more the religion of a book and a building. The Torah and the Temple were the visible symbols of the faith. Nor must it be forgotten that a high order both of religious conduct and of happiness resulted from this two-fold culture.

(3) Absolute monotheism had now been attained. There could be no remnant of a belief in other gods. But if *Jahveh* was the god of Israel and also of all the world, what was the relation of Israel to that world, and how was God himself disposed toward these other nations? From the time of the exile there had been two tempers of mind regarding other nations, as has been already stated. Both find expression in post-exilic days. The date of the books of Joel and Jonah is still an open question, but both may be confidently placed within the limits of this period. (See JOEL.) The former voices the conservative view. The nations exist only for the sake of Zion. When trouble visits the land, *Jahveh* is called into activity by a solemn fast, and at once promises to take vengeance on the nations for their treatment of the chosen people. What are all these nations compared with Judah and Jerusalem? War is declared against them; Egypt and Edom shall be desolated, and all Zion's foes shall perish. Even the beautiful promise of the outpouring of the Divine spirit refers to Israel alone as its recipient. In striking contrast with this attitude is that of the author of Jonah, a book much misunderstood and ridiculed, but one of the most precious in the Old Testament. Jonah represents the narrow and ungracious spirit of those Jews who have no desire to give a message of salvation to other nations. In contrast with the noble-minded mariners and the repentant Ninevites, he plays but a sorry part. (See JONAH.) The book is a forceful protest against the narrower phases of post-exilic Judaism.

(4) But this very conception of God compelled the Jew to adjust the heathen to the Divine and all-ruling law in some manner. Two methods were open. The one was that of proselyting, *i. e.,* admitting the heathen to covenant privileges under the law, through compliance with certain prescribed forms, viz., circumcision, baptism, and the offering of sacrifices. The opening of this door gave rise to an earnest missionary propaganda, especially in the century before Christ. But there were those who looked with disfavor on any efforts to widen the embrace of the national faith, and, while proselytism did not absolutely cease, it lost its force after a time. The second view as to the heathen, or gentiles, was that they should be conquered and brought into subjugation at the period of Messianic supremacy yet ahead. Probably this was the more prevalent view, growing naturally out of the lofty ideas regarding the law and the temple, and the privileges they conferred on the chosen people.

(5) At what period the synagogue came into being, or when Pharisees and Sadducees first arose, remains uncertain; at some time before the Maccabean movement, at any rate. Perhaps as important was the influence of Hellenism upon Jewish thought. Alexander's conquests produced a wide diffusion of Greek ideas, and perhaps no people were more profoundly affected by them than the Jews. This was especially true outside of Palestine. The Dispersion, *i. e.,* those Jews who lived in other parts of the world, Persia, Asia Minor, and Europe, were less under the influence of the conservative party than the Jews of the Holy Land. But even in Jerusalem the liberalizing tendency manifested itself in a decided manner, and it is impossible to say to what lengths it might have gone had not another force interposed. Antiochus IV, called Epiphanes (see ANTIOCHUS), the overlord of Palestine, whose capital was at Antioch, impatient of Jewish customs and religious services in Jerusalem, attempted to force the process of Hellenizing upon the people, and by his profanation of the temple drove the people to a frantic uprising under the leadership of the Maccabees. (See MACCABEES.) In this struggle the older conservatism asserted itself, and a decisive break with Hellenism occurred. That reaction persisted as perhaps the most effective force which the Judaism of the period presents, viz., the Pharisees. The most interesting souvenir of that struggle is the book of Daniel, written about B. C. 165, and intended as an encouragement to the warriors in the struggle, by its portrayals of heroism and deliverance gathered around the character of Daniel in the captivity, and the prophecies of eventual victory put into his mouth. (See DANIEL.)

This period is also marked by the appearance of Chronicles, a work which reconstructs the history from the priestly point of view, reading back into remote times conditions and ideals which, as a matter of fact, were post-exilic. Other books of the time were Ecclesiastes, Sirach, Judith, Tobit, Enoch, 1 Maccabees, etc. (See APOCRYPHA.)

In this period the belief in a future life took form, with the doctrine of rewards and punishments, the belief in a being called the adversary, or Satan, and the more definite forms of the Messianic hope.

(10) The Messianic Hope. (1) Israel was a nation of hope and promise. Unlike other peoples, its Golden Age was in the future, not in the past. From the earliest beginning of national consciousness it was a gradually developing belief that Israel had a special mission, separate from the rest of the world, yet in some important degree connected with the spiritual life of the world. The Divine purpose for humanity was believed to lie implicit in the unfolding history of this people. The Hebrew records preserved the first promise made to the race (Gen. iii:15), a promise that though the struggle between good and evil should be long and bitter, yet in the end the good should triumph. This Divine purpose manifested itself in the selection of certain individuals or tribes through whose life the disclosure of the plans of God was to be made. Such men were Noah (Gen. vi:8; ix:8-17); Shem, (Gen. ix:26, 27), and through him the Semites as a race; Abraham (Gen. xii:1 *sq.*) and his descendants, the Hebrews; Jacob (Gen. xxviii:10-16) and his descendants, called after him Israel; and Judah, as the royal tribe, and the one which should stand as the representative of the nation (Gen. xlix:8-10). This process of selecting men for the special purpose of leadership in this nation continued throughout its history. It was the application of the universal principle of selection. But it was not a selection for favor, but rather for service. Israel was the chosen people of God, but not for its own sake. It had a ministry for the world. Its leaders were prophets, priests, and kings, and these men, especially the prophets, were unique in their character and work. Their counterpart is not to be found in any other history. But in the last analysis the nation as a whole was regarded as royal, as priestly, as prophetic (Exod. xix:6). What these special men did as leaders for the nation, Israel as a unit was to do for the world. Herein lay its unique office.

(2) But from the time of Amos and Hosea it was seen that the nation as a whole was unprepared for such a ministry. (See AMOS and HOSEA.) The religion of Jahveh was set aside too

often for that of other gods, or was mixed with unworthy elements that robbed it of its effectiveness. A purgation was seen to be necessary. A cleansing process alone could purify the people and make them worthy of their high ministry; and the power through which this regeneration was to be wrought was recognized by all the prophets of that period as being Assyria, and later Babylonia. Only such a purification as should come through national disaster and suffering could avail to prepare Israel for its true mission. But after this period of suffering had passed, the remnant would be worthy, and a glorious future would be expected. That future would be the Messianic age, holy and marked by the presence of God. The consecration of kings and priests was signified by their anointing with the holy oil. From this word "Anointed," or "Messiah," grew up the idea of the future glorious time as "Anointed," or "Messianic." The conception of a *person,* who stands as the common denominator of the new period of national salvation and purification, is first presented by Isaiah. In his rebuke of King Ahaz for presumptuous disregard of God and an attempted defense of his capital by resort to arms and alliance with Assyria, the prophet announces the birth of a child, in whose day, soon to dawn (Is. vii:14), and under whose leadership as a conqueror, and yet a Prince of Peace (Is. ix:6, 7), the national deliverance was to be achieved; after which there would come the period of happiness and peace (Is. xi:1 *sq.*). That Isaiah expected this child-king of the house of David in his own day seems certain, otherwise the predictions of deliverance from Assyrian oppression would have been meaningless, and herein is disclosed one of the interesting factors of prophecy. The outlines of the coming order of things were apparent to the eyes of the prophet, but the hour of arrival was not so clear. The drama of redemption was contracted into a single scene, but its larger meaning lay implicit in the slowly unfolding movements upon which they looked. Deliverance from Assyria came, but not through the rise at that time of the Messianic King. Yet the vision was true, for the larger outlines of the Messianic time yet ahead fitted in no small degree the local distress and the certainly foreseen deliverance.

(3) It remained for a later prophet to see with yet clearer vision the true character of the Messianic work and outlines of the Messianic figure. The Evangelical Prophet sets forth the Messianic hope in its fullest light, and he does this under the figure of the Suffering Servant of God. To him at first Israel as a whole is the Servant (Is. xli:8; xliv:1 *sq.*). Though fallen upon unhappy days, yet this very time is one of purification; and now that the process of purgation is reaching its completion, it is time to prepare for larger things to come. Redemption is not to be wrought by war and strife, as was the earlier view, but by peaceful methods (Is. xlii:1-4), and therefore the figure of the King no longer appears, but the Servant in a humble and yet successful work. Presently, however, the idea that the nation as a whole can do the great work appears to be abandoned. Too many are indifferent. The remnant, the best part of the nation, is all that can be counted upon in such an enterprise. This remnant will save not only the apostate part of the nation, but the world at large (Is. xlix:5-7). But even the remnant was weak and unable to accomplish the Divine work; and at last One rises from the remnant, a representative of both it and the whole nation, able to do that which both had failed to accomplish, the Divine Servant, the

Messiah. From Is. lii:13 to liii:12 the success of the Servant's mission is set forth in terms that show the blending of the personal and national ideas about the Messianic figure. That this conception of the Messiah finds its fulfillment in the historic work of Jesus Christ is the teaching of the New Testament.   H. L. W.

HEBRON (hē'bron). *1.* (Heb. חֶבְרוֹן, *kheb-rone'*, a community; alliance).

(1) Location. It was situated in the south of Palestine and in the tribe of Judah, 18 miles south from Jerusalem, in 31 deg. 32 min. 30 sec. N. lat., 35 deg. 8 min. 20 sec. E. long., at the height of 2664 Paris feet above the level of the sea (Schubert). It is one of the most ancient cities existing, having, as the sacred writer informs us, been built 'seven years before Zoan in Egypt,' and being mentioned even prior to Damascus (Num. xiii: 22; Gen. xiii:18; comp. xv:2).

(2) Ancient Names. Its most ancient name was Kirjath-arba, that is, 'the city of Arba,' from Arba, the father of Anak and of the Anakim who dwelt in and around Hebron (Gen. xxiii:2; Josh. xiv:15; xv:3; xxi:11; Judg. i:10). It was peculiarly a Hittite city, although the Hittites and the Amorites were mingled together within its confines. It appears to have been also called Mamre, probably from the name of Abraham's Amoritish ally (Gen. xxiii:9; xxxv:27; comp. xiv:13, 28).

The name of Hebron has the same origin as that of the Khabiri who appear in Ebed-Tob's letters by the side of Labai, Babylonia, and Naharaim as the assailants of Jerusalem and its territory. (See TELL AMARNA, TABLETS OF.) Consult Sayce, *Patriarchal Palestine,* pp. 146-7.

(3) Early History. The ancient city lay in a valley; and the two remaining pools, one of which at least existed in the time of David, serve, with other circumstances, to identify the modern with the ancient site (Gen. xxxvii:14; 2 Sam. iv:12). Much of the lifetime of Abraham, Isaac, and Jacob was spent in this neighborhood, where they were all entombed; and it was from hence that the pariarchal family departed for Egypt by the way of Beersheba (Gen. xxxvii:14; xlvi:1). After the return of the Israelites, the city was taken by Joshua and given over to Caleb, who expelled the Anakim from its territories (Josh. x: 36, 37; xiv:6-15; xv:13-14; Judg. i:20). It was afterwards made one of the cities of refuge, and assigned to the priests and Levites (Josh. xx:7; xxi:11, 13). David, on becoming king of Judah, made Hebron his royal residence. Here he reigned seven years and a half; here most of his sons were born; and here he was anointed king over all Israel (1 Sam. ii:1-4, 11; 1 Kings ii:11; 2 Sam. v:1, 3). On this extension of his kingdom Hebron ceased to be sufficiently central, and Jerusalem then became the metropolis. It is possible that this step excited a degree of discontent in Hebron which afterwards encouraged Absalom to raise in that city the standard of rebellion against his father (2 Kings xv:9, 10). Hebron was one of the places fortified by Rehoboam (2 Chron. xi: 10); and after the exile the Jews who returned to Palestine occupied Hebron and the surrounding villages (Neh. xi:25).

Hebron is not named by the prophets, nor in the New Testament. Hebron is now called el-Khulîl-er-Rahman. We learn from the first book of Maccabees, and from Josephus, that it came into the power of the Edomites, who had taken possession of the south of Judah, and was recovered from them by Judas Maccabæus (1 Macc. v:65; Joseph. *Antiq.* xii:8, 6). During the great war, Hebron was seized by the rebel Simon Giorides, but was recaptured and burnt by Cerealis, an officer of Vespasian (Joseph. *De Bell. Jud.* iv:9; vii:9). Josephus describes the tombs of the patriarchs as existing in his day; and both Eusebius and Jerome and all subsequent writers who mention Hebron down to the time of the Crusades, speak of the place chiefly as containing these sepulchers.

Among the Moslems it is still called by the appellation of *el Khulil*, 'the Friend' (of God), the name which they gave to Abraham. The full name given above, el-Khulîl-er-Rahman, means 'the Friend of the Merciful (God).'

(4) Under Moslem Rule. Since the capture of Jerusalem by Saladin in 1187, Hebron also reverted to the Moslems, and has ever since remained in their possession. In the modern history of Hebron the most remarkable circumstance is the part which the inhabitants of the town and district took in the rebellion of 1834, and the heavy retribution which it brought down upon them. They held out to the last, and gave battle to Ibrahim Pasha near Solomon's Pools. They were defeated; but retired and entrenched themselves in Hebron, which Ibrahim carried by storm, and gave over to sack and pillage. The town has not yet recovered from the blow it then sustained. In the fourteenth century pilgrims passed from Sinai to Jerusalem direct through the desert by Beersheba and Hebron, and it continued to be occasionally visited by European travelers down to the latter part of the seventeenth century; but from that time till the present century it appears to have been little frequented by them.

(5) Present Condition. (1) The town of Hebron lies low down on the sloping sides of a narrow valley (of Mamre), chiefly on the eastern side, but in the southern part stretches across also to the western side. The houses are all of stone, high and well built, with windows and flat roofs, and on these roofs are small domes, sometimes two or three to each house.

(2) The shops are well furnished, better indeed than those of towns of the same class in Egypt, and the commodities are of a very similar description. The only display of local manufactures is the produce of the glass-works, for which the place has long been celebrated in these parts. The articles manufactured consist almost exclusively of glass lamps, many of which are exported to Egypt, and rings of colored glass worn by females on the arms. Gates are placed not only at the entrance of the city, but in different parts of the interior, and are closed at night for the better preservation of order, as well as to prevent communication between the different quarters.

(3) There are nine mosques in Hebron, none of which possess any architectural or other interest, with the exception of the massive structure which is built over the tombs of the patriarchs. This is esteemed by the Moslems one of their holiest places, and Christians are rigorously excluded from it. At an earlier period, however, when the Holy Land was in the power of the Christians, access was not denied; and Benjamin of Tudela says that the sarcophagi above ground were shown to the generality of pilgrims as what they desired to see; but if a rich Jew offered an additional fee, 'an iron door is opened, which dates from the time of our forefathers who rest in peace, and with a burning taper in his hands the visitor descends into a first cave, which is empty, traverses a second in the same state, and at last reaches a third, which contains six sepulchers, those of Abraham, Isaac, and Jacob, and of Sarah, Rebekah, and Leah, one opposite the other. All these sepulchers bear inscriptions, the letters being engraved; thus

upon that of Abraham: "This is the sepulcher of our father Abraham, upon whom be peace;" even so upon that of Isaac and all the other sepulchers' (*Itinerary*, i:77; ed. Asher, Berlin, 1840). The identity of this place with the cave of Machpelah is one of the few local traditions in Palestine which even Dr. Robinson suffers to pass without dispute, and may therefore be taken for granted.

The court in which the mosque stands is surrounded by an extensive and lofty wall, formed of large stones, and strengthened by square buttresses. This wall is the greatest antiquity in Hebron, and even Dr. Robinson supposes that it may be substantially the same which is mentioned by Josephus (*Antiq.* i:14; *De Bell. Jud.* iv:9, 7), and by Eusebius and Jerome (*Onomast.* s. v. *Arboch*) as the sepulcher of Abraham. A common Moslem tomb in the neighborhood of Hebron passes as the tomb of Abner. He was certainly interred in this city (2 Sam. iii:32); and the head of Ishbosheth, after his assassination, was deposited in the same sepulcher (2 Sam. iv:12); but there is slight evidence in favor of the tradition which professes to point out this locality to the modern traveler.

Besides this venerable wall, there is nothing at Hebron bearing the stamp of antiquity, save two reservoirs for rain water outside the town. As these pools are doubtless of high antiquity, one of them is in all likelihood the 'pool of Hebron' over which David hung the assassins of Ishbosheth (2 Sam. iv:12).

(4) The present population of Hebron is about 5000. Most of the inhabitants are Moslems, of fierce and intolerant character. There are no resident Christians. The Jews amount to about one hundred families, mostly natives of different countries of Europe, who have emigrated to this place for the purpose of having their bones laid near the sepulchers of their illustrious ancestors. They have two synagogues and several schools.

(5) The environs of Hebron are very fertile. Vineyards and plantations of fruit trees, chiefly olive trees, cover the valleys and arable grounds; while the tops and sides of the hills, although stony, are covered with rich pastures, which support a great number of cattle, sheep, and goats, constituting an important branch of the industry and wealth of Hebron. The hill country of Judah, of which it is the capital, is indeed highly productive, and under a paternal government would be capable of sustaining a large population. That it did so once, is manifest from the great number and extent of ruined terraces and dilapidated towns. It is at present abandoned, and cultivation ceases at the distance of two miles north of the town. The hills then become covered with prickly and other stunted trees, which furnish Bethlehem and other villages with wood. (See Dr. Robinson, Dr. Olin, Rev. V. Monro, and Schubert; Sayce *Patriarchal Palestine;* Thomson, *The Land and the Book,* vol. ii: pp. 408 *sq.*).

2. A town in the territory of Asher (Josh. xix: 28) on the boundary of the tribe, named next to Hebron, as above. In the original the names are quite different. Kirjath Arba seems to have been the name of this place prior to the Israelitish occupancy (Josh. xv:13, 14). In the time of Abraham it was honored with another name (Gen. xxiii:19; xxxv:27); but its earliest as well as later name was undoubtedly Hebron.

3. The third son of Kohath, and a grandson of Levi; a younger brother of Amram, father of Moses and Aaron (Exod. vi:18; Num. iii:19; 1 Chron. vi:2, 18; xxiii:12), B. C. before 1290. His descendants are called *Hebronites* (Num. iii:27, etc.). (See HEBRONITES.)

4. The son of Mareshah, and apparently, grand-son of Caleb, of the posterity of Judah (I Chron. ii:42, 43), B. C. after 1170.

HEBRONITES (hē′bron-īts), (Heb. חֶבְרֹנִי, *kheb-ro-nee'*), descendants of Hebron, son of Kohath (Num. iii:27; xxvi:58; I Chron. xxvi:23).

HEDGE (hěj), (Heb. גָּדֵר, *gaw-dare´*, and Heb. גְּדֵרָה, *ghed-ay-raw'*, are used of the hedge of a vineyard (Ps. lxxxix:40; I Chron. iv:23.)

The word *mes-oo-kaw'* (Heb. מְסוּכָה) means a thorn hedge (Mic. vii:4). The Gr. φραγμός, tr. 'hedge' in Matt. xxi:33, Mark xii:1, Luke xiv:23, denotes a fence of any kind, whether hedge, or wall, or palings. The purpose of the hedge, as the term is used in the Bible, is either to protect that which is enclosed in it (*e. g.*, Job i:10), or to restrain and hinder (*e. g.*, Job iii:23; Hos. ii: 6). (See FENCE.) From the word *gadare* came the Phœnician name of one of their colonies, Gadir, which has become Cadiz, in Spain.

Figurative. (1) God's protecting providence, government, or whatever defends from hurt and danger, is called a *hedge* (Job i:10; Is. v:2; Ezek. xiii:6). (2) Troubles and hindrances are called *hedges,* as they stop our way and prevent our doing and obtaining what we please (Lam. iii:7; Job xix:8; Hos. ii:6). (3) *The way of the sloth-ful is a hedge of thorns;* he always apprehends great difficulties in the way of doing any good, and often he entangles himself in inextricable dif-ficulties (Prov. xv:19).

Mint.

HEDUOSMON (he-dū′os-mon), (Gr. Ἡδύοσμον, *hay-doo'os-mon,* i. e., having a sweet smell), trans-lated *mint,* is mentioned in Matt. xxiii:23.

'Woe unto you, Scribes and Pharisees, hypo-crites! for ye pay tithe of *mint* and anise (prop-erly *dill*) and cummin, and have omitted the weightier matters of the law;' and, again, in Luke xi:42: 'But woe unto you, Pharisees! for ye tithe *mint* and rue, and all manner of herbs, and pass over judgment and the love of God: these ought ye to have done, and not to leave the other undone.' All the plants mentioned in the above passages belong to the smaller ones culti-vated in gardens in Europe, and which usually come under the denomination of sweet herbs. It is difficult to determine the exact species or va-riety of mint employed by the ancients. There are numerous species very nearly allied to one another. They usually grow in moist situations, and are herbaceous, perennial, of powerful odor, especially when bruised, and have small reddish-colored flowers, arranged in spikes or whorls. The taste of these plants is bitter, warm, and pun-gent, but leaving a sensation of coolness on the tongue; in their properties they are so similar to each other, that either in medicine, or as a condiment, one species may safely be substituted for another. But the species *Mentha sylvestris* and *Mentha arvensis* probably yielded the varie-ties cultivated in Palestine. It is still used there as a food-flavoring. J. F. R.

HEGAI (hē′gai), (Heb. הֵגָי, *hay-gah'ee,* eunuch), or **HEGE** (hē′gē), (Esth. ii:3, Heb. הֵגֶא, *hay-gay',* same), one of the chamberlains of Ahasuerus (or Xerxes), who had charge of the women of the harem (Esth. ii:8, 15), B. C. 479.

HEIFER, RED (hěf′ēr, rěd), (Heb. עֶגְלָה, *eg-law',* פָּרָה, *paw-raw'*). See SACRIFICE.

Figurative. (1) Young wives were called *heifers,* to mark their gaiety, and expected fruitfulness (Judg. xiv:18). (2) Nations are likened to heifers: Egypt to a *fair* one; to mark their glory and prosperity (Jer. xlvi 20). (3) The Chaldeans are compared to a *fat* one, to mark their wealth, wantonness, and unconcern (Jer. l:11). (4) The ten tribes of Israel are lik-ened to a *backsliding* one, to signify their stupid and perverse revolting from God (Hos. iv:16). Also to a *taught* one, loving to tread the corn, over whose *fair neck* God *passed;* they were in-structed by God's oracles and prophets; they were expert and skillful in idolatry; they loved to riot in such plenty as they possessed under Jeroboam the Second; but were quickly after re-duced to slavery and distress by the Assyrians (Hos. x:11). (5) If our version rightly renders Hagla Shalishiah, *a heifer of three years old,* Zoar and Horonaim, cities of Moab, are thus likened to mark their untameable obstinacy; or, rather, their terrible outcries, when the inhabitants fled from the Assyrians and Chaldeans. But perhaps these words may be the names of cities that should share in the ruin (Is. xv:5; Jer. xlviii: 34).

HEIR (âr), (Heb. יָרַשׁ, *yaw-resh',* a primitive root, meaning to occupy), one that succeeds to the inheritance of anything after its present possessor.

In this sense, even enemies succeeding a people driven out of their own land are called their "heirs" (Jer. xlix:2; Mic. i:15).

Figurative. (1) Christ is *"heir of all things;"* as God's Son, he hath an equal right to all things with his Father; as Mediator, he has, by God's sovereign decree, been raised to this dignity; so that his elect, and all things, are given into his hand, to dispose of for their good (Matt. xxi:38; Heb. i: 2). (2) Saints are *"heirs"* of the *prom-ise; "heirs" of righteousness; "heirs" of salva-tion; "heirs" of the grace of life; "heirs" of the kingdom; "heirs" of the world; "heirs of God"* and *"joint-heirs" with Christ* as united to Christ, and by virtue of his death, they have the most free and honorable title to all the promises, bless-ings, creatures, and fullness of God (Rom. iv:13; viii:17; Heb. i:14; vi:17; xi:7; James ii:5; 1

Pet. iii:7). (3) But perhaps Abraham's being *"heir of the world,"* signifies his having Canaan divinely bequeathed to his seed (Rom. iv:13). Perhaps Gal. iii:29 explains this. (4) Christ, the seed of Abraham, is *"heir of all things;"* and his people are *heirs* with him. (5) A handmaid *"heir to her mistress,"* cannot be borne with, because of her intolerable pride (Prov. xxx:23). (See BIRTH-RIGHT; INHERITANCE.)

HELAH (hē'lah), (Heb. חֶלְאָה, *khel-aw'*, rust), one of the wives of Ashur, the ancestor of the men of Tekoah (1 Chron. iv:5), B. C. about 1612.

HELAM (hē'lam), (Heb. חֵילָם, *khay-lawm'*, place of abundance), a place celebrated for a defeat of the Syrians by David, in which he took their horses and chariots (2 Sam. x:16, 17), it would seem to have been not far from the Euphrates. Perhaps it can best be identified with Alamatha.

HELBAH (hĕl'bah), or **CHELBA** (Heb. חֶלְבָּה, *khel-baw'*, fatness, a fertile region), a city of Asher (Judg. i:31); perhaps Helbon in Syria. "It still exists in the village of *Helbôn*, a place with many ruins three and a half miles north of Damascus in the midst of a valley of the same name" (Keil, *Com.*, in loc.)

HELBON (hĕl'bŏn), (Heb. חֶלְבּוֹן, *khel-bone'*, fat), a name which occurs only in Ezek. xxvii:18, where 'the wine of Helbon' is named among the commodities brought to the great market of Tyre.

Helbon is thought to be identical with Chalybon, an old city of Syria, famous for wine.

Now it is generally agreed that the site is at Helbun, thirteen miles north of Damascus. The village is situated in a narrow valley shut in by steep, bare cliffs and long, shelving banks 2,000 to 3,000 feet high. The bottom of the glen is occupied by orchards, and far up the mountain slopes are terraced vineyards. Along the terraces and in the valley below are extensive ruins. The wine was celebrated in Assyria, Babylonia, and Persia (Strabo xv:735; Nebuchadnezzar 1 R. 65, 32).

HELDAI (hĕl'dāi or hĕl'da-ī), (Heb. חֶלְדַּי, *khel-dah'ee*, worldliness).

1. A Netophathite, descendant of Othniel, who had charge of one of the courses in the temple service (1 Chron. xxvii:15), B. C. 1014.

2. One of those returning from captivity. Zechariah was instructed to make certain crowns for him and others as memorials (Zech. vi:10), B. C. 520.

HELEB (hē'leb), (Heb. חֵלֶב, *khay-leb'*, fat, fatness), a Netophathite, son of Baanah, and one of David's guard (2 Sam. xxiii:29).

HELED (hē-led') (Heb. חֵלֶד, *khay'led*, portion of time), the name (1 Chron. xi:30) which appears as Heleb in 2 Sam. xxiii:29.

HELEK (hē'lek), (Heb. חֵלֶק, *khay'lek*, a portion), a descendant of Gilead and founder of a family by his own name (Num. xxvi:30). His descendants were influential in the tribe (Josh. xvii:2), B. C. about 1612.

HELEKITES (hēlek-ītes), (Heb. חֶלְקִי, *khel-kee'*), a family descended from HELEK (which see).

HELEM (hē'lem), (Heb. חֵלֶם, *khay'lem*, dream.

1. Apparently a descendant of Asher (1 Chron. vii:35), B. C. about 1658. See Burrington, i:265.

2. A name given in Zech. vi:14: probably the same as *Heldai* in ver. 10. (Ewald, *Propheten*, i:536).

HELEPH (hē'leph), (Heb. חֶלֶף, *kheh'lef*), one of the boundary marks of the tribe of Naphtali (Josh. xix:33). Perhaps it corresponds to the modern *Beitlif:* Van de Velde, *Memoir*, p. 320: *Syria*, i:233.

HELEZ (hē'lez), (Heb. חֶלֶץ, *khay'lets*, or חֶלֶץ, *kheh'lets*, strength).

1. One of David's "thirty" (2 Sam. xxiii:26; 1 Chron. xi:27). In the last passage he is called an Ephraimite, and captain of the seventh course in the temple worship (1 Chron. xxvii:10), B. C. 1014.

2. Son of Azariah, of the tribe of Judah (1 Chron. ii:39), a descendant of Jerahmeel (B. C. before 1017).

HELI (hē'lī), (Gr. Ἡλί, *hay-lee'*, for Heb. עֵלִי, *ay-lee'*, ascent), the father-in-law of Joseph, and maternal grandfather of Christ, (Luke iii:23). Harvey, *Genealogies*, pp. 130, 138.

HELIOPOLIS (he'lĭ-ŏp'o-lĭs). See ON.

HELKAI (hĕl'ka-ī), (Heb. חֶלְקָי, *khel-kah'ee*, apportioned), a priest in the days of Joiakim the high priest (Neh. xii:15), B. C. after 536.

HELKATH (hĕl'kath), (Heb. חֶלְקַת, *khel-kath'*, smoothness), a town on the boundary of the tribe of Asher (Josh. xix:25), which was allotted to the Gershonite Levites (xxi:31).

HELKATH-HAZZURIM (hĕl'kath-hăz'zu rĭm), (Heb. חֶלְקַת הַצֻּרִים, *khel-khath' hats-tsoo-reem'*, smoothness of the rocks; others, field of the sharp edges), a plot of ground near the pool of Gibeon (2 Sam. ii:16). The name was given from the bloody duel fought there (Van de Velde, *Memoir*, p. 320).

HELL (hĕl), (Heb. שְׁאוֹל, *sheh-ole'*, the unseen state.)

The term used in Old English to designate the world of the dead generally, with all the sad and painful associations of the dark region into which the living disappear. In modern English it has the specific sense of the place and condition of penalty destined for the finally impenitent among the dead. With this it expresses also the abode of evil spirits.

1. Scripture Terms. Much that belongs to this subject has already been considered under the head Hades. It is there shown that hell is represented by the word *Sheol* in the Old and by ᾅδης (*Hades*) in the New Testament. But as both these words mean also the grave or the condition of the dead, hell, as the place of final punishment for sinners, is more distinctively indicated by the term *Gehenna* (γέεννα), which is the word translated 'hell' in Matt. v:22, 29, 30; x:28; xviii:9; xxiii:15, 33; Mark ix:43, 45, 47; Luke xii:5; James iii:6. It is also distinctively indicated by such phrases as 'the place of torment' (Luke xvi:28; 'everlasting fire' (Matt. xxv:41); 'the hell of fire, where the worm dieth not, and the fire is not quenched' (Mark ix:44). The dreadful nature of the abode of the wicked is implied in various figurative expressions, such as 'outer darkness,' 'I am tormented in this flame,' 'furnace of fire,' 'unquenchable fire,' 'where the worm dieth not,' 'the blackness of darkness,' 'torment in fire and brimstone,' 'the ascending smoke of their torment,' 'the lake of fire that burneth with brimstone' (Matt. viii:12; xiii:42; xxii:13; xxv: 30; Luke xvi:24; comp. Matt. xxv:41; Mark ix: 43-48; Jude 13; comp. Rev. xiv:10, 11; xix:20; xx:14; xxi:8). The figure by which hell is represented as burning with fire and brimstone is probably derived from the fate of Sodom and Gomorrah, as well as that which describes the smoke as ascending from it (comp. Rev. xiv:10, 11, with Gen. xix:24, 28). To this coincidence of description Peter also most probably alludes in 2 Pet. ii:6.

2. Figurative Allusions. The names which in many of the other instances are given to the punishments of hell, are doubtless in part figurative, and many of the terms which were commonly applied to the subject by the Jews are retained in the New Testament. The images, it will be seen, are generally taken from death, capital punishments, tortures, prisons, etc. And it is the obvious design of the sacred writers in using such figures, to awaken the idea of something terrible and fearful. They mean to teach that the punishments beyond the grave will excite the same feelings of distress as are produced on earth by the objects employed to represent them. We are so little acquainted with the state in which we shall be hereafter, and with the nature of our future body, that no strictly literal representation of such punishments could be made intelligible to us. Many of the Jews, indeed, and many of the Christian fathers, took the terms employed in Scripture in an entirely literal sense, and supposed there would be actual fire, etc., in hell. But from the words of Christ and his apostles nothing more can with certainty be inferred than that they meant to denote great and unending miseries.

3. Punishments of Sin. The punishments of sin may be divided into two classes: (1) *Natural* punishments, or such as necessarily follow a life of servitude to sin. (2) *Positive* punishments, or such as God shall see fit, by his sovereign will, to inflict.

(1) Natural. Among the natural punishments we may rank the privation of eternal happiness (Matt. vii:21, 23; xxii:13; xxv:41; comp. 2 Thess. i:9); the painful sensations which are the natural consequence of committing sin, and of an impenitent heart; the propensities to sin, the evil passions and desires which in this world fill the human heart, and which are doubtless carried into the world to come. The company of fellow-sinners and of evil spirits, as inevitably resulting from the other conditions, may be accounted among the natural punishments, and must prove not the least grievous of them.

(2) Positive. The positive punishments have been already indicated. It is to these chiefly that the Scripture directs our attention. 'There are but few men in such a state that the merely natural punishments of sin will appear to them terrible enough to deter them from the commission of it. Experience also shows that to threaten positive punishment has far more effect, as well upon the cultivated as the uncultivated, in deterring them from crime, than to announce, and lead men to expect, the merely natural consequences of sin, be they ever so terrible. Hence we may see why it is that the New Testament says so little of natural punishments (although these beyond question await the wicked), and makes mention of them in particular far less frequently than of positive punishments; and why, in those passages which treat of the punishments of hell, such ideas and images are constantly employed as suggest and confirm the idea of positive punishments (Knapp's *Christian Theology*, sec. 156).

(3) Varying. As the sins which shut out from heaven vary so greatly in quality and degree, we should expect from the justice of God a corresponding variety both in the natural and the positive punishments. This is accordingly the uniform doctrine of Christ and his apostles. The more knowledge of the divine law a man possesses, the more his opportunities and inducements to avoid sin, the stronger the incentives to faith and holiness set before him, the greater will be his punishment if he fails to make a faithful use of these advantages. 'The servant who knows his lord's will and does it not, deserves to be beaten with many stripes:' 'To whom much is given, of him much will be required' (Matt. x:15; xi:22, 24; xxiii:15; Luke xii:48). Hence St. Paul says that the heathen who acted against the law of nature would indeed be punished; but that the Jews would be punished more than they, because they had more knowledge (Rom. ii:9-29). In this conviction, that God will, even in hell, justly proportion punishment to sin, we must rest satisfied. We cannot now know more; the precise degrees as well as the precise nature of such punishments are things belonging to another state of being, which in the present we are unable to understand (Knapp's *Christian Theology*, translated by Leonard Woods, Jun., D. D., secs. 156-158; Storr and Flatt's *Biblical Theology*, with Schmucker's Additions, sec. iii. 58; Alger's *Critical Hist. of the Doctrine of a Future Life*, N. Y.)

HELLENIST (hĕl'lĕn-ĭst), (Gr. Ἑλληνιστής, *hel-lay-nis-tace'*, one who talks Greek).

This word is derived from the Greek verb ἑλληνίζω, *hel-lay-nid'zo*, which in Aristotle means 'to talk (good) Greek' (Rhetoric, iii:5,1; 12:1); but, according to the analogy of other verbs in —ίζω, it might mean 'to favor the Greeks,' or 'to imitate Greek manners.' In the New Testament it seems to be appropriated as the name of those persons who, being of Jewish extraction, nevertheless talked Greek as their mother-tongue; which was the case generally with the Jews in Egypt, Syria, Asia Minor, and Greece; and in fact, through the influence of the Greek cities in northern Palestine (Decapolis), it would appear that the Galileans from their childhood learned nearly as much Greek as Hebrew. The appellation *Hellenist* is opposed to that of *Hebrew* in Acts vi:1; in Acts ix:29 the reading is not so certain, yet probably it should there also be 'Hellenists,' meaning unconverted Jews.

The fact that so large a portion of the Jewish nation was Hellenistic was destined to work great results on the Christian cause. Indeed, in some sense, Christianity itself may be said to have had its human birth among Hellenists, since Jesus himself and the majority of his disciples were reared in Galilee, and were probably nearly as familiar with the Greek as with the Hebrew tongue. Nevertheless, during the early times which followed the day of Pentecost, no striking result appears from this, except that it must have facilitated communication with the Jews of the dispersion. The important part which the Hellenists were to sustain, was first indicated by the preaching of Stephen; who discerned the lower place which must be assigned to the national law of Moses in the kingdom of Messiah. Stephen, indeed, was abruptly cut off by the odium which his principles caused; but the same were soon after adopted, and yet more efficiently inculcated, by his persecutor Saul, to whom the high office was allotted of establishing the peculiar system of doctrine which thenceforward distinguished the Gentile from the Jewish church.

The Epistle of James (whether written, as Neander thinks, *before* the development of the Pauline views or not) exhibits to us undoubtedly the state of Christian doctrine in the mother-church of Jerusalem. We see in it the higher spirit of Christ struggling to put down the law into its right place, but having by no means as yet brought out into their full clearness the distinguishing doctrines of the gospel. All of these were preached and established by Paul in his own churches, founded among Gentile proselytes to Hellenistic Judaism, and from them in no long time were imbibed by all Gentile Christendom. But, simultaneously, the struggle began within the church itself between the Hebraic and the Hellenistic spirit.

The (so-called) first council at Jerusalem (Acts xv) decided, for the time at least, that the Mosaic law was not to be enforced upon the Gentiles, but it did not lessen the importance of it to Jewish Christians; and it would appear that the Hebrew spirit became afterwards even stronger still within the Jerusalem church, if we may interpret literally the words of James (Acts xxi:20) : 'Thou seest, brother, how many thousands of Jews there are which believe, and *they are all zealous of the law.*' At any rate it appears certain that the resistance to the Pauline doctrine continued intense in the great body of the Hebrew Christians; for they show themselves in ecclesiastical history only under the names of Nazarenes and Ebionites, and are always regarded as (more or less) heretical by the Gentile churches, since they held only the bare rudimental creed on which the original Pentecostal church was founded; and pertinaciously rejected the distinguishing tenets of Paul, which were confirmed by Peter, and perhaps extended by John. This first and greatest of controversies ended in the extinction of the Hebrew churches, which had refused to grow with the growth of the Christian spirit in its highest and most favored leaders. But long before that event the Hellenistic Jews had been swallowed up in the mass of Gentile believers; and to follow the further development of the Grecian mind within the bosom of Christianity, belongs, not to this article, but to a history of Gentile Christendom.   F. W. N.

HELMET (hĕl'mĕt), (Heb. כּוֹבַע, *ko'bah*), a cap made of brass, iron, or other metal, for protecting the head of a warrior, 1 Sam. xvii:5.

Figurative. (1) The salvation of his people is God's *"helmet;"* the deliverance he intends and works for them, will appear conspicuous as if on his head, and he will have the glory of it (Is. lix:17). (2) Eternal salvation, and the hope of it, are the saints' *"helmet;"* they defend and render them bold and courageous in their spiritual warfare (Eph. vi:17; 1 Thess. v:8). (See ARMS, ARMOR.)

HELON (hē'lon), (Heb. חֵלֹן, *khay-lone'*, strong), the father of Eliab, who was a man of influence in the tribe of Zebulun (Num. i:9; ii:7; vii:24, 29; x:16), B. C. before 1658.

HELP (hĕlp). Besides its usual meaning of *assistance,* a technical application is given the term in the instances below cited:—

"Helps" (Gr. βοήθεια, *bo-ay'thi-ah*), an apparatus for securing a leaking vessel, by means of ropes, chains, etc., forming a process of undergirding (Acts xxvii:17). The helm is now the handle which moves the rudder, but it was formerly used loosely for the whole steering apparatus. Hence in James iii:4 it is translated a rudder. It was Tyndale who introduced 'helm' here, and he was followed by all the versions except Geneva, which has 'rudder,' and Rheims which has 'sterne.' The R. V. follows Geneva.

HELPMEET (hĕlp'mēt'), (Heb. עֵזֶר כְּנֶגְדּוֹ, *heh'-zer keh-neg-dow'*, a help as his counterpart), i. e., an aid suitable and supplementary to him.

A beautiful and delicate designation of a wife (Gen. ii:18-20). (See MARRIAGE.)

HELPS (hĕlps), (Gr. ἀντιλήψεις, *an-til'ape-sis*, aids; supports); Vulg. *opitulationes;* 1 Cor. xii:28).

The Greek word, signifying aids or assistances, has also this meaning, among others, in the classical writers (*e. g.* Diod. Sic. i:87). In the Sept. it answers to the Heb. עֶזְרָה, (*Ez-raw'*), (Ps. xxii:19). It is found in the same sense Ecclus. xi:12; 2 Macc. xi:26; and in Josephus (*De Bell. Jud.* iv:5, 1). In the New Testament it occurs once, viz. in the enumeration of the several orders, or classes of persons possessing miraculous gifts among the primitive Christians (*ut supra*), where it seems to be used by metonymy, the abstract for the concrete, and to mean *helpers;* like the words δυνάμεις, 'miracles,' i. e. *workers* of miracles; κυβερνήσεις, 'governments,' that is, *governors,* etc., in the same enumeration. Great difficulty attends the attempt to ascertain the nature of the office so designated among the first Christians. (Barrington's *Miscellanea Sacra,* i:166; Macknight on 1 Cor. xii:10-28). After all it must be confessed, with Doddridge, that 'we can only guess at the meaning of the words in question, having no principles on which to proceed in fixing it absolutely.'   J. F. D.

HELVE (hĕlv), (Heb. עֵץ, *ates,* wood), the handle or wooden part (Deut. xix:5) of an ax (which see).

HEM (Gr. κράσπεδον, *kras'ped-on,* Matt. ix:20,) R. V., "border." "Entomb'd upon the very *hem* o' the sea."—Shakespeare.

HEMAM (hē'mam), son of Lotan, the eldest son of Seir (Gen. xxxvi:22), in 1 Chron. i:39, the name is Homan which is doubtless correct. (B. C. after 1964.)

HEMAN (hē'man), (Heb. הֵימָן, *hay-mawn',* faithful).

1. A member of the tribe of Judah named with others celebrated for their wisdom, to which that of Solomon is compared (1 Kings iv:31; 1 Chron. ii:6). The considerations stated under Ethan will distinguish this Heman from the following, with whom he is sometimes confounded. (B. C. after 1856.)

2. A Kohathite of the tribe of Levi, and one of the leaders of the temple music as organized by David (1 Chron. vi:33; xvi:41, 42), B. C. 1014. This, doubtless, is the Heman to whom the 88th Psalm is ascribed.

HEMATH (hē'math), (Heb. חֲמָת, *kham-awth',* fortress).

A name found in 1 Chron. ii:55, in the genealogical lists of Judah, but whether of a place or person cannot be determined.

HEMDAN (hĕm'dan), (Heb. חֶמְדָּן, *khem-dawn',* pleasant), son of Dishon, son of Anah the Horite (Gen. xxxvi:26). The name is changed to Hauram (Heb. *Chamram',* 1 Chron. i:41), B. C. about 1964.

HEMLOCK (hĕm'lŏk), a wrong rendering of the Heb. רֹאשׁ, *roshe* (A. V. Hos. x:4) (see GALL), and of לַעֲנָה, *lah-an-aw'* (Amos vi:12), which should be rendered as in the R. V. *Wormwood.*

Figurative. The figurative use of it is explained by comparing the above passage with Deut. xxix:18; Amos v:7; Heb. xii:15. The evils of perverted judgment resemble the springing up of useless and poisonous plants where we look for and expect valuable and nutritious vegetation.

HEM OF A GARMENT (hĕm ŏv a gär'ment), (Heb. שׁוּל, *shool*, to hang down; Gr. κράσπεδον, *kras'ped-on*), the extremity; border of the outer garment; fringe (Exod. xxviii:33; xxxix:24-26; Matt. ix:20; xiv:36).

The importance attached to this by the later Jews, especially Pharisees (Matt. xxiii:5) was founded on Num. xv:38, 39. The fringe owed its origin to the ends of the woof being left in order to prevent raveling.

HEN (hĕn), (Heb. חֵן, *khane*, grace), son of Zephaniah (Zech. vi:14). Apparently the same as Josiah of verse 10. Perhaps we should read "for the favor of the son of Zephaniah."

HENA (hē'nȧ), (Heb. הֵנַע, *hay-nah'*), a city of Mesopotamia, the same, probably, which was afterwards called Ana, situated on a ford of the Euphrates (2 Kings xviii:34; xix:13; Is. xxxvii:13).

HENADAD (hĕn'a-dăd), (Heb חֵנָדָד, *khay-naw-dawd'*, favor of Hadad), Hadad, a Levite, who with his family, helped to rebuild the Temple under Jeshua (Ezra iii:9), B. C. before 535.

HENOCH (hē'nok), (Heb. חֲנוֹךְ, *khan-oke'*, initiated).

1. The form in which *Enoch* appears (1 Chron. i:3). The Hebrew is *Chanoch*, both here and in Genesis.

2. The form in which *Hanoch* appears in 1 Chron. i:33. (See ENOCH.)

HEPHER (hē'pher), (Heb. חֵפֶר, *khay'fer*, a pit, well).

1. A Canaanitish city with a king, subdued by Joshua (Josh. xii:17). Situation unknown.

2. Youngest son of Gilead (Num. xxvi:32), and head of the family by his name. (B. C. before 1618.)

3. Son of Naarah, one of the two of Ashur's wives (1 Chron. iv:6), B. C. 1612.

4. One of David's guard, called the Mecherath-ite (1 Chron. xi:36).

HEPHERITE (hĕ'pher-īte), (Heb. חֶפְרִי, *khef-ree'*, a descendant of Hepher 2 (Num. xxvi:32).

HEPHZIBAH (hĕph'zĭ-bäh), (Heb. חֶפְצִי־בָהּ, *khef-tsee'baw*, my delight is in her).

1. The queen of Hezekiah and mother of King Manasseh (2 Kings xxi:1), B. C. before 690.

2. A name to be borne by the restored Jerusalem (Is. lxii:4).

HERAKLES (hĕr'a-klez), (Ἡρακλῆς, *her-ak-lace*,) is mentioned in 2 Macc. iv:19, as the Tyrian god to whom the Jewish high-priest Jason sent a religious embassy (θεωροί), with the offering of 300 drachmæ of silver.

That this Tyrian Hercules (Herod. ii:44) is the same as the Tyrian Baal, whose worship prevailed in the time of the Judges, and was put down by Samuel (1 Sam. vii:4). The effects of that suppression appear to have lasted through the next few centuries, as Baal is not enumerated among the idols of Solomon (1 Kings xi:5-8; 2 Kings xxiii:13). The power of nature, which was worshiped under the form of the Tyrian Hercules, Melkarth, Baal (see BAAL) Adonis, Moloch, and whatever his other names are, was that which originates, sustains, and destroys life. These functions of the deity, according to the Phœnicians, were represented, although not exclusively, by the *sun*, the influence of which both animates vegetation by its genial warmth, and scorches it up by its fervor. Pliny expressly testifies that human sacrifices were offered up every year to the Carthaginian Hercules (*Hist. Nat.*

51

xxxvi v:12), which coincides with what is stated of Baal in Jer. xix:5 and with the acknowledged worship of Moloch.   J. N.

HERALD (hĕr'ald), (Heb. כָּרוֹז, *kaw-roze'*).

The only occurrence of the mention of this officer in the Old Testament is (Dan. iii:4). In the New Testament "Herald" might be substituted in 1 Tim. ii:7; 2 Tim. i:11; 2 Pet. ii:5 for "preacher."

HERBS, BITTER (ẽrbs, bĭt'tẽr), (Heb. מְרֹרִים, *mer-o-reem'*).

The Israelites were commanded to eat "bitter herbs" with the Passover bread (Exod. xii:8; Num. ix:11) to remind them of the bitterness of their bondage in Egypt (Exod. i:14). "The *Mishnah* mentions these five as falling within the designation of 'bitter herbs,' viz., lettuce, endive, succory, what is called 'Charchavina (urtica, beets?), and horehound' " (Edersheim, *The Temple*, p. 204).

HERD (hẽrd), (Heb. בָּקָר, *baw-kawr'*; Gr. ἀγέλη, *ag-el'ay*).

"The herd was greatly regarded both in the patriarchal and Mosaic period. This word is generic for *oxen*. It is not like *zôu*, applicable to two or more species. Wherever it is used, therefore, it might without loss, and with sensible advantage, be translated *oxen*. Other Hebrew words are translated *herds of cattle*, and *flocks of sheep*.

The ox was the most precious stock next to horse and mule. The herd yielded the most esteemed sacrifice (Num. vii:3; Ps. lxix:31; Is. lxvi:3); also fresh meat and milk, chiefly converted, probably, into butter and cheese (Deut. xxxii:14; 2 Sam. xvii:29), which such milk yields more copiously than that of small cattle. The full-grown ox was hardly ever slaughtered in Syria; but, both for sacrificial and convivial purposes, the young animal was preferred (Exod. xxix:1). The agricultural and general usefulness of the ox, in plowing, thrashing, and as a beast of burden (1 Chron. xii:40; Is. xlvi:1), made such a slaughtering seem wasteful. The animal was broken to service probably in his third year (Is. xv:5; Jer. xlviii:34). In the moist season, when grass abounded in the waste lands, especially in the 'south' region, herds grazed there. Especially was the eastern table-land (Ezek. xxxix:18; Num. xxxii:4) 'a place for cattle.' Herdsmen, etc., in Egypt were a low, perhaps the lowest caste; but of the abundance of cattle in Egypt, and of the care there bestowed on them, there is no doubt (Gen. xlvii:6, 17; Exod. ix:4, 20). So the plague of hail was sent to smite especially the cattle (Ps. lxxviii:48), the first-born of which also were smitten (Exod. xii:29). The Israelites departing stipulated for (Exod. x: 26) and took 'much cattle with them' (xii:38). Cattle formed thus one of the traditions of the Israelitish nation in its greatest period, and became almost a part of that greatness. When pasture failed, a mixture of various grains (Job vi:5) was used, as also 'chopped straw' (Gen. xxiv:25; Is. xi:7; lxv:25), which was torn in pieces by the thrashing machine and used probably for feeding in stalls. These last formed an important adjunct to cattle keeping, being indispensable for shelter at certain seasons (Exod. ix:6, 19)." (Smith, *Bib. Dict.*)

HERDMAN (hẽrd-man), (Heb. בֹּקֵר, *bo-kare'*, a tender of oxen; in distinction from רֹעֵי, a feeder of sheep).

Nothing more strikingly brings out the contrast between the Egyptians and the Hebrews than their different estimation of the pursuit of cattle-raising.

While the latter had large herds and flocks, and considered their possession and keep honorable, the former, quite as dependent upon them for food and labor, despised the herdsman as "an abomination" (Gen. xlvi:34). By the influence of Joseph his brethren were made Pharaoh's chief herdsmen (Gen. xlvii:6). The patriarchs were great herdsmen. The occupation was not inconsistent with state honors; thus, Doeg, "the chiefest of the herdsmen," was high in Saul's favor (1 Sam. xxi:7). David's herdmasters were among his chief officers of state. In Solomon's time, although commerce decreased its relative importance, the pursuit was still extensive (Eccl. ii:7; 1 Kings iv:23). "It must have suffered greatly from the inroads of the enemies to which the country, under the later kings of Judah and Israel, was exposed. Uzziah, however (2 Chron. xxvi:10), and Hezekiah (xxxii:28, 29), resuming the raising of cattle, had great herds; their principal feeding grounds were Sharon (1 Chron. xxvii:29), the Carmel (1 Sam. xxv:2), and Dothan, (Gen. xxxvii:17), but doubtless all the uncultivated lands were used for this purpose. But for food they did not use, as we do, full-grown beeves, but killed the calves. Fattening for beef is indeed not practiced in the East. The oxen were broken for service in the third year (Is. xv:5). When the heat had dried up all the pasture, the oxen were stalled (Hab. iii:17); hence the figure "a stalled ox" for stately magnificence, which is used in Prov. xv:17. "Calves of the stall" were watchfully cared for (Mal. iv:2). Cattle feed upon foliage as well as upon grass (Ps. l:10). A mixture of various grains, as also chopped straw, is fed when the pasture gives out. See Job vi:5, "fodder;" Is. xxx:24, "provender;" Gen. xxiv:25; Is. xi:7; lxv:25. (See AGRICULTURE; FLOCK; PASTURAGE; Ox.) (Schaff, *Bib. Dict.*)

HERES (hē'rēz), (Heb. הַרחֶרֶס, *har-kheh'res*, mountain of the sun), Mount Heres near Aijalon on the borders of Judah and Dan, inhabited by Amorites (Judg. i:35). (See IR-HAHERES.)

HERESH (hē'resh), (Heb. חֶרֶשׁ, *kheh'resh*, work, silence, or artificer), a Levite who, with others, was assigned to look after the tabernacle (1 Chron. ix:15), B. C. 536.

HERESY (hĕr'ē-sy̆). This word is derived from the Greek word αἵρεσις, *hah-ee'res-is*, which originally meant simply choice, for example of a set of opinions, but is generally used to signify some fundamental error adhered to with obstinacy.

In 1 Cor. xi:19, on margin of R. V., the word is rendered "sects, factions." On margin of Gal. v:20, R. V., it is rendered "parties." It is also used to denote a doctrine or a sect consequent upon departure from sound doctrine (2 Pet. ii:1, margin of R. V. "sects of perdition").

The heresies chiefly alluded to in the apostolic epistles are: (1) Those of the Judaizers, or rigid adherents to the Mosaic rites, especially that of circumcision. (2) Those of converted Hellenists, or Grecian Jews, who held the Greek eloquence and philosophy in too high an estimation, and corrupted, by the speculations of the latter, the simplicity of the gospel. (3) Those who endeavored to blend Christianity with a mixed philosophy of magic, demonology, and Platonism, which was then highly popular in the world.

With respect to the latter, the remarks of Hug will tend to illustrate some passages in the writings of St. Paul: Without being acquainted with the notions of those teachers who caused the apostle so much anxiety and so much vexation, a considerable part of these treatises must necessarily remain dark and unintelligible. From the criteria by which the apostle points them out, at one time some deemed that they recognized the Gnostics; others perceived none but the Essenes; and every one found arguments for his assertions from the similarity of the doctrines, opinions and morals. It would, however, be as difficult to prove that the Gnostic school had at that time indeed perfectly developed itself, as it is unjust to charge the Essenes with that extreme of immorality of which St. Paul accused these seducers, since the contemporaries and acquaintances of this Jewish sect mention them with honor and respect, and extol its members as the most virtuous men of their age.

The similarity of the principles and opinions, which will have been observed in both parties, compared with St. Paul's declarations, flows from a common source, from the philosophy of that age, whence both the one and the other have derived their share. We shall therefore go less astray if we recede a step, and consider the philosophy itself as the general modeler of these derivative theories. It found its followers among Judaism as well as among the heathens; it both introduced its speculative propositions into Christianity, and endeavored to unite them, or to adjust them to it, as well as they were able, by which means Christianity would have become deformed and unlike to itself, and would have been merged in the ocean of philosophical reveries, unless the apostles had on this occasion defended it against the follies of men. An oriental, or, as it is commonly called, a Babylonian or Chaldean, doctrinal system had already long become known to the Greeks, and even to the Romans, before Augustus, and still more so in the Augustan age, and was in the full progress of its extension over Asia and Europe. It set up different deities and intermediate spirits in explanation of certain phenomena of nature, for the office of governing the world, and for the solution of other metaphysical questions, which from time immemorial were reckoned among the difficult propositions of philosophy. The practical part of this system was occupied with the precepts by means of which a person might enter into communication with these spirits or demons. But the result which they promised to themselves from this union with the divine natures, was that of acquiring, by their assistance, superhuman knowledge, that of predicting future events, and of performing supernatural works. These philosophers were celebrated under the name of magi and Chaldeans; who, for the sake of better accommodating themselves to the western nations, modified their system after the Greek forms, and then, as it appears, knew how to unite it with the doctrine of Plato, from whence afterward arose the Neo-Platonic and in Christendom the Gnostic school.

HERETIC (hĕr'ē-tĭk). See HERESY.

HERITAGE (hĕr'ĭt-âj). See INHERITANCE.

HERMAS (hēr'mas), (Gr. Ἑρμᾶς, *her-mas'*, Mercury, interpreter), one of the Christians at Rome, to whom Paul addressed special salutations in his Epistle (Rom. xvi:14).

Of his history and station in life nothing is known. By several writers, ancient and modern, he has been reputed to be the author of a work entitled *The Shepherd of Hermas*, which from its high antiquity and the supposed connection of the writer with St. Paul, has been usually classed with the epistles of the so-called Apostolic Fathers. It was originally written in Greek, but we possess it only in a Latin version (as old as the time of Tertullian), a few fragments excepted, which are found as quotations in other ancient authors. It has been divided by modern editors (for in the manuscript copies there is no such division) into three books; the first consisting of four visions, the second of twelve commands, and the third of ten similitudes. It is called the 'Shepherd' (ὁ Ποιμήν, *Pastor*), because the Angel of Repentance (*Nuntius Pœnitentiæ*), at whose dictation Hermas professes that he wrote the second and third books, appeared in the garb of a shepherd. Impartial judges will probably agree with Mosheim, that '*The Shepherd*' contains such a mixture of folly and superstition with piety, of egregious nonsense with momentous truth, as to render it a matter of astonishment that men of learning should ever have thought of giving it a place among the inspired writings.

The Shepherd of Hermas was first published at Paris in 1513, and is included in the editions of the Apostolic Fathers by Cotelerius, Galland, and Hefele. Fabricius also published it in his *Codex Apocryphus*, Hamburgi, 1719. Archbishop Wake's translation is well known. J. E. R.

HERMES (her'mēz), (Gr. Ἑρμῆς, *her-mace'*, i. e., the Greek Mercury), the Mercurius of the Romans, was the messenger of the gods, and was equally characterized by adroitness of action and readiness of speech.

He was also the customary attendant of Jupiter when he appeared on earth (Ovid, *Fast.* v:495). These circumstances explain why the inhabitants of Lystra (Acts xiv:12), as soon as ever they were disposed to believe that the gods had visited them in the likeness of men, discovered Hermes in Paul, as the chief speaker, and as the attendant of Jupiter.

HERMOGENES and **PHYGELLUS**, (her'mŏj'e-nēz ănd fī-gĕl-lus), (Gr. Ἑρμογένης, *her-mog-en'ace*, Mercury-born, Φύγελλος, foog-el-los, a fugitive), disciples cf Asia Minor, and probably companions in labor of St. Paul.

They abandoned him during his second imprisonment at Rome, doubtless from alarm at the perils of the connection (2 Tim. i:15), A. D. 64.

HERMON (her'mon), (Heb. חֶרְמוֹן, *kher-mone'*, the peak).

A mountain which formed the northernmost boundary of the country beyond the Jordan which the Hebrews conquered from the Amorites (Deut. iii:8), and which, therefore, must have belonged to Anti-Libanus.

Since modern travelers have made us acquainted with the country beyond the Jordan, no doubt has been entertained that the Mount Hermon of those texts is no other than the present Jebel Es-sheikh, or the Sheikh's mountain, or, which is equivalent, Old Man's Mountain, a name it is said to have obtained from its fancied resemblance (being topped with snow, which sometimes lies in lengthened streaks upon its sloping ridges) to the hoary head and beard of a venerable sheikh (Elliot, i:317). This Jebel Es-sheikh is a southeastern, and in that direction culminating, branch of Anti-Libanus. It is probably the highest of all the Lebanon mountains, and is thought to rival Mont Blanc, though, as Elliot observes, the high ground on which it stands detracts considerably from its apparent altitude, and makes it a less imposing object than that king of European mountains as viewed from the Italian valley of Aösta.

The mention of Hermon along with Tabor in Ps. lxxxix:12, led to its being sought near the latter mountain, where, accordingly, travelers and maps give us a 'Little Hermon.' But that

passage, as well as Ps. cxxxiii:3, applies better to the great mountain already described; and in the former it seems perfectly natural for the Psalmist to call upon these mountains, respectively the most conspicuous in the western and eastern divisions of the Hebrew territory, to rejoice in the name of the Lord. Besides, we are to consider that Jebel Es-sheikh is seen from Mount Tabor, and that both together are visible from the plain of Esdraelon. There is no reason to suppose that the so-called Little Hermon is at all mentioned in Scripture. Its actual name is Jebel ed-Duhy; it is a shapeless, barren, and uninteresting mass of hills, in the north of the valley of Jezreel and opposite Mount Gilboa. (Thomson, *The Land and the Book,* vol. i, p. 458).

Hermon was perhaps the 'high mountain' of Matt. xvii:1; Mark ix:2 ('the mountain' of Luke ix:28) near Cæsarea Philippi, which was the scene of the Transfiguration and of the cloud which covered the disciples. In the Roman period it was a sacred center, and small temples were built on the slopes on every side, while the highest point was encircled with a masonry wall, and seems to have supported an altar. Close by is a rock-cut chamber on the plateau. In the fourth century A. D. (see *Onomast.* s. v. 'Aermon') there was still a temple at which the people of Paneas and Lebanon worshiped, on the summit of Hermon. In the tenth century it became the center of the Druze religion, and to it Sheikh ed-Derâzi, the founder of the latter creed, retired from Egypt. At Hasbeya, on its western slopes, the sacred books of the sect were found by the French in 1860. Hermon is called *Jebel esh-Sheikh,* or 'mountain of the chief,' for this reason, being the residence of the religious Sheikh of the Druzes. The translation sometimes suggested, 'chief of mountains,' is grammatically impossible. Hermon was visited by the present writer in 1873 (when the height and geographical position were determined) and in 1882. (R. C. Conder, Hastings' *Bib. Dict.*)

Kitto says: "There can be no doubt that one of the southern peaks of Hermon was the scene of the Transfiguration. Our Lord traveled from Bethsaida, on the northwest shore of the Sea of Galilee, to the coasts of Cæsarea Philippi; thence he led his disciples 'into a high mountain apart, and was transfigured before them.' Afterward he returned, going toward Jerusalem through Galilee (comp. Mark viii:22-28; Matt. xvi:13; Mark ix:2-13, 30-33). For many centuries a monkish tradition assigned this honor to Tabor, but it is now restored to its proper locality."

HERMONITES (her'mon-ītes), (Heb. חֶרְמוֹנִים, *kher-mo-neem'*), properly "the Hermons," with reference to the three summits of Mount Hermon (Ps. xlii:6).

HEROD (hĕr'od); this was not a personal name, but the family or surname.

It belonged alike to all the generations of the Herodian house as known to the Scriptures. Much confusion has arisen from not having cognized this simple fact. Hence some have even questioned the inerrancy of Luke in that he called Herod Antipas "Herod," when Josephus uniformly calls him "Antipas." But the point assumed is itself a mistake. For Luke mentions him as "Herod," and "Herod the tetrarch," and as "Herod the tetrarch of Galilee" in the same chapter (iii:1, 19); and Josephus repeatedly calls him "Herod the tetrarch," and "Herod the tetrarch of Galilee," and "that Herod who was called Antipas" (*Ant.* xviii, ch. 2, sec. 3; ch. 7, sec. 1). (See HERODIAN FAMILY.)

HERODIAN FAMILY (he-rō'di-an făm'ĭ-lў), (Gr. Ἡρωδιανοί, *hay-ro-dee-an-oy'*).

Josephus introduces us to the knowledge of the Herodian family in the fourteenth book of his *Antiquities.* He there tells us (ch. i, sec. 3) that among the chief friends of Hyrcanus the high-priest was an Idumæan, named Antipater, distinguished for his riches, and no less for his turbulent and seditious temper. He also quotes an author who represented him as descended from one of the best of the Jewish families which returned from Babylon after the captivity, but adds that this statement was founded on no better grounds than a desire to flatter the pride and support the pretensions of Herod.

(1) Herod the Great was the son of Antipater and Cypros and bore the titles of "Herod the King," "King of Judea," and "Herod the Great." In 47 B. C. Julius Cæsar gave the procuratorship of Judea to Antipater, who divided the territory among his four sons, giving Herod Galilee. He was then only about twenty-five years of age.

His first act was to repress the brigands who were infesting his province, many of whom he executed. Sextus Cæsar appointed him governor of Cœle-Syria, which he also held under Cassius, and for some time was very efficient in raising money for military purposes. In 41 B. C., when Antony came to Syria, Herod made him valuable presents and gained his favor. He and Phasael were appointed tetrarchs of Judea; but war breaking out, Herod fled to Rome, where, by the aid of Antony, he was made king of Judea. He was not acceptable, however, and the Asmonean family contested his right to their kingdom. Herod made preparations to take Jerusalem, and after six months' siege, the Romans entered the city, and the Asmonean dynasty passed away. Herod executed all the members of the Sanhedrim except two, confiscated their property, and put a new priest in power.

After the defeat of Antony at Actium, Herod obtained an audience with Octavius, and obtained assurances of security in his realm; and nearly all of Palestine was added to his territory.

In his domestic life Herod had endless trouble. His father died by poison. The poisoner was assassinated. His brothers Phasael and Joseph fell in wars. His satanic sister Salome urged him to crime. His brother Pheroras, while plotting with Antipater against Herod, was poisoned by his own wife. When Herod went to meet Mark Antony, and again to meet Octavian, he gave orders to put his wife Mariamne, the Asmonean, to death if he should not return. His uncle Joseph in one case, and his minister Sohemus in the other, let the woman worm the secret from them. Both were executed for that. He murdered but one of his wives; others he cast aside. Doris was cast off, recalled, again stripped of honors and wealth, and banished. The first Mariamne learned of his murderous orders concerning her, and of his crafty murder of her brother Aristobulus, a pretended accident. She hated him and flouted him. In a frenzy he charged her with adultery, for he dared not dispose of her secretly. She marched to death with the proud dignity of a Maccabean. Her two sons, Aristobulus and Alexander, were educated at Rome in the imperial family of Augustus. Herod brought them home. He admired them, but found them too popular. A charge of treason put the strangler's cord upon their necks. Antipater, eldest son, had much reason to hate his father, for his mother's sake and his own. He laid plots for assassination. The Roman judge condemned him. Augustus left final sentence to Herod. The son was put to death five days before the father died. The emperor is said to have made the remark, "I had rather be Herod's sow than Herod's son." His diseased body, no doubt, helped to make him the monster of crime that he was.

At the visit of the Magi, and the announcement of the birth of some great personage in his kingdom, he was greatly stirred, and all Jerusalem with him. The massacre of the children in Bethlehem was no strange act for a man who had murdered so many of his own household. When nearing death he gave orders that the principal Jews, whom he had shut up in the hippodrome at Jericho, should be killed immediately after his death; but they were released, and the day was

---

GENEALOGY OF THE FAMILY OF HEROD THE GREAT.

1. Herod the Great, son of Antipater; born B. C. 72; died 4 B. C.; King, B. C. 37 (Matt. ii and Luke i). Nine wives.

Principal Wives.
1. *Doris, mother of Antipater, whom his father executed a few days before his own death.*
2. *Mariamne, daughter of Alexander and Alexandra, both of the Maccabees or Asmoneans; mother of Aristobulus and Alexander. Put to death by Herod, B. C. 29.*
3. *Mariamne, second; daughter of Simon, high-priest; mother of Herod Philip, the disinherited. No. 7, below.*
4. *Malthake, of Samaria, mother of Archelaus and Herod Antipas. (Some say of No. 6 also.)*
5. *Cleopatra, of Jerusalem, mother of Herod Philip, the tetrarch.*

2. Antipater; see *Doris,* above. Not in N. T.

3. Aristobulus, executed B. C. 5 with his brother Alexander Not in N. T.

4. Archelaus, depo. A. D. 6 (?), Matt. ii:22.

5. Herod Antipas, † A.D. 44, Matt. xiv, Mark vi, viii, Luke iii, viii, ix, xiii, xxiii, Acts iv, xiii. Dethroned.

6. Herod Philip, the Tetrarch, Luke iii:1, † A. D. 34. Acts xiii. *Salome, No. 11.*

7. Herod Philip, in private life only, Matt. xiv, Mark vi, Luke iii:19. *Herodias, who deserted him. See Nos. 10 and 5.*

8. Herod Agrippa I. † A. D. 44. Acts xii.

9. Herod of Chalcis, married nieces. 1. *Bernice; she left him* (below). 2. *Salome, the dancer.*

10. Herodias, Matt. xiv, Mark vi, Luke iii:19. 1. *Herod Philip, No. 7. She left him.* 2. *Herod Antipas.*

1. *Dau. of Aretas, the King.*
2. *Herodias, No. 10, wife of No. 7; Antipas and she died exiles in Gaul.*

11. Salome, the dancer, Matt. xiv:6. Mark vi:22,28. *Herod No. 9.*

12. Herod Agrippa II. Acts xxv, xxvi, † A. D. 100.

13. Bernice, Acts xxv, xxvi. *Herod of Chalcis.* (Not in N. T).

14. Drusilla; Acts xxiv. Perished with son in eruption of Vesuvius, A D. 79
1. *Azizus, King of Emesa, whom she deserted.*
2. *Antonius Felix, governor,* Acts xxiii, xxv.

15. Agrippa, son of Felix; † 79 with mother.

*** All other descendants of Herod not noticed in N. T. or concerned with these are omitted from this table, which includes all N. T. references.

S. W.

celebrated as a deliverance rather than as a funeral. He died, aged sixty-nine, a few days before the Passover, B. C. 4, and the death scene, as reported, was awful, both as regards his mind and body. "And so, choking as it were with blood, desiring massacres, as in its very delirium, the soul of Herod passed forth into the night."—*Farrar.*

Though he had married ten wives, had nine sons and five daughters, yet within one hundred years not a relative of the great Herodian family was left to curse the earth. He left three sons as heirs of his immense estates—Archelaus, Antipas, Philip II; and two grandsons, Agrippa I and Agrippa II. Despite all his inhuman villainy, he did much for Judea and his kingdom. His greatest work was the rebuilding of the temple in Jerusalem, the main part of which was completed in less than two years; but additions continued for "forty and six years." It stood complete but a short time, when Herod's great work fell before the legions of Titus; and the beautiful house where the Divine Master walked and talked was no more.

(2) Archelaus ('Αρχέλαος) was the elder of the two sons of Herod by Malthace, a Samaritan woman (*Ant.* xvii, 1, 3). He was brought up at Rome with his own brother Antipas, at a private house. He had been accused by Antipater of disloyalty, and so had been at first kept out of any inheritance. His visit to Rome has been narrated above. After he had acquired the kingdom, there is little related of him. He outraged Jewish sentiment by marrying Glaphyra, widow of his brother Alexander, although she had had children by him, and had another husband (Juba of Mauritania) living, and his own wife was alive. He built a palace at Jericho, and a village in his own honor, of the name of Archelais. He was the worst of all Herod's sons that survived, and, after nine years of his rule, the people of Judæa and Samaria could no longer endure his cruelty and tyranny. They complained to Augustus, who summoned Archelaus to Rome, and, after hearing the case, banished him to Vienne. From this time to the year A. D. 41 Palestine was under Roman procurators.

Archelaus is mentioned once in the New Testament, in Matt. ii:22.

(3) Herod Antipas, of Galilee and Peræa. This Herod was first married to a daughter of King Aretas of Arabia; but forming an unholy attachment for Herodias, the wife of his brother Philip, he soon became involved in a course of guilt which ended in his utter ruin. Aretas, to avenge his daughter, sent a considerable army against Herod, whose generals in vain attempted to oppose its progress. The forces which they led were totally destroyed, and instant ruin seemed to threaten both Herod and his dominions. An appeal to the Romans afforded the only hope of safety. Aretas was haughtily ordered by the emperor to desist from the prosecution of the war, and Herod accordingly escaped the expected overthrow. But he was not allowed to enjoy his prosperity long. His nephew Agrippa having obtained the title of king, Herodias urged him to make a journey to Italy and demand the same honor. He weakly assented to his wife's ambitious representations; but the project proved fatal to them both. Agrippa anticipated their designs; and when they appeared before Caligula they were met by accusations of hostility to Rome, the truth of which they in vain attempted to disprove. Sentence of deposition was accordingly passed upon Herod, and both he and his wife were sent into banishment and died at Lyons in Gaul.

(4) Philip (Φίλιππος) was the son of Herod the Great by Cleopatra, a woman of Jerusalem (*Ant.* xvii:1, 3). He had been educated at Rome, like the remainder of Herod's sons. The territory to which he succeeded on the death of his father and by the decision of Augustus (see above), consisted, according to Josephus, of Batanea, Trachonitis, Auranitis, Gaulanitis, and Paneas (*Ant.* xvii, viii, 1, xi, 4, xviii, iv, 6; *BJ* II, vi:3), according to St. Luke (iii:1) the country of Ituræa and Trachonitis.

Unlike the rest of his family, he was distinguished for justice and moderation. He married his niece Salome, the daughter of Herodias and his brother Herod (Philip), who was the young woman that danced before Herod Antipas. Philip is referred to twice in the New Testament (Luke iii:1; Acts xiii:1).

He ruled for 38 years from his accession in B. C. 4. His character is summed up by Josephus (*Ant.* xviii, iv, 6): 'He was moderate and peaceful in his rule, and spent his whole life in his country. He went out with only a small retinue, always taking with him the throne on which he might sit and judge. Whenever he met any one who had need of him, he made no delay, but set down the throne wherever he might be and heard the case.'

(5) Herod Agrippa, or Agrippa I, alluded to above, was the son of Aristobulus, so cruelly put to death by his father Herod the Great. The earlier part of his life was spent at Rome, where the magnificence and luxury in which he indulged reduced him to poverty. After a variety of adventures and sufferings he was thrown into bonds by Tiberius, but on the succession of Caligula was not only restored to liberty, but invested with royal dignity, and made tetrarch of Abilene, and of the districts formerly pertaining to the tetrarchy of Philip. His influence at the Roman court increasing, he subsequently obtained Galilee and Peræa, and at length Judæa and Samaria, his dominion being thus extended over the whole country of Palestine.

To secure the good-will of his subjects, he yielded to their worst passions and caprices. Memorable instances are afforded of this in the apostolic history, where we are told that 'He stretched forth his hands to vex certain of the church, and he killed James, the brother of John, with the sword; and because he saw it pleased the Jews, he proceeded further to take Peter also' (Acts xii:1-3). His awful death, described in the same chapter, and by Josephus almost in the same words (*Antiq.* xix, 8), occurred in the fifty-fourth year of his age.

(6) Herod Agrippa, or Agrippa II, the son of the above named, was in his seventeenth year when his father died. The emperor Claudius, at whose court the young Agrippa was then residing, purposed conferring upon him the dominions enjoyed by his father. From this he was deterred, says Josephus, by the advice of his ministers, who represented the danger of trusting an important province of the empire to so youthful a ruler. Herod was, therefore, for the time, obliged to content himself with the small principality of Chalcis, but was not long after created sovereign of the tetrarchies formerly belonging to Philip and Lysanias; a dominion increased at a subsequent period by the grant of a considerable portion of Peræa. The habits which he had formed at Rome, and his strong attachment to the people to whose rulers he was indebted for his prosperity, brought him into frequent disputes with his own nation. In Acts xxv and xxvi we have an account of the speech of St. Paul before Agrippa, Bernice, and Festus. St. Paul's compliment, that Agrippa was 'expert in all customs and questions which are among the Jews,' was well deserved, and the somewhat enigmatic 'Almost thou persuadest me to be a Christian' may be interpreted according to our conception of Agrippa's character. He died, at the age of seventy, in the early part of the reign of Trajan. H. S.

HERODIANS (he-rō'di-anz), (Gr. 'Ηρωδιανοί, *hay-ro-dee-an-oy'*), a class of Jews that existed in the time of Jesus Christ, whether of a political or religious description it is not easy, for want of materials, to determine.

The passages of the New Testament which refer to them are the following (Mark iii:6; xii:13; Matt. xxii:16; Luke xx:20). The particulars are these: The ecclesiastical authorities of Judæa having failed to entrap Jesus by demanding the authority by which he did his wonderful works, especially as seen in his expurgation of the temple; and being incensed in consequence of the parable spoken against them, namely, 'A certain man planted a vineyard,' etc., held a council against him, and associating with themselves the Herodians, sent an embassy to our Lord with the express but covert design of ensnaring him in his speech, that thus they might compass his destruction. The question they put to him was one of the most difficult—'Is it lawful to pay tribute to Cæsar?' The way in which Jesus extricated himself from the difficulty and discomfited his enemies is well known.

Do these circumstances afford any light as to what was the precise character of the Herodians? Whatever decision on this point may be arrived at, the general import of the transaction is very clear, and of a character highly honorable to Jesus. That his enemies were actuated by bad faith, and came with false pretenses, might also be safely inferred. Luke, however, makes an express statement to this effect, saying (xx:18-20), 'they sought to lay hands on him; and they feared the people; and they watched him, and sent forth spies which *should feign themselves just men,* that they might take hold of his words, that so they might *deliver him* unto the power and authority *of the governor.*' The aim, then, was to embroil our Lord with the Romans. For this purpose the question put had been cunningly chosen. These appear to have been the several feelings whose toils were around Jesus—the hatred of the priests, the favor of the people towards himself, and their aversion to the dominion of the Romans, their half faith in him as the Messiah, which would probably be converted into the vexation and rage of disappointment, should he approve the payment of tribute to Rome; another element of difficulty had in the actual case been deliberately provided—the presence of the Herodians. Altogether the scene was most perplexing, the trial most perilous. But what additional difficulty did the Herodians bring? Herod Antipas was now tetrarch of Galilee and Peræa, which was the only inheritance he received from his father Herod the Great. As tetrarch of Galilee he was specially the ruler of Jesus, whose home was in that province. The Herodians then may have been subjects of Herod, Galilæans, whose evidence the priests were wishful to procure, because theirs would be the evidence of fellow-countrymen, and of special force with Antipas

as being that of his own immediate subjects (Luke xxiii:7).

Herod's relations with Rome were in an unsafe condition. He was a weak prince, given to ease and luxury, and his wife's ambition conspired with his own desires to make him strive to obtain from the Emperor Caligula the title of king. For this purpose he took a journey to Rome, and was banished to Lyons in Gaul.

The Herodians may have been favorers of his pretensions: if so, they would be partial hearers, and eager witnesses against Jesus before the Roman tribunal. It would be a great service to the Romans to be the means of enabling them to get rid of one who aspired to be king of the Jews. It would equally gratify their own lord, should the Herodians give effectual aid in putting a period to the mysterious yet formidable claims of a rival claimant of the crown.

We do not see that the two characters here ascribed to the Herodians are incompatible; and if they were a Galilæan political party who were eager to procure from Rome the honor of royalty for Herod (Mark vi:14, the name of king is merely as of courtesy), they were chosen as associates by the Sanhedrim with especial propriety.

The deputation were to 'feign themselves just men,' that is, men whose sympathies were entirely Jewish, and, as such, anti-heathen: they were to intimate their dislike of paying tribute, as being an acknowledgment of a foreign yoke; and by flattering Jesus, as one who loved truth, feared no man, and would say what he thought, they meant to inveigle him into a condemnation of the practice. In order to carry these base and hypocritical designs into effect, the Herodians were appropriately associated with the Pharisees; for as the latter were the recognized conservators of Judaism, so the former were friends of the aggrandizement of a native as against a foreign prince. J. R. B.

HERODIAS (he-rō'di-as), (Gr.'Ηρωδίας, *hay-ro-dee'as,* feminine of Herod), the daughter of Aristobulus—one of the sons of Mariamne and Herod the Great—and sister of Herod Agrippa I. (See HERODIAN FAMILY, and Table, page 804.)

HERODION (he-rō'di-ŏn), (Gr. 'Ηρωδίων, *hay-ro-dee'ohn,* derived from *Herod*), a Christian at Rome to whom Paul sent a salutation as his kinsman (Rom. xvi:11). A. D. 55. According to Hippolytus he became Bishop of Tarsus, but according to others, of Patra.

HERON (hĕr'ŭn), (Heb. אֲנָפָה, *an-aw-faw',* Lev. xi:19; Deut. xiv:18).

The original is a disputed name of an unclean bird, which has also been translated kite, woodcock, parrot, and crane. For the first of these see GLEDE; the second is rare and only a momentary visitor in Palestine; the third surely required no prohibition where it was not a resident species, and probably not imported till the reign of Solomon; and, as to the crane, we have already shown it to have been likewise exotic, making only a momentary appearance, and that rarely, in Syria. If the Hebrew name be derived from *anaph,* 'to breathe short,' or 'to sniff through the nostrils with an irritated expression,' the most obvious application would be to the goose, a bird not. perhaps, otherwise noticed in the Hebrew Scriptures: though it was constantly eaten in Egypt it was not held unclean by the Jews, and, at some seasons, must have frequented the lakes of Palestine. The heron, though not so constantly hissing, can utter a similar sound of displeasure with much more meaning, and the common species *Ardea cinerea* is found in Egypt, and is also abundant in the Hauran of Palestine, where it frequents the margins of lakes and pools, and the reedy watercourses in the deep ravines, striking and devouring an immense quantity of fish.   C. H. S.

HESED (he'sed), (Heb. חֶסֶד, *keh'sed*, kindness), a man whose son was Solomon's commissary officer in Aruboth, Sochoh and Hepher (1 Kings iv:10), B. C. 955.

HESHBON (hĕsh'bŏn), (Heb. חֶשְׁבּוֹן, *khesh-bone'*, intelligence), a town in the southern district of the Hebrew territory beyond the Jordan, parallel with, and twenty-one miles east of, the point where the Jordan enters the Dead Sea, and nearly midway between the rivers Jabbok and Arnon.

It originally belonged to the Moabites; but when the Israelites arrived from Egypt, it was found to be in the possession of the Amorites, whose king, Sihon, is styled both king of the Amorites and king of Heshbon, and is expressly said to have 'reigned in Heshbon' (Josh. ix:10; comp. Num. xxi.26; Deut. ii:24). It was taken by Moses (Num. xxi:23-26), and eventually became a Levitical city (Josh. xxi:39; 1 Chron. vi:81) in the tribe of Reuben (Num. xxxii:37; Josh. xiii: 17); but being on the confines of Gad, is sometimes assigned to the latter tribe (Josh. xxi:39; 1 Chron. vi:81). After the ten tribes were sent into exile, Heshbon was taken possession of by the Moabites, and hence is mentioned by the prophets in their declarations against Moab (Is. xv:4; Jer. xlviii:2, 34, 45). Under King Alexander Jannæus we find it again reckoned as a Jewish city (Joseph. *Antiq.* xiii, 15, 4).

At the present day it is known by its ancient name of Heshbon, in the slightly modified form of Hesbân. The ruins of a considerable town still exist, covering the sides of an insulated hill, but not a single edifice is left entire. The view from the summit is very extensive, embracing the ruins of a vast number of cities, the names of some of which bear a strong resemblance to those mentioned in Scripture. (Burckhardt, George Robinson, Lord Lindsay, Harper, *Bib. and Mod. Dis.*, p. 374.)

Figurative. In Cant. vii:4 the eyes of the Shulamite are compared to the "fishpools of Heshbon," by the gate of Bath-rabbim. The bright pools in the stream which runs beneath Hesbân on the west are perhaps intended (Harper).

HESHMON (hĕsh'mŏn), (Heb. חֶשְׁמוֹן, *kheshmone'*, fatness), a city of Judah (Josh. xv:27), in the extreme southern part.

HESRON (hĕs'rŏn). See Hezron.

HESRONITES, THE (hĕs'rŏn-ītes, thŭ). See Hezronites.

HETH (hĕth), (Heb. חֵת, *khayth*, terror, dread), father of the Hittites, was eldest son of Canaan, and dwelt south of the promised land, at or near Hebron (Gen. x:15; xxiii:3, 7; xxv:10).

Ephron, of Hebron, was of the race of Heth; and that city, in Abraham's time, was peopled by the children of Heth. Some think there was a city called Heth; but we find no traces of it in Scripture (Gen. x; 1 Chron. i). (See Hittites.)

HETHLON (hĕth'lŏn), (Heb. חֶתְלֹן, *kheth-lone'*, wrapped up), a city mentioned in Ezek. xlvii:15; xlviii:1; comp. Num. xxxiv:8), as limiting the land of promise, north.

It is not fully identified, though it may be mentioned that Kasteren proposes to identify Hethlon

with the modern *Adlûn* N. of the mouth of the Kasimiyeh, which he takes to have been the ideal northern boundary of Israel. Bertholet (*Hesekiel, ad loc.*) and Buhl are inclined to favor Kasteren's identification.

HEWING (hū'ĭng), (Heb. חָצַב, *khaw-tsab'*).

The Gibeonites, having deceived Joshua, were sentenced to serve as "hewers of wood and drawers of water unto all the congregation" (Josh. ix:21), a service which was performed by the menial portion of the people (Deut. xxix:11). In 1 Kings v:15 it is recorded that Solomon "had fourscore thousand hewers in the mountains."

HEXATEUCH (hĕks'a-tūk), (Gr. ἕξ, six, and Τεῦχος, a book), the first six books of the Old Testament.

Many questions have arisen concerning the six books which are included in the above term, and great liberties have been taken in the direction of speculations upon this subject. Results are one thing and *scientific* results are quite another. There is a form of Higher Criticism which claims to seek "the solution of all questions relating to origin, form and value of literature" chiefly by the examinations of internal phenomena, and especially claims to be able to reconstruct and rearrange compositions, to redetermine authorship, revise statements and rearrange dates of the several portions of the Hexateuch.

(1) Principles of Scientific Criticism. Science, however, consists in the exact observation of certain facts, and a careful interpretation of them without prejudice under the following principles or laws of thought:

1. Facts must be *observed*, not assumed.
2. They must be observed without pre-judgment.
3. All relevant principles must be considered.
4. There must be no forcing of facts by either rejection or assertion.
5. There must be logical inductions from the whole body of facts, and these deductions must be unhampered by theories, and unconfuted by grave exceptions.
6. There must be a substantial agreement in conclusions which exclude conflicting explanations.

How far the criticism in question has conformed to these principles of science will appear from even the casual notice of certain points which brevity requires.

(2) Unwarranted Assumptions. In order to harmonize the facts with certain theories, it is necessary to make unwarranted assumptions, and subordinate methods are often employed, which it is difficult to justify in the light of science:

1. Some critics assume the privilege of reconstructing narratives at their own discretion, and they make peremptory challenge of words and phrases which they claim belong to redactors. This process is too common to require an example.
2. They deny the plain statements of the narrative, as when Wellhausen pronounces Abraham to be "a free creation of unconscious art."
3. They transplant words, phrases, sentences and long paragraphs hither and thither, absolutely without restriction, and assign them to certain writers, which they denominate either J. E. or P.
4. With the same freedom, and for the same purpose, they assert the former existence and loss of considerable portions of the work of these hypothetical writers.

5. They claim the right to identify two transactions which the narratives make entirely distinct, and they also disintegrate a single transaction into two, and in each case they claim to find contradictions or proofs of diverse authorship.

When these results are obtained by speculation, by the forcing of facts, and by unwarranted assumptions without proof, we must inquire wherein such methods differ from that of the miner who introduces ore into his claim by artificial methods, or those of the chemist who adulterates a product before analysis?

(3) **Varied Results.** But even under these principles and processes, there is very little agreement in results, and there is scarcely one important theory which has been advanced by the so-called Higher Critics which has not been more or less discredited by some other member of the same school. This system allows the greatest diversity of opinion on the one hand, and a general copying from each other at the same time.

Dr. Briggs epitomizes "a general agreement of the ablest biblical scholars" as to the following writers: viz., P., J., E., D. and three redactors, making seven, but in the same treatise he finds it "necessary to distinguish" five more, making twelve.

Cornill specifies no less than eighteen writers and editors of the Hexateuch. Wellhausen wants twenty more, while Dillmann, the strongest scholar of them all, sturdily rejects seven or eight of these imaginary personages; for who could surely distinguish the various parts of the work which might have been done by twenty, twelve, or even six, writers in one composition which was fairly well combined?

The whole literary public has been unable to identify the portions of a collaborated novel which was prepared by even two writers, and that, too, in a vernacular whose every shade of meaning was familiar to the critics. What, then, can we think of the success of an effort of this kind after centuries have intervened, and the tongue in which the work was written has become practically a dead language?

(4) **The Polychrome Bible.** The only way in which the Polychrome Bible can furnish its variegated texts is by assigning each book to a single editor. It may be doubted whether Professor Cheyne could find seven scholars of high repute in England, America or Germany who would fully accept his dismemberment of Isaiah into more than one hundred and sixty fragments, with scores of transpositions, numerous lacunæ and rejections, together with the assignment of some twenty dates, ranging over a period of four hundred and sixty-five years. A very striking peculiarity meets us also in the fact that, after this elaborate specification of sources, the fabric which has been so laboriously constructed is demolished at a stroke by some of the leaders of the enterprise, when they declare the alleged writers to be, not individuals, but processes extending through long periods. Some notice should be taken of the liberty which is used in alleging glosses, later text changes, and erroneous statements, in order to maintain the recent theories as to the tribe of Levi and the priesthood, the history of the law and the sanctuary, but for such particulars there must be a resort to more extended discussions. (See *"The Veracity of the Pentateuch,"* by Dr. Samuel Colcord Bartlett, p. 328.)

(5) **Assigned Dates.** In regard to the assigned dates of the alleged constituents of the Hexateuch, it may be said that although there are considerable differences, still there is more or less agreement in the tendency to bring them down to a period some five hundred years later than Moses to the Exile, and even later, with allowances for fragments of earlier origin.

(6) **Contemporaneous History.** But a conclusion, however elaborately argued, is not scientifically established unless it excludes other valid explanations. This complicated and unrestrained, and yet unstable analysis of the Hexateuch has not, in the judgment of many sound and scholarly thinkers, excluded the more simple and formerly accepted view, which is a history substantially contemporaneous with the authorship though in part drawn from previous authentic sources, and inevitably somewhat modified, and perhaps modernized in the transmission through a period of a thousand years. Those earlier sources may also have undergone some changes in the transfer from the tongue which was native to Abraham in Babylonia, into the Hebrew which became the language of Israel.

(7) **Older Documents.** The fact that some older documents were used in the Hexateuch is not a discovery of modern investigators; that it embodies contents hundreds of years older than Moses is not a matter of speculation, but of record. The history itself refers to "The Book of the Wars of the Lord" and also to "The Book of Jasher," although the latter was merely a collection of poems rather than history.

(8) **Opinions of Recent Scientists.** The possibility of the Deluge by the method described, is sustained by such recent scientists as Miller, Howarth, Dawson and Prestwich, De Girard and others, and is still further confirmed, though unintentionally, by the testimony of Le Conte and other specialists to the effect that "a great inland sea" once submerged the whole region that includes the Caspian Sea, Lake Aral and other lakes. (See also *"Deluge, Illustrative Facts Concerning,"* by Sir J. W. Dawson.)

(9) **Archæological Facts.** Increasing attention is also directed to the indications corresponding to the still earlier portions of the biblical narrative. That the fourteenth chapter of Genesis deals with actual persons and conditions at least two thousand years before Christ is now well sustained, in spite of the strenuous opposition of the critics. (See CHEDORLAOMER; ARIOCH; AMRAPHEL, etc.)

(10) **Separate Histories.** The eleven sets of generations in Genesis were well described a century ago by Lord Arthur Hervey as "marking the existence of separate histories from which the Book of Genesis was compiled," not only in accordance with the obvious facts of the case, and the unquestionable fact of Jewish genealogies extending back into very remote times, but with the definite statement in the narrative itself, concerning the genealogical list from Adam to Noah and his sons, "This is the book of the generations of Adam" (Gen. v:1.)

(11) **Founder of the Nation.** That Moses was the great founder and molder of the nation of Israel, of its character and institutions, is necessarily admitted by the critics (with a few sporadic exceptions), and emphatically so by Wellhausen and Driver. This admission is made because of the undeniable historic testimony, and especially the incorporation of his mighty personality into the whole life and composition of the Jewish people. In a word, nothing in the theories of modern criticism has been so proved as to disprove the authenticity of the Hexateuch,

or to exclude the essential features of the view so long held by the Hebrew nation and the Christian world.

(12) Historical Character of the Hexateuch. Every decade is making it more unsafe to impugn the historical character of the Hexateuch.

It is a question of interest whether that which has been announced as "the greatest Biblical work of the age," the Polychrome Bible, so far as it conforms to Professor Cheyne's standard, may not prove to be a heavy ordnance, more effective in the recoil than the aim.

Andrew Lang, in Longman's Magazine, comments upon it as follows: "The method is simple and Teutonic. You have a theory, you accept the evidence of the sacred writers as far as it suits your theory, and when it does not suit, you say that the inconvenient passage is an interpolation. *It must be, for if not, what becomes of* your theory? So you print the inconvenient passage in green, or what not, and then the people know all about it. (See *"The Veracity of the Hexateuch,"* by Samuel Colcord Bartlett, D.D., LL.D.; *The Documents of the Hexateuch,* by W. E. Addis, M. A., 1898.)

HEZEKI (hĕz'e-kī), (Heb. חִזְקִי, *khiz-kee'*, strong), one of the "sons" of Elpael, a chief resident of Jerusalem (1 Chron. viii:17, 18); a Benjamite. In R. V., Hizki.

HEZEKIAH (hĕz'e-kī'ah), (Heb. חִזְקִיָּה, *khiz-kee-yaw'*, strengthened of Jehovah, 2 Kings xviii: 1, 10, 14, 15).

1. Son of Ahaz and Abi (Abijah), born B. C. about 744 (2 Kings xviii:1, 2; 2 Chron. xxix:1).

(1) Inauguration of Reform. From the commencement of his reign the efforts of Hezekiah were directed to the reparation of the effects of the grievous errors of his predecessors; and during his time the true religion and the theocratical policy flourished as they had not done since the days of David. The Temple was cleared and purified; the utensils and forms of service were restored to their ancient order; all the changes introduced by Ahaz were abolished; all the monuments of idolatry were destroyed, and their remains cast into the brook Kedron. Among the latter was the brazen serpent of Moses, which had been deposited first in the Tabernacle, and then in the Temple, as a memorial of the event in which it originated: and it is highly to the credit of Hezekiah, and shows more clearly than any other single circumstance the spirit of his operations, that even this interesting relic was not spared when it seemed in danger of being turned to idolatrous uses. Having succeeded by his acts and words in rekindling the zeal of the priests and of the people, the king appointed a high festival, when, attended by his court and people, he proceeded in high state to the Temple, to present sacrifices of expiation for the past irregularities, and to commence the reorganized services. A vast number of sacrifices evinced to the people the zeal of their superiors, and Judah, long sunk in idolatry, was at length reconciled to God (2 Kings xviii:1-8; 2 Chron. xxix).

The revival of the great annual festivals was included in this reformation. The Passover, which was the most important of them all, had not for a long time been celebrated according to the rites of the law; and the day on which it regularly fell, in the first year of Hezekiah, being already past, the king, nevertheless, justly conceiving the late observance a less evil than the entire omission of the feast, directed that it should be kept on the 14th day of the second month, being one month after its proper time. Couriers were sent from town to town, inviting the people to attend the solemnity; and even the ten tribes which formed the neighboring kingdom were invited to share with their brethren of Judah in a duty equally incumbent on all the children of Abraham. Of these some received the message gladly, and others with disdain; but a considerable number of persons belonging to the *northernmost* tribes (which had more seldom than the others been brought into hostile contact with Judah) came to Jerusalem, and by their presence imparted a new interest to the solemnity. A profound and salutary impression appears to have been made on this occasion; and so strong was the fervor and so great the number of the assembled people, that the festival was prolonged to twice its usual duration; and during this time the multitude was fed abundantly from the countless offerings presented by the king and his nobles. Never since the time of Solomon, when the whole of the twelve tribes were wont to assemble at the Holy City, had the Passover been observed with such magnificence (2 Chron. xxx).

The good effect of this procedure was seen when the people carried back to their homes the zeal for the Lord which had thus been kindled, and proceeded to destroy and cast forth all the abominations by which their several towns had been defiled, thus performing again on a smaller scale, the doings of the king in Jerusalem. Even the 'high places,' which the pious kings of former days had spared, were on this occasion abolished and overthrown; and even the men of Israel, who had attended the feast, were carried away by the same holy enthusiasm, and, on returning to their homes, broke all their idols in pieces (2 Chron. xxxi:1).

The attention of this pious king was extended to whatever concerned the interests of religion in his dominions. He caused a new collection of Solomon's proverbs to be made, being the same which occupy chaps. xxv-xxix of the book which bears that name. The sectional divisions of the priests and Levites were re-established; the perpetual sacrifices were recommenced and maintained from the royal treasure; the stores of the temple were once more filled by the offerings of the people, and the times of Solomon and Jehoshaphat seemed to have returned (2 Chron. xxxi).

(2) Military Ventures. This great work having been accomplished and consolidated (2 Kings xvii:7, etc.) Hezekiah applied himself to repair the calamities, as he had repaired the crimes, of his father's government. He took arms and recovered the cities of Judah which the Philistines had seized. Encouraged by this success, he ventured to withhold the tribute which his father had paid to the Assyrian king; and this act, which the result shows to have been imprudent, drew upon the country the greatest calamities of his reign. Only a few years before, namely, in the fourth of his reign, the Assyrians had put an end to the kingdom of Israel and sent the ten tribes into exile, but had abstained from molesting Hezekiah, as he was already their tributary.

(3) Assyrian Invasion. Seeing his country invaded on all sides by the Assyrian forces under Sennacherib, and Lachish, a strong place which covered Jerusalem, on the point of falling into their hands, Hezekiah, not daring to meet them in the field, occupied himself in all necessary preparations for a protracted defense of Jerusalem, in hope of assistance from Egypt, with which country he had contracted an alliance (Is. xxx:1-7). (See LACHISH.) Such alliances were not favored by the divine sovereign of Israel and his prophets, and no good ever came of them. But this alliance did not render the good king unmindful of his true source of strength, for in quieting the alarms of the people he directed their attention to the consideration that they in fact had more of power and strength in the divine protection than the Assyrian king possessed in all his host. 'There is more with us than with him; with him is an arm of flesh, but with us is the Lord our God to help us and fight our battles.' Nevertheless, Hezekiah was himself distrustful of the course he had taken, and at length, to avert the calamities of war, sent to the Assyrian king offers of submission. Sennacherib, who was anxious to proceed against Egypt, consented to withdraw his forces on the payment of three hundred talents of silver and thirty talents of gold (see SENNACHERIB), which the king was not able to raise without exhausting both his own treasury and that of the Temple, and stripping off the gold with which the doors and pillars of the Lord's house were overlaid (2 Kings xviii:7-16).

But after he had received the silver and gold the Assyrian king broke faith with Hezekiah and continued to prosecute his warlike operations. While he employed himself in taking the fortresses of Judæa, which it was important to secure before he marched against Egypt, he sent three of his generals—Rabshakeh and Rabsaris, besides the Tartan, or commander-in-chief—with part of his forces to threaten Jerusalem with a siege unless it were surrendered, and the inhabitants submitted to be sent into Assyria; and this summons was delivered in language highly insulting not only to the king and people, but to the God they worshiped.

(4) Assyrian Defeat. When the terms of the summons were made known to Hezekiah he gathered courage from the conviction that God would not fail to vindicate the honor of his insulted name. In this conviction he was confirmed by the prophet Isaiah, who, in the Lord's name, promised the utter discomfiture and overthrow of the blasphemous Assyrian: 'Lo, I will send a blast upon him, and he shall hear a rumor and shall return to his own land, and I will cause him to die by the sword in his own land' (2 Kings xix:7). The rumor which Sennacherib heard was of the advance of Tirhakah the Ethiopian to the aid of the Egyptians, with a force which the Assyrians did not deem it prudent to meet; but, before withdrawing to his own country, Sennacherib sent a threatening letter to Hezekiah, designed to check the gladness which his retirement was likely to produce. But that very night the predicted blast —probably the hot pestilential south wind—smote 180,000 men in the camp of the Assyrians, and released the men of Judah from all their fears (2 Kings xviii:17-37; xix:1-34; 2 Chron. xxxii:1-23; Is. xxxvi:37).

(5) Illness of Hezekiah. It was in the same year, and while Jerusalem was still threatened by the Assyrians, that Hezekiah fell sick of the plague; and the aspect which the plague-boil assumed assured him that he must die. In this he was confirmed by Isaiah, who warned him that his end approached. The love of life, the condition of the country—the Assyrians being present in it, and the throne of David without an heir—caused him to grieve at his doom, and to pray earnestly that he might be spared.

(6) Prayer Answered. And his prayer was heard in heaven. The prophet returned with the assurance that in three days he should recover, and that fifteen additional years of life should be given to him. This communication was altogether so extraordinary that the king required some token by which his belief might be justified; and accordingly the 'sign' which he required was granted to him. The shadow of the sun went back upon the dial of Ahaz, the ten degrees it had gone down. (See DIAL.) This was a marvel greater than that of the cure which the king distrusted, for there is no known principle of astronomy or natural philosophy by which such a result could be produced. A cataplasm of figs was then applied to the plague-boil, under the direction of the prophet, and on the third day, as foretold, the king recovered (2 Kings xx:1-11; 2 Chron. xxxii:24-26; Is. xxxviii). (See PLAGUE.)

The destruction of the Assyrians drew the attention of foreign courts for a time towards Judæa, and caused the facts connected with Hezekiah's recovery, and the retrogression of the shadow on the dial, to be widely known.

(7) King of Babylon. Among others Merodach-Baladan, king of Babylon, sent ambassadors with presents to make inquiries into those matters and to congratulate the king on his recovery. Since the time of Solomon the appearance of such embassies from distant parts had been rare at Jerusalem; and the king, in the pride of his heart, made a somewhat ostentatious display to Baladan's ambassadors of all his treasures, which he had probably recovered from the Assyrians, and much increased with their spoil. Josephus (*Antiq.* x, 2, 2) says that one of the objects of the embassy was to form an alliance with Hezekiah against the Assyrian empire; and, if so, his readiness to enter into an alliance adverse to the theocratical policy, and his desire to magnify his own importance in the eyes of the king of Babylon, probably furnished the ground of the divine disapprobation with which his conduct in this matter was regarded. He was reprimanded by the prophet Isaiah, who revealed to him the mysteries of the future, so far as to apprise him that all these treasures should hereafter be in the possession of the Babylonians, and his family and people exiles in the land from which these ambassadors came (see ISAIAH). The intimation was received by the king with his usual submission to the will of God, and he was content to know that these evils were not to be inflicted in his own days. He has sometimes been blamed for this seeming indifference to the fate of his successors; but it is to be borne in mind that at this time he had no children. This was in the fourteenth year of his reign, and Manasseh, his successor, was not born till three years afterwards (2 Kings xx:12, 19; 2 Chron. xxxii:31; Is. xxxix).

(8) Death. The rest of Hezekiah's life appears to have been peaceable and prosperous. No man before or since ever lived under the certain knowledge of the precise length of the span of life before him. When the fifteen years had expired Hezekiah was gathered to his fathers, after a reign of twenty-nine years. He died sincerely lamented by all his people, and the public respect for his character and memory was testified by his corpse being placed in the highest niche of the royal sepulcher (2 Kings xx:20, 21; 2 Chron. xxxii: 32, 33). Dean Stanley, *Hist. of the Jewish Ch.* ii. 505-540.

2. Son of Neariah, of the royal family of Judah (1 Chron. iii:23). B. C. after 536.

3. A person mentioned in connection with Ater (Neh. vii:21). B. C. before 536.

4. An ancestor of the prophet Zephaniah (Zeph. i:1; in A. V. Hizkiah), B. C. before 630.

HEZION (hē'zi-ŏn), (Heb. חֶזְיוֹן, *khez-yone'*, **vision**), a king of Aram and father of Tabrimon (1 Kings xv:18). It is probable that he is identical with Rezon (1 Kings xi:23), as the names in the original are very similar. (B. C. before 928.)

HEZIR (hē'zir), (Heb. חֵזִיר, *khay-zeer'*, swine).

1. A priest who had charge of the seventeenth course in the Temple service, in the time of David (1 Chron. xxiv:15), B. C. 1014.

2. One of those who sealed the covenant with Nehemiah (Neh. x:20), B. C. 410.

HEZRAI (hĕz'ra-ī), (Heb. חֶצְרַי, *khets-rah'ee*, walled in, 2 Sam. xxiii:35), the same as HEZRO (which see).

A native of Carmel and one of David's guard of "thirty" (2 Sam. xxiii:35), B. C. 1046.

HEZRO (hĕz'ro), (Heb. חֶצְרוֹ, *khets-ro'*, enclosure), the form in which Hezrai appears (1 Chron. xi:37). Kennicott gives Hetzrai as the original form of the name. (B. C. 1046.)

HEZRON (hĕz'ron), (Heb. חֶצְרוֹן, *khets-rone'*, enclosed; walled, Gesenius).

1. Son of Reuben (Gen. xlvi:9; Exod.vi:14; 1 Chron. iv:1; v:3). He was the founder of a family by his name (Num. xxvi:6), B. C. 1874.

2. Son of Pharez, and ancestor of David (Gen. xlvi:12; Ruth iv:18), B. C. 1856.

3. A place on the southern boundary of Judah (Josh. xv:3).

HEZRONITES (hĕz'ron-ītes), the descendants of HEZRON, 1 (which see).

HIDDAI (hĭd'da-ī), (Heb. הִדַּי, *hid-dah'ee*, derivation uncertain), one of the "thirty" heroes of David, "of the brooks of Gaash" (2 Sam. xxiii:30). Kennicott (*Dissert.*, p. 194) thinks this a corruption of *Hurai* found in the parallel lists (1 Chron. xi:32).

HIDDEKEL (hĭd'de-kĕl), (Heb. חִדֶּקֶל, *khid-deh'-kel*), one of the rivers of Eden (Gen. ii:14). It seems to be identical with the "Great River" (Dan. x:4). It is identified with the TIGRIS.

HIEL (hī'el), (Heb. חִיאֵל, *khee-ale'*, life from God).

A native of Bethel, who rebuilt Jericho, above 500 years after its destruction by the Israelites, and who, in so doing, incurred the effects of the imprecation pronounced by Joshua (1 Kings xvi:34), B. C. 915.

Accursed the man in the sight of Jehovah,
Who shall arise and build this city, even Jericho,
With the loss of his firstborn shall he found it,
And with the loss of his youngest shall he fix
    its gates (Josh. vi:26).   J. E. R.

HIERAPOLIS (hī'e-răp'o-lĭs), (Gr. Ἱεράπολις, *hee-er-ap'ol-is*, sacred city).

A city of Phrygia, not far from Colossæ and Laodicea, where there was a Christian church under the charge of Epaphros, as early as the time of St. Paul, who commends him for his fidelity and zeal (Coloss. iv:12, 13). The place is visible from the theater at Laodicea, from which it is five miles distant northward.

Smith, in his journey to the Seven Churches (1671), was the first to describe the ancient sites in this neighborhood. He was followed by Pococke and Chandler; and more recently by Richter, Cockerell, Hartley, and Arundell.

The place now bears the name of Pamluck-kale (Cotton-castle), or *Pambouk-Kalessi*, from the white appearance of the cliffs of the mountain on the lower summit, or rather an extended terrace, on which the ruins are situated. It owed its celebrity, and probably the sanctity indicated by its ancient name (Holy City), to its very remarkable springs of mineral water, the singular effects of which, in the formation of stalactites and incrustations by its deposits, are shown in the accounts of Pococke (ii, pt. 2, ch. 13) and Chandler (*Asia Minor*, ch. 68), to have been accurately described by Strabo (xiii, p. 629). A great number and variety of sepulchers are found in the different approaches to the site, which on one side is sufficiently defended by the precipices overlooking the valleys of the Lycus and Mæander, while on the other sides the town walls are still observable. The magnificent ruins clearly attest the ancient importance of the place.

HIEROGLYPHICS (hī'ĕr-ŏ-glĭf'ĭks), (from Gr. ἱερός, *hee-er-os'*, sacred, and γλύφειν, *gloo'fen*, to carve).

Pictures of objects, as of an animal, tree, bird, etc., representing a word, syllable, or single sound, and intended to convey a meaning.

HIGGAION (hĭg-gā'yŏn), (Heb. הִגָּיוֹן, *hig-gaw-yone'*; Ps. ix:16; xix:15; xcii:4; Lam. iii:62). Perhaps the best view is that of Gesenius, who takes it from הָגָה, *haw-gaw'*, to murmur; meditate.

HIGH DAY (hī dā), (Heb. גָּדוֹל, *gaw-dole'*, Gen. xxix:7), great, i. e., broad daylight.

Shakespeare uses the word great in the same way, thus, "It is great morning" ("Troilus and Cressida").

HIGHEST (hī'ĕst) (Heb. עֶלְיוֹן, *el-yone'*, elevated), a title ascribed to Jehovah (Ps. xviii:13; lxxxvii:5), and in the New Testament (Gr. ὕψιστος, *hoop'sis-tos*) of the highest region, i. e., *heaven* (Matt. xxi:9); it denotes rank, as the Most High God (Mark v:7, Luke viii:28).

HIGH MINDED (hī'mīn'dĕd) (Gr. ὑψηλοφρονέω, *hoop-say-lo-fron-eh'-o* Rom. xi:20; 1 Tim. vi:17), lofty in mind; arrogant.

HIGH PLACE (hī plās), (Heb. בָּמָה, *baw-maw'*, elevation).

As high places and groves are almost constantly associated in Scripture, it seems undesirable to separate them in our consideration.

Idolatrous High Place, with Grove and Worshipers.

By 'high places' (*baw-maw'*) we are content to understand natural or artificial eminences, where worship by sacrifice or offering was made, usually upon an altar erected thereon.

By a 'grove' we understand a plantation of trees around a spot in the open air set apart for worship and other sacred services.

(1) After the Deluge. We find traces of these customs so soon *after* the deluge, that it is probable they existed *prior* to that event. It appears that the first altar after the deluge was built by Noah upon the mountain on which the ark rested (Gen. viii :20), Abraham, on entering the Promised Land, built an altar upon a mountain between Beth-el and Hai (xii :7, 8). At Beersheba he planted a grove, and called there upon the name of the everlasting God (Gen. xxi : 33). The same patriarch was required to travel to the mount Moriah, and there to offer up his son Isaac (xxii :2, 4). It was upon a mountain in Gilead that Jacob and Laban offered sacrifices before they parted in peace (xxxi :54). In fact, such seem to have been the general places of worship in those times; nor does any notice of a temple or other covered or enclosed building for that purpose, occur. Thus far all seems clear and intelligible. There is no reason in the mere nature of things why a hill or a grove should be an objectionable, or, indeed, why it should not be a very suitable, place for worship. Yet by the time the Israelites returned from Egypt, some corrupting change had taken place, which caused them to be repeatedly and strictly enjoined to overthrow and destroy the high places and groves of the Canaanites wherever they found them (Exod. xxxiv :13; Deut. vii :5; xii :2, 3). That they were not themselves to worship the Lord on high places or in groves is implied in the fact that they were to have but one altar for regular and constant sacrifice; and it was expressly enjoined that near this sole altar no trees should be planted (Deut. xvi :21).

(2) Iniquity of the Canaanites. It is possible that the Canaanites had not yet fallen into rank idolatry in the time of Abraham, at least, not into such idolatries as defiled the very places in which they worshiped. We know, at all events, that their iniquity was not full in those earlier times, but that when the Israelites invaded the land their iniquity was full to overflowing. As included in this, we may with tolerable certainty infer that their religion had become so grossly erroneous and impure, that it was needful to place under ban even their places of worship, which might otherwise bring the Israelites into danger by the associations which had become connected with them.

(3) Abominable Rites. The groves which ancient usage had established around the places of sacrifice for the sake of shade and seclusion, idolatry preserved not only for the same reasons, but because they were found convenient for the celebration of the rites and mysteries, often obscene and abominable, which were gradually superadded.

(4) Injunctions Imperfectly Obeyed. The injunctions, however, respecting the high places and groves were very imperfectly obeyed by the Israelites; and their inveterate attachment to this mode of worship was such that even pious kings, who opposed idolatry by all the means in their power, dared not abolish the high places at which the Lord was worshiped. And it appears to us likely, that this toleration of an acknowledged irregularity arose from the indisposition of the people living at a distance from the temple to be confined to the altar which existed there; to their determination to have places nearer home for the chief acts of their religion—sacrifice and offering; and to the apprehension of the kings that if they were prevented from having places for offerings to the Lord in their own neighborhood, they would make the offerings to idols.

This view of the case seems to be strongly confirmed by the fact that we hear no more of this proneness to worship in high places and in groves after synagogues and regular religious services had been established in the towns and gave sufficient operation to the disposition among men to create a local interest in religious observances.

It is more difficult to explain how it happens that, in the face of the prohibition against sacrificing at more than one altar, many persons of piety, and even prophets, not only did so, but, in some instances, did so in high places; Gideon, for instance, at Ophrah (Judg. vi :25), Manoah in Dan (Judg. xiii :16-29), Samuel at Mizpeh (1 Sam. vii :10), and at Bethlehem (xvi :5), David in the threshing-floor of Ornan (1 Chron. xxi :22), and Elijah on Mount Carmel (1 Kings xviii :30, sq.).

HIGH-PRIEST (hī'prēst), (Heb. הַכֹּהֵן, *hak-kohane'*, the priest). (See PRIEST.)

HIGHWAY (hī'wā), (usually Heb. מְסִלָּה, *mes-il-law'*). (See ROAD.)

HILEN (hī'len), (Heb. חִילֵן, *khi-layn'*, perhaps fortress), a city of Judah allotted to the priests (1 Chron. vi :58). (See HOLON).

HILKIAH (hil-kī'ah), (Heb. חִלְקִיָּה, *khil-kee-yaw'*, portion of Jehovah), several persons of this name occur in Scripture, of whom the following are the chief:

1. The father of Jeremiah (Jer. i :1), B. C. 628.

2. A high-priest in the reign of Josias (2 Kings xxii :4, 8, 10).

3. The father of Eliakim (2 Kings xviii :18, 26; Is. xxii :20; xxxvi :22), B. C. 713.

4. A Merarite Levite, son of Amzi and ancestor of Ethan (1 Chron. vi :45), before B. C. 1014.

5. A Merarite Levite, son of Hosah, and a doorkeeper in the tabernacle under David (1 Chron. xxvi :11), about B. C. 1014.

6. One of those who assisted Ezra in instructing the people in the law (Neh. viii :4), about B. C. 410.

7. Father of Gemariah (Jer. xxix :3), before B. C. 587.

HILL (hĭl), (Heb. גִּבְעָה, *ghib-aw'*, high), a conspicuous natural elevation of land.

The name is generally applied to a natural eminence smaller than a mountain and larger than a mound; but the terms are relative, the same height being sometimes known by both names (Is. xxxi :4), or called a mountain in one locality and a hill in another (Rev. xvii :9). Hill is chiefly the rendering of the Hebrew *Gib'ah* and the Greek *Bounus*. Not infrequently it is also employed in the A. V., and much less frequently in the R. V. (Ps. ii :6; iii :4; xv :1; xxiv :3; xlii :6; Matt. v :14; Luke iv :29), to translate Hebrew הָר, *karar'*, and Greek *'Oros,* which are usually rendered mountain. (Davis, *Bib. Dict.*)

HILL COUNTRY (hĭl kŭn'trў), the rendering in the Old Testament (Josh. xxi :11) of Har (see HILL); and in the New Testament of the Gr. *or-i-nos'* (ὀρεινὸς, *mountainous;* Luke i :39, 65); and meaning Mount Ephraim.

The rendering "hill country" is misleading. "With their usual exactness the Hebrews saw that these regions (i. e., the mountains of Judah, Ephraim and Naphtali) formed part of one range, the whole of which they called not by a collective name, but singularly—the mountain" (Smith, *Hist. Geog.,* p. 53).

HILLEL (hĭl'lĕl), (Heb. הִלֵּל, *hil-layl'*, praising), a Pirathonite, and father of the judge Abdon (Judg. xii:13, 15), B. C. before 1070.

HIN (hĭn). See WEIGHTS AND MEASURES.

HIND (hīnd), (Heb. אַיָּלָה, *ah-yaw-law'*, Gen. xlix:21; 2 Sam. xxii:34; Job xxxix:1; Ps. xviii:33, etc.), the female of the hart or stag, doe being the female of the fallow-deer, and roe being sometimes used for that of the roebuck.

All the females of the *Cervidæ*, with the exception of the reindeer, are hornless. It may be remarked that the emendation of Bochart on the version of Gen. xlix:21, where for 'Naphthali is a hind let loose, he giveth goodly words,' he, by a small change in the punctuation of the original, proposes to read 'Naphthali is a spreading tree, shooting forth beautiful branches,' restores the text to a consistent meaning, agreeing with the Sept., the Chaldee paraphrase, and the Arabic version. (See HART.)

HINGE (hĭnj), (Heb. פֹּה, *pohth*, an interstice, the female pudenda).

In ancient times in the East heavy doors turned on pivots, which were constructed on the upper and lower corners of one side and inserted in sockets. The socket is probably more especially referred to in 1 Kings vii:50. (See also Prov. xxvi:14.)

HINNOM (hĭn'nom), (Heb. הִנֹּם, *hin-nome'*, perhaps abundant.)

1. An unknown person whose name is given to the "Valley of Hinnom" (Josh. xviii:16; Neh. xi:30); elsewhere (Josh. xv:8; 2 Kings xxiii:10; 2 Chron. xxxiii:6, etc.) called "the valley of the son," or "children of Hinnom."

2. The valley which bounds Jerusalem on the south, below Mount Zion, and which in Scripture is often mentioned in connection with the horrid rites of Moloch, which under idolatrous kings were there celebrated (Josh. xv:8; xviii: 16; Neh. xi:30; Jer. vii:31; xix:2). When Josiah overthrew this idolatry he defiled the valley by casting into it the bones of the dead, the greatest of all pollutions among the Hebrews; and from that time it became the common jakes of Jerusalem, into which all refuse of the city was cast, and where the combustible portions of that refuse were consumed by fire. Hence it came to be regarded as a sort of type of hell, the Gehenna of the New Testament being no other than the name of this valley of Hinnom (Ge-Hinnom); see Mat. v:22, *sq.;* Mark ix:43; Luke vii:5; John iii:6.

The name by which it is now known is *Wâdy Jehennam*, or *Wâdy er Rubeb* (Smith, *Bib. Dict.,* s. v.). (See HADES; JERUSALEM.)

HIP AND THIGH (hĭp and thī), (Heb. שׁוֹק, *shoke*), a proverbial expression for a *great slaughter* (Judg. xv:8), like the Arabic "war in thigh fashion," or the German "cutting arm and leg in two."

HIPPOPOTAMUS (hĭp'pō-pŏt'ȧ-mŭs). (See BEHEMOTH.)

HIRAH (hī'rah), (Heb. חִירָה, *khee-raw'*, splendor), an Adullamite, and friend of Judah (Gen. xxxviii:1, 12; comp. verse 20).

HIRAM (hī'ram), (Heb. חִירָם, *khee-rawm'*, highborn); generally in the Chronicles חוּרָם, *khoorawm'*, "Huram."

1. King of Tyre, who sent an embassy to David after the latter had captured the stronghold of Zion and taken up his residence in Jerusalem. It seems that the sway of this ruler extended over the western slopes of Lebanon; and, when David built himself a palace, Hiram materially assisted the work by sending cedar-wood from Lebanon and able workmen to Jerusalem (2 Sam. v:11; 1 Chron. xiv:1), B. C. about 1055-1044.

2. King of Tyre, son of Abibaal, and grandson of the Hiram who was contemporary with David, in the last years of whose reign he ascended the throne of Tyre. Following his grandfather's example, he sent to Jerusalem an embassy of condolence and congratulation when David died and Solomon succeeded, and contracted with the new king a more intimate alliance than ever before or after existed between a Hebrew king and a foreign prince (1 Kings v:1).

The alliance seems to have been very substantially beneficial to both parties, and without it Solomon would scarcely have been able to realize all the great designs he had in view. In consideration of large quantities of corn, wine, and oil, furnished by Solomon, the king of Tyre agreed to supply from Lebanon the timber required for the temple, to float it along the coast, and deliver it at Joppa, which was the port of Jerusalem (1 Kings v:1, *sq.;* ix:10, *sq.;* 1 Chron. ii:3, *sq.*). The vast commerce of Tyre made gold very plentiful there; and Hiram supplied no less than 500 talents to Solomon for the ornamental works of the temple, and received in return twenty towns in Galilee; which, when he came to inspect them, pleased him so little that he applied to them a name of contempt, and restored them to the Jewish king (2 Chron. viii:2). (See CABUL.) It does not, however, appear that the good understanding between the two kings was broken by this unpleasant circumstance; for it was after this that Hiram suggested, or at least took part in, Solomon's traffic to the Eastern seas—which certainly could not have been undertaken by the Hebrew king without his assistance in providing ships and experienced mariners (1 Kings ix:27; x:11, etc.; 2 Chron. viii:18; ix:10, etc.). B. C. 1007. (See OPHIR; SOLOMON; PHŒNICIANS.)

3. Hiram, or Huram, son of a widow of the tribe of Dan, and of a Tyrian father. He was sent by the king of the same name to execute the principal works of the interior of the temple, and the various utensils required for the sacred services (1 Kings vii:13, 14, 40). It is probable that he was selected for this purpose by the king from among others equally gifted, in the notion that his half Hebrew blood would render him more acceptable at Jerusalem. He is called "Huram" in 2 Chron. ii:13; iv:11, 16; and "Hirom" in the margin of 1 Kings vii:40. (B. C. 1010.)

HIRE (hīr), (Heb. שָׂכָר, *saw-kar'*, wages; hire; reward).

Hire in A. V. is equivalent always to modern *wages*. Thus Gen. xxxi:8, 'The ring-straked shall be thy hire;' Is. xxiii:18, 'And her merchandise and her hire shall be holiness to the Lord' (Delitzsch, 'her gain and her wages become holy unto Jehovah'); Mic. iii:11, 'The heads thereof judge for reward, and the priests thereof teach for hire;' Luke x:7, 'the laborer is worthy of his hire.' Tyndale has the word very much as in the modern use in Mark ii:1, 'And let yt out to hyre unto husbandmen.' The plural 'hires,' now obsolete, occurs once in A. V. (Mic. i:7), 'All the hires thereof shall be burned with fire.'

HIRELING (hīr'lĭng), (Heb. שָׂכִיר, *saw-keer'*; Gr. μισθωτός, *mis-tho-tos'*), a laborer employed on hire for a limited time (Job. vii:1; xiv:6; Mark i:20), as distinguished from one belonging to his master.

"A hireling is a hired servant, and properly carries no suggestion of unfaithfulness. Thus Tyndale, *Works*, i, 146, 'Hereby mayest thou not understand that we obtain the favor of God, and the inheritance of life, through the merits of good works, as hirelings do their wages.' So Rheims has 'hireling' in Luke xv:17, 19, where all the other versions have 'hired servant.'" Hastings' *Bib. Dict.*)

HISS (hĭs), (Heb. שָׁרַק, *shaw-rak'*, to whistle).

This term usually expresses insult and contempt (Job xxvii:23), and mingled wonder and contempt, as by beholders of the ruined temple (1 Kings ix:8; 2 Chron. vii:21).

It is also used in the sense of to *allure*, to *entice*; as a beekeeper, who, by hissing (whistling) to the sound of a flute, induces the bees to come to a hive or settle on a bush or some other object (Is. v:26; vii:18).

HISTORY (hĭs'tŏ-rȳ).

The subject matter contained in the Biblical history is of a wide and most extensive nature. In its greatest length and fullest meaning it comes down from the Creation till near the close of the first century of the Christian era.

The Jewish history contained in the Bible embraces more and less than the history of the Israelites; more, since it begins with the beginning of the earth and narrates with extraordinary brevity events which marked the period terminated by the flood, going on till it introduces us to Abraham, the primogenitor of the Hebrew race; less, since, even with the assistance of the poetical books, its narratives do not come down to a later date than some 400 years before the birth of Christ. The historical materials furnished relating to the Hebrew nation may be divided into three great divisions: 1. The books which are consecrated to the antiquity of the Hebrew nation —the period that elapsed before the era of the judges. These works are the Pentateuch and the book of Joshua, which, according to Ewald (*Geschichte des Volkes Israel*, i, 72), properly constitute only one work, and which may be termed the great book of original documents. 2. The books which describe the times of the judges and the kings up to the first destruction of Jerusalem; that is, Judges, Kings, and Samuel, to which belongs the book of Ruth; 'all these,' says Ewald, 'constitute also, according to their last formation, but one work, which may be called the Great Book of Kings.' 3. The third class comprises the books included under the head of Hagiographa, which are of a much later origin, Chronicles, with Ezra and Nehemiah, forming the great book of general history reaching to the Grecian period. After these books come those which are classed together under the name of Apocrypha, whose use in this country we think unduly neglected. Then the circle of evangelical record begins, which closed within the century that saw it open. Other books found in the Old and New Testaments, which are not properly of a historical character, connect themselves with one or other of these periods, and give important aid to students of sacred history.

(1) Sources of Biblical History. The sources of Biblical history are chiefly the Biblical books themselves. Any attempt to fix the precise value of these sources in a critical point of view would require a volume instead of an article. Whatever hypothesis, however, may eventually be held touching the exact time when these books, or any of them, were put into their actual shape, as also touching the materials out of which they were formed, one thing appears very certain, that (to take an instance) Genesis, the earliest book (probably), contains most indubitable as well as most interesting historical facts; for though the age, the mode of life and the state of culture differ so widely from our own, we cannot do otherwise than feel that it is among men and women, parents and children—beings of like passions with ourselves—and not with mere creations of fancy or fraud, that we converse when we peruse the narratives which this composition has so long preserved. The conviction is much strengthened in the minds of those who, by personal acquaintance with the early profane writers, are able to compare their productions with those of the Hebrews, which were long anterior, and must, had they been of an equally earthly origin, have been at least equally deformed by fable. The sole comparison of the account given in Genesis of the creation of the world with the Cosmogonies of heathen writers, whether Hindoo, Greek or Latin, is enough to assure the impartial reader that a purer, if not a higher, influence presided over the composition of Genesis than that whence proceeded the legends or the philosophies of heathenism; nor is the conclusion in the slightest degree weakened in the writer's mind by any discrepancy which modern science may seem to show as between its own discoveries and the statements in Genesis. The Biblical history, as found in its Biblical sources, has a decided peculiarity and a great recommendation in the fact that we can trace in the Bible more clearly and fully than in connection with any other history, the first crude elements and the early materials out of which all history must be constructed. How far the literature supplied in the Bible may be only a relic of a literary cyclus called into being by the felicitous circumstances and favorable constitution of the great Shemitic family, but which has perished in the lapse of ages, it is now impossible to determine; but had the other portions of this imagined literature been of equal *religious* value with what the Bible offers, there is little risk in affirming that mankind would scarcely have allowed it to be lost.

(2) Other Books Than the Bible. The Bible, however, bears traces that its were not the only books current in the time and country to which it relates; for writing, writers, and books are mentioned without the emphasis and distinction which always accompany new discoveries or peculiar local possessions and as ordinary, well-known and matter-of-course things. And it is certain that we do not possess all the works which were known in the early periods of Israelite history, since in Num. xxi:14 we read of 'the book of the wars of the Lord,' and in Josh. x:13 of 'the book of Jasher.' Without writing, history, properly so called, can have no existence. Under the head WRITING may be traced the early rudiments and progress of that important art; here we merely remark that an acquaintance with it was possessed by the Hebrews at least as early as their Exodus from Egypt—a fact which shows at least the possibility that the age of the Biblical record stands some thousand years or more (see CHRONOLOGY) prior to the earliest Greek historian, Herodotus.

(3) The Bible a Commemorative Book. There is another fact which has an important bearing on the worth and credibility of the Biblical narratives, namely, that the people of which they speak were a *commemorative race,* were, in other words, given to create and preserve memorials of important events. Even in the patriarchal times we find monuments set up in order to commemorate events. Jacob (Gen. xxviii:18) 'set up a pillar' to perpetuate the memory of the divine promise; and that these monuments had a religious import and sanction appears from the statement that 'he poured oil upon the top of the pillar' (see Gen. xxxi:45; Josh. iv:9; 1 Sam. vii: 12; Judg. ix:6). Long-lived trees, such as oak and terebinth, were made use of as remembrancers (Gen. xxxv:4; Josh. xxiv:26). Commemorative names also were given to persons, places, and things; and from the earliest periods it was usual to substitute a new and descriptive for an old name, which may in its origin have been descriptive too (Exod. ii:10; Gen. ii:23; iv:1). Genealogical tables appear, moreover, to have had a very early existence among the people of whom the Bible speaks, being carefully preserved first memoriter, afterward by writing, among family treasures, and thus transmitted from age to age. These, indeed, as might be expected, appear to have been the first beginnings of history—a fact which is illustrated and confirmed by the way in which what we should term a narrative or historical sketch is spoken of in the Bible, that is, as 'the book of the generation' ('of Adam,' Gen. v:1): a mode of speaking which is applied even to the account of the Creation (Gen. ii:4), 'these are the generations of the heavens and the earth when they were created.' The genealogical tables in the Bible (speaking generally) are not only of a very early date, but are free from the mixtures of a theogonical and cosmogonical kind which are found in the early literature of other primitive nations, wearing the appearance of being, so far at least as they go, true and complete lists of individual and family descent (Gen. v:1).

(4) The Use of Poetry. But perhaps the most remarkable fact connected with this subject is the employment of poetry at a very early period to perpetuate a knowledge of historical events. Even in Gen. iv:23, in the case of Lamech, we find poetry thus employed, that is, by the great-grandson of the primitive father. Other instances may be found in Exod. xv; Judge. v; Josh. x:13; 2 Sam. i:18. This early use of poetry, which must be regarded as a considerable step in civilization, implies a still earlier pre-existent culture; confutes the notion that human society began with a period of barbarism; looks favorably on the hypothesis that language had an immediately divine origin; explodes the position that the Hebrews were at first an ignorant, untutored, and unlettered race, and creates a presumption on behalf of their historical literature. Poetry is a good vehicle for the transmission of great leading facts; for, though it may throw over fact a coloring borrowed from the imagination, yet the form in which it appears gives warning that such hues are upon its details, which hues, besides being themselves a species of history, are then easily removed, while the form shuts up and holds in the facts intrusted to the custody of verse, and so transmits them to posterity without additions and without loss. By means of these several forms of commemoration much knowledge would be preserved from generation to generation, and to their existence from the first may be ascribed the brief, but still valuable, notices which the Bible presents of the primitive ages and condition of the world.

(5) Other Sources, Josephus, Etc. Other sources for at least the early Biblical history are comparatively of small value. Josephus has gone over the same periods as the Bible treats of, but obviously had no sources of consequence relating to primitive times which are not open to us, and in regard to those times does little more than add here and there a patch of a legendary or traditional hue which could have been well spared. His Greek and Roman predilections and his apologetical aims detract from his value, while in relation to the early history of his country he can be regarded in no other light than a sort of philosophical interpreter; nor is it till he comes to his own age that he has the value of an independent (not even then an impartial) eyewitness or well-informed reporter. In historical criticism and linguistic knowledge he was very insufficiently furnished. The use of both Josephus and Philo is far more safe for the student of the New Testament than for the expounder of the old.

(6) The Talmud and the Rabbins. The Talmud and the Rabbins afford very little assistance for the early periods, but might probably be made to render more service in behalf of the times of the Savior than has been generally allowed. The illustrations which Lightfoot and Wetstein have drawn from these sources are of great value; and Gfrörer, in his *Jahrhundert des Heils* (Stuttgart, 1838), has made an ample use of the materials they supply in order to draw a picture of the first century, a use which the learned author is at no small pains to justify. The compilations of the Jewish doctors, however, require to be employed with the greatest caution, since the Rabbins were the depositaries, the expounders and the apologists of that corrupt form of the primitive faith and the Mosaic institutions which has been called by the distinctive name of Judaism, which comprised an heterogeneous mass of false and true things, the flood wood of the East as well as truth from the Bible, and which, to a great extent, lies under the express condemnation of Christ himself. How easy it is to propagate fables on their authority, and to do a disservice to the Gospel records, may be learnt from the fact that older writers, in their undue trust of Rabbinical authority, went so far as to maintain that no cock was allowed to be kept in Jerusalem because fowls scratched unclean things out of the earth, though the authority of Scripture (which in the case they refused to admit) is most express and decided (Matt. xxvi:34; Mark xiv: 30, 60, 72). On the credibility of the Rabbins see Ravii *Diss. Phil. Theol. de eo quod Fidei merentur,* etc., in Oelrich's *Collect. Opusc. Hist. Phil. Theol.;* Wolf, *Bibl. Hebr.* ii. 1095; Fabricius, *Bibliog. Antiq.* i:3, 4; Brunsmann, *Diss. de Judaica levitate,* Hafniæ, 1705.

The classic authors betray the grossest ignorance in almost all cases where they treat of the origin and history of the Hebrew people; and even the most serious and generally philosophic writers fall into vulgar errors and unaccountable mistakes as soon as they speak on the subject. What, for instance, can be worse than the blunder or prejudice of Tacitus, under the influence of which he declared that the Jews derived their origin from Mount Ida in Crete; that by the advice of an oracle they had been driven out of Egypt, and that they set up in their temple at Jerusalem as an object of worship the figure of an ass, since an animal of that species had directed them in the wilderness and discovered to them a fountain (Tacit. *Hist.* v:1, 2). Dion Cassius (xxxvii:17) relates similar fables. Plutarch (*Quæst. Sympos.* iv:5) makes the Hebrews pay divine honors to swine, as being their instructors in agriculture, and affirms that they kept the Sabbath and the Feast of Tabernacles in honor of Bacchus. For a collection of these gross misrepresentations, together with a profound and successful inquiry into their origin, and a full exposure of their falsehoods, see articles by Dr. J. G. Müller, *Theologische Studien und Kritiken*, 1843, *viertes Heft.* p. 893.

HITTITES (hĭt′tītes), (Heb. חִתִּי, *khit′tee*).

The fact that the Hittites were unknown to classic history encouraged a certain class of critics in the assertion that there was no truth in the Biblical statements concerning them.

(1) Early Inscriptions. But as soon as the key was found to the hieroglyphs of Egypt and the cuneiforms of Assyria another great people began to emerge from the darkness of secular history. They appeared chiefly as a nation of warriors in constant conflict with the kings around them, and the picture thus presented was

century before Christ, the Hittites are regarded as a formidable power." (Trans. of Soc. Bib. Arch., vol. vii., part 2, p. 261.)

And Mr. Pinches, of the British Museum, has deciphered an inscription which would seem to place the reign of Sargon of Agade or Agane I. about 3800 B. C.

(2) Extent of the Empire. We may estimate the extent of the Hittite Empire from the number of local Hittite names mentioned in the Scriptures and the inscriptions, and also from the vast extent of country over which Hittite inscriptions and sculptures are scattered. In the Egyptian and Assyrian inscriptions there have already been discovered over 300 geographical Hittite names, only a few of which have as yet been identified. We can better realize how much this means when we consider that in the Royal History of England there are only about 133 names of places mentioned in all of England, Scotland and Ireland.

The inscriptions of Egypt and Assyria are comparatively few and fragmentary, and of these few

Monument of a Hittite King, Accompanied by an Inscription in Hittite Hieroglyphics.

in perfect harmony with that found in the Pentateuch. The inscriptions show the Hittite kings to have been rivals of the Pharaohs from the twelfth to the twentieth dynasty. The shock of Egyptian invasion exhausted itself on the frontier cities of Kadesh and Carchemish, and there were still fresh armies and abundance of wealth to enable the Hittite empire to withstand the might of Egypt for a thousand years.

In the British Museum there are many inscribed objects belonging to the library of Assurbani-pal, and some of them are known as the Assyrian Astronomical Tablets. These are the later editions of the clay books which had been prepared for the ancient kings of Babylon. In one of these comparatively modern editions of a much earlier work we find the following statement: "The king of the Hittites lives and on the throne seizes" (*Records of the Past*, i:159). And again we read: "The king of the Hittites plunders and the throne seizes" (Ibid. p. 160).

It is difficult to assign a date to these and other similar documents, but Professor Sayce conjectures that: "Already in the astrological tables of Sargon of Agade or Agane, in the nineteenth

which have come to light many are still unread. They are chiefly concerned with their own national achievements and the glory of conquerors, and yet these stone and clay records preserve for us twice as many names of places in the Hittite empire as are to be found of English geographical names in a thousand pages of our standard geography and history combined.

In the Bible we first meet the Hittites at Hebron, where they are recognized as the rightful owners of the place. Four hundred years later the spies found the sons of Anak in Hebron and the Hittites dwelling in the mountains (Num. xiii:29), whither they had doubtless been driven; and in a parenthetical clause it is stated: "Now Hebron was built seven years before Zoan in Egypt" (Num. xiii:22). This isolated and independent clause, which always seemed out of the way, now comes into prominence and helps us to knit together the scattered fragments of long lost history. Zoan or Tanis was the capital of the Hyksos, invaders and conquerors of Egypt.

According to Mariette one of the Hyksos dynasties was Hittite; and it is proved by an inscription now in the Louvre, which records the destruction of their palaces on the borders of Egypt, that they had once been a settled people in this region.

It would thus appear that, as the Hittites bore down upon Egypt from the north, they occupied the fertile plain of Mamre, and built Hebron seven years before they had secured sufficient foothold in Egypt to found their capital city of Zoan.

When David sent "Joab and the captains of the host" to number the people (2 Sam. xxiv), it is recorded that they came to Gilead, and to the land of Tahtim-hodshi, and this is the Hittite Kadesh on the Orentes, the southern capital of their empire.

The description given in the Book of Joshua (Josh. i:4), which was long thought to be exaggerated, may now be taken as strictly accurate.

In the war with Rameses II., Kheta-sira, the king of the Hittites, had under his command the Dardanians and the Trojans, and ten or more other peoples, either as subjects or allies. It is clear that a mighty host was brought into the field by a voice of command that must be obeyed.

(3) Geographical Position of Hittite Inscriptions. The existence of their inscriptions and sculptures over a very large extent of country bears witness to the wide extent of their empire.

All the inscribed stones in Hamath must have been carved near where they were found, for all but one (the fragment No. H. I.) were very large and could not have been carried from a distance unless at great cost. Even the fragment was large enough to require a camel to carry it, and the Hamathites had not regarded it as of any importance until the attention of scholars gave them an idea that it had a marketable value.

At Jerabis, the ancient Carchemish, on the Euphrates, a number of these inscriptions have been discovered, and the inscribed stones have been obtained for the British Museum.

On the old road from Carchemish and Marash Colonel C. W. Wilson discovered two Hittite inscriptions at Gurum, within the frontiers of Cappadocia. They have been found also far to the north of this point, and in the northwest of Asia Minor.

"That their empire extended," says Dr. Isaac Taylor, "as far as the Euxine and the Ægean, is shown by hieroglyphics and sculptures in the unmistakable style of Hittite art which are scattered over Asia Minor, more especially in Lydia, Lycaonia, Cappadocia, and Cilicia. Scholars are only just beginning to realize the vast extent of their dominion and their important place in primitive history. Until the rise of Assyria they were the most powerful nation of northwestern Asia." (*The Alphabet,* Dr. Isaac Taylor, vol. ii., p. 121.)

(4) Art and Literature. In the Egyptian inscription concerning the great battle the enemy is called "the miserable king of the Hittites," before the battle contest, while afterward he is called "the great king of the Hittites," showing that he won a partial, if not a decided, victory over the Egyptian forces. When the ambassadors of Kheta-sira, "the great king of the Hittites," went down to Egypt to make a treaty with Rameses II they carried with them a silver plate on which the Hittite text of the treaty was engraved in their own language and character. This text has been lost, but a copy of it in hieroglyphics appears on the walls of the temples of Rameses.

This people was well acquainted with silver, and attention has frequently been called to their presence in the vicinity of silver mines. Their bargain with the patriarch Abraham at Hebron

involved the earliest money transaction on record, and the "shekel" referred to in the phrase "current money with the merchant," was doubtless the forerunner of the coin with which we are acquainted. We find among them considerable progress in commerce, law, and civil institutions.

They use silver as the standard of value, balances for weighing it, and a regular recognized form of sale and conveyance.

Professor Sayce says their art was a modification of that of Babylon before the rise of the Assyrian empire. This, somewhat modified by Egypt, was borne by the Hittites throughout Asia Minor. "The art and culture, the deities and rites, which Lydia owed to Babylon, were brought by the hands of the Hittites, and bore upon them a Hittite stamp. This artistic culture and writings were carried by them into Asia Minor, which they overran and subdued." (Sayce, "*Herodotus,*" pp. 426-432).

Their art was characterized by solidity and roundness and work in relief. "The mural crown was a Hittite invention; the animal forms in which their artists especially excelled were frequently combined to form composite creatures, among which may be mentioned the double-headed eagle, afterwards adopted by the Seljukian Sultans. This Hittite art is the source of the peculiar art of Asia Minor, which forms a well-marked element in that of primitive Greece" (Idem. pp. 426-432).

In relation to the science of letters, scholars have long been perplexed by a number of alphabets which existed in different districts of Asia Minor. They were neither Greek nor Phœnician, but they seemed to come from the same source as did the Greek.

Dr. Isaac Taylor recognizes five distinct alphabets—the Lycian, the Carian, the Cappadocian, the Phrygian and the Pamphylian. To these he thinks may be added three more—the Lydian, the Mysian and the Cilician. Inscriptions found by Mr. Hamilton Lang, in Cyprus, supplied the key to the mysterious alphabets of Asia Minor, and they proved to be distantly related even to the whorls discovered by Dr. Schliemann in the lower stratum of Hissarlik.

This and other important discoveries carried the question farther back towards the parent stem, which seems to be recognized by the existence throughout Asia Minor of numerous inscriptions similar to those Hittite records which were found in Hamah.

"These monuments," says Dr. Isaac Taylor, "are those of a people who have been identified with the Hittites of the Old Testament, the Kheta of the Egyptian monuments, the Khattai of the Assyrian records, and the Keteioi of Homer. They were one of the most powerful peoples of the primeval world, their empire extending from the frontier of Egypt to the shores of the Ægean, and, like the Babylonians and the Egyptians, they possessed a culture, an art and a script peculiar to themselves (*The Alphabet,* ii. pp. 115-120).

We learn from the Egyptian records that the Hittites were far in advance of their neighbors in the arts of war as well as of peace. Indeed, they were formidable in making war because they excelled in peaceful pursuits.

(5) Religion. This people, like the Canaanites, imported their gods and goddesses from Babylonia. Wherever the Phœnicians steered their ships and carried their arts and merchandise the rites and worship of Baal and Astarte (see BAAL) accompanied them. In like manner wherever the Hittites extended their empire, there we find under

52

some form the goddess who was called Atargatis (Ashtoreth or Ishtar) at Carchemish.

The Hittite goddess appears in connection with Attys or Sutekh, accompanied by the horrible rites with which Ishtar (see ASHTORETH) and Tammuz (see TAMMUZ) had been honored in Babylon. In the capital of the Hittites we see one of the numerous shrines where Hittite girls were devoted to wickedness in the name of religion. The worship of these deities took many repulsive forms. Devotees surrendered their children to Baal in the flames while the screams of the victims were drowned by trumpet and drum.

(6) Nationality. Who were the Hittites? To what race or people did they belong?

Outside the Bible our two sources of information on this subject are the Hittite names and sculptures.

It is now pretty generally conceded that the language of the Hittites was not Semitic; that is, it was not of the same family as the language spoken in varying dialects by the Jews and other Semitic people.

There are several eminent linguists who believe that the Hittite language was Semitic, and there should be no dogmatism where our certain knowledge is so limited, but with the most careful balancing of the facts the weight of evidence seems to be on the side of the non-Semitic character of this peculiar tongue. This conclusion is supported by the Hittite and also by the Egyptian sculptures.

Captain Conder draws attention to the distinct characteristics of the Hittites and their allies as pictured on the temple at Ibsamboul: "In this picture the Hittites and their allies are represented as distinct races with different kinds of weapons. The one race is bearded, the other beardless, and the Chinese-like appearance of the Hittites is very remarkable" (*Heth and Moab*, p. 22). This would seem to point to a Tartar or Mongolian people. Colonel Sir Charles Wilson, who has recently returned from Asia Minor, says: "The sculptures show that the Hittites did not belong to a Semitic race. The features are rather those of a northern people, and on the temple of Ibsamboul the Hittites have a Scythic character, with shaven head and a single lock of hair on the crown. Hence it would appear from the testimony of the sculptures, as well as of the proper names, that the Hittites were non-Semitic.

(7) Hittites from a Biblical Standpoint. Thus it has been seen that the Biblical statements are fully confirmed by the cumulative evidence of modern discovery.

We find this people among the settled inhabitants of Canaan while as yet Abraham was only a wandering sheikh. They lived in and about Hebron, and Abraham, when he abode in that neighborhood, was treated by them with respect and consideration (Gen. xxiii:3-7, 11, 12).

He obtains his first possession in Canaan by purchasing a grave for Sarah of the sons of Heth (Gen. xxiii). The story as told in Genesis is true in all the formal details which embellish the framework of a shrewd Oriental bargain. "In fact," says Dr. Thomson, "up to the present day, in this very city of Hebron, a purchase thus witnessed is legal, while the best drawn deeds of a modern lawyer, though signed, sealed and attested, would be of no avail without such living witnesses" (*The Land and the Book*, p. 249).

In the Book of Exodus the Hittites had grown in importance. The promised land is described by an enumeration of the peoples who inhabit it, and the Hitties, who are never absent from that enumeration, occupy the place of distinction (Exod. iii:8, 17; xiii:5; xxiii:23).

In the Egyptian hieroglyphics they occupy exactly the same position which is assigned them in the Book of Exodus. They are first in order and first in importance among the peoples in the promised land. (See Rawlinson, *History of Ancient Egypt*, vol. i., p. 111.)

During the weary years spent in Egypt the Israelites were often encouraged by the promise that they should return to the land of the Hittites. Later Jehovah not only promised to send his angel to lead them there, but also declared he would send before them hornets to drive out the Hittites (Exod. xxiii:28). This promise seems to have been largely fulfilled by the devastating border wars between the Pharaohs and the people of Southern Palestine, who were always the first to feel the shock of Egyptian arms. We can trace the march of Seti I on his first campaign, from Khetam (the Etham of the Bible) past Rehoboth to the fortress of Kanaan, which he stormed, and became the subduer of the whole Edomitish Negeb. On the northern side of the great temple of Karnak this conquest is recorded thus: "In the first year of King Seti there took place, by the strong arm of Pharaoh, the annihilation of the hostile Shasu, from the fortress of Khetam of the land of Zalu as far as Kanaan; the king was against them like a fierce lion. They were turned into a heap of corpses. They lay there in blood." (Brugsch's *Egypt Under the Pharaohs*, vol. ii., p. 14.)

In such fierce border encounters the hand of Pharaoh would press heavily upon any Hittite colonies which occupied advance positions. Hence Joshua found the Anakim at Hebron, and the spies found the Amalekites dwelling in the south and the Hittites driven back to the mountains (Num. xiii:29).

(8) Cities Identified. The remains of the Hittite cities have been long buried; but the efforts of Mr. Skene and Mr. George Smith have identified the two chief capitals of the south, Carchemish (to which reference has already been made) and Kadesh; the former on the Euphrates, known as Jerablûs, the latter on the Orontes (see CARCHEMISH; KADESH). These two places were 'Holy Cities,' that is, under the protection of a goddess and wholly devoted to her worship. These 'Holy Cities' were a characteristic peculiar to the Hittite people. Besides being devoted to the goddess, they were places of 'refuge.' The homicide could escape to them, and once within the protection of its deity he was safe from his pursuers and could not be injured or slain. The debtor and political outcast were equally safe.

(9) Hebrew Cities of Refuge. Palestine also contained "cities of refuge." These Hebrew cities of refuge were six in number. One of them was Hebron, once occupied by the Hittites and Amorites. Another was Kedesh, of Galilee, the name of which shows it to have been a 'holy city' like Kadesh. Shechem, too, had been taken from the Amorites by Jacob (Gen. xlviii:22), and the other three cities were in the region long held by the Amorites. These facts might raise the question, as suggested by Mr. Sayce, in *The Story of a Forgotten Empire*, whether these cities had not already been places of refuge long before God enjoined Moses to make them such for the Israelites. (See Sayce, *The Hittites, The Story of a Forgotten Empire*, 1888; *The Mon. and the O. T.*, Ira M. Price.)

(10) Later Biblical Mention. During the history of Israel from the time of Abraham to the captivity, the Hittites are frequently referred to by the sacred writers. Bath-sheba, the wife of Uriah the Hittite (2 Sam. xi:3, 6; 1 Kings ix:20), was the mother of Solomon and a distant ancestress of Christ. In connection with the siege of Samaria, as recorded in 2 Kings vii, we have an important reference to this people. The Israelites, under Jehoram, were hard pressed in their capital by Benhadad of Damascus. Then, according to Elisha's prophecy, deliverance came. "For the Lord made the host of the Syrians to hear the noise of chariots, and a noise of horses, even the noise of a great host; and they said one to another, Lo the king of Israel hath hired against us the kings of the Hittites and the kings of the Egyptians to come upon us. Wherefore they arose and fled in the twilight, and left their tents, and their horses, even their camp as it was, and fled for their life" (2 Kings vii:6, 7).

Usher places the siege of Samaria at about B. C. 892, and Assyriologists agree in fixing the reign of Assur-natsir-pal about B. C. 883-858.

(11) Other Records. Of this king, who added new vigor to the wars against the people of Northern Syria, there are ample records. He levied tribute upon the conquered Hittites. "To Carchemish, in Syria, I directed my steps. The tribute due from the son of Bahiani, swift chariots, horses, silver, tin, * * * I received." (*Records of the Past*, iii:70).

He passed from Carchemish "to Hazazi, the town of Lubarna of the Khatti," and levied tribute.

From these inscriptions and several others it is clear that at the time of the siege of Samaria the Hittites were still a mighty people spread over the north from Carchemish to Lebanon, and so in the time of the siege of Samaria the Hittite chiefs were distinguished among the nations for "their swift chariots, their horses and their engines of war."

The Hittites who appear for the first time in the inscriptions of Sargon I, to whom Mr. Pinches of the British Museum assigns the possible date 3800 B. C., do not disappear from history in the inscriptions until the time of Sargon II, B. C 717.

Lieutenant Conder says: "The veracity of the Old Testament account of the Hittite princes contemporary with Solomon had been deemed as presenting insuperable difficulties, but the indisputable testimony of the granite records of Thothmes and Rameses has left no doubt of the contemporary rule of this powerful race in Northern Syria in the times of the Hebrew Judges and kings" (see *Empire of the Hittites*, by William Wright, D.D., F. R. G. S., 1886, pp. 36-123; *The Hittites*, A. H. Sayce, LL.D., 1888).

(12) A Summary of the names of the individual Hittites mentioned in the Bible as follows is:
Adah (woman), Gen. xxxvi:2.
Ahimelech, 1 Sam. xxvi:6.
Bashemath, accurately Bas'math (woman); possibly a second name of Adah, Gen. xxvi:34.
Beeri (father of Judith, below), Gen. xxvi:34.
Elon (father of Basmath), Gen. xxvi:34.
Ephron, Gen. xxiii:10, 13, 14, etc.
Judith (woman), Gen. xxvi:34.
Uriah, 2 Sam. xi:3, etc.; xxiii:39, etc.
Zohar (father of Ephron), Gen. xxiii:8.
They are all susceptible of interpretation as Hebrew words, which would lead to the belief either that the Hittites spoke a dialect of the Aramaic or Hebrew language, or that the words were Hebraized in their transference to the Bible records.
In addition to the above, Sibbechai, who in the Hebrew text is always denominated a Hushathite,

is by Josephus (*Ant.* vii:12, sec. 2) styled a Hittite (Smith, *Bib. Dict.*).

HIVITES (hī'vītes), (Hebrew always in the form חִוִּי, *hakh-iv-vee'*, "the Hivite").

One of the nations of Canaan, which occupied Palestine before the Israelites (Gen. x:17; 1 Chron. i:15; Exod. iii:8, 17; xxiii:23; Josh. iii:10). They occupied the northern and northeastern part of the country. In Judg. iii:3, it is stated that 'the Hivites dwelt in mount Lebanon, from mount Baal-hermon unto the entering in of Hamath;' and in Josh. xi:3, the Hivites are described as living 'under Hermon in the land of Mizpeh.' The 'cities of the Hivites' are mentioned in 2 Sam. xxiv:7, and, from being associated with Sidon and Tyre, must have been in the northwest. A remnant of the nation still existed in the time of Solomon, who subjected them to a tribute of personal labor, with the remnants of other Canaanitish nations which the Israelites had been unable to expel (1 Kings ix:20). A colony of this tribe was also found in Northern Palestine, occupying the towns of Gideon, Chephirah, Beeroth, and Kirjath-jearim; and these obtained from Joshua a treaty of peace by stratagem (Josh. ix:3-17; xi:19).

The Hivite form of government is not described, but the mention of "our elders and all the inhabitants of our country" (Josh. ix:11) certainly indicates one in which the people had considerable voice, since the sending of an embassy of unconditional peace is one of the highest acts of sovereignty. So Hamor and Shechem "communed with the men of their city" (Gen. xxxiv:20-24), and reasoned, but did not attempt to command.

The scarcity of Hivite names prevents our judging of their language; but it was in all probability like that of the other Canaanite tribes, quite near the Hebrew. It is not probable that they were the same with the KADMONITES (which see), since these, as their name implies, are more likely to have been "children of the East," Bene-kedem; nor with the Avim, since these had been destroyed by the Caphtorim (Rev. W. Haskell, Barnes' *Bib. Dict.*)

HIZKIAH (hiz-kī'ah), (Heb. חִזְקִיָּה, *khiz-kee-yaw'*, strengthened of Jah), an ancestor of Zephaniah the prophet (Zeph. i:1), B. C. before 630.

HIZKIJAH (hiz-kī'jah), (Heb. same as above).
According to the punctuation of the A. V. a man who sealed the covenant of reformation with Ezra and Nehemiah (Neh. x:17). But there is no doubt that the name should be taken with that preceding it, as "Ater-Hizkijah," a name given in the lists of those who returned from Babylon with Zerubbabel (Smith, *Bib. Dict.*). (See HEZEKIAH.)

HOAR (Heb. שֵׂיבָה, *say-baw'*, 1 Kings ii:6; "hoary," Job xli:32; Prov. xvi:31), said of hair, gray. "As *hoor* as an hawethorn." Piers Ploughman.

HOARFROST (hōr'frŏst), (Heb. כְּפוֹר, *kef-ore'*, Exod. xvi:14; Ps. cxlvii:16; Job xxxviii:29,"hoary.") (See FROST.)

HOARY (Heb. כְּפוֹר, *kef-ore'*, Job xxxviii:29), white frost, as covering the ground.

HOBAB (hō'băb), (Heb. חֹבָב, *kho-bawb'*, beloved).
A kinsman of Moses and priest or prince of Midian, a tract of country in Arabia Petræa, on the eastern border of the Red Sea, at no great distance from Mount Sinai. The family of this indi-

vidual seems to have observed the worship of the true God in common with the Hebrews (Exod. xviii:11, 12).

Considerable difficulty has been felt in determining who this person was, as well as his exact relation to Moses; for the word which, in Exod. iii: 1; Num. x:29; Judg. iv:11, is translated *father-in-law*, and in Gen. xix:14, *son-in-law*, is a term of indeterminate signification, denoting simply relationship by marriage; and besides, the transaction which in one place (Exod. xviii:27) is related of Jethro, is in another related of Hobab. (B. C. 1657.) The probability is, that as forty years had elapsed since Moses' connection with this family was formed, his father-in-law (Exod. ii:18) Reuel or Raguel (the same word in the original is used in both places) was dead, or confined to his tent by the infirmities of age, and that the person who visited Moses at the foot of Sinai was his brother-in-law, called Hobab in Num. x:29, Judg. iv:11; Jethro in Exod. iii:1; and קֵינִי in Judg. i:16, which, in chap. iv:11, is rendered improperly 'the Kenite.'

About a year after the Exodus he paid a visit to Moses, while the Hebrew camp was lying in the environs of Sinai, bringing with him Zipporah, Moses' wife, who, together with her two sons, had been left with her family while her husband was absent on his embassy to Pharaoh. The interview was on both sides affectionate, and was celebrated first by the solemn rites of religion, and afterwards by festivities, of which Aaron and the elders of Israel were invited to partake. On the following day, observing Moses incessantly occupied in deciding causes that were submitted to him for judgment, his experienced kinsman remonstrated with him on the speedy exhaustion which a perseverance in such arduous labors would superinduce; and in order to relieve himself, as well as secure a due attention to every case, he urged Moses to appoint a number of subordinate officers to divide with him the duty of the judicial tribunals, with power to decide in all common affairs, while the weightier and more serious matters were reserved to himself. This wise suggestion the Hebrew legislator adopted (Exod. xviii).

When the Hebrews were preparing to decamp from Sinai, the kinsman of Moses announced his intention to return to his own territory; but if he did carry that purpose into execution, it was in opposition to the urgent solicitations of the Jewish leader, who entreated him, for his own advantage, to cast in his lot with the people of God; at all events to continue with them, and afford them the benefit of his thorough acquaintance with the wilderness. 'Leave us not, I pray thee,' said Moses, 'forasmuch as thou knowest how we are to encamp in the wilderness, and thou *mayest be to us instead of eyes;*' which the Septuagint has rendered καὶ ἔσῃ ἐν ἡμῖν πρεσβύτης, — 'and thou shalt be an elder amongst us.' But there can be little doubt that the true meaning is that Hobab might perform the office of a hybeer or guide. (See CARAVAN.)

That Jethro and Reuel (Raguel) were names of the same person seems evident from Exod. ii:18, 21; iii:1. Hobab would, therefore, be the brother-in-law of Moses. When Jethro returned to his home (Exod. xviii:27) Moses prevailed upon Hobab to remain (as seems implied by the absence of any refusal to his second importunity in Num. x:32) and act as guide through the desert; his influence as an Arab chief, his knowledge of the routes, the situation of the wells, the places for fuel, the prognostics of the weather, and the most eligible stations for encamping, rendering him peculiarly qualified to act in that important capacity.

It is true that God was their leader, by the pillar of cloud by day and of fire by night, the advancement or the halting of which regulated their journeys and fixed their encampments. But beyond these general directions the tokens of their heavenly guide did not extend. And as smaller parties were frequently sallying forth from the main body in quest of forage and other necessaries, which human observation or enterprise were sufficient to provide, so Moses discovered his wisdom and good sense in enlisting the aid of a native sheik, who, from his family connection with himself, his powerful influence, and his long experience, promised to render the Israelites most important services.

HOBAH (hō'bah), (Heb. חוֹבָה, *kho-baw'*, hiding place), (Gen. xiv:15), is probably some hollow, between mountains, which effectually secludes those who occupy it.

It lay north of Damascus, and was the place to which Abraham pursued the kings who had plundered Sodom. Perhaps it was the modern Jôbar.

HOD (hŏd), (Heb. הוֹד, *hode*, majesty; splendor; ornament), son of Zophar, descendant of Asher, (1 Chron. vii:37), B. C. before 1017.

HODAIAH (hŏd'a-ī'ah), (Heb. הוֹדַיְוָהוּ, *ho-dah-veh-vaw'hoo*, majesty of Jah), son of Elioënai in the royal line of Judah (1 Chron. iii:24), B. C. about 406.

HODAVIAH (hŏd'a-vī'ah), (Heb. הוֹדַוְיָה, *ho-dav-yaw'*, praise of Jehovah).

1. A head of the half-tribe of Manasseh, east of the Jordan (1 Chron. v:24), B. C. about 720.

2. A Levite who gave his name to a large family (Ezra ii:40), B. C. 536. (See Lord Hervey, *Genealogies*, p. 119.)

3. Son of Hath-sennah, a Benjamite (1 Chron. ix:7), B. C. before 588.

HODESH (hō'desh), (Heb. חֹדֶשׁ, *kho'desh*, a month, new moon or time of the new moon), one of the wives of Shaharaim, in the genealogies of Benjamin (1 Chron. viii:9). Hodesh may have been a second name of one of the wives (ver. 8).

HODEVAH (ho-dē'vah), (Heb. הוֹדְוָה, *ho-dev-aw'*, brightness; ornament of Jehovah), a Levite family which returned with Zerubbabel from captivity (Neh. vii:43). In parallel lists the name is HODAVIAH, 3; and JUDAH (Ezra iii:9).

HODIAH (ho-dī'ah), (Heb. הוֹדִיָּה, *ho-dee-yaw'*, splendor of Jehovah), wife of Ezra, of Judah, and mother of the founders of Keilah and Eshtemoa, (1 Chron. iv:19).

The name is the same as Jehudijah of verse 18 except for the article which the A. V. disregards.

HODIJAH (ho-dī'jah), (Heb. הוֹדִיָּה, *ho-dee-yaw'*, majesty of Jehovah).

1. The name of two Levites in the time of Ezra and Nehemiah. The first is mentioned in Neh. viii:7, and probably ix:5; x:10; the other in Neh. x:13 (B. C. about 410).

2. One of the heads of the people in the time of Ezra and Nehemiah (Neh. x:18). B. C. about 410.

HOG (hŏg), See BOAR; SWINE.

HOGLAH (hŏg'lah), (Heb. חָגְלָה, *khog-law'*, perhaps partridge), third of the four daughters of Zelophehad, for whom the law of inheritance was so altered that a daughter could inherit her father's property if he had no son (Num. xxvi:33; xxvii:1.

xxxvi:11 ; Joshua xvii:3). (See GILEAD AND BASHAN).

HOHAM (hō'ham), (Heb. הֹהָם, *ho-hawm'*, whom Jehovah incites), king of Hebron, one of the five who besieged Gibeon, with Adoni-zedek, and were hanged by Joshua's orders (Josh. x:3). about B. C. 1612.

HOISE (hoiz), (Gr. ἐπαίρω, *ep-ahee'ro*, Acts xxvii:40), to hoist up.

HOLD (hōld), (Heb. מְצוּדָה, *mets-oo-daw'*, fortress, as often rendered), the term especially applied to the lurking places of David (1 Sam. xxii: 4, 5; xxiv:22, etc.)

HOLINESS (hō-lĭ-něs), (Heb. קֹדֶשׁ, *ko'desh*; Gr. ἁγιωσύνη, *hag-ee-o-soo'nay*; in both cases "separation," or "setting apart," holy, from Saxon "halig," "whole," "sound").

(1) **Holiness of God.** By this is meant the purity and rectitude of his nature. It is an *essential* attribute of God, and what is the glory, luster, and harmony of all his other perfections (Ps. xxvii:4; Exod. xv:11). He could not be God without it (Deut. xxxii:4). It is *infinite* and *unbounded;* it cannot be increased or diminished. *Immutable* and *invariable* (Mal. iii:6). God is *originally* holy; he is so of and in himself, and the *author* and *promoter* of all holiness among his creatures. The holiness of God is visible by his *works;* he made all things holy (Gen. i:31). By his *providences,* all which are to promote holiness in the end (Heb. xii:10). By his *grace,* which influences the subjects of it to be holy (Tit. ii:10, 12). By his *word,* which commands it (1 Pet. i:15). By his *ordinances,* which he has appointed for that end (Jer. xliv:4, 5).

"In the absolute sense God alone is holy, and His holiness is the ground of the requirement of holiness in His creatures (1 Pet. i:16). Holiness is the attribute of God, according to which He wills and does only that which is morally good. In other words, it is the perfect harmony of His will with His perfect ethical nature. But the divine holiness is not to be thought of as a mere passive quiescent state. It is an active impulse, a forthgoing energy. In God's holiness, that is, in the expression of His perfect ethical nature, His self-revelation is grounded. Nay, creation itself, as well as redemption, would be inconceivable apart from the divine holiness, the energizing of God's absolutely good will.

"By some theologians holiness and love are identified, more commonly they are sharply distinguished—holiness being regarded as the self-preservative or retributive attribute of God and love as His beneficent self-imparting attribute." (See article on GOD.) (G. B. Stevens, Hastings' *Bib. Dict.*)

(2) **Holiness in Man** is freedom from sin, or the conformity of the heart to God. It does not consist in knowledge, talents, nor outward ceremonies of religion, but hath its seat in the heart, and is the effect of a principle of grace implanted by the Holy Spirit (Eph. ii:8, 10; John iii:v; Rom. vi:22). It is the essence of happiness and the basis of true dignity (Prov. iii:17; iv:8). It will manifest itself by the propriety of our conversation, regularity of our temper, and uniformity of our lives. It is a principle which may be instantaneous in its reception, although progressive in its operation (Prov. iv:18), and absolutely essential to the enjoyment of God here and hereafter (Heb. xii:14). (See SANCTIFICATION.)

(3) **Holy Place, Things, etc.** The Scriptures also ascribe holiness to places (*e. g.,* the Temple,

and the "most holy place therein"). Also to things, as the altars and other accessories of worship. By holiness in such instances is meant "separation" or dedication to holy uses, and of course there is implied no moral quality or inherent sanctity in the objects themselves. They were to be treated with reverence, as should churches and accessories of worship in these days, because of the holiness of God, to whose service they are dedicated. (Dr. E. McChesney, Barnes' *Bib. Dict.*)

HOLON (hō'lon), (Heb. חֹלוֹן or חֹלֹן, *kho-lone'*, sandy).

1. A town in the mountains of Judah (Josh. xv:51) given to the priests (xxi:15). Location is unknown.

2. A city in the plain of Moab upon which judgment was pronounced by Jeremiah (xlviii: 21). Not identified, although named in connection with Jahazah, Dibon, and other known places.

HOLPEN (hōl'p'n), (Heb. זְרֹעָה, *zer-o-aw'*, Ps. lxxxiii:8), helped; Anglo-Saxon helpan.

HOLYDAY (hō'lĭ dā).

1. The rendering of the Heb. חָגַג, *khaw-gag'*, to dance, a festival celebrated by sacred dances (Exod. xxxv:2, and so a public solemnity (Ps. xlii:4).

2. In Col. ii:16 "holyday" is the rendering of the Gr. *heh-or-tay'* (ἑορτή), a feast, and often so translated.

HOLY GHOST (hōly gōst), the third person in the trinity.

1. Scriptural Designations (Heb. רוּם אֱלֹהִים,

roo'akh el-o-heem', spirit of God; or רוּם יְהֹוָה, *roo'-akh yeh-ho-vaw'*, spirit of Jehovah; Gr. τὸ πνεύμα τὸ ἅγιον, *tŏ pnyoo'mah to hag'ee-on*, "the Holy Ghost," or the "Holy Spirit").

(1) Frequently the term is simply "the Spirit," or "the Spirit of the Lord," or "the Spirit of God," or "the Spirit of Jesus Christ" (Matt iii: 16; Luke iii:22; iv:18; Acts v:9; Phil. i:19). (2) He is called "seven Spirits," because of His perfect and diversified fullness of gifts, graces, and operations (Rev. i:4). (3) He is called the "Spirit of God;" His nature is Divine, and He is sent by God to perform His economic operations (2 Chron. xv:1). (4) He is the "Spirit of Christ," as He proceeds from Him as the Son of God, qualifies Him, and rests on Him as Mediator, and is sent by Him to execute the application of our redemption (Rom. viii:9).

2. Theological Statements.

(1) **Procession from the Father and Son.** (a) The orthodox doctrine is, that as Christ is God by an eternal *filiation,* so the Spirit is God by *procession* from the Father and the Son. "And I believe in the Holy Ghost," says the Nicene Creed, "the Lord and Giver of life, who *proceedeth* from the Father and the Son, who, with the Father and the Son together, is worshiped and glorified." And with this agrees the Athanasian Creed, "The Holy Ghost is of the Father and of the Son, neither made, nor created, nor begotten, but *proceeding."* In the articles of the English Church it is thus expressed: "The Holy Ghost, *proceeding* from the Father and the Son, is of one substance, majesty and glory with the Father and the Son, very and eternal God." The Latin Church introduced the term *spiration,* from *spiro,* "to breathe," to denote the manner of this procession; on which Dr. Owen remarks: "As the vital breath of a man has a continual emanation from him, and yet is never separated utterly from

his person, or forsaketh him, so doth the Spirit of the Father and the Son proceed from them by a continual divine emanation, still abiding one with them." On this refined view little can be said which has clear scriptural authority; and yet the very term by which the third Person in the Trinity is designated, *Wind* or *Breath,* may, as to the third Person, be designed, like the term *Son* applied to the second, to convey, though imperfectly, some intimation of that manner of being by which both are distinguished from each other, and from the Father; and it was a remarkable action of our Lord, and one certainly which does not discountenance this idea, that when he imparted the Holy Ghost to his disciples, "He *breathed* on them, and saith unto them, Receive ye the Holy Ghost" (John xx:22). (b) The direct scriptural doctrine rests on such passages as John xv:26; Matt. x:20; 1 Cor. ii:11, 12; John xiv: 26, etc.

(2) Personality and Deity. (a) In establishing the proper personality and deity of the Holy Ghost, the first argument may be drawn from the frequent association, in Scripture, of a Person under that appellation with two other Persons, one of whom, the Father, is by all acknowledged to be Divine; and the ascription to each of them, or to the three in union, of the same acts, titles, and authority, with worship, of the same kind, and, for any distinction that is made, of an equal degree. (b) The manifestation of the existence and divinity of the Holy Spirit may be expected in the law and the prophets, and is, in fact, to be traced there with certainty. The Spirit is represented as an agent in creation, "moving upon the face of the waters," and it forms no objection to the argument, that creation is ascribed to the Father, and also to the Son, but is a great confirmation of it. That creation should be effected by all the three Persons of the Godhead, though acting in different respects, yet so that each should be a Creator, and, therefore, both a Person and a Divine Person, can be explained only by their unity in one essence. On every other hypothesis this scriptural fact is disallowed, and therefore no other hypothesis can be true. (c) If the Spirit of God be a mere influence, then he is not a Creator, distinct from the Father and the Son, because he is not a Person; but this is refuted both by the passage just quoted, and by Ps. xxxiii:6: "By the word of the Lord were the heavens made; and all the host of them by the breath (Heb. *Spirit*) of his mouth." This is further confirmed by Job xxxiii:4: "The Spirit of God hath made me, and the *breath* of the Almighty hath given me life:" where the second clause is obviously exegetic of the former; and the whole text proves that, in the patriarchal age, the followers of the true religion ascribed creation to the Spirit, as well as to the Father; and that one of his appellations was, "the *Breath* of the Almighty." Did such passages stand alone, there might, indeed, be some plausibility in the criticism which resolves them into a personification; but, connected as they are with the whole body of evidence, as to the concurring doctrine of both Testaments, they are inexpugnable. (d) Again: If the personality of the Son and the Spirit be allowed, and yet it is contended that they were but instruments in creation, through whom the creative power of another operated, but which creative power was not possessed by them—on this hypothesis, too, neither the Spirit nor the Son can be said to create, any more than Moses created the serpent into which his rod was turned, and the Scriptures are again contradicted.

(e) To this association of the three Persons in creative acts, may be added a like association in acts of preservation, which has been well called a *continued creation,* and by that term is expressed in the following passage: "These wait all upon thee, that thou mayest give them their meat in due season. Thou hidest thy face, they are troubled: thou takest away their breath, they die, and return to dust: thou sendest forth thy Spirit, they are created; and thou renewest the face of the earth" (Ps. civ:27-30). It is not surely here meant that the Spirit by which the generations of animals are perpetuated is *wind;* and if he be called an attribute, *wisdom, power,* or both united, where do we read of such attributes being "sent," "sent forth from God?"

(3) Office and Work. (1) He is the "Spirit of promise," because promised to men, and he applies the promises of the new covenant to our heart (Eph. i:13). (2) He is the "Spirit of truth;" he is the "true God," and teacheth nothing but truth (John xiv:17). (3) He is a "holy, good, and free Spirit;" being holy and good in himself, he works holiness and goodness in us, of his own sovereign will, and renders us of a noble and benevolent temper (Ps. li:10, 11; cxliii: 10). (4) He is a "Spirit of judgment," counsel, wisdom, and understanding; being infinite in knowledge and wisdom himself, he qualified Christ's manhood, and qualifies his people with wisdom and understanding (Is. xxviii:16; xi:2; Eph. i:17). (5) He is a "Spirit of bondage and fear," when, by the application of the broken law to men's conscience, he fills their mind with great pressure and fear (Rom. viii:15). (6) He is the "Spirit of adoption," that brings us into the family of God, dwells in every one of God's children, and renders them conform to his image (Rom. viii:15). (7) He is the "Spirit of Life in Christ Jesus," as, by uniting men to Christ, he bestows life on them, and by maintaining their fellowship with Christ, he restores, increases, and perfects their spiritual life (Rom. viii:2). (8) He is the "Spirit of Power," and "of faith," and "of love," and "of a sound mind," and "of supplication;" by his almighty power he works faith, love, and sound wisdom in the heart, and he directs and enables to pray and to wait for the answer thereof (Zech. xii:10; Rom. viii:27; 2 Cor. iv:13; 2 Tim. i:7). And the "love of the Spirit," is love of him, or gracious love produced by him (Rom. xv:30). (9) He is the "Spirit of grace" and "of glory;" as, from the fullness of Christ he conveys to the saints their gracious endowments and glorious happiness (Heb. x:29; 1 Pet. iv:14). (10) He is the "Spirit of the living creatures," which is in the wheels, as he actuates angels and ministers, and the church, and the world managed by them (Ezek. i:20). (*Watson; Brown; Buck; Hastings.*)

HOLY GHOST, SIN AGAINST THE. See SIN, 3.

HOLY OF HOLIES. See TABERNACLE; TEMPLE.

HOLY PLACE. See TABERNACLE; TEMPLE.

HOLY SPIRIT. See HOLY GHOST; PARACLETE.

HOMAM (hō'mam), (Heb. הוֹמָם, *ho-mawm'*, destruction), the name of an Edomite (1 Chron. i:39). In Gen. xxxvi:22 it is given HEMAM, incorrectly, Gesenius thinks (*Theo.* p. 385, a).

HOME. See FAMILY; HOUSEHOLD.

HOMEBORN. See SERVICE.

HOMER (hō′mēr), (Heb. חֹמֶר, *kho′mer*, a heap).

A measure for dry substances and liquids. It contained ten baths or ephahs (Ezek. xlv:11, 14), and one hundred omers (Exod. xvi:36). It held about thirty-six pecks, U. S. measure. (See EPHAH; WEIGHTS AND MEASURES.)

HONEST, HONESTY (ŏn′ĕs-tў), (Gr. καλός, *kal-os′*, excellent), "Honest" is generally rendered in the R. V. "honorable" and "seemly." *Sem-not′-ace* (Gr. σεμνότης) has the meaning of *gravity; probity; purity* (1 Pet. ii:12; 1 Tim. ii:2).

These words have greatly deteriorated in the three centuries that lie between us and the issue of A. V. What they mean now we know; then they meant something nearly approaching the meaning of the Latin words from which they come. *Honestus* from *honos*, 'honor,' had two meanings in Latin: (1) 'Regarded with honor,' 'honorable.' (2) 'Bringing honor,' 'becoming,' and those are just the meanings of 'honest' as it is used in A. V. The word had at the time a special, one might almost say technical, meaning when used of women; it meant 'chaste.' Thus in his chapter in *The Profane State* (v. 1, p. 359) on 'The Harlot,' T. Fuller speaks of her crisping and curling and the like, and then adds, 'I must confesse some honest women may go thus, but no whit the honester for going thus.' (Hastings' *Bib. Dict.*)

HONEY (hŭn′ў). In the Scripture there are three words denoting different sweet substances, all of which are rendered by 'honey' in the Authorized Version. These it is necessary to distinguish.

1. יַעַר, *yah′ar*, which only occurs in 1 Sam. xiv:25, 27, 29; Cant. v:1; and denotes the honey of bees and that only.

2. נֹפֶת, *no′feth*, honey that drops, usually associated with the comb, and therefore bee-honey. This occurs in Ps. xix:10; Prov. v:3; xxiv:13; xxvii:7; Cant. iv:11.

3. דְּבַשׁ, *deb-esh′*. This is the most frequent word. It sometimes denotes bee-honey, as in Judg. xiv:8, but more commonly a vegetable honey distilled from trees, and called *manna* by chemists; also the syrup of dates, and even dates themselves. It appears also sometimes to stand as a general term for all kinds of honey.

It is very evident that the land of Canaan abounded in honey. It is indeed described as 'a land flowing with milk and honey' (Exod. iii: 8, etc.); which we apprehend to refer to *all* the sweet substances which the different Hebrew words indicate, as the phrase seems too large to be confined to the honey of bees alone. Yet the great number of bees in Palestine has been noticed by many travelers; and they were doubtless still more common in ancient times when the soil was under more general cultivation.

The wild honey, which, with locusts, formed the diet of John the Baptist, was probably the vegetable honey. (See MANNA.)

Honey was not permitted to be offered on the altar (Lev. ii:11). As it is coupled with leaven in this prohibition, it would seem to amount to an interdiction of things sour and sweet. Aben Ezra and others allege that it was because honey partook of the fermenting nature of leaven, and when burnt yielded an unpleasant smell—qualities incompatible with offerings made by fire of a sweet savor unto the Lord. But Maimonides and others think it was for the purpose of making a difference between the religious customs of the Jews and the heathen, in whose offerings honey

was much employed. The first-fruits of honey were, however, to be presented, as these were destined for the support of the priests, and not to be offered upon the altar.

The remarkable incident related in 1 Sam. xiv: 24-32, requires to be here noticed. Jonathan and his party coming to the wood, find honey dropping from the trees to the ground, and the prince extends his rod to the honeycomb to taste the honey. On this the present writer is unable to add anything to what is said by Kitto (*Pictorial Bible*, in loc.), which is to the following effect: First, we are told that the honey was on the ground, then that it dropped, and lastly, that Jonathan put his rod into the honeycomb. From all this it is clear that the honey was bee-honey, and that honeycombs were above in the trees; from which honey dropped upon the ground; but it was not clear whether Jonathan put his rod into a honeycomb that was in the trees or shrubs, or into one that had fallen to the ground, or that had been formed there.

Where wild bees are abundant they form their combs in any convenient place that offers, particularly in cavities or even on the branches of trees; nor are they so nice as is commonly supposed in the choice of situations. In India particularly, and in the Indian islands, the forests often swarm with bees.

We have good reason to conclude, from many allusions in Scripture, that this was also, to a considerable extent, the case formerly in Palestine.

The woods on the western coast of Africa, between Cape Blanco and Sierra Leone, and particularly near the Gambia, are full of bees, to which the negroes formerly, if they do not now, paid considerable attention for the sake of the wax. They had bee-hives, like baskets, made of reeds and sedge, and hung on the out-boughs of the trees, which the bees easily appropriated for the purpose of forming their combs in them. In some parts these hives were so thickly placed that at a distance they looked like fruit. As to the other supposition, that the honeycomb had been formed on the ground, we think the context rather bears against it; but the circumstance is not in itself unlikely, or incompatible with the habits of wild bees. For want of a better resource they sometimes form their honey in any tolerably convenient spot they can find in the ground, such as small hollows or even holes formed by animals.*

Figurative. (1) Whatever is sweet, delightful, and healing is likened to "*honey;*" as the word of God (Ps. xix:10; cxix:103); the prayers, praises, and edifying talk of the saints— Christ's gospel truths, and his people's graces, and the knowledge of wisdom (Prov. xxiv:13). (2)

*EDITOR'S NOTE:—A distinction should be made, however, between different sorts of bees called wild. The true *Apis mellifica*, the kind whose culture in Italy is described by Vergil in the third book of the *Georgics*, and which has been appropriated by mankind from time immemorial, generally sends forth a swarm from each hive at least once a year. The bee-keeper, if on his guard, captures this swarm and gives it a hive. But swarms escape from man, and following their nature make their homes in hollow trees, in clefts in rocks, in under-roof spaces in houses, in short, in any place that is hive-like to which they may first come. These, although called wild, are identical in habit with their kindred under human care. They *never* occupy holes in the ground. On the other hand, the various species of *Bombus*, familiarly known as the humble-bee or bumble-bee, make their nests on the ground, in clumps of weeds, in wood-piles, or under the surface of the ground. They never make very large communities, nor accumulate great stores of honey. Their cells are large, as is the bee, but few in number, since they lay up nothing for winter. Only the mother-bees of the *Bombus* hibernate, the males and workers all perishing; but of the *Apis*, the mother-bee or queen (Vergil called her the king) and many workers survive; hence their habit of storing honey in numerous combs for winter use. S. W.

The lips of harlots drop as a *"honeycomb,"* and their mouth is smoother than oil; their speech is soft, flattering, and enticing (Prov. v:3). (3) The full soul loatheth the *"honeycomb;"* but to the hungry even bitter things are pleasant; persons full of goodness in their own conceit, or full of worldly cares, loathe the sweetest promises and blessings of God; but such as are sensible of their wants and unworthiness are glad to obtain the very least of God's mercies (Prov. xxvii:7).

HONORABLE (ŏn'ēr-à-b'l), (Gr. ἔντιμος, *en'tee-mos,* Luke xiv:8), having rank in society.

HOOD (hŏŏd), (Heb. צָנִיף, *tsaw-neef',* Is. iii:23). See HEADDRESS.

HOOF (hŏŏf), (Heb. פַּרְסָה, *par-saw',* to split; divide), the cleft foot of neat cattle (Exod. x:26; Lev. xi:3, etc.), and also of the horse, though not cloven (Is. v:28; Jer. xlvii:3). The parting of the hoof is one of the main distinctions between clean and unclean animals.

HOOK, HOOKS (hŏŏks).

1. *Khawkh* (Heb. חָח, literally, thorn), a ring, such as we place in the nose of a bull to lead him (2 Kings xix:28; Is. xxxvii:29).

2. A peg, or pin, upon which the curtains were hung in the tabernacle (See TABERNACLE).

3. A vine dresser's pruning hook (Is. ii:4; xviii:5; Mic. iv:3; Joel iii:10).

The passages in Exod. xxvi:32, 37; xxxviii:19, 'hooks,' the Sept. and Jerome seem to have understood to mean the *capitals of the pillars;* and it has been urged that this is more likely to be the meaning than *hooks,* especially as 1775 shekels of silver were used in making these *capitals,* for the pillars, overlaying the chapiters, and filleting them (ch. xxxviii:28) ; and that the *hooks* are really the *taches* of Exod. xxvi:6, 11, 33, 35; xxxix:33; (comp. Exod. xxvii:10, 11 ; xxxviii:17, 19) ; from a comparison of these two latter passages it would seem that these hooks, or rather *tenters,* rose out of the chapiters or heads of the pillars.

In the allusions in Exod. xxvii:3; 1 Sam. ii:13, 14, and elsewhere, we have evidently in the first passage, a trident 'of three teeth,' a kind of fork, etc., for turning the sacrifices on the fire, and for collecting fragments, etc.

In Ezek. xl:43, we have 'hooks,' which Gesenius explains as meaning broad hooks or large pegs in the courts of the Temple, where the sacrificial victims were fastened to be flayed; our translators give in the margin 'end-irons, or the two hearthstones.'

Dr. Lightfoot, in his chapter on 'The Altar, the Rings, and the Laver,' observes : 'On the north side of the altar were six orders of rings, each of which contained six, at which they killed the sacrifices. Near by were *low pillars* set up, upon which were laid overthwart beams of cedar; on these were fastened rows of *hooks,* on which the sacrifices were hung; and they were flayed on marble tables, which were between these pillars' (See verses 41, 42; *Works,* vol. 11, ch. xxxiv, Lond. 1684-5-6). J. F. D.

Figurative. The passage in 2 Kings xix:28 reads : 'I will put my hook in thy nose.' Sept. θήσω τὰ ἄγκιστρά μου ἐν τοῖς μυκτῆρσί σου; Vulg. *circulum in naribus tuis.* In the parallel passage (Is. xxxvii:29) the Sept. reads, 'I will put my *muzzle,* halter, or noose,' etc. Jehovah here intimates his absolute control over Sennacherib, by an allusion to the practice of leading buffaloes, camels, dromedaries, etc., by means of a cord, or of a cord attached to a *ring,* passed through the nostrils (Shaw's *Travels,* pp. 167, 168, 2d ed.) ; Job xli:1, 2, 'Canst thou draw out Leviathan with a hook? or *his* tongue with a cord which thou lettest down. Canst thou place a reed-cord (*agmon*) in his nose, or bore through his cheek with a thorn? (*clasp,* or possibly bracelet, etc.) In Ezek. xxix:4, the statement is made, 'I will put my hooks on thy jaws,' etc., and 'I will *cause thee to come up out of the midst of thy rivers.'* Here the prophet foretells the destruction of Pharaoh king of Egypt, by allusions to the destruction, possibly, of a crocodile, the symbol of Egypt. (See LEVIATHAN.)

HOPE, the rendering of several Hebrew and Greek words—among these are:

1. *Beh'takh* (Heb. בֶּטַח, *safety*) means both the fact, *security,* and the feeling, *trust* (Ps. xvi:9; xxii:9, etc.).

2. *Keh'sel* (Heb. כֶּסֶל, *fatness*), confidence sometimes unwisely entertained (Job viii:14; xxxi:24, etc.), but not always (Ps. lxxviii:7).

3. *Mib-tawkh'* (Heb. מִבְטָח, *refuge*), firm and certain hope (Prov. xxii:19, A. V. "trust") ; sometimes figuratively of a person or thing in which confidence is placed (Job viii:14, A. V. "trust;" Ps. xlii:5; lxxi:5, etc.).

4. *El-pece'* (Gr. ἐλπίς) denotes favorable expectation in the New Testament.

5. In general hope may be defined as the desire of some good, attended with the possibility, at least, of obtaining it; and is enlivened with joy, greater or less, according to the probability there is of possessing the object of our hope. Scarce any passion seems to be more natural to man than *hope,* and, considering the many troubles he is encompassed with, none is more necessary; for life, void of all hope, would be a heavy and spiritless thing, very little desirable, perhaps hardly to be borne; whereas hope infuses strength into the mind, and, by so doing, lessens the burdens of life. If our condition be not the best in the world, yet we hope it will be better, and this helps us to support it with patience. The hope of the Christian is an expectation of all necessary good both in time and eternity, founded on the promises, relations, and perfections of God, and on the offices, righteousness, and intercession of Christ. It is a compound of desire, expectation, patience, and joy, (Rom. viii:24, 25). It may be considered, 1. *As pure* (1 John iii:2, 3), as it is resident in that heart which is cleansed from sin. 2. *As good* (2 Thess. ii:16, in distinction from the hope of the hypocrite) as deriving its origin from God, and centering in him. 3. It is called *lively* (1 Pet. i:3) as it proceeds from spiritual life, and renders one active and lively in good works. 4. It is *courageous* (Rom. v:5; 1 Thess. v:8) because it excites fortitude in all the troubles of life, and yields support in the hour of death (Prov. xiv:32). 5. *Sure* (Heb. vi:19) because it will not disappoint us, and is fixed on a sure foundation. 6. *Joyful* (Rom. v:2) as it produces the greatest felicity in the anticipation of complete deliverance from all evil.

HOPHNI (hŏph'nī) **and PHINEHAS** (Heb. חָפְנִי, *chof-nee',* a fighter; one strong), the sons of Eli, whose misconduct in the priesthood (as described in 1 Sam. ii:12-17) brought down that doom of ruin and degradation upon the house of Eli which formed the first divine communication through the young Samuel (1 Sam. iii). Hophni and Phinehas were slain in the battle in which the ark of God was taken by the Philistines, B. C. 1141 (1 Sam. iv:11). (See ELI.)

HOPHRA (hŏph'rà), (Heb. חָפְרַע *khoph-ra'*, Pharaoh-hophra), king of Egypt in the time of Zedekiah, king of Judah, and of Nebuchadnezzar, king of Babylon.

He formed alliance with the former against the latter, and his advance with an Egyptian army constrained the Chaldæans to raise the siege of Jerusalem (Jer. xxxvii:5); but they soon returned and took and destroyed the city. This momentary aid, and the danger of placing reliance on the protection of Hophra, led Ezekiel to compare the Egyptians to a broken reed, which was to pierce the hand of him that leaned upon it (Ezek. xxix: 6, 7). This alliance was, however, disapproved by God; and Jeremiah was authorized to deliver the prophecy contained in his 44th chapter, which con-

1. A mountain in Arabia Petræa, on the confines of Idumæa, and forming part of the mountain of Seir or Edom. It is mentioned in Scripture in connection with the circumstances recorded in Num. xx:22-29; xxxiii:37, 41. The Israelites were encamped before it, when Aaron was summoned to its top to die there, in the presence of his brother and son, who alone witnessed his final departure. (See AARON.)

(1) Location. The mountain now identified with Mount Hor is the most conspicuous in the whole range of Mount Seir, and at this day bears the name of Mount Aaron (Jebel Haroun). It is in N. lat. 30 deg. 18 min., E. long. 35 deg. 33 min. about mid-way between the Dead Sea and the Ælanitic Gulf. It may be open to question if this is really the Mount Hor on which Aaron died, see-

The Summit of Mount Hor.

cludes with a prediction of Hophra's death and the subjugation of his country by the Chaldæans (B. C. 588).

This Pharaoh-hophra is identified with the Apries or Vaphres of ancient authors, and he may be the Psamatik III. of the monuments. Under this identification we may conclude that his wars with the Syrians and Cyrenæans prevented him from affording any great assistance to Zedekiah. Ezekiel xxix:3 speaks of this king as 'the great dragon that lieth in the midst of the rivers, which hath said, my river is mine own, and I have made it for myself.' His overthrow and subsequent captivity and death are foretold with remarkable precision by Jeremiah (xliv:30). This was brought about by a revolt of the troops, who placed Amasis at their head, and after various conflicts took Apries prisoner. He was for a time kept in easy captivity by Amasis, who wished to spare his life; but he was at length constrained to give him up to the vengeance of his enemies, by whom he was strangled (Herod. ii:169; Wilkinson, *Anc. Egyptians,* i:168, 182).

HOR, MOUNT (hôr), (Heb. הֹר הָהָר *hore haw-hawr'*, "mountain, the mountain," i. e. the mountain of mountains), the name of two mountains.

ing that the whole range of Seir was anciently called by that name; yet from its height and the conspicuous manner in which it rises among the surrounding rocks, it seems not unlikely to have been the chosen scene of the high-priest's death (Kinnear, p. 127). To this may be added that Josephus affirms Mount Hor to have been near Petra; and near *that* place there is certainly no mountain which can contest the distinction with the one now in view. The base of the highest pinnacle of this mountain is in fact but a little removed from the skirts of the city to the westward. Much juniper grows on the mountain, almost to the very summit, and many flowering plants. On the top there is an overhanging shelf in the rock which forms a sort of cavern. The tomb itself is enclosed in a small building, differing not at all in external form and appearance from those of Mahommedan saints common throughout every province of Turkey. It has probably been rebuilt at no remote period: some small columns are bedded in the walls, and some fragments of granite and slabs of white marble are scattered about. The door is near the southwest angle, within which a constructed tomb, with a pall thrown over it, presents itself immediately upon entering: it is patched together out of fragments of stone and marble that have made part of other fabrics.

Not far from the northwest angle is a passage, descending by steps to a vault or grotto beneath. The roof is covered, but the whole is rude, ill-fashioned, and quite dark. Towards the further end of this dark vault are the two corresponding leaves of an iron grating, which formerly prevented all nearer approach to the tomb; they have, however, been thrown down.

(2) The View. The view from the summit of the edifice is extremely extensive in every direction, and the eye rests on few objects which it can clearly distinguish to give a name to, although an excellent idea is obtained of the general face and features of the country. The chain of Idumæan mountains which forms the western shore of the Dead Sea seems to run on to the southward, though losing considerably in height. They appear in this point of view barren and desolate. Below them is spread out a white sandy plain, seamed with the beds of occasional torrents, and presenting much the same features as the most desert parts of the Ghor.

(3) Geology. "Mount Hor is formed of reddish sandstone and conglomerate ('Nubian sandstone' of Russegger) of Cretaceous age; the beds rising in a precipitous wall of natural masonry tier above tier, and presenting a bold front towards the west. These huge beds of sandstone compose the upper part of the ridge to a depth of about a thousand feet from the summit, where they rest on a solid foundation of granite and porphyry of great geological antiquity, associated with which, in some way not very clear, are masses of agglomerate, beds of ash and dykes of igneous rock, all of volcanic origin, but of an age anterior to the Cretaceous sandstone. This latter formation dips towards the east, and gradually descends in the direction of the Wady Musa, where it forms the cliffs which surround the city of Petra. Along the flanks of the escarpment of the Arabian Desert to the eastward the sandstone formation passes below the white marls and limestones of Upper Cretaceous age, which form the surface of the plain at a level of over 5,000 feet above the sea." (E. Hall, Hastings' *Bib. Dict.*)

2. A mountain named only in Num. xxxiv:7, 8, as one of the marks in the northern boundary of the land of Promise. Its identification is difficult. The Mediterranean was the western boundary; the first point was Mount Hor, and the second "the entrance of Hamath." If Dr. Porter's identification of the latter with the pass at *Kalat el-Husn*, close to Hums, is correct, then Mount Hor can be nothing else than the great chain of Lebanon itself. (Barnes, *Bib. Dict.*) "It is so clearly the natural northern boundary of the country, that there seems no reason to doubt that the whole range is intended by the term Hor." (Smith, *Bib. Dict., s. v.*)

HORAM (hō'ram), (Heb. הֹרָם, *ho-rawm'*, lofty), a king of Gezer, who, assisting the king of Lachish, was defeated and his country ravaged (Josh. x:33), B. C. 1618.

HOREB (hō'reb), (Heb. חֹרֵב, *kho-rabe'*, desert).

1. A mountain or range frequently mentioned in Scripture. The special application of Horeb and Sinai in the Old Testament has been much discussed. Robinson and Hengstenberg think that Horeb is the name for the whole range, Sinai for a particular peak; Gesenius and others hold precisely the opposite view. Stanley suggests that there is more a distinction of usage than of place.

(1) In Leviticus and Numbers, Sinai is exclusively used of the scene of the giving of the Law. (2) In Deuteronomy, Horeb is substituted for Sinai. (3) In the Psalms the two are used indifferently. See *Sinai and Palestine*, p. 31. The Arabs now apply the name *Jebel et-Tur* to the whole central granite region, while the peaks of which it is composed are called by various names. The mountain of Sinai and its wilderness are distinguished as the theater of events that took place in the district of Horeb, and the whole of Horeb is called "the mountain of God" (Exod. iii:1, 12; iv:27; xvii:6; xviii:5; xxxiii:6. Hence, sometimes "Sinai" alone is spoken of (Exod. xix:11, 19, 23; xxiv:16; xxxi:18; xxxiv:29, 32; Lev. vii:38; xxv:1; xxvi:46; xxvii:34; Num. i:1; iii:1, 14; xxxiii:15. But frequently "Horeb" alone is named, and the same events are spoken of as occurring on Horeb which are described as taking place on Sinai (Deut. i:2, 6, 19; iv:10, 15; v:2; ix:8; xviii:16; xxix:1). Later sacred writers employ both names; *e. g.*, "Horeb" (1 Kings viii:9; xix:8; 2 Chron. v:10; Ps. cvi:19; Mal. iv:4; "Sinai," Judg. v:5; Ps. lxviii:8, 17).

2. In the New Testament, "Sinai" became a general name, as at the present day (Acts vii:30, 38; Gal. iv:24, 25). In more modern times, and ever since the Crusades, the application of the names Sinai and Horeb to the particular mountains or peaks has varied greatly among travelers. The range of Horeb spreads over an extensive field, and may be divided into two groups, exhibiting rugged and venerable mountains of dark granite, stern, naked, splintered peaks and ridges, some of them of indescribable grandeur, rising in frowning majesty high above the general level of the range. The following heights of several peaks are given by the British Ordnance Survey: Jebel Musa, 7,375 feet; Jebel Serbal, 6,735 feet; Jebel Katherin, 8,537 feet; Um Shaumer, 8,450 feet. (Schaff, *Bib. Dict.*) (See SINAI).

HOREM (hō'rem), (Heb. חֳרֵם, *khor-ame'*, devoted), one of the fortified towns of Naphtali (Josh. xix:38). Van de Velde identifies it with *Hurah*. Other authorities fail to concur with him.

HOR-HAGIDGAD (hôr'ha-gĭd'găd), (Hebrew, חֹר הַגִּדְגָּד, *khore hag-ghid-gawd'*, hole of the cleft), the thirty-third encampment of the Israelites during their wandering (Num. xxxiii:32, 33). (See WANDERING, THE.)

HORI (hō'rī), (Heb. חֹרִי, or חוֹרִי, *kho-ree'*, cave dweller).

1. Son of Lotan, the son of Seir, and brother of Hemam (Gen. xxxvi:22; 1 Chron. i:39), B. C. about 1964.

2. Gen. xxxvi:30. In the original "the Horite."

3. Father of Shaphat, who represented the tribe of Simeon among the spies sent up to Canaan by Moses (Num. xiii:5), B. C. before 1657.

HORIMS (hō'rimz), (Deut. ii:12, 22). See HORITE.

HORITE (hō'rīte), (Heb. חֹרִי, *kho-ree'*, cave dweller), A. V. sometimes Hori, Horims.

The predecessors of the Edomites in the country of Seir. They were there as early as the time of Abraham (Gen. xiv:6). Jehovah destroyed them before the sons of Esau, and gave the latter their country (Deut. ii:12, 22). There was, however, such a mingling of the family of Esau and his Horite (in Gen. xxxvi:2 read *Horite* for *Hivite*) connections, that the Horite name and descent was preserved (Gen. xxxvi, especially verses 20, 21, 29-30).

The name Horite is supposed to mean 'cave-dweller' (see Driver, *Deut.* p. 38). On the theory that the Horites were *rephaim,* this fact is of interest in its bearing on the character of the *rephaite* civilization; but they did not always remain cave dwellers. (W. J. Beecher, Hastings' *Bib. Dict.*)

Sayce (*High. Crit.,* p. 203) thinks it better to connect the name with a root signifying "white," and considers the Horites as the representatives of a white race whom their neighbors contrasted with the "red"-skinned Edomites. In such a case they would have been members of the Amorite stock. They were the aboriginal inhabitants of Mount Seir (Gen. xiv:6) from which they were driven by the descendants of Esau (Gen. xiv:6; xxxvi:20, 21, 29; Deut. ii:12, 22).

HORMAH (hôr'mah), (Heb. הׇרְמׇה,*khawr-maw'*, devoted to destruction), a city taken from the Canaanites by Judah and Simeon, (Judg. i:17; Num. xxi:3; Josh. xix:4, 1 Chron. iv:30), and originally called Zephath. It was reduced by Joshua (Josh. xii:14; xv:30; 1 Sam. xxx:30).

HORN (hôrn), (Heb. קֶרֶן, *keh'ren;* Gr. κέρας, *horn*).

Its primary use indicates defense in the case of horned animals (whence Anacreon's Φύσις κέρατα ταύροις, *nature gives horns to bulls*), came to acquire several derivative meanings, some of which are connected with the illustration and right understanding of holy writ. As horns are hollow and easily polished, they have in ancient and modern times been used for drinking vessels and for military purposes; and as they are the chief source of strength for attack and defense with the animals to which God has given them, they serve in Scripture as emblems of power, dominion, glory, and fierceness (Dan. viii:5, 9; 1 Sam. xvi: 1, 13; 1 Kings i:39; Josh. vi:4, 5; 1 Sam. ii:1; Ps. lxxv:5, 10; Jer. xlviii:25; Ezek. xxix:21; Amos vi:13). Hence to defile the horn in the dust (Job xvi:15), is to lower and degrade oneself, and, on the contrary, to lift up, to exalt the horn (Ps. lxxv:4; lxxxix:17; cxlviii:14), is poetically to raise oneself to eminent honor or prosperity, to bear oneself proudly.

In the East, at present, horns are used as an ornament for the head, and as a token of eminent

Ornamental Horns of Modern Asiatics.

rank. (Rosenmüller, *Morg.* iv. 85). The women among the Druses on Mount Lebanon wear on their heads silver horns of native make, 'which are the distinguishing badge of wifehood' (Bowring's *Report on Syria,* p. 8).

By an easy transition, horn came to denote an elevation or hill (Is. v:1); in Switzerland mountains still bear this name, thus, Schreckhorn, Buchhorn.

The altar of burnt-offerings (Exod. xxvii:2) and the altar of incense (Exod. xxx:2), had each at the four corners four horns of shittim-wood, the first being overlaid with brass, the second with gold (Exod. xxxvii:25; xxxviii:2; Jer. xvii:1; Amos iii:14). Upon the horns of the altar of burnt-offerings was to be smeared with the finger the blood of the slain bullock (Exod. xxix:12; Lev. iv:7-18; viii:15; ix:9; xvi:18; Ezek. xliii:20). By laying hold of these horns of the altar of burnt-offering the criminal found an asylum and safety (1 Kings i:50; ii:28). These horns are said to have served as a means for binding the animal destined for sacrifice (Ps. cxviii:27); but this use Winer (*Handwörterb.*) denies, asserting that they did not and could not answer for such a purpose.   J. R. B.

The custom of the Druse women of wearing horns seems not to have been referred to in the Scripture. So remarkable an article of dress, had it been in existence, would in all probability have been noticed by many authors who have entered so minutely into such matters. These horns consisted at first of an apparatus designed to finish off the headdress so as to raise the veil a little from the face, and from small beginnings have developed to their present enormous size. Sometimes they are made of pasteboard, of tin, silver, and among the wealthy of gold. The day for these preposterous appendages is about over. After the wars between the Maronites and the Druses (A. D. 1841 and 1845), the Maronite clergy thundered their excommunications against them, and very few Christians now wear them (Thomson, *Land and Book,* i, 101, 102).

Hair of South Africans Ornamented with Buffalo Horns.

Figurative. **1.** As cattle with their horns push their enemies, and defend themselves, horns are the symbol of power and authority. *Joseph's horn* resembled the horn of the unicorn; the power and dominion of his posterity, in the tribes of Manasseh and Ephraim, were vastly great (Deut. xxiii:17).

2. *Wicked men lift up the horn,* when they arrogantly boast of their power and authority, and threaten to destroy others; and *their horns are cut off* when their power and authority are taken from them (Ps. lxxv:4, 10; Jer. xlviii:25).

3. *Hannah's horn was exalted* when God highly honored her and gave her a child to be ruler over Israel (1 Sam. ii:1).

4. *David's horn was exalted* as the horn of the unicorn, when his kingdom was exalted to great honor and his authority was established; and when his soul was eminently advanced in grace and comfort (Ps. xcii:10).

5. David's being *anointed* with a *horn* full of oil, when Saul was anointed with a *vial* of oil, might mark the abundance of gifts, and the stability of government in the one above the other (1 Sam. x:1; xvi:1).

6. *God is the horn of his people's salvation;* by his power and authority he protects and saves them, and thrusts and destroys their enemies.

7. The *horns of the altar* represented Christ's authority, and ability to save sinners from every end of the earth; and, in allusion hereto, he is called a *horn of salvation* (1 Kings ii :28; Luke i :69) ; and his having *seven horns,* denotes the perfection of his power and authority (Rev. v :6).

8. The *horns* coming out of God's hand, in which was the *hiding* of his power, are the rays of the glorious brightness that attended him at Sinai, and the mighty displays of his power, in which his might was nevertheless but very partially displayed (Hab. iii :4).

9. *Horns* also signify kings and kingdoms (Dan. viii).

10. Antichrist's *two horns* as a lamb may denote his civil and ecclesiastic power (Rev. xiii :11).

11. The *four horns* that scattered Judah were their enemies from every place, particularly the Ammonites, Arabs, Samaritans, Philistines, and Syro-Grecians (Zech. i :21).

HORNET, WASP (hôr'nĕt, wŏsp), (Heb. צִרְעָה, *tsir-aw'*, stinging, Exod. xxiii:28; Deut. vii:20, Sept. τὰς σφηκίας, *hornets*; Vulg. *crabrones;* Josh. xxiv:12, τὴν σφηκίαν, *hornet, crabronem;* Wisd. *Sol.* xii:8, σφῆκας, *vespas,* 'wasps').

It being upon the whole most probable that 'the hornet' is the true rendering in these passages of Scripture, the only further question which remains is, whether the word is to be taken as literally meaning this well-known and terrific insect, or whether it is to be understood in a metaphorical and figurative sense for diseases, supernatural terror, etc., by which Jehovah 'drove out the Hivites, Canaanites, and Hittites from before Israel.' Among the moderns, Michaelis has defended the figurative sense. In addition to other reasons for it, he doubts whether the expulsion of the Canaanites *could* be effected by swarms of σφηκίαι, and derives the Hebrew from a root signifying 'scourges,' 'plagues,' *scutica, plagæ,* etc. (*Suppl. ad Lexic. Hebr.* vi, 2154). In favor of the possibility of such an event it is observed, that Ælian relates that the Phaselitæ were actually driven from their locality by such means (*Hist. Anim.* ix :28), and Bochart has shown that these Phaselitæ were a *Phœnician* people (ut supra, p. 412). Even Rosenmüller himself adopts the figurative sense in his *Scholia* on Exod. xxiii :28; but on Josh. xxiv :12 he retracts that opinion, and amply refutes it. His reasonings and refutations have been adopted by numerous writers (among others see Paxton's *Illustrations of Scripture,* i. 303, etc.; Edin. 1819).

Figurative. However, the word "hornet," in Exod. xxiii :28, is parallel with "fear" in verse 27, and similar expressions, such as "to chase as the bees do," are undoubtedly used metaphorically (Deut. i:44; Ps. cxviii:12). It is therefore reasonable to regard this word as expressing by a vivid image the fear which Jehovah would inspire in the enemy of Israel, as declared in Deut. ii :25; Josh. ii :11.

HORONAIM (hŏr'o-nā'im), (Heb. חֹרֹנַיִם, *kho-ro-nah'yim,* double cave town), a town of Moab (Is. xv:5; Jer. xlviii:3, 5, 34; Josephus *Antiq. lib.* xiii, cap. 23; xiv, cap. 2); doubtless the same called HOLON.

HORONITE, THE (hŏr'o-nīte), (Heb. הַחֹרֹנִי, *hakh-ō-ro-nee'*), the appellation of Sanballat, who opposed Nehemiah in his work of restoration (Neh ii:10, 19; xiii:28).

HORSE (hôrs), (Heb. סוּס, *sus;* Gr. ἵππος, *hippos*), Gen. xlvii:17; xlix:17; Exod. xiv:9, 23, and in many other places; James iii:3; Rev. vi:2, etc.

The horse is one of the noblest animals of the brute kind, celebrated for comeliness, swiftness, pride, wantonness, natural fierceness, tameableness, strength and fitness for burden, draught, or war (Job xxxix :19-25).

It appears to be substantiated that the horse was derived from High Asia, and was not indigenous in Arabia, Syria, or Egypt. They are not mentioned among the presents which Pharaoh bestowed upon Abraham, and occur in Scripture for the first time when the patriarch Joseph receives them from the Egyptians in exchange for bread (Gen. xlvii :17)—evidently as valuable animals, disposed of singly, and not in droves or flocks, like cattle and asses. They were still sufficiently important to be expressly mentioned in the funeral procession which accompanied the body of Jacob to his sepulcher in Canaan (Gen. l :9) ; and, for centuries after, it does not appear that, under the domestic management of the Egyptians, unless the murrain had greatly reduced them, horses had multiplied as they would have done in a land more congenial to their habits, since only six hundred chariots appear to have pursued Israel (Exod. xiv :7)—even admitting that there were other chariots and horsemen not included in that number. In the sculptured battle scenes, which are believed to represent victories of Sesostris, or of Thothmes II and III, over nations of Central Asia, it is evident that the enemy's armies, as well as the foreign allies of Egypt, are abundantly supplied with horses, both for chariots and for riders; and in triumphal processions they are shown as presents or tribute—proving that they were portions of the national wealth of conquered states sufficiently valuable to be prized in Egypt.

Bay or red horses occur most frequently on Egyptian painted monuments, this being the primitive color of the Arabian stock; but white horses are also common, and, in a few instances, black—the last probably only to relieve the paler color of the one beside it in the picture.

C. H. S.

The horses of Egypt were reckoned stronger and finer than those of Syria (Is. xxxi :3).

Mountainous Palestine was not well adapted for the use of the horse, and in early times it was principally employed in the maritime plain and in the valley of Jezreel. There were many horses in Egypt (Gen. xlvii:17; Exod. ix:3). When the exodus took place Pharaoh's pursuing army was equipped with chariots and horses (xiv:9; xv:19). They existed also in the force of the northern Canaanites led by Sisera, Jabin's commander-in-chief (Judg. iv:15; v:22).

God prohibited the Hebrews from multiplying horses (Deut. xvii:16; Josh. xi:6). However, Solomon having married the daughter of Pharaoh, procured a fine breed of horses from Egypt, some of them at the rate of 600 shekels of silver, which, according to Prideaux, is £90 sterling, $450.00, and according to Arbuthnot, £68 9s, $340.00 (1 Kings x:26). He, first of the Hebrews, began to multiply horses, and had 4,000 stables, 40,000 stalls, and 12,000 horsemen (1 Kings iv:26; 2 Chron. ix:25). As the eastern heathens, who worshiped the sun, imagined that he rode along the sky in a chariot drawn with fleet horses, to communicate his light and warmth to mankind, they consecrated to him the finest steeds or chariots; with these they either rode to the eastern gates of their cities as the sun rose, or they held them so sacred that none might ride on them. Josiah removed from the Jewish temple the horses, or images of horses, which his father or grandfather had consecrated to the sun (2 Kings xxiii:11). Among the ancient orientals, horses were reckoned a grand present, and riding on them an honor (Eccles. x:7).

Figurative. (1) Horses are sometimes put for warriors on horseback (Ezek. xxxix:20). (2) God's instruments of accomplishing his purpose, and displaying his greatness and might, are represented as his *horses* or chariots (Zech. x:5; xii:4; Jer. li:21). (3) *White horses,* anciently symbols of victory, denote the gospel, whereby Christ shows his glory, conquers, and comes to his people, and whereby they are supported, borne forward in their heavenly journey, and enabled to conquer their foes; or they may be an emblem of warriors' victory, and of great joy and gladness. (4) *Red horses* represent persecution and bloody wars. (5) *Pale horses* denote famines in the church or state, which are followed with death, spiritual or temporal, and with hell. (6) *Black horses* may represent fearful judgments, that fill men with horror and perplexity. (7) And *"grisled, speckled* and *bay horses"* may denote mingled scenes of mercy and judgment (Rev. vi :2-8; xix:11, 14; Zech. i:8; vi:2, 3). (8) Angels appeared under the form of *"horses and chariots"* of fire, to hint, that God by them powerfully executes his purposes, subdues his enemies, protects his people, and conveys them to heaven (2 Kings ii:11; vi:17). (9) Saints are likened to a *"company of horses"* in Pharaoh's chariots. How precious and costly to Christ! How carefully nourished, cleansed, stationed, and cared for by him! How delightfully yoked under His law! and what a glorious means of displaying His power! (Cant. i:9.) Brown.

HORSELEECH (hôrs'lēch), (Heb. עֲלוּקָה, *al-oo-kaw',* sucking, Prov. xxx:15), either one of the leeches, *Hirudo medicinalis,* Sav., or *Hæmopis sanguisorba,* Sav., found in the stagnant waters throughout the land; or a specter like the "night monster."

HORSEMAN (hôrs'man), (Heb. בַּעַל פֶּרֶשׁ *bah'al paw-rawsh',* master of a horse). From Exod. xiv:9, etc., it would appear that cavalry accompanied Pharaoh in his pursuit of Israel — "his horsemen."

HOSAH (hō'sah), (Heb. חֹסָה, *kho-saw',* hopeful).

1. A city of Asher, at a point on the boundary line where it turned from the direction of Tyre toward Achzib (Josh. xix:29); possibly the modern village of *el Ghazieh* or *el Ezziyah,* a little south of Zidon.

2. A Levitical door-keeper of the temple, whose station was by the 'gate of Shallecheth,' 1 Chron. xvi:38; xxvi:10, 11, 16. (B. C. about 988).

HOSANNA (hŏ-zăn'nà), (Gr. ὡσαννά, *ho-san-nah',* from Heb. הוֹשִׁיעָה נָּא, *ho-she-ah'naw,* save now).

A form of acclamatory blessing or wishing well, which signifies, Save now! Succor now! Be now propitious! It occurs in Matt. xxi:9 (also Mark xi:9, 10; John xii:13)—'Hosanna to the Son of David; Blessed is he that cometh in the name of the Lord; Hosanna in the highest.' This was on the occasion of our Savior's public entry into Jerusalem, and fairly construed would mean, 'Lord, preserve this Son of David; heap favors and blessings on him!' It is further to be ob-

served that Hosanna was a customary form of acclamation at the Feast of the Tabernacles. This feast was celebrated in September, just before the commencement of the civil year; on which occasion the people carried in their hands bundles of boughs of palms, myrtles, etc. (Joseph. *Antiq.* xiii, 13, 6; iii, 10, 4). They then repeated the 25th and 26th verses of Ps. cxviii, which commence with the word Hosanna, and from this circumstance they gave the boughs, and the prayers, and the feast itself, the name of Hosanna. They observed the same forms also at the Encænia, that is, the Feast of the reconsecration of the Temple, as instituted by Judas Maccabæus (1 Macc. x:6, 7; 2 Macc. xiii:51; Rev. vii:9) and the Passover. And as they celebrated the Feast of Tabernacles with great joy and gladness, in like manner, on this occasion, did they hail the coming of the Messiah, whose advent they believed to be represented in all the feasts.

HOSEA (ho-zē'a), (Heb. הוֹשֵׁעַ, *ho-shay'ah,* deliverer).

(1) Place of Hosea in the Versions. Hosea is the first in order of the minor prophets in the common editions of the Hebrew Scriptures, as well as of the Alexandrian and Vulgate translations. The arrangement of the other writers in the Greek versions differs considerably from that of the Hebrew copies. Both, however, place Hosea first in the catalogue; yet the reasons often assigned for the priority of place which this prophet enjoys are by no means satisfactory.

By the best computation he seems to have been preceded by Joel, Amos and Jonah. The prophets are thus arranged by De Wette (*Einleitung,* sec. 225):

Hebrew Text.	Greek Text.
1. Hosea.	1. Hosea.
2. Joel.	2. Amos.
3. Amos.	3. Micah.
4. Obadiah.	4. Joel.

Chronological Order.
1. Joel, about 810 B. C.
2. Jonah, about 810 B. C.
3. Amos, about 790 B. C.
4. Hosea, about 785 B. C.

The table given by Rosenmüller (*Scholia in Min. Proph.,* p. 7) differs from this only in placing Jonah before Joel in chronological order. Compare Newcome (*Preface to Minor Prophets,* p. 45). The probable causes of this location of Hosea may be the thoroughly national character of his oracles, their length, their earnest tone and vivid representations; because he discharged the duties of his office for a longer period than any of his prophetic associates, is the less natural conjecture which has been hazarded by Rosenmüller. The contour of Hosea's book has a closer resemblance to the greater prophets than any of the eleven productions by which it is succeeded.

(2) Name and Family. The name of this prophet has been variously interpreted. Jerome erroneously renders it 'Salvator.' It may be either the infinitive absolute, 'Salvando,' or the imperative, 'Salva' (O· Deus). It is ordinarily written in Greek, Ὡσηέ, and once with the initial aspirate, Ὡσηέ (Rom. ix:25). The figments of Jewish writers regarding Hosea's parentage need scarcely be mentioned. His father has been confounded with a prince of the Reubenites (1 Chron. v:6). So, too, Beeri has been reckoned a prophet himself, according to the rabbinical notion that the mention of a prophet's father in the introduction to his prophecies is a proof that sire as well as son was endowed with the oracular spirit.

(3) Nationality. Whether Hosea was a citizen of Israel or Judah has been disputed. The pseudo-Epiphanius and Dorotheus of Tyre speak of him as being born at Belemoth, in the tribe of Issachar (Epiphan. *De Vitis Prophet.* cap. xi; Doroth. *De Proph.* cap. i), Drusius (*Critici Sacri.* in loc. tom. v) prefers the reading 'Beth-semes,' and quotes Jerome, who says, 'Osee de tribu Issachar fuit ortus in Beth-semes.' But Maurer contends strenuously that he belonged to the kingdom of Judah (*Comment. Theol.*, ed. Rosenmüller, vol. ii. p. 391); while Jahn supposes that he exercised his office, not, as Amos did, in Israel, but in the principality of Judah. Maurer appeals to the superscription in Amos as a proof that prophets of Jewish origin were sometimes commissioned to labor in the kingdom of Israel (against the appeal to Amos, vide Credner, *Joel*, p. 66, and Hitzig, *Handb. Kurzge. exeget zum A. T.*, p. 72). But with the exception of the case recorded in 1 Kings xiii:1 (a case altogether too singular and mysterious to serve as an argument), the instance of Amos is a solitary one, and seems to have been regarded as anomalous by his contemporaries (Amos vii:12). Neither can we assent to the other hypothesis of Maurer that the mention of the Jewish kings Uzziah, Jotham, Ahaz and Hezekiah, by Hosea, in his superscription, is a proof that the seer regarded them as his rightful sovereigns, as monarchs of that territory which gave him birth. Hengstenberg has well replied that Maurer forgets 'the relation in which the pious in Israel generally, and the prophets in particular, stood to the kingdom of Judah. They considered the whole separation, not only the religious, but also the civil, as an apostasy from God. The dominion of the theocracy was promised to be the throne of David.' The lofty Elijah, on a memorable occasion, when a direct and solemn appeal was made to the head of the theocracy, took *twelve* stones, one for each tribe—a proof that he regarded the nation as one in religious confederation. It was also necessary for correct chronology that the kings of both nations should be noted. Jeroboam of Israel is mentioned as a means of ascertaining at what period in the long reign of Uzziah Hosea began to prophesy, and Uzziah's successors are named in particular, because the confusion and anarchy of the several interregna in the kingdom of Israel rendered computation by the names of Jeroboam's successors very awkward, difficult and uncertain. The other argument of Maurer for Hosea's being a Jew, viz., because his own people are so severely threatened in his reproofs and denunciations, implies a predominance of national prepossession or antipathy in the inspired breast which is inconsistent with our notions of the piety and patriotism of the prophetic commission (Knobel, *Der Prophetismus der Hebräer*, vol. i, p. 203). So that we can accede to the opinion of De Wette, Rosenmüller, Hengstenberg, Eichhorn, Manger, Uhland and Kuinoel, that Hosea was an Israelite, a native of that kingdom with whose sins and fates his book is specially and primarily occupied.

(4) Personal and National Relations. The years of Hosea's life were melancholy and tragic. The vials of the wrath of heaven were poured out on his apostate people. The nation suffered under the evils of that schism, which was effected by the craft of him who has been branded with the indelible stigma—'Jeroboam, who made Israel to sin.' The obligations of law had been relaxed, and the claims of religion disregarded; Baal became the rival of Jehovah, and in the dark recesses of the groves were practiced the impure and murderous rites of heathen deities; peace and prosperity fled the land, which was harassed by foreign invasion and domestic broils; might and murder became the twin sentinels of the throne; alliances were formed with other nations, which brought with them seductions to paganism; captivity and insult were heaped upon Israel by the uncircumcised; the nation was thoroughly debased, and but a fraction of its population maintained its spiritual allegiance (2 Kings xix:18). The death of Jeroboam II was followed by an interregnum of ten years. At the expiration of this period his son Zechariah assumed the sovereignty, and was slain by Shallum after the short space of six months (2 Kings xv:10). In four weeks Shallum was assassinated by Menahem. The assassin, during a disturbed reign of ten years, became tributary to the Assyrian Pul. His successor, Pekahiah, wore the crown but two years, when he was murdered by Pekah. Pekah, after swaying his bloody scepter for twenty years, met a similar fate in the conspiracy of Hoshea; Hoshea, the last of the usurpers, after another interregnum of eight years, ascended the throne, and his administration of nine years ended in the overthrow of his kingdom and the expatriation of his people. 'The Lord was very angry with Israel, and removed them out of his sight. So was Israel carried out of their own land to Assyria unto this day' (2 Kings xvii:18, 23).

HOSEA, BOOK OF.

(1) Against Whom Directed. The prophecies of Hosea were directed especially against the country whose sin had brought upon it such disasters—prolonged anarchy and final captivity. Israel, or Ephraim, is the people especially addressed. Their homicides and fornications, their perjury and theft, their idolatry and impiety are censured and satirized with a faithful severity. Judah is sometimes, indeed, introduced, warned and admonished. Bishop Horsley (*Works*, iii, 236), reckons it a mistake to suppose 'that Hosea's prophecies are almost wholly directed against the kingdom of Israel.' The bishop describes what he thinks the correct extent of Hosea's commission, but has adduced no proof of his assertion. Any one reading Hosea will at once discover that the oracles having relation to Israel are primary, while the references to Judah are only incidental. In chap. i:7, Judah is mentioned in contrast with Israel, to whose condition the symbolic name of the prophet's son is specially applicable. In verse 11 the future union of the two nations is predicted. The long oracle in chap. ii has no relation to Judah, nor the symbolic representation in chap. iii. Chap. iv is severe upon Ephraim and ends with a very brief exhortation to Judah not to follow his example. In the succeeding chapters allusions to Judah do indeed occasionally occur, when similar sins can be predicated of both branches of the nation. The prophet's mind was intensely interested in the destinies of his own people. The nations around him are unheeded; his prophetic eye beholds the crisis approaching his country, and sees its cantons ravaged, its tribes murdered or enslaved. No wonder that his rebukes were so terrible, his menaces so alarming, that his soul poured forth its strength in an ecstasy of grief and affection. Invitations, replete with tenderness and pathos, are interspersed with his warnings and expostulations. Now we are startled with a vision of the throne, at first shrouded in darkness, and sending forth lightnings, thunders and voices; but while we gaze, it becomes encircled with a rainbow, which gradually expands till it is lost in that universal brilliancy which itself had originated (chap. xi and xiv).

(2) Peculiar Mode of Instruction. The peculiar mode of instruction which the prophet details in the first and third chapters of his oracles has given rise to many disputed theories. We refer to the command expressed in chap. i :2: 'And the Lord said unto Hosea, Go, take unto thee a wife of whoredoms and children of whoredoms,' etc.; chap. iii:1, 'Then said the Lord unto me, Go yet, love a woman beloved of her friend, yet an adulteress,' etc. What was the precise nature of the transactions here recorded? Were they real events, the result of divine injunctions literally understood, and as literally fulfilled'? or were these intimations to the prophet only intended to be pictorial illustrations of the apostasy and spiritual folly and unfaithfulness of Israel? The former view, viz., that the prophet actually and literally entered into this impure connubial alliance, was advocated in ancient times by Cyril, Theodoret, Basil and Augustine; and more recently has been maintained by Mercer, Grotius, Houbigant, Manger, Horsley and Stuck. Fanciful theories are also rife on this subject. Luther supposed the prophet to perform a kind of drama in view of the people, giving his lawful wife and children these mystical appellations. Newcome (*Min. Prophets*) thinks that a wife of fornication means merely an Israelite, a woman of apostate and adulterous Israel. So Jac. Capellus (*In Hoseam; Opera,* p. 683). Hengstenberg supposes the prophet to relate actions which happened, indeed, actually, but not outwardly. Some, with Maimonides (*Moreh Nevochim,* part ii), imagine it to be a nocturnal vision; while others make it wholly an allegory, as the Chaldee Paraphrast, Jerome, Drusius, Bauer, Rosenmüller, Kuinoel and Lowth. The view of Hengstenberg, and such as have held his theory (Markii *Diatribe de uxore fornicationum accipienda,* etc., Lugd. Batav., 1696), is not materially different from the last to which we have referred. Both agree in condemning the first opinion, which the fast and forward mind of Horsley so strenuously maintained. Hengstenberg, at great length and with much force, has refuted this strange hypothesis (Christology, ii, 11-12). Besides other arguments resting on the impurity and loathsomeness of the supposed nuptial contract, it may be argued against the external reality of the event, that it must have required several years for its completion, and that the impressiveness of the symbol would therefore be weakened and obliterated. Other prophetic transactions of a similar nature might be referred to. Jerome (*Comment. in loc.*) has referred to Ezek. iv :4. It is not to be supposed, as has sometimes been argued, that the prophet was commanded to commit fornication. The divine injunction was to marry— '*Scortum aliquis ducere potest sine peccato, scortari non item.*' Drusius (*Comm. in loc. in Critici Sacri,* tom. v). Whichever way this question may be solved, whether these occurrences be regarded as a real and external transaction, or as a piece of spiritual scenery, or only, as is most probable (Witsii *Miscell. Sac.,* p. 90), an allegorical description, it is agreed on all hands that the actions are typical; that they are, as Jerome calls them, *sacramenta futurorum.*

(3) Differences of Views. Expositors are not at all agreed as to the meaning of the phrase 'wife of whoredoms,' whether the phrase refers to harlotry before marriage, or unfaithfulness after it. It may afford an easy solution of the difficulty if we look at the antitype in its history and character. Adultery is the appellation of idolatrous apostasy. The Jewish nation was espoused to God. The contract was formed on Sinai; but the Jewish people had prior to this period gone a-whoring. Josh. xxiv :2-14, 'Your fathers dwelt on the other side of the flood in old time, and they served other gods.' Comp. Lev. xvii :7, in which it is implied that idolatrous propensities had also developed themselves during the abode in Egypt; so that the phrase employed may signify one devoted to lasciviousness prior to her marriage. The marriage must be supposed a real contract, or its significance would be lost. Jer. ii :2, 'I remember thee, the kindness of thy youth, the love of thine espousals, when thou wentest after me in the wilderness, in a land that was not sown.' *Children of whoredoms* refer most naturally to the two sons and daughter afterwards to be born. They were not the prophet's own, as is intimated in the allegory, and they followed the pernicious example of the mother. Spiritual adultery was the debasing sin of Israel.

The Israelites who had been taken into covenant very soon fell from their first love, and were characterized by insatiable spiritual wantonness; yet their Maker, their husband, did not at once divorce them, but exhibited a marvelous long-suffering.

The names of the children being symbolical, the name of the mother has probably a similar signification. It may have the symbolic sense of 'one thoroughly abandoned to sensual delights.'

The names of the children are Jezreel, Loruhamah, and Lo-ammi. The prophet explains the meaning of the appellations. It is generally supposed that the names refer to three successive generations of the Israelitish people. Hengstenberg, on the other hand, argues that 'wife and children both are the people of Israel; the three names must not be considered separately, but taken together.' But as the marriage is first mentioned, and the births of the children are detailed in order, some time elapsing between the events, we rather adhere to the ordinary exposition. Nor is it without reason that the second child is described as a female.

The first child, Jezreel, may refer to the first dynasty of Jeroboam I and his successors, which was terminated in the blood of Ahab's house which Jehu shed at Jezreel. The name suggests also the cruel and fraudulent possession of the vineyard of Naboth, 'which was in Jezreel,' where, too, the woman Jezebel was slain so ignominiously (1 Kings xvi :1; 2 Kings ix :21). But as Jehu and his family had become as corrupt as their predecessors, the scenes of Jezreel were again to be enacted, and Jehu's race must perish. Jezreel, the spot referred to by the prophet, is also, according to Jerome, the place where the Assyrian army routed the Israelites. The name of this child associates the past and future, symbolizes past sins, intermediate punishments and final overthrow. The name of the second child, Loruhamah, 'not-pitied,' the appellation of a degraded *daughter,* may refer to the *feeble, effeminate* period which followed the overthrow of the first dynasty, when Israel became weak and helpless as well as sunk and abandoned. The favor of God was not exhibited to the nation; they were as abject as impious. But the reign of Jeroboam II was prosperous; new energy was infused into the kingdom; gleams of its former prosperity shone upon it. This revival of strength in that generation may be typified by the birth of a third child, a *son,* Lo-ammi, 'not my people' (2 Kings xiv :25). Yet prosperity did not bring with it a revival of piety; still, although their vigor was recruited, they were not God's people (*Lectures on the Jewish Antiquities and Scriptures,* by J. G. Palfrey, vol. ii, 422, Boston, N. A., 1841).

The space we have already occupied precludes more minute criticism; but the general principles we have indicated may be applied to the second and third chapters.

(4) Divisions. Recent writers, such as Bertholdt, Eichhorn, De Wette, Stuck, Maurer and Hitzig, have labored much, but in vain, to divide the book of Hosea into separate portions, assigning to each the period at which it was written; but from the want of sufficient data the attempt must rest principally on taste and fancy. A sufficient proof of the correctness of this opinion may be found in the contradictory sections and allotments of the various writers who have engaged in the task. Chapters i, ii and iii evidently form one division; it is next to impossible to separate and distinguish the other chapters. The form and style are very similar throughout all the second portion.

(5) Style. The peculiarities of Hosea's style have been often remarked. Jerome says of him, *'Commaticus est et quasi per sententias loquens'* (*Præf. ad XII Proph.*) His style, says De Wette, 'is abrupt, unrounded and ebullient; his rhythm hard, leaping and violent. The language is peculiar and difficult' (*Einleitung*, sec. 228). Lowth (*Prælect.*, 21) speaks of him as the most difficult and perplexed of the prophets. Bishop Horsley has remarked his peculiar idioms—his change of person, anomalies of gender and number, and use of the nominative absolute (*Works*, vol. iii). Eichhorn's description of his style was probably at the same time meant as an imitation of it (*Einleitung*, sec. 555): 'His discourse is like a garland woven of a multiplicity of flowers; images are woven upon images, comparison wound upon comparison, metaphor strung upon metaphor. He plucks one flower, and throws it down that he may directly break off another. Like a bee, he flies from one flower-bed to another, that he may suck his honey from the most varied pieces. It is a natural consequence that his figures sometimes form strings of pearls. Often is he prone to approach to allegory—often he sinks down in obscurity' (comp. chap. v :9; vi: 3; vii :8; xiii :3, 7, 8, 16). Unusual words and forms of connection sometimes occur (De Wette, sec. 228). Many examples might be given of the peculiar abruptness of the style; the particles of connection, causal, adversative, transitive, etc., being frequently omitted.

(6) Quoted in New Testament. Hosea, as a prophet is expressly quoted by Matthew (ii :15). The citation is from the first verse of chap. xi. Hosea (vi :6) is quoted twice by the same evangelist (ix :13; xii :7). Quotations from his prophecies are also to be found in Rom. ix :25, 26. References to them occur in 1 Cor. xv :55 and in 1 Pet. ii :10. Messianic references are not clearly and prominently developed (Gramberg, *Religionsid*, ii :298). This book, however, is not without them; but they lie more in the spirit of its allusions than in the letter. Hosea's Christology appears written not with ink, but with the spirit of the living God, on the fleshly tables of his heart. The future conversion of his people to the Lord their God, and David their king, their glorious privilege, in becoming sons of the living God, the faithfulness of the original promise to Abraham, that the number of his spiritual seed should be as the sand of the sea, are among the oracles whose fulfillment will take place only under the new dispensation.

(7) Literature. Besides works on the Minor Prophets as a whole, such as Ewald, Hitzig-Steiner, Keil, Pusey, von Orelli, etc., particular commentaries on Hosea are: Pococke, Oxf. 1685;

Simson, 1851; Wünsche, 1868; Nowack, 1880; and *Kleine Propheten* (Handkom.), 1897; Scholz, 1882; Cheyne (Camb. Bible), 1884. Comp. Valeton, *Amos en Hosea*, 1894; G. A. Smith, *The Book of the Twelve Proph.* (Expositor's Bible), 1896; Wellhausen, *Die Kleinen Proph.* (*Skizzen v.*), 1893; also W. R. Smith, *Prophets*, Lect. iv.; Billeb, *Die wichtigsten Sätze d. Altt. Kritik vom Standp. der Proph. Am. u. Hos. aus betrachtet*, 1893. On the Text, Houtsma, *Th T*, 1875, p. 55 ff.; Oort, *ib.* 1890, pp. 345 ff. 480 ff.; Bachmann, *Alttest. Untersuch.* 1894; Ruben, *Critical Remarks on some passages of O. T.*, 1896; Loftman, *Kritisk undersökning af den Masoretiska texten till prof. Hoseas bok*, 1894, and *Kommentar till prof. Hoseas bok*, 1896.

HOSE, HOSEN (hōz, hōz'n), (Chald. פַּטִּישׁ, *pat-teesh'*), A. V. (Dan. iii:21) of a Chaldee word meaning *tunics*. Hosen is plural of hose, and originally meant any covering for the legs.

HOSHAIAH (hŏsh'a-ī'ah), (Heb. הוֹשַׁעְיָה, *ho-shah-yaw'*, Jehovah has saved).

1. A man who led the princes of Judah in the procession in celebration of the rebuilding of the wall of Jerusalem under Nehemiah (Neh. xii :32), B. C. 446.

2. The father of Jezaniah or Azariah, who was a man of note after Nebuchadnezzar took Jerusalem (Jer. xlii :1; xliii :2), B. C. 587.

HOSHAMA (hŏsh'a-mà), (Heb. הוֹשָׁמָע, *ho-shaw-maw'*, whom Jehovah hears), according to 1 Chron. iii:18 a son of Jeconiah, or Jehoiachim, next to the last King of Judah.

But the sons of Jeconiah are not mentioned with others of the family (2 Kings xxiv :12, 15), and Jer. xxii :30 denounces him as 'a childless man.' For these reasons there is good ground for sustaining the suspicion that there is some corruption of the genealogy of the royal family in 1 Chron. iii (B. C. after 598).

HOSHEA (ho-shē'à), (Heb. הוֹשֵׁעַ, *ho-shay-ah'*, help, or God is help).

1. Son of Elah, and last king of Israel. He conspired against and slew his predecessor Pekah, and seized his dominions. 'He did evil in the sight of the Lord,' but not in the same degree as his predecessors': and this, by the Jewish commentators, is understood to mean that he did not, like former kings of Israel (2 Kings xv :30), restrain his subjects from going up to Jerusalem to worship. The intelligence that Hoshea had entered into a confederacy with So, king of Egypt, with the view of shaking off the Assyrian yoke, caused Shalmaneser, the king of Assyria, to march an army into the land of Israel; and after a three years' siege Samaria was taken and destroyed, and the ten tribes were sent into the countries beyond the Euphrates (B. C. 720) (2 Kings xv :30; xvii: 1-6; xviii:9-12). The chronology of this reign is much perplexed. (See CHRONOLOGY; ISRAEL.)

2. Son of Nun, i. e. Joshua (Deut. xxxii :44). In Num. xiii :8, the A. V. has *Oshea*. It was probably his original name, to which Jah was added later.

3. A ruler of the tribe of Ephraim in the time of King David (1 Chron. xxvii :20).

4. One of the heads of the people who sealed the covenant with Nehemiah (Neh. x :23), B. C. about 410.

HOSPITALITY (hŏs'pǐ-tal'ǐ-tў).

The practice of receiving strangers into one's house and giving them suitable entertainment may be traced back to the early origin of human society. It is not, however, confined to any age or to any country, but has been observed in all parts of the globe wherever circumstances have been such as to render it desirable—thus affording one among many instances of the readiness with which human nature, in its moral as well as in its physical properties, adapts itself to every varying condition. Hospitality is therefore not a peculiarly Oriental virtue. It was practiced, as it still is, among the least cultivated nations (Diod. Sic. v: 28, 34; Cæs. *Bell. Gall.* vi :23; Tac. *Germ.* 21).

(1) Among Greeks and Romans. It was not less observed, in the early periods of their history, among the Greeks and Romans. With the Greeks, *hospitality* (ξένια) was under the immediate protection of religion. Jupiter bore a name (ξένιος, *protector of guests*) signifying that its rights were under his guardianship. In the *Odyssey* (vi, 206) we are told expressly that all guests and poor people are special objects of care to the gods. There were both in Greece and Italy two kinds of hospitality, the one private, the other public. The first existed between individuals, the second was cultivated by one state towards another. Hence arose a new kind of social relation: between those who had exercised and partaken of the rites of hospitality an intimate friendship ensued,—a species of freemasonry, which was called into play wherever the individuals might afterwards chance to meet, and the right, duties, and advantages of which passed from father to son, and were deservedly held in the highest estimation.

(2) In the East. But though not peculiarly Oriental, hospitality has nowhere been more early or more fully practiced than in the East. It is still honorably observed among the Arabs, especially at the present day. An Arab, on arriving at a village, dismounts at the house of some one who is known to him, saying to the master, 'I am your guest.' On this the host receives the traveler, and performs his duties, that is, he sets before his guest his supper, consisting of bread, milk, and borgul, and, if he is rich and generous, he also takes the necessary care of his horse or beast of burden. Should the traveler be unacquainted with any person, he alights at any house, as it may happen, fastens his horse to the same, and proceeds to smoke his pipe until the master bids him welcome, and offers him his evening meal. In the morning the traveler pursues his journey, making no other return than 'God be with you' (good-by).

(3) Early Mention. We find hospitality practiced and held in the highest estimation at the earliest periods in which the Bible speaks of human society (Gen. xviii :3; xix :2; xxiv :25; Exod. ii :20; Judg. xix :16). Express provision for its exercise is made in the Mosaic law (Lev. xix :33; Deut. xiv :29). In the New Testament also its observance is enjoined, though in the period to which its books refer the nature and extent of hospitality would be changed with the change that society had undergone (1 Pet. iv :9; 1 Tim. iii :2; Tit. i :8; 1 Tim. v :10; Rom. xii :13; Heb. xiii :2). The disposition which generally prevailed in favor of the practice was enhanced by the fear lest those who neglected its rites should, after the example of impious men, be subjected by the divine wrath to frightful punishments (Ælian, *Anim.* xi, 19). Even the Jews, in 'the latter days,' laid very great stress on the obligation: the rewards of Paradise, their doctors declared, were his who spontaneously exercised hospitality.

(4) The Guest. The guest, whoever he might be, was on his appearing invited into the house or tent (Gen. xix :2; Exod. ii :20; Judg. xiii :15; xix : 21). Courtesy dictated that no improper questions should be put to him, and some days elapsed before the name of the stranger was asked, or what object he had in view in his journey (Gen. xxiv :33; *Odyss.* i, 123; iii, 69; *Iliad* vi, 175; ix, 222; Diod. Sic. v, 28). As soon as he arrived he was furnished with water to wash his feet (Gen. xviii :4; xix :2; 1 Tim. v :10; *Odyss.* iv, 49; xvii, 88; vi, 215); received a supply of needful food for himself and beast (Gen. xviii :5; xix :3; xxiv :25; Exod. ii :20; Judg. xix :20; *Odyss.* iii, 464); and enjoyed courtesy and protection from his host (Gen. xix :5; Josh. ii :2; Judg. xix :23). The case of Sisera, decoyed and slain by Jael (Judg. iv :18, *sq.*), was a gross infraction of the rights and duties of hospitality. On his departure the traveler was not allowed to go alone or empty-handed (Judg. xix :5; *Iliad,* vi, 217). As the free practice of hospitality was held right and honorable, so the neglect of it was considered discreditable (Job xxxi :32; *Odyss.* xiv, 56); and any interference with the comfort and protection which the host afforded was treated as a wicked outrage (Gen. xix :4, *sq.*)

(5) Enmities. Though the practice of hospitality was general, and its rites rarely violated, yet national or local enmities did not fail sometimes to interfere; and accordingly travelers avoided those places in which they had reason to expect an unfriendly reception. So in Judg. xix :12, the 'certain Levite' spoken of said, 'We will not turn aside hither into the city of a stranger, that is not of the children of Israel.' The quarrel which arose between the Jews and Samaritans after the Babylonish captivity destroyed the relations of hospitality between them. Regarding each other as heretics, they sacrificed every better feeling. It was only in the greatest extremity that the Jews would partake of Samaritan food (Lightfoot, p. 993), and they were accustomed, in consequence of their religious and political hatred, to avoid passing through Samaria in journeying from one extremity of the land to the other. The animosity of the Samaritans towards the Jews appears to have been somewhat less bitter; but they showed an adverse feeling towards those persons who, in going up to the annual feast at Jerusalem, had to pass through their country (Luke ix :53).

(6) National Festivals. At the great national festivals hospitality was liberally practiced so long as the state retained its identity. On these festive occasions no inhabitant of Jerusalem considered his house his own; every home swarmed with strangers; yet this unbounded hospitality could not find accommodation in the houses for all who stood in need of it, and a large proportion of visitors had to be content with such shelter as tents could afford (Helon, *Pilgrim.* i, 228, *sq.*).

J. R. B.

HOST (hōst). 1. In a social sense, *Xen'os* (Gr. ξένος), literally a *stranger*, i. e. one who receives and entertains hospitably (Rom. xvi :23), where "and of the whole Church" is added. (See HOSPITALITY).

2. In a military sense it means an army.

HOSTAGE (hŏs'tăj), (Heb. תַּעֲרֻבָה, *tah-ar-oo-baw'*, suretyship), one delivered into the hand of another as security for the performance of a pledge or engagement. (2 Kings xiv :14.)

HOST OF HEAVEN (hōst ŏv hĕv''n), (Heb. צְבָא הַשָּׁמַיִם, *tseb-aw' hash-shaw-mah'yim*, army of the skies, Gen. ii :1).

The sun, moon, and stars, under the figure of an army; in which the sun is considered as king, the moon as his vicegerent, the stars and planets as their attendants (comp. Judg. v:20). The worship of the host of heaven, though there are traces of it previously, first became prominent in Israel in the seventh century, B. C.: it was patronized by Manasseh, who 'built altars for all the host of heaven in the two courts' of the Temple (2 Kings xxi:5); it is mentioned in Deuteronomy as a form of idolatry which might prove specially seductive to the Israelite; according to Jer. xix:13; Zeph. i:5, it was carried on upon the roofs of houses. Josiah, in his reformation, destroyed the altars built by Manasseh in the Temple, burned the vessels used in the rites, and put down the priests who took part in them (2 Kings xxiii:3, 5, 12). From the terms of 2 Kings xxiii: 12 'the altars which were on the roof of the upper chamber of Ahaz,' taken in conjunction with what is stated in Jer. xix:13; Zeph. i:5, it is difficult to avoid the inference that, though the 'host of heaven' itself is not expressly mentioned, the worship had in fact been introduced into Judah before Manasseh by Ahaz. This systematic worship of the heavenly bodies was in all probability imported from Assyria and Babylonia, where there was a deeply rooted popular belief in the power of the stars to rule the destinies of individuals and nations, and where from a remote antiquity the events which had been observed to follow from given celestial phenomena had been tabulated for future reference (above, vol. i, p. 194; Sayce, *Hibb. Lect.* 396-403.) (See Article by S. R. Driver, Hastings' *Bib. Dict.*)

HOTHAM (hō'tham), (Heb. חוֹתָם, *kho-thawn'*, a signet ring), one of the sons of Heber, the grandson of Asher (1 Chron. vii:32). He is probably the same with *Helem*, whose sons are enumerated in v:35.

HOTHAN (hō'than), (Hebrew same as Hotham), an Aroerite, father of Shama and Jehiel, two of David's "valiant men" (1 Chron. xi:44), B. C. about 1000.

HOTHIR (hō'thir), (Heb. הוֹתִיר, *ho-theer'*, preserver), the thirteenth son of Heman, who, with eleven of his kinsmen, had charge of the twenty-first division of Levitical singers (1 Chron. xxv:4, 28), B. C. after 1000. (See HEMAN.)

For the full significance of the personal names occurring here see Fürst (*Hebr. u. Chald. Wörterb.* i, 244); Ewald (*Lehrbuch der Hebr. Sprache*, p. 502).

HOUGH (hŏk), (Heb. עָקַר, *aw-kar'*, to extirpate, Josh. xi:6, 9; 2 Sam. viii:4), is an obsolete word from the Anglo-Saxon *hoh*, and means to hamstring, *i. e.*, to cut the back sinews, and thus disable animals.

HOURS (ourz), (Chald. שָׁעָה, *shaw-aw'*, properly a look; Gr. ὥρα, *ho'rah*).

The ancient Hebrews, like the Greeks (Homer, *Il*, xxi, 3), were unacquainted with any other means of distinguishing the time of day than the natural divisions of morning, midday, or noon, twilight, and night (Gen. xv:12; xviii:1; xix:1, 15, 23).

(1) **Early Mention.** The earlier mention of hours occurs in Daniel (iii:15; **iv:19**; v:5); and even in the Septuagint ὥρα invariably signifies a season of the year, as in Homer and Hesiod. As the Chaldeans claimed the honor of inventing this system of notation (Herod. ii, 119), it is most probable that it was during their residence in Babylon that the Jews became familiar with their artificial distribution of the day. At all events no trace of it occurs before the captivity of that people; while, subsequently to their return to their own land, we find the practice adopted, and, in the time of Christ, universally established, of dividing the day and night respectively into twelve equal portions (Matt. xx:3-5; John xi:9; Acts v:7; xix:34).

(2) **Jewish Horology.** The Jewish horology, however, in common with that of other eastern nations, had this inherent defect, that the hours, though always equal to one another, were unequal in regard to the seasons, and that as their day was reckoned from sunrise to sunset, and not from the fixed period of noon, as with us, the twelve hours into which it was divided varied, of course, in duration according to the fluctuations of summer and winter. The midday, which with us is the twelfth hour, the Jews counted their sixth, while their twelfth hour did not arrive till sunset. At the equinoxes, their hours were exactly of the same length with ours, and the time from which they began to reckon their day at those seasons corresponded precisely with our six o'clock A. M.; their first hour being our seven o'clock, their third (Acts ii:15), our nine, their ninth (Acts iii:1), our three o'clock P. M., and their eleventh (Matt. xx:6), our five. This equality, however, in the duration of their hours, as well as in their correspondence to ours, was disturbed as the season approached toward the summer or winter solstice. In midsummer, when sunrise in Judæa takes place at five o'clock A. M., and sunset at seven P. M., the Jewish hours were a little longer than ours; and the only one of their hours which answered exactly to ours was the sixth, or twelve o'clock, while in all the rest there was a considerable difference. Their third hour was shortly *before* our nine, and their ninth a little *after* our three. In like manner, in winter, when the sun rises at seven and sets at five, the Jewish hour was proportionately shorter than ours, their third hour not occurring till a little *after* our nine, and their ninth a little *before* our three. Hence, it is evident that in order to determine exactly the duration of Daniel's silence (for instance 'he was astonied one hour,' Dan. iv:19), or the exact time when the darkness at Christ's crucifixion ended, it is necessary to ascertain the particular seasons when these incidents occurred.

Besides these smaller hours, there was another division of the day into larger hours, with reference to the stated periods of prayer, viz., the third, sixth, and ninth hours of the day (Ps. lv:17; Joseph. *Antiq.* iv, 4, 3).

(3) **Divisions of the Night.** The night was divided into twelve equal portions or hours, in precisely the same manner as the day. The most ancient division, however, was into three watches (*Antiq.* lxiii:6; xc:4); the first, or beginning of the watches, as it is called (Lam. ii:19); the middle watch (Judg. vii:19); and the morning watch (Exod. xiv:24). When Judæa became a province of Rome, the Roman distribution of the night into four watches was introduced (see COCKCROWING; DAY); to which division frequent allusions occur in the New Testament (Luke xii:38; Matt. xiv:25; xiii:35), as well as to that of hours (Matt. xxv:13; xxvi:40; Mark xiv:37; Luke xvii:59; Acts xxiii:23; Rev. iii:3).

The word *hour* is sometimes used in Scripture to denote some determinate season, as 'mine *hour* is not yet come,' 'this is your *hour*, and the power of darkness,' 'the *hour* is coming,' etc.   R. J.

HOUSE (hous), (Heb. בַּיִת, *bah'yith*; Gr. οἰκία, *oy-kee'ah*).

Houses are often mentioned in Scripture, several important passages of which cannot be well understood without a clearer notion of the houses in which the Hebrews dwelt than can be realized by such comparisons as we naturally make with those in which we ourselves live. But things so different afford no grounds for instructive comparison without a knowledge of such facts as can be collected from Scripture, ancient writers, and travelers.

Our information respecting the abodes of men in the ages before the Deluge is, however, too scanty to afford much ground for notice. (See ANTEDILUVIANS.)

We may, therefore, leave this early period, and proceed at once to the later times in which the Hebrews flourished.

1. Primary Dwellings. The observations offered under ARCHITECTURE will preclude the expectation of finding among this Eastern people that accomplished style of building which Vitruvius requires, or that refined taste by which the Greeks and Romans excited the admiration of foreign nations. The reason of this is plain. Their ancestors had roved through the country as nomade shepherds, dwelling in tents; and if ever they built huts they were of so light a fabric as easily to be taken down when a change of station became necessary. In this mode of life solidity in the structure of any dwelling was by no means required; much less were regular arrangement and the other requisites of a well-ordered dwelling matters of consideration. Under such circumstances as these, no improvement in the habitation takes place. The tents in which the Arabs now dwell are in all probability the same as those in which the Hebrew patriarchs spent their lives.

2. Buildings. On entering Palestine the Israelites occupied the dwellings of the dispossessed inhabitants; and for a long time no new buildings would be needed. The generation which began to build new houses must have been born and bred in the country, and would naturally erect buildings like those which already existed in the land. Their mode of building was therefore that of the Canaanites whom they had dispossessed. Of *their* style of building we are not required to form any exalted notions. In all the history of the conquest of the country by the Israelites, there is no account of any large or conspicuous building being taken or destroyed by them. It would seem also as if there had been no temples; for we read not that any were destroyed by the conquerors; and the command that the monuments of idolatry should be overthrown specifies only altars, groves, and high places—which seems to lead to the same conclusion; since, if there had been temples existing in the land of Canaan, they would doubtless have been included. It is also manifest from the history that the towns which the Hebrews found in Palestine were mostly small, and that the largest were distinguished rather by the number than by the size or magnificence of their buildings.

It is impossible to say to what extent Solomon's improvements in state architecture operated to the advancement of domestic architecture. He built different palaces, and it is reasonable to conclude that his nobles and great officers followed more or less the models which these palaces presented. In the East, however, the domestic architecture of the bulk of the people is little affected by the improvements in state buildings. Men go on building from age to age as their forefathers built; and in all probability the houses

which we now see in Palestine are such as those in which the Jews, and the Canaanites before them, dwelt—the mosques, the Christian churches, and the monasteries being the only new features in the scene.

There is no reason to suppose that many houses in Palestine were constructed with wood. A great part of that country was always very poor in timber, and the middle part of it had scarcely any wood at all. But of stone there was no want; and it was consequently much used in the building of houses. The law of Moses respecting leprosy in houses (Lev. xiv:33-40) seems to prove this, as the characteristics there enumerated could only occur in the case of stone walls.

3. Building Materials. The principal building materials mentioned in Scripture may be enumerated with reference to their place in the three kingdoms of nature:

(1) **Vegetable Substances.** (a) *Shittim,* or the timber of the acacia tree, which grows abundantly in the valleys of Arabia Petræa, and was therefore employed in the construction of the tabernacle. Not being, however, a tree of Palestine, the wood was not subsequently used in building.

(b) *Shakemim;* that is, the wood of the sycamore fig-tree, mentioned in Is. ix:10, as a building timber in more common use than cedar, or perhaps than any other wood known in Palestine.

(c) *Eres,* or cedar. As this was a wood imported from Lebanon, it would only be used in the higher class of buildings. For its quality as a building timber, and respecting the question of its being really what we call the cedar, see ERES.

(d) *Algum-wood,* which, being imported from the Eastern seas, must have been valued at a high price. It was used by Solomon for pillars for his own palace, and for the Temple (1 Kings x:11, 12).

(e) *Berosh,* or cypress-wood. Boards of this were used for the floor of the Temple, which may suggest the use to which it was ordinarily applied (1 Kings vi:15; 2 Chron. iii:5).

(2) **Mineral Substances.** (a) *Marble.* We find the court of the king of Persia's palace covered with marble of various colors (Esth.i:6). David is recorded to have possessed abundance of marble (1 Chron. xxix:2; comp. Cant. v:15), and it was used by Solomon for his palace, as well as for the Temple.

(b) *Porphyry* and *Granite* are supposed to be 'the glistering stones, and stones of divers colors' named in 1 Chron. xxix:2. If so, the mountains of Arabia Petræa furnished the nearest source of supply, as these stones do not exist in Palestine or Lebanon.

(c) *Bricks.* Bricks hardened by fire were employed in the construction of the tower of Babel (Gen. xi:3), and the hard bondage of the Israelites in Egypt consisted in the manufacture of sun-dried bricks (Exod. v:7, 10-13). This important building material has been noticed under another head. (See BRICK.)

No subsequent notice of bricks as being used by the Hebrews occurs after they had entered Palestine. Yet, judging from existing analogies, it is more than probable that bricks were to a considerable extent employed in their buildings.

(d) *Chalk* and *Gypsum,* which the Hebrews appear to have comprehended under the general name of *sid.* That the Hebrews were acquainted with these materials appears from Deut. xxvii:2; and from Dan. v:5, and Acts xxiii:3, it further appears that walls were covered with them. A highly instructive and curious account of the plasters used in the East may be seen in tome iv of Langles's edition of Chardin's *Voyages*.

(e) *Mortar,* a cement made of lime, ashes, and chopped straw, or of gypsum and chopped straw. This is probably meant in Jer. xliii:9; Ezek. xiii: 10, 11, 14, 15.

(f) *Asphaltum,* or *Bitumen,* which is mentioned as being used for a cement by the builders of Babel. This must have been in the want of lime-mortar, the country being a stoneless plain. But the Israelites, who had no lack of the usual cements, did not employ asphaltum. (See BITU-MEN.)

(g) The metals also must be, to a certain extent, regarded as building materials; lead, iron and copper are mentioned; and even silver and gold were used in combination with wood, for various kinds of solid, plated, and inlaid work (Exod. xxxvi:34, 38).

(3) **Animal Substances.** Such substances can be but in a small degree applicable to building. *Ivory* houses are mentioned in 1 Kings xxii: 39; Amos iii:14; most likely from certain parts of the woodwork, probably about the doors and windows, being inlaid with this valuable substance. Solomon obtained ivory in great quantities from Tyre (1 Kings x:22; 2 Chron. ix:21). (See IVORY.)

4. *Present Conditions.* In describing the houses of ancient Palestine, there is no way of arriving at distinct notions but by taking the texts of Scripture and illustrating them by the existing houses of those parts of Western Asia which have been the least exposed to the changes of time, and in which the manners of ancient days have been the best preserved.

The present writer, having resided for a considerable time in Turkish Arabia, where the type of Scriptural usages has been better preserved than in Egypt, or even in Palestine itself, is enabled to speak on this matter with somewhat more precision. Of four houses in which he there resided, two were first rate and two second rate. One of the latter has always seemed to him to suggest a more satisfactory idea of a Scriptural house than any of the others, or than any he ever saw in other Eastern countries. That one has therefore formed the basis of all his ideas on this subject, and where it seemed to fail, the others have usually supplied the illustration required.

(1) **Exterior.** We may premise that the houses present little more than a dead wall to the street. The privacy of Oriental domestic habits would render our plan of throwing the front of the houses towards the street most repulsive. On coming to a house, one finds a lofty wall, which would be blank but for the low door of entrance (see GATE); over which is usually the kiosk, or latticed window (sometimes projecting like the huge bay windows of Elizabethan houses), or screened balcony of the 'summer parlor.' Besides this, there may be a small latticed window or two high up the wall, giving light and air to upper chambers. This seems to have been the character of the fronts of ancient Egyptian houses.

(2) **The Court.** The buildings which form the house front towards an inner square or court. Small houses have one of these courts, but superior houses have two, and first-rate houses three, communicating with each other, for the Orientals dislike ascending stairs or steps, and prefer to gain room rather by the extent than height of their habitations. It is only when the building-

ground is confined by nature or by fortifications, that they build high houses. None of our four houses had more than one story; but, from the loftiness of the rooms, they were as high as houses of three stories among ourselves. If there are three or more courts, all except the outer one are much alike in size and appearance; but the outer one, being devoted to the more public life of the occupant, and to his intercourse with society, is materially different from all the others. If there are more than two, the second is devoted chiefly to the use of the master, who is there attended only by his eunuchs, children, and females, and sees only such persons as he calls from the third or interior court in which they reside. In the history of Esther, she incurs danger by going from her interior court to that of the king, to invite him to visit her part of the palace; but she would not on any account have gone to the outermost court, in which the king held his public audiences. When there are only two courts, the innermost is the harem, in which the women and children live, and which is the true domicile of the master, to which he withdraws when the claims of business, of society, and of friends have been satisfied, and where no man but himself ever enters, or could be induced to enter, even by strong persuasions.

Entering at the street-door a passage, usually sloping downward, conducts to the outer court; the opening from the passage to this is not opposite the gate of entrance, but by a side turn, to preclude any view from the street into the court when the gate is opened.

(3) **The Guest Chamber.** On entering the outer court through this passage, we find opposite to us the public room, in which the master receives and gives audience to his friends and clients. This is entirely open in front, and, being richly fitted up, has a splendid appearance when the first view of it is obtained. A refreshing coolness is sometimes given to this apartment by a fountain throwing up a jet of water in front of it.

Guest Chamber of an Eastern House.

This is the 'guest-chamber' of Luke xxii:11. A large portion of the other side of the court is occupied with a frontage of lattice-work filled with colored glass, belonging to a room as large as the guest-chamber, and which in winter is used for the same purpose, or serves as the apartment of any visitor of distinction, who cannot of course be admitted into the interior parts of the house.

(4) **Other Apartments.** The other apartments in this outer court are comparatively small, and are used for the accommodation of visitors, retainers, and servants. These various apartments are usually upon what we should call the first floor, or at least upon an elevated terrace. The

ground floor is in that case occupied by various store-rooms and servants' offices. In all cases the upper floor, containing the principal rooms, is fronted by a gallery or terrace, protected from the sun by a sort of penthouse roof supported by pillars of wood.

In houses having but one court, the reception-room is on the ground floor, and the domestic establishment in the upper part of the house. This arrangement is interesting from its showing the use of the 'pillars' so often mentioned in Scripture, particularly 'the pillars on which the house stood, and by which it was borne up' (Judg. xvi:29).

(5) The Kiosk. The kiosk, which has been mentioned above as fronting the street, over the gateway, is connected with one of the larger rooms already described, or forms a separate apartment, which is the summer parlor of Scripture. Here, in the heat of the afternoon, the master lounges or dozes listlessly, refreshed by the air which circulates between the openings of the lattice work; and here he can, if he pleases, notice unobserved what passes in the street. In this we are to seek the summer parlor in which Ehud smote the king of Moab (Judg. iii:20), and the 'chamber on the wall,' which the Shunamite

Upper Room of an Eastern House.

prepared for the prophet (2 Kings iv:10). The projecting construction over the reception chamber is, like the kiosk, towards the street as a summer parlor; but there it belongs to the women's apartments, and looks into the court, and not the street.

(6) The Inner Court. The inner court is entered by a passage and door similar to those by which we entered from the street. This passage and door are usually at one of the innermost corners of the outer court. Here a much more extended prospect opens to us, the inner court being generally much larger than the former. It is lower, the principal apartments standing upon a terrace or bank of earth, and not upon a basement story of offices; and it also wants the veranda or covered gallery in front, which we find in Syro-Arabian houses. The court is for the most part paved, excepting a portion in the middle, which is planted with trees (usually two) and shrubs, with a basin of water in the midst. In our Arabian house the two trees were palm trees, in which a number of wild doves built their nests.

That the Jews had an arrangement of trees in the courts of their houses as did the ancient Egyptians, and that the birds nested in them, appears from Ps. lxxxiv:2, 3. They had also the basin of water in the inner court, or harem;

and among them it was used for bathing, as is shown by David's discovering Bathsheba bathing as he walked on the roof of his palace. This use of the reservoir has now been superseded by the establishment of public *warm* baths in every town, and in private mansions. Cold bathing has all but ceased in Western Asia.

Arabian House.

The arrangement of the inner court is very similar to that of the outer; but the whole is more open and airy. The buildings usually occupy two sides of the square, of which the one opposite the entrance contains the principal apartments. They are upon what we should call the first floor, and open into a wide gallery or veranda, which in good houses is nine or ten feet deep, and covered by a wooden penthouse supported by a row of wooden columns. This terrace, or gallery, is furnished with a strong wooden balustrade, and is usually paved with squared stones, or else floored with boards. In the center of the principal front is the usual open drawing-room, on which the best art of the Eastern decorator is expended. Much of one of the sides of the court front is usually occupied by the large sitting-room, with the latticed front covered with colored glass, similar to that in the outer court. The other rooms, of smaller size, are the more private apartments of the mansion.

Room Showing Draperies of Oriental House.

(7) Curtains. There are usually no doors to the sitting or drawing rooms of Eastern houses. They are closed by curtains, at least in summer, the opening and shutting of doors being odious to most Orientals. The same seems to have been the case among the Hebrews, as far as we may judge from the curtains which served instead of doors to the tabernacle, and which separated the inner and outer chambers of the temple. The curtained entrances to our Westminster courts of law supply a familiar example of the same practice.

(8) The Basement. These observations apply to the principal story. The basement is occupied by various offices, stores of corn and fuel, places for the water jars to stand in, places for grinding corn, baths, kitchens, etc.

(9) The Kitchen. The kitchens are always in this inner court, as the cooking is performed by women, and the ladies of the family superintend or actually assist in the process. The kitchen, open in front, is on the same side as the entrance from the outer court; and the top of it forms a terrace, which affords a communication between the first floor of both courts by a private door seldom used but by the master of the house and attendant eunuchs.

The kitchen is surrounded by a brick terrace, on the top of which are the fireplaces formed in compartments, and separated by little walls of fire-brick or tile. In these different compartments the various dishes of an Eastern feast may be at once prepared at charcoal fires. This place being wholly open in front, the half-tame doves, which have their nests in the trees of the court, often visit it in the absence of the servants in search of crumbs, etc. As they sometimes blacken themselves, this perhaps explains the obscure passage in Ps. lxviii:13, 'Though ye have lain among the pots, ye shall be as the wings of a dove covered with silver,' etc. In Turkish Arabia most of the houses have underground cellars or vaults, to which the inhabitants retreat during the mid-day heat of summer, and there enjoy a refreshing coolness. In the rest of the year these cellars, or *serdaubs,* as they are called, are abandoned to the bats, which swarm in them in scarcely credible numbers (Is. ii:20).

(10) The Gallery. From the court a flight of stone steps, usually at the corner, conducts to the gallery, from which a plainer stair leads to the house top. If the house be large there are two or three sets of steps to the different sides of the

Oriental House Showing Court and Tile Roof.
(A shows recess where a public speaker would probably stand. B shows tile roof which could be easily "broken up" or removed.)

quadrangle, but seldom more than one flight from the terrace to the house top of any one court. There is, however, a separate stair from the outer court to the roof, and it is usually near the entrance. This will bring to mind the case of the paralytic, whose friends, finding they could not get access to Jesus through the people who crowded the court of the house in which he was preaching, took him up to the roof and let him down in his bed through the tiling to the place where Jesus stood (Luke v:17-26).

If the house in which our Lord then was had more than one court he and the auditors were certainly in the outer one; and it is reasonable to conclude that he stood in the veranda addressing the crowd below. The men bearing the paralytic, therefore, perhaps went up the steps near the door, and, finding they could not even then get near the person of Jesus, the gallery being also crowded, continued their course to the roof of the house, and, removing the boards over the

Dirt Covered House.

covering of the gallery, at the place where Jesus stood, lowered the sick man to his feet. But if they could not get access to the steps near the door, as is likely, from the door being much crowded, their alternative was to take him to the roof of the next house and there hoist him over the parapet to the roof of the house which they desired to enter.

(11) The Roof. The roof of the house is, of course, flat. It is formed by layers of branches, twigs, matting, and earth, laid over the rafters and trodden down, after which it is covered with a compost which acquires considerable hardness when dry; but in those parts of Asia where the climate is more than usually moist, a stone roller is usually kept on every roof, and after a shower a great part of the population is engaged in drawing these rollers over the roof.

It is now very common, in countries where timber is scarce, to have domed roofs; but in that case the flat roof, which is indispensable to Eastern habits, is obtained by filling up the hollow intervals between the several domes, so as to form a flat surface at the top.

These flat roofs are often alluded to in Scripture, and the allusions show that they were made to serve the same uses as at present. In fine weather the inhabitants resorted much to them to breathe the fresh air, to enjoy a fine prospect, or to witness any event that occurred in the neighborhood (2 Sam. xi:2; Is. xxii:1; Matt. xxiv:17; Mark xiii:15).

The dryness of the summer atmosphere enabled them, without injury to health, to enjoy the bracing coolness of the night air by sleeping on the house tops, and in order to have the benefit of the air and prospect in the daytime, without inconvenience from the sun, sheds, booths, and tents were sometimes erected on the house tops (2 Sam. xvi:22).

The roofs of the houses are well protected by walls and parapets. Towards the street and neighboring houses is a high wall, and towards the interior courtyard usually a parapet or wooden rail. 'Battlements' of this kind, for the prevention of accidents, are strictly enjoined in the Law (Deut. xxii:8).

Oriental House with Stages upon the Roof for Sleeping.

(12) **The Ceiling.** The ceiling, if of wood and flat, is of curious and complicated joinery, or, if vaulted, is wrought into numerous coves, and enriched with fretwork in stucco; and the walls are adorned with arabesques, mosaics, mirrors, painting, and gold, which, as set off by the marble-like whiteness of the stucco, has a truly brilliant and rich effect. There is much in this to remind one of such descriptions of splendid interiors as that in Is. liv:11, 12.

(13) **Inferior Dwellings.** In the inferior kinds of Oriental dwellings, such as are met with in villages and very small towns, there is no central court, but there is generally a yard attached, either on one side or at the rear. The shaded platform in front is such as is usually seen attached to coffee-houses.

Here the customers sit and smoke their pipes, and sip their coffee. The village cabins and abodes of the peasantry are, of course, of a still inferior description; and, being the abodes of people who live much in the open air, will not bear comparison with the houses of the same class in Northern Europe, where the cottage is the *home* of the owner.

No ancient houses had chimneys. The word so translated in Hos. xiii:3 means a hole through which the smoke escaped; and this existed only in the lower class of dwellings, where raw wood was employed for fuel or cooking, and where there was an opening immediately over the hearth to let out the smoke. In the better sort of houses the rooms were warmed in winter by charcoal in braziers, as is still the practice (Jer. xxxvi:22; Mark xiv:54; John xviii:18).

The windows had no glass. They were only latticed, and thus gave free passage to the air and admitted light, while birds and bats were excluded. In winter the cold air was kept out by veils over the windows, or by shutters with holes in them sufficient to admit light (1 Kings vii:17; Cant. ii:9).

In the East, where the climate allows the people to spend so much of their time out of doors, the articles of furniture and the domestic utensils

have always been few and simple. They are in this work noticed under separate heads. (See BED; LAMP; POTTER; TABLE.)

5. Literature. Porter, *Damascus;* Shaw, *Travels;* Lane, *Mod. Egypt;* Burckhardt, *Syria;* Layard, *Monuments of Nineveh.*

Figurative. (1) Heaven, the church, the tabernacle, temple, and ordinances, are represented as *God's house,* or a *spiritual house;* as God planned, formed, furnished, or owned them, so he did or does dwell in them, and display his glory, power, and grace in a peculiar manner (John xiv: 1; Heb. iii:2; Judg. xviii:31; 2 Chron. v:14; Ps. lxxxiv:10). (2) The saints are a spiritual house, and household of faith, being formed by the Holy Ghost, and furnished with spiritual graces and enabled to believe the truth as in Jesus; God dwells in them, and among them, as their master, parent, and *householder;* and ministers attend them as their servants (1 Pet. ii:5; Gal. vi:10; Matt. xiii:27 and xxi:33). (3) The *house of God,* at which dangerous judgments begin, is either the ruined Jewish temple or the persecuted Christian church (1 Pet. iv:17). (4) The *house of David and inhabitants of Jerusalem* are all ranks, both great and small (Zech. xiii:1). (5) To *join house to house,* and field to field, till there be no place, is to join several farms or occupations together, in order to grow hastily rich, and by which a great many, especially of the poor, are deprived of livings and subsistence (Is. v:8). (6) God made *houses* to the Hebrews, or to the midwives; he prospered and increased their families (Exod. i:22). (7) Such as build their hopes on Christ in his word are *houses founded on a rock;* their hopes cannot be overturned by any temptation, affliction, death, or judgment to come; but such as found their hopes on anything else are like *houses built on the sand,* which, amid temptation and trouble, are easily overthrown or ruined (Matt. vii:24, 25).

HOUSEHOLD (hous'hōld'), the rendering generally of the same Hebrew and Greek words as are rendered "house," and meaning the members of a family, living in the same dwelling, including domestics and dependents.

In Job i:3 the word *ab-ood-daw'* (literally "service"), appears to mean a retinue of servants. The expression "they of Cæsar's household" (Phil. iv:22) seems to refer to some of the servants of the emperor, and not those of the imperial family.

HOUSE OF GOD (hous ŏv gŏd), a translation in the A. V. of the place Bethel. It is the *place* where the ark was, and not the *ark*, which is called "the house of God." (See BETHEL.) (Judg. xx:18, 26; xxi:2; comp. Judg. xx:27).

HOUSE OF ROLLS, THE (hous ŏv rōls), "House of the rolls," Ezra vi:1, and "treasure-house," Ezra v:17, both refer to the same depository of public documents.

HOUSE TOP (hous tŏp), the flat roof of an Eastern house. (See HOUSE.)

Figurative. Some of these roofs were covered with earth rolled hard, which, softened by rain, would cause grass seeds to spring up. When the returning drought and heat came the grass speedily withered, an apt illustration of temporary prosperity followed by ruin (2 Kings xix:26; Ps. cxxix:6; Is. xxxvii:27).

On account of the flat roofs, the *house tops* were used to speak from to neighbors, or to gaze on an approaching enemy (Matt. x:27; Is. xxii: 1).

HUKKOK (hŭk'kok), (Heb. חֻקֹּק, *khoo-koke'*, appointed), one of the boundary marks of Naphtali (Josh. xix:34). It has been identified with the modern Yåkûk, west of the upper end of the Sea of Galilee, seven miles southwest of Safed.

HUKOK (hū'kok), (Heb. same as above), a city of Asher; the same probably as that of Naphtali, (Josh. xix:34) yielded to the Levites, and assigned for a city of refuge, (I Chron. vi:75). It is represented by Helkath, (Josh. xix:25; xxi:31). (See Helkath.)

HUL (hŭl), (Heb. חוּל, *khool*, circle), second son of Aram, and grandson of Shem (Gen. x:23), B.C. 2414. Huleh, the region occupied by this family, is not definitely known, Josephus and Jerome fix it in Armenia; Schulthess (*Parad.* p. 262), in southern Mesopotamia; von Bohlen (*Introd. to Gen.*, ii, 249), in the neighborhood of Chaldæa. Others have argued in favor of the region of Lebanon.

Quite probable seems the identification proposed by Rosenmüller (*Alterthum*, i, 2, p. 253) with the district now called *Huleh,* around Lake Merom (Mc. and S., *Cyc.*).

The various attempts that have been made to establish its identity will be found in Dillmann, who does not consider that any of them has been successful.

HULDAH (hŭl'dah), (Heb. חֻלְדָּה, *khool-daw'*, weasel; (Gr. Ολδα,, *ol'da*).

The wife of Shallum, a prophetess, who, in the reign of Josiah, abode in that part of Jerusalem called the Mishneh, where the book of the Law was discovered by the high-priest Hilkiah. (B. C. 623.) This prophetess was consulted respecting the denunciations which it contained. She then delivered an oracular response of mingled judgment and mercy; declaring the not remote destruction of Jerusalem, but promising Josiah that he should be taken from the world before these evil days came (2 Kings xxii:14-20; 2 Chron. xxxiv:22-28). Huldah is known only by this circumstance. She was probably at this time the widow of Shallum, a name too common to suggest any information; but he is said to have been grandson of one Harhas, 'keeper of the wardrobe,' but whether the priestly or the royal wardrobe is uncertain. If the former, he must have been a Levite, if not a priest. As to her residence in the Mishneh מִשְׁנֶה, which the Auth. Vers. renders 'in the college,' there is no ground to conclude that any school or college of the prophets is to be understood. The name means 'second' or 'double;' and many of the Jews themselves (as Jarchi states) understood it as the name of the suburb lying between the inner and outer wall of Jerusalem. It is safest to regard it as a proper name, denoting some quarter of Jerusalem about which we are not certain, and, accordingly, to translate 'in the Mishneh.'

HUMAN SACRIFICE (hū'man sak'rĭ-fīz). See Sacrifice.

HUMAN SOUL. See Soul.

HUMANITY OF CHRIST (hŭ-măn'ĭ-tȳ). See Incarnation.

HUMBLENESS (hŭm'b'l-nĕs), (Col. iii:12). See Humility.

HUMILIATION OF CHRIST (hŭ-mĭl'ĭ-ā'-shŭn), an expression which refers to the earthly life of the Lord Jesus Christ.

His humiliation was shown in his earthly life from beginning to end. He humbled himself to be born of a virgin; and the lowly circumstances of his birth have ever been the theme of Christian artists and poets. The humility of the thirty years' subjection to his parents, and of the three years of unceasing toil, privation, and opposition, was crowned when he endured the cross, despising the shame (Heb. xii:2). We may notice specially his praying (Luke ix:18, etc.), his admitting weariness, distress, and pain (John iv:6, Mark xiv:34; John xix:28), and the solemn words and acts by which he inculcated humility (Matt. xi: 29;. John xiii:12-16). At the same time, he asserted his authority (*e. g.,* to forgive sins, to judge men, to found an undying Church); he proclaimed himself as the only way to God, etc. (John xiv:6). He claimed that he alone knew the Father aright (Matt. xi:27).

HUMILITY (hŭ-mĭl'ĭ-tȳ), (Heb. עֲנָוָה, *an-aw-vaw'*, gentleness, affliction; Gr. ταπεινοφροσύνη, *tap-i-nof-ros-oo'nay*, lowliness of mind; Prov. xv:33, *et al.*; Acts xx:19 in R. V. is "lowliness of mind").

Humility is the effect of divine grace operating on the soul, and always characterizes the true Christian. The heathen philosophers were so little acquainted with this virtue that they had no name for it; what they meant by the word we use was *meanness* and *baseness* of mind.

To consider this grace a little more particularly, it may be observed: (1) That humility does not oblige a man to wrong the truth, or himself, by entertaining a meaner or worse opinion of himself than he deserves. (2) Nor does it oblige a man, right or wrong, to give everybody else the preference to himself. A wise man cannot believe himself inferior to the ignorant multitude; nor the virtuous man that he is not so good as those whose lives are vicious. (3) Nor does it oblige a man to treat himself with contempt in his words or actions; it looks more like affectation than humility when a man says such things in his own dispraise as others know, or he himself believes, to be false; and it is plain, also, that this is often done merely as a *bait* to catch the praises of others.

Humility consists: (1) In not attributing to ourselves any excellence or good which we have not. (2) In not overrating anything we do. (3) In not taking an immoderate delight in ourselves. (4) In not assuming more of the praise of a quality or action than belongs to us. (5) In an inward sense of our many imperfections and sins. (6) In ascribing all we have and are to the grace of God.

True humility will express itself: (1) By the modesty of our appearance. The humble man will consider his age, abilities, character, function, etc., and act accordingly. (2) By the modesty of our pursuits. We shall not aim at anything above our strength, but prefer a *good* to a *great* name. (3) By the modesty of our conversation and behavior. We shall not be loquacious, obstinate, forward, envious, discontented or ambitious.

The advantages of humility are numerous: (1) It is well pleasing to God (1 Pet. iii:4). (2) It has great influence on us in the performance of all other duties, praying, hearing, conversing, etc. (3) It indicates that more grace shall be given (James iv:6; Ps. xxv:9). (4) It preserves the soul in great tranquillity and contentment (Ps. lxix:32, 33). (5) It makes us patient and resigned under afflictions (Job i:22). (6) It enables us to exercise moderation in everything.

To obtain this excellent spirit we should remember: (1) The example of Christ (Phil. ii:6, 7, 8). (2) That heaven is a place of humility (Rev. v:8). (3) That our sins are numerous, and deserve the greatest punishment (Lam. iii: 39). (4) That humility is the way to honor (Prov. xvi:18). (5) That the greatest promises of good are made to the humble (Is. lvii:15; lxvi: 2; 1 Pet. v:5; Ps. cxlvii:6; Matt. v:5).

Brown.

HUMTAH (hŭm'tah), (Heb. חֻמְטָה, *khoom-taw'*, fortress), a city in the mountain district of Judah (Josh. xv:54). It has not been identified with any modern place.

HUNDREDS (hŭn'drĕds). One of the groups (Exod. xviii:21) into which Moses divided the people of Israel. (See ISRAEL, CONSTITUTION OF.)

HUNGER (hŭn'gẽr), (Heb. רָעֵב, *raw-abe'*), the rendering of the same Hebrew and Greek words that are sometimes rendered FAMINE (which see).

Figurative. (1) To be *burnt* with *hunger* is to be tormented or afflicted (Deut. xxxii:24). (2) To fast is often called to *afflict one's soul* (Lev. xvi:29-31; Is. lviii:5). (3) Spiritual desire after Jesus and his righteousness is called *hunger;* how it pains men, till the blessings desired are obtained (Matt. v:6; Luke i:53). (4) *Such as feed on Christ never hunger nor thirst;* finding enough in him, they never desire anything else as the chief portion of their soul (John v:35). (5) *A man's strength is hunger-bitten* when it decays for want of food (Job xviii:12).

HUNGER-BITTEN (hŭn'gẽr bĭt't'n), (Heb. רָעֵב, *raw-abe'*, Job xviii:12), famished.

The words hunger-starved and winter-starved are used by the old writers. (See HUNGER, *Figurative* 5.)

HUNT, HUNTER, HUNTING (hŭnt'ĭng), (Heb. צַיִד, *tsah'-yid*, to lie in wait; רָדַף *raw-daf'*, to run after).

The pursuit and capture of beasts of the field was the first means of sustenance which the human race had recourse to, this mode of gaining a livelihood having naturally preceded the engagements of agriculture, as it presented food already provided, requiring only to be taken and slaughtered; whereas tillage must have been an afterthought, and a later resource, since it implies accumulated knowledge, skill, and such provision aforehand of subsistence as would enable a clan or a family to wait till the fruits of the earth were matured. Hunting was, therefore, a business long ere it was a sport. And originally, before man had established his empire on the earth, it must have been not only a serious, but a dangerous pursuit. In process of time, however, when civilization had made some progress, when cities were built and lands cultivated, hunting was carried on not so much for the food which it brought as for the recreation it gave and its conduciveness to health.

The East—the cradle of civilization—presents us with hunting in both the characters now spoken of, originally as a means of support, then as a manly amusement. In the early records of history we find hunting held in high repute, partly, no doubt, from its costliness, its dangers, its similitude to war, its capability of combining the energies of many, and also from the relief which it afforded to the stagnant monotony of a court, in the high and bounding spirits that it called forth. Hunting has always borne somewhat of a regal character, and down to the pres-

ent hour has worn an aristocratic air. In Babylon and Persia this attribute is presented in bold relief. Immense *parks* (παράδεισοι) were enclosed for nurturing and preserving beasts of the chase. The monarch himself led the way to the sport, not only in these preserves, but also over the wide surface of the country, being attended by his nobles, especially by the younger aspirants to fame and warlike renown (Xen. *Cyr.* viii, 1, 38).

In the Bible—our chief storehouse of primitive history and customs—we find hunting connected with royalty so early as in Gen. x. The great founder of Babel was in general repute as 'a mighty hunter before the Lord.' The patriarchs, however, are to be regarded rather as herdsmen than hunters, if respect is had to their habitual mode of life. The condition of the herdsman ensues next to that of the hunter in the early stages of civilization; and so we find that even Cain was a keeper of sheep. This and the fact that Abel is designated 'a tiller of the ground,' would seem to indicate a very rapid progress in the arts and pursuits of social life. The same contrast and similar hostility we find somewhat later, in the case of Jacob and Esau; the first, 'a plain man dwelling in tents;' the second, 'a cunning hunter, a man of the field' (Gen. xxv: 27). The account given of Esau in connection with his father seems to show that hunting was, conjointly with tillage, pursued at that time as a means of subsistence, and that hunting had not then passed into its secondary state, and become an amusement.

In Egypt the children of Israel would be spectators of hunting carried on extensively and pursued by different methods, but chiefly, as appears probable, with a view rather to recreation than subsistence (Wilkinson's *Anc. Egypt*, vol. iii). That the land of promise into which the Hebrews were conducted on leaving Egypt was plentifully supplied with beasts of the chase appears clear from Exod. xxiii:29, 'I will not drive them out in one year, lest the land become desolate and the beasts of the field multiply against thee' (comp. Deut. iii:22). And from the regulation given in Lev. xvii:15, it is manifest that hunting was practiced after the settlement in Canaan. and was pursued with the view of obtaining food. Prov. xii:27 proves that hunting animals for their flesh was an established custom among the Hebrews, though the turn of the passage may serve to show that at that time it was penned sport was the chief aim. If hunting was not forbidden in the 'year of rest,' special provision was made that not only the cattle, but 'the beast of the field' should be allowed to enjoy and flourish on the uncropped spontaneous produce of the land (Exod. xxiii:11; Lev. xxv:7).

That the lion and other ravenous beasts of prey were not wanting in Palestine, many passages of the Bible make obvious (1 Sam. xvii: 34; 2 Sam. xxiii:20; 1 Kings xiii:24; Harris, *Natural History of the Bible;* Kitto's *Pictorial Palestine*). The lion was even made use of to catch other animals (Ezek. xix:3), and Harmer long ago remarked that, as in the vicinity of Gaza, so also in Judæa, leopards were trained and used for the same purpose (Harmer, **iv**:358; Hab. i:8). That lions were taken by pitfalls, as well as by nets, appears from Ezek. xix:4, 8 (Shaw, p. 172). In the latter verse the words of the prophet, 'and spread their net over him,' allude to the custom of enclosing a wide extent of country with nets, into which the animals were driven by hunters (Wilkinson, *Anc. Egypt*, iii:4).

The spots thus enclosed were usually in a hilly country and in the vicinity of water brooks; whence the propriety and force of the language of Ps. xlii:1, 'As the (hunted) hart panteth after the water brooks.' These places were selected because they were those to which the animals were in the habit of repairing in the morning and evening. Scenes like the one now supposed are found portrayed in the Egyptian paintings (Wilkinson).

Hounds were used for hunting in Egypt, and, if the passage in Josephus (*Antiq.* iv:8, 9) may be considered decisive, in Palestine as well. From Gen. xxvii:3, 'Now take thy weapons, thy quiver and thy bow,' we learn what arms were employed, at least in capturing game. Bulls, after being taken, were kept at least for a time in a net (Is. li:20). Various missiles, pitfalls, snares, and gins were made use of in hunting (Ps. xci: 3; Amos iii:5; 2 Sam. xxiii:20). That hunting continued to be followed till towards the end of the Jewish state appears from Josephus (*De Bell. Jud.* i:20, 13), where the historian speaks of Herod as 'ever a most excellent hunter, for in one day he caught forty wild beasts.' The same passage makes it clear that horses were employed in the pursuits of the chase (comp. Joseph., *Antiq.* xv:7, 7; xvi:10, 3). J. R. B.

HUPHAM (hū'pham), (Heb. חוּפָם, *khoo-fawm'*, coast man, Gesenius), son of Benjamin, and the founder of the family of Huphamites (Num. xxvi:39). In Gen. xlvi:21 and 1 Chron. vii:12 the name is given as Huppim, B. C. 1856.

HUPHAMITES (hū'pham-ītes), (Heb. הַחוּפָמִי, *hah-khoo-faw-mee'*), descendants of Hupham, (Num. xxvi:39).

HUPPAH (hŭp'pah), (Heb. חֻפָּה, *khoop-paw'*, covering; protection), a priest under David who had charge of the thirteenth course of the temple service (1 Chron xxiv:13), B. C. 1014.

HUPPIM (hŭp'pim). See HUPHAM.

HUR (hûr), (Heb. חוּר, *khoor*, a hole; a prison).

1. A man of Judah mentioned with Moses and Aaron. We know but few particulars concerning his life; but by the little which Scripture relates, we see that Moses had a great affection for him. When he had sent Joshua against the Amalekites, he went up the mountain with Hur and Aaron (Exod. xvii:10), and while he lifted up his hands in prayer, Aaron and Hur supported his arms, to prevent their growing weary. When he ascended Mount Sinai to receive the law, he referred the elders, if any difficulty should arise, to Aaron and Hur (Exod. xxiv:14). (B. C. 1210.) Jewish tradition makes him identical with No. 2.

2. Son of Caleb, of Esron, and, according to Josephus, husband of Miriam, sister of Moses. Hur was the father of Uri, and Uri was the father of Bezaleel, who was chief artificer of the tabernacle (Exod. xxxi:2; xxxv:30; xxxviii:22; 2 Chron. i:5). Besides Uri he had three sons, who founded Kirjath-jearim, Bethlehem and Bath-gader. (B. C. 1210.)

3. A prince of Midian, killed in an encounter between Phinehas and the Midianites (Num. xxxi:8), B. C. 1170.

4. Father of Rephaiah, who was ruler over half the environs of Jerusalem, and repaired a part of the wall under Nehemiah (Neh. iii:9), B. C. 446.

5. A man called the son of Hur was Solomon's commissariat officer in Mount Ephraim (1 Kings iv:8). B. C. before 995.

HURAI (hū'rāi, or hū'ra-ī), (Heb. חוּרַי, *khoo-rah'ee*, linen worker), a man belonging to David's guard (1 Chron. xi:32). Kennicott thinks the name has been corrupted to Hiddai (2 Sam. xxxiii:30), B. C. 953.

HURAM (hū'ram), (Heb. חוּרָם, *khoo-rawm'*, highborn).

1. Eldest son of Bela, a Benjamite (1 Chron. viii:5).

2. The form of the name of the king of Tyre, in the time of David and Solomon, as given in 2 Chron. ii:3, 11; viii:2; ix:10. Elsewhere it is given as Hiram. (See HIRAM.)

3. The name Huram, the artificer, as it appears in 2 Chron. ii:13; iv:11, 16.

HURI (hū'rī), (Heb. חוּרִי, *khoo-ree'*, linen worker), father of Abihail, chief of the Gadite tribe (1 Chron. v:14), B. C. before 781.

HUSBAND (hŭz'band). See MARRIAGE.

HUSBANDMAN (hŭz'band-man), (properly Heb. אִישׁ אֲדָמָה, *eesh ad-aw-maw'*, man of the ground; Gr. γεωργός, *gheh-ore-gos'*, land worker), a farmer or other tiller of the soil. Husbandry is among the most ancient and honorable occupations (Gen. ix:20; xxvi:12, 14; xxxvii:7; Job i:3; Is. xxviii:24-28; John xv:1). (See AGRICULTURE.)

Figurative. (1) God is likened to a *husbandman;* he sows, plants, cultivates, and expects fruit from his church, head, and members (John xv:1); and the church is his *husbandry,* the great object of his care and work (1 Cor. iii:9). (2) The Jewish priests, rulers, and others were the *husbandmen* to whom God let out his vineyard, church, or ordinances; and who abused his prophets and son, and in the end were involved in ruin (Matt. xxi:33-41).

HUSBANDRY (hŭz'band-rў), (Gr. γεώργιον, *gheh-ore'ghee-on*). In 1 Cor. iii:9 'husbandry' is used figuratively in the sense of 'that which is cultivated': 'ye are God's husbandry', lit., as R. V. margin, 'God's field.'

HUSHAH (hū'shah), (Heb. חוּשָׁה, *khoo-shaw'*, haste). A name given (1 Chron. iv:4; xxvii:11) in the genealogies of Judah; but whether of a place or person it is impossible to say.

HUSHAI (hū'shāi, or hū'sha-ī), (Heb. חוּשַׁי, *khoo-shah'ee*, hasty), the Archite, David's friend.

Being informed of Absalom's rebellion, and that David was obliged to fly from Jerusalem, he met him on an eminence without the city, with his clothes rent, and his head covered with earth. David suggested that, if he went with him, he would be a burden to him; but that he might do him important service if he remained, and pretended to be in Absalom's interest, in order to defeat the counsel of Ahithophel (2 Sam. xv:32, etc.) Hushai, therefore, returned to Jerusalem, and, by defeating the counsel of Ahithophel, and gaining time for David, to whom he sent advices, was the cause of Ahithophel's suicide and of Absalom's miscarriage (2 Sam. xvi:16-19; xviii:5, etc.), about B. C. 1023.

HUSHAM (hū'sham), (Heb. חוּשָׁם, *khoo'shawm*, hastily), king of Edom, successor to Jobab, (Gen. xxxvi:34, 35; 1 Chron. i:45, 46). The LXX identify him with the Husham of the book of Job (B. C. bet. 1618 and 1093).

HUSHATHITE, THE (hū'shath-īte), (Heb. הַחֻשָׁתִי, *khu-sha-thee'*).

1. The designation of Sibbechai, one of David's guard (2 Sam. xxi:18; 1 Chron. xi:29; xx: 4; xxvii:11). From the last passage he must have been a descendant of Zerah of the tribe of Judah.

2. The appellation of Mebunñai, one of David's guard (2 Sam. xxiii:27). This is doubtless a corruption of **No. 1.**

HUSHIM (hū'shim), (Heb. חוּשִׁים, *khoo-sheem'*, hasters).

1. The designation of the sons of Dan (Gen. xlvi:23). In Num. xxvi the name appears as Shuham.

2. A name appearing in the genealogy of Benjamin (1 Chron. vii:12). The name probably represents the sons of Asher. (See Berthean in *Exeg. Handb.*)

3. A name of one of the two wives of Shaharaim in the genealogy of Benjamin (1 Chron. viii:8, 11), B. C. about 1618.

HUSKS (hŭsks), (Gr. κεράτιον, *ker-at' ee-on*, horned, Luke xv:16), the pods of *Ceratonia Siliqua*, L., the *carob tree*).

The carob tree is common in Palestine, and is used for food by the poor, and for the fattening of cattle or swine. When ripe it is like a crooked bean-pod, six to ten inches in length, brown, glossy, and filled with seeds. Miss M. E. Rogers says: "I found it when new rather too sweet to suit my taste. Children seem to enjoy it, and they thrive on it, eating the shell as well as the seeds." The carob tree belongs to the same family as the American "locusts," and is often called by that name by English authors. Some suppose that it was upon these "locusts" that John the Baptist subsisted. Hence this fruit is often called "St. John's bread." But the better critics reject this opinion (Schaff, *Bib. Dict.*). An inspissated decoction of them is known as *dibs kharrûb*, i. e., *carob honey*. (See CERATIA for a full treatment of the subject.)

HUZ (hŭz), (trees), eldest son of Nahor and Milcah (Gen. xxii:21). Elsewhere written Uz. (See Uz.)

HUZZAB (hŭz'zab), (Heb. נַצַּב, *naw-tsab,'* to establish), queen of Nineveh in the time of Nahum (Nah. ii:7).

Many modern critics, however, take the word to be the Hophal of a verb (see Buxtorf, *Lex.;* Gesenius, *Lex*, p. 903). But there is no reason why the word should not be a geographical term —the equivalent of Assyria, i. e., the Zab country.

HYACINTH (hī'à-sĭnth), jacinth. (See LESHEM.)

HYENA (hī-ē'nà), (Heb. צָבוּעַ, *tsaw-boo'ah*, speckled, Ecclus. xiii:18).

Excepting in Ecclesiasticus, just noted, the word does not occur in the English Bible, although there are several passages in the Hebrew canonical books, where *tsawbooah*, 'streaked' or 'variegated,' is assumed to designate the hyena. The most noted of these is Jer. xii:9, where the words, σπήλαιον ὑαίνης, 'the cave of the hyena,' modern commentators preferred to translate 'a speckled bird,' as it stands in our version. But Bochart and the continuator of Calmet vindicate what we take to be the true reading, *oith tsawbooah*, 'the striped rusher,' i. e., the hyena, turning round upon his lair—introduced after an allusion in the previous verse to the lion calling to the beasts of the field (other hyenas and jackals) to come and devour. This allusion, followed up,

as it is, by a natural association of ideas, with a description of the pastor, feeder, or rather consumer or devourer of the vineyard, treading down and destroying the vines, renders the natural and poetical picture complete, for the hyena seeks burrows and caverns for a lair; like the dog it

Hyena.

turns round to lie down; howls, and occasionally acts in concert; is loathsome, savage, insatiable in appetite, offensive in smell; and will, in the season, like canines, devour grapes, as the writer has himself ascertained by actual experiment.

Tsawbooah, therefore, we consider proved to be, generically, the hyena. The striped species is one of three or four—all, it seems, originally African, and, by following armies and caravans, gradually spread over Southern Asia to beyond the Ganges, though not as yet to the east of the Bramapootra. It is now not uncommon in Asia Minor.

C. H. S.

HYMN (hĭm), (Gr. ὕμνος, *hum'nos*, a hymn). In the only places of the New Testament where this word occurs, it is connected with two others of very similar import. 'Speaking to yourselves in *psalms* (ψαλμοῖς), and *hymns* (ὕμνοις), and spiritual *s ngs* (ᾠδαῖς), singing and making melody in your heart to the Lord' (Eph. v:19; Col. iii:16).

It has been conjectured that, by 'psalms and hymns,' the poetical compositions of the Old Testament are chiefly to be understood, and that the epithet 'spiritual,' here applied to 'songs,' is intended to mark those devout effusions which resulted from the spiritual gifts granted to the primitive church; yet in 1 Cor. xiv:26 a production of the latter class is called 'a psalm.' Josephus, it may be remarked, uses the terms ὕμνοι, *hymns*, and ᾠδαί, *songs*, in reference to the Psalms of David (*Antiq.* vii:12, 3). Our information respecting the hymnology of the first Christians is extremely scanty: the most distinct notice we possess of it is that contained in Pliny's celebrated Epistle (*Ep.* x:97). (See POETRY, HEBREW.)

The hymn which our Lord sang with his disciples at the Last Supper is generally supposed to have been the latter part of the *Hallel,* or series of psalms which were sung by the Jews on the night of the Passover, comprehending Ps. cxiii-cxviii; Ps. cxiii and cxiv being sung before, and the rest after, the Passover. J. E. R.

HYKSOS (hĭk'sŏs), (compounded according to Josephus, of the Egyptian *hyk*, "king," and *sos*, "shepherd," or "Arab"), a race who invaded Egypt and constituted the 15th and one or both of the two following dynasties. (See EGYPT.)

HYMENÆUS (hȳ'me-næ'us), (Gr. Ὑμεναῖος, *hoo-men-ah'yos*, wedding song), a professor of Christianity at Ephesus, who, with Alexander (1 Tim. i:20) and Philetus (2 Tim. ii:17), had departed from the truth both in principle and practice, and led others into apostasy.

The chief doctrinal error of these persons consisted in maintaining that 'the resurrection was past already.' The precise meaning of this expression is by no means clearly ascertained; the most general and perhaps best founded opinion is that they understood the resurrection in a figurative sense of the great change produced by the Gospel dispensation. Most critics suppose that the same person is referred to in both the epistles to Timothy by the name of Hymenæus. Dr. Mosheim, however, contends that there were two, but his reasoning is not convincing.   J. E. R.

HYPERBOLE (hĭ-pẽr'bŏ-lĕ), a figure of speech in which the expression is an evident exaggeration of the meaning intended to be conveyed, or by which things are represented as much greater or less, better or worse, than they really are.

Any one who carefully examines the Bible must be surprised at the very few hyperbolic expressions which it contains, considering that it is an Oriental book. Some of these few have occasioned so much difficulty to sincere men that we have reason to bless God that the scene of those great events which comprise the history of man's salvation was laid in Western, and not in Eastern Asia, where the genius of hyperbole reigns without limit or control. In Eastern Asia the tone of composition is pitched so high as to be scarcely intelligible to the sober intellect of Europe; while in Western Asia a medium seems to have been struck between the ultra-extravagance of the far East and the frigid exactness of the far West.

But even regarded as a book of Western Asia, the Bible is, as compared with almost any other Western Asiatic book, so singularly free from hyperbolic expressions as might well excite our surprise, did not our knowledge of its divine origin permit us to suppose that even the style and mode of expression of the writers were so far controlled as to exclude from their writings what in other ages and countries might excite pain and offense, and prove an obstacle to the reception of divine truth. Nor is it to be said that the usage of hyperbole is of modern growth. We find it in the oldest Eastern writings which now exist; and the earlier rabbinical writings attest that, in times approaching near to those in which the writers of the New Testament flourished, the Jewish imagination had run riot in this direction, and has left hyperboles as frequent and outrageous as any which Persia or India can produce.

These things being considered, we shall certainly have more cause to admire the rarity of hyperbolic expressions in the Bible than to marvel at those which do occur.

The strongest hyperbole in all Scripture is that with which the Gospel of St. John concludes: 'There are also many other things which Jesus did, the which, if they should be written every one, I suppose that the world itself could not contain all the books that should be written' (John xxi:25). This has so much pained many commentators that they have been disposed to regard it as an unauthorized addition to the sacred text, and to reject it accordingly. Now this is always a dangerous process, and not to be adopted but on such overwhelming authority of collated manuscripts as does not exist in the present case. How much more natural and becoming is it to regard the verse simply as a hyperbole, so perfectly conformable to Oriental modes of expression, and to some other hyperboles which may be found interspersed in the sacred books, that the sole wonder really is that this one should be rare enough to afford ground for objection and remark. Some

claim that the text means that the world could not receive, or accept, the books. The same Greek word is translated "receive" in Matt. xix: 11, 12. We often find sacred and profane authors using hyperboles of the like kind and signification. In Num. xiii:33, the spies who had returned from searching the land of Canaan, say that they saw 'giants there, of such a prodigious size that they were in their own sight as grasshoppers." In Deut. i:28, cities with high walls about them are said to be 'walled up to heaven.' In Dan. iv:7 mention is made of a tree whereof 'the height reached unto heaven, and the sight thereof unto the end of all the earth;' and the author of Ecclesiasticus (xlvii:15), speaking of Solomon's wisdom, says, 'Thy soul covered the whole earth, and thou filledst it with parables.' As the world is here said to be filled with Solomon's parables; so in John xxi:25, by one degree more of hyperbole, it is said that the world could not contain all the books that should be written concerning Jesus' miracles, if a particular account of every one of them were given. In Josephus (*Antiq.* xiv:22) God is mentioned as promising to Jacob that he would give the land of Canaan to him and his seed; and then it is added, 'they shall fill the whole sea and land which the sun shines upon.' Wetstein, in his note on the text in John, and Basnage, in his *Histoire des Juifs* (iii:1-9; v:7), have cited from the ancient rabbinical writers such passages as the following: 'If all the seas were ink, and every reed was a pen, and the whole heaven and earth were parchment, and all the sons of men were writers, they would not be sufficient to write all the lessons which Jochanan composed;' and, concerning one Eliezer, it is said that, 'if the heavens were parchment, and all the sons of men writers, and all the trees of the forest pens, they would not be sufficient for writing all the wisdom which he was possessed of.'

Hyperboles not less strong than that under review find their way into our own poetry, without shocking our judgment or offending our taste, thus:

'And I as rich in having such a jewel
As fifty seas, if all their sands were pearl,
Their rivers nectar, and their rocks pure gold.'
(See Bishop Pearce's *Commentary on the Four Evangelists.*)

HYPOCRISY (hĭ-pŏk'rĭ-sў), (Hebrew from חָנֵף, *khaw-nafe'*, a seeming or professing to be what in truth and reality we are not).

It consists in assuming a character which we are conscious does not belong to us, and by which we intentionally impose upon the judgment and opinion of mankind. The name is borrowed from the Greek ὑπόκρισις, *hoop-ok'ree-sis*, an answer, to play a part, in which it primarily signifies the profession of a stage player, which is to express in speech, habit and action, not his own person and manners, but *his* whom he undertakes to represent. And so it is, for the very essence of hypocrisy lies in apt imitation and deceit; in acting the part of a member of Christ without any saving grace.

HYPOCRITE (hĭp'ŏ-krĭt). The hypocrite is a *double* person; he has one person, which is natural; another, which is artificial; the first he keeps to himself; the other he puts on as he does his clothes, to make his appearance in before men. It was ingeniously said by Basil, "that the hypocrite has not put off the old man, but put on the *new* upon it." Hypocrites have been divided into four sorts: (1) The *worldly* hypocrite, who makes a profession of religion, and pretends to be religious, merely from worldly considerations (Matt. xxiii:5). (2) The *legal* hypocrite, who relinquishes his vicious practices, in order thereby to merit heaven, while at the same time he has no real love to God (Rom. x:3). (3) The *evangelical* hypocrite, whose religion is nothing more than a bare conviction of sin; who rejoices under the idea that Christ died for him, and yet has no desire to live a holy life (Matt. xiii:20; 2 Pet. ii:20). (4) The *enthusiastic* hypocrite, who has an imaginary sight of his sin, and of Christ; who talks of remarkable impulses and high feelings; and thinks himself very wise and good while he indulges in the most evil practices (Matt. xiii: 39; 2 Cor. xi:14). Brown.

HYSSOP (hĭs'sŭp), (Heb. אֵזוֹב, *ay-zobe'*; Gr. ὕσσωπος, *hoos'so-pos*).

A great variety of opinions have been entertained respecting the plant called *esobh,* translated 'hyssop' in the Authorized Version both of the Old and the New Testaments; but as yet no satisfactory investigation has been made, so as to enable us to fix with certainty on the plant intended.

Hyssop.

The first notice of it occurs in Exod. xii:22, where a bunch of hyssop is directed to be dipped in blood and struck on the lintels and the two side-posts of the doors of the houses in which the Israelites resided. It is next mentioned in Lev. xiv:4, 6, 52, in the ceremony for declaring lepers to be cleansed; and again, in Num. xix:6, 18, in preparing the water of separation. To these passages the apostle alludes in Heb. ix: 19: 'For when Moses had spoken every precept to all the people, according to the law, he took the blood of calves, and of goats, with water, and scarlet wool, and hyssop, and sprinkled both the book and all the people.' From *hoossopos* we find that the Greek name *hoossopos* was considered synonymous with the Hebrew *esobh;* and from the preceding that the plant must have been leafy, and large enough to serve for the purpose of sprinkling, and that it must have been found in Lower Egypt, as well as in the country toward Mount Sinai, and onward to Palestine. From the following passages we get the supposed properties of the plant. Thus, in I Kings iv:33, it is said, 'Solomon spoke of trees, from the cedar-tree that is in Lebanon, even unto the hyssop, that springeth out of the wall;' and in the penitential psalm of David (li:7), 'Purge me with hyssop, and I shall be clean; wash me, and I shall be whiter than snow.' In this passage it is no doubt considered by some commentators that hyssop is used in a figurative sense; but still it is possible that the plant may have possessed some general cleansing properties, and thus came to be employed in preference to other plants in the ceremonies of purification. It ought, at all events, to be found growing upon walls, and in Palestine.

In the account of the crucifixion of our Savior, the Apostle John says (John xix:29), 'Now there was set a vessel full of vinegar, and they filled a sponge with vinegar, and put it upon *hyssop,* and put it to his mouth.' In the parallel passages of Matthew (xxvii:48) and Mark (xv: 36), it is stated that the sponge filled with vinegar was put upon a reed or stick. To reconcile these statements some commentators have supposed that both the sponge and the hyssop were tied to a stick, and that one apostle mentions only the hyssop, because he considered it as the most important; while, for the same reason, the other two mention only the stick; but the simplest mode of explaining the apparent discrepancy is to consider the hyssop and the stick to be the same thing—in other words, that the sponge was affixed to a stick of hyssop.

A great variety of plants have been adduced by different authors as that alluded to in the above passages. It has been thought by some to belong to the class of ferns. Some again contend for species of wormwood, as being, from their bitterness, most likely to have been added to the vinegar in the sponge, that it might be more distasteful to our Savior. The majority, however, have selected different kinds of fragrant plants belonging to the natural family of *Labiatæ,* several of which are found in dry and barren situations in Palestine, and also in some parts of the Desert. Of these may be mentioned the rosemary, species of lavender, of mint, of marjoram, of thyme, of savory, of thymbra, and others of the same tribe resembling each other much in characters as well as in properties; but it does not appear that any of them grow on walls, or are possessed of cleansing properties; and with the exception of the rosemary, they are not capable of yielding a stick, nor are they found in all the required situations.

The *Origanum maru,* however, corresponds with the Arabic definition. It has a slender, square stem, and grows on the walls of the terraces throughout Palestine and Syria. The stem is free from thorns and spreading branches, but ends in a cluster of heads. The odor is highly aromatic, which fits it to be made into a branch for the purpose of sprinkling; in fact, no plant in the East is so well suited for such a purpose. (See YSOP.)

I

I, when it relates to God, is expressive of his dignity (Ps. lxxxi:10); his power (Gen. xvii:1); his self-existence and unchangeableness (Exod. iii:14); where his name is given "I AM" (Heb. אֶהְיֶה אֲשֶׁר אֶהְיֶה, *ehyeh asher ehyeh*, God is he who is).

It relates also to the certainty of his promises and threatenings (Exod. vi:2; Num. xiv:35). Referring to men, it expresses their pride (Is. xlvii:8); the certainty of what they say (Gal. v:2; Phil. iv:11), and their readiness to perform their duty (Micah iii:8; Matt. xxi:30).

IBHAR (ĭb'har), (Heb. יִבְחָר, *yib-khar'*, choice).

A son of David mentioned in the lists (2 Sam. v:15; 1 Chron. iii:6; xiv:5), between Solomon and Elishua. He was born in Jerusalem, and his mother was apparently a wife and not a concubine (B. C. post 1044).

IBIS (ī'bĭs), a bird (Lev. xi:19, R. V. margin), related to the herons and storks. It was formerly held in veneration by the Egyptians. (See HERON.)

IBLEAM (ĭb'le-ăm), (Heb. יִבְלְעָם, *yib-leh-awm'*, devouring people), a city of Issachar, which with its suburbs was allotted to Manasseh (Josh. xvii: 11), but from which the Israelites were unable to expel the Canaanites (Judg. i:27).

Its position is given as between Dor and Megiddo, near the pass of Gur (2 Kings ix:27). The name appears as Bileam (1 Chron. vi:70), where it is stated that the city was assigned to the family of Kohath as a Levitical city. The site is probably that of the modern *Jelameh,* two and a half miles north of Jenin (Robinson, *Researches,* iii:161).

IBNEIAH (ib-nē'ya), (Heb. יִבְנְיָה, *yib-neh-yaw'*, built by Jah), son of Jeroham, who was a chief of the Benjamites and returned with them to Jerusalem from Babylon (1 Chron ix:8), B. C. 536.

IBNIJAH (ib-nī'jah), (Heb. יִבְנִיָּה, *yib-nee-yaw'*, building of Jah), a Benjamite, father of Reuel and ancestor of Meshullam, who settled in Jerusalem after the return from captivity (1 Chron. ix:8), B. C. much before 536.

IBRI (ĭb'rī), (Heb. עִבְרִי, *ib-ree'*, an Eberite, or "Hebrew"), a Levite in the time of David, and son of Merari by Jaaziah (1 Chron. xxiv:27), B. C. 1014. The name is the same as the word rendered *Hebrew* in the A. V.

IBZAN (ĭb'zăn), (Heb. אִבְצָן, *ib-tsawn'*, shining), the tenth 'judge of Israel.'

He was of Bethlehem, probably the Bethlehem of Zebulun and not of Judah. He governed seven years. The prosperity of Ibzan is marked by the great number of his children (thirty sons and thirty daughters), and his wealth, by their marriages—for they were all married. Some have held, with little probability, that Ibzan was the same with Boaz, (Judg. xii:8), B. C. 1249-1243.

ICE (īs), (Heb. קֶרַח, *keh'rakh*, smooth, Job vi:16; xxxviii:29; Ps. cxlvii:17), elsewhere *cold*, "frost," but *crystal* in Ezek. i:22.

Snow has fallen at times nearly to a depth of two feet on the Central Range in Palestine, and ice has sometimes been formed on the pools at Jerusalem, but very rarely.

ICHABOD (ĭk'a-bŏd), (Heb. אִי־כָבוֹד, *ee-kaw-bode'*, where is the glory? inglorious), son of Phinehas and grandson of Eli.

He is only known from the unhappy circumstances of his birth, which occasioned this name to be given to him. The pains of labor came upon his mother when she heard that the ark of God was taken, that her husband was slain in battle, and that these tidings had proved fatal to his father Eli. They were death-pains to her; and when those around sought to cheer her, saying, 'Fear not, for thou hast borne a son,' she only answered by giving him the name of Ichabod, adding, 'The glory is departed from Israel' (1 Sam. iv:19-22), B. C. 1141. The name again occurs in 1 Sam. xiv:3. (See ELI.)

ICONIUM (ī-kō'ni-ŭm), (Gr. Ἰκόνιον, *ee-kon'ee-on*, of unknown derivation), a town, formerly the capital of Lycaonia, as it is now, by the name of Konieh, of Karamania, in Asia Minor.

It is situated in N. lat 37° 51', E. long. 32° 40', about 120 miles inland from the Mediterranean. It was visited by St. Paul in A. D. 45, when many Gentiles were converted; but some unbelieving Jews excited against him and Barnabas a persecution, which they escaped with difficulty (Acts xiii:51; xiv:1, 19, 21; xvi:2; 2 Tim. iii:11). He undertook a second journey to Iconium in A. D. 51. The church planted at this place by the apostle continued to flourish until, by the persecutions of the Saracens, and afterward of the Seljukians, who made it one of their sultanies, it was nearly extinguished. But some Christians of the Greek and Armenian churches, with a Greek metropolitan bishop, are still found in the suburbs of the city, not being permitted to reside within the walls.

Konieh is situated at the foot of Mount Taurus, upon the border of the lake Trogitis, in a fertile plain, rich in valuable productions, particularly apricots, wine, cotton, flax, and grain. The circumference of the town is between two and three miles, beyond which are suburbs not much less populous than the town itself. The town, suburbs, and gardens are plentifully supplied with water from streams which flow from some hills to the westward, and which, to the northeast, join the lake, which varies in size with the season of the year. In the town carpets are manufactured, and blue and yellow leathers are tanned and dried. Cotton, wool, hides and a few of the other raw productions which enrich the superior industry and skill of the manufacturers of Europe, are sent to Smyrna by caravans.

The city, like all those renowned for superior sanctity, abounds with dervishes, who meet the passenger at every turning of the streets and demand paras with the greatest clamor and insolence. The bazaars and houses have little to recommend them to notice (Kinneir's *Travels in Asia Minor;* Leake's *Geography of Asia Minor;* Arundell's *Tour in Asia Minor;* Hamilton, *Researches in Asia Minor,* ii:205 *sq.*; Harper's *Classical Dictionary*).

IDALAH (ĭ-dā'lah), (Heb. יִדְאֲלָה, *yid-al-aw'*, probably exalted), one of the cities of Zebulun, near the western border (Josh. xix:15). Schwarz identified it with *Kellah al-Chiré*, which is probably the Kulat el-Kireh of Robinson, six miles southwest of Semunieh in the Kishon valley, exact site unknown.

IDBASH (ĭd'băsh), (Heb. יִדְבָּשׁ, *yid-bawsh'*, perhaps honeyed, *sweet*), a descendant of Judah (1 Chron. iv:3). By the phrase "of the father of Etam" we are probably to understand that he was a descendant of the founder of Etam, as the list here is largely a topographical one (B. C. about 1612).

IDDO (ĭd'do), (Heb. עִדּוֹ, *id-do'*, seasonable).

1. A prophet of Judah, who wrote the history of Rehoboam and Abijah; or rather perhaps, who, in conjunction with Seraiah, kept the public rolls during their reigns (2 Chron. xii:15). It seems from 2 Chron. xiii:22 that he named his book *Midrash*, or 'Exposition.' Josephus (*Antiq.* viii: 9, 1) states that this Iddo was the prophet who was sent to Jeroboam at Bethel, and consequently the same that was slain by a lion for disobedience to his instructions (1 Kings xiii); and many commentators have followed this statement (B. C. after 953).

2. Grandfather of the prophet Zechariah (Zech. i:1; Ezra v:1; vi:14). He was one of the chief priests who returned from the captivity with Zerubbabel (Neh. xii:4), B. C. 536.

3. *Id-do'*, (Heb. אִדּוֹ), chief of the Jews of the captivity established at Casiphia, a place of which it is difficult to determine the position.

It was to him that Ezra sent a requisition for Levites and Nethinim, none of whom had yet joined his caravan. Thirty-eight Levites and 250 Nethinim responded to his call (Ezra viii:17-20), B. C. 457. It would seem from this that Iddo was a chief person of the Nethinim, descended from those Gibeonites who were charged with the servile labors of the tabernacle and temple. This is one of several circumstances which indicate that the Jews in their several colonies under the Exile were still ruled by the heads of their nation, and allowed the free exercise of their worship.

4. *Yid-do'* (Heb. יִדּוֹ, lovely), a chief of the half tribe of Manasseh beyond the Jordan (1 Chron. xxvii:21), B. C. 1014.

5. A Levite, descendant of Gershom through his father Joah (1 Chron. vi:21). In verse 41 the name is *Adaiah*, who is given as an ancestor of Asaph.

6. Father of Abinadab, which latter was a purveyor under Solomon over Mahanaim (1 Kings iv:14), B. C. about 995.

IDLE (i'd'l), (Heb. רָפָה, *raw-faw'*).

The ordinary uses of this word require no illustration. But the very serious passage in Matt. xii:36 may suitably be noticed in this place. In the Authorized Version it is translated, 'I say unto you, that *every idle word* that men shall speak, they shall give an account thereof in the day of judgment.' The whole question depends upon the meaning or rather force of the term ῥῆμα ἀργόν, *rha'ma ar-gon'*, 'idle word,' concerning which there has been no little difference of opinion. Many understand it to mean 'wicked and injurious words,' as if *argon*, *vain*, *empty* were the same as πονηρόν, *pon-ay-ron'*, wicked.

The meaning of the expression seems to be *void of effect, without result, followed by no corresponding event.* Therefore *rha-ma argon* is *empty or vain words* or *discourse, i. e.,* void of

truth, and to which the event does not correspond. In short, it is the empty, inconsiderate, insincere language of one who says one thing and means another; and in this sense *argos* is very frequently employed by the Greeks. This Tittmann confirms by a number of citations, and then deduces from the whole that the sense of the passage under review is: 'Believe me, he who uses false and insincere language shall suffer grievous punishment; your words, if uttered with sincerity and ingenuousness, shall be approved; but if they are dissembled although they bear the strongest appearance of sincerity, they shall be condemned.' (See Tittmann, *On the Principal Causes of Forced Interpretations of the New Testament, in Am. Bib. Repository* for 1831, pp. 481-484.)

IDOL (i'dŏl).

A large number of Hebrew and Greek words have been rendered in the Bible either by idol or image. These embrace: (1) A class of abstract terms, which, with a deep moral significance, express the degradation associated with it, and stand out as a protest of the language against the enormities of idolatry; (2) those words which more directly apply to the images or idols, as the outward symbols of the deity who was worshiped through them; (3) the terms which have regard to the material and workmanship of the idol rather than to its character as an object of worship.

1. Abstract Terms. **1.** *Ay-maw'* (Heb. אֵימָה), horror, or terror, or terrifying shapes, and hence an object of horror or terror (Jer. 1:38), in reference either to the hideousness of the idols or to the gross character of their worship. In this respect it is closely connected with number 2.

2. *Mif-leh'tseth* (Heb. מִפְלֶצֶת), a "fright," "horror," applied to the idol of Maachah, probably of wood, which Asa cut down and burned (1 Kings xv:13; 2 Chron. xv:16), and which was unquestionably the Phallus, the symbol of the productive power of nature and the nature-goddess Ashera. Allusion is supposed to be made to this in Jer. x:5 and Epist. of Jer. 70 (in the Apocrypha). In 2 Chron. xv:16 the Vulg. render "*simulacrum Priapi*" the image of *Priapus*. (Smith).

3. *El-eel'* (Heb. אֱלִיל), the inane, good for nothing (Lev. xix:4).

It is supposed by some to have a sense akin to that of שֶׁקֶר, *sheh-ker'*, "falsehood," with which it stands in parallelism in Job xiii:4, and would therefore much resemble *aw'-ven*, as applied to an idol. It is used to denote the idols of Noph or Memphis (Ezek. xxx:13). In marked contrast with Jehovah it is seen in Ps. xcvi:5; xcvii:7).

4. *Aw'ven* (Heb. אָוֶן, rendered elsewhere "nought," "vanity," "iniquity," "wickedness," "sorrow," etc., and once only "idol," Is. lxvi:3). The primary idea of the root seems to be emptiness, nothingness, as of breath or vapor; and, by a natural transition, in a moral sense, wickedness in its active form of mischief, and then, as the result, sorrow and trouble. Hence *awven* denotes a vain, false, wicked thing, and expresses at once the essential nature of idols, and the consequences of their worship, akin to הֶבֶל, *heh'bel*, the foolish things, vanities, of Acts xiv:15 (comp. Jer. ii:5).

5. *Ghil-loo-leem'* (Heb. גִּלּוּלִים), is used as a term of contempt, but of uncertain origin (Ezek. xxx:13). In Ezek. iv:12, Zeph. i:17, some have favored the interpretation given in the margin of the A. V. to Deut. xxix:17, "dungy gods." (See 1 Kings xv:12.)

6. *Bo'sheth* (Heb. בֹּשֶׁת), "shame," or "shameful thing" (A. V. Jer. xi:13; Hos. ix:10), applied to Baal or Baal-Peor, as characterizing the obscenity of his worship. It is found in close connection with *el-eel'*.

7. *Shik-koots'* (Heb. שִׁקּוּץ), "filth," "impurity," especially applied, like *shekets*, to that which produced ceremonial uncleanness (Ezek. xxxvii:23; Nah. iii:6), such as food offered in sacrifice to idols (Zech. ix:7; comp. Acts xv:20, 29).

As referring to the idols themselves, it primarily denotes the obscene rites with which their worship was associated, and hence, by metonymy, is applied both to the objects of worship and also to their worshipers, who partook of the impurity, and thus "became loathsome like their love," the foul Baal-Peor (Hos. ix:10).

2. Names of Idols. These may be considered as indicating that the images were made in imitation of external objects, and to represent some idea, or attribute; or as they denote the workmanship by which they were fashioned.

1. (Heb. צֶלֶם, *tseh-lem'*, and צֶלֶם, *tsel-em*, shadow).

It is the "image" of God in which man was created (Gen. i:27; comp. Wisd. ii:23), distinguished from דְּמוּת, *dem-ooth*, or "likeness," as the "image," from the "idea" which it represents (Schmidt, *de Imag. Dei in Hom.* p. 84), though it would be rash to insist upon this distinction. But whatever abstract term may best define the meaning of *tselem*, it is unquestionably used to denote the visible forms of external objects, and is applied to figures of gold and silver (1 Sam. vi:5; Num. xxxiii:52; Dan. iii:1), such as the golden image of Nebuchadnezzar, as well as to those painted upon the walls. (Ezek. xxiii:14). "Image" perhaps most nearly represents it in all passages. Applied to the human countenance (Dan. iii:19) it signifies the "expression," and corresponds to the ἰδέα of Matt. xxviii:3, though *dem-ooth'* agrees rather with the Platonic usage of the latter word. (See IMAGE.)

2. (Heb. סֶמֶל, *seh'mel*, or סֵמֶל, *say'mel*, semblance, likeness). In 2 Chron. xxxiii:7 it appears as "carved images," following the LXX τὸ γλυπτόν, *to glupton*. On the whole the Greek εἰκών, *aikone*, of Deut. iv:16, 2 Chron. xxxiii:7, and the "simulacrum" of the Vulgate (2 Chron. xxxiii:15) most nearly resemble the Hebrew *say'mel*.

3. (Heb. תְּמוּנָה, *tem-oo-naw'*), rendered "image" in Job iv:16; elsewhere "similitude" (Deut. iv:12); "likeness," (Deut. iv:16); "form" or "shape" would be better (comp. 2 Kings xvii:16; Exod. xx:4; Num. xii:8).

4. (Heb. מַצֵּבָה, *mats-tsay-baw'*, anything *set up*, a "*statue*", applied to a memorial stone like those erected by Jacob on four several occasions (Gen. xxviii:18; xxxi:45; xxxv:14, 20) to commemorate a crisis in his life, or to mark the grave of Rachel, (comp. Jer. xliii:13).

Such were the stones set up by Joshua (Josh. iv:9) after the passage of the Jordan, and at Shechem (xxiv:26), and by Samuel when victorious over the Philistines (1 Sam. vii:12). When solemnly dedicated they were anointed with oil, and libations were poured upon them. The word is applied to denote the obelisks which stood at the entrance to the temple of the Sun at Heliopolis (Jer. xliii:13), two of which were a hundred cubits high and eight broad, each of a single stone (Her. ii:111). It is also used of the statues of Baal (2 Kings iii:2), whether of stone

(2 Kings x:27) or wood, which stood in the innermost recess of the temple at Samaria. The Palladium of Troy, the black stone in the Kaaba at Mecca, said to have been brought from heaven by the angel Gabriel, and the stone at Ephesus, "which fell down from Jupiter" (Acts xix:35), are examples of the belief, anciently so common, that the gods sent down their images upon earth.

5. (Heb. עָצָב, *aw-tsawb'*).

6. (Heb. עֶצֶב, *eh'tseb*, Jer. xxii:28).

7. (Heb. עֹצֶב, *oh'tseb*, Is. xlviii:5), a "figure." (The three immediately foregoing are derived from a root *aw-tsab'*, signifying "to work," "to fashion.")

8. (Heb. צִיר, *tseer*, once only applied to an idol, Is. xlv:16).

9. (Heb. מַשְׂכִּית, *mas-keeth'*, Lev. xxvi:1; Num. xxxiii:52; Ezek. viii:12).

The opinion is held by some that *Eben maskeeth'* was originally a smooth elevated stone, employed for the purpose of obtaining from it a freer prospect, and of offering prayer in prostration upon it to the deities of heaven. Hence, generally, they conclude it signifies a stone of prayer or devotion, and the "chambers of imagery" of Ezek. viii:12 are "chambers of devotion."

10. (Heb. תְּרָפִים, *ter'aw-feme*, teraphim). See TERAPHIM.

11. (Heb. חַמָּנִים, *kham-maw-neem'*), in the margin of most passages "sun images." It is used in conjunction with the symbols of the nature goddess Asherah (2 Chron. xiv:3, 5; xxxiv:4, 7; Is. xvii:9; xxvii:8), as was otherwise usual with Baal and Asherah.

They are mentioned with the Asherim, and the latter are coupled with the statues of Baal (1 Kings xiv:23; 2 Kings xxiii:14). The *chammânîm* and statues are used promiscuously (comp. 2 Kings xxiii:14 and 2 Chron. xxxiv:4; 2 Chron. xiv:3, 5), but are never spoken of together. They were probably images of the fire god Baal, and seem to have represented a rising flame of fire, being made of either wood or stone.

3. Material, Etc. Terms denoting the material, tools, workmanship, etc.

1. Heb. נֶסֶךְ, *neh'sek*, or נֵסֶךְ, *nay'sek*, and מַסֵּכָה, *mas-say-kaw'*, are evidently synonymous (Is. xli:29; xlviii:5; Jer. x:14) in later Hebrew, and denote a "molten" image. *Mas-say'kaw'* is frequently used in distinction from *peh'sel* (Deut. xxvii:15; Judg. xvii:3, etc).

2. Heb. פֶּסֶל, *peh'sel*, and פְּסִילִים, *pes-eel-eem'*, usually translated in the A. V. "graven" or "carved" images. In two passages the latter is ambiguously rendered "quarries" (Judg. iii:19, 26).

The verb is used to indicate the finished result of the workmanship of the masons (Ex. xxxiv:4; 1 Kings v:18). *Peh-sel* was later employed of a figure cast in metal (Is. xl:19; xliv:10). These "sculptured" images were probably wood, iron, or stone, covered with gold or silver (Deut. vii:25; Is. xxx:22; Hab. ii:19), the more costly being of solid metal (Is. xl:19) brass and clay were employed for the same purpose (Dan. ii:33; v:23).

4. Forms of Idols. Among the earliest objects of worship, regarded as symbols of deity, were the meteoric stones which the ancients believed to have been the images of the gods sent down from heaven; then rough unhewn blocks;

then stone columns or pillars of wood, in which the Divinity worshiped was supposed to dwell, and which were consecrated, like the sacred stone at Delphi, by being anointed with oil and crowned with wool on solemn days.

We have not many traces of the forms of idolatrous images in the Bible. Dagon, the fish-god of the Philistines, was a human figure terminating in a fish (see DAGON). A few bore some symbolical reference to the worship of the true God, and partook of the nature of idolatry; such, for example, as the golden calf of Aaron comp. Neh. ix :18) ; those of Jeroboam; the singular ephods of Gideon and Micah (Judg. viii :27; xvii :5). (Mc. & Str. *Cyc.;* Smith's *Bib. Dict.*)

IDOLATRY (ĭ-dŏl'a-trỹ), (Heb. תְּרָפִים, *ter-aw-feme'*, teraphim, once only, 1 Sam. xv:23).

1. Definition and Classification. Idolatry, strictly speaking, denotes the worship of deity in a visible form, whether the images to which homage is paid are symbolical representations of the true God, or of the false divinities which have been worshiped in his stead. Idolatry may be classified under the following heads : (1) *Fetishism, or low nature* worship of trees, rivers, hills and stones; (2) of animals; (3) of high nature worship, as the sun, moon and stars, and the powers or forces of nature, as fire, air, etc.; (4) hero worship, as of the leaders of a nation, or of deceased ancestors; (5) *idealism* or the worship of mental qualities or abstractions, as *justice,* etc. There may also be added to these: (a) the worship of the true God by images; (b) of false gods by images; (c) of the worship of the images or symbols themselves.

2. Idolatry Through Heathen Nations. The heathen nations who influenced the Israelites were as follows:

(1) Chaldea. The early existence of idolatry is evinced by Josh. xxiv :2, where it is stated that Abram and his immediate ancestors dwelling in Mesopotamia 'served other gods.' The terms in Gen. xxxi :53, and particularly the plural form of the verb, seem to show that some members of Terah's family had each different gods.

(2) Egypt. From Josh. xxiv :14, and Ezek. xx :8, we learn that the Israelites, during their sojourn in Egypt, were seduced to worship the idols of that country; although we possess no particular account of their transgression. In Amos v :25, and Acts vii :42, it is stated that they committed idolatry in their journey through the wilderness; and in Num. xxv :1, *sq.,* that they worshiped the Moabite idol Baal-peor at Shittim.

(3) Canaan. After the Israelites had obtained possession of the promised land, we find that they were continually tempted to adopt the idolatries of the Canaanite nations with which they came in contact. The book of Judges enumerates several successive relapses into this sin. The gods which they served during this period were Baal and Ashtoreth, and their modifications; and Syria, Sidon, Moab, Ammon, and Philistia, are named in Judg. x :6 as the sources from which they derived their idolatries. Then Samuel appears to have exercised a beneficial influence in weaning the people from this folly (1 Sam. vii) ; and the worship of the Lord acquired a gradually increasing hold on the nation until the time of Solomon, who was induced in his old age to permit the establishment of idolatry at Jerusalem. On the division of the nation, the kingdom of Israel (besides adhering to the sin of Jeroboam to the last) was specially devoted to the worship of Baal, which Ahab had renewed and carried to an un-

precedented height; and although the energetic measures adopted by Jehu, and afterward by the priest Jehoiada, to suppress this idolatry, may have been the cause why there has been no later express mention of Baal, yet it is evident from 2 Kings xiii :6, and xvii :10, that the worship of Asherah continued until the deportation of the ten tribes.

(4) Assyria. The deportation of the ten tribes also introduced the peculiar idolatries of the Assyrian colonists into Samaria. In the kingdom of Judah, on the other hand, idolatry continued during the two succeeding reigns; was suppressed for a time by Asa (1 Kings xv :12) ; was revived in consequence of Joram marrying into the family of Ahab; was continued by Ahaz; received a check from Hezekiah; broke out again more violently under Manasseh; until Josiah made the most vigorous attempt to suppress it. But even Josiah's efforts to restore the worship of the Lord were ineffectual; for the later prophets, Zephaniah, Jeremiah, and Ezekiel, still continue to utter reproofs against idolatry. Nor did the capture of Jerusalem under Jehoiachin awaken this peculiarly sensual people; for Ezekiel (viii) shows that those who were left in Jerusalem under the government of Zedekiah had given themselves up to many kinds of idolatry; and Jeremiah (xliv :8) charges those inhabitants of Judah who had found an asylum in Egypt, with having turned to serve the gods of that country. On the restoration of the Jews after the Babylonian captivity, they appear, for the first time in their history, to have been permanently impressed with a sense of the degree to which their former idolatries had been an insult to God, and a degradation of their own understanding—an advance in the culture of the nation which may in part be ascribed to the influence of the Persian abhorrence of images, as well as to the effects of the exile as a chastisement. In this state they continued until Antiochus Epiphanes made the last and fruitless attempt to establish the Greek idolatry in Palestine (1 Macc. i).

3. Forms of Idolatry. The particular forms of idolatry into which the Israelites fell are described under the names of the different gods which they worshiped (see ASHTORETH; BAAL; etc.) ; the general features of their idolatry require a brief notice here. According to Movers (*Die Phönizier,* i. 148), the religion of all the idolatrous Syro-Arabian nations was a deification of the powers and laws of nature, an adoration of those objects in which these powers are considered to abide, and by which they act. The deity is thus the invisible power in nature itself, that power which manifests itself as the generator, sustainer, and destroyer of its works. This view admits of two modifications: either the separate powers of nature are regarded as so many different gods, and the objects by which these powers are manifested—as the sun, moon, etc.—are regarded as their images and supporters; or the power of nature is considered to be one and indivisible, and only to differ as to the forms under which it manifests itself. Both views co-exist in almost all religions. The most simple and ancient notion, however, is that which conceives the deity to be in human form, as male and female, and which considers the male sex to be the type of its active, generative, and destructive power; while that passive power of nature whose function is to conceive and bring forth, is embodied under the female form. The human form and the diversity of sex lead naturally to the different ages of life—to the old man and the youth,

54

the matron and the virgin—according to the modifications of the conception; and the myths which represent the influences, the changes, the laws, and the relations of these natural powers under the sacred histories of such gods, constitute a harmonious development of such a religious system.

Those who saw the deity manifested by, or conceived him as resident in, any natural objects, could not fail to regard the sun and moon as the potent rulers of day and night, and the sources of those influences on which all animated nature depends. Hence star-worship forms a prominent feature in all the false religions mentioned in the Bible. Of this character chiefly were the Egyptian, the Canaanite, the Chaldæan, and the Persian religions. The Persian form of idolatry, however, deserves to be distinguished from the others; for it allowed no images nor temples of the god, but worshiped him in his purest symbol, fire. It is understood that this form is alluded to in most of those passages which mention the worship of the sun, moon and heavenly host, by incense, on heights (2 Kings xxiii:5, 12; Jer. xix: 13). The other form of astrolatry, in which the idea of the sun, moon and planets is blended with the worship of the god in the form of an idol, and with the addition of a mythology (as may be seen in the relations of Baal and his cognates to the sun), easily degenerates into lasciviousness and cruel rites.

4. Sin of Idolatry. Idolatry was the most heinous offense against the Mosaic law, which is most particular in defining the acts which constitute the crime, and severe in apportioning the punishment. Thus, it is forbidden to make any image of a strange God; to prostrate oneself before such an image, or before those natural objects which were also worshiped without images, as the sun and moon (Deut. iv:19); to suffer the altars, images, or groves of idols to stand (Exod. xxxiv:13); or to keep the gold and silver of which their images were made, and to suffer it to enter the house (Deut. vii:25, 26); to sacrifice to idols, most especially to offer human sacrifices; to eat of the victims offered to idols by others; to prophesy in the name of a strange god; and to adopt any of the rites used in idolatrous worship, and to transfer them to the worship of the Lord (Deut. xii:30, 31). As for punishment, the law orders that if an individual committed idolatry he should be stoned to death (Deut. xvii:2-5); that if a town was guilty of this sin, its inhabitants and cattle should be slain, and its spoils burnt together with the town itself (Deut. xiii:12-18). To what degree also the whole spirit of the Old Testament is abhorrent from idolatry, is evident (besides legal prohibitions, prophetic denunciations, and energetic appeals like that in Is. xliv: 9-20) from the literal sense of the terms which are used as synonyms for idols and their worship which have been considered under IDOL (which see).

5. General Rites of Idolatry. The general rites of idolatrous worship consist in burning incense; in offering bloodless sacrifices, as the dough-cakes and libations in Jer. vii:18, and the raisin-cake in Hos. iii:1; in sacrificing victims (1 Kings xviii:26); and especially in human sacrifices (see MOLECH). These offerings were made on high places, hills, and roofs of houses, or in shady groves and valleys. Some forms of idolatrous worship had libidinous orgies (see ASHTORETH). Divinations, oracles (2 Kings i:2), and rabdomancy (Hos. iv:12) form a part of many of these false religions. The priesthood was generally a numerous body; and where persons of both sexes were attached to the service of any god (like that of Ashtoreth), that service was infamously immoral. It is remarkable that the Pentateuch makes no mention of any *temple* of idols; afterward we read often of such. J. N.

Figurative. Covetousness, in which is implied a setting of our heart on worldly things instead of God, and all inordinate care for the appetite, as *gluttony*, or sinful love to, or trust in any creature, is *idolatry* in God's account, and constitutes the person guilty an *idolater*, or *worshiper of idols* (Eph. v:5; Col. iii:5; Phil. iii:19; comp. Rom. xvi:18; 2 Tim. iii:4).

IDUMÆA (ĭd-ū-mē'à), (Gr. Ἰδουμαία, *id-oo-mah'-yah*). We often meet with the phrase *Eretz-Edom*, 'the Land of Edom,' and once with the poetic form *Sedeh-Edom*, 'the Field of Edom' (Judg. v:4). The inhabitants are sometimes styled *Beni-Edom*, 'the Children of Edom,' and poetically *Bath-Edom*, 'the Daughter of Edom' (Lam. iv:21, 22). A single person was called אֱדֹמִי, *Ed-o-mee'*, 'an Edomite' (Deut. xxiii:8), of which the feminine plural, אֲרֹמִיֹּת, *Ed-o-meeth'*, occurs in 1 Kings xi:1.

1. Name. (1) **Edom.** The name was derived from Isaac's son *Edom*, otherwise called Esau, the elder twin-brother of Jacob (see ESAU). It signifies *red*, and seems first to have been suggested by his appearance at his birth, when 'he came out all red,' i. e., covered with red hair (Gen. xxv:25), and was afterward more formally and permanently imposed upon him on account of his unworthy disposal of his birthright for a mess of red lentils (Gen. xxv:30). The region which came to bear his name is the mountainous tract on the east side of the great valleys El Ghor and El Araba, extending between the Dead Sea and the Elanitic Gulf of the Red Sea. Into this district Esau removed during his father's lifetime, and his posterity gradually obtained possession of it as the country which God had assigned for their inheritance in the prophetic blessing pronounced by his father Isaac (Gen. xxvii: 39, 40; xxxii:3; Deut. ii:5-12, 22).

(2) **Mount Seir.** Previously to their occupation of the country, it was called *Mount Seir,* a designation indeed which it never entirely lost (see SEIR; MOUNT SEIR, 2). The word *seir* means *hairy* (being thus synonymous with Esau), and, when applied to a country, may signify *rugged, mountainous,* and so says Josephus (*Antiq.* i: 20, 3): 'Esau named the country "Roughness" from his own hairy roughness.' But in Gen. xxxvi:20 we read of an individual of the name of Seir, who had before this inhabited the land, and from whom it may have received its first appellation.

The first mention made of Mount Seir in Scripture is in Gen. xiv:6, where Chedorlaomer and his confederates are said to have smitten 'the Horim in their Mount Seir.' (See CHEDORLAOMER.) Among the earliest human habitations were caves, either formed by nature or easily excavated, and for the construction of these the mountains of Edom afforded peculiar facilities. Hence the designation given to the aboriginal inhabitants—*Horim,* i. e., cave-dwellers, an epithet of similar import with the Greek *Troglodytes.* Even in the days of Jerome 'the whole of the southern part of Idumæa, from Eleutheropolis to Petra and Aila, was full of caverns used as dwellings, on account of the sun's excessive heat' (Jerome on *Obadiah,* verse 1); and there is reason to believe that the possessors of the country in every age occupied similar habitations, many traces of which are yet seen in or near Petra, the renowned metropolis.

2. History. We are informed in Deut. ii: 12 that 'the children of Esau succeeded (*marg.* inherited) the Horim when they had destroyed them from before them, and dwelt in their stead, as Israel did unto the land of his possession, which Jehovah gave unto them.' From this it may be inferred that the extirpation of the Horim by the Esauites was, like that of the Canaanites by Israel, very gradual and slow. Some think this supposition is confirmed by the genealogical tables preserved in the thirty-sixth chapter of Genesis (comp. 1 Chron. i), where we have, along with a list of the chiefs of Edom, a similar catalogue of Horite chieftains, who are presumed to have been their contemporaries. But for the chronology of these ancient documents we possess no data whatsoever, and very precarious therefore, must be any deductions that are drawn from them. This much, however, we there learn of the political constitution of the Seirite aborigines, that, like the Esauites and Israelites, they were divided into tribes, and these tribes were subdivided into families—the very polity which still obtains among the Arabs by whom Idumæa is now peopled.

(1) Dukes or Chiefs. Each tribe had its own *Alluf,* a term which is unhappily rendered in the English Version by 'Duke,' for though that has, no doubt, the radical meaning of the Latin *dux,* a 'leader,' it now only suggests the idea of a feudal title of nobility. Of these chiefs of the Horites *seven* are enumerated, viz., Lotan, Shobal, Zibeon, Anah, Dishon, Ezer, and Dishan. The only one of these who is spoken of as related to the other is *Anah,* the son of Zibeon. The primitive and pastoral character of the people is incidentally brought out by the circumstance that this Anah, though a chieftain's son, was in the habit of tending to his father's asses. It was when thus employed that he found in the wilderness *eth-ha-yemim,* rendered in the English Version by 'the mules,' but meaning more probably 'the hot springs;' and thus interpreted, the passage seems to be an intimation that he was the first to discover the faculty with which asses and other animals are endowed, of snuffing the moisture of the air, and thus sometimes leading to the opportune discovery of hidden waters in the desert. There is in the country to the southeast of the Dead Sea (which formed part of the Seirite possessions), a place, *Kallirhoë,* celebrated among the Greeks and Romans for its warm baths, and which has been visited by modern travelers (Josephus, *De Bell. Jud.* i:33, 5; Pliny, *Hist. Nat.* v:5, 17; Legh's *Travels*).

(2) Marriage of Esau. Esau first married into two Canaanitish families of the Hittite and Hivite tribes (Gen. xxvi:34; xxxvi:2; in one or other of which places, however, the text seems corrupt); but anxious to propitiate his offended parents, he next formed a matrimonial alliance with one of the race of Abraham, viz., Mahalath, otherwise called Bashemath, daughter of Ishmael, and sister of Nebaioth, whose descendants, the Nabathæans, by a singular coincidence, obtained in after times possession of the land of Edom (Gen. xxviii:9). (See ESAU.) Esau's firstborn (by Adah or Bashemath, of the daughters of Heth) was Eliphaz, whose son *Teman* gave name to a district of the country (Gen. xxxvi:11, 34; 1 Chron. i:45; Ezek. xxv:13; Obad. verse 9).

(3) The Temanites. The Temanites were renowned for their wisdom (Jer. xlix:7, 20; Baruch iii:22, 23). The chief speaker in the book of Job is another Eliphaz, a Temanite—which is one of the circumstances that has led many to place the scene of that story in the land of Edom (see JOB). The name of Teman was preserved to the days of Eusebius in that of Thaiman, a small town five Roman miles from Petra. Another son of the first-mentioned Eliphaz was *Amalek,* who is not to be confounded, however, with the father of the Amalekites, one of the doomed nations of Canaan, of whom we hear so early as the age of Abraham (Gen. xiv:7).

(4) Edomite Emirs. As a modern Arab *sheikh* is often found to exercise influence far beyond the sphere of his hereditary domain, so in the list of Edomite *emirs* preserved by Moses we have perhaps only the names of the more distinguished individuals who acquired more or less authority over all the tribes.

(5) Kings of Edom. This oligarchy appears gradually to have changed into a monarchy, as happened, too, among the Israelites; for in addition to the above-mentioned lists, both of Horite and Esauite leaders, we have in Gen. xxxvi:31, a catalogue of eight kings (Bela, Jobab, Husham, Hadad, Samlah, Saul, Baal-hanan, Hadar or Hadad) who reigned in the land of Edom before there reigned any king over the children of Israel.' It is not necessary to suppose that this was said by Moses *prophetically;* it is one of those passages which may have been inserted by Ezra when finally arranging the canon, inasmuch as it occurs also in the first book of Chronicles, of which he is the reputed compiler. The period when this change to regal government took place in Idumæa can only be matter of conjecture. In the Song of Moses (Exod. xv:15) it is said that at the tidings of Israel's triumphal passage of the Red Sea the rulers or princes (*Alluf*) of Edom trembled with affright, but when, some forty years afterwards, application had to be made by the Israelites for leave to traverse the land of Edom, it was to the king (*Melek*) that the request was addressed (Num. xx:14). The road by which it was sought to penetrate the country was termed 'the *king's* highway' (verse 17), supposed by Robinson to be the Wady el-Ghuweir, for it is almost the only valley that affords a direct and easy passage through those mountains. From a comparison of these incidents it may be inferred that the change in the form of government took place during the wanderings of the Israelites in the desert, unless we suppose, with Rosenmüller, that it was only this northeastern part of Edom which was now subject to a monarch, the rest of the country remaining under the sway of its former chieftains. But whether the regal power at this period embraced the whole territory or not, perhaps it did not supplant the ancient constitution, but was rather grafted on it, like the authority of the Judges in Israel, and of Saul, the first king, which did not materially interfere with the government that previously existed.

(6) Monarchy Not Hereditary. It further appears, from the list of Idumæan kings, that the monarchy was not hereditary, but elective (for no one is spoken of as the son or relative of his predecessor); or probably that chieftain was acknowledged as sovereign who was best able to vindicate his claim by force of arms. Every successive king appears to have selected his own seat of government; the places mentioned as having enjoyed that distinction are Dinhabah, Avith, Pagu or Pai. Even foreigners were not excluded from the throne, for the successor of Samlah of Masrekah was Saul, or Shaul, 'of Rechoboth, on the river.' The word 'Rechoboth' means, literally, *streets,* and was a not uncommon name given to towns; but the emphatic addition of 'the river,' points evidently to the Euphrates, and between Rakkah and Anah, on that river, there are still the remains of a place called by the Arabs Rachabath-Malik-Ibn Tauk. In the age of Solomon we read of one Hadad, who 'was of the king's seed in Edom' (1 Kings xi:14) ; from which some have conjectured that by that period there was a royal dynasty of one particular family; but all that the expression may imply is, that he was a blood relation of the last king of the country. Hadad was the name of one of the early sovereigns 'who smote Midian in the field of Moab' (Gen. xxxvi:35).

(7) **Feud of Esau and Jacob.** The unbrotherly feud which arose between Esau and Jacob was prolonged for ages between their posterity. The Israelites, indeed, were commanded 'not to abhor an Edomite, for he was their brother' (Deut. xxiii:7) ; but a variety of circumstances occurred to provoke and perpetuate the hostility. The first time they were brought into direct collision was when the Edomites, though entreated by their 'brother Israel,' refused the latter a passage through their territories, and they had consequently to make a retrograde and toilsome march to the Gulf of Elath, whence they had to 'compass the land of Edom' by the mountain desert on the east. We do not again hear of the Edomites till the days of Saul, who warred against them with partial success (1 Sam. xiv: 47) ; but their entire subjugation was reserved for David, who first signally vanquished them in the Valley of Salt (supposed to be in the Ghôr, beside *Usdum,* the Mountain of Salt) ; and, finally, placed garrisons in all their country (2 Sam. viii: 14; 1 Chron. xviii:11-13; 1 Kings xi:15; comp. the inscription of Ps. lx and v:8, 9; cviii:9, 10, where 'the strong city' may denote Selah or Petra). Then were fulfilled the prophecies in Gen. xxv:23 and xxvii:40, that the 'elder should serve the younger;' and also the prediction of Balaam (Num. xxiv:18), that Edom and Seir should be for possessions to Israel. Solomon created a naval station at Ezion-geber, at the head of the Gulf of Elath, the modern Akaba (1 Kings ix:26; 2 Chron. viii:18).

(8) **Attempts at Independency.** Towards the close of his reign an attempt was made to restore the independence of the country by one Hadad, an Idumæan prince, who, when a child, had been carried into Egypt at the time of David's invasion, and had there married the sister of Tahpanhes the queen (1 Kings xi:14-23). (See HADAD.) If Edom then succeeded in shaking off the yoke, it was only for a season, since in the days of Jehoshaphat, the fourth Jewish monarch from Solomon, it is said, 'there was no king in Edom; a deputy was king;' *i. e.,* he acted as viceroy for the king of Judah. For that the latter was still master of the country is evident from the fact of his having fitted out, like Solomon, a fleet at Ezion-geber (1 Kings xxii:47, 48; 2 Chron. xx:36, 37). It was, no doubt, his deputy (called *king*) who joined the confederates of Judah and Israel in their attack upon Moab (2 Kings iii:9, 12, 26). Yet there seems to have been a partial revolt of the Edomites, or at least of the mountaineers of Seir, even in the reign of Jehoshaphat (2 Chron. xx:22) ; and under his successor, Jehoram, they wholly rebelled, and 'made a king over themselves' (2 Kings viii:20, 22; 2 Chron. xxi:8, 10). From its being added that, notwithstanding the temporary suppression of the rebellion, 'Edom revolted from under the hand of Judah unto this day,' it is probable that the Jewish dominion was never completely restored. Amaziah, indeed, invaded the country, and having

taken the chief city, Selah or Petra, he, in memorial of the conquest, changed its name to Joktheel (*i. e.,* subdued of God) ; and his successor, Uzziah, retained possession of Elath (2 Kings xiv:7; 2 Chron. xxv:11-14; xxvi:3). But in the reign of Ahaz, hordes of Edomites made incursions into Judah, and carried away captives (2 Chron. xxviii:17). About the same period Rezin, king of Syria, expelled the Jews from Elath, which (according to the correct reading of 2 Kings xvi:6) was thenceforth occupied by the Edomites.

(9) **Fulfillment of Prophecy.** Now was fulfilled the other part of Isaac's prediction, viz.: that, in course of time, Esau 'should take his brother's yoke from off his neck' (Gen. xxvii:40). It appears from various incidental expressions in the later prophets, that the Edomites employed their recovered power in the enlargement of their territory in all directions. They spread as far south as Dedan in Arabia, and northward to Bozrah in the Hhauran; though it is doubtful if the Bozrah of Scripture may not have been a place in Idumæa Proper (Is. xxxiv:6; lxiii:1; Jer. xlix:7, 8- 20; Ezek. xxv:13; Amos i:12). When the Chaldæans invaded Judah, under Nebuchadnezzar, the Edomites became their willing auxiliaries, and triumphed with fiendish malignity over the ruin of their kinsmen the Jews, of whose desolated land they hoped to obtain a large portion to themselves (Obad. verses 10-16; Ezek. xxv:12-14; xxxv:3-10; xxxvi:5; Lam. iv:21). By this circumstance the hereditary hatred of the Jews was rekindled in greater fury than ever, and hence the many dire denunciations of the 'daughter of Edom,' to be met with in the Hebrew prophets (Ps. cxxxvii:7-9; Obad. *passim;* Jer. xlix:7; Ezek. xxv. and xxxv.). From the language of Malachi (i:2, 3), and also from the accounts preserved by Josephus (*Antiq.* x:9, 7), it would seem that the Edomites did not wholly escape the Chaldæan scourge; but instead of being carried captive, like the Jews, they not only retained possession of their own territory, but became masters of the south of Judah, as far as Hebron (1 Macc. v:65; comp. with Ezek. xxxv:10; xxxvi:5).

(10) **Attack by the Maccabees.** Here, however, they were, in course of time, successfully attacked by the Maccabees, and about B. C. 125 were finally subdued by John Hyrcanus, who compelled them to submit to circumcision and other Jewish rites, with a view to incorporate them with the nation (1 Macc. v:3, 65; 2 Macc. x:16; xii: 32; Joseph. *Antiq.* xiii:9, 1; xv:4). The amalgamation, however, of the two races seems never to have been effected, for we afterwards hear of Antipater, an Idumæan by birth, being made by Cæsar procurator of all Judea; and his son, commonly called Herod the Great, was, at the time of Christ's birth, king of Judea, including Idumæa; and hence Roman writers often speak of all Palestine under that name (Joseph. *Antiq.* xiv:1:3; 8:5; xv:7, 9; xvii:11, 4). Not long before the siege of Jerusalem by Titus, 20,000 Idumæans were called in to the defense of the city by the Zealots; but both parties gave themselves up to rapine and murder (Joseph. *De Bell. Jud.* iv:4, 5; vi:1; vii:8, 1).

(11) **Last Mention of the Edomites.** This is the last mention made of the Edomites in history. The author of a work on Job, once ascribed to Origen, says that their name and language had perished, and that, like the Ammonites and Moabites, they had all become Arabs. In the second century Ptolemy limits the name Idumæa to the country west of the Jordan.

But while, during the captivity of the Jews in

Babylon, the Edomites had thus been extending their territory to the northwest, they were themselves supplanted in the southern part of their native region by the Nabathæans, the descendants of Ishmael's eldest son, and to the article NEBAIOTH, we must refer the reader for the subsequent history of the land of Edom.

(12) Scene of the Book of Job. Could the scene of the book of Job be with certainty fixed in Idumæa, we should then possess much curious and valuable information respecting both the country and people soon after it had been colonized by the descendants of Esau (see Mason Good, Wemyss, and others upon Job). But all that we learn directly of the ancient Edomites from the historical books of Scripture represents them as not, indeed, neglecting agriculture or trade (Num. xx:17), yet, on the whole, as a warlike and predatory race, who, according to the prediction of their progenitor Isaac, 'lived by their sword.' The situation of the country afforded peculiar facilities for commerce, which seems to have been prosecuted from a very early period. 'Bordering,' says Volney, 'upon Arabia on the east and south, and Egypt on the southwest and forming, from north to south, the most commodious channel of communication between Jerusalem and her dependencies on the Red Sea, through the continuous valleys of El-Ghor and El-Araba, Idumæa may be said to have long formed the emporium of the commerce of the East.' The era of its greatest prosperity was after the Nabathæans had become masters of the country and founded the kingdom of Arabia Petræa, of which the renowned metropolis was Petra.

(13) Religion and Prophecy. The *religion* of the early Edomites was, perhaps, comparatively pure; but in process of time they embraced idolatry; in 2 Chron. xxv:20, we read of the 'gods of Edom,' one of whom, according to Josephus (*Antiq.* xv:7, 9) was called *Kotzé*. With respect to the striking fulfillment of the prophetic denunciations upon Edom, we need only refer the reader to the well-known work of Keith, who frequently errs, however, in straining the sense of prophecy beyond its legitimate import, as well as in seeking out too literally minute an accomplishment.

(14) Modern Knowledge of the Land of Esau. From the era of the Crusades down to the present century the land of Esau was, to Europeans, a *terra incognita*. Its situation was laid down in the best maps more than a hundred miles from the true position, and as if lying in a direction where it is now known there is nothing but a vast expanse of desert. Volney had his attention drawn toward it when at Gaza, by the vague reports of the Arabs, and in 1807 the unfortunate Seetzen penetrated a certain way into the country, and heard of the wonders of the Wady Mûsa; but the first modern traveler who 'passed through the land of Edom' was Burckhardt, in the year 1812. And it has been well remarked by Dr. Robinson (*Amer. Bib. Reposit.* vol. iii. p. 250), that 'had he accomplished nothing but his researches in these regions, his journey would have been worth all the labor and cost expended on it, although his discoveries thus shed their strongest light upon subjects which were not comprehended in the plan or purpose either of himself or his employers.' Burckhardt entered Idumæa from the north, and in the year 1818 he was followed in the same direction by Messrs. Legh, Bankes, Irby and Mangles. In 1828 Laborde and Linant found access from the south; and since then it has been visited and described by so many that the names of its localities have become familiar as household words.

(15) Present Condition. It is at present occupied by various tribes of Bedouin Arabs. The chief tribe in the *Jebal* is the Hejaya, with a branch of the Kaabineh, while in *esh-Sherah* they are all of the numerous and powerful tribe of the Haweitat, with a few independent allies. The Bedouins in Idumæa have of late years been partially subject to the Pasha of Egypt, paying an annual tribute which in the case of the Beni Sukhr, is one camel for two tents. The fellahin, or peasants, are half Bedouin, inhabiting the few villages, but dwelling also in tents; they, too, pay tribute to the Egyptian government, and furnish supplies of grain.

Among the localities connected with Edom which are mentioned in the Scripture may be noticed Dinhabah, Bozrah, Theman, Maon (now Maan), Kadesh-barnea (which Robinson identifies with el-Weibeh in the Wady el-Jeib), Zephath (which he supposes to be the pass of Es-Sufah), Elath, and Ezion-geber, etc.; but the most celebrated place in all the region was the chief city, Selah or Petra, for a description of which the reader is referred to the latter head. (See PETRA.)

3. Physical Geography. The limit of the wanderings of the Israelites in the desert was the brook Zered, after crossing which they found themselves in the territory of Moab (Deut. ii:13-18). This brook is supposed to be identical with the *Wady-el-Ahsy*, which, rising near the Castle el-Ahsy, on the route to Mecca of the Syrian caravan upon the high eastern desert, penetrates through the whole chain of mountains to near the southeast corner of the Dead Sea. It was thus the southern border of Moab and the northern of Edom, whence the latter region extended southwards as far as to Elath on the Red Sea. The valley which runs between the two seas consists first of El-Ghor, which is comparatively low, but gradually rises into the more elevated plain of El-Arabah to the south. The country lying *east* of this great valley is the land of Idumæa. It is a mountain tract, consisting at the base of low hills of limestone or argillaceous rock, then lofty mountains of porphyry forming the body of the mountain; above these, sandstone broken up into irregular ridges and grotesque groups of cliffs; and again farther back, and higher than all, long elevated ridges of limestone without precipices. East of all these stretches off indefinitely the high *plateau* of the great eastern desert. The whole breadth of the mountainous tract between the Arabah and the eastern desert does not exceed fifteen or twenty geographical miles. Of these mountains the most remarkable is *Mount Hor*, near the Wady Mûsa. (See HOR, MOUNT.) While the mountains on the west of the Arabah, though less elevated, are wholly barren, those of Idumæa seem to enjoy a sufficiency of rain, and are covered with turfs of herbs and occasional trees. The wadies, too, are full of trees and shrubs and flowers, while the eastern and higher parts are extensively cultivated, and yield good crops.

This mountainous region is at present divided into two districts. The northern bears the name of *Jebâl, i. e.*, 'The Mountain,' the Gebal of the Hebrews (Ps. lxxxiii:8), and the Gebalene of the Greeks and Romans. Commencing at Wady el-Ahsy, it terminates, according to Burckhardt, at Wady el Ghuweir, the largest place in it being Tufileh, perhaps the Tophel of Deut. i:1. The southern district is *esh-Sherah*, extending as far as Akabah, and including Shôbak, Wady Mûsa, Maan, etc. Burckhardt mentions a *third* district, *Jebal Hesma;* but Robinson says that, though there is a sandy tract, el-Hismah, with mountains around it, on the east of Akabah, it does not constitute a separate division.   N. M.

IDUMEA (ĭd'u-mē'à), another form of IDUMÆA (which see).

IEZER (ī-ē'zēr).   See ABIEZER.

IEZERITE.   See ABIEZRITE.

IGAL (ī'gal), (Heb. יִגְאָל, *yig-awl'*, avenger).

1. Son of Joseph, and the representative of the tribe of Issachar among the spies sent to explore the land of Canaan (Num. xiii :7; xiv :37), B. C. 1657.

2. Son of Nathan of Zobah and one of David's heroes (2 Sam. xxiii :36), B. C. 1046. The name appears as Joel (1 Chron. xi :38), which Kennicott regards as more likely to be correct.

3. Son of Shemaiah, a descendant of Zerubbabel (1 Chron. iii :22), B. C. before 406.

IGDALIAH (ĭg'da-lī'ah), (Heb. יִגְדַּלְיָהוּ, *yig-dal-yaw'hoo*, magnified of Jah, great is Jehovah), the father of Hanan, in whose chamber Jeremiah proposed the test of the temperance of the Rechabites (Jer. xxxv :4), B. C. before 606.

IGEAL (ĭg'e-ăl), (Heb. יִגְאָל, *yig'awl*, avenger, 1 Chron. iii :22).   See IGAL, 3.

IGNORANCE (ĭg'nŏ-rans), (Heb. שְׁגָה, *shaw-gaw'*, Lev. iv :2, 6), the want of knowledge or instruction.

It is often used to denote illiteracy. The causes of ignorance are chiefly three : (1) Want of ideas; (2) want of a discoverable connection between the ideas we have; (3) want of tracing and examining our ideas. As it respects religion, ignorance has been distinguished into three sorts :—1. An *invincible* ignorance, in which the will has no part (Acts xvii :30).   It is an insult upon justice to suppose it will punish men because they were ignorant of things which they were physically incapable of knowing. 2. There is a *willful* and *obstinate* ignorance; such an ignorance, far from exculpating, aggravates a man's crimes (Acts iii :17). 3. A sort of voluntary ignorance, which is neither entirely willful nor entirely invincible; as when a man has the means of knowledge, and does not use them (Eph. iv :18).   (See SIN.)

Specific Scripture Allusions. Heathen are *"ignorant;"* destitute of the true knowledge of God (Acts xvii :23). Wicked teachers are *"ignorant;"* they know not what they ought to teach others (Is. lvi :10). Paul sinned *"ignorantly"* against Christ before his conversion, not knowing the truth of the Christian religion (1 Tim. i :13). Peter and John were *"ignorant;"* that is, not trained up in the schools of polite learning (Acts iv :13).

I. H. S.   There are three interpretations of this mystic title. One is that the letters are initials of the words "In Hoc Signo" 'in this sign,' which appeared on the luminous cross supposed to have been miraculously displayed before the army of Constantine.

Another is that they are the initials of the words *Jesus Hominum Salvator,* 'Jesus Savior of Men.'

The third is that they are the first three letters of the Greek word IHΣOYΣ, *I-ay-sous, Jesus.* This last explanation is upheld by the Cambridge Camden Society, in a work called, *Argument for*

the Greek Origin of the Monogram I. H. S. (Lond. 1841).

IIM (ī'im), (Heb. עִיִּם, *ee-yeem'*, ruins), a short form of IJE-ABARIM.

IJE-ABARIM (ī'je-ăb'a-rĭm), (Heb. עִיֵּי הָעֲבָרִים, *ee-yay'haw-ab-aw-reem'*, ruins of Abarim).

1. The forty-seventh station of the Israelites in the wilderness, "in the borders of Moab" (Num. xxxiii :44, 45).

2. A city in the south of Judah, probably within the territory of Simeon (Josh. xv :29; Num. xxi :11). Site unknown.

IJON (ī'jon), (Heb. עִיּוֹן, *ee-yone'*, ruin), a city of northern Palestine, captured in Naphtali by Benhadad of Syria (1 Kings xv :20; 2 Chron. xvi :4), and later by Tiglath-pileser of Assyria (2 Kings xv :29).

Robinson identifies it with *Tell Dibbin* (*Bibl. Res.* iii :375), a hill 110 feet high, on the eastern border of Merj Ayûn, meadow of springs, which seems to preserve a trace of the old name. The site is about eight miles north-northwest of Banias.

IKKESH (ĭk'kesh), (Heb. עִקֵּשׁ, *ik-kashe'*, perverse), father of Ira the Tekoite, of one of David's famous guard, and captain of the sixth regiment of his army (2 Sam. xxiii :26; 1 Chron. xi :28; xxvii : 9), before B. C. 1046.

ILAI (ī'lāi), (Heb. עִילַי, *ee-lah'ee*, supreme), an Ahohite, and one of David's guard (1 Chron. xi :29).

He is called Zalmon in the parallel lists (2 Sam. xxiii :28), B. C. 1046.

ILL-FAVORED (ĭl'fā'vērd), (Heb. רַע, *rah*, bad, injured).

"And, behold, seven other kine came up after them out of the river, *ill favored* and leanfleshed; and stood by the *other* kine upon the brink of the river" (Gen. xli :3).

ILLUMINATED (ĭl-lū'mĭ-nā'tĕd), (Gr. φωτίζω, *fo-tid'zo*, to give light), endowed with the saving knowledge of Christ and divine things (Heb. x :32).

It was used in the early Christian church to denote baptized persons.

ILLYRICUM (il-lyr'i-kŭm), (Gr. Ἰλλυρικὸν, *il-loo-ree-kon'*, lit. *Illyrian;* derivation unknown), a country lying to the northwest of Macedonia, and answering nearly to that which is at present called Dalmatia; by which name indeed the southern part of Illyricum itself was known.

It lies on the east of the gulf of Venice, and is about 480 miles in length and 120 in breadth. It has Austria and part of Hungary on the north, Mœsia or Servia on the east, and part of Macedonia on the south. Counting from northwest to southeast, it was divided into Sclavonia, Bosnia, Dalmatia, and Albania; but sometimes it was taken in a more extended sense.   It is traversed from northwest to southeast by the Noric, Carnic, and Julian Alps, constituting the most easterly portion of the great Alpine chain. Along the coast are excellent harbors and numerous islands. The Illyrian race inhabiting the region were wild mountaineers, who were a thorn in the side of their neighbors, the Macedonians; and, when they descended to the seacoast, they so practiced piracy as to bring them into collision with the Romans, who, in B. C. 229, began to conquer them, and finally made Illyricum, or Illyria, a province of the empire. It was to Illyricum that St. Paul informs Timothy that Titus had gone (2 Tim. iv :10). Paul himself preached the Gospel in Illyricum, which was at that time a province of the Roman Empire (Rom. xv :19). (Cramer, *Ancient Greece;* Smith, *Dict. of Class. Geog.*)

IMAGE (im'ăj), (Heb. plural תְּרָפִים, *ter-aw-feme'*, teraphim). *Image* is often taken for a statue, figure, or idol.

The Book of Wisdom, speaking of the causes of idolatry, says that a father, afflicted for the death of his son, made an image of him, to which he paid divine honors. We read (Rev. xiii:14, 15) that God permitted the beast to seduce men, whom it commanded to make an image of the beast, which became living and animated; and that all who refused to adore it were put to death. The images mentioned in Lev. xxvi:30; Is. xxvii:9, were, according to rabbi Solomon, idols exposed to the sun, on the tops of houses. Abenezra says they were portable chapels or temples, in the form of chariots, in honor of the sun. (See IDOL.)

IMAGE OF GOD (ĭm'ăj), (Heb. צֶלֶם, *tseh'lem*, resemblance; accompanied in Gen. i:26; v:1 by דְּמוּת, *dem-ooth'*, "likeness").

(1) **Man.** Man was made in the "image" of God; he resembled God in the spiritual and immortal nature of his soul, and in his true knowledge, righteousness, and holiness, and in his dominion over the creature (Gen. i:26, 27).

(2) **Christ.** Christ is the "image of the invisible God;" as God's son, he has the same nature as his Father, and resembles him in power; and in his person, God-man, and mediatorial office, he is a bright representation of all the perfections of God (Heb. i:3; Col. i:13). (See JESUS CHRIST.)

We are born in the "image" of Adam; like him in our natural form, and in our rebellion against God (Gen. v:3); and we bear the "image" of Christ, and are renewed after it, when our nature is changed, and we are therein made like God in spiritual knowledge, righteousness, holiness, and every other grace (I Cor. xv:49; Col. iii:10).

Literature. See Van Oosterzee, *Dogmatics*, vol. I, p. 359, *sq.*; Laidlaw, *Bible Doctrine of Man*; Martensen, *Christian Dogmatics*, 136-141; Wuttke, *Christian Ethics*, vol. i, 37, *sq.*; *The Place of Christ in Mod. Theol.*, Fairbairn, 1897; *The Christology of Jesus*, Stalker, 1899.

IMAGERY (ĭm'ăj-rў), (Heb. מַשְׂכִּית, *mas-keeth'*, an image, Lev. xxvi:1; picture, Num. xxxiii:52).

"The chambers of his imagery" is an expression found in Ezek. viii:12, in the description given by the prophet of the vision shown him of the Temple. It probably refers to the idol worship introduced from Egypt and the East. The whole passage (verses 7-12) represents a scene of idolatrous worship which was disclosed to the prophet as through a secret door of entrance (verses 7, 8). On the walls of the apartment were portrayed "every form of creeping thing and abominable beasts, and all the idols of the house of Israel" (verse 10, etc.) A similar chamber of imagery is referred to in Ezek. xxiii:14: "Where she saw men portrayed upon the wall, the images of the Chaldæans portrayed with vermilion," etc. Remains found in the ruins of Nineveh and in cities in Egypt illustrate the practices mentioned by the prophet.

IMAGE WORSHIP (ĭm'ăj wûr'shĭp). See IDOL; IDOLATRY.

IMAGINATION (ĭm-ăj'ĭ-nā'shŭn), (Heb. שְׁרִירוּת, *sher-ee-rooth'*, firmness, generally in a bad sense, i. e., hardness of heart, Deut. xxix:19; often in Jeremiah as in iii:17; יֵצֶר, *yay'tser*, form, conception, Gen. vi:5; viii:21; Deut. xxxi:21, etc.; Gr. διαλογισμός, *dee-al-og-is-mos'*, deliberating with one's self (Rom. i:21); διάνοια, *dee-an'oy-ah*, way of thinking (Luke i:51).

Imagination is that faculty or power of the mind by which it conceives and forms ideal pictures of things communicated to it by the organs of sense; the power to create or reproduce an object of sense previously perceived; invention as in painting, sculpture, architecture, new machinery, landscape gardening, decorating, etc.

It is used of corrupt reasonings in 2 Cor. x:5.

IMLA (ĭm'là), (Heb. יִמְלָא, *yeem-law'*, filled, full, or fulfiller), father, or forefather, of Micaiah, the prophet, who ironically foretold Ahab and Jehoshaphat of the defeat of Israel and Judah before their fatal expedition to Ramoth-gilead (2 Chron. xviii:7, 8), B. C. before 896.

IMLAH (ĭm'lah), (Heb. יִמְלָה, *yeem-lah'*, God doth fill, I Kings xxii:8, 9). See IMLA.

IMMANUEL (ĭm-măn'ū-el), (Heb. עִמָּנוּאֵל, *im-maw-noo-ale'*; Sept. Ἐμμανουήλ, *em-man-oo-ale'*), or EMMANUEL.

This word, meaning '*God with us*,' occurs in the celebrated verse of Isaiah (vii:14), 'Behold, a virgin shall conceive and bear a son, and shall call his name Immanuel.' In forty-three MSS. and thirty-nine printed editions the word is given in the separate form עִמָּנוּ אֵל *im-maw-noo ale immanu el*, but, as Dr. Henderson remarks, 'in the orthography of all compound names, the MSS. and editions widely differ.' In the name itself there is no difficulty; but the verse, as a whole, has been variously interpreted. From the manner in which the word God, and even Jehovah, is used in the composition of Hebrew names, there is no such peculiarity in that of Immanuel as in itself requires us to understand that he who bore it must be in fact God. Indeed, it is used as a proper name among the Jews at this day. This high sense has, however, been assigned to it in consequence of the application of the whole verse, by the Evangelist Matthew (i:23), to our Divine Savior. Even if this reference did not exist, the history of the Nativity would irresistibly lead us to the conclusion that the verse—whatever may have been its intermediate signification—had an ultimate reference to Christ.

The state of opinion on this subject has been thus fairly summed up by Dr. Henderson, in his note on the text: 'This verse has long been a subject of dispute between Jews and professedly Christian writers, and among the latter mutually. While the former reject its application to the Messiah altogether—the earlier rabbins explaining it of the queen of Ahaz and the birth of his son Hezekiah, and the later, as Kimchi and Abarbanel, of the prophet's own wife—the great body of Christian interpreters have held it to be directly and exclusively in prophecy of our Savior, and have considered themselves fully borne out by the inspired testimony of the Evangelist Matthew. Others, however, have departed from this construction of the passage, and have invented or adopted various hypotheses in support of such dissent. Grotius, Faber, Isenbiehl, Hezel, Bolten, Fritsche, Pluschke, Gesenius, and Hitzig, suppose either the then present or a future wife of Isaiah to be the עַלְמָה, *al-maw'* (rendered "virgin"), referred to. Eichhorn, Paulus, Hensler and Ammon are of opinion that the prophet had nothing more in view than an ideal virgin, and that both she and her son are merely imaginary personages, introduced for the purpose of prophetic illustration. Bauer, Cube, Steudel, and some others, think that the prophet pointed to a young woman in the presence of the king and his courtiers. A fourth class, among whom are Richard Simon, Lowth, Koppe, Dathe, Williams, Von Meyer, Olshausen, and Dr. J. Pye Smith, admit the hypothesis of a double sense; one, in which the words apply primarily to some female living in the time of the prophet, and her giving birth to a son according to the ordinary laws of nature, or, as Dathe holds, to some virgin, who at that time should miraculously conceive; and the other, in which they received a secondary and plenary fulfillment in the miraculous conception and birth of Jesus Christ.'

IMMATERIALITY (ĭm'mȧ-tē'rĭ-ăl'ĭ-tў), is predicated of mind, to denote that as a substance it is different from *matter*.

Spirituality is the positive expression of the same idea. Simplicity is also used in the same sense. Matter is made up of parts into which it can be resolved. Mind is simple and has no parts, and so cannot be dissolved. The materiality of the soul was maintained by Tertullian, Arnobius, and others, during the first three centuries. At the end of the fourth, the immateriality of the soul was professed by Augustine, Nemesius, and Mamertus Claudianus. This quality of immateriality is predicated of God. The Absolute Being is one with itself and cannot be divided. He is free from the limitations to which matter is subject, i. e. from the limits of time and space. (See article on GOD.)

IMMER (ĭm'mer), (Heb. אִמֵּר, *im-mare'*, talkative).

1. Head of the sixteenth monthly course in sacerdotal division of David (1 Chron. xxiv:14). B. C. 1014.

2. Father of that Pashur who basely misused the prophet Jeremiah (Jer. xx:1). B. C. before 607.

3. The founder of a family which returned with Zerubbabel to Jerusalem to the number of 1052 (Neh. vii:40; Ezr. ii:37). Perhaps identical with the father of Meshillemoth (Neh. xi:13), and Meshillemith (1 Chron. ix:12), whose descendants were conspicuous in the affairs of Jerusalem after the captivity. He is doubtless the same with the one whose descendants put away their foreign wives (Ezra x:20), B. C. before 536. By some he is identified with the two preceding.

4. One of those returning with Zerubbabel from Babylon, but who could not prove his Israelitish descent (Ezra ii:59; Neh. vii:61), B. C. 536. The name may be that of a place in Babylon from which some of those afterwards named came.

5. The father of Zadok, who rebuilt a part of the wall of Jerusalem. Perhaps the same as 3 (Neh. iii:29). B. C. before 446.

IMMORTALITY (ĭm-mŏr-tăl'ĭ-tў). The quality of never ceasing to live or exist; exemption from death and annihilation; life destined to endure without end.

Immortality is one of the doctrines of natural religion. At death the body dies, and is dissolved into its elements. The soul being distinct from the body, is not affected by the dissolution of the body. How long, or in what state it may survive after the death of the body, is not intimated by the term *immortality*. But the arguments to prove that the soul survives the body, all go to favor the belief that it will live forever.

See Plato, *Phædon;* Porteus, *Sermons;* Sherlock, *On the Immortality of the Soul;* Watson, *Intimations of a Future State;* Bakewell, *Evidence of a Future State;* Autenrieth, *On Man, and His Hope of Immortality,* Tubingen, 1815; Fleming, *Vocab. of Phil.*

God is "immortal," and only hath "immortality;" he hath life in and of himself, and is infinitely secure against death, hurt, or ruin of any kind (1 Tim. i:17; vi:16). The eternal blessedness of the saints is called "immortality;" it can never cease, and is free from such pain, corruption, or unsightliness, as attends death (Rom. ii:7); and it is brought to light, that is, more clearly discovered by the gospel dispensation (2 Tim. i:10).

Compare our Savior's teachings regarding a future deathless life, both by express declaration and as illustrated by parables (Matt. v:12; viii:11, 12; xii:32; xiii:36, 43; xviii:8, 9; xxii:11-13; xxv:1-13, 31-46; Mark viii:35-37; Luke xii:4, 5; xiii:24-29; xvi:19-31; xviii:29, 30; John iii:16; v:39, 40; vi:47-58; x:28; xi:25; xiv:1-6, etc.).

Our mortal body shall put on "immortality," when it shall gloriously rise from the dead, and be no more subject to any tendency towards dissolution or wasting (1 Cor. xv:53).

In the Old Testament the doctrine is taught but not so clearly as in the New. The sixteenth psalm, especially as connected with the apostolic comments (Acts ii:27; xiii:35) is a case in point. (See also Ps. xvii:15; Is. xxvi:19; Dan. xii:2, 3.)

IMMUTABILITY (ĭm-mū'tȧ-bĭl'ĭ-tў), is the absence or impossibility of change.

It is applied to the Supreme Being to denote that there can be no inconstancy in his character or government. It was argued for by the heathen. (See Bishop Wilkins, *Natural Religion.*) The full conception, however, of God's unchangeableness is to be derived only from the Scriptures, and the sublimity of the thought contained in them is one of the indications of Divine revelation (see Van Oosterzee's *Christ. Dogmatics,* vol. i, p. 257, *sq.;* Watson's *Institutes,* vol. i, 398; Knapp's *Theology;* Dorner, and other writers on *Systematic Theology*). (See article on GOD.)

IMNA (ĭm'nȧ), (Heb. יִמְנָע, *yim-naw'*, probably God doth restrain), son of Helem, a descendant of Asher, and one of the chiefs of the tribe (1 Chron. vii:35), B. C. about 1618.

IMNAH (ĭm'nah), (Heb. יִמְנָה, *yim-naw'*, probably God doth restrain).

1. Eldest son of Asher, and founder of a family by his own name (1 Chron. vii:30), B. C. 1874.

2. The father of Kore, the Levite, who had charge of the east gate of the Temple, and the freewill offerings under Hezekiah (2 Chron. xxxi:14), B. C. 726.

IMPART (ĭm-pärt'), (Gr. μεταδίδωμι, *met-ad-id'-o-mee,* Luke iii:11; Rom. i:11), to supply or communicate.

To bestow of one's fullness on others (Luke iii:11). The apostles were willing to *"impart their souls,"* spending their strength, exerting their skill, and exposing their life, to edify their hearers (2 Thess. ii:8).

IMPEDIMENT (ĭm-pĕd'ĭ-ment), (Gr. μογιλάλος, *mog-il-al'os*), in speech, something which hinders one from speaking plainly, or which causes him to stutter or stammer (Mark vii:32).

IMPLEAD (ĭm-plēd'), (Gr. ἐγκαλέω, *eng-kal-eh'o,* Acts xix:38), a law term, meaning to accuse or indict.

It is the city-councilor who speaks in that passage and points out to the Ephesians the lawful remedy for their grievances as opposed to one unlawful.

IMPORTUNITY (ĭm'pŏr-tū'nĭ-tў), (Gr. ἀναίδεια, *an-ah-ee'die-ah,* impudence, shamelessness), spoken of an importunate man, persisting in his entreaties (Luke xi:8; comp. Luke xviii:1; 1 Thess. v:17).

IMPOSITION OF HANDS (ĭm'pŏ-zish'ŭn), an ecclesiastical action, by which a bishop lays his hand on the head of a person in ordination, in confirmation, or in uttering a blessing.

This practice is also usually observed by the different churches at the ordination of their ministers; when the clergymen present place their hands on the head of him whom they are ordaining, while one of them prays for a blessing on him, and on his future labors. There is not full agreement, however, as to the propriety of this ceremony. Some suppose it to be confined to those who received extraordinary gifts in the primitive times; others think it ought to be retained, as it was an ancient practice used where no extraordinary gifts were conveyed (Gen. xlviii:14; Matt. xix:15). They do not suppose it to be of such an important and essential nature, that the validity and usefulness of a man's future ministry depend upon it in any degree.

Imposition of hands was a Jewish ceremony, introduced not by any Divine authority, but by custom; it being the practice among those people, whenever they pray to God for any person, to lay their hands on his head. Our Savior observed the same custom both when he conferred his blessing on children and when he healed the sick, adding prayer to the ceremony. The apostles, likewise, laid hands on those upon whom they bestowed the Holy Ghost. The priests observed the same custom when any one was received into their body. And the apostles themselves underwent the imposition of hands afresh every time they entered upon any new design. In the ancient church, imposition of hands was even practiced on persons when they married, which custom the Abyssinians still observe.

IMPOSSIBLE (ĭm-pŏs'sĭ-b'l), what cannot be done.

In respect of God's nature, it is *"impossible"* for him to lie, or deny himself (Heb. vi:19; Tit. i:2). In respect of his power, nothing good is *"impossible"* to him (Luke i:37; xvii:29).

IMPOTENT (ĭm'pŏ-tent), (Lat. *impotens*), signifies "strengthless," "sick," "infirm." It is the rendering of ἀσθενῶν, *as-then-one'*, in John v:3, and in Acts iv:9; but of ἀδύνατος, *ad-oo'nat-os*, in Acts xiv:8.

IMPRECATION (ĭm-prē'kā-shŭn). See CURSE.

IMPRECATORY PSALMS. See PSALMS.

IMPUDENCY (ĭm'pŭ-den-sȳ), a word found in the caption of Is., ch. iii. The old form of impudent, Lat. *impudentia*.

IMPURITY (ĭm-pū'rĭ-tȳ). See UNCLEANNESS.

IMPUTATION (ĭm-pū-tā'shŭn), (Heb. שׂוֹם, *soom;* or שׂים, *seem;* Gr. λογίζομαι, *log-id'zom-ahee*).

The verb impute occurs fifteen times in the Authorized Version; the noun imputation not at all. The Calvinistic doctrine is that Adam's sin of disobedience in Paradise is imputed to all his natural descendants, making each person who comes into the world chargeable with the guilt of Original Sin. On the other hand, God justifies those effectually called, not by counting faith itself, or any other act of obedience, as merit, but by imputing to them as righteousness the obedience and satisfaction rendered by Christ (*Ency. Dict.*) As Brown states it, we have *"righteousness without works imputed"* to us, when the obedience and sufferings of Jesus Christ in our stead are legally reckoned to the account of us guilty sinners, to render us righteous in law before God as a judge (Rom. iv:6-11). Sin is *"imputed,"* when one is charged with it, with a view to his suffering punishment for it (2 Sam.

xix:19; Lev. xvii:5); and the *"not imputing"* it, imports the free and full forgiveness of it (Rom. v:13). In order to warrant such *"imputation,"* the actor and the one to whom it is *imputed* must be one, either really or legally. The Chaldean king *"imputed"* his power to his god, accounted his idol to have assisted him in conquering the nations (Hab. i:11).

The Arminian view denies the Calvinistic idea of imputation, but fully recognizes the benefits which accrue to the believer from Christ's righteousness. It holds firmly to the imputation of faith for righteousness (Rom. iii:21; iv:22). Hodge *Systematic Theol.*, vol. ii, 192, sq.; Miner Raymond, *Systematic Theol.*, vol. ii, 106, 336, sq.)

IMRAH (ĭm'rah), (Heb. יִמְרָה, *yim-raw'*, stubborn, refractory).

Son of Zophah, a descendant of Asher, and one of the chiefs of the tribe (1 Chron. vii:36), B. C. after 1612.

IMRI (ĭm'rī), (Heb. אִמְרִי, *im-ree'*, eloquently).

1. A man of Judah, son of Bani, of the family of Pharez (1 Chron. ix:4), B. C. ante 536.

2. Father or forefather of Zaccur, who assisted in rebuilding the wall of Jerusalem under Nehemiah (Neh. iii:2), B. C. before 446.

INABILITY (ĭn-à-bĭl'ĭ-tȳ), want of power sufficient for the performance of any particular action or design.

It has been divided into *natural* and *moral*. We are said to be naturally unable to do a thing when we cannot do it if we wish, because of some impeding defect or obstacle that is extrinsic to the will, either in the understanding, constitution of the body, or external objects. *Moral* inability consists not in any of these things, but either in the want of inclination, or the strength of a contrary inclination; or the want of sufficient motives in view to induce and excite the act of the will, or the strength of apparent motives to the contrary. It must not, however, be forgotten, that moral inability or disinclination is no excuse for our omission of duty, though want of natural faculties or necessary means would. That God may command though man has not a present moral ability to perform, is evident, if we consider (1) That man once had a power to do whatsoever God would command him, he had a power to cleave to God. (2) That God did not deprive man of his ability. (3) Therefore God's right of commanding, and man's obligation of returning and cleaving to God, remains firm. And, again, man's inability is not an excuse for wrongdoing or the failure to do right, for God's grace has been promised for ability (Phil. iv:13: "I can do all things through Christ, which strengtheneth me.")

INCANTATION (ĭn-kăn-tā'shŭn). See MAGIC.

INCARNATION (ĭn'kär-nā'shŭn), (Lat. *in* and *caro*, "flesh").

The earth life of the Christ must begin with the incarnation as the all-important point which succeeded the Kenosis or voluntary renunciation of the divine functions and prerogatives.

"What think ye of Christ?" demanded the Master, and the question has lost none of its importance during the ages that are gone. This is the keynote of the Christian faith, and the view which we entertain of him must form the basis of our attitude towards all Biblical truth.

The prophecies of the Old Testament point to his work as well as his birth, to his mission as well as his coming; but our theme covers only the beginning of this great historical life.

(1) Conception. Matthew and Luke give in concise and simple language the announcement which the angel made to Mary, to the effect that she should, while yet a virgin, conceive and bring forth a son. *"And thou shalt call his name Jesus, for he shall save his people from their sins"* (Matt. i:21).

These evangelists also record the fulfillment of the angel's prophecy, and give an account of the leading facts connected with this wonderful birth. Paul endorses the statements of both Matthew and Luke, to the effect that the Son of God was "made of a woman" (γενόμενον ἐκ γυναικός).

"When the fullness of time was come God sent forth his son made of a woman, made under the law, that ye might receive the adoption of sons" (Gal. iv:4-5).

Just how this virginal conception and birth were accomplished we do not know. All that we can say is that from a human standpoint it is miraculous. From the Divine point of view there are no miracles.

If this were all the mystery which is beyond our ken, we might have some excuse for doubting it, but the constantly recurring phenomenon of conception, which is the ultimate fact of biology, is in some ways still unexplained.

It is evident, however, that some power brought man into existence from the great unknown, for man is here, and whatever may have been the process employed, or the time occupied, there must have been some point where there was no parent. It is only fair to presume that the Power which produced humanity without the aid of either parent, could, if he chose, produce another man through the agency of the mother alone.

If we cannot fully explain processes which are constantly taking place around us, we may well shrink from the elucidation of a matter which pertains to the higher order of things. The sum of our knowledge on this subject is contained in the words: *"He was conceived of the Holy Ghost and born of the Virgin Mary."*

(2) The Son of God. The Son of God became the son of man by coming into the world as a helpless babe, the heir of human poverty and human pain: *"He took not on himself the nature of angels, but he took on him the seed of Abraham"* Heb. ii:16). Nevertheless, he came of royal stock, both Mary and his reputed father being descendants of King David, for the prophets had foretold that he should belong to the royal line and be born in the city of Bethlehem. *"Though he was rich, yet for your sakes he became poor"* (2 Cor. viii:9) and lay in the manger over which stood "the star in the East" (Luke ii: 7, 12, 16).

The next phase of the subject pertains to the mission of the Son who came from the Father: *"I came down from heaven not to do mine own will, but the will of him that sent me"* (John vi:38).

But there is no contradiction here, no conflict between the will of the Father and of the Son, for he saith: *"My meat is to do the will of him that sent me and to finish his work"* (John iv:34). The Father sends, the Son comes and bears the power of the Father's name: *"I am come in my Father's name"* (John v:43).

He is "the bread of heaven," who giveth life unto the world. *"I proceeded and came forth from God"* (John viii:42). And, again, *"I came forth from the Father and am come into the world"* (John xvii:28).

(3) The Logos. In the prologue to his Gospel, John affirms both the pre-existence and the divinity of the "Word" or "Logos." *"In the beginning was the Logos, and the Logos was Divine."*

It was this Divine Logos who came out of the pre-existent state of glory with the Father into the state of dwelling with man (John xvii:5).

Here again we are at a loss to understand the method of transition, but the text teaches that the Son had glory with the Father "before the world was." *"The Logos was made flesh and dwelt among us"* (John i:14).

It is here distinctly asserted that the Divine Logos who was "with God" assumed the nature of man and took up his abode with humanity.

The statement of John that the Logos was made flesh is his endorsement of the human birth of Jesus the Messiah. Matthew and Luke record only the historical fact, but John goes back of this and represents the conception and birth as being the incarnation of the pre-existent Logos.

(4) Fleshly Nature. Paul teaches that this form which the Logos assumed was sinful flesh —flesh which, like our own, is subject to the rule of sin: *"For what the law could not do in that it was weak through the flesh, God sending his own Son in the likeness of sinful flesh, and for sin (or by a sacrifice for sin) condemned sin in the flesh"* (Rom. viii:3).

We have seen, therefore, that the Apostle teaches that he who knew no sin was made sin for our sakes; that he redeemed us from the curse by becoming the curse in our stead; that he was "made of woman"; that, though he was rich, yet for our sakes he became poor; that God spared not his only Son, but delivered him up for us all; that he who was crucified on Calvary, yet lives to make intercession for us: *"For though he was crucified through weakness, yet he liveth by the power of God"* (2 Cor. xiii:4). (See also 2 Cor. v:21; viii:4, 9; Gal. iii:13; iv:4; Phil. ii:8.)

The general teaching of these texts is in harmony with all the others, and we find that St. Paul conceives of the incarnation as implying a self-emptying of the equality with God, and the assumption of the human nature.

(5) New Testament Teaching. We have, then, the New Testament doctrine of the incarnation under five heads: (1) The Son of God took upon himself the nature of man." *"And was made in the likeness of men: and being found in fashion as a man, he humbled himself and became obedient unto death, even the death of the cross"* (Phil. ii:7, 8). (2) He was sent by the Father. *"For he hath made him to be sin for us, who knew no sin"* (2 Cor. v:21). (3) The coming out of a pre-existent state of glory into a condition in which *"The Son of man hath not where to lay his head"* (Matt. viii:20). (4) The manifestation in the flesh: *"God was manifest in the flesh, justified in the Spirit, seen of angels, preached unto the Gentiles, believed on in the world, received up into glory"* (1 Tim. ii:16). (5) The Kenosis or self-emptying of the Logos in becoming incarnate. *"Who, being in the form of God, thought it not robbery to be equal with God, but made himself of no reputation, and took upon him the form of a servant, and was made in the likeness of men"* (Phil. ii:6, 7).

The history of the Nazarene has shown us that the Son of God who was also the Son of man, shared with us both the physical and mental life.

The Gospels everywhere bear witness to his physical likeness, and show that he felt the bodily weakness of humanity. He was "an hungered," and he asked the woman of Samaria for a drink of water. He was weary, sleeping in the boat even in the midst of the storm. His heart was human in its affections. He loved the young ruler who came to him to inquire the way of life. He loved Lazarus and wept over his grave. His great heart went out in pity for the hungry crowds that waited on his teaching. He felt the throb of righteous indignation, and severely denounced the Scribes and Pharisees. He never concealed his contempt for hypocrisy, and he even drove the money changers out of the temple with a scourge of small cords.

He is represented as "sighing" or "groaning" and "troubled in spirit" (Mark viii:12).

He suffered deeply in the garden and agonized with more than physical pain on Calvary, and even now while we glory in the cross of Christ, and glory in our risen Lord, we still have a great High Priest who can be touched with the feeling of our infirmities. *"Let us therefore come boldly unto the throne of grace, that we may obtain mercy and find grace to help in time of need"* (Heb. iv:14-16). (See JESUS CHRIST; KENOSIS.)

INCENSE (ĭn'sĕns), (Hebrew usually קְטֹרֶת, *ket-o'reth*).

A perfume which gives forth its fragrance by burning, and, in particular, that perfume which was burnt upon the altar of incense. (See ALTAR; CENSER). Indeed the burning of incense seems to have been considered among the Hebrews so much of an act of worship or sacred offering, that we read not of any other use of incense than this among them. Nor among the Egyptians do we discover any trace of burnt perfume but in sacerdotal use; but in the Persian sculptures we see incense burnt before the king. The prohibition of the Hebrews to make any perfume for private use—'to smell to'—like that prepared for the altar, merely implies, we apprehend, that the sacred incense had a peculiarly rich fragrance before being burnt, which was forbidden to be imitated in common perfumes.

Incense is denoted by the words קְטָר, *kit-tare'* (Exod. xxx:1; Jer. xliv:21); and קְטֹרֶת, *ket-o'reth* (Exod. xxx:1; xxxi:11; Ezek. xvi:18); all of which are equally from the root קָטַר, *kaw-tor'*, which in Pihel signifies generally to *raise an odor by burning*, and in the verbal form it is applied not only to the offering of incense, but also of sacrifices, the smoke or effluvium of which is regarded as an acceptable or sweet odor to God. Indeed, the word which denotes an incense of spices in Exod. xxx:1 describes an incense of fat in Ps. lxvi:15.

The ingredients of the sacred incense are enumerated with great precision in Exod. xxx: 34, 35. 'Take unto thee sweet spices, stacte (שְׁחֵלֶת, *shekh-ay'leth*, netaph), and onycha and galbanum, (חֶלְבְּנָה, *khel-ben-aw'*) these sweet spices with pure frankincense (לְבֹנָה, *leb-o-naw'*); of each shall there be a like weight. And thou shalt make of it a perfume, a confection after the art of the apothecary, tempered together, pure and holy.' The further directions are, that this precious compound should be made or broken up into minute particles, and that it should be deposited, as a very holy thing, in the tabernacle 'before the testimony' (or ark). As the ingredients are so minutely specified, there was nothing to prevent wealthy persons from having a similar perfume for private use; this, therefore, was forbidden under pain of excommunication: 'Ye shall not make to yourselves according to the composition thereof; it shall be unto thee holy for the Lord. Whosoever shall make like unto that, to smell thereto, shall even be cut off from his people' (Exod. xxx:37, 38).

According to Maimonides the use of incense was to prevent the stench which would otherwise have been occasioned by the number of beasts every day slaughtered in the sanctuary. God ordained that incense should be burned in it every morning and evening, and thereby rendered the odor of the sanctuary, and of the vestments of those that ministered exceedingly grateful.

Figurative. Incense was a symbol of *prayer.* It was offered at the time when the people were in the posture and act of prayer; and their orisons were supposed to be presented to God by the priest, and to ascend to Him in the smoke of odor of that fragrant offering. This beautiful idea of the incense frequently occurs in Scripture (comp. Ps. cxli:2; Mal. i:11; Acts x:4; Rev. v:8; viii:4).

By it was signified Christ's precious, powerful, and constant intercession within the vail, on the ground of his own righteousness, which renders us and our spiritual services acceptable to God (comp. Exod. xxx:34-38; Lev. xvi:12-14).

INCEST (ĭn'sĕst), an unlawful conjunction of persons related within the degrees of kindred prohibited by God and the church.

In the beginning of the world, and even long after the deluge, marriages between near relations were allowed. God prohibits such alliances in Lev. xviii, and the degrees of consanguinity within which the prohibition applied are detailed in verses 6-18. The prohibition of incest and similar sensual abominations is introduced with a general warning as to the licentious customs of the Egyptians and Canaanites, and an exhortation to walk in the judgments and ordinances of Jehovah. Intercourse is forbidden (1) with a mother; (2) with a stepmother; (3) with a sister or half-sister; (4) with a grand-daughter, the daughter of either son or daughter; (5) with the daughter of a stepmother; (6) with an aunt, sister of either father or mother; (7) with the wife of an uncle on the father's side; (8) with a daughter-in-law; (9) with a sister-in-law, or brother's wife; (10) with a woman and her daughter, or a woman and her grand-daughter; (11) with the sister of a living wife.

Most civilized people have held incest as an abominable crime (see 1 Cor. v:1). Lot's incest with his two daughters can be palliated only by his ignorance, and the simplicity of his daughters (Gen. xix:31).

INCHANTMENTS (ĭn-chant'mẹnts). See WITCHCRAFT.

INCONTINENT (ĭn-kŏn'tĭ-nẹnt),(Gr. ἀκρασία, *ak-ras-ee'a*, want of self-control), given to unchastity and intemperance (2 Tim. iii:3). Unable to refrain from desire of the lawful pleasures of marriage or from concupiscence (2 Cor. vii:5).

INCORPOREALITY OF GOD (ĭn'kôr-pō'rē-ăl'ĭ-tÿ), is his being without a body.

That God is incorporeal is evident; for (1) Materiality is incompatible with self-existence, and God, being self-existent, must be incorporeal. (2) If God were corporeal, he could not be present in any part of the world where body is; yet his presence is necessary for the support and motion of body. (3) A body cannot be in two places at the same time; yet he is everywhere, and fills heaven and earth. (4) A body is to be seen and felt, but God is invisible and impalpable (John i:18). (See IMMATERIALITY.)

INCORRUPTION (ĭn-kŏr-rŭp'shŭn), (Gr. ἀφθαρσία, *af-thar-see'ah*); in general, *unchanging*, ever enduring.

The body is to know no decay after the resurrection (1 Cor. xv:42, 50, 53, 54). In Rom. ii:7 and 2 Tim. i:10 the Greek word is rendered *immortality,* and in Eph. vi:24, *sincerity,* R. V. *uncorruptness.* The crown of the saints is *incorruptible* (1 Cor. ix:25), also their "inheritance" (1 Pet. i:4).

INDEPENDENCE OF GOD (ĭn'dĕ-pĕnd'ens), is his existence in and of himself, without depending on any other.

His being and perfections are underived, and not communicated to him, as all finite perfections are by him to the creature. This attribute of independence belongs to all his perfections. (1) He is independent as to his knowledge. He does not receive ideas from any object out of himself, as intelligent creatures do (Is. lx:13, 14). (2) He is independent in power. As he receives strength from no one, so he does not act dependently on the will of the creature (Job xxxvi:23). (3) He is independent as to his holiness, hating sin necessarily, and not barely depending on some reasons out of himself inducing him thereto; for it is essential to the divine nature to be infinitely opposite to sin, and, therefore, to be independently holy. (4) He is independent as to his bounty and goodness. He communicates blessings not by constraint, but according to his sovereign will (Rom. ix:18). (See article on GOD.)

INDIA (ĭn'dĭ-à), (Heb. הֹדּוּ, *ho'doo*).

This name occurs only in Esther i:1; viii:9, where the Persian king is described as reigning 'from India unto Ethiopia, over a hundred and seven and twenty provinces.' It is found again, however, in the Apocrypha, where India is mentioned among the countries which the Romans took from Antiochus and gave to Eumenes (1 Macc. viii:8). The occurrence of the name in this passage is suspicious. Luther substituted Ionia. At any rate Judas Maccabæus was misinformed if he was told that the Romans had taken India from Antiochus.

It is evident on the face of the above intimations, and indeed from all ancient history, that the country known as India in ancient times extended more to the west, and did not reach so far to the east—that is, was not known so far to the east—as the India of the moderns. When we read of ancient India, we must clearly not understand the whole of Hindostan, but chiefly the northern parts of it, or the countries between the Indus and the Ganges; although it is not necessary to assert that the rest of that peninsula, particularly its western coast, was then altogether unknown. It was from this quarter that the Persians and Greeks (to whom we are indebted for the earliest accounts of India) invaded the country; and this was consequently the region which first became generally known. The countries bordering on the Ganges continued to be involved in obscurity, the great kingdom of the Persians excepted, which, situated nearly above the modern Bengal, was dimly discernible. The nearer we approach the Indus, the more clear becomes our knowledge of the ancient geography of the country; and it follows that the districts of which at the present day we know the least, were anciently best known. Besides, the western and northern boundaries were not the same as at present. To the west, India was not then bounded by the river Indus, but by a chain of mountains which, under the name of Koh (whence the Grecian appellation of the Indian Caucasus), extended from Bactria to Makran, or Gedrosia, enclosing the kingdoms of Candahar and Cabul, the modern kingdom of Eastern Persia, or Afghanis-

tan. These districts anciently formed part of India, as well as, further to the south, the less perfectly known countries of the Arabi and Haurs (the Arabitæ and Oritæ of Arrian, vi:21), bordering on Gedrosia. This western boundary continued at all times the same, and was removed to the Indus only in consequence of the victories of Nadir Shah.

Toward the north, ancient India overpassed not less its present limit. It comprehended the whole of the mountainous region above Cashmir, Baldakshan, Belur Land, the western boundary mountains of Little Bucharia, or Little Thibet, and even the desert of Cobi, so far as it was known. The discovery of a passage by sea to the coasts of India has contributed to withdraw from these regions the attention of Europeans and left them in an obscurity which hitherto has been little disturbed, although the current of events seems likely ere long to lead to our better knowledge.

From this it appears that the India of Scripture included no part of the present India, seeing, that it was confined to the territories possessed by the Persians and the Syrian Greeks, that never extended beyond the Indus, which, since the time of Nadir Shah, has been regarded as the western boundary of India. Something of India beyond the Indus became known through the conquering march of Alexander, and still more through that of Seleucus Nicator, who penetrated to the banks of the Ganges; but the notions thus obtained are not embraced in the Scriptural notices, which, both in the canonical and the Apocryphal text, are confined to Persian India.

INFANT BAPTISM. See BAPTISM.

INFANT SALVATION. See SALVATION.

INFINITY (ĭn-fĭn'ĭ-tў), (Heb. מִסְפָּר, *mis-pawr'*).

Infinity is taken in two senses entirely different, *i. e.,* in a positive and a negative one. *Positive infinity* is a quality being perfect in itself, or capable of receiving no addition. *Negative* is the quality of being boundless, unlimited, or endless. That God is infinite is evident.

If he be limited, it must either be by himself or by another; but no wise being would abridge himself, and there could be no other being to limit God.

Infinity follows from self-existence; for a necessity that is not universal must depend on some external cause, which a self-existent being does not.

Creation is so great an act of power that we can imagine nothing impossible to that Being who has performed it, but must therefore ascribe to him infinite power.

It is more honorable to the Divine Being to conceive of him as infinite than finite.

The Scriptures represent all his attributes as infinite. His understanding is infinite (Ps. cxlvii:5). His knowledge and wisdom (Rom. xi:33). His power (Rom. i:20; Heb. xi:3). His goodness (Ps. xvi:2). His purity, holiness, and justice (Job iv:17, 18; Is. vi:2, 3).

His omnipotence and eternity prove his infinity; for were he not infinite, he would be bounded by space and by time, which he is not.

We must be careful not to conceive of the infinity of God in a material sense, nor hold that it excludes other and finite existences. The infinity of God is that of Spirit. Extension and impenetrability do not apply to spirit as to matter.

Literature. Sir William Hamilton, *Discussions on Philosophy;* Mansel, *Limits of Religious Thought;* Pope, *Compend of Christ. Theol.,* vol. i, 293, *sq.;* Hodge, *Sys. Theol.,* vol. i, 380, *sq.*

INFIRMITY (ĭn-fẽrm'ĭ-tў), (Heb. מַחֲלָה, *makh-al-aw'*, sickness, Prov. xviii:14; Gr. ἀσθένεια, *as-then'i-ah*, weakness or frailty of body).

(1) Disease or weakness of the body (Lev. xii: 2; 1 Tim. v:23).

(2) Outward afflictions, reproaches, persecutions, and temptations (Heb. v:2; 2 Cor. xii:5, 10).

(3) Spiritual weakness, and defects in grace (Rom. vi:19). Failings and mistakes committed through surprise and want of spiritual courage and strength (Rom. xv:1).

The *weakness of God is stronger than men;* the contemned method of salvation through the death of Christ, is more effectual to render men holy and happy, than all the supposedly wise schemes of men (1 Cor. i:25). The *weakness* and *infirmity* of Christ, were his frail human nature, and the various reproaches, temptations, and troubles, he was compassed with (2 Cor. xiii:4; Heb. v:2). The *weakness* of the ceremonial law, which occasioned its abolition, was its insufficiency to justify, sanctify, or save men (Heb. vii:18). Christ took our *infirmities upon him,* and *bare our sickness;* he bare the punishment of our iniquity; he tenderly sympathizes with his people, and testified his affection, by curing the distressed (Matt. viii:17; Heb. iv:15). The Holy Ghost *helps our infirmities;* he gradually heals our spiritual diseases; and notwithstanding them, enables us to worship and serve God (Rom. viii:26). We ought to *bear with the infirmities of the weak,* exercising patience and love towards the weak, notwithstanding their infirmities, and by kindly endeavoring to strengthen them (Rom. xv:1). The saints glory and take pleasure in *infirmities* and troubles, not in themselves, but as they are the means of glorifying God, and the occasions of his communicating strength to them (1 Cor. xii:5, 10).

INFLAMMATION (in'flăm-mā'shŭn). See DISEASES OF THE JEWS.

INFLUENCE (ĭn'flŭ-ens), (Heb. כִּימָה, *kee-maw'*, Job xxxviii:31).

In this passage allusion is apparently made to the controlling influence which the planets exert over each other.

INGATHERING, FEAST OF (ĭn'găth'ẽr-ĭng, fēst ŏv). See FESTIVALS.

INHABITER, INHABITRESS (ĭn-hăb'ĭt-ẽr, ĭn-hăb'ĭt-rĕs), (Gr. κατοικέω, *kat-oy-keh'o*).

Inhabiter is used for 'inhabitant' in Rev. viii: 13; xii:12. It occurs in Coverdale, as Is. xxvi: 9, 'For . . . the inhabitours of the earth lerne righteuousnesse'; and xl:22, 'all the inhabitours of the worlde are in comparison of him but as greshoppers'; comp. Prayer Book, Ps. lxxv:4, 'The earth is weak and all the inhabiters thereof.' The fem. form inhabitress occurs in Jer. x:17, marg., an attempt to show the gender of the Hebrew word used in the passage. Comp. Chapman, *Hymne to Venus*—

'An inhabitresse
On this thy wood-crowned hill."
(Hastings' *Bib. Dict.*)

INHERITANCE (ĭn-hĕr'ĭt-ɑns), (Heb. נַחֲלָה, *nakh-al-aw'*).

The laws and observances which determine the acquisition and regulate the devolution of property are among the influences which affect the vital interests of states; and it is therefore of high consequence to ascertain the nature and bearing of the laws and observances relating to this subject, which come to us with the sanction of the Bible. We may also premise that, in a condition of society such as that in which we now live, wherein the two diverging tendencies which favor immense accumulations on the one hand, and lead to poverty and pauperism on the other, are daily becoming more and more decided, disturbing, and baneful, there seems to be required on the part of those who take Scripture as their guide, a careful study of the foundations of human society, and of the laws of property, as they are developed in the Divine records which contain the revealed will of God.

That will, in truth, as it is the source of all created things, and specially of the earth and its intelligent denizen, man, so is it the original foundation of property, and of the laws by which its inheritance should be regulated. God, as the Creator of the earth, gave it to man, to be held, cultivated and enjoyed (Gen. i:28, *sq.;* Ps. cxv: 16; Eccles. v:9). The primitive records are too brief and fragmentary to supply us with any details respecting the earliest distribution or transmission of landed property; but from the passages to which reference has been made, the important fact appears to be established beyond a question, that the origin of property is to be found, not in the achievements of violence, the success of the sword, or any imaginary implied contract, but in the will and the gift of the common Creator and bountiful Father of the human race. It is equally clear that the gift was made not to any favored portion of our race, but to the race itself—to man as represented by our great primogenitor, to whom the use of the Divine gift was first graciously vouchsafed.

(1) Patriarchal Inheritance. The impression which the original gift of the earth was calculated to make on men, the Great Donor was pleased, in the case of Palestine, to render, for his own wise purposes, more decided and emphatic by an express re-donation to the patriarch Abraham (Gen. xiii:14, *sq.*). Many years, however, elapsed before the promise was fulfilled. Meanwhile the notices which we have regarding the state of property in the patriarchal ages, are few, and not very definite. The products of the earth, however, were at an early period accumulated and held as property. Violence invaded the possession; opposing violence recovered the goods. War soon sprang out of the passions of the human heart. The necessity of civil government was felt. Consuetudinary laws accordingly developed themselves. The head of the family was supreme. His will was law. The physical superiority which he possessed gave him the dominion. The same influence would secure its transmission in the male rather than the female line. Hence, too, the rise of the rights of primogeniture. In the early condition of society which is called patriarchal, landed property had its origin, indeed, but could not be held of first importance by those who led a wandering life, shifting continually, as convenience suggested, from one spot to another. Cattle were then the chief property (Gen. xxiv:35). But land, if held, was held on a freehold tenure; nor could any other tenure have come into existence till more complex and artificial relations arose, resulting, in all probability, from the increase of population and the relative insufficiency of food.

When Joseph went down into Egypt, he appears to have found the freehold tenure prevailing, which, however, he converted into a tenancy at will, or, at any rate, into a conditional tenancy. Other intimations are found in Genesis which confirm the general statements which have just been made. Daughters do not appear to have had an inheritance. If there are any exceptions to this rule they only serve to prove it. Thus Job (the book so called is undoubtedly very old, so that there is no impropriety in citing it in this connection) is recorded (xlii:15) to have given his daughters an inheritance conjointly with their brothers—a record which of itself proves the singularity of the proceeding, and establishes our position that inheritance generally followed the male line.

(2) Privileges of Inheritance. How highly the privileges conferred by primogeniture were valued, may be learned from the history of Jacob and Esau. In the patriarchal age doubtless these rights were very great. The eldest son, as being by nature the first fitted for command, assumed influence and control, under his father, over the family and its dependents; and when the father was removed by death, he readily, and as if by an act of Providence, took his father's place. Thus he succeeded to the property in succeeding to the headship of the family, the clan, or the tribe. At first the eldest son most probably took exclusive possession of his father's property and power; and when, subsequently, a division became customary, he would still retain the largest share—a double portion, if not more (Gen. xxvii:25, 29, 40). That in the days of Abraham other sons partook with the eldest, and that, too, though they were sons of concubines, is clear from the story of Hagar's expulsion. (See HAGAR.) 'Cast out (said Sarah) this bondwoman and her son; for the son of this bondwoman shall not be heir with my son, even with Isaac' (Gen. xxi:10).

(3) Transfer of Property. The few notices left us in Genesis of the transfer of property from hand to hand are interesting, and bear a remarkable similarity to what takes place in Eastern countries even at this day (Gen. xxi:22, sq.; xxiii:9, sq.). The purchase of the Cave of Machpelah as a family burying place for Abraham, detailed in the last passage, serves to show the safety of property at that early period, and the facility with which an inheritance was transmitted even to sons' sons (comp. Gen. xlix:29). That it was customary during the father's lifetime to make a disposition of property, is evident from Gen. xxiv:35, where it is said that Abraham had given all he had to Isaac. This statement is further confirmed by Gen. xxv:5, 6, where it is added that Abraham gave to the sons of his concubines 'gifts, sending them away from Isaac his son, while he yet lived, eastward unto the east country.' Sometimes, however, so far were the children of unmarried females from being dismissed with a gift, that they shared, with what we should term the legitimate children, in the father's property and rights. Thus Dan and Naphtali were sons of Bilhah, Rachel's maid, whom she gave to her husband, failing to bear children herself, So Gad and Asher were, under similar circumstances, sons of Zilpah, Leah's maid (Gen. xxx:2-14). In the event of the eldest son's dying in the father's lifetime, the next son took his place; and if the eldest son left a widow, the next son made her his wife (Gen. xxxviii:7, sq.), the offspring of which union was reckoned to the firstborn and deceased son. Should the second likewise die, the third son took his place (Gen. xxxviii:11).

(4) Rights of Younger Children. While the rights of the firstborn were generally established and recognized, yet were they sometimes set aside in favor of a younger child. The blessing of the father or the grandsire seems to have been an act essential in the devolution of power and property—in its effects not unlike wills and testaments with us; and instances are not wanting in which this (so to term it) testamentary bequest set aside consuetudinary laws, and gave precedence to a younger son (Gen. xlviii:15, sq.). Special claims on the parental regards were acknowledged and rewarded by special gifts, as in the case of Jacob's donation to Joseph (Gen. xlviii:22). In a similar manner, bad conduct on the part of the eldest son (as well as of others) subjected him, if not to the loss of his rights of property, yet to the evil influence of his father's dying malediction (Gen. xlix:3); while the good and favored, though younger, son was led by the paternal blessing to participate, and probably also to reap, the richest inheritance of individual and social happiness (Gen. xlix:8-22).

(5) Inheritance of the Promised Land. The original promise made to Abraham of the land of Palestine was solemnly repeated to Isaac (Gen. xxvi:3), the reason assigned being, because 'Abraham obeyed my voice and kept my charge,' my commandments, my statutes, and my laws; while it is expressly declared that the earlier inhabitants of the country were dispossessed and destined to extermination for the greatness of their iniquity. The possession of the promised land was embraced by Isaac in his dying benediction to Jacob (Gen. xxviii:3, 4), to whom God vouchsafed (Gen. xxviii:15; see also xxxv:10, 11), to give a renewed assurance of the destined inheritance. That this donation, however, was held to be dependent for the time and manner of its fulfilment on the Divine will, appears from Gen. xxxiii:18, where Jacob, on coming into the land of Canaan, bought for an hundred pieces of money 'a parcel of a field, at the hand of the children of Hamor.' Delayed though the execution of the promise was, confidence never deserted the family of Abraham, so that Joseph, dying in the land of Egypt, assured his brothers that they would be visited of God and placed in possession of Canaan, enjoining on them, in this conviction, that, when conducted to their possession, they should carry his bones with them out of Egypt (Gen. l:25).

A promise thus given, thus repeated, and thus believed, easily, and indeed unavoidably, became the fundamental principle of that settlement of property which Moses made when at length he had effected the Divine will in the redemption of the children of Israel. The observances and practices, too, which we have noticed as prevailing among the patriarchs, would, no doubt, have great influence on the laws which the Jewish legislator originated or sanctioned.

(6) Division of the Promised Land. The land of Canaan was divided among the twelve tribes descended through Isaac and Jacob from Abraham. The division was made by lot for an inheritance among the families of the sons of Israel, according to the tribes, and to the number and size of families in each tribe. The tribe of Levi, however, had no inheritance; but forty-eight cities with their suburbs were assigned to the Levites, each tribe giving according to the number of cities that fell to its share (Num. xxxiii:50; xxxiv:1; xxx:1). The inheritance thus acquired was never to leave the tribe to which it belonged; every tribe was to keep strictly to its own inheritance. An heiress, in consequence, was not allowed to marry out of her own tribe, lest property should pass by her marriage into another tribe (Num. xxxvi:6-9). This restriction led to the marriage of heiresses with their near relations; thus the daughters of Zelophehad 'were married unto their father's brother's sons,' 'and their inheritance remained in the tribe of the family of their father' (ver. 11, 12; comp. Joseph. *Antiq.* iv :7, 5). In general cases the inheritance went to sons, the firstborn receiving a double portion, 'for he is the beginning of his father's strength.' If a man had two wives, one beloved, the other hated, and if the firstborn were the son of her who was hated, he nevertheless was to enjoy 'the right of the firstborn' (Deut. xxi :15). If a man left no sons, the inheritance passed to his daughters; if there was no daughter, it went to his brothers; in case there were no brothers, it was given to his father's brothers; if his father had no brothers, it came into possession of the nearest kinsman (Num. xxvii :8).

TABLE SHOWING ORDER OF SUCCESSION AS HEIRS.

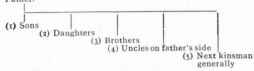

Father.

(1) Sons
   (2) Daughters
      (3) Brothers
         (4) Uncles on father's side
            (5) Next kinsman generally

(7) **The Year of Jubilee.** The land was Jehovah's and could not, therefore, be permanently alienated. Every fiftieth year, whatever land had been sold returned to its former owner. The value and price of land naturally rose or fell in proportion to the number of years there were to elapse prior to the ensuing fiftieth or jubilee-year. If he who sold the land, or a kinsman, could redeem the land before the year of jubilee, it was to be restored to him on his paying to the purchaser the value of the produce of the years remaining till the jubilee. Houses in villages or unwalled towns might not be sold forever; they were restored at the jubilee, and might at any time be redeemed. If a man sold a dwelling house situated in a walled city, he had the option of redeeming it within the space of a full year after it had been sold; but if it remained unredeemed, it belonged to the purchaser, and did not return to him who sold it even at the jubilee (Lev. xxv :8, 23). The Levites were not allowed to sell the land in the suburbs of their cities, though they might dispose of the cities themselves, which, however, were redeemable at any time, and must return at the jubilee to their original possessors (Lev. xxvii :16). (See JUBILEE.)

(8) **Wills.** The regulations which the laws of Moses established rendered wills or a testamentary disposition of (at least) landed property, almost, if not quite, unnecessary; we accordingly find no provision for anything of the kind. Some difficulty may have been now and then occasioned when near relations failed; but this was met by the traditional law, which furnished minute directions on the point (Misch. *Baba Bathra*, iv :3, c. 8, 9) Personal property would naturally follow the land or might be bequeathed by word of mouth. At a later period of the Jewish polity the mention of wills is found, but the idea seems to have been taken from foreign nations. In princely families they appear to have been used, as we learn from Josephus (*Antiq.* xiii :16, 1; xvii :3, 2; *De Bell. Jud.* ii :2, 3); but such a practice can hardly suffice to establish the general use of wills among the people. In the New Testament, however, wills are expressly mentioned (Gal iii :15; Heb. ix :17). Michaelis (*Commentaries*, i :431) asserts that the phrase (2 Sam. xvii :23; 2 Kings xx :i), 'set thine house in order,' has reference to a will or testament. But his grounds are by no means sufficient. J. R. B.

Figurative. (1) God himself, and his everlasting salvation, are the *inheritance* of his people, to which, through Jesus their Savior, they have a free and honorable claim on which they live, and in which they delight and glory (Ps. xvi :5; Jer. iii :19; 1 Pet. i :4). (2) Christ's glorious character of Mediator, and the heathen, or Gentiles, are his *inheritance;* he has an honorable claim to his renown and happiness as God-man, and the Gentiles are given into his hand to be called and converted by him (Heb. i :4; Ps. ii :8). (3) The Jews *took their inheritance in themselves,* when they were forsaken by God, deprived of their civil and ecclesiastic enjoyments, and left to look out for themselves, under the load of their deserved punishment (Ezek. xxii :16). (4) The *inheritance of the congregation of Jacob* is either the Israelites, who were God's *inheritance,* or the law, which God gave them as a valuable inheritance (Deut. xxxiii :4). (5) *God was the Levites' inheritance;* they lived on his offerings (Deut. x :9). (6) *God's testimonies are his people's inheritance;* are of great value, and they delight in and live on them (Ps. cxix :111). (7) *Children are God's heritage* and *reward;* he freely gives them to parents, and cheerfully ought they to devote them to God (Ps. cxxvii :3).

INIQUITY (ĭn-ĭk'wĭ-tў), (Heb. יָוֹן, *aw-vone'*).

This word means not only sin, but the *punishment* of sin, and the expiation of it: "Aaron will bear the iniquities of the people;" he will atone for them (Exod. xxviii :38). The Lord "visits the iniquities of the fathers upon the children" (Exod. xx :5). The priests bear the iniquity of the people; that is, they are charged with the expiation of it (Exod. xxviii :38; Lev. x :17).

INJURIOUS (ĭn-jū'rĭ-ŭs), (Gr. ὑβριστής, *hoo-bris-tace'*, 1 Tim. i :13), insolent, abusive.

INK (ĭnk), (Heb. דְּיוֹ, *deh-yo'*, Jer. xxxvi :18; Gr. μέλαν, *mel'an*, black, 2 Cor. iii :3; 2 John 12; 3 John 13).

The ink of the ancients was composed of powdered charcoal, lampblack or soot, mixed with gum and water. It was intensely black and would retain its color for ages, but was easily removed from the parchments with sponge and water (see Num. v :23). It was not so fluid as ours. Demosthenes reproaches Æschines with laboring in the grinding of ink, as painters do in the grinding of their colors. The substance also found in an inkstand at Herculaneum, looks like a thick oil or paint, with which the manuscripts there have been written in a relievo visible in the letters, when a leaf is held to the light in a horizontal direction. Such vitriolic ink as has been used on the old parchment manuscripts would have corroded the delicate leaves of the papyrus, as it has done the skins of the most ancient manuscripts of Vergil and Terence, in the Vatican library; the letters are sunk into the parchment, and some have eaten quite through it, in consequence of the corrosive acid of the vitriolic ink, with which they were written.

Different colors were used by the Egyptians and Hebrews for writing. They were of red, blue, purple, gold and silver tints.

INKHORN (ĭnk'hôrn), (Heb. קֶסֶת, *keh'seth*, a round *vessel*).

The Oriental inkhorn was a long tube for holding pens, and was carried in the girdle. It was made of brass, copper, silver or hard wood. It was about nine or ten inches long, one and a half or two inches wide, and half an inch deep. To the upper end of this case the inkstand is attached. This is square or cylindrical, with a lid moving on hinges and fastening with a clasp. (See WRITING.)

INN (ĭn), (Heb. מָלוֹן, *maw-lone'*, Gen. xlii:27; xliii:21; Exod. iv:24, a "resting-place for the night"; while the Gr. κατάλυμα, *kat-al'oo-mah*, is used for an "inn," Luke ii:7; an "eating-room," A. V. *guest chamber*, Mark xiv:14; Luke xxii:11). (See CARAVANSARY.)

INNOCENT, INNOCENCY (ĭn'nŏ-sent, ĭn'nŏ-sen-sў), (Heb. נָקִי, or נָקִיא, *nik-kaw-yone'*, literally *clearness*, Gen. xx:5; Ps. xxvi:6).

The signification of these words is well known. The Hebrews considered innocence as consisting chiefly in an exemption from external fault committed contrary to the law; hence they often join innocent with hands (Gen. xxxvii:22; Ps. xxiv:4; xxvi:6). "I will wash my hands in innocency;" and (Ps. lxxiii:13 "Then have I cleansed my heart in vain, and washed my hands in innocency." Josephus admits of no other sins than those which are put in execution. Sins in thought, in his account, are not punished by God. To be innocent, is used sometimes for being exempt from punishment. "I will not treat you as one innocent" (Jer. xlvi:28), literally, "I will not make thee innocent." Calmet.

INNOCENTS, SLAUGHTER OF THE (ĭn'nŏ-sents, sla'tēr), (Matt. ii:16), the slaying of the young children of Bethlehem, by order of Herod, in the hope of killing Jesus. (See HERODIAN FAMILY, I.)

INORDINATE (ĭn-ôr'dĭ-năt), disorderly; excessive, as passions or desires, (Ezek. xxiii:11; Col. iii:5).

INQUISITION (ĭn'kwĭ-zĭsh'ŭn), (Heb. דָּרַשׁ, *daw-rash'*, search; examination, Deut. xix:18). God makes *inquisition* for blood when in his providence he discovers and punishes violent men and oppressors (Ps. ix:12).

INSCRIPTION or SUPERSCRIPTION (ĭn-skrĭp'shŭn, sū'pēr-skrĭp'shŭn), a writing on pillars, altars, marble or coins (Acts xvii:23; Matt. xxii:20).

Anciently the history of nations and the principles of science were thus inscribed. The Grecian history of about 1318 years was inscribed on the Arundelian marbles. Grævius has filled three volumes in folio with inscriptions of the ancient Greeks and Romans. At least an abridgment of the law of Moses, or a copy of the blessings and curses, was inscribed on the altar at Ebal (Deut. xxvii:8). (See WRITING.)

INSPIRATION (ĭn-spĭ-rā-shŭn), (Heb. נְשָׁמָה, *nesh'aw-maw;* Lat. *inspiratio,* a breathing into).

This word is sometimes used to denote the excitement and action of a fervent imagination in the poet or orator. But even in this case there is generally a reference to some supposed divine influence, to which the excited action is owing. It is once used in Scripture to denote that divine agency by which man is endued with the faculties of an intelligent being, when it is said, 'the inspiration of the Almighty giveth him understanding.' But the inspiration now to be considered is that which belonged to those who wrote the Scriptures, and which is particularly spoken of in 2 Tim. iii:16, and in 2 Pet. i:21: 'All Scripture is given by inspiration of God;' 'Holy men of God spake as they were moved by the Holy Ghost.' These passages relate specially to the Old Testament; but there is at least equal reason to predicate divine inspiration of the New Testament.

Inspiration may be best defined, according to the representations of the Scriptures themselves, as *an extraordinary divine agency upon teachers while giving instruction, whether oral or written, by which they were taught what and how they should write or speak.* Or we may say more briefly, that the sacred penmen were completely under the direction of the Holy Spirit, or that they wrote under a plenary inspiration.

1. The Fact of Inspiration. To prove that the Scriptures are divinely inspired we might with propriety refer to the excellence of the doctrines, precepts, and promises, and other instructions, which they contain; to the simplicity and majesty of their style; to the agreement of the different parts, and the scope of the whole; especially to the full discovery they make of man's fallen and ruined state, and the way of salvation through a Redeemer; together with their power to enlighten and sanctify the heart, and the accompanying witness of the Spirit in believers. These are circumstances of real importance, and the discerning advocates of inspiration have not overlooked them. But the more direct and conclusive evidence that the Scriptures were divinely inspired, is found in *the testimony of the writers themselves.* And as the writers did, by working miracles, and in other ways, sufficiently authenticate their divine commission, and establish their authority and infallibility as teachers of divine truth, their testimony, in regard to their own inspiration, is entitled to our full confidence. For who can doubt that they were as competent to judge of, and as much disposed to speak the truth on this subject as on any other? If then we admit their divine commission and authority, why should we not rely upon the plain testimony which they give concerning the divine assistance afforded them in their work? To reject their testimony in this case would be to impeach their veracity, and thus to take away the foundation of the Christian religion. And it is well known that those who deny the justice of the claim which they set up to divine inspiration, do, in fact, give up the infallible truth and authority of the Scriptures, and adopt the principles of deism.

It is, then, of the first importance to inquire what representations are made by the prophets, and by Christ and his apostles, respecting the inspiration, and the consequent authority, of the sacred Scriptures.

(1) Testimony of the Prophets. The prophets generally professed to speak *the word of God.* What they taught was introduced and confirmed by a 'Thus saith the Lord'; or 'The Lord spake to me, saying.' And, in one way or another, they gave clear proof that they were divinely commissioned, and spoke in the name of God, or as it is expressed in the New Testament, *that God spake by them.*

(2) Testimony of Jesus Christ and the Apostles. But the strongest and most satisfactory proof of the inspiration and divine authority of the Old Testament writings, is found in the testimony of Christ and the apostles.

The Lord Jesus Christ possessed the spirit of wisdom without measure, and came to bear witness to the truth. His works proved that he was what he declared himself to be—the Messiah, the great Prophet, the infallible Teacher. The faith which rests on him rests on a rock. As soon then as we learn how *he* regarded the Scriptures, we have reached the end of our inquiries. His word is truth. Now every one who carefully attends to the four Gospels will find, that Christ everywhere spoke of that collection of writings called the Scripture, as the word of God; that he regarded the whole in this light; that he treated the Scripture, and every part of it, as infallibly true, and as clothed with divine authority—thus distinguishing it from every mere human production. Nothing written by man can be entitled to the respect which Christ showed to the Scriptures. This, to all Christians, is direct and incontrovertible evidence of the divine origin of the Scriptures, and is, by itself, perfectly conclusive.

But there is clear concurrent evidence, and evidence still more specific, in the writings of the Apostles. In two texts in particular, divine inspiration is positively asserted. In the first (2 Tim. iii:16) Paul lays it down as the characteristic of '*all Scripture*,' that it '*is given by inspiration of God*' (θεόπνευστος, *theop'neustos*, divinely inspired) ; and from this results its profitableness. '

The other text (2 Pet. i:21) teaches that 'Prophecy came not by the will of man, but holy men of God spake as they were moved by the Holy Ghost.' This passage, which the Apostle Peter applied particularly to the subject of which he was speaking, may be considered as explanatory of what is intended by inspiration. For to say that all Scripture is divinely inspired, and that men of God wrote it as they were moved by the Holy Ghost, is one and the same thing.

The various texts in which Christ and the Apostles speak of Scripture as *the word of God,* and as invested with authority to decide all questions of truth and duty, fully correspond with the texts above considered.

From this view of the subject it follows that the attempt which has been made by a certain class of writers, to account for the production of the whole or any part of the Scriptures by the will or agency, the ingenuity, diligence or fidelity of men, in the use of the means within their reach, without the supernatural influence of the Spirit, is utterly at variance with the teachings of Christ and the Apostles as to the origin of the sacred writings.

(3) Inspiration of the New Testament. As the Christian dispensation surpasses the former in all spiritual privileges and gifts, it is reasonable to presume that the New Testament was written under at least an equal degree of divine influence with the Old, and that it comes recommended to us by equal characteristics of infallible truth. But of this there is clear positive evidence from the New Testament itself.

In the first place, *Jesus Christ,* whose works proved him to be the great unerring Teacher, and to be possessed of all power in Heaven and earth, *gave commission to his Apostles to act in his stead, and to carry out the work of instruction which he had begun,* confirming their authority by investing them with power to perform miracles. But how could such a commission have answered the end proposed, had not the Divine Spirit so guided the Apostles as to render them infallible and perfect teachers of divine truth?

But, secondly, in addition to this, *Jesus expressly promised to give them the Holy Spirit to abide with them continually, and to guide them into all the truth.* He said to them, 'When they shall deliver you up, take no thought how or what ye shall speak; for it shall be given you in the same hour what ye shall speak. For it is not ye that speak, but the Spirit of your Father that speaketh in you.' Storr and Flatt think this is the idea intended: 'The instructions which ye in general give are derived not so much from yourselves as from the Holy Spirit. Hence, when ye are called on to defend your doctrines, ye need feel no anxiety, but may confidently rely on the Holy Spirit to vindicate his own doctrines, by suggesting to you the very words of your defense.' If these promises were not fulfilled, then Jesus was not a true prophet. If they were fulfilled, as

they certainly were, then the Apostles had the constant assistance of the Holy Spirit, and whether engaged in speaking or writing, were under divine guidance, and, of course, were liable to no mistakes either as to the matter or manner of their instructions.

In the third place, *the writers of the New Testament manifestly considered themselves to be under the guidance of the Holy Spirit, and their instructions, whether oral or written, to be clothed with divine authority, as the word of God.*

'We speak,' they say, 'as of God.' Again, 'Which things we speak not in the words which man's wisdom teacheth, but in words which the Holy Ghost teacheth.' They declare what they taught to be *the word of God,* and the things they wrote to be the *commandments of God.* Now the Apostles, being honest, unassuming, humble men, would never have spoken of themselves and their writings in such a manner, had they not known themselves to be under the unerring guidance of the Holy Spirit, and their instructions perfectly in accordance with the mind of God.

(4) Manner of Inspiration. It is perfectly consistent with the plenary inspiration here mentioned, that God operated on the minds of inspired men in a variety of ways, sometimes by audible words, sometimes by direct inward suggestions, sometimes by outward visible signs, sometimes by the Urim and Thummim, and sometimes by dreams and visions. This variety in the mode of Divine influence detracted nothing from its certainty. God made known his will equally in different ways; and, whatever the mode of his operation, he made it manifest to his servants that the things revealed were from him.

But inspiration was concerned not only in making known the will of God to prophets and apostles, but also *in giving them directions in writing the sacred books.* They wrote *as they were moved by the Holy Ghost.* And in this, also, there was a diversity in the mode of divine influence. Sometimes the Spirit of God moved and guided his servants to write things which they could not know by natural means, such as new doctrines or precepts, or predictions of future events. Sometimes he moved and guided them to write the history of events which were wholly or partly known to them by tradition, or by the testimony of their contemporaries, or by their own observation or experience. In all these cases the Divine Spirit effectually preserved them from all error, and influenced them to write just so much and in such a manner as God saw to be best. Sometimes he moved and guided them to write a summary record of larger histories, containing what his infinite wisdom saw to be adapted to the end in view, that is, the benefit of his people in all ages. Sometimes he influenced them to make a record of important maxims in common use, or to write new ones, derived either from their own reason and experience, or from special divine teaching. Sometimes he influenced them to write parables or allegories, particularly suited to make a salutary impression of Divine things on the minds of men; and sometimes to record supernatural visions. In these and all other kinds of writing the sacred penmen manifestly needed special divine guidance, as no man could of himself attain infallibility, and no wisdom, except that of God, was sufficient to determine what things ought to be written for permanent use in the church, and what manner of writing would be best fitted to promote the great ends of revelation.

Some writers speak of different modes and different kinds, and even different degrees, of inspiration. And if their meaning is that God influenced the minds of inspired men in different ways; that he adopted a variety of modes in revealing divine things to their minds; that he guided them to give instruction in prose and in poetry, and in all the different forms of composition; that he moved and guided them to write history, prophecy, doctrines, commands, promises, reproofs, and exhortations, and that he adapted his mode of operation to each of these cases—against this no objection can be made. It is a fact, that the Scriptures exhibit specimens of all these different kinds of writing and these different modes of divine instruction. Still each and every part of what was written was divinely inspired, and equally so. It is all the word of God, and clothed with divine authority, as much as if it had all been made known and written in one way.

Dr. Henderson, who labors perhaps with too much zeal against carrying inspiration to extreme lengths, still says that if those who hold to different modifications of inspiration intend that there are different modifications and degrees of *authority* given to Scripture, their opinion must meet with unqualified reprobation from every sincere believer. He insists that a diversity in the modes and degrees of divine operation did exist in the work of inspiration, and that this diversity was the result of infinite wisdom adapting itself to different circumstances. He thinks that, unless we admit such a diversity, we cannot form correct ideas of the subject. But he is confident that the distinction which he endeavors to establish is not in the slightest degree hostile to the divine authority of Scripture. He affirms that *no part of that holy book was written without miraculous influence; that all parts were equally inspired;* that in regard to the whole volume the great end was infallibly attained, namely, the commitment to writing of precisely such matters as God designed for the religious instruction of mankind; that the sacred penmen wrote what had for its object not merely the immediate benefit of individual persons or churches, but what would be useful to Christians in all future times; and that in regard to the most minute and inconsiderable things which the Scripture contains we are compelled to say, *this also cometh from the Lord.*

(5) Verbal Inspiration. The controversy among orthodox divines respecting what is called *verbal inspiration,* appears to arise, in a great measure, from the different senses affixed to the phrase.

The real question, and the whole question at issue, may be stated thus: *did the work of the Divine Spirit in the sacred penmen relate to the language they used, or their manner of expressing their ideas; and if so, how far, and in what way?*

All those with whom we are concerned in the discussion of this question, hold that Divine inspiration had some respect to the language employed by the inspired writers, at least in the way of general *supervision.* In recording what was immediately spoken with an audible voice by Jehovah, or by an angel interpreter; in giving expression to points of revelation which entirely surpassed the comprehension of the writers; in recording prophecies, the minute bearings of which they did not perceive; in short, in committing to writing any of the dictates of the Spirit, which they could not have otherwise accurately expressed, the sacred writers were supplied with the words as well as the matter.

Even when Biblical writers made use of their own faculties, and wrote each one in his own manner, without having their mental constitution at all disturbed, they were yet always secured by celestial influence against the adoption of any forms of speech, or collocation of words, that would have injured the exhibition of Divine truth, or that did not adequately give it expression. The characteristic differences of style, so apparent among the sacred writers, were employed by the Holy Spirit for the purposes of inspiration, and were called forth in a rational way. The writers, being acted upon by the Divine Spirit, expressed themselves naturally, and while the Divine influence adapted itself to whatever was peculiar in the minds of inspired men, it constantly guided them in writing the sacred volume. The Holy Scriptures were written, not under a partial or imperfect, but under a plenary and infallible, inspiration, and were entirely the result of Divine intervention, and are to be regarded as the oracles of Jehovah.

(6) Plenary Inspiration. (a) The doctrine of a plenary inspiration of all Scripture in regard to the language employed, as well as the thoughts communicated, ought not to be rejected without valid reasons. The doctrine is so obviously important, and so consonant with the feelings of sincere piety, that those evangelical Christians who are pressed with speculative objections against it frequently, in the honesty of their hearts, advance opinions which fairly imply it. This is the case, as we have seen, with Dr. Henderson, who says, that the Divine Spirit guided the sacred penmen in *writing* the Scriptures; that their *mode of expression* was such as they were instructed by the Spirit to employ; that Paul ascribes not only the doctrines which the Apostles taught, but *the entire character of their style,* to the influence of the Spirit. He indeed says, that this does not always imply the *immediate communication of the words* of Scripture; and he says it with good reason. For *immediate* properly signifies, *acting without a medium,* or *without the intervention of another cause or means, not acting by second causes.*

(b) Now those who hold the highest views of inspiration do not suppose that the Divine Spirit, except in a few instances, so influenced the writers of Scripture as to interfere with the use of their rational faculties or their peculiar mental habits and tastes, or in any way to supersede secondary causes as the medium through which his agency produced the desired effect.

In regard to this point, therefore, there appears to be little or no ground for controversy. For, if God so influenced the sacred writers that, either with or without the use of secondary causes, they wrote just *what* he intended, and in the *manner* he intended, the end is secured; and what they wrote is as truly *his word,* as though he had written it with his own hand on tables of stone, without any human instrumentality. The very words of the Decalogue were all such as God chose. And they would have been equally so if Moses had been moved by the Divine Spirit to write them with *his* hand. The expression, that God *immediately imparted* or *communicated* to the writers the very words which they wrote, is evidently not well chosen. The exact truth, is that *the writers themselves* were the subjects of the Divine influence. The Spirit employed them as active instruments, and directed them in writing, both as to matter and manner. They wrote 'as they were moved by the Holy Ghost.' The matter, in many cases, was what they before knew, and the manner was entirely conformed to their habits; it was *their own*. But what was written was none the less inspired on that account. God may have influenced and guided an apostle as infallibly in writing what he had before known, and that guidance may have been as really necessary, as in writing a new revelation. And God may have influenced Paul or John to write a book in *his own peculiar style,* and that influence may have been as real and as necessary as if the style had been what some would call a *divine style.* It *was* a divine style, if the writer used it under Divine direction. It was a *divine* style, and it was, at the same time, a *human style,* and the *writer's own* style, all in one. Just as the believer's exercises, faith and love, are his own acts, and at the same time are the effects of Divine influence.

'In efficacious grace,' says Edwards, 'we are not merely passive, nor yet does God do some and we do the rest. But God does all, and we do all. God produces all, and we act all. For that is what he produces, namely, our own acts. God is the only proper author and foundation; we only are the proper actors. We are, in different respects, wholly passive and wholly active. In the Scriptures, the same things are represented as from God and from us. God is said to convert men, and men are said to convert and turn. God makes a new heart and we are commanded to make us a new heart—not merely because we must use the means in order to the effect, but the effect itself is our act and our duty. These things are agreeable to that text, "God worketh in you both to will and to do."

(c) The mental exercises of Paul and of John had their own characteristic peculiarities, as much as their style. God was the author of John's mind and all that was peculiar to his mental faculties and habits, as really as of Paul's mind and what was peculiar to him. And in the work of inspiration he used and directed, for his own purposes, what was peculiar to each. When God inspired different men he did not make their minds and tastes all alike, nor did he make their language alike. Nor had he any occasion for this; for while they had different mental faculties and habits, they were as capable of being infallibly directed by the Divine Spirit, and infallibly speaking and writing Divine truth, as though their mental faculties, and habits had been all exactly alike. And it is manifest that the Scriptures, written by such a variety of inspired men, and each part agreeably to the peculiar talents and style of the writer, are not only equally from God, but, taken together, are far better adapted to the purposes of general instruction, and all the objects to be accomplished by revelation, than if they had been written by one man, and in one and the same manner.

(d) This view of plenary inspiration is fitted to relieve the difficulties and objections which have arisen in the minds of men from the variety of talent and taste which the writers exhibited, and the variety of style which they used. See, it is said, how each writer expresses himself naturally, in his own way, just as he was accustomed to do when not inspired. And see, too, we might say in reply, how each Apostle, Peter, Paul or John, when speaking before rulers, with the promised aid of the Holy Spirit, spoke naturally, *with his own voice,* and in his own way, as he had been accustomed to do on other occasions were not inspired. There is no more objection to plenary inspiration in the one case than in the other. The mental faculties and habits of the Apostles, their style, their voice, their mode

of speech, all remained as they were. What, then, had the Divine Spirit to do? What was the work which appertained to him? We reply, his work was so to direct the Apostles in the use of their own talents and habits, their style, their voice, and all their peculiar endowments, that they should speak or write, each in his own way, just what God would have them speak or write, for the good of the Church in all ages.

2. Objections from Peculiarities of the Writers.

(1) **Language.** The fact that the individual peculiarities of the sacred penmen are everywhere so plainly impressed on their writings, is often mentioned as an objection to the doctrine, that inspiration extended to their *language* as well as their thoughts. This is, indeed, one of the most common objections, and one which has obtained a very deep lodgment in the minds of some intelligent Christians. It may, therefore, be necessary to take some further pains completely to remove it. And in our additional remarks relative to this and other objections, it will come in our way to show that such a writer as Gaussen, who contends with great earnestness and ability for the highest views of inspiration, does still, on all important points, agree with those who advocate lower views of the subject.

Gaussen says, 'Even if the title of each book should not indicate to us that we are passing from one author to another; yet we could quickly discover, by the change of their characters, that a new hand has taken the pen. It is perfectly easy to recognize each one of them, although they speak of the same master, teach the same doctrines, and relate the same incidents.' But how does this prove that Scripture is not, in all respects, inspired? 'So far are we,' says this author, 'from overlooking human individuality everywhere impressed on our sacred books, that, on the contrary, it is with profound gratitude, and with an ever-increasing admiration, that we regard this living, real, human character infused so charmingly into every part of the Word of God. We admit the fact, and we see in it clear proof of the Divine wisdom which dictated the Scriptures.'

Those who urge the objection above mentioned are plainly inconsistent with themselves. For while they deny the plenary inspiration of some parts of Scripture, *because they have these marks of individuality,* they acknowledge inspiration in the fullest sense in other parts, particularly in the prophecies, where this individuality of the writers is equally apparent.

In truth, what can be more consonant with our best views of the wisdom of God, or with the general analogy of his works, than that he should make use of the thoughts, the memories, the peculiar talents, tastes, and feelings of his servants in recording his Word for the instruction of men? Why should he not associate the peculiarities of their personal character with what they write under his personal guidance? But, independently of our reasoning, this matter is decided by the Bible itself. 'All Scripture is divinely inspired,' and it is all the Word of God. And it is none the less the Word of God, and none the less inspired, because it comes to us in the language of Moses, and David, and Paul, and the other sacred writers. 'It is God who speaks to us, but it is also man; it is man, but it is also God.' The Word of God, in order to be intelligible and profitable to us, 'must be uttered by mortal tongues, and be written by mortal hands, and must put on the features of human thoughts.

This blending of humanity and divinity in the Scriptures reminds us of the majesty and the condescension of God. Viewed in this light, the Word of God has unequaled beauties, and exerts an unequaled power over our hearts.'

(2) Inaccuracy of Translations. (a) The objection to the plenary inspiration of the Scriptures, from the inaccuracy of the translations and the various readings of the ancient manuscript copies, is totally irrelevant. For what we assert is, the inspiration of the *original* Scriptures, not of the translations of the ancient copies. The fact that the Scriptures were divinely inspired, cannot be expunged or altered by any subsequent event. The very words of the Decalogue were written by the finger of God, and none the less so because the manuscripts which transmit it to us contain some variations. The integrity of the copies has nothing to do with the inspiration of the original. It is, however, well known that the variations are hardly worthy to be mentioned.

(b) But if the copies of the Scriptures which we have are not inspired, then how can the inspiration of the original writings avail to our benefit? The answer is that, according to the best evidence, the original writings have been transmitted to us with remarkable fidelity, and that our present copies, so far as anything of consequence is concerned, agree with the writings as they came from inspired men; so that, through the gracious care of Divine Providence, the Scriptures now in use are, in all important respects, the Scriptures which were given by inspiration of God, and are stamped with Divine authority. In this matter, we stand on the same footing with the Apostles. For when they spoke of the Scriptures, they doubtless referred to the copies which had been made and preserved among the Jews, not to the original manuscripts written by Moses and the prophets.

(c) There are some who maintain that all that was necessary to secure the desired results was an infallible guidance of the *thoughts* of the sacred writers; that with such a guidance they might be safely left to express their thoughts in their own way, without any special influence from above.

Now, if those who take this view of the subject mean that God not only gives the sacred penmen the very ideas which they are to write, but, in some way, secures an infallible connection between those ideas and a just expression of them in words, then, indeed, we have the desired result—an infallible revelation from God, made in the proper language of the writers. But if any one supposes that there is naturally such an infallible connection between right thoughts and a just expression of them in language, without an effective divine superintendence, he contradicts the lessons of daily experience. But those to whom we refer evidently do not themselves believe in such an infallible connection. For when they assign their reason for denying that inspiration related to the language of the Scriptures, they speak of the different, and, as they regard them, the contradictory statements of facts by different writers.

(d) But it is easy to see that the difficulty presses with all its force upon those who assert the inspiration of the *thoughts*. For surely they will not say that the sacred writers had *true thoughts* in their minds, and yet uttered them in the language of falsehood. This would contradict their own idea of a sure connection between the conceptions of the mind and the utterance of them in suitable words, and would clearly show that they themselves feel it to be necessary that the Divine guidance should extend to the *words* of inspired men as well as their thoughts. But if an inspired writer, through inadvertence, committed a real mistake as to a statement of fact, it must have been a mistake in his *thoughts* as well as in his words. If, then, there was a mistake, it lay in his *thoughts*. But if there was no mistake, then there is nothing to prove that inspiration did not extend to the language. If, however, there was a real mistake, then the question is not, what becomes of *verbal* inspiration, but what becomes of inspiration *in any sense.*

(e) It is sometimes said that the sacred writers were of themselves generally competent to express their ideas in *proper language,* and in this respect had *no need* of supernatural assistance. But there is just as much reason for saying that they were of themselves generally competent to form their own *conceptions,* and so had no need of supernatural aid in this respect. It is just as reasonable to say that Moses could recollect what took place at the Red Sea, and that Paul could recollect that he was once a persecutor, and Peter what took place on the mount of transfiguration, without supernatural aid, as to say that they could, without such aid, make a proper record of these recollections. We believe a real and infallible guidance of the Spirit in both respects, because this is taught in the Scriptures, and it is obvious that the Bible could not be what Christ and the Apostles considered it to be unless they were divinely inspired.

(3) Diversity in the Narratives. The diversity in the narratives of the Evangelists is sometimes urged as an objection against the position we maintain in regard to inspiration, but evidently without reason, and contrary to reason. For what is more reasonable than to expect that a work of divine origin will have marks of consummate wisdom, and will be suited to accomplish the end in view. Now it will not be denied that God determined that there should be four narratives of the life and death of Jesus from four historians. If the narratives were all alike, three of them would be useless. Indeed, such a circumstance would create suspicion, and would bring discredit upon the whole concern. The narratives must then be different. And if, besides this useful diversity, it is found that the seeming contradictions can be satisfactorily reconciled, and if each of the narratives is given in the peculiar style and manner of the writers, then all is natural and unexceptionable, and we have the highest evidence of the credibility and truth of the narratives.

(4) An Additional Objection. It is by some alleged that writers who were constantly under a plenary divine inspiration would not descend to the unimportant details, the trifling incidents, which are found in the Scriptures. To this it may be replied that the details alluded to must be admitted to be according to truth, and that those things which, at first view, seem to be trifles, may, when taken in their connections, prove to be of serious moment. And it is moreover manifest that, considering what human beings and human affairs really are, if all those things which are called trifling and unimportant were excluded, the Scriptures would fail of being conformed to fact; they would not be faithful histories of human life; so that the very circumstance which is demanded as proof of inspiration would become an argument against it. And herein we cannot but admire the perfect wisdom which guided the sacred writers, while we **mark**

the weakness and shallowness of the objections which are urged against their inspiration.

3. Summary. On the whole, after carefully investigating the subject of inspiration, we are conducted to the important conclusion that 'all Scripture is divinely inspired;' that the sacred penmen wrote 'as they were moved by the Holy Ghost,' and that these representations are to be understood as implying that the writers had, in all respects, the effectual guidance of the Divine Spirit. And we are still more confirmed in this conclusion because we find that it begets in those who seriously adopt it an acknowledgment of the divine origin of Scripture, a reverence for its teachings, and a practical regard for its requirements, like what appeared in Christ and his Apostles. Being convinced that the Bible has, in all parts and in all respects, the seal of the Almighty, and that it is truly and entirely from God, we are led by reason, conscience, and piety to bow submissively to its high authority, implicitly to believe its doctrines, however incomprehensible, and cordially to obey its precepts, however contrary to our natural inclinations. We come to it from day to day, not as judges, but as learners, never questioning the propriety or utility of any of its contents. This precious Word of God is the perfect standard of our faith, and the rule of our life, our comfort in affliction, and our sure guide to heaven.   L. W.

Literature. Dick, *Essay on the Inspiration of the Holy Scriptures* (Glasg. 4th ed., 1840) ; Rennel, *Proofs of Inspiration* (Lond., 1822) ; Carson, *Theories of Inspiration;* Henderson, *Divine Inspiration* (4th ed., 1852) ; Lee, *Inspiration of the Holy Scriptures;* Hannah, *Divine and Human Elements in Holy Scripture* (Bampton Lect. for 1853) ; Westcott, *Introd. to the Gospels,* pp. 5, 383; Maurice, *Theolog. Essays,* p. 314; Denziger, *Die Theol. Lehre v. d. Inspiration,* etc. (in the *Rel. Erklaer.,* ii. 156-242) ; Liddon, *Bampt. Lect.,* 1866, pp. 45, 219; Neander, *Ch. Dogm.,* ii, 433, 442, 607; Pres. Fairchild, *Elements of Theology;* Prof. Warfield, Article on *Inspiration,* (in Pres. and Ref. Review, April, 1893).

INSTANT (ĭn-stănt). **1.** Very eager and earnest; persevering (Rom. xii:12).

2. An *instant* is a moment or short period of time (Jer. xviii:7; Luke ii:38). (See also Rom. xii:12; 2 Tim. iv:2.)

INSTRUCTION (ĭn-strŭk'shŭn). See EDUCATION; SCHOOLS.

INSTRUMENT (ĭn'strų-ment), (Heb. כְּלִי, *kel-ee'*, something *prepared*), a general term for any *apparatus,* as implement, weapon, furniture, utensil, vessel, etc. (Exod. xxv:9).

Figurative. The second causes, whereby God executes his works of mercy or judgment, are his *instruments* (Is. xli:15). Sword, famine, pestilence, and disease are his *instruments of death* (Ps. vii:13). Men's bodies, or members, are *instruments* of righteousness or unrighteousness; are, as it were, tools by which they work the one or the other in outward acts (Rom. vi:13).

INTELLIGENCE (ĭn-tĕl'lĭ-jens), (Heb. בִּין, *bene,* Dan. xi:30), to have an understanding or agreement rather than a quality of mind, with the idea of treachery or double dealing.

INTENT (ĭn-tĕnt'), (Gr. ἵνα, *hin'ah,* John xiii:28), intention or purpose.

INTERCESSION (ĭn'tēr-sĕsh'ŭn), (Heb. פָּגַע, *paw-gah',* to come upon; Gr. ἐντυγχάνω, *en-toong-khan'o,* to meet with, to come between).

(1) Intercession of Christ. His interposing for sinners by virtue of his being a Mediator.

(1) As to the fact itself, it is evident, from many places of Scripture, that Christ pleads with God in favor of his people (Rom. viii:34; Heb. vii:25; 1 John ii:1).

(2) As to the manner of it : the appearance of the high-priest among the Jews, in the presence of God, on the day of atonement, when he offered before him the blood of the sin-offering, is at large referred to by St. Paul as illustrating the intercession of Christ (Heb. ix:11, 14, 22, 26; x:13, 21).

(3) Christ's intercession is not to remind 'the Divine Being of anything which he would otherwise forget, nor to persuade him to anything which he is not disposed to do; but it may serve to illustrate the holiness and majesty of the Father, and the wisdom and grace of the Son; not to say that it may have other unknown uses with respect to the inhabitants of the invisible world. He is represented, also, as offering up the prayers and praises of his people, which become acceptable to God through him (Rev. viii:3, 4; Heb. xiii:15; 1 Pet. ii:5). He there pleads for the conversion of unconverted ones; and for the consolation, preservation, and glorification of his people (John xvii; 1 John ii:1, 2).

(4) Of the properties of Christ's intercession, it may be also observed: (a) That it is authoritative. He intercedes not without right (John xvii:24; Ps. ii:8). (b) Wise; he understands the nature of his work, and the wants of his people (John ii:25). (c) Righteous; for it is founded upon justice and truth (1 John iii:5; Heb. vii:26). (d) Compassionate (Heb. ii:17; v:8; Is. lxiii:9). (e) He is the sole advocate (1 Tim. ii:5). (f) It is perpetual (Heb. vii:25). (g) Efficacious (1 John ii:1, 2; John xi:42).

(2) Intercession of the Holy Ghost. The Holy Ghost makes *intercession* for us with groanings that cannot be uttered; he excites to prayer, directs what to ask, and enables us to offer our requests to God in a duly earnest manner (Rom. viii:26).

(3) Intercession of Believers. We make *intercession* for men, when we plead with God on their behalf, and for his gifts and graces to them (1 Tim. ii:1). In a time of universal apostasy, God wondered that there was no *intercessor,* none to stand up in behalf of religion, and wrestle with him for the turning away of his wrath (Is. lix:16).

INTEREST (ĭn'tēr-ĕst). See USURY.

INTERMARRIAGE (ĭn-tēr măr'rĭj). See MARRIAGE.

INTERMEDDLE (ĭn'tēr-mĕd'd'l), (Heb. עָרַב, *aw-rab',* Prov. 14:10), to take interest in, engage, mingle in, not of necessity in an offensive way, as is generally implied in the use of the word now.

INTERMEDIATE STATE (ĭn'tēr-mē'dĭ-āte stāt), a term made use of to denote the state of the soul between death and the resurrection.

From the Scriptures speaking frequently of the dead as sleeping in their graves, many have supposed that the soul sleeps till the resurrection, *i. e.,* is in a state of entire insensibility. But against this opinion, and that the soul, after death, enters immediately into a state of reward or punishment, the following passages seem to be conclusive: Matt. xvii:3; Luke xxiii:42; 2 Cor. v:6; Phil. i:21; Luke xvi:22, 23; Rev. vi:9. (See HADES.)

INTERPRETATION (ĭn-tēr'prĕ-tā'shŭn) **OF THE OLD TESTAMENT.**

1. Introduction. The science of the interpretation of Scripture has passed through as long and tortuous a course as chemistry or astronomy. As alchemy and astrology led up to these sciences, so the efforts of Jews and Christians to explain the Scriptures have prepared the way for the modern system of interpretation now current in the study of any ancient literature. This consists in giving the plain and obvious meaning of the text, as understood by the men for whom it was first written.

The belief that the Bible was a divine book almost completely closed the eyes of ancient interpreters to its human elements. If they sometimes theoretically admitted them, they practically ignored them. Its literary character, its poetry, its history, were overlooked. It was regarded as an arsenal of divine sayings. Hence, both Jews and Christians sought to find their theories and speculations confirmed by it. They did not ask what the writers intended, but rather what meaning the language would bear. The result of this abuse of Scripture was that the Bible, which we regard as a book for the common people, was sealed; so that among the Jews none but a rabbi was capable of setting forth the sense of the Old Testament, and among the Christians only the Church could determine the significance of the Bible.

2. Ancient Jewish Interpretation. Among the Jews there were two schools of interpreters: the Palestinian, which used the Hebrew consonantal text, and the Alexandrian, which used the Septuagint translation.

(1) The Palestinian School. The character of Palestinian exegesis may be best observed in the Talmud, including the Mishna, or development of the Law; the Gemara, or expansion of the Mishna, and its further modification in the Baraitha. The Jerusalem Talmud was edited A. D. 390; the Babylonian, A. D. 365-427. The Talmudic commentary is called Midrash, investigation, embracing the Halacha, legal enactment, and the Haggada, or illustrations by tales, parables, or allegories. While the rabbis have reduced their mode of interpretation to rules, nothing could seem more lawless, more casuistical, more fantastic, than some of the interpretations in the writings named. In the same connection should be mentioned the KABALA (see article), which regards each letter of Scripture as the source of the greatest mysteries.

(2) The Alexandrian School. The most prominent figure in this school is that of Philo, born about B. C. 20 at Alexandria. Though he found the allegorical method employed in the exegesis of Homer and other Greek writers, as well as in that of the Old Testament, he is worthy of special prominence, because of his pre-eminent ability, his effort to reduce the allegorical interpretation to a system of rules, and on account of his influence, more or less immediately, on the interpretation of the Church Fathers. While retaining the literal sense for the instruction of the common people, he adopted the allegorical for those who were capable, as he thought, of a higher conception of the Scriptures, and turned the plainest narratives into metaphysical abstractions, since it was his belief that the Greek philosophy, of which he was an ardent admirer, could be found in the Old Testament.

(3) The New Testament Writers. As might be expected, Palestinian, and traces of Alexandrian, exegesis are found in the New Testament, both in the Gospels and the Epistles. Paul was brought up at the feet of Gamaliel (Acts xxii:3). He was saturated with Jewish learning and schooled in Jewish modes of thought. When he became a new creature in Christ, he did not cease to think and reason like a Jew; hence, his mode of interpretation is essentially Jewish, but the guiding power of the Divine Spirit has at all times kept him from such extravagances as we find in the Talmud. Now, while we must admit that the human method of interpretation employed was incorrect in form, it was used by Divine wisdom as the only suitable means of conveying truth in New Testament times. An age accustomed to the Jewish mode of interpretation could not make any more use of the modern method than a boy, who has studied only primary arithmetic, could make of a treatise on comic sections. Hence, a New Testament interpretation of the Old is abundantly justified as a necessity of Divine Providence.

3. Medieval Jewish Interpretation. The Middle Ages, which brought no light from the Bible to the Christian church, were marked by distinct progress among the Jews in the interpretation of the Old Testament. Under the inspiration and example of the Arabs, whose language the Spanish Jews spoke, the study of Hebrew grammar at first flourished several hundred years in Spain, beginning with Jehudah Ibn Daud, or Chayuj, and closing with David Kimchi (died 1235), who wrote in Hebrew. Elias Levita (died 1549), a celebrated grammarian, belongs to the period of the Renaissance. Even Rashi (died 1105) shows the influence of the new learning, although abiding by traditional interpretations; and Ibn Ezra (died 1167), who was in some respects a forerunner of the modern critics, is perhaps the most grammatical and historical of the medieval Jewish interpreters. David Kimchi, while subject to philosophical presuppositions, also marks a distinct advance in the history of interpretation.

4. Interpretation by the Church Fathers. The process begun among the Jewish interpreters of putting their own ideas and speculations into the Old Testament, instead of drawing out the meaning of the original writers, was continued by the Church down to the Reformation.

The effort made was to transform the Old Testament into a treasury of New Testament teaching; the instrument used was allegory. In this respect the Church Fathers were following in the footsteps of New Testament writers, especially of Paul and of the author of the Epistle to the Hebrews. Clement of Rome (96 A. D.) sees in the scarlet cord, which Rahab was instructed to bind in her window, a symbol of the atoning blood of Jesus Christ. Barnabas (Epistle between 119 and 126 A. D.) finds in the three hundred and eighteen servants of Abraham a symbol of the name of Jesus and the cross. Indeed, there is scarcely an allusion to wood, or anything which can be tortured into a reminder of the cross, which is not seized upon by Barnabas and other Fathers as a symbol. Justin Martyr's dialogue with Trypho, the Jew (142-148), rests mostly on a use of the Old Testament, which we must consider invalid and superficial, and of which the Jew rightly complained. Such was the uncertainty and subjective character of interpretation in the ancient Church that Tertullian (born about 150) maintained that argument with heretics was useless, because the issue was uncertain. He claims that Apostolic tradition is to be the test of the meaning of Scripture, thus foreshadowing the action of the Council of Trent. Nor did the labors of Origen (born 185, died 254), wonderful as they may be considered, produce sounder methods of interpretation. He sought, as the result of immense labor, through the preparation of his hexaplar text of the Old Testament, by placing the Hebrew text with the various Greek translations in parallel columns, to advance the knowledge of the true text of the Old Testament. Through the errors of subsequent transcribers in disregarding the critical signs, the ancient text of the Septuagint fell into great confusion. Besides, Origen, who may be considered the leading representative of the Alexandrian school, and a great admirer of Philo, sought to systematize the allegorical mode of interpretation. He considered that Scripture had a threefold sense, consisting of body, or literal; soul, or moral; spirit, or mystical. The literal sense was useful for the most simple Christians. Through the allegorical interpretation he found an easy refuge from all difficulties in the Old Testament. The influence of Origen was permanent in the Church, although the Fathers who succeeded him did not go to as great lengths.

There were glimmerings of right principles of interpretation, as appears from the writings of Augustine (born 354, died 430), the great theologian, and Jerome (born 346, died 420), the great Biblical scholar of the ancient Church; but these principles, while recognized, had no controlling effect. Augustine adopted the seven exegetical rules of Tichonius, which were mostly harmful to right interpretation. While his exegetical works contain good comments on Old Testament passages, they are largely composed of fanciful interpretations of Scripture. Among the Church Fathers, Jerome was the only Hebrew scholar worthy of the name. Besides him, with the exception of Origen, none could go back of translations of the Old Testament. Jerome enjoyed the best advantages for the study of the Old Testament that the time afforded. He spared neither pains nor expense to master the Hebrew language. His Latin translation of the Bible was a work of great merit, which, after a test of centuries, displaced its older rivals, and became the Vulgate of the Romish Church. While Jerome had much of the freedom and insight of the modern critic, he was not an original interpreter, and could not break loose from the faults of his time.

Only one of the Fathers earned the title of "the exegete," Theodore of Mopsuestia (born about 350, died 429), the intimate friend and companion, from boyhood, of Chrysostom, to whom in early manhood he owed his conversion. He was the most conspicuous representative of the School of Antioch, which stood for the historical and natural interpretation of Scripture. While he had no knowledge of Hebrew, he had a remarkable intuition of the historical and grammatical mode of exegesis. He was a strong opponent of the methods of Origen. But he was really a thousand years in advance of his time. His works were brought under the suspicion of Nestorianism, and were condemned one hundred and twenty-five years after his death.

The allegorical method, against which Theodore had stoutly contended, continued dominant, and was current among the schoolmen. Nicholas De Lyra (born 1270, died 1340), who was a Hebrew scholar, and who had enjoyed the benefit of the studies of the Spanish Jews of the Middle Ages, does indeed "make the first beginnings of a school of natural exegesis . . . by ascertaining the literal meaning," and, through his influence on Luther, paves the way for the following period;

but, on the whole, the period from the Apostolic Fathers to the Reformation, in the history of exegesis, might be characterized as that of "the misinterpretation of the Old Testament."

5. Interpretation from the Reformation to the Eighteenth Century. Two things are characteristic of the period introduced by the Reformation in the interpretation of the Old Testament; the freeing of Scripture from the bondage of the Church tradition, and the study of it in the original languages. Both were of the greatest importance. Until the Reformation, the Bible for the few who used it could mean to the loyal Romanist only what the Church decreed it should mean; hence the motive was wanting to go behind the official text of the Romish Church as found in the Vulgate. This attitude was entirely changed by the Reformation. The Bible became the source of authority; hence the Reformers did not care for the interpretations of the Fathers. Their sole question was what the Scriptures themselves taught. This rendered necessary a careful study of the Bible in the original languages, for which the way had been prepared by Reuchlin's translation of Kimchi's grammar. Hence we may trace the Bible of Luther and the other reformers back to the studies of Spanish Jews in the Middle Ages, under the tuition of the Arabs. Neither Luther (born 1483, died 1546) nor Calvin (born 1509, died 1564) were profound Hebrew scholars, but they marked an infinite advance over the barren waste of scholastic exegesis. They manifested a free attitude in their judgment of the binding authority of certain parts of the Old Testament, while yielding loyal and unquestioning obedience to Scripture as a whole. Their position in this respect was in sharp contrast to that of the theologians of the Post-Reformation period, who sought, after the manner of an orthodox Jewish scholar of the second century, to make a hedge about the Scriptures. The effort was made by these theologians to find the same infallibility in the Bible which the Fathers had found in the Church as the custodian of Apostolic tradition. This effort extended to defining the limits of the Scripture to claiming, with reference to the vowel points, that they had been supernaturally communicated; that the Old Testament was of equal authority with the New; that the rule of faith was to be found in the clear passages of Scripture, and that the obscure passages were to be interpreted by them. Thus the theologians of the Post-Reformation period brought the Scriptures once more under a yoke of bondage, the rule of faith which was really a barrier to free interpretation. But there were critical tendencies at work, both among Protestants and Catholics. Even Carlstadt (born about 1483, died 1541) had maintained that the Pentateuch could not have been written by Moses, and Luther had asked what difference it would make if he were not the author of it. Yet the main current among Jews, Catholics, and Protestants, during the seventeenth and eighteenth centuries, was to suppress free inquiry about the origin and composition of the Scriptures. But such investigations on the part of individuals could not be kept back.

(1) Spinoza (born 1632, died 1667) may be regarded the father of modern criticism. He was a learned Jew of acute mind who lived in Amsterdam, and who was excommunicated by the Jews because of his critical theories. The principles of interpretation enunciated by him are essentially in accord with those held by the modern critical school.

(2) A little later two French Catholics made important contributions to Old Testament criticism. One, a priest, Richard Simon (born 1638, died 1712), who is sometimes called the father of Biblical introduction, was the author of a *Critical History of the Old Testament.*

(3) Astruc (born 1684, died 1766), a Catholic layman, was the founder of the literary analysis of the Pentateuch in his *"Conjectures Upon the Original Memoirs which Moses Seems to Have Used in Composing the Book of Genesis."*

(4) The condition of the text, which has an important bearing on interpretation, also received great attention in the seventeenth and eighteenth centuries. After a hard fought battle between the Buxtorfs, father (born 1564, died 1629) and son (born 1599, died 1664), on the one hand, and Capellus on the other, it was proved conclusively that the vowel points used in reading Hebrew, far from being original with Moses, were an invention of the Massoretes (after 600 A. D.), the guardians of Jewish text criticism. Kennicott, an English, and De Rossi, an Italian, scholar, devoted great attention to the comparison of Old Testament Hebrew MSS., leading to the negative result, that none of those in existence originated before the Middle Ages, and that the variations in their readings were so slight as to be of no account.

(5) Lowth and Herder were eminent as exegetes, but no scholar arose who effected a general change in the principles of interpretation as introduced by the theologians succeeding the Reformation. They went to the Bible for proof texts to establish the doctrines of the church; and since they sought these by sound, rather than through a historical, interpretation, they found them in the Old Testament as well as the New. Human agency in the production of Scripture was lost sight of, and God was considered the author of Scripture in such a sense that the writers were hardly more than amanuenses of the Divine Spirit.

6. Interpretation During the Nineteenth Century. The last hundred years has marked an epoch in the history of Old Testament interpretation. Ecclesiastical and theological fetters are being struck off from the Old Testament, so that the ancient writers can deliver their message to us in some such way as they sought to deliver it to their contemporaries. Up to the present century, with a few exceptions, the Church was inclined to regard the Old Testament purely as a divine book. Now the critics are teaching the church that the Old Testament is best understood when we give the human element in Scripture its due place; that, as we draw nearer the Master by dwelling on his humanity, so we see God's infinite wisdom in his dealings with Israel more clearly when we recognize the human and dispensational limitations of the Old Testament messengers and those to whom they were sent. Higher criticism cannot disprove the fact of a Divine revelation; indeed, it does not seek to do so; it simply deals with the temporal and natural peculiarities of those who bore it, and to whom it was given through many centuries. While such critics as Kuenen may claim that prophecy in ancient Israel was the product of mere naturalism, the history of ancient religions does not furnish a parallel to any such naturalistic development as is sometimes claimed for the Old Testament. The results of the prophecies demand a supernatural cause. The origin of the Old Testament, in its relation to the New, cannot be explained merely as a human production. No higher critic, so far as he is a careful and conscientious investigator, is to be regarded an enemy of revealed religion on account of his investigations. Whatever

his personal attitude may be to the religion of Israel, his investigations, so far as they are conducted in a scientific spirit, with an honest effort to know the truth, are to be hailed with satisfaction. This may serve to explain a seeming inconsistency in the attitude of evangelical higher critics to results which are sometimes called "destructive." They are not destructive of the authority of the Old Testament, as tested by the New, but of traditional views with respect to its origin and composition. Hence, they claim they do not affect the fact of a Divine revelation, but rather the manner of it.

The Old Testament interpreter, in the closing years of the nineteenth century, has entered into possession of the following most important helps for interpretation, which are mainly the fruit of studies during the last hundred years:

(1) With reference to the text. At least some progress has been made in seeking to determine the original text of the Old Testament. Many of the suggestions in the Hebrew text of the Old Testament edited by Haupt, from which the translation of the Polychrome Bible is being prepared, are doubtless arbitrary and subjective, but it is a step in the right direction which must be followed by others until scholars shall settle with reasonable unanimity on a critical text of the Old Testament.

(2) The discovery of the meaning of words found in the Old Testament is of the utmost importance. Most of these are clear, because they often occur; many are very obscure, because they are found only once. To determine their signification it is not only necessary to compare the different ancient versions, but also to trace them in cognate languages like Arabic, Aramaic, and Assyrian. In some of these respects, Gesenius introduced a new era through his lexicon, which has passed through many editions since his death, and is now being reproduced in this country with all the appliances of modern scholarship.

(3) Not less important is a study of the structure and connection of sentences. In this regard, Gesenius did a conspicuous service, but it was Ewald who unlocked the treasuries of Hebrew syntax, and who has been the inspiration of all subsequent Hebrew grammarians and interpreters through his insight and commanding genius.

(4) It is also of the utmost importance to know the manners and customs and the geography of the country where the Old Testament was produced. The present century has been characterized by the most interesting antiquarian and geographical researches, not only in Palestine itself, but in the seat of the great world powers with which Israel had to do, and in whose domain at different times they found a home, Egypt and Assyria. The value of these researches as aids to interpretation cannot be overestimated. (See EGYPT; ASSYRIA.)

(5) But as exegesis is a historical science, as well as grammatical and critical, it is especially dependent on the researches of the higher critics, because these determine the relative age and succession of documents, and no right interpretation of these documents can be given, as a whole, out of their proper historical setting. No truthful history of Israel's religion or development of it, as a state, can be given without using the results of higher criticism. Its most important discoveries have been made in the Hexateuch (Pentateuch and Joshua), in Psalms, Isaiah, Zechariah, and Daniel. But none are comparable to those brought to light in the Hexateuch. It has been found that the laws of ancient Israel, both civil and relig-

ious, as therein detailed, resting on foundations laid by Moses, and all ultimately gathered in a law book known by his name, were of slow growth, and did not attain their final form until the reorganization of the Jewish state under Nehemiah and Ezra (B. C. 445-444). Reading the Old Testament in the light of this reconstruction of the Pentateuch, there is not a religious or legal institution which does not show traces of development. The critics discovered long ago that the Hexateuch was composed of three main documents. With reference to this there is now almost unanimous agreement among German Old Testament scholars, and the number of those who give their assent to this view in Great Britain and America is constantly increasing. These documents, known as the Jehovistic, B. C. 640, made up of the Yahvistic, written in Judah B. C. 850, and the Elohistic, written in Ephraim, B. C. 750; the Deuteronomic, B. C. 621, including Deuteronomy and the Deuteronomic portions of Joshua; and the Priests' Code were all welded together by some unknown editors, and were published by Ezra, B. C. 444. Even these documents contain others of still greater antiquity. The mode of composition employed is sometimes called "patchwork." It preserves the component parts. It is characteristic of Orientals, and can be easily traced in many places in Chronicles by means of an English reference Bible. Let any one examine the component part of 1 Chron. xvi, cutting out the original passages from an English Bible, and pasting them on cardboard by the side of the corresponding passages of the Chronicles. There is much divergence among critics in details as to the age of the documents named and the editions through which they have passed, but very little as to their literary, legal, and theological characteristics.

The present dominant school of criticism, which considers the Priests' Code the youngest part of the Pentateuch, was founded by Graf, who published in 1866 his *Historical Books of the Old Testament*. But it was the further analysis of Wellhausen (born 1844) and his lucid statement of critical results which won the day in Germany. In Holland the most conspicuous critic of the same school was Kuenen (born 1828, died 1891); in Great Britain, the lamented W. Robertson Smith (born 1846, died 1894), a brilliant scholar and devout Christian, who made a gallant fight for liberty; and in America, C. A. Briggs (born 1841), who has sought a like result. The best summary of the modern critical views of the Old Testament is found in Driver's *Literature of the Old Testament*.

While the Old Testament, in its general teaching, is level with the comprehension of plain, unlettered people, a large proportion of its literature, especially that which is legal and prophetic, gains immeasurably in interest and instructiveness when interpreted in historic light, and with the instruments afforded by modern criticism. The Old Testament, which was primarily designed to be a light to the feet and a lamp to the path of the Jewish congregation, loses nothing in real power or authority through the most searching investigation.   S. I. C.

INTREAT (ĭn-trēt'), (Gr. παρακαλέω, *par-ak-al-eh'o*, 1 Tim. v:1), to exhort in a kindly spirit without rebuking. In the A. V. of 1611 entreat and intreat are used indifferently in both senses of the word. It signifies to deal with.

INWARD (ĭn'wĕrd), (Heb. סוֹד, *sode*, Job xix: 19), intimate, familiar, confidential.

IOTA (ĭ-ō'tà), (Auth. Vers. '*jot*'), the smallest letter of the Greek alphabet (ι); derived from the Hebrew *jod* (י) and the Syriac *judh*, and employed metaphorically to express the minutest trifle.

It is, in fact, one of several metaphors derived from the alphabet—as when *alpha*, the first letter, and *omega*, the last, are employed to express the beginning and the end. We are not to suppose, however, that this proverb was exclusively apposite in the Greek language. The same practical allusion equally existed in Hebrew, some curious examples of which may be seen in Wetstein and Lightfoot. One of these may here suffice:—In the Talmud (*Sanhed*. xx: 2) it is fabled that the book of Deuteronomy came and prostrated itself before God, and said, 'O Lord of the universe, thou hast written in me thy law, but now a testament defective in some parts is defective in all. Behold, Solomon endeavors to root the letter jod out of me,' *i. e.*, in the text, לא ירבה נשים, 'he shall not multiply wives' (Deut. xvii:17). 'The holy, blessed God answered,—Solomon, and a thousand such as he, shall perish, but the least word shall not perish out of thee.' This is, in fact, a parallel not only to the usage but the sentiment, as conveyed in Matt. v:18, 'One jot, or one tittle, shall in no wise pass from the law.'

IPHEDEIAH (ĭph'e-dē'yà), (Heb. יִפְדְיָה, *yifdeh-yaw'*, Jah will liberate), one of the "sons" of Shashak, a descendant of Benjamin (1 Chron. viii: 25); mentioned as chief of the tribe and resident at Jerusalem (B. C. between 1612 and 1588).

IR (ir), (Heb. עִיר, *eer*, a city, town), a Benjamite, father of Shuppim and Huppim (1 Chron. vii:12). He is probably to be identified with a son of Benjamin (Gen. xlvi:21), and not with Iri of 1 Chron. vii:7.

IRA (i'rà), (Heb. עִירָא, *ee-raw'*, citizen, or watchful).

1. A Tekoite, son of Ikkesh, one of David's "thirty" guards (1 Chron. xi:28; 2 Sam. xxiii:26) and commander of the sixth regiment of troops (1 Chron. xxvii:9), B. C. 1046-1014.

2. An "Ithrite," or Jethrite, another of David's famous heroes (2 Sam. xxiii:38; 1 Chron. xi: 40), B. C. 1046.

3. A Zairite, David's chaplain (2 Sam. xx:26), B. C. about 1022. Perhaps identical with **2.**

IRAD (i'răd), (Heb. עִירָד, *ee-rawd'*, fugitive), son of Enoch, and an antediluvian patriarch of the Cainite line (Gen. iv:18), B. C. after 4045.

IRAM (i'ram), (Heb. עִירָם, *ee-rawm'*, city-wise), an Edomite leader in Mount Seir (Gen. xxxvi:43; 1 Chron. i:54), probably contemporaneous with the Horite kings (perhaps B. C. 1618).

IR-HAHERES (ĭr-ha-he'res), (Heb. עִיר הַהֶרֶס, *eer ha-heh'res*, A. V. "the city of destruction"), is the name or epithet of a city of Egypt (Is. xix:18).

If the prophecy is to be taken properly, Ir-haheres must refer to one of the cities partly, at least, inhabited by Jews. Such a one was Onion, which was destroyed by Titus, while Alexandria and perhaps the other three alluded to in the prophecy remained. If the prophecy is to be taken tropically the best meaning can only be determined by verbal criticism.

IRI (i'rī), (Heb. עִירִי, *ee-ree'*, citizen), a Benjamite, the last enumerated of the five sons of Bela (1 Chron. vii:7), B. C. between 1856 and 1658.

IRIJAH (ī-rī'jah), (Heb. יִרְאִיָּה, *yir-ee-yaw'*, fearful of Jah), son of Shelemiah, "a captain of the word" at the gate of Benjamin in Jerusalem where he arrested the prophet Jeremiah, alleging that he was about to desert to the Chaldæans, and conducted him back to the princes (Jer. xxxvii:13, 14), B. C. about 597.

IR-NAHASH (ir-nā'hăsh), (Heb. עִיר־נָחָשׁ, *eer-naw-khawsh'*, city of the serpent), a city of Judah which some supposed to have been named from the abundance of serpents in its neighborhood, but more probably from a person named Nahash, or from an image of the animal worshiped here (1 Chron. iv:12). It has been identified by Schwarz and Van de Velde with *Deir-Nakhaz*, east of Beit-Jibrin.

IRON (ī'ron). **1.** (Heb. יִרְאוֹן, *yir-ohn'*, place of alarm), a city of Naphtali (Josh. xix:38), probably identical with *Zarun* (Saulcy, *Narrat.* ii. 382; Robinson, *Research.*, iii:61, 62, notes).

2. (Heb. בַּרְזֶל, *bar-zele'*), a well-known and serviceable metal.

Much stress has been laid upon the absence of iron among the most ancient remains of Egypt; but the speedy decomposition of this metal, especially when buried in the nitrous soil of Egypt, may account for the absence of it among the remains of the early monarchs of a Pharaonic age (Wilkinson's *Ancient Egypt*, iii:246).

(1) Early Mention. Tubal-Cain is the *first* mentioned smith, '*a forger of every instrument of iron*' (Gen. iv:22). From that time we meet with manufactures in iron of the utmost variety (*some* articles of which seem to be anticipations of what are commonly supposed to be modern inventions); as *iron weapons or instruments* (Num. xxxv:16; Job xx:24); barbed iron, used in hunting (Job xli:7); *an iron bedstead* (Deut. iii:11); *chariots of iron* (Josh. xvii:16, and elsewhere); *iron weights* (shekels) (1 Sam. xvii:7); *harrows of iron* (2 Sam. xii:31); iron armor (2 Sam. xxiii:7); tools (1 Kings vi:7; 2 Kings vi:6); horns (1 Kings xxii:11); nails, hinges (1 Chron. xxii:3); fetters (Ps. cv:18); bars (Ps. cvii:16); iron bars used in fortifying the gates of towns (Ps. cvii:16; Is. xlv:2); a *pen of iron* (Job xix:24; Jer. xvii:1), a pillar (Jer. i:18); yokes (Jer. xxviii:13); pan (Ezek. iv:3); *trees bound with iron* (Dan. iv:15); *gods of iron* (Dan. v:4); threshing instruments (Amos i:3); and in later times, *an iron gate* (Acts xii:10); the actual cautery (1 Tim. iv:2); breastplates (Rev. ix:9).

(2) Plentiful in Palestine. The mineral origin of iron seems clearly alluded to in Job xxviii:2. It would seem that in ancient times it was a plentiful production of Palestine (Deut. viii:9). There appear to have been furnaces for smelting at an early period in Egypt (Deut. iv:20). The requirement that the altar should be made of 'whole stones over which no man had lift up any iron,' recorded in Josh. viii:31, does not imply any objection to iron as such, but seems to be merely a mode of directing that, in order to prevent idolatry, the stones must not undergo any preparation by art. Iron was prepared in abundance by David for the building of the temple (1 Chron. xxii:3), to the amount of one hundred thousand talents (1 Chron. xxix:7), or rather 'without weight' (1 Chron. xxii:14). Working in iron was considered a calling (2 Chron. ii:7). (See SMITH.) Iron seems to have been better from some countries, or to have undergone some hardening prep-

aration by the inhabitants of them, such as were the people called Chalybes, living near the Euxine Sea (Jer. xv:12); to have been imported from Tarshish to Tyre (Ezek. xxvii:12), and 'bright iron' from Dan and Javan (ver. 19). The superior hardness of iron above all other substances is alluded to in Dan. ii:40. It was found among the Midianites (Num. xxxi:22), and was part of the wealth distributed among the tribes at their location in the land (Josh. xxii:8).

Figurative. Iron is *metaphorically* alluded to in the following instances: Affliction is signified by the furnace for smelting it (Deut. iv:20). Under the same figure, chastisement (Ezek. xxii:18, 20, 22). Reducing the earth to total barrenness by turning it into iron (Deut. xxviii:23). Slavery, by a yoke of iron (Deut. xxviii:48). Strength, by a bar of it (Job xl:18); the extreme of hardness (Job xli:27); severity of government, by a rod of iron (Ps. ii:9); affliction, by iron fetters (Ps. cvii:10); prosperity, by giving silver for iron (Is. lx:17); political strength (Dan. ii:33); obstinacy, by an iron sinew in the neck (Is. xlviii:4); giving supernatural fortitude to a prophet, making him an iron pillar (Jer. i:18); destructive power of empires, by iron teeth (Dan. vii:7); deterioration of character, by becoming iron (Jer. vi:28; Ezek. xxii:18), which resembles the idea of the iron age; a tiresome burden, by a mass of iron (Ecclus. xxii:15); the greatest obstacles, by walls of iron (2 Macc. xi:9); the certainty with which a real enemy will ever show his hatred, by the rust returning upon iron (Ecclus. xii:10). Iron seems used, as by the Greek poets, metonymically for the sword (Is. x:34), and so the Sept. understands it, μάχαιρα. The following is selected as a *beautiful comparison* made to iron (Prov. xxvii:17). 'Iron (literally) uniteth iron; so a man uniteth the countenance of his friend,' gives stability to his appearance by his presence. A most graphic *description of a smith at work* is found in Ecclus. xxxviii:28. J. F. D.

IRPEEL (ir'pe-el), (Heb. יִרְפְּאֵל, *yir-peh-ale'*, God will heal), a city of Benjamin mentioned between Rekem and Taralah (Josh. xviii:27). It has been conjecturally identified with *el-Kustul*, situated on a conical hill in the district west of Jerusalem.

IRRIGATION (ir-rĭ-gā-shŭn). See WATER.

IR-SHEMESH (ir'shē'mesh), (Heb. עִיר שֶׁמֶשׁ, *eer sheh'mesh*, city of the sun), a city in Dan (Josh. xix:41) supposed to be the same with Beth-Shemesh, the temple of the sun (1 Kings iv:9).

IRU (ī'ru), (Heb. עִירוּ, *ee-roo'*, citizen), the first named of the sons of the great Caleb, son of Jephunneh (1 Chron. iv:15), B. C. 1618. By some it is claimed that the name should be IR.

ISAAC (ī'zak), (Heb. יִצְחָק, *yits-khawk'*, laughter, i. e., *mockery*; יִשְׂחָק, *yis-khawk'*, he will laugh, in Ps. cv:9; Jer. xxxiii:26; Amos vii:9, 16; Gr. Ἰσαάκ, *ee-sah-ak'*).

The only son of Abraham and Sarah, born in his parents' old age.

The promise of a son had been made to them when Abraham was visited by the Lord in the plains of Mamre, and appeared so unlikely to be fulfilled, seeing that both Abraham and Sarah were 'well stricken in years,' that its utterance caused the latter to laugh incredulously. Being reproved for her unbelief she denied that she had laughed. The reason assigned for the special visitation thus promised was, in effect, that Abraham was pious, and would train his offspring in piety, so that he would become the founder of a great nation, and all the nations of the earth should be blessed in him.

In due time Sarah gave birth to a son, who received the name of Isaac. The reason assigned in Gen. xxi:6 for the adoption of this name, has reference to the laughter occasioned by the announcement of the divine intention—and Sarah said, God hath made me to laugh, all that hear will laugh with me'—the laugh of incredulity being changed into the laugh of joy (comp. Gen. xxi:6; xvii:17; xviii:12).

The first fact that we read of in the history of Isaac, is the command given to his father to offer the youth—'thy son, thine only son Isaac, whom thou lovest'—for a burnt-offering on a mountain in the land of Moriah. Abraham proceeded to obey the divine direction, and was on the point of slaying Isaac, when his hand was withheld by the interposition of God, a ram for sacrifice being provided instead.

(1) Views Regarding the Offering Up of Isaac. This event has found no few detractors. Eichhorn (*Bibl. f. Bibl. Lit.* i. 45, *sq.*) regarded the whole as a vision; Otmar (Henkes' *Mag.* ii. 517), as the explanation of an hieroglyph; Bruns (*Paulus Memorab.* vi:1, *sq.*) finds the source of it in the Phœnician custom of sacrificing children. Some compare (Rosenmüller, *Morgenl.* i. 95) with this narrative the Grecian story of Iphigenia, and other fables of a similar kind. The general aim of certain writers has been, as they consider it, to relieve the Bible from the odium which the narrated circumstances are in their opinion fitted to occasion. That the passage is free from every possible objection, it may be too much to assert; it is, however, equally clear that many of the objections taken to it arise from viewing the facts from a wrong position, or under the discoloring medium of a foregone and adverse conclusion. The only proper way is to consider it as it is represented in the sacred page. The command, then, was especially designed to try Abraham's faith. The trial was made, the fact was ascertained, the victim was not slain. What is there in this to which either religion or morality can take exception? This view is both confirmed and justified by the words of God (Gen. xxii:16, *sq.*), '*because* thou hast not withheld thy only son, in blessing I will bless thee, and in multiplying I will multiply thy seed as the stars of the heaven, and in thy seed shall all the nations of the earth be blessed.'

(2) Marriage. Isaac passed his youthful days under the eye of his father, engaged in the care of flocks and herds up and down the plains of Canaan. At length his father wished to see him married. Abraham therefore gave a commission to his oldest and most trustworthy servant to the effect that, in order to prevent Isaac from taking a wife from among the daughters of the Canaanites, he should proceed into Mesopotamia, and, under the divine direction, choose a partner among his own relatives for his beloved son. Rebekah, in consequence, becomes Isaac's wife, when he was now forty years of age.

In connection with this marriage an event is recorded which displays the peculiar character of Isaac, while it is in keeping with the general tenor of the sacred record regarding him. Probably in expectation of the early return of his father's messenger, and somewhat solicitous as to the result of the embassy, he went out to meditate in the field at the eventide. While there engaged in tranquil

thought, he chanced to raise his eyes, when lo! he beheld the retinue near at hand, and soon conducted his bride into his mother's tent. In unison with all this is the simple declaration of the history, that Isaac 'loved her.' Isaac was evidently a man of kind and gentle disposition, of a calm and reflective turn of mind, simple in his habits, having few wants, good rather than great, fitted to receive impressions and follow a guide, not to originate important influences, or perform deeds of renown.

(3) Children. Isaac having, in conjunction with his half-brother Ishmael, buried Abraham his father, 'in a good old age, in the cave of Machpelah,' took up a somewhat permanent residence 'by the well Lahai-roi,' where, being blessed of God, he lived in prosperity and at ease. One source of regret, however, he deeply felt. Rebekah was barren. In time, two sons, Jacob and Esau, are granted to his prayers. As the boys grew, Isaac gave a preference to Esau, who seems to have possessed those more robust qualities of character in which his father was defective, and therefore gratified him by such dainties as the pursuits of the chase enabled the youth to offer; while Jacob, 'a plain man dwelling in tents,' was an object of special regard to Rebekah—a division of feeling and a kind of partiality which became the source of much domestic unhappiness, as well as of jealousy and hatred between the two sons.

(4) Denies His Wife. A famine compels Isaac to seek food in some foreign land. Divinely warned not to go down to Egypt, the patriarch applies to a petty prince of Philistia, by name Abimelech, who permits him to dwell at Gerar. Here an event took place which has a parallel in the life of his father Abraham. Rebekah was his cousin; afraid lest she should be violently taken from him, and his own life sacrificed to the lust of Abimelech, he represented her as his sister, employing a latitude of meaning which the word 'sister' admits in Oriental usage. The subterfuge was discovered, and is justified by Isaac on the grounds which prompted him to resort to it.

Another parallel event in the lives of Abraham and Isaac may be found by comparing together Gen. xxvi:26, *sq.*, and xxi:22, *sq.* If these parallels should excite a doubt in the mind of any one as to the credibility of the narratives, let him carefully peruse them, and we think that the simplicity and naturalness which pervade and characterize them will effectually substantiate the reality of the recorded events, and explode the notion that fiction has had anything to do in bringing the narrative into its present shape.

(5) Pronounces a Blessing Upon Jacob. Isaac, in his old age, was, by the practices of Rebekah and the art of Jacob, so imposed upon as to give his blessing to the younger son Jacob, instead of to the firstborn, Esau, and with that blessing to convey, as was usual, the right of headship in the family, together with his chief possessions. In the blessing which the aged patriarch pronounced on Jacob it deserves notice how entirely the wished-for good is of an earthly and temporal nature, while the imagery which is employed serves to show the extent to which the poetical element prevailed as a constituent part of the Hebrew character (Gen. xxvii:. 27, *sq.*). Most natural, too, is the extreme agitation of the poor blind old man, on discovering the cheat which had been put upon him: 'And Isaac trembled very exceedingly, and said (to Esau), Who? where is he that hath taken venison and brought it me, and I have eaten, and have blessed him? Yea, and he shall be blessed.' Equally

natural is the reply of Esau. The entire passage is of itself enough to vindicate the historical character and entire credibility of those sketches of the lives of the patriarchs which Genesis presents.

The stealing, on the part of Jacob, of his father's blessing having angered Esau, who seems to have looked forward to Isaac's death as affording an opportunity for taking vengeance on his unjust brother, the aged patriarch is induced, at his wife's entreaty, to send Jacob into Mesopotamia that, after his own example, his son might take a wife from amongst his kindred and people, 'of the daughters of Laban, thy mother's brother.'

This is the last important act recorded of Isaac. Jacob having, agreeably to his father's command, married into Laban's family, returned, after some time, and found the old man at Mamre, in the city of Arbah, which is Hebron, where Abraham and Isaac sojourned.

(6) Death. Here, 'being old and full of days' (180), Isaac 'gave up the ghost, and died, and was gathered unto his people, and his sons Esau and Jacob buried him' (Gen. xxxv:27, *sq.*).

(7) Character. Isaac, the gentle and dutiful son, the faithful and constant husband, became the father of a house in which order did not reign. If there were any very prominent points in his character they were not brought out by the circumstances in which he was placed. He appears less as a man of action than as a man of suffering, from which he is generally delivered without any direct effort of his own. Thus he suffers as the object of Ishmael's mocking, of the intended sacrifice on Moriah, of the rapacity of the Philistines, and of Jacob's stratagem. But the thought of his sufferings is effaced by the ever present tokens of God's favor; and he suffers with the calmness and dignity of a conscious heir of heavenly promises, without uttering any complaint, and generally without committing any action by which he would forfeit respect. Free from violent passions, he was a man of constant, deep, and tender affections. Thus he mourned for his mother till her place was filled by his wife. His sons were nurtured at home till a late period of their lives; and neither his grief for Esau's marriage, nor the anxiety in which he was involved in consequence of Jacob's deceit, estranged either of them from his affectionate care. His life of solitary blamelessness must have been sustained by strong habitual piety such as showed itself at the time of Rebekah's barrenness (xxv:21), in his special intercourse with God at Gerar and Beer-sheba (xxvi:2, 23), in the solemnity with which he bestows his blessing and refuses to change it. His life, judged by a worldly standard, might seem inactive, ignoble, and unfruitful; but the "guileless years, prayers, gracious acts and daily thank-offerings of pastoral life" are not to be so esteemed, although they make no show in history. Isaac's character may not have exercised any commanding influence upon either his own or succeeding generations; but it was sufficiently marked and consistent to win respect and envy from his contemporaries. By his posterity his name is always joined in equal honor with those of Abraham and Jacob; and so it was even used as part of the formula which Egyptian magicians in the time of Origen (*Contra Celsum,* i:22) employed as efficacious to bind the demons whom they adjured (comp. Gen. xxxi:42, 53). (Smith, *Bib. Dict.*).

ISAIAH (ī-zā′yà or ī-zä′yà), (Heb. יְשַׁעְיָהוּ, *yesh-ah-yaw′hoo;* LXX, 'Ησαῖας).

1. Life and Times of the Prophet Isaiah. The heading of this book places the prophet un-

der the reigns of Uzziah, Jotham, Ahaz, and Hezekiah, kings of Judah; and an examination of the prophecies themselves, independently of the heading, leads us to the same chronological results. Chapter vi, in which is related the call of Isaiah, is thus headed: 'In the year in which King Uzziah died [*i. e.,* B. C. 735] I saw the Lord,' etc. Isaiah was accordingly born about 765. His father's name is given as Amoz (not Amos, with which it was confounded by some ancient Fathers).* According to a Jewish rabbinical tradition, Isaiah was either the brother or nephew of King Amaziah, a tradition which has been supported in modern times by pointing to the occurrence of the name of Jehovah as a part of Isaiah's name. This, it has been said, was customary in the earlier periods of Israel's history only in royal circles. But no safe conclusion can be drawn from these data, and, as a matter of fact we must confess that of his earlier personal life nothing is known.

The age in which he lived, however, was critical, and is one of the best understood of all Biblical periods. It is the age in which the great Assyrian monarchs, Tiglath-pileser III, Shalmaneser IV, Sargon, and Sennacherib undertook and carried on extensive campaigns of conquest in Northern Palestine, as well as against Israel and Judah. It was an age in which the true mission of Israel was in need of being specially emphasized. And to this work Isaiah was divinely called. If we assume that he began his prophetic work in B. C. 735, and take into account the data in chapters 36-39 of the book, which indicate that he was active in public life in the fifteenth year of the reign of Hezekiah; *i. e.,* B. C. 713, we shall have a life of public service extending over at least twenty-two years. How much longer he lived and prophesied it is not easy to determine precisely. Some modern scholars, led by Staudlein, Jahn, Bertholdt, and Gesenius, have advanced the opinion that Isaiah lived to a much later period, and that his life extended to the reign of Manasseh, the successor of Hezekiah. For this opinion the following reasons are adduced:

(1) According to 2 Chron. xxxii:32, Isaiah wrote the life of King Hezekiah, It would hence appear that he survived that king.

(2) We find a tradition current in the Talmud, in the Fathers, and in Oriental literature, that Isaiah suffered martyrdom in the reign of Manasseh, by being sawn asunder. It is thought that an allusion to this tradition is found in the Epistle to the Hebrews (xi:37), in the expression, they were sawn asunder (ἐπρίσθησαν), which seems to harmonize, though somewhat vaguely, with 2 Kings xxi:16, 'Moreover Manasseh shed innocent blood very much.'

(3) The authenticity of the second portion of the prophecies of Isaiah being assumed, the nature of this portion would seem to confirm the idea that its author had lived under Manasseh.

These arguments, however, cannot be regarded as conclusive. The first can only prove that Isaiah survived Hezekiah; but even this does not follow with certainty, because in 2 Chron. xxxii:32, where Isaiah's biography of Hezekiah is mentioned, the important words, 'first and last,' are omitted; while in chapter xxvi:22, we read, 'Now the rest of the acts of Uzziah, *first and last,* did Isaiah, the son of Amoz, write.' If

---

*This confusion was due to ignorance of the Hebrew language. The Fathers were accustomed to the use of the Greek Version of the Scriptures, in which Amoz and Amos are precisely the same in spelling.

we take into consideration this important omission, we can easily believe that Isaiah died before Hezekiah, although he wrote his biography up to a certain point; more especially if we bear in mind that, according to the books of Kings and Chronicles, the latter years of the reign of Hezekiah were devoid of important events. We certainly find, in all ages of literature, biographies of persons written during their lifetime.

We may well suppose that the history of Hezekiah terminated with the glorious aid granted to him in his war with the Assyrians, and with the events immediately consequent upon that war.

In reply to the second argument, we observe that it is not certain that the word ἐπρίσθησαν, "they *were sawn asunder*," is used in Hebrews with reference to Isaiah. The statement in the Fathers, and in Oriental writers is entirely deduced from the Jewish tradition, which is throughout of so doubtful a character that no conclusive argument can be based upon it.

With regard to the third argument, we remark, that the differences discernible, if we compare the latter with former portions of Isaiah, can, and ought to be, differently accounted for. Such merely external attempts at explanation always prove unsatisfactory when closely examined.

On the other hand, the superscription of the book indicates that the prophet's public ministry, if not his life, closed either during the life of Hezekiah or very soon after that king's death. According to this superscription, all the prophecies of Isaiah were uttered within the period from Uzziah to Hezekiah. Not one of the prophecies which is headed by a separate superscription of its own is placed after the fifteenth year of Hezekiah; and the internal evidence leads us in none beyond this period. Hence, we infer that the prophetic ministry of Isaiah terminated soon after its fullest development, to which it attained during the period of the Assyrian invasion, in the reign of Hezekiah.

According to these statements Isaiah belongs to the cycle of the most ancient prophets whose predictions have been preserved in writing. He was a contemporary of Hosea and Amos, although younger than those prophets, who belonged to the kingdom of Israel. He was likewise a contemporary and co-worker of the prophet Micah in the kingdom of Judah.

Isaiah was a resident, and perhaps a native, of Jerusalem. He was married, his wife being called "the prophetess" (viii:3). Two of his sons are mentioned, *Shear-jashub* and *Maher-shalal-hash-baz*. These significant names, which he gave to his sons, prove how much the prophet lived in his vocation. He did not consider his children to belong merely to himself, but rendered them living admonitions to the people. In their names were contained the two chief points of his prophetic utterances: one (*Maher-shalal-hash-baz*, "Spoil-speeds-booty-hastes") recalled to mind the severe and inevitable judgment wherewith the Lord was about to visit the world, and especially his people; the other, *Shear-jashub*, which signifies "The-remnant-shall-return," pointed out the mercy with which the Lord would receive the elect, and with which, in the midst of apparent destruction, he would take care to preserve his people and his kingdom.

His wife's name, "the prophetess," cannot mean the wife of a prophet, but indicates that the prophetess of Isaiah had a prophetic gift, like Miriam, Deborah, and Huldah. The appellation here given denotes the genuineness of their conjugal relation.

Even the dress of the prophet was subservient to his vocation. According to chapter xx:2, he wore a garment of haircloth or sackcloth. This seems also to have been the costume of Elijah, according to 2 Kings i:8; and it was the dress of John the Baptist. Hairy sackcloth is in the Bible the symbol of repentance (compare Is. xxii:12; xxxvii:1, 2, and 1 Kings xxi:27). This costume of the prophets was a *sermo propheticus realis*, a prophetic preaching by fact. The prophetic preacher comes forward in the form of personified repentance. What he does, exhibits to the people what they should do. Before he has opened his lips his external appearance proclaims μετανοεῖτε, repent.

2. Lost Writings Ascribed to Isaiah. Besides the prophecies which have been preserved to us, Isaiah also is said to have written two historical works. It was part of the vocation of the prophets to write the history of the kingdom of God, to exhibit in this history the workings of the law of retribution, and to exhort to the true worship of the Lord. History, as written by the prophets, is itself retroverted prediction, and, as such, offers rich materials for prophecy, strictly so-called. Since all the acts of God proceed from his essence, a complete understanding of the past implies also the future; and, *vice versa*, a complete understanding of the future implies a knowledge of the past. Most of the historical books in the Old Testament have been written by prophets. The collectors of the Canon placed most of these books under the head נְבִיאִים, *prophets;* hence, it appears that, even when these historical works were remodeled by later editors, these editors were themselves prophets. The Chronicles are not placed among the נְבִיאִים, *prophets;* this is no sign that they were not written by a prophet. Their author constantly indicates that he composed his work from abstracts taken verbatim from historical monographs written by the prophets; consequently the books of Ruth, Ezra, Nehemiah, and Esther are the only historical books of the Old Testament which did not originate from prophets.

The first historical work of Isaiah was a biography of King Uzziah (comp. 2 Chron. xxvi:22, 'Now the rest of the acts of Uzziah, first and last, did Isaiah the prophet, the son of Amoz, write'). The second historical work of Isaiah was a biography of King Hezekiah, which was subsequently inserted in the annals of Judah and Israel. These annals consisted of a series of prophetic monographs, which were received partly entire, and partly in abstracts, and are the chief source from which the information contained in the Chronicles is derived. In this work of Isaiah, although its contents are chiefly historical, numerous prophecies were inserted. Hence it is called in 2 Chron. xxxii:32, *The Vision of Isaiah.* In a similar manner the biography of Solomon by Ahijah is called in 2 Chron. ix:29, *The Prophecy of Ahijah.* The two historical works of Isaiah were lost, together with the annals of Judah and Israel, into which they were embodied. Whatever these annals contained that was of importance for all ages, has been preserved to us by being received into the historical books of the Old Testament, and the predictions of the most distinguished prophets have been formed into separate collections. After this was effected, less care was taken to preserve the more diffuse annals, which also comprehended many statements, of value only for particular times and places.

3. The Book of Isaiah.

(1) **Structure and Content.** At the very first glance the Book of Isaiah is seen to consist of three very distinct parts. It is divided into 66 chapters. Of these, chapters i-xxxv constitute a more or less homogeneous collection and are distinctly prophetic. Chapters xxxvi-xxxix contain a historical sketch of some events during Hezekiah's reign, and chapters xl-lxvi constitute another homogeneous collection, and are as distinctly prophetic as chapters i-xxxv.

The first of these sections may be further subdivided into five groups of prophetic discourses as follows: (a) Chapters i-xii, dealing generally with the political, social and moral conditions in Judah during the time of the threatened Assyrian and Syrian invasions. Chapter i has been quite properly entitled *The Great Arraignment*. It contains a severe denunciation of the lukewarmness and formalism of the people as well as of the princes and rulers. Chapters ii-iv constitute a connected discourse, opening with a glowing picture of the future exaltation of Zion, then showing by way of contrast its present need and low moral condition, and closing with another picture of its future glory. Chapter v presents in a parable—that of the vine—the care of Jehovah for Judah. Chapter vi gives an account of the vision in the last year of Uzziah's life with which the prophet's ministry began. Chapters vii, x:4, consist of a series of oracles delivered during the reign of Ahaz. The remainder of chapter x (verses 5-34) is a discourse against Assyria. Chapter xi predicts the advent of the Messiah, and chapter xii is a short psalm of thanksgiving to Jehovah. (b) Chapters xiii-xxiii contain a series of so-called "Burdens," *i. e.,* denunciatory oracles on the nations dwelling in Palestine and adjacent countries. The first of these oracles is entitled the Burden of Babylon, and occupies chapters xiii and xiv; the second is the Burden of Moab, in chapters xv and xvi; the third, the Burden of Damascus, in chapter xvii; the fourth, the Burden of Ethiopia, in chapter xviii; the fifth, the Burden of Egypt, in chapter xix. This section is interrupted here by the insertion of a historical fragment, chapter xx, after which come the sixth Burden, *i. e.,* that of the "Wilderness of the Sea," chapter xxi:1, 10; the seventh, *i. e.,* the Burden of Dumah, xxi:11-12; the eighth, *i. e.,* the Burden of Arabia, xxi:13-17; the ninth, *i. e.,* the Burden of the Valley of the Vision (Judah), chapter xxii; and the tenth, *i. e.,* the Burden of Tyre, chapter xxiii. (c) Chapters xxiv-xxvii are of the nature of an eschatological vision. They depict the final judgment and consummation of all things brought about by the confusion, desolation, and collapse of the world, out of which, however, Israel is saved and its dead are raised to life again. (d) Chapters xxviii-xxxiii have been entitled the "Book of Zion." They contain discourses addressed directly to Zion, admonishing and warning it by the example of Samaria (chapters xxviii and xxix), pointing out the folly of an Egyptian alliance (chapters xxx and xxxi), promising a restoration to ideal conditions (chapter xxxii), and denouncing the conquering Assyrian (chapter xxxiii). (e) Chapters xxxiv and xxxv give a picture of the redemption of Israel, the judgment of Edom, and the return of the captives home.

The second main division of the book narrates Sennacherib's invasion and demand for the submission of Hezekiah, and the disastrous ending of the invasion (comp. 2 Kings xvii:30; xx:19), the sickness of Hezekiah (chapter xxxviii), and the mission of Merodach Baladan to Hezekiah (chapter xxxix).

The third division of the book, comprising xl-lxvi, has been called the *Book of Consolations.* Its standpoint is the end of the Babylonian exile, B. C. 550-540, and it is designed evidently to comfort and encourage the captives and assure them of speedy restoration to their native land. The prophecy is continuous and, although capable of minute and detailed analysis, it cannot be subdivided into oracles and discourses as readily as the first section. The best analysis made is that into three parts, i. e. (1) chapters xl-xlviii, (2) chapters xlix-lix, and (3) chapters lx-lxvi.

In the first of these divisions the prophet aims to assure the Jews in exile of the *certainty of restoration.* Chapter xl opens with an exhortation to the people to be of good cheer, for the Great and Divine Deliverer is about to come. The way should be prepared for him. Nothing can hinder him, because no creature can compare with him, nor can any human conception express him (xl: 1-26); hence Jacob is to take courage (27-31). Jacob is Jehovah's favored servant; therefore for his benefit Jehovah stirred up the "righteous man from the east" (Cyrus) (xli:1-9); the servant of Jehovah should fear no ill; Jehovah who protects him knows the end from the beginning (10-29). Jehovah's servant, the Israel of xli:8 is a complex and ideal personality whose head (the Messiah) is at times so prominently before the mind of the prophet that he is spoken of exclusively as "The Servant," whereas at other times, what is said of the servant can only refer to the Israel of God, the people of whom the Messiah is the Head and representative. In chapter xlii:1-12, the Messiah as the Servant of Jehovah is looked to as about to accomplish a double work; i. e. (1) that of enlightening the world and leading it to the true knowledge of God, and (2) that of redeeming Israel, his people, and restoring it to its glory. The mention of Israel leads the prophet to fall back on the more general meaning of the term servant, and, speaking of Israel as the servant, to account for the woes of the Babylonian captivity as caused by the spiritual blindness and deafness of this servant (xlii:13-25). From these woes, however, Jehovah was determined to redeem the people and to enlarge it by the adoption into its fold of the nations of the earth (xliii-xliv:5). In xliv: 6; xlv:25, the greatness and power of Jehovah once more come into the foreground of the prophet's thought. Chapters xlvi and xlvii are occupied with the impending fall of Babylon, the former chapter containing a derisive picture of the downfall of its idols and the latter of the city itself. Chapter xlviii is a recapitulation of the thoughts of chapters xl-xlvii, closing with a triumphant call by the prophet in the name of Jehovah unto his servant Israel to come out of Babylon.

The second section of this great prophecy (xlix-lix) may be entitled *the Servant of Jehovah.* The preceding section had been designed to produce the conviction of the certainty of the restoration. In this one the conviction is assumed to have been formed in the hearts of the people and they are urged to fit themselves for their privileges and enjoy them when they came. The section opens with a dramatic introduction of the Servant of Jehovah and his double work. In chapter l the servant himself declares the character of his work and the difficulties in his way. In chapters li and lii to lv, verse 12, the prophet reverts to the thought of the return, and is filled with the joy of triumph as he realizes the certainty of the event. Chapters lii:13; liii:12, once more present the Servant of Jehovah, but now as the ideal leader, who through humiliation, suffering, and death, not for his own sins but for those of others, is lifted to a higher pedestal of honor and joy. This prophecy has rightly been viewed as fulfilled exhaustively only in the career of Jesus Christ, the true and ideal Servant of Jehovah. In liv-lvi:8 further promises of restoration are addressed to the people. In lvi:9-lviii the prophet reproves Israel and calls for reformation. This is followed by repentance and the people are represented as confessing their sins in chapter lix.

The third and last section of the prophecy (lx-lxvi) depicts in glowing colors the *Future Glory of the Restored Israel*. The darkness of the past is in chapter lx represented as dispelled and the "light" of Zion has dawned upon her. This is followed by an enumeration of Jehovah's favors to the redeemed Zion (lxi, lxii). In chapter lxiii Israel's triumph over her enemies is foreshadowed first in a dramatic dialogue between the prophet and Jehovah as a victor returning from the conquest of Edom, and afterwards in songs of thanksgiving and praise for the conquest of Israel's enemies. In chapter lxv the new relation of God to his people is assured and a new era of prosperity is foreshadowed; and in lxvi the view of the restoration of the temple-service leads to the appreciation of the greatness and majesty of Jehovah, who transcends all earthly temples, and is above visible service. The whole prophecy then closes with a contrasted portraiture of the glory of Zion and the judgment to be visited upon her enemies.

(2) Integrity of the Book of Isaiah. The question of the integrity of Isaiah was first raised by Koppe in his German translation of Lowth's *Isaiah* (pub. 1778). Until this time the title given to the whole collection in chapter i:1 was tacitly accepted as a certificate of the fact that Isaiah, the Son of Amoz, had written the whole book. Koppe denied the validity of this position, and was quickly answered by Kocher (1786). From this beginning the controversy has been carried on involving more and more of the book in its successive stages. At the present day three general views may be distinguished. First, that of those who believe in the unity of the book. Second, that of those who divide it into three parts, ascribing each to one general author; i. e., (1) chapters i-xxxv by Isaiah, the son of Amoz; (2) chapters xxxvi-xxxix reproduced from 2 Kings; (3) chapters xl-lxvi by Deutero-Isaiah, called also the "Great Unknown prophet of the Exile." Third, that of those who find in parts i and iii a multiplicity of authors. The majority of scholars for the present occupies the second of these positions. The reasons for the unity of the book may be given as follows:

First View for Unity of Isaiah.

(a) Isaiah's name is attached to the whole collection (i:1), "The vision of Isaiah, the son of Amoz, which he saw concerning Judah and Jerusalem, in the days of Uzziah, Jotham, Ahaz, Hezekiah kings of Judah." It is here clearly stated that Isaiah was the author of the following prophecies, uttered during the reign of four successive kings. This inscription is of great importance, even if it originated not from Isaiah, but from a later compiler. If we adopt the latest date at which this compilation could have been made, we must fix it at the time of its reception into the canon in the days of Ezra and Nehemiah. Consequently the compiler could not be separated by many years from the Deutero-Isaiah who is said to have prophesied just before Babylon was conquered, or who, according to most critics, wrote even after the fall of Babylon. It is not credible that a compiler living so near the times of the author, should have erroneously ascribed these prophecies to Isaiah, who lived so much earlier, especially if we bear in mind that this so-called Deutero-Isaiah must have been a very remarkable person in an age so devoid of the prophetic spirit as that in which he is said to have lived.

It is still less credible that a Deutero-Isaiah should himself have fraudulently ascribed his prophecies to Isaiah. None of the adversaries of the authenticity of chapters xl-lxvi make such an assertion.

If the compiler lived before the exile, the inscription appears to be of still greater importance. That the collection was made so early is very likely, from the circumstance that Jeremiah and other prophets apparently made use of the prophecies of Isaiah. This fact indicates that the prophecies of Isaiah early excited a lively interest, and that the compiler must have lived at a period earlier than that which is ascribed to the Deutero-Isaiah himself. From all this we infer that the compiler lived before the exile. The opponents of the authenticity of chapters xl-lxvi have felt the weight of this argument. They have therefore attempted to remove it by various hypotheses, which have received a semblance of probability from the circumstance that even the considerate Vitringa has in question the authenticity of the heading. Vitringa has conjectured that this heading originally belonged to the first chapter alone. He has further conjectured that it originally contained only words, *prophecy of Isaiah, the son of Amoz, which he saw concerning Judah and Jerusalem*. The following words, he says, were added by the compiler, who enlarged the particular inscription of the first chapter to a general one of the whole collection. According to Vitringa the inscription does not suit the whole book, the contents of which are not confined to Judah and Jerusalem alone. This had been felt even by Kimchi, who, anticipating the objection, observes, *quaecunque contra gentes profert, ea omnia propter Judam dicit*. "Whatsoever Isaiah utters against the nations, he says on account of Judah." Judah and Jerusalem are the chief subject, and, in a certain sense, the only subject of prophecy. There is no prophecy concerning other nations without a bearing upon the covenant-people. If this bearing should be wanting in any portion of the prophecy, that portion would be a piece of divination and soothsaying. No prophet against foreign nations prophesied concerning them with the view of spreading his predictions among them, because the mission of all prophets is to Israel. The predictions against foreign nations are intended to preserve the covenant-people from despair, and to strengthen their faith in the omnipotence and justice of their God. These predictions are intended to annihilate the reliance upon political combinations and human confederacies. They are intended to lead Israel to the question, 'If they do these things in the green tree, what shall be done in the dry?' If this is the punishment of those who are less intimately allied with God, what shall then become of us to whom He has more clearly revealed Himself? But they are also intended to indicate the future conversion of the heathen, 'and to open to the view of the faithful the future glory of the kingdom of God, and its final victory over the kingdoms of this world; and thus to extirpate all narrow-minded and national particularism. God shall be revealed not only as Jehovah, but also as Elohim. His relation to Israel is misunderstood, if that relation is exclusively kept in view without any regard to the universe. Therefore the whole collection is justly entitled "Prophecies concerning Judah and Jerusalem." No matter whether this inscription originated from Isaiah himself or from an ancient compiler. That the Hebrew word for *"vision"* means not merely a vision, but also a collection of visions and prophecies, may be learned from 2 Chron. xxxii:32, and Nah. i:1. It means a collection of prophecies and visions united like a picture in an historical frame (comp. Jer. xiv:14), although it may also denote the separate prophecy, as in Obadiah, verse 1. The Hebrew for *"vision"* has no plural (comp. Hitzig's *Commentary on chapter* i:1; Ewald, *Propheten,* i, p. 59).

(b) It cannot be proved that there ever existed any so-called prophetic anthology as has been supposed to exist in the book of Isaiah. We find nothing analogous in the whole range of prophetic literature. It is generally granted that the collections bearing the names of Jeremiah and Ezekiel contain only productions of those authors whose name they bear. In the book of the Minor Prophets, the property of each is strictly distinguished from the rest by headings. The authenticity of only the second portion of Zechariah has been attacked; and this with very feeble arguments, which have been refuted. De Wette himself has, in the latest editions of the *Introduction,* confessed that on this point he is vanquished.

But even if it could be proved that the prophecies of Zechariah belonged to two different authors, namely (as Bertholdt and Gesenius suppose), to the two Zechariahs, each of whom happened to be the son of a Barachiah, this identity of names might be considered an inducement for uniting the productions of the two authors in one connection; still this case would not be analogous to what is asserted to be the fact in Isaiah. In Isaiah, it is alleged not only that a series of chapters belonging to a different author was subjoined, commencing about chapter xxxiv, but it is affirmed that, even in the first thirty-three chapters, the genuine and spurious portions are intermixed. Before we admit that the compilers proceeded here in a manner so unreasonable, and so contrary to their usual custom, we must expect some cogent proof to be adduced.

(c) According to the opinion of several critics, all spurious portions of Isaiah belong to one and the same author. But it so happens that the portion which is most emphatically declared to be spurious, namely, chapters xiii and xiv, bear an inscription which expressly ascribes them to Isaiah. Now, as the internal arguments against the authenticity of all the portions which are said to be spurious are nearly identical, if the opposition to chapters xiii and xiv is given up, it cannot with consistency be maintained against the other portions. This argument serves also as an answer to those who ascribe the portions which they consider spurious to several authors. The contents of these portions are similar. They contain predictions of the fall of Babylon, and of the redemption of Israel from captivity. Whatever proves the genuineness of one of these portions indirectly proves the others also to be genuine.

(d) According to Josephus (*Antiq.* xi, c, 1, 1, 2), Cyrus was induced by the prophecies of Isaiah respecting him, to allow the return of the Jews, and to aid them in rebuilding the temple. The credibility of Josephus, who in regard to facts of ancient history is not always to be relied upon, is here supported by two circumstances. First, the favor shown by Cyrus to the Jews, which remains inexplicable except by the fact

mentioned, in combination with the influence of Daniel. In modern times, the favor of Cyrus to the Jews has been called a prudential measure; but it does not appear what he could either hope or fear from a people so enfeebled as the Jews were at that period. It has been added that Cyrus was favorable to the Jews on account of the similarity between the Persian and the Jewish religions; but there is no historical proof that the Persians, on any other occasion, favored the Jews on account of their religion. The favors shown to Nehemiah on behalf of Israel were only personal favors, owing to his position at the Persian court. We allow that all this would be insufficient to prove the correctness of the above statement in Josephus, but it must render us inclined to admit its truth.

The second argument is much stronger; it is that the statement of Josephus is supported by the edict of Cyrus (Ezra i). This edict presupposes the fact related by Josephus, so that Jahn calls the passage in Josephus a commentary on the first chapter of Ezra, in which we read that Cyrus announces in his edict that he was commanded by Jehovah to build him a temple in Jerusalem, and that he received all the conquered kingdoms of the earth as a gift from Jehovah. This cannot refer to any other predictions of the prophet, but only to what are called the spurious portions of Isaiah, in which the Lord grants to Cyrus all his future conquests, and appoints him to be the restorer of his temple (comp. xli:2-4; xliv:24-28; xlv:1-13; xlvi:11; xlviii:13-15). The edict adopts almost the words of these passages (comp. the synopsis in the above-mentioned work of Kleinert, p. 142). In reply to this it is alleged that Cyrus was deceived by pseudo-prophecies forged in the name of Isaiah; but if Cyrus could be deceived in so clumsy a manner, he was not the man that history represents him; and to have committed forgery is so contrary to what was to be expected from the author of chapters xl-lxvi, that even the feelings of our opponents revolt at the supposition that the Deutero-Isaiah should have forged *vaticinia post eventum* in the name of the prophets. Had these prophecies been written, as it is alleged, only in sight of the conquest of Babylon, Cyrus would have been deceived before the eyes of the author, and this could not have been effected without collusion on the part of the author. This collusion would be undeniable, since the author again and again repeats that he was proclaiming unheard-of facts, which were beyond all human calculation.

(a) In the books of the prophets who lived after Isaiah, and before the period of the so-called Deutero-Isaiah, we find imitations of those prophecies which have been ascribed to the latter. Since Gesenius has demonstrated that all the portions which have been considered spurious are to be ascribed to only one author, it can be shown that they were all in existence before the time assigned to the Deutero-Isaiah, although we can produce the imitations of only some of these portions. But even those who ascribe these portions to different authors must grant that their objections are invalidated, if it can be shown that later prophets have referred to these portions, because the arguments employed against them closely resemble each other; consequently these prophecies stand and fall together. This verbal coincidence between Jeremiah and the so-called Deutero-Isaiah is in this respect most important. Jeremiah frequently makes use of the earlier prophets, and he refers equally, and in the same manner, to the portions of Isaiah whose genuineness has been questioned, as to those which are deemed authentic. The most striking is the coincidence of Jeremiah 1:51 with the predictions against Babylon in Isaiah. Jeremiah here gives to God the appellation, *The Holy One of Israel*, which frequently occurs in Isaiah, especially in the portions whose authenticity is questioned, but is found only three times in the other books of the Old Testament. Isaiah uses this appellation with peculiar predilection, because it points out the omnipotent covenant-fidelity of the Lord; which was to be considered, especially as it guarantees the truth of the contents of the prophecies attacked.

(b) Again, the most ancient production of Jewish literature after the completion of the canon furnishes proof of the integral authenticity of Isaiah. The book of Jesus Ben Sirach, commonly called Ecclesiasticus, was written as early as the third century before Christ, as Hug has clearly demonstrated in opposition to those who place it in the second century before Christ. In Ecclesiasticus xlviii:22-25, Isaiah is thus praised: 'For Hezekiah had done the thing that pleased the Lord, and was strong in the ways of David his father, as Isaiah the prophet, who was great and faithful in his vision, had commanded him. In his time the sun went backward, and he lengthened the king's life. He saw by an excellent spirit what should come to pass at the last, and he comforted them that mourned in Zion. He showed what should come to pass forever, and secret things or ever they came.'

This commendation especially refers, as even Gesenius grants, to the disputed portions of the prophet, in which we find predictions of the most distant futurity. The comfort for Zion is found more particularly in the second part of Isaiah, which begins with the words, 'Comfort ye, comfort ye, my people.' The author of this second part himself says (xlviii:3), 'I have declared the former things from the beginning; and they went forth out of my mouth, and I showed them.' Thus we perceive that Jesus Ben Sirach, the learned scribe, confidently attributes the debated passages to Isaiah in such a manner as plainly indicates that there was no doubt in his days respecting the integral authenticity of that book, which has the testimony of historical tradition in its favor. Jesus Ben Sirach declares his intention (Ecclus. xliv:1) to praise the most celebrated men of his nation. The whole tenor of these chapters shows that he does not confine himself to celebrated authors. We therefore say that the praise which he bestows upon Isaiah is not intended for the book personified, but for the person of the prophet. If Ben Sirach had entertained doubts respecting the genuineness of those prophecies on which, in particular, he bases his praise, he could not have so lauded the prophet.

In the Jewish synagogue the integral authenticity of Isaiah has always been recognized. This general recognition cannot be accounted for except by the power of tradition based upon truth; and it is supported as well by the New Testament, in which Isaiah is quoted as the author of the whole collection which bears his name, as also by the express testimony of Josephus, especially in his *Antiquities* (x. 2, 2 and xi. 1. 1).

(c) After such confirmation it would be superfluous to mention the Talmudists.

It is very remarkable that in the far from scanty historical accounts of this period, considering all circumstances, no mention is made of any prophet to whom we could well ascribe these prophecies. This is the more remarkable,

because at that period prophetism was on the wane, and the few prophets who still existed excited on that account the greater attention. What Ewald (p. 57) writes concerning the time about the conclusion of the Babylonian exile, is quite unhistorical. He says, 'In this highly excited period of liberty regained, and of a national church re-established, there were rapidly produced a great number of prophecies, circulated in a thousand pamphlets, many of which were of great poetical beauty.' What Ewald states about a new flood of prophetic writings which then poured forth, is likewise unhistorical. History shows that during the exile prophetism was on the wane. What we read in the books of Jeremiah and Ezekiel proves that these prophets were isolated; and from the book of Ezra we learn what was the spiritual condition of the new colony. If we compare with their predecessors the prophets who then prophesied, Haggai, Zechariah, and Malachi, we cannot say much about a revival of the prophetic spirit towards the conclusion of the exile. Everything concurs to show that the efficiency of prophetism was drawing towards its end. The later the prophets are, the more do they lean upon the earlier prophets; so that we are enabled to trace the gradual transition of prophetism into the learning of scribes. Prophetism dug, as it were, its own grave. The authority which it demands for its earlier productions necessarily caused that the later were dependent upon the earlier, and the more this became the case during the progress of time, the more limited became the field for new productions. It is not only unhistorical, but, according to the condition of the later productions of prophecy, quite impossible, that about the conclusion of the exile there should have sprung up a fresh prophetic literature of great extent. In this period we hear only the echo of prophecy. That one of the later prophets of whom we possess most, namely, Zechariah, leans entirely upon Jeremiah and Ezekiel, as upon his latest predecessors. There is not a vestige of an intervening prophetic literature. The weakness of our opponents' position is manifested by their being obliged to have recourse to such unhistorical fictions in order to defend their opinions.

(d) For those who accept the authority of the New Testament a final argument for the unity of Isaiah is based on the uniform usage of the second part by the Christian canon. Throughout the New Testament Isaiah is quoted by name as the author not only of those parts of the book bearing his name which are conceded by all to be his, but also of those parts which are said to be by another prophet or other prophets (comp. Matt. iii:3; viii:17; xii:17; Mark i:2; Luke iii: 4; iv:17; John i:23; xii:38, 41; Acts viii:30; Rom. x:16, 20). It is evident that the New Testament writers either knew or did not know the truth as to the composition of the passages cited. If they did not know, their authority is proved to be defective; if they knew, they told what they knew to be contrary to fact, in case the critical theory is correct. No such difficulty arises, however, if the traditional theory is true.

As against these considerations, the argument of the advocates of the decisive theory must be examined. It is necessary, however, to single out in this class those who accept the authority of Jesus and the New Testament, and state their views on the attitude of the New Testament towards the question of the authorship of Isaiah.

In general, the apparent citation of a passage under the name of an Old Testament author does not commit the New Testament writer to any view of the authorship of the writing quoted from. If the name of the author be given, it is given simply as a mark of identification, and not necessarily as a definite ascription of the writing to him. In this sense the whole Psalter is credited to David, including anonymous Psalms (such as the second, cited in Acts iv:25 as David's). In accordance with this usage also Matthew quotes from Zechariah ascribing the prophecy to Jeremiah (Matt. xxvii:9). As an identification of an old prophecy the citation was adequately introduced, but as a writing it was not assigned to its own author.

Such usage does not diminish the authority of the New Testament on those matters on which it was designed to give light, but leaves such matters to be distinguished from others by a careful examination of each in its setting and separate intent. The New Testament writers were not omniscient, nor was it necessary that they should be. Their lack of special information on such an unessential matter in no way weakens their trustworthiness on matters which came not only within their province as historians of the life of Jesus and the Apostolic age, but also within their own personal observation.

But if difficulty be found with this standpoint, it may be still further reasoned that even the verbal inerrancy of the New Testament writers need not be affected by the discovery, if it shall prove to be such, of the separate authorship of a portion of Isaiah. The name Isaiah is not such as to show that only the son of Amoz contemporary of Hezekiah, bore it. In its cognates Joshua, Hoshea, etc., it was a favorite one. If therefore another prophet bearing the same name Isaiah lived in the latter part of the period of the exile and uttered the discourses of Is. xl-lxvi it would be very easy for his personality and work to be blended with those of the earlier Isaiah and thus have the books of the two pass under one title and in one volume. In such a case, the evangelists and apostles could speak with strictest accuracy of these utterances as writings or words of Isaiah's. This hypothesis which practically reduces the question into one of the lower or textual criticism, leaves the field clear for an unbiased examination of the grounds on which the divisive theory is based. These grounds are the following:

(e) The distinguishing features of the literary style of chapters xl-lxvi are so different from that of chapters i-xxxix that if Isaiah the son of Amoz was the author of these chapters he could not have been also the author of the others. These differences touch first of all the choice of words. The author of chapters xl-lxvi uses many characteristic and important words never found in the discourses of the son of Amoz. Such are the terms *to choose, to praise, to spring forth, pleasure, to break forth, good will, acceptance, to rejoice.* Besides single words there are characteristic phrases peculiar to Is. xl-lxvi. Such are the expressions *"thy sons"* with a feminine pronoun referring to Zion (xlix:17, 22, 25; li:20; liv:13; lx:4, 9; lxii:5). When Isaiah speaks of the sonship of Israelites it is as God's sons that he thinks of them (i:2, 4; xxx:1, 9). "I am Jehovah and there is none else" (xlv:5, 6, 18, 21, 22). "I am the first and I am the last" (xliv:6); "I am he" (xli:4; xliii:10, 13; xlvi:4; xlviii:12), "I am thy God," "thy Savior" (xli:10, 13; xliii:3; xlviii:17). These phrases never occur in chapters i-xxxix. Besides these words and phrases a series of others occur in chaps. xl-lxvi which, though used in the first part of the

collection, are so used very rarely and in other senses than those here attached to them. (See Driver, *Introd. to the Lit. of the Old Test.,* p. 239). More broadly the second Isaiah has some stylistic characteristics, such as the repetition of words (xl:1; xliii:11; xlviii:11, 15; li:9, 12, 17; lii:1, 11; lvii:1, 14, 19; lxii:10; lxv:1), the repetition of the same word in successive clauses or verses (xi:12, 13; l:7, 9, etc.), the omission of the relative particle. The converse of this is true also, i. e., words, phrases, and stylistic peculiarities found in Isaiah the son of Amoz are never found in the second Isaiah. Such are the words, " the Lord" (not Jehovah, but the Hebrew אֲדֹן, *aw-done'*) "of Hosts" (i:24; iii:1; x:16, 33; xix:4); not-gods (ii:8, 18, 20; x:11; xix:1, 3; xxxi:7); the escaped (iv:2; x:20; xv:9; xxxvii:31, 32); a trampling down (v:5; vii:25; x:6; xxviii:18); and the phrases "In that day," found frequently as shown by examples from two or three chapters (iii:18; iv:1, 2; vii:18, 20, 21, 23—in Is. lxi-lxvi only once, lii:6); "And it shall come to pass" (iv:3; vii:18, 21, 23; x:12; xi:11); "head and tail, palm branch and rush" (ix:14; xix:15); "a consummation and that determined" (x:23; xxviii:22); "flying fiery serpent" (xiv:29; xxx:6); and of habits of thought or style the first Isaiah shows the tendency to draw figures from the harvest (ix:3; xvii:5, 11; xviii:4); the figure of the fat reduced to leanness (x:16; xvii:4); the figure of the scourge (x:26; xxviii:15, 18); the smearing of the eyes of the blind (vi:10; xxix:18). These lists are by no means exhaustive. They simply represent in a few examples the relation of the style of the two authors. In addition it should be remarked that there are rhetorical and poetical characteristics in these writings—such as the construction of sentences, the movement and rhythm of periods—which cannot be presented in lists of examples, but must be observed in the reading of the writings as units.

These differences cannot be accounted for upon the basis of difference of age in the prophet. Isaiah uses the same style in his earliest and his latest writings (comp. ch. vi with xxix-xxxiii and xxxvii). Nor are they to be accounted for on the basis of difference of subject. In i-xxxix the enemies of Judah are the Assyrians, in xl-lxvi the Babylonians. In the first part the fact of preservation from these enemies and the mode of it are the general subjects, in the second part the subject is the liberation from their power and restoration to their own land. Between these two topics no such difference exists as calls for a different phraseology and style. The only reasonable explanation of these facts is difference of authorship.

(f) The historical setting of chapters xl-lxvi is that of the latter part of the exile period (545-535). The prophecy opens with a general call to be of good cheer (xl:1), and seems to be addressed throughout to a people under oppression and away from home. Jerusalem is ruined and deserted (xliv:26; lxiii:18; lxiv:10). This condition of things is not new, but of long standing (lviii:12; lxi:4). The prospect of return is, however, very vivid. In fact restoration is alluded to as if imminent (xl:2; xlvi:13; xlviii:20, etc.). There is no reference of the remotest kind to the times of Ahaz and Hezekiah or even of Manasseh. So clear is the situation and so manifest the adaptation of the prophecy to the conditions of the later period, that those who ascribe it to Isaiah the son of Amoz suppose that the prophet's consciousness was projected into the future, so that while living in the days of Hezekiah he realized the world of the days of Cyrus. This is a hypothesis so much out of analogy with the Biblical idea of prophecy that it must not be resorted to except for the strongest possible reasons. But the chief reason for pressing it seems to be the fact that the predictive element would be eliminated if the view were not accepted. It is alleged that the prophet appeals to the fulfilment of predictive prophecy (xli :26; xlii :9; xliii: 8-10; xlviii :3-8) and such an appeal would have no value if the prophecy dates from the period of the exile. But a close examination of these passages shows that this way of reasoning has no force. The predictions alluded to are such as would be realized very soon. It was not necessary that an interval of more than 150 years should have elapsed in order to give validity to the fulfilment of predictive prophecies. On the other hand, the manner in which these coming events are spoken of indicates that they are in the near future. Cyrus is already "stirred up" (xli:2 25; xlv:13). He is on the horizon not only of the prophetic vision, but also of the historical situation. Upon the whole the prophet speaks as a man in contact with those whom he addresses and if he lived at the time of Hezekiah, his discourses must have remained a sealed and meaningless book for a century and a half.

(g) The content of thought or theology of chapters xl-lxvi is of a different type from that of chapters i-xxxix. The two parts do not contradict each other; neither is it impossible to conceive of the same man's entertaining and expressing the ideas respectively characteristic of each. And yet as a matter of experience differences as marked as are here shown at once produce the impression of difference in personality. The basal thoughts of the two Isaiahs are of course those of the religion of Israel in general. All the writers of the Old Testament hold and teach these thoughts. But the characteristic features of the first Isaiah are absent from the second and vice versa those of the second do not appear in the first. Isaiah the son of Amoz is distinctively a statesman and a reformer. He appears before the kings of his day with a message from Jehovah as to what they should do in view of the political and social situations in which they are implicated. The second Isaiah is an evangelical preacher. His idea of God is that he is the Creator of the Universe, the Life-giver and sustainer of all, the Author of history, the First and the Last, the Incomparable one. The central idea in the conception is his infinitude. Isaiah the son of Amoz dwells rather on the majesty of God and his special care over Israel. The first Isaiah presents the doctrine of the remnant or preservation of a nucleus of Israel through all catastrophes that may be visited on the nation as a result of judgment for their sins. In the second Isaiah this doctrine appears only by implication (lix :20; lxv :8); but in place of it there emerges the doctrine of the call of Israel to a high function and a glorious ultimate destiny. Finally, as regards the Messiah, the two parts of the book differ radically. In the first the Messiah is a glorious King of the line of David, whose reign is marked by peace and prosperity. In the second, the Messiah is the Servant of Jehovah, the head of the people of God (never alluded to by the title of King) whose mission and function are blended with those of the people. He redeems the people by suffering.

(h) As a separate reason for looking on the two sections outlined as the works of two differ-

ent men is given the cumulative force of the occurrence of the above lines of difference. Either the literary, the historical, or the theological differences alone would have pointed to the conclusion claimed by the advocates of the divisive theory. But the concurrence of all the considerations above enumerated, it is said, adds to the force of each, separately taken, and gives the highest degree of probability to the conclusion.

There remains to be considered the third general view of the integrity of Isaiah. This view has been elaborated since 1890 by Duhm (in Nowack's *Handkommentar,* 1892). Hackmann (*Die Zukunftserwartung des Jes.,* 1893), and Cheyne (*Introd. to the Book of Isaiah,* 1895), also in Haupt's *Sacred Books of the Old Testament,* vol. *Isaiah,* 1898. In the judgment of these scholars, the book of Isaiah is neither the work of one man, nor that of two or three, but a compilation of fragments some of which are genuine and some date from as late a period as the second or even first century B. C. The reasons alleged for this view are mainly slight differences of style and grammatical peculiarities, and apocalyptic contact. These reasons have not, however, found favor among expert scholars. They are too subjective and conjectural. Those who hold them seem often to imagine or create the difficulties which they are ostensibly determined to remove. In any case the theory of a multiplicity of authors for Isaiah may be left to be discussed by experts at whose hands it is certain to receive the careful attention it may deserve.

4. Helps to the Study of Isaiah. (1) Commentaries. Of the commentaries on the book of Isaiah, that by J. Addison Alexander (New York and London, 1846) is an almost exhaustive summary of the views propounded to the date of its publication, containing in a compact form the interpretations of all his predecessors, as well as those of the author himself. Of the commentaries that have appeared since the publication of this work, the most important are those of: Delitzsch (1866, 4th ed. 1889; Eng. tr. 1892). Nägelsbach (in Lange's *Bible Work,* 1877; Eng. tr. 1878). T. R. Birks (*Book of Isaiah,* 1878). T. K. Cheyne (*Prophecies of Is. with Com. and App.* 1880). Oreli (1887; Eng. tr. 1889). G. A. Smith (in the *Expositor's Bible,* vol. 1, cc. x-xxxix, 1888; vol. 2, cc. xl-lxvi, 1890). A. Dillmann (in *Kurzgeffasstes Ex. Handbuch zu dem Alt. Testam.,* 1890). Bernhard Duhm (in Nowack's *Handkommentar zu Alt. Testam.,* 1892). J. Skinner (in the *Cambr. Bible,* 1896-98).

(2) Introductions and Critical Discussions. T. K. Cheyne, *The Book of Isaiah Chronologically Arranged,* etc., 1870; *Introduction to the Book of Isaiah,* 1895; G. Douglas, *Isaiah One and His Book One,* 1895; Kennedy, *Argument for Unity of Isaiah,* 1891.

(3) Life and Times of Isaiah. A. H. Sayce, *Life and Times of Isaiah,* 1883; S. R. Driver, *Life and Times of Isaiah (Men of the Bible Series),* 1893; Sinker, *Hezekiah and His Age,* 1898.

A. C. Z.

ISCAH (ĭs'kah), (Heb. יִסְכָּה, *yis-kaw',* watchful), daughter of Abram's brother, Haran, and sister of Lot and Milcah (Gen. xi:29; comp. v:31). According to Jewish tradition and Jerome (*Quaest.* in Genesis) she is identical with Sarah.

ISCARIOT (ĭs-kăr'i-ot), (Gr. Ἰσκαριώτης, *is-kar-ee-o'tace,* perh. from Heb. אִישׁ קְרִיּוֹת, *eesh ker-ee-yōth',* man of Kerioth), a surname of Judas the traitor, to distinguish him from others of the same name (Matt. x:4, etc.). (See JUDAS ISCARIOT.)

ISHBAH (ĭsh'bah), (Heb. יִשְׁבַּח, *yish-bakh'*, he will praise), a descendant of Judah, and "father," or founder of Eshtemoa (1 Chron. iv:17). He was probably a son of Mered by Hodiah. He is perhaps the same as Ishi, ver. 20; and perhaps identical with the Naham of ver. 19 (B. C. after 1612).

ISHBAK (ĭsh'băk), (Heb. יִשְׁבָּק, *yish-bawk'*, leaving), a son of Abraham by Keturah (Gen. xxv:2; 1 Chron. i:32), whose descendants comprised a tribe in northern Arabia. Pool thinks that the location of the settlements of this people may be recovered in the name of the valley called Sabák, or Sibák in the Dahnà, in the highland country of Northeastern Arabia.

ISHBI-BENOB (ĭsh'bi-bē'nob), (Heb. יִשְׁבִּי בְנֹב, *yish-bee'beh-nobe'*, my seat is at Nob), one of the giants, or Rephaim, who carried a spear which weighed 300 shekels, twelve pounds and a half. This giant, being on the point of killing David, who was fatigued in the battle, was himself killed by Abishai, son of Zeruiah (2 Sam. xxi:16, 17), B. C. about 1018. (See GIANTS.)

ISH-BOSHETH (ĭsh'bō'sheth), (Heb. אִישׁ־בּשֶׁת, *eesh-bō'sheth*, man of shame, "bashful"), a son of King Saul, and the only one who survived him.

In 1 Chron. viii:33, and ix:39, this name is given as אֶשְׁבַּעַל, *esh-bah'al;* Baal was the name of an idol, accounted abominable by the Hebrews, and which scrupulous persons avoided pronouncing, using the word *bosheth,* 'shame' or 'vanity,' instead. This explains why the name Eshbaal is substituted for Ish-bosheth, Jerubbaal for Jerubbesheth (comp. Judg. viii:35 with 2 Sam. xi:21), and Merib-baal for Mephibosheth (comp. 2 Sam. iv:4 with 1 Chron. viii:34 and ix:40).

(1) Succeeds Saul. Ishbosheth was not present in the disastrous battle at Gilboa, in which his father and brothers perished; and, too feeble of himself to seize the scepter which had fallen from the hands of Saul, he owed the crown entirely to his uncle Abner, who conducted him to Mahanaim, beyond the Jordan, where he was recognized as king by ten of the twelve tribes. He reigned seven, or, as some will have it, two years—if a power so uncertain as his can be called a reign. Even the semblance of authority which he possessed he owed to the will and influence of Abner, who himself kept the real substance in his own hands.

(2) Quarrels with Abner. A sharp quarrel between them led at last to the ruin of Ish-bosheth. Although accustomed to tremble before Abner, even his meek temper was roused to resentment by the discovery that Abner had invaded the harem of his late father Saul, which was in a peculiar manner sacred under his care as a son and a king. By this act Abner exposed the king to public contempt, if it did not indeed leave himself open to the suspicion of intending to advance a claim to the crown on his own behalf. Abner highly resented the rebuke of Ish-bosheth, and from that time contemplated uniting all the tribes under the scepter of David. Ish-bosheth, however, reverted to his ordinary timidity of character. At the first demand of David, he restored to him his sister Michal, who had been given in marriage to the son of Jesse by Saul, and had afterwards been taken from him and bestowed upon another. It is, perhaps, right to attribute this act to his weakness; although, as David allows that he was a righteous man, it may have been owing to his sense of justice.

(3) Death. On the death of Abner, Ish-bosheth lost all heart and hope, and perished miserably, being murdered in his own palace, while he took his mid-day sleep, by two of his officers, Baanah and Rechab. They sped with his head to David, expecting a great reward for their deed; but the monarch—as both right feeling and good policy required—testified the utmost horror and concern. He slew the murderers, and placed the head of Ish-bosheth with due respect in the sepulcher of Abner (2 Sam. ii:8-11; iii:6-39; iv), B. C. 1048.

(4) Difficulty in Chronology. There is a serious difficulty in the chronology of this reign. In 2 Sam. ii:10 Ish-bosheth is said to have reigned two years; which some understand as the whole amount of his reign. And as David reigned seven and a half years over Judah before he became king of all Israel upon the death of Ish-bosheth, it is conceived by the Jewish chronologer (*Seder Olam Rabba,* p. 37), as well as by Kimchi and others, that there was a vacancy of five years in the throne of Israel. But it is the more usual, and perhaps the better course, to settle this question by supposing that the reigns of David over Judah, and Ish-bosheth over Israel, were nearly contemporaneous, and that the two years are mentioned as those from which to date the commencement of the ensuing events—namely, the wars between the house of Saul and that of David.

ISHI (i'shi), (Heb. יִשְׁעִי, *yish-ee'*, salutary).

1. The son of Appaim, a descendant of Judah, and father of Sheshan (1 Chron. ii:31), of the house of Hezron. (B. C. probably after 1612.)

2. Forefather (father) of several Simeonites who headed an expedition of five hundred men, in which they took Mount Seir from the Amalekites, and possessed it (1 Chron. iv:42), B. C. ante 726.

3. Father of Zoheth and Ben-zoheth (1 Chron. iv:20), B. C. perhaps about 1017.

4. A chief of Manasseh, famous for valor, living east of the Jordan (1 Chron. v:24), B. C. about 720.

5. (Heb. אִישִׁי, *ish'ee*, my husband), a word occurring in Hos. ii:16, and means "my man" or "husband."

ISHIAH (i-shi'ah), (Heb. יִשִּׁיָּה, *yish-shee-yaw'*, Jehovah will lend), the fifth son of Izrahiah, a descendant of Issachar; a chief of his tribe in the time of David (1 Chron. vii:3), B. C. 1618.

ISHIJAH (i-shi'jah), (Heb. as above), a layman of the Israelites among the "sons" of Harim, who gave up his foreign wife (Ezra x:31), B. C. 459.

ISHMA (ĭsh'mà), (Heb. יִשְׁמָא, *yish-maw'*, desolate), a descendant of Judah (1 Chron. iv:3), apparently son of the founder of Etam, and closely connected with Bethlehem (ver. 4), B. C. probably 1612.

ISHMAEL (ĭsh'ma-el), (Heb. יִשְׁמָעֵאל, *yish-maw-ale'*, God hears).

1. Abraham's eldest son, borne to him by Hagar (Gen. xvi:11) fourteen years before the birth of Isaac (B. C. about 2248), the circumstances of whose birth, early history, and final expulsion from his father's tents are related in the articles ABRAHAM and HAGAR (See also ISAAC; INHERITANCE). He afterwards made the desert into which he had been cast his abode, and by attaching himself to, and acquiring influence over, the native tribes, rose to great authority and influence. It would seem to have been the original intention of his mother to have returned to Egypt, to which country she belonged; but this being prevented, she was contented to obtain for her son wives from thence.

(1) Friendship of Ishmael and Isaac. Although their lots were cast apart, it does not appear that any serious alienation existed between Ishmael and Isaac; for we read that they both joined in the sepulchral rites of their father Abraham (Gen. xxv:9). This fact has not been noticed as it deserves. It is full of suggestive matter. As funerals in the East take place almost immediately after death, it is evident that Ishmael must have been called from the desert to the deathbed of his father; which implies that relations of kindness and respect had been kept up, although the brevity of the sacred narrative prevents any special notice of this circumstance. Ishmael had, probably, long before received an endowment from his father's property, similar to that which had been bestowed upon the sons of Keturah (Gen. xxv:6).

(2) Death and Children. Nothing more is recorded of him than that he died at the age of 137 years, and was the father of twelve sons, who gave their names to as many tribes (Gen. xvii:20; xxv:12-16). He had also two daughters, one of whom became the wife of Esau.

(3) Not the Founder of the Arabian Nation. It has been shown, in the article ARABIA, that Ishmael has no claim to the honor, which is usually assigned to him, of being the founder of the Arabian nation. That nation existed before he was born. He merely joined it, and adopted its habits of life and character; and the tribes which sprang from him formed eventually an important section of the tribes of which it was composed. The celebrated prophecy which describes the habits of life which he, and in him his descendants, would follow as recorded in Gen. xvi:11, 12, "A wild man; his hand will be against every man, and every man's hand against him," is, therefore, to be regarded not as describing habits which he would first establish, but such as he would adopt. This passage means that he and his descendants would lead the life of the Bedouins of the Arabian deserts; and how graphically this description portrays their habits, may be seen in the article ARABIA. The last clause, 'He shall dwell in the presence of all his brethren,' is pointedly alluded to in the brief notice of his death, which states that 'he died in the presence of all his brethren' (Gen. xxv:18). Of this expression various explanations have been given, but the plainest is the most probable; which is, that Ishmael and the tribes springing from him should always be located near the kindred tribes descended from Abraham. And this was a promise of benefit in that age of migration, when Abraham himself had come from beyond the Euphrates, and was a stranger and sojourner in the land of Canaan. There was thus, in fact, a relation of some importance between this promise and the promise of the heritage of Canaan to another branch of Abraham's offspring. It had seemingly some such force as this—The heritage of Canaan is, indeed, destined for another son of Abraham; but still the lot of Ishmael, and of those that spring from him, shall never be cast far apart from that of his brethren. This view is confirmed by the circumstance, that the Israelites did, in fact, occupy the country bordering on that in which the various tribes descended from Abraham or Terah had settled—the Israelites, Edomites, Midianites, Moabites, Ammonites, etc. Most interpreters find in this passage, a promise that the descendants of Ishmael should never be subdued. But we are unable to discover this in the text; and, moreover, such has not been the fact, whether we regard the Ishmaelites apart from the other Arabians, or consider the promise made to Ishmael as applicable to the whole Arabian family.

(4) Character. Ishmael appears to have been a wild and wayward child. His training and disposition unfitted him for the tame and unexciting life of a mere shepherd. In his boyhood and early youth he had been the darling of the great Abraham, and had grown impatient of restraint, and overbearing, from the flattery shown him as the heir-apparent of a desert prince. He could never have dreamed of any other than an easy, dignified life, in which he might enjoy himself without a care as the head of a tribe. High-spirited, and fond of listening, at the watch-fires of his father's herdsmen, to their stories of encounters and feuds with hostile neighbors at the wells, or with the freebooters of the desert, he had early given his whole heart to the excitement of border life on the wild wastes. The chase of the gazelle or the wild goat, and the more dangerous pursuit of the bear or the leopard, had inured him to exertion and wild adventure, and the tastes of his youth clung to him through life. If he could not gratify them as the son of a great emir, he would do so as the head of a tribe of his own, and would outrival the bands who had of old so often harried the folds of Abraham. His emblem would be the wild ass of the desert, which no man can tame, with its home in the pathless wilderness. He would live in wild freedom, afar from the hated communities of those who had banished him from their midst.

2. A prince of the royal line of Judah, who found refuge among the Ammonites from the ruin which involved his family and nation. After the Chaldæans had departed he returned, and treacherously slew the too-confiding Gedaliah, who had been made governor of the miserable remnant left in the land. (See GEDALIAH.) Much more slaughter followed this, and Ishmael, with many people of consideration as captives, hastened to return to the Ammonites. But he was overtaken near the pool of Gibeon by Johanan, a friend of Gedaliah, and was compelled to abandon his prey and escape for his life, with only eight attendants, to Baalis, king of the Ammonites, with whom he appears to have had a secret understanding in these transactions (B. C. 588), (Jer. xl:7; xli:15; 2 Kings xxv:23-25).

3. A son of Pashur (Ezr. x:22), who put away his Gentile wife. (B. C. 459.)

4. Father or forefather of Zebadiah (2 Chron. xix:11), B. C. 900.

5. A man of Judah, son of Jehohanan, and captain in the force that assisted Jehoiada in replacing Joash on the throne (2 Chron. xxiii:1), B. C. 877.

6. A Benjamite, son of Azel, and descendant of Saul (1 Chron. viii:38; ix:44), B. C. before 588.

ISHMAELITE (ĭsh'ma-ĕl-īte), (Heb. הַיִּשְׁמְעֵאל, *hah-yish-maw-ay-lee'*, 1 Chron. ii:17; הַיִּשְׁמְעֵאל, *hah-yish-meh-ay-lee'*, xxvii:30; יִשְׁמְעֵאלִים; *yish-meh-ay-leem'*, Gen. xxxvii:25; הַיִּשְׁמְעֵאלִים, *hah-yish-meh-ay-leem'*, Gen. xxxvii:27, 28), a descendant of Ishmael.

The term appears to have been a general name for the Abrahamic peoples of the east country, the Bene-Kedem. The name is applied in its strict sense to the Ishmaelites. It is also applied to Jether, the father of Amasa, by David's sister Abigail (1 Chron. ii:17). (See ITHRA; JETHER.)

The Arabs claim Ishmael to be the firstborn of Abraham, and the majority of their doctors (but the point is in dispute) assert that this son, and not Isaac, was offered by Abraham in sacrifice. The scene of this sacrifice is Mount Arafat, near Mecca, the last holy place visited by pilgrims, it being necessary to the completion of pilgrimage to be present at a sermon delivered there on the 9th of the Mohammedan month Zu-l-Hejjeh, in commemoration of the offering, and to sacrifice a victim on the following evening after sunset, in the valley of Minè. The sacrifice last mentioned is observed throughout the Moslem world, and the day on which it is made is called "The Great Festival" (Mr. Lane's *Mod. Egypt*, ch. iii.).

Mohammed's descent from Ishmael is totally lost, for an unknown number of generations to Adnán, of the twenty-first generation before the prophet; from him downwards the latter's descent is, if we may believe the genealogists, fairly proved. But we have evidence far more trustworthy than that of the genealogists; for while most of the natives of Arabia are unable to trace up their *pedigrees,* it is scarcely possible to find one who is ignorant of his *race,* seeing that his very life often depends upon it. The law of blood-revenge necessitates his knowing the names of his ancestors for four generations, but no more; and this law extending from time immemorial has made any confusion of race almost impossible. (Smith, *Bib. Dict.*).

The Ishmaelites carried on traffic with Egypt (Gen. xxxvii:25, 27; xxxix:1). (See ISHMAEL.)

ISHMAIAH (ĭsh-mā'yà), (Heb. יִשְׁמַעְיָה, *yish-mah-yaw'*, Jah will hear).

1. A Gibeonite, and chief of those who left Saul and came over to David at Ziklag (1 Chron. xii:4), B. C. 1046.

2. Son of Obadiah, and viceroy of the tribe of Zebulun in the time of David and Solomon (1 Chron. xxvii:19), B. C. 1014.

ISHMEELITE (ĭsh'me-el-īte), the form by which the descendants of Ishmael are denominated (1 Chron. ii:17), and in the plural (Gen. xxxvii:25, 27, 28; xxxix:1).

ISHMERAI (ĭsh'me-rāi), (Heb. יִשְׁמְרַי, *yish-mer-ah'ee*, preservative), a chief of the Benjamites, and one of the family of Elpaal residing at Jerusalem (1 Chron. viii:18), B. C. before 588.

ISHOD (ī'shŏd), (Heb. אִישְׁהוֹד, *eesh-hode'*, man of renown), one of the tribe of Manasseh, and son of Hammoleketh, sister of Machir of Gilead (1 Chron. vii:18), B. C. 1658.

ISHPAN (ĭsh'păn), (Heb. יִשְׁפָּן, *yish-pawn'*, he will hide), one of the "sons" of Shashak, resident at Jerusalem, and a chief of the tribe of Benjamin (1 Chron. viii:22), B. C. before 588.

ISHTOB (ĭsh'tŏb), (Heb. אִישׁ־טוֹב, *eesh-tobe'*, man of Tob), apparently a petty kingdom of the country of Aram, mentioned with Zobah, Rehob and Maacah (2 Sam. x:6, 8). Probably the real signification is "the men of Tob," a district mentioned in the history of the Maccabees.

ISHUAH (ĭsh'u-ah), (Heb. יִשְׁוָה, *yish-vaw'*, he will level), the second named of the sons of Asher (Gen. xlvi:17); the A. V. renders the same word ISUAH (1 Chron. vii:30), B. C. bet. 1856 and 1640.

ISHUAI (ĭsh'u-āi), (Heb. יִשְׁוִי, *yish-vee'*, level), the third son of Asher (1 Chron. vii:30), and founder of the family bearing his name (Num. xxvi:44), "Jesuites" (B. C. 1856). Elsewhere the name is ISUI and JESUI (Gen. xlvi:17; Num. xxvi:44).

ISHUI (ĭsh'u-ī), (Heb. יִשְׁוִי, *yish-vee'*, level), the second named of the sons of Saul by Ahinoam (1 Sam. xiv:49). In 1 Sam. xxxi:2 his place is taken by Abinadab, which allows the inference that he died young, or that he is identical with Abinadab.

ISLE, ISLAND (īl, ī'land), (Heb. אִי, *ee*, habitable places).

The Hebrew word is invariably translated, either by the former or by the latter of these English words, which, having the same meaning, will be considered as one. It occurs in the three following senses: First, that of dry land in opposition to water; as 'I will make the rivers islands' (Is. xlii:15). In Is. xx:6, the Isle of Ashdod means the country, and is so rendered in the margin. In Is. xxiii:2, 6, 'the isle' means the country of Tyre, and in Ezek. xxvii: 6, 7, that of Chittim and Elishah. (See also Job xxii:30.) Second, it is used in Hebrew and English according to its geographical meaning, for a country surrounded by water, as in Jer. xlvii:4, 'the isle (margin) of Caphtor,' which is probably that of Cyprus. 'The isles of the sea' (Esth. x:1) are evidently put in opposition to 'the land,' or continent. In Ps. xcvii:1, 'the multitude of the isles' seem distinguished from the earth or continents, and are evidently added to complete the description of the whole world. Third, the word is used by the Hebrews to designate all those countries divided from them by the sea. In Is. xi:11, after an enumeration of countries lying on their own continent, the words, 'and the islands of the sea,' are added in order to comprehend those situate beyond the ocean. The following are additional instances of this usage of the word, which is of very frequent occurrence (Is. xlii: 10; lix:18; lxvi::19; Jer. xxv:22; Ezek. xxvii: 3, 15; Zeph. ii:11). It is observed by Sir I. Newton (on *Daniel*, p. 276), 'By the earth the Jews understood the great continent of all Asia and Africa, to which they had access by land, and by the isles of the sea they understood the places to which they sailed by sea, particularly all Europe.'

J. F. D.

ISMACHIAH (ĭs'ma-kī'ah), (Heb. יִסְמַכְיָהוּ, *yis-mak-yaw-hoo'*, Jah will sustain), a Levite, charged by Hezekiah with the oversight of the sacred offerings (2 Chron. xxxi:13), B. C. 726.

ISMAIAH (ĭs'ma-ī'ah), (Heb. יִשְׁמַעְיָה, *yish-mah-yaw'*, Jehovah hears), one of the chiefs of those warriors who joined themselves to David when he was at Ziklag (1 Chron. xii:4). He is described as "a hero (*Gibbor*) among the thirty and over the thirty"—*i. e.* David's bodyguard; but his name does not appear in the lists of the guard in 2 Sam. xxiii, and 1 Chron. xi. Possibly he was killed in some encounter before David reached the throne (B. C. 1000). (Smith, *Dict. of the Bib.*) (See ISHMAIAH, 1.)

ISPAH (ĭs'pah), (Heb. יִשְׁפָּה, *yish-paw'*, he will scratch), one of the "sons" of Beriah, and a chief of the tribe of Benjamin resident at Jerusalem, originally from the vicinity of Aijalon (1 Chron. viii:16), B. C. before 588.

ISRAEL (ĭz'ra-el), (Heb. יִשְׂרָאֵל, *yis-raw-ale'*).

1. The sacred name, divinely bestowed upon the patriarch Jacob (Gen. xxxii:28) after his wrestling with the angel (Hos. xii:4) at Peniel. It is explained to mean, *a prince with God, a contender with God, or a soldier of God.* Winer (*Heb. Lexicon*) interprets it *pugnator Dei.* Although, as applied to Jacob personally, it is an honorable or poetical appellation, it is the common prose name of his descendants; while, on the contrary, the title Jacob is given to them only in poetry.

2. *Israelites.* (1) The name became the national name of the twelve tribes collectively. They are so called in Exod. iii:16 and afterwards.

(2) It is used in a narrower sense, excluding Judah, in 1 Sam. xi:8. It is so used in the famous cry of the rebels against David (2 Sam. xx: 1), and against his grandson (1 Kings xii:16). Thenceforth it was assumed and accepted as the name of the Northern Kingdom, in which the tribes of Judah, Benjamin, Levi, Dan, and Simeon had no share.

(3) After the Babylonian Captivity, the returned exiles, although they were mainly of the kingdom of Judah, resumed the name Israel as the designation of their nation; but as individuals they are almost always described as Jews in the Apocrypha and New Testament. Instances occur in the Books of Chronicles of the application of the name Israel to Judah (*e. g.,* 2 Chron. xi: 3; xii:6); and in Esther the name Jews to the whole people. The name Israel is also used to denote laymen, as distinguished from priests, Levites and other ministers (Ezra vi:16; ix:1; x: 25; Neh. xi;3, etc.). (Smith, *Bib. Dict.*)

ISRAEL, CONSTITUTION OF.

1. Patriarchal Government. The government of Abraham, Isaac and Jacob was a patriarchal government. So long as they resided in the land of Canaan, they were subject to no foreign power, but tended their flocks and herds wherever they chose to go (Gen. xiii:6-12), and vindicated their wrongs by arms whensoever they had sustained any injury (Gen. xiv). They treated with the petty kings who reigned in different parts of Palestine as their equals in dignity, and concluded treaties with them in their own right (Gen. xiv: 13, 18-24; xxi:22-32; xxvi:16, 27-33; xxxi: 44-54).

The patriarchal power was a sovereign dominion; so that parents may be considered as the first kings, and children the first subjects. They had the power of disinheriting their children (Gen. xlix:3, 4; 1 Chron. v:1), and also of punishing them with death (Gen. xxxviii:24), or of dismissing them from home without assigning any reason (Gen. xxi:14). Further, the patriarchs could pronounce a solemn blessing or curse upon their children, which at that time was regarded as a high privilege and of great consequence. Thus Noah cursed his son Canaan (Gen. ix:25); Isaac blessed Jacob (Gen. xxvii:28, 29, 33); and Jacob blessed his sons (Gen. xlix). On the decease of the father, the eldest son by a natural right of succession inherited the paternal power and dominion, which in those days was one of the rights of primogeniture. To this right the sacerdotal dignity, in the first ages, seems to have been annexed; so that the heads of families not only possessed a secular power, but also officiated as priests in the families to which they belonged (Gen. viii:20; xii:7, 8; xxxv:1-3).

Although the sons of Jacob exercised, each, the supreme power in his own family, during their father's life (Gen. xxxviii:24), yet the latter appears to have retained some authority over them (Gen. xlii:1-4, 37, 38; xliii:1-13; 1:15-17). Afterwards, however, as the posterity of Jacob increased in Egypt, it became necessary to have magistrates or governors invested with more extensive authority; these are termed *Elders* (Exod.

iii:16), being probably chosen on account of their age and wisdom. The *Shoterim* or "officers of the children of Israel" (Exod. v:14, 15, 19), have been conjectured to be a kind of magistrates elected by them; but, from the context of the sacred historian, they rather appear to have been appointed by the Egyptians, and placed over the Israelites in order to oversee their labor.

2. Theocratic. On the departure of the Israelites from the land of their oppressors, under the guidance of Moses, Jehovah was pleased to institute a new form of government, which has been rightly termed a Theocracy; the supreme legislative power being exclusively vested in God or in his oracle, who alone could enact or repeal laws. The Hebrew government appears not only designed to subserve the common and general ends of all good governments—viz., the protection of the property, liberty, safety, and peace of the several members of the community (in which the true happiness and prosperity of states will always consist); but also to set apart the Hebrews or Israelites a holy people to Jehovah and a kingdom of priests.

In the Theocracy of the Hebrews, the laws were given to them by God, through the mediation of Moses, and they were to be of perpetual force and obligation so long as their polity subsisted.

The judges by whom these laws were administered were represented as holy persons, and as sitting in the place of God (Deut. i:17; xix: 17). These judges were usually taken from the tribe of Levi; and the chief expounder of the law was the high priest. In this there was a singular propriety; for the Levites, being devoted to the study of the law, were (as will be shown in a subsequent page) the *literati* among the Israelites. In difficult cases of law, however, relating both to government and war, God was to be consulted by Urim and Thummim and in matters which concerned the welfare of the state. God frequently made known his will by prophets whose mission was duly attested, and the people were bound to hearken to their voice. In all these cases, Jehovah appears as sovereign king, ruling his people by his appointed ministers.

3. The Civil Constitution. This had respect to the classification of the people, succession and right of inheritance of land and property. (See INHERITANCE.)

The nation, from the twelve sons of Israel, formed a great family called "the house of Israel" (Heb. בֵּית יִשְׂרָאֵל, *bayth yis-raw-ale'*). Genealogically it was divided (Josh. vii:14, 16-18) into:

(1) **Heads or Princes of Tribes and Families.** (Heb. מַטֶּה, *mat-teh'*, or שֵׁבֶט, *shay'bet*).

All the various branches of Abraham's descendants, like the ancient Germans or the Scottish clans kept together in a body according to their tribes and families; each tribe forming a lesser commonwealth, with its own peculiar interests, and all of them at last uniting into one great republic. The same arrangement, it is well known, obtained among the Israelites, who appear to have been divided into twelve great tribes, previously to their departure from Egypt.

(2) **Families or Clans.** By Moses, however, they were subdivided into certain greater families, which are called *mish-paw-khoth* (Heb. מִשְׁפָּחוֹת), or *families.*

(3) **Households.** (Heb. בַּיִת, *bah'yith*, house; בֵּית אָב, *bayth awb*, house of father, Num. i:2; Josh. vii:14). A technical term expressing the larger divisions or family groups each of which

again had heads sometimes called *heads of houses of fathers,* and sometimes simply *heads.* These are likewise the same persons, who in Josh. xxiii:2, and xxiv:1, are called *Elders* (Heb. זָקֵן, *zaw-kane'*). (Compare also Deut. xix:12 and xxi: 1-9). It does not appear in what manner these heads or elders of families were chosen, when any of them died. The princes of tribes do not seem to have ceased with the commencement, at least, of the monarchy; from 1 Chron. xxvii:16-22, it is evident that they subsisted in the time of David; and they must have proved a powerful restraint upon the power of the king. (See HEBREWS, RELIGION OF THE.)

ISRAELITE (ĭz'ra-el-īte), (Heb. יִשְׂרָאֵל, *yis-reh-ay-lee',* having power with God, or God's fighter), a descendant of Jacob, and consequently a citizen of the chosen nation of Israel.

The name is applied to the twelve tribes descended from the sons of Jacob while still in Egypt (Exod. iii:16); to the ten northern tribes, after the time of Saul (2 Sam. ii:9, 10, 17, 28), and under David (2 Sam. xix:40); to the tribes, with the exception of Judah, which set up a separate kingdom at Samaria after the reign of Solomon (1 Kings xii:19). The term "Jews" gradually supplanted this term, because, after the return from the captivity of Babylon, the tribe of Judah was the most numerous, and foreigners had scarcely any knowledge of the other tribes. In the New Testament "Israelite" is used to designate those belonging to the true spiritual theocracy (2 Cor. xi:22). (See ISRAEL.)

ISRAELITISH (ĭz'ra-el-i'tish), (Heb. יִשְׂרְאֵלִית, *yis-reh-ay-leeth'*), the designation of a woman whose son was stoned (Lev. xxiv:10 ff).

ISRAEL, KINGDOM OF.

(1) Rivalry of Ephraim and Judah. The separation of the Hebrew nation into two parts, of which one was to embrace ten of the tribes, and be distinctively named Israel, had its origin in the early power and ambition of the tribe of Ephraim. The rivalry of Ephraim and Judah began almost from the first conquest of the land; nor is it without significance that, as Caleb belonged to the tribe of Judah, so did Joshua to that of Ephraim. From the very beginning Judah learned to act by itself; but the central position of Ephraim, with its fruitful and ample soil, and the long-continued authority of Joshua, must have taught most of the tribes west of the Jordan to look up to Ephraim as their head; and a still more important superiority was conferred on the same tribe by the fixed dwelling of the ark at Shiloh for so many generations (Josh. xviii, etc.). Judah could boast of Hebron, Machpelah, Bethlehem, names of traditional sanctity; yet so could Ephraim point to Shechem, the ancient abode of Jacob; and while Judah, being on the frontier, was more exposed to the attack of the powerful Philistines, Ephraim had to fear only those Canaanites from within who were not subdued or conciliated. The haughty behavior of the Ephraimites towards Gideon, a man of Manasseh (Judg. viii:1), sufficiently indicates the pretensions they made. Still fiercer language toward Jephthah the Gileadite (Judg. xii:1) was answered by less gentleness than Gideon had shown; and a bloody civil war was the result, in which their pride met with a severe punishment. This may in part explain their quiet submission, not only to the priestly rule of Eli and his sons, who had their center of authority at Shiloh, but to Samuel, whose administration issued from three

towns of Benjamin. Of course his prophetical character and personal excellence eminently contributed to the result; and it may seem that Ephraim, as well as all Israel besides, became habituated to the predominance of Benjamin, so that no serious resistance was made to the supremacy of Saul.

(2) A National Union. At his death a new schism took place through their jealousy of Judah; yet, in a few years' time, by the splendor of David's victories, and afterwards by Solomon's peaceful power, a permanent national union might seem to have been effected. But the laws of inheritance in Israel, excellent as they were for preventing permanent alienation of landed property, and the degradation of the Hebrew poor into predial slaves, necessarily impeded the perfect fusion of the tribes, by discouraging intermarriage, and hindering the union of distant estates in the same hands. Hence, when the sway of Solomon began to be felt as a tyranny, the old jealousies of the tribes revived, and Jeroboam, an Ephraimite (1 Kings xi:26), being suspected of treason, fled to Shishak, king of Egypt.

(3) Defection of the Ten Tribes. The death of Solomon was followed by a defection of ten of the tribes, which established the separation of *Israel* from *Judah* (B. C. 975). This was the most important event which had befallen the Hebrew nation since their conquest of Canaan. The chief territory and population were now with Jeroboam, but the religious sanction, the legitimate descent, lay with the rival monarch. From the political danger of allowing the ten tribes to go up to the sanctuary of Jerusalem, the princes of *Israel,* as it were in self-defense, set up a sanctuary of their own; and the intimacy of Jeroboam with the king of Egypt may have determined his preference for the form of idolatry (the calves) which he established at Dan and Bethel. In whatever else his successors differed, they one and all agreed in upholding this worship, which, once established, appeared essential to their national unity. Nevertheless it is generally understood to have been a worship of Jehovah, though under unlawful and degrading forms.

(4) Worship of Baal. Worse by far was the worship of Baal, which came in under one monarch only, Ahab, and was destroyed after his son was slain, by Jehu. A secondary result of the revolution was the ejection of the tribe of Levi from their lands and cities in Israel; at least, such as remained were spiritually degraded by the compliances required, and could no longer offer any resistance to the kingly power by aid of their sacred character. When the priestly tribe had thus lost independence, it lost the power to assist the crown. The succession of Jeroboam's family was hallowed by no religious blessing; and when his son was murdered, no Jehoiada was found to rally his supporters and ultimately avenge his cause. The example of successful usurpation was so often followed by the captains of the armies, that the kings in Israel present to us an irregular series of dynasties, with several short and tumultuous reigns. This was one cause of disorder and weakness to Israel, and hindered it from swallowing up Judah; another was found in the relations of Israel towards foreign powers.

(5) The Center of the Monarchy. Jeroboam originally fixed on *Shechem* as the center of his monarchy, and fortified it; moved perhaps not only by its natural suitability, but by the remembrances of Jacob which clung to it, and by the auspicious fact that here first Israel had decided for him against Rehoboam. But the natural delightfulness of *Tirzah* (Cant. vi:4) led him, perhaps late in his reign, to erect a palace there (1 Kings xiv:17). After the murder of Jeroboam's son, Baasha seems to have intended to fix his capital at *Ramah,* as a convenient place for annoying the king of Judah, whom he looked on as his only dangerous enemy; but when forced to renounce this plan (xv:17, 21), he acquiesced in Tirzah, which continued to be the chief city of Israel, until Omri who, since the palace at Tirzah had been burned during the civil war (1 Kings xvi:18), built Samaria, with the ambition not uncommon in the founder of a new dynasty (xvi:24). Samaria continued to the end of the monarchy to be the center of administration; and its strength appears to have justified Omri's choice. (For details, see SAMARIA; also TIRZAH, 2.)

There is reason to believe that Jeroboam carried back with him into Israel the good will, if not the substantial assistance, of Shishak; and this will account for his escaping the storm from Egypt which swept over Rehoboam in his fifth year. During that first period Israel was far from quiet within. Although the ten tribes collectively had decided in favor of Jeroboam, great numbers of individuals remained attached to the family of David and to the worship at Jerusalem, and in the first three years of Rehoboam migrated into Judah (2 Chron. xi:16, 17).

(6) **Rival Sanctuaries.** Perhaps it was not until this process commenced that Jeroboam was worked up to the desperate measure of erecting rival sanctuaries with visible idols (1 Kings xii: 27); a measure which met the usual ill success of profane statecraft, and aggravated the evil which he feared. It set him at war with the whole order of priests and Levites, whose expulsion or subjugation, we may be certain, was not effected without convulsing his whole kingdom, and so occupying him as to free Rehoboam from any real danger, although no peace was made. The king of Judah improved the time by immense efforts in fortifying his territory (2 Chron. xi:5-11); and, although Shishak soon after carried off the most valuable spoil, no great or definite impression could be made by Jeroboam. Israel having so far taken the place of heathen nations, and being already perhaps even in alliance with Egypt, at an early period—we know not how soon—sought and obtained the friendship of the kings of Damascus.

(7) **Union with King of Damascus.** A sense of the great advantage derivable from such a union seems to have led Ahab afterwards to behave with mildness and conciliation towards Benhadad, at a time when it could have been least expected (1 Kings xx:31-34). From that transaction we learn that Benhadad I had made in Damascus 'streets for Omri,' and Omri for Benhadad in Samaria. This, no doubt, implied that 'a quarter' was assigned for Syrian merchants in Samaria, which was probably fortified like the 'camp of the Tyrians' in Memphis, or the English factory at Calcutta; and in it, of course, Syrian worship would be tolerated. Against such intercourse the prophets, as might be expected, entered their protest (vers. 35-43); but it was in many ways too profitable to be renounced. In the reign of Baasha, Asa, king of Judah, sensible of the dangerous advantage gained by his rival through the friendship of the Syrians, determined to buy them off at any price (see JUDAH, KINGDOM OF); and by sacrificing 'the treasures of the house of the Lord and the treasures of the king's house' (xv:18), induced Benhadad I to break his league with Baasha and to ravage all the northern district of Israel. This drew off the Israelitish monarch, and enabled Asa to destroy the fortifications

of Ramah, which would have stopped the course of his trade (xv:17), perhaps that with the seacoast and with Tyre. Such was the beginning of the war *between Israel and Syria,* on which the safety of Judah at that time depended. Cordial union was not again restored between the two northern states until the days of Rezin, king of Syria, and Pekah, the son of Remaliah, when Damascus must have already felt the rising power of Nineveh. The renewed alliance instantly proved so disastrous to Judah, which was reduced to extremest straits (Is. vii:2; 2 Kings xv:37; 2 Chron. xxviii:5, 6), as may seem to justify at least the *policy* of Asa's proceeding. Although it was impossible for a prophet to approve of it (2 Chron. xvi:7), we may only so much the more infer that Judah was already brought into most pressing difficulties, and that the general course of the war, in spite of occasional reverses, was decidedly and increasingly favorable to Israel.

(8) **Wars of Syria and Israel.** The wars of Syria and Israel were carried on chiefly under three reigns, those of Benhadad II, Hazael, and Benhadad III, the first two monarchs being generally prosperous, especially Hazael, the last being as decidedly unsuccessful. Although these results may have depended in part on personal qualities, there is high probability that the feebleness displayed by the Syrians against Jehoash and his son Jeroboam was occasioned by the pressure of the advancing empire of Nineveh.

Asa adhered, through the whole of his long reign, to the policy of encouraging hostility between the two northern kingdoms; and the first Benhadad had such a career of success that his son found himself in a condition to hope for an entire conquest of Israel. His formidable invasions wrought an entire change in the mind of Jehoshaphat (1 Kings xxii:44), who saw that if Israel were swallowed up by Syria there would be no safety for Judah. We may conjecture that this consideration determined him to unite the two royal families; for no common cause would have induced so religious a king to select for his son's wife Athaliah the daughter of Jezebel. The age of Ahaziah, who was sprung from this marriage, forces us to place it as early as B. C. 912, which is the third year of Jehoshaphat and sixth of Ahab. Late in his reign Jehoshaphat threw himself most cordially (1 Kings xxii:4) into the defense of Ahab, and by so doing probably saved Israel from a foreign yoke. Another mark of the low state into which both kingdoms were falling, is, that after Ahab's death the Moabites refused their usual tribute to Israel, and (as far as can be made out from the ambiguous words of 2 Kings iii:27), the united force of the two kingdoms failed of doing more than irritate them. Soon after, in the reign of Jehoram, son of Jehoshaphat, the Edomites followed the example, and established their independence. This event possibly engaged the whole force of Judah, and hindered it from succoring Samaria during the cruel siege which it sustained from Benhadad II, in the reign of Jehoram, son of Ahab. The declining years and health of the king of Syria gave a short respite to Israel; but, in B. C. 885, Hazael, by defeating the united Hebrew armies, commenced the career of conquest and harassing invasion by which he 'made Israel like the dust by threshing.' Even under Jehu he subdued the trans-Jordanic tribes (2 Kings x:32). Afterwards, since he took the town of Gath (2 Kings xii:17) and prepared to attack Jerusalem—an attack which Jehoash, king of Judah, averted only by strictly following Asa's precedent—it is manifest that all the passes and chief forts of the country west of the Jordan must have been in his hand. Indeed, as he is said, 'to have left Jehoahaz only fifty horsemen, ten chariots, and ten thousand footmen,' it would seem that Israel was strictly a conquered province, in which Hazael dictated (as the English to the native rajahs of India) what military force should be kept up.

(9) Delivery of Israel. From this thraldom Israel was delivered by some unexplained agency. We are told merely that 'Jehovah gave to Israel *a savior*, so that they went out from under the hand of the Syrians; and the children of Israel dwelt in their tents as beforetime' (2 Kings xiii: 5). It is allowable to conjecture that the (apparently unknown) deliverer was the Assyrian monarchy, which, assaulting Hazael towards the end of the reign of Jehoahaz, entirely drew away the Syrian armies. That it was some urgent, powerful, and continued pressure, considering the great strength which the empire of Damascus had attained, seems clear from the sudden weakness of Syria through the reigns of Jehoash and Jeroboam II, the former of whom thrice defeated Benhadad III and 'recovered the cities of Israel;' the latter not only regained the full territory of the ten tribes, but made himself master (for a time at least) of Damascus and Hamath. How entirely the friendship of Israel and Judah had been caused and cemented by their common fear of Syria is proved by the fact that no sooner was the power of Damascus broken than new war broke out between the two kingdoms, which ended in the plunder of Jerusalem by Jehoash, who also broke down its walls and carried off hostages; after which there is no more alliance between Judah and Israel. The *empire* of Damascus seems to have been entirely dissolved under the son of Hazael, and no mention is made of its kings for eighty years or more. When Pekah, son of Remaliah, reigned in Samaria, Rezin, as king of Damascus, made a last but ineffectual effort for its independence.

(10) The Assyrian Power. The same Assyrian power which had doubtless so seriously shaken, and perhaps temporarily overturned, the kingdom of Damascus, was soon to be felt by Israel. Menahem was invaded by Pul (the first sovereign of Nineveh whose name we know), and was made tributary. His successor, Tiglath-pileser, in the reign of Pekah, son of Remaliah, carried captive the eastern and northern tribes of Israel (*i. e.,* perhaps all their chief men as hostages?), and soon after slew Rezin, the ally of Pekah, and subdued Damascus. The following emperor, Shalmaneser, besieged and captured Samaria, and terminated the kingdom of Israel, B. C. 721.

This branch of the Hebrew monarchy suffered far greater and more rapid reverses than the other. From the accession of Jeroboam to the middle of Baasha's reign, it probably increased in power; it then waned with the growth of the Damascene empire; it struggled hard against it under Ahab and Jehoram, but sank lower and lower; it was dismembered under Jehu, and made subject under Jehoahaz. From B. C. 940 to B. C. 850 is, as nearly as can be ascertained, the period of depression; and from B. C. 914 to B. C. 830 that of friendship or alliance with Judah. But after (about) B. C. 850 Syria began to decline, and Israel soon shot out rapidly; so that Joash and his son Jeroboam appear, of all Hebrew monarchs, to come next to David and Solomon. How long this burst of prosperity lasted does not distinctly appear; but it would seem that entire dominion over the ten tribes was held until Pekah

received the first blow from the Assyrian conqueror.

(11) Causes of Weakness. Besides that which was a source of weakness to Israel from the beginning, viz., the schism of the crown with the whole ecclesiastical body, other causes may be discerned which made the ten tribes less powerful, in comparison with the two, than might have been expected. The marriage of Ahab to Jezebel brought with it no political advantages at all commensurate with the direct moral mischief, to say nothing of the spiritual evil; and the reaction against the worship of Baal was a most ruinous atonement for the sin. To suppress the monstrous iniquity, the prophets let loose the remorseless Jehu, who, not satisfied with the blood of Ahab's wife, grandson, and seventy sons, murdered first the king of Judah himself, and next forty-two youthful and innocent princes of his house; while, strange to tell, the daughter of Jezebel gained by his deed the throne of Judah, and perpetrated a new massacre. The horror of such crimes must have fallen heavily on Jehu, and have caused a widespread disaffection among his own subjects. Add to this that the Phœnicians must have deeply resented his proceedings; so that we get a very sufficient clue to the prostration of Israel under the foot of Hazael during the reign of Jehu and his son.

Another and more abiding cause of political debility in the ten tribes was found in the imperfect consolidation of the inhabitants into a single nation. Since those who lived east of the Jordan retained, to a great extent at least, their pastoral habits, their union with the rest could never have been very firm; and when a king was neither strong independently of them, nor had good hereditary pretensions, they were not likely to contribute much to his power. After their conquest of the Hagarenes and the depression of the Moabites and Ammonites by David, they had free room to spread eastward; and many of their chief men may have become wealthy in flocks and herds (like Machir, the son of Ammiel, of Lodebar, and Barzillai the Gileadite (2 Sam. xvii:27), over whom the authority of the Israelitish crown would naturally be precarious; while west of the Jordan the agrarian law of Moses made it difficult or impossible for a landed nobility to form itself, which could be formidable to the royal authority. That the Arab spirit of freedom was rooted in the eastern tribes may perhaps be inferred from the case of the Rechabites, who would neither live in houses nor plant vines; undoubtedly, like some of the Nabathæans, lest by becoming settled and agricultural they should be enslaved. Yet the need of imposing this law on his descendants would not have been felt by Jonadab had not an opposite tendency been rising—that of agricultural settlement.

(12) Influence of the Prophets. Although the priests and Levites nearly disappeared out of Israel, prophets were perhaps even more numerous and active there than in Judah, and Abijah, whose prediction first endangered Jeroboam (1 Kings xi:29-40), lived in honor at Shiloh to his dying day (xiv:2). Obadiah alone saved one hundred prophets of Jehovah from the rage of Jezebel (xviii:13). Possibly their extra-social character freed them from the restraint imposed on priests and Levites; and while they felt less bound to the formal rites of the Law, the kings of Israel were also less jealous of them. (See HEBREWS, RELIGION OF THE; see also CHRONOLOGY.)

F. W. N.

ISSACHAR (ĭs'sa-kar), (Heb. יִשָּׂשכָר, *yis-saws-kawr'*, he will bring reward).

1. The Ninth Son of Jacob. Son of Jacob and Leah, born B. C. about 2000, who gave name to one of the tribes of Israel (Gen. xxx:18; Num. xxvi:25).

2. The Tribe of Issachar. (1) **Characteristics.** Jacob, on his deathbed, speaking metaphorically of the character and destinies of his sons, or rather of the tribes which should spring from them, said, 'Issachar is a strong ass couching down between two burdens' (Gen. xlix:14, 15). Remembering the character of the ass in eastern countries, we may be sure that this comparison was not intended in disparagement. The ass is anything but stupid; and the proverbial obstinacy which it sometimes exhibits in our own country is rather the result of ill-treatment than a natural characteristic of the animal. Its true attributes are patience, gentleness, great capability of endurance, laborious exertion, and a meek submission to authority. Issachar, therefore, the progenitor of a race singularly docile, and distinguished for their patient industry, is exhibited under the similitude of the meekest and most laborious of quadrupeds. The descriptive character goes on: 'And he saw that rest was good, and the land that it was pleasant, and he bowed his shoulder to bear, and became a servant unto tribute;' which probably does not imply that reproach upon Issachar, as addicted to ignominious ease, which some commentators find in it. It seems simply to mean that finding itself in possession of a most fertile portion of Palestine, the tribe devoted itself to the labors of agriculture, taking little interest in the public affairs of the nation. Accordingly Josephus says that the heritage of the tribe 'was fruitful to admiration, abounding in pastures and nurseries of all kinds, so that it would make any man in love with husbandry' (*Antiq.* v. 1. 22). But although a decided preference of agricultural over commercial or military pursuits is here indicated, there seems no reason to conclude, as some gather from the last clause, that the tribe would be willing to purchase exemption from war by the payment of a heavy tribute. The words do not necessarily imply this; and there is no evidence that the tribe ever declined any military service to which it was called. On the contrary, it is specially commended by Deborah for the promptitude with which it presented itself in the war with Jabin (Judg. v:15); and in the days of David honorable testimony is borne to its character (1 Chron. xii:32). In this passage the 'children of Issachar' are described as 'men that had understanding of the times, to know what Israel ought to do;' which, compared with Esther i:13, has been supposed to mean that they were skilled in the various practical applications of astronomy. But what need there was of astronomy on the occasion of calling David to the throne of Israel after the death of Abner and Ishbosheth, is not very easy to discover. It more probably means that they were men held in esteem for their prudence and wisdom, and who knew that the time was come when it was no longer safe to delay calling David to the throne of all Israel.

(2) **Numbers.** Quitting Egypt the tribe of Issachar numbered 54,000 adult males, which gave it the fifth numerical rank among the twelve tribes, Judah, Simeon, Zebulun, and Dan being alone above it. In the wilderness it increased nearly 10,000, and then ranked as the third of the tribes, Judah and Dan only being more numerous (Num. i:xxvi).

(3) **Territory.** The territory of the tribe comprehended the whole of the plain of Esdraelon and the neighboring districts—the granary of Palestine. It was bounded on the east by the Jordan, on the west and south by Manasseh, and on the north by Asher and Zebulun. It contained the towns of Megiddo, Taanach, Shunem, Jezreel, and Bethshan, with the villages of Endor, Aphek, and Ibleam, all historical names; the mountains of Tabor and Gilboa, and the valley of Jezreel, were in the territory of this tribe, and the course of the river Kishon lay through it.

3. The seventh son of Obed-Edom; a Korhite Levite, who was doorkeeper in the Temple (1 Chron. xxvi:5), B. C. 1014.

ISSHIAH (is-shī'ah), (Heb. יִשִּׁיָּה, *yish-shee-yaw'*, Jehovah will lend).

1. A Levite; the second son of Uzziel of the house of Kohath (1 Chron. xxiv:25). The context seems to locate him in the time of David.
2. Son of Rehabiah the grandson of Moses through Eliezer. He lived in the time of David and was the head of the large family named after his father (1 Chron. xxiv:21; comp. xxiii:17; xxvi:25). The name is elsewhere given Jeshaiah.

ISSUE (ĭsh'ū), (Heb. מוֹלֶדֶת, *mo-leh'deth*, children, posterity, Gen. xlviii:6; Matt. xxii:25). It is applied also to anything worthless or ignoble (Is. xxii:24).

The *issues from death,* mean, all the means of escape from sin or misery, and all the persons redeemed, belong to the Lord (Ps. lxviii:20). *Out of the heart are the issues of life;* the holy thoughts and good works of men demonstrate spiritual life to be in their heart, and prepare them for eternal life (Prov. iv:23).

ISSUE, RUNNING (Heb. מָקוֹר, *maw-kore'*).

A running of blood, seed, etc. (Lev. xii:7; Ezek. xxiii:20). An issue of this kind was very polluting; but a mother's did not pollute her sucking child. The references in Lev. xv: 2, 3; xxii:4; Num. v:2; 2 Sam. iii:29 are probably to gonorrhœa of the milder form. The virulent forms did not appear until the fifteenth century. (See Chardin, *Voyages en Perse,* ii: 200; Michaelis, *Laws of Moses,* iv:282.)

ISUAH (ĭsh'u-ah), (1 Chron. vii:30). See ISHUAH.

ISUI (ĭs'u-ī), (Heb. יִשְׁוִי, *yish-vee'*, level, Gen. xlvi:17). See ISHUAI.

ITALIAN BAND or COHORT (ĭ-tăl'yan), (Acts x:1), was probably a Roman cohort from Italy, stationed at Cæsarea; so called to distinguish it from the other troops, which were drawn from Syria and the adjacent regions. (Compare Josephus *De Bell. Jud.* iii:42.)

This is the only mention of the word Italian in the Scriptures. (Conybeare and Howson, *Life and Letters of St. Paul,* 1, 143, Am. Ed.)

ITALY (ĭt'a-lỹ), (Gr. Ἰταλία, *ee-tal-ee'ah*), occurs five times in Scripture (Acts xviii:2; xxvii:1, 6; Heb. xiii:24, and *subscription*).

We do not know the ancient name of Italy in the Hebrew language. Jerome has sometimes rendered *Chittim, Italy* (Num. xxiv:24; Ezek. xxvii:6) and in Is. lxvi:19, he translates *Tubal, Italy,* though according to others, the Tiberians are here meant. In the New Testament, written in Greek, there is no ambiguity in the word Italy; it signifies that country including the whole natural peninsula between the Alps and the Straits of Messina, of which Rome is the capital.

ITCH (ĭtch). See PLAGUE.

ITHAI (ĭ'thāi), (1 Chron. xi:31). See ITTAI.

ITHAMAR (ĭth'a-mär), (Heb. אִיתָמָר, eeth-aw-mawr', palm-island), fourth son of Aaron.

He was consecrated to the priesthood along with his brothers (Exod. vi:23; Num. iii:2, 3). Nothing is individually recorded of him, except that the property of the tabernacle was placed under his charge (Exod. xxxviii:21), and that he superintended all matters connected with its removal by the Levitical sections of Gershon and Merari (Num. iv:28). The sacred utensils and their removal were entrusted to his elder brother Eleazar. Ithamar, with his descendants, occupied the position of common priest until the high-priesthood passed into his family in the person of Eli, under circumstances of which we are ignorant. Abiathar, whom Solomon deposed, was the last high-priest of that line; and the pontificate then reverted to the elder line of Eleazar in the person of Zadok (1 Kings ii:34).

ITHIEL (ĭth'i-el), (Heb. אִיתִיאֵל, eeth-ee-ale', God with me).

1. Father of Maaseiah and son of Jesaiah of the tribe of Benjamin. One of his descendants is mentioned as returning from Babylon with a party (Neh. xi:7), B. C. long before 536.

2. A person to whom, with Ucal, Agur Ben-Jakeh addressed his prophecy (Prov. xxx:1), B. C. perhaps about 990.

ITHMAH (ĭth'mah), (Heb. יִתְמָה, yith-maw', orphanage), a Moabite belonging to David's body-guard, according to the supplementary list of 1 Chron. xi:46 (B. C. 1046).

ITHNAN (ĭth'nan), (Heb. יִתְנָן, yith-nawn', extensive), a city in the south of Judah (Josh. xv:23), given between Hazor and Ziph. As it is mentioned with Kedesh and Telem it doubtless lay on the borders of the desert. No trace of it has been found as yet.

ITHRA (ĭth'rà), (Heb. יִתְרָא, yith-raw', excellence), an Ishmaelite (1 Chron. ii:17), but owing to a probable error in transcription he is called an "Israelite" in 2 Sam. xvii:25. He was the father, by Abigail, David's sister, of Amasa, a general under David (1 Kings ii:5), B. C. ante 1023, elsewhere (2 Sam. xvii:25), called JETHER. On the term "Israelite" see: Keil and Delitzsch, Books of Sam. p. 433, Eng. transl.; Wordsworth, Books of Sam. p. 111.

ITHRAN (ĭth'ran), (Heb. יִתְרָן, yith-rawn', excellent).

1. A Horite, son of Dishon and grandson of Seir (Gen. xxxvi:26; 1 Chron. i:41). He was probably, like his father, a commander, "duke," of a tribe of the Horim (Gen. xxxvi:30), B. C. about 1964.

2. Apparently a son of Zophah, a descendant of Asher (1 Chron. vii:37); probably the same as JETHER (ver. 38), B. C. long after 1856.

ITHREAM (ĭth're-ăm), (Heb. יִתְרְעָם, yith-reh-awm', residue of the people), sixth son of David, born to him in Hebron of Eglah, his "wife" (2 Sam. iii:5; 1 Chron. iii:3), B. C. 1045.

ITHRITE (or, better, Jetherite), (ĭth'rīte), (Heb. יִתְרִי, yith-ree'), the descendant of some man named Jether resident in Kirjath-jearim (1 Chron. ii:53).

It was the appellation of Ira and Gareb, two of David's guard (2 Sam. xxiii:38; 1 Chron. xi: 40). According to some, the term "Ithrite" denotes the posterity of Jethro, father-in-law of Moses. Others consider Jether but another form

of Ithra (2 Sam. xvii:25), David's brother-in-law, from whom sprang the family of Ithrites. Still others derive the term from Jattir, a mountain district of Judah, from which the two Ithrite heroes of David may have come.

ITTAH-KAZIN (ĭt'tah-kā'zin), (Heb. עֵת קָצִין, ayth kaw-tseen', time of a judge), a city of Issachar on the boundary of Zebulun (Josh. xix:13), between Gath-hepher and Remmon-methoar. It has not been identified.

ITTAI (ĭt'ta'ī), (Heb. אִתַּי, it-tah'ee, timely).

1. Son of Ribai of Gibeah, a Benjamite hero of David's guard (2 Sam. xxiii:29). In the parallel passage (1 Chron. xi:31) the name is Ithai, Heb. ith-ay'. (B. C. 1046.)

2. A Philistine of Gath in the army of David, commanding the 600 heroes who had made up David's band during his wanderings in Judah (2 Sam. xv:18, 19; comp. 1 Sam. xxiii:13; xxvii: 2; xxx:9, 10). After the organization of the army by David at Mahanaim, Ittai is placed in command of a third part, holding equal rank with Joab and Abishai (2 Sam. xviii:2, 5, 12). No further mention of him occurs, nor of the conduct in battle of the faithful stranger. From the expression, "thy brethren" (2 Sam. xv:20), it is likely that he was not the only Philistine numbered in David's force.

ITURÆA (ĭt'u-ræ'à or rē'à), (Gr. Ἰτουραία, ee-too-rah'yah), a district in the northeast of Palestine, forming the tetrarchy of Philip.

The name is supposed to have originated with yet-oor', or Jetur, enclosure, nomadic camp, one of Ishmael's sons (1 Chron. i:31). In 1 Chron. v:19, this name is given as that of a tribe or nation with which Reuben (beyond the Jordan) warred; and from its being joined with the names of other of Ishmael's sons it is evident that a tribe descended from his son Jetur is intimated.

During the exile this and other border countries were taken possession of by various tribes, whom, although they are called after the original names, as occupants of the countries which had received those names, we are not bound to regard as descendants of the original possessors. These new Ituræans were eventually subdued by King Aristobulus (B. C. 100); by whom they were constrained to embrace the Jewish religion, and were at the same time incorporated with the state (Joseph. Antiq. xiii. 11. 3). Nevertheless the Ituræans were still recognizable as a distinct people in the time of Pliny (Hist. Nat. v. 23). As already intimated, Herod the Great, in dividing his dominions among his sons, bequeathed Ituræa to Philip, as part of a tetrarchy composed, according to Luke, of Trachonitis and Ituræa; and as Josephus (Antiq. xvii: 8. 8) mentions his territory as composed of Auranitis, Trachonitis, and Batanæa, it would appear as if the Evangelist regard Auranitis and Paneas as comprehended under Ituræa. The name is indeed so loosely applied by ancient writers that it is difficult to fix its boundaries with precision. Perhaps it may suffice for general purposes to describe it as a district of indeterminate extent, traversed by a line drawn from the Lake of Tiberias to Damascus; and by different writers, and under different circumstances, mentioned with extensions in various directions, beyond the proper limits of the name. The present Jedur probably comprehends the whole or greater part of the proper Ituræa. This is described by Burckhardt (Syria, p. 286) as 'lying south of Jebelkessoue, east of Jebel es-Sheik (Mount Hermon), and west of the Hadj road.' He adds that it now contains only twenty inhabited villages. By the help of these lights we may discover that Ituræa was a plain country, about thirty miles long from north to south, and twenty-four from east to west, having on the north Abilene and the Damascene district; on the south Auranitis and part of Bashan; on the east the stony region of Trachonitis; and on the west the hill country of Bashan.

IVAH (ī'vah), (Heb. עַוָּה, *iv-vaw'*, or עַוָּא, *av-vaw'*), a city belonging to Assyria whence colonists were deported to Samaria (2 Kings xviii:34; xix:13; Is. xxxvii:13).

In 2 Kings xvii:24, the cognate form "Ava" occurs. Rawlinson identifies it with Hit of Babylonia, the "Is of Herodotus (i:179), which was renowned for its bituminous springs that are still plentiful enough to mark the identity of the place. It is probably the Ahava of Ezra (viii:15). Hit or "Is lay on the east side of the Euphrates between Sepharvaim and Hena, with which it seems to have had a political alliance before the reign of Sennacherib (2 Kings xix:13). Rich. *First Memoir on Babylon*, p. 64; Chesney, *Euphrates Expedition*, i. 55.

IVORY (ī'vŏrў), (Heb. שֶׁנְהַבִּים, *shen-hab-beem'*, ivory tusk, 1 Kings x:22; 2 Chron. ix:21; Rev. xviii:12).

'Elephant's tooth,' or simply 'elephant,' is a common name for ivory, not only in the Oriental languages and in Greek, but also in the Western tongues; although in all of them teeth of other species may be included. The tusks are called *horns* (Ezek. xxvii:15). Elephants' teeth were largely imported as merchandise, and also brought as tribute into Egypt. The processions of human figures bearing presents, etc., still extant on the walls of palaces and tombs, attest by the black crisp-haired bearers of huge teeth, that some of these came from Ethiopia or Central Africa; and by white men similarly laden, who also bring an Asiatic elephant and a white bear, that others came from the East. Phœnician traders had ivory in such abundance that the chief seats of their galleys were inlaid with it. In the Scriptures, according to the Chaldee Paraphrase, Jacob's bed was made of this substance (Gen. xlix: 33); we find King Solomon importing it from Tarshish (1 Kings x:22); and if Ps. xlv:8 was written before his reign, ivory was extensively used in the furniture of royal residences at a still earlier period.

The tusks of African elephants are generally much longer than those of the Asiatic; and it may be observed in this place, that the ancients, as well as the moderns, are mistaken when they assert elephants' tusks to be a kind of horns. They are genuine teeth, combining in themselves, and occupying, in the upper jaw, the whole mass of secretions which in other animals form the upper incisor and laniary teeth. They are used for defense and offense, and for holding down green branches, or rooting up water-plants; but still they are not absolutely necessary, since there is a variety of elephant in the Indian forests entirely destitute of tusks, and the females in most of the races are either without them, or have them very small; not turned downwards, as Bochart states, but rather straight, as correctly described by Pliny. (See ELEPHANT.) C. H. S.

IVY (ī-vў) (Gr. κισσός, *kis-sos'*), is mentioned only once, and that in the Apocrypha (2 Macc. vi:7), where the Temple is described as being desecrated by the Gentiles, and the Jews forced to depart from the laws of their fathers: 'And when the feast of Bacchus was kept, the Jews were compelled to go in procession to Bacchus, carrying ivy.' The term κισσός or κιττός seems to have been applied by the Greeks in a general sense, and to have included many plants, and among them some climbers, as the *convolvulus,* besides the common ivy, which was especially dedicated to Bacchus.

It is well known that in the Dionysia, or festivals in honor of Dionysus, and in the processions called θίασοι, *thee'as-oy*, with which they were celebrated, women also took part, in the disguise of Bacchæ, Naiades, Nymphæ, etc., adorned with garlands of ivy, etc.

IYAR (ē'yâr), (Heb. אִיָּר, *ee-yawr'*), the late name of that month which was the second of the sacred, and the seventh of the civil, year of the Jews, and which began with the new moon of May.

The few memorable days in it are the 10th, as a fast for the death of Eli; the 14th, as the second or lesser Passover, for those whom uncleanness or absence prevented from celebrating the feast in Nisan (Num. ix:11); the 23d, as a feast, instituted by Simon the Maccabee in memory of his taking the citadel Acrai in Jerusalem (1 Macc. xiii:51, 52); the 28th, as a fast for the death of Samuel.

The name Iyar does not occur in the Old Testament, this month being always described as the second month, except in four places in which it is called Ziv (1 Kings v:1, 37; Dan. ii:31; iv:33). Ziv is not considered to be a proper name, but an appellative. It radically means *bright,* an appropriate epithet of the month of flowers. J. N.

IZEHAR (ĭz'e-här), (Num. iii:19). See IZHAR.

IZEHARITES (ĭz'e-har-ītes), (Heb. הַיִּצְהָרִי, *haw-yits-haw-ree'*), a family of Levites descended from Izhar, son of Kohath (Num. iii:27); called elsewhere IZHARITES (which see).

IZHAR (ĭz'här), (Heb. יִצְהָר, *yits-hawr'*, anointing), grandson of Levi, and second son of Kohath (Ex. vi:18, 21; Num. iii:19, xvi:1; 1 Chron. vi:2, 18).

In 1 Chron. vi:22, Amminadab appears in the place of Izhar as the son of Kohath and father of Korah, which must be an error of transcription; for in verse 38 Izhar appears again in the proper place.

IZHARITES (ĭz'här-ītes), (Heb. הַיִּצְהָרִי, *haw-yits-haw-ree'*), same as IZHAR.

Shelomoth was chief of the family in the time of David (1 Chron. xxiv:22), and with his brethren had charge of the Temple treasure (1 Chron. xxiv:22; xxvi:23, 29). The name is Izeharites in Num. iii:27. (See IZEHARITES.)

IZRAHIAH (ĭz'ra-hī'ah), (Heb. יִזְרַחְיָה, *yiz-rakh-yaw'*, Jah will bring forth).

1. A "son" of Uzzi, a descendant of Issachar through Tola (1 Chron. vii:3). B. C. about 1014.

2. A leader of the singers, who joined in the celebration over the completion of the walls of Jerusalem (Neh. xii:42), B. C. 446.

IZRAHITE (ĭz'ra-hīte), (Heb. יִזְרָח, *yiz-rawkh'*), the patronymic appellation of Shamhuth, David's general (1 Chron. xxvii:8). He was probably a descendant of Zerah, son of Judah.

IZRI (ĭz'rī), (Heb. יִצְרִי, *yits-ree'*, the Jezerite), a Levite, leader of the fourth division of singers under David (1 Chron. xxv:11); probably the same as Zeri, son of Geduthun (1 Chron. xxv:3), B. C. 1014.

J

JAAKAN (jā'a-kăn), (Heb. יַעֲקָן, *yah-ak-awn'*, wrestler), father of the Bene-jaakan of Num. xxxiii:30-32; Deut. x:6, and son of Ezer, son of Seir, the Horite (1 Chron. i:42), where his name is given as Jakan, B. C. 1780. He is called Akan in Gen. xxxvi:27.

JAAKOBAH (jā-a-kō'bah), (Heb. יַעֲקֹבָה, *yah-ak-o'baw*, another form of Jacob), one of the prosperous descendants (princes) of Simeon that emigrated to the valley of Gedor in the time of Hezekiah (1 Chron. iv:36), B. C. about 710.

JAALA or JAALAH (ja-ā'là or ja-ā'lah), (Heb. יַעֲלָא, *yah-al-aw'*, wild goat), one of the Nethinim ("servants of Solomon"), whose descendants returned from exile with Zerubbabel (Ezra ii:56; Neh. vii:58), B. C. 536.

JAALAM (ja-ā'lam), (Heb. יַעְלָם, *yah-lawm'*, whom God hides), a son of Esau by Aholibamah, daughter of Anah (Gen. xxxvi:5, 14, 18; 1 Chron. i:35), B. C. 1740.

JAANAI (jā'a-nāi or ja-ā'nāi), (Heb. יַעְנַי, *yah-an-ah'ee*, responsive), a chief Gadite who dwelt in Bashan (1 Chron. v:12), B. C. 1070.

JAARE-OREGIM (jā'a-re-ŏr'e-gĭm),(Heb. אֹרְגִים יַעֲרֵי, *yah-ar-ay' o-reg-eem'*, woods of weavers), the father of Elhanan, belonging to Bethlehem, who slew the brother of Goliath (2 Sam. xxi:19), B. C. 1080. (See JAIR, 4.)

JAASAU (jā'a-sạu), (Heb. יַעֲשׂוּ, *yah-as-oo'* they will do), one of the family of Bani who married a strange wife (Ezra x:37), B. C. 457.

JAASIEL (ja-ā'si-el), (Heb. יַעֲשִׂיאֵל, *yah-as-ee-ale'*, whom God created), son of Abner, in David's time, cousin of Saul (1 Chron. xxvii:21), B. C. 1015, called Jasiel (1 Chron. xi:47), and named among those on the increased list of David's heroes.

JAAZANIAH (ja-ăz'a-nī'ah), (Heb. יַאֲזַנְיָה, *yah-az-an-yaw'*, Jehovah hears).

1. The son of a Maachathite (2 Kings xxv:23; Jer. xl:8). (B. C. 588.)

2. A chief man of the Rechabites (Jer. xxxv: 3). (B. C. 600.)

3. A wicked prince of Judah against whom Ezekiel was told to prophesy (Ezek. xi:1). (B. C. 594.)

4. Son of Shaphan; seen by Ezekiel in a vision worshiping in the "chambers of imagery" (Ezek. viii:11). (B. C. 593.)

JAAZER (ja-ā'zer or jā'zer), (Heb. יַעְזֵיר, *yah-az-ayr'*, helpful. See JAZER.

JAAZIAH (jā'a-zī'ah), (Heb. יַעֲזִיָּהוּ, *yah-az-ee-yaw'hoo*, whom Jehovah consoles), a third son of Merari in the days of Solomon (1 Chron. xxiv:26, 27), B. C. 1010.

JAAZIEL (ja-ā'zi-el), (Heb. יַעֲזִיאֵל, *yah-az-ee-ale'*, comforted by God), one of the Levites of the second order in the time of David (1 Chron. xv:18), B. C. 1015.

JABAL (jā'bal), (Heb. יָבָל, *yaw-bawl'*, a stream).

A descendant of Cain, son of Lamech and Adah, who is described in Gen. iv:20, as 'the father of such as dwell in tents, and have cattle.' This obviously means that Jabal was the first who adopted that nomade life which is still followed by numerous Arabian and Tartar tribes in Asia.

JABBOK (jăb'bok), (Heb. יַבֹּק, *yaw-boke'*, pouring forth).

One of the streams which traverse the country east of the Jordan, and which, after a course nearly from east to west, falls into that river about thirty miles below the lake of Tiberias. It seems to rise in the Hauran mountains, and its whole course may be computed at sixty-five miles. It is mentioned in Scripture as the boundary which separated the kingdom of Sihon, king of the Amorites, from that of Og, king of Bashan (Josh. xii:2); and it appears afterwards to have been the boundary between the tribe of Reuben and the half tribe of Manasseh. The earliest notice of it occurs in Gen. xxxii:22.

The Jabbok now bears the name of Zerka, the blue river. In its passage westward across the plains, it more than once passes underground; and in summer the upper portion of its channel becomes dry. But on entering the more hilly country immediately east of the Jordan, it receives tribute from several springs, which maintain it as a perennial stream, although very low

Jabbok.

in summer. The water is pleasant, and the bed being rocky the stream runs clear (Burckhardt's *Syria*, p. 347; Irby and Mangles, *Travels*, p. 319; Buckingham, *Palestine*, ii. 109; Lindsay, ii. 123).

JABESH (jā'besh), (Heb. יָבֵשׁ, *yaw-bashe'*, dry, parched).

1. Father of Shallum, the fifteenth king of Israel (2 Kings xv:10). (B. C. before 770.)

2. A short form of Jabesh-Gilead (**1 Sam. xi:** 3, 9, 10; xxxi:12, 13; 1 Chron. x:12).

JABESH-GILEAD (jā'besh-gĭl'e-ad), (Heb. יָבֵשׁ גִּלְעָד, *yaw-bashe' ghil-awd'*, Jabesh of Gilead), a town beyond the Jordan, in the land of Gilead.

Jabesh belonged to the half tribe of Manasseh, and was sacked by the Israelites for refusing to join in the war against Benjamin (Judg. xxi: 8). It is chiefly memorable for the siege it sustained from Nahash, king of the Ammonites, the raising of which formed the first exploit of the newly-elected King Saul, and procured his confirmation in the sovereignty. The inhabitants had agreed to surrender, and to have their right eyes put out (to incapacitate them from military service), but were allowed seven days to ratify the treaty. In the meantime Saul collected a large army, and came to their relief (1 Sam. xi). This service was gratefully remembered by the Jabeshites; and, about forty years after, when the dead bodies of Saul and his sons were gibbeted on the walls of Bethshan, on the other side of the river, they made a forced march by night, took away the bodies, and gave them honorable burial (1 Sam. xxxi).

Jabesh still existed as a town in the time of Eusebius, who places it six miles from Pella towards Gerasa; but the knowledge of the site is now lost, unless we accept the conclusion of Mr. Buckingham, who thinks it may be found in a place called Jehaz or Jejaz, marked by ruins upon a hill, in a spot not far from which, according to the above indications, Jabesh must have been situated (*Travels,* ii. 130-134). Robinson (*Bib. Res.* p. 320) supposes it to be the ruins of *ed-Deir* in the Wady *Yabes.*

JABEZ (jā'bez), (Heb. יַעְבֵּץ, *yah-bayts'*, who causes sorrow, possibly a high place).

1. A town of Judah where the families of the scribes dwelt (1 Chron. ii:55).

2. The head of a family of Judah (1 Chron. iv:9, 10). (B. C. 1444.)

JABIN (jā'bin), (Heb. יָבִין, *yaw-been'*, discerner, intelligent).

1. A king of Hazor, and one of the most powerful of all the princes who reigned in Canaan when it was invaded by the Israelites. His dominion seems to have extended over all the north part of the country; and after the ruin of the league formed against the Hebrews in the south by Adonizedek, king of Jerusalem, he assembled his tributaries near the waters of Merom (the lake Huleh), and called all the people to arms. This coalition was destroyed, as the one in the south had been, and Jabin himself perished in the sack of Hazor, his capital. (B. C. about 1169.) This prince was the last powerful enemy with whom Joshua combated, and his overthrow seems to have been regarded as the crowning act in the conquest of the Promised Land (Josh. xi: 1-14).

2. King of Hazor, and probably descended from the preceding. It appears that during one of the servitudes of the Israelites, probably when they lay under the yoke of Cushan or Eglon, the kingdom of Hazor was reconstructed. The narrative gives to this second Jabin even the title of 'king of Canaan;' and this, with the possession of 900 iron-armed war-chariots, implies unusual power and extent of dominion. The iniquities of the Israelites having lost them the Divine protection, Jabin gained the mastery over them; and, stimulated by the remembrance of ancient wrongs,

oppressed them heavily for twenty years. From this thraldom they were relieved by the great victory won by Barak in the plain of Esdraelon, over the hosts of Jabin, commanded by Sisera, one of the most renowned generals of those times, B. C. 1285. The well-compacted power of the king of Hazor was not yet, however, entirely broken. The war was still prolonged for a time, but ended in the entire ruin of Jabin, and the subjugation of his territories by the Israelites (Judg. iv.)

This is the Jabin whose name occurs in Ps. lxxxiii :9.

JABNEEL (jăb'ne-el), (Heb. יַבְנְאֵל *yab-neh-ale'*, built of God).

1. A town on the boundary of Judah near the sea (Josh. xv:11) ; probably the same as JARNEH which see).

2. A city on the border of Naphtali, called "the village by the sea" Josh. xix:33. Site not identified.

JABNEH (jăb'neh), (Heb. יַבְנֶה, *yab-neh'*, a building).

A Philistine town between Joppa and Ashdod (2 Chron. xxvi:6), taken by Uzziah. Its site is probably marked by the modern Yebna, a village about twelve miles distant from Jaffa; in a fine open plain, surrounded by hills and covered with herbage. Northeast of Yebna is a lofty hill, from which is an extensive and pleasing view of Ramla, distant about five miles. On sloping hills of easy ascent, by which the plains are bordered, Yebna, Ekron, Ashdod, and Ashkalon were in sight.

JACHAN (jā'kan), (Heb. יַעְכָּן, *yah-kawn'*, troublesome), the chief of a family of Gad (1 Chron. v:13), B. C. 1100.

JACHIN (jā'kin), (Heb. יָכִין, *yaw-keen'*, he shall establish).

1. A son of Simeon (Gen. xlvi:10; Exod. vi: 15) and founder of the Jachinites (Num. xxvi: 12). (B. C. 1700.)

2. The name of one of the brazen pillars in Solomon's temple (1 Kings vii:21; 2 Chron. iii:17).

3. A priest of Jerusalem after the captivity (1 Chron. ix:10; Neh. xi:10). (B. C. 445.)

4. The head of the family of one of the sons of Aaron (1 Chron. xxiv:17). (B. C. 1015.)

JACHINITES (jā'kin-ītes), (Heb. יָכִינִי, *yaw-kee-nee'*, see above), a family founded by Jachin, Simeon's son (Num. xxvi:12). (See JACHIN, 1).

JACINTH (jā'sĭnth), (Gr. ὑάκινθος, *hoo-ak'en-thos*, hyacinth), a precious stone (Rev. xxi:20); but properly a flower (Rev. ix:17) of deep purple color. (See LESHEM.)

JACOB (jā'kob), (Heb. יַעֲקֹב, *yah-ak-obe'*, heel-catcher, i. e., supplanter).

I. The second son of Isaac by his wife Rebekah. Her conceiving is stated to have been supernatural. Led by peculiar feelings she went to inquire of the Lord, and was informed that she was indeed with child, that her offspring should be the founders of two nations, and that the elder should serve the younger: circumstances which ought to be borne in mind when a judgment is pronounced on her conduct in aiding Jacob to secure the privileges of birth to the exclusion of his elder brother Esau—conduct which these facts, connected with the birth of the boys, may well have influenced.

1. Personal History. As the boys grew, Jacob appeared to partake of the gentle, quiet and retiring character of his father, and was accordingly led to prefer the tranquil safety and pleasing occupations of a shepherd's life to the bold and daring enterprises of the hunter, for which Esau had an irresistible predilection. Jacob, therefore, passed his days in or near the paternal tent, simple and unpretending in his manner of life, and finding in the flocks and herds which he kept, images and emotions which both filled and satisfied his heart. His domestic habits and affections seem to have coöperated with the remarkable events that attended his birth, in winning for him the peculiar regard and undisguised preference of his mother, who probably in this merely yielded to impressions which she could scarcely account for, much less define, and who had not even a faint conception of the magnitude of influence to which her predilection was likely to rise, and the sad consequences to which it could hardly fail to lead.

(1) Buys Esau's Birthright. That selfishness, and a prudence which approached to cunning, had a seat in the heart of the youth Jacob, appears but too plain in his dealing with Esau, when he exacted from a famishing brother so large a price for a mess of pottage as the surrender of his birthright. Nor does the simple narrative of the Bible afford grounds by which this act can be well extenuated. Esau asks for food, alleging as his reason, 'for I am faint.' Jacob, unlike both a youth and a brother, answers, 'Sell me this day thy birthright.' What could Esau do? 'Behold,' he replies, 'I am at the point to die, and what profit (if by retaining my birthright I lose my life) shall this birthright do me?' Determined to have a safe bargain, the prudent Jacob, before he gave the needed refreshment, adds, 'Swear to me this day.' The oath was given, the food eaten, and Esau *went his way,* leaving a home where he had received so sorry a welcome.

The leaning which his mother had in favor of Jacob would naturally be augmented by the conduct of Esau in marrying, doubtless contrary to his parents' wishes, two Hittite women, who are recorded to have been a grief of mind unto Isaac and to Rebekah.

(2) Secures Isaac's Blessing. Circumstances thus prepared the way for procuring the transfer of the birthright, when Isaac, being now old, proceeded to take steps to pronounce the irrevocable blessing which acted with all the force of a modern testamentary bequest. This blessing, then, it was essential that Jacob should receive in preference to Esau. Here Rebekah appears the chief agent; Jacob is a mere instrument in her hands. Isaac directs Esau to procure him some venison. This Rebekah hears, and urges her reluctant favorite to personate his elder brother. Jacob suggests difficulties; they are met by Rebekah, who is ready to incur any personal danger so that her object be gained. Her voice is obeyed, the venison is brought, Jacob is equipped for the deceit; he helps out his fraud by direct falsehood, and the old man, whose senses are now failing, is at last with difficulty deceived. It cannot be denied that this is a most reprehensible transaction, and presents a truly painful picture; in which a mother conspires with one son in order to cheat her aged husband, with a view to deprive another son of his rightful inheritance. Justification is here impossible; but it should not be forgotten in the estimate we form that there was a promise in favor of Jacob; that Jacob's qualities had endeared him to his mother; and that the prospect which arose was dark to her and threatening when she saw the neglected

Esau at the head of the house, and his hateful wives assuming command over herself.

(3) Jacob's Departure. Punishment in this world often follows close upon the heels of transgression. Fear seized the guilty Jacob, who is sent by his father, at the suggestion of Rebekah, to the original seat of the family, in order that he might find a wife among his cousins, the daughters of his mother's brother, Laban the Syrian. Before he is dismissed Jacob again receives his father's blessing, the object obviously being to keep alive in the young man's mind the great promise given to Abraham, and thus to transmit that influence which, under the aid of Divine providence, was to end in placing the family in possession of the land of Palestine, and in so doing to make it 'a multitude of people.'

(4) Dream at Bethel. It appears, from the language which Jacob employs (Gen. xxviii:16) in relation to the dream that he had when he tarried all night upon a certain plain on his journey eastward, that his idea of the Deity was little more than that of a local god—'Surely the Lord is in *this* place, and *I knew it not.*'

(5) Meets Rachel. Jacob, on coming into the land of the people of the East, accidentally met with Rachel, Laban's daughter, to whom, with true eastern simplicity and politeness, he showed such courtesy as the duties of pastoral life suggest and admit. And here his gentle and affectionate nature displays itself under the influence of the bonds of kindred and the fair form of youth: 'Jacob kissed Rachel, and lifted up his voice and wept.'

(6) Serves Laban. After he had been with his uncle the space of a month, Laban inquires of him what reward he expects for his services. He asks for the 'beautiful and well-favored Rachel.' His request is granted on condition of a seven years' service—a long period truly, but to Jacob 'they seemed but a few days for the love he had to her.' When the time was expired, the crafty Laban availed himself of the customs of the country, in order to substitute his elder and 'tender-eyed' daughter Leah. In the morning Jacob found how he had been beguiled; but Laban excused himself, saying, 'It must not be done in our country, to give the younger before the firstborn.' Another seven years' service gains for Jacob the beloved Rachel. Leah, however, has the compensatory privilege of being the mother of the firstborn—Reuben. Three other sons successively follow, namely, Simeon, Levi, and Judah, sons of Leah. This fruitfulness was a painful subject of reflection to the barren Rachel, who employed language on this occasion that called forth a reply from her husband which shows that, mild as was the character of Jacob, it was by no means wanting in force and energy (Gen. xxx:2). An arrangement, however, took place, by which Rachel had children by means of her maid, Bilhah, of whom Dan and Naphtali were born. Two other sons—Gad and Asher—were born to Jacob of Leah's maid, Zilpah. Leah herself bare two more sons, namely, Issachar and Zebulun; she also bare a daughter, Dinah. At length Rachel herself bare a son, and she called his name Joseph.

Most faithfully, and with great success, had Jacob served his uncle for fourteen years, when he became desirous of returning to his parents. At the urgent request of Laban, however, he is induced to remain. The language employed upon this occasion (Gen. xxx:25, *sq.*) shows that Jacob's character had gained considerably during his service both in strength and comprehensiveness;

but the means which he employed in order to make his bargain with his uncle work so as to enrich himself prove too clearly that his moral feelings had not undergone an equal improvement, and that the original taint of prudence, and the sad lessons of his mother in deceit, had produced some of their natural fruit in his bosom.

(7) Departs from Laban. The prosperity of Jacob displeased and grieved Laban, so that a separation seemed desirable. His wives were ready to accompany him. Accordingly he set out, with his family and his property, 'to go to Isaac his father in the land of Canaan.' It was not till the third day that Laban learned that Jacob had fled, when he immediately set out in pursuit of his nephew, and after seven days' journey overtook him in Mount Gilead. Laban, however, is divinely warned not to hinder Jacob's return. Reproach and recrimination ensued. Even a charge of theft is put forward by Laban, 'Wherefore hast thou stolen my gods?' In truth, Rachel had carried off certain images which were the objects of worship. Ignorant of this misdeed, Jacob boldly called for a search, adding, 'With whomsoever thou findest thy gods let him not live.' A crafty woman's cleverness eluded the keen eye of Laban. Rachel, by an appeal which one of her sex alone could make, deceived her father. Thus one sin begets another; superstition prompts to theft, and theft necessitates deceit.

Laban's conduct on this occasion called forth a reply from Jacob, from which it appears that his service had been most severe, and which also proves that however this severe service might have encouraged a certain servility, it had not prevented the development in Jacob's soul of a high and energetic spirit, which when roused could assert its rights and give utterance to sentiments just, striking, and forcible, and in the most poetical phraseology.

Peace, however, being restored, Laban, on the ensuing morning, took a friendly, if not an affectionate farewell of his daughters and their sons, and returned home. Meanwhile Jacob, going on his way, had to pass near the land of Seir, in which Esau dwelt. Remembering his own conduct and his brother's threat, he was seized with fear, and sent messengers before in order to propitiate Esau.

(8) News from Esau. Jacob, informed by his messengers that Esau came to meet him with four hundred men, justly suspected his intentions were murderous, and sent off before him a large present of two hundred and twenty goats, two hundred and twenty sheep, thirty milk-camels with their colts, forty kine, and ten bulls, twenty she-asses and ten foals. These he divided into five droves, and ordered the drivers of each to tell Esau, as they met him, that it was a present to him. By this means he hoped to appease his brother's anger.

(9) Wrestling All Night. Immediately preceding his interview with Esau, Jacob passed the night in wrestling with 'a man,' who is afterwards recognized as the angel of God, and who at length overcame Jacob by touching the hollow of his thigh. His name also was on this event changed by the mysterious antagonist into Israel, 'for as a prince hast thou power with God and with men, and hast prevailed' (Gen. xxxii:28). It is added that on this account his descendants abstained from eating the thigh of slaughtered animals.

(10) Reconciled to Esau. Having crossed the Jabbok, he divided his family into three divisions,

that, if Esau murdered the foremost, the others might flee. The two handmaids, and their children, went foremost; Leah and hers next; and Rachel and Joseph last, that she might have most opportunity to get off, if there was danger. According to Jacob's direction, they all, in the humblest manner, did obeisance to Esau. Partly moved by this deportment, but chiefly by the hand of God, Esau met Jacob with the most tender affection, generously refused his present, because he had much wealth already; but Jacob urged him, because, said he, 'I have everything, and have had the great happiness to meet thee in kindness and love.' So Esau accepted of the present, and they became friends once more.

(11) Departs for Bethel. Having, by the misconduct of Hamor the Hivite and the hardy valor of his sons, been involved in danger from the natives of Shechem in Canaan, Jacob is divinely directed, and under the Divine protection proceeds to Bethel, where he is to 'make an altar unto God that appeared unto thee when thou fleddest from the face of Esau thy brother.' Obedient to the Divine command, he first purifies his family from 'strange gods,' which he hid under 'the oak which is by Shechem;' after which God appeared to him again with the important declaration, 'I am God Almighty,' and renewed the Abrahamic covenant.

(12) Death of Rachel. While journeying from Beth-el to Ephrath, his beloved Rachel lost her life in giving birth to her second son, Benjamin. At length Jacob came to his father Isaac at Mamre, the family residence, in time to pay the last attentions to the aged patriarch.

(13) Loss of Joseph. Not long after this bereavement Jacob was robbed of his beloved son Joseph through the jealousy and bad faith of his brothers. This loss is the occasion of showing us how strong were Jacob's paternal feelings; for on seeing what appeared to be proofs that 'some evil beast had devoured Joseph,' the old man 'rent his clothes, and put sackcloth upon his loins, and mourned for his son many days, and refused to be comforted.'—'I will go down into the grave unto my son mourning' (Gen. xxxvii:35).

(14) Egypt. A widely extended famine induced Jacob to send his sons down into Egypt, where he had heard there was corn, without knowing by whose instrumentality. The patriarch, however, retained his youngest son Benjamin, 'lest mischief should befall him,' as it had befallen Joseph. The young men returned with the needed supplies of corn. They related, however, that they had been taken for spies, and that there was but one way in which they could disprove the charge, namely, by carrying down Benjamin to 'the lord of the land.' This Jacob vehemently refused: 'Me have ye bereaved; Joseph is not, and Simeon is not, and ye will take Benjamin; my son shall not go down with you; if mischief befall him, then shall ye bring down my gray hairs with sorrow to the grave' (Gen. xlii:38). The pressure of the famine, however, at length forced Jacob to allow Benjamin to accompany his brothers on a second visit to Egypt; whence in due time they brought back to their father the pleasing intelligence, 'Joseph is yet alive, and he is governor over all the land of Egypt.' How naturally is the effect of this on Jacob told, 'and Jacob's heart fainted, for he believed them not.' When, however, they had gone into particulars, he added, 'Enough, Joseph my son is yet alive; I will go and see him before I die.'

Encouraged 'in the visions of the night,' **Jacob**

57

goes down to Egypt. (B. C. about 2050.) 'And Joseph made ready his chariot, and went up to meet Israel his father, to Goshen, and presented himself unto him; and he fell on his neck, and wept on his neck a good while (Gen. xlii:46). And Israel said unto Joseph, Now let me die, since I have seen thy face, because thou art yet alive (Gen. xlvi:29). Joseph proceeded to conduct his father into the presence of the Egyptian monarch, when the man of God, with that self consciousness and dignity which religion gives, instead of offering slavish adulation, 'blessed Pharaoh.' Struck with the patriarch's venerable air, the king asked, 'How old art thou?' What composure and elevation is there in the reply, 'The days of the years of my pilgrimage are an hundred and thirty years; few and evil have the days of the years of my life been, and have not attained unto the days of the years of the life of my fathers in the days of their pilgrimage;' and Jacob blessed Pharaoh, and went out from before Pharaoh (Gen. xlvii:8-10).

Jacob, with his sons, now entered into possession of some of the best land of Egypt, where they carried on their pastoral occupations, and enjoyed a very large share of earthly prosperity. The aged patriarch, after being strangely tossed about on a very rough ocean, found at last a tranquil harbor, where all the best affections of his nature were gently exercised and largely unfolded. After a lapse of time Joseph, being informed that his father was sick, went to him, when 'Israel strengthened himself, and sat up in his bed.' He acquainted Joseph with the Divine promise of the land of Canaan which yet remained to be fulfilled, and took Joseph's sons, Ephraim and Manasseh, in place of Reuben and Simeon, whom he had lost.

(15) Death. Then having convened his sons, the venerable patriarch pronounced on them also a blessing, which is full of the loftiest thought, expressed in the most poetical diction, and adorned by the most vividly descriptive and engaging imagery, showing how deeply religious his character had become, how freshly it retained its fervor to the last, and how greatly it had increased in strength, elevation and dignity:—'And when Jacob had made an end of commanding his sons, he gathered up his feet into the bed and yielded up the ghost, and was gathered unto his people' (Gen. xlix:33). (B. C. 1846.)

                                 J. R. B.

2. Character. In Jacob may be traced a combination of the quiet patience of his father with the acquisitiveness which seems to have marked his mother's family; and in Esau, as in Ishmael, the migratory and independent character of Abraham was developed into the enterprising habits of a warlike hunter-chief. Jacob, whose history occupies a larger space, leaves on the reader's mind a less favorable impression than either of the other patriarchs with whom he is joined in equal honor in the New Testament (Matt. viii:11). But in considering his character we must bear in mind that we know not what limits were set in those days to the knowledge of God and the sanctifying influence of the Holy Spirit. A timid, thoughtful boy would acquire no self-reliance in a secluded home. There was little scope for the exercise of intelligence, wide sympathy, generosity, frankness. Growing up a stranger to the great joys and great sorrows of natural life—deaths, and wedlock, and births; inured to caution and restraint in the presence of a more vigorous brother; secretly stimulated by

a belief that God designed for him some superior blessing, Jacob was perhaps in a fair way to become a narrow, selfish, deceitful, disappointed man. But, after dwelling for more than half a lifetime in solitude, he is driven from home by the provoked hostility of his more powerful brother. Then in deep and bitter sorrow the outcast begins life afresh long after youth has passed, and finds himself brought first of all unexpectedly into that close personal communion with God which elevates the soul, and then into that enlarged intercourse with men which is capable of drawing out all the better feelings of human nature. An unseen world was opened. God revived and renewed to him that slumbering promise over which he had brooded for threescore years, since he learned it in childhood from his mother. Angels conversed with him. Gradually he felt more and more the watchful care of an ever present spiritual Father. Face to face he wrestled with the representative of the Almighty. And so, even though the moral consequences of his early transgressions hung about him, and saddened him with a deep knowledge of all the evil of treachery and domestic envy, and partial judgment, and filial disobedience, yet the increasing revelations of God enlightened the old age of the patriarch; and at last the timid "supplanter," the man of subtle devices, waiting for the salvation of Jehovah, dies the "soldier of God" uttering the messages of God to his remote posterity. (Smith, *Bib. Dict.*)

3. Deception of Isaac Palliated. Bishop Horne gives the following considerations on this subject:

The proposition of deceiving Isaac originated not with Jacob, but with Rebekah. Jacob remonstrated against it, as likely to bring a curse upon him, rather than a blessing; nor would consent to perform his part, till she engaged to take all the blame on herself: "On me be thy curse, my son; only obey my voice."

From this speech, and from the earnestness and solicitude discovered by Rebekah, it may not unfairly be presumed that she had some special reason for what she did; that Isaac was about to take a wrong step in a concern of great moment, which ought to be prevented, and could be prevented by no other means.

The rectitude of Rebekah's judgment seems evidently to have been recognized and allowed by Isaac, at the conclusion of the matter. For though he had blessed Jacob, intending to bless Esau, yet, as if recollecting himself, he confirmed and ratified that blessing in the strongest terms: "Yea, and he shall be blessed." Still further—at sending him away, he again repeated the benediction, in the most solemn and affecting manner: "God give thee the blessing of Abraham!" It is difficult to assign any other reason why, if so disposed, upon discovering the fraud, he might not have reversed the proceeding. Nay, by the kind meeting of the brothers afterwards, one should be inclined to suppose that Esau himself acquiesced at length in the propriety of what had been done.

If such were the case, Isaac was only deceived into what was right, and what he himself acknowledged to be so in the conclusion. The deception was like those often practiced by physicians for the benefit of their patients; and casuists must decide upon it in the same manner. The offense of Jacob is certainly alleviated, if not entirely taken off, by the circumstance of Rebekah pledging herself to bear the blame; as the conduct of Rebekah seems justified by that of Isaac ratifying and confirming to Jacob the blessing originally intended for Esau. Upon the whole, if there were any offense, it was one that might be forgiven; and if God, notwithstanding, continued to bless Jacob, he did forgive it, and had reasons for so doing. (Bp. Horne's *Works*, vol. vi. pp. 477, 478.) (See REBEKAH; ESAU; MARRIAGE.)

Figurative. The *"God of Jacob"* (Exod. iii:6; iv:5; 2 Sam. xxiii:1; Ps. xx:1; Is. ii:3) or simply *"Jacob"* (Ps. xxiv:6, where the term אֱלֹהַּ, *el-o'ah*, God, appears to have been dropped from the text), and *"mighty One of Jacob"* (Ps. cxxxii:2), are titles of *Jehovah* as the national deity. For the *house* or *family of Jacob*, i. e., the Israelites, we have the *"House of Jacob"* (Exod. xix:3; Is. ii:5, 6; viii:17, etc.), *"Seed of Jacob"* (Jer. xxxiii:26), *"the sons of Jacob"* (1 Kings xviii:31; Mal. iii:6), *"congregation of Jacob"* (Deut. xxxiii:1), and simply *"Jacob"* (Num. xxiii:7, 10, 21, 23; xxiv:5, 17, 19, etc.); and the expression *"in Jacob"* (Gen. xlix:7; Lam. ii:3), i. e., among the Jewish people. (McC. & Str. *Bib. Cyc.*)

II. Jacob, the father of Joseph, the husband of the Virgin Mary (Matt. i:15, 16). (B. C. before 40.)

JACOB'S WELL (jā-kob's wĕl). See SHECHEM.

JADA (jā'dà), (Heb. יָדָע, *yaw-daw'*, knowing), a brother of Shammai, son of Onam and grandson of Jerahmeel (1 Chron. ii:28, 32), B. C. 1450.

JADAU (jā'dạu or ja-dā'u), (Heb, יַדַּי, *yaddav'*, knowing), one of the Bene-Nebo who had taken a strange wife (Ezra x:43), B. C. 457.

JADDUA (jad-dū'à), (Heb. יַדּוּעַ, *yad-doo'ah*), knowing).

1. A Levite who sealed the covenant with Nehemiah (Neh. x:21). (B. C. 445.)

2. Son of Jonathan, the high priest. The last of the high priests spoken of in the Old Testament (Neh. xii:11, 22). (B. C. 520.)

JADON (jā'dŏn), (Heb. יָדוֹן, *yaw-done'*, judge), called the Meronothite; he assisted in repairing the walls of Jerusalem (Neh. iii:7), B. C. 445.

JAEL (jā'el), (Heb. יָעֵל, *yaw-ale'*, wild goat).

Wife of Heber, the Kenite. When Sisera, the general of Jabin, had been defeated, he alighted from his chariot, hoping to escape best on foot from the hot pursuit of the victorious Israelites. On reaching the tents of the nomade chief, he remembered that there was peace between his sovereign and the house of Heber, and therefore applied for the hospitality and protection to which he was thus entitled. This request was very cordially granted by the wife of the absent chief, who received the vanquished warrior into the inner part of the tent, where he could not be discovered by strangers without such an intrusion as eastern customs would not warrant. She also brought him milk to drink, when he asked only water; and then covered him from view, that he might enjoy repose the more securely. As he slept, a horrid thought occurred to Jael, which she hastened too promptly to execute. She took one of the tent nails, and with a mallet, at one fell blow, drove it through the temples of the sleeping Sisera. (B. C. about 1406.) Soon after, Barak and his people arrived in pursuit, and were shown the lifeless body of the man they sought (Judg. iv:17-22). This deed drew much attention to Jael, and preserved the

camp from molestation by the victors; and there is no disputing that her act is mentioned with great praise in the triumphal song wherein Deborah and Barak celebrated the deliverance of Israel (Judg. v:24).

It does not seem difficult to understand the object of Jael in this painful transaction. Her motives seem to have been entirely prudential, and, on prudential grounds, the very circumstance which renders her act the more odious—the peace subsisting between the nomade chief and the king of Hazor—must, to her, have seemed to make it the more expedient. She saw that the Israelites had now the upper hand, and was aware that, as being in alliance with the oppressors of Israel, the camp might expect very rough treatment from the pursuing force; which would be greatly aggravated if Sisera were found sheltered within it. This calamity she sought to avert, and to place the house of Heber in a favorable position with the victorious party. She probably justified the act to herself by the consideration that as Sisera would certainly be taken and slain, she might as well make a benefit out of his inevitable doom as incur utter ruin in the attempt to protect him. Attempts have been made to vindicate her, because of the usages of ancient warfare, of rude times and ferocious manners. There was not, however, warfare, but peace between the house of Heber and the prince of Hazor. The existence of a set of usages in any civilized society under which the act of Jael would be deemed right is hardly conceivable.

JAGUR (jā'gur), (Heb. יָגוּר, *yaw-goor'*, lodging-place), a town of Southern Judah (Josh. xv:21), which remains unidentified.

JAH (jäh), (Heb. יָהּ, *yawh;* Gr. Κύριος, Lat. *dominus*, Lord), an abbreviated form of Jehovah (Ps. lxviii:4). Jah is also used in the construction of many Hebrew words, and is indicative of some real or supposed excellency of the object of application.

JAHATH (jā'hăth), (Heb. יַחַת, *yakh'ath*, oneness, union).

1. A grandson of Gershom, son of Judah (1 Chron. iv:2). (B. C. 1600.)

2. A descendant of Gershom, son of Levi (1 Chron. vi:20). (B. C. 1450.)

3. A son of Shelomoth, one of the Levite representatives of the Kohathite family of Izhab (1 Chron. xxiv:22). (B. C. 1014.)

4. A Levite who helped oversee the repairing of the Temple (2 Chron. xxxiv:12). (B. C. 623.)

5. Head of the most numerous house of his tribe, the son of Shimei, son of Laadan (1 Chron. xxiii:10, 11). Possibly the same as **2**, the errors having crept in through transcription.

JAHAZ (jā'hăz), (Heb. יַהַץ, *yah'hats*, trodden down, a thrashing floor), a town beyond Jordan where the decisive battle was fought between the Israelites and Sihon, king of the Ammonites (Num. xxi:23; Deut. ii:32; Judg. xi:20). The city was assigned to the Merarite Levites from the tribe of Reuben (Josh. xiii:18; xxi:36; 1 Chron. vi:78). The Babylonian conquerors overran Jahaz, which is involved in the denunciations uttered in Jer. xlviii:21, 34; Is. xv:4. The city was at this time in the hands of the Moabites.

JAHAZA (jā'ha-zà), **JAHAZAH** (jā'ha-zah) **and JAHZAH** (jäh'zah), (Josh. xxi:36; Jer. xlviii:21), other forms of JAHAZ (which see).

JAHAZIAH (jā'ha-zī'ah), (Heb. יַחְזְיָה, *yakh-zeh-yaw'*, whom Jehovah beholds), one of the sons of Tikvah, who with others was appointed by Ezra to determine what Jews had taken foreign wives (Ezra x:15), B. C. 459.

JAHAZIEL (ja-hā'zi-el), (Heb. יַחֲזִיאֵל, *yakh-az-ee-ale'*, beheld by God).

1. One of the heroes who deserted the cause of Saul and joined David at Ziklag (1 Chron. xii:4). (B. C. 1055.)

2. A priest and trumpet blower with Benaiah whose duty it was to appear in the ministrations before the ark after David had brought it to Jerusalem (1 Chron. xvi:6). (B. C. 1043.)

3. A Kohathite Levite whose house is enumerated in the time of David (1 Chron. xxiii:19; xxiv:23). (B. C. between 1618 and 1014.)

4. The son of Zechariah, a Levite, who was inspired by the Holy Spirit to uplift Jehoshaphat by his predictions of decided triumph, when he was anticipating the coming of a great army of Moabites, Ammonites, and Mehunims (2 Chron. xx:14-17). (B. C. about 896.)

5. One of the sons of Jahaziel, chief of the "sons of Shechaniah" who returned from the captivity with Ezra (Ezra viii:5), (B. C. before 459.) The text here is probably corrupt and should read "Sons of Zathoe," or "Zathi."

JAHDAI (jäh'da-ī), (Heb. יֶהְדָּי, *yeh-daw'ee*, Judaistic), a father of six sons spoken of in the genealogy of Caleb (1 Chron. ii:47), B. C. before 612.

JAHDIEL (jäh'di-el), (Heb. יַחְדִּיאֵל, *yakh-dee-ale'*, unity of God), one of the heads of the half-tribe of Manasseh (1 Chron. v:24), B. C. 720.

JAHDO (jäh'do), (Heb. יַחְדּוֹ, *yakh-doe'*, his union), a Gadite, son of Buz and father of Jeshishai (1 Chron. v:14), B. C. between 1093 and 782.

JAHLEEL (jäh'le-el), (Heb. יַחְלְאֵל, *yakh-leh-ale'*, hoping in God), the third of the three sons of Zebulun (Gen. xlvi:14; Num. xxvi:26), and the founder of the family of Jahleelites (B. C. 1700). The name occurs as Jahziel (1 Chron. vii:13).

JAHLEELITES, THE (jäh'le-el-ītes), (Heb. הַיַּחְלְאֵלִי, *hah-yakh-leh-ay-lee'*), the descendants of Jahleel (Num. xxvi:26).

JAHMAI (jäh'ma-ī), (Heb. יַחְמַי, *yakh-mah'ee*, hot), one of the heads of the house of Tola, grandson of Issachar (1 Chron. vii:2), B. C. about 1658.

JAHZAH (jäh'zah), (Heb. יַהְצָה, *yah-tsaw'*, a place stamped, threshing floor, 1 Chron. vi:78). See JAHAZ.

JAHZEEL (jäh'ze-el), (Heb. יַחְצְאֵל, *yakh-tseh-ale'*, God apportions), the first-named of the four sons of Naphtali (Gen. xlvi:24), founder of the family of the Jahzeelites. The name is mentioned in 1 Chron. vii:13 and spelled Jahziel; Heb. *Yachtsiel'* (B. C. 1856).

JAHZEELITES (jäh'ze-el-ītes), (Heb. יַחְצְאֵלִי, *yakh-tseh-a-lee'*, Num. xxvi:48). See JAHZEEL.

JAHZERAH (jäh'ze-rah), (Heb. יַחְזֵרָה, *yakh-zay-raw'*, led back by God), a priest of Immer (1 Chron. ix:12), and son of Meshullam, probably the same as AHASAI (Neh. xi:13), B. C. ante 536.

JAILER (jāl'ēr), (Gr. δεσμοφύλαξ, *des-mof-oo'lax*, guard of a prisoner), the keeper of Paul and Silas when imprisoned at Philippi (Acts xvi:23, 27, 36).

JAIR (jā'ir), (Heb. יָאִיר, *yaw-ere'*, enlightener).

1. A son of Segub, of the tribe of Manasseh by his mother, and of Judah by his father. He appears to have distinguished himself in an expedition against the kingdom of Bashan, the time of which is disputed, but may probably be referred to the last year of the life of Moses (B. C. 1451). It seems to have formed part of the operations connected with the conquest of the country east of the Jordan. He settled in the part of Argob bordering on Gilead, where we find twenty-three villages named collectively Havoth-jair, or 'Jair's villages' (Num. xxxii:41; Deut. iii:14; Josh. xiii:30; 1 Chron. ii:22; 1 Kings iv:13).

2. Eighth judge of Israel, of Gilead, in Manasseh, beyond the Jordan; and therefore, probably descended from the preceding, with whom, indeed, he is sometimes confounded. He ruled twenty-two years, and his opulence is indicated in a manner characteristic of the age in which he lived. 'He had thirty sons, that rode on thirty ass-colts, and they had thirty cities, which are called Havoth-jair, in the land of Gilead.'

The twenty-three villages of the more ancient Jair were probably among the thirty which this Jair possessed (Judg. x:3). (B. C. 1210.)

3. A Benjamite, father of Mordecai, the uncle of Esther (Esth. ii:5). (B. C. before 518.)

4. (Heb. יָעוּר, *yaw-oor*, wooded; marg. text '*yaör'*). Father of Elhanan, a hero of David's army who slew Lahmi, Goliath's brother (1 Chron. xx:5). In the parallel passage (2 Sam. xxi:19) the name is *Jaare-oregim*, through a probable error of transcription. (B. C. before 1018.)

JAIRITE (jāir-īte), (Heb. הַיָּאִרִי, *hah-yaw-e-ree'*), an appellation of Ira, chief ruler or priest of David (2 Sam. xx:26), supposed to have been the descendant of the great Jair of Manasseh. (See JAIR, 2.)

JAIRUS (jā'i-rŭs), (Gr. Ἰάειρος, *ee-ah'i-ros*), a ruler of the synagogue at Capernaum, whose daughter Jesus restored to life (Mark v:22; Luke viii:41), A. D. 27.

JAKAN (jā'kan), (Heb. יַעֲקָן, *yah-ak-awn'*, wrestler, 1 Chron. i:42). The name is identical with JAAKAN (which see).

JAKEH (jā'keh), (Heb. יָקֶה, *yaw-keh'*, obedient, pious), is taken by some to be the name of the father of Agur, author of the Apothegms (Prov. xxx:1 *sq.*). According to the traditional view it is supposed to be a name of mystical import applied to David. Others identify Agur with Solomon, making Jakeh a name of David.

JAKIM (jā'kim), (Heb. יָקִים, *yaw-keem'*, whom God lifts up).

1. At the head of the twelfth course of priests of David (1 Chron. xxiv:12). (B. C. 1014.)

2. A Benjamite, one of the sons of Shimhi resident at Jerusalem (1 Chron. viii:19). (B. C. about 588.)

JALON (jā'lon), (Heb. יָלוֹן, *yaw-lone'*, lodging, abiding), a son of Ezra mentioned in the genealogy of Judah (1 Chron. iv:17), B. C. about 1618.

JAMBRES and JANNES (jăm'brēz and jăn'nēz), (Gr. Ἰαμβρῆς καὶ Ἰαννῆς, *ee-am-brace'* and *ee-an-nace'*, probably of Egyptian etymology), two of the Egyptian magicians who attempted by their enchantments to counteract the influence on Pharaoh's mind of the miracles wrought by Moses.

Their names occur nowhere in the Hebrew scriptures, and only once in the New Testament (2 Tim. iii:8). The Apostle Paul became acquainted with them, most probably, from an ancient Jewish tradition, or, as Theodoret expresses it, *'from the unwritten teaching of the Jews.'* They are found frequently in the Talmudical and Rabbinical writings, but with some variations. The Pythagorean philosopher, Numenius, mentions these persons in a passage preserved by Eusebius (*Præp. Evang.* ix:8), and by Origen (*c. Cels.* iv. p. 198, Ed. Spencer) ; also Pliny (*Hist. Nat.* xxx:1). There was an ancient apocryphal writing entitled *Jannes and Jambres*, which is referred to by Origen (*in Matt. Comment.* sec. 117; *Opera*, v. 29), and by Ambrosiaster, or Hilary the Deacon; it was condemned by Pope Gelasius. (Lightfoot's *Sermon on Jannes and Jambres; Works*, vii. 89; Lardner's *Credibility*, pt. ii. ch. xxxv. in *Works*. vii. 381.)   J. E. R.

JAMES (jāmz), (Gr. Ἰάκωβος, *ee-ak'o-bos*). Three persons of this name are mentioned in the New Testament.

1. James, the Son of Zebedee (Matt. iv: 21) and brother of the evangelist John (Mark v:37). Their occupation was that of fishermen, probably at Bethsaida, in partnership with Simon Peter (Luke v:10). On comparing the account given in Matt. iv:21, Mark i:19, with that in John i, it would appear that James and John had been acquainted with our Lord, and had received him as the Messiah some time before he called them to attend upon him statedly—a call with which they immediately complied. Their mother's name was Salome. We find James, John, and Peter associated on several interesting occasions in the Savior's life. They alone were present at the Transfiguration (Matt. xvii:1; Mark ix:2; Luke ix:28) ; at the restoration to life of Jairus's daughter (Mark v:37; Luke viii:51) ; and in the garden of Gethsemane during the agony (Mark xiv:33; Matt. xxvi:37; Luke xxii:39). With Andrew they listened in private to our Lord's discourse on the fall of Jerusalem (Mark xiii:3). James and his brother appear to have indulged in false notions of the kingdom of the Messiah, and were led by ambitious views to join in the request made to Jesus by their mother (Matt. xx:20-23; Mark x:35).

Character. From Luke ix:54, we may infer that their temperament was warm and impetuous. On account, probably, of their boldness and energy in discharging their Apostleship, they received from their Lord the appellation of Boanerges, or *Sons of Thunder* (For the various explanations of this title given by the fathers see Suiceri, *Thes. Eccles.* s. v. Βροντή, and Lücke's *Commentar*, Bonn, 1840; *Einleitung*, c. i. sec. 2, p. 17). James was the first martyr among the Apostles. Clement of Alexandria, in a fragment preserved by Eusebius (*Hist. Eccles.* i. 9), reports that the officer who conducted James to the tribunal was so influenced by the bold declaration of his faith as to embrace the gospel and avow himself also a Christian; in consequence of which he was beheaded at the same time.

2. James the Less, the Son of Alphæus, one of the twelve Apostles (Mark iii:18; Matt. x:3; Luke vi:15; Acts i:13). His mother's name was Mary (Matt. xxvii:56; Mark xv:40); in the latter passage he is called James *the Less* (ὁ μικρὸς, the Little), either as being younger than James the son of Alphæus, or on account of his low stature (Mark xvi:1; Luke xxiv:10).

3. James, the Brother of the Lord (ὁ ἀδελφὸς τοῦ Κυρίου, Gal. i:19). Whether this James is iden-

tical with the son of Alphæus is a question which Dr. Neander pronounces to be the most difficult in the Apostolic history, and which cannot yet be considered as decided. We read in Matt. xiii:55, 'Is not his mother called Mary, and his brethren James, and Joses, and Simon, and Judas?' and in Mark vi: 3, 'Is not this the carpenter, the son of Mary, and brother of James and Joses, and of Juda and Simon? and are not his sisters here with us?' Those critics who suppose the terms of affinity in these and parallel passages to be used in the more lax sense of near relations have remarked that in Mark xv:40, mention is made of 'Mary, the mother of James the less and of Joses;' and that in John xix:25, it is said, 'there stood by the cross of Jesus his mother and his mother's sister, Mary, the wife of Cleophas, and Mary Magdalene;' they therefore infer that the wife of Cleophas is the same as the sister of the mother of Jesus, and, consequently, that James (supposing Cleophas and Alphæus to be the same name, the former according to the Hebrew, the latter according to the Greek orthography) was a *first cousin* of our Lord, and, on that account, termed his *brother*, and that the other individuals called the brethren of Jesus stood in the same relation.

Objection. Against this view it has been alleged that in several early Christian writers James, the brother of the Lord, is distinguished from the son of Alphæus; that the identity of the names Alphæus and Cleophas is somewhat uncertain; and that it is doubtful whether the words 'his mother's sister,' in John xix:25, are to be considered in apposition with those immediately following. (Lardner's *Supplement*, ch. xvi., *Works*, vi. p. 174; Neander, *History of the Planting*, etc. vol. ii. pp. 9, 22, Eng transl.) Dr. Niemeyer enumerates not less than five persons of this name, by distinguishing the son of Alphæus from James the Less, and assuming that the James last mentioned in Acts i:13 was not the brother, but the father of Judas (*Charakteristik der Bibel*, Halle, 1830, i. 399.)   J. E. R.

JAMES, EPISTLE OF. This is called by Eusebius (*Hist Eccles.* ii. 23) the first of the Catholic Epistles. As the writer simply styles himself *James, a servant of God and of the Lord Jesus Christ*, doubts have existed, both in ancient and modern times, respecting its authorship.

1. Author. It has been ascribed to no less than four different persons, viz., James, the son of Zebedee; James, the son of Alphæus (who were both of the number of the twelve apostles) ; James, our Lord's brother (Gal. i:19) ; and to an anonymous author, who assumed the name of James in order to procure authority to a supposititious writing.

The chief authority for ascribing this epistle to James the son of Zebedee, is the inscription to the Syriac manuscript, published by Widmandstadt, wherein it is termed 'the earliest writing in the New Testament,' and to an Arabic MS. cited by Cornelius a Lapide. Isidore of Seville, and other Spanish writers interested in maintaining that James traveled into Spain (Calmet's *Commentary*) ; assert that James the son of Zebedee visited in person the 'twelve tribes scattered' through that as well as other countries, and afterwards addressed to them this epistle. The Mozarabic liturgy also supports the same view, and the old Italic, published by Martianay, contains the inscription *Explicit Epistola Jacobi fil. Zebedæi*. But this opinion has obtained very few suffrages; for, as Calmet has observed (*Pref. to his Commentary*), it is not credible that so great progress had been made among the dispersed Jews before the martyrdom of James, which took place at Jerusalem about A. D. 42; and if the author, as has been commonly supposed, alludes to St. Paul's Epistles to the Romans (A. D. 58) and Galatians (A. D. 55), it would be a manifest anachronism to ascribe this epistle to the son of Zebedee.

The claim to the authorship of the epistle, therefore, rests between James 'the Lord's brother,' and James the son of Alphæus. In the preceding article the difficult question, whether these names do not, in fact, refer to the same person, has been examined: it suffices, in this place, to state that no writer who regards James 'the Lord's brother' as distinct from James the son of Alphæus, has held the latter to be the author of the epistle: and therefore, if no claim be advanced for the son of Zebedee, James 'the brother of the Lord' remains the only person whom the name at the head of this epistle could be intended to designate.

Hegesippus, cited by Eusebius (*Hist. Eccles.* ii: 23), acquaints us that James, the brother of Jesus, who obtained the surname of the Just, governed the church of Jerusalem along with, or after the apostles. Eusebius (*l. c.*) relates that he was the first who held the episcopate of Jerusalem (Jerome says for thirty years); and both he and Josephus (*Antiq.* xx:9, 1) give an account of his martyrdom. To him, therefore, is the authorship of an epistle addressed to the Jewish Christians with good reason ascribed. The other opinion, which considers the epistle as pseudepigraphical, is treated below.

2. Authenticity and Canonicity. Eusebius, as above, observes that 'James, the brother of Jesus, who is called Christ, is said to have written the first of the Catholic epistles; but it is to be observed that it is considered spurious. Not many of the ancients have mentioned it, nor that called the Epistle of Jude. . . . Nevertheless, we know that these, with the rest, are publicly read in most of the churches.' To the same effect St. Jerome:—'St. James, surnamed the Just, who is called the Lord's brother, is the author of only one epistle, one of the seven called Catholic, which, however, is said to have been published by some other who assumed his name, although in the progress of time it gradually acquired authority.' Dr. Lardner is of the opinion that this statement of St. Jerome is a mere repetition of that of Eusebius. It was also rejected in the fourth century by Theodore of Mopsuestia, and in the sixth by Cosmas Indicopleustes. (See ANTILEGOMENA.) It is, however, cited by Clemens Romanus in his first or genuine *Epistle to the Corinthians* (ch. x., comp. with James ii:21, 23; and ch. xi, comp. with James ii:25, and Heb. xi:31). It seems to be alluded to in the Shepherd of Hermas, 'Resist the devil, and he will be confounded and flee from you.' It is also generally believed to be referred to by Irenæus (*Hær.* iv:16, 2), 'Abraham believed God, and it was,' etc. Origen cites it in his *Comment. on John* i:xix, iv, 306, calling it, however, the *reputed* epistle of James. (See ANTILEGOMENA.) We have the authority of Cassiodorus for the fact that Clemens Alexandrinus commented on this epistle; and it is not only expressly cited by Ephrem Syrus (*Opp. Grœc.* iii:51, 'James the brother of our Lord says "weep and howl,"' together with other references), but it forms part of the ancient Syriac version, a work of the second century, and which contains no other of the *Antilegomena*, except the Epistle to the Hebrews. But though 'not quoted expressly by any of the Latin

fathers before the fourth century' (Hug's *Introduction*), it was, soon after the time of the Council of Nice, received both in the eastern and western churches without any marks of doubt, and was admitted into the canon along with the other scriptures by the councils of Hippo and Carthage. Nor (with the above exceptions) does there appear to have been a voice raised against it since that period until the era of the Reformation, when the ancient doubts were revived by Erasmus (who maintains that the author was not an apostle, *Annot. in New Testament*), Cardinal Cajetan (*Comment.in 7 Canonic. Epist.*, 1532), and Luther. Cajetan observes that 'the salutation is unlike that of any other of the apostolical salutations, containing nothing of God, of grace, or peace, but sending greetings after the profane manner, from which, and his not naming himself an apostle, the author is rendered uncertain.

(1) Luther's Opinion. We have already referred to Luther's opinion (See ANTILEGOMENA), who is generally accused of calling this an *epistle of straw*. The following are his words:—'This epistle in comparison with the writings of John, Paul, and Peter, is a right strawy epistle (*eine rechte stroherne epistel*), being destitute of an evangelic character' (*Præf. to New Testament*). And again (*Præf. to James and John*): 'This epistle, although rejected by the ancients, I notwithstanding praise and esteem, as it teaches no doctrines of men, and strenuously urges the law of God. But, to give my opinion frankly, though without prejudice to any other person, I do not hold it to be the writing of an apostle—and these are my reasons; first, it directly opposes St. Paul and other scriptures in ascribing justification to works, saying that Abraham was justified by works, whereas St. Paul teaches that Abraham was justified by faith without works; . . . but this James does nothing but urge on to the law and its works, and writes so confusedly and unconnectedly that it appears to me like as if some good pious man got hold of a number of sayings from the apostle's followers, and thus flung them on paper; or it is probably written by some one after the apostle's preaching.' The centuriators of Magdeburg follow the same train of thought. 'In addition to the argument derived from the testimony of antiquity, there are other and by no means obscure indications from which it may be collected that the authors of these epistles (James and Jude) were not apostles. The Epistle of James differs not slightly from the analogy of doctrine, in ascribing justification not to faith alone, but to works, and calls the law "a law of liberty," whereas the law "generates to bondage." . . . Nor is it unlikely that it was written by some disciple of the apostles at the close of this (the first) century, or even later' (*Cent.* i. 1. 2, c. 4 col. 54). The same sentiments are followed by Cheunits, Brentius, and others among the Lutherans, and among the Greeks by Cyril Lucaris, patriarch of Constantinople in the seventeenth century (*Lettres Anecdotes de Cyrille Lucar*, Amst. 1718, Letter vii. p. 85).

(2) Arrangement by Luther. As Luther was the first who separated the canonical from the deutero-canonical or apocryphal books in the Old Testament (see DEUTERO-CANONICAL BOOKS), he also desired to make a similar distinction in the New (see ANTILEGOMENA; HAGIOGRAPHA); but the only variation which he actually adopted consisted in his placing the Epistle to the Hebrews between the Epistles of John and James. (See JUDAS OR JUDE.)

(3) Arrangement by Calvinists. The Calvinists, who never questioned the authority of this epistle, followed the arrangement of the Council of Laodicea, in which the Epistle of James ranks as the first of the Catholic epistles; while the Council of Trent followed the order of the Council of Carthage and of the apostolical canons, viz., four Gospels, Acts, fourteen epistles of Paul (viz., Romans, 1 and 2 Corinthians, Galatians, Ephesians, Philippians, Colossians, 1 and 2 Thessalonians, 1 and 2 Timothy, Titus, Philemon, Hebrews), 1 and 2 Peter, 1, 2, and 3 John, James, Jude, Apocalypse. The Lutherans themselves soon acquiesced in the decisions of the universal church in regard to the canon of the New Testament, until the controversy, which had long slept, was again revived in Germany in modern times (De Wette, *Einleitung*).

(4) Opinion of De Wette. De Wette maintains that although this epistle was anterior to the Clementine, it could not have been written so early as the time of James, principally because the degree of tranquility and comfort which appears to have been enjoyed by those to whom the epistle was addressed, seems to him to be inconsistent with the state of persecution which the Christians were subject to during the lifetime of St. James. He conceives it to have been written by some one who assumed the name of James in order to give authority to his arguments against Paul's doctrine of justification.

(5) Opinion of Neander. But no one in modern times has combated this opinion with greater success than Neander (*History of the First Planting of the Christian Church*, vol. ii). Neander (whose reasonings will not admit of abridgment) maintains that there is no discrepancy whatever between St. Paul and St. James; that it was not even the design of the latter to oppose any misapprehension respecting St. Paul's doctrine, but that they each addressed different classes of people from different standpoints, using the same familiar examples. 'Paul,' he says, 'was obliged to point out to those who placed their dependence on the justifying power of the works of the law the futility of such works in reference to justification, and to demonstrate that justification and sanctification could proceed only from the faith of the gospel: James, on the other hand, found it necessary to declare to those who imagined that they could be justified in God's sight by faith in the Jewish sense . . . that this was completely valueless if their course of life were not conformed to it.' And in another place he observes that James 'received the new spirit under the old forms, similarly to many Catholics who have attained to free evangelical convictions, and yet have not been able to disengage themselves from the old ecclesiastical forms; or, like Luther, when he had already attained a knowledge of justification by faith, but before he was aware of the consequences flowing from it as opposed to the prevalent doctrines of the church.'

3. Age of the Epistle. By those who consider James the Just, bishop of Jerusalem, to have been the author of this epistle, it is generally believed to have been written shortly before his martyrdom, which took place A. D. 62, six years before the destruction of Jerusalem, whose impending fate is alluded to in chap. v. Neander fixes its date at a time preceding the separate formation of Gentile Christian churches, before the relation of Gentiles and Jews to one another in the Christian Church had been brought under discussion, in the period of the first spread of Christianity in Syria, Cilicia, and the adjacent regions. It is addressed to Jewish Christians, the descendants of the twelve tribes; but the fact of its being written in Greek exhibits the author's desire to make it generally available to Christians.

4. Contents and Character. This epistle commences with consolations addressed to the faithful converts, with exhortations to patience, humility, and practical piety (ch. i:1-27). Undue respect to persons is then condemned, and love enjoined (ch. ii). Erroneous ideas on justification are corrected (ii. 13-26), the temerity of new teachers is repressed (iii:12); an unbridled tongue is inveighed against, and heavenly wisdom contrasted with a spirit of covetousness (13-18). Swearing is prohibited (v:12). The efficacy of prayer is proved by examples, and the unction of the sick by the presbyters, together with prayer and mutual confession, are enjoined as instruments of recovery and of forgiveness of sins (v:14-18). The approaching advent of the Lord is foretold (v:7).

The style of this epistle is close and sententious, and is characterized by Calmet as consisting of 'expressions thrown together without connection, and adorned by poetical similitudes.' It has, however, been illustrated by no one with greater felicity than by the learned and pious Bishop of Limerick, who has adduced many examples from James of poetical parallelism—which was the principal characteristic of Hebrew poetry. In reference to one of these passages (iii. 1-12) the bishop observes that 'its topics are so various, and, at first sight, so unconnected, not to say incongruous, that it may be thought a rash undertaking to explore the writer's train of thought, and to investigate the probable source and the orderly progress of his ideas—an evidence at once most brilliant and satisfactory that the easy flow of a great mind, when concentrated on a great object, will be found at least as logically just as it may be poetically beautiful.' 'His general manner,' he observes, 'combines the plainest and most practical good sense with the most vivid and poetical conception; the imagery various and luxuriant; the sentiments chastened and sober; his images, in truth, are so many analogical arguments, and if, at the first view, we are disposed to recreate ourselves with the poet, we soon feel that we must exert our hardier powers to keep pace with the logician' (Jebb's *Sacred Literature*). Seiler designates the style of this epistle as 'sometimes sublime and prophetical, nervous, and full of imagery' (*Biblical Hermeneutics*, sec. 315; Wright's translation, p. 548). Wetstein (note to ch. iv:5) conceives the author to have been familiar with the book of Wisdom. The eloquence and persuasiveness of St. James' Epistle, as an ethical composition, are such as must command universal admiration.   W. W.

JAMIN (jā'min), (Heb. יָמִין, *yaw-meen'*, right side or hand).

1. Second mentioned of the sons of Simeon (Gen. xlvi:10; Exod. vi:15; 1 Chron. iv:24). (B. C. 1856.)

2. A son of Ram and a great man in the house of Hezron (1 Chron. ii:27). (B. C. 1650.)

3. A priest who assisted Ezra and Nehemiah in expounding the law (Neh. viii:7). (B. C. 410.)

JAMINITES, THE (jā'min-ītes, the), (Heb. הַיָּמִינִי, *hay-yaw-mee-nee'*), the descendants of Jamin, 1 (Num. xxvi:12). (See Jamin.)

JAMLECH (jăm'lek), (Heb. יַמְלֵךְ, *yam-lake'*, He—i. e. God—makes king), a Simeonite chieftain (1 Chron. iv:34), probably in the time of Hezekiah (see ver. 41), whose family invaded the valley of Gedor (B. C. 711).

JANGLING (jăn'glĭng), (Gr. ματαιολογία, *mat-ah-yol-og-ee'yah*, 1 Tim. i:6), babbling, vain talking, and in Tit. i:10 the noun, "vain talkers," are those who utter senseless, empty things.

JANNA (jăn'nà), (Gr. Ἰαννά, *ee-an-nah'*), father of Melchi and son of Joseph (Luke iii:24), B. C. 200.

JANNES and JAMBRES (jăn'nēz and jăm'-brēz). See JAMBRES AND JANNES.

JANOAH (ja-nō'ah), (Heb. יָנוֹחַ, *yaw-no'akh*, or יָנוֹחָה, *yaw-no'khaw*, quiet).

1. A north Galilee place in the land of Napthali, taken in the first invasion of Tiglath-Pileser (2 Kings xv:29). Hunîn now stands on the spot that would answer to the location of the ancient Jonoah (Porter, *Handbook, Syr. and Pal.* p. 444).

2. A place on the boundary of Ephraim (Josh. xvi:6, 7). It is doubtless the modern Yanûn, about ten miles southeast of *Nablûs* (Neapolis). (Van de Velde ii. 303; Robinson, iii. 297.)

JANOHAH (ja-nō'hah). See JANOAH, 2.

JANUM (jā'num), (Heb. יָנוּם, *yaw-neem'*, asleep), a town of Judah (Josh. xv:53), probably not far from Hebron. It has not been positively identified, though it may be *Jenheh*.

JAPHETH (jā'pheth), (Heb. יֶפֶת, *yeh'feth*, widespread).

A son of Noah. In Gen. v:32 he is mentioned third in order, but some think, from Gen. x:21 (comp. ix:23) that he was the eldest of Noah's sons, begotten one hundred years before the flood. In Gen. x:2, *sq.*, he is called the progenitor of the extensive tribes in the west (of Europe) and north (of Asia), of the Armenians, Medes, Greeks, Thracians, etc. The Arabian traditions (D'Herbelot, *Bibl. Orient.*) rank Japheth among the prophets, and enumerate eleven of his sons, the progenitors of as many Asiatic nations, viz. Gin or Dshin (Chinese), Seklab (Slavonians), Manshuge, Gomari, Turk (Turks), Khalage, Khozar, Ros (Russians), Sussan Gaz, and Torage. In these traditions he is therefore simply called progenitor of the Turks and Barbarians.
E. M.

JAPHIA (ja-phī'à), (Heb. יָפִיעַ, *yaw-fee'ah*, bright, splendid).

1. King of Lachish at the time the Israelites conquered Canaan (Josh. x:3). He was one of the five kings who instigated a confederacy against Joshua and lost his life at Makedah. (B. C. 1618.)

2. One of fourteen sons born unto David in Jerusalem (2 Sam. v:15; 1 Chron. iii:7; xiv:6). (B. C. after 1000.)

3. A town spoken of as the boundary of Zebulon as it ascended from Daberath to Japhia (Josh. xix:12). Robinson identifies the place with *Yafa*, a mile and a half southwest of Nazareth. (*Researches* iii. 194; Porter, *Handbook*. p. 385.)

JAPHLET (jăph'let), (Heb. יַפְלֵט, *yaf-late'*, whom God delivers).

A son of Heber, the son of Asher, and called the father of three sons and a daughter (1 Chron. vii:32, 33). (B. C. between 1856 and 1658.)

JAPHLETI (jăph'le-tī), (Heb. יַפְלֵטִי, *yaf-lay-tee'*).

A branch of the descendants of Japhlet seem to have settled along the boundary between Ephraim and Dan (Josh. xvi:3). Others regard the name as a trace of one of the original Canaanitish settlements.

JAPHO (jā'pho), (Heb. יָפוֹ, *yaw-fo'*, beauty, Josh. xix:46), otherwise called JOPPA, now known as *Yâfa* (2 Chron. ii:16; Ezra iii:7).

"It is 150 *stadia* from Antipatris, six miles west of Rama, and ten hours from Jerusalem at the west end of the mountain road." (Robt. Young, LL.D. *Concordance.*)

JARAH (jā'rah), (Heb. יַעְרָה, *yah-raw'*, honey 1 Chron. ix:42), a short form of JEHOADAH (which see).

JAREB (jā'reb), (Heb. יָרֵב, *yaw-rabe'*, adversary), occurs as a proper name in Hos. v:13; x:6, where a "King Jareb" is spoken of as the false refuge and the final subjugator of the kingdom of Israel.

It is probably a figurative title of the king of Assyria (Hos. v:13; x:6), and from its parallelism with Asshur it is applicable to the country rather than the ruler himself.

JARED (jā'red), (Heb. יֶרֶד, *yeh'red*, descent, low ground).

1. An antediluvian patriarch, father of Enoch (Gen. v:15-20; 1 Chron. i:2; Luke iii:37). (B. C. 3712.) He died at the age of 962. The name appears also as JERED.

2. A man of Judah, apparently the son of Ezra by Jehudijah. He is signalized as the founder of Gedor (1 Chron. iv:18). The A. V. has JERED.

JARESIAH (jăre-sī'ah), (Heb. יַעֲרֶשְׁיָה, *yah-ar-esh-yaw'*, origin uncertain), one of the Bene-Jeroham, a chief of the Benjamites resident at Jerusalem (1 Chron. viii:27), B. C. before 588.

JARHA (jär'hà), (Heb. יַרְחָע, *yar-khaw'*).

The Egyptian slave of a Hebrew named Sheshan, who married the daughter of his master, and was, of course, made free. As Sheshan had no sons, his posterity is traced through this connection (1 Chron. ii:34-41), which is the only one of the kind mentioned in Scripture. Jarha was doubtless a proselyte, and the anecdote seems to belong to the period of the sojourn in Egypt, although it is not easy to see how an Egyptian could there be slave to an Israelite. (B. C. ante 1658.) (See Hervey, *Genealogy*, p. 34.)

Some have supposed that the name of Jarha's wife was Ahlai (ver. 31; comp. 34), but the masculine form of the word, and the use of Ahlai (xi:41) for a man, is opposed to this conclusion.

It has been thought by others that Ahlai was an error in transcription for Attai (ver. 35); still others that Ahlai was a name given to Jarha on his incorporation into the family of Sheshan, while others again suppose that Ahlai was a son of Sheshan, born after the marriage of his daughter.

JARIB (jā'rib), (Heb. יָרִיב, *yaw-rebe'*, adversary).

1. Son of Simeon (1 Chron. iv:24); called *Jachin* (Gen. xlvi:10). (See JACHIN.)

2. One of the "chief heads sent by Ezra to Jerusalem from Babylon to procure a company of priests" (Ezra viii:16). (B. C. 459.)

3. One of the priests of the house of Jeshua who married a foreign wife, whom Ezra forced him to put away (Ezr. x:18). (B. C. 459.)

JARMUTH (jär'muth), (Heb. יַרְמוּת, *yar-mooth'*, height, hill).

1. A town in the low country of Judah (Josh. xv:35); inhabited after the Babylonian captivity (Neh. xi:29). Its king, Piram, was one of the five who were put to death at Makedah, for having planned to slay Gibeon who had formed an alliance with Israel (Josh. x:3, 5, 23; xii:11). It has been identified with *Yarmuk*, seven miles northeast of Beit-Jibrin (Porter, *Handbook*, p. 281).

2. A city of Issachar, given to the Levites of Gershom; it was a city of refuge (Josh. xxi:29), called *Remeth* (Josh. xix:21) and *Ramoth* (1 Chron. vi:73).

JAROAH (ja-rō'ah), (Heb. יָרוֹחַ, *yaw-ro'akh*, new moon), a chief man of the tribe of Gad resident in Bashan (1 Chron. v:14), B. C. before 740.

JASHEN (jā'shen), (Heb. יָשֵׁן, *yaw-shane'*, sleeping), named in 2 Sam. xxiii:32 as the father of several of David's bodyguard. He is called HASHEM in the parallel passage (1 Chron. xi:34), B. C. 1000.

JASHER, BOOK OF (jā'sher, bŏŏk ŏv), (Heb. סֵפֶר הַיָּשָׁר, *say'fer hay-yaw-shawr'*, the book of the righteous).

This work is no longer extant, but cited in Josh. x:13, and 2 Sam. i:18. In the former it is thus introduced: 'And the sun stood still, and the moon stayed, until the people had avenged themselves upon their enemies. Is not this written in the book of Jasher? So the sun stood still in the midst of heaven, and hasted not to go down about a whole day,' etc. And in the passage referred to in 2 Sam. i, it stands thus (ver. 17): 'And David lamented with this lamentation over Saul and over Jonathan his son;' (ver. 18): 'Also he bade them teach the children of Judah the use of the bow; behold, it is written in the book of Jasher.' After which follows the lamentation of David. As the word Jasher signifies *just* or *upright,* by which word it is rendered in the margin of our Bibles, this book has been generally considered to have been so entitled as containing a history of *just men.*

(1) A Poetical Work. Bishop Lowth, however (*Prælect.* pp. 306, 307), conceives, from the poetical character of the two passages cited from it, that it was most probably a collection of national songs written at various times, and that it derived its name from *jashar,* 'he sang.'

(2) Various Conjectures. It is, at the same time, by no means an improbable conjecture that the book was so called from the name of its author. Josephus (*Antiq.* v. 1. 17) speaks of the book of Jasher as one of the 'books laid up in the temple.' Jerome is of the opinion that the book of Jasher is no other than the book of Genesis, which is also the opinion of some Jewish authors. Others suppose it to include the Pentateuch (see Calmet's *Comment. in loc*). Mr. Horne (*Introd.* vol. i.) asserts that 'some understand by the book of Jasher the book of Judges, as mention is therein made of the standing still of the sun.' (?) From the passage above referred to, 2 Sam. i:18—'Also he bade them teach the children of Israel the use of the bow'— it has been supposed by some (see Dr. Adam Clarke's *Comment. in loc.,* and Horne's *Introd.* vol. i.) that the book of Jasher contained a treatise on archery; but it has been observed (see Parker's translation of De Wette's *Introd.* vol. i. p. 301) that, according to the ancient mode of citation, which consisted in referring to some particular word in the document, 'the bow' which the children of Israel were to be taught indicated

the poetical passage from the book of Jasher in which the 'bow of Jonathan' is mentioned (2 Sam. i:22). De Wette's translator supposes that our English translators of the Bible were perhaps ignorant of this manner of reference, and he instances this as a 'ludicrous instance.'

(3) Rabbinical Works. The Book of Jasher is also the title of two Rabbinical works, one of which was written by Rabbi Tham in the thirteenth century, and printed at Cracow in 1617. It is a treatise on Jewish laws. The other was printed in 1625, and contains (see Batolocci's *Bibliotheca Rabbinica,* and Horne's *Introd.* vol. ii., *Bibliogr. App.*) some curious but many fabulous narrations; among other things, that it was discovered at the destruction of the temple in possession of an old man, who was found shut up in some place of concealment, and who had a great number of Hebrew books. It was brought to Spain, preserved at Seville, and published at Naples.

In the year 1751 there was published in London, by a type-founder of Bristol named Jacob Ilive, a book entitled '*The Book of Jasher, with Testimonies and Notes explanatory of the Text: to which is prefixed Various Readings:* translated into English from the Hebrews by Alcuin of Britain, who went a pilgrimage into the Holy Land.' This book was noticed in the *Monthly Review* for December, 1751, which describes it as a palpable piece of contrivance, intended to impose upon the credulous and ignorant, to sap the credit of the books of Moses, and to blacken the character of Moses himself. The reviewer adds that 'the *Book of Jasher* appears to have been constructed in part from the apocryphal writings of the Rabbins; in part from a cento of various scraps stolen from the Pentateuch; and in the remainder from the crazy imaginings of the author' (Ilive). Prefixed to this work is a narrative professing to be from the pen of Alcuin himself, giving a detailed account of his discovery of the Hebrew book of Jasher, in the city of Gazna in Persia, during a pilgrimage which he made from Bristol to the Holy Land, and of his translation of the same into English. This clumsy forgery in modern English, which appeared with the chapters of the thirteenth century, and the numerical versicular divisions of the sixteenth, having been exposed at the time of its appearance, and sunk into well-merited oblivion, was again revived in 1827, when it was reprinted at Bristol, and published in London as a new discovery of the *Book of Jasher.* A prospectus of a second edition of this reprint was issued in 1833 by the editor, who herein styles himself the *Rev.* C. R. Bond. Both Ilive's and Bond's editions contain the following pretended testimony to the value of the work from the celebrated Wycliffe: 'I have read the book of Jasher twice over, and I much approve of it, as a piece of great antiquity and curiosity, but I cannot assent that it should be made a part of the canon of Scripture.'

(4) Sun and Moon Standing Still. The chief interest connected with the Scriptural book of Jasher arises from the circumstance that it is referred to as the authority for the standing still of the sun and moon. There are few passages in Biblical literature the explanation of which has more exercised the skill of commentators than this celebrated one. We shall here give a brief account of the most generally received interpretations.

The first is that which maintains that the passage is to be *literally* understood. According to this interpretation, which is the most ancient, the sun itself, which was then believed to revolve round the earth, stayed its course for a day. Those who take this view argue that the theory of the *diurnal motion of the earth*, which has been the generally received one since the time of Galileo and Copernicus, is inconsistent with the Scripture narrative. Notwithstanding the general reception of the Copernican system of the universe, this view continued to be held by many divines, Protestant as well as Roman Catholic, and was strenuously maintained by Buddeus (*Hist.·Eccles. V. T.*, Halle, 1715, 1744, p. 828, *sq.*) and others in the last century.

But in more recent times the matter has been explained so as to make it accord with the now received opinion respecting the earth's motion, and the Scripture narrative supposed to contain rather an optical and popular, than a literal account of what took place on this occasion. So that it was in reality the earth, and not the sun, which stood still at the command of Joshua.

Another opinion is that first suggested by Spinoza (*Tract. Theolog.-Politic.* c. ii. p. 22, and c. vi.), and afterwards maintained by Le Clerc (*Comment. in loc.*), that the miracle was produced by refraction only, causing the sun to appear above the horizon after its setting, or by some other atmospherical phenomena, which produced sufficient light to enable Joshua to pursue and discomfit his enemies.

(5) Quotation from Poetical Work. Others believe with Wakefield that the book of Jasher was a poetical work written to celebrate the wonderful military achievements of Israel, and that the author of the book of Joshua merely quoted this passage without expecting any one to understand it as history.

It will be seen that the sense of the narrative in Joshua is complete without this quotation which is duly credited to the book of Jasher. Neither historians nor poets expect such descriptions to be cramped within the bonds of literal interpretation. We find often similar expressions in modern verse, and it is frequently noted in the early poets among the Romans and also the Greeks; for instance in the Iliad we find:

"They fought like fire conglob'd; nor hadst thou deemed
The sun exempt from danger, nor the moon."

Yet no one would suppose that Homer intended to convey the idea that the sun or moon was in actual danger of destruction in consequence of the furious fighting before the walls of Troy.

An illustration very similar to that used in the book of Jasher is found in the *Odyssey*, where it is said that:

"Pallas backward held the rising day,
The wheels of night retarding, to detain
The gay Aurora in the wavy main."

When a historian makes a quotation from a poetical work and duly credits it as in the case of Joshua, it is not supposed that his readers will interpret a rhetorical hyperbole as literal history.

(6) Opinion of Maimonides. The last opinion we shall mention is that of the learned Jew Maimonides (*More Nevo.* ii. c. 53), viz. that Joshua only asked of the Almighty to grant that he might defeat his enemies before the going down of the sun, and that God heard his prayer, inasmuch as before the close of day the five kings with their armies were cut in pieces. Grotius, while he admitted that there was no difficulty in the Almighty's arresting the course of the sun,

or making it reappear by refraction, approved of the explanation of Maimonides, which has been since that period adopted by many divines, including Jahn, among the Roman Catholics (who explains the whole as a sublime poetical trope, *Introd.* p. ii. sec. 30), and among orthodox Protestants, by a writer in the Berlin *Evangelische Kirchenzeitung*, Nov. 1832, supposed to be the editor, Professor Hengstenberg (Robinson's *Biblical Repository*, 1833, vol. iii, p. 791, *sq.* See Hopkins' *Plumbline Papers*, Auburn, 1862, ch. vii.).

JASHOBEAM (ja-shō'be-ăm),(Heb. יָשָׁבְעָם, *yaw-shob-awm'*, returning people).

1. The chief of David's captains, who came to him at Ziklag and distinguished himself and his band by slaying 300 men at one time (1 Chron. xi:11). He is the same with Adino the Eznite (2 Sam. xxiii:8), the difference in the Hebrew being slight. (See EZNITE.)

The exploit of breaking through the host of the Philistines to procure David a draught of water from the well of Bethlehem is ascribed to the three chief heroes, and therefore to Jashobeam, who was the first of the three (2 Sam. xxiii:13-17; 1 Chron. xi:15-19).

2. A man named among the Korhites who came to David at Ziklag (1 Chron. xii:6). (B. C. 1053.)

3. There is mention of a Jashobeam who commanded 24,000, and did duty in David's court in the month Nisan (1 Chron. xxvii:2). He was the son of Zabdiel; if, therefore, he was the same as the first Jashobeam, his patronymic of 'the Hachmonite' must be referred to his race rather than to his immediate father.

JASHUB (jăsh'ub), (Heb. יָשׁוּב, *yaw-shoob'*, he who returns).

1. The son of Issachar, who founded the family of the Jashubites (Num. xxvi:24; 1 Chron. vii:1); called JOB (Gen. xlvi:13). (B. C. 1856).

2. One of the "sons" or former inhabitants of Bani whom Ezra forced to put away his foreign wife (Ezra x:29). (B. C. 459.)

JASHUBI-LEHEM (jăsh'u-bī-lē'hem), (Heb. יָשֻׁבִי לֶחֶם, *yaw-shoo'be-leh'khem*, returner of bread), apparently a descendant of Shelah (1 Chron. iv:22), B. C. about 995. By others it is supposed to mean Naomi and Ruth, who returned (from *jashubi* "to return") to Bethlehem after the famine. Perhaps, however, it is a place, and, from its connection with Maresha, situated on the western side of the tribe.

JASHUBITES, THE (jash'ub-ītes), (Heb. יָשֻׁבִי, *yaw-shoo-bee'*), the descendants of JASHUB, son of Issachar (Num xxvi:24).

JASIEL (jā'si-el), (Heb. יַעֲשִׂיאֵל, *yah-as-ee-ale'*, God creates). See JAASIEL.

JASON (jā'son), (Gr. Ἰάσων, *ee-as'oan*, a common Greek name frequently used by the Hellenizing Jews for *Jesus* or *Joshua*), a kinsman of St. Paul and his host at Thessalonica, where the Jews forced his house in order to seize the Apostle.

Not finding the Apostle, they dragged Jason himself and some other converts before the magistrates, who released them with an admonition (A. D. 53). Jason appears to have accompanied the Apostle to Corinth (Acts xvii:5-9; Rom. xvi:21).

JASPER (jăs'pēr).

1. The last stone in the breastplate of the high-priest, and the first in the foundations of the new Jerusalem (Exod. xxviii:20; Rev. xxi:19).

2. Jasper is an opaque species of quartz, of different colors, often banded or spotted, and susceptible of a high polish. The dark green kind is supposed to be the variety of the Bible. From the apparent inconsistency of Rev. iv:3; xxi:11 with the opaque character of this stone, it has been suggested that some transparent gem was denoted by jasper in the New Testament—perhaps the diamond or the translucent chalcedony.

JATHNIEL (jăth'ni-el), (Heb. יַתְנִיאֵל, *yath-nee-ale'*, whom God bestows), fourth son of Meshelemiah, a doorkeeper in the tabernacle (1 Chron. xxvi:2), B. C. 1014.

JATTIR (jăt'tir), (Heb. יַתִּיר, *yat-teer'*, redundant), one of the nine cities which were given out of Judah to the Levites of Kohath's family (Josh. xv:48; xxi:14; 1 Chron. vi:57).

It was here David used to meet his friends in his early wandering days (1 Sam. xxx:27). It was the possible home of his two Ithrite heroes (2 Sam. xxiii:38; 1 Chron. xi:40). It may be identical with the modern Attir, fifteen miles south of Hebron (Robinson, *Researches*, ii. 194, 625).

JAVAN (jā'van), (Heb. יָוָן, *yaw-vawn'*, effervescing).

1. The fourth son of Japheth (Gen. x:2, 4; 1 Chron. i:5, 7). (B. C. post 2514.) The interest connected with his name arises from his being the supposed progenitor of the original settlers in Greece and its isles. (See NATIONS, DISPERSION OF.)

2. A country or city of Arabia Felix from which the Syrians imported stores of iron, cassia, and calamus. The name appears in Is. lxvi: 19, where it is coupled with Tarshish, Pul, and Lud, and more particularly with Tubal and the "isles afar off," as representatives of the Gentile world; again in Ezek. xxvii:13, where it is coupled with Tubal and Meshech, as carrying on considerable commerce with the Tyrians, who imported from these countries slaves and brazen vessels; in Dan. viii:21; x:20; xi:2, in reference to the Macedonian empire; and lastly in Zech. ix: 13, in reference to the Græco-Syrian empire, where Alexander is called the king of Javan. Javan was evidently the name given by the Hebrews to Greece. Sayce, in his *Higher Criticism* states that a Yivâna or "Ionian," is referred to in one of the cuneiform tablets found at Tel-el-Amarna, which corresponds letter for letter with the Hebrew Javan. (See TELL AMARNA, TABLETS OF.)

JAVELIN (jăv'lĭn). See ARMS, ARMOR.

JAW (ja), (Heb., usually לְחִי, *lekh-ee'*, rendered jawbone), jaws, Ps. xxii:15; jaw teeth, Prov. xxx:14.

JAZER (Heb. יַעְזֵר, *yah-zare'*, 1 Chron. vi:81; xxvi:31), a city of Gilead on the east of Jordan, taken from the Amorites (Num. xxi:32), and afterwards given to the Levites. It is now in ruins (Josh. xiii:25, xxi:39; 1 Chron. vi:81; Num. xxxii:1, 3, 35; 2 Sam. xxiv:5). In the time of David it was occupied by the Hebronites (1 Chron. xxvi:31).

JAZIZ (jā'ziz), (Heb. יָזִיז, *yaw-zeez'*, prominent), a Hagarite who had charge of David's flocks, probably east of the Jordan (1 Chron. xxvii:31), B. C. 1014.

JEALOUSY (jĕl'ŭs-ў), (Heb. קִנְאָה, *kin-aw'* ; Gr. ζῆλος, *dzay'los*), properly, suspicion of a wife's fidelity (Num. v:14).

(1) In general it is that particular uneasiness which arises from the fear that some rival may rob us of the affection of one whom we greatly love, or suspicion that he has already done it. The first sort of jealousy is inseparable from love, before it is in possession of its object; the latter is unjust, generally mischievous, and always troublesome. **(2)** It is often used of Jehovah's sensitive regard for the true faith of his people (Exod. xx:5, etc.; 2 Cor. xi:2) ; used for anger or indignation, or intense interest for the welfare of another (Ps. lxxix:5; 1 Cor. x:22; Zech. i:14; viii:2). **(3)** Paul says to the Corinthians that he is jealous over them with a godly jealousy, that he might present them as a chaste virgin to Christ (2 Cor. xi:2). The word, however, is frequently used to express the vindictive acts of dishonored love. Thus the Psalmist (lxxix:5), representing the church as smarting under Divine judgments, occasioned by her infidelity to God, says, "How long, Lord, shall thy jealousy burn like fire?" (See also 1 Cor. x:22).

JEALOUSY, IMAGE OF (jĕl'ŭs-ў ĭm-ăj),(Heb. סֵמֶל הַקִּנְאָה, *say'mel hak-kin-aw'*), the image seen by Ezekiel in the vision of the abominations of Jewish idolatry (Ezek. viii:3, 5).

This was probably the obscene image of Baal or Asherah, which had been placed in the temple by Manasseh (2 Kings xxi:7).

JEALOUSY OFFERING (jĕl'ŭs-ў ŏf'fĕr-ĭng), (Heb. מִנְחַת קְנָאֹת, *min-khath' ken-aw-oth'*, literally, offering of jealousies, an intensive plural).

This was the name of a "meat offering" which a man, who suspected the fidelity of his wife without being able to prove her supposed guilt, had to bring to the priest, when she was to be subjected to the ordeal of the bitter waters (Num. v:11-31). After certain solemn and impressive preparations and actions the woman was given the water to drink upon which the dust of the pavement had been cast and with which a bitter substance had been mingled. (See *Comm*. Dr. Adam Clarke.)

Regarding the Waters of Jealousy Calmet says: "There is something extremely curious, if not inexplicable, in the solemn process prescribed in Num. v:11-31 for the detection and punishment of a woman who had excited her husband's jealousy, without affording him the ordinary means of proving her infidelity."

JEARIM (jē'a-rĭm), (Heb. יְעָרִים, *yeh-aw-reem'*, forests), a mountain named in specifying the northern boundary of the inheritance of Judah. It was a woody mountain, on which the city of Balah, or Kirjath-jearim, was situated (Josh. xv:10). Robinson (*New Researches* p. 154) identifies this with a ridge seven miles west of Jerusalem.

JEATERAI (je-ăt'e-rāi), (Heb, יְאָתְרַי, *yeh-aw-ther-ah'ee*, whom Jehovah leads), a Levite, son of Zerah, of the family of Gershom (1 Chron. vi:21); probably the same as ETHNI (ver. 41).

JEBERECHIAH (je-bĕr-e-ki'ah), (Heb. יְבֶרֶכְיָהוּ, *yeb-eh-rek-yaw'hoo*, whom Jehovah blesses), the father of a Zechariah whom Isaiah made a witness of his marriage to the "prophetess" (Is. viii:2), B. C. about 739.

JEBUS (jē'bus), (Heb. יְבוּס, *yeb-oos'* trodden), one of the names of Jerusalem derived from the ancient Canaanitish city which stood on one of its southwest hills, afterward called Zion (Josh. xv:8; xviii:16, 28; Judg. xix:10; 1 Chron. xi:4, 5). (See JERUSALEM.)

JEBUSI (je-bū'sĭ), (Heb. יְבוּסִי, *yeb-oo-see'*, the Jebusite), the name of the city Jebus (Josh. xv:8; xviii:16, 28). In the first passage the A. V. renders it "Jebusite."

JEBUSITE, JEBUSITES (jĕb'u-sīte, jĕb'u-sītes), (Hebrew always singular הַיְבוּסִי, *hah-yeb-oo-see'*, except that it is הַיְבֻסִי in 2 Sam. v:6; xxiv:16, 18; 1 Chron. xxi:18, and יְבוּסִי in 2 Sam. v:8; 1 Chron. xi:6; Zech. ix:7). The A. V. has "Jebusi" (Josh. xviii:16, 28).

This was one of the most powerful of the nations of Canaan, who settled about Mount Moriah, where they built Jerusalem, and called it Jebus, after the name of their founder (1 Chron. xi:4). They are recounted among the seven Canaanitish cities doomed to destruction (Gen. x:16; xv:21; Exod. iii:8, 17; xiii:5; Deut. vii: 1; xx:17; Josh. iii:10; ix:1; xi:3; xii:8; xxiv: 11; Judg. iii:5; 1 Kings ix:20; 1 Chron. i:14).

Although they were defeated with much slaughter, and Adonizedek, their king, slain by Joshua (Josh. x.), they were not wholly subdued, but were able to retain their city till after his death (Judg. i:8), and were not entirely dispossessed of it till the time of David (2 Sam. v). By that time the inveteracy of the enmity between the Hebrews and such of the original inhabitants as remained in the land had much abated, and the rights of private property were respected by the conquerors. This we discover from the fact that the site on which the temple afterwards stood belonged to a Jebusite named Araunah, from whom it was purchased by King David, who declined to accept it as a free gift from the owner (2 Sam. xxiv:18-25). This is the last we hear of the Jebusites.

In the apocryphal Acts of the Apostles there is an allusion to a cave in Cyprus "where the race of the Jebusites formerly dwelt." Also to "a pious Jebusite, a kinsman of Nero."

JECAMIAH (jĕk-a-mī'ah), (Heb. יְקַמְיָה, *yek-am-yaw'*, he who assembles the people), the fifth named son of King Jeconiah (1 Chron. iii:18) born during the captivity in Babylon (B. C. after 598). In 1 Chron. ii:41 the same name is rendered JEKAMIAH.

JECHOLIAH (jĕk-o-lī'ah), (Heb. יְכָלְיָה, *yek-ol-yaw'*, able through Jehovah), wife of King Amaziah of Judah and mother of his successor, Uzziah (2 Kings xv:2), B. C. 824-807.

JECHONIAS (jĕk-o-nī'as), (Gr. Ἰεχονίας, *ee-ek-o-ni'as*, the Greek form of the name of King JECONIAH, which see (Matt. i:11, 12).

JECOLIAH (jĕk-o-lī'ah), (Heb. יְכָלְיָה, *yek-ol-yaw'*, able through Jehovah, 2 Chron. xxvi:3). See JECHOLIAH.

JECONIAH (jĕk'o-nī'ah), (Heb. יְכָנְיָה, *yek-on-yaw'*, Jehovah establishes), a short form of Jehoiachin, last but one of the kings of Judah (1 Chron. iii:16, 17; Jer. xxiv:1, xxvii:20, xxviii:4; xxix:2; Esth. ii:6). (See JEHOIACHIN.)

JEDAIAH (je-dā'yà), (Heb. יְדָיָה, *yed-aw-yaw'*, praised of Jah).

1. Chief of the second course of priests after they were divided in the reign of David (1 Chron. xxiv:7). (B. C. 1014.)

2. A priest during the time of the high-priest Jeshua (1 Chron. ix:10; Neh. xi:10), and seemed to belong to Jeshua's family (Ezra ii:36; Neh. vii:39); probably identical with the Jedaiah in

Neh. xii:6, and the Jedaiah whom the prophet was directed to honor with a wreath (Zech. vi:10, 14). (B. C. 536-520.)

3. A man spoken of in the history of Simeon as settling in the valley of Gedor; father of Shimri and ancestor of Ziza (1 Chron. iv:37). (B. C. before 711.)

4. Son of Harumaph and one of the builders of the wall of Jerusalem after the return from captivity (Neh. iii:10). (B. C. 446.)

JEDIAEL (je-dī'a-el), (Heb. יְדִיעֲאֵל, *yed-ee-ah-ale'*, known of God).

1. A patriarch of the tribe of Benjamin, 17,-200 of whose descendants are enumerated as warriors in David's census (1 Chron. vii:6, 11): perhaps the same as Ashbel (1 Chron. viii:1).

2. A Korhite Levite, son of Meshelemiah, and doorkeeper of the temple in the reign of David (1 Chron. xxvi:1, 2). (B. C. 1014.)

3. The son of Shimri, a brave chief of Manasseh, who marched with David as he went to Ziklag (1 Chron. xi:45; xii:20). (B. C. before 1000.)

JEDIDAH (jĕd'i-däh), (Heb. יְדִידָה, *yed-ee-daw'*, darling or only one), mother of King Josiah, and daughter of Adaiah; she was the wife of King Amon (2 Kings xxii:1), B. C. 648-639.

JEDIDIAH (jĕd'i-dī'ah), (Heb. יְדִידְיָה, *yed-ee-deh-yaw'*, darling of Jehovah), a name bestowed on David's son Solomon by the Lord, through the prophet Nathan, in token of divine favor (2 Sam. xii:25).

JEDUTHUN (jĕd'u-thŭn), (Heb. יְדוּתוּן, *yed-oo-thoon'*, he who praises), a Levite of Merari's family, and one of the four great masters of the temple music (1 Chron. xvi:41, 42; xxv:1).

This name is also put for his descendants, who occur later as singers and players on instruments (2 Chron. xxxv:15; Neh. xi:17). In the latter signification it occurs in the superscriptions to Ps. xxxix; lxii; lxxvii; but Aben Ezra supposes it to denote here the requiring of a song, and Jarchi, of a musical instrument. (B. C. about 960.)

JEEZER (je-ē'zer), (Heb. אִיעֶזֶר, *ee-eh'zer*, helpless), son of Gilead (Num. xxvi:30); a short form of Abiezer (Josh. xvii:2, etc.). (See ABIEZER).

JEEZERITES (je-ē'zer-ītes), the descendants of JEEZER (which see) (Num. xxvi:30).

JEGAR-SAHADUTHA (jē'gar-sā-ha-dū'thà), (Chald. יְגַר שָׂהֲדוּתָא, *yeg-ar' sah-had-oo-thaw'*, heap of testimony), the Aramæan name given by Laban the Syrian to the heap of stones which he erected as a memorial of the covenant between Jacob and himself, while Jacob commemorated the same by setting up a pillar (Gen. xxxi:47). *Galeed*, a "witness heap," is given as the Hebrew equivalent.

JEHALELEEL (jē-ha-lē'le-el), (Heb. יְהַלֶּלְאֵל, *yeh-hal-lel-ale'*, praiser of God), a descendant of Judah, whose own immediate parentage is not known. Four of his sons are mentioned (1 Chron. iv:16), B. C. about 1618.

JEHALELEL (je-hăl'e-lĕl), (Hebrew same as above), a Merarite Levite, whose son, Azariah, took part in the restoration of the temple in the time of Hezekiah (2 Chron. xxix:12), B. C. 719.

JEHDEIAH (jeh-dē'iah or -yà), (Heb. יֶחְדְּיָהוּ, *yekh-deh-yaw' hoo*, unity of Jah).

1. A representative of the "sons" of Shubael who seems to have had charge of one of the divisions

in the temple service (1 Chron. xxiv:20. (B. C. 1014.)

2. A Meronothite who had charge of breeding stock for David and Solomon (1 Chron. xxvii: 30). (B. C. 1014.)

JEHEZEKEL (je-hĕz'e-kĕl), (Heb. יְחֶזְקֵאל, *yekh-ez-kale'*, God will strengthen).

A priest in David's time who commanded the twentieth course in the service of the house of Jehovah (1 Chron. xxiv:16).

JEHIAH (je-hī'ah), (Heb. יְחִיָּה, *yekh-ee-yaw'*, Jah liveth), one of the porters for the ark when brought by David to Jerusalem (1 Chron. xv:24); elsewhere (ver. 18) JEHIEL (which see).

JEHIEL (je-hī'el), (Heb. יְחִיאֵל, *yekh-ee-ale'*, God lives).

1. One of the rulers of the house of God who contributed to the renewal of the temple service in the time of Josiah (2 Chron. xxxv:8). (B. C. 623.)

2. A Levite "of the second degree," appointed by David to play upon a psaltery on the occasion of the removal of the ark to Jerusalem (1 Chron. xv:18, 20; xvi:5), in which former passage he and those named with him are called "porters." He is apparently the *Jehiah* of ver. 24. By some he is identified with the Gershonite head of the Bene-Laadan in the time of David (xxiii:8), who had charge of the treasures (xxix:8). If so, his descendants were called *Jehieli,* Jehielites (xxvi. 21). (B. C. 982.)

3. "Son of Hachmoni," who seems to have been royal tutor in the later part of David's reign (1 Chron. xxvii:32). (B. C. about 1030.)

4. In the original text, Jehuel, a Levite during the reign of Hezekiah who assisted him in his religious reforms (2 Chron. xxix:14), and had charge later of the sacred offerings (xxxi:13). (B. C. 726.)

5. Father of Obadiah; he with 218 males returned from Babylon with Ezra (Ezra viii:9). (B. C. before 459.)

6. The second named of the six brothers of Jehoram, and son of King Jehoshaphat (2 Chron. xxi:2). These brothers were all murdered by Jehoram upon his accession (ver. 4). (B. C. 850.)

7. Shechaniah's father, of the "sons" of Elam (Ezra x:2); probably the same as the one who put away a foreign wife (Ezra x:26). (B. C. 459.)

8. A priest who also had to put away his wife (Ezra x:21). (B. C. 459.)

9. A forefather of Saul the king (1 Chron. ix: 35). (B. C. about 1618.)

10. One of the sons of Hotham the Aroerite, of the guard of David, included in the supplementary list (1 Chron. xi:44). (B. C. 1046.)

JEHIELI (je-hī'e-lī), (Heb. יְחִיאֵלִי, *yekh-ee-ay-lee'*), Jehielite (1 Chron. xxvi:21).

JEHIZKIAH (jē'hiz-kī'ah), (Heb. יְחִזְקִיָּהוּ, *yekh-iz-kee-yaw'hoo*, same as Hezekiah, whom Jehovah strengthens), son of Shallum, one of the heads of the tribe of Ephraim, who, at the suggestion of the prophet Oded, insisted on clemency towards prisoners from Judah (2 Chron. xxviii:12), B. C. about 738.

JEHOADAH (je-hō'a-dah), (Heb. יְהוֹעַדָּה, *yeh-ho-ad-daw'*, whom Jehovah adorns), son of Ahaz and great grandson to Meribbaal, a descendant of Saul (1 Chron. viii:36), called JARAH in the parallel passage (1 Chron. ix:42), B. C. after 1037.

JEHOADDAN (jē-ho-ăd'dan), (Heb. יְהוֹעַדִּן, *yeh-ho-ad-dawn'*, Jehovah pleased, same as Jehoadah), Queen to King Joash, (2 Kings xiv:2; 2 Chron. xxv:1), B. C. 862-837.

JEHOAHAZ (je-hō'a-hăz), (Heb. יְהוֹאָחָז, *yeh-ho-aw-khawz'*, Jehovah sees).

1. Son of Jehu, king of Israel, who succeeded his father (B. C. 856), and reigned seventeen years (2 Kings x:35). As he followed the evil courses of the house of Jeroboam, the Syrians under Hazael and Benhadad were suffered to prevail over him. Overwhelmed by his calamities, Jehoahaz at length acknowledged the authority of Jehovah over Israel, and humbled himself before him; in consideration of which a deliverer was raised up for Israel in the person of Joash, this king's son, who was enabled to expel the Syrians and re-establish the affairs of the kingdom (2 Kings xiii:1-9, 25).

2. Called Shallum, seventeenth king of Judah, son of Josiah, whose reign began and ended in the year B. C. 608. After his father had been slain in resisting the progress of Pharaoh-necho, Jehoahaz, who was then twenty-three years of age, was raised to the throne by the people (2 Kings xxiii:31, 36). He found the land full of trouble, but free from idolatry. Instead, however, of following the excellent example of his father, Jehoahaz fell into the accustomed crimes of his predecessors; and under the encouragements which his example or indifference offered, the idols soon reappeared. It seems strange that in a time so short, and which must have been much occupied in arranging plans for resisting or pacifying the Egyptian king, he should have been able to deserve the stigma which the sacred record has left upon his name. But there is no limit, except in the greatness of the Divine power, to the activity of evil dispositions. The sway of Jehoahaz was terminated in three months, when Pharaoh-necho, on his victorious return from the Euphrates, thinking it politic to reject a king not nominated by himself, removed him from the throne, and set thereon his brother Jehoiakim. This reign was the shortest in the kingdom of Judah, although in that of Israel there were several shorter. The deposed king was at first taken as a prisoner to Riblah in Syria, but was eventually carried to Egypt, where he died (2 Kings xxiii:30-35; 2 Chron. xxxvi:1-4; 1 Chron. iii: 15; Jer. xxii:10-12).

The anointing of this king has drawn attention to the defect of his title as the reason for the addition of that solemn ceremony. It appears from 1 Chron. iii:15 that Josiah had four sons, of whom Johanan is expressly said to have been 'the firstborn.' But he seems to have died before his father, as we nowhere find his name historically mentioned, while those of the other brothers are familiar to us. If, therefore, he died childless, and Jehoahaz were the next son, his claim would have been good. But he was not the next son. His name, as Shallum, occurs last of the four in 1 Chron. iii:15; and from the historical notices in 2 Kings xxiii and 2 Chron. xxxvi we ascertain that when Josiah died the ages of the three surviving sons were, Eliakim (Jehoiakim) twenty-five years, Jehoahaz (Shallum) twenty-three years, Mattaniah (Zedekiah) ten years; consequently Jehoahaz was preferred by the popular favor above his elder brother Jehoiakim, and the anointing, therefore, was doubtless intended to give to his imperfect claim the weight of that solemn ceremony. It was also probably suspected that, as actually took place, the Egyptian king would seek to annul a popular election unsanctioned by himself; but as the Egyptians anointed their own kings, and attached much importance to the ceremony, the possibility that he would hesitate more to remove an anointed than an unanointed king might afford a further reason for the anointing of Jehoahaz. (See ANOINTING.)

Jehoahaz is supposed to be the person who is designated under the emblem of a young lion carried in chains to Egypt (Ezek. xix :3, 4).

3. A name of the youngest son of Jehoram (2 Chron. xxi:17); Josiah's father (2 Chron. **xxv:** 23); usually called AHAZIAH (which see).

JEHOASH (je-hō'ash), (Heb. יְהוֹאָשׁ, *yeh-ho-awsh'*, Jehovah given). See JOASH.

JEHOHANAN (jē-ho-hā'nan), (Heb. יְהוֹחָנָן, *yeh-ho-khaw-nawn'*, Jehovah favored).

This is at times rendered Johanan and comes to us as John.

1. A Korhite doorkeeper to the house of Jehovah during the reign of David (1 Chron. **xxvi:** 3). (B. C. 1014.)

2. A man of Judah who commanded 280,000 men under Jehoshaphat (2 Chron. xvii:15). In all probability the same as the father of Ishmael, the latter of whom assisted Jehoiada in the restoration of Jehoash (2 Chron. xxiii:1). (B. C. about 910.)

3. One of the Bene-Bebai, whom Ezra forced to put away his Gentile wife after the captivity (Ezra x:28). (B. C. 459.)

4. A priest (Neh. xii:13), who represented the house of Amariah in the time of Joiakim. (B. C. about 406.)

5. One of those who took part in the musical thanksgiving worship at the dedication, by Nehemiah, of the wall of Jerusalem (Neh. xii:42). (B. C. 446.)

JEHOIACHIN (je-hoi'a-kĭn), (Heb. יְהוֹיָכִין, *yeh-ho-yaw-keen'*, Jehovah will establish), by contraction JECONIAH and CONIAH, nineteenth king of Judah, and son of Jehoiakim.

(1) Reign. When his father was slain, B. C. 599, the king of Babylon allowed him, as the rightful heir, to succeed. He was then eighteen years of age according to 2 Kings xxiv:8; but only eight according to 2 Chron. xxxvi:9. Many attempts have been made to reconcile these dates, the most usual solution being that he had reigned ten years in conjunction with his father, so that he was eight when he began his joint reign, but eighteen when he began to reign alone. There are, however, difficulties in this view, which, perhaps, leave it the safest course to conclude that 'eight' in 2 Chron. xxxvi:9 is a corruption of the text, such as might easily occur from the relation of the numbers eight and eighteen.

Jehoiachin followed the evil courses which had already brought so much disaster upon the royal house of David, and upon the people under its sway. He seems to have very speedily indicated a political bias adverse to the interests of the Chaldæan empire; for in three months after his accession we find the generals of Nebuchadnezzar again laying siege to Jerusalem, according to the predictions of Jeremiah (xxii:18). Convinced of the futility of resistance Jehoiachin went out and surrendered as soon as Nebuchadnezzar arrived in person before the city.

(2) Captivity. He was sent away as a captive to Babylon, with his mother, his generals, and his troops, together with the artificers and other inhabitants of Jerusalem, to the number of ten thousand. Thus ended an unhappy reign of three months and ten days. If the Chaldæan king had then put an end to the show of a monarchy and annexed the country to his own dominions, the event would probably have been less unhappy for the nation. But still adhering to his former policy, he placed on the throne Mattaniah, the only surviving son of Josiah, whose name he changed to Zedekiah (2 Kings xxiv:1-16; 2 Chron. xxxvi:9, 10; Jer. xxix:3; xxxvii:1).

(3) Release. Jehoiachin remained in prison at Babylon during the lifetime of Nebuchadnezzar; but when that prince died, his son, Evil-merodach, not only released him, but gave him an honorable seat at his own table, with precedence over all the other dethroned kings who were kept at Babylon, and an allowance for the support of his rank (2 Kings xxv:27-30; Jer. lii:31-34). To what he owed this favor we are not told; but the Jewish commentators allege that Evil-merodach had himself been put into prison by his father during the last year of his reign, and had there contracted an intimate friendship with the deposed king of Judah.

The name of Jeconiah reappears to fix the epoch of several of the prophecies of Jeremiah (Jer. xxiv:1), and of the deportation which terminated his reign (Esth. ii:6). In the genealogy of Christ (Matt. i:11) he is named as the 'son of Josias,' his uncle.

JEHOIADA (je-hoi'a-dà), (Heb. יְהוֹיָדָע, *yeh-ho-yaw-daw'*, God-known).

1. A high-priest in the times of Ahaziah and Athaliah. He is known only from the part which he took in recovering the throne of Judah for the young Joash, who had been saved by his wife Jehoshebah from the massacre by which Athaliah sought to exterminate the royal line of David. The particulars of this transaction are related under other heads. (See ATHALIAH; JOASH.) Jehoiada manifested much decision and forecast on this occasion; and he used for good the great power which devolved upon him during the minority of the young king, and the influence which he continued to enjoy as long as he lived. The value of this influence is shown by the misconduct and the disorders of the kingdom after his death. He died B. C. 834, at the age of 130, and his remains were honored with a place in the sepulcher of the kings at Jerusalem (2 Chron. xxiii. xxiv:16).

2. Father of David's warrior, Benaiah (2 Sam. viii:18; xx:23; xxiii:20, 22; 1 Kings i:8, 26, 32, 36, 38, 44; ii:25, 29, 34, 35, 46; iv:4; 1 Chron. xi:22, 24; xviii:17; xxvii:5). (B. C. before 1046).

3. (Neh. iii:6.) See JOIADA.

4. Son of Benaiah, and a chief adviser of David according to 1 Chron. xxvii:34; but doubtless the son of Jehoiada is meant (2.).

5. A second priest, under Seraiah, the high-priest. He was deposed at the beginning of Zedekiah's reign, and Zephaniah was appointed priest in his stead (Jer. xxix:25-29).

JEHOIAKIM (je-hoi'a-kĭm), (Heb. יְהוֹיָקִים, *yeh-ho-yaw-keem'*, Jehovah established).

1. Name and Family. Jehoiakim was the second son of Josiah and eighteenth king of Judah. His name was originally Eliakim, but its equivalent, Jehoiakim, was bestowed upon him by Pharaoh-necho, the Egyptian king. He was the second son of Josiah by Zebudah, the daughter of Pedaiah of Rumah (2 Kings xxiii:36), born B. C. 633.

2. Personal History.

(1) Made King. On the death of his father the people raised to the throne his younger brother Jehoahaz or Shallum (Jer. xxii:11) but three months after, when the Egyptian king returned from the Euphrates, he removed Jehoahaz, and gave the crown to the rightful heir, Eliakim, whose name he changed to Jehoiakim. This change of name often took place in similar circumstances; and the altered name was in fact the badge of a tributary prince. Jehoiakim began to reign in B. C. 608, and reigned eleven years. He of course occupied the position of a subordinate ruler of the Egyptian empire. However heavy may have been the Egyptian yoke, Jehoiakim was destined to pass under one heavier still.

(2) Vassal to Nebuchadnezzar. In the third year of his reign Jehoiakim, being besieged in Jerusalem, was forced to submit to Nebuchadnezzar, and was by his order laden with chains, with the intention of sending him captive to Babylon (2 Chron. xxxvi:6); but eventually the conqueror changed his mind and restored the crown to him. Many persons, however, of high family, and some even of the royal blood, were sent away to Babylon. Among these was Daniel, then a mere youth. A large proportion of the treasures and sacred vessels of the temple were also taken away and deposited in the idol-temple at Babylon (Dan. i:1, 2). The year following the Egyptians were defeated upon the Euphrates (Jer. xlvi:2), and Jehoiakim, when he saw the remains of the defeated army pass by his territory, could not but perceive how vain had been that reliance upon Egypt against which he had been constantly cautioned by Jeremiah (Jer. xliv:24-30). In the same year the prophet caused a collection of his prophecies to be written out by his faithful Baruch, and to be read publicly by him in the court of the temple.

(3) Destroys the Roll. This coming to the knowledge of the king, he sent for it and had it read before him. But he heard not much of the bitter denunciations with which it was charged, before he took the roll from the reader, and after cutting it in pieces threw it into the brasier which, it being winter, was burning before him in the hall. The counsel of God against him, however, stood sure; a fresh roll was written, with the addition of a further and most awful denunciation against the king, occasioned by this foolish and sacrilegious act. 'He shall have none to sit upon the throne of David; and his dead body shall be cast out in the day to the heat and in the night to the frost' (Jer. xxxvi:30). All this, however, appears to have made little impression upon Jehoiakim, who still walked in his old paths.

(4) Rebellion and Death. After three years of subjection, Jehoiakim, finding the king of Babylon fully engaged elsewhere, and deluded by the Egyptian party in his court, ventured to withhold his tribute, and thereby to throw off the Chaldæan yoke (2 Kings xxiv:1). This step, taken contrary to the earnest remonstrances of Jeremiah, was the ruin of Jehoiakim. It might seem successful for a little, from the Chaldæans not then having leisure to attend to the affairs of this quarter. In due time, however, the land was invaded by their armies, accompanied by a vast number of auxiliaries from the neighboring countries, the Edomites, Moabites, and others, who were for the most part actuated by a fierce hatred against the Jewish name and nation. The events of the war are not related. Jerusalem was taken, or rather surrendered on terms, which Josephus alleges were little heeded by Nebuchadnezzar. It is certain that Jehoiakim was slain, but whether in one of the actions, or, as Josephus says, after the surrender, we cannot determine His body remained exposed and unlamented without the city, under the circumstances foretold by the prophet—'They shall not lament for him, saying, Ah, my brother! or, Ah, sister! They shall not lament for him, saying, Ah, lord! or, Ah, his glory! He shall be buried with the burial of an ass, drawn and cast forth beyond the gates of Jerusalem' (Jer. xxii:18, 19; 1 Chron. iii: 15; 2 Kings xxiii:34-37; xxiv:17; 2 Chron. xxxvi: 4-8).

It was not the object of Nebuchadnezzar to destroy altogether a power which, as tributary to him, formed a serviceable outpost towards Egypt, which seems to have been the great final object of all his designs in this quarter. He therefore still maintained the throne of Judah, and placed on it Jehoiachin, the son of the late king. He, however, sent away another body, a second corps of the nobles and chief persons of the nation, three thousand in number, among whom was Ezekiel, afterwards called to prophesy in the land of his exile.

5. Character. Jehoiakim was from all accounts a vicious and irreligious person (see 2 Kings xxiii:37; xxiv:9; 2 Chron. xxxvi:5, 8). The vindictive pursuit and murder of URIJAH (which see) indicate his cruelty and irreligion (Jer. xxvi:20-23). His daring impiety is evidenced by his treatment of the roll which contained Jeremiah's prophecy. His selfishness is shown by the large sums he squandered in building luxurious palaces for himself when his country was impoverished by the heavy tributes laid upon it both by Egypt and Babylon (Jer. xxii: 17-19). So bitter was the hatred against him that, according to the Rabbins, men whispered that on the dried skin of the corpse, as it lay naked before all, the name of the demon, Codonazer, to whom he had sold himself, appeared stamped in clear Hebrew letters. (See Mc. & Strong's *Cyc.*; Stanley's *His. of the Jewish Church*; Geike's *Hours with the Bible.*)

JEHOIARIB (je-hoi'a-rĭb), (Heb. יְהוֹיָרִיב, yeh-ho-yaw-reeb', Jehovah a defender, or Jehovah impels, or doth contend, 1 Chron. ix:10, xxiv:7, only; elsewhere, both in Hebrew and A. V., the name is abbreviated to JOIARIB), head of the first twenty-four courses of priests during King David's time. (B. C. 1014.) Some of his descendants returned from Babylon (Neh. xi:10), and his course is mentioned as returning (Neh. xii :6).

JEHONADAB (je-hŏn'a-dăb), (Heb. יְהוֹנָדָב, yeh-ho-naw-dawb', Jehovah impels). 2 Kings x:15. See JONADAB.

JEHONATHAN (je-hŏn'a-than), (Heb. יְהוֹנָתָן, yeh-ho-naw-thawn', Jehovah-given).

1. Son of Uzziah, who was superintendent of the treasures and cellars of King David's store-houses (1 Chron. xxvii:25). (B. C. 1014.)

2. A Levite sent by Jehoshaphat to teach the people the Law in the cities of Judah (2 Chron. xvii:8). (B. C. 910.)

3. A priest (Neh. xii:18), representing the family of Shemaiah during the generation after the return from Babylon (ver. 6). (B. C. after 536.)

JEHORAM (je-hō'ram), (Heb. יְהוֹרָם, *yeh-ho-rawm'*, exalted by Jehovah), contracted form JORAM (יוֹרָם, *yo-rawm'*).

The eldest son and successor of Jehoshaphat, and fifth king of Judah, who began to reign (separately) B. C. 853, at the age of thirty-five years, and reigned twelve years (2 Kings i:17; iii:1). He was associated with his father in the later years of his life, but he profited little by this association.

(1) Marriage and Idolatry. He had unhappily been married to Athaliah, the daughter of Ahab and Jezebel; and her influence seems to have neutralized all the good he might have derived from the example of his father. One of the first acts of his reign was to put his brothers to death and seize the valuable appanages which their father had in his lifetime bestowed upon them. After this we are not surprised to find him giving way to the gross idolatries of that new and strange kind—the Phœnician—which had been brought into Israel by Jezebel, and into Judah by her daughter Athaliah (2 Kings viii:18, 19). A prophetic writing from the aged prophet Elijah produced no good effect upon him (2 Chron. xxi: 12-15). For these atrocities the Lord let forth his anger against Jehoram and his kingdom.

(2) Wars. The Edomites revolted, and, according to old prophecies (Gen. xxvii:40), shook off the yoke of Judah. The Philistines on one side, and the Arabians and Cushites on the other, also grew bold against a king forsaken of God, and in repeated invasions spoiled the land of all its substance; they even ravaged the royal palaces; and took away the wives and children of the king, leaving him only one son, Ahaziah (2 Chron. xxii:1).

(3) Sickness and Death. Jehoram was in his last days afflicted with a frightful disease in his bowels, which, from the terms employed in describing it, appears to have been malignant dysentery in its most shocking and tormenting form. After a disgraceful reign, and a most painful death, public opinion inflicted the posthumous dishonor of refusing him a place in the sepulcher of the kings.

(4) Character. Jehoram was by far the most impious and cruel tyrant that had as yet occupied the throne of Judah, though he was rivaled or surpassed by some of his successors (2 Kings viii:16-24; 2 Chron. xxi:4). (See JORAM.)

JEHOSHABEATH (jē'ho-shăb'e-ăth), (Heb. יְהוֹשַׁבְעַת, *yeh-ho-shab-e-ath'*, Jehovah sworn), the form in which the name of JEHOSHEBA (which see) is given in 2 Chron. xxii:11. It is stated there, but not in Kings, that she was the wife of Jehoiada, the high-priest (2 Chron. xxii:11). (See JEHOSHEBA.)

JEHOSHAPHAT (je-hŏsh'a-phăt), (Heb. יְהוֹשָׁפָט, *yeh-ho-shaw-fawt'* Jehovah judged).

1. The fourth king of Judah, and son of Asa, whom he succeeded at the age of thirty-five, and reigned twenty-five years.

(1) Fortifies Kingdom and Resists Idolatry. He commenced his reign by fortifying his kingdom against Israel; and having thus secured himself against surprise from the quarter which gave most disturbance to him, he proceeded to purge the land from the idolatries and idolatrous monuments by which it was still tainted. Even the high places and groves, which former well-disposed kings had suffered to remain, were by the

zeal of Jehoshaphat in a great measure destroyed. The chiefs, with priests and Levites, proceeded from town to town, with the book of the Law in their hands, instructing the people, and calling back their wandering affections to the religion of their fathers. This was a beautiful and interesting circumstance in the operations of the young king.

(2) Enjoys Divine Protection. Jehoshaphat was too well instructed in the great principles of the theocracy not to know that his faithful conduct had entitled him to expect the Divine protection. Of that protection he soon had manifest proofs. At home he enjoyed peace and abundance, and abroad security and honor. His treasuries were filled with the 'presents' which the blessing of God upon the people, 'in their basket and their store,' enabled them to bring. His renown extended into the neighboring nations, and the Philistines, as well as the adjoining Arabian tribes, paid him rich tributes in silver and in cattle. He was thus enabled to put all his towns in good condition, to erect fortresses, to organize a powerful army, and to raise his kingdom to a degree of importance and splendor which it had not enjoyed since the revolt of the ten tribes.

(3) Alliance with Ahab. The weak and impious Ahab at that time occupied the throne of Israel; and Jehoshaphat, having nothing to fear from his power, sought, or at least did not repel, an alliance with him. This is alleged to have been the grand mistake of his reign; and that it was such is proved by the consequences.

After a few years we find Jehoshaphat on a visit to Ahab, in Samaria, being the first time any of the kings of Israel and Judah had met in peace. He here experienced a reception worthy of his greatness; but Ahab failed not to take advantage of the occasion, and so worked upon the weak points of his character as to prevail upon him to take arms with him against the Syrians, with whom, hitherto, the kingdom of Judah never had had any war or occasion of quarrel. However, Jehoshaphat was not so far infatuated as to proceed to the war without consulting God, who, according to the principles of the theocratic government, was the final arbiter of war and peace. The false prophets of Ahab poured forth ample promises of success, and one of them, named Zedekiah, resorting to material symbols, made him horns of iron, saying, 'Thus saith the Lord, with these shalt thou smite the Syrians till they be consumed.' Still Jehoshaphat was not satisfied; and the answer to his further inquiries extorted from him a rebuke of the reluctance which Ahab manifested to call Micah, 'the prophet of the Lord.' The fearless words of this prophet did not make the impression upon the king of Judah which might have been expected; or, probably, he then felt himself too deeply bound in honor to recede. He went to the fatal battle of Ramoth-Gilead, and there nearly became the victim of a plan which Ahab had laid for his own safety at the expense of his too-confiding ally. He persuaded Jehoshaphat to appear as king, while he himself went disguised to the battle. This brought the heat of the contest around him, as the Syrians took him for Ahab; and if they had not in time discovered their mistake, he would certainly have been slain. Ahab was killed, and the battle lost. (See AHAB); but Jehoshaphat escaped, and returned to Jerusalem.

(4) Extended His Reforms. On his return from this imprudent expedition he was met by the just reproaches of the prophet Jehu. The best atonement he could make for this error was by the course he actually took. He resumed his labors in the further extirpation of idolatry, in the instruction of the people, and the improvement of his realm. He now made a tour of his kingdom in person, that he might see the ordinances of God duly established, 'and witness the due execution of his intentions respecting the instruction of the people in the divine law. This tour enabled him to discern many defects in the local administration of justice, which he then applied himself to remedy. He appointed magistrates in every city, for the determination of causes civil and ecclesiastical. Then he established a supreme council of justice at Jerusalem, composed of priests, Levites, and 'the chiefs of the fathers'; to which difficult cases were referred and appeals brought from the provincial tribunals. This tribunal also was inducted by a weighty but short charge from the king, whose conduct in this and other matters places him at the very head of the monarchs who reigned over Judah as a separate kingdom.

(5) Revival of Commerce. The activity of Jehoshaphat's mind was then turned towards the revival of that maritime commerce which had been established by Solomon. The land of Edom and the ports of the Elanitic Gulf were still under the power of Judah; and in them the king prepared a fleet for the voyage to Ophir. Unhappily, however, he yielded to the wish of the king of Israel, and allowed him to take part in the enterprise. For this the expedition was doomed of God, and the vessels were wrecked almost as soon as they quitted port. Instructed by Eliezer, the prophet, as to the cause of this disaster, Jehoshaphat equipped a new fleet, and having this time declined the co-operation of the king of Israel, the voyage prospered. The trade was not, however, prosecuted with any zeal, and was soon abandoned. (See COMMERCE.)

In accounting for the disposition of Jehoshaphat to contract alliances with the king of Israel, we are to remember that there existed a powerful tie between the two courts in the marriage of Jehoshaphat's eldest son with Athaliah, the daughter of Ahab; and, when we advert to the part in public affairs which that princess afterwards took, it may well be conceived that even thus early she possessed an influence for evil in the court of Judah.

(6) Alliance with Joram. After the death of Ahaziah, king of Israel, Joram, his successor, persuaded Jehoshaphat to join him in an expedition against Moab. This alliance was, however, on political grounds, more excusable than the two former, as the Moabites, who were under tribute to Israel, might draw into their cause the Edomites, who were tributary to Judah. Besides, Moab could be invaded with most advantage from the south, round by the end of the Dead Sea; and the king of Israel could not gain access to them in that quarter but by marching through the territories of Jehoshaphat. The latter not only joined Joram with his own army, but required his tributary, the king of Edom, to bring his forces into the field. During seven days' march through the wilderness of Edom, the army suffered much from want of water; and by the time the allies came in sight of the army of Moab, they were ready to perish from thirst. In this emergency the pious Jehoshaphat thought, as usual, of consulting the Lord; and hearing that the prophet Elisha was in the camp, the three kings proceeded to his tent. For the sake of Jehoshaphat, and for his sake only, deliverance was promised; and it came during the

ensuing night, in the shape of an abundant supply of water, which rolled down the exhausted wadies, and filled the pools and hollow ground. Afterwards Jehoshaphat took his full part in the operations of the campaign, till the armies were induced to withdraw in horror, by witnessing the dreadful act of Mesha, king of Moab, in offering up his eldest son in sacrifice upon the wall of the town in which he was shut up.

(7) Renewed Wars. This war kindled another much more dangerous to Jehoshaphat. The Moabites, being highly exasperated at the part he had taken against them, turned all their wrath upon him. They induced their kindred, the Ammonites, to join them, obtained auxiliaries from the Syrians, and even drew over the Edomites; so that the strength of all the neighboring nations may be said to have been united for this great enterprise. The allied forces entered the land of Judah and encamped at Engedi, near the western border of the Dead Sea. In this extremity Jehoshaphat felt that all his defense lay with God. A solemn fast was held, and the people repaired from the towns to Jerusalem to seek help of the Lord. In the presence of the assembled multitude the king, in the court of the temple, offered up a fervent prayer to God, concluding with—'O our God, wilt *thou* not judge them, for *we* have no might against this great company that cometh against us, neither know we what to do; but our eyes are upon thee.' He ceased; and in the midst of the silence which ensued, a voice was raised pronouncing deliverance in the name of the Lord, and telling them to go out on the morrow to the cliffs overlooking the camp of the enemy, and see them all overthrown without a blow from them. The voice was that of Jahaziel, one of the Levites. His words came to pass. The allies quarreled among themselves and destroyed each other; so that when the Judahites came the next day they found their dreaded enemies all dead, and nothing was left for them but to take the rich spoils of the slain. This done, they returned with triumphal songs to Jerusalem. This great event was recognized even by the neighboring nations as the act of God; and so strong was the impression which it made upon them, that the remainder of the good king's reign was altogether undisturbed.

(8) Death. His death, however, took place not very long after this at the age of sixty, after having reigned twenty-five years. (B. C. 896.) He left the kingdom in a prosperous condition to his eldest son Jehoram, whom he had in the last years of his life associated with him in the government.

(9) Character. 'Jehoshaphat, who sought the Lord with all his heart,' was the character given to this king by Jehu, when, on that account, he gave to his grandson an honorable grave (2 Chron. xxii:9). And this, in fact, was the sum and substance of his character. The Hebrew annals offer the example of no king who more carefully squared all his conduct by the principles of the theocracy. He kept the Lord always before his eyes, and was in all things obedient to his will when made known to him by the prophets. Few of the kings of Judah manifested so much zeal for the real welfare of his people, or took measures so judicious to promote it. His good talents, the benevolence of his disposition, and his generally sound judgment are shown not only in the great measures of domestic policy which distinguished his reign, but by the manner in which they were executed. No trace can be found in him of that pride which dishonored some and ruined others of the kings who preceded and followed him. Most of his errors arose from that dangerous facility of temper which sometimes led him to act against the dictates of his naturally sound judgment, or prevented that judgment from being fairly exercised.

2. A priest in the time of David who was appointed to blow the trumpet before the ark when brought up to Jerusalem (1 Chron. xv:24). (B. C. about 1043.)

3. Son of Ahilud, who was recorder or chronicler in the court of David and Solomon (2 Sam. viii:16; xx:24; 1 Kings iv:3; 1 Chron. xviii:15). (B. C. 1014.)

4. Son of Paruah; purveyor of the district of Issachar under Solomon (1 Kings iv:17). (B. C. about 995.)

5. Father of King Jehu (2 Kings ix:2, 14). (B. C. 842.)

JEHOSHAPHAT, VALLEY OF (je-hŏsh'a-phăt, văl'lĭ *uv*), (Heb. יְהוֹשָׁפָט, *yeh-ho-shaw-fawt'*, valley where Jehovah judges), the name now given to the valley which bounds Jerusalem on the east, and separates it from the Mount of Olives. (See JERUSALEM).

In Joel iii:2, 12, we read, 'the Lord will gather all nations in the valley of Jehoshaphat, and plead with them there.' Many interpreters, Jewish and Christian, conclude from this that the last judgment is to take place in the above-mentioned valley. But there is no reason to suppose that the valley then bore any such name; and more discreet interpreters understand the text to denote a valley in which some great victory was to be won, most probably by Nebuchadnezzar, which should utterly discomfit the ancient enemies of Israel, and resemble the victory which Jehoshaphat obtained over the Ammonites, Moabites, and Edomites (2 Chron. xx:22-26). Others *translate* the name Jehoshaphat into *God's judgment,* and thus read, 'the valley of God's judgment,' which is doubtless symbolical, like 'the valley of decision,' *i. e.* of punishment, in the same chapter.

JEHOSHEBA (je-hŏsh'e-bȧ), (Heb. יְהוֹשֶׁבַע, *yeh-ho-sheh'bah,* Jehovah her oath, that is, worshiper of Jehovah), daughter of Jehoram, sister of Ahaziah, and aunt of Joash, kings of Judah. The last of these owed his life to her, and his crown to her husband, the high-priest Jehoiada (2 Kings xi:1, 3; 2 Chron. xxii:11). B. C. 842. (See JEHOIADA.)

JEHOSHUA (je-hŏsh'u-ȧ), (Num. xiii:16). See JOSHUA.

JEHOSHUAH (je-hŏsh'u-ah), (1 Chron. vii:27). See JOSHUA.

JEHOVAH (je-hō'vah), (Heb. יְהֹוָה, *yeh-ho-vaw'*), or rather perhaps JAHVEH (Heb. יַהְוֶה, *yah-veh'*, the existing one), according to the reading suggested by Ewald, Hävernick, and others—the name by which God was pleased to make himself known under the covenant, to the ancient Hebrews (Exod. vi:2, 3). The LXX generally render it by ὁ Κύριος, *ho koo'ree-os,* the Vulgate by *Dominus;* and in this respect they have been followed by the A. V., where it is translated "The Lord."

(1) Pronunciation. The true pronunciation of this name, by which God was known to the Hebrews, has been entirely lost, the Jews themselves scrupulously avoiding every mention of it, and substituting in its stead one or other of the words with whose proper vowel points it may

happen to be written. This custom, which had its origin in reverence, and has almost degenerated into a superstition, was founded upon an erroneous rendering of Lev. xxiv:16, from which it was inferred that the mere utterance of the name constituted a capital offense. In the rabbinical writings it is distinguished by various euphemistic expressions; as simply "the name," or "the name of four letters" (the Greek *tetragrammaton*); "the great and terrible name;" "the peculiar name," *i. e.* appropriated to God alone; "the separate name," *i. e.* either the name which is separated or removed from human knowledge, or, as some render, "the name which has been interpreted or revealed" (Heb. *shem ham'-mee-pho-rawsh*). The Samaritans followed the same custom, and in reading the Pentateuch substituted for Jehovah (שְׁמָא, *shey-maw*) "the name," at the same time perpetuating the practice in their alphabetical poems and later writings.

(2) Meaning. When Moses received his commission to be the deliverer of Israel, the Almighty, who appeared in the burning bush, communicated to him the name which he should give as the credentials of his mission: "And God said unto Moses, I AM THAT I AM (אֶהְיֶה אֲשֶׁר אֶהְיֶה, *eh-yeh' ash-er' eh-yeh'*), and he said, Thus shalt thou say unto the children of Israel, I AM hath sent me unto you." That this passage is intended to indicate the etymology of Jehovah, as understood by the Hebrews, no one has ventured to doubt; it is in fact the key to the whole mystery.

(3) When Revealed. It is distinctly stated in Exod. vi:3, that to the patriarchs God was not known by the name Jehovah. If, therefore, this passage has reference to the first revelation of Jehovah simply as a name and title of God, there is clearly a discrepancy which requires to be explained. In renewing his promise of deliverance from Egypt, "God spake unto Moses and said unto him, I am Jehovah; and I appeared unto Abraham, unto Isaac, and unto Jacob, by (the name of) God Almighty (*El Shaddai*, אֵל שַׁדַּי), but by my name Jehovah was I not known to them." It follows then that, if the reference were merely to the name as a name, the passage in question would prove equally that before this time Elohim was unknown as an appellation of the Deity, and God would appear uniformly as El Shaddai in the patriarchal history. But although it was held by Theodoret (*Quæst.* xv. on Ex.) and many of the Fathers, who have been followed by a long list of moderns, that the name was first made known by God to Moses, and then introduced by him among the Israelites, the contrary was maintained by Cajetan, Lyranus, Calvin, Rosenmüller, Hengstenberg, and others, who deny that the passage in Exod. vi alludes to the introduction of the name. That Jehovah was not a new name Hävernick concludes from Exod. iii:14, where "the name of God Jehovah is evidently presupposed as already in use, and is only explained, interpreted, and applied. . . . It is certainly not a new name that is introduced; on the contrary, the 'I am that I am' would be unintelligible, if the name itself were not presupposed as already known. The old name of antiquity, whose precious significance had been forgotten and neglected by the children of Israel, here as it were rises again to life, and is again brought home to the consciousness of the people." (Smith, *Bib. Dict.*) (See ELOHIM; and article on GOD.)

JEHOVAH-JIREH (je-hō′vah–ji′reh), (Heb. יְהוָה יִרְאֶה, *yeh-ho-vaw′ yir-eh′*, Jehovah will see, i. e., provide). Abraham thus named the altar on which he had been commanded to offer Isaac, and which offering he was so miraculously preserved from making (Gen. xxii:14).

JEHOVAH-NISSI (je-hō′vah–nĭs′sī), (Heb. יְהוָה נִסִּי, *yeh-ho-vaw′ nees-see′*, Jehovah my banner), the name given by Moses to the altar erected upon the hill where he sat with uplifted hands during the successful battle against the Amalekites (Exod. xvii:15).

JEHOVAH-SHALOM (je - hō′vah – shā′lom), (Heb. יְהוָה שָׁלוֹם, *yeh-ho-vaw′ shaw-lome′*, Jehovah is peace), the name Gideon gave to the altar erected in Ophrah. It was called by this name in memory of the words addressed to him by the Angel of Jehovah, " Peace be unto thee " (Judges vi:24).

JEHOVAH-SHAMMAH (je-hō′vah–shăm′mah), (Heb. יְהוָה שָׁמָּה, *yeh-ho-vaw′ shawm′maw′*, Jehovah there, or lit. thither), the name of the city Ezekiel described in his vision (Ezek. xlviii:35).

JEHOZABAD (je-hŏz′a-băd), (Heb. יְהוֹזָבָד, *yeh-ho-zaw-bawd′*, Jehovah endowed).

1. A Levite, son of Obed-edom, a porter of the temple during the reign of David (1 Chron. xxvi:4, 15; comp. Neh. xii:25). (B. C. 1014.)

2. A captain of the tribe of Benjamin, commanding 180,000 armed men during Jehoshaphat's time (2 Chron. xvii:18). (B. C. about 910.)

3. Son of Shomer, the Moabitish woman who conspired against and slew King Joash in his bed (2 Kings xii:21; 2 Chron. xxiv:26). (B. C. 837.)

JEHOZADAK (je-hŏz′a-dăk), (Heb. יְהוֹצָדָק, *yeh-ho-tsaw-dawk′*, Jehovah makes just), son of Seraiah, a high-priest during the reign of Zedekiah (1 Chron. vi:14, 15).

He succeeded his father in the office of high-priest (1 Chron. vi:14, 15); but suffered captivity under Nebuchadnezzar. Elsewhere the name is JOZADAK. (B. C. 588.) He probably died in exile, as his son Joshua (Jeshua) was the first high-priest who officiated after the return from captivity (Hag. i:1, 12, 14; ii:2, 4; Zech. vi:11).

JEHU (jē′hu), (Heb. יֵהוּא, *yay-hoo′*, God is).

1. The eleventh king of Israel, and founder of its fourth dynasty, who began to reign B. C. 884, and reigned twenty-eight years.

(1) Commander in the Army. Jehu held a command in the Israelite army posted at Ramoth-Gilead to hold in check the Syrians, who of late years had made strenuous efforts to extend their frontier to the Jordan, and had possessed themselves of much of the territory of the Israelites east of that river (2 Kings ix:5). The contest was in fact still carried on which had begun many years before in the reign of Ahab, the present king's father, who had lost his life in battle before this very Ramoth-Gilead. Ahaziah, king of Judah, had taken part with Joram, king of Israel, in this war (2 Kings viii:28), and as the latter had been severely wounded in a recent action, and had gone to Jezreel to be healed of his wounds, Ahaziah had also gone thither on a visit of sympathy to him (ver. 29).

In this state of affairs a council of war was held among the military commanders in camp, when very unexpectedly one of the disciples of the prophets, known for such by his garb, appeared at the door of the tent, and called forth Jehu, de-

claring that he had a message to deliver to him (2 Kings ix:1-5). He had been sent by Elisha the prophet, in discharge of a duty which long before had been confided by the Lord to Elijah (1 Kings xix:16), and from him had devolved on his successor.

(2) Anointed King. When they were alone the young man drew forth a horn of oil and poured it upon Jehu's head, with the words, 'Thus saith the Lord God of Israel, I have anointed thee king over the people of the Lord, even over Israel. And thou shalt smite the house of Ahab thy master, that I may avenge the blood of my servants the prophets, and the blood of all the servants of the Lord, at the hand of Jezebel' (2 Kings ix:1-13). Jehu returned to the council, probably with an altered air, for he was asked what had been the communication of the young prophet to him. He told them plainly; and they were obviously ripe for defection from the house of Ahab, for they were all delighted at the news, and taking him in triumph to 'the top of the stairs,' they spread their mantles beneath his feet, and proclaimed him king by sound of trumpet in the presence of all the troops (2 Kings ix:11, 12).

Jehu was not a man to lose any advantage through remissness. He immediately entered his chariot, in order that his presence at Jezreel should be the first announcement which Joram could receive of this revolution.

(3) Stays the Two Kings. As soon as the advance of Jehu and his party was seen in the distance by the watchmen upon the palace-tower in Jezreel, two messengers were successively sent forth to meet him, and were commanded by Jehu to follow in his rear. But when the watchman reported that he could now recognize the furious driving of Jehu, Joram went forth himself to meet him, and was accompanied by the king of Judah. They met in the field of Naboth, so fatal to the house of Ahab. The king saluted him with 'Is it peace, Jehu?' and received the answer, 'What peace, so long as the whoredoms (idolatries) of thy mother Jezebel and her witchcrafts are so many?' This completely opened the eyes of Joram, who exclaimed to the king of Judah, 'There is treachery, O Ahaziah!' and turned to flee. But Jehu felt no infirmity of purpose, and knew that the slightest wavering might be fatal to him. He therefore drew a bow with his full strength and sent forth an arrow which passed through the king's heart. Jehu caused the body to be thrown back into the field of Naboth, out of which he had passed in his attempt at flight (2 Kings ix:16-25).

(4) Death of Jezebel. The king of Judah contrived to escape, but not without a wound, of which he afterwards died at Megiddo. (See AHAZIAH.) Jehu then entered the city, whither the news of this transaction had already preceded him. As he passed under the walls of the palace Jezebel herself, studiously arrayed for effect, appeared at one of the windows, and saluted him with a question such as might have shaken a man of weaker nerves, 'Had Zimri peace, who slew his master?' But Jehu was unmoved, and instead of answering her, called out, 'Who is on my side, who?' when several eunuchs made their appearance at the window, to whom he cried, 'Throw her down!' and immediately this proud and guilty woman lay a blood-stained corpse in the road, and was trodden under foot by the horses. (See JEZEBEL.) Jehu then went in and took possession of the palace (2 Kings ix:30-37).

(5) Destroys House of Ahab. He was now master of Jezreel, which was, next to Samaria, the chief town of the kingdom; but he could not feel secure while the capital itself was in the hands of the royal family, and of those who might be supposed to feel strong attachment to the house of Ahab. The force of the blow which he had struck was, however, felt even in Samaria. When therefore he wrote to the persons in authority there the somewhat ironical but designedly intimidating counsel, to set up one of the young princes in Samaria as king and fight out the matter which lay between them, they sent a very submissive answer, giving in their adhesion, and professing their readiness to obey in all things his commands. A second letter from Jehu tested this profession in a truly horrid and exceedingly Oriental manner, requiring them to appear before him on the morrow, bringing with them the heads of all the royal princes in Samaria (2 Kings x:1-8). A fallen house meets with little pity in the East; and when the new king left his palace the next morning, he found seventy human heads piled up in two heaps at his gate. There, in the sight of these heaps, Jehu took occasion to explain his conduct, declaring that he must be regarded as the appointed minister of the divine decrees, pronounced long since against the house of Ahab by the prophets, not one of whose words should fall to the ground. He then continued his proscriptions by exterminating in Jezreel not only all in whose veins the blood of the condemned race flowed, but also—by a considerable stretch of his commission—those officers, ministers, and creatures of the late government, who, if suffered to live, would most likely be disturbers of his own reign. He then proceeded to Samaria. So rapid had been these proceedings that he met some of the nephews of the king of Judah, who were going to join their uncle at Jezreel, and had as yet heard nothing of the revolution which had taken place. These also perished under Jehu's now fully-awakened thirst for blood, to the number of forty-two persons (verse 14).

(6) Destroys Baalites. On the way he took up into his chariot the pious Jehonadab the Rechabite, whose austere virtue and respected character would, as he felt, go far to hallow his proceedings in the eyes of the multitude. At Samaria he continued the extirpation of the persons more intimately connected with the late government. This, far from being in any way singular, is a common circumstance in eastern revolutions. But the great object of Jehu was to exterminate the ministers and more devoted adherents of Baal, who had been much encouraged by Jezebel. There was even a temple to this idol in Samaria; and Jehu, never scrupulous about the means of reaching objects which he believed to be good, laid a snare by which he hoped to cut off the main body of Baal's ministers at one blow. He professed to be a more zealous servant of Baal than Ahab had been, and proclaimed a great festival in his honor, at which none but his true servants were to be present. The prophets, priests, and officers of Baal assembled from all parts for this great sacrifice, and sacerdotal vestments were given to them, that none of Jehovah's worshipers might be taken for them. When the temple was full, soldiers were posted so that none might escape; and so soon as the sacrifice had been offered, the word was given by the king, the soldiers entered the temple, and put all the worshipers to the sword. The temple itself was then demolished, the images overthrown, and the site turned into a common jakes.

(7) Shortcomings and Death. Notwithstanding this zeal of Jehu in exterminating the grosser idolatries which had grown up under his immediate predecessors, he was not prepared to subvert the policy which had led Jeroboam and his successors to maintain the schismatic establishment of the golden calves in Dan and Bethel. Here Jehu fell short: and this very policy, apparently so prudent and farsighted, by which he hoped to secure the stability and independence of his kingdom, was that on account of which the term of rule granted to his dynasty was shortened. For this, it was foretold that his dynasty should extend only to four generations; and for this the Divine aid was withheld from him in his wars with the Syrians under Hazael on the eastern frontier. Hence the war was disastrous to him, and the Syrians were able to maintain themselves in the possession of a great part of his territories beyond the Jordan. He died in B. C. 856, and was buried in Samaria, leaving the throne to his son Jehoahaz.

(8) Testimony of the Monuments. "Shalmaneser II's own record bears testimony to the existence of Ahab, of Benhadad, and Hazael of Damascus, and of Jehu the son of Omri." (Price, *The Monuments and the Old Testament,* pp. 63, 155, 292.)

(9) Character. He must be regarded, like many others in history, as an instrument for accomplishing great purposes rather than as great or good in himself. With all his remorseless zeal there was no honest enthusiasm for the true God (2 Kings x:31). In the long period during which his destiny though known to others and perhaps to himself lay dormant; in the suddenness of his rise to power; in the ruthlessness with which he carried out his purposes; in the union of profound silence and dissimulation with a stern, fanatic, wayward zeal,—he has not been without his likenesses in modern times. The Scripture narrative, although it fixes our attention on the services which he rendered to the cause of religion by the extermination of a worthless dynasty and a degrading worship, yet on the whole leaves the sense that it was a reign barren in great results. His dynasty, indeed, was firmly seated on the throne longer than any other royal house of Israel (2 Kings x), and under Jeroboam II it acquired a high name amongst the oriental nations. But Elisha, who had raised him to power, as far as we know, never saw him. In other respects it was a failure; the original sin of Jeroboam's worship continued; and in the Prophet Hosea there seems to be a retribution exacted for the bloodshed by which he had mounted the throne: "I will avenge the blood of Jezreel upon the house of Jehu" (Hos. i:4), as in the similar condemnation of Baasha (1 Kings xvi:3). (Smith, *Bib. Dict.*)

2. Son of Hanani, a prophet, who was sent to pronounce upon Baasha, king of Israel, and his house, the same awful doom which had been already executed upon the house of Jeroboam (1 Kings xvi:1-7). The same prophet was, many years after, commissioned to reprove Jehoshaphat for his dangerous connection with the house of Ahab (2 Chron. xix:2). He seems to have been in the office of chronicler during all of Jehoshaphat's reign (2 Chron. xx:34). (B. C. 928-886.)

3. A man of Judah, son of Obed, and father of Azariah (1 Chron. ii:38). (B. C. after 1612.)

4. One of the Benjamite slingers who came over to David at Ziklag (1 Chron. xii:3). (B. C. 1055.)

5. Son of Josibiah, a Simeonite, who migrated to the valley of Gedor, and was one of the chief men of the tribe (1 Chron. iv:35). (B. C. about 711.)

JEHUBBAH (je-hŭb'bah), (Heb. יֶחְבָּה, *yekh-oob-baw'*, he will be hidden).

Son of Shomer, or Shamer, of the tribe of Asher in time of Beriah (1 Chron. vii:34). (B. C. about 1618.)

JEHUCAL (je'hu-kal), (Heb. יְהוּכַל, *yeh-hoo-kal'*, spelled "Jucal" Jer. xxxviii:1), one of the "princes of King Zedekiah" who was sent to Jeremiah to ask advice and prayers on behalf of the kingdom (Jer. xxxvii:3), but on his return he joined those demanding the prophet's death (B. C. 589).

JEHUD (je'hud), (Heb. יְהֻד, *yeh-hood'*, Judah).

A town between Baalath and Bene-berak, of the tribe of Dan (Josh xix:45); perhaps the modern *El-Jehudieh*, seven and a half miles southeast of Jaffa. (Robinson, *Researches,* iii:45.)

JEHUDI (je-hū'dī), (Heb. יְהוּדִי, *yeh-hoo-dee'*, Jew).

Son of Nethaniah, who invited Baruch to read Jeremiah's roll to the princes, and who later read it to the king himself (Jer. xxxvi:14, 21, 23). (B. C. 605.)

JEHUDIJAH (je'hu-dī'jah), (Heb. יְהוּדִיָּה, *yeh-hoo-dee-yaw'*, Jewess), according to the A. V. a woman given as the second wife of Mered (1 Chron. iv:18), B. C. about 1612. The marginal reading, "the Jewess," is undoubtedly correct. She is probably the same as Hodiah (verse 19). She was called the Jewess to distinguish her from the Egyptian.

JEHUSH (je'hush), (Heb. יְעוּשׁ, *yeh-oosh'*, collecting, bringing together), son of Eshek, and descendant of Saul (1 Chron. viii:39), B. C. about 588.

JEIEL (je-ī'el), (Heb. יְעִיאֵל, *yeh-ee-ale'*, treasure of God).

1. A Reubenite of the house of Joel, probably at the time of the census of the trans-Jordanic tribes, taken by Tiglath-pileser (1 Chron. v:7). (B. C. 782.)

2. A Levite doorkeeper at the first establishing of the ark in Jerusalem (1 Chron. xvi:5); probably the same as the one mentioned later (1 Chron. xv:18, 21) as a musician. (B. C. 1043.)

3. A Levite, forefather of Jahaziel, who foretold Jehoshaphat of his victory over the Ammonites and Moabites (2 Chron. xx:14). (B. C. before 890.)

4. One of the scribes who kept the accounts of Uzziah's warriors (2 Chron. xxvi:11). (B. C. 803.)

5. One of those who assisted in restoring the temple under Hezekiah (2 Chron. xxix:13).

6. One of those who assisted in the restoration of the Passover by Josiah (2 Chron. xxxv:9). (B. C. 623.)

7. One who came in the Caravan of Ezra from Babylon to Jerusalem (Ezra viii:13). (B. C. 459.)

8. One of the Bene-Nebo, a layman who, after the exile put aside a foreign wife (Ezra x:43). (B. C. 459.)

JEKABZEEL (je-kăb'ze-el), (Heb. יְקַבְצְאֵל, *yek-ab-tseh-ale'*, God will gather), a city in the remote southern part of Judah (Josh. xv:21; Neh. xi:25), called KABZEEL.

JEKAMEAM (jĕk'a-mē'am), (Heb. יְקַמְעָם, *yek-am-awm'*, the people will rise), a Levite, the fourth in rank of the "sons" of Hebron in the Levitical arrangement established by David (1 Chron. xxiii:19; xxiv:23), B. C. about 960.

JEKAMIAH (jĕk'a-mī'ah), (Heb. יְקַמְיָה, *yek-am-yaw'*, Jehovah will rise).

1. Son of Shallum, a descendant of Judah in the time of King Ahaz (1 Chron. ii:41). (B. C. about 588.)

2. Fifth named son of King Jeconiah (1 Chron. iii:18), born during the Babylonian exile. (B. C. after 598.)

JEKUTHIEL (je-kū'thi-el), (Heb. יְקוּתִיאֵל, *yek-ooth-ee'ale*, reverence for God, piety), a son of Ezra by a Jewish wife, Jehudijah or Hodiah, and in his turn founder of the town of Zanoah (1 Chron. iv:18), B. C. about 1618.

JEMIMA (je-mī'mȧ or jĕm'i-mȧ), (Heb. יְמִימָה, *yem-ee-maw'*, dove), the eldest of the three daughters of Job, born after he was restored to prosperity (Job xlii:14), B. C. about 2200. The name may be contained in the Arabic Jemama (Foster, *Histor. Geog. of Arabia* ii:67).

JEMUEL (je-mū'el), (Heb. יְמוּאֵל, *yem-oo-ale'*, day of God), the first-named son of Simeon (Gen. xlvi:10; Ex. vi:15). Elsewhere NEMUEL (Num. xxvi:12), apparently by error.

JEPHTHAE (jĕfh'tha-ē), (Heb. xi:32). See JEPHTHAH.

JEPHTHAH (jĕfh'thah), (Heb. יִפְתָּח, *yif-tawkh'*, opener).

The ninth judge of Israel, of the tribe of Manasseh. He was the son of a person named Gilead by a concubine. After the death of his father he was expelled from his home by the envy of his brothers, who refused him any share of the heritage, and he withdrew to the land of Tob (Judg. xi: 1-3) beyond the frontier of the Hebrew territories.

(1) A Free Lance. It is clear that he had before this distinguished himself by his daring character and skill in arms; for no sooner was his withdrawment known than a great number of men of desperate fortunes repaired to him, and he became their chief. His position was now very similar to that of David when he withdrew from the court of Saul. To maintain the people who had thus linked their fortunes with his, there was no other resource than that sort of brigandage which is accounted honorable in the East, so long as it is exercised against public or private enemies, and is not marked by needless cruelty or outrage.

Jephthah led this kind of life for some years, during which his dashing exploits and successful enterprises procured him a higher military reputation than any other man of his time enjoyed.

After the death of Jair the Israelites gradually fell into their favorite idolatries, and were punished by subjection to the Philistines on the west of the Jordan, and to the Ammonites on the east of that river. The oppression which they sustained for eighteen years became at length so heavy that they recovered their senses and returned to the God of their fathers with humiliation and tears; and he was appeased, and promised them deliverance from their affliction (B. C. 1143.)

(2) Leader of Israelites. The tribes beyond the Jordan having resolved to oppose the Ammonites, Jephthah seems to occur to every one as the môst fitting leader. A deputation was accordingly sent to invite him to take the command. After some demur, on account of the treatment he had formerly received, he consented. The rude hero commenced his operations with a degree of diplomatic consideration and dignity for which we are not prepared. The Ammonites being assembled in force for one of those ravaging incursions by which they had repeatedly desolated the land, he sent to their camp a formal complaint of the invasion, and a demand of the ground of their proceeding. Their answer was, that the land of the Israelites beyond the Jordan was theirs. It had originally belonged to them, from whom it had been taken by the Amorites, who had been dispossessed by the Israelites: and on this ground they claimed the restitution of these lands. Jephthah's reply laid down the just principle which has been followed out in the practice of civilized nations, and is maintained by all the great writers on the law of nations. The land belonged to the Israelites by right of conquest from the *actual* possessors; and they could not be expected to recognize any antecedent claim of former possessors, for whom they had not acted, and who had rendered them no assistance, and who had themselves displayed hostility against the Israelites. But the Ammonites reasserted their former views, and on this issue they took the field.

(3) Victorious Over Ammonites. When Jephthah set forth against the Ammonites he solemnly vowed to the Lord, 'If thou shalt without fail deliver the children of Ammon into mine hands, then it shall be, that whatsoever cometh forth of the doors of my house to meet me, when I return in peace from the children of Ammon, shall surely be the Lord's, and I will offer it up for a burnt offering'. (Judg. xi:30, 31). He *was* victorious. The Ammonites sustained a terrible overthrow (Judg. xi:3-33). He *did* return in peace to his house in Mizpeh. As he drew nigh his house, the one that came forth to meet him was his own daughter, his only child, in whom his heart was bound up. She, with her fair companions, came to greet the triumphant hero 'with timbrels and with dances.' But he no sooner saw her than he rent his robes, and cried, 'Alas, my daughter! thou hast brought me very low; . . . for I have opened my mouth unto the Lord, and cannot go back.' Nor did she ask it. She replied, 'My father, if thou hast opened thy mouth unto the Lord, do to me according to that which has proceeded out of thy mouth: forasmuch as the Lord hath taken vengeance for thee of thine enemies, the children of Ammon.' But after a pause she added, 'Let this thing be done for me: let me alone two months, that I may go up and down upon the mountains, and bewail my virginity, I and my fellows.' Her father of course assented; and when the time expired she returned, and, we are told, 'he did with her according to his vow.' It is then added that it became 'a custom in Israel, that the daughters of Israel went yearly to lament the daughter of Jephthah the Gileadite four days in the year. (See below.)

(4) Quarrel with Ephraimites. The victory over the Ammonites was followed by a quarrel with the proud and powerful Ephraimites on the west of the Jordan. This tribe was displeased at having had no share in the glory of the recent victory, and a large body of men belonging to it, who had crossed the river to share in the action, used very high and threatening language when they found their services were not required. Jephthah, finding his remonstrances had no effect, re-assembled some of his disbanded troops and

gave the Ephraimites battle, when they were defeated with much loss. The victors seized the fords of the Jordan, and when any one came to pass over, they made him pronounce the word *Shibboleth* (an ear of corn), but if he could not give the aspiration, and pronounced the word as *Sibboleth,* they knew him for an Ephraimite, and slew him on the spot (Judg. xii:1-6).

(5) Rule and Death. Jephthah judged Israel six years (Judg. x:6; xii:7), during which we have reason to conclude that the exercise of his authority was almost if not altogether confined to the country east of the Jordan (B. C. 1080-1074).

(6) Character. Jephthah seems to have had blended opposite characteristics in his nature. He appears to have been ordinarily calm and deliberate notwithstanding his rash vow, as the history of his life clearly shows.

JEPHTHAH'S VOW. Volumes have been written on the subject of 'Jephthah's rash vow:' the question being whether, in doing to his daughter 'according to his vow,' he really did offer her in sacrifice or not. The negative has been stoutly maintained by many able pens, from a natural anxiety to clear the character of one of the heroes in Israel from so dark a stain. But the more the plain rules of common sense have been exercised in our view of biblical transactions, and the better we have succeeded in realizing a distinct idea of the times in which Jephthah lived and of the position which he occupied, the less reluctance there has been to admit the interpretation which the first view of the passage suggests to every reader, which is that he really did offer her in sacrifice. The explanation which denies this maintains that she was rather doomed to perpetual celibacy.

(1) Reasons for Actual Sacrifice. (1) The whole story is consistent and intelligible, while the sacrifice is understood to have actually taken place; but becomes perverted and difficult as soon as we begin to turn aside from this obvious meaning in search of recondite explanations. (2) Again Jephthah vows that whatsoever came forth from the door of his house to meet him 'shall surely be the Lord's, and I will offer it up for a burnt-offering,' which, in fact, was the regular way of making a thing wholly the Lord's. Afterwards we are told that 'he did with her according to his vow,' that is, according to the plain meaning of plain words, offered her for a burnt-offering. (3) Jephthah was a good deal of a heathen, and human sacrifices were customary among the heathen people. (4) The great grief of Jephthah is only accounted for by her devotement to death. (5) People lament the dead not the living; hence the lamentation of the daughters of Israel four days every year. (6) To *live* unmarried was required by no law, custom, or devotement among the Jews: no one had a right to impose so odious a condition on another, nor is any such condition implied or expressed in the vow which Jephthah uttered. (7) There is not the least evidence to show that his conduct was sanctioned by God. (8) The Jewish commentators themselves generally admit that Jephthah really sacrificed his daughter; and even go so far as to allege that the change in the pontifical dynasty from the house of Eleazar to that of Ithamar was caused by the high-priest of the time having suffered this transaction to take place.

(2) Reasons Against Actual Sacrifice. (1) Human sacrifices were most emphatically forbidden by the law (Deut. xviii:10; xii:30, 31; Lev. xviii:21; xx:2; Ps. cvi:37, 38; Jer. vii:

31; xxxii:35; Ezek. xvi:20, 21, etc.). (2) By translating the conjunction "and" by the word "or" in Judg. xi:30, 31, which is justified by the Hebrew idiom and thus given in the margin, all difficulty will disappear. His words would then read, "shall surely be the Lord's, *or* I will offer a burnt offering;" and not unfrequently the sense requires that the Hebrew should be thus rendered (Lev. xxvii:28) where there is a similar meaning of the conjunctive VAU. The vow would then consist of two parts.

(*a*) That what *person* soever met him should be the Lord's or dedicated to his service.

(*b*) That what *beast* soever met him, if clean, should be offered up for a burnt-offering unto the Lord. This rendering, and this interpretation, is warranted by the Levitical law about vows. The *neder*, or *vow*, in general, included either persons, beasts, or things, dedicated to the Lord for pious uses; which, if it were a simple vow, was redeemable at certain prices, if the person repented of his vow, and wished to commute it for money, according to the age and sex of the person (Lev. xxvii:1-8). This was a wise regulation to remedy rash vows. But if the vow was accompanied with *cherem, devotement,* it was irredeemable, as in the following cases:—"Notwithstanding, no devotement which a man shall devote unto the Lord, (either) of man, or of beast, or of land of his own property, shall be sold or redeemed. Every thing devoted is most holy unto the Lord" (Lev. xxvii:28). Here the three *vaus* in the original should necessarily be rendered disjunctively, *or;* as the last actually is in our public translation, because there are three distinct subjects of devotement, to be applied to distinct uses; the *man,* to be dedicated to the service of the Lord, as Samuel by his mother, Hannah (1 Sam. i:11); the *cattle,* if clean, such as oxen, sheep, goats, turtledoves, or pigeons, to be sacrificed; and if unclean, as camels, horses, asses, to be employed for carrying burdens in the service of the tabernacle or temple; and the *lands,* to be sacred property.

(*c*) This law, therefore, expressly applied, in its first branch, to Jephthah's case, who had *devoted* his daughter to the Lord, or opened his mouth unto the Lord, and therefore could not go back; as he declared in his grief at seeing his daughter, and his only child, coming to meet him with timbrels and dances.

(*d*) She was, therefore, necessarily devoted, but with her own consent, to perpetual virginity, in the service of the tabernacle (Judg. xi:36, 37). And such service was customary; for in the division of the spoils taken in the first Midianite war, of the whole number of captive virgins, 'the Lord's tribute was thirty-two persons' (Num. xxxi:35-40). This instance appears to be decisive of the nature of her devotement.

(*e*) Her father's extreme grief on this occasion, and her requisition of a respite of two months to bewail her virginity, are both perfectly natural; having no other issue, he could look forward only to the extinction of his name or family; and a state of celibacy, which is reproachful among women everywhere, was peculiarly so among the Israelites; and was therefore no ordinary sacrifice on her part, who, though she generously gave up, could not but regret the loss of becoming "a mother in Israel." 'And he did with her according to his vow which he had vowed, and she knew no man,' or remained a virgin all her life (Judg. xi:34-49).

(*f*) There is no precedent of any such sacrifice under the law, in the Old Testament. The case of Isaac, before the law, is irrelevant; for Isaac was not sacrificed; and it was only proposed for a trial of Abraham's faith. No father, merely by his own authority, could put an offending, much less an innocent, child to death, upon any account, without the sentence of the magistrates (Deut. xxi:18-21), and the consent of the people, as in Jonathan's case.

(*g*) The Mishna, or traditional law of the Jews, is pointedly against it:—"If a Jew should devote his son or daughter, his man or maid servant, who are Hebrews, the devotement would be void; because no man can devote what is not his own, or of whose life he has not the absolute disposal."

(*h*) That Jephthah could not even have devoted his daughter to celibacy against her will, is evident from the history, and from the high estimation in which she was always held by the daughters of Israel, for her filial duty and her hapless fate, which they celebrated by a regular anniversary commemoration four days in the year (Judg. xi:40).

JEPHUNNEH (je-phŭn'neh), (Heb. יְפֻנֶּה, *yef-oon-neh'*, nimble).

1. The companion of Joshua in his exploration of Canaan; father of Caleb the spy (Num. xiii: 6; xiv:6, 30, 38; xxvi:65; xxxii:12; xxxiv:19; Deut. i:36; Josh. xiv:6, 13, 14; 1 Chron. iv:15; vi: 56). (B. C. 1698.)

2. Eldest son of Jether, or Ithran, a descendant of Asher (1 Chron. vii:38). (B. C. before 1017.)

JERAH (jē'rah), (Heb. יֶרַח, *yeh'rakh*, month), fourth son of Joktan (1 Chron. i:20; Gen. x:26), the founder of an Arabian tribe who probably settled near Hazamaveth and Hadoram. (See JOKTAN.)

JERAHMEEL (je-räh'me-el), (Heb. יְרַחְמְאֵל, *yer-akh-meh-ale'*, God will compassionate).

1. Grandson of Pharez, and great grandson of Judah. His descendants were called Jerahmeelites (1 Chron. ii:9, 26, 27, 33, 42). (B. C. before 1658.)

2. A Merarite Levite of the family of Kish, and representative of his tribe in the organization of the service by David (1 Chron. xxiv: 29). (B. C. 1014.)

3. Son of Hammelech, one of the two appointed by Jehoiakim to arrest Jeremiah (Jer. xxxvi:26). (B. C. 605.)

JERAHMEELITES (je-räh'me-el-ītes), (Heb. יְרַחְמְאֵלִי, *yer-akh-meh-ay-lee'*, patronym, from the above), a tribe descended from JERAHMEEL, 1 (1 Sam. xxvii:10; xxx:29).

JERED (jē'red), (Heb. יֶרֶד, *yeh'red*, descent, going down), (1 Chron. i:2). See JARED, 1; (1 Chron. iv:18). (See JARED, 2.)

JEREMAI (jĕr'e-māi), (Heb. יְרֵמַי, *yer-ay-mah'ee*, dweller on heights), a son of Hashum, who divorced his foreign wife after the exile in Babylon (Ezra x:33), B. C. 459.

JEREMIAH (jĕr'e-mī'ah), (Heb. יִרְמְיָה, *yir-meh-yaw'*, Jah will rise).

1. A native of Libnah, the father of Hamutal, Josiah's wife, who was mother of Jehoahaz (2 Kings xxiii:31) and Zedekiah (xxiv:18; Jer. lii:1). (B. C. before 632.)

2. A Gadite warrior who joined David in the wilderness (1 Chron. xii:10). (B. C. 1061.)

3. Another man of Gad in David's army (1 Chron. xii:13). (B. C. before 1000.)

4. A Benjamite, who joined David at Ziklag (1 Chron. xii:4). (B. C. 1053.)

5. A chief of the trans-Jordanic half-tribe of Manasseh (1 Chron. v:24). (B. C. 782.)

6. Son of Habaziniah, and father of Jaazaniah, the Rechabite, whom the prophet tested with the proffer of wine (Jer. xxxv:3). (B. C. before 606.)

7. A priest, head of one of the courses of temple worship (Neh. xii:1, 34).

8. One of the trumpet players at the celebration of the newly repaired walls of Jerusalem. Apparently the same as the one who signed the covenant with Jeremiah (Neh. x:2), and perhaps identical with (7). (B. C. 446-410.)

9. Jeremiah the Prophet. Son of Hilkiah, a priest of Anathoth, in the land of Benjamin (Jer. i:1). .(See ANATHOTH.) Many have supposed that his father was the high-priest of the same name (2 Kings xxii:8), who found the book of the law in the eighteenth year of Josiah. This, however, seems improbable on several grounds—first, there is nothing in the writings of Jeremiah to lead us to think that his father was more than an ordinary priest ('Hilkiah [one] of the priests,' Jer. i:1); again, the name Hilkiah was common amongst the Jews (see 2 Kings xviii:18; 1 Chron. vi:45; xxvi:11; Neh. viii:4; Jer. xxix:3); and, lastly, his residence at Anathoth is evidence that he belonged to the line of Abiathar (1 Kings ii:26-35), who was deposed from the high-priest's office by Solomon; after which time the office appears to have remained in the line of Zadok.

(1) Early Life. Jeremiah was very young when the word of the Lord first came to him (ch. i:6). This event took place in the thirteenth year of Josiah (B. C. 629), whilst the youthful prophet still lived at Anathoth. It would seem that he remained in his native city several years, but at length, in order to escape the persecution of his fellow townsmen (ch. xi:21), and even of his own family (ch. xii:6), as well as to have a wider field for his exertions, he left Anathoth and took up his residence at Jerusalem.

(2) Ally of Josiah. The finding of the book of the law, five years after the commencement of his predictions, must have produced a powerful influence on the mind of Jeremiah, and king Josiah no doubt found him a powerful ally in carrying into effect the reformation of religious worship (2 Kings xxiii:1-25). During the reign of this monarch, we may readily believe that Jeremiah would be in no way molested in his work; and that from the time of his quitting Anathoth to the eighteenth year of his ministry, he probably uttered his warnings without interruption, though with little success (see ch. xi). Indeed, the reformation itself was nothing more than the forcible repression of idolatrous and heathen rites, and the re-establishment of the external service of God, by the command of the king. No sooner, therefore, was the influence of the court on behalf of the true religion withdrawn, than it was evident that no real improvement had taken place in the minds of the people. Jeremiah, who hitherto was at least protected by the influence of the pious king Josiah, soon became the object of attack, as he must doubtless have long been the object of dislike, to those whose interests were identified with the corruptions of religion.

(3) Relations to Jehoahaz and Jehoiakim. We hear nothing of the prophet during the three months which constituted the short reign of Jehoahaz; but 'in the beginning of the reign of Jehoiakim' the prophet was interrupted in his ministry by 'the priests and the prophets,' who with the populace brought him before the civil authorities, urging that capital punishment should be inflicted on him for his threatenings of evil on the city unless the people amended their ways (ch. xxvi). The princes seem to have been in some degree aware of the results which the general corruption was bringing on the state, and if they did not themselves yield to the exhortations of the prophet, they acknowledged that he spoke in the name of the Lord, and were quite averse from so openly renouncing His authority as to put His messenger to death. It appears, however, that it was rather owing to the personal influence of one or two, especially Ahikam, than to any general feeling favorable to Jeremiah, that his life was preserved; and it would seem that he was then either placed under restraint, or else was in so much danger from the animosity of his adversaries as to make it prudent for him not to appear in public. In the fourth year of Jehoiakim (B. C. 606) he was commanded to write the predictions which had been given through him, and to read them to the people. Because he was 'shut up,' and could not himself go into the house of the Lord (ch. xxxvi:5) he therefore deputed Baruch to write the predictions after him, and to read them publicly on the fast-day. These threatenings being thus anew made public, Baruch was summoned before the princes to give an account of the manner in which the roll containing them had come into his possession. The princes, who, without strength of principle to oppose the wickedness of the king, had sufficient respect for religion, as well as sagacity enough to discern the importance of listening to the voice of God's prophet, advised both Baruch and Jeremiah to conceal themselves, whilst they endeavored to influence the mind of the king by reading the roll to him. The result showed that their precautions were not needless. The bold self-will and reckless daring of the monarch refused to listen to any advice, even though coming with the professed sanction of the Most High. Having read three or four leaves 'he cut the roll with the penknife and cast it into the fire that was on the hearth, until all the roll was consumed,' and gave immediate orders for the apprehension of Jeremiah and Baruch, who, however, were both preserved from the vindictive monarch. Of the history of Jeremiah during the eight or nine remaining years of the reign of Jehoiakim we have no certain account. At the command of God he procured another roll, in which he wrote all that was in the roll destroyed by the king, 'and added besides unto them many like words' (ch. xxxvi:32).

(4) Relations to Jehoiachin. (B. C. 597.) In the short reign of his successor Jehoiachin or Jeconiah, we find him still uttering his voice of warning (see ch. xiii:18; comp. 2 Kings xxiv:12, and ch. xxii:24-30), though without effect.

(5) Relations to Zedekiah. It was probably either during this reign, or at the commencement of the reign of Zedekiah, that he was put in confinement by Pashur, the 'chief governor of the house of the Lord.' He seems, however, soon to have been liberated, as we find that 'they had not put him into prison' when the army of Nebuchadnezzar commenced the siege of Jerusalem. The Chaldæans drew off their army for a time, on the report of help coming from Egypt to the besieged city; and now feeling the danger to be imminent, and yet a ray of hope brightening their prospects, the king entreated Jeremiah to pray to the Lord for them. The hopes of the king were not responded to in the message which Jeremiah received from God. He was assured that the Egyptian army should return to their own land, that the Chaldæans should come again, and that they should take the city and burn it with fire (ch. xxxvii:7, 8). The princes, apparently irritated by a message so contrary to their wishes, made the departure of Jeremiah from the city, during the short respite, the pretext for accusing him of deserting to the Chaldæans, and he was forthwith cast into prison. The king seems to have been throughout inclined to favor the prophet, and sought to know from him the word of the Lord; but he was wholly under the influence of the princes, and dared not communicate with him except in secret (ch. xxxviii:14, 28); much less could he follow advice so obnoxious to their views as that which the prophet gave. Jeremiah, therefore, more from the hostility of the princes than the inclination of the king, was still in confinement when the city was taken.

(6) **Relations to Nebuchadnezzar.** Nebuchadnezzar formed a more just estimate of his character and of the value of his counsels, and gave a special charge to his captain Nebuzaradan, not only to provide for him but to follow his advice (ch. xxxix:12). He was accordingly taken from the prison and allowed free choice either to go to Babylon, where doubtless he would have been held in honor in the royal court, or to remain with his own people. We need scarcely be told that he who had devoted more than forty years of unrequited service to the welfare of his fallen country, should choose to remain with the remnant of his people rather than seek the precarious fame which might await him at the court of the king of Babylon. Accordingly he went to Mizpah with Gedaliah, whom the Babylonian monarch had appointed governor of Judea; and after his murder, sought to persuade Johanan, who was then the recognized leader of the people, to remain in the land, assuring him and the people, by a message from God in answer to their inquiries, that if they did so the Lord would build them up, but if they went to Egypt the evils which they sought to escape would come upon them there (ch. xlii). The people refused to attend to the Divine message, and under the command of Johanan went into Egypt, taking Jeremiah and Baruch along with them (ch. xliii:6). In Egypt the prophet still sought to turn the people to the Lord, from whom they had so long and so deeply revolted (ch. xliv); but his writings give us no subsequent information respecting his personal history.

(7) **Traditions.** Ancient traditions assert that he spent the remainder of his life in Egypt. According to the pseudo-Epiphanius he was stoned by the people at Taphnæ (the same as Tahpanhes), where the Jews were settled (*De Vitis Prophet.* t. ii. p. 239, quoted by Fabricius, *Codex Pseudepigraphus V. T.* t. i. p. 1110). It is said that his bones were removed by Alexander the Great to Alexandria (Carpzov, *Introd.* part iii, p. 138, where other traditions respecting him will be found).

(8) **Character.** Jeremiah was contemporary with Zephaniah, Habakkuk, Ezekiel, and Daniel. None of these, however, are in any remarkable way connected with him, except Ezekiel. The writings and character of these two eminent prophets furnish many very interesting points both of comparison and contrast. Both, during a long series of years, were laboring at the same time and for the same object. The representations of both, far separated as they were from each other, are in substance singularly accordant; yet there is at the same time a marked difference

in their modes of statement, and a still more striking diversity in the character and natural disposition of the two. No one who compares them can fail to perceive that the mind of Jeremiah was of a softer and more delicate texture than that of his illustrious contemporary. His whole history convinces us that he was by nature mild and retiring (Ewald, *Propheten des Alt. Bund.* p. 2), highly susceptible and sensitive, especially to sorrowful emotions, and rather inclined, as we should imagine, to shrink from danger than to brave it. Yet, with this acute perception of injury, and natural repugnance from being 'a man of strife,' he never in the least degree shrinks from publicity; nor is he at all intimidated by reproach or insult, or even by actual punishment and threatened death, when he has the message of God to deliver. He is, in truth, as remarkable an instance, though in a different way, of the overpowering influence of the Divine energy, as Ezekiel. The one presents the spectacle of the power of Divine inspiration acting on a mind naturally of the firmest texture, and at once subduing to itself every element of the soul; whilst the other furnishes an example, not less memorable, of moral courage sustained by the same Divine inspiration against the constantly opposing influence of a love of retirement and strong susceptibility to impressions of outward evil. (See Henderson's *Commentary*, 1851; Cowles, *Notes*, N. Y., 1869; Isaac Taylor, *Spirit of Hebrew Poetry*, p. 272; Stanley, *Jewish Ch.*, ii, pp. 570-622; Noyes, *New Transl. of the Heb. Poets*, Boston, 1866; and others). (See JEREMIAH, BOOK OF; LAMENTATIONS.)　　　　F. W. G.

JEREMIAH, BOOK OF

1. Difficulties and Diversities. Much difficulty has arisen in reference to the writings of Jeremiah from the apparent disorder in which they stand in our present copies, and from the many disagreements between the Hebrew text and that found in the Septuagint version; and many conjectures have been hazarded respecting the occasion of this disorder. The following are the principal diversities between the two texts:

(1) The prophecies against foreign nations, which in the Hebrew occupy chapters xlvi-li at the close of the book, are in the Greek placed after ch. xxv:14, forming chapters xxvi-xxxi; the remainder of ch. xxv of the Hebrew is ch. xxxii of the Septuagint. The following chapters proceed in the same order in both, chapters xliv and xlv of the Hebrew forming ch. li of the Septuagint; and the historical appendix, ch. lii, is placed at the close in both.

(2) The prophecies against the heathen nations stand in a different order in the two editions, as is shown in the following table:

Hebrew.	Sept.
Egypt.	Elam.
Philistines.	Egypt.
Moab.	Babylon.
Ammon.	Philistines.
Edom.	Edom.
Damascus.	Ammon.
Kedar.	Kedar.
Elam.	Damascus.
Babylon.	Moab.

(3) Various passages which exist in the Hebrew are not found in the Greek copies (*e. g.* ch. xxvii: 19-22; xxxiii:14-26; xxxix:4-14; xlviii:45-47). Besides these discrepancies, there are numerous omissions and frequent variations of single words and phrases. To explain these diversities recourse has been had to the hypothesis of a

double recension, an hypothesis which, with various modifications, is held by most modern critics.

2. Genuineness of Writings. The genuineness and canonicity of the writings of Jeremiah in general are established both by the testimony of ancient writers and by quotations and references which occur in the New Testament (2 Macc. ii:1-8; Philo. vol. i. p. 95; Josephus *Antiq.* lib. x:5,1; Matt. ii:17; Matt. xvi:14; Heb. viii:8, 12).

(1) The text in Matt. xxvii:9 has occasioned considerable difficulty, because the passage there quoted is not found in the extant writings of the prophet. Jerome affirms that he found the exact passage in a Hebrew apocryphal book (Fabricius, *Cod. Pseudep.* i. 1103) ; but there is no proof that that book was in existence before the time of Christ. It is probable that the passage intended by Matthew is Zech. xi:12, 13, which in part corresponds with the quotation he gives, and that the name is a gloss which has found its way into the text (see Olshausen, *Comment upon New Testament.*)

(2) The genuineness of some portions of the book has been of late disputed by the critics of the so-called advance school. Movers, whose views have been adopted by De Wette and Hitzig, attributes ch. x:1-16, and cc. xxx, xxxi, and xxxiii to the author of the concluding portion of the book of Isaiah. His fundamental argument against the last-named portion is, that the prophet Zechariah (ch. viii:7, 8) quotes from Jer. xxxi: 7, 8, 33, and in ver. 9 speaks of the author as one who lived 'in the day that the foundation of the house of the Lord of hosts was laid.' He must, therefore, have been contemporary with Zechariah himself. This view obliges him, of course, to consider ch. xxx:1, with which he joins the three following verses, as a later addition. By an elaborate comparison of the peculiarities of style he endeavors to show that the author of these chapters was the so-called pseudo-Isaiah. He acknowledges, however, that there are many expressions peculiar to Jeremiah, and supposes that it was in consequence of these that the prediction was placed among his writings. These similarities he accounts for by assuming that the later unknown prophet accommodated the writings of the earlier to his own use.

(3) Every one will see how slight is the external ground on which Movers' argument rests; for there is nothing in verses 7, 8, of Zechariah to prove that it is intended to be a quotation from any written prophecy, much less from this portion of Jeremiah. The quotation, if it be such, is made up by joining together phrases of frequent recurrence in the prophets picked out from amongst many others. Then, again, the mention of *prophets* is evidence that Zechariah was not referring to the writings of one individual; and, lastly, the necessity of rejecting the exordium, without any positive ground for suspecting its integrity, is a strong argument against the position of Movers. Hitzig (*Jeremia,* p. 230) is induced, by the force of these considerations, to give up the external evidence on which Movers had relied. The internal evidence arising from the examination of particular words and phrases —a species of proof which, when standing alone, is always to be received with great caution— is rendered of still less weight by the evidence of an opposite kind.

Ewald, who is by no means accustomed to acquiesce in received opinions as such, agrees that the chapters in question, as well as the other passage mentioned ch. x:1-16, are the work of Jeremiah. The authenticity of this latter portion is denied solely on internal grounds, and the remarks we have already made will, in substance, apply also to these verses. It seems, however, not improbable that the Chaldee of ver. 11 is a gloss which has crept into the text—both because it is (apparently without reason) in another language, and because it seems to interrupt the progress of thought. The predictions against Babylon in chaps. l and li are objected to by Movers, De Wette, and others, on the ground that they contain many interpolations. Ewald attributes them to some unknown prophet who imitated the style of Jeremiah. Their authenticity is maintained by many critics of acknowledged weight of opinion. The last chapter is generally regarded as an appendix added by some later author. It is almost verbally the same as the account in 2 Kings xxiv:18; xxv:30, and it carries the history down to a later period probably than that of the death of Jeremiah; that it is not his work seems to be indicated in the last verse of ch. li.

3. Disorder of Prophecies. (1) Blayney and Eichhorn. It is impossible, within the limits assigned to this article, even to notice all the attempts which have been made to account for the apparent disorder of Jeremiah's prophecies. Blayney speaks of their present disposition as a 'preposterous jumbling together of the prophecies of the reigns of Jehoiakim and Zedekiah,' and concludes that 'the original order has, most probably, by some accident or other been disturbed' (*Notes* p. 3). Eichhorn says that no other explanation can be given than that the prophet wrote his oracles on single rolls, larger or smaller as they came to his hand, and that, as he was desirous to give his countrymen a copy of them when they went into captivity, he dictated them to an amanuensis from the separate rolls, without attending to the order of time, and then preserved the rolls in the same order (*Einl.* iii, 134). Later critics have attempted in different ways to trace some plan in the present arrangement. Thus Movers supposes the whole collection to have consisted of six books—the longest being that written by Baruch (Jer. xxxvi:2, 32), which was taken by the collector as his foundation, into which he inserted the other books in such places as seemed, on a very slight glance at their contents, to be suitable. All such theories, however, proceed on the presumption that the present arrangement is the work of a compiler, which, therefore, we are at liberty to alter at pleasure; and though they offer boundless scope for ingenuity in suggesting a better arrangement, they serve us very little in respect to the explanation of the book itself.

(2) Ewald. Ewald adopts another principle, which, if it be found valid, cannot fail to throw much light on the connection and meaning of the predictions. He maintains that the book, in its present form, is, from ch. i to ch. xlix, substantially the same as it came from the hand of the prophet, or his amanuensis, and seeks to discover in the present arrangement some plan according to which it is disposed. He finds that various portions are prefaced by the same formula, 'The word which came to Jeremiah from the Lord' (vii:1; xi:1; xviii: 1; xxi:1; xxv:1; xxx:1; xxxii:1; xxxiv:1, 8; xxxv:1; xl:1; xliv:1) ; or by the very similar expression, 'The word of the Lord which came to Jeremiah' (xiv:1; xlvi:1; xlvii:1; xlix:34). The notices of time distinctly mark some other divisions which are more or less historical (xxvi: 1; xxvii:1; xxxvi:1; xxxvii:2). Two other portions are in themselves sufficiently distinct without such indication (xxix:1; xlv:1), while the general introduction to the book serves for the section contained in ch. i. There are left two sections (chaps. ii, iii), the former of which has only the shorter introduction, which generally designates the commencement of a strophe; while the latter, as it now stands, seems to be imperfect, having as an introduction merely the word 'saying.' Thus the book is divided into twenty-three separate and independent sections, which, in the poetical parts, are again divided into strophes of from seven to nine verses, frequently distinguished by such a phrase as 'The Lord said also unto me.'

4. Divisions of the Book. These separate sections are arranged by Ewald so as to form five distinct books: I. The introduction, ch. i. II. Reproofs of the sins of the Jews, cc. ii-xxiv, consisting of seven sections, viz.: (1) ch. ii; (2) cc. iii:vi: (3) cc. vii-x; (4) cc. xi-xiii; (5) cc. xiv-xvii:18; (6) cc. xvii:19-xx; (7) cc. xxi-xxiv. III. A general review of all nations, the heathen as well as the people of Israel, consisting of two sections: (1) cc. xlvi-xlix (which he thinks have been transposed); (2) ch. xxv. And an historical appendix of three sections: (a) ch. xxvi; (b) ch. xxvii; and (c) cc. xxviii, xxix. IV. Two sections picturing the hopes of brighter times: (1) cc. xxx, xxxi; and (2) cc. xxxii, xxxiii, to which, as in the last book, is added an historical appendix in three sections: (a) ch. xxxiv:1-7; (b) ch. xxxiv:8-22; (c) ch. xxxv. V. The conclusion, in two sections: (1) ch. xxxvi; (2) ch. xlv. All this, he supposes, was arranged in Palestine, during the short interval of rest between the taking of the city and the departure of Jeremiah with the remnant of the Jews, to Egypt. In Egypt, after some interval, Jeremiah added three sections, viz.: cc. xxxvii, xxxix, xl-xliii and xliv. At the same time, probably, he added ch. xlvi:13-26 to the previous prophecy respecting Egypt, and, perhaps, made some additions to other parts previously written. VI. The principal predictions relating to the Messiah are found in ch. xxiii:1-8; xxx:31-40; xxxiii:14-26. This arrangement is probably preferable, all things considered.

5. Style. The style of Jeremiah corresponds with the view of the character of his mind; though not deficient in power it is peculiarly marked by pathos. He delights in the expression of the tender emotions, and employs all the resources of his imagination to excite corresponding feelings in his readers. He has an irresistible sympathy with the miserable, which finds utterance in the most touching descriptions of their condition. He seizes with wonderful tact those circumstances which point out the objects of his pity as the objects of sympathy, and founds his expostulations on the miseries which are thus exhibited. His book of Lamentations is an astonishing exhibition of his power to accumulate images of sorrow. The whole series of elegies has but one object—the expression of sorrow for the forlorn condition of his country; and yet he presents this to us in so many lights, alludes to it by so many figures, that not only are his mournful strains not felt to be tedious reiterations, but the reader is captivated by the plaintive melancholy which pervades the whole. (See LAMENTATIONS.)   F. W. G.

JEREMIAH, LAMENTATIONS OF (jĕr-e-mī'ah lăm-ĕn-tā'shŭns). See LAMENTATIONS.

JEREMIAS (jĕre-mi'as), (Gr. Ιερεμίας, hee-er-eh-mee'as), the Greek form of the name of Jeremiah

the prophet, used in the A. V. of Ecclus. xlix:6; 2 Macc. xv:14; Matt. xvi:14. (See JEREMIAH; JEREMY.)

JEREMOTH (jĕr'e-mŏth), (Heb. יְרִימוֹת, yer-ay-mohth', heights).

1. The last mentioned of the sons of Mushi (1 Chron. xxiii:23). The name is JERIMOTH (see JERIMOTH, 4). (1 Chron. xxiv:30.) B. C. after 1856.

2. A Levite who had charge of the fifteenth division of the temple musicians as arranged by David (1 Chron. xxv:22); probably the same as JERIMOTH, 5. (B. C. 1014.)

3. A Benjamite, "son" of Beriah (1 Chron. viii:14). (B. C. about 588.) Probably the same as JEROHAM, 2 (ver. 27).

4. One of the "sons" of Elam who divorced his foreign wife after the captivity (Ezra x:26). (B. C. 459.)

5. A "son" of Zattu who also put away his Gentile wife after the exile (Ezra x:27). (B. C. 459.)

6. (Ezra x:29). (See RAMOTH.)

JEREMY (jĕr'e-my), (Matt. ii:17; xxvii:9), a shortened form of the name of the prophet JEREMIAH (which see).

JERIAH (je-rī'ah). (Heb. יְרִיָּה, yer-ee-yaw', Jah will throw), a Kohathite Levite, the first in rank of the sons of Hebron in the priestly arrangement made by David (1 Chron. xxiii:19; xxiv:23); elsewhere JERIJAH (1 Chron. xxvi:31), B. C. 1014.

JERIBAI (jĕr'i-bāi), (Heb. יְרִיבַי, yer-eeb-ah'ee, contentious), the second named of the sons of Elnaam, and one of David's body-guard (1 Chron. xi:46), B. C. after 1000.

JERICHO (jĕr'i-kō), (Heb. יְרִיחוֹ, yer-ee-kho', fragrant).

A town in the plain of the same name, not far from the river Jordan, at the point where it enters the Dead Sea. It lay before the Israelites when they crossed the river, on first entering the Promised Land; and the account which the spies who were sent by them into the city received from their hostess Rahab, tended much to encourage their subsequent operations, as it showed that the inhabitants of the country were greatly alarmed at their advance, and the signal miracles which had marked their course from the Nile to the Jordan. The strange manner in which Jericho itself was taken must have strengthened this impression in the country, and appears, indeed, to have been designed for that effect.

(1) Destroyed. The town was utterly destroyed by the Israelites, who pronounced an awful curse upon whoever should rebuild it; and all the inhabitants were put to the sword, except Rahab and her family (Josh. vi:25).

In these accounts Jericho is repeatedly called 'the city of palm-trees'; which shows that the hot and dry plain, so similar to the land of Egypt, was noted beyond other parts of Palestine for the tree which abounds in that country, but which was and is less common in the land of Canaan than general readers and painters suppose. It has now almost disappeared even from the plain of Jericho, although specimens remain in the plain of the Mediterranean coast.

(2) Rebuilt. Notwithstanding the curse, Jericho was soon rebuilt (see HIEL), and became a school of the prophets (1 Kings xvi:34; 2 Kings ii:4, 5). Its inhabitants returned after the exile, and it was eventually fortified by the Syrian general Bacchides (Ezra ii:34; Neh. iii:2; 1 Macc. ix:50). Pompey marched from Scythopolis, along the valley of the Jordan, to Jericho, and thence to Jerusalem; and Strabo speaks of the castles Thrax and Taurus, in or near Jericho, as having been destroyed by him (Joseph. *Antiq.* xiv: 4, 1; Strabo, xvi:2, 40).

(3) Varied History. Herod the Great, in the beginning of his career, captured and sacked Jericho, but afterwards strengthened and adorned it, when he had redeemed its revenues from Cleopatra, on whom the plain had been bestowed by Antony (Joseph. *Antiq.* xv:4, 1, 2).

He appears to have often resided here, probably in winter; he built over the city a fortress called Cypros, between which and the former palace he erected other palaces, and called them by the

the word of the Lord which he spake by Joshua, the son of Nun" (1 Kings xvi:34).

Previous to this, however, and almost immediately after the death of Joshua, reference is made to the city of palm-trees, which was captured by Eglon, king of Moab (Judg. iii:13), and it was nearly 100 years before the rebuilding by Hiel that David's ambassadors, who had been so grievously insulted by the king of Ammon, were directed "to tarry at Jericho until their beards were grown" (2 Sam. x:5).

We are to infer, from these several statements, that Jericho was rebuilt soon after its destruction by Joshua, but not upon its ancient foundations —a change by which the penalty was avoided.

Jericho.

names of his friends (Joseph. *Antiq.* xvi:5, 2; *De Bell. Jud.* i. 21, 4, 9). Here also was a hippodrome or circus, in which the same tyrant, when lying at Jericho on his death-bed, caused the nobles of the land to be shut up, for massacre after his death. He died here; but his bloody intention was not executed (Joseph. *Antiq.* xvii: 6, 5; *De Bell. Jud.* i. 33, 6-8). The palace at this place was afterwards rebuilt more magnificently by Archelaus (*Antiq.* xvii:31).

(4) Site Changed. In order to render the several notices of Jericho contained in the Bible consistent with each other, and with the description in Josephus, it seems necessary to suppose more than one change of situation. Joshua "burned the city with fire, and all that was therein," and said, "Cursed be the man before the Lord that riseth up and buildeth this city Jericho; he shall lay the foundation thereof in his firstborn, and in his youngest son shall he set up the gates thereof" (Josh. vi:26). It was about 520 years after this, in the impious reign of Ahab, that Hiel rebuilt the city, and suffered the fearful penalty that had been denounced against such an act of daring impiety. "He laid the foundation thereof in Abiram his firstborn, and set up the gates thereof in his youngest son Segub, according to

The malediction had probably fallen into oblivion, or, if remembered, was likely to be treated with contempt in the infidel and idolatrous age when Hiel restored the original city. It was, according to the common chronology, about thirty years subsequent to this restoration that Elisha healed the fountain from which the city derived its supply of water. It is probable that the accursed site had been again abandoned, upon the catastrophe that followed the impious attempt of Hiel, for the existing city seems to have been at some distance from "the spring of the waters," which produced sterility and disease (2 Kings ii:21). It may have occupied, at the era of Elisha's miracle, the same site as it did when visited by our Savior, and described by Josephus.

(5) In the Time of Christ. By this it will be seen that the Jericho which existed in the time of our Savior was a great and important city—probably more so than it had ever been since its foundation. It was once visited by him, when he lodged with Zaccheus, and healed the blind man (Luke xviii:35-43; xix:1, 7; Matt. xx:29-34; Mark x:46-52).

(6) Subsequent History. Jericho was afterwards made the head of one of the toparchies, and was visited by Vespasian before he left the country, who stationed there the tenth legion in garrison (Joseph. *De Bell. Jud.* iii. 3, 5; iv:8, 1; v:2, 3). Eusebius and Jerome describe Jericho as having been destroyed during the siege of Jerusalem, on account of the perfidy of the inhabitants, but add that it was afterwards rebuilt. The town, however, appears to have been overthrown during the Mohammedan conquest; for Adamnanus, at the close of the seventh century, describes the site as without human habitations, and covered with corn and vines. The celebrated palm-groves still existed. In the next century a church is mentioned; and in the ninth century several monasteries appear. About the same time the plain of Jericho is again noticed for its fertility and peculiar products; and it appears to have been brought under cultivation by the Saracens, for the sake of the sugar and other products for which the soil and climate were more suitable than any other in Palestine. Ruins of extensive aqueducts, with pointed Saracenic arches, remain in evidence of the elaborate irrigation and culture of this fine plain—which is nothing without water, and everything with it—at a period long subsequent to the occupation of the country by the Jews. It is to this age that we may probably refer the origin of the castle and village, which have since been regarded as representing Jericho. The place has been mentioned by travelers and pilgrims down to the present time as a poor hamlet consisting of a few houses. In the fifteenth century the square castle or tower began to pass among pilgrims as the house of Zaccheus, a title which it bears to the present day.

(7) Modern Jericho. The village that now represents the ancient Jericho bears the name of Rihah, and is supposed to date from the ninth century. It is situated about the middle of the plain, six miles west from the Jordan, in N. lat. 31° 57′, and E. long. 35° 33′. Dr. Olin describes the present village as 'the meanest and foulest of Palestine.' It may perhaps contain forty dwellings, formed of small loose stones. The most important object is the castle or tower already mentioned, which Dr. Robinson supposes to have been constructed to protect the cultivation of the plain under the Saracens. It is thirty or forty feet square, and about the same height, and is now in a dilapidated condition.

Rihah may contain about two hundred inhabitants, who have a sickly aspect, and are reckoned vicious and indolent. They keep a few cattle and sheep, and till a little land for grain as well as for gardens. A small degree of industry and skill bestowed on this prolific soil, favored as it is with abundant water for irrigation, would amply reward the labor. But this is wanting; and everything bears the mark of abject, and, which is unusual in the East, of squalid poverty. There are some fine fig-trees near the village, and some vines in the gardens. But the most distinguishing feature of the whole plain is a noble grove of trees which borders the village on the west, and stretches away northward to the distance of two miles or more.

This grove owes its existence to the waters of one of the fountains, the careful distribution of which over the plain by canals and aqueducts did once, and might still, cover it with abundance. One of these fountains is called by the natives Ain es-Sultan, but by pilgrims the Fountain of Elias, being supposed to be the same whose bitter waters were cured by that prophet. Dr. Robinson thinks there is reason for this conclusion. It lies almost two miles N.W. from the village, and bursts forth at the foot of a high double mound, situated a mile or more in front of the mountain Quarantana. It is a large and beautiful fountain of sweet and pleasant water. Beyond the fountain rises up the bold perpendicular face of the mountain Quarantana (Kuruntul), from the foot of which a line of low hills runs out N.N.E. in front of the mountains, and forms the ascent to a narrow tract of table-land along their base. On this tract, at the foot of the mountains, about two and a half miles N. N.W. from the Ain es-Sultan, is the still larger fountain of Duk, the waters of which are brought along the base of Quarantana in a canal to the top of the declivity at the back of Ain es-Sultan, whence they were formerly distributed to several mills, and scattered over the upper part of the plain (Robinson's *Bib. Researches,* ii. 284, 285).

Bishop S. M. Merrill writes of a ride from the ford of the Jordan westward thus: "The fruitful plain that so long ago flourished as the garden of the Lord was a desert. Dry, sandy, and scorched, it is worn out and blighted; and yet it looks as if, with irrigation, it might be easily redeemed to productiveness. The village of Jericho is a cluster of mud houses, with every appearance of poverty and discomfort. The remains of old aqueducts and ruins of buildings indicate that a city of some proportions was once here. It stood close to the mountain range, in fact touched the foot of the mountain. High above the other summits, some three miles away, is the place where Jesus was tempted, and is called the Mount of Temptation, where he fasted forty days and forty nights, tempted of the devil. We left Jericho early in the morning to go up to Jerusalem, probably by the way that was traveled two thousand years ago. We passed the brook Cherith, where Elijah was fed by the ravens when hiding from the wrath of Ahab. On the high ground, above the plain, we struck the old Roman road, with the broad, flat paving stones still covering its bed for quite a distance. Further up, we came to the ruins of an old khan, or caravansary, which is said to be the only spot where an 'inn' ever stood between Jerusalem and Jericho, and therefore, it is the reputed site of the inn to which the good Samaritan took the wounded man who had fallen among thieves in this neighborhood, as related in the Lord's parable. This region has always been famous for robbers.

"After passing the place where Shimei cursed and threw stones at David, when the king was fleeing from the rebellion of Absalom, we arrived at one of the most inviting spots for a rest in all the journey. It is called the Fountain of the Disciples, or Apostles' Fountain. Tradition says it was a favorite stopping place with Christ and his disciples, and it is not difficult to accept the statement; for one can scarcely imagine that a company of weary travelers could come to such a fountain as is here and not be delighted and refreshed. We tarried at this fountain for an hour or two, and after lunch took up our march to Bethany. The hill to ascend after leaving the fountain was a very high one. It was fatiguing to our horses, and we could but feel that to footmen making this journey it would be exhausting indeed. Along these side hills were numerous flocks of sheep and goats, with persons following or watching them quite after the style of the ancients. Almost everything in sight appeared to illustrate some Scriptural allusion or incident." The feet of Jesus must have often been weary as he trod these rugged paths on his missions of mercy to mankind.

JERIEL (jē'ri-el), (Heb. יְרִיאֵל, *yer-ee-ale'*, founded by God), son of Tola; one of the six heads of the tribe of Issachar during David's time (1 Chron. vii:2), B. C. after 1856.

JERIJAH (je-rī'jah), (Heb. יְרִיָּה, *yer-ee-yaw'*, founded by Jehovah), (1 Chron. xxvi:31). See JERIAH.

JERIMOTH (jĕr'i-mŏth), (Heb. יְרִימוֹת, *yer-ee-mohth'*, heights).

1. A son of Bela, and a valiant chief of the Benjamites (1 Chron. vii:7). (B. C. after 1856.)

2. One of the Benjamite archers and slingers with David at Ziklag (1 Chron. xii:5). (B. C. 1055.)

3. Son of Becher, head of a Benjamite house (1 Chron. vii:8). (B. C. 1017.)

4. Head of Merarites during census taken by David (1 Chron. xxiv:30). (See JEREMOTH, 1.)

5. One of the sons of Heman and head of the fifteenth course among the musicians in David's reign (1 Chron. xxv:4, 22). (See JEREMOTH, 2.)

6. Son of Azriel, and captain of the tribe of Naphtali under David and Solomon (1 Chron. xxvii:19). (B. C. 1014.)

7. Son of King David, whose daughter Mahalath was the first wife of Rehoboam, her cousin Abihail being the other (2 Chron. xi:18.) (B. C. before 974.) He is not named in the list of David's children (1 Chron. ch. iii, or xiv:4-7), and it is probable that he was the son of a concubine, and such is the Jewish tradition. The passage, 2 Chron. xi:18, is not quite clear, since the word "daughter" is a correction of the *Keri;* the original text had *bāne*, בן, i. e., "son." (Smith, *Bib. Dict.*)

8. A Levite, one of the overseers of the temple under Hezekiah (2 Chron. xxxi:13).

JERIOTH (jē'ri-ŏth), (Heb. יְרִיעוֹת, *yer-ee-ohth'*, curtains or timidity), according to the A. V. the second wife of Caleb, son of Hezron (1 Chron. ii:18). B. C. after 1856. This seems to be contrary to the Hebrew text, and Jerioth was probably Caleb's daughter.

JEROBOAM (jĕr'o-bō'am), (Heb. יָרָבְעָם, *yaw-rob-awm'*, people will contend).

1. The first king of Israel. He was of the tribe of Ephraim, the son of Nebat, an Ephraimite, by a woman named Zeruiah (1 Kings xi:26).

(1) Noticed by Solomon. He was noticed by Solomon as a very highly gifted and active young man, and was appointed one of the superintendents of the works which that magnificent king was carrying on at Jerusalem (1 Kings xi:28). (B. C. 960.) This appointment, the reward of his merits, might have satisfied his ambition had not the declaration of the prophet Ahijah given him higher hopes.

(2) Future Kingship Foretold. When informed that, by the divine appointment, he was to become king over the ten tribes about to be rent from the house of David, he was not content to wait patiently for the death of Solomon.

(3) Flight Into Egypt. He began to form plots and conspiracies, the discovery of which constrained him to flee to Egypt to escape condign punishment. King Shishak was but too ready to encourage one whose success must necessarily weaken the kingdom which had become great and formidable under David and Solomon, and which had already pushed its frontier to the Red Sea (1 Kings xi:40).

(4) Revolt of the Ten Tribes. When Solomon died (ver. 40) B. C. 934, the ten tribes sent to call Jeroboam from Egypt; and he appears to have headed the deputation which came before the son of Solomon with a demand of new securities for the rights which the measures of the late king had compromised. It may somewhat excuse the harsh answer of Rehoboam, that the demand was urged by a body of men headed by one whose pretensions were so well known and so odious to the house of David.

(5) King of Israel. The imprudent answer of Rehoboam rendered a revolution inevitable, and Jeroboam was then called to reign over the ten tribes, by the style of 'King of Israel' (1 Kings xii:1-20). The general course of his conduct on the throne has already been indicated in the article ISRAEL, and need not be repeated in this place. The leading object of his policy was to widen the breach between the two kingdoms, and to rend asunder those common interests among all the descendants of Jacob which it was one great object of the Law to combine and interlace.

(6) Golden Calves. To this end he scrupled not to sacrifice the most sacred and inviolable interests and obligations of the covenant people, by forbidding his subjects to resort to the one temple and altar of Jehovah at Jerusalem, and by establishing shrines at Dan and Bethel—the extremities of his kingdom—where 'golden calves' were set up as the symbols of Jehovah (1 Kings xii:26, 28), to which the people were enjoined to resort and bring their offerings.

(7) Acting as Priest. The pontificate of the new establishment he united to his crown, in imitation of the Egyptian kings. He was officiating in that capacity at Bethel, offering incense, when a prophet appeared, and in the name of the Lord announced a coming time, as yet far off, in which a king of the house of David, Josiah by name, should burn upon that unholy altar the bones of its ministers.

(8) Smitten with Palsy. He was then preparing to verify, by a commissioned prodigy, the truth of the oracle he had delivered, when the king attempted to arrest him, but was smitten with palsy in the arm he stretched forth. Later, in answer to prayer, it was healed (1 Kings xiii:1-10). At the same moment the threatened prodigy took place, the altar was rent asunder, and the ashes strewed far around. This measure had, however, no abiding effect. The policy on which he acted lay too deep in what he deemed the vital interests of his separate kingdom, to be even thus abandoned; and the force of the considerations which determined his conduct may in part be appreciated from the fact that no subsequent king of Israel, however well disposed in other respects, ever ventured to lay a finger on this schismatical establishment. Hence 'the sin of Jeroboam the son of Nebat, wherewith he sinned and made Israel to sin,' became a standing phrase in describing that iniquity from which no king of Israel departed (1 Kings xii:25-33; xiii).

(9) Extinction of the Dynasty. The contumacy of Jeroboam eventually brought upon him the doom which he probably dreaded beyond all others—the speedy extinction of the dynasty which he had taken so much pains and incurred so much guilt to establish on firm foundations.

(10) His Wife Disguised. His son Abijah being sick, he sent his wife disguised to consult the prophet Ahijah, who had predicted that he should be king of Israel. The prophet, although he had become blind with age, knew the queen, and saluted her with—'Come in, thou wife of Jeroboam, for I am sent to thee with heavy tidings.' These were not merely that the son should die—for that was intended in mercy to one who alone, of all the house of Jeroboam, had remained faithful to his God, and was the only one who should obtain an honored grave—but that his race should be violently and utterly extinguished: 'I will take away the remnant of the house of Jeroboam as a man taketh away dung, till it be all gone' (1 Kings xiv:1-18).

(11) Death of the Son and Father. The son died so soon as the mother crossed the threshold on her return; and as the death of Jeroboam himself is the next event recorded, it would seem that he did not long survive his son. He died about 913 B. C. (1 Kings xiv:20).

(12) Character. Jeroboam was perhaps a less remarkable man in character and ability than the circumstance of his being the founder of a new kingdom might lead us to expect. The tribes would have revolted without him; and he was chosen king merely because he had been pointed out by previous circumstances. His government exhibits but one idea—that of raising a barrier against the reunion of the tribes. Of this idea he was the slave and victim; and although the barrier which he raised was effectual for its purpose, it only served to show the weakness of the man who could deem needful the protection for his separate interests which such a barrier offered.

2. Fourteenth king of Israel, son of Joash, whom (B. C. 783) he succeeded on the throne, and reigned forty-one years. He followed the example of the first Jeroboam in keeping up the idolatry of the golden calves. Nevertheless the Lord had pity upon Israel; the time of its ruin was not yet come, and this reign was long and flourishing. Jeroboam brought to a successful result the wars which his father had undertaken, and was always victorious over the powerful Syrians. He even took their chief cities of Damascus (2 Kings xiv:28: Amos i:3-5) and Hamath, which had formerly been subject to the scepter of David, and restored to the realm of Israel the ancient eastern limits from Lebanon to the Dead Sea. He died B. C. 742 (2 Kings xiv:16, 23-29).

The Scriptural account of this reign is too short to enable us to judge of the character of a prince under whom the kingdom of Israel seems to have reached a degree of prosperity which it had never before enjoyed, and was not able long to preserve. Jonah (2 Kings xiv:25) and Amos prophesied in the reign of Jeroboam II (Amos i:1). Amos draws a melancholy picture of the moral and religious state of Israel at the time (ii:6; v:27; viii:4-6, etc.), for which he predicts judgment from God (vii:1-9; viii:7-10). For these prophecies a complaint was made against him to Jeroboam by Amaziah the priest at Bethel, but it does not seem to have brought any penalty on the prophet (vii:10-17). Hosea also began his prophetic work in the northern kingdom during the lifetime of Jeroboam. The first three chapters pertain to that period. On the death of Jeroboam, his son Zechariah ascended the throne (2 Kings xiv:29).

JEROHAM (jĕr'o-hăm), (Heb. יְרֹחָם, *yer-o-khawm'*, compassionate).

1. Son of Elihu (Eliab, Eliel), and grandfather of Samuel (1 Sam. i:1; 1 Chron. vi:27, 34). (B. C. before 1142.)

2. One of the leaders of the tribe of Benjamin (1 Chron. viii:27). (B. C. probably before 588.) Apparently the same as **3.**

3. Father of Ibneiah, which latter was a Benjamite chief in Jerusalem (1 Chron. ix:8). (B. C. apparently before 536.)

4. Son of Pashur, a descendant of Aaron, of the house of Immer (1 Chron. ix:12). (B. C. before 536.)

5. Son of Pelaliah, and father of the priest Adaiah, who resided in Jerusalem after the exile (Neh. xi:12). (B. C. before 440.) Perhaps he is identical with **4.**

6. A resident of Gedor, father of two Benjamite archers who came to David at Ziklag (1 Chron. xii:7). (B. C. before 1055.)

7. The father of Azareel who was head of the tribe of Dan in the time of David and Solomon (1 Chron. xxvii:22). (B. C. before 1017.)

8. Azariah's father; the latter was one of the two of that name who planned with Jehoiada to restore Joash to the throne (2 Chron. xxiii:1). (B. C. before 76.)

JERUBBAAL (je-rŭb'ba-ăl), (Heb. יְרֻבַּעַל, *yer-oob-bah'al*, Baal will contend), Gideon's surname, after he had destroyed Baal's grove, and his father had said it was Baal's business to avenge it (Judg. vi:31, 32; vii:1; viii:29, 35; ix:1, 2, 5, 16, 19, 24, 28, 57; 1 Sam. xii:11). (See GIDEON.)

JERUBBESHETH (je-rŭb'be-shĕth), (Heb. יְרֻבֶּשֶׁת, *yer-oob-beh'sheth*, contender with shame, i. e., idol).

A name of Gideon (2 Sam. xi:21), given, doubtless, in later times to avoid the necessity of pronouncing the name of a false god (Exod. xxiii:13). Gideon had acquired the name Jerubbaal, "Baal will contend," through his abomination of the worship of Baal.

JERUEL (je-rŭ'el), (Heb. יְרוּאֵל, *yer-oo-ale'*, founded of God).

A wilderness west of the Dead Sea, and south of Judah, where Jehoshaphat obtained a great victory over the Ammonites, Moabites, etc. It was called the valley of Berachah, or blessing; and lay between Engedi and Tekoah (2 Chron. xx:16; compare ver. 26). It corresponds in situation to *el Hasasah*, a tract sloping from Tekoa to Ain-Jidy (Robinson, *Researches*, ii. 212).

JERUSALEM (je-rŭ'sa-lĕm), (Heb. יְרוּשָׁלַםִ, *yer-oo-shaw-lame'*, founded peaceful).

Jerusalem has been the theme for song and story from the earliest ages. "Beautiful for situation, the joy of the whole earth, is Mount Zion, on the sides of the north, the city of the great king" (Ps. xlviii:2). "Jerusalem is builded as a city that is compact together" (Ps. cxxii:3).

1. Names. In the time of Abraham it was called Salem (Gen. xiv:18), but when it fell into the hands of the Jebusites, they called it Jebus; then the two words were united into one, Jerusalem, or "habitation of peace." It is first mentioned as such in Joshua x:1. The Psalmist says (lxxvi:2): "In Salem also is his tabernacle, and his dwelling-place in Zion." After the death of Joshua the tribes of Judah and of Simeon fought against the Canaanites, and captured and burned the city of Jerusalem (Judg. i:1-8). Again, we learn that the "children of Benjamin did not drive out the Jebusites that inhabited Jerusalem" (Judg.

i :21). This statement has reference, doubtless, to the lower city, and not to what was afterwards called Mount Zion. The latter was conquered by David when he led his forces from Hebron to the conquest, and after this brilliant assault it was called the "City of David." This latter name, during the reign of the Maccabees, was sometimes applied to the whole city, but gradually shifted back to the spot still known as Mount Zion, and mentioned so many times in Scripture. In Ezekiel xvi :3; it is written: "Thus saith the Lord God unto Jerusalem; thy birth and thy nativity is of the land of Canaan; thy father was an Amorite, and thy mother a Hittite"—and, indeed, we find a remnant of the Hittite population in the city so late as the time of David. The Latins called it Hierosolyma, and once Ariel; the Greeks had a similar name. In 2 Chron. xxv :28, it is called "the City of Judah." Pharaoh-necho took the "City of Cadytis," which historians believe to be Jerusalem. The "City of God," the "Holy City," "Solima," "Colonia Ælia Capitolina," "Curumobarech," "Leucost," "the Perfection of Beauty," "Princess among the Provinces," are some of the names, while the Arabs speak of it as "El-Khuds"—"the Holy."

2. Situation and Topography. Jerusalem lies near the summit of a broad mountain-ridge, about thirty-five miles east from Joppa on the Mediterranean Sea, eighteen miles west of the north end of the Dead Sea, twenty-two from the Jordan, and with a general elevation of two thousand five hundred feet above the level of the ocean, and three thousand eight hundred and fifty-two higher than the surface of the Dead Sea, the latter being one thousand three hundred and twelve feet below the Mediterranean Sea, and the lowest point on the surface of the globe. "In several respects," says Stanley, "its situation is singular among the cities of Palestine. Its elevation is remarkable; occasioned not from its being on the summit of one of the numerous hills of Judæa, like most of the towns and villages, but because it is on the edge of one of the highest table-lands of the country. Hebron indeed is higher still by some hundred feet, and from the south, accordingly (even from Bethlehem), the approach to Jerusalem is by a slight descent. But from any other side the ascent is perpetual; and to the traveler approaching the city from the east or west it must always have presented the appearance beyond any other capital of the then known world—we may say beyond any important city that has ever existed on the earth—of a mountain city; breathing, as compared with the sultry plains of Jordan, a mountain air; enthroned, as compared with Jericho, or Damascus, Gaza or Tyre, on a mountain fastness" (*S. & P.* p. 170, 171).

The ridge, or mountainous tract, on which Jerusalem stands, extends, without interruption, from the plain of Esdraelon to a line drawn between the south end of the Dead Sea and the southeast corner of the Mediterranean; or, more properly, perhaps, it may be regarded as extending as far south as to Jebel Aráif in the Desert, where it sinks down at once to the level of the great western plateau. This tract, which is everywhere not less than from twenty to twenty-five geographical miles in breadth, is, in fact, high, uneven table-land. It everywhere forms the precipitous western wall of the great valley of the Jordan and the Dead Sea, and is everywhere rocky, uneven, and mountainous; and is, moreover, cut up by deep valleys which run east or west on either side towards the Jordan or the Mediterranean. The line of division, or watershed, between the waters of these valleys—a term which here applies almost exclusively to the waters of the rainy season—follows for the most part the height of land along the ridge; yet not so but that the heads of the valleys, which run off in different directions, often interlap for a considerable distance. Thus, for example, a valley which descends to the Jordan often has its head a mile or two westward of the commencement of other valleys which run to the western sea.

From the great plain of Esdraelon onwards towards the south, the mountainous country rises gradually, forming the tract anciently known as the mountains of Ephraim and Judah; until, in the vicinity of Hebron, it attains an elevation of nearly three thousand Paris feet above the level of the Mediterranean Sea. Further north, on a line drawn from the north end of the Dead Sea towards the true west, the ridge has an elevation of only about two thousand five hundred Paris feet; and here, close upon the water-shed, lies the city of Jerusalem. Its mean geographical position is in latitude 31° 46′ 43″ north, and longitude 35° 13′ east from Greenwich.

The surface of the elevated promontory itself, on which the city stands, slopes somewhat steeply towards the east, terminating on the brink of the valley of Jehoshaphat. From the northern part, near the present Damascus gate, a depression or shallow wady runs in a southern direction, having on the west the ancient hills of Akra and Zion, and on the east the lower ones of Bezetha and Moriah. Between the hills of Akra and Zion another depression or shallow wady (still easy to be traced) comes down from near the Jaffa gate, and joins the former. It then continues obliquely down the slope, but with a deeper bed, in a southern direction, quite to the pool of Siloam and the valley of Jehoshaphat. This is the ancient Tyropœon. West of its lower part Zion rises loftily, lying mostly without the modern city; while on the east of the Tyropœon and the valley first mentioned lie Bezetha, Moriah, and Ophel, the last a long and comparatively narrow ridge, also outside of the modern city, and terminating in a rocky point over the pool of Siloam. These last three hills may strictly be taken as only parts of one and the same ridge. The breadth of the whole site of Jerusalem, from the brow of the valley of Hinnom, near the Jaffa gate, to the brink of the valley of Jehoshaphat, is about one thousand and twenty yards, or nearly half a geographical mile.

The country around Jerusalem is all of limestone formation, and not particularly fertile. The rocks everywhere come out above the surface, which in many parts is also thickly strewed with loose stones; and the aspect of the whole region is barren and dreary; yet the olive thrives here abundantly, and fields of grain are seen in the valleys and level places, but they are less productive than in the region of Hebron and Nabulus. Neither vineyards nor fig-trees flourish on the high ground around the city, though the latter are found in the gardens below Siloam, and very frequently in the vicinity of Bethlehem.

3. History. No city on the globe has suffered more from war and sieges than Jerusalem. No wonder historians claim that not a stone or wall remains of the city of David. And yet, as will be seen from the review of the recent discoveries on the Temple Hill, which accompanies this article, the visitor to Jerusalem can now, if so disposed, see the very stones placed in position

by the masons of Solomon. From walls hanging over shelving cliffs, and valleys filled with more than a hundred feet of debris, the present city stands above the foundations of former cities long since buried in ruin. Storming legions, battering-rams, and catapults have razed it again and again. And yet, the general outline of the city has always been preserved. Zion and Mount Moriah remain in full view from Olivet, and there, on those hills, stretching away toward the west, city after city has come and gone in the passing ages.

(1) Joshua. Joshua took a part of the city about 1,444 years before Christ. After the death of Joshua, when there remained for the children of Israel much to conquer in Canaan, the Lord directed Judah to fight against the Canaanites; and they took Jerusalem, smote it with the edge of the sword, and set it on fire (Judg. i:1-8). After that, the Judahites and the Benjamites dwelt with the Jebusites at Jerusalem; for it is recorded (Josh. xv:63) that the children of Judah could not drive out the Jebusites inhabiting Jerusalem; and we are further informed (Judg. i:21) that the children of Benjamin did not expel them from Jerusalem. Probably the Jebusites were removed by Judah only from the lower city, but kept possession of the mountain of Zion, which David conquered at a later period.

(2) David. Jerusalem is not again mentioned till the time of Saul, when it is stated (1 Sam. xvii:54) that David took the head of Goliath and brought it to Jerusalem. After David, who had previously reigned over Judah alone in Hebron, was called to rule over all Israel, he led his forces against the Jebusites, and conquered the castle of Zion, which Joab first scaled (2 Sam. v:5-9; 1 Chron. xi:4-8). (B. C. 1046.)

(3) City of David. He then fixed his abode on this mountain, and called it 'the city of David.' Thither he carried the ark of the covenant; and there he built unto the Lord an altar in the threshing-floor of Araunah the Jebusite, on the place where the angel stood who threatened Jerusalem with pestilence (2 Sam. xxiv:15-25). The reasons which led David to fix upon Jerusalem as the metropolis of his kingdom have been alluded to elsewhere (see ISRAEL; JUDAH); being, chiefly, that it was in his own tribe of Judah, in which his influence was the strongest, while it was the nearest to the other tribes of any site he could have chosen in Judah. The peculiar strength also of the situation, enclosed on three sides by a natural trench of valleys, could not be without weight. Its great strength, according to the military notions of that age, is shown by the length of time the Jebusites were able to keep possession of it against the force of all Israel. (See DAVID.)

(4) Solomon. After the death of David (B. C. 1010) Solomon built his temple upon Mount Moriah. By him and his father Jerusalem had been made the imperial residence of the king of all Israel: and the temple, often called 'the house of Jehovah,' constituted it at the same time the residence of the King of Kings, the supreme head of the theocratical state, whose vicegerents the human kings were taught to regard themselves. It now belonged, even less than a town of the Levites, to a particular tribe: it was the center of all civil and religious affairs, the very place of which Moses spoke (Deut. xii:5): 'The place which the Lord your God shall choose out of all your tribes to put his name there, even unto his habitation shall ye seek, and thither thou shalt come' (comp. ix:6; xiv:23; xvi:11-16; Ps. cxxii). (See SOLOMON.)

(5) Rehoboam. The importance and splendor of Jerusalem were considerably lessened after the death of Solomon; under whose son, Rehoboam, ten of the tribes rebelled, Judah and Benjamin only remaining in their allegiance. Jerusalem was then only the capital of the very small state of Judah. And when Jeroboam instituted the worship of golden calves in Bethel and Dan, the ten tribes went no longer up to Jerusalem to worship and sacrifice in the house of the Lord (1 Kings xii:26-30).

After this time the history of Jerusalem is continued in the history of Judah, for which the second books of the Kings and of the Chronicles are the principal sources of information.

(6) The Rule of Different Kings. After the time of Solomon, the kingdom of Judah was almost alternately ruled by good kings, 'who did that which was right in the sight of the Lord,' and by such as were idolatrous and evil-disposed; and by the reign of the same king often varied, and was by turns good or evil. The condition of the kingdom, and of Jerusalem in particular as its metropolis, was very much affected by these mutations. Under good kings the city flourished, and under bad kings it suffered greatly.

(7) Destroyed by Shishak, and Restored. Under Rehoboam (B. C. 970) it was conquered by Shishak, king of Egypt, who pillaged the treasures of the temple (2 Chron. xii:9). Under Amaziah it was taken by Joash, king of Israel, who broke down four hundred cubits of the wall of the city, and took all the gold and silver, and all the vessels that were found in the temple (2 Kings xiv:13, 14). Uzziah, son of Amaziah, who at first reigned well, built towers in Jerusalem at the corner-gate, at the valley-gate, and at the turning of the wall, and fortified them (2 Chron. xxvi:9). His son, Jotham, built the high gate of the temple, and reared up many other structures (2 Chron. xxvii: 3, 4). (B. C. about 755.)

(8) Hezekiah. Hezekiah (B. C. 728) added to the other honors of his reign that of an improver of Jerusalem. His most eminent work in that character was the stopping of the upper course of Gihon, and bringing its waters by a subterraneous aqueduct to the west side of the city (2 Chron. xxxii:30). This work is inferred, from 2 Kings xx, to have been of great importance to Jerusalem, as it cut off a supply of water from any besieging enemy and bestowed it upon the inhabitants of the city. (See King, *Recent Discoveries on the Temple Hill.*) Hezekiah's son, Manasseh, in his later and best years, built a strong and very high wall on the west side of Jerusalem (2 Chron. xxxiii:14). The works in the city connected with the names of the succeeding kings of Judah were, so far as recorded, confined to the defilement of the house of the Lord by bad kings, and its purgation by good kings, till about one hundred years after Manasseh, when, for the abounding iniquities of the nation, the city and temple were abandoned to destruction.

(9) Nebuchadnezzar. After a siege of three years, Jerusalem was taken by Nebuchadnezzar, who razed its walls, and destroyed its temple and palaces with fire (2 Kings xxv; 2 Chron. xxxvi; Jer. xxxix). (B. C. 588.) Thus was Jerusalem smitten with the calamity which Moses had prophesied would befall it if the people would not keep the commandments of the Lord, but broke his covenant (Lev. xxvi:14; Deut. xxviii).

(10) Exile of Israel. The ten tribes forming the kingdom of Israel had been already upwards of one hundred and thirty years before transported to Assyria, when Judah also was exiled to Babylon. The castle of David, the temple of Solomon, and the entire city, lay in ruins, and to all appearance there was an end of the people as well as of the holy city, which the Lord had chosen to himself. But God, before whom a thousand years are as one day, gave to the afflicted people a glimpse beyond the present calamity and retributive judgment, into a distant futurity. The same prophets who foretold the destruction of Jerusalem also announced the consolidations of a coming time.

Moses had long before predicted that if in the land of their captivity they repented of their evil, they should be brought back again to the land out of which they had been cast (Deut. xxx:1-5; comp. 1 Kings viii:46-53; Neh. i:8, 9). The Lord also, through Isaiah, condescended to point out the agency through which the restoration of the holy city was to be accomplished, and even named long before his birth the very person, Cyrus, under whose orders this was to be effected (Is. xliv:28; comp. Jer. iii:2, 7, 8; xxiii:3; xxxi:10; xxxii:36, 37). Among the remarkably precise indications should be mentioned that in which Jeremiah (xxv:9-12) limits the duration of Judah's captivity to seventy years. (See CAPTIVITY.)

(11) Daniel and Cyrus. These encouragements were continued through the prophets, who themselves shared the captivity. Of this number was Daniel (Dan. ix:16, 19), who lived to see the reign of Cyrus, king of Persia (Dan. x:1), and the fulfilment of his prayer. It was in the year B. C. 536, 'in the first year of Cyrus,' that in accomplishment of the prophecy of Jeremiah, the Lord stirred up the spirit of this prince, who made a proclamation throughout all his kingdom, expressed in these remarkable words: 'The Lord God of heaven hath given me all the kingdoms of the earth, and *he has charged me to build him a house at Jerusalem, which is in Judah.* Who is there among you of all his people? his God be with him, and let him go up to Jerusalem, and build the house of the Lord God of Israel' (Ezra i:2, 3). This important call was answered by a considerable number of persons, particularly priests and Levites; and the many who declined to quit their houses and possessions in Babylonia, committed valuable gifts to the hands of their more zealous brethren. Cyrus also caused the sacred vessels of gold and silver which Nebuchadnezzar had taken from the temple to be restored to Sheshbazzar, the prince of Judah, who took them to Jerusalem followed by 42,360 people, beside their servants, of whom there were 7,337, (Ezra i:5-11).

(12) Rebuilding of the Temple. On their arrival at Jerusalem they contributed according to their ability to rebuild the temple; Jeshua, the priest, and Zerubbabel, reared up an altar to offer burnt-offerings thereon; and when in the following year the foundation was laid of the new house of God, 'the people shouted for joy, but many of the Levites who had seen the first temple, wept with a loud voice' (Ezra iii:2, 12). When the Samaritans expressed a wish to share in the pious labor, Zerubbabel declined the offer; and in revenge the Samaritans sent a deputation to king Artaxerxes of Persia, carrying a presentment in which Jerusalem was described as a rebellious city of old time, which, if rebuilt, and its walls set up again, would not pay toll, tribute, and custom, and would thus endanger the public revenue. The deputation succeeded, and Artaxerxes ordered that the building of the temple should cease. The

interruption thus caused lasted to the second year of the reign of Darius (Ezra iv:24), when Zerubbabel and Jeshua, supported by the prophets Haggai and Zechariah, again resumed the work, and would not cease though cautioned by the Persian governor of Judæa. (B. C. 520.) On the matter coming before Darius Hystaspis, and the Jews reminding him of the permission given by Cyrus, he decided in their favor, and also ordered that the expenses of the work should be defrayed out of the public revenue (Ezra vi:8). In the sixth year of the reign of Darius the temple was finished, when they kept the Feast of Dedication with great joy, and next celebrated the Passover (Ezra vi:15, 16, 19). (B. C. 516.)

(13) Artaxerxes II. Afterwards, in the seventh year of the second Artaxerxes, Ezra, a descendant of Aaron, came up to Jerusalem, accompanied by a large number of Jews who had remained in Babylon. He was highly patronized by the king, who not only made him a large present in gold and silver, but published a decree enjoining all treasurers of Judæa speedily to do whatever Ezra should require of them; allowing him to collect money throughout the whole province of Babylon for the wants of the temple at Jerusalem; and also giving him full power to appoint magistrates in his country to judge the people (Ezra vii-viii). At a later period, in the twentieth year of King Artaxerxes, Nehemiah, who was his cupbearer, obtained permission to proceed to Jerusalem, and to complete the rebuilding of the city and its wall, which he happily accomplished, despite all the opposition which he received from the enemies of Israel (Neh. i, ii, iv, vi). (B. C. 446.) The city was then capacious and large, but the people in it were few, and many houses lay still in ruins (Neh. vii:4). At Jerusalem dwelt the rulers of the people and 'certain of the children of Judah and of the children of Benjamin'; but it was now determined that the rest of the people should cast lots to bring one of ten to the capital (Neh. xi:1-4). (B. C. about 440.) All strangers, Samaritans, Ammonites, Moabites, etc., were removed, to keep the chosen people from pollution; ministers were appointed to the temple, and the service was performed according to the law of Moses (Ezra x; Neh. viii, x, xii, xiii). Of the Jerusalem thus by such great and long-continued exertions restored, very splendid prophecies were uttered by those prophets who flourished after the exile: the general purport of which was to describe the temple and city as destined to be glorified far beyond the former, by the advent of the long and eagerly expected Messiah, 'the desire of all nations' (Zech. ix:9; xii:10; Hag. ii:6, 7). (See EZRA; NEHEMIAH.)

(14) Josephus and Alexander the Great. It is said by Josephus (*Antiq.* xi:8) that when the dominion of this part of the world passed from the Persians to the Greeks, Alexander the Great advanced against Jerusalem to punish it for the fidelity to the Persians which it had manifested while he was engaged in the siege of Tyre. His hostile purposes, however, were averted by the appearance of the high-priest Jaddua at the head of a train of priests in their sacred vestments. Alexander recognized in him the figure which in a dream had encouraged him to undertake the conquest of Asia. He therefore treated him with respect and reverence, spared the city against which his wrath had been kindled, and granted to the Jews high and important privileges. The historian adds that the high-priest failed not to apprise the conqueror of those prophecies in Daniel by which his successes had been predicted.

The whole of this story is, however, liable to suspicion, from the absence of any notice of the circumstance in the histories of this campaign which we possess.

(15) Ptolemy. After the death of Alexander at Babylon (B. C. 324), Ptolemy surprised Jerusalem on the Sabbath day, when the Jews would not fight, plundered the city, and carried away a great number of the inhabitants to Egypt, where, however, from the estimation in which the Jews of this period were held as citizens, important privileges were bestowed upon them (Joseph. *Antiq.* xii:1). In the contests which afterwards followed for the possession of Syria (including Palestine), Jerusalem does not appear to have been directly injured, and was even spared when Ptolemy gave up Samaria, Acco, Joppa, and Gaza to pillage. The contest was ended by the treaty in B. C. 302, which annexed the whole of Palestine, together with Arabia Petræa and Cœle-Syria, to Egypt.

(16) Ptolemy Euergetes and Ptolemy Philopator. Under easy subjection to the Ptolemies the Jews remained in much tranquillity for more than a hundred years, in which the principal incident, as regards Jerusalem itself, was the visit which was paid to it, in B. C. 245, by Ptolemy Euergetes, on his return from his victories in the East. He offered many sacrifices, and made magnificent presents to the temple. In the wars between Antiochus the Great and the kings of Egypt, from B. C. 221 to 197, Judæa could not fail to suffer severely; but we are not acquainted with any incident in which Jerusalem was principally concerned, till the alleged visit of Ptolemy Philopator in B. C. 211. He offered sacrifices, and gave rich gifts to the temple, but venturing to enter the sanctuary, in spite of the remonstrances of the high-priest, he was seized with a supernatural dread, and fled in terror from the place. It is said that on his return to Egypt he vented his rage on the Jews of Alexandria in a very barbarous manner. (See ALEXANDRIA.) But the whole story of his visit and its results rests upon the sole authority of the third book of Maccabees (chapters i and ii), and is therefore not entitled to implicit credit.

(17) Antiochus. Towards the end of this war the Jews seemed to favor the cause of Antiochus; and after he had subdued the neighboring country, they voluntarily tendered their submission, and rendered their assistance in expelling the Egyptian garrison from Mount Zion. For this conduct they were rewarded with many important privileges by Antiochus.

(18) Seleucus Philopator. Under their new masters the Jews enjoyed for a time nearly as much tranquillity as under the generally benign and liberal government of the Ptolemies. But in B. C. 176, Seleucus Philopator, hearing that great treasures were hoarded up in the temple, and being distressed for money to carry on his wars, sent his treasurer, Heliodorus, to bring away these treasures. But this personage is reported to have been so frightened and stricken by an apparition that he relinquished the attempt; and Seleucus left the Jews in the undisturbed enjoyment of their rights (2 Macc. iii:4-40; Joseph. *Antiq.* xii:3, 3).

(19) Antiochus Epiphanes. His brother and successor, Antiochus Epiphanes, however, was of another mind. He took up the design of reducing them to a conformity of manners and religion with other nations; or, in other words, of abolishing those distinctive features which made the Jews a peculiar people, socially separated from all others. This design was odious to the great body of the people, although there were many among the higher classes who regarded it with favor. Of this way of thinking was Menelaus, whom Antiochus had made high-priest, and who was expelled by the orthodox Jews with ignominy, in B. C. 169, when they heard the joyful news that Antiochus had been slain in Egypt. The rumor proved untrue and Antiochus on his return punished them by plundering and profaning the temple. Worse evils befell them two years after: for Antiochus, out of humor at being compelled by the Romans to abandon his designs upon Egypt, sent his chief collector of tribute, Apollonius, with a detachment of 22,000 men, to vent his rage on Jerusalem. This person plundered the city, and razed its walls, with the stones of which he built a citadel that commanded the temple mount. A statue of Jupiter was set up in the temple; the peculiar observances of the Jewish law were abolished; and a persecution was commenced against all who adhered to these observances, and refused to sacrifice to idols. Jerusalem was deserted by priests and people, and the daily sacrifice at the altar was entirely discontinued (1 Macc. i:29-40; 2 Macc. v:24-26; Joseph. *Antiq.* xii:5, 4). (See ANTIOCHUS, 4.)

(20) Maccabees. This led to the celebrated revolt of the Maccabees, who, after an arduous and sanguinary struggle, obtained possession of Jerusalem (B. C. 163), and repaired and purified the temple, which was then dilapidated and deserted. The sacrifices were then recommenced, exactly three years after the temple had been dedicated to Jupiter Olympius. The castle, however, remained in the hands of the Syrians, and long proved a sore annoyance to the Jews, but at length, in B. C. 142, the garrison was forced to surrender by Simon, who demolished it altogether, that it might not again be used against the Jews by their enemies. Simon then strengthened the fortifications of the mountain on which the temple stood and built there a palace for himself (1 Macc. xiii:43, 52; Joseph. *Antiq.* xiii:6, 6), which was strengthened and enlarged by Herod the Great, who called it the castle of Antonia, under which name it makes a conspicuous figure in the Jewish wars with the Romans.

(21) Pompey. Of Jerusalem itself we find nothing of consequence, till it was taken by Pompey in the summer of B. C. 63, and on the very day observed by the Jews as one of lamentation and fasting, in commemoration of the conquest of Jerusalem by Nebuchadnezzar. Twelve thousand Jews were massacred in the temple courts, including many priests, who died at the very altar rather than suspend the sacred rites (Joseph. *Antiq.* xiv:1-4). On this occasion Pompey, attended by his generals, went into the temple and viewed the sanctuary; but he left untouched all its treasures and sacred things, while the walls of the city itself were demolished. From this time the Jews are to be considered as under the dominion of the Romans (Joseph. *Antiq.* xiv: 4, 5).

(22) Crassus. The treasures which Pompey had spared were seized a few years after (B. C. 51) by Crassus. In the year B. C. 43, the walls of the city, which Pompey had demolished, were rebuilt by Antipater, the father of that Herod the Great under whom Jerusalem was destined to assume the new and more magnificent aspect which it bore in the time of Christ, and which constituted the Jerusalem which Josephus describes.

JERUSALEM

(23) Herod the Great. The temple itself was taken down and rebuilt by Herod the Great, with a magnificence exceeding that of Solomon's (Mark xiii:1; John ii:20). (See TEMPLE.) It was in the courts of the temple as thus rebuilt, and in the streets of the city as thus improved, that the Savior of men walked up and down. Here he taught, here he wrought miracles, here he suffered; and this was the temple whose 'goodly stones' the Apostle admired (Mark xiii:1), and of which Jesus foretold that ere the existing generation had passed away not one stone should be left upon another.

(24) Destruction of the City by Titus. Jerusalem seems to have been raised to this greatness as if to enhance the misery of its overthrow. So soon as the Jews had set the seal to their formal rejection of Christ, by putting him to death, and invoking the responsibility of his blood upon the heads of themselves and of their children (Matt. xxvii:25), the city's doom went forth. Titus, a young, brave and competent Roman general, with an army of sixty thousand trained, victorious warriors, appeared before the city in April, 70 A. D., and the most disastrous siege of all history began. It was Passover week, crowds from the whole land had come to the great annual gathering, and were hopelessly surrounded by the immense army, and driven into the city, swelling the total population to at least a million and a quarter of souls. The assault was commenced on the north and west walls, where, after fifteen days of battering and fighting, a breach was made in the wall of the new city. The Roman army entered and laid siege to the second wall, which was far heavier and stronger than the outer one already passed. Here a most stubborn resistance was made, and the assaulting forces were for a time defeated.

Titus called to his aid the most dreadful of all enemies, that of famine. He encompassed the entire city with a wall five miles in length, which was built within three days. This, with the strictest watch-care, utterly prohibited any food from reaching the doomed city. The distress was so severe that many were crazed by the gnawings of hunger. Mary, daughter of Eleazar, from Perea, a lady of rank, killed her infant child and cooked it for food. The prophecy of Moses, uttered more than fifteen hundred years before, was fulfilled to the letter. "Her children which she shall bear. . . . she shall eat them for want of all things. . . . in the siege and in the straitness, wherewith thine enemies shall distress thee in thy gates" (Deut. xxviii:57, etc.). Bezetha, Akra, Zion, the castle of Antonia, and finally the temple, one by one, all fell before the strong legions of Titus. For three years and a half this most memorable siege continued. Around the great altar of sacrifice lay dead bodies heaped one upon another, and blood flowed into the conduits where before that of the sacrifices ran. Man was the victim now, and the temple, sanctified by the blood of innocence, was defiled by the blood of the guilty. Titus entered the "Holy of Holies," but the Shekinah was gone. He carried away the golden candlestick, and some of the rich furniture; the temple was burned, and thus ended the greatest of sanctuaries.

On the same day of the month, August 15, six hundred and sixty-one years before, Nebuchadnezzar destroyed the holy house, but now the very foundations were razed, after standing eleven hundred and thirty-seven years. The search for gold and silver which had melted in the fire caused the soldiers to dig away the very foundations, until "not one stone was left upon another that was not thrown down." The stronghold of Zion, the city of David, was the last to fall. Then came the order to utterly demolish the walls, leaving three towers, Phasaelus, Hippicus, and Mariamne, as monuments to show the strength with which Titus contended. Micah (iii:12) said: "Therefore shall Zion for your sake be plowed as a field, and Jerusalem shall become heaps."

Thirty-eight years after the Jews had led Christ away to crucify him an avenging army led away as captives all who had cried against the Son of God. Their house was a desolate, a charred ruin, the scepter had departed, the daily sacrifices ceased, the day of vengeance came, and not one tittle of the prophecy of the Divine Master had failed. Over a million persons had perished; ninety-seven thousand were led away as captives, multitudes were sent to the Egyptian mines, thousands were reserved for the triumph of Titus at Rome, and the records on the triumphal arch show us the golden table, the seven-branch golden candlestick, silver trumpets, and other spoils from the temple. Since then the Holy City has lain at the mercy of the Gentiles, and will so remain 'until the times of the Gentiles are fulfilled.'

4. Ancient Jerusalem. Every reader of Scripture feels a natural anxiety to form some notion of the appearance and condition of Jerusalem, as it existed in the time of Jesus, or rather as it stood before its destruction by the Romans. There are unusual difficulties in the way of satisfying this desire, although it need not be left altogether ungratified. The principal sources of these difficulties have been indicated by different travelers. It is a tantalizing circumstance, however, for the traveler who wishes to recognize in his walks the site of particular buildings, or the scenes of memorable events, that the greater part of the objects mentioned in the description, both of the inspired and of the Jewish historian, are entirely razed from their foundation, without leaving a single trace or name behind to point out where they stood.

To the obscurity originating in these causes may be added that which arises from the many ambiguities in the description left by Josephus, the only one which we possess, and which must form the groundwork of most of our notices respecting the ancient city. There are indeed some manifest errors in his account, which the critical reader is able to detect without having the means to rectify.

In describing Jerusalem as it stood just before its destruction by the Romans, Josephus states that the city was built upon two hills, between which lay the valley Tyropœon (Cheesemonger's Valley), to which the buildings on both hills came down. This valley extended to the fountain of Siloam. The hill on which the upper town stood was much higher than the other, and straighter in its extent. On account of its fortifications, David called it the Fortress or Castle; but in the time of Josephus it was known by the name of the Upper Market. The other hill, on which was situated the lower town, was called Akra. It was in the form of a horseshoe or crescent. Opposite to Akra was a third, and naturally lower hill (Moriah), on which the temple was built; and between this and Akra was originally a broad valley, which the inhabitants of Jerusalem filled up in the time of Simon Maccabæus for the purpose of connecting the town with the temple. At the same time they lowered the hill Akra, so as to make the temple rise above it. Both the hills on which the upper and lower towns stood were externally surrounded by deep valleys, and here there was no approach because of the precipices on every side.

(1) The Walls. The first, or most ancient wall, appears to have enclosed the whole of Mount Zion. The greater part of it, therefore, must have formed the exterior and sole wall on the south, overlooking the deep valleys below Mount Zion; and the northern part evidently passed from the tower of Hippicus on the west side, along the northern brow of Zion, and across the valley, to the western side of the temple area. It probably nearly coincided with the ancient wall which existed before the time of David, and which enabled the Jebusites to maintain themselves in possession of the upper city, long after the lower city had been in the hands of the Israelites. Mount Zion is now unwalled, and is excluded from the modern city. The account given by Josephus, of the second wall, is very short and unsatisfactory. But it would seem that it enclosed the whole of the lower city, or Akra, excepting that part of the eastern side of it which fronted the temple area on Mount Moriah, and the southern side, towards the valley which separated the lower from the upper city. In short, it was a continuation of the external wall, so far as necessary, on the west and north, and on so much of the east as was not already protected by the strong wall of the temple area.

Although these were the only walls that existed in the time of our Savior, we are not to infer that the habitable city was confined within their limits. On the contrary, it was because the city had extended northward far beyond the second wall that a third was built to cover the defenseless suburb: and there is no reason to doubt that this unprotected suburb, called Bezetha, existed in the time of Christ. This wall is described as having also begun at the tower of Hippicus: it ran northward as far as to the tower Psephinos, then passed down opposite the sepulcher of Helena (queen of Adiabene), and being carried along through the royal sepulchers, turned at the corner tower by the Fuller's monument, and ended by making a junction with the ancient wall at the valley of the Kidron. It was begun ten or twelve years after our Lord's crucifixion by the elder Herod Agrippa, who desisted from completing it for fear of offending the Emperor Claudius. But the design was afterwards taken up and completed by the Jews themselves, although on a scale of less strength and magnificence. Dr. Robinson thinks that he discovered some traces of this wall, which are described in his great work (*Bibl. Researches,* i. 466).

The same writer thinks that the wall of the new city, the Ælia of Adrian, nearly coincided with that of the present Jerusalem.

We know from Josephus that the circumference of the ancient city was thirty-three stadia, equivalent to nearly three and a half geographical miles. The circumference of the present walls does not exceed two and a half geographical miles; but the extent of Mount Zion, now without the walls, and the tract on the north formerly enclosed, or partly so, by the third wall, sufficiently account for the difference.

The history of the modern walls has already been given in the sketch of the modern history of the city. The present walls have a solid and formidable appearance, especially when cursorily observed from without; and they are strengthened, or rather ornamented, with towers and battlements after the Saracenic style. They are built of limestone, the stones being not commonly more than a foot or fifteen inches square. The height varies with the various elevations of the ground. The lower parts are probably about twenty-five feet high, while in more exposed localities, where the ravines contribute less to the security of the city, they have an elevation of sixty or seventy feet.

(2) Gates. Much uncertainty exists respecting the ancient gates of Jerusalem. Many gates are named in Scripture; and it has been objected that they are more in number than a town of the size of Jerusalem could require—especially as they all occur within the extent embraced by the first and second walls, the third not then existing. It has, therefore, been suggested as more than probable that some of these gates were within the city, in the walls which separated the town from the temple, and the upper town from the lower, in which gates certainly existed. On the other hand, considering the circumstances under which the wall was rebuilt in the time of Nehemiah, it is difficult to suppose that more than the outer wall was then constructed, and certainly it was in the wall then built that the ten or twelve gates mentioned by Nehemiah occur. But these may be considerably reduced by supposing that two or more of the names mentioned were applied to the same gate. If this view of the matter be taken, no better distribution of these gates can be given than that suggested by Raumer.

(a) On the north side.

(1) The *Old Gate,* probably at the northeast corner (Neh. iii:6; xii:39).

(2) The *Gate of Ephraim* or *Benjamin* (Jer. xxxviii:7; xxxvii:13; Neh. viii:16; 2 Chron. xxv:23). This gate doubtless derived its names from its leading to the territory of Ephraim and Benjamin; and Dr. Robinson supposes it may possibly be represented by some traces of ruins which he found on the site of the present gate of Damascus.

(3) The *Corner-gate,* 300 cubits from the former, and apparently at the northwest corner (2 Chron. xxv:23; 2 Kings xiv:13; Zech. xiv:10). Probably the *Gate of the Furnaces* is the same (Neh. iii:11; xii:38).

(b) On the west side.

(4) The *Valley-gate,* over against the dragon-fountain of Gihon (Neh. ii:13; iii:13; 2 Chron. xxvi:9). It was probably about the northwest corner of Zion, where there appears to have been always a gate, and Dr. Robinson supposes it to be the same with the Gennath of Josephus.

(c) On the south side.

(5) The *Dung-gate,* perhaps the same as Josephus' Gate of the Essenes (Neh. iii:13; xii:31). It was 1,000 cubits from the valley-gate (Neh. iii:13), and the dragon-well was between them (Neh. ii:13). This gate is probably also identical with 'the gate between two walls' (2 Kings xxv: 4; Jer. xxxix:4).

(6) The *Gate of the Fountain* nearest to the southeastern corner; the gate of the fountain near the king's pool (Neh. ii:14); the gate of the fountain near 'the pool of Siloah by the king's garden' (Neh. iii:15). The same gate is probably denoted in all these instances, and the pools seem to have been also the same. It is also possible that this fountain-gate was the same otherwise distinguished as the brick-gate (or potter's gate), leading to the valley of Hinnom (Jer. xix:2, where the Auth. Ver. has 'east-gate').

(d) On the east side.

(7) The *Water-gate* (Neh. iii:26).

(8) The *Prison-gate,* otherwise the *Horse-gate,* near the temple (Neh. iii:28; xii:39, 40).

(9) The *Sheep-gate*, probably near the sheep-pool (Neh. iii:1, 32; xii:39).

(10) The *Fish-gate* was quite at the northeast (Neh. iii:3; xii:39; Zeph. i:10; 2 Chron. xxxiii:14).

In the middle ages there appear to have been two gates on each side of the city, making eight in all; and this number, being only two short of those assigned in the above estimate to the ancient Jerusalem, seems to vindicate that estimate from the objections which have been urged against it.

On the west side were two gates, of which the principal was the *Porta David,* gate of David, often mentioned by the writers on the Crusades. It was called by the Arabs *Bab el-Mihrab,* and corresponds to the present Jaffa gate, or *Bab el-Khulil.* The other was the gate of the Fuller's Field, *Porta Villæ Fullonis,* so called from Is. vii:3. This seems to be the same which others call *Porta Judiciaria,* and which is described as being in the wall over against the church of the holy sepulcher, leading to Silo (Neby Samwîl) and Gibeon. This seems to be that which the Arabian writers call *Serb.*

On the north there were also two gates; and all the middle age writers speak of the principal of them as the gate of St. Stephen, from the notion that the death of the protomartyr took place near it. This was also called the gate of Ephraim, in reference to its probable ancient name. Arabic writers called it *Bab 'Amud el-Ghurab,* of which the present name, *Bab el-'Amud,* is only a contraction. The present gate of St. Stephen is on the *east* of the city, and the scene of the martyrdom is now placed near it; but there is no account of the change. Further east was the gate of Benjamin (*Porta Benjaminis*), corresponding apparently to what is now called the gate of Herod.

On the east there seem to have been at least two gates. The northernmost is described by Adamnanus as a small portal leading down to the valley of Jehoshaphat. It was called the gate of Jehoshaphat, from the valley to which it led. It seems to be represented by the present gate of St. Stephen. The present gate of St. Stephen has four lions sculptured over it on the outside, which, as well as the architecture, show that it existed before the present walls.

On the south side were also two gates. The easternmost is now called by the Franks the Dung-gate, and by the natives *Bab el-Mugharibeh.* The earliest mention of this gate is by Brocard, about A. D. 1283, who regards it as the ancient Water-gate. Further west, between the eastern brow of Zion and the gate of David, the Crusaders found a gate which they call the gate of Zion, corresponding to one which now bears the same name.

Of the seven gates mentioned as still existing, three, the Dung-gate, the Golden Gate, and Herod's Gate, are closed. Thus there are only four gates now in use, one on each side of the town, all of which have been enumerated. St. Stephen's, on the east, leads to the Mount of Olives, Bethany, and Jericho. Zion Gate, on the south side of the city, connects the populous quarter around the Armenian convent with that part of Mount Zion which is outside the walls, and which is much resorted to as being the great field of Christian burial, as well as for its traditionary sanctity as the site of David's tomb, the house of Caiaphas, house of Mary, etc. The Jaffa Gate, on the west, is the termination of the important routes from Jaffa, Bethlehem, and Hebron. The Damascus Gate, on the north, is also planted in a vale, which

in every age of Jerusalem must have been a great public way, and the easiest approach from Samaria and Galilee.

(3) Towers. The towers of Jerusalem are often mentioned in Scripture and in Josephus. Most of the towers mentioned by Josephus were erected by Herod the Great, and were, consequently, standing in the time of Christ. It was on these, therefore, that his eyes often rested when he approached Jerusalem, or viewed its walls and towers from the Mount of Olives. Of all these towers, the most important is that of Hippicus, which Josephus, as we have already seen, assumed as the starting-point in his description of all the walls of the city. Herod gave to it the name of a friend who was slain in battle. It was a quadrangular structure, twenty-five cubits on each side, and built up entirely solid to the height of thirty cubits. Above this solid part was a cistern twenty cubits; and then, for twenty-five cubits more, were chambers of various kinds, with a breastwork of two cubits, and battlements of three cubits upon the top. The altitude of the whole tower was consequently eighty cubits.

The above is the only tower which the historian particularly mentions. But in describing the outer or third wall of Agrippa, he states that it had battlements of two cubits, and turrets of three cubits more; and as the wall was twenty cubits high, this would make the turrets of the height of twenty-five cubits or nearly thirty-eight feet. Many loftier and more substantial towers than these were erected on each of the walls at regulated distances, and furnished with every requisite for convenience or defense. Of those on the third or outer wall are enumerated ninety; on the middle or second wall, forty; and on the inner or ancient wall, sixty.

(4) Public Buildings. The temple was in all ages the great glory and principal public building of Jerusalem, as the heathen temple, church, or mosque, successively occupying the same site, has been ever since the Jewish temple was destroyed. That temple is reserved for a separate article (see TEMPLE), and there are few other public edifices which require a particular description. Those most connected with Scripture history are the palace of Herod and the tower of Antonia. The former has already been noticed. In the time of Christ it was the residence of the Roman procurators while in Jerusalem; and as such provincial residences were called by the Romans *Prætoria,* this was the prætorium or judgment-hall of Pilate (Matt. xxvii:27; Mark xv:16; John xviii:28). In front of the palace was the tribunal or 'judgment-seat,' where the procurator sat to hear and determine the causes; and where Pilate was seated when our Lord was brought before him. It was a raised pavement of mosaic work (λιθόστρωτον), called in the Hebrew *gabbatha,* or 'an elevated place.' (See JUDGMENT HALL.)

The tower or castle of Antonia stood on a steep rock adjoining the northwest corner of the temple. It has already been mentioned that it originated under the Maccabees, who resided in it. The name of *Baris* which it obtained was originally the Persian name of a royal palace; but which, according to Jerome (*Epist. ad Princip.* ii. 639), was afterwards adopted in Palestine, and applied to all the large quadrangular dwellings built with turrets and walls. As improved by Herod, who gave it the name of Antonia, after his patron Mark Antony, this fortress had all the extent and appearance of a palace, being divided into apartments of every kind, with galleries and baths, and also broad halls or barracks for soldiers; so that, as having everything necessary within itself, it seemed a city, while in its magnificence it was a palace. At each of the four corners was a tower, one of which was seventy cubits high, and overlooked the whole temple with its courts. The fortress communicated with the cloisters of the temple by secret passages, through which the soldiers could enter and quell any tumults, which were always apprehended at the time of the great festivals. It was to a guard of these soldiers that Pilate referred the Jews, as a 'watch' for the sepulcher of Christ. This tower was also 'the castle' into which St. Paul was carried when the Jews rose against him in the temple, and were about to kill him; and where he gave his able and manly account of his conversion and conduct (Acts xxi: 27-40; xxii). This tower was, in fact, the citadel of Jerusalem.

5. Modern History. The destruction of Jerusalem by the Romans did not cause the site to be utterly forsaken, although for a long period little is heard of it.

(1) **Adrian.** For fifty years the city lay in utter ruin; then it was rebuilt in part by Adrian and again filled with Jews, who were permitted to return from many lands. The idolatrous monarch placed a marble statue of a hog over the gate facing Bethlehem, and erected also a temple to Jupiter. Later the Jews regained command of the city, and unable to endure the idea of their holy city being occupied by foreigners, and that strange gods should be set up within it, broke out into open rebellion under the notorious Barchochebas, who claimed to be the Messiah. His success was at first very great; but he was crushed before the tremendous power of the Romans, so soon as it could be brought to bear upon him; and a war scarcely inferior in horror to that under Vespasian and Titus was, like it, brought to a close by the capture of Jerusalem, of which the Jews had obtained possession. This was in A. D. 135, from which period the final dispersion of the Jews has been often dated.

(2) **A Roman Colony.** The Romans then finished the city according to their first intention. It was made a Roman colony, inhabited wholly by foreigners, the Jews being forbidden to approach it on pain of death; a temple to Jupiter Capitolinus was erected on Mount Moriah, and the old name of Jerusalem was sought to be supplanted by that of Ælia Capitolina, conferred upon it in honor of the emperor, Ælius Adrianus, and Jupiter Capitolinus. This name was applied till the time of Constantine, and passed to the Mohammedans, by whom it was long retained; and it was not till after they recovered the city from the Crusaders that it became generally known among them by the name of El-Khuds—the holy —which it still bears.

(3) **Constantine.** From the rebuilding by Adrian the history of Jerusalem is almost a blank till the time of Constantine, when its history, as a place of extreme solicitude and interest to the Christian church, properly begins. Pilgrimages to the Holy City now became common and popular. Such a pilgrimage was undertaken in A. D. 326 by the emperor's mother Helena, then in the eightieth year of her age, who built churches on the alleged site of the nativity at Bethlehem, and of the resurrection on the Mount of Olives. This example may probably have excited her son to the discovery of the site of the holy sepulcher, and to the erection of a church thereon. He removed the temple of Venus, with which, in studied insult, the site had been encumbered. The holy sepulcher was then purified, and a magnificent church was, by his order, built over and around the sacred spot. This temple was completed and dedicated with great solemnity in A. D. 335. There is no doubt that the spot thus singled out is the same which has ever since been regarded as the place in which Christ was entombed; but the correctness of the identification then made has been of late years much disputed. By Constantine the edict excluding the Jews from the city of their fathers' sepulchers was so far repealed that they were allowed to enter it once a year to wail over the desolation of 'the holy and beautiful house,' in which their fathers worshiped God.

(4) **Julian the Apostate.** When the nephew of Constantine, the Emperor Julian, abandoned Christianity for the old Paganism, he endeavored, as a matter of policy, to conciliate the Jews. He allowed them free access to the city, and permitted them to rebuild their temple. They accordingly began to lay the foundations in A. D. 362; but the speedy death of the emperor probably occasioned that abandonment of the attempt, which contemporary writers ascribe to supernatural hindrances. The edicts seem then to have been renewed which excluded the Jews from the city, except on the day of annual wailing.

(5) **Pilgrimages.** In the following centuries the roads to Zion were thronged with pilgrims from all parts of Christendom. After much struggle of conflicting dignities Jerusalem was, in A. D. 451, declared a patriarchate by the council of Chalcedon. In the next century it found a second Constantine in Justinian, who ascended the throne A. D. 527. He repaired and enriched the former structures, and built upon Mount Moriah a magnificent church to the Virgin, as a memorial of the persecution of Jesus in the temple.

(6) **Persians.** But these prosperous days were soon to end. The Persians, who had long harassed the empire of the East, penetrated into Syria in A. D. 614, and after defeating the forces of the Emperor Heraclius, took Jerusalem by storm. Many thousands of the inhabitants were slain, and much of the city destroyed. The damage occasioned by the Persians was speedily repaired.

(7) **Caliph Omar.** But Arabia soon furnished a more formidable enemy in the Caliph Omar, whose troops appeared before the city in A. D. 636. By his orders the magnificent mosque which still bears his name was built upon Mount Moriah, upon the site of the Jewish temple. Jerusalem remained in possession of the Arabians, and was occasionally visited by Christian pilgrims from Europe till towards the year 1000, when a general belief that the second coming of the Savior was near at hand drew pilgrims in unwonted crowds to the Holy Land.

(8) **The Crusades.** The sight, by such large numbers, of the holy place in the hands of infidels, the exaction of tribute, and the insults to which the pilgrims, often of the highest rank, were exposed from the Moslem rabble, excited an extraordinary ferment in Europe, and led to those remarkable expeditions for recovering the Holy Sepulcher from the Mohammedans which, under the name of the Crusades, will always fill a most important and curious chapter in the history of the world. But by the time the Crusaders, under Godfrey of Bouillon, appeared before Jerusalem, on the 17th of June, 1099, the

Egyptian rulers had recovered possession of Palestine and driven the Saracens beyond the Euphrates. After a siege of forty days, the holy city was taken by storm on the 15th day of July; and a dreadful massacre of the Moslem inhabitants followed, without distinction of age or sex. As soon as order was restored, and the city cleared of the dead, a regular government was established by the election of Godfrey as king of Jerusalem. The Christians kept possession of Jerusalem eighty-eight years. During this long period they appear to have erected several churches and many convents. Of the latter few, if any, traces remain; and of the former, save one or two ruins, the Church of the Holy Sepulcher, which they rebuilt, is the only memorial which attests the existence of the Christian kingdom of Jerusalem.

(9) Saladin. In A. D. 1187 the holy city was wrested from the hands of the Christians by the Sultan Saladin. From that time to the present day the holy city has remained, with slight interruption, in the hands of the Moslems. On the threatened siege by Richard of England in 1192, Saladin took great pains in strengthening its defenses. But in A. D. 1219, the Sultan Melek el Moaddin of Damascus, who then had possession of Jerusalem, ordered all the walls and towers to be demolished, except the citadel and the enclosure of the mosque, lest the Franks should again become masters of the city and find it a place of strength. In this defenseless state Jerusalem continued till it was delivered over to the Christians in consequence of a treaty with the Emperor Frederick II, in A. D. 1229, with the understanding that the walls should not be rebuilt. Yet ten years later (A. D. 1239) the barons and knights of Jerusalem began to build the walls anew, and to erect a strong fortress on the west of the city.

(10) David of Kerek. But the works were interrupted by the emir, David of Kerek, who seized the city, strangled the Christian inhabitants, and cast down the newly erected walls and fortress. Four years after, however, (A. D. 1243), Jerusalem was again made over to the Christians without any restriction, and the works appear to have been restored and completed; for they are mentioned as existing when the city was stormed by the wild Kharisman hordes in the following year; shortly after which the city reverted for the last time into the hands of its Mohammedan masters, who have kept it to the present day.

6. The Early Church. Jerusalem witnessed many scenes connected with the early church. Among them were the day of Pentecost (Acts ii); the first proclamation of the gospel (Acts i:4); the rapid increase of Christian believers (Acts v); and the stoning of Stephen (Acts vii). The first ecclesiastical council was held in the city (Acts xv) under James the Less, bishop of Jerusalem (A. D. 47). Here James was beheaded by Herod (Acts xii). Eleven councils were held in the city at different periods from the year A. D. 47-1632.

7. Modern Jerusalem. **(1) Streets and Apartments.** The streets are narrow, crooked, and generally paved with cobble stones. David street is the Broadway of Jerusalem, and leads from the Joppa Gate, descending eastward, through the center of the city, across the Tyropœon Valley to the west wall of the temple area, having on either side extensive bazaars where all kinds of traffic is carried on. As one enters the city the

Tower of David appears on the right, the foundation of which was doubtless that of Phasaelus. It presents the best specimens of masonry. For twenty feet the foundations slope inwardly at an angle of forty-five degrees, and it was quite unassailable by the battering-rams of the early ages. It was the last place to yield when Jerusalem was captured by the Crusaders, and when the walls of the city were destroyed in the thirteenth century by the Moslems, it withstood the fury of a wasting desolation. Within it are several spacious rooms, and a cistern for water. In one of the apartments, the Mohammedans say, David wrote the Psalms. Near by this tower is the American consulate, while on the left stands the Grand Hotel and the Turkish postoffice. About a block eastward is Christian street, running northward to the Church of the Holy Sepulcher. A little further east is Damascus street, the eastern boundary of the Christian quarter of the city. The Mohammedans' quarters are in the northeast section of the city, the Jewish in the southeast, and the Armenian on the site of Mount Zion, south and west, while the Harem inclosure is on Mount Moriah, further east.

(2) Absalom's Pillar. Near by is Absalom's pillar. The memory of Absalom is so hateful to the Jew that he throws a stone at the monument whenever he passes by it. Near by Absalom's pillar is the burying place of the Jews, and north of this is the garden of Gethsemane, the tomb of the Virgin, and the valley of Jehoshaphat.

(3) Mount Moriah. Directly beyond the valley is Mount Moriah, including the temple area, which the Moslems call Hara es-Sherif. The Mosque of Omar, or "the noble sanctuary," occupies the site of the famous temple of Solomon. Near it, on the north, is the enclosure of Antonia. The quadrangle measures one thousand and forty-two feet on the north, one thousand five hundred and thirty on the east (the front view), nine hundred and twenty-two on the south, and one thousand six hundred and one on the west, embracing about thirty-five acres. Bezetha is on the right, reaching to the extremity of the wall. The Mohammedan cemetery, in the foreground, is near the wall, extending its entire length north and south. Beyond the wall, on the right, is Jeremiah's grotto, where tradition says he wrote the book of Lamentations. It is doubtless one of the openings of the vast system of quarries under this hill, and from which much of the stone used in the construction of the city has been taken. Olive groves and private residences are seen on the northern suburbs of the city. Many fine buildings have lately been erected in this quarter, among which are the Arab Protestant church, the large Russian buildings, the Coptic church, and other modern structures. On the west side of the city is the citadel, and on the southwest the tomb of David.

(4) Church of the Holy Sepulcher. The Church of the Holy Sepulcher, having two domes, is a little to the right of the citadel. It was built, as before stated, by the Empress Helena, mother of Constantine, in 326 A. D., and stands over the traditional place of the Savior's tomb. It was dedicated with great pomp in 335 A. D., Encelius taking part in the gorgeous ceremonies. This building was burnt by the Persians in 614 A. D., but was shortly after rebuilt by Modestus. Muez, of the race of the Fatimites, removed the seat of power from Jerusalem to Cairo, and this church was again destroyed. A third time it fell at the command of a caliph, who razed it to the ground.

A successor of his rebuilt it, completing the building, 1048 A. D.

During the period of the Crusaders the present walls were erected. Fire demolished a part of the structure in 1808 A. D., but the Greek Christians so completely restored it that no traces of the fire remain. The true site of Calvary is now believed to be on the skull-like mound outside the Damascus Gate on the north. The Church of the Holy Sepulcher has two large domes covering several chapels. The sepulcher proper is of marble in the great rotunda under the western dome. The space occupied by the immense pile is three hundred and fifty by two hundred and eighty feet.

(5) **Mosque of Omar.** Just beyond the Golden Gate, near the western wall, stands the famous Mosque of Omar, *Kubbet es Sakhra,* or "dome of the rock," a great octagonal building, each side being sixty-seven feet long, with a diameter of one hundred and forty-eight feet, surmounted by a great dome with a total height of one hundred and seventy feet. It covers the sacred rock on which the old temple stood where Abraham offered Isaac to God; where Araunah, the Jebusite, had his threshing floor, and the spot which David purchased of him on which to build an altar of sacrifice. The building is a poor representative of the temples erected either by Solomon, Nehemiah, or Herod, and yet it has a pleasing effect. Once its dome was plated with gold, and in the morning, reflecting the sunlight from its marble walls and gilded dome, must have been a beautiful picture of oriental magnificence. In the year 680 Caliph Omar found this spot covered with ruins and rubbish, all traces of the former grandeur having been obliterated for ages, and, with naked hands, helped clear the historic site, and proceeded to erect a temporary temple. The work begun was completed by Abdalmelik the tenth caliph, 691 A. D., by immense revenues collected as taxes upon Egypt for seven years. During the rule of the Crusaders it was used as a Christian church, and some marks of violence are shown within. Around the whole interior is a corridor thirteen feet wide, while sixteen marble columns of the Corinthian order lend grace and beauty to the scene. On another inner circle stand twelve larger columns of the same order, with four great intervening piers. The dome is sixty feet in diameter. Within the last circle, and protected by a high iron railing, is the sacred "rock," four feet nine inches higher than the pavement, and forty by sixty feet in dimension. It is certainly a veritable relic. The surface of the rock is rough, bearing marks of the chisel, steps cut, and holes drilled here and there. From this rock, tradition says, Mohammed ascended to heaven, leaving his footprints upon the stone. Underneath this is a small cave, which, undoubtedly, Araunah used as a grain bin. The mosque platform is five hundred and fifty by four hundred and fifty feet, and about ten feet higher than the general area, with beautiful stone ascents made through eight elegant Saracenic gates.

(6) **Mosque el Aksa.** South of the dome of the rock stands a large and beautiful old Basilica, called mosque el Aksa. It was built 798 A. D., is two hundred and seventy-two feet long and one hundred and eighty-four feet wide, having a ground area of fifty thousand square feet; has seven aisles and forty-five columns. It is declared to be in the exact center of the earth.

(7) **Other Features of Interest.** Close by are Solomon's stables and the Tower of David.

On the northwest of the city may be seen the extensive Russian buildings. Here is a large Greek church, a hospice for males, and another for females, where pilgrims are entertained who come to visit the sacred places. There is also a good school building here, and a number of dwelling houses are being built in this quarter outside the city walls. "Talitha Cumi" is a large mission school for girls, on the Joppa road, a little west of the city. Jeremiah's grotto is under the beautiful little hill, covered with Mohammedan graves, outside the northern wall. It is claimed that the prophet lived here for many years, and wrote the book of Lamentations in the small cavern. This hill is now believed to be the true Calvary, and the facts seem to prove the same, both from Biblical and historic authority. Other principal features of the city are elsewhere mentioned.

(8) **The Zionist Movement.** The so-called Zionist movement which is the colonization of Jews in Jerusalem and Palestine is meeting with considerable success. A steady, although at present not a very large, stream of Jewish immigration is setting in that direction. There is now a railroad from Jaffa to Jerusalem, and other roads are under construction.

The visit of the emperor of Germany to Jerusalem in 1898 created great interest in religious circles, and gave an added impetus to the resettlement by the Hebrew people in the land of their fathers.

(9) **Present Population, etc.** The present population of Jerusalem is not far from 40,000. The Mohammedans lead in numbers, about 16,000. The number of Jews is estimated at 15,000, and the Christians at about 9,000. "There is no warm nor bright color here; all is grim and gray except the blue tiles in the Mosque of Omar. The shadow of the Crucifixion rests on the place forever; a strange stillness reigns, and laughter would seem like laughter beside an open grave. Women, veiled in white, glide through the dark, crooked alleys like tenants of a city of specters, and even the children, subdued by the overwhelming gloom, are silent beyond the wont of Orientals. Ruins, ruins at every hand! Well has the prophecy been fulfilled: 'Jerusalem shall become heaps.' The very stones of the streets are dismal, worn away with burdens borne since they rang with the tramp of legions and glittered with the brassy armor of the masters of the earth. Outside the walls—saddest sight where all is sadness—are ancient Jews come merely to die in the land of their love. A few in whom there is much guile offer for sale talismans, gems of magic, rings of occult power. The greater number sit in the sun, motionless as statues, without the dignity that should accompany age, in poverty past telling, dreaming away the day and night—apparently without hope, except to have a little holy dust laid on their eyelids when they shall have closed them to sleep with patriarchs and seers in the Valley of Jehoshaphat."

8. Recent Discoveries. Within the last twenty-nine years excavations have been made on Temple Hill by the engineers of the Palestine Exploration Fund, who have overcome almost insuperable obstacles by their skill, daring, and energy. A brief outline of the great work which they have accomplished is hereby presented.

(1) **Temple Hill.** The massive walls and towers that formed the defense of the Temple Hill have been found intact in many places, the stones resting just as they were placed by the workmen of Solomon and Hiram. Throughout its course the wall rests on a solid foundation of

living rock and rises sometimes to a height of more than one hundred and fifty feet. These "sure foundations" of the massive walls of the Holy City often form the theme of Hebrew poetry and ethics. The Psalmist's words, 'her foundations are upon the holy hills,' are literally true, and Isaiah speaks of the 'sure foundations' of Zion.

At the southeast angle of the wall, the height of the masonry has been found to be one hundred and fifty-six feet and nine inches. In ancient days the wall of the Royal Cloister surmounted this, adding not less than fifty feet to the height, so that at this point in the days of Christ the wall of the temple, from foundation to summit, would be considerably over two hundred feet in height. The valley at this point is now filled with rubbish, covering the wall to a considerable height and raising the bed of the Kedron about forty feet above its true level.

From these interesting discoveries, made by the Rev. James King, of England, it appears that a person in ancient times standing on the Cloister wall would look down into the bed of the Kedron three hundred feet below. Thus recent excavations have proved that the account by Josephus of the astounding height of the southeast wall is not so much exaggerated as it was once thought to be. Doubtless on the top of this wall, at the southeast corner, stood the pinnacle of the temple mentioned in Christ's temptation (Matt. iv: 5, 6).

(2) The East Wall. At the northeast angle of the Harem area stands the so-called Tower of Antonia, which, though having nothing to do with the Tower of Antonia, still retains that name. The part now seen above ground is only a small portion of a once colossal structure, which shows what immense deposits of rubbish must have been made to cover this ancient fortification.

The main east wall crosses a ravine, on the slope of which the Tower of Antonia stands. A hundred and twenty yards from the tower is the

Interior of Golden Gate.

famous Golden Gate (*Porta aurea*) in the eastern wall of the temple area.

(3) The Golden Gate. This occupies a conspicuous place in the east wall. The present structure is no older than the time of Constantine, but the site is doubtless the same as that of the 'Beautiful Gate of the temple' mentioned in Acts, for in the spacious porch may yet be seen two huge monolithic jambs, now used as pillars, which are vestiges of an ancient gateway. Tra-

dition, too, fixes this as the location of the 'Beautiful Gate,' and, strange to say, the Greek word ὡραία, *beautiful*, was incorrectly translated by the Latin *aurea*, golden, perhaps from the resemblance of the two classical words; and usage has perpetuated the error. The Arabs now call the whole gateway Bâb ed Daherîyeh, the Eternal Gate, the northern arch being called Gate of Repentance, the southern, Gate of Mercy.

From the Golden Gate to the southeast corner the length of the wall is a little more than a thousand feet. Here is that part of the Kedron called the Valley of Jehoshaphat, in which both Moslems and Jews believe the Last Judgment will be held. On this account it has been from ancient times a Jewish burial-ground (Joel iii: 2, 12-14).

(4) The Red Heifer Bridge. A hundred feet north of the southeast corner is a break in the continuity of the wall, at a place where a bridge

Remains of Arch of Bridge.

spanned the Kedron Valley. As the Red Heifer Bridge connected the temple precincts with the Mount of Olives in ancient times, and along this the heifer destined for sacrifice was led by the high-priest, to the summit of Olivet, it is justifiable to conjecture that this was the site of the ancient bridge.

(5) Corner Stone. At the southeast corner of the wall is the interesting corner stone of the temple. To the ancient Jews this stone was the emblem of many moral and spiritual truths (Ps. cxviii:22, 23; Is. xxviii:16; Matt. xxi:42; Acts iv:11; Ephes. ii:20, 21; 1 Pet. ii:6). It stands in the same place in which it was set three thousand years ago in the presence of Solomon and his court. It is squared and polished, and measures three feet eight inches high by fourteen feet in length. Three feet east of the angle of the corner stone the excavators found a hole cut out of the native rock, and in this an earthen jar. From its form and evident age it has been conjectured that it was deposited at the laying of the corner stone and contained the holy oil for the consecration of the foundations. The discoveries about this southeast corner have been confirmatory of the account of the building of the temple in 1 Kings v:17, 18. The engineers found "great stones, costly and hewed," and Phœnician fragments of pottery. Phœnician marks painted on the massive blocks proclaim that the stones were prepared in the quarry by the cunning workmen of Hiram, king of Tyre.

(6) The Wall of Ophel. While excavating near the southeast angle of the wall the engineers of the Palestine Exploration Fund found a wall of ancient date, which has been identified with the wall of Ophel, so frequently mentioned in connection with the Roman siege. The stones are small compared with the mighty masses of the wall before mentioned; the foundations rest on clay, and the work bears the marks of haste. Ophel is the name of the ridge south of the Temple Hill. Jotham built much on this wall of Ophel and Manasseh compassed about Ophel (2 Chron. xxxiii:14). This wall seems to have been rebuilt under Nehemiah after the return from captivity. There can be little doubt that this discovery is the wall hastily built up by Nehemiah.

(7) **The South Wall of the Harem.** The south wall of the Harem must at one time have presented a magnificent mass of masonry. It is over nine hundred feet long and had two entrances, known as the Triple Gate, and Double, or Huldah Gate, both now built up. The Double Gate is a very prominent feature in the south wall. It is a hundred yards from the southwest angle and consists of two entrances, each eighteen feet wide. This Double, or Huldah, Gate was the chief entrance to the temple area from the south, and doubtless the Savior passed through it many times during the celebration of the great festival. Modern discoveries show that this wall does not belong to one period of construction, but the portion east of the Double Gate possesses a high antiquity, extending back to the Jewish monarchy, and is, probably, the work of King Solomon; while that to the west, which is a hundred yards in length, belongs to the time of Herod.

A hundred feet west of the southeast angle is a gateway with pointed arch, which, though now closed, seems to have been an entrance in former days to "Solomon's stables." This is called the Single Gate.

(8) **Solomon's Stables.** The vast subterranean vaults, probably known as "Solomon's Stables," extend over an acre of ground. They are forty feet below the Harem area, and more than a hundred feet above the foundation stone of the wall. One hundred square piers arranged in fifteen rows support the ceiling. The Moslems call the place 'The Old Mosque,' but the Frank Kings used it as a stable. It was doubtless originally designed as a support for the temple area, and it is very probable that there are other systems of vaults below these.

(9) **West Wall of the Temple Area.** The west wall of the temple area is over one thousand five hundred feet long. Here are the remains of the Jews' Wailing Place, and Robinson's and Wilson's arches.

(10) **The Jews' Wailing Place.** This is where the Israelites assemble every Friday afternoon. The temple wall visible above ground at this spot is about sixty feet high. The lower courses of stone are magnificent blocks, venerable for their antiquity and for the fact that they are veritable remains of the old Jewish temple. For many generations the Jews have been permitted, at least once a week, to approach the precincts of their temple and kiss the venerable stones of the wall and bathe them with their tears, fulfilling the words in Psalm cii:14. The congregation that gathers here is one of the most solemn gatherings left to the Jewish church. How long this ceremony has been kept up cannot be determined with certainty, although there is historical evidence to prove that they have assembled to mourn over their lost glory and desolate temple since the time of the apostles.

(11) **Robinson's Arch.** A little north of the southwest corner three courses of stone project which have received the name of Robinson's Arch. In ancient times Mount Moriah was separated from Zion by a rugged ravine. On one side of this ravine rose the massive walls of the temple, on the other the palace of the kings of Judah. This valley is now so filled with rubbish from the city that it presents the appearance of a level plain. In the olden times, however, it was spanned by bridges, the most noted being Zion Bridge, which seemed to form a communication between the palace and the temple. Excavating at a point where the next pier of the arch should be, not only the pier itself was found, but arch stones of the fallen arch. How old this viaduct is cannot be stated, but certainly it antedates the Christian era and the Temple of Herod.

(12) **Wilson's Arch,** six hundred feet north of the southwest angle, is also the remains of an ancient bridge, which extended across the valley to the opposite height. Adjoining the arch were discovered a series of arched vaults running westward and evidently connected with the viaduct or bridge which anciently crossed the valley at this place. Probably by this secret way troops were hurried down into the temple area from the barracks on Mount Zion.

(13) **Gate of the Chain.** North of Wilson's Arch is the Gate of the Chain, the principal entrance to the Harem area. It received its name from the tradition that Solomon once stretched a chain across this entrance. A little farther north is the Gate of the Bath, and the Gate of the Cotton Merchants, which a very old tradition identifies with the "Beautiful Gate of the Temple." From this gate to the southwest angle the distance is two hundred yards. The masonry is very ancient and probably dates from the Jewish kings.

(14) **The North Wall of the Harem Area.** Within the northwest angle of the wall stands a pile of buildings used as a barrack. It is situated on a rock twenty feet above the temple area. Here is generally supposed to have been located the ancient Jewish fort of Baris. East of the barracks is a small entrance, called the Gate of the Secretary, and a little farther on the gate called Bab el-Hitta. Just east of this entrance there begins a fosse, which runs along the wall for three hundred and sixty feet, with an average breadth of a hundred and thirty feet. It is called the Pool of Israel, and according to Roman Catholic tradition is the Pool of Bethesda. Near the eastern end of the north wall is the Gate of the Tribes, whose portals adjoin the Castle of Antonia, at the northeast angle.

(15) **The Royal Quarries.** Under Bezetha, the northern hill on which Jerusalem is built, extend vast caverns, reaching far into the bowels of the earth. These are the "Royal Quarries," and their vastness not only throws light upon the stonework of the temple, but impresses the mind with the gigantic character of the sacred edifices that once crowned the summit of Moriah. From its mouth the cave increases rapidly in size; the rock rises perpendicularly from the floor to the ceiling; large fragments of quarried stones lie about, and massive blocks, half cut, still adhere to the wall. All this indicates that the cavern is largely the work of man's hand. The stone was removed by cutting a nick from three to six inches wide on both sides the desired block, also at the bottom and behind. This slow, but simple, process must have been performed by a pick or other instrument with a long handle. By the side of each cutting may be seen a little cup-

shaped hollow, evidently designed to hold oil and wick to give the workmen light. The stone is a hard limestone, which when polished is almost as pure and white as marble. No doubt the Psalmist had this in mind when he expressed the wish that 'our daughters may be as corner stones, polished after the similitude of a palace' (Ps. cxliv: 12). From the fact that all the stonework of Jerusalem, generally, speaking, is of a formation corresponding to the hard, limestone rock of these Royal Quarries, and from their immense size, we are led to the belief that all the stonework of the Holy City, the Temples of Solomon, Zerubbabel, and Herod, the massive walls of Harem, and the encompassing walls of the city, has been excavated from these caverns underneath the northern part of the ancient city. The prevailing, but mistaken notion, that Hiram sent the stone for Solomon's temple from Lebanon or Tyre arose from Solomon's request for cedar and fir trees which Hiram promised to provide (1 Kings v:8).

(16) Waters of Jerusalem. Beneath the Temple Hill are vast cisterns for holding the water that flowed from the hill country of Judæa. Six miles from Jerusalem are the Pools of Solomon, at the head of the Wady Urtâs valley. These pools cover about seven acres, and are capable of holding three million gallons of water. These wonderful architectural remains of the old Jewish monarchy were partly excavated out of the bed of limestone rock, and partly constructed of massive blocks of masonry, by building dams across the valley. They are three in number, connected by conduits, the lower one being the largest and finest of the three. The pools are fed by four natural springs, of which the Sealed Fountain is the largest. According to tradition Solomon shut up this spring and kept the door of it sealed with his signet, so that he might preserve the water for his own drinking in its natural freshness and purity. The Sealed Fountain formed a part of the water system of Solomon and is probably referred to in Canticles (iv:12). These pools and their fountains have an altitude of about two hundred feet above the area of the temple, so that they could have carried water to the highest part of the Sacred City.

From the Sealed Fountain there runs a passage to a vault situated at the northwest corner of the upper pool. At this vault the stream from the Sealed Fountain has recently been found to have been joined by another stream flowing from the south and collecting its supply from the valley of the Arrûb, six miles from Solomon's Pools. It was conducted through a rock-bored tunnel four miles long, passing in its course under another valley called Wady Byar, and thence on to its junction with the Sealed Fountain. With the increased volume from the Sealed Fountain the aqueduct known as the High Level passes along the slope of Wady Urtâs, descending into the valley, west of Bethlehem; it ascends the northern side of the valley again, through an inverted stone syphon, constructed of perforated stone blocks firmly united by cement. This syphon is not only a work of skill in masonry, but shows a knowledge of hydrostatics not possessed by the Romans when they built the great arched structures in the neighborhood of Rome, for conducting water across valleys. The High Level aqueduct has been traced far enough to make it reasonably sure that in olden time it supplied the pool of Upper Gihon, now Birket Mamilla; thence flowing through the channel, still existing at this part, it entered Jerusalem at the Jaffa Gate. It would then supply the Citadel, the Pool of Hezekiah, and all points along the Tyropœon valley until it joined the Pool of Siloam. This aqueduct is of high antiquity, and according to the opinion of the engineers of the Palestine Exploration Fund, dates from the earliest ages of the Jewish occupation. It is without doubt a part of the water system of King Solomon. While it never received any supply from Solomon's Pools, they were a part of the great water system. The skill with which they were constructed would do credit to the nineteenth century, and their massiveness suggests the reign of some energetic king. Expert opinion favors the theory that they were built by Solomon himself and are referred to in Eccl. ii:6. The water of these pools found its way to Jerusalem through the Low Level aqueduct, furnishing Bethlehem on the way. The aqueduct crosses the valley of Gihon on a causeway and enters the city near Burj Al Kibryt. Following along the western slope of the Tyropœon valley it turns eastward and communicates with the great cisterns under the Temple Hill. A few years ago this aqueduct was repaired and for a time the water flowed direct from Solomon's Pools to the cisterns of the Harem as in days of old, but the flow was shortly impeded and at present the water does not get much beyond Bethlehem. This was the main supply of Jerusalem in olden times, and while the aqueduct was repaired by Pontius Pilate its construction was of the period of Solomon and ranks among the most interesting of Biblical antiquities.

The vast cisterns under the Temple Hill are among the most important of modern discoveries. Some are of modern construction, and others, from their form, are very ancient. No less than thirty-five of these cisterns have been explored and examined. Many are of great depth, and their combined capacity is about ten million gallons. They are connected by passages, tunnels and ducts, so that the Temple Hill beneath the surface is honeycombed by a network of vaults and cisterns. The largest and best known is the Great Sea, capable of holding three million gallons. It is mentioned in the book of Ecclesiasticus (i:3). While it is difficult to fix the exact age of these cisterns of the Temple Hill there is abundant evidence to prove that Solomon constructed the reservoirs south of Bethlehem known as Solomon's Pool, the original aqueducts that conveyed their water to the Sacred City, and we may confidently believe that the reservoirs under the Temple area were contemporaneous with these other remains of the water system built by Solomon. (See cut, page 1419.)

(17) The Virgin's Fountain. A spring, called the Virgin's Fountain, in the valley of the Kedron, opposite the village Siloam, flows by a channel cut out of the rock through the Hill of Ophel and issues at the pool of Siloam, the most celebrated of those mentioned in the Scriptures (Neh. iii:15; Luke xiii:4; John ix:7, etc.). This pool is a little lower than the Virgin's Fountain and the excavations about the pool and the tunnel leading to the fountain are likely the work of King Hezekiah. During the reign of that monarch Shalmaneser, of Assyria, threatened Jerusalem. Hezekiah rebuilt the broken-down walls of the city, raised towers, and 'took counsel to stop the waters of the fountains without the city' (2 Chron. xxxii:4). This language applies completely to the diverting of the water from the Virgin's Fountain by the tunnel to Siloam; for before this was done this spring would empty into the valley of the Kedron and could be used by soldiers outside the walls. So that there exists good reason for referring this work to the reign of

Hezekiah. (King, *Recent Discoveries on Temple Hill.*)

JERUSALEM, NEW. The gospel church is called *New Jerusalem* (Rev. xxi:2). In her are found the peculiar presence and ordinances of God; in her the tribes of redeemed men meet, and serve him. How beautiful and compact her form! How firm her foundation! How strongly fortified and protected, by the laws, perfections, and providences of God! How rich, wealthy, and free her true members! How readily they welcome others to reside with them! (Gal. iv:26; comp. Ezek. xl). Perhaps the heavenly state of glory is called *Jerusalem,* or the *New Jerusalem,* for similar reason (Rev. iii:12). Brown.

JERUSHA (je-ru'shà), (Heb. יְרוּשָׁא, *yer-oo-shaw'*, possessed), the daughter of Zadok, and queen of Uzziah. She was the mother of Jotham, king of Judah (2 Kings xv:33), B. C. 738. Called also *Jerushah.*

JESAIAH (je-sā'yà), (Heb. יְשַׁעְיָה, *yesh-ah-yaw'*, Jehovah saves or is opulent).

1. Son of Hananiah, the son of Jerubbabel (1 Chron. iii:21), B. C. after 536.

2. Father of Ithiel, a Benjamite, some of whose descendants were among those chosen by lot to reside in Jerusalem after the exile (Neh. xi:7), B. C. 445.

JESHAIAH (je-shā'iah, or yà), (Heb. יְשַׁעְיָה, *yesh-ah-yaw'*, Jehovah saves).

1. Chief of the eighth division of singers under the tutorship of his father Jeduthun (1 Chron. xxv:3, 15), B. C. 1014.

2. A Levite during David's time; the son of Rehabiah, a descendant of Amram through Moses (1 Chron. xxvi:25), B. C. before 1014.

3. Son of Athaliah, a chief of the house of Bene Elam, who returned with a company of seventy from Babylon (Ezra viii:7), B. C. 459.

4. A Levite of the family of Merari, who returned with Ezra (Ezra viii:19), B. C. 459.

JESHANAH (jĕsh'a-nah), (Heb. יְשָׁנָה, *yesh-aw-naw'*, old).

A town with its suburbs which was taken from Jeroboam by Abijah; it is mentioned as near Bethel and Ephraim (2 Chron. xiii:19). Schwarz locates it at *al-Sanin,* two miles west of Bethel. (*Palestine*, p. 158.)

JESHARELAH (je-shăr'e-lah), (Heb. יְשַׂרְאֵלָה, *yesh-ar-ale'aw*, upright toward God).

Head of the seventh of the twenty-four wards into which the musicians of the Levites were divided (1 Chron. xxv:14); elsewhere (verse 2) called ASARELAH. (B. C. 1014.)

JESHEBEAB (je-shĕb'e-ăb), (Heb. יֶשֶׁבְאָב, *yeh-sheb-awb'*, father's seat), head of the fourteenth course of priests (1 Chron. xxiv:13), B. C. 1014.

JESHER (jē'sher), (Heb. יֵשֶׁר, *yay'sher*, uprightness), the first named of the sons of Caleb, by his wife Azubah (1 Chron. ii:18), B. C. before 1658.

JESHIMON (jĕsh'i-mŏn), (Heb. יְשִׁימוֹן, *yesh-ee-mone'*, a desolation).

A name used in describing the position geographically of Pisgah and Peor. It refers to that portion which lies north of the Dead Sea (Num. xxi:20; xxiii:28; 1 Sam. xxiii:19, etc.). "In the Old Testament the wilderness of Judea is called the Jeshimon, a word meaning devastation, and no term can better suit its haggard and crumbling appearance. It covers some thirty-five miles by fifteen. . . . Short bushes, thorns, and suc-

culent creepers were all that relieved the brown and yellow bareness of the sand, the crumbling limestone, and scattered shingle. Such is Jeshimon, the wilderness of Judea. It carries the violence and desolation of the Dead Sea Valley right up to the heart of the country, to the roots of the Mount of Olives, to within two hours of the gates of Hebron, Bethlehem, and Jerusalem" (Smith, *Hist. Geog.*). (See Tristram, *Land of Israel*, p. 540, 2d ed.).

JESHISHAI (je-shĭsh'a-ī), (Heb. יְשִׁישַׁי, *yesh-ee-shah'ee*, aged), the son of Jahdo and father of Michael, and ancestor of certain of the tribe who lived in Gilead and whose genealogies were made out in the time of Jotham (1 Chron. v:14), B. C. before 782.

JESHOHAIAH (jĕsh'o-hā'iah), (Heb. יְשׁוֹחָיָה, *yesh-o-khaw-yaw'*, Jehovah doth trouble), a chief Simeonite, descendant of Shemei (1 Chron. iv:36), who was engaged in the raid, during Hezekiah's time, upon the Hamites (B. C. about 711).

JESHUA (jĕsh'u-à), (Heb. יֵשׁוּעַ, *yay-shoo'ah*. Jehovah helps).

1. One of the towns in which the people of Judah lived after their return from captivity (Neh. xi:26). According to Schwarz it is *Yesuè,* five miles east of Ekron (*Palest.* p. 116); probably the *Yeshua* of Robinson (*Research.* iii, 145, sq.).

2. A priest during David's reign and head of the ninth sacerdotal order (1 Chron. xxiv: 11); the A. V. has Jeshuah. (B. C. 1014.)

3. Son of Jozedech, and high-priest of the Jews when they returned, under Zerubbabel, from the Babylonian exile (B. C. 536). He was, doubtless, born during the exile. His presence and exhortations greatly promoted the rebuilding of the city and temple. The altar of the latter being first erected, enabled him to sanctify their labor by the religious ceremonies and offerings which the law required. Jeshua joined with Zerubbabel in opposing the machinations of the Samaritans (Ezra iv:3); and he was not found wanting in zeal when the works, after having been interrupted, were resumed in the second year of Darius Hystaspis (Ezra v:2; Hag. i:12). Several of the prophet Haggai's utterances are addressed to Jeshua (Hag. i:1; ii:2), and his name occurs in two of the symbolical prophecies of Zechariah (iii:1-10; vi:11-15). In the first of these passages Jeshua, as pontiff, represents the Jewish people covered at first with the garb of slaves, and afterwards with the new and glorious vestures of deliverance. In the second he wears for a moment crowns of silver and gold, as symbols of the sacerdotal and regal crowns of Israel, which were to be united on the head of the Messiah. He was also called Joshua.

4. (Neh. viii:17). (See JOSHUA.)

5. A Levite who had charge of distributing the sacred offerings in the sacerdotal cities under Hezekiah (2 Chron. xxxi:15), B. C. 726.

6. A descendant of the place or person called Pahath-moab, whose people to the number of 2,812 returned from captivity (Ezra ii:6; Neh. vii:11), B. C. before 536.

7. A Levite whose posterity to the number of 74 returned from Babylon (Ezra ii:40; Neh. vii: 43), B. C. before 536.

8. Father of the Levite Jozabad, whom Ezra appointed to look after the offerings for the sacred services (Ezra viii:33), B. C. before 459.

9. Father of Ezer; the latter repaired a part of the wall of Jerusalem (Neh. iii:19), B. C. before 446.

10. A Levite, head of a house, and an active co-operator with Nehemiah in the reformations he instituted (Neh. viii:7; ix:4, 5; x:9; xii:8). In Neh. (xii:24) "son of Kadmiel" should manifestly read "Jeshua and Kadmiel."

JESHUAH (jĕsh'u-ah), (Heb. יֵשׁוּעַ, *yay-shoo'ah*, Jah is help). (See JESHUA, 2.)

JESHURUN (jĕsh'u-rŭn or jesh-ū'rŭn), (Heb. יְשֻׁרוּן, *yesh-oo-roon'*, upright), a name practically applied to Israel in Deut. xxxii:15; xxxiii:5, 26; Is. xliv:2. It has been variously understood, but it is generally agreed to be a poetical diminutive expressive of affection.

JESIAH (je-sī'ah), (Heb. יִשִּׁיָּה, *yish-shee-yaw'*, lent by Jehovah).

1. One of the Korites who was a mighty helper in battle at Ziklag during David's battle with Saul (1 Chron. xii:6), B. C. 1050.

2. Son of Uzziel, and father of Zechariah (1 Chron. xxiii:20; xxiv:25), B. C. about 1618.

JESIMIEL (je-sĭm'i-el), (Heb. יְשִׂימִאֵל, *yes-eem-aw-ale'*, God will place), one of the thirteen Simeonite princes who, in the time of Hezekiah, migrated to the valley of Gedor for purposes of conquest (1 Chron. iv:36), B. C. about 711.

JESSE (jĕs'se), (Heb. יִשַׁי, *yee-shah'ee*, firm), a descendant of Obed, the son of Boaz and Ruth (Ruth iv:17, 22; Matt. i:5, 6; Luke iii:32; 1 Chron. ii:12).

He was the father of eight sons (1 Sam. xvii: 12); from the youngest of whom, David, is reflected all the distinction which belongs to the name. He seems to have been a person of some note and substance at Bethlehem, his property being chiefly in sheep. It would seem from 1 Sam. xvi:10, that he must have been aware of the high destinies which awaited his son; but it is doubtful if he ever lived to see them realized. The last historical mention of Jesse is in relation to the asylum which David procured for him with the king of Moab (1 Sam. xxii:3), B. C. before 1000.

JESTING (jĕst-ĭng), (Gr. εὐτραπελία, *yoo-trap-el-ee'ah*, pleasantry, humor, facetiousness), is used in a bad sense in Eph. v:4, as ribaldry, low jesting, scurrility.

JESU (je'su), a modern poetical name for JESUS.

JESUI (jĕs'u-ī), (Heb. יִשְׁוִי, *yish-vee'*, level), (Num. xxvi:44). Same as ISHUI (which see).

JESUITES (jĕs'u-ītes), the family of JESUI or ISHUI.

JESURUN (jĕs'u-rŭn), (Heb. יְשֻׁרוּן, *yesh-oo-roon'*), an erroneous form of JESHURUN.

JESUS (jē'zus), (Gr. Ἰησοῦς, *ee-ay-soos'*, Jesu, Jesus, Josue), the Greek form of Joshua or Jeshua, a contraction of Jehoshua (Heb. יְהוֹשֻׁעַ, *yeh-ho-shoo'ah*), that is, "help of Jehovah" or "Savior" (Num. xiii:16).

1. Joshua, son of Nun, the military leader in the wars of Canaan (Acts vii:55; Heb. iv:8). (See JOSHUA.)

2. An ancestor of Christ, who lived about four hundred years after David (Luke iii:29). The A. V. follows a different Greek text and calls him *Jose.*

3. In the Septuagint the name occurs several times in the Apocrypha. The author of Ecclesiasticus was called by this name and twelve persons with the same name are mentioned by Josephus outside of his references to Joshua and to Christ.

It was a common name among the Jews of the Greek-speaking period.

4. A Jewish Christian, also termed Justus, associated with Paul (Col. iv:11). (See JUSTUS.)

5. The name of our Lord. (See JESUS CHRIST.)

JESUS CHRIST (jé-zus krīst), (Gr. Ἰησοῦς Χριστός, Ἰησοῦς ὁ Χριστός), the ordinary designation of the incarnate Son of God, and Savior of mankind.

This double designation is not, like Simon Peter, John Mark, Joses Barnabas, composed of a name and a surname, but, like John the Baptist, Simon Magus, Bar-jesus Elymas, of a proper name, and an official title. Jesus was our Lord's proper name, just as Peter, James, and John were the proper names of three of his disciples. The name seems not to have been an uncommon one among the Jews. The apocryphal book Ecclesiasticus is attributed to Jesus the son of Sirach; and, in the New Testament, we read of Jesus, the father of Elymas the sorcerer (Acts xiii:6), and of 'Jesus, which is called Justus of the circumcision' (Col. iv:11), one of Paul's 'fellow-workers unto the kingdom of God which had been a comfort to him.' To distinguish our Lord from others bearing the name, he was termed Jesus of Nazareth (John xviii:7, etc.), Ἰησοῦς ὁ Ναζωραῖος, and Jesus the son of Joseph (John vi:42, etc.)

(1) Personal Name. There can be no doubt that Jesus is the Greek form of a Hebrew name, which had been borne by two illustrious individuals in former periods of the Jewish history—the successor of Moses and introducer of Israel into the Promised Land (Exod. xxiv:13), and the high-priest who, along with Zerubbabel (Zech. iii:1), took so active a part in the re-establishment of the civil and religious polity of the Jews on their return from the Babylonish captivity. Its original and full form is Jehoshua (Num. xiii: 16). By contraction it became Joshua, or Jeshua; and when transferred into Greek, by taking the termination characteristic of that language, it assumed the form Jesus. It is thus the names of the illustrious individuals referred to are uniformly written in the Sept.; and the first of them is twice mentioned in the New Testament by this name (Acts vii:45; Heb. iv:8).

The conferring of this name on our Lord was not the result of accident, nor of the ordinary course of things, there being 'none of his kindred,' as the 'neighbors and cousins' of his mother said, 'called by that name' (Luke i:61). It was the consequence of a twofold miraculous interposition. The angel who announced to his virgin mother that she was to be 'the most honored of women,' in giving birth to the Son of God and the Savior of men, intimated also to her the name by which the holy child was to be called: 'Thou shalt call his name Jesus' (Luke i:31). And it was probably the same heavenly messenger who appeared to Joseph, and, to remove his suspicions and quiet his fears, said to him: 'That which is conceived in thy wife Mary is of the Holy Ghost, and she shall bring forth a son, and thou shalt call his name Jesus' (Matt. i:20, 21). The pious pair were 'not disobedient to the heavenly vision.' 'When eight days were accomplished for the circumcising of the child, his name was called Jesus, which was so named of the angel before he was conceived in the womb' (Luke ii:21).

The name Jesus, like most of Jewish proper names, was significant; and, as might well be expected, when we consider who imposed it, its meaning is at once important and appropriate. The *precise* import of the word has been a subject of doubt and debate among interpreters. As to its *general* meaning there is all but an unanimous concurrence. It was intended to denote that he who bore it was to be a Deliverer or Savior. This, whatever more, is indicated in the original word; and the reason given by the angel for the imposition of this name on the Virgin's son was 'because he shall save his people from their sins' (Matt. i:21). But while some interpreters hold that it is just a part of the verb signifying to save in the form Hiphil, slightly modified, and that it signifies 'he shall save,' others hold that it is a compound word formed by the addition of two letters of the incommunicable name of the Divinity, יהוה, to that verb, and that it is equivalent to 'The Salvation of the Lord,' or 'The Lord the Savior.' It is not a matter of vital importance. The following circumstances seem to give probability to the latter opinion. It does not appear likely that Moses would have changed the name of his destined successor from Oshea, which signifies 'savior,' into Jehoshua (Num. xiii:16), if the latter signified merely he shall save; whereas, if the word be a compound term, embodying in it the name Jehovah, we see an adequate reason for the change. In the first chapter of the Gospel by Matthew (Matt. i:22, 23), the most natural interpretation of the words (though they admit of another exegesis) seems to imply that the prediction of Isaiah, that the Virgin's son should be called Immanuel, was fulfilled in the imposition of the name Jesus on the Son of Mary. This would be the case only on the supposition that Immanuel and Jesus are equivalent terms, a supposition which cannot be sustained unless *Jesus* can be fairly rendered 'Jehovah will save,' or 'Jehovah the Savior.' In that case, Jesus and Immanuel—God *with* us, *i. e.,* on our side—express the same ideas.

It is right, however, to remark that the merely bearing such a name as either Immanuel or Jesus, even by Divine appointment, is not *of itself* evidence of the divinity of him who bears it. The Hebrews were in the habit of giving names, both to persons and places, which were intended not to describe their distinctive properties, but to express some important general truth. Jacob called an altar built by him El-Elohe-Israel (Gen. xxxiii:20), 'God the God of Israel,' *i. e.,* God is the God of Israel. Moses called an altar he built Jehovah-nissi (Exod. xvii:15), 'Jehovah my banner,' *i. e.,* Jehovah is my banner. The name Jehoshua, as borne by him who brought the people of the Lord into the heritage of the Gentiles, means no more than that by him Jehovah would deliver his people. In many of the proper names in the Old Testament, the name El, or Jehovah, forms a part. Yet when, as in the case before us, he who bears such a name, by express divine appointment, is shown 'by many infallible proofs' to be indeed an incarnation of Divinity, we cannot but perceive a peculiar propriety in this divine appointment, and find in it, if not a new argument, a corroboration of the host of arguments which lead us to the conclusion that He who 'according to the flesh' was the Son of David, 'according to the Spirit of Holiness' was 'the Son of God,' 'God over all, blessed forever' (Rom. i:3, 4; ix:5).

The 'name of Jesus' (Phil. ii:10) is not the name Jesus, but *'the name above every name,'* ὄνομα τὸ ὑπὲρ πᾶν ὄνομα, ver. 9; *i. e.,* the supreme dignity and authority with which the Father has invested Jesus Christ, as the reward of his disinterested exertions in the cause of the divine glory and human happiness; and the bowing ἐν τῷ ὀνόματι Ἰησοῦ *in* or *at the name of Jesus,* is obviously not an external mark of homage when the name Jesus is pronounced, but the inward sense of awe and submission to him who is raised to a station so exalted.

(2) **Official Name.** CHRIST (Gr. Χριστός; *the Anointed One;* Heb. מָשִׁיחַ, *Messiah, the Anointed*). Christ is not, strictly speaking, a proper name, but an official title. Jesus Christ, or rather, as it generally ought to be rendered, Jesus *the* Christ, is a mode of expression of the same kind as John the Baptist, or Baptizer. In consequence of not adverting to this, the force, and even the meaning, of many passages of Scripture are misapprehended. When it is stated that Paul asserted, 'This Jesus whom I preach unto you is Christ' (Acts xvii:3), ὅτι οὗτός ἐστιν ὁ Χριστὸς Ἰησοῦς, etc., that he 'testified to the Jews that Jesus was Christ' (Acts xviii:5), the meaning is that he proclaimed and proved that Jesus was the Christ, τὸν Χριστὸν Ἰησοῦν, or Messiah—the rightful owner of a title descriptive of a high official station which had been the subject of ancient prediction. When Jesus himself says that 'it is life eternal to know the only true God, and Jesus Christ whom he has sent' (John xvii:3), he represents the knowledge of himself as the Christ, the Messiah, as at once necessary and sufficient to make men truly and permanently happy. When he says, 'What think ye of Christ?' περὶ τοῦ Χριστοῦ: 'whose son is he?' (Matt. xxii:42), he does not mean, What think ye of ME, or of my descent? but, What think ye of the Christ—the Messiah—and especially of his paternity. There can be no doubt that the word, though originally an appellative and intended to bring before the mind a particular official character possessed by him to whom it is applied, came at last, like many other terms of the same kind, to be often used very much as a proper name, to distinguish our Lord from other persons bearing the name Jesus. This is a sense, however, of comparatively rare occurrence in the New Testament.

Proceeding, then, on the principle that Christ is an appellative, let us inquire into its origin and signification as applied to our Lord. CHRIST is the English form of a Greek word, Χριστός, corresponding in meaning to the Hebrew word Messiah and the English word Anointed. The Christ is just equivalent to the Anointed One. The important question, however, remains behind, What is meant when the Savior is represented as the Anointed One? To reply to this question satisfactorily it will be necessary to go somewhat into detail.

Unction, from a very early age, seems to have been the emblem of consecration, or setting apart to a particular, and especially to a religious, purpose. Thus, Jacob is said to have *anointed* the pillar of stone, which he erected and set apart as a monument of his supernatural dream at Bethel (Gen. xxviii:18; xxxi:13; xxxv:14). Under the Old Testament economy high-priests and kings were regularly set apart to their offices, both of which were, strictly speaking, sacred ones, by the ceremony of anointing, and the prophets were occasionally designated by the same rite. This rite seems to have been intended as a public intimation of a Divine appointment to office. Thus Saul is termed 'the Lord's anointed' (1 Sam. xxiv:6); David, 'the anointed of the God of Israel' (2 Sam. xxiii:1); and Zedekiah, 'the anointed of the Lord' (Lam. iv:20). The high-priest is called 'the anointed priest' (Lev. iv:3).

From the origin and design of the rite, it is not wonderful that the term should have, in a secondary and analogical sense, been applied to persons set apart by God for important purposes, though not actually anointed, Thus Cyrus, the King of Persia, is termed 'the Lord's anointed' (Is. xlv: 1); the Hebrew patriarchs, when sojourning in Canaan, are termed 'God's anointed ones' Ps. cv: 15); and the Israelitish people receive the same appellation from the prophet Habbakuk (Hab. iii:13). It is probably with reference to this use of the expression that Moses is said by the writer of the Epistle to the Hebrews, to have 'counted the reproach of Christ' (Heb. xi:26), τοῦ Χριστοῦ (λαοῦ), the same class who in the parallel clause are termed the 'people of God,' 'greater riches than the treasures of Egypt.'

In the prophetic Scriptures we find this appellation given to an illustrious personage, who, under various designations, is so often spoken of as destined to appear in a distant age as a great deliverer. The royal prophet David seems to have been the first who spoke of the great deliverer under this appellation. He represents the heathen (the Gentile nations) raging, and the people (the Jewish people) imagining a vain thing, 'against Jehovah, and against his anointed' (Ps. ii:2). He says, 'Now know I that the Lord saveth his anointed' (Ps. xx:6). 'Thou hast loved righteousness and hated iniquity,' says he, addressing himself to 'Him who was to come,' 'therefore God, even thy God, hath anointed thee with the oil of gladness above thy fellows' (Ps. xlv:7). In all the passages in which the great deliverer is spoken of as 'the anointed one,' by David, he is plainly viewed as sustaining the character of a king.

The prophet Isaiah also uses the appellation, 'the anointed one,' with reference to the promised deliverer, but, when he does so, he speaks of him as a prophet or great teacher. He introduces him as saying, 'The Spirit of the Lord God is upon me, because the Lord God hath anointed me to preach good tidings unto the meek; he hath sent me to bind up the broken-hearted, to proclaim liberty to the captives, and the opening of the prison to them that are bound, to proclaim the acceptable year of the Lord, and the day of vengeance of our God; to comfort all that mourn,' etc. (Is. lxi:1, etc.).

Daniel is the only other of the prophets who uses the appellation, 'the anointed one,' in reference to the Great Deliverer, and he plainly represents him as not only a prince, but also a high-priest, an expiator of guilt. 'Seventy weeks are determined upon thy people and upon thy holy city, to finish the transgression, and to make an end of sins, and to make reconciliation for iniquity, and to bring an everlasting righteousness, and to seal up the vision and the prophecy, and to anoint the Most Holy. Know therefore and understand that from the going forth of the commandment to restore Jerusalem unto Messiah the Prince shall be seven weeks, and threescore and two weeks; the city shall be built again, and the wall, even in troublous times; and after threescore and two weeks shall Messiah be cut off, but not for himself' (Dan. ix:24-26).

During the period which elapsed from the close of the prophetic canon until the birth of Jesus, no appellation of the expected deliverer seems to have been so common as the Messiah or Anointed One, and this is still the name which the unbelieving Jews' ordinarily employ when speaking of him whom they still look for to avenge their wrongs and restore them to more than their former honors.

Messiah, Christ, Anointed, is, then, a term equivalent to consecrated, sacred, set apart; and as the record of divine revelation is called, by way of eminence, The Bible, or book, so is the Great Deliverer called The Messiah, or Anointed One, much in the same way as he is termed, The Man, The Son of Man.

The import of this designation as given to Jesus of Nazareth may now readily be apprehended: When he is termed the Christ it is plainly indicated that HE is the great deliverer promised under that appellation, and many others in the Old Testament Scriptures, and that all that is said of this deliverer under this or any other appellation is true of HIM. No attentive reader of the Old Testament can help noticing that in every part of the prophecies there is ever and anon presented to our view an illustrious personage destined to appear at some future distant period, and, however varied may be the figurative representations given of him, no reasonable doubt can be entertained as to the identity of the individual. It is quite obvious that the Messiah is the same person as 'the seed of the woman' who was to 'bruise the head of the serpent' (Gen. iii:15); 'the seed of Abraham, in whom all the nations of the earth were to be blessed' (Gen. xxii: 18); the great 'prophet to be raised up like unto Moses,' whom all were to be required to hear and obey (Deut. xviii:15); the 'priest after the order of Melchizedek;' 'the rod out of the stem of Jesse, which should stand for an ensign of the people to which the Gentiles should seek' (Is. xi:1, 10); the virgin's son whose name was to be Immanuel (Is. vii:14); 'the branch of Jehovah' (Is. iv:2); 'the Angel of the Covenant' (Mal. iii:1); 'the Lord of the Temple,' etc., in the same place. When we say, then, that Jesus is the Christ, we in effect say, 'This is HE of whom Moses in the law, and the Prophets did write' (John i:45); and all that they say of HIM is true of Jesus.

Now what is the sum of the prophetic testimony respecting him? It is this—that he should belong to the very highest order of being, the incommunicable name Jehovah being represented as rightfully belonging to him; that 'his goings forth have been from old, from everlasting' (Mic. v:2); that his appropriate appellations should be 'Wonderful,' 'Counsellor,' 'the Mighty God' (Is. ix:6); that he should assume human nature, and become 'a child born' of the Israelitish nation of the tribe of Judah (Gen. xlix:10), of the family of David (Is. xi:1); that the object of his appearance should be the salvation of mankind, both Jews and Gentiles (Is. xlix:6); that he should be 'despised and rejected' of his countrymen; that he should be 'cut off, but not for himself'; that he should be 'wounded for men's transgressions, bruised for their iniquities, and undergo the chastisement of their peace;' that 'by his stripes men should be healed;' that 'the Lord should lay on him the iniquity' of men; that 'exaction should be made and he should answer it;' that he should 'make his soul an offering for sin;' that after these sufferings he should be 'exalted and extolled and made very high;' that he should 'see of the travail of his soul and be satisfied, and by his knowledge justify many' (Is. liii, throughout); that Jehovah should say to him, 'Sit at my right hand until I make thine enemies thy footstool' (Ps. cx:1); that he should be brought near to the Ancient of Days, and that to him should be given 'dominion, and glory, and a kingdom, that all people, and nations, and languages should serve him—an everlasting dominion which shall not pass away—a kingdom that shall not be destroyed' (Dan. vii:13, 14). All this is implied in saying Jesus is the Christ. In the plainer language of the New Testament 'Jesus is the Christ' is equivalent to Jesus is 'God manifest in flesh' (1 Tim. iii:16)—the Son of God, who, in human nature, by his obedience, and sufferings, and death in the room of the guilty, has obtained salvation for them, and all power in heaven and earth for himself, that he may give eternal life to all coming to the Father through him.

While the statement, 'Jesus is the Christ', is thus materially equivalent to the statement, 'all that is said of the Great Deliverer in the Old Testament Scriptures is true of HIM,' it brings more directly before our mind those truths respecting him which the appellation, 'the Anointed One' naturally suggests. He is a prophet, a priest, and a king. He is the great revealer of Divine truth, the only expiator of human guilt, sole legitimate ruler over the understandings, consciences and affections of men. In his person, and work, and word, by his spirit and providence, he unfolds the truth with respect to the Divine character and will, and so conveys it into the mind as to make it the effectual means of conforming man's will to God's will, man's character to God's character. He has, by his spotless, all-perfect obedience, amid the severest sufferings, 'obedience unto death, even the death of the cross,' so illustrated the excellence of the Divine law and the wickedness and danger of violating it, as to make it a righteous thing in 'the just God' to 'justify the ungodly,' thus propitiating the offended majesty of heaven; while the manifestation of the Divine love in appointing and accepting this atonement, when apprehended by the mind under the influence of the Holy Spirit, becomes the effectual means of reconciling man to God and to his law, 'transforming him by the renewing of his mind.' And now, possessed of 'all power in heaven and earth,' 'all power over all flesh,' 'He is Lord of All.' All external events and all spiritual influences are equally under his control, and as a king he exerts his authority in carrying into full effect the great purposes which his revelations as a prophet, and his great atoning sacrifice as a high-priest, were intended to accomplish.

But the full import of the appellation the CHRIST is not yet brought out. It indicates that He to whom it belongs is the *anointed* prophet, priest, and king—not that he was anointed by material oil, but that he was divinely *appointed, qualified, commissioned,* and *accredited* to be the Savior of men. These are the ideas which the term *anointed* seems specially intended to convey. Jesus was divinely *appointed* to the offices he filled. He assumed them involuntarily, 'he was called of God as was Aaron' (Heb. v:4). 'Behold mine ELECT, in whom my soul delighteth.' He was divinely *qualified:* 'God gave to him the Spirit not by measure.' 'The Spirit of the Lord was upon him, the spirit of wisdom and understanding, the spirit of counsel and might, the spirit of knowledge and of the fear of the Lord, and they made him of quick understanding in the fear of the Lord, so that he does not judge after the sight of his eyes, nor reprove after the hearing of his ears, but he smites the earth with the rod of his mouth, and with the breath of his lips he slays the wicked; and righteousness is the girdle of his loins, and faithfulness the girdle of his reins' (Is. xi:2, 4). He was divinely *commissioned;* 'The Father sent him.' Jehovah said to him, 'Thou art my servant, in thee will I be glorified.' 'It is a light thing that thou shouldst be my servant, to raise up the

tribes of Jacob, and to restore the preserved of Israel; I will also give thee for a light to the Gentiles, that thou mayst be my salvation to the ends of the earth' (Is. xlix:6). 'Behold,' says Jehovah, 'I have given Him for a witness to the people—a leader and commander to the people.' He is divinely *accredited;* 'Jesus of Nazareth,' says the Apostle Peter, was 'a man approved of God among you by miracles, and wonders, and signs which God did by him in the midst of you' (Acts ii:22). 'The Father who hath sent me,' says Jesus himself, 'hath borne witness of me' (John v:37). This he did again and again by a voice from heaven, as well as by the miracles which he performed by that divine power which was equally his as his Father's. Such is the import of the appellation *Christ.*

If these observations are clearly apprehended there will be little difficulty in giving a satisfactory answer to the question which has sometimes been proposed—when did Jesus become Christ? when was he *anointed* of God? We have seen that the expression is a figurative or analogical one, and therefore we need not wonder that its references are various. The *appointment* of the Savior, like all the other Divine purposes, was of course from eternity. 'He was set up from everlasting' (Prov. viii:23); he 'was foreordained before the foundation of the world' (1 Pet. i:20). His qualifications, such of them as were conferred, were bestowed in or during his incarnation, when 'God anointed him with the Holy Ghost and with power' (Acts x:38). His commission may be considered as given him when called to enter on the functions of his office. He himself, after quoting, in the synagogue of Nazareth, in the commencement of his ministry, the passage from the prophecies of Isaiah in which his unction to the prophetical office is predicted, declared, '*This day* is this Scripture fulfilled in your ears.' And in his resurrection and ascension, God, as the reward of his loving righteousness, and hating iniquity, 'anointed him with the oil of gladness above his fellows' (Ps. xlv:7), *i. e.,* conferred on him a regal power, fruitful in blessings to himself and others, far superior to that which any king had ever possessed, making him, as the Apostle Peter expresses it, 'both Lord and Christ' (Acts ii:36). As to his being *accredited,* every miraculous event performed in reference to him or by him may be viewed as included in this species of anointing—especially the visible descent of the Spirit on him in his baptism.

These statements, with regard to the import of the appellation, 'the Christ,' show us how we are to understand the statement of the Apostle John, 'Whosoever believeth that Jesus is the Christ, is born of God' (1 John v:1), *i. e.,* is 'a child of God,' 'born again,' 'a new creature;' and the similar declaration of the Apostle Paul, 'No man can say that Jesus is the Lord,' *i. e.,* the Christ, the Messiah, 'but by the Holy Ghost' (1 Cor. xii:3). It is plain that the proposition, 'Jesus is the Christ,' when understood in the latitude of meaning which we have shown belongs to it, contains a complete summary of the truth respecting the divine method of salvation. To believe that principle rightly understood is to believe the Gospel—the saving truth, by the faith of which a man is, and by the faith of which only a man can be, brought into the relation or formed to the character of a child of God; and though a man may, without divine influence, be brought to acknowledge that 'Jesus is the Lord,' 'Messiah the Prince,' and even firmly to believe that these words embody a truth, yet no man can be brought really to believe and cordially to acknowledge the truth contained in these words, as we have attempted to unfold it, without a peculiar divine influence. That Jesus is ὁ ἐλθών, ὁ Χριστός, is the testimony of God, the faith of which constitutes a Christian, τὸ ἔν, the one thing to which the Spirit, the water and the blood, unite in bearing witness (1 John v :6, 8, 9).

(3) Offices of Jesus Christ. The offices are generally considered as threefold: (a) A prophet to enlighten, warn, and instruct (John vi: 14; iii :2). (b) A priest to sympathize, intercede, and make atonement for his people (Is. liii; Heb. vii). (c) A king to reign in, rule over, protect, deliver, and bless them (Zech. xiv :9; Ps. ii :6). (See articles INTERCESSION; MEDIATOR.) J. B.

JESUS THE CHRIST, LIFE OF.

(1) Records and Chronology. Palestine was a small country on the far eastern edge of the great Roman Empire. The Jewish people were despised and ignored because they were a small Oriental nation, bigoted and exclusive in spirit, austere in morals, and fanatical in religion. The career of Jesus, brief, uneventful and obscure to the general observer of his day, attracted almost no attention outside of his own land. It was nearly thirty-five years after Jesus' death before the Empire came to regard his followers as anything more than a particular Jewish sect. We need not, therefore, expect, nor do we in fact find, much reference to Jesus in the Roman history of this period. The only clear statement about him is contained in Tacitus' "Annals," xv :44: "They called them Christians. Christ, from whom the name was given, had been put to death in the reign of Tiberius, by the procurator Pontius Pilate." There are also some corroborating allusions to Jesus and his followers in other Roman writings. The great Jewish writers of the century, Philo and Josephus, give us practically nothing. Philo nowhere mentions Jesus, perhaps from ignorance of him, although Philo lived until after 40 A. D. Josephus barely mentions "the Christ" in Antiquities xx, ix, 1 (unless some portion of the famous passage xviii, iii, 3 can be called genuine). His silence is intentional, due to Jewish hatred of Jesus. Small, therefore, but very valuable, is the extra-biblical record of Jesus' life.

Within the New Testament, the earliest record is contained in certain epistles of Paul, written not later than the years A. D. 53-63, and whose authorship and historicity is unquestioned. From these letters we learn of his Davidic descent, his unique personality, his exalted character, his preaching of the Kingdom of God, his appointment of apostles, his Messiahship, his betrayal, crucifixion and resurrection. From James, Peter and Hebrews also can be gathered facts about Jesus' life.

But the Gospels have explicitly recorded for us Jesus' life. They contain memorabilia of Jesus. Fragmentary accounts of what Jesus did and said have been brought together for use and preservation. From a time even before his death, the important events, the significant acts, and the weighty teachings of Jesus, were reported among his followers, taught to the new converts (Acts ii :42), and circulated wherever the Gospel was carried. The words and acts of Jesus were the substance of Christianity throughout the apostolic age. For many years this historical material was transmitted orally, according to the Jewish custom of the time. Gradually the records passed from Aramaic, their original language, into Greek, that they might be given also to the Gentiles and to the Jews of the Dispersion. After a time some

of the material was committed to writing, and oral and written tradition went along hand in hand. The first attempt to gather up these fragmentary records was probably made by the apostle Matthew, who collected many of Jesus' sayings in their Aramaic dress, perhaps as early as A. D. 50. This collection is known as the "Logia." Some years later, Mark supplemented Matthew's work by making a collection of the records of the events and deeds of Jesus' public ministry.

And as the generation of eye and ear witnesses of what Jesus had done and said was now passing away, many attempts were made (Luke i: 1-4) to collect the floating material into a more complete and durable form. Our four canonical gospels are such final collections. They came into existence at four different centers of Christian teaching and activity in the apostolic age, and grew out of the cycle of tradition which each center had in its possession. The Gospel of Mark (about 66 A. D.) is the earliest of the four. The Gospel of Matthew is not the "Logia" of the apostle, but an original work in Greek (about A. D. 70-80) by an unnamed author, who used a Greek form of the earlier "Logia" as a source of his material, and drew also from the Gospel of Mark, and from various other sources of oral and written tradition. The Gospel of Luke was also compiled (about A. D. 70-80) from a Greek edition of the "Logia," from Mark's Gospel, and from other sources of oral and written tradition. The fourth Gospel comes from the Apostle John, and contains a cycle of tradition not often parallel to that of the synoptic gospels, but of a peculiar type which John seems to have cherished. This gospel is either directly from the apostle (about A. D. 80-96), or indirectly, through some disciple of his who, after his master's death, collected certain characteristic material from the apostle's teaching and put it forth under John's name (about A. D. 100-130).

Our gospels are therefore compilations. The events, the deeds and the sayings of Jesus which they contain are those which circulated among the Christians from the first. They survived, a few out of a great number, because they most clearly revealed and perpetuated the life, work and teaching of Jesus. The material has passed through a process of wise selection by the disciples, and of practical sifting by time, until we have the choicest and most useful portion, the essence of the history. It must, however, be remembered that the incidents and sayings have, by this process of transmission, lost for the most part their historical setting and their chronological position. This material, when brought together in our gospels, is often grouped topically or illustratively. The arrangement cannot be depended upon in detail. For example, in Matthew the Sermon on the Mount, the Charge to the Twelve, the Parables by the Sea, the Denunciation of the Pharisees, the Eschatological Discourse, and in Luke the long section (chapters x-xix) are all collections of material spoken on various occasions, whose detailed historical setting has been lost, and which are brought together in a topical or literary unity. The same thing can often be seen in the grouping of the incidents as transmitted to us. This feature of the gospels is becoming increasingly clear to all thoughtful scholars, and the recognition of it is essential to a true use of the Gospel histories.

The chronology of Jesus' life is in general certain, but in detail very uncertain. We know that Jesus' death fell in the reign of Tiberius and the procuratorship of Pilate, i. e., somewhere between A. D. 26 and 36. This can probably be narrowed down to A. D. 28-33, but within this range we cannot tell what year. The year A. D. 30 is the date to which it is now commonly assigned, but of this we cannot be at all sure. The beginning of Jesus' public ministry was, presumably, not until after the fifteenth year of Tiberius (Luke iii:1-3), i. e., late in A. D. 28 or 29. Jesus being then "about thirty years of age" (Luke iii:23), his birth goes back a few years into the B. C. period. About the year B. C. 6 is the date toward which we seem now to be trending. Even supposing these data given by Luke to be accurate, there remains an uncertainty of years. We would seem to have a public ministry of Jesus but one full year in length, if he began early in 29 and was crucified in the spring of A. D. 30. Current chronological schemes of the public ministry give it something over three years, on the basis of John ii:13; v: 1; vi:4; xiii:1. But v:1 is not a passover, and vi:4 as a passover is somewhat doubtful (see Westcott and Hort, *"New Testament in Greek,"* vol. ii:Appx. 77-81; and Turner, art. *Chronology of the New Testament in "New Bible Dictionary,"* vol. i, pp: 403-415, the best single article on the whole problem); while the passover in connection with the cleansing of the temple may be the last one, as the synoptic gospels indicate. John's supposed chronological framework is therefore quite questionable. The synoptists mention but one passover, that in connection with Jesus' death. It is sometimes held that they indicate, though they do not name, two others (Mark ii:23 suggests a time of year soon after a passover, and Mark vi:39 is supposed from its reference to "green grass" to indicate a time not long before a passover). But from what we know of the way in which the material of the gospels is put together, we cannot build chronology on such suggestions. Professor Sanday (*"Expositor,"* iv, v: 16) says: "The simple fact is that the synoptic gospels are only a series of incidents loosely strung together, with no chronology at all worthy of the name." The exact dates of Jesus' life cannot at present be known, neither can we know the duration of his public ministry; it was probably either one or two full years, with some portion of a second or third. After all, this matters little; exact chronology is a modern passion, but it is comparatively unimportant. The ethical and religious teaching of Jesus' life is quite independent of precise years, months and days.

(2) Preparation of Jesus for His Work. The Hebrew nation had a genius for morals and religion, as Greece had a genius for science and literature, and Rome a genius for law and administration. Each nation made its essential contribution to the progress of mankind. Naturally, therefore, the greatest religious teacher of the world arose from the Hebrew race, and perfected his people's contribution to human history. Jesus was born of Jewish parents in Palestine. But not at Jerusalem nor in Judea did the Jewish Messiah arise—that honor fell to Galilee. For in Judea, Pharisaism was at its worst. Emphasis upon the letter had crushed out the spirit of religion, righteousness had become a superficial and punctilious observance of formal rules of conduct and empty ceremonies instead of the outworking of a pure heart and a right purpose. The rabbinical schools at Jerusalem were dreary storehouses of Jewish legal lore and factories of casuistical disputations upon the minutiæ of legal obligation. Out of this no good thing could come, least of all the Messiah.

So, in God's providence, Jesus' home was at Nazareth. Galilee breathed a freer, purer religious atmosphere. In fact, was there so favorable a place as Galilee elsewhere in all the earth for the development of the world's greatest teacher? For there he escaped the hollow and hypocritical Pharisaism, and at the same time the gross immorality and barren speculations of the Gentile nations. Jesus' parents were devoted adherents of Judaism in the best prophetic type, genuinely religious. They were simple, quiet, hard-working people of one of the larger Galilean villages. The education which Jesus received was an excellent one for the times. It began in the home, where the greatest care was taken by the best Jewish families to train their children religiously. Then came the assistance also of the synagogue school, where the fundamentals of education were taught. The Old Testament history was thoroughly taught, and then the Old Testament law with its later elaborations, until the child became familiar with the whole canon of Jewish Scriptures. How completely Jesus entered into the spirit of all this appears on his first visit to Jerusalem, at the age of his legal majority, when he eagerly seized the opportunity to ask the rabbis the many great questions of religion and life to which he had found no answers. Jesus probably learned to read the Old Testament Scriptures in Hebrew, and the Aramaic he was of course familiar with, for it was the Jewish vernacular of his day. In addition he knew more or less Greek, for this was the language of commerce with the Gentile world, which had entered largely into Galilee.

Jesus seems never to have gone beyond Syria out into the great Roman Empire, nor to have become familiar with the Gentile type of life, nor to have read the history or literature of any nation besides his own. In morals and religion Judaism was to be the teacher, not the taught. Out of Hebrew history and teaching Jesus drew the truth of God, and it was upon the Old Testament foundation as laid by the greatest of the prophets that he built the everlasting Gospel. That which was good in the religious thought and practice of his day he recognized and cherished, that which was false and harmful he rejected with true spiritual vision. Discrimination of essentials from non-essentials, the fixing of a scale of real values, was characteristic of Jesus. And in addition to all, he loved the world of nature about him, finding everywhere God's workmanship and God's love. No one has seen so much in nature that is beautiful and helpful as Jesus saw. God's own spirit of wisdom, truth and love grew in him to perfect him for his mission. Jesus must have come early to a consciousness of special nearness to God. It was this constraining power which led him safely through the maze of human experience to a complete control over his acts and choices, and to the ultimate approval of God for the Messianic work. He was the normal man; others were abnormal. And yet so unostentatious was Jesus' life during the thirty years at Nazareth, that his townsmen would not believe him extraordinary (Mark iii:20, 21; vi:1-6; Luke iv:16-30).

But however close Jesus felt himself to God, he probably was not yet conscious that he was to be the Messiah. The thirty years was a period of probation for him. When John the Baptist appeared in the district of the Jordan heralding the approach of the Kingdom of God, and calling upon men to prepare therefor, Jesus eagerly responded to the summons. Now was to appear he who should restore pure religion to Israel, and lead men to the glorious realization of their ideal hopes. Jesus would, with the others, receive the symbol of conformity to God's will and of preparation for the kingdom at hand. But with the administering of water baptism to Jesus came God's approval of his Son, and a unique impartation of God's spirit, which was to him at once the announcement of his Messiahship and the endowment for his Messianic work.

The experience which followed upon this, the so-called temptation, was Jesus' self-adjustment to his new office and life. The gospel accounts of this experience came from Jesus himself. In this parabolic language he endeavored to show to his disciples what was the true conception of the Kingdom of God and of the Messiah, as he had determined these at the outset of his ministry. The problem as to what sort of a Messiah he should be, and what methods he should use in the performance of his Messianic mission, was a vital one to Jesus, and the mental anguish of decision was real. God was with him in the choice. He determined to sacrifice himself wholly to the cause, to forego the comforts of life and subject himself to the privations and labors of a traveling ministry. He determined that he would not employ spectacular methods, but quietly and simply would do the work of a preacher of righteousness. And that, however great might be the pressure upon him to become the temporal Messiah of current Jewish expectation, he would insist only and always upon a spiritual kingdom, founded on spiritual truth, composed of spiritual members, and seeking spiritual ends. Then Jesus was ready to begin his public work as Messiah.

(3) Plan and Method of Jesus' Ministry. The decision as to what needed to be done, and how it was to be accomplished, was reached by Jesus before he entered upon his public work. The Kingdom of God, a spiritual and moral kingdom, was to be established upon the earth. It was the nature of this kingdom, first, to transform the individual, second, to dominate and purify the world. Such a kingdom could not be founded from without. All true and effective means must be of an invisible and spiritual kind. There could be no alliance with the political parties and forces already established in Judea, for the Kingdom of God was to take no external, temporal, or local form. It was not to be set up or maintained by any of those instrumentalities upon which human kingdoms depended. "My kingdom is not of this world," said Jesus (John xviii:36). It was to have no officers, no headquarters, no political features, no wordly associations. It was not to be established nor defended by physical force, neither was it to exist in the interest of selfish ends. Nor was it possible for Jesus to carry out the current Messianic programme. The Messiah of the popular hope must establish a temporal kingdom, visible to men, which should give the Jewish nation political supremacy of the world, and so glorify and avenge the down-trodden Israel. This was not the character of the Kingdom of God, as God gave Jesus to see it. "The kingdom of God cometh not with observation," said he, "the kingdom of God is within you" (Luke xvii:20, 21). It was impossible, therefore, for Jesus to coöperate with any of the religious parties which governed the lives and thoughts of his nation. The only means of establishing such a kingdom as he had been commissioned to found was to win to its support individuals who felt its truth and power, waiting patiently until those adherents should attain such numbers and strength as would leaven humanity entire, and transform the whole into the ideal society of perfected individuals.

This plan of Jesus is the most remarkable ever conceived. Rome had united the Mediterranean world by an all-conquering idea of universal political dominion, and men had marveled at the accomplishment of the impossible. Yet how much greater was Jesus' idea of uniting the whole world by the ties of religion into a universal spiritual brotherhood, a union not external, political and selfish, but internal, religious, humanitarian. An invisible kingdom which, planted in a small and obscure country, should expand till it embraced all countries, all men, all time. Such was Jesus' idea of the Kingdom of God. So original was this plan, so independent of all existing thought, that it could have come only from God himself. No other than Jesus could have conceived it, no other than Jesus would have attempted it. Yet Jesus determined upon this plan with full confidence that it was God's will, and with full assurance of its ultimate success. The accomplishment of it he set about with a resolution which carried him through hardships, isolation, reproach, opposition, martyrdom.

The evidence does not seem to justify the view that the plan of Jesus underwent modification during his ministry. His methods, of course, changed with the changing circumstances, his presentation of his message progressed with the developing capacity of his hearers, and his attitude toward the various classes adjusted itself to the attitude which they assumed toward him. It is true that Jesus did not publicly proclaim his Messiahship until the very close of his ministry, and that even to his most intimate disciples he did not make that claim until the latter portion of his work. But this was not because he was not himself certain of his Messiahship. It was due to the fact that if he had at the outset asserted himself as the Messiah, the perverse popular expectation would have demanded its perverse realization, and Jesus would have received no hearing at all for his purely spiritual conception of the kingdom. In every possible way Jesus avoided raising false hopes. He preached the kingdom so that it might appeal to the hearts of men and transform their expectations to accord with the reality. Even this method of superlative wisdom did not succeed with the Jews as a whole, for when they found Jesus would not fulfill their demands, all but a handful of followers deserted him (John vi: 14, 15, 66). But Jesus' failure to win the nation to an acceptance of the real kingdom could not have been a surprise to himself. It did not need a superhuman knowledge to foresee, at the outset of Jesus' public ministry, that a kingdom and a Messiah such as he contemplated would ultimately fail of acceptance by the Jews. It must have seemed quite clear to Jesus at the start that the preaching of such a message would end in its rejection and his own death. The Jewish people had conspicuously stained their history with the blood of their great prophets (Matt. xxiii:29-37), and could their greatest prophet fail to meet a like fate? But even with this probability before him, Jesus went calmly and earnestly about his work of delivering the message and founding the kingdom which God had given into his hands.

His method of procedure was to go about in Galilee, proclaiming the presence of the Kingdom of God, and teaching what were its characteristics, its demands, and its future. In the synagogues he taught upon the Sabbath, but still more every day in the homes, upon the streets, in the fields, by the seaside, wherever and whenever receptive listeners might be found. He gathered about himself disciples whom he trained to carry his message. By his own efforts, which they supplemented, Palestine was made to ring with the Gospel.

And Jesus' teaching was commended to the attention of men, and 'impressed upon their minds, by the mighty works which God gave him to do. Extraordinary operations in the physical world were made to illustrate the powers and blessings of the spiritual world. The divine power manifest in Jesus could heal physical disease, much more could it remove moral disease; it could restore physical sight and hearing, how much more could it open the spirit of man to the eternal truths and beauties of God and his universe; it could supply the physical necessities to man, how much more could it give that spiritual sustenance, that righteousness, which the hungering soul craves; it could remove the physical effects of sin, how much more could it purify the soul; it could quiet the raging waves of the sea, how much more could it soothe the troubled heart; it could restore the dead to life, how much more could it renew the moral and spiritual being. These great works were signs to the people that God was with Jesus, that he was the accredited messenger of the Most High. They were the token of God's presence among them, and the outflowing of his beneficence to humanity.

Then, too, Jesus' own life was the embodiment of his conception of the kingdom, an ideal realization of God's perfect will for men, and so a concrete and living illustration of his teaching. Here, as in all Jesus' teaching, it is the internal, not the external, which has permanent significance. Jesus became for us an example in the spirit of his life. His perfect trust in God, his absolute performance of duty, his unswerving adherence to truth, his serious view of life, his indifference to petty things, his vision into the depths of existence, his complete devotion to a great cause, his willing sacrifice of himself to serve his fellowmen, his patience in privation, adversity and suffering, his purity of character and motive—in all these and many other respects, Jesus was the personification of his own teaching, the pattern of the ideal man, the living example for every sincere soul.

(4) Jesus the Great Religious Teacher. The whole life of a real teacher teaches. The teaching of Jesus is not alone the words which he spoke; it is also the deeds which he did, and the example of his own life. Indeed, one attestation of the truth of his utterances is the beauty of the life which shows that truth in concrete realization. Jesus was recognized by the most receptive minds of his own day to be the great religious teacher (Matt. vii:29; Mark i:27; Luke xxiv: 19) whose coming was to fulfill the ideal hopes of centuries (Luke xxiv:21; John vi:14, 15). It was not his words only that gave them this belief; it was their embodiment in his acts and their illustration in his character. Jesus was sent by God to deliver a divine message to man, a message of life. He revealed religious truth which was to be not only accepted, but lived. The living of truth means the expression of it in one's words, in one's deeds, in one's personality. Jesus not only told men what this divine truth was, but he showed in his own life what it was to live divine truth. Jesus therefore became and continues to be the source of religious belief and practice. He has made known to men that which they practically need to know about God, man, duty, existence; and has shown them how to realize these things in themselves. Teaching is not an end in itself; it is a means to an end. Jesus' teaching was a means for getting God's will done in men individually and collectively. God has a great purpose for the world; we exist as a part of that purpose; we can assist in the realization of that purpose; such assistance consists in living as God would have us live. Jesus came to tell us, and by example to show us, how God would have us live; to make known to us God's love which forgives our failure and patiently awaits our complete success in doing his will; and to proclaim the freely given divine power which is available and sufficient for those whose supreme purpose is set toward realizing God's will in themselves. This was Jesus' mission; all that he did, all that he said, all that he was, belonged to this message. His words announced these truths, his acts embodied them, his character illustrated them. The events of his public ministry were determined by the attitude of the Jews toward him. He was rejected and crucified because the message which he brought, and which he unwaveringly taught, was distasteful to the religious leaders of his nation. He sacrificed himself that men might have the truth of religion.

If, therefore, we wish to know what the religious teaching of Jesus is, we must get the knowledge from him. The essence of Christianity is what Jesus taught, freed from the applications and elaborations of subsequent centuries. He came to make life intelligible and duty clear. His presentation of religious truths was divinely wise. He could omit nothing that was of primary importance. The relation of these truths to each other he perfectly arranged. And thus we have in his Galilean teaching, which was given to untrammeled and receptive minds, the universal presentation of the Gospel. Then can we know what this Galilean teaching was? Yes. God's providence has preserved it in our gospels. Can we trust these records to give us a true account of his teaching? Yes. The reasons for this trust are given above. We can confidently maintain, on historical grounds, that the gospels report to us with substantial accuracy what Jesus did and said and was. In them we get clear back to Jesus, and learn immediately from and of him. The gospel records have been transmitted to us by the first generation of Christians, and contain the apostolic accounts of Jesus' deeds and words. We see him through their eyes, to a certain degree; but there is every reason to think that in the main they saw him clearly and correctly. While the gospels give only excerpts of what he said and did, those sayings and acts have come down to us which most fully and perfectly show his teaching and his life. We of course recognize that the details of the incidents and the *ipsissima verba* of the sayings have been imperfectly preserved. Jesus spoke in Aramaic, and our records of his utterances are only in Greek, so that in every case allowance must be made for translation. Minor variation is everywhere present in the parallel accounts of originally identical incidents or sayings. But these things are unimportant. What we do need is assurance that the facts of Jesus' life and the ideas of Jesus' teaching are contained in our gospel records. And this assurance we have, not on *a priori*, but on strictly historical grounds.

When we endeavor to ascertain from the gospels what the teaching of Jesus was, we find that he centers it all about what he terms the Kingdom of God. This term he derives from his contemporaries, but the content of it he has to modify greatly. The Jews were right in believing in God's kingdom, but his kingdom was different from that which they had conceived it to be. In both views the Kingdom of God meant the realization of God's will in man individually and collectively. The difference lay in the conception of what God's will for man is. To the Jews it meant visible glorification of Israel, temporal power, material blessings; to Jesus it meant the reign of reverence, truth, righteousness, altruism. He set forth clearly and fully what human duty is toward God and toward man. It is to trust and revere God as a Father who loves and cares for his children, to live in dependence upon and communion with him, to lead righteous lives, to be and do good, to love and serve one's fellow men. That is, each must himself do perfectly God's will, and must as far as possible, secure that it be done by others. The outcome of this individual living according to the highest principles of being will be a transformed humanity, a perfected Kingdom of God. Jesus proclaimed this message to men, and exhorted them to accept it and live it. He asserted this to be the divine truth which God had given him to teach to men, in his office as Messiah. This, he taught, was God's answer to the question: What is life, and how shall I live it? It was a very simple and practical religion as Jesus gave it. He expressed it in language unequaled for clearness, beauty and strength, he embodied it in deeds of kindness and sympathy, he illustrated it in his own matchless character and life. Jesus' teaching is the heart of the Bible, the essence of Christianity, the norm of that which is true and useful in religion.

(5) The Jews' Rejection of Their Messiah. The Jewish people in Jesus' day were under the religious domination of the Pharisees. This politico-religious party had arisen some two hundred years earlier to resist the threatening inroads of Hellenism. The aim of the Pharisees was to defend and perpetuate the intensely religious, peculiar and exclusive character of Judaism. They were the political opponents of the Sadducees, that party which was disposed to co-operate with the Roman officials who were their masters, and to take up with the freer life of the Gentiles who surrounded them. In their zeal to maintain the separateness of the Jews from the Gentiles, the Pharisees placed great emphasis upon the law. They extended their legislation by the addition of innumerable ceremonial distinctions and observances, until a hedge was grown about the Jew to prevent his absorption into the great empire of which they unwillingly formed a political part. They looked upon the Romans with unrelenting hatred, and lived in the hope that their long-anticipated Messiah would come to bring them freedom from the odious Gentile yoke. It followed, therefore, that the Pharisees found nothing to their liking in Jesus, for he in no manner responded to their intense, exclusive national pride and expectation. He showed no disposition to undertake the accomplishment of Jewish political independence; on the contrary, he insisted that the obligations to their Roman masters be fulfilled. All the temporal power, national glory, and material prosperity which characterized their Messianic hope, were ignored by Jesus. Generations of misinterpretation of the Old Testament prophecies, and persistent disregard of the spiritual realities of life, had led them astray, until their hearts were set, not upon things which were above, but upon things which were upon the earth. They seem even to have stumbled at the fact that Jesus came from Galilee, and therefore could not be the Messiah of promise (Matt. ii: 5, 6; John i:45, 46; vii:41, 42, 52).

Another important reason for the Pharisaic opposition to Jesus was his open transgression and criticism of their legal regulations. They had en-grossed the religious life of the Jews with rules, forms and ceremonies. The general prohibitions of the Old Testament law were expanded by specific application to all phases of daily life until the individual was enmeshed with external performances. This mass of casuistical legislation was known as "the traditions of the elders" (Mark vii:1-13), and it took precedence over all else. It robbed life of all its freedom, spontaneity and joy. In Galilee little attention was paid to this type of Judaism. Jesus had not been brought up in bondage to it, and he had no sympathy with it. He publicly disregarded this Pharisaic code, and on many occasions emphatically condemned it. The outstanding conflict between Jesus and the Pharisees in this matter was over the observance of the Sabbath. Jesus refused to keep it or to countenance it in the way they demanded. They were enraged by his independence and opposition, and entered upon a course of violent hostility to him (Matt. xii:1-14; Luke xiii:10-17; xiv:1-6; John v:1-18).

But most of all the Pharisees hated Jesus because he tore off their masks, and exposed their despicable characters to the people. Many of the leading Pharisees were hypocrites. Ostentatiously pious, scrupulously observant of religious ceremonies, loud in their professions of goodness, they were in fact guilty of the worst sins. Jesus did not spare them in his denunciations (Matt. v: 20; xxiii:1-33). And there could result nothing but the bitterest enmity and conflict. The Pharisees only awaited the opportunity to get their hands upon him, and they would avenge themselves by assassination (Matt. xii:14; Mark iii:6; John viii:59; x:31, 39; xi:53, 57).

The attitude of the Jewish common people toward Jesus was of quite another sort. They were faithful to their national religion, but did not live under the bondage of Pharisaism. The influence of the Pharisees was strong in Judea, but reached only weakly into Galilee. It was from this environment that Jesus himself arose. He was one of the Galilean common people. He appreciated them and sympathized with them (Matt. ix:10-13; Luke vii:16-18; John i:9-14). His work was mainly among them, for the Pharisee-ridden Judeans would not hear him. The Galileans regarded him as a great prophet and an authoritative teacher (Matt. vii:28, 29; Mark i:27; Luke vii:16). It was from this class of the Jewish nation that Jesus drew his twelve apostles (Judas perhaps excepted). He was eagerly welcomed by the common people when he began his public ministry. Multitudes came to hear him, and he taught and healed them (Matt. v:1; xiii: 1, 2; Mark iii:7, 8; vi:32-44, 53-56). For a considerable time he worked among them, and gained many adherents. But all the time they were hoping that Jesus would proclaim himself the Messiah of their mistaken expectations. They looked anxiously from day to day for the indications that he was about to set up his temporal, visible kingdom, to the freedom and glory of his people. When they had waited until their patience failed, they undertook to force him into this action. This precipitated a crisis, for Jesus could only refuse them (John vi:14, 15). Overwhelming disappointment fell upon his enthusiastic followers, and most of them withdrew (John vi:66-68).

The doors of public teaching were closed against him. There remained the possibility of a last appeal to the nation. This he determined to make in the most impressive manner available to him. Up to this time he had not claimed to be the Messiah, except to his closest disciples, and then with strict charges of secrecy. The proclamation of it would have put a stop to his work by the excitement of false hopes and futile efforts. But now that he could accomplish no more by his public ministry, it only remained to go to Jerusalem, announce himself as Messiah to the passover multitude, claim the allegiance which they would not give (Matt. xxiii:37), and receive the martyrdom which he clearly saw lay at the end of such a course (Mark x:32-34).

The triumphal entry was arranged. The throngs of Galilean celebrants of the passover feast gathered about him and hailed him as Messiah, for it looked now as though their ardent hopes would at last be realized. Jesus accepted their homage, and entered Jerusalem in their company with the demonstrations of a king returning to his city in peace and victory. The enthusiasm and confidence of the multitude was at the highest pitch. The strength of the popular following was so great that both Pharisees and Sadducees became alarmed (Luke xx:6, 19; John xii:19). The Sadducees had paid little attention to Jesus up to this time, for they took small interest in anything but the politics and amenities of life. But now that Jesus seemed to threaten a popular religious uprising, they were aroused to strenuous opposition. The Sadducees were the Jewish office-holders, responsible to the Romans for civic peace in Judea; and if an anti-Roman insurrection took place, as this threatened to do, the Sadducees were liable to be deposed for negligence or inability to preserve the peace (John xi:47-50). The Sanhedrin was, therefore, united in its purpose to put Jesus to death (Matt. xxvi:3-5; John xi:53).

But in the face of the popular support, how could this be accomplished? Only by treachery. A traitor was not lacking. When once Jesus was in the hands of his enemies the people could be turned against him. In fact, the reaction had set in among his followers. For again Jesus was failing them, their Messianic programme was being forgotten. The old disappointment was settling down upon them with fatal force. It was still only a spiritual kingdom that Jesus meant. The Jewish leaders knew how to turn this disappointment into flaming indignation. And when this was done (Matt. xxvii:20-26), the multitude joined hotly in the cry, "Let him be crucified!" Pharisees, Sadducees, common people, all were lost. The rejection was final, and, with the exception of a few hundred faithful souls, complete.

(6) The Crucified But Living Christ. Fear, hatred and vengeance drove the Jewish leaders to swift action against Jesus. Once in their power, by the betrayal of Judas as they supposed, but in fact by his own voluntary surrender of himself to his enemies, the form of a trial before the Sanhedrin was hastily gone through. Prejudged and precondemned, the sentence of death for blasphemy was soon pronounced. The career of this violator of sacred things, this traitor to Judaism, this pretender to Divine honors, this turbulent revolutionist, would now be closed. But the Sanhedrin could only pass, not execute, the death sentence. Jesus, therefore, was hurried before the Roman procurator, Pilate, who alone had the power of capital punishment. Now the charge against Jesus was changed. What cared Pilate for the wrangling of the Jews over their religious superstitions? But if Jesus were an insurrectionist against the Roman government, Pilate would be concerned. This the Jewish leaders tried, but the procurator was not convinced. Indeed, the man was innocent—Pilate would not order his execution. But the Sanhedrists were insistent. If he refused them, they could secure his recall (as a few years later they did) by reporting his misdeeds to the Emperor. Why should Pilate sacrifice himself for this hunted Jew? Throwing the responsibility of the whole affair upon Jesus' Jewish accusers, he gave permission that their demand be carried out. Crucifixion was the common Roman method of executing rebels, and Jesus was put to death as such. With a cry of deep significance he expired upon the cross. It was, indeed, *finished;* he had been obedient even unto death; he had fulfilled his God-given mission to mankind.

Jesus had seen clearly the necessary outcome of this journey to Jerusalem. Even from the entrance upon his public ministry it must have seemed to him probable that he would ultimately be rejected and put to death (Matt. xxiii:29-37; Luke xiii:31-34). The Pharisees opposed him from the first, but when the Galileans gave up their hope and withdrew from him, Jesus saw his work nearing its end. He set about preparing his disciples for his departure. He determined upon a martyrdom for his cause at Jerusalem. He told them that he was going to be put to death by his enemies (Mark x:32-34; Luke xiii:31-34). Deliberately he planned the Jerusalem visit, and calmly he placed himself into the hands of those who sought his life. His teaching would thus be consummated and glorified. But on the other hand, it was an acknowledgment of defeat with his own nation. It was their final rejection of their Messiah (Matt. xxiii:37, 38). The heritage of the Jews was repudiated by them; it must, therefore, be taken from them and given to others (Matt. xxi:28-31, 33-41; Mark xi:12-14). God's chosen people to bear to the world his true and pure religion thus refused to perform their mission. National pride and self-seeking had unfitted them for a universal brotherhood and self-abnegating service. This was the agony of his self-sacrifice.

And yet Jesus realized that his own death at the hands of the Jews did not mean the destruction of his work nor the failure of his cause. Truth, right and goodness cannot fail because men are recreant to their opportunities and trusts. The Kingdom of God would live and triumph, notwithstanding his death—indeed, in a measure because of his death. Jesus' death became the most effective attestation of the truth of his message, and the cross which symbolized his martyrdom became the emblem of his followers. That which was written later (Tertullian, about A. D. 200) of the Christians who died for their faith was primarily and peculiarly true of Jesus himself, "the blood of the martyrs is the seed of the church."

Nor would he by that experience which men call death lay down the work of his life. He knew that shortly, in God's own good time, he would resume it (Matt. xvi:21, 25; comp. Hos. vi:2). The soul which draws its life from God forever lives. "There is no death: what seems so is transition." The crucifixion was an incident in the life of an immortal being. What we term death is but the point at which the relation of the living soul to the physical body changes from that to which we are accustomed. Jesus lived and Jesus lives. He did not die. Shall we deny immortality to him, when we hold to it for ourselves? The Christian does not die: he rises to a larger, better life. Jesus "brought life and immortality to light." He taught us that there is no death, but only transition to a higher sphere of existence. And so Jesus entered through his crucifixion into the life beyond.

The gospels transmit to us the account of his disciples that for a brief time again after the crucifixion Jesus was seen by them as of old. The empty sepulcher supports their statements, while the many evidences of this miracle of the ages are beyond any reasonable dispute and stand incontrovertible. God in his providence gave them to see in familiar outline the risen Christ. This may have been necessary on account of their imperfect apprehension of spiritual truth. Not yet have *we* reached the stage where we at all fully *realize* that the surest and best realities are the spiritual realities. How much more did the first disciples need an objective vision of their risen Master, to give them confidence and courage to carry on his work. It was a living cause; their leader still led on; they found, when they could see again through tear-dimmed eyes, Jesus' presence and power were still with them. Physical vision of him passed into spiritual vision. Invisibly now, but no less really, they felt him near. And in this assurance his disciples set about the spread and upbuilding of the kingdom which he had established, and of which they were now the visible representatives. And Jesus had given them at his departure a memorial of himself, to comfort them, to strengthen them, and to bind them together in love and service. The simple repast of bread and wine, which he had often and now for the last time shared with his disciples, was to call to their remembrance, as often as they ate it together, his own life and death (so called) that men might have religious truth, and truth expressed not only in words, but also in acts and in character. And so the Christ is ever with us, the inspiration and the guide of all who are continuing his work on earth, who are endeavoring to realize in themselves and in this great world the Kingdom of God which he came to make known and to establish among men, which he proclaimed to men in his utterances, and in his deeds, and in his life and death. One is our teacher, leader and example—the Jesus of history, and the living, exalted Christ of faith.   C. W. V.

(7) Literature. Robinson, *Harmony of the Gospels;* Salmon, *Historical Introduction to the New Testament,* 1891; Harman, *Introduction to the Scriptures;* Westcott, *Introduction to the Study of the Gospels;* Gregory, *Why Four Gospels?* Keim, C. T., *The History of Jesus of Nazara,* 1883; Schürer, E., *The Jewish People in the Time of Jesus Christ,* 1891; Strauss, D. F., *The Life of Jesus,* 1892; Weiss, B., *The Life of Christ,* 1883; Watkins, *Modern Criticism of the Four Gospels,* 1890; Barrows, *The Gospels are True Histories;* Geikie, *Life and Words of Christ,* 1878; Neander, *Life of Christ;* Farrar, *Life of Christ;* Andrew, *Life of Christ;* Pressensé, *Jesus Christ, His Life and Times;* Edersheim, *Prophecy and History of the Messiah,* vol. i, 1885; Edersheim, *Jesus the Messiah,* vol. i., 1884; Edersheim, *Life and Times of Jesus the Messiah,* 2 vols., 1884; Cairn, *Christ the Central Evidence of Christianity;* Bruce, *Training of the Twelve; The Place of Christ in Mod. Theol.* Fairbairn, 1897; *The Christology of Jesus,* Stalker, 1899; Dale, *Living Christ and the Four Gospels,* 1890; Genung, *Fourfold Story;* Thompson, *Four Evangelists.*

JESUS THE CHRIST, TESTIMONY OF SCRIPTURE TO.

(1) Concerning Jesus Christ, we are informed that he is, from eternity, begotten by the Father in a manner no creature is (Ps. ii:7; John i:14; Rom. viii:3, 32); that he is equal to him as a Person (Zech. xiii:7; Phil. ii:6, 7), and one with him in essence (John x:30; 1 John v:7).

(2) We find names and titles proper only to God ascribed to him, as JEHOVAH (Jer. xxiii:6,

and xxxiii:16; Is. xlv:23-25, with Rom. xiv:10-12; Is. xl:3, with Luke i:76; Is. vi:1, 9, 10, with John xii:40, 41); and in hundreds of other places where mention is made of the Lord speaking to prophets or others under the Old Testament.

(3) He is called *God* (Matt. i:23; John i:1, 2, and xx:28; 1 Tim. iii:16; 2 Pet. i:1); the *true God* (1 John v:20, 21); the *great* and *mighty God* (Tit. ii:13; Is. ix:6); the *only wise God* (Jude 24, 25; Rom. xvi:27; 1 Tim. i:16, 17); the *God of glory* (Acts vii:2); the *only God* (Is. xlv:15-23, with Rom. xiv:11); *God blessed forever* (Rom. ix:5); the *God of Abraham, Isaac, and Jacob* (Exod. iii:6, with Acts vii:30-32; Hos. xii:3-5); the *Lord of hosts* (Is. viii:13, 14, with 1 Pet. ii:6-8; Ps. cxviii:22, with Matt. xxi:42, and 2 Sam. vi:2, and Is. liv:5, with 2 Cor. xi:2); *Lord of Lords, and King of Kings* (Rev. xvii:14, and xix:13-16, with 1 Tim. vi:14, 15); the *first and the last* (Rev. i:17, 18, and ii:8, with Is. xli:4, and xliv:6).

(4) Divine attributes are ascribed to him; as *omniscience* (Col. ii:3; Rev. ii:23; John xxi:17, and ii:24, 25; John xvi:30); *omnipresence* (Matt. xviii:20, and xxviii:20; Col. i:17; Heb. i:3; John i:18, and iii:13); *almighty power* (Phil. iii:21; Rev. i:8, with chap. i:11, 17, 18; and xxii:12, 13, 20); *eternity* (Rev. i:11, 17, 18; Isa. xli:4; Prov. viii:23; Mic. v:2; John i:1, and viii:56); *unchangeableness* (Heb. i:12, and xiii:8).

(5) Divine works of creation, providence, and redemption are ascribed unto him (John i:1, 2; Col. i:16, 17; 1 Cor. viii:6; Eph. iii:9; Heb. i:3; Acts xx:28).

(6) He is represented as the object of religious worship, without any limitation; as in baptism, by faith, prayer, praise, vows (Matt. xxviii:19; John v:23; xiv:1, and xx:28; Acts vii:5, 9; Heb. i:6; Phil. ii:9-11).

JETHER (jē'ther), (Heb. יֶתֶר, *yeh'ther,* surplus).

1. The father-in-law of Moses. In Exod. iv:18 called JETHRO; margin JETHER.

2. The oldest of the sons of Gideon (Judg. viii:20), who made his age an excuse when his father asked him to kill the Midianite kings, Zebah and Zalmunna (B. C. 1326). He was slain by Abimelech (Judg. ix:24).

3. Father of Amasâ, David's captain (1 Kings ii:5, 32; 1 Chron. ii:17); elsewhere the name is ITHRA.

4. Son of Jada, of the tribe of Judah (1 Chron. ii:32), B. C. after 1856.

5. A son of Ezra, of Judah (1 Chron. iv:17), B. C. about 1618.

6. A chief warrior of the tribe of Asher, and father of Jephunneh (1 Chron. vii:38). Possibly the same as ITHRAN.

JETHETH (jē'theth), (Heb. יְתֵת, *yeh-thayth',* derivation uncertain).

An Edomitish "duke" in Mount Seir who came to Esau (Gen. xxxvi:40; 1 Chron. i:51).

JETHLAH (jĕth'lah), (Heb. יִתְלָה, *yith-law',* suspended, i. e., lofty).

A city of the tribe of Dan given between Ajalon and Elon (Josh. xix:42), therefore probably in the eastern part of the tribe; not identified.

JETHRO (jĕ'thro), (Heb. יִתְרוֹ, *yith-ro',* excellence; superiority), a priest or prince of Midian, both offices probably being combined in one person.

Moses spent the forty years of his exile from Egypt with him, and married his daughter Zipporah (Exod. iii:1; iv:18), B. C. 1250.

It is said in Exod. ii :18, that the priest of Midian, whose daughter Moses married, was Reuel; afterward, in chapter iii :1, he is called Jethro, as also in chapter xviii; but in Num. x :29, "Hobab, the son of Raguel the Midianite," seems to be called Moses' father-in-law (comp. Judg. iv :11). The probability is that Jethro and Reuel or Raguel were but different names of Moses' father-in-law (the former being either a title or a surname showing the rank of Raguel in his tribe), and that the son, Hobab, was his brother-in-law, who may have borne one of the father's names. (See HO-BAB.)

JETUR (jē'tur), (Heb. יְטוּר, *yet-oor'*, encircled), one of the twelve sons of Ishmael (Gen. xxv :15; I Chron. i :31),

His name stands also for his descendants, the Ituræns (1 Chron. v :19), living east of the northern Jordan (Luke iii :1).

JEUEL (jē'u-ĕl), (Heb. יְעוּאֵל, *yeh-oo-ale'*, protected by God), a descendant of Zerath, who, with six hundred and ninety of his kindred, dwelt in Jerusalem after the captivity (1 Chron. ix :6), (B. C. 536).

JEUSH (jē'ush), (Heb. יְעוּשׁ, *yeh-oosh'*, collecting; strong; hasty).

1. Oldest son of Esau, by Aholibamah (Gen. xxxvi :5, 14, 18; I Chron. i :35), born in Canaan, but later he became a "duke" of the Edomites B. C. after 1964).

2. The first mentioned of the sons of Bilhan; he was head of a Benjamite house during David's reign (1 Chron. vii :10, 11), B. C. before 1000.

3. A Levite, one of the four sons of Shimei, of the Gershonites. He, with his brother Beriah, not having many sons, were counted as the third branch of the family (1 Chron. xxiii :10, 11), B. C. about 1014.

4. The first named of the three sons of Rehoboam, apparently by Abihail, his second wife (2 Chron. xi :19), B. C. after 973.

JEUZ (jē'uz), (Heb. יְעוּץ, *yeh-oots'*, counselor), head of a Benjamite house, apparently the son of Shaharaim and Hodesh or Baara (1 Chron. viii :10). B. C. about 1618.

JEW (jū, or jṳ), (Heb. יְהוּדִי, *yeh-oo-dee'*, a Jehudite, i. e., descendant of Judah; Gr. 'Ιουδαῖος, *ee-oo-dah'yos*).

A name formed from that of the patriarch Judah, and applied in its first use to one belonging to the tribe or country of Judah, or rather perhaps to a subject of the separate kingdom of Judah (2 Kings xvi :6; xxv :25; Jer. xxxii :12; xxxviii :19; xl :11; xli :3; lii :28). During the Captivity the term seems to have been extended to all the people of the Hebrew language and country, without distinction (Esth. iii :6, 9; Dan. iii :8, 12); and this loose application of the name was preserved after the restoration to Palestine, when it came to denote not only every descendant of Abraham in the largest possible sense, but even proselytes who had no blood relation to the Hebrews (Acts ii :5; comp. verse 10).

Rabbi D. Philipson explains the meaning of the three names applied to the Jews, as follows:

Broadly speaking, I define the three terms thus: "Hebrew" is the linguistic, "Israelite" the national, "Jew" the religious designation. If we still used the Hebrew as our language in daily life, it would be correct to call us Hebrews; if we were still a nation, the proper appellation would be Israelites, which was the distinguishing term applied to the people when they inhabited

Palestine as a nation, in contrast with the surrounding peoples, Philistines, Moabites, Syrians, Edomites and the like. Since Hebrew is no longer our spoken language, since further we are not a nation, our national existence having ceased with the destruction of Jerusalem by the Romans, it is technically incorrect to apply either of these names to present day Jews. There remains, then, the third, "Jew"; this is primarily the religious term, the name of the professor of Judaism. The distinguishing mark of the Jewish people is their religion; they are a religious community, hence the proper name is "Jew." Our faith is called not Hebraism, nor yet Israelitism, but Judaism, and the corresponding term to Judaism is Jew. (See HEBREW LANGUAGE; ISRAEL; JUDAH.)

JEWEL (jṳ'ĕl), (Heb. חֶלְיָה, *khel-yaw'*, an ornament or trinket, Hos. ii :13), very general in character. (See AMETHYST; RUBY; SAPPHIRE, ETC.)

JEWESS (jū'ess), (Gr. 'Ιουδαία, *ee-oo-dah'yah*,), a woman of Hebrew birth (Acts xvi :1; xxiv :24). In the first passage it refers to Eunice, Timothy's mother; in the second to Drusilla, daughter of Herod and wife of Felix.

JEWISH (jṳ'ĭsh), (Gr. 'Ιουδαϊκός, *ee-oo-dah-ee-kos'*, belonging to the Jews). Paul warns his younger brother against the Rabbinical legends that are designated by this epithet (Tit. i :14).

JEWISH SYNAGOGUE, THE MODERN.

The history of Judaism in America is a record of growth and development, of successive changes in custom and ritual, of large advance in educational and benevolent activity, as the Jewish settlers, chiefly of Spanish origin, coming in scattered numbers previous to the War of Independence, were strengthened by immigration from Germany, Poland, Roumania, and Russia, until at the end of 1896 the Jewish population of the United States reached fully a million.

(1) Doctrine. The customs and doctrines of Judaism which have never been reduced to iron-clad dogmas for all Israel, despite occasional codification, have always admitted of greater or less variation in different lands, according to clime and circumstance. The same conditions were to be experienced in America with similar results. The earlier immigrants of Sephardic stock who settled in the North American colonies, after harsh treatment in South America and varying fortunes in the West Indies, were conservative after the fashion of their fathers, all the memory of martyrdom giving halo and beauty to olden traditions. Many of their descendants two centuries later are no less strict observants of the Spanish and Portuguese ritual and practice. The English and earlier Polish settlers of a subsequent generation have hardly as yet lost their British and Polish conservative associations. The German immigrants of the decade of 1848 who were reared in the school of German liberation were inclined to be less scrupulous of old fashions, and adapted forms and customs to the newer-day environment. Their children have naturally developed along the same progressive lines. The still more recent Jewish landslide from Europe is Russian and Galician in its conception of Jewish doctrine and rite, including a contingent of pronounced radical views.

While, therefore, American Judaism suffers from this stratification, due to successive immigrations of different nationalities, it has never had its authoritative council or synod to promulgate opinion, to ratify or to abolish. There have been associations among rabbis and laymen, but these have not been ecclesiastical in character.

Their views have been simply individual, of interest, of course, as evidencing the trend of thought, but of no binding force. While Jewish congregations may unite and coöperate for education and charity, the autonomy of each is strictly maintained, and every pulpit is purely its own spokesman. Hence there are all shades of sentiment in American Israel, all varieties of interpretations, the two forces of stability and movement being steadily at work and developing phases of conservatism and progress. Considering, however, the essential principles of representative Jewish leaders in pulpit and press, which are practically the same, even if they differ as to observances and the authority of the rabbinical ceremonial code, these may broadly be stated as embracing the unity of God and the unity of mankind. The religious ceremonials in home and synagogue, held more or less strictly, the righteous life impelling to breadth of view, brotherly love to all, and the realization of the highest ideals of American citizenship—such are the corollaries of American Jewish principles.

(2) The Future. The heterogeneous nature of the American Jew and the lack as yet of a distinctly homogeneous class, due to his composite character, in which trait he resembles the American in general, makes it difficult to realize Jewish ideals. The great mass are still foreign, with the atmosphere of Europe and Ghetto conditions; and their Americanization is a slow process, for the parents perhaps impossible. On the other hand, there is a large body of American-born Israelites, apathetic and without sympathy for the synagogue. Yet there are hopeful signs, particularly in educational movements, a more conservative tendency among our representative men, and the awakening of the American Jewess to her duty and opportunity. With co-operation, unselfish effort, and intelligent direction, American Judaism can expect to attain a high degree of usefulness and to realize under providence some of its ideals that will bless and elevate humanity.

(3) Relation to Christianity. As to the question of federal union with other churches, that is impossible so long as church remains church and synagogue, synagogue. The Jew is no propagandist and has no desire to Judaize. He rejoices that the best elements in the church aim to translate into life the ideals of the Jewish prophet. While religious federation is wholly impracticable, church and synagogue do unite for civic purposes, for general educational and charitable progress. In many cities Jew and non-Jew unite on Thanksgiving Day. The Jewish pulpit is freely open to the non-Jewish preacher. Young Men's Hebrew Associations have often called Christian clergymen to their platform. Synagogues have been freely placed at the disposal of Christian congregations whose churches were destroyed by fire, and the courtesy has been reciprocated. These indications of mutual esteem and good will cannot but spread more and more, particularly as national movements for education, charity, civic reform, and congresses of religion increase and rally the broad and thoughtful of all creeds on the same platform. But the most advanced and liberal Jew will not consent to federation, if it means extinction and absorption, and surely the more conservative will be least inclined for such a step. The mission and message of Judaism are not superfluous even in our era. So long as swords are not turned to ploughshares, and idolatries are still practiced, while the nations and creeds are competitors, not partners, the Jew must still be sentinel on the watchtower, however lonely the post, and wait for the dawn. He has survived two thousand years of crucifixion. The Arch of Titus preserves the story of what is termed his nation's fall. But Judaism awoke when the temple vanished; and the Jew, in losing Palestine, has secured the world for the law and the prophet.   A. S. I.

JEWRY (ju̇'rȳ), (Heb. יְהוּד, yeh-hood; Gr. Ἰουδαία, Luke xxiii:5; John vii:1), the Jewish nation, i. e., the kingdom of Judah, later Judea, rendered elsewhere as Judah and Judæa (Dan. v:13).

JEWS, HISTORY OF THE, AND THEIR RELIGION.

(1) From the Fall of Jerusalem to the Middle Ages. The destruction of the temple at Jerusalem meant a crisis for Judaism of even deeper significance than the failure of the Reichstag of Worms to silence the Protestant movement. The belief in the prophecies which had predicted everlasting glory for Jerusalem was shaken; but, as is the case with Adventists, when a prophecy fails to be fulfilled, practical necessity found a way out of the theoretical difficulty. The national calamity began to be considered a transitory condition, after which God's grace would restore the lost glory.

This view was taught by the Pharisaic school. The Pharisees of the first century, A. D., theoretically held the doctrine that the law would be abrogated in the Messianic era; but until then they were just as unwilling to carry this view into practice as the average Christian would be to discard the apostolic creed on the strength of the parable of the Good Samaritan.

The leader of this party was Johanan bon Zakaj. His biography is overgrown with legends. Still so much seems certain that he was a great teacher and a member of the Sanhedrin; that he left Jerusalem before the destruction and established a school in Jabneh, which came to be considered as a substitute for the Sanhedrin. He taught salvation for righteous Gentiles and advocated submission to Rome's political authority. His liturgical institutions meant to preserve as much as possible of the temple worship.

Under the Roman empire the political condition of the Jews was peculiarly sad. The tribute of the half-shekel, the annual sacred gift to the temple, had been confiscated under the name of Fiscus Judaicus—afterwards, however, remitted by Nerva (96-98). During the war of the desolation of Palestine many had been killed, many sold as slaves; great numbers of the survivors were fugitives in the remotest parts of the empire and in Babylonia, then subject to the Parthians; while under Domitian the persecution, especially of proselytes, was most severe; a relative even of the emperor, Flavius Clemens, having been put to death and his wife exiled for this cause. Hadrian (117-138) put an end to the revolution by conciliatory measures, but his despotic syncretism was the cause of another futile rebellion; that of Bar Kokba (132-135), which was the last attempt of the Jews to regain political independence by force of arms.

Their religious life during this period was a consolidation on the basis of changed conditions. Rabban Gamaliel, the Hillelite, under the title of Nassi, or Patriarch, was the recognized successor of the President of the Sanhedrin. His only tangible prerogative was the calendation. He attempted to compile a fixed ritual, but was opposed in his hierarchical tendencies by Eliezer ben Hyrkanos, who had leanings towards Christianity, and by Joshuah ben Hananiah, a strict Congregationalist. Gamaliel and Joshua were united in their opposition to political aspirations, while Rabbi Akiba preached political resurrection and proclaimed Bar Kokba as the Messiah. He supervised the Greek version of the Pentateuch written by the proselyte Akylas.

The defeat of Bar Kokba's uprising was followed by severe measures against the rebels. The name of Jerusalem was changed to Aelia Capitolina, and no Jew was allowed to enter the city. On the site of Jahve's sanctuary a temple of Jupiter Capitolinus was to be erected; over the gate of the city the image of a swine was placed. Circumcision, the observance of the Sabbath, and the study of the law were prohibited.

Under Antoninus (138-161) a complete change took place, and Hadrian's restrictive laws were abolished. From now on until the reign of Constantine we hear nothing of religious persecution. Still, the growing power of Christianity and the devastation of Palestine caused the Jews to emigrate in large numbers to southern Mesopotamia and to western Europe.

The religious development during the period from the Bar-Kokba Revolution up to the Christianization of the Roman empire shows a growing tendency towards legalism. Jehuda Hanassi (i. e., prince, patriarch) (135-216) won an important place in Jewish history by the compilation of the rabbinical law, called Mishna, which, originally intended as a compendium of the rabbinical interpretation of the biblical law, and of other traditional customs, by and by began to be considered part of the Sinaitic revelation.

R. Jehuda met with no serious opposition in his attempt to establish a religious authority, but soon after his death conditions changed. His son, Gamaliel III (A. C. 216-230), was a mere figurehead; and so the position of the patriarch which the son inherited from the father became a shadow, until Theodosius II (A. C. 425) abolished it altogether.

Economic and political adversities drove a great number of Jews to Babylonia, where already during the third century the schools of Sura and Pumbeditha became strong rivals of their sister institutions in Tiberias and Sepphoris. About the middle of the fourth century the last Palestinian authorities died out. Their successors gave all their attention to the edifying explanation of Scripture, called Aggada. At the same time the talmudical law was further developed in Babylonia, where the Rabbis Ashe (died 427) and Abina (died 499) compiled the Talmud of Babylonia. The Talmud consisted of two parts, the Mishna and the Gemara; the former being the law and the latter a discursive commentary on it. Both together form the Talmud. The lectures on the Mishna, compiled in the Palestinian school, formed the Talmud of Jerusalem; those compiled by R. Ashe and R. Abina, form the Babylonian Talmud. The latter always has been the more popular book and was considered a higher authority.

In the Roman empire the Jews from the time of Constantine (312) were subjected to legal discriminations. A very short interval was the reign of Julian (361-363), who, according to ecclesiastical writers, intended to rebuild the temple at Jerusalem. The edict of Ravenna (Feb. 28, 380), promulgated by Theodosius I, which made Rome a Christian empire, affected the condition of the Jews very unfavorably, although the emperor protected them against occasional outbreaks of mobs, stimulated by fanatical ecclesiastics. Because of the dispersion of the Jews the last prerogative of the patriarch, the announcement of the festivals,

was surrendered; Hillel II (A. C. 325) being the last to use it.

In Babylonia the Jews were politically organized under an exilarch, Resh Galutha, who was their representative at the court of the Persian king, and, later on, of the Calif. Their spiritual head was the president of one of the great schools. The religious and national revival following upon the return to power of the Parsees (226) brought great suffering upon the Jews, but their situation was more favorable than that of their brethren under the Christian rule of Rome.

The situation in the Byzantine empire was nowise better than in the western part of the old Roman empire and in the various Germanic states which had formed on its ruins. The greatest sufferings were experienced under the Visigoths in Spain, where church councils decreed the laws which became typical for medieval legislation on the Jews, and it was only the invasion of the Arabs which changed their condition for the better.

The literary activity had from the beginning of the eighth century its seat in the schools of Sura and Pumbeditha. Our rabbinical works, especially the homiletical literature, called the Midrash, date in their present shape from this period, which extends from 750 to 1040, and is called the period of the Geonim, from Gaon, excellency, which was the title of the college-president. At the same time a number of practical guide-books, for civil, liturgical, and dietary laws were written, and the first manual for public worship was compiled by the Gaon Amram (A. C. 850). We also meet at that time the first traces of a theosophical literature (Kabala), of which probably the oldest specimen is a book of creation (Sephar Jezirah.)

The strict adherence to traditional authority which is characteristic of the Babylonian schools of this period aroused a fierce opposition, led by Anan (A. C. 760), who found a great following. The sect, originated by him, called itself Sons of the Bible, Karaites. They rejected all authority outside of the Bible. They still exist in very small numbers, chiefly in southern Russia. Their last literary authority was Abraham Firkowitsch (1786-1874), who has made for himself an unenviable reputation by extensive forgeries of tombstones and manuscripts in the interest of Karaitic glory. At the same time when this schism occurred Judaism made an important conquest by the conversion of the Chazars, a Tartaric nation whose Khan Bulan, with his court and a great majority of his people, embraced the Jewish religion.

The controversy with the Karaites stimulated the neglected study of the Bible amongst the rabbinitic Jews. The ablest apologete of their views was the Gaon Saadjah (892-942), who wrote the first systematic work on philosophy of religion, called "Science and Religion." From that time on the Babylonian schools declined. In 1040 the last Gaon was put to death and no successor appointed.

Babylonian Jews settled in great numbers in northern Africa. Isaac Alfasi, of Fez (1013-1103), emigrated to Spain and founded a school in Lucena. However, previous to his time there was in Cordova a famous seat of learning. Hasdai ibn Shaprut, who occupied a high position at the court of Abderrahman III (912-961), was a patron of Jewish literature. Amongst those whom he supported are the first Jewish grammarians, Dunash ben Labrat and Menahem ben Saruk. A position similar to that of Hasdai was occupied by Samuel ibn Nagrela at the court of the Moorish Calif Habus in Granada. Samuel was not only a patron of Jewish literature, but also a scholar of considerable attainments. He supported one of the best of all New-Hebrew poets, Salomo ibn Gebirol, who also is the author of the philosophical work, "Fountain of Life," which exercised a great influence on the philosophy of Thomas Aquinas. As author of a popular work on religious ethics, "The Duties of the Heart," we have to mention Bahja ibn Pakuda.

In France and Germany the Jewish population increased under Charlemagne (768-814) and his successors. The embassy which Charlemagne sent to Harun Al-Rashid numbered a Jew among its members. With the progress of the German arms the Jews moved eastward to Austria, Bohemia, and Poland.

The literary activity of the Jews in Germany and France is limited to liturgical poetry and to talmudical codes and commentaries. In regard to the latter we mention R. Gershom, called "The Light of the Diaspora," who lived in Mayence (A. C. 960-1020) and who is famous for making monogamy, which up to his time was only a practice, a binding law.

The twelfth century shows the highest development of spiritual life in Judaism. In Spain we have the greatest of all medieval Jewish poets, Jehuda Halevi (1080-1141), who is also famous for his Kusari, an apology for Judaism in the form of a dialogue between the Khan of the Chazars and the rabbi who had converted him. Abraham ibn Esra, also a native of Spain (1092-1167), had in the school of the Karaites, acquired a critical spirit, which he used not only in dissecting and very frequently ridiculing rabbinical interpretations of the Bible, but in criticising the Bible itself. The brightest star in the Jewish literature of the age is Moses Maimonides (1135-1204). Of his numerous works we shall quote only two: Mishneh Thorah, a code of the Jewish law, comprising dogma, ritual, civil, criminal and political law, and Morch Nebuchim, The Guide of the Perplexed, a philosophical apology for Judaism based on Aristotle. His arguments were partly made use of by Thomas of Aquino and Albertus Magnus.

From the thirteenth century on we notice a decline in the intellectual life of Judaism. This decline is typified by a fierce opposition to Maimonides' philosophy. The liberals were represented by David Kimchi (1170-1235), the best known exegete and grammarian of the Middle Ages, while the orthodox party was represented by Solomon ibn Adret (1230-1310), rabbi of Barcelona. He, like the German rabbis, stood for the infallibility of the Talmud. Amongst the German rabbis the highest authority was Meir of Rothenburg (1220-1293), who died in prison because on his advice the Germans refused to pay the high ransom for the extortion of which King Rudolph had imprisoned him.

More spiritual freedom existed in Italy, where we find the poet Immanuel of Rome (1270-1340), who wrote a Hebrew sequel to Dante's Divine Commedia. A very great influence was exercised by the Jews as translators from Arabic into Latin. Persecutions on religious grounds, stimulated by Jewish converts to Christianity such as Nicholas Donin (A. C. 1240), Pablo Christiani (1260), Alfonso of Valladolid (1300), Geronimo da Santa Fe, and Paulus of Burgos (1390-1440), aroused Messianic hopes, based on Kabalistic prophecies. Abraham Abulafia (1280) played the rôle of a Messiah in Sicily and Moses ben Nahman (1200-1270) gave a considerable space to Kabala in his commentary on the Pentateuch.

Like all theosophists, Kabalists claimed to have a very ancient literature. Their fundamental work was the Zohar, Kabalistic homilies on the Pentateuch, written by Moses of Leon (1290), and ascribed to Simeon ben Johaj (2d cent.)

(2) From the Middle Ages to the Present Time. The political condition of the Jews during the latter part of the Middle Ages was very sad, although occasionally some individuals rose to a higher rank as tax-farmers, financiers, physicians, astronomers, astrologists, and authors. The masses were frequently mobbed, not rarely expelled and always outrageously taxed. The German Jews suffered terribly from the crusaders in 1096 and 1147. Many were thrown into burning houses, or hacked to pieces, and thousands were killed under the most cruel tortures. A great number were dragged to churches and baptized, but returned to Judaism in spite of the protest of ecclesiastic dignitaries. Most of the latter, especially St. Bernard, although not favorable to the Jews, condemned these persecutions, but their voices did not prevail with the mob. Similar persecutions of a local character we find all through the Middle Ages, but it would be impossible to enumerate them. Sometimes it is the accusation that they murdered a child to use his blood for their Passover cakes; another time that they perforated a consecrated host which subsequently performed some miracles that lent a semblance of justice to these acts of mob violence. Legislation sanctioned these outbreaks by establishing such discriminations against the Jews as incited passion against them. The council of the Lateran (1215), which represents the highwater mark of papal power under Innocent III, decreed the Jew badge and confirmed all laws tending to degrade the Jews. Under such conditions which, as the pope declared, were part of the divine economy to show by the humiliation of the Jews the glory of Christ, it was of no avail, when Innocent IV (1247) in a bull admonished the rulers to protect the life and property of the Jews, and even protested against the accusation that the Jews committed murder for the sake of their religion. It was also of little avail, when some princes, like Frederick II of Austria (1244), promulgated statutes by which the rights of the Jews, who through the exorbitant taxes imposed upon them were a considerable support of the treasury, were established. Other rulers wantonly disregarded these dearly bought privileges, and the mobs excited by a Good-Friday sermon on Jesus' sufferings, never respected them. Of the innumerable persecutions during the twelfth century, I shall only mention the riots at the time of the coronation of King Richard Cœur de Lion (1190) and the martyrdom of the Jews of Blois (1171) and of Bray (1191). Hundreds died at the stake, singing hymns; hundreds killed themselves with their children to escape the tortures of infuriated mobs. The great plague (1348-1350) added a new pretext for the slaughter of helpless people, who were accused of poisoning the wells. All over western Europe they were persecuted. In Strasburg alone 1,800 Jews were burned on one pyre.

In the fifteenth century the growth of the municipalities had the effect that the Jews, formerly a welcome object for taxation, began to be considered as inconvenient competitors. At the same time the economic crisis, produced by the sudden change of economic conditions due to so many discoveries and inventions, produced the spirit of discontent and restlessness in the masses which always is the prime cause of revolutions and naturally makes the weak suffer first. Legislation and historical conditions having reduced the Jews to the business of money lending, it was only too natural that popular hatred, fomented by religious motives, saw in the Jew the usurer only, and in the usurer the sole cause of the serious economic crisis. They were expelled from almost all the larger cities in Germany, while France, where they had been expelled and called back numerous times before, expelled them peremptorily in 1394, England having done so in 1290. At the same time the increasing perturbation within the church aroused occasional outbreaks against the Jews. In Spain Ferdinand Martinez (1391) had caused a great uprising against the Jews, and a great number, in order to save their lives, professed conversion to Christianity, but secretly practiced Judaism. They formed the large class of the Marannos, whom the church considered as apostates and against whom the inquisition was created which, powerless in its attempt to make the Marannos real Christians, brought about the expulsion of the Jews from Spain (1492) and from Portugal (1495). The council of Basle (1431-43) renewed all the ecclesiastic laws against the Jews. John Capistrano, who failed in his mission to bring the Hussites back into the fold of the Catholic church, triumphed over the Jews. In Breslau he consigned over forty to the stake under the usual allegation of piercing a consecrated host (1454), and from a number of cities they were expelled through his influence. Bernhardin of Feltre, a man of the type which we would call Christian socialists in our days, proved by torture and manipulated testimony that a little boy who was drowned in the Adige had been murdered by the Jews of Trent (1475). A great number were put to death and the rest expelled. As late as 1510 the profaned host caused the death of twenty-nine Jews in Berlin.

The most important event of this epoch was the expulsion of the Jews, about 300,000 in number, from Spain (1492) and Portugal (1496). The refugees settled mostly in Turkey, in northern Africa, in Egypt and in Palestine. The many refugees from Germany turned towards Poland, so that from about 1500 the majority of the Jews lived in eastern countries, debarred from the centers of civilization. The Reformation had only a slight influence on the Jews. Their general condition was not changed. Luther, who, in the beginning of his career, had been favorably inclined to them, spoke in his later days very severely against them, recommending the confiscation of their property and their expulsion. The Renaissance, however, had its influence on the Jews, as it derived some of its impulses from their literature. Johannes Reuchlin (1455-1522), one of the foremost representatives of the Renaissance movement (1510), defended the rabbinical literature against the accusations of John Pfefferkorn, a converted Jew, and his allies, the Dominicans of Cologne, who, by the confiscation of the Talmud, expected to obtain the same power as inquisitors in Germany which their order possessed in Spain. Like many other scholars of that age, Reuchlin had studied Hebrew from Jews. Elijah Levita (1472-1549), a Hebrew teacher of Christians in Italy, came out with the important discovery that the vowel points were a later invention, and that consequently the text of the Hebrew Bible, as we possess it, is of a comparatively late origin. Azariah dei Rossi of Mantua (1511-1578) followed with a series of learned essays in which he proved that the rabbinical writings possessed no authority in scientific matters, a statement which was quite bold in

those days and elicited no small amount of opposition. Meantime in Poland and in the Orient, which had become the seats of rabbinical learning, traditionalism became stronger and stronger. Joseph Karo (1488-1577) *ibn.* Saffed wrote a compendium of Jewish law, *Shulhan Arukh,* which with the annotations of Moses Isserls in Cracow (1520-1573), was considered an authoritative guide-book, and thus became instrumental in perpetuating scholasticism and traditionalism. A rather Utopian scheme of the Maranno Salomo Molcho and his friend, David Reubeni, who posed as a prince of the lost tribes, to establish the Messianic kingdom failed ignominiously. Molcho was burned at the stake (1533), and Reubeni died in prison. A more practical scheme of Don Joseph of Naxos, a Maranno, who had obtained a high position at the court of Constantinople, to establish a Jewish state in the island of Cyprus also failed (1571). The first place where Jews enjoyed full religious freedom was Holland, where after the Netherlands had gained their freedom, Spanish Jews began to settle in considerable numbers. Amsterdam became a mother city for other colonies, which in the course of the seventeenth century settled in England, Sweden, Denmark and America, and were swelled by fugitive Marannos who were fortunate enough to escape from the dungeons of the Inquisition and also by German Jews. At the same time the Jews of Poland were terrible sufferers from the revolution of the Cossacks against their Polish masters (1648). Under their captain Chmelnicki the Cossacks attacked the Jewish settlements, because the Jews as tax-farmers had been instrumental in driving the Cossacks to desperation. Hundreds of thousands were killed, and fugitives flocked into all parts of Europe where they could find co-religionists.

The misery which Jews still endured, even in places where their lives and property were not in constant danger, fomented the Messianic hope, and in 1666 Sabbathai Zebi, a native of Smyrna, announced himself as the Messiah, and succeeded in securing followers all over Europe until, when the Sultan interfered and asked him to prove his Messianic mission by a miracle, he was converted to Islam. This ridiculous result of the Messianic movement showed its effect in a growing aversion to Kabala. At the same time we see some descendants of those who suffered the most cruel martyrdom for their faith break away from Judaism and all positive religions. Both Baruch Spinozas (1632-1677) and Uriel Acosta (1594-1640) were members of the Portuguese Congregation of Amsterdam.

The persecutions, although not as fierce as those of the fifteenth century, continued. In 1670 the Emperor, Leopold I, expelled the Jews from Vienna for no other reason than because his wife, a Spanish princess, desired it for the glory of God. The Marannos in Spain and Portugal were still the victims of the Inquisition. In 1680 Charles II, in order to duly celebrate his nuptials with a French princess, ordered a great *auto da fé* to be held, at which eighteen Jews were burned to death, while a great many others were sentenced to imprisonment and to disgracing acts of penitence.

In consequence of the Messianic movement under Sabbathai Zebi a mystic sect arose which had its followers in the East, who called themselves Hassidim. The Maranno Michael Cardoso (1622-1706); the Italian Mose Hajim Luzzatto (1707-1747), one of the best poets of the New-Hebrew literature, and finally Israel Besht (1696-1760), an ignorant Polish coachman, developed this doctrine. While they never severed their connection with the whole body of Judaism, their doctrinal recognition of theosophy and their belief in miracle workers formed a decided difference between them and the orthodox followers of rabbinical Judaism. The crisis was reached when, in a bitter and protracted controversy between the Rabbi of Altona, Jonathan Eibeschitz (1690-1764) and the celebrated author, Jacob Emden (1696-1776), all belief in Kabala was branded as crypto-Sabbathaism. During this controversy Emden had the boldness to declare the Zohar, the canonical book of the Kabalists, a partial forgery.

This critical view had further consequences. It produced a spiritual independence, which found its most successful exponent in Moses Mendelssohn (1729-1786), who, a consistent deist himself, advocated an amalgamation of the Jews with their surroundings by a general education, but he carefully refrained from advocating any innovations in the religious life. He translated parts of the Bible into pure German (1783), edited the first Hebrew magazine (1784) and was instrumental in the foundation of a Jewish free school. He also advocated the full right of citizenship for the Jews. This became an accomplished fact during the French revolution (1791), and was imitated by other states which, during the revolutionary period, were under French influence, but after the Vienna Congress (1815) a general reaction set in.

Meantime the Jews began to consider the necessity for changing their ritual and revising their dogma. In regard to the latter, the most important move was the declaration against the belief in a personal Messiah. In their ritual the substitution of the vernacular for the Hebrew in some parts of their Prayer Book was the decisive step taken. These reforms were first introduced in the "Tempel" of Hamburg (1817). At the same time rabbinical literature became the object of scientific treatment, and the exclusive dominion of scholasticism was broken. In this respect the merit of the initiation belongs to Leopold Zunz (1794-1886). With him we shall mention: S. L. Rappoport (1791-1867), S. D. Luzzatto (1800-1865), Zacharias Frankel (1801-1875), the representatives of modern conservatism, while Abraham Geiger (1810-1874) represents the liberal theology, within which Samuel Holdheim (1806-1860) and David Einhorn (1809-1879) represent the radical wing. The strictest orthodoxy is represented by Samson R. Hirsch (1808-1888). Of other leading scholars we mention Hirsch Graetz (1817-1891), Leopold Loew (1811-1875) and M. Steinschneider (born 1816).

The present religious condition of the Jews may be described thus: In Asia, northern Africa and Turkey we find strict medievalism, servile practice of ritual laws, superstitious fears of the rabbis, and uncritical acceptance of everything ever taught by anybody in the name of the Jewish religion. In Russia, Roumania and Galicia, strict talmudical orthodoxy is steadily losing ground, to make room for those religious views which are the rule amongst the Jews of western Europe, viz., a liberal attitude to the teachings and the practice of religion very much like that prevailing among the body of German Protestants of the type represented by Harnack and other leading theologians. Their allegiance to Judaism, however, is strengthened by consciousness of the fact that they will remain Jews no matter what their religious position and practice may become.

The revolution of 1848 brought political equality to the Jews all over western Europe, although it was not until 1858 that the first Jew, Lionel de Rothschild, was allowed to take his seat in the English Parliament. The medieval system, which leaves the Jew to the mercy of the mob in occasional outbreaks of violence, reigns still in Morocco and Persia. In Russia and Roumania the Jews are subjected to oppressive laws, such as existed in western Europe up to the eighteenth century. A similar state of affairs exists in Portugal, while in Spain the law granting them liberty of worship has never been carried into effect. In Germany, Austria, and France the anti-Semitic movement for the last twenty years is trying to obtain a repeal of the laws granting the Jews political equality. This renewed hostility, together with the unbearable conditions of Russia, has of late produced the Zionistic movement, which aims to establish a Jewish state in Palestine as an asylum for the persecuted Jews all over the world.

Another notable feature of Jewish history in the nineteenth century is the participation of the Jews in all branches of art, science, literature and public life. France and Italy have had Jewish ministers, Cremieux, Fould, Raynal and Luzatti. All other civilized countries have had influential Jewish politicians. In music we may mention Meyerbeer, Halevy and Goldmark; in literature, Heine, Boerne, Auerbach, Grace Aguilar, Goldsmid (Denmark), Millaud (France), etc. Of great scientists the number is too great for this article to do justice to them.

These facts certainly prove that the admission of the Jews to participation in public life has proven a benefit not only to them, but in no small degree a benefit to the highest interests of humanity.   G. D.

JEWS' LANGUAGE. This phrase is literally "Jewishly," for the Hebrew must be read as an adverb (2 Kings xviii:28; 2 Chron. xxxii:18; Is. xxxvi:11, 13; Neh. xiii:24).

JEZANIAH (jĕz'a-nī'ah), (Heb. יְזַנְיָ֫הוּ, yez-an-yaw'hoo), whom Jehovah hears.

A Maachathite, who co-operated with Johanan in the pursuit of Ishmael (Jer. xl:8). They consulted with Jeremiah as to what the people should do in the disturbed times after the departure of the Babylonians (2 Kings xxv:23; Jer. xl:8; xlii:1), and probably advocated immigration into Egypt (Jer. xliii:4, 5). He is doubtless the same as Azariah (Jer. xliii:2). In 2 Kings xxv:23, the name is written *Jaazaniah* (B. C. 580).

JEZEBEL (jĕz'e-bĕl), (Heb. אִיזֶ֫בֶל, ee-zeh'bel, chaste), daughter of Ethbaal, king of Tyre, and consort of Ahab, king of Israel (B. C. 918).

(1) Induces Idolatry. This unsuitable alliance proved disastrous to the kingdom of Israel; for Jezebel induced her weak husband not only to connive at her introducing the worship of her native idols, but eventually to become himself a worshiper, and to use all the means in his power to establish them in the room of the God of Israel. This was a great enormity. The worship of the golden calves which previously existed was, however mistakenly, intended in honor of Jehovah; but this was an open alienation from him, and a turning aside to foreign and strange gods, which, indeed, were no gods. Most of the particulars of this bad but apparently highly-gifted woman's conduct have been related in the notices of AHAB and ELIJAH. From the course of her proceedings it would appear that she grew to hate the Jewish system of law and religion, on account of what must have seemed to her its intolerance and its anti-social tendencies. She hence sought to put it down by all the means she could command; and the imbecility of her husband seems to have made all the powers of the state subservient to her designs.

(2) Success of Her Policy. She had the reward of her unscrupulous decisiveness of character in the triumph of her policy in Israel, where, at last, there were but 7,000 people who had not bowed the knee to Baal, nor kissed their hand to his image. Nor was her success confined to Israel, for through Athaliah—a daughter after her own heart—who was married to the son and successor of Jehoshaphat, the same policy prevailed for a time in Judah, after Jezebel herself had perished and the house of Ahab had met its doom. It seems that after the death of her husband, Jezebel maintained considerable ascendancy over her son Joram; and her measures and misconduct formed the principal charge which Jehu cast in the teeth of that unhappy monarch before he sent forth the arrow which slew him.

(3) Death. The last effort of Jezebel was to intimidate Jehu as he passed the palace, by warning him of the eventual rewards of even successful treason. It is eminently characteristic of the woman that, even in this terrible moment, when she knew that her son was slain, and must have felt that her power had departed, she displayed herself not with rent veil and dishevelled hair, 'but tired her head and painted her eyes' before she looked out at the window, and called to Jehu as he approached: "Had Zimri peace, who slew his master?" Jehu looked up at the window and said: "Who is on my side? who?" Two or three eunuchs looked out. "Throw her down," he cried, and they unhesitatingly obeyed. She fell in front of his chariot, which he intentionally drove over her, and her blood bespattered the horses and the wall. (See JEHU.) Afterward, when the new monarch bethought him that, as 'a king's daughter,' her corpse should not be treated with disrespect, nothing was found of her but the palms of her hands and the soles of her feet. The dogs had eaten all the rest (1 Kings xvi:31; xviii:4, 13, 19; xxi:5-25; 2 Kings ix:7, 22, 30-37), B. C. 884.

(4) Character. "Jezebel was a woman in whom, with the reckless and licentious habits of an oriental queen, were united the sternest and fiercest qualities inherent in the Phœnician people. The wild license of her life, the magical fascination of her arts or of her character, became a proverb in the nation (2 Kings ix:22). Long afterward her name lived as the byword for all that was execrable, and in the Apocalypse it is given to a church or an individual in Asia Minor, combining in like manner fanaticism and profligacy (Rev. ii:20)." (Smith, *Bib. Dict.*)

JEZELUS (je-zē'lus), (Gr. Ιεξῆλος, *ee-ee-zay'los*).

1. The same as Jahaziel (1 Esdr. viii:32).

2. Jehiel, the father of Obadiah (1 Esdr. viii:35).

JEZER (jē'zer), (Heb. יֵצֶר, *yay'tser*, formation), third named of the four sons of Naphtali (Gen. xlvi:24; Num. xxvi:49; 1 Chron. vii:13), B. C. about 1656.

JEZERITES, THE (jē'zer-ītes).
A family of the tribe of Naphtali descendants of JEZER (Num. xxvi:49).

JEZIAH (je-zī'ah), (Heb. יִזִּיָּה, *yiz-zee-yaw'*, whom Jehovah sprinkles).
One of the "sons" of Parosh, a layman, of the Israelites who put away his foreign wife after the return from Babylon (Ezra x:25), B. C. 458.

JEZIEL (jē'zi-el), (Heb. יְזִיאֵל, *yeh-zee-ale'*, assembly of God), a "son" of Azmaveth, and one

of the skilled Benjamite archers who joined David at Ziklag (1 Chron. xii:3), B. C. before 1000.

JEZLIAH (jěz-lī'ah), (Heb. יִזְלִיאָה, *yiz-lee-aw'*, drawn out, preserved), one of the "sons" (or descendants) of Elpaal, and apparently a chief Benjamite resident at Jerusalem (1 Chron. viii:18), B. C. probably about 590.

JEZOAR (jě-zō'ar), (Heb. יִצְחַר, *yits-khar'*, he will shine), the son of Helah, a wife of Ashur, the father (founder) of Tekoa (1 Chron. iv:7). See ZOAR.

JEZRAHIAH (jěz-ra-hī'ah), (Heb. יִזְרַחְיָה, *yiz-rakh-yaw'*, Jah will shine).
A Levite, superintendent of the choristers at the dedication of the walls of Jerusalem during Nehemiah's time; properly IZRAHIAH (Neh. xii:42), B. C. about 1014.

JEZREEL (jěz're-el), (Heb. יִזְרְעֵאל, *yiz-reh-ale'*, sown by God).

1. A descendant of Judah, one of the family of the father, or founder, of Etam (1 Chron. iv:3). It is probable, from the association of names in this passage that he was the founder of the town in Judah by his name (Josh. xv:56), B. C. about 1612.

2. The eldest son of the prophet Hosea (Hos. i:4), so named in token of the great slaughter predicted by the prophet. He is also, with his brother Lo-ammi, and sister Lo-ruhama, the symbol of the Israelites, restored after their approaching exile (Hos. i:6, 9; ii:22, 23), B. C. about 782.

3. A town in the tribe of Issachar (Josh. xix:18), where the kings of Israel had a palace, and where the court often resided, although Samaria was the metropolis of the kingdom. It is most frequently mentioned in the history of the house of Ahab. Here was the vineyard of Naboth, which Ahab coveted to enlarge the palace-grounds (1 Kings xviii:45, 46; xxi), and here Jehu executed his dreadful commission against the house of Ahab, when Jezebel, Joram, and all who were connected with that wretched dynasty perished (2 Kings ix:14-37; x:1-11).

These horrible scenes appear to have given the kings of Israel a distaste to this residence, as it is not again mentioned in their history. It is, however, named by Hosea (i:4, comp. i:11; ii:22); and in Judith (i:8; iv:3; vii:3) it occurs under the name of Esdraelon.

In the days of Eusebius and Jerome it was still a large village, called Esdraela, and in the same age it again occurs as Stradela (*Itin. Hieros.* p. 586). Nothing more is heard of it till the time of the Crusades, when it was called by the Franks Parvum Gerinum, and by the Arabs Zerin. It ceased to be mentioned by travelers till Turner, Buckingham, and others after them again brought it into notice; and it is still more lately that the identification of Zerin and Jezreel has been restored (Raumer, *Paläst.* p. 155; Schubert, iii:164; Elliot, ii:379; Robinson, iii:164).

Zerin is seated on the brow of a rocky and very steep descent into the great and fertile valley of Jezreel, which runs down between the mountains of Gilboa and Hermon. Lying comparatively high it commands a wide and noble view, extending down the broad valley on the east to Beisan (Bethshean), and on the west quite across the great plain to the mountains of Carmel. It is described by Dr. Robinson (*Researches*, iii:163) as a most magnificent site for a city, which, being itself a conspicuous object in every part, would naturally give its name to the whole region.

Zerin has at present a small number of humble dwellings, mostly in ruins, and with few inhabitants.

(1) Jezreel, Blood of ("I will avenge the blood of Jezreel upon the house of Jehu," Hos. i:4). This probably refers to the murders and outrages committed by Ahab and Jehu at this place. In 2 Kings x:30 God approved of the acts of Jehu in his extermination of the house of Ahab. But very clearly, according to 2 Kings x:29, 31, Jehu did it not for the glory of God, but for his own advancement and interests. He was, therefore, a cruel, relentless murderer, although an instrument of the Divine vengeance.

(2) Jezreel, Ditch of. An entrenchment for the protection of the city, outside of which Naboth was put to death (1 Kings xxi:23).

(3) Jezreel, Fountain of. The waters by which Saul encamped before the battle of Gilboa (1 Sam. xxix:1). There is still a fine spring of water a little east of *Zerin* (Robinson, iii:168), which is probably the one mentioned in the above passage.

(4) Jezreel, Portion of. The field or country adjoining the city, where the crime of Ahab had been committed, and its retribution was to be exacted (2 Kings ix:10, 21, 36, etc.).

(5) Jezreel, Tower of. One of the fortifications of the city (2 Kings ix:17).

(6) Jezreel, Valley of (Josh. xvii:16; Judg. vi:33; Hos. i:5), situated between the ridges of Gilboa and Moreh, now called Jebel ed-Duhy. It was the scene of one of the most glorious victories as well as one of the most bitter defeats by the Israelites. In the time of the Judges it was occupied by the Amalekites and Midianites (Judg. vi:33 *sq.*), who were driven out by Gideon (Judg. vii:1). Two hundred years later Saul was here defeated by the Philistines (1 Sam. xxix:1-11; xxxi:1-6).

4. A city in the mountains of Judah (Josh. xv:56). It was probably from this place that David took his first wife, Ahinoam (1 Sam. xxvii:3; xxx:5). Perhaps identical with the modern *Zurtut* (Robinson, *Researches,* ii:201).

JEZREELITES (jĕz're-el-ītes), inhabitants of JEZREEL, of Issachar, (1 Kings xxi:1, 4, 6, 7, 15, 16; 2 Kings ix:21, 25).

JEZREELITESS (jĕz-re-el-i'tess), (Heb. יִזְרְעֵאלִית, *yiz-reh-ay-leeth'*), a woman of JEZREEL in Judah, one of David's wives (1 Sam. xxvii:3; xxx:5; 2 Sam. ii:2, iii:2; 1 Chron. iii:1).

JIBSAM (jĭb'sam), (Heb. יִבְשָׂם, *yib-sawm'*, fragrant, pleasant), one of the "sons" (posterity) of Tola, the son of Issachar, in David's army (1 Chron. vii:2), B. C. about 1000. He may possibly have been a son of Tola, with descendants in the army of David.

JIDLAPH (jĭd'laph), (Heb. יִדְלָף, *yid-lawf'*, tearful, weeping), the seventh named of the eight sons of Nahor (Abraham's brother) by Milcah (Gen. xxii:22), B. C. perhaps about 2300.

JIMNA (jĭm'nà), (Heb. יִמְנָה, *yim-naw'*, good fortune, luck), firstborn of Asher, and founder of a family by his name (Num. xxvi:44). B. C. 1874. In Gen. xlvi:17 his name is Jimnah.

JIMNAH (jĭm'nah), (Heb. יִמְנָה, *yim-naw'*, prosperity). See JIMNA.

JIMNITES, THE (jĭm'nītes), (Num. xxvi:44), descendants of JIMNA (which see).

JIPHTAH (jĭph'tah), (Heb. יִפְתָּח, *yif-takh'*, he will open), a city in the low country of Judah (Josh. xv:43). Robinson identifies it with *Jimrin* (*Researches*, ii:342, note).

JIPHTHAH-EL (jĭph'thah-ĕl), (Heb. יִפְתַּח־אֵל, *yif-takh-ale'*, opening of God).

A valley mentioned as one of the boundaries of Zebulun (Josh. xix:14, 27), separating it from Asher and Naphtali. It was probably identical with Jotapata, the city that resisted Vespasian so successfully, and the modern *Jefât*, in the hills of Galilee (Robinson, iii:107).

JOAB (jō'ab), (Heb. יוֹאָב, *yo-awb'*, Jehovah his father).

1. One of the three sons of Zeruiah, the sister of David, and 'captain of the host'; generalissimo of the army during nearly the whole of David's reign.

(1) First Appearance. He first appears associated with his two brothers, Abishai and Asahel, in the command of David's troops against Abner, who had set up the claims of a son of Saul in opposition to those of David, who then reigned in Hebron. The armies having met at the pool of Gibeon, a general action was brought on, in which Abner was worsted. In his flight he had the misfortune to kill Joab's brother, the swift-footed Asahel, by whom he was pursued (2 Sam. ii:13-32). The consequences of this deed have been explained elsewhere. (See ABNER; ASAHEL.)

(2) Avenges Asahel. Joab smothered for a time his resentment against the shedder of his brother's blood; but it being whetted by the natural rivalry of position between him and Abner, he afterwards made it the instrument of his policy by treacherously, in the act of friendly communication, slaying Abner at the very time when the services of the latter to David, to whom he had then turned, had rendered him a most dangerous rival to Joab in power and influence (2 Sam. iii:22-27). That Abner had at first suspected that Joab would take the position of blood-avenger (see BLOOD-REVENGE) is clear, from the apprehension which he expressed (2 Sam. ii:22); but that he thought that Joab had, under all the circumstances, abandoned this position, is shown by the unsuspecting readiness with which he went aside with him (2 Sam. iii:26, 27); and that Joab placed his murderous act on the footing of vengeance for his brother's blood, is plainly stated in 2 Sam. iii:30; by which it also appears that the other brother, Abishai, shared in some way in the deed and its responsibilities. At the same time, as Abner was perfectly justified in slaying Asahel to save his own life, it is very doubtful if Joab would ever have asserted his right of blood-revenge, if Abner had not appeared likely to endanger his influence with David. The king, much as he reprobated the act, knew that it had a sort of excuse in the old customs of blood-revenge, and he stood habitually too much in awe of his impetuous and able nephew to bring him to punishment, or even to displace him from his command. 'I am this day weak,' he said, 'though anointed king, and these men, the sons of Zeruiah, be too hard for me' (2 Sam. iii:39).

(3) Appointed to Chief Command. Desirous probably of making some atonement before David and the public for this atrocity, in a way which at the same time was most likely to prove effectual—namely, by some daring exploit, he was the first to mount to the assault at the storming of the fortress on Mount Zion, which had remained so long in the hands of the Jebusites. By this service he acquired the chief command of the army of all Israel, of which David was by this time king (2 Sam. v:6-10).

(4) Serves David Faithfully. It is not necessary to trace the subsequent acts of Joab, seeing that they are in fact the public acts of the king he served. And he served him faithfully.

Although he knew his power over David, and often treated him with little ceremony, there can be no doubt that he was most truly devoted to his interests, and sometimes rendered him good service even against his own will, as in the affair at Mahanaim (2 Sam. xix:5-8).

As Joab was on good terms with Absalom, and had taken pains to bring about a reconciliation between him and his father, we may set the higher value upon his firm adhesion to David when Absalom revolted, and upon his stern sense of duty to the king—from whom he expected no thanks—displayed in putting an end to the war by the slaughter of this favorite son, when all others shrank from the responsibility of doing the king a service against his own will (2 Sam. xviii:1-14). In like manner, when David unhappily resolved to number the people, Joab discerned the evil and remonstrated against it, and although he did not venture to disobey, he performed the duty tardily and reluctantly, to afford the king an opportunity of reconsidering the matter, and took no pains to conceal how odious the measure was to him (2 Sam. xxiv:1-4).

(5) Military Exploits. His great war was that against Ammon, which he conducted in person. It was divided into three campaigns: **(a)** The first was against the allied forces of Syria and Ammon. He attacked and defeated the Syrians, whilst his brother Abishai did the same for the Ammonites. The Syrians rallied with their kindred tribes from beyond the Euphrates, and were finally routed by David himself. (See HADAREZER.) **(b)** The second was against Edom. The decisive victory was gained by David himself in the "valley of salt," and celebrated by a triumphal monument (2 Sam. viii:13). But Joab had the charge of carrying out the victory, and remained for six months, extirpating the male population, whom he then buried in the tombs of Petra (1 Kings xi:15, 16). So long was the terror of his name preserved that only when the fugitive prince of Edom, in the Egyptian court, heard that "David slept with his fathers, and that *Joab the captain of the host was dead,"* did he venture to return to his own country (ch. xi:21, 22). **(c)** The third was against the Ammonites. They were again left to Joab (2 Sam. x:7-19). He went against them at the beginning of the next year "at the time when kings go out to battle"—to the siege of Rabbah. The ark was sent with him, and the whole army was encamped in booths or huts round the beleaguered city (2 Sam. xi:1, 11). After a sortie of the inhabitants, which caused some loss to the Jewish army, Joab took the lower city on the river, and then with true loyalty sent to urge David to come and take the citadel, Rabbah, lest the glory of the capture should pass from the king to his general (2 Sam. xii:26-28). (Smith, *Bib. Dict.*)

(6) Ingratitude of David. David was certainly ungrateful for the service of Joab, when, in order to conciliate the powerful party which had supported Absalom, he offered the command of the host to Amasa, who had commanded the army of Absalom (2 Sam. xix:13).

(7) Murder of Amasa. But the inefficiency of the new commander, in the emergency which the revolt of Bichri's son produced, arising perhaps from the reluctance of the troops to follow their new leader, gave Joab an opportunity of display-ing his superior resources, and also of removing his rival by a murder very similar to, and in some respects less excusable and more foul than, that of Abner (see AMASA). Besides Amasa was his own cousin, being the son of his mother's sister (2 Sam. xx:1-13).

(8) Joins Adonijah. When David lay on his deathbed, and a demonstration was made in favor of the succession of the eldest surviving son, Adonijah, whose interests had been compromised by the preferment of the young Solomon, Joab joined the party of the natural heir. When the prompt measures taken under the direction of the king rendered this demonstration abortive (1 Kings i:7), Joab withdrew into private life till some time after the death of David, when the fate of Adonijah, and of Abiathar—whose life was only spared in consequence of his sacerdotal character—warned Joab that he had little mercy to expect from the new king.

(9) Death. He fled for refuge to the altar; but when Solomon heard this, he sent Benaiah to put him to death; and, as he refused to come forth, gave orders that he should be slain even at the altar. His corpse was removed to his domain in the wilderness of Judah, and buried there (1 Kings ii:5, 28-34), B. C. about 960.

(10) Character. Joab was one of the most accomplished warriors and unscrupulous men that Israel ever produced. But he had no principles apart from what he deemed his duty to the king and the people, and was quite as ready to serve his master's vices as his virtues, so long as they did not interfere with his own interests, or tended to promote them by enabling him to make himself useful to the king. His ready apprehension of the king's meaning in the matter of Uriah, and the facility with which he made himself the instrument of the murder, and of the hypocrisy by which it was covered, are proofs of this, and form as deep a stain upon his character as his own murders (2 Sam. xi:14-25).

2. Son of Seraiah, and a descendant of Kenaz (1 Chron. iv:14). Jerome says that the architects of the temple were selected from among his sons, and for this reason he was called father, or prince, of the valley of Charashim, or smiths.

3. The head of one of the most numerous families which returned from Babylon with Zerubbabel (Ezra ii:6; viii:9; Neh. vii:11), B. C. 445.

JOAH (jō'ah), (Heb. יֹאָח, *yo-awkh'*, Jehovah his brother, friend).

1. Son of Asaph and keeper of the records under Hezekiah. He was one of the embassy sent to the Assyrian general at the conduit of the upper pool (2 Kings xviii:18, 26; Is. xxxvi:3, 11, 22), B. C. 719.

2. Son or descendant of Zimmah (1 Chron. vi:21). The same as Ethan (ver. 42), unless some of the names of one list are omitted in the other (B. C. 719).

3. Son of Obed-edom (1 Chron. xxvi:4). He was a Korhite and one of those appointed by David to keep the southern gate of the Temple, and the house of Asuppim, a storehouse, or court-house in the outer court (ver. 15), B. C. 1014.

4. A Gershonite, son of Zimmah (2 Chron. xxix:12). As a Levite he took a leading part in the purification of the Temple under Hezekiah (B. C. 726).

5. Son of Joahaz and keeper of the records under Josiah. He, with Shaphan and Maaseiah, superintended the repair of the Temple (2 Chron. xxxiv:8), B. C. 623.

JOAHAZ (jō'a-hăz), (Heb. יוֹאָחָז, *yo-aw-khawz'*, Jehovah holds), the father of Joah, who kept the records under Josiah (2 Chron. xxxiv:8), B. C. before 623.

JOANNA (jo-ăn'nà).

1. (Gr. 'Ιωαννᾶς, *ee-o-an-nas'*, Joannas), the son of Rhesa and grandson of Zorobabel, in the lineage of Christ (Luke iii:27).

2. (Gr. 'Ιωάννα, *ee-o-an'nah*, probably feminine of 'Ιωάννης, *John*), wife of Chuza, the steward of Herod Antipas, the tetrarch of Galilee. She was one of those women who followed Christ and ministered to his wants and those of his disciples out of their abundance. They had all been cured of grievous diseases by the Savior, or had received material benefits from him; and the customs of the country allowed them to testify in this way their gratitude and devotedness without reproach. It is usually supposed that Joanna was at this time a widow (Luke viii:3; xxiv:10).

JOASH (jō'ăsh), (Heb. יוֹאָשׁ, *yo-awsh'*, given by Jehovah), a contraction of JEHOASH.

1. Son of Ahaziah and eighth king of Judah, who began to reign in B. C. 878, at the age of seven, and reigned forty-one years.

(1) Saved as an Infant. Joash, when an infant, was secretly saved by his aunt Jehosheba, who was married to the high-priest Jehoiada, from the general massacre of the family by Athaliah, who had usurped the throne (see ATHALIAH; JEHOIADA). By the high-priest and his wife the child was privily brought up in the chambers connected with the temple till he had attained his eighth year, when Jehoiada deemed that the state of affairs required him to produce the youthful heir of the throne to the people, and claim for him the crown which his grandmother had so unrighteously usurped.

(2) Proclaimed King. Finding the influential persons whom he consulted favorable to the design, everything was secretly, but admirably, arranged for producing Joash, and investing him with the regalia, in such a manner that Athaliah could have no suspicion of the event till it actually occurred. On the day appointed, the sole surviving scion of David's illustrious house appeared in the place of the kings, by a particular pillar in the temple-court, and was crowned and anointed with the usual ceremonies. The high-wrought enthusiasm of the spectators then found vent in clapping of hands and exulting shouts of 'Long live the king!' The joyful uproar was heard even in the palace, and brought Athaliah to the temple, from which, at a word from Jehoiada, she was led to her death.

(3) Behavior. Joash behaved well during his youth, and so long after as he remained under the influence of the high-priest. But when he died the king seems to have felt himself relieved from a yoke; and to manifest his freedom, began to take the contrary course to that which he had followed while under pupilage. Gradually the persons who had possessed influence formerly, when the house of David was contaminated by its alliance with the house of Ahab, insinuated themselves into his councils, and ere long the worship of Jehovah and the observances of the law were neglected, and the land was defiled with idolatries and idolatrous usages.

(4) Slays Zechariah. The prophets then uttered their warnings, but were not heard; and the infatuated king had the atrocious ingratitude to put to death Zechariah, the son and successor of his benefactor Jehoiada.

(5) Divine Judgments and Death. For these deeds Joash was made an example of the Divine judgments. He saw his realm devastated by the Syrians under Hazael; his armies were cut in pieces by an enemy of inferior numbers; and he was even besieged in Jerusalem, and only preserved his capital and his crown by giving up the treasures of the temple. Joash was buried in the city of David; but a place in the sepulcher of the kings was denied to his remains (2 Kings xi; xii; 2 Chron. xxiv.)

2. Son and successor of Jehoahaz on the throne of Israel, of which he was the twelfth king.

(1) Reign. He began to reign (B. C. 799), and reigned sixteen incomplete years. He followed the example of his predecessors in the policy of keeping up the worship of the golden calves; but, apart from this, he bears a fair character, and had intervals, at least, of sincere piety and true devotion to the God of his fathers. Indeed, custom and long habit had so established the views of political expediency on which the schismatical establishments at Dan and Bethel were founded, that at length the reprehension which regularly recurs in the record of each king's reign, seems rather to apply to it as a mark of the continuance of a public crime, than as indicative of the character or disposition of the reigning prince, which is to be sought in the more detailed accounts of his own conduct. These accounts are favorable with respect to Joash.

(2) Relations to Elisha. He held the prophet Elisha in high honor, looking up to him as a father. When he heard of his last illness he repaired to the bedside of the dying prophet, and was favored with promises of victories over the Syrians, by whom his dominions were then harassed. These promises were accomplished after the prophet's death. In three signal and successive victories Joash overcame the Syrians, and retook from them the towns which Hazael had rent from Israel.

(3) War and Death. These advantages rendered the kingdom of Israel more potent than that of Judah. He, however, sought no quarrel with that kingdom; but when he received a defiance from Amaziah, king of Judah, he answered with becoming spirit in a parable, which by its images calls to mind that of Jotham (see PARABLE); the cool disdain of the answer must have been, and in fact was, exceedingly galling to Amaziah. In the war, or rather action, which followed, Joash was victorious. Having defeated Amaziah at Beth-shemesh, in Judah, he advanced to Jerusalem, broke down the wall to the extent of 400 cubits, and carried away the treasures both of the temple and the palace, together with hostages for the future good behavior of the crestfallen Amaziah. Joash himself did not long survive this victory; he died in peace, and was buried in Samaria (2 Kings xiii:9-25; xiv:1-17).

3. Father of Gideon, and a man of influence among the Abi-ezrites. During the Midianitish occupation he seems to have yielded to popular opinion, and the exigencies of the time, so far as to have an altar dedicated to Baal (Judg. vi:11, 29, 30, 31; vii:14; viii:13, 29, 32).

4. A younger son of Ahab, who either held a subordinate jurisdiction or was appointed governor while his father was making an attack on Ramoth-Gilead (1 Kings xxii:26; 2 Chron. xviii:25).

5. A descendant of Shelah, son of Judah (1 Chron. iv:22).

6. Son of Shemaah of Gibeah. He was a Benjamite and one of the "helpers" who came to David at Ziklag (1 Chron. xii:3), and with him probably pursued the Amalekites.

7. An officer of David, who had charge of the storehouses of oil and the products of David's possessions in the lowlands (1 Chron. xxvii:28).

8. One of the sons of Becher, and head of a Benjamite house in the time of David (1 Chron. vii:8).

JOATHAM (jō'a-thăm), (Gr. 'Ιωάθαμ, *ee-o-ah'-tham*). JOTHAM, son of Uzziah (Matt. i:9).

JOB (jŏb).

I. (Heb. יוֹב, *yobe*, returning), the third named of the sons of Issachar (Gen. xlvi:13), called Jashub (Num. xxvi:24; 1 Chron. vii:1).

II. (Heb. אִיּוֹב, *ee-yobe'*, persecuted), an Arabian patriarch and the hero of the book which bears his name, mentioned elsewhere only in Ezek. xiv:14, 20; Jas. v:11. The various questions relating to his history are met in the consideration of the poem itself.

1. *Contents of the Book.* In the land of Uz, belonging to the northern part of Arabia Deserta lived an honest, pious man, called Job.

(1) Job's Affliction. For his sincere and perfect devotedness, God had amply blessed him with worldly property and children; but on Satan obtaining leave *to tempt him*, he suddenly lost the good fortune of his life. Ultimately he is smitten with a severe and painful disease; but though his wife *moves* him to forsake God, he still continues true and stanch to the Lord. Three friends, Eliphaz, Bildad and Zophar, hear of his calamities, and come to console him. His distressed state excites their heartfelt compassion; but the view which they take of its origin prevents them from at once assisting him, and they remain silent, though they are sensible that by so doing they further wound his feelings. Seven days thus pass, until Job, suspecting the cause of their conduct, becomes discomposed and breaks silence. His first observations are based on the assertion—not, indeed, broadly expressed—that God acts harshly and arbitrarily in inflicting calamity on men.

(2) Discussion. This causes a discussion between him and his friends, which is divided into three main parts, each with subdivisions, and embraces the speeches of the three friends of Job, and his answers; the last part, however, consists of only two subdivisions, the third friend, Zophar, having nothing to rejoin. By this silence the author of the book generally designates the defeat of Job's friends, who are defending a common cause. Taking a general view of the argument which they urge against him, they may be considered as asserting the following positions:

(a) No man being free from sin, we need not wonder that we are liable to calamities, for which we must account by a reference, not to God, but to ourselves. From the misery of the distressed, others are enabled to infer their guilt; and they must take this view in order to vindicate Divine justice.

(b) The distress of a man proves not only *that he has sinned*, but shows also the degree and measure of his sin; and thus, from the extent of calamity sustained, may be inferred the extent of sins committed; and from this the measure of impending misfortune.

(c) A distressed man may recover his former happiness, and even attain to greater fortune than he ever enjoyed before, if he takes a warning from his afflictions, repents of his sins, reforms his life, and raises himself to a higher degree of moral rectitude. Impatience and irreverent expostulation with God serve but to prolong and increase punishment, for, by accusing God of injustice, a fresh sin is added to former transgressions.

(d) Though the wicked man is capable of prosperity, still it is never lasting. The most awful retribution soon overtakes him; and his transient felicity must itself be considered as punishment, since it renders him heedless, and makes him feel misfortune more keenly.

(3) Job's Answer. In opposition to them, Job maintains:

(a) The most upright man may be highly unfortunate—more so than the inevitable faults and shortcomings of human nature would seem to imply. There is a savage cruelty, deserving the severities of the Divine resentment, in inferring the guilt of a man from his distresses. In distributing good and evil, God regards neither merit nor guilt, but acts according to his sovereign pleasure. His omnipotence is apparent in every part of the creation; but his justice cannot be seen in the government of the world; the afflictions of the righteous, as well as the prosperity of the wicked, are evidence against it. There are innumerable cases, and Job considers his own to be one of them, in which a sufferer has a right to justify himself before God, and to repine at his decrees. Of this supposed right Job freely avails himself, and maintains it against his friends.

(b) In a state of composure and calmer reflection, Job retracts, chiefly in his concluding speech, all his former rather extravagant assertions, and says that, although God generally afflicts the wicked and blesses the righteous, still there are exceptions to this rule, single cases in which the pious undergo severe trials; the inference, therefore, of a man's guilt from his misfortunes is by no means warranted. For the exceptions established by experience prove that God does not always distribute prosperity and adversity after this rule; but that he sometimes acts on a different principle, or as an absolute lord, according to his mere will and pleasure.

(c) Humbly to adore God is our duty, even when we are subject to calamities not at all deserved; but we should abstain from harshly judging of those who, when distressed, send forth complaints against God.

(4) Elihu Appears. The interest of the narrative is kept up with considerable skill, by progressively rising and highly passionate language. At first, Job's friends charge him, and he defends himself, in mild terms, but gradually they are all betrayed into warmth of temper, which goes on increasing until the friends have nothing more to object, and Job remains in possession of the field. The discussion then seems to be at an end, when a fresh disputant, Elihu, appears. Trusting in his just cause, Job had proudly opposed God, with whom he expostulated, and whom he charged with injustice, when the sense of his calamities should have led him to acknowledge the sinfulness of human nature, and humbly to submit to the Divine dispensations. Making every allowance for his painful situation, and putting the mildest construction on his expressions, he is still substantially wrong, and could not therefore be suffered to remain the vanquisher in this high argument. He had silenced his friends, but the general issue remained to be settled. Elihu had waited till Job and his friends had spoken, because they were older than he; but when he saw that the three visitors ceased to answer, he offers himself to reason with Job, and shows that God is just in his ways.

He makes this plain. **(a)** *From the nature of afflictions.* He begins by urging that Job was very wrong in boasting of his integrity, and making it appear that rewards were due to him from God. However righteous he was, he still had no claim to reward; on the contrary, all men are sinners in God's eyes; and nobody can complain that he suffers unjustly, for the very greatest sufferings equal not his immense guilt. Then Elihu explains a leading point on which he differs from the friends of Job: he asserts that from greater sufferings inflicted on a person it was not to be inferred that he had sinned more than others afflicted with a less amount of calamity. Calamities were, indeed, under all circumstances, punishments for sins committed, but at the same time they were correctives also; and therefore they might be inflicted on the comparatively most righteous in preference to others. For he who was most loved by God, was also most in danger of forgetting the sinfulness inherent in all men, and, consequently, also in himself; the rather because sin would in him less strongly manifest itself. If the object of afflictions was attained, and the distressed acknowledged his sinfulness, he would humble himself before God, who would bless him with greater happiness than he ever before enjoyed. But he who took not this view, and did not amend his ways, would be ruined, and the blame would rest wholly with himself. Consequently, if Job made the best of his misfortune, God would render him most happy; but if he continued refractory, punishment would follow his offenses.

(b) *From a clear conception of the nature of God.* 'How darest thou,' says Elihu, 'instead of humbling thyself before God, defy him, and offer to reason with him? The whole creation shows forth his majesty, and evinces his justice. For a man to stand up against him, and to assert that he suffers innocently, is the greatest anthropomorphism, because it *goes* to deny the Divine majesty, evident in all the facts of the created world, and including God's justice. His nature being one and indivisible, it cannot on one side exhibit infinite perfection, and on the other imperfection; each example, then, of God's grandeur in the creation of the world is evidence against the rash accusers of God's justice. Thus it appears that, from the outset, there must have been a mistake in thy calculation, and thou must the rather acknowledge the correctness of my solution of the question.'

(5) **God Decides.** Job had, in a stirring manner, several times challenged God to decide the contest. Elihu suspects the approach of the Lord, when, towards the end of his speech, a violent thunderstorm arises and God answers Job out of the whirlwind, showing how foolishly the latter had acted in offering to reason with him, when his works proved his infinite majesty, and, consequently, his absolute justice. Job now submits to God, and humbly repents of his offense. Hereupon God addresses Eliphaz, Bildad, and Zophar, declaring unto them his displeasure at their unmerciful dealing with their friend, the consequences of which could only be avoided by Job offering a propitiatory sacrifice. This is done, and the Lord grants unto Job ample compensation for his sufferings.

2. **Design of the Book.** All agree that the object of the book is the solution of the question how the afflictions of the righteous and the prosperity of the wicked can be consistent with God's justice. Some assume that the problem could be satisfactorily solved only when the doctrines of immortality and retribution had been first established, which had not been done by the author of the book of Job; a perfect solution of the question was therefore not to be expected from him.

On nearer examination, however, it appears that the doctrine of retribution after death is not of itself alone calculated to lead to a solution of the problem. In contemplating the lives of the righteous, who were perfectly imbued with this doctrine, it will appear that they also struggled with doubts; that a satisfactory solution of the question is to be derived only from the fundamental doctrine on which the faith in retribution rests; and that this faith is shaken where it has not the necessary basis. The belief in a final judgment is firm and rational only when it rests on the belief in God's continued providential government of the world, and in his acting as sovereign Lord in all the events of human life. If God is holy and just, he must also have the will to manifest these qualities in our present life by his bearing toward those who represent his image on earth, as well as toward those who renounce it. If he is omnipotent, nothing can in this life prevent him from exhibiting his justice; but if this is not manifested, and if no reason can be given for which he at times defers his judgments, the belief in retribution after death would be flimsy and shallow. The New Testament holds out to the righteous promises of a future life, as well as of the present, and our Savior himself, in setting forth the rewards of those who, for his sake, forsook everything, begins with this life (Matt. xix:29). A nearer examination of the benedictions contained in the Sermon on the Mount (Matt. v), shows that none of them exclusively refer to future blessings, the judgment of the wicked is in his view proceeding without interruption, and therefore his examples of the distribution of Divine justice in this world, are mingled with those of requital in a future order of things. The Galileans, whose blood Pilate had mingled with their own sacrifices (Luke xiii:1), were in Christ's opinion not accidentally killed; and he threatens those who would not repent that they should in like manner perish. That sickness is to be considered as a punishment for sin we are clearly taught (John v:14; Luke v: 20, 24); in the former passage it is threatened as punishment for sins committed; in the latter it is healed in consequence of punishment remitted. Nay, every patient restored by Christ, who acted not as a superior kind of Hippocrates, but as the Savior of men, is by that very act declared to be a sinner. The passage in John ix: 2, 3, which is often appealed to, in proof that our Lord did not consider sickness as a punishment for sin, does not prove this, but only opposes the Jewish position—founded on the mistaken doctrine of retribution—that all severe sicknesses and infirmities were consequences of crimes. But what is, from this point of view, the solution of the problem regarding the sufferings of the righteous? It rests on two positions:

(a) Calamity is the only way that leads to the kingdom of God.

(b) Calamity, as the veiled grace of God, is with the pious never alone, but manifest proofs of Divine favor accompany or follow it. Though sunk in misery, they still are happier than the wicked, and when it has attained its object, it is terminated by the Lord.

It is this exclusively correct solution of the problem which occurs in the book of Job. All interpreters allow that it is set forth in Elihu's speeches, and, from the following observations, it will appear that they contain the opinion of the author. The leading principle in Elihu's statement is, that calamity in the shape of trial was inflicted even on the comparatively best men, but that God allowed a favorable turn to take place as soon as it had attained its object. Now this is the key to the events of Job's life. Though a righteous man, he is tried by severe afflictions. He knows not for what purpose he is smitten, and his calamity continues, but when he learns it from the addresses of Elihu and God, and humbles himself, he is relieved from the burden which oppresses him, and ample prosperity atones for the afflictions he has sustained. Add to this, that the remaining portion of Elihu's speeches, in which he points to God's infinite majesty as including his justice, are continued in the addresses of God; that Elihu foretells God's appearance; that he is not punished by God as are the friends of Job; in fine, that Job by his very silence acknowledges the problem to have been solved by Elihu; and his silence is the more significant because Elihu had urged him to defend himself (xxxiii:32), and because Job had repeatedly declared he would 'hold his peace,' if it was shown to him wherein he had erred (vi:24, 25; xix:4). This view of the book of Job has among modern authors been supported chiefly by Stäudlin *Beiträge zur Religione und Sittenlehre,* vol. ii, p. 133) and Stickel (*Das Buch Hiob,* Leipzig, 1842), though in both it is mixed up with much erroneous matter; and it is further confirmed by the whole Old Testament giving the same answer to the question mooted, which the speeches of Elihu offer; in its concentrated form it is presented in Ps. xxxvii, xlix, lxxiii.

The object of the book is rather to explain generally the nature and tendency of afflictions, and thereby to contribute towards the attainment of their design, to console the mind, and to cheer the drooping spirits. It is difficult for men to understand that their sufferings, however great, are still under that degree which they deserve. To consider afflictions as proofs of Divine favor, we must first learn to bring them into unison with Divine justice. Upon the doctrine of retribution after death our author does not enter, but that he knew it, may be inferred from several passages with great probability; as, for instance, ch. xiv: 14, 'if a man die shall he live again? All the days of my appointed time will I wait, till my change come.' The *if* here shows that the writer had been before engaged in considering the subject of life after death; and when such is the case a pious mind will necessarily indulge the hope, or will, at least, have an obscure presentiment of immortality. The truth, also, of God's unbounded grace, on which the doctrine of immortality is based, will be found clearly laid down in ch. xix. Still the author does not recur to this hope for the purpose of solving his problem; he would not ground it on something in itself wanting support and a foundation, namely, that which is presented in this book. The doctrine of future retribution, if not sustained by the belief in retribution during this life, is truly a castle in the air. The author did not intend in his discussion to exceed the limits of what God had *clearly revealed,* and this was in his time confined to the vague notion of life continued after death, but not connected with rewards and punishments.

3. Character of Composition. On this subject there are different opinions.

Some contend that the book contains an entirely true history; others assert that it is founded on a true history, which has been recast; while others hold that the book contains a narrative entirely imaginary, and constructed by the author to teach a great moral truth.

The first view, taken by numerous ancient interpreters, is now abandoned by nearly all interpreters. It seems, however, to have been adopted by Josephus, for he places Job in the list of the historical books; and it was prevalent with all the fathers of the church. In its support four reasons are adduced, of which the third and fourth are quite untenable; the first and second are out-

weighed by other considerations, which render it impossible to consider the book of Job as an entirely true history, but which may be used in defence of the second view alluded to. It is said:

(a) That Job is (Ezek. xiv:14-20) mentioned as a public character, together with Noah and Daniel, and represented as an example of piety.

(b) In the Epistle of James (v:11), patience in sufferings is recommended by a reference to Job.

(c) In the Greek translation of the Septuagint a notice is appended to Gen. xxxvi:33, which states that Job was the King Jobab of Edom. This statement is too late to be relied on, and originates in an etymological combination; and that it must be erroneous is to a certain extent evident from the contents of the book, in which Job is not represented as a king.

(d) Job's tomb continues to be shown to Oriental tourists. Now the fact of a Job having lived somewhere would not of itself prove that the hero of our narrative was that person, and that this book contained a purely historical account. Moreover, his tomb is shown not in one place, but in six, and, along with it, the dunghill on which Job is reported to have sat!

Against this view it must be remarked generally, that the whole work is arranged on a well-considered plan, proving the author's power of independent invention. The transactions between God and Satan in the prologue absolutely require that we should distinguish between the subject matter forming the foundation of the work, and its enlargement; which can be only done when a poetical principle is acknowledged in its composition. This argument, which might be further extended without much difficulty, proves the first view above stated of the book of Job to be erroneous, and is meant to support the second; but it does not bear on the third, which contends that the narrative is an entire fiction, without any admixture of real facts; but which is contrary to the practice which anciently prevailed, when writers rarely invented the subject of a narrative and rather took the materials furnished by tradition, digesting, enlarging, and modifying them, so as to make them harmonize with the leading theme. Taking the second view, we must still abstain from undertaking to determine what the poet derived from tradition and what he added himself, since we know how far tradition had already embellished the original fact.

4. Descent, Country and Age of Author. Opinions differed in ancient times as to *the nation* to which the author belonged; some considering him to have been an Arab, others an Israelite; but the latter supposition is undoubtedly preferable. For, first, we find in our book many ideas of genuine Israelite growth; the creation of the world is described, in accordance with the prevailing notions of the Israelites, as the immediate effect of Divine omnipotence; man is formed of clay; the spirit of man is God's breath; God employs the angels for the performance of his orders; Satan, the enemy of the chosen children of God, is his instrument for tempting them; men are weak and sinful; nobody is pure in the sight of God; moral corruption is propagated. There is promulgated to men the law of God, which they must not infringe, and the transgressions of which are visited on offenders with punishments. Moreover, the nether world, or Sheol, is depicted in hues entirely Hebrew.

Proceeding to the inquiry as to *the age* of the author of this book, we meet with three opinions:

(a) That he lived before Moses, or was, at least, his contemporary.

(b) That he lived in the time of Solomon, or in the centuries next following.

(c) That he lived shortly before, or during, or even after, the Babylonian exile. The view of those who assert the book to have been written long after the Babylonian exile, can be supported, as Hirzel justly observes, neither by the nature of its language nor by reasons derived from its historical groundwork, and is therefore now generally rejected.

Against those who refer the composition of the book to the time of the Babylonian exile, militate, first, the references to it in the Old Testament, which prove that it was before this period a generally known writing. Thus, in Ezek. xiv:14-20 are mentioned 'three men, Noah, Daniel, and Job,' as examples of righteousness. Mr. Bernstein, indeed, in defending his hypothesis, rejects this passage as spurious, but it bears every mark of genuineness. Further, in Jer. xx:14, we find evidently imitated Job's cursing of the day of his birth (Job iii). Not only the sentiments but the words are often the same; and that this coincidence is not accidental, or that the author did not imitate Jeremiah, appears from the literary character of each. Jeremiah shows himself throughout dependent on ancient writings, whereas our author is quite original and independent, as proved by Küper (see *Jeremias librorum sacrorum interpres ataque vindex*, p. 164 sq.). There are also in the *Lamentations* of Jeremiah, many passages clearly alluding to our book, which must have eminently suited his taste and interested him (comp. Job xvi:9, 10, with Lam. ii:16; and Job xix:8, with Lam. iii:7, 9). In *Isaiah* the peculiar use of אבא (xl:2) refers us to כֶּפֶל, *keh'fel*, *double*, in Job i (comp. x:17; xiv:14); and *the double* received from God's hand alludes to the end of the history of Job, who is there considered as typifying the future fate of the church. Is. lxi:7, 'In their land they shall have the double,' alludes to the same point; Isaiah li:9 depends on Job xxvi: 13; and Isaiah xix:5 almost literally agrees with Job xiv:11 (see Küper, p. 166). Another example of words borrowed from Job occurs in Ps. cvii:42, where the second part of the verse agrees literally with Job v:16.

A most decisive reason against assigning the composition of Job to the period of the exile is derived from the language, since it is free from *those* Chaldaisms which occur in the books written about that time.

To the view which places the age of the book of Job in the time of the Babylonian exile, is most opposed that which assigns the composition of it to a period prior to Moses. In support of this latter view, only two arguments having a semblance of force can be adduced, and they will not bear the test of strict inquiry. They are: (1) 'There is in the book of Job no direct reference to the Mosaic legislation; and its descriptions and other statements are suited to the period of the patriarchs; as, for instance, the great authority held by old men, the high age of Job, and fathers offering sacrifices for their families—which leads to the supposition that when our book was written no sacerdotal order yet existed.' These points, however, are quite intelligible, if the design of the book, as stated above, is kept in view. The author intended not to rest the decision of the question at issue on particular passages of Scripture, but on religious consciousness and experience. This at once explains why he places the scene without Palestine, why he places it in the patriarchal age, and why he avoids the use of the name Jehovah; of these three items *the first* suffi-

ciently accounts for no reference being made to the Mosaic legislation. (2) 'The language of the book of Job seems strongly to support the opinion of its having been written before Moses.' It has been often said, that no writing of the Old Testament may be more frequently illustrated from the Arabic than this book. Jerome observes (*Præfat. in Dan.*), '*Jobum cum Arabica lingua plurimam habere societatem;*' and Schultens proved this so incontrovertibly that Gesenius was rather too late in denying the fact (see his *Geschichte der Hebräischen Sprache,* p. 33). Now, from this character of its language we might be induced to infer that the work was written in the remotest times, when the separation of the dialects had only begun, but had not yet been completed. This inference would, however, be safe only if the book were written in prose. It is solely from works of this class that the general usage of the language prevailing at the time of the author can be seen. On the contrary, the selection of obsolete and rare words and forms, with the Hebrews, was a peculiar feature of the poetical style, and served to distinguish it from the usual, habitual way of writing. This peculiarity belongs to our book more than to any other.

The most complete statement of the reasons in support of the opinion that the book of Job was written after the age of Moses may be found in Richter's essay, *De Ætate Jobi definienda*, reprinted in Rosenmüller's edition of Lowth's *Prælectiones De Poesi Sacra Hebræorum;* in which he maintains that it was written in the age of Solomon. Most of these reasons, indeed, are either not conclusive at all, or not quite cogent. Thus it is an arbitrary assumption, proved by modern researches to be erroneous, that the art of writing was unknown previous to the age of Moses. The assertion, too, that the marks of cultivation and refinement observable in our book belonged to a later age, rests on no historical ground. Further, it cannot be said that for such an early time the language is too smooth and neat, since in no Semitic dialect is it possible to trace a progressive improvement. The evident correspondence also between our book and the Proverbs and Psalms is not a point proving with resistless force that they were all written at the same time. It is, indeed, sometimes of such a kind, that the authors of the Proverbs and Psalms cannot be exactly said to have copied our book; but it may be accounted for by their all belonging to the same class of writings, by the very great uniformity and accordance of religious conceptions and sentiments expressed in the Old Testament, and by the stability of its religious character.

Summing up the whole of our investigations, we take it to be a settled point that the book of Job does not belong to the time of the Babylonian exile; and it is nearly equally certain that it was not composed prior to the time of Moses. Could it then have been written in some age preceding Samuel and David? It is only with them that a new period of sacred literature began; and our book is related to products of that period, or enlarges on them. But it cannot have been composed later than Isaiah, who alludes to it. Thus we come to this general determination of the age of our book, that it was written, *not before* Samuel and David, but *not later* than the era of Isaiah. With this result we must rest satisfied, unless we would go beyond the indications presented. The intermediate period offers no ground on which we can safely fix the composition of the book of Job. There remains then uncertainty, but it does not concern an important point of religion.

5. Literature. E. W. H. Fry's *New Translation and Exposition*, 1827; Lange, *Das Buch Hiob*, 1831; Knobel, *De Carminis Iobi*, 1835; Ewald, *Das Buch Hiob erklärt*, 1836; Fackens, *Comment. de Jobeide*, 1836; Lee's *Book of Job*, 1837; Wemyss, *Job and his Times*, 1839. Jennings' *Epic of the Inner Life* is one of the latest and best expositions of this ancient poem; Vaihinger, *Erläuter.*, 1842; Noyes, *Notes*, Boston, 1852, 1854; Hengstenberg, *Hiob*, 1856, 1870; Cheyne, *Job and Solomon*, 1887; Bradley, *Lectures on Job*, 1887; R. A. Watson in *Expositor's Bible*, 1892; also Rawlinson in *Public Commentary*, 1891. The section on the book of Job found in each of the chief *Introductions* to the O. T. should, of course, be consulted. The following may be mentioned as representative: Bleek (6th ed. by Wellhausen, 1893), Riehm (ed. Brandt, 1889), Driver (6th ed. 1897), and Cornill (3d and 4th ed. 1896); Wagner, *Sermons;* Davidson, *Commentary*, vol. i; *The Drama of Job*, Rev. Chas. H. Dickinson, *Bib. Sac.*, Jan., 1900, p. 68, *sq.*

There is, perhaps, no book of Scripture of which so many versions and commentaries have been published as Job, or respecting which a greater number of treatises and dissertations have been written. The above are only notable examples.

E. W. H.

JOB'S DISEASE (jŏb's dĭz-ēz').

In this, as in most other Biblical diseases, there is too little distinct description of symptoms to enable us to determine the precise malady intended. But the general character of the complaint under which Job suffered bears a greater resemblance to elephantiasis than to any other disease. (See LEPROSY.) The passages which are considered to indicate this disease are found in the description of his skin burning from head to foot, so that he took a potsherd to scrape himself (ii:7, 8); in its being covered with putrefaction and crusts of earth, and being at one time stiff and hard, while at another it cracked and discharged fluid (vii:5); in the offensive breath which drove away the kindness of attendants (xix:17); in the restless nights, which were either sleepless or scared with frightful dreams (vii:13, 14; xxx:17); in general emaciation (xvi:8); and in so intense a loathing of the burden of life that strangling and death were preferable to it (vii:15).

W. A. N.

JOBAB (jō'băb), (Heb. יוֹבָב, *yo-bawb'*, howling, shouting, trumpet call, a desert).

1. The last of the sons of Joktan (Gen. x:29; 1 Chron. i:23). He has not left his name among the places of Southern Arabia, along with the other sons of Joktan, as far as has been discovered.

2. One of the kings of Edom (Gen. xxxvi:33, 34; 1 Chron. i:44, 45). He was the son of Zerah of Bozrah, and second king on the list.

3. One of the northern chiefs who was routed by Joshua at Meron (Josh. xi:1), B. C. probably before 1210.

4. A Benjamite, and head of a house, the first-named of the sons of Shaharim by his wife Hodesh (1 Chron. viii:9).

5. A "son" of Elpaal, a chief of Benjamin at Jerusalem (1 Chron. viii:18), B. C. about 588.

JOCHEBED (jŏk'e-bĕd), (Heb. יוֹכֶבֶד, *yo-keh'bed*, God-glorified).

Wife of Amram and mother of Miriam, Moses and Aaron. In Exod. vi:20, Jochebed is expressly declared to have been the sister of Amram's father, and consequently the aunt of her husband. As marriage between persons thus related was afterwards forbidden by the law (Lev. xviii:12), various attempts have been made to show that the relationship was more distant than the text in its literal meaning indicates. We see no necessity for this. The example of Abraham (Gen. xx:12) shows the usage of the earlier age. Further it is stated (Exod. ii:1; Num. xxvi:59) that Jochebed was the daughter of Levi, and therefore sister of Kohath, Amram's father.

JOED (jō'ed), (Heb. יוֹעֵד, *yo-ade'*, Jehovah his witness), a Benjamite, son of Pedaiah (Neh. xi:7) and grandson of Sallu, which last was a Benjamite living at Jerusalem after the captivity (B. C. before 536).

JOEL (jō'el), (Heb. יוֹאֵל, *yo-ale'*, Jehovah his God).

1. The Son of Pethuel, a person otherwise unknown to us, prophesied in Judah, probably in Jerusalem (see Joel, Hebrew Version, i:14; ii:1, 15; English Version, ii:32; iii:1, 2, 6, 7, 16, 17, 20, 21—to some of which texts Bleek, p. 525, adds i:9, 13, 16; ii:9, 17). 'Nothing is known of the circumstances of his life. There is a controversy even as to the age in which he lived. But in any case he belonged to the most ancient of the minor prophets, not to the later portion of them. Now, as Amos not only opens his prophecy with an utterance of Joel's (comp. Amos i:2 with Joel iii:16), but also concludes with promises similar to those in Joel (comp. Amos ix:13 with Joel iii:18), Joel must have prophesied before Amos; that is, before the twenty-seven years during which Uzziah and Jeroboam II reigned contemporaneously (apparently a slip of the pen, for the "the twenty-seventh year of Jeroboam, in which Azariah or Uzziah began to reign," 2 Kings xv:1). We are led to assign a still higher antiquity to the prophecies of Joel by the political relations which come into view in them; since neither the Syrians nor the Assyrians had shown themselves hostile to the theocracy, but only the Phœnicians and the Philistines (iii:4), the Egyptians and the Edomites (iii:19). On the one hand, again, there is no mention of the attack upon Jerusalem by the Syrians under Hazael of Damascus, which cost Joash not only the treasures of the palace and of the temple, but also his life (2 Kings xii:18, *sq.*; 2 Chron. xxiv:23, *sq.*; yet for this Amos (i:3-5) prophesies the ruin of the Syrian kingdom, and the carrying away of the people to Assyria. On the other hand, there are the two circumstances, that the Edomites were already punished and brought anew into subjection by Amaziah (2 Kings xiv:7), on account of their revolt from Joram, and that the Philistines had to endure the same at the hands of Uzziah (2 Chron. xxvi: 6, 7), on account of what they had done in the same reign, plundering Jerusalem and carrying away the captive Jews (2 Chron. xxi:16, 17; comp. with Joel iii:4-6). For these two reasons we are justified in concluding that Joel prophesied between Joram's reign and the last years of King Joash. Credner and Winer place him in the time of Joash; Bertholdt, in that of Hezekiah; Cramer and Eckevniaun, in Josiah's reign; Jahn, in Manasseh's, and Schröder still later.

2. The Book of Joel. (1) Occasion. The occasion of the prophecy of Joel was an entire desolation of Judah by an unheard-of plague of locusts, accompanied by a burning drought, which lasted for several years (ii:25). A calamity of this kind was not uncommon in Palestine, and, in ordinary circumstances, would not be made a subject of prophetic discourse. But the visitation described by Joel was exceptionally severe. Successive swarms of locusts swept over the country (i:4), and their devastations went on for years (ii:25). The produce of the fields, vineyards and orchards was destroyed (i:10-12). Food failed for man and beast (i:10-12, 16, 17, 18-20). The daily offering to Jehovah was suspended from lack of the necessary materials (i:9, 13; ii:14). This was equivalent to an interruption of the covenant relation between Jehovah and his people. A calamity which led to such a result was a very serious one. No prophet would have been faithful to his mission as watchman of Israel if he had failed to warn the people of the danger with which such a visitation threatened them. Joel saw in the locust invasion a special judgment from Jehovah, and used it as a text for one of the most interesting and instructive discourses contained in the prophetical books of the Old Testament.

(2) Contents. The book consists of three chapters. (The Hebrew text has four chapters, the last five verses of ch. ii in A. V. forming ch. iii in the Massoretic Text. It divides itself easily into two parts, in the first of which the prophet, and in the second Jehovah, is the speaker. The *first* half of it (i:2-ii:18) contains a call to repentance, urged by the prophet with ever-increasing urgency in the midst of the fearful plague on the land, which had been already threatened in the Law (Deut. xxiii:38, 39) against the transgressors as a punishment from God. The *second* half (ii:19-iv:21) contains the Divine promise, not only of the removal of this judgment, and of the judgment upon all nations hostile to the theocracy, but also of the glorification of the theocracy, through the bestowal of the richest natural blessings, and through the outpouring of the Spirit of God upon all flesh. The two halves are closely bound together into one whole by the historical remark which stands between them (ii:19), "And Jehovah answered, and said unto his people." Accordingly, the prediction of the future does not begin till ii:19 (though the translation in the English version seems quite defensible.

(3) Interpretation. The interpretation of the prophecy depends on the view taken of the locusts. Many of the early Fathers explained the locusts figuratively, following the Chaldee, Ephrem Syrus, Jerome and others. (Bleek, p. 526-7, names also Cyril of Alexandria, Abarbanel, Luther, Grotius and Bertholdt.)

In recent times this view has been supported in his usual fearless fashion by Hengstenberg (*Christ. of O. T.*, Eng. tr., i :296, *sq.*). According to this view, the prophecy refers to future events, and the locusts, in cc. i and ii, represent the world-powers opposed to the Church—such as Jehovah judges on his great day (iii:1, 2; comp. Heb. iv:12).

So Dr. Hengstenberg, while strongly averse to the literal sense, is not disposed to limit the metaphorical meaning to any one event or class of invaders. 'The enemy,' he remarks, 'are designated only as *north countries.* From the north, however, from Syria, all the principal invasions of Palestine proceeded. We have therefore no reason to think exclusively of any one of them. Nor ought we to limit the prophecy to the people of the old covenant. Throughout all centuries there is but one church of God existing in unbroken connection. That this church, during the first period of its existence, was concentrated in a land into which hostile irruptions were made from the north, was purely accidental. To make this circumstance the boundary-stone of the fulfillment of prophecy were just as absurd as if one were

to assert that the threatening of Amos, "by the sword shall all sinners of my people die," has not been fulfilled in those who perished after another manner.

What may be regarded as a modification of the ancient opinion of its purely figurative character has been recently proposed. According to this view the locusts are Apocalyptic—creatures of a supernatural kind, such as may fitly find a place in a vision of the last things, with which the book of Joel closes (comp. the locusts in N. T. Apocalypse).

The third and, in recent times, the most generally accepted opinion is that the locusts are real. The prophet describes an actual locust invasion and makes it the occasion of his prophecy. Keil, *Intr. to O. T.*, voicing this opinion, says: "The prophet does not foretell some future misfortune and some judgment still impending over the theocracy at the hands of armies of hostile nations, under the allegorical veil of a swarm of locusts laying the land waste; but he depicts a present judgment already come, the abiding frightful plague of locusts laying everything waste, in which he beholds the forerunners of the day of Jehovah which is near (i:15; ii:1, 2), though it may still be averted by thoroughgoing repentance (i:13, 14; ii:1, 12, 13, 15, *sq.*)."

(4) Doctrine. The prophet, after describing the approaching judgments, calls on his countrymen to repent, assuring them of the Divine placability and readiness to forgive (ii:12-17). He foretells the restoration of the land to its former fertility, and declares that Jehovah would still be their God (ii:18-26). He then announces the spiritual blessings which would be poured forth in the Messianic age (iii:1-5, Heb. text; ii:28-32, Auth. Vers.). This remarkable prediction is applied by the Apostle Peter to the events that transpired on the day of Pentecost (Acts ii:16-21). In the last chapter (iv Heb. text; iii Auth. Vers.), the Divine vengeance is denounced against the enemies and oppressors of the chosen people, of whom the Phœnicians, Egyptians, and Edomites are especially named. A minute examination of these predictions would exceed our limits; we must refer the reader for further information to the works named at the close of this article.

(5) Style and Canonicity. The style of Joel, it has been remarked, unites the strength of Micah with the tenderness of Jeremiah. In vividness of description he rivals Nahum, and in sublimity and majesty is scarcely inferior to Isaiah and Habakkuk. '*Imprimis est elegans, clarus, fusus, fluensque; valde etiam sublimis, acer, fervidus*' (Lowth, *De Sacra Poesi Hebr.* Præl. xxi).

The canonicity of this book has never been called in question (Keil, *Int. to O. T.*; C. G. Cameron in Hastings' *Bib. Dict.*).

(6) Literature. *A Paraphrase and Critical Commentary on the Prophecy of Joel*, by Samuel Chandler, London, 1745; *Die Weissagung des Propheten Joel, übersetzt und erklärt*, von F. A. Holzhausen, Göttingen, 1829; *Characteristik der Bibel*, von Dr. A. H. Niemeyer, Halle, 1831, vol. v, pp. 295-302; Dr. Hengstenberg's *Christology of the Old Testament, etc.*, transl. by Dr. R. Keith, Washington, 1839, vol. iii. pp. 100-141; Pusey, *Minor Prophets*, 1860; W. R. Smith, art. *Joel* in 9th ed. of *Enc. Brit.*; Farrar, *Minor Prophets*, 113 *sq.*; Ewald, *Prophets*, Eng. tr. i, 107 *sq.*; Reuss *At.* ii, 47 *sq.*; Nowack, *Kl. Proph.*, 1897; G. A. Smith, *Twelve Prophets*, vol. ii, 1898; Cheyne, *Founders of O. T. Crit.*, 312; A. B. Davidson in *Expositor*, March, 1888; Gray, *Expositor*, Sept., 1893.

3. Joel, the Son of the Prophet Samuel
(1 Sam. viii:2; 1 Chron. vi:33; xv:17). With his brother Abiah he was made judge of Beersheba, when old age prevented their father from longer making his circuit; but they were corrupt and their judgments disgraced both them and their father. It was this conduct that brought about the change of the constitution of Israel to a monarchy. In 1 Chron. vi:28 Vashni, mentioned with Abiah, has been substituted for Joel (B. C. 1030).

4. Joel, son of Azariah or Uzziah (1 Chron. vi:36). The name, however, is supposed to be a corruption of Shaul (ver. 24).

5. The head of one of the Simeonite families, who joined the expedition against the Hamites in the time of Hezekiah (1 Chron. iv:35), B. C. 715.

6. A descendant of Reuben, but whether through Hanoch or Carmi is a disputed point (Burrington, *Geneal.* i:53; 1 Chron. v:4, 8).

7. A Gadite chief of Bashan (1 Chron. v:12), B. C. about 1000.

8. Son of Izrahiah of the tribe of Issachar, and one of David's military officers (1 Chron. vii:3), B. C. about 1000.

9. Brother of Nathan and a member of David's guard (1 Chron. xi:38). In 2 Sam. xxiii:36 the name Igal is substituted (B. C. about 1000).

10. Chief of the Gershonites, who brought up the ark from the house of Obed-edom in the reign of David (1 Chron. xv:7, 11).

11. A Gershonite Levite, son of Jehiel (1 Chron. xxvi:22), having charge of the treasures of the Temple under David. Probably the same as Joel, **9.**

12. Son of Pedaiah and chief of the half-tribe of Manasseh on the west of the Jordan in the reign of David (1 Chron. xxvii:20), B. C. about 1000.

13. A Kohathite Levite, one of the two representatives of his tribe in the ceremonies preceding the restoration of the Temple in the time of Hezekiah (2 Chron. xxix:12), B. C. 719.

14. "Son" of Nebo and one of those returning with Ezra, who had taken a foreign wife (Ezra x:43), B. C. 456.

15. A Benjamite, son of Zichri, commanding Judah and his own tribe at Jerusalem after the return from Babylon (Neh. xi:9).

JOELAH (jo-ē'lah), (Heb. יוֹעֵאלָה, *yo-ay-law'*, furthermore), son of Jeroham, of Gedor, who came to David at Ziklag (1 Chron xii:7), B. C. before 1000.

JOEZER (jo-ē'zer), (Heb. יוֹעֶזֶר, *yo-eh'zer*, Jehovah his help), a Korhite captain, who fought by David while he dwelt among the Philistines (1 Chron. xii:6), B. C. before 1000.

JOGBEHAH (jŏg'be-häh), (Heb. יָגְבְּהָה, *yog-beh-haw'*, hillock), one of the "fenced cities" rebuilt by the tribe of Gad when they took possession of their territory east of the Jordan (Num. xxxii:35).

It is mentioned in the account of Gideon's victory over the Midianites (Judg. viii:11). No trace of the place has been found; but it could not have been far from the Jordan, judging from the places with which it is associated.

JOGLI (jŏg'lī), (Heb. יָגְלִי, *yog-lee'*, exiled), of Bukki, a Danite chief (Num. - xxxiv:22), B. C. 1170.

JOHA (jō'hà), (Heb. יוֹחָא, *yo-khaw'*, probably, Jehovah lives).

1. A son of Beriah, a Benjamite chief, dwelling in Aijalon, who had driven out the inhabitants

of Gath (1 Chron. viii:16). Perhaps the same encounter is referred to in viii:13, and 1 Chron. vii: 21 (B. C. about 588).

2. A Tizite, and, according to Kennicott, son of Shimri. He was one of David's guard (1 Chron. xi:45), B. C. 1000.

JOHANAN (jo-hā'nan), (Heb. יוֹחָנָן, *yo-khaw-nawn'*, God-bestowed).

1. One of the officers who came and recognized Gedaliah as governor of Judæa after the destruction of Jerusalem, and who appears to have been the chief in authority and influence among them. He penetrated the designs of Ishmael against the governor, whom he endeavored, without success, to put upon his guard. When Ishmael had accomplished his design by the murder of Gedaliah, and was carrying away the principal persons at the seat of government as captives to the Ammonites, Johanan pursued him and released them. Being fearful, however, that the Chaldæans might misunderstand the affair, and make him and those who were with him responsible for it, he resolved to withdraw for safety into Egypt, with the principal persons of the remnant left in the land. Jeremiah remonstrated against this decision; but Johanan would not be moved, and even constrained the prophet himself to go with them. They proceeded to Taphanes, but nothing further is recorded of Johanan, B. C. 588 (2 Kings xxv: 23; Jer. xl:8-16; xli; xlii; xliii).

2. Son of Azariah, and grandson of Ahimaaz (1 Chron. vi:9, 10). He was high-priest, probably, in the reign of Rehoboam (Hervey, *Geneal.* ch. x).

3. Son of Elioenai in the line of Zerubbabel's heirs (1 Chron. iii:24), B. C. after 400.

4. Eldest son of King Josiah (1 Chron. iii:15). He must have previously died or fallen with Josiah at Megiddo (B. C. after 639).

5. A Benjamite captain, who joined David at Ziklag (1 Chron. xii:4), B. C. 1000.

6. The eighth of the "lion faced" warriors of Gad who joined David (1 Chron. xii:12), B. C. 1000.

7. Father of Azariah, a head of the Ephraimites in the time of Ahaz (2 Chron. xxviii:12), B. C. about 735.

8. Son of Hakkatan, and chief of the sons of Azgad, who came back with Ezra (Ezra viii:12), B. C. about 457.

9. Son of Eliashib (Neh. xii:23). To his chamber Ezra retired and mourned over the sins of the people who had been carried away (Ezra x:6).

10. Son of Tobiah, the Ammonite, who married the daughter of the priest Meshullam (Neh. vi:18), B. C. 445.

JOHN (jŏn), (Gr. Ἰωάννης, *ee-o-an'naçe*, from Hebrew Jehohanan, Jehovah favored).

1. A member of the family of the high-priest. He, with Caiaphas and Annas, heard the case brought against Peter and John for curing the lame man and preaching in the temple (Acts iv:6). Lightfoot (*Cent. Chor. Matth. præf.* ch. 15) identifies him with R. Johanan ben Zaccai, president of the great synagogue after its removal to Jabne.

2. Hebrew name for MARK. In Acts xii:12, 25; xiii:5, 13; xv:37, he is designated by the name under which he was known among his countrymen. (See MARK.)

3. The Apostle John, who was the son of Zebedee, a fisherman, and of Salome. It is probable that he was born at Bethsaida, on the lake of Galilee. His parents appear to have been in easy circumstances; at least, we find that Zebedee employed hired servants (Mark i:20), and that Salome was among the number of those women who contributed to the maintenance of Jesus (Matt. xxvii:56).

The Apostle John.

(1) Belonged to Wealthy Class. We also find that John received Mary into his house after the death of Jesus. Since this house seems to have been situated at Jerusalem ("from that hour," John xix:27), it would appear that he was the owner of two houses. John's acquaintance, also, with the high-priest (xviii:15) seems to indicate that he lived at Jerusalem, and belonged to the wealthier class.

(2) Religiously Inclined. We may suppose that from a tender age he nourished religious feelings, since Salome, who evinced so much love for Jesus, probably fostered at an earlier period those hopes of a Messiah which she expresses in Matt. xx:20; and we find that he entered into communion with the Baptist from pure motives. The occupation, also, of a fisherman was adapted to promote holy meditations, since it would frequently lead him to pass whole nights in stillness upon the water, amid a charming country similar to the environs of the lake of Maggiore.

(3) Called by John the Baptist. On the banks of the Jordan the Baptist directed John to Jesus, and he immediately became the Lord's disciple, and accompanied him on his return to Galilee. Having arrived there, he at first resumed his trade, but was afterwards called to remain permanently with the Redeemer (Luke v:5-10). Jesus was particularly attached to John (John xiii:23; xix:26; xx:2; xxi:7), who was one of the three who were distinguished above the other Apostles (Matt. xvii:1; xxvi:37; Mark v:37).

(4) Apostleship. After the ascension, John abode at Jerusalem, where Paul met him on his third journey, about the year 52 (Gal. ii:3-9). Since he had undertaken the care of the mother of Jesus we cannot well suppose that he left Jerusalem before Mary's death; and, indeed, we find that about the year 58, when Paul was at Ephesus, John was not living there yet. If we consider the great importance of Ephesus among the various churches of Asia Minor, and the dangers arising from false teachers, who were prevalent there as early as the days of Paul (Acts xx:29), it will appear likely that John was sent to Ephesus after Paul had left that scene, about the year 65. During the time of his activity in Asia Minor he was exiled by the Roman emperor to Patmos, one of the sporadic isles in the Ægean Sea, where, according to Revelations i:9, he wrote the Apocalypse. Irenæus (*Adv. Hær.* v. 30) and, following him, Eusebius (*Hist. Eccles.* iii:18) state that John beheld the visions of the Apocalypse about the close of the reign of Domitian.

(5) Exile to Patmos. If this statement can be depended upon, the exile to Patmos also took place under Domitian, who died A. D. 96. Tertullian (*Præscr. adv. Hær.* c. 30) relates that in the reign of Domitian, John was forcibly conveyed to Rome, where he was thrown into a cask of oil; that he was miraculously released, and then brought to Patmos. But since none of the ancient writers besides the rather undiscriminating Tertullian, relate this circumstance, and since this mode of capital punishment was unheard of at Rome, we ought not to lay much stress upon it (compare Mosheim, *Dissertationes ad Historiam Ecclesiasticam*, i, p. 497, *sq.*). It is, however, likely that John was called to suffer for his faith, since Polycrates, bishop of Ephesus, writing about A. D. 200, calls him μάρτυς (*martyr*) (Euseb.

Reputed Tomb of St. John.

Hist. Eccles. v. 24). According to Eusebius (*Hist. Eccles.* iii:20, 23), he returned from exile during the reign of Nerva.

(6) Epistles. The three epistles of John, as also the affecting account concerning his fidelity as a spiritual pastor, given by Clemens Alexandrinus (*Quis Dives Salvus?* ch. 52), testify that he was the pastor of a large diocese. John's second epistle, verse 12, and third epistle, verse 14, indicate that he made journeys of pastoral visitation.

(7) **Death.** John died at Ephesus past the age of ninety, in the reign of the Emperor Trajan. According to Jerome, he was a hundred years old, and according to Suidas, a hundred and twenty.

Jerome (*Comm. ad Gal.* iii, p. 314, mart.) relates that when John had attained a great age he was so feeble that he could not walk to the assemblies of the church; he, therefore, caused himself to be carried in by young men. He was no longer able to say much, but he constantly repeated the words, 'Little children, love one another.' On being asked why he constantly repeated this one saying, he replied: 'Because it is the command of the Lord; and enough is done if this is done.' (French, *Life and Character of John the Evangelist;* Stanley, *Sermons and Essays on the Apost. Age,* iv.)

JOHN THE BAPTIST (Gr.'Ιωάννης ὁ Βαπτιστής, *ee-o-an'ace ho bap-tis-tacé,* John the baptizer), the forerunner of Jesus Christ, or simply 'Ιωάννης, *John,* when the reference is clear, as in Matt. iii:4; iv:12; Lat. Joannes, Tacit. *Hist.* v:12.

(1) **Birth and Early Life.** His parents were Zacharias and Elisabeth, the latter a cousin of Mary, the mother of Jesus, whose senior John was by a period of six months (Luke i). According to the account contained in the first chapter of Luke his father while engaged in burning incense, was visited by the angel Gabriel, who informed him that in compliance with his prayers his wife should bear a son, whose name he should call John—in allusion to the grace thus accorded. Zacharias is slow to believe these tidings and seeks some token in evidence of their truth. Accordingly, a sign is given which acts also as a punishment of his want of faith—his tongue is sealed till the prediction is fulfilled by the event. Six months after Elisabeth had conceived she received a visit from Mary, the future mother of Jesus. On being saluted by her relation, Elisabeth felt her babe leap in her womb, and, being filled with the Holy Spirit, she broke forth into a poetic congratulation to Mary, as the destined mother of her Lord. At length Elisabeth brought forth a son, whom the relatives were disposed to name Zacharias, after his father —but Elisabeth was in some way led to wish that he should be called John. The matter was referred to the father, who signified in writing that his name was to be John. This agreement with Elisabeth caused all to marvel. Zacharias now had his tongue loosed, and he first employed his restored power in praising God.

The parents of John were not only of a priestly order, but righteous and devout. Their influence, in consequence, in the training of their son, would not only be benign but suitable to the holy office which he was designed to fill. More than this— the special aids of God's Spirit were with him (Luke i:66). How thoroughly Zacharias was penetrated with his parental responsibility and the future dignity of his son, appears from the 'divine song' to which he gives utterance. As a consequence of the lofty influences under which he was nurtured, the child waxed strong in spirit. The sacred writer adds that 'he was in the deserts till the day of his showing unto Israel' (Luke i:80).

(2) **Beginning of Ministry.** In the fifteenth year of the Emperor Tiberius, John made his public appearance, exhibiting the austerity, the costume, and the manner of life of the ancient Jewish prophets (Luke iii; Matt. iv). His raiment was camel's hair; he wore a plain leathern girdle about his loins; his food was what the desert spontaneously offered—locusts and wild honey from the rock. The burden of John's preaching bore no slight resemblance to the old prophetic exhortations, whose last echo had now died away for centuries. He called upon the Jewish people to repent (μετανοεῖτε), *to change their minds,* their dispositions and affections, and thus prepared the way for the great doctrine promulgated by his Lord, of the necessity of a spiritual regeneration. That the change which John had in view was by no means of so great or so elevated a kind as that which Jesus required, is very probable; but the particulars into which he enters when he proceeds to address classes or individuals (Matt. iii:7, *sq.,* Luke iii:7, *sq.*), serve fully to show that the renovation at which he aimed was not merely of a material or organic, but chiefly of a moral nature. In a very emphatic manner did he warn the ecclesiastical and philosophical authorities of the land of the necessity under which they lay of an entire change of view, of aim, and of desire, declaring in explicit and awful terms that their pride of nationality would avail them nothing against the coming wrathful visitation, and that they were utterly mistaken in the notion that Divine providence had any need of them for completing its own wise purposes (Luke iii:8, 9). The first reason assigned by John for entering on his most weighty and perilous office was announced in these words—'the kingdom of heaven is at hand.' It was his great work to prepare the mind of the nation, so that when Jesus himself came they might be a people made ready for the Lord. The reference which we have made to John's addresses to his auditors suffices to show that there was an ample and predominant moral element in his conception of this kingdom; and indeed the whole tenor of his teaching seems to our mind intended and fitted to refine, exalt, and expand the ordinary Jewish mind and so to prepare the way for the perfect day of Christ.

The doctrine and manner of life of John appear to have roused the entire of the south of Palestine, and people flocked from all parts to the spot where, on the banks of the Jordan, he baptized thousands unto repentance. Such, indeed, was the fame which he had gained, that 'people were in expectation, and all men mused in their hearts of John, whether he were the Christ or not' (Luke iii:15). Had he chosen, John might without doubt have assumed to himself the higher office, and risen to great worldly power. But he was faithful to his trust, and never failed to declare it in the fullest and clearest manner, that he was not the Christ but merely his harbinger, and that the sole work he had to do was to usher in "the dayspring from on high."

(3) **Meeting with Jesus.** The more than prophetic fame of the Baptist reached the ears of Jesus in his Nazarene dwelling, far distant from the locality of John (Matt. ii:9, 11). The nature of the report—namely, that his divinely predicted forerunner had appeared in Judæa—showed our Lord that the time was now come for his being made manifest to Israel. Accordingly he comes to the place where John is, to be baptized of him, in order that thus he might fulfill all that was required under the dispensation which was about to disappear (Matt. iii:14). John's sense of inferiority inclines him to ask rather than to give baptism in the case of Jesus, who, however, wills to have it otherwise, and is accordingly baptized of John.

Immediately upon the termination of this symbolical act, a divine attestation is given from the opened vault of heaven, declaring Jesus to be in truth the long looked-for Messiah—'This is my beloved Son, in whom I am well pleased' (Matt. iii:17). The events which are found recorded in John i:19, *sq.*, seem to have happened after the baptism of Jesus by John. This appears to us to be implied in the *past* character of the narrative. John is obviously speaking of something over and gone; for instance, "This is he of whom I *said* (not I *say*), 'after me cometh a man,' " etc.

The relation which subsisted between John and Jesus, after the emphatic testimony above recorded had been borne, we have not the materials to describe with full certainty.

It seems but natural to think, when their hitherto relative position is taken into account, that John would forthwith lay down his office of harbinger, which, now that the Sun of Righteousness himself had appeared, was entirely fulfilled and terminated. Such a step he does not appear to have taken. On the contrary, the language of Scripture seems to imply that the Baptist church continued side by side with the Messianic (Matt. xi:2; Luke vii:19; Matt. ix:14; Luke xi:1; Acts xviii:25), and remained long after John's execution (Acts xix:3). Indeed, a sect which bears the name of 'John's disciples' exists to the present day in the East, whose sacred books are said to be pervaded by a Gnostic leaven.

(4) Subsequent Ministry. Still, though it has been generally assumed that John did not lay down his office, we are not satisfied that the New Testament establishes this alleged fact. John may have ceased to execute his own peculiar work, as the forerunner, but may justifiably have continued to bear his most important testimony to the Messiahship of Christ; or he may even have altogether given up the duties of active life some time, at least, before his death; and yet his disciples, both before and after that event, may have maintained their individuality as a religious communion. It was, not improbably, with a view to remove some error of this kind that John sent the embassy of his disciples to Jesus, which is recorded in Matt. xi:3; Luke vii:19. The spiritual course which the teachings of Jesus were more and more taking, and the apparent failure or at least uneasy postponement of the promised kingdom in the popular sense, especially the fact that their esteemed master lay in prison, and was in imminent danger of losing his life, may well have led John's disciples to doubt if Jesus were in truth the expected Messiah. Appearances, to them, were purely adverse. What step so fit on the part of their master, as that he should send them to Jesus himself? No intimation is found in the record that *John* required evidence to give him satisfaction; and all the language that is used is proper and pertinent if we suppose that the doubt lay only in the minds of his disciples. That the terms employed *admit* the interpretation that John was not without some misgivings (Luke vii:23; Matt. xi:6), we are free to allow. And if any doubt had grown up in the Baptist's mind it was most probably owing to the defective spirituality of his views; for even of him Jesus has declared, 'he that is least in the kingdom of heaven is greater than he' (Matt. xi:11). Were this the case it would of itself account not only for the embassy sent by John to Jesus, but also for the continuance and perpetuation of John's separate influence as the founder of a sect.

(5) Imprisonment and Death. The manner of John's death is too well known to require to be detailed here (Matt. iv:12; xiv:3; Luke iii:19;

Mark vi:17; Joseph. *Antiq.* xviii, 5, 2). He reproved a tyrant for a heinous crime, and received his reward in decapitation.

John the Baptist is mentioned in the Koran with much honor, under the name of Jahja.

(6) Literature. Neander, *Life of Jesus;* Taylor, *Life of Christ;* Olshausen, *Com. on the Gospels;* Farrar, *Life of Christ;* Edersheim, *Life of Christ.*

JOHN, GOSPEL OF.

(1) Authenticity and Credibility. During the eighteenth century and the first ten years of the nineteenth, the Gospel of John was attacked, but with feeble arguments, by some English deists and by four German theologians: Bretschneider (*Probabilia de Evangelii et Epistolarum Johannis origine et indole,* 1820); Strauss, (*The Life of Jesus*); Lützelberger (*Die kirchliche Tradition über den Apostel Johannes und seine Schriften,* 1840); and Schwegler (*Der Montanismus und die Christliche Kirche des zweiten Jahrhunderts,* 1841). However, even in Germany, the opponents of its authenticity have not met with much sympathy.

The credibility of the Gospel of St. John is open to attack on account of its differing so much, as well in substance as in form, from the three first Gospels, and on account of its apparent contradiction of them. Among the apparent contradictions may be mentioned the statements that Christ was crucified on the same day on which the Passover was to be eaten (John xviii:28), while according to the other Gospels Jesus ate the Passover with his disciples; and that Jesus, before he went to Gethsemane, offered up a prayer full of sublimity and confidence (xvii), while according to the other Gospels he endured in Gethsemane a very heavy internal conflict, respecting which John is silent. But the most striking difference is that of the speeches. This difference is, perhaps, still more apparent in the form than in the substance of them.

(2) The History and the Speeches. This difference may be accounted for by supposing that John intended to relate and complete the history of the Lord according to his own view of it. We are led to this supposition from the following circumstances; that, with the exception of the history of his passion and his resurrection, there are only two sections in which John coincides with the synoptic gospels (vi:1-21; xii:1); that he altogether omits such important facts as the baptism of Jesus by John, the history of his temptation and transfiguration, the institution of the Lord's supper, and the internal conflict at Gethsemane; and that chapters i:32; iii:24; xi:2, indicate that he presupposed his readers to be already acquainted with the Gospel history. He confined himself to such communications as were wanting in the others, especially with regard to the speeches of Jesus. The historical section in chapter vi he communicated because it is connected with the subsequent speeches of Jesus; and chapter xii:1, because it was of importance for him to relate the history of Judas, so that each event should clearly be understood to be the result of a preceding fact. The history of Christ's sufferings and resurrection, being a prominent part, could not be omitted, although, in the account of these also, John differs in his statements from the writers of the other Gospels Clemens Alexandrinus (Euseb. *Hist. Eccles.* vi: 14) relates, as he says, upon the statement of old Presbyters, that John wrote his Gospel at the request of his friends, in order to place by the side of the σωματικὰ εὐαγγέλια, *bodily gospels*, his πνευματικὸν εὐαγγέλιον, *spiritual gospel*. The same account is confirmed by a Latin fragment of the second century preserved by Muratori, in which it is recorded that the aged apostle was solicited by his co-disciples to commit his Gospel to writing.

Now with regard to the difference of form. In the Gospel of John, Jesus seldom speaks in gnomes, sentences, and parables, but generally in longer speeeches, the parts of which are not closely connected, containing frequent repetitions, and the linguistic characteristics of which strongly resemble those of John's epistles.

The gentle and feminine character of the disciple allows us to suppose that, to a certain degree, he adopted as his own the expressions of the Redeemer, and, consequently, that many terms in which the Epistles agree with the Gospel did not originate with the disciple, but with Christ himself. We find an example of the manner in which the disciple adopted the expressions of his Master in John xii:43, compared with v:41-44. We do not deny that the formation of sentences and expressions is considerably influenced by the peculiar character of the disciple, but with regard to the particular contents of the speeches, we see no reason why we should doubt their authenticity. Strauss himself makes a concession from which much results, namely, that the most characteristic speeches in John are those in which occur the antitheses of σάρξ and πνεῦμα, *flesh* and *spirit*, φῶς and σκότος, *light* and *darkness*, ζωή and θάνατος, *life* and *death*, ἄνω and κάτω, *above* and *below;* and also the mystical expressions of ἄρτος τῆς ζωῆς, *bread of life*, ὕδωρ ζῶν, *living water*. These terms are even by Strauss (vol. i. p. 176) considered to be parts of the original speeches of Christ, and he asserts that the evangelist only developed them in the style of the Alexandrian writers.

(3) Peculiarities. It must be granted that the peculiarities of John's Gospel more especially consist in the four following doctrines:.
(1) That of the mystical relation of the Son to the Father.
(2) That of the mystical relation of the Redeemer to believers.
(3) The announcement of the Holy Ghost as the Comforter.
(4) The peculiar importance ascribed to Love.

Although there can be shown in the writings of the other evangelists some isolated dicta of the Lord, which seem to bear the impress of John, it can also be shown that they contain thoughts not originating with that disciple, but with the Lord himself. Matthew (xi:27) speaks of the relation of the Son to the Father so entirely in the style of John that persons not sufficiently versed in Holy Writ are apt to search for this passage in the Gospel of John. The mystical union of the Son with believers is expressed in Matt. xxviii:20. The promise of the effusion of the Holy Ghost in order to perfect the disciples is found in Luke xxiv:49. The doctrine of Paul with respect to love, in 1 Cor. xiii, entirely resembles what, according to John, Christ taught on the same subject. Paul here deserves our particular attention. In the writings of Paul are found Christian truths which have their points of coalescence only in John, viz., that Christ is Εἰκὼν τοῦ Θεοῦ τοῦ ἀοράτου, *the image of the invisible God*, by whom all things are created (Col. i:15, 16). Paul considers the Spirit of God in the church, *the spiritual Christ*, as Jesus himself does (John xiv:16), frequently using the words εἶναι ἐν Χριστῷ, *ei-nay en Chris-to'*, to be in Christ.

That the speeches of Christ have been faithfully reported may be seen by a comparison of the speeches of the Baptist in the Gospel of John. The Baptist speeches bear an entirely Old Testament character; they are full of gnomes, allusions to the Old Testament, and sententious expressions (John iii:27-30; i:26-36).

(4) Place, Time, and Language. The Fathers supposed that the Gospel of John was written at Ephesus. The author of a synopsis annexed to the works of Athanasius makes an observation which deserves to be noticed on account of the assurance with which it is advanced. It is, that John wrote the Gospel which bears his name in Patmos, but that it was edited by the same Gaius whom Paul in the epistle to the Romans calls ὁ ξένος μου, *mine host* (Athanasii *Opera*, vol. ii, p. 155, Venet.). One might be inclined to explain by this circumstance the postscript contained in John xxi:24, 25.

There is some internal evidence in favor of the statement that this Gospel was written at Ephesus —namely, that the author sometimes alludes to the tenets of Hellenistic theosophy, and that he has in view readers who do not live in Palestine (John ii:6, 13; iv:9; v:1, 2). In addition to this must be mentioned the command of the Hellenistic Greek evinced by the writer. It is, however, not unlikely that John acquired his knowledge of Greek in his native country. The researches of Dr. Paulus, Hug, and Credner, have rendered it highly probable that the knowledge of Greek was then widely spread in Palestine. Even James, the brother of our Lord, although he never left his native country, writes in his epistle tolerably good Greek.

The language of John's Gospel is not very periodic, but moves uniformly on between the particles δέ, *but;* and οὖν, *moreover*. This defect of style may, however, be explained by the mental characteristics of the disciple. John's mind was deficient in the dialectic element; he wanted the logical acuteness of Paul. Even where he reports the speeches of Christ, we often find a want of precision in his representation. The simplicity of John's character is also evinced by the repetition of certain leading thoughts, reproduced in the same words both in the Gospel and in the Epistles; such as μαρτυρία, *testimony;* δόξα, *glory;* ἀλήθεια, *truth;* φῶς, *light;* σκότος, *darkness;* ζωή αἰώνιος, *eternal life;* μένειν, *to abide*.

(5) Interpreters. Among the ancient commentators upon John's Gospel, Chrysostom deserves the first place. The two compilers, Theophylact, who died A. D. 1107, and Euthymius Zigabenus, who died after A. D. 1118, are also worthy of notice. Among the Roman Catholic interpreters, Maldonatus, who died in 1583, is distinguished by originality and accuracy. Calvin is distinguished above the other Reformers for the originality and ease of his interpretation, but his commentary on the Epistles is more carefully worked out than that on the Gospel. Beza is characterized by philological and critical learning. The most complete commentary on the Gospel of John is that of Lampe, (*Commentarius Exegetico-Analyticus in Evangelium Johannis,* Amstelodami, 1637, 3 vols. 4to). The style of this commentary is tasteless and stiff, but in learning the author has not been surpassed by any other interpreter. Lücke (3d ed. 1840) is the most comprehensive of the modern commentators. Shorter commentaries have been written by Tholuck (5th ed.), by Olshausen (3d ed. 1832), and by De Wette (2d ed. 1839).

As introductions to the study of the writings of John, we may mention Frommann's *Johanneischer Lehrbegriff,* 1831, and Neander's *Abriss der Jo-*

hanneischen Lehre in his *Geschichte der Pflanzung der Christlichen Kirche* (3d ed. 1841, p. 75, *sq.*).

Against its Genuineness. See J. J. Taylor, *Attempt to ascertain the Character of the Fourth Gospel*, Lond., 1867; Davidson, *Introd. to the N. T., Lond.*, 1868; *Was John the Author of the Fourth Gospel?* by a layman, Lond., 1868.

For the Genuineness. See Fisher, *The Genuineness of the Fourth Gospel*, in *Essays on the Supernatural Origin of Christianity*, N. Y., 1866; Thenius, *Das Evangelium der Evangelien*, Leipz., 1865; Gage's transl. of *The Origin of the Four Gospels, by* Tischendorf, Am. Tract. Soc., 1868; Row. *Hist. Character of the Gospels tested*, Journal of *Sacr. Lit.*, Oct., 1865, July, 1866; Mombert, *Origin of the Gospels, in Bibl. Sacra*, Oct., 1866; F. Clarke, *The Fourth Gospel and its Author, in Christian Exam.*, Jan., 1868. On doctrine see Westcott, *Introd. to the Study of the Gospels*, Boston, 1862; Scholten, *Das Ev. nach Johannes*, Berl., 1867; Neander, *Pflanzung und Leitung*, Eng. transl. by Robinson, N. Y., 1865.

JOHN HYRCANUS (jŏn hyr'kā-nus). See MACCABEES.

JOHN MARK. See MARK.

JOHN, THE FIRST EPISTLE GENERAL OF.

(1) **Authenticity.** For the authenticity of the first epistle very ancient testimony may be adduced. Papias, the disciple of John, quotes some passages from it. Polycarp, also, another disciple of John, quotes a passage from this epistle (*ad Philipp.*, c:7. So, also Irenæus (*Adv. Hær*, iii: 16; v:8).

The author of the first epistle describes himself, at its commencement, as an eye-witness of the life of our Lord. The style and language manifestly harmonize with those of the author of the Gospel of John. The polemics, also, which in chapter ii: 18-26, are directed against the Docetic Gnostics, in chapter iv:1-3, agree with the sphere of action in Asia Minor in which the Evangelist John was placed. We may, therefore, suppose that the epistle was written to Christian congregations in Asia Minor, which were placed under the spiritual care of the apostle. It is generally admitted that chapter i:2 refers to the Gospel. If this is correct, the apostle wrote this epistle at a very advanced age, after he had written his gospel. The epistle breathes love and devotion, but also zeal for moral strictness (iii:6-8; v:16). There is a remarkable absence of logical connection in the form of separate expressions, and in the transitions from one thought to another. Some writers have been inclined to find a reason for this in the advanced age of the writer. Old age may, perhaps, have contributed to this characteristic, but it is chiefly attributable to the mental peculiarity of the apostle.

(2) **Time and Place of Writing the First Epistle.** On this head nothing certain can be determined. It has been conjectured by many interpreters, ancient and modern, that it was written at the same place as the Gospel. The more ancient tradition places the writing of the Gospel at Ephesus, and a less authentic report refers it to the island of Patmos. Hug (*Introduction*) infers, from the absence of writing materials (3 John 13), that all John's Epistles were composed at Patmos! The most probable opinion is that it was written somewhere in Asia Minor, in which was the ordinary residence of the Apostle (Euseb. *Hist. Eccl.* iii:23), perhaps, according to the tradition of the Greek church, at Ephesus; but for this we have no historical warrant (Lücke's *Commentary*).

It is equally difficult to determine the time of the writing of this Epistle, although it was most probably posterior to the Gospel, which seems to be referred to in 1 John i:4. Some are of opinion that the Epistle was an envelope or accompaniment to the Gosepl, and that they were consequently written nearly simultaneously (Hug's *Introd.*). It has been argued by several, from chapter ii:18 (ἐσχάτη ὥρα ἐστίν, *it is the last time*), that the Epistle was written *before* the destruction of Jerusalem.

Various, indeed, have been the hypotheses regarding the persons to whom this Epistle was written, but it is by no means improbable, from the absence of Old Testament references, that it was addressed to Gentile converts, of which there were several congregations in Asia Minor.

(3) **Object and Design.** The main object and design of this Epistle has been generally perceived to consist in the refutation of certain errors and heresies in the churches subject to St. John's episcopate. But opinions are divided as to who the teachers of these heresies were, whether Jews, Ebionites, Gnostics, Docetæ, Cerinthus and his followers, or finally the disciples of John the Baptist. This polemical object appears, however, to form but a secondary part of the design of John, his main object being rather to enforce the necessity of progressive sanctification, genuine brotherly love, and the renunciation of the world. The design of the Epistle is didactic rather than polemical.

Another portion of this Epistle seems directed against a certain class of antinomian Christians, who perverted Christian liberty into antichristian licentiousness and libertinism, and decided what was sinful or otherwise, not according to the positive law of God, but by their own internal feelings—thus confounding light and darkness, God and the world. This vital error was rather to be found among the heathen than the Jewish Christians, and was probably founded on a perversion of St. Paul's doctrine of justification by faith. (See Augustine, *Tractat. x, in Ep. Johannis ad Parthos;* Luther's *Zwiefache Ausleg.* ed. Walch. vol ix; Whiston's *Commentary on the 3 Cath. Epist. of St. John.*)

There has been no subject connected with Biblical literature which has attracted more attention than this epistle, in consequence of the controversies which have existed since the commencement of the sixteenth century, respecting the once contested but now rejected passage in 1 John v:7, 8. It is sufficient here to say that the disputed passage is found in no Greek manuscript save two, both belonging to the fifteenth century; and that it has not once been quoted by any of the Greek, Latin or Oriental fathers. It is now generally omitted in all critical editions of the New Testament, as it is in the R. V. (See Dean Turton's *Vindication of the Literary Character of Professor Porson from the Animadversions of the Right Rev. Thomas Burgess, D. D., etc.*, published under the name of Crito-Cantabrigiensis, 1827.) The *Memoir of the Controversy Respecting the Heavenly Witnesses* (1830), by the Rev. W. Orme, contains interesting critical notices of the principal writers on both sides of this much agitated question. Dr. Tregelles, in *Journ. Sacr. Lit.*, April, 1858, p. 167, *sq.*, exposes the misstatements of Dr. Turnbull; Candlish, *Lectures.*   W. W.

JOHN, THE SECOND AND THIRD EPISTLES OF.

Authenticity. Eusebius places the second and third epistles of John among the *an-tee-leh-gom-eh'na*, ἀντιλεγομένα, disputed books (*Hist. Eccles.* iii:25).

The second epistle is addressed to a lady, called Κυρία, *koo-ree'ah*, Kuria, *Lady*, which name frequently occurs in ancient writers as that of a woman (comp. Lücke's *Commentar*, p. 351).

The third epistle is addressed to Gaius, a person otherwise unknown. It is remarkable that the writer of this epistle calls himself ὁ πρεσβύτερος, *ho-pres-bu'ter-os*, the elder, or presbyter. Some writers have been inclined to ascribe these letters to the presbyter John, who is sometimes spoken of in the ancient church, and to whom even the Apocalypse has been attributed; but if the presbyter John wrote these epistles, John's Gospel also must be ascribed to the same person, of whom otherwise so little is known. This, however, is inadmissible. We may suppose that the term, πρεσβύτερος, *elder*, expressed in the epistles of John a degree of friendliness, and was chosen on account of the advanced age of the writer. The apostle Paul, also, in his friendly letters to Philemon, abstains from the title Apostle. The circumstances and events in the church, to which the second epistle alludes, coincide with those which are otherwise known to have happened in John's congregation. Here, also, are allusions to the dangers arising from the Gnostic heresy. The admonition, in verse 10, not to receive such heretics as Christian brethren, agrees with the ancient tradition, that John made haste to quit a public bath after Cerinthus the Gnostic entered it, declaring he was afraid the building would fall down.

Rickli's *Johannis erster Brief erklärt und angewendet mit historischem Vorbericht und erklärenden Anmerkungen* (Lucerne, 1828); Lücke's *Auslegung* (2d ed. 1836). Dr. Shepherd's *Notes on the Gospels and Epistles of St. John*, 4to, 1796; and the only separate work on the Epistles is Hawkins' *Commentary on the Epistles of St. John*, 1808. A translation of Lücke's *Commentary on the Epistles of St. John* exists in the Biblical Cabinet, vol. xv. Saml. Cox, *The Private Letters of St. Paul and John*, Lond., 1867. (See also literature cited under JOHN, THE FIRST EPISTLE GENERAL OF.) A. T.

JOIADA (joi'a-dà), (Heb. יוֹיָדָע, *yo-yaw-daw'*, Jehovah knows), contraction of JEHOIADA (which see).

1. A high-priest of the Jews, successor to Eliashib, or Joashib, who lived under Nehemiah, B. C. about 434 (Neh. xii:10, 11, 22; xiii:28).

2. Son of Paseah, and apparently one of the chief priests. He helped to repair the Old Gate, after the captivity (Neh. iii:6).

JOIAKIM (joi'a-kĭm), (Heb. יוֹיָקִים, *yo-yaw-keem'*, Jehovah sets up), a high-priest, the son of that Jeshua who, with Zerubbabel, led the first return from Babylon. His son was Eliashib (Neh. xii:10, 12, 26). Joiakim is a contraction of Jehoiakim. (B. C. before 445.)

JOIARIB (joi'a-rĭb), (Heb. יוֹיָרִיב, *yo-yaw-reeb'*, Jehovah will contend).

1. A Shilonite, which probably means a descendant of Shelah, the son of Judah. He is named in the genealogy of Maaseiah (Neh. xi: 5), B. C. 445.

2. One of those who returned from the captivity with Ezra (Ezra viii:16).

3. Founder of one of the courses of priests (Neh. xii:6). His descendants after the captivity are given in Neh. xi:10; and xii:19, B. C. 536. The name appears also in full. (See JEHOIARIB.)

JOIN (Heb. דָּבַק, *daw-bak'*). (1) To knit or unite together (Job xli:17). (2) To make an alliance or

league (Dan. xi:6). (3) To enter into intimacy with (Acts viii:29). (4) To be reckoned with (Job iii:6).

JOINING (join'ĭng), (Heb. מְחַבְּרוֹת, *mekh-ab-ber-oth'*), binders or cramps in the wall of a building (1 Chron. xxii:3).

The term is applied (1) To *things;* so *house is joined to house*, when one is added to another under the same master (Is. v:8). (2) To *persons*, when they are united in marriage (Eph. v:31); in affinity (2 Chron. xviii:1); in assistance (Exod. i:10); or in church fellowship (Acts ix:26); or in battle, army fighting close with army (1 Sam. iv:2). (3) To *minds*, when people are united in judgment and affection. To be *joined to the Lord*, is to be spiritually espoused to his Son, and solemnly devoted to his service (1 Cor. vi:17; Jer. l:5). To be *joined to idols*, is to be firmly intent on worshiping them (Hos. iv:17). To be *joined to a harlot*, is to have the affections set upon her, and to commit sin with her (1 Cor. vi: 16). Brown.

JOINT (Heb. חַמּוּק, *kham-mook*), a wrapping.

JOINTS are, (1) The uniting of the bones in an animal body (Dan. v:6). (2) The uniting parts of a harness (2 Chron. xviii:33). Joint is employed erroneously in the A. V. (Cant. vii:1) for *drawers*, "a part of the female dress, which, in the case of bridal toilet, are represented as being fringed with a worked edging like lace, or a skillfully chased jewel" (McC. and S., *Cyc.*) It may possibly have reference to a richly embroidered *girdle*.

Figurative. The *joints and bands* which unite Christ's mystical body, are his Spirit, ordinances, and influences and their mutual relations to him, and to one another, and their graces of faith and love fixed on him, and in him loving one another (Col. ii:19; Eph. iv:16). The *joints and marrow* of men's hearts, are their secret dispositions, which the convincing word of God, with no small pain to them, shows and affects them with (Heb. iv:12).

JOKDEAM (jŏk'de-ăm), (Heb. יָקְדְעָם, *yok-deh-awm'*, burning of people), a city in the mountains of Judah (Josh. xv:56). From its connection it must have been south of Hebron.

JOKIM (jō'kim), (Heb. יוֹקִים, *yo-keem'*), contraction of *Joiakim'*, son of Shelah, and grandson of Judah (1 Chron. iv:22). Nothing is positively known of his history. Jerome says he was Elimelech, the husband of Naomi (*Quæst. in Paral*).

JOKMEAM (jŏk'me-ăm), (Heb. יָקְמְעָם, *yok-meh-awm'*, people will be raised), a city of Ephraim, afterwards given to the Levites of Kohath's family (1 Chron. vi:68). In the parallel list in Josh. xxi:22, *Kibzaim* takes its place. From its mention (1 Kings iv:12) it must have been situated in the Jordan Valley on the eastern boundary of the tribe; in this passage the A. V. incorrectly writes JOKNEAM.

JOKNEAM (jŏk'ne-ăm), (Heb. יָקְנְעָם, *yok-neh-awm'*, people will be lamented), a city of Zebulun, given to the Levites of Merari's family (Josh. xxi: 34; xix:11), surnamed Jokneam, of Carmel (Josh. xii:22) because adjacent to that mountain. It has been identified pretty well with the modern *Tell Kaimon*, below the eastern termination of Carmel. The Jokneam of 1 Kings iv:12, according to all the requirements, must be an erroneous form for JOKMEAM.

JOKSHAN (jŏk'shan), (Heb. יָקְשָׁן, *yok-shawn'*, snarer or fowler), second son of Abraham and

Keturah, whose sons Sheba and Dedan appear to have been the ancestors of the Sabæans and Dedanites, who peopled a part of Arabia Felix (Gen. xxv:2, 3; 1 Chron. i:32). (See ARABIA.)

JOKTAN (jŏk'tan), (Heb. יָקְטָן, yok-tawn', small).

The second of the sons of Eber, a descendant from Shem (Gen. x:25, 26, 29; 1 Chron. i:19), and the supposed progenitor of many tribes in Southern Arabia. The Arabians call him Kahtan, and recognize him as one of the principal founders of their nation. See Pocock, *Spec. Hist. Arab.*, pp. 3, 38.) We find traces in Arabia of the names of Joktan's sons, which is a further confirmation of this opinion. These sons were Almohad, Shaleph, Hazarmaveth, Jerah, Hadoram, Uzal, Diklah, Obal, Abimeel, Sheba, Ophir, Havilah, and Jobab (Gen. x:26, etc.). These ancient Arabians lived here without mingling with other people, till Ishmael, son of Abraham and Hagar, and his sons, settled here, who, mixing with them, were called Mos-arabes, or Mostæ-arabes, that is, mixed Arabians.

JOKTHEEL (jŏk'the-el), (Heb. יָקְתְאֵל, yok-theh-ale', veneration of God).

1. A name given by King Amaziah to the city Sela, or Petra, the capital of Arabia Petræa, when he took it from the Edomites (2 Kings xiv:7; 2 Chron. xxv:11-13). (See PETRA.)

2. There was also a city of this name in the tribe of Judah, between Mizpeh and Lachish (Josh. xv:38), possibly preserved in the ruins of *Keitulaneh.*

JONA (jō'nà), (Gr. Ἰωνᾶ, ee-oh-nah', father of the Apostle Peter (John i:42) and hence is addressed as Simon Bar-jona (Matt. xvi:17). In John xxi:15-17 he is called Jonas, which would have been a correct form throughout.

JONADAB (jŏn'a-dăb), (Heb. יוֹנָדָב, yo-naw-dawb', contraction of yeh-ho-naw-dawb', יְהוֹנָדָב, Jehovah impels).

1. A nephew of David, a crafty person, whose counsel suggested to his cousin Amnon the means by which he accomplished his abominable design upon his half-sister Tamar (2 Sam. xiii:4, 5).

2. (1) **Descendant of Rechab.** A son or descendant of Rechab, the progenitor of those nomadic Rechabites, who held themselves bound by a vow to abstain from wine, and never to relinquish the nomadic life. The principle on which the tribe acted may be considered elsewhere. (See RECHABITES.)

(2) **Head of Tribe.** Jonadab was at the head of this tribe at the time when Jehu received his commission to exterminate the house of Ahab, and is supposed to have added to its ancient austerities the inhibition of wine.

(3) **Relation to Jehu.** He was held in great respect among the Israelites generally; and Jehu, alive to the importance of obtaining the countenance and sanction of such a man to his proceedings, took him up in his chariot, when on his road to Samaria to complete the work he had begun at Jezreel. The terms of the colloquy which took place on this occasion are rather remarkable. Perceiving Jonadab, he saluted him, and called out, 'Is thine heart right, as my heart is with thy heart?' Jonadab answered, 'It is.' Then said Jehu, 'If it be, give me thine hand.' And he gave him his hand, and was taken up into the chariot, Jehu inviting him to 'Come and see my zeal for the Lord' (2 Kings x:15-17; Jer. xxxv:6-10).

(4) **Rechabites a Branch of the Kenites.** It would seem that the Rechabites were a branch of the Kenites, over another branch of whom Heber

was chief in the time of Deborah and Barak (Judg. iv:11, 17); and as it is expressly said that Jonadab went out to meet Jehu, it seems probable that the people of Samaria, alarmed at the menacing letter which they had received from Jehu, had induced Jonadab to go to meet and appease him on the road. His venerated character, his rank as the head of a tribe, and his neutral position, well qualified him for this mission; and it was quite as much the interest of Jonadab to conciliate the new dynasty, in whose founder he beheld the minister of the divine decrees, as it was that of Jehu to obtain his concurrence and support in proceedings which he could not but know were likely to render him odious to the people.

JONAH (jō'nah), (Heb. יוֹנָה, yo-naw', a dove; Sept. Ἰωνᾶς, ee-o-nas'), the fifth in order of the minor prophets.

No era is assigned to him in the book of his prophecy, yet there is little doubt of his being the same person who is spoken of in 2 Kings xiv:25. His birthplace was Gath-hepher, in the tribe of Zebulun. Jonah flourished in or before the reign of Jeroboam II, and predicted the successful conquests, enlarged territory, and brief prosperity of the Israelitish kingdom under that monarch's sway. The oracle itself is not extant, though Hitzig has, by a novel process of criticism, amused himself with a fancied discovery of it in chaps. xv and xvi of Isaiah. (Hitzig, *Des Proph. Jon. Orakel. ueber Moab Kritisch-vindicirt, etc.*, Heidelberg, 1831.)

(1) **Ordered to Nineveh.** God ordered this prophet to go to Nineveh, and warn the inhabitants of their approaching destruction. Fearing that the merciful Lord might forbear punishing them if they repented, and so seemingly tarnish his honor, Jonah fled from the presence of the Lord and embarked at Joppa for Tarshish (whether in Cilicia, Africa, or Spain, is uncertain), that, being out of the Promised Land, the spirit of prophecy might forbear to excite him.

(2) **Cast Overboard.** A storm quickly pursued the ship wherein he was. The heathen mariners awaked him, and required him to call on his God for deliverance. Lots being cast, to discern for whose sake the storm rose, the lot fell on Jonah. With shame he confessed his guilt to the mariners. He desired them to cast him into the sea, that the storm might be stayed. With reluctance they were at last obliged to do it, whereon the storm immediately ceased. A large fish swallowed up Jonah, and retained him safe in her belly for three days.

(3) **Ejected by the Whale.** There he earnestly prayed to the Lord, at whose command the fish vomited him alive on the dry land; but whether on the east end of the Syrian sea near Scanderoon we know not, though that is most probable. His orders to warn the Ninevites of their approaching destruction were immediately renewed.

(4) **Warns the Ninevites.** All obedient, he hasted to that vast city. He had not traveled in it above a day's journey, denouncing their ruin, when the king, whom we cannot suppose Pul, but one about fifty or sixty years earlier, and all his people, applied themselves to solemn fasting and prayer. Hereupon God forbore to execute his vengeance upon them, which had been but conditionally threatened. Displeased with the divine mercy, Jonah angrily wished to die, rather than live and see his prediction unfulfilled.

(5) **The Gourd.** While he sat without the city, waiting for his desired view of Nineveh's ruin, God caused a gourd to spring up quickly, to over-

shadow him from the scorching heat of the sun; but next day, a worm having bitten its root, it suddenly withered. The scorching sun and blasting wind vehemently beating on Jonah, he fainted, and angrily wished to die, and averred to God himself that he was right in so doing. The Lord bid him think, if he had pity on the shortlived gourd, was there not far more reason for him and their Maker to pity the penitent inhabitants of Nineveh, where were above 120,000 infants, and much cattle (Jonah i-iv).

Figurative. Did not the fate of this prophet typify our Savior, who was to be cast into the raging sea of wrath; his lying a part of three days in the grave; his glorious resurrection from the dead; and the effectual publication of the gospel to multitudes of sinners, for their everlasting salvation? (See JONAH, BOOK OF.)   Brown.

Tomb of Jonah at Mosul.

JONAH, BOOK OF.

Analysis. The book of Jonah contains an account of the prophet's commission to denounce Nineveh, and of his refusal to undertake the embassy—of the method he employed to escape the unwelcome task (see TARSHISH), and the miraculous means which God used to curb his self-willed spirit, and subdue his petulant and querulous disposition. The third and fourth chapters briefly detail Jonah's fulfillment of the Divine command, and present us with another exemplification of his refractory temper.

(1) Distraction. His attempt to flee from the presence of the Lord must have sprung from a partial insanity, produced by the excitement of distracting motives in an irascible and melancholy heart. The temerity and folly of the fugitive could scarcely be credited, if they had not been equaled by future outbreaks of a similar peevish and morbid infatuation. The mind of Jonah was dark and moody, not unlike a lake which mirrors in the waters the gloomy thunderclouds which overshadow it, and flash over its sullen waves a momentary gleam.

(2) Striking History. The history of Jonah is certainly striking and extraordinary. Its characteristic prodigy does not resemble the other miraculous phenomena recorded in Scripture; yet we must believe in its literal occurrence, as the Bible affords no indication of its being a myth, allegory, or parable.

(3) Reality. On the other hand, our Savior's pointed and peculiar allusion to it is an evidence of its reality (Matt. xii:40). The opinion of the earlier Jews (Tobit xiv:4; Joseph. *Antiq.* ix:10, 2) is also in favor of the literality of the adventure. It requires less faith to credit this simple excerpt from Jonah's biography, than to believe the numerous hypotheses that have been invented to deprive it of its supernatural character, the great majority of them being clumsy and far-fetched, doing violence to the language, and despite to the spirit of revelation.

(4) Vindication of Reality. In vindication of the reality of this striking narrative, it may be argued that the allusions of Christ to Old Testament events on similar occasions are to actual occurrences (John iii:14; vi:48); that the purpose which God had in view justified his miraculous interposition; that this miracle must have had a salutary effect both on the minds of the Ninevites and on the people of Israel. Neither is the character of Jonah improbable. Many reasons might induce him to avoid the discharge of his prophetic duty—fear of being thought a false prophet, scorn of a foreign and hostile race, desire for their utter destruction, a false dignity which might reckon it beneath his prerogative to officiate among uncircumcised idolaters (Jahn, *Introduction to the Old Testament,* translated by S. Turner, pp. 372, 373, translator's notes). Some, who cannot altogether reject the reality of the narrative, suppose it to have had a historical basis, though its present form be fanciful or mythical. Such an opinion is the evident result of a mental struggle between receiving it as a real transaction or regarding it as wholly a fiction. Grimm regards it as a dream produced in that sleep which fell upon Jonah as he lay on the sides of the ship and others regard this book as an allegory.

These hypotheses are all vague and baseless, and do not merit a special refutation. Endeavoring to free us from one difficulty they plunge us into others yet more intricate and perplexing.

(5) Profane Wit. Much profane wit has been expended on the miraculous means of Jonah's deliverance, very unnecessarily and very absurdly; it is simply said, 'The Lord had prepared a great fish to swallow up Jonah.' Now the species of marine animal is not defined, and the Greek *kay-tos, κῆτος sea-monster,* or *whale,* is often used to specify, not the genus whale, but any large fish or sea-monster. All objections to its being a whale which lodged Jonah in its stomach, from its straitness of throat, or rareness of haunt in the Mediterranean, are thus removed. The Scripture thus speaks only of an enormous fish, which under God's direction swallowed the prophet, and does not point out the species to which the voracious prowler belonged. Since the days of Bochart it has been a common opinion that the fish was of the shark species, or 'sea-dog' (Bochart, *Op.* iii: 72; Calmet's *Dissertation sur Jonah*). Entire human bodies have been found in some fishes of this kind. The stomach, too, has no influence on any living substance admitted into it. Granting all these facts as proof of what is termed the economy of miracles, still must we say, in reference to the supernatural preservation of Jonah, Is anything too hard for the Lord?

On what portion of the coast Jonah was set down in safety we are not informed. The opinions held as to the peculiar spot by rabbins and other thaumaturgic expositors need not be repeated. The prophet proceeded, on receiving a second commission, to fulfill it.

(6) Saving of the City. The fearful menace had the desired effect. The city humbled itself before God, and a respite was vouchsafed. The king (Pul, according to Usher) and his people fasted, and their penitence was accepted. The spirit of Jonah was chafed that the doom he had uttered was not executed. He retired to a station out of the city whence he might witness the threatened catastrophe. Under the shadow of a gourd prepared by God he reclined, while Jehovah taught him by the growth and speedy death of this plant, and his attachment to it, a sublime lesson of patient and forgiving generosity.

(7) A Simple Narrative. The book of Jonah is a simple narrative, with the exception of the prayer or thanksgiving in chapter ii. Its style and mode of narration are uniform. There are no traces of compilation, as Nactigall supposed; neither is the prayer, as De Wette (*Einleit.* 237) imagines, improperly borrowed from some other sources. That prayer contains, indeed, not only imagery peculiar to itself, but also such imagery as at once was suggested to the mind of a reverent Hebrew preserved in circumstances of extreme jeopardy. On this principle we account for the similarity of some portions of its phraseology to Ps. lix, xlii, etc. The language in both places had been hallowed by frequent usage, and had become the consecrated idiom of a distressed and succored Israelite. The hymn seems to have been composed after his deliverance, and the reason why his deliverance is noted after the hymn is recorded may be to show the occasion of its composition.

Among the numerous commentators on Jonah may be noticed Martin, *Jonah's mission;* King's *Commentary;* Pusey's *Commentary;* Davidson, On *Prophecy, Dis.* vi. pt. 2. For further literature see HABAKKUK. J. E.

JONAN (jō'nan), (Gr. 'Ιωνάν, *ee-o-nan'*, Jonan), son of Eliakim, in the genealogy of Christ, about the time of Jehoram (Luke iii:30).

The name is probably only another form of Johanan, or JONATHAN.

JONAS (jō'nas), (Gr. 'Ιωνᾶς, *ee-o-nas'*, from the Hebrew Jonah).

1. The form of the name of the prophet Jonah (Matt. xii:39, 40, 41; xvi:4; Luke xi:29, 30, 32).

2. (John xxi:15-17) another form of JONA, which see.

JONATHAN (jŏn'a-than), (Heb. יֹנָתָן, *yo-naw-thawn'*, God-given).

1. A Levite descended from Gershom, the son of Moses (Judg. xviii:30). It is, indeed, said, in our common copies, that the Gershom from whom this Jonathan sprang was 'the son of Manasseh;' but some supposed that in the name of Moses (*mo-seh'*) the single letter (נ) has been interpolated changing it into Manasseh.

The history of this Jonathan is involved in the narrative which occupies Judges xvii, xviii; and is one of the two accounts which form a sort of appendix to that book. The events themselves appear to have occurred soon after the death of Joshua, and of the elders who outlived him, when the government was in a most unsettled state.

Jonathan, who was resident at Bethlehem, lived at a time when the dues of the sanctuary did not afford a livelihood to the numerous Levites who had a claim upon them; and belonged to a tribe destitute of the landed possessions which gave to all others a sufficient maintenance. He, therefore, went forth to seek his fortune. In Mount Ephraim he came to 'a house of gods,' which had been established by one Micah, who wanted nothing but a priest to make his establishment complete. (See MICAH.) This person engaged Jonathan as his priest for his food, a yearly suit of clothes, and ten shekels (twenty-five shillings, about $6.00), a year in money. Here he lived for some time, till the Danite spies, who were sent by their tribe to explore the north, passed this way and formed his acquaintance. When, not long after, the body of armed Danites passed the same way while going to settle near the sources of the Jordan, the spies mentioned Micah's establishment to them; on which they went and took away not only 'the ephod, the teraphim, and the graven image,' but

the priest also, that they might set up the same worship in the place of which they were going to take possession. Micah vainly protested against this robbery; but Jonathan himself was glad at the improvement in his prospects, and from that time, even down to the captivity, he and his descendants continued to be priests of the Danites in the town of Laish, the name of which they changed to Dan.

There is no reason to suppose that this establishment, whether in the hands of Micah or of the Danites, involved an apostasy from Jehovah. It appears rather to have been an attempt to localize or domesticate his presence under those symbols and forms of service which were common among the neighboring nations but were forbidden to the Hebrews. The offense here was two-fold, —the establishment of a sacred ritual different from the only one which the law recognized, and the worship by symbols, naturally leading to idolatry, with the ministration of one who could not legally be a priest, but only a Levite, and under circumstances in which no Aaronic priest could legally have officiated. It is more than likely that this establishment was eventually merged in that of the golden calf, which Jeroboam set up in this place, his choice of which may possibly have been determined by its being already in possession of 'a house of gods.'

2. Eldest Son of Saul, king of Israel, and consequently heir apparent of the throne which David was destined to occupy (1 Sam. xiv:8; 1 Chron. viii:33; ix:39). The war with the Philistines, which occupied the early part of his father's reign, afforded Jonathan more than one opportunity of displaying the chivalrous valor and the princely qualities with which he was endowed. His exploit in surprising the Philistine garrison at Michmash, attended only by his armor-bearer, is one of the most daring which history or even romance records (1 Sam. xiv:1-14). His father came to follow up this victory, and in the ensuing pursuit of the Philistines, Jonathan, spent with fatigue and hunger, refreshed himself with some wild honey which he found in a wood through which he passed. He knew not that his father had rashly vowed to put to death any one who touched a morsel of food before night. When the fact transpired, Saul felt himself bound to execute his vow even upon his gallant son; but the people, with whom the young prince was a great favorite, interposed (1 Sam. xiv:16-52).

(1) Affection for David. The act of David in meeting the challenge of Goliath, and in overcoming that huge barbarian, entirely won his heart; and from that day forward the son of Jesse found no one who loved him so tenderly, who admired his high gifts with so much enthusiasm, or who risked so much to preserve him from harm, as the very prince whom he was destined to exclude from a throne. Jonathan knew well what was to happen, and he submitted cheerfully to the appointment which gave the throne of his father to the young shepherd of Bethlehem. In the intensity of his love and confidence he shrank not to think of David as his destined king and master; and his dreams of the future pictured nothing brighter than the day in which David should reign over Israel, and he be one with him in friendship, and next to him in place and council.

When Saul began to hate David as his intended successor, he was highly displeased at the friendship which had arisen between him and his son. This exposed Jonathan to much contumely, and even to danger of life; for, once at least, the king's passion against him on this account rose so high that he cast a javelin at him 'to smite him to the wall.'

This unequivocal act taught Jonathan that the court of Saul was no safe place for David. He told him so, and they parted with many tears. David then set forth upon those wanderings among strangers and in solitary places which lasted all the time of Saul. The friends met only once more. Saul was in pursuit of David when he was in the wilderness of Ziph; and Jonathan could not forbear coming to him secretly in the wood to give him comfort and encouragement (1 Sam. xxiii:16-18). Nothing more is related of Jonathan till both he and his father lost their lives in the fatal battle of Gilboa, combating the enemies of their country.

(2) David's Lament. There is, perhaps, nothing in Hebrew poetry more beautiful and touching than the lamentation of David for the loss of his friend—nothing more complete as a whole, or more full of fine images and tender thoughts (2 Sam. i:17, *sq.*).

(3) Character. Jealousy and every mean or low feeling were strangers to the generous heart of Jonathan. Valiant and accomplished himself, none knew better how to acknowledge valor and accomplishment in others. He is one of the loveliest personages in Bible history.

3. The son of Abiathar, the high-priest, who gave notice to Adonijah and his party, near the fountain of Rogel, that David had declared Solomon his successor (1 Kings i:42, 43). At the time of David's flight from Absalom he accompanied his father as far as Olivet (2 Sam. xv:36; xvii:15-21). He also appears as a swift and trusted messenger. (B, C. 1000.)

4. Jonathan, or Johanan, or John, high-priest of the Jews, son of Jehoiada, and father of Jeddoa, or Jaddus, celebrated in the time of Alexander the Great (Neh. xii:11). He lived under Ezra and Nehemiah. He died, after having exercised the high-priesthood thirty-two years, and was succeeded by Jeddoa, his son.

5. Son of Shammah, or Shimea, brother of Jonadab, and nephew of David, (2 Sam. xxi:21; 1 Chron. xx:7). He was gifted with both civil and military prowess, and slew a giant Philistine.

6. Son of Shage the Hararite, and one of David's heroes (1 Chron. xi:34; 2 Sam. xxiii: 32).

7. A son of Adin, whose representative, Ebed, returned with Ezra as the leader of fifty males (Ezra viii:6), B. C. 457.

8. Son of Asahel, and one of the four priests who assisted Ezra in the investigation of the foreign marriages that had been contracted in Babylon (Ezra x:15), B. C. 457.

9. A priest in the days of Joiakim, son of Jeshua. He represented the family of Melicu (Neh. xii:14), B. C. 549.

10. The brother of Johanan, the son of Kareah; they were associated in their intercourse with the Babylonian governor (Jer. xl:8), B. C. 588.

11. Father of Zechariah, who blew the trumpet at the dedication of the wall of Jerusalem (Neh. xii:35).

12. Second of the two sons of Jada and grandson of Jerahmeel, of the family of Judah (1 Chron. ii:32, 33), B. C. after 1612.

13. A scribe and keeper of the prisons in Jerusalem under Zedekiah (Jer. xxxvii:15, 20). He was very severe to the prophet Jeremiah, who therefore earnestly desired Zedekiah that he might not be sent back into that dungeon, where his life was in danger. (B. C. 589.)

JONATH-ELEM-RECHOKIM (jō'nath-ē'lem-re-kō'kim), (Heb. יוֹנַת אֵלֶם רְחֹקִים, *yo-nath'ay'lem rekh-o-keem'*, "To the tune of 'The silent dove of those afar'"), the heading of Ps. lvi. There have been many attempts to explain this title, but Aben Ezra seems to come the nearest to the meaning in his explanation that *Jonath Elem Rechokim* indicates the rhythm of the psalm; i. e., "after the melody of the Psalm" which begins *Jonath Elem Rechokim.*

JOPPA (jŏp'på), (Heb. יָפוֹ, or יָפִיא, *yaw-fo'*, beauty; Gr. Ἰόππη, *ee-op'pay*, which name is still preserved in the Arabic Yâfa or Jaffa), a seaport town and haven on the coast of Palestine, situated on an eminence, in a sandy soil, about forty miles northwest of Jerusalem, and nine miles westnorthwest from Ramleh.

(1) Location. The place existed when the Israelites invaded the land of Canaan, and is mentioned as lying on the border of the tribe of Dan (Josh. xix:46). Joppa was the only port possessed by the Israelites till Herod formed the harbor at Cæsarea; and hence it was here that the timber from Lebanon destined for both the first and second temples was landed (1 Kings v:9; 2 Chron. ii:16; Ezra iii:7). It was the place to which Jonah went in expectation of finding a ship bound on some distant voyage, and where he found one going to Tarshish (Jonah i:3). Joppa belonged to the powers which were successively dominant on this shore; and it does not again appear in Jewish history till the time of Judas Maccabæus, when the inhabitants having, contrary to the faith of treaties, thrown 200 Jews into the sea, the hero, to avenge them, surprised the haven by night, and set the shipping on fire (2 Macc. xii:3-7).

(2) Visit of Peter. It is mentioned in the New Testament only in connection with the visit of the Apostle Peter, who here raised Tabitha from the dead, and lodged in the outskirts of the town with Simon the tanner, when favored with the vision which taught him to 'call no man common or unclean' (Acts ix:36-39; x:5, 8; xi:5).

(3) History. During the Jewish war Joppa was taken by surprise by Cestius, when it was plundered and burnt, and 8,400 of the inhabitants were put to the sword (Joseph. *De Bell. Jud.* ii. 18, 10). Its ruins afterwards became the refuge of a great number of persons who had escaped from the destruction of other cities by Vespasian, and who took to piracy for a subsistence. From the first crusade down to our own day Joppa has been the landing-place of pilgrims going to Jerusalem, and is hence mentioned in almost all the innumerable itineraries and books of travels in the Holy Land which have appeared in different languages. There is still here an hospital for pilgrims, dependent on the convent of St. Salvador in Jerusalem, and occupied by Spanish monks. In 1797 the place was taken by storm by the French army under Napoleon, and was sacked without mercy; when the Turkish prisoners, to the number of 500 or 600, were carried to the neighboring sand-hills and put to death by his order.

Josephus describes the natural unfitness of Jaffa for a haven in terms very similar to those which modern travelers employ (*De Bell. Jud.* iii. 9, 3). The port is so dangerous, from exposure to the open sea, that the surf often rolls in with the utmost violence, and even so lately as 1842 a lieutenant and some sailors were lost in pulling to the shore from an English steamer that lay in the harbor (Stent's *Egypt and the Holy Land*, ii:28).

But, however bad, it was the only port which existed within reach of the important district which lay behind it inland; and the miserable state of the ancient roads, or rather perhaps the absence of any roads, made a near harbor, however incommodious, of more immediate consequence than a good one at a greater distance.

(4) Modern Condition. The town is approached on the land side through rich and extensive gardens and orchards, and is very picturesquely situated upon an eminence or promontory, which is crowned by a castle. It chiefly faces the north; and the buildings appear, from the steepness of the site, as if standing upon one another. The most prominent features of the architecture from without are the flattened domes by which most of the buildings are surmounted, and the appearance of arched vaults. The aspect of the whole is mean and gloomy, and inside the place has all the appearance of a poor though large village. There are no public buildings to engage the eye, and the houses are mean and comfortless. No ancient ruins have been observed, nor are any expected to be in a place so often destroyed in war. There are three mosques in Joppa, and Latin, Greek and Armenian convents. The former is that in which European pilgrims and travelers usually lodge. The town still enjoys a considerable trade with the neighboring coasts. Its chief manufacture is soap, which is largely consumed in the baths of Cairo and Damascus; and its excellent fruits are exported in large quantities, especially watermelons, which are very extensively cultivated here and in other parts of the plain of Sharon. The inhabitants are said not to exceed 4,000, of whom one-fourth are reckoned to be Christians. A British consul is now resident in the place. (Raumer's *Palästina;* Volney, i:136, *sq.;* Chateaubriand, ii:103; Clarke, iv:438, *sq.;* Buckingham, i:227, *sq.;* Richter, p. 12; Richardson, ii:16; Skinner, i:175-184; Robinson, i:18; Stent, ii:27; Thomson, *Land and Book,* ii:273.)

JORAH (jō'rah), (Heb. יוֹרָה, *yo-raw'*, sprinkling), one of the descendants of Jorah, who to the number of one hundred and twelve returned with Ezra from Babylon (Ezra ii:18). In Neh. vii:24 their place is taken by the Bene-Hariph, which is probably only a variation caused by a slight confusion of letters (B. C. about 536).

JORAI (jō'ra-ī), (Heb. יוֹרַי, *yo-rah'ee*, rainy, same as JORAH), a Gadite who dwelt in Gilead of Bashan. His genealogies were recorded in the time of Jotham of Judah (1 Chron. v:13), B. C. about 782.

JORAM (jō'ram), (Heb. יוֹרָם, *yo-rawm'*, a shortened form of JEHORAM (which see).

1. The ninth king of Israel, son of Ahab, and successor to his elder brother Ahaziah, who died childless. He began to reign B. C. 896, and reigned twelve years (2 Kings i:17; iii:1). Joram adhered to the sinful policy of Jeroboam in the matter of the golden calves; but, although his mother Jezebel was still alive, he discontinued the dark idolatries of Baal which she had introduced and maintained at such high cost of guilt and blood to the nation.

(1) Revolt of Moabites. The Moabites had been tributary to the crown of Israel since the separation of the two kingdoms. But King Mesha deemed the defeat and death of Ahab so heavy a blow to the power of Israel that he might safely assert his independence. He accordingly did so, by withholding his tribute of '100,000 lambs and 100,000 rams, with the wool.' The short

reign of Ahaziah had afforded no opportunity for any operations against the revolters; but the new king hastened to reduce them again under the yoke they had cast off. The good king of Judah, Jehoshaphat, was too easily induced to take a part in the war. He perhaps feared that the example of Moab, if allowed to be successful, might seduce into a similar course his own tributary, the king of Edom, whom he now summoned to join in this expedition. The deliverance of the allies from perishing for lack of water, and the signal overthrow of the Moabites at the word of Elisha, have been already described under ELISHA and JEHOSHAPHAT.

(2) Benhadad. After this a more redoubtable enemy, Benhadad, king of Syria, occupied for a long time the attention and strength of the king. In the sacred records the more striking events of this war seem to be recorded for the sake of showing forth the great acts of Elisha, and they have therefore been related under his name. It suffices here to indicate that they consisted in the Syrian king being constrained to terminate one campaign in consequence of all his plans being made known by the prophet to the king of Israel (2 Kings vi: 1-23); and in the deliverance of Samaria, according to the prediction of the prophet, from a horrible famine, caused by the city being besieged by the Syrians (2 Kings vi:24-33; vii). An interval of the war also afforded occasion for the remarkable cure of Naaman, the Syrian leper, by the same prophet (2 Kings v), one of the striking incidents of Old Testament history. (See NAAMAN.)

(3) Hazael. After the death of Benhadad, Joram found a new and active enemy in his murderer and successor Hazael. During the illness of Benhadad, the king of Israel seems to have employed himself in strengthening his eastern frontier against the Syrians, and in fortifying Ramoth-Gilead, which had fallen into his hands, and in the attempt to recover which from the Syrians his father had perished. This strong fortress thenceforth became the headquarters of the operations beyond the river. Hazael was scarcely settled on the throne before he took arms and marched against Ramoth, in the environs of which the Israelites sustained a defeat, and the king was wounded. He returned to Jezreel to be healed of his wounds, leaving the army in charge of Jehu, one of his ablest and most active generals. It was in this interval that Jehu was anointed king of Israel by the messenger of Elisha, and immediately proceeded to Jezreel to fulfill his commission to exterminate the house of Ahab. The king, who went forth from the city to meet him when the watchman on the tower of Jezreel announced his approach, was slain under the circumstances described in the article JEHU; and Ahaziah, the king of Judah, who was at Jezreel on a visit to his sick cousin, shared his fate (B. C. 884). With Joram ended the dynasty of Ahab, which reigned forty-four years in Israel (2 Kings viii:25-29; ix:1-20).

2. King of Judah (2 Kings viii:21, 23, 24; 1 Chron. iii:11; 2 Chron. xxii:5, 7; Matt. i:8). (See JEHORAM.)

3. One of the priests sent by Jehoshaphat to instruct the cities of Judah in the law of Moses (2 Chron. xvii:8).

4. A Levite, ancestor of Shelomith, who lived in the time of David (1 Chron. xxvi:25).

5. A messenger sent by his father, King Toi, of Hamath, to congratulate David on his victory over Hadadezer (2 Sam. viii:10), B. C. about 986. (See HADORAM, 2.)

JORDAN, RIVER OF (jŏr'dan), (Hebrew generally with article הַיַּרְדֵּן, *hah-yar-dane'*, the descender, probably from the rapid descent of the stream), the great river of Palestine, as the Nile is of Egypt.

(1) Name. The name "Jordan" is always joined with the article in the Old Testament, with two exceptions (Ps. xlii :6; Job xl :23). The Arabs call it *esh-Sheriah*, or the watering-place." A tradition as old as St. Jerome, A. D. 400, says that the Jordan derived its name from two rivers, the Jor, rising at Banias, and the Dan, rising at Tell el-Kadi. But this tradition seems to be erroneous; for, according to Gen. xiii :10, the river was known to Abraham as the Jordan long before the children of Dan gave their name to Leshem (Josh. xix :47), or Laish (Judg. xviii :29).

(2) Sources. The Jordan rises among the mountains of Anti-Lebanon, and has four sources: (1) *The Hasbâny*, which issues from the large fountain *'Ain Furar*, near Hasbeya, at an altitude of 1,700 feet above the sea. This pool, which the natives say is 1,000 feet deep, Macgregor found to have a depth of 11 feet. (2) *The Banias*, which rises near the ruins of *Banias* (Cæsarea-Philippi), at the base of Mount Hermon, 1,140 feet above the sea-level. (3) *The Leddân* rising in a large fountain on the west side of the *Tell el-Kadi* ("hill of the judge," the site of the city of Dan). In the midst of a thicket of oleander bushes is a large pool, 50 or 60 yards wide, with the water bubbling out of the ground in a full-grown stream. This, which Josephus calls the Little Jordan, is the most copious source. (4) *The Esh-Shar*, a minor tributary, only one or two yards broad. Besides the above four sources, there are numerous small streams from the springs of Lebanon which find their way into the swamp above *Lake Huleh,* and contribute to swell the Jordan.

(3) Course of the Stream. After flowing twelve miles through the valley, it enters a dark defile of six or seven miles, thence through a marsh ten miles, and coming out into the beautiful Lake Merom or Huleh. Taking a south course twelve miles further on it enters the sea of Galilee. Issuing from its southwest corner it flows on some sixty miles till it empties into the Dead Sea.

(4) The Plains of the Jordan. The popular notion that the waters of the river do not seem to mingle with those of the lake, but pass through in a united stream, is a "fable." From the Sea of Tiberias to the Dead Sea there is one deep depression, the hills from the east and west nearly meeting in many places. This depression is filled up to a certain level with an alluvial deposit, forming a vast plain called the Jordan valley, or *Ghôr* (the hollow). This is the "upper plain." It varies in width from one to twelve miles. The river has cut out for itself a plain lower than the preceding by some 50 to 100 feet, and from a quarter of a mile to a mile wide. This is the "lower plain," through which the river, some 60 yards wide, winds its way. During the spring floods this lower plain is inundated. Although the distance in a straight line between Tiberias and the Dead Sea is only 66 miles, the actual distance the stream flows, on account of its many windings, is 200 miles, and the fall 667 feet. Twenty-seven threatening rapids were counted by Lieut. Lynch, besides many others of minor importance. The whole distance from the sources of the river to its mouth is not more than 136 miles in a straight line. The whole descent is 2,999 feet to the Dead Sea, which, according to the latest determination of the British survey, is 1,292 feet below sea-level, although Lynch had reported it at 1,317 feet. (See SALT SEA.) The width of the stream varies from 45 to 180 feet, and its depth from three to twelve feet.

(5) Tributaries. The only living tributaries to the Jordan noticed particularly below Gennesaret were the *Yarmûk* (Hieromax) and the *Zerka* (Jabbok). The mouth of the former of these was passed on the third day, 40 yards wide, with moderate current, while the latter, whose course became visible on the seventh day, was, on the eighth day, discovered to have two distinct outlets into the main stream, one of which was then dry. Older writers had distinguished two beds and banks of the Jordan; the first, that occupied by the river in its normal state; the second, comprising the space which it occupied during its swelling or overflow (Martiniere, *Dict. Geograph.* s. v). Similarly Lieut. Lynch has remarked: "There are evidently two terraces to the Jordan, and through the lower one the river runs its serpentine course. From the stream, *above the immediate banks,* there is, on each side, a singular terrace of low hills, like truncated cones, which is the bluff terminus of an extended table-land, reaching quite to the mountains of Hauran on the eastern and the high hills on the western side" (*Narrat.,* April 3, and comp. what Capt. Newbold says, p. 22).

(6) Bridges and Fords. There are no bridges over the Jordan to which an earlier date has been assigned than that of the Roman occupation; and there are vestiges of Roman roads in different parts of the country—between *Nâbulus* and *Beisân,* for instance—that may well have crossed these bridges. The Saracens afterwards added to their number, or restored those which they found in ruins. Thus the bridge called *el-Ghujan* over the *Hashbeiya* has two pointed arches and one round (Newbold, p. 13), while the entire architecture of the *Jisr Benât Ya'Kôb* (of the daughters of Jacob), two and one-half miles to the south of Little Hûleh, as well as of the khan adjacent to it on the eastern side, is pronounced to be Saracenic (same, p. 20). A Roman bridge of ten arches, *Jisr Semakh*, spans the Jordan near the village bearing that name, and was doubtless on the route from Tiberias and Tarichea to Gadara and Decapolis (Newbold, p. 21; Irby, p. 90). Lastly, the bridge of *Mejâmich*, which crosses the Jordan about six miles from the Lake of Gennesaret, was Saracenic; while that near the ford, *Dâmieh,* was more Roman (Newbold, p. 20, and Lynch, *Narr.,* April 16.)

There are four principal fords over the river: the lower one, opposite Jericho, near the famous bathing place of the pilgrims; another, eastward of *Sakut;* and two others, nearer the Sea of Galilee. At low water there are many other points at which the river might be easily forded, and the British Survey discovered evidences of various fords. During the floods the Arabs are frequently obliged to swim their horses across the river.

(7) Climate and Vegetation. The great depression of the Jordan valley gives to it a semitropical character. "In its natural products it stands unique, a tropical oasis sunk in the temperate zone." Under the intense heat vegetation advances with wonderful rapidity, but is as quickly scorched whenever the water supply is not abundant.

(8) Scripture Reference and History. There is no regular description of the Jordan to be met with in Holy Scripture, and it is only by putting scattered notices of it together that we can give the general idea which runs through the Bible respecting it.

The earliest of these allusions is not so much to the river itself as to the plain or plains which it traversed: "Lot lifted up his eyes, and beheld all the plain of Jordan, that it was well watered everywhere, ... even as the garden of the Lord, like the land of Egypt" (Gen. xiii:10). Abram had just left Egypt (xii:10-20), and therefore the comparison between the fertilizing properties of the Jordan and of the Nile is very apposite, though it has since been pushed much too far, as we shall see. We may suppose Lot to have had his view from one of the summits of those hills that run north in the direction of Scythopolis (*B. J.*, iv:7, Sec. 2), bounding the plains of Jordan on the west; for Lot and Abram were now sojourning between Bethel and Ai (Gen. xiii:3).

Red Sea, where the intermediate agency of a strong east wind is freely admitted (Exod. xiv:21), it is here said, in terms equally explicit, not only that the river was then unusually full of water, but that "the waters which came down from above stood and rose up upon an heap . . . while those that came down toward the sea of the plain . . . failed and were cut off," as soon as ever "the feet of the priests that bare the ark were dipped in the brim of the water" (Josh. iii:15, 16). That it happened in harvest time is seen also from chapter v:10-12. Among those who crossed over the Jordan were Gideon, "faint yet pursuing" after Zebah and Zalmunna (Judg. viii:4, 5); the Ammonites, invading Judah (Judg. x:9); Abner, in flight (2 Sam. ii:29); David in flight (2 Sam.

View of Jordan.

How far the plain extended in length or breadth is not said: other passages speak of "Jordan and his border" (Josh. xiii:27), "the borders of Jordan" (xxii:11), and "the plains of Jericho" (iv: 13; comp. 2 Kings xxv:5); all evidently subdivisions of the same idea, comprehending the east bank equally with the west (Josh. xiii:27).

One of the fords we have mentioned undoubtedly witnessed the first recorded passage of the Jordan in the Old Testament; we say recorded, because there can be little dispute but that Abraham must have crossed it likewise. But only the passage of Jacob is mentioned, and that in remarkable language: "With my staff I passed over this Jordan, and now I am become two bands" (Gen. xxxii:10, and Jabbok in connection with it, verse 22). And Jordan was next crossed—over against Jericho—by Joshua the son of Nun, at the head of the descendants of the twelve sons of him who signalized the first passage. The magnitude of their operations may be inferred from the fact, that—of the children of Reuben and of Gad, and half the tribe of Manasseh only—"about 40,000 prepared for war passed over before the Lord unto battle." . . . . (Josh. iv:12 and 13.)

The ceremonial of this second crossing is too well known to need recapitulation. It may be observed, however, that, unlike the passage of the

xvii:22), and returning to his capital (xix:15, 18) (mention is here made of a ferry-boat, probably only a raft, the only time in Scripture); David, to war with the Syrians; Absalom, in pursuit of his father (2 Sam. xvii:24); Elijah and Elisha, parting the waters with the mantle (2 Kings ii:6-14). As two and a half tribes of Israel dwelt east of the river, the amount of crossing and recrossing must have been considerable, and the best fords were well known (comp. Josh. ii:7; Judg. iii:28; vii:24; xii:5, 6). The river was known to Job (Job xl:23), and Jeremiah speaks of "the swelling of Jordan" (Jer. xii:5; xlix:19; l:44). Noteworthy miracles, in addition to those already mentioned, were the curing of Naaman (2 Kings v:14), and the making the iron to swim (vi:6).

The Jordan is mentioned about 180 times in the Old Testament. In the New Testament it is mentioned 15 times. The chief events noted in connection with it in the New Testament are John's baptism of the multitudes (Matt. iii:6), and especially his baptism of Jesus (Mark i:9). In commemoration of this latter event it is the custom for Christian pilgrims in great numbers to bathe in the Jordan not far from Jericho at Easter.

The Jordan has been several times navigated in a boat in modern times—by Costigan, 1835; by

Molyneaux, 1847; by Lieut. Lynch, 1848; by J. Macgregor (Rob Roy), 1869. "The sight of the Jordan," says Schaff, "is rather disappointing. It bears no comparison in majesty and beauty to the great rivers of Europe and America. Naaman thought the clear rivers of his native Damascus far superior, yet the Abana and Pharpar could not wash away his leprosy. Its chief importance is historic. In this respect the Jordan surpasses the Hudson and the Mississippi, the Rhine and the Danube, and even the Nile. It marks the termination of the wanderings of the children of Israel from the banks of the Nile, and the beginning of their history as an independent nation in their own home. It blends the memories of the old and new Covenants as the culmination of John's testimony and the inauguration of Christ's kingdom."—*Through Bible Lands*, p. 299. "Surely," says Macgregor, "the Jordan is by far the most wonderful stream on the face of the earth, and the memories of its history will not be forgotten in heaven."—*Rob Roy on the Jordan*, p. 406. It is a sacred stream alike to Jew, Ishmaelite, Christian, and Mohammedan, and in this surpasses in interest any other river in the world (Schaff *Bib. Dict.*). (See PALESTINE.)

JORDAN, VALLEY OF (jôr'dan), (Heb. עֲרָבָה, *ar-aw-baw'* ; rendered "the plain," Josh. xviii:18, marg., "the champaign," Deut. xi:30, "the desert," Ezek. xlvii:18). Its modern name is El Ghor. (See JORDAN, RIVER OF.)

JORIM (jō'rim), (Gr. Ἰωρείμ, *ee-o-rime'*), given in the genealogies of Christ as the son of Matthat (Luke iii:29), in the 13th generation from David, or about the time of Ahaz. The name should probably be Joram or Joiarim.

JORKOAM (jôr'ko-ăm), (Heb. יָרְקְעָם, *yor-keh-awm'*, scattered people), either a descendant of Caleb ; or, according to Jarchi, the name of a place in the tribe of Judah, of which Raham was prince (1 Chron. ii:44).

JOSABAD (jŏs'a-băd), (Heb. יוֹזָבָר, *yo-zaw-bawd'*, Jehovah endowed), properly JOZABAD, a Gederathite, one of the warriors of Benjamin who left Saul and came over to David at Ziklag (1 Chron xii:4), B. C. before 1,000.

JOSAPHAT (jŏs'a-phăt), (Gr. Ἰωσαφάτ, *ee-os-ah-fat'*, Matt. i:8, King of Judah). See JEHOSHAPHAT.

JOSE (jō'se), (Gr. Ἰωσή, *ee-oh-say*, Luke iii:29), an incorrect form of JOSES (which see).

JOSEDECH (jŏs'e-dek), (Heb. יְהוֹצָרָק., *yeh-ho-tsaw-dawk'*, justified by Jehovah, Zech. vi:11; Hag. i:1, 12, 14; ii:2, 4), father of Jeshua. Elsewhere the name appears as Josedec (1 Esdr. v:5, 48, etc.)

JOSEPH (jō'sĕf), (Heb. יוֹסֵף, *yo-safe*, increaser, adding).

1. Son of Jacob and Rachel, born under peculiar circumstances, as may be seen in Gen. xxx:24; on which account, and because he was the son of his old age (xxxvii:3), he was beloved by his father more than were the rest of his children, though Benjamin, as being also a son of Jacob's favorite wife, Rachel, was in a peculiar manner dear to the patriarch. The partiality evinced towards Joseph by his father excited jealousy on the part of his brethren, the rather that they were born of different mothers (xxxvii:2).

(1) Hated by His Brothers. Joseph had reached his seventeenth year, having hitherto been engaged in boyish sports, or aiding in pastoral duties, when some conduct on the part of 'the sons of Bilhah and the sons of Zilpah, his father's wives,' seems to have been such as in the opinion of Joseph to require the special attention of Jacob, to whom, accordingly, he communicated the facts. This regard to virtue, and this manifestation of filial fidelity, greatly increased his brothers' dislike, who henceforth 'hated him, and could not speak peaceably unto him' (xxxvii:4). Their aversion, however, was carried to the highest pitch when Joseph acquainted them with two dreams, which appeared to indicate that Joseph would acquire preëminence in the family, if not sovereignty; and while even his father rebuked him, his brothers were filled with envy. Jacob, however, was not aware of the depth of their ill will; so that on one occasion, having a desire to hear intelligence of his sons, who were pasturing their flocks at a distance, he did not hesitate to make Joseph his messenger for that purpose. His appearing in view of his brothers was the signal for their malice to gain head. They began to devise means for his immediate destruction, which they would unhesitatingly have effected but for his half-brother, Reuben, who, as the eldest son, might well be the party to interfere on behalf of Joseph.

(2) Cast Into a Pit. A compromise was entered into, in virtue of which the youth was stripped of the distinguishing vestments which he owed to his father's affection, and cast into a pit. Having performed this evil deed, and while they were taking refreshment, the brothers beheld a caravan of Arabian merchants, who were bearing the spices and aromatic gums of India down to the well-known and much-frequented mart, Egypt. Judah on this feels a bitter emotion arise in his mind, and proposes that, instead of allowing Joseph to perish, they should sell him to the merchants, whose trade obviously from this embraced human beings as well as spicery.

(3) Sold Into Slavery. Accordingly the unhappy young man was sold for a slave, to be conveyed by his masters into Egypt. While on his way thither, Reuben returned to the pit, intending to rescue his brother, and convey him safely back to their father. Joseph was gone. On which Reuben went to the wicked young men, who, not content with selling a brother into slavery, determined to punish their father for his partiality towards the unoffending sufferer. With this view they dipped Joseph's party-colored garment in the blood of a kid and sent it to Jacob, in order to make him believe that his favorite child had been torn to pieces by some wild beast. The trick succeeded, and Jacob was grieved beyond measure.

Meanwhile the merchants sold Joseph to Potiphar, an officer of Pharaoh's, and captain of the royal guard, who was a native of the country.

(4) Member of Potiphar's Household. In Potiphar's house Joseph enjoyed the highest confidence and the largest prosperity. The Hebrew race have always been remarkable for personal beauty, of which Joseph seems to have had an unusual share. This fact explains, if it cannot palliate, the conduct of Potiphar's wife, who tried every means to bring the uncontaminated and pure-minded youth to fulfill her unchaste desires. Foiled in her evil wishes, she resolved to punish Joseph, who thus a second time innocently brings on himself the vengeance of the ill-disposed. Charged with the very crime to which he had in vain been tempted, he is, with a fickleness characteristic of Oriental lords, at once cast into the state prison.

(5) Imprisonment. The narrative states, however, that Joseph was not left without special aid, in consequence of which he gained favor with the keeper of the prison to such an extent that everything was put under his direction.

Two regal officers, the chief of the butlers and the chief of the bakers, had, while in prison with Joseph, each one a dream, which Joseph interpreted correctly. The butler, whose fate was auspicious, promised the young Hebrew to employ his influence to procure his restoration to the free air of day; but when again in the enjoyment of his 'butlership,' he 'forgat' Joseph (Gen. xl). Pharaoh himself, however, had two dreams, which found in Joseph a successful expounder; for the butler remembered the skill of his prison companion, and advised his royal master to put it to the test in his own case. Pharaoh's dream, as interpreted by Joseph, foreboded the approach of a seven years' famine; to abate the evils of which Joseph recommended that some 'discreet and wise' man should be chosen and set in full power over the land of Egypt. The monarch was alarmed, and called a council of his advisers.

(6) Dictator. The wisdom of Joseph was recognized as of divine origin and supereminent value; and the king and his ministers (whence it appears that the Egyptian monarchy—at Memphis —was not despotic, but constitutional) resolved that Joseph should be made (to borrow a term from Rome) Dictator in the approaching time of need.

The highest honors were conferred upon him, and he was made ruler over all the land of Egypt. Pharaoh called Joseph's name Zaphnath-paaneah ('savior of the world;' comp. Jablonski, *Opusc.* i:207, *sq.;* and he gave him to wife Asenath, the daughter of Poti-pherah, priest of On. And 'Joseph went out over all the land of Egypt' (Gen. xli:39, *sq.*).

Seven years of abundance afforded Joseph opportunity to carry into effect such plans as secured an ample provision against the seven years of need. The famine came, but it found a prepared people. The visitation did not depend on any mere local causes, for 'the famine was over all the face of the earth,' 'and all countries came into Egypt to Joseph to buy corn' (verses 56, 57).

(7) Coming of the Sons of Jacob. Among these customers appeared ten brethren, sons of the Hebrew Jacob. They had of necessity to appear before Joseph, whose license for the purchase of corn was indispensable. Joseph had probably expected to see them, and he seems to have formed a deliberate plan of action. His conduct has brought on him the always ready charges of those who would rather impeach than study the Bible, and even friends of that sacred book have hardly in this case done Joseph full justice (Niemeyer, *Charakt.,* ii:366; Heuser, *Diss. non inhumaniter sed prudentissime Josephum cum fratribus fecisse,* Hal. 1773). Joseph's main object appears to have been to make his brothers feel and recognize their guilt in their conduct towards him. For this purpose suffering, then as well as now, was indispensable.

Accordingly Joseph feigned not to know his brothers, charged them with being spies, threatened them with imprisonment, and allowed them to return home to fetch their younger brother, as a proof of their veracity, only on condition that one of them should remain behind in chains, with a prospect of death before him should not their words be verified.

Then it was, and not before, that 'they said one to another, We are verily guilty concerning our brother, in that we saw the anguish of his soul and would not hear; therefore is this distress come upon us. And Reuben said, Spake I not unto you, saying, Do not sin against the child, and ye would not hear? therefore, behold, also his blood is required' (xlii:21). On which, after weeping bitterly, he by common agreement bound his brother Simeon, and left him in custody.

(8) Second Visit. At length Jacob consents to Benjamin's going in company with his brothers, and provided with a present consisting of balm, honey, spices and myrrh, nuts and almonds, and with double money in their hands (double, in order that they might repay the sum which Joseph had caused to be put into each man's sack at their departure, if, as Jacob supposed, 'it was an oversight'), they went again down to Egypt and stood before Joseph (xliii:15); and there, too, stood Benjamin, Joseph's beloved brother. The required pledge of truthfulness was given. If it is asked why such a pledge was demanded, since the giving of it caused pain to Jacob, the answer may be thus: Joseph knew not how to demean himself towards his family until he ascertained its actual condition. That knowledge he could hardly be certain he had gained from the mere words of men who had spared his life for the express purpose of selling him into slavery. How had these wicked men behaved towards his venerable father? His beloved brother Benjamin, was he safe? or had he suffered from their jealousy and malice the worse fate with which he himself had been threatened? Nothing but the sight of Benjamin could answer these questions and resolve these doubts.

Benjamin had come, and immediately a natural change took place in Joseph's conduct; the brother began to claim his rights in Joseph's bosom. Jacob was safe, and Benjamin was safe. Joseph's heart melted at the sight of Benjamin; 'And he said to the ruler of his house, Bring these men home, and slay and make ready, for these men shall dine with me at noon' (xliii:16). But guilt is always the ready parent of fear. Accordingly the brothers expected nothing but being reduced to slavery. When taken to their own brother's house, they imagined they were being entrapped. A colloquy ensued between them and Joseph's steward, whence it appeared that the money put into their sacks, to which they now attributed their peril, was in truth a present from Joseph, designed, after his own brotherly manner, to aid his family in their actual necessities. Noon came, and with it Joseph, whose first question regarded home: 'He asked them of their welfare, and said, Is your father well, the old man of whom ye spake? is he yet alive? And he lifted up his eyes and saw his brother Benjamin, his mother's son, and said, Is this your younger brother? And he said, God be gracious unto thee, my son!' 'And Joseph made haste, for his bowels did yearn upon his brother, and he sought where to weep, and he entered into his chamber and wept there.' Does this look like harshness?

(9) Egyptian Customs. The connection brings into view an Egyptian custom, which is of more than ordinary importance, in consequence of its being adopted in the Jewish polity; 'And they set on (food) for him by himself (Joseph), and for them by themselves (the brethren), and for the Egyptians which did eat with them, by themselves; because the Egyptians might not eat bread with the Hebrews; for that is an abomination unto the Egyptians' (verse 32). This passage is also interesting, as proving that Joseph had not, in his princely grandeur, become ashamed of his origin, nor consented to receive adoption into a strange nation; he was still a Hebrew, waiting, like Moses after him, for the proper season to use his power for the good of his own people.

Other customs appear in this interesting narrative: 'And they (the brothers) sat before him (Joseph), *the first-born according to his birthright,* and the youngest according to his youth.' And he sent messes (delicacies) unto them from before him; but Benjamin's mess was five times so much as any of theirs' (Gen. xliii :32, 33). Fear had now given place to wonder, and wonder at length issued in joy and mirth (comp. verses 18, 33, 34). Thus ended the second act in the drama. Another now opens.

(10) The Silver Cup. Joseph, apparently with a view to ascertain how far his brethren were faithful to their father, hit upon a plan which would in its issue serve to show whether they would make any, and what, sacrifice, in order to fulfill their solemn promise of restoring Benjamin in safety to Jacob. Accordingly he orders not only that every man's money (as before) should be put in his sack's mouth, but also that his 'silver cup, in which my lord drinketh, and whereby he divineth,' should be put in the sack's mouth of the youngest. The brethren leave, but are soon overtaken by Joseph's steward, who charges them with having surreptitiously carried off this costly and highly-valued vessel. They on their part vehemently repel the accusation, adding, 'with whomsoever of thy servants it be found, both let him die, and we also will be my lord's bondmen.' A search is made, and the cup is found in Benjamin's sack. Accordingly they return to the city. And now comes the hour of trial: Would they purchase their own liberation by surrendering Benjamin? After a most touching interview, in which they prove themselves worthy and faithful, Joseph declares himself unable any longer to withstand the appeal of natural affection. On this occasion Judah, who is the spokesman, shows the deepest regard to his aged father's feelings, and entreats for the liberation of Benjamin even at the price of his own liberty. In the whole of literature we know of nothing more simple, natural, true, and impressive (xliv).

(11) Revelation of Identity. Most natural and impressive is the scene also which ensues, in which Joseph, after informing his brethren who he was, and inquiring, first of all, 'Is my father alive?' expresses feelings free from the slightest taint of revenge, and even shows how, under Divine Providence, the conduct of his brothers had issued in good—'God sent me before you to preserve a posterity in the earth, and to save your lives by a great deliverance.' Five years had yet to ensue in which 'there would be neither earing nor harvest;' and therefore the brethren were directed to return home and bring Jacob down to Egypt with all speed. 'And he fell upon his brother Benjamin's neck and wept; and Benjamin wept upon his neck. Moreover, he kissed all his brethren and wept upon them; and after that his brethren talked with him' (xlv :14, 15).

The news of these striking events was carried to Pharaoh, who being pleased with Joseph's conduct, gave directions that Jacob and his family should come forthwith into Egypt. The brethren departed, being well provided for—'And to his father Joseph sent ten asses laden with the good things of Egypt, and ten she asses laden with corn and bread and meat for his father by the way.'

(12) Jacob Goes Down to Egypt. The intelligence which they bore to their father was of such a nature that 'Jacob's heart fainted, for he believed them not.' When, however, he had recovered from the thus naturally told effects of his surprise, the venerable patriarch said, 'Enough; Joseph my son is yet alive; I will go and see him before I die' (xlv :26, 28).

Accordingly Jacob and his family, to the number of threescore and ten souls, go down to Egypt, and by the express efforts of Joseph are allowed to settle in the district of Goshen, where Joseph met his father: 'And he fell on his neck, and wept on his neck a good while.' There Joseph 'nourished his father and his brethren, and all his father's household, with bread, according to their families' (xlvii :12).

(13) Distress in Egypt. Meanwhile the predicted famine was pauperizing Egypt. The inhabitants found their money exhausted, and their cattle and substance all gone, having been parted with in order to purchase food from the public granaries, until at length they had nothing to give in return for sustenance but themselves. 'Buy us'—they then imploringly said to Joseph—'and our land for bread, and we and our land will be slaves unto Pharoah.' 'And Joseph bought all the land of Egypt for Pharaoh, so the land became Pharaoh's.' The people too, 'Joseph removed to cities from one end of the borders of the land to the other end.' Religion, however, was too strong to submit to these political and social changes, and so the priests still retained their land, being supplied with provisions out of the common store gratuitously. The land, which was previously the people's own, was now let to them on a tenancy, at the rent of one-fifth of the produce; the land of the priests being exempted.

(14) Death of Jacob. Joseph had now to pass through the mournful scenes which attend on the death and burial of a father. Having had Jacob embalmed, and seen the rites of mourning fully observed, the faithful and affectionate son—leave being obtained of the monarch—proceeded into the land of Canaan, in order, agreeably to a promise which the patriarch had exacted, to lay the old man's bones with those of his fathers, in 'the field of Ephron the Hittite.' Having performed with long and bitter mourning Jacob's funeral rites, Joseph returned into Egypt. The last recorded act of his life forms a most becoming close. After the death of their father, his brethren, unable, like all guilty people, to forget their criminality, and characteristically finding it difficult to think that Joseph had really forgiven them, grew afraid now they were in his power that he would take an opportunity of inflicting some punishment on them. They accordingly go into his presence, and in imploring terms and an abject manner, entreat his forgiveness. 'Fear not'—this is his noble reply—'I will nourish you and your little ones.'

(15) Death of Joseph.* Joseph lived an hundred and ten years, kind and gentle in his affections to the last; for we are told, 'The children of Machir, the son of Manasseh, were brought up upon Joseph's knees' (1 :23). And so having obtained a promise from his brethren that when the time came, as he assured them it would come, that God should visit them, and 'bring them unto the land which he sware to Abraham, to Isaac,

---

*NOTE.—There is insurmountable difficulty in reconciling the chronology of the patriarchs and the Exodus. The Assyriologists seem to have shown that Abraham was born in the 23d century B. C., and recent research has proved that the Exodus cannot be later than the 13th century B. C. (See CHRONOLOGY.) (Chas. R. Barnes' *Peop. Bib. Cyc.*)

and to Jacob,' they would carry up his bones out of Egypt, Joseph at length 'died, and they embalmed him, and he was put in a coffin' (1:26). This promise was religiously fulfilled. His descendants, after carrying the corpse about with them in their wanderings, at length put it in its final resting place in Shechem, in a parcel of ground that Jacob bought of the sons of Hamor, which became the inheritance of the children of Joseph' (Josh. xxiv :32).

By his Egyptian wife Asenath, daughter of the high priest of Heliopolis, Joseph had two sons, Manasseh and Ephraim (Gen. xli :50, sq.), whom Jacob adopted (Gen. xlviii :5), and who accordingly took their place among the heads of the twelve tribes of Israel.   J. R. B.

(16) Character. Joseph possessed many noble qualities. Piety, a singularly high morality, gentleness, simplicity, patience, fidelity, magnanimity, practical wisdom, firmness and tenacity of purpose were among his characteristics.

2. The Husband of Mary, of whom was born Jesus, who is called Christ (Matt. i :16). By Matthew he is said to have been the son of Jacob, whose lineage is traced by the same writer through David up to Abraham. Luke represents him as being the son of Heli, and traces his origin up to Adam. For the reconciliation of these accounts see GENEALOGY.

(1) Biblical Statements. The statements of Holy Writ in regard to Joseph are few and simple. According to a custom among the Jews, traces of which are still found, such as handfasting among the Scotch, and betrothing among the Germans, Joseph had pledged his faith to Mary; but before the marriage was consummated she proved to be with child. Grieved at this, Joseph was disposed to break off the connection; but, not wishing to make a public example of one whom he loved, he contemplated a private disruption of their bond. From this step, however, he is deterred by a heavenly messenger, who assures him that Mary has conceived under a divine influence, 'And she shall bring forth a son, and thou shalt call his name Jesus; for he shall save his people from their sins' (Matt. i :18, sq.; Luke i :27). To this account various objections have been taken; but most of them are drawn from the ground of a narrow, short-sighted, and half-informed rationalism, which judges everything by its own small standard, and either denies miracles altogether, or admits only such miracles as find favor in its sight.

(2) An Artificer. Joseph was by trade a carpenter, in which business he probably educated Jesus. In Matt. xiii :55, we read, 'Is not this the son of the carpenter?' and in Mark vi :3, 'Is not this the carpenter, the son of Mary?' The Greek term employed, *tech-tone,* is of a general character (from *tech-noh,* 'I form'), and may be fitly rendered by the English word 'artificer,' or 'artisan.' Schleusner (on this subject) asserts that the universal testimony of the ancient church represents our Lord as being a carpenter's son. Hilarius, on Matthew (quoted in Simon's *Dictionnaire de la Bible,* i, 691), asserts, in terms which cannot be mistaken, that Jesus was a smith. Of the same opinion was the Venerable Bede; while others have held that our Lord was a mason, and Cardinal Cajetan, that he was a goldsmith.

The last notion probably had its origin in those false associations of more modern times which disparage hand labor. Among the ancient Jews all handicrafts were held in so much honor that they were learned and pursued by the first men of the nation.

(3) Tradition. Christian tradition makes Joseph an old man when first espoused to Mary (Epiphan. *Hær.* 78, 7), being no less than eighty years of age, and father of four sons and two daughters. The painters of Christian antiquity conspire with the writers in representing Joseph as an old man at the period of the birth of our Lord—an evidence which is not to be lightly rejected, though the precise age mentioned may be but an approximation to fact.

(4) Death. It is not easy to determine when Joseph died. That event may have taken place before Jesus entered on his public ministry. This has been argued from the fact that his mother only appeared at the feast at Cana in Galilee. The premises, however, hardly bear out the inference. With more force of argument, it has been alleged (Simon, *Dict. de la Bible*) that Joseph must have been dead before the crucifixion of Jesus, else he would in all probability have appeared with Mary at the cross. Certainly the absence of Joseph from the public life of Christ, and the absence of reference to him in the discourses and history, while 'Mary' and 'His brethren' not unfrequently appear, afford evidence not only of Joseph's death, but of the inferior part which, as the legal father only of our Lord, Joseph might have been expected to sustain. The traditions respecting Joseph are collected in *Act. Sanct.* iii, p. 4, *sq.;* there is a Life of Joseph written in Italian by Affaitati. (Pearson, *On the Creed;* Mill, *On the Brethren of the Lord;* Alford's *Note on Matt.* xiii :55.)   J. R. B.

3. Father of Igal, who was the spy, sent from the tribe of Issachar to investigate the land of Canaan (Num. xiii :7), B. C. before 1657.

4. An Israelite of the family of Bani, and one of those who put away their foreign wives in the time of Ezra (Ezra x :42), B. C. 456.

5. A priest in the family of Shebaniah in the next generation after the return from captivity (Neh. xii :14), B. C. after 536.

6. An ancestor of Christ (Luke iii :30). He was the son of Jonan, and was in the eighth generation from David, or about contemporary with Ahaziah.

7. An ancestor of Christ (Luke iii :26). He was the son of Judah or Abiud, and grandson of Joanna or Hananiah the son of Zerubbabel.

8. Another ancestor of Christ (Luke iii :24). He was the son of Mattathias, in the seventh generation, before Joseph, Mary's husband.

9. Surnamed CAIAPHAS (which see).

10. Joseph of Arimathea. The name Arimathea denotes probably the place where Joseph was born, not that where he resided.

(1) Location of Arimathea. Arimathea lay in the territory of Benjamin, on the mountain range of Ephraim, at no great distance south of Jerusalem (Josh. xviii :25; Judg. iv :5), not far from Gibeah (Judg. xix :13; Isa. x :29; Hos. v :8).

(2) Begs the Body of Jesus. Joseph was a secret disciple of Jesus—'an honorable counsellor (βουλευτής), who waited for the kingdom of God' (Mark xv :43), and who, on learning the death of our Lord, 'came, and went in boldly unto Pilate, and craved the body of Jesus.' Pilate having learned from the centurion, who commanded at the execution, that 'Jesus was actually dead,' gave the body to Joseph, who took it down and wrapped his deceased Lord in fine linen which he had purchased for the purpose; after which he laid the corpse in a sepulcher which was hewn out of a rock, and rolled a stone unto the door of the sepulcher (Mark xv :43, *sq.*). From the parallel passages in Matthew (xxvii :58, *sq.*), Luke (xxiii :

50, *sq.*), and John (xix:38, *sq.*), it appears that the body was previously embalmed at the cost of another secret disciple, Nicodemus, and that the sepulcher was new, 'wherein never man before was laid;' also that it lay in a garden, and was the property of Joseph himself. This garden was 'in the place where Jesus was crucified.'

(3) **Character.** Luke describes the character of Joseph as 'a good man and a just,' adding that 'he had not consented to the counsel and deed of them,' *i. e.* of the Jewish authorities. From this remark it is clear that Joseph was a member of the Sanhedrim; a conclusion which is corroborated by the epithet 'counsellor,' applied to him by both Luke and Mark. Tradition represents Joseph as having been one of the Seventy, and as having first preached the Gospel in old England (Ittig. *Diss. de Pat. Apostol,* sec. 13; Assemani *Biblioth. Orient.* iii:1, 319, *sq.*). For an attempt to fix the precise spot where Jesus died and was buried, see the article GOLGOTHA.   J. R. B.

11. Joseph ‹called Barsabas was one of the two persons whom the primitive church, immediately after the resurrection of Christ, nominated, praying that the Holy Spirit would show which of them should enter the apostolic band in place of the wretched Judas. On the lots being cast, it proved that not Joseph, but Matthias, was chosen.

Joseph bore the honorable surname of Justus, which was not improbably given him on account of his well-known probity. He was one of those who had 'companied with the Apostles all the time that the Lord Jesus went in and out amongst them, beginning from the baptism of John,' until the ascension (Acts i:23, *sq.*). Tradition also accounted him one of the Seventy (Euseb. *Hist. Eccles.* i:12; Heinrichs, *On Acts* i:23; Ullmann, in the *Theolog. Stud. und Kritik,* i. 377).
J. R. B.

JOSES (jō'sēz), (Gr. 'Ιωσῆς, *ee-oh-sace'*).

1. The son of Mary and Cleopas, and brother of James the Less, of Simon and of Jude, and, consequently, one of those who are called the 'brethren' of our Lord (Matt. xiii:55; xxvii:56; Mark vi:3; xv:40, 47). (See JAMES; JUDAS.) He was the ₀nly one of these brethren who was not an apostle—a circumstance which has given occasion to some unsatisfactory conjecture. It is perhaps more remarkable that three of them were apostles than that the fourth was not.

2. Son of Eliezer in the genealogy of Christ (Luke iii:29). He was in the fifteenth generation from David, which was about the time of Manasseh. Jose of the A. V. is incorrect, being merely the genitive case.

3. (See BARNABAS.)

JOSHAH (jō'shah), (Heb. יֹשָׁה, *yo-shaw'*, Jehovah established), a prince of the house of Simeon, who attacked the Hamite Shepherds in Gedor, without provocation, and, after exterminating them, occupied their country (1 Chron. iv:34), B. C. about 711.

JOSHAPHAT (jŏsh'a-phăt), (Heb. יֹשָׁפָט, *yo-shaw-fawt'*, Jehovah judged), a Mithnite among the guards of David, who evidently came from the east of the Jordan (1 Chron. xi:43), B. C. about 1000.

JOSHAVIAH (jŏsh'a-vī'ah), (Heb. יֹשַׁוְיָה, *yo-shav-yaw'*, Jehovah sufficient), son of Elnaam and one of David's guards (1 Chron. xi:46), B. C. 1000.

JOSHBEKASHAH (josh-bĕk'a-shäh), (Heb. יָשְׁבְּקָשָׁה, *yosh-bek-aw-shaw'*, seat in hardness), a

member of the house of Heman and head of the sixteenth course of musicians (1 Chron. xxv:4, 24), B. C. about 960.

JOSHEB-BASSEBETH (jō'shĕb-băs'sē-bĕth), (Heb. יֹשֵׁב בַּשֶּׁבֶת, *yo-shabe' bash-sheh'beth*, sitting in the council), the chief of David's three leading heroes (2 Sam. xxiii:8), called Jashobeam (1 Chron. xi:11).

JOSHUA (jŏsh'u-à), (Heb. יְהוֹשׁוּעַ, *yeh-ho-shoo'-ah,* Jehovah saves). The name is rendered by Josephus, the Septuagint, and the New Testament, 'Ιησοῦs, *ee-ay-soos, Jesus.*

In the same manner is spelt the name of the author of the apocryphal book Ecclesiasticus. This is the name of four persons in the Old Testament, and means *whose salvation is Jehovah* (compare the German name *Gotthilf*).

1. The most distinguished of the four persons, so called, who occur in the Old Testament, is Joshua the son of Nun, of the tribe of Ephraim, the assistant and successor of Moses. His name was originally Hoshea, *salvation* (Num. xiii:8); and it seems that the subsequent alteration of it by Moses (Num. xiii:16) was significant, and proceeded on the same principle as that of Abram into Abraham (Gen. xvii:5), and of Sarai into Sarah (Gen. xvii:15).

(1) **Commander of Israelites.** In the Bible he is first mentioned as being the victorious commander of the Israelites in their battle against the Amalekites at Rephidim (Exod. xvii:8-16), B. C. 1210.

(2) **On Mount Sinai.** When Moses was on the mount, Joshua tarried somewhere on the side of it, and came down with him (Exod. xxiv:13; xxxii:17).

(3) **In Charge of Tabernacle.** After the defection of Israel and their worship of the golden calf, Moses moved the tabernacle outside of the camp, and, returning to the congregation, left it in charge of Joshua (xxxiii:11).

(4) **Eldad and Medad.** Zealous for Moses' honor, he was for prohibiting Eldad and Medad from prophesying. Moses rebuked him, saying, "Enviest thou for my sake? would God that all the Lord's people were prophets, and that the Lord would put his Spirit upon them" (Num. xi:27-29).

(5) **A Spy.** He was one of the spies that searched the Promised Land (Num. xiii:8, 16; xiv:6, 38; xi:28, 29).

(6) **Appointed Ruler.** A little before Moses' death, Joshua was solemnly installed in the government of the Hebrew nation; and such honor was by' Moses put upon him as tended to make them reverence and obey him (Num. xxvii:18-23; Deut. iii:21; xxxi:14-23).

(7) **With Moses in the Tabernacle.** It was made known to Moses that he was about to die, and that he should appear with Joshua in the tabernacle. And while in the presence of Jehovah Moses gave his devoted minister a "charge," and said, "Be strong and of good courage; for thou shalt bring the children of Israel into the land which I sware unto them; and I will be with thee" (Deut. xxxi:14, 23).

(8) **Takes Charge of Israel.** After Moses' death, God directed and encouraged Joshua to take on him the government of the Hebrews, and promised to give him his continued presence and support. Joshua warned the Reubenites, Gadites, and eastern Manassites, who were settled by Moses, to prepare for crossing the Jordan and

conquering Canaan, along with their brethren. Spies were sent to view Jericho. These, by means of Rahab, were preserved, and returned safe, though no small search had been made for them; they reported that the Canaanites were in the utmost consternation, for fear of the Hebrew invasion.

(9) Crosses the Jordan. At this time, the Jordan overflowed its banks; but, as soon as the feet of the priests, who bare the ark of the Lord, going at the distance of 2,000 cubits, or 3,648 feet, before the host, touched the brim of the waters of Jordan, they parted; those above stood like a mountain, and those below ran off into the Dead Sea, leaving an empty space of about six miles for the Hebrew tribes to pass over. The priests, with the ark, continued in the middle of the channel till all were got over.

(10) In Canaan. To commemorate this event, Joshua erected twelve large stones in the very spot where the ark had stood; and, taking twelve other stones from the mid channel of the river, erected them on the banks. Some days after he ordered that all that had been born for thirty-eight years back to be circumcised; fully assured of God's protecting them, when sore, from their foes. Next, the passover was celebrated. On the morrow after, they began to eat the old corn of Canaan, and the manna fell no more about their tents.

(11) The Angel of Jehovah. Soon after, the angel of Jehovah appeared to Joshua as a glorious man, with a drawn sword, and told him he was come, as chief commander of the Hebrew troops in their approaching wars. He fell on his face, and reverently put off his shoes (Josh. v:13-15).

(12) Capture of Jericho. Directed of God, Joshua made his troops encompass Jericho seven days, and seven times on the seventh, with the ark carried before them, and some sounding with ram's horns. When they had finished the thirteenth circuit, they gave a great shout, and the walls of Jericho, all around, fell flat to the ground. None but Rahab and her family were saved (Josh. vi). The metal found in the city was devoted to the service of God, but everything else to ruin; and a curse was denounced against the rebuilder of the city. Achan, however, coveted and took part of the spoil. (See ACHAN.)

(13) The First Defeat. Advised by some, Joshua, to ease his troops, sent no more but 3,000 to attack Ai. To punish Achan's theft, they were repulsed, and thirty-six of the number slain. This exceedingly grieved Joshua, as he thought it would make the Canaanites triumph over God and his people. After solemn prayer he was informed of the cause, and the sacrilege was punished by the death of Achan and his family (Josh. vii).

(14) Capture of Ai. Next the Lord ordered the whole Hebrew host to attack Ai, and to use stratagems beside. After it was taken, Joshua and the Hebrews seem to have marched northward to Ebal and Gerizim. On Ebal they erected stones, plastered them with plaster, and plainly inscribed thereon a copy of the Mosaic laws, or rather an abridgement, or perhaps no more than the blessings and curses mentioned in Deut. xxvii and xxviii. An altar of rough stones was raised, and the burnt-offerings and peace-offering being finished, the people feasted on the flesh of the last with joy and gladness, that they were thus the covenant people of God. The priests then went down to the valley of Moreh between two hills, and with a loud voice read the blessings and curses. Six of the tribes, descended from

free women, with their wives, and the strangers among them, stood on Gerizim, and echoed Amen to the blessings. Six of the tribes, four of which were descended of bond women, and one of Reuben, who had lost his birthright, with their wives, and the strangers, stood on Mount Ebal, and echoed their Amen to the curses as they were read. After this solemn dedication of themselves to God's service, the Hebrews returned to Gilgal (Josh. vi-viii; Deut. xxvii).

(15) League with the Gibeonites. Next, Joshua and the princes entered into a league with the Gibeonites; and being convinced of his mistake, he devoted that people to the laborious part of the service of God. Enraged that the Gibeonites had made peace with Joshua, Adonizedek, and four of his neighboring princes, entered into a league to destroy them.

(16) Battle of Gibeon. Informed of this, Joshua marched to their assistance and routed the five kings. A little before sunset, Joshua brought these kings out of the cave of Makkedah, where he had shut them up, and after causing his captains to trample on their necks, he hanged them. Joshua proceeded to burn their cities, and slay the inhabitants throughout the south part of the promised land.

(17) Subsequent Conquests. This great battle was followed by the conquest of Makkedah, Libnah, Lachish, Gezer, Eglon, Hebron, and Debir. In this one campaign Joshua subdued the southern half of Palestine, from Kadesh-barnea to Gaza, the eastern and western limit of the southern frontier; and he led the people back to Gilgal (Josh. x:15-43). In another campaign he marched to Lake Merom, where he met and overthrew a confederacy of the Canaanitish chiefs of the north, Jabin, King of Hazor, and in the course of a protracted war he led his victorious soldiers to the gates of Zidon and into the Valley of Lebanon under Hermon. In six years, six nations, with thirty-one kings, swell the roll of his conquests, and amongst others the Anakim—the old terror of Israel—are specially recorded as destroyed everywhere except in Philistia. (Smith, *Dict. of the Bible.*)

(18) Dividing the Inheritance. Joshua, now advanced in years, proceeded, in conjunction with Eleazar and the heads of the tribes, to complete the division of the conquered land; and when all was allotted, Timnath-serah, in Mount Ephraim, was assigned by the people as Joshua's peculiar inheritance. The tabernacle of the congregation was established at Shiloh, six cities of refuge were appointed, forty-eight cities assigned to the Levites, and the warriors of the trans-Jordanic tribes dismissed in peace to their homes.

(19) Assembles the Hebrews. After Joshua had governed the Hebrews seventeen, or perhaps twenty-five years, he, finding his end approaching, assembled the Hebrews, rehearsed to them what God had done for them, and made them renew their solemn engagements to worship and serve him at Shechem, a place already famous in connection with Jacob (Gen. xxxv:4), and Joseph (Josh. xxiv:32).

(20) Death. He died aged one hundred and ten, and was buried at Timnath-serah, his own city (Josh. xxiv:29, 30).

(21) Character. Joshua's life has been noted as one of the very few which are recorded in history with some fullness of detail. In his character have been traced, under an Oriental garb, such features as chiefly kindled the imagination of western chroniclers and poets in the Middle Ages;

the character of a devout warrior, who has been taught by serving as a youth how to command as a man; who earns by manly vigor a quiet, honored old age; who combines strength with gentleness, ever looking up for and obeying the divine impulse with the simplicity of a child, while he wields great power, and directs it calmly, and without swerving, to the accomplishment of a high, unselfish purpose. (Smith, *Bib. Dict.*) (See CANAANITES.)

Figurative. Holy Scripture itself suggests (Heb. iv:8) the consideration of Joshua as a type of Christ. Many of the Christian Fathers have enlarged upon this view. (See Bishop Pearson, who has collected their opinions *On the Creed.* Art. ii, pp. 87-90, and 94-96, ed. 1843).

2. *A Beth-shemite* (1 Sam. vi:14), the owner of the field into which the cart came which bore the ark on its return from the land of the Philistines. (B. C. about 1076.)

3. *The governor of the city of Jerusalem* at the commencement of the reign of Josiah. He gave his name to one of the city gates (2 Kings xxiii:8), B. C. 621.

4. *Joshua or Jeshua*, the son of JOZADAK, or JOSEDECH, was high-priest of the Jews when they returned from Babylon. He assisted Zerubbabel in rebuilding the temple. Zechariah saw him represented as standing before the Lord in filthy garments, and Satan standing at his right hand to accuse and resist him; but the Angel of Jehovah rebuked the devil, and arrayed Joshua in pure raiment. Not long after, Zechariah was directed to make a golden crown for him (Ezra iv:3; Hag. i:1; Zech. iii and vi).

Figurative. Did not he prefigure Jesus, as the High-Priest, Builder, and Savior of his church, who, though once laden with our iniquities, and in the likeness of sinful flesh, is now glorious in his apparel, and crowned with many crowns?

Brown.

JOSHUA, BOOK OF.

(1) Profane Mention of Other Books. There occur some vestiges of the deeds of Joshua in other historians besides those of the Bible. Procopius mentions a Phœnician inscription near the city of Tingis in Mauritania, the sense of which in Greek was:—'Ἡμεῖς ἐσμεν οἱ ψυγόντες ἀπὸ προσώπου Ἰησοῦ τοῦ λῃστοῦ υἱοῦ Ναυῆ—'We are those who fled before the face of Joshua the robber, the son of Nun' (*De Bell. Vandal.* ii, 10). Suidas (sub verbo Χαναάν):—ἡμεῖς ἐσμεν Χαναναῖοι οὓς ἐδίωξεν Ἰησοῦς ὁ λῃστής—'We are the Canaanites whom Joshua the robber drove away.'

A letter of Shaubech, king of Armenia Minor, in the Samaritan book of Joshua (ch. xxvi), styles Joshua *lupus percussor,* 'the murderous wolf;' or, according to another reading in the book *Juchasin* (p. 154, f. 1), and in the *Shalsheleth Rakkabbalah* (p. 96), *lupus vespertinus,* 'the evening wolf.'

(2) Name of the Book. The book of Joshua is so called from the personage who occupies the principal place in the narration of events contained therein, and may be considered as a continuation of the Pentateuch. It commences with the words *now it came to pass,* which may be renderd *thereupon it happened.* Books beginning with what Dr. Samuel Lee calls *the illative vau,* are to be regarded as continuations of earlier works. The Pentateuch, and especially Deuteronomy, are repeatedly referred to in the book of Joshua, the narration of which begins with the death of Moses and extends to the death of Joshua, embracing a chronological period of some-

what less than thirty years. The subject of the book is thus briefly stated in ch. i:5, 6: 'There shall not any man be able to stand before thee all the days of thy life. As I was with Moses, so I will be with thee; I will not fail thee, nor forsake thee. Be strong and of a good courage; for unto this people shalt thou divide for an inheritance the land which I sware unto their fathers to give them.' In these two verses is also indicated the division of the book into two principal portions, with reference to the conquest and the distribution of the land of Canaan. The conquest is narrated in the first twelve, and the distribution in the following ten chapters. In the last two chapters are subjoined the events subsequent to the distribution up to the death of Joshua.

(3) Conquest of Canaan. The history of the conquest of Canaan is a series of miracles, than which none more remarkable are recorded in any part of sacred history. The passage into the Promised Land, as well as that out of Egypt, was through water. Jericho was taken not by might, but by the falling of the walls on the blast of the trumpets of seven priests; and in the war against Gibeon the day was prolonged to afford time for the completion of the victory.

(4) First Twelve Chapters. It is generally granted that the first twelve chapters form a continuous whole; although the author in ch. x:13, refers to another work, he not merely transcribes but intimately combines the quotation with the tenor of his narration. It is certain that there sometimes occur episodes which seem to interrupt the chronological connection, as for instance the portion intervening between chs. i, ii, and iii:1.

The whole tenor of the first twelve chapters bespeaks an eye-witness who bore some part in the transactions, and the expression we *passed over,* in ch. v:1, bears this out, as well as the circumstantial vividness of the narrative, which clearly indicates that the writer was an eye-witness.

(5) Time of Writing. The statement that the monuments which he erected were extant *to this day,* indicates that he did not promulgate the book immediately after the events narrated (comp. iv:9; vii:26; viii:28, 29; x:27). The book could not have been written very long after the time of Joshua, because we find that Rahab was still alive when it was composed (vi:25). The section from chapters xiii to xxii inclusive, which contains an account of the distribution of the land, seems to be based upon written documents, in which the property was accurately described. That this was the case is likely not merely on account of the peculiar nature of the diplomatic contents by which this 'Doomsday Book' is distinguished from the preceding part of Joshua, but also on account of the statement in chapter xviii:4, where Joshua says to the children of Israel, 'Give out from among you three men from each tribe; and I will send them, and they shall rise, and go through the land and describe it according to the inheritance of them; and they shall come again to me.' Compare verse 6, 'Ye therefore shall describe the land into seven parts.' Compare also verses 8 and 9, 'And the men arose and went away; and Joshua charged them that went to *describe* the land, saying, Go, and walk through the land, and *describe* it, and come again to me, that I may here cast lots for you before the Lord in Shiloh.'

(6) Sources. The list of towns granted to the Levites in Josh. xxi differs from that in 1 Chron. vi:39-66 so much that we must suppose the latter to contain abstracts from a source different from that in the book of Joshua. That a change of circumstances might demand changes in such lists becomes evident, if we consider the fate of individual cities. For instance, Ziklag was given to the tribe of Simeon (Josh. xix:5) ; nevertheless we read in 1 Sam. xxvii:6, that Achish gave Ziklag to David.

Since the book of Joshua contains also a description of the territories of Reuben, Gad, and the half tribe of Manasseh, situated on the left bank of the Jordan, which tribes entered into possession before the death of Moses, the Pentateuch itself may be considered as one of the sources from which the second part of the book of Joshua has been compiled. That the author of the book of Joshua derived part of his information from the Pentateuch is evident, if we compare Deut. xviii: 1, 2, and Num. xviii:20, with Josh. xiii:14, 33; xiv:4. Compare also Num. xxxi:8, with Josh. xiii:21 and 22.

The author of the book of Joshua frequently repeats the statement of the Pentateuch in a more detailed form, and mentions the changes which had taken place since the Pentateuch was written. Compare Num. xxxiv:13 and 14, with Josh. xiv: 1-4; Num. xxxii:37, with Josh. xiii:17, sq.; Num. xxxv with Josh. xxi.

(7) Similarities. There is also considerable similarity between the following passages in the books of Joshua and Judges : Josh. xiii:3; Judg. iii:3; Josh. xv:13, sq.; Judg. i:10, 20; Josh. xv: 15-19; Judg. i:11-15; Josh. xv:63; Judg. i:21; Josh. xvi:10; Judg. 1:29; Josh. xvii:12; Judg. i:27; Josh. xix:47; Judg. xviii. The book of Joshua seems to explain the text of the book of Judges by brief notices; as, for instance, the names Sheshai, Ahiman, and Talmai (Josh. xv:14), (comp. Judg. i:10), and makes use of more regular grammatical forms, instead of the more unusual forms in the book of Judges.

(8) Authentic Records. It seems to have been the intention of the author of chapters xiii-xxii to furnish authentic records concerning the arrangements made by Joshua after the conquest of Canaan. Since we do not find in the subsequent history that the tribes, after the death of Joshua, disagreed among themselves about the ownership of the land, it would appear that the object of the book of Joshua, as a 'Doomsday Book,' was fully attained. The circumstance that the book of Joshua contains many Canaanitish names of places to which the Hebrew names are added, seems also to indicate that the second part originated in an early age, when neither the Canaanitish name was entirely forgotten, nor the Hebrew name fully introduced; so that it was expedient to mention both.

(9) Authorship. In the last two chapters occur two orations of Joshua, in which he bids farewell to the people whom he had commanded. In chapter xxiv:26, we read, 'And Joshua wrote these words in the book of the law of God.' The expression, *these words*, seems to refer only to his last address, and the subsequent resolution of the people to follow his example. We are here, however, expressly informed that Joshua did write this much; and consequently, we deem it the more likely that he also committed to writing the other memorable events connected with his career, such as the conquest and the distribution of the land.

Viewing all the circumstances together, we consider it highly probable that the whole book of Joshua was composed by himself up to the twenty-eighth verse of the last chapter; to which a friendly hand subjoined some brief notices, contained in verses 29-33, concerning the death, age, and burial of Joshua; the continuance of his influence upon the people; the interment, in Shechem, of the bones of Joseph, which the children of Israel had brought from Egypt; and the death and burial of Eleazar, the son of Aaron, whom his son Phinehas interred in his allotment on Mount Ephraim.

(10) Authority. The authority of the book of Joshua mainly rests upon the manner in which it is treated in other parts of the Bible.

Besides the above allusions in the book of Judges, we find Joshua referred to in 1 Kings xvi:34:—'In his days did Hiel the Bethelite build Jericho; he laid the foundation thereof in Abiram, his firstborn, and set up the gates thereof in his youngest son Segub, according to the word of the Lord, which he spake by Joshua the son of Nun.' (Comp. Josh. vi:26.) The second and third verses of Psalms xliv contain a brief summary of the whole book of Joshua:—'Thou didst drive out the heathen with thy hand, and plantedst them; thou didst afflict the people, and cast them out. For they got not the land in possession by their own sword, neither did their own arm save them; but thy right hand and thine arm, and the light of thy countenance, because thou hadst a favor unto them.' (Compare Psalm lxviii:12-14; lxxviii:54, 55; cxiv:3 and 5, which refer to the book of Joshua.) Also, Hab. iii:11: 'The sun and moon stood still in their habitation,' etc. Heb. xiii:5: 'For he hath said, I will never leave thee, nor forsake thee.' (Compare Josh. i:5.) Heb. xi:31: 'By faith the harlot Rahab perished not with them that believed not, when she had received the spies with peace;' and James ii:25: 'Likewise also was not Rahab the harlot justified by works, when she had received the messengers, and had sent them out another way?' (Compare Josh. ii and vi:22-25.) Acts vii:45: 'Which (the tabernacle) also our fathers that came after brought in with Jesus into the possession of the Gentiles, whom God drave out before the face of our fathers.' (Compare Josh. iii:14.) Heb. xi:30: 'By faith the walls of Jericho fell down, after they were compassed about seven days.' (Compare Josh. vi:17-23.) Heb. iv:8: 'For if Jesus (Joshua) had given them rest, then would he not afterwards have spoken of another day.'

The quotation from the book of Jasher (Josh. x:13) is said to be contradicted by 2 Sam. i:18, where it appears that this book was written in the days of David. But this is by no means clear from the passage referred to; and even if it were so, it would seem that the book of Jasher was an anthologia, augmented in the days of David. Others have based upon this quotation the inference that the book of Joshua was written after the times of David. De Wette, in his *Einleitung* (Berlin, 1833, p. 219), asserts that the book of Joshua was written after the Babylonian captivity.

The mention of the book of Jasher has given rise to some spurious compilations under that name, as well in Hebrew as in English. (See the article JASHER, BOOK OF.)

(11) Literature. See, besides the *Introductions* of Eichhorn, De Wette, and Hävernick; George Bush, *Notes on Joshua and Judges* (New York, 1838) ; Wordsworth, *Holy Bible with notes*, pt. i:1-74 (Lond., 1865) ; Ewald, *Gesch. des Volkes Israel*, Eng. transl. by Martineau (Lond., 1868) ; Palfrey, *Lectures on the Jewish Scriptures*, ii. 134-183; Davidson, *Introd. to the Old Testament*, i:409-448; Rawlinson, *Hist. Evidences* Lect. iii; Keil, *Introd. to Old Testament*.

JOSIAH (jō-sī'ah), (Heb. יֹאשִׁיָּה, *yo-shee-yaw*, founded by Jah).

1. The seventeenth king of Judah, and son of Amon whom he succeeded on the throne (B. C. 639), at the early age of eight years, and reigned thirty-one years.

(1) Accession to the Throne. As Josiah thus early ascended the throne, we may the more admire the good qualities which he manifested. Avoiding the example of his immediate predecessors, he 'did that which was right in the sight of the Lord, and walked in all the ways of David his father, and turned not aside to the right hand or to the left' (2 Kings xxii:1, 2; 2 Chron. xxxiv: 1, 2).

(2) Purification of the Land. As early as the sixteenth year of his age he began to manifest that enmity to idolatry in all its forms which distinguished his character and reign; and he was not quite twenty years old when he proclaimed open war against it, although more or less favored by many men of rank and influence in the court and kingdom. He then commenced a thorough purification of the land from all taint of idolatry, by going about and superintending in person the operations of the men who were employed in breaking down idolatrous altars and images, and cutting down the groves which had been consecrated to idol worship. His detestation of idolatry could not have been more strongly expressed than by ransacking the sepulchers of the idolatrous priests of former days, and consuming their bones upon the idol altars before they were overturned.

(3) His Action Predicted. Yet this operation, although unexampled in Jewish history, was foretold three hundred and twenty-six years before Josiah was born, by the prophet who was commissioned to denounce to Jeroboam the future punishment of his sin. He even named Josiah as the person by whom this act was to be performed; and said that it should be performed in Bethel, which was then a part of the kingdom of Israel (1 Kings xiii:2). All this seemed much beyond the range of human probabilities. But it was performed to the letter; for Josiah did not confine his proceedings to his own kingdom, but went over a considerable part of the neighboring kingdom of Israel, which then lay comparatively desolate, with the same object in view; and as Bethel, in particular, executed all that the prophet had foretold (2 Kings xxiii:1-19; 2 Chron. xxxiv:3-7, 32). In these proceedings Josiah seems to have been actuated by an absolute *hatred* of idolatry, such as no other king since David had manifested, and which David had scarcely occasion to manifest in the same degree.

(4) Temple Repaired. In the eighteenth year of his reign and the twenty-sixth of his age, when the land had been thoroughly purified from idolatry and all that belonged to it, Josiah proceeded to repair and beautify the temple of the Lord.

(5) Finding of the Law. In the course of this pious labor, the high-priest Hilkiah discovered in the sanctuary a volume, which proved to contain the books of Moses, and which, from the terms employed, seems to have been considered the original of the law as written by Moses. On this point there has been much anxious discussion and some rash assertion. Some writers of the German school allege that there is no external evidence —that is, evidence beside the law itself—that the book of law existed till it was thus produced by Hilkiah. This assertion it is the less necessary to answer here, as it is duly noticed in the article PENTATEUCH. But it may be observed that it is founded very much on the fact that the king was greatly astonished when some parts of the law were read to him. It is indeed perfectly manifest that he had previously been entirely ignorant of much that he then heard; and he rent his clothes in consternation when he found that, with the best intentions to serve the Lord, he and all his people had been living in the neglect of duties which the law declared to be of vital importance. It is certainly difficult to account for this ignorance. Some suppose that all the copies of the law had perished, and that the king had never seen one. This is very unlikely, but however scarce complete copies may have been, the pious king was likely to have been the possessor of one. The probability seems to be that the passages read were those awful denunciations against disobedience with which the book of Deuteronomy concludes, and which from some cause or other the king had never before read, or which had never before produced on his mind the same strong conviction of the imminent dangers under which the nation lay, as now when read to him from a volume invested with a character so venerable, and brought with such interesting circumstances under his notice.

The king in his alarm sent to Huldah 'the prophetess,' for her counsel in this emergency (see HULDAH); her answer assured him that, although the dread penalties threatened by the law had been incurred and would be inflicted, he should be gathered in peace to his fathers before the days of punishment and sorrow came.

(6) Renewal of the Covenant. It was perhaps not without some hope of averting this doom that the king immediately called the people together at Jerusalem, and engaged them in a solemn renewal of the ancient covenant with God. When this had been done, the Passover was celebrated with careful attention to the directions given in the law, and on a scale of unexampled magnificence. But all was too late; the hour of mercy had passed; for 'the Lord turned not from the fierceness of his great wrath, wherewith his anger was kindled against Judah' (2 Kings xxii:3-20; xxiii:21-27; 2 Chron. xxxiv:8-33; xxxv:1-19).

(7) Death. That removal from the world which had been promised to Josiah as a blessing, was not long delayed and was brought about in a way which he had probably not expected. His kingdom was tributary to the Chaldæan empire; and when Pharaoh-necho, king of Egypt, sought a passage through his territories, on an expedition against the Chaldæans, Josiah, with a very high sense of the obligations which his vassalage imposed, refused to allow the march of the Egyptian army through his dominions, and prepared to resist the attempt by force of arms. Necho was very unwilling to engage in hostilities with Josiah; the appearance of the Hebrew army at Megiddo, however, brought on a battle, in which the king of Judah was so desperately wounded by arrows that his attendants removed him from the war-chariot, and placed him in another, in which he was taken to Jerusalem, where he died (B. C. about 680).

(8) Character. Josiah possessed many estimable qualities. No king that reigned in Israel was ever more deeply lamented by all his subjects than he; and we are told that the prophet, Jeremiah, composed on the occasion an elegiac ode, which was long preserved among the people, but which is not now in existence (2 Kings xxiii:29-37; 2 Chron. xxxv:20-27).

2. Son of Zephaniah, whose house Zechariah was commanded to make the assembling place of the chief men of the captivity when Joshua, the high-priest, was crowned (Zech. vi:10), B. C. 519.

JOSIAS (jo-sī'as), (Gr. 'Ιωσίας, *ee-oh-se'os*), the Grecized form of *Josiah*, king of Judah, found Matt. i:10, 11.

JOSIBIAH (jŏs-i-bī'ah), (Heb. יוֹשִׁבְיָה, *yo-shib-yaw'*, *i. e.* Joshibiah, dweller with Jehovah), father of Jehu, a descendant of that branch of the Simeonite tribe of which Shimei was founder, and which later was the most numerous (1 Chron. iv:35), B. C. before 711.

JOSIPHIAH (jos'i-phī'ah), (Heb. יוֹשִׁבְיָה, *yo-shib-yaw'*, dweller with Jehovah), an ancestor, perhaps father, of Shelomith, who returned from the captivity with Ezra (Ezra viii:10), B. C. about 457.

JOT (jŏt), English form of *Iota*, ιῶτα, *ee-oh'ta*, the Greek letter so called, the same in power and place as the English *i*. (See IOTA.)

JOTBAH (jŏt'bah), (Heb. יָטְבָה, *yot-baw'*, pleasantness), given as the native place of Meshullemeth, queen of Manasseh, and mother of Amon, King of Judah (2 Kings xxi:19). The place is not elsewhere mentioned, but it is commonly identified with JOTBATH.

JOTBATH or JOTBATHA (jŏt'băth' or jŏt'ba-thah), (Heb. יָטְבָתָה, *yot-baw'thaw*, pleasantness), the twenty-ninth encampment of Israel in the wilderness, between Gidgad and Ebronah (Num. xxxiii:33, 34; Deut. x:7).

JOTHAM (jō'tham), (Heb. יוֹתָם, *yo-thawm'*, God is upright).

1. The youngest of Gideon's seventy legitimate sons; and the only one who escaped when the rest were massacred by the order of Abimelech (Judg. ix:5). When the fratricide was made king by the people of Shechem, the young Jotham was so daring as to make his appearance on Mount Gerizim for the purpose of lifting up a protesting voice, and of giving vent to his feelings. This he did in a beautiful parable, wherein the trees are represented as making choice of a king, and bestowing on the bramble the honor which the cedar, the olive, and the vine would not accept. The obvious application, which indeed Jotham failed not himself to point out, must have been highly exasperating to Abimelech and his friends; but the speaker fled, as soon as he had delivered his parable, to the town of Beer, and remained there out of his brother's reach. We hear no more of him; but three years after, if then living, he saw the accomplishment of the malediction he had pronounced (Judg. ix:5-21).

2. The tenth king of Judah, and son of Uzziah, whom he succeeded in B. C. 758, at the age of twenty-five; he reigned sixteen years. His father having during his last years been excluded by leprosy from public life (see UZZIAH), the government was administered by his son. Jotham profited by the experience which the reign of his father, and of the kings who preceded him, afforded, and he ruled in the fear of God, although he was unable to correct all the corrupt practices into which the people had fallen.

(1) Prosperous Reign. His sincere intentions were rewarded with a prosperous reign. He was successful in his wars. The Ammonites, who had 'given gifts' as a sort of tribute to Uzziah, but had ceased to do so after his leprosy had incapacitated him from governing, were constrained by Jotham to pay for three years a heavy tribute in silver, wheat, and barley (2 Chron. xxvi:8; xxvii:5, 6).

(2) Public Works. Many important public works were also undertaken and accomplished by Jotham. The principal gate of the temple was rebuilt by him on a more magnificent scale; the quarter of Ophel, in Jerusalem, was strengthened by new fortifications; various towns were built or rebuilt in the mountains of Judah; and castles and towers of defense were erected in the wilderness.

(3) Death. Jotham died greatly lamented by his people, and was buried in the sepulcher of the kings (2 Kings xv:38; 2 Chron. xxvii:3-9), B. C. about 735.

3. A descendant of Judah, son of Jahdai (1 Chron. ii:47).

JOURNEY (jûr'nȳ), (Heb. דֶּרֶךְ, *deh'rek*, a removal from one place to another).

A *day's journey* is reckoned about sixteen or twenty miles. To this distance, around the Hebrew camp, were the quails gathered for food for the people (Num. xi:31). Shaw computes the *eleven days' journey* from Sinai to Kadesh-barnea to be about one hundred and ten miles (Deut. i: 2). A *Sabbath day's journey* is reckoned by the Hebrews at 2000 cubits, or nearly seven hundred and thirty paces; and it is said, that if any Jew traveled above this from the city on the Sabbath, he was beaten; but it is probable they were allowed to travel as far to the synagogue as was necessary (Acts i:12; 2 Kings iv:23). The Hebrews seem to have had fifty-two journeys or marches from Rameses to Gilgal (Num. xxxiii).

JOY (joi), (generally some form of Heb. גִּיל, *gheel*, to spin round, or leap with pleasure); a stronger term than שִׂמְחָה, *sim-khaw'* (Ps. xxx:5, etc.); *Maw-soce'* (מָשׂושׂ, Job viii:19, etc.), rejoicing; *khar-ah'* (Gr. χαρά, Matt. ii:10), gladness; the cause or occasion of joy (Luke ii:10; 1 Thess. ii:20). Joy or gladness in general, is an agreeable mental sensation arising from conscious possession of, or from hope of enjoying, something pleasant or valuable; and the expression thereof in praise, etc.

1. Natural Joy, Etc. We may discriminate between natural *joy, gladness* and *mirth* as follows: What creates *joy* and *gladness* is of a permanent nature; that which creates *mirth* is temporary; *joy* is the most vivid sensation in the soul; *gladness* is the same in quality, but inferior in degree; *joy* is awakened in the mind by the most important events in life; *gladness* springs up in the mind on ordinary occasions; the return of the prodigal son awakened *joy* in the heart of his father; a man feels *gladness* at being relieved from some distress or trouble; public events of a gratifying nature produce universal *joy;* relief from either sickness or want brings *gladness* to an oppressed heart; he who is absorbed in his private distresses is ill prepared to partake of the *mirth* with which he is surrounded at the festive board. *Joy* is depicted on the countenance, or expresses itself by various demonstrations; *gladness* is a more tranquil feeling, which is enjoyed in secret, and seeks no outward expression. (Crabbe's *Synonyms*.)

2. Spiritual Joy. Spiritual joy is excited by the Holy Ghost, and arises from union to, possession of, and hope to enjoy forever, a God reconciled in Christ. This *joy* produces an agreeable earnestness in promoting his honor (Gal. v: 22). Thus the saints *rejoice* in Christ, or in God; they take pleasure in and boast of their connection with him; they praise him for his kindness to them, and for what he is in himself (Luke i:47).

Their *rejoicing in hope,* is their delightful views, holy boasting and cheerful praise, on account of their infallible perseverance and eternal happiness (Heb. iii:6). A saint's *rejoicing in himself,* means his inward satisfaction in the testimony of a good conscience (Gal. vi:4).

Objects and Sources of Spiritual Joy.

The ground or object of one's rejoicing, is called his *joy;* thus God is the *joy,* the *exceeding joy,* of his people; he, as theirs, and as enjoyed by them, is the cause and ground of their eternal and superlative joy (Ps. xliii:4). Christ's exaltation, promised to him, to encourage him in his work, is the *joy set before him* (Heb. xii:2). The heavenly blessedness is called the *joy of the Lord.* It consists in the delightful enjoyment of God in Christ, and it much resembles that pleasure he has in our redemption (Matt. xxv:21, 23). Converts are the "joy" of ministers, who are instrumental in bringing them to Christ (1 Thess. ii:20). Jerusalem and Zion were the "joy of the whole earth;" as God was there present, and peculiarly worshiped, there was more ground of joy than elsewhere; or the words may signify, that they were the joy of the whole land; as all the Jews took pleasure therein, and boasted thereof (Ps. xlviii:2; Lam. ii:15). The church is created a "rejoicing," and her people a "joy," when she is so reformed, settled, purged, and blessed, as to abound with spiritual gladness, and to rejoice the heart of every pious beholder (Is. lxv:18). Falling into temptations, or troubles, is to be accounted "all joy;" as troubles work exceedingly for our real good (James i:2). The "joy of God's salvation," is the heart-exhilarating blessings therein contained, and the spiritual gladness that issues therefrom (Ps. li:12). Spiritual gladness is called "joy in the Holy Ghost," as it proceeds from his dwelling and working in our heart (Rom. xiv:17). Brown.

JOZABAD (jŏz'a-băd), (Heb. זוֹבָד, *yo-zaw-bawd'*, contraction of Jehozabad, Jehovah endowed).

1. One of the captains of Manasseh, who came over to David before the battle of Gilboa, and aided in the rout of the marauding Amalekites (1 Chron. xii:20), B. C. before 1000.

2. A Levite, who, in the reign of Hezekiah, had charge of the offerings and dedicated things in the temple, under Cononiah and Shimei (2 Chron. xxxi:13), B. C. about 719.

3. A captain of Manasseh, who, like (1) came to David (1 Chron. xii:20), B. C. before 1000.

4. A Levite, son of Jeshua. He, with Meremoth and Eleazar, made an inventory of the vessels of gold and silver in the Temple, which were brought from Babylon, and recorded their weight (Ezra viii:33), B. C. about 457.

5. A prince of the Levites, who was an overseer of the offerings and dedicated things in the Temple, and assisted in the great feast of the Passover, held at Jerusalem in the time of Josiah (2 Chron. xxxv:9), B. C. 623.

6. A priest, son of Pashur, and one of those who married foreign wives (Ezra x:22), B. C. 456.

7. A Gederathite, a famous Benjamite archer, who joined David at Ziklag (1 Chron. xii:4), B. C. 1000. (See Josabad.)

JOZACHAR (jŏz'a-kar), (Heb. זוֹזָכָר, *yo-zaw-kawr'*, remembered by Jehovah), the son of the Ammonitess Shimeath, and one of the murderers of Joash, king of Judah (2 Kings xii:21). In 2 Chron. xxiv:26, he is called Zabad, which accord-

ing to Kennicott and others is a clerical mistake for Jozachar (B. C. 839).

JOZADAK (jŏz'a-dăk), (Heb. יוֹזָדָק, *yo-zaw-dawk'*, Jah is great, Ezra iii:2, 8; v:2; x:18; Neh. xii:26), a contracted form of Jehozadak (which see).

JUBAL (jū'bal), (Heb. יוּבָל, *yoo-bawl'*, stream).

One of Cain's descendants, son of Lamech and Adah. He is described as the inventor of the *kinnor,* and the *ugab,* rendered in our version 'the harp and the organ,' but perhaps more properly 'the lyre and mouth-organ,' or Pandean pipe (Gen. iv:21), B. C. 3490. (See Music.)

JUBILEE (jū'bĭ-lē), (Heb. יוֹבֵל, *yo-bale'*, Lev. xxv:8; Vulg. *Annus Jubilei,* or *Jubileus*).

According to some, a period of fifty years, according to others, of forty-nine years, the termination of which led to certain great changes in the condition of the Hebrews, all of which seem to have been designed and fitted to bring about from time to time a restoration of the original social state instituted by Moses, and so to sustain in its unimpaired integrity the constitution of which he was the author.

(1) Sabbatical Year. Intimately connected with the Jubilee was another singular Mosaic institution, namely, the Sabbatical year. On this account, we shall speak briefly of the latter, as preparatory to a right understanding of the former.

While yet wandering in the wilderness, and, therefore, before they had entered 'the land of promise,' the children of Israel received from the lips of their great legislator the following law—six years thou shalt sow thy land, and shalt gather in the fruits thereof; but the *seventh year* thou shalt let it rest; that thine ox and thine ass may rest, and the son of thy handmaid and the stranger may be refreshed' (Exod. xxiii:10, *sq.*). This injunction is repeated in Lev. xxv:1-7, where it stands as proceeding immediately from the Lord. The land is to keep 'a sabbath for the Lord.'

(2) Seven Sabbaths of Years. Then in immediate sequence follows the law relating to the Jubilee (Lev. xxv:8). 'And thou shalt number seven sabbaths of years unto thee, seven times seven years, forty and nine years; then shalt thou cause the trumpet of the Jubilee to sound in the tenth day of the seventh month, in the day of atonement shall ye make the trumpet sound throughout all your land. And ye shall *hallow the fiftieth year,* and proclaim liberty throughout all the land unto all the inhabitants thereof; and ye shall return every man unto his possession and unto his family (Lev. xxv:8-24). Land might be redeemed by a kinsman or by the party who sold it; but in the Jubilee year it must return to its original proprietor. Dwelling-houses within a walled city might be redeemed within the first year; if not redeemed within the space of a full year they became the freehold of the purchaser. The houses of villages were to be counted as the fields of the country. The cities and houses of the Levites were redeemable at any time, and could never be held longer than the ensuing Jubilee; the field of the suburbs of their cities might not be sold (verses 25-38). Israelites who were hired servants (Israelitish *bond*-servants were not allowed) might serve till the year of Jubilee, when they returned to their possessions. A Hebrew sold as a slave to a foreigner, resident in Palestine, was redeemable by himself or relative at any time, by making payment according to the number of years to elapse before the next Jubilee; but at the Jubilee such bondsman was, under all circumstances, to be set at liberty (verses 39-55). The only exception to this system of general restitution was in the case of property set apart and devoted to the divine service—'Every devoted thing is most holy unto the Lord; none devoted shall be redeemed' (Lev. xxvii:28, 29). With these scriptural details, the account given by Josephus (*Antiq.* iii:12, 3) substantially agrees.

The time required by the Sabbatical year and by the Jubilee to be rescued from the labors of the field, was very considerable. Strictly interpreted, the language we have cited would take out of the ordinary course of things every sixth, seventh, and eighth year, during each successive septenary, till the circle of fifty years was in each period completed. Nay, more, the old store, produced in the sixth year, was to last until the ninth year, for the sixth year was to bring forth fruits for three years.

The reader has now before him the whole of this extraordinary power of legislation, which, viewed in all its bearings—in its effects on human labor, on character, on religious institutions and observances, as well as on the general condition of society, no less than on the productiveness of the land, and the means of sustenance to its inhabitants—is wholly unparalleled by any event in the history of the world. It is, however, in perfect concord with the Mosaic economy.

(3) **Restitution of Lands.** The recurring periods of seven years are in keeping with the institution of the seventh day as a Sabbath for man and beast. The aim in both is similar—needful repose. The leading idea involved in the Jubilee —namely, restitution—also harmonizes with the fundamental principles of the Mosaic system. The land was God's, and was entrusted for use to the chosen people in such a way that every individual had his portion. A power of perpetual alienation would have been a virtual denial of God's sovereign rights, while the law of Jubilee was one of continued recognition of them. The conception is purely *theocratical* in its whole character and tendencies. The theocracy was of such a nature as to disallow all subordinate 'thrones, principalities and powers;' and consequently, to demand entire equality on the part of the people. But the power of perpetual alienation in regard to land would have soon given rise to the greatest inequalities of social condition, presenting what modern states have, alas! exhibited but too much of—splendid affluence on one side and sordid pauperism on the other.

(4) **Benevolent Legislation.** A passage in Deuteronomy (xv:4), when rightly understood, as in the marginal translation—'to the end that there be no poor among you'—seems expressly to declare that the aim in view, at least of the Sabbatical release, was to prevent the rise of any great inequality of social condition, and thus to preserve unimpaired the essential character of the theocracy.

Equally benevolent in its aim and tendency does this institution thus appear, showing how thoroughly the great Hebrew legislator cared and provided for individuals, instead of favoring classes. Beginning with a narrow cycle of seven days, he went on to a wider one of as many years, embracing at least seven times seven annual revolutions, seeking in all his arrangements rest for man and beast, and, by a happy personification, rest even for the brute earth; and in the rest which he required for human beings, providing for that more needful rest of mind which the

sharp competitions and eager rivalries of modern society deny to ten thousand times ten thousand. The benign character and tendency of the law of the Sabbatical and Jubilee years is in accordance with the general spirit of the Mosaic legislation, and appears not unworthy of its divine origin.

Warburton adduced this law (*Divine Legation of Moses*) in order to show that Moses was in truth sent and sustained by God, since nothing but a divine power could have given the necessary supplies of food in the sixth year, and no unprejudiced person can well deny the force of his argument.

(5) **Moses the Lawgiver.** But these laws either emanated from Moses, or they did not. If they did not, they arose after the settlement in Canaan, and are of such a nature as to convict their fabricator of imposture, if, indeed, any one could have been found so daring as to bring forth laws implying institutions which did not exist, and which under ordinary circumstances could not find permanence, even if they could ever be carried into operation at all. But if these laws emanated from Moses, is it credible that he would have given utterance to commands which convict themselves of impossibility? or caused the rise of institutions, which, if unsupported of heaven, must come to a speedy termination, and in so doing act to his own discredit as a professed divine messenger?

(6) **Productiveness of Land.** On the possibility of the land's affording sufficient food, we find the following important passage in Palfrey's *Lectures on the Jewish Scriptures,* Boston, 1841, vol. i, p. 303:

'I find no difficulty arising from any inadequacy of the produce of six years to afford sustenance to the people for seven. To say that this was intended would merely be to say that the design was that the consumption of each year should only amount on an average to six-sevenths of its produce. In such an arrangement it cannot be thought that there was anything impracticable.

'There are states of the union which export yearly more than half their produce, and subsist substantially on the remainder, their imports consisting mostly of luxuries. Again, in England nearly three-quarters of the families are engaged in commerce, manufactures, professions, and unproductive pursuits; but in Judea every man was a producer of food, with the advantage of a fine climate and a rich soil.

It may be of some importance to remark that those who believe that these laws were good, and were also executed, are not therefore required to maintain that the regular and intended series of things was never interrupted.

(7) **Conditional Promises.** The promises of God are in all cases conditioned on human obedience. This condition is expressly laid down in the case before us (Lev. xxv:18, 36, 38). At the same time, the silence of the sacred history before the captivity looks as if the law in question was so uninterruptedly, regularly, and as a matter of course, observed from Jubilee to Jubilee, that no occasion transpired for remark. In history, as in every day life, more is said of the exceptional than the periodical and the ordinary.

(8) **Execution of Laws.** The tenor of these observations will probably lead the reader to consider it a somewhat surprising assertion, that these laws were not executed before the Babylonish exile; yet such is the statement of Winer (*Real-wörterb.* under '*Jubeljahr*' and De Wette (*Lehrb. der Archäol.*, p. 158). Some passages of

Scripture are referred to, which are thought to imply the truth of this position, as I Kings xxi: 3; Is. v:8; 2 Chron. xxxvi:21; Lev. xxvi:34).

For the opposite view, there is, in agreement with the general tenor of this article, some positive evidence which must be briefly indicated (see Roman historian Tacitus' *Hist.* v. 4; Josephus *Antiq.* xiv, 10, 6; I Macc. vi:49; Ezek. xlvi:17; Is. lxi:1, 2); and since the essential element of this system of law, namely the Sabbatical year, was, as we have seen, an established institution in the days of Tacitus, Josephus, the Maccabees, Ezekiel, and Isaiah, we think the fair and legitimate inference is in favor of those laws having been long previously observed, probably from the early periods of the Hebrew republic. Their existence in a declining state of the commonwealth cannot be explained without seeking their origin nearer the fountain-head of those pure, living waters, which, with the force of all primitive enthusiasm, easily effected great social wonders, especially when divinely guided and divinely sustained.   J. R. B.

JUCAL (jū'kal), (Heb. יוּכַל, *yoo-kal'*, able), son of Shelemiah (Jer. xxxviii:1). Elsewhere the name is JEHUCAL (which see).

JUDA (jū'dà), (Heb. יְהוּדָה, *yeh-hoo-daw'*, praise; Gr. Ἰούδας, *ee-oo'das*, *Judas;* Juda is only the genitive case).

1. Son of Joseph, in the ninth generation from David in the genealogy of Christ (Luke iii:30), probably the same with Adaiah, the father of Maaseiah (2 Chron. xxiii:1), B. C. before 876. (See GENEALOGY OF JESUS CHRIST.)

2. Son of Joanna (Luke iii:26), or Hananiah (8), and probably the same person as Abiud (Matt. i:13). (See Hervey, *Genealogies,* p. 118, *sq.*). Probably also identical with Obadiah (I Chron. iii:21), B. C. before 406.

3. One of the brethren of Christ mentioned in Mark vi:3. In Matt. xiii:55 the name is Judas. For his identity with Jude, see article JUDAS.

4. The patriarch Judah, thus called in Luke iii:33; Heb. vii:14; Rev. v:5, vii:5.

5. Juda, City of (Luke i:39). Whether this is a town or territory, that is in Judea, is disputed. If a city, it was in the hill country, and perhaps unknown to Luke himself. (See Lightfoot, *Hor. Heb.* ii. 493; Thomson, *Land and Book,* ii. 536; Robinson, *Bib. Res.,* ii. 206.)

JUDÆA (ju-dē'à), (Gr. Ἰουδαία, *ee-oo-dah'yah*), the southernmost of the three divisions of the Holy Land. It denoted the kingdom of Judah as distinguished from that of Israel. But after the captivity, as most of the exiles who returned belonged to the kingdom of Judah, the name Judæa (Judah) was applied generally to the whole of Palestine west of the Jordan (Hag. i:1, 14; ii:2).

(1) Under the Romans. Under the Romans, in the time of Christ, Palestine was divided into Judæa, Galilee, and Samaria (John iv:3, 4; Acts ix:31), the last including the whole of the southern part west of the Jordan. But this division was only observed as a political and local distinction, for the sake of indicating the part of the country, just as we use the name of a county (Matt. ii:1, 5; iii:1; iv:25; Luke i:65); but when the whole of Palestine was to be indicated in a general way, the term Judæa was still employed. Thus persons in Galilee and elsewhere spoke of going to Judæa (John vii:3; xi:7), to distinguish the part of Palestine to which they were proceeding; but when persons in Rome and other places spoke of Judæa (Acts xxviii:21), they used the word as a general denomination for the country of the Jews, or Palestine. Indeed, the name seems to have had a more extensive application than even to Palestine west of the Jordan. It denoted all the dominions of Herod the Great, who was called king of Judæa; and much of these lay beyond the river. After the death of Herod, however, the Judæa to which his son Archelaus succeeded was only the southern province so called (Matt. ii:22); which afterwards became a Roman province dependent on Syria and governed by procurators, and this was its condition during our Lord's ministry. It was afterwards for a time partly under the dominion of Herod Agrippa the elder (Acts xii:1-19), but on his death it reverted to its former condition under the Romans.

(2) Province of Judæa. It is Judæa in the provincial sense only that requires our present notice, the country at large being described in the article PALESTINE. In this sense, however, it was much more extensive than the domain of the tribe of Judah, even more so than the kingdom of the same name. There are no materials for describing its limits with precision; but it included the ancient territories of Judah, Benjamin, Dan, Simeon, and part of Ephraim.

In the rabbinical writings Judæa, as a division of Palestine, is frequently called 'the south,' or 'the south country' to distinguish it from Galilee, which was called 'the north' (Lightfoot, *Chorog. Cent.* xii). The distinction of the tribe of Judah into 'the Mountain,' 'the Plain,' and 'the Vale,' which we meet with in the Old Testament (Num. xiii:30), was preserved under the more extended denomination of Judæa. The *Mountain,* or hill country of Judæa (Josh. xxi:11; Luke i:39), was that 'broad back of mountains,' as Lightfoot calls it (*Chorog. Cent.* xi), which fills the center of the country from Hebron northward to beyond Jerusalem. The *Plain* was the low country towards the seacoast, and seems to have included not only the broad plain which extends between the sea and the hill country, but the lower parts of the hilly region itself in that direction. Thus the rabbins allege that from Bethhoron to the sea is one region (*T. Hieros. Sheviith,* ix:2). The *Vale* is defined by the rabbins as extending from Engedi to Jericho (Lightfoot, *Panergon,* sec. 2).

(3) Topography. Judæa is, as the above intimations would suggest, a country full of hills and valleys. The hills are generally separated from one another by valleys and torrents, and are, for the most part, of moderate height, uneven, and seldom of any regular figure. The rock of which they are composed is easily converted into soil, which being arrested by the terraces when washed down by the rains, renders the hills cultivable in a series of long, narrow gardens, formed by these terraces from the base upwards. In this manner the hills were in ancient times cultivated most industriously, and enriched and beautified with the fig tree, the olive tree, and the vine; and it is thus that the scanty cultivation which still subsists is now carried on. But when the inhabitants were rooted out, and the culture neglected, the terraces fell into decay, and the soil which had been collected in them was washed down into the valleys, leaving only the arid rock, naked and desolate. This is the general character of the scenery; but in some parts the hills are beautifully wooded, and in others the application of the ancient mode of cultivation still suggests to the traveler how rich the country once was and might be again, and how beautiful the prospects which it offered. As, however, much of this was the result of cultivation, the country was probably anciently, as at present, *naturally* less fertile than either Samaria or Galilee. (See Kitto, *Pictorial History of Palestine; Introduct.* pp. 39, 40, 119; Olin, ii:323.)

JUDÆA, THE LAND OF (ju-dæ'à, the lănd ŏv), indicates the country as distinguished from the capital, or Jerusalem (Mark i:5; John iii:22).

Wilderness of Judæa.

JUDÆA, THE WILDERNESS OF.

Here John the Baptist first taught (Matt. iii:1) and Christ was tempted; probably towards the north of it, not far from Jericho. Some parts of it were not absolutely barren or uninhabited.

It lay along the eastern border of Judæa towards the Dead Sea, in which were the six cities mentioned in Josh. xv:61 *sq.* It was a region thinly inhabited, and used mostly as a pasture land.

JUDAH (jū'dah), (Heb. יְהוּדָה, *ye-hoo-daw'*, celebrated).

1. The fourth son of Jacob and Leah (B. C. about 1916). The narrative in Genesis brings this patriarch more before the reader, and makes known more of his history and character than it does in the case of any other of the twelve sons of Jacob, with the single exception of Joseph. It is indeed chiefly in connection with Joseph that the facts respecting Judah transpire; and as they have already been given in the articles JACOB and JOSEPH, 1, it is only necessary to indicate them shortly in this place.

(1) Relation to Joseph. It was Judah's advice that the brethren followed when they sold Joseph to the Ishmaelites, instead of taking his life. By the light of his subsequent actions we can see that his conduct on this occasion arose from a generous impulse, although the form of the question he put to them has been sometimes held to suggest an interested motive: 'What profit is it if we slay our brother and conceal his blood? Come, let us sell him,' etc. (Gen. xxxvii:26, 27).

(2) Domestic Relations. Not long after this Judah withdrew from the paternal tents, and went to reside at Adullam, in the country which afterwards bore his name. Here he married a woman of Canaan, called Shuah, and had by her three sons, Er, Onan, and Shelah. When the eldest of these sons became of fit age, he was married to a woman named Tamar, but soon after died. As he died childless, the patriarchal law, afterwards adopted into the Mosaic code (Deut. xxv:6), required him to bestow upon the widow his second son. This he did; but as Onan also soon

died childless, Judah became reluctant to bestow his only surviving son upon this woman, and put her off with the excuse that he was not yet of sufficient age. Tamar accordingly remained in her father's house at Adullam. She had the usual passion of Eastern women for offspring, and could not endure the stigma of having been twice married without bearing children, while the law precluded her from contracting any alliance but that which Judah withheld her from completing.

Meanwhile Judah's wife died, and after the time of mourning had expired, he went, accompanied by his friend Hirah, to attend the shearing of his sheep at Timnath in the same neighborhood. These circumstances suggested to Tamar the strange thought of connecting herself with Judah himself, under the guise of a loose woman. Having waylaid him on the road to Timnath, she succeeded in her object, and when the consequences began to be manifest in the person of Tamar, Judah was highly enraged at her crime, and, exercising the powers which belonged to him as the head of the family she had dishonored, he commanded her to be brought forth, and committed to the flames as an adulteress. But when she appeared, she produced the ring, the bracelet, and the staff which he had left in pledge with her, and put him to confusion by declaring that they belonged to the father of her coming offspring. Judah acknowledged them to be his, and confessed that he had been wrong in withholding Shelah from her. The result of this painful affair was the birth of two sons, Zerah and Pharez (B. C. about 1893), from whom, with Shelah, the tribe of Judah descended. Pharez was the ancestor of the line from which David, the kings of Judah, and Jesus came (Gen. xxxviii; xlvi:12; 1 Chron. ii:3-5; Matt. 1:3; Luke iii:33).

(3) Later Life. These circumstances seem to have disgusted Judah with his residence in towns; for we find him ever afterwards at his father's tents. His experience of life, and the strength of his character, appear to have given him much influence with Jacob; and it was chiefly from confidence in him that the aged father at length consented to allow Benjamin to go down to Egypt. That this confidence was not misplaced has already been shown (see JOSEPH); and there is not in the whole range of literature a finer piece of true natural eloquence than that in which Judah offers himself to remain as a bond-slave in the place of Benjamin, for whose safe return he had made himself responsible to his father. The strong emotions which it raised in Joseph disabled him from keeping up longer the disguise he had hitherto maintained, and there are few who have read it without being, like him, moved even to tears.

We hear nothing more of Judah till he received, along with his brothers, the final blessing of his father (B. C. 1856), which was conveyed in lofty language, glancing far into futurity, and strongly indicative of the high destinies which awaited the tribe that was to descend from him (Gen. xlix: 8-12).

2. A Levite whose sons assisted in rebuilding the temple after the return from captivity (Ezra iii:9), B. C. 536. (Hervey, *Genealogy*, p. 119.)

3. A Levite who had taken a foreign wife (Ezra x:23). Probably the same person is meant in Neh. xii:8, 36 (B. C. 536).

4. Son of Senuah, a Benjamite (Neh. xi:9), B. C. about 440.

5. One of those who followed half of the Jewish chiefs around the southern section of the newly-erected walls of Jerusalem (Neh. xii:34), B. C. 446.

JUDAH, KINGDOM OF (jū'dah, king'dŭm ŏv). When the territory of all the rest of Israel, except Judah and Benjamin, was lost to the kingdom of Rehoboam, a special single name was needed to denote that which remained to him.

(1) Extended Meaning. And almost of necessity the word *Judah* received an extended meaning, according to which it comprised not Benjamin only, but the priests and Levites, who were ejected in great numbers from Israel, and rallied round the house of David.

(2) The Term Jew. At a still later time, when the nationality of the ten tribes had been dissolved, and every practical distinction between the ten and the two had vanished during the captivity, the scattered body had no visible head, except in Jerusalem, which had been re-occupied by a portion of *Judah's* exiles. In consequence the name Judah (or *Jew*) attached itself to the entire nation from about the epoch of the restoration. But in this article Judah is understood of the people over which David's successors reigned, from Rehoboam to Zedekiah.

(3) Revolt and Invasion. When the kingdom of Solomon became rent with intestine war, it might have been foreseen that the Edomites, Moabites and other surrounding nations would at once refuse their accustomed tribute, and become again practically independent; and some irregular invasion of these tribes might have been dreaded. It was a mark of conscious weakness, and not a result of strength, that Rehoboam fortified fifteen cities (2 Chron. xi:5-11), in which his people might find defense against the irregular armies of his roving neighbors. But a more formidable enemy came in, Shishak, king of Egypt, against whom the fortresses were of no avail (xii: 4), and to whom Jerusalem was forced to open its gates; and, from the despoiling of his treasures, Rehoboam probably sustained a still greater shock in its moral effect on the Moabites and Edomites, than in the direct loss; nor is it easy to conceive that he any longer retained the commerce of the Red Sea, or any very lucrative trade.

(4) Decline. After Jehoshaphat followed the calamitous affinity with the house of Ahab, and the massacres of both families. Under Jehoiada the priest, and Jehoash his pupil, no martial efforts were made; but Amaziah, son of Jehoash, after hiring 100,000 Israelites to no purpose, made war on the Edomites, slew 10,000, and threw 10,000 more down from the top of their rock (xxv:5, 6, 11, 12). His own force in Judah, from twenty years old and upwards, was numbered at only 300,000 choice men, able to handle spear and shield. His son Uzziah had 2,600 military officers and 307,500 men of war (xxvi:12, 13). Ahaz lost, in a single battle with Pekah, 120,000 valiant men (xxviii:6), after the severe slaughter he had received from Rezin, king of Syria; after which no further military strength is ascribed to the kings of Judah.

(5) Army of Rehoboam. It perhaps deserves remark, that in the book of Kings no numbers of such magnitude are found. The army ascribed to Rehoboam (1 Kings xii:21) is, indeed, as in Chronicles, 180,000 men; but if we explain it of those *able* to fight, the number, though certainly large, may be dealt with historically. (See the article on STATISTICS.)

(6) External Relations. As the most important external relations of Israel were with Damascus, so were those of Judah with Edom and Egypt. Some revolution in the state of Egypt appears to have followed the reign of Shishak. Apparently the country must have fallen under the power of an Ethiopian dynasty; for the name of the *Lubim,* who accompanied Zerah in his attack on Asa, is generally regarded as proving that Zerah was from Sennaar, the ancient Meroë. But as this invasion was signally repulsed, the attempt was not repeated; and Judah enjoyed entire tranquillity from that quarter until the invasion of Pharaoh-necho.

(7) Favorable Reaction. In fact, it may seem that this success assisted the reaction, favorable to the power of Judah, which was already begun, in consequence of a change in the policy of Damascus.

Whether Abijah had been in league with the father of Benhadad I (as is generally inferred from 1 Kings xv:19) may be doubted; for the address cannot be rendered, 'Let there be a league between me and thee, *as there was* between my father and thine;' and it possibly is only a hyperbolical phrase of friendship for, 'Let us be in close alliance; *let us count* our fathers *to have been* allies.' However this may be, Asa bought, by a costly sacrifice, the serviceable aid of the Damascene king. Israel was soon distressed, and Judah became once more formidable to her southern neighbors.

(8) Edomites Made Tributary. Jehoshaphat appears to have reasserted the Jewish authority over the Edomites without war, and to have set his own viceroy over them (1 Kings xxii:47). Intending to resume the distant commerce which had been so profitable to Solomon, he built ships suitable for long voyages ('ships *of* Tarshish,' as they are rightly called in 1 Kings xxii:48—a phrase which the Chronicler has misunderstood and translated into 'ships *to go to* Tarshish' (2 Chron. xx:36); but not having the advantage of Tyrian sailors, as Solomon had, he lost the vessels by violent weather before they had sailed. Upon this, Ahaziah, king of Judah, offered the service of his own mariners, probably from the tribe of Asher and others accustomed to the Mediterranean; but Jehoshaphat was too discouraged to accept his offer, and the experiment was never renewed by any Hebrew king.

(9) Revolt of Edomites. The Edomites, who paid only a forced allegiance, soon after revolted from Jehoram, and elected their own king (2 Kings viii:20, 22). At a later time they were severely defeated by Amaziah (2 Kings xiv:7), whose son, Uzziah, fortified the town of Elath, intending, probably, to resume maritime enterprise; but it remained a barren possession, and was finally taken from them by Rezin, in the reign of Ahaz (2 Kings xvi:6). The Philistines, in these times, seem to have fallen from their former greatness, their league having been so long dissolved.

(10) Jerusalem Plundered. The most remarkable event in which the Philistines are concerned is the assault on Jerusalem, in the reign of Jehoram (2 Chron. xxi:16, 17).

It is strikingly indicative of the stormy scenes through which the line of David passed that the treasures of the king and of the Temple were so often plundered or bargained away. First, under Rehoboam, all the hoards of Solomon, consecrated and common alike, were carried off by Shishak (1 Kings xiv:26). Two generations later, Asa emptied out to Benhadad all that had since accumulated 'in the house of Jehovah or in the king's house.' A third time, when Hazael had taken Gath, and was preparing to march on Jerusalem, Jehoash, king of Judah, turned him away by sending to him all 'that Jehoshaphat, Jehoram, Ahaziah and Jehoash himself had dedicated, and all the gold that was found in the treasures of the house of Jehovah and in the king's house (2 Kings xii:18). In the very next reign Jehoash, king of Israel, defeated and captured Amaziah, took Jerusalem, broke down the walls, carried off hostages, and plundered the gold and silver deposited in the temple and in the royal palace (2 Kings xiv:11-14). A fifth sacrifice of the sacred and of the royal treasure was made by Ahaz to Tiglath-pileser (2 Kings xvi:8). The act was repeated by his son Hezekiah to Sennacherib, who had demanded '300 talents of silver and 30 talents of gold.' It is the more extraordinary, therefore, to find expressions used when Nebuchadnezzar took the city, which at first sight imply that Solomon's far-famed stores were still untouched (2 Kings xxiv:13).

The severest shock which the house of David received was the double massacre which it endured from Jehu and from Athaliah (2 Kings x, xi).

(11) Rule of Jehoiada. After a long minority, a youthful king, the sole surviving male descendant of his great-grandfather, and reared under the paternal rule of the priest Jehoiada, to whom he was indebted not only for his throne but even for his recognition as a son of Ahaziah, was not in a situation to uphold the royal authority. That Jehoash conceived the priests to have abused the power which they had gained sufficiently appears in 2 Kings xii, where he complains that they had for twenty-three years appropriated the money, which they ought to have spent on the repairs of the temple. Jehoiada gave way; but we see here the beginning of a feud (hitherto unknown in the house of David) between the crown and the priestly order; which, after Jehoiada's death, led to the murder of his son Zechariah. The execution of the priest of Baal, and of Athaliah (2 Kings xi:13-18), granddaughter of a king of Sidon, must also have destroyed cordiality between the Phœnicians and the kingdom of Judah; and when the victorious Hazael had subjugated all Israel and showed himself near Jerusalem, Jehoash could look for no help from without, and had neither the faith of Hezekiah nor a prophet like Isaiah to support him.

(12) Assassination of Jehoash. The assassination of Jehoash in his bed by 'his own servants' is described in the Chronicles as a revenge taken upon him by the priestly party for his murder of 'the sons' of Jehoiada; and the same fate, from the same influence, fell upon his son Amaziah, if we may so interpret the words in 2 Chron. xxv:27.

(13) Amaziah, Uzziah, and Ahaz. 'From the time that Amaziah turned away from following Jehovah they made a conspiracy against him,' etc. Thus the house of David appeared to be committing itself, like that of Saul, to permanent enmity with the priests. The wisdom of Uzziah, during a long reign, averted this collision, though a symptom of it returned towards its close. No further mischief from this cause followed, until the reign of his grandson, the weak and unfortunate Ahaz; after which the power of the kingdom rapidly moldered away.

The struggle of the crown against priestly control was perhaps the most immediate cause of the ruin of Judah. Ahaz was probably less guided by policy than by superstition, or by architectural taste, in erecting his Damascene altar (2 Kings xvi:10-18).

(14) Ruinous Conduct of Manasseh. But the far more outrageous proceedings of Manasseh seem to have been a systematic attempt to extirpate the national religion because of its supporting the priestly power; and the 'innocent blood very much,' which he is stigmatized for shedding (2 Kings xxi:16), was undoubtedly a sanguinary attack on the party opposed to his impious and despotic innovations. The storm which he had raised did not burst in his lifetime; but two years after it fell on the head of his son Amon; and the disorganization of the kingdom which his madness had wrought is commemorated as the cause of the Babylonish captivity (2 Kings xxiii:26; xxiv:3, 4). It is also credible that the long-continued despotism had greatly lessened patriotic spirit; and that the Jewish people of the declining kingdom were less brave against foreign invaders than against kindred and neighbor tribes or civil opponents.

(15) Fatal Decline. Faction had become very fierce within Jerusalem itself (Ezek. xxii), and civil bloodshed was common. Wealth, where it existed, was generally a source of corruption, by introducing foreign luxury, tastes, manners, superstitions, immorality, or idolatry; and when consecrated to pious purposes, as by Hezekiah and Josiah, produced little more than a formal and exterior religion.

The appointment of Hilkiah to the office of high-priest seems to mark the era at which (by a reaction after the atrocities of Manasseh and Amon) the purer priestly sentiment obtained its triumph over the crown. But the victory came too late. Society was corrupt and convulsed within, and the two great powers of Egypt and Babylon menaced it from without. True lovers of their God and of their country, like Jeremiah, saw that it was a time rather for weeping than for action; and that the faithful must resign themselves to the bitter lot which the sins of their nation had earned.   F. W. N.

JUDAH, TRIBE OF (jū'dăh, trīb ŏv). This tribe sprang from Judah, the son of Jacob.

When the Israelites quitted Egypt, it already exhibited the elements of its future distinction in a larger population than any of the other tribes possessed.

(1) Population. It numbered 74,000 adult males, being nearly 12,000 more than Dan, the next in point of numbers, and 34,100 more than Ephraim, which in the end contested with it the superiority among the tribes. During the sojourn in the wilderness, Judah neither gained, like some tribes, nor lost like others. Its numbers had increased to 76,500, being 12,100 more than Issachar, which had become next to it in population (Num. i:27).

(2) Distribution of Lands. In the first distribution of lands, the tribe of Judah received the southernmost part of Palestine, to the extent of fully one-third of the whole country to be distributed among the nine and a half tribes for which provision was to be made. This oversight was discovered and rectified at the time of the second distribution, which was founded on an actual survey of the country, when Simeon and Dan received allotments out of the territory which had before been wholly assigned to Judah (Josh. xix:9). That which remained was still very large, and more proportioned to the future greatness than to the actual wants of the tribe. When Judah became a kingdom, the original extent of territory assigned to the tribe was more than restored or compensated, for it must have included the domains of Simeon, and we know that Benjamin was included in it.

(3) History of the Judges. The history of the Judges contains fewer facts respecting this important tribe than might be expected. It seems, however, to have been usually considered that the birthright which Reuben forfeited had passed to Judah under the blessing of Jacob; and a sanction was given to this impression when, after the death of Joshua, the divine oracle nominated Judah to take precedence of the other tribes in the war against the Canaanites (Judg. i:2).

It does not appear that any tribe was disposed to dispute the superior claim of Judah on its own account, except Ephraim, although in doing this Ephraim had the support of other tribes. Ephraim appears to have rested its claims to the leadership of the tribes upon the ground that the house of Joseph, whose interest it represented, had received the birthright, or double portion of the eldest, by the adoption of the two sons of Joseph, who became the founders of *two* tribes in Israel.

The existence of the sacerdotal establishment at Shiloh, in Ephraim, was doubtless also alleged by the tribes as a ground of superiority over Judah. When, therefore, Judah assumed the scepter in the person of David, and when the sacerdotal establishment was removed to Jerusalem, Ephraim could not brook the eclipse it had sustained, and took the first opportunity of erecting a separate throne, and forming separate establishments for worship and sacrifice.

Perhaps the separation of the kingdoms may thus be traced to the rivalry of Judah and Ephraim. After that separation the rivalry was between the two kingdoms; but it was still popularly considered as representing the ancient rivalry of these great tribes; for the prophet, in foretelling the repose of a coming time, describes it by saying, 'The envy also of Ephraim shall depart, and the adversaries of Judah shall be cut off; Ephraim shall not envy Judah, and Judah shall not vex Ephraim' (Is. xi:13).

JUDAH UPON JORDAN (jū'dah ŭpŏn jôr'dan), a border town of Naphtali (Josh. xix:34).

While Judah was in the south and Naphtali in the north it is entirely possible that a town in one tribe was named after the country of another.

JUDAISM (jū'dȧ-ĭzm), (Gr. Ἰουδαϊσμός, `ee-oo-day-is-mos'`).

Judaism denotes the Jewish faith in its extravagant form of blind attachment to rites and traditions, and national exclusiveness. This must have been prevalent in the time of Christ, because of his constant exposure of their formalism and self-assumption, and because in John's Gospel "the Jews" is used as synonymous with opposers of Christ and his teachings.

In the eyes of the Jew, Judaism possessed the merit of both piety and patriotism (Gal. i, 13, 14.)

JUDAS or JUDE (jū'das), (Gr. Ἰούδας, `ee-oo'-das`, the Greek form of the Hebrew JUDAH).

1. The patriarch Judah (Matt. i:2, 3).

2. A man who lived in Damascus, and with whom Saul lodged after his conversion (Acts ix:11), in the street, "that is called straight." No further mention of him occurs. It is far from probable that he was a Christian, as none of Saul's company were Christians, nor did they know that he himself had become converted. The so-called "House of Judas" is still shown in an open space called "the Sheik's Place," a few steps out of the Street of Bazaars.

3. Judas, otherwise Jude, surnamed Barsabas, was sent from Jerusalem, with Paul and Barnabas, to the church at Antioch, to report the resolution of the Apostles at Jerusalem, concerning the non-observance of the ways by the Gentiles (Acts xv: 22, 23, 27), A. D. 54. Some think, that this Judas was the brother of Joseph, surnamed also Barsabas, who was proposed, with Matthias, to fill up the place of the traitor Judas (Acts i:23. Luke says that Judas Barsabas was a prophet, and one of the chief among the brethren; and it is also believed that he was one of the seventy disciples.

4. Judas Gaulanitis, or the Gaulanite, opposed the enrollment of the people made by Cyrenius in Judæa (see CYRENIUS) and raised a very great rebellion, pretending that the Jews, being free, ought to acknowledge no dominion besides that of God. His followers chose rather to suffer extreme torments than to call any power on earth lord or master. The same Judas is named Judas the Galilean (Acts v:37) because he was a native of the city of Gamala in the Gaulanitis, which was comprised in Galilee.

5. There were two of this name among the twelve Apostles—Judas, called also Lebbæus and Thaddæus (Matt. x:3, 4; Mark iii:18, which see), and Judas Iscariot. Judas is the name of one of our Lord's brethren, but it is not agreed whether our Lord's brother is the same with the Apostle of this name (See JAMES). We are not informed as to the time of the calling of the Apostle Jude to that dignity. Indeed, the only circumstance relating to him which is recorded in the Gospels consists in the question put by him to our Lord (John xiv:22). 'Judas saith unto him (not Iscariot), Lord, how is it that thou wilt manifest thyself to us, and not unto the world?' Nor have we any account given of his proceedings after our Lord's resurrection, for the traditionary notices which have been preserved of him rest on no very certain foundation. It has been asserted that he was sent to Edessa, to Abgarus, king of Osroene (Jerome, *Annot. in Matt.*), and that he preached in Syria, Arabia, Mesopotamia, and Persia; in which latter country he suffered martyrdom (Lardner's *Hist. of the Apostles*). Jude the Apostle is commemorated in the Western church, together with the Apostle Simon (the name, also, of one of our Lord's brethren) on the 8th of October.

St. Luke (Acts xv:22, 27-33) speaks of Judas, the son of Barsabas, in company with Silas, both of whom he styles 'prophets,' and 'chief men among the brethren.' Schott supposes that Barsabas means the son of Sabas, or Zabas, which he looks upon as an abridged form for Zebedee, and concludes that the Judas here mentioned was a brother of the elder James and of John.

JUDAS ISCARIOT (jū'das is-căr'i-ot).

The object of this article is not to elucidate all the circumstances recorded respecting this person but simply to investigate his motives in delivering up Jesus to the chief priests. The evangelists relate his proceedings, but give no opinion. The subject is consequently open to inquiry. Our conclusions must be guided by the facts of the case, and the known feelings and principles of human nature. Some hypothesis is necessarily formed by every reader.

(1) Motives. The only conceivable motives for the conduct of Judas are a sense of duty in bringing his Master to justice, resentment, avarice, dissatisfaction with the procedure of Jesus, and a consequent scheme for the accomplishment of his own views.

(2) Duty. With regard to the first of these motives, if Judas had been actuated by a sense of duty in bringing his Master to justice for anything censurable in his intentions, words, or actions, he would certainly have alleged some charge against him in his first interview with the chief priests, and they would have brought him forward as a witness against Jesus, especially when they were at so great a loss for evidence; or they would have reminded him of his accusations when he appealed to them after our Lord's condemnation, saying, 'I have sinned in that I have betrayed innocent blood' —a confession which amounts to an avowal that he had never seen anything to blame in his Master, but everything to approve. Moreover, the knowledge of the slightest fault in Jesus would have served, at least for the present, to tranquilize his own feelings, and prevent his immediate despair. The chief priests would also most certainly have alleged any charge he had made against Jesus, as a justification of their conduct, when they afterwards endeavored to prevent his apostles from preaching in his name (Acts iv:15-23; v:27-40).

(3) Resentment. The second motive supposed, namely, that of resentment, is rather more plausible. Jesus had certainly rebuked him for blaming the woman who had anointed him in the house of Simon the leper, at Bethany (comp. Matt. xxvi:8-17; John xii:4, 5); and Matthew's narrative seems to connect his going to the chief priests with that rebuke (verse 14), '*Then* one of the twelve, called Judas Iscariot, went unto the chief-priests'; but closer inspection will convince the reader that those words are more properly connected with verse 3. Besides, the rebuke was general, 'Why trouble *ye* the woman?' Nor was it nearly so harsh as that received by Peter, 'Get thee behind me, Satan' (Matt. xvi:23), and certainly not so public (Mark viii:32, 33).

Even if Judas had felt ever so much resentment, it could scarcely have been his sole motive; and as nearly two days elapsed between his contract with the chief priests and its completion, it would have subsided during the interval, and have yielded to that covetousness which we have every reason to believe was his ruling passion. St. John expressly declares that Judas 'was a thief, and had the bag, and bare (that is, conveyed away from it, stole, ἐβάσταζεν, *eh-bas'tadz-en*) what was put therein' (xii:6; comp. xx:15, in the original, and see a similar use of the word in Josephus, p. 402. 39, ed. Huds.).

This rebuke, or rather certain circumstances attending it, might have determined him to act as he did, but is insufficient, of itself, to account entirely for his conduct, by which he endangered all his expectations of worldly advancement from Jesus, at the very moment when they seemed upon the verge of being fulfilled. It is, indeed, a most important feature in the case, that the hopes entertained by Judas, and all the apostles, from their Master's expected elevation, as the Messiah, to the throne of Judæa, and, as they believed, to the empire of the whole world, were never more steadfast than at the time when they covenanted with the chief priests to deliver him into their hands. Nor does the theory of mere resentment agree with the terms of censure in which the conduct and character of Judas are spoken of by our Lord and the evangelists.

(4) Covetousness. Since, then, this supposition is insufficient, we may consider another motive to which his conduct is more commonly ascribed, namely, covetousness. But if by covetousness be meant the eager desire to obtain 'the thirty pieces of silver,' with which the chief priest 'covenanted with him' (Matt. xxvi:15), it represents scarcely a less inadequate motive. Can it be conceived that Judas would deliberately forego the prospect of immense wealth from his Master, by delivering him up for about four pounds ten shillings sterling, or twenty-two dollars of American money, upon the highest computation, and not more than double the value of a sum which he might easily have purloined from the bag? Is it likely that he would have made such a sacrifice for any further sum, however large, which we may suppose 'they *promised* him' (Mark xiv:11), and of which the thirty pieces of silver might have been the mere earnest (Luke xxii:5)? Had covetousness been his motive, he would have ultimately applied to the chief priests, not to bring again the thirty pieces of silver with the confession, 'I have sinned in that I have betrayed the innocent blood' (Matt. xxvii:4), but to demand the completion of their agreement with him.

(5) Dissatisfaction with the Master. We are now at liberty to consider the only remaining motive for the conduct of Judas, namely, dissatisfaction with the procedure of his Master, and a consequent scheme for the furtherance of his own views. It seems to us likely that the impatience of Judas for the accomplishment of his worldly views, which we conceive to have ever actuated him in following Jesus, could no longer be restrained, and that our Lord's observations at Bethany served to mature a stratagem he had meditated long before. He had no doubt been greatly disappointed at seeing his Master avoid being made a king, after feeding the five thousand in Galilee.

Many a favorable crisis had Jesus seemed to lose, or had not dared to embrace, and now while at Bethany he talks of his burial (John xii:7); and though none of his apostles, so firm were their worldly expectations from their Master, could clearly understood such 'sayings' (Luke xviii:34), yet they had been made 'exceeding sorry' by them (Matt. xvii:23).

At the same time Judas had long been convinced by the miracles he had seen his Master perform that he was the Messiah (John vii:31). He had even heard him accept this title from his apostles in private (Matt. xvi:16). He had promised them that when he should 'sit upon the throne of his glory, they should sit upon twelve thrones judging the twelve tribes of Israel' (Matt. xix:28). Yet now, when everything seemed most favorable to the assumption of empire, he hesitates and desponds. In his daily public conferences, too, with the chief priests and Pharisees, he appears to offend them by his reproofs, rather than to conciliate their favor. Within a few days, the people, who had lately given him a triumphal entry into the city, having kept the passover, would be dispersed to their homes, and Judas and his fellow apostles be, perhaps, required to attend their Master on another tedious expedition through the country. Hence it seems most probable that Judas resolved upon the plan of delivering up his Master to the Jewish authorities, when he would be compelled, in self-defense, to prove his claims, by giving them the sign from heaven they had so often demanded; they would, he believed, elect him in due form as the King Messiah and thus enable him to reward his followers. He did, indeed, receive from Jesus many alarming admonitions against his design; but the plainest warnings are lost upon a mind totally absorbed by a purpose, and agitated by many violent passions. The worst he would permit himself to expect was a temporary displeasure for placing his Master in this dilemma; but as he most likely believed, judging from himself, that Jesus anticipated worldly aggrandizement, he might calculate upon his forgiveness when the emergency should have been triumphantly surmounted.

(6) Hope of a Miracle. Judas could not doubt his Master's ability to extricate himself from his enemies by miracle. He had known him to do so more than once (Luke iv:30; John viii:59; x:39). Hence his directions to the officers to 'hold him fast,' when he was apprehended (Matt. xxvi:48). With other Jews he believed the Messiah would never die (John xii:34); accordingly, we regard his pecuniary stipulation with the priests as a mere artful cover to his deeper and more comprehensive design; and so that he served their purpose in causing the apprehension of Jesus, they would little care to scrutinize his motive. All they felt was being 'glad' at his proposal (Mark xiv:11), and the plan appeared to hold good up to the very moment of our Lord's condemnation; for after his apprehension his miraculous power seemed unabated, from his healing Malchus.

Judas heard him declare that he could even then 'ask, and his father would give him twelve legions of angels' for his rescue. But when Judas, who awaited the issue of the trial with such different expectations, saw that though Jesus had avowed himself to be the Messiah, he had not convinced the Sanhedrim, and, instead of extricating himself from their power by miracle, had submitted to be 'condemned, buffeted and 'spit upon' by his judges and accusers, then it would seem he awoke to a full view of all the consequences of his conduct.

(7) Repentance and Suicide. The prophecies of the Old Testament, 'that Christ should suffer,' and of Jesus, concerning his own rejection and death, flashed on his mind in their true sense and full force, and he found himself the wretched instrument of their fulfilment. He made a last desperate effort to stay proceedings. He presented himself to the chief priests, offered to return the money, confessed that he had sinned in that he had betrayed the innocent blood, and upon receiving their heartless answer was wrought into a frenzy of despair, during which he committed suicide.

There is much significancy in these words of Matt. xxvii:3, 'Then Judas, *when he saw he was condemned,*' not expiring on the cross, 'repented himself,' etc. If such be the true hypothesis of his conduct, then, however culpable it may have been as originating in the most inordinate covetousness, impatience of the procedure of Providence, crooked policy, or any other bad quality, he is certainly absolved from the direct *intention* of procuring his Master's death.

(8) Difference Between Judas and Other Apostles. 'The difference,' says Archbishop Whately, 'between Iscariot and his fellow apostles was, that though they all had the same expectations and conjectures, *he* dared to *act* on his conjectures, departing from the plain course of his known duty to follow the calculations of his worldly wisdom and the schemes of his worldly ambition.' The reader is directed to the Primate's admirable *Discourse on the Treason of Judas Iscariot, and Notes,* annexed to *Essays on Some of the Dangers to Christian Faith,* Lond., 1839; Whitby on Matt. xxvii:3, for the opinions of Theophylact, and some of the Fathers; Bishop Bull's *Sermons,* ii and iii, *On Some Important Points,* vol. i, Lond., 1713; Hales, *New Analysis of Chronology,* vol. ii, b. ii, pp. 877, 878; Mac-

knight's *Harmony of the Gospels,* vol. ii, pp. 427-30, Lond., 1822; Rosenmüller, Kuinoel, *in loc;* Adam Clarke's *Commentary.*   J. F. D.

JUDAS MACCABÆUS. See MACCABEES.

JUDE (jūde). See JUDAS.

JUDE, EPISTLE OF (jūde, ĕ-pĭs' 'l).

(1) Authenticity. Doubts have been thrown upon the genuineness of this Epistle, from the fact that the writer was supposed to have cited two apocryphal books—Enoch and the Assumption of Moses. But, notwithstanding the difficulties connected with this point, this epistle was treated by the ancients with the highest respect, and regarded as the genuine work of an inspired writer. Although Origen on one occasion speaks doubtfully, calling it the 'reputed epistle of Jude,' yet on another occasion, and in the same work (*Com. in Matt.*), he says, 'Jude wrote an epistle, of few lines indeed, but full of the powerful words of heavenly grace, who at the beginning says, "Jude, the servant of Jesus Christ and brother of James."' The same writer (*Com. in Rom.* and *De Princip.* iii:2, i:138) calls it the writing of Jude the *Apostle.*

The moderns are, however, divided in opinion between Jude the Apostle and Jude the Lord's brother, if indeed they be different persons. Hug and De Wette ascribe it to the latter.

(2) Another Brother of James. The author simply calls himself Jude, the brother of James, and a servant of Jesus Christ. This form of expression has given rise to various conjectures.

Hug supposes that he intimates thereby a nearer degree of relationship than that of an apostle.

At the same time it must be acknowledged that the circumstance of his not naming himself an apostle is not of itself necessarily sufficient to militate against his being the apostle of that name, inasmuch as St. Paul does not upon all occasions (as in Philippians, Thessalonians, and Philemon) use this title. From his calling himself the brother of James, rather than the brother of the Lord, Michaelis deduces that he was the son of Joseph by a former wife, and not a full brother of our Lord's, as Herder contends. (See JAMES; JUDAS OR JUDE.)

(3) Coincidence with Epistles of Peter. From the great coincidence both in sentiment and subject which exists between our epistle and the second of St. Peter, it has been thought by many critics that one of these writers had seen the other's work; but we shall reserve the discussion as to which was the earlier writing until we come to treat of St. Peter's Epistle.

(4) When Written. Dr. Lardner supposes that Jude's Epistle was written between the years 64 and 66, Beausobre and L'Enfant between 70 and 75 (from which Dodwell and Cave do not materially differ), and Dr. Mill fixes it at the year 90. If Jude has quoted the apocryphal book of Enoch, as seems to be agreed upon by most modern critics, and if this book was written, as Lücke thinks, after the destruction of Jerusalem, the age of our epistle best accords with the date assigned to it by Mill.

(5) To Whom Addressed. It is difficult to decide who the persons were to whom this epistle was addressed, some supposing that it was written to converted Jews, others to all Christians without distinction. Many of the arguments seem best adapted to convince the Jewish Christians, as appeals are so strikingly made to their sacred books and traditions.

(6) Design. The design of this epistle is to warn the Christians against the false teachers who had insinuated themselves among them and disseminated dangerous tenets of insubordination and licentiousness. The author reminds them, by the example of Sodom and Gomorrah, that God had punished the rebellious Jews; and that even the disobedient angels had shared the same fate. The false teachers to whom he alludes 'speak evil of dignities,' while the archangel Michael did not even revile Satan. He compares them to Balaam and Korah, to clouds without water, and to raging waves. Enoch, he says, foretold their wickedness; at the same time he consoles believers, and exhorts them to persevere in faith and love. The epistle is remarkable for the vehemence, fervor and energy of its composition and style. (See ANTILEGOMENA.)

W. W.

JUDEA (jū-dē′ȧ). See JUDÆA.

JUDGE (jŭj), (Heb. שָׁפַט, *shaw-fat′*).

1. To try and determine a cause (Exod. xviii:13). The manner of giving sentence was different in different nations. The Jewish judges gave sentence by simply declaring to the accused, *Thou art guilty,* or *Thou art innocent.* The Romans did it by casting various tables into a box or urn, marked with an *A,* if they absolved; and with a *C,* if they condemned the accused. Some of the Greeks intimated the sentence of absolution, by giving a white stone; and of condemnation by giving a black one; to this allusion is made in Rev. ii:17.

2. To esteem; account, as if on trial (Acts xvi:15).

3. To rule and govern, as one having power to try and determine causes (Ps. lviii:11).

4. To punish, as in consequence of trial and sentence; and to declare and denounce such punishments (Heb. xñi:4; Ezek. vii:3-8 and xxii:2).

5. To censure rashly (Matt. vii:1).

6. To appear upon one's side, as in consequence of trial of his cause (Prov. xvii:18). (See LAW.)

JUDGES (jŭj′ĕs). This name is applied to fifteen persons who at intervals presided over the affairs of the Israelites during the 350 years (according to Usher's chronology) which elapsed from the death of Joshua to the accession of Saul.

(1) Rulers of the People. The term *Judges,* used in the English Bibles, does not exactly represent the original Heb. שֹׁפְטִים, *sho-phe-tim,* i. e., 'rulers of the people.' The station and office of these *shophetim* are involved in great obscurity, partly from the want of clear intimations in the history in which their exploits and government are recorded, and partly from the absence of parallels in the history of other nations, by which our notions might be assisted.

(2) Singular Institution. In fact the government of the judges forms the most singular part of the Hebrew institutions, and that which appears most difficult to comprehend. The kings, the priests, the generals, the heads of tribes—all these offer some points of comparison with the same functionaries in other nations; but the judges stand alone in the history of the world; and when we think that we have found officers resembling them in other nations, the comparison soon breaks down in some point of importance.

(3) Nature of the Office. It remains to inquire into the nature of the office itself, and the powers and privileges which were connected with it. It is usual to consider them as commencing their career with military exploits to deliver Israel from foreign oppression; but this is by no means invariably the case. Eli and Samuel were not military men; Deborah judged Israel before she planned the war against Jabin; and of Jair, Ibzan, Elon, and Abdon, it is at least uncertain whether they ever held any military command. The command of the army can therefore scarcely be considered the distinguishing characteristic of these men, or military exploits the necessary introduction to the office. In many cases it is true that military achievements were the means by which they elevated themselves to the rank of judges; but in general the appointment may be said to have varied with the exigencies of the times, and with the particular circumstances which in times of trouble would draw the public attention to persons who appeared suited by their gifts or influence to advise in matters of general concernment, to decide in questions arising between tribe and tribe, to administer public affairs, and to appear as their recognized head in their intercourse with their neighbors and oppressors.

(4) Choice of the People. In nearly all the instances recorded the appointment seems to have been by the free, unsolicited choice of the people. The election of Jephthah, who was nominated as the fittest man for the existing emergency, probably resembled that which was usually followed on such occasions; and probably, as in his case, the judge, in accepting the office, took care to make such stipulations as he deemed necessary.

(5) Divine Appointment. The only cases of direct Divine appointment are those of Gideon and Samson, and the last stood in the peculiar position of having been from before his birth ordained 'to begin to deliver Israel.' Deborah was called to deliver Israel, but was already a judge. Samuel was called by the Lord to be a prophet, but not a judge, which ensued from the high gifts which the people recognized as dwelling in him; and as to Eli, the office of judge seems to have devolved naturally, or rather *ex officio,* upon him; and his case seems to be the only one in which the high-priest appears in the character which the theocratical institutions designed for him.

(6) Duties and Privileges. The following clear summary of their duties and privileges is from Jahn (*Biblisches Archäologie,* th. ii. bd. 1, sec. 22; Stowe's translation, ii:86): The office of judges or regents was held during life, but it was not hereditary, neither could they appoint their successors. Their authority was limited by the law alone; and in doubtful cases they were directed to consult the Divine King through the priest by Urim and Thummim (Num. xxvii:21).

They were not obliged in common cases to ask advice of the ordinary rulers; it was sufficient if these did not remonstrate against the measures of the judge. In important emergencies, however, they convoked a general assembly of the rulers, over which they presided and exerted a powerful influence. They could issue orders, but not enact laws; they could neither levy taxes nor appoint officers, except perhaps in the army.

Their authority extended only over those tribes by whom they had been elected or acknowledged: for it is clear that several of the judges presided over separate tribes. There was no income attached to their office, nor was there any income appropriated to them, unless it might be a larger share in the spoils, and those presents which were made them as testimonials of respect (Judg. viii:24).

They bore no external marks of dignity, and maintained no retinue of courtiers, though some of them were very opulent. They were not only simple in their manners, moderate in their desires, and free from avarice and ambition, but noble and magnanimous men, who felt that whatever they did for their country was above all reward, and could not be recompensed; who desired merely to promote the public good, and who chose rather to deserve well of their country than to be enriched by its wealth.

(7) **Exalted Patriotism.** This exalted patriotism, like everything else connected with politics in the theocratical state of the Hebrews, was partly of a religious character, and those regents always conducted themselves as the officers of God; in all their enterprises they relied upon him, and their only care was that their countrymen should acknowledge the authority of Jehovah, their Invisible King (Judg. viii: 22, *sq.;* comp. Heb. xi).

(8) **Character.** Still they were not without faults, neither are they so represented by their historians; they relate, on the contrary, with the utmost frankness, the great sins of which some of them were guilty. They were not merely deliverers of the state from a foreign yoke, but destroyers of idolatry, foes of pagan vices, promoters of the knowledge of God, of religion, and of morality; restorers of theocracy in the minds of the Hebrews, and powerful instruments of Divine Providence in the promotion of the great design of preserving the Hebrew constitution, and, by that means, of rescuing the true religion from destruction.

(9) **Not a Complete History.** The times of the judges would certainly not be considered so turbulent and barbarous, much less would they be taken, contrary to the clearest evidence and to the analogy of all history, for a heroic age, if they were viewed without the prejudices of a preconceived hypothesis. It must never be forgotten that the book of Judges is by no means a complete history. This no impartial inquirer can ever deny. It is, in a manner, a mere register of diseases, from which, however, we have no right to conclude that there were no healthy men, much less that there were no healthy seasons; since the book itself, for the most part, mentions only a few tribes in which the epidemic prevailed, and notices long periods during which it had universally ceased.

(10) **Condition of the People.** Whatever may be the result of a more accurate investigation, it remains undeniable that the condition of the Hebrews during this period perfectly corresponds throughout to the sanctions of the law; and they were always prosperous when they complied with the conditions on which prosperity was promised them; it remains undeniable that the government of God was clearly manifested, not only to the Hebrews, but to their heathen neighbors; that the fulfilling of the promises and threatenings of the law were so many sensible proofs of the universal dominion of the Divine King of the Hebrews; and, consequently, that all the various fortunes of that nation were so many means of preserving the knowledge of God on the earth. The Hebrews had no sufficient reason to desire a change in their constitution; all required was, that they should observe the conditions on which national prosperity was promised them.

(11) **Chronology.** The chronology of the period in which the judges ruled is beset with great and perhaps insuperable difficulties. There are intervals of time the extent of which is not specified; as, for instance, that from Joshua's death to the yoke of Chushan-rishathaim (ii:8); that of the rule of Shamgar (iii:31); that between Gideon's death and Abimelech's accession

(viii:31, 32); and that of Israel's renewal of idolatry previous to their oppression by the Ammonites (x:6, 7). Sometimes round numbers seem to have been given, as forty years for the rule of Othniel, forty years for that of Gideon, and forty years also for the duration of the oppression by the Philistines. Twenty years are given for the subjection to Jabin, and twenty years for the government of Samson; yet the latter never completely conquered the Philistines, who, on the contrary, succeeded in capturing him.

Some judges, who are commonly considered to have been successive, were in all probability contemporaneous, and ruled over different districts. Under these circumstances it is impossible to fix the date of each particular event in the book of Judges; but attempts have been made to settle its general chronology, of which we must in this place mention the most successful.

The whole period of the judges, from Joshua to Eli, is usually estimated at 299 years, in order to meet the 480 years which (1 Kings vi:1) are said to have elapsed from the departure of the Israelites from Egypt to the foundation of the temple by Solomon. But St. Paul says (Acts xiii:20), 'God gave unto the people of Israel judges about the space of 450 years until Samuel, the prophet.' Again, if the number of years specified by the author of our book, in stating facts, is summed up, we have 410 years, exclusive of those years not specified for certain intervals of time above mentioned. In order to reduce these 410 years and upwards to 299, events and reigns must, in computing their years of duration, either be entirely passed over, or, in a most arbitrary way, included in other periods preceding or subsequent.

(*a*) *Of Usher.* This has been done by Archbishop Usher, whose peculiarly faulty system has been adopted in the Authorized Version of the Scriptures. He excludes the repeated intervals during which the Hebrews were in subjection to their enemies, and reckons only the years of peace and rest which were assigned to the successive judges. For example, he passes over the eight years of servitude inflicted upon the Hebrews by Chushan-rishathaim, and, without any interruption, connects the peace obtained by the victories of Othniel with that which had been conferred on the land by the government of Joshua; and although the sacred historian relates on the plainest terms possible that the children of Israel served the king of Mesopotamia eight years, and were afterwards delivered by Othniel, who gave the land rest forty years, the archbishop maintains that the forty years now mentioned began, not after the successes of this judge, but immediately after the demise of Joshua. Nothing certainly can be more obvious than that in this case the years of tranquillity and the years of oppression ought to be reckoned separately.

Again, we are informed by the sacred writer, that after the death of Ehud the children of Israel were under the oppression of Jabin, king of Hazor, for twenty years, and that afterwards, when their deliverance was effected by Deborah and Barak, the land had rest forty years. Nothing can be clearer than this; yet Usher's system leads him to include the twenty years of oppression in the forty of peace, making both but forty years.

(*b*) *Of Hales.* All this arises from the obligation which Usher unfortunately conceived himself under of following the scheme adopted by the Massoretic Jews, who, as Dr. Hales remarks, have by a curious invention included the first four servitudes in the years of the judges who put an end to them, contrary to the express declarations of Scripture, which represents the administrations of the judges, not as synchronizing with the servitudes, but as succeeding them.

The Rabbins were indeed forced to allow the fifth servitude to have been distinct from the administration of Jephthah, because it was too long to be included in that administration; but they deducted a year from the Scripture account of the servitude, making it only six instead of seven years. They sank entirely the sixth servitude of forty years under the Philistines, because it was too long to be contained in Samson's administration; and, to crown all, they reduced Saul's reign of forty years to two years only.

(c) *The necessity* for all these tortuous operations has arisen from a desire to produce a conformity with the date in 1 Kings vi:1, which, as already cited, gives a period of only 480 years from the Exode to the foundation of Solomon's temple. As this date is incompatible with the sum of the different numbers given in the book of Judges, and as it differs from the computation of Josephus and of all the ancient writers on the subject, whether Jewish or Christian, it is not unsatisfactory to find grounds which leave this text open to much doubt and suspicion. We cannot here enter into any lengthened proof; but that the text did not exist in the Hebrew and Greek copies of the Scripture till nearly three centuries after Christ, is evident from the absence of all reference to it in the works of the learned men who composed histories of the Jews from the materials supplied to them in the sacred books. This could be shown by reference to various authors, who, if the number specified in it had existed, could not fail to have adduced it. But our space forbids such reference. (See CHRONOLOGY.)

(12) **Government.** We find that, apart from such offices as those of Moses and Joshua, a very excellent provision existed for the government of the chosen people, both as regarded the interests of the nation generally, as well as of the several tribes. To this latter branch of the government it is important to draw particular attention, because, as it existed before the Law, and is *assumed* throughout as the basis of the theocratical constitution, we hear but little of it in the books of Moses, and are apt to lose sight of it altogether.

The fact is, however, that, through the perversity of the people, this settlement of the general government on theocratical principles was not carried out in its proper form and extent; and it is in this neglect we are to seek the necessity for those officers called Judges, who were from time to time raised up to correct some of the evils which resulted from it.

It is very evident, from the whole history of the judges, that after the death of Joshua the Israelites threw themselves back upon the segregative principles of their government by tribes, and all but utterly neglected, and for long periods did utterly neglect, the rules and usages on which the general government was established. There was, in fact, no human power adequate to enforce them. They were good in themselves, they were gracious, they conferred high privileges; but they were enforced by no sufficient authority. No one was amenable to any tribunal for neglecting the annual feasts, or for not referring the direction of public affairs to the Divine King. Omissions on these points involved the absence of the Divine protection and blessing, and were left to be punished by their consequences.

The people could not grasp the idea of a Divine and Invisible King; they could not bring themselves to recur to him in all those cases in which the judgment of a human king would have determined the course of action, or in which his arm would have worked for their deliverance.

(13) **Reason for Judges.** Therefore it was that God allowed them judges in the persons of faithful men, who acted for the most part as agents of the divine will, regents for the Invisible King; and who, holding their commission directly from him, or with his sanction, would be more inclined to act as dependent vassals of Jehovah than kings, who, as members of royal dynasties, would come to reign with notions of independent rights and royal privileges, which would draw away their attention from their true place in the theocracy. In this greater dependence of the judges upon the Divine King we see the secret of their institutions.

The Israelites were disposed to rest upon their separate interests as tribes; and having thus allowed the standing general government to remain inoperative through disuse, they would in cases of emergency have been disposed 'to make themselves a king like the nations,' had their attention not been directed to the appointment of officers whose authority could rest on no tangible *right* apart from character and services. This, with the temporary nature of their powers, rendered their functions more accordant with the principles of the theocracy than those of any other public officers could be. And it is probably in this adaptation to the peculiar circumstances of the Hebrew theocracy that we shall discover the reason of our inability to find any similar office among other nations. In being thus peculiar it resembled the Dictatorship among the Romans; to which office indeed that of the judges has been compared; and perhaps this parallel is the nearest that can be found. E. W. H.

JUDGES, BOOK OF (jŭj'ĕs, book ŏv), the third in the list of the historical compositions of the Old Testament. It consists of two divisions, the first comprising cc. i-xvi; the second, being an appendix, cc. xvii-xxi.

(1) **Plan of the Book.** That the author, in composing this work, had a certain design in view, is evident from ch. ii:11-23, where he states the leading features of his narrative. He introduces it by relating (ch. i) the extent to which the wars against the Canaanites were continued after the death of Joshua, and what tribes had spared them in consideration of a tribute imposed; also by alluding (ch. ii:1-10) to the benefits which Jehovah had conferred on them, and the distinguished protection with which he had honored them.

Next he states his leading object, namely, to prove that the calamities to which the Hebrews had been exposed since the death of Joshua were owing to their apostasy from Jehovah, and to their idolatry. 'They forsook the Lord, and served Baal and Ashtaroth' (ch. ii:13); for which crimes they were deservedly punished and greatly distressed (ch. ii:15). Nevertheless, when they repented and obeyed again the commandments of the Lord, he delivered them out of the hand of their enemies by the *Shophetim* whom he raised up, and made them prosper (ch. ii:16-23).

To illustrate this theme, the author collected several fragments of the Hebrew history during the period between Joshua and Eli. Some episodes occur; but in arguing his subject he never loses sight of his leading theme, to which, on the contrary, he frequently recurs while stating facts, and shows how it applied to them; the moral evidently being, that the only way to happiness was to shun idolatry and obey the commandments of the Lord. The design of the author was not to give a connected and complete history of the Hebrews in the period between Joshua and the kings; for if he had intended a plan of that kind, he would also have described the state of the domestic affairs and of the government in the several tribes, the relation in which they stood to each other, and the extent of power exercised by a judge; he would have further stated the number of tribes over whom a judge ruled, and the number of years during which the tribes were not oppressed by their heathen neighbors, but enjoyed rest and peace. The appendix, containing two narratives, further illustrates the lawlessness and anarchy prevailing in Israel after Joshua's death.

(2) **Author.** If the first and second divisions had been by the same author, the chronological indications would also have been the same. Now the author of the second division always describes the period of which he speaks thus: 'In those days there was no king of Israel, but every man did that which was right in his own eyes' (cc. xvii:6; xviii:1; xix:1; xxi:25); but this expression never once occurs in the first division. If one author had composed both divisions, instead of this chronological formula, we should rather have expected, 'In the days of the *Shophetim*,' 'At a time when there was no *Shophet*,' etc., which would be consonant with the tenor of the first sixteen chapters.

The style also in the two divisions is different, and it will be shown that the appendix was written much later than the first part. All modern critics, then, agree in this, that the author of the first sixteen chapters of our book is different from him who composed the appendix. (See L. Bertholdt. *Historisch-Kritische Einleitung in die sämmtlichen Schriften des A. und N. T.*, p. 876; Eichhorn's *Einleitung in das A. T.*, iii, sec. 457). The authorship of the first sixteen chapters has been assigned to Joshua, Samuel, and Ezra. That they were not written by Joshua appears from the difference of the method of relating subjects, as well as from the difference of the style.

But though we cannot determine the authorship of the book of Judges, still its age may be determined from internal evidence. The first sixteen chapters must have been written under Saul, whom the Israelites made their king in the hope of improving their condition. Phrases used in the period of the judges may be traced in them, and the author must consequently have lived near the time when they were yet current. He says that in his time 'the Jebusites dwelt with the children of Benjamin in Jerusalem' (ch. i:21); now this was the case only before David, who conquered the town and drove out the Jebusites.

Consequently, the author of the first division of the book of Judges must have lived and written before David, and under King Saul. If he had lived under David he would have mentioned the capture of Jerusalem by that monarch, as the nature of his subject did not allow him to pass it over in silence. The omission, moreover, of the history, not only of Samuel but also of Eli, indicates an author who, living in an age very near that of Eli, considered his history as generally known, because so recent. The exact time when the appendix was added to the book of Judges cannot indeed be determined, but its author certainly lived in an age much later than that of the recorded events.

(3) **Character of the Book.** Parts of the work are undoubtedly taken from ancient records and genealogies, others from traditions and oral information. From ancient authentic documents are probably copied the song of Deborah (ch. v), the beautiful parable of Jotham (ch. ix:8-15), and the beginning of Samson's epinicion, or triumphal poem (ch. xv:16). In their genealogies the Hebrews usually inserted also some historical accounts, and from this source may have been derived the narrative of the circumstances that preceded the conception of Samson, which were given as the parents related them to others (ch. xiii).

(4) **Authority of the Book.** (a) It was published at a time when the events related were generally known, and when the veracity of the author could be ascertained by a reference to the original documents. Several of its narratives are confirmed by the books of Samuel (comp. Judg. iv:2; vi:14; xi, with 1 Sam. xii:9-12; Judg. ix:53 with 2 Sam. xi:21). The Psalms not only allude to the book of Judges (comp. Ps. lxxxiii:11, with Judg. vii:25), but copy from it entire verses (comp. Ps. lxviii:8, 9; xcvii:5; with Judg. v:4, 5). Philo and Josephus knew the book, and made use of it in their own compositions. The New Testament alludes to it in several places (comp. Luke i:13-16 with Judg. xiii:5; xvi:17; Acts xiii:20; Heb. xi:32).

(b) This external evidence in support of the authority of the book of Judges is corroborated by many internal proofs of its authenticity. All its narratives are in character with the age to which they belong, and agree with the natural order of things. We find here that shortly after the death of Joshua the Hebrew nation had, by several victories, gained courage and become valorous (Judg. i and xix); but that it afterwards turned to agriculture, preferred a quiet life, and allowed the Canaanites to reside in its territory in consideration of a tribute imposed on them, when the original plan was that they should be expelled. This changed the Hebrew character entirely; it became effeminate and indolent—a result which we find in the case of all nations who, from a nomadic and warlike life, turn to agriculture.

(c) The intercourse with their heathen neighbors frequently led the uncultivated Hebrews to idolatry; and this, again, further prepared them for servitude. They were consequently overpowered and oppressed by their heathen neighbors. The first subjugation, indeed, by a king of Mesopotamia, they endured but eight years; but the second, more severe, by Eglon, lasted longer; it was the natural consequence of the public spirit having gradually more and more declined, and of Eglon having removed his residence to Jericho with a view of closely watching all their movements (Joseph. *Antiq.* v:5).

When Ehud sounded the trumpet of revolt the whole nation no longer rose in arms, but only the inhabitants of Mount Ephraim (ch. iii:27); and when Barak called to arms against Sisera many tribes remained quietly with their herds (ch. v:14, 15, 26, 28). Of the 30,000 men who offered to follow Gideon, he could make use of no more than 300, this small number only being, as it would seem, filled with true patriotism and courage.

(d) Thus the people had sunk gradually, and deserved for forty years to bear the yoke of the Philistines, to whom they had the meanness to deliver Samson, who, however, loosed the cords with which he was tied, and killed a large number of them (ch. xv). It is impossible to consider such an historical work, which perfectly agrees with the natural course of things, as a fiction; at that early period of authorship no writer could have, from infancy, depicted the character of the Hebrews so conformably with nature and established facts. All in this book breathes the spirit of the ancient world. Martial law we find in it, as could not be but expected, hard and wild. The conquered people are subjected to rough treatment, as is the case in the wars of all uncivilized people; the inhabitants of cities are destroyed wholesale (cc. viii:16, 17; xx). Hospitality and the protection of strangers received as guests is considered the highest virtue (ch. xix; comp. Gen. xix).

(e) In the state of oppression in which the Hebrews often found themselves during the period from Joshua to Eli, it was to be expected that men filled with heroism should now and then rise up and call the people to arms in order to deliver them from their enemies. Such valiant men are introduced by our author, and he extols them indeed highly; but on the other hand he is not silent respecting their faults, as may be seen in the instances of Ehud, whom he reports to have murdered a king to recover liberty for his country (ch. iii:16, sq.); of Gideon, who is recorded to have punished the inhabitants of Succoth and Penuel cruelly, for having refused bread to his weary troops (ch. viii:16, 17); and of Jephthah, who vows a vow that if he should return home as a conqueror of the Ammonites he would offer as a burnt-offering whatever should first come out of the door of his house to meet him (ch. xi:34): in consequence of this inconsiderate vow, his only daughter is sacrificed by a savage father, who thus becomes a gross offender against the Mosaic law, which expressly forbids human immolations. This cannot be a fiction; it is no panegyric on Israel to describe them in the manner the author has done. And this frank, impartial tone pervades the whole work. It begins with displaying the Israelites as a refractory and obstinate people, and the appendix ends with the statement of a crime committed by the Benjamites, which had the most disastrous consequences. At the same time due praise is bestowed on acts of generosity and justice, and valiant feats are carefully recorded.

(5) Authenticity of the Book. This has been questioned, because of the remarkable exploits ascribed to its heroes. But it will be easy to show that, when properly understood, they do not necessarily exceed the limits of human power. Extraordinary indeed they were; but they are not alleged by the Scripture itself to have been supernatural. Those, however, who do hold them to have been supernatural cannot reasonably take exception to them on the ground of their extraordinary character. Considering the very remote period at which our book was written—considering also the manner of viewing and describing events and persons which prevailed with the ancient Hebrews, and which very much differs from that of our age—taking, moreover, into account the brevity of the narratives, which consist of historical fragments, we may well wonder that there do not occur in it more difficulties, and that not more doubts have been raised as to its historical authority. (Bishop Hall, *Contemplations on the O. T.*, bks. x, xi; Milman, *Hist. of the Jews*, N. Y. 1864; Stanley, *Jewish Ch.*, i:315-426, Amer. ed.; Bachman, *Der Buch der Richter*, etc., 1868, i:1-242; Keil, *Iosua*, in *Bibl. Comm.* of Keil and Delitzsch, iii:175-356, trans. by J. Martin, in Clark's *For. Theol. Libr.* Edin. 1865.)

JUDGMENT (jŭj'ment), (Heb. מִשְׁפָּט, *mish-pawt'*).

(1) Wisdom and prudence, whereby one can judge of what is proper or improper, right or wrong (Jer. x:24; Is. xxx:18; Ps. lxxii:1). (2) 'Strict equity,' such as should appear in judging (Luke xi:42). (3) The decision of a judge (1 Kings iii:28). (4) Courts for trying causes (Matt. v:21). (5) Controversies to be tried and decided (1 Cor. vi:4). (6) Sentiment, opinion, advice (1 Cor. i:10 and vii:25). (7) Chastisement inflicted on saints (1 Pet. iv:17). (8) The statutes or commandment of God, or what he has decided in his word, particularly in what relates to civil punishments (Ps. xix:7; Matt. xii:18; Exod. xxi:1). (9) The punishment inflicted for sin (Prov. xix:29; Is. liii:8; Ezek. xxx:14). (10) The power of judging the world: this God has committed to Christ (John v:22 and xvi:8). (11) The solemn trial of men at the last day, that the wicked may be condemned, and the righteous adjudged to everlasting life (Eccl. xii:14; Jude 6, 15).

Examples of Its Use. (1) *God brings forth men's judgment as the noon-day,* when, in his wise and righteous providence, he openly manifests and rewards them according to the goodness and equity of their cause (Ps. xxxvii:6). (2) *Zion shall be redeemed with judgment,* shall be delivered according to the wisdom and equity of God, and through the infliction of punishment on God's Son (Is. i:27). (3) *Christ brings forth judgment to the Gentiles, and sends it forth unto victory,* when he effectually reveals the truths of God, and forms a people to himself (Is. xlii:2, 3; Matt. xii:18, 20). (4) *Now is the judgment of this world come; now shall the prince of this world be cast out.* Now shall God separate multitudes to himself; now shall he bring down their f high looks and imaginations; now shall Satan be cast out from men's hearts, and lose his authority in the world (John xii:31). (5) *The Holy Ghost shall convince men of judgment, because the prince of this world is judged;* by dislodging Satan from men's bodies, and casting him out of their hearts, he shall demonstrate Jesus' power and authority, and evince his future appearance to judgment (John xvi:11). (6) *God's judgments are true and righteous;* his conduct in delivering his people, and punishing his enemies, corresponds with the predictions and threatenings of his word, and the equity of his nature (Rev. xix:2). (7) *Rash judgments* are absolutely forbidden in the sacred Scriptures (Matt. vii:1). (a) We thereby authorize others to requite us in the same kind. (b) It often evidences our pride, envy, and bigotry. (c) It argues a want of charity, the distinguishing feature of the Christian religion. (d) They who are most forward in censuring others are often most defective themselves.

JUDGMENT-HALL (jŭj'ment hall), (Gr. Πραιτώριον, *prahee-to'ree-on*, prætorium, occurs in Matt. xxvii:27; Mark xv:16; John xviii:28, 33; xix:9; Acts xxiii:35; Phil. i:13, in all which places the Vulgate has prætorium.

The English Version, however, uses prætorium once only, and then unavoidably (Mark xv:16), 'The hall called prætorium.' In all the other instances it gives an explanation of the word rather than a translation; thus (Matt. xxvii:27) 'the common hall,' margin, 'or governor's house'; John xviii:28, 33) 'the judgment hall,' margin, 'or Pilate's house'; (Phil. i:13), 'the palace,' margin, 'or Cæsar's court.'

(1) Original Signification. The word prætorium originally signified the general's tent in a camp, and came at length to be applied to the residence of the civil governor in provinces and

cities (Cic. *Verr.* ii, v. 12); and being properly an adjective, as is also its Greek representative, it was used to signify *whatever* appertained to the prætor or governor; for instance, his residence either the whole or any part of it, as his dwelling-house, or the place where he administered justice, or even the large enclosed court at the entrance to the prætorian residence (Bynæus, *De Morte Jes. Christ.* ii:407, Amst., 1696).

(2) Pilate's Residence. Upon comparing the instances in which the evangelists mention the prætorium, it will be seen, first, that it was the residence of Pilate (John xviii:28) which seems to have been the magnificent palace built by Herod, situated in the north part of the upper city, west of the temple (Joseph. *Antiq.* xv:9, 3), and overlooking the temple (Joseph. xx:8, 11).

(3) A Portion of the Palace. Secondly, the word is applied in the New Testament, by synecdoche, to a particular *part* of the prætorian residence. Thus, Matt. xxvii:27, and Mark xv:16, 'And the soldiers led Jesus away into the hall called Prætorium, and gathered unto them the whole band, and they clothed him with purple,' etc.; where the word rather refers to the court or area in front of the prætorium, or some other court where the procurator's guards were stationed. In John xix:9, the word seems applied, when all the circumstances are considered, to Pilate's *private examination room.* In like manner, when Felix 'commanded Paul to be kept in Herod's prætorium' (Acts xxiii:35), the words apply not only to the whole palace originally built at Cæsarea by Herod, and now most likely inhabited by the prætor, but also to the *keep* or *donjon,* a prison for confining offenders, such as existed in our ancient royal palaces and grand baronial castles.

(4) Prætorian Camp. Thirdly, in the remaining instance of the word (Phil. i:13), 'So that my bonds in Christ are manifest in all the prætorium,' 'palace,' it is, in the opinion of the best commentators, used by hypallage to signify the *prætorian camp* at Rome, a select body of troops constituted by Augustus to guard his person and to have charge of the city, the *'cohortes prætorianæ'* (Suet. *Tib.* 37; *Claud.* 10; *Ner.* 8; Tacitus, *Annal.* xii:69); so that the words of the apostle really mean, 'My bonds in Christ are manifest to all the prætorians, and by their means to the public at large.'

JUDGMENT-SEAT (jŭj'ment sēt), (Gr. Βῆμα, *bay'ma,* a step; 1 Cor. vi:2, 4, Κριτήριον, *Kri-tay'-rion,* a court of judgment). See PRÆTORIUM; JUDGMENT-HALL.

Judgments of God are the punishments inflicted by him for particular crimes. The Scriptures give us many striking instances of the display of Divine justice in the punishment of nations, families, and individuals, for their iniquities (see Gen. vi; xix: 25; Exod. xv; Judg. i:6, 7; Acts xii:23; Esther v:14, with ch. vii:10; Lev. x:1, 2; Acts v:1-10; Is. xxx:1-5; 1 Sam. xv:9, 23; 1 Kings xii:25, 33). It becomes us, however, to be exceedingly cautious how we interpret the severe and afflictive dispensations of Providence, in the present world.

Dr. Jortin justly observes that there is usually much rashness and presumption in pronouncing that the calamities of sinners are particular judgments of God; yet, he says, if from sacred and profane, from ancient and modern historians, a collection were made of all the cruel, persecuting tyrants, who delighted in tormenting their fellow-creatures, and who died not the common death of all men, but whose plagues were horrible and strange, even a skeptic would be moved at the evidence, and would be apt to suspect that it was *theion ti,* that the hand of God was in it.

JUDICIAL BLINDNESS OR HARDNESS. A term used to denote moral incorrigibility and spiritual blindness (Mark iii:5). "Being grieved for the *blindness—hardness*—of their hearts." So (Rom. xi:25). "*Blindness—hardness*—in part hath happened to Israel" (Eph. iv:18). "Because of the *blindness—hardness*—of their hearts" (2 Cor. iii:14). "Their minds were *blinded"—hardened;* and elsewhere. In other expressions God is declared to be the cause of such hardness and blindness (John xii:40). He has blinded their eyes and hardened their hearts; which seems to be contradictory to Matt. xiii:15, where the people themselves are said to have closed their own eyes; and so Acts xxviii:27. These seeming contradictions are very easily reconciled by taking the phraseology in its true import:

(a) "Set the eyes of this people"—prophesy such *flowing* times, such abundant jollity, that the people, devoting themselves to gormandizing, may be inebriated with the very idea; and still more with the enjoyment itself when it arrives.

(b) God, by giving plenty and abundance, affords the means of the people's abusing his goodness, and becoming both over-fat with food, and intoxicated with drink; and thus, his very beneficence may be said to make their heart fat, and their eyes heavy.

(c) While, at the same time, the people by their own act, their overfeeding, become unwieldy—indolent—bloated—over-fat at heart; and, moreover, so stupefied by liquor and strong drink that their eyes and ears may be useless to them; with wide open eyes, "staring they may stare, but not perceive; and listening they may hear, but not understand"; and in this lethargic state they will continue; preferring it to a more sedate, rational condition, and refusing to forbear from prolonging the causes of it, lest at any sober interval they should see truly with their eyes, and hear accurately with their ears; in consequence of which they should be shocked at themselves, be converted, be changed from such misconduct, and God should heal them, should cure these blinding effects of dissoluteness (comp. Is. v:11; xxviii).

JUDITH (jū'dith), (Heb. יְהוּדִית, *yeh-hoo-deeth'* Jewess).

I. Daughter of Beeri the Hittite and Esau's wife (Gen. xxvi:34).

II. *Judith* is the name of one of the apocryphal or deutero-canonical books of the Old Testament, is placed in manuscripts of the Alexandrine Version between the books of Tobit and Esther. In its external form this book bears the character of the record of an historical event, describing the complete defeat of the Assyrians by the Jews through the prowess of a woman.

1. Narrative. The following is a sketch of the narrative: Nebuchadnezzar, or, as he is called in the Greek, Nabuchodonosor, king of the Assyrians, having, in the twelfth year of his reign, conquered and taken Arphaxad, by whom his territory had been invaded, formed the design of subduing the people of Asia to the westward of Nineveh, his capital, who had declined to aid him against Arphaxad. With this view he sent his general, Holofernes, at the head of a powerful army, and soon made himself master of Mesopotamia, Syria, Libya, Cilicia, and Idumæa. The inhabitants of the seacoast made a voluntary submission; which, however, did not prevent their territories from being laid waste, their sacred groves burned, and their idols destroyed, in order that divine honors should be paid only to Nebuchadnezzar.

(1) Holofernes. Holofernes, having finally encamped in the plain of Esdraelon (ch. i:3), remained inactive for a whole month—or two, according to the Latin version.

But the Jews, who had not long returned from captivity, and who had just restored their temple and its worship, prepared for war under the direction of their high-priest Joacim, or Eliakim, and the senate. The high-priest addressed letters to the inhabitants of Bethulia (Gr. Βετυλούα) and Betomestham, near Esdraelon (ch. iv:6), charging them to guard the passes of the mountains.

The Jews at the same time kept a fast, and called upon God for protection against their enemies. Holofernes, astonished at their audacity and preparations, inquired of the Moabites and Ammonites who these people were. Achior, the leader of the Ammonites, informed him of the history of the Jews, adding, that if they offended their God he would deliver them into the hands of their enemies, but that otherwise they would be invincible.

Holofernes, however, prepares to lay siege to Bethulia, and commences operations by taking the mountain passes, and intercepting the water, in order to compel the inhabitants to surrender. Ozias, the governor of the city, holds out as long as possible; but at the end of thirty-four days' siege the inhabitants are reduced to that degree of distress from drought that they are determined to surrender unless relieved within five days.

(2) Design of Judith. Meantime Judith, a rich and beautiful woman, the widow of Manasseh, forms the patriotic design of delivering the city and the nation. With this view she entreats the governor and elders to give up all idea of surrender, and to permit the gates of the city to be opened for her. Arrayed in rich attire, she proceeds to the camp of Holofernes, attended only by her maid, bearing a bag of provisions. She is admitted into the presence of Holofernes, and informs him that the Jews could not be overcome so long as they remained faithful to God, but that they had now sinned against him in converting to their own use the tithes, which were sacred to the priests alone; and that she had fled from the city to escape the impending and inevitable destruction which awaited it.

She obtains leave to remain in the camp, with the liberty of retiring by night for the purpose of prayer, and promises that at the proper moment she will herself be the guide of Holofernes to the very walls of Jerusalem.

(3) Holofernes Charmed. Judith is favorably entertained; Holofernes is smitten with her charms, gives her a magnificent entertainment, at which, having drunk too freely, he is shut up with her alone in the tent.

(4) Death of Holofernes. Taking advantage of her opportunity, while he is sunk in sleep, she seizes his falchion and strikes off his head. Giving it to her maid, who was outside the tent door, she leaves the camp as usual, under pretense of devotion, and returns to Bethulia, displaying the head of Holofernes.

The Israelites, next morning, fall on the Assyrians, who, panic-struck at the loss of their general, are soon discomfited, leaving an immense spoil in the hands of their enemies. The whole concludes with the triumphal song of Judith, who accompanies all the people to Jerusalem to give thanks to the Lord. After this she returns to her native city Bethulia, gives freedom to her maid, and dies at the advanced age of 105 years. The

Jews enjoying a profound and happy peace, a yearly festival (according to the Vulgate) is instituted in honor of the victory.

(5) Difficulties of the Story. The difficulties, historical, chronological, and geographical, comprised in the narrative of Judith are so numerous and serious as to be held by many divines altogether insuperable. Events, times, and manners are said to be confounded, and the chronology of the times before and those after the exile, of the Persian and Assyrian, and even of the Maccabæan period, confusedly and unaccountably blended.

The authorship of the book is as uncertain as its date. It is not named either by Philo or Josephus; nor have we any indication whatever by which to form a conjecture respecting its author.

The original language is uncertain. Eichhorn and Jahn (*Introduction*) and Seiler (*Biblical Hermeneutics*), with whom is Bertholdt, conceive it to have been Greek. Calmet states on the authority of Origen (*Ep. ad African.*) that the Jews had the book of Judith in Hebrew in his time. Jerome (*Pref. to Judith*) states that it is written in Chaldee, from which he translated it, with the aid of an interpreter, giving rather the sense than the words.

2. Influence. Although the book of Judith never formed part of the Jewish canon (see Deutero-Canonical), and finds no place in the ancient catalogues, its influence in the Christian church has been very great. (See Apocrypha.)

The book of Judith is supposed by some to be referred to by St. Paul (1 Cor. x:9, 10; comp. with Judith viii:24, 25). Judith, with the other deutero-canonical books, has been at all times read in the church, and lessons are taken from it in the Church of England in course. ("G. B.," in the *Journal of Sac. Lit.*, July, 1856; Cowper, *The Book of Judith and Its Geography*, in the same journal, January 1861.)   W. W.

JULIA (jū'li-à), (Gr. Ἰουλία, *ee-oo-lee'ah*, fem. of Julius, a name common among the Romans), a Christian woman of Rome, to whom St. Paul sent his salutations (Rom. xvi:15); she is named with Philologus, and is supposed to have been his wife or sister.

JULIUS (jū'li-ŭs), (Gr. Ἰούλιος, *ee-oo'lee-os*), the centurion who had the charge of conducting Paul as a prisoner to Rome, and who treated him with much consideration and kindness on the way (Acts xxvii:1, 3, 43).

JUNIA, better JUNIAS (jū'ni-à or jū'ni-as), (Gr. Ἰουνίας, *ee-oo-nee'as*), a person who is joined with Andronicus in Rom. xvi:7: 'Salute Andronicus and Junias, my kinsmen and fellow-prisoners, who are of note among the apostles.' They were, doubtless, Jewish Christians.

JUNIPER (jū'nĭ-pẽr), unquestionably the original intends the rē-tem (*Retama rætam*), a shrub of the broom family, attaining a height of about 12 feet.

This bush grows in the sandy regions of Arabia, Northern Africa, and Spain, but is especially abundant in the desert of Sinai, and is often the only possible shelter. Under its shade travelers are glad to creep on a sultry day for a noontime nap, and thus Elijah lay and slept after his long journey (1 Kings xix:4, 5). The retem has no main trunk, but consists of many stems, mostly small. The roots are disproportionally massive and dense, and from them the Bedouins manufacture charcoal, which is sold in Cairo and other towns, where it brings the highest price, since, of all charcoal, it produces the most intense heat (Ps. cxx:4). In Job xxx:4 we read of hunger so extreme that the bitter roots of this shrub are used for food. During the wanderings of the Israelites one of their stations was named Rithmah, doubtless from the abundance of the retem at that place (Num. xxxiii:18).

JUPITER (jū'pi-ter), (Gr. Ζεύς, *dzyooce*, zeus), the Latin form of the Greek name Zeus, the national god of the Greeks, and the supreme ruler of the heathen world.

In Acts xiv:12, 13, "Jupiter, which was before their city," means that his temple was without the city. In verse 12, the Lystrians call Barnabas 'Jupiter.' Paul, the chief speaker, they thought to be Mercury, the god of eloquence, and the other they thought must be the god whom they worshiped, Jupiter.

JUSHAB-HESED (jū'shăb-hē'sed), (Heb. חֶסֶד יוֹשָׁב, *yoo-shab' kheh'sed*, returner of kindness), son of Zerubbabel (1 Chron. iii:20). It is impossible to tell why the five children here mentioned are separated from the three in verse 19, unless they were born of a different mother, or in Judæa after the return from Babylon.

JUSTICE (jŭs'tĭs) consists in an exact and scrupulous regard for the rights of others, with a deliberate purpose to preserve them on all occasions sacred and inviolate.

(1) Justice and equity may be discriminated as follows: *Justice*, from *jus*, right, is founded on the laws of society. *Equity*, from *æquitas*, fairness, rightness, and equality, is founded on the laws of nature. *Justice* is a written or prescribed law, to which one is bound to conform and make it the rule of one's decisions; *equity* is a law in our hearts; it conforms to no rule but to circumstances, and decides by the consciousness of right and wrong. The proper object of *justice* is to secure property; the proper object of *equity* is to secure the rights of humanity. *Justice* is exclusive, it assigns to every one his own; it preserves the subsisting inequality between men; *equity* is communicative; it seeks to *equalize* the condition of men by a fair distribution.

(2) Dr. Watts gives the following rules respecting justice: (a) "It is just that we honor, reverence, and respect those who are our superiors in any kind (Eph. vi:1, 3; 1 Pet. ii:17; 1 Tim. v:17). (b) That we show particular kindness to near relations (Prov. xvii:17). (c) That we love those who love us, and show gratitude to those who have done us good (Gal. iv:15). (d) That we pay the full due to those whom we bargain or deal with (Rom. xiii:7, 8; Deut. xxiv:14). (e) That we help our fellow-creatures in cases of great necessity (Exod. xxiii:4-7).

JUSTICE OF GOD is that perfection whereby he is infinitely righteous and just in his principles and in all his proceedings with his creatures.

(1) It has been defined thus: "The ardent inclination of his will to prescribe equal laws as the Supreme Governor, and to dispense equal rewards and punishments as the Supreme Judge" (Rev. xvi:5; Ps. cxlv:7; xcvii:1, 2).

(2) It is distinguished into remunerative and punitive justice. Remunerative justice is a distribution of rewards, the rule of which is not the merit of the creature, but God's own gracious promise (James i:12; 2 Tim. iv:8). Punitive or vindictive justice is the infliction of punishment for any sin committed by men (2 Thess. i:6).

(3) That God will not let sin go unpunished is evident: (a) From the word of God (Exod. xxxiv:6, 7; Num. xiv:18.) (b) From the character of God (Is. i:13, 14; Ps. v:5, 6; Heb. xii:29). (c) From sin being punished in Christ, the surety of his people (1 Pet. iii:18). (d) From all the various natural evils which men feel in the present state.

JUSTIFICATION (jŭs'tĭ-fĭ-kā'shŭn), (Heb. צָדֵק' *tsaw-duk'*, to make or declare; Gr. δικαιώνια, *dik-ah-yo'nee-ah*), judicial sentence, declaration of right; thus, judicial acquittal, the opposite of condemnation.

1. Theological Statement. Justification may be defined, in its theological sense, as the nonimputation of sin, and the imputation of righteousness. That there is a reciprocation between Christ and believers, *i. e.* in the *imputation* of their sins unto him, and of his righteousness unto them; and that this forms the ground of the sinner's justification and acceptance with God, it will be the object of the following remarks to demonstrate.

(1) Vicarious Atonements. The *vicarious* nature of the Redeemer's sufferings was set forth under the Mosaic dispensation by very significant types, one of the most expressive of which was the offering of the scapegoat: 'And Aaron shall lay his hands upon the head of the live goat, and confess over him all the iniquities of the children of Israel, and all their transgressions in all their sins, putting them on the head of the goat, and the goat shall bear upon him all their iniquities' (Lev. xvi:21, 22). Abarbanel, in the introduction to his commentary on Leviticus (*De Viel.* p. 301), represents this ceremony as a symbolical translation of the sins of the offender upon the head of the sacrifice, and as a way by which the evil due to his transgression was to be deprecated.

Nachmanides also, commenting on Lev. i, observes, respecting the burnt-offerings and sacrifices for sin: 'It was right the offerer's own blood should be shed, and his body burnt, but that the Creator, in his mercy, hath accepted this victim from him as a *vicarious* substitute and atonement, that its blood should be poured out instead of his blood, and its life stand in place of his life.'

We are informed by Herodotus (ii:39) that the practice of imprecating on the head of the victim the evils which the sacrificer wished to avert from himself was usual also amongst the heathen. The Egyptians, he adds, would not taste the head of any animal, but flung it into the river as an abominataion.

(2) Prophecy and Exposition of Atonement. If this type foreshadowed the vicarious nature of the sufferings and death of Christ—and who with the inspired comment of the author of the Epistle to the Hebrews before him can doubt this?—we may with confidence appeal also to the voice of prophecy, and the expositions of apostles, for the further illustration and enforcement of the same truth.

The fifty-third chapter of Isaiah is so full upon this point that Bishop Lowth says: 'This chapter declares the circumstances of our Savior's sufferings so exactly that it seems rather a history of his passion than a prophecy.' In verses 5 and 6 we are told that God 'laid upon him the iniquities of us all,' that by 'his stripes we might be healed'—that our sin was laid on him, and he bare it (ver. 11). St. Paul, re-echoing the same truth, says, 'He was made sin for us who knew no sin, that we might be made the righteousness of

God in him' (2 Cor. v:21). This is the reciprocation spoken of above.

Again, in Rom. viii:3, 4, the Apostle informs us that God sent his own Son in the likeness of sinful flesh, and for sin condemned sin in the flesh, that the righteousness of the law might be fulfilled in us; that sin was made his, and he bore its penalty; his righteousness is forensically transferred to the believer, and the latter becomes a happy participator of its benefits. This, then, is the change in relation to God from which the soul of a convicted sinner can find peace. Before we notice the objections which have been, and still are, urged against this view of the question, we may inquire *how far* it is confirmed by the earliest and most eminently pious Fathers of the Christian church.

(3) Faith of the Fathers. Amongst these Fathers none could have been better acquainted with the mind of St. Paul than the venerable Clement of Rome, inasmuch as he is honorably recorded by the Apostle as one of his fellow-laborers in the Gospel whose names are written in the book of life (Phil. iv:3). Nothing can be more explicit than this writer is on the point of *forensic justifying righteousness,* and of *intrinsic sanctifying righteousness* (see Clem. Rom. *Epist. ad Corinth.* i. sec. 32, 33). Chrysostom's commentary on 2 Corinthians (ch. v. *Hom.* ii) is also very expressive on this subject: 'What word, what speech is this, what mind can comprehend or speak it? for he (Paul) saith, he made him who was righteous to be made a sinner, that he might make sinners righteous; nor yet doth he (Paul) say so neither, but that which is far more sublime and excellent. For he speaks not of an inclination or affection, but expresseth the quality itself. For he says not he made him a sinner, but sin, that we might be made not merely righteous, but righteousness, and that the righteousness of God, when we are justified not by works (for if we should, there must be no spot found in them), but by grace, whereby all sin is blotted out.'

(4) Roman Catholic View. It was this doctrine of justification which constituted the great ground of controversy between the reformers and the church of Rome (see Luther to Geo. Spenlein, *Epist.* Ann. 1516, tom. i.). That the reader may be able to see in a contrasted form the essential differences upon this head between the two churches, we subjoin what the Tridentine Fathers have stated. In sess. vi. c. xvi. p. 54, they announce the views of their church on justification in the following language:

'Jesus Christ, as the head into the members, and as the vine into the branches, perpetually causes his virtue to flow into the justified. This virtue always precedes, accompanies, and follows their good works; so that without it such good works could in nowise be acceptable to God, and bear the character of meritoriousness.

'Hence, we must believe that to the justified themselves nothing more is wanting which needs to prevent us from thinking both that they have satisfied the divine law, according to the state of this life, by those works which are performed in God, and also that, in their own time, provided they depart in grace, they truly merit the attainment of eternal life.

'Thus neither our own proper righteousness is so determined to be our own, as if it were from ourselves, nor is the righteousness of God either unknown or rejected. For that which is called our righteousness, because through its being inherent in us we are justified, that same is the righteousness of God, because it is infused into us by God through the merit of Christ. Far, however, be it from a Christian man that he should either trust or glory in himself, and not in the Lord, whose goodness to all is so great that what are truly 'his gifts he willeth to be estimated as their merits.'

(5) General Protestant View. Such, so far as the justification and acceptance of man before God are concerned, is the doctrinal scheme of the church of Rome, and nothing can be more foreign than it is from the system set forth by the Protestant church in general. In the view of the latter, justification signifies making *just* in trial and judgment, as sanctification is making holy; but not making just by infusion of grace and holiness into a person, according to the view of the former, thus confounding justification and sanctification together. On the Protestant principle justification is not a real change of a sinner in himself, though a real change is annexed to it; but only a relative change in reference to God's judgment. Thus we find the word used in Rom. iii:23, 24, 25, 26. In fine, the doctrine of Justification by Faith may be expressed in Scriptural language thus: 'All have sinned and come short of the glory of God; every mouth must be stopped, and all the world become guilty before God; therefore by the deeds of the law there shall no flesh living be justified in his sight. But we are justified freely by his grace through the redemption which is in Christ Jesus, whom God hath set forth as a propitiation through faith in his blood, to declare his righteousness for the remission of sins that are past, through the forbearance of God. Where is boasting, then? It is excluded. By what law? of works? Nay; but by the law of faith. Therefore we conclude that a man is justified by faith without the deeds of the law.' For a full exposition of the differences between the two churches, see Möhler's *Symbolik,* translated from the German by Robertson.

2. Objections. We now come to notice the objections which may be urged against this view of justification.

(1) Cruelty and Butler's Answer. It does not consist, say some, with the truth and holiness of God that the *innocent* should suffer for the *guilty.* We answer, that it is no injustice, or cruelty, for an innocent person to suffer for the guilty, as Christ did, provided there be these conditions:

(a) That the person suffering be of the same nature with those for whom he suffers.

(b) That he suffers of his own free will.

(c) That he be able to sustain all that shall be laid upon him.

(d) That a greater amount of glory redound to the divine attributes than if he had not so suffered. Now the Scriptures assure us that all these conditions were realized in the incarnate Savior.

Bishop Butler (*Analogy,* ch. v.) has a striking answer to this objection. He shows that in the daily course of God's natural providence the innocent do often and constantly suffer for the guilty; and then argues that the Christian appointment against which this objection is taken, is not only of the same kind, but is even less open to exception, 'because, under the former, we are in many cases commanded, and even necessitated whether we will or no, to suffer for the faults of others; whereas the sufferings of Christ were voluntary. The world's being under the righteous government of God does, indeed, imply that, finally, and upon the whole, every one shall receive according to his personal deserts; and the general doctrine of the whole Scripture is that this shall be the completion of the Divine government.

'But during the progress, and for aught we know even in order to the completion, of this moral scheme, vicarious punishments may be fit, and absolutely necessary. Men, by their follies, run themselves into extreme distress—into difficulties which would be absolutely fatal to them, were it not for the interposition and assistance of others. God commands by the law of nature that we afford them this assistance, in many cases where we cannot do it without very great pains and labor and suffering to ourselves. And we see in what variety of ways one person's sufferings contribute to the relief of another, and how, or by what particular means, this comes to pass, or follows from the constitution or laws of nature which come under our notice, and, being familiarized with it, men are not shocked by it. So that the reason of their insisting upon objections of the foregoing kind against the satisfaction of Christ is either that they do not consider God's settled and uniform appointments as his appointments at all, or else they forget that vicarious punishment is a providential appointment of every day's experience; and then, from their being unacquainted with the more general laws of nature or Divine government over the world, and not seeing how the sufferings of Christ could contribute to the redemption of it unless by arbitrary and tyrannical will, they conclude his sufferings could not contribute to it any other way. And yet, what has been often alleged in justification of this doctrine, even from the apparent natural tendency of this method of our redemption—its tendencies to vindicate the authority of God's laws, and deter his creatures from sin—this has never yet been answered, and is, I think, plainly unanswerable.'

(2) Contradiction of St. Paul by St. James. Again it is objected, if we are justified on receiving Christ by faith as the Lord our righteousness, and if this be the sole ground of salvation propounded by St. Paul, there is then a palpable discrepancy between him and St. James; for the former states, that a man is justified by faith without the deeds of the law (Rom. iii:8; Gal. ii:16); while the latter says, 'a man is justified by works and not by faith only' (James ii:24). That there is a difficulty here there can be no question, and that it led Eusebius and Jerome, together with Luther and Erasmus, to question the authority of St. James' Epistle, is notable to every reader of ecclesiastical history.

(a) Roman Catholic View. The church of Rome builds her system of man's being justified by reason of inherent righteousness, on the assumption that when St. Paul says 'by the deeds of the law shall no flesh be justified,' he means the *ceremonial* and not the *moral* law. In this way she would establish her own system of human merit, and harmonize the two Apostles. But it is quite clear to the impartial reader of the Epistle to the Romans that the scope of St. Paul's argument must include both the moral and the ceremonial law; for he proves both Jew and Gentile guilty before God, and this with the view of establishing the righteousness of faith in the imputed merits of Christ as the only ground of a sinner's salvation. Leaving, then, this sophistical reconcilement, we come to that which our Protestant divines propose.

(b) Protestant View. This is of a twofold character, viz., first, by distinguishing the double sense of *justification,* which may be taken either for the absolution of a sinner in God's judgment, or for the declaration of his righteousness before men. This distinction is found in Scripture, in which the word *justify* is used in both acceptations. Thus St. Paul speaks of justification *in foro Dei;* St. James speaks of it *in foro hominis.* A man is justified by faith without works, saith the one; a man is justified by works, and not by faith only, declares the other. That this is the true solution of the difficulty appears from the fact that the two Apostles draw their apparently opposite conclusions from the same example of *Abraham* (Rom. iv:9-23; comp. James ii:21-24).

(c) Double Sense of Faith. Another mode of reconciling the Apostles is by regarding *faith* in the double sense in which it is often found in Scripture. St. Paul, when he affirms that we are justified by faith only, speaks of that faith which is true and living, working by love. St. James, when he denies that a man is justified by faith only, disputes against that faith which is false and unproductive; when the true Christian, speaking to the hypocritical boaster of his faith, asks: 'Show me thy faith without thy works, and I will show thee my faith by my works.'

(3) Final Objection Considered. One objection more may be urged against this fundamental doctrine, that sinners are justified by the free grace of God through the imputed righteousness of the Redeemer, namely, that it weakens the obligations to *holiness of life.* This objection the Apostle himself anticipates when he asks, 'What shall we say then? shall we continue in sin that grace may abound?' To which he answers by rejecting the consequence with the utmost abhorrence, and in the strongest manner affirming it to be without any foundation. 'How shall we,' he continues, 'that are dead to sin, live any longer therein?' (Rom. vi:1-2). He who expects justification by the imputed righteousness of Christ, has the clearest and strongest convictions of the obligation of the law of God, and of its extent and purity. He sees in the vicarious sufferings of his Saviour the awful nature of sin and the infinite love of God; and this love of God, being thus manifested, constrains him to deny ungodliness and worldly lusts, and to live soberly, righteously, and godly in this world. In a word, he loves *much* because he feels that God has forgiven him much, because the love of God is shed abroad in his heart by the Holy Ghost which is given unto him. What a practical illustration have we of this in the life of the great Apostle of the Gentiles himself! (See Miner Raymond, *Sys. Theol.;* Hodge, *Sys. Theol.;* Martensen, *Chris. Dogm.;* D'Aubigne, *His. of Ref.*). J. W. D.

JUSTUS (jŭs'tus), (Gr. Ἰοῦστος, ee-ooce'tos).

1. Surname of Barsabas (Acts i:23). (See Joseph.)

2. A Christian at Corinth, with whom Paul lodged (Acts xviii:7), A. D. 54.

3. A surname of Jesus, a believing Jew, who was with Paul at Rome when he wrote to the Colossians (Col. iv:11). The Apostle names him and Marcus as being at that time (A. D. 64) his only fellow-laborers.

JUTTAH (jŭt'tah), (Heb. יוּטָּה, yoo-taw', inclosed), a city of Judah, (Josh. xv:55), in the neighborhood of Carmel.

It was allotted to the priests (Josh. xxi:16). Robinson (*Bib. Res.,* ii, 195, 628), describes a place named *Yutta,* which doubtless represents the ancient town.

K

KABALA or **KABBALAH** (kăb'bă-läh), usually anglicized Cabala (Heb. קַבָּלָה, *kab-baw-law'*).

This word is an abstract, and means *reception*, a doctrine received by oral transmission; so that with mere reference to its etymological signification, it is the correlate of the Hebrew word *tradition*. The term Kabbalah is employed in the Jewish writings to denote several traditional doctrines: as, for example, that which constituted the creed of the patriarchal age before the giving of the law; that unwritten ritual interpretation which the Jews believe was revealed by God to Moses on the mount, and which was at length committed to writing and formed the Mishnah. Besides being applied to these and other similar traditions, it has also been used in, comparatively speaking, modern times, to denote a singular mystical mode of interpreting the Old Testament.

This Kabbalah is an art of eliciting mysteries from the words and letters of the Old Testament by means of some subtle devices of interpretation, or it is an abstruse theosophical and metaphysical doctrine containing the traditional arcana of the remotest times.

(1) Traditional Doctrine. The inartificial or dogmatical Kabbalah consists solely of a traditional doctrine on things divine and metaphysical, propounded in a symbolical form. It treats principally of the mysteries of the doctrine of emanation, of angels and spirits, of the four Kabbalistical worlds, and of the ten Sephiroth or so-called Kabbalistic tree. It is a system made up of elements which are also found in the Magian doctrine of emanation, in the Pythagorean theory of numbers, in the philosophy of the later Platonists, and in the tenets of the Gnostics; but these doctrines are here stated with enigmatical obscurity, and without the coherence and development of a single and entire scheme. Its general tenor may be conceived from the eminent prerogatives which it assigns to the law, and from the consequent latitude of interpretation.

Thus, it is argued in the book of Sohar: 'Alas for the man who thinks that the law contains nothing but what appears on its surface; for, if that were true, there would be men in our day who could excel it. But the law assumed a body; for if angels are obliged, when they descend to this world, to assume a body in order that they may subsist in the world, and it be able to receive them, how much more necessary was it that the law, which created them and which was the instrument by which the world was created, should be invested with a body in order that it might be adapted to the comprehension of man? That body is a history, in which if any man think there is not a soul, let him have no part in the life to come.' Manasseh-ben-Israel, who makes this citation from the book of Sohar, enforces this view with many arguments (*Conciliator*, Amstelod. 1633, p. 169).

(2) Origin. The origin of the Kabbalah is involved in great obscurity. The Jews ascribe it to Adam, or to Abraham, or to Moses, or to Ezra; the last being apparently countenanced by 2 Esdras xiv:20-48. Eichhorn accounts for the origin of that important part of this Kabbalah, the system of allegorical interpretation (by which their occult doctrine was either generated, or, if not, at least brought into harmony with the law), by supposing that the Jews adopted it immediately from the Greeks.

According to him, when the Jews were brought into contact with the enlightened speculations of the Greek philosophers, they felt that their law (as they had hitherto interpreted it) was so far behind the wisdom of the Gentiles, that—both to vindicate its honor in the eyes of the scoffing heathen, and to reconcile their newly adopted philosophical convictions with their ancient creed —they borrowed from the Greek allegorizers of Homer the same art of interpretation, and applied it to conjure away the unacceptable sense of the letter, or to extort another sense which harmonized with the philosophy of the age (*Bibl. Biblioth.* v, 237, *sq.*).   J. N.

KABZEEL (kăb'ze-el), (Heb. קַבְצְאֵל, *kab-tseh-ale'*, God has gathered), a city in the southern part of Judah (Josh. xv:21). It was the native place of the hero Benaiah-ben-Jehoiada (2 Sam. xxiii:20; 1 Chron. xi:22). In Nehemiah the name is written Jekabzeel (Neh. xi:25).

KADESH (kā'desh), (Heb. קָדֵשׁ, *kaw-dashe'*, sanctuary), more fully **KADESH - BARNEA** (kā'desh-bär'ne-ȧ), (Heb. קָדֵשׁ, *kaw-dashe'*, and בַּרְנֵעַ, *bar-nay'ah*; Simon derived the latter word from בַּר, *bar*, desert, and נָע, *nay'ah*, wandering, rendering it " Desert of Wanderings ").

(1) Name and Location. It was a site on the southeastern border of the Promised Land towards Edom, of much interest as being the point at which the Israelites twice encamped with intention of entering Palestine, and from which they were twice sent back; the first time in pursuance of their sentence to wander forty years in the wilderness, and the second time from the refusal of the king of Edom to permit a passage through his territories.

(2) Israelites Driven Back. It was from Kadesh that the spies entered Palestine by ascending the mountains; and the murmuring Israelites afterwards attempting to do the same were driven back by the Amalekites and Canaanites, and afterwards apparently by the king of Arad, as far as Hormah, then called Zephath (Num. xiii:26; xiv: 40-45; xxi:1-3; Deut. i:41-44; comp. Judg. i:7). There was also at Kadesh a fountain (En-mishpat) mentioned long before the exode of the Israelites (Gen. xiv:7); and the miraculous supply of water took place only on the second visit, which implies that at the first there was no lack of this necessary article. After this Moses sent messengers to the king of Edom, informing him that they were in Kadesh, a city in the uttermost part of his border, and asking leave to pass through his country, so as to continue their course round Moab, and approach Palestine from the East. This Edom refused, and the Israelites accordingly marched to Mount Hor, where Aaron died; and then along the Arabah (desert of Zin) to the Red Sea (Num. xx:14-29).

(3) Southern Quarter of Judea. The name of Kadesh again occurs in describing the southern quarter of Judah, the line defining which is drawn 'from the shore of the Salt Sea, from the bay that looked southward; and it went out to the south side of Akrabbim, and passed along to Zin, and ascended up on the south side to Kadesh-barnea' (Josh. xv:1-3; comp. Num. xxxiv:3, 4).

From these intimations the map-makers, who found it difficult to reconcile them with the place usually assigned to Kadesh (in the desert about midway between the Mediterranean and Dead Sea), were in the habit of placing a second Kadesh nearer the Dead Sea and the Wady Arabah. It was left for Dr. Kitto (*Pictorial Bible,* Note on Num. xx:1) to show that one Kadesh would sufficiently answer all the conditions required, by being placed more to the south, nearer to Mount Hor, on the west border of the Wady Arabah, than this second Kadesh. According to this view Kadesh was laid down in the map (in the *Illuminated Atlas*) prepared under his direction, in the same line, and not far from the place which has since been assigned to it from actual observation by Dr. Robinson. This concurrence of different lines of research in the same result is curious and valuable, and the position of Kadesh will be regarded as now scarcely open to dispute.

(4) Discovery of the Fountain. It was clear that the discovery of the fountain in the northern part of the great valley would go far to fix the question. Robinson discovered a fountain called Ain el-Weibeh, which is even at this day the most frequented watering-place in all the Arabah, and he was struck by the entire adaptedness of the site to the scriptural account of the proceedings of the Israelites on their second arrival at Kadesh. 'Over against us lay the land of Edom; we were in its uttermost border; and the great Wady el-Ghuweir afforded a direct and easy passage through the mountains to the table-land above, which was directly before us; while further in the south Mount Hor formed a prominent and striking object, at the distance of two good days' journey for such a host' (*Bib. Researches,* ii, 538). Further on (p. 610) he adds: 'There the Israelites would have Mount Hor in the S.S.E. towering directly before them . . . in the N.W. rises the mountain by which they attempted to ascend to Palestine, with the pass still called Sufah (Zephath); while further north we find also Tell Arad, marking the site of the ancient Arad. To all this comes then the vicinity of the southern bay of the Dead Sea, the line of cliffs separating the Ghôr from the Arabah, answering to the ascent of Akrabbim; and the desert of Zin, with the place of the same name between Akrabbim and Kadesh, not improbably at the water of Hasb, in the Arabah. In this way all becomes easy and natural, and the scriptural account is entirely accordant with the character of the country.'

KADMIEL (kăd'mi-el), (Heb. קַדְמִיאֵל, *kad-mee-ale'*, presence of God).

1. A Levite who returned from Babylon with Zerubbabel, and was apparently a representative of Hodaviah or Judah (Ezra ii:40; Neh. vii:43; xii:8; xii:24). In the first attempt to rebuild the wall Kadmiel and his brother were appointed by Zerubbabel to superintend the workmen and officiate in the ceremonies attending the laying of the foundation (Ezra iii:9). His house was represented in the confession of the people on the day of humiliation. (B. C. 536.)

2. A Levite who assisted in leading the devotion of the people (Neh. ix:4, 5) and with other Levites entered into the covenant to keep God's law (Neh. x:9). Probably a son of **1.** (B. C. 445.)

KADMONITES (kăd'mon-ītes), (Heb. הַקַּדְמֹנִי, *hak-kad-mo-nee'*, the Kadmonite), one of the nations of Canaan, which is supposed to have dwelt in the northeast part of Palestine, under Mount Hermon, at the time that Abraham sojourned in the land (Gen. xv:19).

As the Kadmonites were "Bene-Kedem" (Heb. בְּנֵי־קֶדֶם, Judg. vi:33), A. V. "children of the East," i. e., "tribes who roved in the great waste tracts on the east and southeast of Palestine," they are supposed by Dr. Wells and others to be situated to the east of the Jordan. The name was a term applied collectively, like 'Easterns,' or 'Orientals,' to all the people living in the countries beyond that river. (Thomson, *Land and Book,* i, 242.) Bochart supposes the name to be the same as Cadmus, and identified them with the Hivites (see HIVITES), whose place they fill in the list.

KALI (kä'lĭ), (Heb. קָלִי, *kaw-lee'*). This word occurs in several passages of the Old Testament, in all of which, in the Authorized Version, it is translated *parched corn.* The correctness of this translation has not, however, been assented to by all commentators.

(1) Parched Meal. Some Hebrew writers maintain that flour or meal, and others, that *parched meal,* is intended, as in the passage of Ruth ii:14, where the Septuagint translates *kali* by ἄλφιτον, and the Vulgate by *polenta.* A difficulty, however, occurs in the case of 2 Sam. xvii:28, where the word occurs twice in the same verse. We are told that Shobi and others, on David's arrival at Mahanaim, in the further limit of the tribe of Gad, 'brought beds, and basins, and earthen vessels, and wheat, and barley, and flour, and *parched corn* (kali), and beans, and lentils, and *parched pulse* (kali), and honey, and butter, and sheep, and cheese of kine, for David and for the people that were with him to eat.'

This is a striking representation of what may be seen every day in the East; when a traveler arrives at a village, the common light beds of the country are brought him, as well as earthen pots, with food of different kinds.

(2) Corn and Pulse. The meaning of the above passage is explained by the statement of Hebrew writers, that there are two kinds of kali —one made of *parched corn,* the other of *parched pulse.*

Another principal preparation, much and constantly in use in Western Asia, is *burgoul,* that is, corn first boiled, then bruised in the mill to take the husk off, and afterwards dried or parched in the sun. In this state it is preserved for use, and employed for the same purposes as rice. The meal of parched corn is also much used, particularly by travelers, who mix it with honey, butter, and spices, and so eat it; or else mix it with water only, and drink it as a draught, the refrigerating and satisfying qualities of which they justly extol (*Pictorial Bible,* ii, p. 537).

Parched grain is also, no doubt, very common. Thus, in the bazaars of India not only may rice be obtained in a parched state, but also the seeds of the *Nymphæa,* and of the *Nelumbium Speciosum,* or bean of Pythagoras, and most abundantly the pulse called *gram* by the English, on which their cattle are chiefly fed. This is the *Cicer Arietinum* of botanists, or chick-pea, which is common even in Egypt and the south of Europe, and may be obtained everywhere in India in a parched state, under the name of *chebenne.* We know not whether it be the same pulse that is mentioned in the article Doves' Dung, a sort of pulse or pea, which appears to have been very common in Judæa.

Considering all these points, it does not appear to us by any means certain that *kali* is correctly translated 'parched corn,' in all the passages of scripture. Thus, in Lev. xxiii:14: 'Ye shall eat neither bread, nor parched corn (kali), nor green ears, until . . . .', So in Ruth ii:14, 'And he (Boaz) reached her *parched corn* (kali). and she did eat.' 1 Sam. xvii:17: 'Take now for thy brethren an ephah of *parched corn.*' And again, xxv:18, where five measures of parched corn are mentioned. The name *kali* seems, moreover, to have been widely spread through Asiatic countries.

(3) Field Pea. The present writer found it applied in the Himalayas to the common field-pea, and has thus mentioned it elsewhere: '*Pisum arvense.* Cultivated in the Himalayas, also in the plains of northwest India, found wild in the Khadie of the Jumna, near Delhi; the *corra muttur* of the natives, called *Kullae* in the hills' (*Illust. of Himalayan Botany,* p. 200). Hence we are disposed to consider the pea, or the chick-pea, as more nearly correct than parched corn in some of the above passages of Scripture. (See Parched Corn.)   J. F. R.

KALLAI (kăl'lāi), (Heb. קַלָּי, *kal-lah'ee*, frivolous), a son of Sallai, and a chief priest in the time of the high priest Joiakim (Neh. xii:20), B. C. after 536.

KANAH (kā'nah), (Heb. קָנָה, *kaw-naw'*, reediness).

1. A river which flows into the Mediterranean between Cæsarea and Joppa. It served as a boundary between Ephraim and Manasseh (Josh. xvi:8; xvii:9). It is identified by some as the river Aujeh.

2. A town in the north of Asher (Josh. xix: 28). There are here colossal ruins and figures of persons which are supposed to be of Phœnician origin.

KANEH (kāh'neh), (Heb. קָנֶה, *kaw-neh'*), occurs in several places of the Old Testament, in all of which, in the Authorized Version, it is translated *reed;* as in 1 Kings xiv:15; 2 Kings xviii:21; Job xl:21; Is. xix.6; xxxv:7; xxxvi:6; xlii:3; Ezek. xxix:6.

(1) Reed. The Greek word κάλαμος, *kal'am-os, reed,* appears to have been considered the proper equivalent for the Hebrew *Kaneh,* being the term used by St. Matthew (xii:20), when quoting the words of Isaiah (xlii:3), 'A bruised *reed* (Kaneh) shall he not break.' The Greek word Latinized is well known in the forms of *calamus* and *culmus.* Both seem to have been derived from the Arabic *kalm,* signifying a 'reed' or 'pen,' and forming numerous compounds, with the latter signification, in the languages of the East. It also denotes a weaver's reed, and even cuttings of trees for planting or grafting.

(2) Latitude of Meaning. Such references to the meaning of these words in different languages, may appear to have little relation to our present subject; but κάλαμος, *reed,* occurs very frequently in the New Testament, and apparently with the same latitude of meaning: thus, in the sense of a reed or culm of a grass (Matt. xi:7; Luke vii:24), 'A reed shaken by the wind;' of a pen, in 3 John 13, 'But I will not with *pen* (κάλαμος) and ink write unto thee;' (Matt. xxvii:29), 'Put a reed in his right hand;' (ver. 30), 'took the reed and smote him on the head;'

and in Mark xv:19, it may mean a reed or twig of any kind. So also in Matt. xxvii:48, and Mark xv:36, where it is said that they filled a sponge with vinegar, and put it on a *reed,* while in the parallel passage (John xix:29), it is said that they filled a sponge with vinegar, and put it upon *hyssop,* and put it to his mouth. From which it seems very probable that the term κάλαμος, *reed,* was applied by both the Evangelists to the

Common Egyptian Reed (*Arundo Donax*).

stem of the plant named hyssop, whatever this may have been, in like manner as Pliny applied the term *Calamus* to the stem of a bramble.

In most of the passages of the Old Testament the word *Kaneh* seems to be applied strictly to reeds of different kinds growing in water, that is, to the hollow stems or culms of grasses, which are usually weak, easily shaken about by wind or by water, fragile, and breaking into sharp-pointed splinters. Thus in 1 Kings xiv:15, 'As a reed is shaken in the water;' Job xl:21, 'He lieth in the covert of the reed' (*Kaneh*); Is. xix: 6, 'And they shall turn the rivers far away; and the reeds and flags shall wither.' Also in ch. xxxv:7; while in 2 Kings xviii:21; Ezek. xxix: 6, and Is. xxxvi:6, there is reference to the weak and fragile nature of the reed, 'Lo, thou trustest in the staff of this broken reed, on Egypt, whereon if a man lean, it will go into his hand, and pierce it.'

(3) A Water Plant. From the context of the several passages of scripture in which *Kaneh* is mentioned, it is evident that it was a plant growing in water; and we have seen from the meaning of the word in other languages that it must have been applied to one of the true reeds; as for instance, *Arundo Ægyptiaca* (perhaps only a variety of *A. Donax*), mentioned by M. Bové as growing on the banks of the Nile; or it may have been the *Arundo isiaca* of Delile, which is closely allied to *A. Phragmites,* the *Canna* and *Canne* of the south of Europe, which is found along the banks of pools and marshes in Spain and Italy.

In the New Testament κάλαμος, *reed,* seems to be applied chiefly to plants growing in dry and even barren situations, as in Luke vii:24; 'What went ye into the wilderness to see? a reed shaken by the wind?' To such passages, some of the species of reed-like grasses, with slender stems and light flocculent inflorescence, formerly referred to *Saccharum,* but now separated as distinct genera, are well suited.

Hence, as has already been suggested by Rosenmüller, the noun *Kaneh* ought to be restricted to reeds, or reed-like grasses, while *Agmon* may indicate the more slender and delicate grasses or sedges growing in wet situations, but which are still tough enough to be made into ropes. (See REED.)　　　　　　　　　　　　　J. F. R.

KAREAH (ka-rē'ah), (Heb. קָרֵחַ, *kaw-ray'akh,* bald), father of Johanan and Jonathan, who supported Gedaliah's authority and took vengeance on his murderers (Jer. xl:8, 13, 15, 16; xli:11, 13, 14, 16; xlii:1, 8; xliii:2, 4, 5). Elsewhere the name is CAREAH. (B. C. before 588.)

KARKAA (kär'ka-à), (Heb. קַרְקָע, *kar-kah',* ground floor), a town on the southern confines of the tribe of Judah (Josh. xv:3) between Addar and Azmon. All trace of the place has been lost.

KARKOR (kär'kôr), (Heb. קַרְקֹר, *kar-kore',* foundation), a place, probably on the east of Jordan, where the remnant of the army of Zebah and Zalmunna had encamped after their rout in the Jordan Valley, and from which Gideon dispersed them (Judg. viii:10). Its identification is very uncertain.

KARPAS (kär'pas), (Heb. כַּרְפַּס, *kar-pas',* green), occurs in the book of Esther i:6, in the description of the hangings "in the court of the garden of the king's palace," at the time of the great feast given in the city Shushan, or Susan, by Ahasuerus, who "reigned from India even unto Ethiopia."

We are told that there were white, *green* (*karpas*), and blue hangings fastened with cords of fine linen and purple to silver rings and pillars of marble.

(1) Leek Green. *Karpas* is translated **green** in our version, on the authority, it is said, 'of the Chaldee paraphrase,' where it is interpreted *leek-green.* Rosenmüller and others derive the Hebrew word from the Arabic *kurufs,* which signifies 'garden parsley,' *apium petroselinum,* as if it alluded to the green color of this plant; at the same time arguing that as 'the word *karpas* is placed between two other words which undoubtedly denote colors, viz., the *white* and the *purpleblue,* it probably also does the same.'

(2) Cotton. But if two of the words denote colors, it would appear a good reason why the third should refer to the substance which was colored. This, there is little doubt, is what was intended. The Hebrew *karpas* is very similar to the Sanscrit *karpasum, karpasa,* or *karpase,* signifying the cotton-plant. Celsius (*Hierobot.* i. 159) states that the Arabs and Persians have *karphas* and *kirbas* as names for cotton. These must no doubt be derived from the Sanscrit, while the word *kapas* is now applied throughout India to cotton with the seed, and may even be seen in English prices-current. Nothing can be more suitable than cotton, white and blue, in the above passage of Esther. Hanging curtains usually in stripes of different colors and padded with cotton, called purdahs, are employed throughout India as a substitute for doors. This kind of structure was probably introduced by the Persian conquerors of India, and therefore may serve to explain the object of the colonnade in front of the palace in the ruins of Persepolis. (See COTTON.)
　　　　　　　　　　　　　　　　J. F. R.

KARTAH (kär'tah), (Heb. קַרְתָּה, *kar-taw',* city), a town in the tribe of Zebulun allotted to the Merarite Levites (Josh. xxi:34). Kartah is probably identical with KATTATH (Josh. xix:15).

KARTAN (kär'tan), (Heb. קַרְתָּן, *kar-tawn',* double city), a city of Naphtali allotted to the Gershonite Levites, and made a city of refuge (Josh. xxi:32). The name may be a contraction of KIRJATHAIM (1 Chron. vi:76).

KATTATH (kăt'tath), (Heb. קַטָּת, *kat-tawth',* littleness), the limit of the tribe of Zebulun (Josh. xix:15). In Judg. i:30 called Kithron, which is the same in sense. It is also probably the same as KARTAH.

The Vulgate, LXX, Syriac, and Arabic, render these names, which are from the same root, by *small, trifling, insignificant things:* the Chaldee to the same effect; whence the name of this city, perhaps, might be analogous to our name *littletown,* Littleton. It is quite possible that this is the modern *Katunith,* and the *Cana of Galilee* of the New Testament.

KEDAR (kē'dar), (Heb. קֵדָר, *kay-dawr',* black), a son of Ishmael (Gen. xxv:13; 1 Chron. i:29), and the name of the tribe of which he was the founder.

The name is sometimes used in scripture as that of the Bedouins generally, probably because this tribe was the nearest to them, and was best acquainted with them (Cant. i:5; Is. xxi: 16, 17; lx:7, xlii:11). A great body of speculation founded upon the meaning of the word, namely, 'black,' may be dismissed as wholly useless. The Kedarenes were so called from Kedar, and not because they lived in 'black' tents, or because they were 'blackened' by the hot sun of Southern Arabia; neither of which circumstances could, even if true, have been foreseen at the time that Kedar received his name. The "glory of Kedar" is recorded by Isaiah (xxi:13-17) and Ezekiel (xxvii:21; Ps. cxx:5; Jer. ii:10; xlix: 28), from which we infer that the tribe was one of importance and wealth.

KEDEMAH (kĕd'e-mah), (Heb. קֵדְמָה, *kayd'-maw,* eastward), the youngest son of Ishmael (Gen. xxv:15; 1 Chron. i:31, B. C. after 2061.

KEDEMOTH (kĕd'e-mŏth), (Heb. קְדֵמוֹת, *ked-ay-mothe'*), a city in the tribe of Reuben (Josh. xiii:18), near the river Arnon, which gave its name to the wilderness of Kedemoth, on the borders of that river, from whence Moses sent messengers of peace to Sihon, king of Heshbon (Deut. ii:26), the southern frontier of whose kingdom, and the boundary between the kingdom of the Ammonites and the Moabites, was the Arnon.

KEDESH (kēdesh), (Heb. קֶדֶשׁ, *keh'desh*).

1. A city in the tribe of Judah (Josh. xv: 23). Perhaps it is identical with Kadesh-Barnea (Josh. xv:3; Num. xxxiv:4). (See KADESH.)

2. A city in the tribe of Naphtali (xix:37). It was a Levitical city, and one of the six cities of refuge (Josh. xx:7; xxi:32; 1 Chron. vi:76). Barak was a native of this place (Judg. iv:6), which was taken by Tiglath-Pileser in the reign of Pekah (2 Kings xv:29), where it is mentioned with Hazor.

3. A city of Issachar allotted to the Gershonite Levites (1 Chron. vi:72). As the Kedesh, whose king was slain by Joshua, is mentioned among the cities of the north (xii:22), it was doubtless this Kedesh.

KEDRON (kē'drŏn). See KIDRON.

KEHELATHAH (ke-hĕl'a-thah), (Heb. קְהֵלָתָה, *keh-hay-law'thaw*, convocation), an encampment of the Israelites in the desert of which nothing is known (Num. xxxiii:22, 23).

KEILAH (kēi'lah), (Heb. קְעִילָה, *keh-ee-law'*, inclosed, a citadel), a city of the tribe of Judah (Josh. xv:44), about twenty miles southwest from Jerusalem.

(1) Besieged by Philistines. When this city was besieged by the Philistines, David was commissioned by God to relieve it; notwithstanding which, if he had not made his escape, the ungrateful inhabitants would have delivered him into the hands of Saul (1 Sam. xxiii:1-13). Keilah was a considerable city in the time of Nehemiah (Neh. iii:17, 18), and existed in the days of Eusebius and Jerome, who place it eight Roman miles from Eleutheropolis on the road to Hebron.

(2) Identification. "The site is satisfactorily identified with Khûrbet Kîla, a ruined village seven miles from Beit Jibrin. It is on low ground, which accounts for the expression 'go down,' and it was a key to the hill country, with fertile lands around it." (Harper, *Bib. and Mod. Dic.*, p. 225.)

In the time of Nehemiah Keilah was large enough to have two prefects who assisted in repairing the walls of Jerusalem (Neh. iii:17).

KELAIAH (ke-lā'iah [yà]), (Heb. קֵלָיָה, *kay-law-yaw'*, insignificance), (Ezra x:23). It is the same as KELITA.

KELITA (kĕl'i-tà), (Heb. קְלִיטָא, *kel-ee-taw'*, maiming, dwarf), a Levite who returned from the captivity with Ezra, and had taken a foreign wife (Ezra x:23). He was associated with Nehemiah in expounding the law, and sealing the covenant to follow the law of God (Neh. viii:7; x:10), B. C. 456-410.

KEMUEL (ke-mū'el), (Heb. קְמוּאֵל, *kem-oo-ale'*, assembly of God; Sept. Καμουήλ, Kamuel).

1. The third son of Abraham's brother Nahor, and father of six sons, the first of whom is named Aram, and the last Bethuel (Gen. xxii:21, 23). All these are unknown, except the last, who was the father of Laban and Rebekah (Gen. xxiv: 15). Aram is manifestly no other than a proper name which Kemuel gave to his firstborn; but as it is also the Hebrew name of Syria, some commentators have most strangely conceived that the Syrians were descended from him. This is truly surprising, seeing that Syria was already peopled ere he was born, and that Laban (Gen. xxviii:5) and Jacob (Deut. xxvi:5) are both called 'Syrians,' although neither of them was descended from Kemuel's son Aram.

2. Son of Shiphtan. He was prince of the tribe of Ephraim, and one of the twelve appointed by Moses to divide the land of Canaan (Num. xxxiv:24). (B. C. 1170.)

3. A Levite; the father of Hashabiah, who was prince of the tribe in the reign of David (1 Chron. xxvii:17). (B. C. about 1000.)

KENAN (kē'nan), (Heb. קֵינָן, *kay-nawn'*, fixed), the same as CAINAN, son of Enos (1 Chron. i:2; Gen. v:9, marg.).

KENATH (kē'nath), (Heb. קְנָת, *ken-awth'*, possession), a town of Manasseh, beyond Jordan (Num. xxxii:42), named Nobah, after Nobah, an Israelite, had conquered it. At a later period it was recaptured by Geshur and Aram (1 Chron. ii: 23). Eusebius places it in the Trachonitis, about Bozra; and Pliny in the Decapolis, lib. v, cap. 18.

Its site has been pretty well identified with *Kŭnawât* (Porter, *Damascus*, ii:87-115; *Handbk.* 512-514.

KENAZ (kē'năz), (Heb. קְנַז, *ken-az'*, a hunter).

1. The fifth son of Eliphaz, who was the eldest son of Esau, and one of the "dukes" of Edom (Gen. xxxvi:15, 42; 1 Chron. i:53). He was the founder of the tribe of Kenezites, and doubtless they received their name from him. Caleb and Othniel were of this family. (Josh. xiv:14).

2. The name of a place or tract of country in Arabia Petræa, named after Kenaz **1.** (Gen. xxxvi:11, 15, 42).

3. The younger brother of Caleb, and father of Othniel, who married Caleb's daughter (Josh. xv:17; Judg. i:13; 1 Chron. iv:13).

4. A grandson of Caleb (1 Chron. iv:15).

KENEZITE (kĕn'ez-īte), (Heb. הַקְּנִזִּי, *hak-ken-iz-zee'*, Num. xxxii:12; Josh. xiv:6, 14), an epithet applied to Caleb, son of Jephunneh. (See KENIZZITES.)

KENITES (kĕn'ītes), (Heb. קֵינִי, *kay-nee'*), a tribe of people dwelling among the Amalekites (1 Sam. xv:6; comp. Num. xxiv:20, 21), or occupying in semi-nomadic life the same region with the latter people in Arabia Petræa.

When Saul was sent to destroy the Amalekites, the Kenites, who had joined them, perhaps upon compulsion, were ordered to depart from them that they might not share their fate; and the reason assigned was, that they 'shewed kindness to the children of Israel when they came out of Egypt.'

This kindness is supposed to have been that which Jethro and his family showed to Moses, as well as to the Israelites themselves, in consequence of which the whole tribe appears to have been treated with consideration, while the family of Jethro itself accompanied the Israelites into Palestine, where they continued to lead a nomade life, occupying there a position similar to that of the Tartar tribes in Persia at the present day. According to Judg. i:16; iv:11; Hobab the brother-in-law of Moses, was a Kenite. To this family belonged Heber, the husband of that Jael who slew Sisera, and who is hence called 'Heber the Kenite' (Judg. iv:11). At a later age other families of Kenites are mentioned as resident in Palestine, among them were the Rechabites (1 Chron. ii:55; Jer. xxxv:2); but it is not clear whether these were subdivisions of the increasing descendants of Jethro, as seems most likely, or families which availed themselves of the friendly dispositions of the Israelites towards the tribe to settle in the country. It appears that the tribe of the Kenites possessed a knowledge of the true God in the time of Jethro (see HOBAB); and that those families which settled in Palestine did not afterwards lose that knowledge, but increased it, is clear from the passages which have been cited.

KENIZZITES (kĕn'iz-zītes), (Heb. קְנִזִּי, *ken-iz-zee'*), a Canaanitish tribe, mentioned in Gen. xv:19 along with others over which it was promised that the seed of Abraham should have dominion.

It is supposed that they sprung from Kenaz, the grandson of Edom, and had their dwelling somewhere in Idumæa. The chieftain was known as Kenaz from the tribe which he ruled (Gen. xxxvi:11, 15, 40-42). Individuals of the tribe, on the other hand, united with the sons of Jacob, Jephunneh the Kenizzite apparently taking to wife a woman of the tribe of Judah, and Othniel the Kenizzite becoming the first judge of Israel after the conquest. (See CALEB 2.) The Kenizzites of Num. xxxii:12; Josh. xiv:6, appear, however, to be a different race, the origin of which may without improbability be ascribed to Kenaz. The Kenizzites are not named among the nations whom the Israelites eventually subdued; whence it may be supposed that they had by that time merged into some of the other nations which Israel overcame.

KENOSIS (kĕn-ō'sĭs), (Gr. κένωσις, ken'ō-sis), a Greek term signifying the act of emptying, or self-divesture. It is employed to express the voluntary humiliation of Christ. It is borrowed from the expression of Paul, " But made himself of no reputation," ἑαυτὸν ἐκένωσε, emptied himself (Phil. ii:7).

The New Testament teaching upon this point may be arranged under five heads: (1) The *virginal conception and birth* (Matthew and Luke); (2) The *pempsis*, or mission from the Father (Jesus, John and Paul); (3) The *parousia*, or coming out of the preëxistent state of glory, into the world (Jesus and John); (4) The *assumption of the flesh* (John and Paul); (5) The *Kenosis or self-emptying of the Logos* (Paul).

It is true that these classes overlap, but the arrangement has the recommendation of clearness and convenience.

(1) The first class of passages records the Annunciation, Conception and Birth (Matt. i:18-24; Luke i:26-38; ii:1-10). There is little to add to the Biblical narratives, which are straightforward accounts of historical events. All that we can say is that the conception and birth are both (to us) miraculous, nor can human analogy help us much, as conception, the ultimate fact of human biology, is unexplained and probably unexplainable. And if we thus come—even in a matter of everyday occurrence, and of such apparent simplicity—to the limit of human knowledge, how can we explain the mysteries of a purely spiritual conception?

All that we learn from the account contained in the gospels is the fact that he was "conceived of the Holy Ghost, born of the Virgin Mary." What is important for us is the fact that he whom these two gospels regard as the Son of the living God was born of woman.

This is asserted also in Paul's statement: "When the fullness of time was come, God sent forth His Son made of a woman," etc. (Gal. iv:4).

That the Son of God in becoming the Son of man should submit himself to the regular human method of coming into the world is one of the most sublime proofs of his loving condescension to us. Yet one thing we must not forget,—that this family into which he was born was, on both sides, of royal stock, both Joseph and Mary being descendants of king David. This was a necessity, for the Messiah of prophecy was the descendant of David, born in the royal city of Bethlehem. The attendant circumstances of deep poverty serve to emphasize the humiliation of our Savior; surely he who was rich for our sakes became poor (2 Cor. viii:9).

(2) The second class of passages refers to the *pempsis* the Mission of the Son from and by the Father. Christ here represents his coming as an act dependent upon the will of the Father who sent him. The Father sends, the Son comes, as is attested by numerous passages in the gospel according to John (John iv:34; v:23; vi:39, etc.). The same aspect of his coming is presented in John iii:16 and the Apostle Paul tells us that, "when the fullness of time was come, God sent forth His Son" (Gal. iv:4).

(3) The third class of passages is that large one in which Jesus refers to his coming. The most important of course are those which report his own words. "I am come in the name of my Father" (John v:43).

"For the bread of God is he that cometh down from heaven" (John vi:33). "For I am come forth from God" (John viii:42).

"And now, O Father, glorify thou me with thine own self with the glory which I had with thee before the world was" (John xvii:5).

In the prologue to his gospel (i:1-18) John affirms both the preëxistence and the Divinity of the Logos. It is here distinctly stated the Divine Logos, who was in a preëxistent state with God (a state which, as we learned from John xvii:5, was a state of glory) when he had assumed flesh, became as one of us, making this world his temporary abiding place. Though the method of transition is not directly stated, yet this text teaches as does John xvii:5, a coming out of this preëxistent state of glory, into the earthly life with all that implies.

(4) The fourth class of passages comprises those which refer to the assumption of the flesh. The most important of these is the following: "The Logos became (was made) flesh" (John i:14). This text is the theological statement of the fact of the human birth of the Christ.

That which in the accounts of Matthew and Luke appears as a simple historical fact is by John explained as a process (or episode) within the eternal life of the Divine Logos. *How* the Logos became, or was made flesh, we learn just as little as we learned from Matthew and Luke, *how* the child Jesus was conceived and born.

The celebrated passage in Phil. ii:5-8 teaches that Christ is both Divine and human. Thus we preclude, by comparison with this text, any explanation which might possibly posit an essential change in the eternal life of the Divine Logos. Paul teaches, moreover, that this flesh which the Logos assumed, was "sinful flesh," i. e., flesh which, like our flesh, is subject to the rule of sin.

In 1 Tim. iii:16, Paul speaks of Christ as "manifest in the flesh."

(5) The last class of statements noted comprises those passages in the Epistles of Paul in which the Apostle expounds his conception of Christ's humiliation (Rom. viii:3; 2 Cor. v:21; Gal. iii:13; iv:4, 5; 2 Cor. xiii:4; Rom. viii:32; Phil. ii:5-8).

The general teaching of Paul is that Christ, who knew not sin, was made sin for our sakes; that he was sent in the likeness of sinful flesh; that he redeemed us from the curse, by becoming a curse for our sakes; that he was sent in the fullness of time of the Father, being made of a woman; that though he was rich, yet for our sakes he became poor; that he was crucified through weakness, but liveth by the power of God; that God spared not His own Son; and that though "being in the form of God" considered it not a thing to be eagerly grasped "to be equal with God; but made himself of no reputation, and took upon him the form of a servant, and was made in the likeness of men, and being found in fashion as a man, he humbled himself, and became obedient unto death, even the death of the cross" (Phil. ii:6-8).

We have, then, under these five heads the teaching of the New Testament on this subject. The Son of God, sent of the Father, came upon the earth being born of a woman, in the regular course of nature (yet she was a virgin, and the conception was brought about by the instrumentality of the Holy Spirit). Or, in theological language, the Divine Logos became flesh, i. e. assumed the human flesh, with all its liability to sin, having first emptied himself of equality with God, and the resultant product of this process is Jesus Christ, Son of God, and Son of man.

A careful study of the development of the child, so far as it is possible, fails to show the least trace of duality of consciousness. The boy of twelve in the Temple is just awakening to a great fact of his life, but there is no indication that he is conscious of another *ego* within himself: *"I* must be about my Father's business" (Luke ii:49).

The man Christ Jesus, also, is ever conscious of both his Divinity and his humanity. Thus he says: "I am the living bread that came down from Heaven" (John vi:51). "Before Abraham was, I am" (John viii:58). "Glorify me with the glory which I had with thee before the world was" (John xvii:5).

In these and many similar passages, Jesus Christ distinctly indicates the unity of his theanthropic consciousness, and the continuity of his theanthropic personality upon which the former depends. He does not seem to feel separately conscious of his Divinity and of his humanity, nor does his claim of existence before Abraham, and even before the world was, appear at all strained, but his consciousness of that preëxistence, and of the continuity of his identity, and of his personality since before the foundation of the world, is perfectly natural to him. Both natures intimately united make up the historic Christ of the New Testament records.

We have, then, arrived at the conclusion that the man Jesus Christ shared with us, in the fullest manner, our human constitution, both in the physical and in the psychical life. The gospels everywhere bear witness to his physical likeness to ourselves, and to the reality of his body, which was not exempt from the weaknesses of the flesh.

He was subject to bodily weariness and to thirst (John iv:6-7). He slept in the boat in the midst of the storm, an indication of great weariness (Matt. viii:24. He was "an hungered" (Matt. iv:2; xxi:19).

He was like us also in his soul life. He loved the young ruler who came to him to inquire the way of life (Mark x:21). He is again and again represented as "sighing," "groaning," or "troubled" in spirit (Mark viii:12; John xi:33; xii:27). He has mercy on the crowds that throng him (Matt. xiv:14). He weeps at the grave of Lazarus (John xi:35). He fiercely denounces the Scribes and Pharisees (Matt. xxiii.).

The great turning point in his eternal life of love is the point at which the Son of God, casting aside his pristine glory, and taking unto himself our human nature with all its weaknesses, becomes the Son of Man, the point at which the preëxistent Christ enters into the world's history as the man Jesus Christ for the salvation of the world (John iii:16). (See INCARNATION).

Literature. F. C. H. Wendell, article in *Bib. Sacr.,* Oct. 1897; Lange on *Phil.,* p. 38; Van Oosterzee, *Christ. Dogm.,* vol. ii. secs. xcv. and ci.; Dorner, *Hist. of Doct. of Person of Christ,* i-ii:29; Gore, *Incarnation of the Son of God,* pp. 176-179; 284, 285. E. A. R.

KERCHIEF (kẽr'chĭf), (Heb. מִסְפָּחָה, *mis-paw-khaw'*, a dress for the head).

The word, as used in Ezek. xiii:18, probably means a more than usually splendid headdress,

which the false prophetesses employed to attract attention to themselves, or put on the heads of such as joined them. Woe is denounced against them because "they made kerchiefs on the head of every stature, to hunt souls;" *i. e.* they put them on the head of the idolatrous statures; or they put them on the head of those whom they deluded, and that without respect of age; (*stature* in this passage probably meaning *age.*) It is more than likely that the prophet alludes in the whole passage to the impure worship of Ashtarte the Syrian Venus.

KEREN-HAPPUCH (kẽr'en-hăp'puk), (Heb. קֶרֶן הַפּוּךְ, *keh'ren hap-pook'*, paint-horn, i. e., cosmetic box), the name given to Job's youngest daughter, born during his reviving fortune (Job xlii:14). Her name was probably given on account of her beauty.

KERIOTH (kē'ri-ŏth), (Heb. קְרִיּוֹת, *ker-ee-yoth'*, buildings).

1. A city of Moab, named with Dibon and other places (Jer. xlviii:24). It is supposed to be a synonym of Ar, the ancient capital of Moab, because it seems to be referred to as the capital of Moab, and because in enumerations of the towns of Moab when Kerioth is cited Ar is omitted (Jer. xlviii.; Moabite Stone) and vice versa (Is. xv; xvi; comp. Josh. xiii:16-21). Porter thinks it the modern *Kureiyeh* in the south of *Haurân* (*Five Years*, etc., ii. 191-198; *Handbk.,* pp. 523-524).

2. The name of a town occurring with others in the south of Judah (Josh. xv:25). Robinson would identify it with *el-Kureitein* (*Bibl. Res.,* ii, 101). Formerly Kirioth (Amos ii:2).

KERNEL (kẽr'nĕl), (Heb. חַרְצַן, *khar-tsan'*, sharp, sour), held by the Talmudists to mean the *grape stones*, as opposed to the skin ("husk," Num. vi:4). The ancient versions refer it to the sour or *unripe grapes* themselves. (Mc. & Str. Ency.)

KEROS (kē'ros), (Heb. קֵרֹס or קֶרֶס, *kay-roce'*, curved), the descendants of a man, or a place whose former inhabitants returned as Nethinim. from Babylon after the captivity with Zerubbabel (Neh. vii:47; Ezra ii:44), B. C. before 536.

KETTLE (kĕt't'l), (Heb. דּוּד, *dood*, boiling), a vessel used for culinary or sacrificial purposes (1 Sam. ii:14). The same Hebrew word also means 'basket' (Jer. xxiv:2); 'caldron' (2 Chron. xxxv:13); 'pot' (Job xli:20).

KETURAH (ke-tū'rah), (Heb. קְטוּרָה, *ket-oo-raw'*, incense), the second wife, or, as she is called in 1 Chron. i:32, the concubine of Abraham, by whom he had six sons, Zimran, Jokshan, Medan, Midian, Ishbak and Shuah, whom he lived to see grow to man's estate, and whom he established 'in the East country,' that they might not interfere with Isaac (Gen. xxv:1-6).

As Abraham was one hundred years old when Isaac was given to him by the special bounty of Providence when 'he was as good as dead' (Heb. xi:12) as 'he was one hundred and forty years old when Sarah died; and as he himself died at the age of one hundred and seventy-five years, —it has seemed improbable that these six sons should have been born to Abraham by one woman after he was one hundred and forty years old, and that he should have seen them all grow up to adult age, and have sent them forth to form independent settlements in that last and feeble period of his life.

If, however, God restored his youthful vigor,

there is no reason why he may not afterward have become the father of six sons or even more. Through the offspring of Keturah, Abraham became "the father of many nations."

KETZACH (kĕt'sak), (Heb. קֶצַח, *keh-tsakh'*), written Kezach and Ketsah, occurs only in Is. xxviii:25, 27, and is translated *fitches*, that is, *vetches*, the Authorized Version.

(1) **Different Plants.** It is no doubt from the difficulty of proving the precise meaning of *ketzach*, that different plants have been assigned as its representative. But if we refer to the context, we learn some particulars which at least restrict it to a certain group, namely, to such as are cultivated. Thus, verse 25, 'When he [the ploughman] hath made plain the face thereof, doth he not cast abroad the *fitches* (*ketzach*)?' And again, verse 27, 'For the *fitches* are not threshed with a threshing instrument, neither is a cart-wheel turned about upon the cummin; but *fitches* are beaten out with a staff, and the cummin with a rod.' From which we learn that the grain called *ketzach* was easily separated from its capsule, and therefore beaten out with a stick. The Septuagint

Fitches (*Nigella sativa*).

translates it μελάνθιον, *melanthium*, the Vulgate *git*, and Tremellius *melanthium*, while the Arabic has *shoonez*. All these mean the same thing, namely, a very black-colored and aromatic seed, still cultivated and in daily employment as a condiment in the East.

(2) **Nigella.** Melanthium is universally recognized by botanists to be the Nigella. If we consider that this appears to have been always one of the cultivated grains of the East, and compare the character of nigella with the passages in which *ketzach* is mentioned, we shall find that the former is applicable to them all. The fruit is composed of five or six capsules, which are compressed, oblong, pointed; sometimes said to be hornlike, united below, and divided into several cells, and enclosing numerous, angular, scabrous, black-colored seeds. From the nature of the capsules, it is evident, that when they are ripe, the seeds might easily be shaken out by moderate blows of a stick, as is related to have been the case with the *ketzach* of the text. (See FITCHES.)   J. F. R.

KETZIOTH (kĕtz-ĭ-oth), (Heb. קְצִיעוֹת, *kets-ee'-oth*), is translated CASSIA in the Authorized Version, and is said to be derived from a Hebrew word meaning *to cut off*.

(1) **Cassia.** It therefore denotes 'pieces cut off,' or 'fragments,' and hence is applicable to *cassia*. But many of these derivations have often been traced out in ignorance of the names and properties of the various substances known to the nations of antiquity.

Cassia is mentioned in three places (Exod. xxx:24; Ezek. xxvii:19; and in Ps. xlv:8), in conjunction with myrrh, cinnamon, sweet calamus, and ahalim, or eagle-wood. All these are aromatic substances, and, with the exception of myrrh, which is obtained from Africa, are products of India and its islands. It is probable, therefore, that *ketzioth* is of a similar nature, and obtained from the same countries. Both cinnamon (see KINNAMON) and cassia (see KIDDAH) were no doubt known to the ancients. (See CASSIA.)

(2) **Various Renderings.** It has not been the opinion of several translators and commentators that the *kiddah* of Exod. xxx:24 and Ezek. xxvii:19, and the *ketzioth* of Ps. xlv:8, both signify the same thing; the first having been variously rendered iris, stacte, *costus,* ginger, canna, fistula, amber, *ketziah,* and cassia, while *ketzioth*, or *ketziah,* has been rendered cassia, acacia, amber, ginger, and aloes. *Ketzioth* occurs only once, in Ps. xlv:8: 'All thy garments smell of myrrh, and aloes (*ahalim*), and *cassia* (*ketzioth*).' It has been observed with reference to this passage that 'The garments of princes are often imbued with costly perfumes, those of the high-priests were anointed with holy ointment.'

We have seen above that *ketzioth* has been variously translated, but no one seems to have noticed the resemblance of this word to the *kooth* and *koost* of the Arabs, of which *Kooshta* is said by their authors to be the Syriac name, and from which there is little doubt that the κόστος, *costus,* of the Greeks, and *costus* of the Latins are derived.

Considering, therefore, that *costus* was one of the articles of ancient commerce and is mentioned by Theophrastus as employed in the composition of perfumed unguents, and considering the similarity of the Syriac *kooshta,* and the Arabic *kast,* to the *ketzioth* of scripture, and from their correspondence in properties and uses, the latter appears more likely to be the *costus* of the ancients, than *cassia,* for which there is another name. (See KIDDAH.)   J. F. R.

KEY (kē). The keys of the ancients were very different from ours; because their doors and trunks were generally closed with bands, and the key served only to loosen or fasten those bands. Chardin says that a lock in the East is like a little harrow, which enters half way into a wooden staple, and that the key is a wooden handle with points at the end of it, which are pushed into the staple, and so raise this little harrow.

Figurative. A key was a symbol of power or authority (Is. xxii:22).

1. Christ gives Peter authority in his church (Matt. xvi:19), the key of the kingdom of

heaven, the power of binding and loosing; that is, of opening and shutting; for this frequently consisted only, as we have said, in tying and untying. Isaiah remarks, that Eliakim should wear his key upon his shoulder, as a mark of office, of his power to open and shut with authority.

2. Christ reproaches the scribes and Pharisees with having taken away the key of knowledge (Luke xi:52); that is, with reading and studying the scriptures, without advantage to themselves, and without discovering to others the truth; which in some sort they held captive in unrighteousness (Rom. i:18).

3. He also says (Rev. i:18) that he has the key of death and hell; that is, power to bring to the grave, or to deliver from it; to appoint to life or to death.

KEZIA (ke-zī'à), (Heb. קְצִיעָה, *kets-ee-aw'*, cassia), the second daughter of Job, born after his recovery (Job xlii:14).

KEZIZ (kē'ziz), (Heb. קְצִיץ, *kets-eets'*, abrupt), a city of Benjamin (Josh. xviii:21, A. V. "Valley of Keziz"), the name of which is still preserved in the Wady el Kaziz, on the road from Jerusalem to Jericho, southeast of the Apostles' Well.

KHAN (kän), the Arabic name for the establishments which correspond to our inn. (See INN.)

KIBROTH - HATTAAVAH (kĭb'roth-hat-tā'a-vah), (Heb. קִבְרוֹת הַתַּאֲוָה, *kib-roth' hat-tah-av-aw'*, graves of the longing), an encampment of the Israelites in the wilderness, probably about three days' journey from Sinai (Num. xi:34), thus named because it was the burial place of many who died from overeating the preternatural supply of quail-flesh (Num. xi:35, xxxiii:16, 17; Deut. ix:22). (See WANDERING, THE.)

KIBZAIM (kĭb-zā'im), (Heb. קִבְצַיִם, *kib-tsah'-yim*, a double heap), a city of Ephraim (Josh. xxi:22), which was given up to the Kohathite Levites. In 1 Chron. vi, Jokmeam is substituted for Kibzaim, perhaps through a mistake owing to the similarity in the original.

KID (kĭd). See GOAT; LAMB.

KIDDAH (kĭd'dah), (Heb. קִדָּה, *kid-dawkh'*), as well as KETZIOTH, is rendered CASSIA in our Authorized Version.

The word occurs first in Exod. xxx:24, where cassia (*kiddah*) is mentioned in connection with olive oil, pure myrrh, sweet cinnamon, and sweet calamus; secondly, in Ezek. xxvii:19, where Dan and Javan are described as bringing bright iron, cassia (*kiddah*), and calamus to the markets of Tyre. There is no reason why the substance now called cassia might not have been imported from the shores of India into Egypt and Palestine.

Considerable confusion has, however, been created by the same name having been applied by botanists to a genus containing the plants yielding senna, and to others, as the *cassia fistula*, which have nothing to do with the original cassia. Cassia-buds, again, though no doubt produced by a plant belonging to the same, or to some genus allied to that producing cinnamon and cassia, were probably not known in commerce at so early a period as the two latter substances. There is, certainly, no doubt that some cassia is produced on the coast of Malabar. The name also would appear to be of Eastern origin, as *kasse koronde* is one kind of cinnamon, as mentioned by Burmann in his *Flora Zeylonica;* but it will be preferable to treat of the whole subject in connection with cinnamon. (See KINNAMON.)

J. F. R.

KIDNEY (kĭd'nÿ), (Heb. כְּלָיָה, *kil-yaw';* Gr. νεφρός, *nef-ros'*).

1. Inward part of some animals (Lev. iii:4).

2. The kernel or substantial part of grains of wheat (Deut. xxxii:14).

Figurative. **1.** The inmost powers, thoughts, and desires of the soul are sometimes called *reins;* these being regarded by the Jews as the very innermost parts of the body (Ps. xvi:7; Lam. iii:13; Rev. ii:23).

2. God is *"far from men's reins,"* when they have no true knowledge, fear, love, desire of, or delight in him, and perform no true obedience to him (Jer. xii:2).

3. Men are *"pricked in their reins,"* when their soul is wounded with disquieting thoughts, tormenting passions, envy, sorrow, anger (Ps. lxxiii:21).

4. Men's *"reins instruct"* them, when God, by inspiration or otherwise, stirs up instructive and directive thoughts in their minds (Ps. xvi:7).

KIDRON (kĭd'ron), (Heb. קִדְרוֹן, *kid-rone'*, dusky, gloomy). The brook or winter torrent which flows through the valley of Jehoshaphat (as it is now called), on the east side of Jerusalem.

'The brook Kidron' is the only name by which 'the valley' itself is known in Scripture; for it is by no means certain, nor even probable, that the name 'valley of Jehoshaphat' in Joel (iii:12) was intended to apply to this valley.

(1) Brook. The word rendered 'brook' (2 Sam. xv:23; 1 Kings ii:37, etc.), is נַחַל, *nachal*, which may be taken as equivalent to the Arabic *Wady,* meaning a stream *and* its bed or valley, or properly the valley of a stream, even when the stream is dry. The Septuagint, Josephus, and the Evangelists (John xviii:1), designate it χείμαρρος, *a storm brook,* or *winter torrent.*

The brook Kidron derives all its importance from its vicinity to the holy city, being nothing more than the dry bed of a winter torrent, bearing marks of being occasionally swept over by a large volume of water. No stream flows through it, except during the heavy rains of winter, when the waters descend into it from the neighboring hills. But even in winter there is no constant flow, and the resident missionaries assured Dr. Robinson that they had not during several years seen a stream running through the valley.

(2) Ravine. The ravine in which the stream is collected takes its origin above a mile to the northeast of the city. This ravine deepens as it proceeds, and forms an angle opposite the temple. It then takes a southeasterly direction, and, passing between the village of Siloam and the city, runs off in the direction of the Dead Sea, through a singularly wild gorge, the course of which few travelers have traced (*Pictorial Palestine,* Introd. p. 194). It is in this ravine that the celebrated monastery of Santa Saba is situated. Mr. Madden, who went through the valley to the Dead Sea, thus speaks of the character which it assumes as it approaches the monastery:—'After traversing for the last hour a wild ravine, formed by two rugged perpendicular mountains, the sides of which contained innumerable caverns, which once formed a sort of troglodyte city, in which the early Christians resided, the sight of the convent in this desolate place was like a glimpse of paradise.'

(3) Bed of the Kidron. On leaving the convent the next day he says that he 'marched through the bed of the Kidron, along the horrible ravine which he entered the day before.' (Dr. Robinson, *Biblical Researches,* ii, 249), on passing along the western borders of the lake, came 'to the deep and almost impassable ravine of the Kidron, running down by Mar Saba, and thence called Wady-er-Rahib, "Monk's Valley;" but here also bearing the name of Wady en-Nar, "Fire Valley." At this place it was running east southeast, in a deep, narrow channel, between perpendicular walls of rock, as if worn away by the rushing waters between these desolate chalky hills. There was, however, no water in it then; nor had there apparently been any for a long time.' (Barclay, *City of the Great King*, pp. 302, *sq.*)

At last its dreary course brings the water (when there is any) to the precipice above the Dead Sea, into which it falls. The valley is only twenty miles long, but it has a descent of three thousand, nine hundred and twelve feet.

(4) Recent Explorations. Recent excavations have brought to light the fact that the true bed of the Kidron is about forty feet lower than its present bed, and about seventy feet nearer to the sanctuary wall.

Reference is made to it in 2 Sam. xv:23; I Kings ii:37; xv:13; 2 Kings xi:16; xxiii:4; 2 Chron. xxix:16.

KIKAYON (kī-kay'ŏn), (Heb. קִיקָיוֹן, *kee-kaw-yone'*), occurs only in Jonah iv, where it is several times mentioned, as in verses 6, 7, 9, 1 *.*

(1) Gourd. It is translated *gourd* in our Authorized Version, probably from the *kol-o-kune'-thay*, κολοκύνθη of the Septuagint, often rendered *cucurbita*. In the margin of the English Bible, *Palm-Christ* is given. In the Vulgate *kikayon* is translated *hedera*, 'ivy.' Neither the gourd nor ivy is considered by modern writers to indicate the plant intended. We are told, 'The Lord God prepared a *gourd (kikayon)*, and made it to come over Jonah, that it might be a shadow over his head,' etc. (verse 6). 'But God prepared a worm when the morning rose the next day, and it smote the gourd that it withered' (verse 7). And in verse 10 it is said of the gourd that it 'came up in a night, and perished in a night.' Hence it appears that the growth of the *kikayon* was miraculous, but that it was probably a plant of the country, being named specifically; also that it was capable of affording shade, and might be easily destroyed.

(2) Palma Christi. The Hebrew name *kikayon* is so similar to the *kiki* of Dioscorides, that it was early thought to indicate the same plant. Dioscorides (iv, 164, περὶ κίκεως) states that the *kiki,* or *croton,* is called *wild sesamum.* It has also been called *Pentadactylus* and *Palma Christi,* from the palmate division of its leaves. Having ascertained that the *kiki* of the Greeks is what is now called *Ricinus communis,* we shall find that its characters correspond with everything that is required, except the rapidity of growth, which must be granted was miraculous. From the erect habit, and the breadth of its foliage, this plant throws an ample shade, especially when young. From the softness and little substance of its stem, it may easily be destroyed by insects, which Rumphius describes as sometimes being the case. It would then necessarily dry up rapidly. As it is well suited to the country, and to the purpose indicated in the text, and as its name *kiki* is so similar to *kikayon,* it is doubtless the plant which the sacred penman had in view. (See GOURD; JONAH.) J. F. R.

KIMOSH and KIMSHON (kī'mŏsh, kĭm'shŏn), (Heb. קִמּוֹשׁ, *kim-moshe'*, nettles, and קִמְשׁוֹן, *kim-shone'*), occur, the first in Is. xxxiv:13, and Hos.

ix:6; and the second in Prov. xxiv:31, where it is mentioned along with CHARUL, which we believe to indicate *charlock.*

The field of the slothful is there described as being grown over with thorns (*charullim*), 'and nettles (*kimshon*) had covered the face thereof.' In Isaiah it is said, 'And thorns (*choach*) shall come up in the palaces, nettles (*kimosh*) and brambles in the fortresses thereof.' (Hos. ix:6), 'The pleasant places for their silver, nettles (*kimosh*) shall possess them; thorns (*choach*) shall be in their tabernacles.'

Though different interpretations have been given of this word, as thorns, thistles, wild chamomile, etc., the greatest number of authors have united in adopting nettles, chiefly in consequence of the authority of Jewish writers, and because that meaning is as well suited to the passages in which it occurs as any other which has hitherto been suggested. (See THORNS AND THISTLES.)

J. F. R.

KIN (kĭn). See KINDRED.

KINAH (kī'nah), (Heb. קִינָה, *kee-naw'*, a dirge), a town of Judah (Josh. xv:22) on the extreme south boundary of the tribe, next to Edom.

KINDNESS (kīnd'nĕs), (Heb. חֶסֶד, *kheh'sed,* desire, zeal).

1. Kindness is the quality of being kind, of expressing in words and deeds good will and benevolence and of contributing to the welfare or happiness of others (Gen. xxi:23; 2 Sam. x:2). It denotes compassion for the afflicted (Job vi: 14). A. V. "pity." It is an act of courtesy, good will, benignity and tenderness (Luke vi:35; 1 Cor. xiii:4; 2 Chron. x:7). Kindness and tenderness have been discriminated as follows: *Kindness* and *tenderness* are partial modes of affection, confined to those who know or are related to each other: we are kind to friends and acquaintances, *tender* toward those who are near and dear: *kindness* is a mode of affection most fitted for social beings; it is what everyone can show, and everyone is pleased to receive; *tenderness* is a state of feeling that is occasionally acceptable: the young and the weak demand *tenderness* from those who stand in the closest connection with them, but this feeling may be carried to an excess, so as to injure the object on which it is fixed. Crabbe.

2. Kindness of God towards men is shown in mercies, benefits, blessings, etc. (Ps. xxxi:21; cvii:43; cxvii:2).

KINDRED (kĭn'drĕd). The following are the Hebrew words thus translated in the English Bible:

1. *Mish-paw-khaw'* (Heb. מִשְׁפָּחָה, clan), usually rendered family (Gen. x:18; Ex. vi:14; Num. i:20; Josh. vii:17; Judg. xiii:2). It is rendered 'kindred' (Gen. xxiv:41; Josh. vi:23; Ruth ii:3; Job xxxii:2).

2. *Mo-leh'deth* (Heb. מוֹלֶדֶת, a child, translated 'kindred' (Gen. xxviii:9; Lev. xviii:6, 17). It also means 'persons of the same family' (Gen. xii:1; xxiv:4; xxxi:3; xliii:7; Num. x:30; Esth. ii:10; viii:6).

3. *Mo-dah'ath* (Heb. מוֹדַעַת), is used to express blood relationships (Ruth iii:2).

4. *Gheh-ool-law'* (Heb. גְּאֻלָּה, redemption), designating a relationship so close that it would impose the obligations of a kinsman (Ezek. xi:15).

5. *Awkh* (Heb. אָח, brother, 1 Chron. xii:29). Elsewhere used to express relationship in a wide sense. It comprises all affiliated relationships of consanguinity, affinity, or of the simplest ties.

6. The words which express collateral consanguinity are: (1) uncle; (2) aunt; (3) nephew; (4) niece (not in A. V.); (5) cousin. The terms of affinity are: (1) (a) father-in-law; (b) mother-in-law; (2) (a) son-in-law; (b) daughter-in-law; (3) (a) brother-in-law; (b) sister-in-law. The relations of kindred, expressed by few words, and imperfectly defined in the earliest ages, acquired in course of time greater significance and wider influence. (See FAMILY; MARRIAGE; INHERITANCE; BLOOD-REVENGE.)

KING (kĭng), (Heb. and Chald. בֶּלֶךְ, *meh'lek*, ruler; Gr. Βασιλεύς, *bas-il-yooce'*), a chief ruler, a sovereign, one invested with supreme authority over a tribe, country or nation.

(1) General Use of the Word. In the Scriptures it is used with great latitude of meaning. The kings were local rulers over but one city or large village. Benhadad had thirty-two kings subject to him (1 Kings xx:1, 16). In Canaan, Adonibezek conquered seventy kings, and made them eat bread under his table. Joshua conquered thirty-one (Judg. i:7; Josh. xii). Nimrod of Babylon was the first king we read of; but soon after, we find kings in Egypt, Persia, Canaan, Edom, etc. (Gen. x:10; xiii, xiv, xx, xxxvi).

(2) Relation to Hebrews. Regal authority was altogether alien to the institutions of Moses in their original and unadulterated form. Their fundamental idea was that Jehovah was the sole king of the nation (1 Sam. viii:7): to use the emphatic words in Is. xxxiii:22, 'The Lord is our judge, the Lord is our lawgiver, the Lord is our king.'

(3) Moses. We consider it as a sign of that self-confidence and moral enterprise which are produced in great men by a consciousness of being what they profess, that Moses ventured, with his half-civilized hordes, on the bold experiment of founding a society without a king, and that in the solicitude which he must have felt for the success of his great undertaking, he forewent the advantages which a regal government would have afforded. Such an attempt was singular and novel at a period and in a part of the world in which royalty was not only general, but held in the greatest respect, and sometimes rose to the very height of pure despotism. Its novelty is an evidence of the Divine original to which Moses referred all his polity.

(a) Patriotism. Equally honorable is the conduct of Moses in denying to his lower nature the gratifications which a crown would have imparted —we say denying himself, because it is beyond a question that the man who rescued the Jews from bondage and conducted them to the land of Canaan, might, had he chosen, have kept the dominion in his own hands, and transmitted a crown to his posterity.

Washington, at this late period of human history, after the accumulating experience of above three thousand years, is held deserving of high honor for having preferred to found a republic rather than attempt to build up a throne, and the Hebrew patriot with supreme power in his hands was content to die within sight of the land of promise, a simple, unrewarded, unhonored individual, content to do God's work regardless of self.

It is equally obvious that this self-denial on the part of Moses, this omission to create any human kingship, is in entire accordance with the import, aim, and spirit of the Mosaic institutions, as being Divine in their origin, and designed to accomplish a special work of Providence for man; and, therefore, affords, by its consistency with the very essence of the system of which it forms a part, a very forcible argument in favor of the Divine legation of Moses.

(b) Difficulties to be Met. That great man, however, well knew what were the elements with which he had to deal in framing institutions for the rescued Israelites. Slaves they had been, and the spirit of slavery was not yet wholly eradicated from their souls. They had, too, witnessed in Egypt the more than ordinary pomp and splendor which environ a throne, dazzling the eyes and captivating the heart of the uncultured. Not improbably the prosperity and abundance which they had seen in Egypt, might have been ascribed by them to the regal form of the Egyptian government. Moses may well, therefore, have apprehended a not very remote departure from the fundamental type of his institutions.

Accordingly he makes a special provision for this contingency (Deut. xvii:14), and labors, by anticipation, to guard against the abuses of royal power. Should a king be demanded by the people, then he was to be a native Israelite; he was not to be drawn away by the love of show, especially by a desire for that regal display in which horses have always borne so large a part, to send down to Egypt, still less to cause the people to return to that land. He was to avoid the corrupting influence of a large harem, so common among Eastern monarchs; he was to abstain from amassing silver and gold. He was to have a copy of the law made expressly for his own study—a study which he was never to intermit till the end of his days; so that his heart might not be lifted up above his brethren, that he might not be turned aside from the living God, but observing the Divine statutes, and thus acknowledging himself to be no more than the vicegerent of heaven, he might enjoy happiness, and transmit his authority to his descendants.

(4) Jewish Polity. The Jewish polity, then, was a sort of sacerdotal republic—we say sacerdotal, because of the great influence which, from the first, the priestly order enjoyed, having no human head, but being under the special supervision, protection, and guidance of the Almighty. The nature of the consequences, however, of that Divine influence avowedly depended on the degree of obdience and the general faithfulness of the nation. The good, therefore, of such a superintendence in its immediate results was not necessary, but contingent. The removal of Moses and of Joshua by death soon left the people to the natural results of their own condition and character. Anarchy ensued. Noble minds, indeed, and stout hearts appeared in those who were termed Judges; but the state of the country was not so satisfactory as to prevent an unenlightened people, having low and gross affections, from preferring the glare of a crown and the apparent protection of a scepter, to the invisible and, therefore, mostly unrecognized arm of Omnipotence.

(5) Demand for a King. A king accordingly is requested. The misconduct of Samuel's sons, who had been made judges, was the immediate occasion of the demand being put forth. The request came with authority, for it emanated from all the elders of Israel, who, after holding a formal conference, proceeded to Samuel, in order to make him acquainted with their wish.

Samuel was displeased; but, having sought in prayer to learn the Divine will, he is instructed to yield to the demand on a ground which we should not assuredly have found stated, had the book in which it appears have been tampered with or fabricated for any courtly purposes or any personal ends, whether by Samuel himself, or by David, or any of his successors—'for they have not rejected thee (Samuel), but they have rejected me, that I should not reign over them' (1 Sam. viii:7, 8). Samuel is, moreover, directed to 'protest solemnly unto them, and show them the manner of the king that shall reign over them' (verse 9). Faithfully does the prophet depict the evils which a monarchy would inflict on the people. In vain. They said, 'Nay, but we will have a king over us.'

(6) **Saul the Son of Kish.** Accordingly, Saul the son of Kish, of the tribe of Benjamin, was, by Divine direction, selected, and privately anointed by Samuel 'to be captain over God's inheritance:' thus he was to hold only a delegated and subordinate authority. Under the guidance of Samuel, Saul is subsequently chosen by lot from among the assembled tribes; and though his personal appearance had no influence in the choice, yet when he was plainly pointed out to be the individual designed for the scepter, Samuel called attention to those qualities which in less civilized nations have a preponderating influence, and are never without effect, at least, in supporting 'the Divinity which doth hedge a king:' 'See ye him whom the Lord hath chosen, that there is none like him among all the people' (1 Sam. x: 24), for he was higher than any of the people from his shoulders and upward; 'and all the people shouted, God save the king.'

(7) **Limited Monarchy.** Emanating as the royal power did from the demand of the people and the permission of a prophet, it was not likely to be unlimited in its extent or arbitrary in its exercise. The government of God, indeed, remained, being rather concealed and complicated than disowned, much less superseded. The king ruled not in his own right, nor in virtue of the choice of the people, but by concession from on high, and partly as the servant and partly as the representative of the theocracy. How insecure, indeed, was the tenure of the kingly power, how restricted it was in its authority, appears clear from the comparative facility with which the crown was transferred from Saul to David; and the part which the prophet Samuel took in affecting that transference points out the quarter where lay the power which limited, if it did not primarily, at least, control the royal authority. We must not, however, expect to find any definite and permanent distribution of power, any legal determination of the royal prerogatives as discriminated from the Divine authority; circumstances, as they prompted certain deeds, restricted or enlarged the sphere of the monarch's action. Thus, in 1 Sam. xi:4, *sq.* we find Saul, in an emergency, assuming, without consultation or deliberation, the power of demanding something like a levy *en masse,* and of proclaiming instant war. With the king lay the administration of justice in the last resort (2 Sam. xv:2; 1 Kings iii:16, *sq.*).

He also possessed the power of life and death (2 Sam. xiv.). To provide for and superintend the public worship was at once his duty and his highest honor (1 Kings viii; 2 Kings xii:4; xviii: 4; xxiii:1). One reason why the people requested a king was that they might have a recognized leader in war (1 Sam. viii:20).

The Mosaic law offered a powerful hindrance to royal despotism (1 Sam. x:25). The people also, by means of their elders, formed an express compact, by which they stipulated for their rights (1 Kings xii:4), and were from time to time appealed to, generally in cases of 'great pith and moment' (1 Chron. xxix:1; 2 Kings xi:17; Joseph., *De Bell. Jud.* ii. 1. 2). Nor did the people fail to interpose their will, where they thought it necessary, in opposition to that of the monarch (1 Sam. xiv:45).

The part which Nathan took against David shows how effective, as well as bold, was the check exerted by the prophets; indeed, most of the prophetic history is the history of the noblest opposition ever made to the vices alike of royalty, priesthood, and people.

If needful, the prophet hesitated not to demand an audience of the king, nor was he dazzled or deterred by royal power and pomp (1 Kings xx: 22, 38; 2 Kings i:15). As, however, the monarch held the sword, the instrument of death was sometimes made to prevail over every restraining influence (1 Sam. xxii:17).

(8) **Transfer of the Crown to David.** After the transfer of the crown from Saul to David, the royal power was annexed to the house of the latter, passing from father to son, with preference to the eldest born, though he might be a minor. Jehoash was seven years old when he began to reign (2 Kings xi:21).

This rule was not, however, rigidly observed, for instances are not wanting in which nomination of a younger son gave him a preferable title to the crown (1 Kings i:17; 2 Chron. xi:21). The people, too, and even foreign powers, at a later period, interrupted the regular transmission of royal authority (2 Kings xxi:24; xxiii:24, 30; xxiv:17).

The ceremony of anointing, which was observed at least in the case of Saul, David, and Solomon (1 Sam. ix:14; x:1; xv:1; xvi:12; 2 Sam. ii:4; v:3; 1 Kings i:34, 39, 40), and in which the prophet or high-priest who performed the rite acted as the representative of the will of heaven, must have given to the spiritual power very considerable influence. And both in this particular and in the very nature of the observance directs the mind to Egypt, where the same custom prevailed, and where the power of the priestly caste was immense (Wilkinson's *Ancient Egyptians,* v, 279). Indeed, the ceremony seems to have been essential to constitute a legitimate monarch (2 Kings xi: 12; xxiii:30); and thus the authorities of the Jewish church held in their hands, and had subject to their will, a most important power, which they could use either for their own purposes or the common good. We have seen in the case of Saul that personal and even external qualities had their influence in procuring ready obedience to a sovereign; and further evidence to the same effect may be found in Ps. xlv:3; Ezek. xxviii:12. Such qualities would naturally excite the enthusiasm of the people, who appear to have manifested their approval by acclamations (1 Sam. x:24; 1 Kings i:25; 2 Kings ix:13; xi:13; 2 Chron. xxiii: 11; see also Joseph. *De Bell. Jud.* i, 33, 9). Jubilant music formed a part of the popular rejoicings (1 Kings i:40); thank-offerings were made (1 Kings i:25); the new sovereign rode in solemn procession on the royal mule of his predecessor (1 Kings i:38), and took possession of the royal harem—an act which seems to have been scarcely less essential than other observances which appear to us to wear a higher character (1 Kings ii:13, 22; 2 Sam. xvi:22).

A numerous harem, indeed, was among the most highly estimated of the royal luxuries (2 Sam. v:13; 1 Kings xi:1; xx:3). It was under the supervision and control of eunuchs, and passed from one monarch to another as a part of the crown property (2 Sam. xii:8). The law (Deut. xvii:17), foreseeing evils such as that by which Solomon, in his later years, was turned away from his fidelity to God, had strictly forbidden many wives. But Eastern passions and usages were too strong for a mere written prohibition, and a corrupted religion became a pander to royal lust, interpreting the Divine command as sanctioning eighteen as the minimum of wives and concubines.

(9) Royal Revenues. In the original distribution of the land no share, of course, was reserved for a merely possible monarch; yet the kings were not without several sources of income. In the earlier periods of the monarchy the simple manners which prevailed would render copious revenues unnecessary; and a throne which was the result of a spontaneous demand on the part of the people, would easily find support in freewill offerings especially in a part of the world where the great are never approached without a present. There seems also reason to conclude that the amount of the contributions made by the people for the sustenance of the monarch depended, in a measure, on the degree of popularity which, in any particular case, he enjoyed, or the degree of service which he obviously rendered to the state (1 Sam. x:27; xvi:20; 2 Sam. viii:11; 1 Kings x:11, 25, *sq.*).

That presents of small value and humble nature were not despised or thought unfit for the acceptance of royalty may be learnt from that which Jesse sent to Saul (1 Sam. xvi:20), 'an ass, with bread and a bottle of wine, and a kid.' The indirect detail 'of the substance which was king David's,' found in 1 Chron. xxvii:25, *sq.* (comp. 1 Sam. viii:14; 2 Chron. xxvi:10, *sq.*), shows at how early a period the Israelitish throne was in possession of very large property, both personal and real. The royal treasury was replenished by confiscation, as in the case of Naboth (1 Kings xxi: 16; comp. Ezek. xlvi:16, *sq.;* 2 Sam. xvi:4). Nor were taxes unknown. Samuel had predicted (1 Sam. viii:15), 'He will take the tenth of your seed and of your vineyards,' etc.; and so in other passages (1 Kings v:13; ix:21) we find that levies both of men and money were made for the monarch's purposes; and, in cases of special need, these exactions were large and rigorously levied (2 Kings xxiii:35), as when Jehoiakim 'taxed the land to give the money according to the commandment of Pharaoh; he exacted the silver and the gold of the people of the land, of every one according to his taxation.'

So long, however, as the native vigor of a young monarchy made victory easy and frequent, large revenues came to the king from the spoils of war (2 Sam. viii:2, *sq.*). Commerce also supplied abundant resources (1 Kings x:15).

(10) Oriental Ceremony. According to Oriental custom, much ceremony and outward show of respect were observed. Those who were intended to be received with special honor were placed on the king's right hand (1 Kings ii:19). The most profound homage was paid to the monarch, which was required not merely by common usage, but by the voice of religious wisdom (Prov. xxiv:21)—a requirement which was not unnatural in regard to an office that was accounted of Divine origin, and to have a sort of vice-Divine authority. Those who presented themselves before the royal presence fell with their face towards the ground till their forehead touched it (1 Sam. xxv:23; 2 Sam. ix:6; xix: 18), thus

worshiping or doing obeisance to the monarch, a ceremony from which even the royal spouse was not exempted (1 Kings i:16). A kiss was among the established tokens of reverence (1 Sam. x: 1; Ps. ii:12), as were also hyperbolical wishes of good (Dan. ii:4; iii:9). Serious offenses against the king were punished with death (1 Kings xxi:10).

(11) Hebrew Kings less Despotic than Others. Deriving their power originally from the wishes of the people, and being one of the same race, the Hebrew kings were naturally less despotic than other Oriental sovereigns, mingled more with their subjects, and were by no means difficult of access (2 Sam. xix:8; 1 Kings xx: 39; Jer. xxxviii:7; 1 Kings iii:16; 2 Kings vi: 26; viii:3). After death the monarchs were interred in the royal cemetery in Jerusalem: 'So David slept with his fathers, and was buried in the city of David' (1 Kings ii:10; xi:43; xiv:31). But bad kings were excluded 'from the sepulchers of the kings of Israel' (2 Chron. xxviii:27). In 1 Kings iv will be found an enumeration of the high officers of state under the reign of Solomon (see also 1 Kings x:5; xii:18; xviii:3; 2 Kings viii:16; x:22; xviii:18; xix:2; 1 Chron. xxvii:25; Is. xxii:15; Jer. lii:25). The misdeeds of the Jewish crown, and the boldness with which they were reproved, may be seen exemplified in Jer. xxii:3. 'Thus saith the Lord, Execute judgment and righteousness, and do no wrong; do no violence to the stranger, the fatherless, nor the widow; neither shed innocent blood. But if ye will not hear these words, this house shall become a desolation,' etc. Reference on the subject here treated of may be made to Ewald, *Geschichte des Volkes Israel,* iii. 381; Maurice, *Kings and Prophets of the Old Testament.*

J. R. B.

Figurative. **1.** King is symbolically used in the scriptures, to men: as invested with regal authority by their fellows (Luke xxii:25; 1 Tim. ii:1; 1 Pet. ii:15, 17); to God: as the sole proper sovereign and ruler of the universe (1 Tim. i: 17; vi:15, 16); and to Christ, as the Messiah, the Son of God, the King of the Jews, the sole Head and Governor of his church (1 Tim. vi:15, 16; Matt. xxvii:11; Luke xix:38; John i:49; vi: 15; xviii:32-37).

2. Saints are "kings;" they have the kingdom of God within them; they are heirs of the kingdom of glory; they war against and conquer sin, Satan, and the world; they rule their own spirit, and govern their body, and have no small influence on God's government of nations and churches (Rev. i:6; v:10; xx:4).

3. Leviathan is "king" over all the children of pride, or fierce-looking monsters; in strength or bulk he exceeds all the animals (Job xli:34). (See HISTORY; ISRAEL, KINGDOM OF.)

KINGDOM (kǐng-dŭm), (Heb. מַמְלָכָה, *mam-law-kaw'*).

(1) In General. (1) The country or countries subject to one king (Deut. iii:4). (2) The power of acting as king, or of supreme administration (1 Sam. xviii:8; xx:31).

(2) Kingdom of God. God's universal dominion over all things, is called his "kingdom;" thereby he preserves, protects, gives laws to, and regulates all his creatures, and can dispense favors or judgments as he pleaseth (1 Chron. xxix:11; Ps. cxlv:12. The saints' new-covenant state, and the work of saving grace in their heart, are called the "kingdom" of God, and the "kingdom" of heaven. Therein God erects his throne in their heart, gives laws and privileges to their souls, renders them heavenly-minded and meet to enter the heavenly glory (Matt. vi:33; xiii:31; Luke xvii: 20, 21).

(3) Kingdom of Heaven. (a) The visible church, especially under the New Testament, is called a "kingdom;" Christ and his Father rule in it, and maintain order, safety, and happiness therein. It is called the "kingdom of heaven;" it is of a heavenly original, has a heavenly governor and laws; and is erected to render multitudes fit for heaven (Matt. iii:2; iv:17; xiii:47; xvi:19; Col. i:13).

(b) The state of glory in heaven is called a "kingdom." How great is its glory, happiness, and order! how ready the obedience of all the unnumbered subjects of God and the Lamb therein! (Matt. v:10; Luke xxii:16; 1 Cor. vi:9).

(4) Kingdom of Priests. The Hebrew nation and the saints are a "kingdom of priests;" they were, or are, a numerous and honored body, who have access to offer up sacrifices, prayer, praise, and good works, acceptable to God through Jesus Christ (Exod. xix:6; 1 Pet. ii:9).

(5) The Heathen. Nations are called the heathenish "kingdoms of this world;" their ends, maxims, and manner of government, are carnal and earthly (Rev. xi:15). Brown.

KINGDOM OF ISRAEL. See ISRAEL, KINGDOM OF.

KINGDOM OF JUDAH. See JUDAH, KINGDOM OF.

KINGLY OFFICE OF CHRIST. See JESUS CHRIST.

KINGS, BOOKS OF (kĭngs, bŏŏks ŏv). The two books of Kings formed anciently but one book in the Jewish Scriptures.

But great stress cannot always be laid on the Jewish forms of the sacred books, as they were arranged so as to correspond with the letters of the Hebrew alphabet.

(1) Brief Annals. The books of Kings contain the brief annals of a long period, from the accession of Solomon till the dissolution of the commonwealth. The first chapters describe the reign of Solomon over the united kingdom, and the revolt under Rehoboam. The history of the rival states is next narrated in parallel sections till the period of Israel's downfall on the invasion of Shalmaneser. Then the remaining years of the principality of Judah are recorded till the conquest of Nebuchadnezzar and the commencement of the Babylonish captivity. In the article ISRAEL, the period comprised has been exhibited under the name and reign of the kings who are mentioned there and in these books, and in the article JUDAH, KINGDOM OF, the chronology of the books has been sufficiently considered.

(2) Peculiarities. There are some peculiarities in this succinct history worthy of attention. It is very brief, but very suggestive. It is not a biography of the sovereigns, nor a mere record of political occurrences, nor yet an ecclesiastical register. King, church, and state are all comprised in their sacred relations. It is a theocratic history, a retrospective survey of the kingdoms as existing under a theocratic government.

The character of the sovereign is tested by his fidelity to the religious obligations of his office, and this decision in reference to his conduct is generally added to the notice of his accession. The new king's religious character is generally portrayed by its similarity or opposition to the way of David, of his father, or of Jeroboam, son of Nebat, 'who made Israel to sin.'

Ecclesiastical affairs are noticed with a similar purpose, and in contrast with past or prevalent apostasy, especially as manifested in the popular superstitions, whose shrines were on the 'high places.'

Political or national incidents are introduced in general for the sake of illustrating the influence of religion on civic prosperity; of showing how the theocracy maintained a vigilant and vengeful guardianship over its rights and privileges—adherence to its principles securing peace and plenty, disobedience to them bringing along with it sudden and severe retribution.

(3) Verification of Mosaic Warnings. The books of Kings are a verification of the Mosaic warnings, and the author of them has kept this steadily in view. He has given a brief history of his people, arranged under the various political chiefs in such a manner as to show that the government was essentially theocratic, that its spirit, as developed in the Mosaic writings, was never extinct, however modified or inactive it might sometimes appear.

(4) Religious Form. Thus the books of Kings appear in a religious costume, quite different from the form they would have assumed either as a political or ecclesiastical narrative. In the one case legislative enactments, royal edicts, popular movements, would have occupied a prominent place; in the other, sacerdotal arrangements, Levitical service, music and pageantry, would have filled the leading sections of the treatise.

In either view the points adduced would have had a restricted reference to the palace or the temple, the sovereign or the pontiff, the court or the priesthood, the throne or the altar, the tribute or tithes, the nation on its farms, or the tribes in the courts of the sacred edifice.

But the theocracy conjoined both the political and religious elements, and the inspired annalist unites them as essential to his design. The agency of Divinity is constantly recognized, the hand of Jehovah is continually acknowledged.

(5) Agency of the Prophets. The chief organ of theocratic influence enjoys peculiar prominence. We refer to the incessant agency of the prophets, their great power and peculiar modes of action as detailed by the composer of the books of Kings. They interfered with the succession, and their instrumentality was apparent in the schism. They roused the people, and they braved the sovereign. The balance of power was in their hands; the regal dignity seemed to be sometimes at their disposal; indeed they were his vicegerents by whom his judgments were executed.

In times of emergency they dispensed with usual modes of procedure, and assumed almost unlimited authority with which no subject in an ordinary government can safely be intrusted, executing the law with a summary promptness which rendered opposition impossible or at least unavailing. They felt their Divine commission, and that they were the custodians of the rights of Jehovah. At the same time they protected the interests of the nation, and, could we divest the term of its association with unprincipled turbulence and sedition, we would, like Winer, style them the demagogues of Israel (Winer, *Realwört,* art. *Prophet*).

The Divine prerogative was to them a vested right, guarded with a sacred jealousy from royal usurpation or popular invasion; and the interests of the people were as religiously protected against encroachments, too easily made under a form of government which had not the safeguard of popular representation or aristocratic privilege. The priesthood was in many instances, though there are some illustrious exceptions, merely the creature of the crown, and therefore it became the *prophet-enthum* to assert its dignity and stand forth in the majestic insignia of an embassy from heaven.

(6) Evidence as to Method, Etc. The truth of these sentiments, as to the method, design, and composition of the books of Kings, is confirmed by ample evidence.

(1) Large space is occupied with the building of the Temple—the palace of the Divine Protector—his throne in it being above the mercy-seat and between the cherubim (ch. v-viii). Care is taken to record the miraculous phenomenon of the descent of the Shekinah (ch. viii:10). The prayer of Solomon at the dedication of the house is full of theocratic views and aspirations.

(2) Reference is often made to the Mosaic Law with its provisions; and allusions to the earlier history of the people frequently occur (1 Kings ii:3; iii:14; vi:11, 12; viii:58, etc.; 2 Kings x:31; xiv:6; xvii:13, 15, 37; xviii:4-6; xxi:1-8). Allusions to the Mosaic code are found more frequently toward the end of the second book, when the kingdom was drawing near its termination, as if to account for its decay and approaching fate.

(3) Phrases expressive of Divine interference are frequently introduced (1 Kings xi:31; xii:15; xiii:1, 2, 9; and xx:13, etc.).

(4) Prophetic interposition is a very prominent theme of record. It fills the vivid foreground of the historical picture. Nathan was occupied in the succession of Solomon (1 Kings i:45); Ahijah was concerned in the revolt (xi:29-40). Shemaiah disbanded the troops which Rehoboam had mustered (xii:21). Ahijah predicted the ruin of Jeroboam, whose elevation he had promoted (xiv:7). Jehu, the prophet, doomed the house of Baasha (xvi:1). The reign of Ahab and Ahaziah is marked by the bold, rapid, mysterious movements of Elijah. Under Ahab occurs the prediction of Micaiah (xxii:8). The actions and oracles of Elisha form the marvelous topics of narration under several reigns. The agency of Isaiah is also recognized (2 Kings xix:20; xx:16). Besides 1 Kings xiii presents another instance of prophetic operation; and in xx:35, the oracle of an unknown prophet is also rehearsed. Huldah, the prophetess, was an important personage under the government of Josiah (2 Kings xxii:14). Care is also taken to report the fulfillment of striking prophecies, in the usual phrase, 'according to the word of the Lord' (1 Kings xii:15; xv:29; xvi:12; 2 Kings xxiii:15-18; ix:36; xxiv:2). So, too, the Old Syriac version prefixes, 'Here follows the book of the kings who flourished among the ancient people; and in this is also exhibited the history of the prophets who flourished during their times.'

(5) Theocratic influence is recognized both in the disposition and succession of kings (1 Kings xiii:33; xv:4, 5, 29, 30; 2 Kings xi:17, etc.). Compare on the whole of this view Hävernick, *Einleit.* sec. 168; Jahn, *Introduct.* sec. 46; Gesenius, *Ueber Jes.* vol. i, p. 934. It is thus apparent that the object of the author of the Books of Kings was, to describe the history of the kingdoms, especially in connection with the theocratic element.

(7) Authorship. The authorship and age of this historical treatise may admit of several suppositions. Whatever were the original sources, the books are evidently the composition of one writer. The style is generally uniform throughout. The same forms of expression are used to denote the same thing, *e. g.* the male sex (1 Kings xiv:10, etc.); the death of a king (1 Kings xi:43, etc.); modes of allusion to the law (1

Kings xi:13;); fidelity to Jehovah (1 Kings viii:53, etc.; De Wette, *Einleit,* sec. 184, *a;* Hävernick; *Einleit.* sec. 171). Similar idioms are ever recurring, so as to produce a uniformity of style (*Monotonie der Darstellung,* Hävernick, *l. c.*).

(8) Sources. The sources whence this historic information has been derived have been variously named. That annals contemporary with the events which they describe were written in the early period of the Jewish state, may be at once admitted. Eichhorn supposes that the sources of 'Kings' were private historical works (*Einleit.* sec. 482). De Wette, from the legends related in them, cannot believe them to be official documents. Bertholdt, Hävernick, and Movers hold that the books are extracts from the public annals (comp. Hävernick, sec. 169). The inspired historiographer refers his readers to these sources of evidence in such frequent phrases as 'the *rest* of the acts.' Such a reference is made especially to the sources, when other royal acts than those narrated in the books of Kings are glanced at. These sources are styled the book of the Chronicles of the kings of Judah, or Israel. Similar phraseology is used in Esther x:2; vi:1, to denote the official annals of the Persian empire. Public documents are spoken of in the same way (Neh. xii:23). There is little reason to suppose that the book referred to in this last passage is that styled Chronicles in our copy of the Scriptures (Movers, *Chronik,* sec. 234). So we infer that the 'Book of the Chronicles of the Kings,' so often alluded to, was an authentic document, public and official. Once indeed mention is made of a work entitled 'The Book of the Acts of Solomon.'

(9) Contemporaneous Events Recorded by the Prophets. That the prophets themselves were employed in recording contemporaneous events, is evident from 2 Chron. xx:34; 1 Chron. xxix:29. In the course of the narrative we meet with many instances of description, having the freshness and form of nature, and which are apparently direct quotations from some journal, written by one who testified what he had seen (1 Kings xx:10; 2 Kings xii:15; xiv:8). Thus the credibility of the history contained in these books rests upon a sure foundation.

(10) The Compiler. Now, the compiler from these old documents—he who shaped them into the form they have in our present books of Kings —must have lived in a late age. The Second Book of Kings concludes with an account of the liberation of Jehoiachin, king of Judah, from prison in Babylon—an event which, according to Jahn, happened in the twenty-sixth, or according to Prideaux, in the twenty-eighth year after the destruction of Jerusalem. Jahn and Hävernick place the composition of 'Kings' in the reign of Evil-merodach; and De Wette, towards the end of the Captivity. Instances of later phraseology occurring in the books of Kings are given by De Wette (sec. 115, 6). Jewish tradition makes Jeremiah the author (*Baba-bathra,* fol. 15, 1). Calmet ascribes the authorship to Ezra. The former opinion, adopted by Grotius, and lately revindicated by Hävernick, certainly appears the more probable. It explains the close similarity of the books of Kings and Jeremiah in spirit, style, and tendency, more easily and more satisfactorily than the supposition of De Wette, or any other conjecture of like nature.

The age of the books of Kings may be intermediate between the early work of Samuel and the later treatise of Chronicles.   J. B.

(11) Literature: Hales, *Analysis;* Bunsen, *Egypt's Place in Hist.;* Maurice, *Kings and Prophets;* Keil, *Bücher der Könige;* Wordsworth, *Books of Kings* in his *Holy Bible;* Jahn, *Heb. Commonwealth;* Milman, *Hist. of the Jews;* Newman, *Hist. of the Heb. Monarchy;* Rawlinson, *Monarchies of the Ancient Eastern World,* ii and iii; Cheyne, *Intr. Book of Is.,* 1895, p. 212, sq.; H. Ewald, *Hist. of Isr.*

KING'S DALE (kĭngs dāle), a place where the king of Sodom met Abraham when he returned with the spoil of Sodom (Gen. xiv:17). Also mentioned as the place where Absalom had erected a pillar (2 Sam. xviii:18). It was doubtless close to Jerusalem, but the exact locality has not been agreed upon. The majority take it to be the valley of Jehoshaphat.

KING'S GARDEN (kĭngs gär'd'n), the royal garden near the fortress of Zion (2 Kings xxi:18; xxv:4). It was near Bîr Ayyûb, which is probably En-rogel. (See GARDEN.)

KING'S HOUSE (kĭngs hous), "House of the forest of Lebanon," Solomon's palace (1 Kings vii:1-12). (See PALACE.)

KING'S MOTHER (kĭngs mŭth'ẽr), (1 Kings ii:19). See QUEEN.

KING'S POOL (kĭngs pōōl), (Neh. ii:14). See SILOAM.

KING'S SEPULCHER (kĭngs sĕp'ŭl-kẽr). See BURIAL AND SEPULCHERS.

KINNAMON kĭn'na-mŏn), (Heb. קִנָּמוֹן, *kin-naw-mone'*), translated 'cinnamon,' occurs in three places of Scripture; first, about 1600 years before the Christian era, in Exod. xxx:23, where it is enumerated as one of the ingredients employed in the preparation of the holy anointing oil.

It is next mentioned in Prov. vii:17, 'I have perfumed my bed with myrrh, aloes (*ahalim*), and *cinnamon.*' And again in Cant. iv:14, 'Spikenard and saffron; calamus and *cinnamon*, with all trees of frankincense; myrrh and aloes (*aha-*

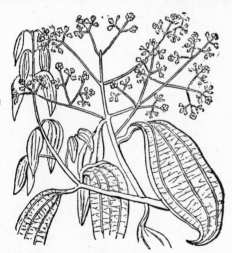

Cinnamon (*Kinnamomum Cassia*).

lim), with all the chief spices. While in Rev. xviii:13, among the merchandise of Babylon, we have 'cinnamon, and odors, and ointments, and frankincense.'

(1) Sweet Cinnamon. In the earliest notice, it is called *kinnamon besem,* or 'sweet cinnamon.' Dr. Vincent is inclined to consider *khennah besem* and *kinnamon besem* as derived from the same

root. Many writers have doubted whether the *kinnamon* of the Hebrews is the same article that we now call cinnamon. If we were to put faith in all these doubts, we should be left without any substances possessed of sufficiently remarkable properties to have been articles of ancient commerce. Galen says that cassia and cinnamon are so much alike that it is not an easy matter to distinguish the one from the other. This is a difficulty that still continues to be experienced.

(2) Cassia Bark. Cassia bark, as we have seen, was distinguished with difficulty from cinnamon by the ancients. In the present day it is

Cinnamon (*Laurus Kinnamomum*).

often sold for cinnamon; indeed, unless a purchaser specify *true* cinnamon, he will probably be supplied with nothing but cassia. It is made up into similar bundles with cinnamon, has the same general appearance, smell, and taste; but its substance is thicker and coarser, its color darker, its flavor much less sweet and fine than that of Ceylon cinnamon, while it is more pungent, and is followed by a bitter taste; it is also less closely quilled, and breaks shorter than genuine cinnamon. There can be no reasonable doubt, as cinnamon and cassia were known to the Greeks, that they must have been known to the Hebrews also, as the commerce with India can be proved to have been much more ancient than is generally supposed. (See CINNAMON; KIDDAH.)

J. F. R.

KINSMAN, KINSWOMAN and KINSFOLK (kĭnz'man, kĭnz'wŏŏm'an, kĭnz'fōk). Several Hebrew words are thus translated. 1. *Sheh-ayr'* (שְׁאֵר, Num. xxvii:11; "kinswoman," Lev. xviii:12, 13; "kinswomen," xviii:17). *Mo-dah'* (מוֹדַע, "kinswoman," Prov. vii:4). *Kaw-robe'*, (קָרוֹב, literally, near, "kinsfolk," Job xix:14; "kinsmen," Ps. xxxviii:11). 2. *Soong-ghen-ace'* (Gr. συγγενής, relative, "kinsfolk," Luke ii:44; xxi:16). 3. The Hebrew word גֹּאֵל, *go-ale'*, redeemer, however, denoted the nearest male blood relation living (Lev. xxv:25,28; Ruth iii:2; iv:1).

(1) Blood Avenger. One of the kinsman's most peculiar offices was that of an avenger of blood. (See BLOOD-REVENGE.)

(2) Redeemer. Another duty of the kinsman was that of *kinsman redeemer.* If his nearest relative had through poverty mortgaged his inheritance, the *goale* was to buy it back. If he had sold himself into slavery, the *goale* was to pay his ransom. If he was murdered, the *goale* was to avenge his blood. If he died childless, the *goale* might espouse his widow, and raise up seed to him; but it does not appear that he was obliged to do this, except he was an unmarried brother (Num. v:8; xxvii:11, and xxxv; Deut. xxv:1-8; Ruth iii, and iv).

Figurative. Did not this *goale* typify Christ's assuming our nature, purchasing our happiness, recovering our liberty, avenging our blood on Satan and his agents, and raising up to our widowed nature a seed of saints and good works? God is called a *Redeemer:* with mighty power and kindness, he rescued the Hebrews from their bondage and trouble, and often delivers the oppressed; and he, through the blood of his Son, saves from deep slavery and woe, under the broken law, to endless glory and happiness (Is. lxiii:19). Christ is a *Redeemer:* by his righteousness, he paid the price of our redemption; by his intercession, he pleads for and procures it; by his Spirit, he applies it to our souls (Is. lix: 20; Job xix:25). Our *redemption* or deliverance from sin, and all its effects, is through his blood, and Spirit (Eph. i:13; Col. i:14; Heb. ix:12), and begins in our forgiveness, is carried on in our sanctification, and perfected in our eternal blessedness, when, at the resurrection, our very bodies shall be delivered from all the deathful effects of sin; and this entrance on eternal glory is called our *redemption,* as it brings the deliverance to its perfection (Luke xxi:28; Rom. viii: 23). Brown.

KIPPOD (kĭp-pôd'), (Heb. קִפּוֹד, *kip-pode'*). This name occurs but three times in Scripture (Is. xiv: 23; xxxiv,11; and Zeph. ii:14), and has been variously interpreted—owl, osprey, tortoise, porcupine, otter, and in the Arabic, bustard.

(1) **Various Translations.** Now, in Is. xiv: 23, 'I will make it a possession for the kippod (bittern), and pools of water,' etc., the words are plain and natural. Marshes and pools are not the habitation of hedgehogs, for they shun water.

(2) **Bittern.** In Is. xxxiv:11, it is said, 'The cormorant (*Sterna caspia*) and kippod (bittern) shall possess it, the owl also and the raven shall dwell in it,' etc.; that is, in the ruins of Idumæa. Here, again, the version is plain, and a hedgehog most surely would be out of place. Zeph. ii:14, 'Both the cormorant (*Sterna caspia*) and the kippod (bittern) shall lodge in the upper lintels of it; and their voice shall sing in the windows,' etc. Surely here kippod cannot mean the hedgehog. a nocturnal, groveling, worm-eating animal, entirely or nearly mute, and incapable of climbing up walls; one that does not haunt ruins, but earthy banks in wooded regions, and that is absolutely solitary in its habits. The Arabian bustard, *Otis houbara,* might be selected, if it were not that bustards keep always in dry deserts and uplands, and that they never roost, their feet not admitting of perching, but rest on the ground.

(3) **Heron.** We think the term most applicable to the heron tribes, whose beaks are formidable spikes that often kill hawks; a fact well known to Eastern hunters. Of these *Nycticorax Europæus,* or common night heron, with its pencil of white feathers in the crest, is a species, not uncommon in the marshes of Western Asia; and of several species of bittern, *Ardea* (*botaurus*) *stellaris* has pointed long feathers on the neck and breast, freckled with black, and a strong pointed bill.

After the breeding season it migrates and passes the winter in the south, frequenting the marshes and rivers of Asia and Europe, where it then roosts high above ground, uttering a curious note before and after its evening flight, very distinct from the booming sound produced by it in the breeding season, and while it remains in the marshes. Though not building, like the stork, on the tops of houses, it resorts, like the heron, to ruined structures, and we have been informed that it has been seen on the summit of Tauk Kesra at Ctesiphon. (See BITTERN; HERON, etc.).

C. H. S.

KIR (kir), (Heb. קִיר, *keer,* fortress), a people and country subject to the Assyrian empire, to which the conquered Damascenes were transplanted (2 Kings xvi:9; Is. xxii:6; Amos i:5), and whither also the Aramæans in the east of Syria once wandered (Amos ix:7).

This is supposed by Major Rennel to be the same country which still bears the name of *Kur*distan or *Kour*distan (*Geog. of Herodot.* 391).

Objections. There are, however, objections to this view, which do not apply so strongly to the notion of Rosenmüller and others, that it was a tract on the river Cyrus, or rather Kuros (Κῦρος and Κύῤῥος), in Zend Koro, which rises in the mountains between the Euxine and Caspian Seas, and runs into the latter after being joined by the Araxes. *Gur*jistan, or Grusia (Grusiana), commonly called Georgia, seems also to have derived its name from this river Kur, which flows through it. Furrer's identification with the district Cyrrhestica, northwest of Antioch, lacks proof.

KIR-HARASETH (kir'hăr'a-sĕth), (Heb. קִיר חֲרֶשֶׂת, *keer-khar-eh'seth*, 2 Kings iii:25; "Kir-hareseth," Is. xvi:7; "Kir-haresh," xvi:11; "Kir-heres," Jer. xlviii:31, 36; and "Kir of Moab," Is. xv:1). See KIR OF MOAB and KIR-MOAB.

KIR-HARESETH (kir'hăr'e-sĕth), (Heb. קִיר חֲרֶשֶׂת, *keer-khar-eh'seth*, Is. xvi:7). See KIR-HARASETH, KIR OF MOAB and KIR-MOAB.

KIR-HARESH (kir'hā'resh), (Is. xvi:11). See KIR-MOAB.

KIR-HERES (kir-hē'res), (Jer. xlviii:31, 36). See KIR-MOAB.

KIRIATH (kir'i-ath). See KIRJATH.

KIRIATHAIM (kir'i-a-thā'im), (Heb. קִרְיָתַיִם, *keer-yaw-thah'yim*), a town beyond Jordan, ten miles from Medaba, west (Josh. xiii:19). It is the same as KIRJATHAIM (which see).

KIRIOTH (kir'i-ŏth). See KERIOTH.

KIRJATH (kir'jath), (Heb. קִרְיַת, *keer-yath'*, city). This word means *town* or *city,* and is much used in the formation of names of places, like our own *town.*

It is also the name of a place in the tribe of Benjamin (Josh. xviii:28). It is probably identical with Kirjath-Jearim (Josh. xv:9, 60; xviii: 14).

KIRJATHAIM (kir'ja-thā'im), (Heb. קִרְיָתַיִם, *keer-yaw-thah'yim,* double town).

1. One of the most ancient towns in the country east of the Jordan, as it was possessed by the gigantic Emim (Gen. xiv:5), who were expelled by the Moabites (Deut. ii:9, 10), who in their turn were dispossessed by the Amorites, from whom it was taken by the Israelites. Kirjathaim was then assigned to Reuben (Num. xxxii:37; Josh. xiii:19). But during the Assyrian

exile, the Moabites again took possession of this and other towns (Jer. xlviii:1-23; Ezek. xxv: 9). Eusebius places it about half an hour west of the ruins of Medeba. Burckhardt found other ruins, called *El Teym*, which he conjectures to have been Kiria*thaim*, the last syllable of the name being retained. This is somewhat doubtful, as the Καριάδα (Καριάθα) of Eusebius is placed ten miles west of Medeba, whereas El Teym is but two miles. Harper and others identified it with the ruins of El Kŭreiyât, between Medeba and Dibon.

2. There was another place of this name in the tribe of Naphtali (1 Chron. vi:76).

KIRJATH-ARBA (kĭr'jath-är'bȧ), (Heb. קִרְיַת אַרְבַּע, *keer-yath' ar-bah'*, city of Arbah), the ancient name of Hebron, but still in use in the time of Nehemiah (xi:25). (See HEBRON.)

that the ancient Kirjath-jearim may be recognized in the present Kuriet-el-Enab.

(2) Name and Position. So close a correspondence of name and position seems to warrant the conclusion of Dr. Robinson in favor of Kuriet-el-Enab. This place is that which ecclesiastical tradition has identified with the Anathoth of Jeremiah, which Dr. Robinson refers to Anata (see ANATHOTH). It is now a poor village, its principal buildings being an old convent of the Minorites, and a Latin church. The latter is now deserted, but not in ruins, and is said to be one of the largest and most solidly constructed churches in Palestine (Robinson, ii, 109; 334-337). Conder argues for the ruins 'Erma, 11 miles west by south of Jerusalem, and two and a quarter south by west of Kesla. But contrary to his opinion Josh. xv:10 is surely against the location pro-

Kirjath-jearim.

KIRJATH-ARIM (kĭr'jath-ä'rim), an abbreviated form of KIRJATH-JEARIM (Ezra ii:25), which see.

KIRJATH-BAAL (kĭr'jath-bā'al), (Heb. קִרְיַת בַּעַל, *keer-yath' bah'al*, city of Baal). This city is more usually called KIRJATH-JEARIM (Josh. xv:60; xviii:14).

KIRJATH-HUZOTH (kĭr'jath-hū'zoth), (Heb. קִרְיַת חֻצוֹת, *keer-yath' khoo-tsoth'*, city of streets), a town in Moab (Num. xxii:39), to which Balak accompanied Balaam after his arrival in Moab. The place has not been identified, though it lay between the Arnon and Bamoth-Baal.

KIRJATH-JEARIM (kĭr'jath-jē'a-rĭm), (Heb. קִרְיַת יְעָרִים, *keer-yath' yeh-aw-reem'*, city of forests).

One of the towns of the Gibeonites (Josh. ix: 17). It was to this place that the ark was brought from Bethshemesh, after it had been removed from the land of the Philistines, and where it remained till removed to Jerusalem by David (1 Sam. vii.; 1 Chron. xiii.).

(1) Ancient Site. This was one of the ancient sites which were again inhabited after the exile (Ezra ii:25; Neh. vii:29). Eusebius and Jerome speak of it as being in their day a village nine or ten miles from Diospolis (Lydda), on the road to Jerusalem. Dr. Robinson thinks it possible

posed by him. 'Erma and Jearim are also radically different, and the site is too remote from the other Gibeonite settlements.

KIRJATH-SANNAH (kĭr'jath-săn'nah), (Heb. קִרְיַת סַנָּה, *keer-yath' san-naw'*, Josh. xv:49), and

KIRJATH-SEPHER (kĭr'jath-sē'pher), (Heb. קִרְיַת סֵפֶר, *keer-yath' say'fer*, both meaning the city of books, or instruction), a city of the tribe of Judah, called also DEBIR (Josh. xv:15, 16; Judg. i:11, 12). (See DEBIR.)

It was situated among the mountains of Judah. It was captured by Joshua and was given to Caleb. It was retaken by the Canaanites only to be captured again by the Israelites, who were led in the attack by Othniel, to whom Caleb for his reward gave his daughter Achsah in marriage (Josh. xv: 15; Judg. i:11).

This city was so called long before Moses; at least it would seem so by the manner of mentioning it, which proves that books were known before that legislator, and that he is not the oldest writer, as the fathers have asserted; a character which, it is to be observed, he never assumes.

It is possible that the Canaanites might lodge their records in this city, and those few monuments of antiquity which they had preserved; or it might be something like the cities of the priests in Israel, the residence of the learned; a kind of college.

This idea receives confirmation from its other name *Debir*, which designates an oracle; and seems to hint at a seat of learning; an establishment, probably, of priests, for the purpose of educating the younger members of their body. The circumstance is very remarkable, because it occurs so early as the days of Joshua; and is evidently an establishment by the Canaanites, previous to the Hebrew invasion.

KIR-MOAB (kĭr-mō'ab), (Heb. קִיר־מוֹאָב, *keer-mo-awb'*, the wall, stronghold, or citadel of Moab), (Is. xv:i), called also KIR-HARESETH and KIR-HERES, meaning brick-fortress (Is. xvi:7, 11; Jer. xlviii:31), a fortified city in the territory of Moab.

Joram king of Israel took the city, and destroyed it, except the walls; but it appears from the passages here cited that it must have been rebuilt before the time of Isaiah.

(1) Fortified Town. Abulfeda describes Karak as a small town, with a castle on a high hill, and remarks that it is so strong that one must deny himself even the wish to take it by force.

(2) During the Crusades. In the time of the Crusades, and when in possession of the Franks, it was invested by Saladin; but after lying before it a month he was compelled to raise the siege (Bohaeddim, *Vita Saladin*, p. 55).

(3) Modern Condition. The first person who visited the place in modern times was Seetzen, who says, 'Near to Karak the wide plain terminates which extends from Rabbah, and is broken only by low and detached hills, and the country now becomes mountainous.

'Karak, formerly a city and bishop's see, lies on the top of the hill near the end of a deep valley, and is surrounded on all sides with lofty mountains. The hill is very steep, and in many places the sides are quite perpendicular. The walls round the town are for the most part destroyed, and Karak can at present boast of little more than being a small country town. The castle, which is uninhabited, and in a state of great decay, was formerly one of the strongest in these countries. The inhabitants of the town consist of Mohammedans and Greek Christians. The present bishop of Karak resides at Jerusalem.'

(4) The Hill of Karak. 'From this place one enjoys, by looking down the Wady Karak, a fine view of part of the Dead Sea, and even Jerusalem may be distinctly seen in clear weather. The hill on which Karak lies is composed of limestone and brittle marl, with many beds of blue, black, and gray flints. In the neighboring rocks there are a number of curious grottoes; in those which are under ground wheat is sometimes preserved for a period of ten years' (Zach's *Monatliche Correspond*. xviii, 434). A fuller account of the place is given by Burckhardt (*Travels in Syria*, pp. 379-387), by whom it was next visited; and another description is furnished by Irby and Mangles (*Travels*, pp. 361-370). From their account it would seem that the caverns noticed by Seetzen were probably the sepulchers of the ancient town. We also learn that the Christians of Karak (which they and Burckhardt call Kerek), are nearly as numerous as the Turks, and boast of being stronger and braver. They were, however, on good terms with the Turks, and appeared to enjoy equal freedom with them.

As the Rev. J. L. Porter surveyed the country of Moab from this eminence as well as from other lofty summits he was led to exclaim: How literal and how true have the words of Jeremiah become! "*O vine of Sibmah, I will weep for thee with the weeping of Jazer: . . . . the spoiler is fallen upon thy summer fruits, and upon thy vintage. And joy and gladness is taken from the plentiful field, and from the land of Moab; and I have caused wine to fail from the wine-presses; none shall tread with shouting*" (Jer. xlviii:32, 33). Nowhere on earth is there such a melancholy example of tyranny, rapacity, and misrule, as here. Fields, pastures, vineyards, houses, villages, cities—all alike deserted and waste. (*Giant Cities of Bashan*.)

KISH (kĭsh), (Heb. קִישׁ, *keesh*, a bow or horn).

1. Son of Ner, and father of king Saul (1 Sam. ix:1; 1 Chron. viii:33; ix:38, 39).

This genealogy may indeed merely register the fact that Kish was a descendant of Ner, without implying that he was his immediate son; and allow of the insertion of Abiel and others between Kish and Ner.

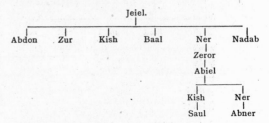

But perhaps only one Kish and one Ner descended from Jeiel. If so, the explanation of the genealogy is that Ner's descendants became two tribal houses, those of Kish and Ner. The former, the important royal family of Saul, looked to Ner's son Kish as its founder, but it was merely a younger branch of the older, but less distinguished, line of Ner. Both houses belonged to the family of Jeiel, and hence Kish as well as Ner is registered, according to the familiar principle, among Jeiel's sons (ix:36). Saul's father, Kish, and Abner's father, Ner, are mentioned as sons of Abiel also (1 Sam. ix:1; xiv: 51), and either Ner or Abner is stated to have been Saul's uncle (xiv:50). Abiel may be, as some expositors suppose, or may not be, another name or the uncorrupted form of Jeiel. (B. C. about 1060.) (Davis, *Bib. Dict.*)

2. Son of Jeiel, and uncle of **1** (1 Chron. ix:36). (B. C. about 1060.)

3. A Benjamite, and great-grandfather of Mordecai, who was carried captive to Babylon (Esth. ii:5). (B. C. before 478.)

4. The son of Abdi, a Levite of Merari's family (2 Chron. xxix:12), and one who assisted Hezekiah in restoring the tribe religion.

5. Second son of Mahli; his sons married the daughters of his brother Eleazar (1 Chron. xxiii: 21, 22). One son was named Jerahmeel (1 Chron. xxiv:29). (B. C. about 1060.)

KISHI (kĭsh'ī), a Merarite, father or forefather of Ethan the minstrel (1 Chron. vi:44). He is called Kushaiah (1 Chron. xv:17). (See KUSHAIAH.)

KISHION (kĭsh'i-ŏn), (Heb. קִשְׁיוֹן, *kish-yone'*, hard ground), a city of the tribe of Issachar, yielded to the Levites of Gershom's family (Josh. xix:20; xxi:28). In the latter passage the A. V. has Kishon incorrectly, as the Hebrew is the same in both. It is also incorrectly called Kedesh (1 Chron. vi:72).

KISHON (kĭ'shon), (Heb. קִישׁוֹן, *kee-shone'*, winding). The incorrect form of Kishion (Josh. xxi:28). In I Chron. vi:72, the name Kedesh appears in its place in the lists.

The most important river in Palestine next to the Jordan. After traversing the plain of Acre, it enters the bay of the same name at its southeast corner. It is celebrated in Scripture for the overthrow of the host of Sisera in its overflowing stream (Judg. iv:13; v:21).

(1) Source of the River. It has been usual to trace the source of this river to Mount Tabor; but Dr. Shaw affirms that in traveling along the southeastern brow of Mount Carmel he had an opportunity of seeing the sources of the river Kishon, three or four of which lie within less than a furlong of each other, and are called Ras el Kishon, or the head of the Kishon. These alone, without the lesser contributions near the sea, discharge water enough to form a river half as large as the Isis.

During the rainy season all the waters which fall upon the eastern side of Carmel, or upon the rising grounds to the southward, empty themselves into it in a number of torrents, at which time it overflows its banks, acquires a wonderful rapidity, and carries all before it.

It was doubtless in such a season that the host of Sisera was swept away, in attempting to ford it. But such inundations are only occasional, and of short duration, as is indeed implied in the destruction in its waters of the fugitives, who doubtless expected to pass it safely.

The course of the stream, as estimated from the sources thus indicated, is not more than seven miles. It runs very briskly till within half a league of the sea; but when not augmented by rains, it never falls into the sea in a full stream, but insensibly percolates through a bank of sand, which the north winds have thrown up at its mouth. It was in this state that Shaw himself found it in the month of April, 1722, when it was crossed by him.

Notwithstanding Shaw's contradiction, the assertion that the Kishon derives its source from Mount Tabor has been repeated by modern travelers as confidently as by their ancient predecessors.

It will probably be found that the remoter source of the river is really in Mount Tabor; but that the supply from this source is cut off in early summer, when it ceases to be maintained by rains or contributory torrents. The copious supply from the nearer springs at Ras el Kishon, with other springs lower down, keep it up from that point, as a perennial stream, even during the drought of summer. Thus during one part of the year the source of the river may appear to be in Mount Tabor, while during another part the source of the diminished stream is at Ras el Kishon.

(2) Overthrow of Sisera. The scriptural account of the overthrow of Sisera's host manifestly shows that the stream crossed the plain, and must have been of considerable size. The above arguments, to show that it did so, and still does so, notwithstanding Dr. Shaw's account, were, in substance, given several years ago in the *Pictorial History of Palestine* (Introd. p. cxci.); and the writer has had the satisfaction of seeing his view since confirmed by Dr. Robinson, who adds that 'not improbably, in ancient times, when the country was perhaps more wooded, there may have been *permanent* streams throughout the whole plain.'

(3) Priests of Baal. The transaction of the prophet Elijah, who, after his sacrifice on Carmel, commanded the priests of Baal to be slain at the river Kishon (I Kings xviii:40), requires no explanation, seeing that it took place at the perennial lower stream. This also explains, what has sometimes been asked, whence, in that time of drought, the water was obtained with which the prophet inundated his altar and sacrifice.

The spot where the priests of Baal were slain was near the foot of Mount Carmel. The location has been almost certainly identified at the east end of the mountain. The place still bears the name *El-Mahraka "the burning."*

KISHUIM (kĭsh-ū-ĭm'), (Heb. קִשֻּׁאִים, *kish-shoo-eem'*), is translated *cucumbers* in the A. V., and the correctness of this rendering has been almost universally admitted.

It first occurs in Num. xi:5, in the verse already quoted in Abattachim, where the Israelites, when in the desert, express their longings for the melons and the *kishuim* or cucumbers of Egypt. Reduced from the plural form, the word *kisha* is so similar to the Arabic *kissa*, that there can be very little doubt of their both meaning the same

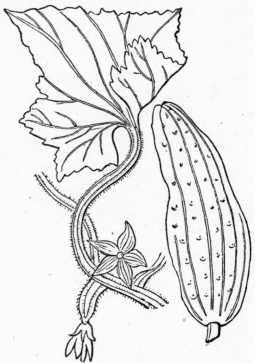

Cucumber (*Cucumis sativus*).

thing. All travelers in the East notice the extensive cultivation and consumption of cucumbers and other vegetables of the same tribe, especially where there is any moisture of soil, or the possibility of irrigation.

Thus even in the driest parts, the neighborhood of a well is often occupied by a field of cucurbitaceous plants, generally with a man or boy set to guard it from plunder, perched up on a temporary scaffolding, with a slight protection from the sun, where he may himself be safe from the attacks of the more powerful wild animals.

That such plants appear to have been similarly cultivated among the Hebrews is evident from Is. i:8, 'The daughter of Zion is left like a cottage in a vineyard, like a lodge in a garden of cucumbers;' as well as from Baruch vi:70, 'As a scarecrow in a garden of cucumbers keepeth nothing, so are their gods of wood.' (See ABAT-TACHIM; CUCUMBER.) J. F. R.

KISON (kī'son), an incorrect form of Kishon (Ps. lxxxiii:9). (See KISHON).

KISS (kĭs), (Heb. נָשַׁק, *naw-shak'*; Gr. φίλημα *fil'ay-mah*). Kissing the lips by way of affectionate salutation was customary among near relatives of both sexes, both in patriarchal and in later times (Gen. xxix:11; Cant. viii:1).

Originally the act of kissing had a symbolical character, and, though this import may now be lost sight of, yet it must be recognized the moment we attempt to understand or explain its signification.

(1) Significance of Action. Acts speak no less, sometimes far more forcibly than words. In the early period of society, when the foundation was laid of most even of our Western customs, action constituted a large portion of what we may term human language, or the means of intercommunication between man and man. Words were then less numerous, books unknown, the entire machinery of speaking being, in its rudimental and elementary state, less developed and called into play. The Oriental character inclined men to general taciturnity, with occasional outbreaks of fervid, abrupt, or copious eloquence. In this language of action, a kiss was naturally the expression and the symbol of affection, regard, respect, and reverence; and if any deeper source of its origin were sought for, it would, doubtless, be found in the fondling and caresses with which the mother expresses her tenderness for her babe.

(2) Biblical Allusions. That the custom is of very early date appears from Gen. xxix:13, where we read—'When Laban heard of the tidings of Jacob, his sister's son, he ran to meet him, and embraced him and kissed him, and brought him to his house': the practice was even then established and recognized as a matter of course.

In Gen. xxvii:26, 27, a kiss is a sign of affection between a parent and a child. It was also, as with some modern nations, a token of friendship and regard bestowed when friends or relations met or separated (Tobit vii:6; x:12; Luke vii:45; xv:20; Acts xx:37; Matt. xxvi:48; 2 Sam. xx:9). The church of Ephesus wept sore at Paul's departure, and fell on his neck and kissed him. When Orpah quitted Naomi and Ruth (Ruth i: 14), after the three had lifted up their voice and wept, she 'kissed her mother-in-law, but Ruth clave unto her.' It was usual to kiss the mouth (Gen. xxxiii:4; Exod. iv:27; xviii:7; 1 Sam. xx: 41; Prov. xxiv:26) or the beard, which was then taken hold of by the hand (2 Sam. xx:9). Kissing of the feet was an expression of lowly and tender regard (Luke vii:38).

(3) Idolatrous Usage. Kissing of the hand of another appears to be an ancient practice: the passage of Job xxxi:27, 'Or my mouth hath kissed my hand,' is not in point, and refers to idolatrous usages, namely, the adoration of the heavenly bodies. It was the custom to throw kisses towards the images of the gods, and towards the sun and moon (1 Kings xix:18; Hosea xiii:2; Minuc. Felix, ii, 5; Tac. *Hist.* iii, 24, 3; Lucian, *De Salt.* c. 17; Plin. *Hist. Nat.* xxviii, 5).

(4) Salutation of Princes. The kissing of princes was a token of homage (Ps. ii:12; 1 Sam. x:1; Xenoph. *Cyrop.* vii, 5, 32). Xenophon says (*Agesil.* v, 4) that it was a natural custom with the Persians to kiss whomsoever they honored; and a curious passage to this effect may be found in the *Cyropædia* (i, 4, 27). Kissing the feet of

princes was a token of subjection and obedience; which was sometimes carried so far that the print of the foot received the kiss, so as to give the impression that the very dust had become sacred by the royal tread, or that the subject was not worthy to salute even the prince's foot, but was content to kiss the earth itself near or on which he trod (Is. xlix:23; Micah vii:17; Ps. lxxii:9; Dion Cass. lix, 27; Seneca, *De Benef.* ii, 12).

(5) Limited by the Rabbins. The Rabbins, in the meddlesome, scrupulous, and falsely delicate spirit which animated much of what they wrote, did not permit more than three kinds of kisses, the kiss of reverence, of reception, and of dismissal (Breschith Rabba *on Gen.* xxix:11).

(6) Custom of Primitive Church. The peculiar tendency of the Christian religion to encourage honor toward all men, as men, to foster and develop the softer affections, and, in the trying condition of the early church, to make its members intimately known one to another, and unite them in the closest bonds, led to the observance of kissing as an accompaniment of that social worship which took its origin in the very cradle of our religion. Hence the exhortation—'Salute each other with a holy kiss' (Rom. xvi:16; see also 1 Cor. xvi:20; 2 Cor. xiii:12; 1 Thess. v:26; in 1 Pet. v:14, it is termed 'a kiss of charity'). The observance was continued in later days, and has not yet wholly disappeared, though the peculiar circumstances have vanished which gave propriety and emphasis to such an expression of brotherly love and Christian friendship.

(7) Literature. Pfanner, *De Osculis Christianor. Veter.;* M. Kempius, *De Osculis,* Francof. 1680; Jac. Herrenschmidius, *Osculogia,* Viteb. 1630; P. Muller, *De Osculo Sancto.* 1674; Boberg, *De Osculis Hebr.* J. R. B.

KITE (kīt). See GLEDE.

KITHLISH (kĭth'lish), (Heb. כִּתְלִישׁ, *kith-leesh'*, wall of man), a city of Judah (Josh. xv:40) in the low country. It has not been identified. Called Chillish in R. V.

KITRON (kĭt'ron), (Heb. קִטְרוֹן, *kit-rone'*, figurative, knotty), a city of Zebulun, which that tribe could not take from the Canaanites (Judg. i:30). Kitron is Sippor, (Sepphoris,) says Bab. Megill. (fol. 6, 1,) a very strong place, and the largest city in Galilee. It is noted in the Talmuds for being a university; in which taught rabbi Judah the Holy, who died here.

KITTIM (kĭt'tim), (Heb. כִּתִּי, *kit-tee'*, כִּתִּיִּי, *kit-tee-ee'*, an islander), son of Javan, and grandson of Noah (Gen. x:4). (See CHITTIM OR KITTIM.)

KNEAD (nēd), (Heb. לוּשׁ, *loosh*), the preparation of dough by working it into a mass with the hands. Kneading was generally performed by women (Gen. xviii:6; 1 Sam. xxviii:24; 2 Sam. xiii: 8, etc.), but occasionally by men (Hos. vii:4). (See BREAD).

KNEADING-TROUGHS (nēd-ĭng-trŏfs), (Heb. מִשְׁאֶרֶת, *mish-eh'reth*). In the description of the departure of the Israelites from Egypt, (Exod. xii: 34) we read that "the people took their dough before it was leavened, their kneading-troughs being bound up in their clothes, upon their shoulders."

Persons who know how cumbersome kneading troughs were, and how much less important they were than many other utensils, may wonder at this statement, and find a difficulty in accounting for it. But this wonder will cease, when it is understood that the vessels which the Arabs make use of, for kneading the unleavened cakes they prepare for those who travel in the very desert through which Israel passed, are only small wooden bowls; and that they seem to use no other in their own tents for that purpose, or any other; these bowls being used by them for kneading their bread, and serving up their provisions when cooked. It will appear, that nothing could be more convenient than kneading troughs of this sort for the Israelites in their journey.

Besides, Dr. Pococke gives us a description of a round leather cover, which the Arabs lay on the ground, from which they eat. This piece of furniture has, he says, rings round it by which it is drawn together with a chain, that has a hook to it, to hang it by. It is drawn together, and in this manner they bring it full of bread, and when the repast is over, carry it away at once, with all that is left. Perhaps this utensil is rather to be understood by the word translated kneading-troughs, than the Arab wooden bowl. There is nothing, in the other three places in which the word occurs, to contradict this explanation. These places are Exod. viii:3; Deut. xxviii:5 and 17; in the last two of which places it is translated *store.* (See BREAD.)

KNEE (nē), (Heb. and Chald. בֶּרֶךְ, *beh'rek ;* Gr. γονύ, *gon-oo'*); **KNEEL** (Heb. בָּרַךְ, *baw-rak ;* Gr. γονυπετέω, *gon-oo-pet-eh'o,* to bend the knee).

Knee not only signifies that part of the body so called, but the whole body, a part being put for the whole (Ps. cix:24). Also for persons; so *weak* and *feeble knees* denote weak and disconsolate persons (Job iv:4; Heb. xii:12; Is. xxxv:3). To bow the knee to one, imports adoration of, or prayer to him (1 Kings xix:18; Eph. iii:14); or to reverence and be in subjection to him (Gen. xli:43; Phil. ii:10). To bring up, or *dandle on the knees,* is affectionately to nourish, as a mother does her own child (Gen. xxx:3 and l:23; Is. lxvi:12). The *smiting of the knees* one against another is expressive of extraordinary terror and amazement (Dan. v:6).

Figurative. Knees are used symbolically for *persons* (Job iv:4; Heb. xii:12).

KNIFE (nīf), (Heb. חֶרֶב, *khee-reb',* sword).

(1) Uses. In their meals the Jews, like other Orientals, made little use of knives, but they were used largely in the preparation of meats and other food, also in preparation of their sacrifices (Gen. xxii:6, 10; 1 Sam. ix:24; Jer. xxxvi:23; Ezek. xxiv:4; Ezra i:9; Matt. xxvi:23). The razor was used frequently for Nazaritic purposes (Num. vi:5, 9, 19; Ezek. v:1; Is. vii:20; Jer. xxxvi:23; Acts xviii:18; xxi:24).

Pruning-hooks were probably curved knives (Is. xviii:5), while the lancets of the priests of Baal were doubtless pointed knives (1 Kings xviii:28).

(2) Material. Knives were generally made of flint (Josh. v:2) and afterwards of iron and steel. The Egyptians when embalming a corpse, used a sharp stone knife for making an incision in the body (Herod. ii:86). The Hebrew scribes sharpened the stylus with a small knife (Jer. xxxvi:23). Herod the Great was accustomed to use a knife for paring fruit, and attempted to kill himself with it (*Antiq.* xvii, 7, 1). These were of metal construction.

KNOCK (nŏk), (Heb. דָפַק, *daw-fak' ;* Gr. κρούω, *kroo'o ;* Cant. v:2, Judg. xix:22, "beat;" Matt. vii:7; Rev. iii:20, etc.).

Missionaries in Oriental countries state that, as in ancient times, Orientals never knock when

about to enter a room, but without warning or ceremony walk in. For scriptural references to knocking in the ordinary sense, see Deut. xxiv: 10; Acts xii:13, 16; Acts x:17, 18.

Figurative. Jesus *knocks* at the door of our hearts; by his word, Spirit, and providence, he awakens, invites, and urges us to receive himself as the free gift of God, the Savior come to seek and save that which is lost (Rev. iii:20; Cant. v:2). Our *knocking* at his door of mercy, is fervent and frequent prayer for his distinguished presence and favors (Matt. vii:7, 8; Luke xi:10). (Brown, *Bib. Dict.*)

KNOP (nŏp), (Heb. כַּפְתּוֹר, *kaf-tore,* a chaplet), that is knob, a word used to translate two terms referring to some architectural object or ornament.

1. *Kaf-tore',* (Heb. כַּפְתּוֹר, a chaplet), (Ex. xxv: 31, 36; xxxvii:17, 22), where the knops are distinguished from the shaft, branches, bowls, and flowers of the candlestick. In Amos ix:1, the same word is translated "lintel," as also in Zeph. ii:14.

2. *Peh-kah'im,* (Heb. פְּקָעִים, (1 Kings vi:18; vii: 24). In the first passage it refers to the carvings on the wainscot of the Temple; in the second, to an ornament cast around the great reservoir of Solomon. The word, no doubt, signifies some round or oval shaped object used in ornamentation.

KNOW (nō), (Heb. יָדַע, *yaw-dah' ;* Gr. γινώσκω, *ghin-oce'ko,* each having a great variety of meaning). Both terms denote *coming to know,* i. e., *gaining a knowledge ;* and *to know,* i. e., *to have knowledge of.* The verb *yawdah* signifies to *perceive, discern, become aware of.*

Know in general signifies: (1) To understand; to perceive (Ruth iii:11). (2) To have the experience of (2 Cor. v:21). (3) To acknowledge, to take particular notice, to approve, delight in, and show distinguished regard to (Is. lv:5; 1 Cor. viii:3; John x:27; Amos iii:2; Gen. xxxix:6; 1 Thess. v:12). (4) To make known, and see discovered (1 Cor. ii:2). (5) To have carnal dealing with (Gen. iv:1 and xix:5; Judg. xix:22). *I know nothing by myself,* means I am not conscious of any allowed wickedness (2 Cor. iv:4). We *make known* our requests unto God, when directed by his Spirit, we express the desires of our hearts in prayer to him (Phil. iv:6). *He that perverteth his way is known,* when God exposes him to shame and punishment on account of it (Prov. x:9).

KNOWLEDGE (nŏl'ĕj), (Heb. דֵעָה, *day-aw'*). The word denotes:

1. The infinite understanding of God, by which he perfectly perceives and comprehends himself, and all things possible or real (1 Sam. ii:3).

2. A speculative knowledge, by which a man has a merely rational perception of things natural or Divine, without any faith in, or love to God produced or strengthened by it (1 Cor. viii:1; Rom. i:28; Eccl. i:18).

3. A spiritual reception of Divine things, by which, through the instruction of God's word and Spirit, we not only perceive, but are powerfully and sweetly disposed to believe in and love God in Christ as our God (2 Cor. vi:6; John xvii:3).

4. The supernatural gift of interpreting dreams, explaining hard passages of Scripture, or foreseeing things to come (Dan. v:12; 1 Cor. xiii:2).

5. Spiritual prudence, and gracious experience in the ways of God (Prov. xxviii:2).

6. The perfect and immediate views of the glory of God in heaven; in this we *know God,*

as we are known; apprehend his existence, and glorious excellencies and work, without any mistake (1 Cor. xiii:12).

7. Instruction, whereby *knowledge is communicated* (Prov. xxii:17).

8. Faith is called *"knowledge,"* as it is supposed knowledge, and is an apprehending of things invisible, on the testimony of God (Is. liii:11), but the text may also mean, that by Jesus' infinitely skillful fulfillment of his work, he shall justify many. **(a)** Saints are enriched with *"all knowledge;"* they are made wise unto salvation, and know everything important concerning it (Rom. xv:14; 1 Cor. i:5; 1 John ii:20). **(b)** *"Through knowledge"* the just shall be delivered; by the infinite wisdom of God, and by means of their faith, spiritual knowledge, and prudence, shall they escape trouble, or get out of it (Prov. xi:9).

KOA (kō'a), (Heb. קוֹעַ, *ko'ah,* perhaps cutting off). Gesenius (*Heb. Lex.,* s. v.) says that "Koa is a *he-camel, stallion,* then figuratively a *prince, noble.*"

It occurs only in Ezek. xxiii:23 and is applied to a people named between Babylonians and Assyrians, located by Friedrich Delitzsch east of the Tigris, south of the lower Zab. The passage reads: "The Babylonians, and all the Chaldeans, Pekod and Shoa, and Koa, and all the Assyrians with them." In the last three words "there is some obscurity, which the older theologians have almost unanimously taken to be the names of different tribes in the Chaldean empire. Ewald also adopts this view, but it is certainly incorrect" (Keil, *Com.* in loc.).

KOHATH (kō'hath), (Heb. קְהָת, *keh-hawth',* allied, assembly), the second son of Levi (Gen. xlvi:11), and father of Amram, Izhar, Hebron, and Uzziel (Num. iii:19).

He went down to Egypt with Levi and Jacob (Gen. xlvi:11). His sister was Jochebed (Exod. vi:20). He lived to the age of one hundred and thirty-three years (Exod. vi:18). (B. C. about 2000.) At the first census in the wilderness, the Kohathite males from a month old and upward were 8,600 (Num. iii:28), and those from thirty to fifty years old 2,750 (Num. iv:34-37). In the subsequent allotment of cities to the family, the priests, the descendants of Aaron, had shares with the other Kohathites, the former obtaining thirteen cities out of the tribes of Judah, Simeon, and Benjamin, and the latter ten cities out of the tribes of Ephraim, Dan, and Manasseh (Josh. xxi: 4, 5; 1 Chron. vi:61, 66-70). In the service of the tabernacle, as settled in the wilderness, the Kohathites had the distinguished charge of bearing the ark and the sacred vessels (Exod. vi:16; Num. iv:4-6).

KOHATHITES (kō'hath-ītes), (Heb. קְהָתִי, *kaw-hawth'ee*), Num. xxvi:57; 1 Chron. vi:54; ix:32; descendants of KOHATH.

KOLAIAH (kŏl'a-ī'ah), (Heb. קֹלָיָה, *ko-law-yaw',* voice of Jehovah).

1. A Benjamite whose descendants lived in Jerusalem after the return from the captivity (Neh. xi:7). (B. C. long before 445.)

2. Father of Ahab, who was burnt by the king of Babylon (Jer. xxix:21). (B. C. about 626.)

KOPH (kōf).

The nineteenth letter of the Hebrew alphabet. English Q comes from the same source; but in anglicized Hebrew names "c" or "k" represents it, as in Cain and Korah. It heads the nineteenth

section of Ps. cxix., in which section each verse of the original begins with this letter.

KOPHER or COPHER (kō'pher), (Heb. כֹּפֶר, *kô-fer'*), occurs twice in Canticles, and is in both places translated *camphire* in the Authorized Version.

(1) Camphor. Thus (i:14), 'My beloved is unto me as a cluster of *camphire (kopher)* in the vineyards of En-gedi;' and in iv:13, 'Thy plants are an orchard of pomegranates, with pleasant fruits, *camphire (kopher),* with spikenard.' It has been supposed to indicate a bunch of grapes (*Botrus kopher*), also *camphor.* The word *camphire* is the old mode of spelling *camphor,* but this substance does not appear to have been known to ancient commerce; at least we cannot adduce any proof that it was so. The word *Kopher* is certainly very like *Kafoor,* the Eastern name for *camphor,* but it also closely resembles the Greek κύπρος, *Cypros.* Indeed, as has been observed, it is the same word, with the Greek pronunciation and termination. The κύπρος of the Greeks is, no doubt, the *Lawsonia inermis* of botanists, and is described by Dioscorides (i, 125) and by Pliny (xii, 24). The Turks and

Camphor (*Lawsonia inermis*).

Moors cultivate these with great care and diligence, because of their sweet-smelling flowers. They also keep their leaves all winter, which leaves they powder and mix with the juice of citrons, and stain therewith on great holidays the hair and nails of their children of a red color, which color may perhaps be seen on the manes and tails of Turkish horses.

(2) Henna. This custom of dyeing the nails and the palms of the hands and soles of the feet, of an iron-rust color, with *henna,* exists throughout the East, from the Mediterranean to the Ganges, as well as in northern Africa. In some parts the practice is not confined to women and children, but is also followed by men, especially in Persia. In dyeing the beard, the hair is turned to red by this application, which is then changed to black by a preparation of indigo. In dyeing the hair of children, and the tails and manes of horses and asses, the process is allowed to stop at the red color which the *henna* produces. Seeing, then, that the *henna* is so universally admired in the East, both on account of the fragrance of its flowers and the dye yielded by its leaves, and as there is no doubt that it is the κύπρος of the Greeks, and as this word is so similar to the *kopher* of the Hebrews, there is every probability of this last being the *henna* of the Arabs, *Lawsonia alba* of botanists.

J. F. R.

KORAH (kō'rah), (Heb. קֹרַח, *ko'rakh*, ice).

1. A Levite, son of Izhar, the brother of Amram, the father of Moses and Aaron, who were therefore cousins to Korah (Exod. vi:21).

(1) Jealousy. From this near relationship we may conjecture that the source of the discontent which led to the steps afterwards taken by this unhappy man lay in his jealousy that the high honors and privileges of the priesthood, to which he, who remained a simple Levite, might, apart from the Divine appointment, seem to have had as good a claim, should have been exclusively appropriated to the family of Aaron. When to this was added the civil authority of Moses, the whole power over the nation would seem to him to have been engrossed by his cousins, the sons of Amram.

(2) Conspiracy. Under the influence of these feelings he organized a conspiracy for the purpose of redressing what appeared to him the evil and injustice of this arrangement. Dathan, Abiram, and On, the chief persons who joined him, were of the tribe of Reuben; but he was also supported by many more from other tribes, making up the number of two hundred and fifty, men of name, rank, and influence, all who may be regarded as representing the families of which they were the heads.

(3) Ostensible Object. The private object of Korah was apparently his own aggrandizement, but his ostensible object was the general good of the people; and it is perhaps from want of attention to this distinction that the transaction has not been well understood. The design seems to have been made acceptable to a large body of the nation, on the ground that the firstborn of Israel had been deprived of their sacerdotal birthright in favor of the Levites, while the Levites themselves announced that the priesthood had been conferred by Moses (as they considered) on his own brother's family, in preference to those who had equal claims; and it is easy to conceive that the Reubenites may have considered the opportunity a favorable one for the recovery of their birthright—the double portion and civil pre-eminence—which had been forfeited by them and given to Joseph.

(4) Complaint. The leading conspirators, having organized their plans, repaired in a body to Moses and Aaron, boldly charged them with their usurpations, and required them to lay down their ill-gotten power. Moses no sooner heard this than he fell on his face, confounded at the enormity of so outrageous a revolt against a system framed so carefully for the benefit of the nation. He left the matter in the Lord's hands, and desired them to come on the morrow, provided with censers for incense, that the Lord himself, by some manifest token, might make known his will in this great matter. As this order was particularly addressed to the rebellious Levites, the Reubenites left the place, and when afterwards called back by Moses, returned a very insolent refusal, charging him with having brought them out of the land of Egypt under false pretences, 'to kill them in the wilderness.'

(5) Destruction. The next day Korah and his company appeared before the tabernacle, attended by a multitude of people out of the general body of the tribes. Then the Shekinah, or symbol of the Divine presence, which abode between the cherubim, advanced to the entrance of the sacred fabric, and a voice therefrom commanded Moses and Aaron to stand apart, lest they should share in the destruction which awaited the whole congregation. On hearing these awful words the brothers fell on their faces, and by strong intercession, moved the Lord to confine his wrath to the leaders in the rebellion, and spare their unhappy dupes. The latter were then ordered to separate themselves from their leaders and from the tents in which they dwelt. The terrible menace involved in this direction had its weight, and the command was obeyed: and after Moses had appealed to what was to happen as a proof of the authority by which he acted, the earth opened and received and closed over the tents of Korah, Dathan, and Abiram (B. C. about 1190). The Reubenite conspirators were in their tents, and perished in them; and at the same instant Korah and his two hundred and fifty, who were offering incense at the door of the tabernacle, were destroyed by a fire which 'came out from the Lord;' that is, most probably, in this case, from out of the cloud in which his presence dwelt.

(6) Sons of Korah. The censers which they had used were afterwards made into plates, to form an outer covering to the altar, and thus became a standing monument of this awful transaction (Num. xvi.). On, although named in the first instance along with Dathan and Abiram, does not further appear either in the rebellion or its punishment. It is hence supposed that he repented in time: and Abendana and other Rabbinical writers allege that his wife prevailed upon him to abandon the cause.

It might be supposed from the Scripture narrative that the entire families of the conspirators perished in the destruction of their tents. Doubtless all who were in the tents perished; but as the descendants of Korah afterwards became eminent in the Levitical service, it is clear that his sons were spared. They were probably living in separate tents, or were among those who sundered themselves from the conspirators at the command of Moses. There is no reason to suppose that the sons of Korah were children when their father perished. The Korahites were appointed by David to the office of guarding the doors of the temple, and of singing praises. They, in fact, occupied a distinguished place in the choral service of the temple, and several of the Psalms (xlii, xliv, xlix, lxxxiv, lxxxv, lxxxvii, lxxxviii) are inscribed to them. Heman, the master of song under David, was of this family, and his genealogy is traced through Korah up to Levi (1 Chron. vi:31-38).

2. Third son of Esau by Aholibamah (Gen. xxxvi:5, 14, 18; 1 Chron. i:35), born before Esau went to Mount Seir (Gen. xxxvi:5-9). (B. C. about 2100.)

3. A "Duke" of Edom, grandson of Esau (Gen. xxxvi:16).

4. A 'son of Hebron' (1 Chron. ii:43), but whether a man or city is meant by 'Hebron' is uncertain. (B. C. long after 1191.)

KORAHITE (kō'rah-ite), that portion of the Kohathite Levites who were descended from Korah (1 Chron. ix:19, 31). (See KORAH.)

KORATHITES (ko'rath-ītes), (Num. xxvi:58). See KORAHITE.

KORE (ko're), (Heb. קוֹרֵא, *ko-ray'*, crier, or a partridge).

1. A Korahite, ancestor of Shallum and Meshelemiah, chief porters in the time of David (1 Chron. ix:19; xxvi:1). (B. C. about 960.)

2. Son of Imnah, a Levite, appointed over the freewill offerings, and gatekeeper of the western side of the temple in the reign of Hezekiah (2 Chron. xxxi:14). (B. C. 719.)

3. The "sons of Kore" (1 Chron. xxvi:19), should probably be "the sons of the Korhite."

KORHITE (kôr'hīte), (Ex. vi:24; 1 Chron. xii:6; xxvi:1; 2 Chron. xx:19). See KORAHITE.

KOTZ (kōtz). See THORNS AND THISTLES.

KOZ (kŏz), (Heb. קוֹץ, *kotse*, a thorn).

1. A descendant of Judah (1 Chron. iv:8), the father of Anub and others. He may have been a son or brother of Ashur (verse 5). (B. C. before 1300.)

2. The head of the seventh division of priests as arranged by David (1 Chron. xxiv:10), where the name is translated *Hak Koz*. (B. C. about 960.) He is probably the same whose descendants returned from Babylon (Ezra ii:61; Neh. vii:63).

KRINON (krī'nŏn). See LILY.

KUSHAIAH (ku-shà'iah), (Heb. קוּשָׁיָהוּ, *kooshaw-yaw hoo*, the bow of Jah), the form of the name of Kish or Kishi, father of Ethan (1 Chron. xv:17). Ethan was appointed a chief assistant in the temple music by David, (B. C. about 900). He is called *Kishi* in 1 Chron. vi:44.

KUSSEMETH (kŭs-sē'meth), (Heb. כֻּסֶּמֶת, *koosseh'meth*), occurs in three places of Scripture.

(1) **Variously Rendered.** In the Authorized Version it is translated *rye* in Exod. ix:32; Is. xxviii:25, and *fitches* in Ezek. iv:9; but its true meaning still remains uncertain. It was one of the cultivated grains both of Egypt and of Syria, and one of those employed as an article of diet. It was also sown along with wheat, or, at least, its crop was in the same state of forwardness; for we learn from Exod. ix:32, that in the seventh plague the hail-storm smote the barley which was in the ear, and the flax which was bolled; but that the wheat and the *Kussemeth* were not smitten, for they were not grown up. Respecting the wheat and the barley, we know that they are often sown and come to maturity in different months.

(2) **Cultivated in Palestine.** That *kussemeth* was cultivated in Palestine we learn from Is. xxviii:25, where it is mentioned along with ketzah (nigella) and cumin, wheat and barley; and sown, according to some translators, 'on the extreme border of the fields,' as a kind of fence for other kinds of corn. This is quite an Oriental practice, and may be seen in the case of flax and other grains in India, at the present day. The rye is a grain of cold climates, and is not cultivated even in the south of Europe. Korte declares (*Travels*, p. 168) that no rye grows in Egypt; and Shaw states (p. 351) that rye is little known in Barbary and Egypt (Rosenmüller, p. 76).

(3) **Used in Making Bread.** That the *kussemeth* was employed for making bread by the Hebrews we know from Ezek. iv:9, where the prophet is directed to 'take wheat, and barley, and beans, and lentiles, and millet, and *kussemeth*, and put them in a vessel, and make bread thereof.' Though it is very unlikely that *kussemeth* can mean rye, it is not easy to say what cultivated grain it denotes. The principal kinds of grain, it is to be observed, are mentioned in the same passages with the *kussemeth*. Though some circumstances seem to point to the *triticum spelta*, or *spelt* as the *kussemeth* of Scripture, the subject is still susceptible of further investigation, and can only be finally determined by first ascertaining the modern agriculture of eastern countries, and comparing it with the ancient accounts of the agriculture of Syria and Egypt. (See RYE.)

J. F. R.

L

LAADAH (lā′a-dah), (Heb. לַעְדָּה, *lah-daw′*, meaning uncertain), the second son of Shelah (son of Judah), and "father" (founder) of Mareshah (1 Chron. iv:21).

LAADAN (lā′a-dăn), (Heb. לַעְדָּן, *lah-dawn′*, as above).

1. An Ephraimite, the son of Tahan, and grandfather of Elishama, which latter was prince of his tribe at the Exodus (1 Chron. vii:26). (B. C. before 1210.)

2. Son of Gershon (1 Chron. xxiii:7, 8, 9; xxvi: 21). Elsewhere and in the margin called Libni. Keil (*Com. in loc.*) is led to believe that Laadan was a later descendant of Gershon than Libni, and that the Shimei of ver. 9 was a descendant of Libni, not elsewhere mentioned.

LAANAH (lā-an′ah), (Heb. לַעֲנָה, *lah-an-aw′*), translated *wormwood*, occurs in several passages of Scripture, in most of which it is employed in a figurative sense.

Thus, in Deut. xxix:18, 'Lest there be among you a root that beareth gall and *wormwood,*' is applied to such Israelites as should worship foreign gods. Prov. v:4, 'But her end is bitter as wormwood.' Jer. ix:15, 'Behold I will feed them, even this people, with wormwood, and give them gall to drink.' So in Jer. xxiii:15, and in Lam. iii:15 and 19, 'Remember mine affliction and my misery, the wormwood and gall,' where it is applied to public and private calamities, and in Amos v:7, it is said of unrighteous judges 'Ye who turn judgment to wormwood'; so in ver. 12, but here the word *laanah* is translated *hemlock*. That *laanah* was a plant of an extreme degree of bitterness, is evident from the various passages in which it occurs; and it has hence, as Celsius observes, been adopted to indicate both the sins and the punishments of men. (See WORMWOOD.)

J. F. R.

LABAN (lā′ban), (Heb. לָבָן, *law-bawn′*, white).

1. Son of Bethuel (Gen. xxviii:5), and grandson of Nahor (Gen. xxix:5), brother of Rebekah (Gen. xxiv:15, 29, 50 *sq.*), and father of Jacob's two wives, Leah and Rachel.

(1) Dealings with Jacob. Dreading the vengeance of Esau his brother, Jacob was compelled to flee from home. Before his departure Isaac sent for Jacob, gave him his blessing, and charged him to go to Padan-aram, and there marry one of his uncle Laban's daughters (Gen. xxviii:2, 5). When Jacob had been with Laban about a month, Laban proposed to give him wages. Jacob offered seven years' service for Rachel his younger, but most beautiful daughter; and with great cheerfulness he fulfilled his engagement, from the great love which he bare to her. When the marriage night came, God, in order to punish Jacob for deceiving his dim-eyed father, permitted Laban to conduct Leah, his elder daughter, whose beauty was far inferior, to Jacob's bed, instead of Rachel. This was easily done, as the bride, when conducted to the bridegroom, was closely veiled. Next morning the cheat was discovered; and Jacob warmly reproached his uncle for it. He pretended that it was contrary to the custom of their country to marry the younger daughter first; but told him he might have Rachel, too, for seven years' more service. This Jacob agreed to (Gen. xxix:15, 30).

Jacob's fourteen years' service for his two wives being finished, he begged that Laban, his father-in-law, would permit him to return to his country, with his family along with him, that he might provide for himself. Sensible of the advantage of his service, Laban offered him what wages he pleased if he would stay. To mark his dependence on the providence of God, Jacob moved that all the spotted cattle and brown sheep afterwards produced should be his hire. Laban, expecting these could not be many, readily consented. To prevent all disputes, and hinder as much as possible the future product of spotted cattle and brown sheep, all of these kinds were removed to the distance of three days' journey, and intrusted to the care of Laban's sons; and the rest were committed to the oversight of Jacob. Instigated by a vision, Jacob employed means by which he increased his portion, and that of the stronger and abler cattle (Gen. xxx: 37-43), so that the wealth of his uncle decreased in proportion as his own was augmented. Laban, therefore, frequently changed his hire; but whatever was allotted to Jacob exceedingly increased, though he also caused Jacob to bear the loss of whatever was missing of his flocks or herds. After Jacob had served other six years, with great labor and fidelity, Laban and his sons began to behave churlishly and rudely towards him, pretending that he had made himself rich at their expense. Meanwhile, God, in a dream, ordered him to return to Canaan. Resolving to do so, he, perhaps when he was shearing his own sheep, at a distance from those of Laban, acquainted his wives that he saw their father's deportment towards him changed, and that he intended to return to Canaan. They, being sensible of their father's injurious behavior, were glad to part with him. So Jacob, his wives and children, and servants, and flocks, moved towards Canaan, and Rachel carried off some of her father's idols. On the third day after, Laban, informed of their departure, pursued them in no small fury; but God, in a dream, charged him to beware of giving Jacob so much as an injurious word. On the seventh day he overtook them on the mountain of Gilead. Some sharp words were exchanged, and Laban heavily complained that they had carried off his gods. Jacob desired him to ransack all his store, and if his gods were found with any, let the person be put to death. Laban searched with the utmost care; but Rachel, having taken the idols and put them into the camel's furniture, sat upon them, pretending that she was in circumstances which prevented her from rising. Nothing of Laban's being found, he and Jacob made a solemn covenant of perpetual friendship, in testimony of which they reared a heap of stones, which Jacob called Galeed, or Gilead, and Laban, Jegar-saha-dutha, both of which designations signified the *heap of witness*. After Jacob had offered sacrifice, and given an entertainment to his friends, Laban and his company affectionately parted, and returned to Padan-aram, while Jacob and his family went forward to Canaan (Gen. xxix, xxx, xxxi). (See JACOB.)

(2) Character. In their mistaken zeal to defend Jacob, Christian writers have unduly depreciated Laban, and even the ready hospitality shown by him to Abraham's servant, and the affectionate reception of his nephew (Gen. xxiv:30, 31; xxix: 13, 14) have been misconstrued into the acts of a selfish man, eager to embrace an opportunity of a lucrative connection. No man, however, is wholly selfish; and even Laban was capable of generous impulses, however mean and unprincipled his general conduct.

2. A city in the desert of Arabia, on the route of the Israelites (Deut. i:1); perhaps identical with their twenty-first halting place, Libnah (Num. xxxiii:20).

LABOR (lā'bẽr), (Heb. עֲבֹרָה, *ab-o-daw'*), is the execution of a definite task.

(1) Not an Evil. In Gen. iii:19, labor is set forth as a part of the primeval curse, 'In the sweat of thy face thou shalt eat bread'; and doubtless there is a view of labor which exhibits it in reality as a heavy, sometimes a crushing burden. But labor is by no means exclusively an evil, nor is its prosecution a dishonor.

(2) Of Herdsman. The Hebrews, like other primitive nations, appear to have been herdsmen before they were agriculturists (Gen. iv:2, 12, 17, 22); and the practice of keeping flocks and herds continued in high esteem and constant observance as a regular employment and a social condition (Judg. v:16; Jer. xxxiii:12; Luke ii:8). The culture of the soil came in course of time, introducing the discovery and exercise of the practical arts of life, which eventually led to those refinements, both as to processes and to applications, which precede, if they do not create the fine arts (Gen. v:29; xxvi:12; xxxiii:19).

(3) Agriculture. Agriculture, indeed, became the chief employment of the Hebrew race after their settlement in Canaan, lay at the very basis of the constitution, both civil and religious, which Moses gave them, was held in great honor, and was carried on by the high as well as the humble in position (Judg. vi:11; 1 Sam. xi:5; 1 Kings xix:19).

(4) Horticulture. No small care was bestowed on the culture of the vine, which grew luxuriously on the hills of Palestine (Is. v:2, 5; Matt. xxi:33; Num. xiii:24). The vintage was a season of jubilee (Judg. ix:27; Jer. xxv:30; Is. xvi:10). The hills of Palestine were also adorned with well cultured olive-gardens, which produced fruit useful for food, for anointing, and for medicine (Is. xvii:6; xxiv:13; Deut. xxiv:20; Ezek. xxvii:17; 1 Kings iv:25; Hos. xiv:6, 7). Attention was also given to the culture of the fig-tree (2 Kings xx:7; 1 Chron. xxvii:28), as well as of the date-palm (Lev. xxiii:40; Judg. i:16; iv:5; iii: 13; Deut. xxxiv:3), and also of balsam (Gen. xliii:11; Ezek. xxvii:17; Jer. viii:22). For the rise and progress of various kinds of hand labor among the people of Israel, see HANDICRAFT.

J. R. B.

LACE (lās), Heb. פָּתִיל, *paw-theel'*, from a verb "to twist," translated *thread* in Judg. xvi:9, *line* in Ezek. xl:3, *wire* (of gold) in Exod. xxxix:3, *ribband* in Num. xv:38, and *bracelets* in Gen. xxxviii:18, 25, where it denotes the string by which the signet-ring was hung about the neck. (See Exod. xxviii:28.)

LACHISH (lā'kish), (Heb. לָכִישׁ, *law-kheesh'*; Sept. Λάχις, *lachis*), a city in the south of Judah, in the plain between Adoraim and Azekah (Josh. x: 3, 5, 31; xv:39).

It was rebuilt and fortified by Rehoboam (2 Chron. xi:9), and seems after that time to have been regarded as one of the strongest fortresses of the kingdom of Judah, having for a time braved the assaults of the Assyrian army under Sennacherib (2 Kings xviii:17; xix:8; 2 Chron. xxxii:9). The site is found by Petrie at Tell el-Hesy, sixteen miles east by north of Gaza and eleven miles west-southwest of Beit Jibrin. Excavation has laid bare the wall of the ancient city, as well as later constructions believed to belong to the times of Rehoboam, Asa, Jehoshaphat, Uzziah, Jotham, and Manasseh. The mound of Tell el-Hesy rises sixteen miles to the east of Gaza. It stands on a natural eminence about forty feet in height, on the summit of which the ruins of ten successive cities are piled sixty feet higher. The lowest is called Amorite, and is reported to be about a quarter of a mile square. It was built on a bluff, about sixty feet above the stream which flowed on the east, and forty feet above the level country on the north. Above the ruins of the primitive Lachish are found fresh walls raised upon those destroyed, and fresh buildings constructed of the old stones. (*Palestine Expl.,* 1900.)

Professor Sayce in *Higher Criticism*, p. 289, says: "In the time of Amenôphis IV, or Khu-n-Aten, Lachish had been the seat of an Egyptian governor. More than one letter from him has been found among the cuneiform tablets of Tell-Amarna, and one of the dispatches of the vassal king of Jerusalem states that Lachish, Ashkelon, and Gezer had furnished the garrison of his city with food and oil." (See LACHISH, EXCAVATIONS AT; LACHISH, SIEGE OF.)

LACHISH, EXCAVATIONS AT.

The importance of the excavations at Lachish is worthy of a separate article. Nearly four thousand years after the founding of the first city the tide of warfare and the passing centuries had left only a great mound called a *tell* and which the Arabs called Tell el-Hesy. The identification of the locality was for a long time undecided, but Major Conder claimed that this must be the site of the original Lachish from the fact that the situation commands the only springs of water in the region except those which lie some three or four miles away, and also because its position corresponds with the account in the "Onomasticon" of the location of Lachish, which was in the district of Daroma, seven miles from Eleutheropolis, or Beit Jibrin. Between April of 1890 and January of 1893, the officers of the Palestine Exploration Fund excavated the great mound and they succeeded in restoring to the original level, a portion of it. The work was begun under the able leadership of Dr. W. M. Flinders Petrie whose "ten years' digging in Egypt" together with his profound scholarship had given him a wonderful adaptability for the work. He was enabled to largely reconstruct the history, and determine the various periods, from remains which to the inexperienced eye would seem entirely without significance. Later the work was pursued by Mr. F. J. Bliss and a portion of the remains of one city after another were slowly uncovered by Arabian workmen, while the women of the tribes carried away the dirt in baskets.

As layer after layer was removed the various forms of pottery were discovered which enabled the explorers to assign the age of each particular city with more or less certainty. In one era the decorations and ornaments indicated the luxurious days of Solomon, and the slabs bearing pilasters in low relief probably date from his time. Much of the pottery which was found belonged to the period of the Jewish kings, and certain forms of idolatrous worship seem to have originated here, for we read that Lachish was "the beginning of sin to the daughter of Zion; for the transgressions of Israel were found in thee" (Micah i:13).

The first city explored was necessarily the last one built, and the scanty remains here found assigned its period to about 400 B. C. The city following this was No. X, and it was assigned to about 500 B. C., on account of the prevalence of polished Greek ware. City IX was assigned to 800 B. C., and VIII to the period between 900 and 1000 B. C.

After all traces of No. VIII had been cleared away they had again a smooth platform to explore, and below it in City VII was a fine range of rooms, but into them the people who built the town above them had dug pits for their ovens, and hence they contained several of the pit ovens which are still so common in Palestine. Below this layer the workmen found a vast amount of debris, and they dug almost ten feet before they came to City VI. It was only about four feet, however, below the foundations of these buildings that they reached the top of the walls of City V.

Still lower than this, in City IV, the walls of a large building were traced by a bed of yellow sand which lay directly under them, never extending either into the rooms or into the streets. In City III the ruins of the rooms were covered with a great bed of ashes which still remain a mystery. Petrie ascribed them to alkali-burners who may have plied their trade on the then deserted hill, while Bliss inclined to a different view based upon the furnace which was found just below. This ruined town lay about fifteen feet lower than the one above it, and covered considerably more ground; indeed the general outline of the whole *Tell* from this point upward was somewhat in the shape of a peak, each city covering less space than did its predecessor. This third city had evidently been sacked as well as destroyed, and the work here was almost barren of results except the few objects which were found in the debris outside of the rooms.

One of the most important of the finds here obtained was a small clay tablet which is now in the Imperial Museum of Constantinople. The finding of this tablet established the fact which had long been suspected by scholars that the pre-Israelitish Canaan possessed their clay libraries as did Babylonia and Assyria. "In size and shape," says Professor Sayce, "it resembles the tablets sent from the south of Canaan. The forms of the cuneiform characters, moreover, which appear on it, are those which we now know to have been used in southern Canaan about 1400 B. C. Lastly, the grammatical forms and formulæ are identical with those employed by the scribes of Southern Canaan when writing to the Egyptian kings. We find them in the tablets of Tell-Amarna as well as in the tablet of Lachish.

"The fact that the original was not accessible made the copying of the cuneiform text somewhat difficult. Indeed, it is sometimes impossible to tell from the impressions what exactly are the characters at the edges of the tablet or where the surface of the tablet is worn. Hence the lacunæ and indications of uncertainty which appear in my copy of the inscription. A translation of the text has been further rendered difficult by the existence in it of words which have not been met with before and which are, therefore, of doubtful meaning. Fortunately enough is clear to show us what the letter—for such it is—is about, and to what period it belongs.

"What makes this letter so particularly interesting is that we already know something about Zimrida, who is twice mentioned in it. Zimrida, or Zimridi, as he is called, was governor of Lachish in the reign of Khu-n-Aten, and a letter from the king of Jerusalem to the Egyptian Pharaoh informs us that he was murdered at Lachish by servants of the Egyptian king. One of the dispatches discovered at Tell-Amarna was sent by him to Egypt and runs thus: 'To the King, my Lord, my God, my Sun-god, the Sun-god who is from heaven, thus (writes) Zimridi, the governor of the city of Lachish, thy servant, the dust of thy feet, at the feet of the King, my Lord, the Sun-god from heaven, bows himself seven times seven. I have very diligently listened to the words of the messenger of the King, my Lord has sent to me and now I have dispatched (a mission) according to his message.'"

Thus the tablet found at Lachish may be part of a correspondence pertaining to similar subjects as that found at Tell-Amarna, or it may be a local letter sent from one Syrian city to another. The discovery of other portions of this correspondence, which we now have a right to expect, would be simply invaluable.

Below this level, in City II, Mr. Bliss made another important discovery which he calls "a sample blast furnace." If his theories concerning it are correct it proves that during the period ranging about 1400 B. C. the hot air blast was used instead of cold air. The hot air blast furnace has been considered a modern improvement in iron manufactures which was due to Neilson and was patented in 1828.

The lowest city in the mound, and the one above it, contained only one class of pottery which Professor Petrie calls "Amorite," and which is plainly distinguishable from the well-known types of Phœnician pottery which begin to appear in City II and continue through both III and IV. "Amorite pottery" is a term which covers the strongly marked types of pre-Israelitish ware, the earliest use of which has not as yet been determined, but which went "out of fashion" as the prevailing type as early as the sixteenth century B. C., although specimens of it are found much later.

Although the remains of a great tower are found in the primitive city we have no direct historical account of the fortification of Lachish until it was done by Rehoboam, king of Judah, in whose list of "fenced cities" it occurs. (See REHOBOAM.) After the Rehoboam period, there was a thin wall built on the front edge of his fortification to heighten and strengthen it. Hence the older wall must by this time have been decayed down to a height of only about six feet, and this fact suggests the passage of considerable time. If the wall had been destroyed by Shishak (2 Chron. xi:9; xii:2) in his subsequent invasion (see SHISHAK) it would have been almost, if not quite, overthrown. This refortification may have been made under Jehoshaphat, who having subdued the Philistines and Arabians (2 Chron. xvii:11, 12) needed a fortress here. And we read that he garrisoned "all the fenced cities" (ver. 2). Amaziah fled to Lachish about 810 B. C. and was killed there (1 Kings xiv:19). When Uzziah attacked the Philistines (2 Chron. xxvi: 11) he doubtless needed a fort at Lachish and probably the fragment left inside the wall of Jehoshaphat may have been his work, for it is said that he built much (ver. 10) and that he raised many cattle in Shephelah; therefore a safe watering place at Lachish would be invaluable.

After this the walls were razed probably by Rezin and Pekah when they beleaguered Jerusalem about 735 B. C. (2 Kings xvi:5).

But another wall was evidently built upon the ruin of the other, and this may have been done by Ahaz, whose passion for building is recorded in Kings (2 Kings xvi:17). Behind the wall of Ahaz and on the north side of the town is the foundation of a thicker wall which had evidently been ruined soon after it was built. On the south side there is a long fortification which is some thirty feet in breadth formed of blocks of stone bedded in the earth and faced with white plaster. These and other details correspond with what we might expect at the time of the siege by Sennacherib. (See LACHISH, SIEGE OF, also SENNACHERIB.)

chish, by W. M. Flinders Petrie. Also *A Mound of Many Cities,* by F. J. Bliss, etc.)

LACHISH, SIEGE OF.

In Old Testament times the besieging army in attacking a fortified city sought first to drive all of its defenders within the walls. They then made choice of three methods of attack. They could either make a bold assault upon the most vulnerable part of the wall, or prepare to invest the city and starve out the defenders, or they might prepare their engines of war for a long and formal siege preparatory to the final battle.

In ancient Nineveh there was an elaborate representation of the siege of Lachish upon the walls of the palace of Sennacherib, and similar bas-reliefs show us the details of the siege of Susa, or Shushan, the capital of Ahasuerus and Esther (see SHUSHAN) and other cities. It was during the siege of Lachish that Sennacherib sent his *tartan* or commander-in-chief to Jerusalem to demand the submission of King Hezekiah as told in 2

Assyrian Sculpture Representing the Capture of Lachish by Sennacherib.

After the destruction of Lachish by Sennacherib there does not appear to have been more than one refortifying of the site. This is the wall on the north which is thin at the east end, but thicker in the middle of the side. This can be traced around the city, and is probably the work of Manasseh, who about 660 B. C. fortified Jerusalem and put commanders in all the fenced cities of Judah. If so these must have been the walls which were besieged by Nebuchadnezzar about 590 B. C. (See Jer. xxxiv:7.) After the siege of Nebuchadnezzar we have little or no data concerning its occupation. Even after the return of the Jews they made their principal settlement in the vicinity of the later site of Umm Lakis, and since the fourth century before Christ the site appears to have been left desolate, or occupied only by the desert tribes and their cattle.

More than twenty-three centuries have passed away and the buried cities still occupy the one great mound, the surface of which was planted with barley and with beans when the spade of the explorer broke the silence of the ages in this tomb of many cities. (See *Tell el-Hesy La-*

Kings xviii. The besieging army consisted of the chariot force which was made up from the military aristocracy of Assyria and consisted largely of men of rank and wealth. The cavalry and infantry came next in importance and finally the great host of common soldiers coming from the tributary peoples.

At Lachish the king himself took command and fought from a chariot, while behind him were two chariots each of which carried a royal standard, the one being the figure of an archer riding a bull, and the other the emblem of the supreme god, Assur on two bulls. The chariots of the king and his standard bearers were covered with gold and silver, while bows, arrows, and battle axes were fastened to the sides. In the rear of each of these chariots was a rich red shield, while above it was a spear from which streamers were flying. The other chariots were similar in construction and general design but they did not bear the royal colors or other insignia of the king.

The cavalry was armed with bows or javelins. The armor of the men was made of scales and consisted of a jacket and greaves. The horses were also protected by a thick leather armor which was fastened around the neck and covered both back and sides. Every cavalry man had a mounted attendant who held the horse by the bridle while his master was fighting.

It appears that the Assyrian infantry also fought in pairs, each archer having a companion who like Jonathan's armor-bearer protected his master as far as possible by holding before him a shield made of wicker work or leather, and in some cases there was also a second armor-bearer whose business it was to carry the arrows.

The higher rank of infantry carried spears and large round shields ornamented with bands of metal. If it was found that no sudden attack could capture a city the besieging army established a fortified camp just outside of bowshot, and if there were danger of a desperate counter-attack this camp would also be protected by a dike. The commander in chief would then slowly move his clumsy war machines forward toward the city walls. This movement was retarded as far as possible by the defenders who threw arrows and stones among the enemy, and also used torches and balls of fire. The fortress was sometimes on the top of a rocky hill as at Susa, and in this case the attacking party must fill up the ditches and raise banks upon which their crude battering-rams could be placed. These rams were made of a beam of wood either with or without a metal covering for the head, and this was carried by a number of men who struck it with all possible force against some weak point in the wall.

A more elaborate machine of the same sort was a ram which was set upon a frame carried upon wheels, and the frame had a covering which protected the men who worked the beam. Upon the highest point of this improved battering-ram a little tower was sometimes built and filled with archers who from this position were enabled to pick off the defenders who stood upon the top of the city wall. If the wall were built of heavy stones and well protected by fighting men it might for a long time defy the attacking party, especially when, as in the case of Tyre, the besieged city had access to the seacoast, and therefore could not be starved into submission. When at last a city was taken the terrible work of slaughter and cruelty really began. The victorious Assyrians often impaled the principal men among their prisoners or skinned them alive. Great piles of the heads of their victims were made at the gates of the city while other prisoners including women and children were driven off into Assyrian slavery. If a prisoner of high degree were saved to grace the triumph of the conqueror, the king would often with his own hands pierce the eyes of his victim with a spear, and lead him back with a thong which had been put through his lips. King Zedekiah was one of these unfortunate victims, and the Assyrian bas-reliefs give many illustrations of this and other barbarities. (William Hayes Ward, *Hom. Rev.*, July, 1895.) (See WAR.)

LAD (lăd), (Heb. נַעַר, *nah'ar*). A general term applied to:

1. An infant just born (Exod. ii:6; Judg. xiii:5, 7; 1 Sam. iv:21).

2. A boy not yet full grown (Gen. xxi:16; xxii:12; Is. vii:16; viii:4).

3. A youth nearly twenty years of age (Gen. xxxiv:19; xli:12; 1 Kings iii:7; 2 Sam. xviii:5, 29).

4. A *girl,* or maiden (Gen. xxiv:14, 16; xxxiv:3, 12; Deut. xxii:15). The A. V. sometimes translates the term "child."

LADAN (lā'dan), A. V. See LAADAN.

LADDER (lăd'dēr), (Heb. סֻלָּם, *sool-lawm'*, staircase), occurs in the account of Jacob's vision at Bethel (Gen. xxviii:12). That it was a contrivance known from the earliest ages is shown by Egyptian monuments.

In Jacob's dream the foot of the ladder stood on the earth, and its top reached unto heaven; the angels of God ascended and descended on the rounds of it. Above the top of it stood the Lord God, and assured him he was the God of his fathers, Abraham and Isaac, and would give him and his seed the land of Canaan for their inheritance, render them numerous as the sand by the seashore, and render all nations blessed in him and his seed. (See JACOB.)

Figurative. This *ladder* represented the providence of God, administered by angels and managed by God, as a God in covenant; and Jesus Christ as the wonder and Lord of angels, and the Mediator between God and man, and the way of access to God, sprung of Jacob in his humanity, but in his divine nature the Lord from heaven, and the means of all blessings from God to sinful men.

LADY (lā'dў).

1. *Gheb-eh'reth* (Heb. גְּבֶרֶת, mistress), a term applied to Babylon as the mistress of the nations (Is. xlvii:5, 7), a mistress in distinction from a maidservant (Gen. xvi:4, 8, 9; 2 Kings v:3; Prov. xxx:23; Ps. cxxiii:2; Is. xxiv:2).

2. *Saw-raw'* (Heb. שָׂרָה), a noble female (Judg. v:29; Esth. i:18).

3. *Koo-ree'ah* (Gr. κυρία, feminine of *master*), found only in 2 John i:1, and applied as an honorable epithet to a Christian woman.

LAEL (lā'el), (Heb. לָאֵל, *law-ale'*, consecrated to God), father of Eliasaph, who was a prince of the Gershonites at the time of the Exodus (Num. iii:24), B. C. before 1607.

LAHAD (lā'had), (Heb. לַהַד, *lah'had*), son of Jahath, of the family of Zerah, a descendant of Judah (1 Chron. iv:2), B. C. after 1612.

LAHAI-ROI, THE WELL (la-hāi'roi), (Gen. xxiv:62). See BEER-LAHAI-ROI.

LAHMAM (läh'mam), (Heb. לַחְמָם, *lakh-mawm'*), a town in the group with Lachish, in the plain of Judah (Josh. xv:40), probably west of the Highlands of Judæa. It is possibly *Beit-Lehai*, a little northeast of Gaza (Robinson, iii, append., p. 118).

LAHMI (läh'mī), (Heb. לַחְמִי, *lakh-mee'*, Beth-lehemite), a brother of Goliath, the Gittite, slain by Elhanan (1 Chron. xx:5). The name is probably a corruption for *Beth-hal-lachmi,* "the Bethlehemite," which occurs in the parallel passage (2 Sam. xxi:19).

LAISH (lā'ish), (Heb. לַיִשׁ, *lah'yish*, a lion).

1. A place in the north of Palestine (Judg. xviii:7, 14), about four miles from Paneas, at the head of the Jordan. It was taken by the Danites and included within their territory. It is called also Leshem and Dan (Josh. xix:47; Judg. xviii:7, 29; Jer. viii:16), now identified with *Tell-el-Kady,* "the mound of the judge," to the north of the waters of Merom (Josh. xi:5). (See DAN.)

2. A place mentioned by the prophet in his description of the Assyrian assault on Jerusalem; from its association it lay north of the city (Is. x:30). The name here translated "unto Laish," should probably be "Laishah." The passage would then read, "listen Laishah," etc. It corresponds to the modern *El-isawiyeh,* a village a mile and a half northeast of Jerusalem (Robinson, *Researches,* ii. 108).

3. A man of the town of Gallim, the father of Phalti, or Phaltiel, to whom Saul gave Michal, the wife of David (1 Sam. xxv:44; 2 Sam. iii: 15). (B. C. before 1062.)

LAKE (lāk), (Gr. λίμνη, *lim'nay,* a pool). The term occurs only in the N. T. regarding the Lake of Gennesaret (Luke v:1, 2; viii:22, 23, 33), and the "lake of fire" (Rev. xix:20; xx:10, 14, 15; xxi:8).

LAKUM (lā'kum), (Heb. לַקּוּם, *lak-koom',* castle, defense), a place on the boundary of Naphtali, probably not far south of Lake Merom (Josh. xix:33).

LAMA (lä'mä), (Gr. λαμά, *lam-ah' ;* λαμμᾶ, *lammah'*), a term signifying *why,* quoted from Ps. xxii:1 by Jesus on the cross (Matt. xxvii:46; Mark xv:34).

LAMB (lăm), the translation of several Hebrew and Greek words:

1. The most frequent are *keh-bes'* (Heb. כֶּבֶשׂ), transposed form *keh'seb* (כֶּשֶׂב), and the feminines *kib-saw'* (כִּבְשָׂה), *kab-saw'* (כַּבְשָׂה) and *kis-baw'* (כִּשְׂבָּה), and respectively denote a male and female lamb from the first to the third year. In sacrifice young rams of corresponding age were offered in almost every sacrifice (Num. vi:14; Lev. iv:32). (See SACRIFICE.)

2. The equivalent Chaldee form for the above is *im-mar'* (Heb. אִמַּר, Ezra vi:9, 17; vii:17).

3. *Taw-leh'* (Heb. טָלֶה, 1 Sam. vii:9; Is. lxv:25), a young sucking lamb; originally the young of any animal.

4. *Kar* (Heb. כַּר, *plump*), a fat ram, or more probably "wether," as the word is generally employed in opposition to *ayil,* which strictly denotes a "ram" (Deut. xxxii:14; Is. xxxiv:6).

5. *Tseh-one'* (Heb. צֹאן, from unused root signifying to *migrate*), rendered "lamb" in Exod. xii:21, is properly a collective term denoting a "*flock*" of small cattle, sheep, and goats, in distinction from herds of the larger animals (Eccles. ii:7; Ezek. xlv:15).

6. *Seh* (Heb. שֶׂה), in opposition to the above collective term, is applied to denote the individuals of a flock, whether sheep or goats (Gen. xxii:7, 8; Exod. xii:3, etc.).

7. In the New Testament we find *ar-nee'on* (Gr. ἀρνίον, diminutive of ἀρήν, *ar-ane',* which latter occurs only in Luke x:3), a lambkin. (Mc. & Str. *Bib. Cyc.*)

For all the principal sacrifices of ordinary occasions a lamb might be used: as a male lamb for a burnt offering (Lev. ix:3; xxiii:12, 18; Num. vi:14; vii:15), a ewe lamb for a sin offering for others than the nation or rulers (Lev. iv: 32, 35; Num. vi:14), and a male or female lamb for a guilt offering (Lev. v:6; xiv:12, 21; Num. vi:12) or for a peace offering (Lev. iii:6, 7; xxiii: 19; Num. vii:17). In every case the lamb must be without blemish.

Figurative. (1) All the sheep offered in the ancient sacrifices represented Christ. He resembled a lamb in his spotless purity (1 Pet. i:19), and was typified by the paschal lamb. (2) He was like a *lamb* also in his gentleness and in his submission to unmerited suffering without murmur or complaint (Is. liii:7 with Luke xxiii:25; Acts viii:32; 1 Pet. ii:21-23). (3) Finally, he, like a *lamb,* was sacrificed for guilt not his own. Hence he is called the LAMB OF GOD, which taketh away the sin of the world (John i:29, 36), *the Lamb slain* from the foundation of the world (Rev. xiii:8), or simply *the Lamb* (Rev. v:6, 8, 12; vii:14, 17; xiv:1, 4). (4) His people are likened to *sheep* and *lambs,* to represent their innocence, patience, harmlessness, usefulness, and exposure to troubles and enemies (Is. liii:7; John x:1-26, and xxi:15-17). (5) Both in the Old Testament and in the New Testament the term *lamb* is at times used figuratively for child (Is. xl:11; John xxi:15). (6) Men in general are compared to *sheep* and *lambs,* to denote their *stupidity,* their weakness, exposure to danger, and need of government (1 Kings xxii:17; Hos. iv: 16; Is. xl:11), or for their *innocency* and harmlessness as to a particular sin (2 Sam. xxiv:17). (7) Sinners are likened to *sheep,* to mark their unthoughtfulness, their proneness to wander, their exposure to ruin, their inability to defend or recover themselves, and their need to be saved, led, and nourished by Jesus the great Shepherd (Ps. xlix:14; Is. liii:6; 1 Pet. ii:25; Luke xv: 4-6). (8) The *rams, goats,* and *lambs,* denote the various classes of people in a country; great and powerful, or poor and weak, and less or more innocent (Is. xxxiv:6, 7, and lx:7; Ezek. xxxiv: 17 and xxxix:18).

LAMB OF GOD (lăm ŏv gŏd), (Gr. ἀμνὸς Θεοῦ, *am-nos'theh-oo'*), a title given to Christ Jesus our Lord (John i:29, 36; comp. Acts viii:32; 1 Pet. i:19). As the *lamb* was the symbol of sacrifice, Jesus Christ is called "*the sacrifice of God,*" or the divine sacrifice (John i:29; comp. Rev. v:12; Is. liii:7, 28; Rom. ix:5; 1 Cor. v:7; 1 Peter i:19).

In the symbolic scenery of the Book of Revelation John beheld "a lamb as it had been slain, having seven horns and seven eyes, which are the seven spirits of God sent forth into all the earth" (Rev. v:6) ; i. e., invested with the attributes of God, omnipotence and omniscience, and sharing the universal empire and homage of the universe. (See LAMB.)

LAME (lām), denotes one maimed, or enfeebled in the limbs (2 Sam. iv:4). *Lameness* disqualified men for officiating in the priesthood, or animals for being offered in sacrifice.

A person thus afflicted might, however, eat of the sacrifices, like other priests (Lev. xxi:17-23).

Figurative. In Jesus, our great Priest and Sacrifice, there is no want of ability to perform his work, and no predisposition to be turned out of the way (Lev. xxi:18; Deut. xv:21). Persons weak in body, or in their intellect and grace, and halting between different opinions, are called *lame* (Is. xxxiii:23; Heb. xii:13).

LAMECH (lā'mek), (Heb. לֶמֶךְ, *leh'mek;* Sept. Λάμεχ, *lamech*).

1. Son of Methusael, and father of Jabal, Jubal, Tubal-cain, and Naamah (Gen. iv:18, 24, etc.). (B. C. probably about 3700.) He is recorded to have taken two wives, Adah and Zillah; and there appears no reason why the fact should have been mentioned, unless to point him out as the author of the evil practice of polygamy. The manner in which the sons of Lamech distinguished themselves as the inventors of useful arts, is mentioned under their several names. (See JABAL; JUBAL; and TUBAL-CAIN.) The most remarkable circumstance in connection with Lamech is the poetical address which he is very abruptly introduced as making to his wives. This is not only remarkable in itself, but is the first and most ancient piece of poetry in the Hebrew Scriptures; and, indeed, the only example of Antediluvian poetry extant:

' Adah and Zillah, hear my voice!
　Wives of Lamech, receive my speech!
If I slew a man to my wounding,
　And a young man—to my hurt:
If Cain was avenged seven times,
　Then Lamech—seventy times seven.'

This exhibits the parallelism and other characteristics of Hebrew poetry, the development of which belongs to another article. (See POETRY, HEBREW.) It has all the appearance of an extract from an old poem, which we may suppose to have been handed down by tradition to the time of Moses. It is very difficult to discover to what it refers, and the best explanation can be nothing more than a conjecture. So far as we can make it out, it would seem to be, as Bishop Lowth explains (Prælect. iv:91), an apology for committing homicide, in his own defense, upon some man who had violently assaulted him, and, as it would seem, struck and wounded him; and he opposes a homicide of this nature to the willful and inexcusable fratricide of Cain. Under this view Lamech would appear to have intended to comfort his wives by the assurance that he was really exposed to no danger from this act, and that any attempt upon his life on the part of the friends of the deceased would not fail to bring down upon them the severest vengeance. Naamah 'the comely one' is fancifully supposed to be perhaps the most ancient Venus of the Pagans (Gen. iv:18-24).

2. Son of Methuselah, and father of Noah (Gen. v:25-31; 1 Chron. i:3; Luke iii:36). (B. C. 3297-2520.)

LAMENT (là-měnt'). See MOURNING.

LAMENTATIONS (lăm'ĕn-tā'shŭns), this book is called by the Hebrews אֵיכָה, *ey-kaw'*, 'how,' from the first word of the book; but sometimes they call it קִינוֹת, *kee-noth'*, tears, or 'lamentation,' in allusion to the mournful character of the work, of which one would conceive, says Bishop Lowth, 'that every letter was written with a tear, every word the sound of a broken heart.' From this, or rather from the translation of it in the Septuagint, *tears*, comes our title of Lamentations.

(1) Ascription. The ascription of the Lamentations in the title is of no authority in itself, but its correctness has never been doubted. The style and manner of the book are those of Jeremiah, and the circumstances alluded to, those by which he is known to have been surrounded. This reference of the Lamentations to Jeremiah occurs in the introductory verse which is found in the Septuagint:—'And it came to pass, after Israel had been carried away captive, and Jerusalem was become desolate, that Jeremiah sat weeping, and lamented with this lamentation over Jerusalem, and said.'

It is disputed whether or not this verse existed in the Hebrew copies from which the translation of the Seventy was made. We are certainly not bound by its authority if disposed to question the conclusion which it supports. But it at least shows the opinion which prevailed as to the author, and the occasion of the book, at the time the translation was made. That opinion, as regards the author, has been admitted almost without dispute. Funeral lamentations, composed by Jeremiah upon the death of King Josiah, are mentioned in 2 Chron. xxxv:25, and are there said to have been perpetuated by an ordinance in Israel. That the lamentations thus mentioned are those which we now possess has been the opinion of many scholars of great eminence. Josephus clearly takes this view (*Antiq.* x:5, 1), as do Jerome (*Comment. in Zech.* iii:11), Theodoret, and others of the Fathers; and in more modern times, Archbishop Usher (*De LXX Interpret.*), Michaelis (Note on Lowth's *Sac. Poet. Hebr.* Prælect. xxii), who afterwards changed his opinion, Datne (*Proph. Major.* ed. 1), and others. De Wette (*Einleit.* sec. 273) is clearly of opinion that the passage in 2 Chronicles refers to the existing book of Lamentations, and that the author considered the death of Josiah as its principal subject. This daring writer uses so little ceremony with the author of the book of Chronicles on other occasions that his own opinion is not to be inferred from this admission; and we are not surprised to find from what follows that he feels at liberty to take a different view from the one which he believes the writer of Chronicles to have entertained.

(2) General View of Commentators. The received opinion, namely, that in accordance with the argument prefixed to the books in the Septuagint, is now quite generally accepted. It is adopted by nearly all commentators who, as they proceed through the book, find that they cannot follow out the details on any other supposition. Indeed, but for the reference suggested by the passage in Chronicles, no one would have been likely to imagine that such expressions as are found in ch. i:17 could point to any other circumstances than those which attended and followed the destruction of Jerusalem by the Babylonians. Besides the prophet speaks throughout the book of the city of Jerusalem and the Temple as ruined, profaned and desolated; and this was not the case during the reign of Josiah or at the time of his death. We may, under this view, regard the first two chapters as occupied chiefly with the circumstances of the siege and those immediately following that event. In the third the prophet deplores the calamities and persecutions to which he had himself been exposed; the fourth refers to the ruin and desolation of the city, and the unhappy lot of Zedekiah; and the fifth and last seems to be a sort of prayer in the name, or on behalf, of the Jews in their dispersion and captivity. As Jeremiah himself was eventually compelled to withdraw into Egypt much against his will (Jer. xliii:6), it has been suggested that the last chapter was possibly written there. Pareau refers ch. i to Jer. xxxvii:5, *sq.*; ch. iii to Jer. xxxviii:2, *sq.*; ch. iv to Jer. xxxix:1, *sq.*, and 2 Kings xxv:1, *sq.*; ch. ii to the destruction of the city and temple; ch. v is admitted to be the latest, and to refer to the time after that event. Ewald says that the situation is the same throughout, and only the time different. In ch. i and ii we find sorrow without consolation; ch. iii consolation for the poet himself; in ch. iv the lamentation is renewed with greater violence; but soon the whole people, as if urged by their own spontaneous impulse, fall to weeping and hoping.

Dr. Blayney, regarding both the date and occasion of the Lamentations as established by the internal evidence, adds, 'Nor can we admire too much the flow of that full and graceful pathetic eloquence, in which the author pours out the effusions of a patriotic heart, and piously weeps over the ruins of his venerable country' (*Jeremiah* p. 376). 'Never,' says an unquestionable judge of these matters, 'was there a more rich and elegant variety of beautiful images and adjuncts, arranged together within so small a compass, nor more happily chosen and applied (Lowth, *De Sacra Poesi Hebr.* Prælect. xxii.).

In the ancient copies this book is supposed to have occupied the place which is now assigned to it, after Jeremiah. Indeed, from the manner in which Josephus reckons up the books of the Old Testament (*Contra Apion.* i:8), it has been supposed that Jeremiah and Lamentations originally formed but one book (Prideaux, *Connection,* i. 332). In the Bible now used by the Jews, however, the book of Lamentations stands in the Hagiographa, and among the five Megilloth, or books of Ruth, Esther, Ecclesiastes, and Solomon's Song. They believe that it was not written by the gift of prophecy, but by the spirit of God (between which they make a distinction), and give this as a reason for not placing it among the prophets. It is read in their synagogues on the ninth of the month Ab, which is a fast for the destruction of the holy city. (Henderson, *Commentary*, London, 1851); Noyes, *Hebrew Prophets*, Boston, 1866; Deutsch, in Kitto's *Cycl. of Bibl. Lit.*)

LAMP (lămp), (Heb. לַפִּיד, *lap-peed'*; whence, perhaps, Gr. λαμπάς, *lampas,* "lamp," the μ being introduced in place of the Hebrew פ; Lat. *lampas,* and our *lamp*).

(1) Oil Used. Lamps are very often mentioned in Scripture; but there is nothing to give any notion of their form. Almost the only fact we can gather is, that vegetable oils were burnt in them, and especially, if not exclusively, olive-oil. This, of the finest quality, was the oil used

Egyptian Lamps.

in the seven lamps of the Tabernacle (Exod. xxvii:20). Although the lamp-oils of the Hebrews were exclusively vegetable, it is probable that animal fat was used, as it is at present by the Western Asiatics, by being placed in a kind of lamp, and burnt by means of a wick inserted in it. This we have often witnessed in districts where oil-yielding plants are not common.

(2) Material and Form. It is somewhat re-markable, that while the golden candlestick, or rather candelabrum, is so minutely described, not a word is said of the shape, or even the material, of the lamps (Exod. xxv:37). This was, perhaps, because they were to be of the common forms, already familiarly known to the Hebrews, and the same probably which were used in Egypt, which they had just quitted. They were in this instance doubtless of gold, although metal is scarcely the best substance for a lamp. The golden candlestick may also suggest, that lamps in ordinary use were placed on stands, and where more than one was required, on stands

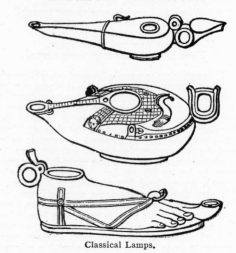

Classical Lamps.

with two or more branches. The modern Orientals, who are satisfied with very little light in their rooms, use stands of brass or wood, on which to raise the lamps to a sufficient height above the floor on which they sit. Such stands are shaped not unlike a tall candlestick, spreading out at the top. Sometimes the lamps are placed on brackets against the wall, made for the purpose, and often upon stools. Doubtless the same contrivances were employed by the Hebrews.

From the fact that lamps were carried in the pitchers of Gideon's soldiers, from which, at the end of the march, they were taken out, and borne in the hand (Judg. vii:16, 20), we may with certainty infer that they were not, like many of the classical lamps, entirely open at top, but so shaped that the oil could not easily be spilled. This was remarkably the case in the Egyptian specimens, and is not rare in the classical. Gideon's lamps must also have had handles; but that the Hebrew lamps were always furnished with handles we are not bound to infer: in Egypt we find lamps both with and without handles.

Cotton wicks are now used throughout Asia; but the Hebrews, like the Egyptians, probably employed the outer and coarser fiber of flax (Pliny, *Hist. Nat.* xix:1); and perhaps linen yarn, if the Rabbins are correct in alleging that the linen dresses of the priests were unraveled when old, to furnish wicks for the sacred lamps. (See CANDLESTICK.)

(3) Use at Night. It seems that the Hebrews, like the modern Orientals, were accustomed to burn lamps overnight in their chambers; and this practice may appear to give point to the expression of '*outer* darkness,' which repeatedly occurs in the New Testament (Matt. viii:12; xxii:13): the force is greater, however, when the contrast implied in the term 'outer' is viewed with reference to the effect produced by sudden expulsion into the darkness of night from a chamber highly illuminated for an entertainment. This custom of burning lamps at night, with the effect produced by their going out or being extinguished, supplies various figures to the sacred writers (2 Sam. xxi:17; Prov. xiii:9; xx:20). And, on the other hand, the keeping up of a lamp's light is used as a symbol of enduring and unbroken succession (1 Kings xi:36; xv:4; Ps. cxxxii:17).

(4) Use at Marriage Ceremonies. It appears from Matt. xxv:1, that the Jews used lamps and torches in their marriage ceremonies, or rather when the bridegroom came to conduct home the bride by night. This is still the custom in those parts of the East where, on account of the heat of the day, the bridal procession takes place in the night time. The connection of lamps and torches with marriage ceremonies, it may be observed, is still preserved in Western Asia, even where it is no longer usual to bring home the bride by night. During two or three, or more nights preceding the wedding, the street or quarter in which the bridegroom lives is illuminated with chandeliers and lanterns, or with lanterns and small lamps suspended from cords drawn across from the bridegroom's house and several others on each side to the houses opposite; and several small silk flags, each of two colors, generally red and green, are attached to other cords (Lane's *Mod. Egypt.* i:201). Lamps of this kind are sometimes hung over doors. There is reason to suppose that the Egyptians had lamps of glass, and if so, there is no reason why the Jews also might not have had them, especially as this material is more proper for lamps intended to be hung up, and therefore to cast their light down from above. The Jews certainly used lamps in other festivals besides those of marriage. If this custom had not been so general in the ancient and modern East, it might have been supposed that the Jews adopted it from the Egyptians, who, according to Herodotus (ii:62), had a 'Feast of Lamps,' which was celebrated at Sais, and, indeed, throughout the country at a certain season of the year. The description which the historian gives of the lamps employed on this occasion, strictly applies to those in modern use already described, and the concurrence of both these sources of illustration strengthens the probable analogy of Jewish usage. He speaks of them as 'small vases filled with salt and olive-oil, in which the wick floated, and burnt during the whole night.' It does not indeed appear of what materials these vases were made; but we may reasonably suppose them to have been of glass.

(5) Feast of Lamps. The later Jews had even something like this feast among themselves. A 'Feast of Lamps' was held every year on the twenty-fifth of the month Chisleu. It was founded by Judas Maccabæus in celebration of the restoration of the temple worship (Joseph. *Antiq.* xii:7, 7), and has ever since been observed by the lighting up of lamps or candles on that day in all the countries of their dispersion (Maimon. *Mish. Hashanah,* fol. 8). Other Orientals have at this day a similar feast, of which the 'Feast of Lanterns' among the Chinese is, perhaps, the best known (Davis' *Chinese,* p. 138).

Figurative. (1) God is likened to a *lamp;* he enlightens, comforts, and honors his people (2 Sam. xxii:29). (2) The *seven lamps* of the golden candlestick, figured out Jesus and his church, as possessed of the fullness of the Holy Ghost, and of Divine oracles and knowledge (Exod. xxv:37). (3) The Holy Ghost is likened to *seven lamps of fire* burning before God's throne, to mark the instructive, comforting, heart-warming, and sin-destroying nature of his influence (Rev. iv:5). (4) The *seven lamps* of the golden candlestick in Zechariah's vision, which received their oil from the bowl or fountain by pipes are a sufficient number of ministers, deriving their light, comfort, gifts, and grace, from Jesus, by the pipes of ordinances, reading the Scriptures, meditation, prayer, and by faith (Zech. iv:2). (5) Christ's eyes of infinite knowledge, and of discovered affection or wrath, are as *lamps of fire,* most penetrating and pure, and yet how terrible to his enemies (Dan. x:6). (6) The Word of God is a *lamp and light:* it discovers manifold mysteries; it directs men's course, and comforts their hearts amidst the darkness of this world (Ps. cxix: 105). (7) The *lamp* ordained for God's anointed, is either Jesus, who is the light of the world, and the continued honor of David's family; or it is the gospel, which from age to age maintains the fame and honor of our Redeemer in the world (Ps. cxxxii:17). (8) A profession of religion is called a *lamp,* it renders men shining and useful, and instructors of others (Matt. xxv:3, 4). (9) Prosperity is a *lamp;* it renders men cheerful, noted, and glorious (Prov. xiii:9; xx:20). (10) The salvation of the church from her troubles is likened to a *"burning lamp";* it is bright and visible, and its effects are instructive and comforting (Is. lxii:1).

LANCE (làns), (Heb. קִידוֹן, *kee-dohn'*), Jer. 1:42; elsewhere "spear." (See ARMS, ARMOR.)

LANCET (lăn′sĕt), (Heb. רמֶח, *ro′makh,* to hurl). This word is found in 1 Kings xviii:28 only; elsewhere "spear." (See ARMS, ARMOR.)

LAND (lănd).

1. The whole continent of the earth, as distinguished from the sea (Matt. xxiii:15).

2. A particular country, especially parts of it which are fit to be plowed (Matt. ix:26; Gen. xxvi: 12; Acts iv:37; Matt. xix:29).

3. The inhabitants of a country (Is. xxxvii: 11). (See AGRICULTURE.)

Figurative. (1) Canaan is called *Immanuel's land,* or the Lord's land. It enjoyed the peculiar care, protection, presence, and ordinances of the Redeemer, and in it he long dwelt in our nature (Is. viii:8). It was a *land of promise,* as given by promise to Abraham and his seed (Heb. xi:9). It was a *land of uprightness;* as there, men having the oracles of God, ought to have behaved uprightly towards God and man (Is. xxvi:10). It is called a *land of unwalled villages,* as it seems, the Jews, at their return, in the beginning of the millennium, will not fortify their cities (Ezek. xxxviii:11). (2) Egypt is called a *land of trouble and anguish,* because there the Hebrews were exceedingly distressed, and it had long been a scene of terrible calamities (Is. xxx:6). (3) Babylon was a *land of graven images;* because idolatry mightily prevailed in it (Jer. 1:38). (4) The *land of the living,* is this world, wherein men are before death, and the heavenly state where no death ever enters (Ps. cxvi:9, and xxvii:13). (5) The grave is the *land of darkness and of the shadow of death* (Job x:21, 22); and of *forgetfulness,* as men are soon forgotten after they are buried (Ps. lxxxviii: 12).

LANDMARK (lănd'märk), (Heb. גְּבוּל, or גְּבֻל, *gheb-ool'*), a mark to designate the boundary of land; a stone, stake, or other monument.

The Mosaic law prohibited the removal of landmarks (Deut. xix:14; xxvii:17, Prov. xxii:28; comp. Job xxiv:2). Landmarks were used in Greece before the age of Homer (*Iliad* xxi:405). They were held so sacred among the Romans that removal was punished with death. They are still used in Persia and in various parts of the East.

LANE (lān). The Greek word ῥύμη, *hroo'may*, street, so rendered in Luke xiv:21, means a narrow alley (comp.Matt. vi:2; Acts ix:11; xii:10), called in A. V. "street."

LANGUAGE (lăn'gwăj).

1. *Saw-faw'* (Heb. שָׂפָה), *sef-eth'* (שְׂפֶת), a lip, and consequently speech (Gen. xi:1, 6, 7, 9; 2 Kings xviii:26, 28; Neh. xiii:24, etc.).

2. *Law-shone'* (Heb. לָשׁוֹן), *lesh-o-naw'* (לִשָׁנָה), *lish-shawn'* (לְשָׁן?), the tongue, and in consequence *language* or *speech* (Esth. i:22; iii:12; viii:9; Dan. iii:29, etc.).

3. *Law-az'* (Heb. לָעֵז), to speak in a foreign tongue (Ps. cxiv:1); *daw-bawr'* (דָּבָר, Ps. xix:3).

4. *Dee-al'ek-tos* (Gr. διάλεκτος), the language peculiar to any people (Acts i:19; ii:6, 8; xxi:40; xxii:2; xxvi:14). (See TONGUES, CONFUSION OF.)

LANTERN (lăn'tĕrn), (Gr. φανός, *fan-os'*, shining, hence *torch*).

This word occurs only in John xviii:3, where the party of men which went out of Jerusalem to apprehend Jesus in the garden of Gethsemane is described as being provided 'with *lanterns* and torches.' In the article LAMP it has been shown that the Jewish lantern, or, if we may so call it, lamp-frame, was similar to that now in use among the Orientals. As the streets of Eastern towns are not lighted at night, and never were so, lanterns are used to an extent not known among us. Such, doubtless, was also formerly the case; and it is therefore remarkable that the only trace

Night Watch Carrying Lantern.

of a lantern which the Egyptian monuments offer, is that in which it seems to be borne by the night watch, or civic guard, and is shaped like those in common use among ourselves. A similar lantern is at this day used in Persia, and perhaps does not materially differ from those mentioned in Scripture. More common at present in Western Asia is a large folding lantern of waxed cloth strained over rings of wire, with a top and bottom of

tinned copper. It is usually about two feet long by nine inches in diameter, and is carried by servants before their masters, who often pay visits to their friends at or after supper-time. In many Eastern towns the municipal law forbids any one to be in the streets after nightfall without a lantern.

LAODICEA (la-ŏd-i-sē'á), (Gr. Λαοδίκεια, *lah-od-ik'i-ah*, justice of the people).

There were four places of this name, which it may be well to distinguish, in order to prevent them from being confounded with one another. The first was in the western part of Phrygia, on the borders of Lydia; the second, in the eastern part of the same country, denominated Laodicea Combusta; the third, on the coast of Syria, called Laodicea ad Mare, and serving as the port of Aleppo; and the fourth, in the same country, called Laodicea ad Libanum, from its proximity to that mountain. The third of these, that on the coast of Syria, was destroyed by the great earthquake of Aleppo in August, 1822, and at the time of that event was supposed by many to be the Laodicea of Scripture, although in fact not less than four hundred miles from it. But the first named, lying on the confines of Phrygia and Lydia, about forty miles east of Ephesus, is the only Laodicea mentioned in Scripture, and is that one of the 'seven churches in Asia' to which St. John was commissioned to deliver the awful warning contained in Rev. iii:14-19. The fulfilment of this warning is to be sought, as we take it, in the history of the Christian church which existed in that city, and not in the stone and mortar of the city itself; for it is not the city, but 'the church of the Laodiceans,' which is denounced.

Laodicea was the capital of Greater Phrygia, and a very considerable city at the time it was named in Scripture (Strabo, p. 578); but the frequency of earthquakes, to which this district has always been liable, demolished, some ages after, great part of the city, destroyed many of the inhabitants, and eventually obliged the remainder to abandon the spot altogether. Laodicea is now a deserted place, called by the Turks Eski-hissar (*Old Castle*). From its ruins, Laodicea seems to have been situated upon six or seven hills, taking up a large extent of ground. To the north and north-east runs the river Lycus, about a mile and a half distant; but nearer it is watered by two small streams, the Asopus and Caprus, the one to the west, and the other to the south-east, both passing into the Lycus, which last flows into the Mæander (Smith, p. 85). Laodicea preserves great remains of its importance as the residence of the Roman governors of Asia under the emperors; namely, a stadium, in uncommon preservation, three theaters, one of which is 450 feet in diameter, and the ruins of several other buildings (*Antiq. of Ionia*, pt. ii. p. 32; Chandler's *Asia Minor*, c. 67).

LAODICEA, CHURCH AT (la-ŏd-i-sē'á, church).

From the passages, Coloss. iv:16; Rev. iii:14, it appears that a Christian church was established at Laodicea by the Apostles. From the epistle to the Colossians iv:15, 16, it would seem that St. Paul himself never visited the church.

LAODICEANS (la-ŏd'i-sē-anz), inhabitants of LAODICEA (Col. iv:16; Rev. iii:14).

LAODICEANS, EPISTLE TO (la-ŏd-i-sē'anz, ĕ-pĭs''l). In Col. iv:16 Paul desires that the epistle from Laodicea "be read at Colosse." (See COLOSSIANS, EPISTLE TO THE.)

LAP (lăp), (Heb. בֶּגֶד, *beh'ged*, 2 Kings iv:39, a garment; חֵיק, *khake*, Prov. xvi:33, the bosom; חֹצֶן, *kho'tsen*, bosom, Neh. v:13; in Is. xlix:22, the Hebrew is translated *armful*). A fold of the garment used by Orientals as a pocket.

The psalmist offered the prayer, "render unto our neighbors sevenfold into their bosom their reproach" (Ps. lxxix:12). The same allusion occurs in the Savior's direction, "Give, and it shall be given unto you; good measure, pressed down, and shaken together, and running over, shall men give into your bosom" (Luke vi:38). (See BOSOM; DRESS.)

LAPIDOTH (lăp'i-dŏth), (Heb. לַפִּידוֹת, *lap-pee-doth'*, torches). Husband of the prophetess Deborah (Judg. iv:4). (B. C. before 1120.)

vinous fawn color, and further embellished with a beautiful fan-shaped crest of the same color, tipped with white and black. Its appellations in all languages appear to be either imitations of the bird's voice or indications of its filthy habits; which, however, modern ornithologists deny, or do not notice. In Egypt these birds are numerous, forming, probably, two species, the one permanently resident about human habitations, the other migratory, and the same that visits Europe. The latter wades in the mud when the Nile has subsided, and seeks for worms and insects; and the former is known to rear its young so much immersed in the shards and fragments of beetles, etc., as to cause a disagreeable smell about its nest, which is always in holes or in hollow trees. Though an unclean bird in the Hebrew law, the common migratory hoopoe is eaten in Egypt, and

Laodicea.

LAPPED, LAPPETH (lăpt, lăp'ĕth), (Heb. לָקַק, *law-kak'*, to lick up as a dog, 1 Kings xxi:19, etc.). Lapping was the test of Gideon's men (Judg. vii:5, 6), and is still in the East supposed to be an evidence of promptitude for active service. (See GIDEON).

LAPWING (lăp'wĭng), in our version, is used for Heb. דּוּכִיפַת, *doo-kee-fath'*, a word which, occurring only in Lev. xi:19, Deut. xiv:18, affords no internal or collateral evidence to establish the propriety of the translation.

It has been surmised to mean double-crest; which is sufficiently correct when applied to the hoopoe; but less so when applied to the lapwing, or the cock of the woods, *Tetrao Urogallus*. The hoopoe is not uncommon in Palestine at this day, and was from remote ages a bird of mystery. The end of the augural rod is said to have been carved in the form of a hoopoe's head; and one of the kind is still used by Indian gosseins, and even Armenian bishops, attention being no doubt drawn to the bird by its peculiarly arranged black and white bars upon a delicate

sometimes also in Italy; but the stationary species is considered inedible.   C. H. S.

LARGE (lärj), (Heb. רָחָב, *raw-khawb'*, roving in every direction). Assyria was a *large* or extensive country, or place, (Is. xxii:18; Hos. iv:16).

David was set in a *large place,* or room, when he had great liberty and comfort, and was advanced to extensive power and authority (Ps. xviii:19; xxxi:8, and cxviii:5).

Gr. ἱκανός, *hik-an-os'*, (Matt. xxviii:12), an ample present of money. "They gave large money to the soldiers."

LASCIVIOUSNESS (lăs-sĭv-ĭ-ŭs-nĕs), (Gr. ἀσέλγεια, *as-elg'i-a*, that which *excites disgust*), unbridled lust, licentiousness, wantonness.

It includes everything tending to promote or fulfill fleshly lusts; and to *give over* one's self to it, is to delight in, and practice it, without shame or remorse (Matt. xv:19; Rom. xiii:13; Gal. v:19; Eph. iv:19). To *turn the grace of God into lasciviousness,* is to use his kindness declared in the gospel as an encouragement in impurity (Jude 4).

LASEA (la-sē'á), (Gr. Λασαία, *las-ah'yah*,) derivation not known, a city of Crete near Fair Havens (Acts xxvii:8). The name is still given to some ruins a few miles east of Fair Havens. (Smith, *Voyage and Shipwreck of St. Paul*, App. iii. pp. 262, 263).

LASHA (lā'shá), (Heb. לֶשַׁע, *leh'shah*), a boundary town of southeast Palestine (Gen. x:19), mentioned by Moses in describing the land of Canaan.

The Chaldee and Jerome take this to be the place Callirrhœ, east of the Dead Sea, where are warm springs, but this cannot be confirmed. It may even be the city of Lasha, Lusa, or Elusa, at nearly an equal distance between the Dead Sea and the Red Sea. Ptolemy mentions this city of Lusa, as do Stephens the geographer, and Josephus. If identified with Callirrhœ as above, the stream from Callirrhœ, now called the Zerka Maein, enters the Dead Sea at the eastern side, about eleven miles in a direct line from the mouth of the Jordan. The springs are about three miles up the stream.

LASHARON (la-shā'ron), (Heb. לַשָּׁרוֹן, *lash-shaw-rone'*, the plain of Sharon), a town of Canaan, whose king Joshua killed (Josh. xii:18); possibly the same as Lasha (Gen. x:19).

LAST DAY. See Judgment.

LASTHENES (lăs'the-nēz), (Gr. Λασθένης, *Lasthen'ace*, 1 Macc. xi:32), an officer who stood high in the favor of Demetrius II Nicator.

LAST TIME. See Eschatology.

LATCHET (lătch'ĕt), (Heb. שְׂרוֹךְ, *ser-oke'*, a binding together), the fastening by which the sandal was held to the foot (Is. v:27; Mark i:7; Luke iii:16; John i:27).

Figurative. It is a proverbial expression for anything of little value (Gen. xiv:23). It is expressive of tightness and durability (Is. v:27). The expression in Matt. iii:11 (comp. Mark i:7; Luke iii:16; John i:27) alludes to slaves who were employed to loosen and carry their masters' shoes.

LATIN (lăt'ĭn), the vernacular language of the ancient Romans, now a dead language, but in part employed as a medium of learned intercourse between the educated of civilized nations (John xix:20).

LATTICE (lăt'tĭs), (Heb. אֶשְׁנָב, *esh-nawb'*), used much in the East in windows to screen the inmates and at the same time admit the air (Judg.v:28, "casement;" Prov. vii:6; Cant. ii:9; 2 Kings i:2). (See House.)

LAUD (lạd), (Gr. ἐπαινέω, *ep-ahee-neh'o*), to praise, extol (Rom. xv:11).

LAUGHTER (lăf'tẽr), (Heb. צְחֹק, *tsekh-oke'*; שָׂחַק, *saw-khak'*; Gr. γέλως, *ghel'oce*). Laughter in Scripture expresses as regards men:

1. Their rejoicing in the blessings promised to or possessed by them, and in their divine security from the calamities of famine, pestilence, etc. (Gen. xvii:17; xxi:6; Job v:22; Luke vi:21).

2. Their sinful mirth, their doubt of God's fulfillment of his promise, or their derision and mockery of other men (Gen. xviii:12, 13; Luke vi:25; Job xxix:24).

3. Conscious security (Job v:22).

4. When predicated of God it means that he disregards their trouble and contemns their opposition (Job ix:23; Ps. ii:4, and xxxvii:13; Prov. i:26).

5. Mockery, folly (Prov. xiv:13; Eccl. ii:2; vii:6).

LAVER (lā'vẽr), (Heb. כִּיּוֹר and כִּיֹר, *kee-yore'*, something *round*, a *basin;* Sept. λουτρόν, *loo-tron'*), a basin to contain the water used by the priests in their ablutions during their sacred ministrations.

Molten Sea or Great Laver.

(1) Tabernacle Laver. There was one of brass (fabricated out of the metal mirrors which the women brought from Egypt, Exod. xxxviii: 8). It had a 'foot' or base, which, from the manner in which 'the laver *and* its foot' are mentioned, must have been a conspicuous feature, and was perhaps separable from the basin itself for the purpose of removal. We are not informed of the size or shape of this laver; but it appears to have been large. It stood between the altar of burnt-offerings and the door of the tabernacle (Exod. xxx:18-21; xl:30-32). The water of this laver seems to have served the double purpose of washing the parts of the sacrifices, and the hands and feet of the priests.

(2) Temple Lavers. But in the temple of Solomon, when the number of both priests and victims had greatly increased, ten lavers were used for the sacrifices, and the molten sea for the personal ablutions of the priests (2 Chron. iv: 6). These lavers are more minutely described than that of the tabernacle. So far as can be made out from the description, they consisted of a square base or stand mounted upon rollers or wheels, and adorned with figures of palm-trees, cherubim, lions, and oxen. The stand doubtless formed a hollow basin for receiving the water which fell from the laver itself, and which appears to have been drawn from it by means of cocks (1 Kings vii:27-39).

(*a*) *Form and Capacity.* The form of the lavers is not mentioned; but it is stated that each of them contained forty baths, or, according to the usual computation, about 300 English gallons.

(*b*) *Brazen Sea.* Solomon made a huge laver supported by twelve brazen or copper oxen, with their heads pointing three and three to the four cardinal points; this was for the priests to wash at, and was called the *brazen sea* (1 Kings vii:22-44; 2 Chron. iv.). From the manner in which the bases of the lavers are described, it is evident that they were regarded as admirable works of art; but it is difficult to follow out the details which are given. This is evinced by the great discrepancy in the different figures, drawn from the descriptions which are given by Lamy, Calmet, and Villalpandus.

(3) Second Temple Laver. In the second temple there appears to have been only one laver. Of its size or shape we have no information, but it was probably like those of Solomon's temple.

LAW (lạ), (Heb. תּוֹרָה, *to-raw'*; Gr. νόμος, *nom'-os*, custom, law), means a rule of conduct enforced by an authority superior to that of the moral beings to whom it is given.

1. Expressive of Moral Connection. The word law is sometimes also employed in order to express not only the moral connection between free agents of an inferior and others of a superior power, but also in order to express the *nexus causalis,* the connection between cause and effect in inanimate nature. However, the expression, *law of nature, lex naturæ,* is improper and figurative. In a wider sense the word νόμος, 'law,' is employed in order to express any guiding or directing power, originating from the nature of anything existing. The apostolic use of the word has been well expressed by Claudius Guilliaud in his work, *In Omnes Pauli Epistolas Collatio,* p. 21. Law is a certain power restraining from some, and impelling to other things or actions. Whatever has such a power, and exercises any sway over man, may be called law, in a metaphorical sense.

2. Mosaical Law. If, however, the word νόμος, 'law,' alone is used, it is almost invariably equivalent to *the law of Moses.* The law is especially embodied in the last four books of the Pentateuch. In Exodus, Leviticus, and Numbers there is perceptible some arrangement of the various precepts, although they are not brought into a system. In Deuteronomy the law or legislation contained in the three preceding books is repeated with slight modifications. The whole legislation has for its manifest object, to found a theocratical hierarchy. In the Mosaical hierarchy the aim is manifest, viz. to make that which is really holy (τὸ ἱερόν) prevail. In the Mosaical legislation the priests certainly exercise a considerable authority as external ministers of holiness; but we find nothing to be compared with the sale of indulgences in the Roman Catholic church.

(1) Taxation by Tithe. Almost the whole amount of taxation was paid in the form of tithe, which was employed in maintaining the priests and Levites as the hierarchical office-bearers of government, in supporting the poor, and in providing those things which were used in sacrifices and sacrificial feasts.

The taxation by tithe, exclusive of almost all other taxes, is certainly the most lenient and most considerate which has ever anywhere been adopted or proposed. It precludes the possibility of attempting to extort from the people contributions beyond their power, and it renders the taxation of each individual proportionate to his possessions; and even this exceedingly mild taxation was apparently left to the conscience of each person. This we infer from there never occurring in the Bible the slightest vestige either of persons having been sued or goods distrained for tithes, and only an indication of curses resting upon the neglect of paying them.

(2) Poll Tax. Besides the tithes there was a small poll-tax, amounting to half a shekel for each adult male. This tax was paid for the maintenance of the sanctuary. In addition to this, the first-fruits and the firstborn of men and cattle augmented the revenue. The firstborn of men and of unclean beasts were to be redeemed by money. To this may be added some fines paid in the shape of sin-offerings, and also the vows and freewill offerings.

(3) Further Development. The Mosaical legislation is the further development of the covenant between Jehovah and Abraham. It is a politico-religious institution given to a nation of freeholders. The fundamental laws of this constitution are:

(1) Jehovah alone is God, and the invisible King of the nation (comp. Josephus, *Contra Apionem,* ii, 16).

(2) The nation is the peculiar property of Jehovah, its King; and it is therefore bound to avoid all uncleanness, as well moral as physical defilement, which must result from intermixture with foreign nations who are not subjects of the theocracy. A confederacy with these nations is accordingly forbidden (Exod. xxiii:32; xxxiv:12).

(3) The whole territory of the state was to be so distributed that each family should have a freehold, which was intended to remain permanently the inheritance of this family, and which, even if sold, was to return at stated periods to its original owners. Since the whole population consisted of families of freeholders, there were, strictly speaking, neither citizens, nor a profane or lay-nobility, nor lords temporal. We do not overlook the fact that there were persons called heads, elders, princes, dukes, or leaders among the Israelites; that is, persons who by their intelligence, character, wealth, and other circumstances, were leading men among them, and from whom even the seventy judges were chosen, who assisted Moses in administering justice to the nation.

(4) Even the inhabitants of towns were freeholders, and their exercise of trade seems to have been combined with, or subordinate to, agricultural pursuits. The only nobility was that of the tribe of Levi, and all the lords were lords spiritual, the descendants of Aaron. The priests and Levites were ministers of public worship, that is, ministers of Jehovah the King; and as such, ministers of state, by whose instrumentality the legislative as well as the judicial power was exercised. The poor were mercifully considered, but beggars are never mentioned. Hence it appears that as, on the one hand, there was no lay nobility, so, on the other, there was no mendicity. We learn from the Epistle of Paul to the Hebrews (ix:16, 17), that the Jews disposed of property by wills; but it seems that in the times of Moses, and for some period after him, all Israelites died intestate. However, the word διαθήκη, as used in Matthew, Mark, Acts, Romans, Corinthians, Galatians, Ephesians, and repeatedly in the Hebrews, implies rather a *disposition, arrangement, agreement* between parties, than a will in the legal acceptation of the term.

(5) There are no laws concerning guardians, and none against luxurious living. The inefficiency of sumptuary laws is now generally recognized, although renowned legislators in ancient times, and in the middle ages, displayed on this subject their wisdom falsely so called. Neither are there any laws against suicide. Hence we infer that suicide was rare, as we may well suppose in a nation of small freeholders, and that the inefficiency of such laws was understood.

(6) The Mosaical legislation recognizes the human dignity of women and of slaves, and particularly enjoins not to slander the deaf nor mislead the blind.

(7) The laws of Moses against crimes are severe, but not cruel. The agony of the death of criminals was never artificially protracted.

(8) Moses expressly enjoined not to reap the corners of fields, in consideration of the poor, of persons of broken fortunes, and even of the beasts of the field.

(9) Punishments were inflicted, in order specially to express the sacred indignation of the Divine Lawgiver against willful transgression of his commandments, and not for any purposes of human vengeance, or for the sake of frightening other criminals.

(10) In lawsuits very much was left to the discretion of the judges, whose position greatly resembled that of a permanent jury, who had not merely to decide whether a person was guilty, but who frequently had also to award the amount of punishment to be inflicted.

(11) In some instances the people at large were appealed to, in order to inflict summary punishment by stoning the criminal to death. This was in fact the most usual mode of execution. Other modes of execution, also, such as burning, were always public, and conducted with the cooperation of the people.

(12) In the Old Testament we do not hear of a learned profession of the law. Lawyers (νομικοί) are mentioned only after the decline of the Mosaical institutions had considerably advanced. As, however, certain laws concerning contagion and purification were administered by the priests, these might be called lawyers. They, however, did not derive their maintenance from the administration of these laws, but were supported by glebe-lands, tithes, and portions of the sacrificial offerings. It is, indeed, very remarkable, that in a nation so entirely governed by law, there were no lawyers forming a distinct profession, and that the *nom-i-koi, lawyers,* of a later age were not so much remarkable for enforcing the spirit of the law, as rather for ingeniously evading its injunctions, by leading the attention of the people from its spirit to a most minute literal fulfillment of its letter.

(13) The present article is, of course, closely interwoven with the contents of a number of others which in this Encyclopædia have preceded, or which follow it in alphabetical order, such as ADULTERY, BLOOD-REVENGE, DECALOGUE, DEUTERONOMY, DIVORCE, EXODUS, GOSPEL, LEVITICUS, MARRIAGE, MOSES, MURDER, PENTATEUCH, ROBBERY, SABBATH, SLAVE, THEFT, etc. It is, indeed, both unnecessary and impracticable to exhaust in this place all that might with propriety be brought under the head of Law. We therefore make no such attempt, but refer our readers to the cognate articles for further information. The chief point here to be considered, is the authority ascribed in the Bible itself to law in general, and to Biblical law in particular. The misconceptions on this subject prevalent in the religious world are the more surprising, since many distinguished ecclesiastical teachers of various periods, and among these St. Augustine of the fourth and fifth, and the Reformers of the sixteenth century, have stated the Biblical doctrine respecting the law with particular clearness.

3. Authority. Christ and the apostles express themselves respecting the authority of the law so variously that in order to reconcile their apparent contradictions the divines of various Christian denominations have usually felt themselves compelled to distinguish between different portions of the law, some of which, they assert, were abolished by Christ, while they maintain that others were established by him. Against this convenient mode of overcoming the difficulty the following observations may be adduced:

(1) Neither Christ nor the apostles ever distinguish between the moral, the ceremonial, and the civil law, when they speak of its establishment or its abolition.

(2) They even clearly indicate that the moral law is by no means excepted when they speak of the abolition of the law in general. Thus, for instance, St. Paul, after having stated that the law is not incumbent upon the righteous, guards us against misunderstanding him, as if this referred to the ceremonial law alone; for he specifies various transgressors to whom the law is given, and who are restrained by the same. The transgressors mentioned by St. Paul are not those of the ceremonial, but of the moral law (1 Tim. i:8-10).

(3) In order to reconcile the apparent contradictions between the various dicta of the New Testament concerning the authority of the law, we must not commence, as is usually done, namely, by distinguishing the matter of the law, but the form of manner in which it is binding or obligatory. He who said that not a jot nor a tittle of the law should perish until all things were fulfilled, certainly could not mean that more than two-thirds of the law were abolished, but intended forcibly to express the idea that, in a certain sense, by his instrumentality, the whole law, without any exception, had obtained an increased authority. We, therefore, conceive that in order to reconcile the apparent, but merely apparent, contradictions of the New Testament, we must distinguish not so much the various materials, ritual, civil, and moral, of which the law is composed, as the various manners in which its *modus obligandi* may exist.

(4) The authority which other beings may exercise upon us is twofold; it is either *nomothetical* or *didactical.* The *nomothetical* authority, which a book, or the living voice of another moral being may exercise upon us, is either such that it precludes the exercise of our own judgment, like that which Pythagoras is said to have exercised upon his disciples, who were in the habit of settling all their disputes, as by a final reason from which there was no appeal, by αὐτὸς ἔφα, *he has said so;* or the authority is such as to excite the faculties of the listener, so that he perceives the necessity of the truth communicated. In this last case the authority exercised is not *nomothetical,* but *didactical.*

(5) So it was also with the human race at large: it was necessary that the law of Moses should exercise *nomothetical* authority by 'Cursed is he who does not continue in the words of this law.' And so it is now with a great portion of Christian religionists, who still require frightful curses and opposite benedictions somewhat similar to those formerly pronounced on the mountains Ebal and Gerizim, in order to keep them in the right direction. But the assertion of this *nomothetical* authority was not the ultimate aim of Christ. His most intimate disciple, whom he especially loved, states strikingly, Ὅτι ὁ νόμος διὰ Μωσέως ἐδόθη· ἡ χάρις καὶ ἡ ἀλήθεια διὰ Ἰησοῦ Χριστοῦ ἐγένετο, *For the law was given by Moses, but grace and truth came by Jesus Christ.*

(6) It is a fact that Christ did not give new laws, but only new motives for keeping the moral precepts more or less clearly known to Jews and Gentiles, by making it a prominent doctrine, that love is due to God and to men in general, even to our enemies, and that intentions are of greater moral importance than outward acts.

(7) The characteristic of the doctrine of Christ does not consist in new laws given, but rather in the forgiveness offered for past transgressions, and in the guidance of the Holy Spirit promised to his true disciples. The authority of this Holy Spirit is described in the Gospel of John, and in the Epistle to the Romans, as superior to the letter of the law. Whosoever is filled with this Spirit is not under the law, although he fulfills the holy aim and intention of the law. The true disciple of Christ, if asked, Why did you not kill such or such a person? cannot answer, Because it is written, 'Thou shalt do no murder.' Christians feel that they are filled with a spirit which prevents them from desiring the commission of crimes.

(8) It is very surprising that the clear perception of the true source of the law, which was fulfilled even by its abrogation, could have been so effectually obscured as is done by the doctrine current in the religious world concerning the abolition of its civil and ceremonial, and the establishment of its moral precepts. The whole aim and scope of the Mosaical legislation have been established as much as the aim of temporary police regulations, enacted in order to meet the emergencies of a commonwealth during a period of rebellion, is established and fulfilled by him who restores perfect peace and public tranquillity, although the natural consequence of this peace is, that those regulations cease to be in force. On the other hand, although the Christian, who is under the guidance of a spirit leading him into all truth, cannot be led by this spirit to the commission of any crime contrary to the moral precepts of Moses, it cannot be said, that by not committing murder and adultery, he obeys the Mosaical law, any more than that he obeys the injunctions of the *Code Napoleon,* in these particular instances.

4. Various Meanings Of. Some think that by *laws, precepts,* or *commandments,* in the books of Moses, is meant the *moral* law; by *statutes,* the *ceremonial,* and that by *judgments* the *judicial* laws are signified; but this observation will not always hold. It is certain, that by law, commandment, precept, statute, and judgment, used in this signification, is often meant one and the same thing. (1) The name *law,* or *commandment,* may denote a thing as the will of a superior; *statute,* represents it as ordained and established by high authority; *judgment* represents it as full of wisdom, and as the standard by which God will judge men. (2) Those passages of Scripture which require any good quality in us, or good work to be performed by us, are the law in a strict sense (John i:17). (3) The ten commandments are called *the law,* or *commandment;* nay, sometimes the last six are so called (James ii:11; Rev. xxii:14; Rom. ii: 25, and vii:7, 8, xiii:8). (4) The commandment of loving one another, is *old,* as it was contained in the moral law ever since the creation; and it is *new,* as enjoined afresh by our Savior, as exemplified in his life, and enforced with the new motive of his dying love (John ii:7, 8, and xiii: 14). (5) The whole constitution of the covenant between God and the Hebrews, and the rites of worship thereto belonging are called a *"law,"* or *"law of ordinances,"* and a *"carnal commandment:"* as, by the authority of God, so many rites, especially relating to carnal sacrifices, washings, and the like, were therein required (Eph. ii:15; Heb. x:1; vii:16). (6) The five books of Moses are called *"the law,"* as they abound with the requirements and prohibitions of God (Mal. iv:4; Matt. v:17); and, for the same reason, the Old Testament is called *"a law"* (John x:34; xv: 25; 1 Cor. xiv:21). (7) The whole word of God is called *"a law," "statutes,"* etc., as it is the sole rule of our faith and practice (Ps. i:2; xix: 7, 8). (8) The doctrines of the gospel are called *"a law,"* and the *"law of faith;"* they teach and instruct men, and when believed by faith, they strongly influence to holy obedience (Is. ii:3; xlii:4; Rom. iii:27), and they are a *"perfect law of liberty,"* proclaim a perfect deliverance and redemption to us through the blood of God's Son,

and prompt to a kindly and free obedience to him; or this perfect *"law of liberty"* may be taken for the law as a rule in the hand of Christ, which is pleasant to his followers (James i:25; ii:12). (9) The commandments and word of God are a "law ordained to life," and are "statutes of life." In believing and obeying these, we receive or possess life temporal and spiritual, and are prepared for life eternal (Ezek. xxxiii:15; Rom. vii:10). (10) One is "without the law," when not under the ceremonial law, or not bound by the law (1 Cor. ix:21); or when he is without the knowledge of it, and destitute of the experience of its convincing power on the conscience (Rom. ii:12; vii:8, 9); or when they have not the word of God revealed to them (Rom. ii:14). (11) Those "under the law," are either Jews under the ceremonial, or sinners under the broken covenant, or saints under the law as a rule. (12) "The law is a schoolmaster to bring us to Christ:" the ceremonial law pointed him out, and led to him as the end and antitype of all its rites (Gal. iii:24). "The law of the Spirit of life in Christ Jesus' makes free from the law of sin and death," whether death, spiritual, temporal, and eternal (Rom. viii: 2). (13) The principle of grace in the saints is called the "law of their mind;" influenced by the views of God in Christ, it reigns, and determines the soul to obedience. (14) The principle of corruption in men is called the "law of sin," as it is altogether sinful; and determines to sinful thoughts, words, and actions; and it is called "the law in the members," as though dislodged from its throne in the heart, it continues strongly to actuate the powers of the soul, and members of the body, to what is impure and wicked (Rom. vii:23, 25). (15) The "law" may sometimes denote men's observance of God's commandments, as that corresponds to the law imposed in the Scripture, or impressed on the heart (Rom. iii: 21; Gal. iii:11; Phil. iii:6, 9).

5. Literature. Compare beside Johann David Michaelis, *Mosaisches Recht,* translated by Alexander Smith, under the title, *Commentaries on the Laws of Moses,* by the late John David Michaelis, London, 1814; Josephus, *Contra Apionem,* ii, 16, *sq.; Mosaicarum et Romanarum legum collatio,* referred usually to the fifth century; Jos. Priestley, *Comparison of the Law of Moses with those of the Hindoos,* etc.; Hugo Grotius, *De Jure Belli et Pacis.*

LAW, CEREMONIAL (lạ sĕr'ĕ-mō'nĭ-al).

(1) The *ceremonial law* regulated the office and conduct of Priests, Levites, Nethinims, Nazarites, and of circumcision, feasts, offerings, tabernacle, temple, and utensils thereof, *vows, purifications,* etc. (See the articles on the above subjects.)

(2) In respect of observance, this law was a heavy yoke, and partition wall; but in respect of the signification of its ceremonies, it was an obscure gospel (Gal. v:1; Eph. ii:14; Col. ii:17). (See LAW.)

LAWFUL (Gr. ἔξεστι, *ex'es-tee*), agreeable to law.

"All things are lawful, but all things are not expedient;" the apostle means that it is lawful, simply considered, to eat any kind of provision; but to eat of meat sacrificed to idols, might, in special circumstances, be injurious to weak consciences, and ought to be avoided (1 Cor. vi:12). In his trance, Paul heard things which were not "lawful to be uttered:" so mysterious and grand, that it was not proper to declare them to men in their embodied state, as they could not be profited thereby, or more truly they were beyond the power of earthly language to express (2 Cor. xii:4).

LAWGIVER (Heb. מְחֹקֵק, *meh-kho-kake'*; Gr. νομοθέτης, *nom-oth-et'ace*), one who prescribes laws.

God or Christ is a "Lawgiver;" his sovereign will is the infallible rule of our conduct; and he has prescribed laws to us in his word (Is. xxxiii:22; James iv:12); and he alone is the Lord of our conscience, the simple expression of his will binds it to obedience, and his laws are subject to no examination, being absolutely supreme and infallible. Moses was a "lawgiver;" by him God gave his system of laws to the Hebrews; the law is called his, and he is said to give its commandments (Num. xxi:18; Deut. xxxiii:21). David and his successors in rule are called "lawgivers;" they had power of enacting laws for the civil government of the Hebrew nation (Gen. xlix:10; Ps. lx:7).

LAW, JUDICIAL.
(1) Regulations. The *judicial law* regulated the affairs of their kings, judges, fields, marriages, punishments, etc. Some laws relative to redeemers, murders, adultery, cities of refuge, malefactors, strangers, etc., seem to have been partly ceremonial and partly judicial.

(2) Preservation of the Laws. Great care was taken to preserve the knowledge of the divine law. Besides the table of the ten commandments deposited in the ark, a copy of the books of Moses was laid up somewhere in the side of the ark. The Jews say that every tribe had a copy of it. From this, other copies were taken. Every king was obliged to transcribe one for himself. The whole law was to be publicly read over at the feast of tabernacles, in the year of release, besides the reading of it on other public occasions. Nay, they were required to have it written on their hearts, and to teach it diligently unto their children (Deut. xvii and xxxi:9-19; vi and x). To this day the Jews have the utmost regard for their law, reading in the ancient manner so much of it every Sabbath, in their synagogues. The book of it publicly used, is written with the greatest exactness, and is carefully preserved from everything tending to defile it. (See LAW; TRADITION.) (W. Smith, *The Pentateuch;* Martensen, *Christian Ethics*, i, vol. i; Hodge, *Sys. Theol.*, vol. iii.)

LAW OF MOSES (Heb. תּוֹרָה מֹשֶׁה, *to-raw' Mo-sheh'*), signifies the whole body of Mosaic legislation.

The *moral law* was most solemnly proclaimed by God himself, after a terrible thunder, lightning, and earthquake, and from the midst of the flames of fire; and was divided into ten precepts, written by God himself upon two tables of stone. Four of these respect our duty to God, and were written on the first, which, in sum require our loving him as the Lord our God with all our heart, soul, mind, and strength; six were written on the second, which in sum require our loving our neighbor as ourselves (Exod. xix, xx, xxxii and xxxiv; Matt. xxii:37-39). (1) More particularly, the first commandment requires that God alone should, both in heart and life, be acknowledged, worshiped, and glorified, as the true God, and our God; and that all Atheism, profaneness, and idolatry, be abstained from. (2) The second requires that all the ordinances of worship instituted by God in his word, should be received, observed, and kept pure and entire; and all carnal conceptions of God, all idolatry and superstition, and monuments, or occasions thereof be detested. (3) The third requires that God's names, titles, attributes, ordinances, words, and works should be, under the severest penalties, used only in a holy and reverent manner. (4) The fourth requires that whatever times God has appointed in his word, particularly one whole day in seven, be carefully observed in spiritual exercises, as holy to the Lord. (5) The fifth requires the preservation of honor, and performance of relative duties between parents and children, husbands and wives, masters and servants, magistrates and subjects, ministers and people; and, in fine, between superiors and inferiors, in age, station, gifts, or grace: and between equals, one to another. (6) The sixth requires that all lawful endeavors shall be used to promote and preserve the life of ourselves and others, temporal, spiritual, or eternal; and prohibits all malice, envy, murder, angry words, drunkenness, and every thing else tending to the hurt of soul or body. (7) The seventh prohibits all kinds of whoredom, fornication, adultery, incest, bestiality, self-defilement, and other uncleanness, and every thing in heart speech, or behavior, tending thereto. (8) The eighth requires, that every thing lawful be done to promote our own and our neighbor's outward estate; and all dishonesty, stealing, robbery, extortion, oppression, sacrilege, etc., be detested. (9) The ninth requires that the utmost care be taken to maintain and preserve truth, and our own and our neighbor's good name; and prohibits all falsehood, lying, dissimulation, flattery, railing, or reproachful language. (10) The tenth prohibits the very root of wickedness in the heart, and first motions thereof, and all discontentment, envy, and inordinate affection towards our neighbor or anything that is his. (See DECALOGUE; LAW.)

LAWYER (la'yẽr), (Gr. νομικός, *nom-ik-os'*, according to law), a term used to signify one who is conversant with the law. An interpreter of the law, a jurist, as in Tit. iii:13.

When, therefore, one is called a lawyer, this is understood with reference to the laws of the land in which he lived, or to which he belonged. Hence among the Jews a lawyer was one versed in the laws of Moses, which he taught in the schools and synagogues (Matt. xxii:35; Luke x:25; xi:45; xiv:3). The same person who is called 'a lawyer' in these texts, is in the parallel passage (Mark xii:28) called a scribe (*gram-ma-toos*); whence it has been inferred that the functions of the lawyers and the scribes were identical. The individual may have been *both* a lawyer and a scribe; but it does not follow that all lawyers were scribes. Some suppose, however, that the 'scribes' were the public expounders of the law, while the 'lawyers' were the private expounders and teachers of it. But this is a mere conjecture; and nothing more is really known than that the 'lawyers' were expounders of the law, whether publicly or privately, or both. Among the Jews the lawyers were generally enemies to our Savior in the days of his flesh, rejected the counsel of God against themselves, and were condemned by him for binding heavier burdens on others than they themselves chose to bear.

LAY (lā), (Heb, שִׂים, *seem*).

1. (Job xli:26). "If one lay at him with the sword," hence to lay at or to strike at; also to lay out and to lay away.

2. (Josh. ii:1). "They came into the house . . . and lay there," R. V., i. e., to lodge or dwell.

LAYING ON OF HANDS.

An act symbolizing dedication to a special purpose. The Israelites placed their hands on the heads of the Levites, dedicating them to the service of the Lord at the tabernacle in the stead of the firstborn of all the tribes. They pressed down their hands upon the heads of the Levites, doubtless with the intention of signifying thereby that with God's permission and by his authority, they transferred their own obligation to service to the Levites (Num. viii:5-20). The Israelite, who brought an animal to the sacrificial altar, placed his hands upon the victim's head, thereby dedicating it to God and making it his own representative and substitute (Lev. i:4; xvi:21). The aged Jacob laid his hands on the heads of Joseph's sons, giving them a place among his own sons, and bestowing upon them the covenant blessing, transferring it from himself as its past possessor to them (Gen. xlviii:5-20). The hands of presbytery were laid upon the head of Timothy. The young man was thereby set apart to official service and grace was bestowed (I Tim. iv:14). Imposition of the hands of presbytery denoted not only commission, but also the bestowal, by those divinely authorized, of official spiritual grace; or at least it signified the authoritative recommendation of the candidate to God as a recipient of grace. (Davis, *Bib. Dict.*) (See IMPOSITION OF HANDS; PRESBYTER; PRESBYTERY.)

LAZARUS (lăz'a-rŭs), (Gr. Λάζαρος, *lad'zar-os*), an abridged form of the Hebrew name Eleazer.

1. An inhabitant of Bethany, brother of Mary and Martha, who was honored with the friendship of Jesus, by whom he was raised from the dead after he had been four days in the tomb. This great miracle is minutely described in John xi. The credit which Christ obtained among the people by this illustrious act, of which the life and presence of Lazarus afforded a standing evidence, induced the Sanhedrim, in plotting against Jesus, to contemplate the destruction of Lazarus also (John xii:10). Whether they accomplished this object or not we are not informed: but the probability seems to be that when they had satiated their malice on Christ they left Lazarus unmolested. According to an old tradition in Epiphanius (*Hær.,* lxvi:34, p. 652), Lazarus was thirty years old when restored to life, and lived thirty years after. (See Ellicott, *Life of Christ;* Watson, *Lazarus of Bethany.*)

2. A beggar represented in the parable of Dives as abjectly poor (Luke xvi:20-25).

LEAD (lĕd), (Heb. עֹפֶרֶת, *o-feh'reth*, a well-known metal, the first Scriptural notice of which occurs in the triumphal song in which Moses celebrates the overthrow of Pharaoh, whose host is there said to have '*sunk like lead*' in the waters of the Red Sea (Exod. xv:10).

Before the use of quicksilver was known, lead was used for the purpose of purifying silver, and separating it from other mineral substances (Plin. *Hist. Nat.* xxxii:31). To this Jeremiah alludes where he figuratively describes the corrupt condition of the people: 'In their fire the lead is consumed (in the crucible); the smelting is in vain, for the evil is not separated' (Jer. vi:29). Ezekiel (xxii:18-22) refers to the same fact, and for the same purpose, but amplifies it with greater minuteness of detail. Compare also Mal. iii:2, 3.

Job (xix:23,24) expresses a wish that his words were engraven 'with an iron pen and lead.' These words are commonly supposed to refer to engraving on a leaden tablet; and it is undeniable that such tablets were anciently used as a writing material (Pausan. ix:31; Plin. *Hist. Nat.* xiii:11). But our authorized translators, by rendering 'an iron pen and lead in the rock for ever,'

seem to have entertained the same view with Rosenmüller, who supposes that molten lead was to be poured into letters sculptured on stone with an iron chisel, in order to raise the inscription.

Although the Hebrew weights were usually of stone, and are indeed called 'stones,' a leaden weight denominated *anach,* which is the Arabic word for lead, occurs in Amos vii:7, 8. In Acts xxvii:28, a plummet for taking soundings at sea is mentioned, and this was of course of lead.

The ancient uses of lead in the East seem to have been very few, nor are they now numerous. One may travel far in western Asia without discovering any trace of this metal in any of the numerous useful applications which it is made to serve in European countries.

We are not aware that any trace of lead has yet been found within the limits of Palestine. But ancient lead-mines, in some of which the ore has been exhausted by working, have been discovered by Mr. Burton in the mountains between the Red Sea and the Nile; and lead is also said to exist at a place called Sheff, near Mount Sinai.

LEAF, LEAVES (lēf, lēvz), (Heb. עָלֶה, *aw-leh'*, a coming up).

Figurative. This word is used either in the singular or plural in three different senses symbolically.

(1) Of Trees (Gen. viii:11; Is. i:30; vi:13; Matt. xxi:19; Mark xi:13; xiii:28, etc).

(2) Of Doors (Heb. צֵלָע, *tsay-law'*, a side), (I Kings vi:32,34), where the Hebrew means "beams," "ribs," "sides." In Ezek. xli:24 "leaves" no doubt means that the doors folded, as in our folding door.

(3) Of a Book (Heb. דֶּלֶת, *deh'leth*), or more properly of the page or column of a roll (Jer. xxxvi:23).

LEAGUE (lēg), (Heb. בְּרִית, *ber-eeth'*), a covenant, or solemn agreement, for peace, protection or assistance, or subjection between nations, or between princes and people (Josh. ix:11, 16; 2 Sam. v:3; I Kings v:12, and xv:19).

After the league made with Antiochus Epiphanes, *he wrought deceitfully;* after a covenant of friendship with Demetrius, his nephew, the true heir, he deceitfully procured the kingdom of Syria to himself; after a covenant of friendship with his other nephew, Philometer, king of Egypt, he deceitfully invaded that country to seize it for himself (Dan. xi:23). To be in *league with the stones of the field,* fowls, or beasts, is, by virtue of an interest in God's new covenant of peace, to be secured by God their proprietor and manager, from receiving any hurt by them (Job v:23; Ezek. xxxiv:25; Hos. ii:18). (See COVENANT.)

LEAH (lē'ah), (Heb. לֵאָה, *lay-aw'*, weary), one of the two daughters of Laban who became the wives of Jacob (Gen. xxix:16).

She was not so beautiful as her sister Rachel, having weak eyes, which probably accounts for Jacob's preference for the younger sister. Leah bore Jacob six sons, Reuben, Simeon, Levi, Judah (xxix:32-35), Issachar, and Zebulun (xxx:17-20), and a daughter, Dinah (verse 21). She appears to have died in Canaan, as she is not mentioned in the migration to Egypt (xlvi:6), and was buried in Hebron (xlix:31).

LEANNOTH (le-ăn'noth), (Heb. לְעַנּוֹת, *le-an-noth'*, for answering), a musical direction in the title of Ps. lxxxviii, showing that it was to be chanted in the manner indicated.

LEASING (lēz'ĭng), (Heb. כָּזָב, *kaw-zawb'*, "falsehood"), is retained in the A. V. of Ps. iv:2; v:6, from the old English versions. The Hebrew word is elsewhere almost uniformly translated "lies" (Ps. xl:4; lviii:3, etc.).

LEATHER (lĕth'ēr), (Heb. עוֹר, *ôre*), 2 Kings i:8; Matt. iii:4; in both these passages the reference is to a girdle. The word "skin" might be translated leather in Lev. xi:32; Num. xxxi:20; also "raiment" (Lev. xiii:48).

LEAVEN and FERMENT (lĕv'n and fēr'mĕnt).

In Hebrew we find two distinct words, both translated *leaven* in the common version of the Bible. This is unfortunate, for there is the same distinction between *Seh-ore'*, שְׂאֹר and *khawmates'*, חָמֵץ, in the Hebrew, as between *leaven* and *ferment* in the English. Chemically speaking, the 'ferment' or 'yeast' is the same substance in both cases; but 'leaven' is more correctly applied to solids, 'ferment' both to liquids and solids.

(1) Process of Fermentation. The organic chemists define the process of fermentation, and the substance which excites it, as follows:— 'Fermentation is nothing else but the putrefaction of a substance containing no nitrogen. *Ferment*, or yeast, is a substance in a state of putrefaction, the atoms of which are in a continual motion.' This definition is in strict accordance with the views of the ancients, and gives point and force to many passages of Sacred Writ (Exod. xii:15; Matt. xvi:6, 11, 12; Mark viii:15; Luke xii:1; xiii:21; 1 Cor. v:5-8; Gal. v:9).

(2) Substances Prohibited. *Leaven,* and fermented or even some readily fermentible substances (as honey), were prohibited in many of the typical institutions both of the Jews and Gentiles. Plutarch (*Rom-Quæst.* cix. 6) assigns as the reason why the priest of Jupiter was not allowed to touch *leaven,* 'that it comes out of corruption, and corrupts that with which it is mingled.' See also Aul. Gellius, viii:15. All fermented substances were prohibited in the Paschal Feast of the Jews (Exod. xii:8, 19, 20) ; also during the succeeding seven days, usually called 'The Feast of Unleavened *Bread,'* though *bread* is not in the original. God forbade either *ferment* or *honey* to be offered to him in his temple (*i. e.* in the symbolical rites), while they were permitted in offerings designed to be consumed as food (Num. xv:20, 21). On the same principle of symbolism, God prescribes that *salt* shall always constitute a part of the oblations to him (Lev. ii:11). Salt prevents corruption or decay, and preserves flesh. Hence it is used as a symbol of incorruption and perpetuity. Thus St. Paul (comp. Col. iv:6; Mark ix:50) uses 'salt' as preservative from corruption, on the same principle which leads him to employ that which is *unfermented* (ἄζυμος) as an emblem of purity and uncorruptedness.

'The usual *leaven* in the East is dough kept till it becomes sour, and which is kept from one day to another for the purpose of preserving leaven in readiness. Thus, if there should be no leaven in all the country for any length of time as much as might be required could easily be produced in twenty-four hours. *Sour dough,* however, is not exclusively used for leaven in the East, the *lees of wine* being in some parts employed as yeast' (*Pictorial Bible,* vol. i, p. 161).

F. R. L.

To commemorate Israel's hasty departure from Egypt, without having time to leaven their dough,

they were prohibited to use any *leaven* at the passover-feast, or to offer it on God's altar in any of their meat-offerings (Exod. xii:15-19; Lev. ii:11).

Figurative. On account of the penetrating and diffusive nature of leaven it is used symbolically of moral influence, good or bad:

(1) The gospel-church of God, which, from small beginnings, gradually spreads in the world; the gospel of Christ, which gradually prevails to reform and convert the nations of the world; and the work of inward grace, which gradually prevails in, and assimilates the hearts of men to its own likeness (Matt. xiii:33).

(2) The erroneous doctrines, corrupt glosses of the Scripture, or vain traditions of the Pharisees, Sadducees, and Herodians, and their corrupt examples, whereby many were infected (Matt. xvi: 6, 12).

(3) Scandal, and scandalous sinners, who infect and cast a blot on the church (1 Cor. v:6).

(4) Malice, hypocrisy, and like corruptions in the heart, which exceedingly defile us, and render us infectious to others (1 Cor. v:7).

LEBANA (lĕb'a-nà), (Neh. vii:48). See LEBANAH.

LEBANAH (lĕb'a-nah), (Heb. לְבָנָה, *leb-aw-naw'*, whiteness), one of the Nethinim whose descendants were among those who returned from captivity under Zerubbabel (Ezra ii:45), B. C. before 536.

LEBANON (lĕb'a-non), (Heb. לְבָנוֹן, *leb-aw-nohn'*, white from the snow on its peaks), a famous mountain in the south of Syria, and north of Canaan. When taken at large, it is about three hundred miles in circumference, and consists of two large mountains, Lebanon or Libanus, and Antilibanus. Hills of less elevation run from it in every direction (Hos. xiv:5). Its streams rendered the rich soil of the valleys extremely productive. The lower zone was covered with vines (verses 6, 7), but the mountains were most noted for their forests of gigantic cedars. Fir trees or cypresses also abounded (1 Kings v:6-10; 2 Kings xix:23; Is. xl:16; lx:13; Zech. xi:1). Lions and leopards roamed in the woods (2 Kings xiv:9; Cant. iv:8).

Lebanon is remarkable for the grandeur and beauty of its scenery, and supplied the sacred writers with many expressive figures (Ps. lxxii: 16; civ:16-18; Cant. iv:15; Is. ii:13; xxxv:2; lx: 13; Hos. xiv:5). (See LIBANUS.)

Figurative. Lebanon is used to symbolize that which is strong, great and beautiful. (1) Jesus Christ, and his church, are likened to *Lebanon,* for their spiritual comeliness and perpetual flourish, and for their fragrancy and fruitfulness (Cant. v:15; Ps. lxxii:16; Is. xxxv:2 and lx:13; Hos. xiv:5-7). (2) Jerusalem, and the temple thereof, are called *Lebanon,* because much built of the cedars of Lebanon; and the houses of Jerusalem were so many and high as to resemble the forest of Lebanon (Hab. ii:17; Zech. xi:1; Ezek. xvii:3; Jer. xxii:23). (3) Sennacherib's army, and the Assyrian empire, are called *Lebanon.* How great was once their glory and strength! but how cut down at last by the axe of God's judgments! (Is. x:34; Ezek. xxxi:3, 15, 16). (4) *"Lebanon shall be turned into a fruitful field, and the fruitful field be esteemed a forest."* The Gentile nations shall become a flourishing church, and the Jews shall be cast out, and live without God, and without Christ, and without hope in the world (Is. xxix:17 and xxxii:15). (5) To *go up to Lebanon and Bashan,* or *Mount*

Gilead, and *cry,* signifies, that the Jews would have none to help them (Jer. xxii :23).

LEBAOTH (lĕb'a-ŏth), (Heb. לְבָאוֹת, *leb-aw-ŏth'*, lions), a place which formed one of the last groups of southern cities possessed by the tribe of Judah (Josh. xv:32); probably the same as BETH-LEBAOTH (Josh. xix:6).

LEBBEUS or LEBBÆUS (leb-bē'us or leb-bæ'us), (Gr. Λεββαῖος, *leb-bah'yos,* courageous), a surname of the Apostle Judas or Jude (Matt. x:3), one of the twelve apostles. He was also called Thaddæus, which perhaps was his regular *apostolic* name.

LEBONAH (le-bō'nah), (Heb. לְבוֹנָה, *leb-o-naw',* frankincense).

A landmark north of Shiloh (Judg. xxi:19). It is no doubt the modern *Lubban,* a little south

LEES (lēz), (Heb. שֶׁמֶר, *sheh'mer* something preserved), the dregs of wine that fall to the bottom of the vessel in which it is refined.

These lees are preserved, and new wine poured on them, and allowed to remain for a long time. It is said this process communicates both strength and flavor to the wine (Is. xxv:6).

Figurative. Men are "*settled on their lees,*" when, through long prosperity, they have arrived at much outward strength, and are fixed in, and delighted with corrupt courses (Jer. xlviii: 11; Zeph. i:12). *To drink the lees* of the cup of wrath means to drain the cup, enduring the punishment to the utmost (Ps. lxxv:8, rendered dregs).

LEFT (lĕft), (Heb. שְׂמֹאול, *sem'ole,* dark; Gr. εὐώνυμος, *hew-o'noo-mos,* of good omen).

The Grand Range of Lebanon.

of Nablûs, on the road to Jerusalem (Wilson, ii. 292, sq.; Porter, p. 330; Robinson, *Researches,* iii, 90).

LECAH (lē'kah), (Heb. לֵכָה, *lay-kaw',* walking, course), a name occurring only in the genealogies of Judah (1 Chron. iv:21), but whether of a place founded by Er, or his son Lecah, the son of Shelah; or whether it is the descendant of Shelah himself that is meant cannot be absolutely stated.

LEDGE (lĕj), (Heb. שָׁלָב, *shaw-lawb'*), an ornament covering the angles at the base of a pedestal, or the angles themselves (1 Kings vii:28, 29).

LEECH (lēch). See HORSE-LEECH.

LEEK (lēk), (Heb. חָצִיר, *khaw-tseer'*), a bulbous vegetable like the onion, a particular species of which has been cultivated in Egypt from a very early period (Num. xi:5).

It is eaten raw with bread. In the passage cited it is supposed that lettuce, salads, or savory herbs generally may be intended, as the original word in the Old Testament is twelve times rendered "grass" and once "herb." (See CHATZIR.)

The left hand was esteemed of ill omen, hence the term *sinister,* as equivalent to unfortunate. This was especially the case among the Greeks and Romans. That which came from the *left* in the auguries was regarded as *sinister;* "the Greek term was used euphemistically in taking auguries; that is for something sinister for which a *good name* was desired." (Grimm *Lex.*) Among other Hebrew uses this indicated the *north* (Job xxiii:9; Gen. xiv:15), the face being understood to be turned to the east.

LEFT-HANDED (lĕft'hănd'ĕd), (Heb. יַד יְמִינ אִטֵּר, *itter yād yeminō,* shut, as to his right hand, Judg. iii:15; xx:16), denotes one who is unable skillfully to use his right hand, and also, perhaps, one who is *ambidexter,* i. e., who can use both hands equally well, although this latter meaning is a doubtful one. (See HAND.)

LEG, the limb of the body by which men and other animals walk. Several Hebrew words in the A. V. are translated by the term leg:

1. *Kaw-raw'* (Heb. כָּרָע), the lower limb, the shank (Exod. xii:9; xxix:17; Lev. i:9, 13; iv:11, etc.)

2. *Shoke* (Heb. שׁוֹק), the shin, but used of the whole limb, e. g., of a person (Deut. xxviii:35; Ps. cxlvii:10; Prov. xxvi:7). It is also used of the "thigh" (Is. xlvii:2) in the phrase "hip and thigh" (Judg. xv:8).

3. *Reh'gel* (Heb. רֶגֶל, properly the *foot*, 1 Sam. xvii:6).

4. Improperly for *show'bel* (Heb. שֹׁבֶל, the train or trailing dress of a woman, Is. xlvii:2), and of *tseh-aw-daw'* (Heb. צְעָדָה, an ornamental chain for the ankle).

The bones of the legs of persons crucified were broken to hasten death (John xix:31). (Mc. & Str. *Bib. Cyc.*) (See CRUCIFIXION.)

Figurative. (1) Men's "*legs*" are taken for their strength (Ps. cxlvii:10), and are called "*strong men*," who bow themselves on becoming feeble in old age (Eccl. xii:3). (2) The "*iron legs*" of Nebuchadnezzar's image, and its feet and toes, partly of iron and clay, not rightly coalescing together, perhaps represented the strong Roman empire, with two consuls at its head; and, after many ages, divided into the eastern and western empires, and which at last was mingled with Goths, Huns, and Vandals, but did not rightly incorporate with them, nor retain its strength, after they had well begun their invasions; and which was divided at last into ten kingdoms (Dan. ii:33). (See DANIEL.) (3) A parable in the mouth of fools, is like the "*unequal legs of the lame*" (Prov. xxvi:7).

LEGERDEMAIN (lĕj'ẽr-dĕ-mān). See MAGI.

LEGION (lē'jŭn), (Gr. Λεγεών, *leg-ee-one'*, a Greek form of the Latin *legio*), a division of the Roman army. It always comprised a large body of men; but the number varied so much at different times that there is considerable discrepancy in the statements with reference to it.

The legion appears to have originally contained about 3,000 men, and to have risen gradually to twice that number, or even more. As all the divisions of the Roman army are noticed in scripture, we may add that each legion was divided into ten *cohorts* or regiments, each cohort into three *maniples* or bands, and each maniple into three *centuries* or companies of 100 each. This smaller division into centuries or hundreds, from the form in which it is exhibited as a constituent of the larger divisions, clearly shows that 6,000 had become at least the formal number of a legion.

The military standard of the Romans was at first a bunch of straw attached to a pole. Later an eagle and four other animals formed the standards of a legion, but after 104 B. C. the eagle alone was employed (Pliny, *Hist. Nat.* x:4). It was committed to the custody of the chief centurion. In addition to the eagle, the standard also commonly bore a small image of the emperor, and the introduction of these images into Jerusalem by Pontius Pilate caused an insurrection of the Jews (*Antiq.* xviii:3, 1; *War* ii:9, 2). But while the great standard of the whole legion was the eagle, each cohort and century had its own standard, and these minor ensigns assumed a variety of forms.

Figurative. The word *legion* came to be used to express a great number or multitude (Matt. xxvi:53). Thus, the unclean spirit (Mark v:9), when asked his name, answers, 'My name is Legion, for *we* are many' (comp. verse 15). The Rabbinical writers even apply it to inanimate objects, as when they speak of 'a legion of olives,' etc.

LEHABIM (lē'ha-bĭm), (Heb. לְהָבִים, *leh-haw-beem'*, fiery, flaming), the third son of Mizraim (Gen. x:13; 1 Chron. 1:11). Some think that Lehabim denotes the Libyans, one of the most ancient peoples in Africa.

In Nah. iii:9, and Dan. xi:43, we find mention of the Lubim, which the Vulgate and LXX every where render Libyans; or, what comes to the same in Nahum and Daniel, they render Nubians. It is clear that this name describes colonies of Egyptians (Calmet). They are undoubtedly the *Re Bu* or *Le Bu* of the Egyptian monuments and are of Midianitish or kindred origin with the Egyptians. "The Lehabim are the fair-haired, blue-eyed Libyans, who as far back as the nineteenth and twentieth dynasties had been incorporated into the Egyptian army. At one time they occupied much the same place in Egyptian history as was subsequently occupied by the Lydians, and it is probable that the twenty-second dynasty, that of Shishak, was of Libyan extraction, and owed its rise to power to the influence of the Libyan troops." (Sayce, *Higher Crit. and Mon.* p. 135.)

LEHI (lē'hī), (Heb. לְהִי, *lekh'ee*, meaning *cheek* or *jawbone*). A place in Judah where Samson, single-handed, conquered the Philistines with a jawbone (Judg. xv:9, 14, 19). It was probably on the border of the Philistine country, but the exact location has not yet been settled.

LEMUEL (lĕm'ū-el), (Heb. לְמוֹאֵל, *lem-oo-ale'*, and לְמוֹאֵל, *lem-o-ale'*).

The maxims written in Proverbs xxxi:1, 19, were addressed to this unknown king by his mother. Most interpreters understand Solomon to be meant; but some, Hezekiah, Eichhorn, Ewald and others consider Lemuel only a poetical appellation of an imaginary king, through whom these maxims were made applicable to all kings.

LEND. See LOAN.

LENTIL (lĕn-tĭl), (Heb. עֲדָשׁ, *aw-dawsh'*).

Lentil.

A cultivated plant, smaller than the garden pea, but of the same family. In the markets of Palestine red lentils are still sold as the best variety, and from them a pottage is made which Dr. Robinson and others who have eaten it affirm would be a savory meal for a weary hunter (Gen.

xxv:29, 34). The "piece of ground full of lentiles" (2 Sam. xxiii:11), is still common in the Holy Land, and the poor not infrequently make lentiles into bread (Ezek. iv:9). This pulse is much used in Roman Catholic countries during Lent, and from it the name of the season is said to be derived. As a crop it is cut and thrashed like wheat. (See ADASHIM.)

Egyptians Cooking Lentils.

LEOPARD (lĕp'ērd), (Heb. נָמֵר, *naw-mare'*, Cant. iv:8; Is. xi:6; Jer. v:6, xiii:23; Hos. xiii:7; Hab. i:8; Dan. vii:6; Rev. xiii:2; Ecclus. xxviii:23).

Though zoologists differ in opinion respecting the identity of the leopard and the panther, and dispute, supposing them to be distinct, how these names should be respectively applied, and by what marks the animals should be distinguished, nevertheless there can be no doubt that the *nimr* of the Bible is that great spotted feline which anciently infested the Syrian mountains, and even now occurs in the wooded ranges of Libanus. The variety of leopard, or rather panther, of Syria, is considerably below the stature of a lioness, but very heavy in proportion to its bulk. Its general form is so well known as to require no description beyond stating, that the spots are rather more irregular, and the color more mixed with whitish, than in the other pantherine felidæ, excepting the Felis Uncia, or Felis Irbis, of High Asia, which is shaggy and almost white. It is a nocturnal, cat-like animal in habits, dangerous to all domestic cattle, and sometimes even to man. In the Scriptures it is constantly placed in juxtaposition with the lion or the wolf; which last, if the hyena be intended, forms a natural association. There is in Asia Minor a species or variety of panther, much larger than the Syrian, not unfrequent on the borders of the snowy tracts even of Mount Ida, above ancient Troy; and the group of these spotted animals is spread over the whole of southern Asia to Africa. From several names of places, it appears that, in the earlier ages of Israelitish dominion, it was sufficiently numerous in Palestine. Leopard skins were worn as a part of ceremonial costume by the superiors of the Egyptian priesthood, and by other personages in Nubia; and the animal itself is represented in the processions of tributary nations. (Wood, *Bible Animals*, p. 29 *sq.*; Thomson, *Land and Book*, ii. 156 *sq.*) C. H. S.

Figurative. (1) God compares himself to a *"leopard;"* with what patience he waits for the manifestation of his judgments (Hos. xiii:7). (2) Wicked men are likened to *"leopards:"* how spotted with corruptions in heart and life! how fierce and untractable to what is good, till God by his grace subdue them (Is. xi:6; Jer. xiii:23). (3) Nebuchadnezzar and his army are likened to *"leopards;"* with what guileful cruelty, and fierce rage, they watched over and besieged the cities of Judah, and nations around, till they took them, and murdered the inhabitants (Jer. v:

67

6; Hab. i:8). (4) The Grecian empire is likened to a *"leopard with four wings and four heads;"* it arose from small beginnings, and was founded with much craft, rapidity, and bloodshed.

LEPER (lĕp'ēr), (Heb. צָרַע, *tsaw-rah'*, intransitive, smitten). See LEPROSY.

LEPROSY (lĕp'rŏ-sy), (Heb. צָרַעַת, *tsaw-rah'-ath*, a smiting; Gr. λέπρα, *lep-rah*, from λεπίς, a scale), is a name that was given by the Greek physicians to a scaly disease of the skin.

A General Term. During the dark ages it was indiscriminately applied to all chronic diseases of the skin, and more particularly to elephantiasis, to which latter, however, it does not bear the slightest resemblance.

1. In Modern Times. The disease, as it is known at the present day, commences by an eruption of small reddish spots slightly raised above the level of the skin, and grouped in a circle. These spots are soon covered by a very thin, semi-transparent scale or epidermis, of a whitish color, and very smooth, which in a little time falls off, and leaves the skin beneath red and uneven. As the circles increase in diameter the skin recovers its healthy appearance towards the center; fresh scales are formed, which are now thicker, and superimposed one above the other, especially at the edges, so that the center of the scale appears to be depressed. The scales are of grayish white color, and have something of a micaceous or pearly luster. The circles are generally of the size of a quarter or half dollar, but they have been known to attain half a foot in diameter. The disease generally affects the knees and elbows, but sometimes it extends over the whole body; in which case the circles become confluent. It does not at all affect the general health, and the only inconvenience it causes the patient is a slight itching when the skin is heated; or, in inveterate cases, when the skin about the joints is much thickened, it may in some degree impede the free motion of the limbs. It is common to both sexes, to almost all ages, and all ranks of society. It is always difficult of treatment, and in old persons, when it is of long standing may be pronounced incurable. It is not uncommonly met with in England, in the United States and in all parts of Europe.

2. In the Time of Moses. (1) **Three Species.** Turning to the Mosaic account, we find three species mentioned, which were all included under the generic term of *Bahéret*, or 'bright spot.' The first is called *Bóhaq*, which signifies 'brightness,' but in a subordinate degree. This species did not render a person unclean. The second was called *Bahéret lebanáh*, or a bright white *Bahéret*. The third was *Bahéret kéháh*, or dusky *Bahéret*, spreading in the skin. These last two were also called *Tsoráat* (*i. e.*, properly, 'a stroke,' as if a chastisement), and rendered a person unclean. The characteristic marks of the *Bahéret lebanáh* mentioned by Moses are a glossy white and spreading scale upon an elevated base, the elevation depressed in the middle, the hair on the patches participating in the whiteness, and the patches themselves perpetually increasing.

(2) **Other Slight Affections.** There are some other slight affections mentioned by name in Leviticus, which the priest was required to distinguish from leprosy, such as *Seét, Shaphál, Neteq, Shechin,* i. e. 'elevation,' 'depressed,' etc.

(3) **Examination by the Priest.** If a person had any of the above diseases he was brought

before the priest to be examined. If the priest found the distinctive signs of a *Tsoráat*, or contagious leprosy, the person was immediately declared unclean. If the priest had any doubt on the subject, the person was put under confinement for seven days, when he was examined a second time. If in the course of the preceding week the eruption had made no advance, he was shut up for another seven days; and if then the disease was still stationary, and had none of the distinctive signs above noticed, he was declared clean (Lev. xiii).

(4) Exclusion. The leper was excluded from the tabernacle and the camp, and when he was healed his restoration to social intercourse with his fellow-men was twofold, performed both in the camp and in the tabernacle (Lev. xiv:3-32). A house for lepers was built outside Jerusalem on the hill of Gareb—*i. e.*, "the hill of scraping" (Jer. xxxi:39, 40; Job ii:8).

(5) Leprosy of Houses and Clothes. With respect to the leprosy of houses and of clothes (Lev. xiv:55), the expression is only analogical, referring to the spots and disfigurations which appeared upon the walls and articles of clothing, resembling the leprous spots, and originating from a species of mold or mildew, indicating a great degree of dampness, corrupting the air, injurious to health, and often the occasion and precursor of fatal diseases. The rites ordained for cleansing and purifying this kind of "leprosy" are in their symbolical bearing strictly analogous to the laws concerning leprosy proper (Lev. xiii:47-59; xiv:33-53).

3. Elephantiasis. It may be useful here to subjoin a description of elephantiasis, or the leprosy of the middle ages, as this is the disease from which most of the prevalent notions concerning leprosy have been derived, and to which the notices of lepers contained in modern books of travels exclusively refer.

(1) Symptoms and Effects. Elephantiasis first of all makes its appearance by spots of a reddish, yellowish, or livid hue, irregularly disseminated over the skin and slightly raised above its surface. These spots are glossy, and appear oily, or as if they were covered with varnish. After they have remained in this way for a longer or shorter time, they are succeeded by an eruption of tubercles. These are soft, roundish tumors, varying in size from that of a pea to that of an olive, and are of a reddish or livid color. They are principally developed on the face and ears, but in the course of years extend over the whole body. The face becomes frightfully deformed; the forehead is traversed by deep lines and covered with numerous tubercles; the eyebrows become bald, swelled, furrowed by oblique lines, and covered with nipple-like elevations; the eyelashes fall out, and the eyes assume a fixed and staring look; the lips are enormously thickened and shining; the beard falls out; the chin and ears are enlarged and beset with tubercles; the lobe and alæ of the nose are frightfully enlarged and deformed; the nostrils irregularly dilated, internally constricted, and excoriated; the voice is hoarse and nasal, and the breath intolerably fetid. After some time, generally after some years, many of the tubercles ulcerate, and the matter which exudes from them dries to crusts of a brownish or blackish color; but this process seldom terminates in cicatrization. The extremities are affected in the same way as the face. The hollow of the foot is swelled out, so that the sole becomes flat; the sensibility of the skin is greatly impaired, and, in the hands and feet, often entirely lost; the joints of the toes ulcerate and fall off one after the other; insupportable fœtor exhales from the whole body. The patient's general health is not affected for a considerable time, and his sufferings are not always of the same intensity as his external deformity. Often, however, his nights are sleepless or disturbed by frightful dreams; he becomes morose and melancholy; he shuns the sight of the healthy, because he feels what an object of disgust he is to them; and life becomes a loathsome burden to him; or he falls into a state of apathy, and after many years of such an existence he sinks either from exhaustion, or from the supervention of internal disease. The Greeks gave the name of elephantiasis to this disease, because the skin of the person affected with it was thought to resemble that of an elephant, in dark color, ruggedness, and insensibility, or, as some have thought, because the foot, after the loss of the toes, when the hollow of the sole is filled up and the ankle enlarged, resembles the foot of an elephant.

(2) Contagious or Hereditary. About the period of the Crusades elephantiasis spread itself like an epidemic over all Europe, even as far north as the Faroe Islands, and henceforth, owing to the above-named mistakes, every one became familiar with leprosy under the form of the terrible disease that has just been described. Leper or lazar houses abounded everywhere; as many as 2,000 are said to have existed in France alone. The disease was considered to be contagious possibly only on account of the belief that was entertained respecting its identity with Jewish leprosy, and the strictest regulations were enacted for secluding the diseased from society. Towards the commencement of the seventeenth century the disease gradually disappeared from Europe, and is now confined to intertropical countries. It existed in Faroe as late as 1676, and in the Shetland Islands in 1736, long after it had ceased in the southern parts of Great Britain. The best authors of the present day who have had an opportunity of observing the disease do not consider it to be contagious. There seems, however, to be little doubt as to its being hereditary. (Good's *Study of Med.*, iii, 421; Rayer, *Mal. de la Peau*, ii, 296; Simpson *On the Lepers and Leper Houses of Scotland and England.*)

W. A. N.

LESHEM (lē'shem), (Heb. לֶשֶׁם, *leh'shem*, strong, fortress), a variation of the name Laish, a city of northern Palestine (Josh. xix:47).

LET (lĕt), (Heb. נָתַן, *naw'than*, to turn; Gr. κατέχω, *kat-ekh'o*). The word is expressive, (1) Of command. (Deut. v:12). (2) Of entreaty. (2 Sam. xiii:6). (3) Of permission. (Gen. xlix:21). (4) Of entrusting, or assigning by lease. (Cant. viii:11). To *let*, also signifies to *hinder*, keep back. (Is. xliii:13; 2 Thess. ii:7).

LETHECH (lē'thĕk), (Heb. לֶתֶךְ, *leh'thek*), a Hebrew measure, half an omer; containing sixteen pecks, or four bushels (Hos. iii:2, marg.).

LETTER (lĕt'tẽr).
1. A mark of sound used in writing.
2. A missive or epistle sent by one person to another (2 Sam. xi:14).
3. Learning, knowledge of the mysterious sense of God's word (John vii:15).

Figurative. The outside of things; so circumcision of the flesh, is called circumcision of the *letter*, as opposed to the spirit (Rom. ii:29; vii:6; 2 Cor. iii:6, 7). The outward observance of Moses' ceremonies, outward service of God, or walking according to our corrupt lusts, is called the *oldness of the letter* (Rom. vii:6).

LETUSHIM (le-tū'shim), (Heb. לְטוּשִׁם, *let-oo-sheem'*, have ground, sharpened).

The second son of Dedan; grandson of Abraham and Keturah (Gen. xxv:3), and progenitor of an Arabian tribe, which has not been traced out. (B. C. after 2024.)

LEUMMIM (le-ŭm'mim), (Heb. לְאֻמִּים, *leh-oom-meem'*, peoples).

One of the descendants of Dedan; grandson of Abraham and Keturah (Gen. xxv:3), and founder of an Arabian tribe, which Fresnel (*Journal Asiat.* iii, série, vi, 217) identifies with the *Ummeiyim*, a very ancient tribe. (B. C. after 2024.)

LEVI (lē'vī), (Heb. לֵוִי, *lay-vee'*, a joining; Sept. Λευεί, *Levi*).

1. The third son of Jacob and Leah, born in Mesopotamia B. C. 1750 (Gen. xxix:34).

(1) Avenges Dinah. No circumstance is recorded of him save the part which he and his full brother Simeon took in the massacre of the Shechemites, to avenge the wrong done to their sister Dinah (Gen. xxxiv:25, 26). This transaction was to his last hour regarded by Jacob with abhorrence, and he failed not to allude to it in his dying declaration.

(2) Simeon and Levi. As Simeon and Levi were united in that act, so the patriarch couples them in his prophecy: 'Accursed be their anger, for it was fierce; and their wrath, for it was cruel! I will divide them in Jacob, and disperse them in Israel.' And, accordingly, their descendants were afterwards, in different ways, dispersed among the other tribes; although, in the case of Levi, this curse was eventually turned into a benefit and blessing.

(3) Children. He had three sons, Gershon, Kohath, and Merari, and a daughter called Jochebed; and his three sons produced three different families.

(4) Goes into Egypt. With these three sons he went down into Egypt (Gen. xlvi:11) where he was probably presented to Pharaoh (Gen. xlvii:2).

(5) Blessing and Death. By the zeal of his descendants on occasion of the golden calf (Exod. xxxii:26-29), the curse pronounced by Jacob was transformed into a blessing. He died in Egypt 137 years old (Exod. vi:16). (See LEVITES.)

2. Son of Simeon and father of Matthat, in the genealogy of Christ between David and Zerubbabel (Luke iii:29). (B. C. after 876.)

3. Son of Melchi, and father of another Matthat (Luke iii:24.) (B. C. before 22.)

4. Son of Alpheus, an apostle elsewhere called Matthew (Mark ii:14; Luke v:27, 29). (See MATTHEW.)

LEVIATHAN (lĕ-vī'á-than), (Heb. לִוְיָתָן, *liv-yaw-thawn'*), Job iii:8; xli:1; Ps. lxxiv:14; civ:26; Is. xxvii:1. (See BEHEMOTH; CROCODILE; DRAGON).

Gesenius very justly remarks that this word, which denotes any twisted animal, is especially applicable to every great tenant of the waters, such as the great marine serpents and crocodiles, and, it may be added, the colossal serpents and great monsters of the desert. In general it points to the crocodile, and Job xli is unequivocally descriptive of that saurian. Probably the Egyptian crocodile is therein depicted in all its magnitude, ferocity, and indolence, such as it was in early days, when as yet unconscious of the power of man, and only individually tamed for the purposes

of an imposture, which had sufficient authority to intimidate the public and protect the species, under the sanctified pretext that it was a type of pure water, and an emblem of the importance of irrigation; though the people in general seem ever to have been disposed to consider it a personification of the destructive principle. At a later period the Egyptians, probably of such places as Tentyris, where crocodiles were not held in veneration, not only hunted and slew them, but it appears from a statue that a sort of Bestiarii could tame them sufficiently to perform certain exhibitions mounted on their backs. The intense musky odor of its flesh must have rendered the crocodile, at all times, very unpalatable food, but breast-armor was made of the horny and ridged parts of its back. We have ourselves witnessed a periodical abstinence in the great saurians, and have known negro women, while bathing, play with young alligators; which, they asserted, they could do without danger, unless they hurt them and thereby attracted the vengeance of the mother; but the impunity most likely resulted from the period of inactivity coinciding with the then state of the young animals, or from the negro women being many in the water at the same time. The occurrence took place at Old Harbor, Jamaica.

LEVIRATE MARRIAGE (lĕv'ĭ-răt măr'rĭj), (from Lat. *Levir*, a *husband's brother*).

A term applied to the practice among the Hebrews that when an Israelite died without leaving male issue his nearest relative should marry the widow, and continue the family of his deceased brother through the firstborn son of such union. The son thus became heir of the former husband. If the brother did not choose to marry the widow she could treat him with great contempt and expose him to ignominy. (See MARRIAGE.)

Levite.

LEVITES (lē'vītes), (Heb. בְּנֵי לֵוִי, *bane lay-vee'*, son of Levi, or simply לֵוִי, *Lăy-vee'*; usually in the plural and with the article הַלְוִיִּם, sons of *Levi*; Sept. Λευῖται, *Levitae*), the descendants of Levi, through his sons Gershon, Kohath, and Merari, whose descendants formed so many sub-tribes or great families of the general body.

In a narrower sense the term Levites designates the great body of the tribe employed in the subordinate offices of the hierarchy, to distinguish them from that one family of their body—the family of Aaron—in which the priestly functions were vested.

1. Appointment to Service. While the Israelites were encamped before Mount Sinai the tribe of Levi, to which Moses and Aaron belonged, was, by special ordinance from the Lord, set specially apart for sacerdotal services, in the place of the firstborn of the different tribes and families to whom such functions, according to ancient usage, belonged; and which indeed had already been set apart as holy, in commemoration of the firstborn of the Israelites having been spared when the firstborn of the Egyptians were destroyed (Num. iii:12, 13, 40-51; Exod. xiii). When it was determined to set apart a single tribe of Levi for this service, the numbers of the firstborn in Israel and of the tribe selected were respectively taken, when it was found that the former amounted to 22,273, and the latter to 22,000. Those of the firstborn beyond the number of the Levites were then redeemed at the rate of five shekels, that is 12s. 6d., or three dollars and twenty-five cents each, and the money assigned to the priests. At the same time the cattle which the Levites then happened to possess were considered as equivalent to all the firstlings of the cattle which the Israelites had; and, accordingly, the firstlings were not required to be brought, as in subsequent years, to the altar and to the priesthood (Num. iii:41-51).

(1) Specific Service. In the wilderness the office of the Levites was to carry the tabernacle and its utensils and furniture from place to place, after they had been packed up by the priests (Num. iv:4-15). In this service each of the three Levitical families had its separate department; the Gershonites carried the hangings and cords of the Tabernacle, for which they were allowed two wains, each drawn by four oxen (Num. iii:25, 26; iv:24-28; vii:7). The Kohathites carried the ark, the table of shew-bread, the candlestick, the two altars, and such of the hangings as belonged to the sanctuary; for this they had no wains or oxen, the whole being carried upon their shoulders (Num. iii:31; iv:4-15; vii:9); the Merarites had charge of the substantial parts of the tabernacle—the boards, pillars, bars, bases, etc., and also all the ordinary vessels of service, for which they were allowed four wains and eight oxen (Num. iii:36, 37; iv:31, 32; vii:8). In this manner they proceeded in all their journeys; and when they settled in a place, and had erected the Tabernacle, the different families pitched their tents around it in the following manner: the Gershonites behind it on the west (Num. iii:23), the Kohathites on the south (iii:29), the Merarites on the north (iii:35), and the priests on the east (iii:38). They all assisted Aaron and his sons in taking care of, and attending on, the Tabernacle, when it was pitched; but they were allowed to take no part in the services of the altar (xviii:2-7).

(2) Duties Changed. This was the nature of their service in the desert: but when they entered the land of Canaan, and the Tabernacle ceased to be migratory, the range of their service was considerably altered. While part attended at the Tabernacle, the rest were distributed through the country in the several cities which were allotted to them. These cities are commonly reckoned forty-eight; but thirteen of them were reserved for the priests, so that only thirty-five belonged to the Levites. The names of these cities, and the tribes in which they were situated, are given in Josh. xxi:20-42; 1 Chron. vi:64-81. Of the forty-eight cities six were cities of refuge for the unintentional homicide, of which one, Hebron, was a priestly city (Deut. iv:41-43; Josh. xx:2-9).

(3) Further Change. In the time of David, when the number of the priests and Levites had much increased, a third and very important alteration was effected, as much, or more, with reference to the Temple, for which he made every possible preparation, as for the existing service at the Tabernacle. While the priests were divided into twenty-four courses that they might attend the Temple in rotation weekly, and only officiate about two weeks in the year, the Levites were also divided into twenty-four courses. In the book of Chronicles we have four times twenty-four courses of Levites mentioned but all their employments are not distinctly stated (1 Chron. xxiii:7-23; xxiv:20-31; xxv:1-31; xxvi:1-12).

(4) Classification and Offices. ⚫The most conspicuous classification is that of twenty-four courses of porters and servitors, and twenty-four of musicians.

The office of the porters was to open and shut the doors and gates of the Temple-courts, at which they also attended throughout the day to prevent the entrance of any harmful or unclean person or thing (1 Chron. xxvi:17, 18). They had also the charge of the treasure-chambers in their respective wards; for we find four of the chief porters holding this trust in 1 Chron. ix:26, and their names and the articles in their charge are given in 1 Chron. xxvi:20-29; 2 Chron. xxxi:12-14.

Besides acting as porters and servants during the day, we learn that they were also the guards of the Temple. Without entering into specific details, it may be remarked that the whole number of guards to the Temple, at night, is stated to have been twenty-four, of whom three were priests. These are described as having been under an overseer, called 'the man of the mountain of the house.' He went his rounds to see that the guards were at their posts: if he found any one seated who should have been standing, he said 'Peace be unto thee;' but if he found any one asleep, he struck him, and sometimes set fire to his clothes. (Maimon. *Beth Habech.* ch. viii.)

(5) Musicians. We have thus seen that one division of the Levites was employed as porters during the day, and another as guards during the night; a third division served as musicians. A catalogue of these is given in 1 Chron. xxi:1-9, according to their employments; and another, according to their courses, in 1 Chron. xxi:9-31. We shall have to speak of Music under that head, and need only here state that on grand occasions, when a full band was formed, the family of Heman sang in the middle (1 Chron. vi:33-38), the family of Asaph on the right hand (vi:39-43), and the family of Ethan on the left. The ordinary place for the musicians, vocal and instrumental, was at the east end of the court of the priests, between the court of Israel and the altar.

It seems that the singers could never be under twelve, because that number was particularly mentioned at their first appointment (1 Chron. xxv:9); but there was no objection to any larger number (*Erachin*, ut supra). The young sons of the Levites were, on such occasions only, allowed to enter the court of the priests with their fathers, that their small voices might relieve the deep bass of the men (*Gemar.* tit. *Succah*, ch. v.); and for this authority was supposed to be found in Ezra iii:9.

(6) No Sacerdotal Functions. The Levites were not at liberty to exercise any properly sacerdotal functions; but on extraordinary occasions they were permitted to assist in preparing the sacrifices, without, however, in any way concerning themselves with the blood (2 Chron. xxix:34; xxx:16, 17; xxxv:1).

(7) Age and Qualifications. In Num. iv:3 the Levites are described as commencing their actual service at thirty years of age; but in Num. viii:24, 25, twenty-five is the age mentioned; and in 1 Chron. xxiii:24, 25, and Ezra iii:8, twenty. The reason of these apparent discrepancies is, that from twenty-five to thirty they were in the state of probationers, doing some things, but excluded from others (Aben Ezra, on Num. viii). At thirty they became qualified for every part of the Levitical service. This was under the Tabernacle; but when the Temple was built, and bodily strength was less required, the age was reduced to twenty. After fifty they were no longer called upon to serve as a matter of obligation, but they might attend if they thought proper, and perform any usual service which was not considered burdensome. Thus, in the wilderness, they ceased at that age to carry any part of the burdens when the ark and Tabernacle were removed (Num. viii:25, 26).

(8) Consecration. When the Levitical body was first set apart for its sacred duties, the existing members were consecrated in the manner particularly described in Num. viii:6, 22. They, and in them their descendants, were thus inducted into their particular office; and, in later times, when any one became of age, it was sufficient for his admission to prove that he belonged to a Levitical family, and, probably, to offer some trifling sacrifice. It does not appear that the Levites, when at home, had any particular dress to distinguish them from their countrymen; nor is there any positive evidence that they had any distinctive garb, even when on actual service at the tabernacle or temple. Josephus (*Antiq.* xx:9) relates, that only six years before the destruction of the Temple by the Romans, the Levites were allowed by Agrippa to wear a linen tunic, like the priests —an innovation with which the latter were highly displeased. This shows that the dress of the Levites, even when on duty, had not previously been in any respect similar to that of the priests.

(9) Subsistence. The subsistence of the Levites was provided for in a peculiar manner.

(1) One-Twelfth of the Land or Forty-eight Cities. It consisted, first, of a compensation for the abandonment of their right to one-twelfth of the land of Canaan; and, secondly, of a remuneration for their services in their official capacity as devoted to the services of the sanctuary. The territorial compensation lay in the forty-eight cities which were granted to the whole tribe, including the priests. These cities were scattered among the different tribes, as centers of instruction, and had 1,000 square cubits, equal to above 305 English acres, attached to each of them, to serve for gardens, vineyards, and pasturage. It is obvious, however, that this alone could not have been an adequate compensation for the loss of one-twelfth of the soil, seeing that the produce of 305 acres could not in any case have sufficed for the wants of the inhabitants of these cities.

(2) The Tithe. The further provision, therefore, which was made for them must be regarded as partly in compensation for their sacrifice of territory, although we are disposed to look upon it as primarily intended as a remuneration for

the dedication of their services to the public. This provision consisted of the tithe, or tenth of the produce of the grounds allotted to the other tribes. The simplest view of this payment is to regard it, first, as the produce of about as much land as the Levites would have been entitled to if placed on the same footing with regard to territory as the other tribes; and also as the produce of so much more land, which the other tribes enjoyed in consequence of its not having been assigned to the tribe of Levi.

In giving the produce of this land to the Levites the Israelites were therefore to be regarded as simply releasing them from the cares of agriculture, to enable them to devote themselves to the service of the sanctuary. The land which produced the tithe was just so much land held by the other tribes in their behalf; and the labor of cultivating this land was the salary paid to the Levites for their official services. The tenth was paid to the whole tribe of Levi; but as the Levites had to give out of this one-tenth to the priests, their own allowance was only nine-tenths of the tenth. A more particular account of tithes belongs to another head. (See TITHES.)

The Levites had also a certain interest in the 'second tithe,' being the portion which, after the first tithe had been paid, the cultivator set apart for hospitable feasts, which were held at the place of the sanctuary in two out of three years, but in the third year at home. This interest, however, extended no further than that the offerer was particularly enjoined to invite the priests and Levites to such feasts.

2. *History, Etc.* **(1) Till Death of Solomon.** The earliest notice we have of the numbers of the Levites occurs at their first separation in the desert, when there were 22,300, of a month old and upwards; of whom 8,580 were fit for service, or between the ages of 30 and 50 (Num. iii:22, 28, 34; iv:2, 34-49). Thirty-eight years after, just before the Israelites entered Canaan, they had increased to 23,000, not one of whom had been born at the time of the former enumeration (Num. xxvi:57, 62-65). About 460 years after the entry into Canaan (B. C. 1015) they were again numbered by David, a little before his death, and were found to have increased to 38,000 men fit for Levitical service—of whom 24,000 were 'set over the work of the Lord,' 6,000 were officers and judges, 4,000 were porters, and 4,000 were musicians (1 Chron. xxiii:3, 4, 5). If the same proportion then existed between those come of age and those a month old which existed when the tribe quitted Egypt, the entire number of the Levitical body, in the time of David, must have been 96,433.

(2) After the Revolt of the Ten Tribes. After the revolt of the ten tribes, those of the Levites who resided in the territories of those tribes, having resisted the request of Jeroboam to transfer their services to his idolatrous establishments at Dan and Bethel, were obliged to abandon their possessions and join their brethren in Judah and Benjamin (2 Chron. xi:12, 13, 14; xiii:9); and this concentration of the Levitical body in the kingdom of Judah must have had an important influence upon its condition and history. That kingdom thus actually consisted of three tribes — Judah, Benjamin, and Levi, — of which one was devoted to sacerdotal uses. This altered position of the Levites—after they had been deprived of most of their cities, and the tithes from ten of the tribes were cut off—presents a subject for much interesting investigation, into which we cannot enter. Their means must have been much reduced; for it cannot be supposed that Judah and Benjamin alone were able, even if willing, to undertake the support of the whole Levitical body on the same scale as when the dues of all Israel flowed into its treasuries. In the subsequent history of Judah the Levites appear less frequently than might have been expected. The chief public measure in which they were engaged was the restoration of the house of David in the person of young Joash (2 Chron. xxiii: 1-11); which may be regarded as mainly the work of the Levitical body, including the priests.

(3) After the Captivity. Under the edict of Cyrus, only 341 Levites, according to Ezra (ii: 40-42), or 350, according to Nehemiah (vii:43-45), returned with Zerubbabel to Jerusalem. This is less surprising than might at first sight appear; for if, before the captivity, the great body of them had been in straitened circumstances and without fixed possessions in Judah, it was only consistent with human prudence that those who had, in all probability, comfortably settled themselves in Babylon, should not be anxious to return in such numbers to Palestine as were likely to produce similar effects. A few more are mentioned in Neh. xii :24-26. Those who did return seem to have had no very correct notion of their obligations and duties; for there were many who formed matrimonial alliances with the idolaters of the land, and thereby corrupted both their morals and genealogies. But they were prevailed upon to reform this abuse, and, as a token of obedience, signed the national covenant with Nehemiah, and abode at Jerusalem to influence others by their authority and example (Neh. x: 9-13; xi:15-19).

(4) In New Testament. The Levites are not mentioned in the Apocryphal books, and very slightly in the New Testament (Luke x:32; John i:19; Acts iv:36); but the 'scribes' and the 'lawyers,' so often named in the gospels, are usually supposed to have belonged to them.

3. General Summary. It would be taking a very narrow view of the duties of the Levitical body if we regarded them as limited to their services at the sanctuary. On the contrary we see in their establishment a provision for the religious and moral instruction of the great body of the people, which no ancient lawgiver except Moses ever thought of attending to. But that this was one principal object for which a twelfth of the population—the tribe of Levi—was set apart, is clearly intimated in Deut. xxxii:9, 10: 'They shall teach Jacob thy judgments and Israel thy law; they shall put incense before thee, and whole burnt sacrifice upon thine altar.' They were to read the volume of the law publicly every seventh year at the Feast of Tabernacles (Deut. xxxi:10-13). 'This public and solemn periodical instruction,' observes Dean Graves (*Lectures*, p. 170), 'though eminently useful, was certainly not the entire of their duty; they were bound from the spirit of this ordinance to take care that at all times the aged should be improved and the children instructed in the knowledge and fear of God, the adoration of his majesty, and the observance of his law; and for this purpose the peculiar situation and privileges of the tribe of Levi, as regulated by the Divine appointment, admirably fitted them.' (Michaelis, *Commentaries on the Laws of Moses*, sec. 52, Eng. transl.)

LEVITICAL CITIES. See LEVITES.

LEVITICUS (lĕ-vĭt′ĭ-kŭs), in the Hebrew canon, is called אֵיקְרָא, *kaw-raw'*, the word with which it begins; the third book of Moses.

1. Contents. Leviticus contains the further statement and development of the Sinaitic legislation, the beginnings of which are described in Exodus. It exhibits the historical progress of this legislation; consequently we must not expect to find the laws detailed in it in a systematic form. There is, nevertheless, a certain order observed, which arose from the nature of the subject, and of which the plan may easily be perceived. The whole is intimately connected with the contents of Exodus, at the conclusion of which book that sanctuary is described with which all external worship was connected (Exod. xxxv-xl).

2. Authenticity. The arguments by which the unity of Leviticus has been attacked are very feeble. Some critics have strenuously endeavored to prove that the laws contained in Leviticus originated in a period much later than is usually supposed. But the following observations sufficiently support their Mosaical origin, and show that the whole of Leviticus is historically genuine.

(1) Mosaic Vestiges. The laws in ch. i-vii contain manifest vestiges of the Mosaical period. Here, as well as in Exodus, when the priests are mentioned, Aaron and his sons are named; as, for instance, in ch. i:4, 7, 8, 11, etc. The tabernacle is the sanctuary, and no other place of worship is mentioned anywhere.

Expressions like the following constantly occur, *before the tabernacle of the congregation*, or *the door of the tabernacle of the congregation* (ch. 1:3; iii:8, 13, etc.). The Israelites are always described as a congregation (ch. iv:13, *sq.*), under the command of the *elders of the congregation* (ch. iv:15), or of a *ruler* (ch. iv:22). Everything has a reference to life in a camp, and that camp commanded by Moses (ch. iv:12, 21; vi:11; xiv: 8; xvi:26, 28). A later writer could scarcely have placed himself so entirely in the times, and so completely adopted the modes of thinking of the age, of Moses: especially if, as has been asserted, these laws gradually sprung from the usages of the people, and were written down at a later period with the object of sanctioning them by the authority of Moses. They so entirely befit the Mosaical age, that, in order to adapt them to the requirements of any later period, they must have undergone some modification, accommodation, and a peculiar mode of interpretation. This inconvenience would have been avoided by a person who intended to forge laws in favor of the later modes of Levitical worship. A forger would have endeavored to identify the past as much as possible with the present.

(2) Law Against Slaughter. In ch. xvii occurs the law which forbids the slaughter of any beast except at the sanctuary. This law could not be strictly kept in Palestine, and had therefore to undergo some modification (Deut. xii). Our opponents cannot show any rational inducement for contriving such a fiction. The law (ch. xvii: 6, 7) is adapted to the nation only while emigrating from Egypt. It was the object of this law to guard the Israelites from falling into the temptation to imitate the Egyptian rites and sacrifices offered to he-goats; which word signifies also demons represented under the form of he-goats, and which were supposed to inhabit the desert (comp. Jablonski, *Pantheon Ægyptiacum*, i, 272, *sq.*)

(3) Concerning Food and Purifications. The laws concerning food and purifications appear especially important if we remember that the people emigrated from Egypt. The fundamental principle of these laws is undoubtedly Mosaical, but in the individual application of them there is much which strongly reminds us of Egypt. This is also the case in Lev. xviii, *sq.,* where the lawgiver has manifestly in view the two opposites, Canaan and Egypt. That the lawgiver was intimately acquainted with Egypt, is proved by such remarks as those about the Egyptian marriages with sisters (ch. xviii :3) ; a custom which stands as an exception among the prevailing habits of antiquity (Diodorus Siculus, i, 27 ; Pausanias, *Attica,* i, 7).

3. A Prophetical Character. The book of Leviticus has a prophetical character. The lawgiver represents to himself the future history of his people. This prophetical character is especially manifest in chapters xxv, xxvi, where the law appears in a truly sublime and Divine attitude, and when its predictions refer to the whole futurity of the nation. It is impossible to say that these were *vaticinia ex eventu,* unless we would assert that this book was written at the close of Israelitish history. We must rather grant that passages like this are the real basis on which the authority of later prophets is chiefly built. Such passages prove also, in a striking manner, that the lawgiver had not merely an external aim, but that his law had a deeper purpose, which was clearly understood by Moses himself. That purpose was to regulate the national life in all its bearings, and to consecrate the whole nation to God. (See especially ch. xxv :18, *sq.*).

But this ideal tendency of the law does not preclude its applicability to matters of fact. The law had not merely an *ideal,* but also a *real* character, evidenced by its relation to the faithlessness and disobedience of the nation. The whole future history of the covenant people was regulated by the law, which has manifested its eternal power and truth in the history of the people of Israel. Although this section has a general bearing, it is nevertheless manifest that it originated in the times of Moses. At a later period, for instance, it would have been impracticable to promulgate the law concerning the Sabbath and the year of Jubilee : for it was soon sufficiently proved how far the nation in reality remained behind the ideal Israel of the law. The sabbatical law bears the impress of a time when the whole legislation, in its fullness and glory, was directly communicated to the people, in such a manner as to attract, penetrate, and command.

The principal works to be consulted with reference to Leviticus will be found under the article PENTATEUCH.   H. A. C. H.

LEVY (lĕv'ўๅ), (Heb. מַם, *mas,* tribute).

1. To raise, by taking a part from among the rest, as tribute is raised from the rest of the incomes of the nation.

2. An army, or number of workmen raised in a nation (1 Kings v :13, 14). The workmen were free Israelites, who to pay tribute (or tax) worked four months in the year, felling trees under the direction of subjects of Hiram. Another *levy* was of Canaanites, who were assigned to tributary labor (ix :15), in this case for the erection of buildings.

LEWD (lūd), (Gr. πονηρός, *pon-ay-ros'*), in a moral sense *evil, wicked, unprincipled* (Acts xvii:5).

LEWDNESS (lūd'nĕs), (Gr. ῥᾳδιούργημα, *hrad-ee-oorg'ay-mah,* literally *doing things easily,* or *boldly*), a piece of knavery, rascality (Acts xviii:14). Elsewhere it is used in its proper sense of *licentiousness* (Heb. זַמָּה, *zam-maw'*), etc., badness, (Judg. xx:6; Jer. xi:15; Ezek. xxiii:44; xxiv:13; Hos. vi:9); once (Hos. ii:10) the *private parts* (Heb. נַבְלוּת, *nab-looth'*).

LIBANUS or LEBANON (līb'a-nus or lĕb'a-non), (Heb. לְבָנוֹן, *leb-aw-nohn*; Gr. Λίβανος, *Libanus,* for the Heb. *Lebanôn'*), the name of a long chain of mountains on the northern border of Palestine.

(1) Name and Location. The term Libanus is more convenient in use than the Hebrew form Lebanon, as enabling us to distinguish the parallel ranges of Libanus and Anti-Libanus, which have no such distinctive names in connection with the Hebrew designation. Lebanon seems to be applied in scripture to either or both of these ranges ; and we shall also use it in this general sense : but Libanus means distinctively the westernmost of those ranges, which faces the Mediterranean, and Anti-Libanus the eastern, facing the plain of Damascus ; in which sense these names will be used in this article. The present inhabitants of the country have found the convenience of distinguishing these parallel ranges ; and give to Libanus the name of 'Western Mountain' (Jebel esh-Sharki), and to Anti-Libanus that of 'Eastern Mountain' (Jebel el-Gharbi) ; although Jebel Libnân (the same name in fact as Lebanon) occurs among the Arabs with special reference to the eastern range.

These two great ranges, which together form the Lebanon of Scripture, commence about the parallel of Tripoli (lat. 34° 28'), run in a general direction from northeast to southwest, through about one degree of latitude, and form, at their southern termination, the natural frontier of Palestine. These parallel ranges enclose between them a fertile and well-watered valley, averaging about fifteen miles in width, which is the Cœle-Syria (Hollow Syria) of the ancients, but is called by the present inhabitants, by way of preëminence, El-Bekaa, or 'the valley,' which is watered through the greater portion of its length by the river Litany, the ancient Leontes.

(2) Hermon. Nearly opposite Damascus the Anti-Libanus separates into two ridges, which diverge somewhat, and enclose the fertile Wady et-Teim. The easternmost of these two ridges, which has already been pointed out as the Hermon of Scripture (see HERMON), Jebel esh-Sheikh, continues its southwest course, and is the proper prolongation of Anti-Libanus. From the base of the higher part of this ridge, a low broad spur or mountainous tract runs off towards the south, forming the high land which shuts in the basin and Lake of el-Huleh on the east. This tract is called Jebel Heish, the higher portion of which terminates at Tel el-Faras, nearly three hours north of Fiek. The other ridge of Anti-Libanus takes a more westerly direction. It is long, low, and level ; and continues to border the lower part of the great valley of Bekaa, until it seems to unite with the higher bluffs and spurs of Lebanon, and thus entirely to close that valley. In fact, only a narrow gorge is here left between precipices, in some places of great height, through which the Litany finds its way down to the sea, north of Tyre. The chain of Lebanon, or at least its higher ridges, may be said to terminate at the point where it is thus broken through by the Litany. But a broad and lower mountainous tract continues towards the south, bordering the basin of the Huleh on the west. It rises to its greatest elevation about Safed (Jebel Safed) ; and at length ends abruptly in the mountains of Nazareth, as the northern wall of the plain of Esdraelon. This high tract may very properly be regarded as a prolongation of Lebanon.

(3) Formation and Height. The mountains of Lebanon are of limestone rock, which is indeed the general constituent of the mountains of Syria. In Lebanon it has generally a whitish hue, and from the aspect which the range thus bears in the distance, in its cliffs and naked parts, the name of Lebanon (which signifies 'white') has been supposed to be derived; but others seek its origin in the snows which rest long upon its summits, and perpetually upon the highest of them.

Of the two ranges, that of Libanus is by far the higher. Its uppermost ridge is marked by a line, drawn at the distance of about two hours' journey from the summit, above which all is barren (Burckhardt, p. 4); but the slopes and valleys below this line afford pasturage, and are capable of cultivation, by reason of the numerous springs which are met with in all directions.

The average height of the Libanus mountains, from the top of which the snow entirely disappears in summer, must be considerably below 11,000 feet, probably about 10,000 feet above the level of the sea. But the higher points, particularly the Sannin, which is the highest of all, must be above that limit.

(4) **Vegetation.** Cultivation is, however, chiefly found on the seaward slopes, where numerous villages flourish, and every inch of ground is turned to account by the industrious natives, who, in the absence of natural levels, construct artificial terraces in order to prevent the earth from being swept away by the winter rains, and at the same time to retain the water requisite for the irrigation of the crops (Burckhardt, pp. 19, 20, 23). When one looks upward from below, the vegetation on these terraces is not visible; so that the whole mountain appears as if composed only of immense rugged masses of naked whitish rock, traversed by deep, wild ravines, running down precipitously to the plain. No one would suspect among these rocks the existence of a vast multitude of thrifty villages, and a numerous population of mountaineers, hardy, industrious, and brave (Robinson, iii, 440). Here, amidst the crags of the rocks, are to be seen the remains of the renowned cedars; but a much larger proportion of firs, oaks, brambles, mulberry-trees, fig-trees, and vines (Volney, i, 272). (Comp. Ezek. xxvii:18.) Its wines are also noticed (Hos. xiv:7); and in Cant. iv:11; Hos. xiv:7, it is celebrated for various kinds of fragrant plants.

It is not easy to determine, with certainty what can be intended by the prophet Isaiah in the phrase, "the glory of Lebanon" (chap. xxxv:2); but very likely it refers to the verdure constantly maintained on it, and to the stately trees which cover it.

(5) **Literature.** Robinson, *Biblical Researches,* iii:344, 345, 439; Kitto, *Pictorial History of Palestine,* Introd. pp. xxxii-xxxv, lv; Reland, *Palæstina,* i, 311; Rosenmüller, *Biblisch. Alterthum,* ii, 236; Raumer, *Palästina,* pp. 29-35; D'Arvieux, *Mémoires,* ii, 250; Volney, *Voyage en Syrie,* i, 243; Seetzen, in Zach's *Monatl. Corresp.,* June, 1806; Burckhardt, *Travels in Syria,* p. i, *sq.;* Richter, *Wallfahrten,* p. 102, etc.; Irby and Mangles, *Travels,* pp. 206-220; Buckingham, *Arab Tribes,* p. 468, *sq.;* Fisk, in *Missionary Herald,* 1824; Elliot, *Travels,* ii, 276; Hogg, *Visit to Alexandria, Jerusalem,* etc., i, 219, *sq.;* ii, 81, *sq.;* Addison, *Palmyra and Damascus,* ii, 43-82; Tristram, *Land of Israel,* 1865; *Reports of the Palestine Exploration Fund.*

LIBATION (lĭ-bā'shŭn), a word used in sacrificial language to express an affusion of liquors, poured upon victims to be sacrificed to the Lord.

The quantity of wine for a libation was the fourth part of a hin; rather more than two pints. Among the Hebrews libations were poured on the victim after it was killed, and the several pieces of it laid on the altar, ready to be consumed by the flames (Lev. vi:20; viii:25, 26; ix:4; xvi:12, 20; xxiii:13). They consisted in offerings of bread, wine and salt. (See OFFERING.)

LIBERAL (lĭb'ēr-al). In Is. xxxii:5, 8, the term *naw-deeb'* (Heb. נָדִיב, voluntary) seems to have been applied to persons of *noble* character or birth. By an easy transition it means one *noble in heart* and action.

A liberal person is one ready to give to the poor and needy. Men stand by "liberal things," as showing kindness to the poor as an especial means of procuring and establishing one's wealth (Prov. xi:25). God giveth "liberally," with a willing and bountiful heart, and in a large abundance (James i:5).

LIBERTINES (lĭb'ēr-tĭns), (Gr. Λιβερτῖνος, *lib-er-tee'nos,* a freedman).

This occurs but once in the New Testament: "Certain of the synagogue, which is called (the synagogue) of the *Libertines,* and Cyrenians, and Alexandrians," etc., are mentioned in Acts vi:9. There has been much diversity in the interpretation of this word.

The most probable opinion, and that which is now generally entertained, is, that the Libertini were Jews, whom the Romans had taken in war and conveyed to Rome, but afterwards freed; and that this synagogue had been built at their expense. Libertini is, therefore, to be regarded as a word of Roman origin, and to be explained with reference to Roman customs. Further, we know that there were in the time of Tiberius many *Libertini,* or 'freed-men,' of the Jewish religion at Rome (Tacit, *Annal.* ii, 85; comp. Suet. *Tib.* 36; and Philo, p. 1014; see Bloomfield, Kuinoel, Wettstein, etc., on Acts vi:9).

LIBERTY (lĭb'ēr-tў). (1) Freedom, to do or forbear a particular action, as one pleases (1 Cor. vii:39; viii:9; x:29). (2) Freedom from human slavery or imprisonment (Lev xxv:10; Heb. xiii: 23). (3) Freedom from the ceremonial and broken covenant of works (Gal. v:1). (4) The happy state of eternal glory, where one is delivered from all misery and servitude (Rom. viii:21).

LIBERTY, CHRISTIAN. "Where the Spirit of the Lord is, there is liberty," that is, freedom from the slavery of sin, Satan, and the broken law, and now under the gospel, from the ceremonial yoke, and great pleasure and boldness in fellowship with God (2 Cor. iii:17). It is wrong to use Christian "liberty," to the hurt of our weak brethren, or to cover a loose practice (Rom. xiv; 1 Cor. viii; 1 Pet. ii:16).

LIBNAH (lĭb'nah), (Heb. לִבְנָה, *lib-naw',* transparency; Sept. Λεβνά, *Lebna*).

1. One of the royal cities of the Canaanites, taken by Joshua immediately after Makkedah (Josh. x:20-30). It lay within the territory assigned to Judah (Josh. xv:42), and became one of the Levitical towns in that tribe (Josh. xxi:13; 1 Chron. vi: 57). It was a strongly fortified place. The Assyrian king Sennacherib was detained some time before it when he invaded Judæa in the time of Hezekiah; and it was before it that he sustained that dreadful stroke which constrained him to withdraw to his own country (2 Kings xix:8; Is. xxxvii:8). In the reign of King Jehoram, Libnah is said to have revolted from him (2 Kings viii:22; 2 Chron. xxi:10). Libnah existed as a

village in the time of Eusebius and Jerome, and is placed by them in the district of Eleutheropolis.

2. A place in the desert between Rimmon-parez and Rissah which marked the twenty-first halting place of the Israelites (Num. xxxiii:20, 21); probably identical with Laban (Deut. i:1).

LIBNATH (lĭb'nath), (for the Heb. see the full form SHIHOR-LIBNATH), a stream near Carmel on the borders of Asher (Josh. xix:26). Michaelis conceives this to be the 'glass-river,' *i. e.*, the Belus, from whose sands the first glass was made by the Phœnicians.

LIBNEH (lĭb'neh), (Heb. לִבְנֶה, *lib-neh'*), occurs in two places of Scripture, viz., Gen., xxx:37; Hos. iv:13, and is supposed to indicate either the *white poplar* or the *storax tree*.

The *libneh* is first mentioned in Gen. xxx:37, as one of the rods which Jacob placed in the watering troughs of the sheep; the *lutz* (the almond) and *armon* (the Oriental plane) being the two others; he 'pilled white strakes in them, and made the white appear which was in the rods.' In Hos. iv:13 reference is made to the shade of trees and the burning of incense:—'They sacrifice upon the top of the mountains, and burn incense upon the hills, under oaks (*allon*, "terebinth tree") and poplars (*libneh*), because the shadow of them is good.' This poplar is said to be called *white*, not on account of the whiteness of its bark, but of that of the under surface of its leaves. It may perhaps be so designated from the whiteness of its hairy seeds, which have a remarkable appearance when the seed covering first bursts. The poplar is certainly common in the countries where the scenes are laid of the transactions related in the above passages of Scripture.

Others, however, have been of opinion that *libneh* denotes the storax tree rather than the white poplar. Thus, in Gen. xxx:37, the Septuagint has ῥάβδον στυρακίνην, 'a rod of styrax;' and the Greek translation of the Pentateuch, according to Rosenmüller, is more ancient and of far greater authority than that of Hosea. From the description of Dioscorides, and his comparing the leaves of the styrax to those of the quince, there is no doubt of the same tree being intended: especially as in early times, as at the present day, it yielded a highly fragrant balsamic substance which was esteemed as a medicine, and employed in fumigation. From the similarity of the Hebrew name *libneh* to the Arabic *lubne*, and from the Septuagint having in Genesis translated the former by *styrax*, it seems most probable that this was the tree intended. It is capable of yielding white wands as well as the poplar; and it is also well qualified to afford complete shade under its ample foliage, as in the passage of Hos. iv:13. We may also suppose it to have been more particularly alluded to, from its being a tree yielding incense. 'They sacrifice upon the tops of the mountains, and burn incense upon the hills, under the terebinth and the storax trees, because the shadow thereof is good.' (See POPLAR.)   J. F. R.

LIBNI (lĭb'nī), (Heb. לִבְנִי, *lib-nee'*, white).

1. The eldest of the two sons of Gershon, son of Levi (Exod. vi:17; Num. iii:18, 21; 1 Chron. vi:17); progenitor of the Libnites. Elsewhere (1 Chron. xxiii:7; xxvi:21) he is called LAADAN. (B. C. post 1856.)

2. The Libni of 1 Chron. vi:29, is in all probability the same man, who is by some error called the son of Mahli and father of Shimei.

LIBNITES (lĭb'nītes), (Heb. לִבְנִי, *lib-nee'*, white), descendants of LIBNI (Num. iii:21; xxvi:58).

LIBYA (lĭb'y-à), (Gr. Λιβύη, *lib-oo'ay*). This name in its largest acceptation, was used by the Greeks to denote the whole of Africa. But Libya Proper, which is the Libya of the New Testament (Acts ii:10), and the country of the Lubim in the Old, was a large tract, lying along the Mediterranean, to the west of Egypt.

Libya is supposed to have been first peopled by, and to have derived its name from, the Lehabim or Lubim. (See NATIONS, DISPERSION OF.) These, its earliest inhabitants, appear, in the time of the Old Testament, to have consisted of wandering tribes, who were sometimes in alliance with Egypt, and at others with the Ethiopians, as they are said to have assisted both Shishak, king of Egypt, and Zerah the Ethiopian in their expeditions against Judæa (2 Chron. xii: 3; xvi:8; Nah. iii:9). They were eventually subdued by the Carthaginians; and it was the policy of that people to bring the nomade tribes of Northern Africa which they mastered, into the condition of cultivators, that by the produce of their industry they might be able to raise and maintain the numerous armies with which they made their foreign conquests. But Herodotus assures us that none of the Libyans beyond the Carthaginian territory were tillers of the ground (Herod. **iv:** 186, 187; comp. Polybius, i:161, 167, 168, 177, Ed. Schweighæuser). Since the time of the Carthaginian supremacy the country, with the rest of the East, has successively passed into the hands of the Greeks, Romans, Saracens, and Turks. The name of Libya occurs in Acts ii:10, where 'the dwellers in the parts of Libya about Cyrene' are mentioned among the stranger Jews who came up to Jerusalem at the feast of Pentecost. (See LUBIM.)

LIBYANS (lĭb'y-anz), (Heb. לֻבִּים, *loo-beem'*). The word thus rendered in Dan. xi:43 should be *Lubim;* in Jer. xlvi:9 it is *Libyans*.

LICE (līc), (Heb. כִּנִּים, *kin-eem'*), occurs in Exod. viii:16, 17, 18; Ps. cv:31; Vulg. *muscas*.

The name of the creature employed in the third plague upon Egypt, miraculously produced from the dust of the land. Its exact nature has been much disputed. Those who reason from the root of the word in the Hebrew text, and assume it to be derived from the Hebrew word to *fix, settle,* or *establish,* infer lice to be meant, from their fixing themselves on mankind, animals, etc. But since it is spoken of as an Egyptian insect, the name for it may be purely Egyptian, and may have no connection with any Hebrew root (Michaelis, *Suppl. ad Lex.* n. 1174).

It is probable, however, that not lice but some species of gnats is the proper rendering. It is not a valid objection, that if this plague were gnats, etc., the plague of flies would be anticipated, since the latter most likely consisted of one particular species having a different destination (see FLY); whereas this may have consisted of not only mosquitoes or gnats, but of some other species which also attack domestic cattle, as the *æstrus,* or *tabanus,* or *zimb* (Bruce's *Travels,* ii:315, 8vo); on which supposition these two plagues would be sufficiently distinct.

But since mosquitoes, gnats, etc., have ever been one of the evils of Egypt, there must have been some peculiarity attending them on this occasion, which proved the plague to be 'the finger of God.' From the next chapter (Ex. ix:31) it appears that the flax and the barley were smitten by the hail; that the former was beginning to grow, and that the latter was in the ear—which, according to Shaw, takes place in Egypt in March

Hence the *kineem* would be sent about February, *i. e.* before the increase of the Nile, which takes place at the end of May, or beginning of June. Since, then, the innumerable swarms of mosquitoes, gnats, etc., which every year affect the Egyptians, come, according to Hasselquist, at the increase of the Nile, the appearance of them in February would be as much a variation of the course of nature as the appearance of the *œstrus* in January would be in England. They were also probably numerous and fierce beyond example on this occasion; and as the Egyptians would be utterly unprepared for them (for it seems that this plague was not announced), the effects would be signally distressing.

For a description of the evils inflicted by these insects upon man, see Kirby and Spence, *Introduction to Entomology*, Lond. 1828, i:115, etc.; and for the annoyance they cause in Egypt, Maillet, *Description de l'Egypte* par l'Abbé Mascrier, Paris, 1755, xc:37; Forskal, *Descript. Animal.* p. 85.

LIEUTENANTS (lŭ-těn'ants), (Heb. אֲחַשְׁדַּרְפְּנִים, *akh-ash-dar-pen-eem'*), the official title of viceroys who governed the provinces of the Persian empire (Esth. iii:12; viii:9; ix:3; Ezra viii:36; called 'prince' in Dan. iii:2; vi:1).

LIFE (līf), (Heb. חַי, *khah'ee*, life or lives; נֶפֶשׁ, *neh'fesh*, breath; Gr. ζωή, *dzo-ay'*, life activity; ψυχή, *psoo-khay'*, breath). The word has several significations in the Scriptures.

1. Physical or animal life (Gen. vi:17; vii:15); or a natural power of acting (Job iii:20; Eccl. ii:17).

2. Spiritual life, consisting in our being reinstated in the favor of God, quickened by his Spirit, and conformed to his image; in consequence whereof, we by supernatural influence, live on God's fullness of grace, enjoy fellowship with him, and act to his glory (Rom. viii:6; Col. iii:3).

3. That eternal holiness and happiness which the saints possess in heaven (Rom. v:17).

4. It is said of Jesus Christ that he is *"the life"* and *"our life;"* he is the source, and maintainer of life to all creatures: he purchased eternal life for his people: he bestows it on them: he, dwelling in their hearts, quickens them, comforts them, and will raise them from the dead, and give them eternal blessedness (John xi:25; xiv: 6; Col. iii:4; 1 John i:2). By *"his life,"* that is, by his resurrection and intercession, we are saved, in consequence of our reconcilement unto God by his death (Rom. v:10). His *"life* is manifested"* in his people's cheerful enduring of suffering for his sake: thereby are clearly evidenced his eternal life in heaven, his intercession for them, and his living in them, as their quickening and comforting head (2 Cor. iv:10); his words are "life," as they, through the Spirit, quicken dead souls, and preserve and restore spiritual life in the saints (John vi:63). And to possess Jesus, the Wisdom of God, is to have the *true fountain of life* in us (Prov. iv:13; John xvii:3).

LIFT (lĭft), (Heb. נָשָׂא, *naw-saw'*; Gr. ἀείρω, *ah'ee-ro*).

1. To raise higher (Gen. vii:17).

2. To render more honorable and conspicuous (1 Chron. xiv:2; 1 Sam. ii:7).

Figurative. (1) God *lifts up* himself, or lifts up his feet, when he hastens to deliver his people (Ps. lxxiv:3); when he displays his power and greatness, and overthrows his and his people's enemies (Ps. xciv:2; Is. xxxiii:3, 10). (2) Christ was *lifted up,* when he hung on the cross,

when exalted to heaven, and when publicly offered in the gospel (John viii:28, and xii:32, 34). (3) He and his people *lift up the head,* when they are filled with joy, glory, and honor (Luke xxi: 28; Ps. cx:7). (4) Men *lift up the eyes,* when they view carefully (Gen. xiii:20; Is. xl:26); or when they pray with expectation of a gracious answer (Ps. cxxi:1). (5) The *lifting up* of the hands, imports swearing (Deut. xxxii:40); threatening (Ezek. xx:15); threatening and oppression (Job xxxi:21); invitation (Is. xlix:22); blessing of others (Lev. ix:22); prayer to God (Ps. xxviii:2; applying earnestly to work (Ps. cxix: 48); rebelling against a sovereign (2 Sam. xviii: 28); or helping, encouraging, and comforting a distressed and disconsolate neighbor (Heb. xii: 12). (6) The *lifting up of the heart or soul* to God, imports solemn dedication to God, joy in his service, and earnest prayer to him (2 Chron. xvii:6; Lam. iii:41; Ps. xxv:1).

LIGHT (līt), (Heb. אוֹר, *ore*), is represented in the Scriptures as the immediate result and offspring of a divine command (Gen. i:3).

The earth was void and dark, when God said, 'Let light be, and light was.' This is represented as having preceded the placing of 'lights in the firmament of heaven, the greater light to rule the day, and the lesser light to rule the night: he made the stars also' (Gen. i:14, *sq.*). Whatever opinion may be entertained as to the facility with which these two separate acts may be reconciled, it cannot be questioned that the origin of light, as of every other part of the universe, is thus referred to the exertion of the Divine will: as little can it be denied that the narrative in the original is so simple, yet at the same time so majestic and impressive, both in thought and diction, as to fill the heart with a lofty and pleasurable sentiment of awe and wonder.

The Divine origin of light made the subject one of special interest to the Biblical nations— the rather because light in the East has a clearness, a brilliancy, is accompanied by an intensity of heat, and is followed in its influence by a largeness of good, of which the inhabitants of less genial climes can have no conception. Light easily and naturally became, in consequence, with Orientals, a representative of the highest human good. All the more joyous emotions of the mind, all the pleasing sensations of the frame, all the happy hours of domestic intercourse, were described under imagery derived from light (1 Kings xi:36; Is. lviii:8; Esth. viii:16; Ps. xcvii: 11). The transition was natural from earthly to heavenly, from corporeal to spiritual things; and so light came to typify true religion and the felicity which it imparts. But as light not only came from God, but also makes man's way clear before him, so it was employed to signify moral truth, and preëminently that divine system of truth which is set forth in the Bible, from its earliest gleamings onward to the perfect day of the Great Sun of Righteousness. The application of the term to religious topics had the greater propriety because the light in the world, being accompanied by heat, purifies, quickens, enriches; which effects it is the peculiar province of true religion to produce in the human soul. Hence its symbolical use.

It is doubtless owing to the special providence under which the divine lessons of the Bible were delivered, that the views which the Hebrews took on this subject, while they were high and worthy, did not pass into superstition, and so cease to be truly religious. Other Eastern nations beheld the sun when it shone, or the moon walking in brightness, and their hearts were secretly enticed, and their mouth kissed their hand in token of adoration (Job xxxi :26, 27). This 'iniquity' the Hebrews not only avoided, but when they considered the heavens they recognized the work of God's fingers, and learnt a lesson of humility as well as of reverence (Ps. viii :3, *sq.*).

Figurative. (1) *God is "light;"* his nature is infinitely pure and glorious; he has all wisdom, excellency and usefulness; and is the author of all knowledge and comfort to his creatures (Ps. xxvii :1; Is. x :17; 1 John i :5). He is *"in the light,"* possesses his own excellencies; is in Christ: and is clearly manifested in his word and works (1 John i :7). (2) Christ is *"the light;"* he is the fountain of all light and knowledge, natural, spiritual, and eternal; and in him we discern everything important (Luke ii :32). (3) The *"light of God's countenance,"* or *"light of the Lord,"* is the instruction given by him; the discoveries of his glory and love; the comforts of his Spirit, and joy of his salvation (Ps. iv :6; Is. ii :5). (4) God's judgments are *"as the light that goeth forth;"* his laws are clear and plain, and his sentences and punishments are righteous, pure, speedy, and irresistible (Hos. vi :5). (5) John the Baptist, and other inspired men, are called *"light,"* or *"lights;"* they are endowed with the knowledge of divine things, and are delightful means of instructing, directing, and comforting others (Matt. v :14; John v :35). (6) Saints are compared to *"light:"* they have the saving knowledge of divine things, and, by their instruction and holy conversation, are agreeable means of conveying knowledge and comfort to others (Luke xvi :8; Eph. v :8). (7) Good kings are called *"light,"* to denote their agreeable splendor, and the counsel and comfort which their subjects receive from them (2 Sam. xxiii :4). (8) A son, or successor, is called *"light,"* as he honors, and keeps his ancestors in view (1 Kings xi :36). (9) The word of God, particularly the gospel, is a *"light,"* or a *"lamp;"* it discovers to us things divine and eternal, and guides us to glory and happiness (Ps. cxix :105; Matt. iv :16). (10) The saving knowledge produced by God's word in our heart is *"light;"* we thereby discern the most glorious and eternal objects, and are wise unto salvation. (11) Prosperity, joy, or comfort, is called *"light."* How pleasant in itself, and it renders men conspicuous (Esth. viii :16; Ps. xcvii :11; Is. lviii :8). (12) The heavenly glory is called *"light,"* and *"light of life,"* to represent its excellency, purity, knowledge, and comfort (Col. i :12).   Brown.

LIGHTEN (līt''n), (Gr. ἀποκάλυψις, *ap-ok-al'oop-sis*).

1. To give light to (Luke ii :32).
2. To make light by unloading (Acts xxvii :18).
3. To make to see or shine ; or to fill with comfort (Ps. lxxvii :18 and xxxiv :5). (See EN-LIGHTEN.)

LIGHTNING (līt'nĭng), (Heb. קָרָק, *baw-rawk'*, gleam; Gr. ἀστραπή, *as-trap-ay'*), flashes of fire that attend thunder. The motion thereof is quick and majestic; and it is called *God's light*, that is, as it were, spread along the sky, as he forms it, and it is grand and glorious (Job xxviii :26 and xxxvi :30).

Figurative. (1) The terrors of the divine wrath are often represented by thunder and lightning; and thunder, on account of its awful impression on the minds of mortals, is often spoken of in Scripture as the voice of the Lord (Exod. ix :28; Job xxviii :26; xxxvii :3, 5; xxxviii :25; xl :9). (2) Divine judgments are likened to *lightning* (Rev. viii :5; xvi :18 and xi :19). (3) Satan falls as *lightning from heaven*, when his power and interest are suddenly ruined (Luke xi :18).

LIGN ALOES (līn' ăl'ōz), (Heb אֲהָלִים, *ă-haw-leem'*; Gr. ἀλοή, *al-ŏ-ay'*). This is doubtless the *lignum aloes* of the ancients, the product of *Aquilaria Agallocha*, and other trees of the same genus growing in India and China according to Roxburg. (See AHALIM; ALOES.)

LIGURE (lĭg'ûr), (Heb. לֶשֶׁם, *leh'shem*), a precious stone in the third row of the high-priest's breastplate (Ex. xxviii :19; xxxix :12). It has been best identified with the Jacinth, a hyacinthine stone, sometimes shading into yellow or brown, and sometimes into imperfect pistachio green. It is harder than the emerald ; but, notwithstanding, the ancients used to engrave upon it.

LIKE (līk), (Heb. כְּמוֹ, *kem-o'*), likely (Jer. xxxviii :9). "He is *like* to die for hunger in the place where he is: for *there is* no more bread in the city."

LIKHI (lĭk'hī), (Heb. לִקְחִי, *lik-khee'*, learned), a Manassite, the third named of the sons of Shemida, the son of Manasseh (1 Chron. vii :19). He left few, if any, descendants, (B. C. after 1950).

LIKING (līk'ĭng), in the A. V. used both as a noun, meaning *condition, plight* (Job xxxix :4), "Their young ones are in good *liking;*" and as a participle meaning "conditioned" (Dan. i :10).

LILY (lĭl'ў), (Gr. κρίνον, *kri'non*). The lily is frequently mentioned in the Authorized Version of the Old Testament as the translation of שׁוּשַׁן, (*shoo-shan'*).

This plant is mentioned in the well-known and beautiful passage (Matt. vi :28) : 'Consider the lilies of the field, how they grow; they toil not, neither do they spin, and yet I say unto you, that even Solomon, in all his glory, was not arrayed like one of these;' so also in Luke xii :27. Here it is evident that the plant alluded to must have been indigenous or grown wild, in the vicinity of the sea of Galilee, must have been of an ornamental character, and from the Greek term κρίνον being applied to it, of a lilaceous nature. Travelers in Palestine mention that in the month of January the fields and groves everywhere abound with various species of lily, tulip, and narcissus.

A species of lily (the *Lilium chalcedonicum* of botanists) is in flower at the season of the year when the sermon on the Mount is supposed to have been spoken, is indigenous in the very locality, and is conspicuous, even in the garden, for its remarkable showy flowers, there can now be little doubt that it is the plant alluded to by our Savior. This is much more likely to be the plant intended than some others which have been adduced, as, for instance, the scarlet *amaryllis*, having white flowers with bright purple streaks, found by Salt at Adowa. Others have preferred the *Crown imperial*, which is a native of Persia and Cashmere. Most authors have united in considering the white lily, *Lilium candidum*, to be the plant to which our Savior referred; but it is doubtful whether it has ever been found in a wild state in Palestine. This opinion is confirmed by a correspondent at Aleppo (*Gardener's Chronicle*, iii. 429), who has resided long in Syria, but is acquainted only with the botany of Aleppo and Antioch: 'I never saw the white lily in a wild state, nor have I heard of its being so in Syria. It is cultivated here on the roofs of the houses in pots as an exotic bulb, like the daffodil.' J. F. R.

LILY WORK (lĭl'ў wûrk), (Heb. שׁוֹשָׁן, *shoo-shan'*, lily; מַעֲשֶׂה, *mah-as-eh'*, work), part of the ornamentation of the two pillars which were erected (2 Chron. iii.15), before the temple (comp. 1 Kings vii:19, 22). (See TEMPLE.)

LIME (līm), (Heb. שִׂיד, *seed*), a material named only three times in the Bible (Deut. xxvii:2, 4; Is. xxxiii:12; Amos ii:1). It is probable that the Jews learned the use of the lime-kiln and lime from the Egyptians.

LINE (līn). One Greek and several Hebrew words are thus rendered. The term is used variously in the Scriptures. It denotes:

1. A cord or instrument to measure and adjust things by (1 Kings vii:15; Is. xxxiv:17; 2 Sam. viii:2).

2. A province or course of motion (Ps. xix: 4). Thus the apostles' line or voice went to the ends of the earth (Rom. x:18); and to boast in another man's *line*, was to go where he had labored, and pretend to have done the work accomplished by him (2 Cor. x:16).

3. A portion, which is as it were measured out by *lines* (Ps. xvi:6).

4. A short instruction, that might be as it were written in one line (Is. xxviii:10).

Figurative. (1) The word of God is a *measuring line;* as our whole conduct, and all the forms and ordinances of the church, must be adjusted thereby (Ezek. xl:3). (2) In a promise the *stretching out of the line upon a place,* imports the measuring of the ground to build houses on it (Jer. xxxi:39; Zech. i:16, and ii:1). (3) But to stretch the *line of confusion and stones of emptiness* on a place, is to render it altogether waste (Is. xxxiv:11, 17). (4) Judgments laid on according to men's deserts, and which lay cities razed on the ground, are called a *line* (Lam. ii: 8). (5) *The line of Samaria, and plummet* of the house of Ahab, is such ruin as Samaria and the family of Ahab met with (2 Kings xxi:13). (6) To lay judgment *to the line,* and righteousness *to the plummet,* is to punish people according to the due desert of their deeds (Is. xxviii:17).

LINEN (lĭn'ĕn). Several Hebrew and Greek words are translated linen, among them the following:

1. *Pish-teh'* (Heb. פִּשְׁתָּה, *carded*) is rendered "linen" in Lev. xiii:47, *sq.;* Deut. xxii:11; Jer. xiii:1, etc.; and "flax" in Josh. ii:6; Judg. xv:14; Prov. xxxi:13; Is. xix:9; Ezek. xl:3; Hos. ii:5, 9. It was used, like our "cotton," to denote not only flax (Judg. xv:14), or raw material from which the linen was made, but also the plant itself (Josh. ii:6), and the manufacture from it. It was used for nets (Is. xix:9), girdles (Jer. xiii:1), measuring lines (Ezek. xl:3), as well as for the dress of the priests (xliv:17, 18). (See FLAX.)

2. *Boots* (Heb. בּוּץ, from root signifying *whiteness*), always translated "fine linen," except in 2 Chron. v:12 ("white linen"), is apparently a late word, and probably the same with the Greek βύσσος, *boos'sos.* It was used for the dresses of the Levite choir in the temple (2 Chron. v:12). It is spoken of as the finest and

most precious stuff worn by kings (1 Chron. xv: 27). The dress of the rich man in the parable was purple and *fine linen* (βύσσος, Luke xvi: 19). "Fine linen," with purple and silk, are enumerated in Rev. xviii:12 as among the merchandise of the mystical Babylon. It is a matter of dispute whether cotton or linen is meant by this word.

3. *Shaysh* (Heb. שֵׁשׁ, *bleached*), an Egyptian word referring chiefly to the Egyptian *byssus,* which was brought to Tyre (Ezek. xxvii:7), and was among the offerings brought out of Egypt by the Israelites (Exod. xxv:4; xxxv:6). The exact material of which *shaysh* was made is difficult to determine, our translators hesitating whether linen or silk should be used (Gen. xli: 42, marg. "silk"; Prov. xxxi:22, "silk" in the text).

4. *Ay-toon'* (Heb. אֵטוּן, *twisted*) occurs only in Prov. vii:16, and there in connection with Egypt. It was probably a kind of thread, made of Egyptian flax, and used for ornamenting the coverings of beds with tapestry work.

5. *Bad* (Heb. בַּד, perhaps from its *separation* for sacred uses) is a word employed in describing the linen dresses worn in religious ceremonies, and may refer to the cloth made from the *shaysh,* or yarn. It occurs in Exod. xxviii: 42; xxxix:28; Lev. vi:10; xvi:4, 23, 32; 1 Sam. ii:18; xxii:18; 2 Sam. vi:14; 1 Chron. xv:27; Ezek. ix:2, 3, 11; x:2, 6, 7; Dan. x:5; xii:6, 7. Celsius is of the opinion that *bad* signifies the finest and best *Egyptian* linen. For fuller discussion of the whole subject see BYSSUS.

Figurative. Fine white linen is in Scripture the emblem of innocence or moral purity (Rev. xv:6), though it is also mentioned as a mark of luxury (Luke xvi:19).

LINTEL (lĭn'tĕl).

1. (Heb. אַיִל, *ah'yil*, a pilaster or pillar in the wall), a beam forming the upper frame of a door (1 Kings vi:31), elsewhere "post."

2. (Heb. כַּפְתּׂר, *kaf-tore'*, a chaplet), Amos ix:1; Zeph. ii:14. The rendering "knop" would be more correct, which is found in all other passages.

3. (Heb. מַשְׁקוֹף, *mash-kofe'*, a projecting cover), Ex. xii:22, 23. The upper door post (Ex. xii:7), which is undoubtedly the correct rendering.

LINUS (li'nus), (Gr. Λίνος, *lee'nos*), one of the Christians at Rome whose salutations Paul sent to Timothy (2 Tim. iv:21).

He is said to have been the first bishop of Rome after the martyrdom of Peter and Paul (Irenæus, *Adv. Hæreus,* iii. 3; Euseb. *Hist. Eccl.* iii. 2, 4; v. 6). (A. D. 64.)

LION (li'ŭn), (Heb. אֲרִי, *ar-ee'*).

The most powerful, daring, and impressive of all carnivorous animals, the most magnificent in aspect and awful in voice. Being very common in Syria in early times, the lion naturally supplied many forcible images to the poetical language of Scripture, and not a few historical incidents in its narratives. This is shown by the great number of passages (about 130) where this animal, in all the stages of existence—as the whelp, the young adult, the fully mature, the lioness—occurs under different names, exhibiting that multiplicity of denominations which always results when some great image is constantly present to the popular mind.

(1) Different Names. Thus we have (1) *gor,* "a suckling," a lion's whelp, a very young lion (Gen. xlix:9; Deut. xxxiii:20; Jer. li:38; Ezek. xix:2; Nahum ii:11, 12, etc.). (2) *Ke-phir',* "the shaggy," a young lion, when first leaving the protection of the old pair to hunt independently (Ezek. xix:2, 3; Ps. xci:13; Prov. xix:12, etc.). (3) *ar-ee',* "the puller in pieces," an adult and vigorous lion, a lion having paired, vigilant and enterprising in search of prey (Nahum ii:12; 2 Sam. xvii:10; Num. xxiii:24). This is the common name of the animal. (4) *Sha'chal,* "the roarer," a mature lion in full strength; a black lion (Job iv:10; x:16; Ps. xci:13; Prov. xxvi: 13; Hos. v:14; xiii:7). This denomination may very possibly refer to a distinct variety of lion, and not to a black species or race, because neither black nor white lions are recorded, excepting in Oppian (*De Venat.* iii:43); but the term may be safely referred to the color of the skin, not of the fur; for some lions have the former fair, and even rosy, while in other races it is perfectly black. An Asiatic lioness, formerly at Exeter Change, had the naked part of the nose, the roof of the mouth, and the bare soles of all the feet pure black, though the fur itself was very pale buff. Yet albinism and melanism are not uncommon in the felinæ; the former occurs in tigers, and the latter is frequent in leopards, panthers, and jaguars. (5) *La'yish,* "the strong," a fierce lion, one in a state of fury (Job iv:11; Prov. xxx: 30; Is. xxx:6). (6) *Labi-ah',* "lowing," "roaring," hence a lioness (Job iv:11), where the lion's whelps are denominated 'the sons of Labiah,' or of the lioness.

(2) Size. The lion is the largest and most formidably armed of all carnassial animals, the Indian tiger alone claiming to be his equal. One full grown, of Asiatic race, weighs above 450 pounds and those of Africa often above 500 pounds. The fall of a fore paw in striking has been estimated to be equal to twenty-five pounds' weight, and the grasp of the claws, cutting four inches in depth, is sufficiently powerful to break the vertebræ of an ox. The huge laniary teeth and jagged molars worked by powerful jaws, and the tongue entirely covered with horny papillæ, hard as a rasp, are all subservient to an immensely strong muscular structure, capable of prodigious exertion, and minister to the self-confidence which these means of attack inspire. In Asia the lion rarely measures more than nine feet and a half from the nose to the end of the tail, though a tiger-skin of which we took the dimensions was but a trifle less than thirteen feet. In Africa they are considerably larger, and supplied with a much greater quantity of mane. Both tiger and lion are furnished with a small horny apex to the tail—a fact noticed by the ancients, but only verified of late years, because this object lies concealed in the hair of the tip and is very liable to drop off. All the varieties of the lion are spotted when whelps; but they become gradually buff or pale yellow. One African variety, very large in size, perhaps a distinct species, has a peculiar and most ferocious physiognomy, a dense black mane extending half way down the back, and a black fringe along the abdomen and tip of the tail; while those of Southern Persia and the Dekkan are nearly destitute of that defensive ornament. The roaring voice of the species is notorious to a proverb, but the warning cry of attack is short, snappish, and sharp. Like all the felinæ, they are more or less nocturnal, and seldom go abroad to pursue their prey till after sunset. When not pressed by hunger, they are

naturally indolent, and, from their habits of uncontrolled superiority, perhaps capricious, but often less sanguinary and vindictive than is expected.

(3) Monogamous. Lions are monogamous, the male living constantly with the lioness, both hunting together, or for each other when there is a litter of whelps; and the mutual affection and care for their offspring which they display are remarkable in animals by nature doomed to live by blood and slaughter. It is while seeking prey for their young that they are most dangerous; at other times they bear abstinence, and when pressed by hunger will sometimes feed on carcasses found dead. They live to more than fifty years; consequently, having annual litters of from three to five cubs, they multiply rapidly when not seriously opposed.

(4) Numerous. In ancient times, when the devastations of Egyptian, Persian, Greek, and Roman armies passed over Palestine, there can be little doubt that these destroyers made their appearance in great numbers. The fact, indeed, is attested by the impression which their increase made upon the mixed heathen population of Samaria, when Israel was carried away into captivity (2 Kings xvii:25, 26).

(5) Scriptural Illustrations. The Scriptures present many striking pictures of lions, touched with wonderful force and fidelity: even where the animal is a direct instrument of the Almighty, while true to his mission, he still remains so to his nature. Thus nothing can be more graphic than the record of the man of God (1 Kings xiii: 28), disobedient to his charge, struck down from his ass, and lying dead, while the lion stands by him, without touching the lifeless body, or attacking the living animal, usually a favorite prey. See also Gen. xlix:9; Job iv:10, 11; Nahum ii: 11, 12. Samson's adventure also with the young lion (Judg. xiv:5, 6) and the picture of the young lion coming up from the underwood cover on the banks of the Jordan, all attest a perfect knowledge of the animal and its habits. Finally, the lions in the den with Daniel, miraculously leaving him unmolested, still retain, in all other respects, the real characteristics of their nature.   C. H. S.

Figurative. (1) God is compared to *"a lion"* in his threatenings, judgments, and chastisements (Hos. v:14; Amos i:2; iii:8). (2) Christ is *"the lion of the tribe of Judah,"* descending from Judah in respect of his manhood; he is the almighty Awakener and Conqueror of souls (Rev. v:5). (3) The church is likened to a *"lion"* strengthened of God; she overcomes, and is terrible to all that oppose her (Mic. v:8); her ministers, especially in the primitive ages, were like *"lions,"* bold, courageous, and active in their work, and conquered multitudes for Christ (Rev. iv:7). (4) The saints are represented as *"lions,"* because of their boldness and activity in the cause of God (Prov. xxviii:1). (5) The tribe of Judah is likened to *"a lion,"* to denote its courage, activity, bravery, and conquests; the tribe of Judah had kings courageous and terrible, who attacked and subdued their enemies. (6) By Samson, the Danites as *"lions,"* mightily mauled their enemies the Philistines (Gen. xlix: 9; Deut. xxxiii:22). (7) The devil is a *"roaring lion";* he furiously goes about to terrify believers and destroy mankind (1 Pet. v:8). (8) Tyrants, oppressors, such as the Assyrian, Chaldean, and Persian conquerors, and the last four kings of Judah are called *"lions"* (Is. xxi:8; Jer. iv:7; v:6; Ezek. xix; Amos iii:8; Nah. ii:12). (9) Men full of wickedness, persecution, oppression, are compared to "*lions,*" as they terrify, tear and murder others around (Is. xi:7; Ezek. xxii:25).

LIP (lĭp), (Heb. שָׂפָה, *saw-faw'*, with the idea of *termination*).

Figurative. (1) To have the "*mouth*" or "*lips covered,*" imports shame and grief (Lev. xiii:45; Ezek. xxiv:17, 22; Mic. iii:7). (2) To "*refrain the lips,*" is to speak little and seasonably; as "the talk of the lips," vain and idle speech, and empty boasting without practice, tends only to poverty (Prov. x:19; xiv:23). (3) To "*open the mouth or lips wide,*" is to talk rashly, boastingly, reproachfully (Ps.xxxv:21; Prov.xiii:3); or to listen with the utmost attention, earnestly desiring instruction (Job xxix:23); or earnestly to desire satisfaction and blessings to our soul (Ps. lxxxi:10). (4) "Uncircumcised of lips" (Exod. vi:12), i. e., not of ready speech, is the same as "slow of speech" (iv:10). (5) The "fruit of the lip" (Heb. xiii:15) is a metaphor for *praise.* (6) By a bolder figure we have "the calves of the lips" (Hos. xiv:2) for a thank offering. (7) To "shoot out the lip" (Ps. xxii:7) has always been an expression of the utmost scorn and defiance. (8) *Unclean lips* are such as are polluted with sinful words (Is. vi:5). (9) *Burning lips* denote fine language, ardent protestations, or words apparently full of love (Prov. xxvi:23).

LIQUOR or LIQUORS (lĭk'ẽr), the translation of three different Hebrew words. One denotes a "tear"—*i. e.,* the juice of the olive and grapes, (Ex. xxii:29); the second denotes "maceration"—*i. e.,* drink prepared by steeping grapes, (Num. vi:3); the last, "mixture"—*i. e.,* highly-flavored wine, (Cant. vii:2). (See WINE.)

LIST (lĭst), (Gr. θέλω, *thel'o*), to please, like, will (Matt. xvii:12; Mark ix:13; John iii:8).

LITTER (lĭt'tẽr). The word translated litter, in Is.lxvi:20, is צָב, *tsawb,* and is the same which, in Num. vii:3, denotes the wains or carts *drawn* by oxen, in which the materials of the tabernacle were removed from place to place.

The *tsawb* was not, therefore, a litter, which is not drawn, but carried. This is the only place in which the word occurs in the Authorized translation. We are not, however, to infer from this that the Hebrews had no vehicles of the kind. Litters, or palanquins, were, as we know, in use among the ancient Egyptians. They were borne upon the shoulders of men, and appear to have been used for carrying persons of consideration short distances on visits, like the sedan chairs of a former day in England. We doubt if the Hebrews had this kind of litter, as it scarcely agrees with their simple, unluxurious habit; but that they had litters borne by beasts, such as are still common in Western Asia, seems in the highest degree probable.

In Cant. iii:9, we find the word *aphiryon,* Sept. πορεῖον, *carriage,* Vulg., *ferculum,* which occurs nowhere else in Scripture, and is applied to a vehicle used by King Solomon. This word is rendered 'chariot' in our Authorized Version, although unlike any other word so rendered in that version. It literally means a *moving couch,* and is usually conceived to denote a kind of sedan, litter, or rather palanquin, in which great personages and women were borne from place to place. The name, as well as the object, immediately suggests that it may have been nearly the same thing as the *takht-ravan,* the *moving throne,* or *seat,* of the Persians. It consists of a light frame fixed on two strong poles, like those of our

sedan chair. The frame is generally covered with cloth, and has a door, sometimes of lattice work. at each side. It is carried by two mules, one between the poles before, the other behind. These conveyances are used by great persons, when disposed for retirement or ease during a journey, or when sick or feeble from age. But they are chiefly used by ladies of consideration in their journeys.

The popular illustrators of Scripture do not appear to have been acquainted with this and the other litters of Western Asia; and have, therefore, resorted to India, and drawn their illustrations from the palanquins borne by men, and from the *howdahs* of elephants. This is unnecessary, as Western Asia still supplies conveyances of this description, more suitable and more likely to have been anciently in use than any which the farther East can produce. If the one already described should seem too humble, there are other *takht-ravans* of more imposing appearance. In Arabia, or in the countries where Arabian usages prevail, two camels are usually employed to bear the *takht-ravan,* and sometimes two horses. When borne by camels, the head of the hindmost of the animals is bent painfully down under the vehicle. This is the most comfortable kind of litter, and two light persons may travel in it.

The *shibreeyeh* is another kind of camel-litter, resembling the Indian *howdah,* by which name (or rather *hódaj*) it is sometimes called. It is composed of a small square platform with a canopy or arched covering. It accommodates but one person, and is placed upon the back of a camel, and rests upon two square camel-chests, one on each side of the animal. It is very evident, not only from the text in view, but from others, that the Hebrews had litters; and there is little reason to doubt that they were the same as those now employed in Palestine and the neighboring countries, where there are still the same circumstances of climate, the same domestic animals, and essentially the same habits of life, as in the Biblical period.

LITTLE OWL (lĭt't'l oul). See OWL.

LIVELY (līv'lĭ), (Heb. חָיֶה, *khaw-yeh',* lively), Exod. i:19, full of life, vigorous, strong; (Gr. ζάω, *dzah'o,* living), Acts vii:38, etc. "This is he who received the lively oracles to give unto us."

LIVER (lĭv'ẽr), (Heb. כָּבֵד, *kaw-bade',* meaning to be heavy), occurs in Exod. xxix:13, 22; Lev. iii:4, 10, 15; iv:9; vii:4; viii:16, 25; ix:10, 19; Prov. vii:23; Lam. ii:11; Ezek. xxi:21; it is applied to the liver, the heaviest of the viscera, as we in English use the word "lights" for lungs, the lightest.

(1) In all the instances where the word occurs in the Pentateuch, it forms part of the phrase translated in the A. V. 'the caul that is above the liver,' but which Gesenius understands to be the great lobe of the liver itself, rather than the caul over it. Jahn thinks the smaller lobe to be meant. It appears from the same passages that it was burnt upon the altar, and not eaten as sacrificial food (Jahn, *Biblisches Archäol.* sec. 378, n. 7). The liver was supposed by the ancient Jews, Greeks, and Romans to be the seat of the passions, pride, love, etc. Thus Gen. xlix:6, 'with their assembly let not' (literally, my liver) 'be united.' (See Heb. of Ps. xvi:9; lvii:9; cviii:2; and Anacreon, *Ode* iii at end; Theocritus, *Idyll* xi:16; Horace, *Carm.* i. 13, 4, 25, 15; iv. 1, 12; and the Notes of the Delphin edition; comp. also Persius, *Sat.* v. 129; Juvenal, *Sat.* v, 647). (2) Wounds in the liver were supposed to be mortal; thus the expressions in

Prov. vii:23, 'a dart through his liver,' and Lam. ii:11, 'my liver is poured out upon the earth,' are each of them a periphrasis for death itself. (3) The passage in Ezekiel contains an interesting reference to the most ancient of all modes of divination, by the inspection of the viscera of animals and even of mankind sacrificially slaughtered for the purpose. It is there said that the king of Babylon, among other modes of divination referred to in the same verse, 'looked upon the liver.' The liver was always considered the most important organ in the ancient art of *Extispicium,* or divination by the entrails. Philostratus felicitously describes it as 'the prophesying tripod of all divination' (*Life of Apollonius,* viii, 7, 5). The rules by which the Greeks and Romans judged of it are amply detailed in Adam's *Roman Antiquities,* p. 261, etc., London, 1834. But divination is coeval and coextensive with a belief in the divinity. We accept the argument of the Stoics, '*sunt Dî : ergo est Divinatio.*' We know that as early as the days of Cain and Abel there were certain means of communication between God and man, and that those means were connected with the sacrifice of animals, and we prefer to consider those means as the source of divination in later ages, conceiving that when the real tokens of the Divine interest with which the primitive families of man were favored ceased, in consequence of the multiplying of human transgressions, their descendants endeavored to obtain counsel and information by the same external observances. We believe that thus only will the minute resemblances be accounted for which we discover between the different methods of divination, utterly untraceable to reason, but which have prevailed from unknown antiquity among the most distant regions. It is further important to remark that the first recorded instance of divination is that of the teraphim of Laban, a native of Padan-aram (Gen. xxxi:19, 30), but by which teraphim both the Septuagint and Josephus understood ἧπαρ τῶν αἰγῶν, 'the *liver* of goats' (*Antiq.* vi:11, 4).

J. F. D.

LIVING CREATURES (lĭv'ĭng krē'tŭrs), (Ezek. cc. i, iii, x; Rev. iv:6-9, A. V. "beasts," but should always be translated as in R. V. "living creatures"). They are identical with CHERUBIM (see CHERUB, CHERUBIM).

LIZARD (lĭz'ērd), (Heb. לְטָאָה, *let-aw-aw',* hiding), a family term, occurring in a list (Lev. xi:30) of six, all of which are rendered in R.V. by names denoting lizards.

Under this denomination the modern zoölogist places all the cold-blooded animals that have the conformation of serpents with the addition of four feet. Thus viewed as one great family they constitute the Saurians, Lacertinæ, and Lacertidæ of authors; embracing numerous generical divisions, which commence with the largest, that is, the crocodile group, and pass through sundry others, a variety of species, formidable, disgusting, or pleasing in appearance—some equally frequenting the land and water, others absolutely confined to the earth and to the most arid deserts; and though in general harmless, there are a few with disputed properties, some being held to poison or corrode by means of the exudation of an ichor, and others extolled as aphrodisiacs, or of medical use in pharmacy; but these properties in most, if not in all, are undertermined or illusory. Of some genera, such as the crocodile and chameleon, we have already made mention. (See CHAMELEON; CROCODILE; DRAGON; LEVIATHAN.) And therefore we shall confine attention to the lizards that are inhabitants of Western Asia and Egypt, and to those more particularly noticed in the Bible.

(1) Of these, commentators indicate six or seven species. Bochart refers *tsab* (Lev. xi:30) to one of the group of Monitors or Varanus, the Nilotic lizard, *Lacerta Nilotica, Varanus Niloticus,* or *Waran* of the Arabs. Like the other of this form, it is possessed of a tail double the length of the body, but is not so well known in Palestine, where there is only one real river (Jordan) which is not tenanted by this species. The true crocodile frequented the shores and marshes of the coast down to a comparatively late period; and therefore it may well have had a more specific name than Leviathan—a word apparently best suited to the dignified and lofty diction of the prophets, and clearly of more general signification than the more colloquial designation. Jerome was of this opinion; and it is thus likely that *tsab* was applied to both, as *waran* is now considered only a variety of, or a young, crocodile. There is a second of the same group, *Lacerta Scincus* of Merrem (*Varanus Arenarius*), Waranel-hard, also reaching to six feet in length; and a third, not as yet clearly described, which appears to be larger than either, growing to nine feet, and covered with bright cupreous scales. This last prefers rocky and stony situations. It is in this section of the Saurians that most of the gigantic fossil species, the real *ben-nephilim,* 'children of the giants,' are found to be located; and of the existing species some are reported to possess great strength. One of the last-mentioned pursues its prey on land with a rapid bounding action, feeds on the larger insects, and is said to attack game in a body, sometimes destroying even sheep. The Arabs, in agreement with the ancients, assert that this species will do fierce and victorious battle with serpents.

(2) We come next to the group of lizards more properly so called, which Hebrew commentators take to be the *letaäh* a name having some allusion to poison and adhesiveness. The word occurs only once (Lev. xi:30), where Saurians alone appear to be indicated. If the Hebrew root were to guide the decision, *letaäh* would be another name for the *gecko* or *anakah,* for there is but one species which can be deemed venomous; and with regard to the quality of adhesiveness, though the *geckos* possess it most, numerous common lizards run up and down perpendicular walls with great facility. We, therefore, take *chomet,* or the sand lizard of Bochart, to be the true lizard, several (probably many) species existing in myriads on the rocks in sandy places, and in ruins in every part of Palestine and the adjacent countries.

(3) We now come to the *Stelliones,* which have been confounded with the noxious *geckos.* They are best known by the bundles of starlike spines on the body. Next we place the *Geckotians,* among which comes the *anakah,* in our version denominated *ferret,* but which is with more propriety transferred to the noisy and venomous *abu-burs* of the Arabs. The particular species most probably meant is the *lacerta gecko* of Hasselquist, the *gecko lobatus* of Geoffroy, distinguished by having the soles of the feet dilated and striated like open fans, from whence a poisonous ichor is said to exude, inflaming the human skin, and infecting food that may be trodden upon by the animal. Hence the Arabic name of *abu-burs,* or 'father leprosy,' at Cairo. To these we add the *Chameleons,* already described (see CHAMELEON); and then follows the *Scincus.*

Of the species of *Seps,* that is, viviparous serpent-lizards, having the body of snakes, with four weak limbs, a species with only three toes on each foot, the *lacerta chalcides* of Linn., appears to extend to Syria.   C. H. S.

LOADEN (lōd'n), (Heb. עָמָשׂ, *aw-mas'*), made a load, laden, burdened (Is. xlvi:1).

LOAF (lōf), (Heb. כִּכָּר, *kik-kawr'*, circle; Gr. ἄρτος, *ar'tos;* occasionally לֶחֶם, *lekh'em,* bread), a biscuit, or round or oval cake, the usual form of bread among the orientals (Exod. xxix:23; Judg. viii:5; 1 Sam. x:3; 1 Chron. xvi:3; Matt. xiv:17; Mark vi:38, etc.). (See BREAD.)

LO-AMMI (lō'ăm'mī), (Heb. לֹא עַמִּי, *lo-am'-mee,* not my people), a name of symbolical significance, given by Hosea (i:9; ii:23) to his second son to indicate that Israel had been rejected by Jehovah, in allusion to the Babylonian Captivity (B. C. 725).

LOAN (lōn), the Mosaic laws which relate to the subject of borrowing, lending, and repaying, are in substance as follows:

(1) Interest. If an Israelite became poor, what he desired to borrow was to be freely lent to him, and no interest, either of money or produce, could be exacted from him; interest might be taken of a foreigner, but not of an Israelite by another Israelite (Exod. xxii:25; Deut. xxiii:19, 20; Lev. xxv:35-38). At the end of every seven years a remission of debts was ordained; every creditor was to remit what he had lent: of a foreigner the loan might be exacted, but not of a brother. If an Israelite wished to borrow, he was not to be refused because the year of remission was at hand (Deut. xv:1-11).

(2) Pledges. Pledges might be taken, but not as such the mill or the upper millstone, for that would be to take a man's life in pledge. If the pledge was raiment, it was to be given back before sunset, as being needful for a covering at night. The widow's garment could not be taken in pledge (Exod. xxii:26, 27; Deut. xxiv: 6, 17).

(3) Biblical Point of View. These laws relating to loans may wear a strange and somewhat repulsive aspect to the mere modern reader, and cannot be understood, either in their bearing or their sanctions, unless considered from the Biblical point of view. The land of Canaan (as the entire world) belonged to its Creator, but was given of God to the descendants of Abraham under certain conditions, of which this liberality to the needy was one. The power of getting loans therefore was a part of the poor man's inheritance. It was a lien on the land (the source of all property with agricultural people), which was as valid as the tenure of any given portion by the tribe or family to whose lot it had fallen. This is the light in which the Mosaic polity represents the matter, and in this light, so long as that polity retained its force, would it, as a matter of course, be regarded by the owners of property. Thus the execution of this particular law was secured by the entire force with which the constitution itself was recommended and sustained. But as human selfishness might in time endanger this particular set of laws, so Moses applied special support to the possibly weak part. Hence the emphasis with which he enjoins the duty of lending to the needy. Of this emphasis the very essence is the sanction supplied by that special providence which lay at the very basis of the

Mosaic commonwealth; so that lending to the destitute came to be enforced with all the power derivable from the express will of God.

That the system of law regarding loans was carried into effect there is no reason to doubt. It formed an essential part of the general constitution, and therefore came recommended with the entire sanction which that system had on, its own behalf; nor were there any predominant antagonistic principles at work which would prevent this from proceeding step by step, in its proper place and time, with the residue of the Mosaic legislation. Nor do the passages of Scripture (Job xxii:6; xxiv:3; Matt. xviii:28; Prov. xxviii:8; Ezek. xviii:8; Ps. xv:5; cix:11) which give us reason to think that usury was practiced and the poor debtor oppressed, show anything but those breaches to which laws are always liable, especially in a period when morals grow corrupt and institutions in consequence decline.

(4) Justice of the Law. While, however, the benign tendency of the laws in question is admitted, may it not be questioned whether they were strictly just? Such a doubt could arise only in a mind which viewed the subject from the position of our actual society. A modern might plead that he had a right to do what he pleased with his own; that his property of every kind—land, food, money—was his own; and that he was justified to turn all and each part to account for his own benefit. Apart from religious considerations this position is impregnable. But such a view of property finds no support in the Mosaic institutions. In them property has a divine origin, and its use is intrusted to man on certain conditions, which conditions are as valid as is the tenure of property itself. In one sense indeed, the entire land—all property—was a great loan, a loan lent of God to the people of Israel, who might well therefore acquiesce in any arrangement which required a portion—a small portion— of this loan to be under certain circumstances accessible to the destitute. This view receives confirmation from the fact that interest might be taken of persons who were not Hebrews and therefore lay beyond the sphere embraced by this special arrangement.

Had the Hebrews enjoyed a free intercourse with other nations, the permission to take usury of foreigners might have had the effect of impoverishing Palestine by affording a strong inducement for employing capital abroad; but, under the actual restrictions of the Mosaic law, this evil was impossible. Some not inconsiderable advantages must have ensued from the observance of these laws. The entire alienation and loss of the lent property were prevented by that peculiar institution which restored to every man his property at the great year of release. In the interval between the jubilees the system under consideration would tend to prevent those inequalities of social condition which always arise rapidly, and which have not seldom brought disaster and ruin on states. The affluent were required to part with a portion of their affluence to supply the wants of the needy, without exacting that recompense which would only make the rich richer and the poor more needy; thus superinducing a state of things scarcely more injurious to the one than to the other of these two parties. There was also in this system a strongly conservative influence. Agriculture was the foundation of the constitution. Had money-lending been a trade, money-making would also have been eagerly pursued. Capital would be withdrawn from the land; the agriculturist would pass into the usurer; huge inequalities would arise; commerce would assume predominance, and the entire commonwealth be overturned—changes and evils which were prevented, or, if not so, certainly retarded and abated, by the code of laws regarding loans. As it was, the gradually increasing wealth of the country was in the main laid out on the soil, so as to augment its productiveness and distribute its bounties.

(5) Teaching of Christ. These views may prepare the reader for considering the doctrine of 'the Great Teacher' on the subject of loans. It is found forcibly expressed in Luke's Gospel (vi:34, 35) : 'If ye lend to them of whom ye hope to receive, what thank have ye? for sinners also lend to sinners, to receive as much again: but love ye your enemies, and do good, and lend, hoping for nothing again; and your reward shall be great, and ye shall be the children of the Highest; for he is kind unto the unthankful and to the evil.' But it can be justly maintained that Christ taught the justice of taking interest in the parable of the Talents and of the Pounds.

J. R. B.

LOAVES (lōvz). See BREAD.

LOCK (lŏk), (Heb. מַנְעֻל, *man-awl'*, lock of door).

The ancient Hebrews had fastenings of wood or iron for the doors of towns, prisons, and fortresses (Is. xlv:2), which were in the form of bolts. The gates of Jerusalem erected by Nehemiah had both bolts and locks (Judg. iii: 23, 24, 25; Neh. iii:3). These bolts, or bars, were almost the only form of locks known. The key was a pin of iron or bronze, or sometimes of wood, to hold the bar in place.

LOCUST (lō'kŭst), (Heb. אַרְבֶּה, *ar-beh'*), generic term; order, *Hemiptera;* species, *Gryllus*, Linnæus.

It is an insect remarkable for numbers and voracity, and hence one of the most dreadful scourges of Eastern countries. Locusts, when mature, can fly to a considerable height, and, occasionally alighting for food and rest, they are often borne by the wind hundreds of miles. The locust is two inches or more in length. It is a winged, creeping thing. Like other insects of the order *Orthoptera*, it has four wings. Those of the anterior pair are narrow, while those of the posterior pair are broader, folded up when not in use, and transparent. It has six legs, on four of which it walks, while the hindmost pair, which are much longer than the others and equal to

Locust (*Œdipoda Migratoria*).

the body in length, it uses for springing (Lev. xi:21, 22). The mouth is furnished with cutting jaws, by means of which it nips off leaves and blades of grass.

There are many species of these insects found in the United States, but none precisely such as live in the Orient. The locusts most destructive and doubtless ordinarily referred to by the Bible are of two kinds, *Acrydium peregrinum* and *Œdipoda migratoria*. In our English Bible seven terms probably describe this insect or allied species—viz., locust, bald locust, beetle, cankerworm, caterpillar, grasshopper, palmer-worm.

68

These seven terms are made to translate nine Hebrew names. The confusion of the entire subject may be seen by the fact that "locust" represents four original words, "grasshopper" two, and "caterpillar" two, while two original words have each a twofold translation. Doubtless the Jews themselves applied some of these terms as loosely and widely as we do such a word as "worm."

It is probable that several of the seven names mentioned describe locusts in their immature state. After leaving the egg this insect passes through changes answering to those of the butterfly, but is never dormant as a chrysalis. From first to last it is voracious, but when it is mature and can fly it lays its eggs and drifts away in vast clouds, perhaps to perish in the ocean. The locusts which the writer saw devastating portions of Syria were fully three inches long when their wings were closed (Lev. xi:22).

Van Lennep in writing of the destruction caused by locusts says: "The ground over which their devastating hordes have passed at once assumes an appearance of sterility and dearth. Well did the Romans call them 'the burners of the land,' which is the literal meaning of our word 'locust.' On they move, covering the ground so completely as to hide it from sight, and in such numbers that it often takes three or four days for the mighty host to pass by. When seen at a distance this swarm of advancing locusts resembles a cloud of dust or sand, reaching a few feet above the ground as the myriads of insects leap forward. The only thing that momentarily arrests their progress is a sudden change of weather, for cold benumbs them while it lasts. They also keep quiet at night, swarming like bees on the bushes and hedges until the morning sun warms and revives them and enables them to proceed on their devastating march (Nahum iii: 17). They 'have no king' nor leader, yet they falter not, but press on in serried ranks, urged in the same direction by an irresistible impulse, and turn neither to the right hand nor to the left for any sort of obstacle (Prov. xxx:27). When a wall or a house lies in their way they climb straight up, going over the roof to the other side, and blindly rush in at the open doors and windows (Exod. x:6; Joel ii:9). When they come to water, be it a mere puddle or a river, a lake or the open sea, they never attempt to go round it, but unhesitatingly leap in and are drowned; and their dead bodies, floating on the surface, form a bridge for their companions to pass over. The scourge thus often comes to an end, but it as often happens that the decomposition of millions of insects produces pestilence and death (Joel ii:20). History records a remarkable instance which occurred in the year 125 before the Christian era. The insects were driven by the wind into the sea in such vast numbers that their bodies, being driven back by the tide upon the land, caused a stench, which produced a fearful plague, whereby 80,000 persons perished in Libya, Cyrene, and Egypt."

The passage in Lev. xi:22 describes four distinct insects of the locust order. "Beetle" is plainly a mistranslation for some one of these leapers, since whatever only crept or flew could be used for food. The locusts were ceremonially clean. John the Baptist ate them, and many others, particularly in Abyssinia, do so still; and being salted and fried, they taste like river cray fish (see as above, Lev. xi:22).

Figurative. The Assyrians were like locusts, for their number and their destructive influence, in the kingdoms of Israel and Judah

(Is. xxxiii:4, 5; Nah. iii:15, 17); and they ruined them, after they had been terribly mowed by the Syrians (Amos vii:1; comp. Joel i:6, 7; ii:2-9).

In the book of Revelation (ix:7) we have a literal description of the symbolical locust, which gives us a terrific impression of their power, and which is curiously illustrated by a passage from an Eastern traveler. An Arab from Bagdad, he says, compared the head of the locust to that of the horse; its breast to that of the lion; its feet to those of the camel; its body to that of the serpent; its tail to that of the scorpion; and so of other parts. In like manner the Italians still call locusts little horses, and the Germans call them hay-horses. (Schaff, *Bib. Dict.*)

LOD (lŏd), (Heb. לֹד, *lode*, 1 Chron. viii:12; Ezra ii:33; Neh. vii:37; xi:35), is doubtless the city of Lydda (Acts ix:32, etc.). (See LYDDA.)

LO-DEBAR (lō'-dē'bar),(Heb. לֹא דְבַר, *lo-deb-ar'*, no pasture).

A town of Gilead, named with places east of Jordan (2 Sam. xvii:27). It was the home of Machir who entertained Mephibosheth and sent food to David (2 Sam. ix:5).

LODGE, TO (lŏj).

1. This word in the A. V. represents the Hebrew verb לוּן, *loon*, or לִין *leen*, which usually has the force of "passing the night" (1 Kings xix:9; 1 Chron. ix:27; Is. x:29; Neh. iv:22; xiii:20, 21; Cant. vii:11; Job xxiv:7; xxxi:32, etc.). The same Hebrew word is otherwise translated in the A. V. by "lie all night" (2 Sam. xii:16; Cant. i:13; Job xxix:19); "tarry the night" (Gen. xix:2; Judg. xix: 10; Jer. xiv:8); "remain" (Ex. xxiii:18).

2. In Josh. ii:1 the word in the original means "to lie," generally in allusion to sexual intercourse.

LOFT (lŏft), (Heb. עֲלִיָּה, *al-ee-yaw'*, lofty), the upper room of a house (1 Kings xvii:19; Acts xx: 9), either over the gate (2 Sam. xviii:24) or built on the roof (2 Kings xxiii:12).

LOG (lŏg), (Heb. לֹג, *lohg*), a liquid measure, two-thirds of an imperial pint. (See WEIGHTS AND MEASURES.)

LOGOS (lŏg'os), (Gr. Λόγος, *logos*, a word), as used in John i:1 it means the Word, symbolically referring to the creative law-giving, revealing activity of God.

(1) It designates especially the mediatorial character of our Redeemer, with special reference to his revelation of the character and will of the Father. It appears to be used as an abstract for the concrete, just as we find this same writer employing *light* for *enlightener*, *life* for *life-giver*, etc.; so that it properly signifies the *speaker* or *interpreter*, than which nothing can more exactly accord with the statement made (John i:18): "No man hath seen God at any time; the only-begotten, who is in the bosom of the Father, hath *declared* him," i. e. communicated to us the true knowledge of his mind and character. (2) That the term is merely expressive of a divine attribute, a position which has been long and variously maintained by Socinians, though abandoned as untenable by some of their best authorities, is in total repugnance to all the circumstances of the context, which distinctly and expressly require personal subsistence in the subject which it describes. (3) He whom John styles the Logos, has the creation of all things ascribed to him; is set forth as

possessing the country and people of the Jews; as the only begotten (son) of the Father; as assuming the human nature, and displaying in it the attributes of grace and truth, etc. Such things could never, with the least degree of propriety, be said of any mere attribute or quality. (4) Nor is the hypothesis of a personification to be reconciled with the universally admitted fact, that the style of John is the most simply historical and the furthest removed from that species of composition to which such a figure of speech properly belongs. To the Logos, the Apostle attributes eternal existence, distinct personality, and strict and proper Deity—characters which he also ascribes to him in his first epistle—besides the possession and exercise of perfections which absolutely exclude the idea of derived or created being.

LOIN (loin), (Heb. חָלָץ, *kha-rats'*), the part of the back and side between the ribs and hip.

The place of the girdle (Job xxxviii:3; xl:7; Is. v:27; xxxii:11): euphemistically for the seat of generation (Gen. xxxv:11; 1 Kings viii:19; 2 Chron. vi:9). Being the pivotal part of the body it was supposed to be most sensibly affected by pain or terror (Deut. xxxiii:11; Job xl:16; Ps. xxxviii:7; lxix:23; Is. xxi:3; Jer. xxx:6; Ezek. xxi:6).

Figurative. The dress of the Oriental nations being loose, it was necessary, when they were traveling or working, to gird up their garments and fasten them about their loins, hence, "to gird up the loins" (1 Kings xviii:46; Job xxxviii:3; xl:7; Prov. xxxi:17, etc.) is used as a figure for vigorous effort. In 1 Pet. i:13, it is used to denote a state of mind in which the soul is prepared to work and exert itself under the influence of divine grace.

LOIS (lō'is), (Gr. Λωΐς, *lo-ece'*, perhaps *agreeable*), the grandmother of Timothy, not by the side of his father, who was a Greek, but by that of his mother.

Hence the Syriac has 'thy mother's mother.' She is commended by St. Paul for her faith (2 Tim. i:5); for although she might not have known that the Christ was come, and that Jesus of Nazareth was he, she yet believed in the Messiah to come, and died in that faith. (A. D. 69).

LONGEVITY (lŏn-jĕv'ĭ-tў). The lengthened ages of some of the ante and postdiluvian fathers, as given by Moses in the Hebrew text, are as follows:

				Years.
Adam	Gen.	v:	5	930
Seth	"		8	912
Enos	"		11	905
Cainan	"		14	910
Mahalaleel	"		17	895
Jared	"		20	962
Enoch	"		23	365
Methuselah	"		27	969
Lamech	"		31	777
Noah	"	ix:	29	950
Shem	"	xi:10,	11	600
Arphaxad	"		12, 13	438
Salah	"		14, 15	433
Eber	"		16, 17	464
Peleg	"		18, 19	239
Reu	"		20, 21	239
Serug	"		22, 23	230
Nahor	"		24, 25	148
Terah	"		32	205
Abraham	"	xxv:	7	175

Infidelity has in various ages attacked revelation because of the supposed absurdity of assigning to any class of men this lengthened term of exist-ence. In reference to this Josephus (*Antiq.* lib. iii.) remarks:—'Let no one upon comparing the lives of the ancients with our lives, and with the few years which we now live, think that what we say of them is false; or make the shortness of our lives at present an argument that neither did they attain to so long a duration of life.' When we consider the compensating process which is going on, the marvel is that the human frame should not' last longer than it does. Some, however, have supposed that the years above named are *lunar,* consisting of about thirty days; but this supposition, with a view to reduce the lives of the antediluvians to our standard, is re-plete with difficulties. At this rate the whole time, from the creation of man to the Flood, would not be more than about 140 years; and Methuselah himself would not have attained to the age which many even now do, whilst many must have had children when mere infants! Be-sides, if we compute the age of the postdiluvians by this mode of calculation—and why should we not?—we shall find that Abraham, who is said to have died in *a good old age* (Gen. xxv:8) could not have been more than *fifteen years* old! Moses must' therefore have meant *solar,* not *lunar* years —not, however, exactly so long as ours, for the ancients generally reckoned twelve months, of thirty days each, to the year.

(1) St. Augustine's Explanation. But it is asked, if Moses meant solar years, how came it to pass that the patriarchs did not begin to be-get children at an earlier period than they are reported to have done? Seth was 105 years old, on the lowest calculation, when he begat Enos; and Methuselah 187 when Lamech was born! St. Augustine (i:15) explains this difficulty in a two-fold manner, by supposing:

(1) Either that the age of puberty was later in proportion as the lives of the antediluvians were longer than ours.

(2) Or that Moses does not record the firstborn sons, but as the order of the genealogy required, his object being to trace the succession from Adam, through Seth, to Abraham.

(2) Josephus' Explanation. As to the prob-able reason why God so prolonged the life of man in the earlier ages of the world, and as to the sub-ordinate means by which this might have been ac-complished, Josephus says (*Antiq.* i, 3): 'For those ancients were beloved of God, and lately made by God himself; and because their food was then fitter for the prolongation of life, they might well live so great a number of years; and because God afforded them a longer time of life on account of their virtue and the good use they made of life in astronomical and geometrical discoveries, for they would not have had the time for foretelling the periods of the stars unless they had lived 600 years; for the great year is completed in that interval.'

(3) Reasons Examined. In the above pas-sage Josephus enumerates *four* causes of the longevity of the earlier patriarchs. As to the first, viz., their being dearer to God than other men, it is plain that it cannot be maintained; for the profligate descendants of Cain were equally long-lived, as mentioned above, with others. Neither can we agree in the second reason he assigns; because we find that Noah and others, though born so long subsequently to the creation of Adam, yet lived to as great an age, some of them to a greater age than he did. If, again,

it were right to attribute longevity to the superior quality of the food of the antediluvians, then the seasons on which this depends must, about Moses' time—for it was *then* that the term of hu-man existence was reduced to its present stand-ard—have assumed a fixed character. But no change at that time took place in the revolution of the heavenly bodies by which the seasons of heat, cold, etc., are regulated; hence we must not as-sume that it was the nature of the fruits they ate which caused longevity.

How far the antediluvians had advanced in scientific research generally, and in astronomical discovery particularly, we are not informed; nor can we place any dependence upon what Josephus says about the two inscribed pillars which re-mained from the old world (see *Antiq.* i, 2, 9). We are not, therefore, able to determine, with any confidence, that God permitted the earlier gen-erations of man to live so long in order that they might arrive at a high degree of mental ex-cellence. From the *brief* notices which the Scrip-tures afford of the character and habits of the antediluvians, we should rather infer that they had not advanced very far in discoveries in natural and experimental philosophy. (See ANTE-DILUVIANS.) We must suppose that they did not reduce their language to alphabetical order; nor was it necessary to do so at a time when human life was so prolonged that the tradition of the creation passed through only two hands to Noah. It would seem that the book ascribed to Enoch is a work of postdiluvian origin (see Jurieu, *Crit. Hist.,* i. 41). Possibly a want of mental employment, together with the labor they endured ere they were able to extract from the earth the necessaries of life, might have been some of the proximate causes of that degeneracy which led God in judgment to destroy the old world.

If the antediluvians began to beget children at the age on an average of 100, and if they ceased to do so at 600 years (see Shuckford's *Connect.,* i. 36), the world might then have been far more densely populated than it is now. Supposing, moreover, that the earth was no more productive antecedently than it was subsequently to the Flood, and that the antediluvian fathers were ignorant of those mechanical arts which so much abridge human labor now, we can easily understand how difficult they must have found it to secure for themselves the common necessaries of life, and this the more so if animal food was not allowed them. The prolonged life, then, of the generations before the Flood would seem to have been rather an *evil* than a blessing, leading as it did to the too rapid peopling of the earth. We can readily conceive how this might conduce to that awful state of things expressed in the words, 'And the whole earth was filled with violence.' In the ab-sence of any well regulated system of govern-ment, we can imagine what evils must have arisen: the unprincipled would oppress the weak, the crafty would outwit the unsuspecting, and, not having the fear of God before their eyes, destruction and misery would be in their ways.

Still we admire the providence of God in the longevity of man immediately after the Crea-tion and the Flood. After the Creation, when the world was to be peopled by one man and one woman, the age of the greatest part of those on record was 900 and upwards. But after the Flood, when there were three couples to repeople the earth, none of the patriarchs, except Shem, reached the age of 500; and only the first three of his line, viz., Arphaxad, Salah, and Eber, who came in the first century after the Flood, lived nearly to that age. In the second century we do not find that any attained the age of 240; and in the third century (about the latter end of which Abraham was born), none, except Terah, arrived at 200; by which time the world was so well peopled, that they had built cities, and were formed into distinct nations under their respective kings (see Gen. xv).

That the common age of man has been the same in all times since the world was well peopled is manifest from profane as well as sacred history. Plato lived to the age of 81, and was accounted an old man; and those whom Pliny reckons up (vii:48) as rare examples of long life may, for the most part, be equaled in modern times. We cannot, then, but see the hand of God in the proportion that there is between births and deaths; for by this means the population of the world is kept up. If the fixed standard of human life were that of Methuselah's age, or even that of Abraham, the world would soon be overstocked; or if the age of man were limited to that of divers other animals, to 10, 20, or 30 years only, the decay of mankind would then be too fast. But on the present scale the balance is nearly even, and life and death keep an equal pace. In thus maintaining throughout all ages and places these proportions of mankind, and all other creatures, God declares himself to be indeed the ruler of the world. (See CHRONOLOGY.)

J. W. D.

LONG-SUFFERING (lŏng'sŭf'fēr-ĭng), (Heb. אֶרֶךְ אַפַּיִם, eh-reh'ap-pah-yeem', slow to anger; Gr. μακροθυμία, mak-roth-oo-mee'ah).

God's "long-suffering," is his patient bearing with manifold affronts, while he forbears to execute deserved wrath upon men, and waits to be gracious to them (Exod. xxxiv:6; Num. xiv: 18; Ps. lxxxvi:15; Jer. xv:15; Rom. ii:4; ix:22; 1 Tim. i:16; 1 Pet. iii:20; 2 Pet. iii:9, 15). The saints' "long-suffering," is their unwearied firmness of mind under manifold trouble, their constant hope of the performance of God's promises, and their patient bearing with others to promote their reformation (Col. iii:12; comp. 2 Cor. vi: 6; Eph. iv:2; 2 Tim. iv:2).

LOOKED (lŏŏkt), (Gr. προσδοκάω, pros-dok-ah'o), to expect (Acts xxviii:6).

LOOKING-GLASS (lŏŏk'ĭng glȧs'). What is thus translated was in fact a plate of metal polished so highly as to produce a very good reflection of objects. Usually these mirrors were of a round shape and provided with a handle (Ex. xxxviii:8; Job xxxvii:18; Is. iii:23). (See MIRROR.)

LOOP (lŏŏp), (Heb. לֻלָאָה, loo-law-aw', winding). The curtains of the tabernacle were fastened by loops to their corresponding knobs. They were probably made of goat's hair cord, and were dyed blue (Exod. xxvi:4, sq.; xxxvi:11). (See TABERNACLE.)

LORD, a Saxon word signifying ruler or governor.

In the A. V. the word Lord is used without much discrimination for all the names applied to God; which cannot be helped, as our language does not afford the same number of distinguishing titles as the Hebrew. When, however, the word represents the dread name of Jehovah, it is printed in small capitals, LORD, and is by this contrivance made a distinguishing term. As the Hebrew name Jehovah is one never used with reference to any but the Almighty, it is to be regretted that the Septuagint, imitated by our own and other versions, has represented it by a word which is also

used for the Hebrew 'Adonai,' which is applied not only to God, but, like our 'Lord,' to creatures also, as to angels (Gen. xix:3; Dan. x:16, 17), to men in authority (Gen. xlii:30, 33), and to proprietors, owners, masters (Gen. xlv:8). The leading idea of the Hebrew, the Greek, and the English words is that of an owner or proprietor, whether God or man; and it occurs in the inferior application with great frequency in the New Testament. This application is either literal or complimentary: *literal*, when the party is really an owner or master, as in Matt. x:24; xx:8; xxi:40; Acts xvi:16, 19; Gal. iv:1, etc.; or when he is so as having absolute authority over another (Matt. ix:38; Luke x:2), or as being a supreme lord or sovereign (Acts xxv:26); and *complimentary*, when used as a title of address, especially to superiors, like the English *Master, Sir;* the French *Sieur, Monsieur;* the German *Herr*, etc., as in Matt. xiii:27; xxi:20; Mark vii:8; Luke ix:54.

It cannot but be deemed desirable that, instead of the extensive use of the word *Lord* which we have described, discriminating terms should be adopted in translation. Apart from the Jewish superstitions which influenced the Seventy in their translation, there can be no good reason why the name Jehovah should not be retained wherever it occurs in the Hebrew. Then 'Lord' might represent *Adonai;* or perhaps 'Sir,' or 'Master,' might be used when that word is applied to creatures; and God would very properly represent *Elohim*.

The different Hebrew words rendered for "Lord," are given, as adapted from Mc. & Str. *Bib. Cyc.,* and Barnes' *Bib. Cyc.*

1. *Yeh-ho-vaw'* (Heb. יְהֹוָה, *self-existent*), Jehovah, the proper name of the God of the Hebrews, and should have been retained in that form by the translators instead of 'Lord.' (See JEHOVAH.)

2. *Aw-done'* (Heb. אָדוֹן), an early word denoting absolute control. It is not properly a divine title, being employed of the master of slaves (Gen. xxiv:14, 27; xxxix:2, 7; A. V. "master"); of kings as the lords of their subjects (Is. xxvi:13); of a husband as lord of the wife (Gen. xviii:12). It is applied to God as the owner and governor of the whole earth (Exod. xxiii:17; Ps. cxiv:7). It is sometimes used as a term of respect, like our *sir;* but with a pronoun attached ("my lord"), and often occurs in the plural.

3. *Ad-o-nai'* (Heb. אֲדֹנָי, *the lord; the master*), regarded by some as plural of the foregoing. It is chiefly used in the Pentateuch (Exod. iv:10, 13; Josh. vii:8); also when God is spoken of (1 Kings xiii:9; xxii:6, etc.). The Jews, out of a superstitious reverence for the name Jehovah, always, in reading, pronounce *Adonai* where *Jehovah* is written. The similar form, *with the suffix*, is also used of men, as of Potiphar (Gen. xxxix: 2, *sq.;* A. V. "master"), and of Joseph (xlii: 30, 33).

4. *Koo'ree-os* (Gr. κύριος, *supreme*), the one who is supreme master whether royal or private subject; "Lord of the vineyard" (Matt. xx:8; xxi:40; Mark xii:9; Luke xx:15); the "Lord of the harvest" (Matt. ix:38; Luke x:2); the "master of the house" (Mark xiii:35); "Lord of the Sabbath" (Matt. xii:8; Mark ii:28; Luke vi:5). This title is given to *God,* the ruler of the universe, both with the article ὁ κύριος (Matt. i:22; v:33; Mark v:19; Luke i:6, *sq.;* Acts vii:33; 2

Tim. i:16, 18) and without the article (Matt. xxi:9; xxvii:10; Mark xiii:20; Luke ii:9; xiii: 25; Heb. vii:21). It is also a title of respect (Matt. xiii:27, A. V. "sir"; Luke xiii:8; xiv:22, etc.); used by a son in addressing his father (Matt. xxi:30, A. V. "sir"); by citizens toward magistrates (Matt. xxvii:63, A. V. "sir"); by anyone wishing to honor a man of distinction (Matt. viii: 2, 6, 8; xv:27; Mark vii:28; Luke v:12, etc.); by the disciples in saluting Jesus their teacher and master (Matt. viii:25; xvi:22; Luke ix:54; John xi:12, etc.). It is a title applied to the exalted and glorified Christ (Acts x:36; Rom. **xiv:** 8; 1 Cor. vii:22; viii:6; Phil. ii:9-11).

5. *Baal* (Heb. בַּעַל, *bah'al*, master), meaning *domination,* applied only to heathen deities, or to human relations, as husband, etc., or to one who was specially skilled in a trade or profession. (See BAAL.)

6. Some other and less important words in the original are translated "Lord" in the A. V. They are: *Shaw-leesh'* (Heb. שָׁלִישׁ, 2 Kings vii:2, 17), an officer of the third rank; *rab* (רַב, Dan. ii: 10), a chief, or captain; *maw'-ray* (מָרֵא, *master*, Dan. ii:10), an official title; *seh'ren* (סֶרֶן), a Philistine term found in Joshua, Judges, and 1 Samuel, where "the *lords* of the Philistines" are mentioned; *rab-reb-awn'* (רַבְרְבָן, *magnate*), used in reference to certain Babylonish nobles (Dan. iv:36; v:1, 9, 10, 23; vi:17), and its Greek equivalent, RABBONI (which see); *sar* (שַׂר, a *head* person), title of nobility (Ezra viii:25). (Barnes, *Peop. Bib. Cyc.*)

LORD'S DAY (lôrd's dā).

(1) The expression so rendered in the Authorized English Version (ἐν τῇ κυριακῇ ἡμέρᾳ, *on the Lord's Day*) occurs only once in the New Testament, viz., in Rev. i:10, and is there unaccompanied by any other words tending to explain its meaning.

It is, however, well known that the same phrase was, in after ages of the Christian church, used to signify the first day of the week, on which the resurrection of Christ was commemorated. Hence it has been inferred that the same name was given to that day during the time of the Apostles, and was in the present instance used by St. John in this sense as referring to an institution well known, and therefore requiring no explanation.

(2) Others, however, have held that it means simply 'the day of the Lord,' the substantive being merely exchanged for the adjective, as in 1 Cor. xi:20, 'the Lord's Supper,' which would make it merely synonymous with 'the day of the Lord' (1 Thess. v:2). But upon the whole, the former interpretation is perhaps the more probable.

(3) We find that immediately after the Feast of Pentecost the disciples met together *daily* for prayer and communion (Acts ii:46); and this practice has been supposed by some to be implied, at a later period, in the expressions used in 1 Cor. xi:21.

But on *one* occasion afterwards we have it specially recorded that they 'came together on the first day of the week to break bread' (Acts xx: 7), when 'Paul preached unto them, and continued his speech till midnight.' It has from this last circumstance been inferred by some that the assembly commenced after sunset on the Sabbath, at which hour the first day of the week

had commenced, according to the Jewish reckoning (Jahn's *Bibl. Antiq.* sec. 398), which would hardly agree with the idea of a commemoration of the resurrection. The regulation addressed to the church of Corinth (1 Cor. xvi:2) with respect to charitable contributions 'on the first day of the week,' is not connected with any *mention* of public worship or assemblies on that day. Yet this has been inferred: and the regulation has been supposed to have a reference to the tenets of the Jewish converts, who considered it unlawful to touch money on the Sabbath (Vitringa, *De Synagogâ*, translated by Bernard, pp. 75-167). In consideration for them, therefore, the Apostle directs the collection to be made on the following day, on which secular business was lawful.

(4) Thus far we cannot say that the evidence for *any particular observance* of this day amounts to much; still less does it appear what *purpose* or object was referred to. We find no *mention* of any *commemoration,* whether of the resurrection or any other event *in the Apostolic records.*

On these points we have no distinct testimony till a later period. The earliest, or Apostolic, Fathers, make no mention whatever of such an institution, unless we except one passage to which we shall presently refer, but which is at most a mere allusion.

(5) The well-known letter of Pliny to Trajan (about A. D. 100) mentions the Christians assembling together for worship on *a stated day.* 'They are accustomed to assemble on a stated day before light, and sing a hymn to Christ as a God' (*Epist.* x. 97).

But it is not till the time of Justin Martyr (A. D. 140) that we find a distinct account of the observance. His statement is clear and circumstantial, to the effect that the Christians were in the practice of assembling for public worship on the first day of the week, as being that on which the work of Creation was commenced, and on which Christ rose from the dead:—'On Sunday we all assemble in common, since that is the first day, on which God, having changed darkness and chaos, made the world, and on the same day our Savior Jesus Christ rose from the dead' (Justin Mart. *Apol.* i. 67).

(6) In the so-called Epistle of Barnabas, probably a forgery of the second century (see BARNABAS), the first day of the week is spoken of as observed with rejoicing in memory of the resurrection. 'We keep the eighth day with joy, on which also Jesus rose from the dead' (Barnab. *Ep.* i. 15).

(7) The earliest authentic instance in which the name of 'the Lord's day' is applied (after the passage in the Apocalypse) is not till A. D. 200, when Tertullian speaks of it as 'die Domini resurrexionis' (*De Orat.* sec. 23); again, 'Domini cum diem' (*De Idol.* 14); and Dionysius of Corinth (probably somewhat later), as *'the Lord's Day'* (quoted by Euseb. *Hist. Eccles.* iv. 23).

Thus far, also, nothing has appeared relative to any observance of the day beyond that of holding assemblies for religious worship, and a festal commemoration of the resurrection and the beginning of the creation.

(8) In the laws of Constantine (A. D. 300), cessation from ordinary work on the Lord's day was first enjoined, but with an express exception in favor of the labors of agriculture. (**See** Jortin's *Remarks on Eccles. Hist.* iii. 236).

(9) Chrysostom (A. D. 360) concludes one of his Homilies by dismissing his audience to their respective ordinary occupations. The Council of Laodicea (A. D. 364), however, enjoined Christians to rest on the Lord's day. To the same

effect is an injunction in the forgery called the *Apostolical Constitutions* (vii:24), and various later enactments from A. D. 600 to A. D. 1100, though by no means extending to the prohibition of all secular business. In fact, in these subsequent ages of the church we find the ceremonial spirit rather displaying itself in the multiplication of religious festivals and solemnities than in any increasing precision in the observance of the Lord's day. This is exemplified in the practice of the unreformed church in modern times, and retained by most of the reformed, with the exception of those formed on the Puritanical model, who have adopted a peculiar view of the entire institution to which we shall refer in another place. (See SABBATH.) We may add, also, that as in the case of Constantine, so in some modern states, where a church has been established *by law,* the same *policy* has prevailed of passing temporal enactments for the cessation of business, and even public amusements, on the Lord's day, especially in more recent times. To those Christians who look to the *written word* as the sole authority for anything claiming Apostolic or Divine sanction it becomes peculiarly important to observe that the New Testament evidence of the observance of the Lord's day amounts merely to the recorded fact that the disciples did assemble on the first day of the week, and the *probable* application of the designation 'the Lord's day' to that day.   B. P.

LORD'S PRAYER (lôrd's prâr), the common title given to the only form of prayer which our Lord himself taught his disciples, and which is recorded in Matt. vi:9-13; Luke xi:2-4.

"The Lord's Prayer is the Prayer of prayers, as the Bible is the Book of books and the Apostles' Creed the Creed of creeds. It is the best and most beautiful, the simplest and yet the deepest, the shortest and yet the most comprehensive, of all forms of devotion. Only from the lips of the Son of God could such a perfect pattern proceed. An ancient Father calls it a summary of Christianity or the gospel in a nutshell. It embraces all kinds of prayer, petition, intercession, and thanksgiving, all essential objects of prayer, spiritual and temporal, divine and human, in the most suitable and beautiful order, commencing with the glory of God, gradually descending to man's needs, then rising to the final deliverance from all evil, and ending in thanksgiving and praise, as all prayer must end at last, in heaven, where all our wants shall be supplied. It accompanies the Christian from the cradle to the grave. It can never be superseded. If we have exhausted the whole extent of our religious wants and the whole vocabulary of devotion, we gladly return to this model prayer as infinitely superior to all our own effusions. It may, indeed, be abused, like every gift of God, and become a dead form—Luther called it in this respect 'the greatest martyr on earth'—but this is no argument against its proper and frequent use. It is not intended, of course, to supersede other forms or extemporaneous prayers, but it should serve as a general pattern and directory to all our devotions, and breathe into them the proper spirit."
          Schaff.

LORD'S SUPPER, THE (lôrd's sŭp'pẽr).
Four distinct accounts are given in the New Testament of our Lord's institution of the Holy Communion. Three of the Gospels contain the narrative in nearly the same terms, while the Apostle Paul, in the first Epistle to the Corinthians, adds his detailed account, derived, as he

emphatically tells us, not from the testimony of eyewitnesses, but from a special revelation made to him. It would seem as if there were little room for any controversy to arise as to the nature of this sacrament, when its original establishment has been so fully described. Nevertheless, the Lord's Supper, designed to be the conservator of peace and harmony, has been made a battle field of polemics.

In studying these accounts, the reader is first of all struck by the singular simplicity of the Lord's Supper. Nothing could be in more complete contrast to the gorgeous ceremonial with which a later and less pure Christianity invested this memorial rite. Not in a splendid sanctuary, but in the upper chamber of a private house in Jerusalem, was the Communion first celebrated. Christ gave to his disciples no "manual of devotion,' no elaborate directions as to postures, and no instructions how to handle the bread and hold the chalice.

It is supposable that some unusual things, difficult to obtain, might have been made the emblems of our Lord's sacrifice. On the contrary, he chose as symbols of his atoning oblation of himself bread and wine, both of which were elements of the Passover, and therefore at the moment on the table at which he gathered his friends. It was an anticipation of St. Paul's language, "Whether therefore, ye eat or drink, or whatsoever ye do, do all to the glory of God." It was a simple meal in commemoration of the death of Christ. There is not even a word to indicate that a minister was necessary to its celebration.

The language used by the Savior in the institution of this sacrament was such as makes it clearly, in its primary significance, a *commemorative* act. He broke the bread, and gave it to them with the words, "Take, eat, this is my body." Now, setting aside for the present the Romish theory of a miraculous change by which the bread was altered in substance into the literal body of Christ, what could he have meant by such an expression?

A simple illustration affords the clearest answer. Passing through a great gallery of art, some one points to a statue, and says, "That is Washington." Or standing before a portrait he says, "That is Lincoln." The language, according to all the ordinary usages of speech, would be perfectly accurate, and no one of intelligence could mistake its significance. The marble or bronze on the one hand, and the canvas and color on the other, *represent* the two great statesmen. In that upper chamber in Jerusalem, with his human body visible to their eyes and tangible to their hands, Christ takes a piece of bread, and says, "This is my body." What possible meaning could those words have had to the disciples, except this, that the bread broken *represented* his body so soon to be broken on the cross?

Such a view of the Supper of the Lord in no way interferes with its efficacy as a means of grace. True, there is no incomprehensible "mystery" about it. The Evangelical Christian does not approach the Lord's table as if it were some magic charm in which he is to find spiritual help, as the Romanist expects to find it in touching a relic of the saints, or the wood of "the true cross." Its philosophy is as clear as the noonday. For what can rekindle the glow of love in the heart like the stirring of the memory? More than once during our Civil War a man drafted for the army was saved by a voluntary substitute, who took his place and died on the field of battle. Could that conscript, thus redeemed from death, ever behold the memento stained with the heart's blood of his substitute and not have his gratitude and love revived?

With that memorial idea another is coupled. The Lord's Supper is a visible Gospel. We cannot see these emblems of the Christ's death without their preaching of his atonement. Perhaps, then, the question might be asked if we do not satisfy all that the sacrament demands when we have looked upon the consecrated symbols of his dying love. Why eat the bread? Why drink the wine? Is not the pictorial representation of our Lord's suffering all that is needed? The answer is that our bodily life is an emblem of our spiritual life. As we sustain bodily existence by eating and drinking, so *by faith* do we feed upon Christ. Even the Old Testament foreshadowed this principle when the prophet, turning from Mosaic rites, cried from the watchtower of vision, "The just shall live by faith." Christ echoed that truth when, long before the night in which he was betrayed, he solemnly declared, "Except ye eat the flesh of the Son of man, and drink his blood, ye have no life in you." That he did not here refer to Communion is clear. He thus spoke at least a year before he instituted the Lord's Supper. He was speaking to an assembly of Jews, who could by no possibility know anything of the ordinance to be established in the future. Moreover, when he found that they gave to his words a gross and unspiritual meaning, he corrected their misapprehension by telling them that in his body he was to ascend to heaven, and that his figurative allusion to his body and blood was only the teaching that the spirit is the support of all spiritual life, as food is the support of physical existence. "What and if ye shall behold the Son of man ascend up where he was before? It is the spirit which quickeneth. The flesh profiteth nothing. The words that I speak unto you, they are spirit and they are life." Nothing seems plainer than that the Communion was instituted to keep ever in mind the fact that partaking of food is not more necessary to the physical than simple faith is to the spiritual existence.

One other principle appears in this rite:

In thus entering into fellowship with his suffering Master, the believer also becomes a member of the vast brotherhood, whatever be the name they bear who partake of Christ by faith, "the blessed company of all faithful people." By faith in Christ "they all eat the same spiritual meat and drink the same spiritual drink." That loving fellowship they symbolize and picture forth by this visible gathering around the same table, and exhibit their common love and common interest in each other, by calling their memorial feast "the Communion."   C. E. C.

LO-RUHAMAH (lō ru'ha-mah), (Heb. לֹא רֻחָמָה, *lo-roo-khaw-maw'*, not pitied, not favored), a symbolical name given to the daughter of Hosea the prophet (Hos. i:6, 8). It was to indicate that the Lord would not continue to show compassion toward the rebellious nation, as he hitherto had done under Jeroboam II (2 Kings xiii: 23). It is rendered in Hos. ii:23 "her that had not obtained mercy." When God restored his favor to the people her name was changed to RUHAMAH (which see).

LOSS, LOSSES (lŏs, lŏs'ĕs). Under the law of Moses, the following were the regulations respecting *losses:* If two men strove together, and as a result one should be disabled from work, the other must pay for the lost time (Exod. xxi: 19); claims for losses from trespass, or for any lost

thing, were to be brought before the judges, and adverse judgment was followed by the payment of double to the other (Exod. xxii:9); a man finding any lost thing, and denying it, was obliged, when he wished to present a trespass offering, to restore the lost thing with an added fifth to the one to whom it belonged (Lev. vi:4, 5). The general principle upon which these enactments were based was that an Israelite's fellow-countrymen were his brothers; and he was always to act the brotherly part. Therefore, whenever he found anything that was lost he was commanded to care for it, and to make diligent search for its owner with a view of restoration (Deut. xxii:3). (Barnes' *Bib. Dict.*) (See LAW OF MOSES.)

LOT (Heb. גּוֹרָל, *go-rawl'*, a pebble; חֵבֶל, *kheh'-bel*, measuring line, portion; Gr. λαγχάνω, *lang-khan'o*, to cast lots, Luke i:9; κλῆρος, *klay'ros*, pebble, bit of wood, to cast lots with (Acts i:26).

The use of lots among the ancients was very general. It was supposed to be employed by the gods themselves (Hom. *Il.* xxii. 209; Cic. *De Div.*, i. 34; ii. 41). The Israelites sometimes had recourse to lots as a means of ascertaining the Divine will. The religious estimate of them may be gathered from Prov. xvi:33. The following are historical or ritual instances:

(1) In the division of the Promised Land among the tribes of Isreal the use of the lot was expressly commanded by God himself, it being understood that the extent of territory should be proportioned to the population of each tribe (Num. xxvi:55).

(2) Choice of men for an invading force (Judg. i:1-3; xx:9).

(3) So the selection of the scapegoat on the day of atonement was to be determined by lot (Lev. xvi:8).

(4) Property was divided in the same way (Ps. xxii:18; Matt. xxvii:35).

(5) The orders of the priests and their daily service were also assigned by lot (1 Chron. xxiv: 5).

(6) The lot was used in the detection of a criminal (Josh. vii:14, 18).

(7) In the choice of the Apostle Matthias (Acts i:26) and in the cases of Saul and Jonathan, and Jonah and his companions, to determine who had offended God (1 Sam. xiv:41, 42; Jonah i:7). (See URIM and THUMMIM.)

(8) That which falls to one by lot, as a *portion* or *inheritance* (Deut. xxxii:9; Josh. xv: 1; 1 Chron. xvi:18; Ps. cv:11; cxxv:3; Is. xvii: 14; lvii:6; Acts viii:21; comp. Acts xiii:19).

As to the manner of casting lots we have no certain information. It is supposed by some that the stones or marks which were used in determining the lot were thrown together into the lap or fold of a garment, or into an urn or vase, and that the person holding them shook them violently, so that there should be a perfect mingling of the whole contents, to prevent all preference by the hand of him who should draw; so that the passage (Prov. xvi:33) is paraphrased thus: "In a lot-vase the lots are shaken in all directions; nevertheless, from the Lord is the whole decision or judgment."

LOT (lŏt), (Heb. לוֹט, *lote*, a covering).

1. Lot was the son of Haran and nephew of Abraham, who by the early death of his father had already come into possession of his property when Abraham went into the land of Canaan (Gen. xi:31). Their united substance, consisting chiefly in cattle, was not then too large to prevent them from living together in one encampment.

(1) Parting of Abraham and Lot. Eventually, however, their possessions were so greatly increased that they were obliged to separate; and Abraham with rare generosity conceded the choice of pasture-grounds to his nephew. Lot availed himself of this liberality of his uncle, as he deemed most for his own advantage, by fixing his abode at Sodom, that his flocks might pasture in and around that fertile and well-watered neighborhood (Gen. xiii:5-13). He had soon very great reason to regret this choice; for although his flocks fed well, his soul was starved in that vile place, the inhabitants of which were sinners before the Lord exceedingly. There 'he vexed his righteous soul from day to day with the filthy conversation of the wicked' (2 Pet. ii: 7).

(2) Prisoner. About eight years after his separation from Abraham, Lot was carried away prisoner by Chedorlaomer, along with the other inhabitants of Sodom, and was rescued and brought back by Abraham (Gen. xiv.), as related under other heads (see ABRAHAM; CHEDORLAOMER). This exploit procured for Abraham much celebrity in Canaan; and it ought to have procured for Lot respect and gratitude from the people of Sodom, who had been delivered from hard slavery and restored to their homes on his account. But this does not appear to have been the result.

(3) Avenging Angels. At length the guilt of 'the cities of the plain' brought down the signal judgments of Heaven. The avenging angels, after having been entertained by Abraham, repaired to Sodom, where they were received and entertained by Lot, who was sitting in the gate of the town when they arrived. While they were at supper the house was beset by a number of men, who demanded that the strangers should be given up to them, for the unnatural purposes which have given a name of infamy to Sodom in all generations. Lot resisted this demand, and was loaded with abuse by the vile fellows outside on that account. They had nearly forced the door, when the angels, thus awfully by their own experience convinced of the righteousness of the doom they came to execute, smote them with instant blindness, by which their attempts were rendered abortive, and they were constrained to disperse. Towards morning the angels apprised Lot of the doom which hung over the place, and urged him to hasten thence with his family.

(4) Escape from Sodom. He was allowed to extend the benefit of this deliverance to the families of his daughters who had married in Sodom; but the warning was received by those families with incredulity and insult, and he therefore left Sodom accompanied only by his wife and two daughters.

(5) Lot's Wife. As they went, being hastened by the angels, the wife, anxious for those who had been left behind, or reluctant to remove from the place which had long been her home, and where much valuable property was necessarily left behind, lingered behind the rest, and was suddenly involved in the destruction, by which —smothered and stiffened as she stood by saline incrustations—she became 'a pillar of salt.' The turning of Lot's wife into a pillar of salt has often been regarded as one of the difficulties of the Bible, but is not so necessarily. "We are not to suppose that she was actually turned into one, but having been killed by the fiery and sulphurous vapor with which the air was filled, and afterward incrusted with salt, she resembled an actual statue of salt" (K. and D., *Com. in loco*).

(6) Departure to Zoar. Lot and his daughters then hastened on to Zoar, the smallest of the five cities of the plain, which had been spared on purpose to afford him a refuge: but, being fearful, after what had passed, to remain among a people so corrupted, he soon retired to a cavern in the neighboring mountains, and there abode.

(7) Daughters' Sin. After some stay in this place, the daughters of Lot became apprehensive lest the family of their father should be lost for want of descendants, than which no greater calamity was known or apprehended in those times; and in the belief that, after what had passed in Sodom, there was no hope of their obtaining suitable husbands, they, by a contrivance which has in it the taint of Sodom, in which they were brought up, made their father drunk with wine, and in that state seduced him into an act which, as they well knew, would in soberness have been most abhorrent to him. They thus became the mothers, and he the father, of two sons, named Moab and Ammon, from whom sprang the Moabites and Ammonites, so often mentioned in Hebrew history (Gen. xix). This circumstance is the last which the Scripture records of the history of Lot; and the time and place of his death are unknown.

(8) Palliation of Daughters' Offense. With respect to Lot's daughters Whiston and others are unable to see any wicked intention in them. He admits that the incest was a horrid crime, except under the unavoidable necessity which apparently rendered it the only means of preserving the human race: and this justifying necessity he holds to have existed in their minds, as they appear to have believed that all the inhabitants of the land had been destroyed except their father and themselves. But it is incredible that they could have entertained any such belief. The city of Zoar had been spared, and they had been there. The wine also with which they made their father drunk must have been procured from men, as we cannot suppose they had brought it with them from Sodom. The fact would therefore seem to be that, after the fate of their sisters, who had married men of Sodom and perished with them, they became alive to the danger and impropriety of marrying with the natives of the land, and of the importance of preserving the family connection. The force of this consideration was afterwards seen in Abraham's sending to the seat of his family in Mesopotamia for a wife for Isaac. But Lot's daughters could not go there to seek husbands; and the only branch of their own family within many hundred miles was that of Abraham, whose only son, Ishmael, was then a child. This, therefore, must have appeared to them the only practicable mode in which the house of their father could be preserved. Their making their father drunk, and their solicitous concealment of what they did from him, show that they despaired of persuading him to an act which, under any circumstances, and with every possible extenuation, must have been very distressing to so good a man.

(9) Character. That Lot was a good man is evinced by his deliverance from among the guilty, and is affirmed by St. Peter (2 Pet. ii:7); his preservation is alluded to by our Savior (Luke xvii:18, etc.); and in Deut. ii:9, 19, and Ps. lxxxiii:9, his name is used to designate the Moabites and Ammonites, his descendants.

2. Lot (Heb. same as foregoing) is mentioned in two passages of Scripture, in both of which it is erroneously translated *myrrh* in the Authorized Version.

In Gen. xxxvii :25, 'Behold a company of Ishmaelites came from Gilead with their camels bearing spicery (*necoth*), and balm (*tzeri*), and *myrrh* (*lot*), going to carry it down to Egypt.' Again, in ch. xliii:11, Jacob directs his sons to take into Egypt 'of the best fruits in the land in your vessels, and carry down the man a present, a little balm (*tzeri*), and a little honey, spices (*necoth*), and *myrrh* (*lot*), nuts (*botnim*), and almonds (*shakadim*).' In this enumeration, in one case, of merchandise, and in the other, of several articles intended for a present, and both destined for Egypt, at that time a highly civilized nation, it is evident that we are to look only for such substances as were likely to be acceptable in that country, and therefore not such as were produced there, or as were more easily procurable from elsewhere than from Syria, as was the case with myrrh, which was never produced in Syria, and could not have been an article of export from thence. This difficulty has been felt by others, and various translations of *lot* have been proposed, as *lotus,* chestnuts, mastiche, stacte, balsam, turpentine, pistachio nuts. Junius and Tremellius render it *ladanum,* which is suitable, and appears to be correct.

Ladanum, or *gum ladanum,* as it is often called, was known to the Greeks as early as the times of Herodotus and Theophrastus, and bore the names of *ledon* and *ladanon,* which are very closely allied to *ladun,* the Arabic name of the same drug. It has been well observed by Rosenmüller, that the proper root and origin of these names is *led,* but that the Hebrew has the hard consonant *t* instead of the softer *d.*

Tournefort, in modern times, has given a detailed description of the mode of obtaining *ladanum,* and relates that it is now gathered by means of a kind of rake with whip-like thongs, which is passed over the plants. When these thongs are loaded with the odoriferous and sticky resin, they are scraped with a knife. It consists of resin and volatile oil, and is highly fragrant, and stimulant as a medicine, but is often adulterated with sand in commerce. *Ladanum* seems to have been produced in Judæa, according to writers in the Talmud (Cels. *l. c.* p. 286.) It is said by Pliny, as long before by Herodotus, to be a produce of Arabia, though this has not been proved to be the case in modern times. Sufficient, however, has been adduced to show that *ladanum* was known to, and esteemed by, the ancients, and as its Greek and Arabic names are similar to the Hebrew, and as it is stated to have been a produce of Syria it was very likely to have been sent to Egypt both as a present and as merchandise. (See MYRRH.) J. F. R.

LOTAN (lō'tan), (Heb. לוֹטָן, *lo-tawn'*, covering), eldest son of Seir, the Horite, and a prince of Idumæa. Through his sister, Timna, he was connected with Esau's eldest son (Gen. xxxvi:12, 20, 22, 29; 1 Chron. i:38, 39).

LOTS, FEAST OF (lŏts, fēst ŏv). See PURIM.

LOVE (lŭv), (Heb. אַהֲבָה, *ă-hab-aw'* ; Gr. ἀγάπη, *ag-ah'pay*).

Love may be regarded either as the internal feeling of good-will and kindness which one intelligent being bears to another, or the expression of that benevolence in words and acts which gratifies and benefits another; but in its full and proper sense, love is the union of these two—of the internal emotion with the outward act: whence it appears that neither doing good nor wishing good to another can in strict propriety be denominated love. The definition also shows that love is restricted to intelligent beings, takes place only between persons, and cannot be predicated of things, being used in a merely derivative and secondary sense whenever we speak of loving aught but rational beings. It also appears that the emotion implies two intelligent existences; indeed, reciprocity seems an almost essential element in the idea of love. Certainly all durable love is mutual; and if love implies two, then, prior to creation, God, however good he might be, could hardly be said to love; so that love is a consequence of creation, a result of the relations in which God was pleased to place himself in regard to man; and since these relations are best declared, if they are not exclusively made known, by the sacred Scriptures, love is a doctrine which takes its source in revelation, where indeed, considered as existing between God and man, it finds at once its highest sanctions and best supports.

(1) Love of God. The New Testament speaks in its great bearings of the love of God towards Christ and towards man. The Son of God, as the most perfect image of the Heavenly Father, is represented as the special object of the divine love; as a consequence of which affection God communicates to Christ all spiritual gifts needful for the redemption of mankind: 'The Father loveth the Son, and showeth him all things whatsoever he doeth' (John v:20) ; 'therefore doth my Father love me, because I lay down my life that I might take it again' (John x:17) ; 'for thou lovedst me before the foundation of the world' (John xvii:24), 'God so loved the world that he gave his only begotten Son, that whoever believeth in him should not perish, but have everlasting life' (John iii:16). And so, 'He that spared not his only Son, but freely gave him up for us all, how shall he not with him also freely give us all things?' (Rom. viii:32) : accordingly 'the love of God is shed abroad in our hearts by the Holy Ghost which is given unto us' (Rom. v:5: see the following verses). The following passages will aid the reader in pursuing this interesting subject into its Scriptural particulars, which want of space compels us to be content with pointing out, namely: Rom. viii:35; 2 Cor. xiii:11; Eph. ii:4; 2 Thess. iii:5; 1 John iv; 1 Tim. i:14, 15; Titus ii:10; John xiii:35; comp. xv:17; Mark xii:30.

(2) Love to Christ. Love to Christ is represented in Scripture as a natural consequence of Christ's love to man, and as a necessary concomitant of the love of God, with which it is kindred in nature, causes, operation, and effects. This holy affection manifests itself not in idle reveries nor warm protestations, but in meek and lowly obedience to Jesus as the Mediator between God and man; and has for its highest reward the love which God displays towards all those who honor his son; which love, springing from God, fills and sanctifies the heart of man (John viii:42; xiv:15, 21, 23, 28; xvi:27).

(3) Love to Man. Love to man ensues from the universal love of God, as the one Creator and Father of all men. The measure and test of love to others is the surrender of personal ambition and the complete abandonment of self in our devotion to others, conformable to the higher and perfect model which Jesus has given in his own life and death (Matt. xxii:39; Mark xii:31; John xv:12; comp. xiii:15; 1 Peter ii:21; 1 John ii:6).

(4) Christian Love. This general good-will and active beneficence may be enhanced and invigorated by those nearer relations which take place between kindred minds, men of 'like precious faith,' whose hearts and aims are one, and who have alike received the gracious and all-prevailing influences of God's spirit; so that Christianity not only places mankind in immediate connection with God, and thus renders all equal and all worthy of each other's love, but creates a new, peculiar, and very intimate relation, making all true disciples one with each other and with the great Head of the church, and thus one, ultimately, with God (John xiii:34, 35; xv:12; Rom. xiii:8, 10; 1 Cor. xiii). And it is this specific Christian affection—the love of man as a brother, purified and enlarged by the consciousness of being an object of Divine mercy and goodness so as to become a properly Christian emotion—which is to actuate the disciples of Christ in their benevolent efforts for the good of others, and specially for their rescue from the evil that is in the world that bringeth death (2 Cor. v:14, 19, 20, 21; Acts xx:24).

LOVE FEASTS (lŭv fēsts). See AGAPE.

LOVING-KINDNESS (lŭv'ĭng-kĭnd'nĕs), (Heb. חֶסֶד, kheh'sed), desire, ardor.

In a good sense *khehsed* is zeal toward any one, *kindness, love.* Of God toward men, *goodness, mercy, grace* (Ps. xvii:7; xxvi:3; xxxvi:7, 10, etc.). Figuratively, it is used of God as a merciful benefactor (cxliv:2, "My goodness"). In the plural, *mercies, benefits* from God (lxxxix:2, "mercy;" ver. 49; xxv:6; Is. lxiii:7). (Barnes' *Peop. Bib. Ency.*)

LOW, LOWER, LOWEST (lō, lō'ẽr, lō'ĕst), (Heb. תַּחְתִּי, takh-tee'). The *lower parts* of the earth means:

(1) The earth itself, which is the lower region of this world (Eph. iv:9). (2) The valleys and their inhabitants; or rather, the Gentile world (Is. xliv:23). (3) The womb; in which the unborn child is hid as in a deep pit (Ps. cxxxix:15). (4) The grave, or state of the dead (Ps. lxiii:9).

Figurative. To be *lowly* is to be meek and humble (Ps. cxxxviii:6; Zech. ix:9). Christ was made for a little while, or in a little degree, *"lower than the angels,"* in his state of humiliation (Ps. viii:5; Heb. ii:7, 9).

LUBIM (lū'bim), (Heb. לוּבִים, loo-beem. See 2 Chron. xii:3; xvi:8; Nah. iii:9; *loob-beem'*, Dan. xi:43, perhaps *thirsty,* thence *inhabitants* of a dry *land),* the Libyans. (See LIBYA.)

LUCAS (lū'cas), (Gr. Λουκᾶς, loo-kas'), the friend and companion of St. Paul during his imprisonment at Rome (Philem. 24). He is the same as Luke, the beloved physician, who is associated with Demas in Col. iv:14, and who remained faithful to the Apostle when others forsook him (2 Tim. iv:11), on his first examination before the emperor (A. D. 64).

LUCIFER (lū'si-fer), (Heb. הֵילֵל, hay-lale').

A word that occurs once in the English Version in the lines—

'How art thou fallen from heaven,
Lucifer, son of the morning!
How art thou felled to the ground,
That didst weaken the nations!'
(Is. xiv:12).

The Hebrew seems to mean 'brilliant,' 'splendid,' 'illustrious,' or, as in the Septuagint, Vulgate, the Rabbinical commentators, Luther, and others, 'brilliant star;' and in this sense was the proper name among the Hebrews of the morn-

ing star. Tertullian and Gregory the Great understood this passage of Isaiah in reference to the fall of Satan; in consequence of which the name Lucifer has since been applied to Satan; and this is now the usual acceptation of the word. But Dr. Henderson, who in his *Isaiah* renders the line, 'Illustrious son of the morning!' justly remarks in his annotation: 'The application of this passage to Satan, and to the fall of the apostate angels, is one of those gross perversions of Sacred Writ which so extensively obtain, and which are to be traced to a proneness to seek for more in any given passage than it really contains, a disposition to be influenced by sound rather than sense, and an implicit faith in received interpretations. The scope and connection show that none but the king of Babylon is meant. In the figurative language of the Hebrews *a star* signifies an illustrious king or prince (Num. xxiv:17; comp. Rev. ii:28; xxii:16). The monarch here referred to having surpassed all other kings in royal splendor, is compared to the harbinger of day, whose brilliancy surpasses that of the surrounding stars. Falling from heaven denotes a sudden political overthrow—a removal from the position of high and conspicuous dignity formerly occupied (comp. Rev. vi:13; viii:10).

LUCIUS (lū'si-ŭs) of Cyrene, (Gr. Λούκιος, loo'-kee-os, illuminative, for Lat. Lucius surnamed the "Cyrenian"), a person named along with Barnabas, Saul, and others, as 'prophets and teachers' in the church at Antioch (Acts xiii:1).

Lucius was probably one of 'the synagogue of the Cyrenians,' and was without doubt one of the men of Cyrene, who went abroad in consequence of the persecution raised on the death of Stephen (Acts vi:9; xi:20). Some suppose that he was one of the seventy disciples; and the tradition is, that he was eventually bishop of Cyrene. This is probably the same Lucius who is mentioned in Rom. xvi:21 as Paul's kinsman; and he has been supposed by some to be the same as Luke the Evangelist. (A. D. 45.)

LUD (lŭd), (Heb. לוּד, lood, Ezek. xxvii:10; xxx: 5), the fourth son of Shem (Gen. x:22). For his descendants, see NATIONS, DISPERSION OF (B. C. after 2513).

LUDIM (lū'dim), (Heb. לוּדִים, loo-deem'), the descendants of (Gen. x:13), concerning whom, see NATIONS, DISPERSION OF.

LUHITH (lū'hith), (Heb. לוּחִית, loo-khoth'; לוּחִית, loo-kheeth', floored).

A town in the land of Moab, between Ar and Zoar, and ravaged by the Assyrians and Chaldeans (Is. xv:5; Jer. xlviii:5). It is evident that it was an elevated station, but whether a town on a hill, or a place for prospect, does not appear. It seems to be associated with other places which we know to be towns.

LUKE (lūke). *1. The Evangelist.* The name Λουκᾶς, loo-kas', Lat. *Lucanus*, indicates that Luke was descended from heathen ancestors, and that he was either a slave or a freedman, *libertus.*

(1) **A Physician.** According to ecclesiastical tradition, the author of the gospel is the same Luke who is mentioned in Paul's Epistles ,(Philem. 24; 2 Tim. iv:11; Col. iv:14), and who is called, in the last-mentioned passage, 'the physician.' This tradition is confirmed by the Acts of the Apostles, according to which the author of that work accompanied the Apostle Paul in his journeys (Acts xvi:10, *sq.;* xx:5-13). Luke accompanied Paul also in his last journeys to Jerusalem and Rome (Acts xxi:1-17; xxvii:28).

The profession of a physician harmonizes also with the condition of a freedman, indicated by the form of the name. It harmonizes with this that Paul (Col. iv:14) distinguishes Luke from the Christians of Jewish descent, whom, in verses 11 and 12, he styles 'being of the Circumcision.' Eusebius (*Hist. Eccles.* iii:4) states that Antioch in Syria was the native city of Luke. In this city there was at an early period a congregation of Christians converted from heathenism. Since Luke was a physician, we must suppose that he was a man of education.

(2) A Scholar. To those skeptics who excuse their disbelief of the miracles recorded in the gospels, by the assertion that their authors were ill-informed Jews, greedy of the marvelous, it must appear of some importance to meet in Luke a well-informed Greek skilled even in the medical sciences. The higher degree of his education is further proved by the classical style in which the prologue to his gospel, and the latter portion of the Acts, are written; and also by the explicit and learned details which he gives in the Acts on various antiquarian, historical, and geographical subjects. Tradition, since the time of Gregory of Nazianzus, makes Luke a martyr; yet not unanimously, since accounts of a natural death slip in. *Where* he died remains a question; certainly not in Rome with Paul, for his writings are far later.

2. The Gospel According to Luke.

(1) Written Documents Used. The classical, connected, periodic, and sustained style of the introduction to the gospel of St. Luke differs so strikingly from the Hellenistic Greek of the history itself, that we clearly perceive that he made use of written documents. The same difference exists, although in a less striking degree, between the portions of the Acts relating to transactions of which Luke himself was not an eye-witness and in which he bore no part, and those where he speaks as a companion of Paul. He did not, however, transcribe verbatim from the documents before him nor did he merely write down verbal traditions; for we find the same characteristic phraseology which belongs to St. Luke's individual style, both in the gospel and in the Acts. Compare, for instance, the peculiar use of the words καὶ αὐτός, Luke i:17, 22; ii:28, 50; iii:23; iv:15, 51; Acts ii:27; v:1, 9, 51, etc.; ἱκανός, Luke vii:12; viii:27, 32; xx:9; Acts v:37; ix:23, 43; xi:24, etc.; παῖς θεοῦ, Luke i:54, 69; Acts iii:13, 16; iv:25, 27, 30, etc.

(2) Other Writers. It is important to notice what he himself says, in his introduction, of the relation borne by his writings to those of others. It is evident that even then 'many,' had attempted to compose a history of our Lord from the statements of eye-witnesses and of the first ministers of the word of God. Luke follows the example of these authors with this difference, that he writes, starting from earlier facts in the history of the Baptist and of the infancy of our Lord, and continuing the narration in uninterrupted succession. Origen, Credner, and Olshausen suppose that the "many," were heretical authors; but this is unlikely, since Luke does not express any blame of them. But it is also unsatisfactory to refer the word "many," merely to Matthew and Mark, as Hug and De Wette have done, especially since the "many" are distinguished from the eye-witnesses. We must therefore suppose that many Christians wrote brief accounts of the life of Jesus, although they had not been eye-witnesses. It is possible that Luke made use of such writings.

(3) Relation to Gospel of Matthew. It appears to be doubtful whether Luke had the gospel of Matthew before his eyes, since, had that been the case, he would probably have been more careful to avoid apparent contradictions, especially in the history of the birth of Jesus, in which he seems to have made use of documents referring to the family of Mary, while the accounts given by Matthew refer more to the family of Joseph. This is also confirmed by the aphoristic mode in which he reports the Sermon on the Mount. We can scarcely imagine that he would have communicated a relation so unusually abrupt, if he had seen the well-arranged and complete statements of Matthew.

The Gospel of St. Luke contains exceedingly valuable accounts, not extant in the books of the other evangelists; for instance, those concerning the childhood of Jesus, the admirable parables in chapters xv and xvi, the narration respecting the disciples at Emmaus, the section from chapter ix:51 to xix:27, which contains particulars mostly wanting in the other evangelists. It has been usual, since the days of Schleiermacher, to consider this portion as the report of a single journey to the feast at Jerusalem; but it is evident that it contains accounts belonging to several journeys, undertaken at different periods.

Some critics of modern times, such as D. Schulz, Schleiermacher, Sieffert, and Schneckenburger, were in the habit of ascribing to the reports of Luke a greater historical accuracy than to those of Matthew; but of late, opinions on this subject have changed, and Strauss, De Wette, and Bruno Bauer find in the reports of St. Matthew more of independent and original information than in those of Luke. There is certainly in the details of the historical account given by St. Luke, more clearness; but many discourses of our Redeemer given by St. Matthew have more of the impress of historical precision, especially the Sermon on the Mount, and the Discourse against the Pharisees in chapters xxiii and xxiv; although it seems that Matthew sometimes brings into connection similar discourses, held at various periods, concerning which we find in Luke more accurately stated the particular circumstances under which they were delivered.

(4) Historical Credibility. The statement of Luke himself, at the beginning of his gospel, must dispose us favorably with regard to its historical credibility. He states that he had accurately investigated the truth of the accounts communicated, and that following the example of the πολλοί, he had made use of the statements of eye-witnesses. Luke had frequent opportunity of meeting these eye-witnesses when he traveled with Paul. He himself reports, in Acts xxi:18, that he met James. He gives also, with greater accuracy than the other evangelists, some chronological notices, such as those at the beginning of chapters ii and iii, and in Acts vii:35, etc. Yet these very dates have been quoted by Strauss and De Wette as being quite incorrect, and as proofs that Luke was destitute of accurate historical information.

This daring assertion has induced some modern apologetical authors to examine the matter more closely, who have triumphantly vindicated the historical character of these statements of Luke.

(5) Date of the Gospel. As to the statements of the ancients concerning the date or time when the Gospel of St. Luke was written, we find in Irenæus (*Adv. Hær.* iii:1) that Mark and Luke wrote after Matthew. According to Eusebius (*Hist. Eccles.* vi:28), Origen stated that

Luke wrote after Matthew and Mark; but Clemens Alexandrinus, according to the same writer (*Hist. Eccles.* vi:14), asserted on the authority of 'the tradition of the earlier elders,' that the gospels containing the genealogies were written before the others. According to this view, Mark was written after Luke. It is however likely that this statement arose from a desire to explain why the genealogies were omitted by Mark and John. Eusebius, at least (*Hist. Eccles.* iii:24), in reference to the Gospel of John, says: 'John properly passed over in silence the genealogy according to the flesh, of our Savior, which was detailed by Matthew and Luke.'

Since the extreme criticism of Strauss and De Wette has been unable to produce even a plausible argument against the authenticity of the Gospel of Luke, attempts have been made to prove at least the very late date of this gospel. De Wette (*Introduction to the New Testament,* 4th edition, p. 176) endeavors to infer from the definiteness with which the destruction of Jerusalem is predicted, and from the circumstance that, according to ch. xxi:25, some time was to intervene between the destruction of Jerusalem and the second advent of Christ, that this gospel was written some time after the destruction of the city had taken place, and after it had become apparent from facts that the second advent was not to be immediately consequent upon that destruction.

We do not here enter into the question whether, according to St. Matthew xxiv:29, it was expected that the second advent should directly follow the destruction of Jerusalem; we merely observe that a *petitio principii* runs through the whole train of this argument, since it sets out with assuming the impossibility of detailed predictions.

3. The Acts of The Apostles. Besides the gospel which bears his name, Luke wrote the Acts of the Apostles. This work contains the history of the foundation of the Christian church in two great sections: the first embracing the spread of Christianity among the Jews, chiefly by the instrumentality of Peter (chapters i-xii); and the second, its spread among the heathen, chiefly by the instrumentality of Paul (chapters xiii-xxviii).

Schneckenburger has strongly endeavored, in his work *Ueber den Zweck der Apostelgeschichte,* 1841, to prove that the Acts had an apologetical tendency, called forth by the particular circumstances of the times. He especially appeals to the manner in which Paul refutes all objections of the Judaizers, who were his enemies.

In those portions of the Acts in which Luke speaks as the companion of Paul, and, consequently, as an eye-witness, his Greek style is more classical than in the rest of the work. This circumstance supports the opinion that Luke followed some written documents in the earlier part of the Acts, as well as in the gospel.

(1) Relation to St. Paul. From the circumstance that the book of Acts leaves St. Paul a captive, without relating the result of his captivity, most critics have, with considerable probability, inferred that Luke accompanied St. Paul to Rome, that he employed his leisure while there in composing the Acts, and that he left off writing before the fate of Paul was decided. Now, since the Gospel of St. Luke was written before the Acts, it seems to follow that it was written a considerable time before the destruction of Jerusalem. De Wette meets this argument merely by his *petitio principii,* that from the detailed nature of the predictions on that head in the gospel, it would follow that they were written after the events to which they refer, and consequently after the destruction of Jerusalem.

It is likely that Luke, during Paul's captivity at Cæsarea, employed his leisure in collecting the accounts contained in his gospel in the localities where the events to which they relate happened. The most ancient testimonies in behalf of Luke's Gospel are those of Marcion, at the beginning of the second century, and of Irenæus, in the latter half of that century.

According to Meyer's opinion, Luke terminates the Acts with Paul's captivity, because the later events were well known to Theophilus, to whom the Acts are dedicated. We do not know who this Theophilus was. Hug, however, infers, from the manner in which Luke mentions Italian localities, that they were well known to Theophilus, and that consequently it was likely he resided in Italy.

(2) Authentic Account. That the accounts of Luke are authentic may be perceived more especially from a close examination of the inserted discourses and letters. The characteristic marks of authenticity in the oration of the Roman lawyer Tertullus, in ch. xxiv, and in the official letters in ch. xxiii:26, *sq.;* xv:23, *sq.;* can scarcely be overlooked. The address of Paul to the elders of the Ephesian church is characteristically Pauline, and even so full of definite allusions and of similarity to the Epistle to the Ephesians, that it furnishes a confirmation of the authenticity of that letter, which has lately been questioned.

Characteristic also are the discourses of Stephen (ch. vii), and those of Peter, concerning which compare Seyler's *Abhandlungen über die Reden des Petrus,* in the *Studien und Kritiken,* 1832, p. 53, *sq.* Even De Wette, in his *Introduction,* sec. 115 a, admits the appropriateness of these discourses.

(3) Chronological Difficulties. It is, however, difficult to reconcile some of Luke's statements with the chronological notices in the Epistles of Paul. Very important investigations on this subject are to be found in the work of Angar, *De temporum in Actis Apostolorum ratione.* As for the testimonies in behalf of the authenticity of the Acts, they are the same as for Luke's Gospel. Clemens Alexandrinus, Irenæus, and Tertullian, expressly mention the Acts, and Eusebius reckons them among the Homologoumena. However, the book of Acts was not read and quoted so often in the early church as other parts of Scripture. Chrysostom, in his first homily *In Actus Apostolorum,* says that many Christians in Asia knew neither the book nor its author. The Manichees rejected it for dogmatical reasons (Augustinus, *De utilitate credendi,* ii:7). So also did the Severiani (Euseb. *Hist. Eccles.* iv:29). Since the book of Acts was not much read, it is surprising that its text is particularly corrupt. It does not, however, by any means appear that these corruptions arose from intentional alterations made for dogmatical purposes (comp. Eichhorn's *Einleitung ins Neue Testament,* ii, 154).

The most complete commentary on the Acts is that of Kuinoel, 2d ed., 1827. There are also some valuable manuals, as Meyer's *Commentary,* 1835, and that of De Wette, 2nd ed., 1841. (See also Lange, *Com.,* and Alford, *Com.*)

LUMP (lŭmp), (Heb. הְבֵלָה, *deb-ee-lawh'*).

1. Bunch of dried figs; a round mass of any kind closely pressed together, especially figs (2 Kings xx:7; Is. xxxviii:21). It is rendered "cake" (1 Sam. xxv:18; xxx:12; 1 Chron. xii:40).

2. A mass of things mixed. In Rom. ix:21, it means "kneaded clay" for moulding; and in 1 Cor. v:6, Gal. v:9, "dough."

LUNATIC (lū′nȧ-tĭk). See DEMONIAC.

LUST (lŭst), was not used formerly in its present restricted sense, but of any strong desire.

In the A. V. it is the translation of three Hebrew and four Greek words. "To lust" appears six times in the A. V. Corruption of nature is called *"lust,"* as it strongly inclines us to evil (Rom. vii:7; James i:14, 15; 2 Pet. i:4). This general lust is distinguished (a) into the *"lust of the flesh,"* such as, unclean desire of carnal pleasure, intemperate desire of liquor or food (Ps. lxxviii:18; Gal. v:17; 1 Pet. ii:11; 2 Pet. ii:10); (b) and the *"lusts of the mind,"* such as pride, covetousness, unbelief, attachment to the law of works (Eph. ii:3; 1 Pet. iv:2).

LUST, GRAVES OF (lŭst, grāvs ŏv). See KIBROTH-HATTAAVAH.

LUSTY (lŭst′y̆), (Judg. iii:29), an old word for "stout."

LUTHERAN CHURCH, EVANGELICAL (lū′thẽr-ạn chûrch, ē′văn-jĕl′ɪ-kạl).

1. Name. In the Great Reformation of the sixteenth century, the adherents of Luther were nicknamed "Lutherans" by the Romanist, Dr. Eck, after the Leipzic Disputation in 1519, and so spoken of by Pope Hadrian VI in 1522. They were first termed "Protestants" at the Diet of Spire in 1529. Luther strongly protested, and disapproved of his name being borne by his fellow confessors; in Europe they were and are called "The Evangelical Church;" in this country they are commonly known as "The Evangelical Lutheran Church."

2. Sources and Growth. **(1) Seventeenth Century.** The first Lutherans who made permanent homes in America came among the colonists from Holland, who settled (1612-1622) for traffic with the Indians on Manhattan Island and the Hudson river. Though brought by the spirit of trade, they were the first in this country to suffer persecution on account of their faith. England's supremacy in 1664 gave them religious liberty. Whilst there are no Dutch Lutheran congregations in the United States to-day, there are a number of Dutch origin, mostly along the Hudson.

Gustavus Adolphus, the king of Sweden, had projected a colony to America, both for the religious welfare of the natives and for the glory of his realm. The glorius victory at Luetzen in 1622, immortalized "The Lion of the North," and left to his great premier, Oxenstiern, the furthering of the colony. In 1638 two shiploads from the Lutheran land of Sweden purchased lands of the Indians and established themselves on the banks of the Delaware. Others followed and all prospered.

They built churches; their pastor, Campanius, translated Luther's catechism into the Delaware dialect, and also gave religious instruction to the Indians. For over forty years previous to the arrival of William Penn they had lived and labored among them in the greatest peace and prosperity, and by their good name and offices greatly promoted the success of Penn's famous treaty with the Indians under the great elm at Philadelphia in 1683. By the close of the following century, through political changes, but mainly from lack of English-speaking Lutheran pastors, these people with their church edifices came into the hands of the Episcopalians.

(2) Eighteenth Century. Not being a sea-going people, previous to the eighteenth century few Germans came to America. During this century, being compelled by persecution and suffering, or encouraged by the plans and prospects of Penn's colony, many thousand German Lutherans sought homes in the New World.

Impoverished by the Thirty Years' War, and in constant dread of invasion, many of the wretched inhabitants of the Rhenish Palatinate sought refuge in England, whence aided by the government and Queen Anne, they came as colonists to New York, Pennsylvania and North Carolina (1707-1712).

Forced into exile in midwinter, 30,000 men, women and children from the Austrian archbishopric of Salzburg went to Prussia, Holland, Sweden and England. The English, by parliamentary aid and public contributions, assisted many of the fellow believers of those who bound themselves in the "covenant of salt" to found the Lutheran colony at Ebenezer, Georgia, under the devoted pastors, Bolzaus and Gronau (1731-1734).

Unscrupulous agents traversed Germany in the interests of shipping companies, and by fabulous tales of plenty, wealth, honor and titles so easily secured in the New World, lured the simple-minded people from their homes. Pennsylvania was the paradise generally sought. In the summer of 1749, 12,000 German immigrants landed at Philadelphia, many of them Lutherans, and for years the tide continued. Many died on the long voyages in the poorly-supplied and overcrowded vessels. On landing the captain advertised the arrival of those too poor to pay the passage charges, and at auction sold men, women and children for three, six, ten or more years, who were taken for service to New England, Pennsylvania and other colonies. Families were separated never again to meet. Whilst character and industry often elevated these servants to the place of masters, and maids betimes married their purchasers, yet, despite the laws for their protection, it was only to protracted slavery, with its wretchedness and abominations, that many of the "redemptorists" were doomed during their enforced labor.

From Waldoboro, Maine, to Ebenezer, Georgia, in 1735 there were but eight pastors for the whole Lutheran population. The people generally were poor, their speech alien, themselves strangers in a strange land. Some made use of devotional books brought from the Fatherland. Here and there an earnest layman assembled his countrymen and read a sermon. Churches were few; barns, mills and stable lofts, carpenter shops, or their rude cabins, were the usual places for worship; the services and ministrations of the church were seldom enjoyed. Clerical impostors, base men, devastated and deceived the congregations. The religious training of the young was sadly neglected. Distressing in the extreme was the general spiritual condition.

"The Patriarch of the Lutheran Church in America," a graduate of the University of Goettingen and sent from Halle, the Rev. Henry Melchoir Muhlenberg, in 1742, reached Philadelphia, Pa. His apostolic life, his faithful, untiring and blessed labors, his piety, ability, tact and sagacity, inspirited the people, reduced chaos to order and laid solid foundations for the future of the church. In 1748, Muhlenberg with five other pastors and lay representatives from twenty pastoral districts, organized the Ministerium or Synod of Pennsylvania and adjacent states. In

1786 the second Synod, that of New York, was organized.

The French and Indian wars, and the War of the Revolution, destroyed churches, devastated communities and scattered congregations. Infidelity, deism and rationalism poisoned by their evil influences. Throughout the colonies religion reached a very low ebb. The German Lutheran population greatly suffered in the general spiritual degeneration and destitution. At the close of the century the New York Synod had decreased in its pastoral roll nearly one-half; in the Carolinas six pastors remained; there were less than seventy in all the United States.

(3) Nineteenth Century. Though diminished by our own Civil War and the wars of Europe a flood-tide of immigration brought multitudes to the United States during the nineteenth century, and a large proportion of the mighty host were Lutherans in their religious faith.

To secure homes and material good brought many; others came to enjoy religious liberty. In Germany the plan of King Frederick William III to bring by law the Lutheran and the Reformed into a "United Church," 1817-1830, worked protest and division. In 1839, under Pastor Grabau, one thousand "Separatists" settled at Buffalo, N. Y., and in 1845 organized the "Synod of Exiles from the Lutheran Church of Prussia," or the Buffalo Synod. Five shiploads of Saxon "Separatists" sailed in 1838. Nothing was ever heard of the "Amalia;" but in 1839 the others located at St. Louis, Mo. Amid perils and poverty unspeakable, in a log cabin they at once established a classical school for the training of ministers, and in 1847 organized at Chicago, Ill., the "German Evangelical Lutheran Synod of Missouri, Ohio, and other States." Prof. Carl F. W. Walther, D. D., was the first president and father of the Missouri Synod. In 1854, at St. Sebald, Iowa, the "German Evangelical Lutheran Synod of Iowa and other States" was founded. A school was instituted, and the ingathering of immigrant Germans and missions among the Indians begun. Other German Synods, the Texas, Wisconsin, Minnesota, Michigan, Wartburg, Augsburg, Nebraska and Immanuel have since been organized.

For nearly two centuries few Swedes found their way to America. Several families came in 1841; in 1850, the Rev. Lars Paul Esbjörn, "the Founder of the Swedish Church," with ten members organized the first regular Swedish Lutheran congregation. Over a million of Swedes are in the United States. The Swedish Lutheran Augustana Synod was founded in 1860. In 1834 a little band of Norwegians came to Rochester, N. Y., finally settling in La Salle Co., Ill. Though not so numerous as the Swedes, Norwegian Lutheran churches have been established from Maine to Oregon, from Manitoba to Texas. Five Synods have been organized; in 1890 three of them joined in forming the "United Norwegian Church," to which The Hague Synod is friendly; the Norwegian inclining toward the Missouri German Synod. In the United States there are more than five score thousand Danes, 10,000 Icelanders, 80,-000 Finlanders, and several thousand Slavonian, Hungarian, French, Scottish, Wendt and Bohemian Lutherans. The Danes have two Synods, the Icelanders and the Finns one each; the others, whilst having congregations, are not in Synodical organizations of their own tongue.

Lutheran pioneers are usually blessed with goodly families. Inured to the hardships and inheriting the spirit of their fathers, as the home hive filled up the hardy sons and daughters swarmed and sought new abodes. Southward and westward they spread. This migration beginning in the eighteenth, grew with the growth of the country in the present century, each successive wave passing beyond its predecessors. Into the rich valleys of Virginia, into the Carolinas and Tennessee, beyond the Alleghenies in Pennsylvania, into Ohio, Indiana, Illinois, Iowa and to the west, descendants of German Lutherans made their way. Pioneer traveling missionaries, self-sustained or sent by the Pennsylvania and other Synods, sought to keep these children of the church supplied with the Word and Sacraments.

Preaching circuits were opened, missions founded, congregations organized, churches built, Synods formed, and schools, colleges and theological seminaries established; the forefathers at the east and the children in the west coöperated in the work. The Synod of New York grew to four Synods; Pennsylvania has eight; Maryland, one; each of the Carolinas, one; Virginia, two; each of the Carolinas, one; Tennessee, two; Mississippi and Georgia, each one; in Ohio there are five; In Indiana, two; in Illinois, four; and one each in Iowa, Wisconsin, Kansas, Nebraska, Colorado and California. English is the usual language for worship and in the transactions of these Synods, except in two, though in these it is much used. The largest share of the membership in nearly all these Synods are descendants of German Lutheran immigrants. They have fifteen or more colleges, ten theological seminaries, and many academies, schools and charitable institutions under their care. They number 2,391 pastors, 3,408 congregations, 355 parochial schools, 517,101 communicant members.

3. Polity and Organization. In its government the Lutheran Church in the United States is not Episcopalian, Congregational, Presbyterian or Methodist, though it has certain terms and usages which are akin to some existing in these ecclesiastical organizations. It is somewhat like the government of the United States.

Jesus Christ is the Supreme Head of the Church. A congregation, consisting of the pastor and his people, joined in organization, constitute the unit. From the Supreme Head the congregation has power to maintain and administer in their purity the Word of Christ and His Sacraments. With the advice and counsel of the Synod, when requested or needed, it manages its own affairs.

Synods are organizations made up of congregations, within the limits prescribed by their constitutions, as agreed upon and subscribed, for the furtherance of the duties and good of the church at large, such as education, the training of pastors, missions, home and foreign, providing books for worship, etc. In the Synod, the congregation is entitled, in addition to its pastor, to at least one lay representative from each parish; in all synodical transactions these laymen have a parity and equal rights and privileges with the pastors. The Synods plan, manage and promote what the single congregation is unable to do, the educational, eleemosynary, mission and general activities of their churches; advise and counsel with them, as constitutionally agreed upon, in some Synods, as with the Swiss referendum, the resolutions of the Synod being in force only when approved by the votes of their congregations. Of the sixty-two Synods in this country, seventeen are independent; the others have united in general bodies. Their relation to the Synods and churches, and their powers, are defined and determined by the constitution agreed to and under which they are established.

Made up of several nationalities, accustomed to various and differing usages in worship and otherwise as Lutherans are, their languages, cults and questions largely of practice have brought about and shaped the union of Synods into these general bodies, as the status also of these bodies toward each other, and also that of the independent Synods and congregations toward each other and to the larger organizations. All agree, however, in accepting the church's historical Augsburg Confession; and there is no just ground for the contention that the church in this country is made up of seventeen different and distinct kinds of Lutherans. Difference in the faith, not in language, cult or practice, makes and marks the separate church.

4. Doctrine and Life. The Lutheran as a historical church accepts the Œcumenical creeds, and her own Unaltered Augsburg Confession; and declares the "Apology of the Augsburg Confession, the Smalcald Articles, the Catechisms of Luther and the Formula of Concord, with the Unaltered Augsburg Confession, to be in the perfect harmony of one and the same scriptural faith." The Canonical books of the Old and of the New Testament she receives as the Word of God, and the only and all-sufficient standard and rule of doctrine and duty. For all men she insists upon and claims the right and obligation to possess, to read and to study this Word.

The Lutheran Church believes in the Trinity; Father, Son and Holy Ghost, three Persons, one God; and in the divine and the human nature forever united in the person of Jesus, the Christ. She teaches, with utmost emphasis, that in Him men are justified by faith alone; and demands good works as fruit of true obedience. The Lutheran Church receives the Sacrament of the Holy Supper and the Sacrament of Baptism; and believes that, in a way not defined, in the Holy Supper the Lord Jesus gives His true Body and His true Blood to the communicant; and that ordinarily Baptism is "necessary to salvation and that by Baptism grace is offered." She confines the rite of Baptism to no one form, and gladly admits infants to this "washing of regeneration and renewing of the Holy Ghost."

The Lutheran Church holds that the Holy Spirit ordinarily reaches and acts upon the souls of men through the Truth, and mediately, through the Word of God and the Holy Sacraments as the only and appointed means of grace. She believes in the spiritual priesthood of all true Christians; but insists that only they who have been rightly called shall teach in her pulpits and minister at her altars. The Lutheran Church in her worship is liturgical; but accords freedom, and does not teach that the unity of the Church depends upon a uniform ritual and service. The Lutheran Church teaches that through the Fall man's nature is changed and debased; that because of sin, mankind is under the sentence of Divine condemnation and spiritually dead; that only through the means of grace, the Word and the Sacraments, by the gracious help of the Holy Spirit, is it possible for man to know and accept God's offered mercy, receive spiritual life, perform acceptable service, and attain the glorious resurrection of the body and eternal salvation.

The passing "isms" of the day but little affect Lutheran pastors and people; steadily and quietly they prosecute the practical duties of a living, loving Christianity, as enjoined and illustrated in the teachings and life of her adorable and exalted Savior and Head. She has prosperous missions among the natives of America and in foreign lands. Her work in these fields has been retarded and weakened by the vast home mission labors forced upon her, in order somewhat to meet the overwhelming demands and necessities of her own immense hosts of spiritual sons and daughters, who by immigration and migration seek homes in the wide borders of the United States. She leads in home-missionary activity; she initiated among the Protestants of America, and successfully promotes deaconess institutions and hospitals, orphanages, homes for the aged, epileptics, etc.

By a few, the Lutheran people of this country have been aided and prayed for; by many they have been assailed and preyed upon. Notwithstanding the humble place which her children took on first reaching these shores, and the extreme difficulties against which they had to contend, the Lutheran Church in the United States has a strong hold upon her people, and secures their hearty support. She makes fair provision and zealous effort for their ingathering and spiritual welfare. She has grown with the years greatly in numbers and good works, so that the Lutheran Church ranks among the foremost in the land; by her conservative positions, by her Scriptural foundation and by her conformity in government and worship to the trend and habit of thought in free America, she has exerted by God's favor and will exert an increasingly powerful influence for good in and among the Christian forces of this land, whether within the family, the community, or the State. By reason of her several nationalities and different tongues, her various cults and diverse customs, the Lutheran Church has within her own wide borders matters of grave measure and greatest moment for the best thought and wisest counsels of her most sagacious, learned and godly leaders. She prays and hopes for, and in God's own good time will realize, full unification in her own household of faith.

The Lutheran Church has sought no alliance with Christians of another name. She holds that not by tolerating or by ignoring positive differences and divergences in faith and practice, but only in and through the Truth can the real unity of the holy Christian Church be found; she assures herself also, that when realized, this blessed unity will have been attained only by the most earnest, devout and prayerful study of the Divine Word, and the honest acceptance of its sacred teachings, through the gracious aid and guidance of the Holy Spirit of God.   H. W. R.

LUTHER LEAGUE OF AMERICA (lū'ther lēg ŏv α-mĕr'ĭ-kα).

This organization is in connection with the Evangelical Lutheran Church, which is the oldest and largest of Protestant communions in the world. (See LUTHERAN CHURCH, EVANGELICAL.)

1. Various Young People's Societies. With the rise and spread of the "Endeavor" movement very many of the English-speaking Lutheran churches immediately followed their example, while others adopted a somewhat similar method, called the "Luther Alliance," and still others continued their young people's societies. Those organized on the line of "Christian Endeavor" have since formed a national association that meets in connection with the International United Society; those of the Synodical Conference organized the "Walther League," which allows male membership only; and a third class, notably those of the larger German churches in New York and Brooklyn, moved in the direction toward a national association that should embrace all the different young people's societies of Lutheran congregations that could at all affiliate on a common platform.

2. Organization of the Luther League of America. Years passed on before an agreement was attained. Neighboring societies and sections of states had meanwhile organized themselves into local associations, and during the year 1895 the call for a general meeting at Pittsburg was cordially responded to. On the thirty-first day of October the delegates from eastern, western, central and southern states met and effected an organization to be henceforth known as The Luther League of America.

(1) **Bond of Union.** As to its faith Art. II provides: "We acknowledge as the bond of our union the Word of God as the only infallible rule of faith and practice and the Unaltered Augsburg Confession as the correct exponent of that Word."

(2) **Objects.** Article III specifies: The objects of this League shall be to encourage the formation of the Young People's Societies in all Lutheran congregations in America, to urge their affiliation with their respective State or Territorial Leagues, and with this League to stimulate the various Young People's Societies to greater Christian activity and to foster the spirit of loyalty to the Church.

(3) **Membership.** The membership is regulated in the fourth article of its constitution thus: Any society of whatever name, connected with a Lutheran congregation or a Lutheran institution of learning, and all District and State organizations, whose admission shall have been in conformity with Article II of this Constitution, and recommended by the committee on credentials, are entitled to membership.

Each society admitted to membership shall be entitled to one delegate, each District Association to three delegates, and each State or Territorial organization to ten delegates in all conventions.

(4) **Officers.** The officers elected under this Constitution were: President, Mr. E. F. Eilert of New York; general secretary, Mr. Leander Trautman of Pittsburgh; recording secretary, Mr. W. C. Stoever of Philadelphia; assistant recording secretary, Miss Vesta E. Severinghaus of Chicago; treasurer, Mr. Cornelius Eckhardt of Washington, D. C.

(5) **Meetings and Relations.** The "Luther League" meets biennially, and has thus far met at Pittsburg, Chicago, New York and Cincinnati. It has not yet succeeded in absorbing all the young people's societies of the Lutheran church, partly because of its conservative character, which keeps many of the existing Endeavor Societies from joining it, and partly because of its Americanism which does not please the "Walther League." As to our synodical divisions there are represented in it most numerously the young people's societies of the General Council, the General Synod, the Norwegian United Church, the United Synod of the South, and the joint Synod of Ohio. All these coöperate in the State Leagues of New York, Pennsylvania, Kansas, New Jersey, Illinois, Ohio, Wisconsin, Minnesota, Indiana, Kentucky, North Carolina, Nebraska, South Dakota; and the District Leagues of Central Connecticut, South Carolina and South Atlantic Region.

(6) **Junior League.** There is also a "Junior League" provided for by a different constitution. This is composed of the younger baptized members, workers and friends of the Evangelical Lutheran Church. In name, faith, object, membership and general programme, it is similar to the former. Meetings of the Junior League may be of a devotional, educational, social, moral, physical or varied character, according to the plans adopted by the Supervising Committee.

(7) **Administrative Board, Etc.** In addition to the official board there is an executive committee which provides a course of topics for the weekly meetings, a general reading course and the necessary literature.

(8) **Official Organ.** The *Luther League Review*, edited by the president, Mr. E. F. Eilert. is the official organ of the Luther League of America. There is a Luther League Hymnal, a Luther League Handbook, Booklets, Pamphlets and Badges. While it is largely managed by laymen and the younger ones of the church, its executive committee has six ministers out of the ten members composing it, and in the list of State Leagues, as quoted in the "Handbook," we meet seven ministers who hold office, as also eight women.   J. D. S.

LUZ (lŭz), (Heb. לוּז, *looz*, almond-tree), the ancient name of Bethel (Gen. xxviii:19). (See BETHEL.) The word Gen. xxx:37 is translated *hazel* in the A. V., and in some others it is rendered by words equivalent to 'walnut'; but 'almond' appears to be its true meaning. (See ALMOND.) It is also the name of several towns.

1. The spot to which the name of Bethel was given appears, however, to have been at a little distance in the environs of Luz, and they are accordingly distinguished in Josh. xvi:2, although the name of Bethel was eventually extended to that town.

2. A small place of the same name in the territory of the Hittites, founded by an inhabitant of Luz of Canaan, who was spared when the place was destroyed by the tribe of Benjamin. Not identified (Judg. i:26); probably the *Luza* of Mt. Gerizim. (Stanley, p. 231, *sq*.)

LYCAONIA (lyk'a-ō'ni-à), (Gr. Λυκαονία, *loo-kah-on-ee'ah'*, from the mythological *Lycaon*, or λύκος a wolf), a province of Asia Minor, having Cappadocia on the east, Galatia on the north, Phrygia on the west, and Isauria and Cilicia on the south.

It extends in length about twenty geographical miles from east to west, and about thirteen in breadth. It was an undulating plain, involved among mountains, which were noted for the concourse of wild-asses. The soil was so strongly impregnated with salt that few of the brooks supplied drinkable water, so that good water was sold for money. But sheep thròve on the pasturage, and were reared with great advantage (Strabo. xii, p. 568; Pliny, *Hist. Nat.* viii:69). It was a Roman province when visited by Paul (Acts xiv:6), and its chief towns were Iconium, Lystra, and Derbe, of which the first was the capital. 'The speech of Lycaonia' (Acts xiv:11) is supposed by some to have been the ancient Assyrian language, also spoken by the Cappadocians (Jablonski, *Disquis. de Lingua Lycaonica*, Opusc. iii, 3, *sq*.); but it is more usually conceived to have been a corrupt Greek, intermingled with many Syriac words.

LYCIA (lÿ'ci-à), (Gr. Λυκία, *loo-kee'ah*, probably from λύκος, a wolf), a province in the southwest of Asia Minor, having Pamphylia on the east, Phrygia on the north, Caria on the west and the Mediterranean on the south.

Great part of the country, however, consists of a peninsula projecting south into the Mediterranean. It is mountainous, and is watered by numerous small rivers which flow from the mountains. Its inhabitants were believed to be descendants of Cretans who came thither under Sarpedon, brother of Minos. Lycia is named in 1 Macc. xv:23, as one of the countries to which the Roman senate sent its missive in favor of the Jews. The victory of the Romans over Antiochus (B. C. 189) gave Lycia rank as a free state, which it retained till the time of Claudius, when it was made a province of the Roman empire (Suet. *Claud,* 25; *Vespas.* 8). Lycia contained many towns, two of which are mentioned in the New Testament; Patara (Acts xxi:1, 2); Myra (Acts xxvii:5); and one, Phaselis, in the Apocrypha (1 Macc. xv:23).

LYDDA (lўd′dà), (Heb. לֹד, *lod*; Gr. Λύδδα, *lud′dah*).

A town within the limits of the tribe of Ephraim, nine miles east of Joppa, on the road between that port and Jerusalem.

It bore in Hebrew the name of Lod, and appears to have been first built by the Benjamites, although it lay beyond the limits of their territory; and we find it again inhabited by Benjamites after the Exile (1 Chron. viii:12; Ezra ii:33; Neh. xi:35).

It is mentioned in the Apocrypha (1 Macc. xi:34), as having been taken from Samaria and annexed to Judæa by Demetrius Nicator; and at a later date its inhabitants are named among those who were sold into slavery by Cassius, when he inflicted the calamity of his presence upon Palestine after the death of Julius Cæsar (Joseph. *Antiq.* xiv. 11. 2; xii. 6). In the New Testament the place is only noticed, under the name of Lydda, as the scene of Peter's miracle in healing Eneas (Acts ix:32, 35). Some years later the town was reduced to ashes by Cestius Gallus, in his march against Jerusalem (Joseph. *De Bell. Jud.* ii, 19, 1); but it must soon have revived, for not long after we find it at the head of one of the toparchies of the later Judæa, and as such it surrendered to Vespasian (Joseph. *De Bell. Jud.* iii:3, 5; iv:8). At that time it is described by Josephus (*Antiq.* xx:6, 2) as a village equal to a city; and the Rabbins have much to say of it as a seat of Jewish learning, of which it was the most eminent in Judæa after Jabneh and Bether (Lightfoot, *Parergon,* sec. 8).

In the general change of names which took place under the Roman dominion, Lydda became Diospolis, and under this name it occurs in coins of Severus and Caracalla, and is often mentioned by Eusebius and Jerome. It was early the seat of a bishopric, and at the different councils the bishops are found to have subscribed their names variously, as of Lydda or Diospolis.

Lydda early became connected with the homage paid to the celebrated saint and martyr St. George, who was not less renowned in the east than afterwards in the west. A church was erected there in honor of him by the Emperor Justinian. This church, which stood outside the town, had just been leveled to the ground by the Moslems when the Crusaders arrived at Lydda; but it was soon rebuilt by them, and they established a bishopric of Lydda and Ramleh. The church was destroyed by Saladin in 1191; and there is no evidence that it was ever rebuilt, although there was in later centuries an unfounded impression that the church the ruins of which were then seen, and which still exist, had been built by King Richard of England. It is now known by the ancient name of Lud. (Robinson's *Bib. Researches,* iii, 55; Pococke, *Description,* ii, 58; Volney, *Voyage,* i, 278.)

LYDIA (lўd′i-à), (Gr. Λυδία, *loo-dee′ah,* derived from Λυδός its founder).

1. A province in the west of Asia Minor, supposed to have derived its name from Lud, the fourth son of Shem (Gen. x:22). (See NATIONS, DISPERSION OF.)

It was bounded on the east by Greater Phrygia, on the north by Æolis or Mysia, on the west by Ionia and the Ægean Sea, and on the south it was separated from Caria by the Mæander. The country is for the most part level. Among the mountains that of Tmolus was celebrated for its saffron and red wine. In the palmy days of Lydia its kings ruled from the shores of the Ægean to the river Halys; and Crœsus, who was its king in the time of Solon and of Cyrus, was reputed the richest monarch in the world. He was able to bring into the field an army of 420,000 foot and 60,000 horse against Cyrus, by whom, however, he was defeated, and his kingdom annexed to the Persian empire (Herod. i, 6). Lydia afterwards formed part of the kingdom of the Seleucidæ; and it is related in 1 Macc. viii:3, that Antiochus the Great was compelled by the Romans to cede Lydia to king Eumenes. In the time of the travels of the Apostles it was a province of the Roman empire. Its chief towns were Sardis (the capital), Thyatira, and Philadelphia, all of which are mentioned in the New Testament, although the name of the province itself does not occur. The manners of the Lydians were corrupt even to a proverb (Herod. i:92).

2. A woman of Thyatira, 'a seller of purple,' who dwelt in the city of Philippi in Macedonia (Acts xvi:14, 15). Lydia was not by birth a Jewess, but a proselyte 'who worshiped God' (σεβομένη τὸν Θεόν). She was converted by the preaching of Paul; and after she and her household had been baptized, she pressed the use of her house so earnestly upon him and his associates that they were constrained to accept the invitation. The Lydians were famous for the art of dyeing purple vests, and Lydia, as 'a seller of purple,' is supposed to have been a dealer in vests so dyed, rather than in the dye itself. (See Kuinoel on Acts xvi:14). (A. D. 47.)

LYDIANS (lўd′i-anz), (Jer. xlvi:9). See LUD; LUDIM; LYDDA.

LYSANIAS (lỹ-sā′ni-as), (Gr. Λυσανίας, *loo-san-ee′as,* ending sadness), tetrarch of Abilene, when John commenced his ministry as the harbinger of Christ (Luke iii:1), A. D. 25.

He is supposed to have been son or grandson of another Lysanias, known in history, who was put to death by Mark Antony, and part of his territories given to Cleopatra. (See ABILENE.)

LYSIAS (lĭs′i-as), (Gr. Λυσίας, *loo-see′as*), or CLAUDIUS LYSIAS, chiliarch and commandant of the Roman troops who kept guard at the temple of Jerusalem, by whom Paul was secured from the fury of the Jews, and sent under guard to the procurator Felix at Cæsarea (Acts xxi:27-38; xxii:24-30; xxiii:17-30; xxiv:7, 22), A. D. 25.

LYSTRA (lỹs′trà), (Gr. Λύστρα, *loos′trah*), a city of Lycaonia in Asia Minor, to which Paul and Barnabas fled from the danger which threatened them at Iconium (Acts xiv:6).

Here, Paul having miraculously cured a cripple, they were both adored as gods; but afterwards, at the instigation of the Jews, Paul was stoned and left for dead (Acts xiv:8-21). Timothy was a native of Lystra (Acts xvi:1; 2 Tim. iii:11). This city was east of Iconium, on the site of the modern Khatyn Serai, as proven by an inscription (Wolfe's *Expedition,* 142; Ramsay, *Hist. Geog.* 332). **M.**

M

MAACAH or MAACHAH (mā'a-kah), (Heb. מַעֲכָה, *mah-ak-aw'*, depression).

1. A city and region at the foot of Mount Hermon, not far from Geshur, a district of Syria (Josh. xiii:13; 2 Sam. x:6, 8; 1 Chron. xix:7). Hence the adjacent portion of Syria is called Aram-Maacah, or Syria of Maachah (1 Chron. xix:6). The Israelites seem to have considered this territory as included in their grant, but were never able to get possession of it (Josh. xiii:13). In the time of David the small state had a king of its own, who contributed 1,000 men to the grand alliance of the Syrian nations against the Jewish monarch (2 Sam. x:6, 8). The lot of the half-tribe of Manasseh beyond the Jordan extended to this country, as had previously the dominion of Og, king of Bashan (Deut. iii:14; Josh. xii:5). The Gentile name is *Maacathite*, which is also put for the people (Deut. iii:14; Josh. xii:5; xiii:11; 2 Kings xv:29). Near, or within the ancient limits of Maacah, was the town called for that reason Abel beth-Maacah. (See ABEL.)

2. The father of Achish, king of Gath (1 Kings ii:39). (B. C. before 1010.)

3. The father of Hanan, one of David's worthies (1 Chron. xi:43). (B. C. before 1046.)

4. The father of Shephatiah, the military chief of the Simeonites in the time of David (1 Chron. xxvii:16). (B. C. before 1014.)

5. A person whose sex does not appear; one of the offspring of Nahor's concubine Reumah (Gen. xxii:24). (B. C. about 2046.)

6. A concubine of Caleb (1 Chron. ii:48). (B. C. before 1656.)

7. Granddaughter of Benjamin, who was married to Machir, son of Manasseh (1 Chron. vii:16). (B. C. after 1856.)

8. Daughter of Talmai, king of Geshur, wife of David, and mother of Absalom (2 Sam. iii:3). In 1 Sam. xxvii:8 we read of David's invading the land of the Geshurites, and the Jewish commentators allege that he then took the daughter of the king captive, and, in consequence of her great beauty, married her, after she had been made a proselyte according to the law in Deut. xxi. But this is a gross mistake, for the Geshur invaded by David was to the south of Judah, whereas the Geshur over which Talmai ruled was to the north, and was regarded as part of Syria (2 Sam. xv:8). The fact appears to be that David, having married the daughter of this king, contracted an alliance with him, in order to strengthen his interest against Ishbosheth in those parts. (B. C. 1053.)

9. Daughter of Abishalom, wife of Rehoboam, and mother of Abijam (1 Kings xv:1, 2). In verse 10 we read that Asa's 'mother's name was Maachah, the daughter of Abishalom.' It is evident that here 'mother' is used in a loose sense, and means 'grandmother,' which the Maachah named in verse one must have been to the Asa of verse 10. It therefore appears to be a great error to make two persons of them, as is done by Calmet and others. The Abishalom who was the father of this Maachah is called Absalom in 2 Chron. xi:20, 21, and is generally supposed by the Jews to have been Absalom the son of David; which seems not improbable, seeing that Rehoboam's other two wives were of his father's family (2 Chron. xi:18). Asa commenced his reforms by 'removing her from being queen, because she had made an idol in a grove' (1 Kings xv:13; 2 Chron. xv:16). B. C. 973-953.

10. Wife of Jehiel and ancestress of king Saul (1 Chron. viii:29; ix:35). B. C. about 1658.

MAACATH (mā'a-kath). See MAACAH, 1.

MAACHATHI (ma-ăk'a-thī), (Deut. iii:14), **MAACHATHITES** (ma-ăk'a-thītes), (Hebrew singular with article, הַמַּעֲכָתִי, *ham-mah-ak-aw-thee'*, once, Josh. xiii:13, מַעֲכָת, *mah-ak-awth'*).

The inhabitants of the kingdom of Maacah, of Syria, or of Beth-maacah in Naphtali (Josh. xii; 5; 2 Sam. xxiii:34). Individual Maachathites are mentioned in 2 Sam. xxiii:34; Jer. xl:8; 2 Kings xxv:23; 1 Chron. iv:19.

MAADAI (ma-ăd'āi), (Heb. מַעְדַי, *mah'ad-ah'-ee*, ornament of Jehovah).

One of the "sons" of Bani, induced by Ezra to put away his foreign wife after the captivity (Ezra x:34). (B. C. 459.)

MAADIAH (mā'a-dī'ah), (Heb. מַעַדְיָה, *mah-ad-yaw'*, ornament of Jehovah).

A chief priest, or one of the families of priests, who returned with Zerubbabel from Babylon (Neh. xii:5, 7). Probably the same as Moadiah (verse 17). (B. C. 536.)

MAAI (ma-ā'i), (Heb. מָעָי, *maw-ah'ee*, compassionate).

A priest, son of Asaph, and one of the musicians at the dedication of the walls of Jerusalem (Neh. xii:36). (B. C. 446.)

MAALEH-ACRABBIM (ma-ăl'eh-a-krăb'bim), (Heb. עַקְרַבִּים מַעֲלֵה, *mah-al-ay' ak-rab-beem'*, ascent of scorpions).

A mountain so called from the multitude of scorpions that infested it, at the southern end of the Salt Sea (Num. xxxiv:4; Josh. xv:3). Identified as the steep pass of *Es Sufah*.

MAARATH (mā'a-răth), (Heb. מַעֲרָת, *mah-ar-awth'*, naked place, desolation).

A town of Judah, in the mountain district north of Hebron, near Halhul (Josh. xv:59), probably. It has not been identified.

MAASEIAH (mā'a-sē'yà), (Heb. מַעֲשֵׂיָה, *mah-as-ay-yaw'*, or מַעֲשֵׂיָהוּ, *mah-as-ay-yaw' hoo*, work of Jehovah).

1. A descendant of Jeshua, the priest, who put away his foreign wife after the captivity (Ezra x:18). (B. C. 459.)

2. A priest, one of the "sons" of Harim, who also divorced his foreign wife (Ezra x:21); perhaps the same as **11.** (B. C. 459.)

3. A priest, one of the "sons" of Pashur, who divorced his wife after the return from Babylon (Ezra x:22). (B. C. 459.)

4. A layman, one of the "sons" of Pahath-moab, who put away his foreign wife after the captivity (Ezra x:30). (B. C. 459.)

5. Father of that Azariah who assisted in repairing the walls of Jerusalem (Neh. iii:23), (B. C. 446.)

6. One of the chiefs of Israel who stood at the right hand of Ezra when the law was read to the people: perhaps he is identical with (**8.**) (Neh. viii:4). (B. C. about 410.)

7. A priest who assisted the Levites in instructing the people in the law as it was read by Ezra (Neh. viii:7). (B. C. about 410.)

8. One of the chiefs who signed the covenant with Nehemiah (Neh. x:25). (B. C. about 410.)

9. Son of Baruch, a descendant of Judah (Neh. xi:5). In 1 Chron. ix:5, he is apparently called ASAIAH. (B. C. 536.)

10. Son of Ithiel, a Benjamite, one of whose descendants lived in Jerusalem after the exile (Neh. xi:7). (B. C. before 536.)

11. Two priests of this name were musicians and participated in the celebration of the rebuilding of the walls of Jerusalem (Neh. xii:41, 42). (B. C. 446.)

12. Father of Zephaniah, who was priest in the time of Zedekiah (Jer. xxix:25). (B. C. before 589.)

13. Father of the false prophet Zedekiah, who was denounced by the prophet (Jer. xxix:21). (B. C. before 589.)

14. One of the Levites appointed by David as gate keeper for the ark (1 Chron. xv:18, 20). (B. C. 1043.)

15. Son of Adaiah; one of the captains of hundreds who helped Jehoiada to overthrow Athaliah and place Joash on the throne (2 Chron. xxiii:1). (B. C. 877.)

16. A military officer of the Levites, in the time of Uzziah (2 Chron. xxvi:11). (B. C. 808.)

17. A prince of the royal house,—probably the son of king Jotham,—who was killed in the invasion of Judah by Zichri, of the tribe of Ephraim (2 Chron. xxviii:7). (B. C. about 738.)

18. A governor of Jerusalem in the reign of Josiah, sent by Josiah to repair the Temple (2 Chron. xxxiv:8). (B. C. 623.)

19. Son of Shallum; a custodian of the Temple (Jer. xxxv:4). (B. C. 606.)

20. A priest, ancestor of Seraiah and Baruch, sons of Neriah (Jer. xxxii:12). (B. C. about 738.)

MAASIAI (ma-ăs'i-āi), (Heb. מַעְשַׁי, *mah-as-ah'ee*, Jehovah's work).

A priest, son of Adiel, resident at Jerusalem after the return from captivity (1 Chron. ix:12). He is apparently the same as AMASHAI (Neh. xi: 13). (B. C. 536.)

MAATH (mā'ath), (Gr. Μαάθ, *mah-ath'*), an ancestor of Jesus, who lived after the time of Zerubbabel (Luke iii:26). The name may be an interpolation of MATTHAT (ver. 24), as no such name as Maath occurs in the Old Testament.

MAAZ (mā'ăz), (Heb. מַעַץ, *mah'ats*, anger), son of Ram, the firstborn of Jerahmeel of the descendants of Judah (1 Chron. ii:27), B. C. after 1658.

MAAZIAH (mā'a-zī'ah), (Heb. מַעַזְיָה, *mah-az-yaw'*, Jehovah's consolation).

1. One of the priests who signed the covenant with Nehemiah (Neh. x:8). (B. C. about 410.)

2. One of the descendants of Aaron, who was head of the twenty-fourth course of priests, as arranged by David (1 Chron. xxiv:18). (B. C. 1014.)

MACCABEES (măk'ka-beez).

1. Name. The etymology of the name is very uncertain. Some have claimed that it was formed from the combination of the initial letters of the Hebrew sentence, "Who among the gods is like unto thee, Jehovah" (Exod. xv:11), which is supposed to have been inscribed upon the banner of the patriots. Another derivation has been given which may be considered as satisfactory: according to this it is formed from the Heb. *mak-kaw-baw'*, מַקְּבָה, "a hammer," giving a sense not altogether unlike that in which Charles *Martel* derived a surname from his favorite weapon: Although the name *Maccabees* has gained the widest currency, that of *Asmonœans*, or *Hasmonœans*, is the proper name of the family. This name probably came from the great-grandfather of Mattathias.

2. Pedigree. The connection of the several members of the family will be seen from the subjoined table:

CHASHMON—THE ASMONÆAN FAMILY.

Chasmon ('of the sons of Joarib,' comp. 1 Chron. xxiv:7).

Johanan ('Ιωάννης).

Simeon (Συμεών, Simon. Comp. 2 Pet. i:1).

Mattathias (Matthias, Joseph. *Ant.* i. 1, § 3).
B. C. 167.

Johanan (Johannes) (Gaddis), ("Joseph" in 2 Macc. viii:22), B. C. 161.	Simon (Thassi), B. C. 135.	Judas (Maccabæus), B. C. 161.	Eleazar (Avaran), B. C. 163.	Jonathan (Apphus), B. C. 143.
Judas, B. C. 135.	Johannes Hyrcanus I, B. C. 106.	Mattathias. B. C. 135.	Daughter ═ Ptolemæus (1 Macc. xvi:11, 12).	

Salome (Alexandra) ═ Aristobulus I. B. C. 105.	Antigonus. B. C. 105.	Jannæus Alexander ═ Alexandra, B. C. 78.	Son.	Son.
	Hyrcanus II, B. C. 30.	Aristobulus II, B. C. 49.		
	Alexandra ═ Alexander. B. C. 28.	B. C. 49.	Antigonus. B. C. 37.	
Mariamne ═ Herod the Great. B. C. 29.	Aristobulus. B. C. 35.			

3. History. As a family, the Maccabees commenced their career of patriotic and religious heroism during the persecution of Antiochus Epiphanes, about the year B. C. 167.

(1) **Mattathias.** At this time the aged Mattathias, a descendant of the Asmonæans, and his five sons, inhabited the town of Modin, to which place Antiochus sent certain of his officers with instructions to erect an altar for heathen sacrifices, and to engage the inhabitants in the celebration of the most idolatrous and superstitious rites. The venerable Mattathias openly declared his resolution to oppose the orders of the tyrant, and one of the recreant Jews approaching the altar which had been set up, he rushed upon him, and slew him with his own hand. His part thus boldly taken, he called his sons and his friends around him, and immediately fled to the mountains, inviting all to follow him who had any zeal for God and the law. A small band of resolute and devoted men was thus formed, and the governor of the district saw reason to fear that a general insurrection would be the consequence of their proceeding. By a sudden attack directed against them on the Sabbath, when he knew the strictness of their principles would not allow them to take measures for their defense, he threw them into disorder, and slew about a thousand of their number, consisting of men, women, and children.

Warned by this event, and yielding to the necessity of their present condition, Mattathias and his sons determined that for the future they would defend themselves on the Sabbath in the same manner as on other days. The mountainhold of the little band was now guarded more cautiously than before. Fresh adherents to the holy cause were continually flocking in; and in a few months the party found itself sufficiently strong to make attacks upon the towns and villages of the neighborhood, throwing down the heathen altars, and punishing the reprobates who had taken part with the enemies of God.

(2) **Judas Maccabæus.** By the death of Mattathias, the leadership of the party devolved upon his son Judas Maccabæus, whose worth and heroic courage pointed him out as most capable of carrying on the enterprise thus nobly begun. Judas lost no time in attacking the enemy. He made himself master of several towns, which he fortified and garrisoned. Apollonius, general of the army in Samaria, hastened to stop the progress of the insurgents. Judas met him on the way, joined battle with him, slew him, and routed his army. The same success attended him in his encounter with Seron, general of the Syrians; and it now became evident to Antiochus that the Jewish nation would soon be delivered from his yoke, unless he proceeded against them with a more formidable force. While, therefore, he himself went into Persia to recruit his treasures, Lysias, whom he left as regent at home, sent an army into Judæa, composed of forty thousand foot and seven thousand cavalry. This powerful array was further increased by auxiliaries from the provinces, and by bands of Jews, who dreaded nothing more than the triumph of those virtuous men of their own nation, who were struggling to save it from reprobation. So unequal did the forces of Judas appear to an encounter with such an army, that in addressing his followers he urged those among them who had any especial reason to love the present world to retire at once; while to those who remained he pointed out the promises of God as the best support of their courage and fidelity. By a forced march he reached a portion of the enemy encamped at Emmaus, while utterly unprepared for his approach. Complete success attended this bold proceeding. The several parts of the hostile army were successively put to flight, a splendid booty was secured, and Judas gained a position which made even the most powerful of his opponents tremble. Another and more numerous army was sent against him the following year, but with no better success. At the head of ten thousand determined followers, Judas defeated the army of Lysias, consisting of sixty thousand. A way was thereby opened for his progress to Jerusalem, whither he immediately hastened, with the devout purpose of purifying the Temple and restoring it to its former glory. The solemn religious rites having been performed which were necessary to the cleansing of the sacred edifice, the Festival of the Purification was instituted, and added to the number of the other national festivals of more ancient date.

Judas had full occupation for his courage and ability in repelling the incursions of those numerous foes who dreaded the restoration of order and religion. But every day added to his successes. Having overthrown the Syrian commanders sent against him, he occupied Samaria, made himself master of the strong city of Hebron, of Azotus, and other important places, taking signal vengeance on the people of Joppa and Jamnia, who had treacherously plotted the destruction of numerous faithful Jews.

Antiochus Epiphanes was succeeded by Antiochus Eupator. At first this prince acted towards the Jews with moderation and tolerance. But he soon afterwards invaded Judæa with a powerful army, and was only induced to make peace with Maccabæus by the fears which he entertained of a rival aspirant to the throne. His caution did not save him. He was put to death by his own uncle, Demetrius, who, obtaining the throne of Syria, made peace with Judas, but took possession of the citadel of Jerusalem, which was occupied by his general Nicanor, and a body of troops. This state of things was not allowed to last long. Demetrius listened to the reports of Nicanor's enemies, and threatened to deprive him of his command unless he could disprove the accusation that he had entered into a league with Judas, and was betraying the interests of his sovereign. Nicanor immediately took measures to satisfy Demetrius, and Judas saw it necessary to escape from Jerusalem, and put himself in a posture of defense. A battle took place in which he defeated his enemy. Another was soon after fought at Beth-horon, where he was again victorious. Nicanor himself fell in this battle, and his head and right hand were sent among the spoils to Jerusalem. But the forces of Demetrius were still numerous. Judas had retired to Laish with about three thousand followers. He was there attacked by overwhelming numbers. Only eight hundred of his people remained faithful to him on this occasion. Resolved not to flee, he bravely encountered the enemy, and was speedily slain, regarding his life as a fitting sacrifice to the cause in which he was engaged.

(3) **Jonathan.** After the death of Judas the patriotic party seems to have been for a short time wholly disorganized, and it was only by the pressure of unparalleled sufferings that they were driven to renew the conflict. For this purpose they offered the command to Jonathan, surnamed Apphus (*the wary*), the youngest son of Mattathias. Jonathan proved himself a worthy successor of his heroic brother, and skillfully evaded the first attack of Bacchides, the Syrian gen-

eral. For two years after this, the brothers were left in tranquillity, and they established themselves in a little fortress called Bethtasi, situated among the rocks near Jericho. The skill and resolution with which they pursued their measures rendered them formidable to the enemy; and the state of affairs in Syria some time after obliged Demetrius to make Jonathan the general of his forces in Judæa, and to invest him with the authority of governor of Jerusalem. To this he was compelled by the rivalry of Alexander Balas; but his policy was too late to secure the attachment of his new ally. Jonathan received offers from Alexander to support his interests among the Jews, and the high-priesthood was the proffered reward. The invitation was accepted; and Jonathan became the first of the Asmonæan line through which the high-priesthood was so long transmitted. Alexander Balas left nothing undone which might tend to secure the fidelity of Jonathan. He gave him a high rank among the princes of his kingdom, and adorned him with a purple robe. Jonathan continued to enjoy his prosperity till the year B. C. 143, when he fell a victim to the treachery of Trypho, who aspired to the Syrian throne.

(4) **Simon.** As soon as Simon, the last remaining brother of the Maccabæan family, heard of the detention of Jonathan in Ptolemais by Tryphon, he placed himself at the head of the patriot party. His skill in war had been proved in the lifetime of Judas (1 Macc. v:17-23), and he had taken an active share in the campaigns of Jonathan, when he was intrusted with a distinct command (1 Macc. xi:59). Tryphon, after carrying Jonathan about as a prisoner for some little time, put him to death, and then, having murdered Antiochus, seized the throne. On this Simon made overtures to Demetrius II (B. C. 143), which were favorably received, and the independence of the Jews was at length formally recognized. The long struggle was now triumphantly ended, and it remained only to reap the fruits of victory. This Simon hastened to do. The prudence and wisdom for which he was already distinguished at the time of his father's death (1 Macc. ii:65) gained for the Jews the active support of Rome (1 Macc. xv: 16-21), in addition to the confirmation of earlier treaties. After settling the external relations of the new state upon a sure basis, Simon regulated its internal administration to the great satisfaction of his subjects.

(5) **John Hyrcanus.** He was succeeded by his son the celebrated John Hyrcanus. (B. C. 135.) At first he was hard pressed by Antiochus Sidetes, and only able to preserve Jerusalem on condition of dismantling the fortifications and submitting to a tribute. (B. C. 133.) The foreign and civil wars of the Seleucidæ gave him afterwards abundant opportunities to retrieve his losses. He reduced Idumæa (Joseph. *Antiq.* xiii: 9, sec. 1), confirmed the alliance with Rome, and at length succeeded in destroying Samaria, the hated rival of Jerusalem. (B. C. 109.) The external splendor of his government was marred by the growth of internal divisions (Joseph. *Antiq.* xii, 10, secs. 5, 6); but John escaped the fate of all the older members of his family, and died in peace (B. C. 106-5) after possessing the supreme authority for thirty years.

(6) **Aristobulus.** He was succeeded by his son, Aristobulus, who added ITURÆA—a district at the base of the Anti-Libanus—to his dominions, but died, after a short reign of one year, of remorse for the murder of his mother, Salome Alex-

andra, to whom the secular dominion had been bequeathed by Hyrcanus, but whom Aristobulus had cast into prison, and caused there to die of hunger.

(7) **Alexander Jannæus.** The son who succeeded him was Alexander Jannæus. Constantly fighting, and generally beaten, this king yet, strange to say, contrived to enlarge his territories; restless and enterprising as he was cruel and sanguinary, he gave his opponents no rest, and his opponents were all his neighbors in turn, excepting Cleopatra, queen of Egypt. Attached to the SADDUCEES (which see), like his father, and probably something of a pagan, he was disliked by the mass of his countrymen, and a civil war of six years' duration ensued. After a brief period of peace, he died (B. C. 78).

(8) **Hyrcanus II** followed Alexander. He did not long retain authority, for Alexander, when dying, had recommended his wife, Alexandra, to throw herself into the arms of the very party who had thwarted him all his life, the Pharisees, as the best way of retaining her authority. This she did; and governed, on the whole, prudently for nine years. The Pharisaic party, however, abused the power which fell into their hands, and a reaction took place. Aristobulus, youngest son of the queen, and a prince of great spirit, placed himself at the head of the movement, marched to Jerusalem, took possession of the city, and ejected his elder brother, Hyrcanus II, from the sovereignty. Afterwards, however, the latter, at the instigation of Antipater, the Idumean, and father of Herod the Great, fled to Aretas, king of northern Arabia, who was induced, by the promise of a cession of the territory which had been acquired by Alexander Jannæus, to take up arms on his behalf. This led to the interference of the Romans, who were then fighting both in Syria and Armenia. After several vicissitudes, Jerusalem was captured (B. C. 63) by Pompey, who had decided in favor of Hyrcanus, and Judæa made dependent on the Roman province of Syria, and Hyrcanus, appointed ethnarch and high-priest. Aristobulus, however, with his two sons, Alexander and Antigonus, and two daughters, were carried captive to Rome. Antigonus was put to death by the common executioner (B. C. 37). Thus ended the Maccabæan dynasty. (Smith, *Bib. Dict.;* Ewald, *Hist. of Israel.*) (See MACCABEES, BOOKS OF.)   H. S.

MACCABEES, BOOKS OF (măk′ka-beez, bŏŏks ŏv). See APOCRYPHA.

1. Number of Books. The books of Maccabees are the titles of certain Jewish histories containing principally the details of the heroic exploits referred to in the preceding article. There were in all four books (to which some add a fifth) known to the ancients, of which three are still read in the eastern, and two in the western church. Of these the *third* is the first in order of time. We shall, however, to avoid confusion, speak of them in the order in which they are commonly enumerated.

(1) **The First Book of Maccabees** contains a lucid and authentic history of the undertakings of Antiochus Epiphanes against the Jews, from the year B. C. 175 to the death of Simon Maccabæus, B. C. 135. This history is confessedly of great value. Although its brevity, observes De Wette (see 1 Macc. i:6; viii:7; xii), renders it in some instances unsatisfactory, defective, and uncritical, and occasionally extravagant, it is upon the whole entitled to credit, chronologically accurate, and advantageously distinguished above all other historical productions of this period. It is the second book in order of time.

(a) *Language*. There is little question that this book was written in Hebrew, although the original is now lost. The Greek version abounds in Hebraisms and errors of translation.

(b) *Author and Age*. Of the author nothing is known; but he must have been a Palestinian Jew, who wrote some considerable time after the death of Simon Maccabæus, and even of Hyrcanus, and made use of several written, although chiefly of traditionary, sources of information. At the same time it is not impossible that the author was present at several of the events which he so graphically describes.

(2) **The Second Book of Maccabees** (the third in order of time) is a work of very inferior character to the first. It is an abridgment of a more ancient work, written by a Jew named Jason, who lived at Cyrene in Africa, comprising the principal transactions of the Jews which occurred during the reigns of Seleucus IV, Antiochus Epiphanes, and Antiochus Eupator. It partly goes over the same ground with the first book, but commences ten or twelve years earlier, and embraces in all a period of fifteen years. It does not appear that the author of either saw the other's work. The second book of Maccabees is divided into two unconnected parts. It commences with a letter from the citizens of Jerusalem and Judæa to the Greek Jews in Egypt, written B. C. 123 (which refers to a former letter written to the same, B. C. 143, acquainting them of their sufferings), and informs them that their worship was now restored, and that they were celebrating the Feast of Dedication. The second part (ii:18) contains a still more ancient letter, written B. C. 159, to the priest Aristobulus, the tutor of king Ptolemy, recounting, besides some curious matter, the death of Antiochus Epiphanes. The third part contains the preface, in which the author states that he is about to epitomize the five books of Jason. The work commences with the attack of Heliodorus on the Temple, and closes with the death of Nicanor, a period of fifteen years. The history supplies some blanks in the first book; but the letters prefixed to it contradict some of the facts recorded in the body of the work, and are consequently supposed to have been added by another hand. Neither are the letters themselves considered genuine, and they were probably written long after the death of Nicanor, and even of John Hyrcanus. This book gives a different account of the place and manner of the death of Antiochus Epiphanes from that contained in the first book.

The narrative abounds in miraculous adventures, historical and chronological errors, extraordinary and arbitrary embellishments, affected descriptions, and moralizing reflections.

(a) *Author and Age*. We are not aware when either Jason himself or his epitomizer lived. Jahn refers the age of the epitomizer to some time previous to the middle of the last century before the birth of Christ, and De Wette maintains that Jason must have written a considerable time after the year B. C. 161.

(b) *Language and Versions*. Jerome (*Prolog. Galeat.*) observes that the phraseology of this book evinces a Greek original. The elegance and purity of the style have misled some persons into the supposition that its author was Josephus.

(3) **The Third Book of Maccabees**, still read in the Greek church, and contained in the Alexandrian and Vatican MSS. (A. & B.) is, as has been already observed, the first in order of time. It contains an account of the persecution of the Egyptian Jews by Ptolemy Philopator, who is said to have proceeded to Jerusalem after his victory at Raphia over Antiochus the Great, B. C. 217, and after sacrificing in the Temple, to have attempted to force his way into the Holy of Holies, when he was prostrated and rendered motionless by an invisible hand. Upon his return to Egypt, he revenged himself by shutting up the Jews in the Hippodrome, and exposing them to be crushed beneath the feet of elephants. This book contains an account of their deliverance by Divine interposition. It is anterior in point of date to the Maccabæan period, and has received its designation from a general resemblance to the first two books in the heroic character of the actions which it describes. Calmet (*Commentary*) observes that this book is rejected as apocryphal in the Latin church; not, however, as not containing a true history, but as not being inspired, as he considers the first two books to be. It is nevertheless regarded by De Wette as a tasteless fable, and notwithstanding the relation which it contains of an annual festival, considered by him as most probably destitute of any historical foundation. Dr. Milman (*Hist. of the Jews*) describes it as a 'romantic story.'

Author, Age, and Versions. The author is unknown. Dr. Allix (*Judgment of the Jewish Church*) considers it to have been written B. C. 200, and by the author of Ecclesiasticus. There is a Syriac version in the Polyglots, but no ancient Latin translation has come down to us.

(4) **The Fourth Book of Maccabees**, which is also found in the Alexandrian and Vatican manuscripts, is generally supposed to be the same as the *Supremacy of Reason*, attributed to Josephus, with which it for the most part accords. It consists of an inflated amplification of the history of the martyrdom of Eleazar, and of the seven brothers, whose torments and death, with that of their mother, form the subject of 2 Macc. chapters vi, vii.

Calmet (*Preface to the Fourth Book of Maccabees*) has pointed out several contradictions between this and the second book, as well as the books of Moses, together with some opinions derived from the Stoics, such as the equality of crimes; which, he supposes, together with its tedious descriptions, have consigned it to the rank of an Apocryphal book.

(5) **Fifth Book of Maccabees.** What has been called the *Fifth Book of Maccabees* is now extant only in the Arabic and Syriac languages.

Author, Age, and Subject. It is impossible to ascertain the author, who could scarcely have been Josephus, as he disagrees in many things with that historian (Calmet's *Preface*).

The work consists of a history of Jewish affairs, commencing with the attempt on the treasury at Jerusalem by Heliodorus, and ending with the tragic fate of the last of the Asmonæan princes, and with the inhuman execution by Herod of his noble and virtuous wife Mariamne, and of his two sons. This history thus fills up the chasm to the birth of Christ.

Dr. Cotton has pointed out among the 'remarkable peculiarities' found in this book the phrases, 'Peace be unto thee,' and 'God be merciful to them,' showing that the practice of prayer for the dead was at this time prevalent. But the most remarkable passage in reference to this subject is 2 Macc. xii:40-45, where Judas forwards to Jerusalem 2,000, or according to the Syriac 3,000, and according to the Vulgate 12,000, drachmas of silver, to make a sin-offering for the Jews slain in action on whose persons were found things consecrated to idols, which they had sacrilegiously plundered in violation of the law of Moses (Deut. vii:25, 26). The author of the book remarks that it was a holy and good thought to pray for the dead, which, he observes, would have been superfluous had there been no resurrection. Calmet observes·that, according to the notions of the Jews and some of the Christian Fathers, the pains of hell for those who died in mortal sin (as appears to have been the case of these Jews) were alleviated by the prayers and alms of the living (Augustine, *De Fide, Spe, et Charitate,* ch. 110), if not entirely removed; and cites a passage from a very ancient Christian liturgy to the same effect. This learned commentator supposes that the ancient and Catholic practice of prayer for the dead had its origin in this usage of the Jews, although he admits it to be a distinct thing from the doctrine of purgatory as held in the Roman Church.

2. Church Authority. The first two books of Maccabees have often been treated with a very high degree of respect in the Christian Church. Origen (*apud Eusebium*), professing to give a catalogue of the twenty-two canonical books, of which, however, he actually enumerates only twenty-one, adds, 'besides, there are the Maccabees.' This has given rise to the notion that he intended to include these books in the Canon, while others have observed that he has omitted the minor prophets from his catalogue. In his preface to the Psalms he excludes the two books of Maccabees from the books of Holy Scripture, but in his *Princip.* (ii, 1), and in his *Comment. ad Rom.* ch. v, he speaks of them as inspired, and as of equal authority with the other books. St. Jerome says that the *Church* does not acknowledge them as canonical, although he elsewhere cites them as *Holy Scripture* (*Com. ad Isa.* xxiii; *ad Eccl.* vii, ix; *ad Dan.* viii). Bellarmine (*De Verbo Dei*) acknowledges that these, with the other deutero-canonical books, are *rejected* by Jerome, as they had not been then determined by any general council. The first councils which included them in the canonical scriptures were those of Hippo and Carthage. They were received with the other books by the Council of Trent. Basnage, cited by Lardner (*Credibility*), thinks that the word 'Canonical' may be supposed to be used here (by the councils of Hippo and Carthage) loosely, so as to comprehend not only those books which are admitted as a rule of faith, but those which are esteemed useful, and may be publicly read for the edification of the people, in contradistinction to such books as were entirely rejected. This is also the opinion of the Roman Catholic Professor Jahn (*Introd.* sec. 29), who expresses himself in nearly the same words. Dr. Lardner conceives that Augustine also, unless he would contradict himself, must be understood to have used the word in the same sense. (See Cotton, *The Five Books of the Maccabees.*)
W. W.

MACEDONIA (măç'e-dō'ni-à), (Gr. Μακεδονία, *mak-ed-on-ee'ah,* from the mythical founder *Macedon*). A country lying to the north of Greece Proper, having on the east Thrace and the Ægæan Sea, on the west the Adriatic and Illyria, on the north Dardania and Mæsia, and on the south Thessaly and Epirus.

The country is supposed to have been first peopled by Chittim or Kittim, a son of Javan (Gen. x:4), (see NATIONS, DISPERSION OF); and in that case it is probable that the Macedonians are sometimes intended when the word Chittim occurs in the Old Testament. Macedonia was the orig-

inal kingdom of Philip and Alexander, by means of whose victories the name of the Macedonians became celebrated throughout the East, and is often used for the Greeks in Asia generally (Esth. Apoc. xviii:10, 14; 2 Macc. viii:20). The rise of the great empire formed by Alexander is described by the prophet Daniel under the emblem of a goat with one horn (Dan. viii: 3-8). As the horn was a general symbol of power, and as the oneness of the horn implies merely the unity of that power, we are not prepared to go the lengths of some over-zealous illustrators of scripture, who argue that if a one-horned goat were not a recognized symbol of Macedonia we should not be entitled to conclude that Macedonia was intended. We hold that there could be no mistake in the matter, whatever may have been the usual symbol of Macedonia. It is, however, curious and interesting to know that Daniel did describe Macedonia under its usual symbol, as coins still exist in which that country is represented under the figure of a one-horned goat. There has been much discussion on this subject—more curious than valuable—but the kernel of it lies in this fact.

(1) Subdued and Divided. When subdued by the Romans under Paulus Æmilius (B. C. 168), Macedonia was divided into four provinces; but afterwards (B. C. 142) the whole of Greece was divided into two great provinces, Macedonia and Achaia. (See GREECE; ACHAIA.) Macedonia therefore constituted a Roman province, governed by a proconsul (*provincia proconsularis;* Tacit. *Annal.* i, 76; Suet. *Claus* 26), in the time of Christ and his apostles.

(2) Paul's Mission. The Apostle Paul being summoned in a vision while at Troas, to preach the gospel in Macedonia, proceeded thither, and founded the churches of Thessalonica and Philippi (Acts xvi:9), A. D. 55. This occasions repeated mention of the name, either alone (Acts xviii:5; xix:21; Rom. xv:26; 2 Cor. i:16; xi:9; Phil. iv:15), or along with Achaia (2 Cor. ix: 2; 1 Thess. i:8). The principal cities of Macedonia were Amphipolis, Thessalonica, Pella, and Pelagonia (Liv. xlv:29); the towns of the province named in the New Testament, and noticed in the present work, are Amphipolis, Thessalonica, Neapolis, Apollonia, and Berea. (See PAUL.)

MACEDONIAN (măs'e-dō'ni-an), an inhabitant of Macedonia (Acts xxvii:2); elsewhere rendered MACEDONIA.

MACHÆRUS (mak-ē'rus), (Gr. Μαχαιρούς, the Black Fortress).

This name is not mentioned in the Bible, but is supposed to be the castle in which John the Baptist was imprisoned and beheaded (Mark vi: 21-29). It was built by Alexander Jannæus as a check against Arab marauders (Josephus, *Wars,* vii, 6, 2), demolished by Gabinius when he made war against Aristobulus, and rebuilt by Herod. It was situated in the gorge of Callirhoe, one of the valleys east of the Dead Sea, three thousand eight hundred and sixty feet above this sea and two thousand five hundred and forty-six feet above the Mediterranean, nine miles east of the Dead Sea. "Its ruins, now called *M'khaur,* are still visible on the northern end of Jebel Attarûs." (See JOHN THE BAPTIST.)

MACHBANAI (măk'ba-nāi), (Heb. מַכְבַּנַּי. *makban-nah'ee,* one fat, thick).

A Gadite warrior who came to David at Ziklag (1 Chron. xii:13). (B. C. about 1061.)

MACHBENAH (măk'bē'nah), (Heb. מַכְבֵּנָא, mak-bay-naw', hillock, hump).

Probably a town of Judah founded by a person of the same name, son of Sheva (1 Chron. ii:49). It is supposed to be the same as Cabbon (Josh xv:40).

MACHI (mā'kī), (Heb. מָכִי, maw-kee', pining).

The father of Geuel, the Gadite representative sent to explore the land of Canaan (Num. xiii: 15). (B. C. before 1657.)

MACHIR (mā'kir), (Heb. מָכִיר, maw-keer', sold, acquired).

1. The eldest son of Manasseh (Gen. 1:23; Josh. xvii:1) by an Aramitess mother (1 Chron. vii:14). He was the founder of the Machirites, who subjugated Gilead, and received their territory as an inheritance (Num. xxxii:39, 40; Josh. xvii:1). Machir was a name at one time applied to the whole tribe of Manasseh (Judg. v:14). (B. C. 1802.)

2. A descendant of Machir **1**, and son of Ammiel, of Lo-debar (2 Sam. ix:4, 5). He supported the lame son of Jonathan, until he was provided for by David, and furnished David himself with provisions while a fugitive during Absalom's rebellion (2 Sam. xvii:27). (B. C. 1037-1023.)

MACHIRITES (mā'kir-ītes), (Heb. הַמָּכִירִי, ham-maw-kee-ree', "the Machirite," only in Num. xxvi:29), descendants of Machir, 1, who was son of Manasseh by an Aramite concubine.

His wife and children are named in 1 Chron. vii:16, 17; but the statement in verse 17, "These are the sons of Gilead, the son of Machir, the son of Manasseh," with the declaration that "Machir begat Gilead" would add Gilead to the list of Machir's sons. (See MACHIR.)

MACHNADEBAI (măk'na-dē'bāi), (Heb. מַכְנַדְבַי, mak-nad-bah'ee, gift of the noble, what is like the liberal?), one of the sons of Bani who divorced his foreign wife at Ezra's command after the exile (Ezra x:40). B. C. 459.

MACHPELAH (mak-pē'lah), (Heb. מַכְפֵּלָה, mak-pay-law', twofold, double).

The name of the plot of ground containing the cave which Abraham bought of Ephron the Hittite for a family sepulcher (Gen. xxiii:9, 17, 19). (See HEBRON.) Here were buried Abraham (Gen. xxv:9, 10), Isaac, Rebekah, and Leah (Gen. xxxv:29; xlvii:28-31; xlix:29-33; l:12, 13). It is no doubt, the cave beneath the great mosque at Hebron. (Stanley, *Jewish Ch.*; Osborn, *Palestine, Past and Present*.)

MAD. See MADNESS.

MADAI (măd'a-ī), (Heb. מָדַי, maw-dah'ee).

A people descended from Japhet. The name is probably Ethnic rather than personal and is only intended to indicate that the Medes were descendants of Japhet. (See GOG; NATIONS, DISPERSION OF.)

MADIAN (mā'di-an), (Gr. Μαδιάν, mad-ee-an', Acts vii:29). See MIDIAN.

MADMANNAH (mad-măn'nah), (Heb. מַדְמַנָּה, mad-man-naw', dunghill).

A city of Simeon (Josh. xv:31), very far south towards Gaza (1 Chron. ii:49), which in the first distribution of lands had been assigned to Judah. Eusebius and Jerome identify it with a town of their time, called Menois, near the city of Gaza (*Onomast.* p. 89). The parallel passage (Josh. xix:5) has BETH-MARCABOTH, with which it is, perhaps, identical. Van de Velde identifies this with *Mikrib*, southwest of the Dead Sea. (*Travels*, ii. 130.)

MADMEN (măd'men), (Heb. מַדְמֵן, mad-mane', dunghill).

A place in Moab named in Jer. xlviii:2, as threatened with destruction by the Babylonians. Not identified.

MADMENAH (mad-mē'nah), (Heb. מַדְמֵנָה, mad-may-naw', dunghill).

A town a little north of Jerusalem, on the line of march of the invading Assyrians (Is. x:31). It doubtless stood between Gibrah and Nob, but has not yet been identified.

MADNESS (măd'nĕs), (Heb. שִׁגָּעוֹן, shig-gaw-one', raving). The epithet mad is applied to several descriptions of persons in Scripture.

1. To one deprived of reason (Acts xxvi:24; 1 Cor. xiv:23).

2. To one whose reason is depraved, and overruled by the fury of his angry passions (Acts xxvi:11).

3. To one whose mind is perplexed and bewildered, so disturbed that he acts in an uncertain, extravagant, irregular manner (Deut. xxviii:34; Eccl. vii:7).

4. To one who is infatuated by the vehemence of his desires after idols and vanities (Jer. 1: 38), folly, deceit and falsehood (Hos. ix:7).

5. To one disturbed by sudden and startling intelligence (Acts xii:15).

6. To utterances of false prophets (Is. xliv: 25; Hos. ix:7).

7. To the effects of inebriety (Jer. xxv:16; li:7).

8. To derision, with reference to the ecstatic utterances of the prophets when in a state of holy exaltation (2 Kings ix:11; Jer. xxix:26).

9. To idolatrous hallucination (Jer. 1:38), or wicked and extravagant mirth (Eccl. ii:2).

10. To a reckless state of mind (Eccl. x:13), bordering on delirium (Zech. xii:4).

11. To overstrained mental effort (Eccl. i:17; ii:12), blind rage (Luke vi:11), or depraved tempers (Eccl. vii:25; ix:3; 2 Pet. ii:16).

It is well known that among oriental, as among most semi-civilized nations, madmen were looked upon with a kind of reverence, as possessed of a quasi-sacred character. This arises partly no doubt from the feeling that one on whom God's hand is laid heavily should be safe from all other harm; but partly also from the belief that the loss of reason and self-control opened the mind to supernatural influence, and gave it therefore a supernatural sacredness. An illustration of it may be seen in the record of David's pretended madness at the court of Achish (1 Sam. xxi:13-15, which shows it to be not inconsistent with a kind of contemptuous forbearance, such as is often manifested now, especially by the Turks, towards real or supposed madmen.

David's madness, however, says Calmet, is by many supposed not to have been feigned, but a real epilepsy or falling sickness.

MADON (mā'don), (Heb. מָדוֹן, maw-dohn', contention, strife).

A city of northern Canaan (Josh xi:1; xii:19), captured by Joshua from its king, Jobab, who was in the confederacy with Hazor. Its site is possibly *Madîn*, a little northwest of Tiberias.

MAGBISH (mag'bish), (Heb. מַגְבִּישׁ, mag-beesh', stiffening, gathering).

Probably the name of a place (Ezra ii:30), as all the names from Ezra ii:20 to 34, except Elam and Harim, are names of places. It is not in the corresponding list in Neh. vii. The place was doubtless in the territory of Benjamin.

MAGDALA (măg'da-là), (Gr. Μαγδαλά, *mag-dal-ah'*, Magdala), a town mentioned in Matt. xv:39, and the probable birthplace of Mary Magdalene, *i. e.*, Mary of Magdala.

It must have taken its name from *a tower* or *castle,* as the name signifies. It was situated on the lake Gennesaret, but it has usually been placed on the *east* side of the lake, although a careful consideration of the route of Christ before he came to, and after he left, Magdala, would show that it must have been on its *western* shore. This is confirmed by the Jerusalem Talmud (compiled at Tiberias), which several times speaks of Magdala as being adjacent to Tiberias and Hamath, or the hot-springs (Lightfoot, *Chorog. Cent.* ch. lxxvi). It was a seat of Jewish learning after the destruction of Jerusalem, and the Rabbins of Magdala are often mentioned in the Talmud (Lightfoot, *l. c.*). A small Moslem village, bearing the name of Mejdel, is now found on the shore of the lake about three miles northwest of Tiberias; and although there are no ancient ruins, the name and situation are very strongly in favor of the conclusion that it represents the Magdala of Scripture. This was probably also the Migdal-el, in the tribe of Naphtali, mentioned in Josh. xix:38 (Burckhardt, *Syria,* p. 559; Seetzen in *Monat. Corresp.* xviii, 349; Fisk, *Life,* p. 316; Robinson, *Researches,* iii, 279).

MAGDALENE (măg'da-lē'ne), (Gr. Μαγδαληνή, *mag-dah-lay-nay'*), a fem. adj. form of *Magdala.*

A surname, indicative of the place of residence, or nativity, of one of the Marys of the New Testament, used for the sake of distinction (Matt. xxvii:56, 61; xxviii:1; Mark xv:40, 47; xvi:1, 9; Luke viii:2; xxiv:10; John xix:25; xx:1, 18).

MAGDIEL (măg'di-el), (Heb. מַגְדִּיאֵל, *mag-dee-ale',* God is renown).

A descendant of Esau (Gen. xxxvi:43; 1 Chron. i:54), and chief among the Edomites in Mount Seir. (B. C. before 1619.)

MAGI (mā'jī), (Heb. מַג, *mag;* Gr. μάγοι, *mag'oy,* A. V. "wise men" in Matt. ii:1, 7, 16; "sorcerer" in Acts xiii:6, 8).

The Magi were originally one of the six tribes (Herod i:101; Plin. *Hist. Nat.* v. 29) into which the nation of the Medes was divided, who, like the Levites under the Mosaic institutions, were intrusted with the care of religion: an office which was held in the highest honor, gave the greatest influence, and which they probably acquired for themselves only after a long time, as well as many worthy efforts to serve their country, and when they had proved themselves superior to the rest of their brethren. As among other ancient nations, as the Egyptians, and Hebrews, for instance, so among the Medes, the priestly caste had not only religion, but the arts and all the higher culture, in their charge. Their name points immediately to their sacerdotal character (from *Mag* or *Mog,* which in the Pehlevi denotes 'priest'), either because religion was the chief object of their attention, or more probably because, at the first, religion and art were so allied as to be scarcely more than different expressions of the same idea.

Little in detail is known of the Magi during the independent existence of the Median government; they appear in their greatest glory after the Medes were united with the Persians. This doubtless is owing to the general imperfection of the historical materials which relate to the earlier periods. So great, however, was the influence which the Magi attained under the united empire, that the Medes were not ill compensated for their loss of national independence. Under the Medo-Persian sway the Magi formed a sacred caste or college, which was very famous in the ancient world (Xenoph. *Cyrop.* viii, 1, 23; Ammian. Marcell. xxiii:6; Heeren, *Ideen,* i, 451; Schlosser, *Universal Uebers,* i, 278).

(1) Divination. According to Strabo (tom. ii, p. 1084, ed. Falcon.) the Magi practiced different sorts of divination—(1) by evoking the dead; (2) by cups or dishes (Joseph's divining cup (Gen. xliv:5); (3) by means of water. By the employment of these means the Magi affected to disclose the future, to influence the present, and to call the past to their aid. Even the visions of the night they were accustomed to interpret, not empirically, but according to such established and systematic rules as a learned priesthood might be expected to employ (Strabo, xvi, p. 762; Cic. *De Divin.* i, 41; Ælian, *V. H.* ii, 17). The success, however, of their efforts over the invisible world, as well as the holy office which they exercised, demanded in themselves peculiar cleanliness of body, a due regard to which and to the general principles of their caste would naturally be followed by professional prosperity, which in its turn conspired with prevailing superstition to give the Magi great social consideration, and make them of high importance before kings and princes (Diog. Laert. ix, 7, 2)—an influence which they appear to have sometimes abused, when, descending from the peculiar duties of their high office, they took part in the strife and competitions of politics, and found themselves sufficiently powerful even to overturn thrones (Herod. iii, 61, *sq.*).

Abuses bring reform; and the Magian religion, which had lost much of its original character, and been debased by some of the lowest elements of earthly passions, loudly called for a renovation, when Zoroaster appeared to bring about the needful change. As to the particulars of his appearance, and in general the particulars of his history, differences of opinion prevail, after all the critical labor that has been expended on the subject. Winer (*Real-wört.*) says he lived in the second half of the seventh century before Christ. He was not the founder of a new system, but the renovator of an old and corrupt one, being, as he himself intimates (*Zendavesta,* i, 43), the restorer of the word which Ormuzd had formerly revealed, but which the influence of Dews had degraded into a false and deceptive magic.

(2) Zoroaster. To destroy this, and restore the pure law of Ormuzd, was Zoroaster's mission. After much and long-continued opposition on the part of the adherents and defenders of existing corruptions, he succeeded in his virtuous purposes, and caused his system eventually to prevail. The Magi, as a caste, did not escape from his reforming hand. He appears to have remodeled their institute, dividing it into three great classes: (1) Herbeds, or learners; (2) Mobeds, or masters; (3) Destur Mobeds, or perfect scholars *Zendav.* ii, 171, 261). The Magi alone he allowed to perform the religious rites; they possessed the forms of prayer and worship; they knew the ceremonies which availed to conciliate Ormuzd, and were obligatory in the public offerings (Herod. i, 132). They accordingly became the sole medium of communication between the Deity and his creatures, and through them alone

Ormuzd made his will known; none but them could see into the future, and they disclosed their knowledge to those only who were so fortunate as to conciliate their good will. Hence the power which the Magian priesthood possessed. The general belief in the trustworthiness of their predictions, especially when founded on astrological calculations, the all but universal custom of consulting the will of the divinity before entering on any important undertaking, and the blind faith which was reposed in all that the Magi did, reported, or commanded, combined to create for that sacerdotal caste a power, both in public and in private concerns, which has probably never been exceeded.

(3) Extent of Functions. Neither the functions nor the influence of this sacred caste were reserved for peculiar, rare, and extraordinary occasions, but ran through the web of human life. At the break of day they had to chant the divine hymns. This office being performed, then came the daily sacrifice to be offered, not indiscriminately, but to the divinities whose day in each case it was—an office therefore which none but the initiated could fulfill. As an illustration of the high estimation in which the Magi were held, it may be mentioned that it was considered a necessary part of a princely education to have been instructed in the peculiar learning of their sacred order, which was an honor conceded to no other but royal personages, except in very rare and very peculiar instances (Cicero, *De Divin.* i, 23; Plutarch, *Themist.*). This Magian learning embraced everything which regarded the higher culture of the nation, being known in history under the designation of the law of the Medes and Persians. It comprised the knowledge of all the sacred rites, customs, usages, and observances, which related not merely to the worship of the gods, but to the whole private life of every worshiper of Ormuzd—the duties which, as such, he had to observe, and the punishments which followed the neglect of these obligations; whence may be learnt how necessary the act of the priest on all occasions was. Under the veil of religion the priest had bound himself up with the entire of public and domestic life. The judicial office, too, appears to have been in the time of Cambyses, in the hands of the Magi; for from them was chosen the college or bench of royal judges, which makes its appearance in the history of that monarch (Herod. iv:31; vii:194; Esther i:13). Men who held these offices possessed this learning, and exerted this influence with the people, may have proved a check to Oriental despotism, no less powerful than constitutional, though they were sometimes unable to guarantee their own lives against the wrath of the monarch (Herod. vii:194; Dan. ii:12). If we turn to the books of scripture we find the import of what has been said confirmed, especially in the book of Daniel, where the great influence of the Magi is well illustrated.

(4) In Various Lands. The Magi were not confined to the Medes and Persians. Since they are mentioned by Herodotus as one of the original tribes of the Medes, they may have been primitively a Median priesthood. If so, they extended themselves into other lands. Possibly Magi may have been at first not the name of a particular tribe or priestly caste, but a general designation for priests or learned men; as Pharaoh denoted not an individual, but generally king or ruler. However this may be, the Chaldæans also had an organized order of Magi, a caste of sacerdotal scholars, which bore the name of 'wise men' (Jer. l:35); 'the wise men of Babylon' (Dan. ii:12), among whom Daniel is classed (ii:18, 24). Among the Greeks and Romans they were known under the name of Chaldæans (Strabo, xvi, p. 762; Diog. Laert. *Præm.* 1), and also of Magi (Diog. Laert. viii, 1, 3). They lived scattered over the land in different places (Dan. ii:14; Strabo, xvi. p. 739), and had possessions of their own. The temple of Belus was employed by them for astronomical observations; but their astronomy was connected with the worship of the heavenly bodies practiced by the Babylonians (Diod. Sic. ii, 31; Ephraem Syr. *Op.* ii, 488; consult Ideler, in the *Transactions of the Berlin Academy* for 1824-5), and was specially directed to vain attempts to foretell the future, predict the fate of individuals or of communities, and sway the present, in alliance with augury, incantation, and magic (Is. xlvii:9, 13; Dan. ii).

It is easy to understand how the lofty science (so called) of these Magi—lofty while its scholars surpassed the rest of the world in knowledge, and were the associates, the advisers, the friends, and the monitors of great and flourishing monarchs, of indeed successively the rulers of the world—might, could indeed hardly fail, as resting on no basis of fact or reality, in process of time, to sink into its own native insignificance, and become either a mere bugbear to frighten the ignorant, or an instrument to aid the fraudulent: thus hastening on to the contempt into which all falsities are sure sooner or later to fall. The decline was indeed gradual; ages passed ere it was completed; but as soon as it ceased to have the support afforded by the mighty and splendid thrones of Asia, it began to lose its authority, which the progress of knowledge and the advent of Christ prevented it from ever regaining.

(5) In New Testament Times. The estimation, however, in which Simon Magus was evidently held, as recorded in the Acts ('some great one,' etc.), gives reason to think that Magianism still retained a large share of its influence at the commencement of our era. It seems, indeed, to have held a sort of middle position, half way between its ancient splendor and its coming degradation: whence we may understand the propriety of the visit paid by the Magi to the newborn King of the Jews (Matt. ii, 'star in the East'). For if the system had been then sunk so low as to correspond in any degree with our conception of these pretended arts, it is difficult to assign, at least to the unbeliever, a sufficient reason why the visit was made, or at any rate why it was recorded; but its credibility is materially furthered if the circumstances of the case are such as to allow us to regard that visit as a homage paid by the representatives of the highest existing influences to the rising Star of a New Day, in the fuller light of which they were speedily to vanish. (See STAR.) (Trench, *Star of the Wise Men;* Rawlinson, *Ancient Monarch.* iii, 125-136, 218, *sq.;* iv, 391-395.) J. R. B.

MAGIC (măg'ĭk), (from Heb. חֶרֶט, *kheh'ret,* to engrave, and so to draw magical lines or circles).

(1) Definition. Magic was the art of influencing future events and changing their course by dark and secret means. The magician was believed to stand in connection with demons, and even with the gods themselves, and to be able to compel them to act according to his will. Of the religion of the Egyptians, Chaldæans, Persians, etc., magic formed an essential element, and of the Egyptian magicians, in their conflict with Moses and Aaron, Exodus gives a vivid account (vii:11, 12, 22; viii:7). Of the religion of the Jews magic did not only not form a part, but the law forbade the consulting of magicians, under penalty of death (Lev. xix:31; xx:6). Nevertheless, from their neighbors magic crept in among the Israelites too, and there were those among the people who believed in it and resorted to it.

(2) Sacrificing Children. It is remarkable that the offering of children should be mentioned in connection with magical arts. The passage in Micah, which has been supposed to preserve a question of Balak and an answer of Balaam, when the soothsayer was sent for to curse Israel, should be here noticed, for the questioner asks, after speaking of sacrifices of usual kinds, "Shall I give my firstborn [for] my transgression, the fruit of my body [for] the sin of my soul" (Micah vi:5-8). Perhaps, however, child-sacrifice is specified on account of its atrocity, which would connect it with secret arts, which we know were frequently in later times the causes of cruelty.

(3) Saul and the Witch of Endor. The account of Saul's consulting the witch of Endor is foremost among those in Scripture which refer to magic (1 Sam. xxviii:3-20). The supernatural terror with which it is full cannot however be proved to be due to this art, for it has always been held by sober critics that the appearing of Samuel was permitted for the purpose of declaring the doom of Saul, and not that it was caused by the incantations of a sorceress. As, however, the narrative is allowed to be very difficult, we may look for a moment at the evidence of its authenticity. The details are strictly in accordance with the age: there is a simplicity in the manners described that is foreign to a later time. The circumstances are agreeable with the rest of the history, and especially with all we know of Saul's character. Here, as ever, he is seen resolved to gain his ends without caring what wrong he does; he wishes to consult a prophet, and asks a witch to call up his shade. Most of all, the vigor of the narrative, showing us the scene in a few words, proves its antiquity and genuineness. We can see no reason whatever for supposing that it is an interpolation. In the New Testament we find it mentioned (Acts viii:9). (See DIVINATION; MAGI; SAUL.)

MAGICIANS (mȧ-jĭsh'ạns). See MAGI.

MAGISTRATE (măj'ĭs-trăt), (Heb. שָׁפַט, *sheh-fat'*, a judge, magistrate).

The word magistrate is used to express general Hebrew and Greek words, relating to a public civil officer. It had a much broader signification among the Hebrews, Greeks and Romans than with us.

1. In Old Testament.
1. In Judg. xviii:7, magistrate means governor.
2. A better translation of Ezra vii:25 would be "judges and rulers," instead of "magistrates and judges."

2. In New Testament.
1. It is used in the sense of rulers, civil officers, in Luke xii:11; Tit. iii:1 (as in the above citation from Ezra).
2. In Acts xvi:20 and following verses it refers to a civic officer or commander who may be called prefect, proctor, or consul. (See PROCONSUL.)
3. *Ar'khone* (Gr. ἄρχων, first), translated *magistrate* (Luke xii:58), signifies *one first in power*. Similar in derivation and meaning is *ar-khay'* (Gr,

ἀρχή, Luke xii:11, "*magistrates;*" Tit. iii:1, "principalities"); ἄρχων is used of Moses as judge and leader of the Israelites. It is also used of the Messiah as supreme king (Rev. i:5).
4. It is used of magistrates of any kind, e. g., the high priest (Acts xxiii:5); of civil judges (Acts xvi:19); a ruler of the synagogue (Matt. ix:18, 23; Mark v:22; Luke viii:41); persons of influence among the sects at Jerusalem, who were also members of the Sanhedrin (Luke xiv:1; xviii:18; xxiii:13, 35; xxiv:20, etc.).
5. Satan the *prince* of the fallen angels (Matt. ix:34; Mark iii:22; Luke xi:15; John xii:31; Eph. ii:2, etc.).

MAGNIFICAL (măg'nĭf'ĭ-kal), (Heb. גָּדַל, *gaw-dal'*, to make great), magnificent, applied to Solomon's Temple (1 Chron. xxii:5).

MAGNIFICAT (măg-nĭf'i-kăt), (Lat. doth magnify), the poem of the Virgin Mary (Luke i:46-55). It is called by this name because "Magnificat" is, in the Vulgate, the first word.

MAGNIFY (măg'nĭ-fī), (Heb. גָּדַל, *gaw-dal'*), to make great, or declare to be great.

(1) God "*magnifies*" his own mercy or name, when, by the fulfillment or powerful application of his word, he discovers the unbounded nature of his mercy and other perfections (Gen. xix: 19; Acts xix:17). (2) He "*magnifies his word above all his name*," when he clearly discovers his mercy and faithfulness therein contained and pledged (Ps. cxxxviii:2). (3) God "*magnifies*" men when he renders them honorable, wealthy, or powerful (Josh. iii:7; iv:14; 1 Chron. xxix: 25; 2 Chron. xxxii:23), or even when, by afflicting them, he shows that he takes much notice of them (Job vii:17). (4) Men "*magnify*" God or his work when they publish and declare his greatness and glory (Job xxxvi:24; Ps. xxxiv:3).

MAGOG (mā'gŏg), (Heb. מָגוֹג, *maw-gogue'*, Magog), son of Japhet (Gen. x:2).
In Ezekiel (xxxviii:2; xxxix:6 it occurs as the name of a nation, coupled with Gog, and is supposed to represent certain Scythian or Tartar tribes descended from the son of Japhet. (See NATIONS, DISPERSION OF.)
Gog and Magog have in a manner passed into a proverb, to express a multitude of powerful, cruel, barbarous and implacable enemies to God and his worship. (See GOG.)

MAGOR-MISSABIB (mā'gor-mĭs'sa-bĭb), (Heb. מָגוֹר מִסָּבִיב, *maw-gore' mis-saw-beeb'*, "a terror on every side"), a name given to Pashur, who abused Jeremiah (Jer. xx:3).

MAGPIASH (măg'pi-ăsh), (Heb. מַגְפִּיעָשׁ, *mag-pee-awsh'*, moth-killer).
One of the chiefs of the people who joined in the sacred covenant with Nehemiah (Neh. x:20). (B. C. about 410.)

MAHALAH (ma-hā'lah or mā'ha-lah), (Heb. מַחְלָה, *makh-law'*, sickness, 1 Chron. vii:18). See MAHLAH, 1.

MAHALALEEL (ma-hā'la-lē'el), (Heb. מַהֲלַלְאֵל, *mah-hal-al-ale'*, praise of God).
1. Son of Canaan; fourth in descent from Adam, according to the Sethite genealogy (Gen. v:12, 13, 15-17; 1 Chron. i:2). (B. C. 3777-2881.)
2. A man of Judah, of the family of Pharez; he was father of Shephatiah and resided in Jerusalem after the captivity. (B. C. before 536.)

MAHALATH (mā'ha-lath), (Heb. מַחֲלַת, *makh-al-ath'*, harp, lyre).

1. A daughter of Ishmael and a wife of Esau (Gen. xxviii:9); also called Bashemath (Gen. xxxvi:3).

2. Daughter of Jerimoth, granddaughter of David, and probably the first of the eighteen wives of king Rehoboam (2 Chron. xi:18). (B. C. 934.)

3. The title of Psalms liii and lxxxviii indicating, perhaps, the manner in which it was to be sung.

MAHALI (mā'ha-lī), (Heb. מַחְלִי, *makh-lee*, sick, infirm, Ex. vi:19). See MAHLI.

MAHANAIM (mā'ha-nā'im),(Heb. מַחֲנַיִם,*makh-an-ah'yim*, two hosts).

A place beyond the Jordan, north of the river Jabbok, which derived its name from Jacob's having been there met by the angels on his return from Padan-aram (Gen. xxxii:2).

The name was eventually extended to the town which then existed, or which afterwards arose in the neighborhood. This town was in the territory of the tribe of Gad (Josh. xiii:26, 30), and was a city of the Levites (Josh. xxi:38). It was in this city that Ish-bosheth, the son of Saul, reigned (2 Sam. ii:8), probably because he found the influence of David's name less strong on the east than on the west of the Jordan. The choice, at least, seems to show that Mahanaim was then an important and strong place. Hence, many years after, David himself repaired to Mahanaim when he sought refuge beyond the Jordan from his son Absalom (2 Sam. xvii:24, 27; 1 Kings ii:8). We only read of Mahanaim again as the station of one of the twelve officers who had charge, in monthly rotation, of raising the provisions for the royal establishments under Solomon (1 Kings iv:14). The site has not yet been identified.

MAHANEH - DAN (mā'ha - neh - dăn), (Heb. מַחֲנֵה־דָן, *makh-an-ay'dawn*).

A place west of Kirjath-jearim where the Danite warriors encamped before they captured Laish (Judg. xviii:12).

MAHARAI (ma-hăr'a-ī), (Heb. מַהְרַי, *mah-har-ah'ee*, hasty, swift).

A Netophathite, one of David's captains from the tribe of Judah (2 Sam. xxiii:28; 1 Chron. xi:30; xxvii:13), B. C. 1014.

MAHATH (mā'hath), (Heb. מַחַת, *makh'ath*, fire-pan, censer).

1. A Kohathite, son of Amasai (1 Chron. vi: 35); apparently the same as Ahimoth (1 Chron. vi:25). (B. C. about 1375.)

2. Another Kohathite Levite in the time of Hezekiah (2 Chron. xxix:12; xxxi:13). He looked after the tithes and offerings (2 Chron. xxxi: 13). (B. C. 726.)

MAHAVITE, THE (mā'ha-vīte), (Heb. מַחֲוִים, *makh-av-eem'*, "the Machavites"), a designation of unknown import applied to one of King David's guard, probably Eliel. The plural is no doubt a corruption (1 Chron. xi:46).

MAHAZIOTH (ma-hā'zi-ŏth), (Heb. מַחֲזִיאוֹת, *makh-az-ee-oth'*, visions), the fourteenth son of Homan, and a Levite musician in the Temple, having charge of the twenty-third division (1 Chron. xxv:4, 30). B, C, 1014.

MAHERSHALALHASHBAZ (mā'her-shăl'al-hăsh'băz), (Heb. מַהֵר שָׁלָל חָשׁ בַּז, *mah-hare'shaw-lawl'khawsh-baz*).

Words prognostic of the sudden attack of the Assyrian army ('he hasteth to the spoil'), which the prophet Isaiah was first commanded to write in large characters upon a tablet, and afterwards to give as a symbolical name to a son that was to be born to him (Is. viii:1, 3). It is, as Dr. Henderson remarks, the longest of any of the scripture names, but has its parallels in this respect in other languages, especially in the English language during the time of Cromwell. Mahershalalhashbaz lived B. C. 739.

MAHLAH (măh'lah), (Heb. מַחְלָה, *makh-law'*).

1. A child of Hamoleketh, a female descendant of Manasseh (1 Chron. vii:18). (B. C. about 1658.) (See MAHALAH.)

2. The first named of the daughters of Zelophehad, of Manasseh (Num. xxvi:33; xxvii:1; xxxvi:11; Josh. xvii:3). (B. C. 1618.)

MAHLI (măh'lī), (Heb. מַחְלִי, *makh-lee'*, sickly, pining).

1. A Levite, son of Merari (Num. iii:20; 1 Chron. vi:19, 29; xxiii:21; xxiv:26; Ezra viii: 18), called Mahali (Exod. vi:19).

2. A Levite, son of Mushi, of the family of Merari; nephew of **1** (1 Chron. vi:47; xxiii: 23; xxiv:30). (B. C. before 1210.)

MAHLITES, THE (măh'lītes), (Heb. מַחְלִי, *makh-lee'*, descendants of Mahli, Num. iii:33; xxvi:58).

MAHLON (măh'lon), (Heb. מַחְלוֹן, *makh-lone'*, pining).

One of the two sons of Elimelech and Naomi, and first husband of Ruth the Moabitess (Ruth i:2, *sq.*). (See RUTH.) (B. C. about 1360.)

MAHOL (mā'hŏl), (Heb. מָחוֹל, *maw-khole'*, a dance).

Father of the four men of fame next to Solomon for wisdom, viz.:—Ethan, Heman, Chalcol, and Darda (1 Kings iv:31). If, however, these are the same as the sons of Zera (1 Chron. ii: 6) the word probably denotes only their pursuit of musical composition.

MAID, MAIDEN (mād, mād''n), the rendering of several Hebrew and Greek words, differing in meaning beyond the mere matter of sex:

1. *Nek-ay-baw'* (Heb. נְקֵבָה, Lev. xii:5 only, a *maid child*), a female from the sexual form. Similar in meaning is *nah-ar-aw'* (Heb. נַעֲרָה, 2 Kings v:2, 4; Ezra ii:4, 9, 13; Prov. ix:3), corresponding to *pahee-dis'kay* (Gr. παιδίσκη, Mark xiv:66; Luke xxii:56), a *girl* from infancy to adolescence.

2. *Beth-oo-law'* (Heb. בְּתוּלָה, Exod. xxii: 16; Judg. xix:24; Job xxxi:1; Ps. lxxviii:63; Jer. ii:32; li:22), a *virgin,* from the idea of *separation.* Similarly *al-maw'* (Heb. עַלְמָה, *veiled,* kept out of *sight,* Exod. ii:8).

3. *Aw-maw'* (Heb. אָמָה, Gen. xxx:3; Exod. xxi:20; Lev. xxv:6, etc.); *shif-khaw'* (Heb. שִׁפְחָה, Gen. xxx:7, *sq.;* Ps. cxxiii:2; Is. xxiv: 2), a *maidservant.* (Barnes *Bib. Dict.*). See VIRGIN.

MAIL, COAT OF. See ARMS, ARMOR.

MAIMED (māmd), (from Heb. חָרַץ, *khaw'rats*, to *wound*, Lev. xxii:22; Gr. κυλλός, *kool-los'*, *rocking about*, Matt. xv:30, 31; xviii:8; Mark ix:43; ἀνάπηρος, *an-ap'ay-ros*, *crippled*, Luke xiv:13, 21), wanting some member of the body or incapacitated from its use by injury.

MAINSAIL (mān-sāl), (Acts xxvii:40.) See SHIP.

MAKAZ (mā'kăz), (Heb. מָקַץ, *maw-kats'*, end).

A district of Ben-Dekar, a purveyor of Solomon, whence he obtained supplies (1 Kings iv: 9). It was probably in Dan; but otherwise unlocated.

MAKE (māk), (Heb. בָּנָה, *baw-naw'*, to build, build up), has the sense of "do," "be occupied with,"—"What *makest* thou in this place" (Judg. xviii:3). The use also of "make" as signifying "pretend," "feign" (Josh. viii:15; ix:4; 2 Sam. xiii: 6; Luke xxiv:28).

1. In general to cause a thing to be that did not before exist; so God at first made all things (Gen. i:31).

2. To put persons or things into such a form, office, or condition as they were not in before (Is. xlv:9).

MAKER (māk'ēr), (Heb. עָשָׂה, *aw-saw'*, to *make* in the widest sense; once only, in Job xxxvi:3, פָּעַל, *paw-al'*, to *do* and so *make;* also צָר, *yaw-tsar'*, to *mold*), a term generally applied to God as creator (Job iv:17; xxxvi:3; Ps. xcv:6; Prov. xxii:2; Is. xvii:7, etc.; Hos. viii:14). It is used of *man* in Is. xxii:11 and Hab. ii:18.

MAKHELOTH (mak-hē'loth), (Heb. מַקְהֵלֹת, *mak-hay-loth'*), the twenty-sixth desert encampment of the Israelites, of which the site is unknown (Num. xxxiii:25).

MAKKEDAH (măk-kē'dah), (Heb. מַקֵּדָה, *mak-kay-daw'*, herdsman's place).

A royal city of the ancient Canaanites (Josh. xii:16), in the neighborhood of which was the cave in which the five kings who confederated against Israel took refuge after their defeat (Josh. x:10-29). It afterwards belonged to Judah (Josh. xv:41). Makkedah is placed by Eusebius and Jerome 8 Roman miles to the east of Eleutheropolis (*Onomast.* s. v. Maceda).

MAKTESH (măk'tesh), (Heb. מַכְתֵּשׁ, *mak-taysh'*; depression).

The name of a quarter or district in or near Jerusalem, perhaps one of the adjacent valleys Zeph. i:11), either Kidron or the one separating the Temple from the city.

MALACHI (măl'a-kī), (Heb. מַלְאָכִי, *mal-aw-kee'*; Sept. Μαλαχίας, *mal-ah-kee'as*).

The last of the minor prophets, and consequently the latest writer in the canon of the Old Testament. Nothing is known of his person or history. It appears that he lived after Zechariah, since in his time the second temple was already built (ch. iii:10); and it is probable that he was contemporary with Nehemiah (comp. ch. ii:11, with Neh. xiii:23-27, and ch. iii:8, with Neh. xiii:10).

(1) Meaning of Name. The name Malachi means, as some understand it, *my angel;* but it seems more correct to regard it as a contracted form of the Hebrew, *angel of Jehovah.* As the word translated 'angel,' however, means also a 'messenger,' angels being, in fact, the messengers of God; and as the prophets are often styled angels or messengers of Jehovah, it is supposed that 'Malachi' is merely a general title descriptive of this character, and not a proper name. It has been very generally supposed that it denotes Ezra, but the weight of opinion is against this.

(2) Date of Prophecy. Although it is well agreed that Malachi was the last of the prophets, the date of his prophecy has been variously determined. Usher makes him contemporary with Nehemiah, in B. C. 416; and the general opinion that this prophet was contemporary with, or immediately followed, Nehemiah, makes most of the proposed alternatives range within a few years of that date.

(3) Character of Prophecy. He censures the same offenses which excited the indignation of Nehemiah, and which that governor had not been able entirely to reform. Speaking of God's greater kindness to the Israelites than to the Edomites, he begins with declaiming against the priests for their profane and mercenary conduct, and against the people for their multiplied divorces and intermarriages with idolatrous nations; he threatens them with punishment and rejection, declaring that God would 'make his name great among the Gentiles' (ch. i:11), for that he was wearied with the impiety of Israel (ch. i, ii). From this the prophet takes occasion solemnly to proclaim that the Lord whom they sought should suddenly come to his temple, preceded by that messenger who, like a harbinger, should prepare his way; that the Lord when he should appear would purify the sons of Levi from their unrighteousness, and refine them as metal from the dross (ch. iii:1-3); that then 'the offering of Judah,' the spiritual sacrifice of the heart, 'should be pleasant to the Lord,' as was that of the patriarchs and their uncorrupted ancestors (ch. iii:4); and that the Lord would quickly exterminate the corruptions and adulteries which prevailed. The prophet then proceeds with an earnest exhortation to repentance; promising high rewards and remembrance to the righteous in that last day when the Lord shall make up his peculiar treasures, and finally establish a distinction of doom and condition between the righteous and the wicked (ch. iii:16-18), Malachi then concludes with an impressive assurance of approaching salvation to those who feared God's name from that 'Sun of Righteousness,' who should arise with healing in his wings, and render them triumphant; enjoining in the solemn close of his exhortation, when uttering as it were the last admonition of the Jewish prophets, an observance of the law of Moses, till the advent of Elijah the prophet (ch. iv:5, or John the Baptist, who came in the spirit and power of Elias, Mark ix:12; Luke i: 17), who before the coming of that 'great and dreadful day of the Lord, should turn the hearts of the fathers to the children, and the heart of the children to their fathers' (ch. iv.). Thus Malachi sealed up the volume of prophecy with the description of that personage at whose appearance the Evangelists begin their gospel history.

(4) Canonicity. The claim of the book of Malachi to its place in the canon of the Old Testament has never been disputed; and its authority is established by the references to it in the New Testament (Matt. xi:10; xvii:12; Mark i:2; ix: 11, 12; Luke i:17; Rom. ix:13).

(5) Style. The manner of Malachi offers few, if any, distinguishing characteristics. The style, rhythm, and imagery of his writings are substantially those of the old prophets, but they possess no remarkable vigor or beauty. This is accounted for by his living during that decline of Hebrew poetry, which we trace more or less in all the sacred writings posterior to the Captivity.

The principal separate works on the subject are: Chytræus, *Explicat. Malach. Prophet.* Rost. 1568; Grynæus, *Hypomnemata in Malach.* Frcf. 1652; Stock, *Commentary upon the whole Prophesye of Malachy,* Lond. 1641; Schlater, *A Brief and Plain Commentary upon the whole Prophecie of Malachy,* Lond. 1650; Ursinus, *Comment. in Malach.* Frcf. 1652; Sal. van Til, *Malach. illustratus,* Lug. Bat. 1701; Wesselius, *Malachias enucleatus,* Lubeck, 1729; *Malachia Propheta c. Turgum Jonathis et Radaki Raschii ac Aben-Esræ Comment. et Interpret.* J. C. Hebenstreit, Lips. 1746; Venema, *Comment. in Malach.* Leovard. 1759; Bahrdt, *Comment. in Malachiam, c. examine verss. vett. et lectt. variant Houbigantii,* Lips. 1768; J. M. Faber, *Comment. in Malachiam,* Onold. 1779; J. F. Fischer, *Observatt. Crit. in Malachiam,* Lips. 1759; J. M. Faber, *Abweischungen der alten Uebersetzer d. Propheten Malachias,* in Eichhorn's *Repert.* vi, 104-124; Moore, *Commentary,* N. Y., 1865; J. Pye Smith, *Scripture Testimony to the Messiah;* Noyes, *Comment.;* Cowles, *Comment.*

MALCHAM (măl'kam), (Heb. מַלְכָּם, *mal-kawm',* thinking), fourth of the seven sons of Shaharaim, by Hodesh (1 Chron. viii:9). B. C. 1612.

MALCHIAH (mal-kī'ah), (Heb. מַלְכִּיָּה, *mal-khee-yaw',* Jehovah's king, i. e., inaugurated by him).

1. A Levite, son of Ethni; one of the ancestors of Asaph, the minstrel (1 Chron. vi:40). (B. C. before 1014.)

2. Two residents, or sons, of Parosh, who divorced their Gentile wives after the exile (Ezra x:25). (B. C. 459.)

3. A resident or son of Harim who assisted in the rebuilding of the walls of Jerusalem (Neh. iii:11), and obeyed Ezra in divorcing his foreign wife (Ezra x:31). (B. C. 459.)

4. Son of Rechab, who assisted in repairing the Dung-gate of Jerusalem after the exile (Neh. iii:14). (B. C. 446.)

5. One of those who assisted Nehemiah in rebuilding the wall of Jerusalem. He was called "the goldsmith's son" (Neh. iii:31). (B. C. 446.)

6. One of those who stood on Ezra's left while he read the law to the people (Neh. viii:4); probably the same as the priest of that name who sealed the covenant with Nehemiah (Neh. x:3). (B. C. about 410.)

7. A priest, father of Pashur (Neh. xi:12; Jer. xxxviii:1). The form is Melchiah (Jer. xxi:1); elsewhere MALCHIJAH (which see).

8. Son of Ham-melech (Jer. xxxviii:6). Hammelech is translated 'king's son' (2 Chron. xxviii: 7; 1 Kings xxii:26), which often means simply an officer of some sort. (B. C. 589.) Perhaps he is identical with MALCHIJAH, 1.

MALCHIEL (măl'ki'el), (Heb. מַלְכִּיאֵל, *mal-kee-ale',* God's king, i. e., appointed by him).

The son of Beriah, son of Ashur (Gen. xlvi: 17). He became the "father," or founder of Birzavith (1 Chron. vii:31), and a tribal family (Num. xxvi:45). (B. C. 1856.)

MALCHIELITE (măl'ki-el-īte), (Heb. מַלְכִּיאֵל, *mal-kee-ay-lee'),* a descendant of Malchiel (Num. xxvi:45).

MALCHIJAH (mal-kī'jah), (Heb. מַלְכִּיָּה, *mal-kee-yaw',* Jehovah's king).

1. Father of Pashur (1 Chron. ix:12); the same as MALCHIAH, 7. (B. C. before 589.)

2. A priest, who had charge of the fifth course as appointed by David (1 Chron. xxiv:9). (B. C. 1014.)

3. An Israelite layman of Parosh who divorced his Gentile wife (Ezra x:25). (B. C. 459.)

4. (Neh. iii:11). See MALCHIAH, 3.

5. (Neh. x:3). See MALCHIAH, 6.

6. A priest among the musicians appointed to assist in the ceremonies in celebration of the completion of the walls of Jerusalem (Neh. xii: 42). (B. C. 446.)

MALCHIRAM (mal-kī'ram), (Heb. מַלְכִּירָם, *mal-kee-rawm',* king of exaltation).

A son of Jeconiah or Jehoiachim (1 Chron. iii:18). (B. C. after 598.)

MALCHISHUA (măl'ki-shụ'à), (Heb. מַלְכִּי־שׁוּעַ, *mal-kee-shoo'ah,* king of help).

A son of king Saul (1 Chron. viii:33; ix:39; 1 Sam. xiv:49), killed in the battle of Gilboa (1 Sam. xxxi:2; 1 Chron. x:2). (B. C. 1053.)

MALCHUS (măl'kus), (Gr. Μάλχος, *mal'khos).*

The servant of the high-priest Caiaphas, whose right ear was cut off by Peter in the garden of Gethsemane (John xviii:10). The name is from the Hebrew *melech,* and corresponds to our title 'king,' or *mallauch,* 'counsellor.'

MALE (māl), (Heb. זָכָר, *zaw-kawr',* remembered, Gen. i:27; vi:19; xxxiv:25), applied to the male of either man or beast.

MALEFACTOR (măl'ĕ-făk'tēr), the translation of two Greek words (κακοποιός, *kak-op-oy-os',* John xviii:30; *evildoers* in 1 Peter ii:12, 14; iii:16; iv:15; and κακοῦργος, *kak-oor'gos,* Luke xxiii:32, *sq.; evildoer* in 2 Tim. ii:9). By the term malefactor is not meant, strictly speaking, thieves or robbers, but insurgents or rebels. (See THIEF, PENITENT, ON THE CROSS.)

MALELEEL (ma-lē'le-el), (Gr. Μαλελεήλ, *mal-el-e-ale',* Luke iii:37). See MAHALALEEL.

MALICE (măl'ĭs), (Gr. κακία, *kak-ee'ah,* badness, 1 Cor. v:8; xiv:20; Eph. iv:31; Col. iii:8; Tit. 3:3; 1 Peter ii:1; *maliciousness,* Rom. i:29; 1 Peter ii:16; *malicious,* from Gr. πονηρός, *pon-ay-ros',* hurtful, 3 John 10), "wicked works."

It denotes in general violent hatred, disposing us to render evil for good, and embraces both Malevolence and Malignity. The three may be discriminated as follows: *Malevolence* has a deep root in the heart, and is a settled part of the character; we denominate the person *malevolent,* to designate the ruling temper of his mind: *maliciousness* may be applied as an epithet to particular parts of a man's character or conduct; one may have a *malicious* joy or pleasure in seeing the distresses of another: *malignity* is not so often employed to characterize the person as the thing; the *malignity* of a design is estimated by the degree of mischief which was intended to be done. (Crabbe's *Synonyms.)*

MALIGNITY (mă-lĭg'nĭ-tў), (Gr. κακοήθεια, *kak-ŏ-ay'thi-ah),* bad character, depravity of heart; used in Rom. i:29 for *malignant subtlety, malicious craftiness.* (See MALICE.)

MALLOTHI (măl'lo-thī), (Heb. מַלּוֹתִי, *mal-lo'-thee,* Jah is speaking or splendid).

One of the fourteen sons of Heman (1 Chron. xxv:4); head of the nineteenth course of musicians, as arranged by David (1 Chron. xxv:26). (B. C. 1014.)

MALLOWS (măl'lŏz), (Heb. מַלּוּחַ, *mal-loo'akh*, saltwort; Gr. ἅλιμα, salted, Job xxx:4 only).

Bochart contends (*Hieroz*, part i, t. iii, c. 16) that the word *malluach* denotes a saltish plant called *ah-lee-mos'* by the Greeks, and which with good reason is supposed to be the *Atriplex Halimus* of botanists, or tall shrubby *Orache*. There is no doubt that species of *Orache* were used as articles of diet in ancient times, and, probably, still are so in the countries where they are indigenous; but there are many other plants, similar in nature, that is, soft and succulent, and usually very saline, such as the *Salsolas*, *Salicornias*, etc., which, like the species of *Atriplex*, belong to the same natural family of *Chenopodeæ*, and which from their saline nature have received their respective names. Some of these are shrubby, but most of them are herbaceous, and extremely common in all the dry, desert, and saline soils which extend from the south of Europe to the north of India. Most of them are saline and bitter, but some are milder in taste and mucilaginous, and are therefore employed as articles of diet, as spinach is in Europe. *Salsola indica*, for instance, which is common on the coasts of the Peninsula of India, Dr. Roxburgh states, saved the lives of many thousands of the poor natives of India during the famine of 1791-2-3; for while the plant lasted, most of the poorer classes who lived near the sea had little else to eat; and indeed its green leaves ordinarily form an essential article of the food of those natives who inhabit the maritime districts.   J. F. R.

MALLUCH (măl'luk), (Heb. מַלּוּךְ, *mal-luke'*, ruler or counselor).

1. A Levite of Merari, son of Hashabiah (1 Chron. vi:44). (B. C. before 1014.)

2. A descendant, or resident of Bani, who divorced his Gentile wife after the exile (Ezra x: 29). (B. C. 459.)

3. A descendant, or son, of Harim, who also put away his foreign wife (Ezra x:32). (B. C. 459.)

4. A priest who returned from the captivity with Zerubbabel (Neh. xii:2), and perhaps identical with the one who signed the covenant in Nehemiah's reign (Neh. x:4). (B. C. between 536 and 410.)

5. One of the chief Israelites who signed the covenant with Nehemiah (Neh. x:27). (B. C. 445.)

6. One of the families of priests who returned from captivity with Zerubbabel (Neh. xii:2), B. C. 536. Perhaps identical with (4).

MAMMON (măm'mŭn), (Gr. μαμμωνᾶς, *mam-mo-nas'*).

A Chaldee word signifying 'wealth' or 'riches,' and bearing that sense in Luke xvi:9, 11; but also used by our Savior (Matt. vi:24; Luke xvi:13) as a personification of the god of riches: 'Ye cannot serve God and Mammon.' "Make to yourselves friends of the mammon of unrighteousness, that, when these riches fail, they may receive you into everlasting habitations:" that is, spend worldly riches, which so many get unjustly, and use as instruments of dishonesty and wickedness, in a pious and charitable manner, that the poor saints, benefited thereby, may be stirred up to pray for you; and that when your riches are no more retained by you, ye may obtain the gracious reward of your charity in heaven; and those poor saints whom you have supported, may with pleas-

ure welcome you into the celestial abodes (Luke xvi:13). (Brown's *Bib. Dict.*)

MAMRE (măm're), (Heb. מַמְרֵא, *mam-ray'*).

1. The name of an Amoritish chief who, with his brothers Aner and Eshcol, was in alliance with Abraham (Gen. xiv:13, 24). (B. C. about 2250.)

2. In the A. V. 'The oaks of Mamre,' 'plain of Mamre' (Gen. xiii:18; xviii:1), or simply 'Mamre' (xxiii:17, 19; xxxv:27), a grove in the neighborhood of Hebron.

Here Abraham dwelt after separating from Lot (Gen. xiii:18), and near by was the cave of Macphelah (Gen. xxiii:17; 19; xxv:9). The spot is still marked by the remains of a building which once, it is said, inclosed the trunk of 'Abraham's tree.' It is about a mile northwest of Hebron. (See Porter, *Handbook*, i, 70.)

MAN (măn). Four Hebrew words are thus translated in the English Version: אָדָם, *aw-dawm'*; אִישׁ, *eesh*; אֱנוֹשׁ, *en-oshe'*; גֶּבֶר, *gheh'ber*.

1. The proper name of the first man, though Gesenius thinks that when so applied it has the force rather of an appellative, and that, accordingly, in a translation, it would be better to render it *the man*. It seems, however, to be used by St. Luke as a proper name in the genealogy (iii: 38); by St. Paul (Rom. v:14; 1 Tim. ii:13, 14); and by Jude (14). St. Paul's use of it in 1 Cor. xv:45 is remarkably clear: 'the first man, Adam.' This derivation is as old as Josephus, who says that 'the first man was called Adam, because he was formed from the red earth,' and adds, 'for the true virgin earth is of this color' (*Antiq.* i, 1, sec. 2).

The truer origin of the word in Gen. i:26; v: 1, is *likeness*, because man was made *in the likeness of God*.

2. It is the generic name of the human race as originally created, and afterwards, like the English word man, person, whether man or woman, equivalent to the Latin *homo*, and Gr. *an-thro-pos*, ἄνθρωπος, (Gen. i:26, 27; v:2; viii: 21; Deut. viii:3; Matt. v:13, 16; 1 Cor. vii:26), and even without regard to age (John xvi:21). It is applied to women only, 'the *human* persons or women' (Num. xxxi:35).

3. It denotes man in opposition to woman (Gen. iii:12; Matt. xix:10), though, more properly, the husband in opposition to the wife (comp. 1 Cor. vii:1).

4. It is used, though very rarely, for those who maintain the dignity of human nature, a *man*, as we say, meaning one that deserves the name, like the Latin *vir* and Greek ἀνήρ, *an'are*, hero: 'One man in a thousand have I found, but a woman,' etc. (Eccles. vii:28.) Perhaps the word here glances at the original uprightness of man.

5. It is frequently used to denote the more degenerate and wicked portion of mankind: an instance of which occurs very early, 'The sons, or worshipers, of God married the daughters of men, or the irreligious' (Gen. vi:2).

6. The word is used to denote other men, in opposition to those already named, as, 'both upon Israel and other men' (Jer. xxxii:20), *i. e.* the Egyptians. 'Like other men' (Ps. lxxiii:5) *i. e.*, common men, in opposition to better men (Ps. lxxxii:7); men of inferior rank, as opposed to men of higher rank. (See Heb. Is. ii:9; v:15; Ps. xlix:3; lxii:10; Prov. viii:4).

7. The phrase 'son of man,' in the Old Testament, denotes man as frail and unworthy (Num.

xxiii:19; Job xxv:6; Ezek. ii:1, 3); as applied to the prophet, so often, it has the force of 'oh mortal!' *Eesh* is a man in the distinguished sense, like the Latin *vir*, and Greek ἀνήρ, 'an *heroic* man.'

8. It is used in all the several senses of the Latin *vir*, and denotes a man as distinguished from a woman (1 Sam. xvii:33; Matt. xiv:21); as a husband (Gen. iii:16; Hos. ii:16); and in reference to excellent mental qualities. A beautiful instance of the latter class occurs in Jer. v:1.

9. It is also used to designate the superior classes (Prov. viii:4; Ps. cxli:4, etc.), a courtier (Jer. xxxviii:7), the male of animals (Gen. vii: 2). Sometimes it means men in general (Exod. xvi:29; Mark vi:44).

10. *Enoshe* denotes *mortals,* as transient, perishable, liable to sickness, etc.: 'Let no man [margin, 'mortal man'] prevail against thee' (2 Chron. xiv:11). 'Write with the pen of the common man' (Is. viii:1), *i. e.* in a common, legible character (Job xv:14; Ps. viii:4; ix:19, 20; Is. li:7; Ps. ciii:15). It is applied to women (Josh. viii:25); *gheh-ber', vir,* man, in regard to strength, etc.

11. It is applied to man as distinguished from woman: 'A man shall not put on a woman's garment' (Deut. xxii:5), like ἀνθρωπος (*male*), in Matt. viii:9; John i:6; to men as distinguished from children (Exod. xii:37); to a male child, in opposition to a female (Job iii:3; Sept. ἀρσεν, *male child*). It is much used in poetry: 'Happy is the man' (Ps. xxxiv:8; xl:4; lii:9; xciv:12). Sometimes it denotes the species at large (Job iv:17; xiv:10, 14).

12. Thus man is also the rendering of the Gr. μηδεις (*may-dice', not one,* Matt. xvi:20; xvii:9; Luke x:4, etc.; of οὐδεις, *oo-dice', none, nobody,* Matt. xi: 27; Mark iii:27; Luke viii:51, etc.; of τις, *tis, some one* or *any,* Matt. xxiv:4; John iii:5; Acts x:47, etc.); and in an inclusive sense πᾶς, (*pas, all,* Rom. ii:10). (See ADAM.)

Common Origin of Man. Scientists are divided into two schools on this subject, namely, Polygenists, or those who say there are more than one species, and monogenists, or those who contend for the unity of the human species. Men of unquestioned scientific repute and ability are found on both sides of the question. Among Polygenists such scholars as Kant, Buffon, Desmoulins, Haeckel, Friedrich Müller, Louis Agassiz, and Peschal; and among monogenists are Blumenbach, Prichard, De Quatrefages, Cuvier, Max Müller, Prof. Owen and Charles Darwin.

The weight of evidence seems clearly to be on the side of the monogenists.

This view is contended for in this article.

To be plain it is very important that the definition of the word species should be understood—for the solution of the whole problem hinges on the meaning of that word.

M. A. de Quatrefages gives the most concise and satisfactory definition of the word "species," as the word is used in reference to vegetables and animals, when he says "The species includes all more or less similar individuals which descend, or may be supposed to descend from a single ancestral pair in unbroken succession" (*Unité de l'Espice Humaine,* p. 54). This definition when applied to a consideration of men allows room for those variations among them resulting in what are called the races of Caucasians, Mongolians, Red Men, Malays and Negroes.

With "species" defined we are prepared to consider briefly the arguments in favor of all men of all races having descended from one ancestral pair.

(1) The first argument is rooted in the facts concerning the habitat of men.

It would militate against the unity of human species were it true that one race of men could live only on a certain section of the globe.

The fact is if the transition is not made too suddenly, and proper precautions are taken, men of any nation can live in the region inhabited by any other nation.

The Chinese illustrate this, for they live on the border of Siberia and are also found on the Island of Singapore almost on the Equator.

(2) The unity of the languages of men in their primitive condition as exhibited in the identity of the roots of many words still in use among the scattered nations.

Max Müller shows by the phenomena of the three great classes of language that it is highly probable that they were originally one. Such eminent philologists as Bopp, Grimm, Klaproth, and Herder agree in this main proposition.

(3) Community of traditions among different and widely separated peoples, such as The Creation of Man; The Garden of Eden or its counterpart; man's temptation and fall; the division of time into weeks; the destruction of man by a deluge; and similar traditions are found to be current among people as widely separated in color, location, and everything else as the Dyaks of Borneo and the North American tribes of Indians.

(4) Another argument quite similar to traditions is that of a community of customs, such as sacrifices to supernatural beings—known to have been offered in all parts of the earth and by all people. Serpent worship in Asia, Africa, Europe and America. Peschal (*Races of Man*, p. 21, *sq.*) calls attention to the following customs: Almost all nations have arrived at a single and double decimal system in mathematics; skin painting, and tattooing; filing the teeth to a point occurs not only in western Africa but in Brazil. The skulls of children have been pressed between boards not only on the steppes of southern Russia but also by the aborigines of South America, by the Tshinuks of British Columbia and by the Flathead tribe of Indians in North America. Many nations have practiced circumcision—the Egyptians, Ethiopians, Hebrews, Phœnicians and tribes of Indians in South America. Greeting by rubbing noses by Eskimos and by aboriginal Australians.

Another custom has extended all over the world —namely, the building of cairns or piles of stones which grow by having additional stones thrown on them by every passer-by. They may be seen in India, Burmah, Borneo, Thibet, the Sinaitic Peninsula, Switzerland and Venezuela.

(5) All men have the same number and kind of bodily organs. The natural position of man is erect. All the nerves, muscles, bones, veins and arteries found in any man of any race are found in every other man of every race regardless of the color of complexion, the character of the hair or the degree of intelligence or culture.

The physical evidence of unity of human species which is most interesting and significant is the prevalence among men of that general law, which runs through the whole of both the vegetable and animal kingdoms, namely, the infertility of hybrids or members of different species, and the fecundity of members of the same species.

Applying this law to the case of men, observation and experiment show that the intermarriage of individuals of different races of men does not reveal sterility but the opposite.

No two races of men exist who cannot intermarry. This would not be true if the different races of men were different species of beings.

(6) The similarity of mental and moral faculties and habits is marked. Intellect, emotion and will, the mental nature of every Caucasian. The same is true of every Mongolian, every Ethiopian, every Malay and every red man. All men have conscience whereby they are sensible of right or wrong.

There are to sum up, then, varieties of men, but all men belong to one species of beings.

If all men are of the same species of being then the brotherhood of man follows. When that is appreciated slavery is not to be thought of. Yet again if all men belong to one species and not to many, then the voice of science harmonizes with that of religion, which proclaims (Gen. iii: 20), "Adam called his wife's name Eve; because she was the mother of all living;" and Mars Hill catches up the proclamation, as Paul stands and says more confidently than science can yet say: "God . . . hath made of one blood all nations of men for to dwell on all the face of the earth" (Acts xvii:24-26). (See *Common Origin of Man* by Rev. Edward M. Deems, A. M., in *Christian Thought*, April 1892, p. 378.)

MANAEN (măn'a-ĕn), (Gr. Μαναήν, man-ah-ane').

A Christian teacher at Antioch (A. D. 44), who had been foster-brother of Herod Antipas (Acts xiii:1). He is supposed to have been one of the seventy disciples, but this is uncertain, as no particulars of his life are known.

MANAHATH (măn'a-hăth), (Heb. מָנַחַת, maw-nakh'ath).

1. A place named in connection with the genealogies of Benjamin (1 Chron. viii:6), whither the Benjamites of Geba, descendants of Ehud, seem to have migrated. The posterity of Salma, of Judah, probably made up half the population (1 Chron. ii:54).

2. Second of the five sons of Shobal, a descendant of Seir, the Horite (Gen. xxxvi:23; 1 Chron. i:40). (B. C. about 1850.)

MANAHETHITES, THE (ma-nā'heth-ītes), (Heb. הַמְּנֻחוֹת, ham-men-oo-khoth', and הַמַּנַחְתִּי, ham-maw-nakh-tee', Manahathites).

The inhabitants of a place, half of whom were descended from Selma, founder of Bethlehem, and half from Shobal, father of Kirjath-jearim (1 Chron. ii:52, 54).

MANASSEH (ma-năs'seh), (Heb. מְנַשֶּׁה, men-ash-sheh', who makes forget, see Gen. xli:51).

1. The Patriarch. The elder of the two sons of Joseph, born in Egypt (Gen. xli:51; xlvi: 20) whom Jacob adopted as his own (xlviii:1) —by which act each became the head of a tribe in Israel. The act of adoption was, however, accompanied by a clear intimation from Jacob, that the descendants of Manasseh, although the elder, would be far less numerous and powerful than those of the younger Ephraim. The result corresponded remarkably with this intimation. (See EPHRAIM.)

2. The Fourteenth King of Judah, son and successor of Hezekiah, who began to reign in B. C. 699, at the early age of twelve years, and reigned fifty-five years.

(1) **Re-established Idolatry.** It appears that the secret enemies of the vigorous reforms of

Hezekiah reappeared, and managed to gain much influence at court during the youth of Manasseh; and he was prevailed upon to reëstablish all the idolatries and abominations which it had taken his excellent father so much pains to subvert. This bent having been unhappily given to the mind of one old enough to listen to evil counsels, but too young to see their danger, the king followed it with all the reckless ardor of youth, and without any of the prudent reservations which older sovereigns, more discreet in evincing the same inclinations, had maintained. Idolatry in its worst forms, and all the abominations connected with its observances, were practiced without stint and without shame, not only in the face of the Temple, but in its very courts, where altars to the heavenly bodies were set up, and rites of idolatrous worship performed. Under this altered state of things, the Judahites, with the sanction of the king's example, rushed into all the more odious observances of Syrian idolatry, with all the ardor which usually attends the outbreak of a restrained propensity, till they became far 'worse than the heathen, whom the Lord destroyed before the children of Israel.' In vain did the prophets raise their voice against these iniquities, and threaten Manasseh and his kingdom with awful tokens of Divine indignation. Instead of profiting by these warnings, the king vented his rage against those by whom they were uttered, and in this, and other ways, filled Jerusalem with innocent blood beyond any king who reigned before him (2 Kings xxi:1-16; 2 Chron. xxxiii:1-10).

(2) **Retribution.** At length the wrath of God burst over the guilty king and nation. At this time there was constant war between Assyria and Egypt, and it would seem that Manasseh adhered to the policy of his father in making common cause with the latter power. This, or some other cause not stated by the sacred historian, brought into Judæa an Assyrian army, under the generals of Esar-haddon, which carried all before it. The miserable king attempted flight, but was discovered in a thorn-brake in which he had hidden himself, was laden with chains, and sent away as a captive to Babylon, which was then subject to the Assyrians, where he was cast into prison (B. C. 677). Here, at last, Manasseh had ample opportunity and leisure for cool reflection; and the hard lessons of adversity were not lost upon him. He saw and deplored the evils of his reign, he became as a new man, he humbly besought pardon from God, and implored that he might be enabled to evince the sincerity of his contrition, by being restored to a position for undoing all that it had been the business of his life to effect. His prayer was heard. His captivity is supposed to have lasted a year, and he was then restored to his kingdom under certain obligations of tribute and allegiance to the king of Assyria, which, although not expressed in the account of this transaction, are alluded to in the history of his successors (2 Chron. xxxiii: 11-13).

(3) **Reformation.** On his return to Jerusalem, Manasseh exerted himself to the utmost in correcting the errors of his early reign, and in establishing the worship of Jehovah in its former purity and splendor. The good conduct of his latter reign was rewarded with such prosperity as enabled him to do much for the improvement and strengthening of his capital and kingdom. He thoroughly repaired the old walls of Jerusalem, and added a new wall on the side towards Gihon; he surrounded and fortified by a separate wall the hill or ridge on the east of Zion, which

70

bore the name of עֹפֶל, Ophel, and he strengthened, garrisoned, and provisioned 'the fenced cities of Judah' (2 Chron. xxxiii:13-17).

(4) Death. He died in peace (B. C. about 664), at the age of sixty-eight, after having reigned longer than any other king of Judah, and was buried in a sepulcher which he had prepared for himself in his own garden (xxxiii:20).

3. In Judg. xviii:30, Manasseh is given as the father of Gershon, the father of Jonathan, the priest of the Danites at Laish. The reading is probably a corruption of "Moses."

4. An Israelite, descendant or resident of Pahath-moab, who divorced his foreign wife at the instance of Ezra (Ezra x:30). (B. C. 459.)

5. A man of Hashum, who also put away his Gentile wife (Ezra x:33). (B. C. 459.)

MANASSEH, TRIBE OF (ma-năs'seh).

When the tribe of Manasseh quitted Egypt, it numbered 32,200 adult males (Num. i:34, 35), being 8,300 less than the tribe of Ephraim, the younger son of Joseph. This was the lowest number of adult males in any tribe at that period; but if we add the two together, the tribe of Joseph, composed of these two tribes, reached to 72,700, which was more than any other tribe contained, except Judah. During the sojourn in the wilderness, the tribe of Manasseh rose to 52,700 (Num. xxvi:34), being an increase of 20,500. This gave it rank in point of population as the sixth of the tribes, Judah, Issachar, Zebulon, Dan, and Asher only being more numerous. In the same period Ephraim had declined to nearly the same position which Manasseh had previously occupied, its numbers being reduced to 32,500. Yet the prophecy of Jacob was fulfilled, and, when settled in Canaan, Ephraim became superior in wealth, power and population, not only to Manasseh, but to all the tribes except Judah. One circumstance tending to weaken Manasseh may have been the division which took place in it on entering Palestine. The pastoral half of the tribe was allowed to establish itself with Reuben and Gad, on the east of the Jordan, where it occupied the northernmost portion, consisting of Argob and Bashan, from the Jabbok to Mount Hermon (Num. xxxii:39; xxxiv:14; Deut. iii:13; Josh. xii:6; xiii:7; 1 Chron. vi:61), while the other half was provided for with the rest of the tribes in Canaan proper, west of the Jordan, where it had a fine tract of country extending from that river to the Mediterranean, with the kindred tribe of Ephraim on the south, and Issachar on the north (Josh. xvi:9; xvii:7-11). The half-tribe west of the river was not, however, for some time able to expel the former inhabitants of the territory, so as to obtain the exclusive possession of it (Josh. xvii:12; Judg. i:27). The tribe of Manasseh makes no figure in the history of the Hebrews. (See PALESTINE.)

MANASSES (ma-năs'sēz), (Gr. Μανασσῆς, *man-as-sace'*, Manasses).

1. The Greek form of Manasseh which is found in Rev. vii:6.

2. The form of Manasseh, 2, found in Matt. i:10, and in the "Prayer of Manasses."

MANASSES, PRAYER OF (ma-năs'sēz, prayer ŏv). See APOCRYPHA.

This pseudepigraphal work has come down to us in the MSS. of the Latin Vulgate, and is found in the early printed editions of that version. Du Pin firmly asserts that the Latin fathers have often cited this prayer; but the earliest reference to it which we know of is in the *Apos-*

tolical Constitutions (sec. 12), attributed to Clemens Romanus, but which are generally believed to be a work of the fourth century. In this work (ii:22) the prayer is cited as if it were an integral portion of the book of Chronicles, together with some traditional accounts of the nature of his imprisonment in shackles of iron, and of his miraculous release: which are also alluded to in the Targum on Chronicles.

It is entitled 'The Prayer of Manasses, king of Judah, when he was holden captive in Babylon,' and had doubtless its origin from 2 Chron. xxxiii:12, 13.

This prayer, however, not being found in the Hebrew, and not being cited by the more eminent fathers, nor contained in any of the catalogues of ancient councils, has not been received in the church as genuine or canonical. It is classed in the Sixth Article of the Church of England among the 'other books read by the church for example of life and instruction of manners;' but the church of Rome classes it with 3d and 4th Esdras (see ESDRAS), removing it to the end of the Bible, and rejecting it from the deutero-canonical, as well as from the proto-canonical books.

MANASSITES (ma-năs'sītes), (Heb. מְנַשֶּׁה, *men-ash-sheh'*, in Judg. xii:4; elsewhere הַמְּנַשִּׁי, *ham-men-ash-shee'*), descendants of Manasseh, the eldest son of Joseph, or some members of the tribe of Manasseh (Deut. iv:43; xxix:8; 2 Kings x:33; 1 Chron. xxvi:32).

MANDRAKE (măn'drāk), (Heb. דּוּדַי, *doo-dah'-ee*, love apples). Modern Bible scholars apply this name to a member of the potato family (*Mandragora officinalis*).

This is a stemless plant with a disk of leaves almost as long, but not nearly as broad, as those of the garden rhubarb, which it somewhat resembles, except in its blossoms. These are of a rich purple, and, appearing among the leaves very early, are followed about wheat-harvest by a round yellow pulpy fruit of the size of a large plum and of a sweet and agreeable flavor. The odor of the plant seems to be enjoyed by Orientals (Cant. vii:13), and by *some* Occidentals. Many strange superstitions are connected with this plant, and the idea of Rachel's time still prevails that conception is ensured by eating the fruit of this plant (Gen. xxx:14-16). For full discussion of the subject see DUDAIM.

MANEH (mā'neh), (Heb. מָנֶה, *maw-neh'*), a weight $\frac{1}{60}$ of a talent. See WEIGHTS AND MEASURES.

MANGER (măn'jēr), (Gr. φάτνη, *fat'nay*, crib, Luke ii:7, 12, 16).

In Luke xiii:15 it is translated "stall." While this is the classical meaning of the word, it has been pretty clearly demonstrated that in the New Testament it means the open courtyard of the inn or *khan*, which was inclosed by a fence of some kind where the cattle were shut up for the night. Mangers in our sense of the word are hardly known in the East.

MANNA (măn'nà) or **MAN**, (Heb. מָן, *mawn*, signifying *what?*).

(1) Substance. The name given to the miraculous food upon which the Israelites were fed for forty years, during their wanderings in the desert. The same name has in later ages been applied to some natural productions, chiefly found in warm, dry countries, but which have little or no resemblance to the original manna. This is first mentioned in Exod. xvi. It is there described as being first produced after the eighth encampment in the desert of Sin, as white like hoar frost (or of the color of *bdellium,* Num. xi:7), round, and of the bigness of coriander seed (*gad*). It fell with the dew every morning, and when the dew was exhaled by the heat of the sun, the manna appeared alone, lying upon the ground or the rocks round the encampment of the Israelites. 'When the children of Israel saw it, they said one to another, *What is it?* for they knew not what it was' (Exod. xvi:15). In the authorized, and some other versions, this passage is inaccurately translated—which indeed is apparent from the two parts of the sentence contradicting each other. In the Septuagint the substance is almost always called *manna* instead of *man.* Josephus (*Antiq.* iii, 1, sec. 10), as quoted by Dr. Harris, says: 'The Hebrews call this food *manna,* for the particle *man* in our language is the asking of a question', *What is this?* (*man-hu*). Moses answered this question by telling them, 'This is the bread which the Lord hath given you to eat.' We are further informed that the manna fell every day, except on the Sabbath. Every sixth day, that is on Friday, there fell a double quantity of it.

(2) **How Gathered.** Every man was directed to gather an omer (about three quarts) for each member of his family; and the whole seems afterwards to have been measured out at the rate of an omer to each person: 'He who gathered much had nothing over, and he who gathered little had no lack.' That which remained ungathered dissolved in the heat of the sun, and was lost. The quantity collected was intended for the food of the current day only; for if any were kept till next morning, it corrupted and bred worms. Yet it was directed that a double quantity should be gathered on the sixth day for consumption on the Sabbath. And it was found that the manna kept for the Sabbath remained sweet and wholesome, notwithstanding that it corrupted at other times, if kept for more than one day. In the same manner as they would have treated grain, they reduced it to meal, kneaded it into dough, and baked it into cakes, and the taste of it was like that of wafers made with honey, or of fresh oil. In Num. xi:6-9, where the description of the manna is repeated, an omer of it is directed to be preserved as a memorial to future generations, 'that they may see the bread wherewith I have fed you in the wilderness;' and in Joshua v:12 we learn that after the Israelites had encamped at Gilgal, and 'did eat of the old corn of the land, the manna ceased on the morrow after, neither had the children of Israel manna any more.'

(3) **Supposed Existence Now.** This miracle is referred to in Deut. viii:3; Neh. ix:20; Ps. lxxviii:24; John vi:31, 49, 58; Heb. ix:4. Though the manna of Scripture was so evidently miraculous, both in the mode and in the quantities in which it was produced, and though its properties were so different from anything with which we are acquainted, yet, because its taste is in Exodus said to be like that of wafers made with honey, many writers have thought that they recognized the manna of Scripture in a sweetish exudation which is found on several plants in Arabia and Persia. The name *man,* or *manna,* is applied to this substance by the Arab writers, and was probably so applied even before their time. But the term is now almost entirely appropriated to the sweetish exudation of the ash

trees of Sicily and Italy (*Ornus Europæa* and *Fraxinus rotundifolia*). These, however, have no relation to the supposed manna of Scripture. Of this, one kind is known to the Arabs by the name of *guzunjbeen,* being the produce of a plant called *guz,* and which is ascertained to be a species of tamarisk. The same species seems also to be called *toorfa,* and is common along different parts of the coast of Arabia. It is also found in the neighborhood of Mount Sinai. In the month of June it drops from the thorns of the tamarisk upon the fallen twigs, leaves and thorns, which always cover the ground beneath the tree in the natural state. The Arabs use it as they do honey, to pour over their unleavened bread, or to dip their bread into; its taste is agreeable, somewhat aromatic, and as sweet as honey. If eaten in any quantity it is said to be highly purgative. When Lieut. Wellsted visited this place in the month of September, he found the extremities of the twigs and branches retaining the peculiar sweetness and flavor which characterize the manna. The Bedouins collect it early in the morning, and, after straining it through a cloth, place it either in skins or gourds; a considerable quantity is consumed by themselves; a portion is sent to Cairo; and some is also disposed of to the monks at Mount Sinai. The latter retail it to the Russian pilgrims. 'The Bedouins assured me that the whole quantity collected throughout the Peninsula, in the most fruitful season, did not exceed 150 wogas (about 700 pounds); and that it was usually disposed of at the rate of 60 dollars the woga' (*Travels in Arabia,* vol. i, p. 511).

(4) **Another Kind.** Another kind of manna, which has been supposed to be that of Scripture, is yielded by a thorny plant very common from the north of India to Syria, and which, by the Arabs, is called Al-haj; whence botanists have constructed the name Alhagi. The *Alhagi maurorum* is remarkable for the exudation of a sweetish juice, which concretes into small granular masses, and which is usually distinguished by the name of Persian manna. The climates of Persia and Bokhara seem also well suited to the secretion of this manna, which in the latter country is employed as a substitute for sugar, and is imported into India for medicinal use through Caubul and Khorassan. These two, from the localities in which they are produced, have alone been thought to be the manna of Scripture. But besides these, there are several other kinds of manna. Burckhardt, during his journey through El-Ghor, in the valley of the Jordan, heard of the Beiruk honey. This is described as a substance obtained from the leaves and branches of a tree called *Gharb* or *Garrab,* of the size of an olive-tree, and with leaves like those of the poplar. When fresh this grayish colored exudation is sweet in taste, but in a few days it becomes sour. The Arabs eat it like honey.

(5) **Not the Manna of Scripture.** One kind, called *Sheer-khisht,* is said to be produced in the country of the Uzbecs. A Caubul merchant informed the author of this article, that it was produced by a tree called *Gundeleh,* which grows in Candahar, and is about twelve feet high, with jointed stems. A fifth kind is produced on *Calotropis procera,* or the plant called *Ashur.* The sweet exudation is by Arab authors ranked with sugars, and called *Shukur-al-ashur.* It is described under this name by Avicenna, and in the Latin translation it is called *Zuccarum-al-husar.* A sixth kind, called *Bed-khisht,* is described in Persian works on Materia Medica, as being pro-

duced on a species of willow in Persian Khorassan. Another kind would appear to be produced on a species of oak, for Niebuhr says, 'At Merdin, in Mesopotamia, it appears like a kind of pollen, on the leaves of the tree called *Ballot* and *Afs* (or, according to the Aleppo pronunciation, *As*), which I take to be of the oak family. All are agreed, that between Merdin and Diarbekir manna is obtained, and principally from those trees which yield gall-nuts.' Besides these, there is a sweetish exudation found on the larch, which is called *Manna brigantiaca,* as there is also one kind found on the cedar of Lebanon. Indeed a sweetish secretion is found on the leaves of many other plants, produced sometimes by the plant itself, at others by the punctures of insects. It has been supposed, also, that these sweetish exudations being evaporated during the heat of the day in still weather, may afterwards become deposited, with the dew, on the ground, and on the leaves of plants; and thus explain some of the phenomena which have been observed by travelers and others. But none of these mannas explain, nor can it be expected that they should explain, the miracle of Scripture, by which abundance is stated to have been produced for millions, where hundreds cannot now be subsisted. (See Tristram, *Nat. Hist. of the Bible,* p. 362; Robinson, *Researches,* i, 470, 550; and other Oriental travelers.)   J. F. R.

Figurative. Manna is called the "corn of heaven" and "angels' food" (Ps. lxxviii:24, 25), perhaps in allusion to the mode by which it was supplied.

The phrase "hidden manna" (Rev. ii:17), figuratively describes the support which Christ furnishes to the true believer, of which the world does not and cannot partake. (Comp. John vi: 49, 51).

MANOAH (ma-nō'ah), (Heb. מָנוֹחַ, *maw-no'akh,* rest).

A native of the town of Zorah, in the tribe of Dan, and the father of Samson, whose birth is recorded in Judg. xiii:1-23. Manoah is again mentioned (Judg. xiv:2-4) at the occasion of Samson's marriage, but seems to have died before the son, whose body was brought up from Gaza by his brethren, not, as Milton has it, by his father (Judg. xvi:31). (See SAMSON.)

MAN OF SIN. See ANTICHRIST.

MAN OF WAR. And Herod with his *men of war* set him at nought (Luke xxiii:11).

Man-of-war, with us, means a *ship* of war; but as here used it signifies just what the composition of the word denotes,—namely, a *warrior,* a *soldier.* This sense of the word is common in old English literature.

What stir
Keeps good old York there with his *men of war?*
                    Shakespeare.

MANSERVANT (măn'sērv'ant). See SLAVE.

MANSIONS (Gr. μοναί, *abodes,* John xiv:2). The word is used in its primary meaning of "dwelling-places," "rooms."

MANSLAYER (măn'slā'ēr), (Heb. רָצַח, *rawtsakh',* to kill; Gr. ἀνδροφόνος, *an-drof-on'os*), one who strikes another so as to kill.

The manslayer was one who was guilty of homicide, having accidentally and without malice slain another. According to the custom of the East, the right and indeed the obligation of revenge lay with the kinsmen of the person slain.

The avenger of blood did not require to consider whether the slaughter had been intentional or not. He was entitled wherever he found the slayer to take vengeance upon him, blood for blood. An important amelioration of this custom was introduced into the Jewish law by the appointment of six Cities of Refuge, in convenient central positions, so that in all parts of the land there might be one within reach. If one had accidentally slain another, he was required to hasten to the nearest City of Refuge and remain there till the death of the high-priest, after which he might return with safety to his home. It was enacted that the roads leading to those cities must be kept in good repair, and absolute security was guaranteed to the refugee. (See BLOOD-REVENGE.)

MAN, SON OF (Gr. ὁ Υἱὸς τοῦ ἀνθρώπου).

This title was evidently taken from Dan. viii: 17, where everlasting dominion is ascribed to the Messiah under that title. It was assumed by Christ himself, and though occurring sixty-one times in the Gospels, is only used by Christ himself. It occurs once in the Acts (vii:56), and is employed by Stephen. It is clear that from the corresponding term, "the Son of God," this title belongs to Christ by virtue of superiority; and that *both* taken together decidedly prove that Christ, in some manner unknown to us, united in his person both the human and the Divine nature. "In this name there surely lies above everything actual humanity. Jesus knew himself to be a perfect personal man, and would not have been able to call himself Son of man if he only knew himself to be a manifest action of God. . . . The phrase must also signify, especially with the definite article, the opposite to imperfection and defacement, the *truth* of man, i. e., the realization of his idea. If he only meant to express by the name that he was a real man like others, the definite article would be inexplicable. The definite article points in that direction, that he was also conscious of his humanity not as a merely ordinary or faulty humanity, but as the perfect manifestation of its truth as well as of its realization" (Dorner, *Christ. Doct.,* iii, 169, *sq.;* also Weiss, *Bib. Theol.* of *New Testament,* 144; Miley, *Sys. Theol.,* ii p. 23, *sq.;* Bloomfield, *Greek Test.,* Matt. viii:20; Barnes, *Bib. Dict.*)

MANTLE (măn't'l). The word employed in the A. V. to translate four Hebrew terms:

1. שְׂמִיכָה, *sem-ee-kaw'.* This word occurs in Judg. iv:18, where it denotes the cloth with which Jael covered Sisera, and which, from all that can be gathered, was a tent-carpet.

2. מְעִיל, *meh-eel',* rendered "mantle" (1 Sam. xv:27; xxviii:14; Ezra ix:3, 5; Job i:20; ii:12; and Ps. cix:29); this word in other passages of the A. V. is rendered "coat," "cloak," and "robe."

3. מַעֲטָפָה, *ma-at-aw-fawh',* (Is. iii:22 only). Apparently an article of female apparel, perhaps an exterior tunic, longer and fuller than the internal one, and provided with sleeves.

4. אַדֶּרֶת, *ad-deh-reth'* (1 Kings xix:13, 19; 2 Kings ii:8, 13, 14); elsewhere "garment" and "robe." It denotes the cape or wrapper which, with a strip of skin or leather round his loins, formed the only garments of the prophet Elijah.

MANUSCRIPTS, BIBLICAL (măn'ū-skrĭpts, bĭb'lĭ-kal). These are either Hebrew or Greek.

1. Jewish Manuscripts. Jewish MSS. are divided into (a) *Synagogue rolls* or *sacred copies;* and (b) *Private* or *common copies.*

(a) The synagogue rolls contain the Pentateuch, the appointed sections of the prophets, or the book of Esther, which last is used only at the Feast of Purim. The three are never put together; but are written on separate rolls. They are in the Chaldee or square Hebrew character, without vowels and accents, accompanied with the *puncta extraordinaria,* and having the unusual forms of certain consonants. The great beauty of penmanship exhibited in these synagogue copies has been always admired. They are taken from authentic exemplars, without the slightest deviation or correction. They seldom fall into the hands of Christians, since, as soon as they cease to be employed in the synagogue, they are either buried or carefully laid aside, lest they should be profaned by coming into the possession of Gentiles.

(b) Private MSS. are written partly in the *square* or *Chaldee* character, partly in the *Rabbinical.* They are held in far less esteem than the synagogue rolls, and are wont to be denominated *profane* (*pesulim*). Their form is entirely arbitrary. They are in folio, quarto, octavo, and duodecimo. Of those written in the *square character,* the greater number are on parchment, some on paper. The ink of the letters is always black, but the vowel points are usually written with ink of a different color from that of the consonants. Initial words and letters are frequently decorated with gold and silver colors. The prose parts are arranged in columns, the poetic in parallel members. Some copies are without columns. The columns are not always occupied with the Hebrew text alone; for a version is frequently added which is either written in the text after the manner of verses or in a column by itself, or in the margin in a smaller character. The number of lines is not prescribed by the Talmud. The upper and lower margins are filled with the Great Masora, and sometimes with a Rabbinical commentary; as also with prayers, psalms, and the like. The external margin is for corrections, *scholia,* variations, notices of the *haphtaroth* (sections from the prophets), *parashoth* (sections from the law), the commentaries of the Rabbins, etc. The inner margin, or that between the columns, is occupied with the little Masora. The single books of the Old Testament are separated from one another by spaces, except the books of Samuel, Kings, Chronicles, Ezra, and Nehemiah, which are written continuously. The sections of the law and prophets are generally marked. In the MSS. of different countries the books are differently arranged. These copies generally pass through various hands before they are finished. The consonants proceed from the *sopher* or scribe. When the same person writes both consonants and vowels, as is frequently the case, he never makes them at the same time; the former are finished before he begins to append the latter. The *K'ris* in the margin uniformly proceed from the vowel-writer. It is probable that these copies were in no instance made by Christians.

Although the square character be employed in all the MSS. of which we have spoken, yet it has varieties. The Jews themselves distinguish in the synagogue rolls, (1) the *Tam* letter, with sharp corners and perpendicular coronulæ, used among the German and Polish Jews; (2) the *Velshe* letter, more modern than the *Tam,* and rounder, with coronulæ, particularly found in the sacred copies of the Spanish and Oriental Jews.

The age of Hebrew MSS. is not easily determined. It is true that they often contain subscriptions giving an account of the time when they were written, and the name of the scribe, or also of the possessor. But these accounts are often ambiguous and occasionally incorrect. Where they are altogether wanting, it is still more difficult to discover the age. In the latter case, the character of the writing, the color of the ink, the quality and yellowness of the parchment, the absence of the Masora, of the vowel-points, of the unusual letters, etc., have been chiefly rested upon. Still, however, such particulars are uncertain marks of age.

The oldest Hebrew MS. at present known belongs to A. D. 1106 (No. 154 of Kennicott). It is true that some others are *supposed* to be older, but simply by conjecture. As far as certainty is concerned, this is certainly the oldest. Loehnis (*Grundzüge der Biblischen Hermeneutik und Kritik,* Giessen, 1839) affirms that some reach as far back as the eighth century, an assertion grounded merely on the conjecture of De Rossi and Kennicott. So much uncertainty attaches to the internal marks adopted by these two Hebraists, that the ages to which they assign several Hebrew MSS. are quite gratuitous. No Hebrew MS. *possessing an indubitably accurate* register of its antiquity, goes farther back than the twelfth century (see the *third* section of Tychsen's *Tentamen de variis Codicum Hebraicorum Vet. Test. MSS. generibus,* etc., Rostock, 1772, 8vo, in which the learned writer examines the marks of antiquity assumed by Simon, Jablonski, Wolf, Houbigant, Kennicott, and Lilienthal, and shows that the *Masora alone* is a certain index for determining the age and goodness of Hebrew MSS).

Private MSS. written in the *Rabbinical character* are much more recent than the preceding; none of them being older than 500 years. They are on cotton or linen paper, in a *cursive* character, without vowel-points or the Masora, and with many abbreviations.

The MSS. found among the Chinese Jews are partly synagogue rolls, partly private copies, whose text does not differ from the Masoretic. The Pentateuch of the Malabar Jews brought from India to England by the late Dr. Buchanan, and described by Mr. Yates, resembles on the whole the usual synagogue rolls of the Jews, except that it is written on red skin. Its text is the Masoretic, with a few unimportant deviations.

Eight exemplars are celebrated among the Jews for their correctness and value. They are now lost, but extracts from them are still preserved. From Jewish writings, and from the margin of some MSS., where a reference is made to them, we learn that they were highly prized for their singular accuracy. They formed the basis of subsequent copies. They are: (1) The codex of Hillel; (2) the Babylonian codex; (3) the codex of Israel; (4) an Egyptian codex; (5) codex Sinai; (6) the Pentateuch of Jericho; (7) codex Sanbuki; (8) the book Taggin. For a more copious account of Hebrew MSS. we refer to Eichhorn's *Einleitung* (Introduction), vol. ii.; Kennicott's *Dissertatio generalis;* Walton's *Prolegomena to the Polyglott,* which have been separately edited by Dathe and Wrangham; Tychsen's *Tentamen;* De Rossi's *Variæ Lectiones Vet. Test.* etc.; and his *Scholia critica in V. T. libros,* etc.; De Wette, *Lehrbuch der Historisch-Kritischen Einleitung;* and Davidson's *Lectures on Biblical Criticism,* in which last the best books are pointed out.

2. Manuscripts of the Greek Testament.

Those that have descended to our time are either on vellum or paper. The oldest material was the Egyptian papyrus; but even so early as the fourth century, the New Testament was written on the skins of animals. This writing material continued in use till the eleventh century, when paper began to be employed. Till the tenth century, MSS. were usually written in *capital* or *uncial* letters; then the cursive character came into use. The most ancient copies have no divisions of words, being written in a continued series of lines. Accents, breathings, and iota subscript are also wanting.

The whole New Testament is contained in very few MSS. Transcribers generally divided it into three parts; the first containing the four gospels; the second, the Acts of the Apostles and the Epistles; the third, the Apocalypse of St. John. The greatest number of MSS. are those which have the four gospels, because they were most frequently read in the churches. Those containing the Acts and epistles are also numerous. Such as have the book of Revelation alone are extremely few, because it was seldom read in public.

A. *Codex Alexandrinus,* presented by Cyril Lucar, patriarch of Alexandria, and afterwards of Constantinople, to Charles I, now in the British Museum. It contains the whole Bible, the Septuagint version of the Old Testament in three folios, and the New Testament in one. It has various chasms. A facsimile of the New Testament portion was published by Dr. Woide, in a folio volume, London, 1786. Mr. Baber of the British Museum executed the Old Testament in the same manner, in four folio volumes, London, 1819. This MS. was probably written at Alexandria, and belongs to the fifth century.

B. *Codex Vaticanus,* 1209, in the Vatican Library at Rome, containing the Old and New Testaments. It is defective in several places; and portions have been supplied by a modern hand. Hug has proved that it belongs to the middle of the fourth century. In regard to the internal value of its readings, it is probably superior to the Codex Alexandrinus.

C. *Codex Regius,* or *Ephraemi.*—This is a *rescript* or *palimpsest* MS., *i. e.* the ancient writing has been erased to make room for some other. The works of Ephrem the Syrian were over the original. In endeavoring to ascertain the character of what was first written on the parchment, and washing off the latter letters, it was found that the MS. contained originally the Old and New Testaments in Greek. In many places it is so faded as to be illegible. There are numerous chasms in it. Several forms of words seem to indicate that it was written in Egypt: it probably belongs to the sixth century, and is now in the Royal Library at Paris, where it is marked 9.

D. *Codex Cantabrigiensis,* or *Bezæ.*—This MS. was presented, in 1581, to the University of Cambridge, by Theodore Beza. It is a **Greek-Latin** MS. of the four gospels, and the Acts of the Apostles, with a single fragment of the Catholic epistles. Its age is probably the *seventh* century, though many have assigned it to the fifth. Kipling, Hug, and Scholz think that it was written in Egypt; but Scholz has given some reasons for assigning it to the south of France, which are not without weight. Credner assents to the latter opinion, as far as the MS. is concerned, while he thinks that the text is of Jewish-Christian origin, and attributes it to Palestine. Great diversity of opinion has prevailed respecting the quality of its readings. Bishop Middleton, at the end of his work on the Greek article, depreciated it. Matthæi had done so before. Both have unduly lessened its value. Dr. Kipling published a facsimile of it at Cambridge, 1793, 2 vols. folio.

D. *Claromontanus,* or *Regius,* 107, a Greek-Latin copy of Paul's epistles, marked with the same letter of the alphabet as the preceding, but containing a different part of the New Testament. It is at present in the Royal Library at Paris: it probably belongs to the eighth century.

E. *Codex Basileensis.*—This MS. has many chasms, and several parts of it have been written by a more recent hand than the rest. It contains the gospels, and belongs to the ninth century.

E. *Laudianus,* having once belonged to Archbishop Laud, and now in the Bodleian Library. It contains the Acts of the Apostles, with a Latin version, and wants from xxvi:29 to xxviii:26. This MS. belongs to the *seventh* or *eighth* century, and was published by *Thomas Hearne* at Oxford in 1715, octavo.

E. *Sangermanensis.*—This is a Greek-Latin MS. of Paul's epistles, but a copy of the *Claromontanus,* with various corrections. It belongs to the eleventh century.

F. *Codex Boreeli,* containing the four gospels. It has been collated no farther than Luke x.

F. *Coislinianus,* a MS. containing part of the Old Testament and Acts ix:24, 25. It belongs to the seventh century.

F. *Augiensis.*—This is a Greek-Latin MS. of Paul's epistles, now in the library of Trinity College, Cambridge. It belongs to the tenth century.

G. *Harleianus,* in British Museum. This is a MS. of the four Gospels, but with many chasms. It belongs to the eleventh century.

G. *Angelicus.*—A MS. containing the Acts of the Apostles, with the Pauline and Catholic epistles, belonging to the Angelican Library at Rome. It is as old as the ninth century. In the Pauline epistles it is marked I.

G. *Boernerianus,* a Greek MS. of Paul's Epistles, with an interlinear Latin version, now in the Electoral Library at Dresden. It wants the Epistle to the Hebrews, and probably belongs to the ninth century. The characters show an approach to the *cursive.*

H. *Wolfii* B, a MS. of the four gospels, with many chasms. It belongs to the eleventh century.

H. *Mutinensis.*—This MS. contains the Acts of the Apostles written in the *ninth* century; but chapters i:1—v:28, were added in the fifteenth century, and xxvii:1 to the end, in the eleventh century. With the Catholic epistles, it contains the Pauline, written in cursive letters (179), and belongs to the twelfth century.

H. *Coislinianus.*—This MS. contains fragments of the Pauline epistles, which have been printed by Montfaucon in the *Bibliotheca Coisliniana.* According to Hug it belongs to the sixth century.

J. *Cottonianus.*—This codex contains fragments of Matthew's and John's gospels. It belongs to the seventh or eighth century.

K. *Codex Cyprius,* formerly *Colbertinus,* 5149, now *Regius,* 63, a MS. containing the gospels. It belongs to the eighth or ninth century, probably the latter, and has been fully collated and described by Scholz at the end of his *Curæ Criticæ,* 4to, Heidelberg, 1820. See, however, Scholz in the prolegomena to Griesbach, vol. i.

L. *Regius,* 62.—This MS. contains the four gospels, with several mutilations. It is of Egyptian origin, as Griesbach has proved; and belongs to the ninth century.

M. *Regius,* 48, containing the gospels, and belonging to the tenth century.

N. *Vindobonensis Cæsareus.*—This fragmentary MS. contains only Luke xxiv:13-21 and 39-49. It belongs to the seventh century.

O. *Montefalconii,* a MS. containing Luke xviii.

P. *Guelpherbytanus,* a codex *rescriptus,* containing fragments of the four gospels, and belonging to the sixth century.

Q. *Guelpherbytanus,* also a rescript MS. containing fragments of the gospels of Luke and John, and belonging to the sixth century. These two MSS. were published and described by Knittel in 1763.

R. *Tubingensis.*—This fragment, containing John i:38-50, has been published by Reuss. It belongs to the seventh century.

S. *Vaticanus,* 354.—This MS. contains the gospels, and belongs to the tenth century.

T. The *Borgian* fragment, part of a Coptic-Greek MS. brought from Egypt. It contains John vi:28-67; vii:6—viii:31. It was printed by George in 1789, and belongs to the fourth or more probably the fifth century.

U. A MS. of the gospels, in St. Mark's Library, Venice. It belongs to the tenth century.

V. *Mosquensis,* a MS. of the four gospels, belonging to the library of the Holy Synod at Moscow. It wants some parts of Matthew, and from John vii:39 is written in cursive characters of the thirteenth century; the first part belongs to the ninth century.

W. *Regius,* a fragment containing Luke ix:36-47; x:12-22; and belonging to the eighth century.

X. *Landshutensis.*—This MS. contains the four gospels, but with numerous chasms and some supplements. It belongs most probably to the tenth century.

Y. *Barberinus,* a fragment in the library of Cardinal Barberini at Rome, containing John xvi:4—xix:28. It belongs to the ninth century.

Z. *Dublinensis,* a rescript, exhibiting the gospel of Matthew, but in a very imperfect state. It was published in facsimile by Dr. Barrett (Dublin. 1801, 4to), and belongs to the sixth century.

Γ. *Vaticanus.*—This fragment contains Matthew xix:6-13; xx:6-22; xx:29—xxi:19. It belongs to the seventh century.

Δ. *Sangallensis.*—This is a Greek-Latin MS. of the gospels, made by the monks in the monastery of St. Gallen. It was published by Rettigus at Turin, in 1836, and belongs to the ninth century.

Such are the *uncial* MSS. hitherto collated. Those written in the *cursive* character are described in the large critical editions of Wetstein, Griesbach, and Scholz; and in the *Introduction* of Michaelis, up to the period when it was published. The other Introductions contain descriptions of several, but not all the MSS.

Three Cursive MSS. deserve mention, from their connection with the much-disputed passage 1 John v:7, which they are usually quoted as containing. As they are written in *cursive* letters they are not older than the tenth century.

(1) *The Codex Montfortianus,* or *Dublinensis,* belonging to the library of Trinity College, Dublin. It was quoted by Erasmus, under the title of *Codex Britannicus.* It is written on paper in 12mo size, and could not have been made earlier than the fifteenth century. It follows the *Vulgate* very closely, not only in the insertion of the much-disputed verse, but in other passages of a remarkable character.

(2) *The Codex Ravianus,* or *Berolinensis.*—This MS. is generally supposed to be a forgery copied in the greater part of it from the Greek text of the *Complutensian Polyglott,* and the third edition of Stephens. It has even their *typographical* errors. It was written in the sixteenth century, and has no *critical value* (see Pappelbaum's *Untersuchung der Ravischen Griechischen Handschrift des Neuen Testaments,* Berlin, 1785, 8vo; and his subsequent treatise, entitled, *Codicis Manuscripti Novi Testamenti Græci Raviani in Biblioth. Reg. Berol. publica asservati examen, quo ostenditur, alteram ejus partem majorem ex editione Complutensi, alteram minorem ex editione Rob. Stephani tertia esse descriptam,* Berlin, 1796, 8vo).

(3) *Codex Ottobonianus,* 298, preserved in the Vatican. This MS. contains the Acts and epistles, with a Latin version. Scholz ascribes it to the fifteenth century. It has no critical value, because it has been altered in many cases to correspond with the *Vulgate.* In it the disputed text is found in a different form from the common reading. Instead of *in heaven,* it has *from heaven;* and instead of *on earth,* it has *from the earth.* (See Davidson, *Biblical Criticism.*)

S. D.

3. Recent Discoveries. The following most important discoveries may be mentioned, all made within a half a century:

1. The Sinaitic manuscript of the New Testament, discovered thirty-five years ago. This is a complete manuscript of the New Testament, and belongs to the fourth century. It is a witness of the very first importance for the history of the New Testament text.

2. Fragments of very early versions of the New Testament, as the Curetonian Syriac, the earliest Syriac known, and portions of Coptic versions.

3. The "Philosophumena," or "Against all Heresies" of Hippolytus, who was martyred in the year 235. This very important work gives an account of the heretical sects of the first and second centuries, and is very valuable for the quotations it makes from such heretics as Valentinus and Basilides, who flourished A. D. 125, and from whom are given quotations from John's gospel.

4. The "Diatessaron" of Tatian. This Syrian Christian father died before A. D. 172. His famous work, discovered and brought to the knowledge of the world not less than twenty years ago, is a harmony of the four gospels, and begins with the first words of John's gospel, and uses that gospel, as well as others, very freely. It is a conclusive proof of the unquestioned acceptance of the gospel as early as the year 170.

5. The Epistle of Barnabas. A complete Greek copy of this epistle, which goes back nearly if not quite, to the beginning of the second century, was discovered in 1859 by Tischendorf. This quotes Matthew under the formula, "It is written." It is of very great value, and was early regarded as itself canonical.

6. The "Shepherd" of Hermas. The Greek text of the most of this important series of Visions and Mandates, which date from as early as the middle of the second century, is also one of the discoveries of the last forty years. It casts much light on the condition of the early church, though the long work does not quote the New Testament.

7. The Epistle of Clement of Rome, probably written A. D. 97. A second copy of this was found by Bryennios, and published several years ago. Such a manuscript cannot but be of the first importance. It gives quotations from Paul.

8. The last of these discoveries, belonging to the last two or three years, is the very important "Teaching of the Apostles," a work which probably goes back to the early years of the second century, and very likely to the last part of the first century, and which gives us the first church manual ever written, on which the so-called Syrian or Coptic Constitutions and the better known Greek Apostolic Constitutions were in considerable part founded. This work, so remarkably preserved and discovered, casts a clearer light than any other on the origin of the officers in the church, and the early character of its services and teachings. It quotes considerable portions of the Sermon on the Mount.

These great discoveries of this century, with others of less importance that might be mentioned, have thrown a full beam of light on the dark interval which separated the day of the Apostles from the days of Irenæus and Clement of Alexandria. They answer most satisfactorily questions of critical doubt raised by skeptical scholars. They remove many difficulties and carry the gospel of John, as well as other portions of the New Testament, back to the very days of the Apostle John, before he died in Ephesus. The condition of the argument is much altered since Norton wrote on the genuineness of the gospels. Every discovery has only confirmed the faith of the church in its accepted Scriptures. To doubt that they are the products of the years to which they assign themselves or have been assigned by the Church, now appears to betray willful skepticism.

MAOCH (mā'ok), (Heb. מָעוֹךְ, maw-oke', poor, a poor one, a breast band).

The father of Achish, king of Gath, to whom David fled for safety (1 Sam. xxvii:2). (B. C. before 1000.)

MAON (mā'on), (Heb. מָעוֹן, maw-ohn').

1. A town in the tribe of Judah (Josh. xv: 55), which gave name to a wilderness where David hid himself from Saul, and around which the churlish Nabal had great possessions (1 Sam. xxiii:24, 25; xxv:2). Jerome places it to the east of Daroma (Onomast. s. v. Maon). The name does not occur in modern times, and Dr. Robinson regards it as one of the sites first identified by himself. Irby and Mangles were in the neighborhood in 1818, but did not detect this and other ancient names. Robinson finds it in the present Tell Maîn, which is about seven miles south by east from Hebron. Here there is a conical hill about 200 feet high, on the top of which are some ruins of no great extent, consisting of foundations of hewn stone, a square enclosure, the remains probably of a tower or castle, and several cisterns. The view from the summit is extensive. This is Tell Maân. The traveler found here a band of peasants keeping their flocks, and dwelling in caves amid the ruins. (Bibl. Researches, ii. 190-196.)

2. Son of Shammai, of the tribe of Judah, and founder of Beth-zur (1 Chron. ii:45). Perhaps the name is here used collectively for the inhabitants of the town of Maon.

MAONITES (mā'on-ītes), (Heb. מָעוֹן, maw-ohn'), a tribe mentioned (Judg. x:12) along with the Amalekites, Zidonians, Philistines, etc. In 2 Chron. xxvi:7, they are called Mehunims, and are mentioned along with the Arabians.

There is still a city Maân with a castle in Arabia Petræa, south of the Dead Sea and near Wady Mousa. Burckhardt's Travels in Syria, etc., p. 437). (See MEHUNIMS, THE.)

MARA (mā'rà), (Heb. מָרָא, maw-raw', bitter), the name chosen by Naomi as symbolical of her bereavements (Ruth i:20).

MARAH (mā'rah), (Heb. מָרָה, maw-raw', bitterness).

(1) The Bitter Waters. The Israelites in departing from Egypt made some stay on the shores of the Red Sea, at the place where it had been crossed by them. From this spot they proceeded southward for three days without finding any water, and then came to a well, the waters of which were so bitter, that, thirsty as they were, they could not drink them. The well was called Marah from the quality of its waters. This name, in the form of Amarah, is now borne by the barren bed of a winter torrent, a little beyond which is still found a well called Howara, whose bitter waters answer to this description. Camels will drink it; but the thirsty Arabs never partake of it themselves; and it is said to be the only water on the shore of the Red Sea which they cannot drink. The water of this well, when first taken into the mouth, seems insipid rather than bitter, but when held in the mouth a few seconds it becomes exceedingly nauseous.

The Hebrews, unaccustomed as yet to the hardships of the desert, and having been in the habit of drinking their full of the best water in the world, were much distressed by its scarcity in the region wherein they now wandered; and in their disappointment of the relief expected from this well, they murmured greatly against Moses for having brought them into such a dry wilderness, and asked him, 'What shall we drink?' On this Moses cried to Jehovah, who indicated to him 'a certain tree,' on throwing the branches of which into the well, its waters became sweet and fit for use.

(2) Was the Change Miraculous? The question connected with this operation is—whether the effect proceeded from the inherent virtue of the tree in sweetening bad water; or that it had no such virtue, and that the effect was purely miraculous. In support of the former alternative, it may be asked why the tree should have been pointed out and used at all, unless it had a curative virtue? And to this the answer may be found in the numerous instances in which God manifests a purpose of working even his miracles in accordance with the general laws by which he governs the world, and for that purpose disguising the naked exhibition of supernatural power, by the interposition of an *apparent* cause, while yet the true character of the event is left indisputable, by the utter inadequacy of the apparent cause to produce, by itself, the resulting effect. This tends to show that the tree, or portion of it, need not be supposed, from the mere fact of its being employed, to have had an inherent curative virtue. It had not *necessarily* any such virtue; and that it positively had not such virtue seems to follow, or, at least, to be rendered more than probable by the consideration —that, in the scanty and little diversified vegetation of this district, any such very desirable virtues in a tree, or part of a tree, could scarcely have been undiscovered before the time of the history, and if they had been discovered, could not but have been known to Moses; and the Divine indication of the tree would not have been needful. And, again, if the corrective qualities were inherent, but were at this time first made known, it is incredible that so valuable a discovery would ever have been forgotten; and yet it is manifest that in after-times the Hebrews had not the knowledge of any tree which could render bad water drinkable; and the inhabitants of the desert have not only not preserved the knowledge of a fact which would have been so important to them, but have not discovered it in the thirty-five centuries which have since passed. This is shown by the inquiries of travelers, some of whom were actuated by the wish of finding a plant which might supersede the miracle. No such plant, however, can be found; and whatever the tree was, it can have had no more inherent virtue in sweetening the bitter well of Marah, than the salt had, which produced the same effect, when thrown by Elisha into the well of Jericho (Lindsay, i. 263-5).

MARALAH (măr'a-lah), (Heb. מַרְעֲלָה, mar-al-aw', earthquake, declivity).

A landmark on the southern boundary of the tribe of Zebulun, but apparently within Issachar (Josh. xix:11). Not identified.

MARAN-ATHA (măr'an-ăth'á), (Gr. μαρὰν ἀθά, mar-an' ath-ah'; Chald. מָרָנָא אֲתָה, our Lord cometh).

An expression used by St. Paul at the conclusion of his First Epistle to the Corinthians: "If any man love not the Lord Jesus Christ, let him be Anathema Maran-atha" (xvi:22). It may have been used as a watchword, common to all believers in the first age. Connected here with an anathema, or curse, it is the Christian's reminder of the advent of the judge to execute the anathema. (See ANATHEMA.)

MARBLE (măr'b'l), (Heb. שַׁיִשׁ, shah'yish, שֵׁשׁ, shesh), white marble or crystalline limestone, was used for columns and costly pavements (Esth. i:6; Cant. v:15), and was the material out of which Solomon's temple was constructed (1 Chron. xxix:2).

It was obtained for the most part from quarries underneath the Temple area. (See JERUSALEM.)

MARCHESHVAN (măr - kĕsh' văn), (Heb. מַרְחֶשְׁוָן, mar-khesh-vawn').

The Macedonian Δῖος, or Zeus, is the name of that month which was the eighth of the sacred, and the second of the civil, year of the Jews; which began with the new moon of our November. There was a fast on the 6th, in memory of Zedekiah's being blinded, after he had witnessed the slaughter of his sons (2 Kings xxv:7).

This month is always spoken of in the Old Testament by its numerical designation; except once, when it is called Bul (בּוּל, 1 Kings vi: 38), supposed to be shortened form of the Hebrew 'rain.' The signification of rain-month is exactly suitable to November in the climate of Palestine. J. N.

MARCUS (măr'kus), (Col. iv:10; Philem. 24; 1 Pet. v:13). See MARK.

MARESHAH (ma-rē'shà), (Heb. מַרְשָׁה, mar-ay-shaw', summit).

1. A town in the tribe of Judah (Josh. xv:44), rebuilt and fortified by Rehoboam (2 Chron. xi: 8). The Ethiopians under Zerah were defeated by Asa in the valley near Mareshah (2 Chron. xiv:9-13). It was laid desolate by Judas Maccabæus, on his march from Hebron to Ashdod (1 Macc. v:65-68; Joseph. Antiq. xii:8, 6). Josephus mentions it among the towns possessed by Alexander Jannæus, which had been in the hands of the Syrians (Antiq. xiii:15, 4) ; but by Pompey it was restored to the former inhabitants, and attached to the province of Syria (xiv. 4. 4). Maresa was among the towns rebuilt by Gabinius (Antiq. xiv. 5. 3), but was again destroyed by the Parthians in their irruption against Herod (xiv. 5. 3). A place so often mentioned in history must have been of considerable importance; but it does not appear that it was ever again rebuilt. The site, however, is set down by Eusebius and Jerome (Onomast, s. v. Morasthi), as within two miles of Eleutheropolis, but the direction is not stated. Dr. Robinson (Bibl. Researches, ii. 422) found, at a mile and a half south of the site of Eleutheropolis, a remarkable tell, or artificial hill, with foundations of some buildings. As there are no other ruins in the vicinity, and as the site is admirably suited for a fortress, this, he supposes, may have been Mareshah. Conder suggested el-Marah, south of the valley of Elah, as Mareshah, but lately has accepted M'erash as the site.

2. The "father" of Hebron; in the line of Judah (1 Chron. ii:42), by which it is apparently meant that he was the progenitor of the inhabitants of Hebron. (B. C. 1190.)

3. Son of Laadah, of the family of Shelah; perhaps the founder of a place by the same name (1 Chron. iv:21). Perhaps identical with **2**. (B. C. about 1612.)

MARINER (măr'ĭ-nēr), (Heb. מַלָּח, mal-lawkh', Ezek. xxvii:9, 27, 29; to shoot, row, xxvii: 8), a sailor. (See SHIP.)

MARISHES (măr'ĭsh-ĕs), an old form of MARSH (which see).

MARK (märk), (Gr. Μάρκος, mar'kos, from the common Latin name Marcus).

According to ecclesiastical testimonies the evangelist Mark is the same person who in the Acts is called by the Jewish name John, whose Roman surname was Marcus (Acts xii:12, 25). This person is sometimes called simply John (Acts xiii:5, 13); and sometimes Mark (Acts xv:39).

Mary, Mark's mother, had a house at Jerusalem, in which the Apostles were wont to assemble (Acts xii:12). In the Epistle to the Colossians (iv:10, 11) Mark is mentioned among the assistants of Paul, and as being one of the converts from Judaism. From this passage we learn also that Mark was a cousin of Barnabas, which circumstance confirms the opinion that he was of Jewish descent. It was probably Barnabas who first introduced him to Paul. He accompanied Paul and Barnabas on their travels as an assistant (Acts xii:25; xiii:5). When they had arrived in Pamphylia, Mark left them and returned to Jerusalem, from which city they had set out (Acts xiii:13). On this account Paul refused to take Mark with him on his second Apostolical journey, 'and so Barnabas took Mark, and sailed unto Cyprus' (Acts xv:37-39). It seems, however, that Mark at a later period, became reconciled to Paul, since, according to Col. iv:10, and Philem. 24, he was with the Apostle during his first captivity at Rome; and according to 2 Tim. iv:11, he was also with him during his second captivity. The passage in Colossians proves also that he was about to undertake for Paul a journey to Colosse.

There is a unanimous ecclesiastical tradition that Mark was the companion and *interpreter* of Peter and either orally or in writing communicated and developed what Peter taught. The testimony in favor of the connection between Mark and Peter is so old and respectable, that it cannot be called in question. It first occurs at the commencement of the second century, and proceeds from the presbyter John (Euseb. *Hist. Eccles.* iii:39); it afterwards appears in Irenæus (*Adv. Hær*, iii. 1. 1, and x. 6); in Tertullian (*Contra Mart.* iv. 5); in Clemens Alexandrinus, Jerome, and others.

The Gospel According to Mark.

(1) Testimony of Eusebius. The same ancient authors who call Mark a disciple and secretary of Peter, state also that he wrote his Gospel according to the discourses of that Apostle. The most ancient statement of this fact is that of the presbyter John and of Papias, which we quote verbatim from Eusebius (*Hist. Eccles.* iii. 39) as follows: "Mark having become secretary to Peter, whatever he put into style he wrote with accuracy, but did not observe the chronological order of the discourses and actions of Christ, because he was neither a hearer nor a follower of the Lord; but at a later period, as I have said, wrote for Peter, to meet the requisites of instruction, but by no means with the view to furnish a connected digest of the discourses of our Lord. Consequently Mark was not in fault when he wrote down circumstances as he recollected them; for he had only the intention to omit nothing of what he had heard, and not to misrepresent anything." Critics usually ascribe all these words to the presbyter. Schmidt especially observes, in his *Einleitung ins Neue Testament Nachträge* (p. 270), that he himself had erroneously quoted this testimony as the words of Papias; but it seems to us that the words ὡς ἔφην do not allow us to consider all this passage as belonging to the presbyter. Papias had not before his eyes a book of the presbyter, and he seems to have alluded to that passage of his own work to which Eusebius refers in his second book (ch. xv.), in which work Papias had given some account respecting the life of this evangelist. According to this view it seems that, with the words οὔτε γὰρ ἤκουσε, there begins an explanation of the words of the presbyter.

(2) Relation to Peter. It has been observed in the article GOSPEL (which see) that this passage has been made use of in order to disprove the existence of an orally fixed evangelium-tradition, since it is here stated that Peter preached as circumstances required. To this we replied that Papias considers the Gospel of Mark to be the reflex of the discourses of Peter, in which character they are described by the presbyter; and since the Gospel of Mark really contains a sketch of the life of Jesus, the account of the presbyter does not imply that the discourses of Peter could not likewise have contained a sketch of his life. The presbyter only says that Peter did not furnish a complete life of Jesus, embracing a history of his infancy, youth, etc.; and that, therefore, the account of Peter was in some respects incomplete, since he, as Papias states, omitted various circumstances. Schleiermacher, and after him Strauss, have turned this into an

argument against the Gospel of Mark. They assert that this gospel is a summary, which, if not chronological, is at least a concatenation according to the subjects. Now the presbyter states that Mark wrote *without order*. By this expression they consider all such arrangement excluded; consequently they infer that the presbyter John, the old disciple of the Lord, spoke of another Mark. We learn, however, from what Papias adds, how Papias himself understood the words of the presbyter; and we perceive that he explains his statement by the term, *writing isolated facts*. Hence it appears that the words οὐ τάξει signify only incompleteness, but do not preclude all and every sort of arrangement.

It would be arbitrary, indeed, to suppose that another Mark had an existence in the earliest times of Christianity, without having any historical testimony for such a supposition. There is no indication that there was any other Mark in the early times of Christianity besides the Mark mentioned in the Acts, who is also reported to have been the author of that gospel which bears his name.

(3) Place among the Gospels. We have mentioned in the article LUKE (which see) that, according to Irenæus, the Gospels of Mark and Luke were written later than that of Matthew; and according to a tradition preserved by Clemens Alexandrinus, the Gospels of Matthew and Luke preceded that of Mark. The chronological order of the gospels is, according to Origen, the same in which they follow each other in the codices. Irenæus (*Adversus Hæreses*, iii. 1) states that Mark wrote after the death of Peter and Paul; but, according to Clemens Alexandrinus (*Hypotypos.* vi.) and Eusebius (*Hist. Eccles.* vi. 14), he wrote at Rome while Peter was yet living. These various data leave us in uncertainty. If the opinions concerning the relation of Mark to Matthew and Luke, which have been current since the days of Griesbach, were correct, we might be able to form a true idea concerning the chronological succession in which the first three gospels were written. Griesbach, Saunier, Strauss, and many others state it as an unquestionable fact, that the Gospel of Mark was merely an abridgment of the Gospels of Matthew and Luke. De Wette, even in the latest edition of his *Einleitung*, 1842, calls this opinion *erwiesen* 'demonstrated' (see pp. 130 and 157). The value of such demonstrations may be learned from what appears to De Wette the most certain proof of the alleged fact, viz., that the statements of Mark concerning the *temptation* of Christ are merely an abridgment of other sources. But we do not perceive why it should be impossible to furnish a condensed statement from oral communications. Weisse, Wolke, and Bauer, on the other hand, have, in recent times, asserted that the Gospel of Mark was the most ancient of all the gospels, that Luke amplified the Gospel of Mark, and that Matthew made additions to both. Weisse and Wolke employ some very artificial expedients in order to explain how it happened that, if Luke and Matthew transcribed Mark, there should have arisen a considerable difference both in words and contents. Wolke especially accuses Luke and Matthew of intentional misrepresentations. In the article GOSPEL we have stated our opinion concerning the relative position in which the evangelists stand to each other. We do not see any reason to contradict the unanimous tradition of antiquity concerning the dependence of Mark upon Peter. We deem it possible, and even probable, that Luke read Mark, and that he also alludes to him by reckoning him among the *many* who had written gospel history before him. This supposition, however, is by no means necessary or certain; and it is still possible that Mark wrote after Luke. Some of the ancient testimonies which we have quoted, namely, those of Irenæus, Clemens Alexandrinus, Jerome, and others, state that Mark's Gospel was written at Rome. Whether this was the case or not, it is certain that it was written for Gentile Christians. This appears from the explanation of Jewish customs (ch. vii:2, 11; xii:18; xiii:3; xiv:12; xv:6, 42). The same view is confirmed by the scarcity of quotations from the Old Testament, perhaps also by the absence of the genealogy of Christ, and by the omission of the Sermon on the Mount, which explains the relation of Christ to the Old Testament dispensation, and which was, therefore, of the greatest importance to Matthew.

(4) Peculiarity of Mark. The characteristic peculiarity of Mark as an author is particularly manifest in two points: (1) He reports rather the works than the discourses of our Savior; (2) He gives details more minutely and graphically than Matthew and Luke; for instance, he describes the cures effected by Jesus more exactly (iv:31, 41; vi:5, 13; vii:33; viii:23). He is also more particular in stating definite numbers (v:13, 42; vi:7, 14, 30), and furnishes more exact dates and times (i:32, 35; ii:1,26; iv:26,35; vi:2; xi:11, 19, 20, etc.). It may be that these characteristics of Mark originated from his connection with Peter.

Most of the materials of Mark's narrative occur also in Matthew and Luke. He has, however, sections exclusively belonging to himself, viz. iii: 21, 31, *sq.;* vi:17, *sq.;* xi:11; xii:28, *sq.*

We mention the conclusion of Mark's Gospel separately, since its genuineness may be called in question. Among the *Codices Majusculi* the Codex B. omits ch. xvi:9-20 altogether, and several of the *Codices Minusculi* mark this section with asterisks as doubtful. Several ancient Fathers and authors of *Scholia* state that it was wanting in some manuscripts. We cannot, however, suppose that it was arbitrarily added by a copyist, since at present all codices, except B, and all ancient versions contain it, and the Fathers in general quote it. We may also say that Mark could not have concluded his gospel with ver. 8, unless he had been accidentally prevented from finishing it. Hence Michaelis and Hug have inferred that the addition was made by the evangelist at a later period, in a similar manner as John made an addition in ch. xxi. of his gospel. Perhaps also an intimate friend, or an amanuensis, supplied the defect. If either of these two hypotheses is well founded, it may be understood why several codices were formerly without this conclusion, and why, nevertheless, it was found in most of them.   A. T.

MARK (märk). This term is variously used.

1. (Heb. בֵּן, *bin*). A sign or brand fixed on the forehead, hand or other part of the body for the purpose of identification (Ezek. ix:4, 6).

2. (Heb. אוֹת, *othe*). Whether God set a "mark" on Cain's person to distinguish him from others, or only gave him some token, as he did Gideon that he would make him conquer the Midianites, and that he would preserve him, we know not (Gen. iv:15).

3. It is used in the sense of a *target* (Heb.

מַטָּרָא, *mat-taw-raw'*, watched, 1 Sam. xx:20; Job xvi:12; Lam. iii:12).

In Gal. vi:17 Paul writes, "Henceforth let no man trouble me, for I bear in my body the marks of the Lord Jesus Christ," *i. e.,* the brand of my master, Jesus Christ. The Greek στίγμα (*stig'mah*) is the common word for the brand or mark with which masters marked their slaves. St. Paul's sufferings and scars were the *marks* or *brands* of Christ, his master.

The mark (Gr. χάραγμα, *khar'ag-mah*, stamp) was stamped on the right hand or the forehead as the badge of the followers of Antichrist (Rev. xiii:16; xiv:9, 11; xvi:2; xix:20; xx:4).

MARKET (mär'kĕt), (Heb. מַעֲרָב, *mah-ar-awb'*, a mercantile term found only in Ezek. xxvii (rendered "merchandise," except in verses 13, 17, 19, 25).

It appears to have been used in several senses: (1) *Barter* (ver. 9, 27); (2) *place* of trade (marg., verses 12, 13, 17, 19); (3) *gain* resulting from trade (ver. 27, 34). In the New Testament see Matt. xxiii:7; Mark xii:38; Luke xi:43; xx:46; Acts xvi:19, etc., and we learn from Matt. xx:3 that not only were all kinds of produce offered for sale here, but hither resorted also the laborers to find employment. The market of an ancient Greek or Roman town occupied generally one side of an area, the other sides being occupied by public buildings, temples, courts, and offices of various kinds. Laws were promulgated here, judicial investigations were instituted; questions of philosophy and public interest were discussed; and all kinds of trade and business were carried on. It was frequented by business-men and by crowds of idlers and loungers. In a strictly Oriental city, such as Jerusalem, the market had not, like the forum, this character of being the center of all public life. Still, it was always a lively place, generally situated just within the gate, and the principal scene of trade and traffic.

Schaff.

MARRIAGE (măr'rĭj), (Heb. עוֹנָה, *o-nawh'*).

(1) Divine Origin. The Divine origin of marriage, and the primitive state of the institution, are clearly recorded in the instance of the first human pair (Gen. ii:18-25), whence it appears that woman was made after man to be 'a helper suited to him.' The narrative is calculated to convey exalted ideas of the institution. It is introduced by a declaration of the Lord God, that 'it is not good that the man should be alone' (ver. 18); of the truth of which Adam had become convinced by experience. In order still further to enliven his sense of his deficiency, the various species of creatures are made to pass in review before him, 'to see what he would call them;' on which occasion he could behold each species accompanied by its appropriate helper, and upon concluding his task would become still more affectingly aware, that amid all animated nature 'there was not found an help meet for himself.' It was at this juncture, when his heart was thus thoroughly prepared to appreciate the intended blessing, that a Divine slumber (Sept. ἔκστασις, *ech'-sta-sis*) or trance, fell upon him—a state in which, as in after ages, the exercise of the external senses being suspended, the mental powers are peculiarly prepared to receive revelations from God (Gen. xv:12; Acts x:10; xxii:17; 2 Cor. xii:2). His exclamation when Eve was brought to him shows that he had been fully conscious of the circumstances of her creation, and had been instructed by them as to the nature of the relation which would thenceforth subsist between them. 'The man said, *this time,* it is bone of my bone, and flesh of my flesh; *this* shall be called woman, for out of man was this taken' (New Translation by the Rev. D. A. De Sola, etc. Lond. p. 8). The remaining words, 'for this cause shall a man leave his father and mother, and shall cleave unto his wife, and they (two) shall be one flesh,' which might otherwise seem a proleptical announcement by the historian of the social obligations of marriage, are by our Lord ascribed to the Divine agent concerned in the transaction, either uttered by him personally, or by the mouth of Adam while in a state of inspiration. 'Have ye not read that he that made them at the beginning, made them male and female, *and said,* for this cause,' etc. (Matt. xix:4, 5).

(2) Monogamous. It is a highly important circumstance in this transaction that God created only *one* female for *one* man, and united them —a circumstance which is the very basis of our Lord's reasoning in the passage against divorce and remarriage; but which basis is lost, and his reasoning consequently rendered inconclusive, by the inattention of our translators to the absence of the article, 'he made them ἄρσεν καὶ θῆλυ,' *a* male and *a* female, 'and said, they shall become one flesh; so that they are no more two, but one flesh. What, therefore, God hath joined together, let no man put asunder.' 'The weight of our Lord's argument,' says Campbell, 'lay in this circumstance, that God at first created no more than a single pair, one of each sex, whom he united in the bond of marriage, and, in so doing, exhibited a standard of that union to all generations. The apostasy introduced a new feature into the institution, namely, the subjection of the wife's will to that of her husband (Gen. iii:16; comp. Num. xxx:6-16). The primitive model was adhered to even by Cain, who seems to have had but one wife (Gen. iv:17).

(3) Polygamy. Polygamy, one of the earliest developments of human degeneracy, was introduced by Lamech, who 'took unto him two wives' (Gen. iv:19). The intermarriage of 'the Sons of God,' *i. e.* the worshipers of the true God, with 'the daughters of men,' *i. e.* the irreligious, is the next incident in the history of marriage. They indulged in unrestrained polygamy, 'they took them wives of all that they chose.' From this event may be dated that headlong degeneracy of mankind at this period, which ultimately brought on them extirpation by a deluge (Gen. vi:3-7). At the time of that catastrophe Noah had but one wife (Gen. vii:7), and so each of his sons (ver. 13). Pursuing the investigation according to chronological arrangement, Job next appears (B. C. 2130) as the husband of one wife (Job ii:9; xix:17). Reference is made to the adulterer, who is represented as in terror and accursed (xxiv:15-18). The wicked man is represented as leaving 'widows' behind him; whence his polygamy may be inferred (xxvii:15). Job expresses his abhorrence of fornication (xxxi:1), and of adultery (ver. 9), which appears in his time to have been punished by the judges (ver. 11). Following the same arrangement, we find Abraham and Nahor introduced as having each one wife (Gen. xi:29). From the narrative of Abraham's first equivocation concerning Sarah, it may be gathered that marriage was held sacred in Egypt. Abraham fears that the Egyptians would sooner rid themselves of him by murder than infringe by adultery the relation of wife even to an obscure stranger. The reproof of

Pharaoh. 'Why didst thou say, She is my sister? so I might have taken her to me to wife: now therefore behold thy *wife,* take her, and go thy way' (Gen. xii:11-19), affords a most honorable testimony to the views of marriage entertained by Pharaoh at that period, and most likely by his court and nation. It seems that Sarah was Abraham's half-sister. Such marriages were permitted till the giving of the Law (Lev. xviii:9). Thus Amram, the father of Moses and Aaron, married his father's sister (Exod. vi:20), a union forbidden in Lev. xviii:12.

(4) Concubinage. The first mention of concubinage, or the condition of a legal though subordinate wife, occurs in the case of Hagar, Sarah's Egyptian handmaid, whom Sarah, still childless, after a residence of ten years in Canaan, prevailed on Abraham, apparently against his will, to receive into that relation (Gen. xvi:1), which was however considered inviolable (Gen. xlix:4; Lev. xviii:8; 2 Sam. iii:8, 16, 21, 22; 1 Chron. v:1). The vehement desire for offspring, common to women in the East, as appears from the histories of Rebecca (Gen. xxv:21), of Rachel (xxx:1), of Leah (ver. 5), and of Hannah (1 Sam. i:6, 7), seems to have been Sarah's motive for adopting a procedure practiced in such cases in that region in all ages. The miseries naturally consequent upon it are amply portrayed in the history of the Patriarchs (Gen. xvi:4-10; xxx: 1, 3, 15).

Lot does not appear to have exceeded one wife (Gen. xix:15). The second equivocation of the same kind by Abraham respecting Sarah elicits equally honorable sentiments concerning marriage, on the part of Abimelech, king of Gerar (Gen. xx:5, 6, 9, 10, etc.), who, it appears, had but one proper wife (ver. 17; see also ch. xxvi: 7-11). Perhaps Abraham relied on the ancient custom, which will shortly be adverted to, of the consent of the 'brother' being requisite to the sister's marriage, and thus hoped to secure his wife's safety and his own.

(5) Marriages, How Brought About. In ancient times the parents chose wives for their children (Gen. xxi:21; xxxviii:6; Deut. xxii:16); or the man who wished a particular female asked his father to obtain her from *her* father, as in the case of Shechem, B. C. 1732 (Gen. xxxiv: 4-6; comp. Judg. xiv:2, 3). The consent of her brothers seems to have been necessary (verses 5, 8, 11, 13, 14; comp. Gen. xxiv:50; 2 Sam. xiii: 20-29). A dowry was given by the suitor to the father and brethren of the female (verses 11, 12; comp. 1 Sam. xviii:25; Hos. iii:2). This, in a common case, amounted to from 30 to 50 shekels, according to the law of Moses (comp. Exod. xxii:16; Deut. xxii:29). Pausanias considers it so remarkable for a man to part with his daughter without receiving a marriage-portion for her, that he takes pains, in a case he mentions, to explain the reason (*Lacon.* iii:12, 2). In later times we meet with an exception (Tobit viii: 23). It is most likely that from some time before the last-named period the Abrahamidæ restricted their marriages to circumcised persons (Gen. xxviii:8; comp. Judg. iii:6; 1 Kings xi:8, 11, 16; Joseph. *Antiq.* xi:8, 2; xii:4, 6; xviii:9, 5).

(6) Various Marriage Accompaniments, Etc. The marriage of Isaac develops additional particulars; for beside Abraham's unwillingness that his son should marry a Canaanitess (Gen. xxiv:3; comp. xxvi:34; xxvii:46; Exod. xxxiv: 16; Josh. xxiii:12; Ezra ix:2; x:3, 10, 11), costly jewels are given to the bride at the betrothal (ver. 22), and 'precious things to her mother and brother' (ver. 53) ; a customary period between espousals and nuptials is referred to (ver. 55) ; and the blessing of an abundant offspring invoked upon the bride by her relatives (ver. 60)—which most likely was the only marriage ceremony then and for ages afterwards (comp. Ruth iv:11-13; Ps. xlv:16, 17) ; but in Tobit vii:3, the father places his daughter's right hand in the hand of Tobias before he invokes this blessing. It is remarkable that no representation has been found of a marriage ceremony among the tombs of Egypt (Wilkinson's *Ancient Egypt,* vol. ii., Lond. 1837). The Rabbins say that among the Jews it consisted of a kiss (Cant. i:2). It is probable that the marriage covenant was committed to writing (Prov. ii:17; Mal. ii:14; Tobit vii:13, 14) ; perhaps, also, confirmed with an oath (Ezek. xvi:8). It seems to have been the custom with the patriarchs and ancient Jews to bury their wives in their own graves, but not their concubines (Gen. xlix:31). In Gen. xxv:1, Abraham, after the death of Sarah, marries a second wife. Esau's polygamy is mentioned in Gen. xxviii: 9; xxxvi:2-13. Jacob serves seven years to obtain Rachel in marriage (Gen. xxix:18-20) ; and has a marriage feast, to which the men of the place are invited (ver. 22; comp. Cant. v:1; viii:33). Samson's marriage feast lasts a week, B. C. 1136 (Judg. xiv:10-12; comp. John ii: 1, etc.) ; in later times it lasted longer (Tobit viii:19). The persons invited to Samson's marriage are young men (Judg. xiv:10) ; called 'sons of the bridal-chamber' (Matt. ix:15). Females were invited to marriages (Ps. xlv:14), and attended the bride and bridegroom to their abode (1 Macc. ix:37) ; and in the time of Christ, if it was evening, with lamps and flambeaux (Matt. xxv:1-10). In later ages the guests were summoned when the banquet was ready (Matt. xxii: 3), and furnished with a marriage garment (ver. 11). The father of the bride conducted her at night to her husband (Gen. xxix:23; Tobit viii: 1). The bride and bridegroom were richly ornamented (Is. lxi:10). In Mesopotamia, and the East generally, it was the custom to marry the eldest sister first (Gen. xxix:26). By the deception practiced upon Jacob in that country, he marries two wives, and, apparently, without any one objecting (ver. 31). Laban obtains a promise from Jacob not to marry any more wives than Rachel and Leah (Gen. xxxi:50). The wives and concubines of Jacob, and their children, travel together (Gen. xxxii:22, 23) ; but a distinction is made between them in the hour of danger (Gen. xxxiii:1, 2; comp. Gen. xxv:6).

(7) Details Regarding Marriages, Etc. It would seem, from the instance of Potiphar's wife, that monogamy was practiced in Egypt (Gen. xxxix:7). Pharaoh gave to Joseph one wife (Gen. xli:45). The Israelites, while in Egypt, seem to have restricted themselves to one. One case is recorded of an Israelite who had married an Egyptian woman (Lev. xxiv:10). The giving of the law (B. C. 1491) acquaints us with many regulations concerning marriage, which were different from the practices of the Jews while in Egypt, and from those of the Canaanites, to whose land they were approaching (Lev. xviii: 3). There we find laws for regulating the marriages of bondmen (Exod. xxi:3, 4), and of a bondmaid (verses 7-12). The prohibition against marriages with the Canaanites is established by a positive law (Deut. vii:3). Marriage is prohibited with any one near of kin, 'of the remainder of his flesh' (Lev. xviii:6-19). A priest

is prohibited from marrying one that had been a harlot, or divorced (Lev. xxi:7). The highpriest was also excluded from marrying a widow, and restricted to one wife (verses 13, 14). Daughters who, through want of brothers, were heiresses to an estate were required to marry into their own tribe, and if possible, a kinsman, to prevent the estate passing into another family (Num. xxvii:1-11 ; xxxvi:1-12). The husband had power to annul his wife's vow, if he heard it, and interfered at the time (Num. xxx:6-16). If a man had betrothed a wife, he was exempt from the wars, etc. (Deut. xx:7; xxiv:5). It was allowed to marry a beautiful captive in war, whose husband probably had been killed (Deut. xxi: 10-14, etc.). Abundance of offspring was one of the blessings promised to obedience, during the miraculous providence which superintended the Theocracy (Lev. xxvi:9; Deut. vii:13, 14; xxviii: 11; Ps. cxxvii:3; cxxviii:3) ; and disappointment in marriage was one of the curses (Deut. xxviii:18, 30; comp. also Jer. vi:12 ; viii:10). A daughter of a distinguished person was offered in marriage as a reward for perilous services (Josh. xv:16, 17; 1 Sam. xvii:25). Concubinage appears in Israel, B. C. 1413. (Judg. xix:1-4). The violation of a concubine is avenged (Judg. xx:5-10). Polygamy (Judg. viii:30). The state of marriage among the Philistines may be inferred, in the time of Samson, from the sudden divorce from him of his wife by her father, and her being given to his friend (Judg. xiv:20), and from the father offering him a younger sister instead (Judg. xv:2). David's numerous wives (2 Sam. iii:3-5). In Ps. xlv., which is referred to this period by the best harmonists, there is a description of a royal marriage upon a most magnificent scale. The marriage of Solomon to Pharaoh's daughter is recorded in 1 Kings iii:1; to which the Song of Solomon probably relates, and from which it appears that his mother 'crowned him with a crown on the day of his espousals' (verses 3, 11; and see Sept. and Vulg. of Is. lxi:10). It would appear that in his time females were married young (Prov. ii:17; comp. Joel i:8) ; also males (Prov. v: 18). An admirable description of a good wife is given in Prov. xxxi:10-31. The excessive multiplication of wives and concubines was the cause and effect of Solomon's apostasy in his old age (1 Kings xi:1-8). He confesses his error in Ecclesiastes, where he eulogizes monogamy (ix:9; ii:10). Rehoboam took a plurality of wives (2 Chron. xi:18-21) ; and so Abijah (2 Chron. xiii:21), and Ahab (1 Kings xx:3), and Belshazzar, king of Babylon (Dan. v:2). It would seem that the outward manners of the Jews, about the time of our Lord's advent, had become improved, since there is no case recorded in the New Testament of polygamy or concubinage among them.

MARRIAGE, CHRISTIAN (măr'rĭj, krĭs'-chan).

(1) Our Lord excludes all causes of divorce, except adultery (Matt. v:32), and ascribes the origin of the Mosaic law to the hardness of their hearts. The same doctrine concerning divorce had been taught by the prophets (Jer. iii:1; Micah ii:9; Mal. ii:14-16).

(2) The apostles inculcate the sacredness of marriage (Rom. vii:3; 1 Cor. vii:4, 10, 11, 39) ; yet St. Paul considers obstinate desertion by an unbelieving party as a release (1 Cor. vii:15).

(3) Our Lord does not reprehend celibacy for the sake of religion, 'those who make themselves

eunuchs for the kingdom of heaven's sake' (Matt. xix:12; comp. 1 Cor. vii:32, 36).

(4) Second marriages not condemned in case of death (1 Cor. vii:39).

(5) Mixed marriages disapproved (Deut. vii:3; 2 Cor. vi:14).

(6) Early marriage not recommended (1 Cor. vii:36).   J. F. D.

Figurative. Both in the Old Testament and in the New Testament the betrothal, marriage feast, and marriage have given rise to numerous allegorical and typical allusions, the relation between Jehovah and his chosen people being the point of comparison in the Old Testament (Is. liv:5; Jer. iii:14; Hos. ii:19, etc.); that of Christ and his Church in the New Testament (Matt. ix:15; John iii:29; 2 Cor. xi:2; Rev. xix:7).

Literature. Evans, *Christian Doctrine of Marriage* (Baltimore, 1860); and magazine articles as cited in Poole's Index; *Holy Matrimony*, Oscar D. Watkins, M. A. Rivington, Percival & Co., (London, 1895).

MARRIAGE, LEVIRATE (măr'rĭj lev'ĭ-răt), the marriage of a childless widow to her husband's brother or nearest of kin, according to ancient Israelitish law.

Judah, Jacob's son by Leah, had married a Canaanitish woman (Gen. xxxviii:2). His firstborn son was Er (ver. 3). Judah took a wife for him (ver. 6). Er soon after died (ver. 7), and Judah said to Onan, 'Go in unto thy brother's wife, Tamar, and marry her, and raise up seed to thy brother.' 'Onan knew that the offspring would not be his.' All these circumstances bespeak a pre-established and well-known law, and he evaded the purpose of it, and thereby, it is said, incurred the wrath of God (ver. 10). It seems from the same account, to have been well understood, that upon his death the duty devolved upon the next surviving brother. No change is recorded in this law till just before the entrance of Israel into Canaan (B. C. 1451), at which time Moses modified it by new regulations to this effect:—'If brethren dwell together (*i. e.* in the same locality), and one of them die, and leave no child, the wife of the dead must not marry out of the family, but her husband's brother or his next kinsman must take her to wife, and perform the duty of a husband's brother, and the firstborn of this union shall succeed in the name of his deceased father, that his name may be extant in Israel;' not literally bear his name, for Ruth allowed her son by Boaz to be called Obed, and not Mahlon, the name of her first husband (Ruth iv:17, yet see Josephus, *Antiq.,* iv. 8, 23). In case the man declined the office, the woman was to bring him before the elders, loose his shoe from off his foot, and spit in, or, as some render it, before his face, by way of contempt (Deut. xxv:9, 10; Josephus understands *in* the face, *Antiq.* v. 9. 4), and shall say, 'So shall it be done unto the man that will not build up his brother's house; and his name shall be called in Israel, the house of him that hath his shoe loosed.' It does not appear that the original law was binding on the brother, if already married; and we may well believe that Moses, who wished to mitigate it, allowed of that exception. The instance of Ruth, who married Boaz, her husband's relation, exhibits the practice of the law under the Judges. Boaz was neither the father of, nor the nearest relation to, Elimelech, father-in-law to Ruth, the wife of Mahlon, and yet he married her after the refusal of him who was the nearest relation (Ruth ii:20; iii, iv).

MARRIAGE PROCESSIONS. The procession accompanying the bride from the house of her father to that of the bridegroom was generally one of great pomp, according to the circumstances of the married couple; and for this they often chose the night. Hence, in the parable of the ten virgins that went to meet the bride and bridegroom (Matt. xxv) it is said the virgins were asleep; and at midnight, being awaked at the cry of the bridegroom's coming, the foolish virgins found they had no oil to supply their lamps; and while they went to buy, the bridegroom and his attendants passed by.

Mr. Taylor has collected very copious information relative to the marriage processions among the Oriental people, in *Fragments,* 49, 557, and 674. Many of the circumstances attending these will be found to contribute aid in the elucidation of two or three passages of Scripture, but their value would not justify us in appropriating to them the space they would occupy. "At a marriage, the procession of which I saw some years ago," says Mr. Ward, (*View of Hist. of Hindoos,* vol. iii. p. 171, 172.) "the bridegroom came from a distance, and the bride lived at Serampore, to which place the bridegroom was to come by water. After waiting two or three hours, at length, near midnight, it was announced, as if in the very words of Scripture, 'Behold! the bridegroom cometh; go ye out to meet him.' All the persons employed now lighted their lamps, and ran with them in their hands, to fill up their stations in the procession; some of them had lost their lights, and were unprepared, but it was then too late to seek them, and the cavalcade moved forward to the house of the bride, at which place the company entered a large and splendidly illuminated area before the house, covered with an awning, where a great multitude of friends, dressed in their best apparel, were seated upon mats. The bridegroom was carried in the arms of a friend, and placed in a superb seat in the midst of the company, where he sat a short time, and then went into the house, the door of which was immediately shut, and guarded by sepoys. I and others expostulated with the doorkeepers, but in vain. Never was I so struck with our Lord's beautiful parable as at this moment:—*and the door was shut.*"

In the beautiful parable of our Lord, there are ten virgins, who took their lamps, and went in a company to meet the bridegroom. Five of them were *wise,* endued with prudence and discretion; the other five were *foolish,* thoughtless and inconsiderate. The thoughtless took their lamps, but were so foolish as to take only a little oil in them to serve the present occasion. But the prudent, mindful of futurity, and knowing that the coming of the bridegroom was uncertain, as well as filling their lamps, prudently took a quantity of oil in their vessels to supply them, that they might be ready to go forth at a moment's warning. Having waited long for the bridegroom, and he not appearing, they all, tired with long watching, and fatigued with tedious expectation, were overcome with sleep, and sunk into profound repose. But lo, at midnight they were suddenly alarmed with a cry "The bridegroom, the bridegroom cometh! Hasten to meet and congratulate him." Roused with this sudden proclamation, they all got up and trimmed their lamps. But the oil in those that belonged to the foolish virgins, being consumed, they were in the utmost confusion when they found them gone out; and having nothing in their vessels to fill them with, they began to see their mistake. In this extremity they entreated their companions to impart to them some of their oil, telling them that their lamps were gone out. To these entreaties the prudent answered, that they had only provided a sufficient quantity for their own use, and therefore advised them to go and purchase oil of those who sold it. They departed accordingly, but while absent on this errand, the bridegroom came, and the prudent virgins, being prepared for his reception, went along with him to the nuptial entertainment, and the door was shut. After some time the others returned, and, knocking loud, supplicated earnestly for admission. But the bridegroom repulsed them, telling them, Ye pretended to be my friends, and to do me honor on this occasion; but ye have not acted as friends, for which reason *I know you not;* I do not acknowledge you as my friends, and will not admit strangers.

From another parable, in which a great king is represented as making a most magnificent entertainment at the marriage of his son (Matt. xxii), we learn that all the guests who were honored with an invitation were expected to be dressed in a manner suitable to the splendor of such an occasion, as a token of just respect to the newly-married couple; and that after the procession, in the *evening,* from the bride's house was concluded, the guests, before they were admitted into the hall where the entertainment was served up, were taken into an apartment and viewed, that it might be known if any stranger had intruded, or if any of the company were appareled in raiment unsuitable to the genial solemnity they were going to celebrate; and such, if found, were expelled from the house with every mark of ignominy and disgrace. From the knowledge of this custom the following passage receives great light and luster. When the king came in to see the guests, he discovered among them a person who had not on a *wedding garment.* He called him and said, Friend, how came you to intrude into my palace in a dress so unsuitable to this occasion? The man was struck dumb; he had no apology to offer for this disrespectful neglect. The king then called to his servants, and bade them bind him hand and foot, to drag him out of the room, and thrust him out into the midnight darkness.　　　Harwood.

MARROW (măr'rŏ), (Heb. מֹחַ, *mo'akh,* Job xxi:24; מָחָה, *maw-khaw',* to mix with marrow, Is. xxv:6; Gr. μυελός, *moo-el-os',* Heb. iv:12; חֵלֶב, *kheh'leb,* Ps. lxiii:5, the richest or choice part, and שִׁקּוּי, *shik-koo'ee,* Prov. iii:8, *moisture*).

Marrow is a soft, oleaginous, and very nourishing substance, contained in the hollow of some animal bones, and which strengthens them, and promotes their healing when broken.

Figurative. To "*marrow*" are compared, (1) The most secret dispositions, thoughts, designs, and desires of our soul (Heb. iv:12). (2) Christ and his fulness of righteousness, grace, and glory, and all the fulness of God in him, which are the delightful nourishment and strength of churches, saints, and their holy dispositions (Ps. lxiii:5; Is. xxv:6). (3) The fear of the Lord, and departing from evil, which greatly promote the health and true welfare of both soul and body (Prov. iii:8).　　　Brown.

MARSENA (mär'se-na), (Heb. מַרְסְנָא, *mar-sen-aw',* worthy), a satrap, or governor of Xerxes (Esth. i:14), B. C. 483.

MARSH (märsh), (Heb. גֶּבֶא, *geh'beh,* a reservoir, Ezek. xlvii:11), a swamp or wet piece of land. The place referred to by Ezekiel is the "Valley of Salt," near the Dead Sea; for there the Kidron, the course of which the prophet describes the holy waters as following, empties. (Barnes, *Peop. Bib. Dict.*)

MARS' HILL (märz hĭll), (Gr. Ἄρειος πάγος, *ar'-i-os pag'os,* Acts xvii:22). See AREOPAGUS.

MART (märt), (Heb. סָחַר, *saw-khar',* to go about as a merchant, Is. xxiii:3. See Prov. iii:14; Is. xlv:14), a trading place or emporium.

Delitzsch says the word cannot have this meaning. (*Com. in loco.*)

MARTHA (mär'thà), (Gr. Μάρθα, *mar'tha;* Heb. מָרְתָא, *mar'thaw,* perhaps *lady*), sister of Lazarus and Mary, who resided in the same house with them at Bethany. (See LAZARUS.)

From the house at Bethany being called 'her house,' in Luke x:38, and from the leading part which Martha is always seen to take in domestic matters, it has seemed to some that she was a widow, to whom the house at Bethany belonged, and with whom her brother and sister lodged; but this is uncertain, and the common opinion, that the sisters managed the household of their brother, is more probable. Luke probably calls it her house because he had no occasion to mention, and does not mention, Lazarus; and when we speak of a house which is occupied by different persons, we avoid circumlocution by calling it the house of the individual who happens to be the subject of our discourse. Jesus was intimate with this family, and their house was often his home when at Jerusalem, being accustomed to retire thither in the evening, after having spent the day in the city. The point which the Evangelists bring out most distinctly with respect to Martha, lies in the contrariety of disposition between her and her sister Mary. The first notice of Christ's visiting this family occurs in Luke x:38-42. He was received with great attention by the sisters; and Martha soon hastened to provide suitable entertainment for the Lord and his followers, while Mary remained in his presence, sitting at his feet, and drinking in the sacred words that fell from his lips. The active, bustling solicitude of Martha, anxious that the best things in the house should be made subservient to the Master's use and solace, and the quiet earnestness of Mary, more desirous to profit by the golden opportunity of hearing his instructions, than to minister to his personal wants, strongly mark the points of contrast in the characters of the two sisters. The part taken by the sisters in the transactions connected with the death and resurrection of Lazarus, is entirely and beautifully in accordance with their previous history. Martha is still more engrossed with outward things, while Mary surrenders herself more to her feelings, and to inward meditation. When they heard that Jesus was approaching, Martha hastened beyond the village to meet him, 'but Mary sat still in the house' (John xi:20, 22). When Martha saw Jesus actually appear, whose presence had been so anxiously desired, she exhibits a strong degree of faith, and hesitates not to express a confident hope that he, to whom all things were possible, would even yet afford relief. But, as is usual with persons of her lively character, when Christ answered, with what seemed to her a vague intimation, 'Thy brother shall rise again,' she was instantly cast down from her height of confidence, the reply being less direct than she expected: she referred this saying to the general resurrection at the last day, and thereon relapsed into despondency and grief. This feeling Jesus reproved, by directing her attention, before all other things, to that inward, eternal, and Divine life, which consists in union with him, and which is raised far above the power even of the grave. This he did in the magnificent words, 'I am the resurrection, and the life: he that believeth in me, though he were dead, yet shall he live: and whosoever liveth and believeth in me shall never die. Believest thou this?' Sorrow and shame permitted the troubled Martha, in whose heart the feeling of an unconditional and entire surrender to his will was re-awakened, to make only the general confession that he was actually the promised Messiah; in which confession she, however, comprised an acknowledgment of his power and greatness. It is clear, however, that she found nothing in this discourse with Christ, to encourage her first expectation of relief. With the usual rapid change in persons of lively susceptibilities, she had now as completely abandoned all hope of rescue for her brother, as she had before been sanguine of his restoration to life. Thus, when Jesus directed the stone to be rolled away from the sepulcher, she gathered from this no ground of hope; but rather objected to its being done, because the body, which had been four days in the tomb, must already have become disagreeable. The reproof of Christ, 'Said I not unto thee, that, if thou wouldest believe, thou shouldest see the glory of God?' suggests that more discourse had passed between them than the Evangelist has recorded, seeing that no such assurance is contained in the previous narrative (John xi:39, 40).

Nothing more is recorded of Martha, save that some time after, at a supper given to Christ and his disciples at Bethany, she, as usual, busied herself in the external service. Lazarus, so marvelously restored from the grave, sat with her guests at table. 'Martha served,' and Mary occupied her favorite station at the feet of Jesus, which she bathed with her tears, and anointed with costly ointment (John xii:1, 2). (See LAZARUS; MARY, 4.)

Character. There are few characters in the New Testament, and certainly no female character, so strongly brought out in its natural points as that of Martha; and it is interesting to observe that Luke and John, although relating different transactions in which she was concerned, perfectly agree in the traits of character which they assign to her. Tholuck has skillfully followed out its development in his *Commentary* on the eleventh chapter of St. John. See also Niemeyer, *Charakt.* i. 66; and Hall's *Contemplations,* vol. iii., b. 4, *Contemp.,* 17, 23, 24.

MARTYR (mär'tēr), (Gr. μάρτυς, *mar'toos,* a witness).

This word means properly *a witness,* and is applied in the New Testament—(1) To judicial witnesses (Matt. xviii:16; xxvi:65; Mark xiv: 63; Acts vi:13; vii:58; 2 Cor. xiii:1; 1 Tim. v:19; Heb. x:28). The Septuagint also uses it for the Hebrew עֵד *ed,* in Deut. xvii:6; Prov. xxiv:28. (2) To one who has testified, or can testify to the truth of what he has seen, heard, or known. This is a frequent sense in the New Testament: as in Luke xxiv:48; Acts i:8, 22;

Rom. i:9; 2 Cor. i:23; 1 Thess. ii:5, 10; 1 Tim. vi:12; 2 Tim. ii:2; 1 Pet. v:1; Rev. i:5; iii:14; xi:3, and elsewhere. (3) The meaning of the word which has now become the most usual, is that in which it occurs most rarely in the Scripture, *i. e.,* one who by his death bears witness to the truth. In this sense we find it only in Acts xxii:20; Rev. ii:13; xvii:6. This now exclusive sense of the word was brought into general use by the early ecclesiastical writers, who applied it to every one who suffered death in the Christian cause (see Suicer, *Thesaurus Eccles. sub voc.).* Stephen was in this sense the first martyr (see STEPHEN); and the spiritual honors of his death tended in no small degree to raise to the most extravagant estimation, in the early church, the value of the testimony of blood. Eventually a martyr's death was supposed, on the alleged authority of the under-named texts, to cancel all the sins of the past life (Luke xii:50; Mark x:39); to supply the place of baptism (Matt. x:39); and at once to secure admittance to the presence of the Lord in Paradise (Matt. v:10-12). In imitation of the family custom of annually commemorating at the grave the death of deceased members, the churches celebrated the deaths of their martyrs by prayer at their graves, and by love-feasts. From this high estimation of the martyrs, Christians were sometimes led to deliver themselves up voluntarily to the public authorities—thus justifying the charge of fanaticism brought against them by the heathen. For the most part, however, this practice was discountenanced, the words of Christ himself being brought against it (Matt. x:23; see Gieseler, *Eccles. Hist.* i. 109, 110).

MARVEL (mär'věl), (Heb. פָּלָא, *paw-law',* to separate, to distinguish).

The word means: **1.** To be struck with surprise at the sight or thought of anything strange and uncommon (Jer. iv:9).

2. To exercise a reverential regard to; or with wonder to adore and serve (Rev. xiii:13).

MARVELS OR WONDERS. **1.** Things strange and astonishing, as the more rare appearances of nature (Ps. cvii:24); or the miracles which God wrought in delivering Israel out of Egypt (Ps. cv:27).

2. A token or sign; thus Isaiah was a "wonder" in Egypt and Ethiopia, as his walking without his upper robe, and barefoot, was a presage of calamities to these countries (Is. xx:3). (See MIRACLES.)

MARY (mā'ry), (Heb. מִרְיָם, *meer-yawm',* rebellion; Gr. Μαρία, *ma-ree'a,* or Μαριάμ, *ma-ree-am').*

1. **The Mother of Jesus.** 'The Mother of Jesus' (Acts i:14), and 'Mary his Mother' (Matt. ii:11), are the appellations of one who has in later times been generally called the 'Virgin Mary,' but who is never so designated in Scripture. Little is known of this 'highly favored' individual, in whom was fulfilled the first prophecy made to man, that 'the seed of the *woman* should bruise the serpent's head' (Gen. iii:15). As her history was of no consequence to Christianity, it is not given at large. Her genealogy is recorded by St. Luke (ch. iii.), in order to prove the truth of the predictions which had foretold the descent of the Messiah from Adam through Abraham and David, with the design evidently of showing that Christ was of that royal house and lineage (comp. Davidson's *Sacred Hermeneutics,* p. 589, sq.).

Eusebius, the early ecclesiastical historian, although unusually lengthy upon 'the name Jesus,' and the genealogies in Matthew and Luke's Gospels, throws no new light upon Mary's birth and parentage. The legends respecting Anne, who is said to have been her mother, are pure fables without the slightest evidence.

(1) The Annunciation. The earliest event in her history, of which we have any notice, was the annunciation to her by the angel Gabriel that she was destined, whilst yet a pure virgin, to become the mother of the Messiah—an event which was a literal fulfilment of the prophecy given centuries before by Isaiah, that 'a *virgin* should conceive, and bear a son, and should call his name Immanuel,' which being interpreted, is 'God with us' (Is. vii:14; Matt. i:23). On this occasion she was explicitly informed that she should conceive by the miraculous power of God, and that her child should be 'Holy,' and be called 'the Son of God.' As a confirmation of her faith in this announcement she was also told by the angel that her cousin Elisabeth, who was the wife of one of the chief priests, and who was now far advanced in years, had conceived a son, and that the time was not far off when her reproach among women should cease (Luke i: 36).

(2) Visit to Elisabeth. Almost immediately on receiving this announcement Mary hastened from Nazareth, where she was when the angel visited her, to the house of her cousin, who was then residing in the hilly district in 'a city of Judah,' supposed to be Hebron. The meeting of these two pious females, on whom such unexpected privileges had been conferred, was one of mutual congratulations, and united thanksgiving to the Author of their blessings. It was on this occasion that Mary uttered the *Magnificat*—that splendid burst of grateful adoration which Christians of all parties have from the earliest times delighted to adopt as expressive of the best feelings of the pious heart towards God (Luke i:39-56). After spending three months with her relative, Mary returned to Nazareth, where a severe trial awaited her, arising out of the condition in which it had now become apparent she was.

(3) Betrothed to Joseph. Betrothed (perhaps in early life) to a person of the name of Joseph, an artificer of some sort (Matt. xiii:55), probably, as our translators suppose, a carpenter, the Jewish law held her exposed to the same penalties which awaited the married wife who should be found unfaithful to the spousal vow. Joseph, however, being a right-hearted man ('one who feels and acts as a man ought to do in the circumstances in which he is placed'), was unwilling to subject her to the evils of a public exposure of what he deemed her infidelity; and accordingly was turning in his mind how he might privately dissolve his connection with her, when an angel was sent to him also to inform him in a dream of the true state of the case, and enjoin upon him to complete his engagement with her by taking her as his wife. This injunction he obeyed, and hence came to be regarded by the Jews as the father of Jesus (Matt. i:18-25).

(4) Census of the People. Summoned by an edict of Augustus, which commanded that a *census* of the population of the whole Roman empire should be taken, and that each person should be enrolled in the chief city of his family or tribe, Mary and her husband went up to Bethlehem, the city of the Davidic family; and whilst there the child Jesus was born.

(5) Subsequent History. After this event the only circumstances in her history mentioned by the sacred historians are her appearance and

offerings in the temple according to the law of Moses (Luke i:22, *sq.*); her return with her husband to Nazareth (Luke ii:39); their habit of annually visiting Jerusalem at the Feast of the Passover (verse 41); the appearance of the Magi, which seems to have occurred at one of these periodic visits (Matt. ii:1-12); the flight of the holy family into Egypt, and their return, after the death of Herod, to Nazareth (verses 13-23); the scene which occurred on another of those periodic visits, when, after having proceeded two days' journey on her way homeward, she discovered that her son was not in the company, and, on returning to Jerusalem, found him sitting in the temple with the doctors of the law, 'both hearing them and asking them questions' (Luke ii:42-52); her appearance and conduct at the marriage feast in Cana of Galilee (John ii:1, *sq.*); her attempt in the synagogue at Capernaum to induce Jesus to desist from teaching (Matt. xii:46, *sq.*); her accompanying of her son when he went up to Jerusalem immediately before his crucifixion; her following him to Calvary; her being consigned by him while hanging on the cross to the care of his beloved apostle John, who from that time took her to reside in his house (John xix:25, *sq.*); and her associating with the disciples at Jerusalem after his ascension (Acts i:14).

(6) Traditions of Death, Etc. The traditions respecting the death of Mary differ materially from each other. There is a letter of the General Council of Ephesus in the fifth century, which states that she lived at Ephesus with St. John, and there died and was buried. Another epistle of the same age says she died at Jerusalem, and was buried in Gethsemane. The legend tells that three days after her interment, when the grave was opened (that Thomas the apostle might pay reverence to her remains), her body was not to be found, 'but only an exceeding fragrance,' whereupon it was concluded that it had been taken up to heaven. The translations of Enoch and Elijah, and the ascension of the Lord Jesus Christ, took place while they were *alive,* and the facts are recorded by the inspiration of God; but when the *dead* body of Mary was conveyed through the earth, and removed thence there were *no witnesses,* and no revelation was ever made of the extraordinary and novel incident, which certainly has no parallel in Scripture. This miraculous event is appropriately called 'the Assumption.'

It is said that Mary died in A. D. 63. The Canon of Scripture was closed in A. D. 96, thirty-three years after her decease; which, however, is never alluded to by any of the apostles in their writings, nor by St. John, to whose care she was entrusted.

In the Roman Catholic church many facts are believed and doctrines asserted concerning the Virgin Mary, which not only are without any authority from Scripture, but many of which are diametrically opposed to its declarations.

It does not appear that Mary ever saw Christ after the resurrection; for she was not one of the 'chosen witnesses' specified in Scripture, as Mary Magdalene was. S. D.

(7) Character. "Her faith and humility exhibit themselves in her immediate surrender of herself to the Divine will, though ignorant how that was to be accomplished (Luke i:38); her energy and earnestness in her journey from Nazareth to Hebron (verse 39); her happy thankfulness in her song of joy (verse 48); her silent, musing thoughtfulness in her pondering over the shepherds' visit (ii:19), and in her keeping her Son's words in her heart (verse 51), though she could not fully understand their import. In a word, so far as Mary is portrayed to us in Scripture, she is, as we should have expected, the most tender, the most faithful, humble, patient and loving of women, but a *woman* still" (Smith, *Dict.*).

(8) Literature. Mrs. Jameson, *Legends of the Madonna* (Lond. 1852); Jones, *On the New Testament*, vol. ii, cc. xiii, xv; Wilberforce, *Rome—Her New Dogma, etc.* (Oxford, 1855).

2. Mary Magdalene. (mā'ry măg'da-lēne), (Gr. Μαγδαληνή, *mag-dal-ay-nay'*), probably so called from Magdala in Galilee, the town where she is supposed to have dwelt. According to the Talmudists, Magdalene signifies 'a plaiter of hair.'

(1) Name. Much wrong has been done to this individual from imagining that she was the person spoken of by St. Luke in ch. vii:39; but there is no evidence to support this opinion. There were two occasions on which Christ was anointed. The first is thus recorded in John xii: 1, 3: 'Six days before the Passover Jesus came to Bethany, where Lazarus was which had been dead, whom he raised from the dead. There they made him a supper; and Martha served. Then took Mary a pound of ointment of spikenard, very costly, and anointed the feet of Jesus, and wiped his feet with her hair.' This Mary was certainly the sister of Martha. The second instance occurred in the house of Simon. 'And, behold, a woman in the city, which was a sinner, when she knew that Jesus sat at meat in the Pharisee's house, brought an alabaster box of ointment, and stood at his feet behind him weeping, and began to wash his feet with tears, and did wipe them with the hairs of her head, and kissed his feet, and anointed them with the ointment' (Luke vii:37). How Mary Magdalene came to be identified with the person here mentioned, it is difficult to say; but such is the case and accordingly she is generally regarded as having been a woman of depraved character. For such an inference, however, there appears to be no just ground whatever.

(2) Personal History. The earliest notice of Mary Magdalene is in St. Luke's Gospel (viii: 2), where it is recorded that out of her 'had gone seven devils,' and that she was 'with Joanna, the wife of Herod's steward, and Susanna, and many others, which ministered unto Christ of their substance.'

This is sufficient to prove that she had not been known as a person of bad character; and it also implies that she was not poor, or amongst the lower classes, when she was the companion of one whose husband held an important office in the king's household.

It is as unjust to say that she who had been so physically wretched as to be possessed by seven devils was dissolute, as to affirm that an insane person is necessarily depraved. In the Savior's last hours, and at his death and resurrection, Mary Magdalene was a chief and important witness. There had followed him from Galilee many women (Matt. xxvii:55, 56), and there stood by the cross several, of whom Mary Magdalene was one; and, after his death, she 'and Mary the mother of Jesus beheld where the body was laid' (Mark xv:47; Luke xxiii:55, 56); 'and they returned and prepared spices and ointments.' 'The first day of the week cometh Mary Magdalene early, when it was yet dark, unto the sepulcher, and seeth the stone taken away from the sepulcher' (John xx:1).

Then she returned to tell Peter and John that the stone was removed. Peter immediately ran to the place with the other disciple, when *they* saw only the napkin and linen clothes lying; and 'the disciples went away again unto their own homes' (John xx:2-11). But she 'who was last at the cross and first at the tomb' 'stood at the sepulcher weeping,' and saw two angels, who said to her, 'Woman, why weepest thou? She saith, because they have taken away my Lord, and I know not where they have laid him.' Her patient waiting was rewarded, for she had scarcely ceased speaking when Jesus himself asked her the same question, and as soon as he said 'Mary,' she turned herself, and then, seeing who it was, said unto him, 'Rabboni,' and at once acknowledged his risen person; when he not only assured her of his resurrection, but also announced his intended ascension (John xx:17). Mary Magdalene then returned and told these things to the apostles (Luke xxiv:10, 11), 'and her words seemed to them as idle tales,' 'and they, when *they* had heard that he was alive, and had been seen of her, believed her not' (Mark xvi: 10). On every occasion Christ selected the most fit and proper persons, and on *this*, his first appearance from the dead, he chose Mary Magdalene to be the only witness of his resurrection; and to other women had been also vouchsafed the vision of angels (Luke xxiv:10). These persons, with the acute perception of their sex, receiving distinct evidence without captious disbelief, at once saw, believed, and 'worshiped' their risen Lord (Matt. xxviii:9); whilst the *men* who had been his daily companions during the whole time of his public ministry, and had heard 'the gracious words which fell from his lips,' entirely refused the testimony of eye-witnesses, to whom, 'by infallible proofs, he had shown himself alive,' and remained unconvinced until 'Jesus stood in the midst of them,' and 'showed them his hands and his feet' (Luke xxiv:36, 40); and even then 'they believed not for joy.'

But the faith of Mary Magdalene is 'in everlasting remembrance,' inasmuch as, when others were 'fools and slow of heart to believe,' she, with less evidence than they possessed, at once acknowledged that 'Christ is risen from the dead, and is become the first-fruits of them that slept,' and to her was granted the honor of being the *first* witness of that great event, the Resurrection, without which Christ would have died in vain (1 Cor. xv.). S. P.

"Nothing is really known to us of the subsequent history of the Magdalene. The Greek Church believed that she died at Ephesus, whither she had followed St. John, and that her relics were removed from thence to Constantinople by the Emperor Leo VI. The story, however, which took root in the West was very different. It was said that she belonged to a wealthy family possessed of great estates at Magdala and Bethany; that she abused all her admirable gifts to tempt others to sin; that after the Ascension she remained at Bethany till the disciples were scattered by the persecution which followed the martyrdom of Stephen. She and her sister with others were placed in a boat by their persecutors, and were providentially carried without oars or sails to Massilia, where, by their preaching and miracles, they converted the heathen, and Lazarus was made bishop, while Mary retired to the wilderness and lived a life of extreme asceticism for thirty years. Finally, she was carried up to heaven in the arms of ascending angels." (J. B. Mayor, Hastings' *Bib. Dict.*)

3. Mary, Wife of Cleophas or Alphæus,
and sister of the Lord's mother (Matt. xxvii:56;
Mark xv:40; John xix:25). This Mary was one
of those holy women who followed Christ, and
was present at the crucifixion; and she is that
'other Mary' who, with Mary Magdalene, attended the body of Christ to the sepulcher when
taken down from the cross (Matt. xxvii:61;
Mark xv:47; Luke xxiii:55). She was also
among those who went on the morning of the
first day of the week to the sepulcher to anoint
the body, and who became the first witnesses of
the resurrection (Matt. xxviii:1; Mark xvi:1;
Luke xxiv:1). James, Joses, Jude, and Simon,
who are called the Lord's brethren (see the
names; also ALPHÆUS; BROTHER, 11), are very
generally supposed to have been the sons of this
Mary, and therefore *cousins* of Jesus, the term
brother having been used with great latitude
among the Hebrews. This is the usual alternative
of those who deny that these persons were sons
of our Lord's mother by her husband Joseph;
although some imagine that they may have been
sons of Joseph by a former wife. The fact seems
to be this: Christ had four 'brethren' called
James, Joses, Simon, and Jude; he had also three
apostles called James, Simon, and Jude, who
were his cousins, being sons of Alphæus and this
Mary; and it is certainly very difficult to resist
the conclusion that the three cousins and apostles
are to be regarded as the same with those three
of the four 'brethren' who bore the same names.

4. The Sister of Lazarus and Martha.
The friendship of our Lord for this family has
been explained in other articles. (See LAZARUS;
MARTHA.) The points of interest in connection
with Mary individually arise from the contrast
of character between her and her sister Martha,
and from the incidents by which that contrast was
evinced. Apart from this view, the most signal
incident in the history of Mary is her conduct
at the supper which was given to Jesus in Bethany, when he came thither after having raised
Lazarus from the dead. The intense love which
distinguished her character then glowed with the
highest fervor, manifesting the depth of her
emotion and gratitude for the deliverance from
the cold terrors of the grave of that brother who
now sat alive and cheerful with the guests at
table. She took the station she best loved, at the
feet of Jesus. Among the ancients it was usual
to wash the feet of guests before an entertainment, and with this the anointing of the feet was
frequently connected. (See ANOINTING.) Mary
possessed a large quantity of very costly ointment; and in order to testify her gratitude she
sacrificed it all by anointing with it the feet of
Jesus. We are told that the disciples murmured
at the extravagance of this act, deeming that it
would have been much wiser, if she had sold the
ointment and given the money to the poor. But
Jesus, looking beyond the mere external act to the
disposition which gave birth to it—a disposition
which marked the intensity of her gratitude—vindicated her deed. Always meditating upon his departure, and more especially at that moment,
when it was so near at hand, he attributed to
this act a still higher sense—as having reference
to his approaching death. The dead were embalmed: and so, he said, have I received, by
anticipation, the consecration of death (John xii:
1-8; Matt. xxvi:6-13; Mark xiv:3-9).

5. The Mother of John, Surnamed Mark,
had a house in Jerusalem, to which it is thought
the apostles retired after the ascension of our
Lord, and where they received the Holy Ghost.

This house was on mount Sion, and Epiphanius
says, it escaped the destruction of Jerusalem by
Titus, and was changed into a very famous
church, which continued several ages. After the
imprisonment of Peter, the faithful were assembled in this house, praying, when Peter, delivered by the ministry of an angel, knocked at the
gate (Acts xii:5, 12). From Col. iv:10 we learn
that she was sister to Barnabas, and they apparently gave up their land and house for the
good of the church (Acts iv:37; xii:12).

6. A Christian woman at Rome greeted by St.
Paul in his Epistle to the Romans (xvi:6). There
is no further notice of her than that she had
treated St. Paul with great kindness. (See
Jowett, *The Epistles of St. Paul.*)

MASCHIL (măs'khil), (Heb. מַשְׂכִּיל, *mas-keel'*,
titles of Ps. xxxii, xlii, xliv, xlv, lii, liii, liv, lv,
lxxiv, lxxviii, lxxxviii, lxxxix, cxlii), probably implies *a poem or song enforcing intelligence, wisdom, piety.*

MASH (măsh), (Heb. מַשׁ, *mash*, meaning unknown), the fourth son of Aram (Gen. x:23), erroneously called Meshech in 1 Chron. i:17. Bochart
believes he inhabited Mount Masius in Mesopotamia, and gave his name to the river Mazecha,
whose source is there. (B. C. 2513.)
"A name corresponding with Mash is found
in Assyrian inscriptions, especially the cylinder
of Assur-bani-pal, who, in describing his Arabian
campaign, says he marched through the desert
of Mash, 'a place of thirst and fainting, whither
comes no bird of the heaven, neither do asses nor
gazelles feed there.' (S. A. Smith, i, pp. 67, 68;
Hastings' *Bib. Dict.*)

MASHAL (mā'shal), (Heb. מָשָׁל, *maw-shawl'*,
depressed, 1 Chron. vi:74). See MISHAL.

MASON (mā's'n), (Heb. חָרָשׁ, *khaw-rash'*).

The Egyptians were skilled in stone-work, and
the Hebrews probably brought much of their
knowledge from there. From 2 Sam. v:11 it has
been inferred that the Hebrews were not so
skilled in masonry as the Tyrians (1 Kings vi:
7; vii:10). Later the Hebrews erected walls,
fortresses, arches, etc. (2 Chron. xxxiii:14;
Ezra iii:10); (comp. 2 Sam. v:11; 2 Kings xii:
12; xxii:6; 1 Chron. xiv:1; xxii:2; 2 Chron.
xxiv:12; Ezra iii:7.)

MASREKAH (măs-rē'kah), (Heb. מַשְׂרֵקָה, *mas-
ray-kaw'*, vineyard), a city in Idumæa, and the
native place of Samlah, an Edomitish king (Gen.
xxxvi:36; 1 Chron. i:47).
The name signifies place or plantation of vines.
Site not identified.

MASSA (măs'sà), (Heb. מַשָּׂא, *mas-saw'*, burden).

A son of Ishmael, who became the founder of
a tribe by the same name (Gen. xxv:14; 1 Chron.
i:30). This tribe is usually identified with the
Masani, on the eastern side of the Arabian desert,
near the borders of Babylon.

MASSAH (măs'sah), (Heb. מַסָּה, *mas-saw'*, trial,
temptation), a name given to the place where the
Israelites murmured for want of water and tempted
Jehovah (Exod. xvii:7; Deut. vi:16; ix:22; xxxiii:8);
called also MERIBAH (which see).
The Arabs point to a rock called Hesy el-
Hattâtîn, in the arid northwestern part of the
Wady Feiran, as the one struck by Moses at
'Massah' (Palmer, *Desert of Exodus*, 159). (See
MERIBAH; REPHIDIM.)

MAST (mȧst). See SHIP.

MASTER (màs'tĕr). The rendering in the A. V. of several Hebrew and Greek words:

1. *Bah'al* (Heb. בַּעַל, owner), master in the prevalent sense, e. g., "the master of the house" (Exod. xxii:8; Judg. xix:23).

2. *Aw-done'* (Heb. אָדוֹן; Gr. κύριος, *koo'ree-os*), properly lord, and usually so rendered.

3. *Oor* (Heb. עוּר, to wake), only so rendered in Mal. ii:12, "the master and the scholar;" marg. "him that waketh and him that answereth."

4. *Rab* (Heb. רַב, abundant, and so great), great or chief (Dan. i:3).

5. *Sar* (Heb. שַׂר, a head person), used only with reference to CHENANIAH, "the master of the song" (1 Chron. xv:27); Greek (ἐπιστάτης, *ep-is-tat'ace*, Luke v:5; viii:24, 45; xvii:13). (See CHENANIAH.)

6. "Master" is the translation of the Gr. κυβερνήτης, *koo-ber-nay'tace* (Acts xxvii:11), a sailing master; rendered "shipmaster" in Rev. xviii:17.

7. *Did-as'kal-os* (Gr. διδάσκαλος, "master"), in the sense of instructor, was often used of Christ, both by his disciples and others.

8. *Oy-kod-es-pot'ace* (Gr. οἰκοδεσπότης, "master of the house"), the head of the family (Matt. x:25; Luke xiii:25; xiv:21).

9. *Ep-is-tat'ace* (Gr. ἐπιστάτης, appointed over), is used of any kind of overseer or superintendent. It is termed RABBI by the disciples when addressing Jesus (Luke v:5; viii:24, 25; ix:33, 49; xvii:13). (See RABBI.)

10. *Kath-ayg-ay-tace'* (Gr. καθηγητής, "one is your master," Matt. xxiii:8, 10). Here "master" is used of a leader in the scholastic sense, i. e., a teacher. (Barnes' *Bib. Dict.;* Strong's *Concordance.*)

11. *Des-pot'ace* (Gr. δεσπότης), a despot or sovereign master (1 Tim. vi:1, 2; Titus ii:9; 1 Peter ii:18).

12. *Koo'ree-os* (Gr. Κύριος, Master, Lord, and Sir). No man can serve two masters (Matt. vi:24; Mark xiii:35; Acts xvi:16; Rom. xiv:4).

Master, then, in general, is one who rules or teaches. It is a title applied (1) to Jesus Christ, who is our great lawgiver and teacher, and who alone can inwardly and powerfully instruct our soul, and in matters of faith and worship is only to be followed (Matt. xxiii:8, 10); (2) to preachers and ministers, who, to assembled congregations, declare and explain the oracles of God (Eccl. xii:11); (3) to such as more privately teach scholars or disciples (Luke vi:40); (4) to such as have and rule over servants (Eph. vi:5); (5) to such as proudly affect vain applause and a superiority above others (Matt. xxiii:10); (6) to such as judge, condemn, censure, and reprove others (James iii:1).

Master in a Christian point of view has duties which relate (1) *To the civil concerns of the family.* To arrange the several businesses required of servants; to give particular instructions for what is to be done, and how it is to be done: to take care that no more is required of servants than they are equal to; to be gentle in our deportment towards them; to reprove them when they do wrong, to commend them when they do right; to make them an adequate recompense for their services, as to protection, maintenance, wages, and character. (2) *To the morals of servants.* Masters must look well to their servants' characters before they hire them; instruct them in the principles and confirm them in the habits of virtue; watch over their morals, and set them good examples.

MATHUSALA (ma-thū'sa-là), (Gr. Μαθουσάλα, *Math-oo-sah'lah,* Luke iii:37). See METHUSELAH.

MATRED (mā'tred), (Heb. מַטְרֵד, *mat-rade',* propelling).

Daughter of Mezahab, and mother-in-law of Hadar, an Edomitish king (Gen. xxxvi:39; 1 Chron. i:50). (B. C. before 1619.)

MATRI (mā'trī), (Heb. מַטְרִי, *mat-ree',* rain of Jehovah, or Jehovah is watching).

The founder of the Benjamite family from which sprang Kish, and his son Saul (1 Sam. x:21). (B. C. about 1612.)

MATRIMONY (mắt-ri-mo-ny). See MARRIAGE.

MATTAN (mắt'tan), (Heb. מַתָּן, *mat-tawn',* a gift).

1. Son of Eleazar, father of Jacob, and grandfather of Joseph, husband to the Virgin Mary. Luke (iii:23) makes Heli, son of Mattan, to be father of Joseph; but it is thought that Heli is the same as Joachim, father of Mary, and father-in-law to Joseph. So that Matthew (i:15, 16) gives the direct genealogy of Joseph, and Luke that of Mary. (Calmet.) (B. C. before 588.)

2. The priest of Baal slain by Jehoiada (2 Kings xi:18; 2 Chron. xxiii:17). This led to the death of Athaliah and the coming of Joash to the throne of Judah. (B. C. 876.)

3. Father of Shephatiah, which latter charged Jeremiah with treason (Jer. xxxviii:1). (B. C. before 589.)

MATTANAH (mắt'ta-nah), (Heb. מַתָּנָה, *mat-taw-naw',* a gift), the fifty-third encampment of Israel (Num. xxi:18, 19), which Eusebius says was on the north side of Arnon, twelve miles from Medaba, southeast.

It was probably in the country of Moab; but the exact site is unknown, although *Maschana,* on the Arnon, twelve miles from Dibon, has been suggested as marking Mattanah.

MATTANIAH (mắt'ta-nī'ah), (Heb. מַתַּנְיָה, *mat-tan-yaw',* gift of Jah.)

1. A Levite, son of Heman, and leader of the ninth course of musicians in David's time (1 Chron. xxv:4, 16). (B. C. 1014.)

2. A Levite, descendant of Asaph, and assistant to Hezekiah in the purification of the temple (2 Chron. xxix:13). (B. C. 726.)

3. The original name of King Zedekiah, which Nebuchadnezzar changed when he raised him to the throne in place of Jehoiachin (2 Kings xxiv:17).

4. A Levite, descendant of Asaph, and great-grandfather of Zechariah (Neh. xii:35). (B. C. before 446.)

5. A Levite, son of Micah, descendant of Asaph. After the exile he lived at Netophathites (1 Chron. ix:16; Neh. xii:28). He was leader of the temple choir (Neh. xi:17; xii:8, 25, 35), and a "keeper" of the "threshold" (1 Chron. xv:18, 21). Probably identical with (4). (B. C. 440.)

6. A Levite, father of Zaccur (Neh. xiii:13). (B. C. before 410.) Perhaps also identical with **5.**

7—10. Four Israelites, the "sons," or residents of Elam (Ezra x:26), of Zattu (Ezra x:27), of Pahath-Moab (Ezra x:30), and of Bani (Ezra x:37), who put away their Gentile wives after the exile. (B. C. 459.)

11. Father of Jeiel, and ancestor of that Jahaziel, the Levite, who foretold the overthrow of the

Moabites at the hands of Jehoshaphat (2 Chron. xx:14). (B. C. 1014.) Perhaps identical with **1**.

MATTATHA (măt′ta-thà) (Luke iii:31). See MATTATHAH, 1.

MATTATHAH (măt′ta-thah), (Heb. מַתַּתָּה, *mat-tat-taw′*, gift of Jehovah).

1. The son of Nathan, the son of David in the genealogy of Christ (Luke iii:31). (B. C. past 1014.)

2. An Israelite, the son of Hashum, who put away his Gentile wife after the exile (Ezra x: 33). (B. C. 458.)

MATTATHIAS (măt′ta-thī′as), (Gr. Ματταθίας, *mat-tath-ee′as*), from the Hebrew for MATTITHIAH (which see).

1. Son of Amos, an ancestor of Christ (Luke iii:25).

2. Son of Semei in the same genealogy (Luke iii:26).

MATTENAI (măt′te-nā′ī), (Heb. מַתְּנַי, *mat-ten-ah′ee*, liberal); probably a contraction of the name MATTANIAH.

1. An Israelite of the family of Hashum, who divorced his foreign wife after the exile (Ezra x:33). (B. C. 459.)

2. One of the family of Bani, who likewise put away his Gentile wife (Ezra x:37). (B. C. 459.)

3. A priest of the house of Joiarib, in the time of Joiakim, the son of Jeshua (Neh. xii:19). (B. C. 536.)

MATTER (măt′tẽr). In James iii:5 the Greek word (ὕλη, *hoo-lay′*) is translated *matter*, i. e., *affair*.

MATTHAN (măt′than), (Gr. Ματθάν, *mat-than′*, Matt. i:15). See MATTAN, 1.

MATTHAT (măt′that), (Gr. Ματθάτ, *mat-that′*), perhaps a form from MATTHAN (which see).

1. A son of Levi, in the genealogy of Christ; between David and Zerubbabel (Luke iii:29). (B. C. after 623.)

2. The son of a later Levi, and grandfather of Mary, the mother of Christ (Luke iii:24). (B. C. before 22.)

MATTHEW (măth′thu), (Gr. Ματθαῖος, *mat-thah′yos*, probably from the Hebrew *Mattathias*, "gift of Jehovah").

(1) Name and Family. According to Mark ii:14, Matthew was a son of Alphæus. It is generally supposed that Jacobus, or James, the son of Alphæus, was a son of Mary, the wife of Cleophas, who was a sister of the mother of Jesus (John xix:25). If this opinion is correct, Matthew was one of the relatives of Jesus.

(2) Collector of Customs. Matthew was a *portitor*, or inferior collector of customs at Capernaum, on the Sea of Galilee. He was not a *publicanus*, or general farmer of customs. We may suppose either that he held his appointment at the port of Capernaum, or that he collected the customs on the high road to Damascus, which went through what is now called Khan Minyeh, which place, as Robinson has shown, is the ancient Capernaum (*Bibl. Res. in Palestine*, vol. iii, pp. 288-295). Thus we see that Matthew belonged to the lower class of people.

(3) Also Called Levi. In Mark ii:14, and Luke v:27, he is called Levi. We hence conclude that he had two names. This circumstance is not mentioned in the list of the apostles (Matt. x and Luke vi); but the omission does not prove the contrary, as we may infer from the fact that Lebbæus is also called Judas in Luke vi:16, in which verse the name Lebbæus is omitted. In Matt. ix:9 is related how Matthew was

called to be an apostle. We must, however, suppose that he was previously acquainted with Jesus, since we read in Luke vi:13, that when Jesus, before delivering the Sermon on the Mount, selected twelve disciples, who were to form the circle of his more intimate associates, Matthew was one of them. After this Matthew returned to his usual occupation; from which Jesus, on leaving Capernaum, called him away. On this occasion Matthew gave a parting entertainment to his friends. After this event he is mentioned only in Acts i:13.

(4) Abstinence from Animal Food. According to a statement in Clemens Alexandrinus (*Pædagog.* ii, 1), Matthew abstained from animal food. Hence some writers have rather hastily concluded that he belonged to the sect of the Essenes. It is true that the Essenes practiced abstinence in a high degree; but it is not true that they rejected animal food altogether. Admitting the account in Clemens Alexandrinus to be correct, it proves only a certain ascetic strictness, of which there occur vestiges in the habits of other Jews (comp. Joseph. *Vita*, cap. ii and iii).

(5) Ministry. According to another account, which is as old as the first century, Matthew, after the death of Jesus, remained about fifteen years in Jerusalem. This agrees with the statement in Eusebius (*Hist. Eccles.* iii, 24), that Matthew preached to his own nation before he went to foreign countries. Rufinus (*Hist. Eccles.* x, 9) and Socrates (*Hist. Eccles.* i, 19) state that he afterwards went into Ethiopia; and other authors mention other countries. There also he probably preached specially to the Jews. According to Heracleon (about A. D. 150), and Clemens Alex. (*Strom.* iv, 9), Matthew was one of those apostles who did not suffer martyrdom.

MATTHEW, THE GOSPEL OF.

The genuineness of the Gospel of St. Matthew has been more strongly attacked than that of any of the three others, as well by external as by internal arguments.

1. External Arguments Against Its Genuineness. We will first consider the external arguments. The most ancient testimony concerning Matthew's Gospel is that of Papias, who, according to Eusebius (*Hist. Eccles.* iii, 39), wrote as follows: 'Matthew wrote the sayings in the Hebrew tongue, but everybody interpreted them according to his ability.' Doubts of three different kinds have been raised whether this testimony could refer to our Greek Gospel of St. Matthew.

(1) Omission by Papias. Papias, the most ancient witness, who was a disciple of John, speaks only about the λόγια of Christ, which were apparently a collection of the remarkable sayings of our Lord.

(2) Possibly Another Tongue. He speaks about a work written in the Hebrew, which here means probably the Aramæan or Chaldee tongue.

(3) Mentions No Translation. His statement seems to imply that there was no translation of this work.

These doubts were particularly brought forward by Schleiermacher in the *Studien und Kritiken*, 1832, Heft 4. The opinion of Schleiermacher was adopted by Schneckenburger, Lachmann, and many others. According to these critics, the apostle wrote only a collection of the remarkable sayings of Jesus; which collection was put into a historical form by a Greek translator. Papias is said to intend the explanation of the sayings of Christ by means of the addition of the historical facts.

2. Unreliability of Evidence Against. Most critics, however, have either never adopted, or have subsequently rejected, the above interpretation. It was first objected by Dr. Lücke, that Papias, in his report, followed the statements of Johannes Presbyter, who said that Peter furnished 'a collection of the sayings of our Lord,' and that Mark stated what he had heard from Peter, and that Papias nevertheless adds that Mark wrote *as well the sayings as the doings of Christ.*

(1) Logia a Comprehensive Term. Hence it follows, according to Dr. Lücke, that λόγια is a term *a parte potiori,* which comprehends the history also. In addition to this, Dr. Lücke observes, that Papias himself wrote a work and that the extracts from this work which Eusebius has furnished prove that its contents were partly historical. According to this view, the testimony of Papias may be considered as referring to our Gospel of St. Matthew; but the force of the two other objections remains still unimpaired.

It has been observed by those who deny the genuineness of this gospel, that in none of the Fathers before Jerome do we find any statement from which we could infer that they had seen the Hebrew Gospel of St. Matthew; and that consequently we may consider as a mere conjecture the opinion of the Fathers, that our gospel is a Greek translation of a Hebrew original.

(2) Testimony of Jerome. Jerome in his *Catalogue of Illustrious Men* (cap. iii), reports that the Hebrew Gospel of St. Matthew was preserved in the library at Cæsarea, and that he took a copy of it. In his commentary on Matt. xii:13, he says that he translated this Hebrew gospel into Greek. In the same passage, and in his book *Contra Pelagianos* (iii, 2), Jerome states that this Hebrew copy was considered 'by most people' (a plerisque) to be the original text of St. Matthew. The cautious expression, 'a plerisque,' is considered by many critics as an indication that Jerome's statement cannot be depended upon. Indeed it appears that the Hebrew copy of St. Matthew was not the mere original of our gospel, for what motive, in that case, could Jerome have had to translate it into Greek?

(3) A Possible Apocryphal Work. The whole difficulty is cleared up if, like most modern critics, we suppose that the *second Gospel to the Hebrews,* about which Jerome speaks, was the Gospel of St. Matthew corrupted by apocryphal additions. This conjecture is confirmed by the fragments of it which have been preserved. Hence many critics are led to suppose that the strictly Judaizing Christians made a translation of St. Matthew, which they endeavored to bring into harmony with their own opinions and legends. Nevertheless Jerome's statement respecting the *second Gospel to the Hebrews* may be taken as a confirmation of the account of Papias, that Matthew wrote his gospel in Hebrew. If this be the fact, the question must arise whether our Greek Matthew is a correct translation of the Hebrew. The words of Papias seem to imply that in his days there was no Greek translation in existence.

(4) Account of Papias Questioned. This has induced many critics to question his account, and to suppose that the original text was Greek. Such is the opinion of Erasmus, Œcolampadius, Calvin, Beza, Lardner, Guerike, Harless, and others.

The authority of Papias has been deemed to be overthrown by the character given of him by Eusebius, according to whose statement he was 'of a very little mind.' Guerike considers also as rather incredible the addition, that "everybody interpreted that gospel according to his ability."

Papias, indeed, proves himself very credulous, by reporting, according to Eusebius, 'many rather fabulous things;' but this does not authorize us to reject his testimony in a mere matter of fact, for the perception of which no extraordinary abilities were required, especially as his account of this fact agrees with the statement of Jerome.

It is by no means improbable, that after several inaccurate and imperfect translations of the Aramæan original came into circulation, Matthew himself was prompted by this circumstance to publish a Greek translation, or to have his gospel translated under his own supervision. It is very likely that this Greek translation did not soon come into general circulation, so that Papias may have remained ignorant of its existence. It may also be, and nothing prevents us from supposing, that Papias, being acquainted with our Greek gospel, spoke, in the passage referred to, of those events only which came to pass soon after the publication of the Aramæan original. We, at least, rather prefer to confess ourselves unable to solve the objections, than to question the direct testimony of Papias; especially since that testimony is supported by other ancient authorities: (1) By Origen (Euseb. *Hist. Eccles.* vi, 25). (2) By the Alexandrian Catechist Pantænus, who, according to Eusebius (*Hist. Eccles.* v, 10), having, in the latter half of the second century, gone on a missionary expedition to India, found there some Christians who possessed the Gospel of St. Matthew in Hebrew. (3) By Irenæus (*Adv. Hær.* iii, 1) and Eusebius (*Hist. Eccles.* v, 8).

To this it has been objected, that Origen and Irenæus probably only repeated the statement of Papias; but it is unlikely that a man of so much learning as Origen should have had no other authority for his account; and the statement of Pantænus, at least, is quite independent of that of Papias. It ought also to be considered that Matthew was not so much known in ecclesiastical antiquity that any partisanship could have prompted writers to forge books in his name.

(5) External Proof of Genuineness. On summing up what we have stated, it appears that the external testimonies clearly prove the genuineness of the Gospel of St. Matthew. The authenticity indeed of this gospel is as well supported as that of any work of classical antiquity. It can also be proved that it was early in use among Christians, and that the apostolical Fathers, at the end of the first century, ascribed to it a canonical authority (see Polycarp, *Epist.* c. ii. 7; Ignatius, *Ad Smyrn.* c. vi; *Ad Rom.* c. vi; Clemens Romanus, *Epist.* i. c. xlvi; Barnabas, *Epist.* c. iv).

3. Internal Arguments Against. But the external arguments against the authenticity of this gospel are less important than the doubts which have been started from a consideration of its internal qualities.

(1) The Claim That Matthew Lacks Clearness. The representations of Matthew (it is said) have not that vivid clearness which characterizes the narration of an eye-witness, and which we find, for instance, in the Gospel of John. Even Mark and Luke surpass Matthew in this respect. Compare, for example, Matt. iv:18 with Luke v:1, *sq.*; Matt. viii:5, *sq.,* with Luke vii:1, *sq.* This is most striking in the history of his own call, where we should expect a clearer representation.

(2) Omissions. He omits some facts which every apostle certainly knew. For instance, he mentions only one journey of Christ to the passover at Jerusalem, namely, the last; and seems to be acquainted only with one sphere of Christ's activity, namely, Galilee. He even relates the instances of Christ's appearing after his resurrection in such a manner that it might be understood as if he showed himself only to the women in Jerusalem, and to his disciples, nowhere but in Galilee (Matt. xxvi:32 and xxviii:7).

(3) Transposition of Events. He relates unchronologically, and transposes events to times in which they did not happen; for instance, the event mentioned in Luke iv:14-30 must have happened at the commencement of Christ's public career, but Matthew relates it as late as ch. xiii: 53, *sq.*

(4) Combines Discourses. He embodies in one discourse several sayings of Christ which, according to Luke, were pronounced at different times (comp. Matt. v-vii, and xxiii).

(5) Errors Claimed. He falls, it is asserted, into positive errors. In ch. i and ii he seems not to know that the real dwelling-place of the parents of Jesus was at Nazareth, and that their abode at Bethlehem was only temporary (comp. Matt. ii:1, 22, 23, with Luke ii:4, 39). According to Mark xi:20, 21, the fig-tree withered on the day after it was cursed, but according to Matt. xxi:19, it withered immediately. According to Matt. xxi:12, Christ purified the temple immediately after his entrance into Jerusalem; but according to Mark he on that day went out to Bethany, and purified the temple on the day following (Mark xi:11-15). Matthew says (xxi: 7) that Christ rode on a she-ass and on a colt, which is impossible. The other gospels speak only of a she-ass.

These circumstances have led Strauss and others to consider the Gospel of St. Matthew as an unapostolical composition, originating perhaps at the conclusion of the first century; while some consider it a reproduction of the Aramæan Matthew, augmented by some additions; others call it an historical commentary of a later period, made to illustrate the collection of the sayings of Christ which Matthew had furnished (comp. Sieffert, *Ueber die Aechtheit und den Ursprung des ersten Evangelii,* 1832; Schneckenburger, *Ueber den Ursprung des ersten Evangelii,* 1834; Schott, *Ueber die Authenticität des Ev. Matth.* 1837).

4. Reply. To these objections we may reply as follows:

(1) Completeness of Narration. The gift of narrating luminously is a personal qualification of which even an apostle might be destitute, and which is rarely found among the lower orders of people: this argument therefore has recently been given up altogether. In the history of his call to be an apostle, Matthew has this advantage over Mark and Luke, that he relates the discourse of Christ (ix:13) with greater completeness than these evangelists. Luke relates that Matthew prepared a great banquet in his house, while Matthew simply mentions that an entertainment took place, because the apostle could not well write that he himself prepared a great banquet.

(2) Omissions by One Witness do not Invalidate Testimony of Others. An *argumentum a silentio* must not be urged against

the evangelists. The raising of Lazarus is narrated only by John; and the raising of the youth at Nain only by Luke, the appearance of five hundred brethren after the resurrection, which, according to the testimony of Paul (1 Cor. xv: 6), was a fact generally known, is not recorded by any of the evangelists. The apparent restriction of Christ's sphere of activity to Galilee, we find also in Mark and Luke. This peculiarity arose perhaps from the circumstance that the apostles first taught in Jerusalem, where it was unnecessary to relate what had happened there, but where the events which had taken place in Galilee were unknown, and required to be narrated: thus the sphere of narration may have gradually become fixed. At least it is generally granted that hitherto no satisfactory explanation of this fact has been discovered. The expressions in Matt. xxvi:32, and xxviii:7, perhaps only indicate that the Lord appeared more frequently, and for a longer period, in Galilee than elsewhere. In Matt. xxviii:16, we are told that the disciples in Galilee went up to a mountain, whither Christ had appointed them to come; and since it is not previously mentioned that any such appointment had been made, the narrative of Matthew himself here leads us to conclude that Christ appeared to his disciples in Jerusalem after his resurrection.

(3) Communications Grouped According to Subjects. There is no reason to suppose that the evangelists intended to write a chronological biography. On the contrary, we learn from Luke i:4, and John xx:31, that their object was of a more practical tendency. With the exception of John, the evangelists have grouped their communications more according to the subjects than according to chronological succession. This fact is now generally admitted. The principal groups of facts recorded by St. Matthew are: (1) The preparation of Jesus, narrated in ch. i—iv:16. (2) The public ministry of Jesus, narrated in ch. iv:17—xvi:20. (3) The conclusion of the life of Jesus, narrated in ch. xvi:21—xxviii.

The second of these groups is subdivided into minor groups. If we consider that Matthew, for the benefit of the Jews, describes Christ as being the promised Messiah of the old covenant, it must appear perfectly appropriate in him to narrate the Sermon on the Mount before the calling of his disciples. The Sermon on the Mount shows the relation in which the Redeemer stood to the old covenant. In cc. viii and ix are given examples of the power which Jesus possessed of performing miracles; after which, in ch. ix:36, is stated the need of 'laborers' to instruct the people. Then naturally follows, in ch. x, the admonition delivered to the apostles before they are sent out on their mission. In ch. xii is recorded how Jesus entered into conflict with the dominant party, etc. (comp. Kern's *Abhandlung über den Ursprung des Evangelii Matthæi,* p. 51, *sq.;* Köster, *Ueber die Composition des Ev. Matth.* in Pelt's *Mitarbeiten,* Heft i; Kuhn, *Leben Jesu,* t. i., *Beilage.*)

But our adversaries further assert that the evangelist not only groups together events belonging to different times, but that some of his dates are incorrect: for instance, the date in Matt. xiii:53 cannot be corrrect if Luke, ch. iv, has placed the event rightly. If, however, we carefully consider the matter, we shall find that Matthew has placed this fact more chronologically than Luke. It is true that the question in Matt. xiii:54, and the annunciation in Luke iv:18-21, seem to synchronize best with the first public appearance of Jesus. But even Schleiermacher, who, in his work on Luke, generally gives the preference to the arrangement of that evangelist, nevertheless observes (p. 63) that Luke iv:23 leads us to suppose that Jesus abode for a longer period in Capernaum (comp. the words κατὰ τὸ εἰωθὸς αὐτῷ in verse 16).

(4) Combination of Harmonious Themes. If the evangelist arranges his statements according to subjects, and not chronologically, we must not be surprised that he connects similar sayings of Christ, inserting them in the longer discourses after analogous topics had been mentioned. These discourses are not compiled by the evangelist, but always form the fundamental framework to which sometimes analogous subjects are attached. But even this is not the case in the Sermon on the Mount; and in ch. xiii it may be doubted whether the parables were spoken at different times. In the discourses recorded in ch. x and xxiii, it can be proved that several sayings are more correctly placed by Matthew than by Luke (comp. especially Matt. xxiii:37-39 with Luke xiii:34, 35).

(5) Sources of Information. It depends entirely upon the mode of interpretation, whether such positive errors as are alleged to exist are really chargeable on the evangelist. The difference, for instance, between the narrative of the birth of Christ, as severally recorded by Matthew and Luke, may easily be solved without questioning the correctness of either, if we suppose that each of them narrates what he knows from his individual sources of information. The history of Christ's childhood given in Luke, leads us to conclude that it was derived from the acquaintances of Mary, while the statements in Matthew seem to be derived from the friends of Joseph. As to the transaction recorded in Matt. xxi:18-22, and Mark xi:11, 15, 20, 21, it appears that Mark describes what occurred most accurately; and we must grant that we should scarcely have expected from an eye-witness the inaccuracy which is observable in Matthew. But we find that there are characters of such individuality that, being bent exclusively upon their main subject, they seem to have no perception for dates and localities.

5. Internal Proof of Genuineness. If these arguments should still appear unsatisfactory, they may be supported by adding the positive internal proofs which exist in favor of the apostolical origin of this gospel.

(1) Harmony of Early Writers with the Book. The nature of the book agrees entirely with the statements of the Fathers of the church, from whom we learn that it was written for Jewish readers. None of the other evangelists quotes the Old Testament so often as Matthew, who, moreover, does not explain the Jewish rites and expressions, which are explained by Mark and John.

(2) Fullness of Accounts. If there is a want of precision in the narration of facts, there is, on the other hand, a peculiar accuracy and richness in the reports given of the discourses of Jesus; so that we may easily conceive why Papias, *a parte potiori*, styled the Gospel of Matthew λόγια τοῦ Κυρίου, *the sayings of the Lord*.

Some of the most beautiful and most important sayings of our Lord, the historical credibility of which no skeptic can attack, have been preserved by Matthew alone (Matt. xi:28-30; xvi:16-19; xxviii:20; comp. also xi:2-21; xii:3-6, 25-29; xvii:12, 25, 26; xxvi:13). Above all, the Sermon on the Mount must here be considered. Even negative criticism grants that Luke's account is

defective as compared with Matthew's; and that Luke gives as isolated sentences what in Matthew appears in beautiful connection. In short, the Sermon on the Mount, according to Matthew, forms the most beautiful and the best arranged whole of all the evangelical discourses. It may also be proved that in many particulars the reports of several discourses in Matthew are more exact than in the other Evangelists; as may be seen by comparing Matt. xxiii. with the various parallel passages in Luke. Under these circumstances it is surprising that the genuineness of this gospel has not yet met with more distinguished advocates. The most important work in defense of the genuineness of Matthew is that of Kern, *Ueber den Ursprung des Evangelii Matthæi*, Tübingen, 1834. Next in value are Olshausen's *Drei Programme*, 1835, and the two *Lucubrationes* of Harless, 1840 and 1843. Even De Wette, in the fourth edition of his *Introduction*, p. 170, has ascribed only a qualified value to the doubts on this head.

6. Early Date. With regard to the date of this gospel, Clemens Alexandrinus and Origen state that it was written before the others. Irenæus (*Adv. Hær.* iii. 1) agrees with them, but places its origin rather late—namely, at the time when Peter and Paul were at Rome. Even De Wette grants (*Einleitung*, sec. 97) that it was written before the destruction of Jerusalem. In proof of this we may also quote ch. xxvii:8.

A. T.

MATTHIAS (mat-thī'as), (Gr. Ματθίας, *mat-thee'as*, gift of Jehovah, equivalent to Matthew), one of the seventy disciples who was chosen by lot, in preference to Joseph Barsabas, into the number of the Apostles, to supply the deficiency caused by the treachery and death of Judas (Acts i:23-26).

This is the sole instance of the lot being employed in the history of the Apostolic Church, and it occurs significantly between the Ascension and Pentecost, when the disciples were 'orphans' (John xiv:18). Stier (*Words of the Apostles, in loc.*) regards this election as premature and unwarranted, the outcome of St. Peter's officious impetuosity. 'The lot fell: not the Lord chose.' He holds that St. Paul was the true successor of Judas, chosen, like the other Apostles, by the Lord himself. It may be granted that the appointment of Matthias stands on a somewhat lower level than that of the original Twelve and of St. Paul; but, in the absence of any direction to the contrary, the procedure was a legitimate exercise of human wisdom in dependence upon Divine guidance; and St. Luke, the 'beloved' friend of St. Paul, appears to endorse the election (representing, doubtless, the general opinion of the Apostolic Church); for after speaking of the eleven Apostles (Acts i:25) he refers (Acts vi: 2) to the 'Twelve.' (H. Cowan, Hastings' *Bib. Dict.*)

According to Grotius, the lot was taken by means of two urns. In one they placed two rolls of paper, with the names of Joseph and Matthias written within them, and in the other, two rolls, one with the word "apostle" and the other blank; and one roll was drawn from each urn simultaneously. Clarke (*Com.*) thinks that the selection was by ballot, the Lord directing the mind of the majority to vote for Matthias. In the case of selection by lot there was no chance, for "the lot is cast into the lap (properly *urn*); but the whole disposing thereof is of the Lord" (Prov. xvi:33).

Nothing sure is known of his subsequent career,

although according to one tradition, he preached in Ethiopia and suffered martyrdom there; according to another, he labored in Judæa and was stoned by the Jews.

Others hold that he was a martyr—by crucifixion—in Ethiopia or Colchis. An apocryphal gospel was published under his name, and Clement of Alexandria quotes from the Traditions of Matthias.

MATTITHIAH (măt'ti-thī'ah), (Heb. מַתִּתְיָה, mat-tith-yaw', gift of Jehovah; prolonged form, מַתִּתְיָהוּ, mat-tith-yaw' hoo).

1. A son of Jeduthun, the Levite, and leader of the fourteenth course of Temple musicians in the time of David (1 Chron. xxv:3, 21). (B. C. 1014.) He was probably the doorkeeper of the ark, appointed by David (1 Chron. xv:18, 21; xvi:5).

2. One of the "sons" of Nebo, who put away his Gentile wife after the exile (Ezra x:43). (B. C. 459.)

3. Son of Shallum, a Korhite Levite, who had charge of the baked offerings of the Temple after the exile (1 Chron. ix:31). (B. C. 440).

4. One of those who stood on Ezra's right when he read the law to the people (Neh. viii:4). (B. C. 410.)

5. Son of Semei in the genealogy of Christ (Luke iii:26); but the name is probably an interpolation of 6.

6. Son of Amos, in the genealogy of Christ (Luke iii:25). (B. C. after 406.)

MATTOCK (măt'tŭk). Three Hebrew words are thus translated:

1. Makh-ar-ay-shaw' (Heb. מַחֲרֵשָׁה), 1 Sam. xiii:20, 21.

2. Kheh'reb (Heb. חֶרֶב). The expression "with their mattocks round about" (2 Chron. xxxiv:6, marg. "mauls."

3. Mah-dare' (Heb. מַעְדֵּר), Isa. vii:25, a weeding hook or hoe.

MAUL (ma̤l), (Heb. מֵפִיץ, may-feets', a breaker). It was a hammer, such as coppersmiths use, found only in Prov. xxv:18.

It is to-day a stick for striking a person on the head as a mark of disgrace, but it may also mean a club. Clubs are always carried by the shepherds of Lebanon, slung from the wrist by a thong or cord. The head of the club is round and heavy and is sometimes studded with iron spikes. Solomon compares a false witness to a "maul," he wounds the reputation, he ruins the health, and takes away the life of his neighbor (see as above Prov. xxv:18). In Jer. li:20, the Hebrew is rendered in R. V. "battle axe," and in the marg. "maul."

MAUZZIM (maüz'zim), (marginal, Dan. xi:38). A word meaning "the God of forces," but by some it is taken as a proper name, though it probably refers to the dedication by Antiochus Epiphanes of a temple in Antioch to Jupiter Capitolinus, or to the family god of the Seleucids to whom there was an altar in the Acropolis at Athens.

MAW (ma̤), (Heb. קֵבָה, kay-baw', hollow), the ventricle, or the second of the four stomachs of ruminating animals, in which the digestion of the food is completed.

It, like tripe, was esteemed a great delicacy among the ancients. This, with the shoulder and the cheeks of a sacrificial animal, was the portion of the priest (Deut. xviii:3).

MAZZAROTH (măz'za-rŏth), (Heb. מַזָּרוֹת, maz-zaw-roth', only in Job xxxviii:32), the name of twelve signs of the zodiac, which were imagined as menazil, i. e., lodging houses; or burug, strongholds, in which one after another the sun lodges as it describes the circle of the year. (See STARS.)

MEADOW (mĕd'ō), the rendering of two words:

1. Aw'khoo (Heb. אָחוּ, Gen. xli:2, 18), probably an Egyptian term. In Job viii:2 this word seems to mean a reed or rush. In Judg. xx:33 the word translated 'meadow' probably means an open plain, or a region stripped of wood, a treeless portion of the country.

2. Mah-ar-eh' (Heb. מַעֲרֵה, stripped), Judg. xx:33, "the meadows of Gibeah."

MEAH (mē'ah), (Heb. מֵאָה, may-aw', a hundred).

A tower on the eastern wall of Jerusalem, probably at the angle of the Temple inclosure (Neh. iii:1; xii:39), between the Sheep Gate and the tower of Hananeel. (See JERUSALEM; HANANEEL.)

MEAL (mēl), the rendering of several words:

1. Keh'makh (Heb. קֶמַח, marrow), the fatness of wheat or barley, i. e., its ground substance (Gen. xviii:6; Num. v:15; 1 Kings iv:22; xvii:12, 14, 16; 2 Kings iv:41; 1 Chron. xii:40; Is. xlvii:2; Hos. viii:7).

2. Keh'makh so'leth (Heb. קֶמַח סֹלֶת, Gen. xviii:6, "fine meal"; Gr. ἄλευρον, al'yoo-ron, Matt. xiii:33; Luke xiii:21), the finest portion of flour.

Figurative. In the prophetic writings 'meal' is used in several figures. The humbling of the Daughter of Babylon was to be shown by her being reduced to the work of grinding meal as a sign of servitude (Is. xlvii:2). Hosea represents the unprofitableness of the evil works of Israel as sowing the wind, reaping the whirlwind, whose bud, having no stalk, makes no meal (Hos. viii:7).

MEAL-OFFERING (mēl ŏf'fēr-ĭng) is the translation substituted by the Old Testament revision for A. V. 'meat-offering.'

The American Revisers further record their preference for 'meal-offering' in Jer. xiv:12; xvii:26; xxxiii:18; xli:5. In these passages our R. V. reads 'oblation' with 'meal-offering' in the margin.

MEALS, MEAL TIME (mēls, mēl tīm).

(1) **When and How Served.** The meals of the Israelites consisted of a simple breakfast in the morning and two other daily meals, one at midday (Gen. xviii:1; xliii:16, 25; Ruth ii:14; 1 Kings xx:16) and the other some time in the evening (Gen. xix:1; Ruth iii:2). In earlier times the midday meal as well as the evening meal was regarded as important and consisted of substantial fare. It was also customary to ask a blessing upon the food (1 Sam. ix:13; Matt. xiv:19; xv:36; Luke ix:16; John vi:11). Meat was served in a solid form, and no soups were used by the Israelites. Portions of flesh, whether boiled or roasted, were lifted by the fingers and placed on a piece of bread, which served as a plate, and also as a fork to lift to the mouth. The food of the poorer classes consisted of bread dipped in vinegar, milk, and parched corn (Ruth ii:14); those in a better position had in addition boiled flesh and a variety of vegetables and fruits; while the wealthy had roasted flesh of fatted cattle, venison and fowls. At feasts honor was shown to guests by the position assigned to them at table, by the

choice pieces and the amount of the portions set before them.

(2) Seasoning of Food. It does not appear that the people were very particular in the seasoning or dressing of their food. Salt was the only seasoning of what was prepared in the temple; if we do not add the oil wherewith meat-offerings were baken. The paschal lamb was eaten with bitter herbs; salt, honey, butter, oil, and perhaps sometimes aromatic herbs were used in their common ragouts.

(3) Various Customs. People of different nations disliked to eat together. The Egyptians hated to eat with shepherds (Gen. xliii:31). The Jews abhorred eating with heathens, particularly the Samaritans (John iv:9); they reproached our Savior for eating with publicans (Matt. ix:11; Luke xv: 2). The Jews washed their hands before and after they partook of their meals (Matt. xv:2; Mark vii:2; Luke xi:33). Anciently, they sat at separate tables, but in after ages they copied after the Persian, Chaldean, and Roman manner of lying on couches at their meals; hence John leaned on Jesus' bosom at his last supper (John xiii:23, 25). The different sexes feasted in different apartments, a common custom in some places of the East. Perfumes on their hair, or on their couches, together with music and dancing, were common at their feasts (Luke vii:37; xv; John xii).

(4) Effect of the Law. The abolishment of the ceremonial law, by the death of Jesus Christ, took away the legal distinction of meats; but to avoid offence of the weak Jews who turned Christians, and were hard to wean from their ancient customs, the synod of Jerusalem required their Christian brethren to abstain from meats offered to idols, and from things strangled, and from blood. This matter, especially that of eating things offered to idols, and which were sometimes, after the oblation, sold in the public markets, occasioned no small disturbance. St. Paul determines, that all food was clean and indifferent in itself; and that whatever was bought in the public market, might be eaten without any scruple of conscience; but warmly inculcates the forbearance of flesh offered to idols, if it tended to lay a stumbling-block before any person, or grieved any tender conscience; and charges such as did otherwise, with being murderers of their Christian brethren, for whom Christ died (Tit. i:15; Rom. xiv; 1 Cor. vi:11-13; viii and x). (See Food.)

MEAN (mēn).

1. The verb to 'mean' (from Anglo-Sax. *maenan* to intend, tell, and connected with 'mind,' the root being *man,* to think) signifies sometimes to design, intend, purpose. Gen. 1:20, 'But as for you, ye thought evil against me; but God meant it unto good;' Is. iii:15, 'What mean ye that ye beat my people to pieces, and grind the faces of the poor?' x:7, 'Howbeit he meaneth not so, neither doth his heart think so;' Acts xxi: 13, 'What mean ye to weep and to break mine heart?' Acts xxvii:2, 'We launched, meaning to sail by the coasts of Asia'; 2 Cor. viii:13; 'For I mean not that other men be eased, and ye burdened.'

2. The noun 'mean' in Prov. xxii:29, signifies that which is *obscure.* (Comp. Acts xxi:39.)

MEARAH (me-ā'rah), (Heb. מְעָרָה, *meh-aw-raw'*, a cave). A place on the northern boundary of Palestine (Josh. xiii:4), near Sidon. Commonly identified with a district of caves on Lebanon, to the east of Sidon, called Jezzim; also with Moghe-iriyeh, northeast of Sidon,

MEASURES (mĕzh'ŭrs). See Weights and Measures.

MEASURING LINE (mĕzh'ŭr-ĭng lĭn). See Weights and Measures.

MEAT (mēt). This word does not appear to be used in the Bible in the sense of animal food, which is denoted uniformly by "flesh."

Perhaps the following may be exceptions: "Savory meat" (Gen. xxvii:4); "corn and bread and meat" (xlv:23).

Figurative. (1) Christ's mediatorial work is represented as his *meat;* it was more delightful to him than his necessary food (John iv:32, 34). He in his person, righteousness, and fullness, and God in him, are represented as *meat;* as true and satisfying food, the receiving and enjoyment of which nourishes up men's souls to eternal life (John vi:55; 1 Cor. x:3; Ps. xxxiv:8). (2) The truths of God in the Scripture are *meat;* they refresh and nourish men's souls; and the deeper mysteries are *strong meat,* which can only edify and nourish strong Christians (Jer. xv:16; Heb. v:12, 14). (3) Ceremonial ordinances are called *meats and drinks;* much of them related to eatables (Heb. xiii:9; Col. ii:16). (4) The kingdom of God consists not *in meat and drink,* but in righteousness, peace, and joy in the Holy Ghost: the gospel-dispensation does not relate to meats and drinks; nor does true inward religion consist in observances of these, but in applying Christ's righteousness, and studying to have fellowship with and conformity to God (Rom. xiv: 17). (5) The fruit of believers is for *meat and medicine;* their instructions and holy examples are edifying (Ezek. xlvii:12). (6) Men are *meat* to others, when they are given up to be destroyed by them (Ps. xliv:11, and liii:4; Num. xiv:9, and xxiv:8). (7) Sin is *meat* to men; they delight in it, and promise themselves nourishment from it; but it becomes the *gall of asps* within them (Job xx:14). (8) *Sorrowful meat,* is coarse provision, which mourners eat (Job vi:7). (9) Tears are *meat,* when sorrow takes away all appetite for meat (Ps. xlii:3). (10) The year of release was *meat* for the Hebrews; they ate what grew of its own accord in it (Lev. xxv:6). (11) Israel's *ordinary food,* which God diminished, was their accustomed prosperity (Ezek. xvi:27).

MEAT-OFFERING (mēt ŏf'fēr-ĭng). See Offering.

MEBUNNAI (me-bŭn'nāi), (Heb. מְבֻנַּי, *meb-oon-nah'ee,* construction).

One of David's bodyguard (2 Sam. xxiii: 27); elsewhere Sibbechai (2 Sam. xxi:18; 1 Chron. xx:4), or Sibbecai (1 Chron. xi:29; xxvii:11).

MECHERATHITE (mĕk'e-rath-īte), (Heb. מְכֵרָתִי, *mek-ay-raw-thee',* from the word meaning a *sword*).

The appellation of Hepher, one of David's heroes (1 Chron. xi:36). The place, Mecherah, is otherwise unknown, but the word may be a corruption of Maachathite (2 Sam. xxiii:34).

MEDAD and **ELDAD** (mē'dăd and ĕl'dad), (Heb. מֵידָד, *may-dawd',* loving).

Two of the seventy elders who were nominated to assist Moses in the government of the people, but who remained in the camp, probably as modestly deeming themselves unfit for the office, when the others presented themselves at the Tabernacle. The Divine spirit, however, rested on them even there, 'and they prophesied in the camp' (Num. xi:24-29). The Targum of Jonathan alleges that these two men were brothers of Moses and Aaron by the mother's side. (B. C. 1657.)

MEDAN or **MADAN** (mē'dan), (Heb. מְדָן, *med-awn'*, contention; Sept. Μαδιάμ, *madiam*).

Son of Abraham, by Keturah (Gen. xxv:2; 1 Chron. i:32). He and his brother Midian are supposed to have peopled the country of Midian, east of the Dead Sea. The word is probably to be identified with *Madān*, the god of some Arab tribe, best known through the proper name '*Abd-Al-Madān*, 'worshiper of Al-Madān.' The seat of the worship of Al-Madān appears to have been Yemen (*Tāj Al-'Arūs, s. v.*), whereas the descendants of Keturah appear to be far away from S. Arabia.

MEDEBA (mĕd'e-bà), (Heb. מֵידְבָא, *may-deb-aw'*, Sept. Μαιδαβάν, *Maedaban*).

A town east of the Jordan, in the tribe of Reuben (Josh. xiii:9, 16), before which was fought the great battle in which Joab defeated the Ammonites and their allies (1 Chron. xix:7). It originally belonged to the Moabites (Num. xxi:30); and after the captivity of the tribes beyond the Jordan, they again took possession of it (Is. xv:2). The *Onomasticon* places it near Heshbon; and it was once the seat of one of the thirty-five bishoprics of Arabia (Reland, *Palæstina*, pp. 217, 223, 226). Medeba, now in ruins, still retains its ancient name, and is situated upon a round hill seven miles south of Heshbon. The ruins are about a mile and a half in circuit, but not a single edifice remains perfect. (Seetzen, in Zach's *Monat. Corresp.*, xviii. 431; Burckhardt, *Syria*, p. 625; Legh. p. 245.)

MEDES (mēdes), (Heb. מָדַי, *maw-dah'ee*, a Mede). The inhabitants in ancient times of one of the most fruitful and populous countries of Asia, called Media.

MEDIA (mē'dĭ-à), (Heb. מָדַי, rendered "Madai," Gen. x:2; 1 Chron. i:5; "Media," Esth. i:3, 14, 18; x:2; Is. xxi:2; Dan. viii:20; "Median," Dan. v:31; מָדְיָא, "Media," R. V. Ezra vi:2).

(1) **Location.** Media lay directly south of Armenia and was bounded on the northeast by the mountains beside the Caspian Sea. To the east and southeast were Hyrcania and Parthia. Elam or Susiana lay on the southern side, and the mighty Assyrian power was on the west.

(2) **Cities.** In Great Media lay the metropolis of the country, Ecbatana (Plin. *Hist. Nat.* vi. 17), as well as the province of Rhagiana and the city Rhagæ, with the plain of Nisæum, celebrated in the time of the Persian empire for its horses and horse-races (Herod. iii. 106; Arrian, vii. 13; Heeren, *Ideen*, i. l. 305). This plain was near the city Nisæa, around which were fine pasture lands producing excellent clover (*Herba Medica*). The horses were entirely white, and of extraordinary height and beauty, as well as speed. They constituted a part of the luxury of the great, and a tribute in kind was paid from them to the monarch, who, like all Eastern sovereigns, used to delight in equestrian display.

(3) **Tribute.** Some idea of the opulence of the country may be had when it is known that, independently of imposts rendered in money, Media paid a yearly tribute of not less than 3,000 horses, 4,000 mules, and nearly 100,000 sheep.

(4) **Products.** The horse-races, once celebrated through the world, appear to exist no more; but Ker Porter saw the Shah ride on festival occasions a splendid horse of pure white. Cattle abounded, as did the richest fruits, as pines, citrons, oranges, all of peculiar excellence, growing as in their native land. Here also was found the Silphium (probably assafœtida), which formed a considerable article in the commerce of the ancients, and was accounted worth its weight in gold. The Median dress was proverbially splendid; the dress, that is, of the highest class, which seems to have gained a sort of classical authority, and to have been at a later period worn at the Persian court, probably in part from its antiquity. This dress the Persian monarchs used to present to those whom they wished to honor, and no others were permitted to wear it. It consisted of a long white loose robe, or gown, flowing down to the feet, and enclosing the entire body, specimens of which, as now used in those countries, may be seen in plates given in Perkin's *Residence in Persia*, New York, 1843. The nature and the celebrity of this dress combine with the natural richness of the country to assure us that the ancient Medians had made no mean progress in the arts; indeed, the colors of the Persian textures are known to have been accounted second only to those of India. If these regal dresses were of silk, then was there an early commerce between Media and India; if not, weaving, as well as dyeing, must have been practiced and carried to a high degree of perfection in the former country (Ammian. Marcell. xxiv. 6. p. 353, ed. Bip.; Xenoph. *Cyrop.* i. 3. 2; *Athen.* xii. pp. 512, 514, *sq.;* Heeren, *Ideen*, i. 205, 307; Herod. vi. 112; Strabo, xi. p. 525; Dan. iii:21).

(5) **Religion.** The religion of the Medes consisted in the worship of the heavenly bodies, more particularly the sun and moon, and the planets Jupiter, Venus, Saturn, Mercury, and Mars (Strabo, xv. p. 732). (See STARS.) The famous Median dress, comprised the miter, as well as the flowing robe. The priestly caste were denominated magi; they were a separate tribe, and had the charge not only of religion, but of all the higher culture.

(6) **Language.** The language of the ancient Medes was not connected with the Semitic, but the Indian; and divided itself into two chief branches, the Zend, spoken in North Media, and the Pehlvi, spoken in Lower Media and Parthia; which last was the dominant tongue among the Parthians.

(7) **Early History.** The Medes originally consisted of six tribes, of which the Magi were one (Herod. i:101). Being overcome by Ninus, they formed a part of the great Assyrian empire, which, however, lost in course of time the primitive simplicity of manners to which its dominion was owing, and fell into luxury and consequent weakness; then Arbaces, who governed the country as a satrap for Sardanapalus, taking advantage of the effeminacy of that monarch, threw off his yoke, destroyed his capital, Nineveh, and became himself sovereign of the Medes, in the ninth century before the Christian era (Diod. Sic., ii. 1, 2, 24, 32). According to Diodorus, this empire extended through nine monarchs, enduring 310 years, until Astyages, son of Cyaxares, was dethroned by Cyrus in the year of the world 3495, when Media became a part of the Persian empire, sinking from the same inevitable causes as those which enabled it to gain over the Assyrian power the dominion of Asia. The account given by Herodotus varies from that now set forth.

We do not propose to subject the diversities to a critical investigation, believing that little, if any, good could result, at least within our narrow space. Dates, names, and dynasties may be more or less uncertain, but the facts we have given are unimpeached.

(8) Extent. The magnitude of the Median empire is another important fact equally well ascertained. Being in their time the most valorous, as well as the most powerful nation of Asia, the Medes extended their power towards the east and the west beyond any strictly definable limits, though, like dominion generally in Oriental countries, it was of a vague, variable, and unstable kind. That they regarded the Tigris as their western boundary appears from the fact that they erected on its banks strongholds, such as Mespila and Larissa (Xenoph., *Anab.* iii. 4, 10) ; but that they carried their victorious arms still farther westward, appears from both Herodotus (i. 134) and Isaiah (xiii:17, 18). The eastern limits of the empire seem to have been different at different periods. Heeren inclines to the opinion that it may have reached as far as the Oxus, and even the Indus (*Ideen,* i. 142). Many, however, were the nations and tribes which were under the sway of its sovereigns.

(9) Government. The government was a succession of satrapies, over all of which the Medes were paramount; but the different nations exerted a secondary dominion over each other, diminishing with the increase of distance from the center of royal power (Herod., i. 134), to which center ultimately the tribute paid by each dependent to his superior eventually and securely came. Not only were the Medes a powerful, but also a wealthy and cultivated people; indeed, before they sank, in consequence of their degeneracy, into the Persian empire, they were during their time the foremost people of Asia, owing their celebrity not only to their valor, but also to the position of their country, which was the great commercial highway of Asia. The sovereigns exerted absolute and unlimited dominion, exacted a rigid court-ceremonial, and displayed a great love of pomp (Heeren, *Ideen,* 143).

(10) Under Persian Rule. Under the Persian monarchs Media formed a province, or satrapy, by itself, whose limits did not correspond with independent Media, but cannot be accurately defined.

To Media belonged another country, namely, Aria, which, Heeren says, took its name from the river Arius (now Heri), but which appears to contain the elements of the name (in the Zend language) which was common to the two, if not to other, Eastern nations who were denominated Indians by Alexander the Great, as dwellers in or near the Indus (which he also misnamed) but who were known in their own tongue as Arians (Arii, Aria, Ariana, also the name of Persia, Iran; see Ritter, *Erdkunde,* v. 458; Manu, 22; x. 45; Herod., vii. 62, who declares that the Medes were of old universally called Arii, Ἄριοι). Subsequently, however, from whatever cause, the Arians were separated from the Medes, forming a distinct satrapy in the Persian empire. Thus the name of a clan, or gens, became the name of a nation, and then of an individual tribe (Strabo, quoted by Heeren, *Ideen,* i. 190).

(11) Scriptural Mention. The Medes are not mentioned in sacred Scripture till the days of Hoshea, king of Israel, about 740 B. C., when Shalmaneser, king of Assyria, brought that monarch under his yoke, and in the ninth year of his reign took Samaria, and carried Israel away into Assyria, placing them in Halah and in Habor, by the river of Gozan, and in the cities of the Medes. Here the Medes appear as a part of the Assyrian empire; but at a later period Scripture exhibits them as an independent and sovereign people (Is. xiii:17; Jer. xxv:25; li:11, 28). In the last passage their kings are expressly named: 'The Lord hath raised up the kings of the Medes; for his device is against Babylon to destroy it.' 'Prepare against her (Babylon) the kings of the Medes, the captains thereof, and all the rulers thereof.'

It has been conjectured that soon after the time of Arbaces they again fell under the dominion of the Assyrians; but availing themselves of the opportunity afforded by the distant expeditions which Sennacherib undertook, they gained their freedom, and founded a new line of kings under Dejoces (Winer, *Realwört.*). Indeed, so sudden and rapid are the changes of government, even to the present day, in Oriental monarchies, that we need not be surprised at any difficulties which may occur in arranging the dynasties or the succession of kings, scarcely in any ancient history, certainly least of all in the fragmentary notices preserved regarding the kings of Media and other neighboring empires.

(12) Medes and Persians. According, however, to other historical testimony, we find the Medes and Persians united as one people in Holy Writ (Dan. v:28; vi:15; viii:20; Esth. i:3, 18; x:2), in the days of Cyrus, who destroyed the separate sovereignty of the former. To the united kingdom Babylon was added as a province.

(13) Conquered by Alexander. After the lapse of about 200 years, Media, in junction with the entire Persian monarchy, fell under the yoke of Alexander the Great (B. C. 330) ; but after the death of Alexander it became, under Seleucus Nicator, the Macedonian governor of Media and Babylonia, a portion of the new Syrian kingdom (1 Macc. vi:56), and, after many variations of warlike fortune, passed over to the Parthian monarchy (1 Macc. xiv:2; Strabo, xvi. p. 745).

(14) The People. The ancient Medes were a warlike people, and much feared for their skill in archery (Herod., vii. 61; Strabo, xi. p. 525.) They appear armed with the bow in the army of the Persians, who borrowed the use of that weapon from them (Herod., *ut supra*). Those who remained in the more mountainous districts did not lose their valor; but the inhabitants of the cities and towns which covered the plains, in becoming commercial lost their former hardy habits, together with their bravery, and, giving way to luxury, became in process of time an easy prey to new aspirants to martial fame and civil dominion. (See Grote, *History of Greece,* iii. pp. 301-312; Rawlinson, *Ancient Monarchies;* Porter, *Travels;* Kinnier, *Persian Empire.*) (See PERSIAN.)

J. R. B.

MEDIAN (mē′dĭ-an), (Chald. מָדַי, *maw-dah′ee*), an appellation of Darius (Dan. ix:1), "the Mede" (xi:1). (See DARIUS).

MEDIATOR (mē′dĭ-ā′tẽr), (Gr. Μεσίτης, *mes-ee′-tace*, mediator), is a word peculiar to the Scriptures (see Beza, *Annot. in Gr. Test.*), and is used, in an accommodated sense, by many of the ancient Fathers, to denote one who intervenes between two dispensations. Hence it is applied to John the Baptist, because he came, as it were, between the Mosaic and Christian dispensations. Thus Greg. Nazianzenus (*Orat.* xxxix. p.633) calls him ὁ παλαιᾶς καὶ νέας μεσίτης. Theophylact, commenting on Matt. iii, gives him the same denomination.

1. Signification. Again, it signifies, in its more proper sense, an *internuncius* or ambassador, one who stands as the channel of communication between two contracting parties.

Some commentators think that the Apostle Paul, in Gal. iii:19, calls Moses *mediator*, because he conveyed the expression of God's will to the people, and reported to God their wants, wishes, and determinations. In reference to this passage of Scripture, Basil (*De Spiritu Sancto*, ch. xiv) says, '*Mosen figuram representásse, quando inter Deum et populum intermedius extiterit.*' Many ancient and modern divines, however, are of opinion that Christ himself, and not Moses, is here meant by the inspired Apostle, and this view would seem to be confirmed by comparing Deut. xxxiii:2 with Acts vii:38-52. Christ it was who, surrounded by angelic spirits, communicated with Moses on Mount Sinai. On this point, the words of the learned and pious Chrysostom, on Gal. iii are very express: 'Here,' says he, 'Paul calls Christ Mediator, declaring thereby that he existed before the law, and that by him the law was revealed.' This application of the passage will be the more evident if we consider the scope of the Apostle's argument, which evidently is, to point out the dignity of the law. How could he present a clearer demonstration of this than by showing that it was the second person of the ever-blessed Trinity who stood forth on the mount to communicate between God the Father and his creature man! Moreover, to contradistinguish Christ's mediation from that of Moses, the former is emphatically styled μεσίτης κρείττονος διαθήκης (Heb. viii:6).

2. Applied to The Christ. Christ is called Mediator by virtue of the reconciliation he has effected between a justly offended God and his rebellious creature man (see Grotius, *De Satisfactione Christi*, ch. viii). In this sense of the term Moses was, on many occasions, an eminent type of Christ. The latter, however, was not *Mediator* merely by reason of his coming between God and his creatures, as certain heretics would affirm (see Cyril Alex. *Dial. 1. de Sancta Trinitate*, p. 410); but because he appeased God's wrath, and made reconciliation for iniquity. 'Christ is the Mediator,' observes Theophylact, commenting on Gal. iii, 'of two, *i. e.*, of God and man. He exercises this office between both by making peace, and putting a stop to that spiritual war which man wages against God. To accomplish this he assumed our nature, joining in a marvelous manner the human, by reason of sin unfriendly, to the Divine nature.' 'Hence,' he adds, 'he made reconciliation.' Oecumenius expresses similar sentiments on the same passage of Scripture. Again, Cyril, in his work before quoted, remarks: 'He is esteemed Mediator because, the Divine and human nature being disjointed by sin, he has shown them united in his own person; and in this manner he reunites us to God the Father.'

(1) Prophet. If, in addition to the above general remarks, confirmed by many of the most ancient and orthodox Fathers of the church, we consider the *three great offices* which holy Scripture assigns to Christ as Savior of the world, viz., those of *prophet, priest,* and *king,* a further and more ample illustration will be afforded of his Mediatorship.

One of the first and most palpable predictions which we have of the prophetic character of Christ, is that of Moses (Deut. xviii:15): 'The Lord thy God will raise up unto thee a prophet from the midst of thee, of thy brethren, like unto me; unto him ye shall hearken.' That this refers to Christ we are assured by the inspired Apostle Peter (Acts iii:22).

Again, in Isaiah lxi:1, 11, Christ's consecration to the prophetic office, together with its sacred and gracious functions, is emphatically set forth: (see Luke iv:16-21, where Christ applies this passage to himself). In order, then, to sustain this part of his mediatorial office, and thus work out the redemption of the world, we may see the necessity there was that Messiah should be both *God* and *man*. It belongs to a prophet to expound the law, declare the will of God, and foretell things to come: all this was done, and that in a singular and eminent manner, by Christ, our prophet (Matt. v:21, etc.; John i:8). All light comes from this prophet. The Apostle shows that all ministers are but stars which shine by a borrowed light (2 Cor. iii:6, 7). All the prophets of the Old, and all the prophets and teachers of the New Testament, lighted their tapers at this torch (Luke xxi:15). It was Christ who preached by Noah (1 Pet. iii:19), taught the Israelites in the wilderness (Acts vii:37), and still teaches by his ministers (Eph. iv:11, 12). On this subject Bishop Butler (*Analogy*, part ii. ch. v.) says: 'He was, by way of eminence, *the prophet*, "the prophet that should come into the world" (John vi:14) to declare the Divine will. He published anew the law of nature, which men had corrupted, and the very knowledge of which, to some degree, was lost amongst them. He taught mankind, taught us authoritatively, to live soberly, righteously, and godly in this present world, in expectation of the future judgment of God. He confirmed the truth of this moral system of nature, and gave us additional evidence of it, the evidence of testimony. He distinctly revealed the manner in which God would be worshiped, the efficacy of repentance, and the rewards and punishments of a future life. Thus he was a prophet in a sense in which no other ever was.' Hence the force of the term ὁ λόγος, by which St. John designates Christ.

But, on the other hand, had the second person of the Trinity come to us in all the majesty of his Divine nature, we could not have approached him as our instructor. The Israelites, terrified at the exhibitions of Deity, cried out that the Lord might not so treat with them again; it was then that he, in gracious condescension to their feelings, promised to communicate with them in future through a prophet like unto Moses. The Son of God, in assuming the form of an humble man, became accessible to *all*. Thus we perceive the connection of Christ's prophetic office—he being both God and man—with the salvation of man. On this subject Chrysostom (*Homil.* cxxxiv. tom. v. p. 860) remarks: 'A mediator, unless he has a union and communion with the parties for whom he mediates, possesses not the essential qualities of a mediator. When Christ, therefore, became Mediator between God and man (1 Tim. ii. etc.), it was indispensable that he should be both God and man.'

Macarius also (*Homil.* vi:97) on this question more pointedly observes: 'The Lord came and took his body from the virgin; for if he had appeared among us in his naked divinity, who could bear the sight? But he spoke as man to us men.'

Again, the Redeemer was not only to propound, explain, and enforce God's law, but it was needful that he should give a practical proof of obedience to it in his own person. Now, if he had not been *man*, he could not have been subject to the law; hence it is said, Gal. iv:4, 'When the fullness of the time was come, God sent forth his son, made of a woman, made under the law;' and if he had not been God, he could not, by keeping the law, have *merited* forgiveness for us, for he had done but what was required of him. It was the fact of his being *very God and very man* which constituted the *merit* of Christ's obedience.

(2) Priest. Moreover, in working out the mighty scheme of redemption the mediator must assume the office of *priest*.

To this office Christ was solemnly appointed by God (Ps. cx:4; Heb. v:10), qualified for it by his incarnation (Heb. x:6, 7), and accomplished all the ends thereof by his sacrificial death (Heb. ix:11, 12); as in sustaining his *prophetic* character, *so in this*, his Deity and humanity will be seen. According to the exhibition of type and declaration of prophecy, the mediator must die, and thus rescue us sinners from death by destroying him who had the power of death. 'But we see Jesus,' says the Apostle (Heb. ii:9), 'who was made a little lower than the angels for the suffering of death, crowned with glory and honor, that he by the grace of God should taste death for every man. Forasmuch, then, as the children are partakers of flesh and blood, he also himself likewise took part of the same, that through death he might destroy him who had the power of death, that is, the Devil.' On the other hand, had he not been *God* he could not have raised himself from the dead. 'I lay down my life (he says, John x:17, 18), and take it up again.' He had not had a life to lay down if he had not been man, for the Godhead could not die; and if he had not been God, he could not have acquired *merit* by laying it down; it must be his own, and not in the power of another, else his voluntarily surrendering himself unto death—as he did on the charge that he, being only man, made himself equal with God—was an act of *suicide,* and consequently an act of blasphemy against God! It was, then, the mysterious union of both natures in the one person of Christ, which constituted the *essential glory* of his vicarious obedience and death.

Nor are the two natures of Christ more apparent in his *death* than they are in the *intercession* which 'he ever liveth to make' in behalf of all who come unto God by him (Heb. vii:25). The author of the Epistle to the Hebrews teaches us (cc. vii, ix) how the high-priest, under the Levitical dispensation, typified Christ in his intercessory character; as the high-priest entered *alone* within the holiest place of the tabernacle once a year with the blood of the sacrifice in his hands, and the names of the twelve tribes upon his heart, so Christ, having offered up himself as a lamb without spot unto God, has gone into glory bearing on his *heart* the names of his redeemed. We may, then, ask, with the Apostle (Rom. viii:33), 'Who shall lay anything to the charge of God's elect? It is God that justifieth, who is he that condemneth? It is Christ that died, yea rather, that is risen again, who is even at the right hand of God, who also maketh *intercession* for us.' In this part of his mediatorial work God's *incommunicable* attributes of *omniscience, omnipresence,* and *omnipotence* are seen. He must therefore have been God, and on the ground of his being able, from personal experience, to sympathize with the suffering members of his mystical body, he must have been man; being perfect God and perfect man, he is, then, a perfect *intercessor.*

(3) King. We come, lastly, to notice Christ's mediatorial character *as king.* The limits of this article will not admit of our even alluding to the varied and multiplied passages of Scripture which delineate Christ as 'Head over all things to the church' (see Ps. ii:6; xlv; Isaiah xxxii: 1; Dan. ix:25; Col. i:17, 18, etc.). Suffice it here to say that Christ could not, without the concurrence of his *Divine* nature, gather and govern the church, protect and defend it against all assailants open and secret, and impart to it his Holy Spirit, to enlighten and renew the minds and hearts of men and subdue Satan—all these are acts of his kingly office.

Such, then, is the work of Christ's mediatorship —salvation revealed by him as prophet, procured by him as priest, and applied by him as king— the work of the whole person wherein both natures are engaged. Hence it is that some of the ancients speaking of it, designate it '*a Divine-human operation*' (see Dionys. Areopag. *Epist. IV. ad Caiam, Damascenus,* iii. 19). For a more ample view of this important subject see Flavel, *Panstratia of Shamier,* vol. iii. fol. Genev. vii. 1, in which the views of the Romish church are ably controverted. See also Brinsley (John), *Christ's Mediation,* 8 vols. Lond. 1657. (See JESUS CHRIST.) J. W. D.

MEDICINE or PHYSIC (mĕd'ĭ-sĭn), (Heb. הֵהָה, *geh-haw'*), is ascribed by Jesus, son of Sirach, to God himself (Eccles. xxxviii:1, etc.).

Scripture makes no mention of physicians before the time of Joseph, who commanded his servants, the physicians of Egypt, to embalm the body of Jacob (Gen. l:2). The art of medicine, however, was very ancient in Egypt. They ascribed the invention of it to Thaut, or to Hermes, or to Osiris, or to Isis; and some of the learned have thought that Moses, having been instructed in all the learning of the Egyptians, must also have known the chief secrets of medicine. It does not appear that physicians were common among the Hebrews, especially for internal maladies, but for wounds, fractures, bruises, and external injuries, they had physicians, or surgeons, who understood the dressing and binding up of wounds, with the application of medicaments. (See Jer. viii:22; xlvi:11; Ezek. xxx:21). Asa, being diseased in his feet, and having applied to physicians, is upbraided with it, as contrary to that confidence which he ought to have had in the Lord (1 Kings xv:23; 2 Chron. xvi: 12). Hezekiah, having a boil, probably a malignant one, was cured by Isaiah, on the application of figs (2 Kings xx:7; Is. xxxviii:21). The low state of the art of medicine, with the persuasion that distempers were effects of God's anger, or were caused by evil spirits, was the reason that in extraordinary maladies the sufferers applied to diviners, magicians, enchanters, or false gods. Sometimes they applied to the prophets of the Lord for cure; or, at least, to know whether they should recover or not. When Ahaziah, king of Israel, by a fall from the roof of his house, was greatly hurt, he sent to consult the false god Baal-zebub at Ekron (2 Kings i:2, etc.). Jeremiah (viii:17) speaks of enchantments used against the biting of serpents, and other venomous animals. Hazael was sent by the king of Syria to consult Elisha the prophet as to the issue of his disease (2 Kings viii:8). Naaman the Syrian came into the land of Israel, to obtain from Elisha a cure for his leprosy (2 Kings v:5, 6). And when our Savior appeared in Palestine, although there can be no doubt that there were physicians in the country, it is evident that the people placed but little confidence in them (comp. Mark v:26; Luke viii:43). They brought to our Savior and his Apostles multitudes of diseased people from all parts of the land, and he laid his hands upon them and healed them.   Calmet.

MEDITATION (mĕd'ĭ-tā'shŭn), is an act by which we consider anything closely, or wherein the soul is employed in the search or consideration of any truth.   In religion it is used to signify the serious exercise of the understanding, whereby our thoughts are fixed on the observation of spiritual things.

Mystic divines make a great difference between meditation and contemplation; the former consists in discursive acts of the soul, considering methodically and with attention the mysteries of faith and the precepts of morality; and is performed by reflections and reasonings which leave behind them manifest impressions on the brain. The pure contemplative, they say, has no need of meditation, as seeing all things in God at a glance, and without any reflection.

(1) A Duty. *Meditation* is a duty which ought to be attended to by all who wish well to their spiritual interests.   It ought to be *deliberate, close,* and *perpetual* (Ps. cxix:97; Ps. i:2-6).

(2) Subjects Of.   The *subjects* which ought more especially to engage the Christian mind are the works of creation (Ps. xix); the perfections of God (Deut. xxxii:4); the excellencies, offices, characters, and works of Christ (Heb. xii:2, 3); the offices and operations of the Holy Spirit (John xv and xvi); the various dispensations of Providence (Ps. xcvii:1, 2); the precepts, declarations, promises, etc., of God's word (Ps. cxix); the value, powers, and immortality of the soul (Mark viii:36); the noble, beautiful, and benevolent plan of the gospel (1 Tim. i:11); the necessity of our personal interest in and experience of its power (John iii:3); the depravity of our nature, and the freedom of Divine grace in choosing, adopting, justifying, and sanctifying us (1 Cor. vi:11); the shortness, worth, and swiftness of time (James iv:14); the certainty of death (Heb. ix:27); the resurrection and judgment to come (1 Cor. xv: 50), etc., and the future state of eternal rewards and punishments (Matt. xxv; Rev. xix:7-9.)

(3) Should Be with Prayer. *To perform this duty aright,* we should be much in prayer (Luke xviii:1); avoid a worldly spirit (1 John ii:15); beware of sloth (Heb. vi:11); take heed of sensual pleasures (James iv:4); watch against the devices of Satan (1 Pet. v:8); be often in retirement (Ps. iv:4); embrace the most favorable opportunities, the calmness of the morning (Ps. v:1, 3), the solemnity of the evening (Gen. xxiv: 63), Sabbath days (Ps. cxviii:24), sacramental occasions, etc. (1 Cor. xi:28).

MEEKNESS (mēk'nĕs), (Heb. from עָנָו, *aw-naw',* to be depressed; Gr. πρᾳότης, *prah-ot'ace,* gentleness).

A state of mind not easily provoked to resentment.   In the Greek language the word signifies also *easiness* of spirit, and thus it may be justly called; for it accommodates the soul to every occurrence, and so makes a man easy to himself, and to all about him.

(1) Specific Results.   The Latins call a meek man *mansuestus,* or *manu assuetus, used to the hand;* which alludes to the taming and reclaiming of creatures wild by nature, and bringing them to be tractable and familiar (James iii:7, 8): so where the grace of meekness reigns, it subdues the impetuous disposition, and teaches it submission and forgiveness.   It teaches us to govern our own anger whenever we are at any time provoked, and patiently to bear the anger of oth-ers, that it may not be a provocation to us.   The former is its office, especially in superiors; the latter in inferiors, and both in equals (James iii:13).

(2) Excellence. *The excellency of such a spirit appears,* if we consider that it enables us to gain a victory over corrupt nature (Prov. xvi: 32); that it is a beauty and an ornament to human beings (1 Pet. iii:4); that it is obedience to God's word, and conformity to the best patterns (Eph. v:1, 2; Phil. iv:8).

It is productive of the highest peace to the possessor (Luke xxi:19; Matt. xi:28, 29).   It fits us for any duty, instruction, relation, condition, or persecution (Phil. iv:11, 12).

(3) How Obtained and Examples. *To obtain this spirit,* consider that it is a Divine injunction (Zeph. ii:3; Col. iii:12; 1 Tim. vi:11). Observe the many examples of it: Jesus Christ (Matt. xi:28); Abraham (Gen. xiii; xvi:5, 6); Moses (Num. xii:3); David (Zech. xii:8; 2 Sam. xvi:10, 12; Ps. cxxxi:2); Paul (1 Cor. ix:19). How lovely a spirit it is in itself, and how it secures us from a variety of evils! What peculiar promises are made to the meek (Matt. v:5; Is. lxvi:2).   Also such give evidence of their being under the influence of Divine grace, and shall enjoy the Divine blessing (Is. lvii:15).

MEGIDDO (me-gĭd'do), (Heb. מְגִדּוֹ, *meg-id-do';* in Zech. xii:11, מְגִדּוֹן, *meg-id-done',* place of troops).

A town belonging to Manasseh, although within the boundaries of Issachar (Josh. xvii:11).   It had been originally one of the royal cities of the Canaanites (Josh. xii:21), and was one of those of which the Israelites were unable for a long time to gain actual possession.   Megiddo was rebuilt and fortified by Solomon (1 Kings ix:15), and thither Ahaziah king of Judah fled when wounded by Jehu, and died there (2 Kings ix:27).   It was in the battle near this place that Josiah was slain by Pharaoh-necho (2 Kings xxiii:29, 30; 2 Chron. xxxv:20-25).   From the great mourning held for his loss, it became proverbial to compare any grievous mourning to it, as 'like the mourning of Hadadrimmon in the valley of Megiddon' (Zech. xii:11).

'The waters of Megiddo' are mentioned in Judg. v:19; and are probably those formed by the river Kishon.   Eusebius and Jerome do not attempt to mark the situation of the place, and it appears that the name Megiddo was in their time already lost.   They often mention a town called Legio, which must in their day have been an important and well-known place, as they assume it as a central point from which to mark the position of several other places in this quarter.   This has been identified with the village now called Lejjun, which is situated upon the western border of the great plain of Esdraelon, where it begins to rise gently towards the low range of wooded hills that connect Carmel with the mountains of Samaria.   This place was visited by Maundrell, who speaks of it as an old village near a brook, with a khan then in good repair (*Journey,* March 22).   This khan was for the accommodation of the caravan on the route between Egypt and Damascus, which passes here.   Having already identified the present village of Taannuk with the ancient Taanach, the vicinity of this to Lejjun induced Dr. Robinson to conceive that the latter might be the ancient Megiddo, seeing that Taanach and Megiddo are constantly named together in Scripture.   (Conder places it at Khurbet el-Mujedda, ten miles southeast from Jezreel.)

MEGIDDON (me-gĭd'don), (Zech. xii:11). See MEGIDDO.

MEHETABEEL (me-hĕt'a-beel), (Neh. vi:10). See MEHETABEL, 2.

MEHETABEL (me-hĕt'a-bĕl), (Heb. מְהֵיטַבְאֵל, meh-hay-tab-ale', bettered of God).

1. Daughter of Matred, and wife of Hadad, king of Edom (Gen. xxxvi:39; 1 Chron. i:50). (B. C. about 1619.)

2. Father of Delaiah and ancestor of the prophet Shemaiah, which latter was hired against Nehemiah (Neh. vi:10). (B. C. before 446.)

MEHIDA (me-hī'dà), (Heb. מְחִידָא, mekh-ee-daw', joining).

Founder of a family of Nethinim, some of whose descendants returned with Zerubbabel (Ezra ii:52; Neh. vii:54). (B. C. before 536.)

MEHIR (mē'hir), (Heb. מְחִיר, mekh-eer', price).

Son of Chelub, of the tribe of Judah, and father, or founder of Eshton (1 Chron. iv:11). (B. C. about 1618.)

MEHOLATHITE (me-hŏl'ath-īte), (Heb. מְחֹלָתִי, mekh-o-law-thee'), probably a native of Abel-Meholah (1 Sam. xviii:19; 2 Sam. xxi:8).

MEHUJAEL (me-hū'ja-el), (Heb. מְחוּיָאֵל, mekh-oo-yaw-ale', smitten of God).

Son of Irad, and father of Methusael, a descendant of Cain (Gen. iv:18). (B. C. about 3840.)

MEHUMAN (me-hū'man), (Heb. מְהוּמָן, meh-hoo-mawn', perhaps, faithful).

One of the eunuchs who served in the palace of Ahasuerus (Esth. i:10). (B. C. 483.)

MEHUNIMS, THE (me-hū'nimz, the), (Heb. מְעוּנָי, meh-oo-naw-ee'; or מְעִינִי, meh-ee-nee').

A people, with a capital city, Maân, twelve miles southeast of Petra, against whom Uzziah was successful in war (2 Chron. xxvi:7). In the reign of Hezekiah the Mehunims (A. V. 'habitations') in the valley of the Gedor were smitten by the Simeonites (1 Chron. iv:39-41). It was probably some of their descendants who served in the Temple as Nethinim after the exile (Ezra ii:50; Neh. vii:52).

ME-JARKON (mē-jär'kon), (Heb. מֵי הַיַּרְקוֹן, may-hah'ee-yar-kone', waters of yellowishness).

A town near Dan, near Joppa (Josh. xix:46). Kiepert and Conder suggest a place on the river Anjah, which flows through a swamp, rendering the waters yellow, as suggested by the name. The stream empties into the Mediterranean a little north of Joppa.

MEKONAH (mĕk'o-nah), (Heb. מְכֹנָה, mek-o-naw', a base, standing place or foundation).

A town reinhabited by men of Judah after the exile (Neh. xi:28). It is mentioned with Ziklag, and therefore probably located far to the south. Not identified.

MELATIAH (mĕl-a-tī'ah), (Heb. מְלַטְיָה, mel-at-yaw', Jah has delivered).

A Gibeonite who helped to repair a part of the northern wall of Jerusalem after the exile (Neh. iii:7). (B. C. 446.)

MELCHI (mĕl'kī), (Gr. Μελχί, mel-khee'; Heb. מַלְכִּי, mal-kee', my king).

1. Son of Addi, an ancestor of Christ (Luke iii:28), probably identical with Maaseiah (2 Chron. xxxiv:8).

2. Son of Janna and father of Levi, in the latter genealogy of Christ (Luke iii:24). (B. C. before 22).

MELCHIAH (mel-kī'ah), (Heb. מַלְכִּיָּה, mal-kee-yaw', Jehovah's king).

A priest, father of Pashur (Jer. xxi:1). Identical with Malchiah (Jer. xxxviii:1; Neh. xi:12), and Malchijah (1 Chron. ix:12).

MELCHISEDEC (mel-kĭz'e-děk), (Heb. v-viii). See MELCHIZEDEK.

MELCHISHUA (mĕl-ki-shu'à), (1 Sam. xiv:49; xxxi:2). See MALCHISHUA.

MELCHIZEDEK (mel-kĭz'e-děk), (Heb. מַלְכִּי־צֶדֶק, mal-kee-tseh'dek, king of righteousness).

A 'priest of the most high God,' and king of Salem, who went forth to meet Abraham on his return from the pursuit of Chedorlaomer and his allies, who had carried Lot away captive. He brought refreshment, described in the general terms of 'bread and wine,' for the fatigued warriors, and bestowed his blessing upon their leader, who, in return, gave to the royal priest a tenth of all the spoil which had been acquired in his expedition (Gen. xiv:18, 20).

This statement seems sufficiently plain, and to offer nothing very extraordinary; yet it has formed the basis of much speculation and controversy. In particular, the fact that Abraham gave a tithe to Melchizedek attracted much attention among the later Jews. In one of the Messianic Psalms (cx:4), it is foretold that the Messiah should be 'a priest after the order of Melchizedek'; which the author of the Epistle to the Hebrews (vi:20) cites as showing that Melchizedek was a type of Christ, and the Jews themselves, certainly, on the authority of this passage of the Psalms, regarded Melchizedek as a type of the regal priesthood, higher than that of Aaron, to which the Messiah should belong. The bread and wine which were set forth on the table of shewbread was also supposed to be represented by the bread and wine which the king of Salem brought forth to Abraham (Schöttgen, *Hor. Heb.* ii. 645). A mysterious supremacy came also to be assigned to Melchizedek, by reason of his having received tithes from the Hebrew patriarch; and on this point the Epistle to the Hebrews (vii:1-10) expatiates strongly, as showing the inferiority of the priesthood represented, to that of Melchizedek, to which the Messiah belonged. 'Consider how great this man was, unto whom even the patriarch Abraham gave a tenth of the spoils;' and he goes on to argue that the Aaronic priesthood, who themselves received tithes of the Jews, actually paid tithes to Melchizedek in the person of their great ancestor. This superiority is, as we take it, inherent in his typical rather than his personal character. But the Jews, in admitting this official or personal superiority of Melchizedek to Abraham, sought to account for it by alleging that the royal priest was no other than Shem, the most pious of Noah's sons, who, according to the shorter chronology, might have lived to the time of Abraham. But such conjectures do not need to be refuted in the light of the discoveries made by the monuments. Prof. A. H. Sayce in his *Patriarchal Palestine* has cleared up the mystery regarding Melchizedek. He says:

It is only since the discovery and decipherment of the cuneiform tablets of Tell Amarna that the story of Melchizedek has been illustrated and explained. Hitherto it had seemed to stand alone. The critics, in the superiority of their knowledge, had refused credit to it, and had denied that the name even of Jerusalem or Salem was known before the age of David. But the monuments have come to our help, and have shown that it is the critics and not the Biblical writer who have been in error.

Several of the most interesting of the Tell Amarna letters were written to the Pharaoh Amenôphis IV, Khu-n-Aten, by Ebed-Tob the king of Jerusalem. Not only is the name of Uru-salim or Jerusalem the only one in use, but the city itself is already one of the most important fortresses of Canaan. It was the capital of a large district which extended southwards as far as Keilah and Karmel of Judah. It commanded the approach to the vale of Siddim, and in one of his letters Ebed-Tob speaks of having repaired the royal roads not only in the mountains but also in the *kikar* or "plain" of Jordan (Gen. xiii:10). The possession of Jerusalem was eagerly coveted by the enemies of Ebed-Tob, whom he calls also the enemies of the Egyptian king.

Now Ebed-Tob declares time after time that he is not an Egyptian governor, but a tributary ally and vassal of the Pharaoh, and that he had received his royal power, not by inheritance from his father or mother, but through the arm (or oracle) of "the mighty king." As "the mighty king" is distinguished from the "great king" of Egypt we must see in him the god worshiped by Ebed-Tob, the "most high God" of Melchizedek and the prototype of the "mighty God" of Isaiah. It is this same "mighty king," Ebed-Tob assures the Pharaoh in another lettter, who will overthrow the navies of Babylonia and Aram-Naharim. Here then as late as the fifteenth century before our era we have a king in Jerusalem who owes his royal dignity to his god. He is in fact a priest as well as a king. His throne has not descended to him by inheritance; so far as his kingly office is concerned, he is like Melchizedek, without father or mother.

Between Ebed-Tob and Melchizedek there is more than analogy; there is a striking and unexpected resemblance; the description given of himself by Ebed-Tob explains what has so long puzzled us in the person of Melchizedek (*Patriarchal Palestine,* pp. 71, sq.).

We may justly conclude that his twofold capacity of king and priest (characters very commonly united in the remote ages) afforded Abraham an opportunity of testifying his thankfulness to God in the manner usual in those times, by offering a tenth of all the spoil. This combination of character happens for the first time in Scripture to be exhibited in his person, which, with the abrupt manner in which he is introduced, and the nature of the intercourse between him and Abraham, render him in various respects an appropriate and obvious type of the Messiah in his united regal and priestly character. Salem, of which Melchizedek was king, is usually supposed to have been the original of Jerusalem (Joseph. *Antiq.* i, 10, 2; Jerome, *Quæst.* on Genes.).

Prof. Sayce also says: The origin of the name of Jerusalem also is now cleared up. It was no invention of the age of David; on the contrary, it goes back to the period of Babylonian intercourse with Canaan. It is written in the cuneiform documents Uru-Salim, "the city of Salim," the god of peace. We can now understand why Melchizedek should have been called the "king of Salem." His capital could be described either as Jeru-salem or as the city of Salem. And that it was often referred to as Salem simply is shown by the Egyptian monuments. One of the

cities of Southern Palestine, the capture of which is represented by Rameses II on the walls of the Ramesseum at Thebes, is Shalam or Salem, and "the district of Salem" is mentioned, between "the country of Hadashah" (Josh. xv:37) and "the district of the Dead Sea" and "the Jordan," in the list of the places which Rameses III at Medînet Habu describes himself as having conquered in the same part of the world.

It may be that Isaiah is playing upon the old name of Jerusalem when he gives the Messiah the title of "Prince of Peace." But in any case the fact that Salim, the god of peace, was the patron deity of Jerusalem, lends a special significance to Melchizedek's treatment of Abraham. The patriarch had returned in peace from an expedition in which he had overthrown the invaders of Canaan; he had restored peace to the country of the priestking, and had driven away its enemies. The offering of bread and wine on the part of Melchizedek was a sign of freedom from the enemy and of gratitude to the deliverer, while the tithes paid by Abraham were equally a token that the land was again at peace. The name of Salim, the god of peace, was under one form or another widely spread in the Semitic world. Salamanu, or Solomon, was the king of Moab in the time of Tiglath-pileser III; the name of Shalmaneser of Assyria is written Sulman-asarid, "the god Sulman is chief," in the cuneiform inscriptions; and one of the Tell Amarna letters was sent by Ebed-Sullim, "the servant of Sullim," who was governor of Hazor. In one of the Assyrian cities (Dimmen-Silim, "the foundation stone of peace") worship was paid to the god "Sulman the fish." Nor must we forget that "Salma was the father of Bethlehem" (1 Chron. ii:51). (*Patriarchal Palestine,* pp. 74-76.)

MELEA (mē'le-à), (Gr. Μελεᾶς, *mel-eh-as'*, signification unknown).

Son of Menan and father of Eliakim in the genealogy of Christ, on the maternal side; but the name is of doubtful authenticity (Luke iii: 31).

MELECH (mē'lek), (Heb. מֶלֶךְ, *meh'lek*, king).

The second of the four sons of Micah, grandson of Jonathan, the son of Saul (1 Chron. viii: 35; ix:41). (B. C. after 1037.)

MELICU (mĕl'i-kū), (Neh. xii:14.) See MALLUCH.

MELITA (mĕl'i-tà), (Gr. Μελίτη, *mel-ee'tay*, Melita), an island in the Mediterranean, on which the ship which was conveying St. Paul as a prisoner to Rome was wrecked, and which was the scene of the interesting circumstances recorded in Acts xxviii:28.

(1) Name. Melita was the ancient name of Malta, and also of a small island in the Adriatic, now called Meleda, and each of these has found warm advocates for its identification with the Melita of Scripture. The received and long-established opinion is undoubtedly in favor of Malta; and those who uphold the claims of Meleda are to be regarded as dissenting from the general conclusion. This dissent proceeds chiefly upon the ground that the ship of St. Paul was 'driven about in (the sea of) Adria,' when wrecked on Melita. But the name Adria was *not*, in its ancient acceptation, limited to the present Adriatic Sea, but comprehended the seas of Greece and Sicily, and extended even to Africa. This seems to have been established beyond dispute, and every one acquainted with the mass of evidence brought to bear on this point, must regard the only strong argument in favor of Meleda as having been entirely overthrown.

(2) St. Paul's Bay. The name of St. Paul's Bay has been given to the place where the shipwreck is supposed to have taken place. This, the sacred historian says, was at 'a certain creek with a shore,' *i. e.* a seemingly practicable shore, on which they purposed, if possible, to strand the vessel, as their only apparent chance to escape being broken on the rocks. In attempting this the ship seems to have struck and gone to pieces on the rocky headland at the entrance of the creek. This agrees very well with St. Paul's Bay, more so than with any other creek of the island. This bay is a deep inlet on the north side of the island, being the last indentation of the coast but one from the western extremity of the island. It is about two miles deep, by one mile broad. The harbor which it forms is very unsafe at some distance from the shore, although there is good anchorage in the middle for light vessels. The most dangerous part is the western headland at the entrance of the bay, particularly as there is

waves. From the headland of the bay the ancient capital of Malta (now Citta Vecchia, Old City) is distinctly seen at the distance of about five miles.

The sacred historian calls the inhabitants βάρβαροι, 'barbarians':—'the barbarous people showed us no small kindness.' This is far from implying that they were savages or uncivilized men: it merely intimates that they were not of Greek or Roman origin. This description applies to the ancient inhabitants of Malta most accurately; and as it could not apply to the inhabitants of Melida, who were Greeks, this is another argument to show that not Melida but Malta is the Melita of Scripture.

(3) Location. The island of Malta lies in the Mediterranean, about sixty miles south from Cape Passaro in Sicily. It is sixty miles in circumference, twenty in length, and twelve in breadth. Near it, on the west, is a smaller island, called Gozo, about thirty miles in circumference. Malta has no mountains or high hills, and makes no figure from the sea. It is naturally a barren rock,

St. Paul's Bay.

close to it a small island (Salamone), and a still smaller islet (Salamonetta), the currents and shoals around which are particularly dangerous in stormy weather. It is usually supposed that the vessel struck at this point.

In 1810 the British frigate Lively went to pieces on those very breakers, at the point of Koura, at the entrance of the bay. The crew, like Paul's shipmen, at the distance of a quarter of a mile, could not see the land, but they saw the surf on the shore. Every ship approaching the land must here pass over twenty fathoms, and not only must this depth be close to the spot where they had the indications of land, but it must bear east by south from the fifteen fathom depth. The fifteen fathom depth is, as nearly as possible, a quarter of a mile from the shore, which is here girt with mural precipices, and on which the sea must have been breaking violently. At the bottom of the Bay of St. Paul's there is a communication with the sea outside by a channel not more than a hundred yards in breadth, formed by the separation of Salamone Island, a long rocky ridge, from the mainland. Near this channel, where "two seas meet," are two *creeks,* into one of which they ran the ship ashore; the forepart stuck fast in the mud and clay, while the stern was dashed to pieces by the force of the

but has been made in parts abundantly fertile by the industry and toil of man.

(4) History. The island was first colonized by the Phœnicians, from whom it was taken by the Greek colonists in Sicily, about B. C. 736; but the Carthaginians began to dispute its possession about B. C. 528, and eventually became entire masters of it. From their hands it passed into those of the Romans, B. C. 242, who treated the inhabitants well, making Melita a municipium, and allowing the people to be governed by their own laws. The government was administered by a proprætor, who depended upon the prætor of Sicily; and this office appears to have been held by Publius when Paul was on the island (Acts xxviii:7). On the division of the Roman empire, Melita belonged to the western portion; but having, in A. D. 553, been recovered from the Vandals by Belisarius, it was afterwards attached to the empire of the East. About the end of the ninth century the island was taken from the Greeks by the Arabs, who made it a dependency upon Sicily, which was also in their possession. The Arabs have left the impress of their aspect, language, and many of their customs, upon the present inhabitants, whose dialect is to this day perfectly intelligible to the Arabians, and to the Moors of Africa. Malta was taken from the

Arabs by the Normans in A. D. 1090, and afterwards underwent other changes till A. D. 1530, when Charles V., who had annexed it to his empire, transferred it to the Knights of St. John of Jerusalem, whom the Turks had recently dispossessed of Rhodes. Under the knights it became a flourishing state, and was the scene of their greatest glory and most signal exploits. The institution having become unsuited to modern times, the Order of St. John of Jerusalem, commonly called Knights of Malta, gradually fell into decay, and the island was surrendered to the French under Bonaparte when on his way to Egypt in 1798. From them it was retaken by the English with the concurrence and assistance of the natives; and it was to have been restored to the Knights of Malta by the stipulations of the treaty of Amiens; but as no sufficient security for the independence of the Order (composed mostly of Frenchmen) could be obtained, the English retained it in their hands; which necessary infraction of the treaty was the ostensible ground of the war which only ended with the battle of Waterloo. The island is still in the hands of the English, who have lately remodeled the government to meet the wishes of the numerous inhabitants.

It has been asserted that no vipers exist in Malta, but Lewin saw a serpent there which he regarded as a viper; but even if not found on the thickly-populated island now, this would not prove that they did not exist in Paul's day and have since been exterminated. (Boisgelin, *History of Malta,* 1804; Bartlett, *Overland Route;* Harper's *Classical Dict.*)

MELODY (mĕl'ŏ-dy̆). See MUSIC.

MELONS (mĕl'ŭnz), (Heb. אֲבַטִּחִים, *ab-at-tee-kheem'*). (Num. xi:5.)

Melons of all kinds have ever been largely cultivated in Egypt, and during the heat of summer often form the chief food and drink of the lower classes. The muskmelon was grown there at the time of the Exodus, and perhaps the watermelon, which came from Persia. "A traveler in the East who recollects the intense gratitude which a gift of a slice of melon inspired while journeying over the hot and dry plains will readily comprehend the regret with which the Hebrews in the Arabian desert looked back upon the melons of Egypt." (See ABATTACHIM.) Kitto.

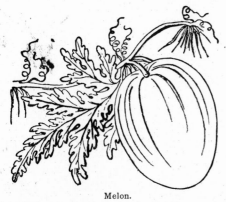

Melon.

MELZAR (mĕl'zar), (Heb. מֶלְצַר, *mel-tsawr'*, from Persian, *butler;* marg. "steward"). The title of the officer in the court of Babylon who had charge of Daniel and the other youths who were candidates for promotion as magi (Dan. i:11, 16).

MEMBER (mĕm'bēr), (Heb. יָצֻר, *yaw-tsoor'*, to mold; Gr. μέλος, *mel'os*, a limb).

A part of an animal body, legs, hands, ears, eyes, etc. (Ps. cxxxix:16). Because our whole man, soul and body is united into one system, the faculties of the soul, as well as the parts of the body, are called "members" (Rom. vi:13, 19).

Figurative. Christ and his people being considered as "a body," the saints are called his *"members,"* and *"members of one another";* they are closely united to him as their head, and joined to one another, as his, by having the same Spirit, engagement, profession, and practice (Eph. iv:25; v:30).

MEMORIAL (me-mō'ri-al), (Heb. אַזְכָּרָה, *az-kaw'raw';* זִכְרוֹן, *zik-rone';* Gr. μνημόσυνον, *mnay-mos'oo-non*), name; report (Prov. x:7; Is. xxvi:14). "Memorial" is that which tends to bring a person or thing to remembrance.

God's name, Jehovah, is his "memorial in all generations"; the name whereby he shall be remembered, called upon, and thought and spoken of (Exod. iii:15). The soul ransom-money, the part of the meat-offering burnt on the altar, and the frankincense set on the shew-bread, are called a "memorial"; they as it were put God in mind of his covenant with, and of the mercies necessary to be shown to, the Hebrews: and they put the Hebrews in mind of Jesus as a ransom, offering, and intercessor for us (Exod. xxx:16; Lev. ii:2; xxiv:7). The stones of the high-priest's breastplate, and shoulder-piece were for a "memorial"; they tended to put him in mind to pray earnestly for the Hebrew tribes; and as it were called down mercies from God upon them (Exod. xxviii:12, 29).

MEMPHIS (mĕm'phis), (Heb. מֹף, *mofe*), a very ancient city, the capital of lower Egypt, standing at the apex of the Delta, ruins of which are still found not far from its successor and modern representative, Cairo.

(1) **Name.** Its Egyptian name, in the *hieroglyphics,* is Menofri; in Coptic, Memfi, Manfi, Membe, Panoufi or Mefi, being probably corrupted from Man nofri, 'the abode,' or, as Plutarch terms it (*Isid. et Osir.* ch. xx), 'the haven of good men.' It was called also Pthah-ei, the abode of Pthah (Wilkinson, *Anc. Egypt.* iii. 278). In Hebrew the city bears the name of *Mofe* (Hos. ix:6), or *Nofe Noph* (Is. xix:13). These several names are obviously variations of one, of which Meph seems to contain the essential sounds. Whether we may hence derive support to the statement that the place was founded by Menes, the first human king of Egypt, or whether we have here a very early instance of the custom which prevailed so extensively among the Greeks and Romans, of inventing founders of cities, having names correspondent with the names of the places they were said to have built, it is impossible, with the materials we possess, to determine with any fair approach to certainty.

(2) **Founder.** Menes, however, is universally reputed to have founded not only Memphis but Thebes; the addition of the latter may seem to invalidate his claim to the former, making us suspect that here, too, we have a case of that custom of referring to some one distinguished name great events which happened, in truth, at different and far distant eras. If, as is probable, Thebes as well as Memphis was, at any early period, the seat of a distinct dynasty, the cradle and the throne of a line of independent sovereigns, they could scarcely have had one founder.

(3) Bed of the Nile. The statement, however, is, that having diverted the course of the Nile, which had washed the foot of the sandy mountains of the Libyan chain, Menes obliged it to run in the center of the valley, and built the city Memphis in the bed of the ancient channel. This change was effected by constructing a dyke about a hundred stadia above the site of the projected city, whose lofty mounds and strong embankments turned the water to the east and confined the river to its new bed. The dyke was carefully kept in repair by succeeding kings, and even as late as the Persian invasion, a guard was always maintained there to overlook the necessary repairs; for, as Herodotus asserts, if the river were to break through the dyke, the whole of Memphis would be in danger of being overwhelmed with water, especially at the period of the inundation. Subsequently, however, when the increased deposit of the alluvial soil had raised the circumjacent plains, the precautions became unnecessary; and though the spot where the diversion of the Nile was made may still be traced, owing to the great bend it takes about fourteen miles above ancient Memphis, the lofty mounds once raised there are no longer visible.

(4) Identification of Site. The site of Memphis was first accurately fixed by Pocock, at the village of Metrahenny. According to the reports of the French, the heaps which mark the site of the ancient buildings have three leagues of circumference; but this is less than its extent in early times, since Diodorus gives it 150 stadia, or six leagues and a quarter. Memphis declined after the foundation of Alexandria, and its materials were carried off to build Cairo (Kenrick, *Egypt of Herodotus,* p. 129; Rennell, ii, 115; Champoll, *Egypte et les Ph.* i, 336).

(5) History. The kingdom of which Memphis was the capital, was most probably the Egypt of the patriarchs (in which Abraham, Jacob, and the Israelites resided. Psammetichus, in becoming sole monarch of all Egypt, raised Memphis to the dignity of the one metropolis of the entire land (Plin. *Hist. Nat.* v, 9), after which Memphis grew in the degree in which Thebes declined. It became distinguished for a multitude of splendid edifices, among which may be mentioned a large and magnificent temple to Vulcan, who was called by the Egyptians Phthah, the demiurgos, or creative power (Wilkinson, i, 96; Herod. ii, 136, 154; Strabo, xvii, p. 807; Plin. *Hist. Nat.* viii, 71; Diod. Sic. i, 57, 67). Under the dominion of the Persians, as well as of the Ptolemies, Memphis retained its preëminence as the capital, though even in the time of the former it began to part with its splendor; and when the latter bestowed their favor on Alexandria, it suffered a material change for the worse, from which the place never recovered. In the days of Strabo many of its fine buildings lay in ruins, though the city was still large and populous. The final blow was given to the prosperity of Memphis in the time of Abdollatif, by the erection of the Arabian city of Cairo.

That the arts were carried to a great degree of excellence at Memphis is proved by the most abundant evidence. Its manufacturers of glass were famed for the superior quality of their workmanship, with which Rome continued to be supplied long after Egypt became a province of the empire. The environs of Memphis presented cultivated groves of the acacia tree, of whose wood were made the planks and masts of boats, the handles of offensive weapons of war, and various articles of furniture (Wilkinson, iii, 92,

168). Memphis was also distinguished as being the place where Apis was kept, and where his worship received special honor. The city's overthrow was predicted (Is. xix:13; Jer. xlvi:19). The latest of these predictions was uttered nearly 600 years before Christ, and half a century before the invasion of Egypt by Cambyses, B. C. 525. The city never recovered from the blow inflicted by Cambyses. The rise of Alexandria hastened its decline. The caliph conquerors founded Old Cairo upon the opposite bank of the Nile, a few miles north of Memphis, and brought materials from the old city to build their new capital, A. D. 638. At length so complete was the ruin of Memphis that for a long time its very site was lost. Recent explorations have brought to light many of its antiquities, and specimens of its relics are now in museums in Europe and America. A little village, Mitrahineh, stands upon a portion of the site of ancient Memphis. "The immense necropolis at the west of Memphis, on the borders of the Libyan desert, still extends from Abu-Rosh in the north to Dashur in the south. The gigantic royal tombs, the pyramids, attract numerous visitors from the whole world. Usually, only the most remarkable group of pyramids (those of *Khufu, Khafre,* and *Menkare* of the fourth dynasty—in Herodotus, *Cheops, Chephren,* and *Mycerinus*) at Gizeh are visited; about fifty other pyramids of smaller size or still more dilapidated are less known (those at Sakkara, belonging to the sixth dynasty, and of Dashur of the fourth dynasty, being most remarkable). The immense sphinx at Gizeh (probably a work of *Khafre—Chephren,* although recently some scholars place it in the twelfth dynasty), and many private tombs, the latter much destroyed, contribute to make the site of ancient Memphis still remarkable." (M. Max Müller, Hastings' *Bib. Dict.*)

(6) Literature. Vyse, *Pyramids of Gizeh;* Wilkinson, *Modern Egypt and Thebes;* Poole, *Englishwoman in Egypt;* Niebuhr, *Travels; Classical Dictionaries.* (See EGYPT.)

MEMUCAN (me-mū'kan), (Heb. מְמוּכָן, *mem-oo-kawn'*).

One of the seven royal counselors at the court of Media and Persia (Esth. i:14, 16, 21), who recommended that Vashti be deposed.

MENAHEM (měn'a-hěm), (Heb. מְנַחֵם, *men-akh-ame',* consoler).

Sixteenth king of Israel, who began to reign B. C. 772, and reigned ten years. Menahem appears to have been one of the generals of king Zachariah. When he heard the news of the murder of that prince, and the usurpation of Shallum, he was at Tirzah, but immediately marched to Samaria, where Shallum had shut himself up, and slew him in that city. He then usurped the throne in his turn; and forthwith marched to Tiphsah, which refused to acknowledge his rule. Having taken this place after a siege, he treated the inhabitants with a degree of savage barbarity, which, as Josephus remarks (*Antiq.* ix, 11, 1), would not have been pardonable even to foreigners. He adhered to the sins of Jeroboam, like the other kings of Israel. In his time the Assyrians, under their king Pul, made their first appearance on the borders of Palestine; and Menahem was only able to save himself from this great invading power at the heavy price of 1,000 talents of silver, which he raised by a tax of fifty shekels from every man of substance in Israel. This was probably the only choice left to him; and he is not therefore to be blamed, as he had not that resource in the treasures of the temple of which the kings of Judah availed themselves in similar emergencies. Menahem died in B. C. 761, leaving the throne to his son Pekahiah (2 Kings xv: 14-22).

MENAN (mē'nan), (Gr. Μαϊνάν, *mahee-nan'*, meaning unknown), the son of Mattatha, a descendant of David and ancestor of Christ (Luke iii:31); the authenticity is doubtful.

MENE, MENE, TEKEL, UPHARSIN (mē'ne, mē'ne, tē'kel', u-phär-sin'), (Chald. מְנֵא, *men-ay'*, מְנֵא, *men-ay'*, תְּקֵל, *tek-al'*, וּפַרְסִין, *u-phar'sin*).

The inscription supernaturally written 'upon the plaster of the wall' in Belshazzar's palace at Babylon (Dan. v:5-25); which 'the astrologers, the Chaldæans, and the soothsayers' could neither read nor interpret, but which Daniel first read, and then interpreted. The sentence reads, when translated literally, *Mene,* "he is numbered;" *Mene,* "he is numbered;" *Tekel,* "he is weighed;" *Upharsin,* "they are divided." "Peres," in the original language, is the same word with "Upharsin," but in a different case or number. It means "he was divided" (Dan. v:25).

The words, as they are found in Daniel, are pure Chaldee, and if they appeared in the Chaldee character could have been read, at least, by any person present on the occasion who understood the alphabet of his own language. To account for their inability to decipher this inscription, it has been supposed that it consisted of those Chaldee words written in another character. Dr. Hales thinks that it may have been written in the primitive Hebrew character, from which the Samaritan was formed, and that, in order to show on this occasion that the writer of the inscription was the offended God of Israel, whose authority was being at that moment peculiarly despised (verses 2, 3, 4), Jehovah adopted the sacred character in which the Decalogue had been written, which Daniel could understand, but which would be unknown to 'the wise men of Babylon' (*New Analysis of Chronology,* vol. i, p. 505, Lond., 1811). This theory has the recommendation that it involves as little as possible of miraculous agency. It has been supposed by some that 'the wise men' were not so much at fault to read the inscription as to explain its meaning, which, it is said, they might sufficiently understand to see its boding import to the monarch, and be unwilling to consider further—like the disciples in regard to the predictions of our Lord's death (Luke ix:45), where it is said, 'this saying was hid from them, they perceived it not, and they feared to ask him of that saying.' And certainly it is said throughout our narrative that 'the wise men could not read the writing, nor make known the interpretation of it,' phrases which would seem to mean one and the same thing; since, if they mean different things, the order of ideas would be that they could not interpret nor even read it, and Wintle accordingly translates 'could not read so as to interpret it' (*Improved Version of Daniel,* Lond. 1807). At all events the meaning of the inscription by itself would be extremely enigmatical and obscure. To determine the application, and to give the full sense, of an isolated device which amounted to no more than 'he or it is numbered, he or it is numbered, he or it is weighed, they are divided.' must surely have required a supernatural endowment on the part of Daniel—a conclusion which is confirmed by the exact coincidence of the event with the prediction, which he propounded with so much fortitude (verses 30, 31).   J. F. D.

MENEPTAH, INSCRIPTIONS OF.

Modern scholars agree with Manetho in the opinion that Meneptah, the son and successor of Rameses II, was the Pharaoh of the Exodus. Manetho calls him "Amenephthes, the son of Rameses," and in the inscriptions found at Bubastis he is represented as the general of the infantry during the reign of his father. The view that he was the Pharaoh of the Exodus is also confirmed by an inscription which was recently discovered.

(1) **Concerning the Israelites.** In the winter of 1895-6, Dr. W. M. Flinders Petrie was working among the ruins of Thebes, and discovered there the remains of a temple which belonged to the Nineteenth Dynasty. Among the inscribed stones he found a large stela of black granite upon which was an inscription, which proved to be a hymn of victory, reciting the glories of Meneptah and his triumphs over his enemies. The record seems to have been made in the fifth year of his reign, and it reads as follows: "Vanquished is the land of the Libyans, and the land of the Hittites tranquilized. Captured is the land of Pa-kana'na with all violence. Carried away is the land of Ashkelon. Overpowered is the land of Gezer. The Israelites (I-s-y-r-a-e-l-u) are minished, so that they have no seed. The land of Kharu is become like the widows of Egypt. All lands are at peace."

Kharu was the southern part of Palestine, and the name was identified by Prof. Maspero with that of the Horites of the Scriptures.

The name of Israel is most distinct, and has been accepted by Prof. Maspero, Dr. Neville, Dr. Spiegelberg and others. This alone of all the people mentioned in the inscription, had no word of explanation concerning the country to which they belonged. They must therefore have been at that time either bond slaves in Egypt, or, as is more probable, they were wanderers in the wilderness, the Exodus having already taken place when the hymn of victory was written.

The word which is here rendered "minished" has the determinative for badness or smallness attached, but it is met with here for the first time. The word which is rendered "seed" is used elsewhere in the sense of offspring. Attempts have been made to explain this statement as referring to the crops in a hypothetical land of Israel, which are supposed to have been destroyed by the Egyptians. But the Israelites were herdsmen, and not agriculturists, and the supposition is also rendered impossible by the fact that they are expressly marked out as having no land of their own upon which crops could be cultivated. The word "seed" must therefore have the meaning which it often bears in other inscriptions—"posterity."

(2) **Invaders.** One of the inscriptions of Meneptah also tells us that a flood of barbarians penetrated as far as Belbeis, in the southern extremity of the land of Goshen, where the country had been "handed over from old kings to foreigners as pasturage for their cattle." These "foreigners" must have been the Israelites, in whom the invaders found sympathizing friends. They are associated also with the land of the Horites, who are said to have become "widows" on account apparently of the destruction of the male seed of Israel. Therefore the author of the poem must have been aware of the fact that Israel had fled towards Edom, which was the territory of their kin.

The cutting off of the male seed lest Israel might ally themselves with an invader was the act of Rameses II, the father and predecessor of Meneptah, but in order to glorify the reigning king, the poet does not hesitate to ascribe to him the deeds of his father, and indeed this was often the custom among the Egyptian kings. They were very willing to erase the inscriptions of their predecessors and inscribe their own victories upon the same stela, or to claim the triumphs for themselves. (See RAMESES II.)

(3) Political Conditions. The narrative in Exodus harmonizes exactly with what we know of the political condition of Egypt in the fifth year of Meneptah, and the geography of the age of Meneptah also harmonizes with the geography of Exodus. For instance, the road from Goshen to the desert at that time lay past Thuku or Succoth and the "Migdol of King Meneptah." Succoth was one of the names of the city of Pithom, and even Baal-Zephon (Ex. xiv:2) is mentioned in a papyrus of the same age. The district which included the land of Goshen appears to have been comparatively unoccupied for a time after it was evacuated by the Israelites, but we have a clay letter which was addressed to the Egyptian court in the eighth year of King Meneptah in which the writer claims that Bedouin tribes from the land of Edom had been allowed to settle and pasture their herds there.

We may therefore conclude that Egyptian tradition is correct in claiming that Meneptah was the Pharaoh of this period, but we need never expect to find any Egyptian monuments recording the escape of the Israelites. The old kings of Egypt and Assyria were enough like modern politicians to preserve a dead silence concerning their defeats and record only their victories. (See PI-BESETH; SENNACHERIB; NEBUCHADNEZZAR.) (*Lectures before Univ. Coll.*, London, by W. M. Flinders Petrie.)

MENES (mēn'ez), **RECENT DISCOVERIES CONCERNING.**

In 1901 Dr. W. M. Flinders Petrie, of the University of London, wrote a most interesting account of his recent work. In a letter from Arabah, Baliana, Upper Egypt, to the London Times he says: "The continuation of the work of the Egypt Exploration Fund on the Royal Tombs of the first Egyptian dynasties has proved in some respects more surprising than that of last year. We are now able to trace out the regular development of civilization during some four hundred years, from the time when writing was but rarely used, and then only in rude pictorial stage, down to the common use of delicately figured hieroglyphs indistinguishable from those used for thousands of years after.

"We have now in our hands the beautifully wrought jewelry and gold works, the minutely engraved ivories, the toilet objects, of Menes, the founder of the monarchy, and his successor, fashioned more than 6,500 years ago.

"The following summary will give an idea of the gain of knowledge during the last three months:

"Of Menes and his predecessors there are about thirty inscriptions and labels in stone and ivory. From these we learn certainly the names of three kings,—Narmer, Ka, and a name written with a fish sign; perhaps also Det and Sam are two other names, but they are more probably word signs. Among these works of Menes are parts of four ebony tables with figures and inscriptions, one apparently showing a human sacrifice. The strangest object is one showing a massive strip of gold of unknown use with the name of Menes (Aha) upon it.

"Of Zer, the successor of Menes, the astonishing find is the forearm of his queen, still in its wrappings, with four splendid bracelets intact. One is a series of figures of the royal hawk perched upon the tomb, thirteen figures in cast and chased gold alternating with fourteen carved in turquoise. The second bracelet is of spiral beads of gold and lazuli in three groups. The third bracelet is of four groups of hour-glass beads, amethyst between gold, with connections of gold and turquoise. The fourth has a center piece of gold copied from the rosette seed of a plant, with amethyst and turquoise beads, and band of braided gold wire. This brilliant and exquisitely finished group of jewelry shows what a high level was already attained at the beginning of the First Dynasty. It is two thousand years older than the jewelry of Dahshur; the oldest yet known, and it has the great advantage of being carefully examined as found, and restrung in its exact arrangement.

"Of the same king there are some forty inscribed pieces of ivory and stone, and two lions carved in ivory. Also the great royal tombstone has been found in pieces and rejoined. About sixty private tombstones give us the names in use in the royal household; many formed from the goddess Neith, but not one from Isis."

Pertaining to the same subject, Prof. A. H. Sayce has an article in the Homiletic Review for March, 1901, entitled "*The New Light from the Ancient Monuments,*" in which he says: "Once more the light which has come from the monuments of the past has been fatal to the pretensions of critical skepticism. The discoveries at Abydos have discredited its methods and results. They have shown that where these can be tested they prove such pretensions to be absolutely worthless.

"Menes and his dynasty were very real and historical personages, in spite of the critics, and the age in which they lived, so far from being mythical, was an age of literary culture and civilization. It is only reasonable to conclude that methods and results which thus break down under the test of monumental discovery must equally break down in other departments of history where no such test can as yet be applied.

"The principles and mode of argument which have turned the Hebrew patriarchs into creatures of myth are precisely the same as those which declared Menes to be unhistorical, and the fate which has overtaken them in the case of Menes may be expected also in the case of the Old Testament.

"It is not the discoveries of higher criticism, but the old traditions, which have been confirmed by archæological research."

MENSTEALER (mĕn-stēl'ẽr), (Gr. ἀνδραποδισ-τής, *an-drap-od-is-tace'*), one who decoys or kidnaps a free person into slavery, or one who steals and sells the slaves of others. St. Paul denounces it as among the highest crimes (1 Tim. i:10).

The stealing of a freeborn Israelite, either to treat him as a slave or sell him into slavery, was by the law of Moses punished by death (Exod. xxi:16; Deut. xxiv:7).

MENUCHAH (mĕn-ū'käh), is regarded as a proper name in the marginal reading (Judg. xx:43; Jer. li:59). If a town it was in Benjamin, on the line of retreat taken by the Benjamites at the siege of Gibeah. (See SERAIAH).

MENUCHITE or MENUCHOTH (men-ū'kite or men-u'koth), (1 Chron. ii:52, 54, marg.). See MANAHETHITES, THE.

MEONENIM (me-ŏn'e-nĭm), (Hebrew from עָנַן, *aw-nan'*, oak of soothsayers, or to act covertly, i. e., to *practice magic*), not "plain," but an oak or terebinth (Judg. ix:37; comp. Deut. xviii:10, 14; Mic. v:12, "soothsayers").

The meaning of the name seems to connect it with some old diviners, probably of the pagan inhabitants. Conder suggests its identity with the plain of *Mŭkhnah*.

MEONOTHAI (me-ŏn'o-thāi), (Heb. מְעוֹנֹתַי, *meh-o-no-thah'ee*, my dwellings), a man of Judah, the founder of Ophrah (1 Chron. iv:14), B. C. after 1612.

MEPHAATH (mĕph'a-ăth), (Heb. מֵיפַעַת, *may-fah'ath*), a city given to the Merarite Levites (Josh. xxi:37; 1 Chron. vi:79), from the tribe of Reuben (Josh. xiii:18), but afterward coming into the possession of Moab (Jer. xlviii:21). Site not known.

MEPHIBOSHETH (me-phĭb'o-shĕth), (Heb. מְפִיבֹשֶׁת, *mef-ee-bo'sheth*, extermination of idols); also in 1 Chron. ix:40, MERIB-BAAL.

1. Son of Jonathan and nephew of Saul (2 Sam. iv:4).

(1) Early Life. He was only five years of age when his father and grandfather were slain in Mount Gilboa; and on the news of this catastrophe, the woman who had charge of the child, apprehending that David would exterminate the whole house of Saul, fled away with him; but in her hasty flight she stumbled with the child, and lamed him for life (B. C. 1055). Under this calamity, which was very incapacitating in times when agility and strength were of prime importance, Mephibosheth was unable to take any part in the stirring political events of his early life. According to our notions, he should have been the heir of the house of Saul; but in those times a younger son of an actual king was considered to have at least as good a claim as the son of an heir apparent who had never reigned, and even a better claim if the latter were a minor. This, with his lameness, prevented Mephibosheth from appearing as the opponent or rival of his uncle Ish-bosheth on the one hand, or of David on the other (2 Sam. ix). He thus grew up in quiet obscurity in the house of Machir, one of the great men of the country beyond the Jordan (2 Sam. ix:4; xvii:27); and his very existence was unknown to David till that monarch, when firmly settled in his kingdom, inquired whether any of the family of Jonathan survived, to whom he might show kindness for his father's sake.

(2) Befriended by David. Hearing then of Mephibosheth from Ziba, who had been the royal steward under Saul, he invited him to Jerusalem, assigned him a place at his own table, and bestowed upon him lands, which were managed for him by Ziba, and which enabled him to support an establishment suited to his rank.

(3) During Absalom's Revolt. He lived in this manner till the revolt of Absalom, and then David, in his flight, having noticed the absence of Mephibosheth, inquired for him of Ziba, and being informed that he had remained behind in the hope of being restored to his father's throne, instantly and very hastily revoked the grant of land, and bestowed it on Ziba (2 Sam. xvi:1-4). Afterwards, on his return to Jerusalem, he was met with sincere congratulations by Mephibosheth, who explained that being lame he had been unable to follow the king on foot, and that Ziba had

purposely prevented his beast from being made ready to carry him; and he declared that so far from having joined in heart, or even appearance, the enemies of the king, he had remained as a mourner, and, as his appearance declared, had not changed his clothes, or trimmed his beard, or even dressed his feet, from the day that the king departed to that on which he returned. David could not but have been sensible that he had acted wrong, and ought to have been touched by the devotedness of his friend's son, and angry at the imposition of Ziba; but to cover one fault by another, or from indifference, or from reluctance to offend Ziba, who had adhered to him when so many old friends forsook him, he answered coarsely, 'Why speakest thou any more of thy matters? I have said, thou and Ziba divide the land.' The answer of Mephibosheth was worthy of the son of the generous Jonathan: 'Yea, let him take all; forasmuch as my lord the king is come again in peace unto his own house' (2 Sam. xix:24-30).

We hear no more of Mephibosheth, except that David was careful that he should not be included in the savage vengeance which the Gideonites were suffered to execute upon the house of Saul for the great wrong they had sustained during his reign (2 Sam. xxi:7). Another Mephibosheth, a son of Saul by his concubine Rizpah, was, however, among those who suffered on that occasion (verses 8, 9).

2. A son of Saul and his concubine Rizpah, who, with his brother Armoni, was delivered by David to the Gibeonites, to be hanged before the Lord (2 Sam. xxi:8, 9), B. C. 1053-1019.

MERAB (mē'răb), (Heb. מֵרַב, *may-rawb*, increase); eldest daughter of king Saul, who was promised in marriage to David; but when the time fixed for their union approached, she was, to the surprise of all Israel, bestowed in marriage upon an unknown personage named Adriel (1 Sam. xiv:49; xviii:17-19). By him she had five sons, who were among those of the house of Saul that were given up to the Gibeonites, who put them to death in expiation for the wrongs they had sustained from their grandfather.

MERAIAH (mĕr'a-ī'ah), (Heb. מְרָיָה, *mer-aw-yaw'*, revelation of Jah), a chief priest of the house of Seraiah, in the days of Joiakim (Neh. xii:12), B. C. after 536.

MERAIOTH (me-rā'yoth), (Heb. מְרָיוֹת, *mer-aw-yohth'*, revelations).

1. A priest of the race of Aaron, son of Zerahiah, and father of Amariah, among the high-priests (1 Chron. vi: 6, 7, 52; Ezra vii:3), B. C. before 1062.

2. A chief priest, father of Hilkai, a contemporary of the high-priest Joiakim (Neh. xii:15).

MERARI (mĕr'ā-rī or me-rā'rī), (Heb. מְרָרִי, *mer-aw'ree*, bitter), youngest son of Levi, born in Canaan (Gen. xlvi:11; Exod. vi:16; Num. iii:17; 1 Chron. vi:1). He is only known from his name having been given to one of the three great divisions of the Levitical tribe. (B. C. 1874.)

MERARITE (mĕr'a-rīte), (Heb. מְרָרִי, *mer-aw'ree*, bitter), descendants of Merari, making one of the three Levitical families (Num. xxvi:57). They were sub-divided into the Mahlites and Mushites (Num. iii:20, 33), at the first census they numbered 6,200 males. Four cities were assigned to them from each of the tribes of Gad, Reuben and Zebulun; of these Ramoth-gilead was a city of refuge (Josh. xxi:34, 40; 1 Chron. vi:63, 77-81). David reorganized the tribe (1 Chron. xxiii:6, 21-23).

MERATHAIM (mĕr'a-thā'im), (Heb. מְרָתַיִם, *mer-aw-thah'yim*, double or rebellion, Jer. l:21), a name given to Babylon because of the double captivity to which it had subjected the Israelites (Jer. l:21).

MERCHANDISE, MERCHANT (mĕr'chan-dīz, mĕr'chant). See COMMERCE.

MERCURY (mĕr'cu-ry). See HERMES.

MERCY (mĕr'sў), (Heb. חֶסֶד, *kheh'sed*, kind-ness; Gr. ἔλεος, *el'eh-os*, compassion).

1. Affectionate pity to such as are in misery and distress, and readiness to do them good (Phil. ii: 1; Col. iii:12; Tit. iii:5).

2. Kind acts proceeding from inward compassion, and desire to relieve such as are in misery and want (Ps. cxlv:9; 1 Tim. i:13, 16). (*a*) Mercy to the sinner is God's sovereign compassion in forgiving him (Rom. ix:15). (*b*) All his dealings with them are the effects of mercy and kindness to them, and are the accomplishment of his promises to them (Ps. xxv:10). (*c*) To "show," "have," or "give" *mercy,* is to discover inward pity and compassion, by acts of kindness to the distressed (Gen. xxxix:21; Exod. xx:6; Ps. iv:1; 2 Tim. i:18). (*d*) To "*find or obtain mercy,*" is to receive acts of kindness, and valuable blessings, proceeding from pity and compassion (Matt. v:7; Heb. iv:16). (*e*) To "*keep mercy,*" is to be in constant readiness to do good freely to the distressed and miserable (Dan. ix: 4). (*f*) To "*remember mercy,*" is to pass injuries unresented, and do acts of undeserved kindness (Hab. iii:2). (*g*) To "*love mercy,*" is to love Christ and take a pleasure in doing undeserved good to such as are in misery and want (Mic. vi:8). (*h*) To "*follow mercy,*" is earnestly to seek after a share in the blessings of the new covenant, and study to exercise acts of pity towards those in mercy (Prov. xxi:21).

MERCY-SEAT (mĕr'sў-sēt), (Heb. כַּפֹּרֶת, *kap-poh'reth*, mercy-seat).

The Hebrew name literally denotes a *cover,* and, in fact, describes the lid of the ark with cherubim, over which appeared 'the glory of God' (Exod. xxv:17, *sq.;* xxx:8; xxxi:7, and elsewhere.) (See ARK OF THE COVENANT.) The word used in the Septuagint and New Testament to translate the term which in Hebrew means simply 'a cover,' is ἱλαστήριον, the 'expiatory' or 'propitiatory,' in allusion to that application of the Hebrew word which we have noted; which application is in this instance justified and explained by reference to the custom of the high-priest once a year entering the most holy place, and sprinkling the lid of the ark with the blood of an expiatory victim, whereby 'he made atonement for the sins of the people.' As this was the most solemn and significant act of the Hebrew ritual, it is natural that a reference to it should be involved in the name which the covering of the ark acquired. By a comparison of the texts in which the word occurs, it will be seen that there would, in fact, have been little occasion to name the cover of the ark separately from the ark itself, but for this important ceremonial. (See TABERNACLE.)

MERED (mē'red), (Heb. מֶרֶד, *meh'red*, rebellion), second son of Ezra of Judah (1 Chron. iv:17). He is said to have married Bithiah, daughter of Pharaoh. Jehudijah, "the Jewess," was probably his second wife. (B. C. 1658). (See BITHIAH.)

MEREMOTH (mĕr'e-mŏth), (Heb. מְרֵמוֹת, *mer-ay-mohth'*, heights, i. e., exaltations).

1. A priest, son of Urijah, descendant of Koz, who returned from captivity with Zerubbabel (Neh. xii:3), and had charge of the gold and silver dishes forwarded by Ezra (Ezra viii:33). He is undoubtedly the same as the one who repaired two sections of the wall of Jerusalem (Neh. iii:4, 21), B. C. 459.

2. A layman of the descendants of Bani, who divorced his foreign wife at Ezra's command (Ezra x:36), B. C. 459.

3. A priest, or better, a family of priests, who sealed the covenant with Nehemiah (Neh. x:5), B. C. 410.

MERES (mē'rēz), (Heb. מֶרֶס, *meh'res*, worthy), one of the seven eunuchs or councillors of the court of Babylon (Esth. i:14), B. C. 483.

MERIBAH (mĕr'i-bah), (Heb. מְרִיבָה, *mer-ee-baw'*, quarrel, strife).

1. One of the names given by Moses to the fountain in the desert of Sin, on the western gulf of the Red Sea, which issued from the rock that he smote by the divine command (Exod. xvii: 1-17). He called the place, indeed, Massa (temptation) *and* Meribah, and the reason is assigned 'because of the *chiding* of the children of Israel, and because they did there *tempt* the Lord.' (See WANDERING, THE; EXODUS, GEOGRAPHY OF THE.)

2. Another fountain produced in the same manner, and under similar circumstances, in the desert of Zin (Wady Arabah), near Kadesh; and to which the name was given with a similar reference to the previous misconduct of the Israelites (Num. xx:13, 24; Deut. xxxiii:8). In the last text, which is the only one where the two places are mentioned together, the former is called Massah only, to prevent the confusion of the two Meribahs, 'Whom thou didst prove at Massah, and with whom thou didst strive at the waters of Meribah.' Indeed, this latter Meribah is almost always indicated by the addition of 'waters,' *i. e., waters of Meribah,* as if further to distinguish it from the other (Ps. lxxxi:8; cvi:32); and still more distinctly 'waters of Meribah in Kadesh' (Num. xxvii:14; Deut. xxxii:51; Ezek. xlvii:19). Only once is this place called simply Meribah (Ps. xcv:8). It is strange, that with all this carefulness of distinction in Scripture, the two places should so rarely have been properly discriminated.

MERIB-BAAL (mĕr'ib-bā'al), (Heb. מְרִיב־בַּעַל, *mer-eeb'bah'al*, contender with Baal), a name given to Mephibosheth, son of Jonathan, in 1 Chron. viii: 34; ix:40. (See MEPHIBOSHETH.)

Of the two latter seems the more correct form. It means 'contender against Baal.' Some think that the difference has arisen from some corruption of the text; but, from the analogy of Ishbosheth, whose original name was Esh-baal, it seems more like a designed alteration, arising probably from the reluctance of the Israelites to pronounce the name of Baal. (See ISH-BO-SHETH.)

MERODACH (me-rō'dak), (Heb. מְרֹדָךְ, *mer-o-dawk'*, death, slaughter).

In conformity with the general character of Babylonian idolatry, Merodach is supposed to be the name of a planet; and, as the Tsabian and Arabic names for Mars are Nerig and Mirrich, 'arrow' (the latter of which Gesenius thinks may be for Mirdich, which is very nearly the same as Merodach), there is some presumption that it may be Mars. As for etymologies of the word, Gesenius has suggested that it is the Persian *mardak,* the diminutive of *mard,* 'man,' used as a term of endearment; or, rather, that it is from the Persian and Indo-Germanic *mord,* or *mort* (which means death, and is so far in harmony with the conception of Mars, as the lesser star of evil omen), and the affix *och,* which is found in many Assyrian names, as Nisroch, etc.

In Jer. 1:2 we read: "Babylon is taken, Bel is confounded, Merodach is broken in pieces. Her idols are confounded, her images are broken in pieces."

Bel Merodach is one of the Babylonian deities, which is not only spoken of in the Scriptures, but which also finds frequent mention on the tablets. According to the inscriptions of Nebuchadnezzar, Marduk or Merodach was the favorite deity of that king. These inscriptions begin by declaring Nebuchadnezzar to be the "King of Babylon, the exalted prince, the worshiper of Marduk, the prince supreme, the beloved of the god Nebo."

Nebuchadnezzar is never weary of extolling his own achievements and the glories of his capital city. The thirty or forty inscriptions of this king which are now in the British Museum all reflect the spirit of the boast: "Is not this great Babylon that I have built, for the house of the kingdom, by the might of my power and for the honor of my majesty?" (Dan. iv:30).

He also describes the splendid temple which he built for Marduk or Bel Merodach, with its costly woods, "its silver and molten gold, and precious stones," and "sea clay" (amber), "with its seats of splendid gold, with lapis-lazuli, and alabaster blocks"; and these have been found in the ruins of Babylon.

And the king made the great festival Lilmuku when the image of Merodach was brought into his temple (4th Col., lines 1-6, Cun. Ins. West. Asia, *Rec. of the Past*).

The inscription also speaks of this idol temple as receiving "within itself the abundant tribute of the kings of the nations, and of all peoples."

This portion of Nebuchadnezzar's inscription is confirmed by the following statement in the book of Daniel: "And the Lord gave the King of Judah into his (Nebuchadnezzar's) hand, with part of the vessels of the house of God, which he carried into the land of Shinar to the house of his god" (Dan. i:2).

MERODACH-BALADAN (me-rō'dak-băl'ā-dăn), (Heb. בְּלַאדָן מְראֹדַךְ, *mer-o-dak' bal-ad-awn'*, Merodach has given a son).

Son of Baladan and king of Babylon. He is mentioned also with the name Berodach-baladan (2 Kings xx:12), which form is due to a confusion of two Hebrew characters which are much alike in their old forms. He is represented as sending messengers to Hezekiah to congraulate him on his recovery from his severe illness, and acquainting himself through them with all the treasures of the Jewish king (2 Chron. xxxii:1; Is. xxxix:1).

Merodach-baladan was by race a Chaldæan, and though the Chaldeans were almost certainly Semites, they were nevertheless quite a different people. (See CHALDÆANS.) He is identified by most modern scholars with Mardokempad, referred to in the inscriptions of Tiglath-pileser, Sargon and Sennacherib. He reigned B. C. 721-710.

If Hezekiah's sickness immediately followed Sargon's campaign against Ashdod (in 711 B. C.), then Merodach-baladan's embassy, nominally to congratulate Hezekiah on recovery from his sickness, but really to ascertain the possibility of an alliance against Sargon, took place in 710 B. C. This order is not impossible, for Sargon's next

two or three years were spent in fully crushing all of his foes in southern Babylonia. After the conquest and organization of all his long-dreamed-of realm, Sargon sought to perpetuate his fame in another way. He established at Khorsabad, several miles above Nineveh, his royal headquarters. Here he built his enormous palace, uncovered by Botta. He entered this magnificent home in 706 B. C., and in the very next summer was assassinated by one of his own soldiers. (See ASSYRIA.)

The assassination of Sargon yielded the throne of Assyria to his son, Sennacherib (705-681 B. C.). Whether this son had anything to do with the intrigue is not known. It is at least significant that the father's name is not found in the records of the son. This king of Assyria, from his frequent mention in the Bible, is most familiar to Bible students. His records of his own campaigns, his conquests, his cruelties, modify in no important respect the character attributed to him by the books of Kings and Isaiah.

The earlier activities of Sennacherib were confined to his eastern and southern boundaries. He measured lances with the irrepressible Chaldeans of the South. His own brother, whom he had put upon the throne of Babylon, was displaced by a usurper; and this usurper, after one month, was deposed by Merodach-baladan. Sennacherib swooped down on the intriguing army of seceders and crushed them, and established his authority in lower Babylonia. To secure himself still further, he captured and pillaged 75 cities and 420 villages; 208,000 captives, with nearly a million large and small cattle, he deported to Assyria. As a kind of figure-head, he placed on the throne of Babylon Bel-ibni, while the country of Chaldæa was under a military governor. With these temporary rulers in power, Sennacherib returned to Nineveh. (Price, *The Monuments and the Old Test.,* pp. 179-181.)

Sennacherib then attacked the west, and while thus engaged a new rebellion began in Babylonia, in which, naturally enough, Merodach-baladan was ready to participate. It was, however, of very short duration, for Sennacherib entered the land again, and again Merodach-baladan fled. He put his goods, his people, and his gods upon boats, and floated them down the Euphrates to the Persian gulf, and settled on its eastern shores in a part of Elam, whither Sennacherib dared not follow. There in exile he soon died. His career is without a parallel among his people. It was filled with contradictions. No man before him of that race has held power so great for so long a time. He had failed ultimately, but his followers would in a later day succeed far beyond his dreams. (Dr. R. W. Rogers, Barnes' *Bib. Cyc.*)

MEROM (mē'rom), (Heb. מֵרוֹם, *may-rome'*, height, or upper waters). The waters of Merom, of Josh. xi:5 are the lake Semechonitis, now called Huleh, the upper or highest lake of the Jordan. (See PALESTINE.)

It is four miles long (some say seven) by three and a half broad, and 270 feet below the Mediterranean Sea. The Jordan passes through it. It was called by the Greeks "Semachonitis," and and by the Arabs "Huleh." Here the confederate kings of North Canaan, under Jabin, king of Hazor, were gathered together, when Joshua fell upon them suddenly, rushing down on them from the mountain slopes, and utterly destroying them. The lake is surrounded by marshes and thickets of papyrus, and abounds in wild duck, pelican, and other fowl. On the north is an impenetrable jungle, the wallowing place of buffaloes. The miasma from the marshes renders the district very unhealthy. Kedesh, an important stronghold of Napthali, lay four miles west of its northern end.

MERONOTHITE (me-rŏn′o-thīte), (Heb. מְרֹנֹתִי, *may-ro-no-thee′*), an appellation of Jehdeiah, the herdsman of David and Solomon (1 Chron. xxvii: 30), and of Jadon, who assisted in repairing the walls of Jerusalem (Neh. iii:7). Meronoth is not otherwise known.

MERORIM (me-rō′rĭm), (Heb. מְרֹרִים, *me-ro-rim′*), occurs in two places in Scripture, and is in both translated *bitter herbs* in our Authorized Version, as well as in several others.

In Exod. xii:8, Moses commanded the Jews to eat the lamb of the Passover 'with unleavened bread, and with *bitter* herbs (*merorim*) they shall eat it.' So at the institution of the second Passover, in the wilderness of Sinai (Num. ix:11).

Succory or endive was early selected as being the bitter herb especially intended; and Dr. Geddes justly remarks, that 'the Jews of Alexandria, who translated the Pentateuch, could not be ignorant what herbs were eaten with the paschal lamb in their days.' Jerome understood it in the same manner; and Pseudo-Jonathan expressly mentions *horehound* and *lettuces*. Forskal informs us that the Jews at Sana and in Egypt eat the lettuce with the paschal lamb. Aben Ezra, as quoted by Rosenmüller, states that the Egyptians used bitter herbs in every meal; so in India some of the bitter *Cucurbitaceæ*, as *kurella*, are constantly employed as food. (See PAKYOTH.) It is curious that the two sets of plants which appear to have the greatest number of points in their favor, are the endive or succory, and one of the fragrant and usually also bitter labiate plants; because we find that the term *marooa* is in the East applied even in the present day both to the bitter wormwood and the fragrant *Ocymum*. Moreover the Chaldee translator, Jonathan, expressly mentions lettuce and *horehound*, or *marrubium*, which is also one of the Labiatæ. It is important to observe that the Artemisia, and some of these fragrant labiatæ, are found in many parts of Arabia and Syria; that is, in warm, dry, barren regions. The endive is also found in similar situations, but requires, upon the whole, a greater degree of moisture. Thus it is evident that the Israelites would be able to obtain suitable plants during their long wanderings in the Desert, though it is difficult for us to select any one out of the several which might have been employed by them. (See BITTER HERBS.)
J. F. R.

MEROZ (mē′rŏz), (Heb. מֵרוֹז, *may-roze′*), a place in the northern part of Palestine, the inhabitants of which are severely reprehended in Judg. v:23, for not having taken the field with Barak against Sisera.

It would seem as if they had had an opportunity of rendering some particular and important service to the public cause which they neglected. The site is not known; Eusebius and Jerome (*Onomast.* under subject 'Merus') fix it twelve Roman miles from Sebaste, on the road to Dothaim; but this position would place it south of the field of battle, and therefore scarcely agrees with the history. Schwarz identifies it with el-Murussus, about four miles northwest of Beth-shean (*Palest.* p. 168).

MESECH (mē′sĕk), (Ps. cxx:5). See MESHECH.

MESHA (mē′shà), (Heb. מֵישָׁא, *may-shaw′*, middle district).

1. A place mentioned in describing that part of Arabia inhabited by the descendants of Joktan (Gen. x:30). Mouza, east of the Red Sea; Bis-

cha, in northern Yemen; and Massa have been suggested as the place referred to. (See NATIONS, DISPERSION OF.)

2. A king of Moab, who possessed an immense number of flocks and herds, and appears to have derived his chief wealth from them. In the time of Ahab, he being then under tribute, 'rendered unto the king of Israel 100,000 lambs and 100,000 rams, with the wool' (2 Kings iii:4). These numbers may seem exaggerated if understood as the amount of yearly tribute. It is, therefore, more probable that the greedy and implacable Ahab had at some one time levied this enormous impost upon the Moabites; and it is likely that it was in the apprehension of a recurrence of such ruinous exactions that they seized the opportunity for revolt which the death of Ahab seemed to offer (2 Kings i:1; iii:5). The short reign of Ahaziah afforded no opportunity for reducing them to obedience; but after his death his brother and successor, Jehoram, made preparations for war; and induced Jehoshaphat to join him in this expedition. The result, with the part taken by Elisha the prophet, has been related under other heads. (See ELISHA; JEHORAM; JEHOSHAPHAT.) King Mesha was at length driven to shut himself up, with the remnant of his force, in Areopolis, his capital. He was there besieged so closely that, having been foiled in an attempt to break through the camp of the Edomites (who were present as vassals of Judah), he was reduced to extremities, and in the madness of his despair sought to propitiate his angry gods by offering up his own son, the heir of his crown, as a sacrifice, upon the wall of the city. On beholding this fearful sight, the besiegers withdrew in horror, lest some portion of the monstrous crime might attach to their own souls. By this withdrawal they, however, afforded the king the relief he desired, and this was, no doubt, attributed by him to the efficacy of his offering, and to the satisfaction of his gods therewith. The invaders, however, ravaged the country as they withdrew, and returned with much spoil to their own land. (See MOABITES.) Mesha was the author and subject of the inscription on the famous Moabite Stone. (See DIBON; MOABITE STONE.)

3. (Heb. as above.) Eldest son of Caleb, of Judah, family of Hezron, and founder of Ziph (1 Chron. ii:42), B. C. 1618.

4. (Heb. as above.) A Benjamite, son of Shaharaim by Hodesh or Baara (1 Chron. viii:9), B. C. about 1612.

MESHACH (mē′shak), (Heb. or Chald. מֵישַׁךְ, *may-shak′*), a name given by the chief of the eunuchs in the court of Babylon to MISHAEL, who was in training for the rank of magi, and was one of the three faithful Jews saved from the fiery furnace (Dan. 1:7; ii:49; iii:12–30).

MESHECH (mē′shĕk), (Heb. מֶשֶׁךְ, *meh′shek*, possession).

Meshech in the Old Testament is nearly always mentioned in connection with his brother Tubal. In the Assyrian inscriptions the names appear as Tublâ and Muskâ. The classical geographers called them Tibareni and Moskhi. At this time, however, they belonged farther to the northward than they had been in the times of the Assyrian monuments.

In the time of Sargon and Sennacherib their territories still extended as far south as Cilicia and the northern half of Komagênê. Afterward they were forced to retreat northward toward the Black Sea, and it was in this region of Asia Minor that Xenophon and his Greek troops found what little remained of this people. (See *Anabasis* v, 5.)

In these two sons of Japheth (Meshech and Tubal) we must see representatives of the so-called Alarodian race, to which the modern Georgians belong. This people were once in possession of the highlands of Armenia, and the cuneiform inscriptions there found were evidently the work of the Alarodian princes who established a kingdom on the shores of Lake Van.

About B. C. 600 the Aryans from Phrygia entered Armenia, overthrew the old monarchy, and imposed their rule upon the indigenous population.

The majority of the Armenians still belong to the older race, although they have long since adopted the language of the invaders. (Sayce, *Races of the Old Testament*). (See NATIONS, DISPERSION OF.)

MESHELEMIAH (me - shĕl' e - mī' ah), (Heb. מְשֶׁלֶמְיָה, *mesh-eh-lem-yaw'*, friendship of Jehovah)> a Korhite Levite, who with his seven sons and ten other relatives had charge of the east gate of the Temple under David (1 Chron. ix:21; xxvi:1). Called SHELEMIAH (1 Chron. xxvi:14), and apparently SHALLUM (1 Chron. ix:19). (See MESHULLAM, 10.) B. C. 1014.

MESHEZABEEL (me - shĕz' a - beel), (Heb. מְשֵׁיזַבְאֵל, *mesh-ay-zab-ale'*, delivered by God).

1. Apparently a priest, the father of Berechiah and ancestor of Meshullam (Neh. iii:4).
2. A chief of the people who sealed the covenant with Nehemiah (Neh. x:21), B. C. about 410.
3. Father of Pethahiah, of Judah (Neh. xi:24), B. C. 410.

MESHILLEMITH (me-shĭl'le-mĭth), (1 Chron. ix:12).

MESHILLEMOTH (me-shĭl'le-mŏth), (Heb. מְשִׁלֵּמוֹת, *mesh-il-lay-mohth'*, reconciliation).

1. An Ephraimite, father of the Berechiah, who opposed reducing his captive brethren of Judah to slavery (2 Chron. xxviii:12), B. C. before 735.
2. A priest, son of Immer (Neh. xi:13). B. C. before 440.

MESHOBAB (me-shō'băb), (Heb. מְשׁוֹבָב, *mesh-o-bawb'*, returned), a chief Simeonite who migrated to Gedor in the time of Hezekiah (1 Chron. iv:34), B. C. about 711.

MESHULLAM (me-shŭl'lam), (Heb. מְשֻׁלָּם, *mesh-ool-lawm'*, allied).

1. A chief Gadite, resident at Jerusalem in the reign of Jotham (1 Chron. v:13), B. C. 781.
2. Grandfather of Shaphan, the scribe (2 Kings xxii:3), B. C. about 623.
3. A priest, son of Zadok, and father of Hilkiah (1 Chron. ix:11; Neh. xi:11). The same as SHALLUM (1 Chron. vi:13; Ezra vii:2).
4. A Kohathite Levite who helped to oversee the repairing of the Temple in the time of Josiah (2 Chron. xxxiv:12), B. C. 623.
5. A Benjamite, descendant of Elpaal, living at Jerusalem (1 Chron. viii:17), B. C. 589.
6. Father of Sallu (1 Chron. ix:7), and son of Joed (Neh. xi:7).
7. Eldest son of Zerubbabel (1 Chron. iii:19), B. C. about 536.
8. A chief priest, of the house of Ezra, in the days of Joiakim (Neh. xii:13), B. C. after 536.
9. Another chief priest, son of Ginnethon, contemporary with Joiakim (Neh. xii:16), B. C. after 536.
10. A chief Israelite, sent with others by Ezra to accompany his party of Levites to Jerusalem (Ezra viii: 16). He seems also to have assisted

in finding out those who had married foreign wives (Ezra x:15), and possibly identical with the Temple warden (Neh. xii:25), B. C. about 440. The last mentioned Meshullam is called *Meshelemiah* (1 Chron. xxvi:1), *Shelemiah* (1 Chron. xxvi:14), and *Shallum* (Neh. vii:45).
11. One of the "sons" of Bani who divorced his foreign wife after the exile (Ezra x:29), B. C. 459.
12. A priest, son of Meshillemith, descendant of Immer (1 Chron. ix:12), B. C. after 440.
13. Son of Berechiah. He helped to repair two sections of the wall of Jerusalem (Neh. iii:4, 30). His daughter married Johanan, the son of Tobiah (Neh. vi:18), B. C. 446.
14. Son of Besodeiah, who helped Jehoiada repair the old gate of the wall of Jerusalem (Neh. iii:6), B. C. 446.
15. One of the princes of Judah who joined in the procession around the walls of Jerusalem at their completion (Neh. xii:33), B. C. 446.
16. A chief Benjamite, dwelling in Jerusalem after the exile (1 Chron ix:8), B. C. about 440.
17. One of the chief Israelites who stood on Ezra's left when he expounded the law to the people (Neh. viii:4), B. C. about 410. Perhaps identical with 10, 13, 14, 15, or 16. Probably identical with the one who sealed the covenant (Neh. x:20).
18. A priest, who sealed the covenant with Nehemiah (Neh. x:7), B. C. about 410. Perhaps identical with 7 or 8.

MESHULLEMETH (me-shŭl'le-mĕth), (Heb. מְשֻׁלֶּמֶת, *mesh-ool-leh'meth*, friend), the wife of Manasseh, and mother of Amon (2 Kings xxi:19). She was the daughter of Haruz of Jotbah. (B. C. 664-642.)

MESOBAITE (mes'o-bā'īte), (Heb, מְצֹבָיָה, *mets-o-baw-yaw'* found of Jah), a title given to Jasiel, one of David's guard (1 Chron. xi:47). If it indicates a place there is no other notice of it.

MESOPOTAMIA (mĕs'o-po-tā'mi-à), (Gr. Μεσοποταμία, *mes-op-ot-am-ee'ah*, the country between the two rivers), the ordinary Greek rendering of the Heb. אֲרַם נַהֲרַיִם, *ar'am nah-har-ah'yim*, the Greek name given after the conquests of Alexander to the region between the Euphrates and the Tigris, excluding the northern part which continued to be known as Babylonia.

The name for this district in the Old Testament is Aram-Naharaim, or "Aram or Syria of the two rivers" (Gen. xxiv:10; Deut. xxiii:4; Judg. iii:8, 10; 1 Chron. xix:6), and Padan-aram or "*Plain of Syria*" Gen. xxv:20; xxviii:2-7; xlvi:15; also Aram or "Syria" (Num. xxiii:7; Gen. xxxi:20, 24; comp. Acts ii:9; vii:2). Under the former name it is referred to as the kingdom of Chushan-Rishathaim, who was conquered by Othniel, son of Kenaz, Caleb's brother (Judg. iii:8). Two great thoroughfares of trade led through Mesopotamia, both starting from Aleppo in Syria and passing, the one to Edessa on the Euphrates, and the other to Carchemish on the same river. This latter road is continued on the east of the Euphrates through Harran to the Tigris. It would therefore be along it, or in that line, that Abraham journeyed on his migration from Ur of the Chaldees to Canaan. From about B. C. 800 Mesopotamia was subject to Assyria and the cities Gozan, Haran, and Rezeph, and Thelasar, are spoken of as among the conquests of Sennacherib (2 Kings xix:12). Jews from Mesopotamia were at Jerusalem at the great Pentecost (Acts ii:9), and

Stephen uses the name in his speech (Acts vii:2). (See Aram.)

MESS (mĕs), (Heb. מַשְׂאֵת, *mas-ayth'*, a raising, as of the hands in prayer, Ps. cxli:2; or of flame, Judg. xx:38, 40), a portion of food (Gen. xliii:34; 2 Sam. xi:8).

MESSIAH (mes-sī'ah), (Heb. מָשִׁיחַ, *maw-shee-akh*; Sept. Χριστός, anointed).

(1) The Anointed. In both languages this word signifies the same thing, viz., *anointed.* Hence Gr. *Khris-tos'*, χριστός, *the anointed priest*, for the Hebrew, *the high priest* (Lev. iv: 3, 5, 16). In order to have an accurate idea of the scriptural application of the term, we must consider the custom of anointing which obtained amongst the Jews. That which was specifically set apart for God's service was anointed, whether *persons* or *things*. (See Anointing.) Thus we read that Jacob poured oil upon the pillar (Gen. xxviii:18, 22). The tabernacle also and its utensils were anointed (Lev. viii:10), being thereby appropriated to God's service.

But this ceremony had, moreover, relation to *persons.* Thus *priests*, as Aaron and his sons, were anointed that they might minister unto God (Exod. xl:13, 15).

Kings were anointed. Hence it is that a king is designated *the Lord's anointed* in the Hebrew, and in the Greek *the anointed of the Lord.* Saul and David were, according to the divine appointment, anointed by Samuel (1 Sam. x:1; xv:1; xvi:3, 13). Zadok anointed Solomon, that there might be no dispute who should succeed David (1 Kings i:39).

We cannot speak with confidence as to whether the prophets were *actually* anointed with the material oil. We have neither an express law nor practice to this effect on record. True it is that Elijah is commanded to anoint Elisha to be prophet in his room (1 Kings xix:16); but no more may be meant by this expression than that he should constitute him his successor in the prophetic office; for all that he did, in executing his divine commission, was to cast his own garment upon Elisha (1 Kings xix:19); upon which he rose and ministered unto him (verse 21). For kings and priests the precept and practice are unquestionable.

(2) Redeemer of Humanity. But the name *Messiah* is, *par excellence*, applied to the Redeemer of man in the Old Testament (Dan. ix:25; Ps. ii:2). The words of Hannah, the mother of Samuel, at the close of her divine song, are very remarkable (1 Sam. ii:10): 'The adversaries of the Lord shall be broken in pieces; out of heaven shall He thunder upon them; the Lord shall judge the ends of the earth; and he shall give strength unto his *king*, and exalt the horn of his Messiah.' The Hebrews as yet had no king; hence the passage may be taken as a striking prophecy of the promised deliverer. In various parts of the New Testament is this epithet applied to Jesus. St. Peter (Acts x:36, 38) informs Cornelius the centurion that God had anointed Jesus of Nazareth to be the *Christ*, and our Lord himself acknowledges to the woman of Samaria that he is the expected Messiah (John iv:25). This term, however, as applied to Jesus, is less a *name* than the expression of his office.

Thus the Jews had in *type*, under the Mosaic dispensation, what we have in *substance* under the Christian system. The prophets, priests and kings of the former economy were types of Him who sustains these offices as the head of his mystical body, the Church. (See Mediator.) As the priests and kings of old were set apart for their offices and dignities by a certain form prescribed in the law of Moses, so was the blessed Savior by a better anointing (of which the former was but a shadow), even by the Holy Ghost. Thus the apostle tells us that God anointed Jesus of Nazareth with the Holy Ghost, and with power (Acts x:38). He was anointed:

First, at his *conception;* the angel tells Mary, 'The Holy Ghost shall come upon thee, and the power of the Highest shall overshadow thee; therefore that holy thing which shall be born of thee shall be called the Son of God' (Luke i:35).

Second, at his *baptism* at the River Jordan (Matt. iii:13; Mark i:9, 10, 11, 12). St. Luke moreover records (Luke iv:17, 21) that our Lord being at Nazareth, he had given unto him the book of the prophet Isaiah; and on reading from ch. lxi:1, 'The Spirit of the Lord is upon me,' etc., he said to his hearers, 'This day is this Scripture fulfilled in your ears.'

(3) Prophecy. But as the Jews will not acknowledge the right of either Jesus or his apostles to apply the prophetic passages which point to the Messiah to himself, it now remains for us to show—

First, That the promised Messiah *has already come.*

Second, That Jesus of Nazareth *is unquestionably the Messiah who has come.*

(a) To prove our first assertion, we shall confine our remarks to *three* prophecies. The first occurs in Gen. xlix:8, 10, where Jacob is giving his sons his parting benediction, etc. When he comes to Judah he says: 'The scepter shall not depart from Judah, nor a lawgiver from between his feet, until Shiloh come; and unto him shall the gathering of the people be.' It is evident that by Judah is here meant, not the *person* but the *tribe;* for Judah died in Egypt, without any preëminence. By *scepter* and *lawgiver*, are obviously intended the legislative and ruling power, which did, in the course of time, commence in David, and which, for centuries afterwards, was continued in his descendants. Whatever variety the form of government—whether monarchical or aristocratical—might have assumed, the *law* and polity *were still the same.* This prediction all the ancient Jews referred to the Messiah. Now, that the scepter has departed from Judah, and, consequently, that the Messiah has come, we argue from the acknowledgments of some most learned Jews themselves. The precise time when all authority departed from Judah is disputed. Some date its departure from the time when Herod, an Idumæan, set aside the Maccabees and Sanhedrim. Others think that it was when Vespasian and Titus destroyed Jerusalem and the Temple, that the Jews lost the last vestige of authority. If, therefore, the scepter *has* departed from Judah—and who can question it who looks at the broken-up, scattered, and lost state of that tribe for ages? —the conclusion is clearly irresistible, that the Messiah *must have long since come.* The tribe of Judah was in a most prosperous state.

The next proof that the Messiah has long since come, we adduce from Dan. ix:25, 26, 27. It is evident that the true Messiah is here spoken of. He is twice designated by the very name. And if we consider what the work is which he is here said to accomplish, we shall have a full confirmation of this. Who but He could finish and take away transgression, make reconciliation for iniquity, bring in everlasting righteousness, seal up the vision and prophecy, confirm the covenants with many, and cause to cease the sacrifice and oblation? If then it be the *true* Messiah who is described in the above prophecy, it remains for us to see how the time predicted for his coming has long since transpired. This is expressly said to be seventy weeks from the going forth of the commandment to restore and build Jerusalem. That by seventy weeks are to be understood seventy sevens of years, a day being put for a year, and a week for seven years, making up 490 years, is allowed by Kimchi, Jarchi, Rabbi Saadias, and other learned Jews, as well as by many Christian commentators. This period of time then *must have long since* elapsed, whether we date its commencement from the first decree of Cyrus (Ezra i:1, 2,), the second of Darius Hystaspes (ch. vi:15), or that of Artaxerxes (ch. viii:11). See Grotius *De Veritat.* v; Josephus, *De Bell. Jud.* vii, 12, 13.

We can only barely allude to one more remarkable prediction, which fixes the time of the Messiah's advent, viz., Hag. ii:7-9: 'I will shake all nations, and the desire of all nations (or the desirable things of all nations shall come—R. V.) : and I will fill this house with glory, saith the Lord of hosts. The silver is mine, and the gold is mine, saith the Lord of hosts. The glory of this latter house shall be greater than of the former, saith the Lord of hosts.' The glory here spoken of *must* be in reference to the Messiah, or on some other account. It could not have been said that the second Temple exceeded in glory the former one; for in many particulars, according to the acknowledgment of the Jews themselves, it was far inferior both as a building (Ezra iii:3, 12), and in respect of the symbols and tokens of God's special favor being wanting (see Kimchi and R. Salomon on Hag. i:8). The promised glory, therefore, must refer to the coming and presence of him who was promised to the world before there was any nation of the Jews, and who is aptly called the '*Desire of all nations.*' This view is amply confirmed by the prophet Malachi (iii:1). Since, then, the very Temple into which the Savior was to enter has for ages been destroyed, *he must*, if the integrity of this prophecy be preserved, *have come*. That there was, at the time of our Lord's birth, a great expectation of the Messiah, both amongst Jews and Gentiles, may be seen from three celebrated historians, as well as from the sacred Scriptures. We may just add that as there was a general expectation of the Messiah at this time, so there were many impostors who drew after them many followers (Joseph. *Antiq.* xx:2, 6; *De Bell. Jud.* lvii:31). See also a full account of the false Christs who appeared by John à Lent *Schediasm,* c:2; Maimon, *Ep. ad Judæos Marsilienses;* Christ prophesies of such persons (Matt. xxiv:24, 29).

(b) The limits of this article will admit of our only touching upon the proofs that Jesus of Nazareth, and none other, is the very Messiah who was to come.

(1) What was predicted of the Messiah was fulfilled in Jesus. Was the Messiah to be of the seed of the woman (Gen. iii:15), and this woman a virgin? (Is. vii:14). So we are told (Gal. iv: 4; Matt. i:18, 22, 23) that Jesus was made of a woman, and born of a virgin. Was it predicted that he (Messiah) should be of the tribe of Judah, of the family of Jesse, and of the house of David? (Mic. v:2; Gen. xlix:10; Is. xi:10; Jer. xxiii:5). This was fulfilled in Jesus (Luke i:27, 69; Matt. i:1). (See GENEALOGY.)

(2) If the Messiah was to be a prophet like unto Moses, so was Jesus also (Deut. xviii:15; John vi:14). If the Messiah was to appear in the second Temple, so did Jesus (Hag. ii:7, 9; John xviii:20).

(3) Was the Messiah to work miracles? (Is. xxxv:5, 6; comp. Matt. xi:4, 5).

(4) If the Messiah was to suffer and die (Is. liii), we find that Jesus died in the same manner, at the very time, and under the identical circumstances, which were predicted of him. The very man who betrayed him, the price for which he was sold, the indignities he was to receive in his last moments, the parting of his garments, and his last words, etc., were all foretold of the Messiah, and accomplished in Jesus.

(5) Was the Messiah to rise from the dead? So did Jesus. How stupendous and adorable is the Providence of God, who, through so many apparent contingencies, brought such things to pass!
J. W. D.

(4) Literature. Harris, *Sermons on the Messiah;* Maclaurine, *On the Prophecies Relating to the Messiah;* Fuller, *Jesus the True Messiah;* Liddon, *Divinity of Christ;* Milman, *History of the Jews,* ii, 432, *sq.,* iii, 366; *Allen, Mod. Judaism.*

MESSIAS (mes-sī'as), (Gr. Μεσσίας, *mes-see'as*), a Greek form of the Hebrew Messiah (John i:41; iv: 25).

METALS (mĕt'als). The principal metals are in this work considered separately under their several names; and a few general observations alone are necessary in this place.

(1) Native Minerals. The mountains of Palestine contained metals, nor were the Hebrews ignorant of the fact (Deut. viii:9); but they do not appear to have understood the art of mining. They therefore obtained from others the superior as well as the inferior metals, and worked them up. They received also metal utensils ready made, or metal in plates (Jer. x:9), from neighboring and distant countries of Asia and Europe. The metals named in the Old Testament are (Heb. בַּרְזֶל) *barzel, iron steel,* (Jer. xv:12) *nekh-o'sheth* (Heb. נְחֹשֶׁת), rendered *brass,* included copper, copper ore, and bronze, and also brass if zinc was then known; *tin,* (בְּדִיל, *bed-eel'*) and *lead* (Heb. עֹפֶרֶת, *o-feh'reth);* (Heb. כֶּסֶף), *keh'sef,* silver; (Heb. זָהָב), *zaw-hawb', gold.* The trade in these metals was chiefly in the hands of the Phœnicians (Ezek. xxvii:12), who obtained them from their colonies, principally those in Spain (Jer. x:9; Ezek. xxvii:12). Some also came from Arabia (Ezek. xxvii:19), and some apparently from the countries of the Caucasus (Ezek. xxvii:13). A composition of several metals is expressed by the Hebrew word *chasmil.* (See CHASMIL.)

(2) Metallic Compositions. In general the ancients had a variety of metallic compositions, and that which the word *chasmil* describes appears to have been very valuable. Whether it was the same as that precious compound known among the ancients as Corinthian brass is uncertain, but it is likely that in later times the Jews possessed splendid vessels of the costly compound known by that name. Indeed, this is distinctly affirmed by Josephus (*Vita,* 13).

The vast quantity of silver and gold used in the temple in the time of Solomon, and which was otherwise possessed by the Jews during the flourishing time of the nation, is very remarkable, under whatever interpretation we regard such texts as 1 Chron. xxii:14; xxix:4, etc. In like manner, we find among other ancient Asiatic nations, and also among the Romans, extraordinary wealth in gold and silver vessels and ornaments of jewelry. As all the accounts, received from sources so various, cannot be founded on exaggeration, we may rest assured that the precious metals were in those ancient times obtained abundantly from mines—gold from Africa, India, and perhaps even then from Northern Asia; and silver principally from Spain.

(3) Metallic Manufactures. The following are the metallic manufactures named in the Old Testament:—Of *iron,* axes (Deut. xix:5; 2 Kings vi:5) ; saws (2 Sam. xii:31) ; stone-cutters' tools (Deut. xxvii:5) ; sauce-pans (Ezek. iv:3) ; bolts, chains, knives, etc., but especially weapons of war (1 Sam. xvii:7; 1 Macc. vi:35). Bedsteads were even sometimes made of iron (Deut. iii:11) ; 'chariots of iron,' *i. e.,* war-chariots, are noticed elsewhere. (See CHARIOTS.) Of *copper* we find vessels of all kinds (Lev. vi:28; Num. xvi:39; 2 Chron. iv:16; Ezra viii:27) ; and also weapons of war, principally helmets, cuirasses, shields, spears (1 Sam. xvii:5, 6, 38; 2 Sam. xxi: 16) ; also chains (Judg. xvi:21) ; and even mirrors (Exod. xxxviii:8). (See COPPER.) *Gold* and *silver* furnished articles of ornament. also vessels, such as cups, goblets, etc. The holy vessels of the temple were mostly of gold (Ezra v:14). Idolaters had idols and other sacred objects of silver (Exod. xx:23; Is. ii:20; Acts xvii:29; xix:24). *Lead* is mentioned as being used for weights, and for plumb-lines in measuring (Amos vii:7; Zech. v:8).

(4) Tools of the Workers. Some of the tools of workers in metal are also mentioned: *Paam,* anvil (Is. xli:7) ; *makkabah* (Is. xliv:12) ; *pattish,* hammer (Is. xli:7) ; *mal kachim,* pincers; and *mappuach,* bellows (Jer. vi:29) ; *matzreph,* crucible (Prov. xvii:3) ; *cur,* melting-furnace (Ezek. xxii:18).

There are also allusions to various operations connected with the preparation of metals. (1) The smelting of metal was not only for the purpose of rendering it fluid, but in order to separate and purify the richer metal when mixed with baser minerals, as silver from lead, etc. (Is. i:25; comp. Plin. *Hist. Nat.* xxxvii:47; Ezek. xxii:18-20). The dross separated by this process is called *sigim,* although this word also applies to metal not yet purified from its dross. For the actual or chemical separation other materials were mixed in the smelting, such as alkaline salts, *bor* (Is. i:25), and lead (Jer. vi:29; comp. Plin. *Hist. Nat.* xxxiii:31). (2) The casting of images (Exod. xxv:12; xxvi:37; Is. xl:19); which are always of gold, silver, or copper. The casting of iron is not mentioned, and was perhaps unknown to the ancients (Hausmann, in *Commentatt. Soc. Goett.* iv:53; *sq.;* Müller, *Archäol.* p. 371.) (3) The hammering of metal and making it into broad sheets (Num. xvi:38; Is. xliv:12; xl:19). (4) Soldering and welding parts of metal together (Is. xli:7). (5) Smoothing and polishing metals (1 Kings vii:45). (6) Overlaying with plates of gold and silver and copper (Exod. xxv:11-24; 1 Kings vi:20; 2 Chron. iii:5; comp. Is. xl:19). The execution of these different metallurgic operations appears to have formed three distinct branches of handicraft before the exile; for we read of the blacksmith, by the name of the *'worker in iron'* Is. xliv:12); the brass founder (1 Kings vii:14); and the gold and silver smith (Judg. xvii:4; Mal. iii:2).

The invention of the metallurgic arts is in Scripture ascribed to Tubal-cain (Gen. iv:22). In later times the manufacture of useful utensils and implements in metals seems to have been carried on to a considerable extent among the Israelites, if we may judge from the frequent allusions to them by the poets and prophets. But it does not appear that, in the finer and more elaborate branches of this great art, they made much, if any, progress during the flourishing times of their commonwealth; and it will be remembered that Solomon was obliged to obtain assistance from the Phœnicians in executing the metal work of the temple (1 Kings vii:13, 14).

The Hebrew workers in iron, and especially such as made arms, were frequently carried away by the different conquerors of the Israelites (1 Sam. xiii:19; 2 Kings xxiv:14, 15; Jer. xxiv:1; xxix:2) ; which is one circumstance among others to show the high estimation in which this branch of handicraft was anciently held.

METEYARD (mēt'yärd), (Heb. מִדָּה, *mid daw,* extension, Lev. xix:35), a yard measure. (See WEIGHTS AND MEASURES.)

METHEG-AMMAH (mē'theg-ăm'mah), (Heb. מֶתֶג הָאַמָּה, *meh'theg haw-am-maw',* bridle of the mother, *i. e.,* curb of the city), a figurative term applied to a city, probably Gath, taken by David from the Philistines (2 Sam. viii:1). A. V. "bit of the metropolis."

METHODISM, EPISCOPAL, IN THE UNITED STATES.

1. The Methodist Episcopal Church.

Small, indeed, the beginnings, but steady the growth and mighty the present stature, of the Methodist Episcopal Church. Figures gathered nearly two years ago (the latest accessible) make the total ministry and lay membership of the church at that time 2,925,629. The same authority (Methodist Year Book, 1901) makes the total value of church and parsonage property $145,759,-844, or in round numbers, at the present time, $150,000,000 for these two items alone.

(1) Introduction to America. This is certainly a sizable tree. From what sort of a seed did it spring, and how did it get rooted? A young Irish carpenter, Philip Embury, is believed to have delivered what may be fairly called the first Methodist sermon in America, to a congregation of five persons in his own humble house in New York. He had been licensed as a local preacher among the followers of Wesley in Ireland, but had made no move religiously during the six years of his residence in the New World, until stirred thereto in 1766 by the strong exhortations of a fellow immigrant, Mrs. Barbara Heck. The start proved to be timely, and in the order of God. The numbers soon increased, a more commodious room was hired, and the excitement rapidly spread. Early in 1767 another Wesleyan local preacher, Capt. Thomas Webb, of the British army, recently appointed barrackmaster at Albany, hearing of the struggling society at New York, hastened to its aid. A stone chapel, the first Methodist meeting-house in America, was dedicated October 30, 1768, and soon crowded with hearers. Thus the movement grew.

(2) Francis Asbury. And now most naturally the eyes of the little company looked for aid to their great father over the sea. Wesley being appealed to sent a couple of preachers, October, 1769, and eight more came in the five years following, but none of them stayed long or were very successful except Francis Asbury. His name is the greatest in the history of Methodism on this side of the water. Dr. Leonard Woolsey Bacon, writing "A History of American Christianity" this year, says of him: "It may reasonably be doubted whether any one man from the founding of the church [meaning the Church of Christ] in America until now has achieved so much in the visible and traceable results of his work." Though only a peasant boy, without education, he proved to be a general of consummate ability, invincible energy and wide-reaching plans. He kept the preachers on the march, and wonderfully aroused the people. Under his wise guidance Methodism passed through the troubled years of the Revolutionary War without a check to its progress, and in 1784 there were 15,000 members, 84 itinerant preachers and probably not less than 200,000 attendants on worship.

(3) Independence Gained. The Methodist Episcopal Church, strictly speaking, in its distinctive organized form as an American institution, began in the closing week of the year 1784. Up to that time the Methodists here had been an offshoot of British Methodism, more or less subject to the control of its founder, John Wesley, and the societies which had been established were in no proper sense a church. This inchoate and unsatisfactory condition of things had been endured with exemplary patience, though not without agitation, until the securement of the independence of the republic. This brought matters to a crisis. Wesley took the right steps. He clearly discerned the signs of the times and believed he had the guidance of the Spirit. He dispatched his right-hand man, Dr. Thomas Coke—having first, in connection with two other presbyters, ordained or set him apart as general superintendent or bishop—to arrange matters. The American Methodist ministers assembled in conference at Baltimore, proceeded, in accordance with the counsel of Wesley, to form themselves into an episcopal church, with superintendents or bishops, elders or presbyters, and deacons, the episcopal office being elective and the elected bishops being amenable to the body of ministers. Coke and Asbury were unanimously elected first incumbents of the office. General rules were adopted, twenty-five Articles of Religion, abridged by Mr. Wesley from the thirty-nine of the Church of England, were accepted, a variety of minor regulations were passed, and the shaping of the new ecclesiastical edifice was, for the time, finished, with remarkable oneness of spirit and great practical wisdom.

(4) The Doctrines. The doctrines of the new church cannot, of course, be stated here with any fullness, yet since they have been one of the main elements, if not chief of all, in its growth, a paragraph must be devoted to them. Calvinism was vigorously repudiated from the start. The doctrines of election, predestination, limited atonement, irresistible grace, and final perseverance of the Saints as set forth by those who accounted themselves the only orthodox, were stoutly opposed in every Methodist pulpit, and the commonsense of the people soon ranged itself with them. On the positive side Methodism gave emphasis in its preaching to the doctrines having closest connection with the spiritual life, and this also powerfully appealed to the people, meeting their needs and capturing their assent. It promoted revivals by preaching strongly the lost condition of humanity without Christ, the freedom of his grace to all who seek and the assurance of present salvation by simple faith in the Savior. It secured thoroughness of religious experience in vast numbers of cases by urging its converts on to complete consecration, which they were taught would be accompanied by a corresponding purification from sin. A bright, joyous, active type of religion was thus produced, very attractive to the multitudes and very effective as a means of church advancement. A free, a full, and a present salvation, which was the early rallying-cry of the Methodist hosts, proved amazingly productive of extensive as well as permanent results. A reasonable religion, being joined with a very earnest religion, swept the country. The freedom of the human will was emphasized rather than the absolute sovereignty of God. God's love was dwelt upon rather than his justice, though by no means to the exclusion of the latter. The depravity of man was not regarded as being total in any ordinary sense of that word, since God's spirit works in all and gracious ability to accept the offers of mercy is freely supplied to all. Methodism is not sacramentative or sacerdotal, but takes a moderate view of the ordinances. It believes that the baptism of infants should be retained in the church, and it offers in theory to all its converts who have not been baptized in infancy their choice as to sprinkling, pouring or dipping; but in practice nearly all are sprinkled.

(5) The Polity. Another large element in the growth of Methodism has been its form of church government. This, therefore, must be briefly sketched. It has a marvelous system of conferences and a complete set of officials carefully graded, all interlocking in a way to secure close supervision and great efficiency of movement, without seriously or needlessly infringing personal liberty. The General Conference, which has supreme jurisdiction over the entire denomination, and is the only legislative body in it, meets on the first Wednesday of May in every fourth year and continues in session about a month. Since 1812 it has been a delegated body, at first wholly of ministers, but since 1872 a part of the delegates have been laymen. It makes such laws, rules and regulations as the interests of the church seem to require, elects the Bishops and other general officers, such as publishing agents, editors and secretaries, supervises all the connectional societies and maintains fraternal relations with other churches. Its powers are somewhat restricted by a constitution, but in most matters it has a free hand. The annual conferences, meeting once a year, are next in order of importance. Including mission conferences and missions, they number now one hundred and forty-five, and are in almost all parts of the world. They are composed entirely of traveling preachers, have only administrative functions, and are presided over by the Bishops. In most Annual Conferences there are several District Conferences, held by the Presiding Elders and composed of the preachers and lay officials of all churches in the districts. Finally, each church or pastoral charge (where several small churches are under one man) has its own Quarterly Conference (consisting of local preachers, exhorters, class leaders, stewards, trustees, Sunday-school superintendents and presidents of Epworth Leagues), which supervises the interests of the charge. The duties of these various lay officers cannot be here specified; but since the most distinctive characteristic of the Methodist economy is the itinerancy of its ministers, a word should be said as to this feature. It sprang up providentially through the necessities of the early days, but it has proved a marvelous labor-saving arrangement. At first the preachers were moved, as a rule yearly, in some instances every six months, though there was no law against their indefinite reappointment to the same place. Then (in 1804) a rule was made that no preacher should be allowed to remain in one station more than two years successively; in 1864 it was changed to three years; in 1888 to five years; and at the General Conference held in Chicago in 1900 the time limit was removed. The

Bishop presiding at the annual conference is authorized to fix the appointments, but he is aided in this arduous duty by information furnished him from both churches and ministers, chiefly through the Presiding Elders, whose business it is to travel all the year, having general oversight, each one of a District comprising from twenty to seventy churches. This system distributes evenly, with very little friction, the talents of the ministry, and supplies every church with a preacher and every preacher with a church all the time.

(6) Growth. After being fully organized, as described, the church proceeded on its widening way, not without difficulties, perplexities, and occasional dissensions, but on the whole with marvelous success. In 1789, Methodism, under the leadership of Jesse Lee, was · introduced into New England, it having previously been confined to the Middle and Southern States. It pushed westward with great vigor, by means of its itinerant, circuit-riding preachers, with their headquarters in the saddle, who kept pace with the advancing tide of emigration. It was the first religious body to congratulate Washington on his inauguration to the presidency in 1789. It was the first to establish, develop and recognize the vast importance of Sunday-schools. It very early laid great emphasis on camp-meetings, and has been more largely identified with this useful means of grace than any other church. Its first literary institution, Cokesbury College, in Maryland, opened in 1787, was burned down in 1795. It was some time before the church, in its poverty, rallied from this blow, but after a while attention was turned anew in this direction, colleges and academies began to be founded, and in the last fifty years (especially the last thirty years) great strides have been made. There are now not far from one hundred and fifty high-class institutions in this country under the various names of university, college, institute, seminary, academy, together with about eighty more of diverse grades in the foreign mission fields. The total value of grounds, buildings and endowments is put in the last reports at $31,385,920, with 46,545 students in attendance. Chief among these institutions are the American University at Washington, the Northwestern University at Chicago, the Boston University at Boston, the Wesleyan University at Middletown, Conn., the Syracuse University at Syracuse, N. Y., the Ohio Wesleyan University at Delaware, Ohio, De Pauw University at Greencastle, Ind., and Dickinson College at Carlisle, Pa. A general Board of Education, chartered in 1869, looks after this interest.

(7) Missions. The Methodist Episcopal Church has been thoroughly missionary from the start so far as the evangelization of this country is concerned, and has expended immense sums on the frontiers, in the cities, among the colored people of the South, the Indians of the West, and the various foreign races that have come to our shores. Its Missionary Society was not regularly organized till 1819, and its first foreign mission, that to Liberia, was not entered upon till 1833. Next it went to South America, 1836; to China in 1847; to Germany in 1849; to India in 1856. It is working now in many parts of Europe (including Sweden, Norway, Finland, Denmark, Russia, Bulgaria, Italy, Switzerland, Germany) in East Africa and Central Africa, as well as Liberia; in Peru, Chili, Paraguay, Uruguay, Brazil and Argentine; in Mexico, Japan, Korea, Malaysia; besides five missions in China and five in India. And in these various fields it has about one hundred and eighty thousand communicants, besides nearly as many adherents. Nearly a million and a quarter of dollars (sometimes more) have been for a few years past annually raised by this society, which covers both foreign and domestic missions. There is in addition a Woman's Foreign Mission Society, begun in 1869, which raises over $300,000 a year, and a Woman's Home Missionary Society, organized in 1880. The total missionary disbursements of the Methodist Episcopal Church through these three societies are about a million and three-quarters a year, and another quarter of a million is expended by the City Missionary Societies.

(8) The Book Concern. The publishing agency of the church (technically called the "Book Concern") was set in motion as early as 1789, and has wonderfully prospered until now it has magnificent headquarters in New York and Cincinnati, and Chicago, with agencies or depositories of large importance at Kansas City, San Francisco, Detroit, Pittsburg and Boston. It publishes a large number of periodicals and papers, makes annual sales of two million dollars, and has a capital of nearly three and a half millions. It has passed all financial panics without the slightest interruption or danger; has cleared profits of six million dollars in the last fifty years and has paid out half of this for various church objects.

(9) Societies. Other organizations dear to the church and employed by it as instrumentalities of wide usefulness are the Sunday School Union (begun in 1827), the Tract Society (organized in 1852), the Board of Church Extension (incorporated in 1865), the Freedmen's Aid and Southern Education Society (started in 1866), and the Epworth League (formed in 1889 by the junction of several young people's societies). This latter has at the present time over twenty thousand senior chapters and over seven thousand junior chapters, or about two million members. The Freedmen's Aid Society has expended nearly $4,500,000 in the South since the war. The Church Extension Board has, during the last twelve years, aided in building nearly twelve thousand new churches, and has a Loan Fund of over $2,500,000. The Hospital and Deaconess work has greatly extended during the past few years.

(10) Secessions. Such are a few of the results which exhibit themselves after something more than a hundred years of effort. The detailed history cannot be given here. As already intimated, it has not been entirely peaceful. This would be too much to expect considering the frailty of human nature. There have been a variety of secessions, none of them, it is worthy of notice, arising from strife over doctrines, but all springing out of differences of opinion over administration. James O'Kelley, a flaming Irishman of great ability and extensive influence in Virginia, led off a small following in 1792, because the Conference refused to restrict the power of the bishops in the appointment of the ministers. In 1816 the colored members of Philadelphia and vicinity withdrew and organized the African Methodist Episcopal Church, and a secession from it in 1820 formed the African Methodist Episcopal Zion Church. In 1830 the Methodist Protestant Church was organized by those who were restive under the power of the bishops, presiding elders and ministers, and had been defeated in their strenuous demand for the incorporation of the lay element in the General Conference. In 1843, many preachers and members, who were dissatisfied with what they deemed the too favorable attitude of the Church toward slavery, withdrew and constituted the American Wesleyan Church. And in 1845 there was organized at Louisville, Ky., the

Methodist Episcopal Church South, embracing nearly all the ministers and members in the slave-holding states (about five hundred thousand) who were dissatisfied with the hostile attitude toward slavery exhibited by the General Conference of 1844. These are all the departures of any consequence. For the last fifty years matters have moved on smoothly. There has been agitation looking towards various changes in polity, some of it successful, some unsuccessful, but there has been no further split, and is not likely to be. The most recent conflicts have been for the purpose of changing the composition of the General Conference so that the laymen shall be as numerous as the ministers, and women delegates may be admitted as well as men. The former has already been won and the last General Conference was composed of an equal number of lay and ministerial delegates. Prevailing sentiment favors the admission of women delegates.

(11) The Last Half Century. The progress in the last half century has been uniform and great. In 1848 there were but six hundred and forty-two thousand nine hundred and twenty-seven communicants lay and ministerial. There are now, as before said, just about three million. And the encouraging feature about it is that the lastest years have shown the most rapid advance. In 1883, eighteen years ago, we had eighteen thousand seven hundred and forty-one churches; there are now about twenty-seven thousand. In 1883 our total membership was one million seven hundred and sixty-nine thousand five hundred and thirty-four; we had in our foreign missions forty-three thousand one hundred communicants; the total value of church and parsonage property was $79,238,085. It will be seen from these figures, compared with those given before for the present, that the Church seems to be just beginning to grow.

Nor do we find on examination that this outward prosperity has been won by any sacrifice of spiritual life or any criminal conformity to worldly folly. Outward methods and habits are different but the heart is no less sound and true. Revivals are still of constant occurrence, and there is very deep interest on all subjects pertaining to the higher Christian life. There has been no lowering of the rigid standard of morals for which from the start Methodism has been nobly conspicuous. It still occupies the foremost position on the temperance question, it still pronounces strongly against demoralizing worldly amusements. Dr. Buckley, one of the latest historians of the church, asking at the close of his volume, "Has Methodism lost to a dangerous degree its original vital impulse?" finds himself able to answer it in the negative. He says, "The flames of pure devotion burn upon many an altar, accessions by conversion are numerous, many preachers deliver truth in the power of the Holy Ghost, and every society contains those who cry continually, 'Wilt thou not revive us again, that thy people may rejoice in thee?'" He thinks that the many institutions which have been superadded to the simpler methods and forms of the fathers are being made tributary to the great work for which Methodism was established. We are quite certain that this is the case, and that the original purposes of the Methodist Episcopal Church are still being carried out under changed conditions. It started, in the language of the Discipline, "to evangelize the continent and spread spiritual holiness over these lands." It is still doing this, and is likely to continue it with unabated efficiency. Its sources of strength, under God, are in itself, its record has been every way

creditable, and its future seems bright. Its progress has not been due to any government aid, nor to members received from emigration, nor to prestige on account of great wealth, social position or superior educational facilities. All these things have been against it. It has been the church of the masses. Its growth has been due to its reasonable doctrines, its earnest piety, its military form of church government. It has been, and still is, a church thoroughly missionary in its organization and well adapted to avail itself promptly of all favorable openings, filled with reverent fire and burning with a zeal to bring men to God, brotherly and social in its spirit, identifying itself with all classes and making them feel at home within its walls, liberal in its opinions yet high-toned in its spiritual life, and admirably adapted every way to the wants of the new nation in which Providence placed it. How could it, being thus, do anything else but thrive as church never throve before.

Dr. J. M. Buckley says, "The most potent forces which account for the numerical increase of Methodism, the mutual labors of pastors and people in the local societies, are incapable of historic description. Yet without them the visible fabric of Methodism would be as the log-hut in which the fathers preached compared with the elaborate ecclesiastical structures which prosperity has made possible."

Bishop Charles H. Fowler says, "What does Methodism mean? It has the fecundity of the acorn. It shall wave on the mountains like the forests of Lebanon. It shall whiten all seas and all worlds with the sails of its spiritual commerce. It has the enlightening power of the school; it shall shine into every dark corner, driving all superstitions and all goblins from the earth's surface. It has the vigilance of the invisible police; it shall expose with the glare of its searchlight every stealthy criminal. It has the compact organization of an army, it shall march with its swing of conquest through every known valley and plain, and plant the cross of the Redeemer on every hilltop and mountain peak."

Dr. Abel Stevens, the principal historian of Methodism in this country, at the close of the last of the four volumes in which he narrates the rise and development of the Methodist Episcopal Church, says: 'This lowly Methodistic story is but the reproduction in substance, of the apostolic history, and presents, in full vitality, that original, that only example of evangelical propagandism, which, when all dogmatic conflicts and hierarchical pretensions, with their wasted passions and pomps, are recorded as historical failures, will bear forward to universal triumph the ensign of the cross by a catholic, living, working church of the common people."   J. M.

2. The Methodist Episcopal Church South. The movement called Methodism originated one hundred and fifty years ago in England, when the Wesleys and Whitfield began their evangelical preaching to the masses. "The field preaching of Wesley and Whitfield, in 1739," says Isaac Taylor, "was the event whence the religious epoch, now current, must date its commencement." The first Methodist Conference was held in the Foundry, London, beginning June 25, 1744. In 1760 Robert Strawbridge came to America, and settled at Sam's Creek, Maryland. Soon after he built the first Methodist church in the United States. In 1766, Philip Embury, a local preacher, organized a Methodist society in New York, being assisted by Barbara Heck. From these beginnings Methodism continued to grow until 1773, when the first annual conference in America was held in the city of Philadelphia. In December, 1784, in Baltimore, at Lovely Lane Chapel, the Methodist Episcopal Church was organized, and Thomas Coke and Francis Asbury were elected and ordained bishops. The Methodist Episcopal Church prospered and grew until 1844, when the agitation on the subject of slavery, which had been going on for some years, culminated in the division of the church. A short time previous to the General Conference of 1844, Bishop James O. Andrew, of Georgia, had married a lady possessed of slaves. Soon after their marriage, in order to free himself from any ownership in these slaves, he had secured them to her by a deed of trust. But the sentiment against his position was so strong among the delegates from the Northern Conferences that when the General Conference met, by a vote of 110 to 68, they passed a resolution that "It is the sense of this General Conference that he [Bishop Andrew] desist from the exercise of this office so long as this impediment remains." The result was a protest from the southern delegates, followed by a long discussion, which resulted in the adoption of a "Plan of Separation." Under the provisions of this plan the delegates from the Southern Conferences met in Louisville, Ky., in May, 1845, and organized the Methodist Episcopal Church South. Since that time this church has gone forward with its work, being faithful to the traditions and principles of Methodism, until now it numbers nearly a million and a half communicants, and 6,000 traveling preachers.

(1) Condition of Membership. While Methodism accepts the great cardinal doctrines of Christianity, such as are crystallized in the Apostles' Creed, there are several distinctive features in her doctrine and polity. Perhaps the most noticeable thing in Methodism is the broad condition of its membership, including all those who desire to flee from the wrath to come. This is the only condition required for admission into the M. E. Church South, the pastor being authorized to receive candidates as soon as he is satisfied of their sincerity.

(2) Witness of the Spirit. Methodism places emphasis on a personal experience and teaches that it is the privilege of every Christian to have a conscious knowledge of the pardon of sin. This doctrine of a conscious conversion, and of a direct witness of the Spirit testifying to the heart of the believer that he is a child of God is, as has been said, "the true key" to Methodist theology.

(3) Free Will. The doctrines of universal redemption and of the freedom of the human will are cardinal principles in Methodism. The M. E. Church South, in common with all other branches of Methodism, teaches that the sacrifice of Christ derived infinite value from the divinity of his person, and is therefore intrinsically sufficient to expiate the sins of the *whole* human race; that he "died for all men," and that salvation does not depend on an arbitrary decree, but upon the willingness or unwillingness of each man to comply with the gospel conditions of salvation. A natural inference from this is the absolute freedom of the human will. Methodists believe in justification by faith. "Justification is the divine judicial act which applies to the sinner believing in Christ the benefit of the atonement, delivering him from the condemnation of his sin, introducing him into a state of favor, and treating him as a righteous person." It is a judicial act, something done *for* the sinner because of his faith, as regeneration is something done *in* him, the two

being part of the one work of conversion. The *originating cause* of justification is the love of God; the *meritorious cause* is the atonement of Christ; the *instrumental cause* is the personal faith of the believer.

(4) The New Birth. Regeneration is an important Methodist doctrine, and is the new birth, a change of heart. All Methodists teach that "Except a man be born again, he cannot see the kingdom of God." It is the work of the Holy Spirit and is a conscious change in the heart and the life.

(5) The Sacraments. Methodism teaches that there are but two sacraments—baptism and the Lord's supper. The Methodist Church holds that the three modes of baptism—pouring, sprinkling, and immersion—are equally valid, but that the vast preponderance of evidence is in favor of pouring or sprinkling. Methodism also teaches the baptism of infants.

(6) The Itinerancy. The chief feature of the Methodist polity is the itinerant system. Every itinerant Methodist preacher is a member of some annual conference, and the bishop presiding over each conference appoints every preacher to some pastoral charge for one year. No preacher can be appointed to the same pastoral charge for more than four consecutive years in the M. E. Church South. From fifteen to twenty pastoral charges constitute a district, over which a presiding elder is appointed, whose duty it is "To travel through his appointed District, in order to preach and to oversee the spiritual and temporal affairs of the Church." No presiding elder can be appointed for more than four years to the same District.

(7) The Conferences. In every pastoral charge a quarterly conference, composed of the official board and local preachers, is held every three months; a conference of all the members of a church may be held monthly; a District Conference, composed of the preachers and delegated laymen of a district is held annually; an Annual Conference, composed of all the preachers and lay delegates in the bounds of that conference, is held once a year, and a General Conference, composed of one preacher and one layman for every forty-eight clerical members of an Annual Conference, is held every four years. The business of the General Conference is: (1) The election of bishops when deemed necessary; (2) To create and readjust the boundaries of the Annual Conference; (3) To revise the laws and rules of Discipline; (4) To superintend the interests of foreign missions; (5) To elect the various connectional officers of the Church.

(8) Principles. The principles and polity of Methodism have borne the test of one hundred and fifty years, and no branch of Methodism has grown more rapidly than the M. E. Church South. She stands to-day for a pure and aggressive Christianity, and claims that her mission is to "Spread scriptural holiness over this land."   W. F. B.

3. The African Methodist Episcopal Church.

(1) Historic Period. The African Methodist Episcopal Church is the oldest and largest organization among the negroes. It has grown up in four distinct periods. The heroic period, beginning in 1787 and continuing until 1816. The organic period, from 1816 to 1868. The developing period, extending from 1868 to 1892, and from 1892 to 1900 has been an expansion period, the borders of the church having extended to the uttermost parts of the earth.

The originating cause of the existence of the African Methodist Episcopal Church was the ill-treatment of the negro members of St. George's Methodist Episcopal Church in Philadelphia, Pa., by the white members of the same in the years 1785, 1786 and 1787.

Richard Allen was a local preacher in the church, and his brethren were denied their rights and were insulted. He organized a class of forty-two persons. This class continued under the care of St. George's Church for several years, but there was much friction between the class and church, which resulted in a call for a convention of all persons and churches having grievances because of ill-treatment received in the Methodist Episcopal Church.

The convention was held in Philadelphia, April 9, 1816. The following persons were present: Richard Allen, Jacob Tapsico, Clayton Durham, James Champion and Thomas Webster, all of Philadelphia, Pa.; Daniel Coker, Richard Williams, Henry Harding, Stephen Hill, Edward Williams and Nicholson Gilliard, of Baltimore, Md.; Peter Spencer, of Wilmington, Del.; Jacob Marsh, Edward Jackson, and William Andrews, of Attleboro, Pa., and Peter Cuff, of Salem, N. J.

(2) Growth and Statistics. Up to the present time thirty bishops have been elected and sixty-eight annual conferences have been organized. Nearly all of these are found upon American soil, but this church also has active forces in Sierra Leone and Liberia, in the Transvaal and South Africa, conferences having been organized in those distant lands during the last ten years.

In the year 1900 there were 5,832 ministers in this connection, and $984,462.84 was devoted to their support, the average annual amount paid to each working pastor being only about $168.20. The membership that year was 672,220, there having been a constant annual increase since the first organization, with only forty-two members, was effected in 1787. Beginning thus in the latter part of the eighteenth century, with only one church, they now have 5,630 churches, and the value of their church property is estimated at $10,310,993.

(3) Educational Work. The first school planted by the A. M. E. Church was in 1847, at Columbus, Ohio. The Rev. John M. Brown was the principal, and Mrs. Frances Allen-Watkins was the assistant principal. It was a manual labor or industrial school. It remained the only school of the church until 1863, when Bishops Daniel Payne and James A. Shorter and Dr. John G. Mitchell purchased Wilberforce University.

The following are the schools now under the control of the A. M. E. Church:
Wilberforce University and Payne Seminary, Wilberforce, Ohio.
Kittrell College, Kittrell, N. C.
Western University, Quindaro, Kan.
Morris Brown College, Atlanta, Ga.
Payne University, Selma, Ala.
Allen University, Columbia, S. C.
Flegler High School, Marion, S. C.
Edward Waters College, Jacksonville, Fla.
Shorter University, North Little Rock, Ark.
Campbell-Stringer College, Jackson, Miss.
Turner N. and T. Institute, Shelbyville, Tenn.
Wayman Institute, Harrodsburg, Ky.
Paul Quinn College, Waco, Texas.
Delhi Institute, Delhi, La.
Sissons High School, South McAlister, I. T.

Total amount of money raised for school purposes during the last quadrennium was $208,-598.28.

There are twenty-eight students from South and West Africa, and South America, who are being educated and making preparations to return

to their homes to begin the work of redeeming their race.

The work of educating the ministry of the Church has long had a special place in the hearts of the leaders. Bishop Daniel A. Payne labored very hard to develop this department of her educational system.

In 1891 Bishop B. W. Arnett promoted the idea of separating the theological department from Wilberforce University by organizing Payne Theological Seminary as a distinct organization.

The school had fifty-eight students the last quadrennium, and is presided over by Bishop Benjamin T. Tanner, as the dean. It is destined to do a good work for the ministers of the A. M. E. Church and other denominations, for the school makes no distinction as to ministerial students.

B. W. A.

4. African Methodist Episcopal Zion Church.

(1) Organization. The African Methodist Episcopal Zion Church was organized in 1796 in New York City by James Varick and a few others, because of proscription on the part of their white brethren in the Methodist Episcopal Church. Twenty-eight years previous (1768) the first Methodist church in America was established in John street, New York; white and colored members contributed of their means to the building and support of the church. As years passed on the colored membership increased, and caste prejudice, the outcome of slavery, began to appear. When the church became rich and influential the color line began to be drawn, and the black members were restricted in their religious privileges until the yoke became unbearable, resulting in the colored members obtaining permission from Bishop Francis Asbury to hold meetings by themselves. In 1796 a cabinetmaker's shop on Cross street, New York City, was hired and fitted up as a house of worship. There services were held until the year 1799, when the membership had so largely increased that a meeting of the colored men of New York was called for the purpose of incorporating themselves into a separate body from the white church. They decided to call their organization the African Methodist Episcopal Church. The word Zion was added some years afterward to distinguish it from the denomination now known as the A. M. E. Church. Nine trustees were appointed to secure a house of worship; two lots were purchased on the corner of Church and Leonard streets, and a small frame building was erected in the year 1800. In 1801 the church was incorporated under the laws of the State of New York. The first annual conference was held in this church June 21, 1821. At this conference a form of limited episcopacy was established and James Varick was elected the first bishop (then called superintendent). This form was continued till 1868, when it was changed to an unlimited (or lifetime) episcopacy.

The first discipline of the Church was adopted October 25, 1820, and in it she declared against slavery; this declaration was the means of keeping her out of the South till 1862.

(2) Growth. During the 105 years of her existence this church has grown to over half a million communicants. She had at the last General Conference nine Bishops, besides other general officers.

(3) Institutions. The church has her own publishing house, located at Charlotte, N. C. The plant is fitted with modern appliances and valued at $30,000. It is controlled by the Bishops and one member from each Episcopal district.

The principal educational institution of the

Church is Livingstone College, Salisbury, N. C. It is well equipped with buildings. Among its departments is an industrial school. This institution is a monument of negro skill and industry. The Church has a missionary department which sustains missions in Africa and the West Indies.

(4) Statistics and Literature. The latest statistics of the A. M. E. Zion Church are as follows:

Number of Ministers	3,155
Number of Churches	2,906
Number of Members	536,271
Number of Sunday Schools	3,200
Number of Pupils	225,000
Value of Property	$6,000,000

A large number of the ministers of this denomination are graduates of some of the best universities of the land. Among the literary production are: *Rise and Progress of the Zion Church in America*, by Bishop Christopher Rush; a brief *History of the Zion Church*, by Bishop J. J. Moore; *Book of Sermons*, by Bishop S. T. Jones; *Book of Sermons*, and a comprehensive *History of the A. M. E. Zion Church, or the Centennial of African Methodism*, by Bishop J. W. Hood, senior bishop of the Church; a *Book of Sermons*, and *A Code on Discipline*, by Bishop J. B. Small.   A. W.

METHUSAEL (me-thū'sa-ĕl), (Heb. מְתוּשָׁאֵל, *meth-oo-shaw-ale'*, man of God), son of Mehujael, of the race of Cain (Gen. iv:18).

METHUSELAH (me-thū'se-lah), (Heb. מְתוּשֶׁלַח, *meth-oo-sheh'lakh*, man of the dart), son of Enoch, and remarkable as being the oldest of those antediluvian patriarchs whose great ages are recorded in Gen. v:21, 22, 25, 27; 1 Chron. 1:3. At the age of 187 years he begat Lamech (the father of Noah); after which he lived 782 years, making altogether 969 years. (See LONGEVITY.)

METROLOGY (me-trŏl'ŏ-jў). See WEIGHTS AND MEASURES.

MEUZAL (me-ū'zăl), in the margin of Ezek. xxvii:19, means perhaps "from Uzal," the later Sanaa, the metropolis of Yemen.

MEZAHAB (mĕz'a-hăb), (Heb. מֵי זָהָב, *may-zaw-hawb'*, waters of gold), father of Matred and grandfather of MEHETABEL, 1, who was the wife of Hadad or Hadar, an Edomite king (Gen. xxxvi:39; 1 Chron. i:50), B. C. before 1619.

MEZUZOTH (mĕz-ū-zŏth'), (Heb. מְזוּזוֹת, *mez-zu-zoth'*). This word is found in Exod. xii:7, 22; Deut. vi:9; and in other places, in all of which it signifies 'doorposts.' It has no other meaning in Scripture. In the texts now referred to, the word occurs in the injunction, 'Thou shalt never forget the laws of the Lord thy God; but shalt write them on the the posts of thy house, and on thy gates.' This, contrary to most Christian interpreters, the Jews understand in the literal sense; and in this sense it might have been followed in the East, where it is at this day not unusual for the Moslems to inscribe on or over the gates, and on other parts of buildings, passages from their sacred book, the Koran. If therefore the Jews, before their dispersion, interpreted this precept literally, they probably applied it in the same manner. But when they came into western countries, where such was not the custom, and where ofttimes it might have proved inconvenient thus to point out their houses as those belonging to Jews, they adopted the custom of writing the precepts on scrolls of parchment, which they inclosed in a case and attached to the doors of their houses and chambers. To the scrolls thus inclosed the name of *mezuzoth* is, not very properly, given. Buxtorf, *Synag. Jud.* p 482; Leo Modena, *Rites and Customs*, pt. I, chapter ii, sec. 3; Allen's *Modern Judaism*, pp. 327-329. (See DOORPOST.)

MIAMIN (mi'a-mĭn), (Heb. מִיָּמִין, *me-yaw-meen'*, from the right hand).

1. A chief priest who returned from Babylon with Zerubbabel (Neh. xii:5), B. C. 536. Probably identical with Miniamin (Neh. xii:17), and perhaps with the one who sealed the covenant with Nehemiah (Neh. x:7).

2. "Son" of Parosh who put away his foreign wife after the exile (Ezra x:25), B. C. 459.

MIBHAR (mĭb'här), (Heb. מִבְחָר, *mib-khawr'*, choice), one of the "sons" of Haggeri and a mighty man of David (1 Chron. xi:38); probably the same as Bani (2 Sam. xxiii:36), B. C. 1046.

MIBSAM (mĭb'sam), (Heb. מִבְשָׂם, *mib-sawm'*, sweet odor).

1. The fourth of the twelve sons of Ishmael, who founded an Arabian tribe of the same name (Gen. xxv:13; 1 Chron. i:29), B. C. after 2061.

2. The son of Shallum, a Simeonite (1 Chron. iv:25), B. C. before 1658.

MIBZAR (mĭb'zär), (Heb. מִבְצָר, *mib-tsawr'*, fortress), one of the petty chiefs of Edom, a descendant of Esau (Gen. xxxvi:42; 1 Chron. i:53), B. C. after 1905.

MICAH (mī'kah), (Heb. מִיכָה, *mee-kaw'*, who is like Jehovah).

1. One of the twelve Minor Prophets who, according to the inscription of the book, prophesied during the reigns of Jotham, Ahaz, and Hezekiah (B. C. 759-699), and was consequently contemporary with Isaiah. It is, however, doubtful whether any accurate separation of the particular prophecies of Micah can be ascertained. He was a native of Moresheth of Gath (i:14,15), so called to distinguish it from another town of the same name, in the tribe of Judah (Josh. xv:44; 2 Chron. xiv:9, 10). Micah is to be distinguished from a former prophet of the same name, called also Micaiah, mentioned in 1 Kings xxii:8 (B. C. 897).

2. An Ephraimite, apparently contemporary with the elders who outlived Joshua. He secretly appropriated 1,100 shekels of silver which his mother had saved; but being alarmed at her imprecations on the author of her loss, he confessed the matter to her, and restored the money. She then forgave him, and returned him the silver, to be applied to the use for which it had been accumulated. Two hundred shekels of the amount were given to the founder, as the cost or material of two teraphim, the one molten and the other graven; and the rest of the money served to cover the other expenses of the semi-idolatrous establishment which was formed in the house of Micah, of which a wandering Levite became the priest, at a yearly stipend; till the Danite army, on their journey to settle northward in Laish, took away both the establishment and the priest, which they afterwards maintained in their new settlement (Judg. xviii:18). (See DAN; JONATHAN, 1). The establishments of this kind, of which there are other instances—as that of Gideon at Ophrah—were, although most mistakenly, formed in honor of Jehovah, whom they thus sought to serve by means of a local worship, in imitation of that at Shiloh. This was in direct contravention of the law, which allowed but one place of sacrifice and ceremonial service; and was something of the same kind, although different in extent and degree, as the service of the golden calves, which Jeroboam set up, and his successors maintained, in Dan and Bethel. The previous existence of Micah's establishment in the former city no doubt pointed it out to Jeroboam as a suitable place for one of his golden calves.

3. Son of Merib-baal, or Mephibosheth, son of Jonathan (1 Chron. viii:34, 35; ix:40, 41), B. C. after 1037. He is called MICHA (2 Sam. ix:12).

4. A Kohathite Levite of the house of Uzziel, and the first in rank according to the arrangement of David (1 Chron. xxiii:20), B. C. 1014. (See MICHAH.)

5. A Reubenite, son of Shimei (1 Chron. v:5), B. C. before 782.

6. A Levite, descendant of Asaph (1 Chron. ix:15). Elsewhere (Neh. xi:17, 22) called MICHA.

7. Father of Abdon (2 Chron. xxxiv:20; 2 Kings xxii:12). In the latter place the form is MICHAIAH, father of Achbor.

MICAH, BOOK OF (mī′kah, book ŏv).

In the book of Micah we do not have the individual discourses which the prophet uttered at different times, but their essential contents united in a collected form and divided into three sections, mutually connected, and referring to one another (cc. i and ii, iii-v, vi and vii). In the form of prophetical discourses they threaten judgments on the theocracy,—namely, the destruction of Samaria and Jerusalem, together with the Temple, and the carrying of the people away captive, on account of the prevalent sins of idolatry, and the covetousness of the powerful classes, the injustice of the judges, and the lying spirit of the false prophets; but they also announce, as coming after the judgment, redemption from the misery, gathering of the delivered remnant of Israel, and glorification of Zion by the Messiah. It follows from the internal unity of the book, that the prophet composed it in the reign of Hezekiah. On account of the frequent rebukes of idolatry (i:5; v:11-13; vi:16), it appears to have been composed before the extermination of idolatry throughout the land, which followed the solemn celebration of the Passover (2 Chron. xxx, xxxi), and before the overthrow of the kingdom of the Ten Tribes, on account of the announcement of the destruction of Samaria (i:6, 7). It is therefore to be dated in the period B. C. 728-722. (Keil, *Int. to O. T.*)

Micah is the third of the minor prophets according to the arrangement of the Septuagint, the sixth according to the Hebrew, and the fifth according to the date of his prophecies.

(1) Analysis. Jahn (*Introd.*) points out the following predictions as contained in the prophet Micah: (1) The destruction of the kingdom of Israel, which was impending when the prophecy was delivered, and which was fulfilled in the taking of Samaria by Shalmaneser, in the sixth year of Hezekiah (2 Kings xvii), and then that of the kingdom of Judah, with the destruction of Jerusalem (iii:12; vii:13). (2) The Babylonian captivity (iv:10, 11; vii:7, 8, 13). These predictions were delivered 150 years before the event, when the Chaldæans, by whom they were accomplished, were scarcely known as a people. (3) The return from the exile, with its happy effects, and the tranquillity enjoyed by the Jews under the Persian and Grecian monarchies, which referred to events from 200 to 500 years distant (iv:18; vii:11; xiv:12). (4) The heroic deeds of the Maccabees, and their victories over the Syrians or Syro-Macedonians, called Assyrians in Micah v, as well as in Zechariah x:11. (5) The establishment of the royal

residence in Sion (iv:8). (6) The birth and reign of the Messiah (v:2). The last three prophecies, observes this learned writer, are more obscure than the others, by reason of the remote distance, in point of time, of their accomplishment from the period of their being delivered.

(2) Bethlehem. There is no prophecy in Micah so interesting to the Christian as that in which the native place of the Messiah is announced. 'But thou, Bethlehem Ephratah (though) thou be little among the thousands of Judah (yet) out of thee shall he come forth unto me (that is) to be ruler in Israel' (Eng. Authorized Version). It is thus translated by the Sept.: 'And thou, Bethlehem, house of Ephratah, although thou be least among the thousands of Judah, out of thee shall come unto me one that shall be a ruler of Israel.' The citation of this passage by the Evangelist differs both from the Hebrew and the Septuagint. "And thou, Bethlehem (in) the land of Judah, are not the least among the princes of Judah; for out of thee shall come a governor, that shall rule (Gr. feed) my people Israel" (Matt. ii:6). The difference, however, is but verbal. Some suppose that the negative (οὐδαμῶς) originally belonged to the Hebrew, and others to the Greek, while many read the Hebrew interrogatively, 'art thou little?' etc. Eichhorn supposes that the Greek translator of St. Matthew's Gospel interchanged *thousands* with *rulers*. Of more importance is the application of the prophecy. It is evident that the Jews in the time of Jesus interpreted this passage to mean the birthplace of the Messiah (Matt. ii:5; John vii:41, 42). The later Rabbinical writers, however, such as Kimchi, Aben Ezra, Abarbanel, etc., have maintained that it had only an indirect reference to the birthplace of the Messiah, who was to be a descendant of David, a Bethlehemite, but not of necessity himself born in Bethlehem. Others, however, as David Ganz (*B. Zemach David*), expressly mention Bethlehem as the birthplace of the Messiah. The interpretation which considered this prophecy as intimating only that the Messiah was to be a descendant of David, was that current among the Jews in the time of Theodoret, Chrysostom, Theophylact and Euthymius Zigabenus, from whom we learn that it was maintained to have been fulfilled in Zerubbabel, the leader of the Jews on their return from Babylon, of which, and not of Bethlehem, he was a native. This interpretation was held among Christians by the celebrated Theodore of Mopsuestia (as we learn from his condemnation by the council at Rome under Pope Vigilius), and afterwards by Grotius (*Comment.*), who, however, regarded Zerubbabel as a type of Christ, and considered Christ's birthplace at Bethlehem as an outward representation of his descent from the family of David. '*Natus ex Bethlehemo Zorobabel recte dicitur, quod ex Davidis familiâ esset, quæ orta Bethlehemi.*' Many of the moderns have been attached to this interpretation of the prophecy, referring it to the general idea of the Messiah rather than to Zerubbabel, while some among them have, after the example of some Jews, ventured to assert that the account of the birth of Christ at Bethlehem was not to be depended on. Some have asserted after Jerome (*Comm. in Mic.*), that the citation in Matt. ii:6 is that of the Sanhedrim only, not of the Evangelist (Hengstenberg's *Christology*). Jahn (*Append. Hermeneut.*) observes that it is evident that the Jews in the time of Christ expected the Messiah's birth to take place at Bethlehem; and although he admits that the prophecy may be understood tropically in the sense applied to it by

Grotius, he contends that the context will not admit of its applicability either to Hezekiah or any other monarch than the Messiah; nor is it possible to apply the prophecy fully and literally to any but him who was not only of the house and lineage of David, but was actually born at Bethlehem, according to the direct testimony of both St. Matthew's and St. Luke's gospels.

(3) Style. The style of Micah is sublime and vehement, in which respects he exceeds Amos and Hosea. De Wette observes that he has more roundness, fullness, and clearness in his style and rhythm than the latter prophet. He abounds in rapid transitions and elegant tropes, and piquant plays upon words. He is successful in the use of the dialogue, and his prophecies are penetrated by the purest spirit of morality and piety. (See especially chapters vi:6-8; and vii:1-10.)

See, besides the works on the minor prophecies collectively in De Wette's *Introduction*, Pococke's *Commentary on Micah;* Groseschopf's *Micah Uebersetzt;* and Jahn's, Eichhorn's and Keil's *Introductions.* **W. W.**

MICAIAH (mī-kā′iȧh) (-yȧ), (Heb. מִיכָיְהָ, *mee-haw-yaw′*, who like Jehovah?), a prophet of the time of Ahab.

He was absent from the mob of false prophets who incited the kings of Israel and Judah to march against the Syrians in Ramoth-gilead; for Ahab, having been offended by his sincerity and boldness, had not called for him on this occasion. But he was sent for at the special desire of Jehoshaphat; and as he declared against the enterprise, which the other prophets encouraged, Ahab commanded him to be imprisoned, and allowed only 'bread and water of affliction' till he returned from the wars in peace. To which the prophet ominously answered, 'If thou return at all in peace, then the Lord hath not spoken by me' (1 Kings xxii:8-28). The event corresponded with this intimation (see AHAB); but we have no further information concerning the prophet.

MICE (mīs). See MOUSE.

MICHA (mī′ka), (Heb. מִיכָא, *mee-kaw′*, who is like Jehovah?).

1. 2 Sam. ix:12. See MICAH, 3.

2. A Levite, or family of Levites, who sealed the covenant with Nehemiah (Neh. x:11), B. C. 410.

3. Neh. xi:17, 22. See MICAH, 6.

MICHAEL (mī′ka-el), (Heb. מִיכָאֵל, *mee-kaw-ale′*, who is like God ?).

1. The name given to one of the chief angels, who, in Dan. x:13-21, is described as having special charge of the Israelites as a nation; and in Jude 9, as disputing with Satan about the body of Moses, in which dispute, instead of bringing against the arch enemy any railing accusation, he only said, 'The Lord rebuke thee, O Satan!' Again, in Rev. xii:7-9, Michael and his angels are represented as warring with Satan and his angels *in the upper regions* (ἐν τῷ οὐρανῷ), from which the latter are cast down upon the earth. This is all the reference to Michael which we find in the Bible.

The passages in Daniel and Revelation must be taken as symbolical, and in that view offer little difficulty. The allusion in Jude 9 is more difficult to understand, unless, with Vitringa, Lardner, Macknight, and others, we regard it also as symbolical; in which case the dispute referred to is that indicated in Zech. iii:1; and 'the body of Moses' is a symbolical phrase for the Mosaical law and institutions. (See JUDAS OR JUDE.) A

comparison of Jude 9 with Zech. iii:1 gives much force and probability to this conjecture.

2. A man of Asher and father of Sethur, who was sent to spy out the land of Canaan (Num. xiii:13), B. C. before 1657.

3. Son of Izrahiah, a descendant of Issachar, of the house of Uzzi (1 Chron. vii:3), B. C. after 1618.

4. A Benjamite, descendant of Elpaal through Beriah (1 Chron. viii:16), B. C. after 1612.

5. A chief Gadite, son of Abihail, who settled in Bashan (1 Chron. v:13), B. C. after 1093.

6. A Gadite ancestor of Abihail (1 Chron. v: 14), B. C. before 782.

7. One of the captains of Manasseh who came to David at Ziklag (1 Chron. xii:20), B. C. 1053.

8. A Levite, father of Shimea, of the house of Gershon, and an ancestor of Asaph (1 Chron. vi:40), B. C. before 1014.

9. Father of Omri, which latter was captain of the people of Issachar in the reign of David and Solomon (1 Chron. xxvii:18), B. C. before 1014.

10. Son of Jehoshaphat, slain by Jehoram (2 Chron. xxi:2), B. C. 887.

11. A descendant of Shephatiah; his son, Zebadiah, returned from Babylon with a company of eighty males (Ezra viii:8), B. C. 459.

MICHAH (mī′kah), (1 Chron. xxiv:24,25). See MICAH, 4.

MICHAIAH (mī-kā′yȧ), another form of MICAIAH (which see).

1. Daughter of Uriel, wife of Rehoboam and mother of Abijah (2 Chron. xiii:2). The name is doubtless a corruption of Maacah (2 Chron. xi:20).

2. One of the princes whom Jehoshaphat sent to 'teach in the cities of Judah' (2 Chron. xvii:7), B. C. 910.

3. 2 Kings xxii:12. See MICAH, 7.

4. Son of Gemariah, who, after having heard Baruch read the terrible predictions of Jeremiah in his father's hall, went, apparently with good intentions, to report to the king's officers what he had heard (Jer. xxxvi:11-13), B. C. 605.

5. Neh. xii:35. See MICAH, 6.

6. One of the priests who played on the trumpet at the celebration of the completion of the walls of Jerusalem (Neh. xii:41), B. C. 446.

MICHAL (mī′kal), (Heb. מִיכַל, *me-kawl′*, brook), youngest daughter of King Saul (1 Sam. xiv:49).

(1) Marriage. She became attached to David, and made no secret of her love, so that Saul, after he had disappointed David of the elder daughter (See MERAB), deemed it prudent to bestow Michal in marriage upon him (1 Sam. xviii: 20-28). Saul had hoped to make her the instrument of his designs against David, but was foiled in his attempt through the devoted attachment of the wife to her husband. Of this a most memorable instance is given in 1 Sam. xix:11-17.

(2) Saves David's Life. When David escaped the javelin of Saul he retired to his own house, upon which the king set a guard over night, with the intention to slay him in the morning. This being discovered by Michal, she assisted him to make his escape by a window, and afterwards amused the intended assassins under various pretenses, in order to retard the pursuit. When they were detected Michal pretended to her father that David had threatened her with death if she did not assist his escape.

(3) Second Marriage. Saul probably did not believe this; but he took advantage of it by canceling the marriage, and bestowing her upon a person named Phalti (1 Sam. xxv :44).

(4) Restored to David. David, however, as the divorce had been without his consent, felt that the law (Deut. xxiv :4) against a husband taking back a divorced wife could not apply in this case; he therefore formally reclaimed her of Ishbosheth, who employed no less a personage than Abner to take her from Phalti and conduct her with all honor to David. It was under cover of this mission that Abner sounded the elders respecting their acceptance of David for king, and conferred with David himself on the same subject at Hebron (1 Sam. iii:12-21).

(5) Reunion Unhappy. The reunion was less happy than might have been hoped. On that great day when the ark was brought to Jerusalem, Michal viewed the procession from a window, and the royal notions she had imbibed were so shocked at the sight of the king not only taking part in, but leading, the holy transports of his people, that she met him on his return home with a keen sarcasm on his undignified and unkingly behavior. This ill-timed sneer, and the unsympathetic state of feeling which it manifested, drew from David a severe but not unmerited retort; and the Great King, in whose honor David incurred this contumely, seems to have punished the wrong done to him, for we are told that 'therefore Michal, the daughter of Saul, had no child to the day of her death' (2 Sam. vi:16-23). It was thus, perhaps, as Abarbanel remarks, ordered by Providence that the race of Saul and David should not be mixed, and that no one deriving any apparent right from Saul should succeed to the throne.

MICHMAS, MICHMASH (mĭk′mas, mĭk′-mash), (Heb. מִכְמָשׁ, *mik-mash'*, something hidden; מִכְמָם, *mik-maws'*), a town of Benjamin (Ezra ii:27; Neh. xi:31; comp. vii:31), east of Beth-aven (1 Sam. xiii:5), and south from Migron, on the road to Jerusalem (Is. x:28).

The words of 1 Sam. xiii:2; xiv:4, and Is. x:29, show that at Michmas was a pass where the progress of a military body might be impeded or opposed. It was perhaps for this reason that Jonathan Maccabæus fixed his abode at Michmas (1 Macc. ix:73); and it is from the chivalrous exploit of another hero of the same name, the son of Saul, that the place is chiefly celebrated (1 Sam. xiii; xiv:4-16). Eusebius describes Michmash as a large village nine Roman miles from Jerusalem on the road to Ramah (*Onomast, s. v.* Μαχμά). Travelers have usually identified it with Bir or El-Bireh; but Dr. Robinson (*Researches*, ii:117) recognizes it in a place still bearing the name of Mukhmas, at a distance and position which correspond well with these intimations. This is a village situated upon a slope to the north of a valley called Wady es-Suweinit. It is small, and almost desolate, but bears marks of having been once a place of strength and importance. There are many foundations of huge stones, and some columns lie among them. The valley es-Suweinit, steep and precipitous, is probably the 'passage of Michmash' mentioned in Scripture. 'In it,' says Dr. Robinson, 'just at the left of where we crossed, are two hills of a conical, or rather spherical, form, having steep rocky sides, with small wadies running up between each so as almost to isolate them. One of them is on the side towards Jeba (Gibeah), and the other towards Mukhmas. These would seem to be the two rocks mentioned in connection with Jonathan's adventure (1 Sam. xiv:4, 5). They are

not, indeed, so "sharp" as the language of Scripture would seem to imply; but they are the only rocks of the kind in this vicinity. The northern one is connected towards the west with an eminence still more distinctly isolated.'

MICHMETHAH or MACHMETHATH (mĭk′me-thah), (Heb. מִכְמְתָת, *mik-meth-awth'*, hiding place), a city of the half-tribe of Manasseh, on the frontiers of Ephraim and Manasseh; over against Shechem (Josh. xvi:6; xvii:7). The site is perhaps indicated by a village called El-Makhua, south of Nablûs (De. Saulcy, *Narrative*, i:93).

MICHRI (mĭk′rī), (Heb. מִכְרִי, *mik-ree'*, prize of Jehovah), a Benjamite, father of Uzzi (1 Chron. ix:8), B. C. before 440.

MICHTAM (mĭk′tăm), (Heb. מִכְתָּם, *mik-tawm'*, a writing, especially a psalm), a word occurring in the title of Psalms xvi, lvi, lvii, lviii, and lx, which means *a writing, poem* or *song*. Some translate it *golden;* and Ewald, *secret, concealed*, that is, a new composition. The best rendering is perhaps *epigram*, a poem intended to record memorable thoughts.

MIDDAY (mĭd′dā), (Heb. צֹהַר יוֹם, *tso' har yome*, double light, 1 Kings xviii:29; מַחֲצִית הַיּוֹם, *makh-ats-eeth' hay-yome'*, half of the day, Neh. viii:3; Gr. ἡμέρα μέσος, *hay-mer'ah mes'os*, middle day, Acts xxvi:13). See TIME.

MIDDIN (mĭd′din), (Heb. מִדִּין, *mid-deen'*, extension), a village in the desert of Judah (Josh. xv:61), probably near the Dead Sea.

MIDDLE WALL (mĭd′d'l wạl), (Gr. μεσότοιχον, *mes-ot'oy-khon*, middle), the *chel*, or sacred partition between the Court of the Gentiles and the inner sanctum of the temple (Eph. ii:14). (See TEMPLE.)

MIDIAN (mĭd′i-an), (Heb. מִדְיָן, *mid-yawn'* strife), fourth son of Abraham by Keturah, and progenitor of the Midianites (Gen. xxv:2; 1 Chron. 1:32), B. C. after 2024.

MIDIANITES (mĭd′i-an-ītes), (Heb. מִדְיָנִים, *mid-yaw-neem'*).

(1) A tribe of people descended from Abraham's son Midian. His descendants must have settled in Arabia, and engaged in trade at an early period, if we identify them with those who in the time of Jacob appear, along with the Ishmaelites, as merchants traveling from Gilead to Egypt, and who, having in their way bought Joseph from his brethren, sold him to the latter country (Gen. xxxvii:28, 36). It is, however, very difficult to conceive that the descendants of a son of Abraham, born so many years after Isaac, had become a tribe of people at the time when the descendants of Isaac himself were so few. One is therefore much inclined to suppose that these Midianites were different and distinct from those descended from Abraham's son; and there appears the more ground for this when at a later period we find two tribes of Midianites, different in locality and character, and different in their feelings towards the Israelites.

(2) If this distinction be admitted, then it would be necessary to seek the earlier Midianites in those dwelling about the eastern arm of the Red Sea, among whom Moses found refuge when 'he fled from Egypt,' and whose priest or sheik was Jethro, who became the father-in-law of the future lawgiver (Exod. iii:1; xviii:5; Num. x:29). These, if not of Hebrew, would appear to have been of Cushite origin, and descended from Midian, the son of Cush. We do not again meet with these Midianites in the Jewish history, but they appear to have remained for a long time settled in the same quarter, where indeed is the seat of the only Midianites known to Oriental authors.

(3) The other Midianites, undoubtedly descended from Abraham and Keturah, occupied the country east and southeast of the Moabites, who were seated on the east of the Dead Sea; or rather, perhaps, we should say that, as they appear to have been a semi-nomad people, they pastured their flocks in the unsettled country beyond the Moabites, with whom, as a kindred, although more settled tribe, they seem to have been on the most friendly terms, and on whose borders were situated those 'cities and goodly castles which they possessed' (Num. xxxi:10). These Midianites, like the other tribes and nations who had a common origin with them, were highly hostile to the Israelites. In conjunction with the Moabites, they designedly enticed them to idolatry as they approached Canaan (Num. xxxi:2, 5; xxv:6, 14-18); on which account Moses attacked them with a strong force, killed all their fighting men, including their five princes or emirs, and made the women and children captives or servants (Num. xxxi). (See SERVICE; SERVANT, etc.) The account of the spoil confirms the view which we have taken of the semi-nomad position of the Midianites—namely, 675,000 sheep, 72,000 beeves, 61,000 asses, 32,000 persons. This was only the 'prey,' or live stock; but besides this there was a great quantity of 'barbaric pearl and gold,' in the shape of 'jewels of gold, chains, and bracelets, rings, earrings, and tablets.'

(4) Some time after the Israelites obtained possession of Canaan, the Midianites had become so numerous and powerful, that, for seven successive years, they made inroads into the Hebrew territory in the time of harvest, carrying off the fruits and cattle, and desolating the land. At length Gideon was raised up as the deliverer of his country, and his triumph was so complete that the Israelites were never more molested by them (Judg. vi: 1-7; vii, viii). To this victory there are subsequent allusions in the sacred writings (Ps. lxxxiii: 9, 12; Is. ix:4; x:26); but the Midianites do not again appear in sacred or profane history.

MIDNIGHT (mĭd'nīt'). See TIME.

MIDWIFE (mĭd'wīf'), (Heb. יָלַד, yaled).

The two midwives mentioned in Exod. i:15 are probably representatives or superintendents of a whole class, as such a number seems to stand in a decided disproportion to the needs of the Jewish nation at that time. The expression "upon the stools," in the following verse, refers to a kind of chair in which the patient sat during the birth, and which is still in use in modern Egypt.

MIGDAL-EL (mĭg'dal-ĕl), (Heb. מִגְדַּל־אֵל, mig-dal-ale', tower of God), a fortified city of Naphtali (Josh. xix:38).

Robinson thinks it may be the modern Mejdel or Mujeidil, ancient ruins being found on the seashore, three miles north of Tiberias.

It lies about twelve miles from Hurah, or Horem, and the same distance from Yarûn or Iron.

MIGDALGAD (mĭg'dal-găd), (Heb. מִגְדַּל־גָּד, mig-dal-gawd', tower of fortune), a city in the low country of Judah (Josh. xv:37). Probably El-Mejdel, about two miles north of Ascalon (Schwarz, Palest. p. 103; Van de Velde, Mem., p. 334).

MIGDOL (mĭg'dol), (Heb. מִגְדֹּל, mig-dole', tower), a place between which and the Red Sea the

Israelites were commanded to encamp on leaving Egypt (Exod. xiv:2; Num. xxxiii:7). (See EXODUS, THE).

The name, which means a tower, appears to indicate a fortified place. In Jer. xliv:1; xlvi:14, it occurs as a city of Egypt, and it would seem to have been the last town on the Egyptian frontier, in the direction of the Red Sea; hence 'from Migdol to Syene,' in Ezek. xxix:10; xxx:6. Among other sites Ebers favors the southern end of Bitter Lakes, where the Gulf of Suez was narrow and liable to be blown back by an east wind. (See EXODUS, GEOGRAPHY OF THE.)

MIGHTIES (mīt'ĭz), (Heb. גִּבּוֹר, ghib-bore', powerful, 1 Chron. xi:12, 24), the term used to denote the three great captains of David, elsewhere called "mighty men" (2 Sam. xxiii:8), and meaning leaders in war, warriors.

MIGRON (mĭg'ron), (Heb. מִגְרוֹן, mig-rone', precipice), a town which, from the historical indications, must have been south or southwest of Ai, and north of Michmas (Is. x:28).

From Michmas northward a narrow valley extends out of and at right angles with that which has been identified as the pass of Michmas. (See MICHMAS.) The town of Migron seems to have been upon and to have commanded the pass through this valley, but the precise situation has not been determined. Saul was stationed at the further side of Gibeah, 'under a pomegranate tree which is by Migron' (1 Sam. xiv:2), when Jonathan performed his great exploit at Michmas; and this is to be explained on the supposition that Migron was on the border, towards Michmas, of the district to which Gibeah gave its name.

MIJAMIN (mĭj'a-mĭn), (Heb. מִיָּמִין, me-yaw-meen', fortunate, or on the right hand).

1. The head of the sixth course of priests as established by David (1 Chron. xxiv:9), B. C. 1014.

2. A family of priests who sealed the covenant with Nehemiah (Neh. x:7); probably descended from 1, and identical with MIAMIN, 1, and MINIAMIN, 2.

MIKLOTH (mĭk'loth), (Heb. מִקְלוֹת, mik-loth', twigs, sticks or rods).

1. An officer of the second division of David's army, under Dodai, the Ahohite (1 Chron. xxvii: 4), B. C. 1014.

2. A Benjamite, son of Jehiel and father of Shimeah or Shimeam, of the family of Saul (1 Chron. viii:32; ix:37, 38), B. C. about 536.

MIKNEIAH (mĭk-nē'iah (-yà), (Heb. מִקְנֵיָהוּ, mik-nay-yaw'hoo, possession of Jehovah), a Levite doorkeeper of the Temple, and musician appointed by David (1 Chron. xv:18, 21), B. C. 1014.

MILALAI (mĭl'a-lā'ī), (Heb. מִלֲלַי, mee-lal-ah'ee, eloquent), a Levite musician who joined the procession about the walls of Jerusalem at their completion after the exile (Neh. xii:36), B. C. 536.

MILCAH (mĭl'kah), (Heb. מִלְכָּה, mil-kaw', advice).

1. Daughter of Haran, and sister of Lot. By her husband Nahor she had eight sons (Gen. xxii: 20, 23). She was the grandmother of Rebekah (Gen. xxiv:15, 24), B. C. about 2047.

2. Daughter of Zelophehad (Num. xxvi:33), who became an heiress, as did her sisters (Num. xxvii: 1; xxxvi:11; Josh. xvii:3), B. C. 1170.

MILCOM (mĭl'kom). See MOLECH.

MILDEW (mĭl'dū), (Heb. יֵרָקוֹן, *yay-raw-kone'*, pale), is properly a species of fungus or parasite which, settling on plants, destroys their leaves, and causes them to wither. Its origin is uncertain. God threatens and sends mildew as a judgment (Deut. xxviii:22; Amos iv:9; Hag. ii:17).

MILE (mīl), (Gr. μίλιον, *mil'ee-on*, the Greek form of the Lat. *milliarium*).

This word is only mentioned in Matt. v:41, where Christ says, 'If any one compel thee to go with him one mile, go with him two.' The mile was originally (as its derivation from *mille,* 'a thousand,' implies) a Roman measure of 1,000 geometrical paces (*passus*) of five feet each, and was therefore equal to 5,000 Roman feet. Taking the Roman foot at 11.6496 English inches, the Roman mile would be 1,618 English yards, or 142 yards less than the English statute mile. By another calculation, in which the foot is taken at 11.62 inches, the mile would be little more than 1,614 yards. The number of Roman miles in a

to have had four havens, one of which was capable of holding a fleet.

It was noted for a famous temple of Apollo, the oracle of which is known to have been consulted so late as the fourth century (Apollodorus, *De Orig. Deor.* iii:130). There was, however, a Christian church in the place, and in the fifth, seventh and eighth centuries we read of bishops of Miletus, who were present at several councils (Magdeburg, *Hist. Eccles.* ii:192; iv:86; v:3; vii:254; viii:4). The city fell to decay after its conquest by the Saracens.

Some take the Miletus where Paul left Trophimus sick (2 Tim. iv:20) to have been in Crete, and therefore different from the above; but there seems no need for this conclusion.

Near the site of the ancient city is a small Turkish village called Melas. The most noteworthy ruins of former grandeur are the theater, with its many tiers of seats in good preservation, and the temple of Apollo, of which a few columns are yet standing. The wandering channels of the

Miletus, Temple of Apollo.

degree of a large circle of the earth is very little more than 75. The Roman mile contained eight Greek stadia (see Smith's *Dict. of Greek and Rom. Antiq.*, art. 'Milliare'). The Greek stade hence bore the same relation to the Roman mile which the English furlong does to the English mile.

MILETUM (mī-lē'tum), (Gr. Μίλητος, *mil'ay-tos*, 2 Tim. iv:20). See MILETUS.

MILETUS (mī-lē'tus), (Gr. Μίλητος, *mil'ay-tos*), a city and seaport of Ionia in Asia Minor, about thirty-six miles south of Ephesus.

St. Paul touched at this port on his voyage from Greece to Syria, and delivered to the elders of Ephesus, who had come to meet him there, a remarkable and affecting address (Acts xx:15-38). Miletus was a place of considerable note, and the ancient capital of Ionia and Caria. It was the birthplace of several men of renown—Thales, Timotheus, Anaximander, Anaximenes, Democritus (Pomp. Mela, i:17; Diog. Laert. *Vit. Philosoph.* pp. 15, 88, 89, 650). Ptolemy (*Geog.* v:2) places Miletus in Caria by the sea, and it is stated

Meander are near by, although the mouth of the river is ten miles away.

MILK (mĭlk). The Hebrew word for milk, חָלָב, *khaw-lawb'*, is from the same root as חֵלֶב, *kheleb'*, 'fatness,' and is properly restricted to new milk, there being a distinct term, חֶמְאָה, *khem'-aw,* for milk when curdled.

(1) Frequent Mention. Milk, and the preparations from it, butter and cheese, are often mentioned in Scripture. Milk, in its fresh state, appears to have been used very largely among the Hebrews, as is usual among people who have much cattle, and yet make but sparing use of their flesh for food. The proportion which fresh milk held in the dietary of the Hebrews must not, however, be measured by the comparative frequency with which the word occurs.

(2) Milch Animals. In reading of milk in Scripture, the milk of cows naturally presents itself to the mind of the European reader; but in Western Asia, and especially among the pastoral and semi-pastoral people, not only cows, but goats, sheep, and camels, are made to give their milk for the sustenance of man. That this was also the case among the Hebrews may be clearly inferred even from the slight intimations which the Scriptures afford. Thus we read of 'butter of kine, and milk of sheep' (Deut. xxxii:14); and in Prov. xxvii:27, the emphatic intimation, 'Thou shalt have goats' milk for food,' seems to imply that this was considered the best for use in the simple state. 'Thirty milch camels' were among the cattle which Jacob presented to his brother Esau (Gen. xxxii:15), implying the use of camel's milk.

(3) Curdled Milk. The word for curdled milk חֶמְאָה, (*khem'aw*) is always translated 'butter' in the A. V. It seems to mean both butter and curdled milk, but most generally the latter; and the context will, in most cases, suggest the distinction, which has been neglected by our translators. It was this curdled milk, highly esteemed as a refreshment in the East, that Abraham set before the angels (Gen. xviii:8), and which Jael gave to Sisera, instead of the water which he asked (Judg. v:25). In this state milk acquires a slightly inebriating power, if kept long enough. Is. vii:22, where it is rendered 'butter,' is the only text in which the word is coupled with 'honey,' and there it is a sign of scarcity, not of plenty as when honey is coupled with fresh milk. It means that there being no fruit or grain, the remnant would have to live on milk and honey; and, perhaps, that milk itself would be so scarce that it would be needful to use it with economy; and hence to curdle it, as fresh milk cannot be preserved for sparing use. Although, however, this word properly denotes curdled milk, it seems also to be sometimes used for milk in general (Deut. xxxii:14; Job xx:17; Is. vii:15).

(4) Idolatrous Use of. The most striking Scriptural allusion to milk is that which forbids a kid to be seethed in its mother's milk, and its importance is attested by being thrice repeated (Exod. xxiii:19; xxxiv:26; Deut. xiv:21). There is, perhaps, no precept of Scripture which has been more variously interpreted than this; it is possible that this was not a common act of cookery, but an idolatrous or magical rite. Maimonides, in his *More Nevochim*, urges this opinion. He says, 'Flesh eaten with milk, or in milk, appears to me to have been prohibited, not only because it affords gross nourishment, but because it savored of idolatry, some of the idolaters probably doing it in their worship, or at their festivals.' This is confirmed by an extract which Cudworth (*Discourses concerning the True Notion of the Lord's Supper*, p. 30) gives from an ancient Karaïte commentary on the Pentateuch. 'It was a custom of the ancient heathen, when they had gathered in all their fruits, to take a kid, and boil it in the dam's milk, and then in a magical way to go about and besprinkle with it all their trees, and fields, and gardens, and orchards, thinking that by this means they should make them fructify, and bring forth more abundantly the following year.' Some such rite as this is supposed to be the one interdicted by the prohibition.

(5) Butter. Butter is not often mentioned in Scripture, and even less frequently than our version would suggest; for, as already intimated, the word *khem'-aw* must sometimes be understood curdled milk. Indeed, it may be doubted whether it denotes butter in any place besides Deut. xxxii:14, 'butter of kine,' and Prov. xxx:33, 'the churning of milk bringeth forth butter,' as all the other texts will apply better to curdled milk than to

butter. Butter was, however, doubtless much in use among the Hebrews, and we may be sure that it was prepared in the same manner as at this day among the Arabs and Syrians. The milk is put into a large copper pan over a slow fire, and a little *leben* or sour milk (the same as the curdled milk mentioned above), or a portion of the dried entrails of a lamb, is thrown into it. The milk then separates, and is put into a goatskin bag, which is tied to one of the tent poles, and constantly moved backwards and forwards for two hours. The buttery substance then coagulates, the water is pressed out, and the butter put into another skin. In two days the butter is again placed over the fire, with the addition of a quantity of *burgoul* (wheat boiled with leaven, and dried in the sun), and allowed to boil for some time, during which it is carefully skimmed. It is then found that the *burgoul* has precipitated all the foreign substances, and that the butter remains quite clear at the top. This is the process used by the Bedouins, and it is also the one employed by the settled people of Syria and Arabia. The chief difference is that in making butter and cheese the townspeople employ the milk of cows and buffaloes, whereas the Bedouins, who do not keep these animals, use that of sheep and goats. The butter is generally white, of the color and consistence of lard, and is not much relished by English travelers. It is eaten with bread in large quantities by those who can afford it, not spread out thinly over the surface, as with us, but taken in mass with the separate morsels of bread. (See BUTTER.)

Figurative. In the greater number of examples it is employed figuratively to denote great abundance, and in many instances it is used as a general term for all or any of the preparations from it.

(1) In its figurative use, the word occurs sometimes alone, as the sign of abundance (Gen. xlix:12; Ezek. xxv:4; Joel iii:18, etc.); but more frequently in combination with honey—*'milk and honey'* being a phrase which occurs about twenty times in Scripture. Thus a rich and fertile soil is described as a *'land flowing with milk and honey';* which, although usually said of Palestine, is also applied to other fruitful countries, as Egypt (Num. xvi:13). Hence its use to denote the food of children.

(2) Milk is also constantly employed as a symbol of the elementary parts or rudiments of doctrine (1 Cor. iii:2; Heb. v:12, 13); and from its purity and simplicity it is also made to symbolize the unadulterated word of God and the blessings of the Gospel. (1 Pet. ii:2; comp. Is. lv:1).

MILL (mĭl), Heb. רֵחֶה, *ray-kheh'*, to pulverize; Gr. μύλων, *moo'lone*, grinder).

The mill for grinding corn had not wholly superseded the mortar for pounding it in the time of Moses. The mortar and the mill are named together in Num. xi:8. But fine meal, that is, meal ground or pounded fine, is mentioned so early as the time of Abraham (Gen. xviii:6); hence mills and mortars must have been previously known. The mill common among the Hebrews differed little from that which is in use to this day throughout Western Asia and Northern Africa. It consisted of two circular stones two feet in diameter, and half a foot thick. The lower is called the 'nether millstone' (Job xli:16, 24), and the upper the 'rider,' רכב (Judg. ix:53; 2 Sam. xi:21). The former was usually fixed to the floor, and had a slight elevation in the center, or, in other words, was slightly convex in the upper surface. The upper stone had a concavity in its under surface fitting to, or receiving, the convexity of the lower stone. There was a hole in the top, through which the corn was introduced by handfuls at a time. The upper stone had an upright stick fixed in it as a handle, by which it was made to turn upon the lower stone, and by this action the corn was ground, and came out at the edges. As there were neither public mills nor bakers, except the king's (Gen. xl:2; Hos. vii:4-8), each family possessed a mill; and as it was in daily use, it was made an infringement of the Law for a person to take another's mill or millstone in pledge (Deut. xxiv:6).

The mill was, as now, commonly turned by two persons, usually women, and these, the work being laborious, the lowest maid-servants in the house. They sat opposite each other. One took hold of the mill-handle, and impelled it half way round; the other then seized it, and completed the revolution (Exod. xi:5; Job xxxi:10, 11; Is. xlvii:2; Matt. xxiv:41). As the labor was severe and menial, enemies taken in war were often condemned to perform it (Judg. xvi:21; Lam. v:13). (Jahn, *Biblisches Archæol.* ix:139.) It will be seen that this millstone does not materially differ from the Highland *quern;* and is, indeed, an obvious resource in those remote quarters, where a population is too thin or too scattered to afford remunerative employment to a miller by trade. In the East this trade is still unknown, the handmill being in general and exclusive use among the corn-consuming, and the mortar among the rice-consuming, nations. (See BREAD; CORN.)

Figurative. (1) Both the millstones were hard, and it seems especially the nethermost, which was fixed; and so the heart of leviathan is likened to a piece of it, to represent his undaunted courage and obstinacy (Job xli:24). (2) The ceasing of the sound of the millstones was a sure sign that a place had been turned into a desolation (Jer. xxv:10; Rev. xviii:22). (3) Christ's falling on men, and grinding them to powder, denotes the final, complete and terrible destruction of those who refuse to yield their wills to him (Matt. xxi:44; Luke xx:18). (4) To "grind the faces of the poor," is cruelly to oppress and afflict them (Is. iii:15). (5) "Let my wife grind to another"; let her become the property of another man, and his slave to work at the mill (Job xxxi:10). Our jaw teeth, which chew our food, are called our "grinders"; and their sound is brought low when they are lost by old age (Eccl. xii:3, 4).

MILLENNIUM (mil-lĕn'nĭ-ŭm), (Lat. *mille,* a thousand, and *annus,* a year).

This word is not found in Scripture; but as it refers to ideas founded on Scripture, a treatment of the doctrine is required. The word denotes the term of a thousand years, and, in a theological sense, that thousand years mentioned in Rev. xx:2, 3, 4, 6, during which Satan is there described as being bound, Christ as reigning triumphant, and the saints as living and reigning with him. The doctrine involved in this view is usually called Millenarianism, but in ecclesiastical history more usually *Chiliasm,* from the Greek word χιλιοι, 'a thousand.' As the world was made in six days, and as, according to Ps. xc:4, 'a thousand years are as one day' in the sight of God, so it was thought the world would continue in the condition in which it had hitherto been for 6,000 years; and as the Sabbath is a day of rest, so will the seventh period of a thousand years consist of this millennial kingdom, as the close of the whole earthly state.

The Jews supposed that the Messiah at his coming would reign as king upon the earth, and would reside at Jerusalem, the ancient royal city. The period of his reign they thought would be very long, and it was therefore put down as a thousand years, which was at first understood only as a round number. This period was conceived by the Jews as a sort of golden age to the earth, and every one formed such a picture of it as agreed with his own disposition, and with the views concerning the highest felicity which were dictated by the degree of intellectual and moral culture to which he had attained. With many these views were very low, being confined to sensual delights, while others entertained better and more pure conceptions of that happy time (Wetstein, *Comment.* in Rev. xxii:2; Knapp, *Christ. Theolog.,* translated by Leonard Woods, Jun., D.D., sec. 154).

This notion was taken up by many of the Judaizing Christians: Jesus had not yet appeared as an earthly king, and these persons were unwilling to abandon an expectation which seemed to them so important. They therefore allowed themselves to hope for a second advent of Christ to establish an earthly kingdom, and to this they transferred most if not all of that which in their unconverted state they had expected of the first. The Apostles generally seem to have entertained this notion till after the ascension of Christ and the outpouring of the Holy Spirit, whereby they were instructed in the higher verities and mysteries of the Gospel; but that they then abandoned it, and expected no other coming of Christ than that at the judgment of the world, appears clear from 1 Cor. xv and other passages. The fact that these Jewish notions had taken deep root in the minds of many Christians, even in the Apostolical age, is, however, manifest from 1 Thess. iv:13, *sq.,* v; and 2 Thess. ii.

The following views are epitomized from *The Seer of Patmos,* by Sir Wm. Dawson:

The millennium which is described in chapter xx of Revelation has attracted much attention from scholars and has become the subject of much controversy, the two centers of criticism being ranged under the heads of "pre-millennial" and "post-millennial" return of our Lord. If, with many able men of our time, we connect the second advent of the Messiah and the resurrection of the saints with the beginning of the millennium, we find these stupendous events very near as indicated by the position which we have reached along the line of events which were foretold by the prophets.

If, on the other hand, we regard the second advent of the Christ as post-millennial, the great event is postponed by the duration of the thousand years and also by the period which is covered by the loosing of Satan, and it is thus connected with the general resurrection and judgment described in chapter xxi and with the New Jerusalem of the closing chapter.

(1) **Nearing Millennial Period.** In either case it would seem that we are now very near the opening of the millennial period. According to the prophecies of Daniel and the statements of the Christ this period is to follow as the next great event after the four successive empires which occupy "the times of the Gentiles."

In order to understand the millennium we must remember that it forms a part of the subject of the prophecies of the things that follow the last septenary of God's judgments on the apostasy and its abettors which are represented by the vials. In the end of chapter xvi these are spoken of as the last plagues, and it is said that men blaspheme God because of them, but the two chapters following contain explanations of this and announce the downfall of the apostasy. Then in chapter xix we have a picture of the marriage of the Lamb and of the bride, the Lamb's wife with her spotless garments.

(2) Final Triumph of the Word. Again the heavens are opened "and behold a white horse; and he that sat upon him was called Faithful and True, . . . and on his head were many crowns; . . . and his name is called The Word of God. . . . And he hath on his vesture and on his thigh a name written, King of kings and Lord of lords."

Here the Lord appears as the "Word of God" and may be considered as representing the final triumph of the "Word" over the three unclean spirits in the sixth vial who have hitherto been going forth "unto the kings of the earth, and to the whole world, to gather them to the battle of that great day of God Almighty," but they are now driven from the field, and their final overthrow, together with that of the beast and the false prophet, is described in unmistakable terms at the close of the chapter.

(3) Binding of the Dragon. In the beginning of chapter xx the angel "laid hold on the dragon, that old serpent which is the Devil and Satan, and bound him for a thousand years." Thus that Satan which has been the instigator of all opposition to God in all ages of the world is shut out from his deceitful work in influencing mankind. The "bottomless pit" or abyss may be a part of the earth, for in a previous passage pertaining to the fifth trumpet, the locusts which typify the Saracen invaders are said to come from the pit or abyss, thus representing the outlying parts of the world— those which are beyond the limits of Christendom.

(4) Revival of the Pure Faith. The description of the millennium plainly indicates a revival of the pure faith and practice of primitive Christianity. It is to be remembered that the Protestant Reformation did not effect this. During the millennial period these will be brought back to their best estate and become dominant, and this state of things will continue during the thousand years. Seated upon the thrones of judgment there are two bodies of judges, the one being "the souls of them that were beheaded for the witness of Jesus and for the Word of God," and the others are those who "had not worshiped the beast, neither his image, neither had received his mark in their foreheads, or in their hands, and they lived and reigned with Christ a thousand years."

(5) A New Heaven and New Earth. At present we are unable to fully comprehend the conditions and details which are connected with any judgment scene, but there must surely be "a new heaven and a new earth, for the first heaven and the first earth were passed away."

The book closes with a description of the New Jerusalem, and its last thought is the promise of the coming of the Christ and John's loving response, "Even so, come Lord Jesus." This is the thought which is presented throughout the New Testament as the sustaining hope of the church, and here it is placed side by side with her final blessedness as the fulfillment of her hopes and prayer and faith. During all her pilgrimage it has been one of the incentives to her loyalty and courage in time of trial, and in the final picture she is reaping the reward of her faith and her patience.

Surely we may well join in the fervent invitation, "Even so, come Lord Jesus."

(See *Enquiry into the Prospects of the Christian Church;* Anderson, *Apolog. for Millen. Doct.,* Glasg. 1830; Irving, *Lect. on the Revelat.,* 1831; Greswell, *Exposition of the Parables,* 1834-35; Pigou, *The Millennium,* 1837; *Millenniarism Unscriptural,* 1838; Jefferson, *The Millennium,* 1840; Bush, *The Millennium,* Salem (N. S.), 1842; Hopkins, *Second Adventism in the Light of Jewish Hist.,* 1873, N. Y.; Carson, *The Personal Reign of Christ,* 1873; see also *Poole's Index* for magazine articles.)

MILLENNIUM, VIEWS ON THE, CONTRASTED.

Two contrasted articles are herein given on the Pre-Millennium and Post-Millennium beliefs.

1. Pre-Millennial View. Millenarian doctrine, known in former years as Chiliasm, has since the foundation of the Church, been the Christian's blessed hope. Throughout her variable history, even when she was seemingly eclipsed, the Church of God never lost sight of this brilliant star in her eschatological sky.

In comparatively recent years, Whitbyism assumed that the millennial era would constitute the period of Christ's spiritual reign, as opposed to literal, and therefore predicated, universal salvation in this age. Accordingly, a conquered world, and an enthroned church, were to be the harbingers of our Lord's return. Pre-millennialists consider Whitby's mode of interpretation akin to Origen's fanciful method of exegesis, and therefore unreliable.

Pre-millennialism is a term of comparative newness. It was not needed in theological discussion for centuries. Post-millennialism having become popularized, it must needs be employed, in order to define the view held by the primitive church, that Christ will literally return from the heavens in order to effect the restitution foretold by the holy prophets (Acts iii:19-21). The re-genesis of nature and restoration of nations included in the promised restitution will occupy one thousand years, the duration of Earth's antitypical Sabbath, including the resurrection of all believers, the imprisonment of Satan, with the destruction of the Antichrist. This hope, as ever imminent, was the strong consolation of early believers, while martyrs in their sufferings were sustained through its constant expectation.

Pre-millennialism has a notable history. During dark days, oft-recurring, when superstition and superficial views of religious life prevailed; when worldliness came in like a flood, and idolatrous practices abounded, this polestar of the church grew dim to the point of evanishment. But yet again its brightness grew apace, until now, when its intensified light shines afar. During the century just ended it was brought into prominent recognition. The highest Biblical scholarship has emphatically indorsed pre-millennialism as an integral part of the gospel scheme, and its profound literature has taken rank among essential theological disquisitions. Many of its living advocates are foremost in Biblical research, are identified with aggressive, world-wide evangelism, and also intensely loyal to orthodox evangelicalism and to inerrant Biblical inspiration.

Pre-millennialism does not base its claims on any single proof-text, or series of texts, but rather on the whole trend of Scripture revelation. The much controverted passage in the Apocalypse (ch. xx:1-6) they explain in the glowing light of multiplied predictions. The learned Alford declared that the whole church for three hundred years understood the above verses in a plain, literal sense. John Albert Bengel, first of exegetes, gave unequivocal testimony to the view that Christ would come before the millennium, and in this hope John Wesley, who was taught it by Bengel, exulted. Prof. Hackett, interpreting Acts iii:19-21, voiced the conviction of many Christian scholars, that the Coming of Christ "was the great consummation on which the strongest desires of their souls (the first believers) were fixed . . . . they lived in expectation of it; they labored to be prepared for it."

Pre-millennialism protests against the application of those parables and discourses of our Lord which clearly point to a new kingdom, introduced and established on his return, to natural phenomena, such as death, war, national calamities and natural convulsions. These frequently recurring events are too superficial as adequate fulfillment of divine prophecy.

Pre-millennialists believe that those Old Testament predictions of the sufferings and glories of Messiah bound the present age. They are as mountain peaks between which lie the Church, and beyond the Millennial Kingdom.

Pre-millennialists believe that the Bible given in the language of men must be interpreted by such rules as govern that language; that the literal meaning of a word be retained until it be determined that the language is figurative. Prophecy frequently appears in symbolic form, but most Scripture symbols are explained in the Scriptures.

In addition to Old Testament predictions is New Testament promise inciting millennial expectation. Several hundred texts emphatically and inferentially teach that our Lord will return visibly, bodily, audibly, gloriously, and that the world's condition at the time of his arrival precludes all possibility of a millennium prior to that event. The age of Noah and the days of Lot prefigure our time-end, thereby harmonizing with parabolic and didactic teaching. The field of wheat and tares, the flock of sheep and goats, the net of good and bad fish prove that evil is not minimized as the age approaches its consummation. Accordingly, the last days, and the latter times are vividly sketched in their woeful degeneracy (1 Tim. iv:1-3; 2 Tim. iii:1-5). Therefore, pre-millennialism holds out no hope of a converted world before the *Parousia*. Results of the Advent will include the resurrection of believers unto glory, life to dead Israel, and liberty for groaning creation. The new kingdom will be clean from Satan's presence when the glory of Jehovah will be revealed, and the will of God be done on the earth, even as it is done in heaven. The shekinah will again appear in the Holy Land when the pierced feet of our glorious Lord shall stand on the Mount of Olives (1 Thess. iv:15-18; Rom. viii:15, 22-23; Rev. xx:1-3; Is. iv:5; Zech. xiv:4).   G. C. N.

2. Post-Millennialism. Ever since the days of the Apostles the Church has looked forward to a better day, when the reigning powers of idolatry and superstition, and all forms of false religion, shall give place to the kingdom of God, and when Jesus Christ will be confessed as Lord among all the nations of the earth. It is impossible to interpret the Scriptures without anticipating a universal diffusion of the knowledge of God and of his Son Jesus Christ, to the extent that the religion of the Bible shall become the religion of mankind throughout the earth. But when shall this better day dawn? By what agencies shall it be brought about?

(1) Difference of Opinion. The great division of the Church is into classes known as Pre-millenarians and Post-millenarians—a division which does not follow denominational lines or imply serious differences upon evangelical doctrines or on questions of vital piety and practical godliness. It is a difference in belief as to whether Christ's second coming will take place at the beginning or the ending of the millennial period; and, of course, it involves different ideas of the character of the millennium—for a millennium with Christ present in person, with the saints of all ages living in the resurrection state, is widely different from one where Christ reigns spiritually in the hearts of his people, who yet live in their mortal bodies while he remains in heaven. It is to this division of sentiment our minds are turned in considering the second coming of the Son of man. Will he come in person and raise the righteous dead, and establish a literal kingdom in this world, and reign a thousand years, and thus subdue the world to himself? Or will he come at the end of time and raise the dead and judge the world, and thus finish the history of earthly life by introducing the eternal state of retribution? Pre-millennialists assert the former, and Post-millennialists the latter.

(2) Basis of Pre-millennial Theory. The Pre-millennial advent theory is based entirely upon a Scripture which is acknowledged by all to be very obscure, in addition to being found in the book of Revelation, in the midst of symbols extremely difficult of explanation and application (Rev. xx:1, 8).

It is assumed by some that the "angel" which had "the key of the bottomless pit, and the great chain in his hand," was none other than Christ himself. But there is absolutely no intimation whatever in this celebrated passage of Scripture, that Christ descends from heaven at the beginning of this "thousand years."

(3) Condition of the World. But what of the millennium, if the idea of the coming of Christ at the imprisonment of Satan be abandoned? To state precisely the condition of the world at the coming of Christ, whether that coming be at the beginning or ending of the millennium in question, is one of the most difficult tasks the expositor of the Scriptures is called to perform. Turn as he will, there are seeming contradictions to be encountered. To admit this is due to candor, and where it is not admitted we suspect the presence of prepossessions unfavorable to impartial exegesis.

(4) Two Classes of Texts. There are two classes of Scripture to be considered—those passages that represent the carelessness and worldliness of the unbelieving and unready, and those that describe the universal triumph of the Gospel, and the prosperity of the Church in the latter days. By looking only at one class we get distorted views.

(1) First Class. Some of the first class look as if the world were never darker or more forgetful of God than in the hour when the Son of man shall come "as a thief in the night." "But as the days of Noah were, so shall also the coming of the Son of man be." "Then shall two be in the field; the one shall be taken, and the other left. Two women shall be grinding at the mill; the one shall be taken, and the other left." This shows that some will be going on in the ordinary pursuits of life, forgetful of spiritual things, as at the present time, and as in the time before the Flood. And that question in the parable of the widow and the unjust judge, "Nevertheless,

when the Son of man cometh. shall he find faith on the earth?" looks in the same direction, and seems to suggest a doubt whether any will be found faithful. But these relate to the unbelieving. They give the worldly side of the picture. There is no doubt that "the day of the Lord" will come unawares upon many, and surprise them in their sins.

(2) *The Other Side.* But there is another side. The Church is to grow, and spread far and wide her holy influences, so as to leave the unthinking worldliness of the age without excuse. "This Gospel of the kingdom shall be preached in all the world for a witness unto all nations." "The mountain of the Lord's house shall be established in the top of the mountains, and all nations shall flow unto it." The name of Christ shall be known from the rising of the sun unto the going down thereof. The knowledge of God shall cover the earth. "For the earth shall be full of the knowledge of the Lord, as the waters cover the sea." The time will come when it shall be said, "The kingdoms of this world are become the kingdoms of our Lord, and of his Christ; and he shall reign forever and ever." What, then, must be the conclusion from this seeming contrariety of description?

In all probability, some of the passages relating to the glory of the latter days, in their ultimate meaning, look to the condition of things in the regenerated earth, beyond the conflagration.

(5) **Better Things.** And yet, as we have said, we cannot explain the Scriptures without anticipating a day of better things for the Church than has been realized. The imprisonment of Satan denotes curtailment of his power, and increased restraint upon his actions, possibly to the extent of hindering his access to men in this world. This will be great gain in advantage for the truth. It will give the Gospel access to the heart, impeded only by the opposition of the depravity within. Under such conditions, the relative power of the Gospel will increase; the accumulated evidences of its divinity will shine out with a luster unseen before; and the quickened activities of Christian people will add to its efficiency, as its conquests are extended, and its victories multiplied. But will every living soul be converted? We dare not assume this. The universal spread of the Gospel neither implies the removal of depravity from human nature nor the submission of every sinner to the sway of divine grace. Men will still be descended from Adam, born after the flesh, and need to be "born again." But Christian intelligence will banish superstition. Idolatry will cease. Apostate churches will be reformed or destroyed. False religions will be overthrown. Enlightened governments, permeated with Christian principles, will displace tyrannies, and religious liberty will become the heritage of all the nations. This much may be expected, and such a millennium will be indescribably glorious. But the old fight with inward corruption will go on. Carnality, and selfishness, and pride, and love of the world, and love of power, will struggle for the mastery, calling for watchfulness and self-denial, and keeping up all the conditions of a real probation. And some will be overborne. Infidelity will find votaries. Men of evil passion will love darkness rather than light. Such will shut their eyes to the brightest beams of the brightest day of Gospel light, and when Satan is loose, they will be ready to join in the battle against the truth. Thus, in the final day of the Lord's coming, will worldliness and sin be found in the earth. So we read

the prophecies. But we "see through a glass darkly." The best lights that reach our vision disclose only the mountain peaks of the land ahead. The valleys and plains of the landscape lie beneath the mists. We must wait till prophecy materializes into history, and then the morning star shall give place to the risen sun.   S. M. M.

MILLET (mĭl'lĕt). See DOKHAN.

MILLO (mĭl'lo), (Heb. with the article, הַמִּלּוֹא *ham-mil-lo'*, heights).

This word denotes 'fullness,' and is applied to a mound or rampart, probably as being filled up with stones or earth. Hence it is the name given to

1. Part of the citadel of Jerusalem, probably the rampart (2 Sam. v:9; 1 Kings ix:15, 24; xi: 27; 1 Chron. xi:8; 2 Chron. xxxii:5). In the last of these texts, where David is said to have restored or fortified Millo 'of' (not 'in') the city of David, the Sept. has τὸ ἀνάλημμα τῆς πόλεως, 'the fortification of the city of David.'

2. The fortress in Shechem. 'All the men of Shechem, and all that dwelt in the house of Millo;' that is, in the castle or citadel (Judg. ix:16, 20), probably the place where Joash was killed (2 Kings xii:20).

MILLSTONE (mĭl'stōn'). See MILL.

MINA (mī'na), so rendered in the margin (Luke xix:13) of the Greek μνα, but in the text as "pound." (See WEIGHTS AND MEASURES.)

MINCHAH (mĭn'kah), the Hebrew name of the bloodless offerings (meal, cakes, etc.), presented in the Temple. (See OFFERING.)

MINCING (mĭn'sĭng), (Heb. טָפַף, *taw-faf'*, Is. iii:16), to take short steps, just putting the heel of one foot against the toe of the other. The prophet condemns the effort of women old in years and sin to imitate the movements of children.

MINES, MINING (mīns, mīn'ĭng), (Job xxviii: 1-11 R. V.). See COPPER; IRON; and other metals.

MINGLED PEOPLE (mĭn'g'ld pē'p'l), (Heb. עֶרֶב, *ay'reb*, mixture).

"Mingled people" are such as originally belonged to different tribes or nations (Jer. xxv:20, 24; l:37; Ezek. xxx:5). The "mixed multitude" that attended the Hebrews in their departure from Egypt were Arabs, Egyptians, Lybians, etc. They first tempted the Hebrews to despise the manna (Num. xi:4). They generally either died in the wilderness, returned to Egypt, or settled in Arabia. The *mixed multitude* which Nehemiah separated from the Jews were the Philistines, Ammonites, Moabites, and others who had come and intermarried among them (Neh. xiii:3).

God *"mingled"* the Jews' adversaries when he raised up many at once (Is. xix:11). His *"mingling the Egyptians with the Egyptians"*, and *"mingling a perverse spirit among them,"* denotes his kindling of civil wars among them (Is. xix:2, 14). The Romans *"mingled themselves with the seed of men,"* but did not cleave to them; they dwelt in the same countries with the Goths, Huns, and other invaders of the empire; but they never had a heartiness of affection for them (Dan. ii:43).

MINIAMIN (mĭn-i-a'mĭn), (Heb. מִנְיָמִין, *min-yaw-meen'*, from the right hand).

1. A Levite who had charge of the free-will offerings in the Temple and distributed them among the families of the sacerdotal order in the time of Hezekiah (2 Chron. xxxi:15), B. C. 726.

2. A priest who returned from captivity with Zerubbabel, and joined in the celebration over the completion of the walls (Neh. xii:17, 41). The name is elsewhere given as *Miamin* (xii:5), or *Mijamin* (x:7).

MINISTER (mĭn'ĭs-tēr), one who acts as a lesser (from *minus* or *minor*) or inferior agent, in obedience or subservience to another, or who serves, officiates, etc., as distinguished from the master, *magister* (from *magis*), or superior.

1. The words so translated in the Old Testament are מְשָׁרֵת, *mesh-aw-rayth'*, and פֶּלַח, *pel-akh'*, (Chald.), and in the New, διάκονος, *dee-ak'o-nos*, servant, and ὑπηρέτης, *hoop-ay-ret'ace*, under-laborer. Moses and his minister, Joshua, are mentioned in Exod. xxiv:13.

2. It is applied to Elisha as minister to Elijah (2 Kings vi:15; Sept. *lei-toor-gos'*, λειτουργός, *public servant;* comp. 2 Kings iii:11; 1 Kings xix:21). Persons thus designated sometimes succeeded to the office of their principal, as did Joshua and Elisha. The word is applied to the angels (Ps. ciii:21, *public servants;* comp. Ps. civ:4; Heb. i:7; and see Stuart's *Comment. in loc.*). Both the Hebrew and Sept. words are applied to the Jews in their capacity as a sacred nation, 'Men shall call you the ministers of our God' (Is. lxi:6); to the priests (Jer. xxxiii:21; Ezek. xliv:11; xlv:4; Joel i:9).

The Greek word is continued in the same sense in Luke i:23, and applied to Christian teachers (Acts xiii:2; Rom. xv:16; and to Christ, Heb. viii:2); to the collectors of the Roman tribute, in consequence of the divine authority of political government, 'they are God's ministers' (λειτουργοί). It was applied by the Athenians to those who administered the public offices (λειτουργίαι) at their own expense (Bœckh).

3. (1) The word διάκονος, *dee-ak'on-os*, 'minister,' is applied to Christian teachers (1 Cor. iii:5; 2 Cor. iii:6; vi:4; xi:23; 1 Thess. iii:2); (2) to false teachers (2 Cor. xi:15); to Christ (Rom. xv:8, 16; Gal. ii:17; (3) to heathen magistrates (Rom. xiii:4); in all which passages it has the sense of a minister, assistant, or servant in general, as in Matt. xx:26; but it means a particular sort of minister, 'a deacon,' in Phil. i:1; 1 Tim. iii:8, 12). The term διάκονοι, *dee-ak-on-oi*, ministers, denotes among the Greeks a higher class of servants than the *doo'loi*, δοῦλοι, slaves (Ahen. x:192; B. comp. Xen. *l. c.* Buttm. *Lexic.* i:220; comp. Matt. xxii:13, and Esth. i:3; ii:2; vi:3). (4) ὑπηρέτης, *hoop-ay-ret'ace*, helper, is applied to Christian ministers (Luke i:2; Acts xxvi:16; 2 Cor. iv:1). Josephus calls Moses τὸν ὑπηρέτην Θεοῦ, *God's helper, Antiq.* iii:1-4. Kings are so called in Wisd. vi:4. (5) The word denotes, in Luke iv:20, the attendant in a synagogue who handed the volume to the reader, and returned it to its place. (6) In Acts xiii:5 it is applied to 'John whose surname was Mark,' in his capacity as an attendant or assistant on Barnabas and Saul. It primarily signifies an under-rower on board a galley, of the class who used the longest oars, and consequently performed the severest duty, as distinguished from the *thran-ee'tace* θρανίτης, the rower upon the upper bench of the three, and from the *hoi-naw'tay*, οἱ ναῦται, sailors, or the *ep-ee-bat'ay*, ἐπιβάται, marines (Dem. 1209. 11, 14; comp. also 1208, 20; 1214, 23; 1216, 13; Pol. i, 25, 3); hence in general a hand, agent, minister, attendant, etc. J. F. D.

MINNI (mĭn'nī), (Heb. מִנִּי, *min-nee'*, division) See ARMENIA.

MINNITH (mĭn'nith), (Heb. מִנִּית, *min-neeth*, distribution), a town in the country of the Ammonites (Judg. xi:33), celebrated for the excellence of its wheat, which was exported to the markets of Tyre (Ezek. xxvii:17).

It still existed in the age of Eusebius four Roman miles from Heshbon, on the road to Philadelphia. The Sept. seem to have found difficulty in this name. In Judg. xi:33 they substitute the name of the Arnon, and in Ezek. xxvii:17 they render it by μύρον, 'myrrh.'

It was probably located about four Roman miles east of Heshbon, now thought to be Mineh, where there are traces of terraces and walls.

MINSTREL (mĭn'strĕl), (Heb. מְנַגֵּן, *men-ag-gayn'*, one striking the harp; Gr. αὐλητής, *ow-lay-tace'*, a musician).

Perhaps the minstrel which Elisha called for, to allay his ruffled spirit with a tune, might be one of the singers of the Temple, who played to him one of David's Psalms (2 Kings iii:15). From minstrels playing at the death of Jairus's daughter, it seems, that the Jews had introduced the heathenish custom of diverting themselves on occasion of mortality; and which still appears in foolish light-wakes and reveling dirges (Matt. ix:23). Brown.

MINT (mĭnt). See HEDUOSMON.

MIPHKAD (mĭph'kăd), (Heb. מִפְקָד, *mif-kawd'*, appointment, census), a gate at Jerusalem (Neh. iii:31), probably identical with the prison gate (Neh. xii:39), under the bridge over the Tyropœon valley.

MIRACLES (mĭr'ȧ-k'ls), (Lat. *miraculum*, from *mirari.* to wonder).

God sees fit to carry on his common operations on established and uniform principles.

(1) The Laws of Nature. These principles, whether relating to the physical or moral world, are called *the laws of nature.* And by the laws of nature the most enlightened philosophers and divines have understood *the uniform plan according to which,* or *the uniform manner in which, God exercises his power throughout the created universe.*

This uniform method of divine operation is evidently conducive to the most important ends. It manifests the immutable wisdom and goodness of God, and, in ways too many to be here specified, promotes the welfare of his creatures. Without the influence of this uniformity, rational beings would have no effectual motive to effort, and the affairs of the universe, intelligent and unintelligent, would be in a state of total confusion. And this general fact may be considered as a sufficient reason why God, in the common course of his providence, has adopted a uniform method of operation in preference to any other.

(2) Divine Interposition. But if, in conducting the affairs of his great empire, God sees, in any particular case, as good a reason for a *deviation* from this uniform order, as there is generally for *uniformity,* that is, if the glory of his attributes and the good of his creatures require it—and no one can say that such a case may not occur—then, unquestionably, the unchangeable God will cause such a deviation; in other words, will work *miracles.*

It is admitted that no man, apart from the knowledge of facts, could ever, by mere reasoning, have arrived at a confident belief, that the conjuncture supposed would certainly occur. But to us, who know that mankind are so depraved and wretched, and that the efforts of human wisdom to obtain relief have been in vain, the importance of a special divine interposition is very apparent. And being informed what the plan is, which a merciful God has adopted for our recovery to holiness and happiness, and being satisfied that this plan, so perfectly suited to the end in view, could never have been discovered by man, and never executed, except by a divine dispensation involving miracles, we conclude that the introduction of a new and miraculous dispensation was in the highest degree an honor to God and a blessing to the world.

(3) Revelation. The method of divine appointment, as set forth in the sacred volume, is that of making a revelation to a number of individuals, who are to write and publish it for the benefit of the world. This revelation to individuals is made in such a manner as renders it certain to their minds, that the revelation is from God. But how can that revelation be made available to others? It will not answer the purpose for those who receive it merely to declare that God has made such a revelation to them, and authorized them to proclaim it to their fellow creatures. For how shall we know that they are not deceivers? Or if their character is such as to repel any suspicion of this kind, how shall we know that they are not themselves deceived?

(4) Attestation. Have we not a right, nay, are we not bound in duty, to ask for evidence? But what evidence will suffice? The reply is obvious. The revelation, in order to be of use to us, as it is to those who receive it directly from God, must not only be declared by them to us, but must have a divine attestation. In other words, those who declare it to us must show, by some incontestable proof, that *it is from God.* Such proof is found in a miracle. If an event takes place which we know to be contrary to the laws of nature, we at once recognize it as the special act of him who is the God of nature, and who alone can suspend its laws, and produce effects in another way. The evidence of a direct interposition of God given in this way is irresistible. No man, no infidel, could witness an obvious miracle, without being struck with awe, and recognizing *the finger of God.*

It is clear that no event which can be accounted for on natural principles, can prove a supernatural interposition, or contain a divine attestation to the truth of a prophet's claim. But when we look at an event which cannot be traced to the laws of nature, and is clearly above them, such as the burning of the wood upon the altar in the case of Elijah's controversy with the false prophets, or the resurrection of Lazarus, we cannot avoid the conviction, that the Lord of heaven and earth does, by such a miracle, give his testimony, that Elijah is his prophet, and that Jesus is the Messiah. The evidence arising from miracles is so striking and conclusive, that there is no way for an infidel to evade it, but to deny the existence of miracles, and to hold that all the events called miraculous may be accounted for according to the laws of nature.

(5) Uniform Experience. Hume arrays *uniform experience* against the credibility of miracles. But the shallow sophistry of his argument has been fully exposed by Campbell, Paley and many others. We inquire what and how much he means by *uniform experience.* Does he mean his own experience? But because *he* has never witnessed a miracle, does it follow that others have not? Does he mean the uniform experience of the greater part of mankind? But how does he

know that the experience of a smaller part has not been different from that of the greater part? Does he mean, then, the uniform experience of all mankind in all ages? How, then, does his argument stand? He undertakes to prove that no man has ever witnessed or experienced a miracle, and his real argument is, that no one *has* ever witnessed or experienced it. In other words, to *prove* that there has never been a miracle, he *asserts* that there never has been a miracle. This is the nature of his argument—an instance of *petitio principii,* to which a man of Hume's logical powers would never have resorted, had it not been for his enmity to religion.

(6) Genuineness. The miraculous events recorded in the Scriptures, particularly those which took place in the times of Moses and Christ, have all the marks which are necessary to prove them to have been matters of fact, and worthy of full credit, and to distinguish them from the feats of jugglers and impostors. This has been shown very satisfactorily by Leslie, Paley, Douglas, and many others. These miracles took place in the most public manner, and in the presence of many witnesses; so that there was opportunity to subject them to the most searching scrutiny. Good men and bad men were able and disposed to examine them thoroughly, and to prove them to have been impostures, if they had been so.

A large number of men of unquestionable honesty and intelligence constantly affirmed that the miracles took place before their eyes. And some of these original witnesses wrote and published histories of the facts, in the places where they were alleged to have occurred, and near the time of their occurrence. In these histories it was openly asserted that the miracles, as described, were publicly known and acknowledged to have taken place; and this no one took upon him to contradict, or to question. Moreover, many persons who stood forth as witnesses of these miracles passed their lives in labors, dangers, and sufferings, in attestation of the accounts they delivered, and solely in consequence of their belief of the truth of those accounts; and, from the same motive, they voluntarily submitted to new rules of conduct; while nothing like this is true respecting any other pretended miracles. (See Paley's *Evidences.*)

(7) Wicked Spirits. It has been a long agitated question, whether miracles have ever been wrought, or can be consistently supposed to be wrought, *by apostate spirits.*

It is sufficient to say here, that it would be evidently inconsistent with the character of God to empower or to suffer wicked beings to work miracles *in support of falsehood.* And if wicked spirits in the time of Christ had power to produce preternatural effects upon the minds or bodies of men, and if those effects are to be ranked among real miracles (which, however, we do not affirm), still the end of miracles is not contravened. For those very operations of evil spirits were under the control of divine providence, and were made in two ways to subserve the cause of Christ. First, they furnished an occasion, as doubtless they were designed to do, for Christ to show his power over evil spirits, and, by his superior miracles, to give a new proof of his Messiahship. Secondly, the evil spirits themselves were constrained to give their testimony, that Jesus was the Christ, the Holy One of Israel.

(8) Close of Dispensation. As to the time when the miraculous dispensation ceased, we can only remark that the power of working miracles, which belonged preëminently to Christ and his apostles, and, in inferior degrees, to many other Christians in the apostolic age, subsided gradually. After the great object of supernatural works was accomplished in the establishment of the Christian religion, with all its sacred truths, and its divinely appointed institutions, during the life of Christ and his apostles, there appears to have been no further occasion for miracles, and no satisfactory evidence that they actually occurred. Wardlaw, *On Miracles,* 1852, N. Y.; Trench, *Miracles of Our Lord;* Evans, *Christian Miracles,* Lond., 1861; McCosh, *The Supernatural in Relation to the Natural;* Mozley, *Lectures on Miracles* (Bampton, 1865); Mountford, *Miracles, Past and Present* (Boston, 1870); Upham, *Star of Our Lord* (N. Y., 1873); Fowle, *Religion and Science* (1873); Christlieb. *Mod. Doubts,* 1874; Smith, *First Lines of Christian Theol.*

L. W.

of Kadesh-barnea (Num. xx:1), where her sepulcher was still to be seen in the time of Eusebius.

2. Son of Mered, a man of Judah, a descendant of Caleb and Ezra (1 Chron. iv:17), B. C. about 1658.

MIRMA (mir'mà), (Heb. מִרְמָה, *meer-maw'*, deceit), a chief of the tribe of Benjamin; the son of Shaharaim by Hodesh (1 Chron. viii:10). B. C. after 1612.

MIRROR (mĭr'rēr), (Heb. מַרְאָה, *mar-aw'*, Exod. xxxviii:8; רְאִי, *reh-ee'*, Job xxxvii:18).

In the first of these passages the mirrors in the possession of the women of the Israelites, when they left Egypt, are described as being of brass; for 'the laver of brass, and the foot of it,' are made from them. In the second, the firmament is compared to 'a molten mirror.' In fact, all the

MIRACLES IN THE APOSTOLIC AGE.

MIRACLES.	PLACE.	RECORD.
The outpouring of the Spirit on the day of Pentecost............	Jerusalem	Acts ii:1-11
Miracles by the apostles..	Jerusalem	Acts ii:43; v:12, 15, 16
Lame man cured..	Jerusalem	Acts iii:7
Death of Ananias and Sapphira.................................	Jerusalem	Acts v:1, 10
Apostles delivered from prison.................................	Jerusalem	Acts v:19
Miracles by Stephen..	Jerusalem	Acts vi:8
Miracles by Philip...	Samaria	Acts viii:6, 7, 13
Æneas made whole..	Lydda	Acts ix:34
Dorcas restored to life..	Joppa	Acts ix:40
Peter delivered from prison....................................	Jerusalem	Acts xii:6-10
Elymas struck blind...	Paphos	Acts xiii:11
Miracles by Paul and Barnabas.................................	Iconium	Acts xiv:3
Lame man cured..	Lystra	Acts xiv:10
Paul restored...	Lystra	Acts xiv:20
Unclean spirits cast out......................................	Philippi	Acts xvi:18
Paul and Silas delivered from prison..........................	Philippi	Acts xvi:25, 26
Special miracles..	Ephesus	Acts xix:11, 12
Eutychus restored to life.....................................	Troas	Acts xx:10-12
Paul unhurt by a viper..	Melita	Acts xxviii:5
Father of Publius and many others healed......................	Melita	Acts xxviii:8, 9

(For Table Miracles of Jesus Christ, see Appendix, p. 54.)

MIRAGE (mĕ'rȧzh'), an optical illusion frequently witnessed in the East (Heb. שָׁרָב, *shaw-rawb'*, "parched ground," Is. xxxv:7; "heat," xlix:10). (See PARCHED GROUND.)

MIRIAM (mĭr'i-am), (Heb. מִרְיָם, *meer-yawm'*, bitterness; Sept. Μαριάμ, *Mariam;* Josephus, Μαριάμνη, *Mariamne*).

1. Sister of Moses and Aaron, and supposed to be the same that watched her infant brother when exposed on the Nile; in which case she was probably ten or twelve years old at the time (Exod. ii:4, *sq.*). When the Israelites left Egypt, Miriam naturally became the leading woman among them. She is called 'a prophetess' (Exod. xv:20). After the passage of the Red Sea, she led the music, dance and song, with which the women celebrated their deliverance (Exod. xv: 20-22). The arrival of Moses' wife in the camp seems to have created in her an unseemly dread of losing her influence and position, and led her into complaints of and dangerous reflections upon Moses, in which Aaron joined. For this she was smitten with leprosy, and, although healed at the intercession of Moses, was excluded for seven days from the camp (Num. xii; Deut. xxiv:9). Her death took place in the first month of the fortieth year after the Exodus, at the encampment

mirrors used in ancient times were of metal; and as those of the Hebrew women in the wilderness were brought out of Egypt, they were doubtless of the same kind as those which have been found in the tombs of that country, and many of which now exist in our museums and collections of Egyptian antiquities. These are of mixed metals, chiefly copper, most carefully wrought and highly polished; and so admirably did the skill of the Egyptians succeed in the composition of metals that this substitute for our modern looking-glass was susceptible of a luster which has even been partially revived at the present day in some of those discovered at Thebes, though buried in the earth for so many centuries. The mirror itself was nearly round, and was inserted in a handle of wood, stone, or metal, the form of which varied according to the taste of the owner. (See Wilkinson's *Ancient Egyptians,* iii:384-386.)

The metal of which the mirrors were composed, being liable to rust and tarnish, required to be constantly kept bright (Wisd. vii:26; Ecclus. xii:11). This was done by means of pounded pumice-stone, rubbed on with a sponge, which was generally suspended from the mirror. The obscure image produced by a tarnished or imperfect mirror appears to be alluded to in 1 Cor. xiii:12. (Smith, *Bib. Dict.*) (See GLASS; LOOKING-GLASS.)

MISCHIEF. Several words in the Scriptures are thus rendered:

1. *Rah* (Heb. רַע, bad, evil, sorrow, adversity, affliction, etc. (Exod. xxxii:12, 22; 1 Sam. xxiii:9; 2 Sam. xvi:8; 1 Kings xi:25, etc).

2. *Aw'ven* (Heb. אָוֶן, perhaps panting), to apply oneself in vain, and applied to idolatry, wickedness, injustice, etc. (Ps. lv:10; lxii:3; Ezek. xi:2).

3. *Aw-sone'* (Heb. אָסוֹן, meaning harm, hurt), (Gen. xlii:4, 38; Exod. xxi:22, 23; xxxii:12, 22).

4. *Aw-mawl'* (Heb. עָמָל, toil, wearing effort), worry of mind, undue strain of the body, or wrong-doing as resulting in sorrow, trouble, etc. (Ps. vii: 14, 16; xciv:20; Prov. xxiv:2; Is. lix. 4).

5. *Hrad-ee-oorg-ee'a* (Gr. ῥᾳδιουργία, ease in doing, cunning, overreaching, unscrupulousness (Acts xiii:10, R. V. "villainy").

Figurative. (1) To imagine *mischief* against God is to contrive methods of dishonoring him (Hos. vii:15). (2) Wicked men have *mischief* under their tongue, in their heart, and are in readiness to utter words, tending to their own or others' hurt (Ps. x:7). (3) They sleep not except they have done *mischief*, and caused some to fall; they daily hurt somebody, and are never more delighted than when so employed (Prov. iv:16 and vi:18 and x:23 and xxiv:2). (4) Their *mischief returns on their head,* and the *mischief of their lips consumes them,* when their purposes, endeavors, and speeches, designed for the hurt of others, turn to their own ruin, as happened in the case of Haman (Ps. vii:16 and lii:2). *Mischievous,* is what tends or intends to hurt (Ps. xxi:11; Prov. xxiv:8).

MISGAB (mĭs'găb), (Heb. מִשְׂגָּב, *mis-gawb'*, height), a city of Moab, on the line of march of the invading Assyrians (Jer. xlviii:1), but not identified.

MISHAEL (mĭsh'a-el), (Heb. מִישָׁאֵל, *mee-shaw-ale'*, who is like God?)

1. One of the three companions of Daniel, who were cast into the burning furnace by Nebuchadnezzar, and were miraculously delivered from it (Dan. iii:13-30). The Chaldæan name was MESHACH (Dan. i:7). B. C. about 580.

2. One of those who stood at Ezra's left when he expounded the law to the people (Neh. viii:4), B. C. 410.

3. A Levite, son of Uzziel, and grandson of Kohath (Exod. vi:22). He, with his brother Elzaphan, were ordered by Moses to bury the bodies of the two men who were struck dead for offering strange fire (Lev. x:4), B. C. 1657. Perhaps the same two are intended in Num. ix:6.

MISHAL (mī'shal), (Heb. מִשְׁאָל, *mish-awl'*, depression).

A city of Asher, yielded to the Levites of the family of Gershom (1 Chron. vi:74), is said by Eusebius to have been in the vicinity of Mount Carmel near the sea. In Josh. xix:26, it is called Misheal, and in xxi:30, Mishal. Not identified.

MISHAM (mī'sham), (Heb. מִשְׁעָם, *mish-awm'*, purification or swift going), a Benjamite, son of Elpaal, and one of the restorers of Ono and Lod (1 Chron. viii:12), B. C. after 1612.

MISHEAL (mī'she-al), (Josh. xix:26). See MISHAL.

MISHMA (mĭsh'mà), (Heb. מִשְׁמָע, *mish-maw'*, fame or report).

1. A Simeonite, son of Mibsam (1 Chron. iv: 25, 26), B. C. before 1053.

2. Fifth son of Ishmael, and head of an Arabian tribe (Gen. xxv:14; 1 Chron. i:30). A trace of the name is perhaps to be found in the *Jebel Misma,* between Damascus and Jarif, or the one 150 miles east of Taima.

MISHMANNAH (mish-măn'nah), (Heb. מִשְׁמַנָּה, *mish-man-naw'*, strength, fatness, vigor), a Gadite who came to David at Ziklag (1 Chron. xii:10). B. C. about 1061.

MISHNAH (mĭsh'nah). See TALMUD.

MISHRAITES (mĭsh'ra-ītes), (Heb. הַמִּשְׁרָעִי, *ham-mish-raw-ee'*), the inhabitants of a place founded by one of the families of Kirjath-jearim, but not otherwise mentioned (1 Chron. ii:53).

MISPERETH (mĭs'pe-reth), (Heb. מִסְפֶּרֶת, *mis-peh-reth'*, writing), one of those who returned from the captivity with Zerubbabel (Neh. vii:7); elsewhere (Ezra ii:2) MIZPAR.

MISREPHOTH-MAIM (mĭs're-phŏth-mā'im), (Heb. מִשְׂרְפוֹת מַיִם, *mis-ref-oth' mah'yim*, burning of waters), a place or district near Sidon (Josh. xi:8; xiii:6). The name means 'burnings of water,' which Kimchi understands of warm baths; but more probably it means burnings *by* or *besides* the water—either lime kilns or smelting furnaces, situated near water (Gesenius). It is probably correctly identified with *el Musheirifeh,* about eleven miles north of Acre, near the sea.

MIST (mĭst), (Heb. אֵד, *ade,* Gen. ii:6), an ascending vapor, fog or cloud suspended in the atmosphere (Job xxxvi:27).

MITE (mīt), (Gr. λεπτόν, *lep-ton'*, thin, scale-like). A small piece of money, two of which made a κοδράντης, a quadrans—four of the latter being equal to the Roman *as.* The *as* was of less weight and value in later than in early times. Its original value was 3.4 farthings, and afterwards 2⅛ farthings. The latter was its value in the time of Christ, and the mite being one-eighth of that sum, was little more than one-fourth of an English farthing, or an eighth of a cent. It was the smallest coin known to the Hebrews (Luke xii: 59). (See WEIGHTS AND MEASURES.)

MITER (mī'tēr).

1. *Mits-neh'feth* (Heb. מִצְנֶפֶת, tiara, Exod. xxviii:4, 37, 39; xxix:6, etc). The turban or headdress of the high priest.

2. *Tsaw-neef'* (Heb. צָנִיף, headdress, Zech. iii:5 only); translated "diadem," (Job xxix:14), "hood," (Is. iii:23). (See CROWN; DRESS.)

MITHCAH (mĭth'kah), (Heb. מִתְקָה, *mith-kaw'*, sweet place, or sweetness), one of the encampments of the Israelites (Num. xxxiii:28, 29). See WANDERING, THE.

MITHNITE (mĭth'nīte), (Heb. מִתְנִי, *mith-nee'*), the appellation of Joshaphat, one of David's bodyguard (1 Chron. xi:43), probably meaning the inhabitant of a place or member of a tribe by the name of Methen of which there is no other notice.

MITHREDATH (mĭth're-dăth), (Heb. מִתְרְדָת, *mith-red-awth'*, given by Mithra, the sun god).

1. The treasurer of Cyrus, king of Persia, who was ordered to return the sacred vessels of the Jews to the chief Sheshbazzar (Ezra i:8), B. C. 536.

2. A Persian governor of Samaria, who joined in urging Artaxerxes Longimanus to prevent the Jews from rebuilding the walls of Jerusalem (Ezra iv:7), B. C. 522.

MITYLENE (mĭt'y-lē'ne), (Gr. Μιτυλήνη, *mit-oo-lay'nay*).

The capital of the isle of Lesbos, in the Ægean Sea, about seven miles and a half from the opposite point on the coast of Asia Minor. It was a well-built town, but unwholesomely situated. It was the native place of Pittacus, Theophanes, Theophrastus, Sappho, Alcæus, and Diophanes. St. Paul touched at Mitylene in his voyage from Corinth to Judæa (Acts xx:14). It does not appear that any Christian church was established at this place in the apostolic age. No mention is made of it in ecclesiastical history until a late period; and in the second century heathenism was so rife in Mitylene that a man was annually sacrificed to Dionysus. In the fifth, sixth, seventh and eighth centuries, we, however, find bishops of Mitylene present at several councils (Magdeburg, *Hist. Eccles. Cent.*, ii:195; v:6; vi:6; vii:4, 253, 254; viii:6). Mitylene still exists, and has given its name, in the form of Mytilni, or Metelin, to the whole island; but it is now a place of no importance under Turkish rule. The people are chiefly Greek. (See Harper, *Class Dict.*)

MIXED MARRIAGES, i. e., between Jews and Gentiles, were strictly forbidden by the Mosaic law. (See MARRIAGE.)

MIXED MULTITUDE (Heb. עֵרֶב, *ay'reb*, mixture). See MINGLED PEOPLE.

MIZAR (mī'zar), (Heb. מִצְעָר, *mits-ar'*, little, small); probably a summit of Lebanon, east of the Jordan, where David retreated from the rebellion of Absalom (Ps. xlii:6). Site not known.

MIZPAH (mĭz'pah), (Heb. מִצְפָּה, *mits-paw'*, watch-tower), is the name of several towns and places in lofty situations whether furnished with a watch-tower or not.

1. A town or city in Gilead (Judg. x:17; xi:11, 34; Hos. v:1). The place originated in the heap of stones set up by Laban, and to which he gave his name (Gen. xxxi:49). Some confound this with the Mizpeh of Gilead in Judg. xi:29; but it is better to distinguish them (see MIZPEH, 3).

2. A city of Benjamin, where the people were wont to convene (Josh. xviii:26; Judg. xx:1, 3; xxi:1; 1 Sam. vii:5-16; x:17, *sq.*). It was afterwards fortified by Asa, to protect the borders against the kingdom of Israel (1 Kings xv:22; 2 Chron. xvi:6). In later times it became the residence of the governor under the Chaldæans (Jer. xl:6, *sq.*; comp. Neh. iii:7, 15, 19). In one place the name occurs with *e,* Mizpéh (Heb. מִצְפֶּה, *mits-peh'*). Its position is nowhere mentioned in Scripture or by Josephus, but it could not have been far from Ramah, since King Asa fortified it with materials taken from that place; and that it was situated on an elevated spot is clear from its name—Neby Samwil (Prophet Samuel)—which, although somewhat distant from Er-Ram, Dr. Robinson (*Researches*, ii:144) inclines to regard as the probable site of Mizpah, especially as in 1 Macc. iii:46 it is described as 'over against Jerusalem,' implying that it was visible from that city, which is true of Neby Samwil. This place is now a poor village, seated upon the summit of an elevated ridge. It contains a mosque, now in a state of decay, which, on the ground of the apparently erroneous identification with Ramah, is regarded by Jews, Christians and Moslems as the tomb of Samuel.

"Grove, Stanley, Bonar, Major Wilson and others would identify Mizpah with Mount Scopus, one of the summits just north of Jerusalem, in the continuation of the Olivet range. From this place the traveler gets a very complete view of the Holy City, and from there the emperor Titus looked down upon it. Not far away is the modern village of *Shafat.* Conder notes that a part of the ridge is called *Arkûb es-Sûffa,* or, "the ridge of the view." Eusebius and Jerome located Mizpah near Kirjath-jearim, and Conder notes a *Shûfa* immediately south of *Kuryet el-Anab* (Kirjath-jearim), a name having exactly the same meaning with Mizpah—viz., "place of view." Conder also says that there is a place called *Umni Sûffa,* equivalent to the Hebrew Mizpah, existing on the road from Samaria to Jerusalem, which would be a suitable position for the Mizpah of Jeremiah (xl, xli), which is not necessarily the Mizpah of Samuel (*Quarterly,* 1876, p. 171). But his final conclusion is that Mizpah and Nob are identical. Whether the Mizpah of Hosea (v:1) was in Benjamin or in Gilead is uncertain" (Schaff, *Bib. Dict.*). (See MIZPEH.)

MIZPAR (mĭz'par), (Ezra ii:2). See MISPERETH.

MIZPEH (mĭz'peh), (Heb. מִצְפֶּה, *mits-peh,* feminine form).

This name has the same meaning and application as Mizpah, and is borne by several places mentioned in Scripture.

1. A town in the plains of Judah (Josh. xv:38). Eusebius and Jerome identify it with a place which, in their time, bore the name of Mapha, on the borders of Eleutheropolis southward, on the road to Ælia or Jerusalem; perhaps the modern *Tell es-Safich* (Robinson, *Researches,* ii:362 ff.).

2. The place more usually called Mizpah, in the tribe of Benjamin, is once called Mizpeh (Josh. xviii:26). (See MIZPAH 2.)

3. Mizpeh of Galilee, through or by which Jephthah passed in his pursuit of the Ammonites

Mizpeh (The Watch-Tower of Benjamin).

(Judg. xi:29). Some think it the same with MIZPAH, 1; and it is possibly the same with the Ramath-mizpeh of Josh. xiii:26.

4. A valley in the region of Lebanon (Josh. xi:8; comp. xi:3). Not identified.

5. A town of Moab, to which David took his parents that they might avoid the persecutions of Saul (1 Sam. xxii:3).

MIZRAIM (mĭz'ra-ĭm), (Heb. מִצְרַיִם, *mits-rah'yim,* or Land of Mizraim), the name by which, in Scripture, Egypt is generally designated, apparently from its having been peopled by Mizraim, the son of Ham (Gen. x). This ancient title is still preserved in Misr, the existing Arabic name of the country. (See EGYPT.)

MIZZAH (mĭz'zah), (Heb. מִזָּה, *miz-zaw'*, fear), son of Reuel, son of Esau by Bashemath; a chief of an Edomite tribe (Gen. xxxvi:3, 4, 13, 17; I Chron. i:37). B. C. after 1927.

MNASON (nā'son), Gr. Μνάσων, *mnah'sohn*, reminding), an 'old disciple' with whom St. Paul lodged when at Jerusalem in A. D. 58 (Acts xxi:16).

He seems to have been a native of Cyprus, but an inhabitant of Jerusalem, like Joses and Barnabas. Some think that he was converted by Paul and Barnabas while at Cyprus (Acts xiii:9); but the designation 'an old disciple,' has more generally induced the conclusion that he was converted by Jesus himself, and was perhaps one of the seventy.

MOAB (mō'ab), (Heb. מוֹאָב, *mo-awb'*, from father), son of Lot and his eldest daughter (Gen. xix:30-38). He was born about the same time as Isaac, and became the founder of the Moabites.

MOABITES (mō'ab-ītes), (Heb. מוֹאָבִי, *mo-aw-bee';* מוֹאָבִים, *mo-aw-beem'*), a tribe descended from Moab, the son of Lot, and consequently related to the Hebrews (Gen. xix:37).

(1) Territory. Previous to the exodus of the latter from Egypt, the former, after expelling the original inhabitants, called *Emims* (Gen. xiv:5; Deut. ii:11), had possessed themselves of the region on the east of the Dead Sea and the Jordan, as far north as the river Jabbok. But the northern, and indeed the finest and best, portion of the territory, viz., that extending from the Jabbok to the Arnon, had passed into the hands of the Amorites, who founded there one of their kingdoms, with Heshbon for its capital (Num. xxi:26). Og had established another at Bashan. Hence at the time of the Exodus the valley and river Arnon constituted the northern boundary of Moab (Num. xxi:13; Judg. xi:18; Joseph. *Antiq.* iv:5, 1). As the Hebrews advanced in order to take possession of Canaan, they did not enter the proper territory of the Moabites (Deut. ii:9; Judg. xi:18), but conquered the kingdom of the Amorites (a Canaanitish tribe), which had formerly belonged to Moab; whence the western part, lying along the Jordan, frequently occurs under the name of 'plains of Moab' (Deut. i:5).

(2) Moab and Israel. The Moabites, fearing the numbers that were marching around them, showed them at least no kindness (Deut. xxiii:4); and their king (Balak) hired Balaam to utter prophetic curses, which, however, were converted into blessings in his mouth (Num. xii *sq.*). The Gadites now took possession of the northern portion of this territory, which the Amorites had wrested from the Moabites, and established themselves there; while the Reubenites settled in the southern part (Num. xxxii:34; comp. Josh. xiii, which, however, differs somewhat in the designation of particular towns).

We see the first hostilities breaking out in the beginning of the period of the Judges, when the Hebrews had been for a long time tributary to the Moabites, but threw off their yoke under Ehud (Judg. iii:12-30). Towards the end of this period, however, peace and friendship were restored, mutual honors were reciprocated (as the history of Ruth shows), and Moab appears often to have afforded a place of refuge to outcasts and emigrant Hebrews (Ruth i:1; comp. I Sam. xxii:

3, 4; Jer. xl:11; Is. xvi:2). After Saul had waged successful war against them (I Sam. xiv: 47), David made them tributary (2 Sam. viii:2, 12; xxiii:20). The right to levy this tribute seems to have been transferred to Israel after the division of the kingdom; for upon the death of Ahab (about B. C. 896) they refused to pay the customary tribute of 100,000 lambs and as many rams (2 Kings i:1; iii:4; comp. Is. xvi:1). Jehoram (B. C. 896), in alliance with Judah and Edom, sought indeed to bring them back to their subjection. The invading army, after having been preserved from perishing by thirst through the intervention of Elisha, defeated the Moabites and ravaged the country; but, through the strange conduct of the king, in offering up in sacrifice his son (MESHA), were induced to retire without completing the object of the expedition. The Moabites deeply resented the part which the king of Judah took in this invasion, and formed a powerful confederacy with the Ammonites, Edomites, and others, who marched in great force into Judæa, and formed their camp at Engedi, where they fell out among themselves and destroyed each other through the special interposition of Providence, in favor of Jehoshaphat and his people (2 Kings iii:4, *sq.;* comp. 2 Chron. xx:1-30). (See ELISHA; JEHORAM; JEHOSHAPHAT.) Under Jehoash (B. C. 849) we see them undertake incursions into the kingdom of Israel, and carry on offensive war against it (2 Kings xiii:20).

Though the subsequent history of Israel often mentions the Moabites, yet it is silent respecting a circumstance which, in relation to one passage, is of the greatest importance, namely, the reconquest of the territory between the Arnon and the Jabbok, which was wrested from the Moabites by the Amorites, and afterwards of the territory possessed by the tribes of Reuben and Gad. This territory in general we see, according to Is. xvi, in the possession of the Moabites again. Even Selah, the ancient capital of the Edomites, seems likewise, from Is. xvi:1, to have belonged to them, at least for a time. The most natural supposition is that of Reland (*Palæstina,* p. 720), Paulus (*Clavis,* p. 110), and Rosenmüller (*in loc.*), that, after the carrying away of those tribes into captivity, the Moabites occupied their territory; as it is expressly stated (Jer. xlix:1-5) that the Amorites intruded themselves into the territory of the captive Gadites, as the Edomites did in respect to the Jews at a later period (Joseph. *De Bell. Jud.* v. 79).

(3) Under Nebuchadnezzar. Still later, under Nebuchadnezzar, we see the Moabites acting as the auxiliaries of the Chaldæans (2 Kings xxiv:2), and beholding with malicious satisfaction the destruction of a kindred people (Ezek. xxv:8-11); yet, according to an account in Josephus (*Antiq.* x:9, 7), Nebuchadnezzar, when on his way to Egypt, made war upon them, and subdued them, together with the Ammonites, five years after the destruction of Jerusalem.

(4) National Hostility. That continual wars and contentions must have created a feeling of national hostility between the Hebrews and the Moabites, may be readily conceived. This feeling manifested itself on the part of the Hebrews, sometimes in bitter proverbs, sometimes in the denunciations of the prophets; on the part of the Moabites in proud boastings and expressions of contempt (Is. xvi:6).

Among the prophecies, however, that of Balaam (Num. xxii-xxiv) is, above all, remarkable, in which this ancient prophet (who withal was not an Israelite), hired by Moab to curse, is impelled by the Divine Spirit to *bless* Israel, and to announce the future destruction of Moab by a mighty hero in Israel (Num. xxiv:17). It is a genuine epic representation worthy of the greatest poet of any age. Nor should we overlook the song of triumph and scorn respecting Moab, suggested by Heshbon, and obscure only as to its origin (Num. xxi:17-30). Among the later prophets, Amos (ii:1-3) predicts their destruction in consequence of their cruelty to the king of Edom; probably with reference to the war recorded in 2 Kings iii, when the Edomites were confederate with the Hebrews; although the particular instance of cruelty is not there specified. Zephaniah (ii:8-10) condemns them to punishment for their scorn and contempt of Israel. Jeremiah repeats the denunciation of evil predicted by Zephaniah, for the most part in the words of Numbers and Isaiah (Jer. xlviii; comp. also ix:26; xxv:21); and Ezekiel threatens them with punishment for their malicious joy at the overthrow of Judæa (xxv:6-11). Moreover, the subjection of Moab finds a place in every ideal description of splendid wars and golden ages predicted for Israel (Is. xi: 14; xxv:10; Ps. lx:8). 'Moab is my wash-pot' (Ps. lxxxiii:6).

(5) After the Exile. After the Exile, an intimate connection between the two nations had found place by means of intermarriages (Ezra ix:1, *sq.;* Neh. xiii:1), which, however, were dissolved by the theocratic zeal of Ezra. The last (chronologically) notice of the Moabites which occurs in Scripture is in Dan. xi:41, which contains an obscure intimation of the escape of the Moabites from the overthrow with which neighboring countries would be visited; but Josephus, in the history of Alexander Jannæus, mentions the cities between Arnon and Jabbok under the title of cities of Moab (*Antiq.* xiii:15). Thenceforth their name is lost under that of the Arabians, as was also the case with Ammon and Edom.

From Burckhardt (*Travels in Syria*), Robinson and others, we learn that in the land of Moab, which lay to the east and southeast of Judæa, and which bordered on the east, northeast and partly on the south of the Dead Sea, the soil is rather more diversified than that of Ammon; and, where the desert and plains of salt have not encroached upon its borders, of equal fertility. There are manifest and abundant signs of its ancient importance. The whole of the plains are covered with the sites of towns on every eminence or spot convenient for the construction of one; and as the land is capable of rich cultivation, there can be no doubt that the country now so deserted, once presented a continued picture of plenty and fertility (Irby and Mangles, p. 378). The form of fields is still visible, and there are remains of Roman highways which are in some places completely paved, 'and on which there are milestones of the times of Trajan, Marcus Aurelius, and Severus, with the numbers of the miles legible upon them. Wherever any spot is cultivated the corn is luxuriant; and the frequency and in many instances the close vicinity of the sites of ancient towns prove that the population of the country was formerly proportioned to its fertility (Irby and Mangles, pp. 377, 378, 456, 460).

(6) Prophecies Fulfilled. It was in its state of highest prosperity that the prophets foretold that the cities of Moab should become desolate, without any to dwell in them; and accordingly we find, that although the sites, ruins and names of many ancient cities of Moab can be traced, not one of them exists at the present day as ten-

anted by man. Porter indicates how completely those various prophecies have been fulfilled, but some of his statements require confirmation. From Salcah he saw upward of thirty deserted towns (Jer. xlviii:15-24). The neglected and wild vineyards and fig trees are rifled by the Bedouins every year in their periodical raids (verses 32, 33). The inhabitants hide themselves in the mountain-fastnesses, oppressed by the robbers of the desert on the one hand and the robbers of the government on the other (verses 28, 44). Cyril Graham, who explored this region, found cities with buildings in a good state of preservation, yet everywhere uninhabited. "In the whole of these vast plains, north and south, east and west, desolation reigns supreme." The long-predicted doom of Moab is now fulfilled, and the forty-eighth chapter of Jeremiah is verified on the spot by the traveler. There are twenty-seven references to Moab in this chapter, and one hundred and twenty-one in the Scriptures.

The argument for the inspiration of the sacred records deducible from this, among other facts of the same kind, is produced with considerable force by Dr. Keith in his work on Prophecy. Gesenius, *Comment. on Is.* xv, xvi; *Introduct.* translated by W. S. Tyler, with *Notes* by Moses Stuart, in *Biblical Repos.* for 1836, vol. vii, pp. 107-124; Keith's *Evidence from Prophecy,* pp. 153-165; and *Land of Israel,* 279-295; *Pictorial Bible,* Notes to Deut. ii:2; Is. xvi, xvii; Jer. xliii. (See Rose, *The Afghans the Ten Tribes;* Schaff *Bib. Dict.*)

MOABITESS (mō'abī-tess), (Heb. מוֹאֲבִיָּה, *mo-aw-bee'*, feminine of Moabite), a Moabitish woman (Ruth i:22; ii:21; iv:5, 19; 2 Chron. xxiv:26).

MOABITE STONE (mō-ab-īte stōn).

(1) How Discovered. This wonderful monument of the times of the events recorded in the

The Moabite Stone.

Book of Kings was discovered by a missionary by the name of F. Klein, in August, 1868. When on his way to the Bekka, a friendly sheik drew his attention to a black basalt stone in the vicinity of his tent at Dibon.

(2) Dimensions. This stone was about three feet and ten inches in height, two feet in breadth, and fourteen and a half inches in thickness. It was rounded both at the top and bottom to nearly the shape of a semicircle, and contained an inscription on one side consisting of thirty-four lines.

(3) Inscription Secured. Mr. Klein tried to obtain it for the museum of Berlin, but negotiations progressed slowly, and in the meantime squeezes were taken of the inscription. This was most fortunate, for the Bedouins of the country, rather than give it up, broke the stone by building a fire under it, and then pouring cold water upon it, after which they distributed the fragments among themselves, to be used as amulets and charms. Happily, however, more than half of the inscription remained intact, and the squeezes and copies which had been obtained nearly supply the lacunæ in the text, as may be seen from an inspection of the original monument now in the museum of the Louvre.

(4) Language. The language of the inscription is almost identical with the ancient Hebrew, and shows that in the tenth century before Christ (the period to which it belongs) the Israelites and Moabites had a common language. This indicates that they sprang from a common ancestry. There was, however, considerable dissimilarity between the characters in which this language was inscribed by the two nations, in consequence of their long separation from each other. Still they bear an essential relationship which may be readily recognized.

(5) By Whom Erected. The tablet tells its own story, and shows that it was erected by MESHA, king of Moab, in order to recount a victory which he obtained over the Israelites. Many of Mesha's exploits are recounted, and the names of various places are given which he claimed to have either built or destroyed (B. C. 900). The Moabites fought many a battle with Israel, but Mesha, like the other heathen kings, records only his victories. This record, however, fills up a gap in the brief account we have in the Books of the Kings concerning the wars between Mesha and Israel especially during the reign of King Omri.

The Moabites had been reduced to subjection by David, but after the separation of the kingdoms, they apparently regained their independence. During the reigns of Jeroboam and Ahab they were again tributaries. But after the death of Ahab, they again rebelled against the king of Israel, as we learn from 2 Kings iii:4. The successful insurrection here referred to, in Biblical history, is recorded by Mesha himself on the Moabite stone, and his victory is ascribed to Chemosh, who is called "the god of Moab," and referred to in 1 Kings xi:7 as "Chemosh the abomination of Moab."

(6) Names Recorded. The stone record gives the names of persons, places and events, which are also given in the Books of Kings and Chronicles, together with others which are supplementary. Jehovah is recognized as the God of Israel. Chemosh is worshiped as the god of Moab, and we find also the names of Dibon (Num. xxxii:34), Nebo, Baal-Meon (Josh. xiii:17), Ataroth (Num. xxxii:34), and others, besides Horonaim (Is. xv:5) and the River Arnon (Josh. xiii:16).

This monument has attracted much attention in the world of scholars, and the literature connected with it is very extensive, there being eight or more volumes devoted to the subject, besides a multitude of papers which have been contributed to various periodicals published in English, French, Italian, German, Hebrew and Greek.

Hopes were entertained that other tablets of that character might be found, but Palmer, who investigated every written stone reported by the Arabs, came to the conclusion that there does not remain *above ground* a single inscribed stone of any importance.

(7) Bibliography. The bibliography connected with the Moabite stone is very extensive. A full translation of the inscription, except the two broken lines, has been made by Dr. A. Neubauer and published in *Records of the Past,* vol. ii (Bagster & Sons, London). See also *Higher Criticism and the Monuments,* by A. H. Sayce. There are books published upon this subject by Clermont, Ganneau, Ginsburg, Hitzig, Kaempf, Schlottman, Vogüe and others, besides an enormous number of contributions by various authors to periodicals in English, French, Italian, German, Greek and Hebrew.

MOABITISH (mō'ab-ī'tish), pertaining to Moab (Ruth ii:6).

MOADIAH (mō'a-dī'ah), (Heb. מוֹעַדְיָה, *moh-ad-yaw*, festival of Jah; Neh. xii:17). (See MAADIAH).

MOCK, MOCKING (mŏk, mŏ'kĭng). Several Hebrew and Greek words are thus translated.

1. *Haw-thal'* (Heb. הָתַל, to deceive; Judg. xvi: 10, 15; Job xiii:9).

2. *Kaw-las'* (Heb. קָלַס, to laugh in scorn or contempt; 1 Kings xviii:27; 2 Kings ii:23; Ezek. xxii:5).

3. *Loots* (Heb. לוּץ; Gr. μυκτηρίζω, *mook-tay-rid'-za;* to scoff, deride, to mock at any one; Prov. xiv: 9; xx:1; Gal. vi:7).

4. *Tsaw-khak'* (Heb. צָחַק, to jest with or play with females, Gen. xix:14; to toy, caress, ravish, or abuse, Gen. xxxix:14, 17).

5. *Law-ag'* (Heb. לָעַג, to scoff, scorn, etc., 2 Chron. xxx:10; Job xxi:3; Prov. i:26).

6. *Aw-lal'* (Heb. עָלַל, to abuse or insult another; Num. xxii:29; Jer. xxxviii:19).

7. *Saw-khak'* (Heb. שְׂחֹק, derision, scorn, derisive laughter; Lam. i:7).

8. *Emp-aheed'zo* (Gr. ἐμπαίζω, to trifle with; Matt. ii:16; xx:19; xxvii:29; Luke xviii:32; xxiii: 11, 36).

9. *Khlyoo-ad'zo* (Gr. Χλευάζω, to shoot out the lip; Acts xvii:32).

Figurative. (1) God "*mocks at men's fear*" when he brings judgment upon them (Prov. i:26). (2) God is "*not mocked;*" he will not be deceived or jested with (Gal. vi:7). (3) Men "*mock*" God, when in words or behavior they jest at his being, his purposes, words, works, ordinances, ministers or people (Job. xiii:9). (4) Wine is a "*mocker,*" and strong drink is "raging;" if drunk to excess, it deceives men, promising them enjoyment, while it lands them in disgrace and violence (Prov. xx:1).

MODERATE, MODERATION (mŏd'ēr-ăt, mŏd'ēr-ā'shŭn), (Gr. ἐπιεικής, *ep-ee-i-kace'*, fairness, gentleness, Phil. iv:5: translated "patient," 1 Tim. iii:3 ; "gentle," Tit. iii:2; 1 Peter ii:18); moderate, in general, is to abate; to keep in due bounds. To "moderate threatening," is to restrain it within due bounds (Eph. vi:9). Our "moderation should be known to all men, because the Lord is at hand;" we should exercise tenderness and gentleness toward all men, and treat them with kindness and respect; and bear injuries (Phil. iv:5).

MOLADAH (mŏl'a-dah), (Heb. מוֹלָדָה, *mo-law-daw'*, birth).

A city first given to Judah, and afterward to Simeon (Josh. xix:2; 1 Chron. iv:28). It was in the southerly part of Judah. The place was re-occupied after the exile (Neh. xi:26). It is identified with *Milh* (Robinson, ii:621), seven and a half miles southwest of Arad, and fourteen southeast of Beersheba. (Stewart, *Tent and Khan*, p. 217). There are ruins of a fortified town, two wells, one with water at the depth of forty feet; and the wells are surrounded with marble troughs. Arab tradition says that Abraham dug these wells and watered his flocks here.

MOLE (mōl), (Heb. חֹפֶר, *khaf-ore'*, Arabic, *khuld*, Lev. xi:30, in our version 'weasel').

Although the similarity of sound in names is an unsafe ground to depend upon when it is applied to specific animals, still, the Hebrew and Syriac appearing likewise to imply creeping into, creeping underneath by burrowing—characteristics most obvious in moles—and the Arabic denomination being undoubted, *chaled* may be assumed to indicate the above animal, in preference to *chinsemeth*, which, in conformity with the opinion of Bochart, is referred to the *chameleon*. This conclusion is the more to be relied on as the animal is rather common in Syria, and in some places abundant. Zoölogists have considered the particular species to be the *Talpa Europœa*, which, under the name of the common mole, is so well known as not to require a more particular description. The ancients represented the mole to have no eyes; which assertion later scientific writers believed they had disproved by showing our species to be possessed of these organs, though exceedingly small. Nevertheless, recent observations have proved that a species, in other respects scarcely, if at all, to be distinguished from the common, is totally destitute of eyes, and consequently has received the name of *Talpa cœca*. It is to be found in Italy, and probably extends to the East, instead of the *Europœa*. Moles must not, however, be considered as forming a part of the Rodent order, whereof all the families and genera are provided with strong incisor teeth, like rats and squirrels, and therefore intended for subsisting chiefly on grain and nuts; they are on the contrary supplied with a great number of small teeth, to the extent of twenty-two in each jaw—indicating a partial regimen; for they feed on worms, larvæ, and underground insects, as well as on roots, and thus belongs to the insectivorous order; which brings the application of the name somewhat nearer to carnivora and its received interpretation 'weasel.'   C. H. S.

MOLECH (mō'lek), (Heb. הַמֹּלֶךְ, *ha-mo'lek*, the ruler), always with the article, except in 1 Kings xi:7.

Molech is chiefly found in the Old Testament as the national god of the Ammonites, to whom children were sacrificed by fire. There is some difficulty in ascertaining at what period the Israelites became acquainted with this idolatry; yet three reasons render it probable that it was before the time of Solomon, the date usually assigned for its introduction. Nevertheless, it is for the first time directly stated that Solomon erected a high-place for Molech on the Mount of Olives (1 Kings xi:7); and from that period his worship continued uninterruptedly there, or in Tophet, in the valley of Hinnom, until Josiah defiled

both places (2 Kings xxiii:10, 13). Jehoahaz, however, the son and successor of Josiah, again 'did what was evil in the sight of Jehovah, according to all that his fathers had done' (2 Kings xxiii:32). The same broad condemnation was made against the succeeding kings, Jehoiakim, Jehoiachin, and Zedekiah; and Ezekiel, writing during the captivity, says, 'Do you, by offering your gifts, and by making your sons pass through the fire, pollute yourselves with all your idols *until this day*, and shall I be enquired of by you?" (xx:31). After the restoration all traces of this idolatry disappear.

It has been attempted to explain the terms in which the act of sacrificing children is described in the Old Testament so as to make them mean a mere passing between two fires, without any risk of life, for the purpose of purification. This theory—which owes its origin to a desire in some Hebrew writers to lessen the mass of evidence which their own history offers of the perverse idolatries of the Jews—is effectually declared untenable by such passages as Ps. cvi:38; Jer. vii:31; Ezek. xvi:20; xxiii:37; the last two of which may also be adduced to show that the victims were slaughtered before they were burnt.

The Rabbins tell us that the idol was made of brass and placed on a brazen throne, and that the head was that of a calf with a crown upon it. The throne and image were made hollow, and a furious fire was kindled within it. The flames penetrated into the body and limbs of the idol; and when the arms were red-hot, the victim was thrown into them, and was almost immediately burned to death, while its cries were drowned by drums.   J. N.

MOLID (mō'lid), (Heb. מוֹלִיד, *mo-leed'*, begetter), a man of Judah, son of Abishur and Abihail (1 Chron ii:29), B. C. after 1612.

MOLOCH (mō'lŏk), (Amos v:26; Acts vii:43). See MOLECH.

MOLTEN IMAGE (mōl't'n ĭm'àj). See CALF; IMAGE.

MOLTEN SEA (mōl't'n sē). See LAVER.

MOMENT (mō'ment), (Heb. רֶגַע, *reh'gah*, wink, Num. xvi:21, 45; Job xx:5; Ps. xxx:5, etc.; Gr. ἄτομος, *at'om-os*, indivisible, 1 Cor. xv:52; παραρρυέω, *par-ar-hroo-eh'o*, to flow by, 2 Cor. iv:17; στιγμή, *stig-may'*, a point, Luke iv:5), an instant, the smallest interval of time.

MONEY (mŭn'ỹ), (Heb. כֶּסֶף, *keh-sef'*, silver).

This term is used to denote whatever commodity the inhabitants of any country may have agreed, or are compelled to receive as an equivalent for their labor and in exchange for other commodities. Etymologists differ respecting its derivation. Bouteroue contends that it is derived from *monere*, because the stamp impressed on the coin indicates its weight and fineness (*Recherches sur les Monnoyes de France*); and Suidas (*s. v.* Μονῆτα), that it originated in the circumstance of silver having been first coined at Rome in the temple of *Juno Moneta*.

(1) Various Commodities. Different commodities have been used as money in the primitive state of society in all countries. Those nations which subsist by the chase, such as the ancient Russians and the greater part of the North American Indians, use the skins of the animals killed in hunting as money (Storch, *Traité d' Economie Politique*, tome i). In a pastoral state of society cattle are chiefly used as money. Thus, according to Homer, the armor of Diomede cost nine oxen, and that of Glaucus one hundred (*Iliad*, vi :235). The etymology of the Latin word *pecunia*, signifying money, and all of its derivatives, affords sufficient evidence that cattle (*pecus*) were the first money of the Romans. They were also used as money by the Germans, whose laws fix the amount of penalties for particular offenses to be paid in cattle (Storch, *l. c.*). In agricultural countries corn would be used in remote ages as money, and even at the present day it is not unusual to stipulate for corn rents and wages. Various commodities have been and are still used in different countries. Smith mentions salt as the common money of Abyssinia (*Wealth of Nations*, i :4). A species of *cyprœa* called the *cowree*, gathered on the shores of the Maldive Islands, and of which 6,400 constitute a rupee, is used in making small payments throughout India, and is the only money of certain districts in Africa. Dried fish forms the money of Iceland and Newfoundland; sugar of some of the West India Islands; and among the first settlers of America corn and tobacco were used as money (Holmes' *American Annals*). Smith mentions that, at the time of the publication of the *Wealth of Nations*, there was a village in Scotland where it was customary for a workman to carry nails as money to the baker's shop or the alehouse (i :4).

(2) Commerce. A long period of time must have intervened between the first introduction of the precious metals into commerce, and their becoming generally used as money. The peculiar qualities which so eminently fit them for this purpose would only be gradually discovered. They would probably be first introduced in their gross and unpurified state. A sheep, an ox, a certain quantity of corn, or any other article, would afterwards be bartered or exchanged for pieces of gold or silver in bars or ingots, in the same way as they would formerly have been exchanged for iron, copper, cloth, or anything else.

Weighing Money.

(3) Values Estimated by Weight. The merchants would soon begin to estimate their proper value, and, in effecting exchanges, would first agree upon the quality of the metal to be given, and then the quantity which its possessor had become bound to pay would be ascertained by weight. This, according to Aristotle and Pliny, was the manner in which the precious metals were originally exchanged in Greece and Italy. The same practice is still observed in different countries. In many parts of China and Abyssinia the value of gold and silver is always ascertained by weight (Goguet, *De l'Origine des Loix*, etc.). Iron was the first money of the Lacedæmonians, and copper of the Romans.

In the sacred writings there is frequent mention of gold, silver, and brass, sums of money, purchases made with money, current money, and money of a certain weight. Indeed, the money of Scripture is all estimated by weight. 'Abraham weighed to Ephron the silver which he had named in the audience of the sons of Heth, four hundred shekels of silver, current money with the merchant' (Gen. xxiii :16). The brethren of Joseph carried back into Egypt the money 'in full weight' which they had found in their sacks (Gen. xliii :21). The golden earring presented by Abraham's steward to Rebekah weighed half a shekel, and the two bracelets for her hands were ten shekels weight of gold' (Gen. xxiv :22). In paying for the field of Hanameel, Jeremiah 'weighed him the money, even seventeen shekels of silver' (Jer. xxxii :9). Amos represents the merchants of Israel as 'falsifying the balances by deceit' (viii :5). The shekel and the talent do not appear to have been originally fixed and stamped pieces of money, but simply weights used in traffic. Hence, 'thou shalt not have in thy bag divers weights, a great and a small' (Deut. xxv :13). It was customary for the Jews to have scales attached to their girdles for weighing the gold and silver they received; but the Canaanites carried them in their hands.

(4) Pieces of Money. There is no direct allusion in the sacred writings to coined money as belonging to the Jewish nation. In Gen. xxxiii :19 Jacob is said to have bought a part of a field 'for an hundred pieces of money;' and the friends of Job are said to have given him each 'a piece of money' (Job xlii :11). The term in the original is *kesitoth*, and is by some thought to denote 'sheep' or 'lamb;' by others a kind of money having the impression of a sheep or lamb; and by others again a purse of money. The most correct translation may be presumed to be that which favors the idea of a piece of money bearing some stamp or mark indicating that it was of the value of a sheep or lamb. The name shekel, first used to indicate a weight, might afterwards be applied to a piece of money. According to Arbuthnot 3,000 of these shekels were equal to a talent. Some allegorical device would naturally suggest itself as the most appropriate for being impressed upon pieces of gold or silver of a given weight and fineness; and as in the patriarchal ages property consisted chiefly of flocks and herds, no better emblem could be used than that of a lamb, with which it is imagined the pieces of money alluded to may have been impressed.

(5) Early Coins. Maurice, in his *Antiquities of India* (vol. vii), bears testimony to the fact that the earliest coins were stamped with the figure of an ox or sheep. In the British Museum there is a specimen of the original Roman As, the surface of which is nearly the size of a brick, with the figure of a bull impressed upon it. Other devices would suggest themselves to different nations as arising out of, or connected with, particular places or circumstances, as the Babylonish lion, Ægina's tortoise, Bœotia's shield, the lyre of Mytilene, the wheat of Metapontum. On some of the reverses of the Roman large brass may be deciphered, 'Valor standing full armed; Honor robed and chapleted; Happiness crowned with obliviscent poppies; Concord with extended hand, and the horn of plenty in her bosom; Hope tripping lightly, and smiling on a flower-bud; Peace offering the olive branch; Fortune resting on a rudder; Military Faith stretching forth his consecrated standard; Abundance emptying her cornucopia; Security leaning on a column; Modesty veiled and sitting; Piety taking her gift to the altar; Fruitfulness in the midst of her nurselings; Equity adjusting her scales; Victory with wings and coronal and trumpet; Eternity holding the globe and risen phœnix; or better, seated on a starry sphere; Liberty with cap and staff; National Prosperity sailing as a good ship before the favoring gale; and Public Faith with joined hands clasping between them the palms of success, and the caduceus of health' (*Quarterly Review*, vol. lxxii, p. 358). Religion would also at an early period claim to be distinguished, and accordingly the effigies of Juno, Diana, Ceres, Jove, Hercules, Apollo, Bacchus, Pluto, Neptune, and many other of the heathen deities are found impressed upon the early coins. The Jews, however, were the worshipers of the one only true God; idolatry was strictly forbidden in their law; and therefore their shekel never bore a head, but was impressed simply with the almond rod and the pot of manna.

(6) Roman Coinage. The first Roman coinage took place, according to Pliny (*Hist. Nat.* xxxiii:3), in the reign of Servius Tullius, about 550 years before Christ; but it was not until Alexander of Macedon had subdued the Persian monarchy, and Julius Cæsar had consolidated the Roman empire, that the image of a living ruler was permitted to be stamped upon the coins. Previous to that period heroes and deities alone gave currency to the money of imperial Rome.

Antiochus Sidetes, king of Syria, is represented to have granted to Simon Maccabæus the privilege of coining money in Judæa (1 Macc. xv:6). This is considered to be the first mention of Hebrew money, properly so called. It consisted of shekels and demi-shekels, the third part of a shekel, and the quarter of a shekel, of silver.

From the time of Julius Cæsar, who first struck a living portrait on his coins, the Roman coins run in a continued succession of so-called Cæsars, their queens and crown-princes, from about B. C. 48 down to Romulus Augustulus, emperor of the West, who was dethroned by Odoacer about A. D. 475 (*Quarterly Review*, ut supra).

After its subjugation by Rome much foreign money found its way into the land of Judæa. The piece of tribute money, or coin mentioned in Luke xx:24, as presented to our Savior, bore the image and superscription of the Roman emperor, and it is reasonable to suppose that a large quantity of Roman coins was at that time in circulation throughout Judæa.   G. M. B.

MONEY CHANGER (mŭn'ў chān'jẽr), Gr. κολλυβιστής, *kol-loo-bis-tace'*, dealer in coin; κερματιστής, *ker-mat-is-tace'*, money broker, from κέρμα, *ker'mah,* a small coin.

It is mentioned by Volney that in Syria, Egypt and Turkey, when any considerable payments are to be made, an agent of exchange is sent for, who counts paras by thousands, rejects pieces of false money, and weigh all the sequins either separately or together. It has hence been suggested that the 'current money with the merchant,' mentioned in Scripture (Gen. xxiii:16), might have been such as was approved of by competent judges whose business it was to detect fraudulent money if offered in payment. The Hebrew word *socher* signifies one who goes about from place to place, and is supposed to answer to the native exchange-agent or money-broker of the East, now called *shroff*. It appears that there were bankers or money-changers in Judæa, who made a trade of receiving money in deposit and paying interest for it (Matt. xxv:27). Some of them had even established themselves within the precincts of the

temple at Jerusalem (xxi:12), where they were in the practice of exchanging one species of money for another. Persons who came from a distance to worship at Jerusalem would naturally bring with them the money current in their respective districts, and it might therefore be a matter of convenience for them to get this money exchanged at the door of the temple for that which was current in Jerusalem, and upon their departure to receive again that species of money which circulated in the districts to which they were journeying. These money-changers would, of course, charge a commission upon all their transactions but from the observation of our Savior, when he overthrew the tables of those in the temple, it may be inferred that they were not distinguished for honesty and fair dealing: 'It is written, my house shall be called the house of prayer, but, ye have made it a den of thieves' (verse 13). G. M. B.

Money Changer.

MONEY, LOVE OF (mŭn'ў, lŭv ŏv), (Gr. φιλαργυρία, *fil-ar-goo-ree'ah*, 1 Tim. vi:10), covetousness or avarice. (See COVETOUSNESS.)

MONEY, PIECE OF (mŭn'ў, pēs ŏv), (Gen. xxxiii:19; Job xlii:11, etc.). See MONEY; WEIGHTS AND MEASURES.

MONOTHEISM (mŏn'ŏ-thĕ-ĭz'm).

(1) The worship of the one God was a primeval principle beginning with the very dawn of human history. As surely as God was first, so surely must the pure worship have preceded the various forms of idolatry. It was man's recognition of a higher Power when dominion was given "over all the earth." But man sinned and went away from God; it was disobedience first, and then murder. Polygamy came next and polytheism was not far behind the other transgressions. There is no instance in the world's history where monotheism has been evolved from polytheism or idol worship. Dr. Frank B. Jevons says: "Indeed, if we base ourselves upon evolutionary principles, we may safely say that whatever may have been the genesis and history of monotheism, one thing is certain, namely, that it cannot have been developed out of polytheism" (*Introduction to the History of Religion*, p. 387).

The further we go back among the earliest mythologies, the nearer we come to the primitive principle. When the Hindus first come within the range of history their devotions are paid to earth and air and sea, the sun is praised, and the rain implored; their gods are few in number. In the early Vedic age there were only seven prominent deities, but polytheism rapidly developed upon the soil of India until her pantheon contained millions of gods.

(2) The more modern polytheism of Rome or even of ancient Greece need hardly be examined, but in Egypt there was at first only one Horus. In later periods, however, this one deity had developed into twelve, each one representing a different conception, but all of them having been evolved from the first. Dr. Wiedmann gives the names of twelve or more different Horuses who were worshiped in different localities, and sometimes several of them were adored in the same temple.

Many eminent Egyptologists, including Mariette, Brugsch, and Renouf, claim that the *earliest* monuments show the primitive religion of the Nile valley to have been monotheism. It is claimed that when the Egyptians moved into the Nile a thousand years before Menes, they had only one God, and that was Nu. Surely this name is very nearly akin to Anu, who is described upon the tablets as the supreme God of ancient Accad.

Maspero and others take exceptions to the monotheistic theory, but all Egyptologists agree that there are comparatively few divinities mentioned in the beginning of monumental history, and that the number steadily increases, until during the Roman era they became almost numberless. All agree that in the earliest forms of worship among the Egyptians there are no such traces of superstition as in the later eras.

Maspero writes as follows: "Ancient tradition affirms that the earliest Egyptian temples contained neither images nor inscriptions, and, in point of fact, the temple of the Sphinx is bare" (Maspero, *Archæology*, p. 86).

Up to this time the temple of the Sphinx was the only one of that earliest time which had been uncovered, but at Medum, in 1891, Dr. Petrie dug up a temple which was even more ancient, and it is a very suggestive fact that in this early sanctuary, so simple and massive in its construction, *"no sign of an idol, or statue, or magical text, was discovered."* (Petrie, *Medum*, London, 1892.) It is also true that the earliest writings of the Egyptians, as *"The Precepts of Phath Hotep,"* are much higher in moral tone than the mass of their later productions.

That the people of Egypt were at one time worshipers of the true God is evident from the prophecy of Isaiah. He says: "And the Lord shall smite Egypt and heal it, and they shall *return* even to the Lord, and he shall heal them" (Is. xix:22). The Hebrew word which is here rendered "return" is translated by the word return, or its equivalents, 815 times in the Old Testament, so there is no room for philological dispute on this important point.

In the valley of the Euphrates the same rule obtains in relation to the multiplication of deities.

(3) It is thought that the worship of Hea, "the god who determines destinies," is a corruption of the worship of the God of Abraham, for Ea is another form of El, and the followers of Ea were evidently monotheists. In relation to monotheism in the valley of the Euphrates, Mr. Hormuzd Rassam, the eminent archæologist, who is a native of Assyria, claims that the early Assyrians were worshipers of the true God, and he bases his claim largely upon his own discoveries. (*Trans. Vic. Inst.*, vol. xiii, pp. 190, 214; also vol. xxv, p. 121.)

This early worship, however, as in the case of the Egyptians, was soon corrupted, and at length the Assyrians counted no less than 300 spirits of heaven and 600 of earth.

These examples among the oldest systems of polytheism show how "development" is related to this subject.

(4) In the *American Journal of Theology* G. M. Grant calls attention to the valued work by Dr. Jevons, above cited, and says: "Totemism, that is, the belief which identified with the divine a species of animals or plants which was regarded as the ancestor of the tribe, is the earliest form of religion known to science. It may be added that the worship originally accorded to the whole species was, after a time, appropriated to one individual of the species. As to this faith, while no authority now accepts Mr. Spencer's theory that it originated in the worship of ancestors, it is admitted that the religious belief in the pre-totemistic stage is entirely a matter of conjecture."

(5) Dr. Jevons, however, argues with great ability that pre-totemism must have been a simple monotheism. He takes issue with those who maintain that, as monotheism is the highest form of belief, it must have developed from the lower forms of totemism and polytheism through intermediate stages.

He strongly insists that the highest must have been implicit in consciousness from the beginning, and also that evolution and progress are two very different things; that evolution is constant but progress very rare. Indeed, "evolution may well be, from a religious point of view, one long process of degeneration." Progress is certainly as exceptional in religion as in other things, and where it takes place it must be due to exceptional causes. "If evolution takes place, something must be evolved; and that something, as being continuously present in all the different stages, may be called the *continuum* of religion."

(6) Again he says. "We must remember that the facts of consciousness were the same for early as for civilized man, but they were not yet discriminated. They swam before man's untrained eye, and ran into one another. But, even so, all was not untrained chaos for man. In the outer world of his experience the laws of nature, which are God's laws, worked with the same regularity then as now. In the world of his inner experience, God was not far from him at any time. If his spiritual vision was dim, his consciousness of God was at least so strong, to start with, that he has never since ceased seeking after Him. The law of continuity holds of religions as of other things."

(7) Dr. Jevons argues that polytheism was developed, not from monotheism, but from totemism. When man realized that the union of the human with the divine had been broken, it was felt that some outward act was needed which would re-establish the connection, and totem animals were offered in sacrifice. The totem being supposed to share the common life of both parties, and to be capable of exercising an influence over both, and the blood covenant being the only means known of effecting a union with any one external to the tribe, the sacrifice of the totem and the common sacramental meal were originated. The universality of the practice is the most conclusive testimony of the ineradicable craving of man's heart for union and communion with God, and to the consciousness that on such union alone can right relations with our fellows be based. Dr. Jevons says: "The whole human race for thousands of years has been educated to the conception that it was only through a divine sacrifice that perfect union with God was possible for man. At times the sacramental conception of sacrifice appeared to be about to degenerate entirely into the gift theory; but then, in the sixth century before Christ, the sacramental conception woke into new life, this time in the form of a search for a perfect sacrifice—a search which led Clement and Cyprian to try all the mysteries of Greece in vain. But of all the great religions of the world, it is the Christian

church alone which is so far heir of all the ages as to fulfill the dumb, dim expectation of mankind; in it alone the sacramental meal commemorates by ordinance of its founder the divine sacrifice which is a propitiation for the sins of all mankind."

(8) Dr. Jevons' argument against the derivation of monotheism from polytheism is very forcible, and even those who dissent from it are forced to acknowledge that Jewish monotheism was due to a peculiar cause, whether that cause be called a special revelation or greater power of insight on the part of the prophets of Israel.

Among this people there was no real development of polytheism, although there were transgressions of God's law by their falling into the customs of the heathen around them; we find evidence of the occasional worship of the powers of nature side by side with the spiritual faith of their fathers. This was Syncretism, or the attempted union of such opposite forces as the worship of God and Baal. Faith in Jehovah as the God of Israel was pure monotheism, and it was connected with that perfect conception of God which was afterwards revealed in the Christ.

Dr. Jevons says: "The monotheism of the Jews is a unique and solitary phenomenon in the history of religion. Nowhere else in the world has the development of religion culminated in monotheism" (p. 388).

"The tendencies which have been supposed in polytheism to make for monotheism have always been purely pantheistic; speculative rather than practical, metaphysical rather than religious; and as being metaphysical speculations have always been confined to the cultured few, and have never even leavened the polytheism of the masses" (p. 389).

"Pantheism is the philosophical complement of

first extending until the Babylonian captivity; the second until one or two centuries after the destruction of Jerusalem by the Romans; and the third from the adpotion of the calendar of Rabbi Hillel the younger (i. e. from about the middle of the fourth century of our era) until the present time.

(1)   First Period.   In the first period the months are, as a rule, mentioned by their numerical designation only—as 'the first month,' 'the second,' etc. We have no explicit indication of the number of days in a month, nor of the number of months in a year; the 27th day and the 11th month being respectively the highest mentioned (Gen. viii:14; Deut. i:3); unless 1 Kings iv:7 be considered to prove that the year had 12 months. Nevertheless, the two Hebrew terms for month —literally new moon, thence month, from a root signifying to be new; and moon, and thence month —afford some proof that the months were measured by the moon (comp. Ps. civ:9).

(2) Second Period. In the second period we find, in part, a continuation of the previous method, with somewhat more definite statements (for instance, 1 Chron. xxvii clearly proves that the year had twelve months), and, in part, the adoption of new names for the months; but the co-existence of both these systems is not easily explained. For, whereas Zechariah, Ezra, Nehemiah, and Esther, introduce the seven new names —Shebat, Chisleu, Adar, Nisan, Elul, Tebeth, and Sivan—all the other canonical books written after the restoration do nothing more than enumerate the months, without any name, in the order of their succession. Although only the above-mentioned seven names occur in the Old Testament, yet there is no manner of doubt that the Jews at the same time adopted the entire twelve names, of which the following is a table:

Civil.	Sacred.	Beginning with the New Moon.
VII............	I. Nisan, or Abib................	March, or April. Neh. ii:1.
VIII............	II. Zif, or Ziv	April, or May. 1 Kings vi:1.
IX............	III. Sivan....................	May, or June. Esth. viii:9.
X............	IV. Tammuz....................	June, or July.
XI............	V. Ab.........................	July, or August.
XII............	VI. Elul......................	August, or September. Neh. vi:15.
I............	VII. Tishri, or Ethanim........	September, or October. 1 Kings viii:2.
II............	VIII. Bul.....................	October, or November. 1 Kings vi:38.
III............	IX. Kisleu, or Chisleu........	November, or December. Neh. i:1.
IV............	X. Tebeth....................	December, or January. Esth. ii:16.
V............	XI. Shebat...................	January, or February. Zech. i:7.
VI............	XII. Adar....................	February, or March. Esth. iii:7.

a pantheon; but the spirit which produced the monotheism of the Jews must have been something very different" (p. 390).

Those who claim that monotheism did generally develop from polytheism will be obliged to reckon with the arguments and with the stubborn facts which are presented by Dr. Jevons and other competent scholars. (See *An Introduction to the History of Religion*, by Frank Byron Jevons, M. A., Litt. D., London, Methuen & Co., 1897; see, also, *The Am. Jour. of Theol.*, p. 1,002, *sq.*) (See SEMITIC RELIGION.)

MONSTERS (mŏn'stẽrs), (Heb. תַּנִּין, *tan-neen'*, stretched out), perhaps the sea serpent or other formidable sea animal. Others suppose it to be the jackal from its running with outstretched neck and body (Lam. iv:3, R. V. "jackal.")

MONTH (mŭnth), (Heb. חֹדֶשׁ, *kho'desh*, the *new moon*).

It is expedient to distinguish three periods in the Jewish mode of denoting dates by months; the

In the same manner as the Old Testament contains no indication of the mode of intercalation, when yet it is certain that some mode must have been used, so also it does not mention by what method the commencement and conclusion of every month were ascertained in either of these periods. According to the Talmud, however, it is certain that, in the second period, the commencement of the month was dated from the time when the earliest visible appearance of the new moon was announced to the Sanhedrim, that, if this happened on the 30th day of the current month, that month was considered to have ended on the preceding 29th day, and was called *deficient;* but, if no announcement was made on the 30th day, that day was reckoned to the current month, which was in that case called *full,* and the ensuing day was at once considered to be the first of the next month. Further, as the cloudy state of the weather sometimes hindered the actual sight of the new moon, it was an established rule that no year should contain less than four, and more than eight, full months. It is generally assumed, although without express warrant, that the commencement of the month was determined in the same way in the first period; but it is very probable, and the Mosaic festivals of the new moon seem to be some evidence for it.

(3) Third Period. With regard to the third period, it is not necessary to say more here than that, as the dispersion of the Jews rendered it impossible to communicate the intelligence of the visible appearance of the new moon, they were obliged to devise a systematic calculation of the duration of their months; but that they retained the above-mentioned names for the months, which are still lunar months, of the mean duration of 29 days, 12 hours, 44 seconds; and that when they were no longer able to regulate the epochs of their festivals by the agricultural year of Palestine, they came, for some such reasons as those assigned by Michaelis, to place every month earlier by one lunation than it had been in the first two periods, so that their Nisan now most nearly coincided with March. The rabbinical writers, therefore, who maintained that the ancient Nisan likewise began with the new moon of March, were mainly led into that opinion by the practice existing in their own time. (See YEAR.)   J. N.

MONUMENTS (mŏn'ŭ-ments), (Heb. סֹבֶךְ, so'-bek, copse), the incorrect translation in Is. lxv:4, for "secret places," as in the R. V.

In general, they denote anything that brings the past to remembrance. The monuments among which idolaters lodged were either tombs or idol temples, by sleeping in which they hoped to have fellowship with the idol or the departed spirit in dreams and visions (Is. lxv:4).

MOON (mōōn), (Heb. יָרֵחַ, yaw-ray'akh, paleness; לְבָנָה, leb-aw-naw', used figuratively in Is. xxiv:23; xxx:26; Gr. σελήνη, sel-ay'nay).

The worship of the heavenly bodies was among the earliest corruptions of religion, which would naturally take its rise in the eastern parts of the world, where the atmosphere is pure and transparent, and the heavens as bright as they are glowing. In these countries the moon is of exceeding beauty. If the sun 'rules the day,' the moon has the throne of night, which, if less gorgeous than that of the sun, is more attractive, because of a less oppressively brilliant light, while her retinue of surrounding stars seems to give a sort of truth to her regal state, and certainly adds not inconsiderably to her beauty.

(1) Early Worship. The moon was therefore worshiped as a goddess in the East at a very early period; in India under the name of Maja; among the Assyrians as Mylitta; with the Phœnicians she was termed Astarte or Ashteroth, who was also denominated the Syrian mother. The Greeks and Romans worshiped her as Artemis and Diana. Job (xxxi:26) alludes to the power of the moon over the human soul: 'If I beheld the sun when it shined, or the moon walking in brightness, and my heart hath been secretly enticed, or my mouth hath kissed my hand; this also were an iniquity, for I should have denied the God that is above.'

The moon, as being mistress of the night, may well have been considered as the lesser of the two great lights of heaven (Gen. i:16). It was accordingly regarded in the old Syrian superstition as subject to the sun's influence, which was worshiped as the active and generative power of nature, while the moon was reverenced as the passive and producing power. The moon, accordingly, was looked upon as feminine. Herein Oriental usage agrees with our own. But this usage was by no means universal.

(2) Egyptian Conception. The Egyptians represented their moon as a male deity, Ihoth; and Wilkinson (*Anc. Egypt.* v:5) remarks that 'the same custom of calling it male is retained in the East to the present day, while the sun is considered feminine, as in the language of the Germans. Ihoth, in the character of Lunus, the moon, has sometimes a man's face, with the crescent of the moon upon his head supporting a disk. Plutarch says the Egyptians 'call the moon the mother of the world, and hold it to be of both sexes; female, as it receives the influence of the sun; male, as it scatters and disperses through the air the principles of fecundity.' In other countries also the moon was held to be hermaphrodite. Another pair of dissimilar qualities was ascribed to the moon—the destructive and the generative faculty—whence it was worshiped as a bad as well as a good power.

(3) Queen of Heaven. The epithet 'queen of heaven' (Horace, *siderum regina*) appears to have been very common. Nor was it, any more than the worship of the moon, unknown to the Jews, as may be seen in a remarkable passage in Jeremiah (xliv:17), where the Israelites (men and women, the latter exert most influence) appear given over to this species of idolatry: 'We will certainly burn incense to the *queen of heaven*, and pour out drink-offerings unto her, as we have done, we and our fathers; for then had we plenty of victuals, and we were well, and saw no evil. But since we left off to burn incense to the queen of heaven, we have wanted all things.' The last verse of the passage adds to the burnt-offerings and drink-offerings, 'cakes to worship her.' Vows were also made by the Jews to the moon, which superstition required to be fulfilled (verse 25).

(4) Baneful Influence. The baneful influence of the moon still finds credence in the East. Moonlight is held to be detrimental to the eyes. In Ps. cxxi:6 we read, 'The sun shall not smite thee by day, nor the moon by night;' so that the impression that the moon may do injury to man is neither partial nor vague. Rosenmüller (*Morgenland.* iv, 108) refers this to the cold of night, which, he says, is very great and sensible in the East, owing, partly, to the great heat of the day. If this extreme (comparative cold is considered in connection with the Oriental custom of sleeping *sub divo*, out of doors, *a la belle étoile*, on the flat roofs of houses, or even on the ground, without in all cases sufficient precautionary measures for protecting the frame, we see no difficulty in understanding whence arose the evil influence ascribed to the moon.

On the influence of the moon on man, see Hayn, *De Planetar. in Corp. hum. influxu;* and Kretschmar, *De Astror. in Corp. hum. Imperio,* Jena, 1820; also Carne, *Leb. und Sitten im Morgenl.* i, 73.   J. R. B.

Figurative. In the figurative language of Scripture the moon is frequently noticed as presaging events of the greatest importance through the temporary or permanent withdrawal of its light (Is. xiii:10; Joel ii:31; Matt. xxiv:29; Mark xiii:24. The church is likened to the *moon;* how comely, useful, and illuminating to the world in the dark night of time! how only illuminated by Jesus the Sun of righteousness shining on her! and how changing her militant state and condition! (Cant. vi:10; Is. lx:20). It is symbolical of coming judgments, becoming as blood (Rev. vi:12). In the passage, "And there appeared a great wonder in heaven; a woman clothed with the sun, and the moon under her feet, and upon her head a crown of twelve stars" (Rev. xii:1), the meaning appears to be that she is clothed with light from head to feet. The whole then becomes the figure of the Church illuminated with the truth and glory of God.

MOON, NEW (mōōn nū). See FESTIVALS.

MOR (mŏr), (Heb. מֹר, *môr*, distilling), sometimes written Mur, is the well-known substance MYRRH.

(1) It is the exudation of a little known tree found in Arabia, but much more extensively in Abyssinia. It formed an article of the earliest commerce, was highly esteemed by the Egyptians and Jews, as well as by the Greeks and Romans, as it still is both in the East and in Europe. The earliest notice of it occurs in Exod. xxx:23, 'Take thou also unto thee principal spices, of *pure myrrh* (*morderor*) 500 shekels.' It is afterwards mentioned in Esther ii:12, as employed in the purification of women; in Ps. xlv:8, as a perfume, 'All thy garments smell of myrrh, and aloes, and cassia;' also in several passages of the Song of Solomon, 'I will get me to the mountain of myrrh, and to the hill of frankincense' iv:6) ; 'My hands dropped with myrrh, and my fingers with *sweet smelling* myrrh' v:5). We find it mentioned in Matt. ii:11, among the gifts presented by the wise men of the East to the infant Jesus—'gold, and frankincense, and myrrh.' It may be remarked as worthy of notice, that myrrh and frankincense are frequently mentioned together. In Mark xv:23, we learn that the Roman soldiers 'gave him (Jesus) to drink wine mingled with *myrrh;* but he received it not.' The Apostle John (xix:39) says, 'Then came also Nicodemus, and brought a mixture of myrrh and aloes (see AHALIM), about an hundred pound weight,' for the purpose of embalming the body of our Savior.

(2) Though myrrh seems to have been known from the earliest times, and must consequently have been one of the most ancient articles of commerce, the country producing it long remained unknown. It is collected in small kid-skins, and taken to Errur, whence the Hurrah merchants, on their way from Shoa, convey it to the great annual market at Berberah from whence great quantities are shipped for India and Arabia.' When the Portuguese first entered these seas, gold dust, ivory, myrrh, and slaves formed the staple commerce of Adal. Though there is no doubt that the largest quantity of myrrh has always been obtained from Africa, yet it is equally certain that some is also procured in Arabia. Mr. Johnson, in his recently published *Travels in Abyssinia* (i. 249), mentions that 'Myrrh and mimosa trees abounded in this place' (Koranhedudah in Adal). The former he describes as being a low, thorny, ragged-looking tree, with bright-green trifoliate leaves; the gum exudes from cracks in the bark of the trunk near the root, and flows freely upon the stones immediately underneath. Artificially it is obtained by bruises made with stones. The natives collect it principally in the hot months of July and August, but it is to be found, though in very small quantities, at other times of the year.

(3) Several kinds of myrrh were known to the ancients, and in modern commerce we have Turkish and East Indian myrrh, and different names used to be, and are still applied to it, as red and fatty myrrh, myrrh in tears, in sorts, and myrrh in grains. In the Bible also several kinds of myrrh are enumerated, respecting which various opinions have been entertained.

(4) Myrrh, it is well known, was celebrated in the most ancient times as a perfume, and a fumi-

gant, as well as for its uses in medicine. Myrrh was burned in their temples, and employed in embalming the bodies of the dead. It was offered in presents, as natural products commonly were in those days, because such as were procured from distant countries were very rare. The ancients prepared a *wine of myrrh,* and also an *oil of myrrh,* and it formed an ingredient in many of the

Myrrh.

most celebrated compound medicines, as the *Theriaca,* the *Mithridata, Manus Dei,* etc. Even in Europe it continued to recent times to enjoy the highest medicinal reputation, as it does in the East in the present day. From the sensible properties of this drug, and from the virtues which were ascribed to it, we may satisfactorily account for the mention of it in the several passages of Scripture which have been quoted. (See MYRRH.)

J. F. R.

MORASTHITE (mō'ras-thīte),(Heb. מֹרַשְׁתִּי, *morash-tee'*), an inhabitant of Moresheth-Gath (Jer. xxvi:18; Mic. i:1).

MORAVIAN CHURCH IN THE UNITED STATES.

(1) **Founding and Characteristics.** This church was known as the United Brethren before the term Moravian Church came into vogue. The latter appellation is derived from the land in which the church in question was formerly the chief representative of the evangelical faith, and from which refugees came to Saxony in 1722, to accomplish its resuscitation after it had been almost extirpated by persecution. Evangelical loyalty to the essentials of the Christian faith, combined with an unwillingness to bind men's consciences to the exact phraseology of a humanly constructed creed in reference to mysteries of the truth, and an exaltation of the value of devout Christian life above professed adherence to symbols apprehended by the intellect, have been characteristic of the Moravian Church from the first, and, since 1732, it has realized that its special calling is to carry the gospel to the neglected hea-

then, whilst in home lands its members fraternize with all who love the Lord Jesus in sincerity.

In accordance with these characteristics and purposes the Moravian Church has consistently shunned every effort at proselytism in Christian lands, though it has freely expended men and means to foster vital religion within state churches in Europe, without seeking to withdraw members from fellowship in those churches.

Founded by spiritual descendants of John Hus in Bohemia in 1457, the Moravian Church was almost extirpated in consequence of the Thirty Years' War, although it had previously spread widely throughout Bohemia, Moravia, Poland and Prussia.

Providentially resuscitated in Saxony during the years from 1722 to 1727 by refugees who were harbored on the estates of Count Zinzendorf, himself destined to become identified with it as a future bishop, its attention was turned to America by two causes: Persecutions at home suggested the wisdom of securing an asylum where religious liberty might be enjoyed; the possibility of inaugurating missions amongst the Indians and the negro slaves became a call of duty. "From the trustees of Georgia Count Zinzendorf obtained a grant of 500 acres of land on the Ogeeche River, and Spangenberg another of fifty acres, forming part of the present site of Savannah. In the spring of 1735, the latter began a settlement, on his tract, with a number of Moravians." (*Moravian Manual*, pp. 38, 39.) This settlement proved a failure, largely owing to the war between England and Spain. The remnant of the Moravian colonists in Georgia, in 1740, came to Philadelphia as passengers in George Whitefield's sloop. "At the invitation of Whitefield they proceeded in May to the Forks of the Delaware, the present Northampton County, where he had purchased a domain of 5,000 acres, embracing what is now Upper Nazareth Township, and began to build a large house destined to be a school for negro children. Ere long, however, doctrinal differences, fostered by the inhabitants of the Scotch-Irish settlements, produced an open rupture between the Moravians and Whitefield, who ordered them to leave his land forthwith. In this extremity Bishop Nitschmann came from Europe commissioned to begin a settlement in Pennsylvania. Ten miles to the south of Whitefield's domain, he purchased an extensive tract, on the Lehigh River." (*Moravian Manual*, p. 40.) The settlement founded here was named Bethlehem. "It was originally intended as a center for the Indian Mission"—begun in 1740 at Shekomeko near the Stissik Mountains, between New York and Connecticut. "But other immigrants having arrived from Germany, a church settlement was organized, June 25, 1742, strictly on the plan of those established by Zinzendorf in his native land, with all their appliances of exclusivism." (*Moravian Manual*, p. 40.) In addition to maintaining an Indian mission, which spread in New York, Connecticut, Pennsylvania, and later in Ohio, an extensive itinerary was undertaken amongst white settlers—Germans, Swedes and English, as well as amongst the negro slaves; but no effort was made to extend the Moravian Church as such amongst those who had not been identified with it in Europe. Rather were applicants for admission to fellowship discouraged, it being the aim of the Moravian evangelists to promote vital Christianity and not to build up a sect. Just here the Moravians failed to recognize the difference between the religious characteristics of this land free from the trammels of a state church and their old conditions of operation in Europe;

and this feature largely accounts for the numerical weakness of the Moravian Church in America to-day. Between the years 1742 and 1748 the Moravians in Pennsylvania devoted themselves, aside from their mission amongst the Indians, to an effort to bring about an organic union amongst the German-speaking Christians of the colony, no German denomination having as yet effected actual organization. But this laudable effort failed.

(2) Denominational Form. Accordingly, the Moravian Church in America was compelled to recognize the leadings of Providence and assume definite denominational form. Its leaders chose to bring the groups of affiliated persons in seven of the original thirteen states into as close an affinity as possible with the German congregations of the church in Europe, and to model their life after the pattern of the exclusive settlements of the Unity there, so as to constitute the Moravian villages spiritual retreats cut off from the rest of the world, where pious souls might cultivate their own Christian life and be mutually helpful in promoting growth in grace. In 1753 a tract was purchased in North Carolina, and here, too, the life in Pennsylvania was duplicated, the chief centers now being Bethlehem, Nazareth and Lititz in Pennsylvania, and after 1766 Salem in North Carolina.

(3) Moravian Villages. The following were the characteristics of the Moravian villages: "None but members were allowed to hold real estate, although others might lease houses. In each settlement there was a public inn and one or more mercantile establishments or trades, belonging to the church, the profits of which went towards its support. This arrangement did not exclude private enterprise and trades, of which there were many. The settlements were governed by a council called the "Board of Overseers," elected by the adult male members of the church. At the head of a council stood a Deacon, who bore the title of 'Warden,' and was its executive officer. On business of importance a general meeting of the adult male members was convened. The purpose of this exclusive system was to keep out of the congregation, as much as possible, the follies and sins of the world, and to promote sober, righteous and holy living. By the blessing of God this was accomplished in a great degree. The peculiar institutions belonging to a settlement were the Brethren's, Sisters' and Widows' Houses. In a Brethren's House unmarried men lived together, and carried on various trades and professions, the profits of which were applied to the support of the establishment and of the church in general. A Sisters' House was inhabited by unmarried women who engaged in different kinds of work. In each house there was a common refectory, dormitory and prayer-hall. Daily religious services were held. There was nothing monastic in the principles underlying these establishments, or in the regulations by which they were governed. The inmates were almost invariably such as had no other homes, and stayed in them at their own option, gaining an honest and decent livelihood, and enjoying the advantage of regular religious instructions. In many instances they were training schools for missionaries. A Widows' House was a home for indigent or other widows, supplying the inmates with all the comforts which they needed at moderate charges, and enabling the poorest to live in a respectable manner. Each house had a spiritual and temporal superintendent—females in the case of Sisters' and Widows' Houses." (*Moravian Manual*, pp. 55 and 56.)

(4) Independence of American Province.
Up to the middle of the present century, when this whole system was abolished, the Moravian Church in America practically formed merely an outpost of the Moravian Church in Germany. Constitutional changes were effected in 1857. Since then the American province of the church is independent so far as its own internal administration is concerned, and has pursued a natural policy of church extension. It now has congregations in Pennsylvania, New York, New Jersey, Maryland, Ohio, Michigan, Indiana, Illinois, Iowa, Missouri, Kansas, Wisconsin, Minnesota, North Dakota, North Carolina, Virginia, Indian Territory, and Alberta Territory, Canada. The entire membership in America numbers 22,345. There are two provincial synods in America, which elect "provincial elders" as the executive boards, having headquarters at Bethlehem, Pa., and Salem, N. C. But the American Moravian Church forms an organic whole in union with the Moravian bodies in Great Britain and on the continent of Europe. The highest legislative body is the General Synod, meeting once in ten years, and constituted of representatives of the three provinces and of the missions among the heathen which constitute the joint enterprise of the entire Moravian Church. The General Synod reviews the life, regulates the statements of doctrine, orders the ritual—liturgical in form, elects bishops, receives a report of the entire management of the missions, and elects the mission board, which has its headquarters at Berthelsdorf.

(5) Missions. The missions amongst the heathen, with an entire membership of about 95,000, are divided into the following missionary provinces: Greenland, Labrador, the Indian mission in North America, Alaska, Jamaica, the eastern islands of the West Indies, Nicaragua, Demerara, Surinam, Cape Colony, Kaffraria, German East Africa, Victoria, North Queensland, the Western Himalayan, and the Leper Hospital in Jerusalem. More than 400 missionaries, foreign and native, are employed. Last year the cost was $404,282.50. In addition a work of evangelization is carried on in Bohemia and Moravia, in which all the "provinces" participate.

(6) Doctrines. The doctrinal standpoint of the Moravian Church is thus set forth by the General Synod:

(1) *The Doctrines of the Moravian Church.* We esteem every truth revealed to us by God as a precious treasure, and heartily believe that such a treasure dare not be let go, even though we could thereby save our body or our life (Luke ix :24). But most especially do we affirm this of *that one* doctrine which the Renewed Brethren's Church has from the beginning regarded as her chief doctrine, and over which she has hitherto, by God's grace, kept guard as a priceless jewel: That "Jesus Christ is the propitiation for our sins, and not for ours only, but also for the whole world" (I John ii:2). For "Him who knew no sin, God made to be sin on our behalf; that we might become the righteousness of God in Him" (2 Cor. v:21) ; or, as we sing in one of our hymns:

Whosoever believeth in Christ's redemption,
Will find free grace and a complete exemption
   From serving sin!

(2) With this our leading doctrine, the following facts and truths, clearly attested by Holy Scripture, are linked in essential connection, and therefore constitute, with that leading doctrine,

the most prominent and main features of our understanding and our proclamation of the way of salvation :

(a) The doctrine of the *total depravity of our human nature; i. e.,* that since the Fall there is no health in man, and that he has no powers left by which to save himself (John iii :6; Rom. iii: 23; vii :18; i :18-32; iii :9-18; Eph. ii :8-13).

(b) The doctrine of the *love of God, the Father, to the fallen human race,* according to which he "chose us in Christ, before the foundation of the world," and "so loved the world that he gave his only begotten Son, that whosoever believeth in Him should not perish, but have eternal life" (Eph. i :3, 4; ii :4; John iii :16; I John iv :9).

(c) The doctrine of the *real Godhead* and the *real humanity of Jesus Christ; i. e.,* that the only begotten Son of God, he by whom all things in heaven and earth were created, forsook the glory which he had with the Father before the world was, and took upon him our flesh and blood, that in all things he might be made like unto his brethren, yet without sin (John i :1-3; i :14; xvii :5; Phil. ii :6, 7; Heb. ii :14, 17; iv :15; Col. i :17-19; I John v :20).

(d) The doctrine of our *reconciliation to God* and our *justification before him through the sacrifice of Jesus Christ, i. e.,* that Christ "was delivered up for our trespasses, and was raised for our justification," and that alone by faith in him "we have through his blood forgiveness of sin," "peace with God," and freedom from the service of sin (Rom. iii :24, 25; v :1; I Cor. i :30; Heb. ii :17; ix :12; I Peter i :18, 19; I John i :9; 2 Cor. v :18, 19).

(e) The doctrine of the *Holy Ghost and the operations of his grace, i. e.,* that without him we are unable to know the truth; that it is he who leads us to Christ, by working in us the knowledge of sin and faith in Jesus, and that he "beareth witness with our spirit that we are children of God" (John xvi :8-11, 13, 14; I Cor. xii: 3; Rom. viii :16).

(f) The doctrine of *good works as the fruit of the Spirit, i. e.,* that in them faith manifests itself as a living acting power, which induces us, out of love and gratitude to him who died for us, willingly to follow the commandments of God (John xiv :15; Rom. vi :11-14; I Cor. vi :20; Gal. v :6, 22-24; I John v :3-5; Eph. ii :8-10; James ii :17).

(g) The doctrine of *the fellowship of believers one with another, i. e.,* that they are all one in Christ Jesus, the Head of his body, and are all members one of another (John xvii :21; Matt. xxiii :8; Eph. iv :4).

(h) The doctrine of the *second coming of the Lord in glory, and of the resurrection of the dead, unto life or unto judgment* (Acts i :11; John vi: 40; xi :25, 26; iii :36; v :25-29; I Thess. iv: 14-17).

(3) Whilst we do not draw up and set forth these truths and our acceptance of them in a strictly formulated creed, our apprehension of the chief substance of Christian doctrine has found in a special way its expression in what has been solemnly declared by our church, year by year, for more than 100 years past, in our Litany on Easter morning.—*Results of the General Synod of the Brethren's Unity,* 1889, pp. 13-15.

(7) No Organic Union. That the American Moravian Church will in the near future unite organically with any other American church is very unlikely. She cannot do so without detriment to her chief form of usefulness, which she shares with the European divisions of the Moravian Church—the work of evangelization amongst the heathen. At the same time she is ready to fellowship with evangelical believers of every name.   J. T. H.

MORDECAI (môr'de-kāi), (Heb. יְרֳכַּדְמָ, *mor-dek-ah'ee,* supposed to come from the Persian word, meaning *little man, mannikin;* or, according to others, from the idol *Merodach,* thus signifying *a votary of Merodach, or a worshiper of Mars.* The last supposition is not unlikely, seeing that Daniel had the Chaldean name of Belshazzar; Sept. Μαρδοχαῖος, *mar-doh-kai'os).*

1. Esther's uncle. He was the son of Jair, of the tribe of Benjamin, descended from one of the captives transported to Babylon with Jehoiachin (Esth. ii:5). He was resident at Susa, then the metropolis of the Persian empire, and had under his care his niece Hadessa, otherwise Esther, at the time when the fairest damsels of the land were gathered together, that from among them a fitting successor to queen Vashti might be selected for king Ahasuerus. Among them was Esther, and on her the choice fell; while, by what management we know not, her relationship to Mordecai, and her Jewish descent, remained unknown at the palace. The uncle lost none of his influence over the niece by her elevation, although the seclusion of the royal harem excluded him from direct intercourse with her.

(1) In the King's Service. He seems to have held some office about the court; for we find him in daily attendance there, and it appears to have been through this employment that he became privy to a plot of two of the chamberlains against the life of the king, which through Esther he made known to the monarch. This great service was however suffered to pass without reward at the time.

(2) Jews Threatened. On the rise of Haman to power at court, Mordecai alone, of all the nobles and officers who crowded the royal gates, refused to manifest the customary signs of homage to the royal favorite. It would be too much to attribute this to an independence of spirit, which, however usual in Europe, is unknown in Eastern courts. Haman was an Amalekite; and Mordecai brooked not to bow himself down before one of a nation which from the earliest times had been the most devoted enemies of the Jewish people. The Orientals are tenacious of the outward marks of respect, which they hold to be due to the position they occupy; and the erect mien of Mordecai among the bending courtiers escaped not the keen eye of Haman. He noticed it, and brooded over it from day to day; he knew well the class of feelings in which it originated, and—remembering the eternal enmity vowed by the Israelites against his people, and how often their conquering sword had all but swept his nation from the face of the earth—he vowed by one great stroke to exterminate the Hebrew nation, the fate of which he believed to be in his hands. The temptation was great, and to his ill-regulated mind irresistible. He therefore procured the well-known and bloody decree from the king for the massacre of all the Israelites in the empire in one day. When this decree became known to Mordecai, he covered himself with sackcloth and ashes, and rent the air with his cries. This being made known to Esther through the servants of the harem, who now knew of their relationship, she sent Hatach, one of the royal eunuchs, to demand the cause of his grief; through that faithful servant he made the facts known to her, urged upon her the duty of delivering her people, and encouraged her to risk the consequences of the at-

tempt. She was found equal to the occasion. She risked her life by entering the royal presence uncalled, and having by discreet management procured a favorable opportunity, accused Haman to the king of plotting to destroy *her* and her people. His doom was sealed on this occasion by the means which in his agitation he took to avert it; and when one of the eunuchs present intimated that this man had prepared a gallows fifty cubits high on which to hang Mordecai, the king at once said, 'Hang him thereon.'

(3) Exaltation. This was, in fact, a great aggravation of his offense, for the previous night, the king, being unable to sleep, had commanded the records of his reign to be read to him; and the reader had providentially turned to the part recording the conspiracy which had been frustrated through Mordecai. The king asked what had been the reward of this mighty service, and being answered 'nothing,' he commanded that any one who happened to be in attendance without, should be called. Haman was there, having come for the very purpose of asking the king's leave to hang Mordecai upon the gallows he had prepared, and was asked what should be done to the man whom the king delighted to honor. Thinking that the king could delight to honor no one but himself, he named the highest and most public honors he could conceive, and received from the monarch the astounding answer, 'Make haste, and do even so to Mordecai that sitteth in the king's gate!' Then was Haman constrained, without a word, and with seeming cheerfulness, to repair to the man whom he hated beyond all the world, to invest him with the royal robes, and to conduct him in magnificent cavalcade through the city, proclaiming, 'Thus shall it be done to the man whom the king delighteth to honor.' After this we may well believe that the sense of poetical justice decided the, perhaps till then, doubtful course of the king, when he heard of the gallows which Haman had prepared for the man by whom his own life had been preserved.

Mordecai was invested with power greater than that which Haman had lost, and the first use he made of it was, as far as possible, to neutralize or counteract the decree obtained by Haman. It could not be recalled, as the kings of Persia had no power to rescind a decree once issued; but as the altered wish of the court was known, and as the Jews were permitted to stand on their defense, they were preserved from the intended destruction, although much blood was, on the appointed day, shed even in the royal city. The Feast of Purim was instituted in memory of this deliverance, and is celebrated to this day (Esth. ii:5; x). (See PURIM). B. C. 479.

2. A Mordecai, who returned from the exile with Zerubbabel, is mentioned in Ezra ii:2 and Neh. vii:7; but this cannot well have been the Mordecai of Esther, as some have supposed. (B. C. 536.)

MOREH (mō'reh), (Heb. הָרֹומ, *mo-reh',* teaching).

1. A name, perhaps derived from a Canaanitish chief, and given to the oak tree or grove near Shechem, where Abraham halted when he entered Canaan (Gen. xii:6; Deut. xi:29, 30). He erected an altar to Jehovah, who appeared to him here. No doubt Jacob here buried the amulets and idols which his family brought from Haran; and here Joshua erected a monument commemorating the covenant which the people renewed there. Here, too, the men of Shechem came to make Abimelech king (Gen. xxxv:4; Josh. xxiv:26).

2. A hill in the valley of Jezreel where the Midianites and Amalekites encamped before the attack by Gideon (Judg. vii:1). It is perhaps the same as Little Hermon, eight miles northwest of Mount Gilboa.

MORESHETH-GATH (mŏr'esh-eth-găth),(Heb. מוֹרֶשֶׁת גַּת, *mo-reh'sheth gath*, possession of Gath), a place named with towns in the low country of Judah, where Micah, the prophet, was born or lived (Mic. i:14; i:1; i:13-15; Jer. xxvi: 18). Jerome locates it near Eleutheropolis. (See Robinson ii, 423).

MORIAH (mo-rī'ah), (Heb. מֹרִיָּה, *mo-ree-yaw'*, seen or chosen of Jehovah), one of the hills of Jerusalem, on which the temple was built by Solomon (2 Chron. iii:1).

The name seldom occurs, being usually included in that of Zion, to the northeast of which it lay, and from which it was separated by the valley of Tyropœon (Joseph. *Antiq.* viii, 3-9). (See JERUSALEM.) The Land of Moriah, whither Abraham went to offer up Isaac (Gen. xxii:2), is generally supposed to denote the same place, and may at least be conceived to describe the surrounding district. The Jews themselves believe that the altar of burnt-offerings in the temple stood upon the very site of the altar on which the patriarch purposed to sacrifice his son. (See KING; JERUSALEM, 8.)

MORNING (môrn'ĭng), (Heb. בֹּקֶר, *bo'ker*, Gen. i:5, *sq.*, Gr. πρωΐα, *pro-ee'ah*, Matt. xxi:18), the early part of the day immediately following sunrise. (See DAY.)

Figurative. (1) The morning is represented as having *eyelids,* to represent the first appearance of the rising light in the reddish sky (Job xli: 18); as having *wings,* to denote the quick spread of light (Ps. cxxxix:9); and as having a *womb* from which the dew is produced (Ps. cx:3). (2) "Every morning," is daily; often (Ps. lxxiii:14). (3) "In the morning," is early; seasonably; earnestly; suddenly (Ps. v:3; xxx:5). (4) To execute judgment "in the morning," is to do it readily, and as seasonably and speedily as possible (Ps. ci:8; Jer. xxi:12). (5) To "eat in the morning," denotes unseasonable and intemperate eating and drinking; luxury (Eccl. x:16; Jer. v:8). (6) The church is likened to the "morning" (Cant. vi:10). (7) A state of grace is called a "morning." It comes after a sad night of sin and misery; and how happily is one awakened, enlightened and refreshed by the gradual increase of its spiritual discoveries, and application of heart-warming love, till it issue in the high day of eternal happiness! (Is. viii:20). (8) A season of prosperity or gospel opportunity, is called a "morning;" it comes after a night of distress, or dark ignorance; and how delightful and refreshing! (Is. xxi:12). (9) The general resurrection is called a "morning;" after a night of darkness and deathful sleep, how shall men be awakened by the last trumpet, enlightened by the glory of, and manifold discoveries made by, the Son of man! and into what an everlasting day it ushers the saints! (Ps. xlix:12). (10) Fearful judgments are likened to the "morning" (Ezek. vii:7, sq.).

MORNING SACRIFICE (môrn'ĭng sak'rĭ-fīz). See PRIEST, HEBREW PRIESTHOOD.

MORNING STAR (môrn'ĭng stär). See ASTRONOMY.

MORNING WATCH (môrn'ĭng wŏch). See WATCH.

75

MORROW (mŏr'rŏ). The translation of several Hebrew and Greek words:

1. *Maw-khar'* (Heb. מָחָר), deferred (Exod. viii:10, *sq.;* ix:6; xix:10; Num. xvi:7, 16; Josh. v:11, 12, etc.).

2. *Bo'ker* (Heb. בֹּקֶר), early dawn, break of day (Lev. xxii:30; Num. xvi:5; xxii:41, etc.).

3. *Hex-ace'* (Gr. ἑξῆς), successive (Acts xxv:17).

4. *Ow'ree-on* (Gr. αὔριον), breeze, i. e., morning air (Matt. vi:30, 34; Luke x:35; xii:28; xiii:32, 33; Acts xxv:17, 22, etc.).

5. *Ep-ow'ree-on* (Gr. ἐπαύριον), the following day (Mark xi:12; Acts x:9, 23; xxiii:32; xxv: 23). (See DAY.)

MORSEL (môr'sĕl), (Heb. פַּת, *path*, bit; Gr. βρῶσις, *bro'sis*, eating, either the act or that which is eaten).

1. A small piece of bread (Ps. cxlvii:17); comp. Judg. xix:5; Ruth ii:14; 1 Sam. xxviii:22; 1 Kings xvii:11).

2. A meal of meat (Heb. xii:16). "Better is a dry morsel with quietness than a house full of sacrifices with strife." Better is the meanest fare, in a state of peace with God, and in the enjoyment of peace of conscience, and of true peace with men, than the most abundant and delicate provision without it (Prov. xvii:1).

MORTAL (môr'tal), (Heb. אֱנוֹשׁ, *en-oshe'*), a term employed to denote a human being (Job iv:17). The Greek θνητός (*thnay-tos'*, liable to die) is applied to man's natural body as compared with the body hereafter to be assumed (Rom. vi:12; 1 Cor. xv:53, 54; 2 Cor. iv:11).

MORTALITY (môr-tăl'ĭ-tў), (Gr. θνητός, *thnay-tos'*, 2 Cor. v:4), subjection to death.

It is the wish of St. Paul that death may be annihilated by life (comp. 2 Tim. i:10). "The appearing of our Savior Jesus Christ, who hath *abolished death,* and hath brought life and immortality to light through the gospel."

MORTAR (môr'tẽr).

1. (Heb. עָפָר, *aw-fawr'*), properly dry earth or dust; from a root עָפַר, *aw-far'*, to be pale or whitish (Lev. xiv:42,45). It may be either a cement of lime and sand (Gen. xi:3; Ex. i:14), or mud or clay used like cement for building purposes (Lev. xiv:42, 45). In Ezek. xiii:10, "untempered mortar" means mortar without straw. In Babylon where clay and lime were scarce bitumen was used in place of mortar.

2. (Heb. מְדֹכָה, *med-o-kaw'*, Num. xi:8; מַכְתֵּשׁ, *mak-taysh'*, hollow, Judg. xv:19; Prov. xxvii:22), a hollow vessel of wood, stone, or metal, used for reducing grain and spices by means of a pestle (Num. xi:8; Prov. xxvii:22). The Arabs of the present day use the stone mortar for grinding grain.

MORTGAGE (môr'găj), (Heb. עָרַב, *aw-rab'*, to give security, to pawn, Neh. v:3), a lien upon real estate for debt. In 1 Sam. xvii:18 it is translated "pledge," and in Prov. xvii:18 "surety."

MORTIFICATION (môr'tĭ-fĭ-kā'shŭn), any severe penance observed on a religious account.

The mortification of sin in believers is a duty enjoined in the sacred Scriptures (Rom. viii:13; Col. iii:5). It consists in breaking the league with sin; declaration of open hostility against it; and strong resistance of it (Eph. vi:10, etc.; Gal. v:24; Rom. viii:13). *The means* to be used in this work are not macerating the body, seclusion from society, our own resolutions; but the Holy Spirit is the chief agent (Rom. viii:13), while faith, prayer and dependence are subordinate means to this end. *The evidences of mortification* are not the cessation from one sin, for that may be only exchanged for another; or it may be renounced because it is a gross sin; or there may not be an occasion to practice it; but if sin be mortified, we shall not yield to temptation; our minds will be more spiritual; we shall find more happiness in spiritual services and bring forth the fruits of the Spirit.

MOSERA (mo-sē'rȧ), (Heb. מוֹסֵרָה, *mo-say-raw'*, chastisement), a station of the Israelites near Mount Hor (Num. xxxiii:30; Deut. x:6). In the last passage the name appears in the plural, *Moseroth*. (See WANDERING, THE.)

MOSEROTH (mo-sē'roth), (Heb. מוֹסֵרוֹת, *moser-othe'*, correction), a station of the Israelites named between Hashmonah and Bene-jaaken (Num. xxxiii:30, 31); same as MOSERA.

MOSES (mō'zez), (Heb. מֹשֶׁה, *mo-sheh'*).

1. Name and Family. The lawgiver of Israel. He belonged to the tribe of Levi, and was a son of Amram and Jochebed (Exod. vi:20). According to Exod. ii:10, the name מֹשֶׁה, *Mosheh*, means *drawn out of water*. Even ancient writers knew that the correctness of this interpretation could be proved by a reference to the Egyptian language (comp. Joseph. *Antiq.* ii, 9, 6; *contra Apionem*, i, 31; Philo, ii, 83, etc., ed. Mang). The name contains also an allusion to the verb to be, *extracted, pulled out*. Hence it appears that *Mosheh* is a significant memorial of the marvelous preservation of Moses when an infant, in spite of those Pharaonic edicts which were promulgated in order to lessen the number of the Israelites. It was the intention of divine Providence that the great and wonderful destiny of the child should be from the first apparent; and what the Lord had done for Moses he intended also to accomplish for the whole nation of Israel.

This table shows the pedigree of Moses:

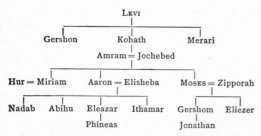

2. **Personal History.** His life falls naturally into three divisions, of forty years each, according to the account preserved in Stephen's speech (Acts vii:23, 30, 36).

(1) Birth. Moses was born in the dark hour of Hebrew story when a son was an object of the murderous search of the Egyptian spies. His father was Amram, his mother Jochebed; his tribe was Levi, and this fact may have determined the choice of Levi for the priesthood. Moses was the youngest child of the family; Miriam was the oldest, and Aaron came between. For three months his parents hid the babe, but at last it was no longer possible, and Jochebed, with a trembling heart, but it may be with a dim consciousness that God had great things in store for him, laid him in the little basket of papyrus she had

deftly woven, pitched with bitumen within and without, and, carrying it down to the brink of one of the canals of the Nile, she hid it among the flags. The child was tenderly watched "afar off" by Miriam, who, less open to suspicion than the mother would be, stood to see what would be done to him. The daughter of the Pharaoh, the oppressor, came to the sacred river to bathe, attended by her maidens, who, surprised to find the basket, which had providentially floated down to the princess' bathing place—or had Jochebed purposely put it there?—call the attention of their mistress to the discovery. The basket is fetched by one of them, and when opened a little babe, evidently one of the Hebrews' children, but exceedingly fair, is revealed to view. The woman-heart of the princess, who was a childless wife according to tradition, yearned over the little one. Her yearning was of God. Then Miriam drew near, gathered from the conversation that the child's life was to be spared, proposed to get a nurse for him among the Hebrew women, and thus it came to pass that Jochebed again had her child at her breast, but this time as his hired nurse.

Pharaoh's daughter called him Mosheh, because she *drew him out* of the water. She took care to have him instructed in all the sciences then known in Egypt. In his earliest years, Jochebed and Amram, no doubt, took care to instruct him in the Hebrew language, and in the principles of the true religion, and in the knowledge of the promises that God had made concerning Israel.

(2) Life in Egypt. The second division of Moses' life was totally different in its character from the first. Moses, at the age of forty, is learned in all the wisdom of the Egyptians. The adopted grandson of the Pharaoh, initiated in the secrets of the priests, to whose order he belonged, he had a brilliant and useful worldly career before him. Had he remained in his advantageous surroundings, he would have been one of the great Egyptian sages—probably the greatest of them all. But God intended him to occupy a much more exalted position. There was needed by him a period of meditation. He must be cut off from books, and by direct contact with nature in all her moods learn what books cannot give. Being divinely instructed that he was to be the deliverer of Israel, he went to visit his brethren at their hard labor. Observing an Egyptian cruelly abusing a Hebrew, and going to murder him, he hastened to them, assisted the Hebrew, killed the Egyptian, and hid his body in the sand. Next day he observed two Hebrews at variance, and begged the faulty person not to hurt his brother. The fellow insolently replied, "Who made you a ruler or judge over us? will you kill me, as you did the Egyptian yesterday?" Finding that his slaughter of the Egyptian was divulged, he fled into the country of Midian, on the Red Sea. It is probable that the murder was intended to impress upon the Hebrews his desire to help them—that he, the king's son, would be their deliverer; for it seems impossible to resist the conclusion that the pious teachings of his mother had not been forgotten, and that many prayers had been put up by him, as he determined to be his brethren's savior. But we see now that it was no wonder that this attempt at an insurrection proved abortive, and likewise that Moses had much to learn before he could properly lead the great Exodus.

(3) In the Wilderness. Moses fled from the prominence, the refinement, and the luxury of the court to the obscurity, the roughness, and the poverty of the wilderness. Sitting down by a well, the seven daughters of Jethro came up to it with their flocks; they had scarcely filled the troughs with the water which they drew, when some barbarous fellows came up, and would have the water to their flocks. Moses assisted the damsels, and drove away the injurious shepherds. Jethro had no sooner heard of his kindness to his daughters, than he ordered him to be called in, and get a refreshment. Moses hired himself to feed Jethro's flock, and received his daughter Zipporah in marriage, by whom he had two sons. The first he called *Gershom,* to denote his being a *stranger* in that place; the other he called *Eliezer,* to denote that his *God was his help* (Exod. ii; Acts vii:20-29; Heb. xi:24, 25, 26).

At last the king of Egypt, by whose daughter Moses had been educated, was dead; but the bondage of the Hebrews still continued under their new tyrant.

(4) The Burning Bush. As Moses one day led his flocks near to the north or west side of Sinai, the Lord appeared to him in a bush burning, but not consumed. Moses, astonished, went near to see the miracle. The Lord spake to him out of the bush, and bade him put off his shoes before he came any nearer, as the spot was sacred by the presence of God. He then declared himself to be the God of Abraham, Isaac, and Jacob; and that from regard to his promise, and to the groans of his oppressed people he now intended to deliver them, and bring them into Canaan, by Moses as the instrument. Moses began to excuse himself, as the Hebrews would not believe that he had a mission. God promised him his presence, and bade him tell the Hebrews that the GREAT I AM, who is being itself, and gives being to his creatures, and fulfills every promise, had sent him to inform them of their approaching deliverance; and assured him that they then would believe him. He ordered him to go to Pharaoh, and, in the name of Jehovah, to require him to let the Hebrews go three days' journey into the Arabian Desert, to offer a solemn sacrifice to the Lord. Meanwhile he told him that Pharaoh would not grant this request, till he and his country should be almost ruined by fearful plagues. Moses still excusing himself, God encouraged him by a fourfold sign: His rod was turned into a serpent, to signify what plagues it would bring on the Egyptians. It was returned to a rod, to mark how useful it would prove for the support of the Hebrews. To mark how easily God would weaken the power of the Egyptians, and strengthen the Israelites, Moses' hand, being put into his bosom, became leprous, white as snow; and again returned into his bosom, became sound as the other. These miracles he was ordered to repeat before the Hebrews, for the confirmation of his mission; and if necessary, to add the taking of water out of the river, and it should become blood. Moses then urged that he had not a ready utterance of speech, and begged to be excused, and urged the Lord would send some more proper person. Offended with his unbelief, God told him that he could qualify him with speech; and that Aaron, who was just coming to meet him, should be his assistant and spokesman. Moses being at last persuaded, went and obtained the leave of his father-in-law to go and visit his parents in Egypt. He took his wife and children along with him. As they were in an inn by the way, an angel threatened to slay Moses, it is supposed on account of his neglect to circumcise his child, or children. To prevent his death, Zipporah took a sharp stone, and having cut off her child's foreskin, cast or laid it at the feet either of her husband or of the child, and said that now she had preserved his life by bloodshed, and he or his son was now her bloody bridegroom. Zipporah and her children returned to her father; but Moses pursued his course into Egypt, and was met by Aaron his brother. They told the Hebrews what God had said, and showed them the signs; the people believed and were filled with joyful expectation of deliverance (Exod. iii, iv).

(5) In Goshen. Arrived at Goshen, Moses and Aaron at once began the discharge of their commission. But their primary efforts only increased the subject people's burdens, and the two brothers were wellnigh in despair. Then began the series of miraculous visitations recounted in Exod. vii-xii. The last of the plagues when the firstborn of the Egyptians were slain caused Pharaoh's servants to influence him to give the Hebrews their dismission. By the sprinkling of the blood of the Passover lambs on the doorposts and upper lintels, they had their families protected from the destroying angel (Exod. v-xii; Deut. iv: 34, and xi:3; Heb. xi:23-29).

3. The Exodus. The third period begins with the Exodus. The Hebrews having taken their departure from Egypt in great haste, and having carried along with them a good part of the wealth of the Egyptians, took their journey to the southeast. Pharaoh and his people repented of letting them go; and with a mighty army pursued them, and almost overtook them on the west of the Red Sea. The Hebrews murmured against Moses, for bringing them out of Egypt. Moses prayed to the Lord for deliverance. By God's direction, he stretched his rod over the Red Sea, and it (where perhaps about eighteen miles broad), parted asunder, and gave the Hebrews an easy passage. By taking off the wheels of their chariots, and darkening their way, the Lord retarded the march of the Egyptians; and when the Hebrews were all over, and the Egyptians all in the channel, Moses, at God's direction, stretched his rod to the sea, and it, moved by a strong wind, suddenly returned, and drowned the host. (See MENEPTAH, INSCRIPTIONS OF.) On the east side of the sea, Moses and the men, and Miriam and the women of Israel, sung a song of praise for their miraculous deliverance.

(1) Waters of Marah. Directing their course to the southeast, the Hebrews were three days without water; and when they found some in Marah, it was so bitter they could not drink it, they murmured against Moses, saying he had brought them into the wilderness to kill them with thirst. Moses cried to God for their relief; and God showed him a tree (perhaps the bitter Ardiphine), and he cast it into the waters and they became sweet. Marching thence, they came to Elim, where were twelve fountains of excellent water, and seventy palm-trees.

(2) Quails and Manna. On the fifteenth day of the second month, which was the thirty-first from their departure, they came to the wilderness of Sin; their food was quite spent, and now they murmured again, saying that Moses had brought them into the wilderness to kill them with hunger. Moses cried to the Lord. That very night a multitude of quails fell about their tents; and next morning the manna, which continued with them forty years, began to fall.

(3) Rephidim. When they came to Rephidim, Moses, by God's direction, smote a rock with his rod, and thence came water, whose streams seem to have followed them about thirty-nine years. Here, chiefly by Moses' intercession, and by his holding up the rod of God in his hand, the

Amalekites were defeated; and to commemorate the victory, Moses reared up an altar, and called it *Jehovah-nissi,* that is *The Lord is my banner.* While they tarried here, Jethro brought Moses his wife and children; and to ease him of his great burden in judging the people, advised him to appoint heads of thousands, hundreds, and fifties, and tens; and let these judge all the lesser causes. This measure, being approved by God, was immediately put in execution (Exod. xiii-xviii; Deut. xi:4; Josh. xxiv:5-7; Neh. ix:9-15; Ps. lxxviii:11-29; cv:26-43; cvi:7-14; cxxxv: 8, 9, and cxxxvi:11-15).

(4) Mount Sinai. On the first day of the third sacred month, the Hebrews came to Sinai. On this mount, God had told Moses the Hebrews would serve him. When Moses first ascended the mount, God told him his intention to enter into a covenant with the people. When Moses rehearsed this to the people, they professed their readiness to do whatsoever the Lord should command them. When Moses returned to the mount, and represented their ready compliance with the divine will, God ordered him down to direct the people to sanctify themselves, and wash their clothes, as, on the third day, God would descend on the mountain, and enter into covenant with them. After they had purified themselves, flames from the top of the mount, and terrible claps of thunder, made all the congregation, Moses not excepted, to tremble and quake; and all the country about shook and was illuminated. Boundaries were fixed around the mount, that neither man nor beast might touch it; and all were commanded not to gaze, as if curious to behold any corporeal similitude of God amidst the fire. With an audible voice, that all Israel might hear, God proclaimed the covenant relation between him and them, and the ten summary precepts of the moral law, in a manner adapted to every particular person. The terrible thunders so frightened the Hebrew assembly that they begged the Lord would speak his mind only to Moses, and Moses declare it to them. Moses returned to the mount, and there received a variety of political and ceremonial laws.

Descending, he erected twelve pillars for the twelve tribes, and offered by the hands of some young men, burnt-offerings and peace offerings on an altar erected of rough stones. The half of the blood he sprinkled on the altar; with the other half he sprinkled the book in which he had written the laws he had received, and the people. After which, he and Aaron, and his sons, and seventy of the elders of Israel, went a little way up the mount, and feasted before the symbols of the presence of God. Thus was the covenant solemnly ratified (Exod. xix-xxiv; Deut. iv-v).

(5) Divine Directions. Leaving Aaron and Hur, and the seventy elders, to govern the people, Moses took Joshua along with him, at least part of his way, and went up to the mount, where they continued without any food for the space of forty days. God then gave Moses directions concerning the formation of the ark, altars, vails, curtains, candlestick, and other things pertaining to the tabernacle; and concerning the priests' garments, and their consecration, and concerning burnt-offerings, incense, and perfume, and concerning the Sabbath; and ordered Bezaleel and Aholiab to frame the work of the tabernacle.

(6) The Golden Calf. After giving to him the two tables of stone, on which the ten commandments had been divinely inscribed, he bade him go down hastily, as the Hebrews had already broken their engagements, and were worshiping a golden calf. He offered to make Moses' family a great nation, if he would but forbear interceding for his guilty brethren. Moses fell on his face before the Lord, and begged he would not destroy them, as they were his covenant people. When he came down from the mount, and observed their idolatry, his holy zeal was so excited, that he threw down the tables of the law, and broke them to pieces before them, as a token of their breaking God's covenant, and exposing themselves to be broken in his wrath. He took their idol-calf and reduced it to powder, and caused the idolaters to drink the water, with the dust mixed with it, as a token that their guilt should be punished.

(7) Destruction of Idolaters. After sharply rebuking Aaron, his brother, for his part in their sin, he placed himself at the door of a tent, which he erected without the camp, and bade all that detested this idolatry to come to him. Three thousand Levites quickly joined him. These he ordered to go through the camp, and slay every man his friend, or near kinsman, who had been active in the idolatry. After representing to the people the greatness of their sin, he returned to the mount, and fasted and prayed for the space of forty days. He begged that if God would not forgive the Hebrews' sin, he himself might be blotted out of the book of providential preservation, and not live to see them ruined, or have the honor of his family established on their ruin. God replied, he would only cut off from life in that quarrel, such as had offended; Moses continued his intercession, till God promised his presence; promised, and gave him a signal manifestation of his mercy, goodness, and equity. Whereupon Moses begged that God would glorify the exceeding riches of his grace, in going up with them, though they were a most rebellious and stiff-necked people.

After hewing two new tables of stone, Moses returned again to the mount; and continuing there forty days, came down with the moral law divinely inscribed on the tables. His face shone with the reflection of the divine glory. When he knew this, he covered his face with a vail, that the Hebrews might converse with him (Exod. xxv-xxxiv; Deut. xi-x).

(8) The Tabernacle. The tabernacle was now to be reared by voluntary contribution. The people brought materials, till Moses restrained them. Every male paid half a shekel as the ransom money of his soul. After six months' work the tabernacle was finished, everything being exactly according to the direction of God by Moses. After divine directions issued therefrom concerning the various offerings, Aaron and his sons were consecrated to the service of it, and then a number of other ceremonial laws were by God uttered therefrom. (See LEVITICUS.)

An account of the Hebrews was then taken, and all were directed in their station and work, and their princes offered the oblations for the dedication of the tabernacle.

(9) Subsequent History. He then received the "spiritual statute book" of Israel as the congregation of Jehovah (Lev. ch. i-vii), and consecrated Aaron and his sons for the priesthood (Lev. ch. viii-ix). Judgment was executed upon Nadab and Abihu (ch. x) and further regulations promulgated (ch. xi-xxvii). After this Moses numbered the people (Num. ch. i), arranged the order of the tribes in the camp and on the march (ch. ii), numbered the Levites and arranged for their special calling (ch. iii-iv), gave directions respecting unclean persons, trespass, Nazarites, etc. (ch. v-vi), received the dedicatory gifts from the princes of the tribes (ch. vii), consecrated the Levites (ch. viii), and prepared for the onward journey (ch. ix-x:10).

Mention is made of Moses securing, by prayer, the quenching of the fire at Taberah (xi:1-3); Moses' complaint of the burden of his charge and the appointment of seventy elders (xi:10-30); the sedition of Miriam and Aaron (ch.xii); the sending out of the spies (ch. xiii-xiv); the rebellion of Korah, Dathan and Abiram (ch. xvi); the death of Miriam and Aaron, and the smiting of the rock at Meribah (ch. xx); the plague of serpents (ch. xxi); the appointment of Joshua by Moses as his successor (ch. xxvii); the assignment of their inheritance to the Reubenites and Gadites (ch. xxxii); the appointment of commissioners to divide the Promised Land.

(10) Final Instructions. The eleventh month of the fortieth year of the Hebrews' travels was now begun. Moses finding that no intercession with God could procure for him an entrance into the Promised Land, and knowing that his end drew near, rehearsed to the Hebrews a summary of what God had done for them, and a number of the laws he had given them, with some additional ones, and caused them to renew their solemn covenant with God. He also set before them the manifold blessings which would attend their obedience, and the curses that would follow on their disobedience. He left a written copy of his law, to be placed at the side of the ark; and ordered the reading of it to the people at their public meetings, especially on the year of release. After giving Joshua a solemn charge with respect to his behavior, he composed a sublime ode that represented the excellency of God, their duty to him, and their danger if they apostatized from it. He then blessed the tribes of Israel; that of Simeon (perhaps because it was the most guilty in the Midianitish whoredom and idolatry) only excepted, and concluded with a lofty commendation of God, as the source of true happiness.

(11) Death. This finished, he went up to the top of Pisgah, where God strengthened his sight to take a clear view of the whole of the western Canaan. His natural strength was no way abated, but, perhaps, in a trance of wonder at the goodness of God, he breathed out his last. To intimate the future burial of his ceremonial law, and to hinder the Hebrews from idolizing his relics, the Lord buried him in the valley over against Bethpeor; but his grave could never be found.

As Thomas Fuller quaintly says, "God buried also his grave." The familiar lines of Mrs. C. F. Alexander's ode, "The Burial of Moses," may be appropriately quoted here:

"And had he not high honor?
   The hillside for his pall,
To lie in state while angels wait,
   With stars for tapers tall;
And the dark rock-pines, like tossing plumes,
   Over his bier to wave;
And God's own hand, in that lonely land,
   To lay him in his grave."

4. Character. Three qualities give him immortal interest and prominence.

(1) Faith. By faith he esteemed "the reproach of Christ greater riches than the treasures in Egypt" (Heb. xi:26). "Never more alluring prospects opened up before any man than those which the world held out to him. The throne of the greatest monarchy of his age was within his reach. All that wealth could procure, or pleasure

bestow, or the greatest earthly power command, was easily at his call. But the glory of these things paled in his view before the more excellent character of those invisible honors which God set before him. This faith sustained him in the solitudes of Midian and animated him amidst all the conflicts attendant on the Exodus and all the difficulties that confronted him in the wilderness. This faith gave him courage in the hour of danger and calmness in the time of trial."

(2) Prayerfulness. "In every time of emergency his immediate resort was to Jehovah. He was not speaking to a stranger, but was like a son making application to his father, and so he never pleaded in vain." His was the prayer of faith.

(3) Humility. "He coveted no distinction and sought no prominence; his greatness came to him, he did not go after it. And his humility was allied with or flowed naturally out into two other qualities, disinterestedness and meekness. (See Num. xi:29 and xii:3 for striking illustrations). He gave up his own ease and comfort to secure the emancipation of his people; and while laboring night and day for them, he had no thought whatever of his own interests. His office brought him no emolument." In this he was like Nehemiah. He was free from all charge of nepotism. His meekness was shown in silently listening to complaints against himself. He appealed unto God for vindication and approval.

In addition must be mentioned his eminent services as lawgiver. It is indeed a vexed question how much credit should be given to him as the publisher of a code marked throughout by "Thus saith the Lord." We are safe in saying that the Law, as we have it recorded in the Scriptures, was divinely inspired, and that Moses made the record as directed of the Lord. The Decalogue is a moral miracle in ancient legislation, and retains its power to this day in all Christian lands. (See Law.)

The only blot upon this beautiful character is a lack of patience or self-control, but this was more evident in the earlier portion of his life, nor was it prominent enough to belie his eulogy.

Dr. Wm. W. Taylor.

5. Writings. To Moses we owe that important portion of Holy Scripture, the Pentateuch, which makes us acquainted with the creation of the world, the entrance of sin and death, the first promises of redemption, the flood, the peopling of the postdiluvian earth, and the origin of nations, the call of Abraham, and the giving of the law. We have, indeed, in it the early history of religion, and a key to all the subsequent dispensations of God to man. The genuineness and authenticity of these most venerable and important books have been established by various writers; but the following remarks upon the veracity of the writings of Moses have the merit of compressing much argument into few words:

(1) Minuteness of Detail. There is a *minuteness* in the details of the Mosaic writings, which bespeaks their truth; for it often bespeaks the eye-witness, as in the adventures of the wilderness; and often seems intended to supply directions to the artificer, as in the construction of the tabernacle.

(2) Touches of Nature. There are *touches of nature* in the narrative which bespeak its truth, for it is not easy to regard them otherwise than as strokes from the life; as where "the mixed multitude," whether half-castes or Egyptians, are the first to sigh for the cucumbers and melons of Egypt, and to spread discontent through the camp

(Num. xi:4); as the miserable exculpation of himself which Aaron attempts, with all the cowardice of conscious guilt: "I cast into the fire, and there came out this calf;" the fire, to be sure, being in the fault (Exod. xxxii:24).

(3) Unexpected Incidents. There are certain little *inconveniences* represented as turning up unexpectedly, that bespeak truth in the story; for they are just such accidents as are characteristic of the working of a new system and untried machinery. What is to be done with the man who is found gathering sticks on the Sabbath day? (Num. xv:32). (Could an impostor have devised such a trifle?) How is the inheritance of the daughters of Zelophehad to be disposed of, there being no male heir? (Num. xxxvi:2)—either of them inconsiderable matters in themselves, but both giving occasion to very important laws; the one touching life, and the other property.

(4) Simplicity of Story. There is a *simplicity* in the manner of Moses, when telling his tale, which bespeaks its truth; no parade of language, no pomp of circumstance even in his miracles, a modesty and dignity throughout all. Let us but compare him in any trying scene with Josephus; his description, for instance, of the passage through the Red Sea (Exod. xiv), of the murmuring of the Israelites and the supply of quails and manna, with the same as given by the Jewish historian, or rhetorician we might rather say, and the force of the observation will be felt.

(5) Candor. There is a *candor* in the treatment of his subject by Moses, which bespeaks his truth; as when he tells of his own want of eloquence, which unfitted him for a leader (Exod. iv:10), his own want of faith, which prevented him from entering the Promised Land (Num. xx:12), the idolatry of Aaron his brother (Exod. xxxii:21), the profaneness of Nadab and Abihu, his nephews (Lev. x), the disaffection and punishment of Miriam, his sister (Num. xii:1).

(6) Disinterested Conduct. There is a *disinterestedness* in his conduct, which bespeaks him to be a man of truth; for though he had sons, he apparently takes no measures during his life to give them offices of trust or profit; and at his death he appoints as his successor one who had no claims upon him, either of alliance, of clanship, or of blood.

(7) Prophetic Passages. There are certain *prophetical* passages in the writings of Moses, which bespeak their truth; as, several respecting the future Messiah, and the very sublime and literal one respecting the final fall of Jerusalem (Deut. xxviii).

(8) Key to Tradition. There is a *simple key* supplied by these writings, to the meaning of many ancient traditions current amongst the heathens, though greatly disguised, which is another circumstance that bespeaks their truth; as, the golden age; the garden of the Hesperides; the fruit-tree in the midst of the garden which the dragon guarded; the destruction of mankind by a flood, all except two persons, and those, righteous persons; the seventh day a sacred day; with many others, all conspiring to establish the reality of the facts which Moses relates, because tending to show that vestiges of the like present themselves in the traditional history of the world at large.

(9) Concurrence with New Testament. The concurrence which is found between the writings of Moses and those of the New Testament bespeaks their truth, the latter constantly appealing to them, being indeed but the completion of the system which the others are the first to put forth. Surely it is a very improbable thing that two dis-

pensations, separated by an interval of some fifteen hundred years, each exhibiting prophecies of its own, since fulfilled, each asserting miracles of its own, on strong evidence of its own, and each with such individual claims to belief, should also be found to stand in the closest relation to one another, and yet both turn out impostures after all.

(10) Purity. Above all, there is a comparative *purity* in the theology and morality of the Pentateuch, which argues not only its truth, but its high origin; for how else are we to account for a system like that of Moses, in such an age and amongst such a people; that the doctrine of the unity, the self-existence, the providence, the perfections of the great God of heaven and earth should thus have blazed forth (how far more brightly than even in the vaunted schools of Athens at its most refined era!) from the midst of a nation of themselves, ever plunging into gross and groveling idolatry; and that principles of social duty, of benevolence, and of self-restraint, extending even to the thoughts of the heart, should have been the produce of an age, which the very provisions of the Levitical law itself show to have been full of savage and licentious abominations? (See Exod. iii:14; xx:3-17; Lev. xix:2, 18; Deut. vi:4; xxx:6.) Such are some of the internal evidences for the veracity of the books of Moses. (See Pentateuch.)

6. Later Scripture Allusions. (1) Moses was a type of Christ. The parallel is readily traced, "As Moses, in the early part of his career, refused the Egyptian monarchy because it could be gained to him only by disloyalty to God, Jesus turned away from the kingdoms of the world because they were offered on condition that he would worship Satan; as Moses became the emancipator of his people, so was Jesus; as Moses, penetrating to the soul of the symbolism of idolatry, introduced a new dispensation wherein symbolism was allied to spirituality of worship, so Jesus, seizing the spirituality of the Mosaic system, freed it from its national restrictions, and ushered in the day when the true worshiper would worship the Father anywhere; as Moses was preëminently a lawgiver, so Jesus, in his Sermon on the Mount, laid down a code which not only expounds but fulfills the Decalogue; as Moses was a prophet, so Jesus is the great Prophet of his Church; as Moses was a Mediator, so Jesus is the Mediator of the new covenant, standing between God and man, and bridging, by his atonement and intercession, the gulf between the two. We cannot wonder, therefore, that in the vision of the Apocalypse they who have gotten the victory over the beast and his image are represented as singing the song of Moses the servant of God, and the song of the Lamb (Rev. xv:3." (2) In Jude 9 is an allusion to an altercation between Michael and Satan over the body of Moses. It probably refers to a lost apocryphal book, mentioned by Origen, called the 'Ascension, or Assumption, of Moses' (Smith, *Bib. Dict.*).

MOSES, BOOKS OF. See Pentateuch.

MOSES, LAW OF. See Law.

MOSES, SONG OF.

This wonderful ode celebrates more fitly the miraculous deliverance of the children of Israel from Egyptian bondage. It is the national anthem, the Te Deum of the Hebrews. It sounds through the psalms of Israel, through the thanksgiving hymns of the Christian Church, through the touching songs of liberated slaves, and it will swell the harmony of the saints in heaven. Allusion to it is made in Rev. xv:2, 3: "They stand on the sea of glass mingled with fire . . . and sing the song of Moses the servant of God."

MOST HIGH (mōst hī), (Heb. יִּלְיוֹן, *el-yone'*, lofty), a name given to Jehovah as supreme and all-glorious (Gen. xiv:18; Ps. vii:17; ix:2, etc.).

MOST HOLY (mōst hōly). See HOLINESS.

MOTE (mōt), a particle of dust, or other matter. Small sins are likened to "motes in the eye"; they are very troublesome to an awakened and tender conscience, and greatly mar our looking on God as our sun and shield (Matt. vii:3).

MOTH (mŏth), (Heb. עָשׁ, *awsh*), occurs in Job iv:19; xiii:28; xxvii:18; Is. l:9; li:8; Hosea v:12; Matt. vi:19, 20; Luke xii:33; Ecclus. xix:3, xlii:13.

There is no Biblical insect whose identity is better ascertained. The following allusions to the moth occur in Scripture: To its being produced in clothes, 'for from garments cometh a moth' (Ecclus. xlii:13); to its well-known fragility, 'mortal men are crushed *before* the moth' (Job iv:19), literally, 'before the face of the moth,' but which words really mean '*like as* the moth is crushed.' The allusion to 'the house of the moth' (Job xxvii:18) seems to refer plainly to the silky spindle-shaped case, covered with detached hairs and particles of wool, made and inhabited by the larva of the *Tinea sarcitella;* or to the felted case or tunnel formed by the larva of the *Tinea pellionella;* or to the arched gallery formed by eating through wool by the larva of the *Tinea tapetzella.* References occur to the destructiveness of the clothes-moth: 'As a garment that is moth-eaten' (Job xiii:28); 'the moth shall eat them up' (Is. l:9); 'the moth shall eat them up like a garment' (li:8); 'I will be to Ephraim as a moth,' *i. e.,* will secretly consume him (Hos. v:12); comp. Matt. vi:19, 20; Luke xii:33; James v:2, metaphorically; and Ecclus. xix:3, 'Moths and worms shall have him that cleaveth to harlots,' but the better reading is σής, 'rottenness.' Since the 'treasures' of the Orientals, in ancient times, consisted partly of 'garments, both new and old' (Matt. xiii:52; and comp. Josh. vii:21; Judg. xiv:12), the ravages of the clothes moth afforded them a lively emblem of destruction. Their treasures also consisted partly of corn laid up in barns, etc. (Luke xii:18, 24); and it has been supposed that the Greek word, translated 'rust,' joined with the σής, *sayce, moth,* in Matt. vi:19, 20, refers also to some species of moth, etc., probably in the larva state, which destroys corn. Kuinoel says the *'curculio,'* or *korn-wurm,'* the larva of the *Tinea granella,* is injurious to corn.

Moths, like fleas, etc., amid other more immediate purposes of their existence, incidentally serve as a stimulus to human industry and cleanliness; for, by a remarkable discrimination in her instinct, the parent moth never deposits her eggs in garments frequently overlooked or kept clean. Indeed, the most remarkable of all proofs of animal intelligence is to be found in the larvæ of the water-moth, which get into straws, and adjust the weight of their case so that it can always float; when too heavy they add a piece of straw or wood, and when too light a bit of gravel (*Transactions of the Royal Society of Edinburgh,* vol. i, p. 42).   J. F. D.

Figurative. (1) Secret influences that insensibly consume men's character or estate are likened to a "moth" (Is. l:9; li:8). (2) God likens himself to a "moth and rottenness," because by his judgments he gradually and insensibly weakened the Jews, and rendered them contemptible (Hos.

v:12). (3) The wicked man builds his house "as a moth"; he builds it by covetousness and anxious care; imagines his lot agreeable but how easily do the judgments of God burn or shake him out of it! (Job xxvii:18). (4) Man's beauty, glory and honor waste like "a moth," are secretly and insensibly, but quickly, consumed (Ps. xxxix: 11).

MOTHER (mŭth'ĕr), (Heb. אֵם, *ame;* Gr. μήτηρ, *may'tare*), the name regarded by many lexicographers as a primitive, imitating the earliest lisping of an infant; they compare it with the Greek μάμμα, *mama;* Sanscrit, *mâ, ambâ;* Copt., *mau;* English and French, *mama;* German, *amme,* (nurse), etc.

The ordinary applications of the word require no illustration; but the following points of Hebrew usage may be noticed: When the father had more than one wife, the son seems to have confined the title of 'mother' to his real mother, by which he distinguished her from the other wives of his father. Hence the source of Joseph's peculiar interest in Benjamin is indicated in Gen. xliii:29, by his being 'his mother's son.' The other brethren were the sons of his father by other wives. Nevertheless, when this precision was not necessary, the stepmother was sometimes styled mother. Thus Jacob (Gen. xxxvii:10) speaks of Leah as Joseph's mother, for his real mother had long been dead. The stepmother was, however, more properly distinguished from the womb-mother by the name of 'father's wife.' The word 'mother' was also, like father, brother, sister, employed by the Hebrews in a somewhat wider sense than is usual with us. It is used of a grandmother (1 Kings xv:10), and even of any female ancestor (Gen. iii:20). (See WOMAN.)

Figurative. The designation of mother is symbolically applied: (1) To the true church; she is Christ's "mother," as he assumed our nature in connection with her, and was one of her members (Cant. iii:11). She is the "mother" of believers; in her, and by her ordinances, they are spiritually born, nourished, protected, and directed (Cant. i:6; iii:4). She "is free," now delivered from the bondage of ceremonies; and her true members are freed from the broken Law, and the slavery of sin and Satan. She is "from above"; is of a heavenly origin, frame and tendency; and her true members have their conversation in heaven (Gal. iv:26; Phil. iii:20). (2) To the kingdom of Judah, or family of David, which produced these wicked oppressors, Jehoahaz, Jehoiakim, Jehoiachin, and Zedekiah (Ezek. xix). (3) To a metropolis, or capital city of a country or tribe; and then the inhabitants, villages, or lesser cities, are called "daughters" (2 Sam. xx: 19; Jer. l:12). (4) 'The *parting* of the way, at the head of two ways' (Ezek. xxi:21) is in the Hebrew 'the mother of the way,' because out of it the two ways arise as daughters. (5) In Job i:21, the earth is indicated as the common 'mother to whose bosom all mankind must return.' (6) To any female superior in age, station, gifts, or grace, or who deals tenderly with one. Deborah was a "mother in Israel;" with tenderness and valor she judged, instructed, and governed that people (Judg. v:7). The mother of Rufus was a mother to Paul; kindly cared and provided for him (Rom. xvi:13). (7) The saints are Christ's "mother," "sisters," and "brethren"; he is formed in their hearts, by their spiritual union to him, and their receiving out of his fullness; and there is a dearer intimacy and relation between him and them than between the nearest relatives on earth (Matt. xii: 49, 50).

MOTIONS (mō'shŭns), (Gr. πάθημα, *path'ay-mah*).

This word signifies suffering, sorrow, misfortune, calamity (Rom. viii:18; 2 Cor. i:6; Col. i:24, etc.), also an affection, passion. The "motions of sin" (Rom. vii:5) are the inward passions of which the sins are the actual consequence.

MOULDY (mōld'ў), (Heb. נִקֻּד, *nik-kood'*, crumbled), Josh. ix:5, 12, refers rather to the crumbling of bread.

MOUNT (mount), (Heb. מָצָב, *moots-tsawb'*, a station, Is. xxix:3; סֹלְלָה, *so-lel-aw'*, Jer. vi:6), a mound or rampart thrown up for a siege.

MOUNTAIN (moun'tĭn).

(1) Dean Stanley gives (*Sinai and Palestine*) the following list, quoted in Ayre's *Treasury of Bible Knowledge*, of Hebrew words used in reference to mountains or hills. It will be noticed the majority are in common use with us:

"Head, *rôsh* (Gen. viii:5; Ex. xix:20; Deut. xxxiv:1; 1 Kings xviii:42; A. V. 'top'). Of a hill, *Gibeah* (Ex. xvii:9, 10).

"Ears, *aznôth*, Aznoth-tabor (Josh. xix:34); possibly in allusion to some projection on the top of the mountain.

"Shoulder, *châtêph* (Deut. xxxiii:12; Josh. xv:8; xviii:16, 'side'), all referring to the hills on which Jerusalem is placed. Josh. xv:10, 'the *side* of Mount Jearim.'

"Side, *tzad* (see the word for the 'side' of a man in 2 Sam. ii:16; Ezek. iv:4, etc.). Used in reference to a mountain in 1 Sam. xxiii:26; 2 Sam. xiii:34.

"Loins or flanks, *chislôth*, Chisloth-tabor, Josh. xix:12, and occurs also in the name of a village, probably situated on this part of the mountain, *Ha-chesulloth, i. e.*, the 'loins' (Josh. xix:18).

"Rib, *tzêlah*. Only used once, in speaking of the Mount of Olives (2 Sam. xvi:13), and there translated 'side.'

"Back, *shechem*. Probably the root of the name of the town Shechem, which may be derived from its situation, as it were, on the back of Gerizim.

"Elbow, *ammah*. The same word as that for 'cubit.' It occurs in 2 Sam. ii:24 as the name of a hill near Gibeon.

"Thigh, *yarchâh* (see the word for the 'thigh' of a man in Judg. iii:16, 21). Applied to Mount Ephraim (Judg. xix:1, 18), and to Lebanon (2 Kings xix:23; Is. xxxvii:24). Used also for the 'sides' of a cave (1 Sam. xxiv:3).

"The word translated 'covert' in 1 Sam. xxv:20 is *sêther*, from *sâthar*, to hide, and probably refers to the shrubbery or thicket through which Abigail's path lay. In this passage 'hill' should be 'mountain.' "

(2) The mountains mentioned in Scripture are noticed under their different names, and a general statement with reference to the mountains of PALESTINE is given under that head.

The most famous mountains mentioned in Scripture are, Seir, in Idumæa; Horeb, near Sinai, in Arabia Petræa; Sinai, in Arabia Petræa; Hor, in Idumea; Gilboa, south of the valley of Jezreel; Nebo, a mountain of Abarim; Tabor, in Lower Galilee; En-gedi, near the Dead sea; Libanus and Anti-Libanus; Gerizim, in Samaria; Ebal, near to Gerizim; Gilead, beyond Jordan; Amalek, in Ephraim; Moriah, where the temple was built; Paran, in Arabia Petræa; Gahash, in Ephraim; Olivet; Pisgah, beyond Jordan; Hermon, beyond Jordan, near Libanus; Carmel, near the Mediterranean sea, between Dora and Ptolemais.

Figurative. In Scripture the governing part of the body politic appears under symbols of different kinds. If the allegory or figurative representation is taken from the heavens, the luminaries denote the governing body; if from an animal, the head or horns; if from the earth, a mountain or fortress; and in this case the capital city or residence of the governor is taken for the supreme power. These mutually illustrate each other. For a capital city is the head of the political body; the head of an ox is the fortress of the animal; mountains are the natural fortresses of the earth; and therefore a fortress or capital city, though seated in a plain, may be called a mountain. Thus the words head, mountain, hill, city, horn, and king are used in a manner as synonymous terms to signify a kingdom, monarchy, or republic, united under *one* government, with only this difference, that it is to be understood in different respects; for the term head represents it in respect of the capital city; mountain or hill in respect of the strength of the metropolis, which gives law to, or is above, and commands, the adjacent territory. When David says, 'Lord, by thy favor thou hast made my mountain to stand strong' (Ps. xxx:7), he means to express the stability of his kingdom.

The detailed symbolical allusions are herewith given: "Mountains" and "hills" are used to represent: (1) The people that dwell in a mountainous and hill country (Ezek. vi:2, 3). (2) The temple which was built on the top of a hill (Is. xxx:29; Jer. xvii:3, 26). (3) The church of God, typified by Mount Zion, and which is firmly settled, conspicuous, and useful in the world (Ps. ii:6; Is. ii:2); and which, as a great "mountain," shall fill the whole earth, when all nations shall be gathered to Christ (Dan. ii:35, 45). (4) The ordinances of Christ, which elevate his people heavenward, and afford them much rich and medicinal provision for their soul (Cant. ii:8; iv:6; Joel iii:18). (5) Men high in station, power and authority, as magistrates in the state, and apostles and ministers in the church (Ps. lxxii:3; Is. xliv:23; lv:12). (6) Powerful hindrances and provocations, and enemies of gospel influence, and of the people of Christ (Is. xl:4; xli:15; xlix:11). (7) The places where idols were worshiped, which were often on hills and high places (Ezek. xviii:6, 11). (8) Idols worshiped in these places, or anything we trust in instead of God (Jer. iii:23). (9) The heavens, which are higher than mountains (Ps. cxxi:1). (10) God, who is likened to the "mountains round about Jerusalem," as he is the sure defense and protector of his people, and the source of all their consolation (Ps. cxxv:2). (11) Samaria is called a "mountain," because built on a hill (Amos iv:1; vi:1). (12) Babylon, or the Chaldean monarchy, is also called a "mountain" because of its lofty building and great power; "a destroying mountain," because it overwhelmed and destroyed the nations around; and a "burning mountain," because at last burnt with fire, and the debris looked like a burnt "mountain" (Jer. li:25; Is. xiii:2). (See BABYLON.)

MOUNTAIN OF THE AMORITES (moun'tĭn ŏv thē ăm'o-rītes), (Heb. הַר הָאֱמֹרִי, *har haw-em-o-ree'*), a place mentioned (Deut. i:19, 20) in connection with the WANDERING. It is probably the place now called *Nukb es-Sufeh* in the range of hills that borders the plateau *et-tih*.

MOUNT EPHRAIM. See EPHRAIM.

MOUNT OF BEATITUDES (mount ŏv bĕ-ăt'ĭ-tūds).

The mount upon which the great sermon was

delivered (Matt. v) may be the heights which are now known as the "Horns of Hattin," Kurun Hattîn, near Capernaum, and on the west of the Lake of Galilee.

MOUNT OF CONGREGATION (mount ŏv kŏn'grĕ-gā'shŭn), (Heb. רַ֫ה מוֹעֵד, *har mo-ade'*), mentioned (Is. xiv:13) in connection with the King of Babylon. It probably corresponds to the Persian *el-Burj*, or the Greek *Olympus* as the home of the gods. (See Congregation, Mount of the.)

MOUNT OF CORRUPTION (mount ŏv kŏr-rŭp'shŭn). See Corruption.

MOUNT OF THE AMALEKITES (mount ŏv thē ăm'a-lek-ītes), (Heb. הַר הָעֲמָלֵקִי, *har haw-am-aw-lay-kee'*), a place in the tribe of Ephraim (Judg. xii:15) where a branch of that clan apparently settled.

MOUNT OF THE VALLEY (mount ŏv thē văl'lǐ), (Heb. הַר הָעֵמֶק, *har haw-ay'mek*), a district in the tribe of Reuben east of the Jordan (Josh. xiii:19), in the "valley" of Ghor or the Jordan.

MOURNING (mōrn'ĭng), (Heb. אָבַל, *aw-bal'*, lament, mourn).

This head embraces both the outward expressions of sorrow for the dead, referred to in the Scriptures, and those expressions which were intended to exhibit repentance, etc. These subjects will be pursued according to Townsend's chronological arrangement, and since they nearly approximate, will be pursued together.

(1) Occasions. The earliest reference to any kind of mourning is that of Job, who, being informed of the destruction of his children as the climax of his calamities, 'arose, rent his mantle, shaved his head, and fell down upon the ground and worshiped' (Job i:20), and uttered sentiments of submission (ver. 21), and sat down among the ashes (ch. ii:8). His friends came to him by an appointment among themselves to mourn with him and comfort him (ver. 11); they lifted up their voices and wept upon seeing his altered appearance; they rent every man his mantle and sprinkled dust upon their heads towards heaven (ver. 12), and sat down with him on the ground seven days and seven nights, waiting till his grief should subside before they commenced their office as mourners. Job then bewails aloud his unhappy condition (ch. iii). In ch. xvi:15, 16, reference is made to the customs of placing sackcloth next the skin, defiling the head with dust, and suffering the face to be begrimed with weeping. Clamor in grief is referred to (ii:12, 13; xix:7); it is considered a wicked man's portion that his widows shall not weep at his death (xxvii:15). Upon Job's recovery from his afflictions all his relatives and acquaintances bemoan and comfort him concerning his past sufferings; which seems to have been a kind of congratulatory mourning, indulged in order to heighten the pleasures of prosperity by recalling associations of adversity (ch. xlii:11). Indeed, the expressions of affectionate joy and grief nearly coincide. Joseph fell upon his brother Benjamin's neck and wept (Gen. xlv:14; comp. Acts xx:37, 38, and Gen. l:1). However it is to be accounted for, in the course of the book of Job nearly all the chief characteristics of Eastern mourning are introduced. This will appear as we proceed. The next instance is that of Abraham, who came to mourn and weep for Sarah (B. C. 1871), words which denote a formal mourning (Gen. xxiii:2). Days of mourning are referred to in regard to the expected death of Isaac (Gen.

xxvii:41). These appear generally to have consisted of seven, as for Saul (1 Sam. xxxi:13; see Judith xvi:24; comp. Ecclus. xxii:12).

(2) Modes. Weeping appears either as one chief expression of mourning or as the general name for it. Hence when Deborah, Rebecca's nurse, was buried at Bethel under an oak, at this period, the tree was called Allon-bachuth, the oak of weeping (Gen. xxxv:8). The children of Israel were heard by Moses to weep throughout their families, every man in the door of his tent (Num. xi:10; comp. xiv:1; xxv:6). So numerous are the references to tears in the Scriptures as to give the impression that the Orientals had them ever ready at command (comp. Ps. vi:6). The woman washed our Lord's feet with tears (Luke vii:38; comp. Ecclus. xxviii:17). Weeping, with lifting up of the voice, occurs in Ruth i:9; 1 Sam. xi:4; 2 Sam. iii:31; xiii:36. Their excitableness appears otherwise; they shout for joy and howl for grief, even the ministers of the altar (Joel i:13; Micah i:8, etc.).

Reuben rends his clothes upon finding Joseph gone (Gen. xxxvii:29) and uttered lamentations (ver. 30). Jacob rends his clothes and puts sackcloth upon his loins, and mourns for his son many days; his sons and his daughters rise up to comfort him, and he gives utterance to his grief; 'thus his father wept for him' (Gen. xxxvii:34, 35). Joseph's brothers rend their clothes (Gen. xliv:13); and this act, as expressive of grief or horror, occurs in multitudes of passages down to the last age of the Jewish empire (Acts xiv: 14).

Scarcely less numerous are the references to sackcloth on the loins as an expression of mourning; we have even lying in sackcloth (1 Kings xxi:27), and sackcloth upon both man and beast at Nineveh (Jonah iii:8).

Joseph's brethren fell to the ground before him in token of grief (Gen. xliv:14); and this, or lying, or sitting on the ground, was a common token of mourning (comp. Ps. xxxv:14; 1 Sam. xxv:24; Is. iii:26; xlvii:1; Ezek. xxvi:16, etc.).

The next incident in the history of the subject is the mourning for Jacob by the Egyptians, which was conducted, no doubt, by professional mourners during threescore and ten days (Gen. l:3), called the days of mourning (ver. 4), though most likely that computation includes the process of embalming (Wilkinson's *Manners and Customs of the Ancient Egyptians*, v. 454, 459). It seems to have amounted to royal mourning, doubtless out of regard to Joseph. The mourning for Joseph's father was renewed by Joseph's command, with a very great and sore lamentation, upon the funeral cavalcade having arrived in Canaan, and continued seven days (ver. 10). The vehemency of that mourning seems to have surprised even the Canaanites, who in consequence named the place where it was held Abel-mizraim, or the mourning of the Egyptians (ver. 11). When the children of Israel mourned under the threat of the Divine displeasure, they did not put on their ornaments (Exod. xxxiii:4; comp. Joel ii:16; Ezek. xxiv:17). At the giving of the law the modes of mourning were regulated by several enactments. The prophet Joel commanded a fast as part of a national mourning. A fast is proclaimed to all the inhabitants or visitors at Jerusalem (Jer. xxxvi:9; comp. Zech. vii:5). Fasting is practiced at Nineveh as part of a public humiliation (Jonah iii:5). In our Lord's language, 'to fast' and 'to mourn' are the same thing (Matt. ix:15). Public humiliations attended with religious assemblies and prayers (Joel ii:16, 17);

with fasts (Is. lviii:3); see all these united (1 Macc. iii:44, 47, 48). The first complete description of mourning for the dead occurs in 2 Sam. iii:31, 35.

(3) Forbidden Modes. It was forbidden the Jews to make cuttings in their flesh for the dead (Lev. xix:28). The ancient Egyptians, according to Herodotus, did not cut themselves (ii:61); it was a Syrian custom, as appears from the votaries of Baal (1 Kings xviii:28); nor were the Jews allowed to make any baldness between their eyes for the dead (Deut. xiv:1). The priests were forbidden to uncover the head in mourning (Lev. x:6), or to rend their clothes, or to contract the ceremonial defilement involved in mourning except for their nearest kindred (Lev. xxi:1, 4); but the high-priest was entirely forbidden to do so even for his father or his mother (ver. 11), and so was the Nazarite (Num. vi:7). These prohibitions respecting the head and the beard (Lev. xix:27) seem to have been restricted to funeral occasions, as the customs referred to were lawfully practiced on other sorrowful events (comp. Ezra ix:3; Job i:20; Is. xxii:12; Jer. vii:29; Micah i:16). Even the food eaten by mourners was considered unclean (comp. Deut. xxvi:14, with Hos. ix:4; Ezek. xxiv:17).

(4) Days of Mourning. The Jews were commanded to afflict their souls on the Day of Atonement (Lev. xxiii:27), and at the Feast of Trumpets (Num. xxix:7). All the house of Israel mourned for Aaron thirty days (Num. xx:29). The beautiful captive, whom the law permitted

Mourning at Grave.

to marry, was required first to bewail her father and mother a full month, and the requisitions that she should shave her head and pare her nails have been by some considered signs of mourning (Deut. xxi:11, 13). The Israelites wept for Moses thirty days, called the days of weeping *and* mourning for Moses (Deut. xxxiv:8), B. C. 1451. Joshua and the elders of Israel put dust upon their heads at the defeat of Ai, and fasted (Josh. vii:6), as did the eleven tribes after the defeat at Gibeah, and wept (Judg. xx:26), as did all the Israelites at the command of Joshua, on which occasion it is said 'they drew water and poured it out before the Lord' (1 Sam. vii:6; comp. Ps. xxii:14).

(5) Elegies by the Prophets. Elegies were composed by the prophets on several disastrous occasions (Ezek. xxvi:1-18; xxvii:1-36; Amos v:1, etc.). In Ps. xxxv, which is ascribed to David, there is a description of the humiliations practiced by the friends of the sick, in order to procure their recovery. Samuel was honored with a public mourning by the Israelites (1 Sam. xxv:1), B. C. 1058. Upon the death of Saul, David wrote an elegy (2 Sam. i:17-27). This, like that upon the death of Abner, seems to be a poetical description of the character of the departed, like the dirge for an Egyptian king.

(6) Various Expressions of Grief. Lifting up hands seems to have been an expression of grief (Ps. cxli:2; Lam. i:17; Ezra ix:5). Messengers were sent to condole with survivors; thus David sent such to Hanun, king of Ammon, upon the death of his father (2 Sam. x:1,2); 'Many of the Jews came to comfort Martha and Mary' (John xi:19); 'A great company of women attended our Lord to the cross, bewailing and lamenting him' (Luke xxiii:27); 'Much people' were with the widow of Nain (Luke vii:12). Indeed, if persons met a funeral procession they were expected to join it—a custom which is thought to illustrate St. Paul's words, 'Weep with them that weep' (Rom. xii:15). Bathsheba mourned for Uriah (2 Sam. xi:26). David, in deprecation of the death of his son by her, prayed to God for the child, fasted, and lay all night upon the earth. Ashes were often laid on the head in token of mourning; thus 'Tamar put ashes on her head, rent her garment, and laid her hand upon her head, and went on crying' (2 Sam. xiii:19, 20; comp. Is. lxi:3; 2 Esdras ix:38). They even wallowed in ashes (Ezek. xxvii:30). Mourning apparel is first mentioned in 2 Sam. xiv:2, where it appears that the wearer did not anoint himself with oil (comp. Matt. vi:17).

(7) Hired Mourners. The first reference to hired mourners occurs in Eccles. xii:5. "The mourners go about the street." They are certainly alluded to in Jer. ix:17-20, 'the mourning women' (probably widows, comp. Ps. lxxviii:64; Acts ix:39), answering to the *Præficæ* of the Romans (comp. Hor. *Ars Poet.* 429). Another reference to them occurs in 2 Chron. xxxv:25; comp. Joseph. *De Bell. Jud.* iii:9, 5. The greater number of the mourners in ancient Egypt were women, as in the modern East. Mourning for the dead was conducted in a tumultuous manner; they also wept and wailed greatly (Mark v:38). Even devout men made great lamentations (Acts viii:2).

(8) Other Signs of Mourning. Among other signs of mourning they shaved the head, and even tore off the hair (Amos viii:10; Micah i:16; Is. xv:2; xxii:12; Jer. vii:29). Ezra plucked off the hair of his head and of his beard (Ezra ix:3;

Wailing with Tabrets.

Joseph. *Antiq.* xvi:7, 5). The Jews went up to the housetops to mourn (Is. xv:2, 3; xxii:1); and so did the Moabites (Jer. xlviii:37, 38; Judith viii:5).

They also made cuttings in their hands (Jer. xlviii:37, 38); they smote upon the thigh (Jer. xxxi:19; Ezek. xxi:12); on the breast (Nahum ii:7; Luke xviii:13; xxiii:48; they smote both hands together (Num. xxiv:10), stamped with the foot (Ezek. vi:11), bowed down the head (Lam. ii:10), covered the lips (Micah iii:7), the face (2 Sam. xix:4), and the head (2 Sam. xv:30), and went barefoot (2 Sam. xv:30). Neighbors and friends provided food for the mourners (2 Sam. iii:35; Jer. xvi:7; comp. Ezek. xxiv:17); this was called 'the bread of bitterness,' 'the cup of consolation.' In later times the Jews had a custom of giving bread to the poor, at funerals, and leaving it for their use at tombs, graves, etc., which resembles the Roman *visceratio* (Tobit iv:17; Ecclus. xxx:8). Women went to tombs to indulge their grief (John xi:31).   J. F. D.

MOUSE (mous), (Heb. עַכְבָּר, *ak-bawr'*, the corn eater), perhaps generically including *aliarbai* or *jerboa*, or *parah* of the Arabs.

The word occurs where, it seems, the nomenclature in modern zoölogy would point out two species of distinct genera (Lev. xi:29; 1 Sam. vi:4, 5, 11, 18; Is. lxvi:17). It is likely that the Hebrews extended the acceptation of the word *ak-bawr,* in the same manner as was the familiar custom of the Greeks, and still more of the Romans, who included within their term *mus,* insectivora of the genus *sorex,* that is 'shrews'; carnivora, among which was the *Mustela erminea,* 'stoat' or 'ermine,' their *Mus ponticus;* and in the systematic order *Rodentia,* the *muridæ,* containing *Myoxus glis* or fat dormouse, *Dipus jaculus* or Egyptian *jerboa; Mus,* rats and mice properly so called, constituting several modern genera; and *cricetus* or hamster, which includes the marmot or Roman *Mus Alpinus.*

Mouse.

In the above texts, all in 1 Sam. vi apparently refer to the short-tailed field-mouse, which is still the most destructive animal to the harvests of Syria, and is most likely the species noticed in antiquity and during the Crusades; for, had they been *jerboas* in shape and resembled miniature kangaroos, we would expect William of Tyre to have mentioned the peculiar form of the de-

stroyers, which was then unknown to Western Europe; whereas, they being of species or appearance common to the Latin nations, no particulars were required. But in Leviticus and Isaiah, where the mouse is declared an unclean animal, the species most accessible and likely to invite the appetite of nations who, like the Arabs, were apt to covet all kinds of animals, even when expressly forbidden, were, no doubt, the hamster and the dormouse; and both are still eaten in common with the *jerboa,* by the Bedouins, who are but too often driven to extremity by actual want of food.   C. H. S.

MOUTH (mouth), (Heb. פֶּה, *peh*).

The ordinary applications of this word, common to all languages, require no explanation; but the following somewhat peculiar uses may be noted: 'Heavy-mouthed,' that is, slow of speech, and so translated in Exod. iv:10; 'smooth mouth' (Ps. lv:21), that is, a flattering mouth; so also 'a mouth of deceit' (Ps. cix:2). The following are also remarkable phrases: 'To speak with one mouth to mouth,' that is, in person, without the intervention of an interpreter (Num. xii:8; comp. 1 Kings viii:15; Jer. xxxii:4). 'With one mouth,' that is, with one voice or consent (Josh. ix:2; 1 Kings xxii:13; 2 Chron. xviii:12). 'With the whole mouth,' that is, with the utmost strength of voice (Job xix:16; Ps. lxvi:17). 'To put words into one's mouth,' that is, to suggest what one shall say (Exod. iv:15; Num. xxii:38; xxiii:5, 12; 2 Sam. xiv: 19, etc.). 'To be in one's mouth,' is to be often spoken of, as a law, etc. (Exod. xiii: 9; comp. Ps. v:10; xxxviii:15). The Hebrew also says, '*upon* the mouth,' where we say, and indeed our translation says, *in* or *into* the mouth (*e. g.* Nahum iii:12); that which is spoken is also said to be '*upon* the mouth,' where we should say, 'upon the lips' (as in 2 Sam. xiv:3). 'To lay the hand upon the mouth' is to be silent (Judg. xviii:19; Job xxi:5; xl:4; comp. Prov. xxx:32), just as we lay the finger on the mouth to enjoin silence. 'To write from the mouth of any one' is to do so from his dictation (Jer. xxxvi:4, 27, 32; xlv:1).

The mouth, as the organ of speech, also signifies the words that proceed out of it, which in the sacred style are the same as commands and actions. Hence, for a person or thing to come out of the mouth of another is to be constituted or commanded to become an agent or minister under a superior power; this is frequent in the Revelation (Rev. xvi:13, 14; i:16; xi:4, 5; xii:15; ix: 19). The term *mouth* is not only applied to a speech or words, but to the speaker (Exod. iv:16; Jer. xv:19), in which sense it has a near equivalent in our expression 'mouth-piece.'

MOWING (mō'ing), (Heb. גֵּז, *gaze;* literally, fleece, something cut; rendered "mown grass" in Ps. lxxii:6). On account of the heat haymaking, as we understand it, is not known in Palestine. The "King's mowings" (Amos vii:1) probably refers to some rights of pasturage. The term "mower" (Heb. קֹצֵר, *kaw-tsar',* to dock off, Ps. cxxix:7) is usually rendered in the A. V. "reaper." (See Shaw's *Travels,* p. 138.)

MOZA (mō'zà), (Heb. מוֹצָא, *mo-tsaw',* going forth).

1. The second mentioned of the three sons of Caleb by a concubine Ephah (1 Chron. ii:46), B. C. after 1037.

2. Son of Zimri, a descendant of Jonathan (1 Chron. viii:36, 37; ix:42, 43), B. C. after 1037.

MOZAH (mō'zȧh), (Heb. מֹצָה, *mo-tsaw'*, an issuing of water).

One of the cities given to Benjamin (Josh. xviii:26). Hac-Chephirah, with which the place is mentioned, has been identified with *Kefir*, two miles east of *Zalo;* but no more accurate location of Mozah has been made.

MUFFLER (mŭf'flēr), (Heb. רְעָלָה, *rah-al-aw'*), long veils, more costly than the ordinary veils (Is. iii:19), covering the whole face except the eyes.

MULBERRY - TREE (mŭl'bĕr-rў-trē), (Heb. בָּכָא, *baw-kaw'*, baka tree). (See BACA.)

MULE (mūl), (Heb. פֶּרֶד, *peh'red*). Two other words are so translated in the A. V., viz.: רֶכֶשׁ, *reh'kesh* (marg., 1 Kings iv:28, R. V., "swift steeds"), and יֵמִם, *yeh'meem* (Gen. xxxvi:24, R.V., "hot springs").

A granivorous animal, the offspring of the horse and the ass. It was used for transportation (2 Sam. xiii:29; 2 Kings v:17; 1 Chron. xii:40). Asses were exported by the Armenians and purchased by the Tyrians (Ezek. xxvii:14).

MUNITION (mŭ-nĭsh'ŭn), (Heb. מָצוֹר, *maw-tsode'*, spying).

1. A watch-tower (Is. xxix:7); spoken symbolically of Mount Zion (verse 8).

2. A stronghold, fortress (Is. xxxiii:16; Heb. מֵצַר, *mets-ad'*, a mountain fastness).

3. A fortress (Nah. ii:1; Heb. מָצוֹר, *maw-tsore'*, something surrounded or hemmed in).

MUPPIM (mŭp'pim), (Heb. מֻפִּים, *moop-peem'*, wavings), according to Gen. xlvi:21, a son of Benjamin, but from parallel accounts he seems to be the son of Becher, son of Benjamin. Probably the same as SHEPHUPHAN (1 Chron. viii:5), SHUPHAM (Num. xxvi:39), and SHUPPIM (1 Chron. vii:12).

MURDER (mûr'dēr), (Heb. רָצַח, *raw-tsakh'*, to kill).

1. The unlawful taking away of a person's life (Mark xv:7).

2. Hatred of, and cruelty to our neighbor, in thought, word, or deed (Matt xix:18; 1 John iii:15). The voluntary killing of any person, except in lawful war, execution of public justice, or necessary self-defense, hath been peculiarly marked out by the vengeance of God. Cain, the first murderer, was preserved as a monument of the divine indignation (Gen. iv:15). No sacrifice was accepted for this sin; no money was to ransom the life of the guilty. Suppose he fled to God's altar for protection, he was to be dragged thence and executed (Gen. ix:6; Num. xxxv:27-31; Ps. li:16).

If a man had ever so involuntarily and accidentally slain his neighbor, the law demanded that the involuntary manslayer be banished from his native abode, and confined to a city of refuge till the death of the high-priest; and if found without it by the slain person's friend, might be put to death (Num. xxxv; Deut. xix). If a body was found murdered in the field, and the murderer unknown, the rulers of the next city slew a heifer, and with washing of hands, solemnly protested their innocence of the crime and their ignorance of the actor; and with the priests or Levites present, begged that the Lord would not lay the sin to the charge of the land (Deut. xxi:1-8).

In regal times the duty of execution of justice on a murderer seems to have been assumed to some extent by the sovereign, as well as the privilege of pardon (2 Sam. xiii:39; xiv:7, 11; 1 Kings ii:34). It was lawful to kill a burglar taken at night in the act, but unlawful to do so after sunrise (Exod. xxii:2, 3), (Smith, *Bib. Dict.;* Jahn, *Arch.;* Keil, *Arch.;* Brown, *Bib. Dict.*).

MURRAIN (mŭr'rĭn). See PLAGUES OF EGYPT.

MUSE (mūz), (Heb. שִׂיחַ, *see'akh*, to dwell in memory upon the past; to ponder, Ps. cxliii:5), to meditate, reflect. In Luke iii:15 the Greek term διαλογίζομαι (*dee-al-og-id'zom-ahee*) means to *judge, reason, deliberate.* (See MUSING.)

MUSHI (mū'shī), (Heb. מוּשִׁי, *moo-shee'*, sensitive), a Levite, second son of Merari, and founder of a house by his name (Ex. vi:19; Num. iii:20; 1 Chron. vi:19, 47; xxiii:21; xxiv:26), through his three sons (1 Chron. xxiii:23; xxiv:30; Num. iii:33; xxvi:58), B. C. after 1856.

MUSHITE (mū'shīte), (Heb. *moo-shee'*, as above), a descendant of MUSHI (Num. iii:33; xxvi:58).

MUSIC (mū'zĭk), (Heb. זְמָר, *zeh-mawr'*).

It seems probable that music is the oldest of all the fine arts. It is more than any other an immediate work of nature. Hence we find it among all nations, even those which are totally ignorant of every other art.

(1) **Early Inventions.** Some instruments of music are named in Scripture even before the deluge, as being invented by Jubal, one of Cain's descendants (Gen. iv:21) ; and some will regard this as confirmed by the common opinion of the Orientals. Chardin relates that the Persians and Arabians called musicians and singers *Kayne*, or 'descendants from Cain.' The instruments invented by Jubal seem to have remained in use after the flood, or at least the names were still in use, and occur in the latest books of the Old Testament. Music, in practical use, is almost constantly mentioned in connection with the song and the dance (Gen. xxxi:27; Exod. xv:20), and was doubtless employed to elevate the former and regulate the latter. Women especially are seen to have employed it in this connection from the earliest times (Exod. xv:20; Judg. xi:34; 1 Sam. xviii:6). At a later period we trace the appearance of foreign girls in Palestine, as in Greece and Italy, who visited the towns like the Bayaderes of the present day (Is. xxiii:16). Music was also through all periods used in social meetings, and in public rejoicings (1 Kings i:40; Is. v:12; xiv:11; xxiv:8; Amos vi:5; Amos v: 23; 1 Macc. ix:39; Judith iii:8).

(2) **Connected with Worship.** By David music was variously and conspicuously connected with the temple worship (1 Chron. xxv:1) ; in particular, the Levites, in their several choirs, performed their music divided into different classes at the great sacrifices (2 Chron. xxix: 25; xxx:21; xxxv:15). The prophets also appear to have regarded music as necessary to their services (1 Sam. x:5) ; and they used it sometimes for the purpose, apparently, of bringing their minds into the frame suited for prophetic inspirations (2 Kings iii:15). In the case of David playing before Saul, we have marked an interesting evidence that the effect of music in soothing the perturbations of a disordered intellect, was well known among the Hebrews (1 Sam. xvi:16).

With respect to the nature of the Hebrew music, it was doubtless of the same essential character as that of other ancient nations, and of all the present Oriental nations; consisting not so much in harmony (in the modern sense of the term), as in unison or melody.

(3) Melody. The old, the young, maidens, etc., appear to have sung one part. The beauty of their music consisted altogether in melody. The instruments by which, in singing, this melody was accompanied, occupied the part of a sustained base; and, if we are disposed to apply in this case what Niebuhr has told us, the beauty of the concerts consisted in this—that other persons repeated the music which had just been sung, three, four, or five notes, lower or higher. Such, for instance, was the concert which Miriam held with her musical fellows, and to which the 'toph,' or tabret, furnished the continued base; just as Niebuhr has also remarked of the Arabian women of the present day, 'that when they dance or sing in their harem, they always beat the corresponding time upon this drum (*Reiseb.* i: 181). To this mode of performance belongs the 24th Psalm, which rests altogether upon the varied representation; in like manner, also, the 20th and 21st Psalms. This was all the change it admitted; and although it is very possible that this monotonous, or rather unisonous music, might not be interesting to ears tuned to musical progressions, modulations, and cadences, there is something in it with which the Orientals are well pleased.

Music of this description could easily dispense with the compositions which mark the time by notes; and the Hebrews do not appear to have known anything of musical notation; for that the accents served that purpose is a position which yet remains to be proved. At the best, the accent must have been an very imperfect instrument for this purpose, however high its antiquity.

The Hebrew music is judged to have been of a shrill character; for this would result from the nature of the instruments—harps, flutes, and cymbals—which were employed in the temple service.

The manner of singing single songs was, it seems, ruled by that of others in the same measure, and it is usually supposed that many of the titles of the Psalms are intended to indicate the names of other songs according to which these were to be sung. (See PSALMS, BOOK OF.)

The allusions to music in the Scriptures are so incidental and concise that it will never be possible to form out of them a complete or connected view of the state of musical science among the ancient Hebrews. The little knowledge which has been realized on the subject has been obtained chiefly through the patient labors and minute investigation of Calmet, Forkel, Pfeiffer, Jahn, Winer, De Wette and others.

MUSICAL INSTRUMENTS (mū'zĭ-kal ĭn'-stru̯-ments).

It is less difficult to determine the general character of the Hebrew instruments of music, than to identify the particular instruments which are named in the Hebrew Scriptures. We see certain instruments different from our own in use among the modern Orientals, and we infer that the Hebrew instruments are probably not unlike these. When, however, we endeavor to identify with these a particular instrument named by the Hebrews, our difficulty begins; because the Hebrew names are seldom to be recognized in those which they *now* bear, and because the Scripture affords us little information respecting the form of the instruments which it mentions.

The matter naturally arranges itself under the following heads—

I. Stringed Instruments.
II. Wind Instruments.
III. Instruments of Percussion.

1. Stringed Instruments. At the head of the stringed instruments we must place the כִּנּוֹר *kinnore',* which is rendered 'harp' in the Authorized Version.

(1) The Harp. The invention and first use of this instrument are ascribed to Jubal (Gen. iv: 21); and Laban names it among the instruments which should have celebrated the departure of his son-in-law (Gen. xxxi :27). In the first ages the *kinnor* was consecrated to joy and exultation; hence the frequency of its use by David and others in praise of the Divine Majesty. It is thought probable that the instrument received some improvements from David (comp. Amos vi:5). In bringing back the ark of the covenant (1 Chron. xvi:5), as well as afterwards, at the consecration of the temple, the *kinnor* was assigned to players of known eminence, chiefly of the family of Jeduthun (1 Chron. xxv:3).

The sorrowing Jews of the captivity, far removed from their own land and the shadow of the sanctuary, hung their *kin-norés* upon the willows by the waters of Babylon, and refused to sing the songs of Zion in a strange land (Ps. cxxxvii:2). Many other passages of similar purport might be adduced in order to fix the uses of an instrument, the name of which occurs so often in the Hebrew Scriptures. They mostly indicate occasions of joy, such as jubilees and festivals. Of the instrument itself the Scripture affords us little further information than that it was composed of the sounding parts of good wood, and furnished with strings. David made it of the berosh wood (see BEROSH); Solomon of the more costly algum (2 Sam. vi:5; 1 Kings x:12); and Josephus mentions some composed of the mixed metal called electrum. He also asserts that it was furnished with ten strings, and played with a plectrum (*Antiq.* vii:12, 3); which, however, is not understood to imply that it never had any other number of strings, or was always played with the plectrum. David certainly played it with the hand (1 Sam. xvi:23; xviii:10; xix:9), and it was probably used in both ways, according to its size.

That this instrument was really a harp is now very generally denied; and Pfeiffer, Winer, and other writers on the subject conclude that it was a kind of guitar, and there is therefore little

Wind Instruments and Sistrum.

room to doubt that the guitar was known to the Hebrews and probably in use among them. Notwithstanding this kind of evidence, the editor of the Pictorial Bible (on Ps. xliii:4) ventured to suggest the greater probability that the *lyre,* in some of its various kinds, was denoted by the word *kin-noré;* and subsequent inquiry has tended to establish this conclusion as firmly perhaps as the nature of the subject admits.

(2) Psaltery. *Nay'-bel* (Heb. נֶבֶל,) is the next instrument which requires notice. The word is rendered 'psaltery' in the Authorized Version. As to when this instrument was invented, and when it came into use among the Hebrews, nothing can be determined with certainty. The first mention of it is in the reign of Saul (1 Sam. x:5), and from that time forward we continue to meet with it in the Old Testament. The use of the instrument prevailed particularly in the public worship of God. David's own instrument was the *kin-noré;* but he neglected not the *nay'-bel.* It was played upon by several persons in the grand procession at the removal of the ark (1 Chron. xv:16; xvi:5); and in the final organization of the temple music it was entrusted to the families of Asaph, Heman, and Jeduthun (1 Chron. xxv:1-7).

Out of the worship of God, it was employed at festivals and for luxurious purposes (Amos vi:5). In the manufacture of this instrument a constant increase of splendor was exhibited. The first we meet with were made simply of the wood of the *berosh* (2 Sam. vi:5; 1 Chron. xiii:8), others of the rarer *algum* tree (1 Kings x:12; 2 Chron. ix: 11); and some perhaps of metal (Joseph. *Antiq.* i:8, 3), unless the last is to be understood of particular parts of the instrument.

Conjectures respecting the probable form of this instrument have been exceedingly various. Passing by the eccentric notion that the *nay'-bel* was a kind of bagpipe, we may assume from the evident tendency of the Scriptural intimations, and from the general bearing of other authorities, that it was composed of strings stretched over a wooden frame. This being assumed or granted, we must proceed to seek some hint concerning its shape; and we find nothing more tangible than the concurrent testimony of Jerome, Isidorus, and Cassiodorus, that it was like the Greek letter Δ inverted ▽.

We are, however, far from thinking that the *nay'-bel* was always of this shape. It appears to us to be a general name for various of the larger stringed instruments of the harp kind, and also to denote, in a more special sense, one particular sort; in other words, that the *nay'-bel* was an instrument of a principal species, the name of which was applied to the whole genus. In fact, we have the names of several instruments which are generally conceived to be different varieties of the *nay'-bel.* Before proceeding to these, we must express an opinion that one of these kinds, if not the principal kind, or the one most frequently denoted by the word, was the

Egyptian Harp.

ancient harp, agreeing more or less with that represented in the Egyptian monuments.

(3) **Awsore** (עָשׂוֹר), occurs as an instrument in only a few places, and never but in connection with the *nay'-bel,* except in Ps. xxxiii:2; Ps. cxliv:9.

(4) **Stringed Instruments** (גִּתִּית, *git'tith*), a word which occurs in the titles to Ps. viii, lxxxi, lxxxiv, and is generally supposed to denote a musical instrument. From the name it has been supposed to be an instrument which David brought from Gath; and it has been inferred from Is. xvi:10 that it was in particular use at the vintage season. If an instrument of music, it is remarkable that it does not occur in the list of the instruments assigned by David to the temple musicians; nor even in that list which appears in verses 1 and 2 of Ps. lxxxi, in the title of which it is found. The supposition of Gesenius, that it is a general name for *a stringed instrument,* obviates this difficulty.

Assyrian Harps.

(5) **Strings** (מִנִּים, *min-neem'*),which occurs in Ps. cl:4 only, is supposed by some to denote a stringed instrument, but it seems merely a poetical allusion to the *strings* of any instrument.

(6) **Sackbut** (שַׂבְּכָא, *sab-bek-aw'*), an instrument rendered 'sackbut,' and which occurs only in Dan. iii:5, 7, 10, 15. It seems to have been a species of harp or lyre, and, as some think, was only a species of the *nay'-bel,* distinguished by the number of its strings.

Stringed Instruments, Cymbals, Etc.

(7) **Greek Psaltery** (פְּסַנְתֵּרִין, *pes-an-tay-reen'*), the ψαλτήριον or psaltery of the Greeks; it occurs only in Dan. iii:7, 10, 15, where it is supposed to represent the Hebrew *nay'-bel.*

(8) **Lute** (Heb. מַחֲלַת, *makh-al-ath'*), which occurs in the titles of Ps. liii and lxxxviii, is supposed by Gesenius and others to denote a kind of lute or guitar, which instrument others find in the *minnim* above noticed. We should not like to affirm that instruments of this kind are represented by either of these words—not that we doubt whether the Hebrews had such instruments, but because we are not satisfied that these are the precise words by which they were denoted.

2. Wind Instruments. There is, happily, less difficulty with respect to instruments of this class than with respect to stringed instruments. The most ordinary division of these is into trumpets and pipes, of which the Hebrews had both, and of various kinds.

(1) **Horn** (קֶרֶן, *keh'ren,* 'horn'), sometimes, but not often, occurs as the name of a musical instrument (Josh. vi:5; 1 Chron. xxv:5; Dan. iii: 5, 7, 10, 15). Of natural horns, and of instruments in the shape of horns, the antiquity and

general use are evinced by every extensive collection of antiquities. It is admitted that natural horns were at first used, and that they at length came to be imitated in metal, but were still called horns. This use and application of the word are illustrated in our 'cornet.' It is generally conceived that rams' horns were the instruments used by the early Hebrews, and these are, indeed, expressly named in our own and many other versions, as the instruments used at the noted siege of Jericho (Josh. vi:5); and the horns are those of the ram, which Josephus assigns to the soldiers of Gideon (*Antiq.* v:6, 5; comp. Judg. vii:16).

(2) Trumpet (שׁוֹפָר, *sho-fawr'*), which is a far more common word than *keren*, and is rendered 'trumpet' in the Authorized Version.

This word seems, first, to denote horns of the straighter kind, including, probably, those of neat

Ancient Horns and Curved Trumpets.

cattle, and all the instruments which were eventually made in imitation of and in improvement upon such horns. It is, however, difficult to draw a distinction between it and the *kehren,* seeing that the words are sometimes used synonymously. Thus that which is called 'a jobel-horn' in Josh. vi:5, is in the same chapter (verses 4, 6, 8, 13) called 'a jobel-horn trumpet.' Upon the whole, we may take the *sho-fawr',* however distinguished from the *kch'ren,* to have been that kind of horn

Assyrian and Egyptian Trumpets.

or horn-shaped trumpet which was best known to the Hebrews. The name *sho-fawr'* means *bright* or *clear,* and the instrument may be conceived to have been so called from its clear and shrill sound, just as we call an instrument a 'clarion,' and speak of a musical tone as 'brilliant' or 'clear.' In the service of God this *sho-fawr'* or trumpet was employed only in making announcements, and for calling the people together in the time of the holy solemnities, of war, of rebellion, or of any other great occasion (Exod. xix:13; Num. x:10; Judg. iii:27; 1 Sam. xiii:3; 2 Sam. xv:10; 2 Chron. xv:14; Is. xviii:3).

(3) Straight Trumpet. Another instrument was *khats-o-tser-aw',* חֲצוֹצְרָה. This was the straight trumpet, different from the *sho-fawr',* which was more or less bent like a horn. There has been various speculation on the name; but we are disposed to assent to the conclusion of Gesenius that it is an onomatopoetic word, imitating the broken pulse-like sound of the trumpet, like the Latin *taratantara,* which this word would more resemble if pronounced as in Arabic, *hadâderah.* Among the Israelites these trumpets were a divine regulation, Moses having been expressly directed how to make them (Num. x:2). They were of pure beaten silver, but the particular form does not appear in Scripture. When, however, riches departed from Palestine, trumpets of baser metal were used (2 Kings xii:13), although probably a certain number of silver were still preserved. They were used in calling the congregation together for sacrifices, and in battle (Hos. v:8). The tone of this trumpet, or rather the noise made by blowing on it, was very variable, and is distinguished by different terms in Scripture.

(4) Jubilee Trumpet. *Yo-bale'* (Heb. יוֹבֵל). There has been much speculation concerning this term, which the reader may find in ample abundance in Bochart (*Hieroz.* i:436). It seems now to be agreed that the word does not denote a separate instrument, but is an epithet applied to the trumpets with which the jubilees were proclaimed, *i. e.,* the 'jubilee-trumpet;' and as the same trumpets were used for signals and alarms, 'the alarm-trumpet, the alarm-horn.' This name for the sound of music is supposed to be derived from Jubal, the inventor of instruments of music.

Wind instruments of softer sound next require attention. The first and principal of these is the

(5) Pipe (חָלִיל, *khaw-leel'*), the meaning of which is *bored through,* and denotes a pipe, perforated and furnished with holes. There are but five places where it occurs in the Old Testament (1 Sam. x:5; 1 Kings i:40; Is. v:12; xxx:29; Jer. xlviii: 36); but the Greek αὐλός occurs in the New Testament (Matt. ix:23), and in the Apocryphal books (1 Macc. iv: 54; ix:39; Judith iii: 8). It would seem to have come rather late into use among the Hebrews, and probably had a foreign origin. The passages to which we have referred will indicate the use of this instrument or class of instruments; but of the form we can only guess by reference to those of the ancient Egyptians, which are very similar to those still in use in Western Asia. The pipe is, however, rarely introduced in the Egyptian sculptures, and does not seem to have been held in much estimation. The principal are the single and double pipes. The single pipe of the Greeks is allowed to have been introduced from Egypt (J. Pollux, *Onom.* iv:10; Athenæus, *Deipnos,* iv), from which the Jews probably had theirs. It was a straight tube, without any increase at the mouth, and when

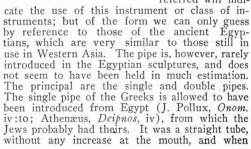

played was held with both hands. It was usually of moderate length, about eighteen inches; but occasionally less, and sometimes so exceedingly long and the holes so low that the player was obliged to extend his arms to the utmost. Some had three holes, others four, and actual specimens made of common reed have been found (Wilkinson, *Ancient Egyptians,* ii:309).

The double pipe was formed with two of such tubes, of equal or unequal lengths, having a common mouth-piece, and each played with the corresponding hand. They were distinguished as the right and left pipes, and the latter, having but few holes and emitting a deep sound, served as a base; the others had more holes and gave a sharp sound (Plin. *Hist Nat.* xvi:36). This pipe is still used in Palestine.

From the references which have been given it will be seen that the pipe was, among the Jews, chiefly consecrated to joy and pleasure. So much was this the case that in the time of Judas Maccabæus the Jews complained 'that joy was taken from Jacob, and the pipe with the harp (κιθάρα) ceased' (1 Macc. iii:45). It was particularly used to enliven the periodical journeys to Jerusalem to attend the great festivals (Is. xxx:29) ; and this custom of accompanying traveling in companies with music is common in the East at this day (Harmer, *Observatt.* ii:197; to which add Tournefort, *Voyage du Levant,* iii:189). Athenæus iv:174) tells us of a plaintive pipe which was in use among the Phœnicians. This serves to illustrate Matt. ix:23, where our Savior, finding the flute-players with the dead daughter of the ruler, orders them away, because the damsel was not dead; and in this we also recognize the regulation of the Jews, that every one, however poor he might be, should have at least two pipes at the death of his wife (Lightfoot *Hor. Hebr. ad Matt.* ix:23). (See MOURNING.)

(6) **Flute** (Chaldee, מַשְׁרוֹקִי, *mash-ro-kee'* ; a musical pipe). This word occurs four times in Daniel (ch. iii:5, 7, 10, 15), but nowhere else, and appears to be the Chaldæan name for the flute with two reeds, of which we have already spoken.

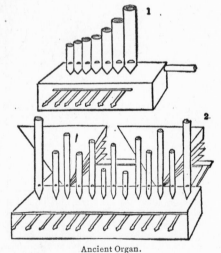

Ancient Organ.

(7) **Organ** (Heb. עוּגָב, *oo-gawb'*), is the word rendered 'organ' in our version. This and the *kinnor* are the instruments whose invention is ascribed to Jubal (Gen. iv:21), and higher antiquity cannot therefore be claimed for any in-

strument. There are only three other places in which it is mentioned in the Old Testament—two in the book of Job (xxi:12, xxx:31), and one in the Psalms (cl:4). The *organon* simply denotes a double or manifold pipe; and hence in particular the Pandæan or shepherd's pipe, which is at this day called a 'mouth-organ' among ourselves. Formerly it was called simply 'organ,' and 'mouth' has been added to distinguish it from the comparatively modern instrument which has usurped the more simple designation of 'organ.' Our translators are thus not chargeable with the obscurity which has since arisen, for they, by the word 'organ,' intended to indicate no other instrument than this.

This antiquity corresponds with the Scriptural intimation concerning the *ugab,* and justifies us in seeking for the *syrinx* among the more ancient instruments of the Orientals, especially as it is still common in Western Asia. Niebuhr saw it in the hands of a peasant at Cairo (*Reisebeschr.* i:181) ; and Russell, in his *Nat. Hist. of Aleppo* (i:155, 156), says that 'the *syrinx* or Pan's pipe is still a festival instrument in Syria; it is known also in the city, but very few performers can sound it tolerably well. The higher notes are clear and pleasing, but the longer reeds are apt, like the dervise flute, to make a hissing sound, though blown by a good player. The number of reeds of which the *syrinx* is composed, varies in different instruments from five to twenty-three.' The classical *syrinx* is usually said to have had seven reeds (Virg. *Ecl.* ii), but we find some in the monuments with a greater number, and the shepherd of Theocritus (*Id.* viii) had one of nine reeds.

3. Instruments of Percussion. *Instruments of percussion,* or such as give forth their sounds on being struck or shaken.

(1) **Timbrel** (תֹּף, *toph,* or *tofe*), seems to have denoted primarily the tambourine, and generally all instruments of the drum kind which were in use among the Israelites. There is not the slightest doubt about this instrument. All the translations and lexicons agree in this one point, and we have, besides, the actual evidence of existing instruments of this kind among the Arabians, bearing the same name in the forms of *doff* and *adufe.* The *toph* was known to the Jews before they quitted Syria (Gen. xxxi:27); it is also mentioned by Job (xxi:12), and it is the first instrument named after the exode, being that with which Miriam led the dances with which the daughters of Israel celebrated the overthrow of Pharaoh (Exod. xv:20). It was employed by David in all the festivities of religion (2 Sam. vi:5). Isaiah adduces it as the instrument of voluptuaries, but left in silence amid wars and desolations (Is. xxiv:8). The occasions on which it was used were mostly joyful, and those who played upon it were generally females (Ps. lxviii: 25), as was the case among most ancient nations, and is so at the present day in the East. It is nowhere mentioned in connection with battles or warlike transactions.

Whether the Israelites had drums or not does not clearly appear, and in the absence of evidence *pro* or *con* it is useless to speculate on the subject. If they had, they must be included under the general name of *toph.* The ancient Egyptians had a long drum, very similar to the tom-toms of India. It was about two feet or two feet and a half in length, and was beaten with the hand. The case was of wood or copper, covered at both ends with parchment or leather, and braced with cords extended diagonally over the exterior of the cylinder. It was used chiefly in war. There was another larger drum, less unlike our own; it was about two feet and a half long by about two feet broad, and was shaped much like a sugar-cask. It was formed of copper, and covered at the ends with red leather, braced by catgut strings passing through small holes in its broad

Timbrel.

margin. This kind of drum was beaten with sticks. It does not appear on the monuments, but an actual specimen was found in the excavations made by D'Athanasi, in 1823, and is now in the museum at Paris.

Another species of drum is represented in the Egyptian paintings, and is of the same kind which is still in use in Egypt and Arabia, under the name of the *darabooka* drum. It is made of parchment stretched over the top of a funnel-shaped case of metal, wood, or pottery. It is beaten with the hand, and when relaxed, the parchment is braced by exposing it for a few moments to the sun, or the warmth of a fire. This kind of drum claims particular attention from its being supposed to be represented on one of the coins ascribed to Simon Maccabæus.

(2) **Bells.** *Pah-am-one'* (Heb. פַּעֲמוֹן). This name nowhere occurs but with reference to the small golden appendages to the robe of the high-priest (Exod. xxviii:33; xxxix:25), which all versions agree in rendering 'bells,' or 'little bells.'

(3) **Cymbals.** Three Hebrew words are translated *cymbals* in most versions, except in Zech. xiv:20, where they are rendered 'bells'—the 'bells of the horses.' If the words, however, denote cymbals in other places, they cannot well denote a different thing here.

There is an important passage (Ps. cl:5), 'Praise him with the clear cymbal, praise him with the resounding cymbal,' which clearly points to two instruments under the same name, and leaves us to conclude that the Hebrews had both hand-cymbals and finger-cymbals (or castanets), although it may not in all cases be easy to say which of the two is intended in particular texts. Cymbals figure in the grand procession at the removal of the ark (1 Chron. xiii:8); other instances occur of their being used in the worship of God (Neh. xii:27; Ps. cl:5; 1 Chron. xv:16); and the illustrious Asaph was himself a player on the cymbal (1 Chron. xvi:5). The sound of these instruments is very sharp and piercing, but it does not belong to fine, speaking, expressive music. Hence Paul could describe it by the word ἀλαλάζον, 'clanging' (1 Cor. xiii:1).

(4) **Triangle** (Heb. שָׁלִישִׁים, *shawl-ish'im*). This word occurs but once, viz., in 1 Sam. xviii:6, and is there uncertainly rendered, in the Authorized Version, 'instruments of music,' and in the mar-

76

gin 'three-stringed instruments.' The word is plural, and means 'threes.' Most writers, proceeding upon this interpretation, identify it with the triangle, which Athenæus (iv:23) alleges to have been a Syrian invention.

(5) **Sistrum** (מְנַעַנְעִים, *men-ah-an-eem'*). This is another word which occurs but once in Scripture (2 Sam. vi:5), where our version translates it by 'cymbals,' although it has appropriated another word to that instrument. It is now more

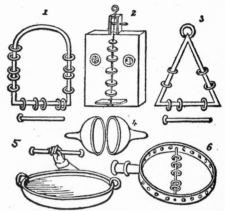

Instruments of Percussion. 1, 3, 6. Rods of metal charged with rings. 2. Supposed Hebrew instrument. 4. A kind of Eastern Cymbal. 5. A pan of sounding metal.

generally thought to denote the *sistrum*, which was generally from eight to sixteen or eighteen

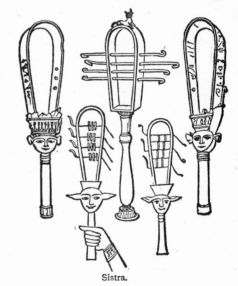

Sistra.

inches in length, and entirely of bronze or brass. It was sometimes inlaid with silver, gilt, or otherwise ornamented, and being held upright was shaken, the rings moving to and fro upon the bars. The last were frequently made to imitate snakes, or simply bent at each end to secure them from slipping through the holes. Several actual specimens of these instruments have been found, and are deposited in the British, Berlin and other museums. They are mostly furnished with sacred symbols, and were chiefly used by the priests and priestesses in the ceremonies of religion, particularly in those connected with the worship of Isis.

MUSING (mūz'ĭng), (Heb. הָגִיג, *haw-gheeg'*, Ps. xxxix:3), a figure borrowed from the fermentation or spontaneous combustion of certain articles. In general it denotes to think, to consider (Ps. cxliii:5).

MUSTARD TREE (mŭs'tērd trē), (Gr. σίναπι, *sin'ap-ee*). See SINAPI.

MUTHLABBEN (mūth-lăb'ben), (Heb. מוּתְלַבֵּן, *mooth-lab-bane'*). This word occurs in the title of Ps. ix, and perhaps the most generally accepted meaning is "with the voice of virgins," indicating that it was to be sung by boys (Ps. ix; title).

MUTTER (mŭt'tēr), (Heb. הָגָה, *haw-gaw'*, Is. viii:19, to speak softly). It seems that anciently wizards muttered or talked in a whispering tone, and peeped to their familiar spirits. (See MAGIC.)

MUZZLE (mŭz'z'l), (Heb. חָסַם, *khaw-sam'* ; Gr. φιμόω, *fee-mo'o*, to stop the mouth).

In the East the grain was thrashed by oxen trampling upon it; and the command was not to put anything in or on the mouth of a beast to restrain it from eating (Deut. xxv:4). St. Paul used it to denote (1 Cor. ix:9; 1 Tim. v:18) that a laborer was not to be deprived of his wages.

MYRA (mȳ'rà), (Gr. Μύρα, *moo'rah*, ointments), one of the chief towns of Lycia, in Asia Minor.

It lay about a league from the sea (in N. lat. 36° 18'; E. long. 30°), upon a rising ground, at the foot of which flowed a navigable river with an excellent harbor at its mouth (Strabo. xiv, p. 665; Pliny, *Hist. Nat.* xxxii:8). The town now lies desolate amid magnificent ruins. When Paul was on his voyage from Cæsarea to Rome he and the other prisoners were landed here, and were re-embarked in a ship of Alexandria bound to Rome (Acts xxvii:5).

MYRRH (mēr), a gum, the thickened sap of a low thorny tree (*Balsamodendron opsobalsamum*), which grows chiefly in Arabia.

Myrrh is sold for medical purposes in small globules of a white or yellow color, of a strong and agreeable smell, but a bitter taste. It was an ingredient of the holy ointment (Ex. xxx:23), and of the embalming substance (John xix:39). It was also used as an agreeable perfume (Esth. ii:12; Ps. xlv:8; Prov. vii:17), and a valuable gift (Matt. ii:11). In Matt. xxvii:34 it is said that they gave Jesus to drink vinegar mixed with gall, which, in Mark xv:23, is called wine mingled with myrrh. It was probably the sour wine which the Roman soldiers used to drink mingled with myrrh and other bitter substances, very much like the *bitters* of modern times. (See MOR.)

MYRTLE (mēr't'l). See HADAS.

MYSIA (mȳ'si-à) (mĭzh'ĭ-à), (Gr. Μυσία, *moo-see'-ah*), a province occupying the northwest angle of Asia Minor, and separated from Europe only by the Propontis and Hellespont ; on the south it joined Æolis, and was separated on the east from Bithynia by the river Æsopus. Paul passed through this province and embarked at its chief port, Troas, on his first voyage to Europe (Acts xvi:7, 8).

MYSTERY (mĭs'tēr-ŷ), (Gr. μυστήριον, *moos-tay'-ree-on*, secret doctrine). The etymology of this Greek word, which seems to be the simplest and most illustrative of its meaning, is that from the Hebrew to 'hide' or 'conceal,' whence a covert or secret place, a secret.

(1) A Revelation. A most unscriptural and dangerous sense is but too often put upon the word, as if it meant something absolutely unintelligible and incomprehensible ; whereas, in every instance in which it occurs in the Septuagint or New Testament, it is applied to something which is *revealed,* declared, explained, spoken, or which may be known or understood. This fact will appear from the following elucidation of the passages in which it is found. First, it is sometimes used to denote the meaning of a symbolical representation, whether addressed to the mind by a parable, allegory, etc., or to the eye, by a vision, etc. Thus our Lord, having delivered to the multitude the parable of the sower (Matt. xiii:3-9), when the disciples asked him (verse 10) why he spoke to them in parables, replied, 'Unto you it is given to know the mysteries of the kingdom of heaven, but unto them which are without it is not given' (Mark iv:11).

(2) Mystery of the Woman. Again, 'the mystery or symbolical representation of the woman upon a scarlet colored beast' (Rev. xvii:3-6), is also explained, 'I will tell thee the mystery of the woman,' etc. (xvii:7). When St. Paul, speaking of marriage, says 'this is a great mystery' (Eph. v:32), he evidently treats the original institution of marriage, as affording a figurative representation of the union betwixt Christ and the church (Campbell, *Dissertation,* p. 10, part iii, sec. 9). The word is also used to denote anything whatever which is hidden or concealed, till it is explained.

(3) Doctrines. Thus the word is used in the New Testament to denote those doctrines of Christianity, general or particular, which the Jews and the world at large did not understand, till they were revealed by Christ and his apostles, 'Great is the mystery of godliness,' *i. e.,* the Christian religion (1 Tim. iii:16), the chief parts of which the apostle instantly proceeds to adduce— 'God was manifest in the flesh, justified by the Spirit, seen of angels,' etc.—facts which had not entered into the heart of man (1 Cor. ii:9) until God visibly accomplished them, and revealed them to the apostles by inspiration (verse 10). The apostle is generally thought here to compare the Gospel with the greater Eleusinian mysteries.

(4) Mystery of Faith. Thus also the Gospel in general is called 'the mystery of the faith,' which it was requisite the deacons should hold with a pure conscience' (1 Tim. iii:9). The same word is used respecting certain particular doctrines of the Gospel, as, for instance, 'the partial and temporary blindness of Israel,' of which mystery 'the apostle would not have Christians ignorant (Rom. xi:25), and which he explains (verses 25-32). He styles the calling of the Gentiles a mystery which, in other ages, was not made known unto the sons of men as it is now revealed unto the holy apostles and prophets by the Spirit' (Eph. iii:4-6; comp. i:9, 10, etc.). To this class we refer the well-known phrase, 'Behold, I show you a mystery (1 Cor. xv:51), we shall all be changed;' and then follows an explanation of the change (verses 51-55). Even in the case of a man speaking in an unknown tongue, in the absence of an interpreter, and when, therefore, no man understood him, although 'by the Spirit he was speaking mysteries,' yet the Apostle supposes that the man so doing understood what himself said (1 Cor. xiv:2-4).

(5) Mystery of Iniquity. And in the prophetic portion of his writings 'concerning the mystery of iniquity' (2 Thess. ii:7), he speaks of it as being ultimately 'revealed' (verse 8) ; and to complete the proof that the word 'mystery' is used in the sense of *knowable* secrets, we add the words, 'Though *I understand all mysteries*' (1 Cor. xiii:2). The Greeks used the word in the same way. Thus Menander, 'Tell not your secret to a friend' (p. 274, line 671, ed. Clerici).

J. F. D.

N

NAAM (nā'am), (Heb. נַעַם, *nah'am*, pleasantness), one of the three sons of Caleb, son of Jephunneh (1 Chron. iv:15), B. C. about 1618.

NAAMAH (nā'a-mah), (Heb. נַעֲמָה, *nah-am-aw'*, pleasant).

1. A daughter of Lamech and Zillah, and sister of Tubal-cain (Gen. iv:22), B. C. about 3549.

2. An Ammonitess, one of the wives of Solomon, and mother of Rehoboam (1 Kings xiv:21).

3. A town in the low country of Judah, which has not been fully identified. It is proposed, however, to identify Naamah with Nä-neh, which is a small mud village on low ground six miles south of *Ludd*, (Lydda). (C. Warren in Hastings' *Dict. of Bib.*)

NAAMAN (nā'a-man), (Heb. נַעֲמָן, *nah-am-awn'*, pleasantness; Sept. Ναιμάν, *naiman*).

1. (1) **Commander of Syrian Armies.** He was the commander of the armies of Damascene Syria, in the time of Joram, king of Israel. Through his valor and abilities Naaman held a high place in the esteem of his king Benhadad.

(2) **A Leper.** Although he was afflicted with leprosy, it would seem that this did not, as among the Hebrews, operate as a disqualification for public employment. Nevertheless the condition of a leper could not but have been in his high place both afflicting and painful; and when it was heard that a little Hebrew slave-girl, who waited upon Naaman's wife, had spoken of a prophet in Samaria who could cure her master of his leprosy, the faint and uncertain hope thus offered was eagerly seized; and the general obtained permission to visit the place where this relief was to be sought. Benhadad even furnished him with a letter to his old enemy, King Joram. But this letter merely stated that Naaman had been sent for him to cure, and the king of Israel rent his clothes in astonishment and anger, suspecting that a request so impossible to grant involved a studied insult or an intention to fix a quarrel upon him with a view to future aggressions.

When tidings of this affair reached the prophet Elisha, he desired that the stranger might be sent to him. Naaman accordingly went, and his splendid train of chariots, horses, and laden camels filled the street before the prophet's house. As a leper, Naaman could not be admitted into the house; and Elisha did not come out to him as he expected, and as he thought civility required; but he sent out his servant to tell him to go and dip himself seven times in the Jordan, and that his leprosy would then pass from him. He was, however, by this time so much chafed and disgusted by the apparent neglect and incivility with which he had been treated, that if his attendants had not prevailed upon him to obey the directions of the prophet, he would have returned home still a leper.

(3) **The Jordan.** But he went to the Jordan, and having bent himself seven times beneath its waters, rose from them clear from all leprous stain. His gratitude was now proportioned to his previous wrath, and he drove back to vent the feelings of his full heart to the prophet of Israel.

(4) **Converted to the God of Israel.** He avowed to him his conviction that the God of Israel, through whom this marvelous deed had been wrought, was great beyond all gods; and he declared that henceforth he would worship him only, and to that end he proposed to take with him two mules' load of the soil of Israel wherewith to set up in Damascus an altar to Jehovah. This shows he had heard that an altar of earth was necessary (Exod. xx:24); and the imperfect notions which he entertained of the duties which his desire to serve Jehovah involved, were natural in an uninstructed foreigner. He had also heard that Jehovah was a very jealous God, and had forbidden any of his servants to bow themselves down before idols; and therefore he expressed to Elisha a hope that he should be forgiven if, when his public duty required him to attend his king to the temple of Rimmon, he bowed with his master. The grateful Syrian would gladly have pressed upon Elisha gifts of high value, but that holy man resolutely refused to take anything, lest the glory redounding to God from this great act should in any degree be obscured.

(5) **Gehazi.** His servant, Gehazi, was less scrupulous, and hastened with a lie in his mouth to ask in his master's name for a portion of that which Elisha had refused. The illustrious Syrian no sooner saw the man running after his chariot than he alighted to meet him, and, happy to relieve himself in some degree under the sense of overwhelming obligation, he sent him back with more than he had ventured to ask (2 Kings v), B. C. about 850. Nothing more is definitely known of Naaman. According to the Midrash, Naaman was the man who 'drew his bow at a venture' at the battle of Ramoth-Gilead (1 Kings xxii:34).

(6) **Character.** "Naaman's appearance throughout the occurrence is most characteristic and consistent. He is every inch a soldier, ready at once to resent what he considers a slight cast either on himself or the natural glories of his country, and blazing out in a moment into sudden 'rage,' but calmed as speedily by a few good-humored and sensible words from his dependents, and after the cure has been effected evincing a thankful and simple heart, whose gratitude knows no bounds, and will listen to no refusal" (McC. and S. *Cyc.*).

2. The second son of Bela, son of Benjamin (Gen. xlvi:21). He was apparently exiled by Bela (1 Chron. viii:4, 7), though head of the family of Naamites (Num. xxvi:40); perhaps the same as Uzzi (1 Chron. vii:7), B. C. after 1856.

NAAMATHITE (nā'a-ma-thīte), (Heb. נַעֲמָתִי, *nah-am-aw-thee'*), an epithet of Zophar, one of Job's friends (Job ii:11; xi:1; xx:1; xlii:9). The name is unknown elsewhere. The place was probably situated in Arabia. It indicates a town in the Shephelah in Josh. xv:41.

NAAMITES (nā'a-mītes), (Heb. נַעֲמִי, *nah-am-ee'*, the Naami), the name given to the family descended from Naaman son of Bela (Num. xxvi:40; 1 Chron. viii:4).

NAARAH (nā'a-rah), (Heb. נַעֲרָה, *nah-ar-aw'*, a girl), the wife of Ashur, of the tribe of Judah, by whom he had four sons (1 Chron. iv:5, 6), B. C. 1618. (See NAARAN and NAARATH.)

NAARAI (nā'a-rāi), (Heb. נֵעֲרָי, *nah-ar-ah'ee*, boyish), son of Ezbai, and one of David's valiant men (1 Chron. xi:37), B. C. about 1015. The name is probably incorrectly written Paarai (2 Sam. xxiii:35).

NAARAN (nā'a-răn), (Heb. נֵעֲרָן, *nah-ar-awn'*, boyish, juvenile, puerile), a town on the southeastern border of Ephraim, between Bethel and Jericho (1 Chron. vii:28). The name is Naarath (Josh. xvi:7).

NAARATH (nā'a-răth), (Heb. נֵעֲרָה, *nah-ar-aw'*, a girl, handmaid).

A city of Ephraim (Josh. xvi:7), about five miles distant from Jericho, the Naaran of 1 Chron. vii:28. Eusebius speaks of it as *Oorath*, a village five miles from Jericho, and Josephus mentions that Herod drew off part of the waters from the village of *Neara* to water the palm trees he had planted. Conder, therefore, suggests that the site of Naarath is to be found in *el'Aüjeh*, near Jericho, where are a ruin and remains of an ancient aqueduct.

NAASHON (na-ăsh'on), (Heb. נַחְשׁוֹן, *nakh-shone'*, oracle), (Ex. vi:23). See NAHSHON.

NAASSON (na-ăs'son), (Gr. Ναασσών, *nah-as-sone'*), Matt. i:4; Luke iii:32; the Greek form of the name NAHSHON.

NAAZUZ or NAATZUTZ (nä'az-uz or nä-atz-utz), (Heb. נַעֲצוּץ, *nah-ats-oots'*), occurs only in two passages of Isaiah, in both of which it is translated 'thorn' in the Authorized Version.

Thus (chap. vii:18, 19), 'Jehovah shall hiss for the fly that is in the uttermost part of the rivers of Egypt, and for the bee that is in the land of Assyria; and they shall come, and shall rest all of them, in the desolate valleys, and in the holes of the rocks, and upon all the *thorns* (*naazuzim*). By some this has been translated *crevices;* but that it is a plant of some kind is evident from chap. lv:13—'Instead of the *thorn* (*naazuz*) shall come up the fir-tree, and instead of the briar shall come up the myrtle-tree.' This might be a species of acacia, of which many species are well known to be abundant in the dry and barren parts of Syria, Arabia and Egypt. (See THORNS AND THISTLES.) J. F. R.

NABAL (nā'bal), (Heb. נָבָל, *naw-bawl'*, stupid, foolish; Sept. Ναβάλ, *nabal'*).

A descendant of Caleb, dwelling at Maon, and having large possessions near Carmel of Judah, in the same neighborhood. He had abundant wealth, being the possessor of 3,000 sheep and 1,000 goats, but his churlish and harsh character had not been softened by the prosperity with which he had been favored. He was holding a great sheepshearing of his numerous flocks at Carmel—which was a season of great festivity among the sheepmasters of Israel—when David sent some of his young men to request a small supply of provisions, of which his troop was in great need. He was warranted in asking this, as, while Nabal's flocks were out in the desert, the presence of David and his men in the neighborhood had effectually protected them from the depredations of the Arabs. But Nabal refused this application, with harsh words, reflecting coarsely upon David and his troop as a set of worthless renegades.' On learning this, David was highly incensed, and set out with his band to avenge the insult. But his intention was anticipated and averted by Nabal's wife Abigail, who met him on the road with a most acceptable supply of provi-

sions, and by her consummate tact and good sense mollified his anger, and indeed caused him in the end to feel thankful that he had been prevented from the bloodshed which would have ensued. When Nabal, after recovering from the drunkenness of the feast, was informed of these circumstances, he was struck with such intense terror at the danger to which he had been exposed that 'his heart died within him, and he became as a stone;' which seems to have been the exciting cause of a malady that carried him off about ten days after. David, not long after, evinced the favorable impression which the good sense and comeliness of Abigail had made upon him by making her his wife, B. C. 1061 (1 Sam. xxv). (See ABIGAIL.)

NABATHÆANS (năb'a-thē'anz), (1 Macc. v:25, ix:35). See NEBAIOTH.

NABOTH (nā'bŏth), (Heb. נָבוֹת, *naw-bŏth'*, fruit, produce).

An inhabitant of Jezreel, who was the possessor of a patrimonial vineyard adjoining the garden of the palace which the kings of Israel had there. King Ahab had conceived a desire to add this vineyard to his ground, to make of it 'a garden of herbs,' but found that Naboth could not, on any consideration, be induced to alienate a property which he had derived from his fathers. This gave the king so much concern that he took to his bed and refused his food; but when his wife, the notorious Jezebel, understood the cause of his trouble, she bade him be of good cheer, for *she* would procure him the vineyard. Some time after Naboth was, at a public feast, accused of blasphemy, by an order from her under the royal seal, and, being condemned through the testimony of false witnesses, was stoned to death, according to the law, outside the town (Lev. xxiv:16; Num. xv:30). By a custom, which had grown up, his estate was forfeited to the crown.

When Ahab heard of the death of Naboth—and he must have known how that death had been accomplished, or he would not have supposed himself a gainer by the event—he hastened to take possession. But he was speedily taught that this horrible crime had not passed without notice by the all-seeing God, and would not remain unpunished by his justice. The only tribunal to which he remained accountable pronounced his doom through the prophet Elijah, who met him on the spot, 'In the place where dogs licked the blood of Naboth, shall dogs lick thy blood, even thine' (1 Kings xxi; xxii:34-38; 2 Kings ix:30-37).

NACHON (nā'chŏn), (Heb. נָכוֹן, *naw-kone'*, prepared).

The floor of Nachon is the name given to the threshing-floor near which Uzzah was slain, for laying his hand upon the ark (2 Sam. vi:6). It is doubted whether this be a proper name, denoting the owner of the floor, or merely an epithet applied to it, *i. e.*, 'the prepared floor,' which in that case it would signify.

NACHOR (nā'chôr), (Gr. Ναχώρ, *nay-kore*, an ancestor of Jesus, Luke iii:34; Josh. xxiv:2). (See NAHOR.)

NADAB (nā'dăb), (Heb. נָדָב, *naw-dawb*, liberal; Sept. Ναδάβ, *nah-dab'*, Nadab).

1. The eldest son of Aaron, who, with his brother Abihu, was slain for offering strange fire to the Lord (Exod. vi:23). (See ABIHU.)

2. Son of Jeroboam, and second king of Israel. He ascended the throne upon the death of his father (B. C. 913), whose deep-laid, but criminal and dangerous policy, he followed. He was engaged in the siege of Gibbethon, a city of the Levites (of which the Philistines had obtained possession), when he was slain in the camp in a conspiracy formed against him by Baasha, one of his officers, who mounted the throne in his stead. He reigned two years (1 Kings xiv:20; xv: 25-28).

3. The first of the two sons of Shammai, of Judah (1 Chron. ii:28, 30), B. C. after 1618.

4. One of the eight sons of Jehiel, founder of Gibeon (1 Chron. viii:30; ix:36), B. C. about 1013.

NADABATH (năd′ā - băth), an unidentified place east of the Jordan (1 Macc. ix:37).

NAGGE (nag′ge), (Gr. Ναγγαί, nang-gah-ee′, for Heb. נֹגַהּ, no′gah, 1 Chron. iii:7), son of Maath, an ancestor of Christ in the maternal line (Luke iii:25), corresponding to Neariah of 1 Chron. iii:22, 23. (B. C. 350.)

NAHALAL (nā-ha′lăl) (Heb. נַהֲלֹל, nah-hal-awl′), a town in the tribe of Zebulun (Josh. xix:15), which was assigned to the Levites (Josh. xxi:35), but of which Zebulun was slow in dispossessing the Canaanites (Judg. i:30). It has been identified with *Mahlul* and *'Ain Mâhil,* four miles northeast of Nazareth.

NAHALIEL (na-hā′li-el), (Heb. נַחֲלִיאֵל, nakh-al-ee-ale′, valley of God), an encampment of the Israelites in the wilderness (Num. xxi:19), probably on one of the northern tributaries of the Arnon. Not identified. (See WANDERING, THE).

NAHALLAL (na-hăl′lal), (Josh. xxi:35). See NAHALAL.

NAHALOL (nā-ha′lŏl), (Heb. נַהֲלֹל, nah-hal-ole′), a form of Nahalal (Judg. i:30). A Levitical city in Zebulun, retained by the Canaanites, near Kattath and Dimnah. Now called *Mahlul.*

NAHAM (nā′hăm), (Heb. נַחַם, nakh′am, consolation), according to the A. V. a brother of Hodiah, the second wife of Mered (1 Chron. iv:19). B. C. after 1612, or else the father of Keilah, the Garmite.

NAHAMANI (na-hăm′a-nī) (Heb. נַחֲמָנִי, nakh-am-aw-nee, comforter or compassionate), one of the Jews or twelve heads of the Jewish community who returned from the captivity with Zerubbabel (Neh. vii:7), B. C. 536.

NAHARAI (na-hăr′a-i), (1 Chron. xi:39). See NAHARI.

NAHARAIM (nā′ha-rā′im). See ARAMNAHARAIM.

NAHARI (nā′ha-rī), (Heb. נַחְרַי, nakh-ar-ah′ee, snorer), a Berothite chieftain under David, and Joab's armor-bearer (2 Sam. xxiii:37; 1 Chron. xi:39), B. C. 1013.

NAHASH (nā′hăsh), (Heb. נָחָשׁ, naw-khawsh, a serpent).

1. A person named only in 2 Sam. xvii:25; and as he is there described as the father of Abigail and Zeruiah, who are elsewhere called the sisters of David, this must have been either another name for Jesse, or, as some suppose, of a former husband of David's mother. Three answers may be given to the puzzling question: (1) The universal tradition of the rabbis, that Nahash and Jesse were identical. (2) The explanation first put forth by Dr. Stanley, that Nahash was the

king of the Ammonites, and that the same woman had first been his wife or concubine—in which capacity she had given birth to Abigail and Zeruiah—and afterward wife to Jesse, and the mother of his children. (3) A third possible explanation is that Nahash was the name, not of Jesse, nor of a former husband of his wife, but of his wife herself (Smith, *Bib. Dict.*).

2. King of the Ammonites, noted for the barbarous terms of capitulation which he offered to the town of Jabesh-Gilead, and for his subsequent defeat by Saul. (See JABESH.) It was natural that the enemy of Saul should be friendly to David; and we find that he did render to the latter, during his persecutions, some acts of kindness, which the monarch did not forget when he ascended the throne of Israel (2 Sam. x:2; 1 Chron. xix:2).

NAHATH (nā′hăth), (Heb. נַחַת, nakh′ath, rest, quiet).

1. The first of the four sons of Reuel, son of Esau, and an Edomite duke or prince (Gen. xxxvi:13, 17), B. C. 1890.

2. A Kohathite Levite, ancestor of the prophet Samuel (1 Chron. vi:26), B. C. 1280. The same as Tohu (1 Sam. i:1) and Toah (1 Chron. vi:34).

3. A Levite who had charge of the sacred tithes and offerings under Hezekiah (2 Chron. xxxi:13). B. C. 725.

NAHBI (näh′bī), (Heb. נַחְבִּי, nakh-bee′, hidden), a son of Vophsi, sent as a representative of the tribe of Naphtali to explore the land of Canaan (Num. xiii:14), B. C. 1657.

NAHOR (nā′hôr), (Heb. נָחוֹר, naw-khore′, snorting).

1. The better form is Nachor, as in Luke iii:34, son of Serug, and father of Terah, the father of Abraham (Gen. xi:22-25). He lived 148 years (B. C. before 2300).

2. Grandson of the preceding, being one of the sons of Terah, and brother of Abraham. Nahor espoused Milcah his niece, daughter of his eldest brother Haran (Gen. xi:27-29). Nahor did not quit his native place, 'Ur of the Chaldees,' when the rest of the family removed to Haran (Gen. xi:30) ; but it would appear that he went thither afterwards, as we eventually find his son Bethuel, and his grandson Laban, established there (Gen. xxvii:43; xxix:5).

NAHOR, CITY OF.

To Biblical students, Haran is best known as the city of Nahor, the designation which it receives in Gen. xxiv:10. It was the city where Abraham's brother Nahor lived with his son Laban, where Terah and Abraham made their home after they left the land of the Chaldees, where Terah died, and whence Abraham was called to go into Canaan. As the city of Abraham's sojourn, it has interest by no means second to Ur of the Chaldees. Assyrian studies have given great interest to this country, and Schrader, Hommel, Delitzsch and Winckler have, during the last few years, devoted much investigation to this region. A paper on Haran, published this year by the latter scholar, is especially important.

Haran is called Charran in the Septuagint, and Harran with the rough H in the Babylonian inscriptions. It was evidently an important place commercially, as its hieroglyph is made by two roads crossing, implying that it was the crossing-place of two caravan routes. It was the chief city of what was called Mesopotamia, not so much because it lay between the Tigris and the

Euphrates, as because it was included in the angle between the two rivers, Euphrates and Habor, the principal affluent of the Euphrates. In its widest extent Mesopotamia did not include the whole of the region between the Tigris and the Euphrates, only this northern, or rather middle part, while the southern part was Babylonia, and we might call Padan-Aram, North Mesopotamia.

We are apt to think of Nineveh and Babylon as the two great capitals of the East, and to suppose that in old times there were no great kingdoms but the two of which they were the capitals. This is a great mistake. Assyria was of importance only for some six or eight hundred years, before and after which it did not exist, nor did its capital city. We now know that, for at least a thousand years before there was any Nineveh, Harran, a more correct form than Haran, was one of the most powerful capitals of the East.

The oldest capital of Southern Babylonia was Ur. Its age goes back perhaps 4000 years B. C. It was nearly or quite 4000 B. C. when the Southern Babylonian power arose, and it extended its power and culture all the way to the Phœnician Coast. Seals belonging to this chiliad have been found even in Cyprus. The astrological tablets ascribed to the ancient Sargas I, whose date is put at 3800 B. C., mention the lands of the West and distinctly refer to Harran. Cedar wood was rafted down the Euphrates in the time of Gudea, about 3500 B. C., brought from the region of Mount Lebanon or Amanus.

From its own monuments we know nothing of the history of Mesopotamia, and its chief city, Harran. None of the mounds in this region have as yet been excavated; what we know of these important sites is wholly from the records of the neighboring kingdoms.

From these we learn that the title "Kings of the World," the favorite designation of the kings of Assyria, was first assumed by the kings of Harran and adopted by Ramman-Niraril, about 1400 B. C. on his conquest of what had been the much more powerful kingdom whose capital was Harran. This was a chiliad of great importance in eastern history. It was between 2000 and 1000 B. C. that the Kassites conquered and held Babylonia, that the Hittites and the Aramians took possession of Syria, that the Assyrian empire was established, and that the Egyptians made their great campaigns in Asia. It was in the latter part of this period that Assyria finally conquered the earlier kingdom of Mesopotamia and took Harran.

To Sin, the moon god of Harran, the Assyrians gave the second place of honor in their pantheon, next after their own god, Assur. This shows the influence of Harran and the honor in which it was held.

When Shalmaneser II (800 B. C.) wished to restore the kingdom of Assyria to the power it had held 500 years before under Shalmaneser I, he rebuilt the temple of Sin at Harran, regarding it as a royal city. A curious illustration of the honor in which Harran was held is supplied by an inscription of the time of Assur-bani-pal, the last great king of Assyria. A scribe, Marduk-sum-usser, writes to the king:

"When the father of the king, my lord, made an expedition into Egypt, he went to the temple in Harran, built of cedar wood. Sin was sitting on his throne with his head bowed. Two royal crowns were on his head. Nusku waited upon him. The father of the king, my lord, entered in.

"Sin raised his head and spoke: 'Go forward, and thou shalt conquer the land.'

"He went forward, and he conquered Egypt. The remaining lands which Assur and Sin have not conquered will the king, the lord of kings, conquer. By the command of Assur, Sin, Shamas (Chemosh) and the other gods shall he sit on a throne of generations."

If Assur, the god of Assur, the first capital of Assyria, was put at the head of the Assyrian pantheon, Sin was put next, because Assyria did not become a kingdom until it had incorporated Mesopotamia, with its capital city, Harran, and adopted its god Sin.

After the fall of Assyria, Mesopotamia, of course, fell to Babylonia. When the last king of Babylon, Nabonidus, was in danger of losing Mesopotamia by the inroad of the Scythians, who had already invaded Media and Assyria, he attempted to propitiate the gods by rebuilding the temple of Sin in its old glory.

We find, then, that in the very oldest times known to us there was in Mesopotamia, or that northern part of Mesopotamia included in the angle of the Euphrates and the Habor valleys, called in Genesis *Padan-Aram*, or Plain of Aram, a kingdom whose capital city was Harran, the Biblical Haran. The difference in spelling comes from the fact that the Hebrew language cannot double the letter *r*. We find its tutelary god worshiped in Babylonia as early as 3500 B. C. We find it mentioned several times in an astrological work which was in existence in the second chiliad B. C. When the Assyrian power arose it became united with the latter, and was so in the time of Shalmaneser I, about 1300 B. C. The advance of the Hittite and other powers reduced the realm of Assyria, but Tiglath-pileser I (about 1100 B. C.) again extended his limits so that Mesopotamia was permanently incorporated with Assyria until the overthrow of the empire by Nabopolassar.

Assyria gave no especial culture to the world, but borrowed what she had from Babylonia and Padan-Aram, both older kingdoms, with established art and religion, and it was by union with the latter and by its help that Assyria conquered all the regions about, north to the Black Sea and west to the Mediterranean. (See ASSYRIA, *Literature;* ASSYRIAN AND BABYLONIAN LIBRARIES.)

This gives us a new point of view to consider the development of civilization in the entire region occupied by the Phœnicians, Syrians and Hittites, including the descendants of Abraham.

We see what a distinguished political ancestry the Hebrew had, coming first from Ur of the Chaldees, the capital of the earliest South Babylonian kingdom, and then from Harran, the capital of the nearly equally old and powerful Mesopotamian kingdom. From these two cities he brought the best education and civilization of the ancient world; and we can see how reasonable it was for Abraham, Isaac and Jacob to seek wives for their sons among their own kindred, instead of among the inferior races around them. (*City of Nahor*, by William Hayes Ward, D. D., Hom. Rev., Oct., 1894.) (See HARAN.)

NAHSHON (näh'shon), (Heb. נַחְשׁוֹן, *nakh-shone'*, enchanter), from which he is called Naason in the genealogies of Christ in Matt. i:4; Luke iii:32, son of Aminadab, and prince or chief of the tribe of Judah, at the time of the exode (Num. i:7; ii:3; vii: 12, 17; x:14).

The chiefs of tribes, of which Nahshon was one, took an important and leading part in the affairs of the Israelites, as described in the article TRIBES. (B. C. 1657.)

NAHUM (nā'hum), (Heb. נחום, *nakh-oom'*, consolation), the seventh of the minor prophets, according to the arrangement of both the Greek and Hebrew, but the sixth in point of date, was a native of Elkosh, a village of Galilee (Jerome's *Pref. to his Comment.*).

He prophesied in Judah after the deportation of the ten tribes, and soon after the unsuccessful irruption of Sennacherib (ch. i:11-13; ii:1, 14), consequently towards the close of the reign of Hezekiah. Attempts have been made to fix the date with precision, from the allusion to the destruction of No-Amnon or Thebes in Egypt (ch. iii:8); but as it is uncertain when this event took place, Eichhorn and others have conjectured that it was near the beginning of the reign of Hezekiah, or about B. C. 735, as about this time Sargon, king of Assyria, waged an unsuccessful war for three years against Egypt (Is. xx). (See EGYPT.)

NAHUM, PROPHECY OF.

(1) Contents. The contents of the prophecy of Nahum are as follows: Chap. i:2-7. The destruction of Nineveh and of the Assyrian monarchy is depicted in the liveliest colors, together with the relief of Judah from oppression. The destruction of Nineveh is detailed with still greater particularity in the third chapter; which has induced some to suppose that the prophet refers to two different events—the sack of Nineveh by the Medes, B. C. 867, in the reign of Sardanapalus, and its second and final destruction, under Chyniladan, by Cyaxares the First and Nabopolassar (B. C. 606). Those who suppose that two events are here alluded to, conclude that Nahum must have prophesied before the first destruction of Nineveh, or about B. C. 877. It is, however, observed by Jahn (Introd.) that it is evident from ch. i:9-11, 14; ii:1, 14, where the Hebrews are represented as oppressed by the Assyrians, and the irruption of Sennacherib is mentioned as having already taken place, that there is but one event referred to, namely, the last destruction of Nineveh. De Wette remarks that Nahum could not have alluded to the historical circumstances under which Nineveh was taken by Cyaxares and Nabopolassar (B. C. 625, 603, or 600), as at that time Babylon, not Assyria, was formidable to the Jews, but that perhaps he was led to prophesy by the liberation of the Medes (from the Assyrians), and 'their election of a king, in the person of Dejoces.'

The beauty of the style of Nahum has been universally felt. It is classic, observes De Wette, in all respects. It is marked by clearness, by its finished elegance, as well as by fire, richness and originality. The rhythm is regular and lively.

(2) Style. The whole book is remarkably coherent, and the author only holds his breath, as it were, in the last chapter. Jahn observes that the language is pure, with a single exception (ch. iii:17), that the style is ornate, and the tropes bold and elegant (rendering it, however, necessary for the reader to supply some omissions; see ii:8; iii:3, 16); and that the descriptions of the divine omnipotence, and of the destruction of Nineveh, are resplendent with all the perfection of oratory. No one, however, has entered more fully into the beauties of the prophet Nahum than the accomplished Eichhorn, who conceives that the most striking characteristic of his style is the power of representing several phases of an idea in the briefest sentences, as in his description of God, the conquest of Nineveh, and the destruction of No-Ammon. 'The variety in his manner of presenting ideas discovers much poetic talent in the prophet. The reader of taste and sensibility will be affected by the entire structure of the poem, by the agreeable manner in which the ideas are brought forward, by the flexibility of the expressions, the roundness of his turns, the delicate outline of his figures, by the strength and delicacy, and the expression of sympathy and greatness, which diffuse themselves over the whole subject. He does not come upon you roaring and violent, nor yet softly and lightly. Here there is something sonorous in his language, there something murmuring; and with both there alternates somewhat that is soft, delicate and melting, as the subject demands. This is not possible for a poet of art, but only for the poet of nature' (De Wette's *Introd.* English transl.). (Edwards, *Notes in Bib. Sacr.* 1848, p. 551 *sq.*; Keil, *Inter. O. T.*)

NAIL (nāil). There are two Hebrew words thus translated in the Auth. Vers., which it may be well to distinguish:

1. (יָתֵד, *yaw-thade'*), which usually denotes a peg, pin, or nail, as driven into a wall (Ezek. xv:3; Is. xxii:25); and more especially a tent pin driven into the earth to fasten the tent (Exod. xxvii:19; xxxv:18; xxxviii:31; Is. xxxiii:20; liv:2). Hence, to drive a pin, or to fasten a nail, presents among the Hebrews an image of a fixed dwelling, a firm and stable abode (Is. xxii:23). It was a tent pin which Jael drove into the temples of Sisera (Judg. iv:21, 22).

2. (מִסְמֵר, *mas-mare'*), which, with some variations of form, is applied to ordinary and ornamental nails. It always occurs in the plural, and is the word which we find in 1 Chron. xxii:3; 2 Chron. iii:9; Is. xli:7; Jer. x:4; Eccles. xii:11. Nails are mentioned in the accounts of the crucifixion (John xx:25; Col. ii:14).

Figurative. (1) Eliakim, and Jesus Christ, as prefigured by him, are likened to a *"nail in a sure place,"* for hanging of vessels on," which is typical of something firm and strong. God made Eliakim the Jewish minister of state, and on him did the subordinate rulers and the people depend. God established Jesus in the office of Mediator, and on him do all the persons of the elect, and all their privileges, graces, and duties, and all the oracles of God, and ordinances and government of the church depend (Is. xxii:23-25). (2) The *"nail"* that came forth of Judah is either Zerubbabel, Nehemiah, or the Maccabees, who established the Jewish state; or rather Jesus Christ, who connects and establishes his church, and bears her and all her concerns (Zech. x:4). (3) The words of the wise are as *"nails fastened;"* the truths of God fixed in the heart remain there perpetually, and make the soul cleave to Jesus, and his church and ordinances (Eccles. xii:11). (4) The *"nails of brass,"* which Daniel's fourth beast had, denotes the covetous robbery and ravage of the Romans, and their power to retain their conquered provinces (Dan. vii:19). (5) Christ's *"nailing"* of the ceremonial law to his cross imports, that by his death he fulfilled the signification thereof, and has abolished its binding force (Col. ii:14).

NAIL OF THE FINGER (nāl ŏv the fin'gĕr,) (Heb. צִפֹּרֶן, *tsip-po'ren*, Deut. xxi:12), like cutting the hair, the paring of the nails—both signs of purification—was a symbol of a captive slave passing out of servitude and being received into communion with the covenant nation.

In Jer. xvii:1 (marg.) "nail" is the rendering of the same Hebrew word, and means the **"point"** of a stylus or a metallic pen. In Dan. iv:33; vii:19 (Chald. שְׁפַר, *tef-ar'*), occurs of the *claws* of a bird or beast (Mc. & S. *Bib. Cy.;* Barnes, *Bib. Dict.*).

NAIN (nā'in), (Gr. Ναιν, *nah-in'*, pleasantness, beauty), a town of Palestine, mentioned only in the New Testament, as the place where Jesus raised the widow's son to life (Luke vii:11-17).

Eusebius and Jerome (*Onomast.* title *"Nain"*) describe it as not far from Endor. As its name has always been preserved, it was recognized by the crusaders, and has been often noticed by travelers up to the present day. It has now dwindled to a small hamlet called *Nein*, which is situated about three miles south by west from Mount Tabor. Another Nain in the south of the land east of the Jordan was fortified by Simon Bar Giora (Joseph. *Wars of the Jews,* iv:9, 4).

"The story of Nain has been told in the simplest and most touching manner by the evangelist. Every word is a picture." (Hugh MacMillan, Hastings' *Bib. Dict.*). The place where the young man was raised to life is beautiful, overlooking the great plains of Esdraelon, the wooded hills of Galilee. The snow-capped Hermon and Lebanon ranges are in full view. A small modern church has been built on the site of the old city.

NAIOTH (nā'yoth), (Heb. נָוִית, *nev-aw-yoth'*, dwellings).

A place in or near Ramah, where Samuel abode with his disciples (1 Sam. xix: 18, 19, 22, 23; xx:1). Naioth does not appear to have been a distinct town or village; and we are willing to accept the explanation of R. Isaiah and other Jewish commentators, who state that Ramah was the name of a hill, and Naioth of the place upon it.

NAKED (nā'kĕd), (Heb. עֶרְוָה, *er-vaw'*, nudity; Gr. γύμνος, *goom'nos*), 'naked' in our Bibles, does not in many places mean absolute nakedness.

(1) Nudity. It has this meaning in such passages as Job i:21; Eccles. v:15; Mic. i:8; Amos ii:16).

(2) Ragged or Poorly Clad. But in other places it means one who is ragged or poorly clad (John xxi:7; Is. lviii:7), in the same sense as γυμνός in James ii:15; which does not indeed differ from a familiar application of the word 'naked' among ourselves.

(3) Slightly Clad. A more peculiar and Oriental sense of the word is that in which it is applied to one who has laid aside his loose outer garment, and goes about in his tunic. When, therefore, Saul is described as having lain down 'naked' (1 Sam. xix:24), we are to understand that he had laid aside his flowing outer robe, by which his rank was most indicated, and was therefore a king 'naked' or undressed.

(4) Naked and Barefoot. It was thus that Isaiah went 'naked' and barefoot (Is. xx:2; comp. John xxi:7). The point of the expression may be the better apprehended when we mention that persons in their own houses freely lay aside their outer garment, and appear in their tunic and girdle; but this is undress, and they would count it improper to appear abroad, or to see company in their own house, without the outer robe.

Figurative. (1) Destitute of innocency, holiness and righteousness, inherent or imputed, and hence exposed to shame and misery (Rev. iii:17, 18). (2) Deprived of the divine favor and protection, and ready to be a prey to their enemies (Exod. xxxii:25; 2 Chron. xxviii:19). Before the fall there was no sinful, shameful, or hurtful *nakedness;* as there were no sinful dispositions, no part of the human body was improper for view; but sin entering, they knew they were naked, that they were become unholy and unrighteous; and they needed a covering for those parts of their body afterwards called *"nakedness"* (Gen. iii:7, 10, 11; ix:22). (3) The *"nakedness"* of the soul lies in being without holiness and righteousness, but sinful before God (Rev. iii:18). (4) The *"nakedness"* of a land, is the poverty, weakness and ruinous condition thereof; or its shameful wickedness (Ezek. xvi:8, 36, 37). (5) Going *"naked,"* or almost so, was an emblem of distress and deprivation of comfort (Is. xx:3; Mic. i:8).

NAMES (nāms), (Heb. שֵׁם, *shame;* Gr. ὄνομα, *on-om-ah*).

It is so interesting, as well as useful, to know the original signification of proper names, that a careful investigation of their nature has many advantages. The chief use, however, which accrues from an accurate knowledge of them is, that we are by their means enabled to attain a more lively apprehension of the truth of ancient history.

1. Two Classes. There are two chief classes of proper names, those of men, and those of everything besides man, as beasts, places and festivals. Those of the latter class are much more durable in their form, as man alone is always changing; they are also important for history, and it is desirable to ascertain, as far as possible, their original signification. But the proper names of the changeable races of men are in a much higher degree those in which history reflects itself in its vicissitudes; they also constitute the more numerous class. For these reasons we confine ourselves at present to the proper names of men, as it is beyond our present scope to treat the entire subject.

2. Simplicity in Use of Names. The first fact that strikes us, on a general view of them all, is that the ancient Hebrews always retained the greatest simplicity in the use of names. In reality, there is always only one single name which distinguishes a person. Where it is necessary, the name of the father is added; sometimes that of the mother instead, in case she happens to be more celebrated; or the line of descent is traced farther back, often to the fourth generation, or even farther. Mere epithets, like 'David the king,' 'Isaiah the prophet,' always express the actual and significant dignity of a man. The instances in which a person receives two names alternately, as Jacob-Israel, Gideon-Jerubbaal (Judg. vi-ix), are casual and rare, and are not to be ascribed to a general custom of the people.

3. Three Periods. When we, then, consider proper names with reference to the grand distinction of times, we are able to discover in their varying use nearly the same three periods as those which mark the history of this people in all other respects. These are the three periods which are most simply defined by the three different names of the nation which prevailed in each—the *Hebrews*, as they were called in early times, gradually adopted the name of *Israelites* in the middle period, and exchanged this name, in the third, for that of *Jews*. It is a remarkable, but nevertheless true, coincidence that, just as the name of the nation varies in these three periods, the color of the names of individuals changes in like manner, according to the different tendencies characterizing the times.

(1) First Period. In the first period, which, for reasons adduced below, we here limit by the commencement of the Mosaic religion, we are able to see the whole process according to which names are formed among this people; the distinct character of the formation of names which was established in this primitive time, continues essentially the same in the succeeding period, while the elements of which names are formed undergo a partial change. For this reason we may explain the laws of this formation in terms of merely general application. Now names are either *simple* or *compound* words, or also words which arise from either of these kinds *by derivation.*

(a) The *simple* names exist in great abundance, and their signification as to the mere word itself, is generally evident; as 'judge;' the Latin *dexter,* an ancient name, according to Gen. xlvi:10; 1 Chron. ii:27; 'desired,' also an ancient name according to Gen. xlvi:10; comp. xxxvi:37; 'hero,' 1 Kings iv:19. Thus most of them express an honorable sense; although examples are not wanting of the direct contrary, as 'crooked' (2 Sam. xxiii: 26).

(b) The *compound* names, however, are more important for history, because they express more complete and distinct ideas than the simple names. Some of them are altogether isolated, as properly 'serpent's mouth,' the grandson of Aaron; the son of Jacob; *Oholiab* (Exod. xxxi:6), 'father's tent,' a name resembling the Greek Patrocles. But most of them bear a general resemblance to each other, and follow in shoals certain dominant opinions and customs; and these last are what we must particularly consider here.

A great number of them owe their origin to the relations of the house, as the sense of the first word of the compound shows. Most of these have the word *abi,* 'father,' for their first member, as *Abiezer, Abital, Abigail.* The prevalent opinion among modern scholars respecting this class is that they are really epithets, which have afterwards, as it were casually, become proper names; that *Abigail,* for example, is literally 'father of joy,' or 'whose father is joy,' that this means *cheerful,* and thus became a proper name.

Another but a smaller class consists of names compounded with עַם, *am,* 'people,' resembling the many Greek compositions with λαός *lah-os',* people, and δῆμος, *day'mos;* and just as in Greek δῆμος, *deme,* is placed first or last (Demosthenes, Aristodemos), so also עַם is at one time found in the first, and at another in the last place; only that, according to the laws of the Semitic language, the sense of one of these positions is exactly the reverse of the other.

Most of the compound names, however, rather endeavor to express a religious sense, and therefore often contain the divine name. As compound names evidently became very general, it is not surprising that, in the infinite multiplication of names to correspond with the infinite multitude of persons, some proper names were at length formed which solely consist of two names of God himself, expressing, as it were, the ineffably holy name to which the person dedicates himself, as *Abiel* and *Eliab,* nay, even *Eliel* (1 Chron. v:24; viii:20; 2 Chron. xxxi:13).

Lastly, many proper names have assumed the derivative syllable *î,* or *ai* (which appears to be only dialectically different from *î,* and is chiefly frequent in the later periods); and we must certainly consider that, in some cases, this syllable may possibly form mere adjectives, and therewith simple names, as 'trueman,' from 'truth,' and *Barzillai,* 'Iron,' or 'Ironman,' the name of a cele-

brated Gileadite family (Ezra ii:61; 2 Sam. xvii: 27).

(2) Second Period. This is the whole principle which regulates the formation of Hebrew names, both as it manifests itself in the earliest times, and as it extends into the succeeding periods, in which it receives new impulses, and undergoes modifications of color but not of substance.

For if we inquire what new element the Mosaic period introduced into names, we find that, on the whole, it is only the influence of the new religion which manifests itself in the strongest characters, and causes extraordinary innovations. It is not in the Psalms only and other books that we discover how deeply this religion affected men; we may also infer it from the names which became current in that period. Nay, it is only these words of common life which render it evident to our senses with what a power this religion penetrated all the depths of the national mind, and how zealously every man in Israel endeavored 'to glory in the name of Jahve,' according to the words of the prophet (Is. xliv:5; comp. Ps. cv:3).

As the whole national life was renovated by so influential a new religion, the mode of giving names returned to its primitive state, since not only were new names created, but entire sentences, of the shortest compass, expressing the mighty thoughts which agitated the times, were also applied as names.

(3) Third Period. This is the type and fashion of the names as late as the times after the first destruction of Jerusalem. The influence of the dispersion among foreign nations may, indeed, be immediately traced in the new names which allude to the captivity, as the name of *Zerubbabel* (the leader of the restoration), which is a contraction of זְרוּ בָּבֶל, *zer-oo-baw-bel,* means 'scattered to Babylon.' Yet this foreign influence is but transient; and in the centuries immediately succeeding the Exile, in which the last books of the Old Testament were written, we find, on the contrary, that the ancient mode of giving names is preserved almost unchanged.

In this respect, however, there is a total difference in the times between the close of the Old and the beginning of the New Testament. For after a purely learned study of the Old Testament had sprung up, and the whole nation only continued to exist in its sacred books, they delighted to give their children the ancient Scriptural names; nay, they sought out such names as had only been common in the times before Moses, and had become obsolete in the long interval: names like *Jacob, Joseph, Maria.* But while these dead names were revived and zealously sought out, the capability for forming new ones became gradually weaker. And, as the love of novelty still operated, and as the people lost their independence more and more, many foreign names became favorites, and were used equally with the old Biblical names. In this manner the form of names had, by the time of the New Testament, reached a state of development which nearly resembles that prevalent among ourselves.

Lastly, with regard to the Biblical names of individuals belonging to the less eminent nations with which the Israelites were surrounded, such as the Edomites, Phœnicians, Damascenes, etc., their formation indeed is generally very like that of the Hebrew names, inasmuch as all these nations spoke a Semitic language; but the materials of which they are formed are so different, that one can almost recognize these foreign nations by their mere names. Thus names like *Hadad, Ben-hadad, Hadad-ezer,* are quite strange to the Israel-ites, and refer to the tribes to the east of Pales-tine, where a god named Hadad was worshiped.

G. H. A. v. E.

4. Words Most Frequently Compounded.

There are some words which appear more fre-quently in compounds of proper names than oth-ers, and to which we will refer in passing. *Beer* means "well" (Beersheba) "well of the oath" (Gen. xxi:31); *Beth* means "house" (Bethlehem, "house of bread"); *En* means "fountain" (En-gedi, "fountain of the kid"); *El* means "God" (Samuel "asked of God," 1 Sam. i:20; Elisha, "God is sal-vation"). On the other hand, *Bath* means "daugh-ter" (Bathsheba), while *Ben* and *Bar* mean "son" (Benjamin, Barjonas).

5. Name of God.

The Name of God was held in a peculiar reverence. To such an extent of superstition is this carried that the modern Jews never pronounce the word "Jehovah," it be-ing considered too sacred. In reading the Old Testament they substitute "Adonai" for it. They misunderstand the passage in Lev. xxiv:16, which forbids the cursing use of "Jehovah," as forbid-ding the mere naming. An abuse of the name of God is expressly forbidden in the Decalogue (Exod. xx:7; Lev. xix:12). In the New Testa-ment miracles are performed in the name of Jesus (Acts iii:6; iv:10), and they who are baptized are baptized in the name of the Trinity (Matt. xxviii:19).

The two special terms used for God by the He-brews were "Elohim" and "Jehovah" (or "Ja-veh"). The first contains an allusion to majesty and power; the second refers to God's absolute existence, his eternity and unchangeableness, and means "I am" Exod. iii:14). God had not been known by this name to Abraham, Isaac, or Jacob (Exod. vi:3).

6. Names of Christ.

The many names used of our Lord are all highly significant. Emmanuel ("God with us") points to his incarnation; Jesus ("Savior") to his mission of salvation; Christ ("Anointed") to his appointment as the promised Messiah; Son of Man to his humility; Son of God to his divine origin and character. Amongst the many other names and titles of Christ are Shiloh (Gen. xl:10), the Wonderful, etc. (Is. ix:6), Prophet, High Priest, King, the Word (John i:1, etc.). (Schaff, *Bib. Dict.*) (See article on JESUS CHRIST; JESUS; GOD.)

7. Names in General.

In general the names of men denote: (1) That particular designation by which they are usually called; (2) The persons themselves (Luke x:20; Rev. iii:4; xiii:8); (3) Reputation, good or evil (Deut. xxii:14; Prov. xxii:1); (4) Honor, glory, renown (Deut. xxvi: 19; 2 Chron. xxvi:8, 15; Zeph. iii:20); (5) Mem-ory or remembrance (Deut. xxix:20); (6) Pos-terity, which keeps up one's name or renown (Deut. xxv:7; Is. lxvi:22).

Figurative. "*Name,*" when ascribed to God or Christ, comprehends whatever he makes him-self known by. *The name of God* signifies: (1) himself (Ps. xxix:2; xxxiv:3; lxi:5); (2) his titles (Exod. iii:13, 14; vi:3); (3) his attributes or properties (Exod. xxxiii:19; xxxiv:6, 7; (4) his word (Ps. v:11; Acts ix:15); (5) his worship and service (1 Kings v:5; Mal. i:6); (6) his will and purpose concerning our salvation, and his grace and mercy therein displayed (Ps. xxii:22; John xvii:6, 26); (7) his power, help, and favor-able assistance (1 Sam. xvii:45; Ps. xx:1, 7); (8) his wisdom, power, and goodness, displayed in the works of creation and providence (Ps. viii:1, 9); (9) his authority, commission (Mic. v:4); (10) his honor, glory, and renown (Ps. lxxvi:1). *The name of Christ* denotes: (1) himself, what he really is, Wonderful, mighty God, God with us (Is. vii:14; ix:6); (2) his titles, as Savior, Prophet, Priest, King, etc. (Matt. i:21; Rev. xix: 16); (3) his authority and commission (Matt. vii: 22; Acts iv:7); (4) his word and gospel, and the profession thereof (Matt. x:22; xix:29; Acts ix: 15; Rev. ii:13); (5) his exaltation to the highest honor, power and glory, as our Mediator (Phil. ii:9, 10).

Other Uses. God's "*name*" is in Christ; his nature and authority are in him; he has sent him to be our Redeemer; and by his execution of his office is his honor chiefly exalted (Exod. xxiii: 21). To be baptized "*in the name*" of the Father, Son, and Holy Ghost, or of Jesus, is to be baptized by the warrant and authority, and into the pro-fession, faith, and obedience of these divine per-sons, as one God (Matt. xxviii:19; Acts xix:5). To trust or believe "*in the name of God*" or "Christ," is to credit his word, and rely on his perfections, titles, and relations, as a certain ground of our receiving all blessings and salvation from him (John iii:18). To "*name the name of Christ,*" is openly to profess that we are his, and to regard his honor and service (2 Tim. ii:19). The "*new name*" that Christ gives, and writes on his people, is the "redeemed of the Lord," the "righteousness of God in him," etc., which an-swers to their new covenant state, and their new nature; and in heaven their character is made gloriously to appear (Rev. ii:17; comp. Is. lxi:6). God's changing the "*name of his church*" denotes his changing her condition from distress and grief, to happiness and joy (Is. lxii:3, 4). The saints pray and do all "*in the name of Christ*" when they do it in the faith of his promise, in obedience to his command, and with a total dependence on his righteousness and intercession for acceptance (John xiv:13; Col. iii:17).

NAOMI (na-ō'mi), (Heb. נָעֳמִי, *nŏ-om-ee'*, my pleasantness, delight), wife of Elimelech of Beth-lehem, and mother-in-law of Ruth, in whose history hers is involved. (B. C. about 1322-1312.)

Her two sons were Mahlon and Chilion. With her husband and sons, because of a famine in her own country, she went to Moab, where they died. Returning to her native land, she was accom-panied by Ruth, who became the wife of Boaz. Upon her return she replied to those asking her, "Is this Naomi?" "Call me not Naomi; call me Mara; for the Almighty hath dealt very bitterly with me." (See RUTH.)

NAPHISH (nā'phish), (Heb. נָפִישׁ, *naw-feesh'* refreshed), one of the twelve sons of Ishmael (Gen. xxv:15; 1 Chron i:31), B. C. after 1077. The clan which he founded is classed among the Hagarites, who were defeated by the tribes east of the Jordan (1 Chron. v:18-22).

"In all probability it is the descendants of this clan who are mentioned among the Nethinim in Ezra ii:50, as 'the children of Nephusim,' and the Nephishesim" (Neh. vii:52). (J. A. Selbie, Hastings' *Bib. Dict.*)

NAPHTALI (năph'ta-lī), (Heb. נַפְתָּלִי, *naf-taw-lee'*, my wrestling).

1. The sixth son of Jacob, and his second by Bilhah, Rachel's handmaid, born B. C. 1747, in Padan-Aram; also the tribe of Israel descended from him. Nothing of his personal history is recorded. In the testamentary blessing of Jacob

Naphtali is described (Gen. xlix:21), as translated in the Auth. Vers., 'a hind let loose, he giveth goodly words.' The Sept. translators, however, must have found the words rendered 'hind' and 'words' different, for they render the verse, 'Naphtali is a goodly tree (terebinth or oak) that puts forth lovely branches.' We certainly incline to this view of the text; the metaphor which it involves being well adapted to the residence of the tribe of Naphtali, which was a beautiful woodland country, extending to Mount Lebanon, and producing fruits of every sort. With this interpretation, better than with the other, agrees the blessing of Moses upon the same tribe: 'O Naphtali, satisfied with favor, and full with the blessing of the Lord, possess thou the west and the south' (Deut. xxxiii:23). When the Israelites quitted Egypt, the tribe of Naphtali numbered 53,400 adult males (Num. i:43), ranking sixth in population among the tribes; but at the census taken in the plains of Moab it counted only 45,400 (Num. xxvi:50), being a decrease of 8,000 in one generation, whereby it became the seventh in point of numbers. The limits of the territory assigned to this tribe are stated in Josh. xix:32-39, which show that it possessed one of the finest and most fertile districts of Upper Galilee, extending from the Lake Gennesareth and the border of Zebulun, on the south, to the sources of the Jordan and the spurs of Lebanon on the north, and from the Jordan, on the east, to the borders of Asher on the west. But it was somewhat slow in acquiring possession of the assigned territory (Judg. i:33). The chief towns of the tribe were Kedesh, Hazor, Harosheth, and Chinnereth, which last was also the name of the great lake afterwards called Gennesareth. In the Hebrew history Naphtali is distinguished for the alacrity with which it obeyed the call to arms against the oppressors of Israel when many other tribes held back (Judg. iv:10; v:18; vi:35; vii:23). In the time of David the tribe had on its rolls 37,000 men fit for military service, armed with shields and spears, under a thousand officers (1 Chron. xii:34).

2. The mountainous district which formed the main part of the territory of Naphtali (Josh. xx:7); answering to "Mount Ephraim" and "Mount Judah."

NAPHTUHIM (naph'tu-hĭm), (Heb. נַפְתֻּחִים, naf-too-kheem', Gen. x:13), a Hamitic race, named third among the seven peoples descended from Mizraim, the second son of Ham (1 Chron. i:11).

NAPKIN (năp'kin), is the translation of the Gr. σουδάριον, soo-dar'ee-on, Luke xix:20; John xi:44; xx:7. It is rendered handkerchief in Acts xix:12, which see.

NARCISSUS (nar-cĭs'sus), (Gr. Νάρκισσος, nar'-kis-sos), a person of Rome, apparently of some consequence, to the believers of whose household St. Paul sent his greetings (Rom. xvi:11).

Many commentators have supposed this person the same Narcissus who was the freedman and favorite of the Emperor Claudius (Suet. Claud. 28; Tacit. Annal. xii:17). A. D. 55. He was said by Pseudo-Hippolytus to be bishop of Athens, but without foundation.

NARD (närd). See NERD; SPIKENARD; STACTE.

NATAF (nā-taf), (Heb. נָטָף, naw-tawf'), occurs only once in Scripture, and is translated 'stacte' in the Authorized Version (Ex. xxx:34).

The Greeks called stakte a species of Storax gum, which Dioscorides describes as transparent like a tear and resembling myrrh. This agrees

well with the Hebrew name. But Storax does not appear to us to be more satisfactorily proved to be nataf than the former; Stacte is probably myrrh, and its Hebrew original in the above passage, naw-tawf', signifying drops, probably refers to myrrh in tears. The same word (Job xxxvi:27) is used for drops of water.

NATHAN (nā'than), (Heb. נָתָן, naw-thawn', given).

1. A Prophet of the Time of David. When that monarch conceived the idea of building a temple to Jehovah, the design and motives seemed to Nathan so good that he ventured to approve of it without the divine authority; but the night following he received the divine command, which prevented the king from executing this great work (2 Sam. vii:2, sq.; 1 Chron. xvii).

(1) Nathan and David. Nathan does not again appear in the sacred history till he comes forward in the name of the Lord to reprove David, and to denounce dire punishment for his frightful crime in the matter of Uriah and Bathsheba. This he does by exciting the king's indignation, and leading him to condemn himself, by reciting to him the very striking parable of the traveler and the lamb. Then, changing the voice of a suppliant for that of a judge and a commissioned prophet, he exclaims, 'Thou art the man!' and proceeds to announce the evils which were to embitter the remainder of his reign (2 Sam. xii:1, sq.; comp. Ps. li). The lamentations of the repentant king drew forth some mitigation of punishment; but the troubled history of the remainder of his reign shows how completely God's righteous doom was fulfilled. The child conceived in adultery died; but when Bath-sheba's second son was born, the prophet gave him the name of Jedidiah (beloved of Jehovah), although he is better known by that of Solomon (2 Sam. xii:24, 25). He recognized in this young prince the successor of David; and it was in a great measure through his interposition that the design of Adonijah to seize the crown was unsuccessful (1 Kings i:8, sq.).

(2) Death. Nathan probably died soon after the accession of Solomon, for his name does not again historically occur. It is generally supposed that Solomon was brought up under his care. His sons occupied high places in this king's court (1 Kings iv:5). He assisted David by his counsels when he reorganized the public worship (2 Chron. xxix:25); and he composed annals of the times in which he lived (1 Chron. xxix:29; 2 Chron. ix:29); but these have not been preserved to us. In Zechariah (xii:12) the name of Nathan occurs as representing the great family of the prophets.

2. Son of Attai, of the house of Jerahmeel of Judah (1 Chron. ii:36), B. C. after 1612.

3. A man of Zobah of Syria, and father of one and brother of another of David's mighty men (2 Sam. xxiii:36; 1 Chron. xi:38).

4. The third child born to David in Jerusalem (2 Sam. v:14). Through him Mary, the mother of Jesus, was descended from David (Luke iii:31). He was perhaps the father of Solomon's officers, Azariah and Zabud (1 King iv:5), B. C. 1032.

5. A chief man in the company which returned from captivity with Ezra on his second expedition (Ezra viii:16), B. C. 459.

6. A son of Bani, who divorced his foreign wife (Ezra x:39).

NATHANAEL (na-thăn'a-el), (Gr. Ναθαναήλ, nath-an-ah-ale', given of God), a person of Cana in Galilee, who, when informed by Philip that the

Messiah had appeared in the person of Jesus of Nazareth, asked, 'Can any good thing come out of Nazareth?'

But he nevertheless accepted Philip's laconic invitation, 'Come and see!' When Jesus saw him coming he said, 'Behold an Israelite indeed, in whom is no guile.' Astonished to hear this from a man to whom he supposed himself altogether unknown, he asked, 'Whence knowest thou me?' And the answer, 'Before that Philip called thee, when thou wast under the fig-tree, I saw thee, wrought such conviction on his mind that he at once exclaimed, 'Rabbi, thou art the son of God, thou art the king of Israel' (John i:45-51). It is clear, from the effect, that Nathanael knew by this that Jesus was supernaturally acquainted with his disposition and character, as the answer had reference to the private acts of devotion, or to the meditations which filled his mind, when under the fig-tree in his garden. It is questioned whether Jesus had actually seen Nathanael or not with his bodily eyes. It matters not to the result; but the form of the words employed seems to suggest that he had actually noticed him when under the fig-tree, and had then cast a look through his inward being. All the disciples of John the Baptist named in the first chapter of St. John became apostles; and St. John does not name Bartholomew, nor the other evangelist Nathanael in the lists of the apostles (Matt. x:3; Mark iii:18; Luke vi:14); besides, the name of Bartholomew always follows that of Philip; and it would appear that Bartholomew (son of Tholmai) is no more than a surname. (See BARTHOLOMEW.)

NATHAN-MELECH (nā′than-mē′lech), (Heb. נְתַן־מֶלֶךְ, neth-an'meh'lek, the king is giver), a eunuch in the court of Josiah dwelling in the precincts of the temple (2 Kings xxiii:11), B. C. 628.

NATIONS, DISPERSION OF (nāshŭns, dispēr-shun ŏv).

Under this or some similar designation, it has been the prevalent opinion that the *outspreading*, which is the entire subject of Genesis, ch. x, and the *scattering* narrated in ch. xi:1-9, refer to the same event, the latter being included in the former description, and being a statement of the *manner* in which the separation was effected. From this opinion, however, we dissent.

1. Two Accounts. An unbiased reading of the text appears most plainly to mark the distinctness, in time and character, of the two narratives. The first was universal, regulated, orderly, quiet, and progressive: the second, local, embracing only a part of mankind, sudden, turbulent, and attended with marks of the divine displeasure.

(1) Of Noah's Sons. The former is introduced and entitled in these words:—'Shem, and Ham, and Japheth;—these are the three sons of Noah; and from them was the whole earth overspread.' After the mention of the sons of Japheth it is added, 'From these the isles of the nations were dispersed, in their lands, each to its language, to their families in their nations.' A formula somewhat differing is annexed to the descendants of Ham: 'These are the sons of Ham, (according) to their families, to their tongues, in their lands, in their nations.' The same phrase follows the enumeration of the house of Shem: and the whole concludes with, 'These are the families of the sons of Noah, (according) to their generations, in their nations; and from these the nations were dispersed in the earth after the Flood' (Gen. ix:19; x:5, 20, 31, 32).

(2) After the Confusion of Tongues. The second relation begins in the manner which often,

in the Hebrew Scriptures, introduces a new subject. We shall present it in a literality even servile, that the reader may gain the most prompt apprehension of the meaning. 'And it was (*col-ha-aretz*) all the earth (but with perfect propriety it might be rendered *the whole land, country, region,* or *district*); lip one and words one (*i. e. the same, similar*). And it was in their going forwards that they discovered a plain in the country Shinar; and they fixed (their abode) there.' Then comes the narrative of their resolving to build a lofty tower which should serve as a signal-point for their rallying and remaining united. The defeating of this purpose is expressed in the anthropomorphism, which is characteristic of the earliest Scriptures, and was adapted to the infantile condition of mankind. 'And Jehovah scattered them from thence upon the face of the whole earth (or land), and they ceased to build the city' ch. xi:2-9. (See ANTHROPOMORPHISM; BABEL, TOWER OF. Also J. Pye Smith's *Scripture and Geology,* lect. vii, where this characteristic of primeval style is investigated).

2. Ancient History. 'The most ancient history of the human race, perhaps in the world, is a work in Hebrew;' of which the initial portions (Gen. i, ii) are 'a preface to the oldest civil history now extant; we see the truth of them confirmed by antecedent reasoning, and by evidence in part highly probable, and in part certain; but the connection of the Mosaic history with that of the gospel, by a chain of sublime predictions unquestionably ancient, and apparently fulfilled, must induce us to think the Hebrew narrative more than human in its origin, and consequently true in every substantial part of it; though possibly expressed in figurative language (referring to the accounts of the creation and the fall). It is no longer probable only, but it is absolutely certain, that the whole race of man proceeded from *Iràn* (the proper and native name of Persia and some connected regions), as from a center, whence they migrated at first in *three great colonies;* and that those three branches grew from a common stock, which had been miraculously preserved in a general convulsion and inundation of this globe (Sir William Jones, *On the Origin and Families of Nations,* Works, ed. by Lord Teignmouth, 8vo. iii:191-196).

From the study of this interesting fragment of antiquity, the following observations have presented themselves:

(1) Nations in Time of Moses. The enumeration comprises only nations existing in the age of Moses, and probably of them only the most conspicuous, as more or less connected with the history of the Israelites. Many nations have been formed in subsequent times, and indeed are still forming, by separation and by combination; these can be considered only as included on the ground of long subsequent derivation. Such are the populations of Eastern Asia, Medial and South Africa, America and Australasia.

(2) Partial Table of Nations. It cannot be affirmed with certainty that we are here presented with a complete *Table of Nations,* even as existing in the time of Moses. Of each of the sons of Noah, it gives the sons; but of their sons (Noah's great-grandsons) it is manifest that all are not mentioned, and we have no possible means of ascertaining how many are omitted. Thus, of the sons of Japheth, the lines of Gomer and Javan only are pursued; Magog, Madai, Tubal, Meshech, and Tiras are dropped without any mention of their issue; yet we have evidence that nations of great importance in the history of mankind have descended from them. Ham had four sons; of three of them the sons, or rather clannish or national descendants, are specified; but to Phut, the fourth, no posterity is assigned. Shem had five sons, but the descendants of only two of them are recorded. It cannot be supposed that those whose sequence is thus cut off, died without children; for, as we shall presently see, nations of great historical interest may be traced up to them.

(3) Tribes or Countries. The immediate descendants of Japheth, Ham, and Shem are, except in the instance of Nimrod and a few more, some of which are doubtful, given by names not personal, but designative of tribes or nations, or their countries. Thus, all those terminating in the plural *im,* and those specified by the gentilitial adjective, the Jebusite, the Hivite, etc.

(4) Uncertainty of Names. In attaching the names of nations to those here given, there is sometimes a deep uncertainty. Resemblances in orthographical appearance, or in similarity of sound, are not to be relied on alone; there must be accessory and confirmatory evidence.

(5) Reasons for Migration. We are not warranted in supposing that the families, or clans, or tribes, or however the groups might have been formed, migrated immediately to their respective seats, by any sort of general breaking up. This would presuppose some kind of compulsory enforcement, which neither the nature of the case, nor any intimation in the narrative, warrants us to assume. We may rather conceive that a diversity of movements took place, excited by general conviction of duty and utility; guided in a great measure by patriarchal directions, and strengthened by circumstances which would inevitably occur; such, on the one hand, as earthquakes, volcanic eruptions, local inundations, landslips, proof of unwholesomeness in marshy districts, the annoyance of winged insects or other noxious animals—urging to depart from disagreeable or dangerous places; and, on the other hand, attractive peculiarities, new and more convenient situations for pasturage, better soils for the various kinds of agriculture, more pleasing sites for dwellings, the formation of towns, and the security of their inhabitants.

(6) Various Results. The acts of separation and journeying would have specific differences of impulse and performance; they would affect one party and another, more or less, as to time, numbers and rapidity of movement.

3. Enumeration of Nations. The enumeration of the nations is as follows:

(1) Sons of Japheth, the Iapetus of the Greeks.

I. GOMER. This name is traced in the Kimmerii of Homer and Herodotus; the Gomares (Γομαρεῖς, Josephus, *Antiq.* i:6), whence Kelts, Gauls, Galatians; the Kymry; all the Celtic and Iberian tribes, Welsh, Gaelic, Irish, Breton; the Cimmerian Bosphorus, Crimea.

Sons of Gomer:

(1) *Ashkenaz,* Axeni, inhabitants of the southern coasts of the Euxine Sea, where we find a country Askania, and a river Askanius, and a large part of Armenia; the Basques in the north of Spain; the Saxons, as the Jews interpret Ashkenaz, in Jer. li :27, to be Germany.

(2) *Riphath* (Diphath, 1 Chron. i :6, a permutation of D and R, not unexampled). Rifou, east of the Euxine; Tobata and other parts of Paphlagonia; Croatia; the Riphæan mountains, a very obscure name in ancient geography (Strabo, Vir-

gil, Pliny, Mela), referring probably to the great chains of mountains from the north of Asia westwards (Hyperboræans, Steph. Byzant.), and therefore including vague knowledge of the Uralian, Hartz, and Alpine regions.

(3) *Togarmah.* Peoples of Armenia and other parts of the Caucasian region. The Armenian traditions assign as their ancestor Haik, the son of Torgon and grandson of Noah.

II. MAGOG. In Ezekiel this seems to be used as the name of a country, and Gog that of its chieftain. The Mongoles, Moguls; the great Tartar nation.

III. MADAI. The Medes; people of Iran, to whom the Sanscrit language belonged; primeval inhabitants of Hindustan.

IV. JAVAN. The Greeks, Asiatic and European. Iaones (Homer, *Iliad,* xiii :685).

Sons of Javan:

(1) *Elisha.* Greeks especially of the Peloponnesus; Hellas; Elis, in which is Alisium ('Αλείσιον, *Iliad,* ii, 617).

(2) *Tarshish.* The east coast of Spain, where the Phœnician Canaanites afterwards planted their colony.

(3) *Kittim.* Inhabitants of the isles and many of the coasts of the Mediterranean, particularly the Macedonians and the Romans, and those farther to the west.

(4) *Dodanim* (Rhodanim, 1 Chron. i :7). Dodona, a colony from which probably settled at the mouths of the Rhone, Rhodanus.

To this Javanian (Ionian) branch is attributed the peopling of 'the isles of the nations' (verse 5), a frequent Hebrew denomination of the western countries to which the Israelites, Tyrians, Egyptians, etc., had access by sea.

(2) Sons of Ham. The word signifies *heat* or *hot,* alluding to the climes which the most of his posterity were to occupy; it was also an indigenous name of Egypt.

I. CUSH. The Ethiopians, first on the Arabian side of the Red Sea, then colonizing the African side, and subsequently extending indefinitely to the west, so that *Cushite* (Jer. xiii :23) became the appellative of a negro.

Sons of Cush:

(1) *Seba.* Joined with Mizraim and Cush (Is. xliii :3), evidently denoting contiguity and affinity. This tribe or class is probably referred to Suba, a native name of Meroe upon the Nile, in the farthest south of Egypt, or the beginning of Ethiopia.

(2) *Havilah.* Of this word vestiges are found in various names of places in Western Arabia, and the adjacent parts of Africa. It is quite distinct from the Havilah (Gen. ii :11) in or near Armenia, and probably from another (verse 29) in Arabia, unless we suppose a union of tribes, or one succeeded by the other.

(3) *Sabtah.* Sabota or Sabbatha is the name of an ancient trading town of Arabia.

(4) *Raamah.* Sept. *Rhegma* (Alex. *Rhegehma*), which, changing ε into η, is the name of a port which the Ægypto-Greek geographer Claudius Ptolemy (who flourished in the earlier part of the second century) places on the Arabian coast of the Persian Gulf. To this place Dr. Baumgarten (Kiel, 1843) refers the name; others take it to be Reama, a town of considerable importance in the southwestern part of Arabia the Happy, whose inhabitants are remarkably black; mentioned along with Sheba in Ezek. xxvii :22, as a place of rich Oriental traffic.

Two sons of this Raamah are mentioned, Sheba and Dedan. We find these in the subsequent

Scriptures distinguished for trade and opulence (Ps. lxxii:10, 15; 1 Kings x:1; Is. lx:6; Ezek. xxvii:15, 20, 22). They both lie in the western part of Arabia. The queen of Sheba came to the court of Solomon. Dedan is not improbably considered as the origin of Aden, that very ancient seaport and island at the mouth of the Arabian Gulf or Red Sea, which has very recently risen into new importance.

(5) *Nimrod*, an individual (See NIMROD). He built, besides Babel, his metropolis, three cities or towns in the great plain of Shinar—Erech, Accad, and Calneh. These were probably Aracca, or Arecha, on the Tigris; (some think Edessa); Sacada, near the confluence of the Lycus and the Tigris; and the third (Calno, Is. x:9) Chalonitis of the Greeks, afterwards called Ctesiphon, but much obscurity lies upon these conjectures.

II. MIZRAIM, literally the *two Egypts,* the upper and the lower; each was called *Misr,* a word even now vernacular in that country. Of his descendants seven are specified under *plural* national names, some of which are well ascertained.

(1) *Ludim.* Ludites, celebrated as soldiers and archers (Is. lxvi:19; Jer. xlvi:9; Ezek. xxvii:10; xxx:5), and in those passages connected with other peoples known to be African. The Ludim probably lay towards Ethiopia. They must not be confounded with the Lydians of Asia Minor (ver. 22).

(2) *Ananim.* Very uncertain. Bochart supposes them to have been wandering tribes about the temple of Jupiter Ammon, where was an ancient people called Nasamones.

(3) *Lehabim.* Perhaps inhabitants of a coast-district immediately west of Egypt. Probably the Lubim of 2 Chron. xii:3 and Nahum iii:9.

(4) *Pathrusim.* The people of the Thebaid (Pathros) in Upper Egypt.

(5) *'Casluhim,* out of whom came Philistim.' A people on the northeast coast of Egypt, of whom the Philistines were a colony, probably combined with some of the Caphtorim.

(6) *Caphtorim.* Inhabitants of the island Cyprus.

III. PHUT. This word occurs in several Scripture passages, always in connection with Africa. Josephus and Pliny mention an African river, Phutes. The great modern archaeologist geographer, Ritter, says that hordes of people have been poured out of Futa, in the interior of Africa.

IV. CANAAN. His descendants came out of Arabia, planted colonies in Palestine, and gradually possessed themselves of the whole country.

His children or posterity:

(1) *Sidon,* his firstborn, founded the city of that name.

(2) *Heth,* the ancestor of the Hittites. The remaining nine are well known, and are here laid down in the singular of the patronymic, or patrial adjective—the Jebusite, the Emorite (Amorite), the Girgashite, the Hivite, the Arkite, the Sinite, the Arvadite, the Zemarite, and the Hamathite. All are assigned to Palestine, and the boundaries of the country are precisely laid down.

(3) **Shem,** though here introduced last, is declared to be the eldest of the three brothers. The reason of this order evidently is the design of the historian to pursue the line of the favored people which the Divine Sovereign would raise up in the posterity of Shem, and in which, 'when the fulness of the time should come,' 'all the families of the earth should be blessed.'

Children of Shem embrace:

I. ELAM. The ancestor of the Elamites, or Elymæans, who possessed Elymais, a region be-

tween Susiana and Media, now called Khusistan. The Japhetian Persians afterwards entered that region and gained the ascendancy, and subsequently they were comprehended under the name of Elam.

II. ASHUR, the ancestor of the Assyrians.

III. ARPHAXAD, a personal name in the Abrahamic line. The word, a remarkable compound, probably denotes *Neighboring to the Chasdim, i. e.,* Chaldæans. The name appears in *Arrhapachitis,* a province in Northern Assyria, the primitive seat of the Chasdim, and near to which, or in it, Abraham was born.

Children of Arphaxad are named below.

These are chiefly personal, and contribute to form the sacred pedigree which leads to the Messiah. In this line are mentioned two grandsons:

(1) *Peleg,* of whom we have treated before, and

(2) *Eber.* The only circumstance that we can attach to him is the very important one (which seems therefore to imply something extraordinary in his personal history) of being the origin of the name Ebrew, or as it is commonly written, on account of the ע, *Hebrew,* the 'ancient and universal name of the nation, including Abraham himself (see Ewald's *Hebr. Gramm.,* translated by Dr. Nicholson, p. 2, and our article HEBER).

Eber's son, Joktan, is recognized as the father of the numerous tribes of Arabs in *Yemen,* Arabia the Happy, so called on account of its spices and other rich products, and to distinguish it from the Rocky and the Desert. Of the founders of those tribes thirteen are specified. The first is evidently *Modad,* with the Arabic article; the second is *Shaleph;* and Ptolemy mentions a people of interior Arabia, the Salapeni. *Hatzarmaveth* is a fruitful district on the south coast, which still bears exactly the same name. That name signifies the *Enclosure, Gate,* or *Court of Death,* on account of its insalubrity, arising from the great abundance and mixture of powerful odors. Jerach signifies the *moon;* and on the west of this region is a gold-producing tract, in which are the Mountains of the Moon, which yet must be distinguished from a group in East Africa, very imperfectly known, and called also by Orientals the Backbone of the World. *Hadoram,* the Adramites of Ptolemy and Pliny, on the south coast. *Uzal,* mentioned in Ezek. xxvii:19, which should be translated 'Vedan and Javan (perhaps Yemen?) from Uzal.' The ancient name of a principal city of Yemen, now Sanaha. *Obal* (Ebal in 1 Chron. i:22), unknown. *Abimael,* unknown; the meaning is, *my father Mael,* and Bochart adduces the Mali of Theophrastus and the Minæi of Strabo, a tribe or tribes in Arabia, as possibly intended. *Sheba,* probably indicating an invasion of this tribe upon the Cushite Sheba and Dedan (Gen. x:7, and see xxv:3). From such mixtures much embarrassment often arises in ethnography. Sheba and Seba (x:7) are often mentioned in the Old Testament as seats of great riches and traffic. *Ophir,* undoubtedly referring to the seaport in South Arabia so celebrated for its traffic in gold, jewelry, and fine woods. The same name was probably given to places in India and East Africa, to which the mercantile ships of this Arabian Ophir resorted. A part of the south coast of Arabia is called Oman, and in it is a town called *El-Ophir,* with the article, *Havilah;* perhaps the Cushite settlers were invaded by this Joktanite tribe. *Jobab;* Ptolemy mentions a people, *Iobaritæ,* on the east coast of Arabia. The *r* may be a mistake, or a dialectic variety, for *b.*

These thirteen tribes seem to have formed the confederacy of the independent and unconquerable Arabs, whose peninsular, desert, and mountainous country defended them from invasion; Ishmael and his descendants were united with them.

Our text concludes with describing a boundary line for the country of these tribes 'from Mesha to Sephar.' The former is probably the country Maishon or Mesene, at the northwest head of the Persian Gulf; and the latter, on the southwest coast of Arabia, where is found a Mount Sabber.

IV. Lud. From him the Lydians in Asia Minor derived their name.

V. Aram. From him the inhabitants of Syria, Chalonitis, and a considerable part of Mesopotamia were descended.

Children or posterity of Aram:

(1) *Uz.* In the northern part of Arábia, bordering upon Chaldæa; the land of Job.

(2) *Hul.* The large flat district in the north of Palestine, through which lies the initial course of the Jordan, even now called the land of Hûleh, and in which is the Lake Hûleh, anciently Merom, amply illustrated by Dr. Robinson, *Researches,* iii:339-357.

(3) *Gether.* East of Armenia; Carthara was a city on the Tigris.

(4) *Mash.* A mountain region branching eastward from the great Taurus ridge: the Masian mountains of the Greeks and Romans.

It seems to follow that the only human family after the flood established themselves in the northern parts of Iràn; that, as they multiplied, they were divided into three distinct branches, each retaining little at first, and losing by degrees the whole of their common primary language, but agreeing severally on new expressions for new ideas; that the branch of Yafet was enlarged in many scattered shoots over the north of Europe and Asia, diffusing themselves as far as the western and eastern seas, and at length, in the infancy of navigation, beyond them both; that they cultivated no liberal arts, and had no use of letters, but formed a variety of dialects, as their tribes were variously ramified. The children of Ham, who founded in Iran itself the monarchy of the first Chaldeans, invented letters, observed and named the luminaries of the firmament, calculated the known Indian period of 432,000 years, or 120 repetitions of the *saros,* and contrived the old system of mythology, partly allegorical and partly grounded on idolatrous veneration for their sages and lawgivers; and they were dispersed at various intervals and in various colonies, over land and ocean. The tribes of Misr, Cush and Rama settled in Africa and India, while some of them, having improved the art of sailing, passed from Egypt, Phœnicia and Phrygia, into Italy and Greece, which they found thinly peopled by former emigrants (Japhetians?), of whom they supplanted some tribes and united themselves with others; whilst a swarm from the same hive moved by a northerly course into Scandinavia, and another, by the head of the Oxus and through the passes of the Imaus, into Cashgar and Eighúr, Khatá and Khoten, as far as the territories of Chin and Tancút (an ancient division of China), where letters have been used and arts immemorially cultivated; nor is it unreasonable to believe that some of them found their way from the eastern isles into Mexico and Peru, where traces were discovered of rude literature and mythology analogous to those of Egypt and India. The old Chaldean empire being overthrown by the Assyrians under Cayúmers, other migrations took place, especially into India, while the rest of Shem's progeny, some of whom had before settled on the Red Sea, peopled the whole

Arabian peninsula, pressing close on the nations of Syria and Phœnicia. From all the three families were detached many bold adventurers of an ardent spirit and a roving disposition, who disdained subordination, and wandered in separate clans till they settled in distant isles or in deserts and mountainous regions. (Sir Wm. Jones, *Discourse on the Origin and Families of Nations;* Works, iii:201.)

Dr. Charles Von Rotteck, Professor of Jurisprudence in the University of Freiburg, published in 1826 the ninth and last volume of *A General History of the World.* This work has been received in Germany with great favor. (See J. Pye Smith's *Scripture and Geology,* and a dissertation by Samuel Forrey, M. D., entitled, *The Mosaic Account of the Unity of the Human Race confirmed by the Natural History of the American Aborigines,* in the *American Biblical Repository,* July, 1843.)   J. P. S.

NATIVITY OF CHRIST (nā-tĭv'ĭ-tў). See Christmas; Jesus Christ.

NATURAL (năt'ū-ral).

1. (Heb. םﬡ, *lay'akh,* freshness; Gr. ψυχικός, *psoo-khee-kos'*), having the nature and characteristics of the principle of animal life. It is that which proceeds from birth and natural causes (1 Cor. xv:44).

2. (Gr. φυσικός, *foo-see-kos',* produced by nature). That which is agreeable to natural design, form, or inclination (Rom. i:26, 27).

It is recorded of Moses that at his death "his eye was not dim, nor his natural force abated" (Deut. xxxiv:7). The meaning is his vigor or strength was fully preserved.

NATURAL HISTORY (năt-yū'ral hĭs-to'ry). See various articles on Tree; Plant; Shrubs, etc., treated under specific heads.

NATURAL MAN, THE. *"The natural man receiveth not the things of the Spirit of God, neither can he know them, because they are spiritually discerned"* (1 Cor. ii:14). (a) Here it is plain that by *"the natural man"* is not meant a person devoid of natural judgment, reason, or conscience, in which sense the expression is often used among men. (b) Nor does it signify one who is entirely governed by his fleshly appetites, or what the world calls a voluptuary, or sensualist. (c) Neither does it signify merely a man in the rude state of nature, whose faculties have not been cultivated by learning and study, and polished by an intercourse with society. The apostle manifestly takes his *"natural man"* from among such as the world hold in the highest repute for their natural parts, their learning and their religion. He selects him from among the philosophers of Greece, who sought after wisdom, and from among the Jewish scribes, who were instructed in the revealed law of God (1 Cor. i:22, 23). These are the persons whom he terms the wise, the scribes, the disputers of this world—men to whom the gospel was a stumbling-block and foolishness (1 Cor. i:20, 23). The natural man is here evidently opposed to ὁ πνευματικός, *"him that is spiritual,"* (1 Cor. ii:15), even as the natural body which we derive from Adam is opposed to the spiritual body which believers will receive from Christ at the resurrection, according to 1 Cor. xv:44, 45. Now the *spiritual man* is one who has the Spirit of Christ dwelling in him (Rom. viii:9), not merely in the way of miraculous gifts, as some have imagined (for these were peculiar to the first age of the Christian Church, and even then not common to all the saints, nor inseparably connected with salvation, 1 Cor. xiv:1-4), but in his saving influences of light, holiness and consolation, whereby the subject is made to discern the truth and excellency of spiritual things, and so to believe, love and delight in them as his true happiness. If therefore a man is called "spiritual" because the Spirit of Christ dwells in him, giving him new views, dispositions and enjoyments, then the "natural man," being opposed to such, must be one who is destitute of the Spirit, and of all his saving and supernatural effects, whatever may be his attainments in human learning and science. It is obviously upon this principle that our Lord insists upon the necessity of the new birth in order to our entering into the kingdom of heaven (John iii:3, 5). (Watson, *Theol. Dict.*)

NATURE (nāt'ūre), (Gr. γένεσις, *ghen'es-is;* φύσις, *foo'sis,* genus; Lat. *nascor,* to be born).

1. Philosophical View. According to its derivation, *nature* should mean that which is produced or born; but it also means that which produces or causes to be born. The word has been used with various shades of meaning, but they may all be brought under two heads—*Natura Naturans, Natura Naturata.*

(1) Natura Naturans. (a) The Author of *nature,* the uncreated Being who gave birth to everything that is. (b) The plastic *nature* or energy subordinate to that of the Deity, by which all things are conserved and directed to their ends and uses. (c) The course of *nature,* or the established order according to which the universe is regulated.

(2) Natura Naturata. (a) The works of *nature,* both mind and matter. (b) The visible or material creation, as distinct from God and the soul, which is the object of *natural science.* "The term *nature* is used sometimes in a wider, sometimes in a narrower extension. When employed in its most extensive meaning, it embraces the two worlds of mind and matter. When employed in its more restrictive signification, it is a synonym for the latter only, and is then used in contradistinction to the former. In the Greek philosophy, the word φύσις was general in its meaning; and the great branch of philosophy styled '*physical* or *physiological*' included under it not only the sciences of matter, but also those of mind. With us, the term *nature* is more vaguely extensive than the terms *physics, physical, physiology, physiological,* or even than the adjective, *natural;* whereas, in the philosophy of Germany, *natur* and its correlatives, whether of Greek or Latin derivation, are, in general, expressive of the world of matter in contrast to the world of intelligence." (Sir Wm. Hamilton, *Reid's Works,* p. 218, note.) (c) *Nature* as opposed to *art,* all physical causes, all the forces which belong to physical beings, organic or inorganic. (d) The *nature* or essence of any particular being or class of beings; that which makes it what it is.

2. Nature Used in Two Senses. 'The word *nature* has been used in two senses—viz., actively and passively; energetic (*forma formans*) and material (*forma formata*).

(1) In the first it signifies the inward principle of whatever is requisite for the reality of a thing as *existent;* while the *essence,* or essential property, signifies the inner principle of all that appertains to the *possibility* of a thing. Hence, in accurate language, we say the essence of a mathematical circle or geometrical figure, not the *nature,* because in the conception of forms, purely geometrical, there is no expression or implication of their real existence.

(2) In the second or material sense of the word *nature,* we mean by it the sum total of all things, as far as they are objects of our senses, and consequently of possible experience—the aggregate of phenomena, whether existing for our outer senses, or for our inner sense. The doctrine concerning *nature* would therefore (the word physiology being both ambiguous in itself, and already otherwise appropriated) be more properly entitled phenomenology, distinguished into its two grand divisions, somatology and psychology.

3. Course of Nature. "There is no such thing as what men commonly call the *course of nature,* or the *power of nature.* The *course of nature,* truly and properly speaking, is nothing else but the *will of God* producing certain effects in a continued, regular, constant, and uniform manner; which course or manner of acting, being in every movement perfectly *arbitrary,* is as easy to be *altered* at any time as to be *preserved.* And if (as seems most probable) this continual acting upon matter be performed by the subserviency of created intelligences appointed for that purpose by the Supreme Creator, then it is easy for any of them, and as much within their natural power (by the permission of God) to *alter* the course of *nature* at any time, or in any respect, as it is to *preserve* or continue it" (Fleming, *Vocab. of Phil.*).

4. Ambiguity in Use of the Term "Nature." "The word nature only gives rise to ambiguity when we are using it in reference to questions which touch theology. It then becomes necessary to ask whether we employ it or understand it in the sense (1) as the complex of the mechanical and chemical forces of the cosmos, or in the sense (2) which reckons man's will and reason as a part of his φύσις, foo'sis), or in the sense (3) of the true religious conception which ultimately refers every operation of phenomenal force to the Agency of the Supreme Mind directing and ordering it in wisdom" (J. H. Bernard, Hastings' *Bib. Dict.*).

5. Scriptural Reference. **(1)** Nature denotes the ordinary course of things which God has ordained in the world (Rom. i:26, 27).

(2) The light of reason naturally implanted in our minds (Rom. ii:14).

(3) Common sense, or the general consent of nations (1 Cor. xi:14).

(4) The substance or essential parts and properties (Heb. ii:16). "For every kind (marg. 'nature') of beasts," etc., "is tamed, and hath been tamed of mankind" (marg. "nature of man") (James iii:7).

(5) Birth, or natural descent (Gal. ii:15). St. Paul in 1 Cor. xiv:10 says: Doth not even *nature* itself teach you that, if a man have long hair, it is a shame unto him? But if a woman have long hair, it is a glory to her: for *her* hair is given her for a covering.

In 4 Macc. v:7 Antiochus recommends Eleazar to eat swine's flesh on the ground that it is given us by *nature.* In both of these cases nature is spoken of as a unity and is personified.

In Eph. ii:3 it is said: We are "*by nature*" children of wrath. Through the gospel promises, we are made "partakers of a *divine nature*"; we have fellowship with the divine nature, and have divinely implanted in our souls a principle or habit of grace, conformed to God, in spiritual knowledge, righteousness, and holiness (2 Pet. i:4). Idols are "*by nature no gods*"; they have no self-existence, nothing of the essential perfections of godhead in them (Gal. iv:8).

NATURE or FORCE PLASTIC (nāt'ūre ôr fôrce plăs'tic), (Gr. πλάσσω, *plas'so*, to form), was the name given by ancient physiologists to a power to which they attributed the formation of the germs and tissues of organized and living beings.

In opposition to the doctrine of Democritus, who explained all the phenomena of *nature* by means of matter and motion, and in opposition to the doctrine of Strato, who taught that matter was the only substance, but in itself a living and active force, Cudworth maintained that there is a *plastic nature,* a spiritual energy, intermediate between the Creator and his works, by which the phenomena of *nature* are produced. To ascribe these phenomena to the immediate agency of the Deity would be, he thought, to make the course of *nature* miraculous; and he could not suppose the agency of the Deity to be exerted directly, and yet monstrosities and defects to be found in the works of *nature.* How far the facts warrant such an hypothesis, or how far such an hypothesis explains the facts, may be doubted. But the hypothesis is not much different from that of the *anima mundi,* or soul of matter, which had the countenance of Pythagoras and Plato, as well as of the school of Alexandria, and later philosophers.

In opposition to this view Boyle maintained that it was absurd to believe that any subordinate energy existed between the Creator and his works.

NAUGHTINESS (na͟'tĭ-nĕs).

1. Heb. רֹעַ, *ro'ah,* badness, 1 Sam. xvii:28, wickedness of heart.

2. הַוָּה, *hav-vaw'* (Prov. xi:6), eagerly desiring. It denotes "nothing, nothingness;" meaning in the A. V. "wicked, wickedness" (Prov. vi:12).

NAUM (nā'um), (Gr. Ναούμ, *nah-oom' ;* for the Hebrew see NAHUM), son of Esli in the maternal ancestry of Christ (Luke iii:25).

NAVE (nāv), (Heb. גַּב, *gab,* hollow or curved), anything curved or arched. It is applied to the back of an animal (Ezek. x:12); to a shield (Job xv:26); to the rim of a wheel (1 Kings vii:33).

NAVEL (nā'v'l), (Heb. שֹׁר, *shore,* שָׁרִיר, *shawreer',* twisted, as a string). The place of attachment of the umbilical cord (Ezek. xvi:4), and used in general for the abdomen (Job xl:16; Prov. iii:8).

Figurative. The *bodice* or vestment of a woman (Cant. vii:2); so the passage is understood by some commentators.

NAVIGATION (năv-i-gā-shun). See SHIP.

NAVY (nā'vy̆), (Heb. אֳנִי, *ŏn-ee',* conveyance, 1 Kings ix:26, etc.) is used in the sense of fleet. (See SHIP.)

NAZARENE (năz-a-rēne'), (Gr. Ναζαρηνός, *nadzar-ay-nos'*).

An epithet constituting a part of one of the names given to our Lord. From the number of times that the epithet is employed, it appears that it became at the very first an appellation of our Lord, and was hence applied to designate his followers. Considering that the name was derived from the place where Jesus resided during the greater part of his life, we see no reason to think that at first it bore with it, in its application to him or his followers, anything of an offensive nature. Such a designation was in this case natural and proper. In process of time, however, other influences came into operation. Nazareth was in Galilee, a part of Palestine, which was held in low esteem for several reasons—its dialect was provincial; lying remote from the

capital, its inhabitants spoke a strange tongue, which was rough, harsh and uncouth, having peculiar combinations of words, and words also peculiar to themselves (Buxtorf, *Lex. Talmud; Mark* xiv:70); its population was impure, being made up not only of provincial Jews, but also of heathens of several sorts, Egyptians, Arabians, Phœnicians (Strabo, *Geog.* xvi:523); its people were in an especial manner given to be seditious, which quality of character they not rarely displayed in the capital itself on occasion of the public festivals (Josephus, Wetstein, as cited in Schleusner, *s. v.* Γαλιλαῖος); whence may be seen the point of the accusation made against Paul as 'ringleader of the sect of Nazarenes' (Acts xxiv:5). As Galilee was a despised part of Palestine, so was Nazareth a despised part of Galilee, being a small, obscure, if not mean, place. Accordingly its inhabitants were held in little consideration by other Galileans, and, of course, by those Jews who dwelt in Judæa. Hence the name Nazarene came to bear with it a bad odor, and was nearly synonymous with a low, ignorant and uncultured, if not un-Jewish person (Kuinoel, in Matt. ii:23). It became accordingly a contemptuous designation and a term of reproach (Wetstein, in Matt. ii:23, 26, 71), and as such, as well as a mere epithet of description, it is used in the New Testament.   J. R. B.

NAZARETH (naz'a-rĕth), (Gr. Ναζαρέθ, *nad-zareth'*).

A town in Galilee, in which the parents of Jesus were resident, and where in consequence he lived till the commencement of his ministry. It derives all its historical importance from this circumstance, for it is not even named in the Old Testament or by Josephus; which suffices to show that it could not have been a place of any consideration, and was probably no more than a village.

(1) History. Nazareth is not mentioned in the Old Testament nor by any classical author, nor by any writer before the time of Christ. It was for some unknown reason held in disrepute among the Jews of Judæa (John i:46). It was situated in a mountain (Luke iv:29) within the province of Galilee (Mark i:9), and near Cana, as John ii:1, 2, 11 seems to imply. There was a precipice near the town, down which the people purposed to cast Jesus (Luke iv:29). It is mentioned twenty-nine times in the New Testament. At Nazareth the angel appeared to Mary at the home of Joseph (Luke i:26; ii:39), and to that place Joseph and Mary returned after their flight into Egypt (Matt. ii:23). The hills and places about the town possess a deep and hallowed interest to the Christian as the home of Jesus during his childhood and youth, until he entered upon his ministry, and had preached in the synagogue, and was rejected by his own townspeople. Even after Capernaum became "his own city" he was known as "Jesus of Nazareth" (Matt. xxvi:71-73; Mark xvi:1-6; Acts ii:22; iii:6; iv:10; vi:14), and his disciples were called "Nazarenes." In the days of Constantine, Nazareth was peopled by Samaritan Jews, but in the sixth century Christian pilgrimages began to be made to the town. In 1109, Tancred held Galilee, and Nazareth became the seat of a Christian bishopric. In 1160 a council was held at Nazareth, which made Alexander III pope of Rome. During the Middle Ages Christian pilgrims frequently visited Nazareth. When the Turks conquered Palestine, in 1517, the Christians were driven from the town. In 1620 the Franciscan monks gained a foothold there, and began to rebuild the village. At the battle of

Mount Tabor, in 1799, Napoleon with his army encamped near Nazareth.

(2) Present Conditions. The town is now called *En-Nâsirah*, or *Nasrah*, and has from 5,000 to 6,000 population, though the Turkish officials estimate it at 10,000. There are about 2,000 Mohammedans, 2,500 Greeks, 800 Latins, and 100 Protestants. The inhabitants pursue farming, gardening and various handicrafts, and the village is quite a center of trade for the adjoining districts. The houses are well built. There are a large Latin church and monastery, a synagogue, a Greek church, a fine Protestant church under the care of the English Church Missionary Society, a Protestant hospital, and a large female orphanage (completed 1874). The synagogue is claimed by tradition to be the one in which Christ taught, but cannot be traced to a date earlier than A. D. 570. Near the Greek Church of the

A Carpenter's Shop in Nazareth.

Annunciation is a spring called "Mary's Well," to which the women resort every evening with their water-jars for their daily supply, and to which Mary with her holy Child may have gone. The women of Nazareth, like those of Bethlehem, are distinguished for beauty above their sisters in the East. The brow of the hill over which the enraged Nazarenes threatened to cast Jesus is probably near the Maronite church, though tradition places it at the "Mount of Precipitation," two or three miles south of the town (Schaff, *Bib. Dict.*) The streets are narrow and crooked, and after rains are often choked with mud and filth. From the top of the hill behind the town a most wonderful panorama of Northern Palestine may be seen. To the north is Lebanon, and high above all, the white tops of Hermon. In the west may be seen Carmel and glintings of the Mediterranean Sea, the bay and the town of Akka; east and south are Gilead, Tabor, Gilboa and the great plain of Esdraelon.

NAZARITE (năz'a-rīte).

(1) Name. (Heb. נָזִיר, *naw-zeer'*, and נְזִיר אֱלֹהִים, *neh-zeer' el-o-heem'*, Nazarite of God).

The term comes from the verb נָזַר, *naw-zar'*, to *separate;* and as such separation from ordinary life to religious purposes must be by abstinence of some kind, so it denotes 'to refrain from anything.' Hence the import of the term Nazarite—one, that is, who, by certain acts of self-denial, consecrated himself in a peculiar manner to the service, worship, and honor of God.

We are here, it is clear, in the midst of a sphere of ideas totally dissimilar to the genius of the Christian system; a sphere of ideas in which the outward predominates, in which self-mortification is held pleasing to God, and in which man's highest service is not enjoyment with gratitude, but privation with pain.

(2) Origin. It may be questioned if at least so much of this set of notions as supposes the Deity to be gratified and conciliated by the privations of the creature is in harmony with the ideas of God which the books of Moses exhibit, or had their origin in the law he promulgated. The manner in which he speaks on the subject (Num. vi:1-21) would seem to imply that he was not introducing a new law, but regulating an old custom; for his words take for granted, that the subject was generally and well known, and that all that was needed was such directions as should bring existing observances into accordance with the Mosaic ritual. Winer, indeed, sees, in the minuteness and particularity of the Mosaic regulations, a proof that the Nazarite vow was of home origin in Mosaism; an argument whose force we cannot discern, for a foreign practice, once introduced, must of necessity be conformed to its new abode.

(3) Meaning of the Vow. It is not least among the merits of Judaism that in general it is eminently of a practical character. Though admitting a multitude of observances, some of which, being of a very minute kind, and relating to everyday life, must have been troublesome, if not vexatious, yet the ordinary current of existence was allowed to run on unimpeded; energy was not directed from its proper channel; and life was spent in the active discharge of those offices which human wants require, and by which human happiness may be best advanced. There was no Indian self-renunciation; there was no monkish isolation; yet the vow of the Nazarite shows that personal privations were not unknown in the Mosaic polity. This vow we regard as an instance and an exemplification of that asceticism which, wherever human nature is left free to develop itself, will always manifest its tendencies and put forth its effects. No age, no nation, no religion has been without asceticism. Self-mortification is, with some minds, as natural as self-enjoyment with others. The proneness to ascetic practices is a sort of disorder of temperament. It is in part a question of original constitution. As some individuals are inclined to melancholy, to brood over their own states of mind, so they tend to become morbid in their feelings, intensely self-dissatisfied, over-thoughtful, full of personal solicitudes; then gloomy; then still more dissatisfied with themselves, till at length they are led to think that nothing but severe mortifications and self-inflicted penalties can atone for their guilt, and placate a justly offended God. This general tendency of a certain physical temperament may be checked or encouraged by religious opinions or social institutions, as well as by the peculiar hue which the fortune of an age or a country may bear. The disease, however, is eminently contagious; and if, owing to unknown circumstances, there was in the days of Moses a tendency, whether borrowed from Egypt or merely strengthened by Egyptian practices, which threatened, in its excess, to become in any degree epidemic, it was wise and patriotic in that lawgiver to take the subject into his own remedial hands, and to restrain and limit to individuals that which might otherwise infect large classes, if not reach and so weaken the national mind.

(4) Law of the Nazarite. The law of the Nazarite, which may be found in Num. vi, is, in effect, as follows: Male and female might assume the vow; on doing so a person was understood to separate himself unto the Lord; this separation consisted in abstinence from wine and all intoxicating liquors, and from everything made therefrom: 'From vinegar or wine, and vinegar of strong drink; neither shall he drink any liquor of grapes, nor eat moist grapes or dried'; he was to 'eat nothing of the vine-tree, from the kernels even to the husks.' Nor was a razor to come upon his head all the time of his vow; he was to 'be holy, and let the locks of the hair of his head grow.' With special care was he to avoid touching any dead body whatever. Being holy unto the Lord, he was not to make himself unclean by touching the corpse even of a relative. Should he happen to do so, he was then to shave his head, and offer a sin-offering and a burnt offering; thus making an atonement for himself, 'for that he sinned by the dead.' A lamb, also, of the first year, was to be offered as a trespass-offering. The days, too, that had gone before his defilement were to be lost, not reckoned in the number of those during which his vow was to last. On the termination of the period of the vow the Nazarite himself was brought unto the door of the tabernacle of the congregation, there to offer a burnt-offering, a sin-offering, a peace-offering, and a meat and a drink offering. The Nazarite also shaved his head at the door of the tabernacle, and put the hair grown during the time of separation into the fire which was under the sacrifice of the peace-offerings. 'And the priest shall take the sodden shoulder of the ram and one unleavened cake out of the basket, and one unleavened wafer, and shall put them in the hands of the Nazarite after the hair of his separation is shaven; and the priest shall wave them for a wave-offering.' 'After that the Nazarite may drink wine.'

(5) Illustrations. There are not wanting individual instances which serve to illustrate this vow, and to show that the law in the case went into operation. Samson's mother took the vow of a Nazarite that she might have a son. Samson himself was a Nazarite from the time of his birth (Judg. xiii). In his history is found a fact which seems to present the reason why cutting the hair was forbidden to the Nazarite. The hair was considered the source of strength; it is, in fact, often connected with unusual strength of body, for the male has it in greater abundance than the female. Delilah urged Samson to tell her where his strength lay. After a time, 'he told her all his heart, and said unto her, There hath not come a razor upon mine head, for I have been a Nazarite unto God from my mother's womb; if I be shaven, then my strength will go from me, and I shall become weak, and be like any other man' (Judg. xvi:15, sq.) The secret was revealed; Samson was shorn and accordingly lost his strength and his life.

From the language employed by Samson, as well as from the tenor of the law in this case, the retention of the hair seems to have been one essential feature in the vow. It is, therefore, somewhat singular that any case should have been considered as the Nazaritic vow in which the shaving of the head is put forth as the chief

particular. St. Paul is supposed to have been under *this* vow, when (Acts xviii:18) he is said to have 'shorn his head in Cenchrea, for he had a vow' (see also Acts xxi:24). The head was not shaven till the vow was performed, when a person had *not* a vow.

Figurative. The vow of the Nazarites indicates an entire consecration of the body to the Lord, and is in the spirit of St. Paul's exhortation to present the body a living sacrifice, holy and acceptable, unto God (Rom. xii:6). It is expressly said that during the days of his separation the Nazarite "is holy unto the Lord" (Num. vi:8).

(1) Were not these Nazarites typical of Jesus Christ? Altogether holy, he was solemnly devoted to the service of God. Never was he defiled with carnal pleasures, nor intoxicated with sinful lusts or earthly cares; never was he defiled by irregular affections towards his nearest relations, nor polluted by his gracious connections with men. His graces and good works increased more and more, and his people rooted in him, grow up and flourish in God's holy place. Never did he break his vow, but finished it in giving himself for an all-comprehensive offering for us; and in his resurrection, laid aside every token of continued subjection to an angry God or broken law, and purges and inflames the hearts of his people, by his bleeding love. (2) Were not these Nazarites emblems of ministers and saints, who, denying themselves, and mortifying the deeds of the body, consecrate themselves to God, renounce this world, and the pleasures of sin? (Brown, *Bib. Dict.*)

NEAH (nē'ah), (Heb. נֵעָה, *nay-aw'*, the shaking or settlement), a town of Zebulun on the southern boundary of Rimmon (Josh. xix:13). Porter suggests 'Ain, about three miles northwest of Nazareth, as its site, but the site is not known.

NEAPOLIS (ne-ăp'o-lĭs), (Gr. Νεάπολις, *neh-ap'o-lis*, new city), a maritime city of Macedonia, near the borders of Thrace, now called Napoli.

Paul landed here on his first journey into Europe (Acts xvi:11). It was situated on a rocky eminence, the most conspicuous object being a temple of Diana, which crowned the top of the hill. The great Roman road *Via Egnatia,* from Macedonia to Thrace, passed through Neapolis, which was eight or ten miles from Philippi. It is now a Turco-Grecian town of 5,000 or 6,000 population, and called *Kavalla;* it has numerous ruins. Another site has been proposed (*Eski*) for Neapolis, but the arguments for it are unsatisfactory. The Roman name of Shechem was also Neapolis, but it is not so named in Scripture.

NEARIAH (nē'a-rī'ah), (Heb. נְעַרְיָה, *neh-ar-yaw'*, servant of Jehovah).

1. A son of Ishi, and captain of 500 Simeonites in the time of Hezekiah (1 Chron. iv:42), B. C. 715.

2. A son of Shemiah, and descendant of David (1 Chron. iii:22, 23), B. C. 350.

NEBAI (nĕb'a-ī), (Heb. נֵיבָי, *nay-baw'*, fruitful), one of the chiefs of the people who signed the covenant with Nehemiah (Neh. x:19), B. C. 410.

NEBAIOTH or NEBAJOTH (ne-bā'yoth), (Heb. נְבָיוֹת, *neb-aw-yoth'*, fruitfulness).

1. *The Firstborn Son of Ishmael* (Gen. xxv: 13; 1 Chron. 1:29) and the prince or *sheik* (rendered by Jerome φύλαρχος) of one of the twelve Ishmaelitish tribes, which, as well as the territory they occupied, continued to bear his name in after times (Gen. xxv:16; comp. xvii:20). One of Esau's wives, Mahalath, otherwise called Bashemath, is expressly designated as 'the sister of Nebaioth' (Gen. xxviii:9; xxxvi:3); and by a singular coincidence the land of Esau, or Edom, was ultimately possessed by the posterity of Nebaioth. In common with the other Ishmaelites, they first settled in the wilderness 'before' (*i. e.*, to the east of) their brethren, the other descendants of Abraham; by which we are probably to understand the great desert lying to the east and southeast of Palestine (Gen. xxv:18; xxi:21; xvi:12; and see the article ARABIA.) From the references of Scripture it is evident that the tribe of Nebaioth followed for ages the nomadic life of shepherds.

2. Nabathæans. This people included a variety of Arab races taking their common name from the progenitor of the largest or most influential tribe, Nebaioth, the firstborn of Ishmael.

(1) Invasion of Western Asia. The successful invasion of Western Asia, first by the Assyrians and afterwards by the Chaldæans, could not but affect the condition of the tribes in Northern Arabia, though we possess no record of the special results. The prophet Isaiah, after his obscure oracle regarding Dumah (ch. xxi:11, 12), introduces a 'judgment upon Arabia,' *i. e.*, Desert Arabia, which some suppose to have been fulfilled by Sennacherib, while others think it refers to the later events that are foretold by Jeremiah (xlix: 28-33) as befalling 'Kedar and the kingdoms of Hazor,' in consequence of the ravages of Nebuchadnezzar. Be this as it may, we know that when the latter carried the Jews captive to Babylon, the Edomites made themselves masters of a great part of the south of Palestine (see IDUMÆA), while either then or at a later period they themselves were supplanted in the southern part of their own territory by the Nabathæans.

The territory occupied by the Nabathæans in its widest sense included the whole of Northern Arabia from the Euphrates to the Elanitic Gulf of the Red Sea; but more strictly taken it denoted (at least in later times) only a portion of the southern part of that vast region (Josephus, *Antiq.* i:12, 4; St. Jerome, *Quæst.* on Is. xxv:13; Ammianus Marcellinus, xiv:8). We first hear of the Nabathæans in history in the reign of Antigonus, who succeeded Alexander the Great in Babylon, and died in the year B. C. 301. He sent two expeditions against them; both were unsuccessful.

(2) Agriculture and Commerce. The Nabathæans were as yet essentially a pastoral people, though they were likewise engaged in commerce, which they afterwards prosecuted to a great extent, and thereby acquired great riches and renown. It was in this way that they gradually became more fixed in their habits; and, living in towns and villages, they were at length united under a regular monarchical government, constituting the kingdom of Arabia, or, more strictly, *Arabia Petræa*, the name being derived not, as some suppose, from the rocky nature of the country, but from the chief city, Petræa.

(3) Kings of Arabia Petræa. The common name of the kings of Arabia Petræa was either Aretas or Obodas. Even in the time of Antiochus Epiphanes (about B. C. 166), we read in 2 Macc. v:8, of an Aretas, king of the Arabians; and from that period downwards they came frequently into contact both with the Jews and Romans, as may be seen in the books of the Maccabees and the writings of Josephus. When Judas Maccabæus and his brother Jonathan had crossed the Jordan, they reached after a three days' march the country of the Nabathæans, who gave them a very friendly reception (1 Macc. v:24, 25; Joseph. *Antiq.* xii. 8. 3; comp. xiii. 13. 5. 15, and *De Bell. Jud.*, i. 4. 4. 7). Long before the kingdom of Arabia was actually conquered by the Romans, its sovereigns were dependent on the Roman power. An expedition was sent thither by Augustus, under Ælius Gallus, governor of Egypt, and a personal friend of the geographer Strabo, who has left us an account of it. After various obstacles he at last reached Λευκή Κώμη or Albus Pagus, the emporium of the Nabathæans, and the port of Petra, which was probably at or near Elath (Strabo, xvi:4, 22, 24; Dion Cassius, liii:27; Arrian, *Periplus Maris Eryth.*). Another friend of Strabo, the Stoic philosopher Athenodorus, had spent some time in Petra, and related to him with admiration how the inhabitants lived in entire harmony and union under excellent laws. The kingdom was hereditary; or at least the king was always one of the royal family and had a *prime minister* or *vizier*, ἐπίτροπος, who was styled *the king's brother*. Pliny also repeatedly speaks of the Nabathæans (*Hist. Nat.* v:11; vi:28; xii:27); and classes along with them the Cedrei, exactly as Kedar and Nebaioth are placed together in Is. lx:7. Another Arabian king of the name of Aretas is the one mentioned by St. Paul (2 Cor. ii:32; comp. Acts vii:24, 25; Joseph. *Antiq.* xviii. 5. 1). We find that a former Aretas had been invited to assume the sovereignty by the inhabitants of Damascus (Joseph. *De Bell. Jud.*, i. 4, 7; *Antiq.* xiii. 15, 1); and now, during the weak reign of Caligula, the same city is seized by another Aretas, and governed through an *ethnarch*, as related by Paul. The kingdom of Arabia Petræa maintained its nominal independence till about A. D. 105, in the reign of the Emperor Trajan, when it was subdued by Cornelius Palma, governor of Syria, and annexed to the vast empire of Rome.

(4) Under the Romans. The Nabathæans had, as we have seen, early applied themselves to commerce, especially as the carriers of the products of Arabia, India, and the far-distant East, which, as we learn from Strabo, were transported on camels from the above-mentioned Λευκή Κώμη to Petra, and thence to Rhinocoloura (El 'Arish) and elsewhere. 'But under the Roman dominion the trade of these regions appears to have widely extended itself, and to have flourished in still greater prosperity; probably from the circumstance that the lawless rapacity of the adjacent nomadic hordes was now kept in check by the Roman power, and particularly by the garrisons which were everywhere established for this specific purpose. The country, too, was now rendered more accessible, and the passage of merchants and caravans more practicable, by military ways.'

From Elath, or Ailah, one great road had its direction northwards to the rich and central Petra; thence it divided, and led on one side to Jerusalem, Gaza, and other ports on the Mediterranean; and on the other side to Damascus. Another road appears to have led directly from Ailah along the Gnor to Jerusalem. Traces of these routes are still visible in many parts.

These facts are derived not from the testimony of historians, but from the specifications of the celebrated *Tabula Theodosiana,* or *Peutingeriana,* compiled in the fourth century. According to this, a line of small fortresses was drawn along the eastern frontier of Arabia Petræa, towards the desert, some of which became the sites of towns and cities, whose names are still extant.

But as the power of Rome fell into decay, the Arabs of the desert would seem again to have acquired the ascendency. They plundered the cities, but did not destroy them; and hence those regions are still full of uninhabited, yet stately and often splendid, ruins of ancient wealth, and taste, and greatness.

(5) Petra. Even Petra, the rich and impregnable metropolis, was subjected to the same fate; and now exists, in its almost inaccessible loneliness only to excite the curiosity of the scholar, and the wonder of the traveler, by the singularity of its site, its ruins, and its fortunes.

In the course of the fourth century this region came to be included under the general name of 'Palestine'; and it then received the special designation of *Palæstina Tertia,* or *Salutaris.* It became the diocese of a metropolitan, whose seat was at Petra, and who was afterward placed under the patriarch of Jerusalem.

With the Mohammedan conquest in the seventh century its commercial prosperity disappeared. Lying between the three rival empires of Arabia, Egypt, and Syria, it lost its ancient independence; the course of trade was diverted into new channels; its great routes were abandoned.

(6) Syria Sobal. At length the entire country was quietly yielded up to the Bedawees of the surrounding wilderness, whose descendants still claim it as their domain. During the twelfth century it was partially occupied by the Crusaders, who gave it the name of *Arabia Tertia,* or *Syria Sobal.* From that period it remained unvisited by Europeans, and had almost disappeared from their maps, until it was partially explored, first by Seetzen in 1807, and more fully by Burckhardt in 1812; and now the wonders of the Wady Mûsa are familiarly known to all. (Vincent's *Commerce of the Ancients;* Forster's *Mohammedanism Unveiled,* and *Geography of Arabia;* Robinson's *Sketches of Idumæa,* in 'Amer. Bib. Repos.', 1833; and *Bibl. Researches,* vol. ii.)   N. M.

NEBALLAT (ne-băl'lat), (Heb. נְבַלָּט, *neb-al-lawt'*, hard, firm, or secret wickedness), a town of Dan, occupied by Benjamites after the captivity (Neh. xi:34). It is now probably Beit Nebâla, four miles northeast of Lydda (Van de Velde, *Memoir* p. 336).

NEBAT (nē'băt), (Heb. נְבָט, *neb-awt'*, regard), a descendant of Ephraim, of the race of Joshua, and father of Jeroboam, the first king of the ten tribes (1 Kings xi:26; 2 Chron. ix:29), B. C. about 1000.

NEBO (nē'bo), (Heb. נְבוֹ, *neb-o'*, height; Sept. Ναβώ, *nah-boh';* Nabium, contracted *nabu* 'the prophet').

1. The interpreter of the will of Bel-Merodach of Babylon. He had a shrine at E-saggilla, the great temple of Bel at Babylon. But his own temple was E-Zida (now *Birs-i-Nimrûd*), in Borsippa, the suburb of Babylon. He was the son of Merodach and Zarpanit, and the husband of Tasmit, 'the hearer.' (A. H. Sayce, Hastings' *Bib. Dict.*)

In later days he was identified with Nusku, a solar deity of fire. He is mentioned in Is. xlvi:1, and supposed to have been the symbol of the planet Mercury, the celestial scribe and interpreter of the gods, answering to the Hermes and Anubis of the Egyptians. He was likewise worshiped by the Sabians in Arabia (Norberg, *Onomast.* p. 95). Gesenius traces the name in the Hebrew word

prophet, an interpreter of the divine will. The divine worship paid to this idol by the Chaldeans and Assyrians is attested by many compound proper names of which it forms a part, as *Nebu*chadnezzar, *Nebu*zar-adan, *Nebu*shasban; besides others mentioned in classical writers—*Nabo*nedus, *Nabo*nassar, *Nabu*rianus, *Nabo*nabus, *Nabo*polassar. (Gesenius and Henderson on Is. xlvi:1.) (See BABYLONIA AND ASSYRIA, RELIGION OF.)

2. A mountain of Moab "over against Jericho," from which Moses beheld the Land of Canaan (Deut. xxxii:49). "And Moses went up from the plains of Moab unto the mountain of Nebo, to the top of Pisgah, . . . and the Lord showed him all the land of Gilead unto Dan" (Deut. xxxiv:1). Nebo was a mountain in the range of mountains called Abarim. Eusebius says it was shown in his day on the other side of Jordan, six miles to the west of Heshbon. If then definitely known, its location was afterward lost. Of the peaks in the Abarim range which have been suggested as Nebo are: *Jebel Attarus,* but this is not "over against Jericho," and is too far south; *Jebel Jil'âd* fifteen miles farther north than Jericho, and therefore not answering to the Scriptural narrative.

The explorations of De Saulcy, Duc de Luynes, Tristram, Warren, Paine, and Merrill have led to the conclusion that Nebo was at the northern end of the Abarim range of mountains, *i. e., Jebel Nebâ.* This mountain was five or six miles southwest of Heshbon, is about 2,700 feet high, and commands a fine view of the country. Paine appears to apply *Jebel Nebâ* to the eastern portion of the northern group of peaks, and *Jebel Siaghah* to the western portion; Dr. Merrill claims that the Arabs use *Jebel Nebâ, Jebel Musa,* and *Jebel Siaghah* indiscriminately for this group. While the discussions respecting Pisgah have been sharp, the majority of explorers and scholars agree in identifying Nebo with the northern end of the Abarim range, *Jebel Nebâ* (Schaff, *Bib. Dict.*). With this identification A. T. Chapman, in Hastings' *Bib. Dict.,* agrees. He says: "It has been questioned whether all the places mentioned in Deut. xxxiv:1 can be seen from any point of the ridge. The 'hinder sea' in this passage probably means the Dead Sea, as being behind Moses when he began his survey, and not the Mediterranean Sea. (*The Prospect from Pisgah,* by W. F. Birch.) (See PISGAH.)

3. A town in the tribe of Judah (Ezra ii:29); or, more fully, in order to distinguish it from the preceding, 'the other Nebo' (Neh. vii:33). The name may have, as in the preceding instance, been derived from that of the idol Nebo; but more probably from the Hebrew word 'to be high.' The site of Nebo has been fixed at *Beit Nubâ,* twelve miles northwest of Jerusalem and eight from Lydda, or at *Nuba,* four miles south of Adullam (Armstrong, *Names and Places,* etc.; W. H. Bennett, Hastings' *Bib. Dict*).

4. A city of Reuben (Num. xxxii:38), taken by the Moabites, who held it in the time of Jeremiah (Jer. xlviii:1). The Moabite stone has an inscription relating to this town. It was eight miles south of Heshbon; perhaps *el Hâbis.*

NEBUCHADNEZZAR (nĕb-u-kad-nĕz'zar), (Heb. נְבֻכַדְנֶאצַּר, *neb-oo-kad-nets-tsar';* and also נְבוּכַדְראֶצַּר, *neb-oo-kad-rets-tsar'.* Gr. Ναβουχοδνόσορ, *Nabouchodnosor;* and also Ναβουκοδρόσορος, *Naboukodrosoros;* Kings, Chronicles, and Daniel; Jer. xxvii; xxviii; xxxiv:1; xxxix:1; Ezek. xxvi:7; and Ezra v:12; written also נְבֻכַדְראֶצַּר, *neb-oo-kad-re-tsar',* Nebuchadrezzar, generally in Jeremiah, and in Ezek. xxx:10).

(1) King of Babylon. The name of the Chaldæan monarch of Babylon by whom Judah was conquered, and the Jews led into their seventy years' captivity. In the Septuagint version he is called Ναβουχοδονοσορ, *Nabuchodonosor*. This name, Nabuchodonosor, has passed from the Septuagint into the Latin Vulgate, and, into the authorized English version of the books of Judith and Tobit. Nabu or Nebo (Is. xlvi:1) was the name of a Chaldæan deity, supposed to be Mercury, and enters frequently into the composition of Chaldæan proper names, as Nabopolassar (*Can. Ptol*); Nabuzar-adan (2 Kings xxv:8, etc.); Samgar-Nebu and Nebushasban (Jer. xxxix:3, 13). The name Nebuchadnezzar has been commonly explained to signify the *treasure of Nebo*, but, according to Lorsbach (*Archiv. f. Morgenl. Literatur*), it signifies *Nebo, the prince of gods.*

The only notices which we have of this monarch in the canonical writings are found in the books of Kings, Chronicles, Daniel, and Ezra, and in the allusions of the prophets Jeremiah and Ezekiel.

From 2 Kings xxiii:29, and 2 Chron. xxxv:20, we gather that in the reign of Josiah (B. C. 610), Pharaoh-necho, king of Egypt, having approached by sea the coast of Syria, made a friendly application to King Josiah to be allowed a passage through his territories to the dominions of the Assyrian monarch, with whom he was then at war. The design of Pharaoh-necho was to seize upon Carchemish (Circesium or Cercusium), a strong post on the Euphrates; but Josiah, who was tributary to the Babylonian monarch, opposed his progress at Megiddo, where he was defeated and mortally wounded. (See JOSIAH.) Necho marched upon Jerusalem, and the Jews became tributary to the King of Egypt.

(2) In the Field. Upon this, Nebuchadnezzar, King of Babylon (2 Kings xxiv:1; 2 Chron. xxxvi:6, where this monarch's name is for the first time introduced), invaded Judah, retook Carchemish, with the territory which had been wrested from him by Necho, seized upon Jehoiakim, the vassal of Pharaoh-necho, and reduced him to submission (B. C. 607). Jehoiakim was at first loaded with chains, in order to be led captive to Babylon, but was eventually restored by Nebuchadnezzar to his throne, on condition of paying an annual tribute. Nebuchadnezzar carried off part of the ornaments of the temple, together with several hostages of distinguished rank, among whom were the youths Daniel and his three friends, Hananiah, Azariah, and Mishael (Dan. i). These were educated at court in the language and sciences of the Chaldeans, where they subsequently filled offices of distinction. The sacred vessels were transferred by Nebuchadnezzar to his temple at Babylon (Is. xxxix; 2 Chron. xxxvi:6, 7). (See BABYLON.)

(3) Opposes Egypt. After the conquest of Judæa, Nebuchadnezzar turned his attention towards the Egyptians, whom he drove out of Syria, taking possession of all the land between the Euphrates and the *river* (2 Kings xxiv:7); which some suppose to mean the Nile, but others a small river in the desert, which was reckoned the boundary between Palestine and Egypt (Prideaux's *Connection*).

(4) Capture of Jerusalem. The fate of Jerusalem was now rapidly approaching its consummation. After three years of fidelity Jehoiakim renounced his allegiance to Babylon, and renewed his allegiance with Necho, when Nebuchadnezzar sent incursions of Ammonites, Moabites and Syrians, together with Chaldæans, to harass him. At length, in the eleventh year of his reign, he was made prisoner, and slain (Jer. xxii). (See JEHOIAKIM.) He was succeeded by his son Jehoiachin, who, after three months' reign, surrendered himself with his family to Nebuchadnezzar, who had come in person to besiege Jerusalem, in the eighth year of his reign (2 Kings xxiv:10-12). (See JEHOIACHIN.) Upon this occasion all the most distinguished inhabitants, including the artificers, were led captive. (See CAPTIVITY.) Among the captives, who amounted to no less than 50,000, were Ezekiel (Ezek. i:1) and Mordecai. (See ESTHER.) The golden vessels of Solomon were now removed, with the royal treasures, and Mattaniah, the brother of Jehoiachin, placed on the throne by Nebuchadnezzar, who gave him the name of Zedekiah, and bound him by an oath not to enter into an alliance with Egypt. Zedekiah, however, in the ninth year of his reign, formed an alliance with Pharaoh-hophra, the successor of Necho. Hophra, coming to the assistance of Zedekiah, was driven back into Egypt by Nebuchadnezzar, who finally captured Jerusalem in the eleventh year of Zedekiah's reign (B. C. 588). (See ZEDEKIAH.) The Temple, and the whole city, with its towers and walls, were all razed to the ground by Nebuzaradan, Nebuchadnezzar's lieutenant, and the principal remaining inhabitants put to death by Nebuchadnezzar at Riblah. Jeremiah was, however, spared, and Gedaliah appointed governor. He was shortly after murdered by Ishmael, a member of the royal family, who was himself soon obliged to take refuge among the Ammonites. Many of the remaining Jews fled into Egypt, accompanied by Jeremiah; those who remained were soon after expatriated by Nebuchadnezzar, who depopulated the whole country.

(5) Siege of Tyre. He next undertook the siege of Tyre (see TYRE), and after its destruction proceeded to Egypt, now distracted by internal commotions, and devastated or made himself master of the whole country from Migdol to Syene (according to the reading of the Seventy, Ezek. xxix:10; xxx:10), transferring many of the inhabitants to the territory beyond the Euphrates.

(6) The Prophet Daniel. We have referred to the captivity of the prophet Daniel, and have to turn to the book which bears his name for the history of this prophet, who, from an exile, was destined to become the great protector of his nation. In the second year of the reign of Nebuchadnezzar, Daniel, who was found superior in wisdom to the Chaldæan magi, was enabled not only to interpret, but to reveal a dream of Nebuchadnezzar, the very subject of which that monarch had forgotten. (See DREAM.)

This was the dream of the statue consisting of four different metals, which Daniel interpreted as four successive monarchies, the last of which was to be the reign of the Messiah. Daniel was elevated to be first minister of state, and his three friends were made governors of provinces.

The history of these events (Dan. ii:4, 8, 9) is written in the Chaldee language, together with the narrative which immediately follows (ch. iii), of the golden statue erected by Nebuchadnezzar in the plain of Dura, for refusing to worship which Daniel's three friends were thrown into a furnace, but miraculously preserved.

(7) Judgment Upon Nebuchadnezzar. The fourth chapter, also written in Chaldee, contains the singular history of the judgment inflicted on Nebuchadnezzar as a punishment for his pride, and which is narrated in the form of a royal proclamation from the monarch himself, giving an account to his people of his affliction and recovery.

This affliction had been, by the monarch's account, predicted by Daniel a year before, in the interpretation of his fearful dream of the tree in the midst of the earth. While walking in his palace, and admiring his magnificent works, he uttered, in the plenitude of his pride, the remarkable words recorded in verse '30: 'Is not this great Babylon that I have built for the house of the kingdom, by the might of my power, and for the honor of my majesty?'

He had scarce uttered the words, when a voice from heaven proclaimed to him that his kingdom was departed from him; that he should be for seven *times* (generally supposed to mean years, although some reduce the period to fourteen months; Jahn, *Introd.*) driven from the habitations of men to dwell among the beasts of the field, and made to eat grass as an ox, until he learned 'that the Most High ruleth in the kingdom of men, and giveth it to whomsoever he will.'

The difficulties attending the nature of the disease and recovery of Nebuchadnezzar have not escaped the notice of commentators in ancient as well as modern times. Origen's supposition that the account of Nebuchadnezzar's metamorphosis was merely a representation of the fall of Lucifer, is not likely to meet with many supporters. Besides Origen's, there have been no less than five different opinions in reference to this subject. Bodin (in *Demonol.*) maintains that Nebuchadnezzar underwent an actual metamorphosis of soul and body, a similar instance of which is given by Cluvier (*Append. ad Epitom. Hist.*) on the testimony of an eye-witness. Tertullian (*De Pœnit.*) confines the transformation to the body only, but without loss of reason, of which kind of metamorphosis St. Augustine (*De Civ. Dei,* xviii:18) reports some instances said to have taken place in Italy to which he himself attaches little credit; but Gaspard Peucer asserts that the transformation of men into wolves was very common in Livonia. Some Jewish Rabbins have asserted that the soul of Nebuchadnezzar, by a real transmigration, changed places with that of an ox (Medina, *De rectâ in Deum fid.*); while others have supposed not a real, but an apparent or docetic change, of which there is a case recorded in the life of St. Macarius, the parents of a young woman having been persuaded that their daughter had been transformed into a mare. The most generally received opinion, however, is that Nebuchadnezzar labored under that species of hypochondriacal monomania which leads the patient to fancy himself changed into an animal, or other substance, the habits of which he adopts. Jerome probably leaned to this opinion. 'Who does not see,' he observes, 'that *madmen* live like brute beasts in the fields and woods, and in what is it wonderful that this punishment should be inflicted by God's judgment to show the power of God, and so humble the pride of kings? Greek and Roman histories relate much more incredible things, as of men changed into Scylla, the Chimæra, and the Centaurs, into birds and beasts, flowers, trees, stars, and stones?' (in Dan. iv:4). To this disease of the imagination physicians have given the name of Lycanthropy, Zoanthropy, or *Insania Canina.* (See DISEASES OF THE JEWS, 8.)

W. W.

NEBUCHADNEZZAR, INSCRIPTION OF. The famous inscription of Nebuchadnezzar which was recovered from the ruins of Babylon is now in the India House in London.

(1) Carved Upon Stone. This long record of his triumphs has been written upon ten stone columns and it contains in all five hundred and eight lines. It was graven apparently by the king's orders, and it is a wonderful exemplification of his boast, "Is not this great Babylon that I have built?"

We have here an authentic relic of the times of this king, and of the period of the fall of the Jewish monarchy.

It gives us a wonderful picture of Nebuchadnezzar with all his pride of position and power, his passionate devotion to his gods, and his untiring labors in the building of his beautiful capital. We now have a corroboration of the statements of Jeremiah and Daniel concerning the gods he worshiped and the city he built, but it is like the records of Sennacherib and other kings, in that it omits the story of royal humiliation, and gives no hint of that severe lesson in which Nebuchadnezzar was taught that: "The Most High ruleth in the kingdoms of men and giveth them to whomsoever he will."

(2) Contents. We have here only the assertion of his greatness and the wonder of his achievements. The following extract will give a general idea of the whole inscription:

"Nebuchadnezzar, king of Babylon, the prince exalted, the favorite of Merodach, the pontiff supreme, the beloved of Nebo . . . . the chiefest son of Nabopolassar, king of Babylon, am I. . . . When Merodach, the great lord, lifted up the head of my majesty, and Nebo, the overseer of the multitude of heaven and earth, a righteous scepter placed in my hands; himself, the leader glorious, the open eyes of the gods, the prince Merodach, my supplications heard and received my prayers.

"I worshiped his lordship. In his high trust, to far-off lands, a road of hardships I pursued, and the unyielding I reduced, I fettered the rebels. The land I ordered aright, and the people I made to thrive, bad and good among the people I removed (or deported).

Silver, gold, precious stones, whatsoever things are precious, a large abundance, a rich present to my city of Babylon, into his presence I brought.

In E-sagilla (the temple of Bel-Merodach) the palace of his lordship, I wrought repairs. Ekua, the cell of the lord of the gods, Merodach, I made to glisten like suns the walls thereof. . . . The great ramparts of Babylon I finished; beside the scarp of its moat, the two strong walls with bitumen and burnt brick I built, and with the wall which my father had constructed I joined them and the city. I carried them round . . . I beautified the road of Ishtar (See ASHTORETH), that hurleth down them that assail her. . . . Strong bulls of copper, and dreadful serpents, standing upright on their thresholds, I erected. Those portals for the gazing of the people, with carven work I caused to be filled. As an outwork, the wall of Babylon, unapproachable, a mighty rampart, at the ford of the sun rising, Babylon I threw around."

There are many glowing descriptions of the work which he did in beautifying his capital city and rebuilding the temples of the gods.

"The cedar of the roofing of the cells of Nebo with gold I overlaid. The silver of the roofing of the gate of Nana, I overlaid with shining silver. The bulls, the leaves of the gate of the cell, with silver I made bright. . . . The house I made gloriously bright, and with carved work I had it filled. The temples of Borsippa I made and filled." (*Ball's Translation.*) (See *Records of the Past* vol. iii, pp. 102-123.)

NEBUCHADREZZAR (nĕb-u-kad-rĕz'zar). See NEBUCHADNEZZAR.

NEBUSHASBAN (nĕb-u-shăs'ban), (Heb. נְבוּשַׁזְבָּן, *neb-oo-shaz-bawn'*, Nebo saves me), Jer. xxxix:13, a follower of Nebu.

The name of one of the Babylonian officers sent by Nebuzar-adan to take Jeremiah out of prison (B. C. 588). W. W.

"The name Nebushasban occurs in the Assyro-Babylonian inscriptions under the form of *Nabû-Swzibanni*, "Nebo Save Me." (T. G. Pinches, Hastings' *Bib. Dict.*).

NEBUZAR-ADAN (nĕb'u-zär-ā'dan), (Heb. נְבוּזַרְאֲדָן, *neb-oo-zar-ad-awn'*, Nebo sends posterity, 2 Kings xxv:8; Jer. xxxix:9; xl:1; lii:12, etc.).

'Nebo is the Lord,' according to the Hebrew; or, according to the Persian, 'Nebo is wise.' The name of the captain of Nebuchadnezzar's guard, who conducted the siege of Jerusalem to a successful issue, the particulars of which are given in 2 Kings xxv:8-21. He treated Jeremiah with generous consideration, as Nebuchadnezzar commanded (Jer. xxxix:11; xl:1). His speech to Jeremiah is preserved in Jer. xl:2, *sq.* When Nebuchadnezzar, five years later, besieged Tyre, Nebuzar-adan came again to Jerusalem, and carried off seven hundred and forty-five Jews more into captivity (Jer. lii:30).

NECHO (nē'ko), (Heb. נְכֹה, *nek-o'*), an Egyptian king, son and successor (according to Herodotus, ii:158) of Psammetichus, and contemporary of the Jewish king, Josiah (B. C. 610).

(1) Army and Fleet. The wars and success of Necho, in Syria, are recorded by sacred as well as profane writers. Studious of military renown, and the furtherance of commerce, Necho, on ascending the throne of Egypt, applied himself to reorganize the army, and to equip a powerful fleet. In order to promote his purposes, he courted the Greeks, to whose troops he gave a post next to his Egyptians. He fitted out a fleet in the Mediterranean, and another in the Red Sea. Having engaged some expert Phœnician sailors, he sent them on a voyage of discovery along the coast of Africa. The honor, therefore, of being the first to equip an expedition for the purpose of circumnavigating Africa belongs to Pharaoh-necho, who thereby ascertained the peninsular form of that continent, twenty-one centuries before the Cape of Good Hope was seen by Diaz, or doubled by Vasco da Gama.

Before entering on this voyage of discovery, Necho had commenced reopening the canal from the Nile to the Red Sea, which had been cut many years before by Sesostris or Rameses the Great. The work, however, if we may believe Herodotus, was abandoned, an oracle warning the Egyptian monarch that he was laboring for the barbarian (Herod. ii:158).

(2) Enters Palestine. Necho also turned his attention to the Egyptian conquests already made in Asia; and, fearing lest the growing power of the Babylonians should endanger the territories acquired by the arms of his victorious predecessors, he determined to check their progress, and to attack the enemy on his own frontier. With this view he collected a powerful army, and entering Palestine, followed the route along the sea-coast of Judæa, intending to besiege the town of Carchemish on the Euphrates. But Josiah, king of Judah, offended at the passage of the Egyptian army through his territories, resolved to impede, if unable to prevent, their march. Necho sent messengers to induce him to desist, assuring him that he had no hostile intentions against Judæa, 'but against the house wherewith I have war; for

God commanded me to make haste.' This conciliatory message was of no avail. Josiah posted himself in the valley of Megiddo, and prepared to oppose the Egyptians. Megiddo was a city in the tribe of Manasseh, between forty and fifty miles to the north of Jerusalem, and within three hours of the coast. It is called Magdolus by Herodotus. In this valley the feeble forces of the Jewish king, having attacked Necho, were routed with great slaughter.

(3) Death of Josiah. Josiah being wounded in the neck with an arrow, ordered his attendants to take him from the field. Escaping from the heavy shower of arrows with which their broken ranks were overwhelmed, they removed him from the chariot in which he had been wounded, and placing him in a 'second one that he had,' they conveyed him to Jerusalem, where he died (2 Kings xxiii:29, *sq.*; 2 Chron. xxxv:20, *sq.*). (See JOSIAH.)

Intent upon his original project Necho did not stop to revenge himself upon the Jews, but continued his march to the Euphrates.

(4) Overthrow of His Successor. Three months had scarcely elapsed, when, returning from the capture of Carchemish and the defeat of the Chaldæans, he learned that, though Josiah had left an elder son, Jehoahaz had caused himself to be proclaimed king on the death of his father, without soliciting Necho to sanction his taking the crown. Incensed at this, he ordered Jehoahaz to meet him 'at Riblah, in the land of Hamath'; and having deposed him, and condemned the land to pay a heavy tribute, he carried him a prisoner to Jerusalem. On arriving there, Necho made Eliakim, the eldest son, king, changing his name to Jehoiakim; and taking the silver and gold which had been levied upon the Jewish nation, he returned to Egypt with the captive Jehoahaz, who there terminated his short and unfortunate career. Herodotus says that Necho, after having routed the Syrians (the Jews) at Magdolus, took Cadytis, a large city of Syria, in Palestine, which, he adds, is very little less than Sardis (ii:159; iii:5). By Cadytis there is scarcely a doubt he meant Jerusalem; the word is only a Greek form of the ancient, as well as the modern, name of that city. (See PHARAOH.) It is, however, to be regretted that the mural sculptures of Egypt present no commemoration of these triumphs on the part of Necho; the sole record of him which they give being the name of Necho, found among the hieroglyphics in the great hall of Karnak. His oval also occurs on vases, and some small objects of Egyptian art.

(5) Defeated by Babylonians. Pleased with his success, the Egyptian monarch dedicated the dress he wore to the deity who was supposed to have given him the victory. He did not long enjoy the advantages he had obtained. In the fourth year after his expedition, being alarmed at the increasing power of the Babylonians, he again marched into Syria, and advanced to the Euphrates. The Babylonians were prepared for his approach. Nebuchadnezzar completely routed his army, recovered the town of Carchemish, and, pushing his conquests through Palestine, took from Necho all the territory belonging to the Pharaohs, from the Euphrates to the southern extremity of Syria (2 Kings xxiv:7; Jer. xlvi:6; 2 Chron. xxxvi:9; 2 Kings xxiv:8).

(6) Death. Nebuchadnezzar deposed Jehoiachin, who had succeeded his father, and carried the warriors and treasures away to Babylon; a short time previous to which Necho died, and was succeeded by Psammetichus II. Wilkinson's *Anc. Egyptians,* vol. i:157, *sq.*).

According to Manetho (Euseb. *Chron. Armen.,* i:219), Necho was the sixth king in the twenty-sixth dynasty, successor to Psammetichus I., and as there had been another of the same name, he was properly Necho the Second. The period of his reign was, according to Manetho, six, according to Herodotus sixteen, years (consult Gesenius, *Isaiah* i:596).
J. R. B.

NECK (něk). (Hebrew usually עֹרֶף, *o-ref'*, as Gen. xlix:8, Lev. v:8, *nape;* צַוָּאר, *tsav-vawr'*, as Gen. xxvii:16; גָּרוֹן, *gaw-rone'*, properly throat, Is. iii:16). That part of an animal body between the head and shoulders (Judg. v:30); both head and neck (Deut. xxi:4).

Figuratíve. It denotes the heart; and so a "hard," "stiff" or "iron neck," signifies men's obstinacy in their love to, and practice of sin (Neh. ix:29; Ps. lxxv:5; Is. xlviii:4).

(1) It stands for the whole man; and so to have a "yoke" or bands on the neck signifies being in slavery and bondage (Deut. xxviii:48; Is. lii:2; Jer. xxvii:2). (2) Transgressions come upon, or are wreathed about, the "neck," when they are punished with bondage and slavery (Lam. i:14). (3) The Assyrians "reached even to the neck"; they almost totally overflowed and ruined Judah, taking all the cities thereof, but Jerusalem the capital (Is. viii:8; xxx:28). (4) The Ammonites "came upon the necks of the slain" Jews, when they were murdered in like manner by the Chaldæans (Ezek. xxi:29). (5) To "lay down the neck," is to be ready to suffer slavery or death (Rom. xvi:4). (6) God "discovers the foundations unto the neck," when he utterly unsettles and almost utterly destroys his enemies (Hab. iii:13).
Brown.

NECKLACE (něk'lāce), (Heb. רָבִיד, *raw-beed'*, binding) is a word which does not occur in the A. V., but was in early times, as now, common in the East.

Necklaces were sometimes made of gold or silver (Exod. xxxv:22), sometimes of pearls or jewels, strung on a ribbon (Cant. i:10), hanging to the breast or girdle. To these were attached golden crescents (Is. iii:18; Judg. viii:21), and amulets (Is. iii:18).

The modern Egyptian ladies are very fond of wearing necklaces of the richest character (Wilkinson, *Anc. Egypt,* i, 339, *sq.*) (See PRECIOUS STONES.)

NECOTH (něk-oth'), (Heb. נְכֹאת, *nek-oth'*), this word occurs twice in the book of Genesis.

(1) **A Syrian Product.** It indicates a product of Syria, for in one case we find it carried into Egypt as an article of commerce, and in another sent as a present into the same country. It occurs in the same passage as *ladanum,* which is translated *myrrh* in the Authorized Version. Many of the same general observations will therefore apply to both. Necoth has unfortunately been rendered *spicery.* This it is not likely to have meant, at least in the present sense of the term, for such commodities were not likely to be transported into Egypt from Gilead, though many Eastern products were, no doubt, carried north by caravans into Asia Minor, up the Euphrates, and by Palmyra into Syria. In the present case, however, all the articles mentioned seem to be products indigenous in Syria. But it is necessary to attend strictly to the original names, for we are apt to be misled by the English translation. Thus, in Gen. xxxvii:25, we read, 'Behold a company of

Ishmaelites came from Gilead with their camels, bearing *spicery* (*necoth*), and balm (*tzeri*), and myrrh (*loth*), going to carry it down to Egypt.' To these men Joseph was sold by his brethren, when they were feeding their flocks at Dothan, supposed to be a few miles to the north of Sebaste, or Samaria. It is curious that Jacob, when desiring a present to be taken to the ruler of Egypt, enumerates nearly the same articles (Gen. xliii:11), 'Carry down the man a present, a little balm, (*tzeri*), and a little honey (*debash*), spices (*necoth*) and myrrh (*loth*)

Bochart (*Hierozoicon,* ii Bk. iv. c. 12) enters into a learned exposition of the meaning of *necoth,* of which Dr. Harris has given an abridged view in his article on spices.

(2) **Various Interpretations.** Bochart shows that the true import of *necoth* has always been considered uncertain, for it is rendered *wax* by the paraphrast Jonathan, in the Arabic version of Erpenius, and in Beresith Rabba (sect. 91, near the end). Others interpret it very differently. The Septuagint renders it Θυμίαμα, *perfume,* Aquila *storax,* the Syrian version *resin,* the Samaritan *balsam,* one Arabic version *khurnoob* or *carob,* another *sumugha* (or gum), Kimchi a *desirable thing.* Rabbi Selomo *a collection of several aromatics.* Bochart himself considers it to mean *storax.* Rosenmüller, in his *Bib. Bot.* p. 165, Eng. transl., adopts *tragacanth* as the meaning of *necoth,* without expressing any doubt on the subject. Tragacanth is an exudation from several species of the genus *Astragalus,* and subdivision *tragacantha,* which is produced in Crete, but chiefly in Northern Persia and in Koordistan in the latter province. Dr. Dickson, of Tripoli, saw large quantities of it collected from plants, of which he preserved specimens, and gave them to Mr. Brant, British consul at Erzeroum, by whom they were sent to Dr. Lindley. One of these, yielding the best tragacanth, proved to be *A. gummifer* of Labillardière. It was found by him on Mount Lebanon, where he ascertained that tragacanth was collected by the shepherds. It might therefore have been conveyed by Ishmaelites from Gilead to Egypt. It has in its favor, that it is a produce of the remote parts of Syria, is described by ancient authors, as Theophrastus, Dioscorides, etc., and has always been highly esteemed as a gum in Eastern countries; it was, therefore, very likely to be an article of commerce to Egypt in ancient times. (See MYRRH; STORAX.)
J. F. R.

NECROMANCER (něk-rŏ-măn'sēr), (from Gr. ν=κρός, *nek-ros'*, the dead, and μαντεία, *man-tee'ah,* divination; Heb. דֹּרֵשׁ אֶל־הַמֵּתִים, *do'rashe el-hammay' theem',* one who inquires of the dead). (See DIVINATION).

NEDABIAH (něd'a-bī'ah), (Heb. נְדַבְיָה, *ned-ab-yaw',* largess of Jah), the eighth son of Jeconiah, in the line of David (1 Chron. iii:18), B. C. about 560.

NEEDLE (nē'd'l), (Gr. ῥαφίς, *hraf-ece'*), occurs in Scripture only in the proverb, "It is easier for a camel to go through the eye of a needle," etc. (Matt. xix:24; Mark x:25; Luke xviii:25). G. M. Mackie, Hastings' *Bib. Dict.,* says:

"An attempt is sometimes made to explain the *needle's eye* as a reference to the small door, a little over 2 feet square in the large heavy gate of a walled city. This mars the figure without materially altering the meaning. There is no custom of calling this small opening 'the eye'; it is usually named 'the small door' 'hole' or 'window.'" (See CAMEL.)

NEEDLEWORK (nē'd'lwûrk), (Heb. רִקְמָה, *rik-maw'*, finely embroidered or variegated work; רֹקֵם, *rok-ame'*, Exod. xxvi:36; xxvii:16; xxviii:39; xxxvi:37; xxxviii:18; Judg. v:30; Ps. xlv:14, a species of weaving). (See EMBROIDERER; WEAVING.)

NEEDY (nē'dȳ). See POOR.

NEESING (nēz'ĭng), (Heb. עֲטִישָׁה, *at-ee-shaw'*). Job xli:18, "By his neesings a light doth shine." *Neesing* is the older form of the word now written *sneezing*. The Anglo-Saxon verb was *niesan*, so that the old form is really nearer the original.

"And waxen in their mirth to *neese* and swear
A merrier hour was never wasted there."
Shakespeare.

"What a *neesing* brake
From my Telemachus."
(Chapman, *Odyssey*, xix:732, 736.)

NEGINAH (nĕg'in-ah), (Ps. lxi). See NEGINIOTH.

NEGINIOTH (nĕg-in'ĭ-oth), (Heb. נְגִינָה, *neg-ee-nawth'*), a word which occurs in the titles of several Psalms. It is a plural form of Neginah, and signifies stringed instruments of music, to be played on by the fingers. The titles of these Psalms may be translated, A Psalm of David to the master of music, who presides over the stringed instruments. (See PSALMS, BOOK OF.)

NEHELAMITE (ne-hĕl'a-mīte), (Heb. הַנֶּחֱלָמִי, *han-nekh-el-aw-mee'*, dreamed), a designation of the false prophet Shemaiah (Jer. xxix:24, 31, 32), derived from his native place or from an ancestor.

NEHEMIAH (nē-he-mī'ah), (Heb. נְחֶמְיָה, *nekh-em-yaw'*, comforted of Jehovah).

1. The Jewish patriot, whose genealogy is unknown, except that he was the son of Hachaliah (Neh. i:1), and brother of Hanani (Neh. vii:2). Some think he was of priestly descent, because his name appears at the head of a list of priests in Neh. x:1-8; but it is obvious, from Neh. ix:38, that he stands there as a prince, and not as a priest; that he heads the list because he was head of the nation. Others with some probability infer, from his station at the Persian court and the high commission he received, that he was, like Zerubbabel, of the tribe of Judah and of the house of David (Carpzov, *Introductio,* etc., P. i, 339).

(1) Appointed Governor. While Nehemiah was cupbearer in the royal palace at Shushan, in the twentieth year of Artaxerxes Longimanus, or 444 years B. C., (see ARTAXERXES), he learned the mournful and desolate condition of the returned colony in Judæa. This filled him with such deep and prayerful concern for his country, that his sad countenance revealed to the king his 'sorrow of heart'; which induced the monarch to ascertain the cause, and also to vouchsafe the remedy, by sending him, with full powers, to rebuild the wall of Jerusalem, and 'to seek the welfare of the children of Israel.' Being furnished with this high commission, and enjoying the protection of a military escort (chapter ii:9), Nehemiah reached Jerusalem in the year B. C. 444, and remained there till B. C. 432, being actively engaged for twelve years in promoting the public good (chapter v:14). The principal work which he then accomplished was the rebuilding, or rather the repairing, of the city wall, which was done 'in fifty and two days' (chapter vi:15), notwithstand-

ing many discouragements and difficulties. These were caused chiefly by Sanballat, a Moabite of Horonaim, and Tobiah, an Ammonite, who were leading men in the rival and unfriendly colony of Samaria (chapter iv:1-3). These men, with their allies among the Arabians, Ammonites, and Ashdodites (chapter iv:7), sought to hinder the refortifying of Jerusalem, first by scoffing at the attempt; then by threatening to attack the workmen —which Nehemiah averted by 'setting a watch against them day and night,' and arming the whole people, so that 'every one with one of his hands wrought in the work, and with the other hand held a weapon' (chapter iv:7-18); and finally, when scoffs and threats had failed, by using various stratagems to weaken Nehemiah's authority, and even to take his life (chapter vi:1-14).

(2) Meets Hindrances. But in the midst of these dangers from without, our patriot encountered troubles and hindrances from his own people, arising out of the general distress, which was aggravated by the cruel exactions and oppression of their nobles and rulers, (chapter v:1-5). These popular grievances were promptly redressed on the earnest and solemn remonstrance of Nehemiah, who had himself set a striking example of retrenchment and generosity in his high office (chapter v:6-19). It appears also (chapter vi: 17-19) that some of the chief men in Jerusalem were at that time in conspiracy with Tobiah against Nehemiah. The wall was thus built in 'troublous times' (Dan. ix:25); and its completion was most joyously celebrated by a solemn dedication under Nehemiah's direction (chapter xii:27-43).

(3) Reforms. Having succeeded in fortifying the city, our reformer turned his attention to other measures in order to secure its good government and prosperity. He appointed some necessary officers (chapter vii:1-3; also chapter xii:44-47), and excited among the people more interest and zeal in religion by the public reading and exposition of the law (chapter viii:1-12), by the unequaled celebration of the Feast of Tabernacles (chapter viii:13-18), and by the observance of a national fast, when the sins of the people and the iniquities of their fathers were publicly and most strikingly confessed (chapter ix), and when also a solemn covenant was made by all ranks and classes 'to walk in God's law' by avoiding intermarriages with the heathen, by strictly observing the Sabbath, and by contributing to the support of the temple service (chapter x). But the inhabitants of the city were as yet too few to defend it and to ensure its prosperity; and hence Nehemiah brought one out of every ten in the country to take up his abode in the ancient capital which then presented so few inducements to the settler, that 'the people blessed all the men that willingly offered themselves to dwell at Jerusalem' (chapter vii:4; also chapter xi:1-19).

(4) Assisted by Ezra. In these important public proceedings, which appear all to have happened in the first year of his government, Nehemiah enjoyed the assistance of Ezra, who is named on several occasions as taking a prominent part in conducting affairs (chapters viii:1, 9, 13; xii:36). Ezra had gone up to Jerusalem thirteen years before according to some, or thirty-three years according to others; but on either reckoning, without supposing unusual longevity, he might well have lived to be Nehemiah's fellow-laborer. (See EZRA).

(5) Return to Babylon. Nehemiah, at the close of his successful administration, 'from the twentieth year even to the thirty-second year of

Artaxerxes the king' (chapter v:14), returned to Babylon (B. C. 432), and resumed, as some think, his duties as royal cupbearer.

(6) **Again at Jerusalem.** He returned, however, after a while, to Jerusalem, where his services became again requisite, in consequence of abuses that had crept in during his absence. His stay at the court of Artaxerxes was not very long (certainly not above nine years); 'for after certain days he obtained leave of the king and came to Jerusalem' (chapter xiii:6, 7).

After his return to the government of Judæa, Nehemiah enforced the separation of all the mixed multitude from Israel (chapter xiii:1-3); and accordingly expelled Tobiah the Ammonite from the chamber which the high-priest, Eliashib, had prepared for him in the temple (chapter xiii:4-9). Better arrangements were also made for the support of the temple service (chapter xiii:10-14), and for the rigid observance of the Sabbath (chapter xiii:15-22). One of the last acts of his government was an effort to put an end to mixed marriages, which led him to 'chase' away a son of Joiada the high-priest, because he was son-in-law to Sanballat the Horonite (chapter xiii:23-29). The duration of this second administration cannot be determined; only it is evident that Joiada was high-priest during that period. Now Joiada, according to some chronologists, succeeded his father Eliashib in the year B. C. 413; and hence we may gather that Nehemiah's second rule lasted at least ten years, namely, from B. C. 424 to 413. It is not unlikely that he remained at his post till about the year B. C. 405, towards the close of the reign of Darius Nothus, who is mentioned in chapter xii:22. (See DARIUS.)

(7) **Death.** At this time Nehemiah would be between sixty and seventy years old, if we suppose him (as most do) to have been only between twenty and thirty when he first went to Jerusalem. That he lived to be an old man is thus quite probable from the sacred history; and this is expressly declared by Josephus, who (*Antiq.* xi:5, 6) states that he died at an advanced age. Of the place and year of death nothing is known.

(8) **Character.** Few men in any age of the world have combined in themselves a more rigid adherence to duty, a sterner opposition to wrong, private or public, a more unswerving faith in God, or a purer patriotism, than Nehemiah. His character seems almost without a blemish.

2. The son of Azbuk (Neh. iii:16), respecting whom no more is known than that he was ruler in Beth-zur (B. C. 445), and took a prominent part in repairing the wall of Jerusalem. (See BETH-ZUR.)

3. Another Nehemiah is mentioned (Ezra ii:2; Neh. vii:7) among those who accompanied Zerubbabel on the first return from captivity (B. C. 445). Nothing further is known of this man, though some writers (see Carpzov, *Introd. ad Lib. Bib. Vet. Testamenti*, P. i, 340, *sq.*) hold him, without valid reasons, to be the same with the well-known Jewish patriot.

NEHEMIAH, BOOK OF (nē'he-mī'ah bŏŏk ŏv), the sixteenth in the order of books in the Old Testament.

(1) **Name.** It bears the title *Nehemiah's Words*, and was anciently connected with Ezra, as if it formed part of the same work (Eichhorn, *Einleitung*, ii, 627). This connection is still indicated by its first words, '*And* it came to pass.' It arose, doubtless, from the fact that Nehemiah is a sort of continuation of Ezra. (See EZRA.)

(2) **Contents.** The work can scarcely be called a history of Nehemiah and his times. It is rather a collection of notices of some important transactions that happened during the first year of his government, with a few scraps from his later history. The contents appear to be arranged in chronological order, with the exception perhaps of ch. xii:27-43, where the account of the dedication of the wall seems out of its proper place; we might expect it rather after ch. vii:1-4, where the completion of the wall is mentioned.

The book is concerned with Nehemiah's great work of rebuilding Jerusalem and the reclamation of the customs and laws of Moses, which had fallen into desuetude. It gives the whole history of this movement in the circumstances which led to it, the elements of opposition which threatened to defeat it, and the complete success which crowned it. Incidentally we are admitted to a glance at the condition, moral and political, of the Jews, at the growing bitterness between them and the Samaritans, and at some scenes in Assyrian life. The account of the walls and gates in ch. iii is among the most valuable documents for the settlement of the topography of ancient Jerusalem. The registers and lists of names are also of value.

(3) **Date.** As to the date of the book, it is not likely that it came from Nehemiah's hand till near the close of his life. Certainly it could not have been all written before the expulsion of the priest, recorded in ch. xiii:23-29, which took place about the year B. C. 413.

(4) **Authorship.** While the book, as a whole, is considered to have come from Nehemiah, it consists in part of compilation. He doubtless wrote the greater part himself, but some portions he evidently took from other works. It is allowed by all that he is, in the strictest sense, the author of the narrative from ch. i to ch. vii:5 (Hävernick, *Einleitung*, ii, 304). The account in ch. vii: 6-73 is avowedly compiled, for he says in ver. 5, 'I found a register,' etc. This register we actually find also in Ezra ii:1-70; hence it might be thought that our author borrowed this part from Ezra; but it is more likely that they both copied from public documents, such as 'the book of the chronicles,' mentioned in Neh. xii:23.

Chapters viii-x were probably not written by Nehemiah, since the narrative respecting him is in the third person (ch. viii:9; x:1), and not in the first as usual (ch. ii:9-20). Hävernick, indeed, (*Einleitung*, ii:305-308) makes it appear, from the contents and style, that Ezra was the writer of this portion. The remaining chapters (xi-xiii) also exhibit some marks of compilation (ch. xii: 26, 47); but there are, on the contrary, clear proofs of Nehemiah's own authorship in ch. xii: 27-43, and in ch. xiii:6-31; and hence Hävernick thinks he wrote the whole except ch. xii:1-26, which he took from 'the book of the chronicles,' mentioned in verse 23.

The mention of Jaddua as a high-priest, in ch. xii:11, 22, has occasioned much perplexity. This Jaddua appears to have been in office in B. C. 332, when Alexander the Great came to Jerusalem (Joseph. *Antiq.* xi:8); how then could he be named by Nehemiah? The common, and perhaps the readiest, escape from this difficulty is to regard the naming of Jaddua as an addition by a later hand. Yet it is just credible that Nehemiah wrote it, if we bear in mind that he lived to be an old man, so as possibly to see the year B. C. 370; and if we further suppose that Jaddua had at that time entered on his office, so that he filled it for about forty years, *i. e.* till B. C. 332. In support of this conjecture, see especially Hävernick's *Einleitung*, ii:320-324. B. D.

L. W. Batten, in Hastings' *Bib. Dict.*, says: "There can be little doubt that the final editor of Ezra-Nehemiah was the author of the Book of Chronicles. He gathered material and prepared a history written according to his own point of view from Adam to Nehemiah. His work was one long piece, Ezra-Nehemiah being a part of Chronicles. But the latter had a considerable struggle to get into the canon."

NEHILOTH (nē'hi-lŏth), (Ps. v), (Heb. נְחִילוֹת, *nekh-ee-loth'*, means wind instruments).

The title of the fifth Psalm may be thus translated, "A Psalm of David, addressed to the master of music presiding over the wind instruments." (See PSALMS, BOOK OF.)

NEHUM (nē'hum), (Heb. נָחוּם, *neh-khoom'*, consoled).

One of the twelve heads of the Jewish community and one of those who returned from the captivity with Zerubbabel (Neh. vii:7), B. C. about 445. The name appears in 1 Esdras v:8, as Roimus.

NEHUSHTA (ne-hŭsh'tà), (Heb. נְחֻשְׁתָּא, *nekh-oosh-taw'*, brass), the daughter of Elnathan of Jerusalem and the mother of King Jehoiachin (2 Kings xxiv:8), B. C. about 616.

NEHUSHTAN (ne-hŭsh'tan), (Heb. נְחֻשְׁתָּן, *nekh-oosh-tawn'*, made of copper), a name given by Hezekiah, king of Judah, to the brazen serpent that Moses had set up in the wilderness (Num. xxi:8), and which had been preserved by the Israelites to that time.

The superstitious people having made an idol of this serpent, Hezekiah caused it to be burnt, and in derision gave it the name of *Nehushtan*—this little brazen serpent (2 Kings xviii:4).

NEIEL (ne-i'el), (Heb. נְעִיאֵל, *neh-ee-ale'*, dwelling-place of God), a village of Asher near the southeastern boundary (Josh. xix:27). Not identified.

NEIGH (nā), (Heb. צָהַל, *tsaw-hal'*, to sound clear), Jer. viii:16; xiii:27; l:11, A. V., "bellow as bulls"; marg. *neigh as steeds*; R. V., *neigh as strong horses.*

Figuratively used to indicate lustful desire in Jer. v:8, of one who "neighed after his neighbor's wife."

NEIGHBOR (nā'bẽr), (Heb. רֵעַ, *ray'ah*, associate; Gr. πλησίον, *play-see'on*, near), signifies a near relation, a fellow countryman, one of the same tribe or vicinage; and generally, any man connected with us by the bonds of humanity, and whom charity requires that we should consider as a friend and relation (Deut. v:20).

At the time of our Savior, the Pharisees had restrained the meaning of the word neighbor to those of their own nation, or to their own friends; holding, that to hate their enemy was not forbidden by the law (Matt. v:43; Luke x:27). But our Lord informed them, that the whole world were neighbors, and illustrated the proposition in the parable of the Good Samaritan who helped the wounded Jew in spite of the bitter feeling existing between the Samaritans and the Jews.

It was because neighborhood was almost exclusively the condition of social contact that the neighbor was specified in connection with the Mosaic provisions of mercy, truth and justice. The stranger was guarded by the law of hospitality. (G. M. Mackie, Hastings' *Bib. Dict.*)

NEKEB (nē'keb), (Heb. נֶקֶב, *neh'keb*, a cavern), a town on the boundary of Naphtali (Josh. xix:33).

The R. V. joins the name with the word preceding, making it *Adami-nekeb*. This name is found, in a corrupt form, of a ruin about three miles northwest of the outlet of the Sea of Galilee.

NEKODA (ne-kō'dà), (Heb. נְקוֹדָא, *nek-o-daw'*, distinguished).

1. The founder of a family of Temple servants, who returned from the captivity with Zerubbabel (Ezra ii:48; Neh. vii:50), B. C. 535.

2. A progenitor of certain persons who after the return from captivity had lost their pedigree (Ezra ii:60; Neh. vii:62), probably the same as 1.

NEMUEL (ne-mū'el), (Heb. נְמוּאֵל, *nem-oo-ale'*, God is spreading, or day of God).

1. A son of Simeon and head of the Nemuelites (Num. xxvi:12), called JEMUEL (Gen. xlvi:10).

2. A Reubenite, son of Eliab and brother of Dathan and Abiram (Num. xxvi:9), B. C. about 1619.

NEMUELITES (ne-mū'el-ītes), (Heb. נְמוּאֵלִי, *nem-oo-ale-ee'*), descendants of Nemuel, son of Simeon (Num. xxvi:12).

NEPHEG (nē'pheg), (Heb. נֶפֶג, *neh'feg*, sprout).

1. One of the sons of Izhar, the son of Kohath (Exod. vi:21).

2. The ninth of David's sons, born to him in Jerusalem (2 Sam. v:15; 1 Chron. iii:7; xiv:6), B. C. after 1000.

NEPHEW (nĕf'ū), is the rendering of Heb. בֵּן, *bane*, Judg. xii:14; נֶכֶד, *neh'ked*, offspring, Job xviii:19; Is. xiv:22; Gr. ἔκγονον, *ek'gon-on*, 1 Tim. v:4; in the old English sense of *grandson* or *descendant.*

"If any widow have children or *nephews*, let them learn first to show piety at home, and to requite their parents" (1 Tim. v:4).

In our present use the word *nephew* is confined to the *son of a brother* or of a *sister;* but formerly it had a less strict meaning, and might denote a *grandson* or even a more remote relation. In the above passage 'children or *nephews*' means, 'children or *grandchildren.'*

Nephew comes to us through the French *neveu*, from the Latin *nepos.*

In the Augustan age *nepos* meant 'grandson'; in the post-Augustan age, sister's or brother's son.

Our word *nepotism,* from *nepos,* and meaning *family favoritism,* retains the original wide signification.

"The warts, black moles, spots and freckles of fathers, not appearing at all upon their children's skin, begin afterwards to put forth and show themselves in their *nephews,* to-wit, the children of their sons and daughters" (Holland's *Translation of Plutarch's Morals.*) (See Swinton's *Bib. Word Book;* Hastings' *Bib. Dict.*)

NEPHILIM (nē'phĭl-ĭm), (Heb. נְפִילִים, *nef-ee-leem'*, Gen. vi:4; Num. xiii:33). See GIANTS.

NEPHISH (nē'phish), (1 Chron. v:19). See NAPHISH.

NEPHISHESIM (ne-phĭsh'e-sĭm), (Heb. נְפוּשְׁסִים, *nef-oo-shes-eem'*, Neh. vii:52). See NEPHUSIM.

NEPHTALIM (neph'ta-lĭm), (Gr. Νεφθαλείμ, *nef-thal-eim'*), the country and tribe of *Naphtali* (Matt. iv:13, 15; Rev. vii:6). (See NAPHTALI.)

NEPHTOAH (nĕph'to-ah), (Heb. נֶפְתּוֹחַ, *nef-to'-akh*, opened).

The name of a place with a fountain and stream of water on the boundary of Judah and Benjamin, west of Jerusalem (Josh. xv:9; xviii:15). It is commonly located at 'Ain Lifta, two miles northwest of Jerusalem, though Porter (*Handbook,* p. 232) places it at 'Ain Yalo, three miles southwest of Jerusalem.

NEPHUSIM (ne-phū'sim), (Heb. נְפִיסִים, *nef-ee-seem'*, expansions), founder of a family of Temple servants who returned from the Captivity with Zerubbabel (Ezra ii:50), B. C. about 535. In Neh. vii:52 the form is *Nephishesim.*

NER (nĕr), (Heb. נֵר, *nare*, a light; Sept. Νήρ, *nare*), grandfather of King Saul (1 Sam. xiv:50, 51; xxvi:5 1 Chron. viii:33). The statement in 1 Chron. ix:36, that Kish and Ner were both sons of *Jeiel* (A V. Jehiel), is explained by the supposition of an elder Kish, uncle of Saul's father, or, rather, Ner's grandfather (B. C. 1140).

J. F. Stenning, Hastings' *Bib. Dict.,* makes Ner the son of Abiel, the father of Abner, and therefore the uncle of Saul (1 Sam. xiv:50, 51). We must render the passage, 'And Kish, the father of Saul, and Ner, the father of Abner, were sons of Abiel.'

NERD or NARD (nĕrd ôr närd), (Heb. נֵרְדְּ, *nayrd*), is mentioned in three places in the Song of Solomon, and by Mark and John in the New Testament, under the name of νάρδος, *nardos, spikenard* or *nerd.*

(1) Spikenard. Both are translated in the Authorized Version by the word *spikenard,* which indicates a far-famed perfume of the East, that has often engaged the attention of critics, but the plant which yields it has only been ascertained in very recent times. That the *nerd* of Scripture was a perfume is evident from the passages in which it occurs. Cant. i: 12: 'While the king sitteth at his table, my spikenard (nard) sendeth forth the smell thereof.' So in Cant. iv:14: 'Spikenard and saffron, calamus and cinnamon, with all trees of frankincense, myrrh and aloes, with all the chief spices.' Here we find it mentioned along with many of the most valued aromatics which were known to the ancients, and all of which, with the exception perhaps of saffron, must have been obtained by foreign commerce from distant countries, as Persia, the east coast of Africa, Ceylon, the northwest and the southeast of India, and in the present instance even from the remote Himalayan mountains. Such substances must necessarily have been costly when the means of communication

Nard.

were defective, and the gains of the successful merchant proportionately great.

(2) Costly. That the nard or νάρδος was of great value we learn from the New Testament (Mark xiv:3). When our Savior sat at meat in Bethany, 'there came a woman having an alabaster box of ointment of (νάρδου) *spikenard* very precious; and she brake the box, and poured it on his head.' So in John xii:3: 'Then took Mary a pound of *ointment of spikenard,* very costly, and anointed the feet of Jesus, and wiped his feet with her hair; and the house was filled with the odor of the ointment.' On this Judas, who afterwards betrayed our Savior, said (verse 5), 'Why was not this ointment sold for three hundred pence, and given to the poor?' This spikenard probably cost the devoted woman about £12, or $62.50.

(3) Possible Identification. The *nard,* νάρδος, was known in very early times, and is noticed by Theophrastus, and by Hippocrates. There can be no doubt that the *jatamansi* of the Hindoos is the *sunbul hindee* of the Arabs, which they compare to the tail of an ermine. This would almost be sufficient to identify the drug. As many Indian products found their way into Egypt and Palestine, and are mentioned in Scripture, indeed in the very passage with nard we have calamus, cinnamon, and aloes (*ahalim*), there is no reason why spikenard from the Himalayas could not as easily have been procured. The only difficulty appears to arise from the term νάρδος, nard, having occasionally been used in a general sense, and therefore there is sometimes confusion between the nard and the sweet cane (*Kaneh-bosem*), another Indian product. Some difference of opinion exists respecting the fragrance of the *jatamansi;* it may be sufficient to state that it continues to be highly esteemed in Eastern countries in the present day, where fragrant essences are still procured from it, as the *unguentum nardinum* was of old. J. F. R.

NEREUS (nē'reūs), (Gr. Νηρεύς, *nare-yoos'*, wet), a Christian living at Rome, to whom Paul sent salutations (Rom. xvi:15), A. D. 55.

The name is found in the inscriptions of the imperial household and is well known in the legends of the Roman church. (*Acta Sanctorum* Bull. *Arch. Christ.* 1874, p. 20; 1875, p. 8; Lightfoot, *Clement,* i, p. 51; A. C. Headlam, Hastings' *Bib. Dict.*)

NERGAL (nĕr'gal), (Heb. נֵרְגַל, *nare-gal'*, a great hero), a deity of the Cuthites (2 Kings xvii:30).

The Rabbinical commentators believe that this idol was in the form of a cock; founding their not very happy conjecture apparently upon the fact that in the Talmud the similar word *tarnegol* means a cock. The more measured researches of Norberg, Gesenius, and other inquirers into the astrolatry of the Assyrians and Chaldeans, lead to the conclusion that *nare-gal'* is the same as the Zabian name for the planet Mars. This name of the planet, both among the Zabians and Arabians means *ill-luck, misfortune;* and it was by no means peculiar to the mythology of the West to make it the symbol of bloodshed and war. Among the people first named, the planet Mars was typified under the figure of a man holding in one hand a drawn sword, and in the other a human head just cut off; and his garments were also red, which, as well as the other ideas attached to this idol, were no doubt founded on the reddish hue which the body of the planet presents to the eye. Among the southern Arabs his temple was painted red; and they offered to him garments stained with blood, and also a warrior (probably a prisoner), who was cast into a pool.

NERGAL-SHAREZER (nẽr'gal-sha-rē'zer). (Heb. נֵרְגַל שַׁרְאֶצֶר, *nare-gal'shar-eh-tser'*, perh, Nergal, prince of fire),

1. A military chieftain under Nebuchadnezzar (Jer. xxxix:3).

2. The chief of the magi (Rab-mag) under the same king, and present in the same expedition (Jer. xxxix:3, 13).

He is generally identified with Neriglissar of profane history, who married Nebuchadnezzar's daughter, and ascended the throne two years after that monarch's death. A palace built by him has been discovered among the ruins of Babylon, and his name found on bricks.

In the Biblical description of the end of the reign of Sennacherib he is said to have been killed by his two sons, Adrammelech and Sharezer (2 Kings xix:37; Is. xxxvii:38). There is little doubt that this name Sharezer is simply the latter part of the name Nergal-sharezer.

The name is given by Abydemus as Nergilos, so that the Old Testament has preserved the latter half of his name and the Greek historian the first half. Abbreviations of names in this manner are common among Assyrians and Babylonians. The Assyrian story of the death of Sennacherib is much more brief in its details, and does not mention the names of his murderers. It is as follows: "On the twentieth day of Tebet, Sennacherib, king of Assyria, was killed by his son during an insurrection. . . . From the twentieth day of Tebet to the second day of Adar, the insurrection continued, and on the eighteenth day of Sivan (of the following year) Esarhaddon ascended the throne." It will be observed that in this account the death of Sennacherib is ascribed to the act of one son, and not to two, as in the Old Testament. There has not yet been found any further allusion to the matter in the inscriptions. It is a probable conjecture that the death of the Assyrian king was due to the jealousy felt for his son Esarhaddon, who succeeded him (Barnes, *Bib. Dict.*)

A. H. Sayce, Hastings' *Bib. Dict.*, inclines to the belief that the supposed two persons are the same individual. He says: "It is hardly doubtful that the Nergal-sharezer who, in Jeremiah, occupies a place so near Nebuchadnezzar, is the Nergal-sharezer who subsequently became king of Babylon. Nergal-sharezer was the son of Belsum-iskum, to whom, in one of his son's inscriptions, is erroneously given the title of king. In B. C. 559 Evil merodach was murdered and Nergal-sharezer seized the throne, which he held for four years."

NERI (nē'rī), (Gr. Νηρί, *nay-ree'*), son of Melchi and father of Salathiel in the genealogy of Christ (Luke iii:27, 28); probably the same as NERIAH (which see) (Jer. li:59).

NERIAH (ne-rī'ah), (Heb. נֵרִיָּה, *nay-ree-yah'*, Jah is light). The son of Maaseiah and father of Seraiah and Baruch (Jer. xxxii:12; xxxvi:4; li:59); probably identical with NERI (Luke iii:27, 28), B. C. about 620.

NERO (nē'rō), (2 Tim., *subscription*), a Roman emperor, born at Antium, probably December 15, A. D. 37 was the son of Cneius Domitius Ahenobarbus by Agrippina, the sister of Caligula, his original name being Lucius Domitius Ahenobarbus.

In the first part of his reign he showed great clemency and justice, pretending to copy after Augustus. In the end of it he became one of the most tyrannical and licentious wretches that ever breathed. He murdered his mother, and almost all his friends and principal subjects. He was the great patron of all fooleries and debaucheries. He is not named in Scripture; but he is indicated by his title of emperor, and by his surname Cæsar. To him St. Paul appealed after his imprisonment by Felix, and his examination by Festus, who was swayed by the Jews. St. Paul was therefore carried to Rome, where he arrived A. D. 61. Here he continued two years, preaching the gospel with freedom, till he became famous even in the emperor's court, in which were many Christians; for he salutes the Philippians in the name of the brethren who were of the household of Cæsar, that is, of Nero's court (Phil. i:12, 13; iv:22). We have no particular information how he cleared himself from the accusations of the Jews, whether by answering before Nero, or whether his enemies dropped their prosecutions, which seems probable (Acts xxviii:21). However, it appears that he was liberated in the year 63.

Nero, the most cruel and savage of all men, and also the most wicked and depraved, began his persecution against the Christian church A. D. 64, on pretense of the burning of Rome, of which some have thought himself to be the author. He endeavored to throw all the odium on the Christians; those were seized first that were known publicly as such, and by their means many others were discovered. They were condemned to death, and were even insulted in their sufferings. Some were sewed up in the skins of beasts, and then exposed to dogs to be torn in pieces; some were nailed to crosses; others perished by fire. The latter were sewed up in pitched coverings, which, being set on fire, served as torches to the people, and were lighted up in the night. Nero gave leave to use his own gardens as the scene of all these cruelties. From this time edicts were published against the Christians, and many martyrs suffered, especially in Italy. St. Peter and St. Paul are thought to have suffered martyrdom, consequent on this persecution, A. D. 65.

The revolt of the Jews from the Romans happened about A. D. 65 and 66, in the twelfth and thirteenth of Nero. The city of Jerusalem making an insurrection, A. D. 66, Florus there slew 3,600 persons, and thus began the war. A little while afterwards, those of Jerusalem killed the Roman garrison. Cestius on this came to Jerusalem to suppress the sedition; but he was forced to retire after having besieged it about six weeks, and was routed in his retreat, A. D. 66. About the end of the same year, Nero gave Vespasian the command of his troops against the Jews. This general carried on the war in Galilee and Judea during A. D. 67 and 68, the thirteenth and fourteenth of Nero. But Nero killing himself in the fourteenth year of his reign, Jerusalem was not besieged till after his death, A. D. 70, the first and second years of Vespasian's reign.

NESER (nē'ser). See EAGLE.

NEST (něst), (Heb. קֵן, *kane*, from קָנַן, *kaw-nan'*, to build; Gr. κατασκήνωσις, *kat-as-kay'no-sis*, encampment, a perch).

1. A small lodgment, where fowls hatch their young (Deut. xxii:6).

2. The eggs or young birds in a nest (Deut. xxii:11; Is. x:14).

Figurative. (1) A habitation seemingly very secure and undisturbed (Jer. xlix:16; Obad. 4; Hab. ii:9). (2) *"To die in one's nest"* (Job xxix:18) seems to mean in the bosom of one's family, with children to succeed him. (3) The Assyrians, Amorites, and other nations are likened to *cedars* in whose boughs all the fowls of heaven made their nests to mark their great strength, pride, and prosperity (Ezek. xxxi:6). (4) A *'nest in cedars,'* is houses built of cedar wood (Jer. xxii:23). (5) The figure of the partridge "gathering young which she hath not brought forth" (Jer. xvii:11, marg.) is applied to one who wrongfully gathers riches. (6) The robbing of a nest in the absence of the parent birds is symbolical of an easy victory (Is. x:14).

NET (nĕt), (Heb. חֶרֶם, *kheh-rem'*, a net, snare, harm).

There are in Scripture several words denoting different kinds of nets, and this, with the frequency of images derived from them, shows that nets were much in use among the Hebrews for fishing, hunting, and fowling. Indeed, for the two latter purposes, nets were formerly used to an extent of which now, since the invention of firearms, a notion can scarcely be formed.

(1) Fishing Nets. We have no positive information concerning the nets of the Hebrews, and can only suppose that they were not materially different from those of the ancient Egyptians, concerning which we now possess very good information. Indeed, the nets of Egypt, the fishers who used them, and the fish caught by them, are more than once mentioned in Scripture (Is. xix: 8). The usual fishing net among this people was of a long form, like the common drag-net, with wooden floats on the upper, and leads on the lower side. It was sometimes let down from a boat, but those who pulled it usually stood on the shore, and landed the fish on a shelving bank. This mode, however, was more adapted to river than to lake fishing; and hence, in all the detailed examples of fishing in the New Testament, the net is cast from and drawn into boats, excepting in one case where, the draft being too great to take into the boat, the fishers dragged the net after their boats to the shore (John xxi:6, 8). Sometimes use was made of a smaller net for catching fish in shallow water, furnished with a pole on either side, to which it was attached; and the fisherman, holding one of the poles in either hand, thrust it below the surface of the water, and awaited the moment when a shoal of fish passed over it.

It is interesting to observe that the fishermen in the boat, excepting the master, are almost naked, as are also those who have occcasion to wade in the water in hauling the net to the shore. Such seems also to have been the practice among his Hebrew fishermen; for Peter, when he left the boat to hasten on shore to his risen Lord, 'girt his fisher's coat unto him, for he was naked' (John xxi:7) ; although, in this case, the word 'naked' must be understood with some latitude. (See NAKED.)

(2) Nets for Birds. Nets were also used in taking birds, to an extent of which we can scarcely form an adequate conception. A clap net was usually employed. This was of different kinds. It consisted of two sides or frames, over which the net work was spread; at one end was a short net, which they fastened to a bush, or a cluster of reeds, and at the other was one of considerable length, which, as soon as the birds were seen feeding in the area within, was pulled by the fowlers, causing the instantaneous collapse of the two sides. In hunting, a space of considerable size was sometimes enclosed with nets, into which the animals were driven by beaters. The spots thus enclosed were usually in the vicinity of the water brooks to which they were in the habit of repairing in the morning and evening; and having awaited the time when they went to drink, the hunters disposed their nets, occupied proper positions for observing them unseen, and gradually closed in upon them. These practices are obviously alluded to in such passages as Job xix:6; Ps. cxl:5; Is. li:20.

Figurative. (1) God's "*net,*" is the entangling afflictions wherewith he chastises or punishes men (Job xix:6). Or the church; or the dispensation of the gospel, whereby many are drawn to Christ. This is cast into the sea of this world, and many are either really, or in appearance drawn by it. At last it will be emptied into the eternal state (Matt. xiii:47-50). (2) The "*net*" of wicked men wherewith they ensnare others, and draw wealth and power to themselves, is their crafty plots, and vigorously executed purposes of mischief (Ps. ix:15; cxl:5; Mic. vii:2; Hab. i:16). (3) The Jewish rulers and priests were a "*net,*" a means of drawing others into sin and ruin (Hos. v:1). 'In vain *the net is spread in the sight of any bird;*' without cause, traps are laid to ensnare and destroy innocent persons (Prov. i:17). (See FISHHOOK.)

NETER (nē'tēr), (Heb. נֶתֶר, *neh'ther;* Sept. and Symmachus, νίτρον, *nit'ron;* Vulg. *nitrum;* English version 'niter'), occurs in Prov. xxv:20; Jer. ii:22; where the substance in question is described as effervescing with vinegar, and as being used in washing; neither of which particulars applies to what is now, by a misappropriation of this ancient name, called 'niter,' and which in modern usage means the saltpeter of commerce, but they both apply to the *natron* or true *nitrum* of the ancients.

The similarity of the names which is observable in this case is considered by Gesenius of great weight in a production of the East, the name of which usually passed with the article itself into Greece. Both Greek and Roman writers describe *natron* by the words given in the Sept. and Vulgate. Jerome, in his note on Prov. xxv:20, considers this to be the substance intended. Natron, though found in many parts of the East, has ever been one of the distinguishing natural productions of Egypt. This substance, according to Herodotus, was used by the Egyptians in the process of embalming (ii:76, 77). The principal natron lakes now found in Egypt, six in number, are situate in a barren valley about thirty miles westward of the Delta, where it both floats as a whitish scum upon the water, and is found deposited at the bottom in a thick incrustation, after the water is evaporated by the heat of summer. It is a natural mineral alkali, composed of the carbonate, sulphate, and muriate of soda, derived from the soil of that region. Forskal says that it is known by the name *atrun,* or *natrun,* that it effervesces with vinegar, and is used as a soap in washing linen, and by the bakers as yeast, and in cookery to assist in boiling meat, etc. (*Flora Ægyptiaco-Arabica,* Hauniæ, 1775, pp. 45, 46). Combined with oil it makes a harder and firmer soap than the vegetable alkali. (See BORITH.) The application of the name niter to saltpeter seems accounted for by the fact that the knowledge of natron, the true niter, was lost for many centuries in this country, till revived by the Hon. R. Boyle, who says he 'had had some of it brought to him from Egypt.' (See NITER.)   J. F. D.

NETHANEEL (ne-thăn'e-el), (Heb. נְתַנְאֵל, *neth-an-ale',* God gives).

1. Son of Zuar and prince of the tribe of Is-

sachar at the time of the exodus (Num. i:8; ii:5; vii:18, 23; x:15), B. C. 1657.

2. Brother of David and the fourth son of Jesse (1 Chron. ii:14), B. C. about 1070.

3. A priest who blew trumpets when David brought up the ark to Jerusalem (1 Chron. xv: 24), B. C. 1043.

4. A Levite, father of Shemaiah, the scribe (1 Chron. xxiv:6), B. C. before 1014.

5. Son of Obed-edom, and a porter in the Temple in the time of David (1 Chron. xxvi:4), B. C. about 1014.

6. One of the five whom Jehoshaphat sent to instruct the cities of Judah in the law (2 Chron. xvii:7), B. C. 912.

7. One of the chief Levites in the reign of Josiah (2 Chron. xxxv:9), B. C. 628.

8. A son of Pashur, who put away his foreign wife (Ezra x:22), B. C. 458.

9. A priest, head of the father's house in the time of Joiakim, the high priest (Neh. xii:21), B. C. about 446.

10. A son of a priest and brother of Zechariah, who blew a trumpet at the celebration dedicating the walls of Jerusalem (Neh. xii:36), B. C. 446. Perhaps the same as **9.**

NETHANIAH (nĕth'a-nī'ah), (Heb. נְתַנְיָה, *neth-an-yaw'*, given of Jehovah).

1. A son of Asaph, and head of the fifth division of Temple singers (1 Chron. xxv:2, 12), B. C. about 961.

2. One of the Levites sent by Jehoshaphat to instruct the cities of Judah in the law (2 Chron. xvii:8), B. C. about 869.

3. Son of Shelamiah and father of Jehudi (Jer. xxxvi:14), B. C. about 606.

4. A man of the family of Judah and father of the Ishmael who killed Gedaliah (2 Kings xxv: 23, 25; Jer. xl:8, 14, 15; xli:1, 2, 6, 7, 9, 10, 11, 12, 15, 16, 18), B. C. about 620.

NETHINIM (nĕth'i-nĭm), (Heb. נְתִין, *naw-theen'*, one given).

(1) Servants of the Temple. This name, which means 'the given,' or 'the devoted,' was applied to the servants of the temple, or temple slaves, who were under the Levites in the ministry of the tabernacle and temple.

(2) Origin and Duties. The first servants whom the Levites obtained were the Gibeonites, on whom devolved the very laborious services of fetching water and collecting wood (Josh. ix: 3-27). The number of such servants appears to have been increased by David; and it seems to have been then, when these servants ceased to be wholly Gibeonites, that Nethinim came into use as a proper name for the whole class (Ezra viii: 20). From that time forward they appear to have been no longer regarded or treated as slaves, but as the lowest order of the servants of the sanctuary; who, although in their origin foreigners and heathen, had doubtless embraced the Jewish religion. These did not all forget their relationship to the sanctuary during the Captivity. Some of them returned to their duties under the decree of Cyrus, and were placed in cities with the Levites (Neh. xi:3; Ezra ii:70; 1 Chron. ix:2).

(3) Number and Position. It was not to be expected that many of them would return to this humble station in Palestine, but 220 accompanied Ezra (Ezra viii:20), and 392 Zerubbabel (ii: 5, 8). The voluntary devotedness which was thus manifested by these persons considerably raised the station of the Nethinim, which was thenceforth regarded rather as honorable than degrading. Their number was, however, insufficient for the service of the temple; whence, as Josephus tells us (*De Bell. Jud.* ii. 17, 6), a festival, called Ξυλοφορία, Xylophoria, was established, in which the people, to supply the deficiency, were obliged to bring a certain quantity of wood to the temple for the use of the altar of burnt-offering.

NETOPHAH (ne-tō'phah), (Heb. נְטֹפָה, *net-o-faw'*, distillation), a town, apparently in Judah, the name of which occurs only in the catalogue of those who returned with Zerubbabel from the Captivity (Ezra ii:22; Neh. vii:26; 1 Esdr. v:18).

Netophah was really an old place. Two of David's guard, Maharai and Heldai (1 Chron. xxvii: 13, 15) were Netophathites. The "villages of the Netophathites" were the residence of the Levites (1 Chron. ix:16). Levites who inhabited these villages were singers (Neh. xii:28). From Neh. vii:26, the town seems to have been in the neighborhood, or closely connected with, Bethlehem. Van de Velde suggests *Antubeh*, two miles northeast of Bethlehem, as the site of Netophah. The Palestine Memoirs note ruins northeast of Bethlehem that were called Metoba, or *Khurbet Umm Tôba*, probably the same as *Antubeh* of Van de Velde, and Conder identifies them as ancient Netophah.

NETOPHATHI (ne-tŏph'a-thī), (Heb. נְטֹפָתִי, *net-o-faw'thee*, inhabitant of Netophah), an inhabitant of Netophah, called the son of Salma (Neh. xii:28), who probably founded the village (2 Sam. xxiii: 28, 29; Jer. xl:8).

NETOPHATHITE (ne-tŏph'a-thīte), (Heb. הַנְּטֹפָתִי, *han-net-o-faw-thee'*, 1 Chron. ii:54). See Netophathi.

NETTLE (net't'l). See Thorns and Thistles.

NETWORK (nĕt'wûrk').

1. (Heb. רֶשֶׁת, *reh'sheth*, net), a broad plate of brass, full of holes, in the manner of a sieve, that was fixed below the fire of the altar, and through which the ashes fell down.

2. (Heb. שְׂבָכָה, *seb-aw-kaw'*), the plaited work around the two court pillars of the temple (1 Kings vii:18, 20, 42). (See Temple.)

3. (Heb. חֹרִי, *khore*, white, Is. xix:9, marg. "white works"), the general name for cotton fabrics, or the different kinds of byssus that were woven in Egypt. (See Byssus.)

NETZ (nĕtz). See Hawk.

NEVER (nĕv'ẽr), (Gr. οὐδέ, *oo-deh'*, Matt. xxvii: 14). "He answered him to never a word," i. e., not at all, in any manner.

NEW, NEWNESS (nū, nū'nĕs), (Gr. καινότης, *kahee-not'ace*). New things or innovations were abhorrent to the people of the Orient, among whom many tendencies converge towards the veneration of use and wont. Of these the following are the most noteworthy:

(1) The uniformity of the rotation in seasons with corresponding climatic changes (Gen. viii: 22; 1 Sam. xii:16-18). (Unseasonable weather was an innovation.)

(2) The conservative influence of the patriarchal government.

(3) The transmission of the same handicraft from father to son, etc.

(4) The remaining upon the land of the inhabitants when it is sold.

(5) The religious conviction that whatever exists is by the will of God. Hence Orientals come to regard Custom as a principle of high authority and to regard whatever is new with profound surprise, etc. (G. M. Mackie, Hastings' *Bib. Dict.*).

Newness in general means different from or more excellent than what went before. Thus are *new* creatures, and have a *new spirit,* a *new heart,* and *all things new;* instead of the old corrupt and carnal views, and dispositions, and manner of life, they have spiritual knowledge, holy dispositions, and pious lives, springing from a conscience purified by the blood of Christ, and a heart actuated by his Spirit, excited by his love, and directed to his glory (Rom. vi:4; vii:6; Gal. vi:15; 2 Cor. v:17; Ezek. xi:19; and xxxvi:26; Rev. xxi:1).

NEW BIRTH (nū bĕrth). See REGENERATION.

NEW JERUSALEM CHURCH.

The New Jerusalem Church originated in the doctrines of the opened Word revealed to mankind in the writings of Emanuel Swedenborg.

(1) The Founder. Emanuel Swedenborg was the son of a Swedish Lutheran Bishop, a scholar, a practical engineer, intrusted with a high official position, a member of the Swedish diet, a man of science, a philosopher, a theologian, and a seer, who lived between 1688 and 1772. This life of over four-score years of untiring energy divides itself upon superficial observation into two periods. The first fifty years of it were devoted to the pursuit of natural learning and independent investigation in science and philosophy; the remaining years to an equally diligent discharge of the "holy office" to which he was called by the Lord Himself. With a thorough academic training, he began with the cultivation of the mathematical and physical sciences, and showed such ability in theoretical science, that he was entrusted with a position in the college of mines that gave him practical control of the development of the mineral wealth of Sweden. While in the faithful discharge of his official affairs he was elaborating in private and publishing from time to time the most sublime and extensive philosophical attempts upon which any single mind ever ventured. Of his philosophical writings, beginning with the *Principia,* devoted to a complete natural philosophy of the elemental world, and continuing with his works on the *Animal Kingdom* or the kingdom of the *Anima,* including a rational physiology as the basis of a rational psychology, it is not enough to say that he anticipated by the application of his analytical and synthetic processes, many of the results of subsequent experimental discovery in every realm of science; it must rather be said that he announced philosophical doctrines, which are far more masterful in explaining the larger field of facts awaiting explanation to-day, than they were appreciable to his own generation.

He was during this entire period the precise type of man which this generation delights to honor; strong, keen, self-reliant, practical. Endowed with a hardy constitution, he had a calm, placid disposition; led an active, laborious, cheerful life, traveling continually and keeping himself posted in the developments of science and contributing to its theoretical and practical achievements; composing his works and conducting his literary business unaided; enjoying the confidence of his king and fellow statesmen; discussing politics in the senate and memorializing the government on finance and other weighty matters; while he was elaborating and publishing a system of universal philosophy, more complete and probably more enduring and controlling than any which bears the name of a human author, and to which the logic of events is compelling the attention of the learned after a century and a half

of marvelous experimental research. Such was Swedenborg the assessor. A more penetrating and practical, and at the same time laborious and comprehensive man of thought never lived.

At the age of fifty-six, in the full maturity of his powers, he was called, as he declares, "to a holy office by the Lord, who most graciously manifested himself to me in person, and opened my sight to a view of the spiritual world, and granted me the privilege of conversing with spirits and angels." "From that day forth," he says, "I gave up all worldly learning and labored only in spiritual things according to what the Lord commanded me to write." Rightly considered, his whole previous career appears to have been a preparation for this work. When he had run the whole circuit of the sciences, he was introduced to a new world of facts and laws by the opening of his spiritual senses, and thus to a spiritual science and philosophy which could never have been discovered without these facts, and can never be understood apart from them.

(2) Doctrines. The fundamental doctrine of his theological writings is the doctrine of the second coming of the Lord. He teaches that the end of God in the creation of the human race is a heaven of angels; and He provides for this by means of the church. It requires three things to constitute a living church: revelation of divine truth adapted to man's reception; understanding on man's part of the truth revealed; and a life in accordance with it. The Lord provides that there shall always be a church with man. He institutes the church by revealing such divine truths as men need to know and can obey in life. When in process of time they pervert this truth and lose the understanding of the revelation committed to them, the Lord makes a new revelation and begins a new church. There have been four such general churches, and a fifth is foretold which is to be the crown of all the churches and is to endure forever. The first great church which was before the flood is called the most ancient, and in the Scriptures Adam, and its consummation is described by the flood. The second, which is called the ancient, and in the Scriptures Noah, was in Asia and partly in Africa, and was consummated by idolatries. The third was the Israelitish, which is historical. The fourth is the Christian, which the Lord established by the Evangelists and Apostles. This church had two epochs; one from the time of the Lord to the Council of Nice, and the other from that council to the year 1757, when the last judgment was effected in the spiritual world, by means of the new revelation of the interiors of the Word, by which at the same time the Lord made his second advent and institutes a new dispensation or church, which is meant by the New Jerusalem, the glorious hope of the apostles and the expectation of Christians from the beginning—the "day of the Lord," which shall have no end.

The second coming of the Lord, therefore, is not in person, as at his first advent; for then he assumed a human nature and glorified it for reasons of redemption and salvation, that he might become in His Humanity the visible God, and acquire to His Humanity "all power in heaven and in earth." What he came to do he perfectly accomplished and needed not to do again; but what was needed was such a revelation of the whole meaning of his Word, as would bring his divine mind spiritually present in power and glory. The Lord, who is the Word, made his second advent by revealing the spiritual sense and genuine meaning of his written Word, in which the divine truth is in its light, and in which he is continually present. This is his coming "in the clouds of heaven with power and great glory;" for the literal sense of the Word is as a cloud, and the spiritual sense as the glory by which the Lord as the Son of Man is revealed in all things of the Word. The Lord has made this revelation by means of a man whom he had prepared for this purpose from his childhood, and whom he filled with his spirit to teach the doctrines of the New Church from the Word. This is Swedenborg's claim, and the writings which contain the doctrines of the Word revealed for the New Church, he published between the years 1749 and 1771. These doctrines may be summarized as follows:

(3) **Summary.** (1) That Jehovah God, the creator and preserver of the universe, is Love itself and Wisdom itself; that he is one both in essence and in person, in whom nevertheless is the Divine Trinity of Father, Son and Holy Spirit, which are the essential divinity, the divine humanity, and the divine proceeding, answering to the soul, the body, and the operative energy in man; and that the Lord and Savior Jesus Christ is that God. The Father is in Him, and the Holy Spirit is from Him.

(2) That the Lord from eternity, who is Jehovah, came into the world and took our nature upon Him; He endured temptations, even to the passion of the cross; He overcame the hells and so delivered man; He glorified His humanity, uniting it with the divinity of which it was begotten; so He became the redeemer of the world, without whom no mortal can be saved; and they are saved who believe in Him and keep the Commandments of His Word.

(3) That the Sacred Scripture, or Word of the Lord, is divine truth itself; containing a spiritual sense, hitherto unknown, whence it is divinely inspired, and holy in every syllable; as well as a literal sense which is the basis of the spiritual sense and in which divine truth is in its fullness, holiness and power. The spiritual and natural senses of the Word are united by correspondence like soul and body, every natural expression and image including a spiritual and divine idea; and thus the Word is the medium of communication with heaven, and of conjunction with the Lord.

(4) That the Lord saves man by the operation of His spirit; but not without man's consent and coöperation. The Lord operates and gives to man to coöperate, that there may be conjunction of the Lord with man and of man with the Lord, and thus salvation. There are two means to this conjunction: the good of love which flows in by an internal way, and the truth of faith which is presented outwardly by means of revelation and instruction. So far as man can be led to accept and live according to the truths of faith as from the Lord, He by an inward and unperceived operation of His spirit conjoins the good of love with those truths, and thus reforms, regenerates and saves.

(5) That charity, faith and good works are unitedly necessary to man's salvation, since charity without faith is not spiritual but natural, and faith without charity is not living but dead, and both charity and faith without good works are perishable, because without use or fixedness.

(6) That immediately after death, which is only a putting off of the material body, never to be resumed, man rises again in a substantial spiritual body in the spiritual world, in which he continues to live to eternity; in heaven if his ruling affections and thence his life have been good, and in hell if his ruling affections and life have been evil.

These doctrines and the whole government of divine love and wisdom in creation and providence, are opened philosophically to the rational faculty from the interiors of the Word and from the facts and laws of the spiritual world, to the end, as Swedenborg affirms, that the man of the church may enter intellectually into the mysteries of faith and by living according to the light of intelligence be conjoined with heaven and the Lord.

Although Swedenborg affirmed a New Church it was no part of his mission to institute an external ecclesiastical body. Those of his own time who understood or cared to read what he had written, were very few. In 1783 a society was formed in London, England, for the study of his works. His books, which were written in Latin, were translated, and the number of believers increased more rapidly, but at first entertained no thought of separate organization. In process of time, however, theological controversies with their old ecclesiastical associates, and the longing for association with those agreed in faith and life, led to the organization of a church. The first society of this kind was formed in London in 1787 and was quickly followed by others in various parts of the kingdom. The name selected was "The Church upon Earth Signified in the Revelation by the New Jerusalem Descending from God Out of Heaven." This cumbrous title has been shortened to "The Church of the New Jerusalem," or "The New Jerusalem Church."

The doctrines were first introduced into America in 1784, and the societies organized from time to time are now grouped into State Associations, and these into a General Convention. The government is practically congregational, with a sort of episcopal advisory supervision. The worship in this country and England, and where the church has a foothold in the continent of Europe, is liturgical.

The church is of the least as to actual membership, but is acknowledged as a formative power by virtue of the rationality and virility of the faith of its members, and by the astonishing activity of its publishing societies in printing and distributing the literature of its doctrinal teaching. L. P. M.

NEW MOON (nū moon), (Heb. שׁדֶח, *khoh-desh'*, new moon, month). See FESTIVALS; MOON.

NEW TESTAMENT (nū tes'ta-ment). See BIBLE; SCRIPTURE, HOLY.

NEW YEAR (nū yēr). See YEAR.

NEZIAH (ne-zī'ah), (Heb. נְצִיחַ, *nets-ee'akh*, preëminent), the progenitor of a family of Nethinim who returned from the captivity with Zerubbabel (Ezra ii:54; Neh. vii:56), B. C. 536.

NEZIB (nĕ'zib), (Heb. נְצִיב, *nets-eeb'*, a statue or idol), a city in the low country of Judah (Josh.xv:43). Beit Nusîb, a little northwest of Hebron, has commonly been thought to represent this place (Robinson, ii·343 *sq.*); but it can scarcely be the place as it is in the hill country.

NIBHAZ (nĭb'hăz), (Heb. נִבְחַז, *nib-chāz'*, barker), an idol of the Avites (2 Kings xvii:31).

In the Zabian books the corresponding name is that of an evil demon, who sits on a throne upon the earth, while his feet rest on the bottom of Tartarus; but it is doubtful whether this should be identified with the Avite Nibhaz. It is supposed that the god was represented by the figure of a dog. It would therefore be allied to Anubis of the Egyptians. A large figure of a dog was found on the road from Beirut to Tripolis.

NIBSHAN (nĭb'shăn), (Heb. נִבְשָׁן, *nib-shawn'*, fertile, light, soft soil), a city of the wilderness of Judah (Josh. xv:62); site not known.

NICANOR (nĭ-kā'nor), (Gr. Νικάνωρ, *nik-an'ore*, conqueror), one of the seven men appointed by the church at Jerusalem to look after the poor, and in particular the Greek-speaking widows (Acts vi:5), A. D. 29.

NICODEMUS (nĭk'o-dē'mus), (Gr. Νικόδημος, *nik-od'ay-mos*, conqueror of the people), a Pharisee and member of the Sanhedrim, who was impressed by what he had heard concerning Jesus, but being unwilling, on account of his station, to commit himself without greater surety than he possessed, repaired by night to the house in which Christ dwelt, and held with him that important discourse which occupies the third chapter of John's Gospel.

(1) Defends Jesus. The effect which was then produced upon his mind may be collected from the fact that subsequently, at one of the sittings of the venerable body to which he belonged, he ventured to let fall a few words in favor of Jesus, whose proceedings were then in question (John vii:50).

(2) At Christ's Burial. He also took part with his colleague, Joseph of Arimathea, in rendering the last honors to the body of the crucified Redeemer (John xix:39). Nothing further is known of Nicodemus from Scripture. Tradition, however, adds that after he had thus openly declared himself a follower of Jesus, and had been baptized by Peter, he was displaced from his office, and expelled from Jerusalem (Phot. *Cod.* p. 171). It is added that he found refuge in a country house of his cousin Gamaliel, and remained there till his death.

(3) Character. Too strong an appreciation of the world's good opinion seems to have been the failing of Nicodemus, although Niemeyer (*Charakt.* i. 113) has lately made a strong effort to clear him from this imputation. We do not lay much stress upon what he ventured to say in the Sanhedrim; for he suffered himself to be easily put down, and did not come forward with any bold avowal of his belief. Winer calls attention to the fact, that although he took part in the sepulchral rites of Jesus, he did not join Joseph in his application to Pilate for the body of his crucified Lord; and justly remarks that such characters usually require a strong external impulse to bring them boldly forward, which impulse was probably in this case supplied by the resurrection of Jesus.

NICOLAITANS (nĭk'o-lā'i-tanz), (Gr. Νικολαΐται, *nikh-ol-ah-ee-tah-ee'*, followers of Nicolas), occurs twice in the New Testament (Rev. ii:6, 15).

(1) Conduct and Doctrine Condemned. In the former passage *the conduct of the Nicolaitans* is condemned; in the latter, the angel of the church in Pergamos is censured because certain members of his church held their doctrine.

(2) Practices. Various traditionary accounts have been given by the fathers of the origin and practices of this sect. Many of the primitive writers believed that Nicholas was rather the occasion than the author of the infamous practices of those who assumed his name, who were expressly condemned by the Spirit of God himself (Rev. ii:6). And, indeed, their opinions and actions were highly extravagant and criminal. They allowed a community of wives, and made no distinction between ordinary meats and those offered to idols. According to Eusebius, they subsisted but a short time; but Tertullian says, that they only changed their name, and that their heresies passed into the sect of the Cainites.

(3) Gnostics. It is evident from these accounts that the Nicolaitans with whom they were acquainted were Gnostics; since they impute to them the distinctive tenets and practices of the Gnostics. But in the short allusion in Rev. ii:6, 15, there is nothing to identify the tenets or conduct alluded to with Gnosticism, even supposing that Gnosticism, properly so called, existed in the Apostolic age, which to say the least, has not been proved to be the case. So that the conjecture mentioned by Mosheim, and which Tertullian appears to favor, may be regarded as probable, that the Nicolaitans mentioned in Revelation had erroneously been confounded with a party of Gnostics formed at a later period by one Nicolas.

The ingenious conjecture of Michaelis is worthy of consideration, who supposes that by Nicolaitans (Rev. ii:6, 15) the same class of persons is intended whom St. Peter (2 Pet. ii:15) describes as *followers of the way of Balaam;* and that their name, Nicolaitans, is merely a Greek translation of their Hebrew designation. The only objection which occurs to us against this very ingenious and probable supposition arises from the circumstance that, in the passage in Rev. ii:14, 15, both 'they that hold the doctrine of Balaam,' and 'the Nicolaitans,' are specified, and are distinguished from each other: 'So hast thou also,' the Nicolaitans, as well as the Balaamites, mentioned in the previous verse. So that whatever general agreement there might be between those two classes of heretics—and their collocation in the passage before us seems to imply that there was such agreement—it appears equally evident that some distinction also must have separated them the one from the other.   R. L.

NICOLAS (nĭk'o-las), (Gr. Νικόλαος, *nik-ol'ah-os*, conqueror of the people), a proselyte of Antioch, and one of the seven deacons (Acts vi:5), A. D. 29. Nothing further is known of him; but a large body of unsafe tradition has been connected with his name, under the supposition that he was the founder of the heresy of the Nicolaitans, stigmatized in Rev. ii:6, 15. (See the preceding article).

NICOPOLIS (ni-kŏp'o-lĭs), (Gr. Νικόπολις, *nik-op'o-lis*, city of victory), a city of Thrace, supposed to be Nicopi, on the river Nessus, now Karasou, which was here the boundary between Thrace and Macedonia; and hence the city is sometimes reckoned as belonging to the latter.

In Titus iii:12, Paul expresses an intention to winter at Nicopolis, and invites Titus, then in Crete, to join him there. There has been some uncertainty in respect to the city intended, as there were four of this name in Asia, five in Europe, and one in Africa. It must have been one of three cities: (1) Nicopolis in Thrace; (2) in Cilicia; or (3) in Epirus. The subscription to the Epistle to Titus calls it "Nicopolis of Macedonia"—*i. e.* Thrace. This subscription, however, is no part of the inspired text, and there is little doubt that the view of Jerome was correct, which identifies the Pauline Nicopolis with the noted city of that name in Epirus. It was built by Augustus Cæsar to commemorate his victory over Antony and Cleopatra at the battle of Actium (B. C. 31). Its modern name is *Paleoprevesa*, or "old Prevesa." The place has extensive ruins of temples, theaters, aqueducts, and a small building in the form of a pagan temple, which tradition says was used by Paul as a house of prayer. Some suppose that Paul was arrested here, and taken to Rome for his final trial. (Kitto and Schaff.) Between A. D. 64-65, or 65-66, or 66-67. "The later history of Nicopolis is short. After falling into decay, it was restored by Julian about

362; and afterwards it was captured by the Goths and destroyed; but again was restored by Justinian, as Procopius, *de Aedif.* iv :2, describes. It is mentioned as the metropolis of Old Epirus by Hierocles about A. D. 530, and retained that position in the ecclesiastical organization; but a late mediæval list of cities that changed their names implies that Prevesa had taken its place and dignity. There are many remains of the ancient city, on which the guide-books of Murray, Baedeker, etc., may be consulted." (W. M. Ramsay, Hastings' *Bib. Dict.*).

NIGER (nī'jer), (Gr. Νίγερ, *neeg'er*, Acts xiii:1).

Surname of Simeon, one of the prophets and teachers of Antioch when Paul and Barnabas returned thither after carrying the contributions of the brethren to the poor saints at Jerusalem. (See SIMEON.)

NIGHT (nīt), (Heb. לַיִל, *lah'yil;* לַיְלָה, *lah'yel-aw;* Gr. νύξ, *nooks*).

Besides representing these properly equivalent Hebrew and Greek words, 'night' stands in A. V. once for 'darkness' (Job xxvi:10; R. V. 'darkness'); thrice for 'twilight' (Is. v:11, R. V. 'night'; Is. xxi:4; lix:10, R. V. 'twilight'); and four times for 'evening' (Gen. xlix:27, R. V. 'even'; Lev. vi:20, R. V. 'evening'; Job vii:4, R. V. 'night'; Ps. xxx:5, R. V. 'night'; R. V. marg. 'even'); 'night season' (Job xxx:17), and 'night seasons' (Ps. xvi:17); 'to pass the night' occurs Dan. vi:18, and in the New Testament we have 'midnight' (Mark xiii:35; Luke xi:5; Acts xvi:25; xx:7); 'to continue all night' (Luke vi:12); 'a night and a day' (2 Cor. xi:25). R. V. omits 'night' on textual grounds from four passages where the word appears in A. V., viz., Matt. xxvii:64; Mark xiv:27; John vii:50; 2 Pet. iii:10. (James Patrick, Hastings' *Bib. Dict.*) (See DAY; TIME.)

Figurative. The term of human life is usually called a day in Scripture; but in one passage it is called *night*, to be followed soon by day, 'the day is at hand' (Rom. viii:12). Being a time of darkness, the image and shadow of death, in which the beasts of prey go forth to devour, it was made a symbol of a season of adversity and trouble, in which men prey upon each other, and the strong tyrannize over the weak (Is. xxi:12; Zech. xiv:6, 7). Hence continued day, or the absence of night, implies a constant state of quiet and happiness, undisturbed by the vicissitudes of peace and war. Night is also put, as in our own language, for a time of ignorance and helplessness (Mic. iii:6). In John ix:4 night represents death, a necessary result of the correlative usage which makes life a day. In the beautiful passage, "There shall be no night there" (Rev. xxi:25; xxii:5), the meaning is that heaven is a place where no sorrow or sin or death finds entrance.

NIGHT HAWK (nīt hak). The Heb. תַּחְמָס, *takh-mawce'*, is uncertain in meaning. Some have rendered it "ostrich," others "owl" (Lev. xi:16; Deut. xiv:15). (See OSTRICH; OWL.)

NIGHT MARCHES (nīt märch'es), (Num. ix:21, "whether it was by day or by night that the cloud was taken up they journeyed"). They made night marches doubtless to escape their enemies.

NIGHT MONSTER (nīt mŏn'stēr), (Heb. לִילִית, *lee-leeth'*, Is. xxxiv:14, marg.). The text has *screech owl*, but the marginal reading is preferable. "The reference is to a nocturnal specter similar to the *Shûl* of the Arabs. All nations have similar apparitions in their legends." (See OWL; NIGHT HAWK.)

NIGHT VISION (nit vīzh'ŭn), (Heb. חֶזְוֹן 2 לַיְלָה, *khaw-zone' lah'yel-aw*, Is. xxix:7; Chald. חֶזְוָא לֵילְיָא, *khez-vaw' lay'leh-yaw*, Dan. ii:19, etc.).

NIGHT WATCH (nīt wŏch). Before the Captivity the night was divided into three parts, or watches, the first extending to midnight, the second to the crowing of the cock, the third to sunrise. During the time of Christ the night was divided into four watches of three hours each.

NILE (nīl). The name Nile, although not occurring in the A. V., is often referred to under different names and titles.

1. *Shee-khore'* (Heb. שִׁיחוֹר, שָׁחוֹר, שָׁחֹר, *dark, turbid*), seems to be indicative of a very dark color (Is. xxiii:3; Josh. xiii:13; 1 Chron. xiii:5; comp. Gen. xv:18).

2. *Yeh-ore'* (Heb. יְאֹר, *channel;* the same as the ancient Egyptian Atur, Aur, and the Coptic *eiero* or *iaro* (Ps. lxxviii:44; Ezek. xxix:3, *sq.;* xxx:12; comp. Is. xxxii:21; Job xxviii:10).

3. "The Nachal of Egypt" (Heb. נַחַל מִצְרַיִם, *nakh'al mits-rah-yim*, stream of Egypt "has generally been understood to mean 'the torrent' or 'brook of Egypt,' and to designate a desert stream at Rhinocorura, now El-'Areesh, on the eastern border. This name must doubtless signify the Nile, for it occurs in cases parallel to those where Shihor is employed (Num. xxxiv:5; Josh. xv:4, 47; 1 Kings viii:65; 2 Kings xxiv:7; Is. xxvii:12), both designating the easternmost or Pelusiac branch of the river as the border of the Philistine territory, where the Egyptians equally put the border of their country toward Kanaan or Kanana (Canaan). It remains for us to decide whether the name signifies the 'brook of Egypt,' or whether Nachal be a Hebrew form of Nile. The Hebrew word *nachal* might have been adopted as very similar in sound to an original proper name" (Smith, *Bib. Dict.*).

4. "The rivers of Cush" (Heb. נַהֲרֵי כוּשׁ, *nah'-ar-ay koosh*), are mentioned only in the perplexing prophecy contained in Is. xviii. By it we must probably conclude "the rivers of Ethiopia" to be the confluents or tributaries of the Nile.

5. "The river of Egypt" (Heb. נַהַר מִצְרַיִם, *nah'ar mits-rah'yim*), mentioned with the Euphrates (Gen. xv:18).

6. The Nile is sometimes poetically called "The Sea" (Heb. יָם, *yawm*, Is. xviii:2; Nah. iii:8; Job xli:31, and perhaps Is. xix:5), so known among the Arabs at the present time. " 'The river' clearly applies to the Nile in Is. xix:5, and there, also, in a parallelism with the Nile as 'the sea.' And the Nile has been smitten in that portion of it which is known as 'the seven streams,' five of those streams being now closed from sight" (Trumbull, *Kadesh-barnea*, p. 348, *sq.*). (Mc. & Str. *Cyc.*; Barnes, *Bib. Dict.*)

This great river of Egypt and of Africa, is probably the second longest river in the world, its entire length being estimated at 4,000 miles. It is connected with the earliest history of the Egyptian and the Israelitish nations (Exod. ii:3; vii:20, 21; Num. xi:5; Ps. cv:29; Jer. xlvi:7, 8; Zech. xiv:17, 18). The Nile is not named in the New Testament. The discovery of the true source of the Nile, and the reason for its annual overflow, are two scientific problems which have been discussed for upward of 2,000 years. The course of the stream is now known for about 3,300 miles, and with two interruptions—the cataract of Syene (Assouan) and the Upper Cataract—it is claimed by Baedeker's *Handbook on Lower Egypt* to be navigable throughout nearly the whole of that distance. But as there are many other cataracts, this statement cannot be correct. The principal stream is now known to be the White Nile, while the *Blue* or *Black* Nile is of greater importance in contributing to the annual inundation of the lower river. The two streams unite at the town of Khartoom, the capital of Nubia, and from this point to the mouths of the stream at Damietta and Rosetta, upward of 1,800 miles, it falls 1,240 feet, and attains its greatest width a little below Khartoom and a little above Cairo, at each of which places it is about 1,100 yards wide. The source of the White Nile is doubtless Lake Victoria Nyanza, the largest part of which lies south of the equator, and from 3,000 to 4,000 feet above the level of the sea. The *White* Nile is so named from the color of the clay with which its waters are stained. The *Blue* Nile resembles a mountain torrent, being liable to rise suddenly with the Abyssinian rains and sweep away whatever it encounters in its rapidly descending course. The source of the Blue Nile is high up in the Abyssinian mountains, from 6,000 to 10,000 feet above the sea level, and in springs which are regarded with superstitious veneration by the neighboring people. A number of festivals were celebrated in connection with the annual rise of the Nile; which appear from the monuments to have been common as early as the fourteenth century B. C. The height of the Nile was measured by the Nilometer, a square well

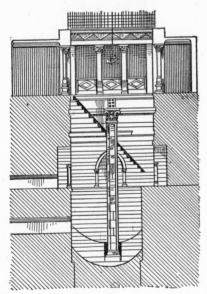

The Nilometer.

having in its center an octagonal column, on which were inscribed the ancient Arabic measures and Cufic inscriptions. This was erected in A. D. 716, and was used to determine the height of the overflow, upon which was based the rate of taxation. The government, however, cheated the poor people by false statements of the overflow, indicated by this measurement. The papyrus reeds—whence paper is designated—the flags, the lotus, and the various colored flowers formerly beautifying the banks of the river have nearly all disappeared, thus fulfilling prophecy (Is. xix:6, 7). This river, so intimately associated with the early

history of the human race, is a favorite resort for tourists, who can go in steamers as far as the First Cataract, near Assouan (Syene), where were the great quarries which supplied stone for ancient Egyptian monuments, and from Philæ up to Aboo-Simbel and the Second Cataract. The Nile voyage, broken by donkey rides and visits to the pyramids, tombs, and ruins of temples and palaces of the Pharaohs, is one of the greatest enjoyments and best recreations of body and mind. (Schaff, *Bib. Dict.*)

"A curious legend in the Targum describes the burial of Joseph's coffin in the Nile and its rediscovery by Moses; the Egyptians never, of course, used the river in this way."

NIMRA (nĭm'ra), (Heb. נִמְרָה, *nim-raw'*, limpid). See BETH-NIMRAH and NIMRIM.

NIMRIM (nĭm'rim), (Heb. נִמְרִים, *nim-reem'*, a stream of the leopards, or limpid, pure), a small stream in the territory of Moab (Is. xv:6; Jer. xlviii:34.)

Its location is not certain. Some identify it with Beth-nimrah in the valley of the Jordan, others with Wady Nemeirah at the south end of the Dead Sea. Tristram places it higher up the valley, where there exists an old Moabite city, Springs of Nemeirah, by name, with many well watered gardens still in cultivation.

NIMROD (nĭm'rŏd), (Heb. נִמְרֹד, *nim-rode'*, Sept. Νεβρώδ, *nee-brode'*), a son of Cush, the eldest son of Ham (Gen. x:8-10).

Five sons of Cush are enumerated in verse 7 in the more usual manner of this chapter; but a change of phrase introduces Nimrod.

(1) Personal Name. This difference may indicate that while, in relation to the other five, the names have a national and geographical reference, this appellation is exclusively personal. It denotes intensively, *the extremely impious rebel.* Hence we conceive that it was not his original proper name, but was affixed to him afterwards, perhaps even after his death, as a characteristic appellative.

No other persons connected with this work must be considered as answerable for the opinion which the writer of this article thinks to rest upon probable grounds, that the earlier part of the book of Genesis consists of several independent and complete compositions, of the highest antiquity and authority, marked by some difference of style, and having clear indications of commencement in each instance. If this supposition be admitted, a reason presents itself for the citation of a proverbial phrase in ch. x:9. The single instance of minute circumstantiality, in so brief a relation, seems to imply that the writer lived near the age of Nimrod, while his history was still a matter of traditional notoriety, and the comparison of any hero with him was a familiar form of speech. It is also supposed that those, not fragments, but complete, though short and separate compositions (of which eight or more are hypothetically enumerated in J. Pye Smith's *Scripture and Geology*, p. 202), were, under divine authority, prefixed by Moses to his own history. Their series has a continuity generally, but not rigorously exact. If we place ourselves in such a point of time, suppose the age succeeding Nimrod, which might be the third century after the Deluge, we may see how naturally the origination of a common phrase would rise in the writer's mind; and that a motive of usefulness would be suggested with it. But both these ideas involve that of nearness to the time; a period in which the country traditions were yet fresh, and an elucidation of them would be acceptable and consonant to general feeling. The following is a close translation of the passage in which Nimrod is mentioned: 'And Cush begat Nimrod: he began [opened a course of action, led the way] to be a hero in the earth [or in the land]: he was a hero at the chase in the presence of Jehovah; on which account the saying is, Like Nimrod, the hero of the chase, in the presence of Jehovah. And the chief [city] of his dominion was Babel; and [he founded] Ezek and Akkad, and Kalneh, in the land of Shinar.'

(2) Strength and Courage. Interpreters, with scarcely an exception, from the Septuagint and the Targums down to our own times, understand the whole case thus: that Nimrod was a man of vast bodily strength, and eminent for courage and skill in the arts of hunting down and capturing or killing the dangerous animals, which probably were both very numerous, and frequently of enormous size; that, by these recommendations, he made himself the favorite of bold and enterprising young men, who readily joined his hunting expeditions; that hence he took encouragement

the same reason that so many places there are named after him. Thus we have the Birs Nimroud, the ancient Borsippa, near the ruins of Babylon, Tel Nimroud, near Baghdad, the dam Suhr el-Nimroud, across the Tigris near Mosul, and the mound of Nimroud, the ancient Calah. To all appearance, he was regarded in later times in his native country as a great builder also. He seems to have been looked upon by the Babylonians as the builder of Babylon, and the bilingual Creation story apparently attributes to him the completion of the E-sagila, the great temple tower in that city, which was certainly of the type of the Tower of Babel, even if it were not that erection itself. This may account for the connection of Nimrod with the catastrophe of the confusion of tongues, ascribed to him in the East both in comparatively ancient and in more recent times."

NIMSHI (nĭm-shī), (Heb. נִמְשִׁי, *nim-shee'*, saved), the grandfather of Jehu (2 Kings ix:2, 14, 20); commonly called "father" (1 Kings xix:16; 2 Chron. xxii:7), B. C. about 950

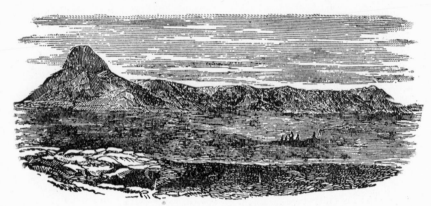

The Great Mound of Nimrod.

to break the patriarchial union of venerable and peaceful subordination to set himself up as a military chieftain, assailing and subduing men, training his adherents into formidable troops, by their aid subduing the inhabitants of Shinar and its neighboring districts; and that, for consolidating and retaining his power, now become a despotism, he employed his subjects in building forts, which became towns and cities, that which was afterwards called Babel being the principal.

(3) Fables and Legends. As a great part of the ancient mythology and idolatry arose from the histories of chiefs and sages, decorated with allegorical fables, it is by no means improbable that the life and actions of Nimrod gave occasion to stories of this kind. Hence, some have supposed him to have been signified by the Indian Bacchus, deriving that name from *Bar-Chus,* 'son of Cush:' and, it is probable, by the Persian giant *Gibber* (answering to the Hebrew Gibbor, 'mighty man,' 'hero,' in Gen. x:8, 9); and by the Greek *Orion,* whose fame as a 'mighty hunter' is celebrated by Homer, in the *Odyssey,* xi:571-4. The Persian and the Grecian fables are both represented by the well-known and magnificent constellation.

J. P. S.

Prof. T. G. Pinches, Hastings' *Bib. Dict.,* says: "The legends that have been preserved concerning Nimrod would seem to show that his fame in the country of his exploits rests more upon what was known of him there than upon the somewhat meager account in Genesis, and it is probably for

NINEVE (nĭn'e-ve), (Gr. Νινευί, *nin-yoo-ee'*), the Greek form of NINEVEH (Luke xi:32).

NINEVEH (nĭn'e-veh), (Heb. נִינְוֵה, *nee-nev-ay'*; Gr. Νινευή, *nin-yoo-ay'*; also Νινευί, *nin-yoo-ee'*), meaning the dwelling of Ninus.

(1) Location. A famous city of the ancient world, capital of the great Assyrian empire, which stood on the eastern bank of the river Tigris, opposite to the present Mosul; its actual site being most probably the same with that of Nunia and the tomb of Jonah, about three-fourths of a mile from the river, in the midst of ruins, north latitude 36° 20' 17''; east longitude 43° 10' 17''.

(2) Name. The Bible makes the city a sort of colony from Babylon or Babel, Shinar (see BABEL, TOWER OF), stating (Gen. x:11), 'out of that land (Babel, etc., in the land of Shinar) went forth Asshur and builded Nineveh.' A similar tradition is indicated in Micah v:6. The native monuments show that the tradition is correct, and that Nineveh was once included in the boundaries of the Babylonian empire. (See Driver in Hogarth's *Authority and Archæology,* pp. 29, *sq.*) In fact it seems to have taken its name from the Babylonian city of Ninâ on the Euphrates, which is mentioned by Diodorus (ii:3, 7), quoting probably from Ctesias.

The name of Nineveh is written *Ninuâ* and *Ninâ* in the cuneiform inscriptions. A popular etymology connected it with the Assyrian *nunu,* 'fish,' at a very early date, since the name is ideographically represented by the picture of a fish inside the enclosure of a city. But it seems really to have been derived from the title of the Babylonian goddess Ninâ, the daughter of Ea, who was identified with the Semitic Istar. Ninâ is the original of the Greek form Ninos." (A. H. Sayce, Hastings' *Bib. Dict.*)

(3) History. After the simple statement in Genesis, the sacred record is for a long time entirely silent respecting Nineveh, which, we may therefore presume, remained inconsiderable for many generations. At length, some fifteen hundred years after the first mention of the place, in the days of Jeroboam II, king of Israel (B. C. 825), Nineveh again enters by name on the biblical record, having meanwhile grown into a mighty power. This reappearance of Nineveh is accidental, and shows that the Bible does not profess to give any orderly and systematic history of the world. Other countries come on the scene and disappear, just as the course of events in the kingdoms of Judah and Israel seem to require or may chance to occasion.

Nineveh is described in the book of Jonah as 'that great city,' 'an exceeding great city of three days' journey,' probably in a straight line through the place, as the large cities of Asia stood on a great extent of country, having gardens, and even fields, in the midst of them; and Jonah is said to 'enter into the city a day's journey' (ch. iii:4) before he began to foretell its overthrow; that is, as is most likely, he penetrated into the heart of the place, as being that which was most suitable for delivering his burden. The magnitude of the place may also be gathered from what is said in the last verse of the book: 'That great city, wherein are more than six score thousand persons that cannot discern between their right hand and their left hand, and also much cattle' (grazing). The population of a place must have been immense in which there were no fewer than 120,000 children—young children, the language employed seems to denote. It also appears from the same book that the state of society was highly complex, organized in divers ranks from the king and the noble to the peasant; and, if we may argue from the exactness with which the number of children is given,

Jewish Captives from Lachish.

we should be justified in asserting that the people were in an advanced stage of civilization, seeing that their social statistics were well attended to and carefully preserved. Civilization, however, had brought luxury, and luxury corruption of morals, for 'their wickedness had gone up before God' (ch. i:2). Yet was not their iniquity of the lowest kind, for the Ninevites repented at the preaching of Jonah.

(4) Prophecies Against Nineveh. A few years later we find the prophet Nahum (B. C.

735) entrusted with 'the burden of Nineveh.' From this book it would appear that the repentance of the city, if sincere, was not durable. Therefore was the anger of Jehovah about to fall upon it and make it a perpetual waste. (See SENNACHERIB.)

Expressions that are employed tend to give a high idea of the size and splendor of the place; it had many strongholds, and many gates with bars, probably of brass; its inhabitants were 'many as the locusts;' it had multiplied its merchants above the stars of heaven; its crowned (princes) were as the locusts, and its captains as the great grasshoppers (ch. iii:12-17). So her wealth was prodigious: 'There is none end of the store and glory out of all the pleasant furniture.' The reason assigned for the destruction of the city shows how great was its wickedness: 'Out of the house of thy gods will I cut off the graven image and the molten image; I will make thy grave; for thou art vile' (ch. i:14). 'Woe to the bloody city! It is all full of lies and robbery' (ch. iii:1). Shortly after (B. C. 713) the delivery of this prophecy Sennacherib, king of Assyria, having invaded Judæa, suffered a signal defeat by the special act of God: 'So Sennacherib departed, and went and returned and dwelt at Nineveh' (2 Kings xix:36). Very brief, however, was his dwelling there, for as he was worshiping in the house of Nisroch, his god, Adrammelech and Sharezer, his sons, smote him with the sword; and Esarhaddon, his son, reigned in his stead (2 Kings xix:37). The predicted punishment of the city was now approaching. Zephaniah gave his authority that it would come (ch. ii:13). (See also Is. xiv:24, *sq.*): 'The Lord will stretch out his hand against the north and destroy Assyria, and will make Nineveh a desolation, and dry like a wilderness.' The language which immediately ensues goes to confirm the view which has been given of the commercial greatness (it was the entrepôt for the trade of Eastern and Western Asia), the surpassing opulence, the high culture, the immense population, and the deep criminality of the city of Nineveh.

Winged Deity.

From Strabo (xvi. p. 737), the place appears to have been much greater than even Babylon; and from Diodorus Sic. (ii:3), that it measured 480 stadia in circumference, having very high and broad walls, which, aided by the river, rendered it impregnable.

This safety was, however, merely imaginary. Sardanapalus, who had a full share of the vices of his subjects, endured in the eighth century before Christ a siege of three years' duration at the hands of the Medes, under Arbaces, which led to the overthrow of the city (Diod. Sic. ii:26). But so large and so powerful a capital was not easily destroyed. Nineveh was the seat of an Assyrian kingdom till the year B. C. 625, when it was taken by Nabopolassar of Babylon and Cyaxares, king of the Medes, which led to the destruction of the

Assyrian kingdom (Herod. i:106). Nineveh flourished no more. Strabo (xvi p. 737) represents it as lying waste; though in the times of the Roman emperors some remains of it seem to have survived, as a Nineveh on the Tigris is mentioned in Tacitus (*Annal.* xii:13), and is characterized as a *castellum*, or fort, probably some small fortification raised out of the ruins of the city for predatory purposes. Something of the kind was found there at a later period, for in the thirteenth century Abulfaragius makes mention of a *castellum* there.

(5) Ruins. The present remains comprise a rampart and foss, four miles in circuit, with a moss-covered wall about twenty feet in height.

Mosul, with which Nineveh is commonly identified, stands on the opposite, or western bank of the Tigris, and lies so near the river that its streets are often flooded—a circumstance which calls to mind some of the terms employed by the prophetic writers before referred to. This place, like its great prototype, carries on a trade (though to a small extent) between the East and the West. The climate is stated to be very healthy; the average temperature of summer not exceeding 66° Fahr.; but in spring, during the floods, epidemics are common, though not fatal.

See Niebuhr, *Reiseb* ii. 353, 368; Ives, *Voyage*, pp. 327, *sq.;* Rosenmüller, *Alterth.* i:2,116; Bruns, *Erdbeschreibung*, ii. 1, 199, *sq.;* Mannert, v, 440,

King Feasting (from Bas-relief).

The ruins at first sight present a range of hills. From these hills large stones are constantly dug out, from which probably a bridge over the Tigris has been built. Vast libraries have been found, and records of a civilization extending far back into the dawn of history.

Jonah's connection with the city is still preserved in a tomb which bears his name; but how far back in antiquity this building runs, it is now impossible to say. The tomb stands on a hill, and is covered by a mosque which is held in great veneration. Bricks, partly whole, partly in fragments, and pieces of gypsum with inscriptions in the arrow-head character, are found from time to time. Landseer, in his *Sabæan Researches*, gives an engraving of cylinders dug up at Nineveh, which he states to be numerous in the East, and supposes to have been employed as signets; they

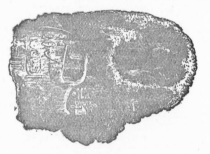

Impressions of the Signets of the Kings of Assyria and Egypt, (Original Size).

are of jasper, chalcedony and jade, and bear astronomical emblems, the graving of which, especially considering the hardness of the materials, shows a high state of art.

sq.; Kinneir's *Persia*, 256-9, Olivier, *Vogaye en Turquie*, iv:265; Ainsworth's *Assyria*, p. 256. (Newman, *Thrones and Palaces of Babylon and Nineveh;* Smith, *Hist. of Assur-bani-pal;* *Assyria from the Earliest Times*, and *Recent Assyrian Discoveries* (in British Museum); *Fresh Light from Ancient Monuments*, A. H. Sayce; *The Monuments and the Old Test.*, Price. (See ASSYRIA.) J. R. B.

NINEVITE (nĭn'e-vīte), (Gr. Νινευῖτης, *nin-yoo-ee'tace*, Ninevite), an inhabitant of Nineveh (Luke xi:30).

NISAN (nī'san), (Heb. נִיסָ֔ן, *nee-sawn*), the first month of the Hebrew civil year Abib, by which name this month is called in the Pentateuch (Exod. xiii:4; xxiii:15; Deut. xvi:1), means an ear of grain, a green ear; and hence 'the month Abib,' is 'the month of green ears.' It thus denoted the condition of the barley in the climate of Egypt and Palestine in this month. Nisan, otherwise Abib, began with the new moon of April or, according to the Rabbins, of March. It is mentioned by name twice only (Neh. ii:1; Esth. iii:7).

NISROCH (nĭs'rŏk), (Heb. נִסְרֹ֔ךְ, *nis-roke'*).

The Hebrew form of the name of a deity of the Assyrians, in whose temple Sennacherib was worshiping when slain by his sons (2 Kings xix:37; Is. xxxvii:38).

There has been much speculation as to the identity of this deity, and many wild theories have been put forward concerning him. Some suggest that the word refers to Noah's dove, which had been made an object of worship. The word is now usually supposed to mean *great eagle*. This bird was held in peculiar veneration by the ancient Persians; and was likewise worshiped by the Arabs before the time of Mohammed. But the word re-

Nisroch.

fers to a divinity represented in the Assyrian tablets by a human form with the wings and head of an eagle, in whose temple at Nineveh Sennacherib was murdered by his sons Adrammelech and Sharezer (NERGAL-SHAREZER, which see) (2 Kings xix:37; Is. xxxvii:38). The etymology of the name, even the Shemitic origin of the word, is doubtful, and nothing definite is known of this deity.

Prof. T. G. Pinches, however, states in Hastings' *Bib. Dict.* that "with regard to the form, *Nisroch,* there are two possible explanations: *Nisroch* (the same as *Esorach*) may be for *Asuraku,* a lengthened form of *Asur* by the addition of *aku*—the same termination as appears in Amaruduk (u), the Marduku (a personal name) of the later contract tablets, in which case the presence of the ending would seem to imply Accadian influence. On the other hand, the name may be really a compound one, *i.e.* the well-known appellation of the god Asur with the Accadian name of the moon-god Aku (compare Eri-Aku, 'servant of the moon-god'=Arioch) attached to it. In support of this second etymology may be cited the fact that Sennacherib's name contains the element *Sin,* the common name of the moon-god in Babylonia and Assyria, and the expression *'his god'* may refer to some such compound deity as Asur-Aku, whom Sennacherib specially worshiped."

NITER (nī'tēr), (Heb. נֶתֶר, *neh'ther;* Gr. νίτρον, *nee'tron*).

Now denotes *saltpeter,* nitrate of potash, but the νίτρον or *nitrum* of the ancients was a different substance, *natron,* carbonate of soda. It occurs as an incrustation on the ground in Egypt, Persia, and elsewhere, and is also a constituent in the water of certain saline lakes. The most famous of the latter are the 'natron lakes' in Egypt. They lie in the 'natron valley' about 60 miles W.N.W. of Cairo. The deposit of these lakes includes an upper layer of common salt and a lower one of natron (Wilkinson, *Modern Egypt,* i. 382, *sq.*). Strabo mentions these Egyptian lakes (*Geog.* xvii, i. 23), and also a similar lake in Armenia (*ib.* xi. xiv:8). See also Pliny, *Nat. Hist.* xxxi:10.

It is found in many other parts of the East. Vinegar has no effect upon common niter, and of course this could not be meant by the wise man, who in Prov. xxv:20 says, "*As* he that taketh away a garment in cold weather, *and as* vinegar upon niter, so is he that singeth songs to a heavy heart." Now, as vinegar has no effect upon niter, but upon *natron* or *soda* its action is very obvious, it seems the English translation should have been "natron." In Jer. ii:22 the same word again is improperly used: "For though thou wash thee with niter, and take thee much soap, yet thine iniquity is marked before me, saith the Lord God." The alkaline earth natron is obviously designed in this passage. It is found as an impure carbonate of soda on the surface of the earth in Egypt and Syria, and is also native in some parts of Africa in hard strata or masses, and is called *trona,* being used for the same purposes as the barilla of commerce. (See NETER.)

NO (nō). See NO-AMON; THEBES.

NOADIAH (nō'ā-dī'ah), (Heb. נוֹעַדְיָה, *no-ad-yaw',* Jehovah convenes, Jah assembles).

1. A Levite, who had charge of the gold and silver vessels brought back by Ezra from Babylon to Jerusalem (Ezra viii:33), B. C. about 459.
2. A prophetess, who attempted to frighten Nehemiah from his purpose of building the wall of Jerusalem (Neh. vi:14), B. C. about 445.

NOAH (nō'ah), (Heb. נֹחַ or נוֹחַ, *no'akh,* rest, quiet), the second father of the human race.

1. He was the son of the second Lamech, the grandson of Methusaleh, and the tenth in descent from Adam.

The father of Noah must not be confounded with the Lamech who was the fourth in descent from Cain. There is another instance of the same name in each line, Enoch; but the periods of each of the two couples must have been very different, though we cannot exactly compare them, for the history does not give the years of life in the line of Cain. The two Lamechs, however, have one remarkable circumstance in common; to each of them a fragment of inartificial poetry is attached as his own composition. That of the Cainitic Lamech is in Gen. iv:23, 24. That of the Sethite now comes before us in ch. v:29, 30: 'Lamech lived 182 years, and then begat a son, and he called his name Noah, saying:

> This shall comfort us
> From our labor,
> And from the sorrowful toils of our hands,
> From the ground,
> Which Jehovah hath cursed.'

The allusion is undoubtedly to the penal consequences of the fall in earthly toils and sufferings, and to the hope of a Deliverer excited by the promise made to Eve. That this expectation was grounded upon a divine communication we infer from the importance attached to it, and the confidence of its expression. (See this subject well argued in Bishop Sherlock's *Use and Intent of Prophecy,* Disc. iv.)

"In Gen. ix:17, Noah appears as the hero of the Flood; in ix:20-29, as the first discoverer of the art of making wine. That these two stories come from different sources is probable, because in the earlier Accadian history of the Flood that event is immediately followed by the translation of Sîtnapisti (Noah), perhaps referred to in chap. vi:9; comp. v:24.

"Amongst the Talmudists (*e. g., Aboda Zara* 64b, *Sanhedrin* 56b) it was customary to speak of 'the seven precepts of the sons of Noah, by which they meant those precepts that were supposed to be already binding upon mankind at large before Abraham and outside of his family. Other enumerations besides seven are also found." (F. H. Woods, Hastings' *Bib. Dict.*)

(1) Sons of God. The descendants of Seth had become designated as 'the sons of God,' faithful and obedient; the women of the Cainite race were called by a term evidently designed to form an appellation of the contrary import, 'daughters of men,' of impious and licentious men. These women possessed beauty and blandishments, by which they won the affections of unwary men, and intermarriages upon a great scale took place. As is usual in such alliances, the worse part gained the ascendancy. The offspring became more depraved than the parents, and a universal corruption of minds and morals took place. Many of them became 'giants, the mighty men of old, men of renown' (*nephilim*), apostates (as the word implies), heroes, warriors, plunderers, 'filling the earth with violence.'

(2) Noah as a Preacher. God mercifully afforded a respite of 120 years (ch. vi:3; 1 Pet. iii: 20; 2 Pet. ii:5), during which Noah sought to work salutary impressions upon their minds, and to bring them to repentance. Thus he was 'a preacher of righteousness,' exercising faith in the testimony of God, moved with holy reverence, obeying the divine commands, and, by the contrast of his conduct, condemning the world (Heb. xi:7) ; and probably he had during a long previous period labored in that benevolent and pious work.

(3) In the Ark. At last the threatening was fulfilled. All humankind perished in the waters, except this eminently favored and righteous man, with his three sons (born about 100 years before) and the four wives. (See DELUGE.)

(4) Noah's Sacrifice. At the appointed time this terrible state of the earth ceased, and a new surface was disclosed to the occupation and industry of the delivered family. In some places that surface would be washed bare to the naked rock, in others sand would be deposited, which would be long uncultivable; but by far the larger portion would be covered with rich soil With agriculture and its allied arts the antediluvians must have been well acquainted. (See ADAM.) The four men, in the vigor of their mental faculties and bodily strength, according to the then existing scale of human life, would be at no loss for the profitable application of their powers. Immediately after the desolating judgment the merciful Jehovah gave intimations of his acceptance of the sacrifice and thanksgivings of Noah and his family, and of his gracious purposes revealed in the form of a solemn covenant for the continual benefit of them and their posterity. The beautiful phenomenon of the rainbow was put to a new and significant use. As infallibly certain as is the production of a rainbow under certain conditions of the atmosphere, so certain and sure of fulfillment are the promises of Jehovah.

(5) Story of the Flood Preserved. As the flood affected equally the common ancestry of mankind, all nations that have not sunk into the lowest barbarism would be likely to preserve the memory of the chief person connected with it; and it would be a natural fallacy that every people should attach to itself a principal interest in that catastrophe, and regard that chief person as the founder of their own nation, and belonging to their own locality. Hence, we can well account for the traditions of so many peoples upon this capital fact of ancient history, and the chief person in it; the *Xisuthrus* of the Chaldæans, with whom is associated a remarkable number of precise circumstances, corresponding to the Mosaic narrative (Alex. Polyhist. in the *Chronicle of Eusebius*, so happily recovered by Mr. Zohrab, in the Armenian Version, and published by him in 1818) ; the Phrygian *Noë* of the celebrated Apamean medal, which, besides Noah and his wife with an ark, presents a raven, and a dove with an olivebranch in its mouth (figured in Bryant's *Anc. Myth.*, vol. iii) ; the *Manes* of the Lydians (Mr. W. J. Hamilton's *Asia Min.*, iii. 383; see NATIONS, DISPERSION OF) ; the *Deucalion* of the Syrians and the Greeks, of whose deluge the account given by Lucian is a copy almost exactly circumstantial of that in the book of Genesis (*Dea Syria; Luciani Opp.* iii:457, ed. Reitz; Bryant iii:28) ; the many coincidences in the Greek mythology in respect of Saturn, Janus, and Bacchus; the traditions of the aboriginal Americans, as stated by Clavigero, in his *History of Mexico;* and many others. (See DELUGE.) J. P. S.

(6) Character. That the conduct of Noah corresponded to the faith and hope of his father we have no reason to doubt. The brevity of the his-

tory satisfies not human curiosity. He was born 600 years before the Deluge. We may reasonably suppose that through that period he maintained the character given of him: 'Noah found favor in the eyes of the Lord. Noah was a just man, and perfect in his generations. Noah walked with God' (Gen. vi:8, 9). These words declare his piety, sincerity, and integrity, that he maintained habitual communion with the Father of Mercies, by the exercises of devotion, and that he was an inspired instrument of conveying the will of God to mankind. The wickedness of the human race had long called upon the wisdom and justice of God for some signal display of his displeasure, as a measure of righteous government and an example to future ages.

2. (Heb. נֹעָה, *no-aw'*, motion), one of the five daughters of Zelophehad (Num. xxvi:33; xxvii:1; xxxvi:11; Josh. xvii:3), B. C. about 1170. She, with her sisters, obtained an inheritance in the Promised Land, as her father had no sons.

NO-AMON (nō-ā'mon), (Heb. נֹא, *no*, the home of Amon, place or portion of Amon).

A populous and celebrated city of Egypt, and the capital of Upper Egypt, named after the god Amon, and called by the Greeks Diospolis, or "city of Zeus," but better known by the name of "Thebes." It was situated on both sides of the Nile, from 400 to 500 miles from its mouth. The only mention of the city in the Bible occurs in the prophecies. It is called No (Ezek. xxx:14-16; Jer. xlvi:25), and, margin, No-amon, rendered 'populous No" (Nah. iii:8).

The Nile valley at Thebes resembles a vast amphitheater, enclosed by the grand forms of the Arabian and Libyan mountains, the river running through nearly the center of this space. The area surrounded by these mountain-bulwarks is filled with ruins—avenues of sphinxes and statues, miles in length, at the end of which were massive columnal structures, the entrances to immense temples and palaces, and colossal images of the ancient Pharaohs, relics of regal magnificence so extensive and stupendous that the beholder might well imagine all the grandest ruins of the Old World had been brought together on this Theban plain. The extent of the city has been variously given by historians. According to Strabo, it covered an area five miles in length and three miles in breadth, and Diodorus makes its circuit about the same. Wilkinson also infers from its ruins that its length must have been about five and a fourth miles and its breadth three miles. Others suppose that the ancient city of Thebes, or No-amon, included the three sites of Luxor, Karnak, and Thebes, and that in the days of its glory, from B. C. 1600 to B. C. 800, it stretched thirty-three miles on both banks of the Nile. Its ruins are the most notable on the banks of that historic river. It became celebrated in the eleventh dynasty, and suffered in the thirteenth because of the invasion of the Hyksos. In the seventeenth century B. C. Amosis liberated the country and it reached its height of magnificence. The splendor of the city departed with the removal of the residence of the Pharaohs to the Delta. In its ruins it is great. Its temple of Karnak is a marvel. Its architecture is a problem of mechanical skill. Its great hall contains 134 columns, the loftiest 75 feet in height and 12 feet in diameter; the hall itself is 175 feet wide by 329 feet long. Every stone a book and every column a library in itself. The R. V. corrects some terms of reference to this place. In Jer. xlvi:25, the "multitude of No" is rendered "Amon of No ;" in Nah. iii:8, the "populous No" is changed to "No-Amon." (See THEBES.)

NOB (nŏb), (Heb. בֹ֗נ, *nobe*; Sept. Νομβᾶ, *nomba*), a city of Benjamin, in the vicinity of Jerusalem, belonging to the priests, and where the tabernacle was stationed in the time of Saul (1 Sam. xxi:2; xxii:9, 11, 19; Neh. xi:32; Is. x:32).

From the last of these texts it would appear that Jerusalem was visible from Nob, which, therefore, must have been situated somewhere upon the ridge of the Mount of Olives, northeast of the city. Dr. Robinson states that he diligently sought along the ridge for some traces of an ancient site which might be regarded as that of Nob, but without the slightest success (*Bibl. Researches*, ii: 150). Kiepert's Map places Nob at *El-Isâ-wîch*, not far from *Anâtâ*, about a mile northwest of Jerusalem. Lieutenant Conder argues (*Quar. Statement* of the "Palestine Exploration Fund," January, 1875, p. 34, *sq.*) that Nob is identical with MIZPEH, and both with the modern *Neby Samwil*.

NOBAH (nō'bah), (Heb. חַבֹ֗נ, *no'bakh*, a bark).

1. A warrior, probably of Manasseh, who during the wars east of the Jordan captured Kenath on the western side of Jebel Hauran and gave the town his own name (Num. xxxii:42), B. C. about 1617.

2. A city mentioned in connection with Jogbehah, of Gad (Judg. viii:11). From the connection its site must be on the boundary between Gad and the Arabian desert.

NOBLE (nō'b'l), the translation of three Hebrew and two Greek words:

1. *Yak-keer'* (Heb. רֹיקָי, *dear, rare*), a term applied (Ezra iv:10) to ASNAPPER (which see).

2. *Par-tam'* (Heb. םֹֽתְּרַפ; Lat. *primus*), a noble, or prince among the Persians (Esth. i:3; iii:1, A. V. "princess"), and the Jews (Exod. xxiv:11; 1 Kings xxi:8, etc.).

3. *So-rake'* (Heb. קֵרֹשׂ, *reddish*), a vine of a finer and richer kind, probably so called from purple grapes (Jer. ii:21).

4. *Yoog-en'aċe* (Gr. εὐγένης, *well-born*), *noble minded, nobly disposed*, and thus inclined to tolerance, spoken of the Bereans (Acts xvii:11); *well-born*, of noble race (1 Cor. i:26).

5. *Krat'is-tos* (Gr. κράτιστος, *strongest*), a term used in addressing men of high rank or office (Acts xxiv:3; xxvi:25; comp. Neh. vi:17).

NOBLEMAN (nō'b'l-man).

The word so rendered in John iv:46 is the Greek βασιλικός, *bas-il-ee-kos'*, which is somewhat varied in signification. It may mean: (1) Descended from a king. (2) Ὑπηρέτης τοῦ βασιλέως, *hoo-pay-ret'aċe too bas-il-eh'oce*, one belonging to the court. (3) *Strat-ee-oh'taċe bas-il-eh'oce*, στρατιώτης βασιλέως, *a soldier of the king*, in which latter sense it often occurs in Josephus. (4) *Yoog-en'aċe* (Gr. εὐγένης, *well-born*, and ἄνθρωπος, *anth'ro-pos*, man), used in the parable of the talents (Luke xix:12) as a title of the person who placed his servants in charge of certain amounts, for which they were to be held accountable, thus testing their fidelity and ability.

This person was, therefore, probably of the court of Herod Antipas, who reigned over Galilee and Peræa (Tholuck, *Commentar zum Johan.* iv: 46). He has been identified with Chuza, Herod's steward (Luke viii:3), and with Manaen, Herod's foster brother (Acts xiii:1). These, of course, are mere conjectures. He was presumably a Jew, and is certainly not to be identified, as he has

sometimes been, with the centurion whose servant Jesus healed (Matt. viii:5; Luke vii:2-10).

NOD (nŏd), (Heb. דֹונ, *node*), the land to which Cain withdrew, and in which he appears to have settled (Gen. iv:16).

While the site of Paradise itself remains undetermined, it is useless to seek for that of the land of Nod. This land, wherever it was, could not have had a name till Cain went to it; and it was doubtless called Nod (which signifies *flight, wandering*, from the circumstance that Cain fled to it. Von Bohlen identifies it with India. Sayce sees in it the *Manda* of the cuneiform inscriptions. To the Rabbis it was sufficient that it lay somewhere in the east and away from Eden, whither Adam had been banished.

NODAB (nō'dăb), (Heb. בָדֹונ, *no-dawb'*, nobility), an Arab tribe, probably belonging to the Syrian desert (1 Chron. v:19).

Delitzsch (*New Com.* on Gen. xxv:15), connects it with Nudébe in the *Wady el-butin* of the Hauran. But it is more likely that we have here a transcription of Nabatean. It would be strange that a powerful kingdom like Nabatea should not have proved a formidable neighbor to the trans-Jordanic Israelites. (See NABAIOTH.)

NOE (nō'e), (Gr. Νῶε, *no'eh*), the Greek form of NOAH (Matt. xxiv:37, 38; Luke iii:36; xvii: 26, 27).

NOGAH (nō'gah), (Heb. הַגֹנ, *no'gah*, a shining), the fourth son born to David in Jerusalem, by other wives than Bathsheba (1 Chron. iii:7; xiv:6), B. C. cir. 1040. The name is wanting in the parallel list (2 Sam. v).

NOHAH (nō'hah), (Heb. הָחֹונ, *no-khaw'*, rest), a son of Benjamin and head of a family in the tribe (1 Chron. viii:2), B. C. about 1850.

He is not mentioned among those who went down with Jacob into Egypt, and was, therefore, probably born after that migration. He is perhaps the same as BECHER (Gen. xlvi:21), or IR (1 Chron. vii:12).

NOISE, NOISED (noiz), (Heb. הָעוּרְתּ, *ter-oo-aw'*; Gr. ἀκούω, *ak-oo'o*).

This term is no longer used of music in a good or neutral sense, as we find it in Ps. xxxiii:3, 'Play skillfully with a loud noise.' Comp. Bunyan, p. 206: 'Mercy—Hark, don't you hear a Noise? Chris.—Yes, 'tis, as I believe, a Noise of Musick, for joy that we are here.' Ps. xlvii:5, Prayer Book, 'God is gone up with a merry noise;' and Milton, *At a Solemn Music*, line 18—

'That we on earth with undiscording voice
May rightly answer that melodious noise.'

Nor is it used of a company or set of musicians, or of a band.

"The king has his *noise* of gypsies as well as of bearwards and other minstrels."   Ben Jonson.

(See article in Hastings' *Bib. Cyc.*, by J. Hastings.)

The verb "to noise," Dr. Hastings says, is no longer in use. But the term in its participle form has not become entirely obsolete, and will again come into active use from its expressiveness, in the sense of "to spread by rumor or report."

It occurs five times in A. V.: Josh. vi:27, 'His fame was noised throughout all the country' (R. V. 'his fame was in all the land'); Judith x:18, 'Her coming was noised among the tents;' Mark ii:1, 'It was noised that he was in the house;' Luke i:65, 'All these sayings were noised abroad;' Acts ii:6, 'When this was noised abroad' (R. V. 'when this sound was heard').

NOISOME (noi'sŭm), (Gr. βλαβερός, *blab-er-os'*, Rev. xvi:2; comp. Ps. xci:3; Ezek. xiv:15, 21; "harmful" in 1 Tim. vi:9), in the early translations was equivalent to noxious, injurious or hurtful. "Foul breath is noisome," Shakespeare.

NON (nŏn), (Heb. נוֹן, *nohn*, continuation).

1. An Ephraimite through Beriah, who was born to Ephraim after the men of Gath had slain some of his sons (1 Chron. vii :27).

2. A form of Nun, which was the name of the father of Joshua. (See NUN.)

NOON (nōōn). See TIME.

NOPH (nŏf), (Heb. נֹף, *nofe*). See MEMPHIS.

NOPHAH (nō'phah), (Heb. נֹפַח, *no'fakh*, blast, windy place), a place in Moab mentioned only in Num. xxi:30. It is possibly the Moabitish form of Mobah.

NOPHECH (nō'fĕk), (Heb. נֹפֶךְ, *no-fekh*), a precious stone, named in Exod. xxviii:18; xxxix: 11; Ezek. xxvii:16; xxviii:13; in all which places it is rendered 'Emerald' in the Authorized Version.

The Sept. and Josephus render it by *an-ah-thrax*, ἄνθραξ, or carbuncle, this name denoting a live coal, the ancients gave to several glowing red stones resembling live coals (Plin. *Hist. Nat.* xxxii :25; comp. Theophrast. *De Lapid.* 18). particularly rubies and garnets. The most valued of the carbuncles seems, however, to have been the Oriental garnet, a transparent red stone, with a violet shade, and strong vitreous luster. It was engraved upon (Theophrast., 31), and was probably not so hard as the ruby, which, indeed, is the most beautiful and costly of the precious stones of a red color, but is so hard that it cannot easily be subjected to the graving-tool. The Hebrew *nophech*, in the breast-plate of the high-priest, was certainly an engraved stone; and there is no evidence that the ancients could engrave the ruby, although this has in modern times been accomplished. Upon the whole, the particular kind of stone denoted by the Hebrew word must be regarded as uncertain (Rosenmüller, *Biblical Mineralogy*, pp. 32, 33). (See CARBUNCLE; EMERALD; RUBY.)

NORTH (nôrth), (Heb. מְזָרֶה, *mez-aw-reh'*, scatterer, Job xxxvii:9).

The Shemite, in speaking of the quarters of the heavens and of the earth, supposes his face turned towards the east, so that the east is before him, the west behind, the south on the right hand, and the north on the left. Hence the words which signify east, west, north, and south signify also that which is before, behind, on the right hand, and on the left. The Hebrew word translated north occurs in the five following senses:

(1) **A Particular Quarter of the Heavens.** It denotes a particular quarter of the heavens; thus, 'fair weather cometh out of the north' (Job xxxvii :22).

(2) **Quarter of the Earth.** It means a quarter of the earth (Ps. cvii:3; Is. xliii:6; Ezek. xx :47; xxxii :30; comp. Luke xiii:29).

(3) **A Northern Aspect.** It occurs in the sense of a northern aspect or direction, etc.; thus, 'looking north' (1 Kings vii:25; 1 Chron. ix:24; Num. xxxiv:7); on 'the north side' (Ps. xlviii :2; Ezek. viii :14; xl :44; comp. Rev. xxi:13).

(4) **Name for Countries.** It seems used as the conventional name for certain countries, irrespectively of their true geographical situation, namely, Babylonia, Chaldæa, Assyria, and Media, which are constantly represented as being to the north of Judæa, though some of them lay rather to the east of Palestine. Thus Assyria is called

the north (Zeph. ii :13), and Babylonia (Jer. i :14; xlvi :6, 10, 20, 24; Ezek. xxvi :7; Judith xvi :4).

(5) **North Wind.** The Hebrew word is applied to the north wind. In Prov. xxvii :16, the impossibility of concealing the qualities of a contentious wife, is illustrated by comparing it to an attempt to bind the north wind. The invocation of Solomon (Cant. iv :16), 'Awake, oh north, and come, thou south, blow upon my garden that the spices may flow out,' and which has occasioned much perplexity to illustrators, seems well explained by Rosenmüller, as simply alluding to the effect of winds from opposite quarters, in dispersing the fragrance of aromatic shrubs (verses 13, 14) far and wide, in all directions. J. F. D.

NORTH COUNTRY (nôrth kŭn'trỹ), a term applied to the countries lying north of Palestine, whence came invaders and foes (Is. xli:25; Jer. i: 14, 15; Ezek. xxvi:7). (See NORTH.)

NOSE, NOSTRILS (nōz, nos'trĭls), (Heb. אַף, *af;* dual אַפָּיִם, *ap-pah-yeem'*, properly, breathing place, Num. xi:20). The Hebrews commonly place the seat of anger in the nose; since the effect of anger is often hard breathing, and in animals, snorting. "There went up a smoke out of his nostrils" (2 Sam. xxii:9; Ps. xviii:8).

Figurative. (1) "*Lo, they put the branch to their nose*" (Ezek. viii :17) appears to be a proverbial expression variously interpreted. Some understand it as the *barsom*, which the Pharisees held in their hand while praying, or rather in front of the mouth as a magical mode of driving demons away. Two other explanations may be given—that it is a proverbial expression, "to apply the twig to anger," in the sense of adding fuel to the fire. The second, that of Hitzig, "They apply the sickle to their nose," *i. e.*, by seeking to injure me they injure themselves (Keil, *Com.*, in loc.).

(2) The words "*they take away thy nose and ears*" (Ezek. xxiii :25) are not to be interpreted, as the earlier expositors suppose, from the custom prevalent among the Egyptians and other nations of cutting off the nose of an adulteress, but depict, by one particular example, the mutilation of prisoners captured by their enemies.

(3) As the Hebrews employed the term signifying nose to denote *anger*, "nose" and "nostrils," ascribed to God, denote his discernment of provocation, and his wrath to be executed on account thereof (Exod. xv:8; Ps. xviii:8; Is lxv:5). "The anger of the Lord and his jealousy shall smoke against that man" (Deut. xxix:20). "Out of his nostrils goeth smoke" (Job xli :20). Camels and oxen were managed by iron rings in their nostrils, and thereto the allusion is made (2 Kings xix:28; comp. Job xli:2; Is. xxxvii:29).

NOSE JEWELS (nōz jū-ĕls), mentioned in Is. iii:21, consisted of a ring of gold or other metal upon which jewels were strung. The nose-rings now worn by the lower classes in Egypt are from one to one and a half inches in diameter and are passed through the right nostril (Schaff).

NOTABLE (nōt'à-b'l), the translation of several words in the Scriptures.

1. (Heb. חָזוּת, *khaw-zooth'*), meaning prominent, conspicuous (Dan. viii:5).

2. (Gr. ἐπιφανής, *ep-if-an-ace'*, Acts ii:20), well-known, conspicuous, clearly seen, illustrious.

3. *Notorious* (Gr. ἐπίσημος, *eh-pis'ay-mos*, Matt. xxvii:16), 'And they had then a notable prisoner, called Barabbas.'

4. *Unmistakable, well known* (Gr. γνωστός, *noce-tos'*, Acts iv:16), 'a notable miracle.'

NOTE (nōt).

1. (Heb. קָקַק, *khaw-kak'*, to engrave), to write (Is. xxx:8).

2. "Who are of note" (Gr. ἐπίσημος, *ep-is'ay-mos*, having a mark) is spoken of Andronicus and Junia, as being highly esteemed by the apostles (Rom. xvi:7).

3. (Gr. σημειόω, *say-mi-ŏ'o*, to distinguish), to mark a man by shunning him (2 Thess. iii:14).

NOTHING, NOUGHT (nŭth'ĭng), (Heb. בֹּל, *kole*).

1. Not anything at all (Gen. xix:8).

2. For no good purpose or end (Matt. v:13).

3. No works truly good and acceptable to God (John xv:5).

4. Of no binding force (Matt. xxiii:16, 18).

5. Entirely false, and without ground (Acts xxi:24).

6. No other means (Mark ix:29).

7. No reward or wages (3 John 7).

8. No new doctrine relative to men's salvation; no new knowledge or authority (Gal. ii:6).

9. No guilt or corruption to work upon (John xiv:30).

Nothing is sometimes taken comparatively: thus our age is *nothing* before God, bears no proportion to his eternal duration (Ps. xxxix:5). All nations are *nothing,* and less than nothing, and vanity; *i. e.,* they bear no proportion to his unbounded excellency and greatness (Is. xl:17). Sometimes it is taken relatively: so Paul was *nothing* valuable in his own estimation of himself (2 Cor. xii:11). Circumcision, or uncircumcision, is *nothing;* is of no avail to render us accepted with God (1 Cor. vii:19). To *come to nought,* is to be ruined, turn out to no good purpose (Job viii:22; Is. viii:10). To *bring to nought,* is to render unsuccessful, base, and contemptible (Ps. xxxiii:10; 1 Cor. i:28). To set at *nought,* is to undervalue, despise (Prov. i:25).

In the phrase *nothing worth* it is probable that 'nothing' is again adverbial, though we have but to transpose the words to find it a substantive. It occurs in Job xxiv:25, 'who will make me a liar, and make my speech nothing worth?'

NOVICE (nŏv'ĭs) or **NEOPHYTE** (Gr. Νεόφυτος, *nee-oh'foo-tos,* one newly converted), (literally *newly planted*), not yet matured in Christian experience (1 Tim. iii:6). The ancient Greek interpreters explain it by 'new-baptized,' νεοβάπτιστος, *nee-oh'bap'tis-tos,* 'proselyte,' προσήλυτος, *pros-ay'lu-tos,* etc.

The word continued to be in use in the early church; but it gradually acquired a meaning somewhat different from that which it bore under the Apostles, when 'newly converted' and 'newly baptized' described, in fact, the same condition, the converted being at once baptized. For when, in subsequent years, the church felt it prudent to put converts under a course of instruction before admitting them to baptism and the full privileges of Christian brotherhood, the term Νεόφυτοι, *Novitii,* Novices, was sometimes applied to them, although more usually distinguished by the general term of Catechumens.

NUMBER (nŭm'bĕr). The following numbers were understood by the Hebrews to have a symbolical or representative significance:

(1) Three was deemed to have a peculiar mystic meaning. It is the number of the Deity (the Trinity), of the thrice-repeated "Holy" (Is. vi:3), of the threefold priestly blessing (Num. vi:23-26), Daniel's three hours of prayer (Dan. vi:10), etc.

(2) Four symbolizes the world or humanity. There are four winds (Ezek. xxxvii:9), four beasts (Rev. iv:6), and four living creatures with four faces, four wings, and four sides (Ezek. i:5-10, etc.).

(3) Five, appears in the tables of requirements and punishments, as Exod. xxii:1; Lev. v:16. Also, five empires (Dan. ii). In the New Testament, five wise and five foolish virgins, etc.

(4) Seven, the union of three and four, is the number of the covenants between God and man. It implies perfection. The number occurs very frequently in connection with both holy things and things unholy. For example, the seven-branched candlestick (Exod. xxv:37; 1 Kings vii:17; Zech. iv:10; comp. Is. xi:2); the sprinkling of the blood seven times (Lev. iv:6; viii:11; xiv:7; xvi:14; Num. xix:4; 2 Kings v:10); seven lambs (Num. xxviii:11; Ezek. xlv:23; 2 Chron. xxix:21); comp. the seven sons of Saul who were hanged before the Lord (2 Sam. xxi:9); the seven locks of the Nazarite Samson (Judg. xvi:13, 19); the seven priests that carried seven trumpets seven times in front of the ark and around the walls of Jericho (Josh. vi:4); the seven days in the week, the seven churches (Rev. i:4), the seven years of plenty in Egypt (Gen. xli:26), the seven angels with seven golden vials (Rev. xv:1); but also the seven heads and seven crowns of the dragon (Rev. xii:3).

(5) Ten, the number of fingers (two hands), symbolizes harmony and completeness. It is the number of the fundamental commandments.

(6) Twelve, the multiple of three and four, is also a covenant number, like seven. Hence we have the twelve tribes, the twelve stones in the high-priest's breastplate (Exod. xxviii:21), twelve apostles, twelve gates in the New Jerusalem, etc.

(7) Forty, four multiplied by ten; as the forty days of our Lord's temptation (Matt. iv), the forty years in the wilderness, etc.

(8) Seventy, seven multiplied by ten; as the seventy elders of Israel (Num. xi:16), the seventy disciples of our Lord (Luke x:1).

It is very difficult, if indeed at all possible, to get the exact and definite meaning of these numbers, and we must not carry the search too far. But that they had a special meaning for the Hebrews there can be little doubt (compare the extended and ingenious treatment of Lange, *Com. on Revelation,* pp. 14, *sq.*). (Schaff, *Bib. Dict.;* Hastings' *Bib. Dict.*).

NUMBERS, BOOK OF (nŭm'bĕrs), is the appellation given to the fourth book of Moses, which in the Septuagint is called Ἀριθμοί, *ar-ith-moi', numbers,* and in the Hebrew canon *be-mid-bar,* 'in the desert.'

1. Contents. This book embraces more especially the continuation of the Sinaitic legislation, the march through the wilderness, the rejection of a whole generation, and the commencement of the conquest of Canaan. Thus we see that it treats on very different subjects, and on this account it has frequently been attempted to resolve it into separate fragments and documents, and to represent it as being composed of the most heterogeneous materials. We will endeavor to refute this opinion, by furnishing an accurate survey of its contents, and by describing the internal connection of its component parts, so that the organization of the book may be clearly understood.

(1) Arrangements for Order. The sum and substance of the law having been stated in the preceding books, that of Numbers commences with the arrangements requisite for preserving good order in the camp of the Israelites. The people are numbered for the express purpose of separating the Levites from those Israelites who had to bear arms, and of thus introducing into practice the law concerning the firstborn, for whom the tribe of Levi became a substitute. For this reason the people are not merely numbered, but also classed according to their descent; the order which each tribe should occupy in the camp is defined; and the Levites are introduced into their respective functions (chapters i-iv).

The camp, having been consecrated, was to be kept pure according to the law of Levitical cleansings; consequently all persons were excluded from it who were afflicted with leprosy, who had become unclean by a flux, and who had touched a corpse (ch. v:1-4).

(2) Authority of Priests. Thus, after civil and sacerdotal life had been brought into a definite form, other laws based upon this form came into force, especially those laws which regulated the authority of the priests in civil affairs (ch. v: 5; vi:27). These regulations conclude with the beautiful form of benediction which indicates the blessing to be expected from the true observance of the preceding directions. The people are impressed with this fact; the hearts of the Israelites are willing to offer the required gifts, and to entrust them to the Levites.

(3) Lamps. Jehovah is faithful to his promise, and gloriously reveals himself to his people (ch. vii). Before the Levites enter upon the discharge of their sacred functions, the law concerning the lamps to be lighted in the sanctuary is significantly repeated (ch. viii). These lamps symbolize the communication of the Holy Spirit and bring to the recollection of the nation the blessings of theocracy to be derived from setting apart the tribe of Levi, which had recently been separated from the rest of the people.

(4) Celebration of Passover. Then follows a description of the celebration of the Passover, preparatory to the departure of the people from Mount Sinai (ch. ix:1-14). Some regulations are connected with the celebration of the Passover, and the whole miraculous guidance of the people is described (ch. ix:15-x).

(5) Entrance Into Canaan. Thus the entrance of Israel into the Holy Land seemed to be fully prepared; and it was of great importance to show how they were prevented from entering it. Accurate details are therefore given of the spirit which pervaded the nation; a spirit which, in spite of the forbearance of God, manifested itself in daring rebellions against the divine authority (chapters xi and xii).

(6) Turning Point of History. Now comes the turning point of the history. Everything seems externally prepared for the conquest of the country, when it appears that the nation are not yet internally ripe for the performance of so important an act (chapters xiii, xiv).

In immediate connection with this are some laws which were given in the desert; the intention of which was to recall to the recollection of the rejected race, which had been justly condemned to suffer severe punishment, that nevertheless they had not ceased to be the people of the covenant, and the depositary of divine revelation (comp. ch. xv:2, 13-16, 22, 23, 37, *sq.*). In this respect the facts mentioned in ch. xv:32-36 and ch. xvi are also of great importance. They show, on the one hand, the continuance of an evil disposition in the people, and, on the other, the majesty of God watching over his holy law.

The contents of chapters xv-xix are of a similar character. The facts there recorded relate to a period of thirty-eight years. The conciseness with which they are stated significantly indicates the strictly legal and theocratical principles of the Mosaical legislation.

(7) Period of Israel's Rejection. The period of Israel's rejection is characterized by the circumstance, that the historian is almost silent respecting it, as being a period not strictly belonging to theocratical history. During this period the striking deeds of God, his miracles and signs, the more prominent operations of his grace, and his peculiar blessings, cease. The rejection of the nation consisted in this suspension of the divine operations. During this period God, as it were, ignored his people. Consequently, the historian also almost ignores the rebellious race. But the period in which the divine promises were to be fulfilled again forms a prominent portion of the history.

(8) Termination of Penal Period. The termination of the penal period is the commencement of the most important era in the Mosaical history. It brings the legislation to a splendid conclusion. The most glorious facts here follow each other in close succession; facts which were intended clearly to demonstrate that the chosen people entered into the land of promise, not by their own power and might, but that this land was given into their hands by the God of promise.

(9) Subsequent History. Miriam was already dead; and the forty years of wandering in the wilderness were accomplished. Israel was again in sight of the Holy Land on the borders of Edom. Then Moses and Aaron also sinned; soon after, Aaron died, and was succeeded by Eleazar. Israel sent ambassadors to the king of Edom to obtain permission to pass through his territory, but was haughtily refused (ch. xx). Everything seemed to be prepared by preceding events already recorded. The dying off of the real emigrants from Egypt might be expected, after the divine decree that this should come to pass, had been mentioned; the unbelief of Moses arose from the protracted duration of the time of punishment, which at length broke his courage; the spirit of Edom arose in overbearing animosity, because it seemed that Jehovah had forsaken his people. It was appointed that Israel should undergo all this in order that they might grow strong in the Lord. Their strength was soon proved against Arad. They vowed to devote all the cities of the Canaanites to Jehovah, who gave them the victory. They were directed to avoid the boundaries of Edom, and to have Canaan alone in view. The people murmured, and the significant symbol of the serpent was erected before them, reminding them of their ancient sin, and how it had been healed and overcome by Jehovah. In all this Israel is constantly directed to Canaan. They march courageously to the boundaries of the Amorites, singing praises to Jehovah, and, by the power of the Lord, defeat the kings of Heshbon and Bashan (ch. xxi).

In the plains of Moab still greater glory awaits the chosen people. The pagan prophet of Mesopotamia, being hired by the king of the Moabites, is overpowered by Jehovah, so that he is compelled to bless Israel instead of cursing them; and also directs them to the ancient blessings granted to the patriarchs. The bitterest enemies of the theocracy are here most deeply humbled, being themselves compelled to contribute to the glory of Jehovah (chapters xxii-xxiv). Not the God, but the people of Israel, were dishonored through the devices of Balaam.

The subsequent account concerning the idolatry into which the people were led, forms a striking contrast with the preceding chapters, and evinces the impotence of the Israelites, whose first attack, therefore, was to be directed against their se-ducers. This was to be the beginning of the con-quest of Canaan, which was essentially a combat against idolatry, and the victory of the kingdom of God over paganism. The conquered country was granted to separate tribes, and for this pur-pose the people were once more numbered, and Joshua appointed their leader.

Jehovah reserves his own rights in the distri-bution of the country, and Israel is directed not to forget the sacrifices to the Lord, the sabbaths, festivals, and vows; the ordinances concerning which are here briefly repeated, inculcated, and completed.

The people shall certainly gain the victory, but only in strict communion with Jehovah. Thus begins the combat against Midian, according to the directions of the law, and forming as it were a prototype of the later combats of Israel against pagan powers (chapters xxv-xxxi).

This was the last external work of Moses. Henceforth his eye is directed only to the internal affairs of his people. An entrance has been effected into the country, and the conquered terri-tory is divided among two tribes and a half-tribe (ch. xxxii).

Moses reminds the people of Jehovah's guid-ance in the wilderness, and of the manner in which the whole land was to be conquered. He com-mands the destruction of the Canaanites and of their idolatry. He appoints to what extent the land is to be conquered, and in what manner it should be divided; also the towns to be granted to the Levites, and the cities of refuge. He es-tablishes also the statute, which was of great im-portance for the preservation of landed property, that an heiress should marry only within her own tribe (chapters xxxiii-xxxvi).

2. Credibility. There have frequently been raised strong doubts against the historical credi-bility of the book of Numbers, although it is im-pressed with indubitable marks of the age to which it refers, and of perfect authenticity.

(1) Author Acquainted with Egypt. The author of the book of Numbers proves himself to be intimately acquainted with Egypt. The pro-ductions mentioned in chapter xi:5 are, according to the most accurate investigations, really those which in that country chiefly served for food.

Narratives like the history of Balaam (xxii, xxiv) furnish also numerous proofs of their high antiquity. These confirmations are of the great-est importance, on account of the many marvelous and enigmatical points of the narrative.

(2) Accurate Geographical Statements. Com-pare, for instance, the geographical statements, which are uncommonly accurate, in chapters xxii: 1, 36, 39; xxiii:14, 15, 27, 28. (See Hengsten-berg's *Geschichte Bileam's,* Berlin, 1842, p. 221, sq.)

The list of stations in chapter xxxiii is an im-portant document, which could not have orig-inated in a poetical imagination. This list con-tains a survey of the whole route of the Israelites, and mentions individual places only in case the Israelites abode there for a considerable period. It is not the production of a diligent compiler, but rather the original work of an author well versed in the circumstances of that period. A later author would certainly have avoided the ap-pearance of some contradictions, such as that in Num. xxxiii:30, 31, comp. with Deut. x:6. This apparent contradiction may best be removed by observing that the book of Numbers speaks of the expedition of the Israelites in the second year of their wanderings, and the book of Deuteronomy of their expedition in the fortieth year. (See DISCREPANCIES, BIBLICAL.) The list of stations contains also important historical notices; those, for instance, in chapter xxxiii:4, 9, 14, 38. These notices demonstrate the accurate historical infor-mation of the author.   H. A. C. H.

NUN (nŭn), (Heb. נוּן, *noon,* in Syr. and Arab., a fish), the father of Joshua, who is hence constantly called Joshua ben-Nun (Exod. xxxiii:11; Num. xi:28; xiii:8, 16; xiv:6, 30, 38; xxvi:65; xxvii:18; xxxii:12, 28, etc.), B. C. before 1210. 'Joshua the son of Nun.' Nothing is known of the person who bore this name.

NURSE, NURSING (nûrs, nûrs'ĭng), (Heb. יָנַק, *yaw-nak',* to give milk; once אָמַן, *aw-man',* to foster, support, Ruth iv:16).

The position of nurse was one of much im-portance and honor. Rebekah's nurse accompa-nied her mistress to Canaan, and was buried with much mourning at Allon-bachuth (Gen. xxiv:59; xxxv:8). The tenderness of a nurse is not infre-quently referred to (Is. xlix:23; 1 Thess. ii:7).

NURSING FATHER (nûrs'ĭng fä'thēr), (Is. xlix:23). A *nursing* father is a *foster father.*

NURTURE (nûr'tŭr), (Gr. παιδεία, *pahee-di'ah,* Eph. vi:4. Training in mind and soul for the duties and responsibilities of life.

Both in LXX and New Testament παιδεία and παιδεύω describe, not 'nurture' in the modern use of that word, but training, especially such train-ing or discipline as involves restraint and even chastisement. Chastise and chastening or chas-tisement are often the best translation, as in Heb. xii:5, 7, 10. In Luke xxiii:16, 22, the verb is used of the scourging of a malefactor; it is rendered 'chastise' in A. V.

NUTS (nŭts), (Heb. בֹּטֶן, *bo'ten*).

Those mentioned in Gen. xliii:11 are doubtless pistachio-nuts, which were produced in Syria, but not in Egypt. The pistachio tree (*Pistacia vera*) resembles the sumac, to whose family it belongs. It is still cultivated in the Levant, and produces thin-shelled nuts resembling almonds, but smaller and with a green meat tasting like that of the wal-nut. The nuts of Cant. vi:11 (אֱגוֹז, *eg-oze'*) are *walnuts.* They are universally cultivated and greatly esteemed in Bible lands.

NYMPHAS (nўm'phas), (Gr. Νυμφᾶς, *noom-fas',* nymph-given), a Christian of Laodicea or Colossæ, to whom Paul sent salutations (Col. iv:15).

O

OAK (ōk). Four Hebrew words are translated oak. Of these, three, אַיִל (ah'yil), אֵלָה (ay-law'), and אַלּוֹן (al-lone'), are uncertain in meaning, and are either *oak* or *terebinth*. The other, אַלָּה (al-law'), probably refers definitely to the *oak*. They are always so translated in A. V. and R. V.

(1) In the following passages, at least, the word probably denotes the terebinth, or the elm of Hos. iv:13 (see TEIL TREE); Gen. xxxv:4, 8; Judg. vi:11, 19; 2 Sam. xviii:9, 10, 14; 1 Kings xiii:14; 1 Chron. x:12; Is. i:30; Ezek. vi:13. In other instances "oak" may denote *any* strong flourishing tree (Amos ii:9), or a grove of such trees.

(2) Botanists find three species of this tree in Palestine. One of the most universal and char-

which are eaten by the poor, while their cups are employed by tanners under the name of valeria, and exported from many parts of the Turkish empire.

Another kind (*Q. infectoria*) sometimes occurs in Samaria and Galilee as a small tree with deciduous leaves, white beneath. Travelers through the uninhabited districts of Gilead and Bashan have found there magnificent forests of all three species.

(3) In the Bible we find these noble trees often mentioned for the purpose of designating the locality of important events as in Gen. xxxv:8; Josh. xxiv:26. Oak wood was used for idols (Is. xliv:14) and idolatry was practiced under oaks (Is. i:30; lvii:5; Ezek. vi:13).

(4) The word translated "plains" in several passages (Gen. xii:6; xiii:18; xiv:13; xviii:1; Deut. xi:30; Judg. iv:11; ix:6, 37; 1 Sam. x:

Abraham's Oak, in the Plains of Mamre.

acteristic bushes of the country is the prickly evergreen-oak (*Quercus pseudo-coccifera*), which has a leaf like the holly, but smaller. This oak now rarely exceeds twelve feet in height, but when the destruction of trees was less universal it doubtless attained great size and age. "Abraham's Oak," in the field of Mamre, near Hebron, the noblest tree of southern Palestine, is of this species, and is twenty-three feet in girth; and there are said to be still finer specimens in the north and east.

The Valonia oak (*Q. ægilops*) sheds its leaves and more resembles some of our own species. The trunk is unusually massive, and the tree often grows to a magnificent size. It is not seen in the south, but abounds in the north, especially about Mount Tabor and also east of the Jordan, and is doubtless the "oak of Bashan" (Is. ii:12, 13; Zech. xi:2). It produces very large acorns,

3) means *places* noted for one or more oaks. (Schaff, *Bib. Dict.*)

(5) It will thus be seen that the several species of oak are among the most widely disseminated trees of Syria and Palestine. The mountains of *Haurân* (Bashan, Is. ii:13; Ezek. xxvii:6; Zech. xi:2) have many oak trees still, mostly *Querecus Coccifera, Querecus Ægilops*, and *Querecus Lusitanica*. Oak trees were planted by tombs (Gen. xxxv:8). Few objects in Palestine or Syria are more striking than the immense oak trees, solitary or grouped near the Welies or tombs of the prophets. (Hastings' *Bib. Dict.*)

The Tyrians made their oars for rowing their ships of the fine "oaks of Bashan" (Ezek. xxvii: 6). (See ALLON.)

Figurative. (1) The Hebrews were like an *"oak whose leaf fadeth;"* stripped of their confidence in themselves and others, and bereaved of their honor, wealth, prosperity, and pleasure (Is. i:30), yet like an *"oak or teil-tree,"* whose substance or life is in it though bare of foliage, could never be utterly destroyed by the Assyrians, Chaldæans, or Romans (Is. vi:13). (2) Governors and great and valiant men, are compared to the tall and strong *"oaks of Bashan,"* to mark their apparent power, strength, and firmness, and their fitness to protect others (Is. ii:13; Zech. xi:2).

OAK, WORSHIP OF (ōk, wûr-shĭp ŏv). Oak groves in ancient times were used as places of religious assembly; altars were set up in them (Josh. xxiv:26); Jacob buried idolatrous images under an oak, which, as a sacred tree, would free them from disturbance (Gen. xxxv:4). (See OAK.)

OATH (ōth), (Heb. שְׁבוּעָה, *sheb-oo-aw'*), an appeal to God in attestation of the truth of what you say, or in confirmation of what you promise or undertake.

The Latin term is *jusjurandum,* or *juramentum.* Cicero (*De Officiis,* iii, 29) correctly terms an oath a religious affirmation; that is, an affirmation with a religious sanction. This appears from the words which he proceeds to employ: that an oath is an appeal to God, as the source and the vindicator of justice and fidelity.

(1) Elements. Hence it appears that there are two essential elements in an oath: first, the human, a declared intention of speaking the truth, or performing the action in a given case; secondly, the Divine, an appeal to God, as a Being who knows all things and will punish guilt. According to usage, however, there is a third element in the idea which 'oath' commonly conveys, namely, that the oath is taken only on solemn, or, more specifically, on juridical occasions. The canon law gives all three elements when it represents *judicium, veritas, justitia,* as entering into the constitution of an oath—*judicium,* judgment or trial on the part of society; *veritas,* truth on the part of the oath-taker; *justitia,* justice on the part of God. An oath is accordingly a religious undertaking either to say (*juramentum assertorium*), or to do (*juramentum promissorium*) something entered into voluntarily with the customary forms. Being a religious undertaking, the appeal will vary according to the religious opinions of the country in which the oath is taken. In some instances it will be an appeal immediately to God; in others, to objects supposed to have Divine power; and by a natural declension, when men have left the only true God, they may appeal in their oaths even to stocks and stones. Accordingly the Roman swore, *'per caput suum vel suorum filiorum,'* or *'per genium principis;'* that is, by his own head or those of his children, or by the genius of the emperor. We shall have by and by to notice similar errors and abuses among the Jews.

(2) Essence. The essence of an oath lies obviously in the appeal which is thereby made to God, or to Divine knowledge and power. The customary form establishes this, 'So help me God.' The Latin words (known to have been used as early as the sixth century), whence our English form is taken, run thus: *'Sic me Deus adjuvet et hæc sancta Evangelia;'* so may God *and these holy Gospels help me;* that is, 'as I say the truth.' The present custom of kissing a book containing the gospels has in England taken the place of the latter clause in the Latin formula. If, then, an appeal to God is the essence of an oath, oath-taking is a practice which cannot be

justified. Such an appeal is wrong, because it is a mere act of a creature's will, being unrequired and unsanctioned by God, in a case in which God is made a party to a certain course, which course may or may not be agreeable to his mind (because a wish on the part of the oath-taker for punishment, should he fail in his undertaking, or any part of the same, is an act unbecoming a frail man, unseemly in its very nature, and awful to think of when man's sinfulness and God's power are rightly apprehended); because it relaxes the general bonds of religion, and morality, and truth; (for in establishing an occasion when justice must be done, it authorizes the idea that its observance is not imperative on other occasions); and because it is founded on an essentially false view of religious obligation; for as God sees, knows, and governs all things, and as all things so each thing, so man is bound universally to speak the truth and perform what he undertakes, bound as much in each and in all the actions of his life, as his dependence and God's sovereignty can bind a rational and accountable being; so that it is radically false to suppose that there is or can be anything special in the obligation of an oath; the tendency of which falsity is not to raise, but to degrade the character, to reduce the general standard of truth and rectitude, to weaken the moral sense, by encouraging the idea that on special occasions, and of course on special occasions *only,* truth is to be spoken and promises performed.

(3) Early Use. It is one among those numerous accordances, small when compared with the dictates of right reason, which will be found to prevail in the Bible the more minutely it is investigated, and which, though now, after a revelation has enlightened the mind, are discoverable thereby, nevertheless are so far beyond its reach, when left to its own resources, that the practice of antiquity bears in the opposite direction—it is one of those very important accordances with truth, that the Mosaic legislation is not answerable for the practice of taking oaths, which existed before the time of Moses. It is found as early as the days of Abraham, who made the oldest servant of his family swear he would select for Isaac a wife of his own kindred (Gen. xxiv:2, 3, 37). It is here observable that the oath is a private, not a judicial one; only that the rectoral authority of Abraham, as patriarch, must be taken into account. The form observed is found in these words: 'Put, I pray thee, thy hand under my thigh; and I will make thee swear by the Lord, the God of heaven and the God of earth, that,' etc.

(4) Occasions. An oath was sometimes a public and general bond, obliging the parties who took it to certain course—a case in which it appears to have been spontaneous and voluntary; as when, in Judg. xxi, the men of Israel swore, saying, 'There shall not any of us give his daughter unto Benjamin to wife' (comp. verse 5). From 1 Kings xviii:10, it appears to have been customary to require on occasions of great concern a public oath, embracing even an entire 'kingdom and nation;' but whether taken individually or by some representative, we have no means of ascertaining. Such a custom, however, implying, as it does, a doubt of the public faith of a people, would hardly be submitted to, unless on the part of an inferior.

Oaths did not take their origin in any Divine command. They were a part of that consuetudinary law which Moses found prevalent, and was bound to respect, since no small portion of the force of law lies in custom, and a legislator can neither abrogate nor institute a binding law of his own mere will. Accordingly, Moses made use of the sanction which an oath gave, but in that general manner, and apart from minute directions and express words of approval; which shows that he merely used, without intending to sanction, an instrument that he found in existence and could not safely dispense with. Examples are found in Exod. xxii:11, where an oath is ordered to be applied in the case of lost property; and here we first meet with what may strictly be called a judicial oath (Lev. vi:3-5).

(5) Forms of Oaths. The forms of adjuration found in the Scriptures are numerous. Saul sware unto Jonathan, 'As the Lord liveth' (1 Sam. xix:6). 'A heap and a pillar' were for a witness between Laban and Jacob, with the ensuing for a sanction, 'The God of Abraham and the God of Nahor, the God of their father, judge betwixt us. And Jacob sware *by the fear of his father Isaac*' (Gen. xxxi:52, *sq.*). A common formula is, 'The Lord do so to me and more also' (Ruth i:17; 1 Sam. iv:44), which approaches nearly to our modern form, 'So help me God,' and is obviously elliptical. Reference appears to be had to the ancient custom of slaying some animal in confirmation of a treaty or agreement. The animal thus slain and offered in a burnt offering to God became an image or type, betokening the fate which would attend that one of the two contracting parties who failed in his engagement; and the words just cited were intended to be a voluntary assumption of the liability thus foreshadowed on the side of those who joined in the covenant: subsequently the sacrifice was in ordinary cases omitted, and the form came in itself, to have the force of a solemn asseveration.

(6) Sanctity. An oath, making an appeal to the Divine justice and power, is a recognition of the Divinity of the being to whom the appeal is made. Hence to swear by an idol is to be convicted of idolatry. Such an act is accordingly given in Scripture as a proof of idolatry and a reason for condign punishment. 'How shall I pardon thee for this? Thy children have forsaken me, and sworn by them that are no gods' (Jer. v:7; xii:16; Amos viii:14; Zeph. i:5).

Other beings besides God are sometimes added in the form of an oath: Elijah said to Elisha, 'As the Lord liveth, and as thy soul liveth' (2 Kings ii:2; 1 Sam. xx:3). The party addressed is frequently sworn by, especially if a prince: 'As thy soul liveth, my lord, I am the woman,' etc. (I Sam. i:26; xvii:55; xxv:26; 2 Sam. xi:11). The Hebrews, as well as the Egyptians, swore also by the head or the life of an absent as well as a present prince: 'By the life of Pharaoh' (Gen. xlii:15). Hanway says that the most sacred oath among the Persians is 'by the king's head.' The oath-taker swore sometimes by his own head (Matt. v:36; see Virg. *Æn.* ix, 300; Ovid, *Trist*, iv, 4, 45; Juven. vi, 17); or by some precious part of his body, as the eyes (Ovid, *Amor.* iii, 3, 13; Tibull. iii, 6, 47); sometimes, but only in the case of the later Jews, by the earth, the heaven, and the sun (Matt. v:34, 35; Eurip. *Hippol.* 1029; Virg. *Æn.* xii, 176); as well as by angels (Joseph. *De Bell. Jud.* ii, 16, 4); by the temple (Matt. xxiii:16; comp. Lightfoot, p. 280); and even by parts of the temple (Matt. xxiii:16; Wetstein). They also swore by Jerusalem, as the holy city (Matt. v:35; Lightfoot, p. 281). The Rabbinical writers indulge in much prolixity on the subject of oaths,

entering into nice distinctions, and showing themselves exquisite casuists.

The levity of the Jewish nation in regard to oaths, though reproved by some of their doctors (Othon. *Lex.* p. 351; Philo, ii, 194), was notorious; and when we find it entering as an element into popular poetry (Martial, xi, 9), we cannot ascribe the imputation to the known injustice of heathen writers towards the Israelites. This national vice, doubtless, had an influence with the Essenes (see ESSENES), in placing the prohibition of oaths among the rules of their reformatory order. J. R. B.

(7) Attitude. It was usual to put the hand under the thigh (Gen. xxiv:2; xlvii:29). The more usual employment of the hand was to raise it towards heaven; designed, probably, to excite attention, to point out the oath-taker, and to give solemnity to the act (Gen. xiv:22, 23). In the strongly anthropomorphitic language of parts of the Scripture, even God is introduced saying, 'I lift up my hand to heaven, and say, I live for ever' (Deut. xxxii:40). It can only be by the employment of a similar license that the Almighty is represented as in any way coming under the obligation of an oath (Exod. vi:8; Ezek. xx:5). Instead of the head, the phylactery was sometimes touched by the Jews on taking an oath (Maimon. *Schebhuoth*, c, xi).

(8) Christian. Our Lord condemned the use of oaths, even when taken with the best intention, declaring that whatever went beyond "yea, yea, or nay, nay," was of the evil one (Matt. v:33-37). He was delivering the Sermon on the Mount and correcting various perversions of the law which the scribes had introduced; and among other evils, he condemned swearing in ordinary communications between man and man. But the judicial oath is lawful; for it was enjoined by God (Exod. xxii:11), and Christ himself did not hesitate to answer when he was put upon his oath by the high-priest (Matt. xxvi:63). The oath was recognized as lawful by the apostles also, for they called on God to witness to the truth of what they said (2 Cor. xi:31; Gal. i:20). The mischief which may arise from a rash oath was well illustrated in that of Herod the tetrarch, which made him, against his will, the murderer of John the Baptist (Matt. xiv:3-12; comp. James v:12). (Davis, *Bib. Dict.;* Raymond, *Sys. Theol.*, vol. iii, p. 161-2.)

OBADIAH (ō-ba-dī'ah), (Heb. עֹבַדְיָה, o-bad-yaw', servant of Jehovah), the name of several persons mentioned in the Scripture.

1. The governor of king Ahab's household, and high in the confidence of his master, notwithstanding his aversion to the idolatries which the court patronized. In the persecution raised by Jezebel, Obadiah hid one hundred of the Lord's prophets in caves, and supplied them secretly with nourishment during the famine. It was this person, when sent out to explore the country in the vain search of pasture unconsumed by the drought, whom Elijah encountered when about to show himself to Ahab, and who was reluctantly prevailed upon to conduct the prophet to his master (1 Kings xviii:4-16). (B. C. 906.)

2. One of the heroes of the tribe of Gad, who joined David at Ziklag (1 Chron. xii:9). (B. C. 1014.)

3. One of the nobles whom Jehoshaphat sent to teach in the cities of Judah (2 Chron. xvii:7). (B. C. 909.)

4. One of the Levites who presided over the restoration of the temple under Josiah (2 Chron. xxxiv:12). (B. C. 623.)

5. The head of a party, consisting of 218 males, with females and children in proportion, who returned with Ezra from Babylon (Ezra viii:9).

6. One of the priests, who sealed the written covenant which Nehemiah caused the people to enter into (Neh. x:5).

7. A man of Issachar of the house of Uzzi (1 Chron. vii:3). (B. C. 1014.)

8. The father of Ishmaiah, which latter was chief of the Zebulunites in the reign of David (1 Chron. xxvii:19). (B. C. 1014.)

9. Son of Azel and a descendant of Jonathan (1 Chron. viii:38; ix:44). (B. C. about 720.)

10. A descendant of David and founder of a family (1 Chron. iii:21). (B. C. about 870.) Probably he is the same as JUDA (Luke iii:26) and ABIHUD (Matt. i:13).

11. A Levite, descendant of Jeduthun, and apparently the founder of a family of porters (1 Chron. ix:16). (B. C. about 446.)

12. *The Prophet Obadiah.* He was the fourth of the minor prophets according to the Hebrew, the fifth according to the Greek, and the eighth according to chronological arrangement, is supposed to have prophesied B. C. about 599. (Jahn's *Introd.*) We have, however, but a small fragment of his prophecies, and it is impossible to determine anything with certainty respecting himself or his history. Several persons of this name occur about the same period, one of whom presided at the restoration of the temple in the reign of Josiah (B. C. 624), and is considered by many to have been the author of the prophecy. Another, who was governor of the house of Ahab, was regarded by the ancient Jews as the author of the book: which opinion is followed by Jerome (Hieron. *Comm. in Abdiam;* Sixtus Senens, *Bib. Sanct.*). Others place the author in the reign of Ahaz (B. C. 728-699); while some think him to have been a contemporary of Hosea, who prophesied B. C. 722.

13. *Obadiah, Prophecy of.*

(1) Time of Prophecy. It is observed by Jahn, Newcome, and others, that it is evident from verse 20 that Obadiah prophesied while Jerusalem was subjected to the yoke of the Chaldæans, and after the expatriation of several of the citizens—which refers him to the period after the seventh year of the Captivity, B. C. 599. Jahn maintains, from the warnings to the Edomites, verses 12-14, that Obadiah prophesied before the destruction of Jerusalem by Nebuchadnezzar; while De Wette infers from the mention of the 'captivity of the children of Israel,' and the 'captivity of Jerusalem' in verse 20, that the composition of the book must be placed after the destruction of that city. From a comparison of Obad. verses 1-4, with Jer. xlix:14-16; Obad. verse 6, with Jer. xlix:9, 10; and Obad. verse 8, with Jer. xlix:7, it is evident that one of these prophets had read the other's work.

(2) Against Whom Directed. His prophecies are directed against the Edomites, and in this respect correspond with Amos i:11; Jer. xlix:22; Ezek. xxv:12-14, and Ps. cxxxvii:7 (Jahn's *Introd.*). He menaces Edom with destruction for their hostile feeling towards Judah, and their insulting conduct towards the Hebrews when Jerusalem was taken (verses 11, 12); but consoles the Jews with a promise of restoration from their captivity, when the Hebrews and the Ten Tribes **(Jahn's *Introd.*)** shall repossess both their land

and that of Edom and Philistia—a prophecy which was fulfilled in the time of the Maccabees, under John Hyrcanus. (B. C. 125.) (Jahn, *l. c.*)

(3) Style, Etc. The language of Obadiah is pure; but Jahn and others have observed that he is inferior to the more ancient prophets in his too great addiction to the interrogatory form of expression (see verse 8). His sentiments are noble, and his figures bold and striking (De Wette's *Introd.,* Eng. transl.). De Wette's translator observes that his hatred towards other nations is not so deep and deadly as that of some of his younger contemporaries. W. W.

Cornill considers that the late prophecies (Is. xxxiv:35), in which, as in Obadiah, eschatological hopes are connected with the downfall of Edom, were certainly known to the author of Obadiah. (Hastings' *Bib. Dict.*)

OBAL (ō'bal), (Heb. עוֹבָל, *o-bawl'*, bare), a son of Joktan, and founder of an Arabian tribe (Gen. x: 28). (B. C. before 2060.)

Bochart, who refers to the fact that Pliny mentions the Avalitæ of the African coast, identifies them with the descendants of Obal.

OBED (ō'bed), (Heb. עוֹבֵד, *o-badé,* serving; Sept. Ὠβήδ, *oh-bade'*).

1. The son of Boaz and Ruth, and father of Jesse the father of David, according to the apparently incomplete genealogical list (Ruth iv:17; 1 Chron. ii:12). The name occurs in the genealogies of Matthew (i:5) and Luke (iii:32).

2. One of David's warriors (1 Chron. xi:47). (B. C. about 1046.)

3. Son of Ephlal and father of Jehu; a descendant of Jerahmeel (1 Chron. ii:37). (B. C. after 1014.)

4. A son of Shemaiah and gate-keeper of the temple (1 Chron. xxvi:7). (B. C. 1017.)

5. Father of Azariah, who lived in the time of Athaliah (2 Chron. xxiii:1). (B. C. before 876.)

OBED-EDOM (ō'bed-ēd'om), (Heb. עבֵד אֱדֹם, *o-bade' ed-ome'*, serving Edom).

1. A Levite in whose premises, and under whose care, the ark was deposited, when the death of Uzzah caused David to apprehend danger in taking it farther. It remained here three months, during which the family of Obed-edom so signally prospered, that the king was encouraged to resume his first intention, which he then happily carried into effect (2 Sam. vi:10-12). We learn from 1 Chron. xvi:38, that Obed-edom's connection with the ark did not then terminate, he and his brethren having charge of the doors of the sanctuary (1 Chron. xv:18, 24).

2. Son of Jeduthun, and warden of the temple (1 Chron. xvi:38). (B. C. 1043.)

3. One of those who had charge of the sacred vessels in the time of Amaziah (2 Chron. xxv: 24). (B. C. 835.)

OBEDIENCE (ŏ-bē'dĭ-ens), (Heb. שָׁמַע, *shawmah'*, to hear intelligently), the fulfillment of a superior's command from regard to his authority.

(1) Characteristics, Etc. (1) Believers' "obedience" lies in believing the truths of the gospel, and therein receiving Jesus and his fullness, as the free gift of God; and, in consequence thereof, sincerely studying conformity to his image, and cheerful fulfillment of his whole law (Rom. vi: 16). This is called "obedience to the faith," because it begins in embracing the truths of the gospel, and is a fulfillment of the Divine law as revealed in the Scripture (Acts vi:7; Rom. i:5). It is an "obedience of faith;" it corresponds with the principles received by faith in the Scripture (Rom. xvi:26). (2) It is an "obedience of Christ;" it flows from his dwelling in, and actuating our heart (2 Cor. x:5). (3) It is an "obedience unto righteousness" (Rom. vi:16). (4) It must spring from a heart renewed, and actuated by his indwelling Spirit (Ezek. xxxvi: 26, 27; Matt. vii:18; Gal. i:16; 1 Tim. i:5; Heb. ix:14). (5) It must be sincere (Ps. li:6; 1 Tim. i:5). (6) Affectionate, springing from love, and not from terror (1 John iv:19; 1 John ii:5; 2 Cor. v:14). (7) Diligent, not slothful (Heb. vi:12; Ps. xviii:44; Rom. xii:11). (8) Conspicuous and open (Phil. ii:15; Matt. v:16). (9) Universal: not one duty, but all must be performed (2 Pet. i:5, 10). (10) Perpetual, at all times, places, and occasions (Rom. ii:7; Gal. vi:9).

(2) Advantages. (1) It adorns the gospel (Tit. ii:10.) (2) It is evidential of grace (2 Cor. v:17). (3) It rejoices the hearts of the ministers and people of God (3 John 2, 3; 1 Thess. ii:19, 20). (4) It silences gainsayers (Titus, i:9). (5) Encourages believers, while it reproves the lukewarm (Matt. v:16). (6) Affords peace to the subject of it (Ps. xxv:12, 13; Acts xxiv:16). (7) It strongly recommends religion, as that which is both delightful and practicable (Col. i: 10). (8) It is the forerunner and evidence of eternal glory (Rom. vi:22; Rev. xxii:14.) (Buck, *Bib. Dict.;* Brown, *Bib. Dict.*)

OBEDIENCE OF CHRIST is generally divided into active and passive. His *active* obedience implies what he did; his *passive* what he suffered. Some divines distinguish these. They refer our pardon to his passive, and our title to glory to his active obedience; though, Dr. Owen observes, that it cannot be clearly evinced that there is any such thing in propriety of speech as *passive obedience;* obeying is doing, to which passion or suffering does not belong. Of the active obedience of Christ the Scriptures assure us that he took upon him the form of a servant, and really became one (Is. xlix:3; Phil. ii:7; Heb. viii). He was subject to the law of God. "He was made under the law;" the judicial or civil law of the Jews: the ceremonial law, and the moral law (Matt. xvii:24, 27; Luke ii:22; Ps. xl:7, 8). He was obedient to the law of nature; he was in a state of subjection to his parents; and he fulfilled the commands of his heavenly Father as it respected the first and second table. His obedience (1) was voluntary (Ps. xl:6); (2) complete (1 Pet. ii:22); (3) wrought out in the room and stead of his people (Rom. x:4; Rom. v:19); (4) well pleasing and acceptable in the sight of God. (Buck, *Bib. Dict.*) (See Martensen, *Christ. Eth.* vol. i, p. 260, *sq.;* Hastings' *Bib. Dict.*)

OBELISK (ŏb-ĕ-lĭsk), (Hos. iii:4. R. V.) See PILLAR.

OBETH (ō'bĕth). (1 Esdras viii:32. Same as EBED, Ezra viii:6).

OBIL (ō'bil), (Heb. אוֹבִיל, o-beel', chief of the camels), Sept. 'Αβίας, a-bee'as, an Ishmaelite, or Arab, doubtless of the nomad tribes, who had charge of the royal camels in the time of David—an exceedingly fit employment for an Arab (1 Chron. xxvii:30).

As Obil means in Arabic 'a keeper of camels' Hieron. (ii, 2), reasonably infers that the person had his name from his office, which has always been a very common circumstance in the East.

OBJECT (ŏb-jĕkt), (Gr. κατηγορέω, kat-ay-gor-eh'-o; to be a plaintiff, to charge with some offense).

This word is rendered *accuse* (Acts xxiv:19); *a public accusation* (Mark xiv:60).

OBLATION (ŏb-lā'shŭn), (Heb. מִנְחָה, min-khaw', a donation). See OFFERING and SACRIFICE.

OBOTH (ō'both), (Heb. אֹבֹת, o-both'), a station of the Israelites near Moab (Num. xxi:10, 11; xxxiii:43, 44). (See WANDERING, THE.)

OBSCURE (ob-skūr'), (Heb. אִישׁוֹן, ee-shone', the little man of the eye, *i. e.,* the pupil or ball); what is dark, little known; and so "obscure darkness," may denote a lone condition of sorrow and misery (Prov. xx:20).

Figurative. (1) Obscurity is much the same as darkness, and denotes what is opposite to the light of knowledge or prosperity, namely, ignorance and misery, calamities (Is. lix:9). (2) The blind "*see out of obscurity, and out of darkness,*" when their natural sight is miraculously given them, or rather when their ignorant minds are enlightened by the spiritual knowledge of Christ, and his truth (Is. xxix:18). (3) Light rises in "*obscurity and darkness,* and is made as the noon-day," when great ignorance and distress are put away, and knowledge, prosperity, and joy, come in their room; or when believers, amidst their outward distress, have fellowship with, and joy in their God; and the church grows greatly amidst distress and persecution (Is. lviii:10).

OBSERVATION (ŏb-zēr-vā'shun), (Gr. παρατήρησις, par-at-ay'ray-sis, that which may be seen) with outward show.

"The kingdom of God cometh not with observation" (Luke xvii:20), *i. e.* it must be viewed as a *spiritual* development and not as a *visible* unfolding as in the case of the kingdoms of men. It must come by *waiting* and *watching.*

OBSERVER OF TIMES (ŏb-zērv'ēr ŏv tīms). See MAGIC.

OBSTINACY (ŏb'stĭ-nà-cy). See HARD, *Figurative.*

OCCUPY (ŏk'kŭ-pī), (Heb. עָשָׂה, aw-saw', Judg. xvi:11), to make use of, to employ.

"If they bind me fast with new ropes that never were *occupied,* then shall I be weak, and be as another man" (Judg. xvi:11).

Occupy now means *to be in present possession, to hold,*—thus one *occupies* a house, a station, etc. But formerly it had a wider sense, and meant not only to have the use of, but to use in general. "Ropes that never were *occupied,*" means ropes that never were *used.* (See also Exod. xxxviii:24).

Its more frequent meaning in our version of the Bible is, to use *in trade,* as money, or to *deal in,* as merchandise (Ezek. xxvii:9); hence, intransitively, *to trade* or *traffic* (Ezek. xxvii:16, 19, 21, 22). In this sense it occurs in Luke xix: 13, "occupy till I come." Compare *occupier.*

Eumenes made as though he had occasion to *occupy* money (that is, to make *use* of money), and so borrowed a great sum.
—North's *Plutarch.*
But now must men *occupy* their goods otherwise.
—Latimer's *Sermons.*
(Swinton, *Bib. Word Book.*)

OCCURRENT (ŏk kûr'rent), (Heb. פֶּגַע, peh'-gah), an occurrence.

"But now the Lord my God hath given me rest on every side, so that there is neither adversary nor evil *occurrent*" (1 Kings v:4). *Occurrent* was the earlier form of the word now written *occurrence.*

OCHIM (ō'kĭm), a species of animal (Is. xiii:21, R. V. "doleful creatures").

OCRAN (ŏk'ran), (Heb. עָכְרָן, *ok-rawn'*, muddler), father of the Pagiel who was chief of Asher about the time of the Exodus (Num. i:13; ii:27; vii:72; x:26), B. C. before 658.

ODED (ō'ded), (Heb. עֹדֵד, *o-dade'*, erecting).

1. The prophet who remonstrated against the detention as captives of the persons whom the army of King Pekah had brought prisoners from Judah, and at whose suggestion they were handsomely treated, and conducted back with all tenderness and care to their own country (2 Chron. xxviii:9). (B. C. 739.)

2. Father of Azariah the prophet, who was commissioned to meet and encourage Asa on his return from defeating the Ethiopians (2 Chron. xv:1-8). It curiously happens that the address which, at the commencement, is ascribed to Azariah, the son of Oded, is at the end ascribed to Oded himself (xv:8). But this is supposed to have been a slip of copyists, and the Alex. MS., the Vulgate and the Peshito-Syriac versions read the latter verse like the former. (B. C. before 953.)

ODEM (ō'dĕm), (Heb. אֹדֶם, *o'dem*; Sept. σάρδιον, *sar'dee-on*), sardius, one of the precious stones in the breastplate of the high-priest (Exod. xxviii:17; xxxix:10, and also mentioned in Ezek. xxviii:13).

In all these places it is rendered 'sardius' in the Authorized Version, following the Septuagint and Josephus (*De Bell. Jud.*, v, 5, 7), who, however, in *Antiq.* iii, 7, 6, makes it the sardonyx (σαρδόνυξ). The sardius is the stone now called the carnelian, from its color (*a carne*), which resembles that of raw flesh. The Hebrew name is derived from a root which signifies being red. The sardius or carnelian is of the flint family, and is a kind of chalcedony. The more vivid the red in this stone, the higher is the estimation in which it is held. It was anciently, as now, more frequently engraved on than any other stone. The ancients called it sardius, because Sardis in Lydia was the place where they first became acquainted with it; but the sardius of Babylon was considered of greater value (Plin. *Hist. Nat.* xxxvii:7). The Hebrews probably obtained the carnelian from Arabia.

ODOR (ō'dẽr), (Heb. נִיחֹחַ, *nee-kho'akh*, restful, Lev. xxvi:31; Dan. ii:46), relating to INCENSE (which see).

It denotes fragrance, a sweet smelling odor and the like (2 Chron. xvi:14; Esth. ii:12; Jer. xxxiv:5; John xii:3; Phil. iv:18).

"The odors of the groves of Lebanon were anciently very famous (Hos. xiv:7; Cant. iv:11); flowers, even exotics, were cultivated in pleasure gardens for this purpose (Cant. i:12; iv:6, 14). Odorous extracts were used sometimes in the form of incense, sometimes as ointments (i:3; iv:10); sometimes in water, with which clothing, bed furniture, etc., was sprinkled (Prov. vii:17)" (McC. & S., *Cyc.*)

Figurative. The prayers and praises of the saints, and their cheerful contributions to fellow-Christians, when in need, are likened to *odors*, to represent how delightful and acceptable they are to God (Rev. v:8; Phil. iv:18).

OF (ŏv), the most frequent preposition in the English language. "And should have been killed *of* them" (Acts xxiii:27), where we should now use *by*, as in Luke xiv:8; 1 Cor. xi:32, and numerous other passages.

Other peculiar uses are, "*of* purpose" (Ruth ii:16), where we should say, *on* purpose; "zeal *of* thine house" (Ps. lxix:9; John ii:17), for zeal *for* thine house; "zeal *of* God" (Rom. x:2), for zeal *for* God.

OFFENSE (ŏf-fens'), three Hebrew words are translated in the A. V. "offenses:"

1. *Mik-shole'* (Heb. מִכְשׁוֹל), an *obstacle*, or *enticement* (1 Sam. xxv:31; Is. viii:14).

2. *Khate* (Heb. חֲטָאָה), *crime*, or its *penalty* (Eccles. x:4).

3. *Aw-sham'* (Heb. אָשַׁם), to *acknowledge* guilt (Hos. v:15).

The Greek words rendered "offense" are: παράπτωμα, *par-ap'to-mah*, to *fall beside or near*, a *lapse*, or deviation from the truth; a *sin*, or *misdeed* (Rom. v:15-20; iv:25, xvi:17; σκάνδαλον, *skan'-dal-on*, the *movable stick of a trap*, any impediment (Matt. xviii:7; Rom. ix:33; Luke xvii:1).

Figurative. In the figurative and moral sense, as an occasion of falling into sin, it means *to cause to offend*, as the Greek word is correctly translated (1 Cor. viii:13), "if meat make my brother to *offend*." So in Matt. v:29, 30, "if thy right eye *offend* thee," *stumble* thee, cause thee to offend, as correctly rendered in the Geneva version, 1560. Luke xvii:2 (Matt. xviii:6; Mark ix:42), "should *offend* one of these little ones," should cause one of them to *offend*, to fall into unbelief; and in the passive, be made to *offend* or *stumble* at unlooked-for difficulties and dangers, and *fall away* from the truth or from duty, as in Matt. xiii:21; xxiv:10; xxvi:31, 33; Mark iv:17; xiv:27, 29; John xvi:1. Rom. xiv:21, "stumbles or is *offended*," is made to offend, led into sin. Thirdly, in the sense of a ground or object of *offense*, of dissatisfaction and aversion, it means *to displease, to give offense;* as in Matt. xv:12, "the Pharisees were *offended* after they heard this saying;" xvii:27, "lest we should *offend* them." So in Matt. xiii:57, "were *offended* in him," found in him (in his humble birth and connections) ground of disapproval and rejection (John vi:61; 2 Cor. xi:29). (Swinton, *Bib. Word Book.*)

OFFERING (ŏf'fẽr-ĭng), (the general name for which in Hebrew is קָרְבָּן), *kor-bawn'*) is anything offered to God as a means of conciliating his favor; which being in the Jewish, as well as in all other religions, considered as the one thing needful, offerings accordingly have always constituted an essential part of public worship and private piety.

Offerings have been divided into three kinds; those which are designed to procure some favor or benefit; the second, those which are expressive of gratitude for bounties or mercies received; the third, those which are meant to atone for sins and propitiate the Deity. Among the Hebrews we find a complex and multiform system of offerings extending through the entire circle of Divine worship, and prescribing the minutest details. A leading distinction separates their offerings into unbloody and bloody.

(1) Meaning and Objects Used. Used in its widest sense the term offering, or oblation, indicates in the Hebrew ritual a very great number of things — as the firstlings of the flock, first fruits, tithes, incense, the shew-bread, the wood for burning in the Temple (Neh. x:34). The objects offered were salt, meal, baked and roasted grain, olive-oil, clean animals, such as oxen, goats, doves, but not fish. The animals were required to be spotless (Lev. xxii:20; Mal. i:8), and, with the exception of the doves, not under eight days old (Lev. xxii:27), younger animals being tasteless and innutritious. The smaller beasts, such as sheep, goats, and calves, were commonly one year old (Exod. xxix:38; Lev. ix:3; xii:6; xiv:10; Num. xv:27; xxviii:9, *sq.*). Oxen were offered at three years of age; in Judges (vi:25) one is offered which is seven years old. As to sex, an option was sometimes left to the offerer, as in peace and sin-offerings (Lev. iii:1, 6; xii:5, 6); at other times males were required, as in burnt sacrifices, for, contrary to classical usage, the male was considered the more perfect. In burnt-offerings and in thank-offerings the kind of animal was left to the choice of the worshiper (Lev. i:3), but in trespass and sin-offerings it was regulated by law (Lev. iv:5). If the desire of the worshiper was to express his gratitude, he offered a peace or thank-offering; if to obtain forgiveness, he offered a trespass or sin-offering.

(2) Burnt-Offerings. Burnt-offerings were of a general kind (Num. xv:3; Deut. xii:6; Jer. xvii:26). Hecatombs or large numbers of cattle were sacrificed on special occasions. In 1 Kings viii:5, 63, Solomon is said to have 'sacrificed sheep and oxen that could not be told or numbered for multitude,' 'two and twenty thousand oxen and an hundred and twenty thousand sheep' (see also 2 Chron. xxix:32, *sq.;* xxx:24; xxxv:7, *sq.;* comp. Herod. vii:43; Xenoph. *Hellen.,* vi:4; Sueton. *Calig.* 14). Offerings were also either public or private, prescribed or free-will. Sometimes they were presented by an individual, sometimes by a family; once, or at regular and periodic intervals (1 Sam. i:24; Job i:5; 2 Macc. iii:32).

Foreigners were permitted to make offerings on the national altar (Num. xv:14; 2 Macc. iii:35; xiii:23; Philo. *Legat.* p. 1014; Joseph. *c. Apion.* ii, 5). Offerings were made by Jews for heathen princes (1 Macc. vii:33; Joseph. *Antiq.* xii, 2, 5).

In the case of bloody offerings the possessor, after he had sanctified himself (1 Sam. xvi:5), brought the victim, in case of thank-offerings, with his horns gilded and with garlands, etc., (Joseph. *Antiq.* xiii:8, 2; Winer, *Real-wörterb.* ii, 212, note 5) to the altar (Lev. iii:1; xii:4; xiv:17), where laying his hand on the head of the animal (Lev. i:4; iii:2; iv:4), he thus, in a clear and pointed way, devoted it to God. Having so done he proceeded to slay the victim himself (Lev. iii:2; iv:4); which act might be, and in later times was, done by the priests (2 Chron. xxix:24; and probably by the Levites.

The blood was taken, and, according to the kind of offering, sprinkled upon the altar, or brought into the temple and there shed upon the ark of the covenant and smeared upon the horns of the altar of incense, and then the remainder poured forth at the foot of the altar of burnt-offerings. Having slain the animal, the offerer struck off its head (Lev. i:6), which when not burnt (Lev. iv:11) belonged either to the priest (Lev. vii:8), or to the offerer (comp. Mishna, *Lebach.* xii:2). The victim was then cut into pieces (Lev. i:6; viii:20), which were either all, or only the best and most tasty, set on fire on the altar by the priests or the offerer, or must be burnt outside the precincts of the holy city. The treatment of doves may be seen in Lev. i:14, *sq.;* v:8. In some sacrifices heaving and waving were usual either before or after the slayings.

(3) Place of Offerings. The place where offerings were exclusively to be presented was the outer court of the national sanctuary, at first the Tabernacle, afterwards the Temple. Every offering made elsewhere was forbidden under penalty of death (Lev. xvii:4, *sq.;* Deut. xii:5, *sq.;* comp. 1 Kings xii:27). The precise spot is laid down in Lev. i:3; iii:2, 'at the door of the tabernacle of the congregation before the Lord.' The object of these regulations was to prevent any secret idolatrous rites from taking place under the cloak of the national ritual; and a common place of worship must have tended considerably to preserve the unity of the people, whose constant disagreements required precautions of a special kind (1 Kings xii:27). The oneness, however, of the place of sacrifice was not strictly preserved in the troubled period of the Judges, nor indeed till the time of David (1 Kings iii:2, 3). Offerings were made in other places besides the door of the Tabernacle (1 Sam. vii:17; Judg. ii:5). High places, which had long been used by the Canaanites, retained a certain sanctity, and were honored with offerings (Judg. vi:26; xiii:19). Even the loyal Samuel followed this practice (1 Sam.), and David endured it (1 Kings iii:2). After Solomon these offerings on high places still continued. In the kingdom of Israel, cut off as its subjects were from the holy city, the national temple was neglected.

(4) Formalism. Under the load and the multiplicity of these outward oblations, however, the Hebrews forgot the substance, lost the thought in the symbol, the thing signified in the sign; and, failing in those devotional sentiments and that practical obedience which offerings were intended to prefigure and cultivate, sank into the practice of mere dead works. Hereupon began the prophets to utter their admonitory lessons, to which the world is indebted for so many graphic descriptions of the real nature of religion and the only true worship of Almighty God (Is. i:11; Jer. vi:20; vii:21, *sq.;* Hos. vi:6; Amos v:22; Micah vi:6, *sq.;* comp. Ps. xl:6; li:17, *sq.;* Prov. xxi:3). All these offerings were typical in various forms of the "full, perfect and sufficient sacrifice, oblation and satisfaction for the sins of the whole world."

The Jewish doctrines on offerings may be found in the treatises *Sebachim, Menachoth,* and *Temura;* a selection from which, as well as from the Rabbins, is given in that useful little work, Othon. *Lex. Talmud.* p. 621, *sq.*　　　　J. R. B.

OFFICER (ŏf'fi-sēr).

The Hebrew and Greek words translated officer are very numerous and indefinite. They are synonymous terms for functionaries known under other and more specific terms, as "eunuch," "scribes," etc.

1. *Saw-reece'* (Heb. סָרִים, to castrate, Gen. xxxvii:36; xxxix:1; xl:2), usually rendered Eunuch (which see).

2. *Sho-tare'* (Heb. שֹׁטֵר, properly a *writer*), from the use of writing in judicial administration, a *magistrate* or *prefect;* the officers set over the Israelites in Egypt (Exod. v:6-19), those appointed with the elders to administer public affairs among the Israelites (Num. xi:16; Deut. xx:5, 8, 9; xxix:10; Josh. i:10, etc.), magistrates in the cities and towns of Palestine (Deut. xvi:18; 1 Chron. xxiii:4; xxvi:29, etc.), and apparently a military chief (2 Chron. xxvi:11, A. V. "ruler," R. V. "officer").

3. *Nits-tsawb'* (Heb. נִצָּב, fixed, 1 Kings iv:5, 7; v:16; ix:23, etc.), general receivers of taxes, or chief tax collectors.

4. Paw-keed' (Heb. פָּקִיד, Gen. xli:34; Judg. rx:28; Esth. ii:3, etc.), a *superintendent*, either civil, military, or ecclesiastical. (McC. & Str. *Bib. Cyc.*)

5. In the New Testament in the case of ὑπηρέτης (*hoop-ay-ret'ace*), the word means bailiffs (Matt. v:25; John vii:32, 45; Acts v:22).

In the case of Πράκτορες (*prak'tor-es*) it denotes those who register and collect the fines imposed by courts of justice (Luke xii:58).

OFFICER THAT STRUCK JESUS. This man struck Jesus on the cheek with his hand or rod, perchance with both. It was the first overt act of personal violence (Luke xxii:63, 64). He was doubtless informed of a Jewish law found in Exodus xxii:28, "Thou shalt not revile God, nor curse a ruler of thy people." But this fellow had a bigoted veneration for the high-priest, and applied this punishment with indiscretion and severe brutality. The blows must have been severe. Jesus had done nothing that merited such a painful insult.

OFFICES OF CHRIST (ŏf'fĭsĕs ŏv krīst), are generally considered as threefold.

(1) A prophet to enlighten and instruct (John vi:14; John iii:2). (2) A priest to make atonement for his people (Is. liii; Heb. vii). (3) A king to reign in, and rule over them (Zech. ix:9; Ps. ii:6).

(1) Prophet. Christ is Prophet because more than all others he has declared to men the truth and will of God. He is himself the revelation of God (see John xiv:9; xvii:25, 26; Heb. i:1, 2, et al.).

(2) High Priest. Christ is the great High Priest. He is the first begotten, an elder brother of God's spiritual family of chosen priests. He directs his people, offers sacrifice for them, and by his blood and Spirit consecrates them to God. How transcendant his unction to, and preparation for his work! He wears his manhood, and executes his office, in the double estate of debasement and glory. How shining his robes of righteousness and garments of salvation! and how fixed forever, as on his shoulder and heart, are all the Israelites indeed! As he espoused a pure and virgin nature into personal union with himself none but virgin saints and churches are really his people. On his head are many crowns; and by him, as our righteousness and sanctification, are we sanctified, and *made holiness to the Lord.* He is the great High Priest of our profession, and of good things to come. His person, as God-man, is infinitely dignified in his sacrificial and intercessory work: his priesthood is the great foundation and object of our gospel-profession, and the cause of all the precious blessings that come upon us in time and eternity (Heb. iii:1, and viii:1). If Christ had remained on earth, he *could not have been a priest:* being descended of the tribe of Judah, he had no right to officiate in the sacerdotal work of the earthly tabernacle or temple; and if he had remained on earth after his oblation of himself, he could not have shewed himself the true Messiah, nor by his intercession finished his work, and rendered the shedding of his blood effectual (Heb. viii:4). (See ATONEMENT.)

(3) King. Christ is *king; King of kings; Lord of lords;* and *King of saints.* By his Father's appointment, he subdues, governs, and defends his church: and has all power in heaven and earth given him for the promoting of her welfare: he restrains and conquers her enemies; and at the last day, he will pass an irreversible sentence of judgment on the whole world (Ps. ii:6, and xlv:1; Matt. xxv:34; Rev. xvii:14, and xix:16). (See JESUS CHRIST; KING; MESSIAH; MEDIATOR.)

OFFSCOURING (ŏf'skour'ĭng), (Heb. סְחִי, *seh-khee'*, refuse, as swept off, Lam. iii:45; Gr. περίψημα *per-ip'say-mah*, I Cor. iv:13, brushed off), used figuratively to express something *vile, worthless*, as the apostles were looked upon by very many in their day.

OFTEN (ŏf''n), (Gr. πυκνός, *pook-nos'*, I Tim. v:23), an old English term for *frequent*. "Often messengers."—Shakespeare.

OG (ŏg), (Heb. עוֹג, *ogue*, giant or long-necked), an Amoritish king of Bashan (Num. xxi:33; xxxii: 33; Deut. iv:47; xxxi:4).

In form he was a giant, so that his bedstead was preserved as a memorial of his huge stature (Deut. iii:11; Josh. xiii:12). (See BED.) He was defeated by the Israelites under Moses (Num. xxi:33; Deut. i:4; iii:3); and his country, which contained many walled cities (Deut. iii:4-10), was assigned to the tribe of Manasseh (Deut. iii:13; Josh. xiii:30). (See AMORITES; BASHAN; GIANTS.)

OHAD (ō'hăd), (Heb. אֹהַד, *o'had*, unity), third son of Simeon and head of a family (Gen. xlvi:10; Ex. vi:15), B. C. 1870.

OHEL (ō'hel), (Heb. אֹהֶל, *o'hel*, tent), the fifth child of Zerubbabel, of the house of David (2 Chron. iii:20), B. C. after 600.

OIL (oil). The Hebrew and Greek words translated oil in the A. V. are as follows: (1) Hebrew שֶׁמֶן, *sheh'men*, grease, sometimes in A. V. "ointment." (2) Heb. יִצְהָר, *yits-hawr'*, shining, clear olive oil (Num. xviii:12; Deut. vii:13; xi:14; xii:17; 2 Kings xviii:32, etc. (3) Chald. מְשַׁח, *mesh-akh'* an *unguent* (only in Ezra vi:9; vii:22). (4) Gr. ἔλαιον, *el'ah-yon*, neuter of word meaning "olive."

Oil amongst the Hebrews, was made from olive berries and from spices (Exod. xxv:6). It was used: (1) In the preparation of food, much as butter and lard are used to-day (1 Kings xvii: 12-15; Exod. xxix:2; Lev. ii:4, etc.); (2) as a cosmetic for anointing the body, the beard, and the head (2 Sam. xiv:2; Ps. xxiii:5; Luke vii: 46, etc.) (see PERFUME); (3) for illuminating purposes in lamps (Exod. xxv:6; xxvii:20; Matt. xxv:3, etc.) (see LAMP); (4) in worship. The first-fruits (Num. xviii:12), and the tithes were dedicated to the Lord (Neh. xiii:5). The meat-offerings were also dipped in oil (Lev. ii:7; vii: 10, etc.) (see OFFERING); (5) in the ritual of consecration of kings and high-priests (1 Sam. x:1; Lev. viii:12, etc.); (6) for medicinal purposes (Mark vi:13; Luke x:34; Is. i:6; James v:14); (7) for anointing the dead (Matt. xxvi:12; Luke xxiii:56) (see ANOINTING).

The practice in the early Church of anointing the bodies of persons whose lives were despaired of was derived from Jas. v:14. The Roman Catholic Church has placed the practice among the sacraments, denominating it "extreme unction."

Figurative. (1) As an ordinary cosmetic, the use of oil is significant of joy and gladness (Ps. xcii:10), and the omission of it betokens sorrow (2 Sam. xiv:2; Matt. vi:17). (2) Oil represents the Holy Ghost's precious and diversified operations and graces, whereby Jesus and his people, and none other, are anointed to the service of God (Exod. xxx:23-33; Cant. i:3; iv:10). (3) Persons *"receive the oil of joy for mourning,"* when, by the comforting gifts and graces of the Holy Ghost, their hearts are healed, purified, invigorated, and honored (Is. lxi:3); but Jesus is *"anointed with the oil of gladness"* above them, having an unmeasurable fullness of the graces and comforts of the Holy Ghost (Ps. xlv: 7). And his name, character, office, and works, are like ointment poured forth, most healing, refreshful, invigorating, and adorning to our soul (Cant. i:3). (4) The *"golden oil emptied"* out of the two olive trees which stand before the Lord, is not the comfort arising to the Hebrews, from the management of Zerubbabel and Joshua, or of Ezra and Nehemiah; but the gracious endowments of the saints, proceeding from Jesus' two natures, or execution of his prophetic and kingly office on and in them (Zech. iv:12); this poured into their wounds, heals them (Luke x: 34). (5) The *"oil"* which true saints have in their lamps, is real grace which abides in them, and makes them shine as lights in the world (Matt. xxv:4). (6) Prosperity, spiritual or temporal, is likened to *"oil:"* it comforts, invigorates, and renders men noted and useful (Ps. xxiii:5). Christian reproof is like *"oil;"* it tends to heal spiritual diseases, restore the character, and render men who regard it honored and agreeable (Ps. cxli:5). (7) Unity among brethren, is like *"ointment;"* it procures delight, honor, cheerfulness, and activity to all concerned (Ps. cxxxiii: 2). (8) God made the river of Egypt run *"like oil;"* that is, very slowly, as in mourning; and when it was so dried up, that it did not make the country fruitful (Ezek. xxxii:14).

OIL, HOLY ANOINTING (oil, hŏ'lў á-noĭnt'-ing). The mode of preparing this oil is prescribed (Exod. xxx:22-25). (See ANOINTING).

OIL-PRESS (oil-prĕs).

"The oil of Palestine is expressed in a rude way. The olive is subjected to pressure in a mill consisting of a great millstone with a hole in its center; this stone is laid on one of its flat surfaces, and a beam of wood fastened upright in the axis. The upper surface of the stone is slightly depressed, except at its margin and around the central hole. Another millstone is set up on its edge in the depression of the upper surface of the lower stone. Through the axis of this stone passes a long beam, which is fastened at one end by a pin to the axis of the horizontal stone, and at the other to a whiffletree, to which a horse or ox is geared when the mill is in operation. The upright stone is moved around the axis of the lower, and crushes the olives by its great weight. The oil which is expressed by this crushing mill is incorporated with the crushed mass, which is then transferred to baskets of flexible structure, eighteen inches wide and six inches deep. A pile of these baskets, eight feet or more in height, is raised within a hollow erect cylinder of stone, which is open in front by a slit, four inches in width, from top to bottom of the cylinder. Into the top of this cylinder passes a piston, which is connected with a lever, to which are attached heavy stones, and by means of the piston the baskets of olives are subjected to as much pressure as is necessary to extract the oil. The quality of oil thus made is quite inferior to that imported from Italy and France. It is largely used in making soap, and was formerly much more used for burning than now." (*Dr. Post, of Beirut,* in Schaff's *Bib. Dict.*) (See OLIVE.)

OIL TREE (oil trē), (Heb. שֶׁמֶן עֵץ, *ates sheh'men*), possibly tree of oil (Is. xli:19).

In 1 Kings vi:23, 31, 32, 33 these words are rendered "olive tree," and represent the material of the cherubim, doors, and posts of Solomon's temple. They are translated "pine" in Neh. viii: 15. But the olive tree is also unmistakably mentioned in this verse. If the oil tree was not the olive tree, what was it? Tristram and others believe it to be the oleaster (*Eleagnus angustifolius*). This shrub has no affinity to the olive, though resembling it in leaf and general appearance and yielding from its berries an inferior oil. It is found plentifully on the highlands of Palestine and about Jerusalem, thus meeting the direction of Neh. viii:15, as the *Balanites Ægyptiaca,* a shrub of the Jordan valley, does not. Dr. Tristram therefore suggests in one place (under "Oil Tree") that its "fine hard wood" was the wood of the cherubim, but in another place (under "Olive") states that material to have been olive wood (as the A. V. reads). The latter opinion has a strong probability in its favor, and it does not appear that the oleaster is more than a large shrub, though the author cited calls it, as compared with the olive, "a smaller tree." For the passage in Nehemiah there would then be no present explanation unless we believe, as is very possible, that the term "oil tree," in later times at least, was extended or restricted to the oleaster.

G. E. Post, Hastings' *Bib. Dict.,* says: "The only trees which fulfill all the necessary conditions are the fatwood trees. The genus Pinus furnishes three species, *Pinus Pinea,* L., the *stone* or *maritime pine, Pinus Halepensis, Mill.,* the *Aleppo pine,* and *Pinus Bruttia, Ten.,* which is perhaps only a variety of the last. Any of these would furnish foliage suitable for booths, and all are constantly used for this purpose in the East. Their massive trunks could easily furnish the log required for the carved image, and the doors and doorposts. They are constantly used in house carpentry. Their heartwood is fat enough to entitle them to be called 'trees of fatness.' They are spontaneous, growing in the wilderness (*i. e.* uncultivated places, and so fit to be associated with the other trees mentioned with them, Is. xli:19). We are inclined with Celsius (*Hierob.* i, 309) to translate *'ez-shemen,* 'fatwood trees,' and to suppose that the reference is to the pines."

OINTMENT (oint'ment).

(1) Name. Ointment is the rendering of the following words in the original: (1) Heb. שֶׁמֶן, *sheh'men* (2 Kings xx:13; Ps. cxxxiii:2; Prov. xxvii:16; Eccles. vii:1; ix:8; x:1; Is. i:6, etc.), probably *oil* (and so elsewhere rendered, except "olive" in 1 Kings vi:23, *sq.*; "pine," in Neh. viii:15; "fatness," in Ps. cix:24; "fat things," in Is. xxv:6; "fruitful," in Is. v:1). (2) Hebrew form רֹקַח, *ro'kakh,* an aromatic (Exod. xxx:25), an odorous compound ("confection," Exod. xxx:35; 2 Chron. xvi:14; "pot of ointment," Job xli:31, etc.). (3) Gr. μύρον, *moo'ron,* myrrh (invariably rendered "ointment"). (McC. & Str. *Bib. Cyc.*)

(2) Nature and Preparation. The holy anointing oil made by Bezalel for Moses (Exod. xxx:23, *sq.*) consisted of one hin of olive oil (about 10 lbs.), 500 shekels of flowing myrrh (about 15 lbs.), 250 shekels of sweet cinnamon (about 7½ lbs.), 250 shekels of sweet calamus, and 500 shekels of cassia (or costus). The Jewish authors who regard the 'shekel of the sanctuary' as twice the ordinary shekel, double these weights. This was to be compounded after the art of the perfumer. Probably these scented substances, or some of them, were brought into the market in powder, as in Cant. iii:6, these spices are called 'the powders of the merchant.' There are different descriptions given by Rabbinical writers of the process whereby the anointing oil was compounded, but most probably it was simple pulverization of the ingredients, and boiling them in the oil; for, as Pliny has remarked, the strength of the ointment is greater when the ingredients are boiled together (xiii:2); but see Otho's *Lexicon*, under the word 'Oleum.' The making of ointment in this way was recognized by Hebrew writers (see Job xli:31). (A. Macalister, Hastings' *Bib. Dict.*)

(3) Uses. Ointment was used among the Hebrew and other nations for cosmetics, for funeral, medicinal and ritual purposes. (See ANOINTING; OIL.)

OLD (ōld). See AGE.

OLD GATE (ōld gāt), a name (Neh. iii:6; xii:9) of a Jerusalem gate; Kitto says probably the gate on the northeast corner. (See JERUSALEM.)

OLD LATIN VERSIONS. See the article VULGATE.

OLD MAN. See REGENERATION.

OLD PROPHET, THE. This prophet lived in Bethel at the commencement of the reign of Jeroboam I. A single incident in his life is narrated (1 Kings xiii:11-32; 2 Kings xxiii:16-18). He desired to entertain as his guest a certain 'man of God' from Judah, who had appeared in Bethel to denounce the royal sanctuary (Possibly on the day of its inauguration?). The stranger was already departing when the prophet overtook him and offered his hospitality. It was refused on the ground that Jehovah had forbidden him to take food in the city. The prophet then falsely declared that he gave his invitation in accordance with a message from Jehovah, and the stranger returned and partook of a meal. He never reached his home again. News came to Bethel that a lion had slain him a short distance from the city. The old prophet recognized this as Jehovah's punishment, saddled his ass, brought in the body, held lamentation over it, and buried it in his own grave. By this he showed his sympathy and respect. (W. B. Stevenson, Hasting's *Bib. Dict.*)

The punishment came upon the old prophet in the way of retribution for not obeying implicitly Jehovah's command. (See *The Speaker's Commentary.* Adam Clarke's *Commentary.* Lange's *Commentary.* The *Expositor's Bible,* Farrar.)

OLD TESTAMENT (ōld tĕs'tà-ment). See BIBLE.

OLIVE (ŏl'ĭv).

1. From ancient times this has been one of the most common fruit trees of Palestine (Deut. vi:11). As the olive stands in the orchard it resembles the apple tree in shape, size, and mode of cultivation. Its leaves are narrow, dull above and silvery beneath, so that the resulting gray-green of these trees becomes beautiful by association (Hos. xiv:6). The white flowers, produced in the greatest profusion, are like those of the lilac, to which the tree is botanically allied; and, though millions are prematurely scattered by the breezes (Job xv:33), enough remain to load down the trees with fruit. This latter is like a plum in shape and color, being first green, then pale, and, when ripe, nearly black. Olives are sometimes plucked in an unripe state and

put into some pickle or other preserving liquid and exported. For the most part, however, they are valuable for the oil they produce, which is expressed from the fruit in various ways, and constitutes an important article of commerce and luxury (Job xxiv:11; Ezek. xxvii:17). The fruit is gathered by beating (Deut. xxiv:20), or shaking the tree (Is. xvii:6); and by Jewish law gleanings were to be left for the poor.

2. The aged olive tree is often surrounded by young and thrifty shoots (Ps. cxxviii:3). Women sometimes adorned themselves with garlands of olives on festal occasions (Judith xv:13), and at the Olympic games in Greece the victor's crown was composed of olive leaves. The olive is still cultivated through nearly every part of Palestine. (See ZAIT OR SAIT.)

Figurative. (1) As olives were emblems of peace, the *olive-leaf* brought to Noah by his dove might mark God's being reconciled to men, and the intimation thereof by the Holy Ghost (Gen. viii:11). (2) To pre-figure Jesus as the peaceful means of our access to God, and supporter of the church, the door and posts of the entrance to the holy of holies, and the posts of the door of the temple were of *"olive-wood:"* and to mark the peaceful illuminating ministration of angels and ministers to the church, Solomon made his two large cherubim, for covering the ark, of *"olive-trees"* (1 Kings vi:23, 31, 33). (3) The *"two anointed olive-trees"* before the Lord, may denote Jesus in his two natures, or in his offices of prophet and priest; or him and his Spirit (Zech. iv:3, 11, 12). (4) Believers and ministers are like *"olive-trees"* for the enlightening, beautifying, softening, and healing of others (Judg. ix:8, 9; Ps. lii:8; Rev. xi:4). (5) The Jews are likened to green, flourishing, and cultivated *"olives"* (Jer. xi:16; Hos. xiv:6). (6) The Gentiles were *"wild olives,"* grafted upon the root of a cultivated olive-tree, while the natural branches were broken off (Rom. xi:17, 24). The apostle does not teach that a wild twig grafted upon a good stock will produce good fruit, for this is not the fact. St. Paul refers rather to the adoption of the Gentiles among God's people as a process "contrary to nature," but accomplished by grace. (7) Wicked men are like *"olives,"* which cast their leaves before their season, and so bear no fruit; their apparent piety and their prosperity come quickly to an end (Job xv:33). (8) Children are like *"olive-plants,"* about their parents' table; how quick their growth! how delightful and fresh their beauty! and what an extensive prospect of their usefulness (Ps. cxxviii:3).   Brown.

OLIVES, MOUNT OF; OLIVET (ŏl'ĭvs, mount ŏv; ŏl'i-vĕt), a noted mountain or range of hills east of Jerusalem.

(1) Name. Its descriptive appellation is "the Mount of Olives" (Heb. הַר הַזֵּיתִים, *harhaz-zay-theem'*, only in Zech. xiv:4; Gr. τὸ ὄρος τῶν ἐλαιῶν).

The mountain derives its name from the olive trees which formerly abounded on its sides, some of which are still found thereon. It is called "Olivet" and "Mount of Olives" in the Old Testament (2 Sam. xv:30; Zech. xiv:4), and is also alluded to as the "mount" (Neh. viii:15), the mount facing Jerusalem (1 Kings xi:7), the "mountain which *is* on the east side of the city" (Ezek. xi:23); and the "mount of corruption" probably refers to a portion of Olivet (2 Kings xxiii:13). The modern Arabic name is sometimes *Jebel ez-Zeitun,* or "mount of olives," but more usually it is *Jebel et-Tôr,* or "mount of the summit."

(2) Physical Features. It faces Jerusalem, lying directly east, is two thousand six hundred and sixty-five feet above sea level, has many beautiful olive trees on its sides, and from these has received its name. It is not a mountain so much as a rounded crown of the broad ridge which runs longitudinally through Palestine. It is the highest spot near the city. Osborn describes six prominent heights in the Olivet range, but he includes Scopus, on the north, and the hill of "Evil Counsel," on the extreme south, of the ridge.

The Olivet range extends north without any marked depression to the portion called Scopus, and the general elevation of the ridge is a little less than 3,000 feet above the sea level. It lies directly east of Jerusalem, and is separated from the city by the valley of the Kedron. The four chief peaks south of Scopus are: (1) The northern summit, called *Viri Galilæi,* from a tradition that the angels stood upon it when they spoke to the disciples (Acts i:11). It is about half a mile northeast from the city, and is 2,682 feet above the sea. (2) The central summit, or the "Mount of Ascension," 2,665 feet in height, is situated directly east of the temple-area, and is the Mount of Olives proper. Three paths lead to this summit—one by a nearly direct ascent, another winding around the southern shoulder, and a third path leading around the northern shoulder. On the top of this peak is a chapel built upon the site of a church erected by Helena, the mother of Constantine, since tradition points out this spot as the place of the ascension of Christ. The monks point out even the footprint made by the ascending Lord, and the spot, a little south of this, where Christ is said to have taught the disciples the model, or Lord's prayer. The true place of the ascension, however, was beyond the summit of Olivet, and near Bethany (Luke xxiv:50). (3) The third summit, about 600 yards southwest of the former, and three-fourths of a mile from Bethany, is called "the Prophets," from a curious catacomb called the "Prophets' Tombs" on its side. (4) The fourth summit, about 1,000 yards from No. 3, is the "Mount of Offense," so-called from the idol-worship which Solomon established there. None of the depressions which separate these summits are very deep; some are to be regarded as quite slight. It is evident that in ancient times this mountain ridge was covered with olives, myrtles, figs, cypresses, and some species of the terebinth or oak, and also abounded in flowers. "The olives and olive-yards," says Stanley, "from which it derived its name must in earlier times have clothed it far more completely than at present, where it is only in the deeper and more secluded slopes leading up to the northernmost summit that these venerable trees spread into anything like a forest. And in those times, as we see from the name of Bethany ('house of dates'), and from the allusions after the Captivity and in the gospel history, myrtle-groves, pines, and palm trees—all of which have now disappeared—must have made it a constant resort for pleasure and seclusion. Two gigantic cedars, probably amongst the very few in Palestine, stood near its summit, under which were four shops where pigeons were sold for purification. The olive and fig alone now remain—the olive still in more or less abundance, the fig here and there on the roadside, but both enough to justify the Mussulmans' belief that in the oath in the Koran, 'By the olive and the

fig,' the Almighty swears by his favorite city of Jerusalem, with this adjacent mountain." (*Sinai and Palestine,* p. 184.) (Schaff, *Bib. Dict.*)

The slopes of Olivet are terraced and cultivated, but the vegetation is not luxuriant. The principal trees now are the olive, fig, and carob, with here and there a few apricot, almond, terebinth, and hawthorn. At the western base of the mountain is Silwan, a miserable little village. Jewish tradition declares that the shekinah, or Divine presence, after retiring from Jerusalem, dwelt three years and a half on Olivet, to see whether the Jews would repent, but when they would not, retired to his own place.

(3) Special Scriptural Notices. On the summit of Olivet God was wont to be worshiped (2 Sam. xv:32). The glory of the Lord appeared there to Ezekiel in a vision (Ezek. xi:23), and Zechariah prophetically portrayed Jehovah standing on the mountain to interpose in behalf of his people (Zech. xiv:4). The mountain is first mentioned in connection with David's flight from Jerusalem to escape from Absalom (2 Sam. xv: 30, 32; xvi:1). Upon it Solomon built high places for the gods of his numerous wives, but these idolatrous places were destroyed by King Josiah (1 Kings xi:7; 2 Kings xxiii:13, 14). When the captive Jews celebrated the feast of tabernacles, the olive, pine, myrtle, and palm branches used in building their booths were brought from this mountain (Neh. viii:15). It is also called, in the New Testament, "Mount of Olives" and "Olivet," and was a scene of several of the most interesting events in the life of our Lord. Jesus went often to this mount (Luke xxi:37; xxii:39; John viii:1). He was descending its slope when the multitude welcomed him to the city with hosannas (Luke xix: 37, 38). He had rounded its shoulder when Jerusalem burst into full view, and he wept over the fate which he knew awaited the city (41-44). He was sitting on the mount with his disciples gazing across the valley at the splendid temple and the city, when he prophesied the destruction of both (Matt. xxiv:3; Mark xiii:3). After his last passover he retired to the mount of Olives (Matt. xxvi:30; Mark xiv:26). The garden of Gethsemane was to the west of it, either at its base or some small distance up its ascent. Bethany and Bethphage were on the eastern side (Matt. xxi:1; Mark xi:1; Luke xix:29). It was near the former of these villages that our Lord's ascension took place (xxiv:50).

(4) Present Appearance, Etc. Of late Olivet has attracted special attention from the Russians. Besides the beautiful temple built on the western slope a large Russian monastery has been erected on the summit, in which are many attractions. "The Pater Noster Chapel, south of the church of the Ascension, was erected in 1865 by the Princess de la Tour d'Auvergne, and is supposed to stand on an old traditional site of the Middle Ages. The intention of the Princess was to have within twenty-four small chambers, in which the 'Lord's Prayer' should be written up in twenty-four different languages, so that pilgrims of all nationalities and all creeds, might unite there in repeating the Lord's Prayer." (Hastings' *Bib. Dict.*)

OLIVE TREE (Heb. רַיִת, *zah'yith,* olive berry, tree, yard). (See OLIVE; ZAIT OR SAIT.)

OLIVE YARD (ŏl'iv yärd), (Heb. רַיִת, *zah'yith,* Exod. xxiii:11; Josh. xxiv:13; 1 Sam. viii:14; 2 Kings v:26; Neh. v:11; ix:25), an orchard or grove of olive trees. (See OLIVE; ZAIT OR SAIT.)

OLIVET (ŏl'i-vĕt). See OLIVES, MOUNT OF.

OLYMPAS (o-lĭm'pas), (Gr. 'Ολυμπᾶς, ol-oom-pas'), a Christian at Rome, whom Paul salutes in his Epistle to the Romans (Rom. xvi:15), A. D. 55.

OMAR (ō'mar), (Heb. אוֹמָר, o-mawr', talkative), son of Eliphaz, and grandson of Esau (Gen. xxxvi: 15; 1 Chron. i:36). He was head of a tribe of Edomites (B. C. about 1900).

OMEGA (ŏ-mē'gà or ō'mĕ-gà), (Gr. ω, fully 'Ωμέγα, i. e., the *long o*, in distinction from the *short o*), the last letter of the Greek alphabet, as Alpha is the first.

Figurative. Omega is used metaphorically to denote the *end* of anything. "I am Alpha and Omega, the beginning and the ending . . . the first and the last" (Rev. i:8, 11; comp. xxi:6; xxii:13, and Is. xli:4; xliv:6). (See ALPHA AND OMEGA.)

OMER (ō'mẽr), (Heb. עֹמֶר, oh-mer', tenth of an ephah, a Hebrew dry measure). See WEIGHTS AND MEASURES.

OMNIPOTENCE OF GOD (ŏm-nip'ŏ-tens ŏv Gŏd) is his Almighty power. This is essential to his nature as an infinite, independent, and perfect being. The power of God is divided into *absolute* and *ordinate* or *actual*. *Absolute* is that whereby God is able to do that which he will not do, but is possible to be done. *Ordinate* is that whereby he does that which he had decreed to do. The power of God may be more especially seen: (1) In creation (Rom. i:20; Gen. i). (2) In the preservation of his creatures (Heb. i:3; Col. i:16, 17; Job xxvi). (3) In the redemption of men by Christ (Luke i:35, 37; Eph. i:19). (4) In the conversion of sinners (Ps. cx:3; 2 Cor. iv:7; Rom. i:16). (5) In the continuation and success of the gospel in the world (Matt. xiii:41-43). (6) In the final perseverance of the saints (1 Pet. i:5). (7) In the resurrection of the dead (1 Cor. xv.). (8) In making the righteous happy forever, and punishing the wicked (Phil. iii:21; Matt. xxv:34), etc.

OMNIPRESENCE OF GOD (ŏm'ni-prĕz'ens ŏv Gŏd), is his ubiquity, or his being present in every place.

This may be argued from his infinity (Ps. cxxxix) his power, which is everywhere (Heb. i:3); his providence (Acts xvii:27, 28), which supplies all. As he is a spirit, he is so omnipresent as not to be mixed with the creatures, or divided part in one place, and part in another; nor is he multiplied or extended, but is essentially present everywhere. From the consideration of this attribute we should learn to fear and reverence God (Ps. lxxxix:7). To derive consolation in the hour of distress (Is. xliii:2; Ps. xlvi: 1). To be active and diligent in holy services (Ps. cxix:168).

OMNISCIENCE OF GOD (ŏm-nĭsh'ens ŏv Gŏd) It is that perfection by which he knows all things, and is (1) Infinite knowledge (Ps. cxlvi: 5). (2) Eternal, generally called fore-knowledge (Acts xv:18; Is. xlvi:10; Eph. i:4; Acts ii: 23). (3) Universal, extending to all persons, times, places, and things (Heb. iv:13; Ps. cxxxix: 12). (4) Perfect, relating to what is past, present, and to come. He knows all by his own essence, and not derived from any other; not successively, as we do, but independently, distinctly, infallibly (Jer. x:6, 7; Rom. xi:33). (5) This knowledge is peculiar to himself (Mark xiii: 32; Job xxxvi:4), and not communicable to any creature. (6) It is incomprehensible to us how God knows all things, yet it is evident that he does; for to suppose otherwise is to suppose him

an imperfect being, and directly contrary to the revelation he has given of himself (Ps. cxxxix: 6; 1 John iii:20; Job xxviii:24; xxi:22).

This attribute of God is constantly connected in Scripture with his omnipresence, and forms a part of almost every description of that attribute; for, as God is a Spirit, and therefore intelligent, if he is everywhere, if nothing can exclude him, not even the most solid bodies, nor the minds of intelligent beings, then are all things naked and opened to the eyes of him with whom we have to do. Where he acts, he is; and where he is, he perceives. He understands and considers things absolutely, and as they are in their own natures, powers, properties, differences, together with all the circumstances belonging to them. "Known unto him are all his works from the beginning of the world," rather (ap'eye-oh'nos, ap' aiōnos), *from all eternity* known, before they were made, in their possible, and known, now they are made, in their actual existence.

OMRI (ŏm'rĭ), (Heb. עָמְרִי, om-ree, God taught).

1. The sixth king of Israel, who reigned twelve years. He was raised to the throne by the army, while it was engaged in the siege of Gibbethon, a Levitical city in Dan, of which the Philistines had gained possession, when the news came to the camp of the death of Elah, and the usurpation of Zimri. On this, the army proclaimed their general, Omri, king of Israel. He then lost not a moment, but leaving Gibbethon in the power of the infidels, went and besieged his competitor in Tirzah. But he was no sooner delivered of this rival (see ZIMRI), than another appeared in the person of Tibni, whom a part of the people had raised to the throne, probably from unwillingness to submit to military dictation. This occasioned a civil war, which lasted six years, and left Omri undisputed master of the throne (B. C. 882). His reign lasted six years more, and its chief event was the foundation of Samaria, which thenceforth became the capital city of the kingdom of Israel (1 Kings xvi:15-28). (See SAMARIA.)

There is a difference between the biblical chronology and that of the Moabite stone regarding the length of Omri's reign. The latter makes the reign of Omri and half of his son Ahab's reign to extend over forty years. The biblical chronology "ascribes to Omri a reign of only twelve years, and to Ahab's entire reign twenty-two years, making the *total* length of *both* reigns only thirty-four years. From these data of the Moabite Stone it is evident that we must extend considerably the reign of Omri. In the scheme set forth in Schrader's cuneiform *Insc. and the Old Testament,* ii, p. 322, *sq.,* Omri's reign is reckoned to be twenty-five years (B. C. 900-875), ten years being deducted from the reign of Baasha."

Owen C. Whitehouse, Hastings' *Bib. Dict.,* says: "These dates harmonize better with (1) the results of Assyriology, (2) with the deep impression which Omri had produced in western Asia by his military prowess. This impression was no fleeting one, but extended over a very long period. We have clear indication of this in the fact that Palestine was called (*mât*) *Bit Humri,* or 'land of the house of Omri,' from the time of Shalmaneser II. (860) to that of Sargon (722-705). The usurper Jehu is called on Shalmaneser's black obelisk *Ja'ua abal Humri,* 'Jehu son of Omri.' And no less deep was the impression produced in Israel and Judah. The reference to the 'statutes of Omri' (Mic. vi:16), is an indication of this, his name being coupled with that of his son Ahab."

2. A Benjamite of the family of Becher (1 Chron. vii :8). (B. C. about 1618.)

3. Son of Imri of the tribe of Judah (1 Chron. ix :4). (B. C. after 1618.)

4. Son of Michael and a captain in the tribe of Issachar in the time of David (1 Chron. xxvii : 18). (B. C. about 1017.)

ON (ŏn), (Heb. וֹן, *one*, strength).

1. A chief of the tribe of Reuben, who was one of the accomplices of Korah in the revolt against the authority of Moses and Aaron. He is mentioned among the leaders of this conspiracy in the first instance (Num. xvi:1), but does not appear in any of the subsequent transactions, and is not by name included in the final punishment. The Rabbinical tradition is, that the wife of On

tion relates that the holy family once rested (Robinson's *Biblical Researches*, i, 36). Heliopolis was the capital of a district or nemos bearing the same name (Plin. *Hist. Nat.* v, 9; Ptolem. iv, 5. The place is mentioned in Gen. xli :45, where it is said that Pharaoh gave to Joseph a wife, Asenath, the daughter of Poti-pherah, priest of On (verse 50).

(2) Sun Worship. From the passage in Jeremiah (as above) it may be inferred that it was distinguished for idolatrous worship: 'He shall break also the images of Beth-shemesh that is in the land of Egypt, and the houses of the gods of the Egyptians shall he burn with fire.' The names, 'City of the Sun,' 'Temples of the Sun,' connected with the place, taken in con-

Plain and Obelisk of Heliopolis.

persuaded her husband to abandon the enterprise. It has been held by some critics that the mention of On is due to a textual corruption.

2. One of the oldest cities in the world, situated in Lower Egypt, about two hours north-northeast from Cairo. The Septuagint translates the name On by Heliopolis, which signifies 'city of the sun;' and in Jer. xliii :13, it bears a name, Beth-shemesh (*oppidum solis*, Pliny, *Hist. Nat.* v, 11), of equivalent import. On is a Coptic and ancient Egyptian word, signifying light and the sun (Ritter, *Erdk.* i, 822).

(1) Location. The site is now marked by low mounds, enclosing a space about three quarters of a mile in length by half a mile in breadth, which was once occupied by houses and by the celebrated Temple of the Sun. This area is at present a plowed field, a garden of herbs; and the solitary obelisk which still rises in the midst of it is the sole remnant of the former splendors of the place. In the days of Edrisi and Abdallatif the place bore the name of Ain Shems; and in the neighboring village, Matariyeh, is still shown an ancient well bearing the same name. Near by it is a very old sycamore, its trunk straggling and gnarled, under which legendary tradi-

junction with the words just cited from the prophet, seem to refer the mind to the purer form of worship which prevailed at a very early period in Egypt, namely, the worship of the heavenly bodies, and thence to carry the thoughts to the deteriorations which it afterwards underwent in sinking to the adoration of images and animals.

"The Sun-god was worshiped at Heliopolis first in the form of Ra; secondly, as Tum, the setting sun; thirdly, as Harakhti, the hawk of the horizon, called by the Greeks Harmakhis; fourthly, as Khepera, figured by a scarabæus, and symbolizing the vivifying and reproductive force of the sun. Of sacred animals here the bull Mnevis was the most important; and the heron, called *bnw,* was the original of the famous phœnix. From the earliest times obelisks were connected with the Sun worship (Jer. xliii :13 [Beth-shemesh]). There was also a sacred pool or spring, mentioned especially by Piankhi, 'in which Ra was wont to wash his face;' hence the Arabian name for this locality is '*Ain esh-shems,*' 'spring of the sun.' In Christian story this is the spring in which the Virgin washed her son while resting in the shade of an acacia tree on her journey into Egypt. The latest successor to the tree is still shown in an enclosure at *Matariyeh*." (Hastings' *Bib. Dict.*) (See EGYPTIANS, RELIGION OF ANCIENT.)

(3) Research. The traces of this city which are found in classic authors correspond with the little of it that we know from the brief intimations of Holy Writ. According to Herodotus (ii. 59), Heliopolis was one of the four great cities that were rendered famous in Egypt by being the centers of solemn religious festivals, which were attended by splendid processions and homage to the gods. In Heliopolis the observance was held in honor of the sun. The majesty of these sacred visits may be best learned now by a careful study of the temples (in their ruins) in which the rites were performed (Wilkinson's *Anc. Egyptians*). Heliopolis had its priesthood, a numerous and learned body, celebrated before other Egyptians for their historical and antiquarian lore; it long continued the university of the Egyptians, the chief seat of their science (Kenrick's *Herod.* ii, 3; Wilkinson); the priests dwelt as a holy community in a spacious structure appropriated to their use. In Strabo's time the halls were to be seen in which Eudoxus and Plato had studied under the direction of the priests of Heliopolis. A detailed description of the temple, with its long alleys of sphinxes, obelisks, etc., may be found in Strabo (xvii; Joseph. *c. Apion.* ii, 2), who says that the mural sculpture in it was very similar to the old Etruscan and Grecian works. In the temple a bullock was fed—a symbol of the god of Mnevis. The city suffered heavily by the Persian invasion. From the time of Shaw and Pocock, the place has been described by many travelers. At an early period remains of the famous temple were found. Abdallatif (A. D. 1200) saw many colossal sphinxes, partly prostrate, partly standing. He also saw the gates or propylæa of the temple covered with inscriptions; he describes two immense obelisks whose summits were covered with massive brass, around which were others one-half or one-third the size of the first, placed in so thick a mass that they could scarcely be counted; most of them thrown down. An obelisk which the Emperor Augustus caused to be carried to Rome, and placed in the Campus Martius, is held by Zoega (*De Orig. et Usu Obelisci*) to have been brought from Heliopolis, and to have owed its origin to Sesostris. This city furnished works of art to Augustus for adorning Rome, and to Constantine for adorning Constantinople. Ritter (*Erdkunde*, i, 823) says that the sole remaining obelisk is from sixty to seventy feet high, of a block of red granite, bearing hieroglyphics which remind the beholder of what Strabo terms the Etruscan style. 'The figure of the cross which it bears (*crux ansata*) has attracted the special notice of Christian antiquaries' (Ritter). J. R. B.

ONAM (ō'nam), (Heb. אוֹנָם, *o-nawm'*, strong).

1. A Horite, son of Shobal (Gen. xxxvi:23; 1 Chron. i:40). (B. C. about 1964.)

2. Son of Jerahmeel and Atarah of the house of Judah (1 Chron. ii:26, 28). (B. C. before 1658.)

ONAN (ō'nan), (Heb. אוֹנָן, *o-nawn'*, strong, stout), second son of Judah by the daughter of Shuah the Canaanite (Gen. xxxviii:4; xlvi:12; Num. xxvi:19; 1 Chron. ii:3), B. C. about 2000.

Being constrained by the obligations of the ancient Levirate law to espouse Tamar, his elder brother's widow, he took means to frustrate the intention of this usage, which was to provide heirs for a brother who had died childless. This crime,

rendered without excuse by the allowance of polygamy, and the seriousness of which can scarcely be appreciated but in respect to the usages of the times in which it was committed, was punished by premature death (Gen. xxxviii: 4, *sq.*)

ONE AND OTHER (Heb. אִישׁ, *eesh*, Jer. xxxvi:16), each, individually, both.

ONESIMUS (o-nĕs'i-mŭs), (Gr. Ὀνήσιμος, *on-ay'-sim-os*, profitable).

A slave belonging to Philemon of Colossæ, who fled from his master, and proceeded to Rome, where he was converted by St. Paul, who sent him back to his master, a friend and convert of the apostle, with an eloquent letter, the purport of which is described in the article PHILEMON. Onesimus, accompanied by Tychicus, left Rome with not only this epistle, but with those to the Ephesians and Colossians (Col. iv:9). It is believed that Onesimus, anxious to justify the confidence which Paul reposed in him, by appearing speedily before his master, left Tychicus to take the Epistle to the Ephesians; and hastened to Colossæ, where he doubtless received the forgiveness which Paul had so touchingly implored for him as 'a brother beloved' (*Canon. Apost.* 73). The part which St. Paul took in this difficult and trying case is highly honorable to him; while for Onesimus himself, the highest praise is, that he obtained the friendship and confidence of the apostle. (A. D. 58.) An uncertain tradition makes Onesimus to have been bishop of Beræa, where he is said to have suffered martyrdom (*Const. Apostol.* vii, 46).

It is probable that various Onesimi have been confused, and it is impossible to extricate any certain fact. His memory was observed by the Latin Church on Feb. 16, by the Greek Church on Feb. 15, and also in conjunction with Philemon, Appia, and Archippus, on Nov. 22: the various traditions will be found in the *Acta Sanctorum* (ii, 855-859) and the Greek *Menæa* (pp. 89-92) for those days. A most interesting modern romance of his life will be found in *Onesimus*, by the author of *Philochristus* (London, 1882). (W. Locke, Hastings' *Bib. Dict.*)

ONESIPHORUS (ŏn'ĕ-sĭf'o-rŭs), (Gr. Ὀνησίφορος, *on-ay-sif'or-os*, profit-bringer), a believer of Ephesus, who came to Rome during the second captivity of St. Paul in that city (A. D. about 64).

And having found out the apostle, who was in custody of a soldier, to whose arm his own was chained, was not ashamed of his chain, but attended him frequently, and rendered him all the services in his power. This faithful attachment, at a time of calamity and desertion, was fully appreciated and well remembered by the apostle, who, in his Epistle to Timothy, carefully records the circumstance; and, after charging him to salute in his name 'the household of Onesiphorus,' expresses the most earnest and grateful wishes for his spiritual welfare (2 Tim. i:16-18). It would appear from this that Onesiphorus had then left Rome.

"It is not perfectly clear whether, at the time when St. Paul wrote, Onesiphorus was alive or dead; but the references to his 'house' rather than to himself in 2 Tim. i:16; iv:19, and still more the words of the prayer in 2 Tim. i:18, 'The Lord grant unto him to find mercy of the Lord in that day,' make it most probable that he was now dead (so De Wette, Huther, Alford, Ellicott, Fairbairn, v. Soden). If so, the passage gains an additional interest from the use that has been made of it in connection with the argument for prayers for the dead. Thus it is appealed to in support of such a practice by Bishop Archibald Campbell in his anonymously published book on *The Intermediate or Middle State of Departed Souls,* 1713, p. 72; and amongst more recent writers by Plumptre (*The Spirits in Prison,* pp. 128, 266) and Luckock (*After Death,* p. 77, *The Intermediate State,* p. 211). Others, as Barrett (*The Intermediate State,* p. 113), find in the words no more than 'a pious wish'." (W. Locke, Hastings' *Bib. Dict.*)

ONION (ŭn'yŭn), (Heb. בֶּצֶל, *beh'tsel,* peeled).

A plant, the bulbous root of which was much used in Egypt as an article of food (Num. xi: 5; Herod. ii, 125). It is *Allium cepa,* called in Hebrew *besel,* in Arabic *basal.* It has been cultivated from an early period in Egypt and other parts of the East. (See CHATZIR.)

ONLY BEGOTTEN (ōn'lỹ bē-gŏt't'n),(Gr. μονο-γενής, *mon-og-en-ace',* single of its kind), an expression used of Jesus Christ (John i:14, 18, etc.) to denote that in the sense in which he is the son of God he has no brethren. (See SONSHIP OF CHRIST.)

ONO (ō'no), (Heb. אֹונֹו, *o-no',* strong), a city of Benjamin; built or rebuilt by the family of Elpaal, of Benjamin (1 Chron. viii:12).

It was five miles from Lod, or Lydda, also built by Benjamites. In Neh. vi:2, we have mention of "The Plain of Ono," which probably was not far from the city. Ono is the modern *Kefr' Anâ,* north of *Ludd* (the ancient Lod or Lydda). Its antiquity is shown by its being noticed, along with the last-named place, in the lists of Tahutmes III. *c.* (B. C. 1600.)

ONYCHA (o-nỹ'ka), (Heb. שְׁחֵלֶת, *shekh-ay'leth,* a scale), a substance mentioned as an ingredient of the holy perfume (Exod. xxx:34).

It is believed to have been the operculum (lid) of a shell mollusk called stromb or wing-shell, which being burnt gave out a certain perfume.

ONYX (ō'nĭks), (Gr. ὄνυξ, *on'ooks* generally for Heb. שֹׁהַם, *sho'ham,* the leek green beryl).

One kind of chalcedony; a precious stone (Exod. xxv:7; Ezek. xxviii:13), exhibiting two or more colors disposed in parallel bands or layers. The Hebrew word *shoham* is uniformly so translated in the Bible. Opinion is divided as to the exact meaning of the term. Josephus says the *onyx* is meant. It was found in the land of Havilah (Gen. ii:12), and was evidently of high value, as it is mentioned among precious stones and metals (Job xxviii:16; Ezek. xxviii:13). It adorned the breastplate of the high priest and the two shoulders of his ephod (Exod. xxviii:9-12, 20). David also gathered such stones for the service of the future temple (1 Chron. xxix:2). The onyx is a cryptocrystalline variety or subvariety of quartz. It is in layers of different colors, which alternate with each other and bear some resemblance to the white and flesh-colored bands of the finger nail.

OPEN (ō'p'n), (Gr. διανοίγω, *dee-an-oy'go,* Luke xxiv:32, to explain, expound, make known, disclose).

Thus Jer. xx:12, 'But, O Lord of hosts, that triest the righteous, *and* seest the reins and the heart, let me see thy vengeance on them: for unto thee have I *opened* my cause.' Acts xvii: 3, 'Paul . . . reasoned with them out of the Scriptures, *opening* and alleging, that Christ must needs have suffered.'

OPEN PLACE (ō-p'n plās), in Gen. xxxviii:14, A. V.

Tamar is said to have taken her seat 'in an open place,' but undoubtedly the correct translation is in the gate of Enaim, R. V.

OPHEL (ō'fel), (Heb. הָעֹפֶל, *haw-ō-fel,* with the article).

1. A place or quarter of Jerusalem near the walls (2 Chron. xxvii:3; xxxiii:44), on the east side (Neh. iii:26; xi:21). Ophel, or, as he calls it, Ophla ('Οφλά 'Οφλάς), is often mentioned by Josephus as adjoining the valley of the Kidron and the temple mount (*De Bell. Jud.* v, 6, 1; vi, 6, 3). He explains himself more precisely in v, 4, 2, where he makes the first wall of the city to extend from the tower of the Essenes over Siloam and the pools of Solomon to Ophel. From these intimations Winer collects that Ophel was a high or ascending place, built over (in the ancient city) with houses. This view is confirmed by Dr. Robinson, who identifies it with the low ridge which extends southward from the temple mount to Mount Zion, between the exterior valley of Jehoshaphat and the interior valley of Tyropœon. The top of this ridge is flat, descending rapidly towards the south, sometimes by offsets of rocks; and the ground is now tilled and planted with olive and other fruit trees. This ridge is considerably below the level of Mount Moriah; its length is 1,550 feet, and its breadth in the middle part, from brow to brow, 290 feet (Winer, title, 'Ophel;' Robinson, ii, 349). (See JERUSALEM.)

2. A place of middle Palestine where Gehazi stowed in a house the presents he took from Naaman (2 Kings v:24). In the A. V. it is rendered wrongly "the tower."

OPHER (ō'fer), (Heb. עֹפֶר, *o'fer*), in Cant. iv:5 it denotes the calf or fawn of a stag (*ail*).

The term occurs in no other book of Scripture, is unknown in the Syriac and Chaldee, and appears to be only a poetical application of a term more strictly belonging to fawn-like animals; for in the above passage it is applied to couples feeding in a bed of lilies—indications not descriptive of young goats or stags, but quite applicable to the Antilopine groups which are characterized in Griffith's Cuvier, in subgenus X. *Cephalophus,* and XI. *Neotragus;* both furnishing species of exceeding delicacy and graceful diminutive structures, several of which habitually feed in pairs among shrubs and geraniums on the hilly plains of Africa. They have always been and still are in request among the wealthy in warm climates for domestication, therefore we may conjecture that a species designated by the name of Opher (perhaps, alluding to Ophir, or even Africa), was to be found in the parks or royal gardens of Solomon and from the sovereign's own observation were alluded to in the truly apposite imagery of his poetical diction (Cant. iv:12). (See ANTELOPE; ROE; ROEBUCK.) C. H. S.

OPHIR (ō'phir), (Heb. אֹופִר, *o-feer',* fat, rich).

1. The proper name of one of the thirteen sons of Joktan, the son of Eber, a great-grandson of Shem (Gen. x:26-29; Vulg. *Ophir*). Many Arabian countries are believed to have been peopled by these persons, and to have been called after their respective names, as Sheba, etc., and among others Ophir (Bochart, *Phaleg,* iii, 15).

2. The name of a place, country, or region, famous for its gold, which Solomon's ships visited in company with the Phœnician. The difficulty is to ascertain where Ophir was situated. The

first theory which appears to be attended with some degree of evidence not purely fanciful is that Ophir was situated in Arabia. In Gen. x: 29, Ophir stands in the midst of other Arabian countries. Still, as Gesenius observes, it is possibly mentioned in that connection only on account of its being an Arabian colony planted abroad. Though gold is not now found in Arabia (Niebuhr, *Description de l'Arabie,* Copenhague, 1773, p. 124), yet the ancients ascribe it to the inhabitants in great plenty (Judg. viii:24, 26; 2 Chron. i; 1 Kings x:1, 2; Ps. lxxii:15). This gold, Dr. Lee thinks, was no other than the gold of Havilah (Gen. ii:11), which he supposes to have been situate somewhere in Arabia, and refers to Gen. x:7, 29; xxv:18; 1 Sam. xv: 7; 1 Chron. i:9 (*Translation of the Book Job, etc.,* Lond. 1837, p. 55). But Diodorus Siculus ascribes gold mines to Arabia (ii, 50). He also testifies to the abundance of 'precious stones' in Arabia (ii, 54), especially among the inhabitants of Sabas (iii, 46; comp. Gen. ii:12; 2 Chron. ix: 1; 1 Kings x:1, 2). Pliny also speaks of the '*Sabæi ditissimi auri metallis*' (*Hist. Nat.* vi, 32). Again, '*Littus Hammæum, ubi auri metalla*' (*ib*). Others suppose that though Ophir was situate somewhere on the coast of Arabia, it was rather an emporium, at which the Hebrews and Tyrians obtained gold, silver, ivory, apes, almug-trees, etc., brought thither from India and Africa by the Arabian merchants, and even from Ethiopia, to which Herodotus (iii, 114) ascribes gold in great quantities, elephants' teeth, and trees and shrubs of every kind. In behalf of the supposition that Ophir was the Arabian port Aphar already referred to, it may be remarked that the name has undergone similar changes to that of the Sept. of Ophir; for it is called by Arrian Aphar, by Pliny Saphar, by Ptolemy Sapphera, and by Stephanus Saphirini. Grotius thinks his to be Ophir. The very name El Ophir has been lately pointed out as a city of Oman, in former times the center of a very active Arabian commerce (Seetzen, in *Zachs. Monatl. Correspond.* xix, 331, *sq.*). In favor of the theory which places Ophir in Africa, it has been suggested that we have the very name in *afri,* Africa. Origen also says, on Job xxii:24, that some of the interpreters understood Ophir to be Africa. Michaelis supposes that Solomon's fleet, coming down the Red Sea from Ezion-geber, coasted along the shore of Africa, doubling the Cape of Good Hope, and came to Tarshish, which he, with many others, supposes to have been Tartessus in Spain, and thence back again the same way; that this conjecture accounts for their three years' voyage out and home; and that Spain and the coasts of Africa furnished all the commodities which they brought back. Strabo indeed says that Spain abounded in gold, and immensely more so in silver (see 1 Macc. viii:3). Others have not hesitated to carry Solomon's fleet round from Spain up the Mediterranean to Joppa. In behalf of the conjecture that Ophir was in India, the following arguments are alleged: that it is most natural to understand from the narrative that all the productions said to have been brought from Ophir came from one and the same country, and that they were all procurable only from India. The Sept. translators also appear to have understood it to be India. Josephus also gives to the sons of Joktan the locality from Cophen, an Indian river; and in part of Asia adjoining it (*Antiq.* i, 6, 4). He also expressly and unhesitatingly affirms that the land to which Solomon sent for gold was 'anciently called

Ophir, but now the Aurea Chersonesus, which belongs to India' (*Antiq.* viii, 6, 4). There are several places comprised in that region which was actually known as India to the ancients (see INDIA), any of which would have supplied the cargo of Solomon's fleet: for instance, the coast of Malabar. Perhaps the most probable of all is Malacca, which is known to be the Aurea Chersonesus of the ancients. It is also worthy of remark that the natives of Malacca still call their gold-mines *ophirs.* Prof. Lassen considers it unnecessary to examine conjectures concerning other localities from the fact that products which are said to come from Ophir have *Indian names,* even in the Hebrew text when they are destitute of genuine Hebrew names. Ritter and Max Müller favor India as the location of Ophir.

On the other hand, some writers give a wider extent to the country in question. Heeren observes that 'Ophir, like the name of all other very distant places or regions of antiquity, like Thule, Tartessus, and others, denotes no particular spot, but only a certain region or part of the world, such as the East or West Indies in modern geography. Hence Ophir was the general name for the rich countries of the south lying on the African, Arabian, or Indian coasts, as far as at that time known' (*Historical Researches, translated from the German,* Oxford, 1833, vol. ii, pp. 73, 74). It remains to be observed, that in Jer. x:9 we have 'the gold from Uphaz,' and in Dan. x:5, 'the fine gold of Uphaz;' and see the Heb. of 1 Kings x:18. In these instances Uphaz is, by a slight change of pronunciation, put for Ophir.   J. F. D.

OPHNI (ōph'nī), (Heb. עָפְנִי, *of-nee',* moldy), a city of Benjamin (Josh. xviii:24) and thought to be the same as Gophni, or Gophna, now *Jufnah,* 2½ miles northwest of Bethel.

OPHRAH (ŏph'rah), (Heb. עָפְרָה, *of-raw',* a fawn).

1. A town of Benjamin (Josh. xviii:23), seemingly in the northeast of that tribe's domain (1 Sam. xiii:17). Accordingly it is placed by Eusebius and Jerome (*Onomast.* title, Aphia) five Roman miles east of Bethel. This corresponds with the position of a place called et-Taiyibeh, which was visited by Dr. Robinson in his excursion to Bethel (*Bibl. Researches,* ii, 120-123). It is now a small village, curiously situated upon a conical hill, on the summit of which is an old tower, whence is commanded a splendid view of the valley of the Jordan, the Dead Sea, and the eastern mountains.

2. A town in the tribe of Manasseh, to which Gideon belonged, and where he continued to reside after he had delivered Israel from the Midianites, establishing there his ephod, which became a snare to Israel (Judg. vi:11-24; viii:27). Josephus calls the place Ephra (*Antiq.* v, 6, 5). It cannot be positively determined from the narrative, whether this Ophrah was in the territory of Manasseh east or west of the Jordan; and no satisfactory attempt to fix the site has yet been made.

3. A son of Meönothai, of Judah (1 Chron. iv:14). (B. C. after 1614.) Probably "father" here should read *founder,* in which case the name would be that of a town. There are certainly names of towns in this list of the Chronicles and this may be one, the Judæan Ephron or even the Benjamite Ophrah. Border towns may be counted at one time to Benjamin, at another to Judah.

ORACLE (ŏr'ȧ-k'l), (Heb. דְּבִיר, *deb-eer'*, from דָּבַר, *daw-bar'*, to speak); (Gr. λόγιον, *log'ee-on*, utterance of God). Among the Jews several sorts of oracles are distinguished.

1. Those delivered *vivâ voce;* as when God spake to Moses face to face, and as one friend speaks to another (Num. xii:8).

2. Prophetical dreams; as those which God sent to Joseph, foretelling his future greatness (Gen. xxxvii:5, 6).

3. Visions; as when a prophet in an ecstasy had supernatural revelations (Gen. xv:1; xlvi:2).

4. The response of Urim and Thummim, which accompanied the ephod, or the pectoral worn by the high-priest (Num. xxvii:21; Joel ii:28). This manner of inquiring of the Lord was often used, from Joshua's time to the erection of the temple at Jerusalem (1 Sam. xxiii:9; xxx:7) after which they generally consulted the prophets.

5. Some of the Jews claimed that upon the ceasing of prophecy, God gave them what they call *Bath-kol,* the daughter of the voice, which was a supernatural manifestation of the Divine will, either by a strong inspiration or internal voice, or by a sensible and external voice, heard by a number of persons sufficient to bear testimony to it; such as the voice heard at the baptism of Christ.

6. The most ancient oracle on record, probably, is that given to Rebekah (Gen. xxv:23), but the most complete instance is that of the child Samuel (1 Sam. iii). The place was the residence of the ark, the regular station of worship. The manner was by an audible and distinct voice.

7. The highest instances of oracles are those voices which, being formed in the air by a power superior to nature, bore testimony to the celestial character of the Divine Messiah; as at his baptism (Matt. iii:17; Mark i:11; Luke iii:22), and again at his transfiguration (Matt. xvii:5; Luke ix:35). "And this voice that came from heaven," says St. Peter, "we heard" (2 Pet. i:18). Nothing can exceed the grandeur and majesty of these oracles; and they could not but forcibly impress the minds of all who witnessed them.

8. By the oracles, in the heathen world, were understood the shrines where utterances concerning the future were given and the utterance itself. The Greeks had many such oracles, of which the most famous was the oracle of Delphi. The priestess, sitting on a tripod over a chasm from which an intoxicating vapor was said to ascend, uttered incoherent words, which were then interpreted by a prophet. These oracles at one time stood in high repute and were consulted by kings. They did not, however, withstand very long the corruptive power of money and bribery.

ORATION (ŏ-rā'shŭn). See ORATOR.

ORATOR (ŏr'a-tēr), (Heb. לָחַשׁ, *law-khash'*, a whisper, Is. iii:3).

1. The rendering of the Hebrew word, as given above is an incantation, preceded by *n'bou,* i. e. skillful in enchantment (Is. iii:3). The R. V. accurately translates the phrase by "skillful enchantment."

2. The rendering of the Greek *Hray'tore* (Gr. ῥήτωρ), is that of a public speaker, pleader. In Acts xxiv:1 it is applied to Tertullus. He was a professional advocate engaged by Paul's Jewish enemies to prosecute the apostle before the Roman procurator.

ORCHARD (ŏr'chĕrd), (Heb. פַּרְדֵּם, *par-dace'*, park), a garden planted with trees (Eccles. ii:5; Cant. iv:13; rendered "forest" in Neh. ii:8).

It is applied by Diodorus Siculus (ii, 10) to the hanging gardens of Babylon. Xenophon (*Anab.* i, 287) describes a park, belonging to Cyrus, like the game preserves of Europe, under this name.

ORDAIN (ôr-dān'), the same as appoint. Ordinances of God are:

1. His fixed purpose and appointment concerning the state and motions of irrational creatures, whether the luminaries of heaven, etc. (Ps. cxix:91; Job xxxviii:33; Jer. xxxi:35).

2. His commandments in general (Lev. xviii: 4).

3. His rules and directions relative to his worship (Heb. ix:10; 1 Cor. xi:2).

4. An office appointed by him (Rom. xiii:2). Forms of magistracy, or their laws for regulating the commonwealth, are called an *ordinance of man* (1 Pet. ii:13; 1 Sam. xxx:25).

"A peculiar use of the word is in the rendering of the Hebrew פָּעַל, *paw-al*, in the passage 'he ordaineth his arrows against the persecutors' (Ps. vii:13), which Gesenius translates 'he maketh his arrows burning,' literally *into* or *for* burning, from a meaning of the Hebrew to *forge*." (Barnes, *Bib. Dict.*)

ORDER (ôr'dẽr), a word with many varieties of meaning, as it is the rendering of several Hebrew and Greek words. It is most frequently the rendering of the Heb. עָרַךְ, *aw-rak'*, to set in a *row*.

1. It denotes position or proper place, (Ezek. xli:6) 'One over another, and thirty in order;' (1 Cor. xv:23) 'Every man in his own order;' (Luke i:8) 'He executed the priests' office before God in the order of his course;' (1 Cor. xiv: 40) 'Let all things be done decently and in order.'

2. Position in office, rank. This is the meaning of Ps. cx:4 'Thou art a priest forever after the order of Melchizedek.' (See Heb. v:6, 10; iii:20).

3. Arrangement or orderly array (Job x:22). 'A land of darkness . . . without any order.'

4. Prescribed custom (1 Chron. vi:32; xv:13), 'we sought him not after the due order' (1 Chron. xxiii:31; 2 Chron. viii:14); 'He appointed, according to the order of David his father, the courses of the priests to their service.'

Figurative. (1) God sets men's sins *in order* before them; he presents them as so many witnesses, or as a well-stated charge against them (Ps. 1:21). (2) Men *order* their cause before God, and fill their mouth with arguments, when they represent it to him truly and in order, and produce and plead manifold reasons for his shewing them favor (Job xxiii:4). (3) To *walk orderly*, or to *order one's conversation aright*, is to endeavor earnestly to perform every duty relative to God or men, in the proper place, time, and manner thereof (Acts xxi:24; Ps. 1:23).

ORDINANCES OF THE GOSPEL (ôr'dĭ-nans-ĕs ŏv thē gŏs'pĕl), are institutions of Divine authority relating to the worship of God; such as: (1) baptism (Matt. xxviii:19); (2) the Lord's Supper (1 Cor. xi:24, etc.); (3) public ministry, or preaching and reading the word (Rom. x:15; Eph. iv:11; Mark xvi:15); (4) hearing the gospel (Mark iv:24; Rom. x:17); (5) public prayer (1 Cor. xiv:15, 19; Matt. vi: 6; Ps. v:1, 7); (6) singing of psalms (Col. iii: 16; Eph. v:19); (7) fasting (James iv:9; Matt. ix:15; Joel ii:12); (8) Solemn thanksgiving (Ps. 1:14; 1 Thess. v:18). (See these different articles.)

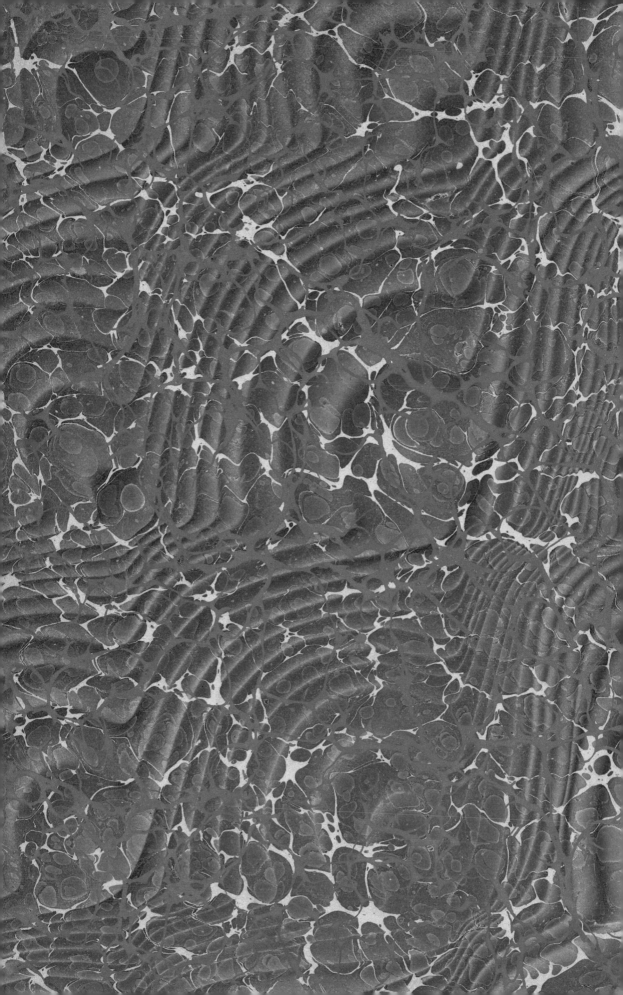